THE ALMANAC OF AMERICAN POLITICS 1998

The Senators, the Representatives and the Governors: Their Records and Election Results, Their States and Districts

Michael Barone and Grant Ujifusa
with Richard E. Cohen

National Journal

Washington, D.C.

NATIONAL JOURNAL INC.

Publishers of:

National Journal
Government Executive, CongressDaily, CongressDaily/A.M.
The Hotline, Greenwire, American Health Line, The Abortion Report
http://www.nationaljournal.com
also
The Capital Source, The Federal Technology Source
also
National Journal Convention Daily, published every four years at the Democratic and Republican National Conventions
and

The Almanac of American Politics

Printed in the United States of America by United Book Press. Composition by Applied Graphics Technologies. Distributed by Times Books, a division of Random House Inc.

Photographs by John Eisele, Susan M. Muniak and Bruce Reedy. For information regarding photographs, contact: National Journal, 1501 M Street, N.W., Washington, D.C. 20005. 202-739-8400. All rights reserved.

ISBN 0-89234-080-0 (Paper)
ISBN 0-89234-081-9 (Cloth)

National Journal Inc. is a wholly-owned subsidiary of the Times Mirror Co.

A Times Mirror
Company

THE ALMANAC OF AMERICAN POLITICS 1998

Authors: Michael Barone, Grant Ujifusa

Editor: Eleanor Evans

Managing Editor: Cathryn M. Newson

Contributing Editor: Richard E. Cohen

Associate Editor & Research Director: Holli Burge

Research Associates: John Gallagher, Richard C. M. Houston, Allan D. Shuldiner

Assistant Editors: Nidhi Agrawal, Tracy McLoone

Research Assistants: Matthew Reed Baker, Blair Campbell, Gary Cohen, Ron Eckstein, Adam Rappaport

Editorial Assistants: Isobel Ellis, Jodie Morris, Greta Waller, Ann Margaret Webb

Photographers: John Eisele, Bruce Reedy

Page Layout: Shirley Yonce, Applied Graphics Technologies

Election Results & State Maps: Election Data Services Inc.

Presidential Election Results: NCEC Services Inc.

Cover Design: Robert Antler

The Almanac especially would like to thank the entire staff of *National Journal* for their invaluable support and assistance during the production of this book.

TABLE OF CONTENTS

GUIDE TO USAGE

The Almanac of American Politics is designed to be self-explanatory. The following guide provides a brief description of each section and a list of sources from which information was derived, both of which serve as a road map to understanding the meaning behind the figures.

The People

Population. All population figures, excluding unemployment rates and voter registration, are from the Bureau of the Census, U.S. Department of Commerce, Washington D.C. 20230, 301-763-4040. Official April 1, 1990, Census figures are used as well July 1, 1996, estimates for each state.

Race and Ethnic Origin. For the 1990 Census, the Census Bureau asked people what their race or ethnic origin was. Race, as defined by the Bureau of the Census, reflects the individual respondents' perception of his or her racial identity and does not reflect any biological or anthropological definition. The basic racial categories are: American Indian or Alaska Native; Asian or Pacific Islander; Black; and White. Hispanic origin is defined as an ethnicity, and includes those who classified themselves in one of three specific Hispanic categories on the census form (Cuban, Mexican, Puerto Rican) or as of "other Spanish/Hispanic origin"; *persons of Hispanic origin may be of any race.* The "Other" category was intended to include those persons who do not consider themselves to be in the basic racial or ethnic categories.

Households and Housing Information. A Household is defined as including all persons occupying a housing unit; a Married Couple Family is a household of persons related by marriage. Owner occupied housing units include only single-family houses on less than ten acres with no business or medical office on the property. The value of a housing unit is the respondent's estimate of how much the unit would sell for if it were for sale, and determines Median House Value. Monthly rent is defined as the per-month contract rent agreed to for a unit, regardless of any goods or services that may be included (e.g. utilities), and determines Median Monthly Rent.

Age. The Bureau of the Census defines age as based on the number of years a person completed as of April 1, 1990. This definition was used to determine the voting age population, the percentage of population over 65 years of age, and the median age. Many people, however, provided their age as of the date they completed the census form rather than the definition provided by the Bureau of the Census.

Education. The level of higher education is measured by the Census from persons over 25 years of age who have pursued vocational, public, or private forms of college education not necessarily leading to graduation.

Unemployment. All unemployment figures are from the Bureau of Labor Statistics, U.S. Department of Labor, Washington, D.C. 20210, 202-606-7828. These figures represent the average rate of unemployment for each state for 1996.

Registered Voters. Registered voter numbers are from the individual states' election bureaus or political parties, and represent the number of voters officially registered as close as possible to the November 1996 election. Some states have no voter registration.

Political Lineup. This block includes the names of top state officials as well as a breakdown by party of the state legislative bodies. The names of U.S. senators and a party breakdown of the state's congressional delegation are also provided.

Presidential Vote. The 1992 and 1996 presidential vote is included for each state and congressional district. Presidential vote by state and by congressional district was derived from state, county and precinct results as compiled by the staff of the National Committee for an Effective Congress (NCEC), 122 C Street, NW, Washington, DC 20001, 202-638-8300. The 1992 presidential vote by congressional district was recalculated in six states to reflect redistricting (remapping) changes. The six states are: Florida, Georgia, Kentucky, Louisiana, North Carolina and Texas. Results of the presidential primaries were provided by the states and the FEC. Caucus results are not provided.

Biography. This section lists when each governor, senator and representative was elected or appointed, date and place of birth, home, college education and degrees obtained (if any), religion, marital status and, if applicable, spouse's name. Also listed is a brief outline of the politician's career, including military service in the Air Force, Army, Marine Corps, Navy, National Guard, or Reserves, and his or her office addresses and telephone numbers. Committee and subcommittee assignments are provided as well. (Note: On many committees, the chairman and ranking minority member are ex officio members of each subcommittee on which they do not hold a regular assignment.)

Ratings

Group Ratings. The congressional rating statistics of 11 interest groups provide an idea of a legislator's general ideology and the degree to which the legislator represents different groups' interests. Not just a record of liberal/conservative voting behavior, these ratings come from a range of groups concerned with everything from single issues (environmental concerns) to the political interests of a particular sector (e.g., consumers). The order of the groups is such that the more "liberal" groups are on the left and the more "conservative" are on the right. Four groups, ACLU, NFIB, NTLC and CHC release ratings only once every two years, the duration of one full congressional session. Following is a general description of each organization, its address and telephone number.

ADA Americans for Democratic Action
1625 K St., N.W., #210, Washington, D.C. 20006, 202-785-5980.

Liberal: Since its founding in 1947, ADA members have pushed for legislation designed to reduce inequality, curtail rising defense spending, prevent encroachments on civil liberties and promote international human rights. The ADA uses a broad spectrum of issues for its vote analysis.

ACLU American Civil Liberties Union
122 Maryland Ave., N.E., Washington, D.C. 20002, 202-544-1681.

Pro-individual liberties: ACLU seeks to protect individuals from legal, executive and congressional infringement on basic rights guaranteed by the Bill of Rights. The ACLU ratings are published for every Congress; the 1992 ratings include the years 1991 and 1992.

AFS American Federation of State, County and Municipal Employees (AFSCME)
1625 L St., N.W., Washington, D.C. 20036, 202-429-5020.
Liberal Labor: As the nation's largest public employee and health care workers union, representing more than 1.3 million members, AFSCME is committed to achieving dignity and improving working conditions through collective bargaining. The AFSCME voting records are based on a representative sample of roll call votes from the First and Second Sessions of the 104th Congress.

LCV League of Conservation Voters
1707 L St., N.W., #750, Washington, D.C. 20036, 202-785-8683.

Environmental: Formed in 1970, LCV is the national, non-partisan arm of the environmental movement. LCV works to elect pro-environmental candidates to Congress. LCV ratings are based on key votes concerning energy, environment and natural resource issues, selected by leaders from major national environmental organizations.

CFA Consumer Federation of America
1424 16th St., N.W., #604, Washington, D.C. 20036, 202-387-6121.

Pro-Consumer: CFA is a group spawned in the mid-sixties as a pro-consumer counterweight to various business-oriented lobbies. Their vote ratings concentrate on pocketbook consumer issues and health and safety concerns.

CON Concord Coalition
1019 19th St., N.W., #810, Washington, D.C. 20036, 202-467-6222.

Pro-Balanced Budget: The Concord Coalition is a nonpartisan, grassroots organization dedicated to eliminating the federal budget deficit by the year 2000. The Coalition, with members and active chapters in all 50 states, is determined to educate the American public about the dangers of the federal deficit.

NFIB National Federation of Independent Business
600 Maryland Ave., S.W., #700, Washington, D.C. 20024, 202-554-9000.

Pro-Small Business: The National Federation of Independent Business represents small and independent business owners—every kind and size of commerical enterprise; high-tech, family farmers, neighborhood retailers and service companies. Founded in 1943, NFIB gives small and independent business a voice in governmental decision making in Washington, D.C. and all 50 states.

COC Chamber of Commerce of the United States
1615 H Street, N.W., Washington, D.C. 20062, 202-659-6000.

Pro-business: Founded in 1912 as a voice for organized business, COC represents local, regional and state chambers of commerce in addition to trade and professional organizations.

ACU American Conservative Union
1007 Cameron St., Alexandria, VA 22314, 703-836-8602.

Conservative: Since 1971, ACU ratings have provided a means of gauging the conservatism of members of Congress. Foreign policy, social and budget issues are their primary concerns.

NTLC National Tax-Limitation Committee
151 North Sunrise Ave., #901, Roseville, CA 95661, 916-786-9400.

Pro-tax limitation: NTLC was organized in 1975 to seek constitutional and other limits on taxes, spending and deficits at the state and federal levels. NTLC actively pursues a balanced budget/tax limitation amendment to the U.S. Constitution. These ratings are based on budget issue votes and bills which would have a major impact on long-term goverment taxing and spending programs.

CHC Christian Coalition
227 Massachusetts Avenue, N.E., #101, Washington, D.C. 20002, 202-547-3600.

Conservative: Pro-family citizen organization and national lobby founded in 1989 working for family-friendly public policy on a local, state and national level with 1.5 million members and activists.

National Journal Ratings. *National Journal*'s rating system establishes an objective method of analyzing congressional voting. A panel of *National Journal* editors and staff initially compiled a list of congressional roll call votes and classified them as either economic, social or foreign policy-related. Professor Garrison Nelson of the University of Vermont provided the computerized roll-call data. The interrelationship of these votes was shown by a statistical procedure called "principal components analysis," which revealed which "yea" votes and which "nay" votes fit a liberal or a conservative pattern. The votes in each of the three subject areas were computer-weighted to reflect the degree they fit the common pattern. All members of Congress who participated in at least half of the votes in each area received ratings; those who missed more that half the votes were not scored (shown as *). Absences and abstentions were not counted.

Members of Congress were then ranked according to relative liberalism and conservatism. Finally, they were assigned percentiles showing their rank relative to others in their chamber. Percentile scores range from a minimum of 0 to a maximum of 99. Because some members voted liberal or conservative on every roll call, however, there are ties at the liberal and conservative ends of each scale. For that reason, the maximum percentiles often turn out to be less than 99.

Election Results

Election Results. Listed for each member of the House are results of the 1996 general, runoff and primary elections, as well as the 1994 general elections (results of any special elections are also listed). Gubernatorial and senatorial results are presented in a like manner. Votes and percentages are included, indicating the margin of victory (due to the process of rounding up and rounding down, some totals may equal more or less than 100%). Candidates receiving less than 4% of the total vote are grouped together and listed as "Other." Dollar amounts listed to the right of the vote totals are campaign expenditures as reported by the candidate to the Federal Election Commission. Election returns were provided by Election Data Services Inc., 1225 Eye Street, N.W., #700, Washington, D.C. 20005, 202-789-2004.

Campaign Finance

All data are derived from candidates' campaign finance reports and party reports available from the Federal Election Commission (FEC), 999 E St., NW, Washington, D.C. 20463, 202-219-3440 (toll free, 1-800-424-9530). The dollar figure, in parentheses to the right of the election results, represent the candidates net disbursements (expenditures) for the period beginning January 1, 1995, and ending December 31, 1996. *These figures may not include any any candidate loans which have been repaid, nor does it include any corrections or amendments filed with the FEC after December 31, 1996.*

Key Votes of the 104th Congress

Key Votes. The Key Votes section attempts to illustrate a legislator's stance on important votes where he or she must vote *for* or *against* a national issue. The process grossly oversimplifies the legislative system where months of debate, amendment, pressure, persuasion, and compromise go into a final floor vote. However, the voting record remains the best indication of a member's general ideologies and position on specific issues.

Following is a list of key votes used. A member who was absent, voted present, or who was not in office at the time of a particular vote receives an asterisk. The votes were drawn from Legi-Slate, a computer system tracking legislation, voting attendance, committee schedules, etc. For information on Legi-Slate or their vote recording process, please contact: Legi-Slate, 777 N. Capitol St., N.E., #900, Washington, D.C. 20002, 202-898-2300.

House Votes, 104th Congress:

1) **Reduce Medicare Growth $** (HR 2425) House voted to reduce projected spending for medicare by $270 billion over the next seven years. October 19, 1995. Vote No. 731: Passed 231-201; (D: 4-194; R: 227-6).

2) **Override Product Liability Veto** (HR 956) House failed to override President Clinton's veto of the bill to limit damages in product liability cases. May 9, 1996. Vote No. 162: Failed two-thirds majority 258-163; (D: 33-157; R: 225-5).

3) **Increase Minimum Wage** (HR 1227) House approved an increase in the minimum wage for most workers to $5.15 per hour as of July 1, 1997. May 23, 1996. Vote No. 192: Passed 266-162; (D: 188-6; R: 77-156).

4) **Welfare Reform** (HR 3734) House passed reform of welfare laws, including imposition of a five-year restriction on welfare benefits and a requirement that beneficiaries find work within two years. July 18, 1996. Vote No. 331: Passed 256-170; (D: 30-165; R: 226-4).

5) **Flag Amendment** (HJRes 79) House passed constitutional amendment to allow Congress and the states to pass laws that prohibit desecration of the U.S. flag. June 28, 1995. Vote No. 431: Passed 312-120; (D: 93-107; R: 219-12).

6) **Drop EPA Limits** (HR 2099) House dropped proposed limitations on the enforcement authority of the Environmental Protection Agency. November 2, 1995. Vote No. 762: Passed 227-194; (D: 163-29; R: 63-165).

7) **Repeal Assault-Weapons Ban** (HR 125) House voted to repeal the ban on the manufacture or sale of certain assault weapons. March 22, 1996. Vote No. 92: Passed 239-173; (D: 56-130; R: 183-42).

8) **Override Partial-birth Abortion Veto** (HR 1833) House overrode President Clinton's veto of the bill barring "partial-birth" abortions. September 19, 1996. Vote No. 422: Passed 285-137; (D: 70-121; R: 215-15).

9) **Cuban Embargo** (HR 927) House tightened the U.S. embargo on trade with Cuba. September 21, 1995. Vote No. 683: Passed 294-130; (D: 67-125; R: 227-4).

10) **Bar Bosnia Troop Funding** (HR 2770) House defeated proposal to prohibit funds for deployment of U.S. troops in Bosnia. December 13, 1995. Vote No. 856: Failed 210-218: (D: 20-175; R: 190-42).

11) **Cut Anti-Missile Defense** (HR 3230) House defeated proposal to cut $109 million from anti-missile defense program to pay for surface-to-air missiles. May 15, 1996. Vote No. 173: Failed 185-240: (D: 182-12; R: 2-228).

12) **Bar U.N. Uniforms** (HR 3308) House voted to prohibit any requirement that U.S. military forces wear a United Nations uniform. September 5, 1996. Vote No. 404: Passed 276-130; (D: 65-118; R: 211-11).

Senate Votes, 104th Congress:

1) **Reduce Medicare Growth $** (HR 2491) Senate voted to reduce projected spending for entitlement programs, including medicare, to balance the federal budget in 2002. October 27, 1995. Vote No. 556: Passed 52-47; (D: 0-46; R: 52-1).

2) **Limit Product Liability Damages** (HR 956) Senate approved the conference report on the bill to limit damages in product liability cases. March 21, 1996. Vote No. 46: Passed 59-40; (D: 12-34; R: 47-6).

3) **Increase Minimum Wage** (HR 3448) Senate approved an increase in the minimum wage for most workers to $5.15 per hour as of July 1, 1997. July 9, 1996. Vote No. 186: Passed 74-24; (D: 47-0; R: 27-24).

4) **Welfare Reform** (HR 3734) Senate passed reform of welfare laws, including imposition of a five-year restriction on welfare benefits and a requirement that beneficiaries find work within two years. July 23, 1996. Vote No. 232: Passed 74-24; (D: 23-23; R: 51-1).

5) **Flag Amendment** (SJRes 31) Senate failed to pass constitutional amendment to allow Congress and the states to pass laws that prohibit desecration of the U.S. flag. December 12, 1995. Vote No. 600: Failed two-thirds majority 63-36; (D: 14-32; R: 49-4).

6) **Endangered Species** (HR 3019) Senate defeated proposal to place a moratorium on the listing of endangered species. March 13, 1996. Vote No. 30: Failed 49-51; (D: 42-5; R: 7-46).

7) **Gay Employment Rights** (S 2056) Senate defeated bill to prohibit job discrimination based on sexual orientation. September 10, 1996. Vote No. 281: Failed 49-50; (D: 41-5; R: 8-45).

8) **Override Partial-birth Abortion Veto** (HR 1833) Senate failed to override President Clinton's veto of the bill barring "partial-birth" abortions. September 26, 1996. Vote No. 301: Failed two-thirds majority 57-41; (D: 12-35; R: 45-6).

9) **Anti-Missile Defense** (S 1026) Senate tabled proposal to cut $300 million from anti-missile defense program. August 3, 1995. Vote No. 354: Tabled 51-48; (D: 4-42; R: 47-6).

10) **Cuban Embargo** (HR 927) Senate tightened the U.S. embargo on trade with Cuba. October 19, 1995. Vote No. 494: Passed 74-24; (D: 23-22; R: 51-2).

11) **Bar Bosnia Troop Funding** (HR 2606) Senate defeated proposal to prohibit funds for deployment of U.S. troops in Bosnia. December 13, 1995. Vote No. 601: Failed 22-77; (D: 1-45; R: 21-32).

12) **Cut Vietnam Aid** (HR 3540) Senate defeated a proposal to strike $1.5 million in economic aid to Vietnam. July 25, 1996. Vote No. 239: Failed 43-56; (D: 10-36; R: 33-20).

ABBREVIATIONS

A.A.	Administrative Assistant
ABC	Americans for Better Childcare Act
ACLU	American Civil Liberties Union
ACP	A Connecticut Party
ACU	American Conservative Union
ADA	Americans for Democratic Action, Americans with Disabilities Act
AFDC	Aid to Families with Dependent Children
AFS	American Federation of State, County & Municipal Employees (AFSCME)
AI	Alaska Independent Party
ANWR	Alaska National Wildlife Refuge
AS	American Samoa
ASI	American Systems Independent Party (PA)
Bd.	Board
BGH	Bovine Growth Hormone
BVP	Brooklyn Voters Party (NY)
C	Conservative Party (NY)
CAB	Civil Aeronautics Board
CAFE	Corporate Average Fuel Economy
CFA	Consumer Federation of America
CCP	Change Congress Party
CHC	Christian Coalition
CHOB	Cannon House Office Building
CIA	Central Intelligence Agency
COC	Chamber of Commerce of the United States
COLA	Cost of Living Adjustment
CON	Concord Coalition
D	Democrat
DCCC	Democratic Congressional Campaign Committee
Dem.	Democratic
DFL	Democratic-Farmer-Labor Party (MN)
DLC	Democratic Leadership Council
DNC	Democratic National Committee
DOE	U.S. Department of Energy
DOT	U.S. Department of Transportation
DSCC	Democratic Senatorial Campaign Committee
DSOB	Dirksen Senate Office Building
EMILY	EMILY's List (Early Money is Like Yeast)
EPA	U.S. Environmental Protection Agency
ERISA	Employee Retirement Income Security Act
FEC	Federal Election Commission
FR	Freedom Party (NY)
FY	Fiscal Year
GATT	General Agreement on Tariffs & Trade
GREEN	Green Party
H	Capitol Building Room—House side
HSOB	Hart Senate Office Building
I, Ind., Indep.	Independent
IC	Independent Conservative
IMF	International Monetary Fund
INF	Independent Fusion Party
INN	Independent Neighbors Party (NY)
IR	Independent-Republican Party (MN)

IRA Individual Retirement Account
ISTEA Intermodal Surface Transportation Efficiency Act
IVP Independent Voters Party

JBS Jobs Party (NY)

L Liberal Party
LCV League of Conservation Voters
LHOB Longworth House Office Building
LIB Libertarian Party
LIF Long Island First Party (NY)
LWV League of Women Voters

MFN Most Favored Nation
MTV Music Television

NAFTA North American Free Trade Agreement
NAP New Alliance Party (MA)
NARAL National Abortion Rights Action League
NEA National Endowment for the Arts
NFIB National Federation of Independent Business
NRCC National Republican Congressional Committee
NRSC National Republican Senatorial Committee
NTLC National Tax-Limitation Committee

PAC Political Action Committee
P&F Peace & Freedom Party (CA)
PDP Popular Democratic Party (PR)
POP Populist Party
PR Puerto Rico
PS Protect Seniors Party (NY)

R, Repub. Republican
RC Rainbow Coalition
Rep./s Representative/s
RHOB Rayburn House Office Building
RLDS Reorganized Church of the Latter Day Saints
RMM Ranking Minority Member
RNC Republican National Committee
RSOB Russell Senate Office Building
RTL Right-to-Life Party

S Capitol Building Room, Senate side
S&L Savings and Loan
SDI Strategic Defense Initiative
Sen./s Senator/s
SIS Staten Island Secession Party (NY)
SM Save Medicare Party (NY)
SOL Solidarity Party (IL)
SWP Socialist Workers Party (MN)

TXB Tax Break Party (NY)

UAW United Auto Workers

VA Veterans' Administration
VNS Voter News Service
VRP Voters Rights Party (NY)

WASP White, Anglo-Saxon, Protestant
WIC Women and Infant Children

INTRODUCTION

The elections of 1996, expected to settle political arguments, instead left them unsettled, to be carried on in different terms, in less focused and frank language—as the country itself continued to change. The Republicans, after their smashing victory in the congressional elections of 1994, hoped to use the same issues to win the presidential contest and to pass their ambitious programs to reform and reduce the size and scope of government. Speaker Newt Gingrich compared 1996 to 1896, when an uncharismatic Republican nominee, William McKinley, built on sweeping Republican congressional gains two years before and established the Republicans as the majority party for the next 34 years. Congressional Democrats, absorbing the shock of unexpected defeat, hoped that the Republican program would be so unpopular that they would sweep back to majorities in the House and Senate, whatever happened in the congressional elections. They compared 1996 to 1948, when after two years of a Republican Congress that cut taxes, restricted labor unions and endorsed an assertive foreign policy, voters swept congressional Democrats back in with large majorities and gave a smaller margin to President Harry Truman as well. President Bill Clinton, reduced in March 1995 to insisting that he was still relevant, hoped to repair the impression voters got from his first two years that his policies would unacceptably increase the size and power of government and that he was a weak and irresolute leader. He may have compared himself to Harry Truman, who after a difficult two years projected an image of steadiness and produced a program that was popular and won a full term despite trailing in the polls for many months.

But 1996 did not turn out to be either 1896 or 1948. Congressional Republicans and President Clinton both won, but not on the terms they hoped. Second-term presidents of both parties in time of perceived peace and prosperity have won between 59% and 61% of the vote—Ronald Reagan in 1984, Richard Nixon in 1972, Lyndon Johnson in 1964. Bill Clinton won reelection with 49%, comfortably ahead of Bob Dole's 41%, but still less than a majority of the vote. Nor did he help his party win majorities in Congress; instead he was the first Democratic president in history elected with a Senate and House controlled by the opposition. But neither did the Republicans continue to make the extraordinary gains they had from the first special election of the first Clinton term to the last, and of course especially in 1994. They did gain two seats in the Senate, but were still five seats short of their goal of 60, enough to defeat a Democratic filibuster. And in the House they lost seats, though not enough to lose control. Republicans went into the 1996 election with 235 House seats, more than the 230 they won in 1994 because of party switches and special election victories; they came out with 227, to 208 for the Democrats and the Vermont Socialist who regularly votes with them. They won more votes than the Democrats, for the first two elections in a row since 1928 and 1930, but not many more: 49.0% to 48.5%.

So in 1996 American voters made essentially the same decisions in presidential and congressional elections as they had the last time they voted for each. They elected Bill Clinton 49%–41% in 1996 just as they elected him 43%–37% in 1992. The results from the two elections resemble each other more closely than any pair of elections since Dwight Eisenhower beat Adlai Stevenson in 1952 and 1956. And they elected a Republican House by 49.0% to 48.5% in 1996 pretty much as they had elected a Republican House by 52%–45% in 1994. Indeed, in popular votes for the House 1996 stood almost precisely midway between 1994 and 1992, when Democrats led 51%–46%.

So what was the mandate? Clinton and congressional Republican leaders talked after the election about how the voters were demanding bipartisan cooperation. But cooperation for what? It is important here to understand one more thing about the election. The Democratic president's victory looked large, but it was contingent. It depended on decisions that could very easily have gone the other way, on a high order of rhetorical and political skills, on the establishment of a distance from his party, not only its historical stands on issues but the stands of most of its current candidates. The Republican Congress's victory looked narrow, but it was fundamental. It was based on a wider than generally appreciated acceptance of its policy thrusts. Congressional Republicans had almost everything working against them: the $35 million AFL-CIO ad campaign, the attack on their Medicare "cuts," hostile and often inaccurate media, polls that may well have been misleading, the great unpopularity of their most visible leader Newt Gingrich and a president of the other party running ahead in times of peace and prosperity. They could have said, as the head of Italy's right Polo coalition Silvio Berlusconi said after his party won the popular vote but lost in legislative seats because of internal splits, "Avevamo tutti contro noi"—we have had everyone against us. If not too many votes had been cast differently, Republicans would have lost the House. Yet their level of support—whether 49% or 48% or 50%—in these circumstances is a sign that the policies they stand for have a large and stubborn base of support in the country.

It is ordinary practice in political discourse to speak of politicians and officeholders as shaping the future, making decisions and setting a course, doing things to or for the country. But in the America of the 1990s, when government does not demand things of us as it does in war or when we do not demand of government great change as we do in depression, politics has been more a matter of the country doing things to or for politicians. To understand what Americans voted for in 1996, we need to see how the people shaped the politicians in 1995 and 1996, and then to step back and take a look at the country that is doing the shaping, and at its increasingly different regions and faiths.

THE 1996 CAMPAIGN

The election of a Republican Congress in 1994 resulted in a restoration of the constitutional order—in the literal sense of the word. For Article I of the Constitution is about the Congress, not the president, and the House of Representatives comes first, not the Senate. Article I is much longer than Article II, about the president, and the powers reserved to Congress are more numerous; it was the expectation of the Founders that in the ordinary course of things, the Congress and in particular the House would set the course of public policy. But for most of the 60 years before 1994 things were not ordinary; the country was on a warlike footing and the president, the commander-in-chief, was in a commanding position in the political arena. Now, with peace and when the president had displayed little sense of command, Congress and the House—or its 230 Republicans—took the lead. Newt Gingrich's September 1994 Contract with America, which almost all Republican House candidates signed, set the agenda. Within weeks the House passed nine of the ten items in the Contract, failing only to muster two-thirds of a congressional term limits constitutional amendment; the Senate moved more slowly and cautiously, rejecting the balanced budget constitutional amendment by one vote. House Republicans worked to produce a budget that they promised would be balanced by 2002 and in fall 1995 announced a plan to cut the projected increase in Medicare spending. Gingrich and other Republicans expected that Clinton would back down and sign these bills.

But Clinton did not behave as they expected. After the bombing of the federal building in Oklahoma City in April 1995, Clinton delivered a moving eulogy, implicitly critical of those who raised angry voices against government programs. In June he abandoned his own budget proposal and agreed to accept the goal of balancing the budget by 2005. But in August 1995 he started running political ads against the Republicans' Medicare plan. All this was part of a strategy pollster Dick Morris called "triangulation," taking positions between liberal Democrats and conservative Republicans so as to elevate the president's stature above both. Clinton was in effect campaigning, not as a backer of liberal congressional Democrats, but as a check and balance on conservative House Republicans. In November and December he negotiated on the budget with Speaker Gingrich and Senate Majority Leader Bob Dole, promising them agreement at times, but he ultimately vetoed most of their appropriations bills. That technically shut down non-emergency functions of the federal government, a step which many Republicans initially welcomed and thought would be popular. This was a stunning miscalculation, as was their lack of a strategy to deal with Clinton's vetoes. They could have argued that it was the president who shut down the government, since Congress passed, though tardily, appropriations bills and Clinton vetoed them. Indeed the press in the 1980s portrayed Ronald Reagan as the one who risked shutting down the government when he vetoed appropriations passed by the Democratic Congress: an example of the media being inconsistent intellectually but consistently anti-Republican. But of course the Republicans seemed to exult in the shutdown, and naturally were blamed by the voters. By the time Republicans backtracked and agreed to Clinton's terms, their ratings were down and they were running behind Democrats in the polls. Beginning in late 1995 Clinton began leading Bob Dole and other Republicans in polls, and when voters were asked which party's candidate they would support for the House—pollsters called this the generic vote—Democrats started coming out ahead of Republicans—results which held up through October 1996. But Republicans had produced a 1996 budget that actually cut domestic discretionary spending, for the first time since 1969.

On the budget battle, and when he dispatched U.S. troops to Bosnia in fall 1995, Clinton showed the decisiveness and sense of command he had seemed to lack in 1993 and 1994. At the same time the stature of his potential Republican opponents was shrinking. Clinton conducted a brilliant behind the scenes campaign in 1995. He started running campaign ads in the spring, to which the media paid little attention partly because early ads had not worked before in presidential races and partly because they were not run in the Washington or New York media markets (most of whose audiences are in states safe for one party or the other anyway). To pay for these he raised very large sums of money early—and in ways, it turned out, which hurt him a little in late October 1996 and then very much more in 1997. Clinton also prevented a challenge in the Democratic primaries. Since 1993 he had courted Senator Edward Kennedy, appearing often at Kennedy events in Massachusetts, subcontracting out Northern Ireland policy to his sister, Ambassador to Ireland Jean Kennedy Smith and former Kennedy aide Nancy Soderberg at the National Security Council. He assigned his deputy chief of staff Harold Ickes, a Jesse Jackson campaign staffer in 1988, to mollify Jackson, who after his son started running in a special election for the House in October 1995 decided not to run. And the Clinton fundraising drive banished any thoughts of running from other Democrats' minds.

Meanwhile, Republican presidential candidates were campaigning furiously, spending much time seeking the support of the religious right who formed as large a part of the Republican base as the feminist left formed of the Democratic base. Seven Republicans ran, of whom the best-known by far was Senate Majority Leader Bob Dole. But his was not the only well-organized campaign; Texas Senator Phil Gramm and former Tennessee Governor Lamar Alexander raised millions of dollars and built organizations aimed at the Iowa caucuses February 12 and the New Hampshire primary February 20. Magazine publisher Steve Forbes spent liberally of his own money on ads touting his flat tax and attacking Dole and others as Washington insider. Columnist and former White House speechwriter Pat Buchanan articulated vividly his opposition to abortion and support of trade restrictions to preserve American jobs—a shift from Reagan Republicans' free market policies which he called "the conservatism of the heart." Senator Richard Lugar ran on his foreign policy expertise and his support of a flat tax. Two other candidates attracted some attention—and proved offputting to many marginal voters—with bombastic speeches, Alan Keyes denouncing America's moral decline and Congressman Robert Dornan denouncing Bill Clinton's morals.

Most of the Republican delegates would be selected quickly, in a process designed mostly by Democrats in party commissions and legislatures. Bob Dole won the nomination not by projecting an attractive persona or presenting a popular program, but by attacking each of his rivals as he was about to make headway: a campaign that did nothing to increase his political capital for the fall campaign. The nomination was decided even between the Louisiana caucus

February 6 and the South Carolina primary March 2. Louisiana was a contest concocted by Phil Gramm, in the hopes that an early win could make him a contender regardless of how he did in Iowa or New Hampshire. But Pat Buchanan came into Louisiana and beat Gramm, whose campaign foundered in Iowa and was over before New Hampshire. Meanwhile, Forbes's heavy advertising in many states made him a threat to Dole, and in Iowa and New Hampshire Dole ran attacks against him. These, plus Forbes's criticism of Christian conservatives just days before the Iowa contests and his weak precinct organization there, left him weak in Iowa and New Hampshire. After Pat Buchanan finished a close second in Iowa, Dole's strategists identified him as their main target. But in New Hampshire they were running ads against Forbes and, starting five days before the primary, against Lamar Alexander, who had a fine campaign organization there. Buchanan, with the militant support of the *Manchester Union Leader*, won in New Hampshire, but Dole finished a close second, edging Alexander by 7,000 votes; without those negative ads, Alexander's organization and walk across New Hampshire might have put him ahead and forced Dole out.

Buchanan hoped to win next in Arizona, but his military metaphors and his campaign costume (black cowboy hat and rifle in Tombstone) put off many voters, and Forbes won there, with Dole second. Buchanan continued his campaign in other states, to dwindling crowds of true believers, hoping to reshape Republican conservatism in his image, but Dole had clinched the nomination in South Carolina five months before the national convention August 12.

The Clinton campaign used that time far more effectively than the Dole campaign. With no primary opponent, the Clintonites could spend millions in federal matching money on messages aimed at general election voters; the Dole campaign, its treasury exhausted, had to use accounting legerdemain to continue bare-bones operation. Dole attracted attention in May when he announced he was resigning from the Senate and in June when he left. But his poll numbers did not rise appreciably, and in July sagged after he told Katie Couric in a TV interview that he wasn't sure if tobacco was addictive.

Then came perhaps the most pivotal moment of the campaign. House Republicans, under withering attack from AFL-CIO ads in marginal seats and for Medicare "cuts" from Clinton and Democrats everywhere, were putting together a budget that increased domestic discretionary spending a bit, and were splitting over raising the minimum wage, a hoary issue that Democrats raised not for policy reasons—they had not bothered with it in the two years they had control—but because it tested well in polls. Now some Republicans wanted to raise the welfare issue again. In 1992 Clinton had campaigned to "end welfare as we know it"; when his poll numbers flagged, his campaign ran welfare spots. But in his first two years, despite pleading from Senator Daniel Patrick Moynihan, he did little on the issue, and in 1995 and 1996 he vetoed two bills which contained Republican-passed welfare reform plans. In July 1996 Congressman Dave Camp of Michigan and John Ensign of Nevada circulated a letter, signed by 100 Republican members, urging Republican leaders to revive the welfare issue, by separating it from their Medicaid plan (which Clinton had said was the reason for his vetoes) and passing it separately. Clinton could either veto it again and give Republicans a campaign issue or he could sign it and give them—congressional Republicans, that is, not Bob Dole—an accomplishment. After the usual angry argument, Congress passed welfare reform, eliminating the federal welfare entitlement after 61 years and giving great leeway to the states. Clinton, after some indecision, signed the bill in August 1996. This was a prime example of the country shaping politics and policy, moving the Republican Congress and the Democratic president to do things they had good tactical political reasons not to do: the political marketplace at work. "The era of big government is over," Clinton said in his January 1996 State of the Union speech, and in August 1996 this Democratic president, with some visible reluctance, hastened its end.

The passage and signing of welfare reform separated the cause of congressional Republicans from Dole and the cause of Clinton from congressional Democrats: it is as if the crews of the two ships were setting off on their own lifeboats, waving an embarrassed goodbye to the passengers as the ship was starting to founder. That was plainly visible at the two party conventions, both scheduled for August so as to avoid conflict with the Atlanta Olympics in July. Like NBC's coverage of the Olympics, the conventions were geared to feminine if not feminist sensibilities, with plenty of dramatic stories of individuals who faced hardship or overcame handicaps and little hard-edged conflict. The week before the Republican convention, Dole came out for a 15% across the board tax cut and named Jack Kemp as his vice presidential nominee; both moves were popular in San Diego, and Dole closed the gap coming out of the convention. Newt Gingrich spoke only briefly, about beach volleyball as an example of American genius; the congressional Republicans were saving their issue offensive for October. Bill Clinton chose to separate himself physically from the campaign, traveling by train through the Midwest in fine August weather, promising to build "a bridge to the 21st Century." On the way he announced many little government plans—tax deductions for college tuition, restrictions on gun sales to spouse abusers, the V-chip to allow parents to restrict children's television viewing—with the common Dick Morris-inspired motif of presenting him as helping parents raise their children. Little was said about electing a Democratic Congress. The well-orchestrated crowd chanted "Four more years!" as House Minority Leader Dick Gephardt spoke, though no member of Congress except the nonvoting delegates from Puerto Rico and Guam has a term of four years. Bill Clinton and Al Gore devoted one sentence each in their acceptance speeches to the need to elect a Democratic Congress. But congressional Democrats saw Clinton as their only chance to victory and praised him with a fulsomeness that would have pleased Lyndon Johnson. The mood was upbeat in Chicago, and Clinton emerged with more than a 10% lead at the end of August.

Relatively little changed in the presidential race during the fall campaign. Dole struggled to find issues that would move voters—the tax cut, teenage drug use, racial quotas and preferences—but none really did. In the two presidential debates, Dole vastly improved on his performances in primary season debates; but he was still far less articulate and empathic than Clinton. In the vice presidential debate Kemp declined, as Dole had, invitations to attack Bill Clinton's character or alleged involvement in scandal. Both candidates kept themselves insulated from the press. During October Clinton started funneling money to Democratic congressional candidates, but said little publicly in their behalf. In the last two weeks a new scandal surfaced, when it was revealed that DNC fundraiser and former Commerce Department appointee John Huang funneled at least one illegal campaign contribution and quite possibly others to the DNC; Huang refused to appear in court as ordered and the DNC initially refused to produce him; then it refused to disclose its contributors to the Federal Election Commission on deadline. It was also revealed that Al Gore attended a fundraiser in a Buddhist temple in California, where monks donated $5,000 each; one monk reported that $5,000 cash was pressed into her hand, but changed her story after the temple hired as her lawyer a former California Democratic chairman. Ross Perot, who had been idling in the polls between 4 and 8 percent, denounced the scandals pithily, and his support increased a bit.

More was happening in congressional races. Republican National Chairman Haley Barbour and Newt Gingrich and his strategists planned to hold up their major spending bills until October. This was resented by many congressional Republicans, who had been under attack from the AFL-CIO and Democratic Party ads going back as far as April 1995. And while Republican candidates had more money to spend than their opponents, Democrats did a fine job of funneling PAC money to endangered incumbents and promising challengers—helped by the fact that even most business PACs are run by former Democratic staffers and operatives. But there were good reasons for waiting, if not for quite so long as Republicans did. Parties of the right, not just in the United States but around the world, have been winning elections by late surges of campaigning: this was true in the 1990 Michigan and 1993 New Jersey governor races, which Republican strategists had very much in mind, and in 1996 in Italy (where the right won more votes but not most seats because of a split vote). There is something fundamental at work here: the free media is staunchly anti-right and so for long months the left has the advantage in the public dialogue; but in the last weeks the right can use money to get its message through with less attention and criticism from the free media.

That is what happened in congressional elections in the United States in 1996. Where the AFL-CIO had been running ads, the Republicans ran ads attacking labor bosses in Washington and criticizing Democrats for taking money from the Laborers Union which the Clinton Labor Department found to be corrupt (while leaving its big contributor Democrat president in office). Where Democrats had been attacking Republican Medicare "cuts"—which is to say just about everywhere—Republicans responded with ads and mail arguing that Clinton's own Medicare trustees said the system was going broke, that the Republican plan would just increase spending more slowly and that the Republican "lockbox" provision would guarantee that savings were devoted to Medicare (not, as Democrats charged, for a tax cut for the rich). The Republicans touted their record of cutting spending, enacting welfare reform, backing the balanced budget and term limits. All of which worked. Republicans' disadvantage among the elderly vanished, and Republicans' standings improved in the polls. The Medicare issue, as Democratic pollster Peter Hart has said, stopped working for Democrats in mid-October. The issue of less government started working again for Republicans, as it had in the congressional elections of 1994 and the presidential elections of 1980, 1984 and 1988. Very few of the AFL-CIO targets lost their seats.

And so in November 1996 Bill Clinton and Al Gore won 49%–41% and congressional Republicans won 49.0%–48.5%. These results leave open many possibilities for the future. The 1992 and 1996 Clinton presidential victories stand for the proposition that a New Democrat beats an Old Republican. The 1994 and 1996 Republican congressional victories stand for the proposition that New Republicans beat Old Democrats. The three decades after the New Deal tell us that Old Democrats beat Old Republicans. But no one can be sure now if New Democrats beat New Republicans, or vice versa. But the basic trends of opinion are clear, and not changed from what they seemed right after 1994. We are moving away from, not toward, an ever-larger government; we are at the least uneasy about our renunciation of traditional moral values, and possibly ready to embrace them again; we cherish an inchoate, mostly unarticulated American nationalism that guides our unfocused, seemingly contradictory impulses on foreign and defense and trade policy.

Those trends have all been strengthened, not weakened, since Bill Clinton was elected in 1992. It has become a firmly established principle, in Washington and in almost every state capital, that taxes must not be increased. Many Democratic and a few Republican politicians believe the country would be better off with higher taxes and more government spending, but few if any dare say so publicly. Welfare policy has been devolved from the federal government to the states, and a decision has been made that healthcare reform will not be federalized but will remain devolved. Telecommunications has been deregulated and electric utilities are in the process of deregulation, with states leading the way. Public schools are escaping centralized control and subjected to more competition and accountability. Most farm subsidies are scheduled to be eliminated over the next seven years. Government spending is no longer expanding faster than the private economy. There are exceptions and qualifications to all these trends, but the basic thrust is unmistakable and unidirectional. Power is flying out of Washington, not because of arbitrary decisions by policymakers or because Democrats had one bad Tuesday in 1994 and another mixed one in 1996, but because it is in accord with the basic character of our society—a character that has changed vastly in the last long generation.

TOCQUEVILLIAN AMERICA

Start with this proposition: that America today more closely resembles the pre-industrial America that Alexis de Tocqueville described in *Democracy in America* in the 1830s than the industrial America in which most of us grew up. Tocqueville's America was egalitarian, individualistic, decentralized, religious, property-loving, lightly governed. Egalitarian, not in economic terms but in the sense that Americans are comfortable with the presumption of the moral equality of every citizen: we are not a servile people, in awe of any elite, respectful of hierarchy, though we are quick to recognize and honor talent. Individualistic, not rejecting common enterprise, but insisting on making personal decisions without interference from others. Decentralized, as the big units that dominated America in World War II and for three decades afterwards—big government, big business, big labor—have lost their hold on the economy and on people's imaginations. Religious, because the United States remains the one economically advanced country in which most people are religious. Property-loving, since ordinary people in the course of a lifetime expect to—and do—accumulate significant wealth, in residential real estate, investments and pensions. Lightly governed, because government leaves to voluntary associations of many kinds social functions which elsewhere and at other times have been performed by the state.

Centralization and hierarchy, which Robert Wiebe in *Self-Rule: A Cultural History of American Democracy* identifies as the dominant characteristics of American life for most of the 20th Century, seem to be yielding to decentralization and equality, as Wiebe shows they were, even more suddenly, in the early 19th Century. Then, when they were released from the threat of Napoleonic wars, Americans liberated religion and medicine from central authorities, stopped working for big employers and surged west in great numbers to become independent farmers and merchants. That America developed a national two-party politics, but as Wiebe puts it, "Politics diffused government power and united a sprawling nation." In the 1990s, Americans once again have been released from the threat of world war. They are rejecting the authority of hierarchies in religion (compare the declining mainline denominations with the surging fundamentalist faiths or the New Age mentality) and medicine (look at the popularity of alternative healing and fads even in a time of great scientific progress).

Geographically, ordinary Americans have been spreading out to edge cities and beyond, in computer-equipped houses in low-priced subdivisions, living comfortably on credit extended in free if seemingly disorderly markets. Economically, they increasingly work for small businesses or hop from one job to another with dexterity and optimism and without generating political demands for economic redistribution or government guarantees. Americans are not a people yearning for security, although the G.I. generation who grew up in the Depression, served in World War II and helped build prosperous postwar America do have a more than economic attachment to Social Security; but there are fewer G.I. generation members in the electorate every day, and more members of Generation X, born after 1965.

Intellectually, Americans take direction not from a cultural and educational elite that seeks to make the country obey abstract rules learned in prestigious universities, but from self-help advisers, television evangelists and radio talk show hosts. The Ivy League elite that Christopher Lasch described in his posthumous *The Revolt of the Elites and the Betrayal of Democracy* no longer captures Americans' imaginations: compare the fascination with the Kennedys in the early 1960s to the now vitriolic dislike by some Americans and mild positive feelings of others toward Bill and Hillary Rodham Clinton.

This 21st Century Tocquevillian America is not necessarily Republican, any more than Tocqueville's 1830s America inevitably voted for the Jacksonian Democrats. The Whigs, when they escaped the thrall of their New England elites, won elections too, and in the 1990s Bill Clinton has shown that Democrats can win by convincing margins. They win when they develop a New Democratic coalition politics that is an acceptable variant of the Republican faith, a set of policies with a more communitarian thrust but not one that attempts to impose centralized, hierarchical solutions on a country that resists centralization and hierarchy. This Clinton did convincingly in 1991 and 1992 and once again in 1995 and 1996; his problem now is whether he can follow that course in 1997 and 1998 as he did not in 1993 and 1994.

In this new-old America the political rules are different from those most readers have grown up with and become accustomed to. Underlying much traditional political analysis is the assumption that the first things voters seek from government are economic—a smooth upward business cycle and redistribution of economic income and wealth. But that is clearly wrong. The first thing voters seek from government is order—not some arbitrary, authoritarian order, but a rational, predictable order in which ordinary people can raise their families, make their livings, participate in their communities and go about their daily lives without fear of physical disorder or economic disaster. Americans have had a happy history during most of which they took this basic order for granted. But they have reacted strongly when order is threatened. The economic disorder of the early 1930s deprived Republicans of the national majority and gave Democrats the chance to become the majority party. The cultural disorder of the late 1960s deprived Democrats of their national majority and gave Republicans the chance to become the majority party.

The fallacy that the first thing most voters seek from government are economic is an idea that grew out of New Deal politics and Keynesian economics—specific responses to an episode of severe economic disorder. Yet even in the 1930s and the generation that followed that idea was never true except at the margins. In different elections 5% and sometimes even 10% of voters would change their minds because of the performance of the macroeconomy or in response to policies of economic redistribution. And in an electorate closely divided between adherents of the two major parties, those 5% and 10% could easily make the difference in election outcomes. But even at the height of what seemed to be class warfare politics—from 1935 to 1963, approximately—the very much larger blocs of the electorate adhered to party preferences based on cultural issues. Southern whites were Democrats because Democrats opposed the Civil War. African Americans, for three generations solidly Republican, became solidly Democratic, because Franklin Roosevelt seemed to back civil rights in the 1930s and 1940s as Abraham Lincoln and the radical Republicans had in the 1860s and 1870s. (Interestingly, the New Dealers who were most favorable to civil rights were former Republicans—Eleanor Roosevelt, Harold Ickes, Henry Wallace.) Voters of New England Yankee stock were heavily Republican, as they had been since they founded the Republican Party in the 1850s; voters of immigrant stock were heavily Democratic, as they had been since they came to the great cities of the East and Midwest and found them run by unsympathetic Yankee Republicans. To these culturally defined blocs were added some defined by their stand on economic issues, most notably the militant members of the industrial CIO unions, which transformed the cities of the industrial Great Lakes—Pittsburgh, Buffalo, Cleveland, Detroit—from Republican strongholds to Democratic bastions. But the politics of economic redistribution even at its height was a driving force to only a minority of voters.

Today it is a driving force to very few. For more than 20 years, since 1973, income distribution has been growing less egalitarian—not only in the United States but in other advanced countries as well. From 1935 to 1963 the CIO unions' heartland in the industrial cities of the Great Lakes were a dependable constituency for the economic redistribution advocated by labor leaders from John L. Lewis to Walter Reuther. But in 1994 these metropolitan areas voted Republican for governor or in some cases for senator—and for Republicans committed to lower taxes and less government spending. In 1996 these areas voted for Bill Clinton, but not necessarily Democratic for Congress, and the Republican governors remain popular. And while the AFL-CIO made a visible splash in national politics, the $35 million spent on ads in House races defeated few targets and total union membership continues to fall. Raising the minimum wage, a favorite AFL-CIO issue, is not very redistributionist in a country where most minimum wage earners are not heads of households and in many booming areas where the market has raised wages well above the statutory minimum already.

So we are moving from what has been an exception in American political life back to what has been the rule: a Tocquevillian politics in a Tocquevillian country. This is a country in which order exists because basic rules are accepted by the people, or insisted upon by them: from a government in which political forces and governmental mechanisms tend to ratchet down the size of government, not ratchet it up as did the political forces and governmental mechanisms operating from the New Deal years up through the 1980s.

One such force is voters' strong conviction that taxes should not be raised, that government already takes a large enough share of what people earn. Voters demonstrated that in the 1990s by doing three unnatural things: in 1990 by giving reduced percentages to House incumbents of both parties, for the first time in 50 years, after most incumbents of both parties voted to raise taxes; in 1992, by lowering George Bush's percentage from 53% to 37% after he broke his "Read my lips—no new taxes" promise; in 1994, by ousting the Democrats' congressional majority at a time when economic indicators were good. Soon after their 1994 victory, House Republicans created another mechanism to hold down government spending, by getting rid of the "current services" budget procedure that gives every department an automatic increase for inflation and lets them argue for more. This system was based on the absurd premise that government, unlike all other large organizations, had achieved the maximum possible efficiency and could not figure out ways to deliver services more cheaply. The Republicans' balanced budget amendment failed to pass in 1995 and 1997, as Democrats encouraged senators who promised to vote for it but were not up for reelection in two years to break their word and vote against it. But politicians of both parties have acted as if it passed. There is considerable fiction in the Clinton plans and some in the Republicans' as well, but both feel obliged to promise a balanced budget, and there is heavy downward pressure on government spending. Another way that politicians used to expand government was by inflating the currency; this was how Richard Nixon pumped up the economy for 1972. But the stagflation of the 1970s made American voters inflationophobic, and the international marketplace now swiftly punishes any attempt to degrade the currency. Bill Clinton has had to go along; he made the most important economic appointment of his second term before it even began, when he renominated Federal Reserve Chairman Alan Greenspan in February 1996, because he knew that an appointment of the kind many Democrats would favor would immediately raise interest rates and hurt his reelection chances. And because Greenspan critic Senator Tom Harkin delayed his confirmation until June 1996, Greenspan's term now extends to June 2000, which means that Republican senators can prevent the confirmation of any successor and leave the selection to the next president.

In any case, arguments about what sound like economic issues are often arguments over cultural issues. Consider welfare. For years the debate on the surface seemed to pit those who wanted to spend less of government's (and their own) money on poor people and those who wanted government to spend more. But the amounts of money involved, if not as trivial as some liberals suggested, were not as enormous as conservative rhetoric implied. The argument is better portrayed as a battle between one side whose cry is "personal responsibility" and another whose belief is "it's society's fault." The complaint of those who wanted to change the welfare system was not so much that it cost too much as that it degraded the morals of society by fostering irresponsibility and the growth of a criminal underclass. Subsidizing single mothers, it was argued, gives sanction to unmarried parenthood by women and irresponsibility by men and creates whole neighborhoods where adolescent boys are unsupervised and are readily drawn into association with the criminals who are the real rulers. Indeed, the same kind of arguments—"personal responsibility" versus "it's society's fault"—have been made on crime issues, and were on vivid display in the debate over the 1994 crime bill. The "personal responsibility" side called for harsher punishments; the "it's society's fault" called for, among other things, midnight basketball and more counseling. It is an argument over discipline versus therapy. Every society, like every family, needs some of both and every society, like every set of parents, will differ how much of each is appropriate.

The Tocquevillian America of the 1990s has opted clearly, on both crime and welfare, for more discipline and less therapy. These were not the decisions of Washington elites or academic experts, who almost uniformly favor therapy; they were forced by the people on their national leaders, or were the product of local officials and citizens acting in disregard of elite opinion. Since the 1960s, liberal elites used the federal government, and the leverage of federal dollars, to impose therapy-type approaches on social work and crime-fighting across the country, with success far greater than the amount of federal spending would suggest. Their secret was to shape the culture of the care-giving and law enforcement professions, through graduate schools, professional organizations and friendly mass media. This was not an invisible process to voters, many of whom understood that programs originally intended to encourage middle-class behavior instead tended to discourage the values that promote stability. They understood that welfare programs increasingly were run by social workers who did not believe in encouraging recipients to work, that schools were run by educators who did not believe in teaching basic skills and information but just in promoting self-esteem, that police departments were sometimes run by leaders who believed that "root causes" rather than individuals were to blame for crime and that prisons were run by penologists who did not believe in keeping people in jail.

Responding to these views, governors in many states sought to change the welfare system and the Clinton Administration, heedful of public opinion, granted some waivers from federal requirements. But the real change seems to have come with passage of the 1996 welfare reform act. Suddenly states were empowered to change the rules and, there is much reason to believe, suddenly recipients and potential recipients decided that welfare was something they could not rely on, and they had better try work. Welfare rolls, which peaked in 1994, started to fall and by late 1996, even before welfare reform was technically in effect, were falling rapidly. Similarly, crime rates in the middle-1990s, after years of staying up near peak levels, started to fall. These were more than responses to a prosperous economy; economic good times in the 1970s and 1980s produced no such result. It is possible, though not yet certain, that we are seeing a decline in welfare and crime beginning around 1994 as sharp and precipitous as the increase in welfare and crime that occurred between 1965 and 1975.

These trends were not uniform across the country. Welfare rolls were down most sharply in Wisconsin—28% between September 1995 and September 1996—and crime rates fell most sharply in New York City—down by one-third since Rudolph Giuliani became mayor in January 1994. Specific individuals were responsible: Governor Tommy Thompson has been devising workfare programs for over 10 years and former New York Police Commissioner William Bratton made New York cops crack down on minor offenders and disturbers of the peace and used computers to isolate high-crime locales so that they could be flooded with police. But in a Tocquevillian America states and cities are laboratories of reform, and an experiment which works in one place can be copied elsewhere. But the successes of Wisconsin and New York City suggest that the culture of the care-giving professions can be changed by determined public officials and that actions by politicians can remove the apparent sanction of fatherless childbearing or criminal behavior.

In Tocqueville's America, politics became a kind of culture war, between a Yankee-led North and a cavalier-led South: indeed, eventually a real Civil War, in which 600,000 Americans lost their lives. Our America is in the midst of a less heated culture war, as Patrick Buchanan called it in 1992 (while showing more relish for it than suited most voters), whose contours are shown in the election results and the exit polls of the 1996 elections. To which let us turn.

The America revealed in the 1996 election results and exit polls is an America deeply divided, more along cultural than along economic lines, and increasingly along regional lines. Those who see economics as the motive force in political decision will find only modest support in the results. The Voter News Service exit poll showed the lowest income group (under $15,000) voted 59%–28% for Clinton and the highest (over $100,000) 54%–38% for Dole, but each of these groups was less than 10% of the electorate; among the other 80%, there was little difference between income groups. On racial lines there were large differences: whites voted 46%–43% for Dole, blacks 84%–12% for Clinton. But there were surprises as well: Hispanics, a disparate group which trended toward Reagan Republicans in the 1980s, voted 72%–21% for Clinton; Asians, portrayed by some activists as a minority in need of special help from government, voted 48%–43% for Dole. Men voted 44%–43% for Dole, women 54%–38% for Clinton: the gender gap that has become familiar since 1980, with an even bigger gap between married women (48%–43% for Clinton) and unmarried women (62%–28% for Clinton).

But the factor which divided voters more than anything else was religion. Definitions here are imprecise, and categories incommensurate between polls, but the overall picture is clear when one interpolates from the VNS and *Los Angeles Times* exit polls. The categories of Jews and those people stating "no religion" voted about 3–1 for Clinton. Traditional white Protestants voted about 2–1 for Dole. A similar pattern was apparent in House races, except that Protestants voted about 3–1 Republican.

Another factor that stands out in the results is education. From the New Deal up through the Reagan years, the pattern was clear: the least educated voters were the most Democratic, the most educated the most Republican. But in the 1990s that has changed. In the VNS poll those who had not graduated from high school voted 65%–35% for Democratic House candidates. But this group was only 6% of the electorate, including many elderly blacks. The three middle groups—high school graduates, those with some college and college graduates—were together 50%–49% Republican, with the former a few points more Democratic and the last a few points more Republican. But those with post-graduate degrees were more Democratic—51%–49% in House races and 52%–40% in the presidential race according to VNS, 49%–43% in the presidential race according to the *Los Angeles Times*. These graduate school degree holders are not just doctors and lawyers, but also teachers and social workers whose credentials earn them higher pay in government jobs under public employee union contracts; they reflect the liberal culture of the care-giving professions; they are now a significant, though nothing like a majority, part of the electorate, numerous enough to have replaced CIO union assembly line workers as the demographic base of the Democratic Party.

One of the striking features of the 1996 elections results is how voters in Democratic regions have become more Democratic, while voters in Republican regions have become more Republican. It was the result perhaps of local responses to national issues, but also a reflection, in a country with enormous social and geographical mobility: people are seeking out their own kind. Many commentators noted on election night that Republicans were becoming a kind of endangered species in the Northeast, and pointed out accurately that there were only four Republican congressmen left in New England, arguably the historic heartland of the Republican Party. True enough, and significant. But these commentators failed to notice that there were only four Democratic congressmen left in the Rocky Mountain states, arguably the heartland of William Jennings Bryan's Democratic Party but not the home base or college site of many of today's media elite. And, one might add, in the 1990s the Rocky Mountain states have more congressmen than New England, so that the Democrats' 19–4 advantage in New England was outweighed ever so slightly by the Republicans' 20–4 advantage in the Rockies. To which one might again add that the Great Plains states running north from Oklahoma to North Dakota elected 13 Republicans and one Democrat to the House.

The interesting point here is that both New England and the Rocky Mountains were becoming more monopartisan. Just four years before, after the 1992 election, both areas were much more evenly divided: the New England delegation was 14–8 Democratic and the Rocky Mountain delegation 13–11 Republican. What we are looking at here is something reminiscent of the realignment shown in the House elections of the 1930s. In 1932, when the economy was in collapse and Franklin Roosevelt was elected on an ambiguous platform, Democrats in House contests made uniform gains in all regions of the country, winning dozens of seats that never went Democratic before—and some that would never go Democratic again. In the 1934 offyear elections, the Democrats actually gained nine seats—the only time the party in power has done so in the offyear—but they did not gain them uniformly. They lost seats in the small towns and rural areas of the East and Midwest, where the centralization of power in the National Recovery Administration and other New Deal agencies was resented as an interference with local arrangements. But they won seats in the industrial, factory districts which had gained population rapidly from 1900 to 1930 and then reeled from huge layoffs and the almost total devaluation of local real estate; in Pennsylvania alone, Democrats gained nine House seats in 1934 that they had not won in 1932—a harbinger of the industrial, unionized base of the Democratic Party for the next 30 years. House Republicans did not do quite so well in 1996; they lost seats on balance, though only eight. But they consolidated gains in the areas where support for their policies was strong, and lost few enough where support for their policies was weak to keep a majority in the House. Which is not to say that they are guaranteed a majority for as long as the New Deal Democrats, but only that they represent a growing force in public opinion, less visible in the precincts of the Washington-New York elite but more widely disseminated across the country as the emerging New Deal majority was in 1934.

To understand the contours of opinion across the country, let us move beyond the Northeast corridor to examine the political responses in all regions of the country, divided along lines that give meaning to the trends of the 1990s. Divide the country into five regions, four of which include about one-sixth of the voters, the other about one-third. The first is New England and the Metroliner Corridor—the six states of New England and the New York, Philadelphia, Baltimore and Washington metropolitan areas, including most of New York, all of New Jersey and Delaware, southeast Pennsylvania, most of Maryland and the District of Columbia. The second is the South Atlantic states from Virginia south to Florida. The third is the Mississippi Valley—a bit more than one-third of the nation—from Upstate New York to Louisiana, from Minnesota to Alabama—the part of America which was first settled from the 1770s to the 1840s and the great industrial base of the nation. The fourth region is the great Interior, the Great Plains and Rocky Mountain states from Texas to Idaho (and including Alaska): the Great American Desert, as it was referred to, during the years just before and after the Civil War. Finally there are the Pacific states, California, Oregon, Washington and Hawaii, those far American outposts in the 19th Century and now our redoubts on the rapidly growing Pacific Rim. Each has its great economic capitals generating commerce and looking to the world beyond—New York, Atlanta, Chicago, Dallas, Los Angeles—and each has its own combination of economic interests and cultural attitudes that sends its politics in different directions. Let us look at each region in turn.

New England/Metroliner Corridor. Throughout the 1996 election cycle, reporters wrote that voters were repelled by the Republican revolutionaries and the religious right, that they were ready to cast an overwhelming though not entirely enthusiastic majority for Bill Clinton, that they were especially annoyed by opponents of abortion, and—while not interested in higher taxes—they were queasy about the prospect of dismantling government. This was an accurate picture—of one-sixth of the nation. The Northeast Corridor voted for Bill Clinton by a rousing 59%–31% margin, producing more than half his popular vote margin—a more one-sided result than any of these regions in the last three presidential elections. And in House elections it voted 58%–41% Democratic, while the rest of the country voted 51%–47% Republican. There is no question that there is an anti-Republican trend at work here. The Northeast Corridor has long been Democratic, but not by so wide a margin: Clinton carried the area 49%–33% in 1992 and Democrats carried the House vote here by a steady 54%–42% in 1990, 52%–43% in 1992, 52%–44% in 1994.

The Northeast Corridor in 1996 voted more like post-Thatcher Britain than like the rest of the United States. Like Prime Ministers Thatcher and Major, Northeast Corridor Governors Weld, Pataki, Whitman and Ridge have been slashing spending and cutting taxes, and since the defeats of Neil Kinnock in Britain in 1992 and Jim Florio in New Jersey in 1993 it has become an article of faith that voters will not countenance a tax increase. But with threat of tax increases removed, other issues come forward. Privatization has not gone as far in the Northeast Corridor as it has in Britain, and many people here, especially in and around New York, have got a government-connected niche which they are loath to give up (note how Long Island Republicans squawked when Newt Gingrich attacked unions). On cultural issues, the Northeast Corridor is not as secular and liberation-minded as Britain, but is getting there. Even nominal Catholics do not take the church's teaching on abortion seriously, and there are very few tradition-minded conservatives here. Nor is American exceptionalism—the idea that this country is special and different, a moral beacon for the world—play especially well in an area where many think most people west of the Hudson wear sheets and hoods. Then there is style. The Northeast Corridor prizes articulateness and doesn't much mind corruption: the tight-lipped, forthright Bob Dole struck no chords here, and Newt Gingrich's denunciations of New York's welfare culture raised hackles, while Bill Clinton's sureness with words and off-and-on relationship with the truth play well.

REGION	PRESIDENT (R-D-I %)	HOUSE (R-D %)
United States 1996	**41-49-8**	**49-49**
Northeast Corridor	31-59-8	41-58
South Atlantic	46-46-7	55-45
Mississippi Valley	41-49-9	49-48
Interior	48-42-8	56-41
Pacific Rim	38-51-8	45-51
United States 1994		**52-45**
Northeast Corridor		44-52
South Atlantic		58-41
Mississippi Valley		54-45
Interior		57-40
Pacific Rim		48-49
United States 1992	**37-43-19**	**46-51**
Northeast Corridor	33-49-17	43-52
South Atlantic	43-41-16	49-49
Mississippi Valley	38-43-18	46-51
Interior	40-36-23	48-49
Pacific Rim	33-45-21	41-55
United States 1990		**45-53**
Northeast Corridor		42-54
South Atlantic		44-55
Mississippi Valley		46-53
Interior		48-51
Pacific Rim		44-52
United States 1988	**53-46**	**45-54**
Northeast Corridor	49-51	42-54
South Atlantic	60-39	48-52
Mississippi Valley	53-46	46-54
Interior	57-42	49-50
Pacific Rim	50-48	43-55

But too much has been made of the Northeast Corridor's anti-Republican trend. This region looms unnaturally large in the minds of the mostly New York- and Washington-headquartered media. In 1944 this area cast 24% of the nation's votes, with New York City by itself accounting for 7%; in 1996 the same area cast just 16% of the national total, with New York City accounting for 2%. Democrats have already won almost every House seat they could hope to win here, and it casts only so many electoral votes—counting New York's but not Pennsylvania's, 99 in 1996 and probably 96 after the 2000 Census. The Northeast Corridor controls the nation's mind less than it thinks—"Home Improvement" has higher ratings than "Seinfeld." And it is in demographic decline: it generates relatively few new jobs and its population has only grown 2.1% in the 1990s, compared to 7.5% for the rest of the country. The Northeast Corridor cannot be ignored, but it is far from the whole story of America.

South Atlantic. A half century ago, there was not much to say about the South Atlantic states and their politics. They were America's backwater, economically far behind the rest of the nation, with low-wage Piedmont textile mills their only major industry, culturally bound by legally-enforced racial segregation, politically so heavily Democratic that few people bothered to pay their poll taxes and vote: they cast only 4% of the nation's votes in 1944. Now very much has changed. The surge of growth in the South Atlantic accelerated after the dismantling of segregation and has grown even faster in the 1990s; the South Atlantic grew 10% between 1990 and 1996 and in the latter year cast 15% of the nation's votes.

Yet the South Atlantic's politics are an outgrowth of deep traditions that go back in some cases to colonial days. Foremost among them is this area's Christian heritage. This is one of the most deeply religious places in any economically advanced country, with churches in every neighborhood and at country crossroads; if tone of daily life in the Northeast Corridor is secular, in the South Atlantic it is religious. The prominence of the religious right in the Republican Party is an asset here, not a liability. Economically, the South Atlantic was within living memory a kind of underdeveloped country, desperate even for low-paying textile mills; politicians here have worked hard to attract industry, keeping taxes down and insisting on right-to-work laws: this is the least unionized part of America. The colonies along the South Atlantic had no large city, unless you count Charleston, and there remains a country atmosphere to life here today. Even in metropolitan Atlanta, in the big urban strips in Florida, in the Northern Virginia suburbs spilling out into the countryside, the look of the place is country: kudzu, swamps, trees and greenery of all kinds dominate the view, and the pleasantry-laden tone of southern life even infects migrants from the North.

Politically, the South Atlantic is one of the two most Republican regions (the other is the Interior). It cast off its Democratic heritage as early as 1952, when most states here went for Dwight Eisenhower; it began electing Republican congressmen in the 1950s, governors in the 1970s. By 1988 it was voting 60%–39% for George Bush; it has been closer since in presidential races, but still more Republican than the nation: 43%–41% for Bush in 1992, 46.1%–45.8% for Clinton in 1996. Clinton owes this carry to his intensive campaigning for Florida's 25 electoral votes; he lost the four other states, including Georgia, which he won in 1992. The underlying Republican trend is stronger. It shows up in House races: the South Atlantic voted 55%–45% Democratic in 1990, a last vestige of its old allegiance, then 49.0%–48.8% Republican in 1992, 58%–41% Republican in 1994, 55%–45% Republican in 1996. Republican strength goes even further downballot: Republicans control four of the area's 10 state legislative chambers and have a tie in another.

The South Atlantic's traditions mix well with 1990s Republicanism, indeed have helped shape it: Newt Gingrich is from Georgia. Hostility to unions and high taxes are deeply ingrained here; strong traditional religious faith comes naturally. Democratic as well as Republican governors here, aware of the need for high skills, have emphasized the need for tough standards even as they have raised teacher pay. And no politician here sees a need to apologize for being tough on crime: the South Atlantic is ready to execute murderers and let law-abiding citizens carry concealed weapons. The major dissenters from this consensus are the South Atlantic's blacks—21% of the population, more than in any other region. Fresh from seeing desegregation imposed from Washington, they have seen a large and interventionist federal government as their agent of change, even as their states have improved local schools and the booming private economy has brought new jobs. But most South Atlantic voters disagree and prefer their regional economic and moral order to liberal Washington's.

The Mississippi Valley. In 1682 the French explorer LaSalle sailed up the St. Lawrence, through the Great Lakes and down the Mississippi Valley: the first man to traverse the region we call the

Mississippi Valley. This land between the Appalachian chains and the Great Plains is the center of America, the heartland, a place of great variety that is likely to be the central battleground in elections to come. It votes almost exactly like the nation as a whole: 49%–41% for Bill Clinton and 49%–48% for Republican House candidates in 1996; 48%–43% for Clinton and 51%–46% for Democratic House candidates in 1992. Clinton carried every state here except Mississippi and Alabama. When the Mississippi Valley does diverge from national patterns, it is worth inquiring the reasons. In 1994 it voted 54%–45% for Republican House candidates at the same time as most of its states were voting lopsidedly for Republican governors who boasted of cutting taxes and spurring economic growth. And while the Republican percentage dropped in 1996, it did not fall to the levels of 1992 and before; Republicans lost some seats here, but kept enough for a majority.

Historically, the Mississippi Valley was divided politically by the Old National Road, later U.S. 40 and Interstate 70, which runs through southwest Pennsylvania, Columbus, Indianapolis, St. Louis and Kansas City. North of the line people voted mostly Republican, south mostly Democratic. Then in the 1930s, with the CIO industrial unions organizing auto, steel and rubber factories, the big metropolitan areas of the Great Lakes became heavily Democratic. In the 1960s, white voters in the South shifted from Democrats toward Republicans, as did some blue collar workers; blacks in both the South and the big cities of the north became heavily Democratic. All these shifts have left the Mississippi Valley pretty close to evenly divided between the parties.

The economy here is mostly industrial, until one gets to the southern reaches of the Mississippi River, and competition between the parties is also a contest between two visions of industrial governance. The Democrats have been allied closely with the big industrial unions, and mostly see government as an instrument of economic redistribution. The constituency for that—blue collar workers in big Great Lakes metro areas—seemed to die out in 1994, but came faintly flickering back to life in 1996. The Republicans, historically allied with big company management, have moved now toward market economics, trusting that lower taxes, less welfare and fewer regulations will invigorate their economies. And in fact manufacturing, in almost terminal condition in the early 1980s, is now thriving, with hundreds of thousands of jobs in small businesses quietly being created—many more than were noisily lost in big company plan closures and layoffs. In 1996 Clinton got some credit for this; in 1994 Republicans did, and they hope to again in 1998.

On cultural issues the Mississippi Valley, like America, is exceedingly diverse. Support for abortion rights seems to be an asset in Illinois and a liability in Louisiana; in other states there are large constituencies for both points of view. Neither of the core cultural constituencies of the two parties—the religious right and the feminist left—dominates the local political dialogue, as the former do in the South Atlantic and Interior and the latter in the Northeast Corridor and Pacific Rim.

The Interior. As farmers moved west across the Great Plains, they came to land with less and less rainfall, until they reached the 100th parallel, which runs through North Dakota south to Texas and has long been considered the boundary between farm fields and grazing land. The land of most of this Interior region is brown and empty today, while farm counties have lost population as fewer hands are needed to harvest the crops. Except for its eastern edge, most of the Interior today is place with large metropolitan areas rising from barren land, with small settlements—resorts, oil drilling towns, county seats—in the vast space in between. Even Kansas, Nebraska and the Dakotas are on their way to becoming city-states.

The original politics of these states revolved around Civil War loyalties and mining and farming interests: Texas voted for the Confederacy, Colorado for the union, Arizona for copper, North Dakota for wheat. But by the 1980s politics in all these states began revolving around the same theme: local interests versus federal control. Texans and Oklahomans were disgusted with federal oil and gas price controls; Nevada was furious at being designated the nation's nuclear waste disposal site; Utah's Mormons disliked the cultural liberalism of Washington bureaucrats; Idahoans and New Mexicans rebelled at the ukases of federal land agencies. Even farm subsidies started to evoke not support but disdain: in 1996 Kansas and Nebraska placidly accepted the phasing out of wheat and corn subsidies. Added to these complaints in many parts of the Interior, though not all, was strong traditional Christian beliefs.

The result is that the once mostly Democratic Interior was in 1996 the most Republican region in the country. The Interior voted 48%–42% for native son Bob Dole over Bill Clinton, and 56%–41% for Republican House candidates in 1996; the latter was almost identical to its 57%–40% support of Republican House candidates in 1994. This was similar to the Interior's 57%–42% vote for George Bush in 1988. The changeover in congressional voting came in 1994; before that the Interior voted Democratic for the House, 51%–48% in 1990, 49%–48% in 1992. Now Democratic congressmen are about as scarce here as Republican congressmen are in the Northeast Corridor. In the House the Interior is represented by 47 Republicans and 22 Democrats, of whom 17 come from Texas, with the cleverest Democratic redistricting plan of the 1990s. (Texans voted 54%–44% Republican for House, but elected 13 Republicans and 17 Democrats.) But Democrats are not likely to control redistricting again here—Governor George W. Bush is highly popular going into 1998 and the state Senate is now Republican—and so the Republicans stand to make redistricting gains in 2002.

Pacific Rim. If the Interior is wide open, the Pacific Rim is densely packed: most people here live in metropolitan areas filling up the narrow interstices between ocean and mountains. Houses are expensive, lots are small, offices are distant over clogged freeways (one reason why so many people work at home). This is the homeland of America's computer creativity and its connection with the surging economies of East Asia; it produced bounteous growth for decades, then foundered as California and Japan went through a deep recession in the early 1990s. California (but not Japan) has now recovered and is rapidly generating jobs and creating new goods and services; Washington and Oregon in the Pacific Northwest are booming; only tourism-dependent Hawaii is lagging. This is the part of America most affected by the vast flows of immigration from Latin America and East Asia. The Pacific Rim cast 10% of the nation's votes in 1944, 16% in 1996.

Ronald Reagan showed Republicans how to carry the Pacific Rim in the 1980s; they have not been able to do it since. George Bush won here in 1988 by only 50%–48%, but lost to Bill Clinton by a resounding 45%–33% in 1992. Clinton carried the Pacific Rim 51%–38% in 1996, while Democratic House candidates were prevailing 51%–45%. Even in 1994 Democrats won 49%–48%. Reagan's success was based on his economic conservatism, his strong defense policy and sunny temperament. The Pacific Rim is quite aware that its growth has come mainly from the private sector, with the important exception in the 1980s of defense. The defense cutbacks of the late 1980s and early 1990s helped trigger southern California's economic collapse, with the upshot that its economy is now less defense-dependent.

Cultural conservatism has never been especially popular here. This is the most secular part of the nation, the place where people are least moored to old communities and folkways (as many still are in the slow-growth Northeast corridor). Exercise, environmentalism, New Age beliefs, gay identity, feminism—all have become religion substitutes for many Pacific Rimmers, and all correlate highly with political liberalism. Traditional religion does have some followers, notably in eastern Washington and Oregon and the Central Valley of California (which might fit in fairly well in the Interior). But the balance is on the other side. Voters here tend to see the religious right as a rebuke and even a threat to their lifestyle. And in the apolitical atmosphere here, so different from the blaring tabloid culture of the Northeast Corridor, voters have been willing to let highly skilled Democratic machine politicians control their legislatures; the California Assembly, briefly Republican, is now back in Democratic hands, as is the Senate. Hawaii's legislature is the most Democratic in the land, and the governorship has been handed down by one faction of Democrats since 1962. A possible countertrend: Washington and Oregon have elected Republican legislatures, perhaps to counterbalance liberal Democratic governors, perhaps because the values of their eastern regions are seeping west.

These regional differences help make some sense of the political trends of the 1990s. There is a seeming paradox here: presidential voting became more Democratic while congressional voting became more Republican. But in fact Americans in the 1990s have been voting more straight tickets than at any time since the 1940s. In the 1970s and 1980s many voters stuck with their ancestral Democratic preference in House races, or voted for the smart young Democratic political entrepreneurs who were so numerous in those years, even while voting Republican for president. In the 1990s such behavior has stopped. In 1992, as a look at the table shows, voters in each region produced about the same margin for each party for president and for the House; this is what we should expect if Perot voters split their House votes evenly. In 1994, voters were plainly responding to national issues in general and Bill Clinton in particular. In 1996, the percentage for Clinton in each region is eerily similar to the Democratic percentage in House races. Some Democrats may take that as evidence that if Clinton's lead was as large as in most polls, they would have won the House. Perhaps. But the fundraising scandals which seem to have lowered his poll numbers were not incidental to the way his campaign raised those numbers in 1995 and early 1996; they were a central part of his campaign strategy, one without which he would probably not have been running so well. In the political marketplace nothing is free; there is some question, however, about when you pay the price. Just as Republicans must worry whether they can again assemble a presidential majority without antagonizing their base, so Democrats must worry whether their 49%s in 1996 were a ceiling rather than a base.

It bears repeating that Clinton's 49% in 1996 was contingent while the House Republicans' 49% was fundamental. Clinton's victory owed much to superior skills and favorable circumstances not all of his making. Other Democrats are not guaranteed those advantages in the future. House Republicans' victory, on the other hand, occurred in unfavorable circumstances and despite the grave unpopularity of the most visible Republican leaders. Not all those disadvantages are guaranteed in the future. Much has been made of the unpopularity of House Republicans in the Northeast Corridor and, to a lesser extent, in the Pacific Rim. Less has been made about their affirmative strength in other regions. In 1990 none of these five regions voted for Republican House candidates. In 1992 only one did, by a fraction of a percentage point. But in 1994 Republican House candidates won 58% in the South Atlantic, 54% in the Mississippi Valley and 57% in the Interior. They held most of that vote in 1996. It would be wrong to say that Republicans are bound to win future congressional elections. But it is wrong to not acknowledge that their victory in 1996 shows that they represent a potential majority coalition capable of asserting itself in presidential as well as congressional contests.

Indeed, one could make the case that the Clinton presidency has been disastrous for the Democratic Party. When Clinton was elected in November 1992 there were 58 Democratic senators. Now there are 45. In November 1992 there were 259 Democratic congressmen. Now there are 208. When Clinton took office in January 1993 there were 28 Democratic governors. Now there are 17, in states with just 25% of the nation's population. There are 500-plus fewer Democratic legislators than there were when Clinton first won. Not all of these losses can be blamed on Bill Clinton, but many can. And there is also clear evidence that the Republican gains in Congress reflect a genuine impulse in the electorate.

THE POLITICAL GOVERNMENT

In the ordinary course of things, incumbents who are reelected to office emerge from the election more powerful and confident than when they went in. But not in early 1997. The 49% president was distracted by scandal. The 49% House Republicans were distracted by something akin to a loss of nerve, a sense that they had somehow lost the election that they actually won. The Senate, looked to for leadership, was hobbled by rules which make it easy to prevent decisive action. Leaders of both parties interpreted the election results as a demand for bipartisan cooperation. But Democrats continued to resent the aggressive tactics Republicans used to win control of the House in 1994, and Republicans continued to resent the mendacity of the Democrats' campaign against Medicare "cuts" in 1996. The voters clearly were in a mood for tranquillity and were tired of what they regarded as bickering. But a free and representative government will have an adversarial politics, and it was the voters themselves who (as in five of the past seven presidential elections) chose a president of one party and a Congress of the other.

Fortunately, the state of the nation was good and the public agenda fairly clear. The United States was the preeminent power around the world, at peace with other nations, with troops on assignment in Bosnia and elsewhere not under concerted attack. The macroeconomy was performing well: steady economic growth, an outpouring of new jobs, low inflation. Indeed, the economy for some time has been performing better than most political rhetoric suggested: the Boskin Commission conclusion that the Consumer Price Index overstates inflation means that wages and incomes have been rising, not falling since 1973. The culture, it is generally conceded, is malfunctional in some ways, but crime rates were falling, welfare rolls were shrinking, the rate of divorce was declining—in many ways things seemed to be moving in the right direction.

The agenda of officeholders in Washington was fairly clear. Congress needed to pass and the president to sign appropriations bills maintaining those parts of government that have been performing well and sending the budget somewhere close to balance by 2002. In a Tocquevillian society where power naturally devolves from the center to local communities, Congress needed to set terms and conditions under which government programs are devolved and commerce deregulated: as the 104th Congress did with welfare reform and telecommunications. And something needed to be done about the looming insolvency of the major entitlement programs, Medicare and Social Security. Ronald Reagan used to say that the solutions to complex problems were simple but not easy. That seemed to be the case again in the wake of the 1996 elections. In our Tocquevillian America, power has been flying out of Washington. But the terms and conditions under which power is devolved can make vast changes in people's lives; and setting those terms and conditions is the job of our elected federal officials in Washington.

THE HOUSE OF REPRESENTATIVES

Article I of the Constitution is not about the president; it is about Congress, and the House of Representatives, not the Senate, comes first. So the Framers expected it to be in government, except in war when the president's power as Commander in Chief would naturally be paramount. The Framers took care to require that all tax laws originate in the House, and by custom appropriations bill originate there too. The power of initiation is the power to frame issues, and as all political consultants know the side that frames the issues usually determines the outcome. That power came to seem less in the wartime conditions of the last 60 years; during the economic emergency of the Depression, during World War II and during the long Cold War, Congresses grew accustomed to waiting for the president's program and the president's budget and then responding to it, usually with changes at the margins.

But then the Cold War ended, and something like the original constitutional order was restored. The Democratic Congress forced George Bush first to drop his capital gains tax cut in 1989 and then to break his "Read my lips" promise and support a major tax increase in 1990. The leaders of the Democratic Congress also pressed Bill Clinton in 1993 to increase taxes, though without any Republican support they had great difficulty rounding up the votes to pass it. Then in 1994 a Republican Congress was elected—the first time voters had chosen a Republican House since 1952. Speaker Newt Gingrich, without whom this historic victory would not have been achieved, had the foresight to prepare an agenda in the form of the Contract with America which he persuaded almost every Republican House candidate to sign in September 1994. And the new Republican House set out writing a budget and enacting tax cuts and setting a goal, embraced by Bill Clinton in June 1995 to the chagrin of many Democrats.

It is widely believed—and by many Republicans—that this strategy was a terrible mistake and resulted in disaster for the House Republicans. To be sure, they did make mistakes. They proposed similar amounts in tax cuts and reduced increases in Medicare, which let Democrats attack them as backing Medicare "cuts" for tax cuts for the rich. And they seemed to take glee in watching the government shut down in December 1995, although in fact it was Bill Clinton's veto that shut it down; they had passed, if tardily in some cases, appropriations bills. But these mistakes aside, the House Republicans' strategy in important ways succeeded. It resulted in cuts in domestic discretionary spending for the first time since 1969—and this was after restoring monies demanded by Bill Clinton. It produced little outcry about programs cut back or eliminated: few people missed them. And it provided part of a platform on which Republicans won control of the House again in 1996.

Chastened by bad poll results, perhaps spooked by hostile press coverage, the Republicans retreated a bit in 1996, allowing domestic discretionary spending and the budget deficit to rise. But they avoided a second showdown with Clinton and won in November. And they mightily affected public policy, in ways that were not always visible: the press reported elaborately on concessions they made to Clinton, but said very much less about the parts of their budget which a Democratic Congress would never have passed but which Clinton accepted.

But in the first months after the 1996 election, the House Republican leaders took a different course. They refused to put forward their own budget proposals, saying they would react to Clinton's. They failed to provide an agenda with anything of the urgency of the Contract with America. They gave up, for a moment anyway, the initiative to shape public policy. Why? One reason was that Newt Gingrich was understandably preoccupied with his case before the ethics committee, from the time the subcommittee report was made public January 17 until the House finally voted January 21. He had little choice: his survival as speaker was a close-run thing. Another reason may be simple weariness. It is far more difficult and time-consuming to write your own budget bills than to make marginal changes in someone else's. And it is hard to summon up the energy to write your own tax bill when it seems sure to be vetoed and then another will have to be written after endless negotiations. Bill Clinton seems to enjoy these marathon sessions; few others do.

There seems to be another reason—many Republicans seemed to have lost their nerve. They seemed to lack the confidence they can take their case to the country, past an articulate, popular president and a hostile, monopartisan media, and prevail. They seem more comfortable responding to the Clinton agenda and waiting until 2001 in the hopes there will be a Republican president. But that is not clear, nor, if they continue their present course, is it clear there will be a Republican House. Republicans assume that the party in power always loses large numbers of seats in its sixth year in the White House, as happened in 1974, 1966, 1958, 1938 and 1918. But it didn't happen in 1986, 1926 or 1902: nothing is inevitable. The 1992 and 1996 presidential elections stand for the proposition that in the 1990s a New Democrat beats an Old Republican. If Republicans in the House seem to stand for nothing, it is conceivable that the Clinton White House could recruit enough activist, innovative New Democrats who could win the 10 seats Democrats need to win the House in 1998.

But the impression of inactivity may not prove lasting. The natural rhythm of congressional sessions is for little activity in the first four months: in January committee and subcommittee assignments are still being made, in February and March and April come the Presidents' Day and Easter recesses, and it ordinarily takes more time to draw up complex legislation—a budget, a telecommunications or electricity deregulation bill—than just a few weeks. Gingrich and the Contract with America set a precedent for early decisive activity which very few Congresses are in a position to follow. In March 1997 Gingrich traveled to China and articulated bluntly to its leaders basic American policies which Vice President Al Gore just days before had been at pains to slough over, and he followed up this show of resolution by returning to Washington and presenting a vision of this Congress making small but significant steps toward the long-term goal of reducing taxes and the size and scope of government.

Moreover, Gingrich had in place a set of committee chairmen committed to moving toward that goal. These chairmen were not necessarily chosen by seniority. Back in December 1992 Gingrich, then still minority whip, backed John Kasich over a more senior member for ranking position on Budget; that is why he is Budget chairman today, and one of the party's most appealing spokesmen. Just days after the 1994 election, Gingrich passed over four more senior members and named Bob Livingston chairman of Appropriations; his confidence that the strong-tempered Livingston would push through spending cuts proved justified. Other major committee chairmen came in with genuine strengths: Bill Archer of Ways and Means, Henry Hyde of Judiciary, Pat Roberts of Agriculture, now a senator, who passed the Freedom to Farm Act phasing out most farm subsidies over seven years. The committee chairmen are also under a deadline: the Republican Conference voted that they can keep their chairmanships only six years. Archer has already announced he will retire in 2000; Kasich seems bent on running for president in that year; the chairmen know that if they want to pass landmark legislation, they must do it while the Clinton-Gore Administration is in office. Important legislation is up before several committees; Transportation must reauthorize ISTEA, Education must reauthorize the Higher Education Act, Commerce has electric utility deregulation, Banking has repeal of Glass-Steagall. Kasich began working up his own budget, Archer began working on tax bills.

The thrust of all these laws, if Republicans do their work, will be to further devolve power from Washington, leaving choices to state and local governments, voluntary associations, parents, consumers and citizens, and leaving competition to be regulated by the market. But very much matters in the terms and conditions of such legislation. Take the familiar example of Social Security, though it is unlikely to be tackled by this Congress or this president. Many have proposed that taxpayers be allowed to invest some or all of their Social Security taxes in the financial markets, which have produced returns much greater than today's FICA taxpayers are scheduled to obtain from the government. On a 1996 commission two proposals attracted significant support. One would let the government invest such funds, with the proviso that it should not interfere in companies' operations. The other would let taxpayers choose between several investment vehicles.

Note that the two alternatives have very different effects on citizens (leaving aside the effect on corporations if the government doesn't obey the proviso). The first leaves citizens as passive objects of government benevolence, with an entitlement and an incentive to seek gains from decisionmakers in Washington. The second encourages citizens to be active shapers of their own future, looking to the private sector for gains. In private pensions and in some public pensions (the state of Michigan, for example) the movement now is away from defined benefit plans, which promise a certain set pension and create a mentality of entitlement, to defined contribution plans, which give the employee a right to make decisions himself and create a mentality of responsibility. Laws do more than appropriate money and forbid bad conduct. They set incentives and cultivate a state of mind. They give sanction to some behaviors and remove sanction from others. As George Will has written, "statecraft is soulcraft." The statecraft of the last Republican Congress performed some soulcraft, notably on welfare reform; the question is whether this Republican Congress can summon up the nerve and energy to do the same.

But what of other House Republicans? And what of House Democrats? It is said often that the Republicans will have a hard time holding their majority together, and it is a fact that only 10 defections will leave them short of a 218-vote majority. But it is often true that a legislative party holds together best when its margin is small, and when the consequences of a defection are readily apparent to all. After the 1958 election, when Democrats gained 13 seats in the Senate and 49 in the House, Senate Majority Leader Lyndon Johnson was exultant over the results; but Speaker Sam Rayburn glumly said, "Too many Democrats," and proved to be right as Democrats felt free to spurn party discipline and he and Johnson had a harder time winning votes than they did when Democrats had a bare majority. House Republican leaders did a fine, though not perfect, job of holding their conference together in the 104th Congress, letting a few members take a bye when they must and rallying the rest; this is hard work, in which they didn't have much practice. It helps that Gingrich has close ties to many Republican moderates, to whom he has paid intellectually serious attention going back to the 1980s. As for conservatives, their chief complaint in early 1997 was that he was not pursuing the Republican agenda enough.

If House Republicans have mostly shown great party unity, so have the diminished numbers of long-fissiparous House Democrats. Many Democrats did support much of the Contract with America in 1995, but in 1996 they united around issues like the minimum wage to split Republicans in turn. Moreover, as of early 1997, nary a peep was heard from House Democrats in criticism of the various Clinton and White House scandals. That is not because House Democrats love Clinton or trust him very much—many cried out in dismay when he accepted the goal of a balanced budget in June 1995 and signed welfare reform in August 1996. But they seem to regard him as the main political force working in their favor: they can't have escaped noting that he won 49% of the vote in November 1996 and they won 48.5%, with results uncannily close in dozens of districts, and that when he was in trouble in November 1994 their percentages were lower. The two major themes virtually all Democratic candidates voiced in 1996—denunciations of Gingrich and Medicare "cuts"—did not win them many districts.

Yet there is clearly no Clinton Democratic Party in the House (or in the Senate either). The two top House Democrats, Minority Leader Richard Gephardt and Minority Whip David Bonior, take a different line on policy—economically less respectful of markets and free trade, culturally somewhat more tradition-minded. Gephardt seems clearly to be running for president against Clinton's choice, Al Gore; Bonior is a committed social democrat who has taken great political risks for his causes. Their opposition to adjustment of the Consumer Price Index in March 1996 scared Clinton off the issue, though his top appointees had told Republicans and Democrats alike that he was in favor. With Clinton's eye on a third term (this time for Gore), Gephardt can—and seems inclined to—cast a kind of veto over policies which require bipartisan support for passage. Only about half the House Democrats share their policy views and Bonior's diehard determination to demonize Gingrich. But they have the levers of party leadership and every incentive to persevere. An interesting question: What kind of Democrats will be persuaded to remain in a House where they seem likely if not certain to be in the minority until at least another term or to run against Republicans or for open seats?

Another interesting question: Can peace be made and compromises worked out by moderate Democrats and Republicans? Certainly there is no lack of volunteers. The Blue Dog Democrats and Lunch Bunch Republicans have active organizations and talented leaders, looking seriously into important policy questions and producing on occasion serious policy proposals. They even have some communication with each other as well as with their parties' leaders. But they are not a perfect fit. The Blue Dogs tend to be economically somewhat liberal and culturally rather conservative; they tend to be from the South and West and many are, to take one important example, against gun control. The Lunch Bunch tend to be economically pretty market-oriented and culturally not so traditional; many are from the big metro areas of the Northeast and industrial Midwest, and are ardent backers of gun control. In a huge and diverse country, in the midst of a kind of culture war, it is hard to amass a majority for any position; the miracle is not that the two parties have trouble holding together their coalitions but that they have any coalition to hold together at all. The Blue Dogs and Lunch Bunch may well be there offering solutions, but it is not clear whether others will take them up.

THE SENATE

The Senate, first on the Sunday talk shows, is second in the constitutional order. As the 105th Congress assembled, there was talk that Senate Majority Leader Trent Lott was going to take charge in setting the policy agenda for Congress—plausible talk given his high skills and the woes then besetting Newt Gingrich. But by mid-March it was apparent that for all Lott's efforts he could not pass the balanced budget amendment and could not produce an agreement on the budget or even a public undertaking by the Clinton Administration to back the adjustment of the Consumer Price Index which Bill Clinton had caused it to be known he would definitely support. The problem was not any mistakes by Lott, but the character of the Senate. For today's

Senate is surely not "the greatest deliberative body in the world," as it likes to style itself; it is very seldom deliberative, and if often scarcely a body at all. This is a legislature where it is every man and woman for him or herself, where the whole is equal to a fair lot less than the sum of its parts, where it is far easier to kill someone else's initiative than it is to sustain one's own. But this is perhaps what the Framers intended. With only one-third of its members elected every two years, with a fair number of its members freed from political pressures because of their personal relationship with voters in small or one-party states, with its rules allowing even the politically weakest and personally least regarded of its members to stop the forward motion of legislation for some precious period of time, the Senate supplies some caution to the enthusiasms of the House.

What else it supplies is open to question. The partisan balance of the Senate has shifted as sharply, in percentage terms, as control of the House since Bill Clinton was elected in 1992. There were 58 Democratic senators then, not quite the 60 needed to stop a filibuster, but a strong Democratic position with a Democratic president. But Democrats lost two seats very quickly—one in the Georgia runoff three weeks after the election, the other in May 1993 when Kay Bailey Hutchison won Lloyd Bentsen's seat in Texas by a 2–1 margin. Democrats then proceeded to lose 10 seats in 1994, all eight open seats plus two incumbents, and two more when Richard Shelby and Ben Nighthorse Campbell switched parties in November 1994 and March 1995. Republicans then lost Bob Packwood's Oregon seat to Democrat Ron Wyden in January 1996. But in November 1996 they gained three seats, in Alabama, Arkansas and Nebraska, while losing one, Larry Pressler's in South Dakota: which leaves the Senate 55–45 Republican.

It is a more partisan, more conservative Senate than the Republican Senate of the 1980s. The 13 states of the South (leaving aside industrial West Virginia) now are represented by 19 Republicans and only 7 Democrats in the Senate; one of the latter has announced his retirement in 1998, and two more may. The nine Rocky Mountain states and Alaska are represented by 14 Republicans and only 4 Democrats, two from Nevada and one each from Montana and New Mexico. Almost all of these are staunch conservatives, dedicated to reducing the power of the federal government and cutting spending and taxes. Conservatives have firm control of the Republican Conference. Yet they do not in any sense control the Senate. The 45 Democrats are more than enough to sustain a filibuster. Half a dozen or so Republicans disagree with conservative positions on many issues.

Harry McPherson, who worked for Lyndon Johnson in the 1950s, writes of a Senate made up of whales and minnows—a dozen or so men of large abilities and concerns, and then the rest who circled around waiting to follow. Today's Senate has very few whales and not so many minnows. Daniel Patrick Moynihan stands out, for the strength of his historic vision and his ability to spot issues before their time. But although he is capable of difficult legislative work, as he showed when he passed the ISTEA transportation bill in 1991 and the Clinton budget and tax package in 1993, he is often the prophet ignored, as on welfare reform in 1996. Most committee chairmen and ranking Democrats are competent men and women, highly skilled and of admirable character in very many cases, but they are more workmanlike than inspirational. On the other hand, there are fewer minnows than there were in the 1950s, fewer weak senators who defer to the leadership of others.

Will the Republicans retain control in 1998? The easy answer is, why not? There are two obviously endangered seats. One is in New York where Alfonse D'Amato is opposed by the brainy and publicity-loving Congressman Charles Schumer; but D'Amato has shown the wiliness to survive before. The other is in Indiana, where Dan Coats is retiring and former Governor Evan Bayh is highly popular; but popular governors of one party running in states heavily favoring the other, in Wyoming, Nebraska, and Massachusetts, have lost in the highly charged partisan atmosphere in recent years. Two Democratic retirements announced in early 1997 have given Republicans excellent chances for pickups in Ohio and Kentucky, and Carol Moseley-Braun in Illinois seemed in trouble. Both parties seemed to have a solid lock on 11 seats, which left four Democrats and three Republicans in some jeopardy. Democrats would have to sweep just about every close contest to win back control; Republicans would have to sweep just about every close contest to win the 60 votes needed to stop a filibuster; both results seemed unlikely.

THE PRESIDENCY

The presidency was not expected to be an important office. Article I of the Constitution is about the Congress, and has 10 long sections; Article II, establishing the Presidency, has just four. The longest sets out how the president is elected—much of this had to be scrapped in 1804—and specifies the oath he must take. Section 2 says that the president is commander-in-chief, that he can require the opinion in writing of officers of government, issue pardons and appoint ambassadors and Supreme Court justices and such other officers as Congress may provide for. Section 3 prescribes that he communicate annually to Congress, recommend laws to them, call Congress into session and "shall take care that the laws be faithfully executed." Section 4 is the impeachment clause. Interesting are the omissions. Article II doesn't say that the president can fire officers of government, or set public policy, much less that he "runs the country." Mostly, his powers are what Congress gives him. The Framers' scheme seems pretty simple. In peacetime the president presides, does what Congress requires and little more. In wartime he has greater powers, unspecified, indeed unlikely to be challenged in the midst of great exigencies.

This, one could argue, is how the Presidency has worked in practice. In wartime the president has terrible powers: Lincoln suspended habeas corpus and expanded federal powers vastly. But 20 years later Woodrow Wilson, then a professor of political science, could argue that Congress runs the government and the president matters hardly at all. As a wartime president, Wilson himself exercised powers that would make us quail and, when peace came, saw his grandest policy frustrated when the Senate declined to ratify the peace treaties he had made. The power of the Presidency subsided again in the 1920s, only to be revived by Franklin D. Roosevelt in the terrible economic disorder of the 1930s. Then came the extended experience of war—World War II, the Cold War, Korea, Vietnam—in which the Presidency became the center of government—indeed, as a symbol of the whole country. We depended on presidents to preserve the nation, to prevent a world war; we were always aware that this one individual had the power to blow up the world. We spoke of "the Eisenhower era" and "the Johnson years"; a president's scandal could give its name to our times, "the Watergate era," or to a set of policies, "the Reagan revolution"; a record parodying the president and his family could soar to number one on the hit parade.

But after the American victories in the long Cold War in 1989 and the brief Gulf war in 1991, is the presidency as important any more? One never hears people talking about "the Bush years" or "the Clinton era." When Bill Clinton was elected president, he like almost all Americans had no living memory of a time when presidents were not utterly central to our politics and government, when the office was swelled up to its wartime dimension. But now it seems to have shrunk back toward the size the Framers envisioned it would have in ordinary times. Clinton seems to understand this; at one point he bemoaned that he did not have a real crisis like World War II on which to exercise his talents and win a large place in history.

Clinton has won at least one place in history: he is one of 15 presidents to have won a second term, and the first Democrat to do so since Franklin Roosevelt, before Clinton was born. It was not at all apparent two years before, after the Republicans' stunning victory in the congressional elections, that Clinton would win, or how. It helped certainly that the nation in 1996 was in a time of peace and prosperity; but the same could have been said of 1994, when Clinton clearly would have lost if he had been on the ballot (as he lost for reelection as governor of Arkansas after his first two years). What got Clinton reelected was a combination of verbal and rhetorical skills of a high order, a perseverance and a discipline not much apparent in his first two years, a well-thought-out political strategy and some wily tactics. First comes rhetoric: Bill Clinton's greatest gift is his way with words: he uses the language eloquently, sinuously, with down-home accents when he wants them and soaring elevation the next moment; when folks are angry at him, he can talk them back to his side, as he has done hundreds of times in Arkansas, a state small enough that he could speak personally to every important person and many thousands not so important. His problem in early 1995 was getting people's attention; in March 1995 he was reduced to asserting that he was still "relevant." But he seized the occasion when the Oklahoma City federal building was blown up in April 1995 to sound authentic notes of consolation and to argue for the worthiness of the enterprise of government, and to suggest if only subliminally that those who criticized government were somehow connected to this crime. From that point he once again had the nation's ear.

Then came the disciplined execution of a shrewd political strategy. The idea, as explained by his constant adviser of 1995 and 1996, pollster Dick Morris, was "Triangulation": Clinton would stand not only between the two parties, as he did in much of the campaign of 1992, but above them both, a healer over the bickerers, a national symbol trying to make peace between petulant partisans. Clinton rationed his public statements as he rationed his food: this naturally weight-gaining middle-aged man actually lost 15 or 20 pounds in a position where he is constantly surrounded by tempting food. Clinton watched as the Republican Congress worked to enact its program, only vaguely threatening to use his veto; he stood apart from his fellow Democrats when in June 1995 he acceded to the Republicans' goal of a balanced budget by 2002. And there was a certain wiliness, even dissimulation, in his negotiations with Republican leaders. He lulled them into believing that he shared their goals and was just inches away from agreement with their plans, and let them believe that he would capitulate to them out of weakness as he had on numerous occasions before. But this time he stood up and opposed their plans, vetoed their appropriations and accused them of shutting the government down. Technically, this was not true: Congress had passed, though in some cases tardily, appropriations to keep the government going; it was Clinton's veto that shut it down. But Republicans gleefully welcomed this clarification, unwisely confident that the voters shared their mistrust of government; and Clinton pressed his advantage for all it was worth.

From January 1996 on, it is apparent in hindsight, Clinton was leading in a presidential race whose course did not much change until November. A more supple opponent might have run better than Bob Dole, and a Clinton veto of welfare reform could well have cost him votes. But a presidential election is usually a referendum on the incumbent, and the verdict was yes. But if Clinton clearly won in politics and at the polls, it is questionable whether he won in governance. His economic policy in 1993 had passed by the barest margin and his healthcare finance reform crashed in ruins in 1994. While he won in the polls over the budget controversy, he lost in substance: the compromise budget he signed in early 1996 actually reduced domestic discretionary spending for the first time since 1969—surely not a result he sought when he ran in 1992. To pursue his triangulation strategy, he signed the Welfare Reform Act of 1996, modified slightly to be sure by his negotiations, but in sum eliminating the federal entitlement to welfare which had existed since 1935—something he had never publicly advocated. Similarly, the foreign policy which he was conducting as he was reelected was diametrically opposed to his earlier policies on American engagement in Bosnia, on trade relations and human rights in China, on NATO expansion in Eastern Europe.

In governance Clinton invites comparison with Richard Nixon. Coming to office as a moderate conservative at a time when the Washington establishment and much of the country was still liberal, Nixon largely acquiesced in liberal policies: his administration recognized China and ended American involvement in the Vietnam war; it produced the first racial quota programs, created EPA and OSHA, took the dollar off the gold standard and put government controls on wages and prices. An argument can be made that in policy terms Nixon was the most liberal president of all time. Similarly, Clinton came to office as a moderate liberal at a time when most of the country and a growing part of the Washington establishment was conservative, and he acquiesced in conservative policies: an expansive foreign policy, cuts in spending, an end to the welfare entitlement and most farm subsidies, deregulation of telecommunications and other industries. An argument can be made that his policies on many if not all issues have been more conservative than Ronald Reagan's. Nixon, unlike Clinton, was able to exert great power in foreign affairs as a president in time of war; but of them both it can be said that in domestic politics they were more creatures of their times than shapers of the future.

On election night 1996 Clinton noted that he had waged his last campaign, and many commentators opined that he would now look not for political gain but to his place in history. But there is little evidence that this man who has been running for public office since he was 27 has suddenly given up a preoccupation with electoral politics. There are very many indications that he is looking for further certification of his worthiness by electoral success, most notably his efforts during the 1996 campaign and convention to increase the stature of his Vice President, Al Gore. Clinton surely knows from history that only two presidents have had the satisfaction of seeing their vice presidents elected as their successors, Andrew Jackson in 1836 and Ronald Reagan in 1988, and that those victories were taken, with some good reason, as validations of those presidents' records and the centrality of their importance in Jacksonian America and the Reagan years. What more fitting way to establish Clinton as a masterful president than to secure the election of his vice president, especially one who shares so much of his approach to policy and who has been an important member of his administration? From the arrangements at his Chicago convention to his backdowns from a fight with likely Gore rival Richard Gephardt over adjusting the Consumer Price Index, Clinton has sought to advance Gore's candidacy and fight for a third consecutive Clinton-Gore victory.

Clinton must hope that the prospects for that are not soured by the scandals over campaign fundraising, the first glints of which became public three weeks before election day and much more of which burst into public view in the first months of 1997. The systematic raising of illegal foreign contributions by John Huang and perhaps others, the decision by the DNC not to vet big contributors for possible ethics problems, the fundraising phone calls from the White House in clear violation of Title 18 U.S. Code, Section 607(a) (which prohibits political fundraising in government buildings), the denials of knowledge and involvement that became inoperative as more information came out: these besmirch Clinton and Gore as well, as does Gore's appearance at the April 1996 Buddhist temple fundraiser. Yet these things were not accidental, but were an integral part of the disciplined Clinton-Gore campaign strategy, which required an unprecedented amount of funds for early television advertising. They paid little price for this before the election; perhaps they will pay more later.

LOOKING AHEAD TO 2000

The office of the Presidency may be diminished in this time of peace and devolution of power, but there is no lack of applicants for the job. And no lack of interest. The spring of 1997 may be just the beginning of a presidential term, but it is only two years and nine months away from the 2000 Iowa caucuses and the New Hampshire primary, and by spring 1997 several candidates were already running. The 2000 contest stacks up to be unusual for two reasons. The first is that it stands to be one of the few in our recent history in which no incumbent president is running. The last such was 1988, and before that 1960 and 1928. The second reason is that the size of the fields in the two parties is at odds with their basic character. The Democratic Party has always been fissiparous, a collection of out-people which at its best amounts to a diverse but fractious majority. But the Democrats had no contest for their nomination in 1996 (the first time that was true since 1944) and, as of early 1997, had only a few plausible candidates for 2000. The Republican Party, in contrast, has always been a party with a central faith and a clear sense of hierarchy and order, which has ended up deferring to seniority in its nominations; most recently with Bob Dole. Yet for 2000 there is no Republican with a plausible claim to precedence, and a very large number who could conceivably run. To winnow among them, the Republicans must operate under a system of primaries and caucuses which was largely contrived by Democrats in response to, if not always turning out to be in harmony with, their perceived needs.

The Democrats. Their frontrunner obviously is Al Gore, who ran for the 1988 presidential nomination before he was 40. His obvious chief rival is Dick Gephardt, whom he outlasted in

1988, though both failed to become Jesse Jackson's main opponent—and therefore the nominee—as Michael Dukakis did. Other possible entrants include Senators Bob Kerrey and John Kerry, both Vietnam war heroes but otherwise not particularly alike. Gore's strategy in 1996 and early 1997 was to emerge so strong among the party's fundraising and activist constituencies as to deter Gephardt from running.

Back in 1960 Theodore H. White identified the Democratic Party's three major constituencies as the big city bosses, the southern governors and organized labor. In the late 1990s there are no big city bosses left (even Chicago Mayor Richard M. Daley can't be described as one), only four southern governors (two of whom must leave office in 1998) and organized labor represents less the old CIO industrial unions than public employees (42% of AFL-CIO members are public employees). The greatest source of energy, enthusiasm and elan in the Democratic Party is the feminist left (just as the greatest source of energy, enthusiasm and elan in the Republican Party is the religious right). About 20% of Democratic primary votes are cast by blacks, who will be represented by leftish black politicians at the convention. It is not clear that any of these candidates has a lock on any of these constituencies.

The Republicans. The following is a list of 27 Republicans who have been mentioned as candidates and whose candidacies, if they ran, would be as plausible as those of Lamar Alexander and Steve Forbes in 1996—and that is said not in jest: both came within a few votes of being positioned to win the nomination. They are, in alphabetical order, Lamar Alexander, John Ashcroft, George W. Bush, Patrick Buchanan, Carroll Campbell, Dick Cheney, Elizabeth Dole, John Engler, Steve Forbes, Phil Gramm, John Kasich, Jack Kemp, Trent Lott, Dan Lungren, Connie Mack, John McCain, Don Nickles, George Pataki, Colin Powell, Dan Quayle, Tom Ridge, Fred Thompson, Tommy Thompson, George Voinovich, Christine Todd Whitman, Pete Wilson. It is not possible that all of them will run, and many pretty clearly will not. But many are thinking about it, and not just wistfully as they fall to sleep at night. And there could be more, emerging from the elections of 1998.

PRESIDENT

President William Jefferson (Bill) **Clinton (D)**

Elected 1992, term expires Jan. 2001; born, August 19, 1946, Hope, AR; home, Little Rock, AR; Georgetown University, B.S. 1968; Rhodes Scholar, Oxford University, 1968–70; Yale University, J.D. 1973; Baptist; married (Hillary Rodham).

Career: Professor, University of Arkansas, 1974–76; Democratic Nominee for U.S. House of Representatives, 1974; Arkansas Attorney General, 1976–78; Practicing attorney, 1981–82; Governor of Arkansas, 1978–80, 1982–92.

Office: The White House, 1600 Pennsylvania Ave., NW, Washington, DC 20500, 202-456-1414;
e-mail: president@whitehouse.gov.

VICE PRESIDENT

Vice President Albert (Al) **Gore, Jr.** (**D**)

Elected 1992, term expires, Jan. 2001; born, March 31, 1948, Washington, DC; home, Carthage, TN; Harvard University, B.A. 1969; Vanderbilt School of Religion, 1971–72; Vanderbilt Law School, 1974–76; Baptist; married (Tipper).

Career: Army, 1969–71 (Vietnam); Homebuilding business; Reporter, *Nashville Tennessean*, 1973–76; U.S. House of Representatives, 1976–84; U.S. Senate, 1984–92.

Office: The White House, 1600 Pennsylvania Ave., NW, Washington, DC 20500, 202-456-1414;
e-mail: vice.president@whitehouse.gov.

1996 Presidential Vote

Clinton (D)	47,401,185	(49%)
Dole (R)	39,197,469	(41%)
Perot (I)	8,085,294	(8%)

1992 Presidential Vote

Clinton (D)	44,908,233	(43%)
Bush (R)	39,102,282	(37%)
Perot (I)	19,741,048	(19%)

The People: Est. Pop. 1996: 265,284,000; Pop. 1990: 248,709,873, up 6.7% 1990–1996. 24.8% rural. Median age: 32.9 years. 12.6% 65 years and over. 75.6% White, 11.7% Black, 2.8% Asian, 1% American Indian, 9% Hispanic origin. Households: 55.1% married couple families; 25.6% married couple fams. w. children; 45.3% college educ.; median household income: $30,056; per capita income: $14,420; 64.2% owner occupied housing; median house value: $79,100; median monthly rent: $374. 5.4% Unemployment. 1996 Voting age pop.: 196,511,000. 1996 Turnout: 96,456,345; 49% of VAP. Registered Voters (1996): 146,211,960.

ALABAMA

Montgomery, the capital of Alabama, is a living shrine to two of the greatest upheavals of American history: the Civil War of the 1860s and the civil rights revolution of the 1960s. The restored Greek Revival Capitol stands on a hill overlooking downtown Montgomery where in February 1861 the Confederate Congress convened and Jefferson Davis took the oath of office as President of the Confederacy. Down the hill is the Dexter Avenue Baptist Church, where in December 1956 the 27-year-old Martin Luther King, Jr., led the boycott that began when Rosa Parks refused to move to the back of the bus. The fires of past controversy are occasionally rekindled, as in 1993 when the Confederate Stars and Bars was raised over the Capitol. But today both the Confederacy and the civil rights movement are celebrated, though as time goes on with less emphasis on the first and more on the latter: Maya Lin's circular Civil Rights Memorial in Montgomery, the Civil Rights Institute across the street from the 16th Street Baptist Church in Birmingham's Civil Rights District, the Pettus Bridge in Selma and the Dexter Avenue Baptist Church are among the many sites of civil rights and black history preserved and promoted by the state.

Yet the classic symmetry of the Capitol and the calm simplicity of the black churches are not the whole story. Nature still seems untamed in Alabama, and the raw passions of the first settlers which gave life to these serene buildings often seem ready to break into anger and even violence. There has been a raucous tone to Alabama's history since the first Jacksonian farmers pushed the Indians west and plowed the steeply inclined red clay hills of northern Alabama and the first plantation owners shipped in hundreds of slaves to grow cotton in the dark Black Belt soil. It was the violent reactions of white Alabamans to desegregation in Tuscaloosa, Freedom Riders in Anniston, schoolchildren on the streets of Birmingham and marchers in Selma that finally turned national opinion in favor of the civil rights revolution. Even in Alabama's peaceful economic development is evidence of the clang of metal on rock: miners hacking away in the 1880s at the solid-iron Red Mountain to feed newly cast steel mills glaring in the valley of Birmingham below; motorists of the 1990s speeding past exposed red earth of gouged-out hillsides to interchanges where the factories and Wal-Mart shopping centers have sprouted up.

There is a similar rawness to Alabama's politics, as it has shifted from one of the nation's most Democratic to one of its most Republican states. In the 1930s and 1940s Alabama elected populist Democrats, crusaders against Wall Street and against the local economic potentates they called the "Big Mules": Hugo Black, a senator until he became a Supreme Court justice in 1937; Lister Hill and John Sparkman, who as senators sponsored landmark health and housing legislation; a House delegation that passed housing, health and public works bills. The dominant governor was Kissin' Jim Folsom, elected in 1946 and 1954, outsized in size and eloquence, whose career ended in 1962 when he appeared drunk in a late campaign appearance on the new medium of television and lost the governor's race to his onetime protege, a young lawyer named George Wallace.

While Wallace was politicking in the Capitol, Martin Luther King was leading what turned out to be a civil rights revolution whose moral force he was among the first to comprehend. In the South of that day what King demanded seemed impossible, and in the short run it helped the politicians who most strongly proclaimed their opposition to desegregation. But in the long run it changed public life in America and in Alabama. But not before George Wallace made himself a national figure. Believing he had lost the 1958 governor's primary because he was "out-segged," he vowed that he never would be again. Elected governor in 1962, he pledged to stand in the schoolhouse door to prevent desegregation—a charade, but a dangerous one, for it encouraged violent resistance. It was the acts of Alabama officials—Birmingham commissioner Bull

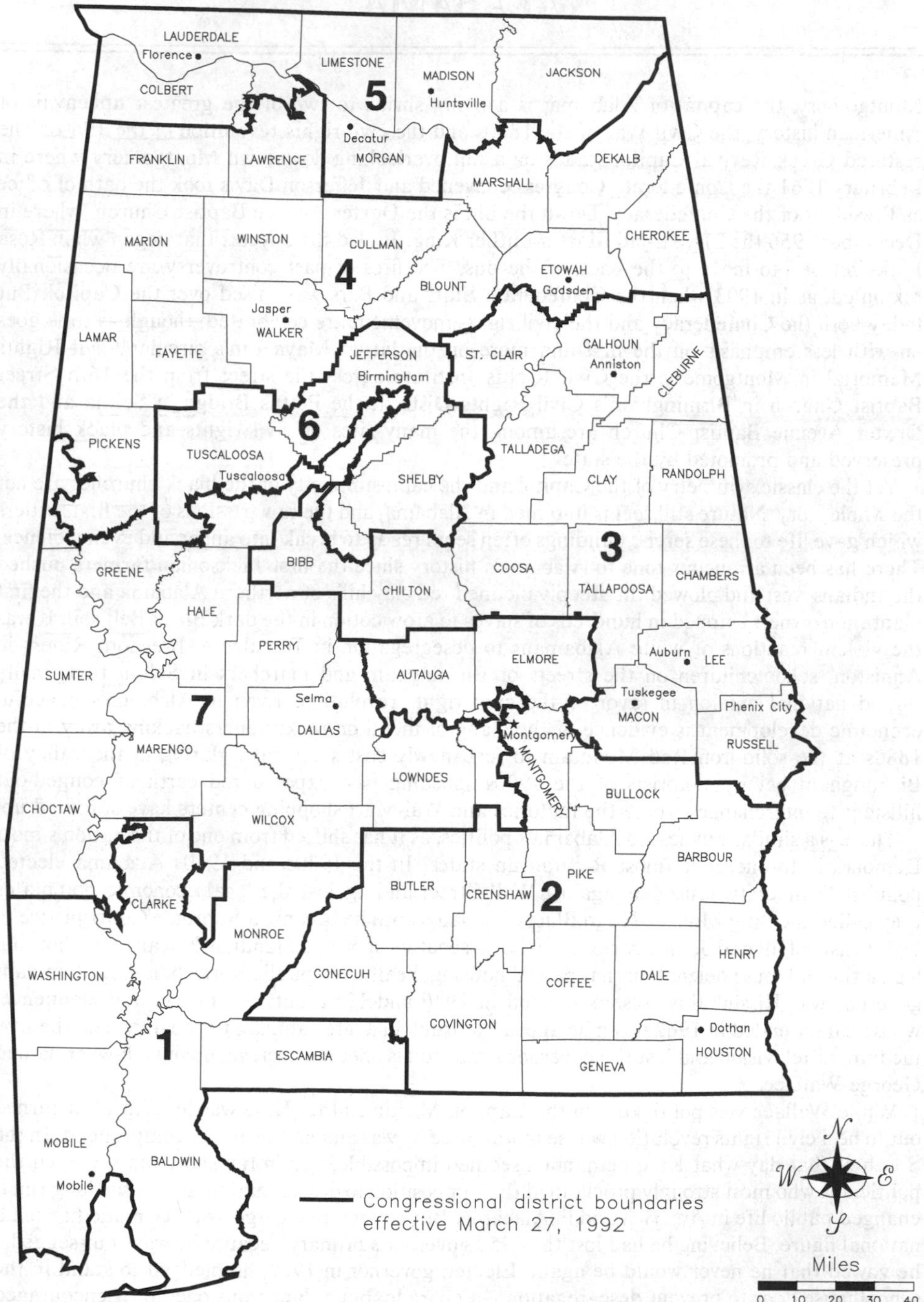
LAUDERDALE
Florence
COLBERT
LIMESTONE
MADISON
Huntsville
JACKSON
5
Decatur
FRANKLIN
LAWRENCE
MORGAN
DEKALB
MARSHALL
MARION
WINSTON
CULLMAN
CHEROKEE
ETOWAH
Gadsden
4
BLOUNT
Jasper
WALKER
LAMAR
FAYETTE
JEFFERSON
Birmingham
ST. CLAIR
CALHOUN
Anniston
CLEBURNE
6
PICKENS
TUSCALOOSA
Tuscaloosa
TALLADEGA
SHELBY
CLAY
RANDOLPH
3
GREENE
BIBB
COOSA
CHAMBERS
TALLAPOOSA
CHILTON
HALE
PERRY
ELMORE
Auburn
LEE
SUMTER
AUTAUGA
Tuskegee
MACON
7
Selma
DALLAS
Phenix City
Montgomery
MONTGOMERY
RUSSELL
MARENGO
LOWNDES
BULLOCK
CHOCTAW
WILCOX
BARBOUR
BUTLER
PIKE
CRENSHAW
2
CLARKE
MONROE
HENRY
WASHINGTON
CONECUH
COFFEE
DALE
COVINGTON
Dothan
1
ESCAMBIA
HOUSTON
GENEVA
MOBILE
BALDWIN
Mobile
N
W
E
S
Congressional district boundaries
effective March 27, 1992
Miles
0 10 20 30 40

Connor's police dogs and fire hoses in 1963, Sheriff Jim Clark's cordons in Selma in 1965—which, transmitted on evening newscasts, made civil rights a national issue. The North was no longer able to turn its eyes away from southern segregation, and most Americans decided they must support the Civil Rights Act of 1964 and the Voting Rights Act of 1965.

Despite his defeat, Wallace went national. With a shrewd sense of ordinary voters' resentment at elites' cultural liberalism, Wallace ran well in the 1964 and 1972 northern Democratic presidential primaries, and as a third-party candidate in the 1968 presidential race won 13.5% of the vote. He was partially paralyzed by a gunshot wound while campaigning in May 1972, and lost all force as a national politician when he lost to Jimmy Carter in the March 1976 Florida primary. But he remained the key figure in Alabama, retiring as governor in 1978 but returning to office in 1982 until his final retirement in 1986. In the 1990s he has been a sad figure, paralyzed and deaf, often in dreadful pain, yet seeking the support of the blacks he had once scorned, meeting with the grown-up student he tried to block in the schoolhouse door. "The South has changed," he said, "and for the better."

Unfortunately, in the Wallace years Alabama lost important ground. While Atlanta was peacefully desegregating and beginning three decades of vibrant white-collar growth, Birmingham was violently resisting the civil rights movement, only to see the shrinkage of its once substantial blue-collar base—the steel industry—and an outflow of talented people of all races. The state's economy, regarded as progressive when manufacturing was the leading edge of growth, seemed backward at the end of the Wallace era. The big steel mills of Birmingham turned cold as demand for steel fell; the shipyards of Mobile scrambled for work; the electric generators of TVA, once hailed as signs of progress, were condemned for burning dirty coal or allegedly hazardous nuclear fuel.

Politically, Wallace probably delayed for a generation the rise of the Republicans in Alabama and the non-metropolitan South. He gave cover to conservative Democratic candidates and preempted campaign money from Republicans. Yet starting at the top of the ticket, Alabama has moved toward Republicans. It has voted for Republicans in five straight presidential elections, with Bob Dole carrying six of seven congressional districts. It has elected Republican governors in the last three contests. By the 1990s it was electing Republicans to downballot state offices. In 1996, when the last congressman, Tom Bevill, elected as a Wallace Democrat retired after 30 years, the Alabama House delegation became 5–2 Republican. The Alabama legislature, elected every four years, is still heavily Democratic, but moving toward Republicans also.

The opposing political forces partly resemble those of 50 years ago. "Big Mules," angry at Alabama's ultraliberal tort law, are pro-Republican, but small business and tradition-minded Protestants are a bigger source of support; Republican enclaves are no longer confined to affluent urban precincts, but have spread out on the Interstates over the hills to sprawling new subdivisions.

Institutionally, Republicans are only beginning to achieve coherence: Governor Fob James and Senator Richard Shelby were first elected to office in the 1970s as Democrats and only in the 1990s became Republicans. The Democrats' institutional base is among teachers' unions and trial lawyers; their 1990 gubernatorial candidate had been a teacher and head of the Alabama Education Association and their 1996 Senate candidate was a leading trial lawyer. But Democratic votes in close races come mostly from blacks, who were excluded from electoral politics until 1965; among whites they are strongest in the TVA counties in the north, though they have been losing these on occasion. Overall the tilt is toward Republicans: the suburbs have been gaining and the Black Belt has been losing population.

Indeed, the Democrats have struggled to stay in power by staging what seem like banana republic coups—and have eventually lost anyway. In 1986, the state Democratic Party stripped a conservative of the gubernatorial nomination after he won the primary by 8,000 votes, and gave it instead to a liberal who lost in the fall to Guy Hunt, a Primitive Baptist preacher and former Amway salesman. Democratic Attorney General Jimmy Evans indicted Hunt for converting to personal use $200,000 from an inaugural fund; he was convicted in April 1993 and removed from office, replaced by Democrat Jim Folsom Jr. But in 1994 Folsom and Evans lost to Republicans Fob James and Jeff Sessions. In another close 1994 race, it appeared that Chief Justice Sonny Hornsby, strongly pro-trial lawyer, had lost to Republican Perry Hooper. But the state Supreme Court decided to count 2,000 absentee ballots that were not properly notarized or witnessed, and declared Hornsby the winner. He stayed in office until a federal court invalidated the absentees and declared Hooper the winner in October 1995. The fighting spirit is still very much alive in Alabama politics.

Governor. Fob James has been an Alabama celebrity off and on for 40 years. He was an All-American halfback at Auburn in 1954, played pro ball for the Montreal Alouettes. At 28 he started an athletic equipment business and made a fortune producing high-density plastic barbells. He was elected governor as a Democrat in 1978, though he had been active in Republican politics two years earlier, and in office claimed credit for raising student test scores and generating business investment. But he did not run for reelection in 1982, when George Wallace won his last term. He moved to the Gulf area and founded a new business and by 1994 was ready to run for governor again, as a Republican. Well known and well financed, James won 40% in a six-candidate primary and then beat Mobile-based state Senator Ann Bedsole in the runoff 62%–38%. In the general he was the underdog to Folsom, holder of a great name and incumbent for 18 months after the conviction of Guy Hunt. Folsom took the Confederate flag off the Capitol, pushed for casino gambling, worked with the legislature on education financing. But in 1994 he was accused of giving a Medicaid contract to a firm co-founded by his father-in-law and incorporated by 7th District Congressman Earl Hilliard. Folsom beat 1990 nominee Paul Hubbert by only 54%–41% in the primary but was edged out by James in November by 10,000 votes.

James blasted Folsom's "Outcomes Based Education," for teaching values rather than skills and costing $1 billion. In 1995 James pushed an education reform through the legislature which called for the rigorous teaching of basics; he opposed Goals 2000, saying it would mean too much federal control. He opposed casino gambling. He opposed any moves to increase taxes for education or other purposes. He instituted chain gangs for prisoners in 1995, but disbanded them a year later. He got changes in the rules for absentee ballots (Republicans claimed Black Belt counties let Chicagoans and Detroiters cast absentees in Alabama). He supports abortion restrictions and issued an executive order banning same-sex marriage. Alabama got Mercedes to build a plant in Tuscaloosa in 1993, with a record $300 million in concessions and incentives; James got a generalized incentive program and in 1996 boasted of attracting $2.7 billion of new investment without such vast incentives.

In 1996 James was frustrated when the legislature rejected a bill to require a three-fifths supermajority to raise taxes and, more important, failed to pass tort reform, probably the largest state issue. In 1991 and 1992 the state Supreme Court overturned the legislature's 1987 tort reform, and Alabama quickly became a trial lawyer's paradise. It was in Alabama that BMW buyer Ira Gore collected $4 million in punitive damages because his car had been repainted; the U.S. Supreme Court actually threw this verdict out as "grossly excessive"—as it did four more Alabama damage awards. Punitive damage awards in Alabama from 1989–96 totalled $80 million, compared to $19 million in Georgia, Tennessee, and Mississippi combined. James came to office determined to change the state Supreme Court, and did, as Chief Justice Sonny Hornsby was finally forced by a federal court to obey the voters' 1994 verdict and leave office in October 1995. But by April 1997 James still could not get a cap on punitive damages and other reforms through the legislature; they passed in the House but were blocked in the Senate by Senator Roger Bedford and Lieutenant Governor Don Siegelman, who had received some $750,000 in contributions from trial lawyers. In 1996 trial lawyers and the Business Council financed expensive campaigns waging another titanic battle. Incumbent pro-trial lawyer Democratic Justice Kenneth Ingram was challenged by Republican Harold See. Trial lawyers claimed that See abandoned his wife and children; Republicans said "rich personal injury lawyers are trying to buy the Alabama Supreme Court." See won 53%–47%, giving the anti-trial lawyer forces a 4–3 margin on the Supreme Court. Some claim Alabama politics has been sidetracked by these debates; but tort law probably channels far more money, to one side or the other, than ordinary state government programs.

In 1998, in contrast to 1982, James has reason to look forward to easy renomination and at least an even chance of winning the general in this increasingly Republican state. Possible Democratic opponents include Don Siegelman and Paul Hubbert. In the meantime James has a weekly radio talk show, "Fob James Live."

Senior Senator. Richard Shelby grew up in Birmingham, the son of a steelworker. He stayed in Tuscaloosa after earning degrees from the University of Alabama, and went into law practice with Walter Flowers, later a conservative Democratic congressman who voted for the impeachment of Richard Nixon; Shelby was well enough politically connected to be elected state senator in 1970, at 36. When Flowers ran for the Senate in 1978, and lost the Democratic primary to Howell Heflin, Shelby ran for his House seat. The critical contest was the Democratic runoff against Chris McNair, a black legislator whose daughter had been killed in the 1963 Birmingham church bombing. The district had the highest black percentage in Alabama at that time, but Shelby compiled a conservative voting record once in office, opposing the Voting Rights Act extension and the Martin Luther King Holiday. In the 1986 Senate race, he won the primary with 51% after getting a liberal to withdraw, then ran TV ads attacking incumbent Jeremiah Denton, a retired admiral who had been a prisoner of war in Vietnam, for voting to cut Social Security and owning two Mercedes (not a likely negative now, with the Mercedes plant in Tuscaloosa); Shelby won by 7,000 votes.

In the Senate Shelby at first attracted little notice. If his vote helped Democrats regain control after six years in the minority, it was usually cast on the conservative side of substantive issues. He voted for the confirmation of Clarence Thomas and for the Gulf war resolution. He voted against the campaign finance bill supported by almost all Democrats and he voted for the Strategic Defense Initiative. He was a major sponsor of a law to enforce court orders on fathers who default on child support payments. After a young Shelby aide was murdered a few blocks from the Capitol, Shelby pushed through a law requiring the District of Columbia to hold a referendum on capital punishment (it lost). In 1992 he beat Republican Richard Sellers easily, 65%–33%; this broke the political jinx on this seat which, before Shelby's election in 1986, had four occupants in ten years.

Shelby's break with the Democratic Party came soon after Bill Clinton took office. In February 1993, angered by Shelby's criticism of the president's just released economic plan—"the taxman cometh"—Clinton strategists ostentatiously decided to make an example of him and Shelby ostentatiously decided to make a display of his independence. At a meeting in which Vice President Al Gore tried to persuade Shelby to support the plan, Shelby turned to the 19 Alabama TV cameras there and, embarrassing Gore, further denounced the Clinton program as "high on taxes, low on spending cuts." As punishment, a multi-million dollar space facility was moved from Alabama to Texas. But, as Clinton's ratings slid downward, this only raised Shelby's popularity ratings to the highest level in the state, making a politician previously known more for his suppleness of maneuver now appear an embattled defender of principle. In retrospect this was a harbinger of the 1994 elections: a state long hungry for federal largess was happy to give up pork in order to get less spending and a lower deficit. Relentlessly but without evident rancor, Shelby voted against the administration again and again and lined up with Republicans on almost every partisan issue, calling for the resignation of Deputy Treasury Secretary Roger Altman and criticizing the Democrats' healthcare plan as "ill-conceived, unworkable and unwanted by the American people."

So it was not much of a surprise when, the day after Republicans regained control of the Senate in 1994, Shelby announced he was switching parties and increased the Republican majority to 53–47. Republicans happily allowed him to keep his seniority on the Banking Committee, ahead of those elected as Republicans in the same year, and gave him seats on

Appropriations and its Defense Subcommittee and on Intelligence as well; he chaired the Treasury-Postal Appropriations Subcommittee, which has jurisdiction over the IRS, and in 1997 moved over to chair the Transportation Subcommittee. He became chairman of Intelligence in 1997 when Arlen Specter rotated off and Richard Lugar chose to remain chairman of Agriculture.

As a Republican, Shelby has maintained his conservative record and has sponsored many conservative measures: the balanced budget amendment, English as the official language, prohibiting takings of land without compensation under the Endangered Species and Wetlands Acts. He was an early supporter of the adoption tax credit passed in 1996. He was the Senate sponsor of House Majority Leader Dick Armey's flat tax. He sought to cut legal immigration to 350,000 annually. On the Banking Committee he backed regulatory relief and was a Clinton critic on Whitewater. He wants to change the 1994 crime act to require 48 hours of work for prisoners before any recreational activities. He wants to stop taxation of state prepaid college tuition funds (Alabama has one). As Intelligence chairman, he criticized Anthony Lake's nomination as CIA director because of his role in allowing Iranian arms sales to Bosnian Muslims in 1994 and his involvement in Demcratic fundraising efforts in 1996; in March 1997, Lake withdrew his name from consideration, calling his confirmation process "nasty and brutish." Shelby presided over the less controversial confirmation of George Tenet in April 1997.

Shelby's seat is up in 1998. Since his party switch he has been a tough partisan, campaigning against Alabama Democratic House members Bud Cramer and Earl Hilliard in 1996. He may have spirited Democratic opposition, perhaps from 1994 nominee Roger Bedford, but recent electoral trends and his fundraising ability make him the favorite to win.

Junior Senator. Alabama's junior senator, Jeff Sessions, had the satisfaction of being elected in 1996 to replace the Democrat who had blocked his nomination to a federal judgeship in 1986, Howell Heflin. They are an interesting contrast, a personification of changes in southern and Alabama politics. Heflin was 75 in 1996, a huge man who styled himself a country judge, a longtime trial lawyer who opposed George Wallace and was elected state Chief Justice, a three-term senator who was conservative on some issues but also cast key votes for the Democratic leadership, such as the vote against Judge Robert Bork. Sessions, elected at 49, is a career prosecutor who has spent most of his life on the public payroll, a thoroughgoing conservative not unacquainted with controversy.

Sessions grew up in Alabama's Black Belt, practiced law in a small town near the Tennessee Valley, became a federal prosecutor and then practiced law in Mobile. He was appointed U.S. Attorney in 1981, at 36, where he became known as a tough, aggressive prosecutor. In 1985 he was nominated for federal judge, but was attacked by some liberals for "gross insensitivity" in racial matters, and defended by conservatives; Heflin voted against him in the Judiciary Committee and his nomination never went to the floor. In 1994 Sessions ran against state Attorney General Jimmy Evans, who had successfully prosecuted Governor Guy Hunt the year before. Sessions won that race 57%–43% and, when Heflin announced his retirement in March 1995, Sessions immediately became the favorite to win the seat.

But he did not win it unopposed. In another era, the leading candidate might well have been Congressman Glen Browder, a political scientist with 14 years in public office, including three as secretary of State and five years as congressman from the 3d District covering both the Birmingham and Montgomery media markets. But in the Democratic primary Browder hesitated before running and was outflanked and outcampaigned by candidates on his left. One was Natalie Davis, a Birmingham-Southern College political scientist and pollster who traveled around the state in a bus. Another was Roger Bedford, state Senator and trial lawyer, with the kind of dramatic past that seemed so resonant in campaign year 1996: in 1989, while running for attorney general, he was diagnosed with terminal cancer; instead he survived and nearly won the Democratic runoff. Bedford raised lots of money from trial lawyers and was endorsed by key public employee unions and black organizations—the heart of today's Alabama Democratic

Party. Bedford won 45% in the June 4 primary, to 29% for Browder and 23% for Davis. Browder won 63% in his home district, but only 22% elsewhere; Davis carried Mobile and Birmingham and came close in Huntsville, with 51% in those areas, but only 15% elsewhere. In the June 25 runoff, Browder attacked Bedford for his support of NAFTA and gambling and his trial lawyer backing. But Bedford had $400,000 to Browder's $75,000 coming out of the primary, and was the better campaigner as well, shaking hands in barbecue festivals and speaking eloquently, placing crisp $100 bills in the collection plates of black churches. Bedford carried everything outside Browder's home district and won 62%–38%.

But major electoral decisions in Alabama are no longer the monopoly of the Democratic primary. In 1986 939,000 Alabamans voted in the Democratic primary for governor and 29,000 in the Republican primary, 3% of the total. In 1996 315,000 Alabamans voted in the Democratic primary for senator and 213,000 in the Republican primary, 40% of the total; seven Republicans and only four Democrats ran. Sessions started running early, avoided debates and controversy, and relied on his base in southern Alabama, territory that not long ago cast almost no Republican primary votes. The strongest competitor was long distance carrier executive Sid McDonald, who ultimately spent more than $1 million, attacking Sessions for office-hopping, accepting a lenient plea bargain for a murderer, and improperly favoring certain tobacco and insurance companies. From Birmingham north, it was a close race: McDonald led Sessions there June 4 by 30%–29%. But in the rest of the state Sessions led 48%–12%, for a 38%–22% statewide margin. In the runoff McDonald continued his attacks and Sessions ducked debates. McDonald extended his lead north from Birmingham, 54%–46%, but almost half the votes were cast to the south, and there Sessions led 73%–27%, for a 59%–41% statewide victory.

Bedford also proved the better campaigner in the general, was competitive in fundraising, and ran close in the polls. "The old liberal days of tax and spend are over," he insisted, and opposed abortion, gun control, and gays in the military. He bragged of his support for tough-on-crime laws and attacked Sessions for the early release of an embezzler who then killed his former mistress. In a state traditionally dependent on federal dollars, he said that "government can't walk away from problems because that will only make them worse," and accused Sessions of backing "the extreme Newt Gingrich agenda." Sessions avoided debates, at which Bedford excelled, and attacked the Democrat as a Ted Kennedy backer and for leading the battle against tort reform in the Alabama Senate in January 1996. He called government "a ball and chain on private enterprise" and signed the Americans for Tax Reform anti-tax pledge, while Bedford didn't. He accused Bedford of steering a $198,000 grant to a lumber company which was his largest source of income. Sessions won 52%–45%, with his largest percentages in the suburbanizing counties surrounding Alabama's cities, leading in five of seven congressional districts; Bedford carried the Black Belt and many rural counties in the north.

Sessions is likely to be one of the most conservative members of the Senate. With help from his Pascagoula, Mississippi, neighbor, Majority Leader Trent Lott, he won seats on Environment and Public Works and Judiciary, which rejected him just a decade before.

Presidential politics. Alabama is pretty firmly established as one of the most Republican states in presidential elections; it was a sign of Bill Clinton's confidence that he stopped there in the last days of the 1996 campaign. Alabama's presidential primary, held on Super Tuesday in the 1980s, was moved to June in 1992. The 662,000 Democrats who turned out in 1996 were about half black; among the 211,000 Republicans who voted, Bob Dole led Pat Buchanan 76%–16%.

Congressional districting. The Voting Rights Act, as revised in 1982, was the engine that drove Alabama's congressional redistricting in 1992. The plan adopted was proposed by Republicans and ordered into effect by a federal court. The 68% black 7th District, stretching from central Birmingham through the Black Belt counties to downtown Montgomery, was the only Clinton district in 1992 and 1996. Republicans in 1992 captured and have since easily held the once competitive 2d and formerly Democratic 6th Districts, from which many blacks were redistricted into the 7th.

The People: Est. Pop. 1996: 4,273,000; Pop. 1990: 4,040,587, up 5.8% 1990–1996. 1.6% of U.S. total, 23d largest; 40% rural. Median age: 34.9 years. 13% 65 years and over. 73.3% White, 25.2% Black, 1% Asian, 1% Hispanic origin. Households: 57.0% married couple families; 27% married couple fams. w. children; 37% college educ.; median household income: $23,597; per capita income: $11,486; 70.5% owner occupied housing; median house value: $53,700; median monthly rent: $229. 5.1% Unemployment. 1996 Voting age pop.: 3,220,000. 1996 Turnout: 1,534,349; 48% of VAP. Registered voters (1996): 2,738,050; no party registration.

Political Lineup: Governor, Fob James (R); Lt. Gov., Don Siegelman (D); Secy. of State, Jim Bennett (R); Atty. Gen., Bill Pryor (R); Treasurer, Lucy Baxley (D); Auditor, Pat Duncan (R); State Senate, 35 (23 D, 12 R); Senate President, Dwayne Freeman (D); State House, 105 (71 D, 34 R); House Speaker, James Clark (D). Senators, Richard C. Shelby (R) and Jeff Sessions (R). Reps., 7 (5 R and 2 D).

Elections Division: 334-242-7210; **Filing Deadline for U.S.Congress**: April 3, 1998.

1996 Presidential Vote

Dole (R)	768,826	(50%)
Clinton (D)	662,066	(43%)
Perot (I)	92,628	(6%)

1992 Presidential Vote

Bush (R)	804,283	(48%)
Clinton (D)	690,080	(41%)
Perot (I)	183,109	(11%)

1996 Republican Presidential Primary

Dole (R)	160,097	(76%)
Buchanan (R)	33,409	(16%)
Other	18,427	(8%)

GOVERNOR

Gov. Fob James (R)

Elected 1994; term expires Jan. 1999. b. Sept. 15, 1934, Lanett; home, Magnolia Springs; Auburn U., B.S. 1955; Episcopalian; married (Bobbie).

Career: Army Corps. of Engineers, 1957–58; Pro football player, Montreal Allouettes, 1956–57; Construction superintendent, 1958–62; Founder & Chmn., Diversified Products Inc., 1962–78; AL Gov., 1979–82; Co-owner, Orange Beach Marina, 1982; CEO, Coastal Erosion Control Inc., 1988; CEO, Escambia Cnty. Environmental Corp., 1992.

Office: Alabama State Capitol, 11 S. Union St., Montgomery 36130, 334-242-7150; Fax: 334-242-4407; Web site: www.alaweb.asc.edu .

Election Results

1994 gen.	Fob James (R)	604,926	(50%)
	James E. Folsom, Jr.(D)	594,169	(49%)
1994 runoff	Fob James (R)	130,233	(62%)
	Ann Bedsole (R)	78,338	(38%)
1994 prim.	Fob James (R)	84,019	(40%)
	Ann Bedsole (R)	54,449	(26%)
	Winton Blount (R)	51,785	(24%)
	Mickey Kirkland (R)	18,538	(9%)
	Others	3,680	(2%)
1990 gen.	Harold Guy Hunt (R)	633,520	(52%)
	Paul R. Hubbert (D)	582,106	(48%)

SENATORS

Sen. Richard C. Shelby (R)

Elected 1986, seat up 1998; b. May 6, 1934, Birmingham; home, Tuscaloosa; U. of AL, B.A. 1957, LL.B. 1963; Presbyterian; married (Annette Nevin).

Career: Practicing atty., 1963–78; AL Senate, 1970–78; U.S. House of Reps., 1978–1986.

DC Office: 110 HSOB 20510, 202-224-5744; Fax: 202-224-3416; e-mail: senator@shelby.senate.gov.

State Offices: Birmingham, 205-731-1384; Mobile, 334-694-4164; Montgomery, 334-223-7303; Tuscaloosa, 205-759-5047.

Committees: *Appropriations* (9th of 15 R): Defense; Foreign Operations; Transportation (Chmn.); Treasury, Postal Service & General Government; VA, HUD & Independent Agencies. *Banking, Housing & Urban Affairs* (3rd of 10 R): Financial Institutions & Regulatory Relief; Housing Opportunity & Community Development; Securities. *Intelligence (Select)* (Chmn. of 10 R). *Aging (Special)* (5th of 10 R).

Group Ratings

	ADA	ACLU	AFS	LCV	CFA	CON	NFIB	COC	ACU	NTLC	CHC
1996	5	12	0	0	21	42	79	77	90	100	100
1995	5	—	0	0	19	54	—	89	91	—	—

National Journal Ratings

	1995 LIB — 1995 CONS			1996 LIB — 1996 CONS		
Economic	26%	—	71%	21%	—	78%
Social	0%	—	88%	0%	—	72%
Foreign	8%	—	81%	32%	—	65%

Key Votes of the 104th Congress

1. Reduce Medicare Growth $	Y	5. Flag Amendment	Y	9. Anti-Missle Defense	Y
2. Lmt. Prod. Liab. Damages	N	6. Endangered Species	N	10. Cuban Embargo	Y
3. Increase Min. Wage	Y	7. Gay Employment Rights	N	11. Bar Bosnia Troop $	N
4. Welfare Reform	Y	8. Ovrd. Part. Birth Veto	Y	12. Cut Vietnam Aid	N

Election Results

1992 general	Richard C. Shelby (D)	1,022,698	(65%)	($2,807,764)
	Richard Sellers (R)	522,015	(33%)	($149,578)
	Other	31,811	(2%)	
1992 primary	Richard C. Shelby (D)	304,957	(62%)	
	Chris McNair (D)	136,836	(28%)	
	Bob Miller (D)	28,432	(6%)	
	Mrs. Frank Ross Stewart (D)	25,956	(5%)	
1986 general	Richard C. Shelby (D)	609,360	(50%)	($2,258,547)
	Jeremiah Denton (R)	602,537	(50%)	($4,621,163)

Sen. Jeff Sessions (R)

Elected 1996, seat up 2002; b. Dec. 24, 1946, Hybert; home, Mobile: Huntingdon Col., B.A. 1969, U. of AL, J.D. 1973; Methodist; married (Mary).

Career: Army Reserves, 1973–86; Practicing atty., 1973–75, 1977–81, 1993–94; Asst. U.S. Atty., 1975–77; U.S. Atty., 1981–93; AL Atty. Gen., 1994–96.

DC Office: 495 RSOB 20510, 202-224-4124; Fax: 202-224-3149; e-mail: senator@sessions.senate.gov.

State Offices: Birmingham, 205-731-1500; Huntsville, 205-747-9303; Mobile, 334-690-3167; Montgomery, 334-265-9507.

Committees: *Environment & Public Works* (10th of 10 R): Clean Air, Wetlands, Private Property & Nuclear Safety; Superfund, Waste Control & Risk Assessment. *Judiciary* (10th of 10 R): Administrative Oversight & the Courts; Youth Violence (Chmn.). *Ethics (Select)* (3rd of 3 R). *Joint Economic Committee* (6th of 10 Sens.).

Group Ratings and Key Votes: Newly Elected

Election Results

1996 general	Jeff Sessions (R)	786,436	(52%)	($3,862,359
	Roger Bedford (D)	681,651	(45%)	($2,284,801)
	Others	31,306	(2%)	
1996 runoff	Jeff Sessions (R)	81,681	(59%)	
	Sid McDonald (R)	56,156	(41%)	
1996 primary	Jeff Sessions (R)	80,694	(38%)	
	Sid McDonald (R)	47,320	(22%)	
	Charles Woods (R)	23,796	(11%)	
	Frank McRight (R)	21,818	(10%)	
	Walter Clark (R)	18,513	(9%)	
	Jimmy Blake (R)	15,305	(7%)	
	Others	7,600	(4%)	
1990 general	Howell T. Heflin (D)	717,814	(61%)	($3,437,073)
	Bill Cabaniss (R)	467,190	(39%)	($1,853,869)

FIRST DISTRICT

Mobile, the port where the Tombigbee and Alabama Rivers flow into the Gulf of Mexico, was long a key point on the American frontier. Spanish until after the Revolutionary War, it was wrested away by threats of war from Secretary of State John Quincy Adams. During the Civil War it was one of the major Confederate ports; here in 1864 Admiral David Farragut, while steaming into the harbor lashed to his mast, cried, "Damn the torpedoes! Full speed ahead." Today, Mobile is full of graceful signs of its slightly exotic past: behind the docks and rail lines are downtown buildings and old houses with Spanish motifs, French accents, or tropical Art Deco lines. Further inland are neighborhoods with spacious houses, often with double porches, overhung by huge live oaks, graced sometimes with Spanish moss. Mobile is a Gulf Coast version of Charleston or a smaller, more comfortable New Orleans, with a taste for shellfish and spicy food and an even older Mardi Gras. As befits a frontier city with a martial past, Mobile is bristling with arms: one of the city's proudest possessions is the battleship *U.S.S. Alabama*, moored at the head of Mobile Bay, with its guns aimed out toward the Gulf.

Mobile's economy was based originally on docks and shipyards, factories and terminals, but with a determination to impose touches of beauty on its hot, flat landscape. For years this southern seaboard of the Confederacy and the Union has been one of the most hawkish parts of America, and today it is solidly Republican in national elections. But its economy is also thriving again; the shipyards and chemical plants have been busy and upriver new timber and paper mills are running.

Mobile is the focus of Alabama's 1st Congressional District, which extends north along the lazily flowing Tombigbee and Alabama rivers, near the old forts and mansions. This was the home of great writers—Harper Lee, whose *To Kill a Mockingbird* is set here, and her childhood playmate Truman Capote; and Winston Groom, author of *Forrest Gump*—and of old-fashioned southern traditions still lovingly maintained. Also here are surviving back-country settlements of blacks and Cajans (who may or may not be descended from Louisiana Cajuns) and Creek Indians. To the south, along the shores of the Gulf of Mexico, are fast-growing condominium communities; the glorious Gulf beaches are one of the South's best-kept secrets and this is one of the fastest-growing—and most Republican— parts of Alabama.

The congressman from the 1st District is Sonny Callahan, a Republican with a rags-to-riches biography, a party-switcher who now chairs one of the key subcommittees in the House. The oldest boy in a family of nine children whose father died young, Callahan went to work at the age of 12, during World War II; fortunately, the boss was his uncle, a warehouse company owner. He served in the Navy during Korea, then rose to become president of the company at 32 and expanded into real estate and insurance. Like so many go-getters, he ran for the state legislature and was elected at 38. As a Democrat, he lost the 1982 primary for lieutenant governor to liberal Bill Baxley. Then 1st District Republican Congressman Jack Edwards decided to retire in 1984 after 20 years and asked Callahan to run as a Republican; he did and won, with 61% in the Republican primary and 51% in the general. He has been reelected easily and has one of the most conservative voting records in the House.

In the House Callahan hip-hopped from one committee to another for a decade, always of course in the minority. In 1993 he got a seat on Appropriations; two years later, after Republicans won control of the House and three more senior Republicans on the panel took other chairmanships, he became part of the "College of Cardinals" as chairman of the Foreign Operations Appropriations Subcommittee, with power over the foreign aid budget. In his first five Congresses, he seldom voted for foreign aid bills. In the 103d Congress he had tried to put conditions on and cut aid to Russia, without much success. In the 104th he insisted he didn't want to cut humanitarian aid, but did want to sharply cut discretionary non-military aid; and he did. The 1996 budget appropriated $12.4 billion in foreign aid, about $2.4 billion less than the Clinton Administration recommended, and 1997's appropriation of $12.2 billion was some $700 million less that the administration sought. This was criticized by international agencies but passed with the support of 167 Democrats.

Like many conservatives, Callahan insists that voters are "sick of being asked to pay more, only to make government bigger, but not necessarily better." But he also tends to local government projects. He helped fund the Orange Beach hurricane evacuation route, the I-10 Mobile Causeway fog detection system, the Weeks Bay estuarine reserve. On environmental issues he has pushed for more lenient recycling standards for paper manufacturers and fought to preserve the Coastal Zone Management program.

Callahan's lightly funded 1996 opponent, Don Womack, called him a "trained seal for Newt Gingrich"—evidently not a telling attack, since Callahan won with 64%. He is now dean of the Alabama delegation, and has voted for term limits though he doesn't share his constituents' support for them. But he may not stay forever: he lives on a houseboat which, he explains, he can take back to the 1st District when he retires.

The People: Pop. 1990: 577,375; 34% rural; 13% age 65+; 69% White; 28% Black; 1% Asian; 1% Amer. Indian; 1% Hispanic origin. Households: 57% married couple families; 27% married couple fams. w. children; 36% college educ.; median household income: $22,881; per capita income: $10,961; median gross rent: $322; median house value: $52,600.

1996 Presidential Vote

Dole (R)	112,999	(53%)
Clinton (D)	83,920	(39%)
Perot (I)	14,660	(7%)

1992 Presidential Vote

Bush (R)	118,420	(51%)
Clinton (D)	84,193	(36%)
Perot (I)	26,749	(12%)

Rep. Sonny Callahan (R)

Elected 1984; b. Sept. 11, 1932, Mobile; home, Mobile; U. of AL; Catholic; married (Karen).

Career: Navy, 1952–54; Finch Cos. 1955–85, Pres., 1964–85; AL House of Reps., 1970–78; AL Senate, 1978–82.

DC Office: 2418 RHOB 20515, 202-225-4931; Fax: 202-225-0562; e-mail: callahan@hr.house.gov.

District Offices: Mobile, 334-690-2811.

Committees: *Appropriations* (13th of 34 R): Energy & Water Development; Foreign Operations, Export Financing & Related Programs (Chmn.); Transportation.

Group Ratings

	ADA	ACLU	AFS	LCV	CFA	CON	NFIB	COC	ACU	NTLC	CHC
1996	0	7	0	15	8	7	97	100	100	98	100
1995	5	—	—	0	0	38	—	100	88	—	—

National Journal Ratings

	1995 LIB — 1995 CONS			1996 LIB — 1996 CONS		
Economic	0%	—	74%	18%	—	80%
Social	0%	—	79%	0%	—	90%
Foreign	36%	—	59%	28%	—	71%

Key Votes of the 104th Congress

1. Reduce Medicare Growth $	Y	5. Flag Amendment	Y	9. Cuban Embargo	Y
2. Ovrd. Product Liab. Veto	Y	6. Drop EPA Limits	N	10. Bar Bosnia Troop $	N
3. Increase Min. Wage	N	7. Repeal Assault-Weap. Ban	Y	11. Cut Anti-Missile Defense	N
4. Welfare Reform	Y	8. Ovrd. Part. Birth Veto	Y	12. Bar U.N. Uniforms	Y

Election Results

1996 general	Sonny Callahan (R)	132,206	(64%)	($402,128)
	Don Womack (D)	69,470	(34%)	($39,826)
	Others	3,741	(2%)	
1996 primary	Sonny Callahan (R)	unopposed		
1994 general	Sonny Callahan (R)	103,431	(67%)	($416,080)
	Don Womack (D)	50,227	(33%)	($55,721)

SECOND DISTRICT

The countryside is everywhere in southern Alabama. Even in Montgomery the stone and brick buildings that rise in the irregular downtown grid do not mask the contours of the hills or hide the lush foliage. You can look downhill from the restored Greek Revival Capitol toward Dexter Avenue Baptist Church where Martin Luther King Jr. was pastor, or out past the impressive theater where the Alabama Shakespeare Festival is held, toward new subdivisions and shopping malls, and easily imagine when this land was covered with pine trees or cotton plants. The atmosphere is even more rural in southeast Alabama's Wiregrass region, named for the stiff native grass, around the town of Dothan, past Daleville and the Army's Fort Rucker to Enterprise, site of the Boll Weevil Monument which commemorates the insect that destroyed two-thirds of the cotton crop here in 1915 and then spread throughout the South. Peanuts are now the Wiregrass's main crop, with 25% of U.S. production within 75 miles of Dothan.

The 2d Congressional District of Alabama covers most of the southeast corner of the state. An 80% black segment of Montgomery County is part of the black-majority 7th District, and the 2d includes 78% white Elmore and Autauga Counties across the Alabama River. Without these adjustments, prompted by the Voting Rights Act, the 2d District would be closely split between the parties. But as now drawn, it is heavily Republican, for politics in southern Alabama remains racially polarized: blacks vote almost unanimously Democratic, whites vote very heavily (but not unanimously) Republican in national elections and state and local contests as well. It would be a mistake to see these preferences as purely racial, however. The civil rights laws of the 1960s have long since been accepted and no one wants to roll them back. Blacks here tend to support a larger and more generous government, and hence vote Democratic. Alabama whites tend to take a hard line on defense and crime, want government to promote traditional cultural values, and hence vote Republican.

The congressman from the 2d District is Terry Everett, a businessman from the Wiregrass first elected in 1992. He is a native son who served in Air Force Intelligence in Germany in the 1950s, learned Russian, worked as a sports and police beat reporter and circulation manager for southern Alabama newspapers, then bought some newspapers himself and sold them for far more, and ended up heading a S&L and owning a large farm and real estate development firm. In 1992, when he decided to run for the seat being vacated by embattled 28-year incumbent Republican Bill Dickinson, he was far from the favorite. But he beat two career politicians, a Montgomery legislator in the Republican primary by 58%–42%, then George Wallace, Jr., state treasurer and son of the former governor, in the general. Everett spent $600,000 of his own money and, echoing an old George Wallace slogan, called on voters to "Send them a message, not a politician." Everett carried the Montgomery area and the Wiregrass and lost the Black Belt and rural counties in between. Redistricting made the difference: within the boundaries of the old district, the Democrat led 48%–46%.

In office Everett has resembled some of Alabama's old conservative Democratic congressmen, except occasionally on economic issues. And he is entirely unbashful in using his committee positions and leverage in the Republican conference to advance his district's interests. In his first term he opposed NAFTA because he thought it would hurt local textile and agricultural businesses, and he traveled to Russia to promote Alabama peanuts. In his second term he formed a Peanut Caucus and was one of three Agriculture Committee members to oppose the Freedom to Farm Act until peanut programs were protected: this was the price Speaker Newt Gingrich and Chairman Pat Roberts had to pay to pass the bill phasing out other farm price supports and restrictions over seven years. On Veterans' Affairs he rose to chair a subcommittee and in October 1996 got an outpatient clinic for the Wiregrass; he also challenged an expensive new V.A. computer system. National Security is his committee assignment with the most important jurisdiction. Everett votes with Republicans on most issues and has worked to save the Army Aviation and Technical Center at Fort Rucker and make housing improvements there, and to build a new medical facility at Maxwell Air Force Base. He boasts of $1.1 billion in defense procurement in southeast Alabama businesses. He secured foreign trade subzone status for the Dothan Sony Magnetic Products plant in April 1996.

Everett has fought hard for reelection though he favors term limits and his family remains in Alabama. In 1994 he won with 74% but decided against running for Howell Heflin's Senate seat in 1996. Instead he spent heavily to beat an Alabama teachers' union lobbyist who accused him of cutting Medicare, Medicaid, and farm programs. He won with a solid 63%, running 2–1 ahead in the Montgomery area and the Wiregrass.

The People: Pop. 1990: 577,203; 42% rural; 13% age 65+; 74% White; 24% Black; 1% Asian; 1% Hispanic origin. Households: 59% married couple families; 28% married couple fams. w. children; 40% college educ.; median household income: $24,374; per capita income: $11,636; median gross rent: $329; median house value: $53,700.

1996 Presidential Vote			1992 Presidential Vote		
Dole (R)	121,306	(56%)	Bush (R)	123,856	(53%)
Clinton (D)	81,148	(37%)	Clinton (D)	82,656	(35%)
Perot (I)	12,691	(6%)	Perot (I)	27,319	(12%)

Rep. Terry Everett (R)

Elected 1992; b. Feb. 15, 1937, Dothan; home, Enterprise; Baptist; married (Barbara).

Career: Air Force, 1955–59; Newspaper reporter, 1959–61, 1966–68; Businessman, 1961–64; Editor & Publisher, 1968–88; Real estate developer, 1988–92.

DC Office: 208 CHOB 20515, 202-225-2901; e-mail: everett@hr.house.gov.

District Offices: Montgomery, 334-277-9113; Dothan 36303, 334-794-9680; Opp, 334-493-9253.

Committees: *Agriculture* (11th of 27 R): Forestry, Resource Conservation & Research; Risk Management & Specialty Crops. *National Security* (14th of 30 R): Military Installations & Facilities; Military Procurement. *Veterans' Affairs* (5th of 16 R): Oversight & Investigations (Chmn.).

Group Ratings

	ADA	ACLU	AFS	LCV	CFA	CON	NFIB	COC	ACU	NTLC	CHC
1996	5	6	0	15	8	17	100	94	100	100	100
1995	0	—	—	6	0	56	—	100	92	—	—

National Journal Ratings

	1995 LIB — 1995 CONS			1996 LIB — 1996 CONS		
Economic	26%	—	67%	0%	—	82%
Social	0%	—	79%	0%	—	90%
Foreign	0%	—	85%	21%	—	72%

Key Votes of the 104th Congress

1. Reduce Medicare Growth $	Y	5. Flag Amendment	Y	9. Cuban Embargo	Y
2. Ovrd. Product Liab. Veto	Y	6. Drop EPA Limits	N	10. Bar Bosnia Troop $	Y
3. Increase Min. Wage	N	7. Repeal Assault-Weap. Ban	Y	11. Cut Anti-Missile Defense	N
4. Welfare Reform	Y	8. Ovrd. Part. Birth Veto	Y	12. Bar U.N. Uniforms	Y

Election Results

1996 general	Terry Everett (R)	132,563	(63%)	($983,814)
	Bob E. Gaines (D)	74,317	(35%)	($171,208)
1996 primary	Terry Everett (R)	unopposed		
1994 general	Terry Everett (R)	124,465	(74%)	($224,606)
	Brian Dowling (D)	44,694	(26%)	($22,742)

THIRD DISTRICT

Forty years ago Lineville, Alabama, in the red hills of Clay County, was Ku Klux Klan country, with whites determined to resist race-mixing and blacks intimidated by threats of violence. Today in Lineville, reports *The Washington Post*'s Eugene Robinson, integrated crowds cheer integrated high school teams, people of all races work amicably together, though they tend to pray separately on Sundays. Interracial dating is getting more common—though a high school principal in Wedowee made national headlines when he canceled the 1994 prom because of it—and Alabamans of both races are wondering how they will adjust to their new Hispanic neighbors. Lineville's progress is not complete, and perhaps it echoes that of America's most integrated institution, the military; for Lineville produced more men and women per capita for Operation Desert Storm than any other community in the nation.

The 3d Congressional District of Alabama is centered geographically and perhaps spiritually in Lineville. There are other places of distinction: Horseshoe Bend, where Andrew Jackson won a climactic battle against the Indians; Tuskegee, home of Booker T. Washington's Tuskegee Institute; Auburn, home of Auburn University and its renowned sports teams and veterinary school; Talladega, home of the Alabama Institute for the Deaf and Blind, turns out to be perhaps America's most user-friendly city for the disabled. From the red clay hills around the manufacturing town of Anniston south to the Black Belt around Tuskegee, this looks and feels like rural country. But few people here make a living off their farms; instead they ride in to work at Tysons Food or Wal-Mart or in dozens of textile mills and small or medium-sized factories. Politically, this was long one of the heartlands of the Democratic Party, the home of populist white Democrats—patriotic supporters of the military, cautious supporters of some domestic programs—who won power so often in the House and Senate. But the towns where the interstates have brought in new businesses and new families—Auburn, Talladega, Pell City—have been trending Republican, and in a 1989 special election it was held only after a spirited campaign by Glen Browder, former political scientist and state legislator, then Alabama Secretary of State. Browder compiled a moderate record in the House, which once would have made him a strong statewide candidate. But when he ran for Howell Heflin's Senate seat in 1996, he finished second in the Democratic primary to Roger Bedford, backed by trial lawyers, teachers' unions, and black organizations. At the same time the 3d District was won by Republican Bob Riley.

Riley grew up in Clay County, where his family lived for six generations; he was at the University of Alabama, watching when George Wallace stood in the schoolhouse door in 1963. Two years later he returned home with a business degree, and at 20 he and his brother started selling eggs door-to-door. That became a large egg-and-poultry company; he also ran a grocery store, airport, pharmacy, sold real estate. He ended up with a car dealership (Midway Ford and Chrysler), a trucking company (Midway Transit), and a cattle farm. He served on the city council in Ashland, near Lineville.

In 1996, when Browder ran for the Senate, Riley ran for the House. He was not the best-known candidate. Three state legislators ran in the Democratic primary, in which turnout was 53,000, compared to 20,000 for the Republicans, and one of them, Braxton Bragg Comer, was the great-grandson of an Alabama governor. But Riley proved a strong and energetic campaigner, a supporter of school prayer, term limits, tax cuts, and a balanced budget amendment, and an opponent of abortion, gun control, and affirmative action. Comer accused him of claiming falsely he had not run for public office before and said he would "go negative." But Comer carried only two counties, and Riley led 39%–20%; in the June 25 runoff Riley won 64%–36%. The leader the Democratic primary was state Senator Ted Little, who opposed NAFTA and promised to "stand up to Newt Gingrich" and opposed cuts in Medicare and education. Little took 46% in the June 4 primary, to 27% for state Senator Gerald Dial and 22% for state Representative Gerald Willis. In the runoff Dial carried his home district, but Little carried the rest and won 61%–39%.

In the general election Riley pounded home his conservative views and assailed Little as a trial lawyer. Little, as vice chairman of the Senate Fiscal Responsibility and Accountability Committee, said he would spend frugally. But there was a clear, if limited contrast; Little said, "It's my nature to stand up for the little people." Riley proclaimed, "The black community are very conservative people. We're going after the black vote and we're going after it big time." Both spent liberally, with Riley putting up more than $200,000 of his own money and Little more than $100,000 of his. Little complained loudly when the Alabama Farmers Federation withdrew its endorsement of him and endorsed Riley at the end of October. The voting patterns were very similar to those in other races. Riley carried the northern half of the district, with big margins in St. Clair County outside Birmingham and his own Clay County. Little won large margins in the Black Belt. As Republicans Bob Dole and Jeff Sessions carried the 3d, so did Riley, 50%–47%.

Other Republicans who have narrowly won formerly Democratic southern districts have held onto them easily, and Riley seems to have views and the skills to do so. With his seat on National Security, he is sure to seek protection of the Anniston Army Depot and is working for the safe storage and disposal of chemical weapons at the now closed Fort McClellan. It remains to be seen if Democrats will be able to field a strong candidate here in 1998.

The People: Pop. 1990: 577,116; 47% rural; 13% age 65+; 73% White; 26% Black; 1% Asian; 1% Hispanic origin. Households: 58% married couple families; 27% married couple fams. w. children; 32% college educ.; median household income: $21,594; per capita income: $10,204; median gross rent: $296; median house value: $46,600.

1996 Presidential Vote

Dole (R)	97,798	(49%)
Clinton (D)	88,156	(44%)
Perot (I)	13,112	(7%)

1992 Pressidential Vote

Bush (R)	104,928	(47%)
Clinton (D)	91,983	(41%)
Perot (I)	23,733	(11%)

Rep. Bob Riley (R)

Elected 1996; b. Oct. 3, 1944, Ashland; home, Ashland; U. of AL, B.A. 1965; Baptist; married (Patsy).

Career: Owner, egg and poultry co.;Rancher; Owner, Midway Transit, 1965–present; Ashland City Council, 1972–76.

DC Office: 510 CHOB 20515, 202-225-3261; Fax: 202-225-5829.

District Offices: Anniston, 205-236-5655; Opelika, 334-745-6222.

Committees: *Banking & Financial Services* (24th of 30 R): Capital Markets, Securities & Government Sponsored Enterprises; General Oversight & Investigations. *National Security* (29th of 30 R): Military Readiness; Military Research & Development.

Group Ratings and Key Votes: Newly Elected

Election Results

1996 general	Bob Riley (R)	98,353	(50%)	($868,833)
	T. D. (Ted) Little (D)	92,325	(47%)	($799,043)
	Others	4,369	(2%)	
1996 runoff	Bob Riley (R)	9,124	(64%)	
	Braxton Bragg Comer (R)	5,163	(36%)	
1996 primary	Bob Riley (R)	7,977	(39%)	
	Braxton Bragg Comer (R)	4,069	(20%)	
	Ben Hand (R)	2,360	(12%)	
	Jack Sexton (R)	2,202	(11%)	
	Rick Hagens (R)	1,643	(8%)	
	Don Sledge (R)	1,275	(6%)	
	Others	692	(3%)	
1994 general	Glen Browder (D)	93,924	(64%)	($171,912)
	Ben Hand (R)	53,757	(36%)	($41,265)

FOURTH DISTRICT

The Appalachians' corduroy ridges, dividing the Atlantic coast from the interior, are America's coal-and-steel industrial spine, from the black coal country of western Pennsylvania to the red hill country of northern Alabama. Here rose America's two premier steel cities, Pittsburgh and Birmingham; around both, and for many miles in between them, is hill country settled by feisty Scotch-Irish farmers in the years between the Revolution and the Civil War. In valley land accessible to railroads are the great steel factories built in the 80 years after the Civil War and smaller factories that produce underwear and tires, glass and chemicals, socks and chickens. Politically, the two regions were separated by the Civil War: western Pennsylvania was overwhelmingly Republican until the 1930s, while northern Alabama was solidly Democratic through the 1950s. But they shared the same political impulses—populist on economics, conservative on culture—which made them both Democratic heartlands during the New Deal and in congressional politics for years afterwards. Now they seem to have traded partisan allegiances. Western Pennsylvania is Democratic, though less solidly so when the Democrats emphasize cultural liberalism. And northern Alabama has moved toward the Republicans, even though it has benefited from massive federal public works programs; the movement is most pronounced in counties close to Birmingham and along the interstates.

Alabama's 4th Congressional District crosses the state and the Appalachian ridges, from the Georgia line near the gritty factory town of Gadsden to the Mississippi line near lightly populated rural counties. It has the lowest black percentage of Alabama's congressional districts and, next to the black-majority 7th district, casts the highest Democratic percentages: it went narrowly for George Bush in 1992 and Bill Clinton in 1996. For 30 years it was represented by Tom Bevill, a pleasant, hard-working, humble man, and one of the strongest and most effective believers in old-fashioned pork barrel politics. From 1977–95 Bevill chaired the Appropriations Subcommittee on Energy and Water Development—a fancy name for public works; in 1995, when Democrats lost their House majority, he worked closely, as he had for years, with the new chairman, John Myers. But in December 1995, after winning reelection easily for years, he announced he would retire, at 75; his last appropriations bill passed easily, but he and Myers were disappointed with funding levels, and Myers retired too. Now Bevill has returned to Alabama, where he can survey his works: the Tennessee-Tombigbee Waterway project, the Jasper Bypass in the hills (its destination: the Tom Bevill industrial park), the University of Alabama at Huntsville's optics research lab and its Tom Bevill Center, the local headquarters of the Army Corps of Engineers, and Corridor X, a freeway project to repair the inexplicable failure of the Interstate Highway system to include a road from Birmingham to Memphis.

The new congressman is Bob Aderholt, a Republican elected at 31, after a contest with

Democrat Bob Wilson Jr. in which each represented a strong northern Alabama tradition. Aderholt is from Winston County, the one ancestrally Republican county in north Alabama, which opposed secession in the Civil War and declared itself the Free State of Winston. Aderholt's father was a circuit judge for over 30 years; his wife's father was a state senator and state commissioner of Agriculture and Industry; Aderholt ran for the legislature in 1990, at 24, and came within 1% of winning. In 1992 he was appointed municipal judge in Haleyville; in 1995 he became a top aide to Governor Fob James. With that pedigree he decided to run for Congress when Bevill retired. Republican primary turnout was only 21,000, a vestige of old party loyalties, and in many counties few votes were cast. But 5,387 Republican ballots were cast in Winston County, and Aderholt won 87% of them, enough to account for just about all his margin over state Representative Kerry Rich. Aderholt led 49%–27%, and Rich decided not to seek a runoff.

In contrast there were four strong candidates and 63,000 votes cast in the Democratic primary. The leader on June 4 was Billy Joe Camp, former press secretary to Governor George Wallace, with 32%. But three legislators had strong local bases. In second place, with 26%, was former state Senator Bob Wilson Jr., whose base was Jasper, in Walker County, the home town of Congressman (1917–40) and House Speaker (1937–40) William Bankhead, one of four Alabama Bankheads to serve in Congress. Wilson's father was a state senator who nominated Wallace for president at the 1972 Democratic National Convention; his campaign manager was a longtime top aide to Tom Bevill. Almost half of Wilson's primary votes came from Walker County, and nearly one-quarter of the June 25 runoff votes were cast in Walker County. Wilson won 71% of them, a margin greater than that in his 52%–48% district-wide victory.

In the general both candidates tried to blur their differences. Wilson called himself a Democrat "in the Tom Bevill tradition" and said he supported family values. He said he was comfortable with Bill Clinton, but "when I come across some of the things in the Democratic Party I don't like, and from time to time I do, I speak out about them." Aderholt recognized Bevill did a lot for the district, and said "I'm going to fight for what we ought to get in this district." To his proposed five-year moratorium on federal highway construction he made an exception for Corridor X. But in this culturally conservative district, he didn't hedge on cultural issues. Against abortion, for school prayer, against gun control, against same-sex marriage, he said, "We want to go to Washington to deliver a message, and that is, don't mess with our traditional family values." On economics, "I think the government of big spending is over . . . the people of this district are interested in more take-home pay and less taxes." He attacked Wilson for his support from unions and trial lawyers, and welcomed Newt Gingrich to come to the district.

This was a nationally targeted race, seriously contested: Aderholt spent $147,000 of his own money and Wilson $527,000 of his. Aderholt won 50%–48%. Wilson carried Gadsden and Walker County, but Aderholt got 70% in Winston County and carried the faster-growing counties northeast from Birmingham on the interstate.

Aderholt is likely to be one of the most conservative freshmen of the 105th Congress. His political position, even in a district Clinton carried, is strong. Few of his stands seem unpopular locally, and with a seat on the powerful Appropriations Committee—a significant feat for a freshman—it is not likely that the Democrats can field another opponent with anything like Wilson's political strengths.

The People: Pop. 1990: 577,058; 66% rural; 15% age 65+; 92% White; 7% Black; 1% Amer. Indian. Households: 65% married couple families; 29% married couple fams. w. children; 26% college educ.; median household income: $20,877; per capita income: $10,170; median gross rent: $262; median house value: $42,800.

1996 Pressidential Vote			**1992 Presidential Vote**		
Dole (R)	101,636	(48%)	Bush (R)	107,064	(44%)
Clinton (D)	91,625	(43%)	Clinton (D)	104,526	(43%)
Perot (I)	17,687	(8%)	Perot (I)	28,558	(12%)

Rep. Robert B. Aderholt (R)

Elected 1996; b. July 22, 1965, Haleyville; home, Haleyville; Birmingham Southern U., B.A. 1987, Samford U., J.D. 1990; Congregationalist; married (Caroline).

Career: Haleyville Municipal Judge, 1992–1996; Asst. Legal Advisor, Gov. Fob James, 1995–96.

DC Office: 1007 LHOB 20515, 202-225-4876; Fax: 202-225-1604.

District Offices: Jasper, 205-221-2310.

Committees: *Appropriations* (34th of 34 R): District of Columbia; Transportation; Treasury, Postal Service & General Government.

Group Ratings and Key Votes: Newly Elected

Election Results

1996 general	Robert B. Aderholt (R)	102,741	(50%)	($763,117)
	Robert T. Wilson (D)	99,250	(48%)	($1,023,515)
	Others	3,926	(2%)	
1996 primary	Robert B. Aderholt (R)	10,410	(49%)	
	Kerry Rich (R)	5,860	(27%)	
	Barry Guess (R)	2,434	(11%)	
	Mickey Moseley (R)	1,596	(7%)	
	Ronny Branham (R)	1,021	(5%)	
1994 general	Tom Bevill (D)	unopposed		($274,164)

FIFTH DISTRICT

The federal government has twice in this century transformed the northern Alabama counties along the Tennessee River. The first time was when it created the Tennessee Valley Authority in 1933. Proposed by Nebraska Senator George Norris, a favorite of President Franklin Roosevelt, TVA took the federal World War I munitions plant at Muscle Shoals on the unnavigable, often-flooding Tennessee River, and built a series of dams to control flooding and produce cheap hydroelectric power. Northern Alabama then was one of the poorest parts of the country—poor white farmers scratched a living out of hardscrabble land, were housed in shacks without electricity or running water, and lived off a diet that produced pellagra and rickets—and TVA was intended to be a showcase of what an enlightened, generous federal government could do. The second major federal project here was the space program. After the Soviets put up Sputnik in 1957, the Redstone Arsenal in Huntsville became our major missile development center. NASA built its Marshall Space Flight Center nearby in the 1960s, and Huntsville changed from a quaint courthouse town of 14,000 in 1950 to a high-tech metro area of 250,000 by the 1990s.

TVA and the space program were primarily Democratic projects, and northern Alabama voters for years remained staunch New Deal Democrats, liberal on economics and not much interested in race, like the longtime Congressman (1937–46) and Senator (1946–79) John

Sparkman, the Democrats' vice presidential nominee in 1952. But the professional and technical people in the space business tend toward Newt Gingrich's combination of high-tech and traditional values, and increasingly vote Republican. This has moved Madison and Morgan Counties, around Huntsville and nearby Decatur, from the Democratic to the Republican column. The 5th Congressional District of Alabama takes in most of the state's TVA and space counties, including Huntsville and Decatur, historically represented by Democratic congressmen. But in presidential elections the 5th has supported Republicans since the departure of Jimmy Carter.

The congressman from the 5th District is Bud Cramer, a Democrat who started off in the TVA tradition. He was born in Huntsville, served as an Army tank officer after law school, beat an incumbent district attorney in 1980, at 33. In 1985 he set up the Child Advocacy Center, a child-friendly environment for abused children; as congressman, he set up a $5 million federal program to encourage such centers across the country. "We are the Mayo Clinic there in Huntsville of child abuse," he boasted. When Congressman Ronnie Flippo ran for governor in 1990, Cramer ran for Congress and won 44% in the Democratic primary and 60% in the runoff. In the general he beat a party-switching former state Agriculture commissioner 67%–33%. In the House, he got on the Transportation and Infrastructure and Science Committees—the better to tend to his district's federal interests—and became a tireless lobbyist for the beleaguered Space Station, which was challenged in seven floor votes and which survived by only a 216–215 margin in June 1993. He won funding to start an Atlanta-Memphis highway. At the same time, he warned people that "a community like this is too tied to federal spending." But Cramer also supported the Democratic leadership on two locally unpopular issues. In July 1993 he voted for the Clinton economic package with its five cent gas-tax increase and opposed the Penny-Kasich budget cuts. And in August 1994 he supported the Clinton crime bill with its gun control provisions. In November 1994 he had serious opposition from Wayne Parker, Huntsville native and son-in-law of Texas Congressman Bill Archer, who called for spending cuts, school choice, tougher sentences and put up billboards saying "Cramer, Clinton, Congress. We won't be fooled again! Vote Parker," while Bill Clinton's job rating was 68% negative. Cramer criticized Parker for living off a trust fund and suggested that Parker, if elected, would move the space-station program to Houston, because of his ties with Archer. (Actually, another local NASA project was transferred to Texas by the Clinton Administration in retaliation for opposition from Alabama Senator Richard Shelby). With $288,000 from PACs, Cramer outspent Parker, and he had massive support from local media. But the issues worked against him, and he barely won, 50%–49%.

Alerted by this close call, and now in the minority, Cramer moved to the right on some issues, voted for the balanced budget amendment and a supermajority to raise taxes in 1995. He stressed his identification with the conservative Blue Dog Democrats, and worked hard on local issues. He got actor Tom Hanks to join him in speaking in 1995 for continued federal funding of the Space Station. He got the National Weather Service to reconsider a proposal to close a radar station in Huntsville and, in October 1996, to break ground on a Next Generation Radar in northeast Alabama to monitor the tornadoes common in the area. On the Transportation Committee he strove to build the Atlanta-Memphis highway and the Keller Memorial Bridge in Decatur. He helped reverse a subcommittee decision and save the NASA Marshall Space Flight Center in Huntsville in July 1995. He worked to bring 2600 Army jobs to the Redstone Arsenal.

Parker continued to dog him with criticism and with help from his father-in-law raised money for a second run in 1996. But primary opponent Hugh McInnish attacked Parker for his Texas support. Parker won the June primary, by 55%–39%, but only 50%–43% in Huntsville's Madison County. Though in the minority, Cramer still raised enough PAC money be financially competitive with Parker and enjoyed strong local media support. In October 1996 he filed a complaint alleging that Archer improperly solicited funds for Parker. The result was a 56%–42% Cramer victory in the November rematch. Cramer ran well ahead of Bill Clinton and Democratic Senate candidate Roger Bedford, who did not carry the 5th District. He seems to have proved that this ancestrally Democratic district is still willing to support a Democratic congressman—although one whose stance toward his party and stands on the issues are pointedly different from those Democrats who have come before.

The People: Pop. 1990: 577,235; 39% rural; 11% age 65+; 83% White; 15% Black; 1% Asian; 1% Amer. Indian; 1% Hispanic origin. Households: 62% married couple families; 29% married couple fams. w. children; 44% college educ.; median household income: $28,364; per capita income: $13,268; median gross rent: $361; median house value: $63,000.

1996 Pressidential Vote			1992 Pressidential Vote		
Dole (R)	111,652	(49%)	Bush (R)	110,268	(44%)
Clinton (D)	98,401	(43%)	Clinton (D)	102,130	(41%)
Perot (I)	18,403	(8%)	Perot (I)	36,921	(15%)

Rep. Robert E. (Bud) Cramer (D)

Elected 1990; b. Aug. 22, 1947, Huntsville; home, Huntsville; U. of AL, B.S. 1969, J.D. 1972; Methodist; widowed.

Career: Army, 1972; Army Reserves, 1976–78; Intructor, U. of AL Law Schl., Dir., Clinical Studies Program, 1972–73; Madison Cnty. Asst. Dist. Atty., 1973–75; Practicing atty., 1975–80; Madison Cnty. Dist. Atty., 1981–1990; Founder, Natl. Children's Advocacy Ctr., 1985.

DC Office: 2416 RHOB 20515, 202-225-4801; Fax: 202-225-4392; e-mail: budmail@hr.house.gov

District Offices: Decatur, 205-355-9400; Huntsville, 205-551-0190; Muscle Shoals, 205-381-3450

Committees: *Science* (6th of 21 D): Space & Aeronautics (RMM). *Transportation & Infrastructure* (11th of 33 D): Aviation; Surface Transportation.

Group Ratings

	ADA	ACLU	AFS	LCV	CFA	CON	NFIB	COC	ACU	NTLC	CHC
1996	40	19	67	69	38	30	81	63	55	66	60
1995	45	—	—	25	23	31	—	71	52	—	—

National Journal Ratings

	1995 LIB — 1995 CONS			1996 LIB — 1996 CONS		
Economic	57%	—	42%	52%	—	47%
Social	55%	—	43%	60%	—	39%
Foreign	36%	—	59%	50%	—	48%

Key Votes of the 104th Congress

1. Reduce Medicare Growth $	N	5. Flag Amendment	Y	9. Cuban Embargo	Y
2. Ovrd. Product Liab. Veto	Y	6. Drop EPA Limits	N	10. Bar Bosnia Troop $	N
3. Increase Min. Wage	Y	7. Repeal Assault-Weap. Ban	Y	11. Cut Anti-Missile Defense	N
4. Welfare Reform	Y	8. Ovrd. Part. Birth Veto	Y	12. Bar U.N. Uniforms	Y

Election Results

1996 general	Robert E. (Bud) Cramer (D)	126,702	(56%)	($1,006,341)
	Wayne Parker (R)	94,330	(42%)	($886,648)
	Others	4,708	(2%)	
1996 primary	Robert E. (Bud) Cramer (D)	unopposed		
1994 general	Robert E. (Bud) Cramer (D)	88,693	(50%)	($565,457)
	Wayne Parker (R)	86,923	(49%)	($430,822)

SIXTH DISTRICT

Once one of America's booming industrial cities, then the site of violence in the civil rights revolution, Birmingham now has prospects for the future far more hopeful than seemed possible even a decade ago. This is a new city by southern standards: before the Civil War there was nothing here but a few creeks running below Red Mountain. But Red Mountain is almost pure iron ore, and by 1890 Birmingham had the South's largest steel mills. In the early 20th Century, as the statue of Vulcan, Roman god of fire and metalworking, looked out over the smokestack-rich valley, Birmingham seemed the most up-to-date and progressive city in the South. But the worldwide overcapacity in steel and technological obsolescence at home sent the American steel industry into long-term decline starting in the 1950s. And in the years when commercial Atlanta was billing itself as "The City Too Busy to Hate," industrial Birmingham's political leaders were plotting to avoid desegregation. Birmingham's violent reaction to civil rights—police commissioner Bull Connor set dogs and firehoses against peaceful demonstrators, and Ku Klux Klansmen bombed the 16th Street Baptist Church killing four young girls in 1963—made a vivid impression over the new medium of television news, helping to pass the Civil Rights Act of 1964, and created a reputation from which Birmingham still suffered a generation later.

But over the years Birmingham developed a new economic base to generate growth and worked to improve race relations. Health care is one major industry: Birmingham has some of the largest and most advanced medical care centers in the South, and is especially reknowned for its sports medicine facilities and specialists that have treated such greats as Bo Jackson and Michael Jordan. Banking is the other: while Atlanta's banks foundered and were acquired by outsiders, Birmingham became the largest southern banking center after Charlotte, North Carolina, with headquarters of SouthTrust, AmSouth Bancorp, First Alabama Bancshares and Central Bancshares of the South. There is still racial polarization: most blacks live in Birmingham itself and the series of factory towns north of Red Mountain; this area is about two-thirds black. A whole new Birmingham has grown up along the freeways south of Red Mountain, starting with the old high-income suburb of Mountain Brook and spreading south into fast-growing Shelby County; this is over 90% white.

The 6th Congressional District of Alabama, which once included all of Birmingham and most of its suburbs, is now, thanks to prevailing interpretations of the 1982 Voting Rights Act amendments, the white Birmingham-area district. It includes only a small part of the city, plus the high-income suburbs south of Red Mountain and in Shelby County and the middle-income suburbs north of Birmingham. It runs south to the white areas of the university town of Tuscaloosa. This is one of the most Republican districts in the nation, 2–1 for Bob Dole in 1996.

The congressman from the 6th District is Republican Spencer Bachus. A Birmingham native, he owned a sawmill company and practiced law, and boasts that he was a good enough trial-lawyer to have produced four straight acquittals in murder trials. He was elected to the state legislature in 1982, at 35, and was an active legislator though one of very few Republicans. He ran for attorney general in 1990 and won 36% of the vote; he was Republican state chairman in 1991 and 1992. But he had serious competition in 1992 the 6th District, first in the primary and runoff, then in the general election against 10-year incumbent Democrat Ben Erdreich, popular for his economically moderate record and because he was, early on, among the few prominent Birmingham whites who supported civil rights at a time when that was not only politically courageous but physically dangerous. Erdreich outspent Bachus nearly 2–1 and led in polls, but Bachus won 52%–45%. This is one seat Democrats lost to racial gerrymandering: Erdreich lost the 6th District portion of Jefferson County by 17,000 votes, but the rest of the county went Democratic by 57,000 votes in the adjacent 7th District race.

Bachus has had a mostly, though not quite totally, conservative voting record and has become an important member in the House far more quickly than he must have expected. In his first term he had a proposal to save 25% of government printing costs. He was the lead questioner of

Treasury Secretary Lloyd Bentsen during the Banking Committee's Whitewater hearings. In his second term, with Republicans suddenly in the majority, he became chairman of a Banking subcommittee. There he spotlighted the threat of offshore counterfeiting of U.S. $100 bills; he got an amendment authorizing more Secret Service agents abroad. He also got a seat on Transportation and Infrastructure where his projects included getting running water for Creswell, a flood control levee for Northport, and a new control tower for the Birmingham airport.

Bachus was reelected without primary opposition and with more than 70% in the general election in 1994 and 1996.

The People: Pop. 1990: 577,170; 23% rural; 12% age 65+; 89% White; 9% Black; 1% Asian; 1% Hispanic origin. Households: 61% married couple families; 28% married couple fams. w. children; 51% college educ.; median household income: $31,864; per capita income: $16,033; median gross rent: $405; median house value: $72,800.

1996 Presidential Vote			1992 Presidential Vote		
Dole (R)	169,870	(68%)	Bush (R)	183,127	(64%)
Clinton (D)	68,545	(27%)	Clinton (D)	73,463	(26%)
Perot (I)	10,995	(4%)	Perot (I)	28,196	(10%)

Rep. Spencer Bachus (R)

Elected 1992; b. Dec. 28, 1947, Birmingham; home, Birmingham; Auburn U., B.A. 1969, U. of AL, J.D. 1972; Baptist; married (Linda).

Career: Natl. Guard, 1969–71; Owner, Lumber Co.; Practicing atty., 1972–92; AL Senate, 1983–84; AL House of Reps., 1984–87; AL Repub. Party Chmn., 1991–92.

DC Office: 442 CHOB 20515, 202-225-4921; Fax: 202-225-2082; e-mail: sbachus@hr.house.gov.

District Offices: Birmingham, 205-969-2296; Northport, 205-333-9894.

Committees: *Banking & Financial Services* (7th of 30 R); Capital Markets, Securities & Government Sponsored Enterprises; General Oversight & Investigations (Chmn.). *Transportation & Infrastructure* (18th of 40 R): Railroads; Surface Transportation. *Veterans' Affairs* (8th of 16 R): Health.

Group Ratings

	ADA	ACLU	AFS	LCV	CFA	CON	NFIB	COC	ACU	NTLC	CHC
1996	5	0	9	23	0	30	97	94	95	100	100
1995	0	—	—	0	8	75	—	100	92	—	—

National Journal Ratings

	1995 LIB — 1995 CONS			1996 LIB — 1996 CONS		
Economic	36%	—	60%	30%	—	68%
Social	30%	—	70%	14%	—	77%
Foreign	0%	—	85%	28%	—	72%

Key Votes of the 104th Congress

1. Reduce Medicare Growth $	Y	5. Flag Amendment	Y	9. Cuban Embargo	Y
2. Ovrd. Product Liab. Veto	Y	6. Drop EPA Limits	N	10. Bar Bosnia Troop $	Y
3. Increase Min. Wage	Y	7. Repeal Assault-Weap. Ban	Y	11. Cut Anti-Missile Defense	N
4. Welfare Reform	Y	8. Ovrd. Part. Birth Veto	Y	12. Bar U.N. Uniforms	Y

Election Results

1996 general	Spencer Bachus (R)	181,336	(71%)	($511,226)
	Mary Lynn Bates (D)	70,081	(27%)	($36,522)
	Others	4,522	(2%)	
1996 primary	Spencer Bachus (R)	unopposed		
1994 general	Spencer Bachus (R)	155,047	(79%)	($332,233)
	Larry Fortenberry (D)	41,030	(21%)	

SEVENTH DISTRICT

Alabama celebrates its black heritage more than any other state, building striking memorials to the civil rights movement in Montgomery and Birmingham, promoting tourism to these and other black history sites, commemorating with dignified restraint a history that was full of raucous hatred and moving sacrifice. Blacks first came here as slaves; the last slave ship to the United States, the *Clotilde*, docked in Mobile in 1859, where its cargo was then set free. Blacks were part of the great migration into the cottonlands after the Jacksonians swept the Indians out of the Southeast and sent them on their Trail of Tears to what is now Oklahoma. Today, Alabama's rural blacks are still clustered in the Black Belt of fertile dark soil across the center of the state: around Montgomery, where Rosa Parks refused to move to the back of a city bus in 1955 and a young minister named Martin Luther King, Jr., led a bus boycott; around Selma, founded by Alabama's one vice president, William Rufus King, and where Sheriff Jim Clark's troops beat up peaceful marchers on the Edmund Pettus Bridge in demonstrations that led to the march on Montgomery and the 1965 Voting Rights Act. All 10 of Alabama's majority-black counties are in the rich farm country of the Black Belt. But most Alabama blacks now live in urban areas, one-quarter in metropolitan Birmingham.

The 7th Congressional District of Alabama, with its convoluted boundaries, was created as a black-majority district. Some 45% of its people live in the narrow valley of Birmingham and Jefferson County where the population is 75% black; another 13% are in an 80% black portion of Montgomery County. The rest of the district includes Black Belt counties where the Alabama and Tombigbee Rivers flow past old plantations, plus part of Tuscaloosa, home of the University of Alabama, and nearby Vance, site of the much sought-after new Mercedes factory. It thus combines the remnants of Alabama's old cotton economy with neighborhoods built in the shadows of Birmingham's once booming steel mills.

The congressman from the 7th District is Earl Hilliard, the first black representative from Alabama since Republican Jeremiah Haralson retired in 1876. Hilliard grew up in segregated Birmingham and was educated in historically black schools—Morehouse, Howard, Atlanta University. In 1974, at 32, he was elected to the Alabama legislature, one of the first blacks there; 10 years later he became a committee chairman. He pushed for horse racing in Birmingham and sponsored tax abatement bills. In 1992 he outmaneuvered others and became the main Birmingham-based candidate for the new 7th District seat. The decisive Democratic primary was a "friends and neighbors" contest reminiscent of the old days of southern white politics. Hilliard led in the primary with 31%, winning 58% in Jefferson County but running far behind elsewhere. In second place with 24%, with solid wins in his home Black Belt, was state Senator Hank Sanders; a Montgomery candidate got 72% there but only 20% districtwide. In the runoff, Hilliard got 71% in Jefferson County and held Sanders to 53% in Montgomery, enough for a 50.5%–49.5% victory.

In the House Hilliard has a largely liberal voting record. But he also backs the school prayer and flag amendments—reminders of the importance of the black church and of the days when the Stars and Stripes overcame the Stars and Bars. He serves on Agriculture and International Relations and is active in the Black Caucus where he is second vice chairman. He pays much attention to local projects—establishing Enterprise Zones for Sumter and Greene Counties and

Smithfield/West End in Birmingham; saving the Marion Aquaculture Center; reinstalling the Gee's Bend Ferry Boat in Wilcox County, which was closed in 1962; stopping Village Creek flooding in Birmingham; authorizing the Selma-to-Montgomery Historic Trail.

Hilliard had no primary opposition in 1994 or 1996. His 1996 Republican opponent, restaurant owner Joe Powell, was 24, the youngest House candidate in the country, and he managed to raise $10,000 more than Hilliard's $213,000. But Hilliard won 71%–27% in the one Alabama district solidly carried by Bill Clinton.

The People: Pop. 1990: 577,430; 27% rural; 14% age 65+; 32% White; 67% Black. Households: 44% married couple families; 20% married couple fams. w. children; 32% college educ.; median household income: $16,560; per capita income: $8,135; median gross rent: $276; median house value: $40,200.

1996 Pressidential Vote			1992 Pressidential Vote		
Clinton (D)	150,271	(72%)	Clinton (D)	151,129	(69%)
Dole (R)	53,565	(26%)	Bush (R)	56,620	(26%)
Perot (I)	5,080	(2%)	Perot (I)	11,633	(5%)

Rep. Earl F. Hilliard (D)

Elected 1992; b. Apr. 9, 1942, Birmingham; home, Birmingham; Morehouse Col., B.A. 1964; Howard U., J.D. 1967; Atlanta U., M.B.A. 1970; Baptist; married (Mary).

Career: Practicing atty., 1972–92; AL House of Reps., 1974–80; AL Senate, 1980–92.

DC Office: 1314 LHOB 20515, 202-225-2665; Fax: 202-226-0772.

District Offices: Birmingham, 205-328-2841; Montgomery 334-281-0513; Selma, 334-872-2684; Tuscaloosa, 205-752-3578.

Committees: *Agriculture* (8th of 23 D): Forestry, Resource Conservation & Research; Livestock, Dairy & Poultry. *International Relations* (15th of 21 D): International Economic Policy & Trade; International Operations & Human Rights.

Group Ratings

	ADA	ACLU	AFS	LCV	CFA	CON	NFIB	COC	ACU	NTLC	CHC
1996	85	80	100	77	62	78	29	31	15	15	7
1995	80	—	—	94	69	8	—	23	12	—	—

National Journal Ratings

	1995 LIB — 1995 CONS	1996 LIB — 1996 CONS
Economic	77% — 23%	76% — 22%
Social	80% — 13%	79% — 18%
Foreign	70% — 28%	72% — 27%

Key Votes of the 104th Congress

1. Reduce Medicare Growth $	N	5. Flag Amendment	Y	9. Cuban Embargo	N
2. Ovrd. Product Liab. Veto	N	6. Drop EPA Limits	Y	10. Bar Bosnia Troop $	N
3. Increase Min. Wage	Y	7. Repeal Assault-Weap. Ban	Y	11. Cut Anti-Missile Defense	Y
4. Welfare Reform	N	8. Ovrd. Part. Birth Veto	N	12. Bar U.N. Uniforms	Y

Election Results

1996 general	Earl F. Hilliard (D)	136,651	(71%)	($223,582)
	Joe Powell (R)	52,142	(27%)	($224,029)
	Others	3,320	(2%)	
1996 primary	Earl F. Hilliard (D)	unopposed		
1994 general	Earl F. Hilliard (D)	116,150	(77%)	($337,772)
	Alfred J. Middleton (R)	34,814	(23%)	

ALASKA

Alaska as it exists today is in very large part a creation of the U.S. government, yet no state is more hostile to and distrustful of Washington. But Alaska would not be part of the United States at all had not Secretary of State William Seward, back in Washington, taken advantage of a fleeting opportunity to create an American Pacific empire by purchasing it from Russia in 1867. The territory started growing feverishly with the Klondike gold rush in 1897, just after American voters reaffirmed the gold standard; Anchorage was established in 1913 as the terminus of the Alaska Railroad, built by the federal government. The Alcan Highway was constructed, like most of Alaska's roads, by the Army, in the grim war days of 1942. And today most travel in Alaska is done in small planes, flown often by pilots originally trained by the U.S. Air Force. Economically Alaska has depended heavily on federal government spending; its private sector is mostly devoted to mineral extraction and fishing, chancy and often dwindling enterprises heavily reliant on government rule-setting. Against all that outside control, Alaskans have usually and perhaps understandably bristled. In this remote place, they like to do as they like, or as Fairbanks banker Gary Roth told *National Journal*'s Margaret Kriz, "We think we live at the end of the highway, and we like to act like renegades a lot of the time."

Statehood was won by Alaska in 1959, after a valiant campaign. But for all its vast size Alaska is in some ways a very small state. Just 607,000 of 265 million Americans live in this gigantic land mass, larger than all the Northeastern and Great Lakes states put together; almost half the population is in the Anchorage area, the rest scattered in a few small towns and Native settlements over an area so vast that, if superimposed on the Lower 48, it would stretch from Florida to southern California to Lake Superior. Alaska was the only part of the nation occupied by the enemy in World War II (Japan held the Aleutian islands of Attu and Kiska) and is the only part of the U.S. to face Russia, just across the Bering Strait. Alaskans are closer to these Siberian neighbors geographically and, for Natives, ethnically and culturally, than to Americans in the Lower 48. Physically, there is something slapdash about Alaska's civilization: much of the housing is flimsily built, garbage is left outside to freeze in the winter, moose nibble shrubbery in suburban Anchorage backyards, and caribou breed in record numbers near the Trans-Alaska oil pipeline. If a whole town, like Kivalina on the Chukchi Sea, runs out of room, it moves somewhere else. In general, this is still a frontier state with few old people and more males than females. Every American has heard of Alaska and has some image of its wildness; but fewer than 10% of Americans have ever been there.

Shaping Alaska even more than statehood has been oil. It began suddenly, accidentally: on the day after Christmas 1967, at Prudhoe Bay on the Arctic coast, an undulating roar as loud as four jumbo jets directly overhead drew a crowd of 40 men, heavily clothed against the 30-below weather, to an oil rig. Suddenly a natural gas flare shot 30 feet straight up: this was the great 11 billion barrel North Slope oil field. Oil companies had drilled seven dry wells on Prudhoe Bay, and ARCO chief executive Robert Anderson wouldn't have ordered this one last try, except that he had a drilling rig nearby. The greatest oil strike ever in the United States has made this country a major (though not self-sufficient) producer during the years after the oil shocks of the 1970s, and has made Alaska what it is—and is not—today. Yet this spurting up of the lifeblood of western civilization in the cold darkness of Arctic winter was not the end of the story of this improbable American commonwealth.

Finding oil in Prudhoe Bay was something like finding it on the moon: it was not clear in 1967 who owned the oil or how it could be taken out. Ownership was in question because the Statehood Act of 1959 provided for the state to choose its own public lands, but only after settling Native land claims. Congress, not Alaska, settled such claims in the 1971 Alaska Native Claims Act which set up 12 regional and 220 village Native corporations, gave them $962 million and time to select their own 44 million acres, and ended the Interior Department's freeze that enabled the state to stake claims to mineral-rich acreage. The only feasible way to get the oil out—the Beaufort Sea remains frozen much of the year—was a pipeline, but that was opposed by environmentalists for fear it would destroy the delicate permafrost and interfere with caribou migrations. Development-minded Alaskans got a pipeline bill through Congress in 1973, by just a one-vote margin in the Senate, but the pipeline had to be built on stilts and wasn't opened until 1977, and Congress banned oil exports to Japan and other obvious East Asian markets. Then in 1980, after brilliant lobbying by environmentalists, Congress passed over the objections of Alaska's two senators and in the face of tears from its Congressman-at-Large Don Young, the Alaska Lands Act, which set aside 159 million acres as wilderness.

The pipeline came on line just as oil prices were approaching their peak, thus generating maximum revenues to the state, which gets 100% of the royalties; the environment was protected and the caribou herd tripled statewide over a period of 20 years; the Natives got more autonomy than the non-Native majority of Alaskans would have given them. With oil providing more than 80% of its revenue, the state abolished its income tax in 1980 and voted lavish benefits, subsidized mortgage interest rates and 25-year residents' housing, granted low-interest college loans and forgave half the debt of students if they would return to Alaska for five years—all for a relatively affluent population, even as the cost-of-living differential from the Lower 48 was shrinking. The state and local tax burden is about one-third of average. In the 1970s, Alaska established a Permanent Fund for most of the oil money, totalling $13.2 billion by 1993, and every one-year resident of Alaska gets an annual check—in 1996, $1,130.

Alaska now faces other tough decisions—which often enough depend on Washington, and therefore on national political trends. With Republican control of Congress, Alaska's three Republican members, with a total of 69 years seniority going into the 105th Congress, are in key positions for the state. Senator Ted Stevens, appointed to fill a vacancy in 1968, ranked second on Appropriations in 1995 and became chairman in 1997. Senator Frank Murkowski, first elected in 1980, chairs the Energy and Natural Resources Committee. And Congressman-at-Large Don Young, first elected in 1973, chairs the Resources Committee. But they have not carried all before them: Bill Clinton, with an administration staffed with environmentalists and no hope of carrying Alaska's electoral votes, frustrated them with vetoes and administrative actions. "This has been the worst administration since Alaska was made a state," Stevens said. And Alaska's Governor Tony Knowles, a Democrat elected in 1994 by 536 votes, proved less development-minded than any governor in at least a dozen years.

The delegation tried but failed to get approval of oil drilling in the Arctic National Wildlife Preserve (ANWR), east of Prudhoe Bay and just west of Canada. Oil companies have wanted to drill on this windy plain since 1987, and Congress seemed headed toward approval until the Exxon *Valdez* went aground in Prince William Sound in March 1989. Environmentalists claimed that drilling would harm the caribou herds (although they have thrived in Prudhoe Bay and amid drilling in Canada) and would hurt the Indians (though some Natives back it). Sale of leases was estimated to bring in $2.6 billion, half to the state and half to the feds, and, with North Slope production declining 7% per year, would provide more American oil. But environmental lobbyists made an emotional appeal—Resources Committee Democrat Bruce

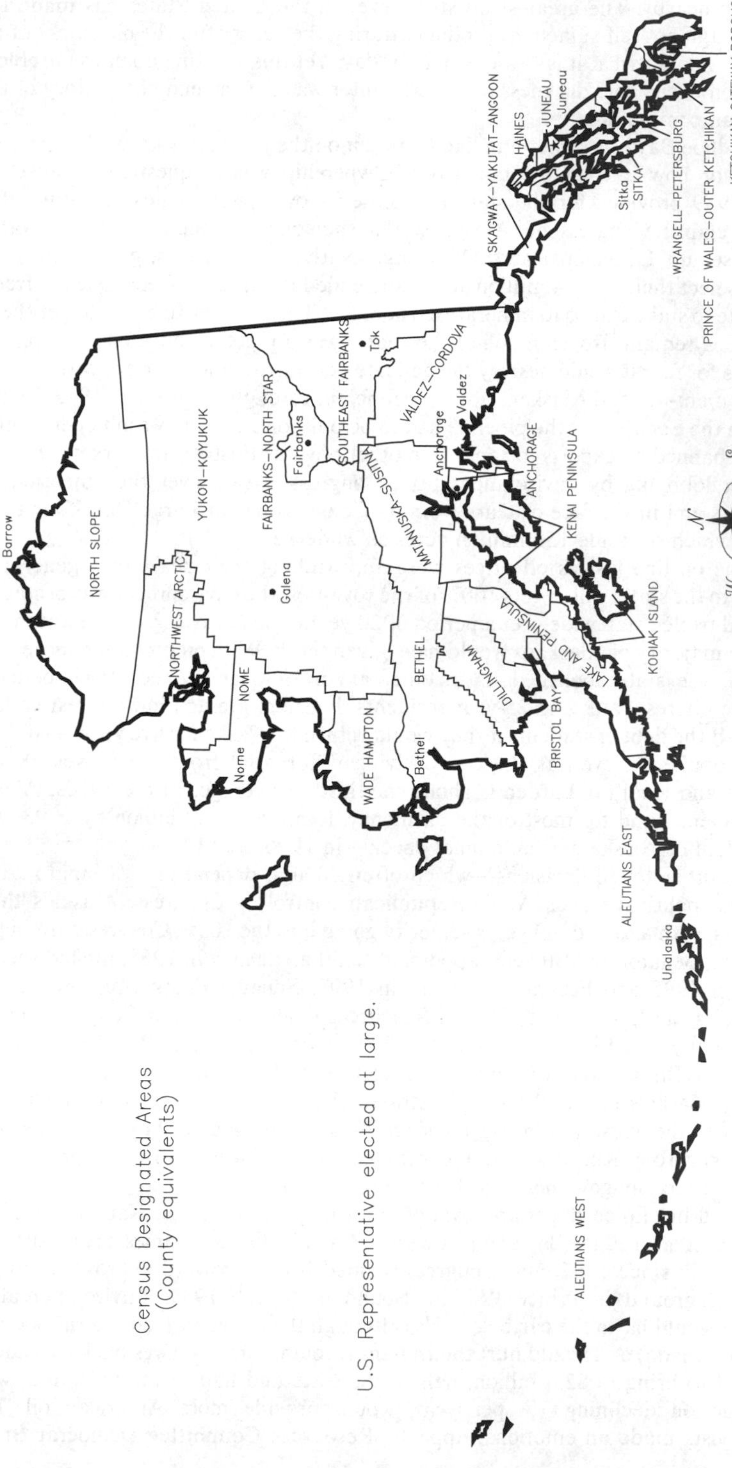

Census Designated Areas
(County equivalents)

U.S. Representative elected at large.

Vento called ANWR "America's Serengeti"—and made the issue a key vote in their Congressional ratings, giving East Coast and Florida Republicans far from Alaska a motive for voting against. Stevens did get ANWR drilling into the 1996 budget reconciliation, but Clinton vetoed the bill and it was dropped afterward.

Another issue on which the delegation strove but failed was logging in the Tongass National Forest, in the southeast panhandle near Ketchikan. In April 1994 the Forest Service canceled a 50-year contract with Louisiana Pacific to harvest 1.7 million acres of old-growth timber at the company's pulp mill, causing the company to eventually close the mill in March 1997. The delegation wants to affirm the contract and extend it 15 years, so the company will modernize and clean up its Ketchikan mill. But different strategies failed. Stevens tried to add an amendment that would have saved the mill to a FY96 Appropriation bill, but when Clinton threatened to veto the bill, Stevens was forced to drop the amendment in return for $110 million in economic aid for southeastern Alaska. Young sought to turn over the whole National Forest to the state—a non-starter. A proposal to transfer 500,000 acres to new Native corporations went no farther. In late September 1996 Murkowski held up the national parks bill, demanding Clinton action on Tongass. He gave in five days later, for a promise that the Forest Service would sell timber to the Ketchikan lumber mill for two years.

The Alaska delegation did achieve some goals. With support from the Clinton Administration, they repealed the economically mindless prohibition on exporting Alaskan oil to its obvious and lucrative markets in Japan and East Asia. And they revised the Magnuson Act to protect seafood stocks from being overfished. With oil exports banned, fish has been Alaska's largest source of export earnings; salmon production was at record highs in 1995 and 1996, but prices tumbled, and limits seem desirable economically and environmentally.

In the middle 1990s there has been an uneasiness in the air in Alaska. The traditional mainstays of the state's economy seem threatened—federal domestic and defense spending are down, the oil business is winding down absent ANWR drilling, fish prices are down—yet in population and jobs Alaska is growing robustly. One reason is that tourism is rising, with 1.2 million visitors in 1996. Alaskans are perhaps less isolated, and the character of this state, with its disproportionate numbers of airplanes and ex-convicts, its earthquakes and surging glaciers, seems slowly to be changing: life on the frontier is becoming more routine and regulated, and the free spirit evidenced in large votes for the Libertarian Party a dozen or more years ago may be vanishing. This is apparent in the 1990 vote to revoke Alaska's 1975 decriminalization of marijuana, in the charging of fees for climbing Mount McKinley in Denali National Park, in the 1994 change from open 48-hour harvests of fish to set quotas, in restrictions against RVs camping out in shopping center parking lots. The Alaska bush in the 1970s attracted hippies and eccentrics looking for elbow room; are the 1990s bringing hotel managers and waiters who introduce themselves by first name? Many of the Native corporations are thriving, but others have fallen on hard times and are selling timber and other resources their creators hoped they would preserve; poverty and alcoholism are high in the bush, and native languages like *Tlingit* are dying out. The U.S. Supreme Court is expected to rule in mid-1997 on whether or not Native Villages have a right to tax businesses on their land—a proposal vehemently opposed by the state but eagerly sought by tribal leaders who believe their sovereignty and economic viability is at stake. Other institutions remain weak. Unions, which were politically pivotal 20 years ago, aren't any more. The oil companies, while not so unpopular as Lower 48ers thought they would be after the oil spill, were not able to stop higher state oil taxes. Political party organizations have never been strong and voters don't follow party lines—Republican Alaska hasn't elected a Republican governor since 1978. As for the legislature—well, just about any kind of candidate can get elected, and has. In national politics, Alaska is solidly Republican, because national Democrats are seen as wanting to lock up Alaska's resources; no Democrat has been elected to Congress here since 1972, though some contests have been close.

Important regional differences persist. Anchorage, with 40% of the population, is much like a prosperous Rocky Mountains' metropolis with longer summer days and winter nights; it is affluent and booming, with 70% of women in the work force, the highest in the country. Politically, it is solidly Republican. So are the smaller settlements in a 200-mile arc around Anchorage, which have been growing even more rapidly—the Matanuska Valley (one of the few places in Alaska where farming is possible), Seward, the Kenai peninsula, the little port of Valdez at the southern terminus of the pipeline, and the town of Wasilla where a local legislator wanted to relocate the state capital—a move defeated in a 1994 referendum 55%–45%. This was strong Ross Perot territory; overall, Alaska cast the nation's second highest Perot percentage, 28%, in 1992, but—less quirky?—voted only 11% for him in 1996. Fairbanks, Alaska's second largest city, is a pipeline and mineral service center deep in the interior, unprotected from Arctic winds in winter and fierce crowds of mosquitoes in the brief but hot summer. Once solidly Republican, it now seems anti-incumbent.

The old Alaska, first settled by Russians, can be seen in the fishing towns of the Panhandle and in the capital of Juneau, located on an inlet of the Pacific up against a steep mountain; Alaskans voted to move the capital to a site near Anchorage in 1974 but defeated referenda to pay for it in 1978 and 1982, and Juneau survived once again in 1994. The Panhandle usually votes Democratic. Far away to the north and west is the Alaska bush, the villages where Natives—Indians, Aleuts, Eskimos—live, often in poverty. Natives make up 16% of Alaska's population and 70% in the vast lands north and west of Anchorage and Fairbanks, but they are only about 90,000 people living in an area larger than the northeast United States.

Governor. Alaska has had a colorful array of governors in its nearly four decades of statehood, from its first governor, Democrat William Egan, through bush pilot Jay Hammond, elected in 1974 and 1978, and Walter Hickel, Anchorage developer, elected in 1966, appointed Richard Nixon's Interior secretary in 1969 (he resigned in 1970 in protest against the invasion of Cambodia) and elected again, as a member of the Alaska Independence Party, at 71 in 1990. None, incidentally, has won an absolute majority of the vote since Egan in 1970; independent and third party candidates have abounded.

The current governor is Tony Knowles, a Democrat who lost to Hickel in 1990 and then, after Hickel retired, was elected by substantially less than a landslide in 1994. Knowles was born in Oklahoma, served in the 82d Airborne in Vietnam, graduated from Yale, and came to Alaska in 1968 and worked as a roughneck. In 1969 he started his first Grizzly Burger, then added two more chains and opened the Downtown Deli; in the mode of local businessmen, he served on the council (the Anchorage Assembly) and as mayor from 1982–87. He boasts of building the Alaska Center for Performing Arts, the Egan Convention Center, and the 11-mile Tony Knowles Coastal Trail. In 1994, with Hickel teasing voters about his intentions, Knowles ran against Republican Jim Campbell and Hickel ally and Lieutenant Governor Jack Coghill on the Alaska Independence ticket. Campbell started out with popular issue stands and a big lead which he squandered by smarmy campaign tactics—a push-poll that implied Knowles supported gay marriage and an ad which hinted that his personal morals were like Bill Clinton's. Knowles surged to a big lead in polls but on election day won by only 41.1%–40.8%, with 13% for Coghill—a 536-vote margin after all the ballots were in. Knowles had huge leads in the bush and Juneau, but ran behind in urban areas.

In office Knowles broke with the Republican legislature, vetoing its welfare reform, teacher tenure reform, and juvenile crime bills, later introducing his own versions; teacher tenure reform passed. His tax proposal was rejected by the legislature. He criticized the legislature for not earmarking Permanent Fund dollars for public education. He did not support the congressional delegation on Tongass logging, but advanced his own initiatives to keep the Ketchikan pulp mill running. He supported the delegation on ANWR drilling but was unable to sway the Clinton Administration. He passed a controversial plan to renegotiate Northstar oil leases. He called for giving rural subsistence users first call on fish and game. He proposed the nation's highest taxes on tobacco and alcohol, but Republicans refused to allow a vote on his $1 cigarette tax.

In 1996 Knowles was disappointed when Republicans added to their margins in the legislature. Republicans gained one seat in the Senate, two in the House—almost enough to override vetoes. But he certainly cannot be counted out for reelection in 1998, when Alaska is likely to have yet another wild and woolly race for governor.

Senior Senator. Few senators occupy as central a place in their state's public and economic life as Ted Stevens has for going on 30 years. "They sent me here," Stevens said in one impassioned debate, "to stand up for the state of Alaska." Stevens is now one of the most senior senators, chairman of the Appropriations Committee and of its Defense Subcommittee; even so, Alaska's special dependence on the federal government makes him more of an ambassador than a run-of-the-mill legislator. "We ask for special consideration," Stevens is not too shy to say, "because no one else is that far away, no one else has the problems that we have or the potential that we have, and no one else deals with the federal government day in and day out the way we do." Stevens spends plenty of time on national issues, but much of his time and energy over most of three decades has been necessarily consumed dealing with parochial Alaska issues. With his often prickly personality, that persistence has not endeared him to many colleagues, but he has demanded the Senate's attention during the many battles over his state's interests.

He has had plenty of training. Stevens grew up in Indiana, served in World War II, went to UCLA and Harvard, then moved to Alaska in 1950. He was U.S. attorney there and worked in the Interior Department in Washington, served in the legislature in Juneau and was appointed to the Senate by Governor Walter Hickel in December 1968, at 45. He quickly gained a seat on Appropriations and worked on Alaska issues of all description. He has not been entirely successful. He could not stop the Alaska Lands Act in 1980 and could not push through ANWR oil drilling in 1991 or 1995. But he did help pass the Native Claims Act in 1971 and got the oil pipeline through by one vote in 1973. And in 1995 he finally secured the repeal of the 1977 law forbidding exports of Alaskan oil, thus opening up the obvious East Asian markets. He managed the oil spill bill of 1989 in response to the *Valdez* accident, requiring double hulls and compensating Alaska. He has worked on fishing legislation: to ban monofilament nets, to reauthorize the 200-mile limit, and most recently to revise the Magnuson Act to reduce bycatch and preserve fish stocks. He has worked for more health and sanitation aid to bush villages and funding for health research on fetal alcohol syndrome and cancers common among Natives. He has tended to the needs of Alaska's Native corporations and has skillfully elicited consensus on Native issues. He got funding for the Alaska Aviation Heritage Museum and the Alaskan Native Heritage Center, for Native cultural programs and for the American Russian Center and restoration of Russian Orthodox churches in Alaska. He secured continuing moratoria on federal control of Alaska's navigable waters and Outer Continental Shelf leasing in Bristol Bay.

In 1997 Stevens became chairman of the Appropriations Committee, replacing Mark Hatfield. He was already chairman of the Defense Subcommittee, where he took quite a different approach from the near-pacifist Hatfield. He has generally supported robust defense spending and he favors a national missile defense that covers Alaska and Hawaii. But he opposed sending U.S. ground troops to Bosnia. He works hard to fund the National Guard, to raise military salaries and to keep troops in readiness. After surgery for prostate cancer in 1991, he has pushed for more funding for breast, cervical and prostate cancer research. He voted against GATT, charging that it would jeopardize Alaska's unitary business tax on oil producers. He is an old-style constitutional literalist: he has opposed all kinds of gun control and has sponsored a Tenth Amendment Enforcement Act to assure states' rights. But he takes some un-Republican stands. He supports the Corporation for Public Broadcasting: Alaska's public TV stations have the nation's largest audience shares. And, with the large government work force in high-cost Alaska, he supports increased salaries and benefits for federal workers and argues volubly for higher salaries for senators and Senate staffers. Stevens served as Republican whip from 1981–84, and ran for majority leader in 1984; he lost 28–25 to Bob Dole. He also lost a bid to head the Commerce Committee in 1995 and seems out of tune in many ways with the Senate's new Republican conservatives. But hard work and seniority make him a player.

Stevens's work on Alaska issues is widely respected and he has not received much serious opposition at home. His 66%–32% margin in 1990 was on the low side for him. In the August

1996 primary he was opposed by former state Representative and millionaire banker David Cuddy, who spent $1.3 million of his own money charging that Stevens was insufficiently conservative on abortion, gun control, state control, and federal spending. He also charged Stevens with illegal spending in 1990—a smear, Stevens backers charged. But Stevens won 59%–278%. The Democratic nominee, former Anchorage school board member Theresa Obermeyer, blamed Stevens for her husband's failure to pass the Alaska bar on 22 separate tries, and she sometimes wore black-and-white prisoner stripes and a ball-and-chain to his public events. Democratic Governor Tony Knowles announced he was voting for Stevens, who won 77%, followed by Green Party candidate Jed Whittaker with 13% and Obermeyer 10%. She is still at large.

Junior Senator. Frank Murkowski stands as a major figure, chairman of the Energy and Natural Resources Committee and his party's point man on one of our stickiest foreign policy problems, North Korea, where he is anxious to facilitate "meaningful dialogue" between North and South Korea. Murkowski grew up in Seattle and Ketchikan, served in the Coast Guard in Alaska, and became a banker in Fairbanks. A department head under Governor Walter Hickel in the 1960s, he ran for Congress and lost in 1970. He was elected to the Senate in 1980 by winning 54% against liberal Democrat Clark Gruening. He got a seat on Energy, which handles many Alaska issues, with many successes and some failures. The former include a ban on driftnet fishing in international waters, the Native Languages Preservation Act, initiating contacts between Alaska and Siberia and a law allowing Native corporation shareholders to retain control of their lands. He sponsored the lifting of the ban on Alaskan oil exports, a 1977 policy that stayed on the books until November 1995. He worked on the Greens Creek land exchange to keep open a silver mine outside Juneau and on dozens of other land exchange details. He led the so-far unsuccessful fight for ANWR oil drilling and losing efforts to continue logging in the Tongass National Forest: both causes frustrated by Clinton vetoes. On many of these matters Murkowski worked harmoniously with Ted Stevens, sometimes one taking the lead, sometimes the other.

On issues farther afield, he passed through the Senate a bill to allow the storage of high-level nuclear waste at Yucca Mountain in Nevada, but the House did not take it up. In 1996 he produced a parks bill, giving legal status to the Presidio trust in San Francisco, Sterling Forest in New York and New Jersey, the Tallgrass Prairie Natural Preserve in Kansas, the New Bedford Whaling National Park, and the Selma-to-Montgomery National Historic Trail. He has worked on East Asia issues, from Taiwan to North Korea, which he visited; in late 1994 he criticized the Clinton Administration's accord with North Korea, but declined to try to overturn it.

Murkowski has been reelected twice in contests that attracted little attention outside Alaska. In 1986 he beat former Alaska Pacific University president Glenn Olds 54%–44%. In 1992, he attracted strong opposition from Native leader Willie Hensley and former commissioner of Economic Development Tony Smith, who attacked Murkowski as ineffective on ANWR and the Exxon clean-up money. Smith edged Hensley in the primary, 45%–40%, but Murkowski ran an ad showing a farmer with a wheelbarrow full of manure, a reference to Smith's allegedly liberal promises; there were some nasty charges and countercharges, and Murkowski greatly outspent Smith, winning 53%–38%. Murkowski has never received as much as 55% of the vote, but his chairmanship is highly valuable to Alaska and his views in line with those of most Alaska voters; he should be in a strong position in 1998.

Representative-At-Large. Alaska's Don Young, onetime tugboat captain on the Yukon and the only licensed mariner in Congress, is, in his words, "not one of these smooth, namby-pamby politicians." He is a hot-tempered, salty-tongued true believer, given to malapropisms ("Pribilof's dog" and "bladderdash") and provocative insults (Republicans soft on the environment are "squishies"). Young grew up in rural California, served in the Army, then moved to Alaska where he became mayor of Fort Yukon. He was elected to the legislature in 1966 and ran for Congress in 1972; his opponent, incumbent Nick Begich, was killed in a plane crash, and Young won the March 1973 special election to succeed him. Young is not a free market conservative, and casts many liberal economic votes; but he is a cultural and foreign policy conservative, and often an angry one. Some of that anger may have come from serving on the Resources Committee, where he was ranking minority member for 10 years before becoming chairman in 1995. This committee, which handles most Alaska issues, has long been packed with environmentalists; indeed, relatively few Lower 48 congressmen see things the way development-minded Alaskans do. The 20 Republican congressmen from Florida and Arizona, for instance, the two states Bill Clinton lost in 1992 and won in 1996, are as eager as some Northeastern Republicans to show their support for the environment; and it often comes at Alaska's, or Young's, expense. Alaska's two senators can use the Senate's dilatory rules to get their way; in the pragmatic House, Young can be efficiently steamrollered, and has been even as chairman.

And the battles are hard to win. The House finally approved oil drilling in ANWR in 1995, but Clinton vetoed it and made it stick. Young's efforts to maintain logging in the Tongass National Forest and, later, to give it to the state of Alaska, have not borne fruit. He was not able to block the 1980 Alaska Lands Act. He was not able to rewrite the Endangered Species Act; as *National Journal*'s Margaret Kriz writes, "Analysts also say that Young's legislative attacks on environmental laws and personal criticisms of environmental activists made the Republicans vulnerable to charges that Congress was pursuing an extremist environmental agenda." And "congressional aides say that Stevens and Young alienated Republican moderates by trying to ram their proposals through." But Young has had his successes, too, some of them endorsed by his environmental enemies: an end to the ban on export of Alaska oil; the driftnet law which would limit foreign fishing techniques and the Magnuson Act revision limiting bycatch; many laws to help the Alaska Natives, including rural sanitation; the 1995 sale of the Alaska Power Administration to Alaska entities; blocking reforms to the 1872 Mining Law which, in Young's view, would make it harder to stake a mining claim here than in Russia. Young can be a consensus legislator more often than he or others may think. He steered a reform of the 30-year-old Arctic National Wildlife Refuge Act to passage, with the help of its original sponsor John Dingell, by 388–37 in October 1995; but the Senate failed to act on it. He is currently the number two Republican on Transportation and Infrastructure, in a position to steer public works projects to Alaska.

If Young is often embattled in Washington, he has been in Alaska as well, where opponents have charged he is ineffective in protecting Alaskan interests. He had significant opposition in 1978, 1984, 1986, 1990, and 1992, with his toughest race the last year, against Valdez Mayor John Devens. The *Anchorage Daily News*'s constant criticisms of Young depressed his vote in that usually Republican city, but his work for Native causes helped him carry the combined rural and bush vote, enough for a statewide victory of 47%–43%. In 1994 Young won by a solid 57%–33% and in 1996 by 59%–36%. After 1994, when he unexpectedly became chairman, he maneuvered around reluctant subcommittee chairmen on wetlands and the Endangered Species Act and said that if environmentalists wouldn't compromise, "I'm just going to ram it down their throats." After 1996, Speaker Newt Gingrich, noting how Democrats used environmental issues against many Republicans, sought to prevent Young from naming all new Republicans to Resources; although most of the committee's Republicans returned for the 104th, Young named at least three development-minded freshmen from Western states to Resources, and he created a new Forests Subcommittee for conservative Helen Chenoweth of Idaho. A move by the Wilderness Society to oust Young as chairman fell flat when New Yorker Sherwood Boehlert, a moderate on environment issues, said he had worked well with Young and supported him. Perhaps the taming of the riverboat captain from Fort Yukon has begun.

Presidential politics. In presidential elections, Alaska votes Alaska issues, but this was not always so: in 1960 and 1968 its vote came eerily close to the national average. Since then, it has voted for development and against the national Democrats: in the year of the Alaska Lands Act, it gave only 26% of its votes to Jimmy Carter, who in some places ran behind Libertarian Ed Clark. In 1992, Ross Perot won 28% here, his second best showing in the country. In 1996, Bob Dole easily led Bill Clinton, 51%–33%, with 11% for Perot.

Alaska has no presidential primary. Party true-believers tend to dominate the caucuses. In the January 1996 straw poll or "beauty contest," Alaska Republicans voted 33% for Pat Buchanan, 31% for Steve Forbes, and 17% for Bob Dole. This gave Buchanan the confidence and verve he showed weeks later in Louisiana, where he beat Phil Gramm, and in other early contests climaxed by his win in New Hampshire February 20.

The People: Est. Pop. 1996: 607,000; Pop. 1990: 550,043, up 10.4% 1990–1996. 0.2% of U.S. total, 48th largest; 33% rural. Median age: 31.9 years. 5% 65 years and over. 73.9% White, 4.0% Black, 3.4% Asian, 15.4% Amer. Indian; 3.2% Hispanic origin. Households: 56.2% married couple families; 34% married couple fams. w. children; 58% college educ.; median household income: $41,408; per capita income: $17,610; 56.1% owner occupied housing; median house value: $94,400; median monthly rent: $503. 7.8% Unemployment. 1996 Voting age pop.: 425,000. 1996 Turnout: 241,620; 57% of VAP. Registered voters (1996): 415,368; 70,173 D (17%), 101,793 R (25%), 243,402 unaffiliated and minor parties (58%).

Political Lineup: Governor, Tony Knowles (D); Lt. Gov., Fran Ulmer (D); Atty. Gen., Bruce M. Botelho (D); Commissioner of Revenue, Wilson Condon. State Senate, 20 (14 R and 6 D); Senate President, Mike Miller (R). State House, 40 (25 R, 15 D); House Speaker, Gail Phillips (R). Senators, Ted Stevens (R) and Frank H. Murkowski (R). Representative, 1 R at large.

Elections Division: 907-465-4611; **Filing Deadline for U.S. Congress:** June 1, 1998.

1996 Presidential Vote

Dole (R)	122,746	(51%)
Clinton (D)	80,380	(33%)
Perot (I)	26,333	(11%)
Other(s)	12,161	(5%)

1992 Presidential Vote

Bush (R)	102,000	(40%)
Clinton (D)	78,294	(30%)
Perot (I)	73,481	(28%)

GOVERNOR

Gov. Tony Knowles (D)

Elected 1994; term expires Jan. 1999. b. Jan. 1, 1943, Tulsa, OK; home, Juneau; Yale U., B.A. 1968; Christian; married (Susan).

Career: Army, 1962–64 (Vietnam). Restaurant owner, 1968–present; Anchorage Assembly, 1975–79; Anchorage Mayor, 1982–87.

Office: P.O. Box 110001, Juneau 99811, 907-465-3500; Fax: 907-465-3532; Web site: www.state.ak.us.

Election Results

1994 gen.	Tony Knowles (D)	87,693	(41%)
	James O. (Jim) Campbell (R)	87,157	(41%)
	John B. (Jack) Coghill (I)	27,838	(13%)
	Jim Sykes (Green)	8,727	(4%)
1994 prim.	Tony Knowles (D)	24,727	(44%)
	Stephen McAlpine (D)	17,482	(31%)
	Sam Cotten (D)	13,899	(25%)
1990 gen.	Walter J. Hickel (AI)	68,181	(39%)
	Tony Knowles (D)	53,998	(31%)
	Arliss Sturgulewski (R)	46,553	(27%)
	Other	6,832	(3%)

SENATORS

Sen. Ted Stevens (R)

Appointed Dec. 1968, seat up 2002; b. Nov. 18, 1923, Indianapolis, IN; home, Girdwood; U.C.L.A., B.A. 1947, Harvard, LL.B. 1950; Episcopalian; married (Catherine).

Career: Army Air Corps, 1943–46 (WWII); Practicing atty., 1950–53, 1961–68; U.S. Atty., 1953–56; U.S. Dept. of Interior, Legis. Cnsl., 1956–58, Asst. to Secy., 1958–60, Solicitor, 1960–61; AK House of Reps., 1964–68.

DC Office: 522 HSOB 20510, 202-224-3004; Fax: 202-224-2354; e-mail: senator_stevens@stevens.senate.gov.

State Offices: Anchorage, 907-271-5915; Fairbanks, 907-456-0261; Juneau, 907-586-7400; Kenai, 907-283-5808; Ketchikan, 907-225-6880; Wasilla, 907-376-7665.

Committees: *Appropriations* (Chmn. of 15 R); Commerce, Justice, State & the Judiciary; Defense (Chmn.); Foreign Operations; Interior; Legislative Branch; VA, HUD & Independent Agencies. *Commerce, Science & Transportation* (2nd of 11 R): Aviation; Communications; Oceans & Fisheries; Science, Technology & Space; Surface Transportation & Merchant Marine. *Rules & Administration* (3rd of 9 R). *Joint Committee on the Library of Congress* (Vice Chmn. of 5 Sens.).

Group Ratings

	ADA	ACLU	AFS	LCV	CFA	CON	NFIB	COC	ACU	NTLC	CHC
1996	20	11	14	0	21	19	82	85	80	86	69
1995	5	—	0	7	13	81	—	94	73	—	—

National Journal Ratings

	1995 LIB — 1995 CONS			1996 LIB — 1996 CONS		
Economic	37%	—	61%	32%	—	67%
Social	39%	—	60%	42%	—	57%
Foreign	19%	—	80%	38%	—	58%

Key Votes of the 104th Congress

1. Reduce Medicare Growth $	Y	5. Flag Amendment	Y	9. Anti-Missle Defense	Y
2. Lmt. Prod. Liab. Damages	Y	6. Endangered Species	N	10. Cuban Embargo	Y
3. Increase Min. Wage	Y	7. Gay Employment Rights	N	11. Bar Bosnia Troop $	N
4. Welfare Reform	Y	8. Ovrd. Part. Birth Veto	Y	12. Cut Vietnam Aid	N

Election Results

1996 general	Ted Stevens (R)	177,893	(77%)	($2,711,710)
	Jed Whittaker (G)	29,037	(13%)	
	Theresa Obermeyer (D)	23,977	(10%)	
1996 primary	Ted Stevens (R)	71,042	(59%)	
	Dave W. Cuddy (R)	32,994	(27%)	
	Others	16,640	(14%)	
1990 general	Ted Stevens (R)	125,806	(66%)	($1,618,098)
	Michael Beasley (D)	61,115	(32%)	($445)
	Other	2,999	(2%)	

Sen. Frank H. Murkowski (R)

Elected 1980, seat up 1998; b. Mar. 28, 1933, Seattle, WA; home, Fairbanks; U. of Santa Clara, Seattle U., B.A. 1955; Catholic; married (Nancy).

Career: Coast Guard, 1955–56; Pacific Natl. Bank of Seattle, 1957–58; Natl. Bank of AK, 1959–67; Commissioner, AK Dept. of Econ. Devel., 1966–70; Pres., AK Natl. Bank, 1971–80.

DC Office: 322 HSOB 20510, 202-224-6665; Fax: 202-224-5301; e-mail: e-mail@murkowski.senate.gov.

State Offices: Anchorage, 907-271-3735; Fairbanks, 907-456-0233; Juneau, 907-586-7400; Kenai, 907-283-5808; Ketchikan, 907-225-6880; Wasilla, 907-376-7665.

Committees: *Energy & Natural Resources* (Chmn. of 11 R). *Finance* (6th of 11 R): International Trade; Long-Term Growth, Debt & Defict Reduction; Taxation & IRS Oversight. *Veterans' Affairs* (3rd of 7 R). *Indian Affairs* (2nd of 8 R).

Group Ratings

	ADA	ACLU	AFS	LCV	CFA	CON	NFIB	COC	ACU	NTLC	CHC
1996	15	6	14	0	14	47	90	92	95	96	100
1995	0	—	0	0	6	26	—	100	91	—	—

National Journal Ratings

	1995 LIB	—	1995 CONS	1996 LIB	—	1996 CONS
Economic	29%	—	70%	18%	—	79%
Social	27%	—	71%	0%	—	72%
Foreign	20%	—	79%	26%	—	70%

Key Votes of the 104th Congress

1. Reduce Medicare Growth $	Y	5. Flag Amendment	Y	9. Anti-Missle Defense	Y
2. Lmt. Prod. Liab. Damages	Y	6. Endangered Species	N	10. Cuban Embargo	Y
3. Increase Min. Wage	Y	7. Gay Employment Rights	N	11. Bar Bosnia Troop $	Y
4. Welfare Reform	Y	8. Ovrd. Part. Birth Veto	Y	12. Cut Vietnam Aid	N

Election Results

1992 general	Frank H. Murkowski (R)	127,163	(53%)	($1,910,759)
	Tony Smith (D)	92,065	(38%)	($910,138)
	Mary Jordan (Green)	20,019	(8%)	($4,091)
1992 primary	Frank H. Murkowski (R)	37,486	(81%)	
	Jed Whittaker (R)	9,065	(19%)	
1986 general	Frank H. Murkowski (R)	97,674	(54%)	($1,514,628)
	Glenn Olds (D)	79,727	(44%)	($412,074)

REPRESENTATIVE

Rep. Don Young (R)

Elected Mar. 1973; b. June 9, 1933, Meridian, CA; home, Fort Yukon; Yuba Jr. Col., A.A. 1952, Chico St. Col., B.A. 1958; Episcopalian; married (Lu).

Career: Army, 1955–57; Fort Yukon City Cncl., 1960–64; Fort Yukon Mayor, 1964–68; AK House of Reps., 1966–70; AK Senate, 1970–73.

DC Office: 2111 RHOB 20515, 202-225-5765; Fax: 202-225-0425.

District Offices: Anchorage, 907-271-5978; Fairbanks, 907-456-0210; Juneau, 907-586-7400; Kenai, 907-283-5808; Ketchikan, 907-225-6880; Mat-Su, 907-376-7665.

Committees: *Resources* (Chmn. of 27 R). *Transportation & Infrastructure* (2nd of 40 R): Coast Guard & Maritime Transportation; Water Resources & Environment.

Group Ratings

	ADA	ACLU	AFS	LCV	CFA	CON	NFIB	COC	ACU	NTLC	CHC
1996	0	21	33	23	8	66	86	81	89	98	100
1995	5	—	—	0	0	75	—	91	91	—	—

National Journal Ratings

	1995 LIB — 1995 CONS			1996 LIB — 1996 CONS		
Economic	51%	—	48%	33%	—	64%
Social	0%	—	79%	10%	—	86%
Foreign	27%	—	72%	0%	—	79%

Key Votes of the 104th Congress

1. Reduce Medicare Growth $	Y	5. Flag Amendment	Y	9. Cuban Embargo	Y
2. Ovrd. Product Liab. Veto	Y	6. Drop EPA Limits	N	10. Bar Bosnia Troop $	Y
3. Increase Min. Wage	Y	7. Repeal Assault-Weap. Ban	Y	11. Cut Anti-Missile Defense	N
4. Welfare Reform	Y	8. Ovrd. Part. Birth Veto	Y	12. Bar U.N. Uniforms	*

Election Results

1996 general	Don Young (R)	138,834	(59%)	($1,176,954)
	Georgianna Lincoln (D)	85,114	(36%)	($245,941)
	Others	9,752	(4%)	
1996 primary	Don Young (R)	70,082	(58%)	
	Georgianna Lincoln (D)	38,105	(32%)	
	Jim Dore (R)	5,936	(5%)	
	Others	6,566	(5%)	
1994 general	Don Young (R)	118,537	(57%)	($930,513)
	Tony Smith (D)	68,172	(33%)	($343,879)
	Jonni Whitmore (Green)	21,277	(10%)	

ARIZONA

Arizona is home to one of America's oldest communities and very many of its youngest. The Hopi Indians, living as shepherds on plateaus east of the Grand Canyon, have not changed much in perhaps 500 years. In 1680 they killed the local Franciscan priests and burned their churches and have spurned Christianity since; more recently they have been involved in land disputes with the far more numerous Navajo. The Hopi are the oldest Arizonans; the newest are moving in every day, into subdivisions rising up out of the empty desert east, north, and west of Phoenix, hemmed in only by dry river beds, upcrops of mountains, and Indian reservation boundaries. Arizona is one of the boom states of the 1990s, with some of the nation's fastest population growth, a state with an economy now sophisticated and decentralized enough that there is no easy explanation, as there once was, of how and why Arizona grows.

The mainstay of Arizona's economy when it was admitted to the Union in 1912 was copper—the Capitol dome is encased in copper; one of its leading public figures was Lewis Douglas, copper heir and congressman, briefly Franklin Roosevelt's budget director and for a longer time Harry Truman's ambassador to Britain. In these years Arizona depended heavily on the federal government, and on politicians like Carl Hayden, Democratic congressman from statehood in 1912 and senator from 1927–69, whose public works projects watered Arizona's cotton, citrus and cattle farms. Then in the decades after World War II businessmen, lawyers, developers, and water companies, notably the Salt River Project, built an Arizona based on something like the opposite of New Deal principles: with minimal government and precious little regulation of business, a welcoming of new technological ideas and shunning of new cultural liberalism; like Disneyland, a more gleaming and spotless embodiment of old values than America had ever been. The state's most visible figure was Barry Goldwater, department store owner and pilot, city council member and senator and the nation's Mr. Conservative for much of the 1950s and 1960s. He helped to make Arizona Republican, the only state to vote Republican for president in every election from 1952–92; though it was volatile enough to vote for Bill Clinton 47%–44% in 1996, even while favoring Republican candidates for the House 59%–38%.

This Arizona has grown phenomenally, from 700,000 people at the end of Word War II to 3.6 million in 1990, and then to 4.3 million in 1996—an increase in six years as large as its whole population in 1945. It is growth based on high-tech and low taxes, the one getting higher and the other lower every year. It is not growth based on an influx of elderly retirees—Arizona may have Sun City, but its proportion of people over 65 is lower than the national average; nor is it based on farming subsidized by cheap water, since thirsty cotton farms are being phased out for urban users who can easily outbid them. More than anything else, the engine of Arizona's growth has been technology: Phoenix has been attracting high-tech industries since Motorola built a research center for military electronics there in 1948, and big employers now include Motorola's semiconductor operation, Allied Signal, Honeywell flight systems, Intel and Tucson's Hughes Aircraft.

Arizona is a place where a relatively unregulated private sector has produced bounteous growth and the change and disorder which are its inevitable byproducts. There is no ancient establishment here, and plenty of sharp dealing: this was the home base of savings and loan crook Charles Keating and Governor (and former developer) Fife Symington, who was indicted for fraud on creditors in 1996; the state legislature in the early 1990s also was laced with corruption. But government does not necessarily determine the course of development. "Shadow governments," to use author Joel Garreau's term, often do—the developers of Sun City issue regulations far more detailed than city zoning commissions, and the Salt River Project, which started off running dams and now provides much of Arizona's water and electricity, does more planning than the city of Phoenix or the state.

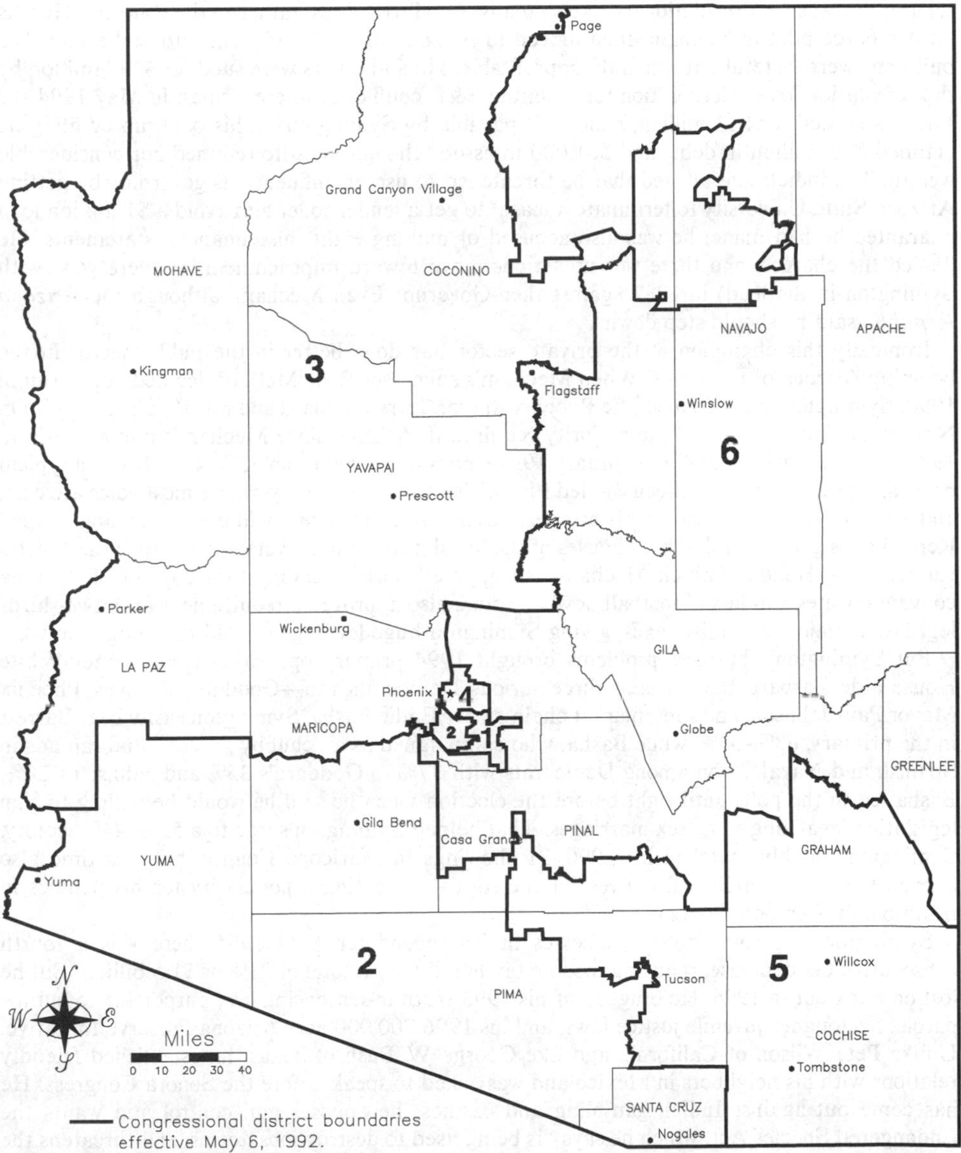
Page
Grand Canyon Village
MOHAVE
COCONINO
NAVAJO
APACHE
3
Kingman
Flagstaff
Winslow
6
YAVAPAI
Prescott
Parker
Wickenburg
LA PAZ
GILA
Phoenix
4
MARICOPA
2
1
Globe
GREENLEE
Gila Bend
Casa Grande
PINAL
GRAHAM
YUMA
Yuma
2
5
Willcox
Tucson
PIMA
N
W
E
S
Miles
0 10 20 30 40
COCHISE
Tombstone
SANTA CRUZ
Nogales
Congressional district boundaries
effective May 6, 1992.

Governor. Arizona's Governor Fife Symington is perhaps the nation's purest free market governor, a tax-cutter whose time in office has been one of surging growth. But he is also beleaguered in his private capacity—a real estate developer who declared bankruptcy in September 1995 and was indicted in June 1996. Like most Arizona voters, Symington grew up somewhere else, the hunt country of Maryland; he is a distant relative of the late Senator Stuart Symington of Missouri and graduated from Harvard in 1968. But he is not a Democrat like the senator nor was he a revolutionary like so many '68 Harvardites: rather to the contrary. He was an Air Force pilot in Vietnam, then moved to Arizona in 1972 and went into real estate. His buildings were tasteful but evidently unprofitable. He and others were sued for $197 million by the Resolution Trust Corporation for violating S&L conflict of interest rules; in May 1994 the suit was settled for $12 million, none of it payable by Symington. In his bankruptcy filing he claimed $25 million in debts and $61,000 in assets, though his wife retained her considerable wealth. The indictment alleged that he threatened to use his influence as governor (by getting Arizona State University to terminate a lease) to get a lender to let him avoid a $1 million loan guarantee he had made; he was also accused of making eight false financial statements. He denied the charges, and there was no serious move toward impeachment, as there was (with Symington in the lead) in 1987 against then-Governor Evan Mecham, although the *Arizona Republic* said he should step down.

Ironically this champion of the private sector has done better in the public sector in the booming Arizona of the 1990s. When Mecham's successor Rose Mofford decided not to run in 1990, Symington faced Democratic Phoenix Mayor Terry Goddard and ran 1% ahead of him in November. But neither had the majority required in Arizona since Mecham's minority win in 1986, and there was a runoff in February 1991 which Symington won 52%–48%. It was a typical partisan pattern: the Republican carried Phoenix's Maricopa County, where most votes are cast, and lost the rest of the state. In his first term Symington cut taxes, held down spending, helped Republicans gain control of both houses of the legislature, and got voters to approve the Martin Luther King Holiday (which Mecham had opposed noisily, leading to a boycott of Arizona convention sites and loss of football bowls). Voters also approved a requirement for a two-thirds legislative majority to raise taxes, giving Symington huge leverage to hold the budget down.

But Symington's business problems brought 1994 primary opposition from former White House aide Barbara Barrett, and three serious Democrats ran—Goddard, the new Phoenix Mayor Paul Johnson, and supermarket chain owner Eddie Basha. Symington easily beat Barrett in the primary, 68%–32%, while Basha, who campaigned as a "chubby grocer," and ran ads in Spanish and Navajo, won among Democrats with 37% to Goddard's 35% and Johnson's 28%. Basha led in the polls until right before the election when he said he would be willing to sign legislation legalizing same-sex marriages. That helped Symington surge to a 52%–44% victory. Symington roughly matched his 1990–91 showings in Maricopa County, but this time also carried the Tucson area and the rest of the state—indicating a popularity for his policies in traditionally Democratic areas.

Symington had some policy successes in his second term. In 1995 there was a fourth consecutive tax decrease, reducing income tax liability by a total of 21% or $1.5 billion. But he lost on a tax cut in 1996. He bragged of his 1993 truth-in-sentencing law, purporting to outlaw parole, his tougher juvenile justice laws, and his 1996 700,000 acre Arizona Preserve Initiative. Unlike Pete Wilson of California and like George W. Bush of Texas, he established friendly relations with his neighbors in Mexico and was asked to speak before the Sonora Congress. He has come out against Indian gambling and casinos; he opposes gun control and wants the Endangered Species Act, which he says "is being used to destroy jobs, towns, and threatens the sustainability of our natural resources," repealed.

Symington seems to have restored the minimalist government tradition identified with Barry Goldwater, which was succeeded by the somewhat more activist approach of Democrat Bruce Babbitt, governor from 1978–1986 and now secretary of the Interior. But his own political fortunes look dim, whatever the outcome of his legal problems. The likelihood for 1998 is a wild and woolly race for governor, which either party and one of several candidates could win, and for a continued Republican legislature.

Senior Senator. John McCain, a junior senator in the minority on the political defensive just a few years ago, is now one of the most respected and powerful senators. His personal story is a dramatic one, told beautifully by Robert Timberg in *The Nightingale's Song*; he is the son and grandson of Navy admirals, a decorated Navy pilot himself who was shot down over Vietnam and who spent five years, most of it in pain and torture, in Communist prisoner of war camps; he refused to be let out ahead of those who had been in longer when he was offered release because of his father's rank.

McCain returned to the United States in March 1973. His final assignment in the Navy was as Senate liaison. In 1980 he retired and move to Arizona, his wife's home state; in 1982 he ran for an open House seat. Attacked as an outsider, he responded, "The longest place I ever lived in was Hanoi." He led 32%–26% in a four-way primary, and won the 1982 and 1984 general elections and then the 1986 Senate contest easily.

McCain got a seat on the Armed Services Committee some 14 years after he left Hanoi; but his most important committee assignment now is Commerce, of which he is, after the defeat of Larry Pressler, chairman. McCain was the only Senate Republican to vote against passage of the 1996 Telecommunications Act, decrying the special intrests that were "driving this train." He advances the causes of deregulation and free markets—a steadfast devotion that at times has raised the ire of Majority Leader Trent Lott and the fear of "K Street" lobbyists. He wants to push for free TV time for candidates who agree to limit campaign spending and he wants to raise revenue through an auction of space in the digital-television spectrum.

As chairman of Indian Affairs, McCain spent much of his time in 1995 and 1996 working on their issues. He obviously feels a responsibility for Indians, who are a larger percentage in Arizona than almost any other state. "Never deceive them," he says. "They have been deceived too many times in the last 200 years." He has worked for Indian self-governance and sovereignty, but has also pushed laws on child abuse on reservations. He has cooperated with the vast expansion in the 1990s of Indian gambling. On adoption issues, he has backed a 90-day limit on the time in which Indian tribes can claim custody of off-reservation adopted children with Indian blood, but he has not fully satisfied those like Republican Congresswoman Deborah Pryce who object to tribal control of children who have been adopted years before by parents who had no knowledge that the birthparents had Indian ancestors. McCain is proud that he was endorsed for reelection in 1992 by every Arizona tribe.

With his military background, McCain is listened to on defense issues—and also because he is not an entirely predictable supporter of armed intervention or increased defense spending. He has criticized the Clinton Administration for stinting on defense but has worked to hold down funding for some projects—the Sea Wolf submarine, B-2 bomber, the Strategic Defense Initiative. He has shown a professional military officer's caution about committing American troops without a clear end in sight, most notably in Bosnia. There he long favored lifting the embargo on arms sales to the Bosnian Muslims, but opposed sending American pilots, arguing that "the use of air power alone has never determined the outcome of a military conflict." But on Korea, in 1994 he called the Clinton Administration's policy "appeasement" and said sanctions against North Korean nuclear proliferation should be backed by explicit threats of airstrikes. And he has criticized relaxation of restrictions on exports of nuclear-sensitive materials and on promoting proliferation for commercial gain. The same combination of caution, boldness and concern about proliferation came out in his comments on Iraq: he urged caution in committing American troops in August 1990, strongly backed the Gulf war resolution in January 1991 and all along threatened a crackdown on Iraq for its nuclear program. He worked hard and closely with Democratic Senator and good friend John Kerry on the special committee investigating charges that American POWs or MIAs remain in Vietnam; they found no evidence of any. With Kerry he supported ending the trade embargo on and initiating diplomatic relations with Vietnam, and has traveled there many times.

McCain's record on most issues tends to be reliably conservative, but with unusual accents. He wants to require a supermajority of 60 Senate votes to raise taxes, backed a tough line-item veto, and wants to end congressional earmarks for highways and public works projects. On environmental issues, McCain favored banning small craft flights in the Grand Canyon and opposed construction of Cliff Dam; his 1992 campaign spots described him as "the Grand Canyon's best friend in Congress." He was one of the leaders of the gifts ban and lobby reform. With Democrat Russ Feingold of Wisconsin, sponsored in 1996 a campaign finance reform bill which in return for agreement to voluntary spending limits would give candidates some free TV time and lower TV ads and postage rates; it would also eliminate PACs and soft money. It was endorsed by Bill Clinton after his reelection, even as he was facing charges of illegal fundraising which McCain called for an independent counsel to investigate.

In early 1996 McCain was among several top Arizona Republicans who endorsed Phil Gramm for president, to no avail. After Gramm dropped out in March 1996, McCain supported Bob Dole and traveled with him often; as a fellow military veteran he buoyed Dole's spirits while, as a usually open and frank politician, he mollified the press. At the San Diego Republican Convention he delivered a seemingly simple yet genuinely elegant nomination speech for Dole.

McCain's standing in Arizona now seems very strong. Prior to the 1992 election he was beset by the Keating Five scandal: he was one of five senators who met with regulators on Keating's case in 1987 and, though he did nothing for Keating, was kept in the case by Democrats on the Ethics Committee because he was the one Republican involved and thus made the scandal bipartisan. McCain's poll ratings moved back upward in 1991. In 1992 he was reelected 56%–32%, with 11% for conservative former Governor Evan Mecham. For 1998 he looks like one of the Republicans' safest senators, and for 2000, perhaps a presidential candidate.

Junior Senator. Jon Kyl, Arizona's junior senator, comes to office almost by inheritance. His father John Kyl was a Republican congressman from Iowa (1959–65, 1967–73), who eventually lost his seat in redistricting; the son moved to a state that, in effect, was gaining the Republican seats Great Plains states like Iowa were losing. The younger Kyl went to college and law school in Arizona, practiced law in Phoenix, worked on Republican campaigns and headed the Phoenix Chamber of Commerce; he won the heavily Republican 4th District seat in 1986 by beating 60%–28% former (1973–77) Congressman John Conlan, who had support from the religious right. In the House, Kyl was a leader among Republicans on the Strategic Defense Initiative, the balanced budget amendment, and for disclosing the names of House members with overdrafts on the House bank—one of the causes that destabilized Democrats' control of the House in 1993 and 1994. But by that time Kyl was running for the Senate seat held for three terms by Democrat Dennis DeConcini, known for casting a critical vote for the Panama Canal Treaties in 1978, casting a critical vote against Judge Robert Bork in 1987, and for interceding with federal regulators on behalf of S&L operator Charles Keating. DeConcini decided to retire, prompting three Democrats to run; Kyl was unopposed in the Republican primary.

He had further luck when the Democrats ran almost even, with one-term Congressman Sam Coppersmith carrying Phoenix, state Senate Minority Leader Cindy Resnick carrying Tucson, and Secretary of State Dick Mahoney carrying the rest of the state; Coppersmith won the September 13 primary, but by only 59 votes of 255,000 cast and after a two-week recount. Kyl, with far more money, ran ads with home movie texture showing him travelling through the desert countryside in a Chevy Suburban, dressed in jeans and working on ranches, while talking about how he and his wife first fell in love with the state. Coppersmith stressed his pro-choice stand on abortion and said he would welcome a campaign visit from President Clinton. Kyl prevailed solidly in the general, winning 54%–40%.

Kyl has a solidly conservative record, with a few exceptions on foreign policy. He continues to support a limit of 19% of gross domestic product on federal spending (something which a balanced budget amendment may produce) and wants to reduce federal controls on western lands. He is the chief sponsor, with Dianne Feinstein, of a constitutional amendment on victims' rights. It would give victims of crime a right to be informed, to be present, and to be heard at critical stages in the judicial process; a right to speedy trial and final conclusion free from unreasonable delay; full restitution from the criminal; and protection from violence or intimidation.

Kyl spent much time in the 104th Congress on immigration. Claiming that 10% of the Arizona workforce is made up of illegal immigrants and that the state government spends $200 million on medical care, education, and incarceration of undocumented immigrants, he was a force on the Immigration Subcommittee for strict border controls. But he was unable to prevent Spencer Abraham's amendment deferring any cuts in legal immigration and Clinton Administration demands that welfare not be cut off entirely for illegals. Kyl did succeed in getting amendments to increase the Border Patrol by 5,000 agents, to develop an entry-exit control system to track legals who overstay their visas, and to require federal reimbursement to states and localities for emergency medical service to illegals. But he supports cuts in legal immigration and new rules for family-based immigration, the kind of measures which in 1996 gravely hurt Republicans among Hispanics and could cost them any chance at their votes in the future.

Kyl does not come up for reelection until 2000, and seems solidly entrenched in still-mostly-Republican Arizona.

Presidential politics. In 1996 Arizona did two unlikely things: it staged one of the decisive presidential primaries in the nation in February, and then in November voted Democratic for president for the first time since 1948, breaking the longest such string in the nation. Governor Fife Symington wanted Arizona to vote the same day as New Hampshire's first-in-the-nation primary; New Hampshire objected and threatened to schedule its primary ever earlier, and Arizona backed down and voted a week later, February 27. Symington, Senator John McCain, and most other Republican politicians were backing Phil Gramm, and hoped to produce an early victory for him. But Gramm was out of the race even before New Hampshire, and Arizona was very much up for grabs.

For months Steve Forbes had been peppering the state with ads boosting his flat tax and attacking Washington politicians. But Pat Buchanan, urging followers to "mount up and ride" after his narrow victory in New Hampshire, appeared at Tombstone's O.K. Corral in black hat and with pistols; he hoped his opposition to illegal immigrants and support of property rights would boost him here. But Buchanan's truculence evidently rubbed many voters wrong. He finished third, with 27%, the end of any serious chance he had; Bob Dole, with Senator John McCain's support, finished second, with 30%; Steve Forbes, after all his ads, took 33% and all the delegates.

But Bill Clinton won all of Arizona's electoral votes in November, by a 47%–44% margin—the first Democrat to carry the state since Harry Truman. Clinton had come close to winning in 1992, losing to George Bush by only 38%–37%. Why was Clinton so competitive in a free enterprise state? Many speculated that elderly voters, fearing for their Medicare, went for him. But Arizona does not have a specially large elderly population, and the air seemed to go out of the Medicare issue in mid-October. More important, perhaps, was the environment issue. Arizona has a much lower percentage of rural and small town voters than other Rocky Mountain states—even Colorado, which switched from Clinton to Republican in 1996. Nearly 80% of Arizonans live in metro Phoenix and Tucson, and they want to preserve the environment that is so visibly being transformed by their own success. Clinton's staging of the announcement of a Utah land preserve at the Grand Canyon may have carried Arizona singlehandedly (it may also have defeated the only Democratic congressman in Utah). Also, Hispanic voters went 10–1 for Clinton in 1996, perhaps out of anger at Republicans' attempts to deny government aid to legal as well as illegal immigrants and to reduce family-based immigration.

Congressional districting. Arizona gained one congressional district in each of the last four censuses, and will surely gain another—perhaps two—after 2000. The current plan was drawn by a federal court to produce a Phoenix-to-Tucson Hispanic majority district, the 2d, which is solidly Democratic. The other five are Republican, though the 1st and 6th went Democratic in 1992 and the 6th almost did again in 1996.

The People: Est. Pop. 1996: 4,428,000; Pop. 1990: 3,665,228, up 20.8% 1990–1996. 1.7% of U.S. total, 21st largest; 12% rural. Median age: 34.4 years. 13% 65 years and over. 71.7% White, 2.9% Black, 1.4% Asian, 5.2% Amer. Indian; 18.8% Hispanic origin. Households: 54.6% married couple families; 25% married couple fams. w. children; 53% college educ.; median household income: $27,540; per capita income: $13,461; 64.4% owner occupied housing; median house value: $80,100; median monthly rent: $370. 5.5% Unemployment. 1996 Voting age pop.: 3,145,000. 1996 Turnout: 1,404,405; 45% of VAP. Registered voters (1996): 2,237,765; 911,024 D (41%), 1,012,282 R (45%), 314,459 unaffiliated and minor parties (14%).

Political Lineup: Governor, Fife Symington (R); Secy. of State, Jane Dee Hull (R); Atty. Gen., Grant Woods (R); Treasurer, Tony West (R); Auditor General, Douglas Norton. State Senate, 30 (18 R and 12 D); Senate President, Brenda Burns (D); State House, 60 (38 R and 22 D); House Speaker, Don Aldridge (R). Senators, John McCain (R) and Jon Kyl (R). Representatives, 6 (5 R and 1 D).

Elections Division: 602-542-8683; **Filing Deadline for U.S. Congress:** June 25, 1998.

1996 Presidential Vote

Clinton (D)	653,288	(47%)
Dole (R)	622,073	(44%)
Perot (I)	112,074	(8%)

1996 Republican Presidential Primary

Forbes (R)	115,962	(33%)
Dole (R)	102,980	(30%)
Buchanan (R)	95,742	(28%)
Alexander	24,765	(7%)
Other	8,033	(2%)

1992 Presidential Vote

Bush (R)	572,086	(38%)
Clinton (D)	543,050	(37%)
Perot (I)	353,741	(24%)

GOVERNOR

Gov. Fife Symington (R)

Elected Feb., 1991, term expires Jan. 1999; b. Aug. 12, 1945, New York, NY; home, Phoenix; Harvard, B.A. 1968; Episcopalian; married (Ann).

Career: Air Force, 1968–71 (Vietnam); Commercial and industrial real estate developer, 1972–91.

Office: 1700 W. Washington, Phoenix 85007, 602-542-4331; Fax: 602-542-7601; Web site: www.state.az.us.

Election Results

1994 gen.	Fife Symington (R)	593,492	(53%)
	Eddie Basha (D)	500,702	(44%)
	Others	35,413	(3%)
1994 prim.	Fife Symington (R)	202,588	(68%)
	Barbara Barrett (R)	94,740	(32%)
1991 runoff	Fife Symington (R)	492,569	(52%)
	Terry Goddard (D)	448,168	(48%)
1990 gen.	Fife Symington (R)	523,964	(50%)
	Terry Goddard (D)	519,653	(50%)

SENATORS

Sen. John McCain (R)

Elected 1986, seat up 1998; b. Aug. 29, 1936, Panama Canal Zone; home, Phoenix; U.S. Naval Acad., B.S. 1958, Natl. War Col., 1973–74; Episcopalian; married (Cindy).

Career: Navy, 1958–80 (Vietnam); Dir., Navy Senate Liaison Ofc., 1977–81; U.S. House of Reps., 1982–1986.

DC Office: 241 RSOB 20510, 202-224-2235; Fax: 202-228-2862; e-mail: senator_mccain@mccain.senate.gov.

State Offices: Mesa, 602-491-4300; Tucson, 520-670-6334; Phoenix, 602-952-2410.

Committees: *Armed Services* (3rd of 10 R): Personnel; Readiness; Sea Power. *Commerce, Science & Transportation* (Chmn. of 11 R). *Indian Affairs* (3rd of 8 R).

Group Ratings

	ADA	ACLU	AFS	LCV	CFA	CON	NFIB	COC	ACU	NTLC	CHC
1996	0	18	0	15	43	38	100	100	95	96	100
1995	0	—	9	7	25	54	—	100	91	—	—

National Journal Ratings

	1995 LIB	—	1995 CONS	1996 LIB	—	1996 CONS
Economic	20%	—	79%	15%	—	84%
Social	19%	—	79%	0%	—	72%
Foreign	48%	—	50%	43%	—	54%

Key Votes of the 104th Congress

1. Reduce Medicare Growth $	Y	5. Flag Amendment	Y	9. Anti-Missle Defense	Y
2. Lmt. Prod. Liab. Damages	Y	6. Endangered Species	N	10. Cuban Embargo	Y
3. Increase Min. Wage	N	7. Gay Employment Rights	N	11. Bar Bosnia Troop $	N
4. Welfare Reform	Y	8. Ovrd. Part. Birth Veto	Y	12. Cut Vietnam Aid	N

Election Results

1992 general	John McCain (R)	771,395	(56%)	($3,766,588)
	Claire Sargent (D)	436,321	(32%)	($287,682)
	Evan Mecham (I)	145,361	(11%)	($86,433)
	Others	28,974	(2%)	
1992 primary	John McCain (R)	unopposed		
1986 general	John McCain (R)	521,850	(60%)	($2,228,498)
	Richard Kimball (D)	340,965	(40%)	($657,908)

Sen. Jon Kyl (R)

Elected 1994, seat up 2000; b. Apr. 25, 1942, Oakland, NE; home, Phoenix; U. of AZ, B.A. 1964, L.L.B. 1966; Presbyterian; married (Caryll).

Career: Practicing atty., 1966–86; Chmn., Phoenix Chamber of Commerce, 1984–85, U.S. House of Reps., 1986–94.

DC Office: 724 HSOB 20510, 202-224-4521; Fax: 202-228-1239; e-mail: info@kyl.senate.gov.

State Offices: Phoenix, 602-840-1891; Tucson, 520-575-8633.

Committees: *Energy & Natural Resources* (7th of 11 R): Forests & Public Land Management; Water & Power (Chmn.). *Judiciary* (6th of 10 R): Administrative Oversight & the Courts; Immigration; Terrorism, Technology & Government Information (Chmn.). *Intelligence (Select)* (5th of 10 R).

Group Ratings

	ADA	ACLU	AFS	LCV	CFA	CON	NFIB	COC	ACU	NTLC	CHC
1996	5	12	0	8	21	51	96	100	100	100	100
1995	0	—	0	0	6	29	—	100	100	—	—

National Journal Ratings

	1995 LIB — 1995 CONS	1996 LIB — 1996 CONS
Economic	0% — 88%	14% — 85%
Social	0% — 88%	0% — 72%
Foreign	22% — 67%	0% — 74%

Key Votes of the 104th Congress

1. Reduce Medicare Growth $	Y	5. Flag Amendment	Y	9. Anti-Missle Defense	Y
2. Lmt. Prod. Liab. Damages	Y	6. Endangered Species	N	10. Cuban Embargo	Y
3. Increase Min. Wage	N	7. Gay Employment Rights	N	11. Bar Bosnia Troop $	Y
4. Welfare Reform	Y	8. Ovrd. Part. Birth Veto	Y	12. Cut Vietnam Aid	Y

Election Results

1994 general	Jon Kyl (R)	600,999	(54%)	($4,138,203)
	Sam Coppersmith (D)	442,510	(40%)	($1,577,556)
	Scott Grainger (Lib)	75,493	(7%)	
1994 primary	Jon Kyl (R)	unopposed		
1988 general	Dennis DeConcini (D)	660,403	(57%)	($2,640,650)
	Keith DeGreen (R)	478,060	(41%)	($238,369)

FIRST DISTRICT

The metropolis of Phoenix is exceedingly young—yet bears traces of a lost Indian civilization a millennium old. Barry Goldwater, born in 1909 and living on into the end of the 20th Century, grew up knowing men and women who remembered when the Valley of the Sun, as some call it today, was virtually empty, with a few parched settlements set above the dry river bed. Phoenix was begun in the years after the Civil War, near the Pueblo Grande Indian ruins and still functioning canals, as a haymarket for cavalry horses at Fort McDowell 40 miles away. On the usually-dry Salt River, Tempe was founded in 1871 as Hayden's Ferry, by the father of future Senator (1927–69) Carl Hayden; it was renamed in 1879 for an ancient Greek vale, and is now home of Arizona State University, founded in 1885, and the Fiesta Bowl. Further east is Mesa, founded by Mormons in 1878 on a square mile, laid out with broad streets with huge blocks holding just four homesites, using Indian canals built 1100 years before; a gleaming white Mormon Temple was built there in 1927, one of the few in the United States. North of the Salt River, directly east of Phoenix and in the shadows of Camelback Mountain, is Scottsdale, founded much more recently, with its trendy shops carefully decked out in Old West style.

For half a century this remained mostly empty land: as late as 1950 only 106,000 people lived in Phoenix and only 331,000 in all of Maricopa County. But in the years after World War II the airconditioner and military technology—in 1948 Motorola built an electronics research center here—transformed Phoenix, from a sleepy whistle-stop, where the small tufa stone turn-of-the-century Capitol was the most prominent building, to today's high-rise studded metropolis, with 1.1 million people in Phoenix and 2.5 million in Maricopa County. This is not, as some think, a giant retirement village; nor is it totally overrun with crooked land salesmen or fast-buck artists, though freewheeling Phoenix has attracted more than its share of both. But the typical cactus-decorated desert-brown adobe tract house here is occupied by a growing family, living a more traditional life than many occupants of more traditional-looking houses back east.

The 1st Congressional District of Arizona includes much of the historic heart of Phoenix: Pueblo Grande and the old Indian School in Phoenix, Arizona State in Tempe (1990 population 142,000) and the Mormon Temple in Mesa (288,000) and Old Town Scottsdale (130,000); it also goes south to include most of Chandler (91,000). Its boundaries are convoluted, designed to maximize the number of Hispanics in the 2d District and Indians (in the Salt River and Gilva River Reservations) in the 6th; geographically, it sits south of Camelback Mountain, west of the Superstition Mountains, east of South Mountain. It includes some high-income neighborhoods, but its cultural tone is resolutely middle class, hard-working, church-going; politically, it has been traditionally heavily Republican.

The congressman from the 1st District is Matt Salmon, one of those freshmen Republicans elected in 1994, replacing a Democrat, Sam Coppersmith, who had upset a Republican incumbent in 1992. Salmon grew up in Utah, went to Arizona State, did Mormon missionary work in Taiwan from 1977–79, then finished school. He worked in public affairs for USWest in the 1980s and was elected to the Arizona Senate, a part-time job, in 1990, where he rose to assistant majority leader. In 1994, when Coppersmith ran for the Senate, Salmon ran for Congress where the real competition turned out to be in the Republican primary. There Salmon won 39% to 22% for cable TV lobbyist Susan Bitter Smith, 19% for attorney Linda Rawles, and 16% for educator Bev Hermon. Salmon was running on the Contract with America even before the Contract was signed, boosting the $500 dependent tax credit, term limits and a buydown of the national debt. "Moses wandered in the desert for 40 years," he said, in an opaque metaphor. "I think the Democratic leadership has been wandering in the desert." He had spirited opposition from Democratic state Senator Chuck Blanchard, a former clerk for Supreme Court Justice Sandra Day O'Connor, who took some moderate stands. But Blanchard was the Arizona head of the 1992 Clinton campaign and defended the national party and the House Democrats' crime bill. Salmon won fairly easily, 56%–39%.

In the House Salmon has been a reliable member of Newt Gingrich's Republican Conference. But he did not get a seat on the Commerce Committee as his former employer must have wished. Pleasant-mannered but with strong views, Salmon supported putting Medical Savings Accounts in Medicare reform and backed tough welfare reforms, like strengthening child support enforcement and forcing birthfathers or their parents to support offspring untill they turn 18. He thinks victims should have a right to view executions, and wants tougher laws for those who assault women and children. As the 104th Congress's only fluent speaker of Mandarin Chinese, and a member of International Relations, he weighed in on China policy. He strongly criticized China's human rights violation, but opposed withdrawal of most favored nation status and other unilateral sanctions. "One thing we don't understand in our culture is the value of saving face and how important that is in their culture. None of this would be fixed if we disengage and withhold MFN."

No one filed to run against Salmon in 1996; he beat Democrat John Cox, nominated by write-ins, 60%–40%. Like many freshmen, Salmon has kept his family back home and commutes to still-strange Washington. But by 1996 he was eschewing some freshmen's angry style: "Both sides need to tone down the rhetoric a little bit."

The People: Pop. 1990: 610,817; 9% age 65+; 80% White; 3% Black; 2% Asian; 2% Amer. Indian; 13% Hispanic origin. Households: 49% married couple families; 24% married couple fams. w. children; 64% college educ.; median household income: $31,288; per capita income: $15,144; median gross rent: $478; median house value: $88,300.

1996 Presidential Vote			1992 Presidential Vote		
Dole (R)	109,137	(46%)	Bush (R)	105,784	(40%)
Clinton (D)	107,698	(45%)	Clinton (D)	88,247	(33%)
Perot (I)	17,048	(7%)	Perot (I)	68,143	(26%)

Rep. Matt Salmon (R)

Elected 1994; b. Jan. 21, 1958, Salt Lake City, UT; home, Mesa; AZ St. U., B.A. 1981, Brigham Young U., M.A. 1986; Mormon; married (Nancy).

Career: Public Affairs Mgr., U.S. West, 1981–94; AZ Senate, 1990–94; Asst. Majority Leader, 1993–94.

DC Office: 115 CHOB 20515, 202-225-2635; Fax: 202-225-3405; e-mail: msalmon@hr.house.gov.

District Offices: Tempe, 602-831-2900.

Committees: *International Relations* (18th of 26 R): Asia & the Pacific; International Operations & Human Rights. *Science* (13th of 25 R): Energy & Environment; Space & Aeronautics.

Group Ratings

	ADA	ACLU	AFS	LCV	CFA	CON	NFIB	COC	ACU	NTLC	CHC
1996	10	12	8	15	54	75	97	88	100	95	92
1995	0	—	—	13	0	75	—	96	92	—	—

National Journal Ratings

	1995 LIB	—	1995 CONS	1996 LIB	—	1996 CONS
Economic	26%	—	67%	0%	—	82%
Social	0%	—	79%	24%	—	72%
Foreign	0%	—	85%	0%	—	79%

Key Votes of the 104th Congress

1. Reduce Medicare Growth $	Y	5. Flag Amendment	Y	9. Cuban Embargo	*
2. Ovrd. Product Liab. Veto	Y	6. Drop EPA Limits	N	10. Bar Bosnia Troop $	Y
3. Increase Min. Wage	N	7. Repeal Assault-Weap. Ban	Y	11. Cut Anti-Missile Defense	N
4. Welfare Reform	Y	8. Ovrd. Part. Birth Veto	Y	12. Bar U.N. Uniforms	Y

Election Results

1996 general	Matt Salmon (R)	135,634	(60%)	($456,089)
	John Cox (D)	89,738	(40%)	
1996 primary	Matt Salmon (R)	unopposed		
1994 general	Matt Salmon (R)	101,350	(56%)	($508,421)
	Chuck Blanchard (D)	70,627	(39%)	($440,372)
	Bob Howarth (Lib)	8,890	(5%)	

SECOND DISTRICT

Although technically part of Mexico for hundreds of years, southern Arizona was never a site of Hispanic civilization like New Mexico. Here the hot desert land was inhabited mainly by Indians who kept their native ways and language until English-speaking whites came in on cavalry horses, miners' wagons and railroad cars in the late 19th Century. Today's Hispanic Arizonans are mostly descendants of later immigrants from Mexico, some who came over the border in the sleepier days before World War II when it was scarcely patrolled and many more who came more recently to partake in the dazzling economic growth which has served as both an attraction and an example to so many *norteno* Mexicans.

The 2d District of Arizona was designed to be the state's Hispanic district; its population is 50% Hispanic and includes nearly two-thirds of the state's Hispanic population. On a map, it looks regularly-shaped, but in fact it is a collection of three distant communities connected by many miles of uninhabited desert. One of these is central Phoenix, including the old downtown, the state Capitol to the west and the skyscraper districts on North Central Avenue out toward Camelback Road. The stereotypical Hispanic neighborhood here is a collection of 1940s and 1950s bungalows, spaced out by empty lots, not far from the railroad or Sky Harbor Airport or nestling within view of South Mountain. In fact, this is a diverse area, with affluent and comfortable neighborhoods, where Hispanics have been moving in scatterings as well as clumps. The west side of Tucson, with about one-third of the people in the 2d, is similar. The 2d also includes Yuma, on a Colorado River crossing, in an irrigated agricultural valley, often the hottest place in the country; also the spring training site for the Yakult Swallows, a Japanese baseball team. A desalination plant, proposed to protect Mexican farmlands, was opened here in 1992, 14 years behind schedule. Across the desert, past the Luke Air Force Base shooting range, the Organ Pipe Cactus National Monument, and the Papago Indian Reservation, is the Mexican border town of Nogales, 75% Hispanic and near many maquiladora plants, and the scene of many illegal crossings until the Border Patrol was beefed up.

The 2d is the one solidly Democratic district in Arizona. The congressman, first elected in a September 1991 special election to replace the ailing Morris Udall, is Ed Pastor, who beat Republican Pat Connor 56%–44%. Pastor grew up in Claypool, a mining town in Gila County, where his parents, he told fellow Democrats in 1996, "taught me the value of education, the need of tolerance and the responsibility of community service. But especially they taught me the reward of a hard day's work." Pastor has been a career politician: after teaching high school, he got a law degree at Arizona State, worked as an assistant to Governor Raul Castro in 1975, then was elected in 1976 to the Maricopa County Board of Supervisors, where he served until elected to Congress. "The fact is I am Hispanic, the fact is there is a lot of pride in the Hispanic community," he said on winning. "And I join in that enthusiasm. But as an elected official for 16 years, you represent the entire community."

As the only Arizona Democrat in Congress, Pastor has been a faithful follower of the Democratic leadership. He supported the Clinton tax increase, family medical leave, minimum wage increase, and national service act. Despite strong labor backing, he supported NAFTA. He vigorously opposes the English Only law and wants to keep bilingual ballots, but says that "everyone acknowledges that English is the common language of our country." He even more vociferously opposed the 1996 Immigration Act, because of its limits on welfare for legal migrants and family unification preference for low-income households. He worked to promote education for the deaf and sponsored Morris Udall Scholarships which focus on environmental and Native American issues at the University of Arizona.

The Democrats' loss of the House has deprived Pastor of the clout he might have expected. It resulted in his rotation off Appropriations in 1995 and the defunding of the Hispanic Caucus just after he was elected its president in 1994. Pastor has worked on many local issues, including consolidation of the Aviation Technical Test Center at the Army's Yuma Proving Ground and Gila River flood control. He has tried to help local farmers when the Yuma area wheat crop was quarantined after an outbreak of Karnal bunt. He was the first Arizona congressman to open an office in Yuma, but nevertheless had opposition from that quarter when state Senator and former Yuma Mayor Jim Buster won the 2d District Republican nomination in 1996. Buster carried Yuma County 58%–39%, but Pastor won the rest of the district 72%–23% for an overall 65%–31% victory.

The People: Pop. 1990: 610,266; 10% rural; 10% age 65+; 38% White; 6% Black; 1% Asian; 4% Amer. Indian; 51% Hispanic origin. Households: 52% married couple families; 28% married couple fams. w. children; 33% college educ.; median household income: $20,258; per capita income: $8,424; median gross rent: $366; median house value: $54,500.

1996 Presidential Vote			1992 Presidential Vote		
Clinton (D)	81,678	(63%)	Clinton (D)	74,588	(51%)
Dole (R)	36,584	(28%)	Bush (R)	41,757	(28%)
Perot (I)	9,292	(7%)	Perot (I)	28,767	(20%)

Rep. Ed Pastor (D)

Elected Sept. 1991; b. June 28, 1943, Claypool; home, Phoenix; AZ St. U., B.A. 1966, J.D. 1974; Catholic; married (Verma).

Career: High schl. teacher, 1966–69; Asst., AZ Gov. Castro, 1975; Maricopa Cnty. Bd. of Supervisors, 1976–91.

DC Office: 2465 RHOB 20515, 202-225-4065; Fax: 202-225-1655; e-mail: edpastor@hr.house.gov.

District Offices: Phoenix, 602-256-0551; Tucson, 520-624-9986; Yuma, 520-726-2234.

Committees: *Appropriations* (23rd of 26 D): Energy & Water Development; Transportation.

Group Ratings

	ADA	ACLU	AFS	LCV	CFA	CON	NFIB	COC	ACU	NTLC	CHC
1996	85	69	92	85	77	11	24	38	5	12	7
1995	95	—	—	88	100	9	—	21	4	—	—

National Journal Ratings

	1995 LIB — 1995 CONS			1996 LIB — 1996 CONS		
Economic	85%	—	12%	65%	—	33%
Social	88%	—	0%	84%	—	12%
Foreign	79%	—	17%	70%	—	29%

Key Votes of the 104th Congress

1. Reduce Medicare Growth $	N	5. Flag Amendment	N	9. Cuban Embargo	N
2. Ovrd. Product Liab. Veto	N	6. Drop EPA Limits	Y	10. Bar Bosnia Troop $	N
3. Increase Min. Wage	Y	7. Repeal Assault-Weap. Ban	N	11. Cut Anti-Missile Defense	Y
4. Welfare Reform	N	8. Ovrd. Part. Birth Veto	N	12. Bar U.N. Uniforms	Y

Election Results

1996 general	Ed Pastor (D)	81,982	(65%)	($405,426)
	Jim Buster (R)	38,786	(31%)	($101,730)
	Alice Bangle (Lib)	5,333	(4%)	
1996 primary	Ed Pastor (D)	unopposed		
1994 general	Ed Pastor (D)	62,589	(62%)	($349,627)
	Robert MacDonald (R)	32,797	(33%)	
	James Bertrand (Lib)	5,060	(5%)	

THIRD DISTRICT

Most of Arizona's physical landscape, for all the vibrant metropolitan growth of Phoenix and Tucson, remains much as it was when white men first settled here. Beneath mountains and along mostly dry creek beds, they built towns that have as Old West a look as anywhere in America, like Prescott, originally a gold mining camp, home since 1888 of America's oldest annual rodeo and now, to the distress of some, the home of many ex-Californians. The landscape retains a beauty that can overpower mere buildings and parking lots: think of the red rocks of Sedona, an esoteric resort between Prescott and Flagstaff, with its own film festival. And some landscape is intentionally preserved, like the sere uplands of the Hopi Indian Reservation. There are some abrupt juxtapositions of settlement and nature: the real London Bridge transplanted to Lake Havasu City, a retirement community on the Colorado River; or Bullhead City, one-third of whose people work in "family gambler" casinos in Laughlin, Nevada, just across the bridge over the rock-lined, piping-hot river. Just west, and a bit north, of Bullhead City is the last known address of Timothy McVeigh, arrested in April 1995 for the Oklahoma City bombing.

All these areas are part of the 3d Congressional District of Arizona, which stretches from the west side of Phoenix to cover most of the northwest quadrant of the state. Most of its people are clustered in its southeast corner, in metro Phoenix. Here, west of the Black Canyon Freeway, is the mushrooming suburb of Glendale, not so long ago just a crossroads but with 148,000 people in 1990; just west are Peoria, as Middle American as its namesake in Illinois, and the huge retirement community of Sun City, with a dozen or so golf courses and many dozens of shuffleboard courts. The 3d District also includes the corridor along the westbound I-10 Papago Freeway, past Litchfield Park and its Wigwam resort to the now open spaces of Goodyear and Buckeye, the likely site of Phoenix's fastest future growth.

This is heavily Republican territory: the retirees here remember—and the upwardly-striving, family-oriented young migrants who have populated these new towns in the desert still try to live—the culturally conservative, Ozzie-and-Harriet lifestyle of the 1950s. Culture, more than affluence, which by national standards is not all that striking here, accounts for their political conservatism. Similarly Republican are the Colorado River new cities and Prescott, where Barry Goldwater used to end all his campaigns.

The 3d District's congressman is Bob Stump, a Republican who quietly and without much notice has become one of the more senior members of the House and is now chairman of the Veterans' Affairs Committee. He grew up in Arizona, enlisted at 17 in the Navy during World War II, raised cotton and grain, and was elected to the legislature in 1958. Like many older Arizonans, he was a "pinto" (conservative) Democrat, elected to Congress as a Democrat in 1976. In 1981, after voting for the Reagan budget and tax cuts, he switched parties, to reflect both his constituency and his convictions. It was one of the smoothest party switches of recent times: he won 64% as a Democrat in 1980 and 63% as a Republican in 1982. When Stump switched, Republicans gave him seats on the National Security and Veterans' Affairs Committees, whose conservatism was compatible with his own. Tight-lipped in public (he has no press secretary), he lets his conservative voting record and style speak for him, as they do eloquently.

Stump's accession to the chair long occupied by Mississippi Democrat Sonny Montgomery did not signal a change in policy. Both are World War II veterans, and they were longtime friends and allies on veterans' issues. Sometimes their work has been innovative, as with the Montgomery G.I. veterans' benefits package of the 1980s. Sometimes it is more retrograde, when they try to resist modernization of the troubled veterans' hospitals—aging facilities for aging beneficiaries. In 1994 Stump angrily insisted that the Republicans' Contract with America wouldn't force sharp cuts in veterans' services despite opponents' arguments otherwise. Stump is also the second ranking Republican, behind South Carolina's Floyd Spence, on the National Security Committee, where he has been cautious about steep defense spending cuts. On other issues, Stump has filed bills to bar states from taxing pension incomes of residents of other states and to repeal the Social Security earnings tax—popular causes in Sun City. He favors four-year terms for representatives, with term limits, and has advocated dropping the anti-abortion plank from the GOP platform.

Stump eschews the common course of seeking pork-barrel projects for his district or backing publicity-worthy causes; but he returns to the district often, spending only one weekend a year in Washington. Except for 1990, when his percentage dipped to 57%, he has been reelected easily in this strongly Republican district. In 1996 he was reelected 67%–33%.

The People: Pop. 1990: 610,424; 18% rural; 20% age 65+; 82% White; 2% Black; 1% Asian; 3% Amer. Indian; 12% Hispanic origin. Households: 63% married couple families; 24% married couple fams. w. children; 49% college educ.; median household income: $27,627; per capita income: $13,185; median gross rent: $457; median house value: $79,700.

1996 Presidential Vote

Dole (R)	130,887	(48%)
Clinton (D)	113,635	(41%)
Perot (I)	26,993	(10%)

1992 Presidential Vote

Bush (R)	109,840	(40%)
Clinton (D)	86,060	(31%)
Perot (I)	73,356	(27%)

Rep. Bob Stump (R)

Elected 1976; b. Apr. 4, 1927, Phoenix; home, Tolleson; AZ St. U., B.S. 1951; Seventh Day Adventist; divorced.

Career: Navy, 1943–46 (WWII); Cotton & grain farmer; AZ House of Reps., 1958–66; AZ Senate, 1966–76, Senate Pres., 1975–76.

DC Office: 211 CHOB 20515, 202-225-4576; Fax: 202-225-6328.

District Offices: Phoenix, 602-379-6923.

Committees: *National Security* (2nd of 30 R): Military Installations & Facilities; Military Procurement. *Veterans' Affairs* (Chmn. of 16 R): Oversight & Investigations.

Group Ratings

	ADA	ACLU	AFS	LCV	CFA	CON	NFIB	COC	ACU	NTLC	CHC
1996	0	6	0	8	8	55	100	94	100	100	100
1995	0	—	—	0	0	56	—	100	92	—	—

National Journal Ratings

	1995 LIB — 1995 CONS			1996 LIB — 1996 CONS		
Economic	0%	—	74%	0%	—	82%
Social	0%	—	79%	10%	—	86%
Foreign	0%	—	85%	0%	—	79%

Key Votes of the 104th Congress

1. Reduce Medicare Growth $	Y	5. Flag Amendment	Y	9. Cuban Embargo	Y
2. Ovrd. Product Liab. Veto	Y	6. Drop EPA Limits	N	10. Bar Bosnia Troop $	Y
3. Increase Min. Wage	N	7. Repeal Assault-Weap. Ban	Y	11. Cut Anti-Missile Defense	N
4. Welfare Reform	Y	8. Ovrd. Part. Birth Veto	Y	12. Bar U.N. Uniforms	Y

Election Results

1996 general	Bob Stump (R)	175,231	(67%)	($233,997)
	Alexander (Big Al) Schneider (D)	88,214	(33%)	($23,567)
1996 primary	Bob Stump (R)	unopposed		
1994 general	Bob Stump (R)	145,396	(70%)	($152,718)
	Howard Lee Sprague (D)	61,939	(30%)	($5,851)

FOURTH DISTRICT

In the late 1990s Barry Goldwater, born on New Year's Day 1909, was still living amid the crags of the Phoenix suburb of Paradise Valley, having seen most of Arizona's history and having turned in his 80s against the cultural conservatism of the Arizona Republican Party he more than anyone else had built. When Goldwater returned from World War II, Paradise Valley was still empty land and Phoenix not much more than a small town, an outpost of American civilization in a sizzling desert. Now it is one of the major metropolises of the country, a diversified high-tech center, an example of how creativity, ingenuity and (on occasion) skullduggery can build a sophisticated city with relatively minimalist government and low taxes.

Today, from Camelback Mountain, 1800 feet above Phoenix and Paradise Valley, or from Frank Lloyd Wright's Taliesin West home and studio, you can with equal awe get a sense of what this land was originally like and an understanding of how impressively Phoenix has grown. South of Camelback, subdivisions were often built with grass and greenery; in the affluent areas north of Camelback and spreading out Scottsdale Road and the Black Canyon Freeway, the natural desert look is more common. Grass is discouraged, and often banned by subdivision covenant; planting anything but desert flora is frowned upon; the architecture of the houses tends toward unadorned stucco with picture windows facing away from the sun; the idea is to suggest that there is a horse corral over in the next lot and sometimes, especially in the northern edges of Phoenix, there is.

The 4th Congressional District of Arizona consists of this northern part of Phoenix, northern Scottsdale, Paradise Valley and part of Glendale, bounded approximately by Camelback Road on the south, Pima Road and the Salt River Indian Reservation on the east, Pinnacle Peak Road on the north and 47th and Grand Avenues on the west. For all its rustic and unplanned air, this is a highly affluent district, and a heavily Republican one; in most elections there is scarcely a Democratic precinct to be found.

The congressman from the 4th is John Shadegg, a freshman elected in 1994, but with a fine Arizona Republican pedigree. His father, Stephen Shadegg, managed Barry Goldwater's first campaign for the Senate in 1952, when he upset Senate Majority Leader Ernest McFarland, and 12 years later wrote *How to Win an Election: The Art of Political Victory*. John Shadegg helped deliver campaign press releases in those pre-fax days. He is a lawyer, served as special assistant in the state attorney general's office and a special counsel to the Arizona House Republican Caucus. When 4th District Congressman Jon Kyl ran for the Senate in 1994, Shadegg ran for the House seat and won 43% in the Republican primary, to 30% for former state Representative Trent Franks, a former aide to controversial conservative Governor Evan Mecham, and 21% for Maricopa Supervisor Jim Bruner, who ran as a tough law-and-order candidate, but was accused by other Republican officials of running up a $62 million county deficit. In November, against a Democrat who backed a balanced budget amendment and took tough stands on crime, Shadegg won 60%–36%.

In the House Shadegg was one of the firebrand leaders of the 1994 Republican freshmen. In January 1995 he tried to insist on a three-fifths supermajority for tax increases in the balanced budget amendment; Speaker Newt Gingrich and Majority Leader Dick Armey disagreed and prevailed. "The freshmen aren't interested in coming here to be reasonable and to settle for what they can get. They don't want to go along to get along," Shadegg said after losing. Shadegg also led the charge to defund the National Endowment for the Arts, even when the leadership compromised, and unsuccessfully tried to cut $12 million from the National Endowment for the Humanities. He was one of 15 freshman to vote against a keep-the-government-open compromise in January 1996. Nevertheless, Shadegg did not become a pariah. He started a small Freshman Breakfast Group to plot strategy and was entrusted with the leadership of GOPAC when Gingrich relinquished it in May 1995. He attracted national attention when he grilled Attorney General Janet Reno in hearings on the Waco massacre. He has sponsored serious conservative bills which may some day pass—an overhaul of the Endangered Species Act, replacing controls on private landowners with financial incentives; a measure to remove federal court jurisdiction over prisoners' habeas corpus petitions unless state court remedies are inadequate or ineffective to test claims of illegal detention; a proposal that legislators state the constitutional authority for every bill, to spotlight the Tenth Amendment reservation of ungranted powers to states and citizens. He was one of the most frugal representatives, spending only 64% of his office allowance.

In 1996 Shadegg won 74% over an environmental activist in the Republican primary. His Democratic opponent, Maria Milton, a follower of Lyndon LaRouche, ran ads saying he "wants to push your parents into the gas ovens of managed care," and "Congressman ValuJet . . . wants to send your Social Security crashing into the Everglades." Democratic leaders repudiated her and Shadegg won 67%–33%.

The People: Pop. 1990: 610,708; 11% age 65+; 88% White; 2% Black; 2% Asian; 1% Amer. Indian; 8% Hispanic origin. Households: 54% married couple families; 24% married couple fams. w. children; 62% college educ.; median household income: $33,681; per capita income: $18,331; median gross rent: $473; median house value: $90,700.

1996 Presidential Vote

Dole (R)	115,094	(48%)
Clinton (D)	103,878	(44%)
Perot (I)	16,547	(7%)

1992 Presidential Vote

Bush (R)	118,927	(43%)
Clinton (D)	86,922	(31%)
Perot (I)	70,682	(25%)

Rep. John Shadegg (R)

Elected 1994; b. Oct. 22, 1949, Phoenix; home, Phoenix; U. of AZ, B.A. 1972, J.D. 1975; Episcopalian; married (Shirley).

Career: Air Natl. Guard, 1969–75; Practicing atty., 1975–present; US Spec. Asst. Atty. Gen., 1983–90; Spec. Cnsl., AZ House Republican Caucus, 1991–92; Cnsl., AZ Wildlife Conservation, 1992.

DC Office: 430 CHOB 20515, 202-225-3361; Fax: 202-225-3462.

District Offices: Phoenix, 602-248-7779.

Committees: *Budget* (14th of 24 R). *Government Reform & Oversight* (16th of 24 R): National Economic Growth, Natural Resources & Regulatory Affairs; National Security, International Affairs & Criminal Justice. *Resources* (18th of 27 R): National Parks & Public Lands; Water & Power.

Group Ratings

	ADA	ACLU	AFS	LCV	CFA	CON	NFIB	COC	ACU	NTLC	CHC
1996	5	12	8	15	23	63	97	88	100	98	100
1995	0	—	—	6	0	75	—	100	92	—	—

National Journal Ratings

	1995 LIB — 1995 CONS			1996 LIB — 1996 CONS		
Economic	0%	—	74%	0%	—	82%
Social	21%	—	72%	10%	—	86%
Foreign	15%	—	73%	0%	—	79%

Key Votes of the 104th Congress

1. Reduce Medicare Growth $	Y	5. Flag Amendment	N	9. Cuban Embargo	Y
2. Ovrd. Product Liab. Veto	Y	6. Drop EPA Limits	N	10. Bar Bosnia Troop $	Y
3. Increase Min. Wage	N	7. Repeal Assault-Weap. Ban	Y	11. Cut Anti-Missile Defense	N
4. Welfare Reform	Y	8. Ovrd. Part. Birth Veto	Y	12. Bar U.N. Uniforms	Y

Election Results

1996 general	John Shadegg (R)	150,486	(67%)	($512,249)
	Maria Elena Milton (D)	74,857	(33%)	($116,003)
1996 primary	John Shadegg (R)	34,306	(74%)	
	Robin Silver (R)	11,944	(26%)	
1994 general	John Shadegg (R)	116,714	(60%)	($590,725)
	Carol Cure (D)	69,760	(36%)	($281,562)
	Others	7,428	(4%)	

FIFTH DISTRICT

Arizona's first frontier was just south of today's Tucson, where Franciscan friars built San Xavier del Bac mission in the 18th Century. To the east the late 19th Century mining towns of Tombstone and Bisbee sprang up on desert mountainsides, where miners dug up gold and silver and, for many years, much of America's copper; Cochise County, including those two towns, was the most populous county when Arizona became the 48th state in 1912. Here the white man last subdued the Indians, when the Apache leader Geronimo faced the U.S. Army in 1900. Southern Arizona remains pioneer country today: this was the site of the Biosphere II project, the greenhouse-like structure in the desert in which eight men and women lived more or less self-sufficiently, sealed from outside contact, from September 1991 until September 1993. Biosphere has now joined Tombstone as a tourist attraction; both are within the orbit of Tucson, Arizona's second metropolis, much smaller, more rough-hewn and politically less conservative than Phoenix. Tucson is a high-tech city, its economy hurt in the early 1990s; it is also home to the University of Arizona. For nearly 40 years, it was the political base of the brothers Udall: Stewart, congressman in the 1950s, Interior Secretary in the 1960s, now an Arizona lawyer again; Morris, congressman for 30 years and Interior Committee chairman, forced to retire in 1991 by Parkinson's disease.

The 5th Congressional District of Arizona includes most, but not all of Tucson and Pima County—the heavily Democratic west side of town, with high Hispanic percentages, is in the 2d District. The 5th also includes much southeastern Arizona desert real estate: all of Cochise County, including Tombstone and Bisbee and Sierra Vista near Fort Huachuca; and some small farming and mining towns in Pinal and Graham Counties. Politically, the cast here is Republican, though if the west side of Tucson were added this would be a potentially Democratic seat.

The congressman from the 5th is Jim Kolbe, a Republican with a moderate record on many issues. He comes originally from Illinois, served in the Navy in Vietnam, became an assistant to Illinois's Republican Governor Richard Ogilvie in 1972, and moved to Arizona shortly thereafter and went into the real estate business. By 1976 he was elected to the Arizona Senate. In 1982 he challenged incumbent Democratic Congressman Jim McNulty, and lost 50%–48%. Two years later he ran again and beat him 51%–48%. He has easily won reelection since.

On economic issues, Kolbe is as conservative and market-oriented as any member of the Arizona delegation. In the legislature he worked on the state Medicaid program, which became the least costly in the nation, and on groundwater legislation with then-Governor Bruce Babbitt. He favored the balanced budget amendment, the line-item veto, and the elimination of baseline budgeting—all passed in the House. He has been a strong ally of Chairman John Kasich on the Budget Committee. He also serves on Appropriations, where he is chairman of the Treasury, Postal Service and General Government Subcommittee. Kolbe strongly opposed the Clinton healthcare plan. His greatest economic cause was the NAFTA, on which he was a leader in the bipartisan coalition for approval. He was one of the three Republicans who pushed their party to provide most of the votes to pass NAFTA in the House in November 1993, and has remained an enthusiast for it since. He has long admired the maquiladora program, through which U.S.-made components shipped to Mexico for assembly can reenter the U.S. without paying full duty, and believes that more trade can boost the economies of both countries. He was also a strong supporter of GATT in November 1994. Separately, he has put pressures on Japan to lower its tariffs on copper and Motorola cellular phones—Arizona products. He favors a dollar coin—another copper cause.

Kolbe's record is more moderate on cultural issues. He is pro-choice on abortion. He voted for the 1994 crime bill. He worked to expand the Saguaro National Monument and make it a national park, and he passed a bill to establish the Cave Creek Canyon Wilderness Area in Cochise County. He voted for the Defense of Marriage Act and in July 1996, apparently pressured by some gay rights group about his vote, announced that he is gay. This has had little political impact. In the September 1996 primary he beat Joe Sweeney 70%–30%; in 1994 he had beaten the same man 80%–20%. In the 1994 general he beat Morris Udall's chiropractor 68%–29%; in 1996, against a retired optometrist, he won 69%–26%.

The People: Pop. 1990: 611,128; 13% rural; 15% age 65+; 78% White; 3% Black; 2% Asian; 1% Amer. Indian; 17% Hispanic origin. Households: 55% married couple families; 23% married couple fams. w. children; 59% college educ.; median household income: $27,047; per capita income: $14,361; median gross rent: $404; median house value: $81,100.

1996 Presidential Vote

Clinton (D)	126,223	(47%)
Dole (R)	116,965	(44%)
Perot (I)	20,732	(8%)

1992 Presidential Vote

Clinton (D)	116,226	(42%)
Bush (R)	104,509	(37%)
Perot (I)	56,516	(20%)

Rep. Jim Kolbe (R)

Elected 1984; b. June 28, 1942, Evanston, IL; home, Tucson; Northwestern U., B.A. 1965, Stanford U., M.B.A. 1967; United Methodist; divorced.

Career: Navy, 1968–69 (Vietnam), Naval Reserves, 1970–77; Asst., IL Bldg. Authority Architect, 1970–72; Asst., IL Gov. Ogilvie, 1972–73; Vice Pres., land planning firm; Real estate consultant; AZ Senate, 1976–82.

DC Office: 205 CHOB 20515, 202-225-2542; e-mail:jimkolbe@hr.house.gov.

District Offices: Tucson, 520-881-3588; Sierra Vista, 520-459-3115.

Committees: *Appropriations* (11th of 34 R): Commerce, Justice, State & Judiciary; Interior; Treasury, Postal Service & General Government (Chmn.).

Group Ratings

	ADA	ACLU	AFS	LCV	CFA	CON	NFIB	COC	ACU	NTLC	CHC
1996	5	19	0	23	23	63	95	94	90	93	67
1995	15	—	—	6	8	75	—	100	60	—	—

National Journal Ratings

	1995 LIB — 1995 CONS	1996 LIB — 1996 CONS
Economic	0% — 74%	0% — 82%
Social	60% — 39%	58% — 41%
Foreign	36% — 59%	44% — 55%

Key Votes of the 104th Congress

1. Reduce Medicare Growth $	Y	5. Flag Amendment	N	9. Cuban Embargo	Y
2. Ovrd. Product Liab. Veto	Y	6. Drop EPA Limits	N	10. Bar Bosnia Troop $	N
3. Increase Min. Wage	N	7. Repeal Assault-Weap. Ban	Y	11. Cut Anti-Missile Defense	N
4. Welfare Reform	Y	8. Ovrd. Part. Birth Veto	N	12. Bar U.N. Uniforms	N

Election Results

1996 general	Jim Kolbe (R)	179,349	(69%)	($415,550)
	Mort Nelson (D)	67,597	(26%)	
	Others	13,952	(5%)	
1996 primary	Jim Kolbe (R)	34,190	(70%)	
	Joe Sweeney (R)	14,704	(30%)	
1994 general	Jim Kolbe (R)	149,514	(68%)	($478,730)
	Gary Auerbach (D)	63,436	(29%)	($113,889)
	Others	7,821	(4%)	

SIXTH DISTRICT

Arizona has one of the nation's largest and fastest-growing Indian populations. There are small, sparsely populated reservations across the state, but by far the largest Indian population is the Navajo, in the northeast corner of the state who form the majority in (ironically) Apache County and a large minority in Navajo County to the west. The Navajo have their own tribal politics, complete with fiercely contested elections for tribal chief; they have been voting in ever increasing numbers in U.S. elections, and heavily Democratic.

The 6th Congressional District of Arizona covers nearly half the state, including the Navajo country and some of northern Phoenix and Scottsdale; household income levels vary from $20,000 in the Indian country to $64,000 in Scottsdale. The 6th also takes in the old mining towns of Globe and Clifton; Flagstaff, south of the Grand Canyon; and the sparsely-populated, wind-swept desert with seven Indian reservations in all; but its erose boundaries exclude the Hopis, who have a long and angry boundary dispute with the Navajo. Closer to Phoenix, the 6th takes in the suburbs of Carefree and Cave Creek, rustic areas where the mile-square grids are far from filled in and the local stores are more likely to feature horse feed than designer clothes, and the Salt River and Gila Valley reservations, their edges now sprouting Wal-marts and Kmarts. Politically, this is a sharply divided district. The Maricopa County portions, which cast 54% of the vote, are usually heavily Republican. The Navajo country is recently, and the copper mining country has been historically, heavily Democratic; Flagstaff is moving that way. The result is that the 6th District has been fiercely contested since it was created in 1992, and could well be again in 1998.

The congressman from the 6th is J.D. Hayworth, a conservative Republican who grew up in North Carolina and made his way upward in the hierarchy of local TV stations as a sportscaster, from Raleigh to Greenville to Cincinnati and then, in 1987, to Phoenix. Hayworth is 6'5", weighs 290, speaks with a booming voice and has a certain resemblance—a help in some quarters, a hindrance in others—to Rush Limbaugh. Certainly he was well known when he entered the race in 1994. He won the Republican primary with 45%, to 21% for former legislative leader David Schweikert and 14% for drug prosecutor Gary Husk. In the general he faced incumbent Democrat Karan English, who won the newly created seat in 1992 by 53%–41% over Doug Wead, a Reagan White House liaison to the religious right, who moved into the district to run. Wead's conservative stand on abortion and other cultural issues moved Barry Goldwater to endorse English, who had strengths of her own; she was a state legislator from Flagstaff who ran as a moderate supporting the line-item veto and a balanced budget amendment. In 1994 Hayworth attacked English for voting for the Clinton tax increase and framed the race as "between a citizen who pays taxes and a career politician who raises them." Hayworth issued his Action Plan for Arizona, full of denunciations of federal programs and praise for state and private initiatives, and enthusiastically signed the Contract with America. Hayworth carried Maricopa County 65%–32%, enough to easily overcome deficits on the Indian reservations and around Flagstaff, and won 55%–41%.

Hayworth has been a solid vote and strong voice in Newt Gingrich's Republican Conference. And with that voice and his sportscaster enthusiasm, he became a spokesman for the freshman in his early months but—like many of the newcomers who lacked previous government experience—he seemed thin on the details. He seemed to irritate Democrats more than just about any other freshman. He got into shouting matches with Democrats, "cursing, and not backing off," *The Hill* reported. Veteran Democrat David Obey told him, "You are one of the most impolite members I have ever seen in my service in this House." He worked on some local issues—to extend the boundaries of the Walnut Canyon National Monument, to transfer some Forest Service land to a local school district, to preserve a 701-acre tract in Scottsdale—and traveled around the district in a Subaru Outback specially designed for his large frame.

Early on Democrats targeted him. Steve Owens, an aide to then-Senator Al Gore in the 1980s and later Arizona Democratic chairman, returned to the district to run against Hayworth; Gore got Owens a speaking spot at the Chicago convention and came out to campaign for him. And the AFL-CIO made Hayworth one of their top targets, spending more than $1 million on ads charging him with cutting Medicare and hurting old folks. Through most of the fall the race was even in the polls. In the summer Hayworth was attacked because an aide had signed his affidavit of candidacy and Hayworth himself signed it only after the filing deadline; but he remained on the ballot. Owens criticized Hayworth on Medicare and the environment. "Hayworth has moved even more toward the right as this campaign has gotten under way," he said, claiming "a clear choice between the followers of Newt Gingrich on the extreme and all the rest of us in the mainstream." The Tribune chain, endorsing Owens, attacked "the bombastic Hayworth" whose "boorish behavior" it called "an affront to his colleagues, an embarrassment for America."

Hayworth kept supporting Gingrich. He called Owens a carpetbagger—a strange charge in a state where most people are from somewhere else—and ran ads pointing out that Owens had taken $5,000 from the Laborers' Union whose "bosses have admitted their connection to organized crime." By mid-October Hayworth had spent $1 million, with $221,000 cash left; Owens had spent only $186,000 but, able to rely on AFL-CIO spending, had $415,000 cash on hand. The Republican National Committee retaliated with pro-Hayworth ads charging that "labor bosses" were trying to take over the seat.

The result was close to a dead heat, and to the average of the 1992 and 1994 results. Hayworth won 48%–46%, carrying Maricopa County 56%–39% and trailing in the rest of the district 56%–38%. After the election Hayworth declined to moderate his views. "Ooh, let's wring our hands and be chastened. Ooh, I'm sorry. I'm not for small government any more. Let's increase government and raise taxes." More seriously, he called his win "a validation, a historic victory." Perhaps, though the closeness of the race suggests the Democrats could make a serious challenge again, if they have a strong candidate, and if they can find the kind of money the AFL-CIO spent.

The People: Pop. 1990: 611,885; 33% rural; 13% age 65+; 64% White; 1% Black; 1% Asian; 21% Amer. Indian; 13% Hispanic origin. Households: 62% married couple families; 28% married couple fams. w. children; 45% college educ.; median household income: $25,710; per capita income: $11,322; median gross rent: $426; median house value: $75,700.

1996 Presidential Vote

Clinton (D)	120,176	(47%)
Dole (R)	113,406	(44%)
Perot (I)	21,462	(8%)

1992 Presidential Vote

Bush (R)	91,269	(38%)
Clinton (D)	91,007	(37%)
Perot (I)	56,277	(23%)

Rep. J. D. Hayworth (R)

Elected 1994; b. July 12, 1958, High Point, NC; home, Scottsdale; NC St. U., B.A. 1980; Baptist; married (Mary).

Career: Sports Reporter/Anchor: WPTF-TV Raleigh, NC, 1980–81; WTFF-TV Greenville, SC, 1981–86; WLWT-TV, Cincinnati, OH, 1986–87; WKTSP-TV Phoenix, AZ, 1987–94; Insurance Agent & PR Consultant, 1994.

DC Office: 1023 LHOB 20515, 202-225-2190; Fax: 202-225-3263; e-mail: hayworth@hr.house.gov.

District Offices: Mesa, 602-926-4151; Flagstaff, 520-556-8760.

Committees: *Veterans' Affairs* (14th of 16 R): Benefits. *Ways & Means* (21st of 23 R): Human Resources; Social Security.

Group Ratings

	ADA	ACLU	AFS	LCV	CFA	CON	NFIB	COC	ACU	NTLC	CHC
1996	0	12	0	23	23	55	100	94	100	98	100
1995	0	—	—	6	0	56	—	100	100	—	—

National Journal Ratings

	1995 LIB — 1995 CONS			1996 LIB — 1996 CONS		
Economic	26%	—	67%	0%	—	82%
Social	0%	—	79%	35%	—	62%
Foreign	0%	—	85%	0%	—	79%

Key Votes of the 104th Congress

1. Reduce Medicare Growth $	Y	5. Flag Amendment	Y	9. Cuban Embargo	Y
2. Ovrd. Product Liab. Veto	Y	6. Drop EPA Limits	N	10. Bar Bosnia Troop $	Y
3. Increase Min. Wage	N	7. Repeal Assault-Weap. Ban	Y	11. Cut Anti-Missile Defense	N
4. Welfare Reform	Y	8. Ovrd. Part. Birth Veto	Y	12. Bar U.N. Uniforms	Y

Election Results

1996 general	J.D. Hayworth (R)	121,431	(48%)	($1,499,443)
	Steve Owens (D)	118,957	(47%)	($762,046)
	Robert Anderson (Lib)	14,899	(6%)	
1996 primary	J.D. Hayworth (R)	unopposed		
1994 general	J.D. Hayworth (R)	107,060	(55%)	($538,650)
	Karan English (D)	81,321	(41%)	($785,765)
	Others	7,687	(4%)	

ARKANSAS

In the 1990s Arkansas has been in the national spotlight as never before. It is the home of Bill Clinton, the president elected to serve most of the decade, the place where he honed his great political skills and the place where he became involved in pecadilloes that may turn out to be his undoing. It is a state attacked by both his Republican opponents as backward and corrupt, and a state that is trending toward Republicans in elections for offices just below the presidency. Arkansas was on display when Bill Clinton announced for president in October 1991 in front of the old State House, its Greek Revival columns were festooned with flags, and when he claimed victory on election night in front of the red-brick Governor's Mansion, bathed in thousands of lights set in place by his Hollywood friends. But Arkansas was also on display in federal court, where Governor Jim Guy Tucker was convicted of fraudulently arranging government loans in May 1996. Which is the real Arkansas? This is like asking which Bill Clinton is authentic—the responsive New Democrat, the cynical insider, the caring campaigner, the indulger in fast food or the articulate intellectual. They are all real, depending on the time, place and circumstances.

Arkansas, like Clinton, began life without many advantages. In area, it's the smallest state between the Mississippi and the Pacific; in population, it's the smallest state in the South; it has not been blessed with any great natural resource or any growing major industry. Arkansas is the land left over when Louisiana and Missouri were carved out of the Louisiana Purchase and what is now Oklahoma was fenced off as Indian Territory. Settled by poor farmers with large families, few slaves and little cash, it has had no Atlanta or Dallas or even Memphis to be a focus of growth. As Arkansas political scientist Diane Blair notes, Arkansas never had a power elite of great plantation owners or economic robber barons. That has left it a heritage without honored traditions or tight standards, but has also made Arkansas a land of great opportunities, where talented people can move up fast—like Blair and her husband, the house counsel at Tyson Foods, who guided the young Hillary Rodham in the commodities trading that resulted in unbelievable profits. Or like Jim McDougal, the onetime political prodigy and proprietor of the now-defunct Madison Guaranty Savings & Loan.

This Arkansas produced old style politicians like John McClellan and William Fulbright, who represented Arkansas in the Senate for a total of 65 years from the 1940s to the 1970s, while chairing the Appropriations and Foreign Relations Committees, and Wilbur Mills, chairman of the House Ways and Means Committee from 1958–74; Governor Orval Faubus, who shamed Little Rock and Arkansas around the world by resisting integration at Central High School in 1957; and Governor Winthrop Rockefeller, who steered the state toward integration a dozen years later. More recently it produced moderate Democrats like Dale Bumpers and David Pryor who each served four years as governor before being elected to the Senate in the 1970s, and Jim Guy Tucker, whose career intersected several times with Clinton's. Arkansas has also produced men who have made huge fortunes by taking break-through ideas and making them work: Sam Walton believed that rural and small town America would support a chain of giant discount stores which, through tough bargaining with vendors and ultra-quick distribution, could undersell competitors, but through demanding management and employee profit-sharing could embody small town friendliness and service; he was the richest American when he died in April 1992. Jack Stephens and his late brother Witt started an investment banking house in Little Rock specializing in underwriting municipal bonds and investing in businesses that are a mix of private enterprise, government subsidies and public regulation; their success—and political connections in Arkansas and elsewhere—amassed a billion dollar fortune. Don Tyson took his father's chicken business and made it one of the biggest food producers in America. Other big Arkansas operations include TCBY (The Country's Best Yogurt) and J.B. Hunt's trucking empire. These business giants have cultivated a down home, laid-back style. But they have also skillfully united their interests with those of the state's politicians, including—especially—Bill Clinton. Three-quarters of the $20 million for the Tyson Center of Excellence for Poultry Science at the University of Arkansas came from the federal and state government.

A case can be made that Arkansas is America in the 1990s in exaggerated form. It has produced in Clinton and in businessmen like Walton, the Stephenses, and Tyson, leaders of unusual ability and outsized personality. At the same time the gulf between the very rich and the rest of Arkansas remains whole magnitudes larger than the oft-lamented (by Democrats in 1992, Republicans in 1996) growth in income disparity in the nation as a whole. Arkansas's economy has grown smartly in the 1990s, with jobs and incomes up about 15% in the first Clinton term; it leads the nation in producing chickens and rice, which have been gaining on beef and potatoes; it has benefited from increased tourism, some of it to the President's birthplace of Hope and boyhood home of Hot Springs.

Politically, Arkansas has resembled the nation in the 1990s, too. It has voted twice for Bill Clinton for president, and at the same time has moved toward the Republican Party in races just below the top of the ticket. In 1996 Clinton beat Bob Dole in Arkansas 54%–47%, almost the same as his 53% in 1992. The Clinton percentages are eerily similar to his vote in his last seriously contested state elections in 1990, when he won the Democratic primary 55%–39% and beat Republican Sheffield Nelson 57%–42%. Clinton had recovered from losing for a second term in 1980 by winning in 1982 and then being reelected with over 60% in 1984 and 1986: Arkansas seemed to have a strong Democratic consensus in the 1980s, but in the 1990s there has been a large stubbornly anti-Clinton vote.

Underneath the totals were numbers signalling trouble for Democrats. Clinton's 1992 margin came primarily from voters over 45, who favored him 70%–26%; those under 45 went for Bush, 43%–41%. And northwest Arkansas, the fastest-growing part of the state, and the home base of the Waltons and Tysons, has become heavily Republican: the 3d Congressional District, where

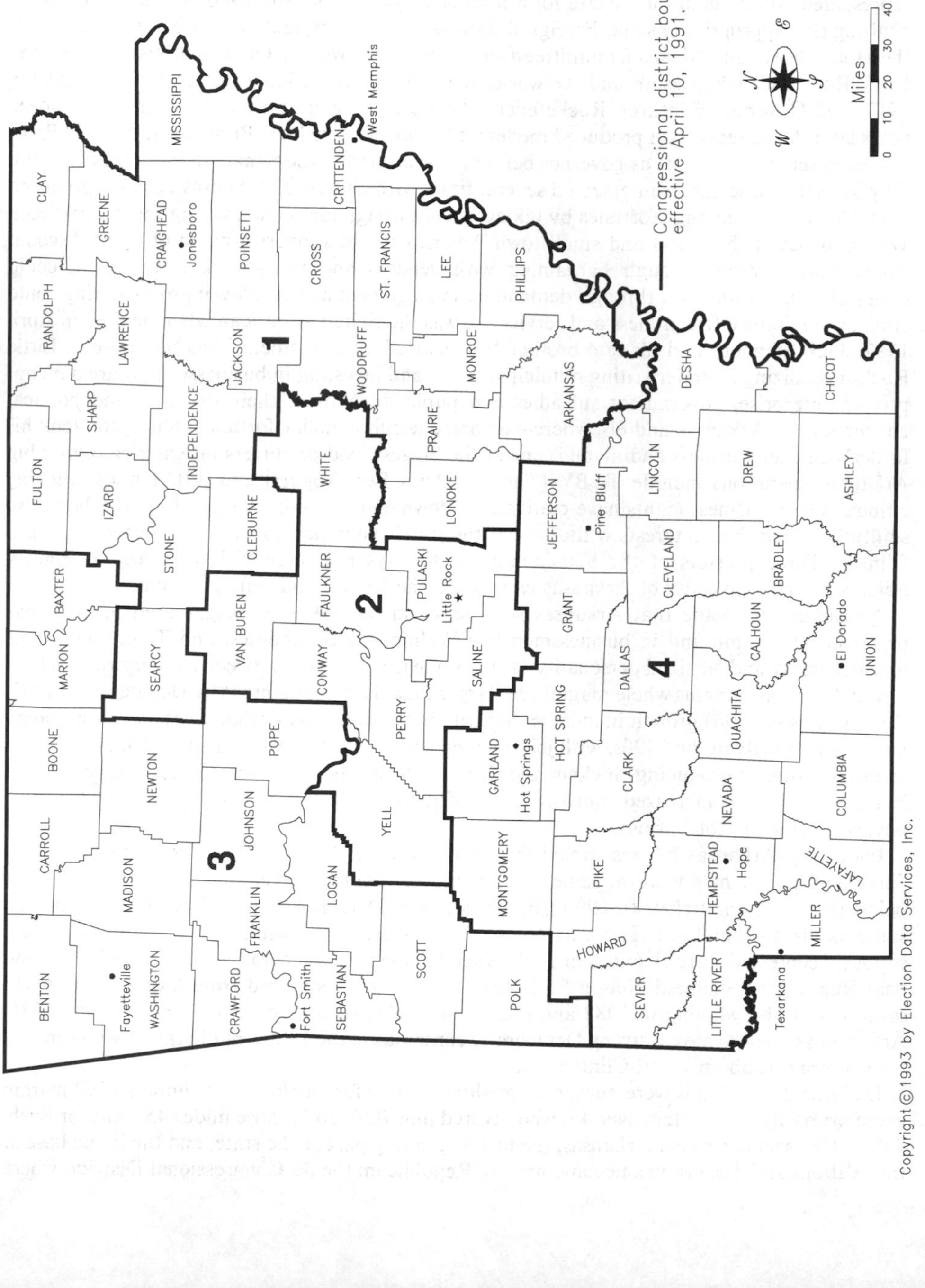
Congressional district boundaries
effective April 10, 1991.
Miles
0 10 20 30 40
N
E
S
W
1
2
3
4
CLAY
GREENE
MISSISSIPPI
CRAIGHEAD
Jonesboro
POINSETT
CRITTENDEN
West Memphis
CROSS
ST. FRANCIS
LEE
PHILLIPS
RANDOLPH
LAWRENCE
JACKSON
WOODRUFF
MONROE
ARKANSAS
DESHA
CHICOT
SHARP
INDEPENDENCE
PRAIRIE
FULTON
IZARD
WHITE
LONOKE
JEFFERSON
Pine Bluff
LINCOLN
DREW
ASHLEY
STONE
CLEBURNE
FAULKNER
PULASKI
Little Rock
GRANT
CLEVELAND
BRADLEY
BAXTER
MARION
SEARCY
VAN BUREN
CONWAY
SALINE
DALLAS
CALHOUN
El Dorado
UNION
BOONE
NEWTON
POPE
PERRY
HOT SPRING
OUACHITA
GARLAND
Hot Springs
CLARK
NEVADA
COLUMBIA
CARROLL
JOHNSON
YELL
MONTGOMERY
PIKE
HEMPSTEAD
Hope
LAFAYETTE
MADISON
FRANKLIN
LOGAN
MILLER
BENTON
Fayetteville
WASHINGTON
CRAWFORD
Fort Smith
SEBASTIAN
SCOTT
POLK
HOWARD
SEVIER
LITTLE RIVER
Texarkana
Copyright © 1993 by Election Data Services, Inc.

Clinton ran his first race in 1974, voted for Clinton in 1992 but for Bob Dole in 1996. On election night 1992 Arkansas Democrats held the governorship and all lower state offices, both Senate seats, and three out of four House seats. In January 1997, Republicans held the governorship, one Senate seat, and two House seats; only in the legislature will they be heavily outnumbered as of yore. Before the 1996 election, Democratic consultant Randy Thompson asked, "Has there been a philosophical shift or have Republicans been elevated by happenstance? That is the question this election will answer." The answer seems to be a tentative yes to both.

There were other signs of a conservative trend—and of lurking scandal. The most popular politician in the state was Mike Huckabee, who was elected lieutenant governor in a 1993 special and reelected easily in 1994; he succeeded to the governorship when Jim Guy Tucker, convicted of fraud, resigned in July 1996. Huckabee had been the favorite to win the Senate seat which David Pryor was vacating; his replacement as Republican nominee, 3d District Congressman Tim Hutchinson, won. In referenda Arkansas rejected casino gambling, with Christian conservatives and Mississippi riverboat casino operators leading the opposition. In 1990 Arkansas voted term limits on its members of Congress; this was the law overturned 5–4 by the Supreme Court in June 1996. But in November Arkansas voted for an initiative requiring opponents of term limits to be so designated on the ballot. And by August 1996, 12 Arkansans had pleaded guilty or been convicted in cases brought by independent counsel Kenneth Starr. Whatever replaces it, the old political order in Arkansas seems on the way out.

Governor. Mike Huckabee became governor of Arkansas in July 1996 at 40, an improbable figure in traditional Arkansas politics but perhaps a prototype of southern politics to come. Like Bill Clinton, Huckabee was born in Hope; unlike Clinton, he grew up there. Clinton was elected governor of Arkansas Boys State in 1963, Huckabee in 1972. Clinton went off to Georgetown and Yale Law School; Huckabee graduated from Ouachita Baptist University at 19 and attended Southwestern Baptist Theological Seminary in Fort Worth for four years. He had a profound spiritual experience at 15, while on a two-week youth fellowship program at Cape Kennedy—the first time he had been outside Arkansas. In the 1980s, while Clinton was governor and was taking the national political stage, Huckabee was a Baptist minister in Pine Bluff and then Texarkana; in both towns he started a 24-hour television station, where he produced documentaries and hosted a program called Positive Alternatives. He became president of the Arkansas Baptist Convention, with a membership of 490,000 in 1989.

In that capacity Clinton asked him to talk to his state health director, Dr. Joycelyn Elders, about some of her more colorful comments she made about Christians. "This was when she was talking about the pro-life people having a love affair with the fetus," Huckabee told *The Hill*. "She gave out condoms in school, and they proved to be defective, for heaven's sake. If you disagreed with her, you were just full of the devil." Afterwards, he told his wife, "We're going to have to get out of the stands and onto the field if people like her are making decisions on public policy." Huckabee ran for the Senate in 1992 and lost to incumbent Democrat Dale Bumpers 60%–40%. Then, after Jim Guy Tucker replaced Bill Clinton as governor, Huckabee ran for lieutenant governor. It was July 1993, the Clinton tax plan and gays in the military had been in the headlines, and Huckabee beat a pro-Clinton Democrat 51%–49%.

That victory changed the Arkansas political landscape. It "sent shock waves because it wasn't supposed to happen. It created disorder and disarray among Democrats," Huckabee said. It also made him the most visible Republican and perhaps the most popular politician in the state. In November 1994 he was reelected 59%–41%. In October 1995, after David Pryor announced he was retiring from the Senate, Huckabee announced he was running; he was already well ahead in the polls. Huckabee discounted then the possibility that Jim Guy Tucker would be forced out by his legal problems. Tucker was another of Arkansas's brilliant Democratic politicians, elected attorney general in 1974, two years before Bill Clinton; elected congressman from Little Rock in 1976; the second place finisher in the 1978 Senate primary and runoff; then elected lieutenant governor in 1990. The success of Clinton, who started off behind him in politics, proved disastrous for Tucker; it's unlikely any prosecutor would have looked at his case but for Clinton's

Whitewater investment.

Tucker's indictment had been thrown out by Judge Henry Woods, a Clinton crony. But in March 1996 the appeals court reversed this decision, and Tucker was convicted on one count of arranging nearly $3 million in fraudulent loans in 1985–87 through Capital Management Services, a government-aided firm run by former municipal Judge David Hale. Tucker promised to resign July 15; on that day, claiming he had a good case on appeal, he hesitated, then finally in early evening resigned—a moment of banana republic politics; and suddenly Arkansas had a popular Republican governor. Huckabee eschewed the Senate race and eventually the Republican Party substituted Congressman Tim Hutchinson, who won in November.

As governor Huckabee acted against stereotype. He backed a tax increase, though a small one—one-eighth of a cent sales tax, in a constitutional amendment, to fund the Games and Fishing Commission and Department of Parks and Tourism, which passed in November 1996. This he presented as an alternative to casino gambling, which he opposed and which was defeated. Faced with a $100 million state surplus, Huckabee proposed a $50 per person rebate of the sales tax on food. He strongly opposes abortion: "I am unapologetically pro-life and feel the government ought to protect citizens, not terminate them." And he defends his participation in politics. "I do not ask people to vote for me because I go to church and am a minister. People never raise questions when Bill Clinton goes to church and stands up in the pulpit and he is not an ordained minister. I have to wonder if there is a double standard." He seems to combine a hard-right stand on issues with a forgiving attitude. He insists that government will never do as much to end poverty as private charity, arguing that the poverty rate has been unchanged since it became a federal responsibility. And on Clinton, he says, "We can attack his healthcare plan, gays in the military, his foreign policy or the lack of one, but we should not attack him personally. He is the embodiment of the American dream, a kid not of a prosperous family with a pedigree through inheritance. He got there the hard way. He gives a lot of people hope."

Huckabee comes up for election to a full term in 1998. He seems likely to be a very strong candidate. Or he might run again for Dale Bumpers's Senate seat, especially if Bumpers decides to retire at 73. If he leaves the governorship, one Republican who may run is Win Rockefeller, son of the late governor.

Senior Senator. Dale Bumpers was once the first of a rising generation of young Democrats in Arkansas politics; now he is dean of the Arkansas delegation and still vital after more than a quarter-century in politics.

Bumpers grew up in the small town of Charleston, in west Arkansas, two decades before Bill Clinton. He served in the Marines during World War II, went to college in Arkansas and law school at Northwestern, then practiced law in Charleston, specializing in jury trials all over the state. In 1970 his eloquence and the skills of consultant Delos Walker elected him governor, over serious competition from Orval Faubus in the primary and Winthrop Rockefeller in the general. In 1974 he ran for the Senate and beat 30-year-incumbent William Fulbright 2–1 in the primary. His political future seemed bright and some thought he was headed to the White House. He certainly was well positioned to run. His issue positions—strong support of civil rights and a sometimes moderate stance on economic issues—was a winning combination for the only two Democrats elected president in the last third of the 20th Century.

Bumpers has the eloquence and gift for the pungent phrase of a trial lawyer who knows how to sway a jury; he can speak the language of ordinary people, reducing complicated arguments to simple statements. But he is also the town iconoclast, with his idiosyncratic, often unpopular ideas, who is nonetheless respected and even loved. Bumpers was raised a Roosevelt liberal Democrat; growing up in the 1930s, he saw FDR's federal government as the one institution working for the common man. But he has bucked organized labor, as when he voted against cloture on filibusters on labor law reform in 1978 and the striker-replacement ban in 1994.

But Bumpers never has run for president, passing up chances in 1984 and 1988 when many urged him to do so. And in the Senate he has had frustrations as well as achievements. He never became a committee chairman; only in 1997 did he become a ranking minority member, on

Energy and Natural Resources. He is on Appropriations, and so does important work quietly on markups, including funding Arkansas projects; but he is still only the fifth-ranking Democrat. At his best Bumpers picks and chooses issues, making him something like a cat: seemingly lazy while he naps but dangerous when he pounces. "Certain senators seem to have an opinion on everything," he says. "I don't like to get involved unless I have very strong feelings and am very prepared." In the rightward moving Senate of the 1990s, he has turned out to be pretty far left on foreign policy issues and even on economics, and often on cultural issues as well. He has vociferously opposed major federal science and defense projects, leading battles to cut funds for the Strategic Defense Initiative, the Space Station, the Supercollider, with varying success: the Supercollider is dead, SDI limited, but the Space Station survived as Bumpers lost 64–36. He also argues for stretching out or canceling defense systems—the Trident submarine, the Milstar II satellite, the F-22, the C-17, the Advanced Neutron Source research reactor. He led unsuccessful attempts to reform the Mining Act of 1872, to require mining companies to pay much higher royalties to the government; he worked more successfully to stop a gold mine near Yellowstone National Park. He has also tried to reform concessions policy for national parks, again attacking well-entrenched interests. He sponsored the 1994 law, sought by Arkansas food producers, to delay nutrition labelling requirements.

Bumpers is capable of swaying colleagues with his oratory, as in 1988 when he made a brilliant speech in favor of preserving the Manassas, Virginia, Civil War Battlefield from a shopping center project. But the newer Republicans seem impervious to his charms. He was early to spot key issues (warning about aerosol cans in 1975, pushing for childhood immunizations in the 1980s) but late in abandoning lost causes (battling against decontrol of energy prices in the early 1980s). He was one of the three senators (Bradley and Hollings were the others) who voted for the 1981 Reagan budget cuts and against the 1981 tax cuts—a set of positions which, if adopted, would have just about eliminated the budget deficits of the 1980s.

Bumpers's phenomenal popularity as governor has cooled a bit in his years in Washington but has not burnt out altogether. He was reelected with 59% in 1980, 62% in 1986, 60% in 1992. His last opponent was Mike Huckabee, now governor, who was preparing to run for the other Senate seat in 1996, until it seemed likely he would succeed Jim Guy Tucker as governor; Huckabee could be a formidable Senate candidate in 1998. "We need to give the people of Arkansas a senator who does more than talk cornbread and catfish in Arkansas, but votes Kennedy and Cranston in Washington," Huckabee proclaimed in 1992. Bumpers remains a strong candidate if he seeks reelection in 1998. But he will turn 73 that year and surely does not enjoy being in the minority, and it would not surprise many if he chooses to retire.

Junior Senator. Tim Hutchinson, elected in 1996, is the first Republican senator from Arkansas since 1879. Hutchinson grew up in northwest Arkansas, attended Bob Jones University and became a Baptist Minister; he also owned and managed a radio station and was founder and administrator of a Christian school in Rogers. In 1984 he was elected to the Arkansas House, where Clinton called him "No-Tax Tim." His brother Asa Hutchinson was the Republican nominee against Senator Dale Bumpers in 1986, later served as Republican state chairman, and ultimately succeeded him in the House. In 1992 Tim Hutchinson ran for Congress and won the three-candidate Republican primary impressively, 53%–32% over a fellow state legislator. In the general, he backed term limits, the balanced budget amendment, the line-item veto—the Contract with America two years early—and called for a base-closings-type commission to curb government spending. He called attacks on him as a religious extremist "scare tactics" reflecting "a kind of intolerance," and in the last week of the campaign was endorsed by local Perot supporters who dismissed Democratic opponent John VanWinkle as a "waffler." But the Democrat raised more money, Bill Clinton was carrying the district, and Hutchinson won by just 50%–47%. In the House he had a very conservative record. He supported NAFTA after watching U.S. exports sell in a Wal-Mart in Mexico City. He was one of the originators of the Contract with America $500 per child tax credit. He was reelected with 68% and seemed headed for a third term when Governor Jim Guy Tucker was convicted of fraud in May 1996 and announced he would resign in July. That elevated Republican Lieutenant Governor Mike Huckabee, who had been the Republicans' very strong candidate for senator and winner of the May 21 primary. Huckabee said May 30 he would leave the Senate race, and Republicans, suddenly afraid they would lose what they had counted as a sure gain, cast around for another candidate. Hutchinson said June 3 he would not run; state Senator John Brown announced June 4 and 4th District Congressman Jay Dickey formed an exploratory committee. But Brown said he would step aside for Hutchinson and Dickey endorsed Hutchinson June 11; a Republican convention June 15 chose Hutchinson as the party nominee.

All this came amidst the Democrats' spirited primary. The seat had been held for 18 years by David Pryor, often called Bill Clinton's best friend in Congress. He was first elected to the House back in 1966, was a nearly successful candidate against Senator John McClellan in 1972, was elected governor in 1974 and 1976 and then senator in 1978. Pryor compiled a mostly liberal record, worked especially on elderly issues and was the driving force behind the 1988 Taxpayer Bill of Rights. The leading Democrat to succeed him since his April 1995 announcement was Attorney General Winston Bryant, the winner of seven consecutive statewide races. But he had three spirited opponents. He led in the May 21 primary with 40% to 22% for liberal state Senator Lu Hardin. Bryant said he would hold the line on taxes and believes in "rural values"; Hardin backers claimed he stood for "less but better government programs that strengthen family values." Bryant won the June 11 runoff 54%–46%.

Hutchinson started his general campaign with an ad showing John Kennedy and saying that his father voted for Kennedy while teaching Tim to have an open mind and open heart. Democrats squawked, and Bryant ran ads tying Hutchinson to Newt Gingrich and accusing him of shutting down the government. But Hutchinson, one of four House Republicans to vote to release the outside counsel's report on Newt Gingrich, brushed aside the attacks saying "The people of Arkansas are going to say, 'No, thumbs down, we don't want a senator who has nothing to offer but criticism.' That's all his campaign has been based on. [Bryant's] criticized Congress. He's criticized me and always with great distortion of the facts." And Hutchinson protested Bryant's increased office budgets: "For 15 years Winston Bryant's been very liberal with your money." Just five days before the election Hutchinson's 22-year-old son was injured in a auto accident; the elder Hutchinson rushed to the hospital to be at his son's side.

On election day Hutchinson won 53%–47%. He carried all of Arkansas west and north of Little Rock and ran just about even in the capital. His brother Asa was elected to his old 3d District House seat, and the two became the second pair of congressional brothers. (The others are Sander and Carl Levin of Michigan.) Tim Hutchinson seems likely to compile a strong voting record and to tend to practical Arkansas needs. He serves on the committee handling public works, as he did in the House, and promises to work to build the 1-69 across the western end of the state. "I don't have a higher priority," he once said. He chaired the Veterans' Subcommittee on Hospitals and Health Care in the House and will continue that work from his seat on Veterans' in the Senate.

Presidential politics. Arkansas was Bill Clinton's strongest state in 1992. Not so in 1996, when he won higher percentages in Massachusetts, Rhode Island, New York, Hawaii, Maryland, Vermont, and Illinois. Arkansas was long one of the least Republican of southern states; now it seems to be moving heavily toward Republicans, and its 1996 showing was more a reflection of Clinton's personal home-state strength than of underlying Democratic allegiance. Al Gore, should he be the 2000 nominee, may have to strain hard to win here, as Clinton did in 1996 to win Gore's Tennessee.

The Arkansas presidential primary is now held in May, and attracts little attention. It didn't when it was held on Super Tuesday, in 1992, either. There is no party registration and Republican turnout has typically been very low; it will be interesting to see if that is still true in 2000.

Congressional districting. Arkansas made only minor changes in its district boundaries to meet the equal-population standard in the 1990s.

The People: Est. Pop. 1996: 2,510,000; Pop. 1990: 2,350,725, up 6.8% 1990–1996. 0.9% of U.S. total, 33d largest; 46% rural. Median age: 35.2 years. 14% 65 years and over. 82.2% White, 15.9% Black, 1% Asian, 1% Amer. Indian, 1% Hispanic origin. Households: 59.2% married couple families; 27% married couple fams. w. children; 34% college educ.; median household income: $21,147; per capita income: $10,520; 69.6% owner occupied housing; median house value: $46,300; median monthly rent: $230. 5.4% Unemployment. 1996 Voting age pop.: 1,873,000; 1996 Turnout: 884,262; 47% of VAP. Registered voters (1996): 1,369,459; no party registration.

Political Lineup: Governor, Mike Huckabee (R); Lt. Gov., Winthrop P. Rockefeller (R); Secy. of State, Sharon Priest (D); Atty. Gen., Winston Bryant (D); Treasurer, Jimmie Lou Fisher (D); Auditor, Gus Wingfield (D). State Senate, 35 (28 D and 7 R); Senate President, Wayne Dowd (D); State House, 100 (86 D and 14 R); House Speaker, Bobby Hogue (D). Senators, Dale Bumpers (D) and Tim Hutchinson (R). Representatives, 4 (2 R and 2 D).

Elections Division: 501-682-5070; **Filing Deadline for U.S. Congress:** March 31, 1998.

1996 Presidential Vote

Clinton (D)	475,171	(54%)
Dole (R)	325,416	(37%)
Perot (I)	69,884	(8%)
Other(s)	13,791	(2%)

1996 Republican Presidential Primary

Dole (R)	32,759	(76%)
Buchanan (R)	10,067	(23%)

1992 Presidential Vote

Clinton (D)	505,823	(53%)
Bush (R)	337,324	(35%)
Perot (I)	99,132	(10%)

GOVERNOR

Gov. Mike Huckabee (R)

Assumed office, July 1996, term expires Jan. 1999; b. Aug. 24, 1955, Hope; home, Little Rock; Ouachita Baptist U., B.A. 1975; Southwestern Baptist Theological Seminary, 1976–80; Baptist; married (Janet).

Career: Advertising Dir., Focus, 1976–80; Baptist Minister, 1980–92; Pres., ACTS-TV, 1983–86; Pres., KBSC-TV, 1987–92; Pres., Cambridge Comm., 1992–96; AR Lt. Gov., 1993–96.

Office: State Capitol, #250, Little Rock 72201, 501-682-2345; Fax: 501-682-3597; Web site: www.state.ar.us.

Election Results

1994 gen.	Jim Guy Tucker (D)	428,936	(60%)
	Sheffield Nelson (R)	287,904	(40%)
1994 prim.	Jim Guy Tucker (D) . unopposed		
1990 gen.	Bill Clinton (D)	400,326	(57%)
	Sheffield Nelson (R)	295,883	(42%)

SENATORS

Sen. Dale Bumpers (D)

Elected 1974, seat up 1998; b. Aug. 12, 1925, Charleston; home, Charleston; U. of AR, Northwestern U., LL.B. 1951; Methodist; married (Betty).

Career: Marine Corps, 1943–46 (WWII); Practicing atty., 1951–70; AR Gov., 1970–74.

DC Office: 229 DSOB 20510, 202-224-4843; Fax: 202-224-6435; e-mail: senator@bumpers.senate.gov.

State Offices: 2527 Fed. Bldg., 700 W. Capitol, Little Rock 72201, 501-324-6286.

Committees: *Appropriations* (5th of 13 D): Agriculture, Rural Development & Related Agencies (RMM); Commerce, Justice, State & the Judiciary; Defense; Interior; Labor, Health & Human Services & Education. *Energy & Natural Resources* (RMM). *Small Business* (2nd of 8 D).

Group Ratings

	ADA	ACLU	AFS	LCV	CFA	CON	NFIB	COC	ACU	NTLC	CHC
1996	85	50	100	85	86	20	34	17	0	7	8
1995	85	—	100	100	88	7	—	32	4	—	—

National Journal Ratings

	1995 LIB — 1995 CONS			1996 LIB — 1996 CONS		
Economic	86%	—	11%	88%	—	11%
Social	73%	—	26%	74%	—	25%
Foreign	97%	—	0%	93%	—	0%

Key Votes of the 104th Congress

1. Reduce Medicare Growth $	N	5. Flag Amendment	N	9. Anti-Missle Defense	N
2. Lmt. Prod. Liab. Damages	N	6. Endangered Species	Y	10. Cuban Embargo	N
3. Increase Min. Wage	Y	7. Gay Employment Rights	Y	11. Bar Bosnia Troop $	N
4. Welfare Reform	N	8. Ovrd. Part. Birth Veto	N	12. Cut Vietnam Aid	N

Election Results

1992 general	Dale Bumpers (D)	553,635	(60%)	($2,016,112)
	Mike Huckabee (R)	366,373	(40%)	($910,212)
1992 primary	Dale Bumpers (D)	322,458	(65%)	
	Julia Hughes Jones (D)	177,273	(35%)	
1986 general	Dale Bumpers (D)	433,092	(62%)	($1,797,370)
	Asa Hutchinson (R)	262,300	(38%)	($939,342)

Sen. Tim Hutchinson (R)

Elected 1996, seat up 2002; b. Aug. 11, 1949, Gravette; home, Bentonville; Bob Jones U., B.A. 1979, U. of AR, M.A. 1990; Baptist; married (Donna King).

Career: Baptist Minister; Founder and Admin., Benton Cnty. Christian Schl., 1975–85; Co-owner and Mgr., KBCV Radio, 1982–89; Prof., John Brown U., 1989–92; AR House of Reps., 1984–92; US House of Reps., 1992-96.

DC Office: 245 DSOB 20510, 202-224-2353; Fax: 202-228-3973; e-mail: senator.hutchinson@hutchinson.senate.gov.

State Offices: Little Rock, 501-324-6336.

Committees: *Environment & Public Works* (8th of 10 R): Clean Air, Wetlands, Private Property & Nuclear Safety; Drinking Water, Fisheries & Wildlife. *Labor & Human Resources* (7th of 10 R): Aging; Children & Families. *Veterans' Affairs* (7th of 7 R).

Group Ratings (As Member of U.S. House of Representatives)

	ADA	ACLU	AFS	LCV	CFA	CON	NFIB	COC	ACU	NTLC	CHC
1996	5	6	0	23	15	42	100	94	100	100	100
1995	0	—	—	0	8	75	—	96	92	—	—

National Journal Ratings (As Member of U.S. House of Representatives)

	1995 LIB — 1995 CONS	1996 LIB — 1996 CONS
Economic	0% — 74%	0% — 82%
Social	0% — 79%	10% — 86%
Foreign	15% — 73%	0% — 79%

Key Votes of the 104th Congress (As Member of U.S. House of Representatives)

1. Reduce Medicare Growth $	Y	5. Flag Amendment	Y	9. Cuban Embargo	Y
2. Ovrd. Product Liab. Veto	Y	6. Drop EPA Limits	N	10. Bar Bosnia Troop $	Y
3. Increase Min. Wage	N	7. Repeal Assault-Weap. Ban	Y	11. Cut Anti-missile Defense	N
4. Welfare Reform	Y	8. Ovrd. Part. Birth Veto	Y	12. Bar U.N. Uniforms	Y

Election Results

1996 general	Tim Hutchinson (R)	445,942	(53%)	($1,604,014)
	Winston Bryant (D)	400,241	(47%)	($1,577,838)
1996 primary	Tim Hutchinson (R)	nominated by convention		
1990 general	David Pryor (D)	unopposed		($622,479)

FIRST DISTRICT

The Delta, the flat, mushy lowlands on both sides of the lower Mississippi River, were some of the country's first industrial farmlands. This land was uncultivated in the 19th Century, when plows were still pulled by mules and muddy flatlands were impassable. Then, around 100 years ago, big landowners used machines to drain the marshlands and used capital to attract poor blacks to tend fields of cotton, rice and later soybeans. The results were bountiful agriculture and impoverished people. Around 1940, the Delta began to change slowly: national minimum wage legislation drew young people out of the Delta and mechanization forced many people off the farms. But this land—stretching flat as far as the eye can see, past rows of telephone poles and ribbons of asphalt that shimmer in the heat—remains poor by national standards and the people undereducated and underemployed.

The 1st Congressional District of Arkansas includes most of the state's Delta lands and stretches west to the cool green Ozarks. The Delta started off heavily Democratic, while some of the hill counties are ancestrally Republican. That changed as partisan preferences oscillated wildly just after the civil rights revolution, but the district returned to its historical norm by the late 1980s, and the Delta provided critical support for, perhaps saving the career of, Bill Clinton in 1990. In 1992, Delta counties voted 58% to 69% for Clinton, some of his best county showings anywhere in the United States.

The congressman from the 1st District is Marion Berry, a Democrat and Clinton supporter who nonetheless only narrowly won this district in 1996. Berry grew up in Bayou Meto in Arkansas County, in the Delta. He earned a pharmacy degree in Little Rock, then ran a pharmacy for two years and has been a family farmer since 1968. He was also active in local politics in Gillett, in Arkansas County, and worked in Bill Clinton's campaigns starting in 1982. Governor Clinton appointed him to the Arkansas Soil & Water Conservation Commission in 1986, and President Clinton appointed him White House liaison to the Agriculture Department in 1993. He returned to Arkansas in 1996, after Congresswoman Blanche Lambert Lincoln announced she would not run for reelection because she was pregnant with twins. Lincoln won the seat in 1992 by beating her former boss, 24-year Congressman Bill Alexander, in the Democratic primary.

Berry turned out to have tough opposition for the seat. Republican Warren DuPwe, former Jonesboro city attorney, who had won 47% against Lincoln in 1994, was running again. And there was Democratic primary opposition that proved surprisingly strong. Tom Donaldson, a 28-year-old deputy prosecutor in Crittenden County, across the river from Memphis, spent little money but ran rural radio ads criticizing Berry for accepting farm subsidies. He held Berry to a 48%–30% lead in the May 21 primary. Lincoln endorsed Berry and he brought in Agriculture Secretary Dan Glickman to campaign for him. Yet he won the June 11 runoff by only 53%–44%.

In the general Berry accused DuPwe over and over of favoring Medicare cuts; DuPwe replied that he favored increasing Medicare spending more slowly. Both candidates opposed abortion rights and gun control and favored a balanced budget. DuPwe got Transportation and Infrastructure Chairman Bud Shuster to hold a hearing on extending I-69 west of the Mississippi River, in Arkansas. But Berry's Washington contacts proved more generous than DuPwe's Washington contacts and he outspent DuPwe nearly 2–1. Berry won 53%–44%, almost the same margin's as his predecessor.

Berry said he wanted a seat on the Agriculture Committee and that his primary goal was to avoid privatization of the Southwest Power Administration, which supplies electricity to city-owned utilities. But such assignments are likely to be less politically rewarding than in the past. The 1996 Freedom to Farm Act phases out agricultural subsidies for cotton and rice over the next seven years, and the nation's electric power industry is being deregulated, which will likely lead to cheaper power through market forces than the SPA can deliver. Given Berry's close margins this historically heavily Democratic district cannot be considered completely safe Democratic territory any more.

The People: Pop. 1990: 588,588; 53% rural; 15% age 65+; 81% White; 18% Black; 1% Hispanic origin. Households: 60% married couple families; 28% married couple fams. w. children; 26% college educ.; median household income: $18,180; per capita income: $9,148; median gross rent: $290; median house value: $39,800.

1996 Presidential Vote

Clinton (D)	116,634	(58%)
Dole (R)	65,707	(33%)
Perot (I)	16,269	(8%)

1992 Presidential Vote

Clinton (D)	131,585	(59%)
Bush (R)	71,160	(32%)
Perot (I)	20,116	(9%)

Rep. Marion Berry (D)

Elected 1996; b. Aug. 27, 1942, Bayou Meto; home, Gillett; U. of AR, B.S. 1965; Methodist; married (Carolyn).

Career: Pharmacist, 1965–67; farmer, 1968–present; AR Soil & Water Conservation Comm., 1986–1994, Chmn. 1992; Special Asst. to the Pres., Domestic Policy Cncl., White House, 1993–96.

DC Office: 1407 LHOB 20515, 202-225-4076; Fax:202-225-5602.

District Offices: Batesville, 501-612-5399; Forrest City, 501-633-4406; Jonesboro, 501-972-4600.

Committees: *Agriculture* (16th of 23 D): Department Operations, Nutrition & Foreign Agriculture; Forestry, Resource Conservation & Research. *Small Business* (16th of 16 D): Tax, Finance & Exports.

Group Ratings and Key Votes: Newly Elected

Election Results

1996 general	Marion Berry (D)	105,280	(53%)	($871,389)
	Warren DuPwe (R)	88,436	(44%)	($574,846)
	Others	5,734	(3%)	
1996 runoff	Marion Berry (D)	30,592	(52%)	
	Tom Donaldson (D)	27,717	(48%)	
1996 primary	Marion Berry (D)	42,195	(48%)	
	Tom Donaldson (D)	26,382	(30%)	
	Kirby J. Smith (D)	19,371	(22%)	
1994 general	Blanche Lambert Lincoln (D)	95,290	(53%)	($505,453)
	Warren DuPwe (R)	83,147	(47%)	($210,360)

SECOND DISTRICT

Little Rock, the capital and central focus of Arkansas for a century and a half, twice in the 20th Century became the central focus of the United States and the world. The first time was in September 1957, when Governor Orval Faubus, eager for a third term, sent in the National Guard to block a desegregation order at Central High School. President Eisenhower sent in U.S. troops and federalized the Guard to enforce the order, and Little Rock became a synonym for bigotry around the world—not quite fairly, since in many ways Little Rock has been more tolerant and less violent than many other places. Little Rock's second, happier moment in the international spotlight came in late 1992, when it was the headquarters of Democratic nominee and President-elect Bill Clinton. Television viewers became familiar with the Old State House and the Governor's Mansion, the Rose Law Firm and McDonald's. Bill Clinton grew up in Hope and Hot Springs, went to school in Washington, Oxford, and New Haven, then lived and ran for Congress in the university town of Fayetteville, in northwest Arkansas; he has lived in Little Rock only in the Governor's Mansion and for two years after he was defeated for governor in 1980. Yet Little Rock is his legal residence and more than anywhere else seems his home.

Little Rock is also the center of Arkansas geographically and, even more, politically. It sets the tone of the public life of its state as do only a few other state capitals—Boston, Providence, Atlanta, Denver, Honolulu. Little Rock is home to the *Arkansas Democrat*, the feistily conservative paper whose editor Paul Greenberg christened "Slick Willie." It is home to the state government and to Jack Stephens's investment banking firm and Worthen Bank, to Dillards department stores and the TCBY yogurt chain, and the defunct Madison Guaranty

Savings & Loan. Little Rock may not be upscale by national standards, but it is in Arkansas. And the bad name it earned internationally when Governor Orval Faubus forcibly resisted the desegregation of Central High School in 1957 has surely been overshadowed by the good name it has won as Bill Clinton's home.

The 2d Congressional District of Arkansas includes Little Rock, with its large black and affluent white neighborhoods, and North Little Rock, a kind of industrial suburb across the Arkansas River known informally for years as Dog Town. (At the turn of the century, Little Rock officials, peeved that North Little Rock was allowed to incorporate separately, dumped all their stray dogs there.) It also includes surrounding counties which have grown rapidly as people move farther out the freeways and a couple of small hill counties. Politically, Little Rock was long a progressive force in a state with widely divergent political tendencies; it provided key support to Clinton when he was in political trouble in the 1990 primary and general, and again in 1992. Yet like much of Arkansas it has been trending Republican since he was elected; in 1996 the 2d District voted for Republican Senator Tim Hutchinson. Over the years its representation has varied widely. In 1958, after the Central High crisis, it elected a segregationist with write-in votes. From 1962–74 its congressman was Ways and Means Chairman Wilbur Mills. For three elections starting in 1984 it elected Tommy Robinson, whose antics as sheriff earned him notoriety and popularity, who switched to the Republican Party in 1989 and ran unsuccessfully for governor in 1990, and later was found to have had 996 overdrafts on the House bank. In 1990, 1992, and 1994 it elected Ray Thornton, a moderate Democrat and pillar of the establishment in Arkansas, who was 2d District congressman in the 1970s, president of Arkansas State University, and nephew of Jack Stephens. He voted for the impeachment of Richard Nixon in 1974, for the Gulf war resolution in 1991 (the only Arkansas Democrat to do so), and against the Clinton budget and tax increase in 1993. In spring 1995 he announced his retirement from Congress and in 1996 was elected to the Arkansas Supreme Court.

The new congressman is Vic Snyder, a Democrat who was not the initial favorite and who came close to losing this historically safe Democratic seat. Snyder grew up in Medford Oregon, dropped out of Willamette University to serve in the Marine Corps in Vietnam, then returned to Oregon for college and medical school and got a law degree in Arkansas. He has been a practicing physician, a general practitioner at the Columbia Family Clinic, who went on medical missions in Thailand, Honduras, Sierra Leone, and Sudan. In 1990 he was elected to the state Senate and made news when he called for repeal of Arkansas's anti-sodomy law and refused to accept his pension.

Snyder ran for Congress as a reformer who believed the system could work; he promised not to accept a congressional pension until the establishment of an equitable system for federal employees. His main Democratic opponents had more political backgrounds. The leader was Mark Stodola, the county prosecutor in Little Rock, a strong Clinton backer who said he would work to solve the root causes of crime. Also running was John Edwards, who handled casework for Senator David Pryor. Snyder cited his work as a doctor and legislator and pressed the attack: "If Stodola has solutions to juvenile crime, he should have introduced those ideas at the local level rather than campaigning on the theme that the current system is broken. He is the system." Stodola replied that "the laws Vic sponsors lets them out." Stodola led the May 21 primary with 48%, to 32% for Snyder and 20% for Edwards. Snyder won the June 11 runoff in an upset 51%–49%. The Republican nomination was won by lawyer Bud Cummins, who beat the 1994 nominee and radio talk show host Ken Powell, who favored decriminalization of hard drugs, 70%–30% in the runoff.

Snyder continued to sound reform themes in the general, but also outspent Cummins overall. Although Bill Clinton was carrying his home district, the Little Rock area was moving toward Republicans lower on the ticket, and Snyder won by a narrow 52%–48% margin. Snyder greeted voters the next morning at 7:30 on a street corner and then lobbied the U.S. Bureau of Prisons on a halfway house in the University Park neighborhood. He announced that he will not begin fundraising for reelection until 90 days before the 1998 primary.

The People: Pop. 1990: 587,412; 31% rural; 12% age 65+; 81% White; 18% Black; 1% Asian; 1% Hispanic origin. Households: 58% married couple families; 27% married couple fams. w. children; 43% college educ.; median household income: $25,142; per capita income: $12,334; median gross rent: $383; median house value: $56,300.

1996 Presidential Vote			**1992 Presidential Vote**		
Clinton (D)	124,545	(55%)	Clinton (D)	130,435	(55%)
Dole (R)	83,218	(37%)	Bush (R)	84,922	(36%)
Perot (I)	14,667	(6%)	Perot (I)	19,348	(8%)

Rep. Vic Snyder (D)

Elected 1996; b. Sept. 27, 1947, Medford, OR; home, Little Rock; Willamette U., B.A. 1975, U. of OR, M.D. 1979, U. of AR, J.D. 1988; Presbyterian; single.

Career: Marine Corps, 1967–69 (Vietnam); Practicing physician, 1982–present; AR Senate, 1991–1996.

DC Office: 1319 LHOB 20515, 202-225-2506; Fax: 202-225-5903.

District Offices: Little Rock, 501-324-5941.

Committees: *National Security* (18th of 25 D): Military Installations & Facilities; Military Procurement. *Veterans' Affairs* (12th of 13 D): Oversight & Investigations.

Group Ratings and Key Votes: Newly Elected

Election Results

1996 general	Vic Snyder (D)	114,841	(52%)	($798,145)
	Bud Cummins (R)	104,548	(48%)	($730,699)
1996 runoff	Vic Snyder (D)	31,435	(51%)	
	Mark Stodola (D)	29,821	(49%)	
1996 primary	Mark Stodola (D)	36,356	(48%)	
	Vic Snyder (D)	24,697	(32%)	
	John Edwards (D)	15,216	(20%)	
1994 general	Ray Thornton (D)	97,580	(57%)	($423,597)
	Bill Powell (R)	72,473	(43%)	($60,918)

THIRD DISTRICT

They once were a synonym for backwardness and isolation; now they are the homes of some of America's most sophisticated and innovative corporations: the Ozarks of northwestern Arkansas. Much of the scenery remains the same: rounded green mountains spotted with farmhouses, little towns and small cities in valleys, man-made lakes glistening in the sunlight. People are still friendly and lifestyles tradition-minded and family-oriented—qualities that have made this one of the nation's favorite retirement areas. Tourists throng to attractions like the Bible Museum and Cosmic Cavern near Eureka Springs. But the Ozarks have also become an engine of economic growth. Sam Walton put the headquarters of his Wal-Mart chain in Bentonville, which has the small town ambience that is so much a part of Wal-Mart's success even though profit-sharing and stock prices have made many Wal-Mart employees millionaires. And down the road near the University of Arkansas in Fayetteville is Don Tyson's Tyson Foods in Springdale, now the leading chicken producer and processor in the nation: once again, an

Arkansas entrepreneur has taken insights gained from his knowledge of Arkansas and enriched the nation as well as the state.

The 3d Congressional District of Arkansas occupies the northwest part of the state, including Bentonville, Fayetteville and the city of Fort Smith on the Oklahoma line, plus several mountain and upcountry counties to the east and south. This is the most Republican part of Arkansas. The 3d voted for Bill Clinton 43%–42% in 1992 but in 1996 it went 45%–44% for Bob Dole, and it has elected Republican congressmen since 1966. Indeed, this was the scene of Bill Clinton's first political race and first defeat; in 1974, at 28, he ran against incumbent John Paul Hammerschmidt and got an impressive but losing 48%. The mountain counties have historically been heavily Republican: they had few slaves and were opposed to secession and remained hostile to the Democratic flatlands. Fort Smith is also a Republican stronghold and, while Wal-Mart had Hillary Rodham Clinton on its board and Don Tyson's house counsel put her in the way of making unbelievable profits in commodities trades, the area around Bentonville and Springdale is very heavily Republican.

The congressman from the 3d District is Asa Hutchinson, elected in 1996 to replace his brother Tim Hutchinson, who represented the 3d since 1992 and in 1996 was elected to the Senate. Both Hutchinsons grew up in Bentonville, went to Bob Jones University, then back to Arkansas—graduate school for Tim, law school for Asa. The younger Hutchinson became Bentonville city attorney, then U.S. Attorney in Fort Smith from 1982–85; his signal achievement was the prosecution of a paramilitary group called the Covenant, the Sword, and the Arm of the Lord. In 1986 he ran for the Senate and lost to Dale Bumpers 62%–38%; in 1990 he ran for attorney general and lost to Democrat Winston Bryant. From 1986–96 he was a partner in a Fort Smith law firm, and in 1990 he became Republican state chairman a post he held until 1995.

In early 1996 Asa Hutchinson wasn't running for Congress; indeed, neither party's ultimate nominees in this district even ran in their party's primary. Tim Hutchinson was nominated for a third term May 21. But that same month Governor Jim Guy Tucker was convicted of fraud and it became clear he would probably resign; Lieutenant Governor Mike Huckabee, who had been nominated for the Senate, announced on May 30 he would leave that race, in order to serve as governor; Tim Hutchinson said on June 3 he would not seek the Senate nomination, but after state Senator John Brown left the race and Congressman Jay Dickey endorsed him, Hutchinson changed his mind and was nominated at the Republican convention June 15. That left the 3d District nomination open. Here Asa Hutchinson had competition. Dickey sent a letter warning that a "dynasty" might be unpopular, Brown ran, and some local politicos had grudges against Hutchinson for his work as state party chairman. But at the July 13 convention Hutchinson beat Brown 93–65.

Hutchinson was the clear favorite in the general. Then on September 4 the Democratic nominee dropped out of the race, saying he had been able to raise only $100,000. State Senators Lu Hardin, who lost the Senate runoff to Winston Bryant, and Jon Fitch both considered the race but decided not to run. The surprise winner at the September 14 convention was University of Arkansas business law professor and former Fayetteville councilmember Ann Henry. "Somebody needed to, and I felt like I could do it." She had close ties to the Clintons—Bill and Hillary Rodham Clinton held their wedding reception in her house and Clinton "bimbo eruption" queller Betsey Wright worked for her campaign—and enough money to contribute $130,000 to her own campaign. She campaigned as a champion of the U.S. Department of Education and an opponent of "the Gingrich agenda."

But Hutchinson's personal strength and party affiliation gave him a 56%–42% victory—far superior to Tim Hutchinson's 50%–47% four years before, when Clinton was also heading the ticket. Asa Hutchinson is likely to have a conservative record similar to his brother's, from support of the $500 per child tax credit to boosting of the I-69 from Bentonville to Texarkana. In November 1996 he said he didn't know if he would vote for Newt Gingrich in the Republican Conference, though he ended up doing so. The two Hutchinsons are one of two brother-brother combinations in the Congress, and they form an interesting contrast. Congressman Sander Levin and Senator Carl Levin of Michigan have mostly liberal voting records and have won strong support from labor unions and in the Jewish community; Senator Tim Hutchinson and Congressman Asa Hutchinson of Arkansas have solidly conservative convictions and have won strong support from small businesses and among Christian conservatives.

The People: Pop. 1990: 589,523; 49% rural; 16% age 65+; 95% White; 2% Black; 1% Asian; 1% Amer. Indian; 1% Hispanic origin. Households: 64% married couple families; 28% married couple fams. w. children; 36% college educ.; median household income: $21,903; per capita income: $10,876; median gross rent: $328; median house value: $48,900.

1996 Presidential Vote			1992 Presidential Vote		
Dole (R)	110,457	(45%)	Clinton (D)	109,111	(43%)
Clinton (D)	107,096	(44%)	Bush (R)	107,351	(42%)
Perot (I)	22,976	(9%)	Perot (I)	35,991	(14%)
Other	4,419	(2%)			

Rep. Asa Hutchinson (R)

Elected 1996; b. Dec. 3, 1950, Gravette; home, Fort Smith; Bob Jones U., B.S. 1972, U. of AR, J.D. 1975; Baptist; married (Susan).

Career: U.S. Atty., AR Western Dist., 1982–85; Practicing atty., 1986–96; Chmn., AR Republican Party, 1990–95.

DC Office: 1535 LHOB 20515, 202-225-4301; Fax: 202-225-5713; e-mail: asa.hutchinson@mail.house.gov.

District Offices: Fayetteville, 501-442-5258; Fort Smith, 501-782-7787; Harrison, 501-741-6900.

Committees: *Judiciary* (18th of 20 R): Constitution; Crime. *Transportation & Infrastructure* (31st of 40 R): Aviation; Surface Transportation. *Veterans' Affairs* (13th of 16 R): Health.

Group Ratings and Key Votes: Newly Elected

Election Results

1996 general	Asa Hutchinson (R)	137,093	(56%)	($366,628)
	Ann Henry (D)	102,994	(42%)	($441,734)
	Others	6,045	(2%)	
1996 primary	Asa Hutchinson (R)	nom. by convention		
1994 general	Tim Hutchinson (R)	129,800	(68%)	($288,412)
	Berta L. Seitz (D)	61,883	(32%)	($61,131)

FOURTH DISTRICT

From the Delta flatlands along the Mississippi River, where the water-soaked fields produce America's largest rice crop, across small cities with antique pasts like Pine Bluff and El Dorado, southern Arkansas runs west to the Ouachita Mountains and the border town of Texarkana, where the main street divides two states and Texan Ross Perot grew up five blocks west of Arkansas. This is the northwestern corner of the Deep South. There is still a large black population here, a reminder that parts of southern Arkansas were once plantation country; but oil is also in production here, a reminder that this is the beginning of the Southwest. The broiler chicken industry looms large in these parts, and the accent is clearly Arkansan: El Dorado, Nevada and Lafayette are all pronounced with long *A*s and penultimate syllable accents, and

Ouachita is, with a bow to the original French, *waSHEEta*. The district also includes the little railroad-crossing, county seat town of Hope, where President Bill Clinton and his first White House chief of staff Mack McLarty were classmates at Miss Mary's kindergarten, and where Arkansas's Republican Governor Mike Huckabee grew up a decade later, and Hot Springs, the spa resort and gambling haven where Bill Clinton's stepfather sold Buicks, his mother bet on the horses and he excelled in high school as he began his climb from southern Arkansas to world eminence.

The 4th Congressional District of Arkansas occupies almost all of the southern geographical half of the state, from the Mississippi River to the Ouachita Mountains, the Delta to Texarkana. It is historically a Democratic district, and one which for most of this century has elected a young man to the House and kept him there for years, to cut deals with the Democratic leadership and bring home the bacon. In 50 years the 4th District had four congressmen, all Democrats. For a while in the 1990s it had a very different congressional politics: bipartisan, with rancorous debates on national issues followed by narrow election victories. But now it seems to have gone back to the old tradition, except with a Republican instead of a Democrat.

The congressman from the 4th District is Jay Dickey, a Republican first elected in 1992. He replaced Beryl Anthony, chairman of the Democratic Congressional Campaign Committee and member of Ways and Means, Washington insider and brother-in-law of the late White House counsel Vincent Foster. Dickey is from Pine Bluff, where his uncle and grandfather were both state Senators; he caught polio in 1960, but recovered and became a top college tennis player and runs 5K races today. Practicing law in Pine Bluff, Dickey represented the Arkansas Fox and Coon Hunters Association challenging state restrictions on running dogs; he won the case in the Arkansas Supreme Court and there are no restrictions on the running of dogs in Arkansas today. In the 1970s and 1980s, Dickey ran Baskin Robbins and Taco Bell franchises and formed an advertising sign company and a travel agency. He won the ordinarily worthless Republican nomination in 1992, but profited from a Democratic schism: 14-year well-connected incumbent Beryl Anthony, despite spending $1 million, lost the primary 51%–49% to Secretary of State Bill McCuen. Dickey attacked McCuen for a $324,000 no-bid contract on computers for his office; McCuen countered by charging that Dickey's pro-life views meant he condoned incest. Dickey won 52%–48%.

In the House Dickey made a mostly conservative voting record and, with seats on Agriculture and Small Business, worked on district projects. He sponsored a crime bill to allow flogging of prisoners and to remove color televisions and other "conveniences for criminals" from prisons. In 1994 he again faced a Democratic insider, state Senator Jay Bradford, who raised as much as Dickey. With majorities from the bigger towns, Dickey won again 52%–48%.

If Dickey's rhetoric in the 103d Congress presaged that of freshmen Republicans in the 104th, his own career took a different, more traditional turn. He got a seat on Appropriations and on its Agriculture, Labor-HHS and Energy Subcommittees, and used them to bring projects to his district—$13 million for the National Center for Toxicological Research in Jefferson, $1.5 million from the Office of Minority Health for the University of Arkansas at Pine Bluff medicine and pharmacy programs. He complained when the Clinton Administration wouldn't accept the state Game and Fish Department offer to keep National Wildlife Reserves open for deer hunting and fishing: "This indifference by the federal government to the rights of Arkansas citizens is intolerable and totally inexcusable." He got Transportation Chairman Bud Shuster into Arkansas for hearings on I-69. In populist tones he called for stripping pension benefits from congressmen convicted of crimes and for barring outside law practice for independent counsel and making them subject to (here one catches the lilt of the turf-protector) the appropriations process.

After his two close elections, Dickey seems to have amassed some political strength. When Senate candidate Mike Huckabee left that race May 30 to replace Jim Guy Tucker as governor, Dickey announced June 4 he was considering the seat; then on June 11 he warmly endorsed 3d District incumbent Tim Hutchinson, who was nominated and elected. But when Hutchinson's brother Asa ran for the 3d District nomination in July, Dickey warned that a "dynasty" might prove unpopular. No well known Democrat chose to run in the 4th District, and so Dickey's November opponent was Vincent Tolliver, a 28-year-old paralegal and poet recently returned from California. In his opening statement in their first debate, Tolliver started by, in the words of *Roll Call*, chanting lines from the poem Maya Angelou wrote for the first Clinton inauguration, then added lines of his own, accusing Dickey of the "morals of a stray cat in a discarded alley," attacking "poorly-managed Taco Bells" he owned, and calling on him to resign. "That's the longest minute-and-a-half I've ever endured," Dickey replied. "I'm not going to resign. Let's get on with the questions." Dickey won 64%–36%, carrying every county, including those with black majorities.

The People: Pop. 1990: 585,202; 52% rural; 16% age 65+; 72% White; 27% Black; 1% Hispanic origin. Households: 59% married couple families; 26% married couple fams. w. children; 30% college educ.; median household income: $19,621; per capita income: $9,723; median gross rent: $299; median house value: $39,900.

1996 Presidential Vote

Clinton (D)	126,896	(60%)
Dole (R)	66,034	(31%)
Perot (I)	15,972	(8%)

1992 Presidential Vote

Clinton (D)	134,692	(57%)
Bush (R)	73,891	(31%)
Perot (I)	23,677	(10%)

Rep. Jay Dickey (R)

Elected 1992; b. Dec. 14, 1939, Pine Bluff; home, Pine Bluff; Hendrix Col., 1958, U. of AR, B.A. 1961, J.D. 1963; Methodist; divorced.

Career: Practicing atty., 1963–92; Pine Bluff City Atty., 1968–70; Small business and franchise owner, 1982–present.

DC Office: 2453 RHOB 20515, 202-225-3772; Fax: 202-225-1314; e-mail: jdickey@hr.house.gov.

District Offices: Hot Springs, 501-623-5800; Pine Bluff, 501-536-3376.

Committees: *Appropriations* (21st of 34 R): Agriculture, Rural Development, FDA & Related Agencies; Energy & Water Development; Labor, Health & Human Services & Education.

Group Ratings

	ADA	ACLU	AFS	LCV	CFA	CON	NFIB	COC	ACU	NTLC	CHC
1996	0	7	0	8	23	38	100	100	100	100	100
1995	0	—	—	6	0	56	—	100	88	—	—

National Journal Ratings

	1995 LIB — 1995 CONS			1996 LIB — 1996 CONS		
Economic	0%	—	74%	0%	—	82%
Social	0%	—	79%	28%	—	72%
Foreign	28%	—	65%	0%	—	79%

Key Votes of the 104th Congress

1. Reduce Medicare Growth $	Y	5. Flag Amendment	Y	9. Cuban Embargo	Y
2. Ovrd. Product Liab. Veto	*	6. Drop EPA Limits	N	10. Bar Bosnia Troop $	Y
3. Increase Min. Wage	N	7. Repeal Assault-Weap. Ban	Y	11. Cut Anti-Missile Defense	N
4. Welfare Reform	Y	8. Ovrd. Part. Birth Veto	Y	12. Bar U.N. Uniforms	Y

Election Results

1996 general	Jay Dickey (R)	125,956	(64%)	($452,572)
	Vincent Tolliver (D)	72,391	(37%)	
1996 primary	Jay Dickey (R)	unopposed		
1994 general	Jay Dickey (R)	87,469	(52%)	($832,117)
	Jay Bradford (D)	81,370	(48%)	($797,708)

CALIFORNIA

California is the great laboratory of America, the place where things—good things and bad things—seem to happen first. In the last third of the 20th Century, California has led the nation toward technology hitherto undreamed of and prosperity greater than the world has ever seen. And it has led the nation away from traditional values and patterns of life and toward a government that grows larger and more dysfunctional regardless of voters' wishes. Yet for all its success and its harbinger status, California is in a sour mood as it heads for the next century. Part of the reason is the economic recession of the early 1990s, spurred by defense cutbacks as the Cold War ended; the cornucopia of California's huge job growth in the 1980s was suddenly empty, and house prices—the personal wealth of ordinary people—plummeted after a giddy rise. But past history should have taught that California's economic pauses are temporary, and by 1995 the high-tech- and small-business-driven economy was generating jobs again, and newcomers kept pouring in with their energy and ingenuity, as they have since the Gold Rush of 1849. But the recession opened people's eyes to other things that were wrong in California. There were disturbing signs that California's children were not being prepared to take their place in a sophisticated economy and a functioning polity, and that the newest immigrant groups were living cordoned off from the larger society. When Ronald Reagan carried California in 1980 and 1984, he did so as a spokesman for the universal culture celebrated and to some extent created by the 1940s movies, the best and most enduring popular culture since Dickens. When Bill Clinton carried California in 1992 and 1996, he did so as a fan of the Hollywood that was addressing a segmented culture, celebrating some groups of society and disparaging others, a Hollywood often more transfixed by the unusual values and lifestyles of its creators than by the universal values and concerns shared by the much larger national and international audience. The California Reagan celebrated was confident that it was a model for success for the nation and the world—and the unexpected prosperity of the 1980s and the American victory in the Cold War were strong evidence it was right. The California Clinton celebrated is unsure that it is a model for the nation and the world, and not very sure that it is a good model for California itself.

This unease is in the air, though California is now as it always has been a place of economic vitality and personal creativity. It has grown partly through luck and through planning by big government and big business. The Gold Rush of 1849 transformed San Francisco from nothing to a great city in just a year, and the Southern Pacific Railroad, the agribusinesses controlling vast chunks of the Central Valley and the architects of the great water engineering projects created a framework in which individuals could work, innovate and prosper, inventing their own technologies and lifestyles. California grew from scratch to 7 million people by World War II, still an "island," as Carey McWilliams said, separated from the rest of the country. Then in World War II California became one of the great defense industry states, building ships and airplanes by the thousands. Millions of Americans came here and millions stayed. California's future was planned by the heads of the big units of government and business—Franklin Roosevelt and Henry J. Kaiser, who built vast shipyards and steel and aluminum factories, Governor Earl Warren, who husbanded tax monies to build schools and freeways in the years after the war, Robert Sproul and Clark Kerr who built the University of California into what Kerr called "the multiversity," Governor Pat Brown who completed the vast system of canals and aqueducts that brought water from the wet north to the thirsty south. But the real engine of growth was the little people who took advantage of this infrastructure and built a humming economy on it. When California's defense plants closed down after World War II, leaders imagined that hundreds of thousands would have to head back east. Instead, as urbanologist Jane Jacobs points out, one-eighth of all the new jobs in the nation in the late 1940s were created in metro Los Angeles. This small scale growth, multiplied thousands of times over, made California into the nation's most populous state by 1963.

Today there are 32 million Californians. Greater Los Angeles, with 15 million people, is the nation's second largest city, behind New York's 20 million but well ahead of Chicago's 8.5 million; San Francisco, with 6.5 million, is fifth. And they owe their current preeminence not to natural advantage but to human ingenuity. Los Angeles, with no natural resources and no natural harbor, is the nation's leading manufacturer and port, as well as the world's entertainment center. San Francisco, which once lived by exporting food, is now the world's leader in computers and high-tech. California has grown not because it had to but because people wanted it to.

All the while California attracted newcomers—until 1965, almost all Americans; after 1965 slowly, at first invisibly, immigrants, mostly from Latin America and the Pacific Rim. Unfortunately, in the process California's leaders abandoned the processes of assimilation which spread universal American values and taught useful skills. California schools in the post-World War II years taught the basics and inculcated students in mainstream American culture, readying them for the rapidly growing network of universities and community colleges and for an expanding and increasingly high-skill private sector. But California's leaders in the years from the Watts riot of 1965 through the Los Angeles riot of 1992 have followed a different path. As affluent families withdrew their children into private schools, conservative elites were content to let school funding drop and liberal elites were content to turn over the education system to teachers' unions. "Multicultural" policies slotted newcomers into quota-fed monocultural enclaves in schools, universities, and big corporations. Public schools, with the pace set by teachers' unions, held students in "bilingual" Spanish-speaking programs long past the age when it is easiest to learn English. The state superintendent of public instruction, Bill Honig, pushed the education school nostrum "whole language" which left a generation unable to read or write standard English at levels acceptable in advanced workplaces—a mistake, he later admitted, which shortchanged perhaps millions of students. Civil liberties-minded legislators hobbled the criminal justice system, leaving teenage gangs to rule large swathes of central cities. Many of the newcomers prospered anyway. Nothing could keep the Asians down, not even the racial quotas which limited rather than increased their places at select high schools and universities. And many Latinos struggled successfully to move out the freeways and up into the working middle class, ignoring the spoils-demanding politicians who claimed to speak in their name and the liberals' concentration on unionizing farm worker jobs which machines have rendered obsolete.

The voting public tried to reimpose the old values, with mixed success. Voters passed Proposition 13 in 1978, holding down property taxes and slowing the growth of welfare-oriented government. To replace the sometimes radical Governor Jerry Brown, they elected conservative Republican George Deukmejian in 1982 and 1986 and the moderate Republican Pete Wilson in 1990 and 1994. But for all but two years liberal Democrats, captained from 1980–95 by Speaker Willie Brown, used their superb political talents to keep control of the California Assembly and, usually outside the public view in a state where most media and especially television pay no attention to politics and government, dominate public policy on education and criminal justice and welfare. During the 1980s, this did not slow down California perceptibly. Private sector

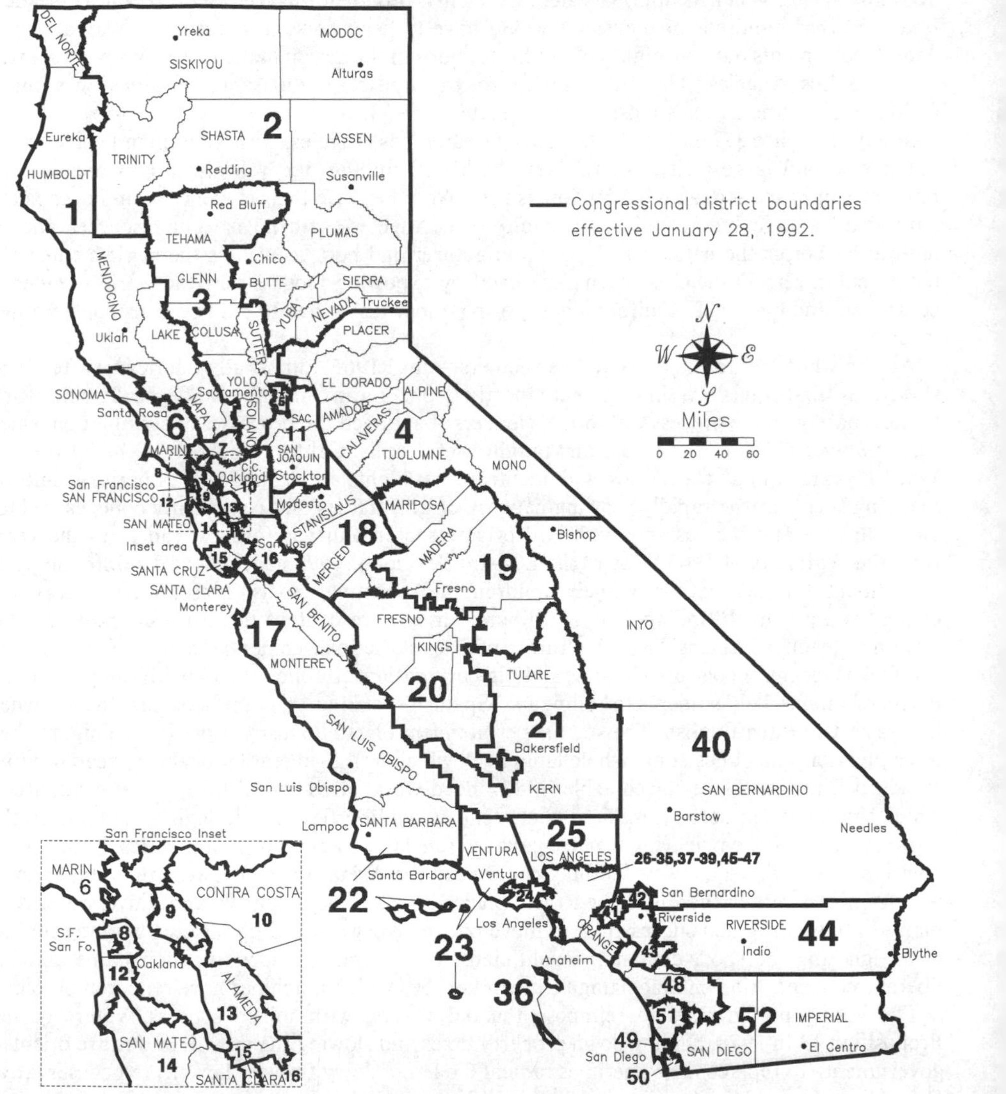

Congressional district boundaries effective January 28, 1992.
N
W
E
S
Miles
0 20 40 60
DEL NORTE
Yreka
SISKIYOU
MODOC
Alturas
Eureka
SHASTA
2
LASSEN
TRINITY
Redding
Susanville
HUMBOLDT
1
Red Bluff
TEHAMA
PLUMAS
Chico
MENDOCINO
GLENN
BUTTE
SIERRA
3
YUBA
NEVADA
Truckee
SUTTER
Ukiah
LAKE
COLUSA
PLACER
YOLO
EL DORADO
SONOMA
Sacramento
ALPINE
NAPA
SOLANO
AMADOR
Santa Rosa
SAC.
6
11
CALAVERAS
4
MARIN
SAN JOAQUIN
TUOLUMNE
MONO
7
C.C.
8
Oakland
Stockton
San Francisco
SAN FRANCISCO
9
10
12
MARIPOSA
Modesto
13
STANISLAUS
SAN MATEO
Bishop
14
18
Inset area
San Jose
MADERA
15
16
MERCED
19
SANTA CRUZ
SANTA CLARA
Fresno
SAN BENITO
Monterey
FRESNO
INYO
17
KINGS
MONTEREY
TULARE
20
SAN LUIS OBISPO
21
40
Bakersfield
San Luis Obispo
KERN
SAN BERNARDINO
Barstow
Lompoc
SANTA BARBARA
25
Needles
VENTURA
LOS ANGELES
26-35,37-39,45-47
Santa Barbara
Ventura
22
24
San Bernardino
42
41
Riverside
RIVERSIDE
44
Los Angeles
ORANGE
Indio
Blythe
23
Anaheim
43
48
36
51
52
IMPERIAL
49
San Diego
SAN DIEGO
El Centro
50
San Francisco Inset
MARIN
6
CONTRA COSTA
10
9
S.F.
San Fo.
8
Oakland
12
ALAMEDA
13
SAN MATEO
15
14
SANTA CLARA
16

growth, fed by defense and high-tech booms and by a vast growth in manufacturing, provided opportunities for those whom the public sector scanted to work their way up anyway. The Los Angeles Olympics of 1984, opened by President Ronald Reagan and producing a series of American triumphs, built confidence that California could show the nation and the world how to grow economically and knit peoples from all over the globe into a single fabric.

But the economic slowdown and the physical and man-made disasters of the early 1990s rent this fabric and destroyed this confidence. Disasters came rapid-fire: the Loma Prieta earthquake in the San Francisco Bay area in October 1989, the Central Valley floods in early 1991, the Los Angeles riot following the acquittal of policemen accused of beating Rodney King in May 1992, the Malibu fires of September 1992, the Northridge earthquake of January 1994, the O.J. Simpson case, starting with the murder in June 1994, the criminal acquittal in October 1995 and the contrary verdict of the civil trial in February 1997. All these things were happening as California was thrust into recession. During the 1980s California's economy created 300,000 new jobs a year; in the early 1990s, it lost 500,000 jobs. Much of the loss came from defense cutbacks, and was heavily concentrated in Los Angeles County; the rest of the state economy lost only 1.2% of jobs—far below the 7–10% of New York or New England. The downturn was exacerbated by tax increases, all proposed by politicians California voted for: George Bush's budget summit in 1990, Pete Wilson's state tax hikes in 1991, Bill Clinton's budget and tax package of 1993. California's nominal incomes (and living costs) are higher than the rest of the country's, and many more people are self-employed or own small businesses, so these soak-the-rich measures were really soak-California. And the impression of economic collapse was increased by the disappearance through merger or bankruptcy of Los Angeles-based big economic units—Hughes Electronics, Carter Hawley Hale, Unocal, Lockheed, Security Pacific and First Interstate Banks—and by the harping of national media back east and by the *Los Angeles Times* on California's supposed collapse.

Yet as the prophets were crying doom, California's economy was recovering, as vibrantly as ever but in different form. No longer were big units, big corporations or big government, leading the way; instead there was small unit growth. As Joel Kotkin of Pepperdine University pointed out, California's knowledge-intensive industries were growing vigorously—telecommunications, biomedical research, computer software, medical equipment, entertainment, international trade. Small factories humming quietly in squat stucco buildings in the Los Angeles basin made California the world's leading manufacturing center, with huge production of apparel, furniture, computer equipment. In the Bay Area, vast numbers of small computer and high-tech companies spawn and grow lustily, financed by the world's largest concentration of sophisticated venture capital. The Central Valley, long the home of the nation's largest and most productive farms, is now also growing industry high-tech and low. Fueling this process are immigrants. If the outflow of native-born Americans from California starting in the recession continued into the mid-1990s, the flow of immigrants into the state never entirely stopped and by the mid-1990s sped up. Their contribution, seldom heralded by the press, is vast. One-third of Silicon Valley engineers are immigrants; most Orange County technicians are Vietnamese; immigrants from Korea, Iran, Armenia and Israel are upgrading inner Los Angeles neighborhoods.

But even as California started growing again, the divisions fostered by government quota policies seemed to widen. They appeared most vividly in response to the O.J. Simpson case, with large majorities of blacks considering him innocent while even larger majorities of non-blacks thought him guilty. Blacks' reaction could not be painted as a response to poverty or political powerlessness. California blacks' incomes are well above the national black average; residential integration in much of California is the norm, and the big growth in black population is in prosperous neighborhoods in southeast Los Angeles. Politically blacks have had more power than their numbers, for they are only 7% of the state's population, 11% in Los Angeles County, and yet the mayor of Los Angeles for 20 years and the Assembly speaker for 15 years were black, as are a disproportionate number of state legislators; blacks were elected to statewide office as early as 1970. The separate mindset symbolized by reactions to Simpson was less the result of overt racism by whites than of the separateness in universities, government employment and the corporate sector which is the proximate result of racial quotas: the natural reaction of those who are stigmatized as inferior and needing help to turn aside from the larger society.

As for Latinos and Asians—two large categories which contain many very different subgroups—they have been poorly served by the civil rights paradigm which sees the central problem as discrimination and the central remedy as government-imposed quotas. Latinos have been badly served by an education system which has lost its capacity to teach basic skills and which insists on holding pupils back in Spanish. Asians have been badly served by quotas which fence them off from opportunity and solicitude for rioters who have destroyed their businesses. The withdrawal of the affluent into hillside subdivisions and distant suburbs, especially in greater Los Angeles, has created a sense of isolation and separateness on all sides. Vast tracts of city and suburb, once peopled by migrants from the Midwest, are now filled with newcomers from Mexico and Korea, El Salvador and Taiwan, Iran and Armenia; young men stand on street corners in affluent areas from dawn, mutely looking for work, sometimes staying all day. The white Anglos who are still the large majority of California's voters watch them uneasily, knowing that most are workers and not criminals, yet fearing that basic rules are no longer being obeyed and that the fundamental order underlying everyday life in any civilized community can no longer be taken for granted.

It is against this context that conservative politicians and the majority of the voters have sought, fumblingly, to reassert old rules and establish a new order. The biggest issues in mid-1990s elections in California were Proposition 187, stating the government does not have to provide non-emergency services for illegal aliens, passed 59%–41% in 1994, and Proposition 209, asserting that state government cannot employ racial preferences or quotas, passed 55%–45%. They were portrayed by articulate liberal opinion as, and believed by most black, many Latino and some Asian voters to be, assaults on immigrants and people of color. But both simply asserted principles taken for granted when Pat Brown and Ronald Reagan were governor: that government has no obligation to serve those who aren't legally here and that government should not decide issues on the basis of race. As Susan Estrich, Michael Dukakis's campaign manager in 1988 and now a Californian, pointed out in the debate over 187, most Californians make a lively distinction between legal and illegal immigrants, and appreciate the contribution of legal immigrants: 187 was not a statement of xenophobia. And as Ward Connerly, the black businessman who was the driving force behind 209, pointed out again and again, racial preferences and quotas are direct violations of the Civil Rights Act of 1964: 209 was not a statement of racism. And the courts agree; in April 1997 a federal appeals court panel upheld 209, reversing a lower court injunction that blocked its enforcement. California may be leading the nation on these issues; the 1996 immigration act, which left legal immigration levels untouched, cracked down on aid programs for illegals, and prominent Californians urged that it crack down more. But if the goal is an orderly and fair system of immigration and racial treatment, the political path is filled with controversy and negative feelings.

California has gone through political as well as economic and ethnic turmoil in the 1990s. From the late 1970s until 1990 California voting behavior was steady: voters chose Republicans, usually seemingly boring middle-aged men, for top political offices, while picking Democrats, often baby boom liberals, for the state legislature and Congress. In effect, voters were ratifying the choices they made during the nation's last period of economic turmoil, when they passed property-tax-cutting Proposition 13 in 1978 and elected Reagan president with a solid 53%–36% margin in 1980 and George Deukmejian governor by 49%–48% in 1982. The Republican executives set the tone, but the Democratic legislators often surreptitiously set the policies, furthering the causes of their clients—teachers' unions, trial lawyers and the criminal defense bar. Such results continued up through 1990, when Pete Wilson beat Dianne Feinstein for governor 49%–46% and Democrats kept control of the legislature and the House delegation.

Then, with the recession, came change. George Bush, never comfortable in California, seemed disengaged from the state's economic problems, while Bill Clinton was busy feeling Californians' pain. Clinton carried California 46%–33% in 1992, and Democrats down the line won as well, carrying the House vote 52%–41% and carrying several districts they had not expected to. Democrats Dianne Feinstein and Barbara Boxer won the two Senate seats in "the year of the woman" (Feinstein won the remaining two years of Wilson's term). In 1994, Clinton's support slumped here, but not nearly as much as nationally, as he visited frequently and tended carefully to state crises and disasters. Wilson, who had been far down in the polls, responded by stressing his support of capital punishment, which was opposed by his Democratic opponent, state Treasurer Kathleen Brown. And he complained loudly about the billions the state was forced to spend on services to illegal aliens and endorsed Proposition 187. Wilson won 55%–41%, as 187 passed by an even wider margin; Republicans edged Democrats in House races 49%–48%. Feinstein prevailed over Republican Michael Huffington by only 47%–45% after the most expensive Senate campaign in history. Republicans won most statewide offices for the first time since 1966.

The wheel turned again in 1996—but perhaps not as much as it first seemed. Bill Clinton carried California over Bob Dole, 51%–38%—the same 13% margin by which he had beaten Bush four years before. But in most parts of the state the Clinton percentage margin fell, as some Perot voters moved back to the Republican column. Where the Clinton percentage margin increased was in areas with many Latino voters, who favored him 71%–20% over Dole and who turned out in significantly larger numbers than in 1992, partly because of Clinton Administration efforts to speed up naturalization of immigrants. One reason may have been the immigration issue, or rather the issue of welfare for legal immigrants: while Wilson and some California Republican congressmen were calling loudly for an end to aid to illegals, and a cutoff of schooling for children of illegals, the Republican welfare bill cut off aid to legal immigrants, which in many cases meant the elderly relatives of young immigrant workers. Ironically, it was mostly Republicans (though also some Democrats, notably California's Howard Berman) who prevented Congress from reducing legal immigration; and it was Democratic administration, building upon the El Paso programs of U.S. Border Patrol agent Silvestre Reyes (now a Democratic Congressman from Texas), which deployed many more INS agents on the border and cut down the illegal migration across the border in California which Wilson's 1994 ads decried. But this was not an unalloyed victory for the political left. Clinton's total was a bare majority. When liberal candidates have come out in the open, they have won less than a majority: Kathleen Brown in 1994, Barbara Boxer (who won 48%–43%) in 1992. In referenda, the same California voters who overwhelmingly favored 187 and 209 rejected single-payer health insurance 73%–27% in November 1994 and the highly regulatory "Big Green" environmental initiative 64%–36% in 1990. Even as Clinton was winning in 1996, Democratic legislative candidates led Republicans, but by a narrower margins than in 1992, 50%–45% for the House, 50%–46% for the Assembly.

Partisan divisions in California, even more than elsewhere, run along cultural rather than economic lines. Non-Hispanic whites voted 46%–42% for Dole over Clinton, while blacks favored Clinton 84%–7%, Hispanics 71%–20% and Asians 53%–42%. Religion, in this relatively secular state, was another sharp divider: for Dole were white Protestants (54%–37%) and other Christians (48%–39%); for Clinton were Jews (74%–12%), those with other religions (61%–19%) and those with no religion (61%–21%). By education, those with graduate school degrees, who are so often unionized teachers, social workers and other government employees, were more for Clinton (52%–36%).

It is as if these groups of voters were living in different Californias. And to some considerable extent they are. The traditional division is between a San Francisco-dominated North and a Los Angeles-dominated South, but that makes little sense today when Los Angeles is leftish and Orange County conservative, or when San Francisco and the Central Valley seem to vote the opposite way on everything. Since the 1970s a more illuminating division has been between coastal and inland California. Coastal California, the big population gainer in the 1970s, tends toward cultural liberalism. The Big Sur coast or the Redwood Empire, San Francisco and Marin

County or Westside Los Angeles—this is the political base of most Democrats. But go inland, even a few miles, and the cultural climate changes as rapidly as the weather. This California is sunnier in summer, colder in winter, more arid. And from the Central Valley and the Sierra foothills to the San Ramon Valley, or the "Inland Empire" at the east end of the Los Angeles basin around San Bernardino, Riverside and the desert beyond, this big growth area of the 1980s has attracted cultural conservatives. While coastal California protected itself from growth with environmental restrictions, new subdivisions and factories and cities proliferated inland. Today's cultural politics turns partisan history on its head. The affluent coastal counties were solidly Republican as late as the 1960s, while the dusty roads of the Central Valley and the inland industrial suburbs were the heartland of the Democratic Party that carried California for Lyndon Johnson in 1964. Another way to understand California is to divide the state into four major political regions, each with about one-quarter of the voters, each of which by itself would be one of the 10 largest states.

Los Angeles County. If no state is culturally more diverse than California, no county is more diverse than Los Angeles County, which is to the America of the 1990s what New York City was to the America of the 1910s: the great entry point for immigrants and the venue of their rapid upward mobility. It is also inevitably, like New York, messy and disorganized, crime-ridden and anxiety-prone. Although there are some suburban tracts here, Los Angeles County increasingly has taken on the function of a central city, but not a population-losing industrial enclave, like most American central cities of the 1960s and 1970s, but a population-surging, economically vital immigrant metropolis. Los Angeles now, like New York then, is the starting point not only of the immigrant but of the small-time entrepreneur—often the same person—who starts a small business in a garage, hires people newly-arrived into town, sells products out of a van, and makes enough money to expand the business and buy a home. Low-lying stucco buildings all over the Los Angeles basin house these businesses, run and staffed by Mexicans, Koreans, Vietnamese, Soviet Jews, Armenians and Iranians. This Los Angeles, like the great surging cities of the past—Dickens's London, Balzac's Paris or Dreiser's New York and Chicago—is not a comfortable place. Traffic is choking; the air has a sour, burnt look. Housing is cramped, with most people living in tightly-packed subdivisions or garden apartments on tiny plots of land that a midwesterner would find claustrophobic. Los Angeles County was hit hard by 1990s defense cutbacks, the 1992 riot and the 1994 earthquake; but like New York after the panic of 1907 and the Triangle fire of 1911, it surges ahead.

Politically, Los Angeles County, like that New York of long ago, leans Democratic but is subject to vast shifts of votes as new ethnic groups take—or change—their places. Unlike the riot-torn cities of the 1960s, Los Angeles County is not headed toward black majorities; it was 11% black in 1990, with a large affluent black population and net outmigration among blacks. The areas where blacks and recent Central American migrants rioted are demographically a small part of LA County, far smaller than heavily Mexican East Los Angeles or affluent black Baldwin Hills or the heavily Asian San Gabriel Valley. Los Angeles's boom, as Joel Kotkin points out, is based less on big defense contractors than on small factories, less on highly visible tenants of downtown office towers than on the self-employed, who are more numerous than union members. The entrepreneurial impulse among Koreans, Armenians, Iranians and many other newcomers remains vibrant; they have not looked to government for aid as Irish-Americans and African-Americans did historically. After blacks, the most reliably Democratic bloc are Westside Jews, exceedingly affluent by national standards, with political clout amplified by many Hollywood figures. Potentially a much larger constituency are Latinos, who were moving toward Republicans in the late 1980s and Democrats in 1996. They still vote in small numbers, because so many are children or non-citizens: in 1996 one central Los Angeles Assembly district cast only 29,000 votes, while a Westside district with the same 1990 population cast 154,000. Latino voters were a key factor in the election of Los Angeles Mayor Richard Riordan, a nominal Republican and the more conservative candidate in 1997; they voted about 60% for him over leftish state Senator Tom Hayden. Latinos have high rates of family formation and work and low rates of divorce and (outside a few central neighborhoods) crime; in some ways they resemble the white Anglo young families who voted for Pat Brown in 1958 and Reagan in 1966, though the schools the education professionals and teachers' unions have provided them are far inferior. Asians have moved around on the political spectrum. In 1992 and 1994 they voted narrowly Republican, presumably in reaction to civic leaders' sympathy for rioters and indifference toward Asian storeowners; in 1996 they voted narrowly Democratic, presumably because the Republican welfare bill cut off aid to legal aliens, including the many aged parents Asians had brought over and put on SSI. Los Angeles County voted solidly for Clinton in 1996, 59%–31%, better than his 53%–29% margin in 1992. But Proposition 209 lost here by only 54%–46%, as most Asians and a large number of Latinos voted against racial quotas and preferences.

Southern California. The rest of southern California outside Los Angeles County looks more like the Los Angeles of the 1940s: predominantly white, middle class, of midwestern origin. But it also has more Asians and Hispanics than East Coast experts usually imagine. Essentially, the old Los Angeles has grown out past the freeways into Orange County and the Inland Empire at the east end of the Los Angeles basin, and out into the desert, past the San Fernando Valley into Ventura County, down south of San Juan Capistrano and Camp Pendleton, where it merges with fast-growing San Diego. Of the four major regions, this is now the most populous, casting 28% of the state's votes, with 413,000 more votes than LA County in 1996. Until the early 1990s Southern California radiated the optimism, the somewhat innocent confidence and the know-how of its pioneers, contemporaries of its natural hero, Reagan, who came out here in hard times and created a new Middle America more tidy and square and cheerful than the original Middle America ever was. Now its leading politician may be San Diego Mayor Susan Golding, who has cut taxes and government payrolls, beefed up police and attracted creative businesses, and may run for the Senate in 1998. In the 1990s southern California soured first on the Republicans for their indifference and next on the Democrats for their indiscipline. In 1992, Southern California outside LA voted only 38%–35%–24% for Bush over Clinton and Perot. In 1994 it voted 68% for Proposition 187 and 65%–31% for Wilson over Brown. In 1996 it voted narrowly, 47%–42% for Bob Dole, but 63%–37% for Proposition 209. But it also voted narrowly for legalizing marijuana for medical purposes: it is more libertarian than culturally conservative.

San Francisco Bay Area. The Bay Area is affluent, preoccupied with the physical environment and identity politics, not propelled by economic necessity. For years San Francisco and the whole Bay Area has attracted those who felt their personal lifestyles were not accepted elsewhere or who relished the atmosphere of counter-culture and revolt that has roots here in the turn-of-the-century artists and writers and the Beat Generation of the 1950s—gays and perpetual graduate students, radicals and perennial rebels. It has lots of voters with graduate degrees, who voted heavily Democratic: California's Democratic base is made up less of blacks and factory workers than it is of teachers, lawyers, nurses, environmental enthusiasts and public sector administrators. Once closely divided politically, the Bay Area is now so overwhelmingly Democratic that most campaigns don't bother to buy ads in the San Francisco media market. The Bay Area voted 55%–27% for Clinton in 1992, voted 63%–30% for Senator Dianne Feinstein when she nearly lost in 1994, and voted 61%–28% for Clinton in 1996. The paradigmatic politician here is Willie Brown, elected mayor of San Francisco in 1995 after being ousted as Assembly speaker after 15 years, a political artist whose canvas has been reduced from state government policy to propitiating San Francisco's homeless lobby.

The rest of California. Little attention is usually given to the rest of California, the lightly populated coastal counties and the huge Central Valley. Yet 8 million people live here, more than in Georgia or Massachusetts; the media markets of Sacramento and Fresno in the Central Valley taken together would be the nation's eleventh largest. This is the most culturally conservative part of the state; many new residents are young families fleeing from the smog and crime of the Los Angeles basin to the cleaner and safer Central Valley or Mother Lode country or Sacramento area. Historically Democratic, this part of California trended against liberal

Democrats in the 1980s. It voted narrowly for Bill Clinton in 1992, 39%–36%, but was 61%–35% for Governor Pete Wilson in 1994. In 1996 it trended Republican, voting 46%–44% for Bob Dole, and 50%–44% and 54%–41% for Republican House and Assembly candidates. It voted 63% for Proposition 209 and 52% against medical marijuana: middle America on the Pacific Rim.

Where is California headed? Economically, California seems headed for growth again; with its creativity, suppleness, Pacific Rim location and brains, it cannot be kept permanently down. Culturally, California seems to want both therapy and discipline, the right to dispense medical marijuana on a casual basis and the liberty to divorce and remarry frequently and to practice different lifestyles, but also stern punishment of criminals, strict enforcement of immigration laws and an end to racial quotas and preferences. In partisan terms, California seems to have settled into a kind of equilibrium after the wild jolts of the first half of the 1990s. Democrats had a slight edge in 1996, Republicans an even slighter one in 1994. It is easy to see either party winning the governorship in 1998; it is possible to concoct plausible scenarios for the reelection of Senator Barbara Boxer in 1998 or her consignment to political oblivion. In all this it is important to keep in mind how almost invisible politics is in California. There is nothing here like the tabloid cultures of the East Coast, with their screaming headlines about the minutiae of local political feuds; California television stations present almost no news of politics or government at all, and the newspapers present leftish-biased coverage which most voters seem blithely to ignore. Much public policy has been made surreptitiously, especially by Democrats in the legislature, sometimes locally, as when the local treasurer bankrupted the government of prosperous Orange County; other important policies have been adopted by the clumsy yet sometimes effective device of initiative and referendum.

Governor. Pete Wilson is beginning his fourth decade in a political career that has taken him from a San Diego Assembly seat to the U.S. Senate and the governorship of the largest state. Like so many Californians, he grew up back East, in the St. Louis suburbs. After attending Yale on scholarship, he went to Camp Pendleton as a Marine and to Boalt Hall in Berkeley as a law student—seeing two very different parts of California—and then settled in San Diego. He was elected to the Assembly in 1966 and became mayor of San Diego in 1971; he was known as a problem solver and moderate, supporting Gerald Ford over Ronald Reagan in 1976, opposing Proposition 13 in 1978. He ran for governor in 1978 and finished fourth in the primary with 9%, about the San Diego media market's share of the statewide vote. In 1982, he ran for senator, won a five-candidate primary with 38%, and beat outgoing Governor Jerry Brown 52%–45%. In the Senate Wilson opposed coastal oil drilling, but favored agribusiness positions inland. He enthusiastically backed the Reagan defense buildup and took up the role of defending California interests that Alan Cranston let slip while running for president in 1983. In 1988 he was reelected 53%–44%.

When Governor George Deukmejian announced he was retiring in 1990, Republican leaders, fearful of giving Democrats full control of redistricting, urged Wilson to run. He agreed: being governor was his first choice all along. He did not get a free ride. The Democratic nominee was Dianne Feinstein, former mayor of San Francisco, a supporter of abortion rights and capital punishment whose ads recalled how she took charge when Mayor George Moscone and Supervisor Harvey Milk were murdered in 1978. Wilson campaigned for "preventive government" programs to help children; both candidates sounded similar. In effect this was a contest to decide whether to strengthen or weaken the hold of liberal Assembly Democrats on public policy, and the decision hinged on referenda which brought such issues out into the open. Wilson supported term limits, which passed 52%–48%; Feinstein backed Tom Hayden's Big Green, which lost 64%–36%; Wilson won 49%–46%.

In his first years Wilson was beleaguered by the recession and the Assembly Democrats' obduracy. They wrangled for months over the budget, which in California must be approved by a two-thirds vote; it included little "preventive government" and a tax increase. Wilson could only attack the legislature for its softness on crime, its obeisance to trial lawyers and the absurdly expensive workmen's comp system which paid benefits (and lawyers' fees) for psychological loss—the logical outgrowth of the goofiness that produced a legislative task force on self-esteem. But redistricting produced plans which, unlike the 1970s and 1980s plans, left open the possibility of Republican majorities. And Wilson's stubborn perseverance kept gaining ground. In 1993 he was able to push Speaker Willie Brown to an agreement on cutting taxes and reforming workmen's comp. He started off the 1994 campaign 23% behind state Treasurer Kathleen Brown, daughter of one governor and sister of another. But her opposition to the death penalty kept her June primary win over Insurance Commissioner John Garamendi to only 48%–33%. Meanwhile, Wilson was fending off a challenge from conservative Ron Unz, a 32-year old computer millionaire, who held Wilson to a 61%–34% majority. But in the general Wilson relentlessly pounded home his support of capital punishment and of Proposition 187, to stop state spending on illegal immigrants. Brown pointed out correctly that the immigration law provision to admit farm workers sponsored in 1986 by Wilson (and then-Congressman Leon Panetta) let many illegals into California in the first place. But Wilson won easily 55%–41%, and Republicans won a 41–39 majority in the Assembly.

In 1995 Wilson went on the offensive in Sacramento and ran for president, with mixed results. He sued the federal government on unfunded mandates while the feds sued him for refusing to spend state money enforcing the federal "motor-voter" act. (California's Democrats had already made voter registration much easier; one result is that the Mexican who murdered presidential candidate Luis Donaldo Colosio turned out to be a registered Democrat in San Pedro.) He tussled with Brown, who got renegade Republicans to serve nominally as speaker while he still ran things; Wilson got two of them recalled, and Brown was elected mayor of San Francisco in December 1995. Wilson pushed through tax cuts and persevered in cutting welfare spending. In December 1994, promoted by Sacramento businessman Ward Connerly, he came out against racial quotas and preferences, which he had supported since the 1970s, and got the University of California Regents to vote to abolish them; this led to Connerly's Proposition 209, which passed 55%–45% in November 1996. Wilson backed, as he had for a decade, English as the official language and supported the legislature on deregulation of electric utilities.

Wilson's presidential candidacy seemed ill-starred from the beginning. He starting running in spring 1995, despite promises earlier not to and despite Republicans' apprehensions about the succession of Democratic Lieutenant Governor Gray Davis, former top aide to Jerry Brown. Throat surgery prevented him from speaking publicly most of the spring; in the summer he withdrew from the Iowa caucuses; despite support from Massachusetts Governor William Weld, he made only a little headway in Massachusetts. Outspokenly pro-choice and pro-gay rights, Wilson infuriated the religious right base of the national Republican Party, while the constituency he targeted has long since moved in many states to the Democratic Party. He withdrew his candidacy in September 1995, and ended up supporting Bob Dole.

In California Wilson continued to set the agenda. In 1996 he attacked teen pregnancy and troubled youths on moral grounds; he pushed for reducing classroom size in kindergarten through third grade. Although Democrats won back control of the Assembly in 1996, by winning narrow margins in several key seats, Wilson called for welfare reform with mandatory work requirements and schedules and for further business tax cuts. Wilson's success in changing the thrust of California's government has been limited, but could prove lasting. The old Democrats who controlled the Assembly for so many years could not successfully defend their policies in public, and term limits have removed many of their stalwarts from action; the speaker elected in December 1996, Cruz Bustamante, is far less adept and more conservative than Willie Brown. But Wilson, who is term-limited, cannot run in 1998, and in early 1997 no one with similar politics was in the race. The Republican nominee seemed sure to be Attorney General Dan Lungren, whose record in that office and as congressman is more conservative than Wilson's, notably on abortion—not a political asset in California. Among Democrats the picture was unclear. In early 1997 Gray Davis was already running; Northwest Airlines magnate Al Checchi was seriously pondering a race; former Clinton White House Chief of Staff Leon Panetta was being mentioned, more perhaps in Washington than in California; and Dianne Feinstein was considering moving from the Senate to Sacramento as Wilson did in 1990. Feinstein has run three though statewide races in 1990, 1992 and 1994, winning two of three; Panetta probably wouldn't run if she did, but Davis ran against her in the 1994 Senate primary and seemed ready to go on the attack again. But none of these Democrats is close to the old liberal apparat, and all seem to have a flexibility and adaptability not dissimilar to Wilson's. The interesting question is not just who wins the governorship, but whether he or she keeps moving it in the direction Wilson has so stubbornly and against such obstacles set. For his part, Wilson has not ruled out a presidential run in 2000, though it is hard to see how he can raise money easily as a non-incumbent and it is not clear that his views can win majorities in most Republican primaries.

Senior Senator. Dianne Feinstein was elected in 1992 with the most votes cast for a senator in U.S. history. She grew up in San Francisco, in lush Presidio Heights, went to Stanford and later studied criminology. She was appointed by Governor Pat Brown to the women's parole board in 1960, at 27. In 1969 she was elected to the San Francisco County Board of Supervisors—the city's council—and twice ran for mayor and lost. As president of the board, she became mayor when Mayor George Moscone and Supervisor Harvey Milk were murdered by former Supervisor Dan White; she discovered Moscone's body and showed steadiness and a sense of command that calmed the city. In 1984, Walter Mondale seriously considered her for vice president, but passed over her for Geraldine Ferraro because of qualms about the business dealings of her husband, Richard Blum. Feinstein presided gracefully that year over the Democratic National Convention in San Francisco—while Ferraro juggled questions about *her* family's business. In fact, Feinstein and Blum's investments have thrived; the Capitol Hill newspaper *Roll Call* estimated their net worth in 1997 at $50 million, the fifth highest in Congress. Ineligible for a third full term in 1987, Feinstein ran for governor in 1990, won the Democratic primary impressively, then lost 49%–46% to Pete Wilson. When Wilson appointed Orange County state Senator John Seymour—an unknown and bland choice—to replace him in the Senate, Feinstein quickly announced for the seat, even though the 1992 race was for only the last two years of Wilson's term, and she could have run for the seat being vacated by Alan Cranston the same year. She had primary competition from Controller (now Lieutenant Governor) Gray Davis, who ran a spot against her campaign finance practices comparing her to Leona Helmsley; Feinstein won 58%–33%. In the general she faced appointed Senator John Seymour, who had just switched to pro-choice and anti-offshore oil drilling. Nothing worked for Seymour—not Feinstein's arguably tricky financing of her 1990 gubernatorial campaign (which resulted in a $190,000 fine), nor fears of immigration, nor Seymour's tending to agricultural interests. Feinstein won 54%–38%, coming close even in Seymour's southern California base.

California has a long tradition of having one senator who expresses ideological views and another who works hard to represent the state's economic interests. Feinstein chose the latter workhorse role, as did Pete Wilson, Alan Cranston and Thomas Kuchel before. She got a seat on Appropriations, where she could funnel money to California, and on Judiciary, where she was one of the women chosen by then-chairman Joseph Biden, who sought to spare himself the flak he got for allowing cross-examination of Anita Hill. Feinstein has a generally but not uniformly liberal voting record; she also has a tough, prosecutorial demeanor, and on the podium she is one of the best speakers in American politics today. She has kept a distance from the Clinton Administration, negotiating for changes before voting for the 1993 budget, voting against NAFTA, withdrawing her support of the Clinton healthcare plan in May 1994. In her first two years she had two major legislative achievements. One was the attachment of the assault weapons ban to the 1994 crime bill—good politics for her and many Democrats in metropolitan states, but a liability to Democrats in much of the West and South. When Idaho's Larry Craig argued that her definition of assault weapons was not rigorous and challenged her knowledge of firearms, she responded by saying: "I know something about what firearms can do; I came to be mayor of San Francisco as a product of assassination." Her other major achievement was a California Desert Protection Act. Similar measures had been stymied by the state's Republican senators as too restrictive, but now that there was no Republican senator, Feinstein managed it through enactment. In October 1994, the retiring Republican Malcolm Wallop of Wyoming tried to kill the bill by end-of-session filibuster, but other senators, apparently sympathetic to Feinstein's case or her political plight, passed it.

Feinstein surely hoped that she would face weak competition in 1994 and that her early and hard work raising money would enable her to win essentially unopposed. But then came Michael Huffington, with the determination and the cash to be the biggest spending Senate candidate of all time. Huffington grew up in Houston, graduated from Stanford and Harvard Business School and made his fortune in his father's oil and natural gas business. In 1991 he moved to Santa Barbara, and immediately ran against 18-year Republican Congressman Robert Lagomarsino, spending over $3 million in the 1992 primary and attacking Lagomarsino for intervening on behalf of a firm selling torture instruments to the Chinese—the kind of constituent service that congressmen usually brag about. Huffington won the primary 49%–43% and the general 53%–35%. Nothing made him a plausible Senate candidate but his money—some $30 million—and his message. Huffington started off with an ad in which he promoted William Bennett's *The Book of Virtues*, addressing Californians' sense of moral deficiency; he followed by attacking Feinstein for providing the deciding vote for the 1993 tax increase. Feinstein ran an ad accusing Huffington of refusing to act as an advocate for Raytheon in Congress, a company located in his district; he responded with an ad showing that Feinstein had received contributions from the same company and that she immediately wrote letters to government agencies on behalf of the company. This was political jujitsu, using her strength of constituency service to prove his claim that she was a "career politician." Feinstein was clearly flustered and angry that a politician who had put in so little time and effort had pulled even with her in the polls by September, and that she could not count on heavily outspending him. By her own standards and those of voters in 1992, she had done an excellent job; shouldn't that be enough? The press took an intense dislike to Huffington and his wife Arianna, attacking her involvement with a religious movement and suggesting that Michael Huffington was some kind of programmed automaton. Actually, he advanced similar ideas in his two campaigns while using separate consultants, and his spending per capita was less than such Democratic senators as Jay Rockefeller and Herb Kohl, who have been spared such hostile scrutiny.

But the result did not hinge on these things. In October, Huffington made a big point of endorsing Proposition 187; Feinstein was opposed to it. Then it was revealed that the Huffingtons had employed an illegal alien as a nanny. Huffington's poll numbers went down. On the Thursday before the election, it was revealed that Feinstein, despite her earlier denials, had employed a woman whose work permit had expired. But the news media ran stories saying that federal officials cast doubt on whether the woman was an illegal. This alibi turned out to be false, but it probably made the difference; it is a sign of Democratic weakness that Feinstein, for all her strength and achievements, was reelected with the help of the Clinton Administration. Feinstein won 47%–45%, carrying the Bay Area 63%–30% and Los Angeles County 52%–40%, while losing the rest of southern California 56%–35% and the north outside the Bay Area 51%–40%.

In the minority for the first time in her career, Feinstein worked on anti-crime legislation, passing the Comprehensive Methamphetamine Control Act of 1996 and proposing a Federal Gang Violence Act (doubling penalties to gang members) and a victim's bill of rights constitutional amendment. She opposed the immigration bill until the Gallegly amendment, allowing states to exclude children of illegal immigrants from schools, was dropped. She opposed the Welfare Reform Act provisions cutting off aid to elderly legal immigrants, and sought in 1997 to repeal that provision; she also said that cutting off welfare recipients after two years cannot work in California. She sought to link trade ties to Mexico with changes in its drug enforcement. Toward China she was more friendly. When San Francisco and Shanghai became sister cities in 1979, Feinstein got to know Mayor Jiang Zemin, now president of China. She supports renewal of MFN status for China; she argues that trade is driving political change in

China and that if trade ties are cut China will just withdraw and remain dictatorial. But her strong stand prompted her husband to give up any profits he makes on investments in China. She co-sponsored the bill to ban denial of hospitalization for mastectomies. She opposed the McCain-Feingold campaign finance bill because it limits ideological PACs like EMILY's List, which gave her much support.

Feinstein's seat comes up in 2000, and in December 1996 she yielded her seat on Appropriations to Barbara Boxer, who runs in 1998. But Feinstein may run that year too, for governor: she was leading polls in early 1997 and like Pete Wilson, who ran for governor after eight years in the Senate and beat Feinstein, she has always been inclined to executive office.

Junior Senator. Barbara Boxer, by most measures, is one of the most liberal members of Congress. Boxer grew up in Brooklyn, where she was a victim of sexual harassment by a college professor and was refused work as a stockbroker; she moved to California in 1965 and worked on civic and political campaigns and ultimately for Democratic Congressman John Burton. In 1972 she ran for the Marin County Board of Supervisors, in the ultra-trendy suburbs nestled between Mount Tamalpais and the Bay, north of the Golden Gate Bridge. She lost, but in 1976, when woman candidates were more accepted, she won a seat on the board. Boxer is energetic, good-humored, unafraid to challenge authority but able to work harmoniously with others. When Burton retired unexpectedly in 1982, she ran for the House and was easily elected. She made many splashes in the House, unearthing the Air Force's $7,622 coffee pot in 1984, denouncing the Persian Gulf war with more ardor than anyone, and leading a march of angry women on the Senate when Anita Hill was testifying against Clarence Thomas. She also compiled the highest-dollar voting record in the House on spending in 1992.

Boxer began the 1992 Senate campaign not as the best-known or best-financed candidate, but as the most distinctive in a year in which the enthusiasm of the feminist left energized the Democratic Party and sped it to victory. In the primary, she faced Lieutenant Governor Leo McCarthy, who had high name identification after four statewide races, and Congressman Mel Levine, who had strong financial backing from Los Angeles's Westside. Levine ran tough ads in favor of the Gulf war resolution and taking a tough stand against the Los Angeles riot, but only managed to alienate liberal voters—who went to Boxer—without winning over moderates who stuck with the better-known but more liberal McCarthy. Boxer, despite 143 overdrafts at the House bank, won with 44% of the vote, to 31% for McCarthy and 22% for Levine. Her general election opponent was Bruce Herschensohn, a Los Angeles TV and radio commentator, Nixon speechwriter and Reagan enthusiast, backer of a flat tax and offshore oil drilling and opponent of abortion. Herschensohn had edged Silicon Valley moderate Congressman Tom Campbell 38%–36% in the primary, with the help of then-Palm Springs Mayor Sonny Bono, who picked up 17% of the vote. The Boxer-Herschensohn race was a battle of opposites, the far left versus the far right of the American electoral spectrum. Herschensohn ran an effective ad attacking Boxer for charging the government $1,565 for limousine service to the airport, and his gentle, friendly persona contrasted with Boxer's avoidance of unguarded public appearances. But Boxer was helped by the collapse of the Bush candidacy in California, by hearty support from Feinstein and by the revelation by the state Democratic political director during the last week of the campaign that Herschensohn attended nude dancer night clubs. In a race where neither candidate won a majority, Boxer won 48%–43%, carrying the Bay Area 61%–30% and Los Angeles County 53%–40%, while losing southern California 52%–38% and the rest of the state 49%–42%.

Boxer's voting record has been strongly liberal, though toned down a bit in 1996. Bob Dole called her "the most partisan senator I've ever known," and she staunchly defends the Clinton White House against scandal charges; her daughter is married to Hillary Rodham Clinton's brother. She has worked to pass a dolphin-safe tuna labeling law and the California Cruise Industry Revitalization Act. She has a bill to require child-proof safety locks on all handguns. She vehemently opposed the partial birth abortion ban and voted against the 1996 welfare reform. She crusaded in 1995 for open Ethics Committee hearings on Bob Packwood. But she has sought out some popular California causes as well. She calls for full reimbursement of border states for the costs of illegal immigration. She has pushed defense reconversion bills and funding, and points with pride to Northrop-Grumman's Stealth Bus, an advanced technology bus made of Stealth Bomber materials. She scored a great success in pushing the public-private trust for the Presidio in the 1996 parks bill, and helped broker a last-minute compromise between the White House and Alaska Senator Frank Murkowski on the Tongass National Forest which enabled the bill to pass. In December 1996 she got Feinstein to yield her a seat on the Appropriations Committee, where she promised to work on California projects. Some of her stands have divided her supporters. She opposed the Defense of Marriage Act, but refused to support government recognition of gay marriages. She sided with writers and directors and against the studios by backing a bill for disclaimers on altered films.

During her first three years in the Senate her job rating was among the chamber's lowest, and Republicans seemed lined up to run against her. But by early 1997 her job rating was up near 50%, and fewer Republicans seemed interested. Congressman Tom Campbell, who nearly won the 1992 nomination, and Michael Huffington, the nearly successful 1994 candidate, have both said they will not run. Running early was state Treasurer Matt Fong, who took a midpoint stance on abortion and said he was neutral on Proposition 187 and supported 209. Congressmen David Dreier and Christopher Cox seemed interested earlier and may still run, but both have important positions in the Republican House and may not want to take a chance at running for the Senate. And Mayor Susan Golding, who has had much success in San Diego, announced her candidacy in May 1997. For abortion rights, pro-environment and fiscally moderate, with a record on attracting business and stopping crime, Golding will make a strong candidate. Another probable Republican is car alarm magnate Darrell Issa, described by *Roll Call* as the "one true conservative," and Sonny Bono is seriously considering the race. This will be the first open primary in California, in which voters can vote for any candidate regardless of party registration; the June primary could turn out to be a good forecast of how Boxer, who says she plans to raise $20 million, will do in November.

Presidential politics. With 54 electoral votes, California is the gorilla of American politics: it may be geographically far away from the rest of the action, but you ignore it at your peril. In the 1970s and 1980s, it was the state that Republicans had to carry to win the White House; they did so handily when they nominated Californians—Richard Nixon in 1972 and Ronald Reagan in 1980 and 1984—but they won only narrowly in 1976 and 1988 when they didn't. Now it is the Democrats who cannot afford to lose California. Bill Clinton, leading in California polls by wide margins, was able to prospect for votes in the Midwest and South in 1992 and 1996. But in two-way races Democrats have been running not much above 50%, and so in 2000 the Democratic nominee may not be so strong here. Clinton was clearly aware of California's importance, visiting the state with businesslike regularity, lavishing it with special aid in disasters and economic distress, paying homage to different subgroups of this culturally diverse state's population. It doesn't seem likely that either party's nominee will carry that kind of advantage into the 2000 election, although Al Gore, as witness his April 1996 trip to the Buddhist temple fundraiser, may try.

California's presidential primary was held for years in June, and it often attracted national attention, as when Robert Kennedy beat Eugene McCarthy in 1968 or when George McGovern edged Hubert Humphrey in 1972. But since 1976, the primary has not mattered much, and for 1996 the legislature rescheduled it to March 26. But even that was too late: the Republican nomination was already decided and the Democratic not even contested. But California could make the difference in 2000.

Congressional districting. California grows so fast and is so populous that redistricting matters here more than anywhere else. The tradition of partisan redistricting goes way back: Republicans drew the lines to their advantage in the 1940s and 1950s, Democrats in the 1960s, 1970s and 1980s, as the California House delegation grew from 23 in the 1940s to 30, 38, 43, 45 and 52, the largest for any state in history. The great genius of redistricting here was Democratic Congressman Phillip Burton, who dominated the line-drawing for House seats and state Senate and Assembly as well; his 1982 plan, slightly revised for 1984–90, left Democrats in secure control of the delegation even though he died in 1983. Thus, in 1984 Democrats had a 27–18 edge in the House delegation, even though Republicans won the popular vote 49%–48%. In contrast, in 1994, when Republicans won the popular vote again 49%–48%, the district lines again produced 27 Democrats but now also 25 Republicans.

The man who made the difference was Governor Pete Wilson, elected in 1990; he was a hard-nosed bargainer with the Democratic legislature in 1991 and persuaded the state Supreme Court (Republican ever since voters threw out three Jerry Brown appointees in 1986) to adopt a plan drawn up by his appointed commission in 1992. This was a relatively evenhanded plan, with generally regular boundaries. There are no black-majority districts (California is only 7% black, and the Los Angeles area's former black ghettos are now heavily Hispanic) and seven Hispanic-majority districts (though in some few Hispanics are registered to vote). The state also includes five districts that are 20% or more Asian—but these are not the districts that elect the state's one Japanese-American and one Korean-American congressmen. California is a nice refutation of the notion that Americans will only elect politicians of their own race.

The People: Est. Pop. 1996: 31,878,000; Pop. 1990: 29,760,021, up 7.1% 1990–1996. 12.0% of U.S. total, 1st largest; 7% rural. Median age: 32.7 years. 11% 65 years and over. 57.2% White, 7.0% Black; 9.1% Asian; 1% Amer. Indian; 25.8% Hispanic origin. Households: 52.7% married couple families; 26% married couple fams. w. children; 54% college educ.; median household income: $35,798; per capita income: $16,409; 55.6% owner occupied housing; median house value: $195,500; median monthly rent: $561. 7.2% Unemployment. 1996 Voting age pop.: 22,826,000. 1996 Turnout: 10,019,484; 44% of VAP. Registered voters (1996): 15,662,075; 7,387,504 D (47%); 5,704,536 R (36%); 2,570,035 unaffiliated and minor parties (16%).

Political Lineup: Governor, Pete Wilson (R); Lt. Gov., Gray Davis (D); Secy. of State, Bill Jones (R); Atty. Gen., Daniel E. Lungren (R); Treasurer, Matt Fong (R); Controller, Kathleen Connell (D). State Senate, 40 (23 D, 16 R, and 1 I); Senate President, Gray Davis (D); State Assembly, 80 (43 D, 37 R); Assembly Speaker, Cruz Bustamante (D). Senators, Dianne Feinstein (D) and Barbara Boxer (D). Representatives, 52 (29 D, 23 R).

Elections Division: 916-654-0365; **Filing Deadline for U.S. Congress:** February 19, 1998.

1996 Presidential Vote

Clinton (D)	5,119,815	(51%)
Dole (R)	3,828,368	(38%)
Perot (I)	697,845	(7%)
Other	372,553	(4%)

1996 Republican Presidential Primary

Dole (R)	1,619,931	(66%)
Buchanan (R)	450,695	(18%)
Forbes (R)	183,367	(7%)
Keyes (R)	93,577	(4%)
Other	104,742	(5%)

1992 Presidential Vote

Clinton (D)	5,121,249	(46%)
Bush (R)	3,630,566	(33%)
Perot (I)	2,296,004	(21%)

GOVERNOR

Gov. Pete Wilson (R)

Elected 1990, term expires Jan. 1999; b. Aug. 23, 1933, Lake Forest, IL; home, San Diego; Yale, B.A. 1955, U. of CA at Berkeley, J.D. 1962; Presbyterian; married (Gayle).

Career: Marine Corps, 1955–58; Practicing atty., 1963–66; CA Assembly, 1966–71, Minority Whip, 1967–69; San Diego Mayor, 1970–83; U.S. Senate, 1982–90.

Office: State Capitol Bldg., Sacramento 95814, 916-445-2841; Fax: 916-445-4633; Web site: www.ca.gov.

Election Results

1994 gen.	Pete Wilson (R)	4,777,674	(55%)
	Kathleen Brown (D)	3,517,777	(41%)
	Others	363,430	(4%)
1994 prim.	Pete Wilson (R)	1,266,832	(61%)
	Ron Unz (R)	707,431	(34%)
	Others	87,528	(4%)
1990 gen.	Pete Wilson (R)	3,791,904	(49%)
	Dianne Feinstein (D)	3,525,197	(46%)
	Other	383,316	(5%)

SENATORS

Sen. Dianne Feinstein (D)

Elected 1992, seat up 2000; b. June 22, 1933, San Francisco; home, San Francisco; Stanford U., B.A. 1955; Jewish; married (Richard C. Blum).

Career: CA Women's Parole Bd., 1960–66; San Francisco Bd. of Supervisors, 1970–78, Pres., 1970–71, 1974–75, 1978; San Francisco Mayor, 1978–88.

DC Office: 331 HSOB 20510, 202-224-3841; Fax: 202-228-3954; e-mail: senator@feinstein.senate.gov.

State Offices: Fresno, 209-485-7430; Los Angeles, 310-914-7300; San Diego, 619-231-9712; San Francisco, 415-536-6868.

Committees: *Foreign Relations* (7th of 8 D): East Asian & Pacific Affairs; International Operations (RMM); Near Eastern & South Asian Affairs. *Judiciary* (5th of 8 D): Immigration; Terrorism, Technology & Government Information (RMM); Youth Violence. *Rules & Administration* (6th of 7 D). *Joint Committee on the Library of Congress* (5th of 5 Sens.).

Group Ratings

	ADA	ACLU	AFS	LCV	CFA	CON	NFIB	COC	ACU	NTLC	CHC
1996	95	35	100	85	79	32	38	38	20	28	7
1995	95	—	100	93	81	15	—	37	13	—	—

National Journal Ratings

	1995 LIB — 1995 CONS			1996 LIB — 1996 CONS		
Economic	62%	—	36%	67%	—	31%
Social	64%	—	35%	72%	—	26%
Foreign	72%	—	24%	58%	—	40%

Key Votes of the 104th Congress

1. Reduce Medicare Growth $	N	5. Flag Amendment	Y	9. Anti-Missle Defense	N
2. Lmt. Prod. Liab. Damages	N	6. Endangered Species	Y	10. Cuban Embargo	N
3. Increase Min. Wage	Y	7. Gay Employment Rights	Y	11. Bar Bosnia Troop $	N
4. Welfare Reform	N	8. Ovrd. Part. Birth Veto	N	12. Cut Vietnam Aid	N

Election Results

1994 general	Dianne Feinstein (D)	3,977,063	(47%)	($14,407,179)
	Michael Huffington (R)	3,811,501	(45%)	($29,969,695)
	Others	714,500	(8%)	
1994 primary	Dianne Feinstein (D)	1,635,837	(74%)	
	Ted Andromidas (D)	297,128	(13%)	
	Daniel O'Dowd (D)	271,615	(12%)	
1992 general	Dianne Feinstein (D)	5,853,621	(54%)	($8,054,222)
	John Seymour (R)	4,093,488	(38%)	($6,849,805)
	Others	832,581	(8%)	

Sen. Barbara Boxer (D)

Elected 1992, seat up 1998; b. Nov. 11, 1940, Brooklyn, NY; home, Greenbrae; Brooklyn Col., B.A. 1962; Jewish; married (Stewart).

Career: Stockbroker, researcher, 1962–65; Journalist, *Pacific Sun*, 1972–74; Dist. aide, U.S. Rep. John Burton, 1974–76; Marin Cnty. Bd. of Supervisors, 1976–82; U.S. House of Reps., 1982–92.

DC Office: 112 HSOB 20510, 202-224-3553; Fax: 415-956-6701; e-mail: senator@boxer.senate.gov.

State Offices: El Segundo, 310-414-5700; Fresno, 209-497-5109; Sacramento, 916-448-2787; San Bernardino, 909-888-8525; San Diego, 619-239-3884; San Francisco, 415-403-0100.

Committees: *Appropriations* (13th of 13 D): District of Columbia (RMM); Interior; Legislative Branch; VA, HUD & Independent Agencies. *Banking, Housing & Urban Affairs* (5th of 8 D): Financial Institutions & Regulatory Relief; Financial Services & Technology (RMM); International Finance. *Budget* (5th of 10 D). *Environment & Public Works* (7th of 8 D): Clean Air, Wetlands, Private Property & Nuclear Safety; Superfund, Waste Control & Risk Assessment; Transportation & Infrastructure.

Group Ratings

	ADA	ACLU	AFS	LCV	CFA	CON	NFIB	COC	ACU	NTLC	CHC
1996	100	59	100	92	86	16	24	23	5	7	7
1995	100	—	100	100	100	19	—	26	0	—	—

National Journal Ratings

	1995 LIB — 1995 CONS			1996 LIB — 1996 CONS		
Economic	95%	—	3%	74%	—	19%
Social	82%	—	15%	78%	—	20%
Foreign	94%	—	3%	77%	—	17%

Key Votes of the 104th Congress

1. Reduce Medicare Growth $	N	5. Flag Amendment	N	9. Anti-Missle Defense	N
2. Lmt. Prod. Liab. Damages	N	6. Endangered Species	Y	10. Cuban Embargo	N
3. Increase Min. Wage	Y	7. Gay Employment Rights	Y	11. Bar Bosnia Troop $	N
4. Welfare Reform	N	8. Ovrd. Part. Birth Veto	N	12. Cut Vietnam Aid	N

Election Results

1992 general	Barbara Boxer (D)	5,173,443	(48%)	($10,415,811)
	Bruce Herschensohn (R)	4,644,139	(43%)	($7,649,072)
	Others	981,781	(9%)	
1992 primary	Barbara Boxer (D)	1,339,126	(44%)	
	Leo McCarthy (D)	935,209	(31%)	
	Mel Levine (D)	667,359	(22%)	
	Charles Greene (D)	122,954	(4%)	
1986 general	Alan Cranston (D)	3,646,672	(50%)	($11,037,707)
	Ed Zschau (R)	3,541,804	(47%)	($11,781,316)

FIRST DISTRICT

The North Coast of California is unlike any other place in America. It is the only part of the Lower 48 states first settled by Russians, who built Fort Ross in 1812; they sold it in 1841 to a Swiss named John Augustus Sutter, whose discovery of gold near Sacramento started the Gold Rush eight years later. It is the only part of the world with large numbers of redwood trees, shooting up in the moist and drizzly air hundreds of feet toward the sky. It is wet country, and for years it has been one of America's prime lumbering areas: Eureka and smaller lumber towns are filled with filigreed Victorian houses and old lumber mills, saloons and waterfront hotels. It has moved on to other crops: in sunny valleys sealed off the from Coast Range ridges grow some of the nation's premium wine grapes, and Mendocino County has been known from the late 1960s for its premier marijuana fields. Twenty years ago, there were only 20 wineries in Napa Valley; today there are more than 200, with another 100 just west of the ridges in Sonoma County. These valleys were some of California's earliest literary haunts: Robert Louis Stevenson took his honeymoon near Calistoga in Napa, and Jack London owned a giant house in Sonoma which mysteriously burned down in 1913.

California's 1st Congressional District consists of most of the North Coast (though just missing Fort Ross), plus much of the wine-growing area inland and just a bit of the vast Central Valley interior. The North Coast lumbering area from Mendocino on north, once filled with rough-hewn working men, was historically Democratic country, but it backlashed toward the Republicans on cultural issues. As veterans of the counterculture settled in Mendocino County and along the coast, it has moved toward the cultural left. In neighboring Humboldt County, voters in the town of Arcata turned control of the city council to a Green Party majority. Inland, the wine-growing country around Healdsburg and in Napa County is politically more conservative, with neither the blue-collar tradition nor the counterculture past of the coast, though there is often partisan competition. The district's inland portion is around Fairfield, home of Travis Air Force Base. The mix of different economies and cultures, of generations with sharply different experiences and outlooks, makes this one of California's politically most unstable districts, and it has changed partisan hands in three of the last four elections.

The congressman from the 1st District is Frank Riggs, a Republican first elected in 1990, defeated in 1992, then elected again in 1994 and 1996. Riggs's background is in law enforcement; he was an MP in the Army and worked for the Santa Barbara and Healdsburg police departments and the Sonoma County sheriff's office. In 1983 he went into real estate in fast-growing Sonoma County and served several years on school boards. In 1990 he ran for Congress, targeting Democrat Doug Bosco, who tended to favor the growth forces in the Redwood Empire more than the Sonoma County enviros. Bosco was also opposed on the left by a Peace & Freedom candidate who took 15% of the vote, and Riggs won 43%–42%. He quickly won attention, first when he reneged on his pledge not to take the "obscene" congressional pay raise and voted against the Gulf war resolution, then as one of the freshman Republican Gang of Seven who insisted on disclosure of the names of House bank check-bouncers. But Riggs then discovered that he had three overdrafts himself.

In 1992 Riggs lost the seat to as different a Democrat as can be imagined. Dan Hamburg moved from Stanford to Mendocino County, founded an "alternative school," served as a supervisor favoring "managed growth," taught Chinese culture and language to foreigners in China. "[Riggs] was a narc. I favor growing your own," Hamburg said; indeed he favored legalization of marijuana. With help from rock stars, Hamburg nearly outraised the incumbent and won 48%–45% in a district Bill Clinton was carrying 46%–29%. Hamburg made an ultraliberal record in the House, which helped him raise money again; he beat Bosco in the June primary, but by only 62%–38%, then lost to Riggs in November by 53%–47%—the only absolute majority for anyone in this culturally fractured district since 1988.

In the House again, Riggs voted for the Contract with America, but broke with the Republican leadership on protecting unionized mass transit workers, Davis-Bacon repeal and the minimum wage. He pushed the timber salvage law, allowing more logging, and from his seat on Appropriations pushed for the $211 million veterans' hospital at Travis Air Force Base, $60 million more for infrastructure improvement to Travis, $15 million for Humboldt Harbor and $22 million for water development projects. But he failed in attempts to lift endangered species protection from a tract around but not including Headwaters Grove. And Senator Christopher Bond's attacks on the veterans' hospital held up funding at least until 1998.

Despite his pro-labor votes, Riggs was targeted by the AFL-CIO and several Democrats vied to run against him. Feminist groups raised money for Monica Marvin of Napa County. But she was outspent by Michela Alioto, 28-year-old granddaughter of former San Francisco Mayor Joseph Alioto and a policy adviser (briefing book compiler, opponents said) of Vice President Al Gore. Alioto, paralyzed at 13 in a ski lift accident, bought a $600,000 house in the Napa Valley a week before filing deadline and eventually spent nearly $600,000 of her own money. She won the March primary 40%–33% over Marvin, and seconded Gore's nomination at the Democratic convention in August. She vowed to "take on Newt Gingrich" and attacked Riggs's support of Medicare "cuts." She was hailed in *People* magazine and attracted campaign visits from Hillary Rodham Clinton and Al and Tipper Gore. But as a candidate she had her deficiencies. In debates she mispronounced town names and mixed up local issues. For all her wealth, she was subject to tax liens for nonpayment of state income taxes. Her campaign staff and family members impersonated a TV news reporter and forged TV station stationery to get hold of Riggs campaign documents. Riggs's campaign was controversial as well. He was attacked for distributing a *Human Events* story comparing Alioto's family to Benito Mussolini's. And a TV ad in which he cited the murder of Polly Klaas and pictured her murderer (to highlight Alioto's opposition to capital punishment) drew protests from Klaas's father. But Alioto's weakness as a candidate prompted most area newspapers to endorse Riggs. Even as Bill Clinton was carrying the 1st 48%–35%, Riggs carried every county but Mendocino and won 50%–43%.

In January 1997 Riggs left Appropriations to chair the education subcommittee with jurisdiction of K-12, special education, school lunches, Head Start and education technology; it is supposed to reauthorize special education and juvenile justice laws. He also has a seat on Transportation and Infrastructure, from which he can help Travis, Eureka Harbor and U.S. 101 in Sonoma County. But the character of the district, and the circumstances of his 1996 victory, almost surely guarantee him serious opposition in 1998. State Senator Mike Thompson has announced he will run and Alioto may make another bid.

The People: Pop. 1990: 572,870; 33% rural; 13% age 65+; 79% White; 4% Black; 3% Asian; 2% Amer. Indian; 11% Hispanic origin. Households: 58% married couple families; 27% married couple fams. w. children; 52% college educ.; median household income: $30,943; per capita income: $14,298; median gross rent: $512; median house value: $136,200.

1996 Presidential Vote

Clinton (D)	113,861	(48%)
Dole (R)	83,669	(35%)
Perot (I)	23,024	(10%)
Other	15,695	(7%)

1992 Presidential Vote

Clinton (D)	119,491	(46%)
Bush (R)	74,597	(29%)
Perot (I)	61,160	(24%)

Rep. Frank D. Riggs (R)

Elected 1994; b. Sept. 5, 1950, Louisville, KY; home, Windsor; Golden Gate U., B.A. 1980; Episcopalian; married (Cathy).

Career: Army, 1972–75; Police officer & Deputy Sheriff, Sonoma Cnty, 1976–83; Owner, Duncan Enterprises, 1985–present; Vice Pres. & Gen. Mr., Learning Tools Educ. Software Co., 1993–94.

DC Office: 1714 LHOB 20515, 202-225-3311; Fax: 202-225-3403; e-mail: repriggs@hr.house.gov.

District Offices: Eureka, 707-441-8701; Napa, 707-254-7308.

Committees: *Education & The Workforce* (14th of 25 R): Early Childhood, Youth & Families (Chmn.); Postsecondary Education, Training & Life-Long Learning. *Transportation & Infrastructure* (23rd of 40 R): Surface Transportation; Water Resources & Environment.

Group Ratings

	ADA	ACLU	AFS	LCV	CFA	CON	NFIB	COC	ACU	NTLC	CHC
1996	10	0	25	23	23	24	95	81	85	100	86
1995	10	—	—	0	0	75	—	100	83	—	—

National Journal Ratings

	1995 LIB — 1995 CONS			1996 LIB — 1996 CONS		
Economic	34%	—	64%	33%	—	64%
Social	35%	—	64%	35%	—	62%
Foreign	35%	—	65%	41%	—	56%

Key Votes of the 104th Congress

1. Reduce Medicare Growth $	Y	5. Flag Amendment	Y	9. Cuban Embargo	Y
2. Ovrd. Product Liab. Veto	Y	6. Drop EPA Limits	N	10. Bar Bosnia Troop $	*
3. Increase Min. Wage	Y	7. Repeal Assault-Weap. Ban	Y	11. Cut Anti-Missile Defense	N
4. Welfare Reform	Y	8. Ovrd. Part. Birth Veto	Y	12. Bar U.N. Uniforms	Y

Election Results

1996 general	Frank D. Riggs (R)	110,242	(50%)	($1,390,399)
	Michela Alioto (D)	96,522	(43%)	($1,228,870)
	Emil Rossi (Lib)	15,354	(7%)	
1996 primary	Frank D. Riggs (R)	unopposed		
1994 general	Frank D. Riggs (R)	106,870	(53%)	($605,185)
	Dan Hamburg (D)	93,717	(47%)	($834,611)

SECOND DISTRICT

Rising 14,000 feet over low foothills and the Central Valley, visible for 100 miles, is the lone snow-capped volcanic cone of Mount Shasta, one of a string of (presumably) burnt-out volcanoes that march up and down the Pacific Coast states. This is the far northern end of California, where truck traffic on Interstate 5 is the only reminder of the choked metropolitan areas where most of the state's people live. It is lumber country mostly, where the mountains that rise on all sides—the Coast Range to the east, the Sierra Nevada to the west, the scattered mountains sealing off the Central Valley north of Redding—are carpeted with trees; rough flannel-shirt, two-lane-road country that was left behind economically when greater Los Angeles and San Francisco boomed after World War II.

In the last dozen years, however, the northern end of California has been attracting people, mostly young families who come here to raise their children in a small town atmosphere, but also retirees looking for a calm atmosphere and low cost of living. There are few minorities here; the population is 88% white Anglo, the highest in any California district.

The 2d Congressional District of California covers most of this area. The district has two major population areas: one around Redding, just below Mount Shasta, and the other farther south, at the edge of the Sierra foothills, around the Butte County communities of Paradise and Chico. (The latter is where Bob Dole fell off a platform in the 1996 campaign; but what was he doing way up here in such Republican country?) Culturally conservative, angry at the diktats of urban environmentalists, this area is heavily Republican now, despite a Democratic heritage: an area which from 1943–80 elected rough-and-ready Democrats who pulled strings in Sacramento and Washington to build roads and dams, now elects abstemious and circumspect Republicans who have solidly conservative voting records and tend to local needs.

The congressman from the 2d District is Wally Herger, a Republican, businessman and rancher first elected to the Assembly in 1980. In 1986 he was elected to Congress after winning solid margins over the mayor of Redding in the primary and a Shasta County supervisor in the general. He has served rather quietly on the Ways and Means Committee and Budget Committees, favoring balanced budgets and lower taxes. "I don't have trouble [making up my mind] on most votes," he has said. He pushed for the timber salvage bill passed in the 104th Congress, to allow 18 months to remove dead and dying trees from federal forests. He pushed successfully for a pilot test of the Quincy Library Project, a plan agreed to by local loggers and environmentalists (the only neutral place to meet was the library in Quincy) to allow the logging of smaller, more crowded trees and leaving more fire-resistant trees in the forest, as a way to reduce wildfires and provide a steady supply of timber for local mills; it was backed as well by Agriculture Secretary Dan Glickman. He tends to local water projects, lamenting in the January 1997 floods the failure to shore up levees and opposing the Central Valley Project water bill for "legislat[ing] a permanent drought." He passed a bill to prevent prisoners in local and state jails from collecting SSI benefits.

Herger seems in a strong position politically. In 1996 he was reelected 61%–34%.

The People: Pop. 1990: 573,226; 40% rural; 16% age 65+; 88% White; 2% Black; 2% Asian; 2% Amer. Indian; 6% Hispanic origin. Households: 58% married couple families; 24% married couple fams. w. children; 51% college educ.; median household income: $24,807; per capita income: $12,458; median gross rent: $429; median house value: $94,000.

1996 Presidential Vote

Dole (R)	126,430	(51%)
Clinton (D)	89,736	(36%)
Perot (I)	22,161	(9%)
Other	10,058	(4%)

1992 Presidential Vote

Bush (R)	101,505	(38%)
Clinton (D)	93,823	(35%)
Perot (I)	67,298	(25%)

Rep. Wally Herger (R)

Elected 1986; b. May 20, 1945, Yuba City; home, Marysville; American River Comm. Col., A.A. 1967; CA St. U., 1968–69; Mormon; married (Pamela).

Career: Rancher; Owner, Herger Gas Inc. 1969–80; CA Assembly, 1980–86.

DC Office: 2433 RHOB 20515, 202-225-3076.

District Offices: Chico, 916-893-8363; Redding, 916-223-5898.

Committees: *Budget* (4th of 24 R). *Ways & Means* (8th of 23 R): Trade.

Group Ratings

	ADA	ACLU	AFS	LCV	CFA	CON	NFIB	COC	ACU	NTLC	CHC
1996	0	7	8	8	0	30	100	100	100	100	100
1995	0	—	—	0	0	75	—	100	92	—	—

National Journal Ratings

	1995 LIB — 1995 CONS			1996 LIB — 1996 CONS		
Economic	0%	—	74%	0%	—	82%
Social	0%	—	79%	24%	—	72%
Foreign	15%	—	73%	0%	—	79%

Key Votes of the 104th Congress

1. Reduce Medicare Growth $	Y	5. Flag Amendment	Y	9. Cuban Embargo	Y
2. Ovrd. Product Liab. Veto	Y	6. Drop EPA Limits	N	10. Bar Bosnia Troop $	Y
3. Increase Min. Wage	N	7. Repeal Assault-Weap. Ban	Y	11. Cut Anti-Missile Defense	N
4. Welfare Reform	Y	8. Ovrd. Part. Birth Veto	Y	12. Bar U.N. Uniforms	Y

Election Results

1996 general	Wally Herger (R)	144,913	(61%)	($536,724)
	Roberts A. Braden (D)	80,401	(34%)	($161,918)
	Others	13,019	(5%)	
1996 primary	Wally Herger (R)	71,452	(84%)	
	Devvy Kidd (R)	13,107	(16%)	
1994 general	Wally Herger (R)	137,863	(64%)	($572,629)
	Mary Jacobs (D)	55,958	(26%)	($167,907)
	Devvy Kidd (AI)	15,569	(7%)	
	Others	5,417	(3%)	

THIRD DISTRICT

California's Sacramento Valley is one of nature's—and man's—miracles. Nature has sculpted a floor of almost perfectly flat land, surrounded on three sides by mountains, alternately purple and brown in the light. To this fertile lush black loam, man has added roads and fences—as straight as the lines in a geometry text—and, most important, water. Pacific clouds pour rain into the mountains, but the water used to run off quickly before it was penned in reservoirs and distributed through a system of canals and aqueducts, levees and pumping plants. The

Sacramento and Central Valleys now produce a marvelous variety of crops—rice, plums, almonds, olives, asparagus, pears, hops, beans, celery, onions, potatoes. The Sacramento Valley has always guarded its water jealously and in the days before one-person-one-vote, it had enough seats in the California Senate to veto water decisions it didn't like; today it must fight to keep enough for its farms against the demands of the cities to the south and to maintain the levees which broke during the floods of January 1997.

The metropolis of this valley is Sacramento. Its historic foundation is apparent, coming into town on the West Sacramento Freeway, elevated above utterly flat rice lands painstakingly drained by a network of canals. As you hurtle over the Sacramento River on the M Street Bridge you see, framed perfectly in its arch, California's glorious golden-domed Capitol. On this landing Sacramento was born, and the state government, along with the agriculture symbolized by those rice fields, were for years its lifeblood. Now Sacramento spreads far to the south, east and north, with 1.5 million people—one of the fastest-growing major metropolitan areas in the last two decades.

The 3d Congressional District of California includes part of metropolitan Sacramento and much of the Sacramento Valley to the north. It takes in many of the suburbs just north of Sacramento and the American River—all or part of Carmichael, Citrus Heights, North Highlands and Foothills Farms. Sacramento is historically Democratic, but these suburbs are increasingly Republican. The 3d also includes heavily Democratic Yolo County, with industrial West Sacramento just across the Sacramento River from the Capitol and, on the flat farmlands, the tree-shaded, bicycle-pathed town of Davis, with its University of California campus. In the Sacramento Valley it extends north along I-5 to Red Bluff.

This is a district that leans Republican in most elections but is represented by one of the leaders of the Democratic Party, Vic Fazio. Fazio grew up and went to college back East; he moved to California in the late 1960s and made his life work politics and legislation. He was a lobbyist in Sacramento, long California's most political locale, a staffer for Assembly Speaker Bob Moretti in the early 1970s and a founder of the *California Journal*. He was elected to the Assembly in 1974, the great breakthrough year for liberal Democrats. In 1978 he was elected to the House, replacing an incumbent who was discovered to have two wives and families, one in California and the other back East. After only two years, Fazio became chairman of the Legislative Appropriations Subcommittee, the panel that handles Congress's own budget—the mayor of Capitol Hill. Fazio is a consummate political insider, always personable and articulate, entirely presentable outside the back rooms and private hallways; knowledgeable without being cynical, a sharp operator who keeps score and remembers friends and enemies, a politician who is anything but an innocent but who retains a certain idealism and a willingness to take serious risks for what he believes. He sponsored congressional pay raises in 1982, 1987 and 1989, and took much heat back home; he served on the Ethics Committee, where in 1989 he found violations of rules by Speaker Jim Wright. After Wright and Tony Coehlo resigned in 1989, Fazio became vice chairman of the Democratic Caucus, technically the number five position in the Democratic leadership. And after the 1994 elections, he easily moved up to become Caucus chairman.

The 1990s have been much more perilous politically for Fazio than the 1970s or 1980s: he became more powerful and more imperiled at the same time. In the late 1980s he headed the Democrats' national redistricting operation and in 1991 he was California House Democrats' chief agent in redistricting negotiations in Sacramento. But he and Speaker Willie Brown were unable to outmaneuver Governor Pete Wilson, and Fazio ended up with a new 3d District that was markedly less Democratic than those he had run in before. After the 1990 elections, he became chairman of the Democratic Congressional Campaign Committee, a post he had sought in 1986; the collapse of George Bush's candidacy on the West Coast helped him avoid great losses, but House Democrats lost 10 seats nationally, even as Bill Clinton was winning the presidency. The institutional advantages that Democrats had enjoyed were deteriorating, despite Fazio's best efforts; the extent of the rot became starkly apparent in his second term as campaign committee chairman, when Democrats lost 52 seats and control of the House in 1994. Despite grumbling about his campaign criticism of the "religious right," few Democrats believed that Fazio could have done much to avoid the debacle.

This same trend was apparent back home. In 1986 Fazio was reelected with 70% of the vote; in 1988 he was unopposed. In 1990 he spent $1 million to his opponent's $40,000 and won 55%–39%. Then came redistricting and in 1992 a better-known opponent, Bill Richardson, a longtime (1966–86) state senator from Southern California who settled in the Sacramento area and was a founder of the Gun Owners of America. But Fazio far outspent him, $1.9 million to $853,000 and argued that he was needed to protect McClellan Air Force Base, to maintain levees and the north's water supply and to promote the proposed Auburn Dam. Fazio won 51%–40%. He carried Yolo County 64%–30% and ran unspectacularly ahead in the Sacramento County suburbs, 49%–41%. But despite his stress on agriculture and water, he lost, 45%–46%, in the Sacramento Valley.

In 1993 and 1994 Fazio became a more visible member of the Democratic leadership as it came increasingly under attack. But his prominence did not always produce success—the Auburn Dam was defeated by a coalition of environmentalists and Republicans—and the demands on his time from the campaign committee and his faraway district became fierce. Fazio got national notice in June 1994 when he attacked Republicans for accepting support from the "radical" and "intolerant" religious right, and in response was attacked for "religious bigotry." At home, his Republican opponent was Tim LeFever, an unheralded 33-year-old real estate broker who attacked him for supporting environmentalism and gun control; he spent only $251,000 while Fazio raised over $1 million from PACs, second only to Speaker Thomas Foley. Fazio again spent $1.9 million, the eighth highest among House candidates. With all that, he won by only 50%–46%, carrying Yolo County 61%–35%, but running only narrowly ahead in Sacramento County (50%–46%) and trailing 53%–43% in the Sacramento Valley.

None of this deterred Fazio from soldiering on. He ran for Caucus chairman, and beat Kweisi Mfume 149–57. He became ranking member on House Oversight and led attempts to embarrass the Republicans into allowing a vote on the lobbyist gift ban. He emphasized his moderate votes, as when he supported the moderate Blue Dog Democrat budget. Despite all his work the 13,000-employee McClellan was on the base-closing list which was approved in September 1995; Bill Clinton, ever mindful of California's electoral votes, promised privatization of the base, and Fazio worked hard to get other uses—a research center on metal-casting, a microelectronics repair facility. But supporters of other Air Force repair bases blocked changes in the 60/40 law that requires 60% of repairs to be made on Air Force bases and thus limits McClellan's chances of survival. Fazio was also frustrated on the Auburn Dam. All four Sacramento area congressmen supported it; Fazio agreed with John Doolittle to allow a multipurpose design since Doolittle's district wants an increased water supply while the other three seek flood protection. But in June 1996 the dam was defeated 35–28 in the Transportation Committee by a combination of environment-minded Democrats and budget-conscious Republicans.

In the 1996 election Fazio was again opposed by LeFever and again raised vast sums of money. Fazio received the most PAC money in the country for House candidates for 1996—$1.3 million; Lefever spent more this time—$650,000, but Fazio again outspent him with $2.3 million, the sixth highest in the House in 1996. Fazio called LeFever an extremist on abortion and assault weapons. LeFever hit Fazio for his longtime opposition to the death penalty and in October 1996 ran an ad accusing him of supporting in the Assembly the determinate sentencing law under which Polly Klaas's murderer Richard Allen Davis gained early release. Arguably a legitimate issue; but LeFever's ad showed Davis's face morphing into Fazio's—a vile slur. There was perceptible recoil, and Fazio won 54%–41%. He carried Yolo 66%–29% and Sacramento 53%–41%, and trailed in the Sacramento Valley 51%–43%. This was Fazio's best showing since 1990. But the special circumstances and Clinton's narrow carry of the district may have given him special help. He is likely to face another tough challenge in 1998, perhaps from Sacramento County Assemblywoman Barbara Alby.

The People: Pop. 1990: 571,545; 18% rural; 11% age 65+; 76% White; 3% Black; 5% Asian; 1% Amer. Indian; 14% Hispanic origin. Households: 56% married couple families; 27% married couple fams. w. children; 53% college educ.; median household income: $30,296; per capita income: $13,786; median gross rent: $498; median house value: $118,300.

1996 Presidential Vote

Clinton (D)	103,507	(45%)
Dole (R)	101,651	(44%)
Perot (I)	15,921	(7%)
Other	7,858	(3%)

1992 Presidential Vote

Clinton (D)	99,781	(41%)
Bush (R)	90,799	(37%)
Perot (I)	53,323	(22%)

Rep. Vic Fazio (D)

Elected 1978; b. Oct. 11, 1942, Winchester, MA; home, West Sacramento; Union Col., B.A. 1965, CA St. U., 1969–72; Episcopalian; married (Judy).

Career: Legis. Consult., 1966–75; Co-founder, *The California Journal*; Consult. & Asst., CA Assembly Speaker, 1971–74; CA Assembly, 1975–78.

DC Office: 2113 RHOB 20515, 202-225-5716; Fax: 202-225-5141; e-mail: dcaucus@hr.house.gov.

District Offices: Red Bluff, 916-529-5629; Woodland, 916-666-5521.

Committees: *Democratic Caucus Chairman. Appropriations* (8th of 26 D): Agriculture, Rural Development, FDA & Related Agencies; Energy & Water Development (RMM); Legislative.

Group Ratings

	ADA	ACLU	AFS	LCV	CFA	CON	NFIB	COC	ACU	NTLC	CHC
1996	80	69	83	77	62	92	41	25	0	21	7
1995	85	—	—	56	77	16	—	38	8	—	—

National Journal Ratings

	1995 LIB — 1995 CONS			1996 LIB — 1996 CONS		
Economic	67%	—	32%	67%	—	33%
Social	80%	—	13%	79%	—	21%
Foreign	67%	—	32%	67%	—	33%

Key Votes of the 104th Congress

1. Reduce Medicare Growth $	N	5. Flag Amendment	N	9. Cuban Embargo	Y
2. Ovrd. Product Liab. Veto	N	6. Drop EPA Limits	Y	10. Bar Bosnia Troop $	N
3. Increase Min. Wage	Y	7. Repeal Assault-Weap. Ban	N	11. Cut Anti-Missile Defense	Y
4. Welfare Reform	N	8. Ovrd. Part. Birth Veto	N	12. Bar U.N. Uniforms	N

Election Results

1996 general	Vic Fazio (D)	118,663	(54%)	($2,320,330)
	Tim Lefever (R)	91,134	(41%)	($645,209)
	Others	11,940	(5%)	
1996 primary	Vic Fazio (D)	51,575	(82%)	
	Rodger McAfee (D)	11,419	(18%)	
1994 general	Vic Fazio (D)	97,093	(50%)	($1,972,033)
	Tim Lefever (R)	89,964	(46%)	($251,369)
	Ross Crain (Lib)	8,100	(4%)	

FOURTH DISTRICT

California sprang suddenly into existence: the Gold Rush of 1849 was followed by statehood and the creation of the first 27 counties in 1850. The new state's first boom area was the Mother Lode country in the foothills of the Sierras above Sacramento. Mining camps the size of eastern cities grew up in vacant valleys locked amid steep hills, with thousands of would-be millionaires gathered to find gold—though most of those who actually got rich did so by catering to miners' needs. In Placerville, John Studebaker had a buggy shop, Phillip Armour ran a butcher shop and Mark Hopkins had a dry goods store. The biggest mine in California was sunk in Grass Valley in 1857 and worked for half a century. But long before that, most of the Mother Lode country emptied out, leaving ghost towns and villages with hundreds of deserted houses—an antique vacation country left behind in time.

In the last 20 years the Mother Lode country has become a boom area again. Thousands of Californians—many of them families from smog-filled, middle-class suburbs of the Los Angeles basin and the San Francisco Bay area—looking for a more pleasant, small-town, orderly environment, found it here along fast-flowing creeks where the '49ers camped. For the first time since the 1860 Census, county populations rose sharply and old Victorian houses were renovated even as new subdivisions were built. Politically, this migration has changed the Mother Lode country from Democrat to Republican. The new migrants are tired of the cultures of therapy of the big metro areas and ready for more discipline. In 1976, nine Mother Lode counties from Sierra to Mariposa cast 118,000 votes, 50% for Jimmy Carter and 47% for Gerald Ford—close to the California average. In 1996 they cast 264,000 votes, 50% for Bob Dole and 37% for Bill Clinton, results closer to Idaho than coastal California.

The 4th Congressional District consists of most of the Mother Lode country plus the northeastern suburbs of Sacramento—Fair Oaks, Citrus Heights, Orangevale—and the old town of Folsom. The district runs northeast along I-80 into Auburn and Roseville in Placer County where the Mother Lode hills start, then up to the crest of the Sierra Nevada and over to the California shore of Lake Tahoe and the arid salt flats around Mono Lake. Politically, this is a solidly Republican area, though in 1992 Ross Perot cut deeply into the Republican vote.

The congressman from the 4th District is John Doolittle, a Republican with one of the most conservative voting records in the House. Doolittle grew up in the Los Angeles area and went to high school in Cupertino, in what now is Silicon Valley. His conservatism was annealed in the fires of adversity: he graduated from the University of California at Santa Cruz in 1972, when the campus was 97% for George McGovern. After law school he moved to Citrus Heights then Rocklin, at the edge of the Sacramento metro area where the foothills begin, and in 1980 was elected at 30 to the state Senate from a district that stretched up to the Oregon border. In Sacramento he made a record against gun control and abortion, and for a crime victims' bill of rights and widespread AIDS testing. When the incumbent retired in 1990 in a district that then stretched from the Mother Lode country to Stockton, Doolittle ran for the seat. He had tougher competition than expected from Democrat Patricia Malberg, a former ski champion and onetime healthcare worker in Africa who was pro-choice on abortion, against nuclear power and for defense spending cuts; Doolittle won by just 50%–46%.

In the 102d Congress Doolittle was one of the less prominent members of the Gang of Seven freshman Republicans who demanded full disclosure of House bank overdrafts. But he was also the House's top user of franked mail, and in 1991 he joined Democrat Maxine Waters in calling for Sacramento-style perks: more staff, $92 daily expense allowances, and more cellular phones for members. He was California House Republicans' point man on redistricting, but he supported a plan that only protected Republican incumbents and gave them no shot at California's seven new seats; this was nixed by Governor Pete Wilson. In 1992 he had a second matchup with Malberg and won again by 50%–46%. In the 103d Congress he made fewer headlines and again had a very conservative record. Perhaps to curry favor with the 25% of the district who voted for Ross Perot in 1992, Doolittle joined his group "United We Stand America." In 1994 he seemed finally to get a firm hold on the district, beating Democrat Katie Hirning, a manager at New Generation Software, 61%–35%.

In the Republican House, Doolittle was given a subcommittee chair the old Democrats who represented this area would have relished: Water and Power Resources. But his agenda resembled theirs only in part. That was the Auburn Dam, which he and other Sacramento area congressmen want built on the American River, 35 miles east of Sacramento. They were interested in flood control; Doolittle insisted on a design that could supply water to the Mother Lode. But in 1996 the dam was rejected in committee, 35–28, by a combination of environmentalists and spending opponents. Doolittle's other plans on the subcommittee are longer range, and also unrealized. He seeks to sell the government's Power Marketing Administrations, which subsidize electric power in some areas because they needed power lines built in the 1930s. But Doolittle's efforts to sell the Southeastern Power Administration was nixed in October 1995 when Speaker Newt Gingrich heeded the plea of the Republican nominee for Governor of Kentucky Larry Forgy (he lost in November anyway). Doolittle also seeks to change the environmental provisions imposed on the Central Valley Project in 1992; he has had some success pressuring the Clinton Administration on this. He also supported the successful timber salvage measure allowing logging of dead or dying timber.

Doolittle was easily reelected in 1996. He started 1997 by proposing funding for the restoration of Yosemite National Park after flooding. He has also proposed a campaign finance reform which would remove existing restrictions on fundraising but provide daily disclosure of contributions: free expression and transparency.

The People: Pop. 1990: 571,027; 38% rural; 12% age 65+; 88% White; 2% Black; 2% Asian; 1% Amer. Indian; 7% Hispanic origin. Households: 63% married couple families; 28% married couple fams. w. children; 58% college educ.; median household income: $35,772; per capita income: $16,263; median gross rent: $569; median house value: $152,400.

1996 Presidential Vote			**1992 Presidential Vote**		
Dole (R)	145,223	(51%)	Bush (R)	117,155	(40%)
Clinton (D)	107,076	(38%)	Clinton (D)	97,501	(34%)
Perot (I)	21,233	(7%)	Perot (I)	73,060	(25%)
Other	9,775	(3%)			

Rep. John T. Doolittle (R)

Elected 1990; b. Oct. 30, 1950, Glendale; home, Rocklin; U. of CA at Santa Cruz, B.A. 1972, U. of the Pacific, J.D. 1978; Mormon; married (Julia).

Career: Practicing atty., 1978–80; CA Senate, 1980–90, Repub. Caucus Chmn., 1987–90.

DC Office: 1526 LHOB 20515, 202-225-2511; Fax: 202-225-5444.

District Offices: Roseville, 916-786-5560.

Committees: *Agriculture* (6th of 27 R): Forestry, Resource Conservation & Research; Risk Management & Specialty Crops. *Resources* (8th of 27 R): Forests & Forest Health; Water & Power (Chmn.). *Joint Economic Committee* (5th of 10 Reps.).

Group Ratings

	ADA	ACLU	AFS	LCV	CFA	CON	NFIB	COC	ACU	NTLC	CHC
1996	5	25	0	15	0	22	97	94	100	100	100
1995	0	—	—	0	0	56	—	96	100	—	—

National Journal Ratings

	1995 LIB — 1995 CONS			1996 LIB — 1996 CONS		
Economic	0%	—	74%	0%	—	82%
Social	0%	—	79%	24%	—	72%
Foreign	15%	—	73%	0%	—	79%

Key Votes of the 104th Congress

1. Reduce Medicare Growth $	Y	5. Flag Amendment	Y	9. Cuban Embargo	Y
2. Ovrd. Product Liab. Veto	Y	6. Drop EPA Limits	N	10. Bar Bosnia Troop $	Y
3. Increase Min. Wage	N	7. Repeal Assault-Weap. Ban	Y	11. Cut Anti-Missile Defense	N
4. Welfare Reform	Y	8. Ovrd. Part. Birth Veto	Y	12. Bar U.N. Uniforms	Y

Election Results

1996 general	John T. Doolittle (R)	164,048	(60%)	($604,778)
	Katie Hirning (D)	97,948	(36%)	($199,179)
	Others	9,319	(3%)	
1996 primary	John T. Doolittle (R)	unopposed		
1994 general	John T. Doolittle (R)	144,936	(61%)	($664,109)
	Katie Hirning (D)	82,505	(35%)	($354,786)
	Others	8,882	(4%)	

FIFTH DISTRICT

Sacramento, capital of the nation's largest state, focus of California's third-largest media market, home of a national sports franchise (the NBA's Sacramento Kings) and an 18-mile light rail system, is no longer just a small city with a lot of civil servants and a vegetable-packing economy. It is a vibrant major American metropolis, with some of the nation's highest job growth. Sacramento started as a river port on the sluggish waters of the Sacramento and American Rivers. It was the destination of many overland migrants, the site of Sutter's Fort where John Augustus Sutter found the gold that set off the Gold Rush of 1849, and the western terminus of the Pony Express in 1860. This was the natural choice to be California's capital, halfway between the San Francisco Bay and the Mother Lode country in the foothills of the Sierras, and in the middle of California's vast valley. Agriculture continues to be important today in Sacra-tomato (as some call it)—it has the world's largest almond processing plant.

In the old days, government was not a big business. Just a few lobbyists hung out in saloons on K or J Streets, the governor's mansion was a musty antique, and the 100-plus degree summers emptied out what there was of the city. But air conditioning has replaced awnings, freeways and shopping malls have followed the city's growth east and north toward the Sierra foothills, and affluence has made this one of America's higher income metropolitan areas. In the 1980s metropolitan Sacramento grew 35%, more than any other large metro area except that other western capital, Phoenix, to more than 1.5 million. Even military base closedowns have not stopped the surge; the city extended benefits to get the computer maker Packard Bell, the number-one U.S. PC retailer to move to the Sacramento Army Depot after its headquarters was destroyed in the 1994 Northridge earthquake. Government expanded, too, even under conservative Republican governors Ronald Reagan and George Deukmejian, and Sacramento is now the home of platoons of lobbyists, lawyers and consultants.

As Sacramento has grown, it has also become more Republican: this once Democratic, pro-government, working-class bastion has become something much closer to an upscale Sun Belt boom town. Sacramento County voted against Ronald Reagan for governor in 1966 and 1970, but voted for him for president in 1980 and 1984; it spurned Richard Nixon and Gerald Ford in the 1970s but voted for George Bush in 1988 and voted for Bill Clinton by about 1% more than his national average in 1992 and 1996. Civil servants and the *Sacramento Bee* once made the city Democratic, but private sector growth and immigration have helped Republicans.

The 5th District consists of the center of metropolitan Sacramento; the metro area now includes parts of three other districts. The 5th contains affluent neighborhoods on older grid streets and scattered low-income black, Mexican-American and Hmong neighborhoods, as well as new condominiums north of the American River and middle-class subdivisions south of downtown. Politically, this includes most of Sacramento's remaining Democratic neighborhoods, and it is now the most Democratic district in the great valley from Bakersfield north to Oregon.

The congressman from the 5th is Robert Matsui, a Democrat first elected in 1978, a member of the Ways and Means Committee and one of the most influential House Democrats on a number of important issues. Born in 1941, the infant Matsui and his family were among the West Coast Japanese Americans forced into internment camps in 1942, and although he has no memory of the experience himself, he does remember the silence his family and others maintained about it. It was Asian shame, when none of the victims had anything to be ashamed about. He was one of the lead sponsors of the 1988 Japanese American redress law which apologized for the internment policy and provided monetary compensation for every survivor of the camps and for so-called "voluntary evacuees." He also sponsored the creation of the Manzanar National Historic Site, near Bishop, California, to preserve the memory of this episode.

Matsui has played a role in national politics, as treasurer of the Democratic National Committee from 1991–95 and deputy chairman in 1995 and 1996; his wife Doris Matsui has been deputy director of public liaison in the White House since 1993. It should be added that as news of Clinton campaign finance scandals came out, no allegation of misconduct appeared about either of the Matsuis. Matsui has also taken a lead on Internet issues. He opposed the Community Decency Act, which allowed government action to keep Internet material from minors; his own Internet Freedom and Empowerment Act, to encourage the private sector to improve user control passed overwhelmingly, but was brushed aside in the Telecommunications Reform Act conference committee for the CDA. Matsui would like to replace it with a law requiring Internet providers to make available software that would allow parents to protect minors from obscene material. He also wants more computers in schools, especially in California, which amazingly enough is a laggard in this regard; in March 1996 he helped organize Congressional involvement for NetDay '96, in which 50,000 volunteers helped wire 3,500 California schools.

Much of Matsui's work has been done on Ways and Means, on which he is now third ranking Democrat. He was a hard-working supporter of the 1986 rate-lowering, preference-cutting tax reform. In 1993 he passed a program to deal with child abuse and neglect and to encourage family preservation. In 1994 he advanced his own welfare reform plan requiring job training and education. As ranking Democrat on the Oversight Subcommittee in 1996, he co-sponsored the Taxpayer Bill of Rights II with Chairman Nancy Johnson. Matsui is one of the strongest proponents of free trade in the Democratic Party; he is now ranking member of the Trade Subcommittee. In early 1993 he took the lead among House Democrats in seeking approval of the North American Free Trade Agreement, even when the Clinton Administration was lukewarm, then-Majority Leader Dick Gephardt was opposed and then-Minority Whip Newt Gingrich was not engaged in the issue. Working with Republican Jim Kolbe of Arizona, he rallied support and let the White House know that NAFTA was foundering and would not pass without a major push. Matsui has always been for MFN status for China, but his stand was reinforced when he was approached in Frank Fat's (the prime politicians' restaurant in

Sacramento) by owner Frank Fat who asked him to support it; Matsui realized that the majority of Asian Americans were leaning toward MFN.

Matsui has also worked on local issues. He seeks to connect the Sacramento and Folsom light rail systems and to get authorization in ISTEA renewal for Sacramento's South Line extension. He has struggled for the Auburn Dam to provide greater flood protection for Sacramento, and supported John Doolittle's version which would also use the dam for water supply; but it was voted down by environmentalists and economizers in the Transportation and Infrastructure Committee in June 1996. He has a bill to preserve healthcare services for military retirees—important locally because Sacramento's McClellan Air Force Base is being closed and possibly privatized. Matsui has flirted with running for other office over the years—against then-Senator Pete Wilson in 1988, for attorney general in 1990, for the Senate seat Alan Cranston vacated in 1992—but decided each time not to; with his seniority now he seems to have no interest in a statewide race. Matsui has remained politically strong in Sacramento. In 1996 his opponent pledged to wage a "polite campaign." Matsui spent much time raising money for Democratic candidates elsewhere, and won by 70%–26%.

The People: Pop. 1990: 573,659; 11% age 65+; 59% White; 12% Black; 13% Asian; 1% Amer. Indian; 15% Hispanic origin. Households: 45% married couple families; 21% married couple fams. w. children; 57% college educ.; median household income: $29,974; per capita income: $14,661; median gross rent: $505; median house value: $121,000.

1996 Presidential Vote

Clinton (D)	119,678	(57%)
Dole (R)	70,925	(34%)
Perot (I)	10,863	(5%)
Other	8,159	(4%)

1992 Presidential Vote

Clinton (D)	120,577	(50%)
Bush (R)	73,562	(31%)
Perot (I)	42,566	(18%)

Rep. Robert T. Matsui (D)

Elected 1978; b. Sept. 17, 1941, Sacramento; home, Sacramento; U. of CA at Berkeley, A.B. 1963, J.D. 1966; United Methodist; married (Doris).

Career: Practicing atty., 1967–78; Sacramento City Cncl., 1971–78.

DC Office: 2308 RHOB 20515, 202-225-7163; Fax: 202-225-0566; e-mail: ca05@hr.house.gov.

District Offices: Sacramento, 916-498-5600.

Committees: *Ways & Means* (3rd of 16 D): Human Resources; Trade (RMM).

Group Ratings

	ADA	ACLU	AFS	LCV	CFA	CON	NFIB	COC	ACU	NTLC	CHC
1996	85	94	100	77	92	91	22	19	0	8	0
1995	90	—	—	94	100	9	—	22	8	—	—

National Journal Ratings

	1995 LIB — 1995 CONS			1996 LIB — 1996 CONS		
Economic	92%	—	6%	82%	—	16%
Social	75%	—	25%	88%	—	0%
Foreign	73%	—	24%	73%	—	26%

Key Votes of the 104th Congress

1. Reduce Medicare Growth $	N	5. Flag Amendment	N	9. Cuban Embargo	Y
2. Ovrd. Product Liab. Veto	N	6. Drop EPA Limits	Y	10. Bar Bosnia Troop $	N
3. Increase Min. Wage	Y	7. Repeal Assault-Weap. Ban	N	11. Cut Anti-Missile Defense	Y
4. Welfare Reform	N	8. Ovrd. Part. Birth Veto	N	12. Bar U.N. Uniforms	N

Election Results

1996 general	Robert T. Matsui (D)	142,618	(70%)	($814,857)
	Robert S. Dinsmore (R)	52,940	(26%)	($18,792)
	Others	6,902	(3%)	
1996 primary	Robert T. Matsui (D)	unopposed		
1994 general	Robert T. Matsui (D)	125,042	(68%)	($929,464)
	Robert S. Dinsmore (R)	52,905	(29%)	($74,212)
	Others	4,649	(3%)	

SIXTH DISTRICT

When the Golden Gate bridge was opened in 1937, San Francisco was one of the nation's best-known cities, but few knew much about the land beyond the bridge's north pierhead. There were fewer than 50,000 people in Marin County then and another 65,000 just to the north in Sonoma County. For San Franciscans, Marin was known for the ferry terminus in Sausalito, a fishing village and art colony, and as the beginning of the Redwood Empire, with its giant trees in Muir Woods; near the Bay was the state prison at San Quentin, with its infamous gas chamber. Farther north, in a sunny valley protected from the fog by the Coast Range, was Santa Rosa, site of agronomist Luther Burbank's laboratory, a town that looked Middle American enough to be the set for dozens of movies. Politically, the area was then typical of the nation: traditionally Republican, but favoring Franklin Roosevelt in the 1930s.

Today this part of California is far more populous, with 230,000 people in Marin and 388,000 in Sonoma, solidly a part of the San Francisco Bay Area, affluent beyond the dreams of the Americans of 50 years ago and extreme in its cultural attitudes. Trendy Marin, with its hot tubs and its fashionable people getting in touch with themselves, became a national caricature in the late 1970s: economically affluent, culturally liberationist. After a while such an image feeds on itself; a place like Marin attracts affluent people who share its values, while those who don't go elsewhere—in the Bay Area to the much more conservative San Ramon Valley, amid the mountains east of Oakland. Indeed the Bay Area as a whole seems to attract liberals and repel conservatives, just as Phoenix does the opposite. And Marin and Sonoma are attracting the most liberal of the liberal—averse to traditional religion, derisive of traditional sexual and marriage mores, viscerally anti-military.

The 6th Congressional District of California includes all of Marin County and most of Sonoma. Republican as recently as 1980, in 1996 the 6th voted 57%–29% for Bill Clinton over Bob Dole. The public dialogue here is increasingly monopartisan, and in this community priding itself on its tolerance nary a dissenting word is heard.

The Congresswoman from the 6th District is Lynn Woolsey, a Democrat elected in 1992 when 10-year incumbent Barbara Boxer was elected to the Senate. Woolsey grew up in the Pacific Northwest, moved to Marin 30 years ago and was a housewife with three children under 6 when her marriage ended in 1968. She went on welfare, got a low-paying job and left her children with 13 different babysitters in a year. Deliverance appeared in the form of a job with a high-tech startup firm where she rose to become a top executive. She remarried and moved to a house in

Petaluma where her mother could live and look after the kids. As she wrote in her campaign literature, "Finally I could concentrate on work. The children had good care at last!" She put herself through business school at night, earned a degree in human resources and started her own personnel service.

In 1984 Woolsey won a seat on the Petaluma Council and is proud of its record in limiting growth (Marin and Sonoma, with their low-growth policies, are becoming less important demographically in California), setting up affirmative action programs and a Women of Color Task Force, requiring that 15% of new housing be reserved for low-income buyers and establishing a voucher system for low-income families' child care. "I know what it means to have an effective safety net to help people get back on their feet," she campaigned. "I know what a bottom line means. I have made the tough decisions to keep our City prosperous in the post-Proposition 13 era." In 1992 she ran for the House. In a nine-candidate primary she faced well-known members of the Marin and Sonoma Boards of Supervisors and the well-financed J. Bennett Johnston III, son of the Louisiana Senator. But in that year of the woman, she ran first in the primary with 26%, well ahead of the next candidate's 19%. In the general she faced liberal Republican Assemblyman Bill Filante. But he had surgery for a brain tumor and stopped campaigning, and she won 65%–34%.

Woolsey has had just about the most liberal voting record in the House. As the only known former welfare recipient in Congress, she co-chaired the Democrats' task force on welfare reform. She opposed the 1996 Welfare Reform Act, and calls for easing work requirements and providing more child care; she wants mothers to be able to stay at home till their children are 11, not 6. With Henry Hyde, she has attacked current child support computer systems and calls for enforcement by the IRS. She lobbied against banning gays in the military, accompanied by her son who is gay. She wants to let school districts use federal aid to provide health services. She has called for a permanent ban on offshore oil drilling. She favors export subsidies for winemakers. Her big local project is to expand the protected area around the Point Reyes National Seashore by purchasing easements from nearby farmers and barring them from selling to nonagricultural users. She has also worked to restore the Russian River and Bolinas Lagoon, to save the Two Rocks Coast Guard training base and to get the Army Corps of Engineers to work on flood control in Petaluma.

Woolsey was reelected by wide margins in 1994 and 1996.

The People: Pop. 1990: 571,360; 19% rural; 13% age 65+; 85% White; 2% Black; 3% Asian; 1% Amer. Indian; 9% Hispanic origin. Households: 53% married couple families; 23% married couple fams. w. children; 67% college educ.; median household income: $40,564; per capita income: $21,603; median gross rent: $709; median house value: $255,900.

1996 Presidential Vote

Clinton (D)	155,513	(57%)
Dole (R)	78,166	(29%)
Perot (I)	18,431	(7%)
Other	21,199	(8%)

1992 Presidential Vote

Clinton (D)	169,301	(56%)
Bush (R)	71,564	(24%)
Perot (I)	60,920	(20%)

Rep. Lynn Woolsey (D)

Elected 1992; b. Nov. 3, 1937, Seattle, WA; home, Petaluma; U. of San Francisco, B.A. 1980; Presbyterian; divorced.

Career: Human Resources Mgr., Harris Digital Telephone, 1969–80; Owner, Woolsey Personnel Svc., 1980–92; Petaluma City Cncl., 1985–92, Vice Mayor, 1986, 1991.

DC Office: 439 CHOB 20515, 202-225-5161; Fax: 202-225-5163; e-mail: woolsey@hr.house.gov.

District Offices: San Rafael, 415-507-9554; Santa Rosa, 707-542-7182.

Committees: *Budget* (7th of 19 D). *Education & The Workforce* (11th of 20 D): Postsecondary Education, Training & Life-Long Learning; Workforce Protections.

Group Ratings

	ADA	ACLU	AFS	LCV	CFA	CON	NFIB	COC	ACU	NTLC	CHC
1996	95	88	100	85	92	42	22	19	0	2	0
1995	100	—	—	100	85	16	—	17	4	—	—

National Journal Ratings

	1995 LIB — 1995 CONS			1996 LIB — 1996 CONS		
Economic	94%	—	0%	89%	—	0%
Social	88%	—	0%	88%	—	0%
Foreign	93%	—	0%	90%	—	0%

Key Votes of the 104th Congress

1. Reduce Medicare Growth $	N	5. Flag Amendment	N	9. Cuban Embargo	N
2. Ovrd. Product Liab. Veto	N	6. Drop EPA Limits	Y	10. Bar Bosnia Troop $	N
3. Increase Min. Wage	Y	7. Repeal Assault-Weap. Ban	N	11. Cut Anti-Missile Defense	Y
4. Welfare Reform	N	8. Ovrd. Part. Birth Veto	N	12. Bar U.N. Uniforms	N

Election Results

1996 general	Lynn Woolsey (D)	156,958	(62%)	($542,131)
	Duane C. Hughes (R)	86,278	(34%)	($292,181)
	Others	10,600	(4%)	
1996 primary	Lynn Woolsey (D)	unopposed		
1994 general	Lynn Woolsey (D)	137,642	(58%)	($649,388)
	Michael J. Nugent (R)	88,940	(38%)	(456,901)
	Others	10,258	(4%)	

SEVENTH DISTRICT

The journey inward from the Pacific Ocean to the vast flatness of California's Central Valley passes through wondrous terrain. The traveler starts at the Golden Gate, with the lush green Presidio on one side and the bluff of the Marin mountains on the other; through the waters of San Francisco Bay, looked down upon by ridges above the East Bay on one side and the cone of Mount Tamalpais on the other; through the narrow Carquinez Strait to Suisun Bay, with its sloughs and marshes, fed by the sluggish waters of the Sacramento and San Joaquin Delta; and finally past the mountains and waters, to the flat, fertile expanse of California's great interior. This is not a journey most tourists make, but it was a familiar route to the first Californians and it passes by much of the industrial base of the Bay Area. On the east side of the bay is Richmond, developed almost instantaneously during World War II when Henry J. Kaiser built a shipyard in its deep water port and 91,000 people from all over the country were put to work building ships for the Pacific theater; it now has a large black population and is attracting high-tech spinoffs. Across Carquinez Strait is Vallejo, named for a Mexican general and member of the first California Senate, the site since 1853 of the giant Mare Island Naval Shipyard. Across the strait are tank farms and factories in Rodeo and Pittsburg and Martinez, the seat of Contra Costa County (literally, the coast opposite San Francisco).

The 7th Congressional District of California includes most of this passage, from Richmond and El Cerrito along both sides of Carquinez Strait and Suisun Bay to Vallejo, Rodeo, Martinez and Pittsburg. It also proceeds inland through the intermountain interstices of Contra Costa County to include most of middle-income Concord, but excludes the heavily Republican and higher-income interior Contra Costa communities around Walnut Hill and the San Ramon Valley. Politically, this industrial area was blue-collar, labor-union Democratic back in the days when San Francisco, with its larger white-collar and professional population, often voted Republican. Today it is heavily Democratic, liberal on most issues, though not so far left as San Francisco or Berkeley.

The congressman from the 7th District is George Miller, one of the few remaining Democrats of the Watergate class of 1974, the first baby-boom liberal to chair a House committee. He is also heir to a tradition of Bay Area working-class politics. His father was chairman of the state Senate Finance Committee; when he died in 1969, Miller lost the race to succeed him, but became a staffer for Senate Leader (and later San Francisco Mayor) George Moscone. Miller was also a protege of the San Francisco Congressman Phillip Burton, who did so much to establish liberal hegemony in the House roundabout 1974; he backed Miller in his first race and saw to it that he served on the same two committees, then called Interior and Education and Labor. To his work Miller brings an aggressiveness and zest for political combat reminiscent of Burton. He is a strong backer of protecting the environment against what he sees as greedy private sector operators and of furthering the causes of labor unions in the private and public sector.

Miller started off the 1990s in a position of power, able to advance his causes forward; in the middle 1990s he found himself defending yesterday's gains and trying to prevent losses. In 1991 he became chairman of Interior (he renamed it Natural Resources in 1993 and Republicans renamed it Resources in 1995) and proceeded, in his words, "to kick ass and take names." He had long crusaded against water reclamation projects that provided cheap water to farmers. In 1992, amid a California drought, he passed a Central Valley Project law that raised farmers' prices closer to urban users and imposed environmental restrictions, over the fierce opposition of Central Valley politicians and Governor Pete Wilson. The victory was sealed when Bill Clinton appointed a top Miller aide as head of the Bureau of Reclamation. But the Clinton Administration was not always helpful on other matters. Miller strongly backed higher mining, grazing and timber fees for companies operating on federal lands, and he was dismayed when Clinton dropped Interior Secretary Bruce Babbitt's proposal for these in March 1993. Nor were his plans for an environmental cleanup of federal lands or expansion of Yellowstone and Rocky Mountain National Parks adopted. He did stand up for the Endangered Species Act in the controversy over the spotted owl and logging in the Pacific Northwest. And he was successful in passing the California desert bill, with Senator Dianne Feinstein: the last major legislation of the Democratic Congress in October 1994. But the month before, Miller had to admit that Senate inaction would prevent revision of the Mining Act of 1872, which he believes allows mining companies to stake claims and extract resources from federal lands for minuscule fees.

Ironically, Miller has had more successes since 1994—but successes in preventing change, not making change. He helped to stymie John Doolittle's attempt to revise the Central Valley Project and with conservative help beat the Auburn Dam sought by Doolittle and other Sacramento area congressmen. He attacked Republicans harshly for trying to change the Endangered Species Act, EPA regulations, Arctic National Wildlife Refuge oil drilling,

Tongass Forest logging and commercial sponsorship of national parks. To make political points, he sponsored bills to make farmers repay the cost of water subsidies and prohibit loan guarantees to Mexico until it cracks down on drugs. In 1995 he became vice-chairman of the House Democratic Policy Committee, and helped initiate attacks on Republican proposals on school lunches and Medicare as well as environmental laws and their initial inaction on the lobbyist gift ban. With no power to hold official hearings, he held ad hoc hearings, including one on Kathie Lee Gifford's unknowing use of child labor, which he used to promote child-labor-free labelling. He worked for the Presidio private-public trust fund and Bay-Delta funding in the successful 1996 parks bill, for the Manzanar National Historic Site commemorating one of the Japanese American detention camps in World War II and for the time waiver so that Congressional Medals of Honor could be granted black heroes from World War II who were unfairly overlooked at the time. Miller's liberalism does take a few unpredictable turns. In the 104th Congress he backed more flexibility in school lunch menus, accusing the USDA of overregulation; in the 1980s, as the first chairman of the Special Committee on Children and Youth he opposed the ABC child care plan sponsored by Marian Wright Edelman and favored a measure with more parent choice and less government supervision.

Miller's district is even safer in the 1990s than in the 1980s, thanks to redistricting, and he is reelected by overwhelming margins.

The People: Pop. 1990: 572,857; 10% age 65+; 56% White; 16% Black; 14% Asian; 1% Amer. Indian; 13% Hispanic origin. Households: 54% married couple families; 26% married couple fams. w. children; 57% college educ.; median household income: $38,608; per capita income: $16,006; median gross rent: $625; median house value: $167,000.

1996 Presidential Vote			**1992 Presidential Vote**		
Clinton (D)	131,707	(65%)	Clinton (D)	140,159	(60%)
Dole (R)	50,140	(25%)	Bush (R)	51,356	(22%)
Perot (I)	12,178	(6%)	Perot (I)	39,038	(17%)
Other	7,321	(4%)			

Rep. George Miller (D)

Elected 1974; b. May 17, 1945, Richmond; home, Martinez; San Francisco St. U., B.A. 1968, U. of CA at Davis, J.D. 1972; Catholic; married (Cynthia).

Career: Legis. aide, CA Sen. Majority Ldr., 1969–74; Practicing atty., 1972–74.

DC Office: 2205 RHOB 20515, 202-225-2095; Fax: 202-225-5609; e-mail: gmiller@hr.house.gov.

District Offices: Pleasant Hill, 510-602-1880; Richmond, 510-262-6500.

Committees: *Education & The Workforce* (2nd of 20 D): Early Childhood, Youth & Families; Workforce Protections. *Resources* (RMM): Water & Power.

Group Ratings

	ADA	ACLU	AFS	LCV	CFA	CON	NFIB	COC	ACU	NTLC	CHC
1996	90	79	100	85	100	81	19	13	0	5	0
1995	95	—	—	94	85	16	—	17	8	—	—

National Journal Ratings

	1995 LIB — 1995 CONS			1996 LIB — 1996 CONS		
Economic	94%	—	0%	82%	—	16%
Social	88%	—	0%	88%	—	0%
Foreign	93%	—	0%	90%	—	0%

Key Votes of the 104th Congress

1. Reduce Medicare Growth $	N	5. Flag Amendment	N	9. Cuban Embargo	N
2. Ovrd. Product Liab. Veto	N	6. Drop EPA Limits	Y	10. Bar Bosnia Troop $	N
3. Increase Min. Wage	Y	7. Repeal Assault-Weap. Ban	N	11. Cut Anti-Missile Defense	Y
4. Welfare Reform	*	8. Ovrd. Part. Birth Veto	N	12. Bar U.N. Uniforms	N

Election Results

1996 general	George Miller (D)	137,089	(72%)	($434,745)
	Norman H. Reece (R)	42,542	(22%)	($41,147)
	Others	11,286	(6%)	
1996 primary	George Miller (D)	unopposed		
1994 general	George Miller (D)	116,105	(70%)	($442,581)
	Charles V. Hughes (R)	45,698	(27%)	($2,432)
	Others	4,798	(3%)	

EIGHTH DISTRICT

On February 20, 1915, Governor Hiram Johnson and Mayor James Rolph led 150,000 people onto the grounds of the Panama-Pacific International Exposition to see the Spanish-Italian baroque style building built on reclaimed land in what became San Francisco's Marina district. The Exposition ostensibly celebrated the completion of the Panama Canal, but it was clearly intended to show off San Francisco's recovery from the 1906 earthquake. It also spotlighted San Francisco as the central focus of an America that was becoming, with its acquisition of Hawaii and the Philippines and its interest in an open door policy with China and trade with Japan, a power in what we now call the Pacific Rim.

The Exposition set the physical style of San Francisco: it encouraged the use of Mediterranean color, accent and detail that characterizes most post-Victorian houses and commercial structures in The City (as the *San Francisco Examiner* still calls it). It created the picturesque Marina district, whose old buildings were among the few damaged in the 1989 earthquake, and today's tourist waterfront around Fisherman's Wharf and Ghirardelli Square. This San Francisco has many facets: on a sunny day it looks almost tropical, with brown mountains baking in the sun and light shining off the pastel stucco buildings; when the clouds scud in from the Pacific, it can look sinister, full of dark corners where a private detective's partner might be ambushed by a pretty girl. The buildings can be majestic, like the monumental Beaux Arts City Hall, or tawdry, like the hotels of the Tenderloin; it is a city that looks exotic at first but, when you look closely, can only be American.

San Francisco has been a dynamic city, capable of great growth, carrying the American tradition of tolerance of diversity to new lengths; it grew from nothing to a major city in the single year of 1850; its American origins are obvious from the regular grids of streets named after politicians and local developers. The San Francisco of 1915 was proud of the writers who had flourished there—Jack London, Ambrose Bierce, Frank Norris—and of the home-town traditions of the arts and crafts movement, just as San Francisco later would have a Herb Caenish pride in the beats of the 1950s North Beach, the hippies who thronged Haight-Ashbury in 1967, and the gays of Castro in the 1970s and 1980s. Over the years, the city's booming economy, based initially on food processing, but now on finance, high-tech and clothing (Levi Strauss, The Gap) has attracted talented newcomers, weighted increasingly toward those who find its liberation-minded cultural attitudes congenial.

Politically, San Francisco was a progressive Republican town, like the two men who led the way into the Exposition. The sour-tempered Hiram Johnson made his name as a reformer throwing out crooked city politicians; his administration gave California primary elections, referenda and recall, and strong civil service laws. "Sunny Jim" Rolph, mayor from 1911–30 and then governor, built the civic center, parks, schools, streetcars and the Hetch Hetchy power lines—the antique infrastructure of San Francisco today. Sympathetic to the conservation movement, willing to deal with organized labor in a union town that had America's only general strike in 1934, as tolerant of the diversity of California as the anti-Chinese working class movements of the 19th Century were not, these progressive Republicans were the recognizable ancestors of, though certainly not identical to, the San Franciscans who in the 1970s and 1980s became increasingly liberal and even radical.

But San Francisco's hipness can be overstated. For if its distinctive style attracted liberal singles and gays in increasing numbers, its economic dynamism on the Pacific Rim has attracted Asians—as indeed San Francisco did from 1850 until immigration was shut off by the Chinese Exclusion Act in 1882. The city has elected strong liberal politicians at least since the 1975 elections of Mayor George Moscone and openly gay Supervisor Harvey Milk, who were shot to death in 1978 by a political opponent who was acquitted of murder by a liberal jury on the bizarre theory that he had been crazed by junk food. Over the next ten years, the city's cultural liberalism was tempered by Mayor Dianne Feinstein, who vetoed a gay marriage ordinance and opposed commercial rent control. When her successor Art Agnos promised shelter to every homeless person in the city and allowed a homeless colony ("Camp Agnos") across from City Hall, he was ousted in 1991 by former police chief Frank Jordan, backed by Asian Americans and white homeowners. Jordan's crackdown on the homeless was attacked by liberals on the Board of Supervisors, and Jordan lost 57%–43% in 1995 to the more liberal Willie Brown, ousted after 15 years as speaker of the Assembly. But the result owed something to Jordan's poor judgment (he posed nude in a shower with two male disc jockeys) and Brown admitted that he didn't want another Camp Agnos and didn't know how to solve the homeless problem in a way acceptable to San Francisco's civil libertarians. Increasingly the key voting bloc in the city are Americans of Chinese, Filipino and other Asian descent, less concerned about living outer lifestyles, more concerned about working their way into the middle class and owning homes in safe and orderly neighborhoods.

The 8th Congressional District of California takes in four-fifths of San Francisco, all but the southwest corner. It has all of San Francisco's high-rise downtown, the increasingly crowded and bustling Chinatown, Telegraph, Nob and Russian Hills, North Beach (which was once really a beach), Pacific Heights (which is still on heights) and the Marina District (which does not have a very big marina). It extends to the ocean to include Sea Cliff overlooking the Golden Gate Bridge, and the Richmond area with its many Asian Americans. In the valleys are the mostly black Fillmore and Western Addition areas, but only 12% of the district's residents are black, as compared to 16% Hispanic and 27% Asian—the highest Asian percentage of any district outside Hawaii. The 8th also has the gay Castro district and Noe Valley, Haight-Ashbury, once the bedraggled center of hippiedom and now another yup-and-coming San Francisco neighborhood, and Portrero Hill with its restored houses overlooking downtown. Farther south are the old residential areas between Candlestick Park, the Cow Palace and I-280, with pastel houses strewn out along grid streets which hug the steep hills.

The 8th District is represented by Nancy Pelosi, a Democrat with deep political roots and a capacity for keeping all parts of her party happy. She has the energy and shrewdness of one who has handled the most delicate political chores and the charm and unflappability of one who has been the parent of five children. Pelosi grew up in Maryland; her father, Thomas D'Alessandro, served in the House from 1939–47 and was mayor of Baltimore for 12 years after that, and her brother, Thomas D'Alessandro Jr., was mayor from 1967–71. Married to a successful San Francisco businessman, she was California Democratic Party chair in the early 1980s, chaired the national party's Compliance Review Commission on delegate rules for 1984, and served as the Democratic Senatorial Campaign Committee's finance chair in 1985. She never considered running for the House when San Francisco's congressional politics was dominated by Phillip Burton, congressman since 1964, an old-fashioned labor-liberal Democrat and opponent of the Vietnam war from the beginning. But Burton died in 1983 and his widow Sala, elected to succeed him, died in 1987. Pelosi ran and won 35%–31% in an April 1987 special primary against gay supervisor Harry Britt.

Pelosi has taken the lead on important issues of local sensitivity. One is China. After the Tienanmen Square massacre, Pelosi sponsored an amendment to give Chinese students the right to remain in the United States; it passed but was vetoed by President Bush. In 1991 she became the lead sponsor of the bill to condition China's Most Favored Nation status on human rights reforms; Bush's veto was overridden in the House but upheld in the Senate. Since then Pelosi has led the fight against MFN status and has sharply criticized China on human rights. She was disappointed in May 1994 when President Clinton renewed MFN status without conditions, and support for denying MFN declined. But in 1997, with news about donations of illegal Chinese money to the Clinton campaign, scrutiny of China increased, and Pelosi seemed likely to assemble a larger bipartisan coalition. "I don't believe in the concept of trickle-down liberty. Economic reform does not necessarily lead to political reform," she has said, arguing the that Chinese make concessions not when the U.S. bows to their wishes but when it threatens to walk away. It should be added that Pelosi's position is by no means universally popular with Asian Americans in her district; many think the U.S. should trade and negotiate quietly with China.

A second Pelosi cause is AIDS funding. She has used her seat on Appropriations to get money for research, treatment and housing for people with AIDS and wants access to new therapies and drugs without regard to ability to pay; she got AIDS spending increased even in the Republican Congress. Another Pelosi cause was the Presidio. Years ago, Burton got a law turning over the Presidio to the Interior Department if it was abandoned by the military; it was on the 1993 base closing list and was transferred to the National Park Service in 1995. There is no more stunning piece of urban property in America, but it is the most expensive Park Service property to maintain ($5 million more than Yosemite) and to restore its dilapidated buildings could absorb most of the Park Service budget when it is cutting elsewhere. Pelosi spent four years trying to devise a private-public trust fund for the Presidio. Her bill passed the House in 1994 but was killed by Senate Republicans. In 1995 and 1996 she worked hard to get Republican support for a trust that would lease out the buildings to provide enough revenue to pay the National Park Service for maintaining the open spaces and renovate the old buildings, with the proviso, insisted on by Republicans, that it be self-supporting in 12 years. The Presidio trust got into the 1996 parks bill, support for which kept falling apart; Pelosi and Bay Area neighbors Barbara Boxer and George Miller worked to get the White House and Alaska Senator Frank Murkowski to compromise on the Tongass National Forest, and the bill passed.

On other issues Pelosi has a perfectly liberal voting record. Although she works well with Republicans on MFN and the Presidio, she is a strong partisan, and, as a member of the Ethics Committee and the subcommittee investigating Newt Gingrich, believed Republicans were obstructing the process and favored censure. As ranking member on the Foreign Operations Subcommittee, she wants aid programs to encourage family planning and environmental protection; she wants to facilitate the naturalization of elderly immigrants deprived of SSI benefits by the 1996 Welfare Reform Act.

Pelosi has shown no interest in statewide office; in 1996 she endorsed Leon Panetta for governor over her San Francisco neighbor, Dianne Feinstein, who stands very much on the other side of the China issue. Pelosi is reelected by huge margins, in 1996, 84%–12% against a Pat Buchanan supporter, Justin Raimondo, who is gay.

The People: Pop. 1990: 573,192; 14% age 65+; 44% White; 12% Black; 27% Asian; 16% Hispanic origin. Households: 31% married couple families; 12% married couple fams. w. children; 58% college educ.; median household income: $31,659; per capita income: $19,377; median gross rent: $631; median house value: $270,100.

1996 Presidential Vote

Clinton (D)	114,906	(66%)
Dole (R)	31,282	(18%)
Perot (I)	7,104	(4%)
Other	20,853	(12%)

1992 Presidential Vote

Clinton (D)	187,201	(75%)
Bush (R)	39,396	(16%)
Perot (I)	21,180	(8%)

Rep. Nancy Pelosi (D)

Elected June, 1987; b. Mar. 26, 1940, Baltimore, MD; home, San Francisco; Trinity College, B.A. 1962; Catholic; married (Paul).

Career: CA Dem. Party, Northern Chmn., 1977–81, St. Chmn., 1981–83; Finance Chmn., DSCC, 1985–87; PR exec., Ogilvy & Mather, 1986–87.

Office: 2457 RHOB 20515, 202-225-4965; e-mail: sfnancy@hr.house.gov.

District Offices: San Francisco, 415-556-4862.

Committees: *Appropriations* (14th of 26 D): Foreign Operations, Export Financing & Related Programs (RMM); Labor, Health & Human Services & Education. *Intelligence (Select)* (4th of 7 D): Human Intelligence, Analysis & Counterintelligence.

Group Ratings

	ADA	ACLU	AFS	LCV	CFA	CON	NFIB	COC	ACU	NTLC	CHC
1996	95	93	100	77	92	48	19	13	0	3	0
1995	89	—	—	88	85	13	—	22	0	—	—

National Journal Ratings

	1995 LIB — 1995 CONS			1996 LIB — 1996 CONS		
Economic	85%	—	15%	89%	—	0%
Social	88%	—	0%	88%	—	0%
Foreign	88%	—	7%	90%	—	0%

Key Votes of the 104th Congress

1. Reduce Medicare Growth $	N	5. Flag Amendment	N	9. Cuban Embargo	N
2. Ovrd. Product Liab. Veto	N	6. Drop EPA Limits	Y	10. Bar Bosnia Troop $	N
3. Increase Min. Wage	Y	7. Repeal Assault-Weap. Ban	N	11. Cut Anti-Missile Defense	Y
4. Welfare Reform	N	8. Ovrd. Part. Birth Veto	N	12. Bar U.N. Uniforms	N

Election Results

1996 general	Nancy Pelosi (D)	175,216	(84%)	($465,863)
	Justin Raimondo (R)	25,739	(12%)	
	Others	6,805	(3%)	
1996 primary	Nancy Pelosi (D)	unopposed		
1994 general	Nancy Pelosi (D)	137,642	(82%)	($370,000)
	Elsa C. Cheung (R)	30,528	(18%)	($19,882)

NINTH DISTRICT

Oakland and Berkeley, on the East Bay opposite San Francisco, stand today on one of the lushest sites in America, overlooking the Bay Bridge and the Golden Gate, basking in the sunshine that is more common here than across the Bay. Both cities are the homes of great institutions, but in different ways they are also museum pieces, antiques from a moment in the 1960s when both, especially Berkeley, gained an identity that is hard to shake. Berkeley was founded as a university town, named after the 18th Century Irish philosopher Bishop George Berkeley, for his proclamation, "Westward the course of empire takes its way." Famous for years as the home of first-rate scholarship at the University of California, Berkeley became famous politically in 1964 as the home of student rebellion when the Free Speech Movement, protesting an administrator's refusal to let students set up a card table to sign up volunteers for Lyndon Johnson's 1964 campaign, led to months of riots, student strikes and classroom confrontation. In 1969, students led protests at "People's Park," a lot owned by the university, and Governor Ronald Reagan sent in the National Guard to protect state property from conversion to a playground: an episode in which both sides relished confrontation more than success. Berkeley in the 1960s gave birth to a street culture that still exists (in 1993, a student went about campus naked and was expelled only when administrators had the ingenuity to charge him with sexual harassment). Its denizens made common cause with the Black Panthers, a violent quasi-political gang from nearby Oakland and smoked marijuana with the Hell's Angels motorcycle gang, also once based in Oakland. Berkeley's city council features bizarre political wars in which Democrats very liberal by national standards are the right wing. The Berkeley campus, with its view of the Bay, remains beautiful, and old buildings like the shingled Claremont Hotel are grand. Undergraduate students, about 40% Asian (a number likely to increase when Governor Wilson's anti-quota legislation goes into effect in the fall of 1997), are studying hard to get ahead in a high-tech economy. But Berkeley has had little commercial development, and its public facilities have a low-maintenance, almost Third World look, as if people want to live forever in 1969.

Oakland has a different history, centered around commerce and building its own civic institutions (Gertrude Stein was wrong: there is a there there). It became the western terminus of the transcontinental railroad in 1870 and was connected by ferry to San Francisco; it has always had heavy industry, and its port today is the busiest on the bay. The docks attracted young roustabouts like the writer Jack London, after whom a downtown square is named; civic affairs were run by the local elite, like the Knowland family who owned the *Oakland Tribune*. With the Bay Area's largest black community, Oakland spawned the Black Panthers in the 1960s; blacks took control of city government in the 1970s and, through the late editor-owner Bob Maynard, the *Tribune* in the 1980s. The city has a high crime rate and more than its share of tragedy, like the firestorm that broke out in the hills in October 1991, killing 25 people and destroying 2,500 homes. But Oakland, more than Berkeley, seems to be looking ahead, with Mayor Elihu Harris pledging better law enforcement and local civic leaders trying to spark new businesses.

The 9th Congressional District consists of Oakland and Berkeley, plus adjacent towns like Alameda, site of an old Navy base on the bay. It has the largest black percentage of any northern California district, but not a majority (31%); it is 15% Asian and 12% Hispanic. Politically, it is leftish Democratic: 75%–13% for Bill Clinton in 1996.

The congressman from the 9th is Ronald Dellums, a product of the radical politics of the late 1960s. Dellums grew up in Oakland, enlisted in the Marine Corps at 18, then became the first member of his family to attend college. He was a psychiatric social worker in San Francisco when friends got him to run for the Berkeley Council in 1967; in 1970 he challenged Congressman Jeffrey Cohelan, a six-term Democrat who had one of the most liberal voting records in Congress but wasn't sufficiently radical to suit the Berkeley left. Dellums has a faith in the domestic public sector which owes something to his career as a social worker and a ramrod-straight bearing and a faithfulness to duty which may come from his service as a Marine. He won a seat on the Armed Services Committee (now National Security) upon arrival in Washington in 1971 but found that he had no place to sit during meetings; the chairman had assigned the same chair to both Dellums and another newcomer. He persevered, though, and in 1993 became chairman; since 1995 he has been ranking Democrat.

"I joined," he has said, "because I knew I would need to become an expert in this field in order to argue successfully for military spending reductions that would free up resources for the desperate human needs that I see every day in my community." Dellums has consistently favored lower defense spending than the House as a whole has supported; he opposed the MX missile, the Pershing II, the Midgetman, B-1 and B-2; he did not vote for a defense authorization bill until 1993. But as chairman first of the Acquisitions Subcommittee and then of the full committee, he never used his power to obstruct projects he opposed, working to see that his bills reflected the views of his colleagues, even when different from his own. His performance is a fine example of how a chairman can preside fairly and with dignity while conscientiously disagreeing with the views of his colleagues. When six local facilities got on the 1993 base closing list, including the Alameda Naval Air Station, with 11,000 employees, Dellums did not fight the list, but instead promoted defense reconversion legislation and pilot programs in Alameda as well as suggesting new research projects for the Lawrence Livermore Labs.

Dellums's views have mellowed a bit over the years, even as on one issue—South Africa—his views have helped to change the world. He first proposed sanctions against South Africa in 1971, finally winning the fight for their passage in 1986; he had the satisfaction of seeing South Africa end apartheid and institute democracy, and of having President Nelson Mandela address Congress. He denounced the U.S. military action in Grenada in 1983 and in the Persian Gulf in 1990 and 1991, leading a lawsuit against President Bush by 54 members of Congress reaffirming that only Congress can declare war. But where he once called for "dismantl[ing] every intelligence agency in this country piece by piece, brick by brick, nail by nail," by 1991, now on the Intelligence Committee, he conceded, "Intelligence acquisition enjoys a rightful place; but responsible agencies must be required to respect both the nation's laws and international laws that we have, by treaty, incorporated into the body of our own jurisprudence." In the 1990s he has come to see the United States as a force for good: he urged the Clinton Administration to take action to restore President Aristide to power in Haiti, though he was cautious about recommending the dispatch of U.S. troops.

Dellums is now ranking Democrat on National Security, where a solid majority has condemned the Clinton Administration for spending too little on defense, and he has lost fights even on the B-2 bomber, which a 1992 amendment he sponsored with then-obscure Republican John Kasich capped production at 20 units. But in 1995 B-2 proponents overcame the opposition of the Clinton Administration, Dellums and now-Budget Chairman Kasich, rejecting their amendment to cut new funding for continued production of the B-2 by 219–203 in June and 213–210 in September. More than a dozen Congressional Black Caucus members, many though not all with B-2 facilities in their districts, voted for the Stealth Bomber. The Clinton Administration accepted it in December 1995 to get funding for the U.S. military mission in Bosnia.

Dellums has a solidly liberal voting record and continues to support measures like national health service and public service jobs for all that are at the far left of the political spectrum. His reelection has never been in doubt, but until 1992 he never won with more than 61% because he lost in the suburbs over the ridge from Berkeley and Oakland. But they were removed and made part of the new 10th District in the 1990s redistricting and Dellums, despite 851 overdrafts on the House bank, has been reelected overwhelmingly ever since.

The People: Pop. 1990: 573,669; 12% age 65+; 41% White; 31% Black; 15% Asian; 1% Amer. Indian; 12% Hispanic origin. Households: 37% married couple families; 17% married couple fams. w. children; 62% college educ.; median household income: $30,067; per capita income: $16,833; median gross rent: $538; median house value: $220,200.

1996 Presidential Vote

Clinton (D)	156,998	(75%)
Dole (R)	26,321	(13%)
Perot (I)	6,277	(3%)
Other	19,498	(9%)

1992 Presidential Vote

Clinton (D)	186,714	(78%)
Bush (R)	29,394	(12%)
Perot (I)	21,207	(9%)

Rep. Ronald V. Dellums (D)

Elected 1970; b. Nov. 24, 1935, Oakland; home, Oakland; Oakland City Col., A.A. 1958, San Francisco St. Col., B.A. 1960, U. of CA, M.S.W. 1962; Protestant; married (Leola).

Career: Marine Corps, 1954–56; Psychiatric social worker, CA Dept. of Mental Hygiene, 1962–64; Prog. Dir., Bayview Community Ctr., 1964–65; Dir., Hunter's Pt. Bayview Youth Oppor. Ctr., 1965–66; Consultant, Bay Area Social Plng. Cncl., 1966–67; Dir., San Francisco Econ. Oppor. Cncl. Employment Prog., 1967–68; Berkeley City Cncl., 1967–71.

DC Office: 2108 RHOB 20515, 202-225-2661; Fax: 202-225-9817.

District Offices: Oakland, 510-763-0370.

Committees: *National Security* (RMM): Military Procurement.

Group Ratings

	ADA	ACLU	AFS	LCV	CFA	CON	NFIB	COC	ACU	NTLC	CHC
1996	100	100	100	77	92	48	11	0	0	5	0
1995	100	—	—	100	100	16	—	0	8	—	—

National Journal Ratings

	1995 LIB — 1995 CONS	1996 LIB — 1996 CONS
Economic	90% — 8%	89% — 0%
Social	88% — 0%	88% — 0%
Foreign	93% — 0%	90% — 0%

Key Votes of the 104th Congress

1. Reduce Medicare Growth $	N	5. Flag Amendment	N	9. Cuban Embargo	N
2. Ovrd. Product Liab. Veto	N	6. Drop EPA Limits	Y	10. Bar Bosnia Troop $	N
3. Increase Min. Wage	Y	7. Repeal Assault-Weap. Ban	N	11. Cut Anti-Missile Defense	Y
4. Welfare Reform	N	8. Ovrd. Part. Birth Veto	N	12. Bar U.N. Uniforms	N

Election Results

1996 general	Ronald V. Dellums (D)	154,806	(77%)	($415,090)
	Deborah Wright (R)	37,126	(18%)	($34,491)
	Others	9,044	(5%)	
1996 primary	Ronald V. Dellums (D)	73,353	(85%)	
	Randal Stewart (D)	12,876	(15%)	
1994 general	Ronald V. Dellums (D)	129,233	(72%)	($482,877)
	Deborah Wright (R)	40,448	(23%)	($18,453)
	Emma Wong Mar (P&F)	9,194	(5%)	

TENTH DISTRICT

In the 1950s, when the streets of San Francisco and Oakland were already crowded, the rolling grasslands on the east of the mountain ridges, over the hill and through the tunnel from Oakland, were still mostly empty. In the years since, they have been filling up. Freeways took the first commuters through the Caldecott Tunnel to the woodsy trail-like roads of Orinda and Lafayette; Interstate 580 brought people east from the southern East Bay towns to the Amador Valley and Livermore, site of one of the nation's nuclear laboratories; Interstate 680 running north-south provided a spine for businesses and shopping centers up and down the San Ramon Valley, from burgeoning Concord through Walnut Creek, Danville and Dublin; BART stations in Walnut Creek and Orinda took commuters to downtown San Francisco. Not all this area is filled in yet, and there is resistance to overdevelopment. But what has evolved in this sunny land, shielded by the mountains from the ocean fogs and rains, is an advanced civilization of highly skilled and educated people. Affluent and generally tolerant of—if a little put off by—what happens in San Francisco, they are respectful of economic markets and wary of government, but concerned about preserving a physical environment that can be one of America's most pleasant. Or as Bruce Cain of Berkeley's Institute of Governmental Studies put it, "These are basically secular professionals."

This is the land of the 10th Congressional District, a seat newly created by the court-ordered redistricting of 1992. It consists almost entirely of the interior portion of the Bay Area, with just a few salients beyond—the suburb of Castro Valley on the East Bay, the working class town of Antioch on the San Joaquin River Delta. This area had been voting Republican for years but was split up between four Democratic districts. It is easily now the most Republican Bay Area district, but not very Republican by national standards.

The congresswoman from the 10th District is Ellen Tauscher, a Democrat who in 1996 beat incumbent Republican Bill Baker. Tauscher grew up in the East, won a seat on the New York Stock Exchange at 25, was a stock trader and investment banker. In 1989 she and her husband, owner of Vanstar (formerly ComputerLand) moved to California. In 1992, after a difficult childbirth, Tauscher started the ChildCare Registry, the first company to offer (for $140) background information on child care providers. "Here we are, on the front porch of the 21st Century, and we don't have standards for caring for the most precious things in the world," she has said. Politically, she raised money for Senator Dianne Feinstein and Superintendent of Public Instruction Delaine Eastin. In 1995 she decided to run against Baker, who won in 1992 and 1994 and had a reputation for knowledgeable fiscal conservatism, but was also a tart-tongued conservative on cultural issues. She ran as a moderate Democrat ("I am not someone who is a typical Bay Area Democrat") but spent liberally of her own money; overall she spent $1.73 million of her own money, second highest in the nation, and $2.6 million total, the fourth highest of any House candidate (after Newt Gingrich, his Democratic opponent, and Richard Gephardt). Baker responded by calling her a "tax-and-spend" liberal and ran ads comparing her to a lottery winner buying a congressional seat. But though he spent $1.4 million, he concentrated on radio and cable TV. Tauscher, in contrast, spent heavily on San Francisco TV stations as well. Her ads called Baker an "extremist" on gun control, abortion and the environment; a brochure opened with, "Did you vote for Newt Gingrich?" She ran one spot in which district resident Steve Sposato, whose wife was killed by a gunman in 1996, complained that Baker wouldn't spend 15 minutes talking to his two-year-old. On issues, Tauscher came out for gun control and tough environmental restrictions, against the Defense of Marriage Act, for the 1996 welfare reform and the death penalty. She came out for national education standards, Baker for local control. In mid-campaign she published *The ChildCare Source Book*. She claimed not to have special interests supporting her, but union workers were out working precincts.

All of this proved a winning combination, though only barely. In by far the highest turnout of any Bay Area district, Tauscher won 49%–47%, slightly ahead of Bill Clinton's 48%–43% margin here. Money made much of the difference; Baker had won when Clinton's margin was wider in 1992. In Washington Tauscher joined the moderate Blue Dogs and New Democratic Coalition; she got a seat on Science and on Transportation and Infrastructure, where she can work for local transit funding. Mentioned as a possible opponent is San Francisco '49er tight end Brent Jones, who lives in Danville, a conservative in the mold of Oklahoma's Steve Largent. But Tauscher's moderate stance and liberal funding make her, despite her narrow margin, a tough target.

The People: Pop. 1990: 571,979; 3% rural; 10% age 65+; 82% White; 2% Black; 6% Asian; 1% Amer. Indian; 9% Hispanic origin. Households: 63% married couple families; 29% married couple fams. w. children; 68% college educ.; median household income: $52,378; per capita income: $23,972; median gross rent: $746; median house value: $273,800.

1996 Presidential Vote

Clinton (D)	138,386	(48%)
Dole (R)	122,296	(43%)
Perot (I)	17,930	(6%)
Other	8,375	(3%)

1992 Presidential Vote

Clinton (D)	127,450	(42%)
Bush (R)	107,191	(35%)
Perot (I)	66,180	(22%)

Rep. Ellen O. Tauscher (D)

Elected 1996; b. Nov. 15, 1951, E. Newark, NJ; home, Pleasanton; Seton Hall U., B.A. 1973; Catholic; married (William).

Career: Wall Street Invest. Banker, 1974–88, NYSE member, 1977–79; Founder & CEO, Registry Cos., 1992–96.

DC Office: 1440 LHOB 20515, 202-225-1880; Fax: 202-225-5914.

District Offices: Antioch, 510-757-7187; Dublin, 510-829-0813; Walnut Creek, 510-932-8899.

Committees: *Science* (21st of 21 D): Technology. *Transportation & Infrastructure* (27th of 33 D): Surface Transportation; Water Resources & Environment.

Group Ratings and Key Votes: Newly Elected

Election Results

1996 general	Ellen O. Tauscher (D)	137,726	(49%)	($2,571,595)
	Bill Baker (R)	133,633	(47%)	($1,398,556)
	Others	11,824	(4%)	
1996 primary	Ellen O. Tauscher (D)	44,106	(75%)	
	Daniel P. White (D)	15,045	(25%)	
1994 general	Bill Baker (R)	138,916	(59%)	($909,065)
	Ellen Schwartz (D)	90,523	(39%)	($440,805)
	Others	4,802	(2%)	

ELEVENTH DISTRICT

People from back East looking for clues about California might consider avoiding Beverly Hills and Nob Hill and taking a look at Stockton. For Stockton, just 50 miles south of Sacramento, is in the middle of the Central Valley, which saw much of California's most rapid growth in the 1980s and is now subject to some growing problems of it own. This is not a new part of the state: Stockton was a Gold Rush trading town founded in 1847, named after Robert Stockton, the second U.S. military governor of California, who captured Santa Barbara and Los Angeles from Mexico and proclaimed California United States territory. The Central Valley, criss-crossed with railroads and canals, became one of the world's greatest agriculture areas; the San Joaquin River channel was deepened to 37 feet and Stockton today is the Central Valley's ocean port. The rich farming attracted immigrants from all over: Mexicans coming up Route 99 joined North Dakotans flocking to the town of Lodi; Italian and Yugoslav immigrants bringing their Old World crops; Yankees and Okies bringing their distinct churches and systems of belief; and now Southeast Asian refugees crowd into the older streets of Stockton. The 1980s growth brought traffic congestion and air quality problems to the Central Valley, and some fear that development will gobble up the best farmland.

The 11th Congressional District includes Stockton and most of surrounding San Joaquin County, plus the southern part of Sacramento County, an area of farms and a few subdivisions, dredge tailings and marshy, rich-soiled islands in the delta of the Sacramento and San Joaquin Rivers. This was once a solidly Democratic area; towns near Stockton were the home base of two House Democratic whips, John McFall, who was defeated for reelection in 1980, and Tony Coelho, who resigned in 1989. But today the Valley has increasingly moved to the right, angry at the intrusiveness of federal environmental regulators, puzzled by the cultural liberalism of Bay Area and Los Angeles Democrats.

The congressman from the 11th District is Richard Pombo, a Republican first elected when the district was created in 1992 and one of the leaders of the property rights movement in Congress. Pombo grew up in Tracy, attended Cal Poly Ponoma, worked on the family cattle ranch; he often wears a cowboy hat. In 1986 he founded the Citizens Land Alliance; in 1990 he was elected to the Tracy City Council and helped bring a Safeway distribution center to town. In 1992, at 31, he ran for the House in this new district. The favorite in the primary was former Sacramento County Supervisor Sandy Smoley, a moderate who lost to Robert Matsui in a Sacramento-based district in 1978. Pombo called Smoley "the surefire choice of the hard-line feminists" and attacked her support of Governor Pete Wilson's gay rights bill; when liberal Massachusetts Congressman Barney Frank called Pombo a "low-rent Pat Buchanan," Pombo embraced the label. Pombo won 36%–27%, with 24% going to a former aide to a former Stockton congressman. In the general, Pombo faced Patti Garamendi, a onetime Peace Corps volunteer, mother of six and wife of Insurance Commissioner and unsuccessful 1994 gubernatorial candidate John Garamendi. She had twice run for the legislature, and lost, in the 1990s, and failed to put Pombo on the defensive. He stressed his opposition to abortion, his support of property rights and opposition to the Endangered Species Act. He denounced the lyrics of rap singer Ice-T's song "Cop Killer," and attacked Garamendi when she accused him of racism for it. Though solidly outspent, Pombo won 48%–46%.

"I'm not going to fit in too well, because I'm anything but politically correct," Pombo said in his first term. His voting record is almost perfectly conservative, yet he tilted with environmentalists on the Resources Committee and with subsidy advocates on Agriculture. He won reelection in 1994 and suddenly was in the majority. Resources Chairman Don Young put him in charge of rewriting the Endangered Species Act; he held hearings with horror stories of absurd regulations (one Fish and Wildlife Service official wanted to reduce the speed limit on a section of I-10 to 15 miles an hour to avoid bothering a rare fly) and produced a bill in the fall which would not prohibit alteration of habitat of an endangered species and would provide compensation to landowners whose property values declined greatly. It passed the committee but, as Republican environmental measures came under attack, was never brought to the floor. Similarly, a Pombo amendment for a new 250,000-worker migrant labor program was defeated in March 1996. Pombo did succeed in passing a reform of the 1930 Perishable Commodities Act, raising fees on farmers for a dispute-resolution procedure. And he worked on many provisions of the Freedom to Farm Act. In 1996 he and liberal Republican Sherwood Boehlert co-chaired a Speaker's Task Force on the Environment, and Pombo points out that the Republican 104th produced more environmental legislation than the Democratic 103d—the Safe Drinking Water, Coastal Zone Management, Food Quality Protection and Water Resources Development Acts, plus Freedom to Farm conservation sections and Everglades protection amendments.

However harshly Pombo is criticized in Washington or San Francisco, he is well thought of in the Central Valley. The *Stockton Record* defended him against the Sierra Club's charge that he is an "eco-thug" and the *Tracy Press* suggested that Pombo, who had just reached the constitutional age of 35, would be a good vice presidential nominee for Bob Dole. In the fall of 1996 he raised money for other candidates and published a book, *This Land is Our Land: How to End the War on Private Property*. He was reelected 59%–36% even as Bill Clinton was carrying the 11th District 46%–45%.

The People: Pop. 1990: 571,650; 15% rural; 11% age 65+; 62% White; 5% Black; 11% Asian; 1% Amer. Indian; 21% Hispanic origin. Households: 58% married couple families; 29% married couple fams. w. children; 46% college educ.; median household income: $31,605; per capita income: $13,299; median gross rent: $499; median house value: $123,000.

1996 Presidential Vote

Clinton (D)	85,117	(46%)
Dole (R)	84,303	(45%)
Perot (I)	12,373	(7%)
Other	4,187	(2%)

1992 Presidential Vote

Clinton (D)	79,432	(40%)
Bush (R)	75,319	(38%)
Perot (I)	41,006	(21%)

Rep. Richard W. Pombo (R)

Elected 1992; b. Jan. 8, 1961, Tracy; home, Tracy; CA Polytechnic Inst., Pomona, 1979–82; Catholic; married (Annette).

Career: Cattle rancher; Co-founder, Citizens Land Alliance, 1986; Tracy City Cncl., 1990–92.

DC Office: 1519 LHOB 20515, 202-225-1947; Fax: 202-225-0861.

District Offices: Stockton, 209-951-3091.

Committees: *Agriculture* (8th of 27 R): Forestry, Resource Conservation & Research; Livestock, Dairy & Poultry (Chmn.); Risk Management & Specialty Crops. *Resources* (11th of 27 R): National Parks & Public Lands; Water & Power.

Group Ratings

	ADA	ACLU	AFS	LCV	CFA	CON	NFIB	COC	ACU	NTLC	CHC
1996	5	19	0	8	8	30	97	94	100	100	100
1995	0	—	—	0	8	38	—	96	100	—	—

National Journal Ratings

	1995 LIB — 1995 CONS	1996 LIB — 1996 CONS
Economic	0% — 74%	0% — 82%
Social	0% — 79%	24% — 72%
Foreign	0% — 85%	0% — 79%

Key Votes of the 104th Congress

1. Reduce Medicare Growth $	Y	5. Flag Amendment	Y	9. Cuban Embargo	Y
2. Ovrd. Product Liab. Veto	Y	6. Drop EPA Limits	N	10. Bar Bosnia Troop $	Y
3. Increase Min. Wage	N	7. Repeal Assault-Weap. Ban	Y	11. Cut Anti-Missile Defense	N
4. Welfare Reform	Y	8. Ovrd. Part. Birth Veto	Y	12. Bar U.N. Uniforms	Y

Election Results

1996 general	Richard W. Pombo (R)	107,477	(59%)	($470,749)
	Jason Silva (D)	65,536	(36%)	($17,862)
	Others	8,083	(4%)	
1996 primary	Richard W. Pombo (R)	unopposed		
1994 general	Richard W. Pombo (R)	99,302	(62%)	($657,627)
	Randy A. Perry (D)	55,794	(35%)	($146,682)
	Others	4,718	(3%)	

TWELFTH DISTRICT

Running south from San Francisco is the Peninsula, which connects the city with the mainland of the United States. This is geologically interesting, and active, country: the San Andreas Fault runs just east of the Coast Range, underneath the reservoirs that store San Francisco's water supply. To the west are green mountains splashing down into the foggy ocean. To the east is a zone of flat land between mountain and bay, an unbroken chain of suburbs and urban settlement, with light industry and salt flats along the bay front, and residential neighborhoods and some commercial strips from the Bayshore Freeway up through the Junipero Serra Freeway atop the mountain ridge. Historically, the Peninsula has seemed separate from San Francisco; Dashiell Hammett, writing before the advent of freeways, gets his detective Sam Spade out of the city for most of a day when he follows a false tip down the Peninsula. But today, the Peninsula suburbs are demographically an extension of the city.

The 12th Congressional District consists of the northern Peninsula suburbs plus the southwest quadrant of San Francisco—the city's middle-income Sunset district, with older houses amid unburied telephone and electric wires, lying on curving hills that were once sand dunes, and affluent St. Francis's Wood. Just to the south, across the San Mateo County line at the southern extension of the BART lines, is Daly City with substantial numbers of Mexican-Americans and Asians; nearby, South San Francisco proclaims itself "the industrial city" in big letters on San Bruno Mountain near the Bayshore Freeway; the streets lined with boxy houses in San Bruno and Pacifica wind over sweeping hillsides facing cemeteries where many San Franciscans and veterans of Pacific wars are buried. That is the view from one side of the Junipero Serra Freeway; from the other, the vista is of San Francisco Bay, broader than one might expect, and the airport next door, connecting this metropolis with others on the Pacific Rim; to the south is the neat suburban city of San Mateo and, on twisting streets in the hills above the Burlingame Country Club, the rich suburb of Hillsborough, home to much of the city's WASP elite.

This is an ethnically diverse and economically prosperous constituency. Fully 26% of its residents are Asian—the second highest of any mainland district, after San Francisco's 8th just to the north—and another 14% are Hispanic. Income levels are, if not among the highest in the country, very far above average. The economic orientation here is more toward San Francisco to the north than south toward Silicon Valley; the political heritage here is Democratic, from ethnic heritage and historic labor union ties. Bill Clinton carried the 12th 70%–21% in 1996.

The congressman from the 12th District, Tom Lantos, has several distinctions, but none more important than the fact that he is the only Holocaust survivor ever to serve in Congress. Lantos was born in Hungary and as a teenager fought in the underground against the Nazis; he was imprisoned and was one of the Jews saved by Swedish diplomat Raoul Wallenberg. So was his wife Annette, his childhood sweetheart and now his unpaid assistant; these two Holocaust survivors have two daughters and 17 grandchildren. Lantos has shown energy and competence throughout his career. He taught economics at San Francisco State, made money as an investor, appeared on television as a foreign policy expert. He had the political insight to challenge a Republican incumbent in the Peninsula in 1980, a Republican year nationally but not so much here, and he has shown great capacity for publicizing his crusades in congressional hearings and on television.

Lantos has spent much of his time in the House on foreign policy. Unlike other Bay Area Democrats, he did not bring to his work an instinctive mistrust of American policy or doubts of American good intentions. He founded the Congressional Human Rights Caucus, focusing on Communist regimes as well as the right-wing dictatorships other liberal Democrats denounced. He is among the most enthusiastic supporters of Israel and called for economic sanctions against Iraq back in 1988 for its gassing of the Kurds. He was an enthusiastic supporter of the Gulf war resolution. Lantos stayed in close touch with Eastern Europe, especially Hungary, as Communism collapsed and new democracies rose up; in 1990 he was the first American official to visit Albania since 1946. He sponsored the first U.S. aid to the newly free countries of Eastern Europe and strongly backed NATO expansion. He advocated a more active American role in Bosnia. He has attacked human rights violations in China and opposes giving them MFN status. He introduced the resolution approving the private visit of President Lee Teng-hui of Taiwan to Cornell University in 1995, prompting the Clinton Administration to issue a visa, and urged U.S. support of Taiwan when China started menacing military maneuvers in early 1996. Lantos has been part of the U.S. delegations to the European Parliament and the United Nations; he became friends with Secretary General Kofi Annan, whose wife Nane Annan is Raoul Wallenberg's niece. He sponsored the bust of Wallenberg which was unveiled in the Capitol in 1995 and the conferring of honorary U.S. citizenship on him—the only person besides Winston Churchill ever so honored.

Lantos has displayed a flair for showmanship on his Government Operations subcommittee investigations. In 1989 and 1990 he conducted hearings on alleged misconduct under Reagan HUD Secretary Samuel Pierce, which resulted in an independent counsel and prosecutions. Unlike almost all other congressional Democrats, he actively pursued Clinton Administration scandals. He aggressively probed into administration actions in the Waco massacre. And he grilled former White House aide Craig Livingstone in the hearing on FBI files in the White House. He sponsored resolutions condemning Louis Farrakhan's antisemitic statements and his meetings with the leaders of Libya, Iran and Iraq, and did not back down when criticized by members of the Congressional Black Caucus. Locally, he has worked to build a tunnel to avoid the hazardous Devil's Slide area where a mudslide closed Route 1 just south of Pacifica in 1983, and for funding of the BART subway to San Francisco Airport.

Lantos raised and spent $1.7 million on his 1980 and 1982 campaigns and has won easily ever since. More recently his fundraising efforts have been directed to help his son-in-law Dick Swett, who was elected congressman from New Hampshire in 1990 and 1992, but lost in 1994 and 1996—and not because of lack of funds.

The People: Pop. 1990: 571,667; 14% age 65+; 56% White; 4% Black; 25% Asian; 14% Hispanic origin. Households: 53% married couple families; 23% married couple fams. w. children; 62% college educ.; median household income: $44,720; per capita income: $20,984; median gross rent: $780; median house value: $320,400.

1996 Presidential Vote

Clinton (D)	191,973	(70%)
Dole (R)	58,260	(21%)
Perot (I)	11,994	(4%)
Other	10,291	(4%)

1992 Presidential Vote

Clinton (D)	139,281	(57%)
Bush (R)	64,984	(27%)
Perot (I)	38,129	(16%)

Rep. Tom Lantos (D)

Elected 1980; b. Feb. 1, 1928, Budapest, Hungary; home, San Mateo; U. of WA, B.A. 1949, M.A. 1950, U. of CA, Ph.D. 1953; Jewish; married (Annette).

Career: Economist, Bank of America, 1952–53; TV Commentator, San Francisco, 1955–63; Dir. of Intl. Programs, CA St. U., 1962–71; Advisor, U.S. Sen. Joseph R. Biden Jr., 1978–79; Mbr., Pres. Task Force on Defense & Foreign Policy, 1976; Prof., San Francisco St. U., 1950–80.

DC Office: 2217 RHOB 20515, 202-225-3531; e-mail: talk2tom@hr.house.gov.

District Offices: San Mateo, 415-342-0300.

Committees: *Government Reform & Oversight* (2nd of 19 D): Human Resources; National Security, International Affairs & Criminal Justice. *International Relations* (3rd of 21 D): International Economic Policy & Trade; International Operations & Human Rights (RMM).

Group Ratings

	ADA	ACLU	AFS	LCV	CFA	CON	NFIB	COC	ACU	NTLC	CHC
1996	95	69	100	77	92	95	30	13	0	7	0
1995	90	—	—	88	85	9	—	25	22	—	—

National Journal Ratings

	1995 LIB		1995 CONS	1996 LIB		1996 CONS
Economic	75%	—	24%	85%	—	11%
Social	80%	—	13%	88%	—	12%
Foreign	69%	—	30%	82%	—	18%

Key Votes of the 104th Congress

1. Reduce Medicare Growth $	N	5. Flag Amendment	Y	9. Cuban Embargo	Y
2. Ovrd. Product Liab. Veto	N	6. Drop EPA Limits	Y	10. Bar Bosnia Troop $	N
3. Increase Min. Wage	Y	7. Repeal Assault-Weap. Ban	N	11. Cut Anti-Missile Defense	Y
4. Welfare Reform	N	8. Ovrd. Part. Birth Veto	N	12. Bar U.N. Uniforms	*

Election Results

1996 general	Tom Lantos (D)	149,052	(72%)	($591,305)
	Storm Jenkins (R)	49,278	(24%)	($4,016)
	Others	9,583	(5%)	
1996 primary	Tom Lantos (D)	unopposed		
1994 general	Tom Lantos (D)	118,408	(67%)	($322,016)
	Deborah Wilder (R)	57,228	(33%)	($146,133)

THIRTEENTH DISTRICT

The East Bay is the workaday, unglamorous side of metropolitan San Francisco—the margin of land perhaps five miles wide between San Francisco Bay and the surprisingly high mountains that rise just to the east. The shoreline is not picturesque, with its closed-down Navy bases, docks, airports and salt evaporators; the skyscrapers of Oakland are unimpressive compared to those of San Francisco; the Bay Bridge, bisected by Yerba Buena Island, cuts an inspiring figure, but the San Mateo Bridge to the south is at best utilitarian. Fifty years ago, when the shipyards of Richmond and the Navy yard in Oakland were buzzing, the East Bay south of Oakland was still largely uninhabited farm fields. In the postwar years, it has filled up, south along Route 17: San Leandro, originally settled by Portuguese, Castro Valley with its Japanese Gardens, Hayward with its Cal State University campus, Union City with its rail yards, and Fremont, home of the famous NUMMI auto plant where Chevrolets and Toyotas are produced together, and of the California School for the Deaf.

The 13th Congressional District is made up of this string of East Bay towns, somewhat lower income than the Peninsula towns across the Bay. The district is racially and ethnically mixed in the California manner—19% Asian, 18% Hispanic, 7% black—and with a Democratic heritage not yet dampened by high crime (crime rates are much lower here than in Oakland) or revulsion toward cultural liberalism (these people are used to TV newscasts from San Francisco). This area looks like much of the Bay Area, with stucco houses and shopping centers, but house prices are below the ridiculously high Bay Area average and the stores are discount chains more than upscale. Still, income levels are well above the national average.

The congressman from the 13th District is Pete Stark, a liberal Democrat and product of the peace movement of the 1960s who in the first half of the 1990s was one of four senior Democratic House committee and subcommittee chairmen elected from four East Bay districts. Now, in the second half of the 1990s, he is only a senior member of the minority party. Stark grew up in Wisconsin, served in the Air Force, got an engineering degree at M.I.T. and an M.B.A. at Berkeley and in 1961 started a bank in Walnut Creek. He first attracted attention all over the Bay Area when he put a giant peace symbol atop the bank headquarters and peace symbols on all checks. In 1972 he ran for Congress, spending his own money freely; he beat an 81-year-old incumbent in the primary 56%–22% and held on in the McGovern undertow to win the general with 53%. He sold his bank stock when he got on the Banking Committee, whose members often used their committee positions to enrich themselves, and by his third term he was on Ways and Means, chairing its Health Subcommittee from 1985–95.

Stark brought to that post a desire to use government powers to make health care more available—and a habit of infelicitous quips that got him into trouble. He was not always successful on policy. His major achievement was the Catastrophic Health Care Act of 1988, which created a new benefit for Medicare recipients but was repealed by an overwhelming vote in 1989 after an outpouring of public protest: the problem was that its tax on the high-income elderly was very unpopular while benefits seemed puny, a reminder that in constructing a healthcare system, even a small mistake can be politically devastating. In 1991 he offered a bill for universal healthcare access, to be financed by higher payroll taxes and a 2% gross income tax; in 1993 he worked toward a "global" budget imposing limits on health costs. All this was overtaken by the Clinton healthcare plan, from whose formulation Stark and other members of Congress complained that they were shut out. In the spring of 1994, Stark worked his subcommittee hard, eventually producing a majority for a bill that modified the Clinton plan with some Stark features; after alterations, it narrowly passed Ways and Means. But, with moderate swing Democrats fearful of its big-government features, it never had majority support in the House and was not brought to the floor. In the 103d Congress Stark also served as chairman of the District of Columbia Committee, now abolished; he seemed to defer its problems to others, as the District plunged into insolvency.

Stark's sharp tongue has gotten him in trouble. In 1990 he called Health and Human Services Secretary Louis Sullivan "a disgrace to his race" for supporting Bush Administration health policies; in 1991, he attacked "Jewish colleagues" for voting for the Gulf war resolution to help Israel. In 1994, when Republican Nancy Johnson, who is married to a physician, attacked Stark's proposals, he said, "The gentlelady got her medical degree through pillow talk and the gentleman from Washington [Jim McDermott, a committee member trained as a psychiatrist] got his medical degree by going to school." Johnson said that was insulting, and 35 Republicans insisted Stark apologize; after an uncomfortable interval he did. Then in March 1995, Stark again insulted Johnson by calling her a "whore" for the insurance industry. This time women members from both sides of the aisle banded together to demand an apology, which he made in writing. His 1996 opponent, James Fay, tried to refer to that with a brochure labelled "Meet Pete Stark's whore," and which went on to say that "If Pete Stark were not a congressman, he would deserve to be sued for sexual harassment."

The Republican capture of Congress in 1994 left Stark with little policy role and more opportunities for invective. He was one of two votes against the 1996 health care bill, on the grounds it did not include mental health coverage and extended patent protection for a drug. He has denounced Columbia/HCA's practice of giving participating physicians stock as a violation of a provision he wrote prohibiting doctors from referring patients to a hospital in which they have an interest, and denounced Blue Cross of California as "a greed-driven vampire" and Newt Gingrich as a "messianic megalomaniac." As for welfare reform, he said, "The President sold out children to get reelected. He's no better than the Republicans." Democrats denouncing their opponents for a lack of civility in politics might want to have a chat with Stark.

Stark has been reelected by wide margins in this Democratic district.

The People: Pop. 1990: 572,333; 9% age 65+; 55% White; 7% Black; 19% Asian; 1% Amer. Indian; 18% Hispanic origin. Households: 59% married couple families; 29% married couple fams. w. children; 55% college educ.; median household income: $43,877; per capita income: $17,335; median gross rent: $726; median house value: $222,700.

1996 Presidential Vote

Clinton (D)	115,633	(62%)
Dole (R)	51,084	(28%)
Perot (I)	13,085	(7%)
Other	5,843	(3%)

1992 Presidential Vote

Clinton (D)	116,829	(54%)
Bush (R)	55,100	(25%)
Perot (I)	43,026	(20%)

Rep. Fortney H. (Pete) **Stark (D)**

Elected 1972; b. Nov. 11, 1931, Milwaukee, WI; home, Fremont; MIT, B.S. 1953, U. of CA at Berkeley, M.B.A. 1960; Unitarian; married (Deborah).

Career: Air Force, 1955–57; Founder, Beacon Savings & Loan Assn., 1961; Founder and Pres., Security Natl. Bank, Walnut Creek, 1963–72.

DC Office: 239 CHOB 20515, 202-225-5065; Fax: 202-226-3805; e-mail: petemail@hr.house.gov.

District Offices: Hayward, 510-247-1388.

Committees: *Ways & Means* (2nd of 16 D): Health (RMM); Human Resources. *Joint Economic Committee* (7th of 10 Reps.). *Joint Committee on Taxation* (5th of 5 Reps.).

Group Ratings

	ADA	ACLU	AFS	LCV	CFA	CON	NFIB	COC	ACU	NTLC	CHC
1996	80	100	100	85	85	60	14	6	0	5	0
1995	100	—	—	94	85	31	—	13	8	—	—

National Journal Ratings

	1995 LIB — 1995 CONS			1996 LIB — 1996 CONS		
Economic	90%	—	8%	89%	—	0%
Social	88%	—	0%	88%	—	0%
Foreign	93%	—	0%	90%	—	0%

Key Votes of the 104th Congress

1. Reduce Medicare Growth $	N	5. Flag Amendment	N	9. Cuban Embargo	N
2. Ovrd. Product Liab. Veto	N	6. Drop EPA Limits	Y	10. Bar Bosnia Troop $	N
3. Increase Min. Wage	Y	7. Repeal Assault-Weap. Ban	*	11. Cut Anti-Missile Defense	Y
4. Welfare Reform	N	8. Ovrd. Part. Birth Veto	N	12. Bar U.N. Uniforms	N

Election Results

1996 general	Fortney H. (Pete) Stark (D)	114,408	(65%)	($630,357)
	James S. Fay (R)	53,385	(30%)	($60,106)
	Terry C. Savage (Lib)	7,746	(4%)	($3,532)
1996 primary	Fortney H. (Pete) Stark (D)	unopposed		
1994 general	Fortney H. (Pete) Stark (D)	97,344	(65%)	($391,319)
	Larry Molton (R)	45,555	(30%)	($26,249)
	Robert Gough (Lib)	7,743	(5%)	

FOURTEENTH DISTRICT

Silicon Valley is a place and a state of mind, an area that had no distinctive identity two decades ago but is now recognized, admired and imitated all over the world. For Silicon Valley has been the center of America's computer and microprocessor industry, a place where creative minds have developed products that large corporations never thought would sell. Its beginnings can be traced back to 1939, when William Hewlett and David Packard started their electronics firm in a Palo Alto garage, or perhaps to 1891, when Stanford University was founded on the estate of a California governor and senator. But Silicon Valley did not achieve critical mass until the late 1970s and early 1980s, when Steve Jobs started Apple in a garage in Cupertino with the idea of making a computer ordinary people could use, and Gordon Moore, Robert Noyce and Andrew Grove started Intel in nearby Santa Clara to make the microchips that let computers process data much faster than almost anyone thought possible. The office parks of Silicon Valley are unremarkable-looking, in Cupertino and Sunnyvale and Mountain View and Palo Alto, the line of towns between the Junipero Serra and Bayshore Freeways running south from San Francisco to San Jose. Yet this is where computer hackers have turned tinkerer's dreams into multi-billion dollar companies and innovators have produced business after business that out-think public planners and out-compete subsidized foreign consortiums.

Ever since there has been much hand-wringing and worrying about Silicon Valley's future; rapidly growing businesses are inherently unstable, but it has proved amazingly adaptable. But Silicon Valley has had enduring advantages. One is Stanford, the students it attracts and produces, and the encouragement of profit-making activity by faculty. Another is venture capital, widely available from innovation-minded San Francisco WASPs. A third, perhaps the greatest, is that Silicon Valley is the kind of place where smart young innovators like to live. Counterculture veterans may cluster around the liberal university towns; elite law and medical school graduates head to the prestigious, high-salary jobs of central cities; but techies are free to live in this pleasant, healthy environment. Sheltered by hills from coastal fogs and rains, Silicon Valley boasts a sunny climate with perceptible but gentle seasons, perfect for year-round outdoor sports; there may well be more jogging trails and bicycle paths here than anywhere else in the country. There is a sort of pure Americana here: these communities were rustic but never poor, rural but never bigoted, country-like but still easily accessible to the luxuries of civilization. People here were ahead of the rest of the nation in fighting to preserve the environment, in favoring natural over processed foods, and in indulging in regular exercise. Innovation extends even to government. The city of Sunnyvale, with its results-oriented management, and flexible job definitions in the semi-conductor, aerospace and biotechnology firms, is the hero of David Osborne's *Reinventing Government*, and President Clinton and Vice President Gore have visited Sunnyvale as well as Silicon Valley for instruction.

The 14th Congressional District coincides almost exactly with Silicon Valley. Though it reaches to the Pacific and homey Half Moon Bay with its pumpkin farms, the 14th's population lies mostly on the San Francisco Bay side of the mountains, in the strip of flat land from Belmont, not far south of San Francisco Airport, through Redwood City, Menlo Park, Palo Alto (home of Stanford), Mountain View, Sunnyvale and Cupertino (home of Apple). There are a few high-income enclaves: Atherton, with its stone-walled lots; Woodside, with its 1850s country store and mansions dotting the hills; Portola Valley and Los Altos Hills, with stark contemporary homes overlooking the Bay. The 14th's political heritage is progressive Republican—a sort of environmentalist, dovish, healthy-lifestyle, but entrepreneurial Republicanism, typified by former Congressmen Pete McCloskey (1967–83), Ed Zschau (1983–87) and Tom Campbell (1989–93), each of whom ran unsuccessfully for the Senate. But absent this kind of Republican, Silicon Valley has become very Democratic. It took immediately to Bill Clinton in 1992, and was not much dismayed when he vetoed the securities litigation bill high-tech entrepreneurs wanted at the behest of trial lawyer William Lerach; anyway, Congress overrode the veto. Silicon Valley is increasingly culturally liberal, has long been dovish on foreign policy and is so rich that it doesn't greatly mind higher taxes and government spending: the 14th voted 58%–31% for Clinton in 1996.

The congresswoman from the 14th District is Anna Eshoo, a Democrat elected in 1992. Born back East, she is the only member of Congress of Assyrian descent. She was a full time homemaker, then chaired the San Mateo County Democratic Party and was elected to the San Mateo Board of Supervisors in 1982. In 1988, she ran for the House, facing Tom Campbell, a Stanford Law professor and economics Ph.D. with high-tech backing. The two spent a total of $2.5 million, and Eshoo was the first congressional candidate to distribute videotapes to voters—a slick video with hip music, showing her in a postmodern office, telling voters that the Silicon Valley, unlike Orange County or Iowa, should be represented by someone special. Campbell won 52%–46%. But in 1992 he ran for the Senate (losing the Republican primary 38%–36% to conservative Bruce Herschensohn), and Eshoo ran for the House. In the primary she beat Assemblyman Ted Lempert, redistricted out of his seat at age 30, by 40%–36%; in the general, she distribute a Tsongas-like 58-page booklet of her issue positions and boasted of her work on setting up a managed-competition health plan for county government; she outspent Republican Tom Huening, and as George Bush was winning only 26% in the district, Eshoo won 57%–39%. (Two of her former opponents are back in office: Campbell won a state Senate seat and then the 15th District House seat in a 1995 special, and Lempert is again in the Assembly.)

In the House Eshoo's voting record is liberal, though somewhat less so on economic issues. She seemed a bit nervous about supporting the Clinton budget and tax package, which hit this high-income area hard, and hesitated long before supporting the North American Free Trade Agreement. She promised to back managed-competition healthcare reform but was not a major player on the issue. In 1994 she was reelected 61%–39%. In the Republican Congress she worked for securities litigation reform, and the veto override. She opposed the Community Decency Act restrictions on the Internet, sponsoring a bill to encourage parental control and replace "indecency" with "harmful to minors." In telecommunications reform she passed an amendment barring the FCC from setting a standard for cable compatibility and from establishing gatekeeper technology for home automation systems. She sought looser controls on high-tech exports and opposed the FASB accounting board proposal to charge stock options against earnings: Silicon Valley stands all. She worked to complete the Phleger estate purchase for the Golden Gate National Recreation Area and got $10 million to purchase Bair Island for the Don Edwards San Francisco Bay National Wildlife Refuge.

Eshoo was easily reelected in 1996.

The People: Pop. 1990: 571,058; 2% rural; 11% age 65+; 69% White; 5% Black; 12% Asian; 14% Hispanic origin. Households: 52% married couple families; 22% married couple fams. w. children; 73% college educ.; median household income: $50,078; per capita income: $26,047; median gross rent: $777; median house value: $401,600.

1996 Presidential Vote

Clinton (D)	137,561	(58%)
Dole (R)	73,302	(31%)
Perot (I)	13,939	(6%)
Other	13,193	(6%)

1992 Presidential Vote

Clinton (D)	143,765	(53%)
Bush (R)	71,754	(26%)
Perot (I)	53,047	(20%)

Rep. Anna G. Eshoo (D)

Elected 1992; b. Dec. 13, 1942, New Britain, CT; home, Atherton; Canada Col., A.A. 1975; Catholic; divorced.

Career: Chmn., San Mateo Cnty Dem. Party, 1980; Chief of Staff, CA Assembly Speaker McCarthy, 1981; San Mateo Cnty. Bd. of Supervisors, 1982–92, Pres., 1986.

DC Office: 308 CHOB 20515, 202-225-8104; Fax: 202-225-8890; e-mail: annagram@hr.house.gov.

District Offices: Palo Alto, 415-323-2984.

Committees: *Commerce* (14th of 23 D): Health & the Environment; Telecommunications, Trade & Consumer Protection.

Group Ratings

	ADA	ACLU	AFS	LCV	CFA	CON	NFIB	COC	ACU	NTLC	CHC
1996	85	73	100	75	100	89	29	29	0	13	7
1995	85	—	—	69	100	38	—	33	16	—	—

National Journal Ratings

	1995 LIB — 1995 CONS			1996 LIB — 1996 CONS		
Economic	76%	—	23%	69%	—	30%
Social	80%	—	13%	88%	—	0%
Foreign	93%	—	0%	90%	—	0%

Key Votes of the 104th Congress

1. Reduce Medicare Growth $	N	5. Flag Amendment	N	9. Cuban Embargo	N
2. Ovrd. Product Liab. Veto	N	6. Drop EPA Limits	Y	10. Bar Bosnia Troop $	N
3. Increase Min. Wage	Y	7. Repeal Assault-Weap. Ban	N	11. Cut Anti-Missile Defense	Y
4. Welfare Reform	N	8. Ovrd. Part. Birth Veto	N	12. Bar U.N. Uniforms	N

Election Results

1996 general	Anna G. Eshoo (D)	149,313	(65%)	($544,566)
	Ben Brink (R)	71,573	(31%)	($432,849)
	Others	9,289	(4%)	
1996 primary	Anna G. Eshoo (D)	unopposed		
1994 general	Anna G. Eshoo (D)	120,713	(61%)	($487,660)
	Ben Brink (R)	78,475	(39%)	($223,118)

FIFTEENTH DISTRICT

The broad valley of Santa Clara County around San Jose a few decades ago was mostly orchards and vineyards. Sheltered by mountains from the chilly ocean fogs, with soil incredibly fertile once it was irrigated, this valley produced peaches, plums, prunes, apricots and grapes and made San Jose half a century ago the nation's biggest fruit-packing center. Today, almost all the orchards have been replaced by subdivisions and shopping centers and office buildings, for Santa Clara County has become a metropolitan area of 1.5 million people. San Jose, with a growing downtown, an arena rising for its own major league hockey team (the San Jose Sharks), and a population of 782,000, has become a major American city. Santa Clara County is also the center of Silicon Valley, site of many creative firms that have made the United States the world's computer and microchip industry center, a phenomenon predicted by few if any national policymakers or corporate leaders a quarter-century ago.

The 15th Congressional District is made up of the central slice of Santa Clara County plus, over the mountains to the south, a portion of Santa Cruz County. Downtown San Jose is in the 16th District to the east, and Silicon Valley towns like Cupertino and Mountain View are in the 14th District to the west; the 15th District lies in between. At its northern end, near the salt evaporators and wetlands around San Francisco Bay, is the Great America theme park, not far from where a huge Lockheed plant was once one of the nation's largest defense contractors. Just to the south is Santa Clara, with its old mission and Santa Clara University. The 15th includes much of the upscale and middle-income neighborhoods of western San Jose, with over 300,000 people. It also has high-income suburbs nestled in what used to be vineyards beneath the encroaching mountains: Saratoga, Los Gatos, Monte Sereno. After all this settlement, the mountains remain surprisingly wild, a haunt of Ken Kesey's Merry Pranksters in the 1960s, now inhabited with rustic cabins and high-income houses in narrow valleys. Prosperous and pleased with its environment, confident in free-market economics and uneasy about the performance of the public sector, people here have been somewhat more conservative than in other quadrants of the Bay Area. There are fewer singles and gays here than farther north, fewer Mexican-Americans than farther east; the 11% who are Asian Americans are far likelier to be high-income producers than to be low-income supplicants. But the 1990s trend here, as elsewhere in the Bay Area and in contrast to most of the country, has been toward the Democrats. This is a place where any traces of cultural conservatism hurt the Republicans.

The congressman from the 15th District is Republican Tom Campbell, chosen in a special election in December 1995; he also was elected in what is now the 14th District in 1988 and 1990. Campbell grew up in Chicago, where his father was a federal judge and an ally of the Daley Democratic machine. He was an outstanding student at the University of Chicago and at Harvard Law School, served as a Supreme Court law clerk and earned an economics Ph.D. at Chicago. A believer in free markets, he worked at the Reagan FTC, then became a law professor at Stanford. In 1988 he ran for the House against a conservative Republican who had unaccountably gotten one term in this alien territory, and beat him in the primary and Anna Eshoo, now congresswoman herself, in the general, 52%–46%. Conservative on economics, liberal on cultural issues, he was easily reelected in 1990 and in 1992 ran for the Senate. In the Republican primary he lost narrowly, 38%–36%, to conservative Bruce Herschensohn, who lost in the general to Barbara Boxer, 48%–43%; many thought Campbell would have won. Campbell went back to California and in 1993 won a special election to the California Senate.

Then in October 1995, 15th District Congressman Norman Mineta, former chairman of the Public Works and Transportation Committee, resigned to become a lobbyist for Lockheed Martin. Under California's special election rules, all candidates would run in December 1995 and if one got a majority he was elected. Campbell was the only Republican and Jerry Estruth, a San Jose Councilman more than a decade before, the only Democrat, and Campbell was the clear favorite. Democrats decided to make this a test case of their strategy of campaigning against Newt Gingrich, who was very unpopular here, and ran anti-Gingrich ads. Campbell, much better financed with his Silicon Valley connections, espoused a reasonable middle in American politics and talked of balancing the budget and improving education; he also blamed Estruth for a $60 million investment loss for San Jose in 1984. Campbell won 59%–36%, a lesson that the get-Gingrich tactic would not sweep all before it, at least against a well-financed candidate who had other things going for him. Campbell's win also cost Democrats a majority in the California delegation for the first time in 37 years; but they won it back in 1996.

"My return is an opportunity to lead. Not be the only leader, but to be a leader in the moderate wing, and that is what I will do," said Campbell on winning. And as the junior member of the House, he did have some achievements: an amendment allowing economic committees to use dynamic scoring, taking effects of taxes on behavior, for informational purposes, and another to allow illegal immigrants to receive federal aid for immunization and treatment of communicable diseases. In California he got passed in March 1996 a referendum allowing voters to choose candidates in primaries regardless of party registration; he figured he might have won the Senate primary in 1992 under this system, and that it would help more moderate candidates and hurt extremes. In November 1996 he was elected to a full term by almost the same margin as 11 months before, 59%–35%. After the election, he called for rules changes, based on his California Senate experience: no legislating on appropriations, a hearing and a vote on one bill for every member every year, and election of committee chairmen by secret ballot (Democrats have a similar method and any Republican could move for a vote in their conference). That made little news. But Campbell made news in January 1997 when he decided he could not vote for Newt Gingrich for speaker because Gingrich had admitting making a misleading statement to the Ethics Committee on a material issue. Campbell went to Gingrich and called on him to withdraw, then voted for Jim Leach. "I've had the most remarkable feeling of a weight lifted from my shoulders." Obviously many Republicans were angry at him, but he reported no retaliations from the leadership.

Campbell's priorities for the 105th Congress include removing regulatory barriers in the housing industry, preemption of state laws on securities litigation, replacing some education aid grants with vouchers and reparations to Japanese of Latin American descent who were in U.S. detention camps in World War II. He has been mentioned often as a candidate against Senator Barbara Boxer in 1998, but in early 1997 was sticking to his 1995 promise not to run.

The People: Pop. 1990: 572,360; 4% rural; 9% age 65+; 76% White; 2% Black; 11% Asian; 1% Amer. Indian; 11% Hispanic origin. Households: 57% married couple families; 25% married couple fams. w. children; 68% college educ.; median household income: $50,823; per capita income: $22,833; median gross rent: $794; median house value: $290,200.

1996 Presidential Vote

Clinton (D)	125,438	(53%)
Dole (R)	83,846	(35%)
Perot (I)	17,506	(7%)
Other	11,155	(5%)

1992 Presidential Vote

Clinton (D)	127,060	(46%)
Bush (R)	83,301	(30%)
Perot (I)	64,192	(23%)

Rep. Tom Campbell (R)

Elected Dec. 1995; b. Aug. 14, 1952, Chicago, IL; home, Campbell; U. of Chicago, B.A., M.A., 1973, Ph.D. 1980, Harvard Law Schl., J.D. 1976; Catholic; married (Susanne).

Career: Law Clerk, Supreme Court, 1977–78; Practicing atty., 1978–80; White House Fellow, 1980–81; Exec. Asst. to Dpty. U.S. Atty. Gen., 1981; Dir., Federal Bureau of Competition, 1981–83; Prof., Stanford U., 1983–95; U.S. House of Reps., 1988–92; CA Senate, 1993–95.

DC Office: 2442 RHOB 20515; 202-225-2631; Fax: 202-225-6788; e-mail: campbell@hr.house.gov.

District Offices: Campbell, 408-371-7337.

Committees: *Banking & Financial Services* (10th of 30 R): Capital Markets, Securities & Government Sponsored Enterprises; Financial Institutions & Consumer Credit. *International Relations* (20th of 26 R): Africa; International Economic Policy & Trade.

Group Ratings (Only Served Partial Term)

	ADA	ACLU	AFS	LCV	CFA	CON	NFIB	COC	ACU	NTLC	CHC
1996	40	25	8	38	85	99	78	88	60	67	40
1995	*	—	—	*	*	*	—	*	*	—	—

National Journal Ratings (Only Served Partial Term)

	1995 LIB — 1995 CONS			1996 LIB — 1996 CONS		
Economic	*	—	*	39%	—	58%
Social	*	—	*	71%	—	28%
Foreign	*	—	*	72%	—	27%

Key Votes of the 104th Congress (Only Served Partial Term)

1. Reduce Medicare Growth $	*	5. Flag Amendment	*	9. Cuban Embargo	*
2. Ovrd. Product Liab. Veto	Y	6. Drop EPA Limits	*	10. Bar Bosnia Troop $	*
3. Increase Min. Wage	N	7. Repeal Assault-Weap. Ban	N	11. Cut Anti-Missile Defense	N
4. Welfare Reform	Y	8. Ovrd. Part. Birth Veto	N	12. Bar U.N. Uniforms	N

Election Results

1996 general	Tom Campbell (R)	132,737	(59%)	($527,125)
	Dick Lane (D)	79,048	(35%)	($64,732)
	Others	15,101	(7%)	
1996 primary	Tom Campbell (R)	unopposed		
1995 special	Tom Campbell (R)	54,372	(59%)	($1,650,740)
	Jerry Estruth (D)	33,051	(36%)	($805,409)
	Linh Kieu Dao (I)	4,922	(5%)	
1994 general	Norman Y. Mineta (D)	119,921	(60%)	($1,009,947)
	Robert Wick (R)	80,266	(40%)	($13,759)

SIXTEENTH DISTRICT

With more people than San Francisco, higher per capita incomes than San Diego, a tradition of high-tech innovation that rivals any on earth, and a major league sports team housed in California's biggest indoor arena, San Jose has great claims on national attention and respect. Yet San Jose—with the 11th largest population within city limits in the United States—does not yet bulk as large in the national consciousness as it should. At the southern end of the Bay, it remains in San Francisco's shadow. San Francisco is every tourist's idea of a city: geographically compact, with picturesque public transportation, old-time immigrant groups and new, an economy historically based on heavy industry and sea trade, a large city bureaucracy symbolized by a monumental city hall. San Jose is quite different. It got its start as a farm-market town, with canneries and fruit-packing operations for the produce from the surrounding fertile plains. It sits not on the Bay, but on the Southern Pacific line above the marshes and salt evaporators; its major transportation arteries are the freeways—U.S. 101, Interstates 280 and 680, California 17—which encircle its revitalized downtown. The main minority group here is Mexican-Americans, who initially came as farm workers but now inhabit every occupational niche and, while concentrated on the east side, are also scattered throughout San Jose and adjacent towns; there are also increasing numbers of Asian Americans. And scattered is the right word to describe San Jose's growth. Starting in the 1950s, San Jose has grown out in every direction, developers hip-hopping across the farmland, putting up subdivisions faster sometimes than the few city employees could update the street map. Economically, San Jose has been sustained by everything from its traditional agriculture to lots of manufacturing to the high-tech businesses that are centered in Silicon Valley towns just to the west but are omnipresent here: an American city, 21st Century style.

The 16th Congressional District consists of the larger part of San Jose, plus its urban fringe to the east and the still agricultural Santa Clara Valley to the south, including Gilroy, the garlic capital of the United States. It includes the old and new downtown and the heavily Mexican-American areas to the east. This is the most heavily Hispanic district in the Bay Area (37%) and is also heavily Asian (20%), with the largest concentration of Vietnamese in the U.S. Politically, it has become Democratic, and its future leanings depend on the trends among Latinos, who are family-oriented and not as favorable to big government as blacks, and Asians, who are more often the victims than the beneficiaries of liberals' quota schemes.

The congresswoman from the 16th District is Zoe Lofgren, a Democrat elected in 1994. Lofgren grew up in the Bay Area, went to Stanford and Santa Clara Law School, worked for eight years as a local staffer to Congressman Don Edwards. In 1980 she was elected to the Santa Clara County Board of Supervisors, where she spearheaded a 1984 ballot proposition to give local governments control of freeway building and moved the jails from the sheriff's office to the local corrections department. In 1994 when Edwards retired after 32 years in the House, Lofgren ran for the seat. Her main primary opponent, former (1983–90) San Jose Mayor Tom McEnery, started off better known. But Lofgren raised almost twice as much money with the support of the National Women's Political Caucus, the National Organization for Women, EMILY's List, Senator Barbara Boxer and Congresswomen Anna Eshoo and Lynn Woolsey. She won the primary 45%–42%. She easily won the general election and looked forward to putting into effect her ideas for early intervention to fight gun violence and drug abuse and to help underprivileged children.

But to her surprise she found herself in the minority. "It has been frustrating because so much of what the Gingrich agenda has been is stuff I don't agree with," she said. "But there is an obligation to try to do something useful. I have had a lot of amendments adopted." They included: on a crime bill, defining children as up to age 14 rather than 11; on immigration reform, restoring protection for battered spouses and children; on regulatory reform, exempting from anti-regulatory rules some FDA procedures on AIDS drugs, FAA actions on unsafe plane and EPA responses to oil spills; on Telecommunications, to help schools get access to the Internet. Her voting record was generally liberal, but somewhat less so on economics. She opposed the Communications Decency Act and tried to encourage screening devices to allow parents to restrict children's access to the Internet. She supported a ban on states' taxing government retirees' pensions when they had moved away to another state.

Lofgren meets with constituents over an ironing board in front of supermarkets. She was reelected easily in 1996.

The People: Pop. 1990: 571,460; 4% rural; 7% age 65+; 38% White; 5% Black; 20% Asian; 1% Amer. Indian; 37% Hispanic origin. Households: 57% married couple families; 32% married couple fams. w. children; 49% college educ.; median household income: $42,223; per capita income: $14,614; median gross rent: $718; median house value: $233,600.

1996 Presidential Vote			1992 Presidential Vote		
Clinton (D)	91,786	(61%)	Clinton (D)	86,418	(52%)
Dole (R)	43,257	(29%)	Bush (R)	44,693	(27%)
Perot (I)	9,659	(6%)	Perot (I)	33,882	(20%)
Other	5,195	(3%)			

Rep. Zoe Lofgren (D)

Elected 1994; b. Dec. 21, 1947, San Mateo; home, San Jose; Stanford U., B.A. 1970, U. of Santa Clara Law Schl., J.D. 1975; Protestant; married (John Collins).

Career: Staff Asst., U.S. Rep. Don Edwards, 1970–78; Practicing atty., 1978–80; Prof., U. of Santa Clara Law Schl., 1981–94; Santa Clara Bd. of Supervisors, 1980–94.

DC Office: 318 CHOB 20515, 202-225-3072; Fax: 202-225-3336.

District Offices: San Jose, 408-271-8700.

Committees: *Judiciary* (9th of 15 D): Courts & Intellectual Property; Immigration & Claims. *Science* (12th of 21 D): Energy & Environment; Space & Aeronautics.

Group Ratings

	ADA	ACLU	AFS	LCV	CFA	CON	NFIB	COC	ACU	NTLC	CHC
1996	85	94	100	77	92	48	27	31	5	7	0
1995	95	—	—	81	92	9	—	21	8	—	—

National Journal Ratings

	1995 LIB — 1995 CONS			1996 LIB — 1996 CONS		
Economic	80%	—	18%	65%	—	33%
Social	88%	—	0%	84%	—	12%
Foreign	79%	—	17%	90%	—	0%

Key Votes of the 104th Congress

1. Reduce Medicare Growth $	N	5. Flag Amendment	N	9. Cuban Embargo	N
2. Ovrd. Product Liab. Veto	N	6. Drop EPA Limits	Y	10. Bar Bosnia Troop $	Y
3. Increase Min. Wage	Y	7. Repeal Assault-Weap. Ban	N	11. Cut Anti-Missile Defense	Y
4. Welfare Reform	N	8. Ovrd. Part. Birth Veto	N	12. Bar U.N. Uniforms	N

Election Results

1996 general	Zoe Lofgren (D)	94,020	(66%)	($191,393)
	Chuck Wojslaw (R)	43,197	(30%)	($77,796)
	Others	5,990	(4%)	
1996 primary	Zoe Lofgren (D)	unopposed		
1994 general	Zoe Lofgren (D)	74,935	(65%)	($646,764)
	Lyle J. Smith (R)	40,409	(35%)	

SEVENTEENTH DISTRICT

The California coast around Monterey Bay is for many a working definition of paradise. This kernel of California history, where Spanish and then Mexicans governed a virtually empty land and Californians set up their first state capital, still makes a fine living, as it has for nearly 150 years, off the land and sea. The fields around Salinas supply much of the nation's lettuce and cauliflower, the fields around Castroville supply almost all of its artichokes, and the vast greenhouses around Watsonville supply a goodly portion of its roses. The fishing fleet and 18 canneries of Monterey are not the major industry they were half a century ago (the last cannery closed 25 years ago), but they have generated a new industry: Cannery Row is refurbished with upscale shops and hotels, and the magnificent Monterey Bay Aquarium has become one of California's top tourist destinations. Monterey Bay has become the language learning capital of the United States, with the Defense Language Institute, the AT&T Language Line and the new Cal State University Monterey Bay Center for Intensive Language and Culture. There are other attractions on the Monterey peninsula as well, like the Pebble Beach golf courses and the Del Monte Lodge, and Carmel, whose restrictive laws—no house numbers, no door-to-door mail delivery, no live entertainment, no stop lights, no cutting trees without city council permission—reflect an effort to maintain the atmosphere of 80 years ago, when it really was an artists' colony.

The 17th Congressional District of California includes all the coast of Monterey Bay and then follows the Big Sur coastline south almost to William Randolph Hearst's castle, San Simeon, past perhaps the most beautiful scenery in America. The district extends inland, into sunny valleys sheltered from ocean mists, and covers some of the nation's richest farmland. This area is a prime example of how the California coast has trended Democratic. The older residents—landowners in Salinas and the townspeople who sympathize with them, retirees in Santa Cruz and the Monterey Peninsula—still vote Republican. But an influx of liberation-minded young people now in their prime years, attracted less by the economy than by the atmosphere, moved the coast to the left. Also, the branch of the University of California at Santa Cruz is so liberal (97% for McGovern in 1972) that it has changed the political balance of the whole county. As late as 1980, Monterey and Santa Cruz Counties were voting less Democratic than the nation. But since 1984 they have been 6% to 10% more Democratic than the nation.

The congressman from the 17th is Sam Farr, a Democrat elected in June 1993. Farr, a fifth-generation Californian, grew up in the area, where his father Fred Farr was a state Senator for many years. Sam Farr after college signed up for the Peace Corps, learned Spanish at the Monterey Institute of International Studies and served two years in Colombia. He was a staffer in the California Assembly for a decade, became a Monterey County supervisor in 1975 and was elected to the Assembly in 1980. There he wrote one of the nation's strictest oil spill liability laws and expanded the state park system. In 1993 the 17th's congressman since 1976, Leon Panetta, resigned to become Office of Management and Budget director, and Farr ran for the House. He entered the race as the overwhelming favorite, and in the all-party primary won 26% to beat two other Democrats who had 19% and 14%. But in the June runoff, after the Clinton budget and tax plan had been introduced, he had trouble against Republican Bill McCampbell, who had been beaten 72%–24% by Panetta seven months before. Farr won, but by just 52%–43%.

In his first years in the House he may have been representing paradise but it sometimes seemed the opposite. The 1991 base closing law closed Fort Ord, site of the Language Institute—one of the biggest closures in the country. Farr worked to get $15 million to help start the California State University campus there (in his second term he got an additional $36 million) and to install a Defense Department finance center. The Clinton Administration legislative agenda, which he mostly supported, got into terrible trouble. In November 1994 Farr again faced McCampell and lost Monterey County, winning by enough in Santa Cruz for a 52%–44% victory. After the election there was terrible flooding. A local official "asked me whether, being in the minority, I was able to handle disasters. I said becoming the minority was a disaster. I am disaster equipped." But Farr had some successes, as well as some failures, in the Republican Congress. He got more funding for Cal State and a new veterans' clinic. He saved 300 jobs at Social Security's Salinas Data Operations Center. On the Agriculture Committee he got two amendments to the Freedom to Farm Act, one with $35 million to help state and local conservation efforts to purchase development rights from farmland owners, one with $1 million to help start community-based produce markets, gardens and other food-access projects—two pet Farr causes. He opposed Richard Pombo's bill to allow 250,000 foreign farm workers in, arguing that growers who pay good wages don't need to import workers; this was a contrast to Panetta's sponsorship in the 1980s of guest worker programs. Farr pushed unsuccessfully to impose a 50-mile off-shore limit on oil tankers and will again try in 1997 to restore the duty on Colombian-grown flowers. Farr produced a campaign finance reform bill, of uncertain constitutionality, which would limit campaign spending to $600,000, PAC spending to $200,000 a cycle, and personal spending to $50,000; it lost on the floor 243–177.

In 1996 Farr faced the director of the Santa Cruz Farm Bureau and won impressively, 59%–38%.

The People: Pop. 1990: 571,077; 15% rural; 10% age 65+; 58% White; 4% Black; 6% Asian; 1% Amer. Indian; 32% Hispanic origin. Households: 57% married couple families; 29% married couple fams. w. children; 54% college educ.; median household income: $33,911; per capita income: $15,006; median gross rent: $643; median house value: $219,100.

1996 Presidential Vote			**1992 Presidential Vote**		
Clinton (D)	109,941	(55%)	Clinton (D)	111,937	(52%)
Dole (R)	64,178	(32%)	Bush (R)	57,990	(27%)
Perot (I)	12,795	(6%)	Perot (I)	42,317	(20%)
Other	12,020	(6%)			

Rep. Sam Farr (D)

Elected June 1993; b. July 4, 1941, San Francisco; home, Carmel; Willamette U., B.S. 1963; Episcopalian; married (Shary).

Career: Peace Corps, Columbia, 1963–65; Staff, CA Assembly, 1965–75; Monterey Cnty. Bd. of Supervisors, 1975–80, Chmn., 1979; CA Assembly, 1980–93.

DC Office: 1117 LHOB 20515, 202-225-2861; Fax: 202-225-6791; e-mail: samfarr@mail.house.gov.

District Offices: Monterey, 408-649-3555; Salinas, 408-424-2229; Santa Cruz, 408-429-1976.

Committees: *Agriculture* (14th of 23 D): Forestry, Resource Conservation & Research; Livestock, Dairy & Poultry. *Resources* (16th of 23 D): Fisheries Conservation, Wildlife & Oceans; Water & Power.

Group Ratings

	ADA	ACLU	AFS	LCV	CFA	CON	NFIB	COC	ACU	NTLC	CHC
1996	90	75	100	85	92	60	17	31	0	7	0
1995	90	—	—	88	100	4	—	17	4	—	—

National Journal Ratings

	1995 LIB — 1995 CONS			1996 LIB — 1996 CONS		
Economic	85%	—	12%	79%	—	18%
Social	88%	—	0%	88%	—	0%
Foreign	93%	—	0%	82%	—	16%

Key Votes of the 104th Congress

1. Reduce Medicare Growth $	N	5. Flag Amendment	N	9. Cuban Embargo	N
2. Ovrd. Product Liab. Veto	N	6. Drop EPA Limits	Y	10. Bar Bosnia Troop $	N
3. Increase Min. Wage	Y	7. Repeal Assault-Weap. Ban	N	11. Cut Anti-Missile Defense	Y
4. Welfare Reform	N	8. Ovrd. Part. Birth Veto	N	12. Bar U.N. Uniforms	N

Election Results

1996 general	Sam Farr (D)	115,116	(59%)	($563,235)
	Jess Brown (R)	73,856	(38%)	($455,239)
	Others	6,573	(3%)	
1996 primary	Sam Farr (D)	52,481	(88%)	
	Art Dunn (D)	6,032	(10%)	
	Others	1,304	(2%)	
1994 general	Sam Farr (D)	87,222	(52%)	($387,872)
	Bill McCampbell (R)	74,380	(44%)	($451,490)
	Others	5,591	(3%)	

EIGHTEENTH DISTRICT

The Central Valley of California is a miraculous man-made landscape, a horizontal factory stretching as far as the eye can see. Nature created the vast flatlands, rimmed by mountains rising surreally in the distant haze. But man in the last century has disciplined the land with a remorseless mile-square grid of roads, and the sluggish-flowing California Aqueduct and dozens of arrow-straight canals; pipes fitted with valves and gauges to pump water and fertilizer and pesticides to the fields in measured quantities give an air of industrial precision. The crops grow in carefully spaced rows, filling the fields, for the rich soil and the irrigated water are too precious to waste on decoration or flower gardens: the Valley is business. Farming here has always been an industrial enterprise; in the 19th Century the land was not given to 160-acre homesteaders but sold to thousands-of-acres capitalist enterprises.

The Central Valley was one of California's surprise boom areas in the 1980s, growing not just crops but people. Middle-wage employees in the San Francisco Bay area drive east at the end of the day on I-580, past surreal windmills whirling on the bare hills of the Altamont pass, across the Westlands fields to modestly priced homes in Modesto, the town immortalized (when it was much smaller) in *American Graffiti*. Water was scarce in the drought years of the late 1980s, and heavily subsidized water was cut off from cultivators of cotton (which after all can be grown in many states where nature provides the water for free), but the towns and countryside of the Central Valley have been generating a well-rounded economy. On the down side, traffic has become a problem, air pollution on bad days has approached coastal metropolitan levels, and the pace of life is getting more hectic and frazzled.

The 18th Congressional District includes a large chunk of the Central Valley from Modesto and Stanislaus County south through Merced almost to Fresno. The political tradition here is Democratic: Democrats in Washington and Democratic Governor Pat Brown built the irrigation canals and authorized the water subsidies; Democrats own the McClatchy newspapers, the predominant Valley chain; Democrats staffed the Bank of America, long the dominant financial force here; on the walls of insider law firms are signed pictures of Franklin Roosevelt and Pat Brown, not Ronald Reagan and Pete Wilson. Today the voters of the 18th District remain fairly heavily Democratic. There are many Latinos here, and an increasing number of Asians, though neither group produces the overwhelming Democratic majorities blacks do; there are some voters of white southern ancestry, used to voting for local Democrats though happy to vote Republican for president. The Central Valley is the part of California with the highest proportion of families and children, and there is a natural cultural conservatism here, shared by successful local Democratic politicians.

The congressman from the 18th District is Gary Condit, a Democrat chosen in a September 1989 special election to replace Democratic Whip Tony Coelho after he resigned, and now one of the key Democrats in a closely-divided House. Condit is a native of Oklahoma and son of a Baptist minister; in 1972, the year he graduated from college, he was elected to the Ceres Council at 24. He was elected to the Stanislaus County Board of Supervisors in 1976 and the California Assembly in 1982. There he made an attractive moderate to conservative record on crime and taxes and was one of the "Gang of Five" Democrats who nearly toppled Speaker Willie Brown in 1988—and were fiercely retaliated against. When Coelho surprised everyone by resigning, Condit seized the chance to run for Congress. Against former state Senator Clare Berryhill, Condit raised money efficiently and ran an absentee voter drive which essentially won the election before it was held. Some 35% of all votes were cast absentee, the large majority Democratic, and Condit won 57%–35%.

Condit has since had the most conservative voting record of any California Democrat: for the balanced budget amendment and line-item veto, against publicly funded abortions, against the 1993 Clinton budget and tax increase, for relaxed environmental restrictions. He had little influence when Democrats were in the majority, but became a key member after the 1994 election. He was the prime Democratic co-sponsor of the unfunded mandates bill, which passed in 1995; when Democratic leader Richard Gephardt refused to appoint him to the conference committee, Speaker Newt Gingrich appointed him instead; the bill Condit helped produce was signed by Clinton. He backed regulatory reform, including risk assessment and cost-benefit analysis. He supported tort reform and product liability reform. He was a founding member of the Coalition, a group of 20-some moderate Democrats widely known as the Blue Dogs; they are not yellow dog Democrats, they said, always faithful to the party, but dogs who were choked till they were blue by liberal Democrats. "We are not a hostile group and we are not mad at anyone. We just want to do what's right for the country and vote our conscience," Condit insists. But "the fact is, our leadership did not want to have a balanced budget and did not want welfare reform. With all due respect, that's unacceptable."

In fall 1995 Condit and the Blue Dogs prepared a budget proposal that balanced in seven years, had no tax cuts, reduced the growth of Medicaid spending but did not block-grant it to the states, did not backload its budget cuts in the sixth and seventh years. But it was opposed by both Democratic and Republican leaderships, even during the government shutdown. Condit cast other conservative votes—for Richard Pombo's guest worker bill, for the June 1996 Republican budget resolution, for scientific risk assessment of government regulation. But he is opposed to school vouchers, NAFTA, the privatization of Social Security. He is a lead sponsor of STEP-21, a transportation spending formula which would guarantee every state 95% of what it puts in.

In the 1996 campaign cycle, the Blue Dogs encouraged like-minded Democrats wherever they could find them; 10 days after the election they formed their group of 23 members including seven freshmen. Their agenda includes a balanced budget, campaign finance reform and tax relief; they agreed to meet regularly with the Lunch Bunch moderate Republicans. Condit, pressed often to switch parties himself, said that party switching was "over with." In a closely divided House he and the Blue Dogs have the potential for great leverage; but there is also the possibility that Gephardt Democrats will move even farther left and Gingrich Republicans even farther right.

That poses few electoral problems for Condit, who rides a Harley when he is back home and is confident enough of reelection that he gives campaign funds to charities. He was reelected with 66% in 1990, 1994 and 1996; in 1992 he had no Republican opponent.

The People: Pop. 1990: 571,358; 19% rural; 10% age 65+; 65% White; 3% Black; 6% Asian; 1% Amer. Indian; 26% Hispanic origin. Households: 61% married couple families; 33 married couple fams. w.

children; 41% college educ.; median household income: $28,324; per capita income: $12,013; median gross rent: $462; median house value: $113,600.

1996 Presidential Vote

Clinton (D)	77,560	(46%)
Dole (R)	76,217	(45%)
Perot (I)	12,161	(7%)
Other	3,470	(2%)

1992 Presidential Vote

Clinton (D)	74,357	(41%)
Bush (R)	67,898	(37%)
Perot (I)	39,645	(22%)

Rep. Gary A. Condit (D)

Elected Sept., 1989; b. Apr. 21, 1948, Salina, OK; home, Ceres; Modesto Jr. Col., A.A. 1970, CA St. U., B.A. 1972; Protestant; married (Carolyn).

Career: Ceres City Cncl., 1972–76; Ceres Mayor, 1974–76; Stanislaus Cnty. Bd. of Supervisors, 1976–82; CA Assembly, 1982–89.

DC Office: 2245 RHOB 20515, 202-225-6131; Fax: 202-225-0819; e-mail: gcondit@hr.house.gov.

District Offices: Merced, 209-383-4455; Modesto, 209-527-1914.

Committees: *Agriculture* (3rd of 23 D): Livestock, Dairy & Poultry; Risk Management & Specialty Crops (RMM). *Government Reform & Oversight* (7th of 19 D): National Economic Growth, Natural Resources & Regulatory Affairs; National Security, International Affairs & Criminal Justice.

Group Ratings

	ADA	ACLU	AFS	LCV	CFA	CON	NFIB	COC	ACU	NTLC	CHC
1996	35	33	50	69	31	95	78	63	70	71	50
1995	40	—	—	6	31	75	—	79	60	—	—

National Journal Ratings

	1995 LIB — 1995 CONS			1996 LIB — 1996 CONS		
Economic	53%	—	47%	52%	—	47%
Social	51%	—	48%	53%	—	45%
Foreign	62%	—	36%	61%	—	37%

Key Votes of the 104th Congress

1. Reduce Medicare Growth $	N	5. Flag Amendment	Y	9. Cuban Embargo	Y
2. Ovrd. Product Liab. Veto	Y	6. Drop EPA Limits	N	10. Bar Bosnia Troop $	Y
3. Increase Min. Wage	Y	7. Repeal Assault-Weap. Ban	N	11. Cut Anti-Missile Defense	Y
4. Welfare Reform	Y	8. Ovrd. Part. Birth Veto	Y	12. Bar U.N. Uniforms	Y

Election Results

1996 general	Gary A. Condit (D)	108,827	(66%)	($678,001)
	Bill Conrad (R)	52,695	(32%)	($75,271)
	Others	4,064	(2%)	
1996 primary	Gary A. Condit (D)	unopposed		
1994 general	Gary A. Condit (D)	91,105	(66%)	($387,494)
	Tom Carter (R)	44,046	(32%)	
	Others	3,901	(3%)	

NINETEENTH DISTRICT

Fresno, in California's Central Valley, between the flat Westlands and the Sierras, is a city agricultural and industrial, middle American and ethnically diverse. It is a creation of the industrial age, founded by the Central Pacific Railroad; its city fathers bred the local wine grape, developed the raisin industry and introduced the Smyrna fig. But these are not all of Fresno County's crops, which include cotton, lima beans, tomatoes, cantaloupes, plums, peaches and alfalfa: Fresno produces more farm products in dollar value than any other county in the United States. Central Valley agriculture is industrial in its precision, its thoroughness and its ownership by large corporations: the vineyards outside Fresno radiate in mechanical precision, with vines just 10 feet apart and exposed to the relentless summer sun—nothing romantic or quaint here. The city of Fresno started off as a farm-marketing center—one high-income neighborhood is called Fig Garden, because that's what it used to be—and as a tourists' stop-off point on the way to Yosemite National Park. But it has long since grown out north, east and west from its old downtown, and its economy has diversified.

Like all the Central Valley, Fresno has always been ethnically diverse, with a telephone book that reads like the United Nations. It has America's second largest Armenian community, after Los Angeles; Fresno's great chronicler was William Saroyan. Its already large Latino population doubled to more than 100,000 in the 1980s; Asians, including Chinese, Filipinos, Vietnamese and Hmong, may number as many as 50,000. Fresno has had its troubles in the 1990s, as immigration continued despite high unemployment, violent teenage gangs and air pollution that made the Sierra Nevada invisible on many days. Local politics was run by Democrats for years, but in 1993 Fresno elected as mayor Republican Jim Patterson, a religious broadcaster who immediately got more policemen out patrolling without increasing taxes and set about reducing burdens on business. Patterson argues that liberals are dividing voters by stressing ethnic differences and conservatives should unite them by stressing common values. It was an anticipation of the state and national trends of 1994, of voters seeking discipline rather than therapy, enforcement of old moral rules rather than erection of new government buildings. Fresno County, long heavily Democratic, voted 63%–33% for Pete Wilson over Kathleen Brown, and in 1996, against the national trend, it favored Bob Dole over Bill Clinton, 47%–45%.

The 19th Congressional District of California includes most of Fresno, all but the old downtown and a Latino area reserved for the Hispanic-majority 20th District. The 19th spreads with an erose boundary over the farm country below the foothills of the Sierras from Visalia, south of Fresno, to mountainous Mariposa County. Most of its land mass is part of the Sierra Nevada, and it contains most of three major national parks, Yosemite, Kings Canyon and Sequoia. Strongly Democratic historically, it trended Republican through the 1980s, and after a pause in 1992 trended even harder that way in 1994 and 1996.

The congressman from the 19th District is George Radanovich, a Republican elected in 1994. Radanovich is the son of Croatian immigrants, with relatives all over the Valley. He worked on the family farm, served on the Mariposa County Planning Commission in the 1980s, won a seat on the Board of Supervisors in 1989. In 1986, after studying the local microclimates, he opened the first winery in Mariposa County and made it work; the Radanovich Winery now ships 4,000 cases of sauvignon blanc, chardonnay, merlot, zinfandel and cabernet sauvignon. In 1992 he ran for Congress, losing the primary 33%–30% to 28-year-old Tal Cloud, who lost to incumbent Democrat Richard Lehman 47%–46%. Lehman was an adept professional politician, an Assembly staffer at 22, assemblyman at 28, congressman at 34; but all his fundraising and skills could not avail him in 1994 as Radanovich, this time an easy winner in the primary, attacked him for supporting the Clinton Administration and for California Democrat George Miller's attempts to raise the price of Valley water. Radanovich won 57%–40%, the widest defeat of a non-freshman incumbent in 1994.

In the House Radanovich was elected president of the 74-member freshman Republicans. A bit moderate on economics, his record was solidly conservative on cultural and foreign issues. He defied conventional wisdom on several counts. He defended the government shutdown, even when it closed Yosemite during the holiday season, and said he would prefer government default before voting to increase the debt limit. In June 1995 he stopped answering constituent mail, sending a form letter explaining how expensive the average member's mail is; the Democratic *Fresno Bee* applauded. He worked on local issues, calling for a light rail in Yosemite even if other parks had to be closed to fund it, and getting 67 families continued access to isolated cabins in Sequoia National Park. In June 1996 his amendment to require Turkey to acknowledge the Armenian genocide of 1915 passed the House 268–153; Turkey spurned aid under such conditions.

This proved to be a highly popular record. Radanovich had weak opposition and was reelected 67%–28%. He opened the 105th Congress by sponsoring with John Doolittle a bill to restore Yosemite after disastrous flood, seeking prompt reopening, cooperation with local governments and businesses, and building a way to prevent future flood damage. He also sponsored a bill to redirect the $22 million in aid for Turkey to Armenia.

The People: Pop. 1990: 573,077; 20% rural; 11% age 65+; 65% White; 3% Black; 7% Asian; 1% Amer. Indian; 24% Hispanic origin. Households: 57% married couple families; 28% married couple fams. w. children; 52% college educ.; median household income: $29,153; per capita income: $13,516; median gross rent: $450; median house value: $90,200.

1996 Presidential Vote

Dole (R)	111,666	(52%)
Clinton (D)	85,744	(40%)
Perot (I)	12,495	(6%)
Other	4,816	(2%)

1992 Presidential Vote

Bush (R)	97,124	(43%)
Clinton (D)	85,049	(38%)
Perot (I)	41,052	(18%)

Rep. George P. Radanovich (R)

Elected 1994; b. June 20, 1955, Mariposa; home, Mariposa; CA Polytechnic U., B.S. 1978; Catholic; married (Ethie).

Career: Farmer; Mariposa Cnty. Planning Comm., 1982–86, Chmn., 1985–86; Mariposa Cnty. Bd. of Supervisors, 1989–92; Founder & Owner, Radanovich Winery, 1986–present.

DC Office: 213 CHOB 20515, 202-225-4540; Fax: 202-225-3402; e-mail: george.radanovich@mail.house.gov.

District Offices: Fresno, 209-248-0800.

Committees: *Budget* (15th of 24 R). *Resources* (15th of 27 R): Forests & Forest Health; National Parks & Public Lands; Water & Power.

Group Ratings

	ADA	ACLU	AFS	LCV	CFA	CON	NFIB	COC	ACU	NTLC	CHC
1996	0	7	0	23	15	59	100	94	100	100	100
1995	0	—	—	0	0	56	—	100	96	—	—

National Journal Ratings

	1995 LIB	—	1995 CONS	1996 LIB	—	1996 CONS
Economic	0%	—	74%	29%	—	70%
Social	0%	—	79%	0%	—	90%
Foreign	15%	—	73%	0%	—	79%

Key Votes of the 104th Congress

1. Reduce Medicare Growth $	Y	5. Flag Amendment	Y	9. Cuban Embargo	Y
2. Ovrd. Product Liab. Veto	Y	6. Drop EPA Limits	N	10. Bar Bosnia Troop $	Y
3. Increase Min. Wage	N	7. Repeal Assault-Weap. Ban	*	11. Cut Anti-Missile Defense	N
4. Welfare Reform	Y	8. Ovrd. Part. Birth Veto	Y	12. Bar U.N. Uniforms	Y

Election Results

1996 general	George P. Radanovich (R)	137,402	(67%)	($618,220)
	Paul Barile (D)	58,452	(28%)	($6,509)
	Others	10,525	(5%)	
1996 primary	George P. Radanovich (R)	unopposed		
1994 general	George P. Radanovich (R)	104,435	(57%)	($468,818)
	Richard H. Lehman (D)	72,912	(40%)	($1,079,999)
	Others	6,579	(4%)	

TWENTIETH DISTRICT

California's Central Valley by car seems a monotonous landscape: mile after mile of farmland with mile-square grid roads, cut across by diagonal railroads and canals, with an occasional cluster town. The land is hilly and gets more water near the Sierra Nevada, and this is where the larger cities cluster. On the other side is the Westlands, where the land is flatter and the water scarcer. Here are huge farming operations, like the J.G. Boswell holdings—the largest farming operation in the world—augmented by purchase of the rival Salyer acreage near Corcoran. This land was always developed and sold in giant plots. And it produces plenty: alfalfa, cantaloupes, cotton, grapes, lima beans, olives, peaches, plums, raisins, sugar beets, tomatoes, walnuts, wheat. The owners are a hardy lot, but like most entrepreneurs they have been happy to use government help: crop price supports, agricultural research, exceptions to the immigration laws, irrigation systems and (most important) subsidized water. They have fought hard against liberals' efforts at change, from Governor Jerry Brown's attempts to encourage Cesar Chavez's United Farm Workers in the 1970s to former House Natural Resources Committee Chairman George Miller's 1992 law to draw off more water to the Sacramento delta and charge higher prices for it in the Valley. But the greatest threats may come from conservatives: in a free market for water, Los Angeles users may outbid the farmers, and restrictions on illegal immigrants, like 1994's Proposition 187, may cut off the supply of farm workers.

The 20th Congressional District includes most of the Westlands of the Central Valley, from south of Bakersfield to north of Fresno. Its irregular boundaries were drawn to maximize the Hispanic population, so the 20th includes the old downtown neighborhoods of both Bakersfield and Fresno, but none of their newer suburbs; it includes heavily Latino towns like Delano, long Chavez's headquarters, but not more Anglo places like Tulare. The 20th's Hispanic percentage is 55%, compared to 20%–26% in other Central Valley districts, but many Latinos don't vote; still, it is the most Democratic seat between Sacramento and Los Angeles.

The congressman from the 20th is Calvin Dooley, a Democrat elected in 1990. He is a farmer, growing cotton, alfalfa and walnuts as his great-grandfather did before him. In the late 1987 he became a staffer for Tulare state Senator Rose Ann Vuich. In 1990, he ran for Congress in a more Republican-leaning district. Luck was with him: incumbent Chip Pashayan had accepted contributions from S&L operator Charles Keating and then interceded with regulators on his behalf. He had also switched off the Resources Committee, which handles so many Valley issues, onto Rules in 1989. Dooley won with a solid 55%. When new district lines were announced in 1992, Dooley avoided a primary with 10-year incumbent Democrat Richard Lehman, who ran in the much more Republican 19th District; Lehman barely won, and was defeated in 1994, while Dooley won 65%–34% in 1992 and 57%–43% in 1994.

That was partly a testimonial to Dooley's somewhat moderate voting record. He tottered before voting for the Clinton budget and tax package, and he supported the balanced budget amendment and the line-item veto. In the Republican 104th Congress, Dooley voted for much of the Contract with America and supported most of welfare reform. In his committee work he tended to district interests. On the Agriculture Committee, he worked on the complex dairy issues, co-sponsoring an amendment with New York Republican Gerald Solomon to phase out butter, cheese and powder price supports and consolidate the 33 milk marketing orders into no more than 14, with a guarantee that California could set its own standard for pricing and milk solids. He was one of three Committee Democrats to vote for Richard Pombo's guest worker bill. In August 1995 he switched his vote on maintaining EPA's powers because he learned that it would force Fresno to spend $197 million and Hanford $30 million to remove radon and arsenic from water; as a result, the amendment failed 210–210 and EPA lost. He came out for eliminating cotton subsidies, a sensitive issue; he had pledged in 1990 not to accept them, but he and his family got $120,000 in cotton subsidies between 1992 and 1994.

In 1996 Dooley got his toughest competition since 1990, from term-limited Assemblyman Trice Harvey. Against gun control, pro-choice on abortion, the Agriculture Committee chairman who preserved the use of the pesticide methyl bromide, Harvey received considerable funding from national Republicans. The campaign got nasty: Dooley accused Harvey of sexual harassment for settling a lawsuit by a state employee. In tribute to conservative feeling here, Dooley stressed welfare reform, the balanced budget and getting tough on crime, meanwhile cultivating Latino voters by coming out against Proposition 209. As Bill Clinton was carrying the 20th 52%–41%, Dooley won 57%–39%. In the 105th Congress, Dooley is one of the co-chairs of the New Democratic Coalition, formerly the Mainstream Forum, a group of moderate Democrats.

The People: Pop. 1990: 573,555; 27% rural; 9% age 65+; 33% White; 6% Black; 5% Asian; 1% Amer. Indian; 55% Hispanic origin. Households: 60% married couple families; 35% married couple fams. w. children; 26% college educ.; median household income: $21,140; per capita income: $8,097; median gross rent: $379; median house value: $63,400.

1996 Presidential Vote			**1992 Presidential Vote**		
Clinton (D)	62,164	(52%)	Clinton (D)	55,942	(47%)
Dole (R)	48,446	(41%)	Bush (R)	44,674	(37%)
Perot (I)	6,617	(6%)	Perot (I)	18,568	(16%)

Rep. Cal Dooley (D)

Elected 1990; b. Jan. 11, 1954, Visalia; home, Visalia; U. of CA at Davis, B.S. 1977, Stanford U., M.A. 1987; Methodist; married (Linda).

Career: Farmer, 1978–91; A.A., CA Sen. Rose Ann Vuich, 1987–89.

DC Office: 1201 LHOB 20515, 202-225-3341; Fax: 202-225-9308.

District Offices: Hanford, 209-585-8171.

Committees: *Agriculture* (5th of 23 D): Forestry, Resource Conservation & Research (RMM); Livestock, Dairy & Poultry. *Resources* (12th of 23 D): Energy & Mineral Resources; Water & Power.

Group Ratings

	ADA	ACLU	AFS	LCV	CFA	CON	NFIB	COC	ACU	NTLC	CHC
1996	55	40	67	54	38	82	70	44	15	43	14
1995	55	—	—	31	31	73	—	71	17	—	—

National Journal Ratings

	1995 LIB — 1995 CONS	1996 LIB — 1996 CONS
Economic	55% — 45%	60% — 40%
Social	65% — 35%	75% — 24%
Foreign	76% — 24%	76% — 22%

Key Votes of the 104th Congress

1. Reduce Medicare Growth $	N	5. Flag Amendment	Y	9. Cuban Embargo	N
2. Ovrd. Product Liab. Veto	Y	6. Drop EPA Limits	N	10. Bar Bosnia Troop $	N
3. Increase Min. Wage	Y	7. Repeal Assault-Weap. Ban	N	11. Cut Anti-Missile Defense	Y
4. Welfare Reform	N	8. Ovrd. Part. Birth Veto	N	12. Bar U.N. Uniforms	N

Election Results

1996 general	Cal Dooley (D)	65,381	(57%)	($662,818)
	Trice Harvey (R)	45,276	(39%)	($505,054)
	Jonathan J. Richter (Lib)	5,048	(4%)	
1996 primary	Cal Dooley (D)	unopposed		
1994 general	Cal Dooley (D)	57,394	(57%)	($275,544)
	Paul Young (R)	43,836	(43%)	($10,346)

TWENTY-FIRST DISTRICT

Bakersfield, at the apex of the southern end of California's Central Valley, has been the focus of great migrations four times—in a gold rush in 1885, when oil was discovered here in 1899, during the 1930s when so-called Okies drove their jalopies from the Dust Bowl of Oklahoma and Kansas and Texas across the Southwest on U.S. 66, and again in the 1980s, when Bakersfield and Kern County grew more rapidly than California's biggest metro areas. Bakersfield's gold is gone, its oil rigs still pump, but the migration that made the deepest imprint was in the 1930s. The Okies drove over one thousand miles of brown landscape, then through the Tehachapi Pass, and found this vast green valley, with its irrigated fields and its eucalyptus-shaded towns, the richest farming country in the world. The story is told vividly in John Steinbeck's *The Grapes of Wrath*, though his vision of the Okies as workers eager to join together with their fellow proletarians and rise up against their bosses did not get the picture quite right. More accurate is Dan Morgan's *Rising in the West*, which shows the strong Pentecostal beliefs which drove many migrants and, unlike Steinbeck, explains how they prospered in California. The area around Bakersfield has become the one southern-accented part of California, the home of country singers Buck Owens and Merle Haggard and a thriving contemporary country music scene, culturally conservative with a strong drive toward discipline and little empathy for the therapy that is so common in Los Angeles, 110 miles south. "I hope you all agree with me that Bakersfield is boring," LA Mayor Richard Riordan said on radio in July 1994—and then came up for a tour in 106-degree heat and heard the Kern County DA tell him that motorists are not fired at on Bakersfield's freeways, its citizens don't riot when they don't like a jury verdict and its celebrities are not on trial for murder.

The 21st Congressional District, the southernmost district in the Central Valley, is centered on Bakersfield and takes in most of Kern and Tulare Counties; it also includes Edwards Air Force Base where Chuck Yeager flew the X-1 and where the space shuttle frequently lands. The district's boundaries are irregular to maximize the Hispanic percentage of the next-door 20th

District. The 21st includes most of Bakersfield and its surroundings, oil fields and high-income subdivisions, and Kern County desert and mountain communities. Politically, this was Democratic territory in the early 1960s—when, for that matter, so was Oklahoma; by the late 1960s, both had become solidly Republican in national politics, and today seem Republican up and down the ticket. In 1996 the 21st District voted 56%–34% for Bob Dole, a showing he matched in only one other California district, the 48th in San Diego County.

The congressman from the 21st, Bill Thomas, is now one of the senior Republicans in the House after years of frustration in the minority. He chairs the House Oversight Committee and is a senior member of Ways and Means and chairman of its Health Subcommittee. Thomas grew up in Orange County; his parents were not high school graduates and he lived for a time in public housing. He graduated from San Francisco State and taught political science from 1965–74 in the community college in Bakersfield. In 1974 he was elected to the Assembly, a conservative in a liberal-run legislature; when Congressman Bill Ketchum died after the 1978 primary, he ran as the relative moderate at the party convention and won the seat. He is bright and testy; he has, wrote Faye Fiore in the *Los Angeles Times*, "an intellect so sharp he is considered one of the brightest members of the House and a temper so mercurial some say he may be one of the meanest." Some of that may come from working on elections issues on what is now Oversight. He lost on the challenge to the Indiana 8th District result in 1985, failed to stop motor voter registration; he worked successfully on bills to encourage uniform poll closings and restricting franked mail. Some younger conservatives considered Thomas too accommodating, and—with the encouragement of then-Minority Whip Newt Gingrich, who had once roomed with Thomas—ran Paul Gillmor of Ohio against him for the ranking-member post on the House Oversight in December 1992, losing by only 12 votes. Thomas fought George Miller's 1992 Central Valley Water Project Act and the 1994 Desert Protection Act, unsuccessfully. He has generally been a free trader, with an eye out for California pistachios; he voted for NAFTA.

Once in the majority, things have been different, though not peaceful. Thomas was given two tough assignments by Gingrich. As Oversight chairman, Thomas managed the Republicans' bills reducing the House budget $50 million, reducing committee staffs by one-third, providing an independent audit of the House, and applying to Congress the laws it applies to others. He opposed Democratic campaign finance measures, and proposed his own reforms: in 1996 to limit both PAC and individual contributions to about $2,500 and to require candidates to raise most of their money in their own districts; in 1997 to ban contributions by non-citizens and to require parties to file preelection reports in general elections.

Thomas was the point man on the Republicans' Medicare reform of 1995. He studied the issue intensively ("I have some knacks, one of them is retention") and reflected on the situation of his parents (his mother was killed and his father gravely injured in a Kern County car crash). He managed to passage in the House the Medicare reform reducing the rate of spending increases and giving seniors more choices. Democrats howled with disapproval; when Thomas postponed one hearing, senior Democrat Sam Gibbons grabbed his tie and yelled, "You're a bunch of dictators, that's all you are. I had to fight you guys 50 years ago." Though Democratic candidates hammered Republicans hard on Medicare, polling showed that after the Republican counteroffensive in October 1996 it was not a net minus for Republican House candidates, who ran even with Democrats among the elderly. On other health issues, he took the lead in establishing 25% deductibility of healthcare insurance for the self-employed in 1995. On other issues he pushed a bill that would stop former members convicted of a felony from continuing to collect their pensions, but allowing them to cash out their savings plan—a response to the more than $100,000 a year that former Ways and Means Chairman Dan Rostenkowski is collecting while in jail for mail fraud. And he promoted a privatized prison in the town of Taft, which turned out to be unpopular with locals who wanted federal jobs. After the 1996 election, Thomas was cool to Clinton's overtures on Medicare. "What happened in the campaign has happened. My lament is that it will be more difficult to do what we must do." Of Clinton, he said, "Republicans look forward to his solution." But he and other Republicans agreed with

Democrats to expand Medicare coverage of diabetes management and early tests for cancer of the breast, cervix, colon, and prostate separately from Medicare reform.

Thomas is a tinkerer who likes to detail cars and take apart computers and admits he is not especially personable. "Other people have other skills, interpersonal maybe, or backslappers, or whatever it is they do. My stock in trade has always been knowledge." He has been reelected by wide margins in the 21st District.

The People: Pop. 1990: 571,143; 19% rural; 11% age 65+; 71% White; 4% Black; 3% Asian; 1% Amer. Indian; 20% Hispanic origin. Households: 59% married couple families; 30% married couple fams. w. children; 47% college educ.; median household income: $29,943; per capita income: $12,983; median gross rent: $454; median house value: $84,600.

1996 Presidential Vote

Dole (R)	109,344	(56%)
Clinton (D)	66,492	(34%)
Perot (I)	15,000	(8%)
Other	3,513	(2%)

1992 Presidential Vote

Bush (R)	94,727	(46%)
Clinton (D)	66,284	(32%)
Perot (I)	43,016	(21%)

Rep. William M. Thomas (R)

Elected 1978; b. Dec. 6, 1941, Wallace, ID; home, Bakersfield; San Francisco St. U., B.A. 1963, M.A. 1965; Baptist; married (Sharon).

Career: Prof., Bakersfield Comm. Col., 1965–74; CA Assembly, 1974–78.

DC Office: 2208 RHOB 20515, 202-225-2915; Fax: 202-225-2908.

District Offices: Bakersfield, 805-327-3611; Visalia, 209-627-6549.

Committees: *House Oversight* (Chmn. of 6 R). *Ways & Means* (3rd of 23 R): Health (Chmn.); Trade. *Joint Committee on the Library of Congress* (Chmn. of 5 Reps.). *Joint Committee on Printing* (Vice Chmn. of 5 Reps.). *Joint Committee on Taxation* (3rd of 5 Reps.).

Group Ratings

	ADA	ACLU	AFS	LCV	CFA	CON	NFIB	COC	ACU	NTLC	CHC
1996	5	6	0	15	8	48	95	94	90	98	66
1995	10	—	—	6	15	38	—	100	72	—	—

National Journal Ratings

	1995 LIB		1995 CONS	1996 LIB		1996 CONS
Economic	0%	—	74%	37%	—	61%
Social	48%	—	51%	53%	—	45%
Foreign	15%	—	73%	30%	—	65%

Key Votes of the 104th Congress

1. Reduce Medicare Growth $	Y	5. Flag Amendment	Y	9. Cuban Embargo	Y
2. Ovrd. Product Liab. Veto	Y	6. Drop EPA Limits	N	10. Bar Bosnia Troop $	Y
3. Increase Min. Wage	N	7. Repeal Assault-Weap. Ban	Y	11. Cut Anti-Missile Defense	N
4. Welfare Reform	Y	8. Ovrd. Part. Birth Veto	Y	12. Bar U.N. Uniforms	Y

Election Results

1996 general	William M. Thomas (R)	125,916	(66%)	($768,689)
	Deborah A. Vollmer (D)	50,694	(27%)	($33,295)
	John Evans (RP)	8,113	(4%)	($5,505)
	Others	6,601	(3%)	
1996 primary	William M. Thomas (R)	53,564	(79%)	
	Karen Gentry (R)	14,030	(21%)	
1994 general	William M. Thomas (R)	116,874	(68%)	($434,146)
	John L. Evans (D)	47,517	(28%)	($31,101)
	Mike Hodges (Lib)	6,899	(4%)	

TWENTY-SECOND DISTRICT

Santa Barbara is one of California's most paradisical cities, a collection of red tile roofs and leafy live oaks, sheltered by towering mountains just above the sea. The impression is a bit misleading, for Santa Barbara has its problems, and its Spanish style is a creation not of 18th-Century Mission culture, but of the 20th Century. Most of its red-tile-roofed, white stucco buildings were put up after a 1925 earthquake leveled much of the town, with the most distinguished of the Spanish Revival buildings designed by an architect with the marvelously un-Latin name of George Washington Smith. Santa Barbara, like Disneyland, does not reproduce the past but presents a bigger, more attractive, cleaner version of it, maintained not by a company but (as in Santa Fe and Nantucket) by an architectural review board. But Santa Barbara's affluence isn't ersatz. This has long been one of the nation's richest retirement communities, and one increasingly devoted to preserving its environment and serenity. Both came under threat spectacularly in 1969, when an underwater oil well ruptured, coating the beach with oil; pictures of the oil slick in the channel and of volunteers trying to wash oil off grounded birds, helped to launch the environmental movement of the 1970s. Almost all the wells are closed now (though some old 19th Century wells still send globs of oil to the beach at nearby Summerland, where the Clintons rested in November 1992) but the oil spill did leave a residue in Santa Barbara's politics—and helped attract high-tech businesses to replace the defense jobs lost in the early 1990s. This is a Republican community, uninterested in redistribution of wealth, but very concerned about the environment (it has built the nation's largest desalination plant) and moderate to liberal on cultural issues like abortion.

The 22d Congressional District consists of all of Santa Barbara County except the town of Carpinteria at its southeast corner, plus San Luis Obispo County to the north. Not all of this area resembles Santa Barbara. The most notable feature in northern Santa Barbara County, across the Santa Ynez Mountains from Ronald Reagan's ranch, is Vandenberg Air Force Base, and the nearby town of Santa Maria is pro-military and conservative. San Luis Obispo County is pleasant and as untrendy a place as you could find on this coast, culturally more Middle American than Santa Barbara.

The congressman from the 22d District is Walter Capps, a Democrat elected in 1996 in the fourth close election here in the last five. Capps grew up in Omaha, went to Yale Divinity School and got a Ph.D., then in 1964 went to teach religious studies at the University of California at Santa Barbara. He was influenced by thinkers like Dag Hammarskjold, Erik Erikson and the Dalai Lama and wrote 14 books, including *The New Religious Right*, of which he does not take a favorable view. In the 1970s he started teaching a class on Vietnam, bringing in Vietnam veterans as speakers, which came to be the largest class on campus; in 1984 he invited Bob Kerrey, then Governor of Nebraska, to teach with him. Capps also set up UC programs in Washington and has visited the Soviet Union and Vietnam. In 1994, the 22d seat came open when Michael Huffington ran for the Senate; Huffington had won it two years before by spending $3 million and beating incumbent Republican Robert Lagomarsino in the primary.

Capps won the three-way Democratic primary with 40% and in the general faced Assemblywoman Andrea Seastrand, a strong conservative. She backed the Contract with America, opposed abortion and gun control, suggested that God may be flashing warning signs to Californians with "floods, drought, fire, earthquakes, lifting mountains two feet high in Northridge." She also campaigned hard for making Vandenberg a spaceport. Capps was described by a local newspaper as invoking "an abstract view of God to encourage a return to community and human relationships." This race was a good example of how politics can become an argument between therapy and discipline. Therapy-minded Santa Barbara County voted 51%–47% for Capps, but discipline-minded San Luis Obispo voted 53%–44% for Seastrand; Seastrand won 49.3%–48.5%, one of the closest races in the nation.

Seastrand compiled an almost perfectly conservative record, defended Newt Gingrich when the national press was savaging him, and Capps ran again. In May 1996 he was injured when a drunk driver struck his car; a broken arm and leg kept him off the campaign trail until August, though he received much favorable publicity in the meantime. "That was really life-defining because I nearly lost it. I wake up every morning and give thanks for that one day," he said. But the tone of the campaign was not so uplifting. The AFL-CIO ran ads attacking Seastrand for Medicare "cuts" and opposition to the minimum wage. Seastrand ran a picture of Richard Allen Davis, Polly Klaas's killer, and said that Capps was the only person besides Davis disappointed when he got the death penalty. She sent out a brochure on immigrants with the headline "Open the door, let 'em in, put 'em on welfare." Capps's daughter worked for George Stephanopoulos in the White House, and Stephanopoulos and his boss both came in to campaign for him. Capps attacked Seastrand on abortion, gun control and the environment, and the Sierra Club ran an independent expenditure against her. Both also had positive issues. Seastrand touted her work on the Vandenberg spaceport. Capps said that education from preschool to college was vital and said he would work for a community college in Paso Robles and to clean up Morro Bay. Bob Dole carried the district by 514 votes, but Capps reversed the 1994 result, losing San Luis Obispo County by only 46%–45% and carrying Santa Barbara County 51%–43%, for a 48%–44% win.

Capps said he wanted to promote conciliation in the House and was put off by partisan confrontations on procedure. "In the world I came from, the world of religion, people don't worry about procedure. They just give you the high ideals." He sought a moral compass: "Then the question is, What will I do? Am I being true to who I am? If I go this way, have I violated anything that is essentially human?" He promised to work on the Science Committee for local educational projects, and with neighboring Republican Elton Gallegly questioned an airborne National Park Services raid on one of the Channel Islands to arrest workers suspected of stealing Chumash artifacts. Capps said he is not likely to serve in Congress for a long time, and against a more moderate Republican might be in trouble; but he represents a large, if not majority, element in the district and could well be reelected.

The People: Pop. 1990: 572,956; 11% rural; 13% age 65+; 72% White; 2% Black; 4% Asian; 1% Amer. Indian; 21% Hispanic origin. Households: 54% married couple families; 24% married couple fams. w. children; 59% college educ.; median household income: $33,680; per capita income: $16,458; median gross rent: $621; median house value: $229,000.

1996 Presidential Vote

Dole (R)	108,722	(44%)
Clinton (D)	108,208	(44%)
Perot (I)	17,311	(7%)
Other	11,656	(5%)

1992 Presidential Vote

Clinton (D)	106,815	(41%)
Bush (R)	92,045	(35%)
Perot (I)	61,030	(23%)

Rep. Walter Capps (D)

Elected 1996; b. May 5, 1934, Omaha, NE; home, Santa Barbara; Portland St. U., B.A. 1961; Yale U., M.A. 1963, Ph.D. 1965; Lutheran; married (Lois).

Career: Prof., U. of CA at Santa Barbara, 1964–96.

DC Office: 1118 LHOB 20515, 202-225-3601; Fax: 202-225-5632.

District Offices: San Luis Obispo, 805-546-8348; Santa Barbara, 805-730-1710.

Committees: *International Relations* (16th of 21 D): Asia & the Pacific; Western Hemisphere. *Science* (16th of 21 D): Basic Research; Space & Aeronautics.

Group Ratings and Key Votes: Newly Elected

Election Results

1996 general	Walter Capps (D)	118,299	(48%)	($904,831)
	Andrea Seastrand (R)	107,987	(44%)	($1,232,118)
	Steven Wheeler (I)	9,845	(4%)	
	Others	8,055	(3%)	
1996 primary	Walter Capps (D)	unopposed		
1994 general	Andrea Seastrand (R)	102,987	(49%)	($630,933)
	Walter Capps (D)	101,424	(49%)	($497,585)
	Others	4,597	(2%)	

TWENTY-THIRD DISTRICT

On a golden mountainside, looking westward over a valley hemmed in by mountains north and south, five United States presidents gathered in November 1991 to dedicate the Ronald Reagan Library. This was the first time in 202 years that five presidents had stood together in one place—one which the Founding Fathers surely did not imagine would ever be American and yet today seems quintessentially so. Simi Valley, famous a few months later as the site of the trial of police officers accused of assaulting Rodney King, is a product of the 1960s, the expansive and still optimistic postwar years, when the vast stream of migrants who had come from all over the United States to Los Angeles spread beyond the city and county limits to fill up barren valleys between golden mountains. To them they brought a willingness to work hard, high competence and high-tech, an appreciation of the local environment and a distaste for the crime and rioting which seemed all too common in the Los Angeles basin they left behind.

Simi Valley is just one of several communities in the valleys and narrow coastal margins of Ventura County, west of Los Angeles, that have been filling up with people leaving the Los Angeles Basin and the San Fernando Valley and building new communities in what had been an agricultural county with a gritty port and Navy base; Simi Valley claims more cars per capita than anywhere else in the United States. After the King trial Simi Valley was criticized for being all-white and racist. In fact it is ethnically diverse: Ventura County, of which Simi Valley is just one town, was 26% Hispanic and 5% Asian in the 1990 Census, and its white Anglo residents include many with names and backgrounds that would have been recognized as ethnic a few years ago. It also has some of the nation's lowest crime rates, a stark contrast with gang warfare in Los Angeles, and some of the highest percentages of intact families in California, a vivid contrast with the showbiz lifestyles of Westside LA. It also has a reminder, where the five presidents met in 1991, that traditional American values are not just material but are also moral: pieces of the Berlin Wall, which President Reagan called on Mikhail Gorbachev to tear down, are on display at the Ronald Reagan Library.

The 23d Congressional District includes almost all of Ventura County except the Thousand Oaks area—Simi Valley, Moorpark, Camarillo, Ventura, Oxnard, and the Point Mugu Navy base—plus just a corner of Santa Barbara County, the town of Carpinteria. Politically, this home of the Reagan Library was strong Reagan country when he was elected governor and president, though it lost some of its cheerful, upbeat optimism in the more downbeat years of his successors, Jerry Brown in California and George Bush in Washington. It has trended conservative in recent local elections, but it is closely enough balanced to go Democratic occasionally, and Bill Clinton carried it narrowly in 1992 and 1996.

The congressman from the 23d District is Elton Gallegly. He grew up in a working class suburb of Los Angeles, dropped out of college and became a real estate broker. He was elected at 35 to the Simi Valley city council, became mayor in 1980, then ran for Congress in 1986 when the incumbent ran for the Senate. Gallegly's local ties and money prevailed 50%–34% in the 1986 primary over Tony Hope, son of comedian Bob Hope, who had spent the previous decade in Washington. In 1992, after redistricting had moved much of fellow incumbent Robert Lagomarsino's district into the new Ventura County-based seat, Gallegly moved fast to push Lagomarsino into running in the 22d District to the north, where he lost the primary to Michael Huffington's $3 million campaign. Gallegly had minimal primary opposition but a spirited challenge from Democrat Anita Perez Ferguson, who raised large sums from the feminist left in "the year of the woman" and held Gallegly to a 54%–41% margin. In 1994 and 1996 he was reelected easily.

Gallegly has had a very solidly conservative voting record and has played a part on major issues. Foremost among them is illegal immigration. In the first weeks of the new Congress he has called for a tougher Border Patrol, a tamperproof identification card for legal aliens and an end to welfare for illegal immigrants. He criticizes the current Immigration and Naturalization Service IDs as easily forgeable, carrying one around himself as evidence. In 1995, Speaker Newt Gingrich named him head of a bipartisan Immigration Reform Task Force. Immigration Subcommittee Chairman Lamar Smith produced a bill with more Border Patrol officers, even as the Clinton Administration, borrowing from an El Paso INS officer (Silvestre Reyes, now congressman from Texas), patrolled the border much more aggressively around San Diego. But Smith and the Judiciary Committee called for only a pilot project on IDs and many Republicans as well as Democrats bridled at even that. In March 1996 Gallegly got the full House to pass his amendment allowing states to deny education to children who are illegal immigrants. This was heartily supported by Bob Dole campaigning in California, and opposed by the Clinton Administration. It was also opposed by Texas Republican Senators Phil Gramm and Kay Bailey Hutchison, and in September 1996, as time was running out, the administration said it would veto the bill with it and Democratic Senators were pressing a filibuster. Republicans agreed to drop it altogether. Gallegly supported another amendment that didn't make it, Richard Pombo's guest worker program, though he tried to impose healthcare costs on farmers and not local government.

Gallegly has worked on other issues as well. He sought to minimize the labeling requirements on vitamins and dietary supplements issued by the Food and Drug Administration in response to a 1990 law sponsored by Los Angeles's Henry Waxman. Gallegly would allow the dietary supplements to make health claims without the documentation required for prescription drugs or foods. Locally, he worked hard to save the Point Mugu Navy base, threatened with closure for six weeks in early 1996, and with 18,000 related jobs, Ventura County's largest employer. To forestall future threats, Gallegly worked to recruit four squadrons of E2-C Hawkeye aircraft for Point Mugu when they leave Miramar in 1997; he even buttonholed an admiral on a refueling stop in San Diego to make his case.

The People: Pop. 1990: 571,562; 5% rural; 9% age 65+; 62% White; 2% Black; 5% Asian; 1% Amer. Indian; 30% Hispanic origin. Households: 63% married couple families; 33% married couple fams. w. children; 54% college educ.; median household income: $42,989; per capita income: $16,617; median gross rent: $733; median house value: $234,200.

1996 Presidential Vote

Clinton (D)	93,046	(45%)
Dole (R)	85,508	(42%)
Perot (I)	19,237	(9%)
Other	6,745	(3%)

1992 Presidential Vote

Clinton (D)	82,613	(38%)
Bush (R)	74,106	(34%)
Perot (I)	58,177	(27%)

Rep. Elton Gallegly (R)

Elected 1986; b. Mar. 7, 1944, Huntington Park; home, Simi Valley; Los Angeles St. Col., 1962–63; Protestant; married (Janice).

Career: Owner, real estate firm; Simi Valley City Cncl., 1979–80; Simi Valley Mayor, 1980–86.

DC Office: 2427 RHOB 20515, 202-225-5811; Fax: 202-225-1100.

District Offices: Oxnard, 805-485-2300.

Committees: *International Relations* (8th of 26 R): Western Hemisphere (Chmn.). *Judiciary* (8th of 20 R): Courts & Intellectual Property; Immigration & Claims. *Resources* (5th of 27 R): National Parks & Public Lands.

Group Ratings

	ADA	ACLU	AFS	LCV	CFA	CON	NFIB	COC	ACU	NTLC	CHC
1996	0	0	0	23	8	34	97	100	100	100	100
1995	0	—	—	0	8	53	—	100	84	—	—

National Journal Ratings

	1995 LIB — 1995 CONS			1996 LIB — 1996 CONS		
Economic	0%	—	74%	0%	—	82%
Social	30%	—	68%	14%	—	77%
Foreign	15%	—	73%	28%	—	71%

Key Votes of the 104th Congress

1. Reduce Medicare Growth $	Y	5. Flag Amendment	Y	9. Cuban Embargo	Y
2. Ovrd. Product Liab. Veto	Y	6. Drop EPA Limits	Y	10. Bar Bosnia Troop $	Y
3. Increase Min. Wage	N	7. Repeal Assault-Weap. Ban	Y	11. Cut Anti-Missile Defense	N
4. Welfare Reform	Y	8. Ovrd. Part. Birth Veto	Y	12. Bar U.N. Uniforms	Y

Election Results

1996 general	Elton Gallegly (R)	118,880	(60%)	($294,940)
	Robert R. Unruhe (D)	70,035	(35%)	($24,642)
	Gail Lightfoot (Lib)	8,346	(4%)	
1996 primary	Elton Gallegly (R)	unopposed		
1994 general	Elton Gallegly (R)	114,043	(66%)	($300,846)
	Kevin Ready (D)	47,345	(27%)	($24,813)
	Others	10,952	(6%)	

TWENTY-FOURTH DISTRICT

The San Fernando Valley, in the early 20th Century when the movie business was young, was a vast expanse of empty land, annexed to Los Angeles in 1915; moviemakers, looking for filming sites for a western, drove past the vacant lots of Westwood, up narrow roads through the Santa Monica Mountains and over into the vast Valley, sheltered from ocean breezes and rain-bearing clouds by the mountains. Over the past 80 years this vast bowl of land has been transformed, first into 1950s suburbia, then into a postmodern city of its own, economically vital and yeastily ethnic. Even in its suburban years the San Fernando Valley was not entirely residential: big factories—the General Motors Van Nuys assembly plant, the Anheuser Busch brewery, Rockwell and Litton defense plants—provided jobs. But in the 1950s and 1960s this was fast-growing, family-friendly territory; politically, turf fought over hard by Republicans and Democrats. By the 1970s young white Anglo families were fleeing, as the Los Angeles Unified School District was hit by a busing order. There is plenty of upscale territory left in the uplands in the rims of the Valley, in heavily Jewish Sherman Oaks and Encino and to the west in Woodland Hills and Chatsworth; and the office blocks and mini-malls along Ventura and Woodland Hills Boulevard show unmistakable signs of affluence. In the inner lowlands of the Valley, new immigrants have moved in. Some old neighborhoods have become rough Latino enclaves, with youth gangs and boarded-up houses and apartments weakened by the Northridge earthquake; in other neighborhoods Iranians and Chinese, Mexicans and Koreans, Israelis and Filipinos are keeping neighborhoods solidly middle-class.

The 24th Congressional District includes most of the southern and western San Fernando Valley, from the hillside mansions of Encino to the gang territory around the Van Nuys plant. Two-thirds of the 24th's people live in the Valley; another one-fifth live directly west, in new communities nestled amid mountains along U.S. 101—ranch-like Agoura, jewel-like Westlake Village and sprawling Thousand Oaks, home of the biotechnology giant Amgen. The 24th also takes in Malibu, with $1 million beach houses five feet from each other and Pepperdine University's campus in the hills. Politically, this is a mixed area. The Jewish precincts are solidly Democratic, and have gotten more so in the 1990s; Thousand Oaks is heavily Republican; the immigrant areas fluctuate and could go any which way; Malibu is trendy showbiz liberal.

The congressman from the 24th is Brad Sherman, a Democrat elected in 1996. Sherman grew up in Monterey Park, in the San Gabriel Valley east of Los Angeles; he started working on Democratic campaigns at age 6, licking stamps and stuffing envelopes, and set up his own stamp wholesaling firm at 14. He graduated with high honors from UCLA, worked as an accountant, then went to Harvard Law and practiced tax law in Los Angeles. But he always had the political bug, and in 1990 cast around for offices to run for and settled on the Board of Equalization. This is a five-member body which is a sort of tax court; Sherman's district was more or less all of Los Angeles County. He sold three condos and spent $400,000 on his campaign, and won. He was known as a stickler for detail, a "tax nerd," as one former staffer said, and while he used the office with a keen scent for political advantage he also disappointed some. He led the fight against Pete Wilson's snack tax in 1991, and got President Clinton to side with his opinion on taxing foreign-owned businesses, which he says saved California $2 billion in revenue. But he irritated cartoonists with a ruling that exempted them from state tax on artwork but not on illustrations; they set up a website, the Sherman gallery, in which they vied in caricaturing the balding and bespectacled Sherman.

Sherman decided to run for Congress, and moved his residence from Santa Monica to Sherman Oaks, when 24th District Congressman Anthony Beilenson announced his retirement in 1995 after 20 years in the House. Beilenson barely won in 1994, beating Republican businessman and lawyer Rich Sybert by only 49%–48%. Sybert is an intense man who worked his way through Berkeley and Harvard Law School, quit law practice to work as Pete Wilson's head of planning, then went into the toy business. He spent large sums of his own money in 1994.

He kept running after 1994, and in March 1996 both he and Sherman won multi-candidate primaries easily—Sherman with 54%, Sybert with 68%. Both stressed their moderation. Sherman ran against Newt Gingrich and the Republican Congress, which was especially unpopular among Jewish voters; but he also supported the death penalty, said he wanted racial quotas and preferences phased out and favored tough measures on illegal immigration. Sybert stressed his independence of Gingrich and the Republican leadership, favoring abortion rights and environmental protections. He also called for a fair and balanced budget, tougher laws on crime, tax cuts and tort reform. Sybert was intense, Sherman a bit humorous (he handed out combs to voters, saying "You can use one more than I can"). It got a bit nasty when in a brochure Sybert claimed the support of Colin Powell. Sherman's campaign material accused him of lying; but Powell, whom Sybert met when he worked as a White House Fellow for Caspar Weinberger, sent Sybert a check for $250.

In the end it came down to something like straight ticket voting. Bill Clinton carried the district 52%–37%, and in this coastal area—unlike the vast stretch of land between the Appalachians and the Sierra Nevada—the Republican Congress was affirmatively unpopular. Sherman won 49%–44%, carrying Los Angeles County 53%–39% and losing the Thousand Oaks area 57%–37%.

The People: Pop. 1990: 572,287; 3% rural; 11% age 65+; 78% White; 2% Black; 6% Asian; 14% Hispanic origin. Households: 55% married couple families; 25% married couple fams. w. children; 66% college educ.; median household income: $48,433; per capita income: $25,767; median gross rent: $779; median house value: $304,300.

1996 Presidential Vote

Clinton (D)	117,724	(52%)
Dole (R)	83,412	(37%)
Perot (I)	16,165	(7%)
Other	8,054	(4%)

1992 Presidential Vote

Clinton (D)	128,572	(48%)
Bush (R)	79,728	(30%)
Perot (I)	57,625	(22%)

Rep. Brad Sherman (D)

Elected 1996; b. Oct. 24, 1954, Los Angeles; home, Sherman Oaks; U.C.L.A., B.A. 1974; Harvard U., J.D. 1979; Jewish; single.

Career: Accountant, 1980–90; CA St. Board of Equalization, 1990–95, Chmn., 1991–95.

DC Office: 1524 LHOB 20515, 202-225-5911; Fax: 202-225-5876.

District Offices: Thousand Oaks, 805-449-2372; Woodland Hills, 818-999-1990.

Committees: *Budget* (17th of 19 D). *International Relations* (17th of 21 D): International Economic Policy & Trade; Western Hemisphere.

Group Ratings and Key Votes: Newly Elected

Election Results

1996 general	Brad Sherman (D)	106,193	(49%)	($1,364,516)
	Rich Sybert (R)	93,629	(44%)	($898,786)
	Others	15,026	(7%)	
1996 primary	Brad Sherman (D)	27,513	(54%)	
	Elizabeth Knipe (D)	7,580	(15%)	
	Jeffrey A. Lipow (D)	5,360	(10%)	
	Michael Jordan (D)	4,786	(9%)	
	Craig Freis (D)	2,540	(5%)	
	Others	3,424	(7%)	
1994 general	Anthony C. Beilenson (D)	95,342	(49%)	($587,641)
	Rich Sybert (R)	91,806	(48%)	($1,687,166)
	Others	6,031	(3%)	

TWENTY-FIFTH DISTRICT

One of the tragedies of the 1994 Northridge earthquake was at the intersection of the I-5 and Route 14 Freeways at the north edge of the San Fernando Valley, where an overpass collapsed and a motorcycle patrolman hurtled to his death. The destruction of the interchange had an economic and personal impact for months afterwards, for the settled area of Los Angeles County no longer ends at the mountains at the northern rim of the San Fernando Valley. It continues along Route 14 past the mountain-surrounded city of Santa Clarita, with 110,000 people in 1990, and 25 miles beyond, where the mountains stop at the San Andreas Fault and the desert stretches out low and flat, divided into mile-square grids—the Antelope Valley, with huge aerospace plants and military bases around the fast-growing towns of Palmdale and Lancaster, where nearly 200,000 people live. Because of the mountain terrain, all these areas are connected by just one freeway, over which thousands commute and travel each day; when the chokepoint intersection was crushed, commuters lined up for hours to get to work.

The 25th Congressional District covers all three of these areas. It includes the northwest quadrant of the San Fernando Valley, Granada Hills and Chatsworth, with 180,000 mostly affluent and Republican white Anglos inside the LA city limits; it takes in Santa Clarita, with its Old West air and its industrial park, spreading subdivisions and Six Flags Magic Mountain theme park, home of a boosterish Republicanism; it includes the aerospace country of the Antelope Valley, with somewhat lower-income. All three parts of the district are heavily Republican, especially the desert area; when the 25th was newly created for 1992 it was assumed the Republican primary would choose the new congressman, and it did.

The congressman from the 25th is Howard "Buck" McKeon, who grew up in Southern California, graduated from Brigham Young University and is the owner of Howard and Phil's Western Wear, a family business which expanded to 55 stores in California, Arizona, Nevada and Utah, then cut back in 1996 to 43. McKeon was the first mayor of Santa Clarita, when it was incorporated by joining several smaller towns, and served five years on the council. He won the 1992 Republican primary 40%–38% over Assemblyman Phil Wyman, who once had a bill to ban the allegedly satanic practice of recording certain words into songs backwards.

McKeon, the 1992 Republican freshman class president, talked about reforming the House and in 1993 helped abolish four select committees. With a seat on the National Security Committee, he worked to save local defense jobs—this is the production base for the B-1 and B-2 bombers, and the F-117 and SR-71 fighter planes. He helped get new contracts for the X-33, the next generation Space Shuttle and the Joint Strike Fighter; he is trying to authorize more B-2s and to get NASA to move Space Shuttle landings to Air Force Base Plant 42 in Palmdale. He opposed the 1994 Desert Protection Act, which, he said, "does little more than create pork projects." He fought an Equal Employment Opportunity Commission religious harassment guideline which, he felt, would bar people from keeping a Bible on their desk or wear religious symbols like the Star of David at work.

After the January 1994 Northridge earthquake, he worked to get some $8 billion in federal aid. After the 1994 election, McKeon got bigger assignments. He is chairman of the Post-Secondary Education, Training and Lifelong Learning Subcommittee, and put together a bill restructuring job training, literacy and youth employment programs which passed the House 345–79 in September 1995, but was never successfully reconciled with the Senate version; he promises to try again. Also, the subcommittee must reauthorize the Higher Education act. On local issues, in 1996 he got the House to pass a bill blocking the Forest Service from transferring land for a proposed dump in Elsmere Canyon, just east of Santa Clarita. He also pressured the Justice Department to get Los Angeles County $13 million and California $225 million for the cost of incarcerating illegal aliens.

McKeon was reelected by wide margins in 1994 and 1996.

The People: Pop. 1990: 573,189; 10% rural; 8% age 65+; 72% White; 4% Black; 6% Asian; 1% Amer. Indian; 16% Hispanic origin. Households: 63% married couple families; 34% married couple fams. w. children; 59% college educ.; median household income: $46,480; per capita income: $18,849; median gross rent: $690; median house value: $213,000.

1996 Presidential Vote

Dole (R)	97,002	(47%)
Clinton (D)	84,212	(41%)
Perot (I)	18,320	(9%)
Other	5,775	(3%)

1992 Presidential Vote

Bush (R)	89,987	(39%)
Clinton (D)	83,305	(36%)
Perot (I)	57,398	(25%)

Rep. Howard P. (Buck) McKeon (R)

Elected 1992; b. Sept. 9, 1939, Los Angeles; home, Santa Clarita; Brigham Young U., B.S. 1985; Mormon; married (Patricia).

Career: Small businessman; Owner, Howard and Phil's Western Wear, 1973–present; William S. Hart School District Bd., 1979–87; Chmn., Valencia Natl. Bank, 1987–88; Santa Clarita Mayor, 1987–88; Santa Clarita City Cncl., 1988–92.

DC Office: 307 CHOB 20515, 202-225-1956; Fax: 202-226-0683; e-mail: tellbuck@hr.house.gov.

District Offices: Palmdale, 805-247-9688; Santa Clarita, 805-254-2111.

Committees: *Education & The Workforce* (8th of 25 R): Oversight & Investigations; Postsecondary Education, Training & Life-Long Learning (Chmn.). *National Security* (16th of 30 R): Military Procurement; Military Readiness.

Group Ratings

	ADA	ACLU	AFS	LCV	CFA	CON	NFIB	COC	ACU	NTLC	CHC
1996	0	0	0	15	8	30	97	100	100	100	100
1995	0	—	—	0	0	38	—	100	88	—	—

National Journal Ratings

	1995 LIB — 1995 CONS			1996 LIB — 1996 CONS		
Economic	0%	—	74%	0%	—	82%
Social	0%	—	79%	23%	—	77%
Foreign	0%	—	85%	0%	—	79%

Key Votes of the 104th Congress

1. Reduce Medicare Growth $	Y	5. Flag Amendment	Y	9. Cuban Embargo	Y
2. Ovrd. Product Liab. Veto	Y	6. Drop EPA Limits	N	10. Bar Bosnia Troop $	Y
3. Increase Min. Wage	N	7. Repeal Assault-Weap. Ban	*	11. Cut Anti-Missile Defense	N
4. Welfare Reform	Y	8. Ovrd. Part. Birth Veto	Y	12. Bar U.N. Uniforms	Y

Election Results

1996 general	Howard P. (Buck) McKeon (R)	122,428	(62%)	($384,011)
	Diane Trautman (D)	65,089	(33%)	($16,434)
	Others	8,686	(4%)	
1996 primary	Howard P. (Buck) McKeon (R)	49,883	(85%)	
	David B. Starr (R)	9,076	(15%)	
1994 general	Howard P. (Buck) McKeon (R)	110,301	(65%)	($474,945)
	James H. Gilmartin (D)	53,445	(31%)	($34,857)
	Others	6,225	(4%)	

TWENTY-SIXTH DISTRICT

A hiker looking north from the crest of the Santa Monica Mountains in 1910 would have seen spread out, almost totally empty and barren, 20 miles wide and 12 miles deep, the San Fernando Valley. Separated by the Cahuenga Pass from rapidly growing Los Angeles and Hollywood, the Valley was bought up in massive tracts by civic leaders even as they were urging city engineer William Mulholland to build a huge 250-mile aqueduct from the Owens Valley to give Los Angeles water and persuading the city in 1915 to annex 200 square miles of the Valley. In the years after World War II, this was modern suburbia, filled with *Leave It to Beaver* families. Today the San Fernando Valley is postmodern urban, with a look you can see in exaggerated form in the Disney headquarters buildings in Burbank or Universal City's CityWalk shopping mall: the driver topping the crest today sees office towers looming out over slightly hazy air, shopping centers and occasional palm trees, lines of grid streets stretching out into the distance beyond stucco subdivisions and the squat factory and warehouse buildings that make Los Angeles County the nation's number one manufacturer.

The people in the Valley have also changed. The white Anglo families with stay-at-home moms in the 1950s have been replaced by hard-working Latino families, with children waiting at the bus stops for schools and parents juggling two jobs. But there is continuity: as in the 1950s, these are places where people work hard and try to raise families who will have better chances and make better livings than they have. Pacoima, at the northern end of the Valley, where Rodney King was pulled over and beaten and arrested, is mostly black and Latino. Farther south, in Canoga Park and Van Nuys and Burbank, are the big aerospace plants and the GM assembly plants which have been shut down since 1989, with thousands of jobs lost; less visible are the hundreds of small factories and multimedia plants where thousands of jobs have been created. The lower income areas here are farther from the central city; the southern rim of the Valley, around Studio City and North Hollywood, is still heavily Jewish and is attracting new families who often send their kids to religious schools.

The 26th Congressional District consists of the Golden State and Hollywood Freeway corridors of the Valley—roughly its eastern half—proceeding as far west as Van Nuys and the San Diego Freeway. Overall, the district was 53% Hispanic in 1990, but as yet Latinos are not the major voting bloc here; many are not citizens, many are children or young people not yet in the voting stream; and the tradition among Latinos in the 1990s, as among Italians in the 1910s, is to trust family and hard work, not politics and government, to get ahead. The high Democratic percentages here are due as much to Jewish as to Latino voters, though the latter also trended Democratic in 1996.

The congressman from the 26th is Howard Berman, one of the most aggressive and creative members of the House—and one of the most clear-sighted operators in American politics. He grew up in Los Angeles in modest circumstances, got involved in politics, and was elected to the Assembly from a formerly Republican Hollywood Hills district in 1972. This was the beginning of the so-called Berman-Waxman political machine—not so much a precinct organization as a group of consultants who raised money, redrew district lines and endorsed candidates through direct mail; their core constituency was liberal Westside Jews. Berman became Assembly majority leader in his first term; in 1980 he tried to unseat Assembly Speaker Leo McCarthy; ultimately both lost out to Willie Brown, who served 15 years. Berman's consolation prize was a Valley-based congressional seat in 1982, which he has held ever since with minimal competition. The Berman-Waxman machine fell on hard times in the 1990s, as Republicans seized control of redistricting, the feminist left became the driving force in the Democratic Party and Berman-Waxman ally Mel Levine lost the 1992 Senate primary to Barbara Boxer.

Berman has been an active legislator even more than a political operator, and on all manner of issues. On foreign policy, he started off less as a Vietnam war dove than as a backer of Israel, and he is not one of those Democrats who think America has habitually been on the wrong side in the world. For a decade he floor-managed foreign aid bills, defending aid to many countries as well as Israel. With Henry Hyde he wrote the law authorizing embargoes on nations that condone terrorism; in April 1990 he called for sanctions on Iraq, four months before Saddam Hussein invaded Kuwait. Berman voted for the Gulf war resolution, but was understandably critical of the administration—if it had followed his advice there might well have been no need for war. More recently, Berman has worked to stop the export of missile and nuclear weapons technology—an uphill battle in the Clinton years.
He passed a law banning the double issuing of U.S. passports to coddle Arab countries who refuse to honor passports with Israeli marks. He pushed through the International Broadcasting Act of 1994, consolidating and downsizing agencies but maintaining Radio Free Europe and establishing Radio Free Asia. He worked hard to save the National Endowment for Democracy. Despite his close ties to organized labor, he voted for NAFTA. He led the successful fight to scuttle the Republicans' Contract With America's call for reducing U.S. participation in UN-led peacekeeping operations. He has worked on reorganizing the State Department and other foreign policy agencies. He co-sponsored a bill for sanctions against foreign investors in key industries in Libya and Iran.

Berman is also a major force on immigration. In 1988 he sponsored the provision allowing 20,000 immigrant visas for migrants without close relatives here, to be selected randomly by computer—"Berman visa applications" they are called. He got into the 1990 law more family reunification slots, to expedite the immigration of Soviet Jews (a vivid presence in L.A. these days), and to pass amnesty provisions allowing more family members to remain in this country. He worked to get the federal government to acknowledge responsibility for state spending on illegal immigrants. On the 1996 immigration bill he made two major contributions. With Republican Dick Chrysler, he sponsored the amendment separating legal and illegal immigration; its passage on the floor by 238–183 in March 1996 and the nearly simultaneous passage of a similar amendment by Republican Spencer Abraham in the Senate Judiciary Committee ended the two immigration subcommittees' chairmen's drive to cut legal immigration. Berman also weighed in heavily against Republican Richard Pombo's amendment to let in 250,000 guest farm workers.

Some of Berman's issues have local angles. He worked to get $8.6 billion in emergency aid after the January 1994 Northridge earthquake. He tried to eliminate the 10% threshold on disaster deductibility. In 1991 he helped establish CALSTART, to produce electric cars in the Valley; in a closed defense plant in Burbank it now produces electric car parts and infrastructure for electric vehicles and electric buses. With Senator Charles Grassley, he sponsored the 1986 False Claims Act rewarding whistleblowers in the government, which collected over $1 billion in civil settlements since its enactment. Berman is not without leverage in the Republican House, but he is clearly frustrated being in the minority. In the spring of 1996 he contemplated running in the April 1997 election for mayor of Los Angeles. But he banked on a Democratic majority returning and made no move to run, and when Republicans held on to the House in November 1996 he judged it was too late. That was not all the bad news: in February 1997 Minority Leader Richard Gephardt prevailed on him to become ranking minority member of the Ethics Committee, badly scarred by partisanship during the investigation of Newt Gingrich. "Condolences are appropriate," Berman said, but added, "In the end I decided that there is an obligation to the House . . . to devote some portion of your time to the institution rather than issues. I was also challenged by the charge to restore some confidence in the ethics process. The Ethics Committee is neither a member-protection agency nor a forum for deciding partisan and ideological battles."

The People: Pop. 1990: 571,538; 8% age 65+; 34% White; 6% Black; 7% Asian; 53% Hispanic origin. Households: 50% married couple families; 28% married couple fams. w. children; 40% college educ.; median household income: $32,134; per capita income: $12,198; median gross rent: $624; median house value: $185,300.

1996 Presidential Vote

Clinton (D)	71,416	(65%)
Dole (R)	27,129	(25%)
Perot (I)	7,930	(7%)
Other	3,150	(3%)

1992 Presidential Vote

Clinton (D)	72,673	(56%)
Bush (R)	31,013	(24%)
Perot (I)	24,167	(19%)

Rep. Howard L. Berman (D)

Elected 1982; b. Apr. 15, 1941, Los Angeles; home, N. Hollywood; U.C.L.A., B.A. 1962, LL.B. 1965; Jewish; married (Janis).

Career: Practicing atty., 1967–72; CA Assembly, 1973–82, Majority Ldr., 1974–79.

DC Office: 2330 RHOB 20515, 202-225-4695; Fax: 202-225-5279.

District Offices: Mission Hills, 818-891-0543.

Committees: *International Relations* (4th of 21 D): Asia & the Pacific (RMM). *Judiciary* (4th of 15 D): Courts & Intellectual Property; Immigration & Claims. *Standards of Official Conduct* (RMM of 5 D).

Group Ratings

	ADA	ACLU	AFS	LCV	CFA	CON	NFIB	COC	ACU	NTLC	CHC
1996	90	77	100	85	100	66	23	19	0	8	0
1995	80	—	—	88	85	15	—	27	5	—	—

National Journal Ratings

	1995 LIB — 1995 CONS			1996 LIB — 1996 CONS		
Economic	75%	—	25%	89%	—	0%
Social	80%	—	13%	88%	—	0%
Foreign	83%	—	16%	90%	—	0%

Key Votes of the 104th Congress

1. Reduce Medicare Growth $	N	5. Flag Amendment	N	9. Cuban Embargo	N
2. Ovrd. Product Liab. Veto	N	6. Drop EPA Limits	Y	10. Bar Bosnia Troop $	N
3. Increase Min. Wage	Y	7. Repeal Assault-Weap. Ban	N	11. Cut Anti-Missile Defense	Y
4. Welfare Reform	N	8. Ovrd. Part. Birth Veto	N	12. Bar U.N. Uniforms	N

Election Results

1996 general	Howard L. Berman (D)	67,525	(66%)	($408,096)
	Bill Glass (R)	29,332	(29%)	($78,469)
	Others	5,658	(6%)	
1996 primary	Howard L. Berman (D)	26,745	(84%)	
	Steven E. Gibson (D)	5,177	(16%)	
1994 general	Howard L. Berman (D)	55,145	(63%)	($432,535)
	Gary E. Forsch (R)	28,423	(32%)	($38,922)
	Erich D. Miller (Lib)	4,570	(5%)	

TWENTY-SEVENTH DISTRICT

In the early years of the 20th Century, when Los Angeles was growing to become one of America's major cities, its richest citizens settled not on the beach (too clammy and cold) or on the west side (too dusty and remote), but in communities they built at the base of the San Gabriel Mountains that rise 10,000 feet above the city, their snow-capped peaks visible most of the year. The premier such community was Pasadena, with its institutions of national stature—the Rose Bowl, Cal Tech—and the premier structures were Pasadena's baroque-domed City Hall and railroader Henry Huntington's house in next-door San Marino, now the Huntington Library, one of the world's great scholarly institutions. Pasadena and South Pasadena have proudly preserved their bungalow neighborhoods, and Pasadena preserved and rebuilt the 80-year old curving Colorado Street Bridge over Arroyo Seco. More middle class is Glendale, north of downtown Los Angeles, site of Forest Lawn Cemetery; just west, beneath the Verdugo Mountains, is Burbank (named not for botanist Luther Burbank but for a local dentist-developer), famous now for the NBC Studios and Disney headquarters and home to many small entertainment multimedia companies as well. With its lower taxes and business-friendly attitude, and despite its earlier loss of aerospace jobs, Glendale and Burbank are booming while inside the city limits of high-tax and high-regulation Los Angeles, Hollywood has become seedy and commercial buildings have huge vacancy rates.

The 27th Congressional District takes in all these affluent foothill communities plus—sandwiched between the Verdugo and San Gabriel Mountains—La Canada, La Crescenta, Sunland and Tujunga. For years these places were traditionally, indeed stereotypically, Republican. But in recent years they have been moving toward the Democrats. The black communities in Pasadena and Altadena, the boyhood home of Jackie Robinson, are expanding. Affluent Asians are moving into San Marino and style-conscious young couples are moving into South Pasadena. Glendale is now the center of Los Angeles's large Armenian community and has many Iranians, Koreans, Filipinos—nearly half its residents are foreign-born. There are also immigrants as well as upscale singles in showbizzy Burbank. The result is a district that votes pretty much the way California does: for Bill Clinton in 1992 and 1996 but for Pete Wilson by a bigger margin in 1994.

The congressman from the 27th is James Rogan, a Republican elected in 1996. He grew up in San Francisco, raised mostly by his grandparents; his mother was a convicted felon and welfare recipient, his stepfather an alcoholic. He dropped out of high school, then worked his way through Berkeley and UCLA Law. He practiced law with a large Los Angeles firm, then became an assistant district attorney, a member of the Hardcore Gang Unit who got death penalties and a resourceful prosecutor whose wordless summation of a drunk driving case was to pour ten cans of beer into ten cups and then snap his fingers. In 1990 he was appointed to the Glendale municipal court and at 33 was the youngest judge in California. In 1993 he won a special election to replace Pat Nolan, once Republican leader in the Assembly, who had pleaded guilty to a federal racketeering charge. In an Assembly bitterly divided on partisan lines he became noted for combining conservative positions with a judicial manner. He was named the best Assembly member by the *California Journal*, and after Republicans, in a 41–39 majority, succeeded in getting rid of three successive Republicans who had been co-opted by Willie Brown to run as his puppet speaker, he was elected majority leader in his first full term. "We cannot be so vain," he said, "as to perceive a bare majority as an overwhelming mandate that would allow us the comfort of ignoring what our friends on that other side have to say." He rallied Republicans to repeal the helmet law, but was less successful on a bill to allow police to spank graffiti vandals, and was unable to pass the Contract with California to roll back business taxes and regulations. But he also supported Democrats' bills on domestic violence, medical marijuana and penalties for carrying concealed weapons. He hosted a February 1996 dinner for Laurence Powell, one of the policemen in the Rodney King case, because he felt he'd been subjected to double jeopardy.

Rogan was an obvious candidate for Congress once 24-year veteran Carlos Moorhead announced his retirement in August 1995; despite his seniority Moorhead had been passed over by Speaker Newt Gingrich for the chairs of both Judiciary and Commerce, and as chairman of the Intellectual Property Subcommittee had been opposed by some Republicans on patent reform. The Democrats had a close primary between Doug Kahn (who held Moorhead to 50%–39% and 53%–42% victories in 1992 and 1994) and Barry Gordon, for seven years president of the Screen Actors Guild. Gordon had endorsements from unions and Congressman Howard Berman, but Kahn attacked him for carpetbagging and condoning sexual harassment (for which Kahn later apologized) and won 51%–49%. Kahn is a computer graphics artist who has lived in Seattle, Miami, New York and Pasadena; his grandmother was a sister of Walter Annenberg and in the mid-1980s, when Annenberg sold his media properties to Rupert Murdoch, Kahn was suddenly rich. He spent $400,000 in the primary and $200,000 more in the general of his own money, and argued that he was the mainstream candidate in the district, while Rogan—against abortion and gun control, for Proposition 187 and school vouchers—was too extreme. "Jim is an attractive candidate who has a winning manner, but his positions on the issues are in the extreme." In debates Rogan responded by comparing his issue positions to Bill Clinton's, promising to save Social Security and Medicare and to deny welfare benefits to drug addicts and alcoholics. He also courted Armenians and other ethnic groups.

Rogan won 50%–43%. In the House he promised to work for education reform, with better standards and less bureaucracy, and said he wanted to be helpful to senior citizens and the poor: it is better to teach a man how to fish than to give him a fish.

The People: Pop. 1990: 572,629; 13% age 65+; 61% White; 8% Black; 10% Asian; 21% Hispanic origin. Households: 49% married couple families; 23% married couple fams. w. children; 61% college educ.; median household income: $37,929; per capita income: $20,344; median gross rent: $671; median house value: $293,200.

1996 Presidential Vote

Clinton (D)	98,348	(49%)
Dole (R)	81,282	(41%)
Perot (I)	13,324	(7%)
Other	7,540	(4%)

1992 Presidential Vote

Clinton (D)	98,057	(44%)
Bush (R)	80,986	(36%)
Perot (I)	42,071	(19%)

Rep. James E. Rogan (R)

Elected 1996; b. Aug. 21, 1957, San Francisco; home, Glendale; U. of CA at Berkeley, B.A. 1979; U.C.L.A., J.D. 1983; Christian; married (Christine Apffel).

Career: Practicing atty., 1983–85; Los Angeles Cnty. Dpty. District Atty., 1985–90; Glendale Municipal Court Judge, 1990—94; CA Assembly, 1994–96. Majority Ldr., 1996.

DC Office: 502 CHOB 20515, 202-225-4176; Fax: 202-226-1279.

District Offices: Pasadena, 818-577-3936.

Committees: *Commerce* (27th of 28 R): Energy & Power; Telecommunications, Trade & Consumer Protection.

Group Ratings and Key Votes: Newly Elected

Election Results

1996 general	James E. Rogan (R)	95,310	(50%)	($763,574)
	Doug Kahn (D)	82,014	(43%)	($1,052,335)
	Others	12,606	(7%)	
1996 primary	James E. Rogan (R)	46,020	(88%)	
	Joe Paul (R)	6,521	(12%)	
1994 general	Carlos J. Moorhead (R)	88,341	(53%)	($968,212)
	Doug Kahn (D)	70,267	(42%)	($581,225)
	Others	8,166	(5%)	

TWENTY-EIGHTH DISTRICT

It is the great route west to California: passengers on the Santa Fe railroad's *Super Chief* or motorists on U.S. 66, after hours and days in barren desert, descended through the El Cajon Pass into the Los Angeles Basin, moving in a stately procession beneath the 10,000-foot snow-capped San Gabriel Mountains, marveling at orange groves and exotic plants. The railroad and highway ran through a line of towns, built by Midwestern Protestants as independent communities and now mostly high-income suburbs with their own civic institutions—Claremont, home of the academically strong Claremont Colleges; La Verne and Glendora; Azusa, named by a Chicago manufacturer for his wife; Duarte, with the City of Hope Medical Center; Monrovia and Arcadia, site of the Santa Anita race track and the Los Angeles County Arboretum. Today, the traveler arriving in Los Angeles can see the same sights, if the air is clear, as the jet glides down the flightpath to LAX.

The 28th Congressional District covers much of this territory, with the exception of Azusa, which is part of the Hispanic-majority 31st District. Its eastern end reaches south from Claremont and Glendora to include Covina and West Covina, classic 1950s suburbs now with many Mexican-Americans, where city ordinances require that lawns be kept watered: 1950s homeowner values continue to govern here. The District's western end reaches south from Monrovia and Arcadia to include Temple City, where many towns are trying to revive their old downtowns. It is far from mono-cultural: 24% Hispanic and 13% Asian in 1990. The 28th has a strong Republican heritage, but it has been trending Democratic lately; Bill Clinton, after losing it by 3% in 1992 carried it by 1% in 1996.

David Dreier, the congressman from the 28th, grew up in Kansas City, Missouri, then spent a decade mostly on the Claremont campus, as a student and administrator, before he was elected to Congress in 1980. He personifies the intellectually rigorous conservatism and free market economics that has thrived in this area and maintains a cheerfulness and good humor characteristic of California—even though he served for 14 years in the minority, and several of those on the Rules Committee, where Republicans were outnumbered 9–4 and lost almost every floor vote. A strong backer of free trade, he was one of the leading Republicans rounding up votes for NAFTA in 1993, was chief Republican negotiator with the Clinton Administration in getting approval for the General Agreement on Tariffs and Trade, has been a leader in extending MFN status to China, and in 1997 was urging fast track status for Chile and other countries in Latin America.

But Dreier's work came in handy when the Republicans won their majority in November 1994. Dreier had been co-chairman of the Joint Committee on the Organization of Congress, and Speaker Newt Gingrich appointed him to realign the committee structure of the House—a task attended with the greatest political and policy sensitivities. Dreier's reform proposals, based on proposals rejected by the joint committee and refined in Republican negotiations and sometimes partisan debate, were introduced on the first day of the 104th Congress and speedily approved. Three committees were abolished, almost half the other panels were renamed and saw some shifting of jurisdictional lines, committee staff was cut by one-third, and term limits were established on chairmen. Dreier got a similar assignment in 1995, but was less venturesome, deciding not to recommend abolition of the Small Business and Science Committees. He encouraged committees to establish websites on the Internet, and held the first interactive subcommittee hearing in May 1996; his reforms adopted in January 1997 include Internet access, allowing members to ask questions for more than five minutes and allowing committees to sit while the House is considering amendments.

Dreier is the second ranking Republican on the Rules Committee, and as such plays an important part on all manner of legislation. He also is on the Republican steering committee; in a sop to the nation's largest GOP delegation, which ended up with no significant committee chairmanship or party leadership post, Gingrich named him head of a Republican task force on California created to respond to the state's legislative priorities. He was spotlighted at the San Diego convention and was the only Republican congressman named by *California Journal* as one of 25 Californians "with the power, influence and ideas to shape the dream for generations to come." His top legislative goals for 1997 were cutting in half the capital gains tax rate and reforming fast track trade procedures.

Dreier lost his first race for Congress in 1978, at 25, against Democrat Jim Lloyd; but he beat Lloyd in 1980 and then fellow Republican Wayne Grisham after they were redistricted together in 1982. At that point, Dreier evidently decided never to be pressed for funds again; he raised plenty of money and spent little, which takes more self-discipline than one might think. After the 1996 campaign he had $2.7 million cash on hand, the second highest in the House (behind Charles Schumer of New York). One possible use of that money would be a 1998 run for the Senate seat held by Barbara Boxer. Dreier has passed up other Senate races and in early 1997 said he might be interested in this one. But others were looking to run—San Diego Mayor Susan Golding, Orange County Congressman Christopher Cox—and Dreier's key position in the House and the relish he has for its work may lead him to run for reelection; he has been reelected easily every two years.

The People: Pop. 1990: 572,189; 11% age 65+; 57% White; 5% Black; 13% Asian; 24% Hispanic origin. Households: 60% married couple families; 30% married couple fams. w. children; 59% college educ.; median household income: $43,508; per capita income: $18,064; median gross rent: $705; median house value: $231,900.

1996 Presidential Vote

Clinton (D)	88,709	(45%)
Dole (R)	86,358	(44%)
Perot (I)	15,215	(8%)
Other	5,441	(3%)

1992 Presidential Vote

Bush (R)	90,644	(41%)
Clinton (D)	82,958	(38%)
Perot (I)	45,623	(21%)

Rep. David Dreier (R)

Elected 1980; b. July 5, 1952, Kansas City, MO; home, San Dimas; Claremont McKenna Col., B.A. 1975, Claremont Graduate Schl., M.A. 1976; Christian Scientist; single.

Career: Corp. Relations Dir., Claremont McKenna Col., 1975–78; Mktg. Dir., Industrial Hydrocarbons, 1979–80; Vice Pres., Dreier Development Co., 1985–present.

DC Office: 237 CHOB 20515, 202-225-2305; Fax: 202-225-7018.

District Offices: Covina, 818-339-9078.

Committees: *Rules* (2nd of 9 R): Rules & Organization of the House (Chmn.).

Group Ratings

	ADA	ACLU	AFS	LCV	CFA	CON	NFIB	COC	ACU	NTLC	CHC
1996	0	0	0	23	8	30	92	100	100	98	93
1995	0	—	—	6	0	53	—	96	80	—	—

National Journal Ratings

	1995 LIB — 1995 CONS			1996 LIB — 1996 CONS		
Economic	0%	—	74%	0%	—	82%
Social	0%	—	79%	0%	—	90%
Foreign	36%	—	59%	0%	—	79%

Key Votes of the 104th Congress

1. Reduce Medicare Growth $	Y	5. Flag Amendment	Y	9. Cuban Embargo	Y
2. Ovrd. Product Liab. Veto	Y	6. Drop EPA Limits	N	10. Bar Bosnia Troop $	N
3. Increase Min. Wage	N	7. Repeal Assault-Weap. Ban	*	11. Cut Anti-Missile Defense	N
4. Welfare Reform	Y	8. Ovrd. Part. Birth Veto	Y	12. Bar U.N. Uniforms	Y

Election Results

1996 general	David Dreier (R)	113,389	(61%)	($396,104)
	David Levering (D)	69,037	(37%)	($50,651)
	Others	4,459	(2%)	
1996 primary	David Dreier (R)	unopposed		
1994 general	David Dreier (R)	110,179	(67%)	($279,050)
	Tommy Randle (D)	50,022	(30%)	($28,905)
	Others	4,076	(2%)	

TWENTY-NINTH DISTRICT

The Westside: the term was not much used 20 years ago, but is now shorthand for what might be the biggest and flashiest concentration of affluence in the world. It is the heartland of one of America's most productive and creative industries—the persistence of the word "industry" here is a charming bit of antiquarianism—and one of the nation's major exports, show business. The first moviemakers came here earlier in the century, looking for a place to shoot silent films where the sunlight was more dependable than Astoria, Queens, or Englewood, New Jersey. They found it in Hollywood, a suburb just annexed by burgeoning Los Angeles when the first movie studio was built in 1911. In 1923 came the Hollywood sign, overlooking the soon-famous intersection of Hollywood and Vine. By the 1930s, the big studio lots were scattered around town, over the mountains in Burbank or out toward the ocean in Westwood and Culver City. Miraculously, the studio bosses of that era—most of them Jewish immigrants with little ancestral experience of America—created a popular culture that was universally accessible and that embodied the American spirit in a way that still captures the imagination. This was the universal American culture of the 1940s movies that Ronald Reagan understood and transferred into politics. Today's showbiz moguls, by contrast, have been absorbed in the enterprise of putting their own personal idiosyncrasies on the screen or the tube or on records or tapes or CDs.

Showbiz still sets the tone for the Westside. It remains tremendously profitable, in large part because it's not run by big business units but by thousands of craftsmen and entrepreneurs who keep it anchored in Los Angeles because so many of them remain here. People on the Westside like to portray themselves as artists in a garret, willing to risk starving to make art and speak truth to bourgeois society. But their disdain for traditional moral values and their yen for fashionable new moral standards—promiscuous sex and drug use are OK, but smoking cigarettes and failing to exercise are wrong—make them disdainful of the ordinary people who are the market of any mass entertainment. The Westside loves to congratulate itself on its moral daring when it makes a movie or TV show revealing businessmen or priests as criminals. But it reacted furiously to Dan Quayle's 1992 remarks about *Murphy Brown*, in which he made the unexceptionable points—later accepted by Bill Clinton—that children are better off with two parents and that glamorizing single motherhood can mislead and harm those less well-off than a fictional newscaster or Hollywood star. And yet the marketplace may be teaching showbiz some lessons. As Michael Medved, movie critic and author of *Hollywood vs. America*, has pointed out, Hollywood's most obscene, anti-business and anti-religious products don't sell nearly as well as its family fare; and television shows and movies started reflecting a wider range of subjects and values. Showbiz rejoiced in the election of Bill Clinton and in his frequent forays into California and obvious fascination with entertainers. But there has also been some recoil from his moderate positions on some issues and his fundraising practices, as witnessed by the dissolution of the Hollywood Women's PAC in April 1997.

Not everyone on the Westside is in show business, of course. This is also the home of thousands of small entrepreneurs, manufacturers, and inventors and marketers of everything imaginable, who sparked the Los Angeles Basin growth of the 1980s, and there are even traces of pre-show business, old Los Angeles money which is also plentiful. There are large numbers of singles and gays here: apartment-renters provided majorities for Santa Monica's radical city government, which thrived when it imposed rent control but foundered when it invited in more homeless. The core of Hollywood itself has gone seedy and is the home now of many Central American immigrants, a high-crime and riot zone, but the Fairfax neighborhood remains solidly middle-class Jewish, and just to the east there are many Russian Jewish migrants. Hancock Park looks as aristocratic as it did when it was built, when Beverly Hills was vacant land. The Westside has been the home of a former president who does not at all exemplify its politics, Ronald Reagan; it is also the home, notably on the former Fox lot that is now Century City where Reagan keeps his office, of some of the largest office buildings in the Los Angeles area. It is the center of the second largest Jewish community in the United States, as well as the focus of the 1980s immigration of Iranians to the United States. It is also the locus of some of America's most expensive residential real estate, where people buy houses for $1 million, knock down the structure and build something new for another million or two, and of one of the world's premier high-priced shopping areas—Rodeo Drive, a quite ordinary shopping street 20 years ago.

The 29th Congressional District contains almost all the major elements of Westside Los Angeles, from old, high-income Los Feliz and the gay neighborhood around Silver Lake through Hollywood and Hancock Park, west through Beverly Hills and Westwood, Bel Air and Brentwood, Santa Monica and Pacific Palisades. It is solidly Democratic, and not just in votes: it probably contributes more money to Democratic candidates and liberal causes than any other district with the possible exception of Manhattan's New York 14th. Its boundaries are carefully sculpted to put blacks in the 32nd District to the south and Hispanics and Asians in the 30th to the east; far from being racially diverse, it has the highest percentage of non-Hispanic whites (76%) of any Los Angeles Basin district except the 24th on the other side of Mulholland Drive.

The congressman from the 29th is Henry Waxman, a Democrat elected in 1974, one of the ablest members of the House and for 16 years was one of the most powerful, a shrewd political operator who is a skilled and idealistic policy entrepreneur. There is no Westside glitz about him: he grew up over his family's store in Watts, his personal demeanor is quiet, he has never attended the Oscars ceremony. He first learned politics at UCLA with Howard Berman, Willie Brown, David Roberti and John Burton. At each stage of his career, he has seen political openings before others did and gone smartly through them. He ran against Assemblyman Lester McMillan in the mostly Jewish Fairfax area in 1968, at 28, and won 64% in the primary. In 1971–72 he chaired the redistricting committee, a good place to make friends, and he went to Congress in 1974 in a district designed, he points out, not by his committee but by a court. Waxman's biggest break came after the 1978 election, when he was elected chairman of the Commerce Committee's Health and Environment Subcommittee. This was one of the first times House Democrats decided not to observe seniority in handing out subcommittee chairs, and Waxman's opponent, Richardson Preyer of North Carolina, was competent and widely respected. Nevertheless, Waxman argued his case on the issues and—in a move quite unprecedented at the time, though common in Sacramento and now also in Washington—made campaign contributions to other Democrats on the full committee, and won the post, 15–12.

The campaign contributions were no accident. Waxman and his friends Howard Berman and former area congressman Mel Levine built their own political machine in Los Angeles. Its power came not from patronage but from fundraising and savvy. Their specialty was targeted direct mail, with hundreds of customized letters and endorsement slates sent out to different lists of people. In the apolitical commonwealth of California, where television advertising is exceedingly expensive and people seem to avoid politics, this made them critical though not always successful players. But in 1992 their machine seemed to founder: Westsider Mel Levine lost the Senate nomination to Barbara Boxer in "the year of the woman," and Tom Hayden beat a Waxman-Berman ally for state senator.

Waxman has been a major national policymaker for nearly 20 years. In 1981 and 1982 he prevented the Reagan Administration and Commerce Committee Chairman John Dingell from revising the Clean Air Act; biding his time, he worked to strengthen it positions in the revision of 1990. He and Dingell—frequent shouting match partners who nevertheless maintained a working relationship—hammered out a compromise, delaying stricter California-type auto standards until 1994 and moving more aggressively on non-auto issues. Another great project of Waxman's has been expanding Medicaid for the poor. His strategy was to expand coverage by threatening to hold up budget reconciliation bills unless they required states to expand Medicaid eligibility. Between 1984 and 1990, he got coverage for all poor children up to 18, all children under seven, and pregnant women in families under 133% of poverty income. This and other Waxman programs helped raise Medicaid from 9% to 14% of state spending in the 1980s, and helps to explain why Waxman is hated by many governors. More than anything else, Waxman's

Medicaid increases and the Republicans' desire to prevent his return to power sparked the demand for the unfunded mandates legislation passed by Congress and signed by former Governor Clinton in 1995.

Waxman had less success on reforming national health care when the issue came out in the open. He wanted to move to something like a single-payer, government-paid program and supported the Clinton plan, but to no avail. He has secured more funding for AIDS research, a burning issue in the 29th District with its large gay population. He passed a law providing damages to children injured by required immunizations, sponsored measures to require testing of mammography devices, expanded the availability of generic drugs, extended patent protection for drugs during part of the regulatory process, and tried unsuccessfully to legalize the use of heroin to reduce the pain of terminal cancer patients. He has worked hard to allow fetal tissue research. In early 1994, in widely publicized hearings, he lined up the chief executive officers of leading tobacco companies and accused them of adding nicotine and other substances to cigarettes and of lying in their testimony; that had no legislative result, and when Thomas Bliley of Richmond, Virginia, became Commerce Committee chair, the hearings stopped. But Waxman brought the tobacco issue out into public view and FDA head David Kessler's election-year proposal to regulate tobacco as a drug proved to be a good campaign issue for Clinton and most Democrats, though not those in tobacco-growing territory.

Waxman reacted with dismay to the Republican takeover of Congress, but with no slackening of effort. "If you believe in things, then you fight for those positions." On some issues he worked to negotiate compromises with Republicans, notably the Safe Drinking Water Act and the pesticide standards in the Food Quality Provision Act of 1996; part of his strategy was "right-to-know" amendments listing contaminants. He led the fight against Republicans' regulatory reform and Medicare and Medicaid changes. He worked for reauthorization of the Ryan White Health Care Act and for mental health insurance coverage. He was the senior Democrat on the Corrections Day Advisory Group, working to prevent liberal laws from being quickly repealed. In December 1996 he promised "the mother of all environmental fights" if cost considerations were introduced into the Clean Air Act standard-setting process. He and Republican Wayne Gilchrest called for bipartisan action on environmental issues. In 1997 he gave up the ranking position on Health to be the lead Democrat on the Government Reform and Oversight Committee. There he sharply attacked Chairman Dan Burton's investigation of Clinton campaign misdeeds, and emerged as perhaps the most articulate defender in the House of Clinton against scandal charges.

Waxman has always won reelection easily, and has contributed generously to other Democrats' campaigns. He hoped the Democrats would win back control of the House in 1996, but showed no inclination to retire when they didn't. His 1996 Republican opponent, Paul Stepanek, denied party funding in this hopeless district, endorsed Bill Clinton and denounced Newt Gingrich and Dick Armey. It availed him nothing; Waxman won 68%–25%.

The People: Pop. 1990: 571,386; 16% age 65+; 76% White; 3% Black; 7% Asian; 13% Hispanic origin. Households: 34% married couple families; 12% married couple fams. w. children; 71% college educ.; median household income: $37,540; per capita income: $34,253; median gross rent: $678; median house value: $500,001.

1996 Presidential Vote

Clinton (D)	150,771	(66%)
Dole (R)	53,354	(24%)
Perot (I)	10,639	(5%)
Other	12,002	(5%)

1992 Presidential Vote

Clinton (D)	183,233	(66%)
Bush (R)	55,924	(20%)
Perot (I)	37,217	(13%)

Rep. Henry A. Waxman (D)

Elected 1974; b. Sept. 12, 1939, Los Angeles; home, Los Angeles; U.C.L.A., B.A. 1961, J.D. 1964; Jewish; married (Janet).

Career: Practicing atty., 1965–68; CA Assembly, 1968–74.

DC Office: 2204 RHOB 20515, 202-225-3976; Fax: 202-225-4099.

District Offices: Los Angeles, 213-651-1040.

Committees: *Commerce* (2nd of 23 D): Health & the Environment; Oversight & Investigations. *Government Reform & Oversight* (RMM of 19 D).

Group Ratings

	ADA	ACLU	AFS	LCV	CFA	CON	NFIB	COC	ACU	NTLC	CHC
1996	90	86	100	85	100	72	9	13	0	2	0
1995	95	—	—	100	100	13	—	13	4	—	—

National Journal Ratings

	1995 LIB — 1995 CONS			1996 LIB — 1996 CONS		
Economic	94%	—	0%	89%	—	0%
Social	79%	—	20%	88%	—	0%
Foreign	93%	—	0%	85%	—	15%

Key Votes of the 104th Congress

1. Reduce Medicare Growth $	N	5. Flag Amendment	N	9. Cuban Embargo	N
2. Ovrd. Product Liab. Veto	N	6. Drop EPA Limits	Y	10. Bar Bosnia Troop $	N
3. Increase Min. Wage	Y	7. Repeal Assault-Weap. Ban	N	11. Cut Anti-Missile Defense	Y
4. Welfare Reform	N	8. Ovrd. Part. Birth Veto	N	12. Bar U.N. Uniforms	N

Election Results

1996 general	Henry A. Waxman (D)	145,278	(68%)	($365,082)
	Paul Stepanek (R)	52,857	(25%)	($135,677)
	John Peter Daly (P&F)	8,819	(4%)	
	Others	7,863	(4%)	
1996 primary	Henry A. Waxman (D)	unopposed		
1994 general	Henry A. Waxman (D)	129,413	(68%)	($186,127)
	Paul Stepanek (R)	53,801	(28%)	($70,777)
	Others	7,162	(4%)	

THIRTIETH DISTRICT

Surrounding downtown Los Angeles are neighborhoods just now becoming antique, as the early 20th Century buildings stop looking familiar and start taking on the patina of the historic. Downtown LA, with its 1980s marble slabs and pink cylinders jutting up to 70 stories from what was once a low-rise business district, seems soulless and detached from the neighborhoods around, which change character with every new immigration flow. Not far east, over the Los Angeles River, is Boyle Heights, once an entry neighborhood for Irish and Jewish immigrants and for the last 30 years predominantly Mexican-American, poor in income terms but with enough community cohesion not to riot in April 1992. To the north of downtown is Lincoln

Heights, a heavily Hispanic area centering on the shopping street of North Broadway, plus the neighborhoods of Highland Park and Eagle Rock, white middle-class 30 years ago, now mostly Hispanic but with Asians as well. West of downtown are lower Sunset Boulevard, the Koreatown strip along Western Avenue, and much of Hollywood and some of South Central. Koreatown was the area worst hurt in the riots, and as elites empathized with the rioters more than the hard-working, law-abiding merchants whose property was destroyed; there is residual bitterness here of unknown proportions. Much of Hollywood has become an entry point for Central American migrants, as has the northern edge of South Central; coming from societies where violence is more common and endemic than in Mexico or the United States, they rioted in large numbers. These are all neighborhoods populated more thickly than they were a quarter-century ago, with small houses and garden apartments full of large families and many children; new migrants stay with those who have been here a few years, with beds assigned to family members working different shifts so they're slept in 24 hours a day. To most American eyes, these look like poverty neighborhoods, but this is the snapshot view; in the video version they are the first frames on the way to prosperity, the first way-station on the Santa Ana and San Bernardino Freeways to middle-income American comfort.

All these areas, centering geographically on Dodger Stadium, are part of California's 30th Congressional District. The population here in 1990 was recorded as 62% Hispanic and 20% Asian. But many of these are recent immigrants; only 34% of registered voters were Latino and 7% Asian. There are some 600,000 people living here, but in 1996 only 21,000 voted in the Democratic primary and only 81,000 in the general election, compared to 62,000 in the primary and 215,000 in the general in the Westside 29th District.

The congressman from the 30th District is Xavier Becerra, a Democrat elected in 1992. He grew up in California, went to college and law school at Stanford, worked for legal services, then worked for state Senator Art Torres and Attorney General John Van de Kamp. In 1990 he was elected to the Assembly, and had a liberal record on the environment and making AIDS drugs available; he backed campaign finance reform and tougher penalties for gang activities near schools. In 1992 the newly-redrawn 30th District was expected to reelect Edward Roybal, California's first Latino congressman, first elected in 1962; his daughter, Assemblywoman Lucille Roybal-Allard, was running in the neighboring 33d District. But Roybal announced late in the game that he was retiring, and Becerra jumped into the race, although his residence was in Monterey Park, outside the district. One competitor, former Roybal aide Henry Lozano, dropped out of the race, and Roybal endorsed Becerra. Becerra's main Latino competitor, Leticia Quezada, was a member of the Los Angeles school board, a powerful engine for publicity, and had the endorsement of Councilman Richard Alatorre and Assemblyman Richard Polanco. But Becerra had the endorsements of Roybal, 34th District Congressman Esteban Torres and County Supervisor Gloria Molina. In a primary in which only 33,000 voters turned out, Becerra won with 32%, to 22% for Quezada 22%, 16% for Albert Lum 16% and 13% for Jeff Penichet. Becerra's 10,417 votes effectively made him the representative of 573,000 people; he won the general in this heavily Democratic district 58%–24%.

The fast-moving Becerra initially was slowed down in the House. He did not get on the Commerce Committee, where he had hoped to work on healthcare reform. But even with Republicans in control, he was legislatively active, if not always successful. On the Judiciary Committee he moved for refunds of the $80 fee paid by the one million visa applicants who would be ineligible under the proposed immigration rules and called for an appeals process for workers denied jobs by errors in the proposed new identification program. He said declaring English as the official language "sends a message of intolerance for those trying to learn English." He worked on the Democrats' welfare reform bill. He opposed a law to allow local law enforcement agents to enter pacts with the Department of Justice to enforce immigration laws. After the 1996 election, he ran for chairman of the Hispanic Caucus and in December 1996 visited Cuba and met with Fidel Castro. He was elected chairman in January 1997 by 12–7, at which point Republican members Ileana Ros-Lehtinen and Lincoln Diaz-Balart resigned because of his trip to, and his refusal to, demand free elections in Cuba. He also became a member of the Ways and Means Committee. Becerra's pleasant and businesslike manner combined with his obvious ambition could make him a force in the House, though his leftish views for the moment anyway make him not very effective.

The People: Pop. 1990: 572,604; 8% age 65+; 15% White; 3% Black; 20% Asian; 62% Hispanic origin. Households: 45% married couple families; 27% married couple fams. w. children; 35% college educ.; median household income: $23,435; per capita income: $9,637; median gross rent: $525; median house value: $187,400.

1996 Presidential Vote

Clinton (D)	61,114	(71%)
Dole (R)	17,053	(20%)
Perot (I)	4,165	(5%)
Other	3,713	(4%)

1992 Presidential Vote

Clinton (D)	56,378	(62%)
Bush (R)	21,750	(24%)
Perot (I)	11,842	(13%)

Rep. Xavier Becerra (D)

Elected 1992; b. Jan. 26, 1958, Sacramento; home, Los Angeles; Stanford U., B.A. 1980, J.D. 1984; Catholic; married (Carolina Reyes).

Career: Staff Atty., Legal Assistance Corp. of Central MA; Dist. Dir., CA Sen. Art Torres, 1986; CA Dep. Atty. Gen., 1987–90; CA Assembly, 1990–92.

DC Office: 1119 LHOB 20515, 202-225-6235; Fax: 202-225-2202.

District Offices: Los Angeles, 213-550-8962.

Committees: *Ways & Means* (15th of 16 D): Health.

Group Ratings

	ADA	ACLU	AFS	LCV	CFA	CON	NFIB	COC	ACU	NTLC	CHC
1996	85	100	100	77	69	22	14	23	0	2	0
1995	85	—	—	94	92	7	—	9	9	—	—

National Journal Ratings

	1995 LIB — 1995 CONS			1996 LIB — 1996 CONS		
Economic	89%	—	11%	89%	—	0%
Social	77%	—	23%	88%	—	0%
Foreign	85%	—	14%	90%	—	0%

Key Votes of the 104th Congress

1. Reduce Medicare Growth $	N	5. Flag Amendment	N	9. Cuban Embargo	N
2. Ovrd. Product Liab. Veto	*	6. Drop EPA Limits	Y	10. Bar Bosnia Troop $	N
3. Increase Min. Wage	*	7. Repeal Assault-Weap. Ban	N	11. Cut Anti-Missile Defense	Y
4. Welfare Reform	N	8. Ovrd. Part. Birth Veto	N	12. Bar U.N. Uniforms	N

Election Results

1996 general	Xavier Becerra (D)	58,283	(72%)	($223,890)
	Patricia Jean Parker (R)	15,078	(19%)	
	Others	7,229	(9%)	
1996 primary	Xavier Becerra (D)	unopposed		
1994 general	Xavier Becerra (D)	43,943	(66%)	($234,096)
	David A. Ramirez (R)	18,741	(28%)	
	R. William Weilberg (Lib)	3,741	(6%)	

THIRTY-FIRST DISTRICT

Anyone interested in the future of America and today's immigrants should drive straight east from downtown Los Angeles on the San Bernardino Freeway, through the string of suburbs that grew up in the 1940s and 1950s. These were once white middle-class communities, with grids of stucco houses above the dry river beds; they were filled with Midwest and East Coast migrants who discovered California during World War II and decided to stay, or who learned of its golden reputation from the new medium of television in the days before smog became part of the language. The atmosphere then was Midwestern, cheerful, busy, with children always underfoot. Over the next generation or so, there has been almost a complete population turnover here, but some things remain the same. Mexican-Americans have spread out from their original East Los Angeles base to become majorities in blue-collar suburbs like El Monte, Baldwin Park and Azusa, all with many more residents than in their Anglo days. Monterey Park and San Gabriel have sprouted Chinese and Korean shopping centers and storefronts, and have become the American center for Taiwanese. In next-door Alhambra, the Asians have made the local high school "an academic giant," reports *The Washington Post*'s Jay Mathews. "Its name is . . . at the top of lists of the leading science and mathematics programs in American education." But these are not mono-ethnic communities, and East Los Angeles has not become a slum. There are no empty storefronts, but busy shops with new signs; no housing riddled with vandalism and neglect, but newly painted homes with carefully tended gardens; these are neighborhoods still filled with children whose parents believe in traditional values. When blacks and Latinos were rioting in South Central and Hollywood, East Los Angeles and the San Gabriel Valley were quiet and orderly. Sometime in the 21st Century, novels will be written describing the by-then vanished atmosphere of these immigrant suburbs, that will surely tell more about the human condition than the 1980s minimalist novels (like the eponymous *Less Than Zero*) did about the horrors of growing up rich in Beverly Hills.

In the 1950s, these were Democratic areas—New Dealers bringing their voting habits west—but the new Latinos and Asians seem up for grabs. They voted strongly for Ronald Reagan in 1984 and were only 5% to 8% more Democratic than average in the 1988 and 1990 elections; in 1992, Latinos moved toward the Democrats, but Asians, dismayed by responses to the riot, trended Republican. In 1996 the move was in the other direction. Latinos, less because of Proposition 209 which prohibited racial quotas than because of Republican immigration and welfare acts removing aid to legal immigrants, moved heavily toward the Democrats; Asians moved a bit in the same direction. The promise of increased government benefits could help the Democrats. But working against them are these new Americans' hard work in building small businesses and their bad experiences with government here and where they came from.

The 31st Congressional District covers much of this territory, from the LA city limit east through East Los Angeles, Alhambra, San Gabriel, Rosemead, El Monte, Baldwin Park and Azusa; it brushes, but excludes, higher-income suburbs up against the San Gabriel Mountains. It was 59% Hispanic in 1990 and 22% Asian, with one of the lowest percentages of non-Hispanic whites (18%) in California, and is solidly Democratic.

The congressman from the 31st is Marty Martinez, a Democrat elected in 1982. The owner of an upholstery company, he was elected to the Monterey Park City Council in 1974, at 45, and became mayor of Monterey Park in 1976. He was tapped in 1980 to run for the Assembly by Howard Berman, who was running for speaker, and the Berman-Waxman machine superintended Martinez's campaign to a win. Their ally, Phil Burton, in the 1982 redistricting plan forestalled a Republican-Hispanic alliance by creating two Hispanic districts in the eastern Los Angeles Basin. One of them was for Martinez, and after a desultory campaign he beat incumbent Republican and onetime John Birch Society organizer John Rousselot 54%–46%.

By 1993 Martinez was a subcommittee chairman and technically the lead sponsor of the Clinton Administration's National Community Service Bill and the reauthorizations of the Older Americans Act and the Juvenile Justice Act and Delinquency Prevention Act, all signed into law. He also passed a Native American Languages Act to record these languages before they die out. His pet cause is regulating private security guards, omnipresent in southern California and on occasion the perpetrators of horrible crimes; he had a bill to require states to set minimum training and screening standards and another to open up FBI crime records to state regulators. Martinez sought to exempt the Census from the English-official-language bill and opposed the Republican bill prohibiting the Labor Department from advising pension fund managers to make investments based on social criteria. In 1997 he and other Eastside congressmen tried to get the next Metro line built in their area rather than on the Westside as favored by appropriator Julian Dixon.

Martinez's hold on the seat does not seem solid: he won only 43% and 55% in primaries in 1992 and 1994. One sometime-critic is his daughter, Diane Martinez, elected to the Assembly in 1992 after breaking with her father and the Berman-Waxman machine, whose sharp tongue and willingness to fight has gotten her labeled "Miss Congeniality" in Sacramento.

The People: Pop. 1990: 572,758; 9% age 65+; 18% White; 2% Black; 22% Asian; 59% Hispanic origin. Households: 57% married couple families; 33% married couple fams. w. children; 36% college educ.; median household income: $30,667; per capita income: $10,264; median gross rent: $622; median house value: $178,400.

1996 Presidential Vote			**1992 Presidential Vote**		
Clinton (D)	70,288	(65%)	Clinton (D)	59,616	(51%)
Dole (R)	27,736	(26%)	Bush (R)	37,250	(32%)
Perot (I)	7,043	(7%)	Perot (I)	18,449	(16%)
Other	2,468	(2%)			

Rep. Matthew G. (Marty) **Martinez (D)**

Elected 1982; b. Feb. 14, 1929, Walsenburg, CO; home, Monterey Park; Los Angeles Trade Tech. Col., 1950; Catholic; married (Elvira).

Career: Marine Corps, 1947–50; Businessman, 1950–70; Monterey Park Planning Cmte., 1971–74; Monterey Park City Cncl., 1974–80; Monterey Park Mayor, 1976, 1980; CA Assembly, 1980–82.

DC Office: 2234 RHOB 20515, 202-225-5464; Fax: 202-225-5467.

District Offices: Alhambra, 818-458-4524.

Committees: *Education & The Workforce* (4th of 20 D): Early Childhood, Youth & Families (RMM); Workforce Protections. *International Relations* (7th of 21 D): Asia & the Pacific; Western Hemisphere.

Group Ratings

	ADA	ACLU	AFS	LCV	CFA	CON	NFIB	COC	ACU	NTLC	CHC
1996	80	81	100	85	69	14	28	31	10	13	7
1995	85	—	—	88	62	31	—	26	12	—	—

National Journal Ratings

	1995 LIB — 1995 CONS			1996 LIB — 1996 CONS		
Economic	89%	—	11%	79%	—	18%
Social	73%	—	27%	76%	—	23%
Foreign	69%	—	31%	52%	—	48%

Key Votes of the 104th Congress

1. Reduce Medicare Growth $	N	5. Flag Amendment	Y	9. Cuban Embargo	N
2. Ovrd. Product Liab. Veto	N	6. Drop EPA Limits	Y	10. Bar Bosnia Troop $	N
3. Increase Min. Wage	Y	7. Repeal Assault-Weap. Ban	N	11. Cut Anti-Missile Defense	N
4. Welfare Reform	N	8. Ovrd. Part. Birth Veto	Y	12. Bar U.N. Uniforms	N

Election Results

1996 general	Matthew G. (Marty) Martinez (D)	69,285	(67%)	($83,015)
	John V. Flores (R)	28,705	(28%)	($39,439)
	Michael B. Everling (Lib)	4,700	(5%)	
1996 primary	Matthew G. (Marty) Martinez (D)	unopposed		
1994 general	Matthew G. (Marty) Martinez (D)	50,541	(59%)	($123,767)
	John V. Flores (R)	34,926	(41%)	($81,517)

THIRTY-SECOND DISTRICT

One of the myths of the Los Angeles riots of 1992 and 1965 is that black Angelenos live in conditions of isolation and poverty. Some do, but in levels of income and in degree of residential integration with non-blacks, Los Angeles blacks rank among the top in the United States, and its black-owned businesses have the highest revenues of any city in the nation. Californians have historically shown less prejudice against blacks than most Americans, and job opportunities in Los Angeles—up to and including the office of mayor for 20 years—have been plenteous for blacks. This is apparent in the hills just west of Crenshaw, an Art Deco neighborhood built in the 1920s and 1930s in vacant flat land southwest of downtown LA. Here, in Baldwin Hills, where on clear days you can see the towers of downtown and the snow-capped San Gabriel Mountains beyond, is a high-income black neighborhood, one of the strongest in the country, and where Magic Johnson has built his fabulously successful multiplex theaters. To the north and west are other comfortable black-majority neighborhoods; on the flatlands south of Beverly Hills and the Fairfax district not far away, many affluent blacks are buying houses.

This part of Los Angeles is the heart of the 32d Congressional District, which runs approximately from the Harbor Freeway west past Baldwin Hills to Culver City almost to the ocean, and south from Olympic Boulevard past the Santa Monica Freeway down almost to Inglewood and the LAX airport. The 32d vies with the Maryland 4th and New York 6th for the largest numbers of affluent blacks. Politically there has been no serious trend toward Republicans. Indeed, affluent, well-educated blacks seem if anything to be culturally more liberal than low-income black voters who may have closer ties to church and tradition. Any affection that upper-income blacks may have for free market economics is tempered by the knowledge that many of them have profited on the way up from some form of government intervention—a student loan, a public sector job, an affirmative action program.

The congressman from the 32d District is Julian Dixon, a Democrat elected in 1978. Dixon went to college and law school in southern California after serving in the Army; he practiced law in Los Angeles and was elected in 1972 to the Assembly, where he was an ally of Henry Waxman; in 1978, when incumbent Yvonne Burke ran for attorney general, Dixon was elected to the House. Intelligent, politically savvy, a team player with high ethics, he got good positions and tough assignments. In 1984 he chaired the rules committee at the Democratic National Convention and dealt effectively with Jesse Jackson's challenges to the rules. In 1989, as chairman of the House Ethics Committee, he had to supervise the task of passing judgment on Speaker Jim Wright. This was as high-pressure an assignment as could be imagined: Republicans led by Newt Gingrich were furiously pursuing Wright, Democrats were nervously defending him. Dixon proceeded deliberately, maintaining bipartisanship on the committee and let the evidence come out that prompted Wright to resign in June 1989.

Early on Dixon got a seat on the Appropriations Committee and rose quickly to become chairman of the District of Columbia Subcommittee—a thankless post. At first he sought to help Mayor Marion Barry obtain plenty of funds for the large District government. But when Barry returned to office in 1995 after serving time in prison, Dixon became a harsh critic and called for privatization of some services and federalization of others, like corrections; but he also sometimes opposed Republican plans as overstringent.

On Appropriations he has been attentive to local issues. On the Defense (now National Security) Subcommittee he worked for Los Angeles area defense contractors, and sponsored a loan guarantee act for small businesses hurt by military base closings and defense contract terminations. His voting record, very liberal on most things, is more moderate on foreign issues. He stepped in with "dire emergency" supplementals for Los Angeles after the riots in 1992 and the Northridge earthquake in January 1994. He has been the chief funder of Los Angeles's Metro subway, an often troubled venture; when Henry Waxman objected to building on the Wilshire Boulevard corridor, one of the most densely populated part of the Los Angeles Basin, because of methane gas deposits, Dixon steered the route farther into his district, though unaccountably no route is planned to nearby LAX. He has pushed for more funding of the INS and Border Patrol guards and for reimbursing states for the costs of jailing illegal aliens. He got a $400 million federal loan for the Alameda Corridor, an underground connection between Los Angeles's huge port and the major east-west rail lines. On the National Security and Commerce Subcommittees (he was rotated off the first in 1995 and 1996) he got funding for the California National Guard/Los Angeles Unified School District program to teach math and science to at-risk youth and funding for the Angel Gate Academy for at-risk middle school students. He works to maintain funding for the Legal Services Corporation, the Clinton police program, Commerce Department technology programs and the Minority Business Development Agency. Since 1993 he has served on the Intelligence Committee; in 1996, after the San Jose Mercury News charged that the CIA financed the crack cocaine trade in Los Angeles, he carefully called for an "airing" of the issue.

Dixon is regularly reelected without significant opposition. He has declined calls to run for the Los Angeles Board of Supervisors (instead his predecessor Yvonne Burke was elected in 1992) and mayor of Los Angeles.

The People: Pop. 1990: 572,630; 11% age 65+; 24% White; 38% Black; 7% Asian; 30% Hispanic origin. Households: 38% married couple families; 18% married couple fams. w. children; 50% college educ.; median household income: $28,332; per capita income: $14,520; median gross rent: $592; median house value: $231,400.

1996 Presidential Vote			1992 Presidential Vote		
Clinton (D)	130,394	(81%)	Clinton (D)	147,623	(77%)
Dole (R)	19,348	(12%)	Bush (R)	23,956	(13%)
Perot (I)	5,764	(4%)	Perot (I)	17,561	(9%)
Other	4,854	(3%)			

Rep. Julian C. Dixon (D)

Elected 1978; b. Aug. 8, 1934, Washington, D.C.; home, Culver City; CA St. U., Los Angeles, B.S. 1962, Southwestern U., LL.B. 1967; Episcopalian; married (Betty).

Career: Army, 1957–60; Practicing atty., 1960–73; CA Assembly, 1972–78.

DC Office: 2252 RHOB 20515, 202-225-7084; Fax: 202-225-4091.

District Offices: Los Angeles, 213-678-5424.

Committees: *Appropriations* (7th of 26 D): Commerce, Justice, State & Judiciary; District of Columbia; National Security. *Intelligence (Select)* (2nd of 7 D): Human Intelligence, Analysis & Counterintelligence (RMM).

Group Ratings

	ADA	ACLU	AFS	LCV	CFA	CON	NFIB	COC	ACU	NTLC	CHC
1996	90	81	100	77	85	48	22	19	0	8	0
1995	95	—	—	94	100	7	—	17	4	—	—

National Journal Ratings

	1995 LIB — 1995 CONS			1996 LIB — 1996 CONS		
Economic	90%	—	8%	89%	—	0%
Social	88%	—	0%	88%	—	0%
Foreign	88%	—	7%	75%	—	24%

Key Votes of the 104th Congress

1. Reduce Medicare Growth $	N	5. Flag Amendment	N	9. Cuban Embargo	N
2. Ovrd. Product Liab. Veto	N	6. Drop EPA Limits	Y	10. Bar Bosnia Troop $	N
3. Increase Min. Wage	Y	7. Repeal Assault-Weap. Ban	N	11. Cut Anti-Missile Defense	Y
4. Welfare Reform	N	8. Ovrd. Part. Birth Veto	N	12. Bar U.N. Uniforms	N

Election Results

1996 general	Julian C. Dixon (D)	124,712	(82%)	($97,495)
	Larry Ardito (R)	18,768	(12%)	
	Neal Donnoer (Lib)	6,390	(4%)	
1996 primary	Julian C. Dixon (D)	unopposed		
1994 general	Julian C. Dixon (D)	98,017	(78%)	($141,941)
	Ernie A. Farhat (R)	22,190	(18%)	($43,910)
	John Honigsfeld (P&F)	6,099	(5%)	

THIRTY-THIRD DISTRICT

A block from Los Angeles's "modern architecture" City Hall, whose 452-foot white tower—long the symbol of the city but now dwarfed by 60- and 70-story postmodern marble slabs and pink cylinders a few blocks away—is the huge retail shopping street of Broadway. The sidewalks are thronged, the signs are mostly in Spanish, the merchandise is often strewn on tables: this could be Mexico City or Lima, Latin America transplanted a block from a gleaming symbol of Yankee propriety and gaudy emblems of North American prosperity. Broadway, now somewhat in decline from its retail hey-day, is neither the geographical nor spiritual center of Los Angeles's Latino communities and it is by no means their only major shopping area. But it is an emblem of the entry-level Latino neighborhoods of the nation's second largest city, the places where many immigrants, not so much from Mexico as from Central and South America, come to find a cheap place to live, doubled and tripled up with other families and single newcomers, close enough to drive an old car to work in factories and warehouses that fill so much of the acreage south and east of downtown.

Broadway and many of these entry-level neighborhoods make up much of the 33d Congressional District. It includes downtown and MacArthur Park, once beautiful and now a drug dealers' hangout, and Pico Union, where many Central and South American immigrants make their first homes; it includes the giant factories south of downtown along the Southern Pacific Railroad and Santa Ana Freeway; it takes in part of East Los Angeles. To the south it includes the garment factories of Vernon and the 1940s working-class, southern-white suburbs—Huntington Park, with its vibrant shopping strip on Pacific Boulevard, South Gate, Bell and Bell Gardens, Commerce, Maywood and Cudahy—which are now heavily Latino. The 33d District in 1990 was 84% Hispanic, by far the highest figure of any California district, and the only district that can be called monocultural. Politically, these neighborhoods are more Democratic than when they were white but less Democratic than when they were black. This is mostly a non-voting constituency: newcomers may not be citizens, many residents are children, workers at two jobs may be too busy to register and Latinos tend to see private sector work, not public sector protections, as their way up in the world. As a result, in 1996 only 14,445 people voted in the 33d District's Democratic primary and only 58,000 in the general election, compared to 215,000 in the Westside 29th District and 103,000, 75,000, 103,000 and 138,000 in the Hispanic-majority 26th, 30th, 31st and 34th Districts. The 33d District looks like a late 20th Century version of a rotten borough, Old-Sarum-on-the-Pacific-Rim; but it is a district where people work hard and play by the American rules, with high rates of family stability and low levels of AFDC dependence, the home of people rising into the middle class.

The 33d District's congresswoman is Lucille Roybal-Allard, first elected in 1992, the daughter of 30-year Congressman Edward Roybal, whose roots were in New Mexico, not Mexico. Roybal-Allard was elected to the Assembly in 1986 and there sponsored bills on sexual assault, domestic violence and such causes as requiring more environmental impact reports for toxic waste incinerators (a move prompted by protests against a proposed incinerator in Vernon.) She entered the 1992 House race even before her father announced his retirement, and she won 75% in the Democratic primary and 63% in the general election. She says she is "dedicated to community empowerment at all levels," and compiled an almost perfectly liberal voting record. She worked for the Violence Against Women Act of 1994 and has sponsored a Battered Women's Economic Protection Act. On the Budget Committee she worked against cuts in the WIC nutrition program and the Earned Income Tax Credit. She favored the Community Development Banking and Financial Institutions Act of 1994, and attacked tobacco companies for targeting women. She has urged that the Los Angeles Metro line be extended in her Eastside area. In 1997 she became the Democratic co-chairman of the California delegation, working with senior Republican Jerry Lewis for bipartisan consensus on California issues where possible.

Back home Roybal-Allard sponsors health fairs and workshops on home-buying and U.S. citizenship. She has been reelected without difficulty.

The People: Pop. 1990: 570,893; 6% age 65+; 8% White; 4% Black; 4% Asian; 84% Hispanic origin. Households: 49% married couple families; 34% married couple fams. w. children; 17% college educ.; median household income: $20,708; per capita income: $6,997; median gross rent: $484; median house value: $154,400.

1996 Presidential Vote

Clinton (D)	48,636	(80%)
Dole (R)	8,538	(14%)
Perot (I)	2,691	(4%)
Other	1,146	(2%)

1992 Presidential Vote

Clinton (D)	33,642	(63%)
Bush (R)	12,607	(23%)
Perot (I)	7,149	(13%)

Rep. Lucille Roybal-Allard (D)

Elected 1992; b. June 12, 1941, Los Angeles; home, Los Angeles; CA St. U., Los Angeles, B.A. 1965; Catholic; married (Edward Allard).

Career: CA Assembly, 1986–92.

DC Office: 2435 RHOB 20515, 202-225-1766.

District Offices: Los Angeles, 213-628-9230.

Committees: *Banking & Financial Services* (12th of 25 D): Capital Markets, Securities & Government Sponsored Enterprises; Financial Institutions & Consumer Credit. *Budget* (8th of 19 D).

Group Ratings

	ADA	ACLU	AFS	LCV	CFA	CON	NFIB	COC	ACU	NTLC	CHC
1996	90	94	100	92	92	6	17	25	0	2	0
1995	95	—	—	100	100	9	—	13	4	—	—

National Journal Ratings

	1995 LIB — 1995 CONS			1996 LIB — 1996 CONS		
Economic	85%	—	12%	89%	—	0%
Social	88%	—	0%	88%	—	0%
Foreign	93%	—	0%	87%	—	10%

Key Votes of the 104th Congress

1. Reduce Medicare Growth $	N	5. Flag Amendment	N	9. Cuban Embargo	N
2. Ovrd. Product Liab. Veto	N	6. Drop EPA Limits	Y	10. Bar Bosnia Troop $	N
3. Increase Min. Wage	Y	7. Repeal Assault-Weap. Ban	N	11. Cut Anti-Missile Defense	Y
4. Welfare Reform	N	8. Ovrd. Part. Birth Veto	N	12. Bar U.N. Uniforms	N

Election Results

1996 general	Lucille Roybal-Allard (D)	47,478	(82%)	($144,278)
	John P. Leonard (R)	8,147	(14%)	($6,208)
	Howard Johnson (Lib)	2,203	(4%)	
1996 primary	Lucille Roybal-Allard (D)	unopposed		
1994 general	Lucille Roybal-Allard (D)	33,814	(81%)	($124,271)
	Kermit Booker (P&F)	7,694	(19%)	

THIRTY-FOURTH DISTRICT

One of the great population surges in the United States is the upward social and outward geographic movement of the hundreds of thousands of immigrants to the Los Angeles Basin in recent decades, from crowded entry-level neighborhoods out freeways to the suburbs. It is visible east and southeast of Los Angeles, in suburbs that over a generation have changed from solidly white Anglo to largely Latino. Many have made their way up working in small smokeless factories along railroad tracks and near river beds, beneath roaring freeways and on grid streets near stucco garden apartment blocks—the factories that have made Los Angeles the nation's number one manufacturing metro area—and in small business offices and stores. These people came to the United States not to re-create their Third World environment but to rise above it, and they see this country not as a land of oppression but of opportunity. Their values resemble those of working-class Americans of the pre-Vietnam 1960s: pro-family and respectful of traditional personal morals (LA-area Latinos have lower than average divorce rates and are more likely to raise children in two-parent families), patriotic and pro-military (they are more likely than average to volunteer for military service).

Vast numbers of these new residents—whose rise through hard work has gone shamefully unnoticed in a mainline press which often seems convinced that only government can produce upward mobility—live in the 34th Congressional District of California. This is a swatch of suburban Los Angeles County anchored by three suburbs. On the northwest is Montebello, a working-class suburb since the 1940s just beyond East Los Angeles, now heavily Latino. To the east is La Puente, a center of the light-manufacturing economy that created hundreds of thousands of jobs in the Los Angeles Basin in the 1980s, and in which increasing numbers of small businesses are owned by Asians, Latinos and blacks. To the south is Whittier, a town founded by Midwestern Quakers, much of which is in the 34th District, where Richard Nixon grew up and went to Whittier College, and Norwalk, farther south astride the Santa Ana Freeway. The first 34th District was drawn in 1982, the result of redistricting politics; in the 1990s it has moved, like its people, outward from the central city; it was drawn not for partisan purposes but to maximize the Hispanic percentage, which was 62% in 1990, the second highest figure in California.

The congressman from the 34th District is Esteban Torres, a Democrat elected in 1982. Torres grew up in the mining town of Miami, Arizona, until his father was deported; he and his mother moved to East Los Angeles, where he joined a gang and dropped out of high school; his science teacher persuaded him to return. He served in the Army, returned and got a job on the assembly line at Chrysler and became active in the United Auto Workers. In the 1960s UAW President Walter Reuther asked him to start an antipoverty agency, TELACU. He worked in the Carter White House, and in 1982, with support from the Waxman-Berman machine, ran in the newly districted 34th. He beat former Congressman Jim Lloyd in the primary and won the general election 57%–43%.

In the House Torres has had a strongly liberal voting record in the UAW tradition, favoring government action to help the poor move up into the middle class. On foreign issues, he is somewhat more moderate—the B-2 is built in a Northrop Grumman plant in Pico Rivera, but the plant will close by the end of 1999, and Torres will surely work on a viable economic alternative for the 200 acres that Northrop will turn back to the city. He served on the Banking Committee, where he passed a bill banning use of the Rule of 78s (an antiquated method of calculating unearned interest) in consumer loans longer than five years. On cultural issues he is mostly liberal. For years he worked on credit agency laws, and finally succeeded in passing the Consumer Credit Reporting Reform Act of 1996, requiring free access to credit reports for those denied apartments or bank accounts, and new tools to opt out of mailing lists. He is proud of a San Gabriel Basin public-private partnership to clean up groundwater "without the costly delays of Superfund." He got a seat on Appropriations in 1993 and has worked on local projects; he got $14 million for flood control projects and $14 million for water recycling.

Torres was torn two ways on NAFTA; his UAW roots against, his Latino heritage in favor. At first he opposed it, then eventually voted for it after the Clinton Administration agreed to create a $225 million North American Development Bank to help workers adversely affected by NAFTA. He sponsored anti-gang sections of the 1994 crime bill. He knocked out of the 1990 immigration law a pilot program to create a forgery-proof driver's license. He opposed the English official language bill and sought unsuccessfully to preserve current aid to illegal immigrants. He wants Los Angeles's Metro extended into the Eastside, tangling on this issue on Appropriations with the more senior Julian Dixon from the Westside. He has a bill to give recycling incentives for spare tires, used oil and lead-acid batteries. Back home he sponsors a Procurement Expo and high school art competition and awards Congressional medals for volunteerism and physical fitness.

Torres has been reelected without difficulty. He considered running for the County Board of Supervisors in 1990, but had already filed for reelection when a vacancy came up there. In December 1996 he was strongly considered by the Clinton Administration for secretary of Labor; he waited by the phone for the call and encouraged his son-in-law to run to succeed him. But President Clinton evidently decided on a different breakdown of minorities in his reshuffled cabinet, and appointed White House aide Alexis Herman instead, and former Transportation Secretary Federico Pena, an Hispanic, became secretary of Energy.

The People: Pop. 1990: 573,456; 9% age 65+; 27% White; 2% Black; 9% Asian; 62% Hispanic origin. Households: 61% married couple families; 33% married couple fams. w. children; 37% college educ.; median household income: $36,224; per capita income: $12,012; median gross rent: $637; median house value: $172,900.

1996 Presidential Vote

Clinton (D)	91,603	(64%)
Dole (R)	39,277	(27%)
Perot (I)	10,396	(7%)
Other	2,930	(2%)

1992 Presidential Vote

Clinton (D)	78,889	(51%)
Bush (R)	48,181	(31%)
Perot (I)	27,944	(18%)

Rep. Esteban E. Torres (D)

Elected 1982; b. Jan. 27, 1930, Miami, AZ; home, West Covina; E. Los Angeles Commun. Col., 1959, CA St. U., 1963, U. of MD, 1965, American U., 1966; No religious affiliation; married (Arcy).

Career: Army, 1949–53; Assembly-line worker, Chrysler Corp., 1953–63; Chief Steward, UAW Local 230, 1961–63; UAW Intl. Rep., Region 6, 1963–64, Inter-Amer. Rep., 1965–68; Dir., E. Los Angeles Commun. Union, 1968–74; UAW Intl. Affairs Dept., 1974–77; U.S. Permanent Rep., UNESCO, 1977–79, Special Asst., Pres. Jimmy Carter, 1979–81; Pres., Intl. Enterprise & Devel. Corp., 1981–82.

DC Office: 2269 RHOB 20515, 202-225-5256; Fax: 202-225-9711; e-mail: arcolris@hr.house.gov.

District Offices: Pico Rivera, 562-695-0702.

Committees: *Appropriations* (17th of 26 D): Foreign Operations, Export Financing & Related Programs; Transportation.

Group Ratings

	ADA	ACLU	AFS	LCV	CFA	CON	NFIB	COC	ACU	NTLC	CHC
1996	100	88	100	85	85	61	22	14	0	0	0
1995	90	—	—	100	100	25	—	21	4	—	—

National Journal Ratings

	1995 LIB — 1995 CONS			1996 LIB — 1996 CONS		
Economic	85%	—	12%	89%	—	0%
Social	88%	—	0%	88%	—	0%
Foreign	77%	—	22%	79%	—	19%

Key Votes of the 104th Congress

1. Reduce Medicare Growth $	N	5. Flag Amendment	N	9. Cuban Embargo	N
2. Ovrd. Product Liab. Veto	N	6. Drop EPA Limits	Y	10. Bar Bosnia Troop $	N
3. Increase Min. Wage	Y	7. Repeal Assault-Weap. Ban	N	11. Cut Anti-Missile Defense	Y
4. Welfare Reform	N	8. Ovrd. Part. Birth Veto	N	12. Bar U.N. Uniforms	N

Election Results

1996 general	Esteban E. Torres (D)	94,730	(68%)	($207,398)
	David G. Nunez (R)	36,852	(27%)	($11,171)
	Others	6,858	(5%)	
1996 primary	Esteban E. Torres (D)	unopposed		
1994 general	Esteban E. Torres (D)	72,439	(62%)	($178,972)
	Albert J. Nunez (R)	40,068	(34%)	($5,115)
	Carl M. (Marty) Swinney (Lib)	4,921	(4%)	

THIRTY-FIFTH DISTRICT

In April 1992, the corner of Florence and Normandie in South Central Los Angeles became for a moment the most famous intersection in America: the epicenter of the Los Angeles riot. This was not, as was commonly said, simply an outpouring of anger at the Rodney King verdict; if it were, there would have been rioting everywhere in the Los Angeles Basin, since few citizens agreed with the Simi Valley jury. It was rather, like the urban riots of the 1960s, a collection of criminal acts suddenly committed by people in the expectation that so many others would be doing the same thing that all would have impunity; and even so, the rioting this time clearly would have been stopped but for the dereliction of LAPD Chief Daryl Gates, who had prepared no contingency plan and spent hours on his way to and from a political fundraiser as the rioting broke out. The rioting did in fact stop once Governor Pete Wilson and President George Bush announced that some 25,000 troops were being ordered to Los Angeles, eliminating potential rioters' expectation that they would not be punished.

The commitment of troops was much greater than in the big 1960s riots, and this riot ended far sooner. But in the meantime great damage was done. Most visible was the harm to individuals: black and Latino onlookers were killed and injured by rioters and law enforcement personnel; a white truck driver was viciously beaten at Florence and Normandie; Asian and Latino storeowners were singled out by black and Central American rioters and treated as oppressors, when in fact they were providing goods and services which no one else—for reasons later painfully apparent—was willing to provide. Even more harmful may be the damage to Los Angeles's civic culture. For in the aftermath of the riot it was widely repeated that blacks were helpless victims of racism and poverty, when in fact most LA area blacks have moved upward economically and out geographically from the old South Central and Watts ghettos in the 27 years since the 1965 riots, and African-Americans are well-represented in LA and California politics.

Among those commenting most vociferously on the riot was Congresswoman Maxine Waters, whose 35th Congressional District includes Florence and Normandie as well as much of the South Central and Watts corridors which formed California's first black-majority district 30 years ago. The 35th also includes the majority-black middle-income suburb of Inglewood, home of the Los Angeles Forum; Hawthorne, birthplace of the Beach Boys; and Gardena, with California's first licensed poker clubs at which some of the most cutthroat games in the country are played. Latinos have been moving for two decades into South Central and Watts, and in 1990 the 35th District was 43% Hispanic. But 40% of its residents and a solid majority of its voters were black, and Waters seems to regard her constituency as essentially black, whatever the Census numbers. Waters came to California in 1961, worked in a garment factory and raised two children, got a sociology degree at California State University in Los Angeles and became an assistant Head Start teacher after the Watts riot of 1965. In 1976 she won a seat in the California Assembly. There she supported Willie Brown and passed minority, women's and tenants' rights laws, limits on police strip searches, and a provision mandating divestiture of state pension funds from South Africa. She became a Democratic National Committeewoman in 1980 and was consulted on the 1982 redistricting by Phillip Burton. When Congressman

Augustus Hawkins retired in 1990 after 28 years in the House and 28 years in the California Assembly, Waters was the obvious choice for the seat and won it easily. She had already made a national name for herself as a vocal supporter of Jesse Jackson in 1984 and 1988 and was probably the most prominent freshman in the 102d Congress.

Waters brings to her work a wrath that is almost palpable, and an insistence that she will assert herself regardless of protocol, partly perhaps a result of anger but also a weapon she uses shrewdly and cynically to get both publicity and results. "I don't have time to be polite," she says, beginning her career by getting herself included in a post-riot White House meeting with George Bush after learning of the meeting on a morning TV show. Sometimes she over-blusters: she missed the chance to demand a roll call for one of her amendments, which was beaten, because she was outside the House participating in a press conference. She comes from a poor background and believes with fervor in federal aid for the poor and for racial preferences to help blacks overcome years of slavery, segregation and discrimination; she favors drastic reductions in defense spending and was one of six members who voted against supporting the Gulf war once it started, asking how urban gang members could be expected to stop fighting when America's own leaders were waging battles.

But she has also produced specific legislation, including the Community Reinvestment Act racial quotas, a "Youth Fair Chance Act" with job training and counseling for unemployed young men 17 to 30, and a Center for Women Veterans within the Department of Veterans Affairs. She was successful in getting legislation passed in 1992 which assures preference to low-income veterans in purchasing foreclosed properties from failed banks and S&Ls. She also succeeded in passing amendments, some of them even making laws more acceptable to conservatives, on Banking. She has worked for many set asides for women and minorities. She was an early but unillusioned supporter of Bill Clinton for the Democratic nomination, and traveled often with Clinton. At the 1992 Democratic convention, insisting that "this is the last time I support an all-white anything," she said she would support the Democratic ticket in 2000 only if it has a black or a woman on it. Her husband, a former professional football player and Mercedes Benz salesman, became President Clinton's Ambassador to the Bahamas. Even so, she voted against the crime bill rule in August 1994 when the administration desperately needed votes, because she said she "could not vote for a crime bill that sweepingly expands the death penalty to include sixty new crimes." In 1994 she protested Clinton's cutoff of Haitian refugees and was arrested at the gates of the White House. In 1996, again opposing Clinton, she denounced his signing of the welfare bill and called for a vast expansion of government spending and powers.

The Los Angeles riot was occasion for both Waters' best and worst moments. She flew home immediately and roused the Department of Water and Power to restore water to the riot area, and was effective in gaining provisions to the post-riot emergency act that eventually made it through Congress and was signed into law. But she also over-emotionally claimed, "Los Angeles is under siege . . . the violence could spill over to many other cities in this country." Which, of course, it didn't. And she made statements suggesting that the rioters were morally justified, that somehow street thugs were speaking for the black community instead of destroying it. She herself spoke in the accents of the street in the summer 1994 Banking Committee Whitewater hearings when Congressman Peter King was interrogating Maggie Williams, Mrs. Clinton's chief of staff, and Waters told King to "Shut up."

In the fall of 1996 Waters continued to make news. She pushed the theory, supported in a story in the *San Jose Mercury News* but by little else, that the CIA had worked with Nicaraguan contras to import crack cocaine into South Central Los Angeles. She continued to push the theory in 1997. And in November 1996 she was elected chairman of the Congressional Black Caucus. She promised a "real war on drugs," an 800 line for complaints of discrimination and a business development initiative for minorities. She may not have many legislative successes in the Republican House, though she is skillful enough to win some, but she has a voice that will be heard.

The People: Pop. 1990: 570,697; 7% age 65+; 10% White; 40% Black; 6% Asian; 43% Hispanic origin. Households: 42% married couple families; 25% married couple fams. w. children; 35% college educ.; median household income: $25,481; per capita income: $9,761; median gross rent: $573; median house value: $148,700.

1996 Presidential Vote			1992 Presidential Vote		
Clinton (D)	92,773	(84%)	Clinton (D)	100,432	(77%)
Dole (R)	12,063	(11%)	Bush (R)	16,685	(13%)
Perot (I)	4,129	(4%)	Perot (I)	11,950	(9%)
Other	1,727	(2%)			

Rep. Maxine Waters (D)

Elected 1990; b. Aug. 31, 1938, St. Louis, MO; home, Los Angeles; CA St. U., Los Angeles, B.A. 1970; Christian; married (Sidney Williams).

Career: Teacher, Head Start, 1966; Deputy, City Councilman David S. Cunningham, 1973–76; CA Assembly, 1976–90.

DC Office: 2344 RHOB 20515, 202-225-2201; Fax: 202-225-7854.

District Offices: Los Angeles, 213-757-8900.

Committees: *Banking & Financial Services* (9th of 25 D): Capital Markets, Securities & Government Sponsored Enterprises; General Oversight & Investigations (RMM). *Judiciary* (11th of 15 D): Constitution.

Group Ratings

	ADA	ACLU	AFS	LCV	CFA	CON	NFIB	COC	ACU	NTLC	CHC
1996	85	100	100	77	100	12	9	19	0	5	0
1995	95	—	—	100	85	9	—	0	9	—	—

National Journal Ratings

	1995 LIB — 1995 CONS			1996 LIB — 1996 CONS		
Economic	90%	—	10%	89%	—	0%
Social	80%	—	13%	83%	—	17%
Foreign	87%	—	12%	86%	—	13%

Key Votes of the 104th Congress

1. Reduce Medicare Growth $	N	5. Flag Amendment	N	9. Cuban Embargo	*
2. Ovrd. Product Liab. Veto	N	6. Drop EPA Limits	Y	10. Bar Bosnia Troop $	N
3. Increase Min. Wage	Y	7. Repeal Assault-Weap. Ban	*	11. Cut Anti-Missile Defense	Y
4. Welfare Reform	N	8. Ovrd. Part. Birth Veto	N	12. Bar U.N. Uniforms	N

Election Results

1996 general	Maxine Waters (D)	92,762	(86%)	($235,851)
	Eric Carlson (R)	13,116	(12%)	($2,428)
	Others	2,610	(2%)	
1996 primary	Maxine Waters (D)	unopposed		
1994 general	Maxine Waters (D)	65,688	(78%)	($177,791)
	Nate Truman (R)	18,390	(22%)	($9,580)

THIRTY-SIXTH DISTRICT

For many southern Californians, there is no better place to be than the beach. It is not a perfect environment: in the morning there may be mists, the winter air is damp and clammy, even in summer the weather can be chilly, the water is never very warm and is sometimes polluted. But for many this is echt-California, and in this democratic polity, there is a beach to suit the taste of just about everyone. The funkiest of all is Venice, with its beach houses jammed together and the long-stagnant canals dug by a developer in 1904, with the boardwalk where skateboarding got its start and where the latest crazes are chainsaw juggling and outdoor massages. Right behind is Marina Del Rey, with sleek modern apartment complexes and expensive yacht moorings. Just south, across an inlet, is LAX, the only American airport commonly known by its three-letter code; the swooping arches of its theme building, intended in 1961 to symbolize the jet era, are now an historic landmark, like Disneyland's Tomorrowland or the *Jetsons*, an antique version of a surpassed future. To the south is El Segundo, named for Socal's second oil refinery. Next are Manhattan Beach, one of the favorites three decades ago of the original Beach Boys who grew up a couple of miles inland in Hawthorne, and tiny Hermosa Beach, with tightly packed frame houses originally the homes of elderly retirees; the current attitude here is suggested by Councilman Robert (Burgie) Benz, who sponsors a beer drinking and vomiting fest every Fourth of July. To the south are the flower-planted rises of Redondo Beach and Torrance, whose vast inland expanse is filled with the American headquarters of Japanese companies. The South Bay beaches end where the Palos Verdes Peninsula looms high over the ocean, seismically active and socioeconomically upscale. Just to the east is the harbor town of San Pedro, once working-class, but moving up as well, overlooking LA's eerily modern containerport.

All this beach territory, from Venice south to San Pedro (both of which technically are part of Los Angeles, though the area in between is not), makes up the 36th Congressional District. Historically Republican, this area is still leery of taxes, but culturally it is libertarian—against restrictions or even aspersions on its various lifestyles. When those issues are paramount, the Beach area trends Democratic, as in the mid-1970s and mid-1980s; when economics or defense are more important, it is solidly Republican, as in the 1960s and 1980s. For this has been one of America's leading defense and aerospace areas, where Howard Hughes built planes half a century ago and where so much of the 1980s defense buildup took place.

The congresswoman from the 36th is Jane Harman, a Democrat elected in 1992. Harman grew up in Los Angeles and remembers sitting as a teenager in the gallery at the 1960 Democratic National Convention in Los Angeles. After law school, she worked on Senator John Tunney's staff and made headlines when she quit a White House job to stay home with her children. Shortly afterwards, she divorced her first husband and in 1980 married Sidney Harman, who made a fortune manufacturing audio equipment; she has maintained a Washington residence ever since. But when she saw the new district lines drawn for 1992, she returned to California and ran for the House—one of seven Democrats and 11 Republicans running. It turned out to be the year of the woman on the macho beach: women got 73% of Democratic and 68% of Republican primary votes in this district. Harman, spending her own money liberally, won with 45%; the second-place finisher, the daughter-in-law of the late Speaker and Treasurer Jesse Unruh, got 16%. In the Republican primary Los Angeles Councilwoman Joan Milke Flores beat Maureen Reagan, daughter of the former President, 34%–31%. In the general Harman campaigned as "pro-choice and pro-change"; Flores was pro-life and had the burden of George Bush's flagging candidacy. Harman also argued that she could do more to protect defense jobs in the area, and supported a targeted capital gains tax cut and the line-item veto. She spent $2.3 million, the fourth highest of any campaign in the country. The Republican registration advantage eroded from 5% to 2% during the campaign, an unusual shift in a short time, and Harman won 48%–42%.

In the House Harman has had a moderate voting record and has been a strong supporter of local defense industries. "Representative. That's my job title. I represent the aerospace center of the universe." She voted for the Clinton budget and tax package and against NAFTA in 1993, for the balanced budget amendment and line-item veto in 1995. She co-authored the Deficit Reduction Lockbox, requiring that spending cuts be used to reduce the deficit; appropriators didn't like it, but it passed 364–59 in September 1995. She supported welfare reform, term limits, the death penalty; she voted to override Clinton vetoes on securities litigation reform and product liability reform. On local issues, Harman pushed for the California Cruise Ship Act and Marina del Rey dredging. She voted against the Clean Water Act, saying it would allow more partially treated sewage to be dumped into Santa Monica Bay.

With a seat on the National Security Committee, she managed the fight for the C-17 cargo plane, kept the Los Angeles Air Force Base off the base closure list, got funding for the F/A-18, the Milstar satellite and the Space Station. She worked to create a defense export loan guarantee program funded by defense contractors. She sponsored dual-use research partnerships between the Defense Department and companies. She worked to make surplus MREs available to food shelters. She led the fight to repeal the provision requiring discharge of HIV-positive service personnel. She was a vigorous supporter of the B-2 Stealth bomber, rushing back from the Beijing women's conference to round up votes, including 10 from California Democrats. "We have a very hard job to explain why this cut—which isn't school lunches or vaccinations—still has a human face. This is how we deter aggression and do war-fighting without putting more human faces at risk." The House voted 213–210 to build 3 more B-2s. More recently, she was one of thirteen members sent in December 1996 to the Aberdeen basic training base to investigate charges of sexual harassment.

Harman had serious competition in 1994 and 1996 from Susan Brooks, a Rancho Palos Verdes council member. The narrow winner of primaries each time, Brooks campaigned on the Contract with America; pro-choice on abortion, she is against gun control and argues that Harman has let spending drop too much: "Overall, she shrinks the loaf and brings us home the crumbs." But Brooks campaigned door-to-door while Harman, very well funded by defense PACs and her many Washington contacts, and undergirded by her great personal wealth, far outspent her, advertising on Los Angeles television. In 1994 this turned out to be one of the closest races in the nation. Brooks was 93 votes ahead on election night, but the absentee ballots went heavily for Harman—the result of good organization—and the state certified Harman as the winner by 812 votes. Brooks challenged the result, but could not persuade either the House or the courts that there were enough votes cast illegally to change the result. Brooks ran again in 1996, winning her primary by just 42%–37%. Harman raised $1.7 million and appeared at local defense installations; when Tim Hannemann of TRW and Kent Kresa of Northrop Grummann supported Harman, Brooks said, "They're a bunch of political whores, and you can quote me on that!" In October 1996 Minority Leader Richard Gephardt got Harman a seat on the Intelligence Committee, which she publicized widely; Brooks argued that her Washington law firm's work for a German company which worked on poison gas factories in Libya and Iraq disqualified her, but Harman and the firm said Harman never did any work for the client. Bill Clinton carried the district 47%–41%, with the same 6% margin as in 1992; Harman won 52%–44%, the first time she has gone over 50%. But this could still be a seriously contested district in 1998.

The People: Pop. 1990: 573,665; 10% age 65+; 69% White; 3% Black; 12% Asian; 15% Hispanic origin. Households: 49% married couple families; 20% married couple fams. w. children; 67% college educ.; median household income: $48,522; per capita income: $25,534; median gross rent: $812; median house value: $369,800.

1996 Presidential Vote

Clinton (D)	109,244	(47%)
Dole (R)	96,872	(41%)
Perot (I)	18,510	(8%)
Other	9,375	(4%)

1992 Presidential Vote

Clinton (D)	111,014	(41%)
Bush (R)	95,646	(35%)
Perot (I)	62,458	(23%)

Rep. Jane Harman (D)

Elected 1992; b. June 28, 1945, New York, NY; home, Rolling Hills; Smith Col., B.A. 1966, Harvard, J.D. 1969; Jewish; married (Sidney).

Career: Legis. Dir., U.S. Sen. John Tunney, 1972–73; Chief Cnsl. & Staff Dir., Senate Judiciary Subcmtee., 1973–77; Dep. Cabinet Secy., White House, 1977; Defense Dept. Special Cnsl., 1979; Harman Intl. Industries, Corp. Secy., 1985–92, Dir., 1990–92; Practicing atty., 1987–92.

DC Office: 325 CHOB 20515, 202-225-8220; Fax: 202-226-0684; e-mail: jharman@hr.house.gov.

District Offices: Torrance, 310-783-8220.

Committees: *Intelligence (Select)* (5th of 7 D): Technical & Tactical Intelligence. *National Security* (12th of 25 D): Military Personnel; Military Research & Development.

Group Ratings

	ADA	ACLU	AFS	LCV	CFA	CON	NFIB	COC	ACU	NTLC	CHC
1996	60	47	58	69	77	70	70	60	26	42	21
1995	65	—	—	31	85	56	—	54	25	—	—

National Journal Ratings

	1995 LIB — 1995 CONS			1996 LIB — 1996 CONS		
Economic	58%	—	41%	58%	—	42%
Social	74%	—	26%	71%	—	29%
Foreign	67%	—	32%	57%	—	42%

Key Votes of the 104th Congress

1. Reduce Medicare Growth $	N	5. Flag Amendment	Y	9. Cuban Embargo	N
2. Ovrd. Product Liab. Veto	Y	6. Drop EPA Limits	Y	10. Bar Bosnia Troop $	N
3. Increase Min. Wage	Y	7. Repeal Assault-Weap. Ban	N	11. Cut Anti-Missile Defense	Y
4. Welfare Reform	Y	8. Ovrd. Part. Birth Veto	N	12. Bar U.N. Uniforms	*

Election Results

1996 general	Jane Harman (D)	117,752	(52%)	($1,579,938)
	Susan M. Brooks (R)	98,538	(44%)	($486,564)
	Others	8,169	(4%)	
1996 primary	Jane Harman (D)	unopposed		
1994 general	Jane Harman (D)	93,939	(48%)	($1,300,855)
	Susan M. Brooks (R)	93,127	(48%)	($580,837)
	Others	8,742	(4%)	

THIRTY-SEVENTH DISTRICT

Los Angeles is the creation not of nature but of man: there is little natural water supply here and no natural port, little in the way of natural resources except for oil which turned out not to be enough for California; it is a place for people who plan big. Nearly a century ago Los Angeles's city fathers decided to build a port where the usually-dry Los Angeles River debouches into the ocean; in 1906 they annexed an eight-mile-long, four-block-wide corridor of land (christened Harbor Gateway in 1984) and the harbor areas of Wilmington and San Pedro, and converted a shallow bay with a few marshy inlets into the biggest port on the West Coast, ahead of the splendid natural harbors of San Francisco and San Diego. Inland, along the rail lines that hug the river bed, heavy and light industry developed—oil tank farms and big factories, small job shops and warehouses. Interspersed were subdivisions and to the north was Watts, the epicenter of the 1965 riot and also the site of one of the strangest made-by-man structures in this made-by-man city, the 107-foot-high Watts Tower, built from 1921–54 by Simon Rodia out of all manner of salvaged material.

The 37th Congressional District takes in a swath of low-income industrial suburbs from Watts and the new Century Freeway, the most expensive road in history, south to Wilmington and the port. Here are Compton and Lynwood, which switched from all-white to all-black in the 1960s and in the 1980s became heavily Latino; here is Carson, with recent subdivisions amid freeway interchanges and tank farms; here is Wilmington, facing a spankingly modern port. Overall, the 37th District in 1990 was 32% black and 45% Hispanic, but blacks far outnumber Latinos as registered voters, but in 1996 55% of registered voters were black and only 16% Latino.

The congresswoman from the 37th District is Juanita Millender-McDonald, chosen in a March 1996 special election. She was born in Alabama, raised a family in Carson and earned a bachelor's degree in 1979, at 40; she worked as a teacher and editor/writer for the Los Angeles Unified School District and was manuscript editor for *IMAGES*, "a textbook designed by the State Department of Education for girls and young women to enhance self-esteem and explore non-traditional careers and vocations." She later became director of gender equity programs for the district and was appointed to the National Commission on Teaching and America's Future chaired by North Carolina Governor Jim Hunt. In April 1990 she was elected to the Carson City Council. In 1992 she ran for the Assembly and beat an incumbent in the primary. She chaired the Insurance and Revenue and Taxation Committees for a year each and sponsored the bill qualifying for designation as a National Transportation Artery the Alameda Corridor—a proposed combination of underground rail lines and freeway lanes connecting the port to major east-west rail lines and freeways. She favored homeless voting rights and domestic violence insurance, sponsored tax incentives for business and workmen's comp reform and opposed the motorcycle helmet law. She supported the state takeover of Lincoln Park Cemetery in Carson amid talk of embezzlement and sponsored a bill to outlaw necrophilia.

Her opening to run for Congress came in December 1995, when two-term Congressman Walter Tucker was convicted of extortion and tax fraud as mayor of Compton and sentenced to 27 months in federal prison. (Tucker's original lawyer was Johnnie Cochran, but he dropped the case to spend all his time representing O.J. Simpson.) A special election was set for March 26, 1996, the same day as the regular primary, and since no Republicans ran, it would determine the winner. Already running for months was Assemblyman Willard Murray, chief of staff to former (1981–93) Congressman Mervyn Dymally. But with help from EMILY's List Millender-McDonald raised much more money. Also running were Compton Mayor Omar Bradley, Lynwood Mayor Paul Richards and Tucker's wife Robin. Murray may have started off best known, but he had problems: he favored building a prison for Compton, which voters turned down 87%–13%, and he favored the state takeover of Compton's public schools. Millender-McDonald won the nine-candidate special with 27% to 20% for Murray, 14% for Bradley and 12% for Richards. The regular primary on the same ballot was a bit closer because of the presence of another candidate, Susan Carrillo, who got 15%. Millender-McDonald won this contest by just 24%–21%. Robin Tucker got just 6% of the vote. The victory was a bit bittersweet, since Millender-McDonald's son Keith McDonald lost the primary for her Assembly seat to her predecessor Richard Floyd.

In the House the Democratic leadership gave Millender-McDonald a seat on the Transportation and Infrastructure Committee, and she promised that her first priority would be the Alameda Corridor. But she made national news on another issue, when after the *San Jose Mercury News* charged that the CIA aided Nicaraguan contras in smuggling crack cocaine to Los Angeles, Millender-McDonald invited CIA Director John Deutsch to a public meeting in her district weeks after the November election. Astonishingly, he accepted, and was denounced by dozens of speakers and booed and interrupted with obscenities by many others despite Millender-McDonald's pleas for order.

The People: Pop. 1990: 572,191; 7% age 65+; 12% White; 32% Black; 10% Asian; 45% Hispanic origin. Households: 51% married couple families; 30% married couple fams. w. children; 32% college educ.; median household income: $27,127; per capita income: $9,104; median gross rent: $548; median house value: $140,800.

1996 Presidential Vote

Clinton (D)	88,877	(81%)
Dole (R)	13,874	(13%)
Perot (I)	4,798	(4%)

1992 Presidential Vote

Clinton (D)	90,523	(73%)
Bush (R)	19,299	(16%)
Perot (I)	12,905	(10%)

Rep. Juanita Millender-McDonald (D)

Elected March 1996; b. Sept. 7, 1938, Birmingham, AL; home, Carson; U. of Redlands, B.S. 1979, CA St. U., M.Ed. 1981; Baptist; married (James).

Career: Teacher/Schl. Admin., 1981–90; Carson City Cncl., 1990–92; Carson Mayor Pro-Tem, 1991–92; CA Assembly, 1993–96.

DC Office: 419 CHOB 20515, 202-225-7924; Fax: 202-225-7926.

District Offices: Carson, 310-549-0537.

Committees: *Transportation & Infrastructure* (23rd of 33 D): Aviation; Surface Transportation. *Small Business* (8th of 16 D): Empowerment; Tax, Finance & Exports.

Group Ratings (Only Served Partial Term)

	ADA	ACLU	AFS	LCV	CFA	CON	NFIB	COC	ACU	NTLC	CHC
1996	83	75	100	100	90	74	20	20	0	14	0
1995	*	—	—	*	*	*	—	*	*	—	—

National Journal Ratings (Only Served Partial Term)

	1995 LIB — 1995 CONS	1996 LIB — 1996 CONS
Economic	* — *	89% — 0%
Social	* — *	* — *
Foreign	* — *	78% — 22%

Key Votes of the 104th Congress (Only Served Partial Term)

1. Reduce Medicare Growth $	*	5. Flag Amendment	*	9. Cuban Embargo	*
2. Ovrd. Product Liab. Veto	N	6. Drop EPA Limits	*	10. Bar Bosnia Troop $	*
3. Increase Min. Wage	Y	7. Repeal Assault-Weap. Ban	*	11. Cut Anti-Missile Defense	Y
4. Welfare Reform	N	8. Ovrd. Part. Birth Veto	N	12. Bar U.N. Uniforms	N

Election Results

1996 general	Juanita Millender-McDonald (D)	87,247	(85%)	($113,081)
	Michael E. Voetee (R)	15,399	(15%)	($42,972)
1996 primary	Juanita Millender-McDonald (D)	10,213	(24%)	
	Willard H. Murray Jr. (D)	8,999	(21%)	
	M. Susan Carrillo (D)	6,681	(15%)	
	Omar Bradley (D)	5,746	(13%)	
	Paul H. Richards (D)	5,523	(13%)	
	Robin Tucker (D)	2,632	(6%)	
	Charles Davis (D)	2,131	(5%)	
	Others	1,256	(3%)	
1996 special	Juanita Millender-McDonald (D)	13,868	(27%)	($214,176)
	Willard H. Murray Jr. (D)	10,396	(20%)	($144,748)
	Omar Bradley (D)	6,975	(14%)	($34,056)
	Paul Richards (D)	6,035	(12%)	($113,490)
	Robert Sausedo (D)	4,495	(9%)	
	Robin Tucker (D)	3,661	(7%)	($29,096)
	Charles Davis (D)	2,555	(5%)	($55,905)
	Others	2,896	(6%)	
1994 general	Walter R. Tucker III (D)	64,166	(77%)	($269,976)
	Guy Wilson (Lib)	18,502	(22%)	($34,640)

THIRTY-EIGHTH DISTRICT

Long Beach, founded in 1888, with 434,000 people in 1990, would be a major metropolis anywhere but in Los Angeles County where it seems just the largest of many suburbs. But it has an identity of its own. Started as a beach resort, it soon became a port when Los Angeles civic leaders decided that if their town were to be a world-class city it must have a world-class harbor; nature not having provided one, they built it where the Los Angeles River merges into the ocean at Long Beach. By 1909, Los Angeles had annexed the harbor towns of San Pedro and Wilmington next to Long Beach; over the next decades the two cities persuaded the government to dredge channels and build a breakwater and turning basins. Long Beach was developing other businesses as well: it sprouted oil derricks in the 1920s and briefly became one of the nation's big oil producers; it was the site of major aircraft plants in the 1940s and after. By the 1980s, the Los Angeles-Long Beach port was the nation's largest, the fastest-growing major cargo center in the world, with huge steel-gray container ships pulling quietly up to enormous automated loading facilities—a 21st Century contrast to the rotting docks of New York and San Francisco. Long Beach even acquired the *Queen Mary*, which became its biggest tourist attraction, and, until it was sawed apart and taken to a museum in Oregon, Howard Hughes's *Spruce Goose*, the huge cargo seaplane that was piloted just once across this harbor in 1946. Long Beach's downtown, once full of rundown 1920s buildings and pawn shops, now has an array of glittering 1980s high-rises and the area has become a favorite for Japanese and Asian companies' American headquarters. Long Beach was hurt by closure of its naval shipyard and cutbacks at the huge McDonnell Douglas plant, but small businesses have grown. Long Beach's school system is the third largest in California, and the first in the state to make school uniforms mandatory; three-quarters of students go on to college.

The 38th Congressional District includes most of Long Beach, the beachfront and harbor and airport. It extends north and inland to include the post-World War II suburbs of Lakewood, Paramount, Bellflower and Downey. This is middle-class country, but not monochromatic; the 38th excludes some black areas of Long Beach but in 1990 was 26% Hispanic and 9% Asian; it has a large Cambodian communities, a core of union members, a large gay population. Defense contracts and bases are important in Long Beach, and Downey has the Boeing (formerly Rockwell) plant that built the space shuttle. Politically, the 38th is marginal, voting for Bill Clinton in 1992 and 1996 and Pete Wilson in 1990 and 1994.

The congressman from the 38th is Steve Horn, a Republican first elected in 1992. Horn grew up on a farm near San Juan Bautista, California, worked his way through Stanford and Harvard. He was an aide to President Eisenhower's labor secretary in the 1950s and to California Senator Thomas Kuchel in the 1960s. He was in Everett Dirksen's office helping draft the language of the Voting Rights Act in those stirring days of 1965, and he served on the U.S. Commission on Civil Rights from 1969–82. Horn is also a political scientist, who has written books on parliamentary procedures, the Senate Appropriations Committee and campaign finance. He worked at the Brookings Institution, was a dean at American University in Washington, and then from 1970–88 was president of Cal State at Long Beach, leaving the job when he first ran for Congress. That race was in a district that stretched from Long Beach far into Orange County, and he ran third, with 20%, behind the more conservative and flamboyant Dana Rohrabacher. In 1992 he ran in the newly drawn 38th. In the primary the pro-choice Horn beat pro-life former Assemblyman Dennis Brown by 105 votes out of 45,000 cast, 29.8%–29.5%. In the general he faced Long Beach Councilman Evan Anderson Braude, stepson of 22-year incumbent and Public Works Chairman Glenn Anderson. Horn accepted no PAC money and ran his campaign out of his son's apartment, sending out 50,000 15-minute videos to voters. He won 49%–43%.

In the House Horn has a mostly moderate voting record, but was downright liberal on cultural issues (for abortion rights, gun control, gays in the military). He opposes non-emergency health care for illegal aliens, sought more Border Patrol guards, and favors a tamperproof Social Security card. With Jane Harman of the 36th District, he worked to save the C-17 transport plane assembled at Long Beach. He obtained flood control projects for the Los Angeles and Rio Hondo Rivers. He plays a key role in obtaining funds for the Alameda Corridor, the $1.8 billion underground rail connection from the port to the main east-west rail lines.

In 1995 Horn became chairman of the Subcommittee on Government Management, Information and Technology. Working often in bipartisan fashion with Democrat Carolyn Maloney, he produced a Debt Collection Act, aimed at getting back some $2 billion the government is owed but is not able to collect, a Single Audit Act, electronic transfer and direct deposit programs (which he says will have consumers $1.6 billion and taxpayers $90 million a year). He is concerned about the year 2000 problem on computers, and like an old-time professor took to grading government agencies for a while on how they're handling it: 4 As, 3 Bs, 3 Cs, 10 Ds, 4 Fs in July 1996. He has done oversight on oil companies' failure to pay $2 billion in royalties to governments.

Horn's moderate record and taste for bipartisanship appeals to many voters but sparks opposition in several quarters. He was comfortably reelected in 1994. Rick Dykema, an aide to Dana Rohrabacher, started to challenge him from the right, but was talked out of running by Tom DeLay and Bill Paxon. His Democratic opponent was Rick Zbur, an environmental lawyer for a big Los Angeles law firm who won the nomination 51%–49%; he said he counseled big companies on how to obey the law, but Horn, endorsed by the Sierra Club as well as the Chamber of Commerce, said a bit sharply, "I assume they are major polluters in southern California or they wouldn't be going to Latham & Watkins." Zbur is part Hispanic (his mother is from New Mexico) and also announced that he is gay, which attracted some attention and support; he outspent Horn by $1 million to $470,000. Zbur attacked Horn for supporting Newt Gingrich and Medicare "cuts." Horn, just turned 65, flashed his own Medicare card and said he would not destroy a program he had worked on passing with Kuchel in 1965. Bill Clinton made several appearances for Zbur and carried the district 53%–36%. But Horn won 53%–43%. Footnote: the Green Party candidate won 3% although he was in jail for failing to register as a sexual offender.

The People: Pop. 1990: 572,676; 12% age 65+; 58% White; 7% Black; 9% Asian; 1% Amer. Indian; 26% Hispanic origin. Households: 46% married couple families; 21% married couple fams. w. children; 53% college educ.; median household income: $34,364; per capita income: $16,497; median gross rent: $636; median house value: $222,700.

1996 Presidential Vote

Clinton (D)	91,673	(53%)
Dole (R)	62,053	(36%)
Perot (I)	14,310	(8%)
Other	5,472	(3%)

1992 Presidential Vote

Clinton (D)	88,728	(44%)
Bush (R)	66,647	(33%)
Perot (I)	43,596	(22%)

Rep. Stephen Horn (R)

Elected 1992; b. May 31, 1931, San Juan Bautista; home, Long Beach; Stanford U., A.B. 1953, Harvard U., M.P.A. 1955, Stanford U., Ph.D. 1958; Protestant; married (Nini).

Career: Army Reserves, Strategic Intelligence, 1954–62; A.A., U.S. Labor Secy. James Mitchell, 1959–60; Legis. Asst., U.S. Sen. Thomas Kuchel, 1960–66; Sr. Fellow, Brookings Inst., 1966–69; Dean, Grad. Studies, American U., 1969–70; Vice Chmn./Mbr., U.S. Commission on Civil Rights, 1969–82; Pres., CA St. U. at Long Beach, 1970–88; Chmn., Amer. Assn. of State Cols. and Universities, 1985–86; Prof., CA St. U. at Long Beach 1988–92.

DC Office: 438 CHOB 20515, 202-225-6676; Fax: 202-226-1012.

District Offices: Lakewood, 310-425-1336.

Committees: *Government Reform & Oversight* (10th of 24 R): District of Columbia; Government Management, Information & Technology (Chmn.). *Transportation & Infrastructure* (12th of 40 R): Surface Transportation; Water Resources & Environment.

Group Ratings

	ADA	ACLU	AFS	LCV	CFA	CON	NFIB	COC	ACU	NTLC	CHC
1996	40	20	36	54	69	34	89	80	63	93	53
1995	25	—	—	25	46	87	—	88	58	—	—

National Journal Ratings

	1995 LIB	—	1995 CONS	1996 LIB	—	1996 CONS
Economic	26%	—	67%	48%	—	51%
Social	69%	—	30%	65%	—	35%
Foreign	42%	—	58%	38%	—	60%

Key Votes of the 104th Congress

1. Reduce Medicare Growth $	Y	5. Flag Amendment	*	9. Cuban Embargo	Y
2. Ovrd. Product Liab. Veto	Y	6. Drop EPA Limits	Y	10. Bar Bosnia Troop $	Y
3. Increase Min. Wage	*	7. Repeal Assault-Weap. Ban	N	11. Cut Anti-Missile Defense	N
4. Welfare Reform	Y	8. Ovrd. Part. Birth Veto	N	12. Bar U.N. Uniforms	Y

Election Results

1996 general	Stephen Horn (R)	88,136	(53%)	($470,077)
	Rick Zbur (D)	71,627	(43%)	($1,011,672)
	Others	7,882	(5%)	
1996 primary	Stephen Horn (R)	unopposed		
1994 general	Stephen Horn (R)	85,225	(58%)	($442,982)
	Peter Mathews (D)	53,681	(37%)	($433,706)
	Others	6,863	(5%)	

THIRTY-NINTH DISTRICT

When Walt Disney began planning Disneyland in the late 1940s, he did not have to drive far southeast of downtown Los Angeles before coming into agricultural land. Dairy farms and orange groves covered most of southeast Los Angeles County and Orange County, which had only 216,000 people in 1950, five years before Disneyland opened there in 1955. As Disneyland became a vast success, the area around it, a mass of flat land surrounded by mountains and sea, found itself directly in the path of settlement of the most explosively growing metropolitan area in the United States. Orange County's population rose to 703,000 in 1960, 1.4 million in 1970, 1.9 million in 1980 and 2.4 million in 1990—the fifth largest in the nation.

Always Republican, Orange County became a symbol of conservatism first in California and then nationally: in the 1988 election Orange County cast the largest plurality, 317,000, for George Bush; even in 1996, it gave Bob Dole a 119,000-vote margin. Orange County's conservatism reflected a belief in technological progress and traditional values as unyielding as the mile-square grid the county's founders imposed on most of its land, a belief in the market economics that had produced such wonders as Disneyland and the area's advanced military technologies. These faiths have been tried on occasion, in the recession and amid the defense cutbacks of the early 1990s, and in December 1994, the county government declared bankruptcy because of the county treasurer's sloppy investment and bookkeeping practices. Shortly afterwards, Walt Disney shelved plans for a $2 billion resort development that would have doubled the size of Disneyland, a further blow to local officials and businesses.

The 39th Congressional District consists of an area that was mostly farmland when Disneyland was being laid out. In Los Angeles County, its largest community is Cerritos, once all dairy farms, now a suburb with a harmonious Angeleno mix: 45% Asian, 36% white Anglos, 12% Hispanic. La Mirada to the north is more upscale, as are the La Habra communities which span the LA-Orange County line. The biggest Orange County city here is Fullerton, with its own branch of Cal State University; to the southwest are Buena Park, home of the earliest theme park (c. 1940), Knott's Berry Farm, plus Cypress, Los Alamitos and Rossmoor. The 39th also pushes east of Fullerton to include, by just a few blocks, the Richard Nixon Library and birthplace in Yorba Linda.

The 39th District's congressman, Ed Royce, was four years old and growing up in Anaheim when Disneyland opened; his life almost precisely covers the post-World War II growth of Orange County. Like Orange County, he has long been conservative: he was in the Young Americans for Freedom at Cal State Fullerton; he worked several years as a tax and capital projects manager for a cement company. In 1982, a bunch of conservative legislators known as "the Cave Men" took him to a Black Angus restaurant—no avocado and bean sprout sandwiches for them—and after a few beers persuaded him to run for the state Senate. He did and at age 31 won. There he sponsored the 1990 law making stalking a crime, now copied in every other state. When the legislature refused to pass his legislation allowing crime victims to object to trial delays, giving grand juries more power and ending shopping for juries, he put it on the ballot as an initiative and it passed by a wide margin in 1990. Many Vietnamese have moved to Orange County, and Royce passed a law making it easier for University of Saigon medical graduates to practice in California.

In 1992 Royce ran for the House when the 39th's incumbent made a quixotic run for the Senate. With the blessing of Orange County Republican leaders and his own strength, Royce had no opposition in the decisive Republican primary and easily won the general. In the House Royce has a conservative voting record, though a bit less so on foreign issues; he surprised some by voting against NAFTA. He worked to pass anti-stalking legislation, first in the 1994 crime bill, then as part of a defense appropriation in September 1996; in the signing ceremony Royce was shunted off to the side and was not mentioned by Clinton. He continues to push a victim's rights constitutional amendment. Another amendment he has pressed without success is a ban on retroactive taxation. He is co-chairman, with Democrat David Minge, of the House "porkbusters," risking others' wrath by opposing appropriations bills with dubious projects. In 1995, for example, he targeted the Puget Sound Naval Shipyard gym ("there is a YMCA less than a mile away") and worked with appropriator Frank Wolf to stop highway "demonstration projects," which do not necessarily coincide with state highway priorities. Appropriations Democrat David Obey attacked him for seeking $12 million for the Los Alamitos Reserve Center. As an offshoot of porkbusters, he backed the deficit lockbox amendment, requiring spending cuts to be applied to the deficit; it passed 364–59 in September 1995, but was not acted on by the Senate; he got a rules change requiring unauthorized spending to be listed separately in appropriations bills. He is also a crusader against what he considers corporate welfare. He tried to abolish OPIC, which guarantees foreign investments by corporations, and managed to prevent a doubling of its loan authority. In May 1996 he proposed repeal of the 1993 4.3 cent gas tax increase; Democrats barraged him with angry objections.

Royce has been reelected easily. His agenda for the 105th Congress includes the deficit lockbox, corporate welfare reductions and a second Grace Commission to recommend spending cuts. Also he was tapped to become chairman of the International Relations Subcommittee on Africa. This comes at a time when, after three decades of economic stagnation and dictatorship, several African countries are moving toward democracy and market economics. Royce will presumably try to help them along.

The People: Pop. 1990: 573,941; 9% age 65+; 61% White; 3% Black; 13% Asian; 23% Hispanic origin. Households: 62% married couple families; 29% married couple fams. w. children; 58% college educ.; median household income: $46,196; per capita income: $18,190; median gross rent: $736; median house value: $236,600.

1996 Presidential Vote

Dole (R)	97,247	(48%)
Clinton (D)	83,246	(41%)
Perot (I)	15,909	(8%)
Other	4,841	(2%)

1992 Presidential Vote

Bush (R)	100,669	(44%)
Clinton (D)	78,305	(34%)
Perot (I)	50,834	(22%)

Rep. Edward R. Royce (R)

Elected 1992; b. Oct. 12, 1951, Los Angeles; home, Fullerton; CA St. U., Fullerton, B.A. 1977; Catholic; married (Marie).

Career: Tax Manager, 1979–82; CA Senate, 1982–92.

DC Office: 1133 LHOB 20515, 202-225-4111; Fax: 202-226-0335.

District Offices: Fullerton, 714-992-8081.

Committees: *Banking & Financial Services* (11th of 30 R): Capital Markets, Securities & Government Sponsored Enterprises; Financial Institutions & Consumer Credit. *International Relations* (13th of 26 R): Africa (Chmn.); Asia & the Pacific.

Group Ratings

	ADA	ACLU	AFS	LCV	CFA	CON	NFIB	COC	ACU	NTLC	CHC
1996	15	7	0	23	38	84	95	88	100	100	100
1995	0	—	—	0	0	75	—	96	100	—	—

National Journal Ratings

	1995 LIB		1995 CONS	1996 LIB		1996 CONS
Economic	0%	—	74%	33%	—	64%
Social	0%	—	79%	0%	—	90%
Foreign	45%	—	52%	52%	—	47%

Key Votes of the 104th Congress

1. Reduce Medicare Growth $	Y	5. Flag Amendment	Y	9. Cuban Embargo	Y
2. Ovrd. Product Liab. Veto	Y	6. Drop EPA Limits	N	10. Bar Bosnia Troop $	Y
3. Increase Min. Wage	N	7. Repeal Assault-Weap. Ban	Y	11. Cut Anti-Missile Defense	N
4. Welfare Reform	Y	8. Ovrd. Part. Birth Veto	Y	12. Bar U.N. Uniforms	Y

Election Results

1996 general	Edward R. Royce (R)	120,761	(63%)	($489,076)
	Bob Davis (D)	61,392	(32%)	
	Jack Dean (Lib)	10,137	(5%)	
1996 primary	Edward R. Royce (R)	unopposed		
1994 general	Edward R. Royce (R)	113,037	(66%)	($403,335)
	Bob Davis (D)	49,459	(29%)	($3,755)
	Jack Dean (Lib)	7,862	(5%)	

FORTIETH DISTRICT

Over the last two decades the great American movement west has turned back east, at least in California. As settlement reached the Pacific Coast, young families looking for affordable houses and neighborhoods and schools, where traditional values are respected, moved away from the liberation-minded and high-crime coast and toward the sunny, often hot, valleys inland. This impulse has resulted in rapid growth in the Central Valley, the repopulation of the Mother Lode country in the foothills of the Sierras and the startling growth in the eastern end of the Los Angeles Basin, around San Bernardino and Riverside, and east and north past the mountain rims into the desert. This "Inland Empire" of San Bernardino grew so robustly in the 1980s, from 1.6 million to 2.6 million, that it increased from three congressional districts to five in 1992.

One of these is the 40th Congressional District, which covers most of the land area of continental America's physically largest county, San Bernardino, though its population is concentrated in just a few places. About one-third of its people live on the eastern edge of San Bernardino itself, or around Loma Linda, Redlands and Yucaipa—small towns formed by pious Midwesterners at the base of 10,000-foot mountains, now part of the expanding Los Angeles suburban strip. North of the mountains, out beyond the wind-torn El Cajon Pass in the scorching desert, are Victorville and Apple Valley, once tiny gas station stops on the road to Las Vegas; Roy Rogers and Dale Evans lived for years on a ranch here, with their stuffed Trigger, Buttermilk and Bullet in a nearby museum. Now vast subdivisions and the new city of Hesperia have grown up here, housing more than 150,000 people. The rest of the people of the 40th are scattered across the desert, in ghost towns and weapons testing sites, in Twentynine Palms and its Marine base. The 40th has some of the nation's hottest temperatures and some of its lowest rainfall, the lower 48 states' highest point at Mount Whitney and lowest point in Death Valley.

The congressman from the 40th is Jerry Lewis, a House member since 1978, an assemblyman for 10 years before that and a House Republican leader from 1984–92. Up to that point his career followed the usual path of House Republican leaders of earlier generations. He was an insurance agent in Redlands, a joiner in civic causes, when he was elected to the Assembly at 34. In the House, he got a seat on the Appropriations Committee, where bipartisan cooperation was the norm, enabling even minority members to confer favors on their districts. He eventually became ranking Republican on the Legislative Subcommittee, working amicably on Congress's budget with fellow Californian, Chairman Vic Fazio. Lewis seemed to be following Robert Michel's route to the minority leadership: chairman of the Republican Research Committee in 1984, chairman of the Republican Policy Committee in 1986, Conference chairman in 1988. But conservatives resented Lewis's cooperation with Democrats and his support of the 1990 budget summit tax increases. In 1990 California Republicans voted him out as their representative on the committee on committees. In December 1992 Dick Armey opposed him for reelection as Conference chairman and won 88–84. That narrow margin, plus Newt Gingrich's 87–85 victory for whip in March 1989 put in place the two top leaders of the Republican majority that emerged after November 1994.

Lewis was unhappy with that setback, but has rebounded well. He has a mostly conservative voting record and supported the Contract with America except for term limits. He is a member of the "college of cardinals," as chairman of the VA-HUD Appropriations Subcommittee, with jurisdiction over the VA, HUD, EPA, NASA, the National Science Foundation and FEMA. He boasts that his subcommittee has reduced spending by $14.8 billion, more than any other. "It is this moderate who is doing some major cutting." But he will be challenged by proposed increases in HUD spending as Section 8 housing comes up for renewal in 1997 and 1998. He worked hard for relief appropriations after the Northridge earthquake of 1994 and has worked for the Alameda Corridor rail connection between the Los Angeles-Long Beach port and main east-west rail lines. He inserted a rider releasing California from a proposed EPA smog reduction plan. He worked for a medical facility at Loma Linda University and on behalf of a national bone marrow transplant registry; he wants to widen I-15 and I-40 in fast-growing desert areas. He sought to reverse the IRS's sudden withdrawal of tax exemption from the California Earthquake Authority in June 1996.

Lewis is now chairman of the California Republican delegation and has tried to promote cooperation on some state issues with the California Democrats, chaired by Lucille Roybal-Allard. He has many friends among Democrats, and once saved Speaker Jim Wright from drowning in Hawaii and asked the Pope to pray for the cancer-stricken daughter of Vic Fazio. He retains a certain aggressiveness: one evening in May 1994 he saw a thief driving his 1984 Oldsmobile away from a parking place on Capitol Hill and chased the car down Pennsylvania Avenue until it crashed and police arrested the man two blocks away.

One cause on which Lewis has fought fiercely is against the Desert Protection Act sponsored by Dianne Feinstein and George Miller and passed over his opposition, but with some of his limiting amendments, in 1994. In 1995 Lewis reduced the appropriation for National Park Service management to $1 and transferred authority to the Bureau of Land Management, who is less inclined to close off roadways to the hunters, grazers and four-wheel drive enthusiasts who are permitted to use the area under the 1994 law. But this was threatened with a veto by Bill Clinton, and House Republican leaders withdrew the provision in 1996.

Lewis has been reelected easily in this Republican district.

The People: Pop. 1990: 573,939; 18% rural; 12% age 65+; 74% White; 5% Black; 3% Asian; 1% Amer. Indian; 16% Hispanic origin. Households: 60% married couple families; 30% married couple fams. w. children; 49% college educ.; median household income: $30,408; per capita income: $13,568; median gross rent: $507; median house value: $110,300.

1996 Presidential Vote

Dole (R)	94,916	(49%)
Clinton (D)	73,316	(38%)
Perot (I)	20,719	(11%)
Other	5,467	(3%)

1992 Presidential Vote

Bush (R)	86,453	(39%)
Clinton (D)	76,363	(35%)
Perot (I)	53,955	(25%)

Rep. Jerry Lewis (R)

Elected 1978; b. Oct. 21, 1934, Seattle, WA; home, Redlands; U. of CA, B.A. 1956; Presbyterian; married (Arlene).

Career: Insurance exec., 1959–78; Field rep., U.S. Rep. Jerry Pettis, 1968; CA Assembly, 1968–78.

DC Office: 2112 RHOB 20515, 202-225-5861; Fax: 202-225-6498.

District Offices: Redlands, 909-862-6030.

Committees: *Appropriations* (5th of 34 R): National Security; VA, HUD & Independent Agencies (Chmn.). *Intelligence (Select)* (3rd of 9 R): Technical & Tactical Intelligence (Chmn.).

Group Ratings

	ADA	ACLU	AFS	LCV	CFA	CON	NFIB	COC	ACU	NTLC	CHC
1996	5	12	8	31	0	1	92	94	83	95	73
1995	5	—	—	13	0	38	—	95	68	—	—

National Journal Ratings

	1995 LIB — 1995 CONS			1996 LIB — 1996 CONS		
Economic	36%	—	64%	39%	—	61%
Social	37%	—	63%	44%	—	56%
Foreign	36%	—	59%	21%	—	72%

Key Votes of the 104th Congress

1. Reduce Medicare Growth $	Y	5. Flag Amendment	Y	9. Cuban Embargo	Y
2. Ovrd. Product Liab. Veto	Y	6. Drop EPA Limits	N	10. Bar Bosnia Troop $	N
3. Increase Min. Wage	Y	7. Repeal Assault-Weap. Ban	*	11. Cut Anti-Missile Defense	N
4. Welfare Reform	Y	8. Ovrd. Part. Birth Veto	Y	12. Bar U.N. Uniforms	Y

Election Results

1996 general	Jerry Lewis (R)	98,821	(65%)	($239,448)
	Robert Conaway (D)	44,102	(29%)	($12,085)
	Others	9,338	(6%)	
1996 primary	Jerry Lewis (R)	46,108	(77%)	
	George Craig (R)	13,836	(23%)	
1994 general	Jerry Lewis (R)	115,728	(71%)	($209,763)
	Donald M. Rusk (D)	48,003	(29%)	($39,544)

FORTY-FIRST DISTRICT

One of the areas of explosive growth in the 1980s boom years in California was in the eastern end of the Los Angeles Basin—the Inland Empire, as it is now called. Mostly orange groves a couple of decades ago, this territory now is the site of rapid economic growth, personal upward mobility and ethnic and cultural harmony. The secret of the economic growth is small entrepreneurial businesses, usually started by people with no particular connections or advantages—increasingly, of Asian or Latino immigrant background. California has never been a land of leisure, as stereotype would have it, but rather a place for hard work, where neither the amazing fertility of the soil nor the amazing productivity of the people has happened without a lot of effort and a tolerant and welcoming attitude toward newcomers. California hasn't always welcomed people from strange places—a strain of anti-Asian feeling expressed itself in the Chinese Exclusion Act of 1882 and the Japanese American relocation camps of 1942–44—but certainly since World War II this has been one of the least prejudiced and most welcoming places on earth, one reason why it has been receiving more immigrants than any other American state.

The 41st Congressional District, in the Inland Empire, is one place where such trends are visible. The 41st is centered on the point where Los Angeles, San Bernardino and Orange Counties come together. In San Bernardino County it includes most of Ontario and its airport and industrial zone, plus the higher income towns of Montclair and Upland; it includes the old town of Pomona, now much expanded, site of the Los Angeles County Fair, and fast-growing Diamond Bar; it includes Chino, site of a low security prison, and subdivisions below the Chino Hills; over the hills in Orange County, it includes Yorba Linda, site (just beyond the district line) of the birthplace of Richard Nixon in 1913 (when Orange County had only 40,000 residents), and the site of the Richard Nixon Library now (when Orange County has 2.5 million and Yorba Linda 52,000). This was all rapidly growing country in the 1980s, filling up with two-worker households. Ethnically diverse, in the 1990s its residents were 32% Hispanic and 10% Asian, believers still in traditional values, working their way up through the private sector—and leaning toward Republicans.

The congressman from the 41st, a new district created after the 1990 Census, is Jay Kim, a Republican elected in 1992 and the first Korean American member of Congress. He was born in Korea, where his father was a lawyer; their house was destroyed in the Korean war and they had to walk 90 miles to safety. He came to California in 1961, got an engineering degree from Southern California in 1967 and became city engineer for Ontario and Compton. In 1976, with a Small Business Administration loan, he started Jaykim Engineers, designing highways, water reclamation plants and other big projects—mostly government contracts, some minority set-asides. In 1984 he got an Army Corps of Engineers contract for the Los Angeles district and later an $8.7 million contract for Los Angeles's Metro Rail. In 1990 he built a $1 million dream house in Diamond Bar and immediately ran for City Council, placing first in a nine-candidate race, and serving as mayor from 1991–92. This was perhaps characteristic: friends remember he was always interested in politics. In 1992, even while his firm was having problems, he ran for Congress. He campaigned for lower taxes and privatizing government services, against illegal immigration and for abortion rights. He loaned his campaign $169,000 and raised about an equal amount, outspending two primary opponents, an assemblyman and a former Washington lawyer. Kim won the primary 30%–28%–27%; in the general he prevailed 60%–34%.

Then a cloud appeared: in July 1993 the *Los Angeles Times* reported that his company had spent $400,000 on his campaign, a supposedly illegal corporate contribution. But $300,000 of that was his salary, which is not extraordinary: candidates can be paid salaries when they run and usually are, and he wholly owned the company anyway, though he sold it after he was elected. He did admit that he should have paid the company rent for office facilities and subsequently reimbursed them. No legal or ethics charges were brought. But in late 1995 and early 1996 five Korean companies—Korean Air Lines, Hyundai, Samsung, Daewoo International and Haitai America—pled guilty to making illegal contributions and were fined a total of $1.6 million. They admitted to reimbursing employees for contributions to Kim's 1992 campaign; Kim said he had not known this. In May 1996 Hyundai executive Paul Koh was acquitted of conspiring to make illegal contributions. In April 1997 Kim's 1994 campaign treasurer Seokuk Ma was convicted of concealing illegal contributions. Is all this evidence of a "pattern of dishonesty and lack of integrity," as Kim's 1996 primary opponent Bob Kerns said? Or is it evidence of media bias, as Kim says? "Number one, I'm a Republican. Nine out of ten reporters are registered Democrats. Number two, I'm an Asian. And some media people just don't like to see a conservative Asian American." In any case as of early 1997 no charges had been filed against Kim.

In the House Kim has had a strongly conservative voting record, and he has disagreed with the many leftish Asian American activist groups. He strongly opposes illegal immigration and backed Proposition 187 in 1994. "America's still the richest country. But all the political leadership led the country in the wrong direction. We have all the freebies, and we don't have to do anything. The government will hand out everything for you. I think all the Big Brother concepts, government-can-take-care-of-you kind of mentality, have ruined our society. People have lost incentive." He serves on the Transportation and Infrastructure Committee and has sought aid for local projects—shuttle buses in north Orange County, $151 million for Orange County sewer recycling. He wants federal reimbursement for maintaining roads overstressed by Mexican truck traffic after NAFTA; some such monies were included in the 1997 Clinton budget. He sought to allow repair shops as well as car dealers to operate on-board diagnostic systems under the Clean Air Act. He declined to join the International Relations Committee in 1993, then joined in 1995; in 1996 he called for cutting off food aid to North Korea until it entered talks with South Korea.

Kim's hold on the district does not seem entirely solid. In the 1994 primary he won just 41% in a primary against four opponents; he beat the closest by 2–1 but a less-than-majority vote for an incumbent is a danger sign. The general he won easily, 62%–38%. In 1996 primary opponent Kerns, a Pat Buchanan backer, spent almost no money, but sent out mailers attacking Kim's ethics; his phone message machine answered, "Truth and integrity. The American way." The much better financed Kim beat him by only 58%–42%. Kim won the general 58%–33%, against attorney Richard Waldron. Kim has pledged to serve only three terms and so presumably will not run in 1998; if he does, he could have serious competition.

The People: Pop. 1990: 572,529; 1% rural; 6% age 65+; 52% White; 6% Black; 10% Asian; 32% Hispanic origin. Households: 65% married couple families; 38% married couple fams. w. children; 55% college educ.; median household income: $44,607; per capita income: $16,002; median gross rent: $656; median house value: $202,700.

1996 Presidential Vote

Dole (R)	76,867	(47%)
Clinton (D)	71,393	(43%)
Perot (I)	13,007	(8%)
Other	3,732	(2%)

1992 Presidential Vote

Bush (R)	78,902	(42%)
Clinton (D)	64,666	(35%)
Perot (I)	41,112	(22%)

Rep. Jay Kim (R)

Elected 1992; b. Mar. 27, 1939, Seoul, Korea; home, Diamond Bar; U. of Southern CA, B.S. 1967, M.S., 1973, CA St. U., M.P.A. 1980; Methodist; married (June).

Career: City Engineer, Ontario & Compton; Founder & Pres., Jaykim Engineers, 1976–93; Diamond Bar City Cncl., 1990–91, Diamond Bar Mayor, 1991–92.

DC Office: 227 CHOB 20515, 202-225-3201; Fax: 202-226-1485.

District Offices: Ontario, 909-988-1055; Yorba Linda, 714-572-8574.

Committees: *International Relations* (15th of 26 R): Asia & the Pacific; Western Hemisphere. *Transportation & Infrastructure* (11th of 40 R): Public Buildings & Economic Development (Chmn.); Water Resources & Environment.

Group Ratings

	ADA	ACLU	AFS	LCV	CFA	CON	NFIB	COC	ACU	NTLC	CHC
1996	0	6	0	23	15	30	97	100	100	100	100
1995	0	—	—	6	8	38	—	100	92	—	—

National Journal Ratings

	1995 LIB — 1995 CONS			1996 LIB — 1996 CONS		
Economic	0%	—	74%	0%	—	82%
Social	21%	—	72%	29%	—	68%
Foreign	15%	—	73%	0%	—	79%

Key Votes of the 104th Congress

1. Reduce Medicare Growth $	Y	5. Flag Amendment	Y	9. Cuban Embargo	Y
2. Ovrd. Product Liab. Veto	Y	6. Drop EPA Limits	N	10. Bar Bosnia Troop $	Y
3. Increase Min. Wage	N	7. Repeal Assault-Weap. Ban	Y	11. Cut Anti-Missile Defense	N
4. Welfare Reform	Y	8. Ovrd. Part. Birth Veto	Y	12. Bar U.N. Uniforms	Y

Election Results

1996 general	Jay Kim (R)	83,934	(58%)	($579,673)
	Richard L. Waldron (D)	47,346	(33%)	
	Richard G. Newhouse (Lib)	7,135	(5%)	
	Others	5,150	(4%)	
1996 primary	Jay Kim (R)	24,321	(58%)	
	Bob Kerns (R)	17,461	(42%)	
1994 general	Jay Kim (R)	81,854	(62%)	($810,211)
	Ed Tessier (D)	49,924	(38%)	($73,244)

FORTY-SECOND DISTRICT

The gateway to the Los Angeles Basin for decades was San Bernardino, situated on flat land where the route through the twisting, windy El Cajon Pass took passengers on the Santa Fe Railroad and motorists on U.S. 66 from the hot and dusty desert to the greener, tree-lined basin. There were orange groves around the little railroad towns and vineyards to the west; this was an agricultural zone until World War II, when Henry J. Kaiser built the West Coast's first major steel mill between the Santa Fe and Southern Pacific lines in Fontana, just west of San Bernardino. Today, these lands have largely filled up. This Inland Empire, as it is called, may be where the smog piles up against the mountains, but it also has some of the lowest real estate prices in the Los Angeles Basin and a thriving small business economy.

The 42d Congressional District consists of most of San Bernardino and the towns running west—low-income Rialto, Fontana with many other businesses replacing the closed steel mill (the blast furnaces were dismantled in 1994 and reassembled in China), fast-growing Rancho Cucamonga. It is 34% Hispanic, 11% black and 4% Asian. Politically this area trended Republican in the 1980s, as the cultural liberalism of California Democrats repelled family-oriented residents, but when the economy slowed and real estate prices plummeted in the early 1990s, it swung toward Bill Clinton and the Democrats.

The congressman from the 42d District is George Brown, a Democrat who in 1997 was serving his 33d year in the House. An engineer with a Quaker upbringing who has long cared about arms control issues, Brown worked for 17 years for the city of Los Angeles. In 1958 he was mayor of Monterey Park, far to the west; in that banner Democratic year, he was elected to the California Assembly and served on the redistricting committee. Lo and behold, he got one of California's eight new districts in 1962. He ran for the Senate in 1970 and almost beat John Tunney in the primary; if he had, he might well have won the general. Brown found a new district in 1972 in the Inland Empire, and Phillip Burton redrew the lines in 1982 to help him through another decade. But Brown has not won by landslides: against a religious fundamentalist, a small town businessman and a San Bernardino County supervisor, he won between 53% and 57% in the 1980s. His military dovishness over the years has moderated into support for local defense installations, and he has long been a supporter of space exploration. In 1990 he inherited the chairmanship of the House Science Committee. There he supported both manned and unmanned space exploration, backing a new space launch vehicle and the space shuttle. He worked to restructure the national weapons laboratories and maintain the Landsat remote-sensing system. He supported federal aid for emerging technologies and development of electric vehicles and solar energy. He looked forward to working with Vice President Albert Gore, a former Science Committee member, as "heaven on earth," and he had the pleasure of seeing Science become a sought-after assignment in 1993. But after 1994 he reverted to the minority and in July 1995 voted against the space station, arguing that space science programs have deteriorated and that given budget constrictions the program may have to be sacrificed for other, presumably unmanned, space projects.

Brown has continued to have serious challenges at home in the 1990s, as the new district lines were not as favorable as the old. In 1992 he faced Dick Rutan, pilot of the *Voyager* plane which circled the earth without refueling in 1986; with gobs of PAC money, Brown outspent him 2–1 and won 51%–44%. In 1994 he was opposed by Rob Guzman, owner of a workplace training business called Templo Calvario Legalization & Education; Brown outspent him by a narrower margin and won 51%–49% in a Republican year.

In 1996 five Republicans lined up to run against Brown. Guzman ran again, and finished fourth in the primary, with 15%; retired Air Force officer Chuck Williams had 16%; youthful Rancho Cucamonga Mayor pro tem Rex Gutierrez had 23%. The winner, with 34%, was Linda Wilde, a Superior Court Judge on leave of absence to run. Wilde, a lawyer and wife of a police officer, had defeated an 18-year incumbent judge on a tough-on-crime platform in 1992; she was encouraged to run by friends at the Claremont Institute and was endorsed by Orange County Congressmen Dana Rohrabacher and Ed Royce. Brown "clings to his beliefs that he's held for a long time regardless of the fact that the area's changed around him," she said, citing his opposition to the death penalty (though he voted for some crime bills), welfare reform, the flag amendment. She called for a three strikes law, tough penalties for drug dealers and repeat offenders. A Wilde radio ad said Brown was "guilty as charged" of votes against welfare reform and voting to lower penalties for crack cocaine on the grounds they were racially discriminatory. She lamented that illegal immigrants are "crowding our schools, filling our jails and stretching our social services to the breaking point."

Brown argued that he worked hard to put more police on the street and fight drugs, to invest money in schools and protect Social Security. He said his support of solar energy and electric-powered vehicles show he is future-oriented. He attacked Wilde's opposition to gun control with a radio ad featuring staccato gunfire. He made one *faux pas* when in a debate in Salvatore's Restaurant in Fontana he said, "I imagine Linda, because she is a lady, is afraid of math." He quickly apologized, but Wilde responded that she had completed five advanced statistics courses in graduate school.

This was one of the closest races in the nation, and the closest in Brown's long career. He won 50.48%–49.52%, by just 996 votes. His manager said, "We would like more, but you win with 51%." But Brown seems likely to have serious competition in 1998.

The People: Pop. 1990: 571,595; 7% age 65+; 51% White; 11% Black; 4% Asian; 1% Amer. Indian; 34% Hispanic origin. Households: 58% married couple families; 35% married couple fams. w. children; 46% college educ.; median household income: $33,737; per capita income: $12,308; median gross rent: $562; median house value: $125,600.

1996 Presidential Vote			1992 Presidential Vote		
Clinton (D)	76,745	(53%)	Clinton (D)	76,964	(45%)
Dole (R)	51,106	(36%)	Bush (R)	54,978	(32%)
Perot (I)	12,342	(9%)	Perot (I)	35,828	(21%)
Other	3,329	(2%)			

Rep. George E. Brown, Jr. (D)

Elected 1972; b. Mar. 6, 1920, Holtville; home, San Bernardino; U.C.L.A., B.A. 1946; United Methodist; married (Marta).

Career: Army, 1942–46 (WWII); Monterey Park City Cncl., 1954–58, Monterey Park Mayor, 1955–56; Personnel, Engineering and Mgmt. Consult., City of Los Angeles, 1957–61; CA Assembly, 1958–62; U.S. House of Reps., 1962–70.

DC Office: 2300 RHOB 20515, 202-225-6161; Fax: 202-225-8671; e-mail: talk2geb@hr.house.gov.

District Offices: Colton, 909-825-2472.

Committees: *Agriculture* (2nd of 23 D): Department Operations, Nutrition & Foreign Agriculture; Forestry, Resource Conservation & Research. *Science* (RMM of 21 D).

Group Ratings

	ADA	ACLU	AFS	LCV	CFA	CON	NFIB	COC	ACU	NTLC	CHC
1996	90	88	100	85	77	48	24	25	0	5	0
1995	85	—	—	100	85	37	—	29	8	—	—

National Journal Ratings

	1995 LIB — 1995 CONS			1996 LIB — 1996 CONS		
Economic	79%	—	21%	89%	—	0%
Social	79%	—	20%	84%	—	12%
Foreign	88%	—	7%	90%	—	0%

Key Votes of the 104th Congress

1. Reduce Medicare Growth $	N	5. Flag Amendment	N	9. Cuban Embargo	N
2. Ovrd. Product Liab. Veto	N	6. Drop EPA Limits	Y	10. Bar Bosnia Troop $	N
3. Increase Min. Wage	Y	7. Repeal Assault-Weap. Ban	N	11. Cut Anti-Missile Defense	Y
4. Welfare Reform	N	8. Ovrd. Part. Birth Veto	N	12. Bar U.N. Uniforms	N

Election Results

1996 general	George E. Brown, Jr. (D)	52,166	(50%)	($722,544)
	Linda M. Wilde (R)	51,170	(50%)	($685,623)
1996 primary	George E. Brown, Jr. (D)	24,930	(78%)	
	Alfred Palazzo (D)	7,133	(22%)	
1994 general	George E. Brown, Jr. (D)	58,888	(51%)	($485,455)
	Rob Guzman (R)	56,259	(49%)	($308,574)

FORTY-THIRD DISTRICT

Riverside was a sleepy town of 34,000, a couple hours' drive from Los Angeles, when Richard and Pat Nixon were married in 1940 in the gaudy Mission Inn, with its bell towers, altars, fountains, rotunda, stained-glass windows and wrought-iron grilles. Riverside was not much larger, with 46,000 people, when Ronald and Nancy Reagan spent their honeymoon at the Mission Inn a dozen years later, in 1952. Riverside then was a citrus center, a market town amid orange groves, where the local agricultural college developed among other things the navel orange. Today the Mission Inn is still doing business, but Riverside has changed completely. The city has expanded to 226,000 people, and Riverside County, which had 105,000 people in 1940, had 663,000 in 1980 and 1.17 million in 1990—a 76% increase in one decade. Riverside County stretches east to Arizona, so some of this increase was in the desert, but much was in the Inland Empire around Riverside, where the flat Los Angeles Basin plains are interrupted by odd-shaped hills and ridges and the vegetation has an other-worldly air. There are odd by-products from such rapid development, like the dozens of 300-pound pigs that live in the river bed just outside Riverside. This was one of the boom parts of California in the 1980s, where modest-income families found new houses in inexpensive developments and small businesses expanded mightily; it was hit hard by the recession of the early 1990s and now has rebounded and is growing again.

The 43d Congressional District is one of two that were formed from the old 37th District which included most of Riverside County and was the fastest-growing in the country in the 1980s. This was a seat without an incumbent and with great political volatility—not accidental in an area where few voters have deep roots, where neither ethnic ties nor economic security produces strong commitment to either party, and where the economy has changed so sharply. The 43d District includes all of Riverside and the towns immediately around; another population node just to the west, around Corona; and new subdivisions scattered around I-215 and I-15, which run south from Riverside and Corona until they join at Murietta Hot Springs, just north of the new town of Temecula.

The congressman from the 43d is Ken Calvert, a Republican elected in 1992. Calvert grew up in Corona; after college, he ran a restaurant there and in 1980 started in the commercial real estate business. In 1982, at 29, he ran for Congress and in the old Riverside County district lost a nine-candidate primary to Al McCandless by a 25%–24% margin: 868 votes kept him out of Congress for 10 years. He continued to be active in civic affairs and chaired the local Republican Party. In 1992 he ran for Congress in the new 43d—one of seven Republicans and seven Democrats—and won the primary with 28%, followed by business professor Joseph Khoury (who ran ads featuring Milton Berle), with 21%, and Larry Arnn, president of Claremont Institute, with 18%. His Democratic opponent was Mark Takano, a 33-year-old eighth grade teacher and Riverside Community College trustee with institutional support from teachers' unions and financial support from Japanese Americans, who also won his primary narrowly. The 43d is a good example of the return of straight ticket voting in the 1990s: George Bush beat Bill Clinton in the district by 797 votes and Calvert beat Takano by 519 votes.

In the House, Calvert has compiled a conservative voting record and served quietly in the minority on the Science and Resources Committees. But he ran into trouble back home. In

November 1993 he was stopped by the Corona police with a convicted prostitute in his car; not much was reported about the incident but the *Riverside Press-Enterprise* brought suit to recover police records, and in April 1994 it revealed the police reports, which showed that Calvert had been partly undressed. Calvert responded that he was upset because his wife had divorced him the month before and his father had recently committed suicide. "I realize now that this, or a similar incident, was probably inevitable," he said. "My conduct that evening was inappropriate. It was inappropriate, not because it was illegal or violated the office I hold, but because it violated the values of the person I strive to be." Also, it was reported that Calvert and his ex-wife owed $16,000 in back taxes on a nine-acre lot. He argued that the tax liability had been overlooked during his divorce, and his ex-wife defended him against charges of intentional tax avoidance. But it was, as he said, "an extremely embarrassing situation," which his opponents rushed to take advantage of. Joseph Khoury, running again, was already attacking Calvert as insufficiently conservative and chimed in on the scandal. Calvert won the primary 51%–49%, with only an 884-vote margin. Mark Takano, running again in the general, ran an ad with the song "The Liar" and accused him of "flagrant womanizing." At a public meeting, Republican Assemblyman Ray Haynes called Takano a "nutzoid" liberal homosexual. Calvert was rated the most endangered incumbent by *Roll Call*. But the Republican tide of the year showed up in the election results, with Calvert winning by a thumping 55%–38%.

In 1995 Calvert found himself, after several political near-death experiences, chairman of the Energy and Mineral Resources Subcommittee. He produced a bill to reform the Mining Law of 1872, which allows mining companies to stake claims on federal lands for absurdly low fees; he would have required them to pay fair market value and a royalty of 3%. But Democrats and some Republicans like Fred Upton and John Kasich called 3% "anemic" and wanted an 8% royalty; no legislation passed. He also sponsored a toll-free verification number to check on the immigration status of job applicants and, inspired by the subdividing of March Air Force Base near Riverside, sponsored a bill to allow unused military bases to be used by police and firefighters.

In 1996 Calvert still was bedeviled by personal problems; his former wife sued for nonpayment of alimony, and he in turn sued her. He refused to speak to the *Press-Enterprise* on campaign issues because, a spokesman said, the paper continued to "rehash the incident of a few years ago." But no serious opposition arose. He called for cutting taxes, ending racial quotas and preferences and curtailing illegal immigration and was reelected by a solid 55%–38% as Bob Dole ran slightly better against Bill Clinton than George Bush had. He lost his seat on Agriculture and switched subcommittee chairs, to the Energy and Environment Subcommittee of Science. He questioned proposed EPA standards on ozone and particulate emissions; "I simply asked EPA to base their regulations on sound scientific evidence."

The People: Pop. 1990: 571,090; 14% rural; 8% age 65+; 65% White; 6% Black; 4% Asian; 1% Amer. Indian; 25% Hispanic origin. Households: 63% married couple families; 35% married couple fams. w. children; 50% college educ.; median household income: $37,806; per capita income: $14,449; median gross rent: $595; median house value: $153,200.

1996 Presidential Vote			1992 Presidential Vote		
Dole (R)	82,940	(45%)	Bush (R)	76,837	(38%)
Clinton (D)	78,384	(43%)	Clinton (D)	76,040	(38%)
Perot (I)	16,406	(9%)	Perot (I)	48,197	(24%)
Other	4,687	(3%)			

Rep. Ken Calvert (R)

Elected 1992; b. June 8, 1953, Corona; home, Corona; San Diego St. U., B.A. 1975; Protestant; divorced.

Career: Restaurant Owner, 1975–80; Real estate broker, 1980–92; Chmn, Riverside Cnty. Repub. Party, 1984–88.

DC Office: 1034 LHOB 20515, 202-225-1986; Fax: 202-225-2004.
District Offices: Riverside, 909-784-4300.

Committees: *Resources* (10th of 27 R): Energy & Mineral Resources; Water & Power. *Science* (9th of 25 R): Energy & Environment (Chmn.); Space & Aeronautics.

Group Ratings

	ADA	ACLU	AFS	LCV	CFA	CON	NFIB	COC	ACU	NTLC	CHC
1996	0	12	0	15	8	17	97	100	95	100	100
1995	0	—	—	0	0	38	—	100	84	—	—

National Journal Ratings

	1995 LIB — 1995 CONS			1996 LIB — 1996 CONS		
Economic	0%	—	74%	0%	—	82%
Social	0%	—	79%	32%	—	67%
Foreign	0%	—	85%	0%	—	79%

Key Votes of the 104th Congress

1. Reduce Medicare Growth $	Y	5. Flag Amendment	Y	9. Cuban Embargo	Y
2. Ovrd. Product Liab. Veto	Y	6. Drop EPA Limits	N	10. Bar Bosnia Troop $	Y
3. Increase Min. Wage	N	7. Repeal Assault-Weap. Ban	*	11. Cut Anti-Missile Defense	N
4. Welfare Reform	Y	8. Ovrd. Part. Birth Veto	Y	12. Bar U.N. Uniforms	Y

Election Results

1996 general	Ken Calvert (R)	97,247	(55%)	($594,665)
	Guy C. Kimbrough (D)	67,422	(38%)	($46,590)
	Others	13,055	(7%)	
1996 primary	Ken Calvert (R)	39,364	(74%)	
	David Davis (R)	13,517	(26%)	
1994 general	Ken Calvert (R)	84,500	(55%)	($768,290)
	Mark A. Takano (D)	59,342	(38%)	($562,401)
	Gene L. Berkman (Lib)	9,636	(6%)	

FORTY-FOURTH DISTRICT

From the air two decades ago, a night flight east from Los Angeles showed the lights of 10 million people's streets and houses and then almost perfect darkness: a vast metropolis surrounded by almost uninhabited territory. Today the sprinkled pattern of white lights has spread into the Inland Empire around Riverside and San Bernardino and is multiplying outward into the desert. The Inland Empire has filled up with instant towns like Moreno Valley, which did not exist in 1980 and had 118,000 people in 1990. The surreal landscape to the south and east, around the old towns of Perris and Hemet, is filling up with new places like Sun City and Valle Vista. Over the 10,000-foot San Jacinto Mountains, desert communities have boomed:

Palm Springs, once the lone winter resort for the stars, is now one of a string of communities along Highway 111 and Frank Sinatra and Bob Hope Drives. Among rich retirees, the vogue for the coast lessened as beach cities filled up with enviro-activists and rent control crusaders; the clean, dry, roomy desert, where the days are almost always crystal clear and the sky usually blue and cloudless, became more attractive, and, with everything air-conditioned, a comfortable year-round home for more than 150,000 in 1990. That's 200,000 if you count Indio, the heavily Latino center of the Coachella Valley which has 98% of the country's date palms and which features camel races at its annual date festival. Two presidents have retired to the desert, Dwight Eisenhower in Palm Desert for the winters and Gerald Ford in nearby Rancho Mirage.

The 44th Congressional District is one of two that were created from the fastest-growing district in the United States in the 1980s, which included all the desert and most of the rest of Riverside County. The 44th covers all the desert and proceeds west to Moreno Valley, including most of the region around Perris and Hemet. It is heavily Republican in most elections, but trended Democratic and voted for Bill Clinton in 1992. Then, unlike coastal California but like inland California and most of the Rocky Mountain area, moved toward Republicans and voted for Bob Dole in 1996.

The congressman from the 44th District is Sonny Bono, onetime showbiz celebrity and mayor of Palm Springs, a 1992 U.S. Senate candidate, elected to the House as a Republican in 1994. Bono, born in Detroit, moved with his Sicilian-American family to southern California in World War II; after high school he became a songwriter and drove a meat delivery truck to make money. He wrote *Needles and Pins*, worked with Phil Spector and the Righteous Brothers and in 1964 borrowed $175 to record *Baby Don't Go* with his then-girlfriend Cherilyn Sarkisian: Sonny and Cher. By 1965, Sonny had recorded five songs ranked in the Billboard Top 100, an achievement unmatched by anyone except the Beatles. As rock went drugward, they called for abstinence and named their daughter Chastity, made a couple of flop movies, then developed the mainline *Sonny and Cher* TV show. After they were divorced in 1974, Bono dropped out of showbiz, started restaurants and settled in Palm Springs, where he got angry when city bureaucrats stalled his building plans; he ran for mayor and was elected in 1988. He claimed credit for erasing a $2.5 million deficit without new taxes and for starting a local film festival. He survived controversies over development and a recall attempt and ran for the Senate in 1992. He got 17% of the vote, behind conservative Bruce Herschensohn with 38% and moderate Tom Campbell with 36%. Afterwards, he became friends with the good-natured Herschensohn and started to run for lieutenant governor. Then, when 44th District Congressman Al McCandless announced his retirement, Bono ran for the House. He won a six-candidate primary with 49% and in the general beat former Assemblyman Steve Clute 56%–38%.

In his showbiz days, Bono always portrayed himself as a worse singer than Cher and the object of her putdowns; he carried that image over into his political career. "I feel kind of like the black sheep in Congress, but here I am," he once said. But behind his seeming klutziness is a sense of humor that suggests a shrewdness as well. When asked to talk about illegal immigration, he replied, "What's to talk about? It's illegal"—a response that nicely anticipated the success of Proposition 187. Bono has worked to get federal aid to preserve the habitats of various endangered species in Riverside County, but when the Endangered Species Act required millions from local government and property owners to protect Stephens's Kangaroo rat in Riverside County, he said, "We all love the environment, but we have placed creatures above people. A rat is a rat." On the Judiciary Committee he promoted his bill to require three-judge courts to consider challenges to voter-passed referenda; it passed the House in 1995 and seemed likely to again in 1997 after a single judge overturned California's Proposition 209.

Bono has played a role on several other issues. Influenced perhaps by the local Agua Caliente Band of Cahuilla Indians, who own every other square mile in Palm Springs, he got an amendment requiring that an Indian serve on the commission set up to study gambling and tried to bar it from investigating Indian gambling or gambling addiction. In 1996 he came out for a national sales tax and abolition of the IRS.

In the culture wars, Bono stands in a place where he can talk to both sides. He convened a summit of House Republicans and Hollywood denizens in 1995. He voted for the Defense of Marriage Act, but apologetically, telling Barney Frank, "I simply can't handle it yet, Barney. I wish I was ready, but I can't tell my son it's OK." He pushed an amendment to allow senior citizen housing to ban families with children. He passed a bill allowing the Torres-Martinez tribe to open a casino near the Salton Sea; it was stopped by Nevada's senators.

Bono remains a celebrity, one of the most sought-after speakers for other Republicans. He can fly off the handle; he apologized in October 1996 after calling Bill Clinton a "criminal" and saying he had sent CIA hit squads to Haiti. His campaign at home did not demand much; he spent part of late October 1996 in Washington with a bleeding ulcer and still won 58%-39%. After the election he got Robert Dornan's seat on National Security, and will stay on Judiciary. He has been mentioned as a possible candidate for the Senate seat held by Barbara Boxer in 1998, and says he will announce by mid-1997.

The People: Pop. 1990: 571,843; 14% rural; 18% age 65+; 64% White; 5% Black; 3% Asian; 1% Amer. Indian; 28% Hispanic origin. Households: 58% married couple families; 25% married couple fams. w. children; 45% college educ.; median household income: $29,049; per capita income: $14,417; median gross rent: $545; median house value: $121,800.

1996 Presidential Vote

Dole (R)	86,414	(45%)
Clinton (D)	85,397	(44%)
Perot (I)	17,830	(9%)
Other	3,914	(2%)

1992 Presidential Vote

Clinton (D)	87,180	(40%)
Bush (R)	76,772	(36%)
Perot (I)	50,867	(24%)

Rep. Sonny Bono (R)

Elected 1994; b. Feb. 16, 1935, Detroit, MI; home, Palm Springs; Catholic; married (Mary).

Career: Entertainer, Songwriter, Producer, 1959–88; Restaurateur, 1982–92; Palm Springs Mayor, 1988–92.

DC Office: 324 CHOB 20515, 202-225-5330; Fax: 202-225-2961.

District Offices: Moreno Valley, 909-653-4466; Palm Springs, 760-320-1076.

Committees: *Judiciary* (13th of 20 R): Courts & Intellectual Property; Immigration & Claims. *National Security* (26th of 30 R): Military Personnel; Military Procurement.

Group Ratings

	ADA	ACLU	AFS	LCV	CFA	CON	NFIB	COC	ACU	NTLC	CHC
1996	0	0	8	15	8	17	94	94	95	100	92
1995	0	—	—	6	0	56	—	100	96	—	—

National Journal Ratings

	1995 LIB — 1995 CONS			1996 LIB — 1996 CONS		
Economic	26%	—	67%	20%	—	76%
Social	40%	—	60%	42%	—	58%
Foreign	15%	—	73%	21%	—	72%

Key Votes of the 104th Congress

1. Reduce Medicare Growth $	Y	5. Flag Amendment	Y	9. Cuban Embargo	Y
2. Ovrd. Product Liab. Veto	Y	6. Drop EPA Limits	N	10. Bar Bosnia Troop $	Y
3. Increase Min. Wage	Y	7. Repeal Assault-Weap. Ban	Y	11. Cut Anti-Missile Defense	N
4. Welfare Reform	Y	8. Ovrd. Part. Birth Veto	Y	12. Bar U.N. Uniforms	Y

Election Results

1996 general	Sonny Bono (R)	110,643	(58%)	($458,527)
	Anita Rufus (D)	73,844	(39%)	($116,240)
	Others	7,141	(4%)	
1996 primary	Sonny Bono (R)	unopposed		
1994 general	Sonny Bono (R)	95,521	(56%)	($731,238)
	Steve Clute (D)	65,370	(38%)	($340,587)
	Donald Cochran (AI)	10,885	(6%)	

FORTY-FIFTH DISTRICT

In the 1950s, when the Beach Boys were at Hawthorne High School, surfers would drive far down the coast to the vast expanse of Huntington Beach in Orange County to catch a wave. This was empty country then, vegetable fields and orange groves, with nary a freeway or shopping center in sight. Today the beach itself is eerily empty, with swampland across the highway where surfers' pickups are parked; but the rest of Orange County is pretty much filled in. Huntington Beach is a city of 181,000, a mixture of family subdivisions and garden apartments. To the north are Stanton and Westminster, the latter the center of the biggest Vietnamese-American community in the nation. South along the San Diego Freeway is Fountain Valley, the central focus now of many Asian-owned high-tech businesses, an engine of Southern California growth. Near the coast again is Costa Mesa, site of South Coast Plaza, with its luxury stores, and Newport Beach, with its large harbor and expensive mansions a block or two from the ocean.

The 45th Congressional District includes all this territory. Politically, it is heavily Republican, though Democrats have sometimes been competitive in Stanton and Westminster. The Vietnamese here are conservative, angry with America—not for going into Vietnam but for leaving it. There is confidence here in free enterprise despite the early 1990s recession and despite the Orange County bankruptcy of December 1994 (the work of the county's one Democratic officeholder, Treasurer Robert Citron, but accepted by local government Republicans greedy for revenue). There is also a desire, despite the wildness of the beach and the seeming anarchy of the freeway, for discipline to supplant therapy and reassert the order that seemed so solid when Orange County was starting to grow in the 1950s.

The congressman from the 45th is Dana Rohrabacher, a Republican elected in 1988. Rohrabacher calls himself a surfer Republican, wears a Reagan baseball cap and sports an American flag surfboard—a Reaganite with *Saturday Night Live* attitude. He grew up in southern California, went to college and experimented with drugs and once had a folk band called the "Goldwaters." He worked on the 1976 and 1980 Reagan presidential campaigns, wrote editorials for *The Orange County Register* and served in the Reagan White House speechwriting shop. He returned to Southern California in 1988 when Long Beach-based Congressman Dan Lungren decided not to run again (Lungren went on to be elected attorney general in 1990). Rohrabacher, with fundraising help from Oliver North, won the primary with 35%, compared to 22% for an Orange County supervisor who had padded her resume and 20%

for Steve Horn, now congressman from the Long Beach-based 38th District. After redistricting, Rohrabacher tussled with Robert Dornan and won, running in this heavily Republican district while Dornan ran in the marginal 46th, where he lost in 1996. Rohrabacher persuaded the mayor of Huntington Beach not to run and won the primary with 48% of the vote, to 28% 28% and 24% for Costa Mesa and Huntington Beach councilmen.

Rohrabacher has made waves—or is that an inapt surfer metaphor?—on several issues in the House. One is the subsidization of obscene and religiously offensive art by the National Endowment for the Arts. That may seem out of sync with his libertarian spirit, but why should the government pay for *Piss Christ*? On the Science Committee he worked for the single stage-to-orbit vehicle and the national aerospace plane. His third major issue is illegal immigration, which he says is "going to bankrupt America," and he vocally supported Proposition 187 in 1994. At the same time he insists on a sharp distinction between legals and illegals: he is not against government benefits for aliens legally resident in the United States, and he opposed the forcible return of refugees to Haiti when many liberals as well as conservatives were demanding it. He sharply criticized the dispatch of U.S. troops to Bosnia in October 1995. He is one of the few coastal congressmen not to pay homage to environmental shibboleths: offshore oil platforms make "our coastline pretty at night" and global warming is "liberal claptrap."

In the 104th Congress he took on the issue of patent protection. GATT requires the United States to extend the life of patents from 17 to 20 years, and subcommittee chairman Carlos Moorhead's bill would have dated the 20 years from the time the application for patent was filed. Rohrabacher objected that that would leave inventors at the mercy of dilatory bureaucrats and wanted to reinstate the old law which gave 17-year protection after the patent was granted. The result was deadlock, and the House leadership killed both bills. But Moorhead retired and Rohrabacher is back. He is also a leader in the move to deny MFN status to China. "China has gobbled up every economic carrot we've offered and their behavior hasn't improved one bit. It's time to kick the weasel out of the garden. Deny MFN and we'll have the undivided attention of China's rulers." In similar tones, he argued in January 1997 that Guam and other territories are "economic basket cases . . . backward and economically depressed."

In 1996 Rohrabacher's opponent was 82-year-old Sally Alexander; he said he would not challenge her to his usual surfing contest, but she went out surfing anyway. Rohrabacher won 61%-33%. But he is embroiled in local political controversy nonetheless. In 1996 and 1997 he attacked Orange County District Attorney Michael Capizzi for prosecuting Assemblyman Scott Baugh and Rhonda Carmony, his surfing partner, fiance and 1996 campaign manager, for falsifying election documents in an Assembly special election. In early 1997, both Baugh and Carmony remain under indictment and in April 1997 the defense tried and failed to disqualify Capizzi in Carmony's case.

Rohrabacher has been mentioned as a candidate for the Senate in 1998, but has said he will not run if Orange County colleague Christopher Cox does, and is not expected to in any case.

The People: Pop. 1990: 570,991; 10% age 65+; 73% White; 1% Black; 11% Asian; 15% Hispanic origin. Households: 52% married couple families; 23% married couple fams. w. children; 63% college educ.; median household income: $45,074; per capita income: $21,046; median gross rent: $815; median house value: $264,200.

1996 Presidential Vote

Dole (R)	108,240	(50%)
Clinton (D)	81,299	(38%)
Perot (I)	17,831	(8%)
Other	6,972	(3%)

1992 Presidential Vote

Bush (R)	105,893	(42%)
Clinton (D)	80,646	(32%)
Perot (I)	63,609	(25%)

Rep. Dana Rohrabacher (R)

Elected 1988; b. June 21, 1947, Coronado; home, Huntington Beach; Long Beach St. Col. B.A. 1969, U. of S. CA, M.A. 1971; Baptist; single.

Career: Radio & print journalist, 1970–80; Sr. Speechwriter, Special Asst. to Pres. Reagan, 1981–88.

DC Office: 2338 RHOB 20515, 202-225-2415; Fax: 202-225-0145.

District Offices: Huntington Beach, 714-847-2433.

Committees: *International Relations* (11th of 26 R): Asia & the Pacific; International Economic Policy & Trade. *Science* (6th of 25 R): Energy & Environment; Space & Aeronautics (Chmn.).

Group Ratings

	ADA	ACLU	AFS	LCV	CFA	CON	NFIB	COC	ACU	NTLC	CHC
1996	15	6	0	23	31	75	95	93	100	100	100
1995	0	—	—	6	0	38	—	96	100	—	—

National Journal Ratings

	1995 LIB — 1995 CONS			1996 LIB — 1996 CONS		
Economic	0%	—	74%	24%	—	76%
Social	30%	—	68%	0%	—	90%
Foreign	45%	—	52%	49%	—	50%

Key Votes of the 104th Congress

1. Reduce Medicare Growth $	Y	5. Flag Amendment	Y	9. Cuban Embargo	Y
2. Ovrd. Product Liab. Veto	Y	6. Drop EPA Limits	N	10. Bar Bosnia Troop $	Y
3. Increase Min. Wage	N	7. Repeal Assault-Weap. Ban	Y	11. Cut Anti-Missile Defense	N
4. Welfare Reform	Y	8. Ovrd. Part. Birth Veto	Y	12. Bar U.N. Uniforms	Y

Election Results

1996 general	Dana Rohrabacher (R)	125,326	(61%)	($272,859)
	Sally J. Alexander (D)	68,312	(33%)	($51,491)
	Mark F. Murphy (Lib)	8,813	(4%)	
1996 primary	Dana Rohrabacher (R)	unopposed		
1994 general	Dana Rohrabacher (R)	124,006	(69%)	($187,656)
	Brett Williamson (D)	55,489	(31%)	($85,803)

FORTY-SIXTH DISTRICT

Orange County is the fifth most populous county in the United States, having grown from 130,000 in 1940 to 216,000 in 1950, 703,000 in 1960, 1.4 million in 1970, 1.9 million in 1980 and 2.4 million in 1990. It is now a mature community with the patina of maturity—and in some ways an aging community, fraying around the edges. The county is no longer capable of its early growth, when Disneyland sprung up on empty land and mile-square grids of orange groves and bean fields were transformed into one suburban subdivision and shopping center and office tower after another. A distinctive civilization was implanted here: mostly white and middle-class, confident of its traditional values and its market capitalism, proud of American principles and American military might. Orange County has been troubled in years since, transformed by its own openness to economic and ethnic change. Its economy was constantly being reshaped by the inevitable upheavals of capitalism: there is no single industry here—not even defense—which is totally responsible for the prosperity of Orange County, and people here must be ready to adapt almost as deftly as the Taiwanese on the other side of the Pacific Rim. It was hit hard by the defense cutbacks and recession of the early 1990s but seems to be bouncing back, pitched forward by new startups and small entrepreneurial successes not anticipated by government or corporate planners. It also was shaken by the bankruptcy of the county government in December 1994, caused by the improvident investments of County Treasurer Robert Citron. Orange County's position on the Pacific Rim is apparent in its people: widely perceived as homogeneously white, Orange County has for years been home to large numbers of Latinos and Asians. Quietly, without political hubbub, they have moved out along the freeways, building ethnic cores like the Mexican-American precincts of Santa Ana and the Vietnamese corridor in Westminster and Garden Grove, working hard at jobs, commuting on freeways and living in stucco subdivisions like anyone else. By 1990 Orange County was about one-quarter Hispanic and one-tenth Asian—scarcely homogeneous. These changes have made for some political wobble—but not very much: Asians tend to vote Republican and Latinos have been registered in very small numbers.

The 46th Congressional District is the geographic heart of Orange County. About half its people live in the county seat of Santa Ana, now heavily Latino, full of large families and many workers. It also includes most of Garden Grove, with many Latinos and some Vietnamese—though the main Vietnamese shopping area is across the line in Westminster—and most of Anaheim, including the site of Disneyland and territory just across the street from Orange County landmarks Anaheim Stadium, Knott's Berry Farm and John Wayne Airport. Overall, the district is 50% Hispanic and 12% Asian. For years this has been the least Republican part of Orange County, and from 1962–82 redistricters carefully sculpted Democratic districts here. But in the mid-1980s the Vietnamese tilted the district toward the Republicans; now in the mid-1990s increasing numbers of Latinos seem to be tilting it toward the Democrats.

The congresswoman from the 46th District is Loretta Sanchez, a Democrat who in 1996 upset one of the loudest voices of American conservatism, Robert Dornan. Sanchez grew up in Anaheim, graduated from Chapman University in Orange. She worked as a financial analyst, providing advice to public agencies and private businesses; she established her own firm in the early 1990s, though it had no listed phone number. For a time she and her husband lived in Palos Verdes Estates, but in 1994 she ran for the city council in Anaheim under her married name, Loretta Sanchez-Brixey, and lost. She ran for the House in 1996 against three Anglo male Democrats (she had registered as a Democrat in February 1992), and won with 35% of the vote; she carried the Latino vote heavily, winning 72 of 85 precincts in Santa Ana. She ran her primary campaign out of the office of sometime business associate Howard Kieffer, who went to prison for tax fraud and was ordered to pay $213,000 in restitution in 1989—something for which Dornan attacked her later.

Sanchez's primary victory in March 1996 attracted little attention, not even from Dornan. But she shrewdly counted on increasing Latino turnout ("Latinos will vote for Latinos," she said) and also dropped Kieffer as an advisor, and must have calculated that if she could make her candidacy plausible she could attract contributions from many of Dornan's political enemies. For Dornan had made many over a long political career. He was first elected to the House in 1976 from a Westside Los Angeles district and won three highly expensive and acrimonious races; in 1982 he ran for the Senate and lost dismally; in 1984 he journeyed down to Orange County and beat an incumbent Democrat in a similarly-shaped district. Dornan attacked Bill Clinton as a draft-dodger and "multiple womanizer"; he called feminists "lesbian spear chuckers"; he attacked gay rights activists vitriolically. In February 1995 he started running for president, and continued for more than a year, obviously enjoying the debates on the campaign trail. But this did not play well at home: he won only 1,029 primary votes for president in the 46th District. In previous elections he had raised as much as $2 million, most of it from sustained direct mail drives; but in 1996 he neglected fundraising and had almost no money in July, and not enough time to raise much by mail. Meanwhile, Sanchez was running close to even in polls, was being touted by national Democrats and was raising large sums from labor unions, Hollywood liberals, feminists and gays; she outspent Dornan by $811,000 to $742,000. The campaign was acrimonious: Dornan would not debate Sanchez because of her past association with Kieffer; Sanchez's husband tore down two Dornan signs and was prosecuted and fined $640. Dornan predicted he would win 50%-41%, as he had in 1992 against another Latino; but this time Latino turnout was up from 14% to 20% of the total, and it went heavily against him. Bill Clinton came to Santa Ana late in the campaign to stump for Sanchez, and this may have made the difference. She won by 984 votes, 47%-46%.

There was great cheering in the White House and in many liberal precincts at Dornan's defeat. From Dornan there were bellows of rage and charges of vote fraud; if he had put as much effort into his congressional campaign earlier as he did in fighting his loss later, he probably would have won. Dornan brought his case to the House Contested Elections Task Force, which in February 1997 issued many subpoenas and promised a hearing in Orange County. Dornan argued that there were 1,789 illegal voters and by spring 1997 Dornan came up with proof that 547 non-citizens voted in Orange County and that 303 ineligibles had been registered to vote in the 46th District by a group called Hermandad Mexicana Nacional; this fell short of proving the result was wrong, but raised questions about the netherworld of voter registration in Orange County. California's registration laws make it easy to get anyone on the voter rolls (the accused assassin of Mexican presidential candidate Luis Donaldo Colosio was a registered Democrat in San Pedro), and the Clinton Administration INS made great efforts to process new citizens and dispensed with the usual check for criminal records if the FBI did not respond within sixty days. It is possible that Dornan has a case, though in early 1997 it seemed unlikely that Sanchez would be unseated and a new election called.

The People: Pop. 1990: 570,963; 7% age 65+; 36% White; 2% Black; 12% Asian; 50% Hispanic origin. Households: 58% married couple families; 33% married couple fams. w. children; 38% college educ.; median household income: $35,416; per capita income: $11,297; median gross rent: $719; median house value: $187,900.

1996 Presidential Vote

Clinton (D)	51,330	(49%)
Dole (R)	42,780	(41%)
Perot (I)	8,229	(8%)
Other	2,609	(2%)

1992 Presidential Vote

Bush (R)	47,689	(40%)
Clinton (D)	44,352	(37%)
Perot (I)	27,542	(23%)

Rep. Loretta Sanchez (D)

Elected 1996; b. Jan. 7, 1960, Lynwood; home, Garden Grove; Chapman U., B.A. 1982; American U., M.B.A. 1984; Catholic; married (Stephen Brixey).

Career: Mgr. & Financial Analyst, Orange Cnty. Transp. Auth., 1984–87; Asst. Vice Pres., Fieldman, Rolapp & Assoc., 1987–90; Assoc., Booz, Allen & Hamilton, 1990–93; Principal, Amiga Advisors, 1993–present.

DC Office: 1529 LHOB 20515, 202-225-2965; Fax: 202-225-5859.

District Offices: Garden Grove, 714-621-0102.

Committees: *Education & The Workforce* (18th of 20 D): Oversight & Investigations; Postsecondary Education, Training & Life-Long Learning. *National Security* (22nd of 25 D): Military Research & Development.

Group Ratings and Key Votes: Newly Elected

Election Results

1996 general	Loretta Sanchez (D)	47,964	(47%)	($811,219)
	Robert K. (Bob) Dornan (R)	46,980	(46%)	($741,984)
	Others	7,540	(7%)	
1996 primary	Loretta Sanchez (D)	7,142	(35%)	
	Michael P. Farber (D)	6,125	(30%)	
	James Prince (D)	5,574	(27%)	
	Robert J. Brennan (D)	1,758	(9%)	
1994 general	Robert K. (Bob) Dornan (R)	50,126	(57%)	($2,261,696)
	Michael P. Farber (D)	32,577	(37%)	($302,747)
	Richard G. Newhouse (Lib)	5,018	(6%)	

FORTY-SEVENTH DISTRICT

As one drives southeast in Orange County, there are still large patches of vacant land, places where one can see what this metropolis must have looked like before the vast growth starting in the 1950s. The Irvine Ranch, originally stretching 10 miles along the Pacific Coast and 22 miles inland to the mountains, was sold to developers by the Irvine family in the late 1970s but is still not entirely inhabited. Arrayed at the edges of the Irvine Ranch are Orange County landmarks. One is John Wayne Airport, named after the movie star who lived in Newport Beach and who symbolized patriotism though he never served in the military himself. Another is South Coast Plaza, the highest-volume upscale shopping center in southern California, standing in what not too long ago was a lima bean field. Another is University of California-Irvine, with 1,000 acres donated by the Irvine Ranch developers. On all sides are comfortable settlements—Orange, an orderly community, within sight of the hills, where even the street signs are orange; Newport Beach around its harbor; Irvine, with its planned communities, handsome clusters of office towers, landscaped shopping plazas and groups of houses and condominiums (but no cemeteries); artsy-craftsy Laguna Beach between mountains and the sea. Orange County is assailed by some as monotonous and sterile and boring, but for most of its residents it is a promised land, orderly without being authoritarian, crowded perhaps but with privacy, sunny without being too hot.

The 47th Congressional District is centered geographically on the Irvine Ranch lands. On the coast it includes about half of Newport Beach as well as most of Irvine and runs south to Laguna Beach. It includes the growing subdivisions of El Toro and Laguna Hills near the now closed El Toro Marine Corps Air Station. About half its residents live to the north, in and around Orange; the other half are split between the ocean communities and those inland. Politically, this is a conservative area, one of the most Republican districts in the United States. Its people like the sense of order conveyed by its grid street patterns and the feeling of protection imparted by the subdivision walls. They have felt comfortable as well with the military nearby. Although there are some distinctively rich communities here, the people do not feel that they are some kind of elite; they tend to see themselves as ordinary Americans with classic values who have worked hard and are entitled to enjoy their comfort.

The congressman from the 47th is Christopher Cox, a Republican elected in 1988, one of the intellectual leaders of his party in the House. Cox grew up in St. Paul, Minnesota, graduated from Southern California in three years, went to Harvard Law and Business Schools jointly, practiced law at Latham & Watkins in Orange County, then was part of the counsel's staff in the Reagan White House. In 1988, when the local incumbent retired, he ran for the House—one of 14 candidates in the Republican primary. With the support of Oliver North, Robert Bork and members of the Irvine family, he won with 31%. He has won since without difficulty. Cox's intellect and range of interests are impressive: from the former Soviet Union (he and his father published an English translation of *Pravda* from 1984–88) to lobbying for more local control of highway funds and a proposed monorail system in Orange County. As a low-seniority member of the minority party, he forced the first vote on term limits in 1991. He called for the abolition of the Interstate Commerce Commission and teamed up with law school classmate Barney Frank to eliminate the helium program: both goals were accomplished in 1995 and 1996. He killed a proposal to require companies to deduct the inherently speculative value of stock options from their statements of current earnings. Cox did more than lament Orange County Treasurer Robert Citron's reckless investments, which bankrupted the county government; he backed local Republican John Moorlach against the Democrat when Moorlach criticized Citron's practices and afterwards proposed that public sector investors be required to make the same disclosures as private.

With the Republican victory in 1994, Cox came into his own, becoming chairman of the Republican Policy Committee and a leading legislator on many fronts. On the first day of the new Congress, he led the move to end baseline budgeting, which gave every agency department either an inflation increase or the previous year's increase, whichever was more, and an opportunity to argue for even more: this practically insured that government grew faster than the private economy. His radical idea was to state budget totals in dollar terms, so that an increase is an increase and a cut is a cut. Later in the year he proposed a new budget procedure, in which the President and the Congress would agree first on total spending in each of 19 different functions, then work out the numbers within each. Another specialty is tort reform. Cox passed through the House bills limiting "injured feelings" recovery to $250,000 and repealing joint and several liability. He wrote the securities litigation reform, to prevent predatory suits against high-tech and other companies, which got two-thirds support in both houses and was the only bill passed over Bill Clinton's veto in his first term. His bill to limit appeals of death penalties became law in April 1995.

Cox's interests extend abroad as well. His response to the Mexico bailout was a bill that passed the House in July 1995 barring the president from spending Exchange Stabilization Funds to bolster a currency. Opposed to renewal of MFN status to China, he wrote a bill requiring four committees to hold hearings on Chinese human rights and economic practices. His 1996 bill got the House on record in favor of NATO expansion to Poland, Hungary and the Czech Republic, and favoring it as well for Estonia, Latvia, Lithuania, Slovakia, Slovenia and Romania. Cox is an Internet surfer and, with Ron Wyden of Oregon, passed the Internet Freedom and Family Empowerment Act, which protects on-line providers who try to clean up their pages against tort liability and bars the FCC from content or economic regulation of the Internet. In January 1997 he was working with Wyden, who is now in the Senate, to ban state and local taxes on the Internet. And he was designated to take the lead role on the Government Reform Committee investigating the Clinton White House's FBI files scandal.

Amid all these big issues he works on small ones. He passed a Corrections Day bill easing requirements for metric conversion in federal projects to what is practical. He passed a law allowing FedEx, UPS or other private delivery services to meet the IRS "timely-mailing-as-timely-filing" requirement. He sponsored a law to allow deputization of state and local law enforcement officers to enforce immigration law. And he pushed through a land exchange between the Orange County Boy Scouts Council and the U.S. Forest Service.

Cox has been reelected easily in the 47th District. He considered running for the Senate in 1994 against Dianne Feinstein, but decided not to enter the primary against Michael Huffington, who was prepared to spend freely of his own money. He has been mentioned as a candidate against Senator Barbara Boxer in 1998, and has the potential to win wide support. But he may decide that he can influence national policy more from the House—and national politics too: George Will has suggested he would be a good choice for vice president.

The People: Pop. 1990: 571,605; 11% age 65+; 75% White; 2% Black; 9% Asian; 13% Hispanic origin. Households: 58% married couple families; 27% married couple fams. w. children; 72% college educ.;

median household income: $51,554; per capita income: $25,268; median gross rent: $845; median house value: $279,900.

1996 Presidential Vote		
Dole (R)	137,024	(54%)
Clinton (D)	91,916	(36%)
Perot (I)	17,680	(7%)
Other	7,206	(3%)

1992 Presidential Vote		
Bush (R)	127,700	(46%)
Clinton (D)	86,279	(31%)
Perot (I)	64,227	(23%)

Rep. Christopher Cox (R)

Elected 1988; b. Oct. 16, 1952, St. Paul, MN; home, Newport Beach; U. of Southern CA, B.A. 1973, Harvard, M.B.A., J.D., 1977; Catholic; married (Rebecca).

Career: Clerk, U.S. Court of Appeals, Judge Hebert Choy, 1977; Practicing atty., 1978–86; Lecturer, Harvard Bus. Schl., 1982–83; Sr. Assoc. Cnsl., White House, 1986–88.

DC Office: 2402 RHOB 20515, 202-225-5611; Fax: 202-225-9177; e-mail: chriscox@hr.house.gov.

District Offices: Newport Beach, 714-756-2244.

Committees: *Republican Policy Committee Chairman. Commerce* (15th of 28 R): Oversight & Investigations (Vice Chmn.); Telecommunications, Trade & Consumer Protection. *Government Reform & Oversight* (7th of 24 R): Civil Service.

Group Ratings

	ADA	ACLU	AFS	LCV	CFA	CON	NFIB	COC	ACU	NTLC	CHC
1996	5	0	0	15	15	79	100	88	100	100	100
1995	0	—	—	0	0	56	—	96	100	—	—

National Journal Ratings

	1995 LIB — 1995 CONS			1996 LIB — 1996 CONS		
Economic	0%	—	74%	0%	—	82%
Social	0%	—	79%	0%	—	90%
Foreign	0%	—	85%	0%	—	79%

Key Votes of the 104th Congress

1. Reduce Medicare Growth $	Y	5. Flag Amendment	Y	9. Cuban Embargo	Y
2. Ovrd. Product Liab. Veto	Y	6. Drop EPA Limits	N	10. Bar Bosnia Troop $	Y
3. Increase Min. Wage	N	7. Repeal Assault-Weap. Ban	*	11. Cut Anti-Missile Defense	N
4. Welfare Reform	Y	8. Ovrd. Part. Birth Veto	Y	12. Bar U.N. Uniforms	Y

Election Results

1996 general	Christopher Cox (R)	160,078	(66%)	($527,738)
	Tina Louise Laine (D)	70,362	(29%)	($73,980)
	Others	13,337	(5%)	
1996 primary	Christopher Cox (R)	unopposed		
1994 general	Christopher Cox (R)	152,413	(72%)	($246,400)
	Gary Kingsbury (D)	53,035	(25%)	($60,846)
	Others	7,175	(3%)	

FORTY-EIGHTH DISTRICT

The California coast between Los Angeles and San Diego has never entirely filled up with development and never will as long as the Marine Corps retains custody of Camp Pendleton, the giant training base just south of the Orange-San Diego County line. But on both sides of Pendleton up and down the coast and for miles inland on the pleasant hills and in sunny valleys, there has been tremendous growth over the past two decades. Little wonder: this area has perhaps the most agreeable climate in the continental United States, beautiful scenery, the physical infrastructure typical of California and much lower crime rates than Los Angeles or even San Diego. A quarter century ago, this was largely empty territory—never fertile enough to produce a large farm community, never endowed with much manufacturing, never actively promoted as a retirement community. In 1990 there were half a million people just north and south of Pendleton, and the Interior Department was struggling to come up with a district plan that would protect the ecosystem of the 4-inch gnat-catcher bird and other endangered species in the area.

The 48th Congressional District occupies the southernmost portion of Orange County, the North County part of San Diego County and a small slice of Riverside County, the instant town of Temecula. It includes the seaside communities of San Clemente, where Richard Nixon lived just after leaving the White House, and San Juan Capistrano, to which the swallows famously return every year. Inland, there are the newer condominium communities of Mission Viejo and Laguna Niguel; just south of Pendleton in San Diego County are Oceanside and Vista. Farther inland amid the hills are Fallbrook and, in Riverside County, Temecula, in the mid-1980s a corner-grocery town serving a vineyard district, now the center of an area with 100,000 people, mostly commuters to Orange County and Riverside attracted by low house prices and traditional values. People in all these areas tend to be Republicans; they are affluent enough to identify with the party of property, conventional enough in their personal lives to identify with what describes itself as the party of the family, undivided enough by ethnic differences to identify with the party that fancies it is made up of an unethnic majority.

The congressman from the 48th, Ron Packard, is a Republican who first won when a new district was created for this area in 1982. Packard is a Mormon from Idaho, a dentist who served in the Navy Dental Corps in Camp Pendleton in the 1950s, then moved his growing family (now 7 children and 33 grandchildren) to Carlsbad. There he served on the school board, the Chamber of Commerce and city council, was a director of the North County Transit District and mayor: one of the people who keeps things working in these growing communities. He was mayor of Carlsbad in 1982 when he ran for Congress in the new district, losing an 18-candidate Republican primary by 92 votes to Johnnie Crean, who spent his own money on ads fraudulently claiming President Reagan's endorsement. Packard promptly ran as a write-in and won with 37% to 32% for the Democrat and 31% for Crean. He has been easily reelected since, winning 66%–27% in 1996.

Relegated to the minority, Packard had been a conservative backbencher; but since 1994 he has been chairmen of two Appropriations subcommittees. The first was Legislative Branch, which cut spending on Congress by 9% and would have cut more but for resistance by the Senate. He spurred privatization of services by the Architect of the Capitol and worked to create a "cyber-Congress" with up-to-date computer systems in all offices; the latter created pressure for more spending. In 1997 Packard switched to chair the Military Construction Subcommittee, on which he says his first priority is improving base housing, including at Camp Pendleton. One big problem is what to do with El Toro Marine Corps Air Station, scheduled to be closed in 1999. North Orange Countians want to make it a civilian airport, but south Orange Countians and Packard don't, and it will be expensive to clean up its hazardous waste.

Packard's big crusade in the 104th Congress was against the INS checkpoints in North County on I-5 and in Temecula on I-15. For years he has wanted them expanded and manned around the clock; the INS has resisted. In July 1995 he said that he would favor closing them unless changes were made; given his position as an appropriator, the INS in July 1996 agreed to 24-hour manning and expansion.

The People: Pop. 1990: 573,211; 11% rural; 10% age 65+; 74% White; 4% Black; 4% Asian; 1% Amer. Indian; 17% Hispanic origin. Households: 63% married couple families; 30% married couple fams. w. children; 65% college educ.; median household income: $42,389; per capita income: $19,435; median gross rent: $696; median house value: $237,300.

1996 Presidential Vote

Dole (R)	132,545	(56%)
Clinton (D)	80,646	(34%)
Perot (I)	18,731	(8%)
Other	6,462	(3%)

1992 Presidential Vote

Bush (R)	108,581	(44%)
Clinton (D)	71,621	(29%)
Perot (I)	65,980	(27%)

Rep. Ron Packard (R)

Elected 1982; b. Jan. 19, 1931, Meridian, ID; home, Oceanside; Brigham Young U., 1948–50; Portland St. U., 1952–53; U. of OR, D.M.D. 1957; Mormon; married (Jean).

Career: Navy, 1957–59; Practicing dentist; Carlsbad Sch. Dist. Bd., 1962–74; Carlsbad City Cncl., 1976–78; Carlsbad Mayor, 1978–82.

DC Office: 2372 RHOB 20515, 202-225-3906; Fax: 202-225-0134; e-mail: rpackard@hr.house.gov.

District Offices: San Clemente, 714-496-2343; Vista, 619-631-1364.

Committees: *Appropriations* (12th of 34 R): Foreign Operations, Export Financing & Related Programs; Military Construction (Chmn.); Transportation.

Group Ratings

	ADA	ACLU	AFS	LCV	CFA	CON	NFIB	COC	ACU	NTLC	CHC
1996	0	13	0	23	8	13	97	93	94	100	100
1995	0	—	—	0	0	38	—	100	92	—	—

National Journal Ratings

	1995 LIB		1995 CONS	1996 LIB		1996 CONS
Economic	0%	—	74%	33%	—	67%
Social	21%	—	72%	14%	—	77%
Foreign	0%	—	85%	21%	—	72%

Key Votes of the 104th Congress

1. Reduce Medicare Growth $	Y	5. Flag Amendment	Y	9. Cuban Embargo	Y
2. Ovrd. Product Liab. Veto	Y	6. Drop EPA Limits	N	10. Bar Bosnia Troop $	Y
3. Increase Min. Wage	N	7. Repeal Assault-Weap. Ban	Y	11. Cut Anti-Missile Defense	N
4. Welfare Reform	*	8. Ovrd. Part. Birth Veto	Y	12. Bar U.N. Uniforms	Y

Election Results

1996 general	Ron Packard (R)	145,814	(66%)	($264,625)
	Dan Farrell (D)	59,558	(27%)	($10,645)
	Others	16,019	(7%)	
1996 primary	Ron Packard (R)	unopposed		
1994 general	Ron Packard (R)	143,275	(73%)	($210,125)
	Andrei Leschick (D)	43,446	(22%)	($3,726)
	Donna White (P&F)	8,520	(4%)	

FORTY-NINTH DISTRICT

When the United States was dictating the terms of the Treaty of Guadalupe Hidalgo in 1848, after its successful war with Mexico, it made sure the southern boundary of its new California territory was just south of the port of San Diego. This is one of three splendid natural harbors on the Pacific Coast and the major West Coast U.S. Navy base for more than 50 years. The port and Navy base in the sheltered harbor are still the central focus of a metropolis which has grown tenfold over that time span and now stretches far inland and to the north. On one side is its downtown, blooming with post-modern buildings like the Horton Plaza amid a few well-preserved early 20th Century relics like the Spreckels Theatre. Across the harbor, on the sand spit that guards it against the ocean, is the white frame castle of the Hotel Del Coronado, with its surprisingly dark wooden interior, the world's largest wooden structure and a favored resort of past American presidents; the town of Coronado has long been a favorite retirement place for Navy admirals and captains.

But San Diego is not all harbor and Navy. To the north, the Pacific waves pound against the beach beneath erose cliffs of unique rock formations that stride up and down the coast on which stand some of San Diego's great cultural institutions: the Scripps Institute of Oceanography, the University of California San Diego campus, the Salk Institute and the Torrey Pines reserve, home of this unique, wide-spreading pine tree. They look out over the ocean through clear and gentle air south to La Jolla, the city's highest-income neighborhood, and north toward Del Mar and the race track that made San Diego a tourist mecca 50 years ago when the track was owned by Bing Crosby and friends. The weather—sunny 70% of the time—has lured people to San Diego; the informal resort atmosphere of La Jolla and Mission Beach appeal to tourists—and those attending the 1996 Republican National Convention. But this is a working town as well, a sophisticated high-tech center with nearly 200,000 full- and part-time students at its colleges and universities and growing biotech, electronics, software and telecommunications industries; someone who looks like a professional surfer may turn out to be a high-tech engineer. And it is a manufacturing center as well, with maquiladora factories clustering near the Mexican border.

The 49th Congressional District, which includes about half the population of San Diego plus Coronado and Imperial Beach, takes in most of the harbor and Navy bases and much of its high-tech businesses and workers. It reaches as far south as the Mexican border and includes most of downtown San Diego and Balboa Park, with its justly famous zoo. It reaches inland where the city's freeway network, denser and more practical than San Francisco's or even Los Angeles's, efficiently shuttles commuters from scattered employment centers to their homes on hilltop subdivisions. San Diego under then-Mayor (1971–82) Pete Wilson wouldn't let developers build on the sides of the hills, so San Diego doesn't have the picturesque but precarious hillside streets of the Hollywood Hills or Pacific Heights—but rather the natural landscape that the Portuguese explorer Cabrillo saw in the 1500s and the American adventurer Richard Henry Dana saw three centuries later, though the hills are now topped unobtrusively by subdivisions. It includes Ocean Beach and Mission Bay and La Jolla and reaches as far north as Torrey Pines and as far inland as the outer boundary of Miramar Naval Air Station.

With its climate, scenery and friendliness, this should be paradise, but politically San Diego was in a foul temper in the early 1990s, kicking out incumbents of both parties all over town. Voters here tend to be Republican and free market on economics but liberal on cultural issues like abortion and the environment—much like Pete Wilson, who was elected U.S. Senator in 1982 and 1988 and governor in 1990 and 1994, and Susan Golding, elected mayor in 1992 and reelected with 78% in 1996. Her brand of governance—lower taxes, slimmer but more proactive government—has made her a strong and viable Senate candidate against Barbara Boxer in 1998, and did much to attract the Republican National Convention here in 1996. "If the the GOP wants to present itself as the party for the 21st Century," she said to National Journal's *Convention Daily* "there's no better city than San Diego. We are at the center of the Pacific Rim, and we target the fastest-growing markets in the world."

The congressman from the 49th is Brian Bilbray, a Republican who was born in Coronado and grew up on naval bases and in Imperial Beach. He owns a tax service business and was elected to the Imperial Beach Council in 1976, at 25, then mayor two years later, and to the San Diego County Board of Supervisors in 1984, where he worked for environmental protections and economic development. He made his first big splash in 1980 when he mounted a skiploader and built a berm to keep the sewage-polluted Tijuana River from seeping into San Diego County beaches. An experienced surfer, he made news again in 1984 when he paddled out on his surfboard to battle a fire raging on the city pier. In 1994 he ran for the House seat won two years earlier by Democrat Lynn Schenck. Schenk had a moderate voting record and had worked hard on the base closure issue and aiding high-tech businesses, but she voted for the 1993 Clinton budget and tax increase. Bilbray attacked her for that and supported the Contract with America, and won 49%–46%.

In the House Bilbray got a seat on the Commerce Committee and, as the only member living within sight of the Mexican border, worked on many immigration-related issues. He got the Republican budget to include funds for hospitals treating illegal immigrants; by 1996 a $3.5 billion trust fund was set up to reimburse states, including $1.6 billion for California. He also worked to get 1,400 new Border Patrol agents and $425 million to reimburse states for costs of incarcerating illegal immigrants. He backed reduced levels of legal immigration and a pilot program for an electronic verification system. On the first Corrections Day, in July 1995, he passed 269–156 a permanent waiver for San Diego of federal sewage treatment requirements; San Diego's output meets federal standards, but without the waiver it would have had to spend far more. He sponsored a bill to allow customs inspectors at the border to impose fines and seize vehicles for violations of emission standards or failure to meet California insurance requirements. He helped pass the California Cruise Ship Industry Revitalization bill, which allowed ships with gambling to stop in more than one California port; they had been skipping San Diego. He deleted the saccharine warning requirement on retailers (since the warnings are required on products) and called for prohibiting employment discrimination on any other basis than things pertaining to job performance.

This was naturally a Democratic target seat. Schenk waited until the last minute and then decided not to run; the Democratic nominee was Peter Navarro, who lost to Golding in 1992 and then lost races for City Council in 1993 and Board of Supervisors in 1994. (Two candidates ran for the Reform Party nomination; phone sex dominatrix Mistress Madison was beaten by Kevin Hambsch.) Navarro hit Bilbray for supporting Newt Gingrich on abortion, environmental regulations, Medicare and education funding. Bilbray lampooned Navarro for changing residence and party and running so many times and said he stood up to Gingrich on hospital funding and the assault weapons ban. He campaigned as "San Diego's independent voice for change" and his radio ads proclaimed "Brian has been there when we needed him." When Navarro was supported by Bill Clinton, Bilbray replied, "I'll match the support of Susan Golding with anyone in Washington." Unlike 1994, when he was outspent almost 2–1, Bilbray had a money advantage: $1.1 million to $450,000. Clinton carried the district 49%–40%, almost exactly his national average, but Bilbray won 53%–42%.

Bilbray says his goals for the 105th Congress include legal immigration reform, protecting

California's electric utility deregulation, restoring former funding levels for disproportionate share hospitals and starting up the International Wastewater Treatment plant at the border to end the health threat from Mexican sewage.

The People: Pop. 1990: 573,437; 12% age 65+; 75% White; 5% Black; 6% Asian; 1% Amer. Indian; 13% Hispanic origin. Households: 41% married couple families; 16% married couple fams. w. children; 67% college educ.; median household income: $32,562; per capita income: $19,184; median gross rent: $607; median house value: $224,200.

1996 Presidential Vote

Clinton (D)	110,920	(49%)
Dole (R)	91,478	(40%)
Perot (I)	15,084	(7%)
Other	9,514	(4%)

1992 Presidential Vote

Clinton (D)	114,081	(43%)
Bush (R)	82,834	(31%)
Perot (I)	65,856	(25%)

Rep. Brian P. Bilbray (R)

Elected 1994; b. Jan. 28, 1951, Coronado; home, San Diego; Southwestern Commun. Col., 1972; Catholic; married (Karen).

Career: Imperial Beach Council, 1976–78; Imperial Beach Mayor, 1978–85; San Diego Cnty. Supervisor, 1985–94; Tax consultant, 1972–present.

DC Office: 1530 LHOB 20515, 202-225-2040; Fax: 202-225-2948; e-mail: bilbray@hr.house.gov.

District Offices: San Diego, 619-291-1430.

Committees: *Commerce* (19th of 28 R): Finance & Hazardous Materials; Health & the Environment; Oversight & Investigations.

Group Ratings

	ADA	ACLU	AFS	LCV	CFA	CON	NFIB	COC	ACU	NTLC	CHC
1996	20	12	8	54	62	58	92	94	74	90	66
1995	15	—	—	6	31	85	—	96	72	—	—

National Journal Ratings

	1995 LIB — 1995 CONS			1996 LIB — 1996 CONS		
Economic	0%	—	74%	47%	—	53%
Social	47%	—	52%	52%	—	47%
Foreign	15%	—	73%	41%	—	59%

Key Votes of the 104th Congress

1. Reduce Medicare Growth $	Y	5. Flag Amendment	Y	9. Cuban Embargo	Y
2. Ovrd. Product Liab. Veto	Y	6. Drop EPA Limits	Y	10. Bar Bosnia Troop $	Y
3. Increase Min. Wage	Y	7. Repeal Assault-Weap. Ban	N	11. Cut Anti-Missile Defense	N
4. Welfare Reform	Y	8. Ovrd. Part. Birth Veto	Y	12. Bar U.N. Uniforms	Y

Election Results

1996 general	Brian P. Bilbray (R)	108,806	(53%)	($1,122,073)
	Peter Navarro (D)	86,657	(42%)	($450,424)
	Others	11,305	(5%)	
1996 primary	Brian P. Bilbray (R)	unopposed		
1994 general	Brian P. Bilbray (R)	90,283	(49%)	($750,654)
	Lynn Schenk (D)	85,597	(46%)	($1,392,948)
	Others	10,238	(6%)	

FIFTIETH DISTRICT

San Diego, at one corner of the continental United States, not so long ago a small Navy town known for its good harbor and splendid weather, is now a major metropolis, a city of 1.1 million people and the center of a metro area of 2.5 million. It is also, to its increasing discomfort, one of the largest cities anywhere directly on an international border and between countries with strikingly different economic conditions, political systems and cultural traditions. Not many other Americans think about it, but Mexican presidential candidate Luis Donaldo Colosio was murdered in March 1994 just a few blocks from the border in Tijuana.

This is, in fact, the busiest border crossing in the world, but most of San Diego seems to look away, toward the ocean. Tijuana, inland, looks to the United States, to the lower-income part of San Diego—the industrial zone on brown hills in Otay Mesa and San Ysidro, the industrial suburbs of Chula Vista and National City toward the bay and the grid streets south of downtown and behind the harbor in San Diego itself. Latinos are scattered in various parts of the city, in the southern corridor and in Encanto and Chollas Park in the east. Oddly, there is not much evidence of Mexican style in San Diego—less even than in Los Angeles, as if the border city was insisting on its Yanqui origins, just as San Diego's civic leaders bridle at the idea of a bi-national airport on the border. Even San Diego's favorite symbol, the red Tijuana Trolley that takes tourists from downtown to the San Ysidro-Tijuana border station, is as resolutely American as Main Street in Disneyland.

The 50th Congressional District—the first 50th district in the history of the House—covers the southern and eastern ends of San Diego and includes National City and Chula Vista down toward the border. The district was 41% Hispanic in 1990, and in partisan terms it is by far the most Democratic district in the San Diego area. Even so, districts in this general territory ousted incumbent Democratic congressmen in 1980 and again in 1990, both times electing Republicans who after the ensuing redistricting chose to run in more heavily Republican seats farther from the central city: Duncan Hunter, who now represents the 52d District, and Duke Cunningham, who represents the 51st.

The congressman from the 50th District is Bob Filner, a Democrat elected in 1992, the close winner of primaries that year and in 1996. Filner grew up in New York and was a Freedom Rider in 1961, imprisoned for two months in Mississippi. He earned a Ph.D. at Cornell and taught history at San Diego State and directed the Lipinsky Institute for Judaic Studies; he took time off to work on Senator Hubert Humphrey's staff in the 1970s and was elected to the San Diego school board in 1979 and to the city council in 1987. On the school board he worked for mandatory homework, tougher graduation requirements, stricter discipline and attendance regulations. He gave up the seat to run for council in 1983 and lost. But in 1987, when Councilman Uvaldo Martinez pleaded guilty to misusing credit cards, Filner ran again and won; in 1991 he won reelection 70%–26%, despite a heavy Latino majority. In the 1992 primary he had strong backing from blacks and Latinos although he had two better-known rivals. Filner won with 26%, to 23% for Waddie Deddeh, state senator and assemblyman since 1966, but 71 and recovering from heart surgery; 20% for Jim Bates, four-term congressman beaten in 1990 after being disciplined for sexual harassment; and 19% for Juan Carlos Vargas, returned to San Diego after training to be a Jesuit priest and then switching to Harvard Law School. In the general, Filner won 57%–29% over Republican Tony Valencia, who made pointed references to his religion before Latino audiences.

Filner is politically savvy, with some original ideas about policy, aggressive to the point of abrasiveness. He told the 1993 Democratic freshmen they should vote as a bloc for reform; they did not, and many lost, as Filner foresaw. He killed the proposed bi-national Otay Mesa Airport by cutting funds for planning. Filner won handily in 1994 and said "The shaking up of the system probably helped me more than hurt me." He worked with freshman Republican Brian Bilbray to get funding for the international sewage treatment center (taking too much of the credit Bilbray thought) and supported the permanent waiver Bilbray obtained from the sewage treatment standards. At the same time, Filner worked to get San Diego exempted from the Clean Water Act standards; that was accomplished by the Republican Congress in 1995. He crashed a Newt Gingrich press conference in Mission Valley to attack him on Medicare even as he conceded that the Republicans' $2.2 billion reimbursement of hospitals for treatment of illegal immigrants was "needed and appreciated." He was frustrated on his own proposal for a "Jobs Train" to reopen the now-defunct San Diego and Arizona Eastern Railroad, providing a connection between the port of San Diego and the East. He wanted only $490,000 so as to trigger a $7.9 million loan guarantee, but his proposal, supported also by Bilbray, lost 238–162 when the other three San Diego Republicans voted against it; it would dip into Mexico and, Duncan Hunter said, be a conduit for Mexican drug smugglers. Filner also raised some hackles when he challenged the $1 billion or so tax advantage enjoyed by mutual life insurance companies.

In the March 1996 primary Filner was challenged by Vargas, who had been elected to succeed him on the Council in 1993, where he made a name favoring graffiti removal and expansion of Jack Murphy Stadium. Vargas ran as a moderate and could expect support from many Latinos. Filner, with more money, ran some sharp ads against him, saying he was "anti-choice" and "supports extremists who threaten patients and doctors," accusing him of doing nothing to protect Medicare and cutting spending for sewage treatment and graffiti cleanup. He bragged of fighting Gingrich on Medicare and saving taxpayers $3 billion on sewage treatment. Vargas responded with an ad showing his wife praising his positive, door-to-door campaign ("a candidate who doesn't throw mud to win elections") and with him saying, "It's wrong to cut Medicare and veterans' benefits, and it's wrong to burn the American flag"—a reference to Filner's vote against the flag amendment. This was one of the closest primaries for an incumbent in 1996: Filner won, but by just 55%–45%.

Filner won 62%–32% in November and afterward started working on local issues, opposing the transfer of allegedly noisy helicopters from Orange County to Miramar Naval Air Station, saying they should go to March Air Force Base near Riverside instead, where congressmen would welcome them. Asked if he was interested in running to succeed term-limited Mayor Susan Golding, he responded with his own detailed economic plan for the city. Golding has announced her intention to run against Barbara Boxer in 1998, so a vacancy could occur before 2000. But it's also possible that there will be another tough primary contest in the 50th District again.

The People: Pop. 1990: 573,244; 1% rural; 8% age 65+; 32% White; 14% Black; 14% Asian; 41% Hispanic origin. Households: 54% married couple families; 30% married couple fams. w. children; 44% college educ.; median household income: $27,655; per capita income: $10,577; median gross rent: $540; median house value: $136,200.

1996 Presidential Vote

Clinton (D)	78,881	(60%)
Dole (R)	42,730	(32%)
Perot (I)	7,764	(6%)
Other	2,765	(2%)

1992 Presidential Vote

Clinton (D)	69,546	(48%)
Bush (R)	42,830	(30%)
Perot (I)	30,267	(21%)

Rep. Bob Filner (D)

Elected 1992; b. Sept. 4, 1942, Pittsburgh, PA; home, San Diego; Cornell U., B.A. 1963, U. of DE, M.A. 1969, Cornell U., Ph.D. 1973; Jewish; married (Jane).

Career: Prof., San Diego St. U., 1970–92; Legis. Asst., U.S. Sen. Hubert Humphrey, 1974; Legis. Asst., U.S. Rep. Don Fraser, 1975; San Diego Schl. Bd., 1979–83, Pres., 1982–83; San Diego City Cncl., 1987–92, Dpty. Mayor, 1990.

DC Office: 330 CHOB 20515, 202-225-8045; Fax: 202-225-9073.

District Offices: Chula Vista, 619-422-5963.

Committees: *Transportation & Infrastructure* (19th of 33 D): Railroads; Surface Transportation. *Veterans' Affairs* (3rd of 13 D): Benefits (RMM).

Group Ratings

	ADA	ACLU	AFS	LCV	CFA	CON	NFIB	COC	ACU	NTLC	CHC
1996	90	93	100	85	77	38	19	29	0	5	7
1995	80	—	—	88	100	13	—	17	9	—	—

National Journal Ratings

	1995 LIB		1995 CONS	1996 LIB		1996 CONS
Economic	94%	—	0%	78%	—	21%
Social	88%	—	0%	84%	—	12%
Foreign	88%	—	7%	87%	—	10%

Key Votes of the 104th Congress

1. Reduce Medicare Growth $	N	5. Flag Amendment	N	9. Cuban Embargo	N
2. Ovrd. Product Liab. Veto	N	6. Drop EPA Limits	Y	10. Bar Bosnia Troop $	N
3. Increase Min. Wage	Y	7. Repeal Assault-Weap. Ban	N	11. Cut Anti-Missile Defense	Y
4. Welfare Reform	N	8. Ovrd. Part. Birth Veto	N	12. Bar U.N. Uniforms	N

Election Results

1996 general	Bob Filner (D)	73,200	(62%)	($1,142,370)
	Jim Baize (R)	38,351	(32%)	($120,562)
	Others	6,789	(6%)	
1996 primary	Bob Filner (D)	18,809	(55%)	
	Juan Vargas (D)	15,673	(45%)	
1994 general	Bob Filner (D)	59,214	(57%)	($818,051)
	Mary Alice Acevedo (R)	36,955	(35%)	($352,091)
	Others	8,282	(8%)	

FIFTY-FIRST DISTRICT

When FBI director J. Edgar Hoover came to the races at Del Mar for two weeks every summer in the 1940s and 1950s, the rest of north San Diego County, from the track north to the Marine Corps's Camp Pendleton, was mostly uninhabited: there were a few thousand people in the beach towns of Oceanside and Carlsbad and a few thousand more scattered over the dry, brownish hills that rolled inland. Today about 650,000 people live in North County, and who can blame them? For this is one of America's most beautiful and comfortable environments, with ocean and mountain scenery, sunny and warm weather, no rural poverty and low crime. Here, amid dry but not desert landscape, you can see miles of rolling hills, with occasional surrealistic trees and sagebrush-like bushes; mountains clump up not in ridges, but here and there, seemingly at random. This land has attracted thousands of new migrants, many, but by no means all, retirees. Outside the Los Angeles media market, not frequented by many entertainment celebrities, North County does not have a high media profile, which probably suits the quietly successful people who have moved here just fine.

The 51st Congressional District covers much of North County. It includes some 200,000 people in San Diego itself—not in its urbanized core, but in land it annexed during Governor Pete Wilson's long tenure as mayor, including the Rancho Bernardo planned community and Miramar Naval Air Station, whose Navy fliers were made famous in *Top Gun* and infamous in the Tailhook scandal. It also includes Rancho Sante Fe where 39 members of the Heaven's Gate cult—under the direction of New Age philosophist Marshall Applewhite—committed mass suicide in March 1997, apparently in an attempt to hitch a ride on the "spaceship" trailing Comet Hale-Bopp. The 51st takes in the beach communities from Del Mar north to Carlsbad and the nearby La Costa resort. Inland, with its red-tile roofs filling a sunny valley and its splendid arts center, is fast-growing Escondido, with 108,000 people in 1990. Politically, this is overwhelmingly Republican territory, though with a taste for Ross Perot in 1992; rather conservative on cultural issues, against bigger government, patriotic and nationalistic on foreign policy.

The congressman from the 51st is Randy (Duke) Cunningham, a Republican elected in 1990. Born the day after Pearl Harbor, he taught and coached swimming in Hinsdale, Illinois, and San Diego; in 1966, at 25, he joined the Navy and became one of the most decorated pilots in the Vietnam war. He then trained pilots at Miramar in the Top Gun program; he retired from the Navy in 1987 and started a business in San Diego. In 1990 he ran in a Democratic district against Democratic Congressman Jim Bates, who was charged with sexual harassment; Cunningham beat a former ambassador to Qatar in the Republican primary 46%–30%, and in the general beat Bates 46%–45%. In 1992, faced with a choice of districts to run in, he passed up the marginal and culturally more liberal 49th on the coast and ran in the 51st in North County. Incumbent Bill Lowery, a Republican who had 300 overdrafts at the House bank, withdrew from the race in April 1992, and Cunningham won the primary and general by wide margins.

Cunningham was immediately assigned two committees reflecting both his professional experience and local concerns: National Security and Merchant Marine and Fisheries. He arrived just time for the Gulf war debate and in his first years worked to make Filipino Gulf war veterans eligible to apply for U.S. citizenship and to prevent base closings in the San Diego area. He voted for the North American Free Trade Agreement. He was one of four congressmen who in October 1992 met with George Bush and prompted him to ask questions about Bill Clinton's student trip to Moscow and Eastern Europe, an issue that hurt the Republican ticket. In 1995 he sought to repeal the dolphin-safe tuna act, since NAFTA and GATT outlaw the embargo on foreign tuna and new nets have reduced the dolphin kill to 1% of what it was in 1972. He cautioned that U.S. air strikes in Bosnia were a dangerous business.

With Republican control, Cunningham moved to the Education and the Workforce Committee and became chairman of the Early Childhood, Youth and Families Subcommittee. He sought more freedom for states to experiment and less federal regulation; at the prompting of his wife, a principal in the Encinitas Union School District, he emphasized equipping schools with high-tech capacity; he sought money for high-tech equipment also for libraries and museums. On welfare reform, he sought to give states control of the school lunch program, but was rebuffed by Senator Richard Lugar's insistence on federal control. Cunningham was the lead sponsor of the English-as-official-language bill passed by the House in August 1996. "We must take this defining step to avoid our nation becoming divided into many ethnic enclaves." He has pressed for stricter enforcement of immigration laws and criticized the Operation Gatekeeper program of the INS and San Diego U.S. Attorney Alan Bersin. He sponsored a "no frills prison act." Cunningham has a gift for pungent comments; at one National Security hearing, he said, "I do not believe they [troops] can be well led when they have a commander-in-chief who has turned his back on them." After he said Jim Moran "switched his vote and turned his back on Desert Storm," Moran pushed him in the hall, then apologized. Cunningham opposed incarcerating illegal immigrants at Miramar in March 1996 and in September 1996 opposed stationing helicopters there, saying they would be too noisy and would be better off at March Air Force Base near Riverside, whose local congressmen wanted them.

Cunningham has been reelected easily since 1992. In 1997 he switched to the Appropriations Committee, and promised to continue to push English-as-official-language and a Sunset Act that would repeal every government program in five years unless reauthorized. He has sponsored a Community Protection Act to allow current and former law enforcement officers to carry concealed weapons in any jurisdiction. In January 1997 his 27-year-old son was arrested and charged with flying a plane to Boston with 400 pounds of marijuana. He said, "As a parent this is the most anguishing thing that can happen to you. We love him. If the charges are true, we are disappointed, and he must face his responsibilities."

The People: Pop. 1990: 572,850; 3% rural; 11% age 65+; 76% White; 2% Black; 8% Asian; 14% Hispanic origin. Households: 61% married couple families; 28% married couple fams. w. children; 68% college educ.; median household income: $45,186; per capita income: $20,586; median gross rent: $730; median house value: $230,200.

1996 Presidential Vote

Dole (R)	130,459	(52%)
Clinton (D)	97,128	(38%)
Perot (I)	16,963	(7%)
Other	7,918	(3%)

1992 Presidential Vote

Bush (R)	108,470	(40%)
Clinton (D)	86,870	(32%)
Perot (I)	73,580	(27%)

Rep. Randy (Duke) **Cunningham (R)**

Elected 1990; b. Dec. 8, 1941, Los Angeles; home, San Diego; U. of MO, B.A. 1964, M.S. 1966, National U., M.B.A. 1979; Baptist; married (Nancy).

Career: Navy, 1966–87 (Vietnam); Businessman, 1987–90.

DC Office: 2238 RHOB 20515, 202-225-5452; Fax: 202-225-2558.

District Offices: Escondido, 619-737-8438.

Committees: *Appropriations* (29th of 34 R): District of Columbia; Legislative; National Security.

Group Ratings

	ADA	ACLU	AFS	LCV	CFA	CON	NFIB	COC	ACU	NTLC	CHC
1996	10	6	0	15	31	71	97	81	100	100	100
1995	0	—	—	6	8	38	—	100	92	—	—

National Journal Ratings

	1995 LIB — 1995 CONS			1996 LIB — 1996 CONS		
Economic	33%	—	67%	0%	—	82%
Social	32%	—	68%	0%	—	90%
Foreign	28%	—	65%	0%	—	79%

Key Votes of the 104th Congress

1. Reduce Medicare Growth $	Y	5. Flag Amendment	Y	9. Cuban Embargo	Y
2. Ovrd. Product Liab. Veto	Y	6. Drop EPA Limits	Y	10. Bar Bosnia Troop $	Y
3. Increase Min. Wage	N	7. Repeal Assault-Weap. Ban	*	11. Cut Anti-Missile Defense	N
4. Welfare Reform	Y	8. Ovrd. Part. Birth Veto	Y	12. Bar U.N. Uniforms	Y

Election Results

1996 general	Randy (Duke) Cunningham (R)	149,032	(65%)	($425,525)
	Rita Tamerius (D)	66,250	(29%)	($19,935)
	Others	13,742	(6%)	
1996 primary	Randy (Duke) Cunningham (R)	65,268	(86%)	
	Donald J. Pando (R)	10,502	(14%)	
1994 general	Randy (Duke) Cunningham (R)	138,547	(67%)	($395,144)
	Rita Tamerius (D)	57,374	(28%)	($65,035)
	Others	11,067	(5%)	

FIFTY-SECOND DISTRICT

San Diego began as a port, but today most metropolitan area residents live out of sight of the sea, in hilltop neighborhoods inland that look out over distant ridges and freeways or in warm, sunny valleys amid the mountains which become denser and higher as one travels east from the Pacific. There is a discernible difference in attitudes and values between those who have settled inland and those nearer the ocean, part of the coastal-inland split which became critical in California's political struggles and culture wars since the 1980s. In San Diego, both groups tend to identify as Republicans, and coastal people may be more affluent. But those who settle inland are more likely to be conventionally religious and to have traditional moral values; they tend to be more supportive of the military and of an assertive foreign policy; they are more dubious about the ability of government to shape poor citizens' lives. They are more conservative on most of the cultural and foreign issues of recent times, and therefore more reliably Republican: when oceanfront voters in San Diego shifted sharply toward Democrats in 1992, those in inland suburbs shifted morc to Ross Perot but stayed Republican in other races.

The 52d Congressional District—the highest-numbered House district in American history—takes in many of the inland San Diego suburbs and proceeds eastward across mountains and desert and the man-made Salton Sea to the drained-dry Colorado River on the Arizona border. More than half its people are clustered in suburbs directly east of San Diego, off I-8 and Routes 94 and 67: Lemon Grove, La Mesa, Spring Valley, El Cajon, Santee. The rest are scattered in pockets around rural San Diego County and in the Imperial Valley, irrigated desert land where low-paid farm workers harvest some of America's most bounteous crops.

The congressman from the 52d is Duncan Hunter, who came to the House in 1980 as an upset winner in the Reagan landslide and now is the leader of a strain of Republicanism which is not represented in large numbers in the House but which Hunter thinks has greater support among ordinary voters. Hunter served in the Army in Vietnam, in helicopter combat assaults, and was an antipoverty lawyer afterwards. In 1980, at 32, he beat an incumbent Democrat and came to the House brash and confident he had the right answers. In the 1980s he was part of the group of young conservative Republicans around Newt Gingrich. On the National Security Committee, he was an ardent backer of the Strategic Defense Initiative and of the buildup of the Navy. He worked to block relaxation of export controls on high-tech products. He called for greater willingness to receive Vietnamese refugees and worked for U.S. citizenship for the 4,000 Filipinos who served with U.S. forces in the Persian Gulf. But as the 1980s wore on into the 1990s, he developed on his own a politics very much like Patrick Buchanan's. He has continued to work for higher defense expenditures on particular programs. But he has strongly opposed free trade measures. And, representing a district with hundreds of miles of the Mexican border, he has prosecuted a crusade for more fences and barriers along the border.

On National Security he remains in line with the Republican leadership. He is a strong backer of Republican proposals to keep U.S. troops out from under U.N. command. He led the fight for more missile defense spending than the Clinton Administration wanted but was beaten in February 1995—the first Contract With America item that failed to win a majority. As chairman of the Subcommittee on Military Procurement, he called for accelerated development of the F-22 because of its stealth capabilities even though the F-15 has a long shelf life; he notes that the F-117s that Congress provided over the Pentagon's objections worked well in the Gulf war. He supported building 20 more B-2s, but also has tried to push the Pentagon to change its requirements so that it can build more nuclear submarines and match apparent Russian gains in quiet technology.

Hunter's most open break with the Republican leadership came in the debate over NAFTA, of which he was one of the most ardent opponents. He decried Mexican abuses of human rights and in 1996 said that NAFTA cost the United States 250,000 jobs. He also vociferously opposed GATT in 1994 and the Mexico bailout in 1995. "We're engaged in what I call dumb trade." When the World Trade Organization in January 1996 ruled that U.S. clean air regulations on gasoline discriminate against gasoline imports, he demanded withdrawal from the organization. In October 1995 he warned that he would vote against the Republican budget unless fast track authority for extending NAFTA to Chile was removed; it was.

In the early 1990s Hunter called for a 10-foot steel wall to replace the chain link fence between San Diego and Tijuana, and worked to use military personnel to repair border fences and improve border roads. And he enacted a "return-to-sender" system to intercept sewage flows from across the border in Tijuana and return them to Mexico before sewage can enter the Tijuana River and pollute San Diego beaches. More recently, he has pushed for a three-layer fence, with barriers 30 feet apart, along the border. The House version of the 1996 immigration bill included $12 million for the triple fence, but the INS resisted the proposal and Dianne Feinstein made it optional in the Senate version; Hunter's view prevailed. Hunter noted that the INS had also resisted his proposal for 14 miles of single fence, but that agents became enthusiastic for it when they saw that it forced border crossers into chokepoints where they could easily be apprehended. Under pressure from Hunter, the Border Patrol agreed in July 1996 to build a compromise barrier with a third layer of fence along two miles of the Tijuana River in San Ysidro, whose crossing Hunter has called a "cocaine freeway." Border concerns also prompted Hunter's opposition to funds to secure a federal loan guarantee to rebuild the San Diego & Arizona Eastern Railroad. San Diego Democrat Bob Filner argued that it would provide the port of San Diego with a direct connection to an east-west railroad. But Hunter noted that the railroad dips into Mexico and said it would attract Mexican bandits, border crossers and cocaine smugglers, and the proposal lost 238–162 in June 1996.

Hunter has usually been reelected without difficulty. In 1992 he was troubled by 399 overdrafts on the House bank totalling $129,000, and for three days set up a card table in front of the El Cajon courthouse with copies of his checks, ready to explain each one to any voter. He was reelected with a closer than usual 53%–41%. In 1994 and 1996 he won by better than 2–1.

The People: Pop. 1990: 573,355; 11% rural; 11% age 65+; 71% White; 3% Black; 3% Asian; 1% Amer. Indian; 23% Hispanic origin. Households: 58% married couple families; 29% married couple fams. w. children; 52% college educ.; median household income: $33,046; per capita income: $14,075; median gross rent: $566; median house value: $155,100.

1996 Presidential Vote

Dole (R)	94,035	(48%)
Clinton (D)	81,401	(41%)
Perot (I)	16,657	(8%)
Other	5,531	(3%)

1992 Presidential Vote

Bush (R)	81,421	(37%)
Clinton (D)	74,913	(34%)
Perot (I)	63,176	(29%)

Rep. Duncan Hunter (R)

Elected 1980; b. May 31, 1948, Riverside; home, Alpine; U. of MT, U. of CA, Western St. U., B.S.L & J.D. 1976; Baptist; married (Lynne).

Career: Army, 1969–71 (Vietnam); Practicing atty., 1976–80.

DC Office: 2265 RHOB 20515, 202-225-5672; Fax: 202-225-0235.

District Offices: El Cajon, 619-579-3001; Imperial, 619-353-5420.

Committees: *National Security* (3rd of 30 R): Military Procurement (Chmn.); Military Readiness.

Group Ratings

	ADA	ACLU	AFS	LCV	CFA	CON	NFIB	COC	ACU	NTLC	CHC
1996	10	0	0	15	0	17	88	94	100	97	93
1995	0	—	—	6	0	25	—	91	88	—	—

National Journal Ratings

	1995 LIB		1995 CONS	1996 LIB		1996 CONS
Economic	0%	—	74%	20%	—	76%
Social	28%	—	70%	14%	—	77%
Foreign	0%	—	85%	0%	—	79%

Key Votes of the 104th Congress

1. Reduce Medicare Growth $	Y	5. Flag Amendment	Y	9. Cuban Embargo	Y
2. Ovrd. Product Liab. Veto	Y	6. Drop EPA Limits	*	10. Bar Bosnia Troop $	Y
3. Increase Min. Wage	N	7. Repeal Assault-Weap. Ban	Y	11. Cut Anti-Missile Defense	N
4. Welfare Reform	Y	8. Ovrd. Part. Birth Veto	Y	12. Bar U.N. Uniforms	Y

Election Results

1996 general	Duncan Hunter (R)	116,746	(65%)	($632,305)
	Darity Wesley (D)	53,104	(30%)	($40,178)
	Others	8,471	(5%)	
1996 primary	Duncan Hunter (R)	unopposed		
1994 general	Duncan Hunter (R)	109,201	(64%)	($559,926)
	Janet M. Gastil (D)	53,024	(31%)	($181,855)
	Others	8,461	(5%)	

COLORADO

Colorado, at the Front Range of the Rocky Mountains and at the front edge often of cultural change, can claim to be the typical American state, but in so many ways is atypical. Colorado is far away from just about any other population center, an island of nearly 4 million people surrounded by the sea of the Great Plains and the ramparts of the Rockies. With vistas of vast emptiness, it is mostly an urban state: more than half its people live in metropolitan Denver and four-fifths in the urban strip paralleling the Front Range, where the Rockies rise suddenly from the mile-high plateau. And despite the sturdiness of its peaks and the sublimity of its plains, as a society it has been subjected to bouts of unsettling change—indeed, may be in the midst of one today.

Colorado started off with a boom, with the discovery of gold and silver in the crevasses of the Rockies. Evidence of this mining boom can be seen still in the opera houses and storefronts of Cripple Creek and Central City, Aspen and Telluride, built when Denver was just a village on the creek that is the South Platte River. Then Denver grew, as a meatpacking, banking and manufacturing center, and also as the state capital and regional headquarters of the federal government: growth that is evident in the orderly neighborhoods and lush trees and pleasant parks of older Denver neighborhoods. Then came the booms of the 1960s and the high-energy-priced 1970s, when the Denver skyline sprouted new buildings overlooking the Capitol's golden dome and sports entrepreneurs built ever more ski resorts and year-round mountain condominiums. Young people looking for a splendid environment settled where the Front Range of the Rockies rears dramatically up over the High Plains; for them Colorado "represented the geography of hope," as then-newcomer Dick Lamm said (he went on to be elected governor three times).

These Denver liberals, who included Lamm, Gary Hart, Patricia Schroeder, Tim Wirth—none of them natives of Colorado—set the tone for Colorado civic life and political struggles for most of two decades. They took prosperity for granted, opposed the war in Vietnam and looked askance at American power abroad, wanted to preserve the environment and set limits on development. Their first success came in 1972, when they persuaded voters to reject the 1976 Winter Olympics; in quick succession Schroeder and Wirth were elected to Congress, Lamm was elected governor and Hart senator, and Democrats won the legislature. Republicans surged back to take the legislature in 1976 (they have held it ever since) and to retain an open Senate seat in 1978, as Colorado partook thirstily of the gushings of the energy boom of 1974–82.

It was a time of business success and excess: Denver was the base of several billionaires and also of the now infamous Silverado Savings and Loan; the environment was cleaned up in many ways, but Denver tends to have bad air quality ("brown cloud") and the government's plutonium plant at Rocky Flats just north of Denver was shut down in 1989 for safety violations. The original Denver liberals gave way to other Democrats who worked in cooperation with the private sector—Roy Romer, elected governor in 1986 and reelected to serve until 1998, and former Denver Mayor Federico Pena (now secretary of Energy), who promoted a new convention center, Coors Field baseball stadium, and the giant Denver International Airport 25 miles from downtown.

Airports can serve as a metaphor for Colorado's course in the 1990s. Up through the 1980s the state's prime airport was Stapleton, named after the man who brought Western Slope water over the mountains to thirsty Denver, a typical product of the combination of business leaders and government operators who ran Colorado until the Denver liberals came along. It was one of the nation's busiest airports, and most convenient, a mere five miles from downtown. But the Denver Democrats, notably Pena, thought they could do better. Using projections from a few years

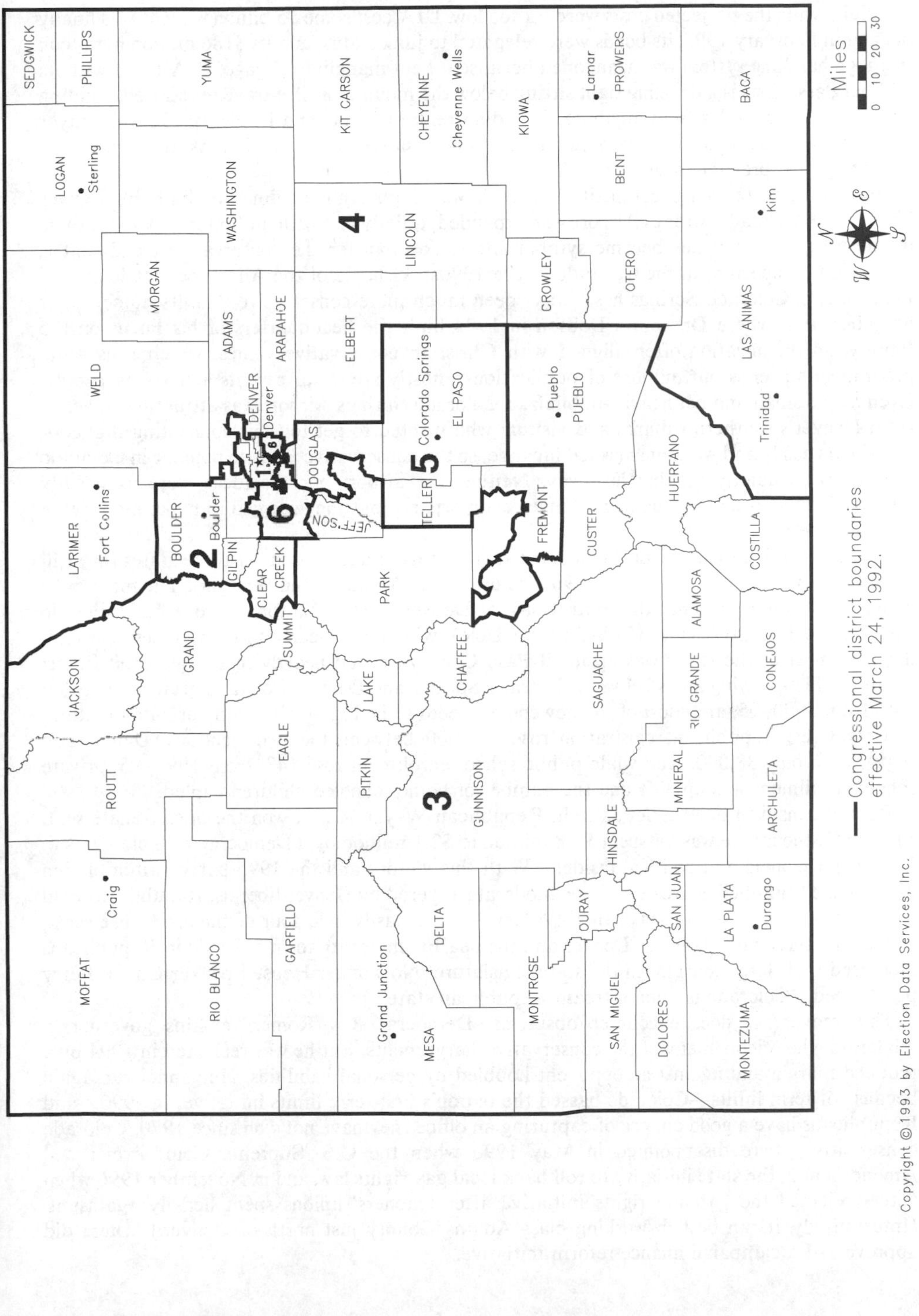
SEDGWICK
PHILLIPS
YUMA
KIT CARSON
CHEYENNE
Cheyenne Wells
KIOWA
Lamar
PROWERS
BACA
Miles
0 10 20 30
LOGAN
Sterling
WASHINGTON
4
LINCOLN
BENT
Kim
MORGAN
CROWLEY
OTERO
ADAMS
ARAPAHOE
ELBERT
LAS ANIMAS
WELD
DENVER
Denver
DOUGLAS
Colorado Springs
EL PASO
Pueblo
PUEBLO
Trinidad
1
5
HUERFANO
LARIMER
Fort Collins
BOULDER
Boulder
6
JEFF'SON
TELLER
FREMONT
CUSTER
COSTILLA
2
GILPIN
CLEAR CREEK
PARK
ALAMOSA
JACKSON
GRAND
SUMMIT
LAKE
CHAFFEE
SAGUACHE
RIO GRANDE
CONEJOS
EAGLE
PITKIN
GUNNISON
MINERAL
ROUTT
3
HINSDALE
ARCHULETA
MOFFAT
Craig
RIO BLANCO
GARFIELD
DELTA
OURAY
SAN JUAN
LA PLATA
Durango
Grand Junction
MESA
MONTROSE
SAN MIGUEL
DOLORES
MONTEZUMA
Congressional district boundaries effective March 24, 1992.
Copyright © 1993 by Election Data Services, Inc.

when both United and Frontier operated hubs here, they proclaimed that Stapleton could not handle future traffic and persuaded voters in 1990 to build DIA at a predicted cost of $1.7 billion. But after United and Frontier merged, the projections for future traffic proved to be way too high, while the projected costs were far too low. DIA cost some $5 billion when it was finally opened in February 1995, its bonds were relegated to junk status, and its $186 million high-tech baggage handling system was abandoned because it kept mangling luggage. DIA's roof with its 34 fiberglass masts is a dazzling sight sitting below the mountains. But travelers started avoiding it because it was miles from anything, including rental car lots and hotels. As Denver Mayor Wellington Webb said, with perhaps unintentional understatement, "I think the age of the megaproject is probably over."

Into the gap stepped a competitor. If DIA was a government dinosaur built by Denver liberals, the Colorado Springs Airport was expanded, quietly and without fanfare, by the fathers of the same city that has become symbol and spokesman for the conservative trend that is increasingly important in the Colorado of the 1990s. As home of the Air Force Academy and Fort Carson, Colorado Springs has always been much more conservative than its much larger neighbor. It is where Dr. James Dobson in 1994 built the headquarters of his Focus on the Family, an organization often aligned with Christian conservative values, which runs radio programs and sends out millions of publications, mostly advice to parents and young people. Even as the small and not heavily-publicized Colorado Springs Airport was attracting travelers from Denver's southern suburbs and visitors who wanted to get to their connecting flights or rental cars easily and without smashed luggage, so the conservative ideas so popular in Colorado Springs were quietly making headway. Neither the airport nor the ideas were as heavily publicized or as prominent as their Denver counterparts, but they seemed to make more sense and produce better results.

The most visible evidence of this was the fact that Colorado was one of three states that Bill Clinton carried in 1992 and lost in 1996 (the others are Montana and Georgia). The metropolis which set the tone was not the central city of Denver (62%–30% for Clinton) but Colorado Springs and El Paso County (59%–32% for Dole), which cast nearly as many votes. Turnout, down in most of the state, was up in El Paso County and up heavily in Douglas and Elbert Counties, fast-growing areas between Colorado Springs and Denver. Colorado grew robustly, up 14% from 1990–95, and most of the newcomers seem to be high-tech, family-oriented cultural conservatives: Republican registration rose 156,000 between the two elections, Democratic registration only 38,000. And while public school enrollment rose 14% from 1990–95, private school enrollment was up 33% and the number of home-schooled children tripled.

Republicans won downballot as well. Republican Wayne Allard won the open Senate seat, 51%–46%, though he was outspent $2.8 million to $2.1 million by a Democrat with close ties to Denver developers and political insiders. With this victory and the 1995 party switch of Ben Nighthorse Campbell, a Western Slope moderate angered by Denver liberals, Republicans hold both of Colorado's Senate seats. In 1996 Republicans easily held four of the six House seats, losing only those dominated by Denver and the nearby university town of Boulder. Republicans increased their large margins in the state legislature. No wonder House Speaker Chuck Berry proclaimed, "Colorado is a mainstream Republican state."

This movement does encounter obstacles. Democrat Roy Romer remains governor, a moderate who rejects many of the conservatives' arguments. But he was reelected in 1994 by a reduced margin and against an opponent hobbled by personal liabilities. He cannot run again because of term limits—Colorado passed the nation's first term limits initiative, in 1990—and Republicans have a good chance of capturing an office they have not won since 1970. Colorado conservatives were disappointed in May 1996 when the U.S. Supreme Court overturned Amendment 2, the state initiative to roll back local gay rights law, and in November 1996 when voters rejected the parental rights initiative after teachers' unions spent heavily against it. (Interestingly, it ran best in working class Adams County just north of Denver.) Voters did approve 2–1 a campaign finance reform initiative.

It is not clear what is ahead for Colorado. Its growth may slow since big construction projects like DIA, Coors Field, and the Colorado Springs Airport are finished. Its political pendulum may stop swinging; in 1997 both the Democratic and Republican National Committees chose Coloradans to head their parties—Democrat Roy Romer and Republican Jim Nicholson. But increasingly Colorado voters, especially newcomers to the state, seem to be looking to Colorado Springs, not Denver, for leadership. Voter approval is now required for tax increases, thanks to a 1992 initiative, and voters have turned down those put before them. This was one of Ross Perot's best states in 1992: he was leading in Colorado polls when he left the race July 16 and he won 23% here in November. But he got only 7% in 1996, and most of his old voters went to Bob Dole. As Colorado continues to grow and attracts yet another generation of newcomers, the reverence for the environment and insouciance toward traditional values and market economics of the Denver liberals seems to be on the way out.

Governor. Governor Roy Romer is one of the nation's oldest and politically most experienced governors, but he remains refreshingly brusque, forceful, energetic, a man of impressive capacity and force of character. He grew up in a small town four miles from the Kansas border, built a chain of construction equipment stores and went into politics early on. He was elected to the legislature in 1958 and, as an opponent of the Vietnam war, ran for and lost a Senate seat against Republican Gordon Allott in 1966. In 1975 he became chief of staff to Governor Dick Lamm, who was younger and skeptical of growth. In 1976 Romer was elected state treasurer and in 1986 won his first term as governor. Unlike some Democrats, Romer does not see economic growth solely as a menace to the environment. He has sought foreign investment and was a big booster of the troubled Denver International Airport.

Despite a lifetime in state and national politics, Romer increasingly seems to see solutions in community and individual action. He is a member and former chairman of the National Education Goals Panel, a bipartisan body set up between President Bush and the governors (led by Bill Clinton) as a result of a 1989 education summit, and has called for higher standards. But he says, "There is no way we can be assured of progress toward reaching the goals until states and communities develop and use rigorous standards." Back in 1992 Romer sought voter approval of an education tax; they rejected that and passed a measure instead requiring voter approval of future tax increases. In response Romer has sought reforms which don't require additional taxes; for example, he backs charter schools. And the thrust towards local control continues: he sought $22 million for K-12 schools, with a teacher training program required; he applauded the legislature for increasing school funding by 3%. He worked on the "virtual university" project with Utah Governor Mike Leavitt to provide alternative higher education access in remote areas.

Romer's biggest priority recently has been his "Bright Beginnings" childcare plan, launched in 1995, community-based and run by volunteers; it targets new and teen parents and seeks to improve child health care. To help this effort, Romer got the legislature in 1996 to pass a childcare tax credit and a voluntary checkoff on state income tax forms to allocate a portion of taxes to childcare facility improvement. He also convened a Task Force on Responsible Fatherhood. His second biggest priority was transportation. He launched a "smart growth development" initiative and asked for $100 million; the legislature granted $158 million for projects. Romer has also been tough on crime, signing a bill over Democrats' protests to allow children as young as 12 to be tried as adults. He wants to direct all welfare recipients into jobs or training by mid-1997.

Romer won reelection in 1994 over businessman Bruce Benson. The incumbent was trailing in polls, when it was revealed that Benson had previous drunk driving arrests and had made threats against his former wife; also, in October Romer's car was mysteriously chased at over 100 mph on I-25 until a policeman finally shook the pursuer. Romer won 55%–39%. Term limits prevent him from running in 1998, but the demands of the governorship and his appointment by Clinton in January 1997 to chair the Democratic National Committee will keep him busy nonetheless. Romer inherits a public relations nightmare in trying to restore the DNC's tarnished image from charges of receiving illegal contributions from foreign sources. Among those mentioned as possible gubernatorial candidates are three top state legislators: Republican Speaker Chuck Berry and Senate President Tom Norton and Democrat Senate Minority Leader Mike Feeley.

Senior Senator. Ben Nighthorse Campbell is the only Native American Indian in the Senate—only the eighth to serve in Congress, and a former Democrat who switched to the Republican Party in March 1995. He is a distinctive figure, with his bolo ties and his pony tail, riding a motorcycle as he did in a parade at the 1996 Republican National Convention, or riding a horse wearing full Indian headdress as he did at the 1993 Presidential Inaugural Parade. Campbell had a rough early life; he was placed in an orphanage, dropped out of high school, joined the Air Force and served in Korea. He studied judo for four years in Japan and was captain of the 1964 U.S. Olympic judo team and carried the American flag in the opening ceremonies. He settled not in one of the trendy "granola belt" ski resorts but in the small town of Ignacio, on the plain below Durango, near the New Mexican border, where he bred horses and built a successful jewelry-making business. He is a member of the Northern Cheyenne tribe and attends tribal ceremonies every year in Montana. He got into politics serendipitously. One day in 1982 his plane was grounded and he attended a Democratic Party meeting for a friend being nominated for sheriff; Campbell spoke briefly and was soon drafted to run for the legislature. He spent $13,000 of his own money and won. Four years later he ran for Congress and beat a Republican incumbent who had personal financial problems. In the House he had a moderate record, showing more interest in economic growth than in preserving the environment. When Tim Wirth surprised just about everyone by announcing his retirement from the Senate in 1992, Campbell plunged into the race.

Campbell had to beat two tough Denver-based candidates. First was Dick Lamm, Ross Perot's competitor for the Reform Party nomination in 1996 but then known as a three-term governor and sponsor of one of the first legalized abortion laws, proponent of zero population growth and immigration restrictions and a believer that the terminally ill have "a duty to die" rather than undergo elaborate medical treatment. They ran just about even in the Democratic state convention, packed with liberal activists. In the primary Campbell, with backing from the Western Slope and other non-upscale areas, had 46%, while Lamm, carrying Denver, its affluent suburbs, and the "granola belt," had 36%; 1990 nominee Josie Heath won 18%. In the general election Campbell faced entrepreneur Terry Considine, a former state senator who started the national term limits campaign. Campbell was put on the defensive by charges he'd accepted an oil company's plane ride to Alaska and stated falsely that he was trapped behind enemy lines for five weeks in Korea. In the weeks before his election, Campbell kept with him a ceremonial eagle feather tuft and Northern Cheyennes held a series of ritual ceremonies and prayer meetings on his behalf. Campbell benefited from Bill Clinton's victory in Colorado, from the endorsement of the active Colorado Perot organization and from the fact that he backed some of Considine's conservative reforms, notably term limits and the balanced budget amendment. Campbell won 52%–43%.

Campbell started his Senate career by taking up Indian causes, passing a law for labelling Indian crafts and getting the Custer Battlefield Monument renamed as Little Bighorn. He criticized Clinton environmental policies and had his own version of grazing fee reform and Mining Act revision. In Colorado he pushed for the Animas-LaPlata water project (in his local area) to fulfill an Indian treaty, and sought to open the Naval Oil Shale Reserves for drilling—all projects opposed by environmentalists. But the most startling thing he did was to switch parties. He acted the day after the balanced budget amendment failed in the Senate by one vote, and expressed irritation with the Denver liberals he had so often opposed in Colorado and Washington. Their environmental stands may have irked him, and so may their reformism: he was upset when he was denied an exemption from congressional income limits on his jewelry making, even though book royalties and investment income is exempted. As he explained at the convention in San Diego, "I apologize for being a slow learner. I have to tell you, I should have changed years ago. The Democratic Party has become a party of special interests, not the people's interests," while Republicans are "the party that will protect private property rights and your right to use the public lands."

As a Republican, he has had some legislative successes—$9 million for Animas-LaPlata, for example, and a study on Naval Oil Shale Reserves drilling. He got a seat on Appropriations in October 1995, when Phil Gramm rotated off. Some of his stands dissent from his new party's positions. As a Democrat he was a key sponsor of midnight basketball in the crime program; he wants troubled kids to have a second chance as he did. And he was one of three Republicans to vote against nuclear waste storage in Nevada and for adding $6 billion for child care to the 1996 welfare bill. But he has a strong conservative record on foreign and defense issues, and supports such conservative causes as the flag-burning amendment and the partial birth abortion ban (he switched after voting against). With Maine's Olympia Snowe he sponsored a repeal of the federal law penalizing states without mandatory motorcycle helmet laws.

Campbell is a distinctly visible senator, and not just on his motorcycle. He appeared in ads for Banana Republic and, using his judo training, wrestled down a man who attacked a Capitol Police officer. In the 105th Congress, after Slade Gorton and other more senior senators waived seniority, he became chairman of the Indian Affairs Committee; it is not clear if this independent-minded Indian will be as independent of professional Indian lobbyists as he is of almost everyone else. He also chairs the Appropriations subcommittee with jurisdiction over the Treasury and White House—a fast rise. He has pledged to serve no more than two terms in the Senate, but if as expected he runs again in 1998 it will be the first time since 1984 that a Colorado senator has run for reelection (Gary Hart retired in 1986, Bill Armstrong in 1990, Tim Wirth in 1992, Hank Brown in 1996, all in their 50s). His chances for reelection seem good, but he will surely not lack serious competition.

Junior Senator. Wayne Allard is a Republican elected in 1996. He grew up in the northern end of the Front Range, attended veterinary school, and built a veterinary practice in Loveland—a lively business in an area with vast feedlots. In 1982 he was elected to the state Senate, where he succeeded in limiting the length of legislative sessions—so legislators would be more in touch with their constituents, he said. In 1990, when Congressman Hank Brown, a moderate on cultural issues but a workfare advocate and porkbuster in the House, ran for the Senate, the solidly conservative Allard ran for the House in the 4th District, which covered much of the High Plains and the northern end of the Front Range. Against a former local university president and legislator, Allard barely carried the Front Range, but he won 61% on the conservative High Plains, for a solid 54% victory. In 1992, Allard's opponent tried to capitalize on anti-incumbent feeling by running a TV spot showing pigs at the trough and an old farmer who said he would vote for Allard "when pigs fly." But Allard won with 58% and celebrated by showing off inflatable pigs with wings. He was easily reelected in 1994 and, when Brown retired from the Senate after just one term ("I never thought of this job as a lifetime career"), Allard ran for the Senate.

Allard's voting record was one of the most conservative in the House. He returned more than $1 million in unspent office funds, and sponsored a Citizens Congress Act, to abolish the congressional pension system, require votes on pay raises, ban personal use of frequent flier miles, and ban unsolicited mailings. "I have always felt it was important that whoever serves in the House and Senate be able to walk in the shoes of the people they represent." He moved to defund the National Biological Survey in 1994, charging that it leads to misuse of the Endangered Species Act, and the Commerce Department's Technology Administration. He sponsored a bill for regulatory relief for the farm credit system and a bill to improve the process of approving drugs for animals, both of which passed. He was less successful in challenging a new Forest Service policy to impose new bypass requirements on existing water supplies, even if it meant cutting off water users without compensation. Nor was he able to pass a bill to give farmers greater leeway to drain small wetlands, requiring the government to sign 15-year contracts with property-owners rather than buying permanent easements.

Many of Colorado's biggest political names stayed out of the 1996 Senate race—former

Senator Gary Hart, Governor Roy Romer, former Governor Dick Lamm. Probably the best known candidate was Attorney General Gale Norton, Allard's strongest competition in the Republican primary. But she lost in the Supreme Court defending Colorado's anti-gay rights Amendment 2 a month before the June 1996 nominating convention, and her support of abortion rights rankled many Republican activists and voters; she took a more moderate stance on environmental issues than Allard. With strong support from religious conservatives, Allard led 40%–31% at the convention. With more money, he ran a blitz of ads before the primary, stressing his background as a veterinarian: "Four candidates for the U.S. Senate. Three more lawyers and Wayne Allard." In the August 13 primary Norton ran close to even in metro Denver, but Allard took 62% in the rest of the state, and won 57%–43%. The Democratic race was between two insiders. University of Colorado law dean Gene Nichol ran as a campaign finance reformer, refusing PAC money; he won 53% at the June convention and got Gary Hart's endorsement. But Tom Strickland, law partner of Phil Brownstein, one of the key fundraisers and political insiders in Colorado, raised far more money and had the support of Roy Romer and Denver Mayor Wellington Webb; he ran away with the primary, 66%–34%.

The matchup between Allard and Strickland typified the contrast between Denver liberals and rural conservatives. Strickland was better funded, spending $600,000 more than Allard's $2.2 million, and far more articulate. He held fundraisers with Robert Redford, Gloria Steinem, and musician Don Henley. "I'm the mainstream moderate," he said. "He's the extremist." Allard saw the contrast another way. "He's a lobbyist, and I'm a veterinarian," he said. Strickland attacked Allard's "Neanderthal" positions on the environment; Allard said he was interested in "sound science" rather than emotional appeals and just wanted less bureaucracy and more local decision-making. Allard went on to run ads attacking Strickland for defending clients with environmental problems, including one company trying to build a medical waste incinerator in a poor Denver neighborhood. Allard's most embarrassing moment came when during a debate he came out in favor of public hangings; he quickly retracted. Strickland delayed releasing his tax records, then revealed he made $886,000 in 1995; in October he loaned his campaign $387,000. His image as a lobbyist hurt; as one former Romer aide said, "Tom's OK with me, but I don't like the people around Tom. I don't believe you can swim with the sharks and say you're a trout." Allard won 51%–46%, trailing only narrowly in metro Denver (47%–51%) and winning solidly in the rest of the state (56%–41%).

Allard will surely be among the most conservative of senators, working hard and unassumingly, paying heed to the details of Colorado water and land use law, returning frequently to Colorado. He has seats on the Environment and Public Works and Banking Committees.

Presidential politics. Colorado has been one of the most closely contested states in presidential elections in the 1990s; a reporter could do worse than cover the race from the Denver media market. In 1988 and 1992 it voted close to the national average; in 1996, with the rising voice of Colorado Springs and family-oriented conservatism here, it switched and voted for Bob Dole.

Colorado in the 1990s has had an early March presidential primary. It has produced one interesting result, the victory of Jerry Brown in March 1992, but has otherwise been mostly predictable, with easy victories for George Bush in 1992 and Bob Dole in 1996.

Congressional districting. Colorado did not gain a new House seat out of the 1990 Census, for the first time in three decades, because of sagging population growth in the mid-1980s. Redistricting by the Republican legislature and Democratic Governor Roy Romer didn't change the districts much. Faster growth in the 1990s means that Colorado may gain a seat in 2002, a prospect that undoubtedly many young Colorado politicians have an eye on.

The People: Est. Pop. 1996: 3,823,000; Pop. 1990: 3,294,394, up 16.0% 1990–1996. 1.4% of U.S. total, 25th largest; 18% rural. Median age: 35 years. 10% 65 years and over. 80.7% White, 3.9% Black, 1.7% Asian, 1% Amer. Indian, 12.9% Hispanic origin. Households: 53.8% married couple families; 27% married couple fams. w. children; 58% college educ.; median household income: $30,140; per capita income: $14,821; 62.2% owner occupied housing; median house value: 82,700; median monthly rent:

$362. 4.2% Unemployment. 1996 Voting age pop.: 2,862,000. 1996 Turnout: 1,510,704; 53% of VAP. Registered voters (1996): 2,285,503; 719,230 D (31%), 824,222 R (36%), 742,051 unaffiliated and minor parties (32%).

Political Lineup: Governor, Roy Romer (D); Lt. Gov., Gail Schoettler (D); Secy. of State, Victoria Buckley (R); Atty. Gen., Gale A. Norton (R); Treasurer, Bill Owens (R). State Senate, 35 (20 R and 15 D); Senate President, Tom Norton (R); State House, 65 (41 R and 24 D); House Speaker, Charles Berry (R). Senators, Ben Nighthorse Campbell (R) and Wayne Allard (R). Representatives, 6 (4 R and 2 D).

Elections Division: 303-894-2680; **Filing Deadline for U.S. Congress:** June 5, 1998.

1996 Presidential Vote

Dole (R)	691,846	(46%)
Clinton (D)	671,150	(44%)
Perot (I)	99,628	(7%)
Other	45,646	(3%)

1992 Presidential Vote

Clinton (D)	629,681	(40%)
Bush (R)	562,850	(36%)
Perot (I)	366,010	(23%)

1996 Republican Presidential Primary

Dole (R)	108,065	(44%)
Buchanan (R)	53,314	(22%)
Forbes (R)	51,557	(21%)
Alexander (R)	24,164	(10%)
Keyes (R)	9,049	(4%)

GOVERNOR

Gov. Roy Romer (D)

Elected 1986, term expires Jan. 1999; b. Oct. 31, 1928, Garden City, KS; home, Denver; CO St. U., B.S. 1950, U. of CO, LL.B. 1952, Yale, 1954; Presbyterian; married (Bea).

Career: Air Force, 1952–53; CO House of Reps., 1958–62; CO Senate, 1962–1966, Asst. Minority Ldr., 1964–66; Practicing atty., businessman, 1966–75; CO Ag. Commissioner, 1975; Chief of Staff, Gov. Richard D. Lamm, 1975–1977, 1982–1983; CO Treasurer, 1977–1986.

Office: 136 State Capitol, Denver 80203, 303-866-2471; Fax: 303-866-2003; Web site: www.state.co.us.

Election Results

1994 gen.	Roy Romer (D)	619,205	(55%)
	Bruce Benson (R)	432,042	(39%)
	Others	65,060	(6%)
1994 prim.	Roy Romer (D)	unopposed	
1990 gen.	Roy Romer (D)	626,032	(64%)
	John Andrews (R)	358,403	(36%)

SENATORS

Sen. Ben Nighthorse Campbell (R)

Elected 1992, seat up 1998; b. Apr. 13, 1933, Auburn, CA; home, Ignacio; San Jose St. U., B.A. 1957, Meiji U., Japan, 1960–64; no religious affiliation; married (Linda).

Career: Air Force, 1951–53 (Korea); Rancher, horse trainer, jewelry designer; CO House of Reps., 1982–86; U.S. House of Reps, 1987–92.

DC Office: 380 RSOB 20510, 202-224-5852; Fax: 202-224-1933.

State Offices: Denver, 303-866-1900; Pueblo, 719-542-6987; Colorado Springs, 719-636-9092; Grand Junction, 303-241-6631; Ft. Collins, 303-224-1909.

Committees: *Appropriations* (12th of 15 R): Commerce, Justice, State & the Judiciary; Foreign Operations; Interior; Treasury, Postal Service & General Government (Chmn.); VA, HUD & Independent Agencies. *Energy & Natural Resources* (5th of 11 R): Energy Research, Development, Production & Regulation; National Parks, Historic Preservation & Recreation Subcommittee (Vice Chmn.); Water & Power. *Indian Affairs* (Chmn. of 8 R). *Veterans' Affairs* (5th of 7 R).

Group Ratings

	ADA	ACLU	AFS	LCV	CFA	CON	NFIB	COC	ACU	NTLC	CHC
1996	45	18	50	15	29	64	86	82	78	100	75
1995	30	—	27	21	19	68	—	94	59	—	—

National Journal Ratings

	1995 LIB — 1995 CONS			1996 LIB — 1996 CONS		
Economic	48%	—	50%	46%	—	53%
Social	51%	—	48%	51%	—	48%
Foreign	36%	—	62%	0%	—	74%

Key Votes of the 104th Congress

1. Reduce Medicare Growth $	Y	5. Flag Amendment	Y	9. Anti-Missle Defense	*
2. Lmt. Prod. Liab. Damages	Y	6. Endangered Species	N	10. Cuban Embargo	Y
3. Increase Min. Wage	Y	7. Gay Employment Rights	N	11. Bar Bosnia Troop $	Y
4. Welfare Reform	Y	8. Ovrd. Part. Birth Veto	*	12. Cut Vietnam Aid	Y

Election Results

1992 general	Ben Nighthorse Campbell (D)	803,725	(52%)	($1,561,347)
	Terry Considine (R)	662,893	(43%)	($2,215,791)
	Others	85,671	(6%)	
1992 primary	Ben Nighthorse Campbell (D)	117,634	(46%)	
	Richard D. Lamm (D)	93,599	(36%)	
	Josie Heath (D)	47,418	(18%)	
1986 general	Timothy E. Wirth (D)	529,449	(50%)	($3,787,202)
	Ken Kramer (R)	512,994	(48%)	($3,785,577)

Sen. Wayne Allard (R)

Elected 1996, seat up 2002; b. Dec. 2, 1943, Fort Collins; home, Loveland; CO St. U., D.V.M. 1968; Protestant; married (Joan).

Career: Veterinarian, 1968–present; Owner, Allard Animal Hosp., 1970–90; Loveland City Health Officer, 1970–78; CO Senate, 1982–90; US House of Reps., 1990–96.

DC Office: 716 HSOB 20510, 202-224-5941; Fax: 202-224-6471.

State Offices: Colorado Springs, 719-634-6071; Englewood, 303-220-7414; Grand Junction 971-245-9553; Greeley, 970-351-7582; Pueblo, 719-545-9751.

Committees: *Banking, Housing & Urban Affairs* (8th of 10 R): Financial Institutions & Regulatory Relief; Housing Opportunity & Community Development; Securities. *Environment & Public Works* (9th of 10 R): Clean Air, Wetlands, Private Property & Nuclear Safety; Superfund, Waste Control & Risk Assessment. *Intelligence (Select)* (9th of 10 R).

Group Ratings (as Member of U.S. House of Representatives)

	ADA	ACLU	AFS	LCV	CFA	CON	NFIB	COC	ACU	NTLC	CHC
1996	10	12	0	8	8	63	97	100	100	95	93
1995	0	—	—	6	8	75	—	96	88	—	—

National Journal Ratings (as Member of U.S. House of Representatives)

	1995 LIB — 1995 CONS			1996 LIB — 1996 CONS		
Economic	0%	—	74%	24%	—	73%
Social	0%	—	79%	33%	—	65%
Foreign	27%	—	73%	0%	—	79%

Key Votes of the 104th Congress (as Member of U.S. House of Representatives)

1. Reduce Medicare Growth $	Y	5. Flag Amendment	Y	9. Cuban Embargo	Y
2. Ovrd. Product Liab. Veto	Y	6. Drop EPA Limits	N	10. Bar Bosnia Troop $	Y
3. Increase Min. Wage	N	7. Repeal Assault-Weap. Ban	Y	11. Cut Anti-missile Defense	N
4. Welfare Reform	Y	8. Ovrd. Part. Birth Veto	Y	12. Bar U.N. Uniforms	Y

Election Results

1996 general	Wayne Allard (R)	750,325	(51%)	($2,233,429)
	Tom Strickland (D)	677,600	(46%)	($2,894,916)
	Others	41,686	(3%)	
1996 primary	Wayne Allard (R)	115,064	(57%)	
	Gale Norton (R)	87,394	(43%)	
1990 general	Hank Brown (R)	569,048	(56%)	($3,684,020)
	Josie Heath (D)	425,746	(42%)	($1,943,422)
	Others	27,233	(3%)	

FIRST DISTRICT

One mile above sea level, (as the plaque on the 14th step of the gold-domed Capitol reads), a few miles from where the High Plains yield to the sharp peaks of the Front Range of the Rockies, on no historic trade route and with a fresh water supply adequate for a town one-tenth of its size, stands the great metropolitan center of Denver. With nearly 2 million people, it has been the economic and cultural capital for 100 years of the whole Rocky Mountain region. Denver still has a Western air. It hosts the National Western Stock Show every year, but it is not roughneck. Its neat grid of streets, slanted on a 45-degree angle in downtown to align with the South Platte

River and the railroad lines next to it, its array of parks, the trees which line so many of its streets, a lush contrast with the dried landscape of the high plains—all these give Denver a burnished, sedate air, despite the unembellished skyscrapers of the 1970s energy boom and the 1990s Coors Stadium and Elitch Gardens amusement park. Three-quarters of the metro area's people now live in the suburbs, and Denver itself has become a sort of Rocky Mountain San Francisco, with large minorities and singles populations. The black neighborhoods of northeastern Denver are filled with well maintained 1950s bungalows; the Hispanic quarter northwest of downtown has a certain vitality and has enjoyed upward mobility; gentrified areas south of the Capitol include the elegant elite neighborhood where the Tattered Cover, long the nation's largest independent book store, sits opposite posh Cherry Creek Shopping Center.

Denver increasingly is the liberal heart of Colorado, heavily Democratic in partisan elections, strongly liberation-minded on cultural issues, cautiously liberal on economic issues. Though it remains majority white Anglo, it has elected Hispanic and black mayors since 1983—Federico Pena, who became Bill Clinton's Transportation and then Energy secretary, and Wellington Webb who—out of funds—campaigned for 41 days in 1991 without going home or getting into an automobile, walking the streets and staying at homes of supporters. Denver's liberalism in the early 1970s took the form of skepticism about growth and boosterism, at a time when growth seemed likely to go on forever. By the 1980s the energy boom had collapsed, so Denver's leaders decided to use public monies to spur private growth—with disappointing results. The new convention center had a hard time getting bookings, and Denver International Airport, Pena's pet project, may be one of the greatest public sector fiascoes of all time: it opened 14 months late, at almost triple its originally estimated cost, and its fees were so high that critics said it was sure to have fewer flights than the supposedly obsolescent Stapleton.

The 1st Congressional District of Colorado includes all of Denver and extends northeast toward DIA, taking in Commerce City and the northern part of Aurora, places with warehouses and trucking terminals on main streets and curved-street subdivisions behind. The 1st remains a heavily Democratic district, including most of metro Denver's blacks and Hispanics, singles and gays: the percentage of households with married couples and children is among the lowest in America. In an era when cultural attitudes are a better clue to voting behavior than economic status, this once politically marginal area has become a solidly Democratic constituency.

The congresswoman from the 1st District is Diana DeGette, a Democrat elected in 1996 to replace Patricia Schroeder. A reluctant candidate in 1972, Schroeder changed the substance and style of American politics, dubbing Ronald Reagan the "Teflon president" and, from her seat on the Armed Services Committee, exerting vast influence toward feminizing the American military. She even may have made it respectable for presidential candidates to cry, as she did when she announced she was not running for that office in September 1987; in 1995 she announced she was retiring when "my age hit the 55 speed limit."

DeGette grew up in Denver, went to law school, and worked on Federico Pena's 1983 campaign. In 1992, at 35, she was elected to the Colorado House, where she was surprisingly productive for a member of the minority. She sponsored a "bubble" bill placing a zone of protection around abortion clinics and their clients; she worked on rewriting domestic violence laws; she developed a Voluntary Cleanup and Redevelopment Act to encourage businesses and citizens to clean up the environment; she passed a bill protecting families of accident victims from being contacted by lawyers within 30 days.

When Schroeder ran for Congress in 1972, it was at the suggestion of a friend that she would attract more attention than her husband, who was thinking of running. Now in a place like Denver the feminist left is the heart of the Democratic Party (as the religious right is the heart of the Republican Party in Colorado Springs) and a candidate like DeGette—feminist, organizationally adept and legislatively creative—seems a natural candidate. In June black organizer Les Franklin withdrew from the race, which helped DeGette capture a 57% majority at the nominating convention over former Denver Councilman Tim Sandos with 44%.

In the general DeGette faced Joe Rogers, a black 31-year-old former aide to Senator Hank

Brown. He waged a vigorous campaign, but DeGette far outraised him. She was one of the major beneficiaries of EMILY's List, the feminist group which bundles members' donations and has become a major force in congressional and statewide elections. DeGette spent $889,000 to Rogers's $423,000, and it was hardly a surprise when DeGette won 57%–40%. Interestingly, some of DeGette's issue positions contrasted with Schroeder's. Schroeder first won as an opponent of the Vietnam war; DeGette said she supported U.S. intervention in Bosnia. Schroeder and other Democrats harshly attacked House Republicans for Medicare "cuts." DeGette called for considering entitlement reform, although she also came out against "the wholesale conversion of diverse social programs." In the House she got a seat on the Commerce Committee and became a Democratic whip for the Western region.

The People: Pop. 1990: 549,053; 13% age 65+; 62% White; 12% Black; 2% Asian; 1% Amer. Indian; 22% Hispanic origin. Households: 39% married couple families; 16% married couple fams. w. children; 54% college educ.; median household income: $24,870; per capita income: $14,942; median gross rent: $382; median house value: $74,900.

1996 Presidential Vote			1992 Presidential Vote		
Clinton (D)	133,032	(61%)	Clinton (D)	135,016	(55%)
Dole (R)	66,427	(31%)	Bush (R)	63,283	(26%)
Perot (I)	10,367	(5%)	Perot (I)	43,245	(18%)
Other	7,676	(4%)			

Rep. Diana DeGette (D)

Elected 1996; b. July 29, 1957, Tachikawa, Japan; home, Denver; CO Col., B.A. 1979; N.Y.U., J.D. 1982; Presbyterian; married (Lino Lipinsky)

Career: Practicing atty., 1982–96; CO House of Reps., 1992–96, Asst. Minority Leader, 1994–95.

DC Office: 1404 LHOB 20515, 202-225-4431; Fax: 202-225-5657.

District Offices: Denver, 303-844-4988.

Committees: *Commerce* (23rd of 23 D): Finance & Hazardous Materials; Health & the Environment.

Group Ratings and Key Votes: Newly Elected

Election Results

1996 general	Diana DeGette (D)	112,631	(57%)	($889,219)
	Joe Rogers (R)	79,540	(40%)	($423,755)
	Others	5,668	(3%)	
1996 primary	Diana DeGette (D)	21,523	(56%)	
	Tim Sandos (D)	16,952	(44%)	
1994 general	Patricia Schroeder (D)	93,123	(60%)	($502,466)
	William F. Eggert (R)	61,978	(40%)	($117,935)

SECOND DISTRICT

Boulder, Colorado, nestled right up against the Front Range of the Rockies, the home of the University of Colorado, is billed by its convention bureau as "a combination of lycra-clad athletes, New Age artists, and thoughtful intellectuals sipping cappuccinos." It was called the nation's number one town for outdoor sports by *Outdoor* magazine, and an "international mecca for people who thrive on physical challenge and risk" by the *Rocky Mountain News*'s Clifford May. Boulder is the nation's leading center for bungee jumping, mountain biking, snowshoe running, rock and ice climbing, downhill skiing, land surfing and hot-air ballooning, plus the home of the Buddhist Naropa Institute and the Boulder School of Massage Therapy. All of which is suggested by the terrain: Boulder literally looks up at erose rows of peaks rising to 14,000 feet from a mile-high plain laid out in mile-square grids much farther than the eye can see. Just to the south is another high-risk site, the government's Rocky Flats nuclear weapons plant, closed down in 1989 after revelations of mismanagement and unsafe practices.

The 2d Congressional District of Colorado is centered on this part of metro Denver. It includes all of Boulder County, Rocky Flats, some lightly-populated but picturesque Rocky Mountains acreage, including Central City with its new gambling casino, and lower-middle to middle-income suburbs north and northwest of Denver—Arvada, Wheat Ridge, Westminster, Thornton, Northglenn, Broomfield. Here families of comfortable affluence and struggling finances, of fundamentalist religion and environment-loving liberalism, live in subdivisions with views of the mountains, close to metro Denver's biggest shopping malls. In the 1990s, greater Boulder grapples with the effects of commercial and residential "growth management," as development is restricted to just one percent annually and open space is protected by a "blue line" barrier, causing housing prices to soar. This Metro North area is politically marginal, while Boulder is typically heavily Democratic; overall, despite occasional Republican speculation to the contrary, this is basically a Democratic district.

The congressman from the 2d District is David Skaggs, a Democrat who grew up in New Jersey and came to Colorado after serving as a Marine in Vietnam. He was one of those baby boom liberals who came to the fore in the 1970s; like the California Gold Rush generation who held most major offices there from 1850 when they were in their 30s to the 1890s when they were in their 70s, this generation of politicians held most of Colorado's top posts for two decades. Now Skaggs is one of the last in office. Skaggs was an aide to Congressman Tim Wirth in the 1970s; in the 1980s he was elected to the Colorado legislature. In 1986 when Wirth ran for the Senate, Skaggs won the House seat, beating Democratic National Committee Vice-chair Polly Baca in the primary and hard-campaigning Republican Mike Norton in the general.

Skaggs has worked aggressively on local issues while taking a role in the Democratic leadership in fighting for principles. He was one of the first to call for the closing of Rocky Flats, though it was a major employer, and in late 1996 he was pressing for the Clinton Administration to produce a plan for disposing of its used plutonium. He worked to pass the Colorado wilderness bill in 1993 and, with a seat on Appropriations, successfully worked to ban flights over Rocky Mountains National Park, but failed to get 91% of it declared a wilderness. He worked to pass a federal-Gilpin County land transfer and passed a ban on new dams on North St. Vrain Creek; he also worked to fund the National Institute of Standards and Technology in Boulder.

Overall, Skaggs's voting record is well to the left of the House, although he did vote for the final version of the welfare reform bill in 1996. He ran for chairman of the Democratic Study Group in 1995 against Rosa DeLauro of Connecticut; the vote was 93–93, after which she withdrew in his favor. A Democratic deputy whip, he rounded up votes for the 1990 and 1993 tax increases; he led opposition to the supermajority tax bill in 1996 and challenged the line-item veto in court in 1997, along with Senators Robert Byrd and Daniel Patrick Moynihan; in April a federal judge struck down the line-item veto, calling it unconstitutional. On the Intelligence Committee he attacked secrecy classifications as enormously and unduly costly. He has led moves to defund TV Marti, which attempts to broadcast to Cuba; the House zeroed it out in 1996 but it was restored in conference. In retaliation to an earlier move to defund Radio Marti, Florida Republican Lincoln Diaz-Balart killed a $23 million appropriation for NIST.

Skaggs's opponent in 1994 and 1996 was former legislator Pat Miller, a strong opponent of abortion. In 1994 she ran a lightly funded campaign, and held Skaggs to 57%. In 1996 she spent much more—$458,000, though not enough to compete with Skaggs's $778,000—and campaigned heavily in Denver suburbs while avoiding Boulder. The Boulder *Daily Camera* printed a transcript of her telling a citizen militia group in 1994 that she supported their agenda and that elected sheriffs will not protect the people; naturally all the local papers attacked her and endorsed Skaggs. Skaggs won again, but only with the same 57% he had in 1994—a sign perhaps that this district is becoming more marginal. Now Skaggs is one of only four Democratic congressmen from the Rocky Mountain states; the others are from Denver and Hispanic-majority districts in Arizona and New Mexico. He continues to be an active partisan, but also seems bent on encouraging civility in the House; he and Republican Ray LaHood originated the idea of the bipartisan House retreat in Hershey, Pennsylvania, in March 1997.

The People: Pop. 1990: 548,953; 8% rural; 8% age 65+; 87% White; 1% Black; 2% Asian; 1% Amer. Indian; 10% Hispanic origin. Households: 56% married couple families; 28% married couple fams. w. children; 61% college educ.; median household income: $35,117; per capita income: $15,823; median gross rent: $477; median house value: $89,700.

1996 Presidential Vote

Clinton (D)	127,702	(49%)
Dole (R)	102,107	(40%)
Perot (I)	16,605	(6%)
Other	12,074	(5%)

1992 Presidential Vote

Clinton (D)	123,144	(45%)
Bush (R)	83,209	(30%)
Perot (I)	66,678	(24%)

Rep. David E. Skaggs (D)

Elected 1986; b. Feb. 22, 1943, Cincinnati, OH; home, Boulder; Wesleyan U., B.A. 1964, Yale, LL.B. 1967; Congregationalist; married (Laura).

Career: Marine Corps, 1968–71 (Vietnam), Marine Corps Reserves, 1971–77; A.A., Rep. Timothy E. Wirth, 1975–77, Campaign Dir., 1976; Practicing atty., 1977–86; CO House of Reps., 1980–86, Minority Ldr., 1982–85.

DC Office: 1124 LHOB 20515, 202-225-2161; Fax: 202-226-3806; e-mail: skaggs@hr.house.gov.

District Offices: Westminster, 303-650-7886.

Committees: *Appropriations* (13th of 26 D): Commerce, Justice, State & Judiciary; Interior. *Intelligence (Select)* (3rd of 7 D): Human Intelligence, Analysis & Counterintelligence; Technical & Tactical Intelligence (RMM).

Group Ratings

	ADA	ACLU	AFS	LCV	CFA	CON	NFIB	COC	ACU	NTLC	CHC
1996	90	94	100	85	77	93	22	19	0	7	0
1995	85	—	—	88	100	31	—	21	0	—	—

National Journal Ratings

	1995 LIB — 1995 CONS			1996 LIB — 1996 CONS		
Economic	85%	—	12%	89%	—	0%
Social	88%	—	0%	79%	—	18%
Foreign	79%	—	17%	82%	—	16%

Key Votes of the 104th Congress

1. Reduce Medicare Growth $	N	5. Flag Amendment	N	9. Cuban Embargo	N
2. Ovrd. Product Liab. Veto	N	6. Drop EPA Limits	Y	10. Bar Bosnia Troop $	N
3. Increase Min. Wage	Y	7. Repeal Assault-Weap. Ban	N	11. Cut Anti-Missile Defense	Y
4. Welfare Reform	N	8. Ovrd. Part. Birth Veto	N	12. Bar U.N. Uniforms	N

Election Results

1996 general	David E. Skaggs (D)	145,894	(57%)	($778,880)
	Patricia Miller (R)	97,865	(38%)	($458,442)
	Others	12,025	(5%)	
1996 primary	David E. Skaggs (D)	unopposed		
1994 general	David E. Skaggs (D)	105,938	(57%)	($576,719)
	Patricia Miller (R)	80,723	(43%)	($83,999)

THIRD DISTRICT

On a clear night from the air they look like tiny mottled veins with small clots here and there, thicker near Denver but never very bright: the lights of the civilization Americans have built on the Western Slope of the Rockies in Colorado. The lights follow the trails of valley roads and mountainside switchbacks; the nodes mark the dozens of little towns built during mining boom years—the gold rush of the 1870s, the uranium boom of the 1950s, the oil shale boomlet of the 1970s. The Western Slope—everything west of the Front Range, with dozens of peaks over 14,000 feet—has always blocked east-west movement; but for mining and now skiing, no one would have followed the Ute Indians and settled here. The miners who tracked gold and silver and lead ores also built Victorian towns with opera houses and gingerbread storefronts in Leadville and Salida in valleys and defiles scarcely accessible to the outside world. Now many of these towns have been restored by ski resort operators and joined by dozens of new condominiums and shopping malls.

The political map of the Western Slope is as diverse as its history. Aspen and Telluride, with Victorian houses and counter-cultural substrata, are liberal and Democratic: the "granola belt." Vail and Crested Butte, with contemporary condominiums, formerly Republican, are trending left. The rough-handed mining area around Grand Junction, where piles of tailings still crackle with radioactivity and people remember the oil shale boom with nostalgia, is hostile to environmentalists, while the small Hispanic communities in the south are heavily Democratic.

The 3d Congressional District of Colorado includes all the Western Slope plus the small industrial city of Pueblo. There, on the banks of the Arkansas River, the Rockefellers built large steel factories before World War I to make barbed wire and rails; now this blue-collar town has attracted new plants from McDonnell Douglas, Unisys and B.F. Goodrich. Pueblo is heavily Democratic and so are Hispanic Conejos and Costilla Counties just to the south. Hispanic, not Mexican-American: Spanish-speaking people have been living here, as in northern New Mexico, for 350 years. Politically, the 3d District was a bellwether in the 1980s and has been moving toward the right in the 1990s; it voted for Bob Dole and Wayne Allard in 1996.

The congressman from the 3d District is Scott McInnis, a Republican elected in 1992, when then-Democratic Congressman Ben Nighthorse Campbell was elected to the Senate. McInnis grew up in Glenwood Springs, in a crevassed valley west of Aspen and Vail. He worked as a local policeman and went to law school, practiced law and was elected to the legislature in 1982, at 29. Colorado was one of the few states in the 1980s with a Republican legislature, and McInnis became House majority leader in 1991. In 1992, McInnis won the 3d District Republican nomination unopposed and outworked and outcampaigned Lieutenant Governor Mike Callihan to win 55%–44%. In his campaign, he called for cutting both entitlements and defense spending and was the beneficiary of a $127,000 independent expenditure by the American Medical

Association PAC and by Campbell's refusal to endorse Callihan.

McInnis's voting record has been conservative on economics, mixed on cultural and foreign issues. He is much involved in local issues. He worked with David Skaggs on a federal-Gilpin County land transfer and, with Wayne Allard and Campbell, fought proposals to sell off federal ski resort land for deficit reduction. He worked for the Animas-La Plata project, a favorite of Campbell's, which lost in the House but was saved in the Senate. He also travelled far afield, as a party spokesman on problems in Korea and in Bosnia after the Dayton accords. In 1995 he became a member of the Rules Committee, from which he can advance many local issues and legislative projects. McInnis returns to his district every weekend, and spends the night in his Capitol Hill office during the week.

McInnis was mentioned as a candidate for Hank Brown's Senate seat in 1996, but decided not to run. He was reelected by wide margins in 1994 and 1996. He has made it plain he is interested in running for Campbell's Senate seat in 1998 if Campbell does not run.

The People: Pop. 1990: 549,120; 46% rural; 13% age 65+; 80% White; 1% Black; 1% Asian; 1% Amer. Indian; 17% Hispanic origin. Households: 57% married couple families; 27% married couple fams. w. children; 49% college educ.; median household income: $24,521; per capita income: $12,115; median gross rent: $361; median house value: $62,000.

1996 Presidential Vote

Dole (R)	122,826	(45%)
Clinton (D)	116,628	(43%)
Perot (I)	23,571	(9%)
Other	8,711	(3%)

1992 Presidential Vote

Clinton (D)	107,227	(40%)
Bush (R)	92,292	(34%)
Perot (I)	67,210	(25%)

Rep. Scott McInnis (R)

Elected 1992; b. May 9, 1953, Glenwood Springs; home, Grand Junction; Ft. Lewis Col., B.A. 1975, St. Mary's U., J.D. 1980; Catholic; married (Lori).

Career: Glenwood Springs police officer, 1976; Practicing atty., 1980–92; CO House of Reps., 1982–92, Majority Ldr., 1990–92.

DC Office: 215 CHOB 20515, 202-225-4761; Fax: 202-226-0622.

District Offices: Durango, 303-259-2754; Glenwood Springs, 303-928-0637; Grand Junction, 303-245-7107; Pueblo, 719-543-8200;

Committees: *Rules* (7th of 9 R): Rules & Organization of the House.

Group Ratings

	ADA	ACLU	AFS	LCV	CFA	CON	NFIB	COC	ACU	NTLC	CHC
1996	5	19	0	31	23	73	100	88	100	100	86
1995	5	—	—	0	8	75	—	96	88	—	—

National Journal Ratings

	1995 LIB — 1995 CONS	1996 LIB — 1996 CONS
Economic	0% — 74%	0% — 82%
Social	44% — 56%	45% — 55%
Foreign	45% — 55%	48% — 52%

Key Votes of the 104th Congress

1. Reduce Medicare Growth $	Y	5. Flag Amendment	Y	9. Cuban Embargo	Y
2. Ovrd. Product Liab. Veto	Y	6. Drop EPA Limits	N	10. Bar Bosnia Troop $	*
3. Increase Min. Wage	N	7. Repeal Assault-Weap. Ban	Y	11. Cut Anti-Missile Defense	N
4. Welfare Reform	Y	8. Ovrd. Part. Birth Veto	Y	12. Bar U.N. Uniforms	Y

Election Results

1996 general	Scott McInnis (R)	183,523	(69%)	($270,892)
	Albert L. Gurule (D)	82,953	(31%)	($79,406)
1996 primary	Scott McInnis (R)	unopposed		
1994 general	Scott McInnis (R)	145,365	(70%)	($387,210)
	Linda Powers (D)	63,427	(30%)	($241,305)

FOURTH DISTRICT

The High Plains of eastern Colorado are dusty brown, gently rolling grasslands that seem flat but actually slope imperceptibly downward toward the Mississippi River. The land is fertile but dry: rainfall is rare, the rivers are just a trickle most of the year, and in many places groundwater is equally scarce. It is fine wheat country when irrigated and one of the foremost beef cattle regions. But it has been squeezed in recent decades between declining prices for wheat and declining demand for beef on the one hand, and increased prices for water because of high demand in Denver and along the Front Range. The prairie lands and small towns of the High Plains have small reminders of their past—the Pawnee National Grasslands near Greeley, where antelope, coyotes, and prairie dogs still roam, and Burlington's 1905 carousel, one of the few with the original paint. But the free market that once peopled the High Plains with farmers and ranchers and made it the scene of farm protests and revolts is now causing it to empty out and revert to untamed land, ready again for now increasingly numerous buffalo.

The 4th Congressional District of Colorado contains almost all of the High Plains plus the medium-sized towns of Greeley, Fort Collins and Loveland—the northern end of the densely populated Front Range. By heritage and usually by inclination, this is Republican territory: it was evenly split in 1992 but gave solid margins to Bob Dole and Wayne Allard in 1996. The only Democratic parts are the working-class Adams County suburbs north of Denver and Las Animas County on the New Mexico border.

The congressman from the 4th District is Bob Schaffer, a Republican elected in 1996 to replace Senator Wayne Allard. Schaffer grew up in Cincinnati and went to the same high school as House Republican Conference Chairman John Boehner; after college in Ohio, he moved to Fort Collins and bought and managed rental property. In 1986, at 24, he was elected to the state Senate, where he favored tax cuts, education reform, tougher sentences, and welfare reform. A solid conservative, he seized AIDS pamphlets on display at the Capitol in 1993 as unsuitable for children and supported a bill to enable parents to take children out of sex education classes more easily. He sponsored a law to end judicial review of initiatives passed by the voters. In 1994 he was a Republican candidate for lieutenant governor.

In 1996, when Allard ran for the Senate, Schaffer was one of three Republican legislators running for the House. Schaffer portrayed himself as a "true conservative" and gun control opponent whose first priority was balancing the budget. Pat Sullivan, a urologist from Fort Collins, focused on the budget and agriculture, calling himself a "mainstream conservative." He and Don Ament, a farmer and rancher, both supported limited abortion rights. Ament won 30%, carrying his base in northeast Colorado, and Sullivan won 29%, barely carrying the Fort Collins area. Schaffer, with support from all over the district, won with 40%.

In the general Schaffer faced University of Colorado Regent Guy Kelley. Schaffer ran on the balanced budget amendment and a plan to eliminate the Commerce, Education, and other departments; in the aftermath of the Republicans' phasing-out of farm subsidies, he called for lower taxes on farmers, opening up foreign markets to agricultural exports, and revision of the Endangered Species Act. Kelley accused Schaffer of running on a right-wing agenda undermining public education, abortion rights, and gun control. In October Kelley played a tape of Schaffer talking in 1994 on KHNC, a radio station that provided a platform for "patriot" militias; Schaffer replied that he was just boosting his candidacy for lieutenant governor and told Fort Collins Rotarians in 1996 that militias have no place in a mainstream society.

The argument that Schaffer was too right-wing apparently did not appeal to many voters. Schaffer won 56%–38%, carrying the Adams County suburbs and losing only two southern counties to Kelley; he nearly lost another to Wes McKinley, a rancher and foreman of the grand jury investigating the Rocky Flats plutonium plant, who rode a mule 1,200 miles up and down the district and won 3% of the votes. Schaffer remained bitter at Kelley's tactics: "Issues and attacks were outright invented by the Democrats, and the media took charges with absolutely no foundation and wrote about it as if it were credible." Schaffer serves on the Republican Policy Committee and seems likely to be a solid conservative in the Republican Congress.

The People: Pop. 1990: 549,216; 35% rural; 11% age 65+; 83% White; 1% Black; 1% Asian; 1% Amer. Indian; 15% Hispanic origin. Households: 60% married couple families; 30% married couple fams. w. children; 50% college educ.; median household income: $26,577; per capita income: $12,387; median gross rent: $379; median house value: $70,100.

1996 Presidential Vote

Dole (R)	122,840	(49%)
Clinton (D)	102,355	(41%)
Perot (I)	18,644	(7%)
Other	6,683	(3%)

1992 Presidential Vote

Bush (R)	96,638	(38%)
Clinton (D)	94,234	(37%)
Perot (I)	63,203	(25%)

Rep. Bob Schaffer (R)

Elected 1996; b. July 24, 1962, Cincinnati, OH; home, Fort Collins; U. of Dayton, OH, B.A. 1984; Catholic, married (Maureen).

Career: Legis. Researcher, OH Senate, 1984–85; Press Secy., CO Senate, 1985–87; CO Senate, 1986–96; Owner, Northern Front Range Mktg. Co., 1989–94.

DC Office: 212 CHOB 20515, 202-225-4676; Fax: 202-225-5870.

District Offices: Fort Collins, 970-493-9132; Greeley, 970-353-3507; LaJunta, 719-384-7370; Sterling, 970-522-1788.

Committees: *Agriculture* (24th of 27 R): Forestry, Resource Conservation & Research. *Education & The Workforce* (20th of 25 R): Postsecondary Education, Training & Life-Long Learning; Workforce Protections. *Resources* (25th of 27 R): Forests & Forest Health.

Election Results

1996 general	Bob Schaffer (R)	137,012	(56%)	($464,165)
	Guy Kelley (D)	92,837	(38%)	($261,425)
	Others	14,218	(6%)	
1996 primary	Bob Schaffer (R)	15,138	(40%)	
	Don Ament (R)	11,474	(30%)	
	Pat Sullivan (R)	11,124	(29%)	
1994 general	Wayne Allard (R)	136,251	(72%)	($267,997)
	Cathy Kipp (D)	52,202	(28%)	($19,344)

FIFTH DISTRICT

In 1893 Katherine Lee Bates took the cog railway up from Colorado Springs to the top of 14,100-foot Pikes Peak and, looking out at the purple mountain's majesty above amber waves of grain, wrote the lines of "America the Beautiful." Pike's Peak, first especied by Zebulon Pike in 1806, and Colorado Springs, with the Garden of the Gods and the Broadmoor Hotel, have been tourist attractions ever since. In the second half of the 20th Century, Colorado Springs, safe in the fastness of North America, has also become a great American military fortress, the home of Fort Carson, the site of the Air Force Academy, and, most recently, at Falcon Air Force Base, site of space-based defense research. Around them Colorado Springs has built a high-tech, innovative economy—"silicon mountain." And with the arrival of Dr. James Dobson's Focus on the Family, it has been a center of conservative Christianity, the home base for ideas and ideals which have found an increasing welcome in the rest of Colorado and the nation as a whole.

Politically, Colorado Springs is the home of Colorado's young conservatism, the counterpoint to Denver's aging liberalism, and one which prevailed statewide in 1996 as Bob Dole carried Colorado after Bill Clinton had carried it four years before. The 5th Congressional District of Colorado includes all of Colorado Springs and reaches north through fast-growing Douglas County (from 8,000 to 60,000 in the 1980s). It is by any measure Colorado's most Republican district, and one of the nation's.

The congressman from the 5th District, Joel Hefley, originally came to Colorado seeking work as a cowboy. He moved to Colorado Springs in 1965, became a professional civic leader, served 7 years in the state Senate and was elected to Congress in 1986. He has maintained a highly conservative voting record and an interest in military issues, especially missile defense. His early work foreshadows the 1994 Contract with America: he sought spending cuts, like zeroing out the National Endowment for Democracy and Economic Development Administration; he issued a Porker of the Week award for colleagues; he sought to abolish the Interstate Commerce Commission; he sought to end unfunded mandates and require a three-fifths supermajority vote for new taxes.

Hefley is now chairman of the National Security Subcommittee on Military Installations and Facilities, where he staunchly supports missile defense and has pushed to maintain 12 active Army divisions. In November 1995 his bill to bar U.S. troops from Bosnia absent Congressional approval of funds passed the House 243–171, but was ignored by the Senate; a similar fate in 1996 befell his bill to allow Interior and Agriculture Departments to use private firms to build housing for land-management workers. He has long tried to create a base-closing-like commission on national parks, arguing that Congress has designated new parks without merit and then not funded existing parks adequately.

Hefley won a contested primary in 1986 and has held the seat easily since. In 1996 he had primary opposition from former state Senator Bill Hughes, who called for a national sales tax, and was angry that Hefley voted against the term limits constitutional amendment. Hughes won 31% at the 5th District convention, just over the 30% needed to get on the ballot. Hefley, who pledged he would vote for future term limits measures, beat Hughes 77%–23% and then won the general 72%–28%. His greatest priorities, he says, are the balanced budget amendment, replacing the Internal Revenue Service with a flat tax, and funding defense: "I don't make any apologies for supporting the defense establishment."

The People: Pop. 1990: 549,264; 11% rural; 7% age 65+; 85% White; 5% Black; 2% Asian; 1% Amer. Indian; 7% Hispanic origin. Households: 63% married couple families; 33% married couple fams. w. children; 65% college educ.; median household income: $33,348; per capita income: $15,370; median gross rent: $432; median house value: $90,200.

1996 Presidential Vote

Dole (R)	158,790	(59%)
Clinton (D)	88,057	(33%)
Perot (I)	16,583	(6%)
Other	5,928	(2%)

1992 Presidential Vote

Bush (R)	125,749	(49%)
Clinton (D)	71,185	(28%)
Perot (I)	57,488	(22%)

Rep. Joel Hefley (R)

Elected 1986; b. Apr. 18, 1935, Ardmore, OK; home, Colorado Springs; OK Baptist U., B.A. 1957, OK St. U., M.S. 1962; Baptist; married (Lynn).

Career: Exec. Dir., Community Planning & Research Cncl., 1966–86; CO House of Reps., 1976–78; CO Senate, 1978–86.

DC Office: 2230 RHOB 20515, 202-225-4422; Fax: 202-225-1942.

District Offices: Colorado Springs, 719-520-0055; Englewood, 303-792-3923.

Committees: *National Security* (8th of 30 R): Military Installations & Facilities (Chmn.); Military Research & Development. *Resources* (7th of 27 R): National Parks & Public Lands. *Small Business* (3rd of 19 R).

Group Ratings

	ADA	ACLU	AFS	LCV	CFA	CON	NFIB	COC	ACU	NTLC	CHC
1996	10	6	8	8	8	38	95	94	100	92	87
1995	5	—	—	13	8	56	—	92	84	—	—

National Journal Ratings

	1995 LIB — 1995 CONS			1996 LIB — 1996 CONS		
Economic	0%	—	74%	20%	—	76%
Social	35%	—	64%	14%	—	77%
Foreign	0%	—	85%	0%	—	79%

Key Votes of the 104th Congress

1. Reduce Medicare Growth $	Y	5. Flag Amendment	Y	9. Cuban Embargo	Y
2. Ovrd. Product Liab. Veto	Y	6. Drop EPA Limits	N	10. Bar Bosnia Troop $	Y
3. Increase Min. Wage	N	7. Repeal Assault-Weap. Ban	Y	11. Cut Anti-Missile Defense	N
4. Welfare Reform	Y	8. Ovrd. Part. Birth Veto	Y	12. Bar U.N. Uniforms	Y

Election Results

1996 general	Joel Hefley (R)	188,805	(72%)	($329,794)
	Mike Robinson (D)	73,660	(28%)	($16,017)
1996 primary	Joel Hefley (R)	36,994	(77%)	
	Bill Hughes (R)	11,236	(23%)	
1994 general	Joel Hefley (R)	unopposed		($137,960)

SIXTH DISTRICT

A generation ago, most people in metro Denver lived in the city itself; at the city limits the tree-shaded sidewalks gave way to the empty High Plains. Today, three-quarters of metro Denver residents live outside the city. Just south of Denver, in Arapahoe County, Englewood, Littleton and Cherry Hills, pioneered in the 1940s and 1950s, are comfortable and affluent suburbs. Aurora, to the east, benefited at first from the growth around now-closed Stapleton Airport, but has grown big enough—from 50,000 in 1965 to 220,000 in 1990—to support its own regional mall. West in Jefferson County, which since 1992 has cast more votes than Denver, are Lakewood and Wheat Ridge, creations of the 1960s and 1970s, affluent but not elite suburbs with winding streets and office complexes, notably Lakewood's gigantic Denver Federal Center. Up against the Front Range is Golden, the headquarters of Coors beer and the Coors family which funds so many conservative causes, and of the National Renewable Energy Laboratory, which develops solar energy exports.

The 6th Congressional District of Colorado covers most of this suburban territory. This is almost entirely Republican domain. The dominant tone is technical and managerial, and many people here yearn for the certainty of traditional limits. They value their environment, but they also see the need for economic growth and scientific innovation—both of which they think liberals tend to underrate.

The congressman from the 6th District, its only one since its creation in 1982, has been Republican Dan Schaefer. He was first elected in March 1983 to replace astronaut Jack Swigert, who had been elected in 1982 but died before taking office. Like many Colorado politicians, Schaefer grew up elsewhere—in South Dakota, was educated in Upstate New York, served in the Marine Corps, came to Colorado and worked as a public relations consultant. In 1978 he was elected to the Colorado legislature.

In the House he maintained a conservative voting record and got a seat on the Commerce Committee. This was anonymous service for some years: Schaefer worked with Chairman John Dingell on the cleanup of the Rocky Flats plutonium plant, and wrote a law giving states power to impose environmental regulations on the federal government. He opposed the 1992 cable reregulation bill, the only law passed over George Bush's veto; not surprisingly, since Denver is the headquarters of John Malone and TCI. And he supported telecommunications deregulation, to let regional Bells compete with cable and vice versa; telecom was the most-lobbied issue in the 104th Congress and finally passed in February 1996.

By that time Schaefer was already a power in the House, in his second year as chairman of the Commerce Subcommittee on Energy and Power. He was co-author, with Texas Congressman Stenholm, of the balanced budget amendment which passed the House 300–132 in January 1995 and came within one vote of receiving the required two-thirds in the Senate; he resisted the demands of some conservatives to include a provision requiring a three-fifths supermajority for tax increases. He also passed other laws, of national and sometimes local importance. One was a measure to open a Waste Isolation Pilot Project in Carlsbad, New Mexico, which could receive transuranic waste from Rocky Flats. Another was a law to improve safety and regulation of oil and natural gas pipelines. He twice restored funding, with a $42 million increase, of federal renewable energy research and development, much of which is done at the NREL in Golden. He successfully fought attempts to sell off part of the Strategic Petroleum Reserve.

His next big project is electric utility deregulation. Some states have already started allowing a free market in electric power. Schaefer's bill would end state-granted monopoly franchises for electric utilities and would give consumers the right to choose their own suppliers of electricity. Advocates argue this would lower cost and increase efficiencies; opponents argue it would be unfair to big utilities with their fixed costs. This may well be the most lobbied issue of the 105th Congress. Schaefer has also proposed giving states 85% of the funds in the Leaking Underground Storage Tank Trust Fund to clean up solid waste. Schaefer has also co-sponsored a national retail sales tax that would replace the income tax and abolish the need for the IRS.

Despite his conservative record, Schaefer has worked with Democrats on some issues. He is a founder of the Mainstream Conservative Alliance, some 39 Republicans who call themselves Blue Dogs, after the moderate Democrats, to advance civility and bipartisan cooperation. He has been reelected easily every two years, in 1996 against Jefferson County Clerk Joan Fitzgerald, who called this busy and productive legislator "sluggish and inactive."

The People: Pop. 1990: 548,788; 5% rural; 8% age 65+; 87% White; 3% Black; 2% Asian; 1% Amer. Indian; 6% Hispanic origin. Households: 56% married couple families; 28% married couple fams. w. children; 68% college educ.; median household income: $37,333; per capita income: $18,289; median gross rent: $473; median house value: $92,200.

1996 Presidential Vote

Dole (R)	118,856	(49%)
Clinton (D)	103,376	(43%)
Perot (I)	13,858	(6%)
Other	4,574	(2%)

1992 Presidential Vote

Bush (R)	101,679	(38%)
Clinton (D)	98,875	(37%)
Perot (I)	68,186	(25%)

Rep. Dan Schaefer (R)

Elected Mar. 1983; b. Jan. 25, 1936, Guttenberg, IA; home, Lakewood; Niagara U., B.A. 1961, Potsdam St. U., 1963; Catholic; married (Mary).

Career: Marine Corps, 1955–57; Educator, 1961–67; PR consultant, 1967–83; CO House of Reps., 1977–78; CO Senate, 1979–83.

DC Office: 2160 RHOB 20515, 202-225-7882; Fax: 202-225-7885; e-mail: schaefer@hr.house.gov.

District Offices: Englewood, 303-762-8890.

Committees: *Commerce* (5th of 28 R): Energy & Power (Chmn.); Telecommunications, Trade & Consumer Protection. *Veterans' Affairs* (10th of 16 R): Benefits.

Group Ratings

	ADA	ACLU	AFS	LCV	CFA	CON	NFIB	COC	ACU	NTLC	CHC
1996	0	0	0	8	8	42	100	100	100	100	100
1995	5	—	—	0	8	38	—	96	92	—	—

National Journal Ratings

	1995 LIB — 1995 CONS	1996 LIB — 1996 CONS
Economic	40% — 60%	0% — 82%
Social	0% — 79%	0% — 90%
Foreign	15% — 73%	0% — 79%

Key Votes of the 104th Congress

1. Reduce Medicare Growth $	Y	5. Flag Amendment	Y	9. Cuban Embargo	Y
2. Ovrd. Product Liab. Veto	Y	6. Drop EPA Limits	N	10. Bar Bosnia Troop $	Y
3. Increase Min. Wage	N	7. Repeal Assault-Weap. Ban	Y	11. Cut Anti-Missile Defense	N
4. Welfare Reform	Y	8. Ovrd. Part. Birth Veto	Y	12. Bar U.N. Uniforms	Y

Election Results

1996 general	Dan Schaefer (R)	146,018	(62%)	($760,648)
	Joan Fitzgerald (D)	88,600	(38%)	($119,224)
1996 primary	Dan Schaefer (R)	unopposed		
1994 general	Dan Schaefer (R)	124,079	(70%)	($495,506)
	John Hallen (D)	49,701	(28%)	($52,171)
	Others	3,929	(2%)	

CONNECTICUT

Connecticut, the nation's highest-income state and quite possibly the wealthiest, through most of its history has been isolated and insular, without significant natural resources, an odd duck of a state that was one of the last to renounce an established church (in 1818) and one of the last to impose an income tax (in the 1990s). Most of Connecticut's residents today trace their ancestry to the Catholic groups who came over in the late 19th or early 20th Centuries. But life here still bears the imprint of its original 17th Century settlers. Connecticut was founded by Puritans who found Massachusetts too lenient and backsliding, and Connecticut Yankees for years have been flintier and more exacting than their Boston brethren—a type readily recognized by readers of Mark Twain's *A Connecticut Yankee in King Arthur's Court*.

They have also turned these characteristics to economic advantage. For Connecticut's affluence has come not from any windfall but from a knack for tinkering. In 1831, Alexis de Tocqueville was struck by how this spot on the map gave America "the clock-peddler, the schoolmaster, and the senator. The first gives you time, the second tells you what to do with it, and the third makes your law and civilization." Connecticut made clocks of wood and metal and hats of felt and invented vulcanized rubber; it produced combs, cigars, clocks, silk thread, pins, matches, furniture; it invented and still manufactures Pez candy in Orange, Pepperidge Farm bread and Nivea cream in Norwalk, the Stanley Powerlock tape measure in New Britain and the Wiffle ball in Shelton. Most importantly, Connecticut—one of the least violent parts of America—has always specialized in arms. The quintessential Connecticut Yankee, Eli Whitney, was the inventor not only of the cotton gin—which may have been the proximate cause of the Civil War—but also of the rifles with interchangeable parts with which so many were killed in that tragic and bloody conflict. For more than a century, ever since Samuel Colt won a War Department contract to manufacture guns for the Mexican-American War, Connecticut has had a close relationship with the military—and at no time more than during the Reagan defense buildup of the 1980s. The state boomed as United Technologies' various subsidiaries made Air Force jets and the Army's Sikorsky helicopters; General Dynamics's Electric Boat Shipyard in New London made the Navy's nuclear submarines.

These arms industries, like Connecticut's civilian manufacturers, depend heavily on precision work. For years, the state was the center of the brass industry, the nation's main producer of precision instruments, a center for machine tools, and the home of high-tech machinery-maker Perkin Elmer. And if Connecticut workers today are more likely the descendants of Irish and Italian immigrants than of Yankee tinkerers, they have not lost the Yankee knack: Connecticut ranks among the highest in new patents per capita. Connecticut also has the skill of cannily assessing risk: that is the foundation for its great insurance companies, Aetna, Connecticut Mutual and ITT Hartford. This business requires not just managing money but understanding people. The poet Wallace Stevens, a Hartford resident in his adult life, worked for The Hartford

Company investigating whether claims were valid or bogus.

But Connecticut has had its tough times. The insurance industry was hit by large casualty losses in the 1990s and has been consolidating. The end of the Cold War and decline of defense spending cost Connecticut nearly 150,000 manufacturing jobs, down from a peak of 420,000 in 1982. Four of the country's 10 fastest shrinking cities are in Connecticut—New Haven, Hartford, Bridgeport, Waterbury—and have lost 51,000 jobs in 10 years. Accordingly, the nation's highest-income state has lost population in the 1990s. But Connecticut is adapting. Its biggest growth industry recently comes from the tiny Mashantucket Pequot tribe and its battery of lawyers and lobbyists that enabled it to set up the Foxwoods Casino, the nation's most profitable, in 1992. Small high-tech businesses burgeoned as well, and by 1993 Connecticut's unemployment rate was again below the national average. But has it lost its knack for tinkering?

Politically, Connecticut has been stubbornly retrograde through much of its history. This was the last state to favor the moribund Federalist Party; it voted for Herbert Hoover in the depression year of 1932. For most of the 20th Century, Connecticut politics was an ethnic struggle between Yankee Republicans and Catholic Democrats, with the latter very slowly but steadily gaining ground. The key figure was John Bailey, state Democratic Party chairman from 1946–75. A master legislative strategist and ticket-balancer, Bailey's power was augmented by Connecticut's strong party and straight ticket voting traditions; he was one of the earliest endorsers of John F. Kennedy, seeing electoral advantage in his Catholicism when most other old-line bosses saw peril. Connecticut also had a vital Republican Party which generated national party chairmen and swept occasional elections from 1950–70. Since then, the straight ticket lever has been abolished and Connecticut has been all over the lot politically. The Protestant-Catholic divide seems less important as memories have faded of the 17th Century religious wars and the immigration surge of the 19th Century, and the guiding political temperament of Connecticut seems to be one of *laissez faire*, a hostility to taxes on the one hand and an aversion to imposition of old moral codes. All of which makes a certain sense in a state which is affluent economically and in which the orthodoxies of Puritan Protestantism and Roman Catholicism no longer claim many adherents. This Connecticut has voted happily for Bill Clinton twice in the 1990s; elected two governors by plurality, former Republican Lowell Weicker who imposed an income tax and Republican John Rowland who opposed it; and an increasing number of Democratic congressmen and legislators who seem unlikely to raise taxes or to challenge Rowland's radical welfare reform.

Governor. Republican John Rowland elected governor in 1994, at 37, was already a grizzled veteran of Connecticut's political wars, with some scar tissue and some muscular strength he didn't have when he started. Rowland grew up in Waterbury, the high-skill factory town that had America's highest percentage of Italian-Americans in the 1990 Census, where his family has owned an insurance agency for four generations and where his father and grandfather were City Comptrollers. He was elected to the state House from a Democratic district, in 1980, at 23, and voted against taxes and for welfare reform. He ran for Congress in 1984, at 27, the youngest member of the House, upsetting a Democratic incumbent. In 1990, at 33, Rowland ran for governor. State government, used to vast spending increases, had fallen deep into deficit with the defense slowdown and recession, despite a 1989 tax increase. It was a three-way race in which Democratic Congressman Bruce Morrison was shoved aside by Lowell Weicker, smarting from defeat in 1988 after three terms as a liberal Republican senator, now running on his own party line. Rowland was against instituting an income tax; Weicker refused to take a position and won 40%–37%. In August 1991 Weicker pushed through the legislature a 4.5% income tax, with mostly Democratic votes; in October 1993 he withdrew from the 1994 race.

Rowland ran again in 1994, this time against Democrat Bill Curry, who ran as an outsider and a moderate, Lieutenant Governor Eunice Groark, the candidate of Weicker's A Connecticut Party, and independent Tom Scott, an anti-tax crusader. Curry said he would keep the income tax and guarantee college educations without increasing taxes. Rowland called for eliminating the income tax and, when President Clinton came to campaign for Curry, warned that,

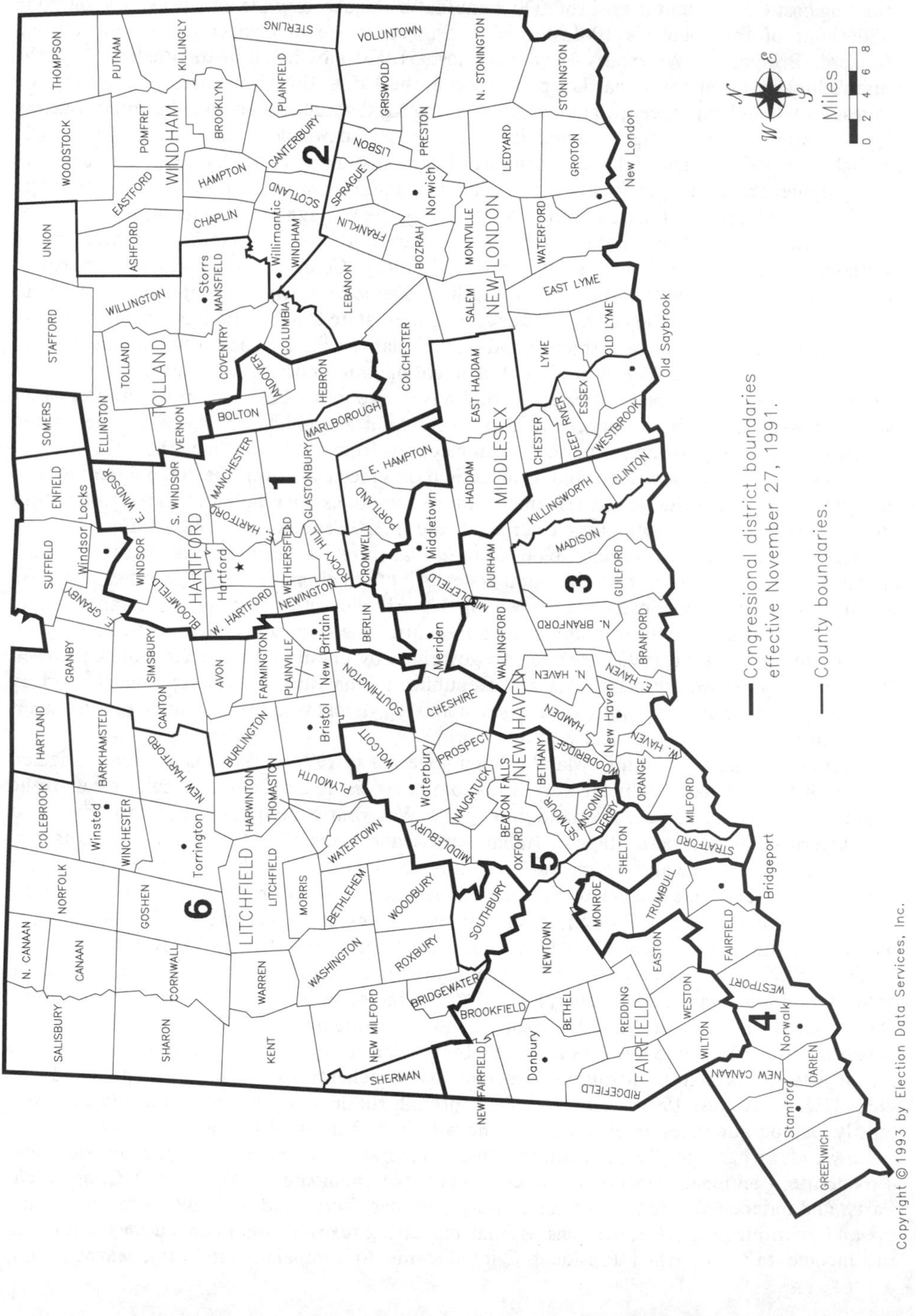

Congressional district boundaries effective November 27, 1991.
County boundaries.
Miles
0 2 4 6 8
Copyright © 1993 by Election Data Services, Inc.
1
2
3
4
5
6
WINDHAM
TOLLAND
HARTFORD
NEW LONDON
MIDDLESEX
NEW HAVEN
LITCHFIELD
FAIRFIELD
THOMPSON
PUTNAM
KILLINGLY
STERLING
VOLUNTOWN
N. STONINGTON
STONINGTON
WOODSTOCK
POMFRET
BROOKLYN
PLAINFIELD
GRISWOLD
PRESTON
LEDYARD
GROTON
New London
CANTERBURY
LISBON
EASTFORD
HAMPTON
SCOTLAND
SPRAGUE
Norwich
UNION
ASHFORD
CHAPLIN
Willimantic
WINDHAM
FRANKLIN
BOZRAH
MONTVILLE
WATERFORD
Storrs
MANSFIELD
WILLINGTON
STAFFORD
LEBANON
SALEM
EAST LYME
COLUMBIA
COVENTRY
TOLLAND
ANDOVER
COLCHESTER
LYME
OLD LYME
Old Saybrook
HEBRON
EAST HADDAM
ESSEX
DEEP RIVER
CHESTER
WESTBROOK
SOMERS
ELLINGTON
VERNON
BOLTON
MARLBOROUGH
E. HAMPTON
HADDAM
CLINTON
KILLINGWORTH
ENFIELD
E. WINDSOR
S. WINDSOR
MANCHESTER
GLASTONBURY
PORTLAND
MADISON
SUFFIELD
Windsor Locks
WINDSOR
E. HARTFORD
Hartford
WETHERSFIELD
ROCKY HILL
CROMWELL
Middletown
DURHAM
GUILFORD
E. GRANBY
BLOOMFIELD
W. HARTFORD
NEWINGTON
MIDDLEFIELD
N. BRANFORD
GRANBY
SIMSBURY
AVON
FARMINGTON
PLAINVILLE
New Britain
BERLIN
Meriden
WALLINGFORD
BRANFORD
N. HAVEN
E. HAVEN
HARTLAND
BARKHAMSTED
CANTON
BURLINGTON
Bristol
SOUTHINGTON
CHESHIRE
HAMDEN
New Haven
NEW HARTFORD
HARWINTON
THOMASTON
PLYMOUTH
WOLCOTT
Waterbury
PROSPECT
BETHANY
WOODBRIDGE
W. HAVEN
COLEBROOK
Winsted
WINCHESTER
Torrington
NAUGATUCK
BEACON FALLS
SEYMOUR
ANSONIA
DERBY
ORANGE
MILFORD
LITCHFIELD
WATERTOWN
MIDDLEBURY
OXFORD
SHELTON
STRATFORD
NORFOLK
GOSHEN
MORRIS
BETHLEHEM
WOODBURY
SOUTHBURY
MONROE
TRUMBULL
Bridgeport
N. CANAAN
CANAAN
CORNWALL
WARREN
WASHINGTON
ROXBURY
NEWTOWN
EASTON
FAIRFIELD
WESTPORT
SALISBURY
SHARON
KENT
NEW MILFORD
BRIDGEWATER
BROOKFIELD
BETHEL
REDDING
WESTON
Norwalk
SHERMAN
NEW FAIRFIELD
Danbury
RIDGEFIELD
WILTON
NEW CANAAN
DARIEN
Stamford
GREENWICH

"Connecticut can't afford another double-talking Bill." This time, in this four-way race, 36% was enough to win. Rowland's strength was in western Connecticut, where Republican leanings, home-town strength and the fact that he was the only candidate able to buy much New York TV time all helped him corral half the vote. Curry carried the Hartford area, central cities and college and mill towns, for 33%; Groark, strongest in WASP areas, had 19%, and Scott, taking almost all his votes from Rowland, had 11%. Republicans also won the state Senate, 19–17. Curry got a job on the White House staff.

In his first year as governor Rowland had surprising success. Connecticut passed a "tough love" welfare bill limiting payments to 21 months and encouraging recipients to get a job and work their way up instead of taking job training courses while collecting benefits. By October 1995 the number of employed welfare parents had doubled. The income tax was cut marginally. Business taxes were lowered and unemployment and workmen's compensation were made more business-friendly. Parents delinquent with child support were denied all state licenses. A new death penalty law and Megan's law to inform communities of released sex offenders were passed. Enterprise zones were passed for the lagging central cities. State art grants were doubled. The state payroll was cut by 2,500. The lottery was privatized.

Rowland's job rating hovered above 50% in fall 1996. But the local Clinton sweep helped Democrats gain seats in the legislature and take over the state Senate 19–17, with wins in marginal areas north and east of Hartford. Rowland had said it would be a "disaster" if Democrats won, but afterward noted blandly that "nobody was really debating our record here in Hartford." Others argued that Democratic control of the legislature would give Rowland an excuse for not eliminating the income tax. Rowland has considerable strength, but his party seemed very weak in 1996, and he is likely to have serious opposition in 1998, perhaps from Curry again, perhaps from Attorney General Richard Blumenthal.

Senior Senator. Christopher Dodd was almost born into politics. His father Thomas Dodd, a prosecutor at the Nuremberg trials, was elected to the House in 1952, when Chris was eight; he lost a Senate race to Prescott Bush, George Bush's father, in 1956, and then won in 1958. Chris Dodd served in the Peace Corps in the Dominican Republican from 1966–68. In 1967, the older Dodd was censured by the Senate for misuse of funds; he ran as an independent in 1970 and Chris Dodd managed his campaign, in which he finished behind Republican Lowell Weicker and Democrat Joseph Duffey, for whom Yale Law School student Bill Clinton was working as a volunteer. Almost immediately after law school, Christopher Dodd ran for Congress in an open seat and, in the Watergate year of 1974, won comfortably. He was reelected easily and in 1980 outmaneuvered fellow Watergate Democrat Toby Moffett to get the Democratic nomination to succeed Senator Abraham Ribicoff, and won that race by a wide margin.

Much of Dodd's work in the Senate has centered on the Western Hemisphere Subcommittee, where he regularly opposed U.S. military aid to El Salvador's government and aid to the Nicaraguan contras; alert to any human rights violations by these forces, he was muted in his criticisms of the pro-Communist Salvador rebels and Sandinistas. Events have not entirely vindicated Dodd's judgment: the El Salvador government has become more observant of human rights than the rebels, and Nicaraguan voters, when given the chance, have voted twice against the Sandinistas. Dodd also worked on the never-passed ABC child care bill, supported by the AFL-CIO and the Children's Defense Fund, which sought to put preschooling into much the same institutional mold as elementary and secondary school, with federal aid aimed at national standards and promoting a corps of teachers trained in education schools and represented by teachers' unions. It passed the Senate but was rejected in the House in the late 1980s.

Other Dodd legislation has been more successful—and often more moderate. He sponsored the Family and Medical Leave Act vetoed by George Bush and signed by Bill Clinton. He worked on the Interstate Banking Act that became law in 1993. He put an Ounce of Prevention Council, which helps local groups cut through the red tape of government crime prevention programs, into the 1994 crime bill. He sponsored a "truth in savings" bill passed in the 1980s and reauthorized in 1995. He wrote a "safe schools" section of the Goals 2000 education law. He fought hard in 1992 to save the Seawolf submarine, built by Electric Boat in Groton.

On voting charts Dodd's record shows up as very liberal (*National Journal* ranked him in the top 20 most liberal Senators for 1995). But he has also supported important legislation sought by business. He was the chief Democratic sponsor of the securities litigation bill sought by high-tech companies and fought by trial lawyers; "people shouldn't make a business out of ambulance chasing when a stock simply fluctuates on the market," he said. When Clinton vetoed it, he immediately started lobbying Senate and House Democrats, and both houses voted to override—the only veto override in the first Clinton term. He was a lead sponsor of the product liability bill vetoed by Clinton in May 1996. He worked with Alfonse D'Amato and Phil Gramm to pass a Securities Promotion Act backed by the SEC and securities industry and signed into law in October 1996. He supported Nancy Kassebaum's FDA reform bill in 1996 and promised to fight for it in 1997. He has supported the McCain-Feingold campaign finance reform plan, also unpassed, and opposed the Helms-Burton law for sanctions on Cuba, managing to drop a provision that would allow lawsuits in U.S. courts.

Dodd's greatest strength is his easy, confident articulateness; in his third decade in Congress and fifth decade of proximity to high office, he seems unfazed by opposition and approaches debates with an affable air, deflating opponents' indignation and suggesting that they are all in this game together. He is fond of mixing with politicians; he has been a close friend to many colleagues, including Ted Kennedy and Bill Clinton. After the 1994 election, he launched a quick and nearly successful campaign for Senate Democratic leader: Jim Sasser, his original choice, had lost in Tennessee, and after a month-long campaign Dodd lost to Tom Daschle by 24–23. (A crucial vote was cast by Ben Nighthorse Campbell, who in March 1995 switched parties.) Dodd was promptly asked by Bill Clinton to be Democratic national chairman and accepted after arranging that the organizational work would be done by Donald Fowler. Dodd performed ably in public debates and set-tos with Republican Chairman Haley Barbour, but was embarrassed in the last weeks of the 1996 campaign when he followed White House orders to stonewall on charges that DNC top-level fundraiser John Huang raised hundreds of thousands in illegal foreign contributions. He later said, "We mades mistakes at the DNC and I was general chairman. I accept responsibility."

Dodd dropped the national chairmanship in January 1997, and now has senior positions now on Foreign Relations and Labor, where he ranks second behind Ted Kennedy. The last time he came up for reelection, in 1992, he easily outspent a wealthy Republican and won 59%–38%. Bill Clinton's strong showing, and Republicans' weak showings, in Connecticut in 1996 make Dodd a heavy favorite for reelection in 1998, barring any serious opposition. Dodd has been mentioned as a presidential candidate, and might some day be one, though he is unlikely to challenge seniority and run against Al Gore in 2000.

Junior Senator. Joseph Lieberman in a decade in the Senate has exerted influence out of proportion to his seniority, committee position or political clout, an influence that came from respect for his independence of mind, civility of spirit and fidelity to causes in which he believes. Yet he is anything but a political innocent. He grew up in Stamford, the son of a liquor store owner, went to Yale, became chairman of the *Yale Daily News*, worked summers for Senator Abraham Ribicoff and the Democratic National Committee. In college he wrote a biography of that quintessential political boss John Bailey, which was both revealing and admiring. He helped found the Caucus of Connecticut Democrats, with liberal reformers and antiwar activists; in 1970 he ran for state Senate in New Haven against the Senate majority leader, and won with volunteer help from a Yale Law student named Bill Clinton. In 1980 he ran for an open House seat and lost 52%–46%; in 1982 he was elected attorney general, where he took action against fake charities, crooked car dealers and gouging merchants.

In 1988 he ran against Senator Lowell Weicker. Both were party mavericks, in different ways—Weicker well to the left of most Republicans on government spending and cultural issues, Lieberman more conservative than most Democrats on cultural issues and foreign policy. Lieberman is an orthodox Jew—he didn't attend the convention that nominated him because it was held on Saturday—and a believer that "we in government should look to religion as a partner, as I think the Founders of our country did." On many issues he ran to Weicker's right, favoring the death penalty and a moment of silence in schools, and opposing Weicker's proposed 30-cent gas tax increase. He ran witty ads, one showing a bear sleeping through work—a nice take-off on the growling but erratic Weicker. Lieberman won 50%–49%; the contest cut across party lines, with Lieberman running especially well in industrial towns and Weicker in Hartford, college towns and tony towns in Litchfield County.

In the Senate Lieberman has been a major force on defense and foreign policy. He was one of the leaders in the fight for the Gulf war resolution in January 1991, "a defining moment," he said—and without his earnest but vehement support it might not have passed. Presciently, he called for "final victory" over Saddam Hussein. He is a strong supporter of Israel but favored F-15 sales to Saudi Arabia in 1992 and interceded with the Clinton campaign to get a hearing for Arab-American Institute head James Zogby. More recently he has favored U.S. ground troops in Bosnia and action against Serb atrocities. He has strongly backed NATO expansion in Eastern Europe. He worked hard to keep funding for the Seawolf submarine and the adjacent Groton submarine base. On economic issues, he has backed capital gains tax cuts for small business ("you can't be pro-jobs and anti-business") and urged President Clinton to sign the 1996 welfare reform bill—both stands opposed by many Democrats. He favors product liability reform, enterprise zones, and tax incentives to clean up brownfields. From a seat on the Environment Committee, he has opposed Republicans' property rights "takings" and changes in wetlands laws. He opposed oil drilling in the Arctic National Wildlife Refuge.

"If you're not speaking the language of values in American politics today, you're not speaking to the minds and hearts of the American people," Lieberman once said. In October 1995 he and *Book of Virtues* author William Bennett and Democrat Sam Nunn criticized by name 10 daytime TV talk shows as "trash TV" and called on corporate heads to quit advertising on them. This had some major impact: several shows were canceled, others became less offensive, and new, more acceptable shows were developed. Also, in June 1995 Lieberman and Bennett and Democratic Party activist C. Delores Tucker criticized "gangsta rap" records for glamorizing violence and degrading behavior; again, there was a corporate response: Time Warner at first bristled, then sold its gangsta rap label.

Lieberman was reelected by a 67%–31% margin in 1994—an extraordinary margin, and in a Republican year. As DLC chairman, he felt considerable satisfaction with the changes in the second two years of the Clinton Administration. He had supported the 1993 tax increase and 1994 crime bill but had called the Clinton healthcare plan "a top-down, welfare-state kind of program." In 1996 he was pleased that Clinton signed the welfare bill, supported the V-chip and other means of increasing parental authority, but criticized the TV rating system announced in December 1996 as "a turkey"; the Democratic Party, he said, was moving his way. Others Democrats of course disagree, and many will try to move it in another direction. But Lieberman says that Franklin Roosevelt, with his skill at adaptation and belief in experimenting with new policies, would be a New Democrat today, and, with his skill and transparent goodheartedness, Lieberman has made some impact on his party.

Presidential politics. Connecticut voted Democratic for president in the 1960s and 1990s, Republican in the 1970s and 1980s. The shifts from party to party have resulted from fractures of old coalitions: the Democrats split in the culture wars of the Nixon years, the Republicans split amid the economic turmoil—more of loss of wealth than of income—in the 1990s. Both splits were symbolized by independent candidacies—Thomas Dodd's independent candidacy for the Senate in 1970, Lowell Weicker's successful third-party candidacy for governor in 1990, followed by Ross Perot's strong 22% here in 1992. Bill Clinton's margin here was solid in 1996, though not as large as suggested in most state polls.

Connecticut's presidential primary, held fairly early in the process, hasn't made much difference in recent races. In March 1992, in a low-turnout primary, Jerry Brown eked out a 37%–36% victory over Bill Clinton; like Gary Hart's 1984 win here, it made little difference. In

1996 Connecticut voted on March 5 and gave Bob Dole a solid 54%–20% lead over Steve Forbes. But that was three days after the primary in South Carolina, where the race already was decided.

Congressional districting. Connecticut's six districts were drawn by a nine-member commission appointed by legislative leaders that made only minimal changes for the 1990s.

The People: Est. Pop. 1996: 3,274,000; Pop. 1990: 3,287,116, down 0.4% 1990–1996. 1.2% of U.S. total, 28th largest; 21% rural. Median age: 36.2 years. 14% 65 years and over. 83.8% White, 7.9% Black, 1.5% Asian, 6.5% Hispanic origin. Households: 55.6% married couple families; 25% married couple fams. w. children; 50% college educ.; median household income: $41,721; per capita income: $20,189; 65.6% owner occupied housing; median house value: $177,800; median median monthly rent: $510. 5.7% Unemployment. 1996 Voting age pop.: 2,479,000. 1996 Turnout: 1,392,614; 56% of VAP. Registered voters (1996): 1,869,913; 668,247 D (36%), 470,774 R (25%), 730,892 unaffiliated and minor parties (39%).

Political Lineup: Governor, John Rowland (R); Lt. Gov., M. Jodi Rell (R); Secy. of State, Miles S. Rapoport (D); Atty. Gen., Richard Blumenthal (D); Treasurer, Christopher Burnham (R); Comptroller, Nancy Wyman (D). State Senate, 36 (19 D and 17 R); Senate President, M. Jodi Rell (R); State House, 151 (96 D and 55 R); House Speaker, Thomas Ritter (D). Senators, Christopher J. Dodd (D) and Joseph I. Lieberman (D). Representatives, 6 (4 D and 2 R).

Elections Division: 860-566-3106; **Filing Deadline for U.S. Congress:** nominated by convention.

1996 Presidential Vote

Clinton (D)	735,740	(53%)
Dole (R)	483,109	(35%)
Perot (I)	139,523	(10%)
Other(s)	34,237	(2%)

1996 Republican Presidential Primary

Dole (R)	70,998	(54%)
Forbes (R)	26,253	(20%)
Buchanan (R)	19,664	(15%)
Alexander (R)	6,985	(5%)
Other	6,518	(5%)

1992 Presidential Vote

Clinton (D)	682,318	(42%)
Bush (R)	578,313	(36%)
Perot (I)	348,771	(22%)

GOVERNOR

Gov. John G. Rowland (R)

Elected 1994, term expires Jan. 1999; b. May 24, 1957, Waterbury; home, Hartford; Villanova U., B.S. 1979; Catholic; married (Patricia).

Career: Insurance Agent, 1979–84; CT House of Reps., 1980–84; U.S. House of Reps., 1984–90.

Office: Executive Chamber, State Capitol, Hartford 06106, 860-566-4840; Fax: 860-566-4677; Web site: www.state.ct.us.

Election Results

1994 gen.	John G. Rowland (R)	415,201	(36%)
	Bill Curry (D)	375,133	(33%)
	Eunice Strong Groark (ACP)	216,585	(19%)
	Tom Scott (I)	130,128	(11%)
1994 prim.	John G. Rowland (R)	78,051	(68%)
	Pauline R. Kezer (R)	37,010	(32%)
1990 gen.	Lowell P. Weicker, Jr. (ACP)	460,576	(40%)
	John G. Rowland (R)	427,840	(37%)
	Bruce Morrison (D)	236,641	(21%)

SENATORS

Sen. Christopher J. Dodd (D)

Elected 1980, seat up 1998; b. May 27, 1944, Willimantic; home, East Haddam; Providence Col., B.A. 1966, U. of Louisville, J.D. 1972; Catholic; divorced.

Career: Peace Corps, Dominican Republic, 1966–68; Army Reserves, 1969–75; Practicing atty., 1972–74; U.S. House of Reps., 1974–80.

DC Office: 444 RSOB 20510, 202-224-2823; Fax: 202-224-1083; e-mail: sen_dodd@dodd.senate.gov.

State Offices: Wethersfield, 203-240-3470.

Committees: *Banking, Housing & Urban Affairs* (2nd of 8 D): Financial Services & Technology; Housing Opportunity & Community Development; Securities (RMM). *Foreign Relations* (3rd of 8 D): European Affairs; International Operations; Western Hemisphere & Peace Corps Affairs (RMM). *Labor & Human Resources* (2nd of 8 D): Children & Families (RMM); Employment & Training. *Rules & Administration* (5th of 7 D).

Group Ratings

	ADA	ACLU	AFS	LCV	CFA	CON	NFIB	COC	ACU	NTLC	CHC
1996	85	39	100	77	71	0	34	38	10	7	7
1995	95	—	91	100	69	19	—	32	4	—	—

National Journal Ratings

	1995 LIB — 1995 CONS	1996 LIB — 1996 CONS
Economic	84% — 15%	89% — 5%
Social	85% — 7%	80% — 8%
Foreign	65% — 31%	61% — 38%

Key Votes of the 104th Congress

1. Reduce Medicare Growth $	N	5. Flag Amendment	N	9. Anti-Missile Defense	N
2. Lmt. Prod. Liab. Damages	Y	6. Endangered Species	Y	10. Cuban Embargo	N
3. Increase Min. Wage	Y	7. Gay Employment Rights	Y	11. Bar Bosnia Troop $	N
4. Welfare Reform	N	8. Ovrd. Part. Birth Veto	N	12. Cut Vietnam Aid	N

Election Results

1992 general	Christopher J. Dodd (D-ACP)	882,569	(59%)	($4,553,792)
	Brook Johnson (R)	572,036	(38%)	($2,395,262)
	Others	46,104	(3%)	
1992 primary	Christopher J. Dodd (D-ACP), nom. by convention			
1986 general	Christopher J. Dodd (D)	632,695	(65%)	($2,276,764)
	Roger W. Eddy (R)	340,438	(35%)	($183,632)

Sen. Joseph I. Lieberman (D)

Elected 1988, seat up 2000; b. Feb. 24, 1942, Stamford; home, New Haven; Yale, B.A. 1964, LL.B. 1967; Jewish; married (Hadassah).

Career: CT Senate, 1970–80, Majority Ldr., 1974–80; CT Atty. Gen., 1983–88.

DC Office: 706 HSOB 20510, 202-224-4041; Fax: 202-224-9750; e-mail: senator_lieberman@lieberman.senate.gov.

State Offices: Hartford, 860-549-8463.

Committees: *Armed Services* (7th of 8 D): Acquisition & Technology (RMM); Airland Forces; Sea Power. *Environment & Public Works* (6th of 8 D): Clean Air, Wetlands, Private Property & Nuclear Safety; Drinking Water, Fisheries & Wildlife. *Governmental Affairs* (3rd of 7 D): Oversight of Government Management, Restructuring & the District of Columbia (RMM); Permanent Subcommittee on Investigations. *Small Business* (5th of 8 D).

Group Ratings

	ADA	ACLU	AFS	LCV	CFA	CON	NFIB	COC	ACU	NTLC	CHC
1996	75	28	86	77	64	30	46	54	35	31	7
1995	95	—	100	100	81	2	—	33	10	—	—

National Journal Ratings

	1995 LIB — 1995 CONS	1996 LIB — 1996 CONS
Economic	85% — 14%	55% — 44%
Social	76% — 18%	63% — 34%
Foreign	22% — 67%	51% — 45%

Key Votes of the 104th Congress

1. Reduce Medicare Growth $	N	5. Flag Amendment	N	9. Anti-Missile Defense	Y
2. Lmt. Prod. Liab. Damages	Y	6. Endangered Species	Y	10. Cuban Embargo	Y
3. Increase Min. Wage	Y	7. Gay Employment Rights	Y	11. Bar Bosnia Troop $	N
4. Welfare Reform	Y	8. Ovrd. Part. Birth Veto	N	12. Cut Vietnam Aid	N

Election Results

1994 general	Joseph I. Lieberman (D)	723,842	(67%)	($4,017,520)
	Jerry Labriola (R)	334,833	(31%)	($166,064)
	Others	20,989	(2%)	
1994 primary	Joseph I. Lieberman (D)	nominated by convention		
1988 general	Joseph I. Lieberman (D)	688,499	(50%)	($2,570,779)
	Lowell P. Weicker, Jr. (R)	678,454	(49%)	($2,609,902)

FIRST DISTRICT

In 1871, Mark Twain moved to Hartford to become director of an insurance company, and in time became the Connecticut capital's most famous citizen. Hartford, already more than two centuries old, home of the nation's longest circulating newspaper (since 1764), the *Hartford Courant*, was becoming the nation's best-known insurance center. This was not a role envisioned by the harsh Puritans who established Hartford as a haven from backsliding Bostonians, but Connecticut's Yankees turned out to be shrewd businessmen. Thanks to the broad Connecticut River, Hartford became a seaport; its merchants, prevented from trading and writing marine insurance by Thomas Jefferson's Embargo Act of 1807, turned to writing fire insurance and using the capital they'd accumulated in the Napoleonic Wars to finance their ventures. They were also ready to finance tinkerers like Samuel Colt, whose gun factory just south of downtown Hartford became one of the nation's great arms plants—and whose company became a symbol of Connecticut's recession when it went into Chapter 11 in 1992.

Insurance and arms are still economic mainstays of Hartford, Connecticut's capital and the center of its largest metropolitan concentration. Though their economic clout and workforce have diminished, Hartford-headquartered Aetna, CIGNA and ITT Hartford are among the nation's biggest insurers, with some $200 billion in assets. Just across the river is the Pratt and Whitney jet engine plant in East Hartford, cornerstone of Connecticut-based defense contractor United Technologies. Surrounding the downtown Hartford now are slums; the central city is troubled by high crime and poor schools (contracted out to a private firm and declared unconstitutionally segregated by the state Supreme Court) and many neighborhoods have emptied out.

The 1st Congressional District of Connecticut is centered on Hartford, but it now casts only 12% of its votes—fewer than West Hartford and not much more than Manchester or East Hartford. Politically, the Hartford area has long been more Democratic than the rest of Connecticut: Hartford in Connecticut is something like Boston in Massachusetts, a great commercial metropolis more statist than is its surroundings. But Hartford had a political leader more effective over a longer period than any in Boston—John Bailey, longtime state (1946–75) and national (1961–68) Democratic chairman, an old-fashioned political boss with a scandal-free career who promoted a raft of first-class candidates.

Representing the 1st District in the House today is Barbara Kennelly, John Bailey's daughter and widow of a former speaker of the Connecticut House. She grew up in Hartford, served on the Hartford Court of Common Council in the 1970s, was elected secretary of State in 1978 and won her seat in the House in a January 1982 special election. In 1983 she got a seat on Ways and Means, whose jurisdiction over taxes is vital to the insurance industry. She fought successfully during the 1986 tax reform against Chairman Dan Rostenkowski to save single-premium insurance policies from what the insurance companies consider overtaxation. She won passage of a law eliminating taxes on accelerated life insurance death benefits to the terminally ill. She sponsored a bill to get annual mammograms for women over 65. In the Clinton healthcare plan, she supported maintaining a role for private insurers and permitting premiums based on experience rating rather that community rating. She managed the revision of the "nanny tax" in 1994. She passed the historic preservation tax credit and child support enforcement laws.

Kennelly has been a team player among House Democrats, and was elected vice chairman of the Democratic Caucus in November 1994, a position she still holds. She was co-chairman of the Democrats' 1996 Platform Committee. On the 1996 welfare bill she successfully prevented reductions in federal foster care and child protection spending, but failed to require states to spend 85% of current spending. She was a leader in the fight for most favored nation status for China, a big customer for Pratt and Whitney jet engines, and helped get Export-Import Bank financing for the sale of such engines to Russia. At home she has funneled money to the Old State House renovation, Riverfront Recapture and Children's Hospital.

Kennelly passed up the chance to run for governor in 1990, but in early 1997 seemed to be exploring a race in 1998; although she has become a national leader of her party, she does not seem happy serving in the minority. In the 1st District she has been reelected by impressive margins. In 1996 her Republican opponent, Webster Brooks, withdrew in July after local Republicans failed to invite him to a Bob Dole appearance in Hartford; given Dole's 59%–30% loss in the district, he might better have thanked them. The substitute candidate, a former Glastonbury school board member, lost 74%–25%.

The People: Pop. 1990: 547,979; 11% rural; 14% age 65+; 75% White; 13% Black; 2% Asian; 10% Hispanic origin. Households: 51% married couple families; 22% married couple fams. w. children; 49% college educ.; median household income: $39,961; per capita income: $18,644; median gross rent: $572; median house value: $170,700.

1996 Presidential Vote

Clinton (D)	136,775	(59%)
Dole (R)	68,483	(30%)
Perot (I)	20,862	(9%)
Other	5,204	(2%)

1992 Presidential Vote

Clinton (D)	133,686	(50%)
Bush (R)	82,086	(31%)
Perot (I)	52,154	(19%)

Rep. Barbara B. Kennelly (D)

Elected 1982; b. Jul. 10, 1936, Hartford; home, Hartford; Trinity Col. (DC), B.A. 1958, Trinity Col. (Hartford), M.A. 1971; Catholic; widowed.

Career: Vice Chmn., Hartford Comm. on Aging, 1971–75; Hartford Court of Common Cncl., 1975–79; CT Secy. of State, 1979–82.

DC Office: 201 CHOB 20515, 202-225-2265; Fax: 202-225-1031.

District Offices: Hartford, 860-278-8888.

Committees: *Democratic Caucus Vice Chairman. Ways & Means* (4th of 16 D): Social Security (RMM).

Group Ratings

	ADA	ACLU	AFS	LCV	CFA	CON	NFIB	COC	ACU	NTLC	CHC
1996	80	56	100	77	85	96	35	25	10	10	7
1995	85	—	—	81	100	16	—	33	12	—	—

National Journal Ratings

	1995 LIB	—	1995 CONS	1996 LIB	—	1996 CONS
Economic	74%	—	25%	73%	—	25%
Social	75%	—	23%	84%	—	12%
Foreign	73%	—	24%	66%	—	33%

Key Votes of the 104th Congress

1. Reduce Medicare Growth $	N	5. Flag Amendment	Y	9. Cuban Embargo	Y
2. Ovrd. Product Liab. Veto	Y	6. Drop EPA Limits	Y	10. Bar Bosnia Troop $	N
3. Increase Min. Wage	Y	7. Repeal Assault-Weap. Ban	N	11. Cut Anti-Missile Defense	Y
4. Welfare Reform	N	8. Ovrd. Part. Birth Veto	N	12. Bar U.N. Uniforms	N

Election Results

1996 general	Barbara B. Kennelly (D)	158,222	(74%)	($543,033)
	Kent Sleath (R)	53,666	(25%)	($8,459)
	Others	3,248	(2%)	
1996 primary	Barbara B. Kennelly (D). nominated by convention			
1994 general	Barbara B. Kennelly (D)	138,637	(73%)	($579,121)
	Douglas T. Putnam (R)	46,865	(25%)	($24,693)
	Others	3,405	(2%)	

SECOND DISTRICT

Eastern Connecticut, where small rivers run past flinty hills down toward Long Island Sound, is one of those little-known parts of America which have contributed quietly to the nation's heritage. Historically this was high-tech country. New London and Norwich were among the 13 colonies' leading workshops and ports, and in the 19th Century, factories sprang up around mills in little villages on the fast-flowing Quinebaug and Shetucket Rivers. Sandbars kept oceangoing ships out of the rivers, but they docked at New London. In the mid-20th Century four nuclear power plants were built here, more than in any similarly-populated part of the United States. And in Groton, across the Thames River from New London, is General Dynamics' Electric Boat Company, the major producer for four decades of nuclear submarines, with a much smaller work force but kept in operation, lest we lose the capacity to produce these marvels of engineering and science which may very well have deterred nuclear war.

Today eastern Connecticut seems to be moving from technology to entertainment. It has six of the state's leading tourist destinations, including Mystic Seaport and the Coast Guard Academy, and Six Flags amusement park has proposed building a $200 million facility in North Stonington. Electric Boat has yielded its place as the area's biggest employer to the Foxwoods Casino, the largest in the East, with hotels and golf courses and a convention center, which has 10,000 employees and attracts 50,000 visitors a day. Foxwoods was built by the 370-member Mashantucket Pequot tribe and the legions of managers and lawyers and lobbyists it has hired. The tribe has reaped enormous profits, donating $10 million to the National Museum of the American Indian and $500,000 to the Democratic Party before the 1994 elections; right afterwards, they ponied up some $300,000 to the Republicans. Despite its efforts, Foxwoods now has competition, from the Mohegan Sun Casino down the road in Montville which opened in October 1996.

The 2d Congressional District includes most of eastern Connecticut, centering on New London and Norwich, including mill towns and the university town of Storrs nestled in the rocky hills to the north, and stretching west to Middletown, once ethnic and now a college town, and picturesque resort towns like Old Lyme and Old Saybrook on Long Island Sound. For many years this was a politically marginal district, with close battles between Yankee Republicans and Catholic Democrats. In the 1990s it has been the scene of political rebellions. The 2d District voted 27% for Ross Perot in 1992—his best showing in New England after the two Maine districts—and in 1994 it came within 21 votes of defeating a Democratic congressman who won by large margins in the 1980s. In the 105th Congress only four Democratic congressmen—the two from Maine, Texas conservative Ralph Hall, and Minnesota's David Minge—represent districts with a higher 1992 Perot percentage.

The congressman from the 2d is Sam Gejdenson, one of the leading liberal Democrats now in the House, who was first elected in 1980 at 32. Gejdenson was born in a German displaced persons camp, the son of concentration camp inmates, and grew up on a dairy farm in Bozrah, Connecticut; he likes to refer to himself wryly as "just a farm boy who spends his week in Washington." He was elected to the legislature in 1974, at 26, served as a staffer to Governor Ella Grasso, then ran for the House when then-Congressman Christopher Dodd ran for the Senate. Gejdenson brings to his work good-humored energy and a set of beliefs characteristic of many of the liberals first elected in the Watergate year of 1974. He believes that an energetic and expanding government can help ordinary people, he has generally been suspicious about the assertion of American power abroad, and he tends to champion liberal cultural values. Of course he has worked hard and with considerable success to keep Electric Boat operating and is an active supporter of the Coast Guard. He was a strong supporter of Speaker Thomas Foley, and in December 1992 Foley put him in charge of campaign finance reform for the party. This was an example of the fox guarding the chicken coop—Gejdenson had just won reelection over Republican Ed Munster by a 51%–49% margin after outspending Munster $1,014,000 to $140,000. In 1994, he faced Munster again, and this time—after the state Supreme Court's six-day hearing and final count—won by the less-than-landslide margin of 21 votes. In this contest Gejdenson spent $1,422,000 and Munster $426,000.

Neither of these close calls stopped Gejdenson from compiling one of the most liberal voting records in the House. In 1995 he became second ranking Democrat on the International Relations Committee, where he has worked to relax export controls on countries like China and Russia, strongly supported Israel, and has said the U.S. commitment to Taiwan was greater than to Saudi Arabia or Kuwait (he voted in 1991 against the Gulf war resolution). He supported direct student loans and led a highly-publicized crusade against high breakfast cereal prices which resulted in 10% to 20% price decreases. He worked on a National Heritage Corridor and for nuclear plant worker safety. In 1996 with Minority Leader Dick Gephardt he produced a pension bill to increase portability and encourage small business pension plans.

Munster, a biostatistician at Pfizer in Groton, has now run three losing races against Gejdenson, in different political climates. In 1992 he was on the attack, charging that Gejdenson voted "against every weapons system except the bow and arrow" and that "Sam greased the wheels for Saddam." In 1994 it was a three-way race, with obstetrician and ice cream store owner David Bingham, a grandson of Connecticut Governor and Senator Hiram Bingham, running as an environmentalist and pro-choicer; he took 15%, probably most of it from Gejdenson. Initial returns had Gejdenson ahead by 2 votes, out of 186,000 cast; recounts raised his margin to 4 and finally, before the state Supreme Court, 21. But House Republicans decided not to examine the results for themselves and overturn them, as House Democrats, with Gejdenson taking a lead role on the then-House Administration Committee, had done in a similar case in 1987.

In 1996 Gejdenson was more on the attack and Munster more on the defensive. Munster won his primary by only 60%–40% over state Representative Andrew Norton, who called for new blood. And Gejdenson sharply attacked Speaker Newt Gingrich's "extreme agenda" and charged that Republicans were trying to cut Medicare. Munster criticized Gejdenson with some effect for voting against welfare reform and term limits, but his attacks on Gejdenson's 51 overdrafts on the House bank may have sounded stale. Interestingly, even with Republicans in control of the House, Gejdenson got the lion's share of PAC money, outraising Munster $398,000 to $75,000 among them in 1996. Also Gejdenson raised $650,000 in individual contributions, many of them undoubtedly from Jewish contributors across the country; he was the nation's number one recipient of pro-Israel PAC money in 1987–95, with $126,000, according to *Congressional Quarterly*. And the political terrain was much more favorable for Gejdenson than in 1994. The Perot vote dropped to 13% (still the highest of any Connecticut district), there was no serious third candidate, and Bill Clinton was running far ahead here, and came in to help Gejdenson. The result was a 48%–45% Gejdenson victory.

That was hardly a landslide, but it may be enough to discourage Munster or another serious Republican, and it at least gives Gejdenson another term as a leading Democrat in the House. As ranking minority member on the House Oversight Committee, he will take a leading role for Democrats on campaign finance reform bills. As second ranking Democrat on International Relations he is in position to affect American policy in many parts of the world. But he must also spend time shoring up his position in the ornery-minded 2d District.

The People: Pop. 1990: 548,018; 45% rural; 12% age 65+; 92% White; 4% Black; 1% Asian; 3% Hispanic origin. Households: 59% married couple families; 27% married couple fams. w. children; 48% college educ.; median household income: $38,524; per capita income: $16,946; median gross rent: $564; median house value: $150,900.

1996 Presidential Vote			1992 Presidential Vote		
Clinton (D)	123,595	(53%)	Clinton (D)	113,553	(43%)
Dole (R)	73,863	(32%)	Bush (R)	79,110	(30%)
Perot (I)	29,790	(13%)	Perot (I)	72,782	(27%)
Other	6,991	(3%)			

Rep. Samuel Gejdenson (D)

Elected 1980; b. May 20, 1948, Eschwege, Germany; home, Bozrah; Mitchell Col., A.S. 1966, U. of CT, B.A. 1970; Jewish; married (Betsy Henley-Cohn).

Career: CT House of Reps., 1974–78; Legis. Liaison to CT Gov. Ella Grasso, 1979–80.

DC Office: 1401 LHOB 20515, 202-225-2076; Fax: 202-225-4977; e-mail: bozrah@hr.house.gov

District Offices: Middletown, 203-346-1123; Norwich, 203-886-0139.

Committees: *International Relations* (2nd of 21 D): International Economic Policy & Trade (RMM). *House Oversight* (RMM of 3 D). *Joint Committee on the Library of Congress* (5th of 5 Reps.). *Joint Committee on Printing* (5th of 5 Reps.).

Group Ratings

	ADA	ACLU	AFS	LCV	CFA	CON	NFIB	COC	ACU	NTLC	CHC
1996	90	88	100	85	100	38	16	20	0	5	0
1995	90	—	—	94	92	4	—	13	4	—	—

National Journal Ratings

	1995 LIB — 1995 CONS			1996 LIB — 1996 CONS		
Economic	85%	—	12%	79%	—	18%
Social	88%	—	0%	88%	—	0%
Foreign	84%	—	15%	76%	—	22%

Key Votes of the 104th Congress

1. Reduce Medicare Growth $	N	5. Flag Amendment	N	9. Cuban Embargo	N
2. Ovrd. Product Liab. Veto	N	6. Drop EPA Limits	Y	10. Bar Bosnia Troop $	N
3. Increase Min. Wage	Y	7. Repeal Assault-Weap. Ban	N	11. Cut Anti-Missile Defense	Y
4. Welfare Reform	N	8. Ovrd. Part. Birth Veto	N	12. Bar U.N. Uniforms	N

Election Results

1996 general	Samuel Gejdenson (D)	115,175	(52%)	($1,177,355)
	Edward W. Munster (R)	100,332	(45%)	($423,658)
	Others	7,740	(3%)	
1996 primary	Samuel Gejdenson (D), nominated by convention			
1994 general	Samuel Gejdenson (D)	79,188	(43%)	($1,422,126)
	Edward W. Munster (R)	79,167	(43%)	($426,390)
	David Bingham (ACP)	27,716	(15%)	

THIRD DISTRICT

Two centuries ago, in 1798, Eli Whitney, a young Yale graduate, won an order from the federal government to produce 10,000 muskets at $13.40 each: the beginning of Connecticut's defense industry. Six years before, Whitney had invented the cotton gin, which revolutionized the South but for years only embroiled him in a patent suit. On the musket contract, he was determined to make a profit right off, so he set up a system of interchangeable parts and invented a milling machine and gauges: the beginning of standardized American manufacturing. It was also the beginning of New Haven, Connecticut, as a manufacturing center, for Whitney set up his factory along a small, rapidly flowing river just north of this town established more than 150 years before as a religious haven for strict Puritans. For the next 150 years or so, the town mass-produced rifles, clocks, locks, hardware and toys—anything its tinkerers and entrepreneurs could fashion. Manufacturing is less important than it used to be, and there is not a large white collar employment center as exists in Hartford. Yale, with its gothic spires, redbrick halls and modernist skating rink, has always been the visual focus of the city; now Yale is New Haven's largest employer, while the city's population is far below its historic peak.

The 3d Congressional District of Connecticut covers the New Haven metropolitan area, which has long since spread beyond the narrow city limits over the hills of what were once Yankee villages and countryside; the population-losing city of New Haven cast only 15% of its votes in 1996. Politics in the New Haven area for years was a three-cornered battle, between Yankee Republicans, Irish Democrats, and Italians who became its largest ethnic group and usually voted Republican: in effect each group joined the party not supported by the people who welcomed them at the docks. Though often regarded as a Democratic seat, the 3d has been marginal, changing partisan hands in the 1980s as well as the 1940s and 1950s.

Rose DeLauro, congresswoman from the 3d District, is well connected in New Haven and Washington. She grew up in New Haven's Wooster Square, where her father Ted was alderman; today her mother, Luisa DeLauro, is New Haven's longest-serving alderman and her husband Stanley Greenberg was Bill Clinton's chief pollster from 1991–94, and a thoughtful academic and author of *Middle Class Dreams*. Rosa DeLauro has been in politics for years: she was a development administrator in New Haven in the 1970s, chief of staff to Senator Christopher Dodd from 1980–87, then spent a year working to stop U.S. military aid to Nicaraguan contras before going on to become director of EMILY's List, the spectacularly successful liberal women's fundraising group; in 1996 it raised more money than any other PAC—more than $12 million. In 1990, when 3d District incumbent Bruce Morrison ran for governor, DeLauro ran for Congress, and won 52%–48% over anti-tax and anti-abortion legislator Tom Scott after spending an impressive $957,000.

DeLauro is now a chief deputy whip, part of the Democratic leadership that meets every morning at 8:30 and then again at 5:00 when the House is in session. She has supported the Clinton Administration faithfully for the most part, though she, like most House Democratic leaders, voted against NAFTA. She has cheerfully joined other Democrats in bringing ethics charges against Speaker Newt Gingrich, all but one of which were dismissed. She has been an active and enthusiastic supporter of feminist causes. In 1991 she was formally called down for demanding the Senate hold "a full and public hearing" on Anita Hill's charges (House rules forbid urging the Senate to do anything). More recently her amendment to end the ban on abortions in military hospitals abroad failed 20–25 in the National Security Committee, of which she is a junior member. She has proposed that HMOs be banned from requiring women to be discharged from hospitals until 48 hours after mastectomies.

DeLauro lost a seat on Appropriations when Democrats lost their majority in 1994, but regained a seat there in 1996. She has worked on local projects: helping Longshoremen's Local 1398 to buy the bankrupt New Haven Terminal port facilities; getting federal money to purchase the Great Meadows Salt Marsh to complete the Stewart McKinney Wildlife Reserve; starting, with Attorney General Richard Blumenthal, a "Kick Butts Connecticut" campaign against juvenile smoking; sponsoring a New Haven Truancy Court with Mayor John DeStefano.

DeLauro's last serious competition in the 3d District came in 1992, when she outspent Scott $1,022,000 to $219,000 and beat him 66%–34%. She won easily in 1994 over a black Republican who attacked her as an insider and in 1996 over a Republican who said he would spend no more than $40,000, and didn't. As Bill Clinton was easily winning the district where he attended law school, DeLauro won 71%–28%.

The People: Pop. 1990: 547,904; 12% rural; 15% age 65+; 82% White; 12% Black; 2% Asian; 5% Hispanic origin. Households: 54% married couple families; 23% married couple fams. w. children; 48% college educ.; median household income: $39,815; per capita income: $18,243; median gross rent: $623; median house value: $173,300.

1996 Presidential Vote

Clinton (D)	129,756	(57%)
Dole (R)	71,009	(31%)
Perot (I)	22,916	(10%)
Other	5,531	(2%)

1992 Presidential Vote

Clinton (D)	121,163	(44%)
Bush (R)	96,085	(35%)
Perot (I)	54,147	(20%)

Rep. Rosa L. DeLauro (D)

Elected 1990; b. Mar. 2, 1943, New Haven; home, New Haven; Marymount Col., B.A. 1964, London Sch. of Economics, 1962–63, Columbia U., M.A. 1966; Roman Catholic; married (Stanley Greenberg).

Career: Exec. Asst., New Haven Mayor Frank Logue, 1976–77; Exec. Asst. and Development Admin., City of New Haven, 1977–79; Chief of Staff, U.S. Sen. Christopher Dodd, 1980–87; Exec. Dir., Countdown '87, 1987–88; Exec. Dir., EMILY's List, 1989.

DC Office: 436 CHOB 20515, 202-225-3661; Fax: 202-225-4890.

District Offices: New Haven, 203-562-3718.

Committees: *Chief Deputy Minority Whip. Appropriations* (20th of 26 D): Agriculture, Rural Development, FDA & Related Agencies; Labor, Health & Human Services & Education.

Group Ratings

	ADA	ACLU	AFS	LCV	CFA	CON	NFIB	COC	ACU	NTLC	CHC
1996	85	69	100	85	100	38	22	19	0	7	7
1995	85	—	—	94	100	4	—	25	4	—	—

National Journal Ratings

	1995 LIB — 1995 CONS	1996 LIB — 1996 CONS
Economic	80% — 18%	79% — 18%
Social	80% — 13%	84% — 12%
Foreign	79% — 17%	76% — 22%

Key Votes of the 104th Congress

1. Reduce Medicare Growth $	N	5. Flag Amendment	N	9. Cuban Embargo	N
2. Ovrd. Product Liab. Veto	N	6. Drop EPA Limits	Y	10. Bar Bosnia Troop $	N
3. Increase Min. Wage	Y	7. Repeal Assault-Weap. Ban	N	11. Cut Anti-Missile Defense	Y
4. Welfare Reform	N	8. Ovrd. Part. Birth Veto	N	12. Bar U.N. Uniforms	N

Election Results

1996 general	Rosa L. DeLauro (D)	150,798	(71%)	($424,582)
	John Coppola (R)	59,335	(28%)	
1996 primary	Rosa L. DeLauro (D), nominated by convention			
1994 general	Rosa L. DeLauro (D)	111,261	(63%)	($655,245)
	Susan E. Johnson (R)	64,094	(37%)	($8,297)

FOURTH DISTRICT

The hilly land rising from Long Island Sound in the southwest corner of Connecticut has long been the site of some of America's most affluent suburbs; today it is the site also of an edge city that is the biggest office center between Manhattan and Boston. Little in its early history suggested this prominence; this was lightly populated Yankee farm country in the 17th and 18th Centuries, which in the 19th became industrial as Bridgeport became a factory town, famous as the home of P. T. Barnum. By the early 20th Century, Greenwich and other Yankee villages clustered around commuter railroad stations became the home of some of New York's elite. Greenwich's beautifully manicured hills, its elaborately simple boat docks, its carefully casual roads, its good manners and dull haircuts, 16 private clubs and 10 private schools, give it a plainly American—and affluent—look. New York's corporate leaders, eager as always to minimize their own commutes, have moved their headquarters out to Greenwich and Stamford and Fairfield and points inland: General Electric, American Brands, Union Carbide, Champion International, Pitney Bowes, and Olin. The real estate bust of the 1990s left edge city Stamford with high vacancy rates, and some corporate headquarters have been downsized. But small businesses surged into the vacuum and this is still affluent country.

The 4th Congressional District of Connecticut covers all of Connecticut along Long Island Sound from industrial Bridgeport to Greenwich, plus several inland towns. It includes Stamford, chock full of office complexes; woodsy Darien and New Canaan; Norwalk, with its industrial zone and modest neighborhoods down by the tracks; artsy-craftsy Westport; Fairfield, home of GE; Bethel, where Duracell opened its $70 million headquarters in 1995; and Bridgeport, an odd duck, industrial and low-income, where the Mashantucket Pequots tried and failed to build an $875 million gambling casino. The basic political balance has been the same since the 1940s, when the heavily affluent suburbs attracted enough people to outvote Bridgeport and elect Republican Clare Boothe Luce to the House in 1942 and 1944. More than the rest of Connecticut, the 4th is oriented to New York rather than Hartford or Boston. People here watch New York TV stations: they are Yankee, not Red Sox, fans; their political attitudes are shaped by what is happening in the City as much as in Hartford. Hatred of the state income tax enabled Republican gubernatorial candidate John Rowland to carry this area heavily in 1990 against Greenwich native Lowell Weicker and again in 1994. But the specter of religious right domination of the Republican Party eroded the Episcopalian Republican vote and helped Bill Clinton make a dead heat of the race here against Greenwich native George Bush in 1992 and to beat Bob Dole 51%–40% in 1996.

The 4th District's congressman, Christopher Shays, is a product of the upscale towns and one of the most influential—and unusual—Republicans in the House. Shays grew up in Stamford. After college he and his wife volunteered for the Peace Corps and served in Fiji; after graduate school he was elected to the Connecticut House at 29 and served for 12 years, working with Common Cause on rules reform. He won the U.S. House seat in a 1987 special election by beating a culturally conservative Democrat from Bridgeport after incumbent Stewart McKinney, a liberal Republican who left his name on an act to help the homeless, died of AIDS. Shays is a pleasant man with a stubborn streak and considerable legislative savvy. In 1985, he went to the length of going to jail for seven days to protest judicial system corruption. He is middle-of-the-road on economics, rather liberal on cultural issues, mixed on foreign policy. Yet when they were in power the Democratic leadership had little to do with him, and he is an admirer and dedicated ally of Newt Gingrich. He is pro-gun control, in favor of many environmental regulations, against term limits, a sponsor of the McCain-Feingold campaign finance reform bill, and pro-choice on abortion, although he switched his vote in 1997 to support a ban on partial birth abortion. But, as he put it in January 1996, "I am very much a part of the Republican revolution—and I do think it is a revolution—but I am still an independent person."

In 1994 and 1995 Shays played a critical role in unraveling the Democratic majority and establishing Republican working control of the House. In August 1994, although he had voted for the Clinton Administration crime bill, he withdrew his support in protest at Democratic tactics, and at Gingrich's behest led a team of Republican moderates to negotiate with the administration. When the new Republican House assembled on January 4, 1995, the first major bill was managed by Shays, the Congressional Accountability Act, imposing on Congress the laws it imposes on others; it passed unanimously. Shays was also chief sponsor of the gift ban law and the Lobby Disclosure Act(with Charles Canady). As chairman of the Human Resources and Intergovernmental Relations Subcommittee, he sponsored with Steven Schiff a law making healthcare fraud a federal crime and held hearings on Gulf war syndrome. He was not always working in tandem with the Republican leadership. With Jack Quinn of Buffalo, he rallied support for the minimum wage increase Republican leaders opposed but Democrats pushed forward in 1996. And his amendment to freeze 1997 defense spending at 1996 levels failed by only a 219–193 margin, as party discipline on both sides withered. But Shays's Republican loyalties continued. He deeply resented Democrats' charges that Republicans were cutting school lunches ("blatant falsehood" he characterized a charge by his Connecticut neighbor Rosa DeLauro) and cutting Medicare (he chaired the Republican Medicare working group on the Budget Committee). Over the years, he has worked on a bipartisan basis on other efforts, including Tom Lantos's extensive investigation of HUD, cable reregulation and the Clinton Administration's National Service legislation.

Before 1996 Shays had been reelected by wide margins. But in 1996 Bridgeport Councilman Bill Finch attacked him for supporting Newt Gingrich. Shays's response was, "It's not about Newt Gingrich. It's not about Bill Clinton. It's about whether I've done the job. I think I've been tremendously effective." But his percentage dropped from 74% in 1994 to a still comfortable 60% in 1996; he carried Bridgeport with 55% in the earlier year and lost it 64%–33% two years later. Reporters were happy to quote him after the election when he said he wouldn't vote for Gingrich for speaker until the report of the Ethics Committee's outside counsel was made public. But he voted for him in the Republican Conference and seems likely to continue working with—often backing, sometimes opposing—the Republican leadership.

The People: Pop. 1990: 547,561; 4% rural; 14% age 65+; 74% White; 13% Black; 2% Asian; 11% Hispanic origin. Households: 55% married couple families; 23% married couple fams. w. children; 54% college educ.; median household income: $47,636; per capita income: $27,130; median gross rent: $706; median house value: $275,500.

1996 Presidential Vote

Clinton (D)	113,411	(51%)
Dole (R)	88,181	(40%)
Perot (I)	14,825	(7%)
Other	5,355	(2%)

1992 Presidential Vote

Bush (R)	110,072	(42%)
Clinton (D)	109,122	(42%)
Perot (I)	40,802	(16%)

Rep. Christopher Shays (R)

Elected Aug. 1987; b. Oct. 18, 1945, Stamford; home, Stamford; Principia Col., B.A. 1968, NYU, M.B.A. 1974, M.P.A. 1978; Christian Scientist; married (Betsi).

Career: Peace Corps 1968–70; Aide, Trumbull Mayor, 1971–72; CT House of Reps., 1974–87.

DC Office: 1502 LHOB 20515, 202-225-5541; Fax: 202-225-9629; e-mail: cshays@hr.house.gov.

District Offices: Bridgeport, 203-579-5870; Norwalk, 203-866-6469; Stamford, 203-357-8277.

Committees: *Budget* (3rd of 24 R). *Government Reform & Oversight* (5th of 24 R): Human Resources (Chmn.); National Security, International Affairs & Criminal Justice.

Group Ratings

	ADA	ACLU	AFS	LCV	CFA	CON	NFIB	COC	ACU	NTLC	CHC
1996	30	25	33	54	77	97	70	69	60	81	46
1995	40	—	—	31	100	95	—	79	40	—	—

National Journal Ratings

	1995 LIB — 1995 CONS			1996 LIB — 1996 CONS		
Economic	52%	—	48%	51%	—	48%
Social	67%	—	32%	58%	—	41%
Foreign	59%	—	39%	72%	—	27%

Key Votes of the 104th Congress

1. Reduce Medicare Growth $	Y	5. Flag Amendment	N	9. Cuban Embargo	Y
2. Ovrd. Product Liab. Veto	Y	6. Drop EPA Limits	Y	10. Bar Bosnia Troop $	Y
3. Increase Min. Wage	Y	7. Repeal Assault-Weap. Ban	N	11. Cut Anti-Missile Defense	N
4. Welfare Reform	Y	8. Ovrd. Part. Birth Veto	N	12. Bar U.N. Uniforms	Y

Election Results

1996 general	Christopher Shays (R)	121,949	(60%)	($552,597)
	Bill Finch (D)	75,902	(38%)	($183,061)
	Others	3,861	(2%)	
1996 primary	Christopher Shays (R), nominated by convention			
1994 general	Christopher Shays (R)	109,436	(74%)	($438,259)
	Jonathan D. Kantrowitz (D)	34,962	(24%)	
	Others	2,664	(2%)	

FIFTH DISTRICT

The stony hills of central Connecticut are physically isolated, the climate is forbidding, local manners are frosty, there is nothing to suggest lavishness: this might be the Switzerland of America. Yet in the last 200 years, the mountains of Switzerland and the hills of Connecticut have been transformed from subsistence farmland to some of the most productive and affluent places on earth. Their secrets have been thrift, hard work, inventiveness and an intolerance for imprecision. Keeping time is a common motif: Switzerland was long the world's leading watchmaker, and Connecticut has long been America's leading clockmaker. The comparison at some point breaks down: Switzerland has prospered by closing others out, its political neutrality and financial probity reassuring investors and undergirding its banking industry. Connecticut, like the rest of America, is an open society, welcoming newcomers and imbuing immigrants with the Yankee knack for tinkering and precision work. It has also been quick to adapt to market changes. Danbury was once the nation's leading producer of hats; now it cuts almost no felt but is a major corporate headquarters. Meriden once made ivory combs, clocks, cutlery, and silver; now it produces electrical signalling equipment, jewelry, biotech filters, and nuclear instruments. Waterbury, once the nation's largest producer of brass, saw the last of its big three brass fabricators shut down in 1985, but has replaced that with health care and now two local hospitals are the city's biggest employers. (The old Scovill brass factory is now a shopping mall.)

The 5th Congressional District of Connecticut is an irregularly shaped slice of central Connecticut, entirely inland, from Meriden west through Waterbury to Danbury and the high-income havens of Ridgefield and Wilton. This was the Federalist heartland in the early 19th Century. It voted Republican for nearly a century, then became Democratic as Catholics started outnumbering Protestants. Now, cultural conservatism and economic growth have tilted it toward Republicans again; it produced the lowest Clinton margin of any Connecticut district in 1996. But it is closely balanced enough to be marginal often, and has voted out incumbent congressmen of both parties in 1972, 1978, 1984, and 1996.

The congressman now is James Maloney, a Democrat who beat Republican Gary Franks in 1996. Maloney grew up in Danbury, and after college and law school spent a year as a Vista volunteer. From 1974–78 he headed Danbury's antipoverty agency. In 1986 he was elected to the state Senate, where he worked on a family leave act, voted against the state income tax, and supported business tax cuts. In 1994 he decided to run against Franks, then the only black Republican in the House. Franks had won the seat in 1990, compiled a solid conservative record, and was reelected in a three-way race in 1992. Maloney held him to a 52%–46% margin in 1994, the second lowest margin for a Republican incumbent that year, and in early 1996 decided to run again. Maloney was helped when a primary candidate dropped out in July; this was the first uncontested Democratic primary here since 1990.

Maloney ran on a somewhat conservative platform—for the balanced budget amendment, favoring job opportunities and not cash payments for welfare recipients. Meanwhile, Franks was being lambasted by AFL-CIO ads for Medicare "cuts." Maloney also criticized Franks for receiving a $100,000 advance from HarperCollins (also Newt Gingrich's publisher) for his book *Searching for the Promised Land*, in which he described his four years in the Congressional Black Caucus whose leaders did not want him as a member. Unperturbed, Franks spent much of summer 1996 on a 17-city book tour. And he made it no secret that he was thinking of running against Senator Christopher Dodd in 1998. Maloney said, "I don't think Gary Franks is running for the Senate in 1998 because he's not going to be in Congress after this year. How about paying attention to the needs of the 5th district?" Franks responded, "We're not forgetting about '96. But we're serious as a heart attack about running for the Senate in '98."

Although a July poll showed Franks ahead 48%–33%, he claimed later that he never got much more support from the national party. The real problem was that Bob Dole was running poorly and that Franks failed to run far ahead of him as Chris Shays and Nancy Johnson did in their

Connecticut districts. Maloney won 52%–46%, as labor bosses cheered. Missouri Congressman Bill Clay, in a graceless note after the election, called Franks "a foot-shuffling, head-scratching 'Amos and Andy' brand of 'Uncle Tomism' " and a "Negro Dr. Kevorkian" who "gleefully assists in suicidal conduct to destroy his own race." "Obviously, Bill Clay is not a supporter of mine," Franks said, "but I wish him godspeed."

Maloney favors comprehensive restructuring of the healthcare, welfare and political systems and wants to expand educational programs; he would like especially to cut the high shcool dropout rate as he claims his program in Danbury did, by 50%. That is perhaps a tall order for a minority-party freshman congressman, and most likely much of Maloney's time will be devoted to strengthening his position in this often marginal district.

The People: Pop. 1990: 547,907; 21% rural; 13% age 65+; 88% White; 5% Black; 1% Asian; 6% Hispanic origin. Households: 61% married couple families; 28% married couple fams. w. children; 50% college educ.; median household income: $44,056; per capita income: $20,316; median gross rent: $574; median house value: $182,500.

1996 Presidential Vote

Clinton (D)	110,596	(48%)
Dole (R)	92,570	(40%)
Perot (I)	24,265	(10%)
Other	4,694	(2%)

1992 Presidential Vote

Bush (R)	111,327	(42%)
Clinton (D)	93,966	(35%)
Perot (I)	60,891	(23%)

Rep. Jim Maloney (D)

Elected 1996; b. Sept. 17, 1948, Quincy, MA; home, Danbury; Harvard U., B.A. 1972, Boston U., J.D. 1980; Catholic; married (Mary Draper).

Career: Danbury Anti-Poverty Agency, exec. dir., 1974–78; Practicing atty., 1980–96; CT Senate, 1986–95.

DC Office: 1213 LHOB 20515, 202-225-3822; Fax: 202-225-5746.

District Offices: Waterbury, 203-573-1418.

Committees: *Banking & Financial Services* (22nd of 25 D): Housing & Community Opportunity. *National Security* (23rd of 25 D): Military Personnel; Military Procurement.

Group Ratings and Key Votes: Newly Elected

Election Results

1996 general	James H. Maloney (D-ACP)	111,974	(52%)	($614,440)
	Gary A. Franks (R)	98,782	(46%)	($644,293)
	Others	4,374	(2%)	
1996 primary	James H. Maloney (D)	nominated by convention		
1994 general	Gary A. Franks (R)	93,471	(52%)	($574,024)
	James H. Maloney (D)	81,523	(46%)	($896,785)
	Others	4,059	(2%)	

SIXTH DISTRICT

Connecticut, from its Yankee past to its Ellis Islander present and ahead to its third wave of immigrants future, has been a land of tinkerers specializing in precision work, of inventors able to transform vagrant ideas into profitable products. Over the years this stony soil has become the home of some of the most affluent people in the nation and the world. This is true even in the hills of northwest Connecticut, off the interstates and far from Connecticut's small urban capital of Hartford and its sometime booming edge city of Stamford. Here are exquisite Yankee towns like Washington and Kent, prosperous once in the post-Revolutionary era when Connecticut's ship owners accumulated capital and invested it in factories and mills, and now a country-home mecca for ultra-rich New Yorkers seeking to avoid the glitz of Sag Harbor. Not far away are small industrial cities like New Britain, America's ball bearing capital for years, and Bristol, where sports announcer Bill Rasmussen dreamed up the idea of transmitting satellite feeds of UConn games to his neighbors by cable TV—an idea which became ESPN.

The 6th Congressional District of Connecticut covers approximately the northwest corner of the state, stretching from Enfield and Windsor Locks, north of Hartford on the Connecticut River, across the affluent Farmington valley suburbs of Hartford to industrial New Britain and Bristol, and includes all of Litchfield County. Historically, this was rock-ribbed Federalist and Republican territory; in the 20th Century, with Italian immigrants heading to Enfield and Windsor Locks and Poles to New Britain, it moved toward marginal territory.

The congresswoman from the 6th District is Nancy Johnson, a Republican first elected in 1982. She came east to school, then lived in New Britain as a doctor's wife and a teacher, raising three children while active in charitable and community affairs. She was elected to the Connecticut Senate in 1976 from a heavily Democratic district. When 6th District Congressman Toby Moffett ran against Senator Lowell Weicker in 1982, Johnson won the House seat, beating Bill Curry, then a 30-year-old nuclear freeze organizer and later the 1994 Democratic candidate for governor and a Clinton White House aide.

Johnson has become one of the most active and productive legislators in the House, and was on her way to being so even before Republicans won control. Her record has been mostly market-oriented on economics, fairly liberal on foreign policy and cultural issues. She is pro-choice but has opposed what she considers statist legislation, from the Children's Defense Fund childcare bill in the 1980s to the Clinton healthcare package in 1994. She voted for the 1994 crime bill and was one of the few Republican dissenters from the Contract with America crime package. On Ways and Means she took the lead on eliminating the old childcare tax credit, which tended to help high-income parents, and replaced it with $300 million in vouchers to low-income working mothers. And she also has worked on the unemployment benefits program, to get states to pay partial benefits for part-time workers. She is a strong proponent of Superfund reform, eager to cut payments to lawyers and quicken the pace of cleanup at polluted sites. She works on local projects—redevelopment in New Britain, the Bradley Airport tower, a UConn biotech center, preserving the Farmington Wild and Scenic River, building the Black Revolutionary War Patriots Memorial.

In the Democratic 103d Congress Johnson was a major force on healthcare finance; in the Republican 104th Congress she was a major force on welfare reform. She backed the Bush proposal for tax credits for low-income people to buy insurance, and in 1993 met often with the Clinton healthcare task force and participated in markups in the Ways and Means Health Subcommittee, despite gratuitous and sexist insults from then-Chairman Pete Stark. In command of facts and arguments, she continued attacking as Stark and Ways and Means Chairman Sam Gibbons tried to paste a bill together, and her efforts contributed to its demise later in the summer. Johnson's bill to continue low-cost health care for seniors was the only healthcare law passed by Congress in 1994. On welfare reform in 1995, Johnson was part of the majority putting a bill together. Back in 1991 she had called for a job requirement after two years on the rolls—a radical proposal then. But she opposed Newt Gingrich when he called for permanently denying AFDC to women who have additional children while on welfare. In 1995 she worked with Clay Shaw and pushed successfully for a child support enforcement amendment and for guaranteed Medicaid benefits for welfare recipients with no private health insurance. She also helped put together the healthcare portability law in 1996 and long-term care deductibility, which she co-sponsored with Connecticut Democrat Barbara Kennelly. And she was involved in constructing the Republican Medicare plan—"Medicare Select" she called it. She also worked on community health centers, orphan drugs, funding for academic health centers, spousal IRAs, and expanding the Taxpayer Bill of Rights. She was one of the Republicans who worked actively to increase the minimum wage in 1996

But most of this work was overshadowed, in the stridently anti-Gingrich press and in the campaign in the 6th District, by Johnson's role as chairman of the Ethics Committee. This was a hot seat, given the bevy of charges Democrats filed against Newt Gingrich—many of them utterly baseless, only a few of them found by the evenly-divided committee to merit serious consideration. Johnson and Gingrich, despite her moderate record, had long been allies: he has consulted her often on issues; she gave him key support in his 1989 race for Republican whip, which he won by two votes, and shares much of his partisan aggressiveness. So critics honed in on her, charging conflict of interest because she had contact with GOPAC, which Gingrich headed—which is like saying there was a conflict because they were both Republicans. In September 1995 she agreed to have one charge (the financing of his college course) considered by outside counsel, James Cole, but over the next year Johnson and ranking Democrat Jim McDermott seemed to lose trust for each other, and even small differences reportedly triggered lengthy battles on the committee. In September 1996 Cole finished the report and submitted it to subcommittee; Johnson, in line with the precedent set during the investigation of Speaker Jim Wright, did not make it public. That sparked Democratic cries of coverup and back home in Connecticut her Democratic opponent Charlotte Koskoff called her "Stonewall Johnson."

Johnson had beaten Koskoff 64%–32% in 1994 and in 1996 outspent her by about 4–1. But Bill Clinton ended up carrying the 6th District 50%–36%, and Newt Gingrich was highly unpopular there. The National Organization of Women, which had endorsed Johnson in six races and was neutral in 1994, endorsed the Democrat. The election was so close the result was not known until Thursday. The networks reported on election night that Johnson was beaten; in fact she ended up winning 50%–49%. Johnson carried most of the small towns; Koskoff carried New Britain, Bristol, and her home town of Plainville in between, plus Enfield, Windsor Locks and several towns in Litchfield County. This was a major switch: from 1984–94 Johnson had carried every town in every election, except Plainville in 1994. For her narrow win Johnson blamed Koskoff's distortion of her record on Medicare and health care and labor ads saying "scaring worked." But she readily admitted that her role on the Ethics Committee "absolutely hurt me."

Although the Ethics Committee agreed just before Christmas on the Gingrich reprimand, Johnson did not make public the counsel's report until after Gingrich's reelection as speaker in January. Democrats harshly criticized her for truncating to one day the public hearings on Gingrich, though their own tactics led to the delay. Johnson made it known she wanted to rotate off the committee, having served the six years the rules allow, but followed through as chairman until the ethics probe was complete. Cole's report, made public during the hearings January 17, found that Gingrich had intentionally misled the investigation and that he should have consulted a tax attorney, and the committee voted 7–1 for a House reprimand and an unprecedented $300,000 penalty, both of which were approved on the House floor January 21 by a vote of 395–28—evidence that, in the end, Johnson helped to bring consensus to the House. Utah's James Hansen replaced Johnson as chairman and she resumed her chair of the Ways and Means Oversight Subcommittee. She also serves on the Health subcommittee where she will focus once again on the healthcare issues that brought her so much success in 1994. She reemerged into the policy spotlight in the spring as the leading House sponsor of healthcare legislation for children, and seemed far more comfortable working again in a bipartisan spirit. Koskoff voiced interest in a third bid, but Johnson's handling of the Gingrich ethics case may be old news and not quite the stinging attack it proved to be in the 1996 race. Bristol defense consultant and 1988 Democratic nominee James Griffin has pledged to challenge Johnson in 1998.

The People: Pop. 1990: 547,747; 32% rural; 14% age 65+; 93% White; 2% Black; 1% Asian; 4% Hispanic origin. Households: 60% married couple families; 26% married couple fams. w. children; 49% college educ.; median household income: $42,817; per capita income: $19,863; median gross rent: $571; median house value: $165,900.

1996 Presidential Vote

Clinton (D)	121,607	(50%)
Dole (R)	89,003	(36%)
Perot (I)	26,865	(11%)
Other	6,462	(3%)

1992 Presidential Vote

Clinton (D)	110,828	(40%)
Bush (R)	99,633	(36%)
Perot (I)	67,995	(24%)

Rep. Nancy L. Johnson (R)

Elected 1982; b. Jan. 5, 1935, Chicago, IL; home, New Britain; U. of Chicago, 1951–53, Radcliffe Col., B.A. 1957, U. of London, 1957–58; Unitarian; married (Theodore).

Career: Pres., Sheldon Community Guidance Clinic; Adjunct Prof., Central CT St. Col., 1968–71; CT Senate, 1976–82.

DC Office: 343 CHOB 20515, 202-225-4476; Fax: 202-225-4488.

District Offices: New Britain, 860-223-8412.

Committees: *Ways & Means* (5th of 23 R): Health; Oversight (Chmn.).

Group Ratings

	ADA	ACLU	AFS	LCV	CFA	CON	NFIB	COC	ACU	NTLC	CHC
1996	20	6	33	31	46	80	74	81	55	78	40
1995	21	—	—	19	62	87	—	78	56	—	—

National Journal Ratings

	1995 LIB		1995 CONS	1996 LIB		1996 CONS
Economic	44%	—	53%	48%	—	52%
Social	65%	—	33%	67%	—	32%
Foreign	15%	—	73%	44%	—	56%

Key Votes of the 104th Congress

1. Reduce Medicare Growth $	Y	5. Flag Amendment	Y	9. Cuban Embargo	Y
2. Ovrd. Product Liab. Veto	Y	6. Drop EPA Limits	Y	10. Bar Bosnia Troop $	Y
3. Increase Min. Wage	Y	7. Repeal Assault-Weap. Ban	N	11. Cut Anti-Missile Defense	N
4. Welfare Reform	Y	8. Ovrd. Part. Birth Veto	N	12. Bar U.N. Uniforms	Y

Election Results

1996 general	Nancy L. Johnson (R)	113,020	(50%)	($931,406)
	Charlotte Koskoff (D)	111,433	(49%)	($273,133)
1996 primary	Nancy L. Johnson (R), nominated by convention			
1994 general	Nancy L. Johnson (R)	123,101	(64%)	($597,703)
	Charlotte Koskoff (D)	60,701	(32%)	($105,290)
	Patrick J. Danford (CC)	8,915	(5%)	($16,025)

DELAWARE

Delaware, the first state to ratify the Constitution, the second smallest state in area, fifth smallest in population, has a fair claim to being typical of the country, despite a peculiar history. Delaware was explored by Henry Hudson, and the Dutch and Swedes built settlements there in the 1630s. But the three counties of Delaware owe their separate existence to the politics of the proprietors of William Penn's colony of Pennsylvania, and to Delawareans' own speed in ratifying the Constitution which made it literally the "First State." Delaware has not been typical in every way. Over much of its history, Delaware has been unusually affluent, with some of the nation's highest income levels during the early 20th Century; two-thirds of its people live in the mostly-upscale, mostly-suburban county of New Castle. It houses, in beautiful cobblestone mansions in its chateau country, many members of the most numerous and wealthy family in America, the du Ponts. Yet the United States today, after all, is mostly suburban and throughout its history has been by world standards affluent, and the du Ponts don't elevate the median income any more than a couple thousand more lawyers would. Delaware's ethnic and racial mixture is much like that along the rest of the East Coast and not that much different than the nation's, though with fewer than average Hispanics and Asians; there is a mixture here of suburbs, old immigrant neighborhoods, poor black neighborhoods and farmlands. If not all parts of the nation can follow Delaware's exact path to continued prosperity, perhaps they can get an idea of the direction to travel.

The central focus of Delaware's economy for two centuries has been the business started when Eleuthere Irenee du Pont, the practical business-minded son of a dreamy, idealistic French immigrant, built a gunpowder mill on the banks of Brandywine Creek in 1802. This was the first enterprise of the family du Pont, and it expanded to become one of America's great munitions and chemical companies. It grew especially rapidly during World War I, generating so much capital that the Du Pont Company bought control of General Motors in the 1920s and held GM for thirty years while it was America's largest corporation. That capital also financed what was arguably the world's finest research and development program. In the years during and after World War II, Du Pont prospered by bringing to the consumer and industrial market new synthetics and plastics like rayon, nylon, cellophane, polyethylene, lucite and teflon: "Better Living Through Chemistry." Delaware's other major business of note has been creating other businesses. In the late 19th Century, it pioneered liberal laws of incorporation, giving more flexibility and power to managers and owners. A large share of the nation's big companies are incorporated in Delaware—their legal births take place in a federal-style building near the Capitol in Dover—which means that much of the nation's corporate law, especially on mergers and acquisitions and unfriendly takeovers, is made in Delaware courts.

In recent years Delaware has continued to prosper thanks to the skills and ingenuity of its citizens and thanks to political decisions and economic incentives that have created a favorable business climate. Chemical manufacturing, always more capital- than labor-intensive, remains important, but now accounts for fewer than 10% of Delaware's jobs. More jobs were created in the 1980s after Governor Pete du Pont's successful fight for liberalizing Delaware's banking laws to encourage out-of-state banks to locate operations here. And du Pont's systematic lowering of the income tax rate has also contributed mightily; his successors, Republican Mike Castle and Democrat Tom Carper, have continued in the path he set. Delaware's economy grew robustly in the 1980s, and unemployment did not rise or housing values fall nearly as markedly as in other East Coast states in the recession of the early 1990s. In the mid-1990s it is growing again; its population jumped 9% between 1990 and 1996, more than any other Northeastern or Midwestern state.

Despite Delaware's mostly metropolitan character, there is still an intimacy to politics here. Most of Delaware is reached (though politically ignored) by Philadelphia TV, so personal campaigning is still important. The Thursday after the election is "Return Day," when winning and losing candidates—opponents ride in the same car—come back to the lower Delaware town of Georgetown to receive the bipartisan cheers of the voters.

Governor. Tom Carper grew up in southside Virginia and went to college in Ohio. But out-of-state origins are not uncommon here: Delaware's two senators were born in Montana and Pennsylvania. Carper first came to Delaware as an ensign in the Navy, then returned after service in Southeast Asia to get his M.B.A. In 1976, he was elected state treasurer, at 29; he ran for Congress in 1982 and beat a scandal-tarred incumbent. In the House, Carper had a moderate voting record and worked to let banks into the securities business and to prevent ocean sludge dumping, both causes supported by Delaware constituencies. In 1992, when Republican Mike Castle had served his two allotted terms and ran for Congress, Carper ran for governor and won the general with 65%.

In office Carper pursued an agenda in many ways more conservative than liberal. He continued du Pont's policy of cutting taxes, reducing income tax rates about 10% and also cutting small business and utility taxes. Revenues kept gushing in from Delaware's strong economy, and he increased the "rainy day" fund and boosted the state's credit rating to an historic high. He inherited Mike Castle's standard-based education reform, and raised standards. In 1996 he pushed through his own education reform with public school choice and charter schools. He worked to keep current industries and attract others; jobs rose 30,000 in four years. His June 1995 welfare reform imposed four-year time limits on welfare payments, required recipients to work, and discouraged teen pregnancy by denying additional welfare aid to families which increase in size. He built more prisons, saw that violent criminals served 89% of their sentences, and helped pass Megan's Law requiring those guilty of assaulting children to register their addresses upon release from prison. His major defeat came when the legislature voted to allow slot machines at harness racing tracks over his opposition.

In the 1996 election Republican state Treasurer Janet Rzewnicki accused Carper of raising spending 45% and called for a 30% income tax cut. In late October Republican consultant Ann Stone accused Carper of abusing his wife and said she was seeking a divorce. Rzewnicki called for disclosure of court records, but none had been filed and Martha Carper held a press conference to refute the charges. Senator Joseph Biden, Congressman Mike Castle, the state Republican chairman, and the Wilmington *News Journal* came to the defense of Carper, and he ended up winning 70%–31%. In his second term Carper promises to reform state land use laws, and strengthen environmental regulations. He could easily be a candidate for William Roth's Senate seat in 2000.

Senior Senator. Senator William Roth, the sixth most senior Republican in the Senate, has now held high statewide office for longer than anyone else in Delaware's history. He served in the Army in World War II, settled in Delaware and practiced law, became Republican state chairman in 1961 and ran for the state's at-large House seat in 1966, a marvelous Republican year, and won. In 1970, when Senator John Williams retired after four terms, Roth was the obvious Republican choice. With his moderate voting record, friendly demeanor and frequent

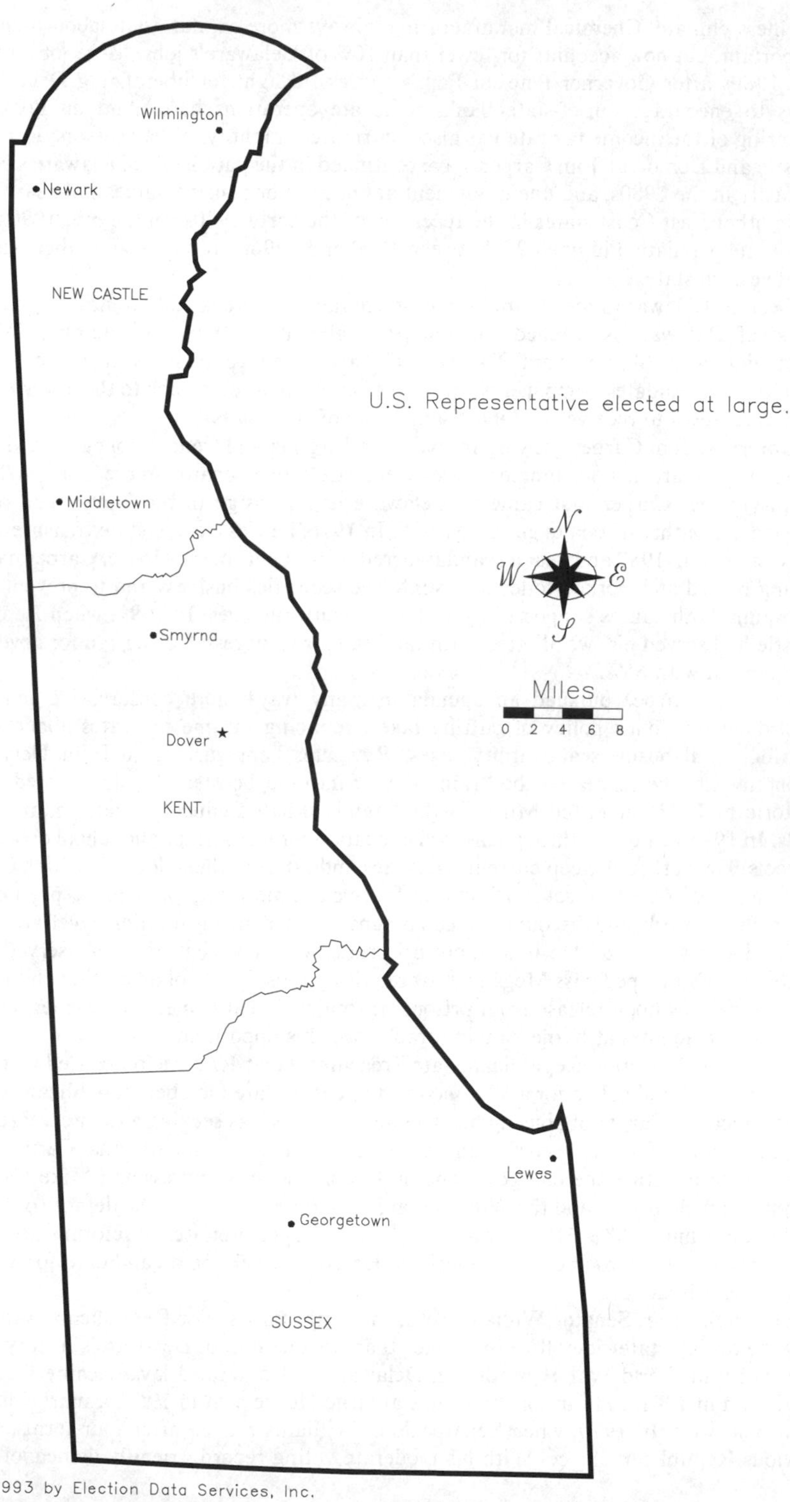
Wilmington
Newark
NEW CASTLE
U.S. Representative elected at large.
Middletown
N
W
E
S
Smyrna
Miles
0 2 4 6 8
Dover
KENT
Lewes
Georgetown
SUSSEX

presence in Delaware with a St. Bernard by his side, he has been politically strong ever since. He remains an elusive figure to many in Washington: he is not stylish or dazzlingly articulate, and his wife is a federal judge back in Delaware. Yet he has sponsored important legislation and advanced powerful political ideas with considerable success and, since Bob Packwood's resignation in December 1995, he has held one of the key power positions on Capitol Hill, the chairmanship of the Senate Finance Committee. He is also vice-chairman of the Joint Committee on Taxation. In May 1997, Roth dropped his seat on Governmental Affairs and its Permanent Subcommittee on Investigations, both of which he chaired before taking over Finance.

Roth's overall voting record is middle-of-the-road in the Republican Senate, but his key initiatives have been in the direction of reducing taxes and giving citizens more leeway in spending what they earn. One major initiative was the Kemp-Roth tax cut, of which he was the chief Senate sponsor, the 30% across-the-board cut in income tax rates first proposed and backed by almost every Republican in 1978 and then largely enacted in 1981 after Ronald Reagan won in 1980. Another major Roth cause is promoting IRAs—adapting the Individual Retirement Accounts to allow tax-free savings for college educations and making IRAs available to homemakers. He has also called for replacing the income tax with a value-added tax, a cause which has gone nowhere, and for a $5,000 adoption tax credit, which was passed in the Republican Congress and signed by President Clinton in August 1996. When Roth took over the Finance Committee he sought consensus within his party and in the Senate, retaining some key staffers, modulating the House tax bill by denying the $500-per-child tax credit to single earners over $75,000 and couples earning over $110,000; even so, the measure was vetoed by Clinton, but has resurfaced for 1997. He worked hard for Medicare reform, and opposed separating it from welfare reform, as House Republicans and Trent Lott, in search of a campaign issue, did in July 1996.

Even bolder was Roth's action on the Consumer Price Index. With ranking Democrat (and former chairman) Daniel Patrick Moynihan, he appointed an expert commission headed by Bush economist Michael Boskin which announced in December 1996 that the CPI overstated inflation by 1.1% a year. If acted upon, this could have major economic impact: it would reduce Social Security and other cost-of-living adjustments and would increase revenues since tax rates are indexed, thus vastly lowering future deficits. More important is what it tells us about the economy, that rather than stagnating for the last 25 years, as most politicians have been saying, it has been growing fairly robustly, with rising living standards for just about everyone. But Roth shied away from unilateral Republican congressional action, and called for bipartisan consensus, even as the Bureau of Labor Statistics announced it would be reluctant to tamper with the CPI and the AFL-CIO promised to campaign against any change. Other areas where Roth will be busy are Medicare, Medicaid, and trade, the first two hyperpartisan up through 1996, the last more bipartisan if Roth gets his way.

On Governmental Affairs, Roth had been a reformer for some time, pressing for government performance audits and in 1993 passing the legislation authorizing Vice President Al Gore's reinventing government initiative. Roth's version of regulatory reform in 1995 was supplanted by a version sponsored by Bob Dole and Bennett Johnston; neither passed. On a few issues Roth tends to be liberal. He opposes ocean dumping and incineration of toxic waste, backs the Coastal Zone Management Act and wants to protect the striped bass; he is a leading Republican opponent of oil drilling in Alaska's Arctic National Wildlife Refuge; he pushed to allow women to serve as combat pilots. He voted for the Brady bill and the 1994 crime bill and supported the nomination of Henry Foster for surgeon general. He has been a tireless advocate of Amtrak and with Biden's help was able to get additional funds for the railroad in the 1997 transportation bill.

Roth was reelected by comfortable margins in 1976, 1982, and 1988. He once promised not to run after he turned 70, but he ran anyway in 1994. Attorney General Charles Oberly, the Democratic nominee, spent over $1.5 million, competitive with Roth's $2.3 million. But Oberly never got much traction in that Republican year, and Roth mostly stayed above the fray, winning 56%–42%. He will be 79 when his seat comes up in 2000. Two obvious candidates to succeed him are Democrat Tom Carper, governor and former congressman, and Republican Mike Castle, congressman and former governor.

Junior Senator. Joseph Biden is in his third decade as a senator and even in the minority has had influence on important policies. Biden grew up in 1950s white collar suburbia (his father was a car salesman and one grandfather was a state senator in Pennsylvania), a Catholic when it was still assumed that only a Protestant could be president, and a teenager with a stutter who taught himself to deliver a speech to his whole school. Born just a few years before the baby boom, he married and had children while still in law school. He moved to the Wilmington suburbs, practiced law, and in 1970, at 27, was elected to the New Castle County Council. In 1972 he ran for the Senate, against a popular incumbent who seemed ready to retire, while this young challenger had energy, an attractive extended family and an ability to connect with voters' emotions. He won 51%–49%, though his victory was tempered a month later by the auto accident which killed his wife and daughter. He began his practice, kept up to this day, of commuting every day from his home near Wilmington on the Amtrak Metroliner 80 minutes to and from Washington. He remains a familiar figure in, and one familiar with, his constituency.

In the Senate Biden has had a by no means entirely liberal voting record, with distinct suburban middle-class accents. Reconciling these two has not been easy work, especially on the Judiciary Committee, which he chaired from 1987–1995 and served as ranking Democrat on in 1981–87 and 1995–97, and on which he has done much of his most visible work. For the issues that arise here—abortion, flag-burning, capital punishment, crime control—cut deeply, and for years the cultural liberals in the Democratic Party differed sharply on most of them from the constituents Biden saw in Delaware every day.

Biden also presided over probably the most contentious Supreme Court confirmation hearings in history. The 1987 hearings on Robert Bork set a high standard for intellectual seriousness; Bork spoke candidly about difficult constitutional issues, and Biden among others asked serious questions. But many of Bork's opponents used his candor to vote against him for disgracefully dishonest reasons, from which Biden's attempts to construct an honestly based, anti-Bork rationale proved politically indistinguishable; and no other nominee since has testified so frankly. The 1991 hearings on Clarence Thomas exploded when someone leaked charges of sexual harassment by Anita Hill against the nominee. Biden was bitterly criticized for covering up this information, but he had shared it with committee members, who agreed that Hill's initial unwillingness to testify publicly meant that any reference to it would be monstrously unfair to Thomas. Once the story was out though, Hill and then Thomas testified to fascinated television audiences. Most voters, most women and most blacks believed Thomas over Hill, despite the strong pro-Hill bias of the press, and Thomas was confirmed, over Biden's opposition.

In the middle of the Bork hearings came a climactic moment for Biden's presidential candidacy. He announced in 1987, hoping to inspire a new generation as John Kennedy had inspired his. But Biden decided to leave the race when a Michael Dukakis staffer leaked an "attack video" showing similarities between Biden's stump speech about his background and a speech by British Labour Party leader Neil Kinnock. Paraphrasing someone else's words is not a political crime—most political discourse is conducted in familiar shorthand terms—but Biden in dramatizing his background actually distorted it, for unlike Kinnock he did not rise from working class roots and in the United States unlike Britain upward social mobility is a common experience. In 1988 Biden nearly died of an aneurysm, but recovered fully.

After the Thomas hearings, Biden seemed defensive about attacks from the feminist left, the greatest source of activism in the Democratic Party as the religious right is in the Republican Party; he sought out women to serve on Judiciary and pressed hard for a Violence Against Women Act. Most of his energies in the early Clinton years were devoted to what became the 1994 crime bill, which included provisions for federal payment for additional (nominally 100,000) police officers, aid for building prisons and boot camps, drug courts combining punishment and therapy for first-time drug offenders, juvenile prevention programs (like the much maligned midnight basketball), and gun control measures. The bill came very close to being whipsawed between liberals who disdain harsh punishment and conservatives opposed to gun control and therapy for offenders, and it was only after a characteristically eloquent and angry performance by Biden, and after tough negotiations between the Clinton Administration and House Republican moderates led by Delaware's Mike Castle, that the bill passed.

In the Republican Congress Biden had a mixed record on crime. A Biden-Hatch Methamphetamine Control Act, a Biden-Gramm nationwide tracking system for sex offenders, and a bill to crack down on Rohypnol, the so-called "date rape" drug were passed. But a Biden-Thompson bill to reform juvenile justice stalled in committee. Interestingly, on the main crime measure of 1995 and 1996, the antiterrorism bill, the positions of conservatives and liberals seemed reversed from what Biden was used to. Conservatives stopped the wiretapping, dynamite-tagging provisions, and anti-racketeering positions, evoking loud protests from Biden and many Democrats.

On foreign policy there was also some turning of the tables. In the 1970s Biden was part of a Democratic majority on Foreign Relations that, wary of another Vietnam, tended to oppose the extension of American military power overseas and sought accommodation and propitiation of the Soviets and their allies. In the 1990s, after the U.S. victory in the Cold War, Biden has sought to maintain American involvement in the world. His stated goals at first were to promote democracy, contain nuclear weapons, rely on multilateral forces like the U.N. and protect the global environment. But when democracy in the former Yugoslavia was thwarted by state-led terrorism and when multilateral instrumentalities proved ineffective, Biden was among the strongest voices—and the best positioned, with his high-ranking seat on Foreign Relations—to call for lifting the arms embargo on Bosnia and training Bosnian Muslims, demanding that the United States and NATO investigate war crimes there, and arguing for NATO air strikes. Eventually Biden's lead was followed, with results much as he predicted. Biden has spoken out for freedom elsewhere. He has worked hard to preserve Radio Free Europe and Radio Liberty inside a new international broadcast organization and has been the real father of Radio Free Asia: he argues that these broadcast services can provide accurate information when little else is available. With the retirement of Claiborne Pell, he became ranking minority member on Foreign Relations, relinquishing the same position on Judiciary, and his voice will surely be heard even more on foreign policy.

Biden's most visible gift is an articulateness that can verge on the mellifluous; he can inspire, but can also drone on at great length (being elected a senator at 29 does not curb a tendency to verbosity). But this has not reduced the appreciation most Delawareans have for his admirable personal qualities. He was reelected by wide margins in 1984 (60%–40%) and 1990 (63%–36%). He said that he came close to retiring in 1996, a year when a record 14 incumbent senators decided not to seek reelection. "All the things I fought for were under siege." But his wife persuaded him otherwise: "You're not so special. But you're at the top of your game. You're not going to get any better. If you're going to quit now, why did you run in the first place?" His opponent was Raymond Clatworthy, a Naval Academy graduate and businessman (a radio station and restaurants), who called Biden a big government booster and said, "His best days are over." Clatworthy walked, rode a bicycle, and rollerbladed through the state to reach voters, but even raising $1 million could not break Biden's lead. Biden pledged to seek middle class tax relief and to fight drug abuse and drug trafficking, and won 60%–38%—very similar to the last two races. He turns 60 just after his seat next comes up, in 2002.

Representative-At-Large. In 1992, Mike Castle was elected to the House after eight years as governor, where he was proud of starting a program to make health care services available to all children, developing an "Environmental Legacy" program to address issues in the coming decade, and increasing teacher salaries, even while lowering tax rates. He won the primary by 56%–30% over state Treasurer Janet Rzewnicki in what many called the "year of the woman," and he won the general 55%–43% over former Lieutenant Governor and Senate candidate S. B. Woo, beating the man who raised more in individual contributions (mostly from Chinese-

Americans) than any other non-incumbent in 1992. In the House, it seemed hardly likely that Castle, as a moderate member of a conservative minority party, could be influential; yet he was. He was a leader of the bipartisan freshmen who offered their own budget cuts. And in August 1994 he withdrew his support from the crime bill when he thought Democrats overreached, then at Newt Gingrich's suggestion led a group of moderate Republicans to negotiate with the administration. This delivered a stinging rebuke to Democrats—broke their majority apart, in fact—and yet ultimately produced a crime bill with less spending on prevention but with the gun control provisions which Castle unlike many Republicans supported.

Castle played the same role as "middle man," in *Congress Daily*'s phrase, in the Republican 104th Congress: "Take almost any contentious issue this Congress and at the center you will find Representative Michael Castle, like a magnet, attracting a bipartisan coalition of moderates just strong enough to give GOP leaders a headache. But he always seems to carry a remedy all sides are able to swallow." Thus he removed riders to an appropriation limiting EPA's powers, softened some education cuts, and insisted that tax cuts could only take effect upon enactment of a deficit reduction plan. In August 1996, when Republicans revived their twice-vetoed welfare reform, Castle and Tennessee Democrat John Tanner proposed an alternative. It was rejected, but several of its provisions were included in the final bill—requiring states to spend 80% of previous budgets, allowing states to use their own funds for vouchers, continuing Medicaid benefits—and Castle voted for it. Castle uses the skills he developed as a governor in Dover and at governor's conferences, including a working relationship with Bill Clinton. But the results of his efforts tilt more to the Republicans than the Democrats.

Castle chairs the Banking Subcommittee on Domestic and International Monetary Policy, holding hearings on the new $100 bill, the future of the penny, the proposed dollar coin, and regulation of electronic banking. He opposed a moratorium on regulators to give insurance powers to banks, very important in Delaware; it was rejected, but so was the bill. He has waged war on some congressional perks, and his amendment now requires franked mail to say "prepared, published, and mailed at the taxpayers' expense." Castle himself ranks 433d of 435 in spending on franked mail.

That has not damaged his political standing in Delaware. He was reelected with 71% in 1994 and 70% in 1996. He is a likely candidate for William Roth's Senate seat in 2000.

Presidential politics. Delaware has been competitive in presidential elections since the Federalists were battling the Jeffersonians. Today it can claim to be the nation's presidential bellwether: it has voted for every winner starting with 1952; the second longest streak is held by Missouri, which has voted for winners starting with 1960. Wilmington is heavily Democratic, the two lower counties lean Republican these days, and the balance is struck by the New Castle County suburbs. Yet Delaware with its three electoral votes gets little national attention, and its two presidential candidates, Pete du Pont and Joseph Biden in 1988, got nowhere.

In 1996 Delaware vied for attention by holding its presidential primary February 24, just four days after New Hampshire. But New Hampshire Republicans put pressure on candidates to ignore Delaware, and only Steve Forbes and Alan Keyes showed up here. Forbes advertised heavily on Philadelphia TV and won the contest with 33% of the vote, to 27% for Bob Dole, 19% for Pat Buchanan, and 13% for Lamar Alexander. Now Delaware must decide whether it wants to compete with New Hampshire again.

The People: Est. Pop. 1996: 725,000; Pop. 1990: 666,168, up 8.8% 1990–1996. 0.3% of U.S. total, 46th largest; 27% rural. Median age: 35. 13% 65 years and over. 79.3% White, 16.7% Black, 1.3% Asian, 2.4% Hispanic origin. Households: 55.8% married couple families; 26% married couple fams. w. children; 45% college educ.; median household income: $34,875; per capita income: $15,854; median house value: $100,100; median monthly rent: $425. 5.2% Unemployment. 1996 Voting age pop.: 548,000. 1996 Turnout 270,810; 49% of VAP. Registered voters (1996): 419,695; 177,810 D (42%), 148,866 R (35%); 93,019 unaffiliated and minor parties (22%).

Political Lineup: Governor, Thomas R. Carper (D); Lt. Gov., Ruth Ann Minner (D); Secy. of State, Edward J. Freel; Atty. Gen., M. Jane Brady (R); Treasurer, Janet C. Rzewnicki (R); Auditor, R. Thomas Wagner Jr. (R); Comptroller General, Russell Larson. State Senate, 21 (13 D and 8 R); Senate President, Ruth Ann Minner (D); State House, 41 (27 R and 14 D); House Speaker, Terry Spence (R). Senators, William V. Roth, Jr. (R) and Joseph R. Biden, Jr. (D). Reps., 1 R at large.

Board of Elections: 302-379-4277; **Filing Deadline for U.S. Congress:** July 31, 1998.

1996 Presidential Vote

Clinton (D)	140,355	(52%)
Dole (R)	99,062	(37%)
Perot (I)	28,719	(11%)

1996 Republican Presidential Primary

Forbes (R)	10,709	(33%)
Dole (R)	8,909	(27%)
Buchanan (R)	6,118	(19%)
Alexander (R)	4,375	(13%)
Keyes (R)	1,729	(5%)
Other	933	(3%)

1992 Presidential Vote

Clinton (D)	126,054	(44%)
Bush (R)	102,313	(35%)
Perot (I)	59,213	(20%)

GOVERNOR

Gov. Thomas R. Carper (D)

Elected 1992, term expires Jan. 2001; b. Jan. 23, 1947, Beckley, WV; home, Wilmington; OH St. U., B.A. 1968, U. of DE, M.B.A. 1975; Presbyterian; married (Martha).

Career: Navy, 1968–73 (Vietnam), Naval Reserves, 1973–91; Industrial Devel. Specialist, DE Div. of Econ. Devel., 1975–76; DE Treasurer, 1976–82; U.S. House of Reps., 1982–92.

Office: Legislative Hall, Dover 19901, 302-739-4101; Fax: 302-739-2775; and 820 N. French St., Wilmington 19801, 302-577-3210; Fax: 302-577-3118; Web site: www.state.de.us.

Election Results

1996 gen.	Thomas R. Carper (D)	188,300	70%
	Janet C. Rzewnicki (R)	82,654	31%
1996 prim.	Thomas R. Carper (D)	unopposed	
1992 gen.	Thomas R. Carper (D)	179,365	(65%)
	B. Gary Scott (R)	90,725	(33%)
	Others	6,944	(3%)

SENATORS

Sen. William V. Roth, Jr. (R)

Elected 1970, seat up 2000; b. July 22, 1921, Great Falls, MT; home, Wilmington; U. of OR, B.A. 1944, Harvard U., M.B.A., LL.B. 1947; Episcopalian; married (Jane).

Career: Army, 1943–46 (WWII); Practicing atty., 1950–66; Chmn., DE Repub. State Cmte., 1961–64; U.S. House of Reps., 1966–70.

DC Office: 104 HSOB 20510, 202-224-2441; Fax: 202-224-0354.

State Offices: Dover, 302-674-3308; Georgetown, 302-856-7690; Wilmington, 302-573-6291.

Committees: *Finance* (Chmn.): Health Care; International Trade; Taxation & IRS Oversight. *Joint Economic Committee* (2nd of 10 Sens.). *Joint Committee on Taxation* (Vice Chmn. of 5 Sens.).

Group Ratings

	ADA	ACLU	AFS	LCV	CFA	CON	NFIB	COC	ACU	NTLC	CHC
1996	10	6	14	62	36	51	79	85	85	97	84
1995	5	—	0	50	13	88	—	68	74	—	—

National Journal Ratings

	1995 LIB	—	1995 CONS	1996 LIB	—	1996 CONS
Economic	46%	—	53%	40%	—	58%
Social	45%	—	54%	44%	—	55%
Foreign	52%	—	47%	30%	—	68%

Key Votes of the 104th Congress

1. Reduce Medicare Growth $	Y	5. Flag Amendment	Y	9. Anti-Missile Defense	Y
2. Lmt. Prod. Liab. Damages	N	6. Endangered Species	Y	10. Cuban Embargo	Y
3. Increase Min. Wage	Y	7. Gay Employment Rights	N	11. Bar Bosnia Troop $	N
4. Welfare Reform	Y	8. Ovrd. Part. Birth Veto	Y	12. Cut Vietnam Aid	N

Election Results

1994 general	William V. Roth, Jr. (R)	111,088	(56%)	($2,310,474)
	Charles M. Oberly III (D)	84,554	(42%)	($1,561,440)
	Others	3,387	(2%)	
1994 primary	William V. Roth, Jr. (R)	unopposed		
1988 general	William V. Roth, Jr. (R)	151,115	(62%)	($1,942,119)
	S.B. Woo (D)	92,378	(38%)	($2,235,318)

Sen. Joseph R. Biden, Jr. (D)

Elected 1972, seat up 2002; b. Nov. 20, 1942, Scranton, PA; home, Wilmington; U. of DE, B.A. 1965, Syracuse U., J.D. 1968; Catholic; married (Jill).

Career: Practicing atty., 1968–72; New Castle Cnty. Cncl., 1970–72.

DC Office: 221 RSOB 20510, 202-224-5042; Fax: 202-224-0139; e-mail: senator@biden.senate.gov.

State Offices: Dover, 302-678-9483; Georgetown, 302-856-9275; Wilmington, 302-573-6345.

Committees: *Foreign Relations* (RMM of 8 D): European Affairs (RMM); International Economic Policy, Export & Trade Promotion. *Judiciary* (3rd of 8 D): Terrorism, Technology & Government Information; Youth Violence (RMM).

Group Ratings

	ADA	ACLU	AFS	LCV	CFA	CON	NFIB	COC	ACU	NTLC	CHC
1996	80	39	71	92	71	35	38	46	20	29	15
1995	95	—	91	100	75	19	—	37	17	—	—

National Journal Ratings

	1995 LIB — 1995 CONS	1996 LIB — 1996 CONS
Economic	80% — 17%	57% — 39%
Social	52% — 47%	60% — 38%
Foreign	61% — 38%	89% — 7%

Key Votes of the 104th Congress

1. Reduce Medicare Growth $	N	5. Flag Amendment	N	9. Anti-Missile Defense	N
2. Lmt. Prod. Liab. Damages	N	6. Endangered Species	Y	10. Cuban Embargo	*
3. Increase Min. Wage	Y	7. Gay Employment Rights	Y	11. Bar Bosnia Troop $	N
4. Welfare Reform	Y	8. Ovrd. Part. Birth Veto	Y	12. Cut Vietnam Aid	N

Election Results

1996 general	Joseph R. Biden, Jr. (D)	165,465	(60%)	($2,466,499)
	Raymond J. Clatworthy (R)	105,088	(38%)	($1,126,427)
	Others	5,038	(2%)	
1996 primary	Joseph R. Biden, Jr. (D)	unopposed		
1990 general	Joseph R. Biden, Jr. (D)	112,918	(63%)	($2,550,061)
	M. Jane Brady (R)	64,554	(36%)	($240,669)
	Other	2,680	(1%)	

REPRESENTATIVE

Rep. Michael N. Castle (R)

Elected 1992; b. July 2, 1939, Wilmington; home, Wilmington; Hamilton Col., B.A. 1961, Georgetown U., LL.B. 1964; Catholic; married (Jane).

Career: DE Dep. Atty. Gen., 1965–66; DE House of Reps., 1966–68; DE Senate, 1968–76, Minority Ldr., 1975–76; DE Lt. Gov., 1980–84; DE Gov., 1984–92.

DC Office: 1227 LHOB 20515, 202-225-4165; Fax: 202-225-2291; e-mail: delaware@hr.house.gov.

District Offices: Dover, 302-736-1666; Wilmington, 302-428-1902.

Committees: *Banking & Financial Services* (8th of 30 R): Domestic & International Monetary Policy (Chmn.); Housing & Community Opportunity. *Education & The Workforce* (9th of 25 R): Early Childhood, Youth & Families (Vice Chmn.); Postsecondary Education, Training & Life-Long Learning. *Intelligence (Select)* (6th of 9 R): Human Intelligence, Analysis & Counterintelligence.

Group Ratings

	ADA	ACLU	AFS	LCV	CFA	CON	NFIB	COC	ACU	NTLC	CHC
1996	25	12	8	54	69	73	86	88	60	85	66
1995	5	—	—	13	54	56	—	92	56	—	—

National Journal Ratings

	1995 LIB — 1995 CONS	1996 LIB — 1996 CONS
Economic	41% — 56%	50% — 49%
Social	59% — 40%	55% — 43%
Foreign	36% — 59%	53% — 46%

Key Votes of the 104th Congress

1. Reduce Medicare Growth $	Y	5. Flag Amendment	Y	9. Cuban Embargo	Y
2. Ovrd. Product Liab. Veto	Y	6. Drop EPA Limits	Y	10. Bar Bosnia Troop $	N
3. Increase Min. Wage	Y	7. Repeal Assault-Weap. Ban	N	11. Cut Anti-Missile Defense	N
4. Welfare Reform	Y	8. Ovrd. Part. Birth Veto	Y	12. Bar U.N. Uniforms	N

Election Results

1996 general	Michael N. Castle (R)	185,576	(70%)	($376,350)
	Dennis E. Williams (D)	73,253	(27%)	($6,437)
	Others	7,996	(3%)	
1996 primary	Michael N. Castle (R)	unopposed		
1994 general	Michael N. Castle (R)	137,960	(71%)	($400,083)
	Carol Ann DeSantis (D)	51,803	(27%)	($45,863)
	Others	5,274	(3%)	

DISTRICT OF COLUMBIA

Washington, D.C., the capital of the most successful democracy in the history of the world, is itself a dysfunctional polity, a city with above-average incomes and a vibrant commercial property base but with a local government so bloated with employees yet so indifferent to its duties that it is destroying one marginal neighborhood after another. The problem is not new—in the 1790s the framers of the Constitution, familiar with contemporary London and Paris mobs and remembering how crowds had threatened Congress in Philadelphia, purposely gave the new federal government control of the 10-mile-square enclave that came to be called the District of Columbia—but in the 1990s the irresponsibility of District officials, primarily of Mayor Marion Barry, led a reluctant Congress to turn control of the capital's city finances over to a federal financial control board.

This sad episode came some 20 years after Congress relinquished the direct control of the District which it had exercised over most of its history, for its own advantage and out of distrust of the city's large black population. For blacks have consistently made up at least one-quarter of metropolitan Washington's population since the 1790s, and the city was a center for free blacks before and after the Civil War and Emancipation. Radical Republicans gave the District self-government in the era of Reconstruction in 1871, but Governor Alexander "Boss" Shepherd built great public works and spent the District into bankruptcy, and local self-government ended in 1874. Washington's vast growth, starting during the New Deal and World War II, resulted in the springing up of large, mostly white suburbs, and blacks formed a larger part of the city's population—a majority in the 1960 Census. During the civil rights revolution of the 1960s, it began to seem absurd to deny the vote to Washington. So in 1964, Washingtonians began to cast three electoral votes for president; in 1968 they were allowed to vote for their board; in 1971, they finally got to elect a non-voting delegate to Congress; in 1974, they got home rule and could vote for a mayor and city council. Now the movement seems to be in the other direction. The control board exerted superintending power over District finances in 1995 and took over the school board in 1996. Statehood, an option pressed to a roll call vote by congressional Democrats as recently as 1993 (it lost 277 153), is a dead cause, and self-government continues in form only. And the percentage of blacks is decreasing, as middle- and modest-income blacks leave for the suburbs: the District's population fell 10% from 1990 to 1996, an astonishing drop that leaves once functional neighborhoods now empty and crumbling.

The lead actor in this tragedy has been Marion Barry, elected mayor in 1978, 1982 and 1986, then disgraced in January 1990 when he was videotaped and arrested in a D.C. hotel using crack cocaine, a crime for which he was eventually convicted and imprisoned—and then, astonishingly, elected mayor again in 1994. Barry is a man of great competence and charm, a Ph.D. candidate in chemistry from Tennessee who became a dashiki-clad protest leader in Washington in the 1960s. He inherited a government that was already overlarge and undermanaged, and increased the first tendency while eventually, as he came to spend too much of his time drinking, womanizing and taking drugs, increasing the latter as well. There is no serious party competition here; Washington is overwhelmingly Democratic, more Democratic than any county in the United States; the District voted 85% for Bill Clinton over Bob Dole in 1996. So Barry developed his own coalition of public employee unions and big real estate developers who ponied up votes and money and, until his arrest, seemed to have made him Mayor-for-life.

Barry's downfall produced a surge for reform, and the election in 1990 of Sharon Pratt Dixon (Sharon Pratt Kelly, after her 1991 marriage). She won the September 1990 primary with 35% to 25% for Councilman John Ray and 21% for Councilwoman Charlene Drew Jarvis. She promised to cut a District government which had about 46,000 employees with outlays approaching nearly $5 billion (about $8,000 per person) and a bureaucracy famously indifferent to the citizens it was supposed to serve, an attitude surely nourished by Barry's increasingly flagrant behavior. It had public schools so weak that the incoming Clintons did not even consider them for their daughter, even though per-pupil spending was among the highest in the country. But when it came time to make cuts, Kelly flinched, and started relying on the usual alibis: the federal payment the District receives in lieu of taxes on federal buildings wasn't large enough; Congress would not let the District tax suburbanites working in the city; Congress would not vote for statehood. But the federal payment is actually generous; the city has plenty of affluent white and black residents to soak with high taxes, and does; and Congress is not going to vote greater powers to a government plainly incompetent to handle those it has.

Under Barry the District developed—and Kelly did little to change—a public sector of Soviet magnitude and social problems of Third World dimensions—two facts that are surely related. The crime rate in the District is very high, and if it is not the nation's murder capital any more, there are many parts of the city which drug dealers rule, where murder is commonplace and women are routinely abused. The capital of the United States has a level of infant mortality twice the national average, and in poor neighborhoods the level is worse than in Sri Lanka, Panama or Jamaica. Drinking, drug use and simple neglect by unmarried mothers are the primary causes: the fatherless underclass seems in large parts of the District to have created a society which is literally hellish. Washington has a far lower percentage of people living in families than any state, or almost any central city, despite income levels well above the average (raised by affluent whites in Ward 3, west of Rock Creek Park, and affluent blacks in Ward 4, just east of the Park). The District government does deliver some services adequately—the Metro remains clean and efficient—but most are carried out poorly, in vivid contrast to the high civic competence of suburban Maryland and Virginia jurisdictions (including majority-black Prince Georges County, Maryland). The result is a city whose electorate increasingly is made up of public employees and welfare recipients, plus white liberals who are not averse to paying high taxes even for a dysfunctional government.

Marion Barry, emerging from prison, immediately began running for office. In 1992 he was elected to the Council from Ward 8 east of the Anacostia River, the poorest part of the city, with many single mothers on welfare and very high rates of crime. Then in 1994 he ran again for mayor. Barry energetically built an organization in Anacostia and other poor areas, corralled support from public employees and built networks of families with imprisoned relatives. He won the September primary with 47% of the vote, to 37% for John Ray and only 13% for Kelly; their combined vote would have beat him. The vote was highly uneven. Barry won 83% in Ward 8 and 66% in Ward 7, also in Anacostia; Ray beat him in Ward 3, 83% to 3%. Councilman Bill Lightfoot, who said he would run as an Independent if Ray lost to Barry, changed his mind after the primary. In the general, Republican Carol Schwartz, a former councilwoman, ran a gallant campaign, but Barry won 56%–42%.

Barry's narrow but decisive victories may have come from the same impulse that is producing large numbers of nullification verdicts in D.C. criminal trials: older black jurors who, regardless of the evidence presented, are reluctant to send another black male to jail. Voters, especially in Anacostia where the large majority are older, often expressed a desire to forgive Barry and honor his "redemption." All societies need some balance between love and discipline, and so do all families; but voters in Washington's poorest areas, almost all from homes where men are conspicuously absent, seem full of motherly therapy and lacking in fatherly discipline. The result is a dysfunctional polity: streets controlled by thugs let loose by nullifying jurors, the mayor's office in the hands of Marion Barry.

But not governmental power. The District's credit rating was so poor it could not borrow in the marketplace and its cash plunged toward zero. No one knew exactly how many people it employed—around 36,000—or how much money it was spending. To the rescue came not the Clinton Administration, which showed scant interest in the District, but a pair of Republicans and D.C.'s Delegate Eleanor Holmes Norton. The Republicans were Speaker Newt Gingrich, who met with Barry and talked of making the District a cherished capital like London or Paris, and Tom Davis, the suburban Virginia congressman who was formerly chairman of the Fairfax County Board of Supervisors and whom Gingrich named chairman of the Government Reform and Oversight's District Subcommittee (the old District Committee was eliminated by the Republicans). They agreed on setting up the five-member financial control board, which was voted without roll call votes in the House or Senate in April 1995. Under Chairman Andrew Brimmer the control board analyzed the District budget, demanded cuts in spending and a reduction of 5,600 government jobs. Barry oscillated from cooperation to demagogic attacks, with fewer of the latter than many expected; he was on a trip to China and Korea when the control board took over the schools in November 1996, noting that schools for 3,000 pupils did not open in September because of fire code violations and giving the system "an absolute F." The board also produced a major shake-up in the police department which had been troubled by the hiring of subgrade recruits in 1989. There were occasional criticisms of the board by Norton, and Appropriations subcommittee chairman Jim Walsh, who used to serve on the Syracuse city council, tried to rein in funding.

What else should be done? Norton and Barry have proposed a residency requirement for D.C. employees and income taxes on suburbanites commuting to the city; neither will be enacted as long as Maryland and Virginia are represented in Congress. Nor does a larger general-purpose federal payment seem to be in the works. If overlarge government has caused the problems of the District, perhaps overgenerous tax relief will lead toward their solution. By May 1997, even the control board realized that it could point to relatively few improvements over the past two years, that spending cuts alone would not restore the District, and a substantial increase in federal aid might be necessary. With Marion Barry's approval ratings at a record low—63% of residents disapproved of his performance and 78% said he should not run again—the control board made a radical proposal to appoint a professional city manager to take over the day-to-day operations of the city. This would essentially nullify home rule and strip Barry of most all governing powers.

D.C. Delegate. Eleanor Holmes Norton was first elected Delegate in 1990. She was criticized during that campaign because her husband hadn't filed their income taxes for several years and in the primary beat Councilwoman Betty Anne Kane by only a 39%–33% margin. But she has won easily since and has proved herself to be hard-working, competent, intellectually honest, able to get along with opponents as well as fellow partisans, willing to take personal and political risks in the long-term interests of her community and constituency. a splendid representative. She established good relations with Republicans active on District matters long before they got their majority, and even though she led the drive, much resented by Republicans in 1993 and repealed by them in 1995, to give her and the four territorial delegates to the House—all of whom were then Democrats—votes on most legislation in the House. She also got on the good side of Bill Clinton, whose nomination she supported in 1992. In 1995 and 1996 she showed candor and creativity, taking great political risks, for Barry could easily choose to blame her as well as the Republican Congress for any cuts.

Norton did come up with specific grants or borrowing authority for specific purposes: $200 million for street repairs, $75 million on the water system (there was a health scare about D.C. water in summer 1995), $15 million for police, and $12 million for schools. Norton has also proposed, and received impressive bipartisan support for, a tax bill that would exempt incomes under $25,000 for heads of household, would establish a flat 15% federal income tax for District residents, and a $5,000 tax credit for first time home buyers. In May 1997, Majority Leader Trent Lott introduced a bill in the Senate mirroring many of Norton's proposals, but Ways and Means Chairman Bill Archer has not even scheduled a hearing in the House on Norton's bill. This radical measure is akin to, but far more sweeping than, Jack Kemp's proposals for enterprise zones, and no one can be sure what its effect could be, or whether the windfall for the city's affluent whites can be justified. But as Norton said in September 1996, "What is demoralizing residents and sending them out of the city is the absence of visible change for the better. If people have no example of improvement to hang their hat on, they will hang their hat in Prince George's County."

Norton has not had serious electoral competition, and was easily reelected in 1996.

The People: Est. Pop. 1996: 543,000; Pop. 1990: 606,900, down 10.5% 1990–1996. 0.2% of U.S. total, 50th largest. Median age: 35.6 years. 14% 65 years and over. 27.4% White, 65.1% Black, 1.8% Asian, 5.4% Hispanic origin. Households: 25.3% married couple families; 10% married couple fams. w. children; 52% college educ.; median household income: $30,727; per capita income: $18,881; 38.9% owner occupied housing; median house value: $123,900; median monthly rent: $441. 8.5% Unemployment. 1996 Voting age pop.: 422,000. 1996 Turnout: 185,726; 44% of VAP. Registered voters (1996): 361,419; 288,475 D (79%); 25,979 R (7%); 46,366 unaffiliated and minor parties (13%).

Political Lineup: Delegate, 1 D at large.

1996 Presidential Vote

Clinton (D)	158,220	(85%)
Dole (R)	17,339	(9%)
Perot (I)	3,611	(2%)
Other	6,566	(4%)

1992 Presidential Vote

Clinton (D)	192,619	(85%)
Bush (R)	20,698	(9%)
Perot (I)	9,681	(4%)

1992 Republican Presidential Primary

Dole (R)	2,256	(76%)
Buchanan (R)	283	(9%)
Uncommitted, other	448	(15%)

DELEGATE

Del. Eleanor Holmes Norton (D)

Elected 1990; b. June 13, 1937, Washington, D.C.; home, Washington, D.C.; Antioch Col., B.A. 1960, Yale, M.A. 1963, LL.B. 1964; Episcopalian; divorced.

Career: Asst. Legal Dir., ACLU, 1965–70; New York City Comm. on Human Rights, 1970–77; Equal Empl. Oppor. Comm., 1977–81; Sr. Fellow, The Urban Inst., 1981–82; Prof., Georgetown U. Law Ctr., 1982–90.

DC Office: 1424 LHOB 20515, 202-225-8050; Fax: 202-225-3002; Web site: www.house.gov/norton.

District Offices: Washington, 202-783-5065; Washington, 202-678-8900; Web site: www.dchomepage.net.

Committees: *Government Reform & Oversight* (10th of 19 D): Civil Service; District of Columbia (RMM). *Transportation & Infrastructure* (12th of 33 D): Public Buildings & Economic Development; Surface Transportation.

Election Results

1996 general	Eleanor Holmes Norton (D)	134,996	(90%)	($119,818)
	Spraque Simonds (R)	11,306	(8%)	
	Others	3,696	(2%)	
1996 primary	Eleanor Holmes Norton (D)	unopposed		
1994 general	Eleanor Holmes Norton (D)	154,988	(89%)	($72,830)
	Donald A. Saltz (R)	13,828	(8%)	
	Others	4,848	(3%)	

FLORIDA

Florida, for much of its history a forgotten swamp, the only Atlantic Coast state not among the original 13 states, is now almost an empire of its own, America's fastest-growing megastate and most popular tourist destination, with an international flavor and sometimes almost with its own foreign policy. This is one of the places where America is meeting its future. For many years, Florida was the place which millions of retirees looked forward to: the sunny year-round warmth after eternal gray skies over winter factories and rain pounding on office windows. More recently, for millions of young families, from the South and various points north, Florida has been a booming economy, with jobs and opportunities in communities that did not exist a generation ago. For refugees from Cuba and Haiti and immigrants from all over the Caribbean and Latin America, Florida has been a land of freedom and security from the armed thugs that control everyday life in police states; for immigrants from all over the Caribbean and Latin America, it has been a land of opportunity and upward mobility. For Americans and foreigners of all kinds—some 43 million of them in 1996, up from 23 million a dozen years before—Florida is the place to visit, with attractions, year-round swimming, restaurants and rooms to suit every taste and pocketbook. Yet there can be trouble here as well: what seemed like paradise for some can be dystopia to others; a retirement haven can turn out to be a crime capital; a showplace of American creativity can turn out to be the breeding grounds of con men and swindlers.

Florida is a creation not of America's elite—though a few millionaires like Henry Flagler and Marcus Plant pioneered tourism here—but a place for which ordinary people have voted with their feet. Half a century ago, it was the least populous state in the South, with 1.4 million people, isolated, disease-ridden, bigoted, with no mineral resources but phosphate mines, not much agriculture outside its citrus groves and hardly any manufacturing at all. Today it is America's fourth most populous state, with 14 million people (it passed Ohio, Illinois, and Pennsylvania in the 1980s and is now closing in on New York). Florida is not a replica of the nation but an exaggeration: a state one-fifth of whose economy is based on tourism in a country where tourism is one of the great growth industries; a state with an economy based on services in a country increasingly service-oriented; the state with the largest proportion of elderly and retired citizens in a country where an increasing percentage will live many years in retirement; a state also with a growing number of school children in a country which, replenished by immigration, is growing faster and more robustly than any other advanced nation. Florida's architectural style once seemed exotic—Flagler's vast luxury hotels, the pink stucco motels of the 1940s and 1950s, the art deco hotels of Miami Beach—but now they have become leading edge: the Disney World Dolphin Hotel and Arquitectonica's Miami towers. And Florida is becoming a show business center, with actual movie production on the lots at the Universal and Disney World theme parks near Orlando: tourist attractions becoming workplaces, life imitating art imitating life.

Florida in the mid-1990s has had one of America's most buoyant economies, though its economic base may seem a mystery to outsiders—it can't all be tourism and retirees, can it? The answer is that it is also services and trade. Miami for two decades has been the economic and commercial capital of Latin America, as well as its mecca for political exiles. It is the one place from where you can fly nonstop to just about any place in Latin America, and the one place where you can be sure your money and your person are safe from government takeover. It is the one major city where both English and Spanish are commonly understood.

What may be fragile in Florida is civil society; Florida can be disorderly and chaotic. Most people here do not have deep roots in the state, most communities sprang into existence within living memory and, if Florida gives people more freedom and options than they may ever have

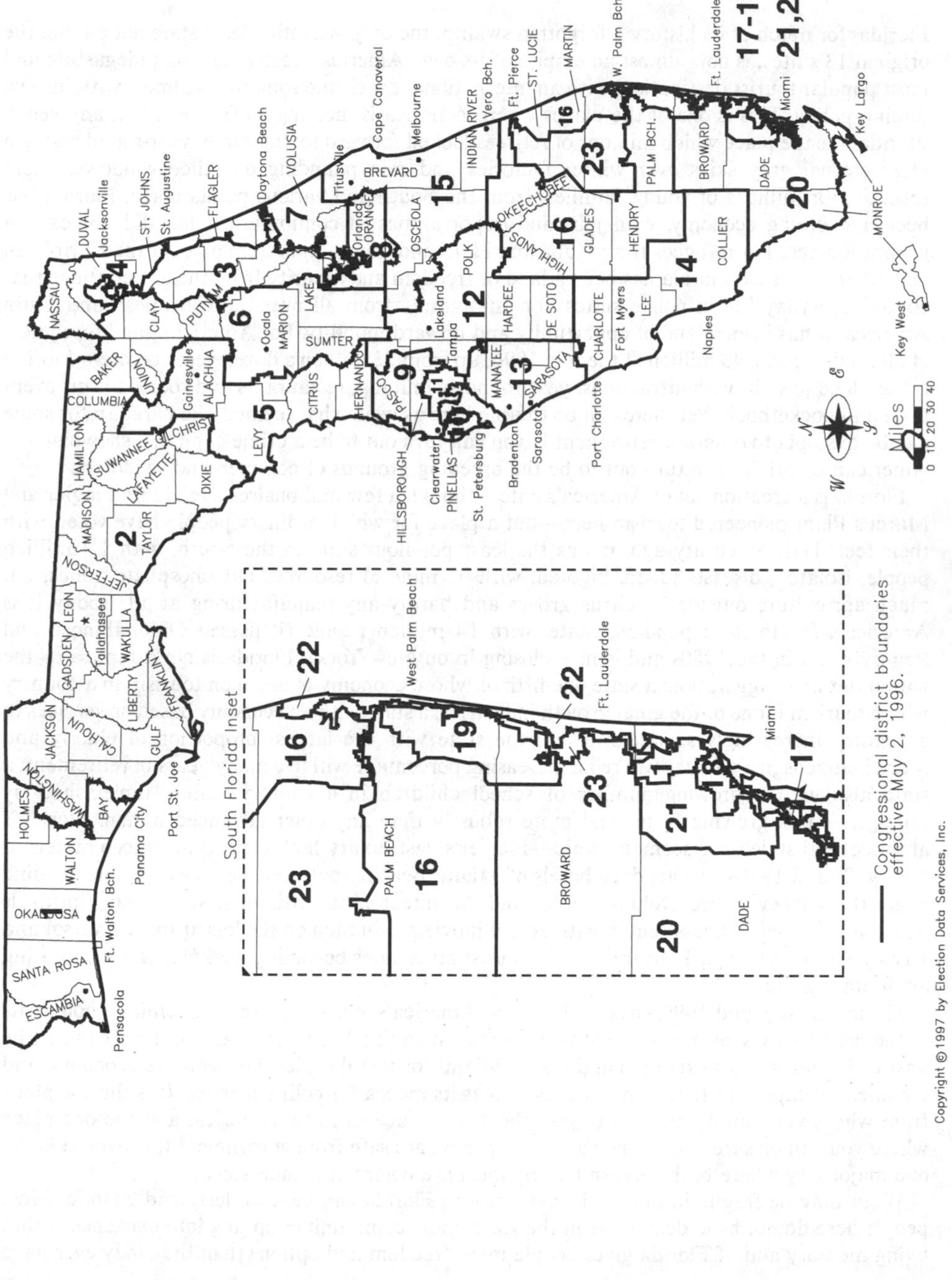
South Florida Inset
Congressional district boundaries effective May 2, 1996.
Copyright © 1997 by Election Data Services, Inc.
Miles
0 10 20 30 40
ESCAMBIA
SANTA ROSA
OKALOOSA
WALTON
HOLMES
WASHINGTON
JACKSON
BAY
CALHOUN
GULF
LIBERTY
GADSDEN
FRANKLIN
WAKULLA
LEON
JEFFERSON
MADISON
TAYLOR
HAMILTON
SUWANNEE
LAFAYETTE
DIXIE
COLUMBIA
GILCHRIST
BAKER
UNION
NASSAU
DUVAL
CLAY
ST. JOHNS
PUTNAM
FLAGLER
ALACHUA
LEVY
MARION
VOLUSIA
CITRUS
SUMTER
LAKE
HERNANDO
PASCO
ORANGE
SEMINOLE
BREVARD
OSCEOLA
POLK
HILLSBOROUGH
PINELLAS
MANATEE
HARDEE
DE SOTO
HIGHLANDS
OKEECHOBEE
INDIAN RIVER
ST. LUCIE
MARTIN
SARASOTA
CHARLOTTE
GLADES
LEE
HENDRY
PALM BCH.
COLLIER
BROWARD
DADE
MONROE
PALM BEACH
Pensacola
Ft. Walton Bch.
Panama City
Port St. Joe
Tallahassee
Jacksonville
St. Augustine
Gainesville
Ocala
Daytona Beach
Titusville
Cape Canaveral
Orlando
Melbourne
Vero Bch.
Ft. Pierce
W. Palm Bch.
West Palm Beach
Ft. Lauderdale
Miami
Key Largo
Key West
Naples
Fort Myers
Port Charlotte
Sarasota
Bradenton
St. Petersburg
Clearwater
Tampa
Lakeland
1
2
3
4
5
6
7
8
9
10
11
12
13
14
15
16
17
18
19
20
21
22
23
17-19,
21,22

imagined, it has also given them more disruption and crime than they surely anticipated. Many of Florida's great fortunes were made elsewhere, and brought here partly because the state has no income or inheritance taxes. And the real estate developers and trial lawyers who are the main sources of political money may be admirable as smart operators who made fortunes from their wits, but most lack roots and a broad sense of community responsibility. Government is weak here, and even in fighting crime Florida has let citizens take the lead. This was the first major state with a carrying-concealed-weapons law, which allows law-abiding citizens to routinely be licensed to carry guns. The result has been lower crime rates because, backers say, criminals hesitate to attack people who may be armed. Instead, muggers target foreign tourists who don't have guns—to the point that at Frankfurt Airport in Germany you can buy a kit with American bumper stickers and a Florida State decal for your rental car.

This new Florida, like today's America, has no real center; the state, says Governor Lawton Chiles, is "more of a crowd than a community." Its largest urban center, Miami, is geographically off to one corner and culturally uniquely Cuban, with its eyes increasingly on Latin America. The rest of the Gold Coast, north past West Palm Beach, while containing almost one-third of Floridians is also atypical, with a population drawn heavily from New York (the largest migration between any two states is from New York to Florida) and other Northeastern metro areas, with large numbers of Jews, and huge retiree condos lining the ocean front. Even faster growing is central Florida, the I-4 corridor from Tampa-St. Petersburg through citrus and tourist country and Orlando, then finally to the Space Coast. This is mostly family, not retiree, country, living off high-tech industries as much as tourism, a year-round rather than seasonal civilization. There is also the Gulf Coast, the affluent and burgeoning communities south of Tampa Bay and the more modest retirement counties to the north, and the hard-sand-beach Atlantic Coast along Jacksonville and Daytona Beach, all culturally more southern. Very southern culturally is the western Panhandle, the "Redneck Riviera" around Pensacola and Panama City, which has Florida's most luxuriant white sand beaches. These areas are growing robustly, and with a confidence and optimism hard to find in mature parts of the Gold Coast.

Politically, this all adds up to a Florida that has been moving in two different directions for the 1990s. It is becoming more Democratic at the top of the ticket: Democratic Governor Lawton Chiles won reelection over the strong challenge of Republican Jeb Bush in 1994, and this is one of two states (Arizona is the other) which Bill Clinton lost in 1992 but carried in 1996, and by a solid 48%–42% margin. At the same time Florida is becoming more Republican in downballot elections. Republicans represent 15 of Florida's 23 congressional districts, and Republicans have been winning state offices for some years. Florida is the first former Confederate state with a Republican legislature: in 1994 Republicans won control of the Senate and in 1996 the House, even as Chiles and Clinton were winning. Working for Republicans in these races are the same issues that made Florida seem a solid Republican state in presidential contests in the 1980s: taxes, crime, and reinforcing traditional values. Working for Democrats at the top of the ticket have been the environment, Cuban issues, and, though they have not been nearly as important as generally assumed, Medicare and Social Security. This is not for want of trying. In 1994 Democrats ran a phone campaign to seniors charging that Jeb Bush would cut Social Security; Chiles disavowed any connection with it, but in 1995 newspapers revealed it was run by James Krog, a top Democratic Party official. And in such a close race this knowledge might have made a difference.

But in 1996 the Democrats' oft-trumpeted charges that Republicans favored "cuts" in Medicare seemed to have only a marginal effect. Bob Dole actually ran better than George Bush in Gulf Coast counties heavily peopled by retirees, while he ran worse in the Gold Coast, especially in Dade County, and in the Orlando area, which has relatively few retirees. Clinton made great gains among Cuban-Americans and other Hispanics, partly because of his support of Radio Marti and the Helms-Burton Act, his condemnation of the shooting down of the Brothers to the Rescue planes in February 1996, and the Republicans' welfare bill which cut aid to legal immigrants—which the two Cuban-American congressmen from Miami voted against. The

Clinton Administration also worked hard to naturalize record numbers of citizens—1996 was the top year for this in American history—who seem to have voted heavily for the President.

Then there is the environment. Migrants from New York or Illinois may not have cared much about environmental issues when they lived there. But they came to Florida in large part because of the climate and setting, and they don't want to see oil drilled on the Gulf coast or the Everglades paved over. This "river of grass" is actually a shallow sheet of water that flows slowly from Lake Okeechobee south to Florida Bay; dense sawgrass gives it the appearance of a vast, waterlogged field. In February 1996 Vice President Al Gore announced an Everglades cleanup plan and sought a 1-cent-per-pound tax on Everglades sugar and a commitment by farmers to reduce phosphorus fertilizer runoff. Also there was a "Save Our Everglades" ballot initiative for the penny tax, with heavy advertising on both sides; it was rejected by voters, but popular among many environment-minded migrants, and the publicity undoubtedly helped the Clinton-Gore ticket. The Cuban and environmental issues helped Clinton raise his lead in the Gold Coast from 48%–36% in 1992 to a whopping 60%–33% in 1996 and to convert a 36%–42% loss in the I-4 Corridor in 1992 to a 46%–43% carry in 1996. In contrast the margin in the rest of the state was 44%–35% Republican in 1992 and 48%–41% Republican in 1996.

Now the political balance of Florida seems fairly well set. The Gold Coast, with about one-quarter of the votes, is heavily Democratic; heavily pro-Democratic Jewish voters are one major reason. The I-4 corridor, with three-eighths of the votes, is marginal territory: the Tampa-St. Petersburg area was narrowly for Clinton and the Orlando area narrowly for Dole in 1996. The rest of the state, with three-eighths of the votes, is mostly Republican, though for different reasons. The panhandle and north Florida are culturally part of the South. They were historically Democratic and now are heavily Republican, except for black-majority enclaves and the capital of Tallahassee and the university town of Gainesville. The Gulf Coast is mixed, heavily Republican in affluent areas south of Tampa Bay, more marginal in the working class retirement havens to the north. The historic trend favors the Republicans. From 1978–96 total registration in Florida rose from 4.2 million to 8 million, with Republican registration up 2 million and Democratic registration up only 788,000. The Democrats' registration edge dropped from 64%–30% in 1980 to 51%–41% in 1992 and 46%–41% in 1996. Counterbalancing this trend is the Florida media, which is generally liberal and pro-Democratic, which may be especially important in a state with eight media markets and dozens of newspapers, and hundreds of thousands of new voters unacquainted with Florida government or politics and no established civic ladders for developing political talent. And Florida's political season is brief, tucked into hurricane season, with a primary in September, a runoff in October (and there often are runoffs), and then the November election. It's over in a flash: the wonder is that the results are as rational as they have been.

Governor. Lawton Chiles in 1998 is completing his second term as governor of Florida and his 40th year in Florida politics. He grew up in Lakeland, in the citrus and phosphate country of central Florida, attended the University of Florida and served in Korea, then practiced law and was elected to the state House in 1958. In 1970 he ran for the U.S. Senate, and set out to walk 1,000 miles across the state from the Panhandle to the Keys—the country's first walking campaign. He finished second in the primary, won an upset in the runoff, then upset a conservative Republican in the general. He made a moderate record, chaired the Budget Committee for a time and became frustrated with the federal deficit, and declined to run for reelection in 1988. In spring 1990 he suddenly jumped into the race for governor. He beat then-Congressman (and now Insurance Commissioner) Bill Nelson in the primary. In the general he faced Bob Martinez, the only Republican governor elected since 1970, widely unpopular for pushing through a tax on services that had to be repealed; Chiles beat him 57%–43%.

As governor, Chiles technically has few powers. Many appointments and budget decisions must be approved by a cabinet made up of six separately elected officials. And one option is ruled out: the state Constitution forbids an income tax, which in any case would be unpopular since out-of-staters provide one-third of sales tax revenue. But a governor does set the agenda and tone of state government. Chiles, working closely with Lieutenant Governor Buddy MacKay, has sounded a Democratic Leadership Council note. He reduced spending increases, called for "right-sizing" the bureaucracy, settling a federal suit on the Everglades. He was proud of requiring "Healthy Start" to screen every pregnant woman for health risks and pushed a mandatory work program that he said cut state welfare rolls. MacKay worked on "reinventing government." But Chiles also called for $1.3 billion in new taxes in 1992, at which point his job rating plummeted. And in 1994 his healthcare reform plan was rejected by the legislature.

In 1995 Chiles had fierce opposition from Jeb Bush, Miami businessman and son of President George Bush. Bush presented a program of thoroughgoing conservative reform. "We need to change our entire relationship with government [until it plays] a useful but smaller role in our lives," he said. He called for fewer appeals for death row inmates and speedier executions; said Florida should withdraw from Aid to Families with Dependent Children (AFDC) and replace it with limited temporary assistance; called for school choice and demanded voter approval of all state and local tax increases. Chiles responded that he had already started reforming welfare and education and had approved as many executions as Martinez. But his campaign only got revved up in October when he ran negative ads about Bush's ties with savings and loans and attacked a Bush ad which showed a mother, whose daughter had been murdered, accusing Chiles of not speeding executions. Chiles also got credit for calling on the federal government in August to stop the flow of refugees from Cuba to Florida, in response to which Bill Clinton confined refugees at the Guantanamo Naval Base. He limited contributions from individuals to $100. And Chiles started emphasizing his "cracker" roots and calling himself "the he-coon [who] always walks before the light of day."

The result was a 51%–49% Chiles victory. The controversial crime ad may have hurt Bush, who otherwise ran no negative ads. But even more important may have been the mentions of savings and loans, as beloved by many older voters as Social Security. Chiles clearly cut into the elderly vote on the Gulf Coast and won big on the Gold Coast. Exit polls showed voters over 65 were 54% for Chiles and voters under 65 gave Bush a majority. Blacks were 94% for Chiles, Jews were 79% for Chiles, Cubans 74% for Bush. But Republicans won three of the six lower statewide offices, captured control of the state House and increased their seats in the Senate.

"Government can't work. People work," Chiles said in his inaugural address, and called for reducing government regulations by 50% in two years. But he was still looking around for things for government to do. His prime initiative was a lawsuit, authorized by a 1994 state law, against the tobacco companies, suing them for Medicaid expenses caring for people with smoking-related illnesses. While Republicans talked of changing the 1994 law, Chiles pursued the suit with relish, and also made a well-publicized initiative against children smoking. Meanwhile, the legislature voted for large increases in spending on prisons and for a plan encouraging charter schools. But Chiles's moderate tone was not enough to stop Republicans from gaining the House and keeping the Senate in 1997. The Republican Speaker Dan Webster said, "We're for less taxes, less regulation, and more personal freedom," and the legislature was expected to push tort reform—trial lawyers are one of the financial mainstays of Florida Democrats—and changes in the tobacco suit law.

The 1998 governor race seems almost certain to be a battle—a titanic battle—between Buddy MacKay, representing the moderate activist government policies of Chiles, and Jeb Bush, representing the intellectually rigorous paring back of government—an interesting experiment in one of the nation's most important laboratories of political experimentation.

Senior Senator. Bob Graham is careful, methodical, thorough, hard-working, reliable—always wearing his Florida ties, recording every meeting and meal in notebooks, scheduling meetings with every member of the Florida House delegation and with lobbyists on both sides of environmental, banking and crime issues. He comes from a prominent Florida family. His father started out with a Miami area dairy farm and developed the planned mini-city of Miami Lakes; his half-brother Philip Graham was publisher of *The Washington Post*. He has been in politics almost all his adult life; he was elected to the state House in 1966, at 30, and to the state Senate in 1970. In 1978, after a come-from-behind win in the Democratic runoff and a solid 56% win in the general, he began the first of two terms as governor. The attention-getting device in that campaign (invented by Senator Tom Harkin for his 1974 House race) was work days: Graham worked one day a week at some local job, from bagging groceries to construction. He keeps it up still, once a month, and in March 1997 logged his 321st work day; it was at a work day rebuilding a school in Opalocka, the Monday after the November 1996 election, that he announced he would run for reelection to the Senate and not for governor in 1998.

Graham's voting record in the Senate has been middle-of-the-road, though it moved a bit to the left, as the Senate median moved to the right after the 1994 election. He has been a hardliner on crime legislation, supporting capital punishment, seeking federal reimbursement to states which jail criminal aliens, opposing a higher minimum wage for prisoners. A staunch opponent of Fidel Castro, Graham has argued for the embargo on Cuba, although he bucked his state's Cuban-American leaders in supporting Clinton's May 1995 deal to send additional refugees back to Guantanamo. He wanted to stem the flow of Haitian refugees to Florida, and backed the dispatch of U.S. troops to Haiti. He has proposed a Step-21 new highway funding formula, to guarantee states 95% of what they put in to the highway trust fund; he wants to change the Veterans' funding formula because Florida's veteran population is increasing rapidly. He urged action on Clinton Administration officials when a "surge" of tomato exports from Mexico threatened Florida growers' markets. He opposed taxation of prepaid college tuitions. He has worked hard to restore the Kissimmee River to its natural state, to ban oil drilling off the southwest Florida coast and get the federal government to buy up existing leases, to expand the Everglades park and to make the Suwanee in north Florida a National Wild and Scenic River.

On national issues he often supports Democratic policy butis willing to buck both party and constituency on some issues. He voted unhesitatingly for the Gulf war resolution. He supports the balanced budget amendment. He supports the McCain-Feingold campaign finance reform. But he . In 1996 he called for means-testing Medicare and slightly reducing automatic increases in Social Security, in order to balance the budget—even as the Clinton campaign and AFL-CIO were excoriating Republicans for suggesting such things. But Graham coolly said that "it is appropriate to ask those able to contribute more to their health care premiums to do so" and, before the Bosking Commission report, that "there is ample evidence that the Consumer Price Index has overstated inflation."

Graham won the Senate seat in 1986 as he was leaving the governorship by beating Paula Hawkins, a sometimes eccentric but often popular Republican elected in 1980, 55%–45%. In 1992, he won easily. Graham's moderate stance and strong intellect have led some to call on him to run for national office, and he was on Bill Clinton's short list of vice presidential possibilities in 1992. But there seems little chance he will run. He is regarded as a strong favorite for reelection, even in Republican-trending Florida.

Junior Senator. Connie Mack III is an important leader of Senate Republicans. He grew up with a famous name: his paternal grandfather was the longtime owner and manager of the Philadelphia Athletics from 1901–50; his maternal grandfather was Morris Sheppard, Texas senator from 1913–41. Connie Mack III moved to Florida after school and became a banker in the Gulf Coast town of Cape Coral. In 1982, at 40, when he was president of the Florida National Bank of Lee County, he won a multi-candidate Republican primary for the House in a newly created Gulf Coast district. In the House, Mack became a supply-sider and one of the leaders of Newt Gingrich's Conservative Opportunity Society. He was the lead House sponsor of the Gramm-Rudman deficit-cutting measure that originated in the Senate; pro-choice on abortion, he switched when contemplating the 1988 Senate race. He entered that contest in October 1987, before incumbent Lawton Chiles and former Governor Reubin Askew decided not to run. Against the Democratic nominee, Congressman (and now Lieutenant Governor) Buddy MacKay, Mack's campaign theme was, "Hey, Buddy, you're liberal." Mack called for "less taxing, less spending, less government, and more freedom" and attacked MacKay for opposing contra aid and the balanced budget amendment. Worries about social security clearly helped MacKay, who carried St. Petersburg and ran far ahead of most Democrats in Mack's own retiree-heavy House district. But Mack ran far ahead of other Republicans in the heavily military Jacksonville area and in the family-oriented I-4 corridor. Mack lost among those who went to the polls on election day, but with a big absentee margin won 50.4%–49.6%.

Mack has a solidly conservative voting record, with special attention to issues of importance in Florida. He is a staunch opponent of Fidel Castro and pushed for tightening of the Cuba embargo, helped set up TV Marti, and called for murder indictments against the Cuban pilots who shot down the Brothers to the Rescue in February 1996. He is a strong supporter of Israel and continues to be wary of the PLO. He opposes offshore oil drilling and sponsored the Florida Coastal Zone Protection Act. He was a sponsor of the 1996 Everglades cleanup law which authorized $300 million for converting sugar cane farms into buffer and water filtration zones. He was successful in helping Florida get two more baseball teams—the Florida Marlins in Miami and the Devil Rays in Tampa Bay who start playing in 1998..

Mack has given special attention to health care issues—which have tended to go his way. He was one of the few to oppose the catastrophic health care act of 1988, when he was running for the Senate, and which proved so unpopular it was repealed in 1989. He was one of three Republicans who responded on national television to Bill Clinton's healthcare speech in September 1993. He has given special attention to early detection of cancer—both he and his wife are cancer survivors—and he sponsored the 1996 Health Insurance Portability Act that bars insurers from denying coverage because of preexisting conditions or charging higher premiums because of genetic information.

Mack's other specialty is economics. His collaborators in the House in the mid-1980s, notably Newt Gingrich and Trent Lott, were in a hopeless minority, and they unsuccessfully opposed George Bush's tax increase in 1990 and Bill Clinton's in 1993. Now they are better positioned. Mack chaired the Joint Economic Committee in the 104th Congress and made a major change by dropping the "current services budget" concept—the procedure which lets every government department get all the money it spent last year, plus more if it can claim more beneficiaries, plus the rate of inflation, all of which is based on an assumption that there can be no more efficient way of delivering government services than we have at present. Mack also chaired a Republican task force on committees. His new rules added several oversight and investigations subcommittees—always a useful tool for a majority congressional party which doesn't control the White House—and prohibits committee chairmen from chairing subcommittees and allows a maximum of two subcommittee chairs per person, with the result that just about everybody gets to be a chairman.

In 1994 Mack was reelected easily. Democrats failed to recruit a well-known candidate and their nominee was Hugh Rodham, a Miami public defender who had never voted until 1992, and the brother of Hillary Rodham Clinton. Mack won 71%–29%. In August 1996 Mack evidently made the very short list for Bob Dole's vice presidential nomination, but was passed over for Jack Kemp; the Clinton White House let it be known that Mack was the candidate they feared most, but that was probably disinformation. Mack's seat does not come up until 2000, and he seems an excellent prospect for reelection.

Presidential politics. Florida, solidly Republican in presidential contests in the 1980s, has become a fierce battleground in the 1990s: in 1992 and 1996 this was the only one of the four largest states to be seriously contested. George Bush carried it in 1992, but only by 41%–39%, and after Lawton Chiles edged Jeb Bush in 1994, 51%–49%, Bill Clinton's strategists targeted Florida for 1996. It was a shrewd decision. Why has Florida changed from the most Republican megastate in 1988 to a 48%–42% Clinton state in 1996? The Medicare and Social Security issues helped, though not nearly to the extent generally thought. It may be that environmental issues switched more votes: people come to Florida looking for a kind of paradise, and are more concerned about the environment than they were when they lived in New York or Ohio or Illinois. Then there are Cuban-Americans, carefully cultivated by Clinton for years, helping him to be the first Democratic presidential nominee to carry Miami's Dade County since 1976. But there cannot be entire confidence in predicting Florida's presidential vote in the future, for this is a state whose population is changing, whose cohorts of elderly turn over fast, where there are vast internal migrations like the movement of Jews northward from Miami to Broward and Palm Beach Counties. Democrats have carried Florida's electoral votes four times since World War II—1948, 1964, 1976, 1996—and each time with a different geographic base and different electoral coalition.

Florida's early March presidential primary is the one around which Southern Super Tuesday was built for the 1988 cycle; by 1996, Florida was one of the mid-season states, and its influence diluted from what it was, in 1976, when Jimmy Carter's victory here ended the presidential candidacy of George Wallace. Florida's Democratic turnout peaked that year, at 1.3 million; increasingly the Democratic electorate is liberal, with large numbers of blacks, Jews, teachers and other unionized public employees. The Republican electorate has grown from 609,000 in 1976 to 901,000 in 1988, maintaining that level for the 1990s, and is hawkish, anti-tax, but with a soft spot for the environment.

Congressional districting. Florida gained four new House seats from the 1990 Census, going from 19 to 23, and redistricting was naturally fiercely contested. Democrats were so conflicted that they could not produce a plan even though they controlled both houses of the legislature and the governorship. So in May 1992, a federal court adopted a plan drawn by a Tulane University professor which created three black-majority (two of them new) and two Hispanic-majority districts (one new), some with very peculiar shapes; boundaries of the other 18 districts were not so driven by politics, but sometimes ended up grotesque because of next-door minority districts. The result was the election of three black congressmen, and a Republican edge that increased from 10–9 in 1990 to 15–8 after 1994 and 1996. In April 1996 the 3d District, which meandered through half the swamps of north Florida, was ruled unconstitutional, and redrawn amicably by a split-party legislature; its black percentage fell from 51% to 40%, but incumbent Democrat Corinne Brown was reelected. Florida will gain several representatives after the 2000 Census—something which surely has not escaped the attention of any number of Florida politicians.

The People: Est. Pop. 1996: 14,400,000; Pop. 1990: 12,937,926, up 11.3% 1990–1996. 5.4% of U.S. total, 4th largest; 15% rural. Median age: 37.6 years. 19% 65 years and over. 73.2% White, 13.1% Black, 1.1% Asian, 12.2% Hispanic origin. Households: 54.4% married couple families; 21% married couple fams. w. children; 44% college educ.; median household income: $27,483; per capita income: $14,698; 67.2% owner occupied housing; median house value: $77,100; median monthly rent: $402. 5.1% Unemployment. 1996 Voting age pop.: 11,043,000. 1996 Turnout: 5,300,927; 48% of VAP. Registered voters (1996): 8,077,877; 3,728,513 D (46%), 3,309,105 R (41%), 1,040,257 unaffiliated and minor parties (13%).

Political Lineup: Governor, Lawton Chiles (D); Lt. Gov., Buddy MacKay (D); Secy. of State, Sandra Mortham (R); Atty. Gen., Robert A. Butterworth (D); Treasurer and Insurance Commissioner, Bill Nelson (D); Comptroller, Robert Milligan (R); Auditor General, Charles L. Lester (D). State Senate, 40 (23 R and 17 D); Senate President, Tony Jennings (R); State House, 120 (61 R and 59 D); House Speaker, Daniel Webster (R). Senators, Bob Graham (D) and Connie Mack III (R). Representatives, 23 (15 R, 8 D).

Elections Division: 904-488-7697; **Filing Deadline for U.S. Congress:** May 8, 1998.

1996 Presidential Vote

Clinton (D)	2,546,870	(48%)
Dole (R)	2,244,536	(42%)
Perot (I)	483,870	(9%)

1996 Republican Presidential Primary

Dole (R)	511,108	(57%)
Forbes (R)	181,708	(20%)
Buchanan (R)	162,713	(18%)
Other	42,541	(6%)

1992 Presidential Vote

Bush (R)	2,158,914	(41%)
Clinton (D)	2,062,579	(39%)
Perot (I)	1,047,341	(20%)

GOVERNOR

Gov. Lawton Chiles (D)

Elected 1990, term expires Jan. 1999; b. Apr. 3, 1930, Lakeland; home, Tallahassee; U. of FL, B.S. 1952, LL.B. 1955; Presbyterian; married (Rhea).

Career: Army, 1953–54 (Korea); Practicing atty., 1955–71; Instructor, FL Southern Col., 1955–58; FL House of Reps., 1958–66; FL Senate, 1967–70; U.S. Senate, 1970–88; Dir., LeRoy Collins Ctr. for Pub. Policy, 1989–90.

Office: The Capitol, Tallahassee 32399, 904-488-7146; Fax: 904-487-0801; Web site: www.state.fl.us.

Election Results

1994 gen.	Lawton Chiles (D)	2,135,008	(51%)
	Jeb Bush (R)	2,071,068	(49%)
1994 prim.	Lawton Chiles (D)	603,657	(72%)
	Jack Gargan (D)	232,757	(28%)
1990 gen.	Lawton Chiles (D)	1,988,341	(57%)
	Bob Martinez (R)	1,526,738	(43%)

SENATORS

Sen. Bob Graham (D)

Elected 1986, seat up 1998; b. Nov. 9, 1936, Coral Gables; home, Miami Lakes; U. of FL, B.A. 1959, Harvard, J.D. 1962; United Church of Christ; married (Adele).

Career: The Graham Cos., Sengra Development Corp., 1962–66; FL House of Reps., 1966–70; FL Senate, 1970–78; FL Gov., 1978–1986.

DC Office: 524 HSOB 20510, 202-224-3041; Fax: 202-224-2237; e-mail: bob_graham@graham.senate.gov.

State Offices: Miami, 305-536-7293; Tallahassee, 904-422-6100; Tampa, 813-228-2476.

Committees: *Energy & Natural Resources* (6th of 9 D): Energy Research, Development, Production & Regulation; Forests & Public Land Management; National Parks, Historic Preservation & Recreation. *Environment & Public Works* (5th of 8 D): Clean Air, Wetlands, Private Property & Nuclear Safety (RMM); Superfund, Waste Control & Risk Assessment; Transportation & Infrastructure. *Finance* (6th of 9 D): Health Care; International Trade; Long-Term Growth, Debt & Deficit Reduction (RMM). *Veterans' Affairs* (2nd of 5 D). *Intelligence (Select)* (4th of 9 D).

Group Ratings

	ADA	ACLU	AFS	LCV	CFA	CON	NFIB	COC	ACU	NTLC	CHC
1996	85	39	86	77	64	85	43	46	15	28	15
1995	95	—	91	100	88	29	—	47	13	—	—

National Journal Ratings

	1995 LIB — 1995 CONS	1996 LIB — 1996 CONS
Economic	64% — 35%	57% — 39%
Social	71% — 28%	70% — 28%
Foreign	65% — 31%	62% — 36%

Key Votes of the 104th Congress

1. Reduce Medicare Growth $	N	5. Flag Amendment	Y	9. Anti-Missile Defense	N
2. Lmt. Prod. Liab. Damages	N	6. Endangered Species	Y	10. Cuban Embargo	Y
3. Increase Min. Wage	Y	7. Gay Employment Rights	Y	11. Bar Bosnia Troop $	N
4. Welfare Reform	N	8. Ovrd. Part. Birth Veto	N	12. Cut Vietnam Aid	N

Election Results

1992 general	Bob Graham (D)	3,245,565	(65%)	($3,318,473)
	Bill Grant (R)	1,716,505	(35%)	($242,251)
1992 primary	Bob Graham (D)	968,618	(84%)	
	Jim Mahorner (D)	180,405	(16%)	
1986 general	Bob Graham (D)	1,877,231	(55%)	($6,173,663)
	Paula Hawkins (R)	1,551,888	(45%)	($6,723,729)

Sen. Connie Mack III (R)

Elected 1988, seat up 2000; b. Oct. 29, 1940, Philadelphia, PA; home, Cape Coral; U. of FL, B.A. 1966; Catholic; married (Priscilla).

Career: Banker, 1966–82; U.S. House of Reps., 1982–88.

DC Office: 517 HSOB 20510, 202-224-5274; Fax: 202-224-8022; e-mail: connie@mack.senate.gov.

State Offices: Ft. Meyers, 941-275-6252; Jacksonville 904-268-7915; Miami 305-530-7100; Pensacola, 904-479-9803; Tallahassee, 904-425-1995; Tampa, 813-225-7683.

Committees: *Republican Conference Chairman. Banking, Housing & Urban Affairs* (4th of 10 R): Financial Institutions & Regulatory Relief; Financial Services & Technology; Housing Opportunity & Community Development (Chmn.). *Finance* (11th of 11 R): International Trade; Long-Term Growth, Debt & Defict Reduction (Chmn.); Taxation & IRS Oversight. *Joint Economic Committee* (Vice Chmn. of 10 Sens.).

Group Ratings

	ADA	ACLU	AFS	LCV	CFA	CON	NFIB	COC	ACU	NTLC	CHC
1996	0	31	0	0	8	51	100	100	100	100	100
1995	0	—	0	7	0	29	—	100	91	—	—

National Journal Ratings

	1995 LIB — 1995 CONS	1996 LIB — 1996 CONS
Economic	0% — 88%	0% — 94%
Social	22% — 74%	41% — 58%
Foreign	21% — 78%	32% — 65%

Key Votes of the 104th Congress

1. Reduce Medicare Growth $	Y	5. Flag Amendment	Y	9. Anti-Missile Defense	Y
2. Lmt. Prod. Liab. Damages	Y	6. Endangered Species	N	10. Cuban Embargo	Y
3. Increase Min. Wage	N	7. Gay Employment Rights	N	11. Bar Bosnia Troop $	N
4. Welfare Reform	Y	8. Ovrd. Part. Birth Veto	Y	12. Cut Vietnam Aid	N

Election Results

1994 general	Connie Mack III (R)	2,894,726	(71%)	($5,729,359)
	Hugh E. Rodham (D)................	1,210,412	(29%)	($617,190)
1994 primary	Connie Mack III (R)	unopposed		
1988 general	Connie Mack III (R)	2,049,329	(50%)	($5,181,639)
	Buddy MacKay (D)	2,015,717	(50%)	($3,714,852)

FIRST DISTRICT

The "Redneck Riviera" is the affectionate local name for the Gulf Coast beaches of Florida's Panhandle, from Pensacola east to Destin. This has been military country ever since John Quincy Adams persuaded Spain to sell Florida to the U.S. in 1819 to get the port of Pensacola. The Navy has been there ever since—this was the site of the nation's first naval aviation training base and the birthplace of carrier aviation—and the Air Force has a massive presence in Eglin Air Force Base, which spreads over the lion's share of three counties. Culturally part of Dixie, this was economically backward land for years, dependent in the 1940s and 1950s on the military bases for growth. More recently, as the South has become more prosperous, this American Riviera has become a major vacation and retirement spot for southerners who enjoy its vast, fine-grained white sand beaches, perhaps the finest in the country, and its pleasant inlet-filled bays. Its cultural conservatism has remained ingrained from that earlier era, and it has become economically more conservative as well, while militarily it is supportive of assertive American policies around the world.

The 1st Congressional District of Florida includes the end of the Panhandle, so far west it's in the Central time zone. It stretches from Pensacola and the Alabama border east to include part of Panama City. Politically, this is Republican territory. George Bush and Bob Dole may not have run well elsewhere, but they carried the 1st District smartly against Bill Clinton in 1992 and 1996. The Panhandle has become reliably Republican in statewide races and now elects mostly Republicans to the legislature.

The congressman from the 1st is Joe Scarborough, a Republican first elected in 1994. Scarborough grew up in Pensacola and after school ran a beauty contest company and then practiced law and was active in community affairs. In October 1993 he helped collect 3,000 signatures to protest the city government's 65% property tax increase. He had never run for office, but had long been interested in politics: his family remembers him at five, in 1968, coloring in states red and blue depending on whether they went Democratic or Republican. When Democratic Congressman Earl Hutto, a conservative elected with only 52% in 1990 and 1992, decided to retire, Scarborough ran for Congress. He was one of five Republicans in the race, and far from the best known. The best-known Republican was Lois Benson, a one-term legislator and four-year Pensacola Council member, generally conservative but pro-choice on abortion. She won 31.4% in the primary, but Scarborough, conservative and anti-abortion, built on petition contacts and bought 30-minute cable broadcasts and received 30.6%; in October he won the runoff 54%–46%.

His Democratic opponent, Vince Whibbs Jr., was just the kind of politician who had held such conservative seats for years—the son of a long-time Pensacola mayor, a Marine veteran and local businessman and lawyer, an opponent of gun control, supporter of school prayer and the balanced budget amendment. "I've never voted for a Democrat," Whibbs said, but added that he could do more for the district as part of the Democratic majority. Scarborough, in contrast, said, "The federal government should protect our shores and get out of citizens' way." He talked about "retaking America" and returning to the small government of Jefferson and Madison. "We need to send someone who will say 'no' when everyone else is saying 'yes.'" He advocated a five-year federal spending freeze, school vouchers and tax credits for home schoolers and a ban on offshore oil drilling. Voters here were looking not for favors from a Democratic Congress but for new policies from a Republican Congress. Scarborough won by the whopping margin of 62%–38%.

Scarborough fit in happily in the new Republican Congress. His fellow freshmen elected him their political director and new Speaker Newt Gingrich named him to head a Republican task force on education. He continued prodding Gingrich and other leaders to be more aggressive, casting one of 10 Republican protest votes against the FY96 budget and urging intransigence in budget negotiations in December 1995. Scarborough was not all stereotype. One of the youngest freshmen, he kept a coonskin cap in his office and liked to wear jeans on Fridays. He called for ending corporate welfare, including royalty relief for offshore oil drillers and aid to large tobacco and sugar companies. He sponsored a bill to force the United States to leave the United Nations after a four-year transition, saying it was "a passive bystander, an expensive toy but hardly a critical tool." He opposed offshore oil drilling in the Gulf of Mexico.

In 1996 Scarborough had desultory opposition and won with 73% of the vote, the second highest for a House Republican in a contested race. Unchastised, it would seem, by the 1996 results, he was elected co-chairman of the New Federalists in the 105th Congress.

The People: Pop. 1990: 562,575; 26% rural; 11% age 65+; 83% White; 13% Black; 2% Asian; 1% Amer. Indian; 2% Hispanic origin. Households: 59% married couple families; 26% married couple fams. w. children; 49% college educ.; median household income: $25,866; per capita income: $12,505; median gross rent: $390; median house value: $61,800.

1996 Presidential Vote

Dole (R)	146,794	(59%)
Clinton (D)	77,070	(31%)
Perot (I)	24,322	(10%)

1992 Presidential Vote

Bush (R)	117,809	(51%)
Clinton (D)	59,316	(26%)
Perot (I)	53,250	(23%)

Rep. Joe Scarborough (R)

Elected 1994; b. Apr. 9, 1963, Atlanta, GA; home, Pensacola; U. of AL, B.A. 1985; U. of FL, J.D. 1990; Baptist; married (Melanie).

Career: Dir., Miss American Co-ed Beauty Schl., 1985–87; Practicing atty., 1990–94.

DC Office: 127 CHOB 20515, 202-225-4136; Fax: 202-225-3414; e-mail: fl01@hr.house.gov.

District Offices: Pensacola, 904-479-1183; Ft. Walton Beach, 904-664-1266.

Committees: *Education & The Workforce* (25th of 25 R): Oversight & Investigations. *Government Reform & Oversight* (15th of 24 R): Government Management, Information & Technology; National Economic Growth, Natural Resources & Regulatory Affairs. *National Security* (23rd of 30 R): Military Installations & Facilities; Military Research & Development.

Group Ratings

	ADA	ACLU	AFS	LCV	CFA	CON	NFIB	COC	ACU	NTLC	CHC
1996	10	27	8	15	54	9	92	94	95	88	86
1995	15	—	—	6	15	38	—	88	96	—	—

National Journal Ratings

	1995 LIB — 1995 CONS			1996 LIB — 1996 CONS		
Economic	0%	—	74%	36%	—	63%
Social	37%	—	63%	33%	—	65%
Foreign	15%	—	73%	0%	—	79%

Key Votes of the 104th Congress

1. Reduce Medicare Growth $	Y	5. Flag Amendment	Y	9. Cuban Embargo	Y
2. Ovrd. Product Liab. Veto	Y	6. Drop EPA Limits	N	10. Bar Bosnia Troop $	Y
3. Increase Min. Wage	N	7. Repeal Assault-Weap. Ban	Y	11. Cut Anti-Missile Defense	N
4. Welfare Reform	Y	8. Ovrd. Part. Birth Veto	Y	12. Bar U.N. Uniforms	Y

Election Results

1996 general	Joe Scarborough (R)	175,946	(73%)	($428,856)
	Kevin Beck (D)	66,495	(27%)	($30,613)
1996 primary	Joe Scarborough (R)	unopposed		
1994 general	Joe Scarborough (R)	112,901	(62%)	($345,687)
	Vince Whibbs Jr. (D)	70,389	(38%)	($271,953)

SECOND DISTRICT

Tallahassee seems an odd choice to be the capital of the nation's fourth largest state. Until recently it was not much more than a Spanish-mossed county seat with a handsome creole capitol, built in 1845 and preserved opposite its 1977 skyscraper replacement, and two state universities—sited here in the days when almost all Floridians lived along the state's northern edge and Tallahassee was near the population center. Ralph Waldo Emerson, visiting Tallahassee in the 19th Century, said it was a "grotesque place, rapidly settled by public officers, land speculators and desperadoes." The countryside around it is distinctly Dixie: cotton fields, soft pine stands, catfish farms, large families, small towns with big churches, both black and white. Madison County, 50% black, with Florida's lowest per capita income and losing population since 1930, is a noteworthy example. But Tallahassee itself and the subdivisions spreading beyond it are bringing to the state's north end some of the new urbanized Florida, with an additional pro-government tilt: 42% of Tallahassee area jobs are now in city and state government, compared to 15% statewide. Tallahassee has not attained the critical mass of the capitals of the three more populous states (Sacramento, Austin, and Albany), but it is on its way.

The 2d Congressional District of Florida is centered on Tallahassee, but extends westward to Panama City and eastward almost to Jacksonville. Historically, this was Democratic country, Jeffersonian and segregationist. Today, it is still Democratic, though for different reasons; there is a large black percentage (23%, the fourth largest in Florida) and a strong Democratic preference among state employees and those dependent on them. Tallahassee's Leon County gave solid margins twice to Bill Clinton and voted very solidly 63%–37% for Democratic Governor Lawton Chiles over Republican challenger Jeb Bush in 1994. This is one of the few white-majority districts in the South which solidly favors national and statewide Democrats.

The congressman from the 2d District is Allen Boyd, a Democrat first elected in 1996, and one who seems sure to join the dwindling but sometimes still lively band of Democratic conservatives in the South. A life-long farmer, Boyd grew up in Monticello in Jefferson County. He served in Vietnam and received his degree from Florida State. His political career began in 1989 when he was elected to the state House. There, he formed the Conservative Democratic Caucus, which he likened during his congressional campaign to the coalition of conservative Democrats in Congress known as the Blue Dogs.

Boyd decided to run for the House in 1995, when incumbent Pete Peterson, a moderate Democrat and Vietnam prisoner-of-war, decided to retire after three terms, saying he believed in term limits; later, in March 1996, Bill Clinton named Peterson our first ambassador to Vietnam. A huge 141,000 people voted in the Democratic primary and 117,000 in the runoff. Boyd ran well ahead, with 48% to 26% for Leon County Commissioner Anita Davis and 25% for retired Gulf County Judge David Taunton. Boyd then easily prevailed in the runoff 64%–36%. Republicans, with less than 23,000 voters in the primary and 15,000 in the runoff, had a contest between economic and moral conservatives: former state Commerce Secretary Bill Sutton finished ahead of Christian Coalition-backed Carole Griffin by 48%–36% in the primary, but by only 51%–49% in the runoff. In the general, Boyd campaigned with Blue Dog conservative House Democrats Pete Geren (who was retiring from Congress) and Bud Cramer. More important, he spent $807,000 to $287,000 for Sutton.

The result was a solid victory 59%–40% for Boyd. In the House he immediately joined five southern newcomers—Jim Davis, Chris John, Mike McIntyre, Jim Turner, Virgil Goode—to raise the ranks of the Blue Dogs to 21, with hopes for more. They want, of course, to become a pivotal group, more conservative on cultural issues and often more liberal on economics than moderate Republicans. But their position is less critical now, since Republicans can conceivably, and in the 104th Congress often did, achieve majorities without significant Democratic support.

The People: Pop. 1990: 562,410; 46% rural; 12% age 65+; 74% White; 23% Black; 1% Asian; 2% Hispanic origin. Households: 54% married couple families; 25% married couple fams. w. children; 42% college educ.; median household income: $23,388; per capita income: $11,491; median gross rent: $375; median house value: $57,500.

1996 Presidential Vote			**1992 Presidential Vote**		
Clinton (D)	114,601	(47%)	Clinton (D)	95,198	(43%)
Dole (R)	99,487	(41%)	Bush (R)	80,447	(37%)
Perot (I)	25,455	(11%)	Perot (I)	42,921	(20%)

Rep. F. Allen Boyd, Jr. (D)

Elected 1996; b. June 6, 1945, Valdosta, GA; home, Monticello; N. FL Jr. Col., A.A. 1966; FL St. U., B.S. 1969; Methodist, married (Cissy).

Career: Army 1969–71 (Vietnam); Farmer; FL House of Reps., 1989–96.

DC Office: 1237 LHOB 20515, 202-225-5235; Fax: 202-225-5615.

District Offices: Panama City, 904-785-0812; Tallahassee, 904-561-3979.

Committees: *National Security* (20th of 25 D): Military Installations & Facilities; Military Procurement. *Small Business* (11th of 16 D): Government Programs & Oversight; Regulatory Reform & Paperwork Reduction.

Group Ratings and Key Votes: Newly Elected

Election Results

1996 general	Allen Boyd (D)	138,151	(59%)	($807,103)
	Bill Sutton (R)	94,122	(40%)	($287,292)
1996 runoff	Allen Boyd (D)	75,587	(64%)	
	Anita L. Davis (D)	41,677	(36%)	
1996 primary	Allen Boyd (D)	68,588	(48%)	
	Anita L. Davis (D)	37,050	(26%)	
	David L. Taunton (D)	36,027	(25%)	
1994 general	Douglas (Pete) Peterson (D)	117,404	(61%)	($334,740)
	Carole Griffin (R)	74,011	(39%)	($102,221)

THIRD DISTRICT

Before the Civil War, most of Florida was still an unchartered watery wilderness, festooned with exotic greenery, inhabited by unusual animals: a part of the United States so far out of the experience of most Americans as to seem foreign. As late as 1940, Florida had the smallest population of all the southern states, and most of the people here lived in classic Dixie rural counties with small courthouse towns, where civic affairs were run by the richest white men; blacks lived in poorly-constructed unpainted shotgun houses propped up on blocks, having little money and no vote. This was a land of swamps and lakes and orange groves, of Marjorie Kinnan Rawlings's Cross Creek, where she wrote the great children's classic *The Yearling*, and the Florida of the broad St. Johns River, one of the few rivers in North America that flows (if only sluggishly) north, through the orange grove country to the port of Jacksonville, for many years Florida's largest city.

The 3d Congressional District occupies much of this old Florida terrain. The district was created in 1992 to be north Florida's black-majority seat, and was modified for 1996, by an almost unanimous vote of the legislature, when it was overturned by a court order, and is now about 40% black. The district as drawn in 1992 collected the descendants of the slaves who worked on the plantations and farms of northern Florida over a century ago, plus blacks who have settled in the state since then. As redrawn in 1996, it no longer has a tentacle reaching out to Gainesville and Ocala, but extends more or less straight north and south, from Jacksonville to Orlando. Almost half of the district's population lives in Jacksonville, almost one quarter in and near Orlando (including all-black Eatontown, home of author Zora Neale Hurston). Much of it follows Florida watercourses: it touches on Cross Creek as well as the St. Johns river and numerous swamps.

The congresswoman from the 3d District is Corrine Brown, a Democrat first elected in 1992. She grew up in Jacksonville, taught at the community college and was a guidance counselor, and in 1982 was elected to the Florida House. With her Jacksonville base, she was the obvious favorite in the new 3d in 1992. In the Democratic primary she faced Andy Johnson, a white talk radio host who proclaimed himself "the blackest candidate in the race." Brown led Johnson 43%–31% in the primary, then polished him off 64%–36% in the runoff, and won the general 59%–41%. Johnson attempted revenge when he brought the case challenging the district boundaries, and his lawyer did not accept the legislature's new plan, claiming that the new 3d is a "landslide-safe district for an African-American Democrat" and arguing that "any plan that draws together Jacksonville and Orlando is still a racial gerrymander.

Brown has compiled a liberal record on most issues, though she supports more defense spending than many on the left; she stresses that the military can be a source of opportunity, a lesson many black Americans have learned from personal experience. She worked very hard, and used her seats on Transportation and Veterans' Affairs to bring economic development to her district, working to secure a $100 million federal courthouse for Jacksonville, to keep district facilities off the base closure list, to promote LYNX in Orlando and cross-Florida high-speed rail, to make "investments that protect and promote our children, education, the environment and our communities." As the only woman on the Veterans' Committee until 1997, she spearheaded a law to provide better health care for women in veterans' hospitals and clinics. On broader issues, she strongly supported the Clinton crime bill (and claimed it brought 200 new policemen to the 3d District) and the earned income tax credit. She favors the Step-21 highway trust fund allocation formula and changing the funding formula for aviation.

For a hard-working, practical-minded congresswoman, Brown has had some serious political struggles. In 1994 she faced a spirited primary challenge from Alvin Brown, a former appointee in the Clinton Administration Commerce Department; she won 67%–33%. In the general black Republican talk-show host Marc Little advocated a 2% cap on domestic spending increases and lower levels of immigration; he carried some counties, but was forced to change his registration back to the 4th District and lost 58%–42%. Then in 1996 she faced the challenge to the district's boundary lines. But instead of resisting change, she embraced it, endorsing the legislature's new boundaries warmly, and winning a solid 61%–39% victory here in the fall.

In the 105th Congress Brown can be counted on to continue her work on practical issues. Also, in November 1996 she was elected secretary of the Congressional Black Caucus, where she might be a counterweight to the fiery and angry Maxine Waters.

The People: Pop. 1990: 563,079; 16% rural; 12% age 65+; 42% White; 55% Black; 1% Asian; 3% Hispanic origin. Households: 43% married couple families; 19% married couple fams. w. children; 32% college educ.; median household income: $19,780; per capita income: $9,419; median gross rent: $372; median house value: $46,800.

1996 Presidential Vote

Clinton (D)	110,701	(58%)
Dole (R)	66,057	(35%)
Perot (I)	12,633	(7%)

1992 Presidential Vote

Clinton (D)	85,964	(52%)
Bush (R)	56,593	(34%)
Perot (I)	22,397	(14%)

Rep. Corrine Brown (D)

Elected 1992; b. Nov. 11, 1946, Jacksonville; home, Jacksonville; FL A&M, B.S. 1969, M.S., 1971; Baptist; divorced.

Career: Prof., FL Commun. Col., 1977–82, Guidance Counselor, 1982–92; FL House of Reps., 1982–92.

DC Office: 1610 LHOB 20515, 202-225-0123; Fax: 202-225-2256.

District Offices: Jacksonville, 904-354-1652; Orlando, 407-872-0656.

Committees: *Transportation & Infrastructure* (17th of 33 D): Aviation; Surface Transportation. *Veterans' Affairs* (6th of 13 D): Health.

Group Ratings

	ADA	ACLU	AFS	LCV	CFA	CON	NFIB	COC	ACU	NTLC	CHC
1996	90	75	100	85	85	55	19	31	0	8	7
1995	100	—	—	94	85	0	—	13	12	—	—

National Journal Ratings

	1995 LIB — 1995 CONS			1996 LIB — 1996 CONS		
Economic	94%	—	0%	79%	—	18%
Social	79%	—	20%	79%	—	18%
Foreign	70%	—	28%	63%	—	36%

Key Votes of the 104th Congress

1. Reduce Medicare Growth $	N	5. Flag Amendment	Y	9. Cuban Embargo	Y
2. Ovrd. Product Liab. Veto	N	6. Drop EPA Limits	Y	10. Bar Bosnia Troop $	N
3. Increase Min. Wage	Y	7. Repeal Assault-Weap. Ban	N	11. Cut Anti-Missile Defense	Y
4. Welfare Reform	N	8. Ovrd. Part. Birth Veto	N	12. Bar U.N. Uniforms	N

Election Results

1996 general	Corrine Brown (D)	98,085	(61%)	($330,201)
	Preston James Fields (R)	62,196	(39%)	($38,413)
1996 primary	Corrine Brown (D)	unopposed		
1994 general	Corrine Brown (D)	63,845	(58%)	($383,017)
	Marc Little (R)	46,895	(42%)	($212,235)

FOURTH DISTRICT

With nearly one million people in the surrounding area, Jacksonville is one of Florida's major cities, with a National Football League franchise (the Jaguars) and bold new skyscrapers looming above a wide river and a shopping mall overshadowing grid streets of tiny shotgun houses. The wide freeways leading to huge beachfront subdivisions are not far from primeval wetlands and citrus groves. Mayport, one of the Navy's biggest bases, and other military installations are nearby. But Floridians tend to overlook Jacksonville. While its gleaming downtown is just one of a dozen in a state that had no commercial office development a generation ago, Jacksonville was known not long ago as a smelly, slow-growing insurance and paper mill town. Attracting big installations from AT&T, Brockway International, Prudential, Sears, UPS, American Express and the Mayo Clinic, Jacksonville grew in the 1980s, while still maintaining its big military bases and insurance headquarters. The city is solidly southern, with a large number of blue-collar whites with southern accents, a large black population, lots of children and comparatively few retirees; the area has less tourism and high-tech industry than the rest of Florida. Like much of north Florida, it has a vivid Democratic political tradition and solidly Republican voting habits.

The 4th Congressional District of Florida includes most of Jacksonville (minus the mostly black areas in the 3d District) and the beach areas to the north and south as far as St. Augustine, the oldest European-founded city in the United States, settled by the Spanish in the 16th Century, and Daytona Beach, made famous by racing cars and its hard-sand beach. The beaches were mostly vacant during the 1940s, when Jacksonville was the largest city in the state, but have now filled up with large subdivisions and giant developments.

The congresswoman from the 4th District is Tillie Fowler, a Republican elected in 1992 after the retirement of 44-year Democratic incumbent Charles Bennett. Fowler grew up in Milledgeville, Georgia—where writer Carson McCullers lived; her father was a druggist who served in the legislature. After law school she worked in Washington for Georgia Congressman Robert Stephens and the Nixon Administration—in the Office of Consumer Affairs with Elizabeth Dole. After marrying a Jacksonville businessman, she raised a family, did volunteer work and was elected to the City Council in 1985. In line with her support of Florida's successful term limit initiative, she believed that "eight is enough," and planned to retire from the council by 1992. Then Bennett retired and she ran for the House, leaving no doubt about her priorities: two retired admirals attended her announcement and she was armed with a promise from House Republican leaders that if elected she would get a seat on the National Security Committee. She pledged to make Mayport her top priority, while supporting abortion rights and the balanced budget amendment. Her Democratic opponent, Mattox Hair, hailed from rural Florida, served in the Army and in the legislature from 1972–88. He resigned a judgeship and campaigned as a conservative Democrat. But Fowler, bolstered by a strong showing in Jacksonville, won with 57%. She was unopposed in 1994 and 1996.

Fowler got her seat on National Security, long chaired by Carl Vinson who was also from Milledgeville. She was elected co-chair of the Freshman Republican Task Force on Reform, and in her second term she became a deputy whip and member of the Republican Steering Committee. She worked on an eight year term limits amendment based on Florida's "eight is enough" initiative; but she was denied the chance to present her amendment to the House. She continues, however, to pledge to serve no more than four terms.

On National Security, Fowler argued against additional defense cuts, accusing the Clinton Administration of "ignoring the lessons of history." She also fought hard and knowledgeably about the Clinton Administration's relaxation of export controls, which allowed proliferation of dangerous high-tech weapons systems. She is part of the Depot Caucus, arguing against full privatization and for preserving 40% of depot work for the military. In late 1996 Newt Gingrich gave Fowler and Democrat Jane Harman the tough assignment of investigating sexual harassment in the Army. On Transportation and Infrastructure, she worked on local projects and won authorization to replace Jacksonville's Fuller Warren Bridge, one of the last two drawbridges on I-95. (The other is the Wilson Bridge, outside of Washington, D.C., on the Maryland-Virginia line.)

Fowler's record is not totally conservative, with some moderate positions. She is a strong partisan, however, and on the gender gap said, "I think [Republicans] have gotten a bum rap. We're not an uncaring, unfeeling party." Her district has been moving her way: when she first ran in 1992, the 4th District registration was 52%–41% Democratic; in 1996, when the 4th's boundaries were changed slightly to accommodate changes in the 3d, the 4th registration was 45%–43% Republican.

The People: Pop. 1990: 562,154; 13% rural; 14% age 65+; 89% White; 6% Black; 2% Asian; 3% Hispanic origin. Households: 58% married couple families; 25% married couple fams. w. children; 53% college educ.; median household income: $31,707; per capita income: $16,845; median gross rent: $483; median house value: $80,700.

1996 Presidential Vote

Dole (R)	145,760	(56%)
Clinton (D)	94,843	(36%)
Perot (I)	19,071	(7%)

1992 Presidential Vote

Bush (R)	129,267	(53%)
Clinton (D)	74,878	(31%)
Perot (I)	40,093	(16%)

Rep. Tillie K. Fowler (R)

Elected 1992; b. Dec. 23, 1942, Milledgeville, GA; home, Jacksonville; Emory U., A.B. 1964, J.D. 1967; Episcopalian; married (Buck).

Career: Legis. Asst., U.S. Rep. Robert Stephens, 1967–70; White House Office of Consumer Affairs, 1970–71; Jacksonville City Cncl., 1985–92, Pres., 1989–90.

DC Office: 109 CHOB 20515, 202-225-2501; Fax: 202-225-9318.

District Offices: Jacksonville, 904-739-6600; Ormond Beach, 904-672-0754.

Committees: *National Security* (11th of 30 R): Military Installations & Facilities; Military Readiness. *Transportation & Infrastructure* (16th of 40 R): Railroads; Surface Transportation.

Group Ratings

	ADA	ACLU	AFS	LCV	CFA	CON	NFIB	COC	ACU	NTLC	CHC
1996	10	13	0	38	15	5	100	92	95	95	73
1995	5	—	—	19	0	38	—	100	79	—	—

National Journal Ratings

	1995 LIB	—	1995 CONS	1996 LIB	—	1996 CONS
Economic	26%	—	67%	36%	—	63%
Social	45%	—	54%	42%	—	58%
Foreign	0%	—	85%	0%	—	79%

Key Votes of the 104th Congress

1. Reduce Medicare Growth $	Y	5. Flag Amendment	Y	9. Cuban Embargo	Y
2. Ovrd. Product Liab. Veto	Y	6. Drop EPA Limits	N	10. Bar Bosnia Troop $	Y
3. Increase Min. Wage	N	7. Repeal Assault-Weap. Ban	Y	11. Cut Anti-Missile Defense	N
4. Welfare Reform	Y	8. Ovrd. Part. Birth Veto	Y	12. Bar U.N. Uniforms	Y

Election Results

1996 general	Tillie K. Fowler (R)	unopposed		($280,593)
1996 primary	Tillie K. Fowler (R)	42,047	(89%)	
	Gregg R. Trude (R)	4,957	(11%)	
1994 general	Tillie K. Fowler (R)	unopposed		($103,233)

FIFTH DISTRICT

Over the past quarter century, Florida's urban areas have grown in every unlikely direction, occupying the high ground between the swamps and wetlands that still take up much of the state's peninsula. The pattern of development is clear in the Gulf Coast counties north of St. Petersburg and Tampa, where subdivisions and trailer parks and shopping centers with Eckerd drug stores and Publix and Winn Dixie supermarkets sprang up in what were sleepy little towns with low brick buildings baking in the Florida sun. More than a half million people live in the towns starting with Clearwater and Tampa's northern suburbs that run up the spines of U.S. 19, just off the Gulf Coast, or U.S. 41 and I-75 inland near the orange groves. Though there are plenty of working people here, this is retirement country. People are comfortable though not usually affluent here, and if the existence of such communities is taken for granted by most Americans, their construction—the creation of an infrastructure of water and sewer lines, underground electricity, and phone and TV cables—is an example of the miracles of modern technology.

The 5th Congressional District of Florida, created after the 1990 census, occupies much of the fast-growing area, including the New Port Richey area on the Pasco County coast and fast-growing Citrus and Hernando Counties to the north. The 5th travels northward to include Gainesville, home of the University of Florida, where students from the more wealthy urban corridors of central and south Florida study in a town occupied by flimsy houses from the impoverished South of 50 years ago; here they can become part of a Florida elite bonded by shared memories of the Gator Growl festivities. In 1990 there were 562,000 people in land that held about 129,000 in 1960. Three decades ago, this area was typically southern Democratic. Now the voting patterns reflect the presence of the newcomers. Today the Gulf Coast counties are marginal territory, Democratic at the top of the ticket in 1996, and Gainesville is liberal and Democratic.

The congresswoman from the 5th District is Karen Thurman, a Democrat who has shown something like perfect political pitch while spending most of her adult lifetime in political office. An Air Force brat, she grew up in Florida and elsewhere, worked as a middle school math teacher for eight years before being elected to the Dunnellon Council and then became mayor. Elected to the Florida Senate in 1982, at 31, she was reelected in 1986 with more votes than any other state senator. She sponsored an average of 60 bills a year on issues like education, the environment and agriculture, and, most important, as chairman of the reapportionment committee was careful to include her home town in the new 5th District for 1992. She easily won the primary and in the general faced a former prosecutor who called her a "professional, big money politician." She outraised him 2–1 and won 49%–43%.

In the Democratic House Thurman has compiled a middle-of-the-road voting record; when the House shifted right after 1994, without changing her positions she was somewhat farther to the left of the median. She casts conservative votes on many issues but has supported at some risk the Democratic position on some key votes, like the 1993 tax increase and term limits. One of her chief causes is regulatory relief: she was a lead Democrat for requiring EPA to conduct risk-assessment studies before issuing regulations and worked with Republicans even in the Democratic 103d Congress on this. In the Republican 104th she was one of four Democrats on the Government Reform Committee to vote to freeze new federal regulations until Congress can review the underlying statutes. She has also worked for local water and sewer projects, like a $29 million Tampa Bay water reuse project, and got a $13 million grant for equipment for the University of Florida Brain Institute. She opposes offshore oil drilling and has pushed for changes in the formulas for federal high way funds. She wants the federal government to assume financial responsibility for criminal aliens.

Thurman was targeted for defeat by Republicans in 1994 and their candidate received national attention. But it wasn't very favorable: former drag racing champion Don "Big Daddy" Garlits called for "medieval-style prisons," advocated public paddling of juveniles in town squares for truancy, and said Americans who do not believe the country is great should be charged with subversion. Thurman raised more money and won more votes, carrying all but one county and winning 57%–43%.

In the 104th Congress Thurman continued to fight for risk assessment and came up with an ingenious amendment to the line-item veto which passed with bipartisan support: to avoid giving the president too much leverage over members of Congress by threatening to veto their favorite projects, it calls for a separate override vote on one or more projects if 50 members agree. But she supported Bill Clinton in his budget showdown with Congress ("it was the worst thing I have ever seen. I watched a lot of people get hurt") and adroitly refused contributions from tobacco companies. In May 1996 a redistricting case overturning the grotesquely-shaped, black-majority 3d District helped her, because the legislature's redistricting bill removed 69,000 voters from rural conservative counties from the 5th District and added black and white liberal precincts in Gainesville and Alachua County. This made the 5th definitely more Democratic, and Republican state Senator Ginny Brown-Waite, who was preparing to run, quit the race. The eventual Republican nominee, Dave Gentry, campaigned hard on crime issues, but it turned out he was arrested in 1995 in Gainesville for carrying a concealed weapon without a permit. Thurman vastly outraised him and won 62%–38%, carrying every county. Gentry ended the race by filing a lawsuit charging that Thurman's staff burglarized his headquarters and promised to run again in 1998.

Thurman's political shrewdness makes that race appear a long shot. And immediately after the election she secured a seat on the Ways and Means Committee, only its sixth woman member in history.

The People: Pop. 1990: 562,936; 42% rural; 26% age 65+; 90% White; 6% Black; 1% Asian; 3% Hispanic origin. Households: 58% married couple families; 17% married couple fams. w. children; 38% college educ.; median household income: $21,374; per capita income: $11,987; median gross rent: $403; median house value: $62,200.

1996 Presidential Vote			1992 Presidential Vote		
Clinton (D)	135,496	(50%)	Clinton (D)	109,258	(42%)
Dole (R)	100,603	(37%)	Bush (R)	87,759	(34%)
Perot (I)	34,973	(13%)	Perot (I)	61,416	(24%)

Rep. Karen L. Thurman (D)

Elected 1992; b. Jan. 12, 1951, Rapid City, SD; home, Dunnellon; U. of FL, B.A. 1973; Episcopalian; married (John).

Career: Middle schl. teacher, 1974–82; Dunnellon City Cncl., 1974–82; Dunnellon Mayor, 1979–81; FL Senate, 1982–92.

DC Office: 440 CHOB 20515, 202-225-1002; Fax: 202-226-0329; e-mail: kthurman@hr.house.gov.

District Offices: Gainesville, 352-336-6614; Inverness, 352-344-3044; New Port Richey, 813-849-4496.

Committees: *Ways & Means* (16th of 16 D): Oversight.

Group Ratings

	ADA	ACLU	AFS	LCV	CFA	CON	NFIB	COC	ACU	NTLC	CHC
1996	75	53	92	77	69	78	43	25	15	25	7
1995	60	—	—	50	62	4	—	39	23	—	—

National Journal Ratings

	1995 LIB — 1995 CONS			1996 LIB — 1996 CONS		
Economic	64%	—	35%	70%	—	28%
Social	73%	—	27%	73%	—	26%
Foreign	61%	—	39%	64%	—	35%

Key Votes of the 104th Congress

1. Reduce Medicare Growth $	N	5. Flag Amendment	Y	9. Cuban Embargo	Y
2. Ovrd. Product Liab. Veto	N	6. Drop EPA Limits	Y	10. Bar Bosnia Troop $	N
3. Increase Min. Wage	Y	7. Repeal Assault-Weap. Ban	Y	11. Cut Anti-Missile Defense	Y
4. Welfare Reform	N	8. Ovrd. Part. Birth Veto	N	12. Bar U.N. Uniforms	Y

Election Results

1996 general	Karen L. Thurman (D)	161,050	(62%)	($521,859)
	Dave Gentry (R)	100,051	(38%)	($62,164)
1996 primary	Karen L. Thurman (D)	unopposed		
1994 general	Karen L. Thurman (D)	125,780	(57%)	($564,265)
	Don Garlits (R)	94,093	(43%)	($308,963)

SIXTH DISTRICT

The flat rolling grasslands of central Florida, once bypassed by southbound tourists heading for the coast, in the 1980s had become a prime growth area in the nation's prime growth state. In earlier decades, these areas depended economically on farming, on state institutions (the University of Florida in Gainesville, the big state prison in Raiford) and on passing tourists getting off the interstate to see attractions like Silver Springs, the world's largest formation of clear artesian springs. But as time went on, retirees began settling in places like the bluegrass country around Ocala (one of America's prime horse breeding grounds) and the plenteous lakes in Lake County to the south. These are not necessarily affluent developments: this part of central Florida has the highest percentage of mobile homes in the United States.

The 6th Congressional District of Florida takes up much of this territory. Before redistricting in 1996, its boundaries were a bit odd, since it was almost seven-eighths surrounded by the former black-majority 3d District. But a new congressional map eliminated the 3d's black precincts west of the Jacksonville area and smoothed out the 6th District's eastern border with the 3d. Now the 6th takes in all of Union and more of Baker and Marion Counties and picks up Sumter County, formerly in the 5th District. About half of its people live around Ocala or in Lake County, marginal political territory. Another one-third live on the west side of Jacksonville or in suburban communities in Clay County, just to the south, both heavily Republican.

The congressman from the 6th District is Cliff Stearns, a Republican first elected in 1988 when incumbent Democrat Buddy MacKay ran for the Senate (he lost but is now Lieutenant Governor). Stearns grew up and attended public schools in Washington, D.C., and served in the Air Force; he worked as an aerospace engineer, but then went into real estate and ended up owning five motels, three restaurants and other property—"someone who works in the community, goes to church with his neighbors, and doesn't live in Tallahassee," as he put it in his 1988 campaign, when he beat the favorite, state House Speaker Jon Mills, 54%–46%.

"I was elected to put the federal government on a diet," Stearns has said, and he has compiled an almost perfectly conservative voting record. He first became noticed on Capitol Hill for cutting congressional staff pay raises; now most of those fuming staffers are off the public payroll altogether. He sponsored a free market healthcare reform bill, pushed for funding cuts in the National Endowment for the Arts, chaired a Republican task force on gays in the military which surveyed generals and admirals and found 97% of them opposed to lifting the ban. In June 1994, he penned the letter signed by 87 Republicans calling for the resignation of then-Surgeon General Joycelyn Elders. He worked out a consensus for a return to Florida state government of 77,000 acres set aside for the now-canceled Cross-Florida Barge Canal. He was able to convince HUD to issue rules protecting seniors-only housing developments from discrimination suits. But Stearns is also interested in funds which mean jobs for north Florida. He took credit for siting a new 3,000-bed federal prison in Sumter County and a new veterans' psychiatric facility and a VA ambulatory care center in Gainesville—both now just slightly outside the district. He got funding for novel uses of closed military bases: a veterans' cemetery in the closed Cecil Field Naval Air Station, a $34 million project to store Titan rocket motors at Camp Blanding. He is one of the leaders in urging recognition of Gulf war syndrome.

After Republicans won a majority in 1994, he was unable to get into the party leadership; he lost the race for vice chair of the House Republican Conference to Susan Molinari of New York by 124–100. But he played an important role on legislation. On the Commerce Committee, he worked on the 1996 Telecom Act, installing amendments to relax prohibitions on multiple ownership of TV and radio stations and providing for fair use of telephone poles. He sees deregulation as promoting competition, greater choice, lower prices, and more freedom. On the 1996 Health Care Act he proposed a successful amendment prohibiting insurers from discriminating by genetic testing. He has called for a bipartisan commission to reform Medicare.

Stearns is a prototype of the 1994 freshmen Republicans, capturing a Democratic district and holding it easily ever since against weak opposition.

The People: Pop. 1990: 561,464; 48% rural; 18% age 65+; 89% White; 7% Black; 1% Asian; 3% Hispanic origin. Voting age pop.: 427,270; 6% Black; 3% Hispanic origin. Households: 65% married couple families; 26% married couple fams. w. children; 37% college educ.; median household income: $26,025; per capita income: $12,274; median gross rent: $417; median house value: $66,400.

1996 Presidential Vote

Dole (R)	124,489	(50%)
Clinton (D)	96,135	(39%)
Perot (I)	27,762	(11%)

1992 Presidential Vote

Bush (R)	110,712	(46%)
Clinton (D)	78,681	(32%)
Perot (I)	52,215	(22%)

Rep. Clifford B. Stearns (R)

Elected 1988; b. Apr. 16, 1941, Washington, DC; home, Ocala; George Washington U., B.S. 1963; Presbyterian; married (Joan).

Career: Air Force, 1963–67; Data Control Systems Inc., 1967–68; Negotiator, CBS, 1969–70; Pres., Stearns House Inc., 1972–present.

DC Office: 2352 RHOB 20515, 202-225-5744; Fax: 202-225-3973; e-mail: cstearns@hr.house.gov.

District Offices: Ocala, 352-351-8777; Orange Park, 904-269-3203; Leesburg, 352-326-8285.

Committees: *Commerce* (9th of 28 R): Energy & Power; Telecommunications, Trade & Consumer Protection. *Veterans' Affairs* (9th of 16 R): Health (Chmn.).

Group Ratings

	ADA	ACLU	AFS	LCV	CFA	CON	NFIB	COC	ACU	NTLC	CHC
1996	5	6	0	8	15	73	100	88	100	100	100
1995	0	—	—	0	0	56	—	96	96	—	—

National Journal Ratings

	1995 LIB — 1995 CONS	1996 LIB — 1996 CONS
Economic	0% — 74%	0% — 82%
Social	0% — 79%	24% — 72%
Foreign	0% — 85%	0% — 79%

Key Votes of the 104th Congress

1. Reduce Medicare Growth $	Y	5. Flag Amendment	Y	9. Cuban Embargo	Y
2. Ovrd. Product Liab. Veto	Y	6. Drop EPA Limits	N	10. Bar Bosnia Troop $	Y
3. Increase Min. Wage	N	7. Repeal Assault-Weap. Ban	Y	11. Cut Anti-Missile Defense	N
4. Welfare Reform	Y	8. Ovrd. Part. Birth Veto	Y	12. Bar U.N. Uniforms	Y

Election Results

1996 general	Clifford B. Stearns (R)	161,527	(67%)	($301,045)
	Newell O'Brien (D)	78,908	(33%)	($38,183)
1996 primary	Clifford B. Stearns (R)	unopposed		
1994 general	Clifford B. Stearns (R)	unopposed		($189,905)

SEVENTH DISTRICT

In ever-changing Florida, new communities and towns continue to spring up on the landscape, replacing older town centers with which tourists have been familiar. Just down the road from Daytona Beach, where motorcyclists gather in February for Hog Week, is New Smyrna Beach, a new town established on the site of an old settlement. Fifteen miles inland, close to Sanford, where Amtrak's Auto-Train unloads its Florida-bound travelers, is Deltona, a vast five-mile square development that drained a part of Florida swamp and designed curving streets meandering around small lakes and golf courses, set aside land for shopping centers and office space, and then marketed the place nationwide. It created an instant city: in 1990, 51,000 people lived in Deltona—where there were 15,000 in 1980 and 4,800 in 1970.

The 7th Congressional District of Florida includes Deltona, New Smyrna Beach and part of Daytona Beach, as well as most of Sanford. Stretching from Daytona across the marshy St. Johns River basin to Seminole County, it includes large Orlando suburbs like Altamonte Springs and small old towns like Oviedo, and goes south to include part of Orlando itself. In most elections, this is a solidly Republican district, although the area around Daytona has a conservative Democratic heritage and was the site of two close legislative races in 1996, where Democrats failed to take Republican seats and lost control of the state House.

The congressman from the 7th is John Mica, a spirited Republican and a political veteran who campaigns as an opponent of the status quo. He grew up in south Florida, in a bipartisanly political family: his younger brother Dan Mica was a Democratic congressman from Palm Beach County from 1978–88, when he lost a primary for U.S. Senate, and another brother worked for Democratic Governor Lawton Chiles. But John Mica has always been a conservative Republican. He made a small fortune by turning 360 feet of New Smyrna beachfront into a real estate business, then served as a staffer to Florida Senator Paula Hawkins from 1981–85, then became a lobbyist, representing American Specialty Chemical, Coopers & Lybrand and Harris computers. When attacked in the 1992 Republican primary as an insider representing special interests, Mica lobbied pro bono for the Daytona airport and got a runway extension, and won 53%–34%. Democrat Dan Webster attacked Mica as "the epitome of the professional politician," but Mica responded accurately that Webster was a liberal backed by trial lawyers and labor unions. Mica started his campaign with a $100,000 loan, raised plenty from former clients and outspent Webster, and won 56%–44%.

Mica started off as a brash reformer, leading the charge to abolish House select committees and to make public the names of those signing petitions to discharge legislation. In 1993, Mica also pushed a plan to require the EPA to subject new regulations to a cost-benefit analysis. That stalled the bill to elevate EPA to cabinet status; similar provisions were passed as part of the Contract with America and incorporated into the 1996 Safe Drinking Water Act. He has sponsored a global environment cleanup act, to monitor other countries' environmental laws and encourage laggards to do better or risk losing U.S. aid.

Mica's brashness came out during the 1995 welfare reform debate, when he compared welfare recipients with alligators: "If left in their natural state, alligators can take care of themselves"—a metaphor that was denounced by many Democrats and caused many Republicans to wince. But he was successful on risk assessment and cost benefit clauses in environmental legislation and on the unfunded mandates bill as well. He chaired the Government Reform and Oversight's Civil Service Subcommittee and helped pass the White House Accountability Act of 1996, imposing on the White House, as a Republican-pushed 1995 law imposed on Congress, the laws the legislative and executive branches impose on others. Mica works on smaller issues as well—a law authorizing a National Archives public/private partnership; and on local projects—the I-4/Greeneway interchange and the one mile "missing link" of Miner Road north of Orlando, preserving the St. Johns River, new buses for Orlando's LYNX, legislation sought by Daytona Speedway and NASCAR to standardize race car transporters.

"I've made a lot of money," Mica has said. "I don't need the salary and I don't need the title." But in fact he has thrived politically. In 1994, against a Democratic TV ballroom dance instructor, he was reelected with 73%; in 1996, against former state Senator and 1990 gubernatorial candidate George Stuart, he was reelected with 62%.

The People: Pop. 1990: 563,552; 11% rural; 16% age 65+; 89% White; 4% Black; 1% Asian; 6% Hispanic origin. Households: 60% married couple families; 25% married couple fams. w. children; 51% college educ.; median household income: $30,921; per capita income: $15,132; median gross rent: $529; median house value: $80,400.

1996 Presidential Vote

Dole (R)	108,636	(47%)
Clinton (D)	100,603	(43%)
Perot (I)	22,863	(10%)

1992 Presidential Vote

Bush (R)	105,059	(45%)
Clinton (D)	80,602	(34%)
Perot (I)	49,476	(21%)

Rep. John L. Mica (R)

Elected 1992; b. Jan. 27, 1943, Binghamton, NY; home, Winter Park; Miami-Dade Comm. Col., A.A. 1965, U. of FL, B.A. 1967; Episcopalian; married (Patricia).

Career: Exec. Dir., Palm Beach & Orange Cnty. Govt. Charter Study Commissions, 1970–74; Pres., MK Development, 1975–92; FL House of Reps., 1976–80; A.A., U.S. Sen. Paula Hawkins, 1981–85; Partner, Mica, Dudinsky & Assoc., 1985–92;

DC Office: 106 CHOB 20515, 202-225-4035; Fax: 202-226-0821: e-mail: mica@hr.house.gov.

District Offices: Casselberry, 407-657-8080; Deltona, 407-860 - 1499; Port Orange, 904-756-9798.

Committees: *Government Reform & Oversight* (11th of 24 R): Civil Service (Chmn.); National Security, International Affairs & Criminal Justice. *House Oversight* (6th of 6 R). *Transportation & Infrastructure* (14th of 40 R): Railroads; Surface Transportation.

Group Ratings

	ADA	ACLU	AFS	LCV	CFA	CON	NFIB	COC	ACU	NTLC	CHC
1996	0	12	0	8	15	30	100	100	100	100	100
1995	0	—	—	0	0	56	—	100	92	—	—

National Journal Ratings

	1995 LIB — 1995 CONS			1996 LIB — 1996 CONS		
Economic	0%	—	74%	0%	—	82%
Social	0%	—	79%	24%	—	72%
Foreign	0%	—	85%	0%	—	79%

Key Votes of the 104th Congress

1. Reduce Medicare Growth $	Y	5. Flag Amendment	Y	9. Cuban Embargo	Y
2. Ovrd. Product Liab. Veto	Y	6. Drop EPA Limits	N	10. Bar Bosnia Troop $	Y
3. Increase Min. Wage	N	7. Repeal Assault-Weap. Ban	Y	11. Cut Anti-Missile Defense	N
4. Welfare Reform	Y	8. Ovrd. Part. Birth Veto	Y	12. Bar U.N. Uniforms	Y

Election Results

1996 general	John L. Mica (R)	143,667	(62%)	($539,973)
	George Stuart Jr. (D)	87,832	(38%)	($165,921)
1996 primary	John L. Mica (R)	unopposed		
1994 general	John L. Mica (R)	131,711	(73%)	($300,058)
	Edward D. Goodard (D)	47,747	(27%)	($28,075)

EIGHTH DISTRICT

Who would have supposed that the most popular tourist destination in the world would rise in the swamps and orange groves of central Florida? The answer is: Walt Disney, and just about no one else. In the middle 1960s Disney looked at the map and decided that the intersection of I-4 and Florida's Turnpike, the "crossroads of Florida," just a few miles southwest of Orlando, was the perfect place for the vast theme park he was planning. Metro Orlando in 1960 had about as many people—88,000—as the Orlando area has hotel rooms today, as Walt Disney World's Magic Kingdom, opened in 1971, EPCOT Center, Disney/MGM Studios, Sea World, Universal Studios, Splendid China and dozens of other attractions bring in millions of visitors from all over the world. Orlando is the center of a one million-plus metropolitan area, with the biggest job gain, 74%, in the 1980s of any major metro area. And the economy has diversified beyond tourism: Martin Marietta built a big defense plant here way back in 1956, and greater Orlando has a high-tech economy and a population weighted toward young families with children rather than retirees.

The spirit of this place has been set by a man who never lived here but created something now taken for granted. Walt Disney conceived the first theme park in the flatlands of Orange County, California, but he perfected it in the 17,000 acres of swamp and lakes in Florida's Orange County. And with the invention of the theme park, Disney also pioneered sophisticated communications, utility, and waste disposal methods—all out of sight and underground. Yet Disney World is not just an engineering marvel; it requires some 36,000 people with know-how and unfailing cheerfulness. Disney's vision of a future that was labor-intensive as well as high-tech—in which the critical ingredient is the provision of services—accurately forecast the service-driven economy that has grown so lustily for decades now.

The 8th Congressional District of Florida includes most of Orlando and surrounding Orange County. It excludes most heavily black neighborhoods and towns placed in the 3d District—boundaries that, for the most part, survived redistricting in 1996. It includes central and eastern Orlando and all its suburbs directly to the east, plus most to the south and west. It also takes in most of the Kissimmee area in Osceola County just to the south and Disney World's Magic Kingdom. Politically, this Orange County is less Republican than the Orange County where the original Disneyland was built; it was historically Democratic, like all of central Florida, and can sometimes be persuaded to vote for Democrats. It voted narrowly for George Bush in 1992, gubernatorial candidate Jeb Bush in 1994, and Bob Dole in 1996—though each ran better in the 8th District portion, because so many area blacks live in the 3d.

The congressman from the 8th District is Bill McCollum, one of the most active and articulate Republicans in the House, involved in one issue after another, and now chairman of Judiciary's Crime Subcommittee. McCollum is a native Floridian who after law school and Navy service practiced law in the Orlando area and was Seminole County Republican chairman. In 1980, he ran for the House, in a district that went west to the Gulf of Mexico, and with his Orlando area base won the runoff and general. In the Democratic House he often lost on issues but was a force to be reckoned with. He led the fight against the Brady bill, winning in 1988 but losing in 1993. On immigration he was not happy with the higher quotas in the 1990 bill. He served on the Iran-contra Committee, where he was a vocal critic of majority Democrats. He led the unsuccessful fight in 1992 to allow S&Ls to count goodwill as an asset. He led the fight in the House against the so-called "racial justice" provision, which would impose something like racial quotas on executions by allowing capital defendants to use statistics to challenge a death sentence as biased based on race; he lost 217–212 in one vote but many House Democrats, under the spotlight, switched and by a 264–149 vote took it out of the 1994 crime bill. On all these unfashionable controversies, McCollum showed attention to detail and bulldog perseverance.

Now that the House has moved well to the right, McCollum has had to fight on both flanks. In 1992 and 1993 he fought uphill battles for term limits; then in 1995 he was harshly criticized by some national term-limits backers for his plan, which would allow House members to serve 12 years. Three other alternatives were offered, but McCollum's amendment was the Contract With America version and won 227 votes. That was well short of the two-thirds required (290) but it was still astonishing that a majority of House members voted to limit their own terms. McCollum was less successful in his own leadership race. Since 1988 he had been vice chair of the Republican Conference. In 1994 he contributed over $1 million he raised to House Republican candidates, while making many local appearances on their behalf, and ran for majority whip. But he got only 28 votes, as Tom DeLay won with 119 and Bob Walker had 80. McCollum nonetheless remained legislatively active, sponsoring anti-terrorism legislation, serving as number two Republican on the Banking Committee just behind Chairman Jim Leach.

McCollum has been reelected easily; his most serious competition came in 1992 from an advocate of Florida's "eight is enough" term limits, and McCollum won with 69%. On election night 1996, he said he might run for Bob Graham's Senate seat in 1998. Graham was widely assumed to run for governor; but six days later Graham announced for reelection, and in early 1997 it was not expected that McCollum will run against him.

The People: Pop. 1990: 562,244; 9% rural; 11% age 65+; 81% White; 5% Black; 2% Asian; 11% Hispanic origin. Households: 55% married couple families; 25% married couple fams. w. children; 52% college educ.; median household income: $31,251; per capita income: $15,464; median gross rent: $531; median house value: $84,600.

1996 Presidential Vote

Dole (R)	95,300	(47%)
Clinton (D)	88,306	(44%)
Perot (I)	17,231	(9%)

1992 Presidential Vote

Bush (R)	101,758	(47%)
Clinton (D)	70,143	(33%)
Perot (I)	43,109	(20%)

Rep. Bill McCollum (R)

Elected 1980; b. July 12, 1944, Brooksville; home, Altamonte Springs; U. of FL, B.A. 1965, J.D. 1968; Episcopalian; married (Ingrid).

Career: Navy, 1969–72, Naval Reserves, 1972–92; Practicing atty., 1973–81; Chmn., Seminole Cnty. Repub. Cmte., 1976.

DC Office: 2266 RHOB 20515, 202-225-2176; Fax: 202-225-0999.

District Offices: Orlando, 407-872-1962.

Committees: *Banking & Financial Services* (2nd of 30 R): Financial Institutions & Consumer Credit (Vice Chmn.). *Judiciary* (3rd of 20 R): Courts & Intellectual Property; Crime (Chmn.). *Intelligence (Select)* (5th of 9 R): Human Intelligence, Analysis & Counterintelligence (Chmn.).

Group Ratings

	ADA	ACLU	AFS	LCV	CFA	CON	NFIB	COC	ACU	NTLC	CHC
1996	0	6	0	15	15	30	95	100	95	98	93
1995	5	—	—	0	8	38	—	100	84	—	—

National Journal Ratings

	1995 LIB	—	1995 CONS	1996 LIB	—	1996 CONS
Economic	0%	—	74%	27%	—	71%
Social	21%	—	72%	29%	—	68%
Foreign	15%	—	73%	0%	—	79%

Key Votes of the 104th Congress

1. Reduce Medicare Growth $	Y	5. Flag Amendment	Y	9. Cuban Embargo	Y
2. Ovrd. Product Liab. Veto	Y	6. Drop EPA Limits	N	10. Bar Bosnia Troop $	Y
3. Increase Min. Wage	N	7. Repeal Assault-Weap. Ban	Y	11. Cut Anti-Missile Defense	N
4. Welfare Reform	Y	8. Ovrd. Part. Birth Veto	Y	12. Bar U.N. Uniforms	Y

Election Results

1996 general	Bill McCollum (R)	136,515	(67%)	($421,409)
	Al Krulick (D)	65,794	(33%)	($34,066)
1996 primary	Bill McCollum (R)	unopposed		
1994 general	Bill McCollum (R)	unopposed		($448,334)

NINTH DISTRICT

Half a century ago, the land north of St. Petersburg and Tampa was scarcely inhabited. The Gulf is lined with swamps and inland the terrain is spotted with lakes and was covered with dense semitropical forests. Over the years, development has moved up the coast and up the major highways inland. Much of this area originally was designed for retirees—condominiums, garden apartments, trailer parks. But this is working country as well. Businesses grew up around Clearwater in northern Pinellas County and inland in Pasco County off I-75. And people brought their ancestral political beliefs with them. In the 1950s and 1960s, only white-collar retirees could afford to buy new places in Florida, and they were heavily Republican. As blue-collar workers and union members became more affluent in the 1970s and 1980s, they came with their traditional Democratic Party identification and cultural conservatism. Those cross-currents have made this area prime marginal territory in Florida politics.

The 9th Congressional District of Florida covers much of this area north of St. Petersburg and Tampa. About half its population is in northern Pinellas County around Clearwater and Tarpon Springs, an old resort first settled by Greek sponge divers early in the 20th Century. Another quarter is in northern Hillsborough County, on the suburban fringe of Tampa. The final quarter is the inland portion of Pasco County, north of Tampa, where former crossroads like Zephyr Hills have become significant population centers.

The congressman from the 9th District is Michael Bilirakis, a Republican who grew up in Pittsburgh; he served in the Air Force, and then worked his way through college toiling in a steel mill. He also worked for the government in Washington and an aerospace contractor in Florida, then practiced law. He believes strongly that Americans can work their way up, with occasional government assistance (like the G.I. Bill that helped him through school). Originally a Democrat, he switched to the Republican Party in 1980 and in 1982, when this district was created, he won, though it had been designed for a Democrat. He has had a mostly, but not always, conservative voting record, and does not approach issues with the fervor of younger Republicans. He has made something of an environmental record, opposing western water subsidies and offshore oil drilling on the Gulf Coast.

Early in his career Bilirakis won a seat on the Commerce Committee, and today he holds one of the most powerful chairmanships in Congress, that of the Health Subcommittee headed for 16 years by Democrat Henry Waxman. Over the years Bilirakis supported increased federal elderly home care money, research on Alzheimer's disease, and drug discounts for the VA and other federal purchasers. But he was one of the few to vote against the Catastrophic Health Care Act in 1988. In 1993, with Democrat Roy Rowland, he sponsored a Health Care Reform Consensus Act, which tried to make health insurance portable and to stop insurers from denying coverage for pre-existing conditions. After Bill Clinton wrote him a letter rejecting "piece by piece" legislation, the Bilirakis-Rowland bill became the chief vehicle of conservatives and indeed could clearly have passed had Democrats allowed it to come to a vote. But they held out for the Clinton plan, until it died in fall 1994. In 1995 Bilirakis came forth again with a similar Health Coverage Availability and Affordability Act. This was the vehicle, usually named after its Senate sponsors Nancy Kassebaum and Edward Kennedy, which congressional Republicans and the Clinton Administration seized on, hoping for some positive achievements, in summer 1996; and it became law. Bilirakis also sponsored the 1996 Safe Drinking Water Act, which had bipartisan support, and the Food Quality Protection Act, which eliminated the Delaney clause and substituted a provision allowing pesticides only when there is a reasonable certainty of no harm to the consumer. Also he sponsored reauthorization of the Ryan White Act and, as vice chairman of the Veterans' subcommittee on hospitals, passed a law prorating VA disability checks for spouses (the government had demanded their return the month the beneficiary died).

Back in 1994, Bilirakis had said he would retire unless he had legislation pending. He didn't retire, and became one of the most legislatively productive members of the 104th Congress. Against spirited competition in 1990 and 1992 he won with 58% and 59%; in 1994 and 1996 he was easily reelected.

The People: Pop. 1990: 562,814; 19% rural; 22% age 65+; 91% White; 3% Black; 1% Asian; 4% Hispanic origin. Households: 60% married couple families; 21% married couple fams. w. children; 48% college educ.; median household income: $29,293; per capita income: $15,797; median gross rent: $485; median house value: $84,800.

1996 Presidential Vote

Dole (R)	119,658	(45%)
Clinton (D)	118,996	(44%)
Perot (I)	27,335	(10%)

1992 Presidential Vote

Bush (R)	113,853	(41%)
Clinton (D)	94,662	(34%)
Perot (I)	68,167	(25%)

Rep. Michael Bilirakis (R)

Elected 1982; b. July 16, 1930, Tarpon Springs; home, Palm Harbor; U. of Pittsburgh, B.S. 1959, U. of FL, J.D. 1963; Greek Orthodox; married (Evelyn).

Career: Air Force, 1951–55; Steelworker, 1955–59; Govt. contract negotiator, 1959–60; Petroleum engineer, 1960–63; Practicing atty., 1969–83.

DC Office: 2369 RHOB 20515, 202-225-5755; Fax: 202-225-4085; e-mail: fl09@hr.house.gov.

District Offices: Clearwater, 813-441-3721; Land O'Lakes, 813-996-7441.

Committees: *Commerce* (4th of 28 R): Energy & Power; Health & the Environment (Chmn.). *Veterans' Affairs* (3rd of 16 R): Health.

Group Ratings

	ADA	ACLU	AFS	LCV	CFA	CON	NFIB	COC	ACU	NTLC	CHC
1996	5	0	8	23	46	55	92	94	90	95	100
1995	5	—	—	6	23	56	—	96	84	—	—

National Journal Ratings

	1995 LIB — 1995 CONS			1996 LIB — 1996 CONS		
Economic	0%	—	74%	20%	—	76%
Social	0%	—	79%	14%	—	77%
Foreign	45%	—	52%	0%	—	79%

Key Votes of the 104th Congress

1. Reduce Medicare Growth $	Y	5. Flag Amendment	Y	9. Cuban Embargo	Y
2. Ovrd. Product Liab. Veto	Y	6. Drop EPA Limits	N	10. Bar Bosnia Troop $	Y
3. Increase Min. Wage	Y	7. Repeal Assault-Weap. Ban	Y	11. Cut Anti-Missile Defense	N
4. Welfare Reform	Y	8. Ovrd. Part. Birth Veto	Y	12. Bar U.N. Uniforms	Y

Election Results

1996 general	Michael Bilirakis (R)	161,708	(69%)	($846,392)
	Jerry Provenzano (D)	73,809	(31%)	($84,370)
1996 primary	Michael Bilirakis (R)	45,183	(80%)	
	Pamela Mills Corbino (R)	11,236	(20%)	
1994 general	Michael Bilirakis (R)	unopposed		($191,717)

TENTH DISTRICT

St. Petersburg, established in the 1888 and named for the then-Russian capital, known for decades as the American city with the largest percentage of elderly residents, has in the 1990s finally reached a certain balance. It started off promoting itself as a retirement center, in the early 1900s when *St. Petersburg Times* editor W. L. Straub tried to stop the industrialization of the waterfront, setting the city's character by establishing parks and park benches. By the 1950s, St. Petersburg had become a national cliche, bringing to mind old folks trying to drum up a game of shuffleboard. Starting off on the grid streets facing Tampa Bay, spreading later toward the beaches on the Gulf Coast, St. Petersburg filled up to a greater extent than any other American city with retirees, mostly from the North and modestly affluent. They adapted easily to a city whose civic tone was set by the *St. Petersburg Times* and its longtime owners Nelson and Henrietta Poynter: sober, good-humored, supportive of clean government and civil rights.

Like any retirement center, St. Petersburg has had rapid population turnover, reflected in its political trends. White-collar Yankee retirees in the 1940s and 1950s made St. Petersburg the first Republican center in ancestrally Democratic Florida; it voted for Thomas Dewey in 1948 and elected a Republican congressman in 1954. Then, as more blue-collar workers could afford Florida retirement and the affluent moved farther down the Gulf Coast, St. Petersburg trended Democratic in the 1970s and 1980s. Also, St. Petersburg developed more businesses, attracted more young families with children, and its black and Hispanic communities grew larger, as retirees flocked more to the Gulf Coast communities to the south and north. It became a kind of central city, even hosting the 1996 vice presidential debate. In the process St. Petersburg became contested territory politically, casting narrow margins for Bill Clinton in 1992 and 1996 and for Governor Lawton Chiles in 1994.

St. Petersburg and southern Pinellas County, including Largo and the string of barrier island beach towns from Mullet Key to Belleair Beach, make up the 10th Congressional District of Florida. In this decade it has been voting Democratic at the top of the ticket, Republican for most other offices.

The congressman from the 10th District is Bill Young, a Republican first elected in 1970, who is tied for third in seniority among House Republicans. Interestingly, neither he nor the two more senior—Joseph McDade and Philip Crane—is a full committee chairman; two others elected in 1970, Bill Archer and Floyd Spence are. Young, originally from Pennsylvania, worked in the 1950s for St. Petersburg's first Republican congressman, William Cramer; was elected to the state Senate in 1960, at 29; then, when Cramer ran for the Senate in 1970 (and lost to Lawton Chiles), Young ran for the St. Petersburg House seat and won. In the early 1970s, Social Security was vastly increased and indexed to inflation and St. Petersburg basked in prosperity; Young delivered constituency services and had a moderate to conservative voting record, and was easily reelected.

Early on, Young got a seat on Appropriations, where he, like many Republicans, worked closely with the Democratic chairmen. Young's special project was the bone marrow donor program, originated by Dr. Robert Good of All Children's Hospital in St. Petersburg. Young was successful in a three-year effort to transfer authority for the program to the National Institutes of Health. He has backed child health research centers, juvenile diabetes centers, more money for pediatric AIDS, and the University of Florida Brain Institute. In 1980, he got on the National Security Appropriations Subcommittee, where he mostly supported the Reagan and Bush Administrations but had his own pet projects.

The Republican capture of the House in 1994 did give Young a subcommittee chairmanship—he now chairs the National Security Subcommittee, and thus has great leverage over military spending and policy—but not a full committee chair, at least not yet. In November 1994 Speaker-designate Newt Gingrich passed over the four senior Appropriations Republicans—Joseph McDade because he was under indictment, John Myers because he opposed the Penny-Kasich tax cuts vigorously, and Young and Ralph Regula because they seemed too pro-spending and accommodationist—to pick the aggressive Bob Livingston as chairman. Gingrich had the votes in the Republican conference to sustain his choices, and there was no open protest. Myers chose to retire in 1996, but McDade after being acquitted on the charges that had hung over him for eight years said during the 1996 campaign that he would seek the full committee chairmanship. Again the House leadership said no, that Livingston had done a fine job of cutting $53 billion in domestic discretionary spending under tough circumstances; at which point McDade demanded the National Security subcommittee chair. Livingston vetoed that, saying that Young had performed well and that his ouster would touch off a highly destructive domino effect on the committee; McDade got the vacant Energy and Water subcommittee and Young seems secure at National Security. But his chances at the full committee chair seem problematic.

Young has mostly been reelected without serious competition. But in 1992 he was criticized in a series of articles in the *Tampa Tribune* for speech honoraria he received and trips he took, and Democrat Karen Moffitt, an expert on children with special health needs, ran as a New Democrat. She held Young to a 57%–43% margin. In 1994 he was unopposed and in 1996 won easily, citing his work on bone marrow transplants and his funding of medical research and Pinellas County beaches.

The People: Pop. 1990: 562,301; 26% age 65+; 87% White; 9% Black; 1% Asian; 2% Hispanic origin. Households: 49% married couple families; 15% married couple fams. w. children; 44% college educ.; median household income: $25,145; per capita income: $15,124; median gross rent: $448; median house value: $68,700.

1996 Presidential Vote

Clinton (D)	120,716	(51%)
Dole (R)	89,928	(38%)
Perot (I)	23,579	(10%)

1992 Presidential Vote

Clinton (D)	107,121	(40%)
Bush (R)	96,956	(36%)
Perot (I)	63,765	(24%)

Rep. C. W. (Bill) **Young (R)**

Elected 1970; b. Dec. 16, 1930, Harmarville, PA; home, Indian Rocks Beach; United Methodist; married (Beverly).

Career: Aide, U.S. Rep. William Cramer, 1957–60; FL Senate, 1960–70, Minority Ldr., 1966–70.

DC Office: 2407 RHOB 20515, 202-225-5961; Fax: 202-225-9764.

District Offices: St. Petersburg, 813-893-3191; Largo 813-581-0980.

Committees: *Appropriations* (3rd of 34 R): Labor, Health & Human Services & Education; Legislative; National Security (Chmn.). *Intelligence (Select)* (2nd of 9 R): Technical & Tactical Intelligence.

Group Ratings

	ADA	ACLU	AFS	LCV	CFA	CON	NFIB	COC	ACU	NTLC	CHC
1996	5	0	13	15	15	57	92	85	88	95	100
1995	10	—	—	13	23	38	—	100	72	—	—

National Journal Ratings

	1995 LIB	—	1995 CONS	1996 LIB	—	1996 CONS
Economic	0%	—	74%	27%	—	73%
Social	38%	—	60%	39%	—	60%
Foreign	28%	—	72%	21%	—	72%

Key Votes of the 104th Congress

1. Reduce Medicare Growth $	Y	5. Flag Amendment	Y	9. Cuban Embargo	Y
2. Ovrd. Product Liab. Veto	Y	6. Drop EPA Limits	Y	10. Bar Bosnia Troop $	Y
3. Increase Min. Wage	Y	7. Repeal Assault-Weap. Ban	N	11. Cut Anti-Missile Defense	N
4. Welfare Reform	*	8. Ovrd. Part. Birth Veto	Y	12. Bar U.N. Uniforms	Y

Election Results

1996 general	C. W. (Bill) Young (R)	114,443	(67%)	($265,355)
	Henry Green (D)	57,375	(33%)	($36,554)
1996 primary	C. W. (Bill) Young (R)	unopposed		
1994 general	C. W. (Bill) Young (R)	unopposed		($146,246)

ELEVENTH DISTRICT

Tampa is one of America's boom towns whose history goes back just a little more than a century. Its industrial past goes back to 1886, when Cuban cigar-makers left Key West for what became the Ybor City neighborhood of Tampa. Soon after, it was the major takeoff spot for U.S. troops in the Spanish-American War of 1898. It also became a major citrus distribution center. The old industrial city developed along the waterfront, where today you can find the world's longest sidewalk (6.5 miles along Bayshore Boulevard) and still see the 13 minarets of Tampa pioneer Henry B. Plant's 1890s Arabian-style Tampa Bay Hotel (long since taken over by the University of Tampa). For a time, Tampa was Florida's one industrial city. Now, with a diversified economy, a fast-growing service sector, tourist attractions led by Busch Gardens, and a famously pleasant and convenient airport, it has moved ahead, with subdivisions and condominiums, office towers and low-rise commercial buildings spreading inland across swamps and lowlands.

Through all this, and in contrast to St. Petersburg with its many retirees, Tampa has remained a city of families and young people, a place with a blue-collar past which is quickly moving upscale as it expands. To be sure, it has had some setbacks: defense contractors here have been hurt by cutbacks. But the Tampa Bay area in 1995 finally won a new major league baseball franchise (the Devil Rays) to fill the Thunderdome across Tampa Bay. And the local defense industry seems to have stabilized and may feel less at risk with a Republican Congress. The smell of cigars still wafts over Ybor City (though pollution controllers want to get rid of it) and Tampa is still an important military command center: Central Command, which ran the Gulf war, is headquartered at the still-thriving MacDill Air Force Base, and General Norman Schwarzkopf remains a Tampa area resident.

The 11th Congressional District of Florida consists of Tampa and two-thirds of surrounding Hillsborough County. Tampa was historically Democratic as St. Petersburg was Republican, but in fact the two sides of Tampa Bay seem to have come together politically; if anything, they have both changed parties. Bill Clinton won a higher percentage in Hillsborough County in both 1992 and 1996, and in the 1994 governor race Pinellas County voted for Democrat Lawton Chiles and Hillsborough went to Republican Jeb Bush. But the 11th District does have most of Tampa's heavily Democratic precincts.

The congressman from the 11th District is Jim Davis, a Democrat first elected in 1996 on the retirement of Sam Gibbons after 34 years in the House and a frustratingly brief seven months as Ways and Means chairman in 1994; Gibbons was one of the House's strongest free traders and a bellowing opponent of Newt Gingrich's 104th Congress freshmen ("a bunch of dictators," he once said, and "I had to fight you guys 50 years ago"). Davis grew up in Tampa, returned after law school, was elected in 1988, at 31, to the state House. There he showed insider skills and interests, favoring a requirement that criminals serve 85% of their sentences and rewriting the education formula to help Hillsborough County. After the 1992 election he was elected House majority leader, a job it turns out he could not have kept—Republicans won the Florida House in 1996. Of the five candidates who ran in the 11th District, Davis was probably only the third or fourth best known. In the Democratic primary he faced Sandy Freedman, Tampa's mayor from 1986–95, Hillsborough County Commissioner Phyllis Busansky, and former state Senator Pat Frank. But Davis showed great skill at raising money and was the only candidate running TV ads for the September 3 primary. Freedman led that contest, with 35%, but Davis came in second with 25%, just 274 votes ahead of Busansky. Freedman promptly attacked Davis for converting

$9,000 in office funds for personal use, but he was able to prove he hadn't; on black radio, Freedman charged that Davis opposed restitution for two blacks pardoned for a 1963 murder. Davis attacked her for causing the deaths of two police officers because of a city policy requiring them to carry shotguns in their trunks. More interesting than this rat-a-tat was what they agreed on: both supported the balanced budget amendment, the 1996 welfare reform, called for more managed care—proposals advanced by the House Republicans so bitterly denounced by Gibbons.

Davis won the runoff 56%–44% and faced Republican Mark Sharpe in the general. Sharpe was born at MacDill, where his father was stationed, and spent eight years in the Navy as an intelligence officer. In 1992, he ran against Gibbons and held him to a 53%–41% margin—startling, considering that Gibbons outspent him $960,000 to $51,000. In 1994 he ran again, this time spending $472,000; Gibbons spent $1.1 million, and won by only 52%–48%. For 1996 Sharpe had a tougher target. He attacked Davis as a fan of higher taxes and a career politician. But Sharpe got some unfavorable publicity. The *St. Petersburg Times* wrote that he admitted to making up poll numbers in his 1992 primary. The *Tampa Tribune* printed the shocking news that he had been teaching history at a Presbyterian school without certification. And it reported that some Sharpe contributors associated with Outback Steakhouse didn't divulge their Outback connection. Meanwhile, the candidates debated defense spending (Sharpe wanted more, Davis didn't), property "takings" legislation (Sharpe for, Davis against), school vouchers (ditto). Davis insisted he was a New Democrat, supporting the Defense of Marriage Act and opposing the penny-per-pound sugar tax on the Florida ballot; he also called for more education spending.

Davis, spending about the same amount as Sharpe, won by a very solid 58%–42%, perhaps because his moderate views were more popular than Gibbons's, or he was more in touch with the district, or Sharpe did not show up well under the microscope. Davis promptly joined the Blue Dog Democrats and will be one of the more conservative Democratic voices on the Budget Committee.

The People: Pop. 1990: 562,293; 1% rural; 12% age 65+; 68% White; 17% Black; 1% Asian; 14% Hispanic origin. Households: 47% married couple families; 20% married couple fams. w. children; 46% college educ.; median household income: $26,166; per capita income: $13,578; median gross rent: $439; median house value: $66,000.

1996 Presidential Vote

Clinton (D)	98,028	(52%)
Dole (R)	75,004	(40%)
Perot (I)	14,849	(8%)

1992 Presidential Vote

Clinton (D)	81,849	(41%)
Bush (R)	77,942	(39%)
Perot (I)	39,148	(20%)

Rep. Jim Davis (D)

Elected 1996; b. Oct. 11, 1957, Tampa; home, Tampa; Wash. & Lee U., B.A. 1979; U. of FL, J.D. 1982; Episcopalian; married (Peggy).

Career: Practicing atty., 1982–96; FL House of Reps., 1988–96, Majority Ldr. 1994–96.

DC Office: 327 CHOB 20515, 202-225-3376; Fax: 202-225-5652.

District Offices: Tampa, 813-354-9217.

Committees: *Budget* (16th of 19 D). *International Relations* (22d of 22 D): Africa.

Group Ratings and Key Votes: Newly Elected

Election Results

1996 general	Jim Davis (D)	108,500	(58%)	($935,314)
	Mark Sharpe (R)	78,856	(42%)	($755,184)
1996 runoff	Jim Davis (D)	23,633	(56%)	
	Sandy Warshaw Freedman (D)	18,434	(44%)	
1996 primary	Sandy Warshaw Freedman (D)	23,505	(35%)	
	Jim Davis (D)	16,753	(25%)	
	Phyllis Busansky (D)	16,479	(24%)	
	Pat Frank (D)	10,586	(16%)	
1994 general	Sam M. Gibbons (D)	76,814	(52%)	($1,155,373)
	Mark Sharpe (R)	72,119	(48%)	($472,871)

TWELFTH DISTRICT

With their skyscrapers rising over bays and rivers, the great gleaming cities of Florida are found near the Atlantic or Gulf coasts. Inland are parts of the state that were most heavily settled half a century ago. One is Polk County, the biggest inland county south of Orlando, with its small lakes and small cities of Lakeland, Bartow, Lake Wales and Winter Haven scattered about. The citrus business is still a mainstay of the local economy and orange groves abound, although periodic freezes have convinced some growers to move south or to produce tomatoes instead. Turpentine distilleries, dependent on the big stands of pine, and phosphate mining businesses can be found also; there are more manufacturing jobs here proportionately (though not that many) than almost anywhere else in Florida. Retired *Ladies Home Journal* editor Edward Bok—father of former Harvard President Derek Bok—built the most prominent landmarks here, the gothic Bok Tower and the surrounding Mountain Lake Sanctuary and gardens. But little of Bok's prestige remains here and the area has not become a major retiree haven.

Polk County historically was Democratic, the home of successive Governor-Senators Spessard Holland and Lawton Chiles; Holland was senator 1946–71, after serving as governor, and Chiles was senator 1970–88 and then was elected governor in 1990 and 1994. But as in most of the Deep South, Republicans have picked up strength in Polk County. Chiles kept it in the Democratic column and stopped Republicans from picking up the two seats they needed for a state Senate majority in 1990. But it voted for George Bush in 1992, against Chiles and for Republican Jeb Bush in 1994, and for Bob Dole in 1996.

The 12th District of Florida encompasses all but the northeast edge of Polk County, plus the western, rapidly suburbanizing edge of Tampa's Hillsborough County. It extends into old-fashioned Florida agricultural country north of Polk County, around Dade City in Pasco County, and to the south, in Hardee, DeSoto and a slice of Highlands Counties. This was long a Democratic seat, until Congressman Andy Ireland switched parties in 1984; ever since it has been Republican.

The congressman from the 12th is Charles T. Canady. He grew up in Lakeland, went to Haverford College and Yale Law School, then practiced law in Lakeland; his father, Charles E. Canady, served for 18 years as Lawton Chiles's top staffer in Florida and Washington. The younger Canady was elected to the Florida House in 1984, at 30, served as majority whip, and switched parties in 1989, saying he had little in common with liberal Democrats. In 1990 he ran for the state Senate and, as Chiles swept Polk County, lost. In 1992, Canady ran for Congress, unopposed in the Republican primary, and faced Democratic legislator Tom Mims in the general, who started off ahead in the polls. But Canady attacked Mims sharply in mailings and in the end with TV spots calling him pro-tax and antibusiness, and won 52%–48%. Feelings between the two remained amicable enough for them to lunch together, as promised, the Friday after the election.

In just two terms Canady has become one of the most productive and effective members of the House. In his first two years he compiled a conservative voting record, opposing NAFTA because of citrus and tomato growers' concerns, voting for the 1994 crime bill. But after the 1994 elections, Judiciary Chairman Henry Hyde named him chairman of the Constitution Subcommittee, one of the busiest in the House. Canady is hard-working and soft-spoken ("when he was a kid, what he did for fun was read the encyclopedia," his father once said), strong in his convictions but businesslike in demeanor, bright enough to keep up with the subcommittee's ranking Democrat, Barney Frank, a strong partisan Republican but willing to work with Frank and other Democrats when the occasion arises. His first major bill was the private property protection bill, passed by the House as part of the Contract with America in March 1995, but never acted on by the Senate. He controlled debate on the Housing for Older Persons Act to allow seniors-only housing; it passed the House in April 1995 and became law in December. Perhaps his biggest achievement was lobby reform, where he worked with Frank and other Democrats, struggling to keep out maximalist amendments which would have doomed the bill while retaining its substance. As *National Journal*'s Eliza Newlin Carney wrote, "Canady's success on the lobby legislation, which was threatened with myriad roadblocks, reflected a combination of skilled coalition-building and legislative elbow grease." It was passed in November 1995 and signed in December. In April 1996 Canady also led the fight for two key prison reforms, discouraging court-imposed limits on prison populations and curbing frivolous prisoner lawsuits; it was signed that month. Canady also managed the Defense of Marriage Act, grudgingly signed by Bill Clinton in September 1996.

Not all his legislation passed. In July 1995 he co-sponsored with Bob Dole a ban on race and gender preference in federal hiring, contracting, and program administration; but other Republicans, including for some time Dole, wanted to steer clear of the issue, and it never got serious legislative consideration. Canady's English-as-the-official-language bill did pass the House in August 1996, but not the Senate. And the partial birth abortion ban, of which Canady was chief House sponsor, was vetoed by Bill Clinton in April 1996; the House voted to override, but the Senate did not.

Canady was reelected easily in 1994 and 1996; his opponent in 1996 was Michael Canady, a 61-year-old construction consultant and distant cousin, whose campaign spent less than $13,000.

The People: Pop. 1990: 562,381; 34% rural; 17% age 65+; 81% White; 12% Black; 1% Asian; 6% Hispanic origin. Households: 62% married couple families; 25% married couple fams. w. children; 35% college educ.; median household income: $25,315; per capita income: $12,277; median gross rent: $381; median house value: $61,800.

1996 Presidential Vote

Dole (R)	96,140	(46%)
Clinton (D)	89,296	(43%)
Perot (I)	20,770	(10%)

1992 Presidential Vote

Bush (R)	90,694	(45%)
Clinton (D)	68,487	(34%)
Perot (I)	39,770	(20%)

Rep. Charles T. Canady (R)

Elected 1992; b. June 22, 1954, Lakeland; home, Lakeland; Haverford Col., B.A. 1976, Yale Law Schl., J.D. 1979; Presbyterian; married (Jennifer).

Career: Practicing atty., 1979–92; FL House of Reps., 1984–90.

DC Office: 2432 RHOB 20515, 202-225-1252; Fax: 202-225-2279; e-mail: canady@hr.house.gov.

District Offices: Lakeland, 941-688-2651.

Committees: *Agriculture* (9th of 27 R): Department Operations, Nutrition & Foreign Agriculture. *Judiciary* (9th of 20 R): Constitution (Chmn.); Courts & Intellectual Property.

Group Ratings

	ADA	ACLU	AFS	LCV	CFA	CON	NFIB	COC	ACU	NTLC	CHC
1996	5	6	8	31	15	17	95	94	85	95	86
1995	5	—	—	0	0	38	—	100	76	—	—

National Journal Ratings

	1995 LIB	—	1995 CONS	1996 LIB	—	1996 CONS
Economic	0%	—	74%	42%	—	56%
Social	30%	—	68%	38%	—	61%
Foreign	15%	—	73%	0%	—	79%

Key Votes of the 104th Congress

1. Reduce Medicare Growth $	Y	5. Flag Amendment	Y	9. Cuban Embargo	Y
2. Ovrd. Product Liab. Veto	Y	6. Drop EPA Limits	N	10. Bar Bosnia Troop $	Y
3. Increase Min. Wage	Y	7. Repeal Assault-Weap. Ban	Y	11. Cut Anti-Missile Defense	N
4. Welfare Reform	Y	8. Ovrd. Part. Birth Veto	Y	12. Bar U.N. Uniforms	Y

Election Results

1996 general	Charles T. Canady (R)	122,584	(62%)	($213,131)
	Michael Canady (D)	76,513	(38%)	($12,818)
1996 primary	Charles T. Canady (R)	unopposed		
1994 general	Charles T. Canady (R)	106,123	(65%)	($333,623)
	Robert Connors (D)	57,203	(35%)	($192,849)

THIRTEENTH DISTRICT

Everyone else followed the circus to Sarasota. When the Ringling Brothers made a success of the circus they founded in the 1880s, they needed a place for performers and animals to rest during the winter months. They settled on the bayfront village behind a barrier island along the Gulf of Mexico. It was just far enough north to be reachable by railroad, just far enough south to be semitropical so the elephants would not get sick and die. Here, John Ringling established the Ringling Museum of Art, with its huge sculpture garden and built his own Venetian palace, the Ca'd'Zan. After World War II, when people began spending their retirement years in warmer climates, the Gulf Coast started attracting new settlers—affluent, WASPy Republicans from upper crust suburbs of northern cities. The population exploded, with Manatee and Sarasota Counties growing from 63,000 in 1950 to 489,000 in 1990.

The 13th Congressional District of Florida includes Sarasota County and Manatee County and slivers of Tampa's Hillsborough County on the north and Charlotte County on the south. It is mostly a collection of Gulf Coast towns, from Tampa Bay south past Venice (where the circus now has its winter quarters). It is retiree country: 30.5% of the people here are 65 or older (the highest, with 31.5%, is the 22d, the Gold Coast beachfront). The 13th is also very heavily Republican, with the second highest Republican registration of any Florida district (the highest is the 14th, just to the south).

The congressman from the 13th District is Dan Miller, a Republican elected in 1992 when new boundaries were drawn and Andy Ireland, who had represented most of the 12th and 13th, was retiring. Miller is a native of Michigan, with an M.B.A. and a Ph.D., who taught economics at Georgia State and then moved to Bradenton in the 1970s and practiced economics, starting small businesses—the Memorial Pier Restaurant, the Suncoast Manor Nursing Center, the Barnett Bank Building and Riverview Center. He served on local commissions, the hospital board of directors and the judicial nominating commission. He was one of five Republicans and two Democrats running for the seat. Calling for less government, fewer regulations, and lower taxes, he ran second in the primary, 143 votes behind former Bush Administration appointee Brad Baker; in the runoff, with Ireland's endorsement, Miller won 53%–47%. Against Democrat Brad Snell, a former top staffer for Lawton Chiles and director of a congressional study on "Biotechnology in a Global Economy," he won 58%–42%.

Miller's has had a conservative voting record,with a few exceptions on cultural issues: he voted for the assault weapons ban and has supported abortion rights. As an economist he has seats on money committees, Appropriations and Budget. He has taken some political risks. He spearheaded opposition to the AARP's endorsement of the Clinton health reform plan in the 103d Congress and in the 104th helped put together the Republican Medicare proposal. One area of spending he looks favorably on is medical research: he worked to appropriate more than Bill Clinton requested for the National Institutes of Health and for Central for Disease Control programs for breast and cervical cancer research, AIDS education and prevention, and polio eradication. "We are on the verge of finding cures to our most deadly diseases," he predicts. He strongly supported the Contract with America plank to reduce the tax on Social Security recipients' earnings.

Miller's great crusade has been to repeal the sugar program, which he calls "corporate welfare." It increases prices to consumers $1.4 billion a year, grants favored foreign nations a $200 million subsidy, and stimulates overproduction of sugar—and pollution—in the Everglades; and all for a program 40% of whose benefits go to 1% of recipients. On the Appropriations Committee, with Democrat Charles Schumer, he challenged the sugar program on the 1995 farm bill, and lost narrowly, 217–208. In April 1997, Miller and Schumer unveiled a bill which would repeal the program.

Miller had little difficulty winning reelection in 1994 and 1996.

The People: Pop. 1990: 562,501; 11% rural; 31% age 65+; 90% White; 5% Black; 1% Asian; 4% Hispanic origin. Households: 59% married couple families; 16% married couple fams. w. children; 45% college educ.; median household income: $27,616; per capita income: $16,254; median gross rent: $512; median house value: $81,300.

1996 Presidential Vote

Dole (R)	133,005	(46%)
Clinton (D)	122,884	(43%)
Perot (I)	29,634	(10%)

1992 Presidential Vote

Bush (R)	124,394	(43%)
Clinton (D)	100,831	(35%)
Perot (I)	65,283	(22%)

Rep. Dan Miller (R)

Elected 1992; b. May 30, 1942, Highland Park, MI; home, Bradenton; U. of FL, B.S./B.A. 1964, Emory U., M.B.A. 1965, Louisiana St. U., Ph.D. 1970; Episcopalian; married (Glenda).

Career: Businessman, Miller Enterprises, 1973–present; Asst. Prof., Georgia St. U., 1969–73; Adjunct Prof., U. of S. FL, 1975–83.

DC Office: 102 CHOB 20515, 202-225-5015; Fax: 202-226-0828.

District Offices: Bradenton, 941-747-9081; Sarasota, 941-951-6643.

Committees: *Appropriations* (20th of 34 R): Interior; Labor, Health & Human Services & Education. *Budget* (7th of 24 R).

Group Ratings

	ADA	ACLU	AFS	LCV	CFA	CON	NFIB	COC	ACU	NTLC	CHC
1996	10	6	0	23	46	68	92	88	95	90	93
1995	5	—	—	6	15	87	—	96	80	—	—

National Journal Ratings

	1995 LIB		1995 CONS	1996 LIB		1996 CONS
Economic	34%	—	64%	24%	—	73%
Social	38%	—	60%	50%	—	48%
Foreign	15%	—	73%	30%	—	65%

Key Votes of the 104th Congress

1. Reduce Medicare Growth $	Y	5. Flag Amendment	Y	9. Cuban Embargo	Y
2. Ovrd. Product Liab. Veto	Y	6. Drop EPA Limits	N	10. Bar Bosnia Troop $	Y
3. Increase Min. Wage	N	7. Repeal Assault-Weap. Ban	N	11. Cut Anti-Missile Defense	N
4. Welfare Reform	Y	8. Ovrd. Part. Birth Veto	Y	12. Bar U.N. Uniforms	Y

Election Results

1996 general	Dan Miller (R)	173,671	(64%)	($387,149)
	Sanford Gordon (D)	96,098	(36%)	($73,500)
1996 primary	Dan Miller (R)	unopposed		
1994 general	Dan Miller (R)	unopposed		($278,042)

FOURTEENTH DISTRICT

On the edge of the Tropics, in a physical environment once teeming with diseases and inhospitable to advanced civilization only a generation ago, Florida's Gulf Coast has sprung up as a model of what America will be for many when they retire. The wide white sand beaches with gentle breakers, the inlets and broad estuaries that abound for boating, the wetlands filled with exotic birds, eventually made this prime resort country: Thomas Edison had his winter home in Fort Myers, Henry Ford used to visit here, Walter Reuther, after his gunshot wound, recuperated by building a modest house near the Caloosahatchee River. But the local economy could not support many permanent residents, and at the beginning of World War II, there were only 68,000 people living on the Gulf Coast from Sarasota south to Naples.

By 1990 there were 1.1 million: the climate and environment attracted affluent suburbanites from the Midwest and Northeast, with the added lure of no state income or inheritance taxes.

Developers like Barron Collier, who built the Tamiami Trail across the Everglades and designed Naples with the wealthy in mind (and gave his name to Collier County, the richest in Florida), were determined to avoid the high-rise canyons that line the Atlantic from Miami to Palm Beach. The alternative has been low-rise, city-sized developments like Cape Coral and Port Charlotte, with canals in most backyards, and thinly paved roads along the sand spits next to the sultry, lapping waves of the Gulf, or the luxurious town of Naples set amid preserved coastal islands and interior swamps. This is very much retirement country, with more than one in four residents over 65. Florida's 14th Congressional District occupies the southern half of this Gulf Coast, from Charlotte County past Cape Coral and Fort Myers south to Naples. This district has the highest Republican registration of any in Florida, and continually casts among the highest Republican percentages.

The congressman from the 14th is Porter Goss, a Republican first elected in 1988, who worked 10 years in the CIA's Clandestine Services and then moved to Sanibel Island (whose famous shells are now scarce), where he founded a prize-winning newspaper, served on the city council and passed growth management laws and was appointed to the Lee County Commission by then-Governor Bob Graham. When incumbent Connie Mack III ran for the Senate in 1988, Goss ran for this seat and effectively won it in the Republican primary, leading 38%–29%–19% former Congressman Skip Bafalis and retired General Jim Dozier.

Goss has a moderate voting record among House Republicans and has presented proposals suggesting an active and original mind. In line with Gulf Coast opinion, he is something of an environmentalist; he has helped extend, and wants to make permanent, the moratorium on oil drilling in the Outer Continental Shelf of the Gulf—and bucked an important regulatory segment of the Contract with America. He has also worked to increase Everglades funding above the $200 million voted in the 1995 farm bill. Goss is also something of a reformer. He pushed for the gift ban and has his own campaign finance reform proposal. He proposed charging members $600 from their office accounts for each insertion of extraneous matter into the *Congressional Record*. He introduced legislation to repeal the Ramspeck Act, a measure passed in 1940 to make it easier for displaced Hill staffers to enter the civil service system. He is willing to take risks with elderly constituents: he served on Nebraska Senator Bob Kerrey's 1994 entitlements commission. But he also calls for raising the Social Security earnings limit. He has been a lead sponsor of the line-item veto and of the lock-box provision, which states that any money saved on eliminated federal projects must be applied to deficit reduction. He is the chief sponsor of the Ricky Ray Hemophilia Relief Fund Act, to compensate hemophiliacs who contracted AIDS from what was presented as safe blood.

Goss is the number three Republican on the Rules Committee and has taken on some unpleasant assignments as well. He chairs the Intelligence Committee—a difficult place these days. In March 1995 with Democratic Senator Bob Graham he inspected Cuban refugee camps in Guantanamo Bay, which he called a "tinderbox"; weeks later the Clinton Administration allowed all 21,000 people there into the United States. From 1991–96, Goss served on the Ethics Committee, where of course the most contentious issue has been the charges Democrats have brought against Speaker Newt Gingrich. Without quite saying so, he charged that committee Democrats have made the process partisan. "Politics is destroying the process," he told *National Journal*. "I think we are going to have to make some procedural changes in order to get the politics out of the ethics process, or we are going to have to give up trying to pretend that we are conducting an efficient and responsible ethics oversight role amongst ourselves." And in 1997 Goss was asked to serve on a task force set up to re-examine the Ethics Committee process. He has proposed a jury system so that randomly chosen panel members would investigate ethics complaints.

Goss has been reelected without difficulty.

The People: Pop. 1990: 562,489; 18% rural; 26% age 65+; 87% White; 5% Black; 1% Asian; 7% Hispanic origin. Households: 62% married couple families; 18% married couple fams. w. children; 44%

college educ.; median household income: $29,620; per capita income: $17,165; median gross rent: $519; median house value: $90,500.

1996 Presidential Vote			1992 Presidential Vote		
Dole (R)	140,921	(51%)	Bush (R)	129,493	(46%)
Clinton (D)	105,027	(38%)	Clinton (D)	87,978	(31%)
Perot (I)	29,735	(11%)	Perot (I)	63,175	(22%)

Rep. Porter Johnston Goss (R)

Elected 1988; b. Nov. 26, 1938, Waterbury, CT; home, Sanibel; Yale, B.A. 1960; Presbyterian; married (Mariel).

Career: Army Intelligence, 1960–62; CIA Clandestine Svcs. 1960–71; Businessman, Newspaper publ., 1973–78; Sanibel City Cncl., 1974–82; Sanibel Mayor, 1974–77, 1980; Lee Cnty. Commissioner 1983–88.

DC Office: 108 CHOB 20515, 202-225-2536; Fax: 202-225-6820.

District Offices: Fort Myers, 941-332-4677; Naples, 941-774-8060; Punta Gorda; 941-639-0051.

Committees: *Rules* (3rd of 9 R): Legislative & Budget Process (Chmn.). *Intelligence (Select)* (Chmn. of 9 R).

Group Ratings

	ADA	ACLU	AFS	LCV	CFA	CON	NFIB	COC	ACU	NTLC	CHC
1996	10	0	0	23	46	63	89	88	95	90	93
1995	11	—	—	13	54	56	—	88	80	—	—

National Journal Ratings

	1995 LIB — 1995 CONS	1996 LIB — 1996 CONS
Economic	41% — 56%	39% — 58%
Social	42% — 57%	38% — 61%
Foreign	28% — 65%	0% — 79%

Key Votes of the 104th Congress

1. Reduce Medicare Growth $	Y	5. Flag Amendment	Y	9. Cuban Embargo	Y
2. Ovrd. Product Liab. Veto	Y	6. Drop EPA Limits	Y	10. Bar Bosnia Troop $	N
3. Increase Min. Wage	N	7. Repeal Assault-Weap. Ban	Y	11. Cut Anti-Missile Defense	N
4. Welfare Reform	Y	8. Ovrd. Part. Birth Veto	Y	12. Bar U.N. Uniforms	Y

Election Results

1996 general	Porter Johnston Goss (R)	176,992	(73%)	($372,563)
	Jim Nolan (D)	63,842	(27%)	($19,596)
1996 primary	Porter Johnston Goss (R)	unopposed		
1994 general	Porter Johnston Goss (R)	unopposed		($142,940)

FIFTEENTH DISTRICT

When Cape Canaveral was chosen as the nation's rocket testing site in the 1940s, there were only 20,000 people in all of Brevard County, which stretches along 60 miles of the coast and includes the Cape. It was a backward place with no industry, picked because it was the sunny Atlantic coast: rockets here have to be launched eastward so spent parts fall into the ocean. Today, Brevard County north and south of the cape has 400,000 people. It is a prototype of America's future, with no city center but plenty of shopping centers along strip highways, with a white-collar, service economy, knit together by interest in the space program.

The 15th Congressional District of Florida includes all of the Space Coast and Brevard County and extends south into Indian River County and the fast-growing retirement areas around Vero Beach. It continues west past the vast new town of Palm Bay, now the district's largest city, to what is left of primeval Florida. But more may come: the Army Corps of Engineers, which straightened out the Kissimmee River in the early 1970s, is now seeking to restore it to its natural snake-like course, while nearby in the Three Lakes Wildlife Management Area, whooping cranes were released to propagate in the wild. The Space Coast is heavily Republican, distrustful of many national Democrats' disdain for the space program. But from 1978–92, it elected Democratic congressmen: for 12 years, Bill Nelson, the first House member to go up in space, now Florida Insurance Commissioner; and for four years moderate Jim Bacchus.

The congressman from the 15th now is Dave Weldon, one of the most conservative of the 1994 freshmen. Weldon grew up on Long Island, went to medical school in Buffalo, served in the Army in Fort Stewart Georgia, then in 1987 joined Melbourne Internal Medicine Associates in Florida. In 1989 he founded the Space Coast Family Forum, "to promote family-friendly issues and positions." Weldon ran for the House in 1994, and was considered a weak candidate because of his strong conservative views on cultural issues. He led the seven-candidate Republican primary, but with only 24% of the vote, and in the runoff won 54%–46% over Carole Jordan, who campaigned as a pro-choice moderate. Democrats ran former Space Coast Chamber of Commerce head Sue Munsey, a former Republican, who also campaigned as pro-choice on abortion. Weldon called for phasing out welfare and banning abortion; Munsey said Speaker Thomas Foley promised her a seat on the Science Committee.

Weldon won 54%–46%, and it was Speaker Newt Gingrich, whom he called an "idol," who gave him a seat on Science and made him vice chairman of the Space and Aeronautics Subcommittee; he was also freshman representative on the Steering and Policy Committee.

Naturally Weldon defended the Kennedy Space Center and promoted the Space Shuttle, protecting their funding even when NASA funding was going down. He also called for restoration of Brevard County beaches. But the most interesting issue revolved around a veterans' hospital. Bacchus was able to move a veterans' hospital proposed for Orlando to the Space Coast instead. But Weldon insisted that only an outpatient clinic was necessary, and that for other needs veterans could be authorized to seek care in existing local hospitals. This struck hard at the rationale for the separate existence of a VA hospital system, not to mention the conventional wisdom that politicians should seek every available federal dime for their local districts. Weldon was attacked sharply on this in 1996 by Democratic nominee John Byron, who as a former Navy submarine captain and former employee of space contractor Johnson Controls, had fine credentials for the race. Byron brought in Veterans' Secretary Jesse Brown to attack Weldon on the hospital and called him "an extremist with a narrow agenda." But Weldon outspent and, evidently, outargued him, and won 51%–43%–6%. This was a strong endorsement of Weldon's views, in a difficult year, and yet the strength of his conservative convictions may mean he will have serious competition again.

The People: Pop. 1990: 562,542; 18% rural; 19% age 65+; 88% White; 7% Black; 1% Asian; 3% Hispanic origin. Households: 61% married couple families; 22% married couple fams. w. children; 49%

college educ.; median household income: $29,755; per capita income: $15,225; median gross rent: $485; median house value: $74,800.

1996 Presidential Vote			1992 Presidential Vote		
Dole (R)	125,430	(46%)	Bush (R)	117,206	(43%)
Clinton (D)	111,263	(41%)	Clinton (D)	83,507	(31%)
Perot (I)	34,594	(13%)	Perot (I)	69,605	(26%)

Rep. David J. Weldon (R)

Elected 1994; b. Aug. 31, 1953, Amityville, NY; home, Palm Bay; S.U.N.Y. Stonybrook, B.A. 1978, S.U.N.Y. Buffalo, M.D. 1981; Christian; married (Nancy).

Career: Army Medical Corps, 1981–87, Army Reserves, 1987–92; Practicing physician, 1987–94.

DC Office: 216 CHOB 20515, 202-225-3671; Fax: 202-225-3516; e-mail: fla.15@hr.house.gov.

District Offices: Melbourne, 407-632-1776.

Committees: *Banking & Financial Services* (20th of 30 R): Domestic & International Monetary Policy; Financial Institutions & Consumer Credit. *Science* (12th of 25 R): Space & Aeronautics (Vice Chmn.).

Group Ratings

	ADA	ACLU	AFS	LCV	CFA	CON	NFIB	COC	ACU	NTLC	CHC
1996	5	0	0	15	23	17	100	100	100	100	100
1995	0	—	—	0	0	38	—	100	96	—	—

National Journal Ratings

	1995 LIB — 1995 CONS			1996 LIB — 1996 CONS		
Economic	0%	—	74%	20%	—	76%
Social	0%	—	79%	29%	—	68%
Foreign	0%	—	85%	0%	—	79%

Key Votes of the 104th Congress

1. Reduce Medicare Growth $	Y	5. Flag Amendment	Y	9. Cuban Embargo	Y
2. Ovrd. Product Liab. Veto	Y	6. Drop EPA Limits	N	10. Bar Bosnia Troop $	Y
3. Increase Min. Wage	N	7. Repeal Assault-Weap. Ban	Y	11. Cut Anti-Missile Defense	N
4. Welfare Reform	Y	8. Ovrd. Part. Birth Veto	Y	12. Bar U.N. Uniforms	Y

Election Results

1996 general	David J. Weldon (R)	139,014	(51%)	($774,408)
	John L. Byron (D)	115,981	(43%)	($332,687)
	David Golding (I)	15,355	(6%)	
1996 primary	David J. Weldon (R)	unopposed		
1994 general	David J. Weldon (R)	117,027	(54%)	($478,303)
	Sue Munsey (D)	100,513	(46%)	($494,364)

SIXTEENTH DISTRICT

Urban Florida has fanned far across the swamplands from its original nuclei in beachfront resort communities. Thus Palm Beach has spread out from its original locus at the Breakers Hotel, across Lake Worth and well beyond the less fashionable city of West Palm Beach: these are now just neighborhoods in a vast metropolitan area. Old beach towns, such as Hobe Sound, located northward along the ocean, have become the hub of extremely affluent developments that stretch all the way to Stuart in Martin County. Farther north, near the old town of Fort Pierce are larger, but more modest developments like Port St. Lucie. Entire square miles west and northwest of West Palm Beach have been reclaimed from swampland and made into condo communities surrounded by golf courses or tracts of factories and warehouses. Once, metro Palm Beach was a narrow stretch along Lake Worth; now it runs inland halfway to Lake Okeechobee.

The 16th Congressional District of Florida includes much of greater West Palm. Its boundaries include the beach towns from Jupiter north to Port St. Lucie, but they are convoluted to avoid the black-majority 23rd District. The district also takes in many recently and soon-to-be developed parcels in inland Palm Beach County. One sixth of the district's residents live in citrus and vegetable growing areas around Lake Okeechobee, and as far away as Sebring, site of an auto racing track: here is the source of the Everglades, the 50-mile-wide and six-inch-deep "river of grass" that flows so slowly to the Gulf of Mexico. This is a Republican-leaning district, though much of Palm Beach County has been trending Democratic, and it can be competitive.

The congressman from the 16th District is Mark Foley, a Republican first elected in 1994. Foley was born in Massachusetts, moved to Florida at age three, dropped out of Palm Beach Community College and opened a restaurant in Lake Worth at 20. He was active in politics, working for Democratic Congressman Paul Rogers and was also a real estate broker. Foley was elected to the Lake Worth City Commission at 23, to the state House as a Republican in 1990 and the state Senate in 1992. In 1994, when Republican Congressman Tom Lewis decided to retire after 12 years, he and the local Republican organization supported Foley, who won a three-way primary with 61% of the vote. The Democratic opponent, John Comerford, had worked in the Carter Administration, and accused Foley of being beholden to special interests. But Foley outraised him and won 58%–42%, though only 52%–48% in Palm Beach County.

In the House Foley's political skills caught the leadership's eye, and he was named one of 14 deputy whips and a member of task forces to abolish government departments. But Foley also displayed an independent streak and concentrated on issues with local ramifications—immigration and agriculture. He proved capable of shifting on issues, voting in 1995 to cut EPA monies and in 1996 against; his 1996 vote for repeal of the assault weapons ban contrasted with his support of some gun control measures in Florida. He supported funding of AIDS research, family planning, and public broadcasting. He tried to speed up deportation of illegal immigrants and was angry when he found the INS had cleared inmates out before he and other members inspected the Krome Avenue detention facility in Miami. He wants to amend the Constitution so that children born here are not automatically citizens. But he also worked to increase the number of immigrants admitted as farmworkers, although many overstay their visas and never return.

Much of his work focused on the Everglades. He persuaded Speaker Newt Gingrich to support $300 million for Everglades restoration, and he helped get Bob Dole to support $200 million for it in the Senate farm bill. He opposed the penny-per-pound sales tax proposed by the Clinton Administration arguing that it would cut sugar use. In response, he was the target of a slashing attack by financier Paul Tudor Jones, the referendum's chief moneygiver, which won sympathy for Foley among constituents in the farm area inland from Palm Beach.

That area was his bulwark when he campaigned for reelection in 1996 and described his record as "moderate, moderate, modcrate," and said, "I think we did go too far" in 1995. He heavily outspent his Democratic opponent, who favored the sugar tax, and won 64%–36%. Afterwards, he predicted "a much more temperate Congress," and added, "Among most freshmen, I think, there is more flexibility. Compromise, we've found, is not a dirty word."

The People: Pop. 1990: 561,856; 22% rural; 24% age 65+; 89% White; 4% Black; 1% Asian; 6% Hispanic origin. Households: 62% married couple families; 21% married couple fams. w. children; 45% college educ.; median household income: $30,582; per capita income: $16,952; median gross rent: $575; median house value: $87,900.

1996 Presidential Vote

Clinton (D)	131,252	(47%)
Dole (R)	116,630	(42%)
Perot (I)	29,321	(11%)

1992 Presidential Vote

Bush (R)	108,503	(39%)
Clinton (D)	98,154	(36%)
Perot (I)	68,543	(25%)

Rep. Mark Foley (R)

Elected 1994; b. Sept. 8, 1954, Newton, MA; home, West Palm Beach; Palm Beach Comm. Col., 1974; Catholic; single.

Career: Restauranteur, 1974–84; Real estate broker, 1984–90; Lake Worth City Comm., 1977–83; Vice Mayor, 1983–84; FL House of Reps., 1990–92; FL Senate, 1992–94.

DC Office: 113 CHOB 20515, 202-225-5792; Fax: 202-225-3132; e-mail: mfoley@hr.house.gov.

District Offices: Palm Beach Gardens, 561-627-6192; Port St. Lucie, 561-878-3181.

Committees: *Agriculture* (17th of 27 R): Department Operations, Nutrition & Foreign Agriculture; Risk Management & Specialty Crops. *Banking & Financial Services* (29th of 30 R): Domestic & International Monetary Policy; General Oversight & Investigations. *Science* (16th of 25 R): Energy & Environment; Space & Aeronautics.

Group Ratings

	ADA	ACLU	AFS	LCV	CFA	CON	NFIB	COC	ACU	NTLC	CHC
1996	10	6	8	38	46	52	89	94	90	93	73
1995	10	—	—	13	23	75	—	96	84	—	—

National Journal Ratings

	1995 LIB — 1995 CONS	1996 LIB — 1996 CONS
Economic	0% — 74%	39% — 58%
Social	51% — 49%	49% — 50%
Foreign	36% — 59%	45% — 54%

Key Votes of the 104th Congress

1. Reduce Medicare Growth $	Y	5. Flag Amendment	Y	9. Cuban Embargo	Y
2. Ovrd. Product Liab. Veto	Y	6. Drop EPA Limits	Y	10. Bar Bosnia Troop $	Y
3. Increase Min. Wage	Y	7. Repeal Assault-Weap. Ban	Y	11. Cut Anti-Missile Defense	N
4. Welfare Reform	Y	8. Ovrd. Part. Birth Veto	Y	12. Bar U.N. Uniforms	Y

Election Results

1996 general	Mark Foley (R)	175,714	(64%)	($613,392)
	Jim Stuber (D)	98,827	(36%)	($84,523)
1996 primary	Mark Foley (R)	unopposed		
1994 general	Mark Foley (R)	122,734	(58%)	($629,406)
	John Comerford (D)	88,646	(42%)	($163,311)

SEVENTEENTH DISTRICT

North from downtown Miami, alongside the railroad tracks that Henry Flagler built shortly after Miami was founded in 1896 and alongside Interstate 95, Miami's main north-south artery, is Miami's largest black community, stretching from the Orange Bowl near downtown Miami north through Allapattah and Liberty City toward the suburb of Opalocka. This has been a kind of frontierland in Miami, the scene where hostilities between Miami's blacks and its Cuban-American majority have been played out. In 1980, 18 people died in a riot after the acquittal of a police officer charged with killing a black insurance salesman; this was the first public crisis for Janet Reno, then in her first term as Dade County Attorney and now U.S. Attorney General. Another riot broke out in 1989, after a Colombian-born police officer shot a black motorcyclist; the police officer, originally convicted of manslaughter, won an appeal and was acquitted in May 1993. Many Miami blacks have resented the economic upward mobility and political strength of the Cubans, the first generation of which rose while still speaking mostly Spanish, and of other Latins—including the Haitians in little Haiti—who have been moving upward as well. There is a political dimension as well: blacks are Miami's most Democratic voting group, while Cuban-Americans, at least until the 1996 presidential election, have been heavily Republican.

The 17th Congressional District of Florida covers all of this territory, running along the I-95 and 27th Avenue corridors from the Miami River north to the Dade County line. The mostly white high-rise gated condominiums on the shore of Biscayne Bay and heavily Cuban Hialeah were carefully excluded from the district. It extends south along a narrow corridor on either side of Dixie Highway, expanding here and there to bring in heavily black areas all the way south to Homestead, site of Hurricane Andrew's worst damage.

The congresswoman from the 17th is Carrie Meek, one of the most politically experienced of the freshman Democratic class of 1992. The granddaughter of a slave, Meek was born in 1926 in Tallahassee and grew up near the old Capitol in a neighborhood called the Bottom. She was a gifted athlete when she attended Florida A&M's lab school; she went to Florida A&M and the University of Michigan (Florida government paid the tuition because its graduate schools were segregated). When she came back to Miami, she taught physical education at Miami-Dade Community College. Here she became active in politics and, when pioneer black legislator Gwen Cherry died in an auto accident, Meek was elected to the Florida House in 1978. Particularly effective in the legislature, Meek passed legislation to criminalize stalking, a Minority Business Enterprise law, and promoted literacy and dropout prevention programs. In the State Senate for a decade, she helped to draw the district she would eventually serve. When the 17th was drawn with a black majority, she was clearly the best-known and best-liked politician in the Miami area and was nominated with 83% of the vote in the primary and elected with no Republican opposition.

Meek has had a very liberal record, except on some foreign policy issues; she is a strong critic of Fidel Castro. In her first term, she demonstrated her own determination and savvy by being the only freshman Democrat to win a seat on the Appropriations Committee. She said her first priority was creating jobs through federal programs and private initiatives to help blacks develop their own businesses and banks as, she notes, Cuban-Americans have. She worked on projects ranging from changing the rules for Social Security for household employees, to setting up women's VA clinics. The Republican capture of the House cost her her seat on Appropriations.

In January 1995, she unexpectedly found herself as the vocal center of Democrats' anger at how House Speaker Newt Gingrich's Republicans were running the House. In a floor speech, Meek criticized Gingrich's book deal with Rupert Murdoch's HarperCollins publishing company. "News accounts tell us that while the speaker may have given up the $4.5 million advance, he stands to gain that amount and much more . . . That is a whole lot of dust where I come from." Republicans demanded that her words be stricken from the record. They had a point regarding House rules, but they aroused a furor among Democrats, who started a two-hour shouting match on the floor. Meek was undaunted and will surely continue her attacks on Republican policy and politicians. After the 1996 election, Meek made her way back onto Appropriations.

The People: Pop. 1990: 563,284; 10% age 65+; 20% White; 56% Black; 1% Asian; 23% Hispanic origin. Households: 42% married couple families; 21% married couple fams. w. children; 32% college educ.; median household income: $21,899; per capita income: $9,157; median gross rent: $426; median house value: $63,900.

1996 Presidential Vote			1992 Presidential Vote		
Clinton (D)	115,732	(85%)	Clinton (D)	99,422	(73%)
Dole (R)	16,802	(12%)	Bush (R)	25,873	(19%)
Perot (I)	3,944	(3%)	Perot (I)	9,913	(7%)

Rep. Carrie P. Meek (D)

Elected 1992; b. April 29, 1926, Tallahassee; home, Miami; FL A&M U., B.A. 1946, U. of MI, M.S. 1948; Primitive Baptist; divorced.

Career: Admin., Miami-Dade Comm. Col., 1949–92; FL House of Reps, 1978–82; FL Senate 1982–92.

DC Office: 401 CHOB 20515, 202-225-4506; Fax: 202-226-0777.

District Offices: Miami, 305-381-9541.

Committees: *Appropriations* (24th of 26 D): Treasury, Postal Service & General Government; VA, HUD & Independent Agencies.

Group Ratings

	ADA	ACLU	AFS	LCV	CFA	CON	NFIB	COC	ACU	NTLC	CHC
1996	85	87	100	77	77	58	16	33	5	5	0
1995	95	—	—	81	100	9	—	13	8	—	—

National Journal Ratings

	1995 LIB — 1995 CONS			1996 LIB — 1996 CONS		
Economic	94%	—	0%	79%	—	18%
Social	88%	—	0%	88%	—	0%
Foreign	73%	—	24%	60%	—	39%

Key Votes of the 104th Congress

1. Reduce Medicare Growth $	N	5. Flag Amendment	N	9. Cuban Embargo	Y
2. Ovrd. Product Liab. Veto	N	6. Drop EPA Limits	Y	10. Bar Bosnia Troop $	N
3. Increase Min. Wage	Y	7. Repeal Assault-Weap. Ban	N	11. Cut Anti-Missile Defense	Y
4. Welfare Reform	N	8. Ovrd. Part. Birth Veto	N	12. Bar U.N. Uniforms	N

Election Results

1996 general	Carrie P. Meek (D)	114,638	(89%)	($257,039)
	Wellington Rolle (R)	14,525	(11%)	
1996 primary	Carrie P. Meek (D)	unopposed		
1994 general	Carrie P. Meek (D)	unopposed		($166,452)

EIGHTEENTH DISTRICT

The hum of orange and pink neon signs in hot night air, moonlight reflecting off Biscayne Bay onto surrealistic high rises, the pastel, random-shaped, sharp-angled style of clothes and furniture and the air of menace in streets where many are armed and vast quantities of drugs and cash regularly change hands—the *Miami Vice* image of Miami lingers on. A resort city known for pseudo-Spanish mansions and art deco beach hotels two generations ago, on its way to becoming a fairly typical American metropolitan area one generation ago, Miami today cannot be mistaken for any other American—or Latin American—city. It lives on the cusp of two civilizations: Anglo and Latino, with different traditions, styles and sensibilities, converging here in Miami, despite some friction, toward an amalgam with many strengths of both. Miami has become commercially and economically the capital of Latin America, the one place from which it is easiest to fly directly to any other part of Latin America, where top business and banking services are available to a sophisticated Spanish-speaking (and usually also English-speaking) clientele. With NAFTA ratified, and other Latin nations eager for free trade with the United States, Miami stands to be at the center of the largest free-trade zone in the history of mankind, uniquely able to connect all sides.

In the meantime, there are inevitably frictions in a community divided between culturally defined groups with distinct histories and styles. Miami's Dade County in 1990 was 49% Hispanic (mostly Cuban), 32% white Anglo and 19% black. There is tension on the streets between blacks and Cubans, and a resentment by some blacks of the success the hardworking, anything-but-fatalistic Cubans have achieved. And there is resentment, also, by many Cuban-Americans of white liberals, reflected in Cuban activist Jorge Mas Canosa's charges that the *Miami Herald* "manipulates information just like *Granma*," the Castro paper in Havana. On its face, the charge is absurd, yet it should be added that many goodhearted liberals, for which the *Herald* is a proxy, have failed to appreciate the totalitarianism of Castro's regime and glossed over the brutality that has been its steady conduct.

Typical is the liberal Miami politician who calls the city's Cuban-Americans "emigres," the term leftists have used to disparage supposedly rich and selfish opponents of progressive revolutions since the French Revolution 200 years ago. Anglo-Americans, after years of politics in which the shades of difference between candidates are often subtle and in which basic liberties and property are not threatened, have a hard time understanding the enthusiasm of Americans with backgrounds in Latin America, where the differences between political creeds can be enormous and where liberties have frequently been in danger. In U.S. politics, that has led to a friction between the Cuban-Americans, heavily Republican for 30-some years since John F. Kennedy refused to send air cover to the Bay of Pigs invasion, and Miami's blacks and Jews, overwhelmingly Democratic since they first came to the city.

The 18th Congressional District of Florida is one of two Hispanic-majority districts in Dade County, about two-thirds Cuban-American, and usually heavily Republican. It includes the corridor along Southwest 8th Street—Calle Ocho—which was the original Cuban-American commercial strip when the first exiles from Castro's Communist regime came over in the early 1960s. Dade County's Latino population has increased from 50,000 in 1960 to 953,000 in 1990, and Calle Ocho remains a major Cuban-American thoroughfare, humming with commerce and activity. The 18th District spreads south and west toward Miami Airport and the suburb of Kendall. It stretches all the way down to Homestead, site of Hurricane Andrew's worst damage, and then extends back north, around the black-majority 17th, to include the neighborhoods of Coconut Grove and Miami Beach's South Beach, the hottest and hippest place in America at the moment, with old art deco hotels that used to house elderly retirees now a temporary home to the world's glitziest celebrities.

The representative from the 18th District is Ileana Ros-Lehtinen, the first Cuban-American elected to Congress. She was born in Cuba, became a teacher in Miami, then was the owner of a private school. She was elected to the Florida House in 1982, at 30, and to the state Senate in 1986. She ran for the House in the special election called after the death in May 1989 of Claude Pepper, one of the most enduring liberals in American politics, who served in the Senate from 1936–50 and in the House from 1962–89, was a great defender of Social Security and staunch opponent of Castro. The contest made news when Democratic nominee Gerald Richman proclaimed, "This isn't an Anglo seat, it isn't a Jewish seat, it isn't a Cuban-American seat. It's an American seat." Voting ran almost entirely on ethnic lines: exit polls showed that 96% of blacks and 88% of non-Hispanic whites voted for Richman, while 90% of Hispanics voted for Ros-Lehtinen. Hispanic turnout was 58%, compared to 42% for non-Hispanic whites, and Ros-Lehtinen won with 53%. She was reelected in 1990 by a 60%–40% margin. Redistricting has given her a much more solidly Cuban-American—and Republican—district, in which her only serious opposition could be in the Republican primary.

Ros-Lehtinen has a fairly moderate voting record, and often supports government spending. But one might add that free market economics has not had strong supporters in the Latin tradition until very recently. Despite the long-term local economic benefit, she opposed NAFTA (which extends only to Mexico), and spoke out against it. She harshly criticized the Clinton Administration for its decisions to route Cuban refugees to Guantanamo and then to force them back to Castro. But she also refused to sign the Contract with America in 1994, and in 1995 and 1996 was a harsh critic of Republican attempts to pass English-only legislation, to cut off welfare for legal immigrants, and to reduce the immigration quota for relatives of U.S. citizens. "I wish our party would be more aggressive in courting this Hispanic vote but because of welfare and immigration reform and English-only issues we are afraid to try and solicit their support," she said. She believes that with Republicans' pro-family, pro-business, anti-tax philosophy, Hispanic votes "could be a gold mine for us if we could shed our fears." But she had to watch glumly as Bill Clinton, with his support of Brothers to the Rescue and TV Marti, cut deeply into the Cuban-American vote which had gone over 80% for Ronald Reagan and George Bush.

Ros-Lehtinen was reelected herself without opposition in 1994 and 1996.

The People: Pop. 1990: 562,394; 17% age 65+; 29% White; 3% Black; 1% Asian; 67% Hispanic origin. Households: 50% married couple families; 20% married couple fams. w. children; 42% college educ.; median household income: $25,537; per capita income: $14,779; median gross rent: $460; median house value: $95,000.

1996 Presidential Vote

Clinton (D)	71,673	(43%)
Dole (R)	86,005	(52%)
Perot (I)	7,788	(5%)

1992 Presidential Vote

Bush (R)	93,870	(57%)
Clinton (D)	54,113	(33%)
Perot (I)	16,988	(10%)

Rep. Ileana Ros-Lehtinen (R)

Elected Aug. 1989; b. July 12, 1952, Havana, Cuba; home, Miami; Miami-Dade Comm. Col., A.A. 1972, FL Intl. U., B.S. 1975, M.S. 1986; Catholic; married (Dexter).

Career: Teacher, Principal & Owner, Eastern Academy Elem. Schl., 1978–85; FL House of Reps., 1982–86; FL Senate, 1986–89.

DC Office: 2240 RHOB 20515, 202-225-3931; Fax: 202-225-5620.
District Offices: Miami, 305-262-1800.

Committees: *Government Reform & Oversight* (8th of 24 R): District of Columbia; National Security, International Affairs & Criminal Justice. *International Relations* (9th of 26 R): International Economic Policy & Trade (Chmn.); International Operations & Human Rights; Western Hemisphere.

Group Ratings

	ADA	ACLU	AFS	LCV	CFA	CON	NFIB	COC	ACU	NTLC	CHC
1996	30	33	40	54	38	3	89	73	60	90	86
1995	15	—	—	19	38	56	—	88	76	—	—

National Journal Ratings

	1995 LIB — 1995 CONS			1996 LIB — 1996 CONS		
Economic	53%	—	46%	55%	—	45%
Social	38%	—	60%	52%	—	47%
Foreign	28%	—	65%	21%	—	72%

Key Votes of the 104th Congress

1. Reduce Medicare Growth $	Y	5. Flag Amendment	Y	9. Cuban Embargo	Y
2. Ovrd. Product Liab. Veto	Y	6. Drop EPA Limits	Y	10. Bar Bosnia Troop $	Y
3. Increase Min. Wage	Y	7. Repeal Assault-Weap. Ban	N	11. Cut Anti-Missile Defense	N
4. Welfare Reform	N	8. Ovrd. Part. Birth Veto	Y	12. Bar U.N. Uniforms	Y

Election Results

1996 general	Ileana Ros-Lehtinen (R) .... unopposed		($163,902)
1996 primary	Ileana Ros-Lehtinen (R) .... unopposed		
1994 general	Ileana Ros-Lehtinen (R) .... unopposed		($148,341)

NINETEENTH DISTRICT

When the first millionaires came to Palm Beach in the 1920s to winter in their new Palm Beach Addison Mizner pseudo-Mediterranean mansions and as the first real estate speculators arrived in Miami, there was virtually nothing man-made between these two cites. In 1920, Dade, Broward and Palm Beach Counties had some 66,000 residents. Now, more than 4 million are wedged almost entirely in the 5- to 15-mile strip between the Atlantic Ocean and the protected Everglades. The contrast between the 1920s and today's vast state is especially glaring in Boca Raton, where Mizner built what is now the Boca Raton Hotel and Club in 1926. Its azure-tiled fountains and red-tiled roofs, its pseudo-Moorish columns and pink stucco walls bespeak a vision of a holiday Florida, a bit mannered and antique to today's eye, but still exuberant. Today, Boca Raton has grown inland and is still solidly affluent, but also is more functional and workaday. Affluent retirees from the Northeast and Canada ("snowbirds") live in unadorned high-rise towers, enjoying the weather and the lack of a state income tax. But there are also major corporate headquarters here—W.R. Grace and an IBM-Intel joint venture: high-tech and big money at work in what used to be just paradise.

The 19th Congressional District of Florida includes former swampland and citrus groves in Palm Beach and Broward Counties. It does not touch the ocean at all, kept from it by the majority-black 23d District which collects the black neighborhoods just inland from the Intracoastal Waterway. It stretches from the edge of West Palm Beach, travels through the Lantana headquarters of the *National Enquirer* to Boynton Beach, Boca Raton, Deerfield Beach and Sunrise. With the growth in northern Broward and southern Palm Beach Counties during the 1970s and 1980s, the district's largest communities are no longer the beach towns, but new inland communities: Coral Springs, Margate, Tamarac. Liberal condominium associations, mobilized by "condo commandos," are political powers.

The congressman from the 19th is Robert Wexler, a Democrat first elected in 1996. Wexler grew up in Florida, and after law school went into practice in Boca Raton. In 1990, at 29, he was elected to the state Senate, where he sponsored tough prison sentencing guidelines, a cap on money taxpayers contributed to Everglades cleanup, and more funds for education. When eight-year incumbent Democrat Harry Johnston announced his retirement, decrying the rightward bent of the Republican 104th Congress, Wexler was one of three Democratic legislators who sprang into the race. It was a close three-way race in Broward County, but in Palm Beach County, which casts about two-thirds of the votes, Wexler led going away; overall he won 47% to 29% for state Senator Peter Weinstein and 21% for state Representative Benjamin Graber. The October 1 runoff was bitter. Wexler won 65%–35%, carrying Palm Beach County 83%–17% and losing Broward County 59%–41%; but afterwards Weinstein filed a $10 million defamation suit against him, due to an unflattering picture of Weinstein in a Wexler TV ad.

In the general Wexler outspent by 10–1 Republican talk show host Beverly Kennedy, who had run against Peter Deutsch in the neighboring 20th District in 1992 and 1994. Wexler called for more education spending, preserving Medicare, fighting crime, and protecting the environment and consumers. He called for a federal healthcare plan for children and for keeping affirmative action programs. Wexler won unsurprisingly, 66%–34%. "Americans want moderates. They want Republican moderates and Democratic moderates," he said after the election, though his proposals suggest he will be among the more liberal members of the House. He promised that his first piece of legislation would be to require Medicare to cover long-term health care. It sounds similar to a proposal advanced by the late Claude Pepper in a Democratic Congress with no success; it is unlikely to fare well in a Republican Congress now. Wexler has a safe seat, but in a Democratic Congress he would be considerably more effective.

The People: Pop. 1990: 562,978; 2% rural; 28% age 65+; 90% White; 3% Black; 1% Asian; 6% Hispanic origin. Households: 60% married couple families; 19% married couple fams. w. children; 50% college educ.; median household income: $34,396; per capita income: $20,029; median gross rent: $672; median house value: $107,100.

1996 Presidential Vote			**1992 Presidential Vote**		
Clinton (D)	189,336	(65%)	Clinton (D)	159,284	(54%)
Dole (R)	81,020	(28%)	Bush (R)	89,698	(30%)
Perot (I)	20,094	(7%)	Perot (I)	46,946	(16%)

Rep. Robert Wexler (D)

Elected 1996; b. Jan. 2, 1961, Queens, NY; home, Boca Raton; U. of FL, B.A. 1982; George Washington U., J.D. 1985; Jewish; married (Laurie).

Career: Practicing atty., 1985–96; FL Senate, 1990–96.

DC Office: 1609 LHOB 20515, 202-225-3001; Fax: 202-225-5974.

District Offices: Boca Raton, 561-988-6302; Margate, 954-972-6454.

Committees: *International Relations* (18th of 21 D): Asia & the Pacific; International Operations & Human Rights. *Judiciary* (14th of 15 D): Crime; Immigration & Claims.

Group Ratings and Key Votes: Newly Elected

Election Results

1996 general	Robert Wexler (D)	188,766	(66%)	($872,367)
	Beverly Kennedy (R)	99,101	(34%)	($121,117)
1996 runoff	Robert Wexler (D)	23,439	(65%)	
	Peter Weinstein (D)	12,580	(35%)	
1996 primary	Robert Wexler (D)	21,142	(47%)	
	Peter Weinstein (D)	13,073	(29%)	
	Benjamin Graber (D)	9,206	(21%)	
	Others	1,214	(3%)	
1994 general	Harry A. Johnston (D)	147,591	(66%)	($288,073)
	Peter J. Tsakanikas (R)	75,779	(34%)	($615,927)

TWENTIETH DISTRICT

Fort Lauderdale, back when Connie Francis first made it famous in the 1960 spring break movie *Where the Boys Are*, was just a small town with a strip of motels along the beach and some nice houses fronting canals. Now it is the center of a vast metropolitan area with its own major airport. Fort Lauderdale and Broward County had fewer than 100,000 people in 1950; by 1990 it was up to 1.3 million. The land from the strip of beach along the Atlantic Ocean west to the Sawgrass Expressway and the Everglades Wildlife Management Area has filled up with subdivisions, shopping centers, office complexes, warehouses and trucking terminals. Broward County is no longer just vacation country; it is also a major port and business center with high-tech companies and startups that have become national giants, including Blockbuster Video. As it has grown, the ethnic composition of Broward County has changed. In the 1950s, it was understood that Jews couldn't buy houses or rent hotel rooms this far north of Miami. Today, after three decades of Cubans moving into the Miami area and many Jews moving out, Broward County is the most heavily Jewish part of Florida, indeed one of the most heavily Jewish parts of the United States. Nearer the coast, especially in the huge high-rises of Hollywood and Hallandale, most of Broward's Jews are retirees from New York and other northeastern metro areas. But inland, in towns like Pembroke Pines and Davie, and Plantation and Sunrise that didn't exist a few decades ago, there are many young Jewish parents raising families in communities that pride themselves on fine schools and high property values.

The 20th Congressional District of Florida includes most of southern Broward County, though not the precincts nearest the beach, which are in the 22d and 23d Districts. The district also includes much of the unpopulated Everglades west of the Sawgrass, connecting Broward County with southern Dade County, the outlying parts of the Miami area, and the Florida Keys. At the end of the Overseas Highway is Key West, now a bustling tropical outpost that echoes its historic seafaring roots. This southern-most city in the continental United States was long accessible only by sea, and shipwrecks along the miles of coral reefs once gave its residents the highest per capita income in the nation. Key West has attracted famous residents—Ernest Hemingway, Tennessee Williams, Jimmy Buffett—and a large gay population, many living in restored "conch houses"—quaint clapboard bungalows. In 1982, some Key West citizens proclaimed the town as a separate Conch Republic. Politically, the Keys are Democratic; so is Broward County. The Miami area in between, with many Cuban-Americans, leans Republican.

The congressman from the 20th District is Peter Deutsch, a Democrat first elected in 1992. Deutsch grew up in New York, graduated from Yale Law School in June 1982, moved to Florida and by November was elected to the state legislature. Two years later, he was reelected with the largest vote in Florida and was unopposed in the next three elections. A *Miami Herald* reporter said Deutsch was "viewed by colleagues as bright but abrasive, and an expert at using procedural rules to advance or torpedo legislation." The newly drawn 20th District looked as if it were drawn for Deutsch. He became the first congressional candidate in Florida history to get on the ballot by petition, started off his campaign by loaning it $350,000, and allowed himself to be taped making fund-raising calls while in the presence of a reporter: "I raise money from special interests because they have a role to play in the process." He openly challenged incumbent and fellow Democrat and Foreign Affairs Committee chairman Dante Fascell, who, faced with the prospect of seeking reelection in a district dominated by unfamiliar Broward County, decided to retire after 38 years in the House. Deutsch won the primary nearly 2–1 and the general election 55%–39%.

Deutsch is pro-Israel, pro-choice and pro-universal health care. He is also a politician who does not waste time. On his first day in Congress, while most freshmen were attending swearing-in ceremonies, Deutsch held a press conference to announce he had introduced a bill to increase flood insurance benefits. He has a mostly liberal voting record—to the left of about 70% of the House and the right of about 30%. In the 1994 Republican House, Deutsch got the Commerce Committee seat that eluded him as a freshman. His chief achievements were passage of a law to protect the healthcare benefits of police officers and fire fighters injured in the line of duty, named after Plantation fire fighters James Alu and Jim O'Hara who were injured in a 1995 Plantation explosion, and a $1.5 million law enforcement training program on missing children, named after 9-year-old Jimmy Ryce of Miami Beach who was abducted and murdered.

Deutsch won reelection easily in 1994 and 1996. In 1996 he was the number one fundraiser in the Florida delegation: he raised over $1.1 million, but left most of it unspent. Evidently he was accumulating a war chest to run for Bob Graham's Senate seat if, as then widely expected, Graham ran for governor in 1998. But Republicans won control of both houses of the legislature on election day 1996 and six days later Graham announced he would run for reelection to the Senate. Deutsch, who appears to have no opening for the Senate, now has a large campaign treasury and little to do with it—though this talented political entrepreneur will surely think of something.

The People: Pop. 1990: 562,673; 9% rural; 16% age 65+; 82% White; 4% Black; 2% Asian; 12% Hispanic origin. Households: 59% married couple families; 24% married couple fams. w. children; 51% college educ.; median household income: $35,378; per capita income: $18,285; median gross rent: $624; median house value: $102,300.

1996 Presidential Vote

Clinton (D)	148,289	(59%)
Dole (R)	78,699	(31%)
Perot (I)	23,296	(9%)

1992 Presidential Vote

Clinton (D)	116,568	(47%)
Bush (R)	83,485	(33%)
Perot (I)	48,687	(20%)

Rep. Peter Deutsch (D)

Elected 1992; b. Apr. 1, 1957, New York, NY; home, Lauderhill; Swarthmore Col., B.A. 1979, Yale Law Schl., J.D. 1982; Jewish, married (Lori).

Career: FL House of Reps., 1982–92; Practicing atty., 1983–92.

DC Office: 204 CHOB 20515, 202-225-7931; Fax: 202-225-8456; e-mail: pdeutsch@hr.house.gov.

District Offices: Pembroke Pines, 954-437-3936.

Committees: *Commerce* (12th of 23 D): Energy & Power; Health & the Environment; Oversight & Investigations.

Group Ratings

	ADA	ACLU	AFS	LCV	CFA	CON	NFIB	COC	ACU	NTLC	CHC
1996	70	44	82	69	92	52	34	53	18	20	20
1995	85	—	—	50	100	31	—	42	28	—	—

National Journal Ratings

	1995 LIB	—	1995 CONS	1996 LIB	—	1996 CONS
Economic	68%	—	31%	64%	—	36%
Social	72%	—	27%	70%	—	29%
Foreign	73%	—	24%	79%	—	19%

Key Votes of the 104th Congress

1. Reduce Medicare Growth $	N	5. Flag Amendment	Y	9. Cuban Embargo	Y
2. Ovrd. Product Liab. Veto	N	6. Drop EPA Limits	Y	10. Bar Bosnia Troop $	N
3. Increase Min. Wage	Y	7. Repeal Assault-Weap. Ban	N	11. Cut Anti-Missile Defense	Y
4. Welfare Reform	Y	8. Ovrd. Part. Birth Veto	N	12. Bar U.N. Uniforms	*

Election Results

1996 general	Peter Deutsch (D)	159,256	(65%)	($435,604)
	Jim Jacobs (R)	85,777	(35%)	($29,928)
1996 primary	Peter Deutsch (D)	unopposed		
1994 general	Peter Deutsch (D)	114,615	(61%)	($1,011,936)
	Beverly Kennedy (R)	72,516	(39%)	($111,869)

TWENTY-FIRST DISTRICT

As the Cuban-American and other Latino populations of Miami and Dade County increased from 50,000 in 1960 to 953,000 in 1990, Cuban-American neighborhoods centered along 8th Street—Calle Ocho—expanded to the southwest, west and northwest. Development moved out in the 1960s and 1970s, filling up the land all the way to the Palmetto Expressway; in the 1980s, development reached outward to the Homestead Extension of Florida's Turnpike. The Cuban-Americans moved out and beyond Hialeah, whose now-closed race track was constructed in the 1920s beyond the edge of urban development, and which now has the highest percentage of Cuban-Americans in the Miami area. To the south, Westwood and Kendall Lakes—southwest suburbs of Miami with large Cuban-American populations—have been growing outwards into what once was swampland. Here, planned communities and subdivisions often have just one guarded entrance, with streets fanning out around lakes and golf courses.

The 21st Congressional District of Florida includes most of these new Cuban-American communities, taking in Hialeah and, just to the north, the planned community of Miami Lakes developed in 1962 by Senator Bob Graham and his father. To the south, it is centered on Kendall Lakes, and its boundaries go out to the Everglades Wildlife Management Area. The district is 70% Hispanic—almost all of it Cuban-American—and usually heavily Republican. Knowing first hand the evils of Communism, Cuban-Americans appreciate the blessings of free enterprise, cherish traditional moral values, and for years preferred Republicans to Democrats on all these counts. But in 1996 Bill Clinton cut into the Cuban vote by condemning the Cubans who shot down the Brothers to the Rescue pilots, supporting the Helms-Buron Act, and opposing cutoffs of welfare to legal aliens.

Lincoln Diaz-Balart is congressman from the 21st District, a Republican first elected when the district was created in 1992. Diaz-Balart was born in Cuba where his grandfather and father served in the Cuban Congress; the family left Cuba in 1959, shortly after Castro took over and their house was looted and burned. His aunt was the former wife of Fidel Castro and the mother of Castro's only recognized child. Lincoln Diaz-Balart started off as a poverty lawyer and a Democrat, but switched parties. He was elected to the state House as a Republican in 1986 with 78% of the vote and to the state Senate in 1989 with 82%, a year after his younger brother Mario was elected to the state House. In the legislature Lincoln Diaz-Balart sponsored laws toughening sentences for crimes against law enforcement officers, increasing penalties for drug money-laundering, providing low-interest home construction loans, creating a statewide substance abuse program, and requiring prospectuses of Florida firms issuing securities to disclose whether they do business with Cuba.

In 1989, Jorge Mas Canosa's Cuban American National Foundation convinced Diaz-Balart not to run against Ileana Ros-Lehtinen in the then-18th District special election to replace Claude Pepper. In 1992, the organization endorsed Diaz-Balart to run in the new 21st. But fellow Senator Javier Souto, also Cuban-born, opposed him in the primary, charging that Diaz-Balart was backed by wealthy contributors and was not a lifelong Republican. Diaz-Balart won 69%–31%.

Diaz-Balart has a voting record that is rather liberal on economics, veering far from market principles on issues from the minimum wage to NAFTA, though he has said he believes a hemispheric common market is inevitable. Naturally he has favored sanctions against Cuba, and when the Clinton Administration announced in May 1995 that it would no longer give automatic safe haven in the U.S. to Cuban refugees and instead would return them to Cuba—a reversal of previous U.S. policy—Diaz-Balart was one of two people arrested while protesting this policy switch. When Colorado Democrat David Skaggs tried to cut funding for Radio Marti and TV Marti broadcasts to Cuba, Diaz-Balart moved successfully to cut $23 million in funding for the National Institute of Standards and Technology in Skaggs's district.

When Republicans took over the House, Speaker Newt Gingrich named Diaz-Balart to the Rules Committee. But he has not always followed the party line. He was one of three Republican incumbents who refused to sign the Contract with America in 1994, and he voted against the Republican welfare bills because of their provisions denying welfare to legal immigrants. Republicans stuck to the provision, because it saves some $23 billion over six years. But Diaz-Balart in August 1996 pointed to the many elderly Cuban and other immigrants in south Florida who are dependent on SSI. "This is a disaster for my district. We're in crisis mode. I've been getting calls by the hour, I've been hearing stories from people in restaurants about the elderly, the disabled, who are going to be affected by this."

Diaz-Balart was reelected without opposition in 1994 and 1996.

The People: Pop. 1990: 562,402; 1% rural; 10% age 65+; 26% White; 3% Black; 1% Asian; 70% Hispanic origin. Households: 61% married couple families; 31% married couple fams. w. children; 45%

college educ.; median household income: $32,043; per capita income: $13,173; median gross rent: $592; median house value: $91,100.

1996 Presidential Vote			1992 Presidential Vote		
Dole (R)	82,384	(50%)	Bush (R)	85,292	(58%)
Clinton (D)	72,844	(45%)	Clinton (D)	45,778	(31%)
Perot (I)	7,901	(5%)	Perot (I)	15,545	(11%)

Rep. Lincoln Diaz-Balart (R)

Elected 1992; b. Aug. 13, 1954, Havana, Cuba; home, Miami; U. of S. FL, B.S. 1977, Case Western Reserve U., J.D. 1979; Catholic; married (Cristina).

Career: Practicing atty., 1979–92; Asst. St. Atty., 1983–84; FL House of Reps., 1986–89; FL Senate 1989–92.

DC Office: 404 CHOB 20515, 202-225-4211; Fax: 202-225-8576.

District Offices: Miami, 305-470-8555.

Committees: *Rules* (6th of 9 R): Rules & Organization of the House.

Group Ratings

	ADA	ACLU	AFS	LCV	CFA	CON	NFIB	COC	ACU	NTLC	CHC
1996	30	31	42	46	23	4	78	60	60	93	86
1995	20	—	—	31	38	38	—	79	72	—	—

National Journal Ratings

	1995 LIB — 1995 CONS			1996 LIB — 1996 CONS		
Economic	55%	—	44%	55%	—	45%
Social	38%	—	60%	49%	—	50%
Foreign	0%	—	85%	21%	—	72%

Key Votes of the 104th Congress

1. Reduce Medicare Growth $	Y	5. Flag Amendment	Y	9. Cuban Embargo	Y
2. Ovrd. Product Liab. Veto	N	6. Drop EPA Limits	Y	10. Bar Bosnia Troop $	Y
3. Increase Min. Wage	Y	7. Repeal Assault-Weap. Ban	Y	11. Cut Anti-Missile Defense	N
4. Welfare Reform	N	8. Ovrd. Part. Birth Veto	Y	12. Bar U.N. Uniforms	Y

Election Results

1996 general	Lincoln Diaz-Balart (R)	unopposed	($130,085)
1996 primary	Lincoln Diaz-Balart (R)	unopposed	
1994 general	Lincoln Diaz-Balart (R)	unopposed	($125,082)

TWENTY-SECOND DISTRICT

The barrier islands of Florida's Gold Coast have been developed in spasms of speculative frenzy, not just as vacation places and retirement homes but as embodiments of dreams and fantasies, bearing about the same relation to people's everyday lives as MTV videos. Consider Palm Beach, the great beach resort of the 1920s, where rich WASPs would leave their snow-covered Tudor or Georgian mansions and live in Addison Mizner's pseudo-Mediterranean confections. Consider also Miami Beach: the great resort of the 1950s, where Jews who had grown up amid prejudice and made their fortunes in ebullient postwar America vacationed in surrealistically curved and embellished skyscraper hotels—like Morris Lapidus's Fontainebleau and Eden Roc—giant variations on the themes set out in the much smaller Art Deco hotels at the beach's south end. Or think of the 1970s and 1980s, as the coastline of Dade, Broward and Palm Beach Counties were lined with one high-rise condo after another, a promised land for retirees, free from winter frost and state and city income taxes.

Almost all of this beach area is now gathered together into Florida's 22d Congressional District, a thin strip of land 91 miles long and never more than three miles wide, along the barrier islands from Juno Beach in the north through Palm Beach south to the northern half of Miami Beach. Palm Beach has been maintained as if under glass by great wealth, while the Fort Lauderdale beach has gone downhill and rich people have fled to gorgeous condos north of Palm Beach. Today's 22d District has the highest percentage of over-65 residents and quite possibly the highest percentage of high-rise dwellers, of any district in America. Politically, it is marginal territory, more Republican than not, but with many heavily Democratic condos.

The congressman from the 22d District is Clay Shaw, first elected in 1980, and now a senior Republican. Shaw grew up in Fort Lauderdale, practiced law and served as a judge and councilman; in 1975, at 36, he became the city's mayor. In 1980 he ran for the House, and had the good fortune of seeing the Democratic incumbent lose his primary to a Miami lawyer. He won the seat handily and held it despite the Fort Lauderdale area's Democratic tilt. For eight years he served on the Judiciary Committee, working on drug and crime bills; he backed the death penalty for major drug dealers, a federal drug czar, and the use of the military to interdict drug smuggling, which became law in 1988. In July 1988 he switched to Ways and Means. There he drafted an alternative to the statist ABC child care bill, first supported and then in 1989 opposed the Catastrophic Health Care Act, worked on the nanny tax bill in 1993–94 and opposed taxes on Social Security earnings. He has sponsored bills on Medical Savings Accounts and FDA reform to make drugs available to the terminally ill.

But Shaw has really made his mark as his party's leader in the House on the subject of welfare reform. In 1993 he introduced a bill to end the federal entitlement to welfare and take most recipients off the rolls and require them to work after two years. This attracted little notice, but it found its way into the Contract With America and became one of House Republicans' major priorities in 1995. Shaw's bills were passed twice in 1995 and vetoed twice in somewhat different form, and were not completely without strings: cash benefits were barred for mothers under 18 and the two-year-and-work rule could not be dropped. But the principle remained important. In early 1996 House Republicans hoped that Bob Dole could use the issue against Bill Clinton. By July 1996 they decided that Dole was likely to lose anyway, and so decided to pass welfare reform a third time, giving Dole an issue if Clinton vetoed it again and giving House Republicans an accomplishment if Clinton signed it. They had no idea what he would do, but in the end he signed, and a major change in American public policy was made.

Shaw's job now is to monitor how welfare reform works—or doesn't. He has said he is open to modifications, and that the federal government has some continuing responsibility for the "toxic waste dump of humanity" created in central cities by federal programs; but "I'm not going to tear out the heart and soul of the program which is the requirement of work after two years." At the same time he is on the lookout for ways in which states may shift responsibilities to the federal government; "we've got to be sure there's legitimacy to the way those things happen." On Hillary Rodham Clinton's possible role, he said, "She doesn't look like she is going to be on the bridge to the 21st century with us on welfare reform."

Shaw has not carried the 22d District, with its ardently liberal Democratic Jewish residents balanced off against its ardently conservative Republican gentiles, without serious competition. In 1992, after the district was created in its present form, he had well-financed opposition from Florida Senate President Gwen Margolis and won 52%–37%. In 1994 and 1996 he won by wider margins.

The People: Pop. 1990: 560,959; 31% age 65+; 83% White; 3% Black; 1% Asian; 13% Hispanic origin. Households: 44% married couple families; 11% married couple fams. w. children; 51% college educ.; median household income: $29,595; per capita income: $24,663; median gross rent: $545; median house value: $117,300.

1996 Presidential Vote

Clinton (D)	124,715	(54%)
Dole (R)	86,668	(38%)
Perot (I)	17,418	(8%)

1992 Presidential Vote

Clinton (D)	115,912	(45%)
Bush (R)	96,986	(38%)
Perot (I)	44,845	(17%)

Rep. E. Clay Shaw, Jr. (R)

Elected 1980; b. Apr. 19, 1939, Miami; home, Ft. Lauderdale; Stetson U., B.A. 1961, U. of AL, M.B.A. 1963, Stetson U., J.D. 1966; Catholic; married (Emilie).

Career: Practicing atty., 1966–68; Ft. Lauderdale Chf. City Prosecutor, 1968–69; Assoc. Municipal Judge, 1969–71; Ft. Lauderdale City Comm., 1971–73; Ft. Lauderdale Vice Mayor, 1973–75, Mayor, 1975–80.

DC Office: 2408 RHOB 20515, 202-225-3026; Fax: 202-225-8398.

District Offices: Ft. Lauderdale, 954-522-1800.

Committees: *Ways & Means* (4th of 23 R): Human Resources (Chmn.); Trade.

Group Ratings

	ADA	ACLU	AFS	LCV	CFA	CON	NFIB	COC	ACU	NTLC	CHC
1996	10	0	8	23	46	45	95	94	95	93	80
1995	15	—	—	13	23	56	—	96	68	—	—

National Journal Ratings

	1995 LIB — 1995 CONS			1996 LIB — 1996 CONS		
Economic	26%	—	67%	30%	—	68%
Social	48%	—	51%	45%	—	54%
Foreign	28%	—	65%	21%	—	72%

Key Votes of the 104th Congress

1. Reduce Medicare Growth $	Y	5. Flag Amendment	Y	9. Cuban Embargo	Y
2. Ovrd. Product Liab. Veto	Y	6. Drop EPA Limits	Y	10. Bar Bosnia Troop $	Y
3. Increase Min. Wage	Y	7. Repeal Assault-Weap. Ban	*	11. Cut Anti-Missile Defense	N
4. Welfare Reform	Y	8. Ovrd. Part. Birth Veto	Y	12. Bar U.N. Uniforms	Y

Election Results

1996 general	E. Clay Shaw, Jr. (R)	137,098	(62%)	($548,109)
	Kenneth D. Cooper (D)	84,517	(38%)	($85,040)
1996 primary	E. Clay Shaw, Jr. (R)	unopposed		
1994 general	E. Clay Shaw, Jr. (R)	119,690	(63%)	($808,984)
	Hermine L. Wiener (D)	69,215	(37%)	($522,269)

TWENTY-THIRD DISTRICT

In the morning shadow of the high-rise condominiums that line the Atlantic Ocean from Palm Beach to Miami Beach, behind the waterways that separate the barrier islands from the mainland, usually a few blocks off the coast and often off old U.S. 1, are the black neighborhoods of South Florida's Gold Coast. They are gatherings of older stucco homes and commercial storefronts, ranging from enclaves of upper-middle-class residents to rundown slums. These are neighborhoods overlooked by most tourists and feared by most local residents.

The 23d Congressional District of Florida, created by the May 1992 court redistricting, gathers together many of these black neighborhoods in a constituency that is geographically grotesque but ethnically defined. A little more than half its residents live in Broward County, with a little more than onc-third living in Palm Beach County and the rest scattered—some in north Dade County, more in a geographically expansive but lightly populated segment that includes migrant worker camps around Lake Okeechobee and the old black neighborhood of Fort Pierce, a small city 120 miles north of Miami.

The congressman from the 23d District is Alcee Hastings, a former federal judge and the only member of the House previously impeached and removed from the bench by Congress. Hastings is articulate and charming, the son of a hotel maid, who rose to an appointment as a federal judge by President Carter. He was impeached by the House of Representatives by a vote of 426–3 in 1988 and convicted and removed from office by the Senate by a vote of 69–26. The impeachment arose from allegations that Hastings conspired with a friend to accept $150,000 for giving two convicted swindlers a break in sentencing. Hastings was acquitted in a criminal trial in 1983, but the friend was convicted. In the House the case for impeachment was made by John Conyers, senior member of the Congressional Black Caucus. Removed from the bench, Hastings was unapologetic. In 1990, he ran an abortive campaign for governor, then lost in the primary for Florida secretary of state. When the 23d District was created, he sprang into that race.

This is a heavily Democratic district, and the primary and runoff were decisive. In the primary Hastings, with 28%, barely edged out another black candidate who had 27%; the leader was Palm Beach County legislator Lois Frankel. In the runoff Hastings was helped by a ruling by federal Judge Stanley Sporkin that his removal from office was invalid since the charges were not heard by the full Senate; the Supreme Court ruled to the contrary in a case involving another federal judge in January 1993, but by that time, Hastings was in Congress. Frankel blasted Hastings for his record, and he responded "The bitch is a racist," and won the runoff 58%–42%, with voting closely following racial lines. He won the general election 59%–31%.

As a judge, Hastings had sometimes acted like a politician, called President Reagan a racist and a liar; as a congressman, he has acted more like a judge, treating colleagues pleasantly and respectfully. "I'm not a vengeful person." he said in 1993. "I get on with life. I didn't enter here with my arms and my elbows flying. I came here to work . . . I've met with nothing but pleasant exchanges." He had amiable relations with Conyers and with John Bryant, who conducted his prosecution in the Senate. He has compiled a very liberal voting record on most issues except Cuba. He has worked to improve black-Jewish relations. He became vice chairman of the Congressional Black Caucus in 1993, but in 1994 lost a run for the chair to Donald Payne 23–15. He was elected to the Democratic Steering and Policy Committee, and as a member of the International Relations Committee traveled to Haiti, Bosnia, and Israel. There is still some firebrand in him, though. He was arrested in 1994 while protesting the Clinton Administration's repatriation of Haitian refugees.

Hastings has not had serious competition in the 23d District since 1992. In 1996 he said he wanted to serve three more terms, then retire to teach.

The People: Pop. 1990: 563,645; 5% rural; 13% age 65+; 39% White; 50% Black; 1% Asian; 9% Hispanic origin. Households: 43% married couple families; 19% married couple fams. w. children; 32%

college educ.; median household income: $23,039; per capita income: $10,511; median gross rent: $486; median house value: $67,200.

1996 Presidential Vote

Clinton (D)	107,884	(74%)
Dole (R)	27,531	(19%)
Perot (I)	9,193	(6%)

1992 Presidential Vote

Clinton (D)	94,873	(62%)
Bush (R)	35,265	(23%)
Perot (I)	22,084	(14%)

Rep. Alcee L. Hastings (D)

Elected 1992; b. Sept. 5, 1936, Altamonte Springs; home, Miramar; Fisk U., B.A. 1958, Howard U., 1958–60, FL A&M, J.D. 1963; Methodist; divorced.

Career: Practicing atty., 1964–77; Broward Cnty. Circuit Court Judge, 1977–79; Federal Judge, U.S. District Court, 1979–89.

DC Office: 1039 LHOB 20515, 202-225-1313; Fax: 202-226-0690; e-mail: hastings@hr.house.gov.

District Offices: Ft. Lauderdale, 954-733-2800.

Committees: *International Relations* (13th of 21 D): Africa; Asia & the Pacific. *Science* (10th of 21 D): Energy & Environment; Space & Aeronautics.

Group Ratings

	ADA	ACLU	AFS	LCV	CFA	CON	NFIB	COC	ACU	NTLC	CHC
1996	95	87	100	69	92	55	16	20	0	3	0
1995	95	—	—	94	100	0	—	8	4	—	—

National Journal Ratings

	1995 LIB — 1995 CONS			1996 LIB — 1996 CONS		
Economic	94%	—	0%	89%	—	0%
Social	88%	—	0%	82%	—	17%
Foreign	78%	—	21%	73%	—	26%

Key Votes of the 104th Congress

1. Reduce Medicare Growth $	N	5. Flag Amendment	N	9. Cuban Embargo	*
2. Ovrd. Product Liab. Veto	N	6. Drop EPA Limits	Y	10. Bar Bosnia Troop $	N
3. Increase Min. Wage	Y	7. Repeal Assault-Weap. Ban	N	11. Cut Anti-Missile Defense	Y
4. Welfare Reform	N	8. Ovrd. Part. Birth Veto	N	12. Bar U.N. Uniforms	N

Election Results

1996 general	Alcee L. Hastings (D)	102,161	(73%)	($276,708)
	Robert Paul Brown (R)	36,907	(27%)	($13,417)
1996 primary	Alcee L. Hastings (D)	unopposed		
1994 general	Alcee L. Hastings (D)	unopposed		($217,742)

GEORGIA

Without much warning or many predictions, Georgia has emerged as the boom state of the 1990s—in population, in economy, and in spirit. In 1990 Georgia was the 11th largest state, with 6.4 million people; by 1996 it was just under 7.4 million, with the fastest growth rate east of the Rockies, and had passed fast-growing North Carolina to be the tenth largest state: the first time Georgia has been among the top 10 since the 1850 Census. Almost all this growth has come in the booming Atlanta metropolitan area, not in the core city, but amid the hills of suburban counties for almost 100 miles around, many of them until recently rural. Atlanta was long the capital of the South—spiritually, financially, and in its central role in the civil rights movement. But now it has become a world city, a status suitably memorialized when it hosted the 1996 Olympics and re-emphasized every day as travelers all over the world watch the news from the CNN Broadcast Center next door to the World Congress Center.

Atlanta's growth is not immediately apparent to the busy traveler: on the approach to Hartsfield Airport, one of the busiest in the world, you see trees and muddy fields, and on the traffic-filled Route 400 toll road in the booming northern suburbs you see what looks like forest all around. There is still something messy and not yet finished about the urban landscapes of greater Atlanta; the landscape has what author John Brinckerhoff Jackson called the disorderliness characteristic of the South, and even the gleaming malls and office towers are never out of sight of kudzu vines and muddy creeks.

If Atlanta's rise to world eminence was not widely foreseen, its rise as the capital of the South was far from inevitable. It was, after all, only a small railroad crossroads when it was burned by General William Tecumseh Sherman's troops as they began their "march to the sea." Richmond, Charleston, and New Orleans all had stronger claims to being the central focus of the South a century ago. But in the 20th Century two figures imprinted Atlanta on the national imagination. One was Margaret Mitchell, whose 1936 novel *Gone with the Wind* inspired the 1939 movie in which Tara was improbably sited near a burning Atlanta. The other was Martin Luther King, Jr., reared in Atlanta and based there during most of his career, as a leader and ultimately the national symbol of the civil rights revolution that changed the South and the nation. Linking the two was Atlanta's business community, notably Robert Woodruff, who headed Coca-Cola from 1932–60 and made Coke a worldwide enterprise. Perhaps aware that a world company could not indefinitely be associated with racial segregation, Woodruff and William Hartsfield, mayor from 1937–61, cooperated with blacks and promoted Atlanta as "the city too busy to hate." Hartsfield's successor Ivan Allen, elected in 1961 and 1965, supported the Civil Rights Act of 1964, as Peachtree Center and the first atriumed Hyatt Regency were going up in downtown Atlanta.

This new Atlanta was growing up amid a mostly rural, deeply segregationist Georgia that as late as 1960 cast the second highest Democratic percentage of any state for president: memories of General Sherman were still strong. Political contests typically matched Atlanta-supported moderates against rural-supported segregationists, and the latter invariably won: Georgia's electoral votes were cast for Barry Goldwater in 1964 and George Wallace in 1968. Then came change in the person of Jimmy Carter, former nuclear submarine officer and one-term state Senator, who ran and was elected governor in 1970 with a rural base but also with conspicuous black support. On taking office he proclaimed a reconciliation of the races and installed a portrait of Martin Luther King Jr. in the Capitol. Carter thus became one of the first politicians from the rural South to celebrate and honor the civil rights revolution, and set himself on the road to being elected President in 1976. Today he remains a prominent figure in Atlanta, promoting Habitat for Humanity, and around the world, monitoring elections and negotiating

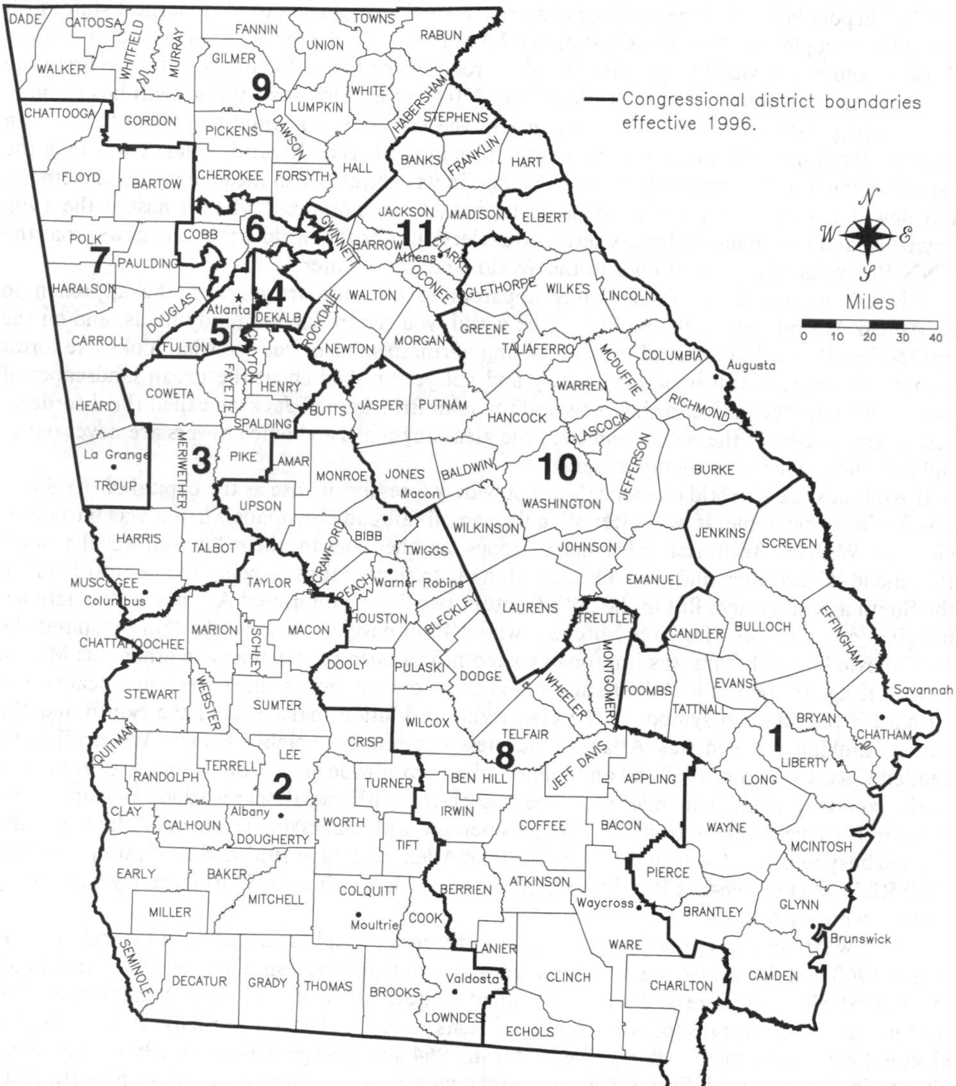
Congressional district boundaries effective 1996.
N
W
E
S
Miles
0 10 20 30 40
1
2
3
4
5
6
7
8
9
10
11
DADE
CATOOSA
WHITFIELD
MURRAY
FANNIN
TOWNS
RABUN
UNION
GILMER
WALKER
WHITE
HABERSHAM
LUMPKIN
STEPHENS
CHATTOOGA
GORDON
PICKENS
DAWSON
BANKS
FRANKLIN
HART
HALL
FLOYD
BARTOW
CHEROKEE
FORSYTH
JACKSON
MADISON
ELBERT
GWINNETT
COBB
BARROW
Athens
CLARKE
POLK
PAULDING
OCONEE
OGLETHORPE
WILKES
LINCOLN
HARALSON
Atlanta
DEKALB
WALTON
DOUGLAS
ROCKDALE
GREENE
CARROLL
FULTON
CLAYTON
NEWTON
MORGAN
TALIAFERRO
MCDUFFIE
COLUMBIA
Augusta
FAYETTE
HENRY
WARREN
COWETA
RICHMOND
HEARD
BUTTS
JASPER
PUTNAM
SPALDING
HANCOCK
GLASCOCK
MERIWETHER
La Grange
PIKE
LAMAR
MONROE
JONES
BALDWIN
JEFFERSON
BURKE
TROUP
Macon
UPSON
WASHINGTON
HARRIS
TALBOT
CRAWFORD
BIBB
WILKINSON
JENKINS
SCREVEN
TWIGGS
JOHNSON
MUSCOGEE
Columbus
TAYLOR
PEACH
Warner Robins
EMANUEL
EFFINGHAM
LAURENS
TREUTLEN
BLECKLEY
HOUSTON
CANDLER
BULLOCH
MARION
MACON
SCHLEY
CHATTAHOOCHEE
MONTGOMERY
STEWART
WEBSTER
DOOLY
PULASKI
DODGE
WHEELER
TOOMBS
EVANS
Savannah
TATTNALL
SUMTER
WILCOX
BRYAN
CHATHAM
QUITMAN
TELFAIR
CRISP
LEE
LIBERTY
JEFF DAVIS
TERRELL
RANDOLPH
TURNER
BEN HILL
APPLING
LONG
CLAY
Albany
CALHOUN
IRWIN
WORTH
COFFEE
BACON
WAYNE
DOUGHERTY
TIFT
MCINTOSH
EARLY
BAKER
PIERCE
ATKINSON
COLQUITT
BERRIEN
MITCHELL
Waycross
GLYNN
MILLER
BRANTLEY
Moultrie
COOK
Brunswick
WARE
LANIER
SEMINOLE
DECATUR
GRADY
THOMAS
BROOKS
Valdosta
CLINCH
CHARLTON
CAMDEN
LOWNDES
ECHOLS

conflict resolution in places from Korea to Haiti. Without exactly saying so, Georgia has developed what Charles Moskos and John Sibley Butler in their book on races in the Army, *All We Can Be*, call an Anglo-African culture, a merger of traditions that were long associated intimately in private life but rigidly and even violently separated in public. This is the dominant culture of the Army, Moskos and Butler argue, and increasingly of the nation; and if they are not yet right about the nation, they surely are about Georgia.

Over the past 20 years Georgia has developed new political patterns, which arguably have been echoed in the country as a whole. The Democratic Party has lost its easy natural majority, and depends increasingly on the black votes. But the party is still capable of winning here: If Bill Clinton lost Georgia to Bob Dole 47%–46% in 1996, he won it over George Bush 43.5%–42.9% in 1992. All of Georgia's top three officeholders won their posts by the narrowest of margins: Democratic Governor Zell Miller won a second term in 1994 by 51%–49%; Republican Senator Paul Coverdell was elected 51%–49% in a November 24, 1992, runoff; Democratic Senator Max Cleland won 49%–48% in 1996 over Guy Millner, the same Republican who lost to Zell Miller. Had Georgia's runoff law not been repealed by the Democratic legislature, Millner might have overtaken Cleland in a second contest as Coverdell did incumbent Wyche Fowler four years earlier.

At other levels Georgia has been moving strongly toward the Republicans. Its best-known downballot statewide official is former Attorney General Michael Bowers, who switched to the Republican Party and won overwhelmingly in 1994. Bowers announced his retirement in early May, presumably to prepare for a run for governor in 1998; Bowers makes a strong candidate and is already considered to be a front runner in the race. Republicans also have made some big gains in Georgia's legislature, long run by Democratic Speaker Thomas Murphy. The Democrats' lead in the House was reduced from 114–66 in 1994 to 106–74 in 1996, and they picked up a seat in the Senate. The transformation has already taken place in the state's U.S. House delegation. Going into the 1992 election, Georgia's House delegation consisted of eight white Democrats, one black Democrat and one Republican, Newt Gingrich. By mid-1995 Georgia was represented by zero white Democrats (after the last one switched parties), three black Democrats and eight Republicans, including the Speaker of the House; Republicans received 53% of the vote for the House in 1996, even while leaving one district uncontested.

What are the lines of division? The central city of Atlanta and suburban areas of south Fulton and DeKalb Counties are black and heavily Democratic; there are similar Democratic cores in the state's smaller cities, some economically thriving, some not. But the suburbs of Atlanta, plus the city's Buckhead and Northside neighborhoods, are heavily Republican; a pattern replicated around well-off growing cities up and down the interstates. It is no good to ascribe this to some lingering segregationist sentiment; many of these neighborhoods were empty land when Jimmy Carter was elected governor, and support for reimposing legal segregation is all but extinct; the sentiment if anything is to get rid of what some see as the discrimination inherent in racial setaside and quota programs. All around the state there are pockets of white areas that vote Democratic—university precincts, farming communities, some textile mill towns—and enough white Democrats scattered here and there to keep statewide elections close.

Governor. Zell Miller in 1998 completes his eighth year as governor and his 28th year in public office. He grew up in the mountains of north Georgia in the town of Young Harris (of which his mother was mayor), and joined the Marines after high school; his 1997 book is titled *Corps Values: Everything You Need to Know, I Learned in the Marines*. He returned home, went back to school, and was elected to the Georgia Senate in 1960, at 28; he worked for Lester Maddox in his last two years as governor, and ran the state Democratic Party when Jimmy Carter was governor. Miller was elected lieutenant governor in 1974 and held the office, which carries some power in Georgia, for 16 years. In 1990 he finally ran for governor. In the Democratic primary he beat Andrew Young, longtime Atlanta mayor, congressman and ambassador to the United Nations, by 62%–38%. In the general he beat Republican Johnny Isakson 53%–45%.

Miller's major issue in 1990 was a state lottery, with funds dedicated to education. He can reasonably claim to have kept his promise, and then some. The lottery passed, and Miller dedicated the proceeds to specific education programs. One was expanding pre-kindergarten for four-year-olds and making it available to any parent in the state; Georgia now claims the nation's highest percentage of four-year-olds in pre-K. Another was funding computers and high-tech learning aids. His most original program was his HOPE (Helping Outstanding Pupils Educationally) Scholarship Program, which as expanded up through 1996 provides free tuition at any eligible Georgia college, private or public, to freshmen, regardless of family income, who maintain B averages in high school. Further HOPE money is available to those who get B averages in college or study to be teachers. By 1996, 97% of instate freshmen at the University of Georgia and Georgia Tech were HOPE scholars. Miller also sponsored a charter schools program.

Miller took tough stances on spending, taxes, and crime. Coming into office he cut $700 million in spending and in 1996 got the legislature to cut $600 million in taxes, phasing out the sales tax on groceries and zeroing out the business tax on intangibles. On crime, he produced boot camps for troubled youth and, inspired by the drive for three-strikes-and-you're-out laws in other states, passed two-strikes-and-you're-out. He also got the legislature to pass a victims' bill of rights. He took on lost causes as well: in 1993, looking ahead to the Olympics, he tried to get the legislature to remove the Confederate stars and bars from the Georgia flag, but the legislature refused.

Miller speaks in populist tones that come naturally in north Georgia but may also have been inspired by—or helped inspire—his 1990 consultant James Carville. Perhaps prodded by Carville, Miller became an early backer of Bill Clinton for president, and got the 1992 Georgia primary rescheduled from Super Tuesday to a week earlier, March 3; Clinton won a big victory here, getting Paul Tsongas and Bob Kerrey to use up their resources. Miller was one of three keynoters at the 1992 Democratic National Convention and helped Clinton carry, narrowly, Georgia's 13 electoral votes that November. But Miller's association with Clinton and his earlier vow to serve just one term hurt him when he ran for reelection in 1994. The Republican nominee, Guy Millner, founder of the Norrell temporary employee firm, spent some of his estimated $84 million on the campaign and won 48% in the first primary and 59% in the runoff. In the general, Millner attacked Miller for paroling too many prisoners, called for tough welfare reform, and charged that Miller's workfare rules exempted 86% of eligibles. Miller criticized Millner for having mutual fund investments in casinos while opposing the state lottery. Miller won, 51%–49%. As if in response, he accelerated HOPE and advanced tough positions on crime and welfare in his second term. In early 1997 he opposed a gas tax increase and proposed a four-year time limit on welfare. Interestingly, Miller appointed Johnny Isakson, his former gubernatorial opponent, to be chairman of the State Board of Education in 1996.

In December 1996 Miller told a radio audience, "I will never be a candidate ever again, and we might as well go further and say that I will not take a job or an appointment in Washington." He plans to teach at Emory University near Atlanta and at Young Harris College. There should be serious competition to succeed him. The best known Republican candidates are former Attorney General Michael Bowers, a party-switcher, and Millner, who narrowly lost the 1996 Senate race. Other possibilities include Fulton County Commission Chairman Mitch Skandalakis and Congressmen Saxby Chambliss and Charlie Norwood. Leading Democratic candidates include Lieutenant Governor Pierre Howard and state Representative and 1990 gubernatorial candidate Roy Barnes.

Senior Senator. Georgia's senior Senator, Paul Coverdell, won his seat by the narrowest margin and in the last election of 1992, and quickly moved to the leading edge of political change. Coverdell grew up in Kansas City and went to University of Missouri journalism school, then served in the Army in Okinawa, Taiwan and Korea. In 1960, at 21, he started working in his parents' insurance marketing business in Atlanta. In 1970, when the Republican Party seemed to be rising in the South, he was elected to the state Senate; in 1974, when the Republican rise seemed stalled, he became minority leader (of 5 Republicans versus 51 Democrats). He was Republican state chairman in the mid-1980s, supported George Bush in 1988 and served as Peace Corps Director from 1989–91, leading the Peace Corps into Eastern Europe and Russia.

In 1992 Coverdell ran for the Senate, and battled through four elections before winning by barely more than 1%. In the July primary he ran first, with former U.S. Attorney and now 7th District Congressman Bob Barr just ahead of Waycross Mayor John Knox. In the August runoff, Coverdell beat Barr by 1,500 votes. In the general he faced incumbent Wyche Fowler, a politically savvy liberal who had represented the black-majority 5th District and then won statewide over Republican incumbent Mack Mattingly in 1986. Fowler had beaten Coverdell once before—in a 1977 House special election in which Fowler had 40%, John Lewis, 29%, and Coverdell, 22%. Coverdell attacked Fowler in the Senate race for opposing the Gulf War, supporting defense cuts, backing the congressional pay raise and defending the House bank. Coverdell's most memorable tactic was his "grandmother" ad showing 73-year-old Margie Goode Lopp of Cuthbert, Georgia, sitting on a swing and singing a jingle she composed after being repelled by Fowler's ads: "Let's put Paul Coverdell in the Senate and put Wyche Fowler out," it began. Fowler led in November, but only by 49%–48%, less than the absolute majority then required by Georgia law; so there was a runoff November 24. Bill Clinton and Al Gore campaigned for Fowler; Coverdell got enthusiastic support from national and local Republicans, the Libertarian candidate who had deadlocked the first race, the Georgia Ross Perot organization, from elite suburban Republicans who liked his pro-choice stand on abortion and from the Christian Coalition pleased by his pledge to vote against the federal Freedom of Choice Act. Both national parties poured $1 million of soft money into the race, but Coverdell had the momentum. The runoff was the fourth straight time in which Georgia was almost evenly split on this Senate seat, as it was in the 1992 presidential race—and turned out be in the 1994 gubernatorial and 1996 Senate races. This time the Republican won, 51%–49%. Coverdell carried the suburban ring around Atlanta and also most of rural north Georgia and the rural counties in the southeast—economically booming areas like next-door South Carolina. He lost in the central and southwest parts of the state, economically ailing like Alabama.

In the Senate Coverdell has had a strong conservative voting record and become part of the Republican leadership. "The American people," he said, "want the federal government to be their partner and not their boss." He supported the balanced budget amendment and line-item veto; inspired by the Clinton budget and tax package, he sponsored a constitutional amendment to ban retroactive tax increases. He opposed the Clinton healthcare plan and worked to include medical savings accounts in the 1996 healthcare portability law. He successfully stopped the Postal Service from "bullying" people with inspection audits. He led the fight for release of Clinton healthcare task force documents. He was early in opposition to U.S. troops serving under United Nations command and supported the fall 1996 air strikes against Iraq. Coverdell became a deputy whip in December 1994 and was elected Republican Conference secretary, number four in the leadership, by 41–14 over Conrad Burns in December 1996. Coverdell's major miscue was his early support for Phil Gramm for president in 1996; by the time Georgia voted, Gramm was out and Coverdell endorsed Bob Dole.

Much of Coverdell's work in the Senate has revolved around drugs and peanuts (he is against the former and for the latter). Starting in 1995 he used his chairmanship of the Western Hemisphere Subcommittee on Foreign Relations to work against imports of illegal drugs. He worked successfully with Joseph Biden to get tough penalties for felons who use drugs, such as the so-called date rape drug Rohypnol, to commit crimes. He worked to amend the 1996 Immigration Act to get more money to pay for tougher sentences for drug smugglers. He also amended the immigration bill to allow deportation of immigrants who commit crimes of domestic violence, stalking, or rape. He was part of the successful move to preserve peanut programs in the 1996 Freedom to Farm Act, and in 1997 became chairman of the Agriculture Committee's Marketing, Inspection and Product Promotion Subcommittee, which will allow him to protect peanut programs. Coverdell also chairs the Senate Republican Education Task

Force; he introduced a school choice bill in 1997 to allow parents of kids in high-violence schools to send them elsewhere. He works on local projects as well: $7 million for the Sidney Lanier Bridge in Brunswick; a $2.5 million beach project on Tybee Island, and more than $16 million in funding of Savannah and Brunswick harbors.

Will Coverdell win reelection in 1998? The close margin in both of Georgia's last two Senate races makes prediction risky. But he was surely glad to hear in December 1996 that Governor Zell Miller, Georgia's strongest Democrat, will not run for the seat. And if Coverdell is not a household word, he has shown the political skills to wage an aggressive campaign against long odds, and in a state which seems increasingly to hew to his views.

Junior Senator. Max Cleland was first elected in 1996, after a long career in public life and having overcome grievous injuries sustained during the Vietnam War. Cleland grew up in Lithonia, now a suburb in DeKalb County but then a country town that could have been hundreds of miles from Atlanta. After college and a master's degree in American History at Emory, he volunteered for the Army and went to Vietnam in 1967, at 25; when he tried to pick up a loose grenade it exploded and he lost both legs and one arm. In 1970 Cleland was elected to the Georgia Senate, where he wrote a law to make public facilities accessible to the handicapped. In 1977 Jimmy Carter appointed him head of the Veterans' Administration. In 1982 he was elected Georgia secretary of state, and was reelected by wide margins in 1986, 1990, and 1994. In October 1995, Senator Sam Nunn surprised Georgians when he announced he would retire from the Senate in 1996, at 58, after 24 years there and with every prospect of reelection; Nunn's moderate voting record, his recognition as a military expert, and his slot as ranking Democrat on the Armed Services Committee made him unbeatable. Cleland promptly announced he would run for the seat and had no primary opposition.

There was plenty of fight on the Republican side: just the opposite of the old days when Democrats had raucous primary fights and Republicans considered themselves lucky to have one plausible candidate. Nearly as many votes were cast in the Republican primary (446,000) as the Democratic (517,000). The leading Republican candidates were Guy Millner, the 1994 gubernatorial nominee whose fortune from the Norrell temporary employee firm is estimated at $100 million; Johnny Isakson, 1990 gubernatorial nominee and state Senator for 17 years; and Clint Day, scion of the Days Inn family. Day ran as a Christian conservative, Millner as a conservative on most issues, and Isakson took a chance with ads on abortion: "I trust my wife, my daughter and the women of Georgia to make the right choice." Millner, to show he was closer to people, took a 13-day bus tour through 87 counties. The election was further complicated by the Olympics, which started 10 days after the July 9 primary and ended just two days before the August 6 runoff. In the primary Millner led with 42%, to 35% for Isakson and 19% for Day. Isakson carried the Atlanta area narrowly, where about two-thirds of the votes were cast. Millner won the August 6 runoff 53%–47%.

Cleland's campaign was mostly positive, making folksy, self-deprecating speeches, running soft-focus positive ads showing him shaving, putting on a tie, driving, saying, "I was raised to believe you can't expect help if you don't help yourself." His issue stands were mostly conservative: for a balanced budget amendment, term limits, the 1996 welfare reform bill, the death penalty for drug dealers, victims' rights, a constitutional amendment allowing limits on campaign spending. Millner spent over $9 million altogether. He ran tough ads charging that Cleland sought parole for a killer with a politically connected father who, when released, committed another murder, and criticizing Cleland for a $300,000 settlement paid to a worker in his office when she blew the whistle on his use of state computers for political purposes. Cleland attacked Millner for his membership in a discriminatory country club. Millner attacked Cleland for ducking debates and said he was politically close to Ted Kennedy. The result was exceedingly close. Cleland won 49%–48%; Millner had a microscopic edge in metro Atlanta and ran well in north Georgia, but he carried few counties south of Atlanta. These percentages were identical to four years before, when Democrat Wyche Fowler led Republican Paul Coverdell, triggering a runoff three weeks later which Coverdell won. But in the meantime, the legislature, led by Speaker Tom Murphy, repealed the runoff law, and Millner did not have a second chance.

Cleland now is one of no more than half a dozen moderate southern Democratic senators remaining. He serves on the Armed Services and Governmental Affairs Committees, where he will likely pursue a moderate agenda and, as did his predecessor, will watch over the interests of Georgia's military bases.

Presidential politics. Georgia used to be an outlier in presidential politics—the second most Democratic state in 1960, for Barry Goldwater in 1964 and George Wallace in 1968, heavily Republican in 1972, strongly for native son Jimmy Carter in 1976 and 1980. In the 1990s it has emerged as one of the prime marginal states—for Bill Clinton by 13,000 votes in 1992, for Bob Dole by 27,000 votes in 1996. With many new voters every cycle, Georgia is likely to remain seriously contested and unpredictable.

Georgia's 1992 presidential primary was scheduled one week before Super Tuesday at the insistence of Governor Zell Miller, who wanted to help Bill Clinton, and did: Clinton won smartly to balance losses in Maryland and Colorado the same day. George Bush's 64%–36% victory here over Pat Buchanan showed the Buchanan Brigades were not about to overrun the South. Bob Dole similarly defeated Buchanan 41%–29%. Turnout here has been a gauge of changing partisan balance: Republican turnout increased from 200,000 in 1980 to 400,000 in 1988, 454,000 in 1992 and 561,000 in 1996. Democratic primary turnout fell from 684,000 in 1984 to 612,000 in 1988 and 454,600 in 1992; the 1996 primary was uncontested.

Congressional districting. Georgia is one of three southern states which were forced by the Supreme Court to redraw its congressional districts for 1996. Its 1992 redistricting plan, manufactured by Speaker Tom Murphy, misfired on both its major aims. Murphy had hoped to end the career of Newt Gingrich, who first ran for Congress from Carrollton, 12 miles from Murphy's home in Bremen. But Gingrich was reelected, and Democrats lost ground: they had a 9–1 edge in the delegation when Murphy's plan was drawn but now the delegation is 8–3 Republican. The other purpose, the creation of three black-majority districts, was foisted on the legislature by the Bush Justice Department. But the Supreme Court in June 1995 ruled the convoluted 11th District, which extended from Atlanta to Savannah, was a "racial gerrymander" and violated the Constitution; the legislature failed to produce a new plan in a five-week special session and so a three-judge federal court drew new lines in December 1995. They proved cleaner, following county lines everywhere outside the Atlanta area. Congresswoman Cynthia McKinney complained loudly that her new 4th District including most of DeKalb County did not have a black majority; but she won in November anyway, as did 2d District Congressman Sanford Bishop. McKinney later argued that she won only because of her incumbency and that she never could have won initially in the new district. But her 1996 victory shows that she and many black potential candidates can win in non-black-majority districts, and that they have only themselves to blame if they do not try. The Justice Department and minority rights activists nonetheless contested the lines in a case the Supreme Court heard in December 1996.

The People: Est. Pop. 1996: 7,353,000; Pop. 1990: 6,478,216, up 13.5% 1990–1996. 2.8% of U.S. total, 10th largest; 37% rural. Median age: 33.3 years. 10% 65 years and over. 70.1% White, 26.8% Black, 1% Asian; 1.7% Hispanic origin. Households: 55.2% married couple families; 27% married couple fams. w. children; 41% college educ.; median household income: $29,021; per capita income: $13,631; 64.9% owner occupied housing; median house value: $71,300; median monthly rent: $344. 4.6% Unemployment. 1996 Voting age pop.: 5,418,000. 1996 Turnout: 2,298,899; 42% of VAP. Registered voters (1996): 3,811,284; no party registration.

Political Lineup: Governor, Zell Miller (D); Lt. Gov., Pierre Howard (D); Secy. of State, Lewis Massey (D); Atty. Gen., Thurbert Baker (D); Auditor, Claude L. Vickers. State Senate, 56 (34 D and 22 R); Senate President, Pierre Howard (D); State House, 180 (106 D and 74 R); House Speaker, Thomas B. Murphy (D). Senators, Paul Coverdell (R) and Max Cleland (D). Reps., 11 (8 R and 3 D).

Elections Division: 404-656-2871; **Filing Deadline for U.S. Congress:** May 1, 1998.

1996 Presidential Vote

Dole (R)	1,080,840	(47%)
Clinton (D)	1,053,848	(46%)
Perot (I)	146,337	(6%)

1996 Republican Presidential Primary

Dole (R)	226,732	(41%)
Buchanan (R)	162,627	(29%)
Alexander (R)	75,855	(14%)
Forbes (R)	71,278	(13%)
Other	22,577	(4%)

1992 Presidential Vote

Clinton (D)	1,004,295	(43%)
Bush (R)	991,139	(43%)
Perot (I)	309,202	(13%)

GOVERNOR

Gov. Zell Miller (D)

Elected 1990, term expires Jan. 1999; b. Feb. 24, 1932, Young Harris; home, Young Harris; U. of GA, A.B. 1957, M.A. 1958; Methodist; married (Shirley).

Career: Marine Corps, 1953–56; Young Harris Mayor, 1960–63; GA Senate, 1960–64; Dir., St. Board of Probation, Personnel Officer, GA Dept. of Corrections, 1965–66; Exec. Secy., Gov. Lester Maddox, 1969–71; Exec. Dir., GA Dem. Party, 1971–73; GA Lt. Gov., 1974–90.

Office: 203 State Capitol, Atlanta 30334, 404-656-1776; Fax: 404-657-7332; Web site: www.state.ga.us.

Election Results

1994 gen.	Zell Miller (D)	788,926	(51%)
	Guy W. Millner (R)	756,371	(49%)
1994 prim.	Zell Miller (D)	321,963	(70%)
	Jim Boyd (D)	78,444	(17%)
	Mark Tate (D)	30,749	(7%)
	Charles Poag (D)	28,623	(6%)
1990 gen.	Zell Miller (D)	766,662	(53%)
	Johnny Isakson (R)	645,625	(45%)
	Other	37,365	(3%)

SENATORS

Sen. Paul Coverdell (R)

Elected 1992, seat up 1998; b. Jan. 20, 1939, Des Moines, IA; home, Atlanta; U. of MO, B.A., 1960; Methodist; married (Nancy).

Career: Army, 1962–64; Businessman, Coverdell & Co. Inc., 1964–89; GA Senate, 1970–89, Minority Ldr., 1974–89; Chmn., GA Repub. Party, 1985–87; Dir., Peace Corps, 1989–91.

DC Office: 200 RSOB 20510, 202-224-3643; Fax: 202-228-3783; e-mail: senator_coverdell@coverdell.senate.gov.

State Offices: Atlanta, 404-347-2202; Augusta, 706-722-0032; Columbus, 706-322-7920; Dalton, 706-226-1925; Macon, 912-742-0205; Moultrie, 912-985-8113; Savannah, 912-238-3244.

Committees: *Republican Conference Secretary. Agriculture, Nutrition & Forestry* (5th of 10 R): Forestry, Conservation & Rural Revitalization; Marketing, Inspection & Product Promotion (Chmn.). *Foreign Relations* (3rd of 10 R): East Asian & Pacific Affairs; International Economic Policy, Export & Trade Promotion; Western Hemisphere & Peace Corps Affairs (Chmn.). *Small Business* (3rd of 10 R).

Group Ratings

	ADA	ACLU	AFS	LCV	CFA	CON	NFIB	COC	ACU	NTLC	CHC
1996	5	22	0	0	7	51	100	92	100	100	100
1995	0	—	0	7	0	29	—	100	96	—	—

National Journal Ratings

	1995 LIB — 1995 CONS	1996 LIB — 1996 CONS
Economic	0% — 88%	0% — 94%
Social	12% — 81%	0% — 72%
Foreign	8% — 81%	0% — 74%

Key Votes of the 104th Congress

1. Reduce Medicare Growth $	Y	5. Flag Amendment	Y	9. Anti-Missile Defense	Y
2. Lmt. Prod. Liab. Damages	Y	6. Endangered Species	N	10. Cuban Embargo	Y
3. Increase Min. Wage	N	7. Gay Employment Rights	N	11. Bar Bosnia Troop $	N
4. Welfare Reform	Y	8. Ovrd. Part. Birth Veto	Y	12. Cut Vietnam Aid	Y

Election Results

1992 runoff	Paul Coverdell (R)	635,114	(51%)	($3,193,774)
	Wyche Fowler (D)	618,877	(49%)	($4,894,620)
1992 general	Wyche Fowler (D)	1,108,416	(49%)	
	Paul Coverdell (R)	1,073,282	(48%)	
	Others	69,889	(3%)	
1992 runoff	Paul Coverdell (R)	80,435	(50%)	
	Bob Barr (R)	78,887	(50%)	
1992 primary	Paul Coverdell (R)	100,016	(37%)	
	Bob Barr (R)	65,471	(24%)	
	John Knox (R)	64,514	(24%)	
	Charles Tanksley (R)	32,590	(12%)	
	Other	7,352	(1%)	
1986 general	Wyche Fowler (D)	623,705	(51%)	($2,779,297)
	Mack Mattingly (R)	601,235	(49%)	($5,119,249)

Sen. Max Cleland (D)

Elected 1996, seat up 2002; b. Aug. 24, 1942, Atlanta; home, Lithonia; Stetson U., B.A. 1964; Emory U., M.A. 1968; Methodist; single.

Career: Army, 1965–68 (Vietnam); GA Senate, 1970–75; Staff Mbr., Senate Veterans' Affairs Cmte., 1975–77; Admin., U.S. Veterans' Admin., 1977–81; GA Secy. of State, 1982–96.

DC Office: 461 DSOB 20510, 202-224-3521; Fax: 202-224-0072; e-mail: senator_max_cleland@cleland.senate.gov.

State Offices: Atlanta, 404-331-4811.

Committees: *Armed Services* (8th of 8 D): Airland Forces; Personnel (RMM); Readiness. *Governmental Affairs* (7th of 7 D): International Security, Proliferation & Federal Services; Oversight of Government Management, Restructuring & the District of Columbia; Permanent Subcommittee on Investigations. *Small Business* (7th of 8 D).

Group Ratings and Key Votes: Newly Elected

Election Results

1996 general	Max Cleland (D)	1,103,993	(49%)	($2,926,391)
	Guy Millner (R)	1,073,969	(48%)	($9,858,955)
	Others	81,270	(4%)	
1996 primary	Max Cleland (D)	unopposed		
1990 general	Sam Nunn (D)	unopposed		($1,214,695)

FIRST DISTRICT

Georgia's South Atlantic coast, long one of the poorest parts of the country, has been booming in recent years. The area was settled by James Oglethorpe as Britain's 13th coastal colony in the 1730s as a refuge and reformatory for convicts. It did not take long for the sea islands and lowlands along the wide rivers and inlets to become plantation country. Savannah, the state's first capital, was by the 1830s one of America's booming cotton ports; it languished after the Civil War, living off paper mills and chemical plants in the 20th Century, with impoverished blacks on the islands still speaking Gullah dialects. Then, a few decades ago, preservationists started restoring houses and churches on the grid punctuated by 24 squares that Oglethorpe had laid out more than 200 years before. Today Savannah is one of the most graciously preserved cities in the country, and a major tourism mecca thanks to the popularity of John Berendt's *Midnight in the Garden of Good and Evil*, a somewhat-based-on-facts story of eccentricity and murder that has been on the bestseller lists since 1994. Some of the islands have been preserved as well, for years by rich private owners, more recently by government; one such is Cumberland Island, where John F. Kennedy Jr. married Carolyn Bessette in a private ceremony in September 1996. Other islands have old resorts and new condominiums, and literary fame of their own; in 1995 St. Simons Island was the home of three authors with bestsellers: William Diehl, Eugenia Price, and George Dawes Green.

The 1st Congressional District of Georgia includes all the state's Atlantic coast and goes 50 or so miles inland, through cotton and tobacco fields and softwood forests. There are more exotic products here as well: Toombs County is the home of the fragrant Vidalia onions that folks say are so sweet you can eat 'em like an apple, while Claxton in tiny Evans County has for nearly a century been home to two of the nation's prime fruitcake makers. The boundaries were changed a bit in the 1996 court-mandated redistricting, in which the 1st lost some rural counties and gained black neighborhoods in Savannah; the black percentage rose from 23% to 31%. Though the counties in the 1st District are ancestrally Democratic, most voters here are conservative on cultural and military issues. That, plus coastal prosperity, has made this area Republican at the top of the ticket and even in some statewide contests; in 1996 the 1st gave narrow margins to Republican Bob Dole for president and Democrat Max Cleland for the Senate.

The congressman from the 1st District is Jack Kingston, a Republican first elected in 1992. Kingston grew up in Texas, Ethiopia, and Athens, Georgia, the son of a professor; after college he moved to Savannah in 1977 and became a commercial insurance agent. In 1984 he was elected to the Georgia House, at 29, and served eight years. In 1992, when incumbent Democrat Lindsay Thomas retired to work on the Atlanta Olympics, Kingston ran for Congress. Against Democrat Barbara Christmas, a school principal in four counties over the years, Kingston won decisively—58%–42%, with a 2–1 margin in his home base of Savannah and Chatham County.

In the House Kingston has had a mostly conservative voting record and has tended to district interests as have Democratic congressmen of yore. He has parted company with the Republican leadership on some issues, notably NAFTA and GATT, decrying the World Trade Organization. He serves on the Agriculture Subcommittee of Appropriations, where he has used his vote and lobbied his colleagues for district interests. One is sugar. The nation's largest sugar refinery, Savannah Foods, is in the 1st District, and in May 1996 he tried to get a cap of 21 cents a pound on the price of raw sugar, but faced spirited opposition from lawmakers from cane-producing states: Appropriations Chairman Bob Livingston of Louisiana and several members from Florida. Kingston ultimately accepted a compromise in August requiring regular reports of sugar prices from the Department of Agriculture. He also failed in his push for an amendment to the 1996 immigration reform bill to allow farmers to hire foreign workers to harvest crops like Vidalia onions, withholding 25% of their wages until they are ready to return home.

More successful was a Kingston amendment to an FY97 spending bill barring requests for FBI files except for those of presidential appointees or regarding clear threats to national security, as attested by the Attorney General or White House Counsel; this was prompted by the fact that one of Kingston's top aide's files was among those found in the Clinton White House. On local issues, Kingston has fought for historic preservation and looked after Fort Stewart, with its 24,500 military and civilian employees. He has worked to bring in $7 million for replacing the Sidney Lanier drawbridge in Brunswick, $3.5 million for dredging Savannah and Brunswick harbors and $1.5 million for land acquisition in Cumberland Island.

This has proved to be a winning political formula. Kingston was reelected with 77% in 1994 over a Democrat who called for abolition of the income tax and with 68% in 1996 over a more serious opponent, Rosemary Kaszans. These were equivalent showings given the changes in district lines, and he ran far ahead of other Georgia Republicans.

The People: Census data not available due to 1996 redistricting.

1996 Presidential Vote			**1992 Presidential Vote**		
Dole (R)	87,895	(48%)	Bush (R)	81,443	(44%)
Clinton (D)	81,804	(45%)	Clinton (D)	76,900	(42%)
Perot (I)	11,491	(6%)	Perot (I)	26,023	(14%)

Rep. Jack Kingston (R)

Elected 1992; b. Apr. 24, 1955, Bryan, TX; home, Savannah; U. of GA, B.S. 1978; Episcopalian; married (Libby).

Career: Insurance agent, 1979–92; GA House of Reps., 1984–92.

DC Office: 1507 LHOB 20515, 202-225-5831; Fax: 202-226-2269.

District Offices: Brunswick, 912-265-9010; Savannah, 912-352-0101; Statesboro, 912-489-8797.

Committees: *Appropriations* (22nd of 34 R): Agriculture, Rural Development, FDA & Related Agencies; Foreign Operations, Export Financing & Related Programs; Military Construction.

Group Ratings

	ADA	ACLU	AFS	LCV	CFA	CON	NFIB	COC	ACU	NTLC	CHC
1996	5	12	0	15	46	81	100	86	100	95	100
1995	0	—	—	6	15	75	—	100	96	—	—

National Journal Ratings

	1995 LIB — 1995 CONS			1996 LIB — 1996 CONS		
Economic	26%	—	67%	0%	—	82%
Social	30%	—	68%	0%	—	90%
Foreign	28%	—	65%	35%	—	65%

Key Votes of the 104th Congress

1. Reduce Medicare Growth $	Y	5. Flag Amendment	Y	9. Cuban Embargo	Y
2. Ovrd. Product Liab. Veto	Y	6. Drop EPA Limits	Y	10. Bar Bosnia Troop $	Y
3. Increase Min. Wage	N	7. Repeal Assault-Weap. Ban	Y	11. Cut Anti-Missile Defense	N
4. Welfare Reform	Y	8. Ovrd. Part. Birth Veto	Y	12. Bar U.N. Uniforms	*

Election Results

1996 general	Jack Kingston (R)	108,616	(68%)	($452,178)
	Rosemary D. Kaszans (D)	50,622	(32%)	($46,023)
1996 primary	Jack Kingston (R)	unopposed		
1994 general	Jack Kingston (R)	88,788	(77%)	($296,202)
	Raymond Beckworth (D)	27,197	(23%)	

SECOND DISTRICT

The southwest corner of Georgia, plantation country before the Civil War, still is mostly agricultural land today: cotton fields, peanut acreage, pine lands. In the south, near the Florida border, is the Plantation Trace area around Thomasville, where rich northerners have come to shoot quail and ducks in winters since the 1880s; a bit to the north is Albany, the largest city in these parts, with several factories, and the site of civil rights protests in the 1960s; two counties north is the village of Plains, the home since childhood of Jimmy Carter, and the center of the Free World during his presidency 20 years ago. This is hardscrabble country: as recently as World War II, most rural residents lived in clapboard cabins without power or running water, eking a living out of over-tilled soil. Today this remains one of the low-income quarters of America. But rural electrification and then air-conditioning made homes and workplaces comfortable; automobiles and good roads have given people options they never had before (think of outlet malls); racial desegregation has given dignity to all in a way few dreamed possible thirty-some years ago.

This is the land of Georgia's 2d Congressional District. For the 1992 and 1994 elections this was a seat with ragged boundaries designed to make it black-majority; it included black neighborhoods in Columbus, Macon, and Valdosta, as well as Albany and the heavily black counties along the Alabama border. But the Supreme Court overturned the Georgia districting, and a three-judge federal court drew new boundaries along county lines that excluded Columbus, Macon, and Valdosta, and reduced the black percentage from 57% to 39%.

The congressman from the 2d District is Sanford Bishop, a Democrat first elected in 1992 and reelected impressively in 1996. Bishop grew up in Mobile, Alabama, where his father was a state college president. He went to Morehouse College in Atlanta and was an award-winning student at Emory Law School, then served in the Army. After a year in New York, he settled in Columbus, practiced law, joined the church choir and many civic organizations, and was elected to the state legislature in 1976, at 29. He served there until 1990, when he was elected to the Georgia Senate. He had prime positions in both, helping to push through an ethics law, a training program for welfare recipients, and establishing the Commission on Equal Opportunity and the Office of Child Support Receiver. In 1992 he ran for the House against incumbent Charles Hatcher, who gained his greatest public notice when it was revealed he had 819 overdrafts on the House bank. Bishop was urged into the race by Columbus business leaders, and in the primary he edged another Hatcher challenger by 21%–19% for a runoff slot. Hatcher had 40%, but could not get many more votes, and Bishop won the runoff 53%–47%. He won the general election 64%–36%.

Bishop describes himself as "a moderate conservative on fiscal issues and a 'traditionalist' on so-called family issues." His style is not confrontational and his voting record is far more moderate than that of Georgia's two other black Democrats, John Lewis and Cynthia McKinney. He serves on the Agriculture Committee and on its Risk Management and Specialty Crops Subcommittee, which has jurisdiction over peanuts and tobacco. In the the 1996 farm bill debate, he realized he could not save the old peanut program and fashioned what he calls a "market-oriented, no-net cost" peanut program. Working with 8th District Republican Saxby Chambliss, Bishop lobbied hard to pass it, and it prevailed on the House by three votes; he points out that 23 members of the Congressional Black Caucus voted for it, and suggests his work was crucial in getting these votes. As a member of the Veterans' Affairs Committee in the 104th Congress, he worked on eligibility reform for veterans' hospitals. In the 105th Congress, he gained a seat on Intelligence.

On national issues, he emphasizes his support of the balanced budget, anti-flag desecration, school prayer amendments, and the Defense of Marriage Act. He supported the 1993 Clinton budget and tax increase, but supported neither the Clinton nor the Republican budget in 1995. Instead, as part of the Blue Dog Democrats, he supported a more moderate budget which favored deeper Democratic spending cuts and less Republican tax cuts. He voted against the Republicans' original welfare program in 1995, saying it lacked funding for critical services, but for the Welfare Reform Act of 1996. He voted for the crime bill in 1994, but against the Brady bill, and in the 104th Congress voted to repeal the ban on so-called assault weapons. He voted against NAFTA but for GATT, saying he was satisfied with concessions on peanuts. He is against the creation of tougher penalties for crack than cocaine, but wants to increase the penalty for cocaine. After 9th District Congressman Nathan Deal switched parties and became a Republican, there was talk that Bishop might, and he certainly would have been welcomed by Newt Gingrich. Bishop said he wasn't considering any change but added, "No one can speak about the future."

On local projects, Bishop claims to have brought $300 million in federal funds to the district, including relief from the disastrous floods of 1994, anti-crime and -drug programs, transportation projects, housing, and education. He intervened to settle a dispute between FEMA and the local government in Albany over trailers to house flood victims. He worked out a funding mechanism for modernization of the Valdosta Regional Airport.

Bishop won reelection easily in 1994, winning 2–1 in both the primary and general. But the change in boundaries and the reduction in black percentage produced stronger opposition. He lost not only many black and therefore solidly Democratic voters but also his home base of Columbus; he moved his residence to Albany for the 1996 election. When the district lines were announced, Georgia House Speaker Tom Murphy touted the candidacy of former University of Georgia football coach Ray Goff, even though no one knew to which party Goff belonged. But in April 1996 Goff decided not to run. Then Bishop faced opposition in the primary from his former staffer, W. T. Gamble, who attacked him on GATT and the assault weapons ban. But Bishop carried every county and won 59%–33%.

In the general Republican Darrel Ealum ran ads calling Bishop "shockingly liberal," hitting his votes for the 1996 tax increase and on the crack versus cocaine distinction. In the final debate, Ealum flung a computer printout across the stage, claiming Bishop got 92% of his money from outside the district. But Bishop stayed cool and ran ads mentioning job security, the balanced budget amendment, and his work promoting local military bases. Bishop also outspent Ealum by about a 2–1 margin. This time, Bishop's victory was narrower, 54%–46%, but impressive nonetheless. He lost seven counties, most with relatively well-off towns, ran up big margins in the black-majority counties, and won solidly in counties filled up with white farmers—the kind of people it was thought 30 years ago would never vote for a black congressman. As much as any contest in the nation, this election showed that white voters in the Deep South, and therefore perhaps anywhere else in America, are ready and willing to vote for a black candidate if he works hard and favorably represents their interests.

The People: Census data not available due to 1996 redistricting.

1996 Presidential Vote			1992 Presidential Vote		
Clinton (D)	82,429	(49%)	Clinton (D)	82,220	(46%)
Dole (R)	72,934	(44%)	Bush (R)	71,749	(40%)
Perot (I)	11,494	(7%)	Perot (I)	23,278	(13%)

Rep. Sanford D. Bishop, Jr. (D)

Elected 1992; b. Feb. 4, 1947, Mobile, AL; home, Albany; Morehouse Col., B.A. 1968, Emory U., J.D. 1971; Baptist; divorced.

Career: Army, 1970–71; Practicing atty., 1971–92; GA House of Reps., 1976–90; GA Senate, 1990–92.

DC Office: 1433 LHOB 20515, 202-225-3631; Fax: 202-225-2203.

District Offices: Albany, 912-439-8067; Dawson, 912-995-3991; Valdosta, 912-247-9705.

Committees: *Agriculture* (12th of 23 D): Department Operations, Nutrition & Foreign Agriculture; Risk Management & Specialty Crops. *Intelligence (Select)* (7th of 7 D): Human Intelligence, Analysis & Counterintelligence.

Group Ratings

	ADA	ACLU	AFS	LCV	CFA	CON	NFIB	COC	ACU	NTLC	CHC
1996	60	50	75	62	46	66	43	44	30	33	7
1995	85	—	—	75	46	16	—	41	13	—	—

National Journal Ratings

	1995 LIB — 1995 CONS			1996 LIB — 1996 CONS		
Economic	67%	—	33%	64%	—	36%
Social	80%	—	13%	68%	—	31%
Foreign	72%	—	28%	47%	—	52%

Key Votes of the 104th Congress

1. Reduce Medicare Growth $	N	5. Flag Amendment	Y	9. Cuban Embargo	Y
2. Ovrd. Product Liab. Veto	N	6. Drop EPA Limits	Y	10. Bar Bosnia Troop $	N
3. Increase Min. Wage	Y	7. Repeal Assault-Weap. Ban	Y	11. Cut Anti-Missile Defense	Y
4. Welfare Reform	Y	8. Ovrd. Part. Birth Veto	N	12. Bar U.N. Uniforms	Y

Election Results

1996 general	Sanford D. Bishop, Jr. (D)	88,256	(54%)	($774,474)
	Darrel Ealum (R)	75,282	(46%)	($329,309)
1996 primary	Sanford D. Bishop, Jr. (D)	56,660	(59%)	
	W. T. Gamble (D)	31,615	(33%)	
	Walter H. Lewis (D)	7,116	(7%)	
1994 general	Sanford D. Bishop, Jr. (D)	65,383	(66%)	($473,931)
	John Clayton (R)	33,429	(34%)	($9,736)

THIRD DISTRICT

Running south from Atlanta, within an hour or so's travel you can see the most modern part of Georgia and some of the most traditional. The modern is Atlanta's Hartsfield Airport, built by Mayor William Hartsfield on the site of Candler Racetrack eight miles south of Atlanta's Five Points. Hartsfield was the mayor whose moderation on racial issues made Atlanta known as "the city too busy to hate," and whose airport, totally rebuilt in the 1980s, is one of the busiest anywhere and the link between Atlanta's world corporations—Coca-Cola, CNN—its celebrations—the 1996 Olympics—and the world. Not far south are the old courthouse towns of Jonesboro and Fayetteville, now surrounded by new suburbs, but both with claims to be the spiritual homes of *Gone With the Wind*; near Jonesboro is the mansion long owned by Senator (1957–81) Herman Talmadge, which looks a lot like Tara.

Eventually—farther south each year, it seems—the suburbs thin out, and you are in rural Georgia; a county past Sprayberry's Barbecue in booming Newnan is the village of Warm Springs and the faded hotel and pool where Franklin Roosevelt recuperated from polio in the 1920s, and where he died in 1945. Roosevelt liked to look over the wooded hills of Meriwether County, where few dwellings had central heat or indoor plumbing and almost everyone voted Democratic, as they had since General Sherman marched his troops not too many miles away from Atlanta to the sea. Farther south is another Georgia, the small industrial city of Columbus and next-door Fort Benning, long the home of the Army's Infantry School, the place where George Marshall's brilliant talents were first noticed and where he kept his little book on the brilliant officers whom he would make generals in World War II.

The 3d Congressional District of Georgia, in its new boundaries set for the 1996 election, takes in all this territory, starting just south of the airport, passing through suburbs and fields to Columbus. The bulk of the votes here are cast in the Atlanta communities. These new communities are affluent but not dominated by any establishment, liberation-minded in much of their lifestyles but often tradition-minded in their yearnings. Politically this is conservative country, full of young families moving up who prefer the relatively bucolic culture of the smaller counties. Mostly white, their ancestral politics may be Democratic but their current preferences lean Republican; these areas voted heavily for Bob Dole in 1996. The 3d's boundaries, imposed by a federal court, removed some rural counties and added Warm Springs and black neighborhoods in Columbus; this increased the black percentage from 18% to 25%, and made the 3d somewhat more Democratic.

The congressman from the 3d is Mac Collins, a switcher to the Republican Party in the 1980s. Collins grew up in Jackson and started his trucking company at age 18, hauling logs for Georgia-Pacific; he is known, a local paper said, for "his lumbering stature and signature boots." He served as a Democrat on the Butts County Commission in the late 1970s, lost in 1980 then convinced the Butts County Republicans to elect him chairman. In 1988, he was elected to the state Senate, where he worked on welfare and ethics reforms and bills to fight drug dealing. In 1992, Collins capitalized on a fierce primary battle between the two Democrats Speaker Tom Murphy had in mind for the seat, incumbent Congressman Richard Ray and David Worley, who came close to beating Gingrich in the old 6th District in 1990. Ray won the Democratic primary 51%–32%. But Collins, like Worley, attacked Ray as an insider; Ray spent 10 years as an aide to Senator Sam Nunn before running for Congress himself. Ray, with a seat on Armed Services, spent $1.1 million. But Collins won 55%–45%.

Collins has one of the most conservative voting records in the House, plus a constituent-based agenda. Hartsfield Airport was his chief early focus; he pushed for a repeal of the airline fuel tax slated for fall 1995, arguing the levy would cripple the industry. He voted to pare spending at almost every opportunity, except for defense and 3d District projects—and made a point of opting out of the congressional pension plan. Collins is not a pure free marketeer, however: he voted against NAFTA and GATT.

In his first term Collins was a minority backbencher; in his second, a majority member of Ways and Means. He backed welfare reform, the 1996 health care bill, a lower tax on earnings by Social Security recipients, the Freedom to Farm Act, telecommunications reform. He voted against the minimum wage increase. His down-home style comes through loud and clear: when Sam Gibbons charged that Republicans were gutting Medicare, Collins said, "You're spouting bull."

In 1994 Collins beat by 2–1 a Democrat who outspent him by $1.28 million to $503,000. But he did shift one course when redistricting made the 3d more Democratic: he dropped his opposition to PAC contributions and collected $289,000 from PACsHis Democratic opponent, former B-52 pilot Jim Chafin, said he could advance the conservative agenda better and charged that Collins was attacking the Clean Air Act and Medicare. Collins won only 53% in the Columbus and Warm Springs area, but won 64% in the rest of the district—about the same as in 1994—for a 61%–39% victory overall. After the election, he showed some independence when he was one of 28 House Republicans who initially would not commit to voting for Newt Gingrich for speaker because of his ethics problems, though Gingrich once represented much of this district; but he voted for Gingrich January 7 nonetheless.

The People: Census data not available due to 1996 redistricting.

1996 Presidential Vote

Dole (R)	104,286	(50%)
Clinton (D)	87,911	(42%)
Perot (I)	13,550	(7%)

1992 Presidential Vote

Bush (R)	94,957	(47%)
Clinton (D)	80,583	(40%)
Perot (I)	27,914	(14%)

Rep. Mac Collins (R)

Elected 1992; b. Oct. 15, 1944, Jackson; home, Hampton; Methodist; married (Julie).

Career: Army Natl. Guard, 1964–70; Founder & Pres., Collins Trucking Co., 1965–92; Chmn., Butts Cnty. Comm., 1977–80; Chmn., Butts Cnty. Repub. Party, 1981–82; GA Senate, 1988–92.

DC Office: 1131 LHOB 20515, 202-225-5901; Fax: 202-225-2515; e-mail: rep3mac@hr.house.gov.

District Offices: Columbus, 706-327-7228; Jonesboro, 770-603-3395.

Committees: *Ways & Means* (15th of 23 R): Human Resources; Social Security.

Group Ratings

	ADA	ACLU	AFS	LCV	CFA	CON	NFIB	COC	ACU	NTLC	CHC
1996	5	12	0	23	8	17	97	94	100	100	100
1995	0	—	—	6	0	73	—	100	92	—	—

National Journal Ratings

	1995 LIB — 1995 CONS			1996 LIB — 1996 CONS		
Economic	26%	—	67%	0%	—	82%
Social	0%	—	79%	0%	—	90%
Foreign	0%	—	85%	0%	—	79%

Key Votes of the 104th Congress

1. Reduce Medicare Growth $	Y	5. Flag Amendment	Y	9. Cuban Embargo	Y
2. Ovrd. Product Liab. Veto	Y	6. Drop EPA Limits	N	10. Bar Bosnia Troop $	Y
3. Increase Min. Wage	N	7. Repeal Assault-Weap. Ban	Y	11. Cut Anti-Missile Defense	N
4. Welfare Reform	Y	8. Ovrd. Part. Birth Veto	Y	12. Bar U.N. Uniforms	Y

Election Results

1996 general	Mac Collins (R)	120,251	(61%)	($485,354)
	Jim Chafin (D)	76,538	(39%)	($122,393)
1996 primary	Mac Collins (R)	unopposed		
1994 general	Mac Collins (R)	94,717	(66%)	($503,867)
	Fred Overby (D)	49,828	(34%)	($1,284,414)

FOURTH DISTRICT

In 1920, when Gutzom Borglum began sculpting Jefferson Davis, Robert E. Lee and Stonewall Jackson into the side of Stone Mountain, the huge outcropping of granite was a day's drive into the country from central Atlanta. Even when the memorial (the largest single piece of sculpture in the world) was completed in 1972, suburban development barely reached this far. But today, after two decades of some of the most explosive metropolitan growth in the country, DeKalb

County, which Stone Mountain overlooks, is part of the core of the Atlanta metropolitan area, and this monument to the Confederacy sits in one of the most cosmopolitan and liberal constituencies in the South. Not far from Stone Mountain is Emory University, just beyond the old mansions of Druid Hills, where *Driving Miss Daisy* was filmed. A few miles away are the Centers for Disease Control and Prevention, one of the federal government's superb research institutions. All around in north DeKalb County are affluent suburbs, including much of Atlanta's Jewish community, with voting habits somewhat more liberal than other suburbs. Also, southern DeKalb is being transformed from mostly rural territory 25 years ago to one of the nation's largest collection of affluent black neighborhoods, rivalled only by Prince George's County, Maryland. This has pushed DeKalb County's percentages well to the left: this was a Republican county when rural Georgia was almost all Democratic in the 1960s; now it is the most heavily Democratic major county in Georgia, even more than next-door Fulton County which includes central Atlanta.

The 4th Congressional District of Georgia consists of almost all of DeKalb County plus a small slice of the newer, more Republican Gwinnett County to the northeast. It is the product of the 1996 redistricting, in which a federal court, enforcing a Supreme Court decision, reduced the number of black-majority districts in Georgia from three to one. It also produced some nimble district-hopping. Cynthia McKinney, elected in 1992 and 1994 from the old black-majority 11th District which stretched from DeKalb County all the way to Savannah, decided to run here, albeit with a white majority; south DeKalb is her political base. And Republican John Linder, who represented most of DeKalb in the old 4th District, who had been held to a 58%–42% victory by Democrat Comer Yates in the Republican year of 1994, decided to run in the new 11th District, which includes most of Gwinnett County plus many smaller counties running east to South Carolina.

Cynthia McKinney grew up in Atlanta, just long ago enough to remember many of the great events of the civil rights revolution; she recalls riding on her father's shoulders as a child in civil rights marches. Her father, Billy McKinney, was elected to the legislature in 1973, just one year after Andrew Young was elected to Congress from a white-majority Atlanta district. Cynthia McKinney went to college in California, studied international relations in graduate school, taught at Spellman College, Clark Atlanta University, and Agnes Scott College, and is a doctoral candidate in international relations at the Fletcher School at Tufts. In 1988 she was elected to the Georgia House from south DeKalb County, and became part of the only father-daughter legislative team in the country. She got a seat on the Georgia legislature's 1991 redistricting committee and worked long and hard to craft the two new black-majority districts. In 1992 she ran in the 11th, one of the districts she had helped create. The real contest was for the Democratic nomination: with her DeKalb base, she led the primary with 31%, then won the runoff over George DeLoach 56%–44%.

McKinney has had one of the most liberal voting records in the House—what one might expect from her outspokenness. "I'm attracted to fights," she said when she insisted on wearing pants on the floor of the House. "I don't think that anybody as different as me will ever be an insider. But I know how to get things done. I deliver." She supported the Clinton budget and tax increase in 1993, and the 1994 crime bill. On national issues her major cause is an international "code of conduct" which other countries must adhere to before receiving American arms transfers—promoting democracy, respecting human rights, not engaging in aggression, participating in the United Nations Register of Conventional Arms. On local issues she sought an investigation of price-fixing by local miners of kaolin, the white clay used in china, stationery and paint, and in 1994 the Justice Department started an antitrust probe; later she blamed Kaolin producers for instigating the redistricting case. Against her Atlanta neighbor Newt Gingrich she became one of the most fiery opponents; she attacked his lucrative book deal and told a satirical "children's tale" about him called "a little piglet who spent most of his days rolling around in a filthy ditch." She was one of three members who brought the ethics complaint charging Gingrich with violating anti-gift rules by accepting free cable-TV time to broadcast his college course. She harshly attacked Republican budget and welfare proposals.

Then came the redistricting case. In June 1995 the Supreme Court ruled the lines McKinney had helped draw were an unconstitutional "racial gerrymander." McKinney was their most visible defender, arguing that blacks can't get elected in majority-white districts (although Young had done so in Atlanta more than 20 years before). In December 1995 a three-judge federal court came down with new lines, and McKinney who had represented a 60% black district was placed in the new 4th which was 33% black in 1990 (and probably higher by 1996, because many middle-class blacks are moving out of Atlanta into south DeKalb). Now it was in her interest to disprove her own arguments. Into this awkward situation she moved with the verve that characterizes her colorful clothes and incendiary rhetoric.

McKinney's first tough challenge came in the Democratic primary. Running again was 1994 nominee Comer Yates, with the endorsement of notables including former DeKalb (1974–84) Congressman Elliott Levitas, who said that no one could win the district without moderate positions. "I offer the idea of common ground," Yates said. "The skin color or gender could not be less relevant." But he ran a poll mentioning that she voted against John Lewis's resolution to condemn Louis Farrakhan. McKinney carried south DeKalb almost unanimously and won many votes in liberal university and Jewish north DeKalb precincts for a 67%–24% victory. Her general election opponent was John Mitnick. He attacked McKinney for opposing school vouchers while sending her son to the elite Paideia school and for attending a panel discussion at Howard University in 1995 with Louis Farrakhan and for her vote on the Farrakhan resolution. She called Mitnick a Gingrich clone, although he favored gun control and took a pro-choice stand on abortion. In October 1996 Billy McKinney called Mitnick "a racist Jew." She asked him to apologize publicly—"he's my dad and I love him, but I am with him when he's right and I tell him when he's wrong"—and he withdrew from her campaign. Her TV ads stressed her efforts to pass the crime bill, her support of the minimum wage increase and her efforts to stop "the extremists who tried to cut Medicare to fund tax breaks for the wealthy"—pretty standard 1996 Democratic stuff.

The result was a thumping 58%–42% victory for McKinney. Again she carried south DeKalb overwhelmingly and ran well in north DeKalb. Overall she ran about 6% behind Bill Clinton and Democratic Senate candidate Max Cleland—a dropoff, but of similar magnitude to many across the country. McKinney argued that her victory was the result of incumbency, that she could not have won an initial election in such a district. Not, perhaps, if she had run the identical campaign she had in 1992, when she pitched her appeal entirely to black voters; but if she had taken the more moderate tone of her 1996 ads she might well have won then within the lines of the current district. She argues that single-member districts are unfair to black candidates and calls for proportional representation, so that they would have to appeal to blacks only. But the fact that she won many white votes undercuts her argument, which in any case is not likely to go anywhere in the current political climate. In the House she continues to be one of the most vitriolic opponents of Newt Gingrich and the Republican majority.

The People: Census data not available due to 1996 redistricting.

1996 Presidential Vote			**1992 Presidential Vote**		
Clinton (D)	141,078	(64%)	Clinton (D)	124,831	(55%)
Dole (R)	69,912	(32%)	Bush (R)	80,229	(35%)
Perot (I)	8,014	(4%)	Perot (I)	23,040	(10%)

Rep. Cynthia A. McKinney (D)

Elected 1992; b. Mar. 17, 1955, Atlanta; home, Lithonia; U. of Southern CA, B.A. 1978; Catholic; divorced.

Career: Diplomatic Fellow, Spelman Col., 1984; GA House of Reps., 1988–92; Atlanta Bd. of Health Svcs. Plng. Cncl., 1990–92; Adjunct Prof., Agnes Scott Women's Col., 1991–92.

DC Office: 124 CHOB 20515, 202-225-1605; Fax: 202-226-0691.

District Offices: Decatur, 404-377-6900.

Committees: *Banking & Financial Services* (20th of 25 D): Financial Institutions & Consumer Credit; General Oversight & Investigations. *International Relations* (12th of 21 D): International Operations & Human Rights; Western Hemisphere.

Group Ratings

	ADA	ACLU	AFS	LCV	CFA	CON	NFIB	COC	ACU	NTLC	CHC
1996	100	80	100	77	92	40	8	20	0	5	0
1995	85	—	—	81	92	8	—	4	13	—	—

National Journal Ratings

	1995 LIB	—	1995 CONS	1996 LIB	—	1996 CONS
Economic	89%	—	10%	84%	—	15%
Social	80%	—	13%	88%	—	0%
Foreign	93%	—	0%	90%	—	0%

Key Votes of the 104th Congress

1. Reduce Medicare Growth $	N	5. Flag Amendment	Y	9. Cuban Embargo	N
2. Ovrd. Product Liab. Veto	N	6. Drop EPA Limits	Y	10. Bar Bosnia Troop $	N
3. Increase Min. Wage	Y	7. Repeal Assault-Weap. Ban	N	11. Cut Anti-Missile Defense	Y
4. Welfare Reform	N	8. Ovrd. Part. Birth Veto	N	12. Bar U.N. Uniforms	N

Election Results

1996 general	Cynthia A. McKinney (D)	127,157	(58%)	($1,015,197)
	John Mitnick (R)	92,985	(42%)	($654,287)
1996 primary	Cynthia A. McKinney (D)	42,508	(67%)	
	Comer Yates (D)	15,126	(24%)	
	Ron Slotin (D)	3,993	(6%)	
	Others	1,370	(2%)	
1994 general	Cynthia A. McKinney (D)	71,560	(66%)	($274,232)
(GA 11)	Woodrow Lovett (R)	37,533	(34%)	($12,091)

FIFTH DISTRICT

Venture out of the quiet of the Ebenezer Baptist Church or the shade of Martin Luther King Jr.'s boyhood home two blocks away and into the steamy heat of the sun on Auburn Avenue—Sweet Auburn—and you can see, a mile away, downtown Atlanta's atrium-skyscrapers towering in their glory. They are evidence of the wealth and vibrant growth of "the city," as it boasted in the 1960s, "too busy to hate," the commercial capital of the South, the metropolis that has grown up where there was little more than a railroad junction at the time of the War Between the States. But the awesome achievement that is downtown Atlanta is overshadowed by the revolution made in very large part by a man who grew up on Auburn Avenue, where people who never felt air-conditioning moved slowly in the sweltering heat, and around Morehouse and Spelman Colleges, where proud professionals struggled and worked hard and raised their families. Atlanta's white establishment, led by Mayors William Hartsfield and Ivan Allen and Coca-Cola's Robert Woodruff, deserve credit for abandoning segregation, but it was King and other civil rights leaders who took the risks that led them to do so. Atlanta's city fathers acted out of good will, but also with an eye for the economic growth of their city, which they knew would be hurt by violent resistance. White Atlanta's decision to desegregate has helped Atlanta prosper, but King's vision and movement to change the way Americans behave have made it possible for a nation to live up to its ideals.

Yet, sadly, not all is entirely well in Atlanta—on Peachtree Street or on Sweet Auburn. Downtown Atlanta's primacy in office buildings is being eclipsed by north side Edge Cities in Buckhead and along I-285. Many of Atlanta's black neighborhoods today have been abandoned by families who have headed to subdivisions in DeKalb County, leaving the central city with abandoned housing and street crime. Atlanta has its glories: the headquarters of world-girdling Coca-Cola and CNN, the gigantic Hartsfield Airport, the modern Martin Luther King Center that depicts the triumphs of the civil rights movement and the antique Cyclorama that shows Atlanta burning during the Civil War, the stadiums and sports facilities built for the 1996 Olympics. As the world turned its attention to Atlanta for the Summer Games, officials scurried to repave streets, build new parks, and revitalize inner-city neighborhoods such as Summerhill and Mechanicsville, spending more than $2 billion. But the bombing which killed one person at Centennial Olympic Park and complaints about run-down housing for athletes and inefficient transportation marred the festivities, and Atlanta was left with $500 million in new sports facilities but scant profits.

The 5th Congressional District of Georgia includes most of Atlanta and a few suburbs, from posh white Sandy Springs in the north to middle-class and increasingly black East Point in the south, plus rural southwest Fulton County and a black neighborhood around the airport in Clayton County. About 62% of its residents are black and it was little changed by redistricting for 1996.

The congressman from the 5th District is John Lewis, who made history a generation ago as a hero of the civil rights movement. A sharecropper's son from Troy, Alabama, he was seized by religious fervor as a child, preaching in the barnyard, determined to be a minister. He was the first in his family to finish high school; he wrote to Ralph Abernathy for help in suing for the right to enter Troy State College; he met Martin Luther King when he was 18. In 1959, at age 19, he helped organize the first lunch-counter sit-in, which was received with open hostility hard to imagine today. In 1960, the day after John Kennedy was elected, Lewis sat in the Krystal Diner in Nashville while a waitress poured cleansing powder down his back and water over his food; after eating, he went to talk to the manager, who turned a fumigating machine on him. In May 1961, he was on the first of the Freedom Rides, riding buses as they were attacked and burned; he was viciously beaten in Rock Hill, South Carolina, and Montgomery, Alabama. He spoke at the 1963 March on Washington, criticizing Kennedy liberals for inaction on civil rights and calling for massive help for the poor. In 1964, he helped coordinate the Mississippi Freedom Project. In 1965, he led the Selma-to-Montgomery march to petition for voting rights and was beaten by policemen who fractured his skull. Modestly, quietly, maintaining his poise and good judgment under harsh circumstances, Lewis was one of the people who risked their lives many times to make the civil rights revolution happen.

Lewis responded to these beatings with a stubborn determination to persevere with actions, not just words. He worked for Robert Kennedy for president in 1968, and was with him in Indianapolis when they heard Martin Luther King was killed and in Los Angeles just before

Kennedy himself was shot.

Lewis's tenure as head of the Voter Education Project in Atlanta and his work at ACTION during the Carter Administration did not give him the publicity and fame, however, that made a national celebrity of Jesse Jackson, whose civil rights movement credentials are much thinner. Lewis's first foray into electoral politics was unsuccessful: he ran in 1977 to replace Andrew Young in the House and was soundly beaten by Wyche Fowler (but ran ahead of Republican Paul Coverdell, who beat Fowler in the 1992 Senate election). After winning a seat on the Atlanta Council in 1981, Lewis ran for Congress in 1986, and trailed Julian Bond 47%–35% in the primary. But even though Bond won over 60% of the black vote, Lewis won the runoff by assembling a coalition of poor blacks and affluent whites: "vote for the tugboat, not the showboat" was his slogan, stressing his hard work on local issues like zoning and ethics. He has been reelected easily since, running unopposed in 1996.

Lewis has been a strong partisan, with one of the most liberal voting records in the House, committed to working with members of all races. Usually quiet, he is capable of eloquence, as in his speech opposing the Gulf war resolution in January 1991. He is one of the Democrats' four chief deputy whips, an integral part of the leadership, and has a seat on Ways and Means. He has defected from his party occasionally, as when he opposed the 1994 crime bill because of his opposition to capital punishment; he cast a key vote against the rule in August 1994, then under pressure switched later. A believer in the possibility of a bi-racial liberal majority, he reacted vehemently to the Republicans' capture of the House in 1994. His formerly pleasant relationship with Newt Gingrich ended in early 1995 as he attacked him for his book contract and called for an independent counsel on the issue. Later he filed ethics complaints against Gingrich for the financing of his college course and use of GOPAC funds. Lewis argued passionately against the Republican welfare bills: "They're coming for the children. They're coming for the poor. They're coming for the sick, the elderly, and the disabled." And he implicitly compared the Republicans to Nazis by quoting an anti-Nazi German theologian against them.

Lewis has worked to commemorate the civil rights revolution in which he played such a large part. He got a federal building in Atlanta named for Martin Luther King and got the route from Selma to Montgomery designated a National Historic Trail. His vision remains clear. "You can have an integrated society without losing diversity. But you can also have a society that transcends race, where you can lay down the burden of race—I'm talking about just *lay it down*—and treat people as human beings, regardless of the color of their skin." But he has diverged from other black leaders. He has attacked Louis Farrakhan: "The means by which we struggle must be consistent with the end we seek." He called the court decision that overturned Georgia's congressional district lines a setback to black participation in politics (even though both black incumbents threatened ended up winning), but would prefer lower black percentages, to encourage bi-racial coalitions. Affirmative action should move from race to class as a criterion, he believes, but for now he tenaciously defends today's racial quotas and setasides.

The People: Pop. 1990: 586,526; 3% rural; 10% age 65+; 35% White; 62% Black; 1% Asian; 2% Hispanic origin. Households: 35% married couple families; 15% married couple fams. w. children; 49% college educ.; median household income: $25,892; per capita income: $15,831; median gross rent: $461; median house value: $74,800.

1996 Presidential Vote

Clinton (D)	134,597	(74%)
Dole (R)	41,346	(23%)
Perot (I)	4,980	(3%)

1992 Presidential Vote

Clinton (D)	140,547	(69%)
Bush (R)	47,479	(23%)
Perot (I)	14,784	(7%)

Rep. John Lewis (D)

Elected 1986; b. Feb. 21, 1940, Troy, AL; home, Atlanta; Amer. Baptist Theological Seminary, B.A. 1961, Fisk U., B.A. 1963; Baptist; married (Lillian).

Career: Chmn., Student Nonviolent Coord. Cmte., 1963–66; Field Foundation, 1966–67; Community Organization Dir., Southern Regional Cncl., 1967–70; Exec. Dir., Voter Educ. Project, 1970–76; Assoc. Dir., ACTION, 1977–80; Community Affairs Dir., Natl. Coop. Bank, 1980–82; Atlanta City Cncl., 1981–86.

DC Office: 229 CHOB 20515, 202-225-3801; Fax: 202-225-0351.

District Offices: Atlanta, 404-659-0116.

Committees: *Chief Deputy Minority Whip. Ways & Means* (10th of 16 D): Health.

Group Ratings

	ADA	ACLU	AFS	LCV	CFA	CON	NFIB	COC	ACU	NTLC	CHC
1996	100	94	100	85	100	21	17	19	0	2	0
1995	100	—	—	94	100	13	—	9	9	—	—

National Journal Ratings

	1995 LIB	—	1995 CONS	1996 LIB	—	1996 CONS
Economic	94%	—	0%	89%	—	0%
Social	88%	—	0%	88%	—	0%
Foreign	93%	—	0%	87%	—	10%

Key Votes of the 104th Congress

1. Reduce Medicare Growth $	N	5. Flag Amendment	N	9. Cuban Embargo	N
2. Ovrd. Product Liab. Veto	N	6. Drop EPA Limits	Y	10. Bar Bosnia Troop $	N
3. Increase Min. Wage	Y	7. Repeal Assault-Weap. Ban	N	11. Cut Anti-Missile Defense	Y
4. Welfare Reform	N	8. Ovrd. Part. Birth Veto	N	12. Bar U.N. Uniforms	N

Election Results

1996 general	John Lewis (D)	unopposed		($207,661)
1996 primary	John Lewis (D)	unopposed		
1994 general	John Lewis (D)	85,094	(69%)	($323,725)
	Dale Dixon (R)	37,999	(31%)	($47,726)

SIXTH DISTRICT

In the red clay hills north of Atlanta, over the last three decades, an almost wholly new metropolitan quarter has grown up as affluent Atlanta has spread out from Ansley Park, just north of downtown, and the rolling hills of Buckhead, within the city limit, past the I-285 Perimeter into territory that was once just farms, small towns and little factory cities. Where there were perhaps 100,000 people in the 1950s, there are one million today. No longer is downtown Atlanta the only focus: the Edge Cities of Buckhead, Perimeter Center and the area near Cumberland Mall are now not just shopping but major office centers, rivaling downtown Atlanta in square footage. Cobb County around Marietta is the headquarters of Home Depot and the Weather Channel; Dunwoody in northern DeKalb County is the home of Holiday Inns. Yet physically this Golden Crescent north of the Perimeter and between I-75 in Cobb County and I-85 in Gwinnett County seems not to have changed greatly: the buildings are tree-shaded and lush foliage and large-lot requirements have given most of the communities a woodsy look.

The 6th Congressional District of Georgia occupies a large portion of this Golden Crescent north of Atlanta, including most of Cobb County, Fulton County north of the Perimeter, and to the east northern DeKalb County and a slice of Gwinnett. Its creation for the 1992 election was a recognition of the explosive growth of affluent suburban Atlanta. It would surely surprise Georgians a generation or two ago to learn that one of their congressional districts would rank among the nation's richest and most educated. The 6th ranks 11th of 435 districts in percentage of adults with a college degree, at 40%; it ranked 23d in median family income in 1990, behind districts all in larger metro areas. It is easily the most Republican district in Georgia, and by some measures one of the most heavily Republican districts in the country.

The congressman from the 6th District is Newt Gingrich, first elected in 1978, for years Georgia's lone Republican congressman, now speaker of the House of Representatives. In less than six years Gingrich moved from being a backbencher despised by Democratic House leaders and mistrusted by Republicans in the Executive Branch to a guiding figure in American politics. Gingrich grew up as the son of a Army officer, part of the career military world that in so many ways is more American than America itself. His political career, he says, dates from a visit to the ossuary at Verdun, France, where the sight of the bones of thousands of soldiers convinced him that politics matters. Gingrich went to college at Emory, got a Ph.D. in European history at Tulane, then in 1970 started teaching at West Georgia College in Carrollton. A Republican who favored civil rights, was something of an environmentalist and who was fascinated by space travel and science fiction, he ran for Congress in 1974 in a still mostly rural district south and west of Georgia, challenging the conservative Democratic incumbent as unethical. He lost narrowly, ran again in 1976 and lost again as Jimmy Carter swept rural Georgia; he persevered and won in 1978, just as House Republicans were embracing the Kemp-Roth 30% tax cut.

Although Gingrich has changed positions on a few issues like the environment, over a long career he has steadily advocated a coherent and consistent set of ideas. Gingrich is an American exceptionalist, a believer in the idea widely shared by American voters—but widely rejected by American intellectuals—that this is a uniquely good nation with a special mission in world history. While his liberal contemporaries disparaged traditional America in struggles over civil rights, he was living in the most integrated part of America, the career military, and during Vietnam he was married with children and saw no need to justify his lack of military service. He is a cultural conservative who believes that liberal values are destroying the lives of the poor, a market capitalist who celebrates technological innovation.

As a young Republican in a House that had been dominated by Democrats for four decades, Gingrich argued that ranking Republicans should fight Democratic bills, not try to compromise with them for a few crumbs in return, and should frontally challenge Democratic ideas. In the early 1980s he formed the Conservative Opportunity Society—the opposite, he said, of the liberal welfare state—and organized colleagues to give special orders speeches directed not at the House but at the C-SPAN audience. Gingrich dared to challenge Speaker Jim Wright in December 1987 by bringing the ethics charges against him which, after bitter controversy, brought Wright's resignation in June 1989. In March 1989, after Dick Cheney was appointed secretary of Defense, Gingrich ran for whip against Edward Madigan, who was next in line in the leadership and had the support of fellow Illinoisan, Minority Leader Robert Michel. But Gingrich rounded up support from conservatives, younger members, even some moderates, and won 87–85. The ranks of his opponents soon started to thin, starting with Madigan who became secretary of Agriculture.

As a child Gingrich told people his goal was to become speaker of the House, and he worked steadily and shrewdly toward that goal for 20 years, though almost no one else thought it was attainable. His courtship of Republican moderates, for example, was not just momentary but continual; he listened respectfully to their views and engaged in intellectually serious interchange. His use of ethics issues helped erode the Democrats' moral authority, but only because he was careful to make charges that stuck. Democrats attacked him for doing almost no work on legislation and dismissed his goal of achieving Republican control as ridiculous—an argument that is obsolete now. Colleagues mistrusted him because he seemed indifferent to the professional and sometimes personal ruin he inflicted on politicians who got in his way. But Gingrich kept planning his way ahead. In 1992 he helped to engineer the ouster of Jerry Lewis and election of Dick Armey as chairman of the Republican Conference and the selection of John Kasich over Alex McMillan as ranking Republican on the Budget Committee: both would become key leaders of his Republican majority. He used the GOPAC organization, which he inherited from Delaware Governor Pete duPont to raise money to help candidates when the National Republican Congressional Committee was in financial trouble; Democrats attacked him for not disclosing donors, though the law did not require it. With logistical help from the Progress and Freedom Foundation, he taught his course "Renewing American Civilization," for three years first at Kenesaw State College, then at Reinhardt College—both in Georgia. It was in arranging these matters that he made the mistakes which led to his House reprimand on ethics charges in January 1997. The offense stemmed from his failure to hire a tax attorney to review the unique financing of his course and from the inconsistent information he later gave the Ethics Committee, according to the panel's 7–1 ruling. GOPAC contended that the financing of the course was entirely legal, but facing a threat that he might lose his speakership if he contested the findings, Gingrich signed a statement admitting the violations. All of this led to an unprecedented $300,000 payment which Gingrich agreed to pay by January 1999, with help from a loan provided by Bob Dole. Ironically, Gingrich's aim all along was to use the college course to change the American mind; he may have had some success in his ends, but in his means he helped to turn many Americans' minds against him.

After Minority Leader Robert Michel announced his retirement in October 1993, Gingrich effectively became party leader a year before the 1994 election. He worked closely with the Clinton White House and rounded up the promised number of votes for NAFTA, which passed with 132 Republicans and 102 Democrats. But he took a tough stand against the Clinton healthcare plan. He worked hard to recruit and raise money and campaign for 1994 Congressional candidates who shared his views. Although he received a lot of organizational help from other Republicans, chiefly Dick Armey, the Contract With America was Gingrich's initiative, more than anyone else's. Against conventional wisdom and the scorn of most reporters, he committed Republicans to voting on specific issues and bills; by staging a big Capitol rally September 27 and then stressing the Contract when Democrats criticized it, he helped nationalize the election and reduce the already declining political skills and institutional advantages of the Democrats. In May he thought Republicans might win House control; by August, with the Democrats' debacle on the crime and healthcare bills, he predicted they would; in November he seemed unsurprised by victory—Republicans gained 52 seats for a 230–204 majority.

By 1996 the consensus in the press was that the Contract was highly unpopular and a big mistake. But the fact is that it enabled Gingrich to control the agenda of the new congressional majority, which otherwise would have flailed about in dozens of different directions. Ironically, for all Gingrich's ambitions to shape the national mind, he had more success as an inside-the-House legislative leader than as an outside-the-House shaper of public opinion. It should always be remembered that one possible result of legislative activity is no result at all, that majorities are not automatically assembled, that entropy is more natural than concerted action. Gingrich used the Contract, the budget process, the appropriations bills to lead the House to purposeful action. He established a good working relationship with Bob Dole—something that was by no means inevitable—and with Republican governors. He made one very major miscalculation when he assumed that Bill Clinton would cave in and accept the Congress's budget in 1995 and that a four-week government shutdown would not hurt Republicans politically; he had no fallback when Clinton was suddenly able to characterize himself as the purposeful, decisive preserver of government against those who would wreck it. This caused Republicans to abandon their sweeping plans as they dropped about 10% behind Democrats in generic polls (which party's candidate would you vote for for Congress?) and led to schisms with hard-line Republicans over issues such as the minimum wage and environmental laws in 1996. But the appropriations bills Clinton eventually signed that year cut non-defense discretionary spending for the first time since 1971—a decisive change in the trajectory of government. His Medicare reform—routinely called "cuts" by Democrats and the press, though they would still increase spending—is widely thought to be a political failure. Still, he predicted at the time that Medicare would make the 1996 House elections hard-fought and close, but that Republicans would win, which is what happened; and no serious student of public policy believes that Medicare can indefinitely continue on its current course without disaster. He has undeniably been a constructive force on foreign policy, trade, scientific research: policies that are important for society's long-range interests.

In July 1996, pushed by backbench Republicans, Gingrich brought forward the welfare reform package which Clinton had twice vetoed along with other bills. In doing so, he severed the cause of House Republicans from that of the lagging Dole campaign, and invited Clinton to sever his campaign's fate from that of congressional Democrats by signing the bill, an invitation Clinton, after some dithering, accepted. But more important than the transitory political effect was the effect on public policy and the public mind. By ending the entitlement to welfare, the Republican Congress and Democratic President sent a message that welfare was no longer a guarantee, and that a lifetime of dependency was no longer possible. It is probably no accident that welfare rolls peaked in 1994 and started falling with the election of the Republican Congress, just as it is no accident that interest rates peaked and then started falling again in November 1994.

"I think I am a transformational figure," Gingrich has said. But he is also a highly unpopular one. Some of this reflects the bias of a press which routinely portrays him unfairly, but not all. What is it that so many people dislike about him? A cocksureness, a professorial abstractness about policy, a more than occasional petulance and high self-regard. America after all is not a Gaullist country. Gingrich is sometimes politically tone-deaf, as when he accepted a $4.5 million book contract from Rupert Murdoch's HarperCollins or when he seemed to whine that Bill Clinton left him in the back of Air Force One, unconsulted. The real problem may be that Gingrich is addicted to what *The Economist* calls "crunchiness"—making plain the sharp differences between his views and those of his opponents, forcing clear choices over issues that most voters would prefer to slough over. His insistence on proclaiming traditional moral stands that would have been entirely noncontroversial in the Eisenhower era now enrages a media and educated elite—and probably a majority of the American people—who have staked their lives on the proposition that these moral standards can be ignored or waived, and are understandably reluctant to look at evidence of the harm that has been done. His insistence on rubbing people's noses in the failure of big government is resisted by people who have, after all, supported such big government for many years. He is a teacher, and not an entirely steady or pleasant one, whose lessons many in his audience would prefer to ignore.

Interestingly, this same popular resistance to a politician who claims with some justice to be representing the views of the people has shown up in his different districts in Georgia. The 6th District which he represented in the 1970s and 1980s covered south Atlanta suburbs near Hartsfield Airport and traditionally Democratic counties out in the country. In 1990 he nearly lost there, as Democrat David Worley attacked him for supporting the congressional pay raise and opposing government intervention in the Eastern Airlines strike; Gingrich won by only 974 votes after spending $1.5 million. In 1992, Speaker Tom Murphy tried to beat Gingrich by putting him in a new 3d District farther out from Atlanta with incumbent Democrat Richard Ray. Gingrich decided to run in the new, heavily Republican 6th District instead, but faced primary opposition from Herman Clark, who had resigned his seat in the legislature to run. Democrats joined in and urged Gingrich haters to cross party lines and vote for Clark, who attacked Gingrich for his 22 House bank overdrafts and for his "carpetbagging"; Gingrich won by only 980 votes, 51%–49%. In the general election Gingrich was also attacked on personal grounds. He won 58%–42%, comfortably but behind normal party lines. In 1994 he was opposed by former Congressman Ben Jones, running in his third district in three elections; Gingrich won 64%–36%, a wide margin but again below the party line vote here. In 1996 millionaire Michael Coles, of the Great American Cookie Company, spent liberally, $3.3 million, against Gingrich, who spent $5.5 million—the most exepensive 1996 House race; Gingrich repeated his 1992 percentage, winning 58%–42%.

It is interesting to ponder how history would have been different if Gingrich had received 1,000 fewer votes in either 1990 or 1992. It is likely that without his vision, determination and hard work Republicans would not have won their majority. Yet now that they have achieved it and despite his sweeping power, his role is not quite so essential: the machine is in motion and others have shown they are capable of taking the controls. This is why Republicans could seriously consider dumping him as speaker in early January 1997 (nine actually did vote against him), and why even after his settlement of the $300,000 payment many still wonder whether they wish to go into the election of 1998 with the burden of his unpopularity on their backs. But the fact is that Gingrich in or out of office will be a target of Democratic attacks, just as Republicans didn't stop attacking Jimmy Carter after 1980 or Democrats Herbert Hoover after 1932. Under Republican rules change, Gingrich can serve no more than four terms as speaker, and has looked forward publicly to working with a Republican president in 2001 and 2002; he has tried to combine incrementalist tactics in negotiating budget and other bills with Bill Clinton with a visionary strategy for governing which he hopes Republicans will be in a position to implement after 2000. It was not at all clear in early 1997 that Gingrich could carry out any or all of these plans. But he has far exceeded expectations before, and even if he does nothing else he will have uniquely changed the course of American politics.

The People: Pop. 1990: 586,641; 11% rural; 5% age 65+; 90% White; 6% Black; 2% Asian; 2% Hispanic origin. Households: 62% married couple families; 32% married couple fams. w. children; 70% college educ.; median household income: $46,997; per capita income: $22,181; median gross rent: $600; median house value: $120,500.

1996 Presidential Vote

Dole (R)	186,084	(61%)
Clinton (D)	100,714	(33%)
Perot (I)	15,416	(5%)

1992 Presidential Vote

Bush (R)	155,469	(55%)
Clinton (D)	84,064	(30%)
Perot (I)	41,959	(15%)

Rep. Newt Gingrich (R)

Elected 1978; b. June 17, 1943, Harrisburg, PA; home, Marietta; Emory U., B.A. 1965, Tulane U., M.A. 1968, Ph.D. 1971; Baptist; married (Marianne).

Career: Asst. Prof., W. GA Col., 1970–78.

DC Office: 2428 RHOB 20515, 202-225-4501; Fax: 202-225-4656; e-mail: georgia6@hr.house.gov.

District Offices: Marietta, 770-565-6398.

Committees: *Speaker of the House.*

Group Ratings and Key Votes: Speaker does not usually vote

Election Results

1996 general	Newt Gingrich (R)	174,155	(58%)	($5,577,715)
	Michael Coles (D)	127,135	(42%)	($3,325,030)
1996 primary	Newt Gingrich (R)	unopposed		
1994 general	Newt Gingrich (R)	119,432	(64%)	($1,817,792)
	Ben Jones (D)	66,700	(36%)	($321,774)

SEVENTH DISTRICT

The red clay hills of north Georgia, home of the Cherokee Nation before they were sent west in the 1830s on the Trail of Tears, have been manufacturing country for the last century. There are hundreds of textile mills and dozens of carpet mills located near the supply of natural cotton and along the railroad lines heading southwest at the base of the southern Appalachian chain. Factories were hailed as the vanguard of technological progress by the late 19th Century propagandists of the New South, and in fact the factories produced a higher standard of living than farms on this stubborn land. But mill work put scant premium on education or the cultivation of civic virtues and did little to bring in higher-skill white-collar work. All-white hiring practices maintained racial segregation in mostly white north Georgia. Today north Georgia is developing a different kind of economy, as the example of Atlanta shines to the south and spreads out interstate highways north into what used to be mill towns. Cobb County, once centered on the Lockheed aircraft factory in Marietta, has been transformed into an upscale suburb and office center; places like the textile mill town of LaGrange or the carpet mill town of Rome are seeing change as well.

The 7th Congressional District of Georgia includes much of this part of north Georgia. It extends along the state's western boundary from LaGrange to Rome, and extends east to Cartersville, where U.S. 41 starts its four-lane roll toward Atlanta, and takes in part of western Cobb County, including the old center of Marietta. This was Democratic territory from the time of General Jackson and General Sherman until the civil rights revolution of the 1960s. In the 1970s Carrollton, in the western part of the 7th, was the home of a West Georgia College professor who, in his third try, became a Republican congressman: Newt Gingrich. Now north Georgia is solidly Republican and Gingrich is Speaker of the House.

The congressman from the 7th is Bob Barr, a Republican elected in 1994 and already prominent on national issues. Like most members of the Georgia delegation, Barr grew up elsewhere; his father, like Gingrich's, was in the Army and he went to high school in Tehran and college at the University of Southern California. In the 1970s he worked as a CIA analyst while he went to law school at Georgetown University. In 1978 he left the agency and moved to Georgia to practice law; in 1986 he became U.S. Attorney in Atlanta. That was a high-profile job in which he successfully prosecuted, among others, Republican Congressman Pat Swindall.

In 1992 Barr ran for the Senate, and with 24% in the primary just made it into a runoff with Paul Coverdell. He lost the runoff 50.5%–49.5%. Undaunted, in 1994 Barr ran for the House. Against a less conservative primary opponent he won 57%–43%. In the general election, he faced incumbent Buddy Darden, a Democrat with a mixed voting record who stayed in office in a Republican-leaning district. Barr's campaign gave out t-shirts showing Darden jogging with Bill Clinton and attacked Darden for voting for the Clinton tax increase and the crime bill. Darden replied that he voted against the Clinton healthcare plan and for the balanced budget amendment, but he could not deny he was a Clinton supporter. Darden lost, 52%–48%.

Barr has a strongly conservative voting record, is a stern opponent of gun control and proponent of family values, though he is not a gun enthusiast and has been divorced twice. "It's really come to the point of no return with government taking so much power. I really have a tremendous fear of government taking away our freedoms." Though as a freshman he ranked 20th of 20 Republicans on the Judiciary Committee, Gingrich named him head of the Republican Firearms Legislation Task Force, where he took a lead role on two major pieces of legislation. The first was the anti-terrorism bill sought after the April 1995 Oklahoma City bombing. Barr led a fight to amend the bill produced by Judiciary Chairman Henry Hyde and stitched together a coalition of conservative Republicans angry at government misconduct at Waco and Ruby Ridge and liberal Democrats long opposed to government infringements of civil liberties. His amendment deleted the government's authority to designate chosen foreign groups as terrorist and withhold entry visas to their members, and the provision to allow illegally obtained wiretap evidence in terrorism cases. It also struck the provisions lowering the standard of proof for prosecution when the guns used in crimes are provided in court, and restricted proposed smokeless powder and armor-piercing bullet studies. In March 1996 the amendment passed 246–171, with support from most Republicans and about one-third of Democrats.

Two months later Barr introduced the Defense of Marriage Act, allowing states to refuse to recognize same-sex marriages and to define marriage for federal benefit purposes as the legal union of one man and one woman. This was a response to the Hawaii court case that seemed likely to legalize same-sex marriages there, which ordinarily would cause them to be honored in every state by the Constitution's full faith and credit clause. Barr's fury at liberal proponents of gay marriage was unmistakable: "This is an issue being shouted at us by extremists intent, bent on forcing a tortured view of morality on the rest of the country." The bill passed overwhelmingly and a reluctant but reelection-minded Bill Clinton signed it in the dark of night in September 1996. Another Barr cause, not passed: a constitutional amendment to deny automatic citizenship to people born to foreign parents in the United States. In January 1997, Barr was one of 26 Republicans to vote against the $300,000 penalty and reprimand handed to House Speaker Gingrich by the Ethics Committee.

Georgia Democrats would have loved to beat Barr in 1996, and Georgia Speaker Tom Murphy, a resident of the 7th District, helped recruit Charlie Watts, Banking Committee Chairman in the Georgia House. But Barr's positions proved far from anathema, and his fundraising prowess was impressive: he spent $1.2 million to Watt's $300,000. Barr won with 58%, carrying every county, even beating Watts in his home county 55%–45%.

The People: Pop. 1990: 587,917; 46% rural; 11% age 65+; 85% White; 13% Black; 1% Asian; 1% Hispanic origin. Households: 62% married couple families; 30% married couple fams. w. children; 31% college educ.; median household income: $28,831; per capita income: $12,428; median gross rent: $403; median house value: $64,300.

1996 Presidential Vote

Dole (R)	99,320	(51%)
Clinton (D)	77,741	(40%)
Perot (I)	16,603	(9%)

1992 Presidential Vote

Bush (R)	92,652	(46%)
Clinton (D)	76,355	(38%)
Perot (I)	30,080	(15%)

Rep. Bob Barr (R)

Elected 1994; b. Nov. 5, 1948, Iowa City, IA; home, Smyrna; U. of Southern CA, B.A. 1970, George Washington U., M.A. 1972, Georgetown U., J.D. 1977; Methodist; married (Jeri).

Career: CIA Analyst, 1971–78; Practicing atty., 1978–86, 1990–94; U.S. Atty., N. GA District, 1986–90; Dir., SE Legal Foundation, 1990–92; U.S. Senate candidate, 1992.

DC Office: 1130 LHOB 20515, 202-225-2931; Fax: 202-225-2944; e-mail: bbarr@hr.house.gov.

District Offices: Carrollton, 770-836-1776; LaGrange, 706-812-1776; Marietta, 770-429-1776; Rome, 706-290-1776.

Committees: *Banking & Financial Services* (16th of 30 R): Domestic & International Monetary Policy; Financial Institutions & Consumer Credit. *Government Reform & Oversight* (23rd of 24 R): National Economic Growth, Natural Resources & Regulatory Affairs; National Security, International Affairs & Criminal Justice. *Judiciary* (16th of 20 R): Constitution; Crime.

Group Ratings

	ADA	ACLU	AFS	LCV	CFA	CON	NFIB	COC	ACU	NTLC	CHC
1996	5	0	0	15	8	30	97	94	100	100	100
1995	0	—	—	0	0	38	—	96	92	—	—

National Journal Ratings

	1995 LIB — 1995 CONS	1996 LIB — 1996 CONS
Economic	0% — 74%	27% — 71%
Social	0% — 79%	0% — 90%
Foreign	0% — 85%	0% — 79%

Key Votes of the 104th Congress

1. Reduce Medicare Growth $	Y	5. Flag Amendment	Y	9. Cuban Embargo	Y
2. Ovrd. Product Liab. Veto	Y	6. Drop EPA Limits	N	10. Bar Bosnia Troop $	Y
3. Increase Min. Wage	N	7. Repeal Assault-Weap. Ban	Y	11. Cut Anti-Missile Defense	N
4. Welfare Reform	Y	8. Ovrd. Part. Birth Veto	Y	12. Bar U.N. Uniforms	Y

Election Results

1996 general	Bob Barr (R)	112,009	(58%)	($1,272,303)
	Charlie Watts (D)	81,765	(42%)	($308,368)
1996 primary	Bob Barr (R)	unopposed		
1994 general	Bob Barr (R)	71,265	(52%)	($846,821)
	George (Buddy) Darden (D)	65,978	(48%)	($622,336)

EIGHTH DISTRICT

South Georgia has been under attack and enemy occupation more than almost any other part of America. Most famously, of course, when General William Tecumseh Sherman's troops set out from Atlanta, without supplies or lines of communication, to march through Georgia to the sea, burning its antebellum mansions, destroying its crops, capturing its leader (the Jefferson Davis Memorial in Ocilla marks the spot where Union troops took him in May 1865), leaving memories of slaves freed, handed down as family lore for over a century. But the land bears, if only on its road signs, the memory of another invasion, when poor white farmers aided by Andrew Jackson's troops drove the Cherokees and other Indians off this land, where Indians had lived for perhaps thousands of years, west over the Trail of Tears to what is now Oklahoma. And there was the oppression of blacks by whites under the old systems of slavery and legal segregation, the latter not long dead—a past recalled by Macon's Harriet Tubman Historical and Cultural Museum. More recently, many south Georgians, black and white, find themselves threatened by drug dealers heading north on I-75 from Florida, spreading addiction and AIDS to Macon and smaller towns that once thought they were immune to these scourges.

The 8th Congressional District runs down the center of Georgia, roughly along these lines of occupation, past immense stands of soft lumber pines, through counties where 60% of the world's kaolin (used for china and ceramics) is mined, all the way from Macon to the Okeefenokee Swamp and the Florida line. The district lines were more regular for 1996 than for 1992 and 1994, thanks to a federal court-ordered plan handed down in 1995 after the Supreme Court overturned the former lines as a "racial gerrymander." The 8th now includes all of Macon, home of music legends Otis Redding, Little Richard and the Allman Brothers, a city proud of its restored houses and Japanese cherry trees (it has 20 times as many as Washington). The 8th no longer includes white areas in and around Albany, Moultrie or Valdosta; Dougherty, Worth, Colquitt, and Lowndes Counties are now in the new 2d, while the 8th reaches northward into the former 3d District counties of Lamar, Upson, Monroe, and Crawford. This has been Democratic country since Sherman's troops came through, and the 1995 redistricting made the 8th more Democratic, primarily by increasing the black percentage from 21% to 31%. Bill Clinton lost the old 8th in 1992 but narrowly carried the new 8th in 1996, the same year Democratic Senator Max Cleland carried all but two of its counties.

The congressman from the 8th District is Saxby Chambliss, a Republican elected in 1994 to replace a retiring conservative Democrat. Chambliss grew up in Shreveport, Louisiana, the son of an Episcopalian minister, went to college in Georgia, and had practiced business and agriculture law in Moultrie since 1968. In 1992 he ran for the House and lost the Republican primary; in 1994 he was the sole Republican candidate, while Democrats, as in days of yore, had a multi-candidate contest, the ultimate winner of which was Craig Mathis, 32-year-old son of onetime (1971–81) Congressman Dawson Mathis and a former staffer for Congressmen Ed Jenkins and Sonny Callahan. In Chambliss's favor were public antipathy toward Clinton and Chambliss's own sports credentials. For two decades he had coached Little League; one of his former players is now the University of Georgia football coach. Chambliss called for targeting repeat offenders and reducing the deficit; he opposed Dick Armey's proposal to zero out peanut subsidies. He dismissed Mathis: "He's a nice young man. But as soon as he gets elected, he becomes an integral part of the Clinton team." Chambliss won 63%–37%.

"Saxby's chief concerns are strengthening and building upon Georgia's military tradition and agricultural heritage," his office brochure states. In the House, Newt Gingrich saw that Chambliss had the committee assignments he needed most—National Security to look after Robins Air Force Base near Macon, and Agriculture to protect subsidies for peanut farmers in the counties to the south. In his first term Chambliss toured every military base in Georgia (80-plus years of Carl Vinson, Richard Russell, and Sam Nunn is a tough legacy to follow) and worked with locals to remove Robins, an air logistics center, from the final Base Closing Commission list in 1995. To protect peanut farmers, he voted in committee against the Freedom to Farm Act in 1995 with four other Republicans, which defeated it temporarily; he opposed a provision to end the cotton marketing program as well. When the leadership folded the farm bill into the budget, Chambliss threatened not to support it but backed down under pressure. With Sanford Bishop of the 2d District, he devised a new "no-net-cost, market-oriented" peanut program, with a quota set at the projected domestic demand for edible peanuts; this was put into the final Freedom to Farm Act, passed by the House in February 1996 and signed by Bill Clinton in April.

On other issues, Chambliss almost always votes with the Republican leadership, but was one of the 1994 freshman class members who wanted a lower income cap on the $500-per-child tax credit. He staunchly opposed Clinton proposals for regulating tobacco like a drug. He opposes gun control and has become vice chairman of the Sportsmen's Caucus, which sponsored the first Congressional Shoot-out. An avid outdoorsman, he said "On one of those rare outdoor occasions when my mind turns to a pending issue in Congress, I have found no better place to be alone with my thoughts than my favorite fishing hole," he said. He hailed the National Wildlife Refuge Improvement Act passed in April 1996, which legalized hunting and fishing in numerous national wildlife refuges, and supported revision of the "outdated" Endangered Species Act.

Redistricting put the 8th District within range of Democratic targeters for 1996. Chambliss's home town was removed from the district, and he moved to an apartment in Macon. But he vastly outspent Democrat Jim Wiggins, a Vietnam veteran and prosecutor, by $1.08 million to $277,000 by October 16. Chambliss won in November 53%–47%, running ahead of Bob Dole and Senate candidate Guy Millner, benefiting from his achievements as Democratic incumbents had benefited from local issues in the past. In December 1996 he was one of two sophomores on the Republican Steering Committee.

The People: Census data not available due to 1996 redistricting.

1996 Presidential Vote

Clinton (D)	90,662	(47%)
Dole (R)	85,224	(45%)
Perot (I)	14,643	(8%)

1992 Presidential Vote

Clinton (D)	95,225	(46%)
Bush (R)	79,079	(39%)
Perot (I)	30,144	(15%)

Rep. Saxby Chambliss (R)

Elected 1994; b. Nov. 10, 1943, Warrenton, NC; home, Macon; U. of GA, B.A. 1966; U. of TN, J.D. 1968; Episcopalian; married (Julianne).

Career: Practicing atty., 1968–94.

DC Office: 1708 LHOB 20515, 202-225-6531; Fax: 202-225-3013; e-mail: saxby@hr.house.gov.

District Offices: Macon, 912-475-0665; Waycross, 912-287-1180.

Committees: *Agriculture* (18th of 27 R): Forestry, Resource Conservation & Research; General Farm Commodities; Risk Management & Specialty Crops. *National Security* (21st of 30 R): Military Readiness; Military Research & Development.

Group Ratings

	ADA	ACLU	AFS	LCV	CFA	CON	NFIB	COC	ACU	NTLC	CHC
1996	0	0	0	15	8	17	100	100	100	100	100
1995	0	—	—	6	0	56	—	100	96	—	—

National Journal Ratings

	1995 LIB — 1995 CONS	1996 LIB — 1996 CONS
Economic	33% — 66%	0% — 82%
Social	0% — 79%	0% — 90%
Foreign	0% — 85%	30% — 65%

Key Votes of the 104th Congress

1. Reduce Medicare Growth $	Y	5. Flag Amendment	Y	9. Cuban Embargo	Y
2. Ovrd. Product Liab. Veto	Y	6. Drop EPA Limits	N	10. Bar Bosnia Troop $	Y
3. Increase Min. Wage	N	7. Repeal Assault-Weap. Ban	Y	11. Cut Anti-Missile Defense	N
4. Welfare Reform	Y	8. Ovrd. Part. Birth Veto	Y	12. Bar U.N. Uniforms	Y

Election Results

1996 general	Saxby Chambliss (R)	93,619	(53%)	($1,081,914)
	Jim Wiggins (D)	84,506	(47%)	($277,400)
1996 primary	Saxby Chambliss (R)	unopposed		
1994 general	Saxby Chambliss (R)	89,591	(63%)	($680,075)
	Craig Mathis (D)	53,408	(37%)	($352,437)

NINTH DISTRICT

In the last years of the 20th Century, the hills and mountains of north Georgia have suddenly become one of the boom areas of the South. This is a sharp turn in their history. Since the Cherokee were driven out early in the 19th Century, this has been poor country, where small farmers scratched a living off rocky land. It was devastated by the Civil War, by General Sherman's troops and because so many young men who left to fight for the Confederacy (and a few who left from mountain counties long Republican to fight for the Union) never returned. After the war not much changed for a while. Most communities lived in isolation; roads with hairpin curves led to remote hills where until very recently moonshine stills were more common than summer cabins. In time textile mills began springing up along the railroads, around Gainesville poultry production became a big business, and in Dalton the craft tradition of tufted bedspread handiwork was transformed into the world's largest carpet industry. But these were low-wage industries, and all-white; there had never been many slaves here, and in 1912 Forsyth County made headlines when it drove out its few black residents. It is only more recently, with the surging growth of greater Atlanta which began in the 1960s and accelerated in the 1990s, that prosperity and growth have made their way here. Forsyth and next-door Cherokee County are fast-growing, affluent suburban areas; Gainesville is surging; even the reservoirs near Gainesville and the mountains near North Carolina are filling up with summer homes and mountain cabins.

The 9th Congressional District of Georgia consists of the northern end of the state, from the Georgia suburbs of Chattanooga and Dalton in the west to the old Republican and new resort counties in the east. It extends south to include Forsyth County and part of Cherokee. A few counties here have always been Republican, many started switching in the 1970s and 1980s, and Cherokee and Forsyth now are among the most heavily Republican counties in the South—or anywhere. Economic prosperity and cultural traditionalism have sent politics here in one direction, even against national tides: despite north Georgia native Governor Zell Miller's strong support for Bill Clinton, every county in the 9th District voted for Bob Dole in 1996.

The congressman from the 9th District is Nathan Deal, first elected in 1992, who switched parties and became a Republican in April 1995. Deal grew up in Gainesville, went to Mercer University, then served in the Army from 1966–68; he returned home to practice law and hold public offices a young lawyer takes as civic duty—assistant district attorney, juvenile court judge, county attorney. In 1980, at 38, he was elected to the state Senate, as a Democrat; Jimmy Carter was still president, the legislature was overwhelmingly Democrat, and it would have been quixotic to run as a Republican. He proved a capable legislator and was elected Senate president pro tem in 1989 and 1991. In 1992, with the retirement of 16-year Congressman Ed Jenkins, a power on the Ways and Means Committee, Deal ran, and beat a Republican abortion opponent with 59% of the vote.

In the House, Deal helped found the Fiscal Caucus, a group of 26 freshman Democrats who supported the line-item veto and a balanced budget amendment. He opposed the Clinton budget and tax increase in August 1993, and in 1994 co-sponsored a version of the "A to Z" spending cuts plan, which called for a special session of the House to consider lopping off additional parts of the federal budget. Many saw Deal as a potential party-switcher, but while campaigning in 1994 he said, "If I choose to switch during the term, I think the honest thing to do is resign and have a special election." He beat an underfunded Republican, but with only 58%—a sign of increasing Republican sentiment.

In early 1995 he soldiered on as a Democrat, becoming co-chairman of The Coalition, a newly formed group of moderate-to-conservative House Democrats seeking bipartisan legislation. He worked with other Democrats to offer an alternative to the Republicans' welfare reform package, which got the votes of every Democrat and a few Republicans as well. He then moved quickly. On Monday, April 3, he was saying how pleased he was by Democrats' support for his welfare reform package. On Wednesday, April 5, he found himself at odds with Democrats' opposition to tax cuts and with senior Democrats' criticisms of Clean Water Act revision proposals he and Louisiana's Jimmy Hayes (later a party-switcher himself) had gotten approved on a bipartisan committee vote. On Monday, April 10, back home in Gainesville for the congressional recess, he announced he was switching to the Republican Party—the first party-switcher in the 104th Congress. He said the national Democratic Party was unwilling to admit it was "out of touch with mainstream America" and "I think that it is important that at some point you get away from the schizophrenia I have had to deal with." Democrats were stunned and Newt Gingrich was clearly delighted; Deal was rewarded with a seat on the Commerce Committee. Despite his earlier statements, Deal did not resign to run as a Republican in a special election.

Deal has not proved to be a totally party-line Republican. In July 1996 he backed the minimum wage increase and bucked the leadership by leading successful opposition to cost-of-living increases in the salaries for congressmen and staffers. But his voting record was mostly conservative, and constituents did not protest vehemently at the Tailgate Talk public meetings he held in town squares every summer. Some local Republicans were irritated by his switch, and threatened primary opposition in 1996, but no one ran. In the general he faced state Representative Ken Poston, his best-funded and most articulate opponent. Poston ran town hall meetings on the Internet and called for political reform; Deal attacked him for supporting trial lawyers and opposing a measure to require inmates to serve 85% of their sentences. Deal was reelected 66%–34%, his best performance so far, carrying every county and running especially strong among suburbanites in Cherokee (73%) and Forsyth (79%) Counties. He promises to work on national issues like welfare and immigration, as well as local matters like the Chickamauga-Chattanooga road.

The People: Pop. 1990: 586,310; 78% rural; 12% age 65+; 94% White; 4% Black; 2% Hispanic origin. Households: 66% married couple families; 31% married couple fams. w. children; 30% college educ.; median household income: $26,581; per capita income: $12,027; median gross rent: $365; median house value: $62,200.

1996 Presidential Vote

Dole (R)	115,306	(55%)
Clinton (D)	73,861	(35%)
Perot (I)	20,809	(10%)

1992 Presidential Vote

Bush (R)	94,744	(48%)
Clinton (D)	70,717	(36%)
Perot (I)	32,698	(16%)

Rep. Nathan Deal (R)

Elected 1992; b. Aug. 25, 1942, Millen; home, Lula; Mercer U., B.A. 1964, J.D. 1966; Baptist; married (Sandra).

Career: Army, 1966–68; Hall Cnty. Atty., 1966–70; Asst. Dist. Atty., NE Judicial Circuit, 1970–71; Hall Cnty. Juvenile Court Judge, 1971–72; Practicing atty., 1971–92; GA Senate, 1980–92, Pres. Pro Tem, 1989–90, 1991–92.

DC Office: 1406 LHOB 20515, 202-225-5211; Fax: 202-225-8272.

District Offices: Dalton, 706-226-5320; Gainesville, 770-535-2592; Lafayette, 706-638-7042.

Committees: *Education & The Workforce* (23rd of 25 R): Postsecondary Education, Training & Life-Long Learning. *Commerce* (16th of 28 R): Finance & Hazardous Materials; Health & the Environment; Telecommunications, Trade & Consumer Protection.

Group Ratings

	ADA	ACLU	AFS	LCV	CFA	CON	NFIB	COC	ACU	NTLC	CHC
1996	5	0	17	31	38	24	89	81	90	88	93
1995	0	—	—	13	15	38	—	96	80	—	—

National Journal Ratings

	1995 LIB		1995 CONS	1996 LIB		1996 CONS
Economic	36%	—	60%	20%	—	76%
Social	0%	—	79%	0%	—	90%
Foreign	45%	—	52%	30%	—	65%

Key Votes of the 104th Congress

1. Reduce Medicare Growth $	Y	5. Flag Amendment	Y	9. Cuban Embargo	Y
2. Ovrd. Product Liab. Veto	Y	6. Drop EPA Limits	N	10. Bar Bosnia Troop $	Y
3. Increase Min. Wage	Y	7. Repeal Assault-Weap. Ban	Y	11. Cut Anti-Missile Defense	N
4. Welfare Reform	Y	8. Ovrd. Part. Birth Veto	Y	12. Bar U.N. Uniforms	Y

Election Results

1996 general	Nathan Deal (R)	132,532	(66%)	($865,898)
	Ken Poston (D)	69,662	(34%)	($429,454)
1996 primary	Nathan Deal (R)	unopposed		
1994 general	Nathan Deal (D)	79,145	(58%)	($368,648)
	Robert L. Castello (R)	57,568	(42%)	($22,953)

TENTH DISTRICT

Augusta, Georgia, is one of those small American cities that pops up now and again in our history. Founded in 1735 on the site of a fur-trading post, it is far older than Atlanta and just about as old as coastal Savannah. It was missed, fortunately, on General Sherman's march through Georgia; in those same years it was the boyhood home of Woodrow Wilson. Its antique Medical College of Georgia dates back to 1835. It is best known for its Augusta National golf course, where President Eisenhower used to tee off, and where the Masters Tournament is held every year; in 1997 Tiger Woods amazed the world with his record-breaking score at that prestigious event and attracted thousands of new fans to the sport.

Augusta was once a cotton port on the Savannah River, with its own Cotton Exchange; now it has a Riverwalk on the site of the old levee. The paper industry, stoked by the pines that grow in profusion on the flat Piedmont land, is important here; so are nuclear weapons, produced until 1989 and now under disarmament downriver in South Carolina at the Savannah River site.

The 10th Congressional District of Georgia includes Augusta and its fast-growing suburbs—they account for more than half the population and votes—plus 22 mostly rural counties in every direction. This district was very much changed by the redistricting of December 1995, which followed a Supreme Court decision overturning the boundaries used in 1992 and 1994 as a "racial gerrymander." The old 10th District did not include the black neighborhoods of Augusta, and most of its other counties were to the north and west, toward the Gwinnett County suburbs of Atlanta. Only 18% of its residents were black, and most of its smaller counties had been trending Republican for years. The new 10th includes all of Augusta, plus several black-majority counties to the south—once big plantation country; the district lost 12 of its 19 counties and gained 17 new ones. Its population now is 38% black, and even the majority-white counties mostly vote Democratic.

The congressman from the 10th District is Charlie Norwood, a Republican elected by a smashing margin in 1994 and reelected narrowly in 1996. Norwood grew up in Valdosta, went to college and dental school, served in the Army in Vietnam, then practiced dentistry in Augusta. He was president of the Georgia Dental Association and also started small businesses—Northwood Tree Nursery, Park Avenue Fabrics. In 1993 he decided to sell his dental practice and run against Congressman Don Johnson, who had just been elected in 1992. Johnson was the kind of Democrat who had held such southern seats for years: a former congressional staffer and state Senator, with strong local connections and good political instincts. But he came under scathing criticism when he broke a campaign promise to vote against any tax increase and supported the Clinton budget and tax package in 1993. Norwood's toughest race in 1994 turned out to be the primary; he came from behind to beat Ralph Hudgens in the runoff 51%–49%. When Johnson said he wanted Bill Clinton or Al Gore to visit the 10th District only if "they are coming down to endorse my opponent," Norwood invited Clinton and offered to pay his plane fare. Norwood won 65%–35%, as Johnson took one of the worst lickings of a non-scandal-tarred incumbent in recent history.

In the House Norwood has a conservative voting record, with seats on the Commerce and Education and The Workforce Committees. His one major dissent from the leadership was his successful opposition in 1995 to the sale of the Southeastern Power Administration for the purpose of deficit reduction; he was afraid private utilities would charge higher rates. He was strongly for a three-fifths supermajority requirement for all federal tax increases and denounced the IRS for delaying tax refunds. His own bills to set standards for healthcare plans and to reform OSHA were held up in committee.

One area in which Norwood has excelled is fundraising. In 1995 he ranked fifth among the 73 Republican freshmen in raising PAC money, and collected $664,000 in PAC contributions for the 1996 election. Altogether he ended up spending $1.6 million, to a healthy but outclassed $604,000 for his Democratic opponent, state legislator David Bell. Bell campaigned as a conservative, said he would support the Blue Dog Democrats in the House, but criticized Norwood and the Republicans on education, the environment, Medicare and the minimum wage (Norwood voted against the minimum wage increase). The AFL-CIO also targeted Norwood, running ads accusing him of cutting Medicare and college loans. But Norwood did not sit idly by. He challenged the accuracy of the AFL-CIO ads and persuaded all but one Augusta station not to run them; he purchased his own ads, to be run right after the AFL-CIO spots, calling them lies and urging viewers to switch channels. And when Bell ran an ad in which a cartoon fish said, "Sorry, Charlie," Norwood's campaign alerted StarKist Tuna, which called it a trademark infringement on their Charlie the Tuna ads and demanded it be yanked. Off the air, Bell attacked Norwood for taking tobacco PAC money; Norwood attacked Bell for "all the dirty labor money that you have collected that has the Mafia print on it," referring to the Laborers' Union which the Clinton Labor Department found to be mob-controlled.

This was the closest House election in Georgia in 1996. Overall Norwood won 52%–48%. He won 55%–45% in the Augusta area, a big falloff from 1994, but mostly explained by the addition of black precincts. In the rest of the district, Bell won narrowly. The result is not likely to change Norwood's style or voting record, but this district could easily see a serious contest in 1998.

The People: Census data not available due to 1996 redistricting.

1996 Presidential Vote

Clinton (D)	94,968	(48%)
Dole (R)	90,213	(46%)
Perot (I)	11,669	(6%)

1992 Presidential Vote

Clinton (D)	91,995	(46%)
Bush (R)	83,748	(42%)
Perot (I)	25,257	(13%)

Rep. Charlie Norwood (R)

Elected 1994; b. July 27, 1941, Valdosta; home, Evans; GA Southern U., B.S. 1964; Georgetown U., D.D.S. 1967; Methodist; married (Gloria).

Career: Army, 1967–69 (Vietnam); Small businessman, 1969–present; Practicing dentist, 1969–93; Pres., GA Dental Assn., 1983.

DC Office: 1707 LHOB 20515, 202-225-4101; Fax: 202-225-0279; e-mail: ga10@hr.house.gov.

District Offices: Augusta, 706-733-7066; Dublin, 912-275-2814; Milledgeville, 912-453-0373.

Committees: *Commerce* (22nd of 28 R): Energy & Power; Health & the Environment. *Education & The Workforce* (18th of 25 R): Oversight & Investigations (Vice Chmn.).

Group Ratings

	ADA	ACLU	AFS	LCV	CFA	CON	NFIB	COC	ACU	NTLC	CHC
1996	0	6	0	15	0	17	100	100	100	100	100
1995	0	—	—	6	0	56	—	100	100	—	—

National Journal Ratings

	1995 LIB — 1995 CONS			1996 LIB — 1996 CONS		
Economic	26%	—	67%	0%	—	82%
Social	0%	—	79%	0%	—	90%
Foreign	15%	—	73%	0%	—	79%

Key Votes of the 104th Congress

1. Reduce Medicare Growth $	Y	5. Flag Amendment	Y	9. Cuban Embargo	Y
2. Ovrd. Product Liab. Veto	Y	6. Drop EPA Limits	N	10. Bar Bosnia Troop $	Y
3. Increase Min. Wage	N	7. Repeal Assault-Weap. Ban	Y	11. Cut Anti-Missile Defense	N
4. Welfare Reform	Y	8. Ovrd. Part. Birth Veto	Y	12. Bar U.N. Uniforms	Y

Election Results

1996 general	Charlie Norwood (R)	96,723	(52%)	($1,622,486)
	David Bell (D)	88,054	(48%)	($604,043)
1996 primary	Charlie Norwood (R)	unopposed		
1994 general	Charlie Norwood (R)	96,099	(65%)	($787,441)
	Don Johnson (D)	51,192	(35%)	($773,927)

ELEVENTH DISTRICT

Greater Atlanta has grown out in every direction, south past the airport, west over the Chattahoochee, north past Buckhead and the Perimeter Mall and, to an extent generally unpredicted, to the east past Stone Mountain. Gwinnett County, on I-85, has become an urban community of its own: it cast 21,000 votes in 1972 and 162,000 in 1996, a level approaching Fulton County, which includes central Atlanta, or DeKalb just to the east. Now similar growth is heading east to Walton and Barrow Counties, the then-rural home of Senator (1933–71) Richard Russell, and south to Rockdale County, where spiritualist Nancy Fowler channel messages said to be from the Virgin Mary. Politically, these new growth areas favor market forces over government regulation on economic issues and traditional values over liberal ones on cultural issues; they vote overwhelmingly Republican.

But there is another Georgia in the counties beyond, a state of still rural communities, and Athens, home of the University of Georgia, the country's oldest chartered state university. Athens is the site of one of America's finest collection of Greek Revival buildings—gleaming white columns, perfectly proportioned little Parthenons, flat-roofed square houses surrounded by fluted columns with Corinthian capitals, all dating from the 1830s–50s. Politically, Athens remains liberal and Democratic, though neighboring Oconee County has been, Gwinnett-like, trending Republican.

The 11th Congressional District of Georgia consists of much of this territory, from Gwinnett County east to Athens, then northeast to the Savannah River. Gwinnett and the other counties in metro Atlanta cast 70% of the votes here in 1996, a share that will probably rise; Athens and Oconee County another 14%, the rural counties 16%. The current 11th District was created when the Supreme Court in 1995 declared Georgia's district lines a "racial gerrymander." The former 11th was a black-majority district that snaked from heavily black south DeKalb County across the state to black precincts in Savannah and Augusta; none of the new 11th is contained within these lines. Athens and most of the rural counties were formerly part of the 10th District.

The congressman from the 11th District is John Linder, a Republican elected in 1992 and 1994 in the old 4th District, which combined north DeKalb County and half of Gwinnett. Like most of the Georgia delegation, Linder grew up elsewhere, in his case in Minnesota, where he went to college and dental school. Then after two years in the Air Force he moved to greater Atlanta and practiced dentistry for 13 years. In 1977 he started Linder Financial Corporation, a lending institution for entrepreneurial ventures in the South. In 1974, at 32, he was elected to the Georgia House, where he served all but two of the next 14 years. In 1990 he challenged Democratic Congressman Ben Jones, known to TV watchers as Cooter in the *Dukes of Hazzard*, and lost 52%–48%. When 1992 redistricting removed black middle- and upper-income south DeKalb from the 4th, Jones decided to run in the new 10th, where he lost the Democratic primary. Linder ran again in the 4th, where he finished first in a six-candidate primary with 38%, then won the runoff with 62%. In the general he faced Democratic state Senator Cathey Steinberg and, in a race that ran along national party lines, won by just 51%–49%.

Linder is a longtime ally of Newt Gingrich; back in 1975 he, Gingrich and Paul Coverdell began meeting to try to build a strong Georgia Republican Party, surely not imagining that within 20 years they would be congressman, Speaker and Senator. Linder has little of Gingrich's articulateness, but shares most of his views. His legislative priorities, he says, "include lowering taxes to put those dollars back in the hands of working people and families and eliminating the cumbersome regulations that hinder free enterprise"; his "over-arching ideology [is] that individuals will make better decisions for their families than the government." His demeanor is calm and quiet; he made few waves in his first term except for sponsoring the Republicans' three-term limit on service as a committee's ranking minority member—an important procedural change now that Republicans are chairmen. After Republicans won control, Gingrich gave Linder a seat on the Rules Committee and called on him often to preside over contentious debates, and his quiet Minnesota-nice manner helped make things go smoothly. He differed from Gingrich only occasionally: he wanted a more powerful line-item veto and a balanced budget amendment with a three-fifths vote to raise taxes, and called term limits "a bad idea whose time has come." But he works hard to devise and support leadership positions.

Linder also became the informal head of a group of Republicans determined to defend Gingrich on ethics charges. In September 1996 he introduced a resolution demanding a special counsel in the ethics probe against Democratic Leader Dick Gephardt, whom the Ethics Committee found had filed an inaccurate statement on the ownership of a beach house. That same month he attacked Ethics Committee ranking Democrat Jim McDermott as "the least ethical person in the House." Linder revealed that Gingrich had reached a settlement with the committee in December 1996 when he said that Gingrich had provided inaccurate information because of an error by his former lawyer—a claim the committee neither accepted nor rejected; Gingrich accepted the Ethics Committee's report in January 1997, which recommended a House reprimand, and he agreed to pay the $300,000 penalty with his personal funds.

Linder has also been a key Gingrich lieutenant on electoral politics. After the 1996 election, Gingrich chose him to succeed Bill Paxon as chairman of the National Republican Congressional Committee. Linder said he wanted to build on Paxon's success in helping produce the first two consecutive Republican House majorities since 1926 and 1928. On campaign finance reform, he favored barring union dues from being used for political purposes, raising the contribution limits set in 1974, and requiring greater disclosure.

Linder has won reelection himself fairly easily. In 1994, against an opponent who was supported by national Democrats and who attacked him as a tool of the National Rifle Association and as an opponent of abortion, Linder won 58%–42%. He narrowly lost DeKalb County, but won 69% in Gwinnett. For 1996 he quickly decided not to run in the new Democratic-leaning 4th District, and ran in the solidly Republican 11th even though he still resides outside its boundaries in Tucker. In one debate he attacked his Democratic opponent, state House Majority Whip Tommy Stephenson, for going into bankruptcy, having his car repossessed and his electricity and telephone service cut off; Stephenson called Linder "the meanest man in America." Linder had a huge financial advantage, and won 64%–36%. He lost Athens and one rural county, but carried 73% of the vote in Gwinnett, and over 60% in Barrow, Walton, and Rockdale.

The People: Census data not available due to 1996 redistricting.

1996 Presidential Vote

Dole (R)	128,320	(54%)
Clinton (D)	88,083	(37%)
Perot (I)	17,668	(7%)

1992 Presidential Vote

Bush (R)	109,590	(49%)
Clinton (D)	80,858	(36%)
Perot (I)	34,025	(15%)

Rep. John Linder (R)

Elected 1992; b. Sept. 9, 1942, Deer River, MN; home, Tucker; U. of MN, B.S. 1964, D.D.S., 1967; Presbyterian; married (Lynne).

Career: Air Force, 1967–69; Practicing dentist, 1969–82; Founder & Pres., Linder Financial Corp., 1977–92; GA House of Reps., 1974–80, 1982–90.

DC Office: 1005 LHOB 20515, 202-225-4272; Fax: 202-225-4696; e-mail: jlinder@hr.house.gov.

District Offices: Athens, 706-355-9909; Duluth, 770-931-9550.

Committees: *National Republican Congressional Committee Chairman. Rules* (4th of 9 R): Legislative & Budget Process.

Group Ratings

	ADA	ACLU	AFS	LCV	CFA	CON	NFIB	COC	ACU	NTLC	CHC
1996	0	6	0	23	15	24	100	100	100	100	100
1995	0	—	—	0	0	38	—	100	88	—	—

National Journal Ratings

	1995 LIB — 1995 CONS			1996 LIB — 1996 CONS		
Economic	0%	—	74%	0%	—	82%
Social	0%	—	79%	14%	—	77%
Foreign	0%	—	85%	36%	—	63%

Key Votes of the 104th Congress

1. Reduce Medicare Growth $	Y	5. Flag Amendment	Y	9. Cuban Embargo	Y
2. Ovrd. Product Liab. Veto	Y	6. Drop EPA Limits	N	10. Bar Bosnia Troop $	Y
3. Increase Min. Wage	N	7. Repeal Assault-Weap. Ban	Y	11. Cut Anti-Missile Defense	N
4. Welfare Reform	Y	8. Ovrd. Part. Birth Veto	Y	12. Bar U.N. Uniforms	Y

Election Results

1996 general	John Linder (R)	145,821	(64%)	($780,653)
	Tommy Stephenson (D)	80,940	(36%)	($58,200)
1996 primary	John Linder (R)	unopposed		
1994 general	John Linder (R)	90,063	(58%)	($671,801)
(GA 4)	Comer Yates (D)	65,566	(42%)	($521,432)

HAWAII

The turning point in Hawaii's history—the moment when it broke with Polynesian religion and culture, and started on its way to becoming American—came almost 200 years ago, in 1819. But a thousand or so years before that moment, this volcanic island chain was settled by Polynesians who paddled across vast Pacific expanses in small outrigger canoes. In this hospitable archipelago, teeming with food and seldom inconvenienced by bad weather, Hawaiians built a fierce civilization, with harsh taboos and cannibalism as well as alluring music and dance. The islands were united politically in 1779 by King Kamehameha I, who ate one of his rivals and maintained the old culture. But in 1819, within a year of Kamehameha's death, his consort Kaahumanu outlawed the Hawaiian religious taboos and welcomed the American missionary Hiram Bingham. The New England missionaries and their trader cousins came—while British and Russian ships occasionally put into port—and established the predominant culture. By the 1850s they were importing laborers from China and Japan and Portugal and the Philippines to work their sugar and pineapple plantations. American planters and businessmen bridled at the caprices of the royal line and, in January 1893, with the help of U.S. Marines, ousted Queen Liliuokalani from the Iolani Palace and called on the United States to annex Hawaii. President Grover Cleveland demurred, and Hawaii for five years was a republic; it was annexed by President William McKinley in July 1898.

This history is a source of regret for some; an *Onipa'a* ceremony remembering Liliuokalani's overthrow was staged by John Waihee, the first governor of native Hawaiian descent, in January 1993, with the American flag conspicuously absent. Yet Hawaii, with all its oddness and some of its recent discomforts, is a civilization both American and Pacific which has created a better life for its citizens than almost any island or native commonwealth of 100 years ago. Its ethnic mixing had already begun a century ago: disease reduced the native Hawaiians to 45,000 by the late 19th Century and they shared Liliuokalani's Hawaii with 3,000 Americans, 20,000 Chinese, 25,000 Japanese. Hawaii was well on it way to being "the gathering place of peoples," as Walter McDougall called it in his 1993 history of the North Pacific, *Let the Sea Make a Noise.*

To that Americanness, each group has made a positive contribution. The Asian migrant laborers brought traditions of hard work, family loyalty and group solidarity that found expression most vividly in the performance of the 442d "Go for Broke" Regimental Combat Team, made up mostly of sons of Japanese immigrants, which became the most decorated unit in U.S. military history. The Yankee spirit has been evident in Hawaii's commercial success, as a port and a tourist center, and in its attachment to the rule of Anglo-American law. The Hawaiian spirit is alive in the vitality of the *aloha* ambience, the welcoming of others despite their differences and a willingness to absorb the teachings of others while maintaining a certain Polynesian attitude toward life. When Pearl Harbor was attacked by the Japanese in December 1941, no one in Hawaii or on the Mainland doubted that this was part of America. Ironically, it was Hawaii's super-American tolerance that inspired segregationist southern Democrats to block its admission to the Union for years. Today, Hawaiians retain pride in their ethnic heritage—or heritages: 44% of non-military weddings are "out" marriages and 60% of babies born are of mixed ethnicity; in 1989, the state gave up trying to tabulate the ethnic origin of its legislators.

The sensible future for Hawaii is not to create enclaves or racial preference for the 12% who call themselves Hawaiians or the 21% who have some Hawaiian ancestry—and few proposals for "native sovereignty" go so far—but to nurture the special strengths of all the peoples who have made Hawaii tolerant and affluent—just as Hawaii, to protect its 10,000 unique biological and botanical species, needs not to put them under glass but to maintain the environment in which

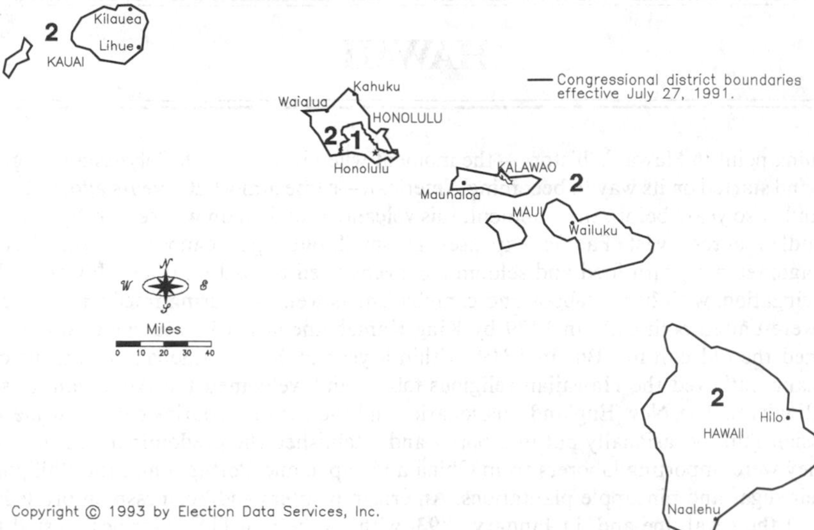

they have flourished.

Hawaii's economy was built first on agriculture, by the Big Five trading companies that shipped out sugar and pineapple and shipped in almost anything else; then on the military, important for nearly 100 years in this strategic site in the middle of the world's largest ocean. But the sugar and pineapple plantations are uneconomic, and are being closed; and military spending is down. The real engine of Hawaii's economy today is tourism: like Nevada this is a million-person commonwealth that lives on serving tourists. It is a major business far beyond the dreams of the proprietors of the cruise ships and low stucco hotels of the Waikiki of the 1950s; but it is also unstable, heavily dependent on the economies of California and Japan. Tourism peaked in 1990, with 7 million visitors, and fell to 6.1 million in 1993, then rebounded a bit to 6.9 million in 1996; unemployment doubled from 1989–95, and Hawaii, like Japan, has had zero economic growth this decade. Moreover, many tourism jobs are low-wage, and Hawaiians worry that educated young people will go to the Mainland to find high-skill work. Living costs here are one-third higher than on the Mainland; Hawaii got its first discount store, a K-mart, only in 1992. And real estate prices, though they have fallen from the astronomic levels to which Japanese buyers inflated them in the late 1980s, are still beyond the reach of many local wage earners.

Governor Ben Cayetano has called for making Hawaii more business-friendly, which means changing some of the policies of this long-Democratic-ruled state, strengthening education, building a big convention center, relaxing immigration rules to attract immigrant-investors as Vancouver, British Columbia, has done. Possibilities for diversification beyond tourism do exist: ocean research, from these islands specks surrounded by miles of water; astronomy, in this land of clear air; securities markets, in one of the few inhabited places where it's daytime during the four hours when the New York Stock Exchange has closed and Tokyo has not yet opened; "health tourism," wherefore East Asians are attracted to first-class American medical facilities. After all, Hawaii has American political stability and is sensitive to East Asian ways; it has first-rate transportation and communication facilities. Almost too good: Hawaii's island ecology means there are few species here and that the islands can be overrun by new intruders; Hawaiians are desperate to keep out the tree snake that has infested Guam and the Miconia calvescens plant that has overrun Tahiti.

As it seeks new growth, Hawaii needs to avoid being hurt by two special characteristics it shares with no other state. The first is its large concentrations of economic power, a product of its native and royal past. Eight public and private entities own 70% of Hawaii's land: the federal government 16%, the state 29%, and six private landowners 25%. The Bishop Estate (Mrs. Bishop was the last surviving member of the Hawaiian royal family) owns 8%; its five trustees, appointed by the state Supreme Court, which is to say by the long-dominant Democratic machine, and paid some $800,000 a year, are supposed to spend all the Estate's huge income on the Kamehameha School whose students are all native Hawaiians and whose teachers are supposed to be all Protestants. Most of this land is held on long-term leaseholds; since a state law forcing outright sales was upheld by the U.S. Supreme Court in 1984, the Bishop Estate has made vast outside investments, including a $500 million stake in the investment firm of Goldman Sachs and buying other businesses, but avoiding taxes by seeking favorable IRS rulings to use losses from some operations to offset profits from others.

The second peculiar characteristic of Hawaii is its *aloha* spirit. This great asset could become a liability if Hawaii goes too far on Native Hawaiian sovereignty. The commemoration of the overthrow of Liliuokalani has led the state government to set up a process for Native Hawaiians to decide if they want sovereignty, though no one is quite sure what that means. In September 1996, 30,000 eligibles with some Native blood (there are only a few hundred pure native Hawaiians left) voted 73% yes on the question, "Shall the Hawaiian people elect delegates to propose a native Hawaiian government?" It seems unlikely they will want to be a separate nation, or that Congress will let them; some leaders of native groups call for "nation within a nation" status, with dual citizenship, limited return of lands, and restoration of Hawaiian culture, which also seems a nonstarter. Others want the same status as recognized Indian tribes, which would allow Native gambling—a bonanza in the one of two American states (Utah is the other) which allows no gambling of any kind. Cayetano says sovereignty will be fine if it is "acceptable to the non-Hawaiians, as well as the United States government"; the four-member Hawaiian congressional delegation promised to abide by the results of the referendum.

But it is by no means clear why Hawaii's basic character should be changed by 20% of its citizens, many of them with little Hawaiian blood, most of them well assimilated to American culture. One sovereignty booster says, "Hawaiians are reasserting who they are and are beginning to prevail over western ideology." But western ideology has made Hawaii a free, tolerant, and prosperous state, and the stability of being an unquestioned part of the United States is one of the assets Hawaii can deploy to diversify its economy beyond tourism. Hawaiians have learned that their cultural attitudes can certainly influence the cultural debate on the Mainland, as national lawmakers scurried to pass the Defense of Marriage Act in 1996 in response to Hawaii's recognition of same-sex marriages. It is one thing to celebrate a cultural heritage and a sometimes tragic history, but it is another, as Canadians have learned, to widen splits and schisms in a state that more than almost any place in the world has proved that diverse people can live amicably and successfully together.

Hawaii's dominant political institution is the Democratic Party which, under a single chain of leadership, has welded Hawaii's disparate groups together to win elections since territorial days. It had its beginning in the 1950s when returning World War II veterans like Daniel Inouye, Spark Matsunaga and George Ariyoshi joined forces with former Mainlander John Burns, who as a policeman during the war helped prevent persecution of Japanese Americans. They allied themselves with the then-powerful International Longshoremen's and Warehousemen's Union, and cemented the allegiance of Japanese American voters. In the 1950s, Hawaii, resenting Mainland southern Democratic senators who delayed statehood, tended to vote Republican. But Inouye was elected to the House as a Democrat in 1959 and the Senate in 1962, and Republicans have won few elections since. In time, the ILWU's power waned; the machine became centered on the governor's office and the patronage it controlled, from state judgeships to the board of the Bishop Estate. There are some noticeable ethnic splits: Japanese Americans, used to working together in unions and government, have tended to be the heart of the Democratic Party; whites, with relatively high incomes, tend toward Republicans; Filipinos, often in menial jobs, are heavily Democratic. But in the Democratic organization's dominance there are echoes of a Pacific Rim political style—cool, competent, tough, unsentimental; Hawaii is one of the few states to prohibit write-in votes, a law the Supreme Court upheld in 1992.

Governor. Ben Cayetano is Hawaii's first Filipino-American governor. He grew up in Honolulu, went to college and law school in Los Angeles, then went into private practice in Hawaii; he was elected to the legislature in 1974, at 34, and served 12 years, working on low-income housing loans and auto insurance premium rollbacks and Agent Orange compensation. He was elected lieutenant governor in 1986 and was former Governor John Waihee's choice to succeed him. But Cayetano had serious competition in 1994. In the September primary he beat state healthcare program director Jack Lewin by only 55%–38%. In the general he faced former Congresswoman Pat Saiki, a strong though losing candidate against Senator Daniel Akaka in 1990, and of Japanese descent, and Frank Fasi, who formed his own The Best Party, using as his symbol the Hawaiian good luck gesture of a raised thumb and little finger. Fasi is the termagent of Hawaii politics, mayor of Honolulu for all but four years from 1968–94, several-time candidate for governor as a Democrat and a Republican, accusing Democratic machine politicians of corruption and accused by them of it in turn. It was a corker of a race. Cayetano said he was concerned about education and ran a half-hour ad telling his personal story; Saiki ran an unfocused campaign; Fasi rallied his supporters in Honolulu and came near to winning. Cayetano won with 37%,to 31% for Saiki and 29% for Fasi.

In office Cayetano started to reverse the thrust of politics Democrats had been following for more than 30 years. Their impulse was to centralize government, and provide generous services: Hawaii is one statewide school district; it has four county governments, which perform most local functions; in the 1970s it pioneered a state healthcare plan that aimed at universal coverage, which was not too difficult since more than 80% of Hawaiians were already insured by Blue Cross/Blue Shield or Kaiser Permanente. But in 1995 state government faced a huge deficit. Cayetano cut spending, by 10% to 22% in all departments except education, overall to below the level in 1993; he laid off state employees and cut the state work force by 2,750. To improve the business climate he reformed workmen's comp, proposed—though failed—to abolish the Hawaii Labor Relations Board, and called for running civil service on merit as well as seniority. More autonomy was given to public school authorities and School Community Based Management Councils were set up. Telecom was deregulated. He ended the state's 60–40 affordable housing rule and let the county governments negotiate with developers. As his ally Lieutenant Governor Mazie Hirono noted, they were moving to cut programs they had entered into politics to promote. To attract more tourists and business, Cayetano called for building a $350 million convention center which is scheduled to open in mid-1998, sprucing up the Honolulu waterfront, and attracting a big medical clinic for "health tourism," as East Asians are attracted to first-class American medical facilities. It remains to be seen whether Hawaii can become as big a center of commerce as it has been of tourism.

Senior Senator. The largest figure in Hawaii's public life remains Senator Daniel Inouye, who has held statewide elective office since Hawaii attained statehood in 1959—longer than many Hawaii voters can remember. Inouye was a severely wounded veteran of the 442d Regimental Combat Team in World War II, then became a lawyer, and was elected to the state legislature in 1954, the House in 1959 and the Senate in 1962. He was keynoter at the turbulent 1968 Democratic National Convention, a tenacious member of the Senate Watergate Committee in 1973–74 and the first chairman of the Senate Intelligence Committee, in 1976.

What does he believe in? The Senate, the Democratic Party, Hawaii, the armed services, Native Americans—among other things. He is the fourth most senior member of the Senate, and a stickler for its prerogatives. He went out of his way to defend senators in his view unjustly attacked—Harrison Williams during the Abscam scandal, Dennis DeConcini of the Keating Five—but was also quick to call for the resignation of Bob Packwood after the Senate voted in 1993 to subpoena his diaries.

Inouye is ranking democrat on the Appropriations Defense Subcommittee; the committee's chairman is Ted Stevens of Alaska, which gives enormous clout to two senators in office since the 1960s from the two states most recently admitted to the Union, both with their own special claims on the federal government. Inouye's record on most issues is liberal, but he shared little of the liberals' skepticism or hostility to American foreign and defense policies in the 1970s and 1980s. On the contrary, he says he fears that the Pentagon budget is "bare bones," stretched to the breaking point and that the Army is "eating its seed corn." He has always strongly favored aid to Israel. Inouye has long used his seat on Appropriations to fund projects he finds worthy, from his alma mater of George Washington University to the Pacific Island Technical Assistance Program to native Hawaiian education. For years he earmarked money for projects in Hawaii; when Republicans attacked that process in 1995, and removed earmarked projects from the FY96 defense spending bill. Inouye saw to it that earmarks were listed in the Senate committee report. And he sent out press releases enumerating the amount of defense spending going into Hawaii—$263 million in 1995, $176 million in 1996, $255 million in 1997. He is pleased to note that he funded an oceanography vessel the Navy officially says it doesn't want and that the Navy decided that the *U.S.S. Missouri*'s final berth would be in Pearl Harbor. Inouye was successful in getting the island of Kahoolawe, a federal target range for many years, turned back to the state, with $445 million earmarked for cleanup. He pushed for $1.2 billion in aid after Hurricane Iniki struck Kauai in September 1991. And, after Hurricane Emilia, the strongest Pacific storm ever, narrowly missed Hawaii in August 1994, Inouye proposed a federal natural disaster reinsurance program to protect insurance companies whose reserves would be wiped out by such disasters. He has supported many appropriations for Native Hawaiian organizations, like the Papa Ola Lokahi healthcare program, which supports traditional healing methods for natives, and he weighed in to allow shipment of Hawaiian avocados to the Mainland in early 1996. He helped get funding for the Spark Matsunaga Medical Center, named after his Senate colleague of 14 years.

On the Commerce Committee, Inouye was long involved in communications issues and tended to favor government regulation over markets. He backed cable reregulation and was pleased that the Telecommunications Act of 1996 imposed a competition checklist for local services on the Regional Bells before they could enter the long-distance market. Inouye wanted to set aside up to 20% of the information superhighway for libraries, schools, state and local governments and nonprofits, but the provision was not included in the final bill.

He chaired the Indian Affairs Committee from 1989–94, where he worked to authorize a new building on Washington's Mall to house part of the American Indian Museum collection and in 1990 got Indian reservations exempted from the federal death penalty. He backed Indian gaming in 1988 but has sponsored legislation which would tighten federal control over it. He sponsored a 1993 bill in which the United States apologized for overthrowing the Hawaiian monarchy, and is sympathetic to the claim of native Hawaiians for some form of sovereignty. On cultural issues, he voted against the partial birth abortion ban, against the Defense of Marriage Act (though he opposes same-sex marriage), and against the 4-cent gas tax repeal.

Honolulu is a long two flights from Washington, and Inouye's local influence has varied. In 1986 and 1990, he supported John Waihee for governor and Daniel Akaka for senator; both won close races. But Inouye was subjected to attacks in his 1992 campaign as never before. He was opposed by brash Republican legislator Rick Reed, who started a newspaper in Maui in the 1970s and defended himself successfully in a libel suit by an alleged organized crime figure. Reed called Inouye a Washington insider and defender of the Keating Five and ran an ad with tapes of Inouye's long-time woman barber, Lenore Kwock, accusing Inouye of forcing himself on her sexually some 17 years ago. Kwock said she was taped without her consent and demanded the ad be pulled, and it was. But on election day Inouye won with a much reduced percentage, 57%, to 27% for Reed and 14% for the Green Party's Linda Martin.

After the 1996 election, Inouye said he would ask Hawaii voters for one more term in 1998. He must be considered a heavy favorite. Mentioned as possible Republican candidates have been Maui Mayor Linda Crockett Lingle and Kauai Mayor Maryanna Kuska.

Junior Senator. Daniel Akaka is the first native Hawaiian senator. He served in the Army Corps of Engineers in the 1940s, went to college, taught school and became a principal. In 1971, at 47, he became director of the Hawaii antipoverty program; in 1975, he became an assistant to Governor George Ariyoshi. The next year, when both of Hawaii's congressmen ran for the Senate, he was elected to the House, where he served quietly on the Appropriations Committee. In May 1990, after the death of Senator Spark Matsunaga, Governor John Waihee appointed him to the Senate. Akaka has thus been an integral part of the dominant Democratic organization and a quiet but diligent worker on Hawaii issues.

Akaka had one tough election in 1990—indeed the only Senate election in Hawaii that has generated any suspense since 1976. His opponent was Republican Congresswoman Pat Saiki, who conceded that Akaka was congenial, but suggested he was ineffective and not too bright. Akaka struck back hard with ads stressing his crime bill amendment putting stiff penalties on "ice," a drug originating in Korea and Taiwan, and his defense bill amendment banning use of the island of Kahoolawe as a target range. The Democratic organization worked hard and Akaka won 54%–45%, carrying not just the Democratic Neighbor Islands and poorer areas of Honolulu, but most of Oahu as well.

One of Akaka's major causes is to stop nuclear waste and chemical weapons dumping in the Pacific. In 1991 he got a ban on German chemical weapons dumping on Johnston Island, 700 miles southwest of Hawaii; the dump is scheduled to be dismantled and closed in 2000. In 1996 he opposed the building of a nuclear waste dump in Palmyra Island, 1,000 miles southwest of Hawaii, which had been bought by what he called "nuclear entrepreneurs," and he is opposing a similar dump on the Marshall Islands, though the local government seems to want it. Akaka vehemently opposed French nuclear testing in the South Pacific.

He passed a Hawaiian Home Lands Recovery Act in 1995, to reclaim Native lands in Lualualei unlawfully withdrawn from the home lands when Hawaii was a territory. He fought successfully to reauthorize the sugar program in the 1996 Freedom to Farm Act. He has worked on veterans programs, especially for native Hawaiians, and set up a Pacific Center for Post-Traumatic Stress Disorder.

Akaka was easily reelected in 1994, by 72%–24%.

Presidential politics. Hawaii's presidential voting over the years has been the product of two sometimes countervailing forces. One is the Islands' strong Democratic partisan preference, since voters tend to favor big government and value racial tolerance and diversity. This helps explain why Hawaii voted Democratic when most states didn't in 1980 and 1988. The other is an inclination to support incumbents in a state that takes patriotism very seriously, in part because the patriotism of so many of its citizens was once unjustly questioned and in part because, in these heavily fortified Pacific islands, foreign threats seem more menacing. This helps explain why Hawaii supported President Reagan solidly in 1984 and came close to voting for President Ford in 1976, though it wasn't nearly enough to help George Bush in 1992: Ross Perot's military background, and the presence of Hawaiian Orson Swindle among his top leaders, gave him 14% and helped Bill Clinton carry Hawaii 48%–37%. But Bush ran behind by only 50%–43% among Asians, the largest number of whom are Japanese; Filipinos and native Hawaiians were 73% and 61% for Clinton.

In 1996, as in 1968 and 1980, both forces were moving in the same direction, and Bill Clinton, as the incumbent and as the Democratic nominee, won easily, 57%–32% over Bob Dole. Clinton won higher percentages only in the District of Columbia, Massachusetts, Rhode Island, and New York. This time his percentage among Asians was 65%.

Hawaii chooses presidential delegates by caucus. Sometimes insurgents have been able to swamp thinly-attended meetings and win, as Jesse Jackson and Pat Robertson did in 1988. But in the 1990s Hawaii's caucus-goers went for the frontrunners, Bill Clinton on the Democratic side and George Bush and Bob Dole among Republicans.

Congressional districting. Hawaii has two congressional districts: the 1st includes urban Honolulu (city elections now cover all of Oahu) and extends westward to Pearl Harbor and the rural area beyond; the 2d includes the rest of Oahu and the Neighbor Islands. Both districts are represented by liberal Democrats who had served in the past, then lost elections, ran again and won in 1990 and have been reelected since.

The People: Est. Pop. 1996: 1,184,000; Pop. 1990: 1,108,229, up 6.8% 1990–1996. 0.4% of U.S. total, 41st largest; 11% rural. Median age: 35.1 years. 13% 65 years and over. 31.4% White, 2.3% Black; 58.3% Asian; 7.3% Hispanic origin. Households: 59.1% married couple families; 29% married couple fams. w. children; 51% college educ.; median household income: $38,829; per capita income: $15,770; 53.9% owner occupied housing; median house value: $245,300; median monthly rent: $599. 6.4% Unemployment. 1996 Voting age pop.: 890,000. 1996 Turnout: 360,120; 40% of VAP. Registered voters (1996): 544,916; no party registration.

Political Lineup: Governor, Benjamin J. Cayetano (D); Lt. Gov. & Secy. of State, Mazie Hirono (D); Atty. Gen., Margery Bronster (D); Comptroller, Sam Callejo. State Senate, 25 (23 D and 2 R); Senate President, Norman Mizuguchi (D); State House, 51 (39 D and 12 R); House Speaker, Joseph Souki (D). Senators, Daniel K. Inouye (D) and Daniel K. Akaka (D). Representatives, 2 (2 D).

Elections Division: 808-453-8683; **Filing Deadline for U.S. Congress:** July 21, 1998.

1996 Presidential Vote

Clinton (D)	205,012	(57%)
Dole (R)	113,943	(32%)
Perot (I)	27,362	(8%)
Other	13,807	(4%)

1992 Presidential Vote

Clinton (D)	179,310	(48%)
Bush (R)	136,822	(37%)
Perot (I)	53,003	(14%)

GOVERNOR

Gov. Benjamin J. Cayetano (D)

Elected 1994, term expires Jan. 1999. b. Nov. 14, 1939, Honolulu; home, Honolulu; U. of CA, B.A. 1968; Loyola Law Schl., J.D. 1971; Christian; married (Lorraine).

Career: Practicing atty., 1971–86; HI House of Reps., 1974–78; HI Senate 1978–86; HI Lt. Gov., 1986–90.

Office: State Capitol, Executive Chambers, Honolulu 96813, 808-586-0034; Fax: 808-586-0006; Web site: www.state.hi.us.

Election Results

1994 gen.	Benjamin J. Cayetano (D)	134,978	(37%)
	Frank F. Fasi (Best)	113,158	(31%)
	Patricia F. Saiki (R)	107,908	(29%)
	Others	12,969	(4%)
1994 prim.	Benjamin J. Cayetano (D)	110,489	(55%)
	John (Jack) Lewin (D)	76,606	(38%)
	Others	14,305	(7%)
1990 gen.	John D. Waihee III (D)	203,491	(60%)
	Fred Hemmings (R)	131,310	(39%)
	Others	5,331	(2%)

SENATORS

Sen. Daniel K. Inouye (D)

Elected 1962, seat up 1998; b. Sept. 7, 1924, Honolulu; home, Honolulu; U. of HI, B.A. 1950, George Washington U., J.D. 1952; United Methodist; married (Margaret).

Career: Army, 1943–47 (WWII); Honolulu Dep. Public Prosecutor, 1953–54; HI House of Reps., 1954–58; HI Senate, 1958–59; U.S. House of Reps., 1959–62.

DC Office: 722 HSOB 20510, 202-224-3934; Fax: 202-224-6747; e-mail: senator@inouye.senate.gov.

State Offices: Hilo, 808-935-0844; Honolulu, 808-541-2542.

Committees: *Appropriations* (2nd of 13 D): Commerce, Justice, State & the Judiciary; Defense (RMM); Foreign Operations; Labor, Health & Human Services & Education; Military Construction. *Commerce, Science & Transportation* (2nd of 9 D): Aviation; Communications; Oceans & Fisheries; Surface Transportation & Merchant Marine (RMM). *Rules & Administration* (3rd of 7 D). *Indian Affairs* (Vice Chmn.). *Joint Committee on Printing* (5th of 5 Sens.).

Group Ratings

	ADA	ACLU	AFS	LCV	CFA	CON	NFIB	COC	ACU	NTLC	CHC
1996	85	35	100	77	86	16	30	33	11	14	7
1995	95	—	100	57	75	1	—	41	0	—	—

National Journal Ratings

	1995 LIB	—	1995 CONS	1996 LIB	—	1996 CONS
Economic	89%	—	10%	86%	—	13%
Social	85%	—	7%	92%	—	0%
Foreign	53%	—	44%	57%	—	42%

Key Votes of the 104th Congress

1. Reduce Medicare Growth $	N	5. Flag Amendment	N	9. Anti-Missile Defense	N
2. Lmt. Prod. Liab. Damages	N	6. Endangered Species	Y	10. Cuban Embargo	N
3. Increase Min. Wage	Y	7. Gay Employment Rights	Y	11. Bar Bosnia Troop $	N
4. Welfare Reform	*	8. Ovrd. Part. Birth Veto	N	12. Cut Vietnam Aid	N

Election Results

1992 general	Daniel K. Inouye (D)	208,266	(57%)	($3,515,722)
	Rick Reed (R)	97,928	(27%)	($438,851)
	Linda B. Martin (Green)	49,921	(14%)	($6,687)
	Other	7,547	(2%)	
1992 primary	Daniel K. Inouye (D)	94,827	(79%)	
	Wayne K. Nishiki (D)	25,782	(21%)	
1986 general	Daniel K. Inouye (D)	241,887	(74%)	($1,039,418)
	Frank Hutchinson (R)	86,910	(26%)	($31,843)

Sen. Daniel K. Akaka (D)

Appointed May, 1990, seat up 2000; b. Sept. 11, 1924, Honolulu; home, Honolulu; U. of HI, B.A. 1953, M.A. 1966; Congregationalist; married (Mary Mildred).

Career: Army Corps of Engineers, 1945–47 (WWII); Public schl. teacher, principal and admin., 1953–71; Dir., HI Office of Econ. Oppor., 1971–74; Asst., HI Gov. Ariyoshi, 1975–76; Dir., Progressive Neighborhoods Program, 1975–76; U.S. House of Reps., 1976–90.

DC Office: 720 HSOB 20510, 202-224-6361; Fax: 202-224-2126.

State Offices: Hilo, 808-935-1114; Honolulu, 808-522-8970.

Committees: *Energy & Natural Resources* (4th of 9 D): National Parks, Historic Preservation & Recreation; Water & Power (RMM). *Governmental Affairs* (4th of 7 D): International Security, Proliferation & Federal Services; Permanent Subcommittee on Investigations. *Veterans' Affairs* (3rd of 5 D). *Indian Affairs* (4th of 6 D).

Group Ratings

	ADA	ACLU	AFS	LCV	CFA	CON	NFIB	COC	ACU	NTLC	CHC
1996	95	44	100	85	86	16	29	31	5	4	8
1995	95	—	100	86	88	19	—	24	0	—	—

National Journal Ratings

	1995 LIB — 1995 CONS			1996 LIB — 1996 CONS		
Economic	94%	—	5%	89%	—	5%
Social	85%	—	7%	92%	—	0%
Foreign	97%	—	0%	64%	—	34%

Key Votes of the 104th Congress

1. Reduce Medicare Growth $	N	5. Flag Amendment	N	9. Anti-Missile Defense	N
2. Lmt. Prod. Liab. Damages	N	6. Endangered Species	Y	10. Cuban Embargo	N
3. Increase Min. Wage	Y	7. Gay Employment Rights	Y	11. Bar Bosnia Troop $	N
4. Welfare Reform	N	8. Ovrd. Part. Birth Veto	N	12. Cut Vietnam Aid	N

Election Results

1994 general	Daniel K. Akaka (D)	256,189	(72%)	($1,017,872)
	Maria M. Hustace (R)	86,320	(24%)	($29,293)
	Richard O. Rowland (Lib)	14,393	(4%)	
1994 primary	Daniel K. Akaka (D)	unopposed		
1990 general	Daniel K. Akaka (D)	188,901	(54%)	($1,691,384)
	Patricia Saiki (R)	155,978	(45%)	($2,398,961)

FIRST DISTRICT

Tourists in Honolulu see the airport and adjacent Hickam Air Force Base, the Arizona monument in Pearl Harbor, perhaps the downtown with its wondrously Victorian Iolani Palace, and of course Waikiki, with its 40-story hotels rising within a few feet of one another. But few of Hawaii's 1st District voters live in any of these places and, as a result, traffic jams have become a way of life for commuters who must share the road with some 600,000 vehicles to and from Honolulu's urban center. An aging road system with little room to expand and the location of the island's more affordable housing, puts most workers a clogged freeway drive from their jobs.

The neighborhoods around Honolulu's downtown and the university campus are lower income and usually Democratic. To the west, around the harbor, are many military families in modest neighborhoods who may vote for Democrats but can be attracted to Republicans. To the east, past Waikiki, around Diamond Head and out to the Kahala and Koko Head beach areas, is higher-income territory, voting for Republicans when they seriously contest a race.

The 1st District is represented by Neil Abercrombie, a Democrat with a graying beard and pony tail; his home is decorated with leis and a Buddha statue; he debates with an aggressiveness and bombast tempered by enthusiasm and good humor. After college in Upstate New York, he taught school, moved to Hawaii, earned a Ph.D. in sociology; he was elected to the Hawaii legislature in 1974 and served 12 years. Abercrombie first came to the House in 1986, when he won a special election, and served only three months; he lost a primary for the full term to a Democrat who then lost to Republican Pat Saiki. When she ran for the Senate, Abercrombie won a three-way primary for the House seat and won the 1990 and 1992 general elections easily. Abercrombie is one of the distinctive and often delightful figures in the House. He is enthusiastic and humorous and sometimes aggressive. He has the '60s liberal's visceral skepticism about military spending, but he has used his National Security Committee seat to work for $50 million in military housing at Schofield Barracks and Kaneohe. He wants to stop a nuclear waste dump on Palmyra Island, 1,000 miles from Hawaii, and make it easier for Koreans to get U.S. tourist visas. He co-sponsored a $13 million National Oceanographic Partnership Act included in the 1997 defense spending bill. After the Republican takeover of the House, he co-authored *Blood of Patriots*, a thriller in which two terrorists disguised as staffers walk into the House during a vote and murder 125 members of Congress.

In the last two elections Abercrombie had serious competition from Republican Orson Swindle, Marine Corps pilot and Vietnam POW, who as a Reagan appointee blew the whistle on then-Speaker Jim Wright's favor-seeking and who served as national leader of Ross Perot's United We Stand America in 1992. In 1994 Swindle campaigned hard against Abercrombie's pro-Clinton and dovish voting record, and carried Republican areas and made serious inroads elsewhere. But Abercrombie raised over $200,000 from PACs, compared to $20,000 for Swindle, and won 54%–43%. In the much less Republican year of 1996 Swindle ran again. During the campaign, Swindle labeled Abercrombie a far left hippie and called for serious cuts to wasteful government social programs that he said Abercrombie had always been willing to support. Swindle was helped by strong backing from the 1st District military community. Abercrombie narrowly outspent him, and outraised him among PACs $437,000 to $62,000, though Democrats no longer control the House. But Swindle narrowed the gap with the voters, and Abercrombie won by only 50%–46%, even as Bill Clinton was smashing Bob Dole locally.

Abercrombie can be counted on to advance his causes spiritedly in the 105th Congress. But he may have to face another spirited contest at home in 1998.

The People: Pop. 1990: 554,174; 12% age 65+; 28% White; 2% Black; 64% Asian; 6% Hispanic origin. Households: 58% married couple families; 26% married couple fams. w. children; 54% college educ.; median household income: $40,257; per capita income: $17,508; median gross rent: $659; median house value: $307,800.

1996 Presidential Vote

Clinton (D)	99,351	(57%)
Dole (R)	58,906	(34%)
Perot (I)	10,741	(6%)
Other	5,521	(3%)

1992 Presidential Vote

Clinton (D)	87,664	(47%)
Bush (R)	72,182	(39%)
Perot (I)	23,442	(13%)

Rep. Neil Abercrombie (D)

Elected 1990; b. June 26, 1938, Buffalo, NY; home, Honolulu; Union Col., B.A. 1959, U. of HI, M.A 1964, Ph.D. 1974; no religious affiliation; married (Nancie Caraway).

Career: Elem. and high schl. teacher, 1959–63; Probation Officer, Marin Cnty., CA, 1964–67; Sociologist, 1967–74; HI House of Reps., 1974–78; HI Senate, 1978–86; Asst. prof., HI Loa Col., 1979–80; Consultant, 1983–87, 1989–90; U.S. House of Reps., 1986–87; Asst., HI Superintendent of Educ., 1987–88; Honolulu City Cncl., 1988–90.

DC Office: 1233 LHOB 20515, 202-225-2726; e-mail: neil@abercrombie.house.gov.

District Offices: Honolulu, 808-541-2570.

Committees: *National Security* (9th of 25 D): Military Installations & Facilities; Military Research & Development. *Resources* (8th of 23 D): Fisheries Conservation, Wildlife & Oceans (RMM).

Group Ratings

	ADA	ACLU	AFS	LCV	CFA	CON	NFIB	COC	ACU	NTLC	CHC
1996	90	94	100	85	92	1	16	25	0	5	0
1995	90	—	—	88	92	9	—	8	8	—	—

National Journal Ratings

	1995 LIB	—	1995 CONS	1996 LIB	—	1996 CONS
Economic	82%	—	18%	85%	—	11%
Social	88%	—	0%	84%	—	12%
Foreign	84%	—	15%	64%	—	35%

Key Votes of the 104th Congress

1. Reduce Medicare Growth $	N	5. Flag Amendment	N	9. Cuban Embargo	N
2. Ovrd. Product Liab. Veto	N	6. Drop EPA Limits	Y	10. Bar Bosnia Troop $	N
3. Increase Min. Wage	Y	7. Repeal Assault-Weap. Ban	N	11. Cut Anti-Missile Defense	Y
4. Welfare Reform	N	8. Ovrd. Part. Birth Veto	N	12. Bar U.N. Uniforms	N

Election Results

1996 general	Neil Abercrombie (D)	86,732	(50%)	($674,404)
	Orson Swindle (R)	80,053	(46%)	($627,839
	Others	5,421	(3%)	
1996 primary	Neil Abercrombie (D)	65,732	(72%)	
	Richard Thompson (D)	25,905	(28%)	
1994 general	Neil Abercrombie (D)	94,754	(54%)	($391,451)
	Orson Swindle (R)	76,623	(43%)	($276,355)
	Others	5,329	(3%)	

SECOND DISTRICT

The 2d District of Hawaii includes not only the Neighbor Islands but most of Oahu's acreage beyond Honolulu. It has Wheeler Air Force Base, still looking much as it did in December 1941, and the farmlands north of Pearl Harbor, between two jagged chains of mountains that lift the island out of the sea. Over the mountains to the west is the Leeward Coast—calm, sultry and lightly populated; over the mountains to the northeast is the Windward Coast—windy, as its name implies—with many prosperous and Republican subdivisions in and around Kaneohe and Kailua. The Neighbor Islands have distinct personalities. Hawaii, the Big Island, is large enough to boast huge cattle ranches, the active volcano of Kilauea, and Mauna Kea, the highest mountain in the world if you count from its base far under the ocean to the peak. On the north shore, with heavy rainfall and tropical foliage, is the old port of Hilo and Hawaii's macadamia nut industry; this is a blue-collar Democratic area. On the Kona Coast, where there is little rainfall and the landscape is dominated by lava flows, there are retirement condominiums and a higher-income, more Republican population. Maui in recent years has been the fastest-developing island, with dozens of luxury condominiums and vast upscale resorts. Kauai, much of which was devastated by Hurricane Iniki in 1991, is the least-developed and most agricultural of the main islands; parts of it have the nation's highest rainfall, while others seldom get wet. Its large farm work force makes it the most Democratic of the islands.

The 2d District is represented by Patsy Mink, still exuberant and enthusiastically liberal after a long congressional career. She grew up in Hawaii, went to law school in Chicago, then practiced law in Honolulu starting in 1953. She was first elected to the House in 1964, gave up the seat to run unsuccessfully for the Senate in 1976, then, after losing races for governor in 1986 and mayor of Honolulu in 1988, won the House seat again in 1990 after incumbent Daniel Akaka was appointed to the Senate. She helped feminism grow from a fringe cause to one of the main rallying cries for Democrats, and sponsored a gender equity act, which passed the House and then the Senate—though in a more diluted form—and women's health care measures. She spoke with special vehemence in March 1995 against product liability reform. (She sued a drug company and hospital 44 years ago after she was given the anti-miscarriage drug DES during pregnancy; but it was later thought to expose children to a greater risk of cancer, and Mink collected $250,000 in a settlement.) And, after the French resumed nuclear testing in the South Pacific, she made news by boycotting a February 1996 speech by President Jacques Chirac before a joint session of Congress.

Mink won the seat in 1990 by narrowly edging former 1st District incumbent (1986–88) Mufi Hannemann in the primary; she won easily in 1992 and 1994. But in 1996 she had primary opposition from four Democrats, principally state Senator Robert Bunda, a Honolulu insurance broker running as a "moderate alternative." "I am committed to breaking the inertia of timeworn thinking that keeps Hawaii a place whose vast promise we always seem to recognize but never seem to realize," he said. Controversy ensued when Bunda cited Mink's vote against the Defense of Marriage Act; Mink ran newspaper ads saying she voted that way because she thought the measure was unconstitutional, but that she was against the principle of same-sex marriage. Mink won the primary by 60%–32%, a wide margin. Nevertheless, as Neil Abercrombie's near-loss in the 1st District shows, it can be difficult keeping in close touch in Hawaii when you are working ten hours' flight time away.

The People: Pop. 1990: 554,055; 22% rural; 10% age 65+; 35% White; 2% Black; 53% Asian; 9% Hispanic origin. Households: 64% married couple families; 33% married couple fams. w. children; 48% college educ.; median household income: $37,247; per capita income: $14,032; median gross rent: $633; median house value: $189,700.

1996 Presidential Vote

Clinton (D)	105,661	(57%)
Dole (R)	55,037	(30%)
Perot (I)	16,621	(9%)
Other	8,286	(4%)

1992 Presidential Vote

Clinton (D)	91,646	(49%)
Bush (R)	64,640	(34%)
Perot (I)	29,561	(16%)

Rep. Patsy T. Mink (D)

Elected Sept., 1990; b. Dec. 6, 1927, Paia, Maui; home, Hilo; U. of HI, B.A. 1948, U. of Chicago, J.D. 1951; Protestant; married (John Francis).

Career: Practicing atty., 1953–64, 1987–90; HI House of Reps., 1956–58; HI Senate, 1959, 1963–64; U.S. House of Reps., 1964–76; U.S. Asst. Secy. of State for Oceans and Intl. Environment and Scientific Affairs, 1977–78; Pres., Americans for Democratic Action, 1978–81; Honolulu City Cncl., 1983–87.

DC Office: 2135 RHOB 20515, 202-225-4906; Fax: 202-225-4987.

District Offices: Hilo, 808-935-3756; Honolulu, 808-541-1986; Mavai 808-242-1818.

Committees: *Budget* (5th of 19 D). *Education & The Workforce* (7th of 20 D): Early Childhood, Youth & Families; Oversight & Investigations (RMM).

Group Ratings

	ADA	ACLU	AFS	LCV	CFA	CON	NFIB	COC	ACU	NTLC	CHC
1996	95	94	100	85	92	45	16	25	5	7	0
1995	95	—	—	94	100	16	—	8	8	—	—

National Journal Ratings

	1995 LIB — 1995 CONS			1996 LIB — 1996 CONS		
Economic	94%	—	0%	76%	—	22%
Social	88%	—	0%	88%	—	0%
Foreign	88%	—	7%	79%	—	19%

Key Votes of the 104th Congress

1. Reduce Medicare Growth $	N	5. Flag Amendment	N	9. Cuban Embargo	N
2. Ovrd. Product Liab. Veto	N	6. Drop EPA Limits	Y	10. Bar Bosnia Troop $	N
3. Increase Min. Wage	Y	7. Repeal Assault-Weap. Ban	N	11. Cut Anti-Missile Defense	Y
4. Welfare Reform	N	8. Ovrd. Part. Birth Veto	N	12. Bar U.N. Uniforms	Y

Election Results

1996 general	Patsy T. Mink (D)	109,178	(60%)	($315,187)
	Tom Pico Jr. (R)	55,729	(31%)	($88.935)
	Nolan Crabbe (I)	7,723	(4%)	
	Others	8,333	(5%)	
1996 primary	Patsy T. Mink (D)	64,371	(60%)	
	Robert Bunda (D)	33,886	(32%)	
	Others	8,428	(8%)	
1994 general	Patsy T. Mink (D)	124,431	(70%)	($157,523)
	Robert H. Garner (R)	42,891	(24%)	
	Larry R. Bartley (Lib)	10,074	(6%)	

IDAHO

Idaho is one of America's leading states in the 1990s—leading in population growth, in technological progress, and leading at least part of the nation in cultural attitudes and politics, in a direction that other parts of the nation, and especially the national media, resent and resist. Idaho has first of all a robust and growing economy: from 1990–96 employment rose 18% and population rose 22%—among the fastest rates in the nation. Most of Idaho's biggest businesses—J. R. Simplot's potato empire, Micron Technology and Albertson's supermarkets—have expanded (though Morrison Knudsen is struggling to recover from mismanagement) and dozens of new high-tech and service businesses have sprung up. From California a few highly publicized liberal entertainment personalities and a much larger number of conservative engineers and entrepreneurs have come to Idaho for a fresh environment and fresh start, clean air and few crowds and no cumbersome and expensive regulations, where family lifestyles are still prevalent, traditional values respected and traditional rules enforced.

In Idaho the wilderness is never far away here, nor is the experience of the first settlers. Towering over the state Capitol in Boise is the vast peak of Shafer Butte, and a few miles away are impassable mountains; Idaho ranks third in National Wilderness lands behind California and Alaska. This was the last North American area European pioneers—fur traders—set eyes on. The first farmers in Idaho were New England Yankees led by ministers wending their way west on the Oregon Trail into the broad Snake River Valley. Idaho's northern panhandle, an extension of Washington's Columbia Valley, was first settled by miners seeking gold and silver; loggers followed. Mormons moved north from Utah and settled in eastern Idaho. But what brought the most settlers were federal water reclamation projects first authorized in 1894, which transformed the barren Snake River Valley into some of the nation's best volcanic soil-enriched farmland. With in recent memory are the people who pioneered this state, built the first towns and farms, established the first churches and schools and became its community leaders. Yet while Idaho remains close to its roots, it is also cosmopolitan. Its potato-based agriculture which uses more water per capita than any other state—a fact of political significance—makes this an exporting state, shipping food as well as lumber to the other side of the Pacific Rim. Add Idaho's high-tech development, and you have a state very much connected to the world beyond.

Idaho politics for years was run by two bosses—Democrat Tom Boise from the panhandle and Republican Lloyd Adams from the Mormon east—who could patch together statewide alliances from the regional divisions still apparent today. Overall, Idaho is heavily Republican. Bob Dole was in trouble in the rest of the country in 1996, but he carried Idaho 52%–34% over Bill Clinton, winning all but four counties—Sun Valley with its trendy newcomers and three northern panhandle counties, with university professors and mill hands. Dole carried the Boise area comfortably 52%–37%, ran up large margins in the heavily Mormon east, and even carried the panhandle, which had voted for Clinton over George Bush in 1992.

This is a major switch from the historic norm. Although its first settlers had a Republican heritage, silver-mining Idaho went for William Jennings Bryan and free silver in 1896, and then supported Woodrow Wilson and Franklin D. Roosevelt; as late as 1960, John F. Kennedy won 46% of the vote here. Idaho produced prominent national politicians of both parties—notably, Senate Foreign Relations Committee Chairmen William Borah, a Republican, and Frank Church, a Democrat. Then, ahead of the national trend, Idaho turned right. Idahoans began to think of themselves less as downtrodden employees of absentee corporations needing a protective federal government, and more as pioneering entrepreneurs who needed to get a bloated, bossy federal government off their backs. The federal government owns 65% of Idaho's land; when regulatory measures block exploitation of local resources to protect the environ-

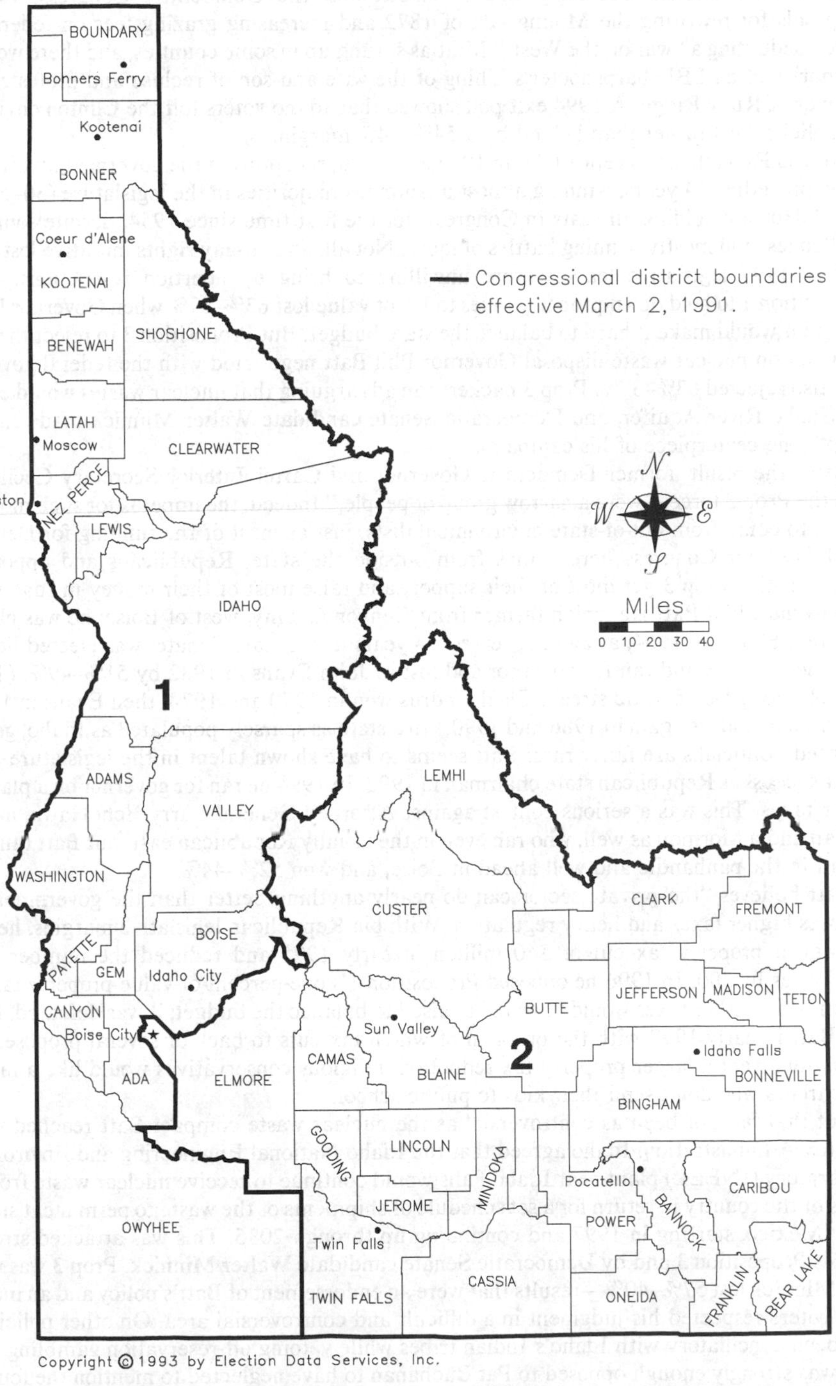
Congressional district boundaries effective March 2, 1991.
Miles
0 10 20 30 40
N
E
S
W
1
2
BOUNDARY
Bonners Ferry
Kootenai
BONNER
Coeur d'Alene
KOOTENAI
SHOSHONE
BENEWAH
LATAH
Moscow
CLEARWATER
Lewiston
NEZ PERCE
LEWIS
IDAHO
ADAMS
VALLEY
LEMHI
WASHINGTON
CUSTER
CLARK
FREMONT
PAYETTE
BOISE
GEM
Idaho City
JEFFERSON
MADISON
TETON
CANYON
BUTTE
Boise City
Sun Valley
Idaho Falls
CAMAS
ADA
ELMORE
BLAINE
BONNEVILLE
BINGHAM
GOODING
LINCOLN
MINIDOKA
Pocatello
CARIBOU
JEROME
POWER
BANNOCK
OWYHEE
Twin Falls
CASSIA
ONEIDA
FRANKLIN
BEAR LAKE
TWIN FALLS

ment—vetoing a logging operation or preventing sheep ranchers from destroying coyotes—Washington can arouse fierce resentment here. In the early 1990s, opinion simmered. Idahoans shouted that Interior Secretary Bruce Babbitt and the Democratic Congress, with their proposals for rewriting the Mining Act of 1872 and increasing grazing fees on federal lands, were conducting a "war on the West." Militias sprung up in some counties, and there were bitter memories of an FBI sharpshooter's killing of the wife and son of recluse and protester Randy Weaver at Ruby Ridge. A 1994 exit poll showed that Idaho voters felt the Clinton environmental policies hurt rather than helped by a 54%–14% margin.

And so Republicans swept Idaho in 1994 and 1996, recapturing the governorship after losing it the preceding 24 years, winning almost unanimous majorities in the legislature (30–5 Senate, 59–11 House); holding all seats in Congress, for the first time since 1954, despite some strong challenges; and mostly winning battles of ideas. Not all: an anti-gay rights initiative lost in 1994, and in 1997 legislative leaders were unwilling to bring up abortion restrictions. In 1996 Proposition 1 to hold down property taxes to 1% of value lost 63%–37% when Governor Phil Batt argued it would make it hard to balance the state budget. But Proposition 3 to reject the 40-year compact on nuclear waste disposal Governor Phil Batt negotiated with the federal government was also rejected 63%–37%. Prop 3 backers ran ads arguing that nuclear wastes would endanger the Snake River Aquifer, and Democratic Senate candidate Walter Minnick made support of Prop 3 the centerpiece of his campaign.

After the result, former Democratic Governor and Carter Interior Secretary Cecil Andrus said the Prop-3 forces "were a narrow group of people." Indeed, the impetus for such movements seems to come from out-of-state environmentalists, just as most of the funding for Democratic candidates for Congress here comes from outside the state; Republicans and opponents of measures like Prop 3 get most of their support and raise most of their money in Idaho.

Governor. Phil Batt is an onion farmer from Canyon County, west of Boise; he was elected to the state House in 1964, at age 37, served 14 years in the state Senate, was elected lieutenant governor in 1978 and ran for governor and lost to John Evans in 1982 by 51%–49%. (This was part of a long Democratic streak: Cecil Andrus won in 1970 and 1974, then Evans in 1978 and 1982, then Andrus again in 1986 and 1990.) In a state as sparsely populated as Idaho, genuinely talented politicians are fairly rare; Batt seems to have shown talent in the legislature and had great success as Republican state chairman in 1992. In 1994 he ran for governor on a platform of lower taxes. This was a serious contest against Attorney General Larry EchoHawk, a Pawnee Indian and a Mormon as well, who ran even in the usually Republican east; but Batt ran slightly ahead in the panhandle and well ahead in Boise, and won 52%–44%.

Batt believes "the private sector can do nearly anything better than the government," and opposes higher taxes and heavy regulation. With big Republican legislative margins, he pushed through a property tax cut of $40 million in early 1995 and reduced the number of state employees by 300. In 1996 he opposed Proposition 1's one-percent-of-value property tax on the grounds that other taxes would have to be raised to balance the budget; it was defeated. But that left Batt in early 1997 with the problem of which tax cuts to back of several proposed. Some legislators want a larger property tax reduction; religious conservatives would like a tax credit for parents who don't send their kids to public school.

But that has not been as controversial as the nuclear waste compact Batt reached with the Clinton Administration. Idaho agreed that the Idaho National Engineering and Environmental Laboratory (INEEL) plant near Idaho Falls would continue to receive nuclear waste from other parts of the country in return for a set schedule of shipments of the waste to permanent storage in New Mexico, starting in 1997 and continuing up through 2035. This was attacked strongly in 1996's Proposition 3 and by Democratic Senate candidate Walter Minnick. Prop 3 was rejected and Minnick lost 57%–40%—results that were an endorsement of Batt's policy and an indication that voters respected his judgment in a difficult and controversial area. On other policies, Batt has been conciliatory with Idaho's Indian tribes while vetoing off-reservation gambling casinos, and was strongly enough opposed to Pat Buchanan to have neglected to mention the four Idaho delegate votes during the roll call at the 1996 Republican Convention in San Diego.

In early 1997 it was not clear whether Batt will run for reelection in 1998, when he turns 71. If he does, he must be considered the favorite. If he doesn't some locals expect Senator Dirk Kempthorne, a former mayor of Boise, to return home and run. The best known Democratic officeholder is state Controller J. D. Williams.

Senior Senator. Larry Craig brings to politics stentorian argumentation and a controlled fervor in support of his conservative positions. Born on a ranch homesteaded by his grandfather in 1899, he was elected to the state Senate in 1974, at 29, and to the U.S. House in 1980, at 35. In Washington he started off very much in the minority, co-sponsoring with Charles Stenholm of Texas the balanced budget amendment. It got just 153 votes in 1982 but Craig plugged away first in the House and then, after being elected to succeed retiring Senator Jim McClure in 1990, even more in the Senate, working with Democrat Paul Simon, conceding it would not be "a cure-all" but arguing it would be "a fundamental change in the budget environment." In February 1995 the amendment, which would require a three-fifths vote to raise the debt ceiling but would not require a super-majority to raise taxes, passed with 300 votes in the House; in March 1995, the Senate on a cliff-hanger 65–35 vote fell barely short of gaining the two-thirds vote required to pass the amendment, with all of the 53 Republicans except for Mark Hatfield voting in favor, and with six Democrats who had previously supported versions switching to oppose it. (The bill actually had 66 votes, one short of the two-thirds required, but Bob Dole switched to vote against it so that he could call it up for reconsideration.)

By that time Craig had become a leading conservative force in the Republican Party, chairman of the informal conservative Steering Committee, whose members seem to win most of the leadership positions, then after Dole's resignation in June 1996, Craig became chairman of the Republican Policy Committee, the number four leadership position. He was, Idaho reporter Dan Popkey wrote, "poised to become the fourth face on Idaho's Mount Rushmore, joining Senators William Borah, Frank Church, and Jim McClure."

What Craig seems to relish most is his battle against what he calls "environmental extremism." With seats on Appropriations, Agriculture, and Energy, he is well positioned for these fights. He supported the 1996 Freedom to Farm Act: "There's a legitimate role for government, but it's not to tell you what to plant and it's not to tell you how to plant it." He strongly opposed the Clinton Administration proposal to revise the Mining Act of 1872 and to increase grazing fees, and he has long sought to revise the Endangered Species Act. Now he is chairman of the Forests and Public Land Management Subcommittee, where his major project is revision of forest management laws. Craig's legislation would streamline planning procedures, limit court challenges to people who commented during the planning process, and forbid deviations from the plan once adopted; most controversially, he would allow states, with congressional approval, to take over management of National Forest and Bureau of Land Management lands. That will be fiercely fought in committee and on the floor; but even if he loses, Craig could make an end run from the Appropriations Interior Subcommittee by authorizing a pilot program.

Another Craig cause is nuclear waste: he backs Governor Phil Batt's compact with the federal government and wants to open an interim nuclear waste storage site at Yucca Mountain in Nevada, so that the federal government can start taking commercial nuclear waste, especially from Idaho's INEEL. But for all his fervor, Craig has sometimes compromised with critics, as on the "share the risk" initiative, under which half of Idaho salmon would be allowed to spill over dams and the other half would ride to the ocean in barges. Craig tends to local matters as well, like expanding the Nez Perce National Historic Park. And he served on the Ethics Committees in both House and Senate, sitting in judgment on Jim Wright and Bob Packwood.

Craig won the seat relatively easily in 1990, with 59% in the primary against Attorney General Jim Jones and with 61% in the general. For a while the 1996 race looked tougher. Democratic Senatorial Campaign Committee Chairman Bob Kerrey put Idaho on his target list and recruited building materials millionaire Walt Minnick to run. Minnick had testified against

Craig's plans for deficit timber sales and road building in the national forests: "I was the industrialist on the Wilderness Society board and the conservationist in industry groups." Minnick spent $945,000 of his own money, and his total spending of $2.2 million almost equalled Craig's $2.9 million. He attacked Craig sharply for backing the nuclear waste compact, and ran "Lying Larry" ads associating him with nuclear pollution, clear-cutting, gill-netting, and national parks destruction. Craig responded by rafting down the river with his family and running ads predicting toxic desolation if the nuclear waste compact was not carried out. In time Minnick's party affiliation worked against him and Craig's Republican conservatism and hard work paid off: he won 57%–40%, with Minnick carrying only three counties.

Junior Senator. Senator Dirk Kempthorne seems to lack Craig's sharp edges; he seems more easygoing and some Democrats say he is easier to work with; but he is a solid conservative all the same. Kempthorne grew up in Spokane, Washington, and has spent most of his adult life in the political arena, if not always in electoral politics: as Idaho public affairs director for FMC Corporation, an executive at the Idaho Home Builders Association, manager of Phil Batt's 1982 gubernatorial campaign and as mayor of Boise for seven boom years from 1986–93. Kempthorne won the Senate seat in 1992 after two-term incumbent Republican Steve Symms announced his retirement in August 1991. He easily won the Republican primary, but had tough competition in the general from Democratic Congressman Richard Stallings, a Mormon and a conservative on abortion and gun control, who won the 2d District seat in eastern Idaho three times. Kempthorne attacked Stallings for having eight overdrafts on the House bank, pledged never to vote to give away Idaho's water rights, called for a capital gains tax cut and for additional compensation to property owners for federal takings. Kempthorne was in the lead by June 1992; Stallings's charges that Kempthorne raised taxes in Boise didn't turn it around. Kempthorne won with 57%, barely carrying the panhandle, but running far ahead in the Boise market and carrying the Mormon areas in the east.

In January 1993 he was 100th in seniority in the Senate, and in the minority party; his first major issue, unfunded mandates—laws passed by Congress requiring states to spend money—seemed a nonstarter and didn't pass either chamber. But in January 1995 Kempthorne was part of the majority and Majority Leader Bob Dole made his unfunded mandates bill S.1, the first order of legislative business. Kempthorne impressed colleagues with his knowledge of detail and his willingness to face off with Robert Byrd, who fought mightily against the bill as an infringement of congressional prerogatives; it passed the Senate easily with bipartisan support. "To go from being told you will never get a public hearing to then being invited to the Rose Garden where the president signed the bill indicates we went the full spectrum on this." Kempthorne also worked hard on the Safe Drinking Water Act, which passed with bipartisan support in 1996.

On other issues, he has paid attention to state interests. He and Larry Craig voted against NAFTA and GATT because of its effect on Idaho sugar beet farmers. On the Armed Services Committee, he looked after INEEL and worked to improve the quality of life for U.S. troops stationed in danger zones abroad. The latter led to his chairmanship of the Personnel Subcommittee in the 105th Congress. He also chairs Environment's Drinking Water, Fisheries and Wildlife Subcommittee with jurisdiction over the Endangered Species Act, and has not been as confrontational as many Republicans were on this issue in 1995. "We've surprised people on all sides of this issue," he said, "as to the progress we've made so far in creating a balanced, bipartisan bill."

Kempthorne is a heavy favorite to win reelection in 1998, though he has also been mentioned as a candidate for governor if Phil Batt retires.

Presidential politics. Idaho remains one of the most Republican states in national politics. It was carried easily by George Bush and Bob Dole; in 1992 Bill Clinton only narrowly beat out Ross Perot for second place, 28%–27%. Since 1988, Idaho's presidential primary has been held in late May, but is not binding for the state's Democrats, who select their presidential nominee in the early March caucus. Bob Dole easily won here in May 1996.

Congressional districting. Idaho has two congressional districts; redistricting for 1992 just shuffled nine Boise precincts between them.

The People: Est. Pop. 1996: 1,189,000; Pop. 1990: 1,006,749, up 18.1% 1990–1996. 0.4% of U.S. total, 40th largest; 43% rural. Median age: 33 years. 11% 65 years and over. 92.2% White, 1% Asian; 1.2% Amer. Indian; 5.3% Hispanic origin. Households: 62.2% married couple families; 32% married couple fams. w. children; 49% college educ.; median household income: $25,257; per capita income: $11,457; 70.1% owner occupied housing; median house value: $58,200; median monthly rent: $261. 5.2% Unemployment. 1996 Voting age pop.: 858,000. 1996 Turnout: 489,481; 57% of VAP. Registered voters (1996): 700,430; no party registration.

Political Lineup: Governor, Phil Batt (R); Lt. Gov., C. L. (Butch) Otter (R); Secy. of State, Pete T. Cenarrusa (R); Atty. Gen., Alan Lance (R); Treasurer, Lydia Justice Edwards (R); State Controller, J. D. Williams (D). State Senate, 35 (5 D and 30 R); Senate President, Jerry Twigs (R); State House, 70 (11 D and 59 R); House Speaker, Michael Simpson (R). Senators, Larry Craig (R) and Dirk Kempthorne (R). Representatives, 2 (2 R).

Elections Division: 208-334-2852; **Filing Deadline for U.S. Congress:** April 3, 1998.

1996 Presidential Vote

Dole (R)	256,595	(52%)
Clinton (D)	165,443	(34%)
Perot (I)	62,518	(13%)

1992 Presidential Vote

Bush (R)	202,645	(42%)
Clinton (D)	137,013	(28%)
Perot (I)	130,395	(27%)

1996 Republican Presidential Primary

Dole (R)	74,011	(62%)
Buchanan (R)	26,461	(22%)
Other	12,339	(10%)
Keyes (R)	5,904	(5%)

GOVERNOR

Gov. Phil Batt (R)

Elected 1994, term expires Jan. 1999; b. Mar. 4, 1927, Wilder; home, Boise; U. of ID, 1944–48; Baptist; married (Jacque).

Career: Army, 1945–46; Onion farmer; ID House of Reps., 1964–66; ID Senate, 1966–70, 1972–78, 1984–88; ID Lt. Gov., 1978–82.

Office: State House, Boise 83720, 208-334-2100; Fax: 208-334-2175; Web site: www.state.id.us.

Election Results

1994 gen.	Phil Batt (R)	216,123	(52%)
	Larry EchoHawk (D)	181,363	(44%)
	Ronald D. Rankin (I)	15,793	(4%)
1994 prim.	Phil Batt (R)	57,066	(48%)
	Larry Eastland (R)	38,664	(33%)
	Charles L. Winder (R)	16,063	(14%)
	Doug Dorn (R)	7,098	(6%)
1990 gen.	Cecil D. Andrus (D)	217,801	(68%)
	Roger Fairchild (R)	101,885	(32%)

SENATORS

Sen. Larry Craig (R)

Elected 1990, seat up 2002; b. July 20, 1945, Midvale; home, Payette; U. of ID, B.A. 1969; United Methodist; married (Suzanne).

Career: Army Natl. Guard, 1970–74; Rancher, farmer; ID Senate, 1974–80; U.S. House of Reps., 1980–90.

DC Office: 313 HSOB 20510, 202-224-2752; Fax: 202-228-1067; e-mail: larry_craig@craig.senate.gov.

State Offices: Boise, 208-342-7985; Coeur d'Alene, 208-667-6130; Idaho Falls, 208-523-5541; Lewiston, 208-743-0792; Pocatello, 208-236-6817; Twin Falls, 202-734-6780.

Committees: *Republican Policy Committee Chairman. Agriculture, Nutrition & Forestry* (10th of 10 R): Forestry, Conservation & Rural Revitalization; Research, Nutrition & General Legislation. *Appropriations* (13th of 15 R): Energy & Water Development; Labor, Health & Human Services & Education; Legislative Branch; Military Construction; VA, HUD & Independent Agencies. *Energy & Natural Resources* (4th of 11 R): Energy Research, Development, Production & Regulation; Forests & Public Land Management (Chmn.); Water & Power. *Veterans' Affairs* (6th of 7 R). *Aging (Special)* (3rd of 10 R).

Group Ratings

	ADA	ACLU	AFS	LCV	CFA	CON	NFIB	COC	ACU	NTLC	CHC
1996	0	22	0	0	21	22	100	100	95	100	100
1995	0	—	0	0	0	29	—	100	96	—	—

National Journal Ratings

	1995 LIB — 1995 CONS	1996 LIB — 1996 CONS
Economic	0% — 88%	6% — 91%
Social	12% — 81%	0% — 72%
Foreign	0% — 92%	0% — 74%

Key Votes of the 104th Congress

1. Reduce Medicare Growth $	Y	5. Flag Amendment	Y	9. Anti-Missile Defense	Y
2. Lmt. Prod. Liab. Damages	Y	6. Endangered Species	N	10. Cuban Embargo	Y
3. Increase Min. Wage	N	7. Gay Employment Rights	N	11. Bar Bosnia Troop $	Y
4. Welfare Reform	Y	8. Ovrd. Part. Birth Veto	Y	12. Cut Vietnam Aid	Y

Election Results

1996 general	Larry Craig (R)	283,532	(57%)	($2,992,451)
	Walt Minnick (D)	198,422	(40%)	(2,140,878)
	Others	15,279	(3%)	
1996 primary	Larry Craig (R)	unopposed		
1990 general	Larry Craig (R)	193,641	(61%)	($1,620,304)
	Ron J. Twilegar (D)	122,295	(39%)	($544,419)

Sen. Dirk Kempthorne (R)

Elected 1992, seat up 1998; b. Oct. 29, 1951, San Diego, CA; home, Boise; U. of ID, B.A. 1975; Methodist; married (Patricia).

Career: Exec. Asst. to the Dir., ID Dept. of Public Lands, 1976–78; Exec. V.P., ID Home Builders Assn., 1978–81; Campaign Mgr., Phil Batt for Governor, 1982; ID Public Affairs Mgr., FMC Corp., 1983–86; Boise Mayor, 1986–93.

DC Office: 304 DSOB 20510, 202-224-6142; Fax: 202-224-5893; e-mail: dirk_kempthorne@kempthorne.senate.gov.

State Offices: Boise, 208-334-1776; Caldwell, 208-455-0360; Coeur d'Alene, 208-664-5490; Idaho Falls, 208-522-9779; Lewiston, 208-743-1492; Moscow, 208-883-9783; Pocatello, 208-236-6775; Twin Falls, 208-734-2515.

Committees: *Armed Services* (6th of 10 R): Airland Forces; Personnel (Chmn.); Strategic Forces. *Environment & Public Works* (4th of 10 R): Drinking Water, Fisheries & Wildlife (Chmn.); Transportation & Infrastructure. *Small Business* (4th of 10 R).

Group Ratings

	ADA	ACLU	AFS	LCV	CFA	CON	NFIB	COC	ACU	NTLC	CHC
1996	0	22	0	0	21	22	100	100	95	100	100
1995	0	—	0	0	0	29	—	100	96	—	—

National Journal Ratings

	1995 LIB		1995 CONS	1996 LIB		1996 CONS
Economic	0%	—	88%	6%	—	91%
Social	12%	—	81%	0%	—	72%
Foreign	0%	—	92%	0%	—	74%

Key Votes of the 104th Congress

1. Reduce Medicare Growth $	Y	5. Flag Amendment	Y	9. Anti-Missile Defense	Y
2. Lmt. Prod. Liab. Damages	Y	6. Endangered Species	N	10. Cuban Embargo	Y
3. Increase Min. Wage	N	7. Gay Employment Rights	N	11. Bar Bosnia Troop $	Y
4. Welfare Reform	Y	8. Ovrd. Part. Birth Veto	Y	12. Cut Vietnam Aid	Y

Election Results

1992 general	Dirk Kempthorne (R)	270,468	(57%)	($1,305,338)
	Richard Stallings (D)	208,036	(43%)	($1,222,222)
1992 primary	Dirk Kempthorne (R)	67,001	(57%)	
	Rod Beck (R)	26,977	(23%)	
	Milton Erhart (R)	22,682	(19%)	
1986 general	Steven D. Symms (R)	196,958	(52%)	($3,229,939)
	John V. Evans (D)	185,066	(48%)	($2,135,537)

FIRST DISTRICT

The 1st District, which stretches from the Nevada border to Canada, includes most of usually Republican Boise and the panhandle which has recently been known as the home of militias, where the dominant voice is Coeur d'Alene newspaper baron and resort developer Duane Hagadone. In statewide elections, it is the less Republican of the two districts because of the Democratic tradition of the panhandle, which goes back to its mining days but thrives more now in the university town of Moscow; though it is solidly Republican by national standards.

This is the district that has twice elected Congressman (she doesn't use congresswoman) Helen Chenoweth, one of the most distinctive of Republican conservatives. Chenoweth is a divorced grandmother, a medical office manager and lobbyist for timber and mining industries who lived for years in Orofino, a small mining town deep in the mountains. Idaho's Public Utilities commissioner once described how she drove a Cadillac up a steep embankment, comparing her to a mountain goat—stubborn, impulsive, utterly self-confident. She worked in political campaigns for former Senator Steven Symms and former Lieutenant Governor David Leroy, but left after disagreements. In 1992 she ran against incumbent Democrat Larry LaRocco, a former aide to Frank Church who won the seat as a moderate in 1990 and 1992. Chenoweth's core support came from religious conservatives, sympathizers with militia and patriot movements, and from believers in Wise Use, an organization she helped found to combat what she considers environmental extremism. In the primary she beat Leroy 42%–28%, carrying all but one remote county. In the general she attracted attention when she held "endangered salmon bakes" throughout the district, ridiculing the listing of Idaho salmon as an endangered species. Chenoweth led in a poll after the May primary—a harbinger of the Republican tsunami—and survived LaRocco's attacks on her "out-of-state extremist agenda." She talked more about mining, timber and the "Clinton war on the West." Chenoweth won with 55% of the vote, carrying 58% in Boise's Ada County and losing the panhandle by only 51%–49%.

Serving in Congress has not moderated Chenoweth's views. She voted against some measures even other Idaho Republicans supported—Sawtooth Recreation Area funding, Governor Phil Batt's "share the risk" salmon initiative, MFN status for China despite pressure from big Boise employer Hewlett-Packard. She refused to meet with leaders of Indian tribes. She was one of 15 Republicans who voted against the bill to get the government running again in January 1996. She declined to distance herself from her extremist supporters. In March 1995 Chenoweth met with militia members and supporters in Boise and proclaimed, "We have democracy when government is afraid of the people." To the Oklahoma City bombing in April 1995 she reacted, "While we can never condone this, we still must begin to look at the public policies that may be pushing people too far." One of her pet pieces of legislation, written with the FBI misuse of power at Ruby Ridge in mind, is a bill to require federal agents to get written authorization from local sheriffs before enforcing federal law.

In the meantime she made not an impeccably conservative voting record—she seems to sign up on no one else's team—but a strong one on Idaho issues on the Agriculture and Resources Committees, where she chairs the new Forests and Forest Health Subcommittee. Not surprisingly, she had a strong Democratic opponent in 1996, former Frank Church staffer Dan

Williams. She seemed in trouble in 1995 when she admitted (just one day after the deadline for bringing House ethics charges before the election) after an FEC investigation that she had failed to report an unsecured $50,000 loan after the 1994 campaign and when it was suggested that land she sold near the end of her 1994 campaign was worth only one-sixth of its $60,000 price, which helped finance a last-minute ad blitz. Chenoweth won her 1996 primary by only 68%–32% over a challenger sent to a mental institution after removing most of his clothes during a TV interview.

But the general election campaign seemed to revolve on issues rather than ethics. Williams opposed gun control, favored a capital gains tax cut, called for limiting government—all popular in this district. And he argued to upwardly mobile Boiseans that Chenoweth was too rural, wacky, extreme. Chenoweth raised more money, but Williams had help from ads paid for by the AFL-CIO. And while Chenoweth clearly lost some Republican votes to Williams, leading him by only 50%–48% in Boise and Ada County, she carried all but five counties and won overall by the same margin. But the narrowness of the margin did not cause Chenoweth to blanch. "We're seeing a trend all over the nation. Those conservative Republicans who stood up for the principles that were of great consequence to the American people survived the election. Those who tried to moderate lost." She surely will continue to be a provocative politician.

The People: Pop. 1990: 503,141; 46% rural; 13% age 65+; 93% White; 1% Asian; 1% Amer. Indian; 5% Hispanic origin. Households: 63% married couple families; 30% married couple fams. w. children; 47% college educ.; median household income: $25,086; per capita income: $11,530; median gross rent: $332; median house value: $60,000.

1996 Presidential Vote

Dole (R)	134,783	(51%)
Clinton (D)	91,297	(35%)
Perot (I)	33,130	(13%)
Other(s)	4,142	(2%)

1992 Presidential Vote

Bush (R)	101,787	(41%)
Clinton (D)	75,499	(30%)
Perot (I)	67,677	(27%)

Rep. Helen Chenoweth (R)

Elected 1994; b. Jan. 27, 1938, Topeka, KS; home, Boise; Whitworth Col., B.A. 1962; Christian; divorced.

Career: Legal/Medical Mgmt. Consultant, 1964–75; Exec. Dir., ID Republican Party, 1975–77; Chief of Staff, U.S. Rep. Steve Symms, 1977–78; Founder & Pres., Consulting Associates Inc., 1978–94.

DC Office: 1727 LHOB 20515, 202-225-6611; Fax: 202-225-3029; e-mail: askhelen@mail.house.gov.

District Offices: Boise, 208-336-9831; Coeur d'Alene, 208-667-0127; Lewiston, 208-746-4613.

Committees: *Agriculture* (14th of 27 R): Forestry, Resource Conservation & Research. *Resources* (13th of 27 R): Forests & Forest Health (Chmn.); National Parks & Public Lands; Water & Power. *Veterans' Affairs* (15th of 16 R): Health.

Group Ratings

	ADA	ACLU	AFS	LCV	CFA	CON	NFIB	COC	ACU	NTLC	CHC
1996	10	20	8	0	0	17	97	88	95	98	100
1995	5	—	—	6	0	56	—	92	91	—	—

National Journal Ratings

	1995 LIB — 1995 CONS			1996 LIB — 1996 CONS		
Economic	36%	—	60%	0%	—	82%
Social	28%	—	70%	35%	—	65%
Foreign	15%	—	73%	0%	—	79%

Key Votes of the 104th Congress

1. Reduce Medicare Growth $	Y	5. Flag Amendment	Y	9. Cuban Embargo	Y
2. Ovrd. Product Liab. Veto	Y	6. Drop EPA Limits	N	10. Bar Bosnia Troop $	Y
3. Increase Min. Wage	N	7. Repeal Assault-Weap. Ban	Y	11. Cut Anti-Missile Defense	N
4. Welfare Reform	Y	8. Ovrd. Part. Birth Veto	Y	12. Bar U.N. Uniforms	Y

Election Results

1996 general	Helen Chenoweth (R)	132,344	(50%)	($1,129,263)
	Dan Williams (D)	125,899	(48%)	($659,753)
	Others	6,535	(2%)	
1996 primary	Helen Chenoweth (R)	38,616	(68%)	
	William A. Levinger (R)	18,054	(32%)	
1994 general	Helen Chenoweth (R)	111,728	(55%)	($796,149)
	Larry LaRocco (D)	89,826	(45%)	($845,902))

SECOND DISTRICT

The 2d District of Idaho, from central Boise east to the Utah border, is one of America's most Republican districts in presidential elections and, after several competitive years, in House elections as well. The congressman is Mike Crapo, first elected in 1992 when Democratic incumbent Richard Stallings ran for the Senate. Crapo grew up in Idaho Falls, went to Harvard law school, is a faithful Mormon who became a bishop in the church at 31; he was elected to the state Senate in 1984, at 33, became state Senate leader in 1988, was described by an Idaho Falls *Post Register* reporter as "intelligent, approachable and even-tempered." Crapo won the 1992 primary 68%–32% and campaigned against all tax increases, for spending cuts, a balanced budget amendment and the line-item veto—the Contract with America two years early. "Cowboy Democrat" J. D. Williams, the state controller, ran on a "put America first" stand on industrial policy and trade. Crapo won 61%–35%.

Crapo came to Washington with "a passion for reform," he said, to change both the institution and government. In 1993, freshmen Republicans voted him their class leader, he crusaded hard to make it easier for Members to sign the discharge petition in order to get bills out of recalcitrant committees, and he opposed the select committees, closed rules and closed committee meetings. On broader national issues, like many Republicans he favors simple, hard-and-fast rules—a balanced budget, term limits, across-the-board spending cuts (excluding social security)—to force tough decisions. He came into his own with the Republican victory in 1994, and became a deputy whip, with seats on Commerce and Agriculture, which he dropped for a seat on Resources in the 105th. By Washington standards he is a solid conservative, but he is a bit more moderate than his Idaho Republican colleagues. He opposed a bill that the other three co-sponsored to transfer 270 million acres of Bureau of Land Management land to private ownership: "Benefits available to all Idahoans include the scenic, recreational, economic, hunting, fishing and other opportunities afforded by our public outdoors." He got funding for the Sawtooth Recreation Area, opposed by colleague Helen Chenoweth. He wants decisions on issues like grazing, water quality, and grizzly bear management to be made at local forums. "Will we maintain the national standards but move the decision-making back to the local communities? I think we can make progress." He is on a task force to save Idaho salmon and steelhead while maintaining the flow of Snake River water to Idaho farms. He wants to restructure the Northwest electric utility industry; utility deregulation is a key item on the Commerce Committee agenda in the 105th Congress. He favors Governor Phil Batt's nuclear waste compact with the federal government, allowing waste to be transported now to INEEL in the 2d District in return for a promise of later shipment to waste sites in New Mexico and Nevada.

Crapo was hit on that issue and for his contributions from tobacco PACs by his 1996 Democratic opponent, Boise builder John Seidl, who decided to run when the government shutdown delayed a VA loan for a client. Crapo defended the nuclear waste compact, which was upheld when voters rejected Proposition 3, and angrily replied that he had never smoked and opposed all tobacco subsidies. He was reelected 69%–30%, carrying even left-leaning Sun Valley's Blaine County.

The People: Pop. 1990: 503,608; 39% rural; 11% age 65+; 92% White; 1% Asian; 1% Amer. Indian; 6% Hispanic origin. Households: 63% married couple families; 33% married couple fams. w. children; 51% college educ.; median household income: $25,446; per capita income: $11,384; median gross rent: $327; median house value: $55,900.

1996 Presidential Vote

Dole (R)	121,812	(53%)
Clinton (D)	74,146	(32%)
Perot (I)	29,388	(13%)

1992 Presidential Vote

Bush (R)	100,858	(43%)
Perot (I)	62,718	(27%)
Clinton (D)	61,514	(26%)
Other	8,925	(4%)

Rep. Michael Crapo (R)

Elected 1992; b. May 20, 1951, Idaho Falls; home, Idaho Falls; Brigham Young U., B.A. 1973, Harvard, J.D. 1977; Mormon; married (Susan).

Career: Practicing atty., 1977–92; ID Senate, 1984–92.

DC Office: 437 CHOB 20515, 202-225-5531; Fax: 202-225-8216.

District Offices: Boise, 208-334-1953; Idaho Falls, 208-523-6701; Pocatello, 208-236-6734; Twin Falls, 208-734-7219.

Committees: *Resources* (27th of 27 R): Fisheries Conservation, Wildlife & Oceans; Water & Power. *Commerce* (14th of 28 R): Energy & Power (Vice Chmn.); Finance & Hazardous Materials; Oversight & Investigations.

Group Ratings

	ADA	ACLU	AFS	LCV	CFA	CON	NFIB	COC	ACU	NTLC	CHC
1996	0	19	0	8	0	30	100	100	95	100	100
1995	5	—	—	6	0	56	—	100	92	—	—

National Journal Ratings

	1995 LIB — 1995 CONS			1996 LIB — 1996 CONS		
Economic	33%	—	66%	0%	—	82%
Social	28%	—	70%	33%	—	65%
Foreign	0%	—	85%	0%	—	79%

Key Votes of the 104th Congress

1. Reduce Medicare Growth $	Y	5. Flag Amendment	Y	9. Cuban Embargo	Y
2. Ovrd. Product Liab. Veto	Y	6. Drop EPA Limits	N	10. Bar Bosnia Troop $	Y
3. Increase Min. Wage	N	7. Repeal Assault-Weap. Ban	Y	11. Cut Anti-Missile Defense	N
4. Welfare Reform	Y	8. Ovrd. Part. Birth Veto	Y	12. Bar U.N. Uniforms	Y

Election Results

1996 general	Michael Crapo (R)	157,646	(69%)	($755,679)
	John D. Seidl (D)	67,625	(30%)	($163,532)
	Others	3,977	(2%)	
1996 primary	Michael Crapo (R)	51,778	(86%)	
	Peter Rickards (R)	8,382	(14%)	
1994 general	Michael Crapo (R)	143,593	(75%)	($352,461)
	Penny Fletcher (D)	47,936	(25%)	($26,862)

ILLINOIS

One hundred years ago America seemed destined to center on Chicago. This brash new city on the lake had grown from 112,000 in 1860, when it was host to the Republican Convention that nominated Illinois's Abraham Lincoln, to 1,400,000 people when it hosted the Columbian Exposition in 1893. "Make no little plans," Chicago architect Daniel Burnham exhorted, and Chicago was making vast plans, building grand parks on the lakefront, erecting America's first downtown of skyscrapers, building expansive retail palaces, becoming the headquarters of the new American Medical and American Bar Associations, creating a great university from scratch on the Exposition's Midway Plaisance, housing the union agitators and their liberal advocate Clarence Darrow as well as the corporate leaders and attorneys who bested them, hosting the Democratic Convention of 1896 that nominated 36-year-old William Jennings Bryan after his "cross of gold" speech and becoming the headquarters of the brilliant campaign Marcus Hanna waged for William McKinley which beat Bryan in the fall. Chicago started with the advantage of a great location, where the Great Lakes met the prairies of the vast Mississippi Valley, and Chicago's entrepreneurs made it the hub of the nation's railroad network and the center of the nation's trade in lumber, grain and meat, as William Cronon describes in *Nature's Metropolis*.

A century later, Chicago is the nation's third largest metropolis, sometimes overshadowed by and often ignored by the media of coastal New York and Los Angeles; but it is still a productive and creative world-city. In commerce, Chicago remains a prime producer and processor of food products, a great manufacturing center with the strongest white-collar and service economy between the coasts, the home of the world's greatest commodities exchanges and futures markets. O'Hare Airport, built with care by longtime (1955–76) Mayor Richard J. Daley, is the nation's busiest, a center of commerce and travel rivalled only by London's Heathrow.

Politically, Chicago and Illinois have not produced any presidents in the 20th Century, but they have produced crucial votes and pivotal politicians. Start with Charles Dawes, a 30-year-old lawyer sent to Chicago by Hanna to manage McKinley's campaign; later he was a World War I general, the first Budget Bureau (now Office of Management and Budget) director, and vice president under Calvin Coolidge. Or Chicago lawyer Harold Ickes, who was Franklin Roosevelt's great Interior secretary. Prominent Illinois Republicans have included Speaker Joseph Cannon, Senate Republican Leader Everett Dirksen, Senator Charles Percy and House Republican Leader Robert Michel; prominent Democrats have included Governor Adlai

Stevenson, Mayor Richard J. Daley and Ways and Means Chairman Dan Rostenkowski. As for votes, Illinois has 22 electoral votes and, with percentages near the national average of blacks and Hispanics, immigrants and pioneers, city-dwellers and suburbanites and farmers, the affluent and the impoverished, heavy industry and high-tech, they tend to reflect national divisions. Illinois is furiously contested in close presidential elections and, since Bryan orated and Dawes set up shop, it has voted for the losing presidential candidate only twice, in 1916 and 1976. Increasingly, its aberrations from the national average reflect the views of the Chicago suburbs which cast 40% of the state's vote, pro-market on economics and *laissez faire* on cultural issues: these sent Illinois toward Gerald Ford when Jimmy Carter was winning and toward Bill Clinton in the 1990s, when Illinois was by a significant margin his best Midwestern state.

But politics has not always been central to life in Illinois, or America. This was a state of farmers, whose families, communities and churches absorbed more of their energies than politics or government. Chicago was established not by government but by markets; it has always been a free enterprise city, settled by pioneers from New England and Kentucky, by immigrant Irishmen who dug the first canal connecting Lake Michigan and the Illinois River, and by railroad promoters who saw its potential as the great connecting point between East and West and the Great Lakes and the Mississippi Valley. Its factories, built where iron ore from Great Lakes freighters and coal from inland hills came together, attracted migrants from near and far. To meet the demands of these masses and referee their cultural struggles, political machines sprang up, allied with the Republicans who predominated in northern Illinois and the Democrats who usually prevailed from Springfield south. Not until the Depression of the 1930s did Chicago become reliably Democratic, and that was in part because so many Republicans had moved to the Cook County suburbs and the Collar Counties surrounding Chicago.

Illinois's political trends have also been set by reactions to the political officeholder most visible to the voters, who is not usually the governor off in remote Springfield and certainly not the senators who have to work "out of town" in Washington, but the mayor of Chicago—even though Chicago itself now casts only 20% of the state's votes. During the years in which Richard J. Daley was "Da Mare," politics here was a contest between Chicago and Downstate, typified by the 1960 presidential race when Daley helped John F. Kennedy carry Illinois by exactly (or so it was reported) 8,858 votes out of 4.7 million cast. (Only twice since then, in 1984 and 1992, has Illinois cast more votes; the 1996 turnout of 4.3 million was the lowest since 1948.) Then in 1968 the terrible schisms in the Democratic Party were displayed in vivid form in the 1968 Democratic Convention in Chicago, when demonstrators attacked police and police, in one episode captured on videotape, attacked them and anyone nearby; in Illinois and nationwide Democrats had trouble for a generation rallying the middle-class voters who were their historic base. In the 1980s, with the election of black Mayor Harold Washington and the ensuing "council wars," politics in the Chicago area was racially polarized; despite a farm recession Downstate, Illinois was mostly Republican in the Reagan years. Then with the election of Richard M. Daley in 1989, racial animosities lessened and the Democrats projected an appealing image in the suburbs. This, together with national issues, helped Bill Clinton carry Illinois twice by effective margins—49%–34% over George Bush in 1992 and 54%–37% over Bob Dole in 1996, when Clinton carried the suburbs 48%–43% as well as the city 79%–16%. This was a sharp improvement for Clinton in the suburbs, which he lost 42%–39% in 1992. But Clinton's margin Downstate shrunk a bit: he carried it 45%–36% over Bush and 48%–41% over Dole. The suburbs—anti-tax, secular if not liberal on cultural issues—seemed largely satisfied with Clinton by 1996; while Downstate—culturally more conservative, less in need of government public works or farm programs as their economy recovered from the recession of the 1980s—if anything moved a bit away from Clinton and his party.

Yet the Republicans have also on occasion done well in the 1990s. Governor Jim Edgar, elected by a narrow margin in 1990, was reelected by a huge 64%–34% in 1994, with Republicans winning up and down the ticket and taking control of both houses of the legislature.

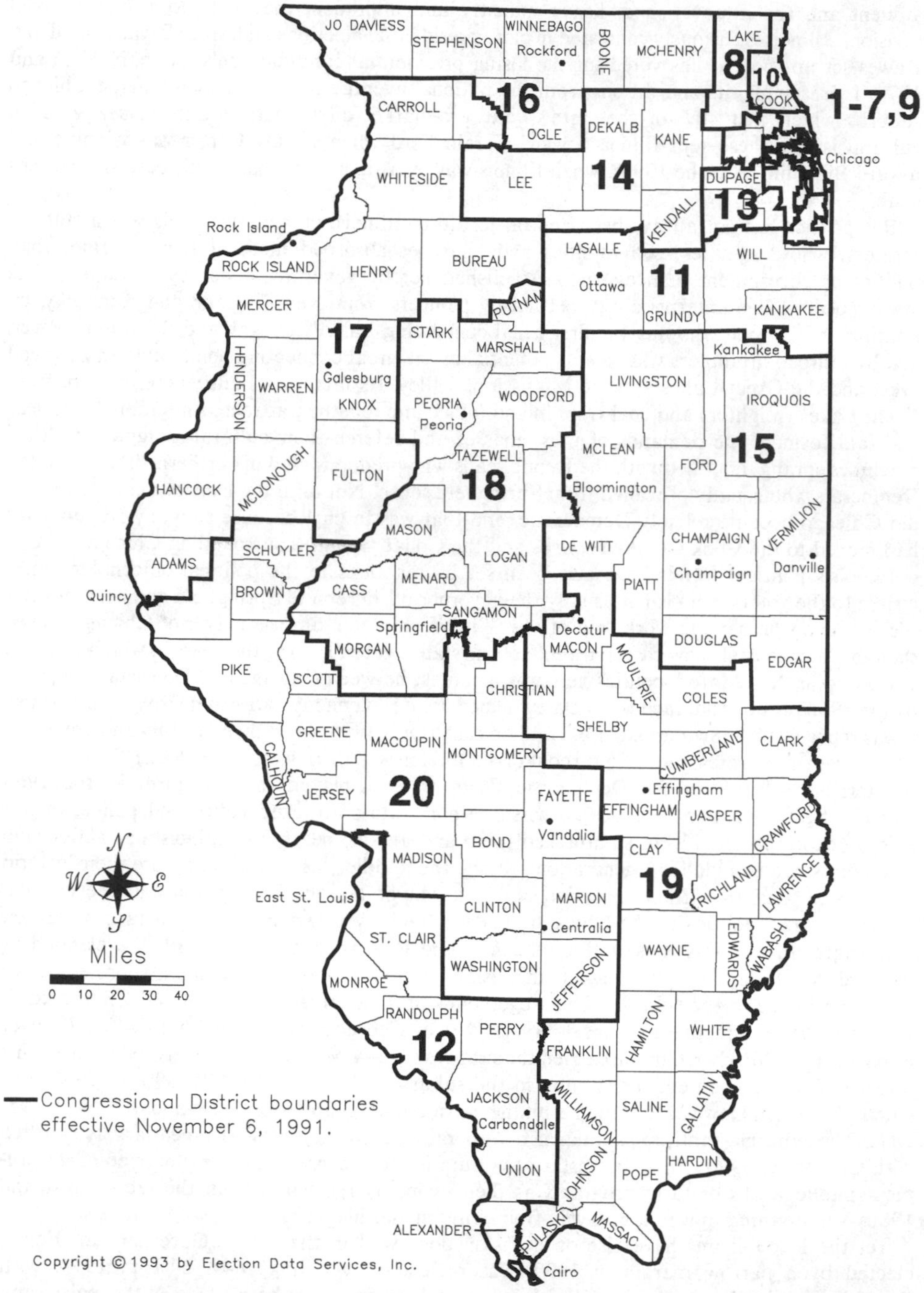
JO DAVIESS
STEPHENSON
WINNEBAGO
Rockford
BOONE
MCHENRY
LAKE
8
10
COOK
1-7,9
Chicago
CARROLL
16
OGLE
DEKALB
KANE
WHITESIDE
LEE
14
DUPAGE
13
KENDALL
WILL
Rock Island
ROCK ISLAND
HENRY
BUREAU
LASALLE
Ottawa
11
GRUNDY
KANKAKEE
Kankakee
MERCER
PUTNAM
STARK
MARSHALL
17
Galesburg
KNOX
WARREN
HENDERSON
LIVINGSTON
IROQUOIS
PEORIA
Peoria
WOODFORD
TAZEWELL
MCLEAN
Bloomington
FORD
15
HANCOCK
MCDONOUGH
FULTON
18
MASON
DE WITT
CHAMPAIGN
Champaign
VERMILION
Danville
ADAMS
SCHUYLER
LOGAN
MENARD
Quincy
BROWN
CASS
PIATT
SANGAMON
Springfield
Decatur
MACON
MORGAN
DOUGLAS
EDGAR
PIKE
SCOTT
CHRISTIAN
MOULTRIE
COLES
SHELBY
GREENE
MACOUPIN
MONTGOMERY
CUMBERLAND
CLARK
CALHOUN
JERSEY
20
FAYETTE
Effingham
EFFINGHAM
JASPER
CRAWFORD
Vandalia
BOND
MADISON
CLAY
19
RICHLAND
LAWRENCE
East St. Louis
CLINTON
MARION
Centralia
ST. CLAIR
WAYNE
EDWARDS
WABASH
WASHINGTON
JEFFERSON
MONROE
RANDOLPH
PERRY
12
HAMILTON
WHITE
FRANKLIN
JACKSON
Carbondale
WILLIAMSON
SALINE
GALLATIN
UNION
JOHNSON
POPE
HARDIN
PULASKI
MASSAC
ALEXANDER
Cairo
N
W
E
S
Miles
0 10 20 30 40
Congressional District boundaries effective November 6, 1991.

In 1996 Democrats recaptured the state House but not the Senate, and took one U.S. House seat away from the Republicans while narrowly losing another, all of which suggests a certain equipoise once one gets below the top of the ticket. There will be stirring contests again in 1998. Republicans are by no means assured of holding onto the governorship, at least if Edgar retires or runs for the Senate; while the Democrats' hold on Carol Moseley-Braun's Senate seat is tenuous given her problems. Illinois's political battles are fought more fiercely the closer they relate to issues that are local; but they have exemplary value as well for the nation.

That is even more true of Illinois's primaries. Illinois has the earliest filing deadline in the country: Robert Michel's decision not to run for reelection had to be made by December 1993, giving Newt Gingrich plenty of time to consolidate his leadership of House Republicans before the 1994 campaign. And its state primary is held in March in off years as well as presidential years: the March 1992 defeat of Senator Alan Dixon and four incumbent congressmen (two of whom had been redistricted to run against other Democratic lawmakers), and Dan Rostenkowski's close shave were an early warning of that year's anti-incumbent trend. Illinois's presidential primary, held fittingly on or around St. Patrick's Day, has played a decisive role in most recent contests. As the first big northern state to vote, Illinois signalled the dismal fate of Edward Kennedy's candidacy in 1980; in 1984, it clinched the Democratic nomination for Walter Mondale; in 1988, George Bush's victory here eliminated any doubt that he would win the Republican nomination, while Michael Dukakis would probably have cinched the nomination or Al Gore would have ignited his candidacy here but for the dominance of two Illinois candidates, Senator Paul Simon and then-Chicago resident Jesse Jackson. In 1992, Bill Clinton clinched the Democratic nomination in Illinois, angrily dismissing in a Chicago TV studio Jerry Brown's attempt to raise the Whitewater scandal against him. Only in 1996, when Bill Clinton was unopposed and Bob Dole's primary victory in South Carolina March 2 clinched the nomination, did Illinois's March 19 primary occur too late to determine the result. But it may again, especially if there is a crowded Republican field, in 2000.

Governor. In his second term as governor of Illinois, Jim Edgar seems modest and quiet; yet he admits he has been ambitious to succeed in politics since the second grade. He grew up in the Downstate town of Charleston; his father died young, the victim of a drunk driver. In 1968, at 22, Edgar wangled a job in Springfield with state Senate President Russell Arrington, a bright old-style legislator who was learning to play new policy games; he worked for Speaker Robert Blair in the years when Republican Governor Richard Ogilvie pushed through a politically disastrous tax increase. Edgar won a seat in the state legislature in 1976, and in 1981, Governor James Thompson appointed him secretary of state, where he garnered attention by pushing through an anti-drunk-driving law. In 1990, Edgar ran to succeed Thompson, with strong opposition from Democratic Attorney General Neil Hartigan. Ironically, Hartigan talked of cutting taxes and running government like a business; Edgar promised to make permanent the 1989 tax surcharge for education. Both favored an initiative requiring a 60% state House and Senate vote for a tax increase. Edgar narrowly won, 51%–48%, becoming the first Downstater elected governor since the 1920s.

In office Edgar has maintained high job ratings while winning important policy successes, especially after Republicans won both houses of the legislature in 1994. He has held the line on taxes, cut government payrolls, installed property tax caps. His "Earnfare" program encouraged welfare mothers to work and required mothers 18 and under to stay in high school to qualify for welfare benefits; in 1995 he signed a bill eliminating AFDC by 1999 and capping other welfare benefits. He has had some major tussles with Mayor Richard M. Daley, though they have cooperated on occasion. Daley outflanked Edgar's plans to build a new airport at Peotone, 45 miles south of Chicago, by entering into an interstate compact with Gary, Indiana; but when Daley closed Meigs Field airstrip on the lakefront in 1996, Edgar engineered a lame duck session of the legislature in which the Republican majority voted to keep it open. Edgar has so far successfully opposed Daley's plan for a Chicago gambling casino and has sought a domed stadium to replace Soldier Field. But Edgar and the legislature cooperated by voting to turn over control of the Chicago schools to Daley.

In 1994 Edgar was opposed by state Senator Dawn Clark Netsch, a lakefront liberal who called for a big increase in the state income tax and opposed capital punishment; she won the primary after a clever ad showing her shooting pool and making a tough shot. But being "a straight shooter" was not enough, given her issue positions and Edgar's great popularity, even after Edgar had quadruple bypass surgery in July 1994 and had to persuade his Lieutenant Governor, Bob Kustra, to stay on the ticket after he said he was leaving to become a talk radio host. Edgar won 64%–34%, carrying 101 of 102 counties (he lost one Downstate county by 3 votes) and helped Republicans sweep to legislative control and victories for all statewide offices.

Edgar used that victory to achieve tort reform (limits on civil liability awards), a $250 million cut in unemployment taxes and a $400 million increase for education, charter schools and high school senior exit exams; by early 1997 his budget was in surplus and unemployment was well below the national average. But he was not successful in everything. His constitutional amendment to allow a rise in state taxes and lower property taxes was blocked by Democrats. And in 1996 Democrats regained control of the state House.

In early 1997 Edgar said he was undecided about running for reelection. His job rating is high, and he would be the favorite if he runs. Neil Hartigan announced he was not running in November 1996, and some looked to retired Senator Paul Simon (who ran for the office, and lost the Democratic primary, in 1972). Other interested Democrats include John Schmidt, former top Daley staffer, who left the number three post in the Clinton Justice Department in early 1997 to return to Chicago, U.S. Attorney Jim Burns, former Attorney General Roland Burris, and Representative Glenn Poshard. If Edgar retires or runs for the Senate, Republican possibilities include Lieutenant Governor Bob Kustra, Secretary of State George Ryan, and Attorney General Jim Ryan.

Mayor. Richard M. Daley, mayor of Chicago since 1989, who came to office with a reputation as an inarticulate heir, has proved to be an innovative, thoughtful and effective mayor—one of the most successful Democratic public officials in the country. His father of course was Richard J. Daley, first elected in 1955 and mayor until his death in December 1976—and boss of the fabled Chicago machine. Richie Daley, as he is often called, was a state senator and Cook County state's attorney whose one major setback was his defeat in the 1983 mayoral primary by Harold Washington, an able mayor who was vociferously opposed by white politicians in "the council wars"; after Washington's death no qualified black successor appeared, and Daley was elected by winning the white "bungalow wards" plus Hispanic and lakefront wards his opponents took for granted. Daley's first achievement was racial reconciliation; his approval ratings among blacks run around 50% and among others, including suburbanites, are up around 80%. His second step was to downsize and privatize city government, eliminating 1600 jobs and privatizing 40 functions. The old Daley machine, in which city employees were expected to be Democratic precinct and ward committeemen, producing votes for the machine on election day, was rendered defunct by a 1970s court case that prohibited firing employees for political reasons, and it became obvious that the government bureaucracy was so inefficient that continuing to rely on it would mean ever-higher taxes and municipal ruin. Daley has hired 1,000 new police officers, but held the line on property taxes.

Daley then entered upon an era of great projects, not all of which have come to fruition. His plans for a new airport around Lake Calumet were abandoned when the legislature would not meet his terms; he in turn blocked the Republicans' plans to build a new airport at Peotone, 45 miles south of Chicago. O'Hare is the grand project of the Daleys, father and son, and the current mayor wants to expand it, over the opposition of the mostly Republican constituencies that live under the flightpaths; Daley closed down Meigs Field, on the lakefront in October 1996, only to have Governor Jim Edgar and the lame-duck Republican legislature pass a law to re-open it in December 1996. (The "council wars" of the 1980s have been replaced by the airport wars of the 1990s.) Daley was also frustrated by Edgar's veto of a lakefront casino in Chicago. And he was besieged when an ancient Chicago Water Tunnel collapsed and flooded much of the

Loop in April 1992.

More recently, Daley has turned from grand projects to delivering services better. The legislature was happy to turn over control of the dreadful Chicago public school system to him, and he installed his own people to get the system working better again. Like his father, he seems to know the city block by block, and he has worked to improve both struggling and rising neighborhoods; and the fact is that, even as some of Chicago's big units—big companies like Sears, the big housing projects—leave or decay, the city as a whole has marvelous vitality. Small businesses are replacing large; old factories far from the lakefront are being rebuilt as luxury condominium complexes; immigrant communities are vibrant in precincts that once seemed to be dying; South Side black neighborhoods, with help from Daley's SNAP (Strategic Neighborhood Assistance Program) zones, are well maintained and growing rather than being abandoned; the new United Center, replacing Chicago Stadium, is bringing signs of life to the bedraggled West Side, even as the old open-air Maxwell Street Market is moved and divided. Symbolic of Daley's approach is his zest for wrought-iron fences, in parks, around new developments, in neighborhoods: strong fences making good neighbors. "People care about what they see out their front windows. The big projects always have the same players; you either get them done or you don't because of politics and money. But the detail work, the wrought iron, the streets, crime, the schools. That's what you do." Mayor Daley and his brother William Daley, one of the smartest political strategists everywhere, were courted by Bill Clinton in 1992 and then mostly abandoned, with Bill Daley being edged out for secretary of Transportation. But Daley returned to help Clinton pass NAFTA in November 1993, and in December 1996 William Daley became Commerce secretary. The Democratic National Convention was given to Chicago, and the city and the Daleys shined amid appropriately perfect weather.

There is no "Daley machine" any more, only a city with diverse neighborhoods packed with aspiring politicians. Mayor Daley's endorsement, public or silent, is worth something but not everything; it could help Dan Rostenkowski in the 1992 primary, for instance, but not in the 1994 general election, nor could the Daleys help him out in his legal troubles. Mayor Daley was reelected by a wide margin in spring 1995, beating a competent black opponent overwhelmingly in the primary; his prospects for reelection in 1999 are excellent.

Senior Senator. Carol Moseley-Braun, the nation's first black woman senator, is charming, politically experienced, well spoken, grounded in the reality of urban life. She grew up in a middle-class neighborhood, the daughter of a policeman and a medical technician. She was elected to the legislature in 1978, at 31, and performed creditably even according to Republicans. She wanted to be slated for lieutenant governor in 1986 and, failing that, got elected Cook County Recorder of Deeds in 1989. Her political intuition told her that Senator Alan Dixon, up for reelection in 1992 after 40 years in public office, would be vulnerable, and that an attractive candidate who built on the 25% of primary voters who are black could beat him. Dixon and Al Hofeld, a free-spending trial lawyer also in the race, traded charges; Moseley-Braun (she inserted the hyphen in 1993—in the campaign her last name was Braun) stayed, as consultant David Axelrod said, "really below the fray," and came on strong in the final week to win with 38% of the vote to 35% for Dixon and 27% for Hofeld. In the 1992 general, Chicago area voters were in a mood for racial reconciliation, and there was no easier way to signal that than to vote for the intelligent, always smiling Moseley-Braun. Meanwhile, her opponent, former Reagan aide Rich Williamson, was fending off attacks for switching his position on abortion just about the time he announced his candidacy. So strong was support for Moseley-Braun that she weathered the storm in September 1992 when it was revealed that in 1989 she split among herself and siblings a $28,750 timber royalty inheritance owed to her mother, a nursing home resident who was supposed to have reimbursed Medicaid with the money. Moseley-Braun's explanations were unconvincing at best, and a candidate of other race and gender might have lost the election right there. But she did well in debates and won 53%–43%, losing the suburbs by only 52%–44% and carrying Downstate 50%–45%.

Her record since has been a mixture of some legislative accomplishments and much-criticized exercises in bad judgment. Her voting record has been generally liberal but is also supportive of Illinois business interests. In 1993 she helped delete a commodities futures-exchange tax from the Clinton tax package. She won Finance Committee approval and enactment of a plan to allow a team including composer Quincy Jones and the Tribune Company to use a minority-ownership preference to purchase a group of television stations. She supported product liability reform and the balanced budget amendment. In the 1996 farm bill she sponsored an amendment to set the soybean loan rate at 85% of a moving average, and she sought to have biodiesel declared an alternative fuel: pet causes of Dwayne Andreas and Archer-Daniels-Midland, which is based in Downstate Decatur. She showed Chicago-style political acumen in getting Tom Daschle to give her his Finance Committee seat in return for her support in his race for minority leader, which he won by one vote.

Moseley-Braun won favorable notice in July 1993 when she confronted and defeated Jesse Helms when he sought to renew a patent for the insignia of the United Daughters of the Confederacy. And she spoke out eloquently against the 1996 welfare reform. She sponsored a measure creating a corporation to help schools borrow to buy computers and other high-tech items. She secured more favorable pension benefits for widows and divorced women. Another successful amendment allowed state and local governments to set retirement ages for police officers and fire fighters. She worked for historic preservation of buildings at historically black colleges and universities.

But these may have been overshadowed by her missteps. In her 1992 campaign 138 contributors exceeded the $1,000 limit and $249,000 of expenditures were not accounted for: unusual sloppiness, at the least. Her campaign manager and then-fiance, Kgosie Matthews, was accused of sexual harassment by female campaign workers and criticized for taking a month-long trip to Africa with her after the 1992 election. Then in August 1996, she and Matthews, a former registered agent of the Nigerian government, paid a "private" visit to Nigeria where they met with dictator General Sani Abacha. Moseley-Braun had once signed a letter criticizing the Nigerian regime on human rights; in 1996 she was defending the regime, as on the road to democracy. She returned to the 1996 Democratic convention in Chicago, where she was criticized by many Democrats including Mayor Daley. A month later she admitted she "erred in the handling of the whole issue of my private travel."

Moseley-Braun's job rating has not been high, and after the 1996 Nigeria visit one consultant said she was politically "DOA." Speculation abounded on possible opponents. Congressman Jesse Jackson Jr. said he would not run and would discourage opposition to the first black woman senator. Other Democrats were mentioned as possible candidates—former gubernatorial candidate Michael Bakalis, Chicago Congressman Luis Gutierrez, 1994 lieutenant governor candidate Sheila Smith, Chicago Treasurer Miriam Santos—though it's not clear any of them will risk alienating blacks or feminists by running. Meanwhile, Republicans are probably hoping that Moseley-Braun will run. Senate Majority Leader Trent Lott was trying to entice Edgar to run against Moseley-Braun; if he does, other Republicans are not likely to give him a primary challenge. If Edgar does not run, possibilities include Secretary of State George Ryan, Attorney General Jim Ryan, Lieutenant Governor Bob Kustra, State Comptroller Loleta Didrickson and 1996 nominee Al Salvi.

Junior Senator. Richard Durbin, a faithful Democratic Party follower, won the seat vacated by Paul Simon in 1996. Durbin grew up in East St. Louis, and for almost all his adult life has been in politics. Right out of law school he joined Paul Simon's staff when he was lieutenant governor (1969–73), then was a state Senate staffer in the 1970s. He taught in medical school and lost two races for office in the 1970s, but in 1982 won the nomination to oppose Republican Congressman Paul Findley, who had characterized himself as Yasir Arafat's best friend in Congress; that helped Durbin raise large sums from Israel supporters and to attack Findley for concentrating on issues of no importance at home. Durbin won that race, got a seat on the Agriculture Committee, and then moved to Appropriations, where in January 1993 he became chairman of the Agriculture Appropriations Subcommittee, succeeding Jamie Whitten of

Mississippi who had held the job since 1949 (except for 1953–55 when Republicans were in control). As part of the "college of cardinals" (the Appropriations subcommittee chairmen), Durbin proceeded to work for Illinois projects—not just Downstate projects like the research center at the Lincoln home, but the $750 million Chicago Circulator trolley project as well. He worked to promote ethanol and soybean-based ink in government documents—big causes in the homeland of Dwayne Andreas's Archer-Daniels-Midland. Durbin's father died of lung cancer when he was 14, and Durbin's most prominent achievement was the 1988 ban on smoking on domestic airline flights; he followed that up by trying to limit tobacco subsidies. His amendment to direct the FDA to regulate tobacco as a health hazard was killed in 1994, but was revived by FDA Administrator David Kessler and the Clinton-Gore campaign in 1996.

Frustrations may have impelled Durbin to run for the Senate in 1996. The Republican victory of 1994 deprived him of his subcommittee chair, and his own recent races were uncomfortably close: he won against a serious opponent with 57% in 1992, then won with just 55% in 1994 against a construction worker and John Birch Society member who spent only $55,000. So in June 1995, after his old mentor Paul Simon announced his retirement from the Senate after two terms, Durbin decided to run. Simon would probably have easily won: his country-newspaper-editor demeanor (he had started out as a crusading editor of the *Troy Tribune* in 1948, at 19) plus his statewide durability (he was elected lieutenant governor in 1968) and his brief fame as a presidential candidate in 1988 gave him strength beyond party lines. Simon immediately endorsed Durbin, which surely helped him Downstate. That left as Durbin's chief problem an almost total lack of name identification in Chicago, which would cast 46% of the primary votes. That problem was solved with money: Durbin raised more that $1 million for the March 19 primary, vastly outspending his only serious opponent, former state Treasurer Pat Quinn. Durbin went on TV in early February, talking of his working class roots and fights against tobacco and gun lobbies. The result was an overwhelming 65%–30% Durbin win. Meanwhile, the Republican primary was won in an upset. Governor Jim Edgar and other insiders had worked to persuade a reluctant Lieutenant Governor Bob Kustra to run. But Kustra, who at one point in 1994 announced he was retiring from politics to be a talk radio host, seemed to have little fire in his belly. His opponent, trial lawyer and abortion opponent Al Salvi, did, and spent more than $1 million of his own money in the primary. Salvi argued that he led the fight against tax increases while Kustra voted for them. Despite a meek demeanor and total lack of name identification, Salvi came from behind to edge Kustra 48%–43%.

The general election was a battle of broad-brush charges in a state where few voters knew much about either candidate. Salvi called Durbin a tax-raiser, hit him for opposing the balanced budget amendment; a bartender in one of his ads called Durbin "a big-taxin', big-spendin', pay-grabbin' liberal congressman." Durbin constantly called Salvi an "extremist," and hit him for opposing the assault weapon ban and taking tobacco money. Polls throughout showed Durbin with small leads, but under 50%. Perhaps the leading issue was gun control. Salvi's opposition to the assault weapons ban was undoubtedly unpopular, especially in the suburbs, and an October endorsement from gun control activists Jim and Sarah Brady undoubtedly helped Durbin. But more important was an astonishing mistake by Salvi: in late October, someone he met at a rally told him that Jim Brady used to sell machine guns and, without checking out the story, Salvi repeated it on a radio interview. It was totally untrue and Salvi had to apologize, but any chance of his overtaking Durbin was gone. Durbin won 56%–41%, with a huge margin in Chicago and narrow edges in the suburbs and Downstate. Durbin's 56% was almost exactly identical to Bill Clinton's 54% and Democratic House candidates' 55%. After his victory, Durbin said he would push for campaign finance reform and targeted middle-class tax cuts. He serves on the Judiciary, Governmental Affairs, and Budget Committees.

Presidential politics. Illinois is a presidential bellwether: it has voted for every presidential winner for 100 years except for southerners Jimmy Carter in 1976 and Woodrow Wilson in 1916 (the latter was the first year women voted here; Protestant women turned out more than Catholics, tipping the state Republican). In the 1990s Illinois is perhaps less of a bellwether, since it has tilted so heavily toward Bill Clinton; he has dipped heavily into the ordinarily Republican vote in the suburbs, one of which, Park Ridge, is the childhood home of Hillary Rodham Clinton.

Illinois's mid-March primary arguably decided the party's nominee for the Republicans in 1976, 1980 and 1988 and for the Democrats in 1980, 1984 and 1992. In 1996, it was held on March 19, the same day as Ohio, Michigan and Wisconsin. But the nomination had already been decided March 2 in South Carolina, and Bob Dole's 65%–23% victory over Pat Buchanan was icing on his cake. Illinois's Republican primary voters, by the way, are about evenly split between the suburbs, with their affluent free-marketeer dislike for taxes, and Downstate, with their old-fashioned, practical-minded Midwestern politics. Illinois's Democratic primary voters are more evenly split between Chicago, the suburbs, and Downstate.

Congressional districting. A federal court redistricted Illinois's House seats in 1991, choosing a plan favoring Republicans; this was a counterbalance to the court decision 10 years before which favored Democrats. The 1991 plan caused a quick revolution in Illinois politics, for the filing deadline here is in December, the earliest in the nation. It forced two primaries between pairs of Democratic incumbents, one Downstate and one mostly in the Chicago suburbs, and might have forced another, in a Chicago area district if the incumbent had not retired. Four Democratic incumbents were defeated in the primary, two by other incumbents. A new Hispanic-majority seat was created, but has now come under fire for racial gerrymandering; the Supreme Court in 1996 sent the case back to a Chicago panel of judges, which had not taken action by early 1997. The 1996 election saw a reshuffle: Democrats recaptured Rostenkowski's district easily, but narrowly lost successful Senate candidate Richard Durbin's Downstate seat.

The People: Est. Pop. 1996: 11,847,000; Pop. 1990: 11,430,602, up 3.6% 1990–1996. 4.5% of U.S. total, 6th largest; 15% rural. Median age: 34.3 years. 13% 65 years and over. 74.8% White, 14.6% Black, 2.4% Asian; 7.9% Hispanic origin. Households: 54.1% married couple families; 26% married couple fams. w. children; 46% college educ.; median household income: $32,252; per capita income: $15,201; 64.2% owner occupied housing; median house value: $80,900; median monthly rent: $369. 5.3% Unemployment. 1996 Voting age pop.: 8,754,000. 1996 Turnout: 4,311,391; 49% of VAP. Registered voters (1996): 6,663,301; no party registration.

Political Lineup: Governor, Jim Edgar (R); Lt. Gov., Bob Kustra (R); Secy. of State, George H. Ryan Sr. (R); Atty. Gen., James E. Ryan (R); Treasurer, Judy Baar Topinka (R); Comptroller, Loleta A. Didrickson (R). State Senate, 59 (28 D and 31 R); Senate President, James (Pate) Phillip (R); State House, 118 (60 D and 58 R); House Speaker, Mike Madigan (D). Senators, Carol Moseley-Braun (D) and Richard J. Durbin (D). Representatives, 20 (11 D and 9 R).

Elections Division: 217-782-4141; **Filing Deadline for U.S. Congress:** December 18, 1997.

1996 Presidential Vote

Clinton (D)	2,341,744	(54%)
Dole (R)	1,587,021	(37%)
Perot (I)	346,408	(8%)

1996 Republican Presidential Primary

Dole (R)	532,467	(65%)
Buchanan (R)	186,177	(23%)
Forbes (R)	39,906	(5%)
Keyes (R)	30,052	(4%)
Other	29,762	(4%)

1992 Presidential Vote

Clinton (D)	2,453,350	(49%)
Bush (R)	1,734,096	(34%)
Perot (I)	840,515	(17%)

GOVERNOR

Gov. Jim Edgar (R)

Elected 1990, term expires Jan. 1999; b. July 22, 1946, Vinita, OK; home, Springfield; E. IL U., B.A. 1968; American Baptist; married (Brenda).

Career: Staff Aide, IL House of Reps. & IL Senate, 1968–76; IL House of Reps., 1976–79; Legis. Affairs Dir., IL Gov. Thompson, 1979–81; IL Secy. of State, 1981–90.

Office: 207 State House, Springfield 62706, 217-782-6830; Fax: 217-524-1676; Web site: www.state.il.us.

Election Results

1994 gen.	Jim Edgar (R)	1,984,318	(64%)
	Dawn Clark Netsch (D)	1,069,850	(34%)
	Others	52,398	(2%)
1994 prim.	Jim Edgar (R)	521,590	(75%)
	Jack Roeser (R)	173,742	(25%)
1990 gen.	Jim Edgar (R)	1,653,126	(51%)
	Neil F. Hartigan (D)	1,569,217	(48%)

SENATORS

Sen. Carol Moseley-Braun (D)

Elected 1992, seat up 1998; b. Aug. 16, 1947, Chicago; home, Chicago; U. of IL, B.A., 1969, U. of Chicago, J.D. 1972; Catholic; divorced.

Career: Asst. U.S. Atty., 1973–77; IL House of Reps., 1978–88, Asst. Majority Ldr., 1983; Cook Cnty. Recorder of Deeds, 1989–92.

DC Office: 324 HSOB 20515, 202-224-2854; Fax: 202-228-1318; e-mail: senator@moseley-braun.senate.gov.

State Offices: Chicago, 312-353-5420; Fairview Heights, 618-632-7242; Springfield, 217-492-4126.

Committees: *Banking, Housing & Urban Affairs* (6th of 8 D): Financial Institutions & Regulatory Relief; Housing Opportunity & Community Development; International Finance (RMM). *Finance* (7th of 9 D): Health Care; International Trade; Social Security & Family Policy. *Aging (Special)* (6th of 8 D).

Group Ratings

	ADA	ACLU	AFS	LCV	CFA	CON	NFIB	COC	ACU	NTLC	CHC
1996	90	78	86	77	64	27	45	46	5	7	7
1995	100	—	82	93	63	19	—	32	9	—	—

National Journal Ratings

	1995 LIB	—	1995 CONS	1996 LIB	—	1996 CONS
Economic	73%	—	23%	70%	—	27%
Social	76%	—	18%	92%	—	0%
Foreign	86%	—	7%	89%	—	7%

Key Votes of the 104th Congress

1. Reduce Medicare Growth $	N	5. Flag Amendment	N	9. Anti-Missile Defense	N
2. Lmt. Prod. Liab. Damages	Y	6. Endangered Species	Y	10. Cuban Embargo	N
3. Increase Min. Wage	Y	7. Gay Employment Rights	Y	11. Bar Bosnia Troop $	N
4. Welfare Reform	N	8. Ovrd. Part. Birth Veto	N	12. Cut Vietnam Aid	Y

Election Results

1992 general	Carol Moseley-Braun (D)	2,631,229	(53%)	($6,699,942)
	Richard S. Williamson (R)	2,126,833	(43%)	($2,300,924)
	Nine Others	181,496	(4%)	
1992 primary	Carol Moseley-Braun (D)	557,694	(38%)	
	Alan J. Dixon (D)	504,077	(35%)	
	Albert F. Hofeld (D)	394,497	(27%)	
1986 general	Alan J. Dixon (D)	2,033,926	(65%)	($1,928,750)
	Judy Koehler (R)	1,053,793	(34%)	($851,305)

Sen. Richard J. Durbin (D)

Elected 1996, seat up 2002; b. Nov. 21, 1944, East St. Louis; home, Springfield; Georgetown U., B.S. 1966, J.D. 1969; Catholic; married (Loretta).

Career: Staff, Lt. Gov. Paul Simon, 1969–72; Legal Cnsl., IL Sen. Judiciary Cmte., 1972–82; Prof., S. IL Schl. of Medicine, 1978–82; U.S. House of Reps., 1982–96.

DC Office: 364 RSOB 20510, 202-224-2152; Fax: 202-228-0400.

State Offices: Chicago, 312-353-4952; Springfield, 217-492-4062.

Committees: *Budget* (10th of 10 D). *Governmental Affairs* (5th of 7 D): International Security, Proliferation & Federal Services; Permanent Subcommittee on Investigations. *Judiciary* (7th of 8 D): Administrative Oversight & the Courts (RMM); Immigration; Terrorism, Technology & Government Information.

Group Ratings (as Member of U.S. House of Representatives)

	ADA	ACLU	AFS	LCV	CFA	CON	NFIB	COC	ACU	NTLC	CHC
1996	80	69	100	77	69	68	24	27	0	14	7
1995	85	—	—	100	92	16	—	25	8	—	—

National Journal Ratings (as Member of U.S. House of Representatives)

	1995 LIB — 1995 CONS			1996 LIB — 1996 CONS		
Economic	79%	—	20%	78%	—	22%
Social	80%	—	13%	83%	—	16%
Foreign	69%	—	31%	86%	—	14%

Key Votes of the 104th Congress (as Member of U.S. House of Representatives)

1. Reduce Medicare Growth $	N	5. Flag Amendment	N	9. Cuban Embargo	Y
2. Ovrd. Product Liab. Veto	N	6. Drop EPA Limits	Y	10. Bar Bosnia Troop $	N
3. Increase Min. Wage	Y	7. Repeal Assault-Weap. Ban	N	11. Cut Anti-Missile Defense	Y
4. Welfare Reform	N	8. Ovrd. Part. Birth Veto	N	12. Bar U.N. Uniforms	N

Election Results

1996 general	Richard J. Durbin (D)	2,384,028	(56%)	($4,966,804)
	Al Salvi (R)	1,728,824	(41%)	($4,696,065)
	Others	137,870	(3%)	
1996 primary	Richard J. Durbin (D)	512,520	(65%)	
	Pat Quinn (D)	233,138	(30%)	
	Others	44,397	(6%)	
1990 general	Paul Simon (D)	2,115,377	(65%)	($8,665,789)
	Lynn Martin (R)	1,135,628	(35%)	($4,921,613)

FIRST DISTRICT

The South Side of Chicago has been the nation's largest urban black community for nearly a century now. At first there were just a few blocks where black families from the South would settle; this ghetto grew rapidly with the first influx of blacks from the Mississippi Delta in the 1910s. By the 1920s, the South Side was well established, a center of blues music in America and of black-owned businesses. Politically, the South Side was a heavily Republican constituency throughout those years; the comfortable white Protestants who settled in solid brick houses here believed in the party of Yankee propriety, and the blacks had faith in the party of Lincoln. This was one of the heartlands of the Republican Party, represented in Congress by Republican Leader James Mann, and then Appropriations Chairman Martin Madden. After Madden died in the Appropriations Committee room in 1928, the 1st District elected Oscar DePriest, the first black elected to the House in the 20th Century. Blacks remained faithful to the party of Lincoln even during the Depression, voting for Herbert Hoover and DePriest in 1932.

The New Deal and the racial liberalism of New Dealers like Eleanor Roosevelt and Interior Secretary Harold Ickes (a former Chicago Republican himself) attracted blacks to the Democratic Party, and DePriest was beaten by a black Democrat in 1934. The South Side has been Democratic ever since. For 40 years, it was a cooperative part of Chicago's Democratic machine; then, after the death of longtime Congressman William Dawson, it rebelled against Mayor Richard J. Daley. Then the South Side seemed to take over the city when Congressman Harold Washington was elected mayor in 1983 and 1987. But control of political office does not mean what it once did. Patronage jobs became fewer as a result of court decisions. After Washington died in December 1987, other South Side black politicians flailed at each other, even though Chicago's electorate is only 40% black and a black candidate needs non-black voters to win. As these leaders fell, gang members came to fill the vacuum; the Gangster Disciples gang has a PAC called 21st Century VOTE (Voices of Total Empowerment) and in 1995 two candidates backed by the gangs ran and lost races for city council. But the gangs do not rule everywhere and many South Side neighborhoods are showing signs of vitality and growth. Citizens have banded together to fight crime using high-sodium streetlights and roadblocks. The South Shore Development Bank, much touted by Bill Clinton, has provided loans to minority business owners.

The 1st Congressional District of Illinois includes about half of Chicago's South Side black community within its oddly shaped boundaries. It also extends out into the suburbs, and is no longer the nation's highest-percentage black district, but is by most measures Illinois's most Democratic. It includes the Gothic spires of the University of Chicago and the mansions of Kenwood, once the home of Chicago's Jewish aristocracy and more recently the headquarters of the Nation of Islam and home to its leader, Louis Farrakhan. Miles and miles of the district are made up of bungalow neighborhoods, with single-family houses lining arrow-straight streets. The 1st's odd shape follows historic patterns: the eastern half of the district roughly approximates the boundaries of 1st Districts going back to the 1960s; the western half, to which it is connected by a strip a mile wide, has some all-black neighborhoods, but also includes the high-income Irish-

American neighborhoods of Morgan Park and Beverly, where the annual South Side Irish St. Patrick's Day Parade is held. It goes as far south as the industrial suburbs of Alsip and Blue Island.

The congressman from the 1st District is a man who has gone through several transformations. Bobby Rush grew up on the North Side, a Boy Scout whose mother was a Republican precinct captain. In the Army, he became involved in Student Non-Violent Coordinating Committee in the South, then founded the Illinois Black Panthers, where he recruited Fred Hampton, later killed in a raid by police in 1969. Rush served six months in prison for illegal possession of firearms, but also during his time with the Black Panthers he had run a medical clinic which developed the nation's first mass sickle cell anemia testing program. In 1983, he was elected 2d Ward alderman and became a strong Harold Washington supporter; after 1989, he worked amicably with Mayor Richard M. Daley as well. In 1992, with the district expanded, he decided to challenge the incumbent, Charles Hayes, an older generation politician with a more conventional background. Just before the March 1992 primary it was revealed that Hayes had 716 overdrafts on the House bank. In a big primary turnout of 128,000, Rush beat Hayes 42%–39%, carrying eight of 12 black wards plus Morgan Park and Beverly, where many white police veterans live and where Rush was helped by House Speaker and 13th Ward Committeeman Michael Madigan.

Rush's rhetoric has toned down over the years. "Most African-Americans just want a comfortable, middle-class lifestyle," he said in 1992. "Twenty-five years ago, I didn't know that." On crime, he said, "Blacks are killing blacks. Young blacks are killing other young blacks. We don't need to make excuses for our young people. We need to challenge them." He called for laws to reduce crime in high schools, increase youth employment and establish community-based organizations: articulating surely the yearnings of constituents struggling to keep safe neighborhoods where they can raise their families and work their way up.

In office Rush has risen up the ladder: he is 2d Ward Committeeman and a deputy Democratic whip. He has a seat on Commerce and served on the conference committee on telecom. His voting record is liberal on most issues—against Republican budget cuts, strongly against the 1996 welfare reform, against the Republican crime bill. But he also voted for the securities litigation reform bill that was passed over President Clinton's veto. On locally oriented issues, he sought to ban handguns in housing projects and to get federal penalties for drug dealing near schools. He got $6 million in emergency relief for Chicago in July 1995 when many people died during the extraordinary heat wave, and a new zip code for Evergreen Park. He is not entirely a team player. He was so angry that Clinton signed the welfare bill that he would have thrown away his delegate credential for the 1996 Democratic National Convention but for his wife's urging. He did however host a "Red, White and Blues Cruise" sponsored by Ameritech and Comsat. And he has criticized Daley on housing, education, and development and has been mentioned as a candidate against him in 1999.

He was mentioned as a possible candidate in 1995 as well. But a week before the 1994 election his Republican opponent crashed a Rush press conference and accused him of owing $55,000 in back taxes. This was a civil case, and Rush had already paid off tax liens of $27,000. He also settled $6,000 of back parking tickets with the city of Chicago for $2,500 and claimed with some plausibility that state computer records erred in saying he owed $13,500 in child support. These charges did not hurt him too much in the 1st District— Harold Washington owed back income taxes, and won anyway—and Rush was easily reelected in 1994 and 1996.

The People: Pop. 1990: 571,908; 14% age 65+; 26% White; 70% Black; 1% Asian; 4% Hispanic origin. Households: 35% married couple families; 15% married couple fams. w. children; 45% college educ.; median household income: $24,140; per capita income: $11,709; median gross rent: $425; median house value: $72,400.

1996 Presidential Vote

Clinton (D)	179,767	(85%)
Dole (R)	22,914	(11%)
Perot (I)	6,378	(3%)

1992 Presidential Vote

Clinton (D)	214,104	(81%)
Bush (R)	32,803	(12%)
Perot (I)	17,355	(7%)

Rep. Bobby Rush (D)

Elected 1992; b. Nov. 23, 1946, Albany, GA; home, Chicago; Roosevelt U., B.A. 1973, U. of IL, M.A. 1994; Protestant; married (Carolyn).

Career: Army, 1963–68; Student Non-Violent Coor. Cmtee., 1966–68; Co-founder, IL Black Panther Party, 1968; Chicago City Alderman, 1983–92; Committeeman, 2d Ward, 1984–present.

DC Office: 131 CHOB 20515, 202-225-4372; Fax: 202-226-0333; e-mail: brush@hr.house.gov.

District Offices: Chicago, 773-224-6500; Evergreen Park, 708-422-4055.

Committees: *Commerce* (13th of 23 D): Energy & Power; Telecommunications, Trade & Consumer Protection.

Group Ratings

	ADA	ACLU	AFS	LCV	CFA	CON	NFIB	COC	ACU	NTLC	CHC
1996	95	87	100	85	77	45	15	25	0	5	7
1995	85	—	—	75	92	24	—	15	4	—	—

National Journal Ratings

	1995 LIB — 1995 CONS	1996 LIB — 1996 CONS
Economic	88% — 12%	89% — 0%
Social	88% — 0%	83% — 17%
Foreign	88% — 7%	90% — 0%

Key Votes of the 104th Congress

1. Reduce Medicare Growth $	N	5. Flag Amendment	N	9. Cuban Embargo	N
2. Ovrd. Product Liab. Veto	N	6. Drop EPA Limits	Y	10. Bar Bosnia Troop $	N
3. Increase Min. Wage	Y	7. Repeal Assault-Weap. Ban	N	11. Cut Anti-Missile Defense	Y
4. Welfare Reform	N	8. Ovrd. Part. Birth Veto	N	12. Bar U.N. Uniforms	N

Election Results

1996 general	Bobby Rush (D)	174,005	(86%)	($156,219)
	Noel Naughton (R)	25,659	(13%)	($20,220)
	Others	3,449	(2%)	
1996 primary	Bobby Rush (D)	74,281	(89%)	
	Caleb A. Davis Jr. (D)	8,894	(11%)	
1994 general	Bobby Rush (D)	112,474	(76%)	($195,833)
	William J. Kelly (R)	36,038	(24%)	($37,066)

SECOND DISTRICT

Chicago is a great center of both commerce and industry, and if its white collar offices are heavily concentrated in the Loop, its blue collar heavy industries are most visible on the far south side. This heavy industry Chicago, diminished in importance economically now, is historically significant and, with the remnants of its great hulking factories around Lake Calumet and the nearby rail yards, has a certain undeniable majesty. Thomas Geoghegan, who writes more poetically than a lawyer ought to be able to, has told in his book, *Whose Side Are You On?*, of the fights to wrest severance benefits and pension rights for the workers whose steel mills shut down, of the decline in the labor movement in a place where it got much of its inspiration. For this is where the Pullman strike of 1894 was broken by federal troops and where policemen killed 10 union supporters in the Little Steel strike of 1937. Over the years, Chicago grew around the tight ethnic neighborhoods where workers went home at shift break each afternoon or midnight; today, they are mostly empty buildings that suburbanites speed by on the Calumet and Dan Ryan Expressways.

The 2d Congressional District of Illinois includes much of Chicago's old South Side industrial area plus many suburbs to the south. About two-thirds of its people live in Chicago, in widely separated neighborhoods. Some are in the old factory towns around Lake Calumet, some in the once heavily Jewish South Shore neighborhood, some in black wards west of Halsted Street. The Chicago portion of the 2d is overwhelmingly black; many blacks, especially young parents fleeing Chicago public schools, are moving into suburbs directly to the south—Harvey, Dolton, Posen (a reminder of its Polish origin), Markham. Farther south are Homewood and Flossmoor, with significant Jewish populations, high-income Olympia Fields, the planned town of Park Forest, and Chicago Heights, home town of America's premier political reporter for three decades now, David Broder. Two-thirds of the district's voters are black, and most are middle class. But there are signs everywhere of crime: a PAC called 21st Century VOTE (it stands for Voices of Total Empowerment) was run, according to ABC News and the *Los Angeles Times*, by the Gangster Disciples, a 30,000-member gang.

The 2d District is represented by Jesse Jackson Jr., son of civil rights activist and 1984 and 1988 presidential candidate Jesse Jackson. The younger Jackson was born in Greenville, South Carolina, while his father was marching to Selma; he went to St. Albans School in Washington (as did Vice President Al Gore), then to North Carolina A&T (as did his father), and got a masters degree at Chicago Theological Seminary and a law degree at the University of Illinois. He worked for his father's Rainbow Coalition and did not run for office until the spectacular rise and fall of 2d District Congressman Mel Reynolds, who was hailed nationally when he defeated the anti-Semitic Gus Savage in the 1992 primary and then lobbied Dan Rostenkowski for a seat on Ways and Means. Reynolds was disgraced when he was convicted and sentenced to five years in prison for having sexual relations with a teenage campaign worker; he resigned in October 1995, and was charged in 1996 with personal and campaign finance fraud. When Reynolds announced he would resign, Jackson promptly decided to run. He faced serious opposition in Emil Jones, a 23-year legislator and state Senate minority leader who had the support of Mayor Richard M. Daley, and two other legislators as well. Jones boasted of his clout and political experience; Jackson said being his father's son was a lifetime of political experience. He talked of bringing dollars to the South Side and, echoing the argument Dan Rostenkowski made to Mayor Richard J. Daley in 1957, said, "The only way one grows into leadership in Congress is to get elected young enough that you become speaker of the House or chairman of the Ways and Means Committee." The November 1995 primary was a close contest, but Jackson won with 46% to Jones's 37%; state Senator Alice Palmer had 10% and state Representative Monique Davis, endorsed by Louis Farrakhan and Gus Savage, won only 2%. Jackson easily won the special general election with 76%.

In office Jackson combined advocacy of left-wing positions with the exercise of shrewd political instincts. He called for a law to create full employment through job training and a single-payer universal health care system—both nonstarters even in a Democratic Congress. And he supported Chicago Urban League chief James Compton's alliance with VOTE in a registration drive, and had nothing to say when Compton broke it off. But he also made one of his main issues advocacy of a third Chicago area airport in Peotone, 45 miles south of the Loop and just south of the 2d District along Interstate 57. This has been a pet project of Republican Governor Jim Edgar and has been blocked by Mayor Daley; but Jackson disregarded partisan ties and argued that Chicago needed the airport and that it would bring thousands of jobs to the 2d District.

Kept off the Transportation Committee by 3d District Congressman Bill Lipinski, a strong opponent of Peotone, Jackson made the best of a seat on Banking; at the December 1996 caucus, he nominated 80-year-old former Chairman Henry Gonzalez for "one more term" as ranking member. Jackson also shrewdly attacked Rules Committee Chairman Gerald Solomon for putting up a portrait of former Chairman Howard Smith, a Democrat and staunch segregationist; Solomon would have been wiser to memorialize Clarence Brown of Ohio, ranking Republican during Smith's tenure and a strong backer of civil rights. Jackson took another interesting step by working with Budget Committee Chairman John Kasich to deny reauthorization of the Overseas Private Investment Corporation as "corporate welfare." "We just ended welfare—government assistance of millions of poor people in our own communities. Yet we are providing government assistance to companies to invest in foreign countries." At the same time, he adhered closely to Clinton-Gore campaign discipline; his candidacy in 1995 may have softened his father's obvious antagonism toward Clinton then and have contributed to his team player posture in 1996.

All of which suggests that Jesse Jackson Jr. is planning on a long career in the House; he became ranking member of a Small Business subcommittee in early 1997. As middle-class blacks, the heart of his constituency, are moving in large numbers from Chicago to the suburbs, any hope he has of being elected mayor recede, but as congressman he enjoys more attention from major media than most newcomers receive and has handled himself well in the spotlight. He can count on easy reelection: he had no primary opposition in March 1996 and his Republican opponent withdrew from the race in September.

The People: Pop. 1990: 572,188; 10% age 65+; 25% White; 68% Black; 1% Asian; 7% Hispanic origin. Households: 46% married couple families; 22% married couple fams. w. children; 42% college educ.; median household income: $30,217; per capita income: $11,468; median gross rent: $449; median house value: $64,200.

1996 Presidential Vote

Clinton (D)	170,819	(85%)
Dole (R)	22,204	(11%)
Perot (I)	6,395	(3%)

1992 Presidential Vote

Clinton (D)	194,639	(80%)
Bush (R)	31,634	(13%)
Perot (I)	16,950	(7%)

Rep. Jesse L. Jackson, Jr. (D)

Elected Dec. 1995; b. Mar. 11, 1965, Greenville, SC; home, Chicago; NC A&T, B.S. 1987, Chicago Theological Seminary, M.A. 1990, U. of IL, J.D. 1993; Baptist; married (Sandra).

Career: Civil rights activist; Pres., Keep Hope Alive PAC, 1989–90; V.P., Operation PUSH 1991–95; Field Dir., Natl. Rainbow Coalition 1993–95.

DC Office: 313 CHOB 20515, 202-225-0773; Fax: 202-225-0899.

District Offices: Homewood, 708-798-6000.

Committees: *Banking & Financial Services* (19th of 25 D): Domestic & International Monetary Policy; Housing & Community Opportunity. *Small Business* (7th of 16 D): Regulatory Reform & Paperwork Reduction (RMM).

Group Ratings (Only Served Partial Term)

	ADA	ACLU	AFS	LCV	CFA	CON	NFIB	COC	ACU	NTLC	CHC
1996	100	93	100	92	85	60	22	19	0	6	0
1995	*	—		*	*		—	*	*	—	—

National Journal Ratings (Only Served Partial Term)

	1995 LIB — 1995 CONS	1996 LIB — 1996 CONS
Economic	* — *	89% — 0%
Social	* — *	88% — 0%
Foreign	* — *	90% — 0%

Key Votes of the 104th Congress (Only Served Partial Term)

1. Reduce Medicare Growth $	*	5. Flag Amendment	*	9. Cuban Embargo	*
2. Ovrd. Product Liab. Veto	N	6. Drop EPA Limits	*	10. Bar Bosnia Troop $	*
3. Increase Min. Wage	Y	7. Repeal Assault-Weap. Ban	N	11. Cut Anti-Missile Defense	Y
4. Welfare Reform	N	8. Ovrd. Part. Birth Veto	N	12. Bar U.N. Uniforms	N

Election Results

1996 general	Jesse L. Jackson, Jr. (D)	172,648	(94%)	($260,163)
	Frank H. Stratman (Lib)	10,880	(6%)	
1996 primary	Jesse L. Jackson, Jr. (D)	unopposed		
1995 spec. gen.	Jesse L. Jackson, Jr. (D)	48,145	(76%)	($469,536)
	Thomas Joseph Somer (R)	15,171	(24%)	($443,717)
1995 spec. prim.	Jesse L. Jackson, Jr. (D)	30,017	(46%)	
	Emil Jones Jr. (D)	24,097	(37%)	
	Alice Palmer (D)	6,343	(10%)	
	Others	1,771	(3%)	
1994 general	Mel Reynolds (D)	unopposed		($427,562)

THIRD DISTRICT

A century ago, Finley Peter Dunne's fictional Mr. Dooley pontificated on matters political in a saloon on Archer Avenue. This was, and is, Archer Avenue on the South Side of Chicago, one of the radial streets that cuts across what was once open prairie near the Loop and out the Chicago River and the Chicago and Sanitary Ship Canal. Archer Avenue was one of the paths of outward migration and upward mobility for the children and grandchildren of Chicago's different ethnic and cultural groups; and still is. Italians from the river wards along the Canal moved west; the

South Side Irish moved west and south along Cicero Avenue toward Oak Lawn; the Bohemians (as they were called then; now Czechs) were heavily concentrated in the neat bungalows of the industrial suburbs of Berwyn and Cicero, famous as a haven for Al Capone's mobsters in the 1920s. Today, Hispanics of varying origin are driving these same avenues, up before dawn to arrive at large factories and small, or heading to the Loop on the CTA or to edge city jobs out the expressways or the Tollway, then home to old bungalows carefully refurbished and tended by kids home from school.

The 3d Congressional District of Illinois consists of much of this territory, criss-crossed by the Canal, the radial streets and the railroad lines and switching yards so common in this, the center of the nation's rail network. It includes the far west edge of Chicago and most of Cicero and Berwyn; Riverside, with its early 20th Century prairie-style houses; a few older affluent suburbs like Western Springs and the more recent and middle-income expanses of Oak Lawn and Palos Heights. Politically, this is marginal territory. Ancestral political preferences are mostly Democratic, but this is a culturally conservative area, with a sense of patriotism; Cicero, hostile to blacks in the 1960s, is now growing with an influx of Hispanic families. The conflict here now is between Democratic machine tradition and new Republican faith in traditional values.

The congressman from the 3d District, Democrat William Lipinski, grew up in southwest Chicago, started off as a patronage employee with the Parks District, was elected 23d Ward alderman and ward committeeman in 1975; he still holds that position in the ward that includes Midway Airport and Chicago's westernmost stretch of Archer Avenue). He ran for Congress and beat an aging incumbent in the 1982 primary 61%–36%. His credo: "I know the people of the 3d District—what they believe in, what they want for their future and their children's future . . . I have never been so involved in what was happening in Washington that I lost sight of my constituents and their needs."

Lipinski's views on issues seem a mirror of those of his constituents. He is anti-abortion, and lobbied to have the 1996 Democratic platform include "toleration" of pro-life views. He was strongly against gays in the military and for the Defense of Marriage Act. He favors the death penalty and opposed NAFTA and GATT. He voted for family medical leave and the minimum wage increase and against Republican budget cuts but was one of nine Democrats to vote for the Republican welfare bill. He was proud of the passage of his amendment, co-sponsored by two Republicans, denying welfare benefits to fugitive criminals (previously, it barred benefits only to those in jail; those who escaped were entitled; Mr. Bumble would have known what to make of this). He voted for the 1996 healthcare portability bill, but also spoke out for medical savings accounts. He supported restrictions on welfare for legal immigrants, but also got an amendment to help 832 refugees, who had left Poland and Hungary before fall 1989, gain permanent resident status.

Lipinski sees his main role as providing transportation facilities to the 3d District. He serves on the Transportation and Infrastructure Committee and is proud that he helped complete the CTA Orange Line. He is a staunch advocate of Midway Airport, which generates more jobs than any other site in the 3d District, and of O'Hare: "Aviation is our ride into the future." His battles on their behalf range from pressuring Britain and Japan to enter open skies agreements to backing a facility charge enabling Mayor Richard M. Daley to expand O'Hare and Midway to keeping the 2d District's Jesse Jackson Jr. off Transportation because he favors a new airport at Peotone, 45 miles south of Chicago. Few projects are small enough to escape his attention. In 1996 he got $204 million for Chicago Shoreline Protection and money to repair leakage at the O'Brien and Chicago Harbor locks, which prevents Chicago from diverting the allowed amount of Lake Michigan water downriver. For 1997 he wants to use the ISTEA reauthorization to build the Central Avenue Bypass and to rebuild the intersection of Cicero Avenue and 127th Street (moving the interchange with I-294 farther away). In the 1996 FAA reauthorization he included a provision allowing local communities to regulate train whistles: it may not sound like much, but when your district has (probably) the largest number of freight yards and surface crossings in the nation and whistle-blowing is mandatory, you will hear about it.

Despite all this hard work and his views on issues, Lipinski has had serious competition in the 3d District in the 1990s. Redistricting put him in a 1992 primary contest with fellow incumbent Marty Russo, a member of Ways and Means, who vastly outspent him (over $1 million to $375,000). But Lipinski had the support of the committeemen from the 13th and 23d Wards (House Speaker Michael Madigan and himself) and ran as "a neighborhood guy" against a luxury-loving Washington insider. Mayor Richard Daley quietly and the *Chicago Tribune* openly endorsed Lipinski as "more important to the future of Illinois," and Lipinski won 58%–37%. In 1994, Lipinski had a serious Republican opponent, Jim Nalepa, a retired Army officer and real estate developer. He put Lipinski's picture on a poster that said "WANTED for attempted robbery by trying to raise your property taxes" and attacked Lipinski's wife for working as a Washington lobbyist for the Chicago Transit Authority. Lipinski attacked Nalepa for paying low child support while spending much more on his campaign, and Lipinski profited from his own vociferous opposition to the Clinton budget in 1993 and to gays in the military. Lipinski, according to his office literature, is "not afraid to break from the Democratic Party when his views and the views of his neighbors diverge from the party's position." Lipinski won 54%–46%.

In 1996 Nalepa ran again, and Republicans had great hopes of winning the seat. But the trend in the suburbs and the bungalow wards was strongly toward the once-again-moderate Bill Clinton; Lipinski worked the district hard and won 65%–32%.

The People: Pop. 1990: 570,902; 16% age 65+; 89% White; 2% Black; 1% Asian; 7% Hispanic origin. Households: 58% married couple families; 25% married couple fams. w. children; 40% college educ.; median household income: $36,250; per capita income: $15,854; median gross rent: $489; median house value: $92,100.

1996 Presidential Vote		
Clinton (D)	114,089	(53%)
Dole (R)	78,853	(37%)
Perot (I)	19,441	(9%)

1992 Presidential Vote		
Clinton (D)	108,342	(41%)
Bush (R)	102,632	(39%)
Perot (I)	52,905	(20%)

Rep. William O. Lipinski (D)

Elected 1982; b. Dec. 22, 1937, Chicago; home, Chicago; Loras Col., 1956–57; Catholic; married (Rose Marie).

Career: Army Reserves, 1961–67; Chicago Parks & Recreation Dept., 1958–75; Chicago 23d Ward Committeeman, 1975–present; Chicago City Alderman, 1975–83.

DC Office: 1501 LHOB 20515, 202-225-5701; Fax: 202-225-1012.

District Offices: Chicago, 312-886-0481; Palos Heights, 708-371-7460.

Committees: *Transportation & Infrastructure* (4th of 33 D): Aviation (RMM); Railroads.

Group Ratings

	ADA	ACLU	AFS	LCV	CFA	CON	NFIB	COC	ACU	NTLC	CHC
1996	70	25	83	85	62	13	37	38	40	28	53
1995	50	—	—	69	62	31	—	35	36	—	—

National Journal Ratings

	1995 LIB — 1995 CONS			1996 LIB — 1996 CONS		
Economic	64%	—	36%	61%	—	39%
Social	52%	—	47%	45%	—	55%
Foreign	54%	—	45%	59%	—	40%

Key Votes of the 104th Congress

1. Reduce Medicare Growth $	N	5. Flag Amendment	Y	9. Cuban Embargo	Y
2. Ovrd. Product Liab. Veto	N	6. Drop EPA Limits	Y	10. Bar Bosnia Troop $	Y
3. Increase Min. Wage	Y	7. Repeal Assault-Weap. Ban	N	11. Cut Anti-Missile Defense	N
4. Welfare Reform	Y	8. Ovrd. Part. Birth Veto	Y	12. Bar U.N. Uniforms	Y

Election Results

1996 general	William O. Lipinski (D)	137,153	(65%)	($455,967)
	Jim Nalepa (R)	67,214	(32%)	($202,334)
	Others	5,549	(3%)	
1996 primary	William O. Lipinski (D)	unopposed		
1994 general	William O. Lipinski (D)	92,353	(54%)	($366,804)
	Jim Nalepa (R)	78,163	(46%)	($277,772)

FOURTH DISTRICT

Just west of the Loop, the Chicago River splits into North and South Branches, both penetrating the heart of old neighborhoods where immigrants fresh off the boat first got their start in Chicago. The South Branch is the guts of Chicago, the site of one of western civilization's astonishing engineering feats: here in 1900, the course of the river was reversed so that sewage flowed Downstate through a canal rather than out into Lake Michigan. Just blocks away was Maxwell Street, thronged with market stalls (now closed), long the arrival neighborhood for Chicago's Jews; not far away, in an Italian-American neighborhood on Halsted Street, was Jane Addams's Hull House, the original settlement house, where social workers told new immigrants not how to rebel against middle-class American mores but how to live them. To the south were Bridgeport, home of the Irish and of the mayors of Chicago from 1933–79 and again from 1989 until recently, when the Richard M. Daleys moved to the South Loop, and Pilsen, arrival neighborhood for the Bohemians (Czechs). Off the North Branch of the River was Milwaukee Avenue, the main street of Polish-Americans and Ukrainian-Americans for a century now.

Today, many of these places are arrival neighborhoods again, mostly for Chicago's wide variety of Hispanic immigrants. On the South Side, in the old river wards, is Chicago's Mexican-American community, extending west into the once Bohemian suburb of Cicero; on the North Side are many Puerto Ricans and other Hispanics. Altogether, the 1990 Census counted 545,000 Hispanics in Chicago, by far the largest Latino concentration north of Texas and Florida and between the two coasts. They have been attracted, as immigrants were 100 years ago, by a vibrant economy that provides opportunity to those who work hard, and by a culture which can be portrayed as unwelcoming only because of its own high standards.

The 4th Congressional District of Illinois is the Hispanic-majority district which was deemed mandatory under the Voting Rights Act amendments of 1982. The problem was that the South Side Mexican-American and the North Side Puerto Rican communities were separated by the West Side black ghetto. The solution was today's 4th Congressional District, with arguably the most convoluted shape of any district in the country: essentially these two Latino communities, defined by erose boundaries to maximize the Hispanic percentage, are connected by a thin line of territory which stretches around the West Side black-majority 7th District to meet at the Cook-DuPage County line. Most of this salient consists of parkland, railroad yards and cemeteries; more than 95% of the votes are in Chicago or Cicero. As a consequence of this creativity, the district has bcome caught up in the battle over racial gerrymandering. In November 1996, the Supreme Court sent back the case that challenged the challenged the lines to a three judge panel in Chicago; a ruling was pending as of June 1997. The 4th's population is about two-thirds Hispanic, with Mexican-Americans outnumbering Puerto Ricans more than 2–1; but eligible voters are 58% white anglo and 39% Latino, with Mexican-Americans and Puerto Ricans about equally split. This is a solidly Democratic district, though by no means as Democratic as the black-majority 1st, 2d or 7th.

The congressman here, Luis Gutierrez, was effectively chosen in the 1992 Democratic primary. He is a politician who in his decade-long career has shown great skill at political maneuvering. Gutierrez grew up, the son of a cab driver and factory worker, in both Chicago, where he was a social worker, and Puerto Rico, where he taught school. He started off politically as a supporter of Harold Washington by defiantly running—and losing—against Dan Rostenkowski for 32d Ward Committeeman in 1983. Then Washington hired him as a staffer, and backed Gutierrez in a crucial 1986 special election for City Council in one of two new Hispanic seats. Gutierrez won and, with Juan Soliz on the South Side, gave control of the Council to Washington. Then Washington died in 1987 and, in the 1989 election to succeed him, Gutierrez backed (and Soliz opposed) Richard M. Daley. For that, Gutierrez was richly rewarded: he became chairman of the Housing Committee, pushed through his "New Homes for Chicago" plan authorizing the city to sell vacant lots to developers of affordable housing for $1; he also authored a bill prohibiting discrimination against gays and the disabled. In both cases, he helped Daley cement his support with crucial groups in the middle 20% of the electorate, Latinos and gays.

Another "payback," as Gutierrez called it, came in the 1992 race for the new 4th District. Gutierrez and Soliz were again rivals. Gutierrez called crime the number one problem and bragged of his council record; Soliz talked about trade and health care and called Gutierrez a machine candidate. Certainly Gutierrez seemed a multi-ethnic candidate: "There is a Hispanic agenda . . . it's the same as the Polish, Irish and Lithuanian agenda. If you work hard, sweat and toil and play by the rules, you will be rewarded . . . with clean streets, safer and better schools, the opportunity to send your kids to college. Tell me who in America and in the 4th Congressional District doesn't want these things?" Gutierrez said, and won 60%–40%. The 1994 primary was a rematch and Gutierrez won again, 64%–36%; in 1996 he won 71% against three little-known candidates. Gutierrez has a high profile in the district, running recycling drives, a Gutierrez Community Corps to paint out graffiti and citizenship enrollment meetings.

Gutierrez's in-your-face style produced mixed results in the House. His past independence kept him from a seat on the Ways and Means Committee, of which Dan Rostenkowski was still chairman; Gutierriez' call for a congressional pay freeze was not heeded. In February 1994, he was the subject of a *60 Minutes* profile, in which he called the House "the belly of the beast," charging that chairmen intimidated members and that the House Democratic leadership stifled reform, and that some freshmen Democrats "sold out" or "reneged on their reformist promises." These arguably accurate observations were not appreciated by Democratic colleagues, to put it mildly. "I've gotten my rear end kicked around here," Gutierrez told *The Washington Post*. A leadership staffer said Gutierrez "will never get a choice committee assignment . . . He will always end up on the Banking Committee." And at least for now, he has not been very successful legislatively. Gutierrez amendments to make abortions an available service in veterans' hospitals and to limit public housing tenants' rent to 30% of income were rejected. So were Gutierrez causes like lobbying reform and single-payer health insurance. Since November 1994 he has been in the minority, with even less clout. But if he is a pariah on Capitol Hill, he remains a strong backer of Mayor Daley and a vocal political force in Chicago, and is already speculating about the possibility of a second Hispanic district after the 2000 Census.

The People: Pop. 1990: 571,162; 8% age 65+; 27% White; 6% Black; 2% Asian; 65% Hispanic origin. Households: 49% married couple families; 31% married couple fams. w. children; 24% college educ.;

median household income: $23,083; per capita income: $8,352; median gross rent: $393; median house value: $64,300.

1996 Presidential Vote

Clinton (D)	82,225	(80%)
Dole (R)	14,661	(14%)
Perot (I)	5,160	(5%)

1992 Presidential Vote

Clinton (D)	82,271	(65%)
Bush (R)	29,093	(23%)
Perot (I)	15,272	(12%)

Rep. Luis V. Gutierrez (D)

Elected 1992; b. Dec. 10, 1953, Chicago; home, Chicago; Northeastern IL U., B.A. 1975; Catholic; married (Soraida).

Career: Teacher, Puerto Rico, 1977–78; Social Wkr., Chicago Dept. of Children & Family Svcs., 1979–83; Advisor, Chicago Mayor Harold Washington, 1984–86; Chicago City Alderman, 1986–92, Pres. Pro Tem, 1989–92.

DC Office: 2438 RHOB 20515, 202-225-8203; Fax: 202-225-7810; e-mail: luisg@hr.house.gov.

District Offices: Chicago, 773-509-0999; Chicago, 773-579-0902.

Committees: *Banking & Financial Services* (11th of 25 D): Capital Markets, Securities & Government Sponsored Enterprises; Housing & Community Opportunity. *Veterans' Affairs* (4th of 13 D): Health (RMM).

Group Ratings

	ADA	ACLU	AFS	LCV	CFA	CON	NFIB	COC	ACU	NTLC	CHC
1996	100	75	100	92	85	4	22	14	0	8	0
1995	95	—	—	100	92	16	—	21	16	—	—

National Journal Ratings

	1995 LIB — 1995 CONS	1996 LIB — 1996 CONS
Economic	84% — 15%	89% — 0%
Social	74% — 25%	88% — 0%
Foreign	79% — 17%	87% — 10%

Key Votes of the 104th Congress

1. Reduce Medicare Growth $	N	5. Flag Amendment	Y	9. Cuban Embargo	Y
2. Ovrd. Product Liab. Veto	N	6. Drop EPA Limits	Y	10. Bar Bosnia Troop $	N
3. Increase Min. Wage	Y	7. Repeal Assault-Weap. Ban	N	11. Cut Anti-Missile Defense	Y
4. Welfare Reform	N	8. Ovrd. Part. Birth Veto	N	12. Bar U.N. Uniforms	N

Election Results

1996 general	Luis V. Gutierrez (D)	85,278	(94%)	($261,252)
	William Passmore (Lib)	5,857	(6%)	
1996 primary	Luis V. Gutierrez (D)	27,140	(71%)	
	John Joseph Holowinski (D)	8,206	(21%)	
	William Garcia (D)	2,234	(6%)	
	Others	736	(2%)	
1994 general	Luis V. Gutierrez (D)	46,695	(75%)	($367,811)
	Steven Valtierra (R)	15,384	(25%)	($12,603)

FIFTH DISTRICT

No place in America today has more variety, ethnic and cultural, than the North Side of Chicago. From the air, the geometric grid streets lit by high-sodium lamps seem monotonous; on the ground, on a winter's day with snow swirling, its brick buildings look stolid and forbidding. This has been the homeland of one immigrant group after another and the chosen neighborhoods of all manner of successful middle-class people. Wooden workingman's cottages from the late 19th Century give way to sturdy huge brick houses of the early 1900s and then to the prairie bungalows of the 1920s and white-shuttered, orange-brick colonials of the 1950s. Chicago was America's number one immigrant destination for Poles, Lithuanians, Czechs, Slovaks, Ukrainians and Romanians; something about the heavy dull clouds of the long winters, the short hot summers, a climate suited to potatoes and cabbage and other hardy vegetables, may have reminded them of central and eastern Europe. By the late 1980s, new upwardly mobile immigrants from Mexico and Guatemala, Korea and the Philippines, refugees and recent arrivals from Eastern Europe and the former Soviet Union moved into these melting pot precincts. Family ties, webs of acquaintance that reach back to ancestral villages, have made the North Side of Chicago a natural port of entry for Eastern bloc migrants coming to America.

The 5th Congressional District of Illinois covers an oddly-shaped slice of Chicago's North Side, running from the Lakefront all the way to the suburbs directly south of O'Hare Airport. Its boundaries were carefully drawn to put most Hispanics in the 4th District just to the south, but otherwise it reflects the full variety of the North Side. It includes Chicago's most glamorous lakefront apartments facing the Oak Street beach and the gentrified neighborhoods of Old Town, where old houses and factories are being converted into upscale condominiums. It takes in the Polish-American and Ukrainian-American neighborhoods around Milwaukee Avenue, and the old Italian neighborhoods running west on Grand Avenue. It includes, a couple of blocks from the Chicago River, the old church of St. Stanislaus Kostka, a traditional center of the Polish community since the 19th Century, and the residence across Pulaski Park of a man who from 1980–94 was one of America's most powerful politicians, Dan Rostenkowski, who as congressman represented this district and its predecessors from 1958 until his surprise defeat in 1994.

The congressman from the 5th District now is Rod Blagojevich, a Democrat elected in 1996 over the Republican who upset Rostenkowski, Michael Flanagan. Blagojevich is of Serbian descent; he was a Golden Gloves boxer who graduated from Northwestern and Pepperdine Law School. He was an assistant State's Attorney and in 1992, at 30, was elected state Representative. Politics in Chicago is often a matter of genealogy, and it did not hurt that Blagojevich is the son-in-law of 33d Ward Committeeman Dick Mell, one of the lead supporters of Mayor Richard M. Daley over the years. In the legislature Blagojevich pushed a law taking away gun permits of those convicted of domestic violence or stalking; he sought to lengthen the amount of prison time served, to raise the minimum age for handgun permits from 18 to 21, and to make a felony of threatening anyone for refusing to join a gang. Blagojevich was surely as surprised as anyone when Flanagan beat Rostenkowski 54%–46%, and he immediately began eyeing the seat. The 5th District is ancestrally, if not always behaviorally, Democratic; and except for voting against the 1993 Republican budget resolution Flanagan had a near-perfect record of supporting the Contract with America and Speaker Newt Gingrich.

Not surprisingly, Blagojevich had primary opposition, the strongest from state Representative Nancy Kaszak. They had similar records, except on the death penalty—Blagojevich blasted her for switching from opposition to endorsement—but different bases of support. Blagojevich had Mell's organization, one of the more active ward operations in the city, and the backing of Mayor Daley; Kaszak had fundraising help from EMILY's List and roughly matched him in money. But Blagojevich had more votes, winning 50%–38%.

In the general Blagojevich focused on guns and tobacco, saying that Flanagan might as well be a lobbyist for the National Rifle Association and the American Tobacco Institute. He campaigned with a Republican state representative at one stop, arguing he could bring more to the district, and with Hillary Rodham Clinton during convention week, denouncing the Republican Medicare reform at a senior citizens' center. To lakefront voters Blagojevich introduced himself as the pro-choice candidate; to others he promised to seek laws to help cities fight crime and gang violence. Flanagan, who had conducted dozens of town meetings, boasted of never supporting a tax increase and of bringing federal projects to the district. He also argued, a bit lamely, that "most people in this district like what this majority's doing," except when they "go out on the fringe every once in a while." Rostenkowski, meanwhile, had disappeared from the scene: a month after the primary, in April 1996, he pleaded guilty to mail fraud and agreed to a sentence of 17 months which he began serving in the summer.

The result in retrospect seems preordained. Bill Clinton ran far ahead in this district, Blagojevich outspent and out-organized Flanagan, and the Democrat won by a 64%–36% margin. It seems unlikely he will receive a strong challenge, at least until redistricting takes effect in 2002.

The People: Pop. 1990: 571,053; 15% age 65+; 79% White; 1% Black; 6% Asian; 13% Hispanic origin. Households: 44% married couple families; 18% married couple fams. w. children; 47% college educ.; median household income: $33,262; per capita income: $19,242; median gross rent: $514; median house value: $109,200.

1996 Presidential Vote

Clinton (D)	120,132	(63%)
Dole (R)	56,532	(30%)
Perot (I)	12,915	(7%)

1992 Presidential Vote

Clinton (D)	124,273	(51%)
Bush (R)	80,036	(33%)
Perot (I)	39,113	(16%)

Rep. Rod R. Blagojevich (D)

Elected 1996; b. Dec. 10, 1956, Chicago; home, Chicago; Northwestern U., B.A. 1979; Pepperdine U., J.D. 1983; Eastern Orthodox; married (Patti).

Career: Practicing atty., 1984–96; Asst. Cook County Atty., 1986–88; IL House of Reps., 1992–96

DC Office: 501 CHOB 20515, 202 225 4061; Fax: 202-225-5603.

District Offices: Chicago, 773-868-3240.

Committees: *Government Reform & Oversight* (15th of 19 D): Government Management, Information & Technology; National Security, International Affairs & Criminal Justice. *National Security* (15th of 25 D): Military Procurement; Military Research & Development.

Group Ratings and Key Votes: Newly Elected

Election Results

1996 general	Rod R. Blagojevich (D)	117,544	(64%)	($1,552,073)
	Michael Patrick Flanagan (R)	65,768	(36%)	($724,124)
1996 primary	Rod R. Blagojevich (D)	33,907	(50%)	
	Nancy Kaszak (D)	26,115	(38%)	
	Ray Romero (D)	8,001	(12%)	
1994 general	Michael Patrick Flanagan (R)	75,328	(54%)	($112,638)
	Dan Rostenkowski (D)	63,065	(46%)	($2,495,222)

SIXTH DISTRICT

The nation's busiest airport today was half a century ago an airstrip in an apple orchard (hence its current three-letter code: ORD); to the east was the Forest Preserve along the Des Plaines River, to the west little suburban villages strung along rail lines, separated by cornfields. But in the 1950s, Mayor Richard J. Daley decided that Chicago needed a new airport, annexed the orchard, and named it after a World War II Medal of Honor winner from a good Chicago Irish Catholic Democratic family. Today, O'Hare is surrounded on all sides by suburbs as densely settled as the bungalow wards of the city, with hotels and office buildings clustered near the interchanges in Rosemont, and characteristic Chicago yellow-orange brick houses in orderly rows in suburbs like Park Ridge, where Hillary Rodham Clinton grew up at 235 Wisner, just three blocks west of Chicago. Politically, these suburbs have long been solidly Republican, as were the Rodhams, convinced that civic virtues could best be realized by opposing the party of City Hall in Chicago and economic growth could best be assured by opposing the party that backed stifling government regulation. Indeed, Maine Township, which includes Park Ridge, has remained true to the principles which its most famous daughter has renounced, voting for Paul Tsongas over Bill Clinton in the 1992 Illinois primary and for Bush/Quayle, and in 1996 Dole/Kemp over Clinton/Gore.

The 6th Congressional District of Illinois includes much of this suburban area. It includes Park Ridge and Des Plaines just north of O'Hare and to the west the newer suburb of Elk Grove Village, the headquarters of United Airlines. The larger part of the district is over the line in DuPage County, including the string of long-settled suburbs directly west of the Loop: Elmhurst, Villa Park, Lombard, Glen Ellyn, Wheaton. It also takes in the newer suburbs along I-290 and Lake Street: Bensenville, Addison, Wood Dale, Bloomingdale. Economically, this is high income territory; culturally, it is cautiously moderate; politically, it is one of the most Republican districts in Illinois.

The congressman from the 6th is Henry Hyde, one of the most senior Republicans in Congress, chairman of the House Judiciary Committee. He also is one of the most respected and intellectually honest members of the House. Hyde springs from Chicago earth, was raised a Catholic and a Democrat, but came to see a widening gulf between his core beliefs and his ancestral party. He was elected to the Illinois legislature in 1966 and in the Democratic year of 1974 was elected to the House. He first made his name in the House as an opponent of abortion, attaching to Appropriations subcommittee bills his Hyde Amendments prohibiting the use of federal funds to pay for abortions in various circumstances. Hyde is unhappy that efforts to overturn *Roe v. Wade* have failed. But the Hyde amendment banning federal funding of most Medicaid abortions has been law since 1978, and in 1993, over the opposition of the incoming Clinton Administration, it was passed again in the House and the Senate by solid margins of 255–178 and 59–40. The exceptions are limited, to save the woman's life and, starting again in 1993, for victims of rape and incest.

Hyde's voting record is one of the most conservative in the House, but with some interesting variations. He is concerned about born as well as unborn children and was one of the few Republicans who supported the family leave bill; he felt it was logical to help mothers care for children. He worked to outlaw commercial surrogate motherhood contracts and to facilitate adoption of Romanian children. Hyde also joined the bipartisan effort on the 1995 welfare bill to add tough measures against "deadbeat dads" who fail to support their family, proposing that the IRS collect child support through wage withholding, a step resisted by Ways and Means chairman Bill Archer. His stands seem to stem from deep religious beliefs combined with a trial lawyer's combative instincts, a respect for rules combined with a certain compassion.

Hyde is one of the most eloquent members of the House. His speeches against term limits and in favor of the flag-burning amendment are classics; his evisceration of the nuclear freeze resolution helped turn the tide on foreign policy in the House in the 1980s. He defended the

Reagan Administration on Iran-contra and called early for a ban on arms sales to terrorist nations like Iraq. But he has not been entirely in sync with Contract With America Republicans: he opposed term limits, though he reported the amendment to the floor, supported reauthorization of the independent counsel bill (frowned on by some Republicans then and in the Clinton White House now), and voted for the Brady bill waiting period for gun purchases.

Hyde chose to become Judiciary chairman when Republicans gained their majority; he might have stayed in the leadership as Republican Policy Committee chairman or might have chaired International Relations. But on Judiciary he was able to achieve many long-sought goals as well as respond creatively to events. In the latter category was the antiterrorism legislation of 1995 (divested of its wiretapping provisions by a combination of liberal Democrats and conservative Republicans), enforcing in the U.S. the international treaty against war crimes, and the church arson law of 1996. He fought through to passage a victim restitution law, an act limiting death penalty appeals, Megan's Law (requiring released sex offenders to report their addresses), a law allowing senior citizen housing to discriminate by age, a law banning state taxes on pensions of nonresidents, and the Lobbying Disclosure Act of 1995. He also led the moves to authorize $10 billion for prison expansion, to make commercial counterfeiting subject to RICO, and to protect property rights in digital recordings and biotech patents. He was frustrated on the balanced budget amendment, which passed the House but was defeated when six Democratic senators not up for reelection in 1996 switched their votes. Three major measures passed both houses but were vetoed by Clinton: the partial-birth abortion ban, product liability, and tort reform. He decided not to bring forward a constitutional amendment allowing prayer in school. Hyde continued to play a role on foreign policy issues as well. He failed to repeal the dead-letter War Powers Act when some Republicans demurred. But he headed a select subcommittee on the U.S. policy of secretly allowing shipment of Iranian arms to Bosnia: not a scandal, he said, but "ineptitude in foreign policy." He chaired the Republican platform committee in San Diego and preserved the party's anti-abortion plank.

Hyde's integrity and intellectual honesty are universally respected. That was one of the reasons he was suggested by *National Review*'s Kate O'Beirne as interim speaker while Newt Gingrich's ethics case was being investigated; but Hyde would have nothing of it. As Judiciary chairman he may play some role in unfolding Clinton Administration scandals: he pushed a bill to reimburse the fired employees of the White House travel office for legal expenses and in late 1996 said he wanted to investigate whether the FBI has become too political. In 1993 the FDIC brought suit against Hyde and other directors of a bankrupt savings and loan; in November 1996 a settlement was announced in which Hyde had to pay nothing.

Hyde wins reelection every two years without difficulty.

The People: Pop. 1990: 572,268; 12% age 65+; 88% White; 1% Black; 5% Asian; 5% Hispanic origin. Households: 62% married couple families; 29% married couple fams. w. children; 57% college educ.; median household income: $44,216; per capita income: $19,405; median gross rent: $605; median house value: $129,800.

1996 Presidential Vote			**1992 Presidential Vote**		
Dole (R)	105,797	(48%)	Bush (R)	121,868	(47%)
Clinton (D)	93,358	(42%)	Clinton (D)	86,448	(33%)
Perot (I)	18,796	(9%)	Perot (I)	52,734	(20%)

Rep. Henry J. Hyde (R)

Elected 1974; b. Apr. 18, 1924, Chicago; home, Wooddale; Georgetown U., B.S. 1947, Loyola U., J.D. 1949; Catholic; widowed.

Career: Navy, 1944–46 (WWII); Naval Reserves, 1946–68; Practicing atty., 1950–75; IL House of Reps., 1966–74, Majority Ldr., 1971–72.

DC Office: 2110 RHOB 20515, 202-225-4561; Fax: 202-225-1166.

District Offices: Addison, 630-832-5950.

Committees: *International Relations* (4th of 26 R): International Operations & Human Rights. *Judiciary* (Chmn. of 20 R): Constitution.

Group Ratings

	ADA	ACLU	AFS	LCV	CFA	CON	NFIB	COC	ACU	NTLC	CHC
1996	10	0	0	31	15	9	97	100	90	98	93
1995	0	—	—	13	0	38	—	96	68	—	—

National Journal Ratings

	1995 LIB — 1995 CONS			1996 LIB — 1996 CONS		
Economic	0%	—	74%	33%	—	64%
Social	32%	—	65%	35%	—	62%
Foreign	15%	—	73%	21%	—	72%

Key Votes of the 104th Congress

1. Reduce Medicare Growth $	Y	5. Flag Amendment	Y	9. Cuban Embargo	Y
2. Ovrd. Product Liab. Veto	Y	6. Drop EPA Limits	N	10. Bar Bosnia Troop $	Y
3. Increase Min. Wage	N	7. Repeal Assault-Weap. Ban	N	11. Cut Anti-Missile Defense	N
4. Welfare Reform	Y	8. Ovrd. Part. Birth Veto	Y	12. Bar U.N. Uniforms	Y

Election Results

1996 general	Henry J. Hyde (R)	132,401	(64%)	($434,160)
	Stephen De La Rosa (D)	68,807	(33%)	($11,139)
	Others	4,746	(2%)	
1996 primary	Henry J. Hyde (R)	53,720	(84%)	
	Bob Bailie (R)	6,200	(10%)	
	Robert L. Wheat (R)	4,315	(7%)	
1994 general	Henry J. Hyde (R)	115,664	(73%)	($423,027)
	Tom Berry (D)	37,163	(24%)	($14,449)
	Others	4,551	(3%)	

SEVENTH DISTRICT

The cross-country flyer on a lucky day can get a clear view of the biggest man-made cityscape between the Atlantic and Pacific Oceans: Chicago's Loop. High-rise buildings were pioneered a century ago in the Loop—named in 1897 for the circle the "El" train forms around the city's center—by architects like Louis Sullivan and Daniel Burnham. International School modernists built their most impressive collection of buildings here and along Lakeshore in the years after World War II; in the last dozen years, postmodernists have decorated the Chicago River and reinvented the skyscraper. The Loop now spreads beyond the El, up the wondrous shopping street of North Michigan Avenue with a peak at the John Hancock Tower, and west beyond the commodities exchanges to the Sears Tower on the Chicago River. This is the face Chicago likes to present to the world: giant structures rising where the prairies meet the inland sea, a vast concentration of brains and muscle, the nerve center of the markets of the nation and the world.

Behind the lakefront, where the air traveler sees the grid spread out below with occasional radials, is the muscle and sinew, gristle and fat of the city. And also the parts that do not work so well: houses and apartment buildings are abandoned; commercial space stands empty and vandalized; giant housing projects, like the Robert Taylor Homes off the Dan Ryan Expressway, rise starkly, their playgrounds empty because of the ever-present threat of gunfire. The West Side of Chicago, the vast acres directly west of the Loop, for years was a dreadful slum; some of it was nicely spruced up for the Democratic Convention held here at the United Center in 1996. And the decay has spread west to the Austin neighborhood, just before the border of upper income—and for two decades racially integrated—Oak Park.

The 7th Congressional District of Illinois contains the Loop and most of the North Michigan corridor and the Near North Side, with the infamous Cabrini-Green housing project. It also goes south, past 19th Century Prairie Avenue mansions to the Taylor homes and takes in a few heavily black South Side neighborhoods. Its heart, demographically and spiritually, is the black ghetto of the West Side, far more depopulated and socially disorganized than the South Side. To the west are Oak Park and River Forest, and the much more modest Maywood, which is black-majority, and Broadview and Hillside. About two-thirds of the people here are black; there are few Hispanics since they were confined by painstaking boundary-drawing to the 4th District, which practically encircles the 7th on three sides.

The congressman from the 7th District is Danny Davis, a Democrat first elected in 1996 after two unsuccessful tries in 1984 and 1986. Davis grew up on a cotton farm in Arkansas, graduated from college there, then moved to Chicago, and worked as a teacher, assistant principal, and guidance counselor in Chicago public schools. He was elected alderman in the 29th ward on the boundary of Oak Park in 1979 and supported Mayor Harold Washington in the 1980s; he is also 29th Ward committeeman. In 1990 he was elected a Cook County commissioner; in 1991 he made a quixotic run against Mayor Richard M. Daley.

In 1996, when Cardiss Collins retired after nearly 24 years in the House, Davis decided to run. Perhaps his toughest opponent, Alderman Percy Giles, was hurt when he was linked to the "Operation Silver Shovel" waste-dumping kickback scandal; the other major contenders were 3d Ward Aldermen Dorothy Tillman, an ally now of Mayor Daley, and 37th Ward Alderman Ed Smith. They sounded different accents. The fiery Tillman told one crowd she had a "contract" on Newt Gingrich; Smith was for reform of welfare which he said "ought to be a temporary solution, not a permanent one" and once called for martial law on the West Side. Davis campaigned as a big-government liberal, calling for a $7.60 minimum wage, affirmative action, and a national healthcare plan; he said his goal was "the development of an urban strategy, and urban agenda, that reclaims the inner cities of America." Like teacher unions, he opposed school vouchers and favored more money to local districts, even ones like Chicago which have performed poorly.

The March 1996 Democratic primary was decisive here. Davis finished well ahead with 33%, followed by Tillman with 20%, Smith with 12%, Bobbie Steele with 12%, and Giles with 11%. Davis won the general election with ease. In Congress, he has seats on the Government Reform and Small Business Committees, and has taken a stance against sugar subsidies—favored by Downstate corn growers—which he views as corporate welfare.

The People: Pop. 1990: 572,039; 10% age 65+; 27% White; 65% Black; 3% Asian; 4% Hispanic origin. Households: 33% married couple families; 15% married couple fams. w. children; 43% college educ.; median household income: $25,220; per capita income: $13,056; median gross rent: $449; median house value: $89,300.

1996 Presidential Vote

Clinton (D)	152,606	(82%)
Dole (R)	25,757	(14%)
Perot (I)	5,037	(3%)

1992 Presidential Vote

Clinton (D)	184,966	(78%)
Bush (R)	35,530	(15%)
Perot (I)	15,992	(7%)

Rep. Danny K. Davis (D)

Elected 1996; b. Sept. 6, 1941, Parkdale; home, Chicago; AR AM&N Col., B.A. 1961; Chicago St. U., M.S. 1968; Union Inst., Ph.D. 1977; Protestant; married (Vera).

Career: Teacher, Chicago Public Schls., 1962–69; Health Care Planner 1969–79; Chicago City Alderman, 1979–90; Cook County Commissioner, 1990–96;

DC Office: 1218 LHOB 20515, 202-225-5006; Fax: 202-225-5641.

District Offices: Chicago, 773-533-7520.

Committees: *Government Reform & Oversight* (16th of 19 D): Government Management, Information & Technology; Postal Service. *Small Business* (10th of 16 D): Empowerment; Tax, Finance & Exports.

Group Ratings and Key Votes: Newly Elected

Election Results

1996 general	Danny K. Davis (D)	149,568	(83%)	($410,662)
	Randy Borow (R)	27,241	(15%)	($33,155)
	Others	4,286	(2%)	
1996 primary	Danny K. Davis (D)	22,188	(33%)	
	Dorothy J. Tillman (D)	13,433	(20%)	
	Ed H. Smith (D)	8,215	(12%)	
	Bobbie L. Steele (D)	8,148	(12%)	
	Percy Z. Giles (D)	7,378	(11%)	
	Joan Powell (D)	2,753	(4%)	
	Joan A. Sullivan (D)	2,751	(4%)	
	Others	3,174	(5%)	
1994 general	Cardiss Collins (D)	93,457	(80%)	($200,544)
	Charles (Chuck) Mobley (R)	24,011	(20%)	

EIGHTH DISTRICT

Schaumburg may not be nationally known, but it is one of America's major corporate headquarters cities and one of several edge cities northwest of Chicago. Fifty years ago, this was farmland, half a dozen miles beyond the orchard which is now O'Hare Airport. Today Schaumburg, near the intersection of the Northwest Tollway and I-290, with lots of office space and Woodfield Mall and miles of subdivisions, with moderately-priced apartments and with some black residents, is the site of the headquarters of Motorola, one of the most innovative large corporations, which has done much to wrest the technological edge from the Far East, and of Zurich American Life Insurance; nearby are the headquarters of Sears and Kemper Insurance. Yet Schaumburg yearns for traditions: it built a performing arts center, formed an orchestra for young people, and is now building from scratch a traditional downtown, to be ready by 1998.

The 8th Congressional District of Illinois is made up of Schaumburg and dozens of communities something like it, on the prairies and hilly lakelands northwest of Chicago. Near Schaumburg are Streamwood, Hoffman Estates, Arlington Heights, Rolling Meadows, Palatine: over 60% of the district's population is in the far northwest extremity of Cook County. The 8th also includes the filling-up western half of Lake County, with little lake communities being surrounded by new suburbs. The tone of life here is not elite, but it is highly affluent; culturally, this is part of the great rural Midwest as much as—perhaps more than—it is of yeasty, lusty Chicago. Economically, it is suspicious of government spending, which it associates with the corrupt big city of yore. By most measures, this is the most Republican district in Illinois, and one of the most Republican in the nation.

The congressman from the 8th District is Philip Crane, a conservative Republican first elected in a 1969 special election, and now the second most senior Republican in the House. Crane grew up in Indiana, one of several sons of a doctor who had his own radio program; he went to college at Hillsdale, got a Ph.D. at Indiana University, was a conservative intellectual when that seemed an oxymoron. He moved to the Chicago area in 1967, and then, at 39, won a November 1969 special election to the House, replacing Donald Rumsfeld, who was then Richard Nixon's poverty program director, before he was chief of staff and Defense secretary under Gerald Ford. Crane supported a set of ideas which then seemed backward-looking but which have been on the ascendant in the nation and the world since—free market economics, a strong national defense, traditional values. In his first years in the House he sat largely unnoticed on the back benches and had meager influence. In 1980 he ran for president, hoping, as the truer libertarian, to cut in on the elderly Ronald Reagan's support and then take it over when the Reagan candidacy faded. But his strategy totally failed, and through the 1980s he seemed embittered and unfocused; he was never a part of the young conservative movement led by Jack Kemp, Newt Gingrich, and Trent Lott. By the early 1990s he was in trouble back home. In 1992 he had primary opposition from Gary Skoien, a former aide to then-Governor James Thompson, who hit hard at congressional perks and criticized Crane for opposing a highway bill with many Illinois projects and for his anti-abortion stance; Crane, who declined the PAC money he could easily collect as a member of Ways and Means, won by only 55%–45%. That fall, Democrat Sheila Smith, a onetime champion swimmer and owner of a lamp manufacturing company, waged a vigorous campaign and was endorsed by the *Chicago Tribune*, once (though no longer) the voice of conservative Republicanism. Crane won unimpressively, 56%–40%. In 1994 Crane once again had serious primary opposition, from Skoien again and from state Senator Peter Fitzgerald, a young conservative whose father was a well-known bank president. Fitzgerald spent plenty of his own money and did little to conceal statewide ambitions, but Crane won 40% of the vote to Fitzgerald's 33% and Skoien's 21%. Fitzgerald plans to run for Moseley-Braun's Senate seat in 1998.

After those close scrapes Crane suddenly found himself part of a Republican majority. He was not a committee chairman—Bill Archer had seniority over him on Ways and Means, and no one thought of pushing him aside—but Crane did chair the Trade Subcommittee, and seemed to become engaged in legislation. Most of the Republican Ways and Means tax plan—the $500 per child tax credit, repeal of the alternative minimum tax for corporations—was vetoed by President Clinton. But Crane did work to insert in the unvetoable minimum wage bill several provisions—the adoption tax credit, expanding Employee Stock Ownership Plans, Subchapter S changes to help small businesses, and various insurance provisions. On the Trade Subcommittee, he pushed for extending the General System of Preferences and shepherded through Most Favored Nation status for Bulgaria, Romania, and Cambodia. He also supported renewal of MFN status for China;"Illinois exports to China grew 25% last year," he pointed out in 1996. He supported NAFTA and GATT, which were passed largely with Republican votes.

Crane also tended, as he had not much in the past, to local projects. He boasted that he called Appropriators Bob Livingston and Bill Young and got money for ALQ-135 radar jammers for F-15s restored; they account for 1300 jobs at the Rolling Meadows Northrop plant. He worked with John Porter to get reauthorization for the Des Plaines River Wetlands Demonstration Project and with Don Manzullo to get more floodgates in the Fox River region.

All of which didn't hurt and might have helped in 1996. Crane beat his one primary opponent

75%–25% and won the general election 62%–36% though Bill Clinton was running relatively strongly in the 8th District. He continues to head the Trade Subcommittee and has promised to push to extend NAFTA to Chile and to seek closer trade relations with countries in sub-Saharan Africa. He has advocated a flat tax since the 1970s, and may weigh in on that as well, though the decision as to whether to seek major tax reform will presumably be Bill Archer's. And he will continue his longstanding battle to defund the National Endowment for the Arts. Archer has said he will retire in 2000; Crane now seems to have a good chance to remain in the House past that time, if he chooses, and to become Ways and Means chairman, if Republicans maintain control.

The People: Pop. 1990: 571,464; 6% rural; 7% age 65+; 89% White; 2% Black; 4% Asian; 6% Hispanic origin. Households: 65% married couple families; 33% married couple fams. w. children; 61% college educ.; median household income: $47,374; per capita income: $20,488; median gross rent: $667; median house value: $131,900.

1996 Presidential Vote

Dole (R)	105,742	(49%)
Clinton (D)	86,907	(41%)
Perot (I)	19,482	(9%)

1992 Presidential Vote

Bush (R)	118,714	(47%)
Clinton (D)	76,327	(31%)
Perot (I)	54,269	(22%)

Rep. Philip M. Crane (R)

Elected Nov., 1969; b. Nov. 3, 1930, Chicago; home, Wauconda; DePauw U., Hillsdale Col., B.A. 1952, IN U., M.A. 1961, Ph.D. 1963; Protestant; married (Arlene).

Career: Army, 1954–56; Instructor, IN U., 1960–63; Asst. Prof., Bradley U., 1963–67; Dir., Westminster Academy, 1967–68.

DC Office: 233 CHOB 20515, 202-225-3711; Fax: 202-225-7830.

District Offices: Lake Villa, 847-265-9000; Palatine, 847-358-9160.

Committees: *Ways & Means* (2nd of 23 R): Health; Trade (Chmn.). *Joint Committee on Taxation* (2nd of 5 Reps.).

Group Ratings

	ADA	ACLU	AFS	LCV	CFA	CON	NFIB	COC	ACU	NTLC	CHC
1996	0	12	0	15	8	44	100	100	100	100	100
1995	0	—	—	0	0	53	—	100	100	—	—

National Journal Ratings

	1995 LIB — 1995 CONS			1996 LIB — 1996 CONS		
Economic	0%	—	74%	0%	—	82%
Social	0%	—	79%	24%	—	72%
Foreign	15%	—	73%	0%	—	79%

Key Votes of the 104th Congress

1. Reduce Medicare Growth $	Y	5. Flag Amendment	Y	9. Cuban Embargo	Y
2. Ovrd. Product Liab. Veto	Y	6. Drop EPA Limits	N	10. Bar Bosnia Troop $	Y
3. Increase Min. Wage	N	7. Repeal Assault-Weap. Ban	Y	11. Cut Anti-Missile Defense	N
4. Welfare Reform	Y	8. Ovrd. Part. Birth Veto	Y	12. Bar U.N. Uniforms	Y

Election Results

1996 general	Philip M. Crane (R)	127,763	(62%)	($534,151)
	Elizabeth Anne Hull (D)	74,068	(36%)	($30,804)
	Others	3,474	(2%)	
1996 primary	Philip M. Crane (R)	40,489	(75%)	
	Don Huff (R)	13,364	(25%)	
1994 general	Philip M. Crane (R)	88,225	(65%)	($722,267)
	Robert C. Walberg (D)	47,654	(35%)	($66,960)

NINTH DISTRICT

"Make no little plans," commanded architect Daniel Burnham, who made no little plans for the Chicago lakefront: the glorious parks he designed are still among America's urban jewels, and the row of high-rise apartment buildings—some austere works of masters of the international style, some in traditional styles evocative of some other place and time, some sleek Art Deco works of the 1920s and 1930s—are a splendid accompaniment. Behind the lakefront is all the diversity of Chicago. In sturdy brick houses, with scarcely a shoe horn's space between them, or in stubby apartment buildings, are ethnic and racial groups of all sorts, from Argentinians to Slavs, Plains Indians to Indian plainsmen. Two decades ago, the neighborhoods behind the lakefront seemed to be getting grimier and heading downhill. In the past dozen years, they have been busy gentrifying, as young marrieds and gays, professionals and entrepreneurs renovate old houses and open new businesses.

The lakefront has long been the most heavily Jewish part of Chicago. Chicago's Jewish community, prominent for more than a century, has never been as much a force for big government as in New York, nor is it connected as much to a glamorous industry as in Los Angeles. Yet among Jewish voters liberal impulses have been strong: the 19th Century impulse to resist state authority and imposition of cultural uniformity and the 20th Century impulse to increase state responsibility for individuals' lives. Chicago's North Side Jews, on the lakefront or in neighborhoods like Rogers Park and nearby suburbs like Skokie and Niles, have been a solidly Democratic voting bloc, involved with—but skeptical of—the old Democratic machine. In the racial city politics of the 1980s, as in state politics, Jewish voters and lakefront liberals of all backgrounds have been a key swing group.

The 9th Congressional District of Illinois covers most of Chicago's lakefront, from Diversey Harbor north to Evanston, the home of Northwestern University and a city which has moved gracefully from historic Yankee Republican-ness to trendy postgraduate Democratic-ness. The 9th presses inland from the Rogers Park neighborhood at the north end of Chicago west into Polish-American areas at the northwest edge of the city; from Evanston it reaches west through heavily Jewish Skokie to Morton Grove and Niles.

The 9th District's congressman, Democrat Sidney Yates, is the only member of the House who can remember having served in a Republican Congress. His father was a Jewish immigrant from Lithuania who drove a truck in Chicago; two of his brothers were vaudeville booking agents there. Yates went to the University of Chicago, practiced law mostly in public sector jobs, joined the Navy at 35 in 1944 and was elected to Congress from the Lakefront wards in 1948. In his second term, he helped save the career of Admiral Hyman Rickover, whose nuclear submarine program helped maintain nuclear deterrence and produce American victory in the Cold War. Recalling the last time the Republicans took over the House, 42 years ago, he said in 1994: "Republicans fought what they called the socialistic measures of Democrats, and we tried just to stay alive in that Congress and come back . . . In that session Republicans were much tougher on Democrats than the present Republicans say we were on them. There was no bipartisanship except on foreign policy." But Democrats did come back in 1954. Yates ran for the Senate in 1962, losing to Everett Dirksen 53%–47%; he returned to the House in 1964.

In Chicago and in Washington, Yates has combined liberal idealism and practical political sense. Back home he has been cordially supported by liberal reformers even while maintaining a cooperative relationship with Democratic machine politicians. When he had a tough primary challenge in 1990, both lakefront reformers and Mayor Richard M. Daley stood at his side. In the House, Yates has long been on the Appropriations Committee, where he has quietly furthered liberal causes while getting along with practical-minded colleagues. Had he not run for the Senate, he would have been in line to become chairman of Appropriations after Jamie Whitten was replaced in 1992, and perhaps sooner; instead, from 1975–94 he chaired the Interior Subcommittee. Here he exerted great influence over important public policies—and has channeled billions to Chicago and Illinois. Local projects range from $3.8 million for the Midewin Tallgrass Prairie visitors' center to $12.3 million for the Chicago Deep Tunnel sewage system, including $2.9 million for a Chicago Wilderness Project (to restore prairies on public lands), $1.4 million for the Chicago Greenstreets program, $3.2 million for the Chicago-based Municipal Management Consortium, $8 million for the Chicago Shoreline Project, $45 million for the purchase of low-income apartment complexes, and $3.7 million for Indiana Dunes Lakeshore land acquisition. Over many years he nurtured projects like the Chicago Cultural Center and Navy Pier park restorations, and responded rapidly to the flooding of Chicago's old water tunnels in 1993. Nationally, Yates is known as an environmentalist with a detailed knowledge of government land use policy, who used his appropriating power to create new national parks, wildernesses, seashores, lakeshores, wild and scenic rivers—a kind of pork many members and voters regard as particularly kosher. In the 104th Congress, he twice moved to recommit the Interior appropriation because it preserved timber harvesting in the Tongass National Forest in Alaska and lifted a moratorium on mining in some western states.

Yates for years was a kind of Maecenas, the House's chief defender of the National Endowments for the Arts and Humanities and the National Trust for Historic Preservation. The NEA has been attacked for years because of the fecklessness of administrators who fund artists whose work might be considered obscene by the taxpayers whose funds are being used. Yates has seen his duty as preserving the NEA budget, and has tried to sidestep both the dubious claims that a denial of grants would restrict artistic freedom (since artists may do whatever they like on their own dollar) and the graceless task of writing a code of conduct for the agency. His political maneuvering kept the NEA alive during the Bush years, thriving during the first two Clinton years, and still alive but with reduced appropriations in 1995 and 1996. He will surely be fighting for it again in 1997 and 1998.

Yates has shown great hardiness in the polls. In the 1990 primary, against wealthy 31-year-old Alderman Edwin Eisendrath, he won 70%–27%. In later primaries he won 65% against two candidates in 1992, 75% against one in 1994, 84% against three in 1996. His percentages in general elections declined, though only slightly, in the 1990s. In 1996 34-year-old Republican Joseph Walsh held an 87th birthday party for Yates and paid $1,000 to Yates' doorman for being the first to see him in his district. But Yates, who won with 66% in 1994, won 63%–37% in 1996. In October 1996, however, he announced this would be his last campaign, and so he will retire in 1998, 50 years after he was first elected. The race to succeed him will probably be decided in the Democratic primary; Evanston state Senator Jan Schakowsky has said she will run and Hyatt hotel chain scion J. B. Pritzker is a possible candidate.

The People: Pop. 1990: 571,611; 16% age 65+; 68% White; 12% Black; 10% Asian; 10% Hispanic origin. Households: 42% married couple families; 17% married couple fams. w. children; 60% college educ.; median household income: $32,183; per capita income: $18,691; median gross rent: $508; median house value: $145,000.

1996 Presidential Vote

Clinton (D)	139,166	(69%)
Dole (R)	52,263	(26%)
Perot (I)	9,732	(5%)

1992 Presidential Vote

Clinton (D)	155,446	(61%)
Bush (R)	68,418	(27%)
Perot (I)	29,294	(12%)

Rep. Sidney R. Yates (D)

Elected 1964; b. Aug. 27, 1909, Chicago; home, Chicago; U. of Chicago, Ph.D. 1931, J.D. 1933; Jewish; married (Adeline).

Career: Navy, 1944–46; Practicing atty.; Asst. Atty., IL St. Bank Receiver, 1935–37; Asst. Atty. Gen., IL Commerce Comm., 1937–40; U.S. House of Reps., 1948–62; U.N. Rep., Trusteeship Cncl., 1963–64.

DC Office: 2109 RHOB 20515, 202-225-2111; Fax: 202-225-3493.

District Offices: Chicago, 312-353-4596; Evanston, 847-328-2610.

Committees: *Appropriations* (2nd of 26 D): Foreign Operations, Export Financing & Related Programs; Interior (RMM).

Group Ratings

	ADA	ACLU	AFS	LCV	CFA	CON	NFIB	COC	ACU	NTLC	CHC
1996	85	94	100	92	77	51	21	7	0	3	15
1995	85	—	—	100	85	8	—	17	4	—	—

National Journal Ratings

	1995 LIB — 1995 CONS			1996 LIB — 1996 CONS		
Economic	94%	—	0%	89%	—	0%
Social	70%	—	30%	83%	—	16%
Foreign	93%	—	0%	90%	—	0%

Key Votes of the 104th Congress

1. Reduce Medicare Growth $	N	5. Flag Amendment	N	9. Cuban Embargo	N
2. Ovrd. Product Liab. Veto	N	6. Drop EPA Limits	Y	10. Bar Bosnia Troop $	N
3. Increase Min. Wage	Y	7. Repeal Assault-Weap. Ban	N	11. Cut Anti-Missile Defense	Y
4. Welfare Reform	N	8. Ovrd. Part. Birth Veto	N	12. Bar U.N. Uniforms	N

Election Results

1996 general	Sidney R. Yates (D)	124,319	(63%)	($184,005)
	Joseph Walsh (R)	71,763	(37%)	($115,401)
1996 primary	Sidney R. Yates (D)	44,259	(84%)	
	Terrence R. Gilhooly (D)	5,725	(11%)	
	Seth Tillman (D)	2,763	(5%)	
1994 general	Sidney R. Yates (D)	94,404	(66%)	($217,952)
	George Edward Larney (R)	48,419	(34%)	($48,121)

TENTH DISTRICT

Since 1855, when the first Chicago & Northwestern opened the railroad line from downtown Chicago north along the lakeshore, the North Shore suburbs along Lake Michigan have been the favorite residence for Chicago's elite. The North Shore starts in Evanston, founded by Methodists to promote temperance (a cause that has never prospered in Chicago), and goes on to Wilmette, Winnetka, Glencoe, Highland Park, Lake Forest—each with a slightly different personality and character, each long established, mightily prosperous and with a patina of age. Not far from the gritty, monosyllabic city, these are communities of pleasant, affluent, well-educated people living in an environment whose natural beauty—the long water vista and blue light off the Lake, the gentle hills and fine trees—is kept carefully disciplined.

The 10th Congressional District of Illinois is the North Shore district, starting at the Baha'i Temple on the Wilmette lakefront, just north of Evanston, reaching up past Fort Sheridan (which was closed in 1993) to the city of Waukegan (once famous as the home of comedian Jack Benny) and the Wisconsin border beyond. The district also goes inland to what for many years was just cornfields (some still are) to Northbrook and Deerfield, just west of Glencoe and Highland Park. Farther inland are suburbs like Arlington Heights, developed in the 1950s and 1960s on the Northwestern railroad line, and Wheeling, developed in the 1960s and 1970s near Interstate 294. To the north are Long Grove and Libertyville, near where the Adlai Stevensons, the late presidential candidate and his son the former senator, have what is now one of the last farms only a few miles from Lake Michigan and the Onwentsia Club.

The congressman from the 10th District is John Porter, a Republican who has long seemed to fit the district well. He is a North Shore native, the son of an Evanston judge, a graduate of Northwestern, a Republican who is against tax increases and looks with favor on free markets, but who takes liberal stands on some foreign and cultural issues. Elected in 1980, he is chairman of the Labor-HHS-Education Appropriations Subcommittee, with much say about vast flows of money: one of the key members of the 104th and 105th Congresses.

When Republicans gained control in 1994, Porter suddenly had the responsibility of managing an appropriation's bill slated for most of the Republicans' reductions in domestic discretionary spending—on the order of $9 billion of a $70 billion total—and to navigate between the subcommittee's very able and aggressive ranking Democrat, David Obey, and its strong conservative Republicans, like Ernest Istook. All this Porter proved able to do. He held out against increased education funding, on the grounds that however popular this is primarily a state and local responsibility, and instead increased spending for the National Institutes of Health (up 6.9% for 1997) and biomedical research, where the federal government plays a unique role which he has compared to Prince Henry the Navigator's encouragement of ocean exploration in 15th Century Portugal. Against many Republicans, he maintained support for family planning programs and Medicaid funding of abortions in cases of rape and incest. He voted against the Republican tax cut, saying that spending should be cut first, and against the balanced budget amendment with a supermajority required to raise taxes. He was the number two Republican in opposition on Contract votes, though he supported it 80% of the time; his support of spending cuts plus opposition to tax cuts gave him the second best Concord Coalition rating over 1995–96. On other issues, he led opposition to repeal of the assault weapons ban and of the 1993 gas tax, opposed term limits and the defunding of public broadcasting. He opposed EPA riders restricting its regulatory authority and has an environmental record which won the support of the Sierra Club. He is a House reformer, sponsor of the limit on ranking Republican committee positions to six years which now limits their service as chairmen. He has opposed the B-2 bomber, the Seawolf submarine, and the space station; he is a strong supporter of Radio Free Asia and has denounced Turkey and Iran for their persecutions of Armenians, Kurds, and Baha'i. He tends to local matters as well, such as the Great Lakes Naval Training Center and the Wisconsin Central commuter rail line.

Porter's combination of carrying important Republican policies on some issues and opposing them on others has inspired both strong support and strong opposition within the party. He had articulate conservative opponents in the last three primaries, who attacked him for favoring abortion rights, gun control, and the National Endowment for the Arts. Against Kathleen Sullivan, founder of a high school program counseling sexual abstinence, he won with 60% in 1992 and 66% in 1994; against businessman Richard Rinaolo, he won with 68% in 1996. Porter briefly considered a run for the Senate seat Paul Simon vacated but ruled it out, but after the 1996 election Porter took a "hard look" at challenging Senator Carol Moseley-Braun in 1998. In March 1997, Parter decided against running, however, saying he did not want to relinquish his post as one of the College of Cardinals on the Appropriations Committee.

The People: Pop. 1990: 571,501; 1% rural; 10% age 65+; 83% White; 6% Black; 4% Asian; 7% Hispanic origin. Households: 66% married couple families; 33% married couple fams. w. children; 66% college educ.; median household income: $50,355; per capita income: $26,405; median gross rent: $605; median house value: $180,200.

1996 Presidential Vote

Clinton (D)	112,105	(50%)
Dole (R)	97,434	(43%)
Perot (I)	13,418	(6%)

1992 Presidential Vote

Bush (R)	112,401	(43%)
Clinton (D)	108,149	(41%)
Perot (I)	40,719	(16%)

Rep. John E. Porter (R)

Elected 1980; b. June 1, 1935, Evanston; home, Wilmette; M.I.T., 1953–54, Northwestern U., B.S.B.A. 1957, U. of MI, J.D. 1961; Presbyterian; married (Kathryn).

Career: Army Reserves, 1958–64; Atty., U.S. Dept. of Justice, 1961–63; Practicing atty., 1963–80; IL House of Reps., 1972–78.

DC Office: 2373 RHOB 20515, 202-225-4835.

District Offices: Arlington Heights, 847-392-0303; Deerfield, 847-940-0202; Waukegan, 847-662-0101.

Committees: *Appropriations* (6th of 34 R): Foreign Operations, Export Financing & Related Programs; Labor, Health & Human Services & Education (Chmn.); Military Construction.

Group Ratings

	ADA	ACLU	AFS	LCV	CFA	CON	NFIB	COC	ACU	NTLC	CHC
1996	25	7	0	38	54	100	78	75	80	73	60
1995	25	—	—	25	77	98	—	75	48	—	—

National Journal Ratings

	1995 LIB — 1995 CONS			1996 LIB — 1996 CONS		
Economic	49%	—	49%	44%	—	55%
Social	55%	—	43%	58%	—	42%
Foreign	54%	—	45%	50%	—	48%

Key Votes of the 104th Congress

1. Reduce Medicare Growth $	Y	5. Flag Amendment	N	9. Cuban Embargo	Y
2. Ovrd. Product Liab. Veto	Y	6. Drop EPA Limits	Y	10. Bar Bosnia Troop $	Y
3. Increase Min. Wage	N	7. Repeal Assault-Weap. Ban	N	11. Cut Anti-Missile Defense	N
4. Welfare Reform	Y	8. Ovrd. Part. Birth Veto	Y	12. Bar U.N. Uniforms	N

Election Results

1996 general	John E. Porter (R)	145,626	(69%)	($726,615)
	Philip R. Torf (D)	65,144	(31%)	($54,367)
1996 primary	John E. Porter (R)	33,530	(68%)	
	Richard Rinaolo (R)	15,563	(32%)	
1994 general	John E. Porter (R)	114,884	(75%)	($538,716)
	Andrew M. Krupp (D)	38,191	(25%)	($10,214)

ELEVENTH DISTRICT

South of Chicago, sluggishly flowing rivers run circles around industrial sites. This low-lying land is a great divide, over which French explorers portaged, the easiest path from the inland oceans of the Great Lakes to the widened-out channels of communication through North America, the Mississippi River and all its tributaries. Today, there is still a kind of borderland here, as the factories and shopping centers and subdivisions stop around the Cook County line and Downstate Illinois prairies begin, cornfields bisected by highways and railroads radiating out from the Loop and the railyards of the nation's transportation hub. Politically, this is a borderland as well, between the traditionally Democratic Chicago metropolitan area, with its hard-bitten machine politics, and heavily Republican Downstate Illinois, with its tradition of governance by local civic leaders that stretches back to the days of Abraham Lincoln.

The 11th Congressional District of Illinois covers much of this borderland. It includes the old 10th Ward of Chicago plus the suburbs of South Holland, Calumet City and Lansing near the Indiana line. This is heavy industry country; many of the factories around Lake Calumet are empty now—if not torn down—but the rows of workers' houses on the grid streets remain. This is the home of the struggling white working class, ancestrally Democratic. To the west is Joliet. Once a canal boat town, and later the producer of one-third of America's wallpaper, Joliet now has two big prisons; the federal Joliet Arsenal recently lost its last industrial operation, and Joliet owes its current prosperity to the four riverboat casinos built since 1992, generating $100 million in payrolls and $90 million in tax revenue. To the south is Kankakee, a Downstate county seat amid rich prairie earth on the Illinois Central main line; this is heavily Republican territory. Farther west, on bluffs above the Illinois River heading down to the Mississippi, are the factory towns of Ottawa and LaSalle and, to the south, Streator; this is LaSalle County, the only sometimes Democratic part of heavily Republican northern Downstate Illinois.

The congressman from the 11th District is Jerry Weller, a hard-working, politically savvy Republican who won the seat in 1994 and held it in 1996—one of the politically competent young Republicans who have made the difference between a Democratic and a Republican House. Weller grew up on a Grundy County farm, where his family still raises hogs; out of college, he was a staffer to Congressman Tom Corcoran and Agriculture Secretary John Block; in the mid-1980s he returned to Illinois and was elected to the state House in 1988. In 1994, when Democratic Congressman George Sangmeister retired "to smell the proverbial roses," Weller was one of six Republicans and seven Democrats to run for the seat. He boasted of reforming health care via market-based principles, holding criminals accountable and promoting markets for ethanol fuels and soybean inks; he was proud of replacing the "granny tax" on nursing home residents with a cigarette tax as a way to pay for health care. In the Republican primary he edged 1992 nominee Robert Herbolsheime, 32%–29%; in the general, against Democrat Frank Giglio who had been a legislator for 20 of the previous 22 years, and said of Congress, "Wouldn't this be a nice way to finish my career?" Weller won 61%–39%.

In the House Weller showed impressive insider skills. With the help of Chief Deputy Whip Dennis Hastert of the 14th District, he was named one of three freshmen on the Republican Steering Committee. On the Veterans' Committee he steered to passage a law allowing the Veterans' Administration to contract outpatient care with private clinics and hospitals—making possible a revolution in veterans' healthcare policy. On Transportation and Infrastructure, he worked to upgrade the Aurora FAA center and exempt airlines for three more years from the 1993 gas tax increase; he also promotes the third Chicago airport proposed for Peotone, 45 miles south of the Loop and a few miles north of Kankakee. He passed a bill authorizing federal aid to local juvenile detention centers in places like Will, Kankakee, and LaSalle Counties. He got money for the conversion of the 23,500-acre Joliet Arsenal into a 19,000-acre Midewin National Tallgrass Prairie, the biggest east of the Mississippi. He also worked on the Thornton Reservoir Project and a proposed Calumet Ecological Park in Chicago.

In fall 1996 Weller waged two campaigns, both narrowly successful. The first was for reelection. Bill Clinton ran well in the southern suburbs of Chicago, and Democrats picked up several crucial state House seats there. Democrat Clem Balanoff made a late TV buy, excoriating Weller for supporting Newt Gingrich and Medicare "cuts." Balanoff carried the Cook County portion of the district and ran even in LaSalle; Weller was not declared the winner election night until a computer glitch in Will County was fixed, and his margin was a narrow 52%–48%. But early the next morning he was running his other campaign, for a seat on the Ways and Means Committee. He called Majority Leader Dick Armey and reminded him that with the defeat of Michael Flanagan the committee had no one representing Chicago, "a world economic center." And he called in chits from fellow Republicans who had benefited from the PAC he had formed. With help from Hastert and acquiescence from Ways and Means Chairman Bill Archer and Vice Chairman Phil Crane, he won one of the four open Ways and Means seats.

Neither of these victories was anything like assured, and Weller's skill in gaining them suggests he could remain an influential House member for some time.

The People: Pop. 1990: 571,050; 20% rural; 13% age 65+; 84% White; 8% Black; 1% Asian; 7% Hispanic origin. Households: 62% married couple families; 30% married couple fams. w. children; 39% college educ.; median household income: $33,632; per capita income: $13,838; median gross rent: $414; median house value: $66,900.

1996 Presidential Vote

Clinton (D)	112,110	(51%)
Dole (R)	83,648	(38%)
Perot (I)	23,162	(11%)

1992 Presidential Vote

Clinton (D)	108,456	(43%)
Bush (R)	90,058	(36%)
Perot (I)	50,186	(20%)

Rep. Jerry Weller (R)

Elected 1994; b. July 7, 1957, Streator; home, Morris; U. of IL, B.A. 1979; Christian; single.

Career: Farmer; Aide, U.S. Rep. Tom Corcoran, 1980–81; Aide, U.S. Agriculture Secy. John Block, 1981–85; IL House of Reps., 1988–94.

DC Office: 130 CHOB 20515, 202-225-3635.

District Offices: Joliet, 815-740-2028; Ottawa, 815-433-0085.

Committees: *Ways & Means* (22nd of 23 R): Oversight; Social Security.

Group Ratings

	ADA	ACLU	AFS	LCV	CFA	CON	NFIB	COC	ACU	NTLC	CHC
1996	5	0	42	15	31	30	94	87	84	100	100
1995	0	—	—	0	0	38	—	100	92	—	—

National Journal Ratings

	1995 LIB		1995 CONS	1996 LIB		1996 CONS
Economic	34%	—	64%	33%	—	64%
Social	0%	—	79%	24%	—	72%
Foreign	15%	—	73%	41%	—	56%

Key Votes of the 104th Congress

1. Reduce Medicare Growth $	Y	5. Flag Amendment	Y	9. Cuban Embargo	Y
2. Ovrd. Product Liab. Veto	Y	6. Drop EPA Limits	N	10. Bar Bosnia Troop $	Y
3. Increase Min. Wage	Y	7. Repeal Assault-Weap. Ban	Y	11. Cut Anti-Missile Defense	N
4. Welfare Reform	Y	8. Ovrd. Part. Birth Veto	Y	12. Bar U.N. Uniforms	Y

Election Results

1996 general	Jerry Weller (R)	109,896	(52%)	($1,116,062)
	Clem Balanoff (D)	102,388	(48%)	($481,979)
1996 primary	Jerry Weller (R)	unopposed		
1994 general	Jerry Weller (R)	97,241	(61%)	($877,429)
	Frank Giglio (D)	63,150	(39%)	($614,142)

TWELFTH DISTRICT

The nation's two mightiest streams, the Mississippi and Missouri Rivers, their waters roiling together, join just a few miles above St. Louis and just a few miles below Alton, Illinois. Most views of this center of the Mississippi Valley focus on the Gateway Arch and the buildings of downtown St. Louis. But the Mississippi shoreline of Illinois is worthy of attention as well. Alton's 19th Century buildings recall its turbulent history, when it was the home of the anti-slavery agitator Elijah Lovejoy, murdered by a mob; more recently it was the longtime home of conservative crusader and columnist Phyllis Schlafly. Just across from the Gateway Arch is East St. Louis, where dozens of rail lines and highways funnel into bridges over the river. Once a rail and stockyards center second only to Chicago, East St. Louis is now one of America's poorest and most troubled cities, a half-abandoned slum with one of the nation's highest crime rates and a rapidly declining tax base. South of East St. Louis and the industrial area around Belleville, the river counties are lightly inhabited, but they were not always unimportant: this was the site of the French Kaskaskia settlement that became Illinois's first capital in 1818. Farther south, the river abuts the coal country and the town of Carbondale, once a coal center but now as the home of Southern Illinois University bustling with students from Downstate Illinois and Chicago and the retirement base of former Senator Paul Simon. The land here is sometimes known as Egypt, the southern end of Illinois where the Ohio River meets the Mississippi: flat, fertile farmland, protected by giant man-made levees because it is susceptible to yearly floods. There is more than a touch of Dixie here: the unofficial capital of Egypt, Cairo (pronounced *KAYroh*), is a declining town closer to Mississippi than to Chicago with its own occasional racial violence.

The 12th Congressional District of Illinois covers all of this riverfront from Alton south to Cairo, with some inland territory as well. Most of its population is in St. Clair (East St. Louis and Belleville) and Madison (Alton) Counties, but one-third of the votes are cast in counties running south to Cairo. The congressman from the 12th District is Jerry Costello, a Democrat from an old St. Clair County political family who first won the seat in 1988, when it was vacated after 44 years by Democrat Mel Price. Costello has worked in the public sector just about all his adult life; in 1980, he became chairman of the St. Clair County Board of Supervisors. Experienced, well-connected, supported by organized labor, he was the obvious successor when Price finally retired. Costello won the three-way special primary 46%–27%–25%, then by 53%–47% won the general election.

Costello is as practical- and district-minded as any member of the House, with a liberal record on economics and a mixed record on cultural and foreign issues, a lawmaker who places loyalty to party leadership as a relatively low priority. He opposed George Bush's Clean Air Act and Bill Clinton's North American Free Trade Agreement, bucked Clinton on the balanced budget amendment and House Republicans on public works votes. He trumpets his accomplishments without subtlety. He has worked to build a Clean Coal Technology Center in Carterville, to rebuild the Len Small Levee, to fund the Super Max prison. Bridges are important in a river district: Costello has worked to replace the Clark Bridge in Alton and, with the late Congressman Bill Emerson of Missouri, to build a new bridge to Cape Girardeau to be named after Emerson. His biggest ongoing project has been developing a Mid-America Airport at Scott Air Force Base near Belleville which is scheduled to open in the summer of 1997; he also got funding to extend a light rail line from East St. Louis to Scott and helped to keep Scott and the Mel Price Army Support Center in Granite City off the 1995 base-closing list.

Costello has won reelection without difficulty, and for a time seemed to be bent on running for Illinois secretary of State in 1998. But in September 1996 Amiel Cueto, a longtime friend and former business partner of Costello, was indicted for obstruction of justice for trying to stop an investigation of a gambling operation run by a former business partner and client; the indictment alleged that an "undisclosed business partner" who was also a "public official" offered to use his influence to install Cueto as St. Clair County state's attorney. The *St. Louis Post-Dispatch* identified the public official as Costello, and more accusations were brought up at Cueto's trial. The revelations have damaged his plans to run for secretary of State in 1998.

The People: Pop. 1990: 571,441; 22% rural; 14% age 65+; 81% White; 17% Black; 1% Asian; 1% Hispanic origin. Households: 54% married couple families; 25% married couple fams. w. children; 40% college educ.; median household income: $25,032; per capita income: $11,547; median gross rent: $360; median house value: $47,400.

1996 Presidential Vote			1992 Presidential Vote		
Clinton (D)	120,389	(56%)	Clinton (D)	132,570	(54%)
Dole (R)	72,652	(34%)	Bush (R)	69,829	(28%)
Perot (I)	19,777	(9%)	Perot (I)	42,169	(17%)

Rep. Jerry F. Costello (D)

Elected Aug. 1988; b. Sept. 25, 1949, East St. Louis; home, Belleville; Belleville Area Col. A.A. 1970, Maryville Col. B.A. 1972; Catholic; married (Georgia).

Career: Dir., IL Court Svcs. & Probation, 1973–80; Chmn., Region's Cncl. of Govts., 1980–84; Chmn., St. Clair Cnty. Bd. of Supervisors, 1980–88.

DC Office: 2454 RHOB 20515, 202-225-5661; Fax: 202-225-0285; e-mail: jfcil12@hr.house.gov.

District Offices: Belleville, 618-233-8026; Carbondale, 618-529-3791; East St. Louis, 618-397-8833; Granite City, 618-451-7065.

Committees: *Budget* (4th of 19 D). *Transportation & Infrastructure* (9th of 33 D): Aviation; Surface Transportation.

Group Ratings

	ADA	ACLU	AFS	LCV	CFA	CON	NFIB	COC	ACU	NTLC	CHC
1996	70	50	91	69	62	63	39	25	30	15	40
1995	70	—	—	88	46	25	—	33	32	—	—

National Journal Ratings

	1995 LIB		1995 CONS	1996 LIB		1996 CONS
Economic	65%	—	35%	68%	—	31%
Social	52%	—	47%	46%	—	52%
Foreign	62%	—	36%	61%	—	37%

Key Votes of the 104th Congress

1. Reduce Medicare Growth $	N	5. Flag Amendment	Y	9. Cuban Embargo	Y
2. Ovrd. Product Liab. Veto	N	6. Drop EPA Limits	Y	10. Bar Bosnia Troop $	N
3. Increase Min. Wage	Y	7. Repeal Assault-Weap. Ban	Y	11. Cut Anti-Missile Defense	Y
4. Welfare Reform	N	8. Ovrd. Part. Birth Veto	Y	12. Bar U.N. Uniforms	Y

Election Results

1996 general	Jerry F. Costello (D)	150,005	(72%)	($506,257)
	Shapley R. Hunter (R)	55,690	(27%)	($4,261)
	Others	3,824	(2%)	
1996 primary	Jerry F. Costello (D)	unopposed		
1994 general	Jerry F. Costello (D)	101,391	(66%)	($499,844)
	Jan Morris (R)	52,419	(34%)	($43,779)

THIRTEENTH DISTRICT

Most residents of Chicagoland now live not in the city but in the suburbs, and increasingly not even in Cook County but in the Collar Counties all around. DuPage County, straight west of Chicago, had 103,000 residents in 1940; in 1990, there were 781,000, with new subdivisions still springing up. Nor are these just bedroom communities. Here in Oak Brook are the headquarters of Ace Hardware, Federal Signal, Waste Management, the Spiegel catalogue and, most prominently, McDonald's and its Hamburger University. One out of eight young Americans has worked at McDonald's, and millions have learned from this corporation the basics of arithmetic and literacy, good work habits and cheerful service, lessons not always taught in today's public schools. Nearby are gracefully older railroad commuter towns like Hinsdale and Downers Grove, but also Naperville, once a country village, now an edge city. And vast government laboratories have sprung up, sparking private research firms, the Argonne National Laboratory along the Sanitary and Ship Canal and the Des Plaines River.

The 13th Congressional District of Illinois includes the southern slice of DuPage County, including Oak Brook, Downers Grove and Naperville, the southwest corner of Cook County around Palos Hills, and the northern slice of Will County north of Joliet. Politically, this is a heavily Republican area, suspicious of the motives and operations of Chicago's Democrats, devoted to free enterprise and hostile to higher taxes. DuPage County has indeed become Illinois's Republican powerhouse, the home base of state Senate President Pate Philip and House Minority Leader (and former Speaker) Lee Daniels.

The congressman from the 13th is Harris Fawell, a son of DuPage County who was elected to the Illinois Senate in 1962, at 33, and served for 14 years; in 1984, when an incumbent retired, he was elected to the House. He is a fiscal conservative who spent a decade tilting at Democratic windmills; but even in the minority he had some effect. In 1990, with Democrats Charles Stenholm and Tim Penny, he formed "Porkbusters," to attack pork barrel spending in Appropriations bills; Fawell claimed credit for $2.4 billion in rescissions from 1992–94, including the honey subsidy that eventually was voted out. More important, "pork" became a rallying cry with the public, to the point that Republicans were able to discredit a Democratic crime bill by calling it pork.

But not all government action is pork in Fawell's book, and on the Education and The Workforce and Science Committees he has worked to pass important legislation. He chairs the Employer-Employee Relations Subcommittee, and was chief sponsor of the TEAM act, encouraging worker-management cooperation; it was vetoed by Bill Clinton at the behest of labor unions. His bill to allow flextime by letting employees accept compensatory time off passed the House but was not acted on in the Senate; the Clinton Administration threatened a veto of it in any case. He was a supporter of CAREERS Act, to consolidate education and training programs and of the bills to allow employers not to have to pay wages for the hours employees commute in company-owned cars and to let local governments set retirement ages for police officers and firefighters. He is the chief sponsor of bill to enforce the Supreme Court's Beck decision, which allows union members to opt out of paying dues if the money is used for politics and which the Clinton Administration has refused to enforce. One of Fawell's major causes has been a healthcare bill to allow small businesses to form purchasing cooperatives to buy health insurance; he favored the 1996 portability law. Another is repeal of the Davis-Bacon Act, which increases federal construction costs by mandating that government contractors pay local prevailing wages to construction workers. He wants OSHA to allow more flexibility for total quality management in the workplace. He is a champion of the ERISA pension law and is against efforts to get private pension plans to invest in "socially correct" firms.

On the Science Committee Fawell is a strong backer of Argonne National Laboratory and FermiLab, and he favors Impact Aid education funds for nearby communities. On Education he favors special needs funding and increased support of college grants and loans. He seeks reform of grazing laws in the West and conservation of open land in metro Chicago. He claims credit for helping to pass a law allowing seniors to deduct costs of long-term care over 7.5% of income and increasing the healthcare deductibility of the self-employed from 30% to 40% in 1997 and up a scale to 80% by 2006.

Fawell is reelected routinely every two years, but by a lower-than-usual 60% in 1996.

The People: Pop. 1990: 571,344; 4% rural; 8% age 65+; 90% White; 3% Black; 4% Asian; 3% Hispanic origin. Households: 68% married couple families; 37% married couple fams. w. children; 65% college educ.; median household income: $50,087; per capita income: $20,912; median gross rent: $619; median house value: $139,800.

1996 Presidential Vote

Dole (R)	126,594	(50%)
Clinton (D)	104,713	(41%)
Perot (I)	21,701	(9%)

1992 Presidential Vote

Bush (R)	128,612	(47%)
Clinton (D)	88,314	(32%)
Perot (I)	58,123	(21%)

Rep. Harris W. Fawell (R)

Elected 1984; b. Mar. 25, 1929, West Chicago; home, Naperville; North Central Col., B.A. 1949, Chicago-Kent Col. of Law, J.D. 1953; United Methodist; married (Ruth).

Career: Practicing atty., 1953–84; IL Senate, 1962–76.

DC Office: 2368 RHOB 20515, 202-225-3515; Fax: 202-225-9420; e-mail: hfawell@hr.house.gov.

District Offices: Clarendon Hills, 630-655-2052.

Committees: *Education & The Workforce* (4th of 25 R): Employer-Employee Relations (Chmn.); Oversight & Investigations; Workforce Protections (Vice Chmn.). *Science* (3rd of 25 R): Energy & Environment.

Group Ratings

	ADA	ACLU	AFS	LCV	CFA	CON	NFIB	COC	ACU	NTLC	CHC
1996	10	6	0	38	46	48	95	100	85	93	60
1995	20	—	—	25	23	56	—	96	60	—	—

National Journal Ratings

	1995 LIB		1995 CONS	1996 LIB		1996 CONS
Economic	0%	—	74%	27%	—	71%
Social	55%	—	43%	50%	—	48%
Foreign	42%	—	55%	44%	—	55%

Key Votes of the 104th Congress

1. Reduce Medicare Growth $	Y	5. Flag Amendment	Y	9. Cuban Embargo	Y
2. Ovrd. Product Liab. Veto	Y	6. Drop EPA Limits	Y	10. Bar Bosnia Troop $	Y
3. Increase Min. Wage	N	7. Repeal Assault-Weap. Ban	N	11. Cut Anti-Missile Defense	N
4. Welfare Reform	Y	8. Ovrd. Part. Birth Veto	Y	12. Bar U.N. Uniforms	Y

Election Results

1996 general	Harris W. Fawell (R)	141,651	(60%)	($537,449)
	Susan W. Hynes (D)	94,693	(40%)	($130,612)
1996 primary	Harris W. Fawell (R)	unopposed		
1994 general	Harris W. Fawell (R)	124,312	(73%)	($278,469)
	William A. Riley (D)	45,709	(27%)	

FOURTEENTH DISTRICT

A few dozen miles beyond Chicago's Loop there is an invisible line marking two different Chicagos. One is the Chicago dominated by blacks and descendants of the vast immigrations of 1840–1924 and 1970s–90s, a Chicago where certain loyalties are taken for granted: loyalty to ethnic group, to church (usually the Catholic Church, often with an ethnic prefix), and to party (almost always the Democrats). This Chicago is a gritty city, where personal cheerfulness and courtesy lighten up days otherwise as cold and impersonal as the gray Chicago winter sky. The other Chicago is the beginning of the Great Plains, originally a white Anglo-Saxon Protestant Chicago, a place whose residents are products of the first great wave of immigration to America. The tone of this Chicago is lighter, its streets and highways cleaner and neater, its daily life generally free from evidence of unpleasantness and deprivation. People in this Chicago think of themselves as typical Americans, and their geographical vision takes in the vast plains. Ronald Reagan grew up in Downstate Illinois within the orbit of this Chicago (though he did live in the city briefly), and its spirit helped to characterize his presidency. His migration to southern California, incidentally, is not atypical: you can see in the geometric grids and Republican voting patterns of Orange County or Phoenix almost exact replicas of the grids and patterns in Chicago's suburban "Collar Counties," transported to the once-empty Southwest on the Atchison, Topeka & Santa Fe or out U.S. 66 from their beginnings in Chicago's Loop.

The 14th Congressional District of Illinois straddles this line between metropolitan Chicago and Downstate Illinois. It gets as close as 30 miles to Chicago's Loop, in western DuPage County, with two great Chicagoland landmarks: Cantigny, the estate of Colonel Robert McCormick, longtime publisher of the *Chicago Tribune*, and FermiLab, the world's fastest energy particle accelerator and employer of some 2,000 people: icons of political conservatism and high technology within two miles of each other. The 14th also contains the Fox River Valley, and its industrial cities of Elgin and Aurora, and antique St. Charles in the heart of the Collar Counties. Farther west, amid what may be the world's richest cornfields, the 14th passes through

DeKalb, long the world's leading manufacturer of barbed wire, and goes on to Kendall and Lee Counties, including Reagan's boyhood home in Dixon. This is some of the most heavily Republican territory in the country. Northern Illinois was settled, when Chicago was just a frontier village, by Yankees from Ohio, Indiana, Upstate New York and New England: people who formed the heart of the Republican Party from its founding in 1854, and who would form the core of the Grand Army of the Republic a few years later. Their descendants, in this Anglo-Saxon extension of Chicagoland, remain solidly Republican today.

The congressman from the 14th is Dennis Hastert, a Republican who like many congressmen from high-income districts full of entrepreneurs and professionals are politicians from relatively modest backgrounds. After college he taught government and history and coached wrestling for 16 years at Yorkville High School in Kendall County. Starting in 1980, he served six years in the Illinois Assembly; he was chosen by the party to run for Congress after the March 1986 primary when the incumbent was fatally stricken with cancer. Hastert was attacked by some Republicans as insufficiently conservative and won with only 52%.

In the 1990s Hastert emerged as one of the leaders of House Republicans. Even before the Republican takeover in 1994 he worked to produce a Republican healthcare plan—experience that was valuable once they were the majority. His healthcare package passed the House in March 1996, and included removal of preexisting conditions, allowing small businesses to use pools to buy insurance, creating Medical Savings Accounts, increasing on a sliding scale tax deductibility of health insurance for the self-employed, and reforming malpractice laws. He also helped put together the Republicans' Medicare proposals, which were designed to offer more choices and did not "cut" total Medicare spending as Democrats insisted. Another Hastert cause was inserted into the Contract with America: repealing the Social Security "earnings tax"—the deduction of benefits among senior citizens who earn over a certain figure.

Hastert was involved in many other issues. After managing Tom DeLay's successful campaign for whip, Hastert was appointed chief deputy whip after the 1994 election and spent much time creating united Republican positions, holding together the party's majority, and negotiating with the Senate. On occasion he substituted for DeLay, as when DeLay refused to support term limits. Hastert was active on the Commerce Committee as well, notably on the tortuous negotiations which ultimately produced the Telecommunications Act of 1996. He also worked to restore funds to the White House Office of Drug Control Policy and to free employers in high pollution zones from a Clean Air Act obligation to reduce employees' car trips.

Hastert has been politically secure in the 14th District, enough so that in 1992 he declined to try to get his Democratic opponent off the ballot for insufficient signatures—"We thought people ought to hear the issues." In 1996 he won with 64% of the vote.

The People: Pop. 1990: 571,540; 21% rural; 9% age 65+; 84% White; 4% Black; 2% Asian; 10% Hispanic origin. Households: 65% married couple families; 35% married couple fams. w. children; 50% college educ.; median household income: $39,815; per capita income: $15,769; median gross rent: $484; median house value: $100,100.

1996 Presidential Vote			**1992 Presidential Vote**		
Dole (R)	103,773	(48%)	Bush (R)	105,700	(44%)
Clinton (D)	89,939	(41%)	Clinton (D)	83,109	(34%)
Perot (I)	22,148	(10%)	Perot (I)	52,914	(22%)

Rep. J. Dennis Hastert (R)

Elected 1986; b. Jan. 2, 1942, Aurora, IL; home, Yorkville; Wheaton Col., B.A. 1964, N. IL U., M.A. 1967; Protestant; married (Jean).

Career: High schl. teacher & coach, 1965–80; IL House of Reps., 1980–86.

DC Office: 2241 RHOB 20515, 202-225-2976; Fax: 202-225-0697; e-mail: dhastert@hr.house.gov.

District Offices: Batavia, 630-406-1114.

Committees: *Chief Deputy Majority Whip. Commerce* (7th of 28 R): Energy & Power; Health & the Environment (Vice-Chmn.); Telecommunications, Trade & Consumer Protection. *Government Reform & Oversight* (3rd of 24 R): National Economic Growth, Natural Resources & Regulatory Affairs; National Security, International Affairs & Criminal Justice (Chmn.).

Group Ratings

	ADA	ACLU	AFS	LCV	CFA	CON	NFIB	COC	ACU	NTLC	CHC
1996	0	0	0	15	15	30	100	100	100	100	100
1995	0	—	—	0	0	38	—	100	92	—	—

National Journal Ratings

	1995 LIB	—	1995 CONS	1996 LIB	—	1996 CONS
Economic	0%	—	74%	0%	—	82%
Social	0%	—	79%	0%	—	90%
Foreign	15%	—	73%	21%	—	72%

Key Votes of the 104th Congress

1. Reduce Medicare Growth $	Y	5. Flag Amendment	Y	9. Cuban Embargo	Y
2. Ovrd. Product Liab. Veto	Y	6. Drop EPA Limits	N	10. Bar Bosnia Troop $	Y
3. Increase Min. Wage	N	7. Repeal Assault-Weap. Ban	Y	11. Cut Anti-Missile Defense	N
4. Welfare Reform	Y	8. Ovrd. Part. Birth Veto	Y	12. Bar U.N. Uniforms	Y

Election Results

1996 general	J. Dennis Hastert (R)	134,432	(64%)	($968,055)
	Doug Mains (D)	74,332	(36%)	($125,997)
1996 primary	J. Dennis Hastert (R)	unopposed		
1994 general	J. Dennis Hastert (R)	110,204	(76%)	($696,217)
	Steve Denari (D)	33,891	(24%)	($54,330)

FIFTEENTH DISTRICT

South from Chicago the Illinois Central Railroad heads to the city of New Orleans on a railbed elevated a few feet above the rich black soil of the Illinois prairie, topsoil reaching down not just inches but feet. This land dazzled its first settlers, who were used to the land further east that had to be cleared of trees and stumps before it could be plowed; this treeless prairie could be cultivated almost immediately, and with bounteous results. Today, this remains farming country, made up not of small family farms but of large commercial operations, typically of 1,000 acres or more. Cultivating this soil is a business, requiring informed decisions about crop selection (soybeans and corn are the current favorites), maximizing yields, proper pesticides, marketing decisions, watching farm export prospects and, until the 1996 Freedom to Farm Act, taking advantage of government programs. The landscape on the prairies of eastern Illinois is marked by only a few towns, the largest of which, Champaign-Urbana and Bloomington-Normal, are the sites of universities (the University of Illinois and Illinois Normal). Politically, these prairie lands have been Republican, often very Republican; they incline much more to the politics of former Speaker Joseph Cannon, a Republican from the manufacturing city of Danville east of Urbana, than to that of Vice President Adlai Stevenson, a Democrat from Bloomington, who served under *laissez-faire* Democrat Grover Cleveland and was the grandfather of the Adlai Stevenson nominated by the Democrats for president in 1952 and 1956.

The 15th Congressional District of Illinois occupies much of this prairie, beginning 60 miles from Chicago, where the Illinois Central heads toward Kankakee, and moving over 150 miles of prairie to the courthouse town of Monticello. It includes Bloomington, Champaign-Urbana and Danville, and runs south almost to the National Road and U.S. 40, traditionally the line between northern Republican and southern Democratic Illinois. Today, the area is strongly Republican and has been represented for years by Republicans who have been active in local businesses, civic affairs and state legislative politics.

The congressman from the 15th, Thomas Ewing, fits that description. He served in the Army in the 1950s, then headed the Pontiac and Harvey Chambers of Commerce, got a law degree and became an assistant state's attorney, then was elected to the Illinois House in 1974, at 39. Ewing owes his election to Congress indirectly to Newt Gingrich, for Gingrich beat Ewing's predecessor, Edward Madigan, 87–85 in the race for minority whip in March 1989, and in late 1990 Madigan was happy to accept George Bush's appointment as secretary of Agriculture. (Madigan died in December 1994, as Gingrich was preparing to become speaker.) Ewing, assistant and deputy minority leader in Springfield from 1982, quickly became the overwhelming favorite. He beat the Democrat 66%–31% in the July 1991 special election.

Ewing has compiled an almost impeccably conservative voting record, but seems to have concentrated on issues of local import. Thanks to then-Minority Leader Robert Michel, he got a seat on the Agriculture Committee; thanks to then-Minority Whip Newt Gingrich, and the work he did to enable Republicans to win a majority, Ewing became just three years later a chairman, of the Agriculture Subcommittee on Risk Management and Specialty Crops. This has jurisdiction over commodity futures, crop insurance, and the crops other than cotton, wheat, corn, soybeans, rice, which traditionally have had their own subcommittees. Ewing is a promoter of ethanol, produced from Illinois prairie grain and by Decatur-based Archer-Daniels-Midland; in the 104th Congress he objected when Ways and Means lowered the ethanol tax subsidy from 54 to 51 cents a gallon and barred new entrants from the program. He fought hard against eliminating sugar price supports; high sugar prices guarantee a market for manufacturers of high-fructose syrup (ADM again). Ewing and Mark Foley of Florida led the sugar coalition to a 217–208 victory, and sugar joined cotton as the crop subsidies which the Republicans were not able to wipe out in the Freedom to Farm Act. Ewing also used the Corrections Day procedure to exempt vegetable oils from the strict safety requirements mandated for shipping oil by the 1993 law passed in response to the Exxon *Valdez* oil spill. Like most farm state congressmen, Ewing favors Most Favored Nation status for China every year; he would go a step farther with his Export Stabilization Act to declare permanent MFN status for China and 16 former Communist countries.

Despite all this Ewing had vigorous opposition from Democrat Laurel Prussing, former Champaign County Auditor. She attacked Newt Gingrich and Medicare "cuts," and called Ewing "Tornado Tom" for allegedly twisting his position on term limits. Ewing won, but with just 57% of the vote, his lowest percentage.

The People: Pop. 1990: 571,292; 34% rural; 13% age 65+; 89% White; 7% Black; 2% Asian; 2% Hispanic origin. Households: 55% married couple families; 26% married couple fams. w. children; 45% college educ.; median household income: $26,760; per capita income: $12,709; median gross rent: $372; median house value: $52,300.

1996 Presidential Vote			1992 Presidential Vote		
Clinton (D)	100,016	(45%)	Clinton (D)	107,914	(42%)
Dole (R)	98,926	(45%)	Bush (R)	98,378	(39%)
Perot (I)	19,478	(9%)	Perot (I)	47,280	(19%)

Rep. Thomas W. Ewing (R)

Elected July 1991; b. Sept. 19, 1935, Atlanta, GA; home, Pontiac; Milliken U., B.S. 1957, John Marshall Law Schl., J.D. 1968; Methodist; married (Connie).

Career: Army, 1957–59; Army Reserves, 1959–63; Exec. Dir., Pontiac & Harvey Chambers of Commerce, 1963–68; Asst. State Atty., Livingston Cnty., 1968–73; IL House of Reps., 1974–91.

DC Office: 2417 RHOB 20515, 202-225-2371; Fax: 202-225-8071.

District Offices: Bloomington, 309-662-9371; Danville, 217-431-8230; Pontiac, 815-844-7660; Urbana, 217-328-0165.

Committees: *Agriculture* (5th of 27 R): Department Operations, Nutrition & Foreign Agriculture (Vice Chmn.); Risk Management & Specialty Crops (Chmn.). *Science* (17th of 25 R): Basic Research; Technology. *Transportation & Infrastructure* (9th of 40 R): Aviation; Surface Transportation.

Group Ratings

	ADA	ACLU	AFS	LCV	CFA	CON	NFIB	COC	ACU	NTLC	CHC
1996	0	12	0	15	38	24	100	100	100	100	100
1995	0	—	—	6	15	53	—	96	96	—	—

National Journal Ratings

	1995 LIB — 1995 CONS	1996 LIB — 1996 CONS
Economic	0% — 74%	0% — 82%
Social	30% — 68%	0% — 90%
Foreign	15% — 73%	30% — 65%

Key Votes of the 104th Congress

1. Reduce Medicare Growth $	Y	5. Flag Amendment	Y	9. Cuban Embargo	Y
2. Ovrd. Product Liab. Veto	Y	6. Drop EPA Limits	Y	10. Bar Bosnia Troop $	Y
3. Increase Min. Wage	N	7. Repeal Assault-Weap. Ban	Y	11. Cut Anti-Missile Defense	N
4. Welfare Reform	Y	8. Ovrd. Part. Birth Veto	Y	12. Bar U.N. Uniforms	Y

Election Results

1996 general	Thomas W. Ewing (R)	121,019	(57%)	($664,934)
	Laurel Lunt Prussing (D)	90,065	(43%)	($369,185)
1996 primary	Thomas W. Ewing (R)	unopposed		
1994 general	Thomas W. Ewing (R)	108,857	(68%)	($511,926)
	Paul Alexander (D)	50,874	(32%)	($144,040)

SIXTEENTH DISTRICT

The far northwest corner of Illinois is one of the heartlands of the Republican Party. Here, in the town square of Freeport, some 15,000 people came to hear Abraham Lincoln and Stephen Douglas in one of their seven debates, and on terrain most partial to Lincoln. Settled by New England Yankees, northern Illinois was one of the strongest Republican constituencies in 1860 and for years after. Not far away, on a little river once navigable by Mississippi River steamboats, is Galena, one of the earliest settlements in northern Illinois, the home of Ulysses S. Grant before he became general and then president; not far away are Tampico and Dixon, birthplace and boyhood home of Ronald Reagan. Farther up on the Rock River is Rockford, the home town of John Anderson, a conservative Republican for most of the 20 years he served in Congress before he became known as the liberal reformist independent candidate for president in 1980, and of Lynn Martin, congresswoman for 10 years and George Bush's secretary of Labor. During all these years, northern Illinois, perhaps inspired by Democratic Chicago, remained steadfastly Republican; it backed Herbert Hoover in 1932, Barry Goldwater in 1964 and George Bush in 1992 when most of America and Illinois were going the other way.

The 16th Congressional District consists of much of northwest Illinois; the largest city here is Rockford, headquarters of the paleo-conservative Rockford Institute. The district extends west to the hilly, almost mountainous country around Galena and the Mississippi River, and east to McHenry County, full of new subdivisions surrounding old towns, where Motorola has been opening new cellular phone plants to supply Japan and affluent young families make their way up through free enterprise and have conservative cultural values. This is not atypical; according to the current congressman, "This quiet northern Illinois district is responsible for between one-third and one-half of the state's manufactured exports and is a leader in agricultural and processed food exports."

That congressman is Don Manzullo, an unsuccessful candidate in the 1990 primary who won the seat in 1992. Manzullo grew up in Rockford, where his family owns Manzullo's Drive-In Restaurant and Italian Villa. While in college in Washington in the mid-1960s, he worked for Republican candidates, and he has practiced law in Illinois since 1970. He lives on a cattle-breeding farm, writes poetry and books on constitutional law, and ran a radio talk show; he and his wife home-school their three young children. He lost the 1990 primary 54%–46% to a moderate, who after revelations of personal problems then lost the general to Democrat John Cox. Cox favored increased taxes, opposed capital punishment and was hurt when ultra-Republican McHenry County was added in redistricting. Manzullo ran again and, with support from conservative Christians, beat a moderate 56%–44% in the primary, attacking him for supporting gasoline, cigarette and computer software tax increases in the legislature. Cox campaigned for higher taxes; Manzullo for a 10% across-the-board income tax cut. Manzullo lost narrowly in Rockford and in Winnebago County but he won nearly 2–1 in McHenry County and won overall with 56%.

Manzullo's focus in the House has been on increasing manufactured exports. He supported NAFTA and GATT: "opening new markets benefits the United States." He got a seat on International Relations and on its Subcommittee on International Economic Policy & Trade, where he hopes to spur more exports. He opposed cutting off Export-Import Bank financing to China, saying that Illinois's Caterpillar would be replaced on the Three Gorges Dam with Japanese heavy equipment manufacturers. On a variety of legislation he has taken what might be considered common sense initiatives. He attacked the relocation to the U.S. of Iraqi prisoners of war when the needs of some Gulf war veterans were being ignored. He amended the Clean Air Act to make the car pooling provisions voluntary. He got the Navy to stop giving away deactivated ships to allies; it now leases or sells them, generating $600 million in revenue. He wants to limit the power of federal judges to raise state and local taxes by requiring judges to take their decisions' impact on the community into account before they are issued.

Manzullo was reelected with a resounding 71% in 1994—the best showing in this district since 1972—and with 60% in 1996/

The People: Pop. 1990: 571,488; 26% rural; 12% age 65+; 91% White; 5% Black; 1% Asian; 3% Hispanic origin. Households: 63% married couple families; 31% married couple fams. w. children; 43% college educ.; median household income: $34,668; per capita income: $15,107; median gross rent: $392; median house value: $73,300.

1996 Presidential Vote

Dole (R)	111,641	(47%)
Clinton (D)	99,397	(42%)
Perot (I)	24,153	(10%)

1992 Presidential Vote

Bush (R)	108,949	(42%)
Clinton (D)	95,103	(36%)
Perot (I)	56,169	(21%)

Rep. Donald Manzullo (R)

Elected 1992; b. Mar. 24, 1944, Rockford; home, Egan; American U., B.S. 1967, Marquette U. Law Schl., J.D. 1970; Baptist; married (Freda).

Career: Practicing atty., 1970–92; author.

DC Office: 409 CHOB 20515, 202-225-5676; Fax: 202-225-5284.

District Offices: Crystal Lake, 815-356-9800; Rockford, 815-394-1231.

Committees: *Banking & Financial Services* (28th of 30 R): Domestic & International Monetary Policy. *International Relations* (12th of 26 R): Asia & the Pacific; International Economic Policy & Trade. *Small Business* (4th of 19 R): Government Programs & Oversight; Tax, Finance & Exports (Chmn.). *Joint Economic Committee* (2nd of 10 Reps.).

Group Ratings

	ADA	ACLU	AFS	LCV	CFA	CON	NFIB	COC	ACU	NTLC	CHC
1996	5	12	0	15	31	76	100	94	100	98	100
1995	0	—	—	0	0	56	—	100	100	—	—

National Journal Ratings

	1995 LIB — 1995 CONS	1996 LIB — 1996 CONS
Economic	0% — 74%	0% — 82%
Social	30% — 68%	24% — 72%
Foreign	28% — 65%	30% — 65%

Key Votes of the 104th Congress

1. Reduce Medicare Growth $	Y	5. Flag Amendment	Y	9. Cuban Embargo	Y
2. Ovrd. Product Liab. Veto	Y	6. Drop EPA Limits	N	10. Bar Bosnia Troop $	Y
3. Increase Min. Wage	N	7. Repeal Assault-Weap. Ban	Y	11. Cut Anti-Missile Defense	N
4. Welfare Reform	Y	8. Ovrd. Part. Birth Veto	Y	12. Bar U.N. Uniforms	Y

Election Results

1996 general	Donald Manzullo (R)	137,523	(60%)	($786,063)
	Catherine M. Lee (D)	90,575	(40%)	($391,414)
1996 primary	Donald Manzullo (R)	unopposed		
1994 general	Donald Manzullo (R)	117,238	(71%)	($579,059)
	Pete Sullivan (D)	48,736	(29%)	($214,715)

SEVENTEENTH DISTRICT

Illinois's western prairies are some of America's richest agricultural land. This land was first settled by Yankees coming overland from northern Indiana and Ohio and Upstate New York. After 1848, Germans, who left their homeland in search of better opportunities, settled this land that in so many ways resembles the flat, orderly plains of northern Germany. All these migrants farmed quarter-sections and built small towns, with banks and stores, community churches and libraries. In time, investors built farm machinery factories, and the Quad Cities of the Mississippi—Davenport, Iowa, and Rock Island, Moline and East Moline, Illinois—became one of the nation's biggest agricultural equipment manufacturing centers. These plants were unionized in the 1930s and 1940s, and in post-World War II America their wages went up as the demand for ever more sophisticated machines rose among the Midwest's government-subsidized farmers. But eventually the cost of subsidies rose too high and the market had its revenge. In the early 1980s, farm profits vanished, land values declined and orders for new machinery and equipment dried up. The result was a depression in western Illinois and neighboring Iowa, and a political swing toward the Democrats and away from the Republicans who had been the ancestral party in most of this area. Now Republicanism seems to be returning, but not with the speed of the Democratic trend a dozen years ago.

The 17th Congressional District includes most of Illinois's Mississippi River border with Iowa plus half a dozen more prairie counties to the east. For years, its Democratic base in the Quad Cities was outvoted by Republican counties elsewhere. But in 1982, longtime Republican congressman Tom Railsback lost to a conservative in the primary; ready to take advantage of this opening was Democrat Lane Evans, a local legal services attorney angry at the Reagan recession who took a gamble in running and ended up winning with 53%. Evans has represented the district ever since. He brings to his work an earnestness that is almost square, a pleasant, boyish demeanor which will never be mistaken for East Coast slick. He served in the Marine Corps from 1969–71, then went to college and law school and did most of his lawyering for the poor. He calls himself a "populist" rather than a liberal; by most standards, his voting record is one of the most liberal and pro-union in the House. He was a strong opponent of NAFTA and GATT. He fervently favored higher agricultural subsidies during his 5-year tenure on the Agriculture Committee, but left that post to take a seat on National Security in 1988, even as farm subsidies were cut back in 1985 and 1990 and phased out in 1996.

Evans is ranking Democrat on the Veterans' Committee and has devoted much time to veterans' issues. He worked hard for years to get compensation for veterans who claimed they were harmed by their exposure to Agent Orange, and ultimately succeeded. In 1996 he passed a bill providing benefits to children of Vietnam veterans exposed to Agent Orange who were born with spina bifida—the first entitlement for children of veterans. In 1992, he passed measures to provide mental health services for women veterans who are sexually traumatized on active duty. In 1994 he began to investigate what he and others have characterized as Gulf war syndrome, despite lack of evidence of causal connection between the variety of ailments complained of and Gulf war conditions. Evans's approach to traditional veterans' organizations and to Agent Orange was very different from that of longtime Chairman Sonny Montgomery, whom Evans challenged in the Democratic Caucus after the 1992 election; Montgomery won by only 127–123, but Evans did not challenge him for the ranking minority position in 1994 and Montgomery retired in 1996.

From his National Security post, Evans has concentrated on finding alternatives to tritium production; he has also questioned how much export controls should be relaxed on critical weapons materials. His major cause on the committee has been a ban on land mines, which continue to injure thousands years after wars are over. In 1996 he sponsored a law designed to encourage an international ban on land mines by imposing a one-year moratorium three years hence on U.S. land mines except on international borders and calling on the president to negotiate similar moratoria, which may end up saving many thousands of lives and limbs.

In the years of agricultural unrest in western Illinois, Evans was reelected by wide margins, and he won with 66% and 60% in 1990 and 1992; in the more prosperous mid-1990s, his margins have been narrower. In 1994 against an underfunded candidate he won with 55%. In 1996 he faced Mark Baker, a former TV anchor in Quincy, in the southern end of the district, who had good financing and high-level Republican support. Baker argued that Evans was ignoring the area's agricultural and transportation needs, and promised to serve on those committees, and accused him of "a far-left social agenda and tax-and-spend record." Evans campaigned against

Newt Gingrich and Medicare "cuts" and attacked Baker's opposition to gun control and abortion. The final result was a 52%–47% Evans victory. He carried Rock Island and the central part of the district, but lost the northern end and the area around Quincy by wide margins.

On election night Evans said, "About the only way I can think to pay you back is to keep the pledge I made when you sent me to Washington in 1982: to work for the seniors who built this country, the veterans who defended it, and the children who inherited it." Democrats claimed that he had survived the toughest challenge Republicans could make, and can hold the seat indefinitely. Republicans claimed that Evans's declining percentages showed he was on the way out; Baker said he had not decided whether to run again. The likelihood is for a serious contest in the 17th District again in 1998. When Senator Paul Simon announced his retirement in 1995, Evans gave serious consideration to the race, but decided not to run; in early 1997 there was speculation he might run in the primary against Senator Carol Moseley-Braun in 1998, but decided against this too.

The People: Pop. 1990: 571,585; 38% rural; 17% age 65+; 93% White; 3% Black; 1% Asian; 3% Hispanic origin. Households: 59% married couple families; 26% married couple fams. w. children; 38% college educ.; median household income: $25,195; per capita income: $12,052; median gross rent: $309; median house value: $41,200.

1996 Presidential Vote

Clinton (D)	119,918	(51%)
Dole (R)	89,447	(38%)
Perot (I)	23,176	(10%)

1992 Presidential Vote

Clinton (D)	124,175	(47%)
Bush (R)	95,554	(36%)
Perot (I)	45,566	(17%)

Rep. Lane Evans (D)

Elected 1982; b. Aug. 4, 1951, Rock Island; home, Rock Island; Augustana Col., B.A. 1974, Georgetown U., J.D. 1978; Catholic; single.

Career: Marine Corps, 1969–71; Practicing atty., 1978–82.

DC Office: 2335 RHOB 20515, 202-225-5905; Fax: 202-225-5396.

District Offices: Galesburg, 309-342-4411; Moline, 309-793-5760.

Committees: *National Security* (7th of 25 D): Military Procurement; Military Readiness. *Veterans' Affairs* (RMM of 13 D).

Group Ratings

	ADA	ACLU	AFS	LCV	CFA	CON	NFIB	COC	ACU	NTLC	CHC
1996	95	94	100	85	92	9	19	19	0	9	7
1995	95	—	—	100	100	9	—	8	12	—	—

National Journal Ratings

	1995 LIB		1995 CONS	1996 LIB		1996 CONS
Economic	92%	—	6%	85%	—	11%
Social	88%	—	0%	75%	—	24%
Foreign	84%	—	15%	90%	—	0%

Key Votes of the 104th Congress

1. Reduce Medicare Growth $	N	5. Flag Amendment	N	9. Cuban Embargo	N
2. Ovrd. Product Liab. Veto	N	6. Drop EPA Limits	Y	10. Bar Bosnia Troop $	Y
3. Increase Min. Wage	Y	7. Repeal Assault-Weap. Ban	N	11. Cut Anti-Missile Defense	Y
4. Welfare Reform	N	8. Ovrd. Part. Birth Veto	N	12. Bar U.N. Uniforms	N

Election Results

1996 general	Lane Evans (D)	120,008	(52%)	($629,624)
	Mark Baker (R)	109,240	(47%)	($506,793)
1996 primary	Lane Evans (D)	unopposed		
1994 general	Lane Evans (D)	95,312	(55%)	($270,939)
	Jim Anderson (R)	79,471	(45%)	($15,583)

EIGHTEENTH DISTRICT

Old vaudeville bookers, presented with a new act, used to ask, "Will it play in Peoria?" The implication was that if an act went over in this small city on the bluffs above the Illinois River, 154 miles from Chicago and 171 miles from St. Louis, it would go over just about anywhere. In the first half of this century, Peoria did seem pretty typical of America. If its citizens were mostly of British or German descent, with a small percentage of blacks, that was the image of ordinary America that prevailed up through the 1960s, despite the great immigrations of 1880–1924 and the northward urban migrations of southern rural blacks of 1940–1965. And for years, Peoria was a good test market for commercial products. But Peoria's economy, arguably typical at mid-century, is less so today. For this is still a heavy manufacturing town, dominated by big plants that produce farm machinery and earth-moving equipment. Its biggest employer is Caterpillar, the world's standard producer of earth-moving and construction equipment, and one of America's major exporters. And there are more than just memories here of the sharp divide between blue collar and white collar, union and management, Democrat and Republican—the basis of the class warfare politics that was the norm in the heavy industrial metropolises of the Great Lakes region for three or four decades starting with the sitdown strikes of the late 1930s. But the blue collar workers now are not as numerous and the unions not as strong. The Peoria area went through terrible times in the 1980s, as big farm machinery plants laid off workers and even closed down; now employment seems permanently down. And Caterpillar, struck by the United Auto Workers in 1992, hired replacement workers and continued to operate—not without some friction and inefficiency, but profitably—something unheard of a dozen or more years before.

The 18th Congressional District of Illinois, variously configured, has been the Peoria district since the 1940s. It has been represented by two national Republican leaders: from 1934–48 by Everett McKinley Dirksen, who was elected senator in 1950 and was Senate Republican leader from 1959–69, and Robert Michel, congressman from 1956–94 and Republican House leader from 1980–94. The 18th's boundaries have changed considerably over that time; currently they extend south along the Illinois River and almost to Springfield, away from historically Republican Peoria toward the historically margin counties of central Illinois.

The congressman from the 18th District is Ray LaHood, a Republican elected in 1994. LaHood grew up in Peoria, the grandson of an immigrant from Lebanon and son of a restaurant manager. He worked his way through school, spent six years teaching in Catholic schools, then moved to Rock Island where he worked with delinquent teens and became a staffer for Congressman Tom Railsback. He served in the Illinois House in 1982, then worked for Congressman Robert Michel in Peoria and, from 1990–94, as his chief of staff in Washington. Michel had represented the 18th district since 1956, a pleasant and decent man who could be a tough partisan on occasion but always maintained amicable relations with Democratic leaders.

It was an approach very different from that of Newt Gingrich, whose election as minority whip in March 1989 Michel opposed; and although they worked together there was also tension. Gingrich pointedly declined to rule out running against Michel for Republican leader after the 1994 election; Michel, faced with a December 1993 filing deadline, decided to retire. LaHood ran to replace his boss, and in the Republican primary beat state Representative Judy Koehler 50%–40%, carrying the Peoria area but running behind in the rest of the district. In the general, LaHood's Democratic opponent was Douglas Stephens, a labor lawyer and small businessmen, who held Michel to 52% and 55% in 1982 and 1988. Stephens favored school prayer, term limits and abortion limits, and called for House members to debate and vote from their districts via interactive television. As for LaHood's experience with Michel, Stephens said, "I'm not sure being Arnold Palmer's caddy makes you as good a golfer as he is." He put on an energetic campaign, but in this Republican year LaHood carried all but one county and won 60%–39%.

LaHood did not sign the Contract with America and did not seem to fare well at first in Newt Gingrich's House. He lost his bid for a seat on the Appropriations Committee, on which Michel had served for years, and he voiced objection to the Republicans' tax cuts—an old-time Republican voice for fiscal responsibility out of tune with the Contract melody. His voting record verged to the moderate. Yet he ardently defended Republican budget-cutting, championed strongly the Republican approach to Medicare, and voted for the Republican welfare reform. He supported the balanced budget amendment, decried continuing deficits, and supported cuts in domestic discretionary spending. He worked on the 1996 Freedom to Farm Act, which phased out most farm subsidies, and went after food stamp fraud as well; he also worked to reform the soybean checkoff program to make it fairer to applicants. And he was often chosen to preside over the House, a tribute to his knowledge of its procedures and his capacity for fairness to all. He looked after local issues as well: the silt problem in Peoria Lake, TCI's decision to cut WGN from central Illinois cable, federal funding for a highway directly from Chicago to Peoria.

Still there were differences in emphasis. He was skeptical about the strategy of letting the government be shut down by Clinton vetoes, and in January 1996 he realized that the public opposed the shutdown and Clinton had won the PR battle. After being reelected with a comfortable 59%, he was still strong for Medicare reform, dismissing the idea of a commission and saying that Congress should address it. He was eager to attack the trial lawyers and seek tort reform. And he advanced two original ideas. One was a nonstarter, banning the Electoral College: "It's kind of nonsensical in an era when every other election goes to the winner of the popular vote." The other was embraced by most other members and hailed by editorial writers: he and Colorado Democrat David Skaggs proposed a bipartisan retreat in Hershey, Pennsylvania, in March 1997, not to discuss issues, but for members to get to known each other, "to foster a Congress that is more civil and to create better communication among members."

The People: Pop. 1990: 572,238; 37% rural; 14% age 65+; 93% White; 5% Black; 1% Asian; 1% Hispanic origin. Households: 61% married couple families; 28% married couple fams. w. children; 43% college educ.; median household income: $30,189; per capita income: $13,792; median gross rent: $352; median house value: $51,600.

1996 Presidential Vote

Dole (R)	118,572	(47%)
Clinton (D)	112,678	(44%)
Perot (I)	20,975	(8%)

1992 Presidential Vote

Clinton (D)	117,483	(42%)
Bush (R)	114,090	(41%)
Perot (I)	47,087	(17%)

Rep. Ray LaHood (R)

Elected 1994; b. Dec. 6, 1945, Peoria; home, Peoria; Canton Jr. Col., 1963–65, Bradley U., B.S. 1971; Catholic; married (Kathy).

Career: Jr. High Schl. Teacher, 1971–77; Dir., Rock Island Youth Svcs., 1972–74; Chief Planner, Bi-state Planning Comm., 1974–76; Dist. A.A., U.S. Rep. Tom Railsback, 1977–82; IL House of Reps., 1982; Dist. A.A., U.S. Rep. Bob Michel, 1983–90, Chief of Staff, 1990–94.

DC Office: 329 CHOB 20515, 202-225-6201; Fax: 202-225-9249.

District Offices: Jacksonville, 217-245-1431; Peoria, 309-671-7027; Springfield, 217-793-0808.

Committees: *Agriculture* (19th of 27 R): Department Operations, Nutrition & Foreign Agriculture; Forestry, Resource Conservation & Research. *Transportation & Infrastructure* (21st of 40 R): Aviation; Surface Transportation. *Veterans' Affairs* (16th of 16 R): Benefits.

Group Ratings

	ADA	ACLU	AFS	LCV	CFA	CON	NFIB	COC	ACU	NTLC	CHC
1996	10	12	25	31	38	79	86	88	80	88	73
1995	10	—	—	6	23	31	—	88	72	—	—

National Journal Ratings

	1995 LIB — 1995 CONS			1996 LIB — 1996 CONS		
Economic	36%	—	60%	33%	—	64%
Social	41%	—	58%	35%	—	62%
Foreign	27%	—	72%	41%	—	56%

Key Votes of the 104th Congress

1. Reduce Medicare Growth $	Y	5. Flag Amendment	Y	9. Cuban Embargo	Y
2. Ovrd. Product Liab. Veto	Y	6. Drop EPA Limits	Y	10. Bar Bosnia Troop $	Y
3. Increase Min. Wage	Y	7. Repeal Assault-Weap. Ban	Y	11. Cut Anti-Missile Defense	N
4. Welfare Reform	Y	8. Ovrd. Part. Birth Veto	Y	12. Bar U.N. Uniforms	Y

Election Results

1996 general	Ray LaHood (R)	143,110	(59%)	($699,963)
	Mike Curran (D)	98,413	(41%)	($113,363)
1996 primary	Ray LaHood (R)	unopposed		
1994 general	Ray LaHood (R)	119,838	(60%)	($697,727)
	G. Douglas Stephens (D)	78,332	(39%)	($345,701)

NINETEENTH DISTRICT

Southern Illinois is a land of prairies, of flat, treeless land sloping imperceptibly down to the Ohio and Mississippi Rivers. It was settled almost entirely from the south by farmers coming overland from Kentucky, such as Abraham Lincoln's family. Just beyond the Ohio River, they found hilly terrain, some of which turned out to have coal deposits. To the north they must have been astonished, after miles of thick forest, to see the great American prairie stretch before them, a vast sea of empty land extending past the horizon. The prairie lands proved wondrously rich, and were soon criss-crossed by rail lines taking their produce away and bringing in products of industrial civilization from Chicago and St. Louis and points east. About the same time, vast coal deposits were found in southern Illinois, producing one mining town after another: this was the home turf of John L. Lewis, the imperious leader of the United Mine Workers for half a century and, in the late 1930s and early 1940s, one of the most powerful and eloquent figures in American politics.

The 19th Congressional District of Illinois covers most of the eastern half of southern Illinois. Mostly it is south of the old National Road, which became U.S. 40 and is paralleled by Interstate 70, the traditional boundary between the part of Downstate Illinois settled by southerners and the Downstate settled by Yankees—a boundary also between traditional Democrats and traditional Republicans. North of that line, the 19th includes Decatur, a small city that is home of the giant Archer-Daniels-Midland company, the major producer and promoter of government-subsidized ethanol. About a third of the 19th is prairie, straddling or south of the National Road line; the other third is far Downstate, the Egypt region as it is called, where people speak with what Yankees regard as southern accents and southern mores prevail, including an attachment to a conservatively inclined Democratic Party.

The congressman from the 19th District is Glenn Poshard, a Democrat first elected in 1988. Poshard's parents' first home was a corn crib, and at 16 he was a $1-an-hour farm laborer; he joined the Army at 17 and served in Korea in the early 1960s; he graduated from Southern Illinois University in 1970. He taught history and government and coached high school sports in the coal country towns of Galatia and Thompsonville and got an education Ph.D. He was elected to the state Senate in 1984 and 1986, where he chaired a committee and worked to cut down on pollution from coal use. When longtime (1954–74, 1984–88) and colorful incumbent Ken Gray retired a second time, the earnest and hard-working Poshard was elected to the House in 1988. In 1992 Poshard was redistricted in with another Democratic incumbent, Terry Bruce, and one much better financed. But Poshard ran a campaign of lawn signs and personal appearances, attacked his opponent for a memo on the House bank scandal ("we need to protect our privacy and wrap up the investigation quickly"). He ran well in the Decatur area with 40%, and cut deeply into Bruce's old district with 44% and won in his own old district areas 90%–10%, for a 62%–38% victory.

Poshard is a moderate on the issues and an earnest reformer whose sincerity is not in doubt. He favors "the citizen-legislator, not the career legislator" type of government, he says; he has a 100% voting record and returns home every weekend, spending half his time in the north part of the district and half in the south. Early in his career, he had a crisis of conscience about a PAC contribution, and hasn't accepted any since; he would like to limit PAC contributions to $1,000 per campaign cycle and accepts no more than $500 on individual contributions. He also supports the McCain-Feingold bill. He pledged early on to serve only five terms and return home, and in early 1997 announced he was keeping his word and would retire from Congress in 1998. He favors the balanced budget amendment, has supported the Blue Dog (conservative Democratic) budget, and says that everything must be on the table; "that includes entitlements too." "I hope, as a moderate Democrat, we continue to hold both parties' feet to the fire and get this balanced budget thing going." While other Democrats have been demagoging the issue, he has called for Medicare reform.

Poshard serves on the Transportation Committee and is co-chair of the Rural Health Coalition and of the Congressional Oil and Gas Forum. Southern Illinois has many abandoned oil wells, and the state can't afford to cap them any time soon; Poshard would like a federal solution but confesses he is not sure exactly what. He is opposed to abortion and spoke eloquently against partial-birth abortion. He voted for welfare reform in 1996, but only after satisfying himself that the needs of children were addressed. He opposed NAFTA but got an amendment to protect the domestic broom industry; there are many small broom factories here. He favors government subsidies of ethanol and federal government purchase of soybean-based ink.

Poshard has won impressive margins in the 1990s, and won with 67% in 1996. In March 1997, Poshard announced that he would run for governor, though his lack of statewide name recognition will hinder his chances. The race to succeed him in this district is likely to be seriously contested on both sides.

The People: Pop. 1990: 571,390; 51% rural; 17% age 65+; 95% White; 4% Black; 1% Hispanic origin. Households: 60% married couple families; 27% married couple fams. w. children; 34% college educ.; median household income: $22,979; per capita income: $11,333; median gross rent: $295; median house value: $38,500.

1996 Presidential Vote

Clinton (D)	113,635	(47%)
Dole (R)	97,977	(41%)
Perot (I)	28,653	(12%)

1992 Presidential Vote

Clinton (D)	131,396	(47%)
Bush (R)	95,759	(34%)
Perot (I)	50,706	(18%)

Rep. Glenn Poshard (D)

Elected 1988; b. Oct. 30, 1945, Herald.; home, Marion; Southern IL U., B.A. 1970, M.S. 1974, Ph.D. 1984; Southern Baptist; married (Jo).

Career: Army, 1962–65; High schl. teacher, 1970–74, Dir., Regional Educ. Svc. Ctr. for Educators of the Gifted, 1974–84; IL Senate 1984–88.

DC Office: 2334 RHOB 20515, 202-225-5201; Fax: 202-225-1541.

District Offices: Decatur, 217-362-9011; Effingham, 217-342-7220; Lawrenceville, 618-943-6036; Marion, 618-993-8532; Mattoon, 217-234-7032; West Frankfort, 618-937-6402.

Committees: *Small Business* (4th of 16 D): Government Programs & Oversight (RMM). *Transportation & Infrastructure* (10th of 33 D): Aviation; Water Resources & Environment.

Group Ratings

	ADA	ACLU	AFS	LCV	CFA	CON	NFIB	COC	ACU	NTLC	CHC
1996	70	56	75	69	62	89	57	44	45	39	46
1995	60	—	—	44	31	75	—	54	44	—	—

National Journal Ratings

	1995 LIB		1995 CONS	1996 LIB		1996 CONS
Economic	59%	—	41%	62%	—	36%
Social	50%	—	50%	46%	—	52%
Foreign	70%	—	28%	64%	—	35%

Key Votes of the 104th Congress

1. Reduce Medicare Growth $	N	5. Flag Amendment	N	9. Cuban Embargo	Y
2. Ovrd. Product Liab. Veto	N	6. Drop EPA Limits	N	10. Bar Bosnia Troop $	N
3. Increase Min. Wage	Y	7. Repeal Assault-Weap. Ban	Y	11. Cut Anti-Missile Defense	Y
4. Welfare Reform	N	8. Ovrd. Part. Birth Veto	Y	12. Bar U.N. Uniforms	Y

Election Results

1996 general	Glenn Poshard (D)	158,668	(67%)	($237,030)
	Brent Winters (R)	75,751	(32%)	($100,055)
1996 primary	Glenn Poshard (D)	unopposed		
1994 general	Glenn Poshard (D)	115,045	(58%)	($164,541)
	Brent Winters (R)	81,995	(42%)	($57,702)

TWENTIETH DISTRICT

Springfield, the capital of Illinois, has changed rather little since its great moment in history—when it was the home of Abraham Lincoln, lawyer, unsuccessful candidate for Congress and 16th President of the United States. Today, beyond the suburban fringe, the prairie countryside outside Springfield is still mostly farmland with few towns. Farming technology has changed vastly, but the patterns of cultivation, the contours of the land, even the shape of the ribbons of back country roads, cannot be entirely different from what Lincoln saw as a lawyer making his way from one county seat to another on the circuit. Nor has downtown Springfield changed as much since Lincoln's time as have downtown Columbus or Indianapolis or even Des Moines. If most of the officefronts and houses captured in the old photographs are gone, some remain; and the scale has not changed utterly. Lincoln's clapboard house is still in Springfield, and so is the courtroom where he argued cases before federal judges; the Greek revival downtown bloc where Lincoln & Herndon kept their law offices is open for inspection, as is the state Capitol building built here in 1839. Much of today's Springfield is tawdry, but unlike other state capitals it has not lost its 19th Century scale.

The 20th Congressional District of Illinois is one of only 19 districts which can claim to be the lineal descendant of a district whose representative also became a president of the United States. The 20th District includes the southern half of Springfield and much of the Downstate Illinois prairie, which in 1846 elected a 37-year-old railroad lawyer and Whig opponent of the Mexican War named Abraham Lincoln to his single term in the House. Lincoln's denunciation of the Mexican War was so strong that he gave up any chance of a second term, for the countryside south and west of Springfield, straddling the National Road and along the Illinois River, both avenues of migration from the South, were strongly supportive of that war. Similar sentiments—a cultural conservatism, strong national pride—are still apparent here today.

The congressman from the 20th District is John Shimkus, a Republican elected by a narrow margin in 1996. Shimkus grew up in Collinsville, a county seat in Madison County, on the other side of the Mississippi River from St. Louis. He graduated from West Point, served in the Army, studied in California, then came back to Collinsville to teach high school. In 1988 he ran for the Madison County Board, and lost; in 1990, at 32, he beat a 12-year incumbent and was elected Madison County treasurer, the only Republican countywide officer. In 1992 he ran against Congressman Richard Durbin, who first won the seat as a moderate in 1982 but increasingly voted with the party leadership and, though heavily outspent ($921,000 to $278,000) held him to a 57%–43% victory. In 1995, when Durbin decided to run for the Senate seat being vacated by Paul Simon, Shimkus decided to run for Congress again.

He had plenty of competition. He was one of eight Republicans in the March primary, which he won with 51%, far ahead of the 19% of his nearest rival. In the general election he faced Jay Hoffman, a 34-year-old state Representative since 1990. Both were anti-abortion, anti-gun control, and pro-balanced budget amendment. But Shimkus took and Hoffman refused to take Americans for Tax Reform's pledge not to raise taxes. Shimkus supported the Republican budget; Hoffman attacked Newt Gingrich and decried Medicare "cuts." Hoffman bragged of his legislative record as Democratic floor leader and on child welfare, victim's rights, and truth-in-sentencing laws. Shimkus called for tougher border control to keep out drugs, more access to health insurance for the self-employed and employees of small business. He called Hoffman a big government spender and predicted, "Jay will move left. It's just a matter of time." Shimkus led in early polls, but Hoffman raised more money and had the benefit of AFL-CIO ads run against Shimkus.

This turned out to be one of the closest races in the country: Shimkus won 50.3%–49.7%, a margin of 1,238 votes. Hoffman carried the Democratic counties between Springfield and Madison County and the coal country in the southeast; Shimkus, campaigning in a Winnebago complete with his wife and two infant sons, did well in the farthest rural corners of the district and, critically, carried both Madison County and Springfield. Shimkus can be expected to have a mostly conservative voting record. He serves on the Commerce Committee, a good perch for the fundraising that will be necessary if, as seems quite possible, this district is seriously contested in 1998.

The People: Pop. 1990: 571,138; 48% rural; 16% age 65+; 95% White; 4% Black; 1% Hispanic origin. Households: 60% married couple families; 27% married couple fams. w. children; 36% college educ.; median household income: $26,173; per capita income: $12,289; median gross rent: $337; median house value: $47,000.

1996 Presidential Vote			1992 Presidential Vote		
Clinton (D)	117,775	(47%)	Clinton (D)	129,865	(46%)
Dole (R)	101,634	(41%)	Bush (R)	94,038	(34%)
Perot (I)	26,431	(11%)	Perot (I)	55,712	(20%)

Rep. John Shimkus (R)

Elected 1996; b. Feb. 21, 1958, Collinsville; home, Collinsville; West Point Military Acad., B.S. 1980; Christ Col., Teaching Cert., 1990; S. IL U., 1991–present; Lutheran; married (Karen).

Career: Army 1980–86; Teacher, Metro-East Lutheran H.S., 1986–90; Madison Cnty. Treasurer, 1990–96

DC Office: 513 CHOB 20515, 202-225-5271;

District Offices: Collinsville, 618-344-3065; Springfield, 217-492-5090.

Committees: *Commerce* (28th of 28 R): Energy & Power; Telecommunications, Trade & Consumer Protection.

Group Ratings and Key Votes: Newly Elected

Election Results

1996 general	John Shimkus (R)	120,926	(50%)	($647,796)
	Jay C. Hoffman (D)	119,688	(50%)	($812,397)
1996 primary	John Shimkus (R)	23,218	(51%)	
	Carl Oblinger (R)	8,786	(19%)	
	Bill Owens (R)	6,344	(14%)	
	Rick Angel (R)	4,436	(10%)	
	Others	2,857	(6%)	
1994 general	Richard J. Durbin (D)	108,034	(55%)	($692,886)
	Bill Owens (R)	88,964	(45%)	($55,337)

INDIANA

Every Memorial Day the nation's eyes turn to Indianapolis, to the center of a state with the nation's most distinctive nickname and some of its least distinctive borders, for a sports spectacle celebrating the knack for tinkering and the taste for powerful machines that make the Midwest the nation's manufacturing center: the Indianapolis 500. The combination of sports and manufacturing is symbolic of Indiana's strengths and its successes; and if its manufacturing base and sports heritage seems as antique as the bricks with which the Indianapolis Speedway was originally paved, it should be noted that all but one yard at the start/finish line have long since been ashpalted over, and that Indiana's manufacturing economy, after rough years in the early 1980s, is now humming, high-skill and high-tech. The Speedway is literally at the center of American manufacturing: almost precisely half the country's manufacturing jobs are east of Indiana and the other half west, almost half are north and half south. Indiana itself has the second highest percentage of workers in manufacturing in the nation. It is the number one steel producer in the nation, in the giant, heavily automated steel mills on the south shore of Lake Michigan. It leads the world in making compact discs and elevators, and leads the nation in televisions, refrigerators, engine electrical equipment, recreational vehicles, mobile homes and musical instruments. It gave the world canned pork and beans, tomato juice, the Coca-Cola bottle, and Alka-Seltzer.

Nor are Indiana's days of innovation over. Just as it has attracted new teams and events to Indianapolis's new sports facilities, so the small factories set amidst farm landscape or at the edge of small cities are centers of advanced manufacturing innovation. Indiana's job growth was slow in the 1980s, as it shed low-wage, low-skill jobs; and its income levels are slightly less than the national average now, and well below those not only of the coasts but also of the Chicago area just over the state line. But housing and healthcare costs are also lower than average, and the tax burden far lower and tort laws less onerous.

Culturally, Indiana is like an older America, with low levels of social pathology—violent crime, unwed mothers, and divorce. It retains some of the old norms that in the 1920s and 1930s brought sociologists Robert and Helen Lynd in their search for the typical American place to "Middletown" (actually Muncie). The major metropolitan area, Indianapolis, now has 1.5 million people, but still doesn't have the big singles and gay neighborhoods of larger cities. Ethnically, Indiana seems older too: except for the steel area around Gary—really an extension of the Chicago metropolitan area—Indiana has relatively few descendants from the 1840–1924 wave of immigration, and few recent Hispanic or Asian migrants. Finally, Indiana is transfixed by American sports: Indianapolis's civic leaders have made sports the focus of their development plans, attracting the Colts professional football team to the Hoosier Dome, hosting the Pan-American games in 1987, several trials for the 1996 Olympics and the NCAA Final Four in 1991, the pro basketball Pacers, the Big Ten Women's Basketball Championship in 1995, and of course the Indianapolis 500 at the Speedway every Memorial Day. When high school athletic departments decided in 1996 to institute four-class basketball, Hoosiers remembered how tiny Milan High School won the state championship in 1954; a bill proposing a statewide referendum on the issue failed, but Indiana introduced a "Tournament of Champions" where the four-class champions will face each other.

Politically, Indiana is also typical of an older America, with partisan preferences anchored in the Civil War era and a small overlay of change from the union-organizing days of the 1930s. Indiana's cultural conservatism has kept it Republican in presidential elections for the last generation, but for many years before, it was a fulcrum point in partisan politics, a crucial state from the Civil War to the New Deal in the struggles between Republicans and Democrats. Party

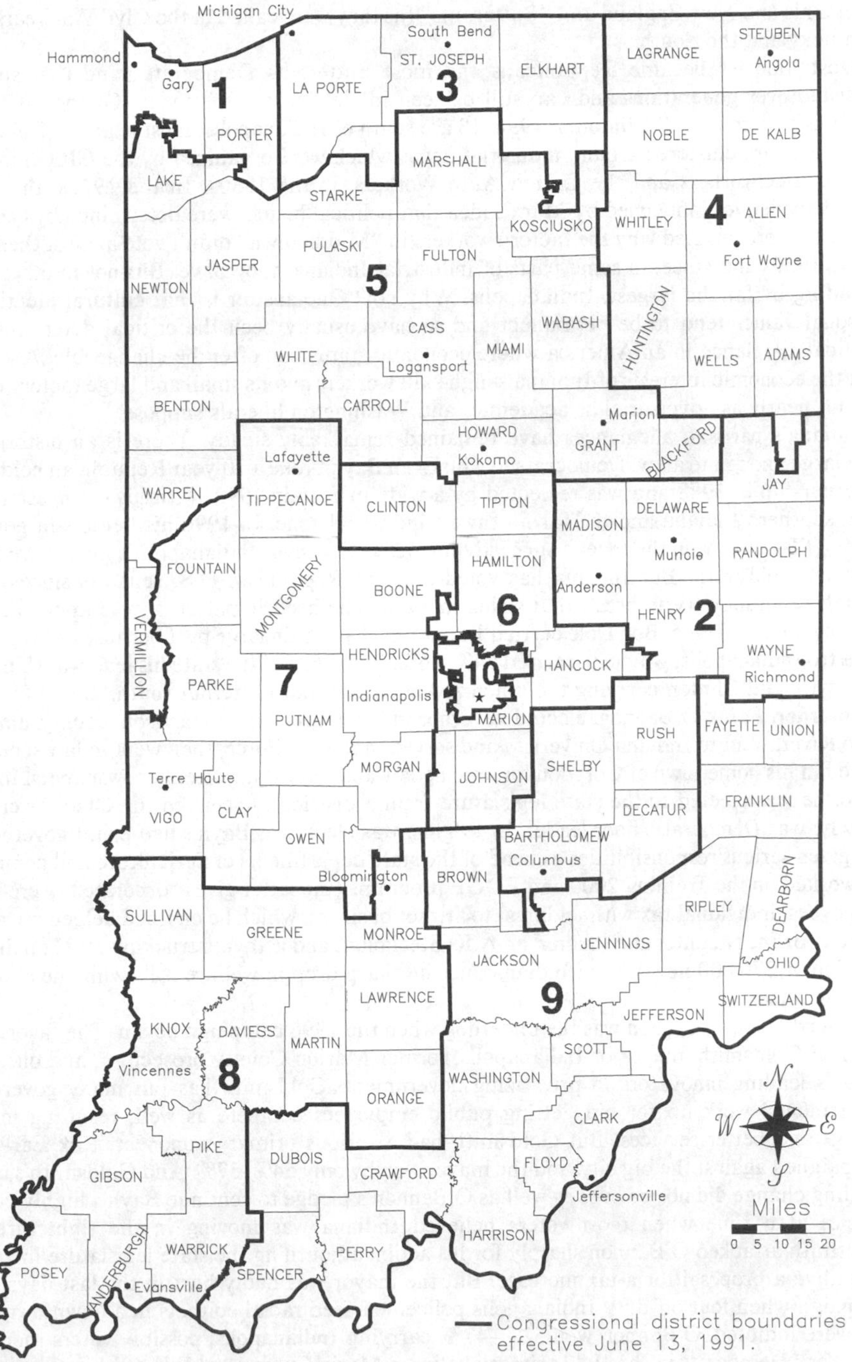
Michigan City
Hammond
Gary
1
LAKE
PORTER
LA PORTE
South Bend
ST. JOSEPH
3
ELKHART
LAGRANGE
STEUBEN
Angola
NOBLE
DE KALB
MARSHALL
STARKE
KOSCIUSKO
WHITLEY
4
ALLEN
Fort Wayne
JASPER
NEWTON
PULASKI
FULTON
5
CASS
Logansport
WHITE
MIAMI
WABASH
HUNTINGTON
WELLS
ADAMS
BENTON
CARROLL
HOWARD
Kokomo
Marion
GRANT
BLACKFORD
JAY
Lafayette
WARREN
TIPPECANOE
CLINTON
TIPTON
MADISON
DELAWARE
Muncie
RANDOLPH
FOUNTAIN
MONTGOMERY
BOONE
HAMILTON
Anderson
6
HENRY
2
VERMILLION
PARKE
7
HENDRICKS
Indianapolis
10
MARION
HANCOCK
WAYNE
Richmond
PUTNAM
RUSH
FAYETTE
UNION
Terre Haute
VIGO
CLAY
MORGAN
JOHNSON
SHELBY
FRANKLIN
DECATUR
OWEN
BARTHOLOMEW
Columbus
Bloomington
BROWN
DEARBORN
RIPLEY
SULLIVAN
GREENE
MONROE
JENNINGS
JACKSON
OHIO
9
SWITZERLAND
LAWRENCE
JEFFERSON
KNOX
DAVIESS
MARTIN
SCOTT
Vincennes
8
WASHINGTON
ORANGE
CLARK
PIKE
DUBOIS
FLOYD
GIBSON
CRAWFORD
Jeffersonville
HARRISON
WARRICK
PERRY
POSEY
VANDERBURGH
Evansville
SPENCER
N
W
E
S
Miles
0 5 10 15 20
Congressional district boundaries effective June 13, 1991.

identification was handed down with religious affiliation—the Lynds noted that the Presbyterians had little to do with Methodists, but that was nothing next to divisions between Republicans and Democrats—in a state still peopled largely by descendants of its original settlers, Yankees from Ohio and New England and "Butternuts" (as they were called in the Civil War years) from Kentucky and the South.

Most Yankees became Republicans and most Butternuts Democrats., and that split has persisted over generations and can still be seen in election returns today. Of the 26 Indiana counties carried by Bill Clinton in 1996, 18 are south of Indianapolis, most near the Ohio River. The others are clustered around industrial towns which were organized by the CIO unions, the United Steelworkers and the United Auto Workers, in the 1930s. In the 1920s, the Lynds, liberal academics influenced by Marx's idea that political beliefs were determined by economic interests, were puzzled why the factory workers in "Middletown" didn't vote against the bosses; in the 1930s and since, in some parts of industrial Indiana, they have. But not in other cities, including by far the largest, Indianapolis. Why not? One answer is that cultural identity and personal values tend to be permanent and so have usually been the critical determinants of political allegiance in an America where economic status can often be changeable. Another is that the economic interests of Indiana's high-skill workers and its small and large factory owners are not nearly as adversarial as academics and Washington liberals suppose.

Indiana's partisan allegiances have remained remarkably steady. There is an historic base here large enough to allow Democrats to win: Evan Bayh broke a 20-year Republican hold on the governorship in 1988 and was reelected by a wide margin in 1992, with his strongest support from southern Indiana and the far northwest industrial zone. In 1996 his lieutenant governor, Frank O'Bannon, won the race to succeed him, 52%–47%, over Indianapolis's innovative Mayor Stephen Goldsmith. But Indiana has voted only for Republican U.S. senators since 1976—though Bayh may try to break that string in 1998. The historic patterns were apparent in the 1996 presidential race. Bob Dole carried Indiana 47%–42%, in large part because of his strength in metro Indianapolis, which he carried 54%–36%. In the rest of the state his lead was thin, 45%–43%, with Bill Clinton carrying the unionized north and the Butternut south.

Governor. Frank O'Bannon, elected governor in 1996, grew up in Harrison County, along the Ohio River, went to Indiana University and served in the Air Force, then went to law school. He settled in his home town of Corydon, practicing law and publishing weekly newspapers. In 1970, at 40, he was elected to the state legislature from a district adjacent to the Ohio River; from 1979 he was Democratic floor leader. In 1988 he was elected as Bayh's lieutenant governor and was given serious responsibilities as head of the state departments of agriculture and commerce. He worked on the Training 2000 and EDGE programs (the latter gives corporate tax credits for employees' individual tax withholdings) to attract business, which he claimed helped attract the United Airlines maintenance center, an A.K. Steel plant and a Toyota truck plant. He hailed the creation of 370,000 new jobs in Indiana and the sharp drop in welfare rolls while he and Bayh were in office.

Nevertheless, O'Bannon was the underdog when the 1996 campaign began. The favorite was Stephen Goldsmith, mayor of Indianapolis, former Marion County prosecutor, and one of the nation's leading innovators in privatizing government. Goldsmith has put many government departments' work up for bid, letting public employees compete as well, resulting in large savings and better services. But Goldsmith had a serious primary opponent, Rex Early, who campaigned against the big city, and the mayor won by only 54%–37%. And Goldsmith's call for startling change did not go over as well as O'Bannon's pledge to continue Bayh's highly popular policies at a time when most voters believed Indiana was moving in the right direction. Goldsmith attacked O'Bannon sharply for his action adjourning the state legislature in 1993 to keep alive a proposal for a tax increase. But the mayor was badly hurt in the last days of the campaign when four off-duty Indianapolis policemen used racial epithets in a downtown brawl and were indicted. O'Bannon won 52%–47%, carrying Indianapolis; possibly voters there (like New York Democrats in the 1982 primary between Mario Cuomo and Edward Koch) wanted to support a popular candidate for governor and keep a popular mayor.

In office O'Bannon proposed to continue the course he and Bayh had set. He called for cutting educational regulations and changing state emphasis on monitoring bureaucracy to measuring results. "Local control must go hand in hand with accountability for higher performance." He called for forgiving college loans for students with at least a B-average, a property tax credit for families, a welfare-to-work income tax credit, and 500 new police in four years.

Senior Senator. Richard Lugar, fresh and undaunted after an unsuccessful presidential campaign in 1996, has a career in public life going back four decades to the late 1950s, when as a young Navy officer he prepared intelligence briefings for chief of Naval Operations Arleigh Burke and briefed President Eisenhower over closed-circuit television. Now he is the first Indiana senator ever elected to a fourth term, chairman of the Senate Agriculture Committee and a leading power on Foreign Relations. Lugar grew up in Indianapolis, where his family had a farm and a food machinery firm, founded in 1893; he was an Eagle Scout, a straight-A student, and a Rhodes scholar. After the service he returned to the family business, was elected to the school board in 1964, then was elected mayor of Indianapolis in 1967, at 35. As mayor, he consolidated the city and county into Unigov, which brought in tax resources and suburban voters, keeping the city both solvent and Republican. In the late 1960s, Lugar bucked fashion and called for fewer rather than more federal programs, and became known as Richard Nixon's favorite mayor—not a political asset in 1974, when Lugar ran against Senator Birch Bayh and lost 51%–46%. But in the more favorable climate of 1976 and against a weaker Democratic incumbent, Vance Hartke, Lugar won 59%–40%.

Throughout his public life, Lugar's strength has been that he has followed where his stubborn convictions and his considerable intellect led, regardless of political risk or reward—and he has plenty of accomplishments but also some disappointments to show for it. His lone course has served him well in Indiana, but has had mixed results in the Senate and in the national arena. He is a conservative in many ways, though not on all the hot button issues of today's conservative activists; he is an internationalist, at a time when the president's attention to foreign issues is episodic and some in Lugar's own party are tempted to revert to isolationism. Lugar started off in the Senate leading the 1978 filibuster to defeat the AFL-CIO's labor law reform bill, although unions were then big in Indiana. He strongly supported NAFTA in 1993, in a midwestern state where many thought foreigners were taking their jobs. In 1994, he doggedly raised questions about the ethical conflict posed by the investment in Lloyds of London by Supreme Court nominee Stephen Breyer. He voted against the Civil Rights Act of 1990, saying it imposed racial quotas. He ran for president in 1996 on his own platform and without any concessions to the political shorthand or the TV sensibility of the day.

But even amid his ill-fated presidential campaign, he achieved a staggering legislative success in the passage of the Federal Agriculture Improvement and Reform Act of 1996—The Freedom to Farm Act. Lugar is a farmer himself, raising corn, soybeans and wheat on a 600-acre spread outside Indianapolis. But for years he had opposed the complex system of farm subsidies which had many farmers responding to government regulations and subsidies rather than to the market. As ranking Republican on the Agriculture Committee since 1987, he formed a coalition of Republicans and non-subsidy Democrats who took the lead in fashioning a 1990 farm bill that froze target prices and dairy supports, allowed farmers more flexibility, ended land-idling schemes and cut spending. In 1992 he led a crusade to close some of the 11,000 USDA field offices in nearly all the nation's 3,000-plus counties. As chairman in 1995, he set forth a series of tough questions for incoming Agriculture Secretary Dan Glickman, critically examining the need for current subsidies and calling for reduced target prices annually until they are zeroed out in five years. That set the stage for the 1996 farm bill. Lugar's stance, and the House Republican budget which set tight limits on farm spending, helped convince House Agriculture Chairman Pat Roberts, now Kansas senator, that subsidies must be phased out. Lugar in the meantime moved his bill in the Senate. In late January 1996 he left the campaign trail in Iowa and returned to Washington to outmaneuver Dakota Democrats Tom Daschle and Byron

Dorgan, and pass a bill phasing out most subsidies over seven years, thus encouraging farmers to produce for growing foreign markets. He was especially proud of its environmental provisions—$200 million for the Everglades, an expansion of the Conservation Reserve program for wetlands, and an incentive program for waste containment facilities. The bill became law in April 1996—and probably never would have come close to passage without Lugar. He had other legislative accomplishments in 1996. He worked on the Safe Drinking Water Act and the food stamp provisions of welfare reform. And he co-sponsored the Gambling Study Commission, with a two-year charter and subpoena power.

Lugar's other great interest has been foreign policy. For 1985–86, he was chairman of the Foreign Relations Committee, where he quickly took command over a committee sharply divided between Jesse Helms of North Carolina, inclined to conduct his own foreign policy, and liberal Democrats. Lugar was in the middle, backing contra aid and favoring sanctions on South Africa. On the Philippines, he took the lead, quickly concluding that Ferdinand Marcos's 1986 "victory" over Corazon Aquino was fraudulent and, at a decisive point, called on Marcos to leave office; the Reagan Administration followed. After Republicans lost control of the Senate in 1986, Helms invoked seniority to take the ranking minority position on Foreign Relations, and after 1994 became chairman. But Lugar has staked out certain issues on which he has played a major role. He worked for ratification of the INF Treaty in 1988, START I in 1992, and START II in 1996; he supported the Chemical Weapons Convention in 1997. In 1991 he joined with Democrat Sam Nunn to encourage the dismantling and conversion of the Soviet nuclear stockpile. Their Nunn-Lugar Cooperative Threats Reduction program provided billions to Russia, Ukraine, and Belarus to dismantle and destroy their nuclear weapons and some chemical and biological weapons as well, to prevent them from falling into the hands of hostile powers or terrorists. In June 1992, Lugar called for the use of U.N. and, if necessary, U.S. military force in Bosnia. But by 1994 he was critical of those who would lift the arms embargo on the Bosnian Muslims, and in early 1995, said the United States should have intervened when Yugoslavia split into separate states in 1991. He remains a major force for international engagement and a bipartisan approach; in early 1997 he urged Bill Clinton to increase spending on international affairs.

Lugar's disappointments include his loss to Bob Dole in the race for majority leader in 1984 as well as being elbowed aside by Helms in 1986. In August 1988, George Bush picked not Lugar, but his junior and less experienced Hoosier colleague, Dan Quayle, to be his vice president. But Lugar is a long-distance runner (literally) and does not quit. In Indiana he has remained vastly popular. He was reelected in 1988 with 68% of the vote, a state record, and in 1994 won with 67%. Right after that victory, Lugar started thinking about running for president again. He had enough home state and Washington support to raise almost $10 million and he proceeded to emphasize the issues he thought important. "Only the president can deal with the two challenges on which our future really depends—nuclear security and fiscal sanity." He emphasized his work on deterring nuclear terrorism, running a series of four ads showing a president having to respond to such a threat; but critics said many voters simply didn't understand them. And he showcased his April 1995 proposal for a 17% national sales tax to replace the income tax and abolish the IRS. But Lugar got little coverage from journalists and never caught many voters' attention. He made a disappointing showing in the Iowa caucuses—7th place with 4%—and did only slightly better in New Hampshire, taking 5th place with 5%. His high point came in Vermont, where he campaigned hard and got 14%. On March 6 he withdrew from the race and endorsed Bob Dole.

Junior Senator. Republican Dan Coats grew up in Jackson, Michigan, about an hour south of Lansing, joined the Army after college, went to law school, worked for an insurance company and in 1976 was an Indiana staffer for a young congressman named Dan Quayle. Coats was elected to succeed Quayle in the House in 1980, was appointed to succeed him in the Senate in December 1988 and elected in his own right for the remainder of the term in 1990 by 54%–46% and for a full term in 1992 by 57%–41%.

Coats has worked hard on several issues in the Senate. One cause, dating back to his House days, is limiting shipment of out-of-state waste. His bill passed the Senate in the 104th Congress but died in the House, and Coats reintroduced another bill to deal with the problem in March 1997. Another Coats cause was the line-item veto, passed in the 104th Congress, a useful reduction in his view of Congress's power. Coats serves on Armed Services and Labor and Human Resources and, starting in 1997, the Intelligence Committees, and is a strong supporter of the military service. He currently chairs the Armed Services Committee Airland Forces Subcommittee, and is supportive enough of defense needs to have acquiesced when Indiana's only two active bases were included on the 1991 base closure and realignment list. In 1993, he was the lead Republican seeking to block Clinton's plans to end the ban on gays in the military. Coats insisted he was not anti-gay and that the Clinton plan would lead to harm for many gays; in fact, the number of discharges for homosexuality has risen.

But most important, Coats is motivated by a devotion to traditional values rooted in religious faith. That is manifest in a very conservative voting record, but one also attentive to the needs of parents and children; he supported the Family Leave Act. Coats is strongly against abortion—a leader on the fetal tissue research ban, an opponent of RU-486 and the Henry Foster for surgeon general nomination. He sponsored a law allowing parents to block dial-a-porn phone numbers and one banning "indecent or lewd" material on the Internet. Most interestingly, he has proposed a series of laws designed to strengthen families and faith-based institutions. "Is it enough to cut spending or do we have a vision for the country that goes beyond fiscal accountability and responsibility?" he asked fellow conservatives. In 1995 he announced The Project for American Renewal, and with William Bennett proposed a list of 19 bills, including reserving 15% of public housing for intact families, more money for abstinence education, grants for neighborhood anti-crime groups, an adoption tax credit, a school mentoring program, a model residential academy for at-risk youth. Its centerpiece was a $500 per person tax credit for charitable contributions to organizations that help the poor. Coats wants to shift power, money and influence from Washington to families, grassroots community organizations, private and religious charities. He believes that private, faith-based counseling often works better than public, secular counseling. Coats was disappointed that of the 1996 presidential candidates only Lamar Alexander sounded similar notes, but on the other hand Bill Clinton pulled Coats aside at a White House reception to compliment his ideas and included similar language in his State of the Union address. In 1997 Coats announced a different Renewal Alliance, stressing similar ideas; this time he and House Budget Chairman John Kasich were proposing that the $500 tax credit be paid for by reducing current welfare spending and eliminating what they called corporate welfare.

In December 1996, Coats announced he would not run for reelection in 1998. "If politics is not your life, when do you leave? I want to leave when I am young enough to contribute somewhere else—young enough to resume a career outside government. I want to leave when there is still a chance to follow God's leading to something new." He admitted that a 1998 campaign would be onerous, and indeed recent Indiana polls showed him trailing outgoing Governor Evan Bayh, who immediately became the favorite to win the seat. Bayh seems almost certain to run; he had raised $1.3 million by mid-1996, while he was still in office, and his record as governor has remained highly popular, enough so to help elect Democratic successor Frank O'Bannon in this mostly Republican state. But Republican states in recent years have shown an unwillingness to elect even the most popular of Democratic governors to the Senate, where they may vote with Ted Kennedy and in support of Bill Clinton; notable examples are Nebraska in 1996 and Wyoming in 1994. A likely list of candidates includes Fort Wayne Mayor Paul Helmke, Indianapolis lawyer and former Reagan speechwriter Peter Rusthoven and conservative attorney John Price.

Presidential politics. In presidential elections, Indiana remains among the most Republican of the larger states; the only larger states with higher percentages for Bob Dole in 1996 were Texas and North Carolina. The cultural liberalism of Democratic presidential candidates simply does not sell well here. So Indiana sees little of those candidates in election year autumns.

Indiana's May presidential primary has not been influential since 1968, and native son Richard Lugar did not stay in the race long enough to win what surely would have been an impressive victory here in 1996.

Congressional districting. Indiana's 1991 districting plan is a mild revision of a 1981 plan enacted by Republicans and upheld in a Supreme Court decision important to redistricting law. The 1980s districts surprised and disappointed Republicans by electing at one point eight Democrats and only two Republicans. When it came time for redistricting in 1991, legislative control was split between the parties and the lines were changed only marginally. The plan is now, quite belatedly, having its intended political effect, as six out of ten seats are held by Republicans.

The People: Est. Pop. 1996: 5,841,000; Pop. 1990: 5,544,159, up 5.3% 1990–1996. 2.2% of U.S. total, 14th largest; 35% rural. Median age: 34.8 years. 13% 65 years and over. 89.6% White, 7.7% Black, 1% Asian; 1.8% Hispanic origin. Households: 58.2% married couple families; 28% married couple fams. w. children; 37% college educ.; median household income: $28,797; per capita income: $13,149; 70.2% owner occupied housing; median house value: $53,900; median monthly rent: $291. 4.1% Unemployment. 1996 Voting age pop.: 4,374,000. 1996 Turnout: 2,135,431; 49% of VAP. Registered voters (1996): 3,484,033; no party registration.

Political Lineup: Governor, Frank O'Bannon (D); Lt. Gov., Joe Kernan (D); Secy. of State, Sue Ann Gilroy (R); Atty. Gen., Jeff Modisett (D); Treasurer, Joyce Brinkman (R); Auditor, Ann DeVore (R). State Senate, 50 (19 D and 31 R); Senate President, Robert Garden (R); State House, 100 (50 R and 50 D); House Speaker, John Gregg (D). Senators, Richard G. Lugar (R) and Daniel R. Coats (R). Representatives, 10 (6 R and 4 D).

Election Commission: 317-232-3939; **Filing Deadline for U.S. Congress:** January 21, 1998.

1996 Presidential Vote

Dole (R)	1,006,632	(47%)
Clinton (D)	887,454	(42%)
Perot (I)	224,280	(11%)

1996 Republican Presidential Primary

Dole (R)	365,860	(71%)
Buchanan (R)	100,245	(19%)
Forbes (R)	50,802	(10%)

1992 Presidential Vote

Bush (R)	939,375	(43%)
Clinton (D)	848,420	(37%)
Perot (I)	455,934	(20%)

GOVERNOR

Gov. Frank O'Bannon (D)

Elected 1996, term expires Jan. 2001; b. Jan. 30, 1930, Louisville, KY; home, Indianapolis; IN U., B.A. 1952, J.D. 1957; Methodist; married (Judy).

Career: Air Force, 1952–54; Practicing atty., 1957–88; Dir. & Chmn., O'Bannon Publishing Co., 1970–88; IN Senate, 1971–88; IN Lt. Gov., 1989–96.

Office: 206 State House, Indianapolis 46204, 317-232-4567; Fax: 317-232-3443; Web site: www.state.in.us.

Election Results

1996 gen.	Frank O'Bannon (D)	1,087,128	(52%)
	Stephen Goldsmith (R)	986,982	(47%)
	Others	35,937	(2%)
1996 prim.	Frank O'Bannon (D)	unopposed	
1992 gen.	Evan Bayh (D)	1,382,151	(62%)
	Linley E. Pearson (R).........	822,853	(37%)

SENATORS

Sen. Richard G. Lugar (R)

Elected 1976, seat up 2000; b. Apr. 4, 1932, Indianapolis; home, Indianapolis; Denison U., B.A. 1954; Rhodes Scholar, Oxford U., M.A. 1956; Methodist; married (Charlene).

Career: Navy, 1957–60; Mgr., family farm; V.P. and Treas., Thomas L. Green & Co., 1960–67; Indianapolis Bd. of Schl. Commissioners, 1964–67; Indianapolis Mayor, 1968–75; Prof., U. of Indianapolis, 1976.

DC Office: 306 HSOB 20510, 202-224-4814; e-mail: senator_lugar@lugar.senate.gov.

State Offices: Evansville, 812-465-6313; Fort Wayne, 219-422-1505; Indianapolis, 317-226-5555; Jeffersonville, 812-288-3377; Merrillville, 219-937-5380.

Committees: *Agriculture, Nutrition & Forestry* (Chmn. of 10 R). *Foreign Relations* (2nd of 10 R): East Asian & Pacific Affairs; European Affairs; Western Hemisphere & Peace Corps Affairs. *Intelligence (Select)* (3rd of 10 R).

Group Ratings

	ADA	ACLU	AFS	LCV	CFA	CON	NFIB	COC	ACU	NTLC	CHC
1996	5	17	0	15	29	92	100	85	95	93	82
1995	5	—	11	7	13	81	—	100	77	—	—

National Journal Ratings

	1995 LIB		1995 CONS	1996 LIB		1996 CONS
Economic	26%	—	71%	22%	—	76%
Social	38%	—	61%	28%	—	68%
Foreign	46%	—	53%	30%	—	68%

Key Votes of the 104th Congress

1. Reduce Medicare Growth $	Y	5. Flag Amendment	Y	9. Anti-Missile Defense	Y
2. Lmt. Prod. Liab. Damages	Y	6. Endangered Species	N	10. Cuban Embargo	Y
3. Increase Min. Wage	N	7. Gay Employment Rights	N	11. Bar Bosnia Troop $	N
4. Welfare Reform	Y	8. Ovrd. Part. Birth Veto	Y	12. Cut Vietnam Aid	N

Election Results

1994 general	Richard G. Lugar (R)	1,039,625	(67%)	($4,688,326)
	James Jontz (D)	470,799	(31%)	($472,788)
	Others	33,144	(2%)	
1994 primary	Richard G. Lugar (R)	unopposed		
1988 general	Richard G. Lugar (R)	1,430,525	(68%)	($3,244,601)
	Jack Wickes (D)	668,778	(32%)	($314,233)

Sen. Daniel R. Coats (R)

Appointed Jan. 1989, seat up 1998; b. May 16, 1943, Jackson, MI; home, Fort Wayne; Wheaton Col., B.A. 1965, IN U., J.D. 1971; Presbyterian; married (Marcia).

Career: Army Corps of Engineers, 1966–68; Asst. V.P. & Cnsl., Mutual Security Life Insurance Co., 1972–76; Dist. Rep., U.S. Rep. J. Danforth Quayle, 1976–80; U.S. House of Reps., 1980–88.

DC Office: 404 RSOB 20515, 202-224-5623; Fax: 202-228-4745; Web site: www.senate.gov/coats.

State Offices: Evansville, 812-465-6313; Fort Wayne, 219-422-1505; Indianapolis, 317-226-5555; Jeffersonville, 812-288-3377; Merrillville, 219-736-9084.

Committees: *Armed Services* (4th of 10 R): Airland Forces (Chmn.); Personnel; Readiness. *Labor & Human Resources* (2nd of 10 R): Children & Families (Chmn.); Public Health & Safety. *Intelligence (Select)* (10th of 10 R).

Group Ratings

	ADA	ACLU	AFS	LCV	CFA	CON	NFIB	COC	ACU	NTLC	CHC
1996	10	18	0	23	21	89	100	100	100	100	100
1995	0	—	0	14	0	68	—	95	96	—	—

National Journal Ratings

	1995 LIB — 1995 CONS			1996 LIB — 1996 CONS		
Economic	0%	—	88%	25%	—	74%
Social	12%	—	81%	0%	—	72%
Foreign	8%	—	81%	0%	—	74%

Key Votes of the 104th Congress

1. Reduce Medicare Growth $	Y	5. Flag Amendment	Y	9. Anti-Missile Defense	Y
2. Lmt. Prod. Liab. Damages	Y	6. Endangered Species	N	10. Cuban Embargo	Y
3. Increase Min. Wage	N	7. Gay Employment Rights	N	11. Bar Bosnia Troop $	N
4. Welfare Reform	Y	8. Ovrd. Part. Birth Veto	Y	12. Cut Vietnam Aid	Y

Election Results

1992 general	Daniel R. Coats (R)	1,267,972	(57%)	($3,802,077)
	Joseph H. Hogsett (D)	900,148	(41%)	($1,584,173)
	Others	43,306	(2%)	
1992 primary	Daniel R. Coats (R)	unopposed		
1990 general	Daniel R. Coats (R)	806,048	(54%)	($3,662,672)
	Baron P. Hill (D)	696,639	(46%)	($1,077,074)

FIRST DISTRICT

At the southernmost shore of Lake Michigan is a part of America made by steel. Here, in the northwest corner of Indiana, where the water highway of the Great Lakes comes closest to the steel highway of the transcontinental railroads, America's leading capitalists nearly a century ago recognized the best possible site for manufacturing steel. On empty sand dunes, United States Steel, then the nation's largest corporation, created only a few years before by financier J. P. Morgan, established the city of Gary in 1906 and named it for the company's chairman, Chicago Judge Elbert Gary. For nearly 70 years, the steel mills attracted a diverse work force, like Chicago and quite unlike the rest of Indiana—Irish, Poles, Czechs, Ukrainians and blacks from the American South. Politics here has always been turbulent, from the Communist-led long and unsuccessful steel strike of 1919 to the racially polarized politics of the 1960s and 1970s. The tone of public life—the clash between union stewards and management foremen, between blacks and eastern European ethnics, between the stalwarts of different factions vying for control of Gary's massive City Hall—was always abrasive, like the clash of steel on steel.

Steel brought sudden growth and sudden depression to northwest Indiana. The massive storefronts built on Gary's aptly named Broadway bear witness to the confidence and exuberance of the 1920s. But today they stand vacant, vandalized, sometimes burnt down—witness to the steel layoffs and crime waves of the 1970s. The steel mills went cold during the Depression of the 1930s, but were thronged with workers in World War II, and in the years afterwards their massiveness helped create the illusion that life in the steel towns of Gary, Hammond, and East Chicago would go on forever pretty much like it was in the 1950s. The companies granted generous union contracts, confident they could sell as much steel as they could make for any price they chose to charge. But technological advances inevitably replaced increasingly expensive workers with increasingly efficient machines. And the efforts to seal off the U.S. steel market from the world inevitably failed. The oil crunch of 1979 was the catalyst for change, reducing the demand for large-sized autos, the biggest customer for steel. Steel employed 70,000 workers in northwest Indiana in 1979, and just 35,000 a few years later. Obsolete mills were closed, old mills modernized and new ones built which cut the number of man-hours needed by two-thirds; just-in-time methods were introduced; management and high-skill workers cooperated to engineer higher-quality, less expensive steel to meet customers' needs. By 1989, Indiana was the number one steel producing state in the nation, but with only about 30,000 steel workers in northwest Indiana.

As the steel industry was rebuilding, Gary was falling almost into ruins. As long ago as 1967, Gary elected a black mayor, Richard Hatcher, who was determined to use city government to cure poverty; but high crime rates produced a flight to the suburbs and left Broadway's storefronts empty, and Gary's publicly financed convention center and airport do little business. In 1993 and 1995, Gary was the nation's murder capital, with Governor Evan Bayh dispatching 50 state troopers to help Gary police for three months in 1995. In 1995 Gary responded by electing a Democratic white mayor, Scott King, with 78% of the vote. The city's hope now is for salvation by riverboat (actually, lakeboat) gambling. But most of northwest Indiana's people have long since scattered out to suburbs and countryside, making it part of the greater Chicago area, distinctive mainly for its lower sales tax.

Indiana's 1st Congressional District stretches from Gary and Hammond along the Lake Michigan shore, east almost to Michigan City. Politically, this has been a heavily Democratic area since the Depression of the early 1930s and the United Steelworkers organizing drives of the late 1930s. It is the most Democratic part of mostly Republican Indiana.

The congressman from the 1st District is Pete Visclosky, a Democrat first elected in 1984. Visclosky grew up in northwest Indiana, went to college there and law school at Notre Dame, not far away. He practiced law, then worked for six years for 1st District Congressman Adam Benjamin. Benjamin died suddenly in 1982 and Visclosky returned to Indiana. In 1984 he ran against Katie Hall, a black state senator who had been given the 1982 nomination—and thus the election, in this area—by Richard Hatcher, then district party chairman. But Hall was able to win only 33% of the 1984 primary vote; Visclosky had 34% and another white candidate 31%. Visclosky beat Hall again 57%–35% in 1986 and 51%–30% in 1990. He has not had serious primary opposition since.

Visclosky has a somewhat moderate voting record and concentrates much of his effort on projects to help the local economy. He supports the balanced budget amendment and has his own bill to force a balanced budget by 2002 with strict timelines. He was one of only six Democrats to vote for the Republicans' $17 billion recission bill in March 1995. Though he supported welfare reform, he voted against the final bill that passed the House in 1996. He has voted against programs like the Market Promotion Program as corporate welfare. He has a solid pro-union voting record, opposing Bacon-Davis repeal, the TEAM Act (which would allow businesses to form company unions), and the Republican measure to allow workers to choose compensatory time instead of premium overtime pay. He pays attention to ethnic constituencies, as when he stopped $25 million in aid to Turkey in 1996 because of its blockade of Armenia.

Visclosky serves on Appropriations and its National Security and Energy & Water Development Subcommittees. There he has pushed for $32 million in flood control and harbor reconstruction for the Little Calumet River, Burns Harbor, Cady Marsh Ditch and Mondaldi Barons; $2.2 million for beach renourishment at the Indiana Dunes National Lakeshore; brownfield grants for Gary, East Chicago and Hammond. He got northwest Indiana declared a High Intensity Drug Trafficking Area and secured funding for 82 additional policemen, 600 bulletproof vests, 2 military helicopters and night-vision goggles. Over the opposition of Senator Dan Coats, he pushed through an exception to the Johnson Act, making Lake Michigan state waters eligible for gambling and thus allowing riverboat casinos for Gary. He worked to fund a 760-job postal encoding facility in Gary, and to stop the FAA from closing its air tower at Gary Regional Airport, which he had once tried to make Chicago's third major airport.

Visclosky has usually been reelected easily. In 1994 he faced for the first time a Republican who spent more than $100,000; small business owner John Larson carried Porter County, east of Gary, and some conservative southern suburbs; Visclosky won by just 56%–44%. Against weaker opposition in 1996 he won 69%–29%.

The People: Pop. 1990: 554,514; 9% rural; 12% age 65+; 70% White; 21% Black; 1% Asian; 9% Hispanic origin. Households: 57% married couple families; 27% married couple fams. w. children; 37% college educ.; median household income: $31,300; per capita income: $13,161; median gross rent: $399; median house value: $56,400.

1996 Presidential Vote

Clinton (D)	116,355	(58%)
Dole (R)	62,595	(31%)
Perot (I)	19,530	(10%)

1992 Presidential Vote

Clinton (D)	117,115	(52%)
Bush (R)	68,392	(31%)
Perot (I)	37,129	(17%)

Rep. Peter J. Visclosky (D)

Elected 1984; b. Aug. 13, 1949, Gary; home, Merrillville; IN U. Northwest, B.S. 1970, U. of Notre Dame, J.D. 1973, Georgetown U., LL.M. 1982; Catholic; married (Anne Marie).

Career: Practicing atty., 1973–76, 1983–84; Aide, U.S. Rep. Adam Benjamin, 1976–82.

DC Office: 2313 RHOB 20515, 202-225-2461; Fax: 202-225-2493.

District Offices: Gary, 219-884-1177; Portage, 219-763-2904; Valparaiso, 219-464-0315.

Committees: *Appropriations* (15th of 26 D): Energy & Water Development; National Security.

Group Ratings

	ADA	ACLU	AFS	LCV	CFA	CON	NFIB	COC	ACU	NTLC	CHC
1996	85	69	92	92	77	97	19	19	15	13	26
1995	70	—	—	88	85	75	—	25	8	—	—

National Journal Ratings

	1995 LIB — 1995 CONS			1996 LIB — 1996 CONS		
Economic	67%	—	32%	65%	—	35%
Social	73%	—	26%	63%	—	37%
Foreign	66%	—	33%	63%	—	36%

Key Votes of the 104th Congress

1. Reduce Medicare Growth $	N	5. Flag Amendment	N	9. Cuban Embargo	N
2. Ovrd. Product Liab. Veto	N	6. Drop EPA Limits	Y	10. Bar Bosnia Troop $	N
3. Increase Min. Wage	Y	7. Repeal Assault-Weap. Ban	N	11. Cut Anti-Missile Defense	Y
4. Welfare Reform	N	8. Ovrd. Part. Birth Veto	Y	12. Bar U.N. Uniforms	Y

Election Results

1996 general	Peter J. Visclosky (D)	133,553	(69%)	($318,769)
	Michael Edward Petyo (R)	56,418	(29%)	($47,379)
	Others	3,142	(2%)	
1996 primary	Peter J. Visclosky (D)	43,140	(84%)	
	Daniel C. Langmesser (D)	8,216	(16%)	
1994 general	Peter J. Visclosky (D)	68,612	(56%)	($290,049)
	John Larson (R)	52,920	(44%)	($172,531)

SECOND DISTRICT

Muncie, Indiana, became famous as the "Middletown" that sociologists Robert and Helen Lynd lived in and reported on in 1924–25 and again in 1935, and where a team of sociologists investigated again in 1976–78. The Lynds were attracted to Muncie by its typicalness—"every small city from Maine to California," *Life* said—but it wasn't exactly: it was a factory town in a country still almost half rural, it was almost entirely Protestant and northern in a country one-quarter Catholic and one-third southern. It was more typical in being culturally homogeneous but economically riven. In the 1920s, Muncie celebrated its common values and was loath to admit its economic disparities; in the 1930s, the latter came out into the open when Muncie, like most of the industrial Midwest, was unionized in what were sometimes violent uprisings. The business elite—local bankers, merchants, executives at General Motors and the Ball family's glass company—was fiercely opposed by workers who were joining CIO unions and voting Democratic. Partisan politics took on the sharp, bitter tone of a struggle for wealth between two rival classes whose claims seemed irreconcilable. Echoes of this class warfare politics remain today, even after decades of rising incomes and a shift of political focus from economics to culture. Indiana manufacturing towns with strong union traditions, like Muncie and Anderson, still lean toward Democrats while Indiana manufacturing towns without strong union traditions, like Richmond and Kokomo, vote strongly Republican.

The 2d Congressional District of Indiana covers most of east central Indiana. It includes Muncie and Anderson, with its big General Motors factories, in the north; Richmond, founded by a major branch of American Quakers and the home of their Earlham College; Columbus, the home of Cummins Engine, whose longtime head J. Irwin Miller paid major national architects to design most of the town's important buildings, public and private. This is a Republican district in presidential politics, a swing district in Indiana races.

The congressman from the 2d District is David McIntosh, a Republican first elected in 1994. McIntosh was born in California, moved to Kendallville, north of Fort Wayne, when his mother returned home after his father's death; his mother became a Democratic city judge. His interest in politics began in 1976, at 18, when he saw 29-year-old Dan Quayle in his first campaign for Congress. McIntosh went to Yale and the University of Chicago Law School, where he studied under Antonin Scalia and was one of the founders of the conservative Federalist Society. McIntosh worked in the Reagan Justice Department and White House, then became director of the White House Council on Competitiveness headed by Vice President Quayle. After 1992, McIntosh worked for the Hudson Institute in Indianapolis and lived in Muncie, with a view of running against Philip Sharp, a Democrat who had held the seat for 20 years despite some very close races. When Sharp announced his retirement in February 1994, McIntosh was not the only Republican interested in the race: State Auditor Ann DeVore was already running. But astonishingly, her candidacy failed in February when she missed a noon deadline for filing nominating papers, though the office was down the hall from her own. Bill Frazier, Sharp's opponent in 1976, 1978 and 1980, also ran. While McIntosh showcased big-name endorsers like Robert Bork and Boyden Gray, Frazier spent $616,000 of his own money and attacked McIntosh as a Washington insider who only returned to Indiana to run. McIntosh won 43%–42%, with his biggest margin in Richmond.

The Democratic nominee was Secretary of State Joe Hogsett, Governor Evan Bayh's campaign manager in 1988 and Senator Dan Coats's opponent in 1992; he raised and spent nearly as much money as McIntosh. But McIntosh tied him to Bill Clinton—he called the 1994 crime bill "the Clinton/Hogsett hug-a-thug bill"—and the Democratic House leadership: "Joe says he's against taxes and for prayer in schools. But that first vote [that is cast at the start of each Congress] elects a speaker and chairs who are on the other side of those issues." Hogsett carried his home base, Rush County, but otherwise the vote went pretty much down straight ticket lines, and McIntosh won 54%–46%.

McIntosh very quickly became a leader in the House, the freshman liaison to the Republican leadership and chairman of the Government Reform and Oversight Subcommittee on National Economic Growth, Natural Resources and Regulatory Affairs. McIntosh promptly called for a moratorium on new regulations retroactive to November 1994, some 4,300 of them, and wrote a bill requiring agencies like EPA and OSHA to make cost-benefit analyses and risk assessments and stand for court challenges before issuing regulations: placing on government the same kind of burdens it delighted in placing on business. McIntosh floor-managed this to passage in

February 1995. It was an impressive feat, although it died in the conference committee and was attacked by Democrats as an assault on the environment and workplace safety.

On this and other issues McIntosh was one of the most aggressive and effective of House Republican freshmen. "Closing down parts of government isn't that much of a problem," he said in 1995, and in January 1996 was one of 15 Republican freshmen to vote against the bill to reopen the government, criticizing Newt Gingrich in the process. He called for reform of Superfund, and total repeal of retroactive liability. He called for periodic review of regulations costing more than $100 million. He took the lead on Ernest Istook's bill to limit non-profit organizations that receive federal funds from spending more than 5% of their budgets on lobbying. This was attacked as an abridgement of free speech. "All we are asking is that these groups make a choice. Be a lobbying organization or be a grant recipient." When opponents said it would ban the Red Cross from testifying before Congress, McIntosh offered to exempt statutorily recognized "patriotic organizations." But he got in trouble when he handed out a news release prepared by his staff but produced on the letterhead of the leftish Alliance for Justice, and had to apologize; the measure did not pass.

McIntosh had greater, though quieter, success when he amended the March 1996 debt limit bill to give Congress power to veto or change proposed regulations within 60 legislative days. "The act is the most significant change in regulatory law in 50 years . . . yet no one noticed. Most observers failed to read it carefully," he said. He showed a flair for legislative responses to Democratic arguments, calling for cash rather than IOUs to be deposited in the Social Security trust fund and exempting minimum wage workers from the income tax. He was even more adroit in finding Hoosier examples of people hurt by regulation and helped by his deregulatory work. He cited the case of an Anderson girl in need of a drug awaiting FDA approval; McIntosh called the FDA head and the drug was approved. Another case was asphalt layers required by a federal regulation to wear long pants in the summer; McIntosh got a rider deleting funds for enforcement of the regulation.

In addition, he used these examples as part of his positive ad campaign for reelection. McIntosh raised $1.3 million for the campaign, and spent $1.1 million. Democrat Marc Carmichael, a former state legislator and gas company lobbyist, who said he would work to create jobs and balance the budget "compassionately," spent only $183,000. McIntosh won by the convincing margin of 58%–40%, losing Muncie's Delaware County narrowly, but winning by 2–1 in the southern end of the district.

McIntosh is likely to be one of the busiest and most aggressive House Republican sophomores in the 105th Congress. He was the first to focus attention on the Clinton White House's 200,000-name database, allegedly not used for political purposes. When Senator Dan Coats announced his retirement in December 1996, McIntosh was looked to as a possible candidate; in February 1997 he said he was "testing the waters." McIntosh has pulled back from his statement, however, saying in late March 1997, "chances are that I will not run for the Senate," and will instead seek reelection to the House, where his future looks bright.

The People: Pop. 1990: 554,321; 43% rural; 14% age 65+; 95% White; 4% Black; 1% Hispanic origin. Households: 60% married couple families; 27% married couple fams. w. children; 32% college educ.; median household income: $26,185; per capita income: $12,311; median gross rent: $331; median house value: $43,000.

1996 Presidential Vote			1992 Presidential Vote		
Dole (R)	97,406	(45%)	Bush (R)	101,370	(43%)
Clinton (D)	89,038	(42%)	Clinton (D)	82,008	(35%)
Perot (I)	26,483	(12%)	Perot (I)	50,458	(22%)

Rep. David M. McIntosh (R)

Elected 1994; b. June 8, 1958, Oakton, CA; home, Muncie; Yale U., B.A. 1980; U. of Chicago Schl. of Law, J.D. 1983; Episcopalian; married (Ruthie).

Career: Spec. Asst., U.S. Atty Gen., 1986–87; White House Spec. Asst., Domestic Affairs, 1987–88; Spec. Asst., Vice Pres. Dan Quayle, 1989–91; Exec. Dir., Cncl. of Competitiveness, 1989–92; Sr. Fellow, Hudson Inst., 1993–94.

DC Office: 1208 LHOB 20515, 202-225-3021; Fax: 202-225-3382; e-mail: mcintosh@hr.house.gov.

District Offices: Anderson, 765-640-2919; Columbus, 812-372-3637; Richmond, 765-962-2883; Muncie, 765-747-5566.

Committees: *Education & The Workforce* (17th of 25 R): Early Childhood, Youth & Families; Postsecondary Education, Training & Life-Long Learning. *Government Reform & Oversight* (13th of 24 R): Human Resources; National Economic Growth, Natural Resources & Regulatory Affairs (Chmn.). *Small Business* (15th of 19 R): Regulatory Reform & Paperwork Reduction.

Group Ratings

	ADA	ACLU	AFS	LCV	CFA	CON	NFIB	COC	ACU	NTLC	CHC
1996	0	20	0	15	15	51	100	100	100	95	100
1995	0	—	—	6	0	84	—	100	100	—	—

National Journal Ratings

	1995 LIB — 1995 CONS			1996 LIB — 1996 CONS		
Economic	0%	—	74%	29%	—	70%
Social	21%	—	72%	24%	—	72%
Foreign	0%	—	85%	0%	—	79%

Key Votes of the 104th Congress

1. Reduce Medicare Growth $	Y	5. Flag Amendment	Y	9. Cuban Embargo	Y
2. Ovrd. Product Liab. Veto	Y	6. Drop EPA Limits	N	10. Bar Bosnia Troop $	Y
3. Increase Min. Wage	N	7. Repeal Assault-Weap. Ban	Y	11. Cut Anti-Missile Defense	N
4. Welfare Reform	Y	8. Ovrd. Part. Birth Veto	Y	12. Bar U.N. Uniforms	Y

Election Results

1996 general	David M. McIntosh (R)	123,113	(58%)	($1,050,616)
	R. Marc Carmichael (D)	85,105	(40%)	($182,508)
	Others	4,665	(2%)	
1996 primary	David M. McIntosh (R)	52,812	(85%)	
	Gregory Lunsford (R)	9,418	(15%)	
1994 general	David M. McIntosh (R)	93,592	(54%)	($973,209)
	Joseph H. Hogsett (D)	78,241	(46%)	($794,684)

THIRD DISTRICT

When Notre Dame University was founded in 1842, Catholics were still a rarity in most of America, and certainly rare on the limestone-bottomed plains of northern Indiana. This was still farm country and South Bend no more than a crossroads on the St. Joseph River. By the 1920s, both had grown. Notre Dame, thanks to its football team, "the Fighting Irish," was the most famous Catholic university in the land, and South Bend was a significant industrial city, home of Studebaker and Bendix and dozens of other factories. In the last 50 years, Notre Dame has grown in size and reputation, without giving up football; but South Bend has not done so well. Studebaker went out of business in the 1960s; other major factories closed; high-wage unionized jobs disappeared, replaced by lower-wage jobs with less protection. Elkhart, in the next county to the east, is still the nation's largest maker of "manufactured housing," i.e., trailers, and band instruments, but other plants have closed. The industrial swath from Michigan City on the Lake through South Bend to Elkhart is one of the few parts of the industrial Midwest that has suffered early 1980s-style job losses in the early 1990s.

The 3d Congressional District of Indiana has centered for decades on South Bend. This is an industrial and ethnic city—with the nation's largest percentage of Hungarian-Americans—which has long been Democratic; so is LaPorte County around Michigan City. Elkhart County, with more management people, is decidedly Republican.

The congressman from the 3d District is Tim Roemer, a Democrat first elected in 1990. Roemer grew up in South Bend and went to college in San Diego, then received a masters and Ph.D. from Notre Dame; he worked for 3d District Congressman John Brademas and Arizona Senator Dennis DeConcini and is married to the daughter of former Louisiana Senator Bennett Johnston. Roemer returned to South Bend and ran for Congress in 1990, raised more PAC money than Republican incumbent John Hiler and sounded outsider themes with insider skill.

Roemer has a moderate voting record, though more liberal on foreign affairs issues; he stresses his support of the balanced budget amendment, votes against pork barrel projects and supported much of the Contract With America. Counting the costs of the bills he has sponsored, the National Taxpayers Union Foundation rated him among the thriftiest in Congress. In 1994, even before Republicans took control, he angered organized labor, long an important factor in South Bend, on an OSHA bill; at the same time he started a Children's Working Group and called for more spending on Head Start, immunizations and WIC.

In 1995, with Republicans in control, Roemer voted for the conservative Democrat Blue Dog balanced budget and moved to cut one-third of the employees in Energy Department labs. He called for much smaller tax cuts and for adjusting the Consumer Price Index, and he sought Medicaid reform with higher spending than the Republicans' bill and more flexibility for the states. In November 1995 he and Fred Upton, a Republican from next-door St. Joseph, Michigan, wrote Speaker Gingrich and called for temporary appropriations, with the lower of Senate or House figures; he was booed and hissed by fellow Democrats when he spoke for it on the floor and was paid little heed by Gingrich. And he decried the harsh partisan atmosphere of the House. "You can't talk about family values and balancing the budget without having bipartisanship and civility. And so little of that has been laid on the table so far." In 1996 Roemer supported welfare reform and was one of 37 House Democrats who wrote Clinton urging him to sign the August 1996 Welfare Reform Act.

Roemer has run well ahead of his party in a district that was always marginal between 1980 and 1990. He won with 57% in 1992 when George Bush was carrying the district, and with 55% in 1994 when Republicans carried it for all statewide offices. In 1996, against state Senator Joe Zakas, he paraded his moderate views and survived a last minute Zakas charge that he voted for a sex survey of teenagers; Roemer lost only narrowly in Elkhart County and carried the district 58%–41%. Right after the election he formed, with Jim Moran and Calvin Dooley, a New Democrats organization, for moderate Democrats uncomfortable with the mostly southern Blue Dogs' stands on gun control and environmental measures. "If your experience on the campaign trail has been anything like ours, you have probably found that advocating traditional Democratic policies did not get you elected," he wrote fellow Democrats, seeking recruits. He seems likely to be a player in any bipartisan coalition in the 105th Congress.

The People: Pop. 1990: 554,482; 29% rural; 13% age 65+; 90% White; 7% Black; 1% Asian; 2% Hispanic origin. Households: 59% married couple families; 28% married couple fams. w. children; 37% college educ.; median household income: $29,470; per capita income: $13,385; median gross rent: $395; median house value: $55,000.

1996 Presidential Vote			**1992 Presidential Vote**		
Dole (R)	91,427	(46%)	Bush (R)	91,708	(42%)
Clinton (D)	86,715	(43%)	Clinton (D)	82,483	(38%)
Perot (I)	20,374	(10%)	Perot (I)	41,358	(19%)

Rep. Tim Roemer (D)

Elected 1990; b. Oct. 30, 1956, South Bend; home, South Bend; U. of CA at San Diego, B.A. 1979, U. of Notre Dame, M.A., 1981, Ph.D. 1985; Catholic; married (Sally).

Career: Staff Asst., U.S. Rep. John Brademas, 1980; Legis. Advisor, U.S. Sen. Dennis DeConcini, 1985–89; Instructor, American U., 1988.

DC Office: 2348 RHOB 20515, 202-225-3915; Fax: 202-225-6798; e-mail: troemer@hr.house.gov.

District Offices: South Bend, 219-288-3301.

Committees: *Education & The Workforce* (9th of 20 D): Early Childhood, Youth & Families; Postsecondary Education, Training & Life-Long Learning. *Science* (5th of 21 D): Energy & Environment (RMM).

Group Ratings

	ADA	ACLU	AFS	LCV	CFA	CON	NFIB	COC	ACU	NTLC	CHC
1996	60	44	83	69	62	86	57	56	40	37	40
1995	75	—	—	31	46	87	—	50	32	—	—

National Journal Ratings

	1995 LIB		1995 CONS	1996 LIB		1996 CONS
Economic	59%	—	40%	58%	—	42%
Social	47%	—	53%	42%	—	56%
Foreign	62%	—	36%	75%	—	25%

Key Votes of the 104th Congress

1. Reduce Medicare Growth $	N	5. Flag Amendment	Y	9. Cuban Embargo	N
2. Ovrd. Product Liab. Veto	Y	6. Drop EPA Limits	N	10. Bar Bosnia Troop $	N
3. Increase Min. Wage	Y	7. Repeal Assault-Weap. Ban	N	11. Cut Anti-Missile Defense	Y
4. Welfare Reform	Y	8. Ovrd. Part. Birth Veto	Y	12. Bar U.N. Uniforms	Y

Election Results

1996 general	Tim Roemer (D)	114,288	(58%)	($525,727)
	Joe Zakas (R)	80,699	(41%)	($310,084)
1996 primary	Tim Roemer (D)	unopposed		
1994 general	Tim Roemer (D)	72,497	(55%)	($350,594)
	Richard Burkett (R)	58,878	(45%)	($64,373)

FOURTH DISTRICT

The northeast corner of Indiana, in the center of a flat agricultural area, can claim to be the center of Middle America. Its first settlers were of New England Yankee stock, establishing orderly communities with public schools and even colleges; they were joined by German immigrants, who built tidy farms and their own civic institutions. In the northern part of the state there are hills and lakes, and the strange swamp that is the central focus of Gene Stratton

Porter's children's classic, *Girl of the Limberlost*. The one large city here, Fort Wayne, was built on the flat terrain along the Maumee River that flows to Toledo, Ohio; it grew as a factory town, surging ahead and then falling back as large factories, often tied to the auto industry, opened and closed over the years. Now, Fort Wayne has more white collar jobs.

Politically, this area is ancestrally Republican since the Civil War years. Since the New Deal, it has sometimes veered Democratic in times of economic distress. This part of Indiana is also a cradle of vice presidents. Thomas Marshall, Woodrow Wilson's vice president, was born in North Manchester and practiced law in Columbia City; Dan Quayle spent his high school years and later practiced law in Huntington.

The 4th Congressional District of Indiana consists of nine counties in northeast Indiana, plus a bit of one other. It includes Fort Wayne, Huntington and Columbia City but not North Manchester. This is the district that Dan Quayle won in 1976 and represented for two terms; he was among the few who saw early on the potential of the anti-government, lower-taxes trend that dominated the 1980s, but was almost nowhere predicted in the 1970s.

The congressman from the 4th District is Mark Souder, a Republican first elected in 1994. Souder grew up in Grabill, 10 miles from Fort Wayne, where his Amish great-great-grandfather's family settled and started Souder's of Grabill in 1907, originally a harness shop and now a furniture store and manufacturer of store fixtures. Souder worked in the furniture business, returned to Grabill, went to work in 1984 for Dan Coats, Quayle's successor in the House, as minority staff director of the Select Committee on Children, Youth and Families. He moved with Coats to the Senate in 1989, where he served as his legislative director and deputy chief of staff. In 1993 he returned to Fort Wayne and started running against Jill Long, a Democrat elected to replace Coats. With a moderate record and a farm background, she was not an easy target. But Souder raised more money and easily won the six-candidate Republican primary with 40% of the vote; the state Republican ticket was also running far ahead of the Democrats in the 4th District. The result was a 55%–45% Souder victory.

In the House, Souder was elected vice president of the freshman class and became one of its more outspoken advocates of change. He was one of only two Republicans—the other was another Hoosier freshman, John Hostettler—who voted against the balanced budget amendment, because it did not require a supermajority to raise taxes. "I'm skeptical of the spending cuts and certain of the tax hikes." As Majority Leader Dick Armey once said, "Tell Souder I always assume that if there's trouble, it's him." In the 1995–96 budget showdown, Souder urged holding out for bigger cuts. When he and Hostettler were two of the 17 votes against a continuing resolution in January 1996, Gingrich announced that he would not appear at fundraisers for them. Said Souder, "This is a test of whether you can vote your conscience." Later in 1996, angry that the Republican budget increased domestic discretionary spending, he pushed for 1.9% cuts in every appropriation.

Souder spent much time and effort on trying to stop the flow of drugs into the United States. Noting that Fort Wayne police seized $1.4 million of drugs in 1995 versus $184,500 in 1990, he proposed an amendment to cut off foreign assistance to Mexico if it did not stop the drug flow. It passed the House in June 1996, and the conference committee included a modified version, calling for $2.5 million to be withheld. Interestingly, the DEA promised to set up a Fort Wayne office in 1997. Other Souder proposals were put forward without much hope of passage, but to stimulate thought. In July 1995 he proposed a GIVE Act, which would give a 120% deduction for charitable contributions, allow non-itemizers to deduct contributions of $1,000 or more, exclude charities from the overall limit on itemized deductions, and extend the deadline for deductions to April 15. Later that year he also proposed a McFlat tax, with deductions for mortgage interest and charitable contributions. Upset with graphic music lyrics, he said, "There may be some attempt at a V-chip for music."

In September 1996 Souder called for an investigation of the INS program Citizenship USA, charging, presciently, that the Clinton Administration was seeking to naturalize new citizens unduly quickly so they could vote in November.

Souder was reelected by a handsome 58%–39% margin against a poorly funded challenger. Despite qualms about Newt Gingrich's ethics problems, Souder announced on January 2, 1997, that he would back him for speaker. Later that month he and fellow Hoosier sophmore David McIntosh proposed a Social Security Preservation Act, requiring the government to put cash—not IOUs—in the Social Security trust fund.

The People: Pop. 1990: 554,577; 40% rural; 12% age 65+; 92% White; 6% Black; 1% Asian; 2% Hispanic origin. Households: 62% married couple families; 31% married couple fams. w. children; 40% college educ.; median household income: $30,859; per capita income: $13,436; median gross rent: $373; median house value: $56,200.

1996 Presidential Vote

Dole (R)	110,538	(53%)
Clinton (D)	75,185	(36%)
Perot (I)	19,641	(9%)

1992 Presidential Vote

Bush (R)	102,779	(46%)
Clinton (D)	69,292	(31%)
Perot (I)	49,565	(22%)

Rep. Mark Edward Souder (R)

Elected 1994; b. July 18, 1950, Fort Wayne; home, Grabill; IN U., B.S. 1972; Notre Dame U., M.B.A. 1974; Protestant; married (Diane).

Career: Furniture salesman, 1976–83; Staff Dir., U.S. House Select Cmte. on Children, Youth & Families, 1984–89; Legis. Dir., U.S. Sen. Dan Coats, 1989–91, Dep. Chief of Staff, 1991–93.

DC Office: 418 CHOB 20515, 202-225-4436; Fax: 202-225-3479; e-mail: souder@hr.house.gov.

District Offices: Ft. Wayne, 219-424-3041.

Committees: *Education & The Workforce* (16th of 25 R): Early Childhood, Youth & Families; Postsecondary Education, Training & Life-Long Learning. *Government Reform & Oversight* (14th of 24 R): Human Resources; National Security, International Affairs & Criminal Justice (Vice Chmn.). *Small Business* (9th of 19 R): Empowerment (Chmn.).

Group Ratings

	ADA	ACLU	AFS	LCV	CFA	CON	NFIB	COC	ACU	NTLC	CHC
1996	10	25	17	23	23	87	97	75	95	93	93
1995	5	—	—	6	8	25	—	92	100	—	—

National Journal Ratings

	1995 LIB — 1995 CONS			1996 LIB — 1996 CONS		
Economic	36%	—	60%	30%	—	68%
Social	21%	—	72%	33%	—	65%
Foreign	42%	—	55%	0%	—	79%

Key Votes of the 104th Congress

1. Reduce Medicare Growth $	Y	5. Flag Amendment	Y	9. Cuban Embargo	Y
2. Ovrd. Product Liab. Veto	Y	6. Drop EPA Limits	N	10. Bar Bosnia Troop $	Y
3. Increase Min. Wage	N	7. Repeal Assault-Weap. Ban	Y	11. Cut Anti-Missile Defense	N
4. Welfare Reform	Y	8. Ovrd. Part. Birth Veto	Y	12. Bar U.N. Uniforms	Y

Election Results

1996 general	Mark Edward Souder (R)	121,344	(58%)	($438,384)
	Gerald L. Houseman (D)	81,740	(39%)	($65,093)
	Others	4,796	(2%)	
1996 primary	Mark Edward Souder (R)	44,853	(82%)	
	Phillip D. Marx (R)	10,118	(18%)	
1994 general	Mark Edward Souder (R)	88,584	(55%)	($422,161)
	Jill L. Long (D)	71,235	(45%)	($410,299)

FIFTH DISTRICT

Across the plains of northern Indiana runs the Hoosier Heartland Corridor—the HHC, a publicist's name for U.S. 24 as it runs west from Fort Wayne along the Wabash River through Wabash, Peru and Logansport, and then overland toward the Illinois prairie. Scattered on the major east-west railroad and highway lines that connect the East Coast and Chicago, the Hoosier Heartland's small cities and large towns display a geometric order and heartland American values. It is also an economically creative place. Here in Kokomo, Elwood Haynes built one of the first gas-powered automobiles and invented stainless steel. And if this area was hit heavily by recession in the early 1980s, it has rebounded smartly. Its large factories, like Delco and Chrysler, are expanding, and its small manufacturers have proved high-skill and adaptive. This is a part of America with little immigrant heritage from the early waves of immigration, relatively few blacks, and only a handful of the more recent Latin and Asian immigrants. Basic values have not been shaken so much here as in other parts of the nation: this area has one of the nation's highest percentages of households with families, married couples and children. It is also a place that has given America such icons as James Dean, who grew up in Fairmount (and would be in his 60s today if he had not smashed up his Porsche near the Pacific), and Cole Porter, who grew up in Peru.

The 5th Congressional District of Indiana occupies most of the land on either side of the HHC. There are no big cities within the district: it just skirts Indianapolis, Fort Wayne, South Bend and Gary. And, though farming is important here, factories large and small employ many more people: this is one of the centers of American manufacturing. Since the Civil War, this has mostly been Republican country, and the western part of the district was the home base of House Minority Leader (1959–65) Charles Halleck. But in much of the 1970s and 1980s, Democrats were competitive.

The 5th District's congressman is Steve Buyer (pronounced BOOyer), a Republican elected in 1992. Buyer grew up in White County, graduated from The Citadel and served in the Army, worked in Indianapolis and started a family law practice in Monticello, where he joined all the civic organizations. A major in the military reserves, he was called to active duty in fall 1990, serving as legal adviser at a prisoner-of-war camp in the Persian Gulf. Buyer was enraged that two-thirds of House Democrats, including the 5th District's Democratic Congressman Jim Jontz, voted against the war. After he returned to Indiana, where he was White County Republican vice chairman, he began appearing in uniform around the Hoosier Heartland, attacking Jontz on his Gulf war stand. In October 1991, Buyer met with all of Jontz's former opponents, and then launched his campaign. In 1992 he focused on the House bank and post office scandals and called for term limits and application of laws passed by Congress to Congress itself: an anticipation of the Contract with America. He attacked Jontz for switching committees in order to protect the spotted owl in Oregon. Jontz was a skilled politician, but Buyer won 51%–49%, carrying the Hoosier Heartland but losing counties at the edge of the district.

In the House Buyer compiled a conservative voting record and got seats on National Security and Veterans' Affairs. He served on the Republican task force on health care, favoring incremental reform. He worked with Senator Dan Coats on trying to get states authority to limit import of out-of-state solid waste; a measure passed the Senate in the 104th Congress but died in the House.

Buyer has done much of his legislative work on the Veterans' Affairs Committee. He worked on the Benefits Improvement Act of 1996 and on the measure to extend veterans' preferences (to the federal judiciary, for the first time). One pet cause has been investigating "Gulf war syndrome." Since his return from the Gulf, Buyer has suffered from flu, pneumonia, spastic colon, kidney infection, bronchitis and a constant cough. He investigated and discovered there may have been chemical weapons in a bunker destroyed by U.S. Army troops at Khamisiyay, Iraq. In 1994 he successfully cosponsored legislation that allows the VA to compensate Gulf war veterans suffering from a chronic disability resulting from an undiagnosed illness that became manifest to a degree of 10% or more within a year of the Gulf war—a real departure in veterans' law. While Buyer does not claim to have identified a single Gulf war syndrome, he is insisting on further investigation.

Buyer is now chairman of the Military Personnel Subcommittee of National Security—significant because he looks askance at U.S. troop deployment in Bosnia. In October 1995 he sponsored with fellow Gulf war veteran Paul McHale a resolution saying that U.S. deployment should not be a requisite for a peace agreement; it passed 315–104. In December 1995 he and Ike Skelton wrote a resolution reiterating opposition to deployment; it passed 287–141. Ultimately, House Republicans failed to block the Bosnian mission, as the Senate opposed a similar resolution and U.S. troups were already on their way.

Buyer seems politically very strong in this formerly Democratic-held district. He was reelected with 70% of the vote in 1994 and 65% in 1996.

The People: Pop. 1990: 554,240; 58% rural; 13% age 65+; 96% White; 2% Black; 1% Hispanic origin. Households: 64% married couple families; 30% married couple fams. w. children; 31% college educ.; median household income: $27,893; per capita income: $12,252; median gross rent: $335; median house value: $46,400.

1996 Presidential Vote

Dole (R)	105,906	(50%)
Clinton (D)	78,270	(37%)
Perot (I)	27,469	(13%)

1992 Presidential Vote

Bush (R)	103,124	(45%)
Clinton (D)	70,891	(31%)
Perot (I)	52,354	(23%)

Rep. Steve Buyer (R)

Elected 1992; b. Nov. 26, 1958, Rensselaer; home, Monticello; The Citadel, B.S. 1980; Valparaiso U., J.D. 1984; Methodist; married (Joni).

Career: Army, 1984–87, 1990–91 (Persian Gulf); Army Reserves, 1980–84, 1988–present; IN Dep. Atty. Gen., 1987–88; Vice Chmn., White Cnty. Repub. Party, 1988–90; Practicing atty., 1988–92.

DC Office: 326 CHOB 20515, 202-225-5037.

District Offices: Kokomo, 317-454-7551; Monticello, 219-583-9819.

Committees: *National Security* (10th of 30 R): Military Installations & Facilities; Military Personnel (Chmn.). *Judiciary* (12th of 20 R): Crime. *Veterans' Affairs* (6th of 16 R): Oversight & Investigations.

Group Ratings

	ADA	ACLU	AFS	LCV	CFA	CON	NFIB	COC	ACU	NTLC	CHC
1996	5	6	9	23	31	22	97	94	95	100	100
1995	0	—	—	6	0	56	—	100	88	—	—

National Journal Ratings

	1995 LIB — 1995 CONS	1996 LIB — 1996 CONS
Economic	36% — 60%	30% — 68%
Social	28% — 70%	14% — 77%
Foreign	0% — 85%	0% — 79%

Key Votes of the 104th Congress

1. Reduce Medicare Growth $	Y	5. Flag Amendment	Y	9. Cuban Embargo	Y
2. Ovrd. Product Liab. Veto	Y	6. Drop EPA Limits	N	10. Bar Bosnia Troop $	Y
3. Increase Min. Wage	Y	7. Repeal Assault-Weap. Ban	Y	11. Cut Anti-Missile Defense	N
4. Welfare Reform	Y	8. Ovrd. Part. Birth Veto	Y	12. Bar U.N. Uniforms	Y

Election Results

1996 general	Steve Buyer (R)	133,627	(65%)	($227,204)
	Douglas L. Clark (D)	66,628	(32%)	($6,764)
	Others	5,253	(3%)	
1996 primary	Steve Buyer (R)	unopposed		
1994 general	Steve Buyer (R)	111,031	(70%)	($501,287)
	J.D. Beatty (D)	45,224	(28%)	($181,780)
	Others	3,403	(2%)	

SIXTH DISTRICT

Indianapolis is one of America's most symmetric cities, sited in almost the exact center of Indiana, centered on Monument Circle with eight avenues radiating like wheel spokes, with the city occupying most of almost perfectly square Marion County. In the seven surrounding suburban counties, the irregularities of the physical landscape and the asymmetries of the original settlers' boundaries intrude; but a respected order has been established here. The more affluent areas are typically farther out, starting on the north side somewhere north of the home of Benjamin Harrison, Indiana's one president, and the 1920s-era Governor's Mansion built on North Meridian Street by the same man who more or less invented the gas station. Here are comfortable in-town neighborhoods built in the 1940s and 1950s, the cul-de-sac subdivisions and condominiums of the 1970s and 1980s, and new developments set out on hills in the once rural counties beyond.

The 6th Congressional District of Indiana includes most of the suburban territory around the core of Indianapolis, which forms the 10th District. The exception is to the west of the city, where most of Hancock and Boone Counties are in the 7th District. But the 6th includes the north side of Indianapolis and the affluent Hamilton County suburbs of Carmel and Fishers; it includes Hancock County to the east and takes in the less affluent but still conservative suburban territory to the south. This is by far the most Republican in Indiana and indeed one of the most Republican districts in the country.

The congressman from the 6th District is Dan Burton, an active and enthusiastic Republican who has been running for office since he was in his 20s. He had a horrific childhood: his father was abusive and left the family; his mother worked as a waitress and bought the kids' clothes at Goodwill; his father ultimately kidnapped his mother and went to jail and the kids were sent to the county home. Dan earned money as a teenager shining shoes and at 18 enlisted in the Army. He never finished college but made his way up as a real estate broker and insurance salesman.

He also ran for public office, often unsuccessfully. He was elected to the Indiana House in 1966, 1976 and 1978 and to the Indiana Senate in 1968 and 1980; he lost races for Congress in 1970 and 1972 and was first elected to the House in 1982 when the legislature created this heavily Republican suburban seat.

Burton is an enthusiastic conservative, confrontation-minded long before most of today's feisty young House Republicans appeared on the scene (or started shaving). He is chairman of the Government Reform and Oversight Committee now and in the 104th Congress was chairman of the Western Hemisphere Subcommittee of International Relations. He is head of the 70-member Conservative Action Team, a force independent of and sometimes at odds with the Republican leadership. He was regarded for years by many Democrats as a nut, excitably pursuing lost causes. He opposed sanctions on South Africa, backed UNITA in Angola and Renamo in Mozambique, offered dozens of spending cuts that were overwhelmingly defeated, pushed for universal mandatory AIDS testing. But he has also been vindicated by events for some stands which were widely scorned, from his hard-line opposition to the Soviet Union to his lonely vote against the Catastrophic Health Care Act of 1988. And through his tirades shines an uncynical sincerity and a certain friendliness.

Burton had substantial legislative successes in the Republican 104th Congress. He deserted the leadership on the first rule it lost, in July 1995, because he wanted to strike the National Endowment for the Arts appropriation; but the NEA was cut back and put on its way to extinction. He co-sponsored the V-chip legislation with Massachusetts Democrat Edward Markey; it passed as part of the Telecommunications Act, over the strong objection of the broadcast lobby. He opposed any changes in campaign finance rules; none were made. An avid participant in charity golf tournaments, he reluctantly supported a strict gift ban, backed by many Republican freshmen, which passed 422–6. He rounded up signatures on a letter insisting on at least $245 billion in tax cuts, which is in line with Republican positions. He backed the adoption tax credit and provided for explosive-sniffing dogs in the FAA authorization bill. He protected the pensions of the privatized Naval Air Warfare Center in Indianapolis.

His biggest achievement was the Helms-Burton Act. It was a response to the shooting down of the Brothers to the Rescue planes by the Cuban Air Force, and stated that foreign companies could be sued in American courts if as part of business deals with Fidel Castro's regime they took over property expropriated from American owners. Canada and European allies yelped, but why should they have a moral entitlement to property unlawfully seized by a dictator? Helms-Burton passed the House in September 1995 and the Senate in October and was signed by Bill Clinton, who may have been casting an eye at the Cuban-American vote in Florida, into which he did make inroads. But the bill allows the president to delay implementation, which Clinton did into early 1997. On other foreign issues Burton has strong views which he is unafraid to utter. He opposed normalization of relations with Vietnam. He opposed cutoff of aid to Turkey: "I'm awfully tired of watching Turkey get kicked in the teeth on the floor and in this committee," On troop deployments to Bosnia in December 1995 he said resignedly, "We have no choice but to go along." He moved to reduce aid to India, because of its treatment of the Sikhs and Kashmiris, whose American counterparts contributed heavily to his 1996 campaign.

In late 1996, when it became clear his committee would investigate the various misdeeds of the Clinton White House, some Republicans talked of getting another chairman. They felt Burton was too excitable and vulnerable to attack by Democrats; they remembered with dismay his 1994 speech questioning whether White House counsel Vincent Foster had been murdered and his body moved and recounting his reenactment of the shooting at his home. But Burton had played a much more measured role in questioning Clinton White House officials in the 1995 and 1996 hearings before then-Chairman Bill Clinger. And Burton promised to be judicious. "The perception of me . . . is an ax-wielding serial killer. I would describe myself as an individual congressman who felt compelled to pursue truth aggressively. But as chairman, people will be pleasantly surprised with the bipartisan approach I'm going to take. I'm not going to be warm and fuzzy, but I'm going to be fair." In early 1997, Burton wanted to keep the investigation focused on the Clinton White House and threatened to charge it with contempt of Congress. House Democrats attacked him for not expanding the investigation to include Republican misdeeds, and the ranking Democrat on the committee, Henry Waxman, called Burton's investigation "a partisan witch hunt." Ironically, Burton had his own campaign finance troubles: he had to return contributions to Sikh temples in April 1997 and to a lobbyist for Zaire President Mobutu a month later, and faced allegations from a former Pakistani lobbyist who accused Burton of threatening to cut off his access to other Republicans unless he raised money for Burton's campaign.

In this heavily Republican district Burton has been reelected easily, and no serious primary opposition has appeared. In 1996 he was reelected 75%–23%, winning 81% of the vote in Hamilton County. He also ended the race with $961,000 cash on hand. He was mentioned as a candidate for governor in 1996 and senator in 1998, but made no move to run.

The People: Pop. 1990: 553,865; 24% rural; 11% age 65+; 97% White; 1% Black; 1% Asian; 1% Hispanic origin. Households: 65% married couple families; 32% married couple fams. w. children; 52% college educ.; median household income: $38,644; per capita income: $17,971; median gross rent: $452; median house value: $81,200.

1996 Presidential Vote			**1992 Presidential Vote**		
Dole (R)	168,497	(63%)	Bush (R)	153,269	(57%)
Clinton (D)	75,285	(28%)	Clinton (D)	61,030	(23%)
Perot (I)	22,404	(8%)	Perot (I)	54,909	(20%)

Rep. Dan Burton (R)

Elected 1982; b. June 21, 1938, Indianapolis; home, Indianapolis; IN U., 1958–59, Cincinnati Bible Seminary, 1959–60; Protestant; married (Barbara).

Career: Army, 1956–57, Army Reserves, 1958–63; Real estate broker; Founder, Dan Burton Insurance Agency, 1968; IN House of Reps., 1966–68, 1976–80; IN Senate, 1968–70, 1980–82.

DC Office: 2185 RHOB 20515, 202-225-2276; Fax: 202-225-0016.
District Offices: Greenwood, 317-882-3640; Indianapolis, 317-848-0201.

Committees: *Government Reform & Oversight* (Chmn. of 24 R). *International Relations* (7th of 26 R): International Operations & Human Rights; Western Hemisphere.

Group Ratings

	ADA	ACLU	AFS	LCV	CFA	CON	NFIB	COC	ACU	NTLC	CHC
1996	10	6	0	15	0	22	94	94	100	100	100
1995	0	—	—	0	0	56	—	96	100	—	—

National Journal Ratings

	1995 LIB — 1995 CONS			1996 LIB — 1996 CONS		
Economic	0%	—	74%	20%	—	76%
Social	21%	—	72%	0%	—	90%
Foreign	0%	—	85%	0%	—	79%

Key Votes of the 104th Congress

1. Reduce Medicare Growth $	Y	5. Flag Amendment	Y	9. Cuban Embargo	Y
2. Ovrd. Product Liab. Veto	Y	6. Drop EPA Limits	N	10. Bar Bosnia Troop $	Y
3. Increase Min. Wage	N	7. Repeal Assault-Weap. Ban	Y	11. Cut Anti-Missile Defense	N
4. Welfare Reform	Y	8. Ovrd. Part. Birth Veto	Y	12. Bar U.N. Uniforms	Y

Election Results

1996 general	Dan Burton (R)	193,193	(75%)	($491,08
	Carrie Jean Dillard-Trammell (D)	59,661	(23%)	($11,27
	Others	5,003	(2%)	
1996 primary	Dan Burton (R)	unopposed		
1994 general	Dan Burton (R)	136,876	(77%)	($455,09
	Natalie M. Bruner (D)	40,815	(23%)	

SEVENTH DISTRICT

Of the railroad passenger trains that used to run on the lines criss-crossing the township grids o the Midwest, none had a more romantic name than the Wabash Cannonball that rumbled alon the Wabash River, across the rolling farmland of northern Indiana on its way from Detroit to St Louis, crossing the old National Road, now U.S. 40, which runs in a nearly straight line fron Indianapolis to St. Louis. The landscape here is some of the most prosaic in the United States mostly flat, with neat farms and frame-bungalowed towns, looking unchanged from years ago Today the Cannonball no longer runs; people bounce around the Midwest on commuter airline from small city to hub; and the National Road and U.S. 40 have been replaced for throug traffic by Interstate 70.

The 7th Congressional District of Indiana covers much of the routes of the Wabas Cannonball and the National Road in western Indiana, starting from the Indianapolis city limits Its two largest towns are quite different in character. Terre Haute is an old manufacturing towr the boyhood home of Socialist Eugene Debs, and now has a Sony compact disc plant. It has nc gained population in years and tends to vote Democratic—a lonely stand in central Indiana. Th other major town is Lafayette, where the main business is Purdue University, Indiana's lanc grant college and the alma mater of C-SPAN founder Brian Lamb. Growing and prosperou Lafayette tends to vote Republican. Even more Republican are the small counties and th suburban territory in Hendricks and Boone Counties outside Indianapolis.

The congressman from the 7th district is Edward Pease, a Republican elected in 1996 t replace 30-year incumbent John Myers. Pease grew up in Terre Haute, where he was an Eagl Scout and high school valedictorian. After college and law school at Indiana University, h practiced law in Brazil, the Clay County seat; he was active in many charities, including the Bo Scouts. In 1980 he was elected to the state Senate, where he served 12 years. In 1984 he went t work as Indiana State University's general counsel in Terre Haute, then became Vice Presider in 1993. Myers's retirement was not unexpected; he was the third most senior Republican bu was passed over for the Appropriations chair by Newt Gingrich, who thought him to accommodationist; he also had two serious primary opponents in 1994.

Pease was one of 15 Republicans and four Democrats who ran for the seat. At first the chi competition seemed to be state Senator Dick Thompson and former county party chairman Da Pool, who got 22% and 18% against Myers in 1994. But also emerging was former prosecut John Meyers, whose name was just one "e" away from the incumbent's. John Myers initially ha said he would not endorse anyone. But his daughter was supporting Pease and his son-in-law wa Pease's communications and finance director. In late April Myers endorsed Pease for the Ma primary; Pease immediately began running radio and TV ads featuring the endorsement. It ma have made the difference: Pease won with 30% of the vote; Meyers had 17%; Thompson an

Pool 15% and 11%; state Representative Kathy Willing, 9%. Thompson, Pool, and Willing carried their home counties; Pease carried pretty much everything else.

In the general election Pease faced Democrat Robert Hellmann, a Terre Haute neighbor, longtime (1982–96) state legislator, and a self-described conservative. They differed sharply on one issue, abortion, with Hellmann saying, "The Fourth Amendment prohibits government intrusion into those healthcare decisions"—an odd statement inasmuch as the Fourth Amendment barring illegal searches and seizures has never been cited by abortion rights backers. Hellmann attacked Pease for selling his house to a cousin for $350,000, renting it back, and donating $155,000 to his own campaign. Pease called for getting the government out of agriculture and increasing Pell grants and student loans.

Pease won 62%–35%, carrying every county but Vigo, which includes Terre Haute, where he lost by only 159 votes, and next-door Vermillion. He had 57% in the county that includes Lafayette and 73% and 70% in Hendricks and Boone, outside Indianapolis. Pease serves on the Judiciary Committee as well as Transportation and Infrastructure where, as the only Hoosier on the committee, he will work to get funding for projects throughout the state as Congress reauthorizes ISTEA, the Intermodal Surface Transportation Efficiency Act.

The People: Pop. 1990: 554,500; 48% rural; 12% age 65+; 96% White; 2% Black; 1% Asian; 1% Hispanic origin. Households: 62% married couple families; 29% married couple fams. w. children; 39% college educ.; median household income: $28,080; per capita income: $12,536; median gross rent: $358; median house value: $54,300.

1996 Presidential Vote			**1992 Presidential Vote**		
Dole (R)	111,500	(52%)	Bush (R)	103,801	(46%)
Clinton (D)	75,150	(35%)	Clinton (D)	71,273	(32%)
Perot (I)	25,773	(12%)	Perot (I)	48,916	(22%)

Rep. Edward A. Pease (R)

Elected 1996; b. May 22, 1951, Terre Haute; home, Seelyville; IN U., A.B. 1973, J.D. 1977; Methodist; single.

Career: Practicing atty., 1977–84; IN Senate, 1980–92; Gen. Cnsl., IN State U., 1984–93, Vice Pres., 1993–96.

DC Office: 226 CHOB 20515, 202-225-5805.

District Offices: Danville, 317-718-0307; Lafayette, 765-423-1661; Terre Haute, 812-238-1619.

Committees: *Judiciary* (19th of 20 R): Courts & Intellectual Property; Immigration & Claims. *Transportation & Infrastructure* (28th of 40 R): Aviation; Surface Transportation.

Group Ratings and Key Votes: Newly Elected

Election Results

1996 general	Edward A. Pease (R)	130,010	(62%)	($586,448)
	Robert F. Hellmann (D)	72,705	(35%)	($340,816)
	Others	7,125	(3%)	
1996 primary	Edward A. Pease (R)	22,095	(30%)	
	John Meyers (R)	12,487	(17%)	
	Richard Thompson (R)	10,792	(15%)	
	Dan L. Pool (R)	8,157	(11%)	
	Katherine Willing (R)	6,724	(9%)	
	Pete Ross (R)	5,020	(7%)	
	John Lee Smith (R)	3,732	(5%)	
	Others	5,228	(7%)	
1994 general	John T. Myers (R)	104,359	(65%)	($543,967)
	Michael M. Harmless (D)	55,941	(35%)	($480,693)

EIGHTH DISTRICT

"Evansville," wrote John Bartlow Martin in 1947, "called the Pocket City (though not by loyal natives), is the capital of a tri-state area comprising the neglected tag ends of Indiana, Kentucky and Illinois." It was a factory town then, building car parts and refrigerators, drawing workers from Kentucky, Tennessee and the picturesque but not very fertile hills of southern Indiana, the lowland soaked by the terrible flood of March 1997. It was a town of hard-bitten politics, with plenty of partisan conflict. This was the boyhood home of Senator William Jenner, a McCarthy ally who once said General George Marshall would sell out his grandmother to the Communists, and the political base of Senator Vance Hartke.

Evansville is one of two major focuses of the 8th Congressional District of Indiana which, within irregular borders, covers most of the southwest portion of the state. The other is Bloomington, quite a different place, the home of Indiana University and a limestone quarrying center. This southwest corner of Indiana was the first part of the state settled by whites. Vincennes, now a small town on the banks of the Wabash River, was once the metropolis of Indiana, and Scottish philanthropist and visionary Robert Owen established the town of New Harmony downstream. Owen's son was the first congressman from the area, elected in 1842 and 1844. Since then, it has been represented by both parties, at one point in the 1970s electing four different congressmen in four successive elections, the only congressional district in the country to do so in that decade. The overall partisan tradition here has been Democratic since the Civil War, but the Democrats' cultural liberalism has cost them votes.

The congressman from the 8th District is John Hostettler, a Republican elected in 1994, an ingenuous and idealistic man who seems miscast in politics. Hostettler is from Posey County, just west of Evansville; he went to Rose-Hulman Institute of Technology in Terre Haute and in 1983 became a Southern Indiana Gas & Electric Company engineer. He had never run for office, but in 1994, at 33, he was one of six Republican candidates vying to run against 12-year incumbent Democrat Frank McCloskey. Hostettler's great strength was his support from anti-abortion and Christian fundamentalist groups; he also had obvious regional strength in the western edge of the district, along the Wabash. He won the primary with 35%, to 23% for his next competitor. In the general, Hostettler refused to take PAC money; McCloskey collected $368,000 of it, and outspent the Republican $565,000 to $309,000; Hostettler's biggest fund raiser was a $100-per-family fried chicken dinner with Marilyn Quayle. Hostettler attacked McCloskey on taxes, gay rights, gun control, environment, school prayer, his 65 overdrafts at the House bank, and constantly referred to him as Frank McClinton. McCloskey accused Hostettler of wanting to outlaw all abortions and called him John McGingrich. McCloskey carried Evansville and Bloomington by microscopic margins. But Hostettler carried most of the rural counties and won 52%–48%.

In the House Hostettler was a not entirely predictable conservative. He and fellow Indiana freshman Mark Souder were the only two Republicans to vote against the balanced budget amendment in 1995, because it did not require a supermajority to raise taxes. Hostetler also opposes changing the Constitution except where there is no alternative. For the same reason he opposed term limits. He is strongly opposed to abortions, especially partial-birth abortions. In January 1996 he was one of 15 Republican members to vote against the continuing resolution to reopen the federal government. In response Newt Gingrich cancelled his appearance at a Hostettler fundraiser. Hostettler wrote Gingrich, "I cannot allow my fund-raising to be tied in any way to specific votes," and invited Dick Armey instead.

Hostettler has taken on some quixotic causes for principle and come tantalizingly close to success. In June 1996 he sponsored an amendment to zero out AmeriCorps—"This demeans the entire notion of citizenship since it pays people to volunteer"—and lost 240–183. In the same month Hostettler teamed with Joe Kennedy to eliminate the federal subsidy (timber road purchaser credits) for logging in national forests. "If private companies don't think it is economically feasible to pay for the roads, why should taxpayers have to?" The amendment passed late one night, 211–210, then was brought up the next afternoon (after a request from the floor for a revote) and was rejected on a tie vote, 211–211. Hostettler formed the Interstate 69 Mid-Continent Highway Caucus, with 20 congressmen and 10 senators, to promote the development of I-69 southwest from Indianapolis to Evansville. He also seeks to change the highway aid formula, to give states at least 95% of what they pay in taxes, when ISTEA comes up for reauthorization in 1997.

With his narrow margin, his unpolitical ways, and the Democratic heritage of the district, Hostettler became one of the targets of the AFL-CIO ad campaign in 1996. Two Democrats ran against him, both with connections to McCloskey. McCloskey endorsed state Representative Rick McConnell, but the winner, by 40%–39% in the Democratic primary, was Jonathan Weinzapfel, a former McCloskey aide now working as a bank public relations manager in Evansville. Weinzapfel, like Hostettler, was from Posey County just west of Evansville; in the primary he concentrated on the Evansville area and Bloomington, and carried them while losing in the smaller rural counties. Weinzapfel was a good fundraiser, and got $185,000 from PACs and party committees, while Hostettler, true to his promise, raised no PAC money at all but still managed to outspend Weinzapfel, $528,000 to $470,000. Hostettler attacked Weinzapfel for taking labor PAC money, especially from the Laborers' Union, which the Clinton Justice Department said had "ties to organized crime." And the National Republican Congressional Committee attacked Weinzapfel for a $10,000 loan from his employer which it claimed was not backed by collateral. Hostettler looked like one of the most endangered Republican freshmen. But he eked out a 50%–48% victory, carrying most of the rural counties, some by handsome margins, while losing narrowly in the Evansville and Bloomington areas. In the 105th Congress Hostettler continued his candid ways, voting "present" in the election for speaker. He started his term by attacking EPA's proposed ozone standards and calling for income averaging for farmers.

The People: Pop. 1990: 554,347; 42% rural; 14% age 65+; 95% White; 3% Black; 1% Asian; 1% Hispanic origin. Households: 58% married couple families; 27% married couple fams. w. children; 37% college educ.; median household income: $25,242; per capita income: $12,153; median gross rent: $341; median house value: $48,800.

1996 Presidential Vote			**1992 Presidential Vote**		
Clinton (D)	100,171	(45%)	Clinton (D)	103,844	(42%)
Dole (R)	96,956	(43%)	Bush (R)	97,062	(40%)
Perot (I)	23,905	(11%)	Perot (I)	43,177	(18%)

Rep. John N. Hostettler (R)

Elected 1994; b. July 19, 1961, Evansville; home, Wadesville; Rose-Hulman Inst. of Tech., B.S. 1983; Baptist; married (Elizabeth).

Career: Mechanical Engineer, S. IN Gas & Electric Co., 1983–94.

DC Office: 431 CHOB 20515, 202-225-4636; Fax: 202-225-3284; e-mail: johnhost@hr.house.gov.

District Offices: Bloomington, 812-334-1111; Evansville, 812-465-6484.

Committees: *Agriculture* (15th of 27 R): Forestry, Resource Conservation & Research; Livestock, Dairy & Poultry. *National Security* (20th of 30 R): Military Installations & Facilities; Military Research & Development.

Group Ratings

	ADA	ACLU	AFS	LCV	CFA	CON	NFIB	COC	ACU	NTLC	CHC
1996	20	7	8	15	31	71	89	88	95	85	80
1995	5	—	—	19	0	31	—	83	84	—	—

National Journal Ratings

	1995 LIB	—	1995 CONS	1996 LIB	—	1996 CONS
Economic	41%	—	56%	33%	—	64%
Social	0%	—	79%	33%	—	67%
Foreign	28%	—	65%	30%	—	65%

Key Votes of the 104th Congress

1. Reduce Medicare Growth $	Y	5. Flag Amendment	Y	9. Cuban Embargo	N
2. Ovrd. Product Liab. Veto	Y	6. Drop EPA Limits	N	10. Bar Bosnia Troop $	Y
3. Increase Min. Wage	N	7. Repeal Assault-Weap. Ban	Y	11. Cut Anti-Missile Defense	N
4. Welfare Reform	Y	8. Ovrd. Part. Birth Veto	Y	12. Bar U.N. Uniforms	Y

Election Results

1996 general	John N. Hostettler (R)	109,860	(50%)	($528,325)
	Jonathan Weinzapfel (D)	106,201	(48%)	($470,027)
	Others	3,803	(2%)	
1996 primary	John N. Hostettler (R)	38,807	(82%)	
	Michael Allen McCamish (R)	8,537	(18%)	
1994 general	John N. Hostettler (R)	93,529	(52%)	($309,484)
	Frank McCloskey (D)	84,857	(48%)	($565,810)

NINTH DISTRICT

The southeastern corner of Indiana, now in the national eye only during the awful flood of March 1997, was a busy place when white settlers rafted down the Ohio River in the early 19th Century. They were mostly southerners, "Butternuts," from across the river in Kentucky or over the mountains in Virginia, and they built the first large Indiana settlements. Today, you can see their work in the marvelous old buildings of Madison, now quiet but once one of the busiest ports on the Ohio River. Farther down the river is Corydon, from 1816–25 the state capital, home town of Indiana's current Governor, Frank O'Bannon. The early 19th Century buildings here have been well preserved because these towns were bypassed first by the railroads, then by U.S. routes and interstate highways, and they certainly are remote from major airports. The river is still an artery of commerce, but utilitarian barges have replaced steamers.

Butternut Indiana retained its affection for things southern into the Civil War and beyond. Local politician Jesse Bright was expelled from the U.S. Senate in 1862 for "supporting the rebellion." To this day, the hills along the Ohio River typically vote Democratic, as do the Indiana suburbs of Louisville. But to the east Indiana is now filling up with migrants from Cincinnati—a Yankee and German abolitionist bastion in Jesse Bright's time, an overwhelmingly Republican stronghold in ours—who are moving the southeast corner of Indiana away from its ancestral party.

The 9th Congressional District of Indiana is made up of most of the state's Ohio River counties and an oddly shaped collection of lightly populated counties to the north. Ancestrally Democratic, culturally conservative, recently Republican and idiosyncratically creative.

The congressman from the 9th District is Lee Hamilton, a Democrat first elected in 1964, former chairman of the International Relations and Intelligence Committees. Hamilton grew up in Evansville, studied at DePauw, in postwar Germany and at Indiana University, worked for a while for a big Chicago law firm but decided that he liked small town life and moved to Columbus; after eight years of law practice, he ran for the House in 1964, and beat a Republican in the LBJ landslide. Hamilton seems folksy and without urban savvy, has a strong intellect and capacity for hard work plus a sense of moral imperative. For a decade until the 1994 election, he was one of the leaders of the Democratic House—chairman of the Intelligence Committee in 1985–87; House chairman of the Iran-contra Committee in 1987–88, in which capacity he sternly denounced Oliver North and the Reagan Administration; chairman of the Joint Economic Committee in 1989–90; chairman of International Relations in 1993–95. In 1992 he was co-chairman of the Joint Committee on the Organization of Congress, whose recommendations were ignored, perhaps to the electoral detriment of the Democrats then in control; it is only since the Republicans took control that Hamilton proposals were adopted, like the gift ban, congressional staff cuts, strengthening lobbyist regulation, and applying workplace laws to Congress. Hamilton was seriously considered by both Michael Dukakis and Bill Clinton for the vice presidential nomination and was mentioned as a possible Clinton secretary of state.

To his work Hamilton brings a small town demeanor and the gravity of concern about the long term that is the hallmark of the bipartisan foreign policy establishment that thrived in the years before he came to Congress. He was long an advocate of tax increases, and supported them in 1990 and 1993; he now supports the balanced budget amendment and supported the moderate Democratic, but not the Republican, balanced budget proposals in 1995 and 1996. He voted for the Welfare Reform Act but strongly criticized the Republicans' Medicare reform.

On foreign affairs, Hamilton in the late 1990s has been trying to revive the post-World War II tradition of bipartisan foreign policy. But before then, he was more partisan, strongly criticizing the Reagan Administration on Iran-contra, opposing the Gulf war resolution with dire predictions—massive American casualties, a fracturing of the allied coalition, rising anti-Americanism—that almost entirely failed to come true. Like the Clinton Administration in its early years, he saw weapons proliferation as a major problem and included among major goals "the fight against hunger, disease and rapid population growth." He has advocated most favored nation status for China, in line with both Bush and Clinton Administrations, though he held out the possibility of sanctions because of Chinese missile sales. On Bosnia, in February 1993, he called American participation in a multi-national peacekeeping force "a prudent commitment of American power," and in December 1995 offered a resolution that declared support for American troops deployed there and avoided condemning the Clinton policy; it was rejected, 237–190, for an alternative that opposed deployment. In the Middle East, he has long taken an evenhanded view frustrating to many backers of Israel; in October 1995 he said the bill recognizing Jerusalem as the capital of Israel was being advanced "for reasons of domestic politics, not foreign policy." On Cuba, he opposed the Helms-Burton Act in 1996 and the Cuba Libertad bill in 1995. He opposed the foreign policy reorganization proposed by Senate Foreign Relations Chairman Jesse Helms.

In February 1997 Hamilton announced that he would not run for reelection in 1998—the tenth Democratic former committee chairman to retire since the Republicans won the House. He had at least the prospect of a serious challenge. After winning reelection easily in the 1970s and 1980s, he won by only 52%–48% over state Senator Jean Leising in 1994; she waged an aggressive campaign against him on abortion, gun control, and welfare reform, and mocked his failure to achieve congressional reform in the Democratic House; and she carried the eastern counties near Cincinnati. In 1996 Leising ran again. This time both candidates spent nearly twice as much money, with Hamilton raising $426,000 from PACs, and Hamilton ran significantly better, winning 56%–42%. Leising will run again in 1998 and may face Kevin Kellems, a former aide to Senate Richard Lugar. On the Democratic side, former state Senator Baron Hill, who lost a close race for the Senate against Dan Coats in 1990, despite being vastly outspent, announced that he will run.

The People: Pop. 1990: 554,516; 59% rural; 13% age 65+; 97% White; 2% Black. Households: 64% married couple families; 31% married couple fams. w. children; 29% college educ.; median household income: $26,900; per capita income: $11,727; median gross rent: $325; median house value: $49,200.

1996 Presidential Vote			1992 Presidential Vote		
Clinton (D)	101,434	(44%)	Clinton (D)	97,970	(41%)
Dole (R)	99,915	(44%)	Bush (R)	97,412	(40%)
Perot (I)	26,154	(11%)	Perot (I)	44,839	(19%)

Rep. Lee H. Hamilton (D)

Elected 1964; b. Apr. 20, 1931, Daytona Beach, FL; home, Nashville; DePauw U., B.A. 1952, Indiana U., J.D. 1956, Goethe U., Frankfurt, Germany, 1952–53; United Methodist; married (Nancy).

Career: Practicing atty., 1956–64; Instructor, American Banking Inst. 1960–61.

DC Office: 2314 RHOB 20515, 202-225-5315; Fax: 202-225-1101; e-mail: hamilton@hr.house.gov.

District Offices: Jeffersonville, 812-288-3999.

Committees: *International Relations* (RMM of 21 D). *Joint Economic Committee* (8th of 10 Reps.).

Group Ratings

	ADA	ACLU	AFS	LCV	CFA	CON	NFIB	COC	ACU	NTLC	CHC
1996	45	25	75	77	62	68	62	56	45	32	26
1995	70	—	—	44	54	87	—	42	12	—	—

National Journal Ratings

	1995 LIB — 1995 CONS			1996 LIB — 1996 CONS		
Economic	61%	—	38%	57%	—	43%
Social	60%	—	39%	41%	—	58%
Foreign	79%	—	17%	59%	—	40%

Key Votes of the 104th Congress

1. Reduce Medicare Growth $	N	5. Flag Amendment	Y	9. Cuban Embargo	N
2. Ovrd. Product Liab. Veto	Y	6. Drop EPA Limits	Y	10. Bar Bosnia Troop $	N
3. Increase Min. Wage	Y	7. Repeal Assault-Weap. Ban	Y	11. Cut Anti-Missile Defense	Y
4. Welfare Reform	Y	8. Ovrd. Part. Birth Veto	Y	12. Bar U.N. Uniforms	Y

Election Results

1996 general	Lee H. Hamilton (D)	128,123	(56%)	($967,859)
	Jean Leising (R)	96,442	(42%)	($451,475)
	Others	3,307	(1%)	
1996 primary	Lee H. Hamilton (D)	52,737	(86%)	
	E. Joe Finke (D)	8,435	(14%)	
1994 general	Lee H. Hamilton (D)	91,459	(52%)	($578,468)
	Jean Leising (R)	84,315	(48%)	($241,854)

TENTH DISTRICT

Indianapolis, radiating outward from the Soldiers and Sailors statue in Monument Circle, is precisely at the center of Indiana, dominating it as few other cities do a state. It is the political and governmental capital, industrial and financial center, and the intellectual center of Indiana as well. It is symmetrically laid out: just to the west of the circle is the state Capitol, to the north is the American Legion headquarters, to the east is the City-County building, to the south is the redeveloped Union Station, and the Hoosier Dome. The local papers are owned by former Vice President Dan Quayle's family, the Pulliams. Farther out is the huge and growing Indiana University Medical Center, and the state park along the creek-sized White River which is attracting new museums. Indianapolis has the world's biggest children's museum and has become one of the nation's top centers for religious conventions. In the 1990s it has attracted a $1 billion United Airlines repair center, a $67 million Postal Service overnight mail hub, and the Hudson Institute, a leading conservative think tank. Indianapolis has tried to make itself the amateur sports capital of the United States, and may have succeeded. It showed off its amateur athletic facilities, probably the best in the nation, in the 1987 Pan American Games: a state-of-the-art natatorium, a track and field stadium, a velodrome for cycling, a soccer center, a horse park, plus the Hoosier Dome (renamed the RCA Dome) and Market Square Arena. And of course Indianapolis has its U.S. Track and Field Hall of Fame and the Speedway where the Indianapolis 500 is held every Memorial Day weekend.

Politically, Indianapolis has long had robust competition in national as well as local races. In 1996 Indiana voted for Republican Bob Dole for president and Democrat Frank O'Bannon for governor. There is a Democratic core here in Indianapolis, made up mostly of blacks in Center Township; Indianapolis lacks the hearty ethnic mix of most midwestern cities, and has never had really big CIO unions nor large singles or gay communities. Almost all of this core is in the 10th Congressional District, which went strongly for Bill Clinton in 1992 and 1996, bounded by an irregular line which runs about five miles out from Monument Circle in all directions.

The congresswoman from the 10th District is Julia Carson, a Democrat elected in 1996. Carson was born to a teenage mother and grew up in poverty, working as a waitress, newspaper deliverer and summer farm laborer; she can remember going to the welfare office for a ration of cornmeal and lard. As a divorced mother she raised two children and then two grandchildren. In

1965 she was hired away from her job as a secretary at UAW Local 550 by newly elected Congressman Andy Jacobs to do casework in his Indianapolis office. When his election prospects looked dim in 1972 (he did lose, but won the seat back two years later), he encouraged Carson to run for the state House; she won, then was elected to the state Senate in 1976. In 1990 she ran for Center Township Trustee, the position responsible for running welfare in central Indianapolis; the agency was $17 million in debt and accused of mismanagement of taxpayer funds and mistreatment of welfare applicants. As Trustee, she instituted a workfare program, requiring recipients to work cleaning the streets, highways and riverbanks. The debt was paid off and property taxes lowered; the Republican Marion County Auditor said, "Julia Carson wrestled that monster to the ground."

In 1996 Jacobs decided to retire after spending 30 of 32 unorthodox and humor-filled years in the House, and Carson decided to run. She won Jacobs's endorsement and that of the local Democratic organization. Her primary opponent, former prosecutor and party chairman Ann DeLaney outspent her on radio and TV ads; but Carson won 49%–31%. Something similar happened in the Republican primary, where Marvin Scott, a Butler University professor who held Jacobs to 53% in 1994, got the party endorsement after a tough battle with William Hudnut, longtime Indianapolis mayor and the victor over Jacobs in 1972. But Virginia Blankenbaker, a stockbroker and state Senator from 1980–92, won out 51%–40%, despite Scott's his attempt to liken her to Hillary Rodham Clinton. So in this youth-prone age, this turned out to be a race between two grandmothers.

Both were also more liberal than many in their parties, pro-choice on abortion and against the death penalty. Carson cited her work as Center Township Trustee and said she supported welfare reform, though not the 1996 act; she was for "universal" health care but not "nationalized" medicine. "Every poor kid in the country ought to have a laptop computer. I don't think you respond effectively to juvenile delinquency when you keep your foot on the neck of children who are not responsible and shouldn't be held accountable," she said. Many commentators wondered whether a black Democrat could beat a white Republican in this 30% black district, and Blankenbaker led in an early October poll, 41%–36%. But Carson raised and spent almost as much as Blankenbaker and was probably helped by the indictment late in the campaign of four policemen involved in a downtown brawl with a black man. "I am not your African-American candidate, I am the Democratic candidate for Congress. I don't allow my opponents to stereotype me and confine me to a certain segment of the population," Carson said. She won a solid 53%–45% victory in November.

Unhappily, Carson was not able to take her seat on schedule. On January 4, 1997, technically a day after her term began, she had heart surgery in Indianapolis, and on swearing-in day was recovering in the hospital. She had additional surgery in mid-February on an artery in her neck. She kept up with events by watching C-SPAN from her hospital bed before finally arriving in Washington on March 5, where she got seats on the Banking and Veterans' Affairs Committees, and has come out in favor of making restrictions to NAFTA.

The People: Pop. 1990: 554,797; 11% age 65+; 68% White; 30% Black; 1% Asian; 1% Hispanic origin. Households: 43% married couple families; 20% married couple fams. w. children; 40% college educ.; median household income: $25,304; per capita income: $12,562; median gross rent: $394; median house value: $45,700.

1996 Presidential Vote

Clinton (D)	89,851	(54%)
Dole (R)	61,892	(37%)
Perot (I)	12,547	(8%)

1992 Presidential Vote

Clinton (D)	92,514	(47%)
Bush (R)	70,458	(36%)
Perot (I)	33,229	(17%)

Rep. Julia Carson (D)

Elected 1996; b. July 8, 1938, Louisville, KY; home, Indianapolis; Baptist; divorced.

Career: Secy., UAW, 1962–63; Legis. Aide, U.S. Rep. Andy Jacobs, 1965–72; IN House of Reps., 1972–76; IN Senate, 1976–90; Center Township Trustee, 1991–96.

DC Office: 1541 LHOB 20515, 202-225-4011; Fax: 202-225-5633.

District Offices: Indianapolis, 317-226-7331.

Committees: *Banking & Financial Services* (24th of 25 D): Housing & Community Opportunity. *Veterans' Affairs* (10th of 13 D): Health.

Group Ratings and Key Votes: Newly Elected

Election Results

1996 general	Julia Carson (D)	85,965	(53%)	($572,617)
	Virginia Blankenbaker (R)	72,796	(45%)	($638,275)
	Others	3,612	(2%)	
1996 primary	Julia Carson (D)	17,950	(49%)	
	Ann Delaney (D)	11,310	(31%)	
	Jocelyn-Tandy Adande (D)	3,747	(10%)	
	Mmoja Ajabu (D)	1,492	(4%)	
	Others	2,272	(6%)	
1994 general	Andy Jacobs, Jr. (D)	58,573	(53%)	($27,544)
	Marvin Bailey Scott (R)	50,998	(47%)	($69,852)

IOWA

Corny and quirky, corn-producing and computer-literate, Iowa is a state that longs to lead America, and not just by holding the first presidential contest of the season (well, almost the first, and treated as first by almost all candidates). As Americans were surging westward in the 1840s, Iowa was filling up with Yankee farmers and German immigrants, watching as wagon trains headed to the Oregon Trail and the Mormon thousands mustered by Brigham Young headed from the Mississippi across the rolling hills to Council Bluffs on the Missouri and then west. Iowa was a young state then, proud of its hundreds of schools and dozens of colleges, sending more than its share of young men to fight for the cause of the Union back east. After that war Iowans built a solid civilization based on farming and farm machine making and meat processing that resisted the blandishments of William Jennings Bryan's populism and cheap money and became one of the most solidly Republican states in the nation. And then, starting around 1900, Iowa grew old. Its commercial and financial center remained stuck in the railroad hub of Chicago, its economy failed to diversify and develop the dense manufacturing base of the Great Lakes states, and its young people started to move away to make their fortunes. Iowa's population, up from 674,000 in 1860 to 2.2 million in 1900 increased only slowly, and has not reached 3 million to this day. Its solid Capitol and courthouses, its sturdy but mostly old housing stock, give testimony to Iowa's strengths but also bespeak its lack of dynamism. Even its great economic achievement—the development of high-tech, ever-more-productive, but also less labor-intensive agriculture—has made this a state that did not grow much.

A century ago Iowa could claim to be the typical state; but for much of the 20th Century it has been culturally and politically countercyclical, headed in just the other direction as the rest of the nation—determinedly, with confidence in its own chipper rectitude, unembarrassedly out of step. In the industrial New Deal era, it stayed mostly agricultural and Republican, even as onetime Des Moines radio announcer, Ronald Reagan, became an enthusiastic Roosevelt Democrat and headed to Hollywood. It partook little of postwar economic growth. It was dovish during the Vietnam war and dubious about Watergate. In the 1980s, as Reagan, now a conservative Republican, became president, Iowans watched helplessly as farm prices and land values plummeted downward, farm implement factories closed, and 7% of its citizens left, as its population fell more than any other state but West Virginia. Self-pity became the dominant note of Iowa's politics, as voters sought protection from the vagaries of the market even as elsewhere commercial real estate and stock prices boomed. In the 1988 presidential cycle Iowa became one of the most Democratic states in the nation, sending 1988 caucus winner Dick Gephardt's politics solidly to the left and producing the second highest percentage for Michael Dukakis in November.

Now Iowa has swung back again, and so perhaps has the nation. If its economic rebellion against America's move toward free markets failed in the 1980s, its cultural qualms about America's move away from traditional values may be setting an example for the rest of the country in the 1990s. For Iowa has managed to combine over the years steady habits and tolerance of diversity. It has one of the lowest rates of divorce and very low rates of crime; yet it has led the way in welcoming refugees from southeast Asia and visiting students from all quarters of the world. Iowans' incomes dropped in the 1980s, but in the 1990s its high level of literacy and good work habits have produced white-collar and high-tech growth in and around its pleasant small cities, even as the old factories have closed. Iowa's unemployment rate is now among the nation's lowest, its farm land values have revived even as Congress voted in 1996 to phase out most crop subsidies, and Iowa's community spirit enabled it to rebound from the disastrous floods in 1993.

Politically, Iowa seems to have led the way. At the top of the ticket it has voted twice for Bill Clinton, 43%–37% in 1992, almost precisely at the national average, and 50%–40% in 1996, a little more Democratic. But down the ballot it has moved toward Republicans. Republican Senator Charles Grassley was reelected overwhelmingly in 1992, Democratic Senator Tom Harkin by a narrow margin in 1996. Republican Governor Terry Branstad survived serious challenges in both the primary and general election in 1994 to become the nation's longest-serving governor. Plus, Republicans won most U.S. House elections in the 1990s and won control of the state House in 1994 and the state Senate in 1996. Collectively, these results bespeak a sort of steady moderation, a desire to accept the verdict of the markets and to honor traditional values with some hedging on both counts. Iowa remains quirky in some respects. It is still probably one of the most dovish, isolationist-prone states, though very much aware of its role as an international exporter. It is thrift-minded, seeing a balanced budget more as a badge of moral rectitude than as a prudent economic policy. It pioneered legal riverboat gambling in 1989, but is not as dependent on it as some Mississippi Valley states. It is of two minds on some cultural issues, to the point that some of its politicians like to portray themselves as both pro-life and pro-choice. But much the same can be said of much, perhaps most, of America.

Governor. Iowa's Terry Branstad, first elected in 1982, is now the most senior governor in the nation, though he only turned 50 after the 1996 election. Branstad was born on a farm in northern Iowa, "a country kid that grew up learning about hard work"; he has never claimed to be an intellectual, but he has been running for things, and winning, since eighth grade. He was a conservative at the leftish University of Iowa in the late 1960s, then spent two years in the Army as an MP; he returned to his Lake Mills farm, started a family, and graduated from law school.

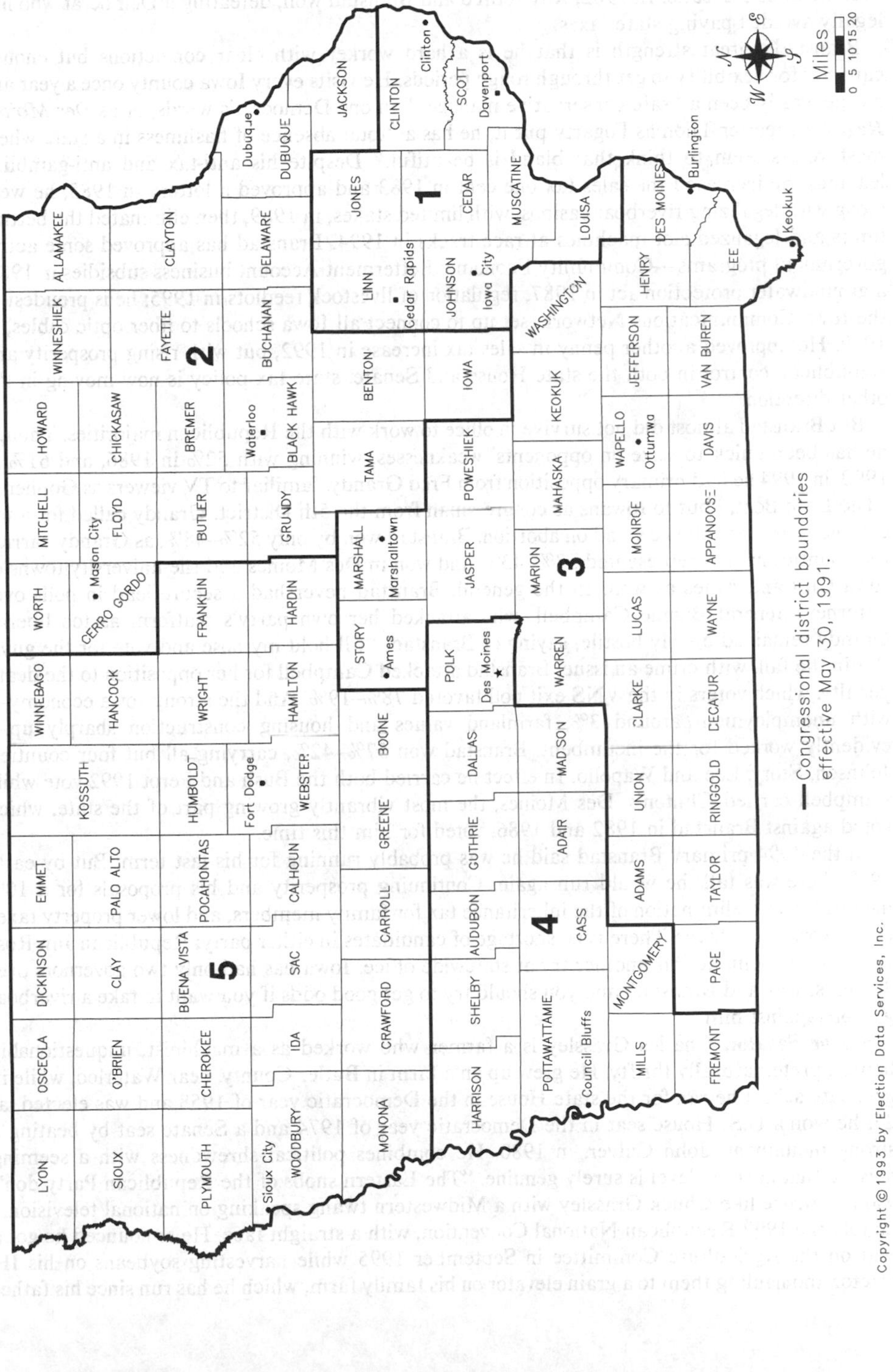
LYON
OSCEOLA
DICKINSON
EMMET
WINNEBAGO
WORTH
MITCHELL
HOWARD
WINNESHIEK
ALLAMAKEE
SIOUX
O'BRIEN
CLAY
PALO ALTO
KOSSUTH
HANCOCK
CERRO GORDO
Mason City
FLOYD
CHICKASAW
FAYETTE
CLAYTON
PLYMOUTH
CHEROKEE
BUENA VISTA
POCAHONTAS
HUMBOLDT
WRIGHT
FRANKLIN
BUTLER
BREMER
Sioux City
WOODBURY
IDA
SAC
CALHOUN
WEBSTER
Fort Dodge
HAMILTON
HARDIN
GRUNDY
BLACK HAWK
Waterloo
BUCHANAN
DELAWARE
DUBUQUE
Dubuque
MONONA
CRAWFORD
CARROLL
GREENE
BOONE
STORY
Ames
MARSHALL
Marshalltown
TAMA
BENTON
LINN
Cedar Rapids
JONES
JACKSON
CLINTON
Clinton
HARRISON
SHELBY
AUDUBON
GUTHRIE
DALLAS
POLK
Des Moines
JASPER
POWESHIEK
IOWA
JOHNSON
Iowa City
CEDAR
SCOTT
Davenport
MUSCATINE
POTTAWATTAMIE
Council Bluffs
CASS
ADAIR
MADISON
WARREN
MARION
MAHASKA
KEOKUK
WASHINGTON
LOUISA
MILLS
MONTGOMERY
ADAMS
UNION
CLARKE
LUCAS
MONROE
WAPELLO
Ottumwa
JEFFERSON
HENRY
DES MOINES
Burlington
FREMONT
PAGE
TAYLOR
RINGGOLD
DECATUR
WAYNE
APPANOOSE
DAVIS
VAN BUREN
LEE
Keokuk
1
2
3
4
5
N
E
S
W
Miles
0 5 10 15 20
—Congressional district boundaries effective May 30, 1991.

Even before that, he was elected to the state House in 1972, just before turning 26, and served three terms. In 1978 he was elected lieutenant governor, winning the primary with conservative support and coasting into office under the coattails of moderate Republican Bob Ray, who had been in office a decade. In 1982, Ray retired and Branstad won, defeating a Democrat who had legally avoided paying state taxes.

Branstad's great strength is that he is a hard worker with clear convictions but enough capacity for flexibility to get through rough periods. He visits every Iowa county once a year and has generally been a "safe conservative manager," in one Democrat's words; or as *Des Moines Register* reporter Thomas Fogarty put it, he has a "total absence of flashiness in a state where most voters seem to think that bland is beautiful." Despite his anti-tax and anti-gambling leanings, he increased the sales tax one cent in 1983 and approved a lottery in 1985; he went along with legalizing riverboat casinos, with limited stakes, in 1989, then eliminated the betting limits and legalized slot machines at race tracks in 1994. Branstad has approved some active government programs—Community Economic Betterment Account business subsidies in 1985, a groundwater protection act in 1987, regulation of livestock feedlots in 1995; he is proudest of the Iowa Communications Network, set up to connect all Iowa schools to fiber optic cables, in 1989. He approved another penny in sales tax increase in 1992, but with rising prosperity and Republican control in both the state House and Senate, state tax policy is now moving in the other direction.

But Branstad almost did not survive in office to work with the Republican majorities. Though he has been quick to seize on opponents' weaknesses, winning with 52% in 1986, and 61% in 1990, in 1994 he had primary opposition from Fred Grandy, familiar to TV viewers as Gopher in "The Love Boat," but to Iowans as congressman from the 5th District. Grandy called for a tax cut and took a pro-choice stand on abortion. Branstad won by only 52%–48%, as Grandy carried the counties he had represented 57%–43%, and won in Des Moines and the university towns of Iowa City and Ames as well. In the general, Branstad never had a secure lead in polls over Attorney General Bonnie Campbell, who attacked her own party's platform as too liberal; Grandy remained openly hostile, saying of Branstad, "I'll hold my nose and vote for the guy." But in the fall, with crime an issue, Branstad attacked Campbell for her opposition to the death penalty, which voters in the VNS exit poll favored 78%–19%. And the strong Iowa economy—with unemployment around 3%, farmland values and housing construction sharply up—evidently worked for the incumbent. Branstad won 57%–42%, carrying all but four counties: Johnson, Story, Lee and Wapello. In effect he carried both the Bush and Perot 1992 vote while Campbell carried Clinton's. Des Moines, the most vibrantly growing part of the state, which voted against Branstad in 1982 and 1986, voted for him this time.

In the 1994 primary Branstad said he was probably running for his last term. But by early 1997 there was talk he would run again. Continuing prosperity and his proposals for a 10% income tax cut, elimination of the inheritance tax for family members, and lower property taxes could work in his favor. There is no shortage of candidates in either party; Republican Jim Ross Lightfoot may make this another try at statewide office. Iowa has had only two governors over 30 years, Ray and Branstad, and you should try to get good odds if you want to take a riverboat gamble against him.

Senior Senator. Charles Grassley is a farmer who worked as a machinist, unquestionably honest, preternaturally thrifty. He grew up on a farm in Butler County, near Waterloo; while in graduate school he ran for the state House in the Democratic year of 1958 and was elected, at 25; he won a U.S. House seat in the Democratic year of 1974 and a Senate seat by beating a strong incumbent, John Culver, in 1980. He combines political shrewdness with a seeming naivete that at some level is surely genuine. "The Eastern snobs of the Republican Party don't want someone like Chuck Grassley with a Midwestern twang speaking on national television," he told the 1992 Republican National Convention, with a straight face. He announced he got a seat on the Agriculture Committee in September 1995 while harvesting soybeans on his IH tractor and hauling them to a grain elevator on his family farm, which he has run since his father died in 1960.

Grassley's record in Congress has been guided by three issues: thrift, agriculture and dovishness on defense; he is ever alert for abuse of power. His first major legislation was the 1986 Federal False Claims Act, which allows whistleblowers to bring suits for fraud on behalf of the government. He long sponsored the bill to apply to Congress the laws it applies to others, and was the chief sponsor of the Congressional Accountability Act of 1995. With David Pryor he has long worked on the Taxpayer Bill of Rights. He is usually a pretty partisan Republican but does not hesitate to vote against other Republicans on issues he thinks important: he was one of two Republicans who voted against the Gulf war resolution in 1991. And Grassley can be flexible. In 1995 he commissioned a GAO report on AmeriCorps, and charged it was more expensive than promised; but in 1996 he worked with AmeriCorps director Harris Wofford to make changes in the program and then supported its continuation.

Grassley has not always supported ever-higher farm price supports as some Democrats have. He pushed to limit cuts in commodity programs to 20% of total cuts in the 1996 Freedom to Farm Act, and he worked with Republicans to soften the "swampbuster" laws and wetlands regulations. He chairs the International Trade Subcommittee on Finance, and is a strong supporter of free trade, backing NAFTA and its extension to Chile; he worked to get Europeans to accept genetically engineered corn without labeling. He says the Freedom to Farm Act "ensures a safety net for family farmers, while enabling them to respond to the demands of the world marketplace. It sends a clear signal to the rest of the world that American farmers will compete for every sale in every market."

Grassley is a stern critic of the defense budget. He grilled Defense Secretary William Perry hard on "$33 billion of costs that can't be tracked," and in 1995 said, "The defense budget should be leveling off, not going up." He questioned why the Marine Corps needed 12 new generals when it had fewer enlisted men. He shellacked the Pentagon when he found out that an Air Force general, his wife, and cat were flown from Italy to Colorado in an otherwise empty 200-seat plane, and he criticized Speaker Newt Gingrich for having military aides.

He has used his seat on Judiciary to take on lawyers and judges. He correctly skewered the American Bar Association as blatantly political in its ratings of judges, worked to block a 12th judgeship for what he considered the underworked D.C. Circuit, and sent a questionnaire to federal judges to see how they spend their money. "Some of these people should get out of their offices and they would see the poor John Deere worker in Waterloo, Iowa, is as concerned about judges wasting his money as the generals wasting his money."

Grassley always makes his points soberly and stolidly; he is plainly sincere, yet surely cannot be unaware of his influence. Since 1980 he has been the most popular politician in Iowa. In 1986 he became the first Iowa senator to win reelection in 20 years, with a record 66% of the vote. In 1992, against state Senator Jean Lloyd-Jones who had started a peace institute, he pointed out that she had declined to probe the senate president's involvement in a banking scandal. Grassley carried even her home base, the university town of Iowa City, and all the state's 99 counties, for a 70%–27% victory, a new record. Grassley's seat comes up in 1998, and he can easily be reelected. He contemplated running for governor, but has decided that he won't.

Junior Senator. Tom Harkin has also proved a durable political figure who has had his political setbacks but also considerable accomplishments, and against some odds. He is one of the Democrats' Watergate babies, first elected in 1974, but there is no smooth Ivy League smugness to him. He has a craggy and almost worn look; he grew up poor in a rural town, where his father was a coal miner and his mother, a Slovenian immigrant, died when he was 10. His desire to use government to help those who are struggling comes not from academic theory but from tough personal experience. He worked his way through college and law school, spent five years in the Navy during the 1960s, ferrying planes from Vietnam for repair. Returning there in 1970 as an aide to Congressman Neal Smith, he discovered the infamous "tiger cages" prison cells. After a narrow loss in 1972, Harkin ran for Congress again in 1974 and invented "work days," a campaign technique widely imitated since: he spent a day working at each of a dozen or so local jobs. He won solidly and held the seat with good percentages. Well before the 1984 election, he cornered the Democratic nomination to run against Senator Roger Jepsen, who was gravely weakened by, among other things, insisting he was entitled to commute to work alone in the highway lane reserved for multiple passenger cars. In a tough year for Democrats elsewhere, Harkin was elected to the Senate with 55%.

Harkin's record in the Senate may fairly be characterized as liberal, though not always on economic issues; he voted for the balanced budget amendment in 1995. His biggest disappointment has surely been on farm policy. He came to the Senate as a self-styled populist, eager to expand government farm programs, and a decade ago his big initiative was the 1987 Harkin-Gephardt supply management farm bill, which would have raised overall food costs in order to benefit small farmers. But it was a nonstarter even in the 1980s, when Iowa farmers were hurting, and farm policy since has gone in the other direction: in 1996 Harkin voted—to no avail—against the Freedom to Farm Act which phases out most subsidies over seven years. In those years Harkin has supported food aid and exports. With some reluctance, he voted for NAFTA: Iowa is the nation's leading producer of corn and pork, the staples of Mexican cuisine.

Harkin's biggest success came from his work on the Americans with Disabilities Act (ADA). Harkin's brother Frank became deaf at age nine, and Harkin has long been a champion of the disabled, using his chairmanship of the Labor-HHS Appropriations Subcommittee for that purpose; he has implemented grants for "assistive technology" for the handicapped and a new NIH Institute on Deafness and Other Communications Disorders. The ADA was a great achievement, one that required overcoming resistance based on cost and qualms about the real-world effect of regulations. At Gallaudet University in Washington, D.C., a noted school for the hearing impaired, Harkin gave part of his speech in sign language when he withdrew from the 1992 presidential race. Harkin's Appropriations seat has made him a major force on medical research, with specific interests. He created an Office of Alternative Medicines at NIH, after he got relief from allergies by eating morsels of bee pollen; then in 1994 essentially got its head to leave because he was dissatisfied with his performance. The office was dismantled a year later.

On foreign policy, Harkin is very much a product of the Vietnam experience, an opponent of U.S. military intervention and aid on behalf of right-wing governments, but in favor of aid to the left-wing government of Haiti. He opposed contra aid and verged on being an apologist for the Nicaraguan Sandinista government in the 1980s and fervently opposed the Gulf war in 1991, bringing a lawsuit against President Bush to try to prevent him from using force without congressional approval. But Harkin was just as fervent a sponsor of an embargo on Haiti in 1994 when the military was in power and of threatening to use force to install then-exiled President Aristide.

In 1990, Harkin won reelection with 54% against a tough Republican opponent, Congressman Tom Tauke, a knowledgeable critic of government programs and a smart political operator. Then, in 1991, Harkin surprised many by running for president. In angry phrases, with a Trumanesque zest, Harkin preached that George Bush and the Republicans helped only the rich and that government must get involved to help the poor and middle class. But organized labor withheld an early endorsement despite his 90%-plus AFL-CIO voting record—a great tactical victory for Bill Clinton, governor of a right-to-work state. Harkin's sweep of the Iowa caucuses February 10, actually an impressive testimonial to his home state popularity, was mostly discounted by the media. And he failed to strike a chord with voters in low-tax New Hampshire, winning only 10% there February 18. He won the Minnesota and Idaho caucuses March 3, but got only 7% in South Carolina March 7 after campaigning there with Jesse Jackson. In debt and ineligible for matching funds, Harkin quit the race.

But Harkin didn't sulk in his tent. He endorsed Clinton March 26 and campaigned gamely for him in primaries and with union audiences. This brought out the best side of Harkin. He showed none of the defensiveness he does when he's running himself; instead, he was a genuinely happy warrior. Clinton ultimately returned the favor by appointing his wife Ruth Harkin, a Washington lawyer who combines good humor, competence and strong beliefs, to head the Overseas

Private Investment Corporation. In the Senate Harkin tried to salvage the Clinton healthcare plan by calling for insurance for children, but it was too late. He fought on Appropriations for more money for education and health care and conducted a campaign against Medicare waste, getting HCFA to monitor the Medicare billing system in Iowa. He got immigration agents permanently assigned to Iowa and sponsored bills to require "child labor free" labeling on products not produced with child labor and to establish "pay equity"—comparable worth setting of wages by government. These were not successful, and neither was his great cause in 1996. He put a hold on Federal Reserve Chairman Alan Greenspan's renomination for four months, denouncing his "insistence on high interest rates, despite the non-existent threat of inflation [which] hurts real people." But after a few days of debate, Greenspan was easily confirmed in June 1996—which means that his term extends to June 2000, when it will be difficult for an outgoing President Clinton to appoint a different-minded Fed chairman and get him confirmed.

In 1996 Harkin became the first Iowa Democrat to win three full Senate terms, narrowly. In 1995 he had no well-known opponent, but in 1996 3d District Congressman Jim Ross Lightfoot decided to run; Lightfoot won 61% in the June primary to 25% and 14% for legislators Maggie Tinsman and Steve Grubbs. "We're going to light this place up and liberalism is going to die in Washington," Lightfoot exclaimed, and his ads argued that Harkin was too liberal, had voted for pay raises and higher taxes, and lived in a big house in northern Virginia and was out of touch with Iowa. The polls tightened up in summer, and Harkin used his heavy financial advantage—he ended up spending $6.1 million to $2.5 million for Lightfoot—to widen his lead. Then the race seemed to narrow again in October; "we're in danger of winning this thing," Lightfoot quipped. But Harkin ended up winning 52%–47%—a narrow victory which he called a "character-building experience."

In the 105th Congress Harkin remains on Appropriations and is the ranking Democrat on the Agriculture Committee—the first time an Iowan has held the top position for his party on Agriculture since Jonathan Dolliver died in 1910.

Presidential politics. On a frosty evening in early February upwards of 150,000 Iowans troop to caucuses in 2,142 precincts and begin the process of choosing a president of the United States. (In 1996, there were caucuses earlier in Louisiana and Alaska, but few paid them much heed.) The precinct caucuses were scheduled early in the cycle for 1972 by Democratic doves who wanted more leverage for their views, and that year they started George McGovern on his way to the Democratic nomination. But the caucuses have had other, unanticipated consequences. In 1976, Jimmy Carter's strategist Hamilton Jordan determined that intensive campaigning could produce a surprise victory that could make a little-known candidate a national contender: without Iowa and the next-week New Hampshire primary, Carter would never have become president. By 1980, Iowans were so used to candidates courting them that when Ronald Reagan ducked an Iowa debate he was beaten by George Bush, even as Carter, still profiting from his 1976 contacts, was trouncing Edward Kennedy. But Reagan recovered in New Hampshire, where he did show up for a debate ("I paid for this microphone") and Carter lost in November: a forecast of Iowa's irrelevance in cycles to come.

Iowa's economic angst in the 1980s made George Bush, the 1980 winner here, a third-place finisher in 1988, behind Bob Dole and Pat Robertson—a sign of the increasing presence of Christian conservatives in the Republican Party. Iowa's leftish economic policies had a substantial effect on Dick Gephardt, who won the Democratic contest in 1988. But Democrats have not had a contest since: Iowa's Tom Harkin preempted the field in 1992 and Bill Clinton was unopposed in 1996. Indeed there were no contests here at all in 1992, for Pat Buchanan started his insurgent campaign in New Hampshire, where he had the strong backing from the Manchester *Union Leader*; he would have been staunchly opposed by the *Des Moines Register*. In 1996 Bob Dole had the support of leading Republicans, led by Governor Terry Branstad and Senator Charles Grassley, and farm state roots as well: his very narrow victory was an omen of the weakness of his candidacy later, and the negative ads run against him by Steve Forbes and others may have contributed to his weak showing in Iowa in November (he did worse than was generally expected in other states subjected to Forbes ad barrages: New Hampshire, Arizona, Delaware). But no one pays close attention to Iowa in the fall, with its seven electoral votes, even though the state has voted close to the national average in the 1990s; in 1996 Bill Clinton won solidly, 50%–40%, carrying 80 of 99 counties.

So a case can be made that the Iowa caucuses haven't determined a nomination since 1984. Will they matter for the future? It is by no means clear that their first-in-the-nation status can be preserved. It is enshrined in the rules of the Democratic Party, and Iowa might be the biggest obstacle for Al Gore, who ducked out of the caucuses in 1988, if he were running against Dick Gephardt, who spent 144 days campaigning in the state in 1988, or Bob Kerrey, who is from next-door Nebraska. Republicans have no rules favoring Iowa, but in 1996 most Republican candidates avoided other early contests because Iowa Governor Terry Branstad and New Hampshire Governor Steve Merrill threatened them with attacks if they competed elsewhere. Now New Hampshire has a Democratic governor and Branstad, first elected in 1982, may not be governor in 2000. Outgoing Republican Chairman Haley Barbour set up a commission to rethink the presidential selection process, and it could decide that it is time Americans stopped giving voters in two small and atypical states such a major say in who their nominee will be. But in the meantime putative candidates have been spied disembarking in Iowa airports and attending fundraising dinners for obscure Iowa politicians. Don't bet the farm against Iowa.

Congressional districting. In May 1991, Iowa's Democratic legislature and Governor Branstad approved congressional district lines drawn by the non-partisan Legislative Services Bureau. These lines hurt the Democrats in the short run—incumbent Republican Jim Nussle beat incumbent Democrat Dave Nagle in the new 2d District; Republican Jim Ross Lightfoot held on in the Democrat-leaning 3d, while veteran Democrat Neal Smith, given much new territory, lost in 1994. But when Lightfoot ran for the Senate in 1996, Democrat Leonard Boswell took the seat, and as Bill Clinton swept the state three of the four incumbent Republicans won with only 52% or 53%. Iowa could be a target state for House Democrats in 1998 as it was in 1996.

The People: Est. Pop. 1996: 2,852,000; Pop. 1990: 2,776,755, up 2.7% 1990–1996. 1.1% of U.S. total, 30th largest; 39% rural. Median age: 36.1 years. 15% 65 years and over. 95.9% White, 1.7% Black, 1% Asian, 1.2% Hispanic origin. Households: 59.2% married couple families; 28% married couple fams. w. children; 42% college educ.; median household income: $26,229; per capita income: $12,422; 70.0% owner occupied housing; median house value: $45,900; median monthly rent: $261. 3.8% Unemployment. 1996 Voting age pop.: 2,138,000. 1996 Turnout: 1,234,075; 58% of VAP. Registered voters (1996): 1,757,493; 578,997 D (33%), 604,185 R (34%), 574,302 unaffiliated and minor parties (33%).

Political Lineup: Governor, Terry E. Branstad (R); Lt. Gov., Joy Corning (R); Secy. of State, Paul Danny Pate (R); Atty. Gen., Tom Miller (D); Treasurer, Michael L. Fitzgerald (D); Auditor, Richard D. Johnson (R). State Senate, 50 (21 D and 28 R, 1 vacancy); Senate President, Mary Kramer (R); State House, 100 (46 D and 54 R); House Speaker, Ron Korbett (R). Senators, Charles E. Grassley (R) and Tom Harkin (D). Representatives, 5 (1 D and 4 R).

Elections Division: 515-281-5865; **Filing Deadline for U.S. Congress:** March 13, 1998.

1996 Presidential Vote

Clinton (D)	620,258	(50%)
Dole (R)	492,644	(40%)
Perot (I)	105,159	(9%)

1992 Presidential Vote

Clinton (D)	586,353	(43%)
Bush (R)	504,891	(37%)
Perot (I)	253,468	(19%)

GOVERNOR

Gov. Terry E. Branstad (R)

Elected 1982, term expires Jan. 1999; b. Nov. 17, 1946, Leland; home, Des Moines; U. of IA, B.A. 1969, Drake U., J.D. 1974; Catholic; married (Christine).

Career: Army, 1969–71; IA House of Reps., 1972–78; Practicing atty., Farmer, 1974–1982; IA Lt. Gov., 1978–82.

Office: State Capitol, Des Moines 50319, 515-281-5211; Fax: 515-281-6611; Web site: www.state.ia.us.

Election Results

1994 gen.	Terry E. Branstad (R)	566,395	(57%)
	Bonnie J. Campbell (D)	414,453	(42%)
	Others	16,400	(2%)
1994 prim.	Terry E. Branstad (R)	161,228	(52%)
	Fred Grandy (R)	149,809	(48%)
1990 gen.	Terry E. Branstad (R)	591,852	(61%)
	Donald D. Avenson (D)	379,372	(39%)

SENATORS

Sen. Charles E. Grassley (R)

Elected 1980, seat up 1998; b. Sep. 17, 1933, New Hartford; home, New Hartford; U. of N. IA, B.A. 1955, M.A. 1956, U. of IA, 1957–58; Baptist; married (Barbara).

Career: Farmer; IA House of Reps., 1958–74; U.S. House of Reps., 1974–80.

DC Office: 135 HSOB 20510, 202-224-3744; Fax: 202-224-6020; e-mail: chuck_grassley@grassley.senate.gov.

State Offices: Cedar Rapids, 319-363-6832; Council Bluffs, 712-322-7103; Davenport, 319-322-4331; Des Moines, 515-284-4890; Sioux City, 712-233-1860; Waterloo, 319-232-6657.

Committees: *Agriculture, Nutrition & Forestry* (8th of 10 R): Forestry, Conservation & Rural Revitalization; Production & Price Competitiveness. *Budget* (2nd of 12 R). *Finance* (3rd of 11 R): Health Care; International Trade (Chmn.); Taxation & IRS Oversight. *Judiciary* (3rd of 10 R): Administrative Oversight & the Courts (Chmn.); Immigration; Youth Violence. *Aging (Special)* (Chmn.). *Joint Committee on Taxation* (3rd of 5 Sens.).

Group Ratings

	ADA	ACLU	AFS	LCV	CFA	CON	NFIB	COC	ACU	NTLC	CHC
1996	15	17	0	15	21	67	90	92	90	97	100
1995	5	—	0	7	6	88	—	100	91	—	—

National Journal Ratings

	1995 LIB — 1995 CONS			1996 LIB — 1996 CONS		
Economic	43%	—	54%	26%	—	69%
Social	12%	—	81%	0%	—	72%
Foreign	58%	—	41%	50%	—	49%

Key Votes of the 104th Congress

1. Reduce Medicare Growth $	Y	5. Flag Amendment	Y	9. Anti-Missile Defense	N
2. Lmt. Prod. Liab. Damages	Y	6. Endangered Species	N	10. Cuban Embargo	Y
3. Increase Min. Wage	Y	7. Gay Employment Rights	N	11. Bar Bosnia Troop $	Y
4. Welfare Reform	Y	8. Ovrd. Part. Birth Veto	Y	12. Cut Vietnam Aid	Y

Election Results

1992 general	Charles E. Grassley (R)	899,761	(70%)	($2,486,030)
	Jean Lloyd-Jones (D)	351,561	(27%)	($410,894)
	Others	40,879	(3%)	
1992 primary	Charles E. Grassley (R)	unopposed		
1986 general	Charles E. Grassley (R)	588,880	(66%)	($2,513,319)
	John P. Roehrick (D)	299,406	(34%)	($255,673)

Sen. Tom Harkin (D)

Elected 1984, seat up 1996; b. Nov. 19, 1939, Cumming; home, Cumming; IA St. U., B.S. 1962, Catholic U., J.D. 1972; Roman Catholic; married (Ruth).

Career: Navy, 1962–67; Naval Reserves, 1969–72; Practicing atty., 1972–74; Staff Aide, House Select Cmte. on U.S. Involvement in SE Asia, 1973–74; U.S. House of Reps., 1974–84.

DC Office: 731 HSOB 20510, 202-224-3254; Fax: 202-224-9369; e-mail: tom_harkin@harkin.senate.gov.

State Offices: Cedar Rapids, 319-365-4504; Davenport, 319-322-1338; Des Moines, 515-284-4574; Dubuque, 319-582-2130; Sioux City, 712-252-1550.

Committees: *Agriculture, Nutrition & Forestry* (RMM of 8 D). *Appropriations* (7th of 13 D): Agriculture, Rural Development & Related Agencies; Defense; Foreign Operations; Labor, Health & Human Services & Education (RMM); VA, HUD & Independent Agencies. *Labor & Human Resources* (3rd of 8 D): Employment & Training; Public Health & Safety. *Small Business* (4th of 8 D).

Group Ratings

	ADA	ACLU	AFS	LCV	CFA	CON	NFIB	COC	ACU	NTLC	CHC
1996	80	39	71	85	64	38	34	38	10	17	15
1995	95	—	91	93	69	68	—	44	9	—	—

National Journal Ratings

	1995 LIB — 1995 CONS			1996 LIB — 1996 CONS		
Economic	62%	—	36%	67%	—	31%
Social	85%	—	7%	80%	—	8%
Foreign	94%	—	3%	93%	—	0%

Key Votes of the 104th Congress

1. Reduce Medicare Growth $	N	5. Flag Amendment	N	9. Anti-Missile Defense	N
2. Lmt. Prod. Liab. Damages	N	6. Endangered Species	Y	10. Cuban Embargo	N
3. Increase Min. Wage	Y	7. Gay Employment Rights	Y	11. Bar Bosnia Troop $	N
4. Welfare Reform	Y	8. Ovrd. Part. Birth Veto	N	12. Cut Vietnam Aid	N

Election Results

1996 general	Tom Harkin (D)	634,166	(52%)	($6,070,137)
	Jim Ross Lightfoot (R)	571,807	(47%)	($2,439,679)
1996 primary	Tom Harkin (D)	unopposed		
1990 general	Tom Harkin (D)	529,571	(54%)	($5,628,242)
	Thomas J. Tauke (R)	453,273	(46%)	($5,060,104)

FIRST DISTRICT

A century and a half ago settlers surged west of the Mississippi River into the fertile, hilly lands that became Iowa. There New England Yankees built on the strange, open terrain their characteristic farmhouses, barns, town halls, church spires and small colleges; Germans, after crossing the ocean, stopped at the river bluffs reminiscent of their native land and built neat farmhouses and substantial towns; railroad builders, headquartered in Chicago, extended their networks of steel rails over the plains and rivers. Today some of the distinctiveness of these settlers remains in eastern Iowa, though the old ethnic folkways have faded, the old river craft have been replaced by giant barges and riverboat casinos and the old rail lines have been modernized and employ fewer men. Davenport, on the hills over the Mississippi River (which, with Rock Island, Moline and East Moline, Illinois, are called the Quad Cities) still has the look of the city where Ronald Reagan got his first radio announcing job more than 60 years ago. Cedar Rapids, a couple of counties west of the river, looks more up-to-date, with big high-tech employers (Rockwell has large avionics and electronics operations here); in 1992, PMX Industries, a metalworking company, opened a plant here, the largest single South Korean investment in the country. Iowa City, to the south, is a university town complete with trendy bookstores and vegetarian eateries.

Eight counties in eastern Iowa, with Davenport in one corner and Cedar Rapids in another, make up Iowa's 1st Congressional District. Historically, it has been Republican; in the 1970s and 1980s, it became Democratic, though not as much as the rest of the Quad Cities across the River in Illinois; now it can be labeled marginal.

The congressman from the 1st District for 20 years has been Jim Leach, now chairman of the House Banking Committee, and one of the most senior and most independent Republicans in the House. Leach grew up in Davenport, where his family owns propane gas and wholesale businesses, attended Princeton, studied Soviet politics at Johns Hopkins and the London School of Economics. He became a Foreign Service Officer in 1968, worked for Donald Rumsfeld when he was head of the Office of Economic Opportunity, then was assigned to the Arms Control and Disarmament Agency and served in the United Nations when George Bush was U.S. Ambassador there. In 1973 he resigned out of dismay when Richard Nixon fired special prosecutor Archibald Cox and returned to the family businesses in Davenport and in 1976 ran for the House and beat incumbent Democrat Edward Mezvinsky.

A believer in free enterprise with hands-on experience in a regulated business, Leach remains market-oriented on most economic issues. On cultural issues, almost in the tradition of mainline Protestants, he looks with some favor on liberal-minded changes such as supporting international family planning. On foreign policy, like many Iowa Republicans, he has been cautious about asserting U.S. military power, but he strenuously supported the Gulf war resolution.

Leach distinguished himself in the 1980s as the most trenchant and persistent critic of the mess Congress made of the savings and loan industry. From his seat on the Banking Committee, he warned early on that allowing the states to liberate S&Ls from their investment limits without increasing capital requirements would leave the federal government open to huge losses on federal deposit insurance. In 1989, he voted against the S&L bailout measure when the House wouldn't accept his higher capital requirements; by then he had gained a considerable moral authority as it became apparent he had been solitarily right when so many others were so wrong, at a cost of hundreds of billions to the taxpayers.

On the Whitewater scandal he was also on top of the facts and ahead of his time. As ranking minority member of Banking in 1993 and 1994, he pointed to evidence of serious misconduct in which the Clintons were deeply involved. Democratic Chairman Henry Gonzalez refused Leach's demand for an investigation and subpoena of records. Then, after the 1994 Republican victory made him chairman, Leach charged that Resolution Trust Company regulators looking at Madison Guaranty S&L were being "gagged" by superiors. Leach behaved in a dignified and serious manner in public hearings in July, while Democrats clowned and blustered and tried to make a mockery of them. Unwilling to encroach on independent counsel Kenneth Starr, Leach was unable to provide a tidy conclusion, though he clearly did demonstrate some abuse of power on the Clintons' behalf.

But Whitewater was not the only major issue before the Banking Committee. When investments in derivatives became controversial, Leach argued for caution by banks on such high-risk investments, but resisted the calls to ban or heavily regulate them. He rejected the Clinton Administration attempt to consolidate banking regulation, preferring to leave some of that power in the hands of the independent Federal Reserve. He sought to overhaul the Glass-Steagall Act, which keeps banks out of the investment business. That was stymied by insurance interests in the 104th Congress, and in November and December 1996 the Comptroller of the Currency and the Fed moved to tear down some of the firewalls between these businesses. In early 1997 Leach introduced a bill to make it easier for banks to underwrite securities and to allow securities firms to affiliate with banks and with insurance companies; the aim is to open up all these businesses to each other.

Until 1996 Leach had won reelection easily, even though he doesn't accept PAC contributions or money from outside Iowa or contributions over $500. But in 1996 he had spirited opposition from Cedar Rapids lawyer and former state Senator Bob Rush, who said he was an old friend of Leach; Leach was incredulous when he heard that and did not have a high regard for him. Rush said Leach used to be a "nonpartisan, independent thinker" but had become more conservative and partisan. "Leach's high-profile role in the Whitewater investigation and his unwavering support for the Gingrich agenda has [sic] alienated him from voters in the 1st District," a Rush brochure read. Leach responded unaggressively. As Banking chairman, he could easily have raised money for an high-pressure campaign, but spent only $370,000 to $420,000 for Rush, who collected $129,000 from PACs. The 1st District went solidly for Bill Clinton in 1992 and again in 1996, and Leach said resignedly that he was "at peace" with himself whatever the result. He won, but narrowly, 52%–47%. Rush carried the counties around Cedar Rapids (narrowly) and Iowa City; Leach's 61% in Davenport's Scott County saved him.

Leach is willing to take other risks. In January 1997 he was the second Republican (after Michael Forbes) to announce he would not vote for Newt Gingrich for speaker and said that Gingrich's defense against ethics charges was "simply inadequate for a maker of laws." Other Republicans groused and there was talk he might lose the Banking chair. Though Leach said that Gingrich made no threats he refused to say whether others in the leadership had. "No one knows more than I the risks implied when one goes against the leadership. So, if I lose a position, so be it. I'm comfortable with that as a possibility. I have no idea what's going to occur." His decision probably played well in Iowa; the *Des Moines Register*'s James Flansburg wrote that Leach "has a moral compass and follows its directions when it would be far easier to be blown along by the political winds." But there was speculation that Leach would not run again in 1998, while Rush seemed poised to make another well-financed race. If Leach does not run, a possible Republican nominee is Iowa House Speaker Ron Korbett.

The People: Pop. 1990: 555,229; 24% rural; 12% age 65+; 94% White; 3% Black; 1% Asian; 2% Hispanic origin. Households: 58% married couple families; 27% married couple fams. w. children; 49% college educ.; median household income: $29,544; per capita income: $13,660; median gross rent: $365; median house value: $55,500.

1996 Presidential Vote			**1992 Presidential Vote**		
Clinton (D)	135,839	(54%)	Clinton (D)	128,655	(46%)
Dole (R)	92,207	(37%)	Bush (R)	95,660	(34%)
Perot (I)	19,027	(8%)	Perot (I)	52,983	(19%)
Other	4,409	(2%)			

Rep. James A. Leach (R)

Elected 1976; b. Oct. 15, 1942, Davenport; home, Davenport; Princeton U., B.A. 1964, Johns Hopkins U., M.A. 1966, London Schl. of Econ., 1966–68; Episcopalian; married (Elisabeth).

Career: Staff Asst., U.S. Rep. Donald Rumsfeld, 1965–66; U.S. Foreign Svc., 1968–69, 1971–72 (Arms Control & Disarmament Agency); A.A. to Dir. of U.S. Office of Equal Opp., 1969–70; Pres., Flamegas Co., 1973–75; Dir., Fed. Home Loan Bank Bd., Midwest Reg., 1975–76.

DC Office: 2186 RHOB 20515, 202-225-6576; Fax: 202-226-1278; e-mail: talk2jim@hr.house.gov.

District Offices: Cedar Rapids, 319-363-4773; Davenport, 319-326-1841; Iowa City, 319-351-0789.

Committees: *Banking & Financial Services* (Chmn. of 30 R). *International Relations* (3rd of 26 R): Asia & the Pacific.

Group Ratings

	ADA	ACLU	AFS	LCV	CFA	CON	NFIB	COC	ACU	NTLC	CHC
1996	40	19	33	54	77	99	86	69	37	83	53
1995	30	—	—	31	46	87	—	96	40	—	—

National Journal Ratings

	1995 LIB		1995 CONS	1996 LIB		1996 CONS
Economic	26%	—	67%	52%	—	48%
Social	60%	—	39%	63%	—	35%
Foreign	59%	—	39%	52%	—	47%

Key Votes of the 104th Congress

1. Reduce Medicare Growth $	Y	5. Flag Amendment	N	9. Cuban Embargo	Y
2. Ovrd. Product Liab. Veto	Y	6. Drop EPA Limits	Y	10. Bar Bosnia Troop $	N
3. Increase Min. Wage	Y	7. Repeal Assault-Weap. Ban	N	11. Cut Anti-Missile Defense	N
4. Welfare Reform	Y	8. Ovrd. Part. Birth Veto	Y	12. Bar U.N. Uniforms	N

Election Results

1996 general	James A. Leach (R)	129,242	(53%)	($369,864)
	Bob Rush (D)	111,595	(46%)	($419,647)
	Others	3,759	(2%)	($6,027)
1996 primary	James A. Leach (R)	22,041	(99%)	
1994 general	James A. Leach (R)	110,448	(60%)	($268,937)
	Glen Winekauf (D)	69,461	(38%)	($82,447)
	Others	3,552	(2%)	

SECOND DISTRICT

Northeast Iowa, along the Mississippi River and westward, has some of the loveliest landscape in America. Here bluffs rise above the Mississippi, which broadens out in great quiet pools and then flows fast in constricted narrows. Inland from the Mississippi are the rolling hills portrayed with surprisingly little exaggeration in the paintings of Iowa's Grant Wood. These were lands settled by immigrants in the late 19th Century. German Catholics settled Dubuque, whose giant Victorian courthouse looks down on the Mississippi and up at the Fenelon Place Elevator that rides up the bluff. North are the tiny towns of Allamakee County, settled by Swiss Germans, where former Senator John Culver restored his ancestral family home in McGregor. Just west of Dubuque is Dyersville, where *Field of Dreams* was filmed and to which baseball buffs now repair: "If you build it, they will come." Farther west is Waterloo, which grew rapidly after 1900 as the John Deere tractor factory expanded and the eight-floor Rath factory became the largest meatpacking plant in the world; Rath closed in 1984 and Deere had thousands of layoffs, but Waterloo has rebounded somewhat with new businesses from a dog track to telemarketing to a high-tech Iowa Beef Processing (IBP) factory. To the south are the Amana colonies, settled in the 1850s by the Community of True Inspiration, German pietists, who have retained many of their old customs even as they have built businesses like Amana appliances.

The 2d Congressional District of Iowa covers most of northeast Iowa, including Dubuque and Waterloo, Allamakee County and Dyersville and the Amana colonies. There is considerable political variation here. Dubuque, heavily German Catholic, was for years Iowa's most Democratic city, and still often is unless abortion is the issue. But the rural counties along the river and farther west—more German Protestant, Scandinavian and Yankee—were traditionally Republican. Waterloo, originally Republican, trended sharply Democratic as the Rath plant shut down and Deere had big layoffs.

The congressman from the 2d District is Jim Nussle, first elected in 1990, at 30 the youngest member of the 102d Congress, who has prevailed against serious competition in every election since. Nussle grew up in Chicago, attended a Lutheran college (he is Danish-American and speaks Danish) and law school and then moved back to his native Iowa. In the small town way, he soon became Delaware County attorney, known for prosecuting a local day care employee for child abuse. He coupled his anti-abortion stance with support for helping expectant mothers with the expenses of parenthood. When Republican Congressman Tom Tauke ran for the Senate in 1990, Nussle ran for his seat, narrowly winning the Republican primary and then facing a better-financed Democrat. Nussle emphasized his experience in law enforcement, called for more informed parental involvement in the drug war as well as in choosing day care. This was enough for him to win 50%–49%, one of the closest margins in the country that year.

Nussle quickly became one of the leaders of the nascent Republican revolution. He was one of the Gang of Seven, a group of freshman Republican reformers who attacked the Democratic leadership. In October 1991 he made national news by coming into the House with a paper bag over his head to protest Democratic leaders' refusal to make full disclosure of House bank overdrafts. He voted against agricultural appropriations, to the dismay of senior Iowa Democrats and moved to cut congressional salaries 5% every year the federal budget is not balanced. For 1992, redistricting put Nussle into a district with incumbent Dave Nagle, a Democratic who had helped organize the defense of Speaker Jim Wright against Newt Gingrich's charges in 1989. Nagle had represented more of the new district and had won three elections by wider margins. But in a race in which both incumbents spent over $850,000, Nussle won, again by 50%–49%, with Nussle winning 56% in his old district and Nagle only 51% in his.

Still in the minority, Nussle continued to go his own way, excoriating the Democratic leadership and holding up a flood relief measure after the 1993 Iowa floods because it didn't have offsetting spending cuts. That prompted Nagle to run again in 1994, but this time as a challenger he could raise only about half as much money. Nussle won this time 56%–43%, carrying his old district with 61% and winning 54% in counties that were in Nagle's old district as well.

After the election, Newt Gingrich appointed Nussle as the director of the transition to Republican rule: from paper bag to power in just three years. Nussle froze hiring, demanded detailed accountings, and supervised an overhaul of House administration. He also got a seat on Ways and Means, where he again took risks, voting in September 1995 for a bill that reduced subsidies of ethanol. He then tried to persuade Gingrich to save the program, but told Iowans they would be hard to keep. He also defended Republican changes in Medicare: "We can bury our heads in the sand or suck it up and say it's time to do something with Medicare." At the same time he tried to raise Medicare reimbursements for rural healthcare providers. And he sponsored a bill to make northeast Iowa a National Park Service "agricultural heritage area," to help the voluntary group Silos & Smokestacks to promote 60 sites as a single tourism destination.

Nussle at first looked to have an easy time of it in the 1996 election. Democrat Donna Smith, a 17-year Dubuque County Supervisor, spent only $70,000 to his $680,000. But she hammered home his closeness to Gingrich, attacked "Georgia Jim" for supporting big hog feedlots, and, when he announced he was getting divorced, Smith said that he "divorced" Iowans by voting for the tax bill cutting the ethanol subsidy. Nussle continued to sound his conservative themes; of the Freedom to Farm Act he said, "By and large farmers make much better decisions than Washington can." But he added defensively that his ties to Gingrich "allowed us to save several programs." Though not targeted by Democrats, this turned out to be a close election. Nussle won by just 53%–46%, losing Dubuque County and Waterloo's Black Hawk County. It is likely that Nussle will continue to be a stalwart part of the Republican majority, but also quite possible that he will have serious competition in 1998.

The People: Pop. 1990: 555,494; 49% rural; 16% age 65+; 97% White; 2% Black; 1% Hispanic origin. Households: 62% married couple families; 28% married couple fams. w. children; 36% college educ.; median household income: $25,010; per capita income: $11,611; median gross rent: $300; median house value: $42,400.

1996 Presidential Vote

Clinton (D)	129,148	(53%)
Dole (R)	91,155	(37%)
Perot (I)	21,377	(9%)

1992 Presidential Vote

Clinton (D)	120,228	(44%)
Bush (R)	95,005	(35%)
Perot (I)	55,279	(20%)

Rep. Jim Nussle (R)

Elected 1990; b. June 27, 1960, Des Moines; home, Manchester; Luther Col., B.A. 1983, Drake U., J.D. 1985; Lutheran; divorced.

Career: Delaware Cnty. Atty., 1986–90.

DC Office: 303 CHOB 20515, 202-225-2911; Fax: 202-225-9129; e-mail: nussleia@hr.house.gov.

District Offices: Dubuque, 319-557-7740; Manchester, 319-927-5141; Mason City, 515-423-0303; Waterloo, 310-235-1109.

Committees: *Budget* (12th of 24 R). *Ways & Means* (12th of 23 R): Trade.

Group Ratings

	ADA	ACLU	AFS	LCV	CFA	CON	NFIB	COC	ACU	NTLC	CHC
1996	5	0	0	15	8	66	100	94	95	100	100
1995	0	—	—	6	8	85	—	100	84	—	—

National Journal Ratings

	1995 LIB — 1995 CONS	1996 LIB — 1996 CONS
Economic	0% — 74%	0% — 82%
Social	0% — 79%	29% — 68%
Foreign	45% — 55%	44% — 55%

Key Votes of the 104th Congress

1. Reduce Medicare Growth $	Y	5. Flag Amendment	Y	9. Cuban Embargo	Y
2. Ovrd. Product Liab. Veto	Y	6. Drop EPA Limits	N	10. Bar Bosnia Troop $	N
3. Increase Min. Wage	N	7. Repeal Assault-Weap. Ban	Y	11. Cut Anti-Missile Defense	N
4. Welfare Reform	Y	8. Ovrd. Part. Birth Veto	Y	12. Bar U.N. Uniforms	Y

Election Results

1996 general	Jim Nussle (R)	127,827	(53%)	($679,904)
	Donna L. Smith (D)	109,731	(46%)	($69,796)
1996 primary	Jim Nussle (R)	unopposed		
1994 general	Jim Nussle (R)	111,076	(56%)	($876,142)
	Dave Nagle (D)	86,087	(43%)	($491,552)
	Others	1,324	(1%)	

THIRD DISTRICT

As the pioneers did a century and a half ago, the rolling farmland of southern Iowa heads west, from the railroad towns perched below the bluffs on the Mississippi River to the dusty plains above the Missouri River looking over to Nebraska and the West. The southern two tiers of Iowa's counties have none of the state's large cities; the accent here sounds like rural Missouri, with a touch of the South. Population here has been declining for many years, as the numerous children of large farm families seek opportunity elsewhere, since mechanization and technology require fewer people on the land.

The 3d Congressional District covers 27 counties in southern Iowa, including almost all of the southern tier, from the Mississippi River border with Illinois almost to the Missouri River border with Nebraska. The 3d also juts north as far as Ames, the home of Iowa State University. There are dozens of notable towns here: Pella, home of the Pella window firm; Newton, home of Maytag appliances; Grinnell, with Grinnell College; Marshalltown, memorialized in *The Music Man*; and Fairfield, the home of Maharishi University and national headquarters of the Natural Law Party, whose presidential nominee John Hagelin got 21% of the vote in surrounding Jefferson County. The historical preference here is mostly Republican, but there are Democratic counties as well, next to heavily Democratic counties in northern Missouri.

The congressman from the 3d District is Leonard Boswell, a Democrat elected in 1996, and the first Democratic freshman from Iowa in 10 years. He is not the stereotypical freshman, however; he was elected at 62. Boswell grew up on farms in Ringgold and Decatur Counties, near the Missouri border. He was drafted in 1956, at 22, as a private in the Army. He reenlisted, graduated first in both fixed wing and helicopter flying school, served two years in Vietnam, and retired as a lieutenant colonel in 1976. He settled down on his farm in Decatur County and became head of the local Farmers' Coop. He managed to keep it out of bankruptcy during the farm depression of the 1980s, and decided to go into politics. He was elected state Senator from a six-county Republican district in 1984, served as chairman of Appropriations and, after 1992, Senate president, and was the Democratic nominee for lieutenant governor in 1994.

In 1996, when 3d District conservative Republican Congressman Jim Ross Lightfoot ran for the Senate, Boswell ran for the House. He had a serious primary opponent in Charles Krogmeier, state deputy attorney general. But he won a 93%, 3,180-vote margin in his state Senate district, and while losing Ames and the counties on the Mississippi, broke better than even elsewhere, to win a 58%, 4,341-vote victory. Republican Mike Mahaffey, Poweshiek County attorney, showed similar home strength (90% in Poweshiek) and won all but one county, to win his three-way primary with 59%. The general election was very much a contest of nice guys. Boswell flew his four-seater Piper Comanche 250 around the district and called for balancing the budget, higher education aid, and protections against reductions in Medicare, all to be financed with Pentagon cuts and elimination of Medicare waste. Mahaffey ran as a moderate Republican, budget-balancer, term limits advocate. Boswell drew on his experience in Des Moines: "I'm a farmer, he's a lawyer. I have experience in budgeting. I've been there, done it." He talked of being a congressman-as-facilitator: "if you get a roomful of knowledgeable and honorable people together, a good solution will surely emerge." That, he said, was what happened when Iowa faced a $400 million deficit in the early 1990s, and the legislature's solutions produced a $400 million surplus.

But Boswell was not a political naif. He was endorsed by the Farm Bureau, which usually backs Republicans. He raised more money and spent $634,000 to Mahaffey's $439,000, with most of the difference being a $100,000 edge in PAC money. And when Republicans attacked him for not backing enough inheritance tax relief, he retaliated with his first negative ad, an attack on Newt Gingrich and Republican Medicare policy. This looked all along like one of the closest races in the country, and was. Mahaffey ran well ahead of Lightfoot's showing in the Senate race in the eastern and northern part of the district. But Boswell ran nearly 20 points ahead of Senator Tom Harkin's showing in his old state Senate district. The result was a 49%–48% Boswell victory, with a margin of 4,019 votes.

Boswell sought a seat on Appropriations, in vain, but serves on Transportation and Infrastructure and the Agriculture Committee. Regarding the Freedom to Farm Act, Boswell remarked, "I find farmers are still enthused about this bill. Individuals have talked to me about staying alert to this bill and to ensure a level playing field is maintained as we compete against foreign markets and treasuries."

The People: Pop. 1990: 555,299; 46% rural; 16% age 65+; 97% White; 1% Black; 1% Asian; 1% Hispanic origin. Households: 61% married couple families; 27% married couple fams. w. children; 39% college educ.; median household income: $24,767; per capita income: $11,567; median gross rent: $315; median house value: $41,200.

1996 Presidential Vote

Clinton (D)	123,246	(50%)
Dole (R)	95,308	(39%)
Perot (I)	21,408	(9%)
Other	4,576	(2%)

1992 Presidential Vote

Clinton (D)	120,495	(45%)
Bush (R)	96,515	(36%)
Perot (I)	47,028	(18%)

Rep. Leonard L. Boswell (D)

Elected 1996; b. Jan. 10, 1934, Harrison Co., MO; home, Davis City; Graceland Col., B.A. 1969; Reorganized Latter Day Saints; married (Dody).

Career: Army, 1956–76 (Vietnam); Farmer; IA Senate, 1984–96, Pres., 1992–96.

DC Office:1029 LHOB 20515, 202-225-3806; Fax: 202-225-5608.

District Offices: Osceola, 515-342-4801.

Committees: *Agriculture* (23rd of 23 D): Livestock, Dairy & Poultry; Risk Management & Specialty Crops. *Transportation & Infrastructure* (30th of 33 D): Aviation; Water Resources & Environment.

Group Ratings and Key Votes: Newly Elected

Election Results

1996 general	Leonard L. Boswell (D)	115,914	(49%)	($634,351)
	Mike Mahaffey (R)	111,895	(48%)	($439,269)
	Others	7,066	(3%)	($24,830)
1996 primary	Leonard L. Boswell (D)	15,349	(58%)	
	Charles J. Krogmeier (D)	11,008	(42%)	
1994 general	Jim Ross Lightfoot (R)	111,862	(58%)	($709,487)
	Elaine Baxter (D)	79,310	(41%)	($374,500)

FOURTH DISTRICT

Iowa, which today seems very much in the middle of the country, was once part of the West. Iowa was home to sober farmers and pious burghers, but it was also the eastern terminus of the first Transcontinental Railroad, a waystop for people in a hurry to get to Nebraska and the Rockies and the Pacific or the Dakotas and the fastness of Montana. Those who stayed behind were determined to use the wealth accumulated by methodical husbandry of their fertile farmlands to implant firmly the glories of western civilization. You can feel that impulse today in Des Moines when you look across the river from downtown at the Victorian Capitol, its gold dome above a Corinthian pediment, or Terrace Hill, the beautifully restored governor's mansion, atop a hill overlooking the Raccoon River. The nearby Living History Farms, which recreate Indian villages, frontier towns and turn-of-the-century farms, show the effort the new settlers made to put their imprint on the environment. The same civilizing impulse can be seen farther west, in the city of Council Bluffs, in the mansion of General Grenville Dodge. Here in 1859, General Dodge lobbied Illinois lawyer Abraham Lincoln on the need for a transcontinental railroad; Lincoln got it through Congress in 1863, Dodge became its chief engineer, and Council Bluffs became its eastern terminus when it was completed in 1869.

Today Iowa is, as one voter said with satisfaction, "in the heart of middle America." In the 1980s, when farm prices plummeted and meatpacking factories closed and main street storefronts were vacant, it seemed to be emptying out. But around 1987 the economy turned around, and Iowa started growing again. Now growth is centered in and around its cities, especially Des Moines, now spreading around the countryside even as farm counties' population continues to decline. Insurance and printing and service businesses are expanding in office centers downtown and at freeway interchanges; Iowans are driving 100 miles or more to fill the shopping malls at cities' edge. Missing perhaps is the heady confidence of Iowans when they were pushing the frontier west; but missing also is the bedraggled feeling of the 1980s: Des Moines is leading Iowa deliberately into the future.

The 4th Congressional District of Iowa includes Des Moines and most of its expanding suburban fringe, into fast-growing Dallas County and even into Madison County, site of the famous novel and movie about covered bridges. It also proceeds west to Council Bluffs and the Missouri River, along the Interstate where communities are growing again. Historically Des Moines, with its unionized workers and in the midst of corn and hog country, with the liberal *Des Moines Register* setting the tone, yearned after farm subsidies and voted heavily Democratic; now, with an increasing white collar work force, it is trending mildly toward Republicans. Council Bluffs, surrounded by beef grazing territory, where federal intrusion has long been resented, looks west to Omaha, taking on the culturally more conservative tone of Nebraska and the conservative politics of the *Omaha World-Herald*.

The congressman from the 4th District is Greg Ganske, a Republican first elected in a stunning upset in 1994 and then reelected after a titanic struggle in 1996. Ganske grew up in Manchester (the home now of 2d District Congressman Jim Nussle), where he worked in his father's grocery store; he worked his way through the University of Iowa. After medical school he served in the Army Reserves and started a plastic surgery practice in Des Moines, specializing in reconstructive surgery for birth defects and victims of accidents, burns and crimes. He and his wife, a physician, made plenty of money, raised a family, and bought a farm.

Then Ganske decided to run for Congress in 1994. The incumbent was Neal Smith, a Democrat first elected in 1958, chairman of an Appropriations subcommittee and a stickler for rectitude and procedure. Redistricting had removed some Democratic territory and added Republican Council Bluffs and nearby rural counties, but Smith won easily, 62%–37%, in 1992. But Ganske put his own money, ultimately $618,000, into the campaign and, at Newt Gingrich's suggestion, bought a rusty beige 1958 DeSoto, made in the year Smith first won, and drove it around the district with a sign reading, "'58 Nealmobile—WHY is it still running?" Ganske opposed the Clinton healthcare plan and attacked Smith for "logrolling," saying, "What do 36-year career politicians like Neal Smith always do? They blame each other, spend more money and then raise your taxes." Smith raised and spent more than $1 million, but had a hard time speaking in the idiom of 1994, and his claims of clout were undermined when Appropriations Chairman William Natcher died in February 1994 and Smith lost 152–106 in the race to succeed him to the younger and less senior David Obey. Ganske was leading in polls as early as June 1994, and in November he won 53%–46%, winning 65% in Council Bluffs and 62% in rural counties, and losing to Smith in the Des Moines area by only 48%–51%.

In the House Ganske has charted his own course, with moderate votes on many issues; early on he irritated the Republican leadership by seeking to scale back the Contract with America's tax cut by denying the $500 per child tax credit to upper-income taxpayers. But he has been an enthusiastic follower of Newt Gingrich on many issues. He serves on the Commerce Committee where he can weigh in on health care as well as many economic issues.

Not surprisingly, Ganske had serious competition in 1996. Two Democrats vied to run against him, with former nurse and Des Moines weathercaster Connie McBurney edging out Jack Hatch, former legislator and aide to Senator Tom Harkin, in the June primary, 58%–42%. Even before that the AFL-CIO started running TV ads against Ganske, and in the summer he was trailing in the polls. But he was not defenseless. He persuaded TV stations not to run ads charging that he voted to "cut" Medicare (the Republican plan increased spending more slowly than the Democrats wanted), and when the Teamsters ran an ad charging that he took tobacco money, he roared in protest. "I took care of a lot of patients who had serious complications from tobacco like throat cancer and lung cancer," he said, and got the ad pulled when he demonstrated that he never took money from tobacco interests. He was not underfunded, however. He spent $2.3 million, some $553,000 of it his own money; he also raised $668,000 from PACs and over $1 million from individuals. That more or less evened spending out, counting the labor ads together with McBurney's $853,000.

But the key event may have come during the August 1996 recess. Ganske traveled to Peru, not to junket, but to do charity medical work, operating on children with cleft palates and other disfigurements. In the process he contracted post-viral encephalitis, and was hospitalized in Des Moines and off the campaign trail for weeks. It became difficult to portray him as a picture of greed or indifference. He regained the lead in polls, and won 52%–47% on election day. Compared to 1994, he lost ground in Council Bluffs and the rural counties, which he carried with 57% and 58% of the votes. But he gained a point in metro Des Moines, running even there, 49%–49%, trailing by just 28 votes.

This does not guarantee Ganske a free ride in 1998, but it does show impressive strength for a conservative Republican in what had long been the stronghold of Iowa's Democrats. He seems unlikely to be daunted in his conservatism, though neither he nor anyone else is likely to pursue exactly the same strategy—contracting a dangerous disease—again.

The People: Pop. 1990: 555,276; 26% rural; 14% age 65+; 94% White; 3% Black; 1% Asian; 2% Hispanic origin. Households: 58% married couple families; 27% married couple fams. w. children; 46% college educ.; median household income: $28,591; per capita income: $13,813; median gross rent: $405; median house value: $52,500.

1996 Presidential Vote

Clinton (D)	127,250	(49%)
Dole (R)	107,359	(42%)
Perot (I)	20,296	(8%)

1992 Presidential Vote

Clinton (D)	117,863	(43%)
Bush (R)	107,745	(39%)
Perot (I)	47,835	(17%)

Rep. Greg Ganske (R)

Elected 1994; b. Mar. 31, 1949, New Hampton; home, Des Moines; U. of IA, B.S. 1972; M.D. 1976; Catholic; married (Corrine).

Career: Army Reserves, 1986–present; Farmer; Practicing surgeon, 1976–94;

DC Office: 1108 LHOB 20515, 202-225-4426; Fax: 202-225-3193; e-mail: greg.ganske@mail.house.gov.

District Offices: Council Bluffs, 712-323-5976; Des Moines, 515-284-4634.

Committees: *Commerce* (21st of 28 R): Finance & Hazardous Materials; Health & the Environment; Oversight & Investigations.

Group Ratings

	ADA	ACLU	AFS	LCV	CFA	CON	NFIB	COC	ACU	NTLC	CHC
1996	20	6	8	23	38	52	95	94	83	95	86
1995	10	—	—	0	0	85	—	100	72	—	—

National Journal Ratings

	1995 LIB		1995 CONS	1996 LIB		1996 CONS
Economic	0%	—	74%	30%	—	68%
Social	45%	—	54%	42%	—	56%
Foreign	50%	—	49%	66%	—	33%

Key Votes of the 104th Congress

1. Reduce Medicare Growth $	Y	5. Flag Amendment	Y	9. Cuban Embargo	Y
2. Ovrd. Product Liab. Veto	Y	6. Drop EPA Limits	N	10. Bar Bosnia Troop $	Y
3. Increase Min. Wage	Y	7. Repeal Assault-Weap. Ban	N	11. Cut Anti-Missile Defense	N
4. Welfare Reform	Y	8. Ovrd. Part. Birth Veto	*	12. Bar U.N. Uniforms	*

Election Results

1996 general	Greg Ganske (R)	133,419	(52%)	($2,334,251)
	Connie McBurney (D)	119,790	(47%)	(853,104)
1996 primary	Greg Ganske (R)	unopposed		
1994 general	Greg Ganske (R)	111,935	(53%)	($1,195,525)
	Neal Smith (D)	98,824	(46%)	($1,005,498)

FIFTH DISTRICT

Sioux City, one of the oldest market towns on the Great Plains, is situated picturesquely, nestled below and running up the loess bluffs above the Missouri River. Although still the largest city on the Plains west of Des Moines and north of Omaha, Sioux City has not grown much in the last five decades. Its original economic base has become obsolete, and so has some of the city itself: the waterfront, once raucous with boatmen and stockyard workers, is now quiet; stockyards have been replaced by IBP's modern (and low-wage) beef factory across the river in Dakota City, Nebraska; downtown stores have been replaced by shopping malls at the edge of town where people will still drive for 100 miles to spend a day doing a season's shopping. Yet many neighborhoods still look the same as they did during the childhood days of the Friedman twins, Eppie and Popo, better known these last 40 years as Ann Landers and Abigail Van Buren.

Sioux City is the largest city in the 5th Congressional District of Iowa, which covers most of northern and northwest Iowa, politically an area that, on balance, is a few points more Republican than the rest of the state. Its biggest population centers are Sioux City and Fort Dodge, northwest of Des Moines, to the east. The counties on the gently rolling landscape in between are an ethnic melange: Irish Catholics in Palo Alto, Dutch in Sioux (the most heavily Republican county in Iowa), and the descendants of the English lords who built huge cattle ranches around Le Mars in Plymouth County.

The congressman from the 5th District is Tom Latham, a Republican first elected in 1994. Latham grew up on a farm in Franklin County, where his family has owned a seed company—a very Iowa business!—since 1947. For years Tom Latham was active in Republican politics, contributing, attending the national convention, and serving as a farm adviser to Congressman Fred Grandy. In 1994 Grandy ran for governor, an unhappy enterprise since he lost to incumbent Terry Branstad in the June primary 52%–48% and sounded sour notes against Branstad and Newt Gingrich in the months afterward. But Latham fared more happily. Running as an opponent of the Clinton healthcare plan and supporting Contract with America principles before the Contract existed, he easily beat Sioux City state Senator Brad Banks 62%–38% in the primary and in the general easily outpolled Democrat Sheila McGuire, a Boone health consultant trained as a dentist and with a doctorate in epidemiology, who was one of 47 medical care professionals selected to sit on a White House advisory panel to review the Clinton healthcare program. Latham contrasted his farm and business background to McGuire's, noting that she had never been in a private practice of dentistry or medicine. "Professor McGuire helped write the Clinton healthcare plan that would put a bureaucrat between you and your doctor, raise your taxes and close many rural hospitals," a Latham ad said. "Everyone agrees the Clinton-McGuire plan was a bad idea." Not quite everyone; but enough that Latham won 61%–39%. McGuire carried her home county with 52% and lost every other county; Latham won 87% in rural Sioux County and carried the Sioux City and Fort Dodge areas.

In the House Latham had a solidly conservative record. He served on the Agriculture Committee and supported the Freedom to Farm Act which phased out subsidies for most crops—which evidently have little support left in northwest Iowa. Inspired by the gruesome murder of a 19-year-old in Hawarden, he sponsored a successful amendment to allow local law enforcement officers to enter into agreements with the INS to detain illegal immigrants. On the Transportation Committee he sponsored a bill to establish a system for government and relief organizations to help the families of disaster victims. He favored campaign finance reform that would require candidates to raise most of their money from contributors in their home districts and would require union members to give consent for political use of their dues money. Overall his record was solidly conservative on just about everything but foreign and defense issues. He held hearings on abuses of regulatory power and hailed Republican attempts to save Medicare.

In 1996 Latham was not seriously challenged and won reelection with 65%. He got a seat on the Appropriations Committee and on its subcommittees on Agriculture, Commerce-Justice-State-Judiciary, and the Legislative Branch.

The People: Pop. 1990: 555,457; 52% rural; 18% age 65+; 98% White; 1% Black; 1% Asian; 1% Hispanic origin. Households: 62% married couple families; 28% married couple fams. w. children; 38% college educ.; median household income: $24,150; per capita income: $11,461; median gross rent: $285; median house value: $37,000.

1996 Presidential Vote			1992 Presidential Vote		
Dole (R)	106,615	(45%)	Bush (R)	109,966	(42%)
Clinton (D)	104,775	(44%)	Clinton (D)	99,112	(38%)
Perot (I)	23,051	(10%)	Perot (I)	50,343	(19%)

Rep. Tom Latham (R)

Elected 1994; b. July 14, 1948, Hampton; home, Alexander; Wartburg Col., 1966–67; IA St. U., 1967–70; Lutheran; married (Kathy).

Career: Farmer; Bank Teller/Bookkeeper, 1970–72; Independent Insurance Agent, 1972–74; Hartford Insurance Mktg. Rep., 1974–76; Co-Owner, Latham Seed Co., 1976–present.

DC Office: 516 CHOB 20515, 202-225-5476; Fax: 202-225-3301.

District Offices: Dodge, 515-573-2738; Orange City, 712-737-8708; Sioux City, 712-277-2114; Spencer, 712-262-6480.

Committees: *Appropriations* (32nd of 34 R): Agriculture, Rural Development, FDA & Related Agencies; Commerce, Justice, State & Judiciary; Legislative.

Group Ratings

	ADA	ACLU	AFS	LCV	CFA	CON	NFIB	COC	ACU	NTLC	CHC
1996	0	6	0	23	8	17	100	100	95	100	93
1995	5	—	—	0	8	87	—	96	84	—	—

National Journal Ratings

	1995 LIB — 1995 CONS			1996 LIB — 1996 CONS		
Economic	0%	—	74%	27%	—	71%
Social	0%	—	79%	14%	—	77%
Foreign	48%	—	50%	30%	—	65%

Key Votes of the 104th Congress

1. Reduce Medicare Growth $	Y	5. Flag Amendment	Y	9. Cuban Embargo	Y
2. Ovrd. Product Liab. Veto	Y	6. Drop EPA Limits	N	10. Bar Bosnia Troop $	N
3. Increase Min. Wage	N	7. Repeal Assault-Weap. Ban	Y	11. Cut Anti-Missile Defense	N
4. Welfare Reform	Y	8. Ovrd. Part. Birth Veto	Y	12. Bar U.N. Uniforms	Y

Election Results

1996 general	Tom Latham (R)	147,576	(65%)	($477,173)
	MacDonald Smith (D)	75,785	(34%)	($126,516)
1996 primary	Tom Latham (R)	unopposed		
1994 general	Tom Latham (R)	114,796	(61%)	($742,308)
	Sheila McGuire (D)	73,627	(39%)	($719,811)

KANSAS

"Like everyone else," James Dickenson writes of his grandmother Mary Phipps, who lived her 91 years in Kansas, "she was taught that the earth and the other planets circled the sun, but deep down she had the feeling that the sun and the rest of the cosmos really revolved around western Kansas. If anyone had suggested this in so many words, she'd have laughingly denied it, but it was implicit in her worldview. She took as the First Principle that bread, the staff of life, was one of the bases of existence itself, along with air and water. From this flowed the inescapable conclusion that wheat farmers were truly engaged in the Lord's work." These words open the book *Home on the Range*, in which Dickenson, for three decades a top national political reporter, starts with his own family and boyhood in Rawlins County to explain how Kansas came to be what it was, and how it is ceasing to be that and becoming something else. But Kansas has always been quintessentially American, which is not to say entirely placid or entirely unflavorful. Recall that in 1989 when Russian leader Yevgeny Primakov wanted to see "real Americans," he flew out with Bob Dole to Dodge City, to visit Boot Hill Museum and the Long Branch Saloon—and was questioned about, among other things, why his country continued to occupy the Baltic States. Kansas, like so much of Russia, may look quiet, full of solid farmers who work hard and have deep roots in the soil, the place around which the cosmos revolves. But Kansas's history, like Russia's, has also been punctuated by uprisings, intellectual and violent, by moments of anger and rage sweeping through the tall sheaves like a tornado wind. The difference, of course, is that Russian traditions of law and liberty, culture and civility are weak, while in Kansas as in all America they are remarkably strong.

Kansas literally began in a moment of violence, the Bleeding Kansas of the 1850s, that led proximately to the terrible war that split the whole nation. The trigger was the Kansas-Nebraska Act of 1854, which left to local settlers the question of whether this new Kansas Territory would be a free or slave state. Pro-slavery "bushwhackers" rode over the line from Missouri, stealing elections and writing a pro-slavery constitution. But much larger numbers of free-soil "jayhawkers" from New England and the New England-Yankee-settled Great Lakes states put down roots and, despite the massacres of the mad John Brown, prevailed and established their own law and order. The effect on national politics was tumultuous: the Democratic Party was split, the Republican Party was created, the nation was plunged into Civil War. The effect on Kansas was calming: the anti-slavery majority bent the soil to the plow and built small towns thick with schools, churches and colleges, to the point that in the 1939 color movie, *Wizard of Oz*, Kansas was shot in dreary black and white as the image of dull, prim, old-fashioned Middle America.

But the rebellious impulse did not totally die out. Kansas lived almost entirely on farming, and its livelihood was always at risk; hailstorms, grasshopper invasions, dry seasons or a drop in world farm prices could mean disaster for thousands of Kansans. The high-rainfall 1880s attracted hundreds of thousands of new settlers to Kansas; the low-rainfall 1890s produced a bust and a populist rebellion. "What you farmers should do," said orator Mary Ellen Lease, "is to raise less corn and more hell." For a few years in the 1890s, and then in farm rebellions of the 1930s, 1950s and 1970s, Kansans did, but afterwards always returned to jayhawker Republicanism.

At least a whiff of rebellion can be sniffed in the air of the 1990s. Kansas is still Republican—but not in quite the same way as before. Bob Dole has been the largest figure here, a congressman first elected in 1960 and Senator until his resignation in June 1996, and for most of those years he epitomized Main Street Kansas Republicanism: wary of budget deficits, unselfconsciously traditional on cultural issues, converted from the isolationism of the years before World War II to a willingness to shoulder the burden of advancing freedom and democracy around the world, a burden for whom Dole himself paid an excruciatingly high price. But Kansans in the 1990s have experimented with other forms of politics. In 1992 they cast 27% of their votes for Ross Perot—his fifth highest percentage in the nation. This was not a wheat country rebellion or an urban uprising: Perot ran strongest in counties just at the edge of metropolitan expansion and in the sparsely populated Flint Hills, places where young families live, commuting to jobs and shopping malls 50 or even 100 miles away.

Then in 1996, Kansas's two leading officeholders stepped away from the scene. Bob Dole, having secured the Republican presidential nomination, shocked everyone when he decided to retire from the Senate in June 1996, some two years before his term expired, as a way of showing the earnestness of his candidacy. Senator Nancy Kassebaum, first elected in 1978, had already announced her retirement; a moderate Republican, with nuanced views on foreign and domestic issues, her final achievement was the healthcare portability legislation passed and signed in August 1996. Replacing them, and taking all four seats in the Kansas House delegation, were Republicans running as strong conservatives and strong reformers. Pat Roberts, the longtime 1st District congressman and chairman of the House Agriculture Committee, had long tended to the intricacies of farm subsidies; but he shepherded to passage the Freedom to Farm Act of 1996, which phased out most subsidies over seven years. He was easily elected to the Senate. The other seat was won by freshman 2d District Congressman Sam Brownback, one of the most aggressive conservative reformers in the House. Though Democrats ran serious candidates in most contests, the results were decisive: Dole carried Kansas 54%–36%, losing only four of 105 counties; Roberts won 62%–34%, losing only one county; Brownback won 54%–43%, losing only four counties; Republican House candidates won the popular vote 56%–41%, losing only six counties. The conservative Republicanism associated with Newt Gingrich and the 1994 House Republican freshmen, may have been a product of the suddenly booming metropolises of the South and the ridges of the Rocky Mountains, but it seems, at least for the moment, to have found a congenial home in deep-rooted Kansas.

Governor. Kansas's governor is Bill Graves, a Republican elected in 1994. Graves grew up in Salina, where his family had a trucking firm, Graves Truck Lines; he worked in the business from loading dock to management, even though he moved to a suburb of Kansas City (his wife practiced law in Missouri). In 1986 he was elected secretary of State. In 1994 he ran for governor. But Republican Kansas has elected Democratic governors more often than not over the last 30 years, and the initial favorite was Democratic Congressman Jim Slattery, a 12-year moderate who in spring 1994 cast a decisive vote against Democratic healthcare plans in the Commerce Committee. Slattery won a five-candidate primary with an impressive 53%. Graves meanwhile was winning a six-candidate Republican primary with 41%. "Load 'em high and tight," he repeated over and over again, as his family had loaded the trailers of 18-wheelers with cartons of goods. Graves called Slattery a "double-dealing Washington congressman" and pledged to keep spending down, to rein in government. The race blew open in the last weeks, and Graves won 64%–36%—the widest margin in over 20 years—carrying 102 of 105 counties.

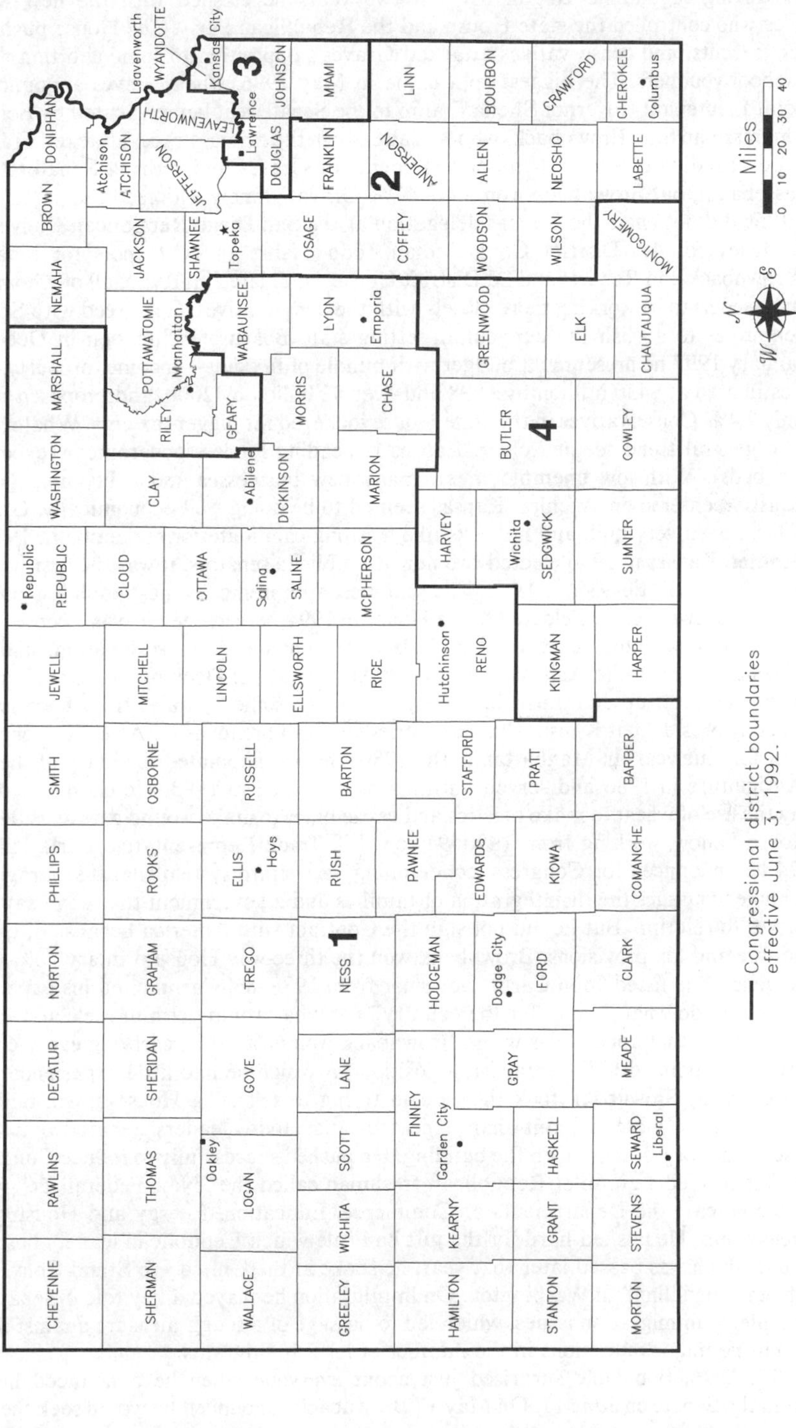
CHEYENNE
RAWLINS
DECATUR
NORTON
PHILLIPS
SMITH
JEWELL
REPUBLIC
Republic
WASHINGTON
MARSHALL
NEMAHA
BROWN
DONIPHAN
SHERMAN
THOMAS
SHERIDAN
GRAHAM
ROOKS
OSBORNE
MITCHELL
CLOUD
CLAY
RILEY
POTTAWATOMIE
Manhattan
JACKSON
ATCHISON
Atchison
JEFFERSON
LEAVENWORTH
Leavenworth
WYANDOTTE
Kansas City
WALLACE
LOGAN
Oakley
GOVE
TREGO
ELLIS
Hays
RUSSELL
LINCOLN
OTTAWA
Salina
SALINE
DICKINSON
Abilene
GEARY
WABAUNSEE
SHAWNEE
Topeka
DOUGLAS
Lawrence
JOHNSON
3
GREELEY
WICHITA
SCOTT
LANE
NESS
1
RUSH
BARTON
ELLSWORTH
RICE
MCPHERSON
MARION
MORRIS
CHASE
LYON
Emporia
OSAGE
FRANKLIN
MIAMI
HAMILTON
KEARNY
FINNEY
Garden City
HODGEMAN
PAWNEE
STAFFORD
RENO
Hutchinson
HARVEY
BUTLER
GREENWOOD
COFFEY
ANDERSON
2
LINN
STANTON
GRANT
HASKELL
GRAY
FORD
Dodge City
EDWARDS
KIOWA
PRATT
KINGMAN
SEDGWICK
Wichita
4
ELK
WOODSON
ALLEN
BOURBON
MORTON
STEVENS
SEWARD
Liberal
MEADE
CLARK
COMANCHE
BARBER
HARPER
SUMNER
COWLEY
CHAUTAUQUA
MONTGOMERY
WILSON
NEOSHO
LABETTE
CRAWFORD
CHEROKEE
Columbus
Miles
0 10 20 30 40
Congressional district boundaries effective June 3, 1992.

By most criteria Graves has been a conservative governor, backing tax cuts, a spending cut in one year, reducing regulation. But in his first two years he clashed with the new Kansas conservatives who controlled the state House and the Republican Party. The House pushed for even bigger tax cuts, and conservatives attacked Graves's opposition to some abortion restrictions and school vouchers. The biggest split came in May 1996, when Graves announced he would appoint Lieutenant Governor Sheila Frahm to the Senate seat being vacated by Bob Dole in June. Congressman Sam Brownback, who was already in the primary race, attacked Frahm as a "status quo" candidate. She had the endorsements of Graves and retiring Senator Nancy Landon Kassebaum, but Brownback won 55%–42%. Graves gamely endorsed the party ticket, even though he did not chair the Kansas delegation at the San Diego Republican Convention. He raised money for 4th District Congressman Todd Tiahrt and cut spots for senatorial nominees Brownback and Roberts and 2d District House candidate Jim Ryun, all of whom won.

Graves now seems to be working more closely with the conservatives. He agreed with Speaker Tim Shallenburger to abolish the curriculum-setting state Board of Education in December 1996. In January 1997 he presented a budget with bundle of tax cuts—income, property, sales, business—estimated at $436 million by 1998 and over $2 billion by 2000, and proposed raising spending only 2.4%. Conservatives in the state House jockeyed for bigger tax cuts. Whatever the outcome, the general trend seemed clear: Kansas is heading for less government (except for more prison beds). With low unemployment, many new businesses and a booming general aviation industry centered on Wichita, Kansas seemed to be doing well economically. Graves's job ratings have been very high and he looks like a strong candidate for reelection in 1998.

Senior Senator. Kansas in 1996 elected two new Republican senators; it was the first time the state had two Senate elections since 1962. The senior senator, ironically, has much less political experience: Sam Brownback was elected to the House in 1994, served one term as a conservative reformer, then plunged into the race when Bob Dole announced his resignation, and beat appointee Sheila Frahm in the August primary and Democrat Jill Docking in November.

Sam Brownback grew up on a farm in Anderson County, some 50 miles from Kansas City, was student body president at Kansas State and briefly a farm broadcaster. After law school, he practiced law for four years in Manhattan in the 1980s; he was appointed secretary of the state Board of Agriculture in 1986 and served until it was abolished in 1993. He claims credit for encouraging the use of wheat to make plastics and cattle hides to make wound dressings. He was a White House Fellow, working from 1990–91 for U.S. Trade Representative Carla Hills. In March 1994 he announced for Congress, condemning "a welfare system that discourages the work ethic and encourages the disintegration of families and a government that can't say no to spending or yes to reform." But he did not sign the Contract with America because of qualms about its welfare and tax provisions. Brownback won the three-way House primary 48%–35%–16%. In the general he faced John Carlin, governor from 1978–86. Carlin cited his experience and said he would "do what is right for the country" not what would get him reelected. But in anti-incumbent 1994 that appeal was weak. Brownback won 66%–34%, carrying every county. Carlin oddly was appointed U.S. Archivist, a position for which he had little experience.

After the election, Brownback took the lead in trying to sell off a House annex building, though it proved even more difficult than expected, and House leaders debated options on whether to sell, lease or just tear down the building. He pushed successfully to reduce Congress's own budget. He headed a group of Republican freshman called the "New Federalists," whose mission is to eradicate the Departments of Commerce, Education, Energy and Housing and Urban Development. He pushed hard for the gift ban rule which Republican leaders hesitated on in 1995 but which was passed later that year; he spoke at the United We Stand Convention against "influence peddling" in Washington. On immigration he played a key role in separating the legal and illegal immigration issues, which led to passage of a tough measure against illegal immigrants but no major reductions in the number of legal immigrants.

On May 15, 1996, Bob Dole surprised just about everyone when he announced he was resigning from the Senate on June 11. On May 17 Brownback announced he would seek the seat, noting "They are size 25 shoes that even Michael Jordan couldn't fill." Meanwhile, Governor Bill Graves's choice to fill the vacancy, Lieutenant Governor Sheila Frahm, delayed ten days before accepting. Though both labeled conservative, Frahm and Brownback presented a strong contrast. As Brownback put it, "This race is a microcosm of what is going on nationally in the Republican Party. Do you stay with the status quo and nip and tuck around the edges? Or do you make real changes to get the country going in the right direction?" Frahm meanwhile proclaimed she was comfortable with compromise. She was pro-choice on abortion, he anti-abortion. Brownback accused her of voting as a state legislator to raise taxes $500 million; she criticized his "slash and burn" approach to federal spending. He criticized her for voting against cloture on a campaign finance bill. She rejected his call for debates. Graves and Kassebaum endorsed Frahm; William Bennett of Empower America and James Dobson of Focus on the Family endorsed Brownback. The August primary resulted in a 55%–42% Brownback win.

In the general election Brownback faced a Democrat with a great political name, Wichita stockbroker Jill Docking, wife of a former lieutenant governor whose father and grandfather both served as governor. In the Democratic primary she convincingly beat former Governor Joan Finney, an abortion opponent, 74%–26%. Docking promised "Kansas common sense," likened herself to Kassebaum, and when charged with being a Ted Kennedy liberal asked: "Did you ever meet a liberal stockbroker?" Brownback campaigned on the 3 Rs: "Reduce, reform and return. Reduce the size and scope of the federal government. Reform the Congress. Return to the basic values that built the country: work and family and the recognition of a higher moral authority." He promised to serve only two terms (presumably two full terms); this election was for the last two years of Dole's term.

Both candidates spent liberally, and some fall polls showed the race close. But Brownback won by the convincing though not overwhelming margin of 54%–43%. In the Senate he serves on the Commerce, Governmental Affairs and Foreign Relations Committees, and continues to be an outspoken conservative and sometimes maverick reformer who insists on a more confrontational leadership style than was demonstrated by Brownback predecessor Bob Dole. In January 1997, he was the only member of the Commerce Committee to vote against William Daley for Secretary of Commerce. Brownback faces a 1998 contest for a six-year term. But his 1996 win and GOP strength in Kansas should give him an easy ride.

Junior Senator. Kansas's junior but highly experienced senator is Pat Roberts, elected to succeed Nancy Landon Kassebaum in 1996. Roberts comes from a fine Kansas Republican background: his great-grandfather founded Kansas's second oldest newspaper and his father, Wes Roberts, was briefly Republican National Committee chairman during the Eisenhower years. Pat Roberts has spent most of his adult life preparing for the place he is in now. After four years in the Marine Corps and five years running an Arizona newspaper, he worked for two years as an aide to Senator Frank Carlson and 12 years as chief aide to 1st District Congressman Keith Sebelius. When Sebelius retired in 1980, Roberts won the seat with 56% in a three-candidate Republican primary. For 14 years, in the minority in the House, he concentrated on farm issues, learning their intricacies and minutiae, traveling in a van to keep in touch with constituents in a district so large that it took two weeks to visit every county seat.

Then, in January 1995, Roberts became chairman of the House Agriculture Committee. He had long understood that the huge subsidies of the early 1980s would never return; "Farm programs have declined an average of 9% since 1986 and are going to go on declining." Faced with Republican budget parameters, Roberts fashioned a Freedom to Farm bill which would phase out subsidies over seven years. In September 1995 his bill failed in committee when southern Republicans eager to protect cotton, rice and peanut subsidies voted against it. But in November 1995 Roberts persuaded Agriculture conferees to include most of his bill in the 1996 budget reconciliation bill, which Clinton vetoed. He agreed to maintain cotton and rice marketing loans and managed to preserve the conservation reserve program popular in Kansas. But the overall thrust of his bill was revolutionary, the biggest change in agriculture policy since the New Deal act of 1933. Roberts's new bill passed the Agriculture Committee 29–17 in

January 1996, the full House in February, and became law in April. In the process, there was much acrimony between Roberts and appropriators, led by Appropriations Chairman Bob Livingston and Agriculture Subcommittee Chairman Joe Skeen; they resented the mandatory nature of payments in Roberts's bill, and he resented the budget limits which they imposed. But without that tension, it's quite possible that nothing like the Freedom to Farm Act would have passed at all.

Roberts has worked for other programs as well—for a more aggressive U.S. farm exports policy, against cargo preference provisions which increase export prices to help the maritime unions, for rural healthcare programs, against environmental regulations that infringe on property rights—like the Endangered Species Act and the wetlands act. "It's time we protect the wetlands of true importance to the environment, not some low spot in your field where no self-respecting duck would ever land." He worked to keep food stamps flowing to states and not block-granted in welfare reform. And he was something of a House reformer, leading the successful fights to investigate abuses at the House Post Office and to defund House caucuses.

When Kassebaum announced her retirement in November 1995, Roberts at first backed away from the race; but as the Freedom to Farm Act's fortunes improved, he announced in January 1996 that he was running. He won the August primary with an overwhelming 78% in a four-way race and in the general election faced state Treasurer Sally Thompson. She called Roberts a Washington insider who had lost touch with Kansas and who profited personally in Washington. Roberts responded, "My experience is the right kind to continue getting government out of our lives and pocketbooks," and he charged that she mismanaged funds in the Municipal Investment Pool, losing $20 million. Roberts won easily, 62%–34%, losing only the county that contains Kansas City and carrying the 104 others.

In the Senate he continues his peppery conservatism, although he is more of an accommodationist than his freshman colleague, Sam Brownback. As the most experienced of the 16 Republican newcomers elected in 1994 and 1996, he is positioned to serve as a liaison to the party's establishment wing. Roberts will continue to pursue his farm policy interests in the Senate with a seat on the Agriculture Committee; he chairs the Production and Price Competitiveness Subcommittee. But, with the freedom of a six-year term and the Senate's open operations, Roberts has also added a national-security focus to his work from seats on Armed Services and Intelligence Committees.

Presidential politics. Kansas is heavily Republican in presidential politics. It voted for Lyndon Johnson over Barry Goldwater, barely, in 1964, but has otherwise backed Republicans over the last 60 years. It was also one of Ross Perot's best states in 1992. In 1996 Kansans were so elated with Dole's early success in wrapping up the Republican nomination that the state legislature voted to cancel the April primary, ensuring unanimous support for their native son at the San Diego Republican Convention.

Congressional districting. Kansas lost one of its five seats in the 1990 Census. A freshman Republican was beaten in the 1992 primary after he was redistricted, but in 1994 Democrat Jim Slattery left to make an unsuccessful race for governor, and Democrat Dan Glickman, who was later named secretary of Agriculture, was narrowly defeated. So Kansas now is one of the seven states with an all-Republican congressional delegation (the others are Alaska, Idaho, New Hampshire, Oklahoma, Utah and Wyoming). And, with five of its six members new to their seats and the other a second-termer, it is the most junior delegation in Congress—a far cry from 1995, when it included three committee chairmen and the Senate majority leader.

The People: Est. Pop. 1996: 2,572,000; Pop. 1990: 2,477,574, up 3.8% 1990–1996. 1.0% of U.S. total, 32d largest; 31% rural. Median age: 34.7 years. 14% 65 years and over. 88.4% White, 5.7% Black, 1.2% Asian; 1% Amer. Indian; 3.8% Hispanic origin. Households: 58.5% married couple families; 28% married couple fams. w. children; 48% college educ.; median household income: $27,291; per capita income: $13,300; 67.9% owner occupied housing; median house value: $52,200; median monthly rent: $285. 4.5% Unemployment. 1996 Voting age pop.: 1,897,000. 1996 Turnout: 1,063,452; 56% of VAP. Registered voters (1996): 1,436,418; 423,595 D (30%), 650,566 R (45%); 362,257 unaffiliated and minor parties (25%).

Political Lineup: Governor, Bill Graves (R); Lt. Gov., Gary Sherrer (R); Secy. of State, Ron Thornburgh (R); Atty. Gen., Carla Stovall (R); Treasurer, Sally Thompson (D); Commissioner of Insurance, Kathleen Sebelius (D). State Senate, 40 (13 D and 27 R); Senate President, Richard Bond (R); State House, 125 (48 D and 77 R); House Speaker, Tim Shallenburger (R). Senators, Sam Brownback (R) and Pat Roberts (R). Representatives, 4 (4 R).

Elections Division: 913-296-4561; **Filing Deadline for U.S. Congress:** June 10, 1998.

1996 Presidential Vote

Dole (R)	583,245	(54%)
Clinton (D)	387,659	(36%)
Perot (I)	92,639	(9%)

1992 Presidential Vote

Bush (R)	449,469	(39%)
Clinton (D)	389,704	(34%)
Perot (I)	311,316	(27%)

GOVERNOR

Gov. Bill Graves (R)

Elected 1994, term expires Jan. 1999; b. Jan. 9, 1953, Salina; home, Lenexa; KS Wesleyan U., B.A. 1975, U. of KS, 1976–79; Methodist, married (Linda).

Career: Graves Truck Line; KS Deputy Secy. of State, 1980–84; KS Asst. Secy of State, 1984–85; KS Secy. of State, 1986–94.

Office: State Capitol, 2d Fl., Topeka 66612, 913-296-3232; Fax: 913-296-7973; Web site: www.state.ks.us.

Election Results

1994 gen.	Bill Graves (R)	526,113	(64%)
	Jim Slattery (D)	294,733	(36%)
1994 prim.	Bill Graves (R)	115,608	(41%)
	Gene Bicknell (R)	79,816	(28%)
	Fred Kerr (R)	63,495	(22%)
	Others	23,706	(8%)
1990 gen.	Joan Finney (D)	380,609	(49%)
	Mike Hayden (R)	333,589	(43%)
	Christina Campbell-Cline (I)	69,127	(9%)

SENATORS

Sen. Sam Brownback (R)

Elected 1996, seat up 1998; b. Sept. 12, 1956, Garnett; home, Topeka; KS St. U., B.S. 1978; U. of KS, J.D. 1982; Methodist; married (Mary).

Career: Radio broadcaster, KKSU, 1978–79; Practicing atty., 1982–86, 1993; Prof., KS St. U. Law Schl., 1982–86; Ogden & Leonardville City Atty., 1983–86; KS Secy. of Agriculture, 1986–93; White House Fellow, Office of USTR, 1990–91; U.S. House of Reps., 1994–96.

DC Office: 303 HSOB 20510, 202-224-6521; Fax: 202-228-1265; e-mail: sam_brownback@brownback.senate.gov.

State Offices: Overland Park, 913-492-6378; Pittsburg, 316-231-6040; Topeka, 913-233-2503; Wichita, 316-264-8066.

Committees: *Commerce, Science & Transportation* (11th of 11 R): Aviation; Communications; Consumer Affairs, Foreign Commerce & Tourism; Manufacturing & Competitiveness. *Foreign Relations* (10th of 10 R): International Operations; Near Eastern & South Asian Affairs (Chmn.); Western Hemisphere & Peace Corps Affairs. *Governmental Affairs* (3rd of 9 R): Oversight of Government Management, Restructuring & the District of Columbia (Chmn.); Permanent Subcommittee on Investigations. *Joint Economic Committee* (5th of 10 Sens.).

Group Ratings (as Member of U.S. House of Representatives)

	ADA	ACLU	AFS	LCV	CFA	CON	NFIB	COC	ACU	NTLC	CHC
1996	5	20	0	15	46	84	100	93	100	100	93
1995	0	—	—	13	8	75	—	100	92	—	—

National Journal Ratings (as Member of U.S. House of Representatives)

	1995 LIB — 1995 CONS			1996 LIB — 1996 CONS		
Economic	26%	—	67%	0%	—	82%
Social	21%	—	72%	35%	—	62%
Foreign	36%	—	59%	38%	—	60%

Key Votes of the 104th Congress (as Member of U.S. House of Representatives)

1. Reduce Medicare Growth $	Y	5. Flag Amendment	Y	9. Cuban Embargo	Y
2. Ovrd. Product Liab. Veto	Y	6. Drop EPA Limits	N	10. Bar Bosnia Troop $	N
3. Increase Min. Wage	N	7. Repeal Assault-Weap. Ban	Y	11. Cut Anti-Missile Defense	N
4. Welfare Reform	Y	8. Ovrd. Part. Birth Veto	Y	12. Bar U.N. Uniforms	Y

Election Results

1996 general	Sam Brownback (R)	574,021	(54%)	($2,269,550)
	Jill Docking (D)	461,344	(43%)	($1,125,844)
	Others	29,351	(3%)	
1996 primary	Sam Brownback (R)	187,914	(55%)	
	Sheila Frahm (R)	142,487	(42%)	
	Christina Campbell-Cline (R)	12,378	(4%)	
1992 general	Robert Dole (R)	706,246	(63%)	($3,542,989)
	Gloria O'Dell (D)	349,525	(31%)	($249,359)
	Christina Campbell-Cline (I)	45,423	(4%)	
	Other	25,253	(2%)	

Sen. Pat Roberts (R)

Elected 1996, seat up 2002; b. Apr. 20, 1936, Topeka; home, Dodge City; KS St. U., B.A. 1958; United Methodist; married (Franki).

Career: Marine Corps, 1958–62; Co-owner, editor, *The Westsider* (AZ newspaper) 1962–67; A.A., U.S. Sen. Frank Carlson, 1967–68; A.A., U.S. Rep. Keith Sebelius, 1968–80; U.S. House of Reps., 1980–96.

DC Office: 116 DSOB 20510, 202-224-4774; Fax: 202-224-3514.

State Offices: Dodge City, 316-227-2244; Prairie Village, 913-648-3103; Topeka, 913-295-2745; Wichita, 316-263-0416.

Committees: *Agriculture, Nutrition & Forestry* (7th of 10 R): Forestry, Conservation & Rural Revitalization; Production & Price Competitiveness (Chmn.). *Armed Services* (10th of 10 R): Acquisition & Technology; Airland Forces; Readiness. *Ethics (Select)* (2nd of 3 R). *Intelligence (Select)* (8th of 10 R).

Group Ratings (As Member of U.S. House of Representatives)

	ADA	ACLU	AFS	LCV	CFA	CON	NFIB	COC	ACU	NTLC	CHC
1996	5	13	8	31	8	17	95	94	95	95	92
1995	0	—	—	13	8	73	—	96	80	—	—

National Journal Ratings (as Member of U.S. House of Representatives)

	1995 LIB — 1995 CONS			1996 LIB — 1996 CONS		
Economic	26%	—	67%	24%	—	73%
Social	0%	—	79%	23%	—	76%
Foreign	0%	—	85%	0%	—	79%

Key Votes of the 104th Congress (as Member of U.S. House of Representatives)

1. Reduce Medicare Growth $	Y	5. Flag Amendment	Y	9. Cuban Embargo	Y
2. Ovrd. Product Liab. Veto	*	6. Drop EPA Limits	N	10. Bar Bosnia Troop $	Y
3. Increase Min. Wage	Y	7. Repeal Assault-Weap. Ban	Y	11. Cut Anti-Missile Defense	N
4. Welfare Reform	Y	8. Ovrd. Part. Birth Veto	Y	12. Bar U.N. Uniforms	Y

Election Results

1996 general	Pat Roberts (R)	652,677	(62%)	($2,305,898)
	Sally Thompson (D)	362,380	(34%)	($659,066)
	Others	37,243	(4%)	
1996 primary	Pat Roberts (R)	245,411	(78%)	
	Tom Little (R)	25,052	(8%)	
	Thomas L. Oyler (R)	23,266	(7%)	
	Richard L. Cooley (R)	20,060	(6%)	
1990 general	Nancy Landon Kassebaum (R)	578,605	(74%)	($521,140)
	Dick Williams (D)	207,491	(26%)	($16,627)

FIRST DISTRICT

"A prairie is not any old piece of flatland in the Midwest," writes Kansas-born reporter Dennis Farney. "No, a prairie is wine-colored grass, dancing in the wind. A prairie is a sun-splashed hillside, bright with wild flowers. A prairie is a fleeting cloud shadow, the song of the meadowlark. It is the wild land that has never felt the slash of the plow." This prairie once covered almost all of Kansas. Now only a little virgin prairie can still be found, in the Flint Hills region west and south of Topeka, where the waist-deep sea of grass still waves in the wind as it did when the pioneers on the Santa Fe Trail went west through here some 150 years ago; the

Tallgrass Prairie National Preserve was created in 1996 to protect this unique landscape. Most of the Kansas prairie has long since been transformed by agriculture. Much of it was grazing land, first for buffalo, then for the cattle driven to Kansas railheads like Abilene and Dodge City in the 1870s and 1880s, a brief moment in history recaptured with varying accuracy in movies over a much longer span, and commemorated in Dodge City's Boot Hill Museum.

Then, after the harsh winter of 1886–87 wiped out the cattle herds, came the plow and barbed wire (commemorated in LaCrosse's Barbed Wire Museum), which enabled farmers to keep livestock out of their wheatfields. The farmers also brought to this vacant landscape Yankee civilization, with its schools and churches and colleges, and some foreign traditions as well, like the Cathedral of the Plains built by German Catholics. Now this civilization is threatened. "My great-grandparents and grandparents were part of the stream of settlers who migrated to western Kansas after the Civil War to become wheat farmers," writes James Dickenson in his elegiac *Home on the Range*. "They broke the virgin sod, erected houses, barns, schools, churches and towns, and made the area one of the most agriculturally productive in the world. A little more than a century later, the population has ebbed away from this area and many of the farms, schools, churches and towns lie vacant, dilapidated and boarded up like old boomtowns."

The 1st Congressional District of Kansas consists of most of this expanse of the state, almost everything from the Flint Hills and Abilene west. Its 66 counties (only the Nebraska 3d and South Dakota at-large have more) increased from 76,000 people in 1870 to 570,000 in 1890; then growth slowed to 666,000 in 1940 and dropped to 619,000 in 1990. Population here has dropped since 1980 almost everywhere except the natural gas exploration areas around Dodge City, its largest town, Salina, and German-Catholic Ellis County, with the high birth rates most Catholic communities had 30 years ago. Life isn't dismal in the "Big First," but community institutions are threatened by slow growth, and talented young people move elsewhere to get ahead in life. Politically, the 1st remains heavily Republican—indeed in the prosperous middle 1990s more so than in the economically troubled 1890s.

The congressman from the 1st District is Jerry Moran, elected in 1996. Moran grew up in Plainville in Rooks County and got his start in politics as an intern for Representative Keith Sebelius, where Moran's predecessor, now Senator, Pat Roberts, was a long-time aide. He worked as a banker for four years before attending law school at the University of Kansas. Moran was elected to the state Senate in 1988 where he fought to cut taxes and, as chairman of the Judiciary Committee, pushed to give judges greater flexibility on juvenile crime. In 1995 he became state Senate majority leader, succeeding Sheila Frahm who became lieutenant governor and then U. S. senator from June to November 1996. When Pat Roberts announced in January 1996 that he would not seek reelection for the House seat but would run for the Senate, Moran stepped into the 1st District race and, with the help of other Republicans, avoided serious primary competition. He won 76% of the vote in the August primary, which was tantamount to election; in November he was elected 73%–24%.

In the House Moran will pursue farm interests on both the Agriculture Committee and the International Relations Committee, which also deals with trade issues. He typifies the more experienced newcomers in contrast to the 1994 Republican freshman class. "This Congress has a lot of folks who had experience in state legislatures as speakers and majority leaders, as chairmen of committees. That lends itself to an ability to accomplish things," said this former state Senate majority leader. He says he wants less government, less taxes, fewer regulations but he also thinks "we're looking to get things done. It seems to me there's a great desire among Republicans to work together."

The People: Pop. 1990: 619,371; 51% rural; 17% age 65+; 92% White; 1% Black; 1% Asian; 5% Hispanic origin. Households: 62% married couple families; 28% married couple fams. w. children; 43% college educ.; median household income: $23,433; per capita income: $11,328; median gross rent: $297; median house value: $38,000.

1996 Presidential Vote			**1992 Presidential Vote**		
Dole (R)	167,237	(62%)	Bush (R)	122,621	(42%)
Clinton (D)	75,840	(28%)	Perot (I)	85,004	(29%)
Perot (I)	25,055	(9%)	Clinton (D)	81,423	(28%)

Rep. Jerry Moran (R)

Elected 1996; b. May 29, 1954, Great Bend; home, Hays; U. of KS, B.S. 1976, J.D. 1981; Methodist, married (Robba).

Career: Operations Officer, Consolidated State Bank, 1975–77; Mgr., Farmers State Bank & Trust Co., 1977–78; Practicing atty., 1981–96; Instructor, Fort Hays St. U., 1986; KS Senate, 1988–96, Majority Ldr., 1995–97.

DC Office: 1217 LHOB 20515, 202-225-2715; Fax: 202-225-5124.

District Offices: Hays, 913-628-6401; Hutchinson, 316-665-6138.

Committees: *Agriculture* (21st of 27 R): Forestry, Resource Conservation & Research; General Farm Commodities; Risk Management & Specialty Crops. *International Relations* (25th of 26 R): International Economic Policy & Trade. *Veterans' Affairs* (11th of 16 R): Health.

Group Ratings and Key Votes: Newly Elected

Election Results

1996 general	Jerry Moran (R)	191,899	(73%)	($430,261)
	John Divine (R)	63,948	(24%)	($82,631)
	Others	5,298	(2%)	
1996 primary	Jerry Moran (R)	79,119	(76%)	
	R. W. Yeager (R)	15,376	(15%)	
	Bert Fisher (R)	9,887	(9%)	
1994 general	Pat Roberts (R)	169,531	(77%)	($309,950)
	Terry L. Nichols (D)	49,477	(23%)	

SECOND DISTRICT

The green plains of eastern Kansas have seen more than their share of American history. Here, on bluffs above the Missouri River, Fort Leavenworth was built in 1827, famous for years for its war college and military prison and now the oldest U.S. fort west of the Mississippi. In the 1850s, newly founded towns along the Kansas River and along the Missouri line were the centers of "Bleeding Kansas," where the pro-slavery bushwhackers set up a state capital in tiny Lecompton and anti-slavery New Englanders set up their stronghold down the river at Lawrence. Farther up the river is Fort Riley, once an outpost against the Indians, now a major Army base threatening, even after the end of the Cold War, to expand into adjacent farm fields, and Manhattan, home of Kansas State University. Topeka, the state capital, sits here on a low bluff above the river; it was this city whose system of legal segregation was overturned in the 1954 landmark case, *Brown v. Board of Education.* Farther south, on the Missouri border, are the hills called "the Balkans." Here coal miners, often of Eastern European origin, lived in and near towns like Pittsburg and Girard, once a center of American socialism, where Clarence Darrow and Upton Sinclair made pilgrimages, and its paper, *Appeal to Reason*, had a nationwide 750,000 circulation.

These disparate areas, Topeka and Manhattan, Fort Riley and Fort Leavenworth, wheat-growing counties and the Balkans—most of eastern Kansas except the Kansas City metropolitan area—make up the 2d Congressional District of Kansas. The heritage here has been Republican ever since jayhawk Republicans defeated bushwhack Democrats once the votes were counted honestly in the 1850s. Yet Democrats in recent decades have been competitive here in state and local races, especially in Topeka. For 20 of the 24 years from 1970–94 Democrats were elected to fill the 2d District seat. But Kansas's strong conservate Republicanism now seems to have taken root. Despite some controversy, the 2d has elected two solidly conservative Republican congressmen in the last two elections—in 1994, Sam Brownback, who went on to fill Bob Dole's seat in the Senate and in 1996 Jim Ryun.

Jim Ryun had been famous for more than 20 years before he ran for Congress. He grew up in Wichita, where in 1965 he was the first high-schooler to break the four-minute mile; his 3:55.3 time is still the world record for high schoolers. He was a star runner at the University of Kansas, and ran in the Olympics of 1964, 1968, and 1972, winning a silver medal and setting world records for the 880-yard dash and the 1500-meter run. After his competitive athletic career, he operated a sports camp, was a motivational speaker for corporations and Christian groups, wrote two books, started a sports management firm and worked with a hearing aid company that produced a "Sounds of Success" program to help hearing-impaired children achieve their potential.

In May 1996, when Brownback decided to run for the Senate seat suddenly vacated by Bob Dole, Ryun decided to run for Congress. He was opposed by former Topeka Mayor Douglas Wright and Cheryl Brown Henderson, whose father was the plaintiff in *Brown v. Board*. Wright called Ryun an "extremist" and proclaimed, "This is clearly a battle over the direction of the Republican Party in Kansas," and predicted Ryun couldn't win the general. Both Wright and Henderson favored abortion rights; Ryun was strongly opposed. Ryun campaigned for tax cuts and elimination of unnecessary government regulation. While the press treated Ryun as something of an oddity, Republican primary voters didn't: he won 62% to 25% for Wright and 14% for Henderson.

Ryun faced another tough test in the general. His Democratic opponent John Frieden was a trial lawyer, and amateur long distance runner, who spent $200,000 of his own money and outspent Ryun by nearly 2–1. Frieden was pro-choice, opposed to the Dole-Kemp tax cut; he berated Newt Gingrich and Republican Medicare "cuts." He sounded just a bit condescending when he said, "Ryun clearly falls short of being the kind of person we should send to the United States Congress." Ryun replied that Frieden was lying about his record, was maligning his character and was trying to buy the office. To charges that his strong religious views made him "extreme," Ryun replied, "I go to church once a week. I do pray over my meals, and so do a lot of people in my district. I don't think that's extreme. I love people, I love God, I love my family . . . And I will tell you that our family prayed about my decision to run for office. Maybe that makes me an extremist."

In the fall Democrats circulated "Courtship Makes a Comeback," written by Ryun and his wife for Focus on the Family. It recounted their practice that any young man wanting to date Ryun's daughters—the Ryuns have four children, ages 21 to 26— has to call him and ask permission. "At this very first meeting or phone call, the father explains that the family believes in courtship, which means that the young man must be spiritually and financially prepared to marry her if they fall in love. Otherwise, don't even bother starting a relationship." Again there was ridicule, with the press calling Dr. Ruth to mock the Ryuns' practices. Frieden also charged that the Ryuns stated that the husband is the "high priest" of the family; Ryun said he wrote that he and his wife were "co-workers in whatever God calls us to do."

But however absurd the Ryuns' beliefs may seem to Manhattan or Malibu sophisticates, they were not political poison in Kansas. Ryun won 52%–45%, losing Topeka and Shawnee County 52%–46%, but carrying the rest of the district 55%–43%. Having triumphed decisively over an aggressive, high-spending opponent, he should be in good shape to hold the district. And the fact that Ryun won a seat on the National Security Committee—a more prestigious slot than those received by the two other Republican freshmen from Kansas, each of whom had been a state legislative leader—shows that he is off to a quick start in his Capitol Hill career.

The People: Pop. 1990: 619,385; 41% rural; 14% age 65+; 89% White; 6% Black; 1% Asian; 1% Amer. Indian; 3% Hispanic origin. Households: 60% married couple families; 29% married couple fams. w. children; 44% college educ.; median household income: $24,903; per capita income: $11,662; median gross rent: $344; median house value: $44,000.

1996 Presidential Vote			1992 Presidential Vote		
Dole (R)	125,087	(49%)	Bush (R)	98,884	(36%)
Clinton (D)	100,110	(39%)	Clinton (D)	98,457	(36%)
Perot (I)	27,748	(11%)	Perot (I)	75,549	(28%)

Rep. Jim Ryun (R)

Elected 1996; b. May 29, 1947, Wichita; home, Topeka; U. of KS, B.A. 1970; Presbyterian; married (Anne).

Career: U.S. Olympian, Track & Field, 1964, 1968, 1972; Founder & Dir., Jim Ryun Running Camps, 1976–present; Rancher, 1983–present.

DC Office: 511 CHOB 20515, 202-225-6601; Fax: 202-225-7986.

District Offices: Pittsburg, 316-232-6100.

Committees: *National Security* (27th of 30 R): Military Personnel; Military Procurement. *Banking & Financial Services* (21st of 30 R): Financial Institutions & Consumer Credit. *Small Business* (11th of 19 R): Regulatory Reform & Paperwork Reduction.

Group Ratings and Key Votes: Newly Elected

Election Results

1996 general	Jim Ryun (R)	131,592	(52%)	($415,606)
	John Frieden (D)	114,644	(45%)	($757,637)
	Others	5,928	(2%)	
1996 primary	Jim Ryun (R)	48,602	(62%)	
	Douglas S. Wright (R)	19,410	(25%)	
	Cheryl Brown Henderson (R)	10,923	(14%)	
1994 general	Sam Brownback (R)	135,725	(66%)	($749,330)
	John Carlin (D)	71,025	(34%)	($526,315)

THIRD DISTRICT

Though the central city is in Missouri, one-third of metropolitan Kansas City's residents now live west of the state line in Kansas. Some are in Kansas City, Kansas, where the low-lying land near the Missouri River used to house one of the nation's largest stockyards; and home now to Gates Barbeque, one of Bill Clinton's favorite rib joints. This is still a working-class town with a few dilapidated looking streets and lots of modest frame houses, the largest black neighborhood and oldest Catholic ethnic neighborhoods in Kansas, and an old Democratic machine politics. But Kansas City is losing population, while Johnson County, just to the south, is gaining rapidly, and now has nearly three times as many people. Its older neighborhoods are separated from the affluent Kansas City, Missouri, neighborhood around the old Country Club Plaza shopping center by just a single small street; the newer neighborhoods are arrayed along the interstates, and have grown to the point that Overland Park, Olathe, Shawnee and Lenexa—unfamiliar names to most Kansans—are among the largest municipalities in the state. Politically, Johnson County is heavily Republican, but not sympathetic to all the causes of rural Kansas, and with plenty of voters more moderate or even liberal on cultural issues.

The 3d Congressional District consists of Johnson County, Kansas City and surrounding Wyandotte County, the town of Lawrence which is the home of University of Kansas and one rural county to the south. A few decades ago Kansas City would have made this the most Democratic-leaning district in the state. But the balance has changed. Over the last 50 years, working-class Kansas City has hardly grown at all (and cast fewer votes in 1996 than in 1940), while Johnson County has grown explosively. In 1940, Kansas City's Wyandotte County cast 66,000 votes to Johnson's 16,000; in 1960, Wyandotte cast 76,000 to Johnson's 65,000; in 1996, Wyandotte's 49,000 was overwhelmed by Johnson's 189,000. All of which means that the 3d leans heavily Republican.

The congressman from the 3d District is Vince Snowbarger, a Republican elected after a close contest in 1996. Snowbarger grew up in Downstate Illinois and then in Johnson County, when his father was transferred to the world headquarters of the Nazarene Church in Kansas City. He graduated from Southern Nazarene University and got a masters at the University of Illinois and a law degree at the University of Kansas. He settled in Olathe, became active civically and served on the planning commission, then was elected to the Kansas House in 1984, at 35. There he opposed gambling and less strict liquor laws, supported the death penalty and abortion restrictions and called for lower taxes. In 1993 he became House majority leader and pushed for even greater tax cuts than other Republicans wanted. He was clearly a strong conservative but was also skilled at mollifying all factions; one pundit said, "His smile is quicker than his scowl." He decided to run for Congress even before incumbent Republican Jan Meyers announced her retirement. She chaired the Small Business Committee, but won against conservative primary challengers with only 56% in 1992 and 59% in 1994; in November 1995 she decided to retire for "mostly personal" reasons.

Snowbarger had tough opposition in both the primary and general elections. In the primary he faced Ed Eilert, mayor of Overland Park, the largest city in Johnson County. Eilert ran as a moderate, pro-choice on abortion. Snowbarger emphasized tax cuts, in Kansas and Washington: while in the state house, he sponsored bills cutting automobile taxes in half, granting the largest tax cut in Kansas history, and he backed a balanced budget amendment and capital gains tax cut on the federal level. Eilert attacked Snowbarger because of his high approval rating from the Christian Coalition; Snowbarger charged that Eilert raised spending in Overland Park 88% in five years. Eilert was endorsed by Meyers and retiring Senator Nancy Landon Kassebaum, and had a major lead in fundraising; Snowbarger was barred by state law from raising money from PACs and lobbyists until May 23, when the legislative session was over. But conservatives turned out strongly in the August primary, and Snowbarger edged Eilert 44%–40%.

The Democratic nomination was won by Judy Hancock, Meyers's opponent in 1994. She grew up on a farm in Kansas and attended Harvard Law School, practiced law on Wall Street and worked for the Carter trade office. She showed great skill at fundraising, spending $840,000 altogether, almost twice Snowbarger's spending; much of it she raised from EMILY's List and labor unions. Hancock, like other Democrats in Kansas in 1996, tried to appeal to moderate Republicans whose candidates lost in their primaries. "This is the clearest choice in this district in a generation. This district has been represented by moderate Republicans, fiscally conservative, but socially moderate . . . he [Snowbarger] is a complete departure from that." One such issue was abortion; he was anti-abortion, she pro-choice. Another was gun control: she criticized his opposition to the assault weapons ban and his support of a carrying-concealed-weapon (CCW) law in Kansas. Snowbarger defended the CCW law as the best kind of gun control (enactment of such laws in other states has been followed by drops in violent crime) and said that the abortion issue, though helpful to him in the primary, was "not my motivation for running." Hancock was endorsed by some prominent Republicans, though not by Meyers or Kassebaum, whose example she often evoked, and argued that she was a moderate Democrat, for NAFTA, for some form of a balanced budget amendment, for some form of welfare reform. She campaigned strongly against Newt Gingrich, mentioning him 22 times in her first debate with

Snowbarger.

Hancock ran about even or ahead in some late polls, and the newspapers wrote up the race as a mass desertion of moderate Republicans from a supposedly extreme Snowbarger. The election results tell a different story. In 1994 Hancock lost to Meyers by 57%–43%; in 1996 she lost to Snowbarger by 50%–45%. The desertion by Republican voters, if any, went not so much to Hancock as to the Libertarian and Reform Party candidates, and those voters in a two-way race might well have preferred Snowbarger. Hancock's increase of just 2% between the two elections was actually less than that of the average Democratic House candidate across the country. Given Hancock's money advantage and the coverage in the local press, Snowbarger showed considerable strength in winning this seat, and must be considered the favorite to hold it in 1998.

The People: Pop. 1990: 619,445; 7% rural; 10% age 65+; 86% White; 9% Black; 2% Asian; 1% Amer. Indian; 3% Hispanic origin. Households: 57% married couple families; 28% married couple fams. w. children; 60% college educ.; median household income: $34,275; per capita income: $16,585; median gross rent: $454; median house value: $75,300.

1996 Presidential Vote

Dole (R)	144,924	(50%)
Clinton (D)	121,152	(42%)
Perot (I)	18,176	(6%)

1992 Presidential Vote

Clinton (D)	116,396	(38%)
Bush (R)	113,963	(37%)
Perot (I)	75,413	(25%)

Rep. Vince Snowbarger (R)

Elected 1996; b. Sept. 16, 1949, Kankakee, IL; home, Olathe; S. Nazarene U., B.A. 1971; U. of IL, M.A. 1974; U. of KS, J.D. 1977; Nazarene; married (Carolyn).

Career: Instructor, Mid-America Nazarene Col., 1973–77; Practicing atty., 1977–96; KS House of Reps., 1984–96, Majority Ldr., 1993–96.

DC Office: 509 CHOB 20515, 202-225-2865; Fax: 202-225-5897

District Offices: Kansas City, 913-621-0832; Lawrence, 913-842-9313; Miami County, 913-294-4122; Overland Park, 913-383-2013.

Committees: *Banking & Financial Services* (23rd of 30 R): Capital Markets, Securities & Government Sponsored Enterprises. *Government Reform & Oversight* (22nd of 24 R): Human Resources (Vice-Chmn.); National Economic Growth, Natural Resources & Regulatory Affairs. *Small Business* (12th of 19 R): Tax, Finance & Exports.

Group Ratings and Key Votes: Newly Elected

Election Results

1996 general	Vince Snowbarger (R)	139,169	(50%)	($465,869)
	Judy Hancock (D)	126,848	(45%)	($840,595)
	Others	13,296	(5%)	
1996 primary	Vince Snowbarger (R)	31,341	(44%)	
	Ed Eilert (R)	28,453	(40%)	
	Others	11,851	(16%)	
1994 general	Jan Meyers (R)	102,218	(57%)	($376,484)
	Judy Hancock (D)	78,401	(43%)	($340,859)

FOURTH DISTRICT

Wichita is the largest Kansas-only metropolitan area, smaller than million-plus metro Kansas City, but a Great Plains metropolis of the magnitude of Omaha or Tulsa. It began as a farm market town and grew with local oil and gas discoveries in the 1920s. But its real impetus came during World War II and the years just after, when aircraft factories sprouted up here on the Kansas plains and Wichita suddenly became the nation's major producer of small planes. Today the big three—Cessna, Beechcraft and Learjet—are all located here; so is the bulk of Boeing's military business. This is the general aviation center of America. Wichita has also become a regional health center in the common Great Plains pattern, as rural counties are unable to attract new doctors or maintain hospitals, and people from miles around come to the metropolis for treatment. Wichita has also become home to franchising giant, Thorn Americas Inc. (formerly Rent-A-Center) and many telemarketing companies. In the early 1990s general aviation was hurt by the recession and by liability suits which held manufacturers liable for planes they had produced years, even decades, before. But now Wichita has recovered: the demand for small planes is robust, and a federal limit on liability pushed through by, among others, former Wichita area Congressman Dan Glickman, has enlivened the industry.

Kansas's 4th Congressional District is centered around Wichita, covering wheat-growing areas to the east and west, but with most of its people in Wichita and Sedgwick County. Politically, it has voted Republican most years; in 1992 and 1996 it voted for George Bush and Bob Dole. It has had a recent history, however, of sharply contested House elections, first in 1994, when Democrat Dan Glickman was upset after 18 years, and then in 1996 when his challenger was reelected after another tough race.

The congressman from the 4th District is Todd Tiahrt, a Republican first elected in 1994. He grew up on a farm in South Dakota, went to the same high school as South Dakota Senator Tim Johnson, played football for the South Dakota School of Mines and Technology and graduated from Evangel College. In 1976 he moved to the Wichita area to be closer to his wife's family and worked at Zenith as a project engineer and at Boeing as a proposal manager on the Space Station, Air Force One, KC-135, B-52, B-1, B-2, A-67, YF-22 and Comanche helicopter programs. In 1990, he went to the courthouse to file to run for the Kansas House, and decided he was a Republican; he lost that race by only eight votes. His grandfather had raised him to be a Democrat, but he found his strong religious views—"to me, liberty is the freedom to do the right thing, not the freedom to do anything"—were more in line with Republicans. "When my great, great, great-grandfather came from Prussia to Whitewater, Kansas, he didn't come for the entitlements. He came for the opportunity."

In 1992 Tiahrt was elected to the Kansas Senate, where his great cause was a concealed weapons law allowing citizens on application to carry firearms. In 1994 he got it into his head to run against Glickman, a task all the more daunting because Glickman seemed to be having a good ninth term: he was chairman of the House Intelligence Committee and, with Senator Nancy Kassebaum, passed legislation reducing the product liability of general aviation manufacturers in 1994. Tiahrt attacked Glickman for supporting the Clinton Administration, ran ads showing his face morphing into Clinton's, and targeted his vote for the 1994 crime bill with its gun control provisions. "I am a working man who cares about the financial bottom line," Tiahrt said. "I'm sick and tired of all the hype and all the waste. I don't have the Clinton Administration breaking their necks to get me into office."

Tiahrt's base was among Wichita's numerous religious conservatives, who have taken over the local Republican Party. Tiahrt assembled a corps of 1,800 volunteers, many from church contacts. "I moved below radar and stayed low-key, so my opponent wouldn't start raising lots of money," he said. In fact, he was vastly outspent; Glickman spent $694,000, Tiahrt $200,000. On election day Glickman ran relatively well, as he had for years, in high-income Republican precincts; but he suffered serious losses in middle-income areas in Wichita and Sedgwick

County and beyond. Tiahrt won a solid 53%–47% victory, and on election night his volunteers sang "What a Mighty God We Serve." Glickman went on to become secretary of Agriculture.

In the House Tiahrt was an enthusiastic supporter of the Contract with America and boasted that he voted with Newt Gingrich 97% of the time. When Democrats attacked him for that, "My response was simply to point out that Kansans agree with a balanced budget, welfare reform, tax relief for families, term limits and a real crime bill." He has failed to achieve his principal legislative goal, abolition of the Department of Energy, but he argued the issue on many TV appearances with Energy Secretary Hazel O'Leary. He tried to zero out AmeriCorps as well, but proposed spending some of its money for veterans' health care and the rest for reducing the budget deficit. He was more successful in introducing the Adoption Promotion and Stability Act of 1996, which gives tax breaks for adoptive parents and ends the ban on transracial adoptions; introduced by Republicans, it was embraced by Bill Clinton and passed nearly unanimously. For a solid economic conservative, he did keep his eye on local economic issues, sponsoring an amendment to allow USDA money to be used for value-added products like wheat flour, and building up the Winfield and Arkansas City levees.

Given the narrowness of his victory and the strength of his religious views, Tiahrt was naturally targeted by Democrats, unions, environmentalists and abortion rights advocates. Starting in March 1996 the AFL-CIO spent somewhere upwards of $500,000 on ads against Tiahrt, charging him with favoring "cuts" in Medicare and student loans and complicity in raids on union pensions funds. Some TV stations refused to run the union ads on the basis they were misleading, and even the *Wichita Eagle*'s cartoonists called them a "sort of an escape from reality kind of thing, fictitious, unreal, but big-budget and well-made." Democrats had a serious candidate in Randy Rathbun, U.S. Attorney in Kansas. Tiahrt attacked Rathbun as a liberal, a big spender, a bumbling prosecutor, a pawn of Democratic special interests. He challenged Rathbun to come up with his own plan to balance the budget; Rathbun refused. He outspent Rathbun by only $903,000 to $608,000, not counting the huge AFL-CIO ad campaign. But he turned that against the Democrat with a late ad attacking Rathbun as "in the pocket" of organized labor which was being infiltrated by organized crime: this a reference to the Laborers' Union, which the Clinton Justice Department found to be mob-ridden while allowing its leader Arthur Coia, a big Democratic contributor, to avoid any tougher action such as removal from office.

Democrats hoped that Rathbun's moderate stances and Tiahrt's strong conservatism could reverse the 1994 result. Tiahrt's share of the vote did drop, from 53% to 50%. But Rathbun won the same losing percentage (47%) Glickman had; the difference was the Libertarian. "I want to thank you for trusting me," said Tiahrt on election night. "And I will trust you to love your children more than the government loves them. And to spend your money more wisely than the government spends it." He will get his chance to make some of those decisions. After heavy-duty lobbying and at least one disappointment, the loyal Tiahrt in November 1996 was rewarded with a seat on the Appropriations Committee.

The People: Pop. 1990: 619,373; 24% rural; 14% age 65+; 87% White; 7% Black; 2% Asian; 1% Amer. Indian; 4% Hispanic origin. Households: 59% married couple families; 28% married couple fams. w. children; 48% college educ.; median household income: $28,308; per capita income: $13,623; median gross rent: $376; median house value: $52,000.

1996 Presidential Vote

Dole (R)	145,997	(56%)
Clinton (D)	90,557	(35%)
Perot (I)	21,660	(8%)

1992 Presidential Vote

Bush (R)	114,001	(40%)
Clinton (D)	93,428	(33%)
Perot (I)	75,350	(27%)

Rep. Todd Tiahrt (R)

Elected 1994; b. June 15, 1951, Vermillion, SD; home, Goddard; Evangel Col., B.A. 1975; SW MO St. U., M.B.A. 1989; Assembly of God; married (Vicki).

Career: Project Engineer, Zenith Corp., 1976–84; Proposal Mgr., Boeing Co., 1985–94; KS Senate 1992–94.

DC Office: 428 CHOB 20515, 202-225-6216; Fax: 202-225-3489; e-mail: tiahrt@hr.house.gov.

District Offices: Independence, 316-331-8056; Wichita, 316-262-8992.

Committees: *Appropriations* (30th of 34 R): District of Columbia; Military Construction; Transportation.

Group Ratings

	ADA	ACLU	AFS	LCV	CFA	CON	NFIB	COC	ACU	NTLC	CHC
1996	5	12	8	15	8	42	100	94	100	98	100
1995	0	—	—	0	0	56	—	100	100	—	—

National Journal Ratings

	1995 LIB — 1995 CONS	1996 LIB — 1996 CONS
Economic	0% — 74%	0% — 82%
Social	0% — 79%	14% — 77%
Foreign	28% — 65%	38% — 60%

Key Votes of the 104th Congress

1. Reduce Medicare Growth $	Y	5. Flag Amendment	Y	9. Cuban Embargo	Y
2. Ovrd. Product Liab. Veto	Y	6. Drop EPA Limits	N	10. Bar Bosnia Troop $	Y
3. Increase Min. Wage	N	7. Repeal Assault-Weap. Ban	Y	11. Cut Anti-Missile Defense	N
4. Welfare Reform	Y	8. Ovrd. Part. Birth Veto	Y	12. Bar U.N. Uniforms	Y

Election Results

1996 general	Todd Tiahrt (R)	128,486	(50%)	($903,348)
	Randy Rathbun (D)	119,544	(47%)	($608,355)
	Other	8,361	(3%)	
1996 primary	Todd Tiahrt (R)	unopposed		
1994 general	Todd Tiahrt (R)	111,653	(53%)	($199,973)
	Dan Glickman (D)	99,366	(47%)	($693,534)

KENTUCKY

Kentucky today remains very much what it was at its beginning—a Jeffersonian commonwealth. Literally: it is one of four commonwealths (the others are Virginia, Pennsylvania and Massachusetts) and when the first settlers came here, in the years when Jefferson was writing his *Notes on Virginia*, it was part of Virginia. Kentucky was admitted to the Union in 1792, when Jefferson was Secretary of State; and when Jefferson was aroused at the Federalists' anti-sedition acts, he ghost-wrote the Kentucky Resolutions in 1798. Kentucky's one large county is named after Jefferson and its one large city after the monarch to whom he was credentialed as ambassador to France, Louis XVI. To this day Kentucky still has a constitution informed by a Jeffersonian jealousy of power. Its one-term limit on governors was raised to two only in 1995, and even then the incumbent chose not to run; it has strict limits on when the legislature can meet; every governor must swear that he or she has not participated in a duel (remember what Jefferson thought of Aaron Burr). Kentucky has long favored the Democratic Party, which can trace its ancestry at least tenuously back to Jefferson; Republicans have had their successes here of late, but the state voted twice, though by diminishing margins, for William Jefferson Clinton.

The agrarian Jefferson would approve of Kentucky's demography, which is still largely rural, with well under half its population in the big metropolitan areas of Louisville, Lexington and the Kentucky towns across the Ohio River from Cincinnati. And the tobacco planters who once presided over what one historian called "the alcoholic republic" might not entirely disapprove of a Kentucky economy that remains heavily dependent on century-old industries such as tobacco (Kentucky's burley crop makes it the nation's number two producer), whiskey (Bourbon County is in Kentucky) and coal. Many of the buildings here are old: the small-town 19th Century courthouses, the cabins in the coal mining Appalachians, the unpainted houses in the soggy lowlands beneath the levees by the Mississippi River.

Satellite dishes and four-lane highways have brought modern civilization into hollows and lowland farms which lacked indoor plumbing and electricity within living memory, but people in this state still have a strong attachment to place and family. The continuity is real. Kentucky's population has grown just over 30% in the past 50 years; few outsiders have moved in, so today's Kentuckians are mostly descendants of settlers who poured over the mountains in the 40 years after Daniel Boone made his way through the Cumberland Gap in 1775, when Kentucky's population rose from 73,000 in the Census of 1790 to 564,000 in 1820.

There has long been hearty, though lopsided, political competition here; with most of the 120 counties voting today as they did in the Civil War era. The eastern mountains were pro-Union and remain Republican, except for counties where coal miners were organized by the United Mine Workers in the 1930s; the Bluegrass region and the western end of the state were slaveholding territory and Democratic. Louisville, with many German immigrants, was an anti-slavery town, and supported a strong Republican organization. These patterns, which have more or less prevailed for more than 100 years, were apparent in the returns for governor in 1995, senator in 1996, and president in 1992 and 1996.

For years, all this meant control by the Democratic Party, with the real battle in the Democratic primary. There was almost a party system within the dominant party, with factions that go back to the 1938 primary when Senate Majority Leader (and later Vice President) Alben Barkley was challenged by Governor (and later Senator and Baseball Commissioner) Happy Chandler. Barkley's faction was later led by Governor (1959–63) Bert Combs and Chandler's by Governor (1971–74) and Senator Wendell Ford, who were arrayed prominently on opposite sides in the 1987 primary. Chandler and Combs both died in 1991, and it is getting harder to trace the continuity, though the current governor, Democrat Paul Patton, comes from the

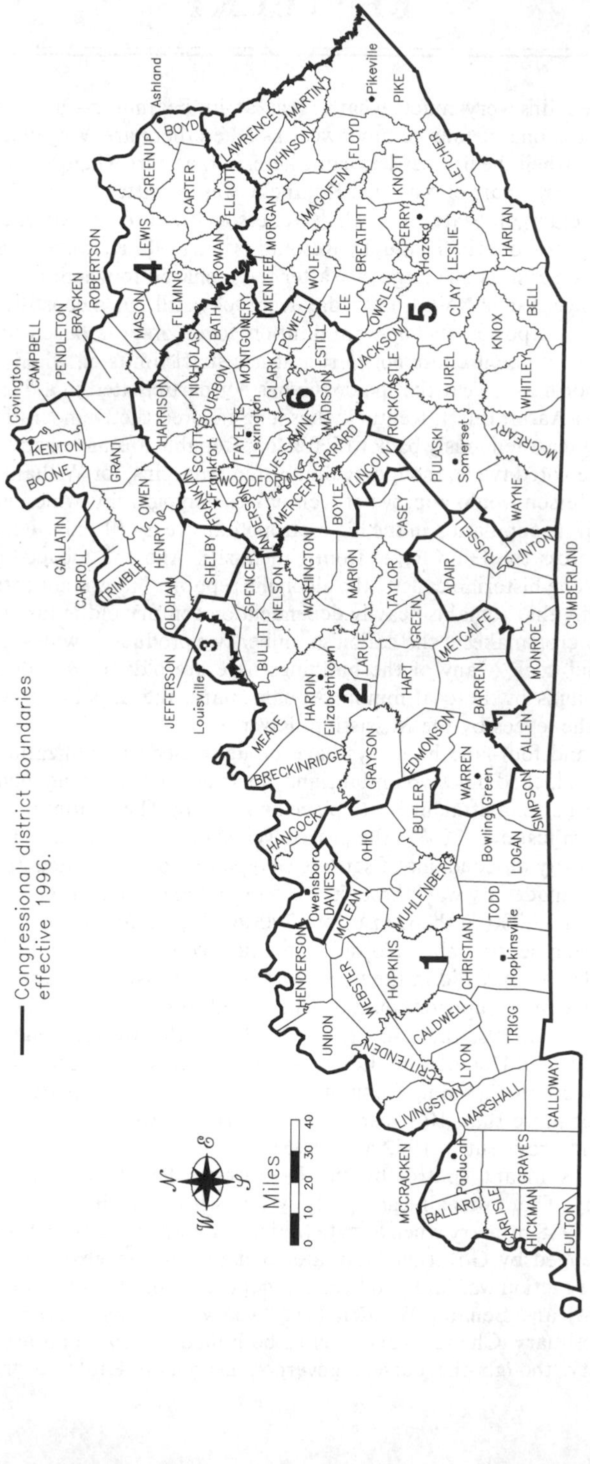
Congressional district boundaries effective 1996.
Miles
0 10 20 30 40
N
S
E
W
Copyright © 1997 by Election Data Services, Inc.
1
2
3
4
5
6
Covington
Ashland
Pikeville
Hazard
Lexington
Frankfort
Louisville
Elizabethtown
Owensboro
Bowling Green
Hopkinsville
Paducah
Somerset
BOONE
KENTON
CAMPBELL
GRANT
PENDLETON
BRACKEN
ROBERTSON
MASON
LEWIS
GREENUP
BOYD
CARTER
ELLIOTT
LAWRENCE
MARTIN
JOHNSON
FLOYD
PIKE
KNOTT
LETCHER
MAGOFFIN
MORGAN
ROWAN
FLEMING
BATH
MENIFEE
WOLFE
BREATHITT
PERRY
LESLIE
HARLAN
OWSLEY
LEE
CLAY
BELL
KNOX
LAUREL
JACKSON
ESTILL
POWELL
MONTGOMERY
NICHOLAS
HARRISON
BOURBON
CLARK
MADISON
ROCKCASTLE
WHITLEY
MCCREARY
PULASKI
WAYNE
CLINTON
RUSSELL
CUMBERLAND
ADAIR
CASEY
LINCOLN
GARRARD
JESSAMINE
FAYETTE
SCOTT
WOODFORD
FRANKLIN
ANDERSON
MERCER
BOYLE
OWEN
GALLATIN
CARROLL
TRIMBLE
HENRY
OLDHAM
SHELBY
SPENCER
NELSON
WASHINGTON
MARION
TAYLOR
GREEN
METCALFE
MONROE
BARREN
HART
LARUE
BULLITT
JEFFERSON
HARDIN
MEADE
BRECKINRIDGE
GRAYSON
EDMONSON
ALLEN
WARREN
SIMPSON
BUTLER
LOGAN
HANCOCK
OHIO
DAVIESS
MCLEAN
MUHLENBERG
TODD
CHRISTIAN
HOPKINS
HENDERSON
WEBSTER
UNION
CALDWELL
TRIGG
CRITTENDEN
LYON
LIVINGSTON
MARSHALL
CALLOWAY
MCCRACKEN
BALLARD
CARLISLE
GRAVES
HICKMAN
FULTON

eastern mountains as Combs did, and the current attorney general is Ben Chandler, Happy Chandler's grandson.

Now in the 1990s there has been more two-party competition, as there was around 30 years ago: Republicans even held the governorship and both Senate seats then (1967–71). But the great prize of the governorship has eluded the Republicans since that time; Democrat Paul Patton, with labor and eastern Kentucky support and denunciations of Newt Gingrich and Medicare "cuts," overcame early perils and won in November 1995, and Democrats held all statewide downballot offices. But Patton's 51% was far below the 59% to 65% Democrats won in four of the last five gubernatorial races. Bill Clinton did carry the state 45%–41% in 1992; but in 1996 his margin was just 46%–45%, as opposition to his tobacco stand cost him votes in south central and western Kentucky. Meanwhile Republicans picked off one House seat after another, the 2d in a May 1994 special election, the 1st in November 1994, the 3d in November 1996, to hold a 5–1 edge in the delegation. After 1996 Democrats held a solid lead in the state House, but were even, 20–20, in the state Senate. And Republican Senator Mitch McConnell, after seeming to be in some trouble, won 55%–43% in 1996, his best margin in three elections.

Governor. There is no question who stands at the apex of Kentucky politics: the governor. The governor's appointment powers are wide; the legislature meets only 60 days every two years and the governor can then shift around line items in the state budget. The governor has almost always been the undisputed leader of his party. For 100 years a one-term limit was imposed on all statewide officials after Treasurer "Honest Dick" Tate absconded in 1888 with $250,000. In 1995 the limit was raised to two terms, but Governor Brereton Jones decided not to run anyway.

Kentucky's governor is now Democrat Paul Patton, formerly lieutenant governor under Brereton Jones and elected in 1995 to succeed him. Patton grew up in Lawrence County on the West Virginia border in a house converted from a silo. He was a 1959 graduate of the University of Kentucky's College of Engineering, and went on to become a coal company executive. He began his public service career as deputy state transportation secretary from 1979–80 and made a successful first run for public office in 1982 as Pike County judge-executive. In 1991 he was elected Lieutenant Governor and worked on the law granting tax credits to firms that create jobs. The 1995 gubernatorial race was an uphill battle. In the Democratic primary he won 45%—enough to avoid a runoff—to 24% for Secretary of State Bob Babbage and 21% for legislator John "Eck" Rose. In the general he faced Larry Forgy, who campaigned hard against the KERA education reform. Passed in 1990 after the state Supreme Court outlawed the school finance laws, KERA vastly raised per pupil spending, moved toward equalizing spending in districts, mandated ungraded classes for kindergarten through third grade and a teacher assessment system based on written portfolios. Unfortunately test scores have not risen and, in the words of *New York Times* reporter Peter Applebome, "There is little definitive evidence it is working." Forgy blasted KERA as an experimentation; Patton said he would fix KERA.

On other issues Forgy sounded conservative notes and Patton often echoed them, calling for school prayer and boot camps. When the Clinton Administration threatened to regulate tobacco as a drug, Patton filed a lawsuit, lit up a cigarette and said he wouldn't support Clinton in 1996 if the FDA acted. Forgy attacked 24 years of one-party rule, corruption (the state House speaker was indicted for taking a $500 bribe in 1992), called for tough action on welfare and crime. In the fall the campaign took a different turn. As House Republican job approval fell, Patton began to attack Newt Gingrich and Medicare "cuts," even as Forgy had attacked Bill Clinton on tobacco. Patton hired a Clinton Administration staffer, who was later charged with campaign theft, to run a black voter turnout drive and called Forgy a "two-headed extremist." "We're going to save Kentucky from Newt the Second," Patton proclaimed.

It was enough to prevail. Patton won 51%–49%, not a dazzling margin; Brereton Jones had won 65%–35% four years before. But it was the first major Democratic success in stalling Republican advances since Clinton took office, and Democrats all over the country took heart. In office Patton proceeded cautiously, appointing Republicans to his cabinet, signing an anti-concealed weapons law, appointing a drug task force to handle "crank," signing a law making it easier to charge a juvenile offender as an adult. He appointed a task force to review KERA to "lay a foundation for building on what is in my judgment one of Kentucky's finest achievements." Despite earlier talk, he ran a full-bore campaign for the Clinton-Gore ticket, hand-picked former Lieutenant Governor Steve Beshear to run for the Senate and backed him strongly, and tried to win back the 1st District House seat and Republican seats in the legislature. His efforts were only partly successful. Clinton won by 1%, Beshear lost by a wide margin, the Republicans gained rather than lost a House seat, pulled even in the state Senate, and lost just one seat in the state House. Patton's response was to guard his right flank: he called a special session of the legislature in December and passed workmen's comp reform, over the opposition of unions and lawyers. 1997, unusually, is not an election year in Kentucky: the 1998 legislative races may be an indicator of how Patton will fare running for reelection in 1999.

Senior Senator. Wendell Ford is a canny veteran of Kentucky and Washington political wars who has usually been on the winning side, but now is in the minority. Ford grew up in Owensboro, served in the Army during World War II, went back home and ran a family insurance business and got into politics. He was chief aide to Governor Bert Combs from 1959–63, was elected lieutenant governor in 1967, ran for governor in 1971 and beat Combs in the primary and the hand-picked successor of Republican Governor Louie Nunn in the general. In 1974 he pondered long before giving up one year of the governorship to run for the Senate, but did and beat incumbent Republican Marlow Cook in 1974.

Ford has a moderate but partisan voting record and has fought fiercely for what he regards as Kentucky's interests. He chaired the Democratic Senatorial Campaign Committee from 1976–82, chaired the Rules Committee for eight years after 1986, in which capacity he presided at the inaugurations of George Bush and Bill Clinton. He was elected Democratic whip in 1990, the number two position in the leadership; but Majority Leader George Mitchell effectively made freshman Tom Daschle his deputy, and Daschle, now Democratic Leader, does not often delegate to Ford. Ford's power is more often exerted through committees. On Commerce, he has long been a leader on aviation issues; with Oregon's Ron Wyden, he called for more disclosure of airline safety data after the May 1996 ValuJet crash. He has taken care to fund Kentucky aviation projects, including the greater Cincinnati airport in northern Kentucky and the airport in Owensboro. In 1996 he was one of 15 Democrats who voted against cloture on an aviation bill one provision of which would reassert FedEx's status as an "express company," making it harder for unions to organize, but would not benefit UPS, which uses Louisville as a hub. He weighed in on the telecom bill to guarantee universal service for rural areas. On Energy, he has worked for clean coal technologies and research on alternatives to high-temperature burnings. He has worked to promote eastern coal and once threatened "blood on the floor of the Senate" to backers of a coal slurry pipeline which would compete with Kentucky coal.

Ford is now ranking Democrat on the Rules Committee where he was chief sponsor of the Democrats' motor voter bill, signed soon after Clinton was inaugurated, which has vastly increased voter rolls but, so far at least, not turnout. He spurned requests to set up a House bank-type operation in the Senate and used the issue in a 1992 campaign spot: "I said no way, we're not going to have a bank on our side. If it ain't good for Kentucky, it ain't good for Wendell Ford." More recently he blocked Washington Republican Rick White's bill to allow candidates free access to the Internet.

Ford has worked hard on tobacco issues, from his first term when he got cigarettes excluded from the Consumer Product Safety Act to the Clinton years when he fought hard against the tobacco tax proposed to finance the Clinton healthcare plan. When Clinton proposed FDA regulation, he responded sharply, "We're all for reversing the current trends in teen smoking. But the FDA plan is the wrong response, with the wrong agency at the wrong level of government." He hailed U. S. Tobacco and Philip Morris for their programs against teen smoking and, days after Al Gore's emotional speech about his sister's death from lung cancer, Ford quoted his daughter, a breast cancer survivor, as saying, "Why do we have to zero in politically on one company or one state, when all these other things are out there we need to get after?" Ford has worked hard for breast cancer research and many local causes as well: the $7.4 million William Natcher Bridge, the Atomic Vapor Laser Isotope Separation facility in Paducah, and making sure that horses qualify for business expensing under Section 179 of the tax code.

Ford has a middle-of-the-Senate voting record combined with Democratic Party loyalty; he surprised people by voting for the assault weapons ban in 1994 and pleased unions by voting against NAFTA. "In the 104th Congress we saw our lives pass before our eyes," he told a union audience in 1996; he called a Republican plan to privatize four Kentucky lakes a "ridiculous proposal." Ford has won reelection by wide margins in 1980, 1986, and 1992. He holds some records: the first opposed candidate to carry all 120 counties, in 1980, and the highest number of votes cast for any Kentucky candidate, in 1992. That year his opponent attacked him for opposing the Gulf war resolution and "waffling" on the balanced budget amendment (a criticism that later seemed prescient, given Ford's support of the amendment when it failed by several votes in the Senate in 1994, and his vote against a slightly different version in the 1995 razor-thin defeat); his 63% in 1992 was lower. For the 105th Congress, Ford said his goals were a balanced budget, campaign finance reform, and education investments such as making $10,000 of college tuition deductible or providing $1,500 HOPE scholarships for two years of college. These sound like an attractive campaign platform, but in February 1997 Ford announced he would retire in 1998. Republican 4th District Congressman Jim Bunning and Democrat 6th District Congressman Scotty Baesler have both announced they will run.

Junior Senator. Mitch McConnell, the only Republican to win a statewide race in Kentucky since 1968, is one of the most partisan Republicans in the Senate and often one of the most effective, a hard-working defender of Republican causes and an assiduous attacker of Democrats. He grew up in Louisville and overcame polio as a child; he has been in politics most of his adult life. On finishing law school, he became a staffer for Senator Marlow Cook, then moved back to Louisville and in 1977, at 35, won the office that had been Cook's political stepping stone, Jefferson County judge-executive. In 1984 McConnell ran for the Senate, highlighting the weakness in incumbent Democrat Dee Huddleston's low profile.

McConnell has a mostly conservative voting record and high party loyalty. Yet he was willing to penalize a fellow Republican when as Ethics Committee chairman he led the investigation of Bob Packwood for sexual harassment; the committee seized Packwood's diaries and ultimately recommended expulsion, at which point, in September 1995 Packwood resigned. McConnell has been a strong backer of product liability and medical malpractice reform, seeking to cap trial lawyers' contingent fees. He sponsored a Pornography Victims Act, to let victims of sex crimes sue producers of hard-core pornography that motivated the offenders. He successfully kept horse shows operating despite criticism by animal rights activists—an issue he used in his 1990 campaign. He split with other Republicans and opposes term limits. He works on local issues—saving $170 million for the Appalachian Regional Commission, getting a $6 million operating subsidy for Land Between the Lakes, obtaining $6.6 million for Louisville's Printing House for the Blind.

McConnell served on the Foreign Affairs Committee for years, then switched to Appropriations, where he chairs the Foreign Operations Subcommittee. There he strongly supports aid to Israel and has been skeptical about aid to Russia. In February 1994 he rallied 31 Republicans to vote against the confirmation of Strobe Talbott, Bill Clinton's Oxford roommate and longtime skeptic about tough policies toward Russia.

But perhaps McConnell's greatest expertise is on campaigns and elections. He has fought one battle after another against campaign finance proposals that in his view limit free speech and vigorous electoral competition. "Spending is speech. That is the law," he says, and when challenged for his willingness to limit speech by supporting the flag burning amendment changed his position and opposed it. "I am a First Amendment hawk." Throughout the 1990s he has led Republicans in opposing campaign finance measures—earlier David Boren's bill limiting PAC contributions and instituting some public financing, more recently the McCain-Feingold bill to provide other financing for candidates who accept limits. He has persevered through floor fights in 1990 and 1991, a conference report in 1992, a floor fight in 1993, a filibuster in 1994, and a floor fight in 1996. He has made some headway: by early 1997 public financing had become unthinkable and McConnell's arguments and court rulings were raising doubts that campaign spending can be constitutionally limited. His own proposals are for enforcing the Supreme Court decision banning unions from using mandatory dues for politics, discouraging out-of-state financing, and providing ever more disclosure.

McConnell is now chairman of the National Republican Senatorial Committee for the 105th Congress where his views on campaign finance have already brought success. A letter to potential donors averring the White House had been "sold for illegal foreign cash" produced a rush of giving. McConnell has had great successes in Kentucky also, particularly with creative TV ads. In 1990, he ran a spot showing a bottle of pills; his opponent Harvey Sloane, a physician, had prescribed sleeping pills for himself after his DEA permit expired. Sloane was a formidable opponent, but McConnell outspent him and outcampaigned him, and won 52%–48%.

McConnell has worked hard to build up Kentucky's chronically ailing Republican Party, and has met with success. He oversaw Ron Lewis's capture of the 2d District House seat in a May 1994 special election, plus another House seat and several Republican legislative pickups in historically Democratic counties in Western Kentucky that November. Then, when Democrat Paul Patton was narrowly elected governor in November 1995, it seemed McConnell might be in trouble. Patton and Senator Wendell Ford backed former Attorney General and Lieutenant Governor Steve Beshear who beat former Congressman Tom Barlow 66%–24% in the Democratic primary. Encouraged by Patton's attacks on Newt Gingrich and the Republican Medicare plan, Beshear sounded the same themes, and attacked McConnell for stopping campaign finance reform, for refusing to release his tax returns, for seeking to delay voting on the minimum wage increase and for supporting NAFTA. McConnell, he said, was part of "the extremist agenda of Newt Gingrich, Bob Dole and the rest of the Republican-controlled Congress."

McConnell did not need to respond creatively when Bill Clinton proposed that the FDA regulate tobacco as a drug. Beshear, obviously on the defensive, said that there are ways to fight teenage smoking "without stepping on our necks in burley country." But McConnell made other interesting arguments. He argued that Beshear was a lobbyist and a political insider. One example was Beshear's law firm's $10.6 million in fees for representing the state insurance commissioner as liquidator of a bankrupt insurance company. Other ads attacking Beshear were for contributions from trial lawyers, for representing foriegn companies, for investing in companies that exploit foreign labor. "Steve's been pretending to be a folksy, shotgun-toting, pickup-driving defender of the working class," McConnell said, while running an ad saying that Beshear could not relate to people because he belonged to a fox hunting club. Beshear protested it was a club anyone could join. But he was followed on the campaign trail by a character dressed in riding regalia and carrying a sign reading "Fox Hunters for Beshear."

To make these arguments McConnell spent $5 million over the six-year cycle; Beshear, well financed by most standards, spent $2 million. McConnell, running even in polls earlier in the year, in November won 55%–43%. He carried the Louisville and Lexington areas, won 2–1 in northern Kentucky, and lost only handfuls of counties in the eastern mountains and in the far western end of the state.

Presidential politics. In presidential elections, Kentucky is competitive when Democrats run a southerner or two, as it was in such widely separated years as 1952, 1976, 1980, 1992 and 1996; otherwise it has gone pretty solidly Republican. Attacks on tobacco caused Bill Clinton to lose many votes in rural Kentucky, while turnout in heavily Democratic mountain counties declined by as much as 29%; he ended up carrying the state 46%–45% in 1996 only by improving his vote in Lexington and the Bluegrass and the Louisville and northern Kentucky suburbs. Was the difference made by the appearance at a November 4 Clinton-Gore rally in Lexington of University of Kentucky basketball coach Rick Pitino? Maybe so: Kentucky takes basketball very seriously, and under Pitino UK won its first national championship in two decades in 1996.

Kentucky was part of the Super Tuesday primary in March 1988, but switched back to a May date for 1992 and 1996, so that state and presidential contests can be held on the same day. It has had no effect on the outcome of the presidential contest.

Congressional districting. Kentucky lost one district in the 1990 Census. Redistricting moved the 4th District out of the Jefferson County suburbs and east into the mountains and merged most of the old 5th and 7th mountain Districts, one very Republican and the other very Democratic, into a new 5th. Scandal, death, retirement and political upheaval have produced great turnover in what in the 1980s was one of the House's most stable delegations: Kentucky's six districts have been represented by 12 congressmen already in the 1990s.

The People: Est. Pop. 1996: 3,884,000; Pop. 1990: 3,687,000, up 5.3% 1990–1996. 1.5% of U.S. total, 24th largest; 48% rural. Median age: 35.1 years. 13% 65 years and over. 91.7% White, 7.1% Black. 1% Asian; 1% Hispanic origin. Households: 59.2% married couple families; 29% married couple fams. w. children; 33% college educ.; median household income: $22,534; per capita income: $11,153; 69.6% owner occupied housing; median house value: $50,500; median monthly rent: $250. 5.6% Unemployment. 1996 Voting age pop.: 2,928,000. 1996 Turnout: 1,387,999; 47% of VAP. Registered voters (1996): 2,391,190; 1,473,323 D (62%), 744,612 R (31%), 173,255 unaffiliated and minor parties (7%).

Political Lineup: Governor, Paul Patton (D); Lt. Gov., Steven L. Henry (D); Secy. of State, John Y. Brown III (D); Atty. Gen., Albert B. (Ben) Chandler III (D); Treasurer, John Kennedy Hamilton (D); Auditor, Ed Hatcher (D). State Senate, 40 (20 D and 20 R); Senate President, Don Byers (D); State House, 100 (53 D, 46 R, and 1 I); House Speaker, Thomas Moss (D). Senators, Wendell H. Ford (D) and Mitch McConnell (R). Representatives, 6 (1 D and 5 R).

Elections Division: 502-573-7100; **Filing Deadline for U.S. Congress:** January 27, 1998.

1996 Presidential Vote

Clinton (D)	636,614	(46%)
Dole (R)	623,283	(45%)
Perot (I)	120,396	(9%)

1996 Republican Presidential Primary

Dole (R)	76,669	(74%)
Uncommitted & Other	14,822	(14%)
Buchanan (R)	8,526	(8%)
Keyes (R)	3,822	(4%)

1992 Presidential Vote

Clinton (D)	665,095	(45%)
Bush (R)	617,196	(41%)
Perot (I)	203,968	(14%)

GOVERNOR

Gov. Paul E. Patton (D)

Elected 1995, term expires, Dec. 1999; b. May 26, 1937, Fallsburg; home, Pikeville; U. of KY, B.S. 1959; Presbyterian; married (Judi).

Career: Coal Co. Exec., 1959–79; KY Dpty. Transportation Secy., 1979–1980; KY Dem. Party Chmn., 1981–83; Pike Cnty. Judge-Executive, 1982–91; KY Lt. Gov., 1991–95; KY Economic Develop. Secy., 1991–95.

Office: Office of the Governor, State Capitol, Frankfort 40601, 502-564-2611; Fax: 502-564-2735; Web site: www.state.ky.us.

Election Results

1995 gen.	Paul Patton (D)	500,787	(51%)
	Larry Forgy (R)	479,227	(49%)
1995 prim.	Paul Patton (D)	152,203	(45%)
	Bob Babbage (D)	81,352	(24%)
	John (Eck) Rose (D)	71740	(21%)
	Gatewood Galbraith (D)	29,039	(9%)
1991 gen.	Brereton C. Jones (D).	540,648	(65%)
	Larry J. Hopkins (R)	294,452	(35%)

SENATORS

Sen. Wendell H. Ford (D)

Elected 1974, seat up 1998; b. Sep. 8, 1924, Thruston; home, Owensboro; U. of KY, MD Schl. of Insurance; Baptist; married (Jean).

Career: Army, 1944–46 (WWII); Army Natl. Guard 1949–62; Family insur. business; Chief A.A., Gov. Bert Combs, 1959–63; KY Senate, 1965–67; KY Lt. Gov., 1967–71; KY Gov., 1971–74.

DC Office: 173-A RSOB 20510, 202-224-4343; Fax: 202-224-0046; e-mail: wendell_ford@ford.senate.gov.

State Offices: Covington, 606-491-7929; Lexington, 606-233-2484; Louisville, 502-582-6251; Owensboro, 502-685-5158.

Committees: *Minority Whip. Commerce, Science & Transportation* (3rd of 9 D): Aviation (RMM); Communications; Consumer Affairs, Foreign Commerce & Tourism. *Energy & Natural Resources* (2nd of 9 D): Energy Research, Development, Production & Regulation (RMM); Water & Power. *Rules & Administration* (RMM). *Joint Committee on Printing* (4th of 5 Sens.).

Group Ratings

	ADA	ACLU	AFS	LCV	CFA	CON	NFIB	COC	ACU	NTLC	CHC
1996	70	17	86	62	86	2	38	38	40	24	38
1995	80	—	91	57	63	0	—	47	13	—	—

National Journal Ratings

	1995 LIB — 1995 CONS			1996 LIB — 1996 CONS		
Economic	71%	—	27%	57%	—	39%
Social	49%	—	50%	48%	—	51%
Foreign	57%	—	42%	51%	—	45%

Key Votes of the 104th Congress

1. Reduce Medicare Growth $	N	5. Flag Amendment	Y	9. Anti-Missile Defense	N
2. Lmt. Prod. Liab. Damages	N	6. Endangered Species	N	10. Cuban Embargo	Y
3. Increase Min. Wage	Y	7. Gay Employment Rights	N	11. Bar Bosnia Troop $	N
4. Welfare Reform	Y	8. Ovrd. Part. Birth Veto	Y	12. Cut Vietnam Aid	N

Election Results

1992 general	Wendell H. Ford (D)	836,888	(63%)	($2,321,131)
	David L. Williams (R)	476,604	(36%)	($335,304)
1992 primary	Wendell H. Ford (D)	unopposed		
1986 general	Wendell H. Ford (D)	503,755	(75%)	($1,201,624)
	Jackson M. Andrews (R)	173,330	(25%)	($58,572)

Sen. Mitch McConnell (R)

Elected 1984, seat up 2002; b. Feb. 20, 1942, Sheffield, AL; home, Louisville; U. of Louisville, B.A. 1964, U. of KY, J.D. 1967; Baptist; married (Elaine Chao).

Career: Chief Legis. Asst., U.S. Sen. Marlow Cook, 1967–70; Dep. Asst. Atty. Gen., 1974–75; Jefferson Cnty. Judge Exec., 1977–1984.

DC Office: 361-A RSOB 20510, 202-224-2541; Fax: 202-224-2499.

State Offices: Bowling Green, 502-781-1673; Fort Wright, 606-578-0188; Lexington, 606-224-8286; London, 606-864-2026; Louisville, 502-582-6304; Paducah, 502-442-4554.

Committees: *National Republican Senatorial Committee Chairman. Agriculture, Nutrition & Forestry* (4th of 10 R): Marketing, Inspection & Product Promotion; Research, Nutrition & General Legislation (Chmn.). *Appropriations* (7th of 15 R): Agriculture, Rural Development & Related Agencies; Commerce, Justice, State & the Judiciary; Defense; Energy & Water Development; Foreign Operations (Chmn.). *Labor & Human Resources* (10th of 10 R): Children & Families; Employment & Training. *Rules & Administration* (4th of 9 R). *Joint Committee on Printing* (3rd of 5 Sens.).

Group Ratings

	ADA	ACLU	AFS	LCV	CFA	CON	NFIB	COC	ACU	NTLC	CHC
1996	10	22	14	0	14	32	97	85	95	100	100
1995	0	—	0	0	6	29	—	100	91	—	—

National Journal Ratings

	1995 LIB — 1995 CONS			1996 LIB — 1996 CONS		
Economic	21%	—	74%	26%	—	69%
Social	12%	—	81%	0%	—	72%
Foreign	22%	—	67%	0%	—	74%

Key Votes of the 104th Congress

1. Reduce Medicare Growth $	Y	5. Flag Amendment	N	9. Anti-Missile Defense	Y
2. Lmt. Prod. Liab. Damages	Y	6. Endangered Species	N	10. Cuban Embargo	Y
3. Increase Min. Wage	Y	7. Gay Employment Rights	N	11. Bar Bosnia Troop $	N
4. Welfare Reform	Y	8. Ovrd. Part. Birth Veto	Y	12. Cut Vietnam Aid	Y

Election Results

1996 general	Mitch McConnell (R)	724,794	(55%)	($5,031,293)
	Steven L. Beshear (D)	560,012	(43%)	($2,073,794)
	Others	22,240	(2%)	
1996 primary	Mitch McConnell (R)	88,620	(89%)	
	Tommy Klein (R)	11,410	(11%)	
1990 general	Mitch McConnell (R)	478,034	(52%)	($5,229,296)
	G. Harvey I. Sloane (D)	437,976	(48%)	($2,929,641)

FIRST DISTRICT

Where the Ohio River flows into the Mississippi—the intersection Huckleberry Finn and Jim missed in the fog—must have struck early settlers as a site for a great city. But no Pittsburgh or St. Louis grew up on this fertile black soil. Instead, the Kentucky land west of the dammed-up Tennessee and Cumberland Rivers, bought from the Chickasaw Indians by General Andrew Jackson and Governor Isaac Shelby in 1818—the Jackson Purchase, it is still called—was settled by farmers. Most people here today are the descendants of these farmers, with memories of earlier generations retained in family lore. Just to the east of the Tennessee and the Cumberland Rivers is the Pennyrile (after pennyroyal, a common variety of local wild mint), a land of low hills and small farms, where you find the west Kentucky coal fields, the site of much strip mining in recent years.

The 1st Congressional District of Kentucky is made up of the Jackson Purchase and much of the Pennyrile, plus a line of counties stretching some 200 miles east of the Mississippi along the Tennessee border. There is a distinctive southern atmosphere here—in the crops that are grown, in the accents of the people, in historically low wage levels and in the fact that the big city people look to is more often Nashville than Louisville. The Jackson Purchase and the Pennyrile have long been Democratic; Paducah, the 1st's largest city, produced one of the most enduring Democratic politicians of this century, Alben Barkley, whose career from 1912–56 included 14 years in the House, 24 in the Senate and four as vice president; he was Senate majority and minority leader and he keynoted four Democratic National Conventions and died while delivering the peroration at Washington and Lee University's mock political convention in 1956. But the hills far from the Mississippi are Republican country and this, combined with the Republican trend which reached north from Dixie to Paducah in 1994, has made the 1st District seriously contested political territory, a district that has so far had three congressmen in the 1990s.

The congressman now, and the first to be reelected since 1990, is Ed Whitfield, a longtime Democrat turned Republican. He grew up in Hopkinsville and Madisonville, in a family with Pennyrile roots going back before 1800. He served in the Army, practiced law in Hopkinsville, and was elected to the legislature in 1973 as a Democrat where he was something of an insider; former Governor (1963–67) Edward Breathitt was best man at his wedding. After one term in Frankfort, Whitfield ran an oil distributorship in the west Kentucky coal fields, then in 1979 moved to Washington to become an executive for the Seaboard and CSX railroads. He was legal counsel to the chairman of the ICC from 1991–93, when he returned to west Kentucky and ran for Congress as a Republican.

He was returning to a district which since Barkley's time had been represented by quiet, long-serving, conservative Democrats. But Congressman Carroll Hubbard, first elected in 1974, got himself in terrible trouble when he was exposed as having used his Banking Committee post to raise money and pocket speaking fees while doing lobbyists' bidding, and to have pressured banking interests to raise money for his wife Carol Hubbard, who in 1992 was running in the 5th District in eastern Kentucky. All of this was revealed just before election day, and both Hubbards lost their primaries. His successor in the 1st District was Tom Barlow who won the seat in 1992 by beating the Republican 61%–39%, and proceeded to generally support the Clinton Administration. In the May 1994 primary Whitfield beat Barlow's 1992 opponent by only 53%–47%. Then, with help from Senator Mitch McConnell, Whitfield raised nearly twice as much money as the incumbent. He won 70% in the mountain counties added after redistricting, but also carried traditionally Democratic areas around Hopkinsville in the Pennyrile, and Murray in the Jackson Purchase, for a 51%–49% victory.

In the House Whitfield had a moderate voting record and got a seat on the Commerce Committee. He had two significant legislative achievements. He sponsored the "lock box" amendment on Medicare, prohibiting savings from being used for other purposes; this was to blunt Democratic charges that Republicans were "cutting" Medicare to pay for a tax cut for the rich. And he blocked TVA's five development proposals for the Land Between the Lakes recreation area between the Tennessee and Cumberland Rivers. But Whitfield was very much a target of the Democrats and the AFL-CIO. The 1996 Democratic nomination was won by Dennis Null, a former law partner of Carroll Hubbard, who admitted he "more or less evaded (legally) the draft." Null traveled around the district in Old Blue, an aging Lincoln Town car, constantly changing the oil. The media buy against Whitfield came from the AFL-CIO, which attacked him on tax cuts, pension security, and Medicare.

But Whitfield had a huge money advantage, $897,000 to $479,000. Whitfield campaigned as a "compassionate conservative," attacking the Clinton Administration proposal for FDA regulation of tobacco, a big crop here; Whitfield was the only politician at an October 1996 "tobacco appreciation dinner" in Mayfield. Whitfield brushed off Null's attacks on him for not owning a house in the district (an insult to renters, the incumbent said) and for holding a fundraiser with Newt Gingrich in California (just raising money to battle Null's money from the union bosses). Whitfield ads attacked Null as a "liberal trial lawyer" who represented drug dealers. Null hit Whitfield on the minimum wage, the unions' pension issue and student loans; but he lacked the money to buy time in the eastern media markets. The Democratic heritage in the Jackson Purchase and Pennyrile is strong. Senator Mitch McConnell, on his way to a big victory, lost 13 of the district's 31 counties, and Whitfield lost 13 too. But Whitfield carried Paducah, which he lost in 1994, and won overall 54%–46%. It was a solid win in a difficult year, but does not guarantee Whitfield an easy race in 1998.

The People: Pop. 1990: 614,212; 61% rural; 15% age 65+; 91% White; 8% Black; 1% Hispanic origin. Households: 62% married couple families; 29% married couple fams. w. children; 28% college educ.; median household income: $20,331; per capita income: $10,238; median gross rent: $278; median house value: $40,200.

1996 Presidential Vote			**1992 Presidential Vote**		
Clinton (D)	105,150	(47%)	Clinton (D)	116,648	(48%)
Dole (R)	96,356	(43%)	Bush (R)	96,605	(39%)
Perot (I)	22,727	(10%)	Perot (I)	30,871	(13%)

Rep. Edward Whitfield (R)

Elected 1994; b. May 25, 1943, Hopkinsville; home, Hopkinsville; U of KY, B.S. 1965, J.D. 1969; Methodist; married (Connie).

Career: Army Reserves, 1967–73; Practicing atty., 1969–79; KY House of Reps. 1973–75; Owner, Rhodes Oil Co., 1975–79; Cnsl., Seaboard System Railroad, 1979–83; Vice Pres., CSX, 1983–91; Cnsl., Interstate Commerce Comm., 1991–93.

DC Office: 236 CHOB 20515, 202-225-3115; Fax: 202-225-3547; e-mail: edky01@hr.house.gov.

District Offices: Henderson, 502-826-4180; Hopkinsville, 502-885-8079; Paducah, 502-442-6901; Tompkinsville, 502-487-9509.

Committees: *Commerce* (20th of 28 R): Energy & Power; Health & the Environment.

Group Ratings

	ADA	ACLU	AFS	LCV	CFA	CON	NFIB	COC	ACU	NTLC	CHC
1996	5	6	8	23	15	24	92	94	85	95	93
1995	10	—	—	13	8	75	—	100	92	—	—

National Journal Ratings

	1995 LIB — 1995 CONS			1996 LIB — 1996 CONS		
Economic	36%	—	60%	20%	—	76%
Social	28%	—	72%	14%	—	77%
Foreign	42%	—	55%	44%	—	55%

Key Votes of the 104th Congress

1. Reduce Medicare Growth $	Y	5. Flag Amendment	Y	9. Cuban Embargo	Y
2. Ovrd. Product Liab. Veto	Y	6. Drop EPA Limits	N	10. Bar Bosnia Troop $	Y
3. Increase Min. Wage	Y	7. Repeal Assault-Weap. Ban	Y	11. Cut Anti-Missile Defense	N
4. Welfare Reform	Y	8. Ovrd. Part. Birth Veto	Y	12. Bar U.N. Uniforms	Y

Election Results

1996 general	Edward Whitfield (R)	111,473	(54%)	($897,338)
	Dennis L. Null (D)	96,684	(46%)	($479,210)
1996 primary	Edward Whitfield (R)	unopposed		
1994 general	Edward Whitfield (R)	64,849	(51%)	($349,472)
	Tom Barlow (D)	62,387	(49%)	($621,279)

SECOND DISTRICT

In the 1770s and 1780s Americans began settling the limestone-soiled country of central Kentucky, staking out towns like Bardstown and Harrodsburg and starting academies and colleges; they were well-settled when Stephen Collins Foster wrote "My Old Kentucky Home" just before the Civil War. That conflict tore deeply here: this part of Kentucky gave birth to both Abraham Lincoln and Jefferson Davis (Davis was actually born in the 1st), and in the Civil War it lost thousands of soldiers, Union and Confederate, and would suffer disproportionate casualties in the wars of the 20th Century as well. This area is also the home of several Kentucky landmarks—Fort Knox, the nation's gold depository; several of the nation's largest bourbon distilleries; and Mammoth Cave, the world's largest accessible cavern, in the south near Bowling Green.

The 2d Congressional District of Kentucky consists of much of the territory south and southwest of Louisville, starting with the southern Jefferson County suburbs and proceeding south to Bowling Green and west along the Ohio River to Owensboro. This is rural and small town country, where most people have family roots that go back generations and a connection with the past not often found in big metropolitan areas. Civil War loyalties are reflected in the election returns here; Kentucky was deeply split on secession, and a color-coded map of the current 2d District would show various splotches of counties pro-South and splotches pro-Union. But the bits of color would only hint at the deep and often bitter feelings caused by the splits over the War and the losses people suffered—feelings of which current partisan preferences are a dim but persistent reflection. And growing dimmer, for in the 1990s opinion has moved toward the Republicans in what was for 129 years a Democratic district.

The congressman from the 2d District is Ron Lewis, a Republican first elected in a May 1994 special election that had national implications. Lewis was born in a log cabin and raised in eastern Kentucky; he worked his way through Morehead State as a laborer at Armco Steel. He worked in the highway department, at a state hospital, then served in the Navy. He worked in sales, and in 1980 became a Baptist minister; in 1985 he started a Christian book store in Elizabethtown, two counties south of Louisville; he was the opposite of a political insider.

Then, in March 1994, Democratic Congressman William Natcher died. He was chairman of the Appropriations Committee, and a politician of a very old school, so hard-working and conscientious that he never missed a roll call vote from the time he won a special election in 1953 until he was mortally ill 41 years later. An incumbent who hired only a small staff, he refused all political contributions, and campaigned by driving around the district and talking to voters while avoiding reporters. Democratic leaders were clear on who should succeed him: former state Senate President Joe Prather, who had managed Governor Brereton Jones's campaign; before the election, Prather even flew to Washington to go apartment hunting. But Democrats failed to account for the national and local conservative trend. Lewis ran for the open seat, and the National Republican Congressional Committee contributed $200,000 for the May 1994 special. Lewis ran ads showing Prather's face morphing into Bill Clinton's and saying that Prather had increased taxes and fees 40 times in the Kentucky legislature. Prather only belatedly raised campaign money and asserted that he was quite a different sort of Democrat than Clinton. Lewis won a solid 55%–45% victory, carrying Bowling Green heavily and running ahead in Owensboro and outside Louisville: the first Democratic loss of this seat in 129 years.

In the House Lewis voted a predictably conservative line and got seats on the National Security and Agriculture Committees. He made news in August 1994 when he attended a smokers' rights rally where Hillary Rodham Clinton was burned in effigy—"inappropriate," he said, but "kind of a desperate act to get some attention to their cause." His November 1994 Democratic opponent, Owensboro Mayor David Adkisson, called it "an act of hate." It was widely assumed that Lewis's victory was aberrational and that Adkisson, a protege of Senator Wendell Ford, would win in November. But Lewis projected sincerity, and his strong religious views and opposition to the Clinton tax increase and healthcare plan were pluses. "Simply put, I'm very much for reducing the size and intrusiveness of the federal government," he said. Lewis won by a resounding 60%–40% margin, even carrying Owensboro's Daviess County.

In 1996 Lewis had another opponent with strong political credentials, former state Senate Majority Leader Joe Wright, who retired from office in 1992 and became head of the Burley Tobacco Growers Association. While Bill Clinton was proposing that the FDA regulate tobacco as a drug, Wright was taking his cutting knife around the district and helping farmers cut tobacco. Wright raised lots of money from highway contractors, lobbyists, and Breckinridge County neighbors; but national Democrats, looking at polls that showed the 2d District solidly Republican now on national issues, gave him very little. As a result, Lewis outspent Wright, $639,000 to $480,000. Lewis's theme was "promises made, promises kept"; he campaigned hard against Clinton on tobacco issues and called on him to spend more time fighting illegal drugs than legal ones. A Lewis ad showed him holding a staffer's 23-month-old son Cooper: "My opponent thinks this election is about scaring seniors, distorting my record, and Newt Gingrich. This campaign isn't about the next election. It's about the next generation. And Cooper's."

Lewis, who has pledged to serve no more than four full terms, won 58%–42%, carrying all but three counties. Wright's response was, "Some years I've worked like a dog trying to get a crop out, and some years it just doesn't rain. It just didn't rain this year on my political efforts, and I accept that." Lewis said, "I think it really comes down to the fact that this is a very conservative district, what I call mainstream America, and I think I represent the values of this district."

The People: Pop. 1990: 615,184; 56% rural; 11% age 65+; 93% White; 5% Black; 1% Asian; 1% Hispanic origin. Households: 65% married couple families; 33% married couple fams. w. children; 30% college educ.; median household income: $23,212; per capita income: $10,609; median gross rent: $310; median house value: $47,900.

1996 Presidential Vote

Dole (R)	113,923	(49%)
Clinton (D)	95,530	(41%)
Perot (I)	22,021	(9%)

1992 Presidential Vote

Bush (R)	107,401	(45%)
Clinton (D)	98,999	(41%)
Perot (I)	33,232	(14%)

Rep. Ron Lewis (R)

Elected May 1994; b. Sept. 14, 1946, McKell; home, Stephensburg; U. of KY, B.A. 1969, Morehead State U., M.A. 1981; Baptist; married (Kayi).

Career: Navy OCS, 1972; Heavy Equip. Sales Rep., 1975–80; Baptist Minister, 1980-present; Prof., Watterson Col., 1980–85; Owner, Alpha Christian Bookstore, 1985–94.

DC Office: 223 CHOB 20515, 202-225-3501.

District Offices: Bowling Green, 502-842-9896; Elizabethtown, 502-765-4360; Owensboro, 502-688-8858.

Committees: *Agriculture* (13th of 27 R): Forestry, Resource Conservation & Research; Livestock, Dairy & Poultry; Risk Management & Specialty Crops. *National Security* (17th of 30 R): Military Personnel; Military Procurement.

Group Ratings

	ADA	ACLU	AFS	LCV	CFA	CON	NFIB	COC	ACU	NTLC	CHC
1996	5	19	0	23	0	17	100	94	100	100	100
1995	0	—	—	6	0	38	—	96	96	—	—

National Journal Ratings

	1995 LIB		1995 CONS	1996 LIB		1996 CONS
Economic	26%	—	67%	0%	—	82%
Social	0%	—	79%	24%	—	72%
Foreign	0%	—	85%	0%	—	79%

Key Votes of the 104th Congress

1. Reduce Medicare Growth $	Y	5. Flag Amendment	Y	9. Cuban Embargo	Y
2. Ovrd. Product Liab. Veto	Y	6. Drop EPA Limits	N	10. Bar Bosnia Troop $	Y
3. Increase Min. Wage	N	7. Repeal Assault-Weap. Ban	Y	11. Cut Anti-Missile Defense	N
4. Welfare Reform	Y	8. Ovrd. Part. Birth Veto	Y	12. Bar U.N. Uniforms	Y

Election Results

1996 general	Ron Lewis (R)	125,433	(58%)	($639,397)
	Joe Wright (D)	90,483	(42%)	($480,101)
1996 primary	Ron Lewis (R)	unopposed		
1994 general	Ron Lewis (R)	90,535	(60%)	($393,266)
	David Adkisson (D)	60,867	(40%)	($493,564)

THIRD DISTRICT

At the falls of the Ohio River, Americans more than 200 years ago founded one of their first inland metropolises, the river port and industrial city of Louisville (pronounced *LOOuhv'l*). It is one of two major American cities today named for a man who was executed, King Louis XVI of France (the other is St. Paul). Far enough north for a midwestern climate, Louisville has always retained an air of the South; when Kentucky decided not to secede in 1861, the decision was not unanimous, and the culture of tidewater Virginia is still visible in the Louisville lawn party. Steamboats are still tied up in front of Louisville's downtown, primed to follow the channel around the falls of the Ohio which prompted George Rogers Clark to found the town in 1778. Mint juleps are served on the verandas of mansions, especially (but not only) during Kentucky Derby week in May; horse racing is a preoccupation throughout the year. Although the Ohio River is crossed with many bridges and the accent across the river in Indiana may sound the same to outsiders, Louisville partakes of the cavalier culture that second sons of big landowners from the west of England brought to Virginia in the 17th Century and their heirs brought over the Appalachians to the valleys of Kentucky in the 18th Century.

Though Louisville's economy is not particularly southern, tobacco and cigarettes are a major business here, and so is distilling whiskey. Louisville still specializes in assembling large, clunky things like appliances and automobiles, and Louisville airport is the hub for UPS. But its biggest business now is health: Columbia-HCA Healthcare, the nation's largest operator of for-profit hospitals, has its headquarters here a few blocks from the riverfront in a Michael Graves building which is one of the monuments of post-modern architecture, and the headquarters of Humana is just a few blocks away. Politically, Louisville has always had some un-southern aspects and has often voted against the rest of Kentucky; if its elite were Virginia cavaliers, many of its burghers were Germans and Pennsylvanians who made this river town a Republican and anti-slavery island in a secessionist and pro-slavery sea. Locally, Louisville and Jefferson County have long had a robust two-party politics, with Jefferson County judge-executives often running for statewide office, notably Republican Senator Mitch McConnell.

The 3d Congressional District of Kentucky includes all of Louisville and almost all of the Jefferson County suburbs—the strip highway zone running south toward Fort Knox, then blue-collar factory zones south of Churchill Downs and the affluent suburbs in the hills to the east heading out toward Bluegrass country. Historically Louisville has had a strong Republican tradition, among its German and black voters; it also has a tradition of activist Democratic politics, personified in Mayors Wilson Wyatt, who served in the 1940s, Harvey Sloane, elected in 1973 and 1981, and Jerry Abramson, the highly popular current incumbent. The 3d District has had periods when it was closely contested, from 1958–64, in 1970, when it had the closest race in the nation, and again in 1994 and 1996.

The 3d District is currently represented by Ann Northup, a Republican elected in 1996. Northup grew up in a large Catholic family in Louisville—she has nine sisters and one brother—and has raised six children of her own. Her husband is a small business owner and she volunteered and served on the boards of many charities and associations—Leadership Louisville, Foster Grandparents, DePaul School for Dyslexic Children, Lexington Road Preservation. In 1986, at 36, she was elected to the Kentucky House, where she worked to hold down taxes and reduce regulatory burdens, and became the number one critic of tobacco in the capital of the nation's number two tobacco state.

In 1996 she decided to run for Congress. The incumbent Democrat, Mike Ward, called himself an "old Democrat" and continued to be inspired by liberal ideas from the 1960s and 1970s; he compiled a liberal voting record and waffled back and forth on 1996 welfare reform. He had won by narrow margins in 1994: he beat a cable TV millionaire in the primary 27%–24%, and in the general edged a pro-choice Republican by 44.4%–44.1%, a margin of 425 votes, with 12% voting for an anti-abortion third candidate. Plus, in a year when almost all Democrats and most Republicans ran cookie-cutter identical campaigns, Northup showed originality in strategy and tactics. First, she outraised him: Ward raised more from PACs, $452,000 to $283,000, but Northup raised an amazing $868,000 from individuals and spent $1,182,000 to Ward's $880,000. Second, she started TV spots in August three weeks before Ward got on the air. Third, she used unusual issues, such as Ward's vote against making English the official language, a vote considered obviously enlightened in liberal circles but inexplicable to most ordinary citizens. "In some states in the U.S., you can take the driver's exam in 35 languages. But if you can't read English, how can you read the traffic signs?" Both candidates opposed FDA regulation of tobacco, but her criticisms of tobacco companies— "I'm very disappointed that the Republicans have not been more forthcoming about kids not smoking"—moderated her image. She argued that government should handle money like the family checkbook: "Hey, if you can't afford it, you can't afford it." Ward's ads saying that she wanted to "steal" from Medicare and attacking her support of restrictions on abortion probably helped him, but not enough; he ran behind Democratic legislative candidates. Northup won 50.3%–49.7%, a margin of 1,299 votes.

In Washington Northup arrived an unabashed supporter of Newt Gingrich and enthusiast for most Republican stands. She certainly showed great electoral competence, and the Republican leadership has recognized the value of having someone of her caliber in their ranks: she received a seat on the coveted Appropriations Committee, where she has already stood out as a team player. But she is likely still to get serious opposition in 1998. Among the names mentioned as candidates are former Attorneys General Fred Cowan and Chris Gorman, Secretary of State John Y. Brown III, state Representative Eleanor Jordan and Kentucky Commission on Women director Virginia Woodward.

The People: Pop. 1990: 613,266; 2% rural; 14% age 65+; 80% White; 18% Black; 1% Asian; 1% Hispanic origin. Households: 50% married couple families; 22% married couple fams. w. children; 44% college educ.; median household income: $26,614; per capita income: $14,072; median gross rent: $344; median house value: $56,300.

1996 Presidential Vote

Clinton (D)	134,975	(53%)
Dole (R)	101,977	(40%)
Perot (I)	17,230	(7%)

1992 Presidential Vote

Clinton (D)	143,824	(50%)
Bush (R)	105,520	(37%)
Perot (I)	35,902	(13%)

Rep. Anne M. Northup (R)

Elected 1996; b. Jan. 22, 1948, Louisville; home, Louisville; St. Mary's Col., B.A. 1970; Catholic; married (Robert).

Career: KY House of Reps., 1986–96.

DC Office: 1004 LHOB 20515, 202-225-5401; Fax: 202-225-5776; e-mail: rep.northup@mail.house.gov.

District Offices: Louisville, 502-582-5129.

Committees: *Appropriations* (33rd of 34 R): District of Columbia; Labor, Health & Human Services & Education; Treasury, Postal Service & General Government.

Group Ratings and Key Votes: Newly Elected

Election Results

1996 general	Anne M. Northup (R)	126,625	(50%)	($1,181,546)
	Mike Ward (D)	125,326	(50%)	($880,073)
1996 primary	Anne M. Northup (R)	unopposed		
1994 general	Mike Ward (D)	67,663	(44%)	($565,022)
	Susan B. Stokes (R)	67,238	(44%)	($580,409)
	Richard A. Lewis (TXP)	17,591	(12%)	($25,472)

FOURTH DISTRICT

The commonwealth of Kentucky has gone to court more than once to assert its claim to all of the Ohio River up to its northern bank: this is the northernmost extension of the South. The Ohio sees many different parts of Kentucky. Ashland, near the West Virginia border, is industrial, the home of Ashland Oil; the river here is bound in by tight hills which hold smoke and soot close in the air. Farther down the river, the country is more bucolic: here Eliza fled across the ice floes in Harriet Beecher Stowe's *Uncle Tom's Cabin.* Farther west, between Louisville and Cincinnati, are counties which still look like they're in the 19th Century. But metropolitan growth obtrudes. Oldham County, just upriver from Louisville, has some of Kentucky's oldest homes, but the horse country is also sprouting affluent subdivisions. And the three northern Kentucky counties across the river from Cincinnati, saw rapid population growth and a sharp rise in incomes in the 1990s, with old cities on the river like Covington, connected to Cincinnati by a suspension bridge built by John Roebling 16 years before the Brooklyn Bridge, and Newport, once known for its gambling, and new subdivisions sprouting on the hills to the south.

The 4th Congressional District of Kentucky spans all these variations of Ohio River country, from Ashland west to Oldham County; it also includes the typically less populated counties just inland. Economically, it runs the gamut from coal mining towns to rich suburbs. Politically, it has some of the most Democratic counties in America, like Elliott County (65%–21% for Bill Clinton in 1996) in the mountains south of Ashland, and then some of the most Republican territory in Kentucky, like Oldham County with its new affluent migrants from Louisville (57%–34% for Bob Dole). This district was substantially changed by 1990s redistricting and lost the Jefferson County suburbs of Louisville. A few decades ago this would have been a Democratic district; now on balance it leans Republican.

The congressman from the 4th District is Jim Bunning, who may go down in history first as a great baseball pitcher, but now has become a congressman of some power. Bunning threw a no-hitter for the Detroit Tigers in 1958 and pitched a perfect game for the Philadelphia Phillies in 1964; he also played for the Pittsburgh Pirates and the Los Angeles Dodgers and retired in 1971 with a 224–184 record, a 3.24 ERA, 2,855 strikeouts and one of the highest totals in baseball history for hitting batters. He was inducted into the Baseball Hall of Fame in August 1996. Unlike some baseball players, he is a college graduate; unlike most celebrities, he is a family man, with nine children (with two sets of twins) and at last count 30 grandchildren. The skill, energy and aggressiveness he showed in baseball he brought to politics in his native northern Kentucky (no, he never played for the Cincinnati Reds). He was elected to the state Senate in 1979 and won a respectable 44% against Martha Layne Collins in the 1983 race for governor (the best showing for a Republican gubernatorial candidate from 1971–95). When incumbent 4th District Congressman Gene Snyder retired in 1986, Bunning won the seat with 55%.

In the House Bunning has a well-nigh perfect conservative voting record and has become a deputy whip, a high-ranking member of Ways and Means and chairman of its Social Security Subcommittee. One of his major causes there has been raising the earnings limit for Social Security beneficiaries; part of the Contract With America was his successful amendment to raise it to $30,000 by 2002. He also sponsored the 1994 law to make the Social Security Administration an independent agency. He has promised to hold hearings in 1997 on the recommendations of the Social Security advisory commission that reported in December 1996: a political hot potato. But Bunning is unafraid of controversy. He served six years on the Ethics Committee, starting off in March 1992 by leading the charge against the House bank overdraft scandal, and ending in January 1997 by resigning from the committee out of disgust with the partisanship of ranking Democrat Jim McDermott. Nor is he a respecter of Bill Clinton, whom he called in September 1993 "the most corrupt, the most amoral, the most despicable person I've ever seen in the presidency."

On other Ways and Means issues, Bunning fought the Clinton healthcare plan and the tobacco tax proposed to help finance it. He worked with Democrats on making the nanny tax less oppressive—and Congress finally raised the limit to trigger coverage, which had not been changed since the 1930s. He passed bills to grant certain tax benefits for troops in Bosnia, as if their services were performed in combat, and to accelerate life insurance benefits for the terminally ill. He preserved expensing for horses (very important in Kentucky) and enacted tax credits for elderly purchasers of long-term care health insurance. He was the principal House sponsor of the adoption tax credit and the law to stop the ban on transracial adoptions.

Bunning has been reelected by wide margins. In 1992, with new mountain counties added, and against former gubernatorial candidate Dr. Floyd Poore (he changed his name legally so that the "Dr." appears on the ballot), he won with 62%. His 1996 opponent, Covington Mayor Denny Bowman, called for "a balanced budget with an education kicker," whatever that means; but he raised little money and Bunning won 68%–32%.

Bunning had been mentioned as a candidate for governor in 1999, but when Wendell Ford announced his plans to retire from the Senate, Bunning jumped into the race. Recognizing the need for a broader message for a statewide audience, Bunning began to sound more moderate notes. But the entry of 6th District Congressman Scotty Baesler into the race increases the likelihood of a spirited and expensive campaign.

The People: Pop. 1990: 614,410; 46% rural; 12% age 65+; 97% White; 2% Black. Households: 62% married couple families; 31% married couple fams. w. children; 34% college educ.; median household income: $26,362; per capita income: $11,863; median gross rent: $336; median house value: $56,700.

1996 Presidential Vote

Dole (R)	115,187	(49%)
Clinton (D)	95,070	(41%)
Perot (I)	20,733	(9%)

1992 Presidential Vote

Bush (R)	105,023	(44%)
Clinton (D)	92,207	(39%)
Perot (I)	39,900	(17%)

Rep. Jim Bunning (R)

Elected 1986; b. Oct. 23, 1931, Campbell County; home, Southgate; Xavier U., B.S. 1953; Catholic; married (Mary).

Career: Pro baseball player, 1950–71; Investment broker & agent, 1960–86; Ft. Thomas City Cncl., 1977–79; KY Senate, 1979–83.

DC Office: 2437 RHOB 20515, 202-225-3465; Fax: 202-225-0003; e-mail; bunning4@hr.house.gov.

District Offices: Ashland, 606-325-9898; Ft. Wright, 606-341-2602.

Committees: *Budget* (5th of 24 R). *Ways & Means* (6th of 23 R): Social Security (Chmn.).

Group Ratings

	ADA	ACLU	AFS	LCV	CFA	CON	NFIB	COC	ACU	NTLC	CHC
1996	5	12	0	15	15	63	100	81	100	98	100
1995	0	—	—	13	0	38	—	96	92	—	—

National Journal Ratings

	1995 LIB — 1995 CONS			1996 LIB — 1996 CONS		
Economic	0%	—	74%	0%	—	82%
Social	0%	—	79%	0%	—	90%
Foreign	0%	—	85%	0%	—	79%

Key Votes of the 104th Congress

1. Reduce Medicare Growth $	Y	5. Flag Amendment	Y	9. Cuban Embargo	Y
2. Ovrd. Product Liab. Veto	Y	6. Drop EPA Limits	N	10. Bar Bosnia Troop $	Y
3. Increase Min. Wage	N	7. Repeal Assault-Weap. Ban	Y	11. Cut Anti-Missile Defense	N
4. Welfare Reform	Y	8. Ovrd. Part. Birth Veto	Y	12. Bar U.N. Uniforms	Y

Election Results

1996 general	Jim Bunning (R)	149,135	(68%)	($886,717)
	Denny Bowman (D)	68,939	(32%)	($55,239)
1996 primary	Jim Bunning (R)	unopposed		
1994 general	Jim Bunning (R)	96,695	(74%)	($560,590)
	Sally Harris Skaggs (D)	33,717	(26%)	($20,141)

FIFTH DISTRICT

The mountains of eastern Kentucky have been a special place since Daniel Boone came through the Cumberland Gap in 1775. As Virginians poured through and created their version of a Tidewater civilization in the Bluegrass country, the people who settled the mountain counties and the Cumberland Plateau, most of them of Irish Protestant or Border Scots descent, brought different values—an assertive egalitarianism, loyalty to family and community and passionate willingness to settle differences by feuds or violence. Most of the people in the mountains today are descendants of families who settled there in the two or three generations after Boone. Handed down are living memories of the old ways of doing things from the time not so far distant when there was little contact here with the outside world and the ties to the rest of American civilization were secured mainly by school primers and the King James Bible.

Only when people's lives have been changed and uprooted by outside events and institutions have their basic political attitudes been changed—and in each case, changed with a lasting imprint. The first agent of such change was the Civil War; the second was the great United Mine Workers organizing drives in the coal mines around the 1930s. The Civil War made the mountains and the Cumberland Plateau a stronghold of the Republican Party. For this was never slave territory—hardly any blacks have ever lived here—and yet communities and families were riven by the rebellion of the South. People have not forgotten: the counties around Somerset and Corbin in south central Kentucky cast some of the highest Republican percentages in the nation in election after election.

Then came coal. Early in this century, vast seams of coal were discovered under the Kentucky mountains; representatives of eastern capitalists began prowling through these hills, hiring courthouse town lawyers to buy up mineral rights from unsuspecting farmers, building tiny industrial slum towns in hollows and creek beds beneath glowering, heavily forested mountainsides. The mines kept mountaineers home, but coal mining is harsh and deadly work: mine accidents, black lung disease and simple exhaustion killed tens of thousands of miners, while low wages and company stores kept them poor. Then John L. Lewis's United Mine Workers came in and something like open warfare followed, with neither mine operators nor union organizers loath to use violence and threats. The union mostly won in eastern Kentucky and in the short run raised wages and built hospitals for miners and their families; in the longer run, the UMW phased out many jobs in the mines, in return for job security and health benefits, as use of oil expanded. Politically, the UMW counties in the eastern part of the state became heavily Democratic and have remained so even as underground mine jobs lost out to the strip mining boom of the 1970s, and as UMW membership declined in the 1980s and 1990s.

The 5th Congressional District of Kentucky includes much of the Cumberland Plateau and most of the eastern mountains, a mixture of heavily Republican and heavily Democratic territory. It basically split its vote between Bill Clinton and Bob Dole in 1996, but with huge internal differences. The eastern mountain counties, with diminished turnout, were heavily for Clinton; Knott County gave him a 73%–18% margin. The Cumberland Plateau counties to the west were heavily Republican; Jackson County, a few mountain ridges away from Knott, voted 70%–22% for Dole. The current 5th District was created in 1991 by combining most of the old 5th, long one of the most Republican districts in the nation even though it also has had some of the lowest income levels, and the old 7th, reliably Democratic and represented for 35 years by Carl Perkins, chairman of the Education and Labor Committee from 1967–84.

The congressman from the 5th District now is Harold Rogers, a Republican first elected in the old 5th in 1980. He grew up in Wayne County, went off to the University of Kentucky and served in the National Guard, then practiced law in Somerset; in 1969, at 34, he was elected Pulaski-Rockcastle Commonwealth's Attorney. In 1980, when the 5th District Congressman retired, he was one of 11 Republicans in the primary; he won easily in November. His toughest race came in 1992, with redistricting. It first looked like he would have to face 7th District incumbent Chris Perkins, Carl Perkins's son; but the younger Perkins retired at 37, before it was revealed he had 514 overdrafts on the House bank. So Rogers ended up facing state Senator John Doug Hays of Pike County, whose grandfather Doug "Sawloggin" Hays was state senator before him. Hays attacked Rogers for supporting trickle-down economics and argued that as a Democrat he could get more money for the district in Bill Clinton's Washington. Rogers countered by pointing to his ongoing efforts to build the $250 million Cumberland Gap twin tunnels and Harlan County flood projects. Rogers won with 55%. He had 71% in his old 5th

District, which cast 52% of the new district's votes; he lost 64%–36% in the old 7th District. The returns show the strength of partisan feelings in eastern Kentucky: Owsley County was 78% for Rogers; next-door Breathitt County was 68% for Hays.

Rogers has done most of his work in the House on the Appropriations Committee, where he is now a senior member. He chairs the Commerce-Justice-State-Judiciary subcommittee and, much more important in Kentucky, is number two on Energy and Water Development. His voting record is mostly but not always conservative. Representing a low-income district, he is sympathetic to some spending bills; he was one of three Republicans to vote for the Clinton stimulus package in March 1993. He keeps a skeptical eye on international institutions, especially those who seek U.S. taxpayers' money. He has long advocated cuts in American support for the United Nations and sharply criticized Secretary General Boutros Boutros-Ghali. After he was denied a second term by the U.S., Rogers said, "The United States had to drag Boutros-Ghali screaming into the reform century despite the fact that the U.N. payroll is clearly bloated and patronage-ridden, and it wastes far too much money. If the U.N. can't accomplish even the minimal reforms that have been discussed, I'm not sure that the organization is doing us much good."

But Rogers spends the most time on domestic and Kentucky projects. Of Appropriations, he has said, "It's like a car. It's a practical place where you have to work out practical problems." Since the Republicans gained their majority and Rogers his subcommittee chairmanship, his challenge has been to resist conservatives' demands for zeroing out programs he supports. His approach is to be straightforward, negotiate a deal, then stick with it. He stoutly opposed the proposal to abolish the Appalachian Regional Commission; the ARC lives. When Republicans proposed to zero out the Legal Services Corporation, Rogers refused and negotiated with Majority Leader Dick Armey a cut from $400 million to $278 million. When the Senate put in a higher number, Rogers stuck to his $278 million, though his personal preference would be for more. Rogers resisted dismantling the Commerce Department, but he accepted a cut of more than $500 million. Meanwhile, he supported all of the Contract with America except the tax cuts. "Leadership knows on the big, important issues I have been there and will be there. But they also know that if they try to do something that will have an unfair impact on my people, I'll come out fighting." As freshman leader David McIntosh of Indiana said, "I think most freshmen would view Hal as one of the good guys."

More to the point, so do voters in eastern Kentucky. Rogers claims credit for flood control projects in the Cumberland and Big Sandy River Basins, new business and education development projects in Somerset, Whitesburg, and Hazard, the musical arts center in Prestonburg, reconstruction of key highways, the weather station in Jackson. He has also created regional development organizations, including the education program "Forward in the Fifth" and the Southern Kentucky Tourism Development Council. Since his tough race in 1992, Rogers has become well known in the eastern counties. Against a respectable opponent in 1994 he won with 79%, carrying counties a Republican never had won. In 1996 he was unopposed in both primary and general elections.

The People: Pop. 1990: 613,979; 87% rural; 12% age 65+; 99% White; 1% Black. Households: 65% married couple families; 34% married couple fams. w. children; 20% college educ.; median household income: $15,052; per capita income: $7,717; median gross rent: $243; median house value: $35,400.

1996 Presidential Vote			1992 Presidential Vote		
Clinton (D)	95,633	(47%)	Clinton (D)	111,600	(48%)
Dole (R)	87,692	(43%)	Bush (R)	97,432	(42%)
Perot (I)	18,260	(9%)	Perot (I)	24,344	(10%)

Rep. Harold D. Rogers (R)

Elected 1980; b. Dec. 31, 1937, Barrier; home, Somerset; U. of KY, B.A. 1962, J.D. 1964; Baptist; widowed.

Career: Army Natl. Guard, 1957–64; Practicing atty., 1964–69; Pulaski-Rockcastle Commonwealth atty., 1969–80.

DC Office: 2468 RHOB 20515, 202-225-4601; Fax: 202-225-0940.

District Offices: Hazard, 606-439-0794; Pikeville, 606-432-4388; Somerset, 606-679-8346.

Committees: *Appropriations* (7th of 34 R): Commerce, Justice, State & Judiciary (Chmn.); Energy & Water Development; Transportation.

Group Ratings

	ADA	ACLU	AFS	LCV	CFA	CON	NFIB	COC	ACU	NTLC	CHC
1996	10	0	8	15	0	30	89	81	95	95	93
1995	0	—	—	19	0	75	—	92	80	—	—

National Journal Ratings

	1995 LIB		1995 CONS	1996 LIB		1996 CONS
Economic	41%	—	56%	33%	—	64%
Social	0%	—	79%	14%	—	77%
Foreign	27%	—	72%	21%	—	72%

Key Votes of the 104th Congress

1. Reduce Medicare Growth $	Y	5. Flag Amendment	Y	9. Cuban Embargo	Y
2. Ovrd. Product Liab. Veto	Y	6. Drop EPA Limits	N	10. Bar Bosnia Troop $	Y
3. Increase Min. Wage	Y	7. Repeal Assault-Weap. Ban	Y	11. Cut Anti-Missile Defense	N
4. Welfare Reform	Y	8. Ovrd. Part. Birth Veto	Y	12. Bar U.N. Uniforms	Y

Election Results

1996 general	Harold D. Rogers (R)	unopposed		($132,717)
1996 primary	Harold D. Rogers (R)	unopposed		
1994 general	Harold D. Rogers (R)	82,291	(79%)	($348,243)
	Walter (Doc) Blevins (D)	21,318	(21%)	($52,377)

SIXTH DISTRICT

With its white picket fences, horse farms and Georgian brick house-filled small towns, the Bluegrass country almost plumb in the middle of Kentucky is the longest-settled part of interior America: Lexington was founded in 1775; the town of Hopewell was renamed Paris in 1789 out of gratitude for French help during our Revolution and in a salute to theirs (though the county name remained Bourbon even after Louis XVI was executed). Tobacco farming started here in the 1770s, horse racing in 1787, and the first whiskey distillery, in Bourbon County, was built in 1790. Tobacco, whiskey and race horses remained the staples of the Bluegrass economy for six generations until 1956, when IBM built its typewriter plant and headquarters in Lexington. IBM's arrival "really was the beginning of Lexington's industrial revolution," as University of Kentucky historian Carl Cone put it. You imagine a Kentucky colonel sitting on the porch, dressed in a white suit and string tie and sipping a mint julep, as IBM engineers in their dark suits and white shirts file into their offices. But capitalism, as Joseph Schumpeter wrote, is a process of creative destruction. The typewriter was eventually outclassed by the PC, and the IBM plant put on the block. Meanwhile, in the 1980s Toyota, lured by lush subsidies, built a $2 billion assembly plant in Georgetown, a town with early 19th Century houses and lush countryside, just one county north of Lexington and west of Paris. Some of the most famous horse farms—Spendthrift, Calumet—went bankrupt or were sold; Toyota doubled the size of its plant. From IBM to Toyota to even the Bluegrass horse farms, Lexington seems to be a focus of innovation and certainly of economic growth.

Lexington was the home base of the Whig Party's great leader Henry Clay, but in the century and a half since his death the Bluegrass country has been mostly Democratic. Bush edged out Clinton here in 1992 (there was a strong Perot vote), but Clinton picked up the 6th in 1996. He bought more time on Lexington TV than in just about any other media market in America, and raised his percentages 2% to 8% in Lexington and Bluegrass counties; the last day of the campaign he came to Lexington and appeared with University of Kentucky basketball coach Rick Pitino. All of which was just enough to give him a 46%–45% victory over Bob Dole in the 6th and in Kentucky, despite the president's proposal that the FDA regulate tobacco as a drug.

The 6th Congressional District of Kentucky includes Lexington and the counties all around—a natural unit, unlike some other Kentucky districts. Historically Democratic, from 1978–92 it was represented by Republican Congressman Larry Hopkins who retired after a disastrous run for Governor in 1991.

The congressman from the 6th District now is Democrat Scotty Baesler, a celebrity in Lexington and the Bluegrass country for many years. He grew up in Athens, Kentucky, where he still has a tobacco farm: he is the only tobacco grower in Congress. Baesler was captain of the University of Kentucky basketball team, class of 1963—the days of the legendary Coach Adolph Rupp. He went on to law school, then became administrator of Fayette County Legal Aid. He was elected Lexington mayor in 1982, where he created a statewide scholarship program called Sweet 16 Academic Showcase, brought the DARE program into schools to teach kids about drugs, sponsored downtown redevelopment, developed a Family Care Center for poor families, chaired a state commission to develop tourism and the arts and hosted major sports tourneys. In 1991 Baesler ran for governor and finished second in the Democratic primary, trailing Brereton Jones 38%–30%; if there had been a runoff, as there is now, he might have won. Baesler was the obvious candidate for the 6th District seat in 1992; he won 82% in a five-candidate primary and then beat a little-known Republican 61%–39%.

In the House Baesler has had a moderate voting record, just a bit to the left of midpoint on economic, cultural and foreign issues most years. He serves on Agriculture where he naturally looks after the interests of tobacco. He has questioned the chemical weapons incineration proposal for Bluegrass Army Depot, established a 150-store "Country Store" rural communications network, put small-town amendments into the 1994 crime bill, gotten funding for the Perryville Civil War battlefield.

Baesler seems clearly unhappy with the leaders of his party in the House and the White House. He makes a point of noting that he supported North Carolina's Charlie Rose for minority leader in 1995 over Dick Gephardt. In 1994 he refused support from the Democratic Congressional Campaign Committee after its chairman, Vic Fazio, criticized the religious right. He opposed the Clinton healthcare plan's tobacco tax and criticized Surgeon General Joycelyn Elders for proposing to legalize marijuana but to outlaw tobacco. After Vice President Al Gore's denunciations of tobacco in Chicago in 1996, a Baesler aide made a point of saying Baesler "does not appreciate Gore's contradictory statements on tobacco." And when Clinton came to Lexington the day before the election, Baesler decided to keep commitments to campaign in country stores and could not attend the Clinton rally. "I agree with him on education and a whole lot of things like that. I think he's wrong on tobacco, and I'm very upset about it."

Baesler's electoral strength has slipped a bit since he first won. He was embarrassed in April 1994 when it was revealed that on his last day as mayor he used two city employees to load furniture from his home onto a rental truck bound for Washington. After Republicans won the 2d District special election in May 1994, he decided to accept PAC money. Baesler won with 59%, a solid win but 2% less than in 1992, and against a weaker opponent. After considerable speculation, he declined to run for governor in 1995. In 1996 he was challenged by conservative Ernest Fletcher, a one-term legislator who is also a physician, a former Air Force pilot, and a Baptist minister; Fletcher won his primary by exactly four votes. National Republican Congressional Committee Chairman Bill Paxon targeted this race and poured money in; Baesler outspent Fletcher by only $574,000 to $435,000, not much of an edge for an incumbent. Fletcher's campaign sounded a bit incoherent: he accused Baesler of being a liberal, then said that he didn't have "a seat at the table" because he was a Blue Dog Democrat at odds with his party's leadership. He hit Baesler for stands on parental consent for abortion, midnight basketball, balancing the budget and even, despite Baesler's high-profile opposition to FDA regulation, tobacco. Baesler quickly ran negative spots against Fletcher. "If I'm going to win a basketball game, I'm not going to let them come down and shoot. I'm going to get in their face." He charged that Fletcher was an extremist and that one of his bills in the legislature would have gutted Kentucky's healthcare reforms.

Baesler won with a solid 56%, carrying Lexington and Fayette County with 53%, and running behind in only three small counties. Yet his showing trailed the Democratic legislative ticket and he is now the only remaining Democrat in the Kentucky House delegation. Baesler has good committee assignments—a new seat on Budget, plus Agriculture—but he has clearly expressed disgust with top Democrats and it's not clear that he's comfortable with his party or in the House. When Wendell Ford announced his retirement in March 1997, Baesler wasted no time in announcing he would run for the seat.

The People: Pop. 1990: 614,245; 37% rural; 11% age 65+; 90% White; 8% Black; 1% Asian; 1% Hispanic origin. Households: 58% married couple families; 27% married couple fams. w. children; 41% college educ.; median household income: $25,377; per capita income: $12,419; median gross rent: $352; median house value: $61,200.

1996 Presidential Vote			1992 Presidential Vote		
Clinton (D)	110,256	(46%)	Bush (R)	105,215	(42%)
Dole (R)	108,148	(45%)	Clinton (D)	101,817	(41%)
Perot (I)	19,425	(8%)	Perot (I)	39,719	(16%)

Rep. Scotty Baesler (D)

Elected 1992; b. July 9, 1941, Athens; home, Lexington; U. of KY, B.S. 1963, J.D. 1966; Christian; married (Alice).

Career: Army Reserves, 1966–72; Tobacco farmer; Practicing atty., 1966–67; Fayette Cnty. Legal Aid Admin., 1967–73; Lexington Vice Mayor, 1974–78; Fayette Cnty. District Judge, 1978–82; Lexington Mayor, 1982–92.

DC Office: 2463 RHOB 20515, 202-225-4706; Fax: 202-225-2122.

District Offices: Lexington, 606-253-1124.

Committees: *Agriculture* (11th of 23 D): Forestry, Resource Conservation & Research; Risk Management & Specialty Crops. *Budget* (14th of 19 D).

Group Ratings

	ADA	ACLU	AFS	LCV	CFA	CON	NFIB	COC	ACU	NTLC	CHC
1996	60	38	67	77	46	76	59	40	25	37	20
1995	65	—	—	50	54	56	—	54	28	—	—

National Journal Ratings

	1995 LIB — 1995 CONS	1996 LIB — 1996 CONS
Economic	57% — 42%	60% — 39%
Social	58% — 41%	65% — 34%
Foreign	64% — 34%	55% — 43%

Key Votes of the 104th Congress

1. Reduce Medicare Growth $	N	5. Flag Amendment	Y	9. Cuban Embargo	N
2. Ovrd. Product Liab. Veto	N	6. Drop EPA Limits	N	10. Bar Bosnia Troop $	N
3. Increase Min. Wage	Y	7. Repeal Assault-Weap. Ban	N	11. Cut Anti-Missile Defense	Y
4. Welfare Reform	Y	8. Ovrd. Part. Birth Veto	Y	12. Bar U.N. Uniforms	Y

Election Results

1996 general	Scotty Baesler (D)	125,999	(56%)	($574,074)
	Ernest Fletcher (R)	100,231	(44%)	($435,065)
1996 primary	Scotty Baesler (D)	unopposed		
1994 general	Scotty Baesler (D)	70,085	(59%)	($223,327)
	Matthew Eric Wills (R)	49,032	(41%)	($23,190)

LOUISIANA

Louisiana often seems to be America's banana republic, with its charm and inefficiency, its communities interlaced by family ties and its public sector laced with corruption, with its own indigenous culture and its tradition of fine distinctions of class and caste. It is a state with an economy uncomfortably like that of an underdeveloped country, based on pumping minerals out of soggy ground, shipping grain produced in the vast hinterland drained by its great river, and increasingly dependent in recent years on businesses typical of picturesque Third World countries—tourism and gambling. Its politics too has a third world quality, with its own peculiar election laws and a heritage of no-holds-barred conflict and demagoguery no other state can match: what other state has produced a Huey Long, or an Edwin Edwards? With a hereditary rich class and a large low-wage working class, conservative cultural attitudes (Louisiana and Utah have the most conservative abortion laws in the U.S.) and a lazy tolerance of rule-breaking, Louisiana feels more like the Caribbean or the Mediterranean than the North Atlantic or the Pacific Rim. This is not an entirely original observation. Three decades ago, A. J. Liebling described Louisiana as an outpost of the Levant along the Gulf of Mexico. Most of the United States faces east toward the vast Atlantic Ocean or west toward the vast Pacific; Louisiana faces south, to the Gulf of Mexico and the steamy heat and volatile societies of Latin America.

New Orleans preserves the look and feel it had as a French and Spanish outpost in the New World. Traditions of centralized control and easygoing corruption—classic traits of colonialism—are part of this heritage. The *dirigiste* tradition comes from the fact that Louisiana is the only state that operates on the Napoleonic Code of France (which until 1990 required parents to leave a large percentage of their estates to their children), not the common law of England; the concept of civil liberties has shallower roots in Louisiana than in the other 49 states. Here abstract ideals have been overshadowed by the practical need for centralized action. This delta land—much of it below sea level, soggy, swampy, laced with tributaries and offshoots of the Mississippi and other major rivers like the Atchafalaya—requires vast capital expenditures for levees and drainage and causeways. Even today, houses in New Orleans don't have basements, people are buried in above-ground cemeteries in grandiose crypts, and swamp lands begin abruptly at the edges of subdivisions where people find alligators in their backyards.

The economy that grew up in these rich Delta lands has always been based on raw materials. Antebellum Louisiana produced and exported sugar, rice and cotton in enough abundance to generate the wealth which built grand plantation houses behind alleys of oaks running in from the Mississippi, and to make New Orleans the nation's fifth largest city by the time of the Civil War. Then came oil, found in the great Spindletop strike just over the Texas line in 1901 and in salt domes in Louisiana not long after; Jersey Standard (now Exxon) built the huge Baton Rouge refinery that became the training ground for generations of its top executives. When energy prices boomed after the oil shocks of 1973 and 1981, Louisiana, like an oil-rich Third World country, boomed too, reaching up toward national income levels, generating 500,000 new jobs between 1972 and 1981, only to lose 150,000 in the next six years as oil prices crashed and the rig count dropped from a peak of 455 in 1981 to 166 in 1996. Energy produced 41% of state government revenues in 1982, but a meager 9% in 1996. Louisiana's economy has never regained much forward momentum. In the 1990s its great savior was supposed to be gambling, especially the casino authorized for New Orleans in 1992. But in November 1995 the temporary casino closed down for lack of business, and the huge new casino under construction at the little-used Rivergate Convention Center at the foot of Canal Street was left partly finished—with something of the shabby grandeur of the French Quarter's many unrenovated houses; construction has since resumed and the state's only "land-based" casino is scheduled to open by 1998.

Louisiana has greater income disparities than almost anywhere else in the United States, an economy more typical of a Caribbean sugar colony than an American state. New Orleans's rich are notoriously unventuresome and tight-knit, determined to hold on to their wealth against the grasp of the impecunious and unlearned masses. The most enduringly famous, and by far the most talented, was Huey P. Long, who in less than a single term each as governor (1928–32) and senator (1932–35), left an imprint on the state's public life and imposed an organization to its politics that have faded into history only in the last decade. Long's genius was not that he promised to tax the rich to help the poor—hundreds of idealists and demagogues in America have done that—but that, to an amazing extent, he actually delivered. He dominated the legislature so thoroughly that, as governor, he roamed the floors of both chambers at will, bringing to the podium bills he insisted be passed without changing a comma—and they were. He was ready to use bribery, intimidation and physical violence, to the point that his machine reminded many Americans of contemporary dictatorships in Europe. He built a new skyscraper Capitol, a new Louisiana State University, and more miles of roads than any state but rich New York and huge Texas. He also built a national following, and by 1935, he was planning to run for president on the platform of "Share the wealth, every man a king," when he was assassinated at age 42 in the hallway of the Capitol, where the bullet holes can still be seen in the marble.

For America, the Long threat may have moved Franklin Roosevelt to embrace the liberal programs—the Wagner Labor Act, social security, steeply graduated taxes—of the second New Deal. For Louisiana, Long delivered a political structure that revolved around him long after he was dead—and a class of political leaders who, lacking his talents, treated the state as Long's incompetent doctors had treated his fatal wound, leaving Louisiana without either a fully developed economy or a fully competent public sector. For 50 years, until Huey's son Senator Russell Long retired in 1986, Longs and Long proteges held high political office in Louisiana and elections were run along pro- and anti-Long lines. The Long experience has strengthened Louisiana's already strong predispositions—tolerance of corruption, disinterest in abstract reform, and taste for colorful extremists regardless of their short-term means or long-term ends—in a way that helps explain the rise and fall of such unlikely politicians as the four-term

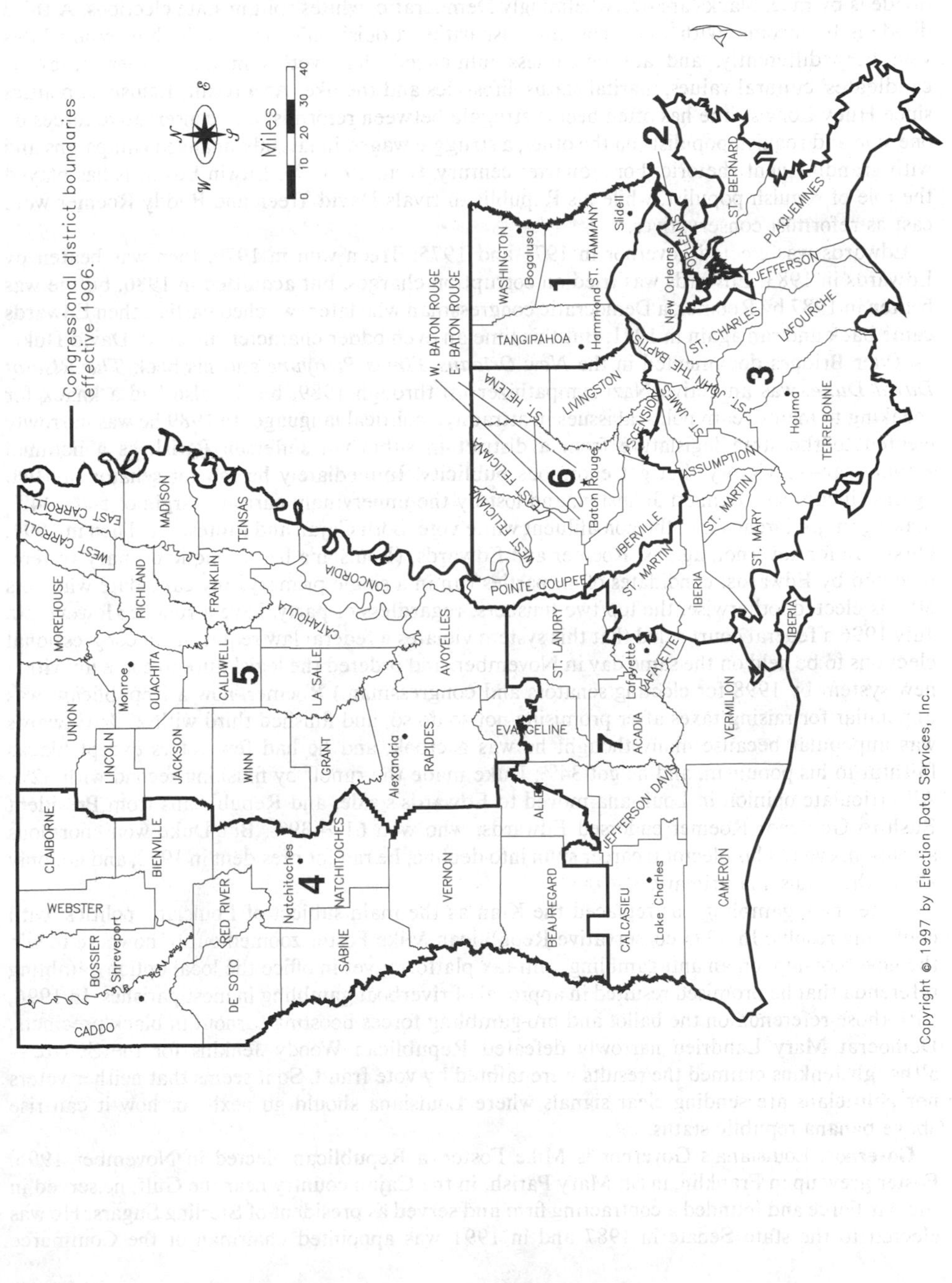
Congressional district boundaries effective 1996.
Miles
0 10 20 30 40
N
E
S
W
1
2
3
4
5
6
7
CADDO
BOSSIER
WEBSTER
CLAIBORNE
Shreveport
DE SOTO
RED RIVER
BIENVILLE
SABINE
NATCHITOCHES
Natchitoches
LINCOLN
UNION
MOREHOUSE
WEST CARROLL
EAST CARROLL
Monroe
OUACHITA
JACKSON
WINN
GRANT
CALDWELL
RICHLAND
FRANKLIN
MADISON
TENSAS
LA SALLE
CATAHOULA
CONCORDIA
VERNON
Alexandria
RAPIDES
AVOYELLES
BEAUREGARD
ALLEN
EVANGELINE
CALCASIEU
Lake Charles
CAMERON
JEFFERSON DAVIS
ACADIA
ST LANDRY
Lafayette
LAFAYETTE
VERMILION
ST. MARTIN
IBERIA
ST. MARY
POINTE COUPEE
WEST FELICIANA
EAST FELICIANA
ST. HELENA
WEST BATON ROUGE
E. BATON ROUGE
Baton Rouge
IBERVILLE
ASCENSION
ASSUMPTION
LIVINGSTON
TANGIPAHOA
Hammond
WASHINGTON
Bogalusa
ST. TAMMANY
Slidell
ST. JAMES
ST. JOHN THE BAPTIST
ST. CHARLES
LAFOURCHE
Houma
TERREBONNE
JEFFERSON
New Orleans
ORLEANS
ST. BERNARD
PLAQUEMINES
Copyright © 1997 by Election Data Services, Inc.

Governor Edwin Edwards and the onetime Ku Klux Klan leader and state legislator David Duke.

Louisiana has natural political divides. One divide is between Cajuns and north Louisiana Baptists; the Cajun parishes cast about 30% of the state's vote, the New Orleans area around 25% or so, with about 45% in Protestant parishes from Baton Rouge on north. White Protestants for years wanted nothing to do with national Democrats, while Cajuns mulled it over. Another divide is by race: blacks are overwhelmingly Democratic, whites split in state elections. A third divide is by income: with wide economic disparities, Louisiana's low- and high-income whites vote very differently, and are much less influenced than voters in most other states by candidates' cultural values, marital status, lifestyles and the like. As a result, Louisiana politics since Huey Long's time has often been a struggle between reformist and conservative forces on one side and roguish populists on the other, a struggle waged in lavishly financed campaigns and with grandiloquent rhetoric. For a quarter century, from 1971–95, Edwin Edwards has played the role of roguish populist, while his Republican rivals David Treen and Buddy Roemer were cast as reformist conservatives.

Edwards was elected governor in 1971 and 1975; Treen won in 1979, then was beaten by Edwards in 1983; Edwards was tried on corruption charges, but acquitted in 1986; but he was beaten in 1987 by Roemer, a Democratic congressman who later switched parties; then Edwards came back and ran again in 1991. But this time an even odder character surfaced. David Duke, as Tyler Bridges documented in the *New Orleans Times-Picayune* and his book *The Rise of David Duke*, was an active Nazi sympathizer up through 1989, but he also had a knack for speaking to mainstream political issues in attractive political language. In 1989 he was narrowly elected to the state legislature from a district in suburban Jefferson Parish as a nominal Republican—a victory that got enormous publicity. Immediately he ran for senator in 1990 against incumbent Bennett Johnston, and lost by the unnervingly narrow margin of 54%–44%, making major inroads into the non-affluent white vote, both Cajun and Protestant. Then in 1991, Duke ran for governor, against Roemer and Edwards. (Louisiana has a unique primary system, invented by Edwards: candidates of all parties run in a single primary; any candidate who gets 50% is elected; otherwise, the top two finishers, regardless of party, have a runoff. However, in July 1996 a federal court ruled that this system violates a federal law requiring all congressional elections to be held on the same day in November, and ordered the legislature to come up with a new system by 1998 for electing senators and congressman.) Roemer, now a Republican, was unpopular for raising taxes after promising not to do so, and finished third with 27%; Edwards was unpopular because many thought he was a crook, and he had few voters except blacks faithful to his populism, and he got 34%; Duke made the runoff by finishing second with 32%. All articulate opinion in Louisiana moved to Edwards's side, and Republicans from President Bush to Governor Roemer endorsed Edwards, who won 61%–39%. But Duke won enormous attention, even as his electoral career spun into decline; he ran for president in 1992, and got only 9% in the Louisiana primary.

Since then, gambling has replaced the Klan as the main subject of Louisiana politics, with confusing results. In 1995 conservative Republican Mike Foster zoomed out of nowhere to win the governorship, on an anti-gambling, anti-tax platform; yet in office the local-option gambling referenda that he promised resulted in approval of riverboat gambling in most parishes. In 1996, with those referenda on the ballot and pro-gambling forces boosting turnout in black precincts, Democrat Mary Landrieu narrowly defeated Republican Woody Jenkins for the Senate—although Jenkins claimed the results were tainted by vote fraud. So it seems that neither voters nor politicians are sending clear signals where Louisiana should go next—or how it can rise above banana republic status.

Governor. Louisiana's Governor is Mike Foster, a Republican elected in November 1995. Foster grew up in Franklin, in St. Mary Parish, in the Cajun country near the Gulf; he served in the Air Force and founded a contracting firm and served as president of Sterling Sugars. He was elected to the state Senate in 1987 and in 1991 was appointed chairman of the Commerce

Committee. He portrays himself as an amateur in politics, convincingly, given his penchant for blunt, impolitic statements. But he had a political pedigree: his grandfather Murphy Foster was governor from 1892–1900, and played a part in abolishing Louisiana's graft-ridden lottery. Mike Foster ran in 1995 as an opponent of gun control and critic of gambling. He pledged to hold a referendum on video poker (operators had been caught bribing legislators), riverboat gambling (allowed in many parishes) and the New Orleans land-based casino. At first he did not attract much attention in the 16-candidate field. Former Governor Buddy Roemer seemed to be the leading Republican candidate, brandishing a Contract with Louisiana, criticizing New Orleans as "Cape Fear" and calling for chain gangs. Congressman Cleo Fields was the one well-known black candidate, as Congressman Bill Jefferson decided not to run; but Fields did not have unequivocal support: New Orleans Mayor Marc Morial, who is black, endorsed both him and Democratic State Treasurer Mary Landrieu. Landrieu, whose father was once mayor of New Orleans, called for cleaning up Louisiana; she was running ahead of Lieutenant Governor Melinda Schwegmann, whose family owned New Orleans's biggest supermarket chain. (The business was sold in 1997.)

Foster surged ahead in fall campaigning, even after TV cameras caught him meeting with top Edwin Edwards cronies. Foster attracted much media attention when he switched parties in September; he got Pat Buchanan's endorsement in October and in the October 21 primary led with 26%. There was almost a three-way tie for second place. Fields edged into second place with 19.0%, to 18.4% for Landrieu and 17.8% for Roemer. In the runoff against Fields, Foster called for a vast consolidation of state agencies and reform of state education and welfare. Fields said he would get tough on juvenile crime and accused Foster of "race baiting" after Foster referred to "that jungle in New Orleans." Foster won 64% to Fields' 37% and took 84% of the white vote, while Fields took 96% of the black vote.

In office Foster pushed through a food tax cut and a $25 per child tax credit, increased teacher salaries and initiated a school-based accountability system. He obtained some changes in civil tort law and enacted new ethics laws. Foster announced he was voting for Pat Buchanan just before the February 6 caucus; he pressed Bill Clinton for a tariff on Chinese crawfish. He failed to get a statewide referendum on gambling, but in September 1996 voters chose to let each parish vote on gambling within its limits. Those referenda boosted turnout in November; 33 parishes rejected video poker, but voters approved all 14 riverboat casinos and the New Orleans land casino. Foster created a new gaming control board and after Harrahs went bankrupt during construction of the New Orleans casino, he led negotiations for a new, stricter deal with the company which guarantees $100 million for the state in the event of another bankruptcy. Foster's job rating has been very high; he comes up for reelection in 1999.

Senior Senator. John Breaux grew up in the fertile political soil of the county seat of Crowley in Cajun country, the home town also of Edwin Edwards. After law school and a year of law practice, he worked four years for Edwards, then a junior congressman. When Edwards was elected governor in 1972, Breaux ran for Congress and won the seat, at 28. Quietly in the House, more publicly in the Senate, he has become a natural dealmaker, with contacts developed everywhere from the tennis court (he is one of Congress's best players) to the Democratic Leadership Council (where he followed Bill Clinton as chairman in 1992). His views on issues have a Louisiana Cajun accent: market-oriented with populist twists on economics, rather conservative on cultural issues. But he is not heavily encumbered with narrow principles. As he told the *Los Angeles Times*, "I see myself not as a philosopher, but somebody who is interested in making government work. More and more people in Congress . . . have an all-or-nothing attitude. All-or-nothing attitudes generally wind up getting nothing."

Breaux used his committee seats in the House to get money to battle coastal wetlands erosion and defeat the Law of the Sea Treaty; to get sugar and natural gas concessions for Louisiana in the 1981 tax bill he uttered his famed statement that his vote was not for sale "but it is available for rent." He ran for the Senate in 1986, initially trailing his Republican House colleague Henson Moore, but holding him to under 50% in the primary and then overtaking him in the general.

In the Senate Breaux has had a middle-of-the-road voting record and a bent toward bipartisan coalitions. He was also active in national campaigns, as head of the Democratic Senatorial Campaign Committee in 1990 (the last time they ended up with more seats than they started) and the Democratic Leadership Council in 1992. On the Commerce Committee he worked on issues with local impact: creating in 1990 the $50 million per year Breaux Fund to protect wetlands, and phasing out by 1995 the recreational boat user fee. He worked with Bennett Johnston to get a $2.5 billion royalty relief package as an incentive to offshore drilling, which once again is booming off Louisiana's coast. He was less successful in influencing the Clinton Administration. In 1992 he said presciently, "I worry that people in the interest groups will try to pull him away from the mainstream positions that got him elected." He opposed the 1993 Clinton stimulus package and the Btu tax, and helped defeat both, and voted against the 1993 budget and tax increase. In 1994 he was the chief Senate sponsor of Tennessee Congressman Jim Cooper's managed care healthcare bill and struggled to come up with bipartisan compromises.

Breaux was mentioned as a candidate for majority leader when George Mitchell announced his retirement in 1994; instead he supported Tom Daschle and, after the Democrats came back as the minority, became chief deputy whip in 1995. He backed an alternative to the Republican Medicare plan and introduced amendments to the welfare reform bill which did not pass but helped shape debate; he voted for the 1996 Welfare Reform Act. His leading bipartisan initiative was the Breaux-Chafee alternative budget, with smaller tax cuts and smaller adjustments to Medicare than the Republican plan and an adjustment to the Consumer Price Index; it lost by only 53–46, winning the votes of 24 Democrats and 22 Republicans. On Louisiana issues he won continuation of rice subsidies in the Freedom to Farm Act and successfully opposed shipping deregulation. In 1997 he became ranking Democrat on the Special Committee on Aging and the Finance Subcommittee on Social Security, fine posts from which to seek a bipartisan compromise on Medicare.

Breaux attracted only desultory opposition in 1992, and won reelection with 73% in the September primary. He is a favorite to win reelection in 1998.

Junior Senator. With the election of Mary Landrieu, Louisiana is now the last state in Dixie with two Democratic senators. She grew up in New Orleans, one of nine children of Moon Landrieu, mayor of New Orleans in the 1970s. She was educated at Ursuline Academy and LSU and in 1979, at 23, became the youngest woman ever elected to the Louisiana state legislature. In 1987 she was elected state treasurer; she opened bond contracts for bid and restructured the state investment portfolio. She also became a sharp critic of Governor Edwin Edwards and opposed gambling. In 1995 she ran for governor, and in the September primary finished third, just 1% and 8,983 votes behind second-place finisher Congressman Cleo Fields. In 1996, with Senator Bennett Johnston, a moderate Democrat, retiring after 24 years, Landrieu decided to run for the Senate as a Democratic Leadership Council centrist: for a balanced budget amendment and capital gains tax cut, promising to make education a top priority.

It was a crowded field, with 15 candidates. But all summer the polls showed Landrieu and another well-known Democrat, Attorney General Richard Ieyoub, ahead, and it seemed likely they would finish that way in the September primary, thus guaranteeing that Democrats would hold the seat. In August Republican Woody Jenkins stepped forward, claiming his party's endorsement by virtue of a resolution adopted by the Republican National Convention that said that the candidate endorsed by the usually ignored Republican state convention should have official endorsement. Jenkins was no political neophyte. He has served for 25 years in the state legislature, where he has been the floor leader in opposing abortion, and he ran twice for the Senate as a Democrat, losing in primaries to Bennett Johnston in 1978 by 59%–41% and to Russell Long in 1980 by 58%–39%. In early September Congressman Bob Livingston, worried that a runoff might include two Democrats or David Duke, rallied other Republicans around Jenkins, and House colleagues abandoned Jimmy Hayes, a party-switching Cajun country congressman who had not raised enough money to get statewide name recognition. Meanwhile, the National Republican Senatorial Committee started running ads attacking Ieyoub on ethics charges for past campaign spending practices. Jenkins surged in the polls, and led the September 21 primary with 26%, to 22% for Landrieu and 20% for Ieyoub; Duke got only 12%.

At this point Jenkins looked like the favorite; Republican candidates had won 55% of the total votes and Democrats only 44%. But he had little money left, and Landrieu, who ultimately outspent him, ran ads attacking him as an extremist. Jenkins was a strong conservative, totally against abortion, calling for elimination of the Internal Revenue Service; he attacked her for opposing abortion restrictions and supporting gay rights, while she attacked him for never voting for a tax in 25 years. Landrieu had to spend much time getting support from blacks, since many were unhappy that she had given only nominal support to Cleo Fields for governor in 1995; but eventually Fields and Congressman Bill Jefferson and New Orleans Mayor Marc Morial backed her. So did gambling interests, who were busy trying to increase black turnout in New Orleans and elsewhere for their gambling referenda. At the end of October—in uncustomary fashion—Archbishop Philip Hannan basically came out for Jenkins, saying if "a person actually believes in Catholic doctrine, then I don't see how they can vote for Landrieu without a feeling of sin."

The result was an exceedingly close election. Landrieu carried New Orleans by more than 100,000 votes and heavily Protestant northwest Louisiana around Shreveport; Jenkins carried his home base around Baton Rouge only narrowly, but also won in the heavily Catholic but often Democratic Cajun country. The official results showed Landrieu ahead by 5,788 votes, 50.2%–49.8%. Jenkins filed a lawsuit claiming vote fraud, but withdrew it, and submitted his case to the Senate. At the behest of Majority Leader Trent Lott, whose Mississippi home town is just east of New Orleans, the Senate seated Landrieu "without prejudice" to Jenkins's challenge. The Senate Rules Committee appointed two outside counsels, one Republican and one Democrat, to consider the evidence Jenkins submitted in early 1997. It seemed serious: he presented affidavits showing that more votes were counted in many New Orleans precincts than the number of voters who signed in, and testimony of campaign operatives, apparently from Morial's L.I.F.E. organization, ferrying people around to vote in one precinct after another. Jenkins asked either to be seated or for a new election to be held. In April 1997, the Rules Committee approved, by a 9–7 party-line vote, to broaden the investigation. Senators will presumably be reluctant to declare a new winner in what is at best a murky situation and to override Louisiana's official declaration of Landrieu as the winner; they might be less reluctant to order a new election, although Democrats are obviously not eager to risk losing a seat and could filibuster any Republican-only attempt to do so. But many senators of both parties will not want to countenance massive vote fraud if it can be proven.

Presidential politics. Louisiana has become arguably the southern state most Democratic in presidential politics. It was Michael Dukakis's strongest southern state in 1988, ranked behind only Bill Clinton's Arkansas and Al Gore's Tennessee in 1992, and behind only Arkansas in 1996 in support of the Democratic ticket. Clinton's 1996 margin of 52%–40% was especially impressive.

Louisiana's presidential primaries in 1992, producing big victories for Bill Clinton and George Bush, got lost in the Super Tuesday shuffle. Not so the February 6 Republican caucuses in 1996. These had been set up by allies of Phil Gramm, who was seeking here as elsewhere early victories that he hoped would strengthen him regardless of what Iowa and New Hampshire did. Instead Louisiana destroyed his campaign. Gramm, relying on polls of active Republicans, was cocksure that he would win. But Pat Buchanan crisscrossed the bayous and upcountry parishes, meeting with voters, talking on cell-phones with any radio show that would have him, dropping in on editorial boards of weekly newspapers. He talked issues national and local, emphasizing his opposition to NAFTA and the need to block imports of Chinese crawfish. It paid off handsomely. Buchanan won more votes than Gramm and took 13 of the 21 delegates. Gramm's campaign in Iowa faltered, and after his poor finish there he had to leave the race without even contesting New Hampshire. Buchanan surged into the public eye, finishing second in Iowa and first in New Hampshire, and surviving long past his loss to Bob Dole in the Super Tuesday Louisiana primary.

Congressional districting. Louisiana is the only state to have had three sets of congressional district lines following the 1990 Census. For 1992, the state, under pressure from the Bush Justice Department and a federal court, produced a plan with two black-majority districts, one compact enough in New Orleans, the other a Z-shaped monstrosity trekking from the Atchafalaya swamp to the northern edge of the state and black precincts in Shreveport. That plan was ruled unconstitutional in federal court in December 1993. In April 1994 the legislature passed a plan with a new 4th extending from the Mississippi River parishes south of Baton Rouge northwest to Shreveport. In July 1994 that new plan was disallowed by a federal court, but the Supreme Court kept it in effect for the 1994 elections. In January 1996 a federal court came up with a new plan, then adopted by the legislature, that cut through few parish boundaries and had much more regular lines; it was upheld by the Supreme Court in June 1996. As a result, Louisiana is left with only one black-majority district, the 2d in New Orleans. Cleo Fields, having lost a bid for governor in 1995 against Foster, announced he would not seek a third term in the newly drawn 4th which dropped from about 55% to 28% black.

The People: Est. Pop. 1996: 4,351,000; Pop. 1990: 4,219,973, up 3.1% 1990–1996. 1.6% of U.S. total, 22d largest; 32% rural. Median age: 33 years. 11% 65 years and over. 65.8% White, 30.6% Black, 1% Asian, 2.2% Hispanic origin. Households: 53.6% married couple families; 28% married couple fams. w. children; 37% college educ.; median household income: $21,949; per capita income: $10,635; 65.9% owner occupied housing; median house value: $58,500; median monthly rent: $260. 6.7% Unemployment. 1996 Voting age pop.: 3,131,000. 1996 Turnout: 1,783,959; 57% of VAP. Registered voters (1996): 2,559,352; 1,666,024 D (65%); 540,216 R (21%); 353,112 unaffiliated and minor parties (14%).

Political Lineup: Governor, Murphy J. (Mike) Foster (R); Lt. Gov., Kathleen B. Blanco (D); Secy. of State, W. Fox McKeithen (R); Atty. Gen., Richard P. Ieyoub (D); Treasurer, Ken Duncan (D). State Senate, 39 (25 D and 14 R); Senate President, Randy Ewing (D); State House, 105 (78 D and 27 R); House Speaker, Hunt Downer Jr. (D). Senators, John B. Breaux (D) and Mary L. Landrieu (D). Representatives, 7 (5 R and 2 D).

Elections Division: 504-342-4970; **Filing Deadline for U.S. Congress:** July 24, 1998.

1996 Presidential Vote

Clinton (D)	927,836	(52%)
Dole (R)	712,586	(40%)
Perot (I)	123,292	(7%)

1996 Republican Presidential Primary

Dole (R)	37,170	(48%)
Buchanan (R)	25,757	(33%)
Forbes (R)	10,265	(12%)
Other	4,597	(6%)

1992 Presidential Vote

Clinton (D)	815,968	(46%)
Bush (R)	733,386	(41%)
Perot (I)	211,477	(12%)
Other	29,185	(2%)

GOVERNOR

Gov. Murphy J. (Mike) Foster (R)

Elected 1995, term expires January 2000; b. July 11, 1930, Shreveport; home, Franklin; LA St. U., B.S. 1951; Episcopalian; married (Alice).

Career: Air Force, 1952–55 (Korea), Air Force Reserves; Farmer; Pres., M.J. Foster Inc.; Pres., Sterling Sugars, Inc.; Partner, Maryland Corp.; Owner, Oaklawn Manor; LA Senate, 1987–95.

Office: State Capitol, P.O. Box 94004, Baton Rouge 70804, 504-342-7015; Fax: 504-342-7099; Web site: www.state.la.us.

Election Results

1995 gen.	Murphy J. (Mike) Foster (R)	984,499	(64%)
	Cleo Fields (D)	565,861	(37%)
1995 prim.	Murphy J. (Mike) Foster (R)	385,267	(26%)
	Cleo Fields (D)	280,921	(19%)
	Mary L. Landrieu (D)	271,938	(18%)
	Buddy Roemer (R)	263,330	(18%)
	Phil Preis (D)	133,271	(9%)
	Melinda Schwegmann (D)	71,288	(5%)
	Ten Others	69,881	(5%)
1991 gen.	Edwin W. Edwards (D)	1,057,031	(61%)
	David Duke (R)	671,009	(39%)

SENATORS

Sen. John B. Breaux (D)

Elected 1986, seat up 1998; b. Mar. 1, 1944, Crowley; home, Lafayette; U. of S.W. LA, B.A. 1964, LA St. U., J.D. 1967; Catholic; married (Lois).

Career: Practicing atty., 1967–68; Legis. Asst. & Dist. Mgr., U.S. Rep. Edwin W. Edwards, 1968–72; U.S. House of Reps., 1972–87.

DC Office: 516 HSOB 20510, 202-224-4623; Fax: 202-228-2577; e-mail: senator@breaux.senate.gov.

State Offices: Lafayette, 318-262-6871; Monroe, 318-325-3320; New Orleans, 504-589-2531.

Committees: *Commerce, Science & Transportation* (6th of 9 D): Aviation; Communications; Consumer Affairs, Foreign Commerce & Tourism (RMM); Oceans & Fisheries; Surface Transportation & Merchant Marine. *Finance* (4th of 9 D): International Trade; Social Security & Family Policy (RMM); Taxation & IRS Oversight. *Aging (Special)* (RMM).

Group Ratings

	ADA	ACLU	AFS	LCV	CFA	CON	NFIB	COC	ACU	NTLC	CHC
1996	60	17	71	38	71	79	45	62	20	28	46
1995	70	—	73	29	50	29	—	56	22	—	—

National Journal Ratings

	1995 LIB — 1995 CONS	1996 LIB — 1996 CONS
Economic	56% — 43%	54% — 45%
Social	43% — 55%	49% — 49%
Foreign	62% — 36%	49% — 50%

Key Votes of the 104th Congress

1. Reduce Medicare Growth $	N	5. Flag Amendment	Y	9. Anti-Missile Defense	N
2. Lmt. Prod. Liab. Damages	N	6. Endangered Species	N	10. Cuban Embargo	Y
3. Increase Min. Wage	Y	7. Gay Employment Rights	Y	11. Bar Bosnia Troop $	N
4. Welfare Reform	Y	8. Ovrd. Part. Birth Veto	Y	12. Cut Vietnam Aid	N

Election Results

1992 primary	John B. Breaux (D)	616,021	(73%)	($2,007,675)
	Jon Khachaturian (I)	74,785	(9%)	($94,919)
	Lyle Stockstill (R)	69,986	(8%)	($34,711)
	Nick Accardo (D)	45,839	(6%)	
	Fred Clegg Strong (R)	36,406	(4%)	
1986 general	John B. Breaux (D)	723,586	(53%)	($2,958,313)
	W. Henson Moore (R)	646,311	(47%)	($5,986,460)
1986 primary	W. Henson Moore (R)	529,433	(44%)	
	John B. Breaux (D)	447,328	(37%)	
	Samuel B. Nunez (D)	73,505	(6%)	
	J.E. Jumonville (D)	53,394	(5%)	
	Sherman A. Bernard (D)	52,479	(5%)	

Sen. Mary L. Landrieu (D)

Elected 1996, seat up 2002; b. Nov. 23, 1955, Arlington, VA; home, New Orleans; LA State U., B.A. 1977; Catholic; married (Frank Snellings).

Career: LA House of Reps., 1979–88; LA Treasurer, 1987–96.

DC Office: 702 HSOB 20510, 202-224-5824; Fax: 202-224-9735; e-mail: senator@landrieu.senate.gov.

State Offices: Baton Rouge, 504-389-0395; New Orleans, 504-589-2427; Shreveport, 318-676-3085.

Committees: *Agriculture, Nutrition & Forestry* (7th of 8 D): Marketing, Inspection & Product Promotion; Production & Price Competitiveness. *Energy & Natural Resources* (9th of 9 D): Energy Research, Development, Production & Regulation; Forests & Public Land Management; National Parks, Historic Preservation & Recreation. *Small Business* (8th of 8 D).

Group Ratings and Key Votes: Newly Elected

Election Results

1996 general	Mary L. Landrieu (D)	852,945	(50%)	($2,504,815)
	Louis (Woody) Jenkins (R)	847,157	(50%)	($1,878,242)
1996 primary	Louis (Woody) Jenkins (R)	322,244	(26%)	
	Mary L. Landrieu (D)	264,268	(22%)	
	Richard P. Ieyoub (D)	250,682	(20%)	
	David Duke (R)	141,489	(12%)	
	Jimmy Hayes (R)	71,699	(6%)	
	Bill Linder (R)	58,243	(5%)	
	Others	119,934	(10%)	
1990 primary	J. Bennett Johnston (D)	752,902	(54%)	($5,389,624)
	David Duke (R)	607,391	(44%)	($2,615,267)
	Others	35,820	(3%)	

FIRST DISTRICT

New Orleans, founded in 1718, the nation's fifth largest city at the outbreak of the Civil War, is ancient for an American metropolis; yet it is still closely girded by the peculiar wilderness of the mushy delta lands of the sluggish Mississippi River. Climb the levee overlooking the Mississippi and you will see an expanse of water with untidy clumps of trees and disorganized-looking, seemingly abandoned docks—what Mark Twain had in his mind's eye while writing *Life on the Mississippi* in the 1870s. Or drive just past the last block of a suburban subdivision, and you are in unreclaimed swamp, vegetation and wetness, thick with herons and alligators, flat as far as the eye can see. For years the river funneled the products of half a continent down to a single port with an international heritage and flair; the New Orleans metropolitan area is still living off that geography and history, with an inward-looking elite preoccupied with who is in which Mardi Gras krewe and interested more in old families' genealogy than in Oil Patch geology. The old buildings of New Orleans are finely proportioned and its old neighborhoods charming, like those in France; and its early 20th Century improvements, like Olmstead's City Park, are grand. But its middle and late 20th Century streetscapes and subdivisions, like those of France, are without ornament or charm, utilitarian works of man made to master the below-sea-level environment.

The 1st Congressional District of Louisiana includes much of the newer part of the New Orleans metropolitan area, spread over the soggy lands of the lower Mississippi and Lake Pontchartrain. Most of its people live in affluent white neighborhoods in New Orleans and the vast suburb of Metairie in Jefferson Parish, divided by slanting grids and elevated only where bridges jut out over the many canals. The 1st extends across the 26-mile Lake Pontchartrain Causeway to include fast-growing St. Tammany Parish, with old towns lush with trees and clusters of new growth around giant intersections, and north and west to Washington and Tangipahoa Parishes, still mostly rural country. This is the most upscale, affluent, highly educated district in Louisiana, and also the most Republican, supportive of political reform and against economic redistribution.

The congressman from the 1st District is Bob Livingston, a Republican first elected in 1977, now chairman of the House Appropriations Committee. Livingston bears the name of the New York aristocrat who as chancellor administered the oath of office to George Washington 200 years ago and who as ambassador to France helped negotiate the Louisiana Purchase, and some of whose relatives became Louisiana planters and politicians. But this Livingston grew up in modest circumstances, enlisting in the Navy after high school, working his way through school at the Avondale Shipyard. He spent most of his pre-congressional career as a prosecutor and approaches politics with a prosecutorial—aggressive, conservative—frame of mind. He won the seat in a 1977 special election, after a Democrat was forced to resign (and eventually jailed) due to fraud, and Livingston went on to be a tough judge of his colleagues while on the House Ethics

Committee during the Abscam investigation. He ran for governor and lost in 1987.

Livingston's rise to the chairmanship of Appropriations was rapid and unexpected. He started the 103d Congress as the fifth ranking Republican on the committee, and ranking minority member on the Foreign Operations Subcommittee. Much of his work was on Louisiana projects—Navy sealift vessels and Navy/Marine amphibious ships built in Jefferson Parish's Avondale shipyard, the Harvey Canal flood control levee on the west bank, the 12-plane fleet stationed at Keesler Air Force Base for hurricane reconnaissance flights. Then Republicans won control of the House, and Speaker-to-be Newt Gingrich passed over Joseph McDade, then under indictment and so ineligible under Republican rules, and the next three Republicans who like McDade had been used to working cooperatively with Democrats. Livingston was then running for Republican Conference chairman, the post being vacated by Dick Armey; Gingrich persuaded him to withdraw, and to become Appropriations chairman instead.

Livingston turned out to be a tough, angry, competent chairman, fighting Democrats who want higher appropriations, fellow Republicans who want to use riders to help their districts or push pet causes, and the Republican leadership which often wanted to use catchall continuing resolutions instead of bringing up each of the 13 appropriations bills separately. He angered conservatives by keeping much of the old Democratic committee staff and angered his new subcommittee chairmen by accepting the money limits set by the Republican leadership. He established a working relationship with ranking Democrat David Obey, a stickler for detail capable of outbursts of temper himself. Livingston got angry with the Clinton Administration when it spent lots of money without authorization or notice—transferring $170 million of F-16s to Jordan, trading federal lands in California in return for the closing of a gold mine near Yellowstone National Park. Livingingston nearly sunk Agriculture Chairman Pat Roberts' farm reform because he thought the mandatory phaseout payments to previously subsidized farmers limited appropriators' discretion; he was the only Louisiana congressman to vote against the Freedom to Farm Act.

Yet for all the *sturm und drang*—he brought an alligator skinning knife, a "Cajun scalpel," to his first meeting—he got quite a job done. Appropriations started the 104th Congress by cutting the Democrats' FY95 spending bills, then cut non-defense discretionary FY96 spending by $5.5 billion—very much contrary to precedent. After the bruising battle over the budget, when Bill Clinton vetoed many appropriations bills, Livingston and his committee allowed spending increases for FY97. But comparing the Democrats' last bills (FY95) and Livingston's latest, non-defense discretionary spending fell from $246 billion to $235 billion, while defense rose only from $262 billion to $265 billion. Total discretionary spending was something like $50 billion less than what it would have been under Democratic projections. The FY96 bills were mostly late, with the final one not approved till March 1996. But he moved the 13 FY97 bills out of committee by August 1996 and got them passed before October 1, only the fourth time such a feat has been accomplished since 1948, the others being 1976, 1988, 1994. He had his narrow escapes—nearly losing the Treasury-Postal Services bill in July 1996—but overall steered his bills through with solid majorities.

After the 1996 election, there was a brief threat to Livingston's chairmanship. McDade was acquitted on bribery charges in August 1996, and said he'd like to invoke seniority and become chairman. But Newt Gingrich decided otherwise: "The core question is, if Livingston had run the team brilliantly for two years, did everything we asked him to, saved $53 billion and got the spending bills through on time this year, how could you demote him?" Livingston negotiated with McDade, naming him vice-chairman of the full committee, and giving him the empty chair of the Energy and Water Subcommittee (instead of Defense, which would have meant displacing Bill Young.) For 1997 Livingston hopes to clear all 13 FY98 appropriations bills before October 1, without riders setting policy, but also warned that the May balanced budget resolution would not prevent him from "attempting to terminate or cut programs of questionable worth," specifically mentioning the National Endowment for the Arts and Americorps. Livingston also took on the formidable mission of chairing a bipartisan task force appointed to reform the House Ethics Committee process and hasten the pace of future investigations.

At home, Livingston's district is solidly Republican; he was reelected in 1996 without opposition in the September primary. That will not happen again, at least if a federal court decision is upheld requiring Louisiana to change its laws so that all members are elected in November; but Livingston, who has kept active on Louisiana issues, is an overwhelming favorite for reelection.

The People: Pop. 1990: 602,848; 28% rural; 12% age 65+; 85% White; 10% Black; 1% Asian; 4% Hispanic origin. Households: 58% married couple families; 28% married couple fams. w. children; 46% college educ.; median household income: $27,877; per capita income: $13,860; median gross rent: $420; median house value: $74,500.

1996 Presidential Vote			**1992 Presidential Vote**		
Dole (R)	152,655	(56%)	Bush (R)	154,662	(56%)
Clinton (D)	100,655	(37%)	Clinton (D)	86,540	(31%)
Perot (I)	16,325	(6%)	Perot (I)	33,419	(12%)

Rep. Robert L. (Bob) Livingston (R)

Elected Aug., 1977; b. Apr. 30, 1943, Colorado Springs, CO; home, Metairie; Tulane U., B.A. 1967, J.D. 1968; Catholic; married (Bonnie).

Career: Navy, 1961–63; Practicing atty., 1968–70, 1976–77; Asst. U.S. Atty., 1970–73; Chief Special Prosecutor, Orleans Parish Dist. Atty.'s Ofc., 1974–75; Chief Prosecutor, LA Atty. Gen.'s Ofc. Organized Crime Unit, 1975–76.

DC Office: 2406 RHOB 20515, 202-225-3015; Fax: 202-225-0739.

District Offices: Metairie, 504-589-2753.

Committees: *Appropriations* (Chmn. of 34 R).

Group Ratings

	ADA	ACLU	AFS	LCV	CFA	CON	NFIB	COC	ACU	NTLC	CHC
1996	0	0	0	15	0	35	95	88	95	95	86
1995	0	—	—	6	0	38	—	96	80	—	—

National Journal Ratings

	1995 LIB — 1995 CONS			1996 LIB — 1996 CONS		
Economic	0%	—	74%	44%	—	55%
Social	32%	—	65%	29%	—	68%
Foreign	36%	—	59%	21%	—	72%

Key Votes of the 104th Congress

1. Reduce Medicare Growth $	Y	5. Flag Amendment	Y	9. Cuban Embargo	Y
2. Ovrd. Product Liab. Veto	Y	6. Drop EPA Limits	N	10. Bar Bosnia Troop $	N
3. Increase Min. Wage	N	7. Repeal Assault-Weap. Ban	Y	11. Cut Anti-Missile Defense	N
4. Welfare Reform	Y	8. Ovrd. Part. Birth Veto	Y	12. Bar U.N. Uniforms	Y

Election Results

1996 primary	Robert L. (Bob) Livingston (R)	unopposed		($1,042,853)
1994 primary	Robert L. (Bob) Livingston (R)	83,928	(81%)	($348,081)
	Forest McNeir (D)	12,336	(12%)	
	Clark Simmons (I)	7,139	(7%)	

SECOND DISTRICT

New Orleans, founded by the French in 1718, ruled by the Spanish from 1763 to just days before the French took over to sell it in 1803, was a Creole city—part French, a bit Spanish, more than a touch Caribbean—when the American flag was raised over what is now Jackson Square. The statue of Andrew Jackson still seems an alien intrusion in a square set off by a French Market, the Cabildo, the Presbytere, the Pontalba apartments and Cathedral St. Louis. New Orleans was the fifth largest American city from 1840 until the Civil War and the only sizable city in the South; yet even as it was sending southern cotton out to the mills of Lancashire, it was an alien cultural force in both the nation and region. Urbanized, yet poor and in many ways primitive, New Orleans had yellow fever epidemics late in the 19th Century, even as it was installing electric lights; it had a riot in which Italian immigrants were massacred, even as it was laying streetcar tracks and telephone lines. This was one of the most corrupt American cities during Reconstruction and the Gilded Age, when its votes were regularly bid for and bought; like other southern cities, it became rigidly segregated after 1890.

For a time during the oil boom in the 1970s New Orleans seemed to be a fast-growing Sun Belt city; but more recently it seems to be moving back to some of its unprincipled traditions. Its port has lost business to others, the oil business is now centered in Houston, it has long since lost Latin American trade to Miami, and it seems beset by crime and corruption more than any other great American city. Horrific crimes have become commonplace, with even policemen committing robberies and shooting innocent victims. The tourist-thronged French Quarter also no longer seems safe, though as long as Mardi Gras and the New Orleans Jazz Festival survive here, thousands of tourists will continue to witness the city's unique culture and colorful blend of traditions.

In 1992 Governor Edwin Edwards and the legislature authorized the state's only land-based casino to be built at the foot of Canal Street, a project that was barely salvaged after Harrahs went bankrupt during construction in November 1995; the state brokered a new deal with the company and the casino is scheduled to open by 1998. And in February 1997, the 128-year-old Schwegmann Giant Supermarket chain, a business long associated with the New Orleans tradition of "makin' groceries," was sold to a New York investment firm. And the terrible crash in late 1996 of a river freighter into the Riverwalk tourist area seemed yet another symbol of New Orleans' broken image as a thriving port city.

The 2d Congressional District of Louisiana includes almost all of the city of New Orleans, everything except a few affluent white neighborhoods, plus the west bank towns of Jefferson Parish—Gretna, Harvey, Westwego, Waggaman—industrial enclosures between levee and swamp. Here is the French Quarter—the *Vieux Carre*—its 19th Century homes still intact because the Americans who moved here after 1803 wanted to stay away from the snobbish Creoles and then built a new downtown across Canal Street. North of the Quarter is the site of Storyville, where prostitution was legal until 1918 and where jazz was probably first played; the old frame houses have long since been torn down and replaced by half-empty and crime-ridden housing projects. But many similar neighborhoods remain, where blacks and some working-class whites live in rickety frame houses which are not always strong enough to keep the rain out and never tight enough to keep out the summer humidity or the damp winter chill, along the vividly named streets—Elysian Fields, Spain, Desire, Arts—that go north from the river wharves. But some 37,000 houses stand empty. South of the quarter is the downtown flecked with skyscrapers and the ominous Superdome, and to the east is the old slum known as the Irish Channel—a reminder that New Orleans had more foreign immigrants than any other part of the South. Up St. Charles Avenue is the Garden District. This was the home of the rich, early American settlers, and its antebellum homes are still covered with vines and Spanish moss. Quaintly named trolley cars still roll out St. Charles to Tulane University and Audubon Park. New Orleans, for many years a speckled black-and-white city, now has a solid black majority, and the 2d District is overwhelmingly Democratic.

The congressman from the 2d District is Bill Jefferson, first elected in 1990 after the retirement of Lindy Boggs, a charming Louisiana lady with perfect manners and perfect political pitch, who won majorities from blacks and whites alike. Jefferson grew up in the northeast corner of Louisiana in Lake Providence. After attending Southern University, he went to Harvard Law, clerked for a well-respected federal judge, worked for Senator Bennett Johnston and finally settled in New Orleans to set up what became the largest black law firm in the South; he received an LL.M. from Georgetown in February 1996 while serving in Congress. Jefferson was elected to the state Senate in 1979; he twice ran for mayor and lost. In 1990, when Boggs retired, he was endorsed by then-Mayor Sidney Barthelemy, and in the primary won 25% of the vote to 22% for Marc Morial, whose father was New Orleans's first black mayor and who was elected mayor himself in March 1994. In the November runoff, charges flew: Jefferson was dogged by reports of defaults on outstanding loans and mortgages, while Morial admitted he was the father of an eight-year-old girl living in the Ivory Coast. Jefferson won with 52% and became the first Louisiana black elected to Congress since Reconstruction.

In the House Jefferson has shown impressive political skills. He was active in the Democratic Leadership Council and got to know its chairman, a young southern governor named Bill Clinton. In November 1991, Jefferson and Mississippi Congressman Mike Espy endorsed Clinton, and both began campaigning hard for him across the country, including a southern bus tour in August—early and important black support. In December 1992, Jefferson won a seat on the Ways and Means Committee. There he succeeded in cutting inland waterway tolls and getting Bill Clinton to help him save a tax break for venture capital companies dealing solely with minority-owned small businesses. In 1994 he sponsored a compromise eliminating employer mandates for health insurance on four million small businesses, which became part of Ways and Means's healthcare package. In 1996 he opposed economic sanctions against Nigeria for its human rights violations.

The Republican majority in 1995 downsized Ways and Means, and Jefferson temporarily lost his seat; but he is back on now. A quiet, conciliatory man, he is also a member of the Democratic Steering Committee and a Deputy Whip at large. But in November 1996 he lost a race for chairman of the Congressional Black Caucus to the much more fiery Maxine Waters. For the moment, anyway, Jefferson seems to have put aside his ambitions for higher office. In 1991 he filed to run for governor, but withdrew; in 1995, he began running for governor again, but withdrew in favor of Cleo Fields, and said he would run for Senate; in May 1996 he bowed out of that race. Jefferson has had no trouble winning reelection in the 2d District.

The People: Pop. 1990: 602,774; 11% age 65+; 34% White; 60% Black; 2% Asian; 4% Hispanic origin. Households: 38% married couple families; 19% married couple fams. w. children; 40% college educ.; median household income: $18,367; per capita income: $9,790; median gross rent: $372; median house value: $61,800.

1996 Presidential Vote

Clinton (D)	169,930	(78%)
Dole (R)	40,739	(19%)
Perot (I)	5,400	(2%)

1992 Presidential Vote

Clinton (D)	152,975	(69%)
Bush (R)	54,833	(25%)
Perot (I)	13,898	(6%)

Rep. William J. Jefferson (D)

Elected 1990; b. Mar. 14, 1947, Lake Providence; home, New Orleans; Southern U., B.A. 1969, Harvard, J.D. 1972; Georgetown U., LL.M. 1996; Baptist; married (Andrea).

Career: Army Reserves, 1969–78, Army Judge Advocate Corps, 1975; Law clerk, U.S. Dist. Judge Alvin Rubin, 1972–73; Legis. aide, U.S. Sen. Bennett Johnston, 1973–75; Practicing atty., 1975–90; LA Senate, 1979–90.

DC Office: 240 CHOB 20515, 202-225-6636; Fax: 202-225-1988.

District Offices: New Orleans, 504-589-2274.

Committees: *Ways & Means* (13th of 16 D): Social Security; Trade.

Group Ratings

	ADA	ACLU	AFS	LCV	CFA	CON	NFIB	COC	ACU	NTLC	CHC
1996	85	81	100	77	69	74	21	31	5	8	14
1995	70	—	—	56	85	7	—	11	9	—	—

National Journal Ratings

	1995 LIB — 1995 CONS			1996 LIB — 1996 CONS		
Economic	84%	—	16%	73%	—	25%
Social	79%	—	20%	75%	—	24%
Foreign	86%	—	13%	60%	—	39%

Key Votes of the 104th Congress

1. Reduce Medicare Growth $	N	5. Flag Amendment	Y	9. Cuban Embargo	N
2. Ovrd. Product Liab. Veto	N	6. Drop EPA Limits	Y	10. Bar Bosnia Troop $	N
3. Increase Min. Wage	Y	7. Repeal Assault-Weap. Ban	N	11. Cut Anti-Missile Defense	Y
4. Welfare Reform	N	8. Ovrd. Part. Birth Veto	Y	12. Bar U.N. Uniforms	N

Election Results

1996 primary	William J. Jefferson (D)	unopposed		($301,082)
1994 primary	William J. Jefferson (D)	60,906	(75%)	($608,567)
	Robert (Bob) Namer (R)	15,113	(19%)	($3,789)
	Others	5,549	(7%)	

THIRD DISTRICT

Below sea level, veined with bayous and creeks and wide streams of water, crossed by only an occasional road or railroad, the wetlands of southern Louisiana are one of America's unique landscapes. Technically, most of this waterlogged land rests on islands in a broad river mouth, through which the waters of the Mississippi and its tributaries drain into the Gulf of Mexico. It is rich with animal life, herons and egrets, shrimp and crawfish, muskrats and alligators. Yet it supports more people than one might think, in surprisingly sturdy small towns, with shopping malls on high ground, and in cabins along the bayous and crossroad towns where Cajun French remains the first language and roadside diners feature crawfish etouffe. But the steep-roofed Cajun houses are not the only structures: here and there, jutting out of the swampy land, are huge elaborate metal sculptures—refineries and petrochemical plants, processing the oil and natural gas trapped under these wetlands and the shallow continental shelf of the Gulf, and released through 20th Century oil rig technology. In the 1960s and 1970s, the oil industry, by providing good jobs for young people here, helped preserve Cajun culture and built a Cajun pride that was seldom articulated a generation ago. Then oil payrolls plummeted and the wetlands were threatened by coastal erosion and battered by Hurricane Andrew in August 1992. But now offshore drilling is booming again, unemployment is low, and the outlook for the Cajun country looks good.

The 3d Congressional District of Louisiana includes about half the Cajun country, plus St. Bernard and Plaquemines Parishes downriver from New Orleans. It then spreads west over the swamplands, covering Houma, where seven bayous converge; St. Charles, St. John the Baptist, St. James and Ascension Parishes on both sides of the Mississippi, once the greatest sugar producers in America, now studded with refineries and petrochemical plants and giving rise to the nickname "cancer alley"; roughneck Morgan City, which services many offshore oil rigs; and Iberia Parish, the home of McIlhenny's Tabasco sauce. The ancestral language here is Cajun French, the ancestral religion Roman Catholic, and the ancestral politics Democratic, but very conservative: in 1996 the 3d District voted for Bill Clinton and for Republican Senate candidate Woody Jenkins.

The congressman from the 3d District is Billy Tauzin, first elected as a Democrat and now a Republican, who brings Cajun caginess and charm to his work. Tauzin grew up in Chackbay, worked on an oil rig to put himself through Nicholls State University and LSU Law School. He was first elected to the legislature in 1971, at 28; he won the 3d District seat in a May 1980 special election. Tauzin ran for governor in 1987, but was doomed when Edwin Edwards entered the race, squeezing him out in Cajun country; he finished fourth, with 10%. In 1989, Tauzin inherited a Merchant Marine subcommittee chairmanship, just in time to handle legislation inspired by the Exxon *Valdez* oil spill in Alaska. In 1990 he drew up plans to allow a drawdown of the Strategic Petroleum Reserve in southern Louisiana to help pay for the Gulf war and then got the Reserve built back up afterwards. Tauzin is both knowledgeable and eloquent. His floor speech for a 1992 Cable Act amendment allowing wireless cable companies access to cable-originated programming carried 338–68 over the opposition of Democratic leaders and the Bush White House. He was a co-sponsor of the securities litigation reform which was passed in 1996 over Bill Clinton's veto. He can also be wily. Defeated in committee and on the House floor, he and Senator Bennett Johnston inserted in conference committee on the Alaska Oil Export Act of 1995 a provision for royalty relief for deep-water oil drilling; that, plus advances in technology, led to the resurgence in offshore drilling in 1996.

Tauzin's voting record has always been conservative. In November 1994 he mulled over switching parties, and decided not to. He was one of two Democrats who supported all provisions of the Contract with America and in February 1995 he and 22 other Democrats formed The (conservative) Coalition. He was the lead Democrat in pushing property rights legislation, requiring the government to compensate landowners if the value of their property was reduced by 20% by the wetlands laws or the Endangered Species Act; that did not become law, but remains a major Tauzin cause. In August 1995 he finally switched parties. He was expected to run for Bennett Johnston's Senate seat in 1996, but when Jack Fields announced his retirement, Tauzin bowed out after being promised by the Republican leadership Fields's spot as chairman of the Telecommunications and Finance Subcommittee. That proved not to be automatic. Mike Oxley, the next Republican in line, wanted the chairmanship also. As a compromise, Telecommunications lost its Finance jurisdiction to Oxley's subcommittee, and in return received the less important Trade and Consumer Protection portfolios. Tauzin was reelected in September 1996, the only party-switcher to win without opposition; he is also the only House member in history to have served in the leadership, as chief deputy whip, of both parties.

Tauzin lists as his top priority oversight of the Telecommunications Act of 1996, which he strongly supported. In line with his pro-competition philosophy, he opposes auctioning the digital TV spectrum, regulating liquor advertising and any campaign finance bill giving free or discounted air time to candidates (in his view, unconstitutional, unfair and ineffective). He also promised to act against cellular phone eavesdropping and to monitor electronic commerce under NAFTA and GATT. Tauzin has other causes: repeal of retroactive liability in Superfund, requiring the government to use the best science in regulation, passing a 15% retail sales tax and abolishing the IRS, putting a tariff on Chinese crawfish.

Tauzin seems not much interested in statewide office these days. In the 3d District he seems very strong, with $664,000 in the bank after the 1996 election.

The People: Pop. 1990: 603,258; 34% rural; 9% age 65+; 74% White; 22% Black; 1% Asian; 2% Amer. Indian; 2% Hispanic origin. Households: 63% married couple families; 34% married couple fams. w. children; 27% college educ.; median household income: $23,813; per capita income: $9,911; median gross rent: $338; median house value: $57,900.

1996 Presidential Vote

Clinton (D)	153,925	(51%)
Dole (R)	120,605	(40%)
Perot (I)	22,182	(7%)

1992 Presidential Vote

Clinton (D)	118,463	(45%)
Bush (R)	102,699	(39%)
Perot (I)	35,462	(13%)
Other	7,118	(3%)

Rep. W. J. (Billy) Tauzin (R)

Elected May 1980; b. June 14, 1943, Chackbay; home, Chackbay; Nicholls St. U., B.A. 1964, LA St. U., J.D. 1967; Catholic; married (Cecile).

Career: Practicing atty., 1968–70; LA House of Reps., 1971–79.

DC Office: 2183 RHOB 20515, 202-225-4031; Fax: 202-225-0563.

District Offices: Chalmette, 504-271-1707; Gonzales, 504-621-8490; Houma, 504-876-3033; New Iberia, 318-367-8231.

Committees: *Commerce* (2nd of 28 R): Finance & Hazardous Materials (Vice-Chmn.); Telecommunications, Trade & Consumer Protection (Chmn.). *Resources* (2nd of 27 R): Energy & Mineral Resources; Fisheries Conservation, Wildlife & Oceans.

Group Ratings

	ADA	ACLU	AFS	LCV	CFA	CON	NFIB	COC	ACU	NTLC	CHC
1996	0	0	8	23	0	75	92	93	90	90	100
1995	5	—	—	0	0	75	—	100	83	—	—

National Journal Ratings

	1995 LIB — 1995 CONS			1996 LIB — 1996 CONS		
Economic	44%	—	53%	33%	—	64%
Social	0%	—	79%	0%	—	90%
Foreign	36%	—	59%	0%	—	79%

Key Votes of the 104th Congress

1. Reduce Medicare Growth $	Y	5. Flag Amendment	Y	9. Cuban Embargo	Y
2. Ovrd. Product Liab. Veto	Y	6. Drop EPA Limits	N	10. Bar Bosnia Troop $	Y
3. Increase Min. Wage	Y	7. Repeal Assault-Weap. Ban	Y	11. Cut Anti-Missile Defense	N
4. Welfare Reform	Y	8. Ovrd. Part. Birth Veto	Y	12. Bar U.N. Uniforms	Y

Election Results

1996 primary	W. J. (Billy) Tauzin (R)	unopposed		($612,332)
1994 primary	W. J. (Billy) Tauzin (D)	90,536	(76%)	($680,211)
	Nick Accardo (I).	28,250	(24%)	

FOURTH DISTRICT

Northwestern Louisiana, south of Arkansas and just east of Texas, is part of the Deep South. Most people here are Protestants, often very tradition-minded, not Catholics, with names that are English or Scots, not French. The tone is set not by wide-open New Orleans but by the much smaller Shreveport, which could be just another East Texas oil town. The countryside is agricultural, though there are few vestiges of large riverfront plantations or backward farm country. Oil provided the basis for much of the economic growth of the 20th Century; defense facilities also helped; more recently there has been some high-tech and local entrepreneurialism. Politically, northern Louisiana voters for more than 100 years have been voting against cosmopolitan New Orleans and the Catholic Cajun south, sometimes for riproaring populists, and more often, as the economy grows more sophisticated, for market-oriented Republicans.

The 4th Congressional District of Louisiana consists of the northwest quadrant of the state. More than half the votes here are cast in Caddo and Bossier Parishes around Shreveport, with the rest scattered around rural areas, picturesque old towns like Natchitoches and strip-highway towns like Leesville near the Army's giant Fort Polk. This area seemed to be trending Republican in the 1980s, but in the 1990s it has gone the other way. Black voters, about one-quarter of the vote, are heavily Democratic, but more than one-third of whites have been voting for Democrats, at least at the top of the ticket. Bill Clinton carried the district in 1992 and had an absolute majority in 1996, and Democrat Mary Landrieu also carried the 4th, a critical factor in her narrow 5,788-vote statewide margin.

The congressman is Jim McCrery, a Republican first elected in April 1988 to represent the 4th District after Roemer's run for governor; after a court ordered redistricing, McCrery represented the 5th District from 1992–96; after a *third* attempt to get the lines right, McCrery is back representing the 4th District. He grew up in Leesville, graduated from Louisiana Tech in Ruston (next door to Grambling, site of the football-famous historically black college) and LSU Law School, and practiced law in Leesville and Shreveport. In 1981 he went to work for Congressman Buddy Roemer, then a Democrat, then worked for Georgia Pacific in Louisiana; after Roemer was elected governor in 1987, McCrery ran as a Republican and won the special election 51%–49%; that fall he won with 68%, beating Roemer's mother. McCrery's toughest race came in 1992, when the creation of the new black-majority 4th District put him in the 5th District with 16-year incumbent Jerry Huckaby, a conservative Democrat. But the district, with few black voters, was heavily Republican and Huckaby had 88 overdrafts on the House bank; McCrery weathered some negative personal attacks. McCrery led in the October primary 44%–29% and won the November runoff 63%–37%.

McCrery has compiled a mostly conservative voting record and has built considerable expertise in two of the hot issues of the 1990s—healthcare financing and welfare reform. From his seats on the Ways and Means Committee and Health and Human Services Subcommittee, and armed with the intuition that made him one of only 72 House members to vote against the disastrous 1988 catastrophic healthcare bill, in 1994 he advanced a Republican alternative to the Clinton healthcare plan, capping deductibility of health insurance, opposing the Democrats' cost control measures, limiting medical malpractice and instituting medical savings accounts. Prompted by complaints from constituents that parents were coaching kids to act out in order to qualify for SSI payments for handicapped children, he has worked to replace the SSI cash benefit with vouchers. He seeks to exempt family-owned businesses and farms from the estate tax. His most visible work in the 104th Congress came as the co-author of the Republicans' Medicare Preservation Act, on which he has shown impressive knowledge and skill.

Louisiana's third redistricting in three elections changed the boundaries in northwest Louisiana significantly. McCrery in 1996 decided to run in the new 4th District—a greater challenge, since the new district's population is 28% black. But in the September 21 primary he won easily, beating a Democrat 71%–29%. In the 105th Congress he serves on the Ways and Means bipartisan task force on transportation taxes and as vice chairman of the National Republican Congressional Committee.

The People: Census data not available due to 1996 redistricting.

1996 Presidential Vote

Clinton (D)	122,729	(52%)
Dole (R)	92,741	(39%)
Perot (I)	17,525	(7%)

1992 Presidential Vote

Clinton (D)	106,737	(45%)
Bush (R)	96,708	(40%)
Perot (I)	30,741	(13%)

Rep. Jim McCrery (R)

Elected Apr. 1988; b. Sept. 18, 1949, Shreveport; home, Shreveport; LA Tech. U., B.A. 1971, LA St. U., J.D. 1975; Methodist; married (Johnette).

Career: Practicing atty. 1975–78; Asst. Shreveport City Atty., 1979–80; Legis. Dir., U.S. Rep. Buddy Roemer, 1981–84; Regional Mgr., Georgia-Pacific Corp., 1984–88.

DC Office: 2104 RHOB 20515, 202-225-2777; Fax: 202-225-8039.

District Offices: Shreveport, 318-798-2254; Leesville, 318-238-0778.

Committees: *Ways & Means* (9th of 23 R): Health; Human Resources. *Joint Economic Committee* (6th of 10 Reps.).

Group Ratings

	ADA	ACLU	AFS	LCV	CFA	CON	NFIB	COC	ACU	NTLC	CHC
1996	0	0	0	23	0	7	100	100	95	100	100
1995	0	—	—	0	0	38	—	100	92	—	—

National Journal Ratings

	1995 LIB — 1995 CONS			1996 LIB — 1996 CONS		
Economic	0%	—	74%	32%	—	67%
Social	21%	—	72%	14%	—	77%
Foreign	15%	—	73%	21%	—	72%

Key Votes of the 104th Congress

1. Reduce Medicare Growth $	Y	5. Flag Amendment	Y	9. Cuban Embargo	Y
2. Ovrd. Product Liab. Veto	Y	6. Drop EPA Limits	N	10. Bar Bosnia Troop $	Y
3. Increase Min. Wage	N	7. Repeal Assault-Weap. Ban	Y	11. Cut Anti-Missile Defense	N
4. Welfare Reform	Y	8. Ovrd. Part. Birth Veto	Y	12. Bar U.N. Uniforms	Y

Election Results

1996 primary	Jim McCrery (R)	94,822	(71%)	($823,121)
	Paul M. Chachere (D)	38,015	(29%)	
1994 primary	Jim McCrery (R)	106,204	(80%)	($459,098)
(LA 5)	Paul Henry Kidd (D)	21,467	(16%)	
	E. Austin Simmons (I)	5,365	(4%)	

FIFTH DISTRICT

Northeast Louisiana is perhaps the least known part of the state. Along the Mississippi River and the Red River and their dozens of tributaries, it was plantation country before the Civil War, with black majorities still in many parishes. Away from the larger rivers, it is hill country, places where small farmers scratched out a living on land connected to parish courthouses by dusty lanes. Such was Winn Parish, where Huey P. Long, the pivotal figure in modern Louisiana politics, was born in 1893, and from which he began his meteoric political career—elected governor in 1928, senator in 1932, a national figure threatening both parties when he was assassinated in his new high-rise Capitol in Baton Rouge in 1935.

The 5th Congressional District of Louisiana contains much of this country, from the river parishes to the hills of Winn Parish. The biggest urban areas here, with under 100,000 people each, are Monroe in the north and Alexandria in the south; Alexandria in Rapides Parish sits at the northernmost extension of Cajun, Catholic Louisiana, while Monroe is heavily WASP and Baptist. This district was newly created for the 1996 election; the 1992 and 1994 districting plans each had a black-majority 4th District whose boundaries jutted here and there throughout northern Louisiana. This new 5th district has geographically regular boundaries and a black population in 1990 of 31%. Politically, it has trended Republican in the 1980s, but there are pockets of Democratic strength in rural as well as urban areas. In 1992 the 5th was even in the presidential race; in 1996 it produced a small margin for Bill Clinton while voting for Republican Woody Jenkins in the close Senate race.

The congressman from the 5th District is John Cooksey, a Republican elected in 1996. Cooksey grew up next to his father's sawmill in Olla, and claims to have lived all his life within a mile of U.S. 165, which runs north and south through the 5th District. He attended LSU and medical school, served in the Air Force and was sent to northern Thailand during the Vietnam war. After a year of medical residency in New Orleans, he moved to Monroe in 1972 and practiced as an ophthamalogist. He also traveled on medical missions five times to Kenya and raised money to set up an eye clinic there. He was a politically active Republican for years, but never ran for office until the new 5th District was created in 1996. It had no incumbent: Jim McCrery chose to run in the 4th, and Cleo Fields, at one time Louisiana's youngest legislator and the youngest member of Congress when he was elected in 1992, unsuccessful candidate for governor in 1995, decided not to run; Fields had won twice in two black-majority districts but the odds against him seemed strong in this 31% black district. Two other serious candidates ran: Democrat Francis Thompson, a state Representative for 22 years, and Clyde Holloway, a Republican elected to the House in 1986, 1988, and 1990 from the old 8th District which extended from Alexandria south toward Baton Rouge and the Cajun country, and who ran unsuccessfully in the 6th District in 1992 and the 7th District in 1994. Holloway carried the area around Alexandria in 1996, and got 27% of the vote; Thompson carried the heavily black Mississippi River parishes, and got 28%; Cooksey carried Monroe and the northern parishes inland from the river, and won 34%. Under Louisiana's unique multiparty primary system (which a federal court says must be changed for 1998 congressional elections), that put Cooksey in the November 5 runoff with Thompson.

With two-thirds of the votes cast September 21 going to Republicans, Cooksey was the obvious favorite. He was happy to bring Speaker Newt Gingrich to the district, and offered to take him out on U.S. 165 to show him it needed to be widened to four lanes. "I want to make sure that they know where Monroe is and Alexandria is and every point in between, because we have a lot of things we have to do for this district." While supporting most conservative positions, he also took some original stands—tax credits to encourage people to buy American-made products, business tax credits for developing and creating vocational and technical training programs. He attacked Thompson for voting for millions in tax increases in his years as a legislator. Thompson described himself as a conservative and called Cooksey a "rich doctor" who is out of touch. "He's sort of a Grey Poupon sort of guy. I've been in the trenches here for over 30 years." Thompson also favored incentives for business in depressed areas and reducing regulatory burdens. Cooksey outspent Thompson, $898,000 to $511,000, with just $107,000 of his own money. Cooksey won 58%–42%, carrying every parish except those near the river, and winning especially big margins in Monroe and Alexandria.

In the House Cooksey got the committee assignments he wanted—Transportation and Infrastructure, Agriculture, Veterans' Affairs. Although he called for cutting spending generally, he was not bashful about widening U.S. 165. He eschewed pomp and ceremony, disliked being called Doctor or Congressman. His description to *The Washington Post* of his recreational activity—"I go to the gym at 4:30 in the morning with a group of other old guys with pot bellies, I ride quarter horses, cutting horses. I fly a plane to keep my instrument rating current. And I do serious whitewater canoeing in Arkansas"—suggests he is not likely to be a career congressman.

The People: Census data not available due to 1996 redistricting.

1996 Presidential Vote

Clinton (D)	132,407	(48%)
Dole (R)	113,846	(42%)
Perot (I)	22,994	(8%)
Other	4,601	(2%)

1992 Presidential Vote

Clinton (D)	106,604	(42%)
Bush (R)	106,449	(42%)
Perot (I)	31,449	(12%)
Other	8,261	(3%)

Rep. John Cooksey (R)

Elected 1996; b. Aug. 20, 1941, Alexandria; home, Monroe; LA St. U., B.S. 1962, M.D. 1966; U. of TX, M.B.A. 1994; Methodist; married (Ann).

Career: Air Force, 1967–69 (Vietnam); Air National Guard, 1970–72; Ophthalmologist, 1972–96.

DC Office: 317 CHOB 20515, 202-225-8490; Fax: 202-225-5639.

District Offices: Alexandria, 318-448-1777; Monroe, 318-330-9998.

Committees: *Agriculture* (27th of 27 R): Forestry, Resource Conservation & Research; General Farm Commodities. *Transportation & Infrastructure* (33rd of 40 R): Aviation; Public Buildings & Economic Development (Vice Chmn.). *Veterans' Affairs* (12th of 16 R): Health.

Group Ratings and Key Votes: Newly Elected

Election Results

1996 general	John Cooksey (R)	135,990	(58%)	($898,479)
	Francis D. Thompson (D)	97,363	(42%)	($511,183)
1996 primary	John Cooksey (R)	60,853	(34%)	
	Francis D. Thompson (D)	50,144	(28%)	
	Clyde Holloway (R)	48,226	(27%)	
	Michael Jordan Caire (D)	9,286	(5%)	
	Others	12,374	(7%)	
1994 primary	Cleo Fields (D)	88,288	(70%)	($271,463)
(LA 4)	Patricia Slocum (R)	37,935	(30%)	($25,978)

SIXTH DISTRICT

Baton Rouge is the central node of Louisiana, on the boundary between the French-speaking, Catholic Cajun country and the heavily Baptist Deep South, its skyscraper Capitol and Exxon (formerly Jersey Standard) refinery sitting just beyond the levees that line the Mississippi River. Baton Rouge still bears the impress of the man who dominated Louisiana politics for much of the 20th Century, Huey Long. Here Long became governor at 36 in the old (and still-standing) Gothic Capitol, when Baton Rouge had only 30,000 people, and was assassinated in 1935 in the hallway of the 34-story Art Deco Capitol he built. To the south are the buildings of Louisiana State University, much of which he built, in an amazingly short time; to the north is the Jersey Standard refinery, which he taxed to finance his public works. Today Baton Rouge is the center of a metro area of half a million, almost all on the east bank of the Mississippi, and reaching far inland to Livingston Parish. Baton Rouge tries to maintain all of Louisiana's traditions; according to political consultant James Carville, who comes from nearby Carville in Iberville Parish, it has "the best restaurants per capita of any city in the United States."

The 6th Congressional District of Louisiana is centered on Baton Rouge, running south to the "petroleum alley" parishes along the Mississippi and east to the Florida Parishes—so called because, even after the United States purchased Louisiana, they were part of the West Florida colony retained by Spain until it was annexed in 1810. And it includes plantation parishes north along the Mississippi, with high black populations. Historically, all of this territory was Democratic. Baton Rouge in the 1980s moved toward the Republicans, and the Baton Rouge area has been politically marginal in the middle 1990s; in 1996 it gave a comfortable margin to Bill Clinton and to Republican Senate candidate Woody Jenkins.

The congressman from the 6th District is Richard Baker, a Republican first elected in 1986. Baker is one of those instinctive politicians who has spent most of his adult life in public office; he came to Baton Rouge to attend LSU, then in 1972, at 23, was elected as a Democrat to the Louisiana House from a blue-collar district in Baton Rouge. He rose to become chairman of the roads committee and also worked as a commercial real estate broker. He became a Republican in 1985, and in 1986, when Baton Rouge Republican Congressman Henson Moore ran for the Senate, Baker ran for the House and beat a Democratic state senator 51%–46%. His toughest race came in 1992, when he was redistricted in the same district with Republican Congressman Clyde Holloway and was opposed as well by the Democratic mayor of Alexandria. The new district lines put Baker at a disadvantage. Holloway had represented much of the new district, had run for governor in 1991, and was endorsed by New Orleans suburban Congressman Bob Livingston. Baker trailed 37%–33% in the primary, but in the November runoff, with 71% in East Baton Rouge and Livingston Parishes, won 51%–49%.

Baker has a conservative voting record and has played an important role on legislation in favor of deregulation. As chairman of the Banking Subcommittee on Capital Markets, Securities and Government Sponsored Enterprises, he favors repeal of the Glass-Steagall Act of 1933, which separates banks and other financial institutions. He sponsored an amendment to a 1995 bank modernization bill to allow affiliations of banks and insurance companies; it passed in committee but was withdrawn in October 1995 because of opposition by insurance agents. Baker's position was strengthened by a March 1996 Supreme Court decision that national banks can sell insurance in small towns despite state laws; the issue will likely be revisited in the 105th Congress. He worked to restructure the regulation of thrift institutions after the S&L crisis. He favored raising the FHA home mortgage loan limit and opposed the requirement that public housing units be replaced one-for-one.

But he has not always been a force for deregulation. On the Agriculture Committee in 1995 he voted against ending a cotton marketing loan program. The final version of the Freedom to Farm Act, which he voted for, did not abolish key programs for cotton, sugar, and rice—all important local products. In the 105th Congress, Baker shifted to Transportation and Infrastructure, which must reauthorize the ISTEA transportation bill; he will likely pay heed to Louisiana highway needs. Baker has also worked on local projects like expansion of the Port Hudson National Cemetery and recognition of the Jena Band of Choctaw Indians.

Baker was mentioned as a possible candidate for governor in 1995 and senator in 1996, but did not run. He was reelected easily in 1994 and 1996.

The People: Census data not available due to 1996 redistricting.

1996 Presidential Vote			1992 Presidential Vote		
Clinton (D)	142,156	(50%)	Bush (R)	120,875	(45%)
Dole (R)	121,851	(43%)	Clinton (D)	116,935	(43%)
Perot (I)	19,222	(7%)	Perot (I)	30,198	(11%)

Rep. Richard H. Baker (R)

Elected 1986; b. May 22, 1948, New Orleans; home, Baton Rouge; LA St. U., B.A. 1971; United Methodist; married (Kay).

Career: Real estate developer, 1972–86; LA House of Reps., 1972–86.

DC Office: 434 CHOB 20515, 202-225-3901; Fax: 202-225-7313.

District Offices: Baton Rouge, 504-929-7711.

Committees: *Banking & Financial Services* (5th of 30 R): Capital Markets, Securities & Government Sponsored Enterprises (Chmn.); Housing & Community Opportunity. *Transportation & Infrastructure* (22nd of 40 R): Surface Transportation; Water Resources & Environment.

Group Ratings

	ADA	ACLU	AFS	LCV	CFA	CON	NFIB	COC	ACU	NTLC	CHC
1996	0	0	0	23	8	9	97	100	95	98	93
1995	0	—	—	6	8	53	—	96	80	—	—

National Journal Ratings

	1995 LIB — 1995 CONS			1996 LIB — 1996 CONS		
Economic	0%	—	74%	29%	—	70%
Social	21%	—	72%	14%	—	77%
Foreign	0%	—	85%	21%	—	72%

Key Votes of the 104th Congress

1. Reduce Medicare Growth $	Y	5. Flag Amendment	Y	9. Cuban Embargo	Y
2. Ovrd. Product Liab. Veto	Y	6. Drop EPA Limits	N	10. Bar Bosnia Troop $	Y
3. Increase Min. Wage	N	7. Repeal Assault-Weap. Ban	Y	11. Cut Anti-Missile Defense	N
4. Welfare Reform	Y	8. Ovrd. Part. Birth Veto	Y	12. Bar U.N. Uniforms	Y

Election Results

1996 primary	Richard H. Baker (R)	117,598	(69%)	($554,968)
	Steve Myers (D)	52,092	(31%)	
1994 primary	Richard H. Baker (R)	103,174	(81%)	($518,945)
	Darryl Paul Ward (D)	24,033	(19%)	

SEVENTH DISTRICT

More than 200 years ago, French-speaking settlers were forced to leave their land of Acadie, which the British had taken over and renamed Nova Scotia, and make their way to the wetlands of southern Louisiana. Here, without much notice, they built steep-roofed houses to slough off nonexistent snow and adapted French cuisine to the crawfish and muskrat they found in abundance in the pelican-tended swamps. The heart of the Cajun country is around Lafayette, just west of the Atchafalaya Basin, where Mississippi waters pour through bayous and canals, with only occasional bits of solid land visible on the 30-mile section of Interstate 10 built on elevated stilts. For half a century the Cajun country thrived, thanks to the oil and gas plentiful here and just off shore in the Gulf of Mexico; oil rigs are common, and every once in a while the swampy foliage parts to reveal a giant refinery or petrochemical plant. In the past two decades, Cajun pride has grown; Cajun French is being kept alive and Cajun cooking has become a tourist attraction here and, in watered-down form, familiar all over the United States. Both Cajun culture and the oil business are particularly evident in Lafayette, with its Acadian Village and plethora of oil exploration firms.

The oil price crash of the middle 1980s hit the Cajun country hard. Rising expectations, and the giddy sense that the oil industry promised lasting prosperity, suddenly collapsed, leaving borrowers overextended and ordinary homeowners unable to maintain the standard of living they expected. Politically, the Cajun country seemed to move then toward national Democrats, whom it had shunned because their cultural liberalism seemed alien to the Cajun tradition of respecting the authority of Church and state while tolerating a certain amount of *laissez les bons temps rouler* spirit. The Cajun country voted for Bill Clinton in 1992 and 1996, as it had voted for Louisiana's foremost Cajun politician, Edwin Edwards, who was elected governor in 1972, 1975, 1983 and 1991.

The 7th Congressional District of Louisiana covers much of the Cajun country, from Lafayette and the Atchafalaya west along I-10 to Lake Charles and the Texas border. Redistricted three times in the 1990s, its boundaries have now smoothed out. It is the descendant of the district represented from 1965–72 by Edwin Edwards and from 1972–86 by John Breaux, both from the small city of Crowley in Acadia Parish, who became governor and Senator respectively.

The congressman from the 7th District now is Chris John, a Democrat elected in 1996. John grew up in Crowley, which may have produced more prominent politicians per capita than any other place in America. After graduating from LSU he went into the family trucking business. In 1987, at 27, he was elected to the seat in the Louisiana House his father had once held, and served two four-year terms, chairing the Acadiana delegation. It is a background that suggests a lack of naivete and an ability to operate politically, to say the least. In 1996 the 7th District seat came open when Jimmy Hayes, a 10-year incumbent who had switched to the Republican Party in December 1995, decided to run for the Senate; his candidacy never caught fire, and he finished fifth with 6% after leading Republicans, including House colleagues, endorsed Republican state legislator Woody Jenkins.

A field of eight candidates ran in the September 21 open primary; Louisiana's system (due to change for 1998) sends the top two finishers, regardless of party, enter a run off in November if no one receives 50% or better in the primary. His chief opponents turned out to be David Thibodaux, an English professor at the University of Southwestern Louisiana and the most prominent Republican running, and Democrat Hunter Lundy, a maritime lawyer from Lake Charles, a religious conservative, well-known for representing the plaintiff in the defamation suit against evangelist Jimmy Swaggert. Thibodaux called for abolishing the Internal Revenue Service and the Department of Education; Lundy emphasized his strong opposition to abortion. John said he was tough on crime and wanted to prepare children to get jobs in the global economy. On September 21 John led with 26% of the vote, and Thibodaux seemed to come in second, 29 votes ahead of Lundy. But rechecking of the voting machines gave second place to Lundy, by 8 votes; Thibodaux protested and filed suit, to no avail. This meant that two Democrats would face off in November, and that Democrats had picked up one House seat even before the voters went to the polls in November—and in a district that, probably because of the abortion issue, voted for Republican Woody Jenkins over Democrat Mary Landrieu in the Senate race.

Neither candidate showed much endorsement of national Democratic principles. Lundy attacked John for supporting legislative pensions and his vote on an abortion amendment; John said he would not benefit from the pension and was described as "pro-life, unequivocally." John was endorsed in October by the House Blue Dog Democrats and in the closing days by Republican Congressmen Jimmy Hayes and Billy Tauzin (whose wife is from Crowley). The result may have come down to geography. The Lake Charles newspaper noted sadly that no candidate from west of the Mermenteau River had won since Vance Plauche in 1940. Some 56 years later Lundy led 63%–37% in the parishes west of the Mermenteau, but they cast only 36% of the district's votes, and John led 62%–38% in the parishes to the east, for a 53%–47% win.

John's endorsement by leading Republicans led some to think he might switch parties, but in January 1997 he joined the Blue Dogs and became co-chair of their task force on regulatory reform, and said he'd continue as a Democrat (of course, Hayes and Tauzin had once said the same thing, and then switched). He is a member of the Agriculture Committee, where he says he wants to encourage exports and will certainly look after rice farmers (his family owns two rice farms) and on Resources, where he says he, as a member of the Congressional Sportsmen's Caucus, wants to protect estuaries, fishlands and marshlands.

The People: Census data not available due to 1996 redistricting.

1996 Presidential Vote

Clinton (D)	106,034	(54%)
Dole (R)	70,149	(35%)
Perot (I)	19,644	(10%)

1992 Presidential Vote

Clinton (D)	127,714	(48%)
Bush (R)	97,160	(37%)
Perot (I)	36,310	(14%)
Other	4,087	(2%)

Rep. Chris John (D)

Elected 1996; b. Jan. 5, 1960, Crowley; home, Crowley; LA St. U., B.A. 1982; Catholic; married (Payton).

Career: Co-owner, John N. John Truckline, 1983–96; Crowley City Council, 1983–87; LA House of Reps., 1987–95.

DC Office: 1504 LHOB 202-225-2031; Fax: 202-225-5724.

District Offices: Lafayette, 318-235-6322; Lake Charles, 318-433-1747.

Committees: *Agriculture* (21st of 23 D): Forestry, Resource Conservation & Research; General Farm Commodities. *Resources* (20th of 23 D): Energy & Mineral Resources.

Group Ratings and Key Votes: Newly Elected

Election Results

1996 general	Chris John (D)	128,449	(53%)	($604,865)
	Hunter Lundy (D)	113,351	(47%)	($513,344)
1996 primary	Chris John (D)	45,398	(26%)	
	Hunter Lundy (D)	38,598	(22%)	
	David Thibodaux (R)	38,590	(22%)	
	Tyron Picard (D)	25,914	(15%)	
	Jim Slatten (R)	12,466	(7%)	
	Charlie Buckels (R)	8,301	(5%)	
	Others	7,792	(4%)	
1994 primary	James A. (Jimmy) Hayes (D)	72,424	(53%)	($436,254)
	Clyde C. Holloway (R)	54,253	(40%)	
	Ron Ceasar (I)	9,937	(7%)	

MAINE

Maine is a state with a distinctive personality—ornery, contrary-minded, almost bullheaded, rough-hewn. It is the state closest geographically to Europe, but it was not heavily settled until the mid-19th Century, and then by people coming from the south and west—the opposite of America's usual thrust. In an urbanizing and rapidly changing country, Maine was famous for its pointed firs and steady habits, with a few dozen small factory and mill towns but nothing like a major metropolis. Maine grew in a rush and then mostly stopped: there were 600,000 people here in 1860 and its population did not top one million until the 1970s. Then, in the 1980s, the New England high-tech boom reached up Interstate 95 and the simple, back-to-nature Yankee style came into vogue; for a moment Maine boomed. The antique dockside buildings on Portland's waterfront were restored and filled with ferns; the Maine Mall expanded and saw office parks spring up nearby, a miniature edge city; real estate prices rose by hundreds of percents, not just in vacation coves, but in Portland and small towns that had never considered themselves picturesque. The L.L. Bean headquarters in Freeport, open 24 hours a day, 365 days a year, symbolized the boom: the Anglo-Saxon monosyllable and two chaste initials suggesting the dry understatement of archetypical Down East Yankees; the 24-hour-a-day schedule recalling the hard work needed to eke out a living from the cold waters of the North Atlantic to the pine-covered north woods; the commercial success of the enterprise a prime example of Maine's unexpected 1980s boom.

The boom didn't help everyone. Maine's manufacturing sector withered as service jobs increased; its principal roads were suddenly jammed with cars waiting for the green arrow so they could turn into the mall. The Grand Banks and lobster grounds have been overfished, and scratching small Maine boiling potatoes out of the soil of Aroostook County has become harder: Maine's potato production in 1995 was less than half of 1980, while Idaho's doubled. Many paper mills have grown musty, with less woodpulp to process since the spruce budworm infestation of the late 1970s. Not far from neat town squares and picturesque seascapes you can find tarpaper- and plastic-clad homes of poor, uneducated, ill-clothed swamp Yankees. In the early 1990s Maine lost 40,000 jobs and saw real estate values crash. It saw the state budget cut three times and humiliating stoppages of state services. People wondered if they had let their forest and coast environments and their town Main Streets deteriorate because of development whose benefits now seemed ephemeral.

Politically, Maine responded with anger and by flailing out in all directions. For decades this state has been an odd duck, often running contrary to national cycles. Up through 1958, it held state elections in September, a date originally chosen because it followed the state's early harvest; in the days before polls, the results here were taken as a gauge of national partisan movement—hence the saying, "As Maine goes, so goes the nation." However in September 1936, Maine voted 56% for Republican Governor Lewis Barrows and in November only Maine and Vermont voted for Alf Landon over Franklin Roosevelt, prompting Roosevelt's campaign manager to observe, "As Maine goes, so goes Vermont." Maine's adherence to flinty Yankee Republicanism and Prohibition was echoed almost nowhere else in the nation. Since then, it has voted for the loser in the close presidential elections of 1948, 1960, 1968 and 1976, and nearly again in 1980—a record equalled by no other state. It cast the nation's highest percentages for Ross Perot in 1992 (30%) and 1996 (14%); it was carried twice by Bill Clinton, but by 1996 elected two Republican women to the Senate and two Democratic men to the House. In 1994 Maine elected an independent candidate as governor—as it did also in 1974; the first was a former Republican, the second a former Democrat.

If Maine's tradition-minded Yankees kept the state Republican long after the nation embraced the New Deal, the sons and daughters of its ethnics—Irish, French Canadian, Greek and Arab immigrants have come to equal the numbers of pure WASPs, though these new state of Mainers in many ways share traditional Yankee traits and values—made the Democrats competitive, perhaps even dominant, here in the 1970s and 1980s as they were losing ground in the rest of the nation. Now those ethnic differences are less important: in 1996 Bill Clinton won between 46% and 54% in every county, Bob Dole between 26% and 37%, Ross Perot between 10% and 19%—uniform results that suggest that ethnic differences and partisan traditions matter less than a Maine consensus, shared by most of those who grew up in Maine or chose to move here. The environment-conscious newcomers of the 1980s, who passed up urban Massachusetts and low-tax New Hampshire because they loved the Maine lifestyle, have made this a good market for natural toothpaste, organic baby food and canvas bags rather than paper or plastic at the supermarket. It was the first state to ban the juicebox as insufficiently biodegradable; it now recycles liquor bottles; above the Ben and Jerry's in Brunswick is the Buddhist Dharma Study Center.

But both old and new Maine voters must worry about how to make a living. The 1980s drop in manufacturing and blue-collar jobs ended the era when high school seniors could go into the woods or to the shoe factory and earn more than their teachers. The biggest private employer in the state is Bath Iron Works, a shipbuilder heavily dependent on defense spending, and is under current contract to build 21 "Arleigh Burke" Class Naval destroyers. Its latest trends are telemarketing, despite the Maine accent, and guiding tourists to view moose (they really are

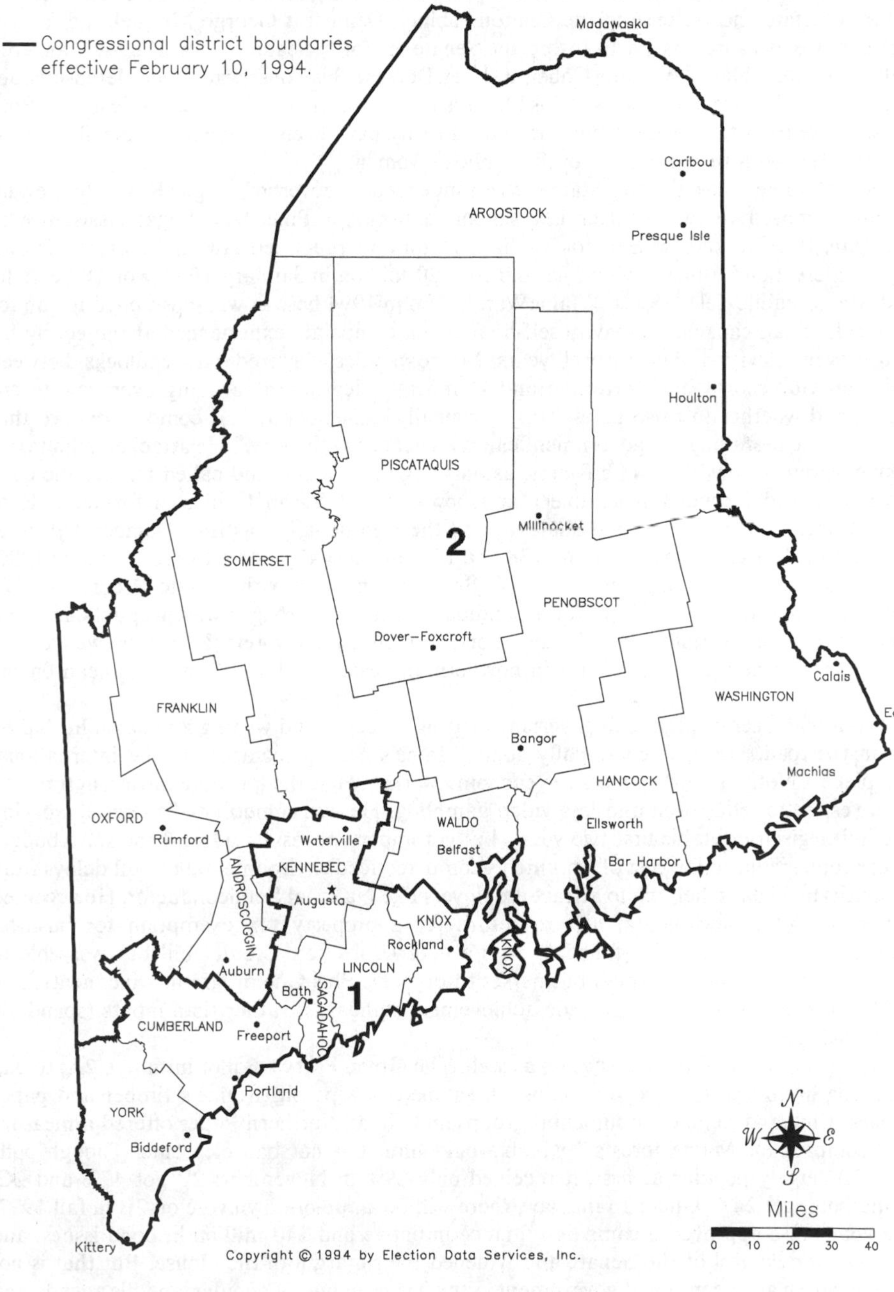
Congressional district boundaries effective February 10, 1994.
Madawaska
Caribou
AROOSTOOK
Presque Isle
Houlton
PISCATAQUIS
Millinocket
2
SOMERSET
PENOBSCOT
Dover–Foxcroft
Calais
WASHINGTON
Eastport
FRANKLIN
Bangor
Machias
HANCOCK
OXFORD
Rumford
Waterville
WALDO
Ellsworth
Belfast
ANDROSCOGGIN
KENNEBEC
Bar Harbor
Augusta
KNOX
Rockland
KNOX
Auburn
LINCOLN
Bath
1
SAGADAHOC
CUMBERLAND
Freeport
Portland
YORK
Biddeford
N
W
E
S
Miles
0
10
20
30
40
Kittery
Copyright © 1994 by Election Data Services, Inc.

big). The Green Party, despite high hopes, did poorly here in 1996; its candidates won few votes and the referendum on its initiative 2A, to ban clearcutting, was defeated. There are limits, it seems, to Maine's quirkiness.

From 1980–94 Maine had two senators prominent enough to have been considered for secretary of State and Defense in the Clinton cabinet; Democrat George Mitchell did not get State, perhaps because his partisanship as Senate majority leader from 1989–94 angered Republicans; Republican William Cohen did get Defense, his conservatism on defense issues reassuring Republicans ill at ease with his liberalism on cultural and some economic issues. Both chose to retire from the Senate when they could easily have been reelected, Mitchell in 1994, Cohen in 1996; both were replaced by Republican women.

Governor. Maine is now the only state with an Independent governor, Angus King. He grew up in Virginia, moved to Maine after law school to work for Pine Tree Legal Assistance in Skowhegan, then worked for Senator William Hathaway, practiced law, and started his own energy conservation business, which he sold for $20 million in January 1994. For 18 years he hosted Maine Public Television's "MaineWatch." So in 1994 he was well-positioned to run for governor: familiar, capable of heavily self-financing a campaign, experienced at projecting his message over television. For several years Maine politics centered on deadlocks between Republican Governor John McKernan and Democratic legislators, arguing over how to cut spending and whether to raise taxes. King, originally a Democrat, had come to believe that "sometimes the best thing the government can do is get out of the way." He attacked high taxes, clumsy government meddling in business, astonishing inefficiency, and called for specific cuts. He overshadowed Republican nominee (and now senator) Susan Collins, a former aide to Senator Cohen, and he contrasted sharply with the traditionally partisan Democrat, former Governor Joseph Brennan, who won in 1978 and 1982 and lost 47%–44% to McKernan in 1990. King pulled even in the polls, then overtook Brennan, and won with 35% to Brennan's 34%, Collins's 23% and 6% for a Green Party candidate. King ran stronger with Republicans than Democrats and did his best with high-education and high-income voters. He scored well among Perot supporters; he ran behind Perot in northern and eastern Maine, and well ahead on the coast.

King is a high-energy, high-tech governor, wearing a beeper and writing a book on his laptop while on the road. He talks continually about Maine's need to compete in the international marketplace: "Nothing works unless the economy works." He calls for more infrastructure and lower taxes, better education and less video gambling. He was sometimes frustrated working with a split legislature in his first two years, but got important results. He cut the state budget and work force, reduced the cost of workmen's comp, reduced environmental permit delays from nine months to 45 days, helping to attract employers like National Semiconductor. He accepted Republicans' future income tax cut in return for a property tax exemption for business machinery and equipment. He failed to pass a "New Jobs Tax Credit" bill but was able to streamline state regulation of small businesses through his Plus One program. On education he called for measuring outputs (statewide achievement standards) rather than inputs (spending, teachers' salaries).

On the environment King had success as well. The Green Party's Ballot initiative 2A, to ban clearcutting in all unorganized townships, threatened to wipe out Maine's timber and paper industries; King and some environmental groups and Great Northern Paper offered a measure 2B, a "compact for Maine forests," which would limit but not ban clearcuts. Though polls showed 2A hugely popular at first, it received only 29% in November; 2B got 47% and 2C, rejecting both, got 24%. Under Maine law, there will be an up-or-down vote on 2B in fall 1997. Maine voters also approved a campaign finance initiative and $40 million in bond issues, and Democrats won control of the Senate and widened their margin in the House. But that is not likely to result in an expansion of government. King has been highly popular, and his agenda and his veto seem likely to keep Maine's government on the course he has set. Is this a formula for success in a wider arena?

Senior Senator. Olympia Snowe is relatively new to the Senate but a veteran in Maine politics. Snowe grew up in Auburn and worked as a legislative staffer after college; in 1973, after her husband state Representative Peter Snowe died in an auto accident, she was elected to his seat in the legislature. In 1978, when then-Congressman Bill Cohen ran for the Senate, she ran for the House in the northern 2d District, and won. She made a moderate record on issues and won by large margins in the 1980s but more narrowly in the 1990s; in 1989 she married Governor John McKernan, her former House colleague. Her voting record has been fairly conservative on economics, rather liberal on cultural issues, a tough partisan on many Republican issues.

Snowe decided instantly to run for the Senate when George Mitchell announced his retirement in March 1994. Immediately she went on the attack against her obvious Democratic opponent, 1st District Congressman Tom Andrews. Two years before, Andrews's margin had been 107,000 votes and hers only 22,000. Snowe attacked him hard for voting for the base-closing bill that closed Loring Air Force Base in northern Maine and for opposing the balanced budget amendment. Andrews attacked her for anti-education votes, but made no impact. Snowe won 60%–36%, carrying every county, losing only Portland, Lewiston and a few mill towns.

In the Senate she was the least conservative of the 11 freshman Republicans elected in 1994. She has supported Republican positions on most economic issues, calling for a balanced budget, but also has backed abortion rights and family leave. She accused Democrats of practicing the "politics of fear" on Medicare. "Our vision for America in the next century is one of fiscal responsibility combined with compassion and vision," she said. She worked on many local issues, establishing a pilot $25 million fishing vessel buyback, passing a "Maine Lights" program to preserve historic Maine lighthouses, working to ban lobster dragging. To the telecommunications bill she and Nebraska's two senators added an amendment for affordable access to telecommunications for rural hospitals and health clinics. She proposed a tax credit for those who care for people with Alzheimer's disease.

Child support enforcement is one of Snowe's major causes, and on the welfare bill she called for retaining some federal role in Medicaid, and helped insert a provision requiring states to spend at least 80% of their old budgets and some $3 billion for childcare programs. She dissented on some other party positions; she was one of eight Republicans to vote for cloture on the Republican filibuster of a campaign finance reform bill in June 1996. She called for public Ethics Committee hearings on Bob Packwood in July 1995. At the 1996 Republican National Convention she was one of the most outspoken opponents of the party's abortion plank, protesting when Bob Dole agreed to drop the "toleration" language. In a 55–45 Republican Senate, Snowe obviously has important leverage to modify party positions with which she disagrees, and on many issues could have great influence. In 1996 Snowe was appointed "counsel" to Majority Whip Don Nickles, a new leadership position which puts her on a par with Chief Deputy Whip Judd Gregg. With her new assignment on Armed Services, she will continue to look out for Maine's defense interests. Snowe does not come up for reelection until 2000.

Junior Senator. Susan Collins, elected in 1996, brings to the Senate little experience in elective office and had not shown great vote-getting prowess. She won the seat held for 18 years by Republican William Cohen, moderate on economics, sometimes liberal on cultural issues, a hardliner on defense, who surprised almost everyone when he announced in January 1996 that he was retiring from what was a very safe seat, and then surprised many again in December 1996 when he agreed to become Bill Clinton's Secretary of Defense.

Susan Collins grew up in Caribou, Maine, in potato-growing Aroostook County, about as far northeast as you can get in the United States. Right after college, she got a job as an intern with Senator Cohen, and stayed on his staff for 12 years and served as the staff director for the Senate Sucommittee on Oversight Government Management, which Cohen chaired from 1981–87. Collins returned to Maine to work five years for Governor John McKernan as a financial regulation commissioner. In 1992 she was New England administrator of the Small Business Administration, and by 1994 she had announced her candidacy for governor. It was a disastrous campaign: she won the Republican nomination, but was overshadowed by Independent Angus

King, and ran third, with only 23% of the vote. Afterwards, Collins became the executive director of the Husson College Center for Family Business.

There is a precedent in Maine for a third-place gubernatorial finisher to be elected senator: George Mitchell was similarly humiliated in 1974, then, after being appointed senator in 1980, won smashing victories in 1982 and 1988. In 1996, Collins had a chance to repeat Mitchell's feat in what some considered an odd race. If Collins and several other contenders seemed to have thin credentials, two others had faces that were perhaps too familiar. The most visible candidate in the Republican primary was Robert Monks, an entrepreneur and business owner who had run against two senators, Margaret Chase Smith in the 1972 primary and Edmund Muskie in the 1976 general; he lost with 67%–33% and 60%–40% respectively. In 1996 he spent $2.1 million—a huge sum for a Maine primary—but got nowhere. He made his biggest headlines when he brought up the fact that another Republican candidate, state Senator W. John Hathaway, had been investigated in Alabama for improper sex with a young babysitter; Hathaway bellowed in outrage, but the incident seems to have hurt both he and Monks. Meanwhile Collins was proclaiming, "I'm similar to Olympia Snowe and Bill Cohen." She supported the balanced budget amendment, line-item veto, term limits (and pledged to serve no more than two terms), welfare run by the states (this was before Congress passed its third welfare reform bill and Clinton signed it). She was also pro-choice on abortion. Collins won the primary with 56%, carrying at least 50% in every county, to 31% for Hathaway and only 13% for Monks.

The other familiar face belonged to Democrat Joseph Brennan, a product of working class Portland, first elected to the legislature in 1964, elected governor in 1978 and 1982, then to Congress in 1986 and 1988. But he lost races for governor in 1990, with 44%, and 1994, with 34%, though finishing well ahead of Collins. One Democratic activist was quoted as calling him "an old-time, backroom Democratic politician"—somewhat unfairly, since he had been on the ballot and in the public eye for years—and the state party chairman asked him not to run. State Senator Sean Faircloth attacked him as a two-time loser no longer capable of winning a statewide election. But he could win a primary: he led Faircloth 57%–25%. And he argued that he was a fiscal conservative, backing the balanced budget amendment, the line-item veto, and term limits.

But for Brennan the going was uphill. More votes were cast in the Republican primary than the Democratic, for the first time since 1982; with the single exception of 1986, Democrats had not topped 50% in a governor race since 1966, and Independent King had won in 1994 with a platform much more Republican than Democratic. Brennan attacked Collins for backing only a 50-cent minimum wage increase and wanting to increase estate tax exemptions from $600,000 to $1 million and for favoring repeal of the assault weapons ban; he charged that Collins was supported by, and her position at Husson College endowed by, a principal in a firm manufacturing assault weapons. Collins responded by reiterating her stands and citing her experience with Cohen, and said "The next time you hear Joe speak, just close your eyes and ask yourself what year you're in. It could be 1964, the year he first ran. The world has changed, but Joe Brennan's ideas haven't." Both brought in luminaries to campaign—Barbara Bush and Hillary Rodham Clinton; Bill Clinton came in the night after a presidential debate. But Collins raised much more money and finished a bit ahead, winning 49%–44%, losing very narrowly the counties around Portland, Lewiston, and Augusta, and carrying everything else. Interestingly, she led among men and he led among women; Brennan ran strongly among the elderly, Collins among college graduates—suggesting that she had the wave of the future.

With Collins, Olympia Snowe, and Kay Bailey Hutchison of Texas, there are enough for a caucus of moderate Republican women in the Senate. Collins sought a seat on the Armed Services Committee, but was assigned to Labor and Human Resources and the Governmental Affairs Committees. She can be expected to vote much as Cohen did.

Presidential politics. Bill Clinton has now carried Maine twice, the second time with 52%; it seems that many of the 1980s Republican voters Ross Perot chipped away from George Bush have become Democrats. Or it may be that Maine, like the rest of the Northeast, simply doesn't like the southernness of the 1990s Republican Party. After all, it inflicted the humiliation on George Bush of having him finish third in 1992 in the state where he has spent every summer of his life except during World War II. Yet in races for governor and senator Maine now seems to be leaning toward Republicans. It is obviously risky to predict anything about the state which twice in a row has been Ross Perot's best state in the nation.

Maine held its first-ever presidential primary on March 5 in 1996, in an attempt to generate an early contest to which candidates would pay attention. But they didn't, much. Bill Clinton had no competition and Bob Dole clinched the Republican nomination three days earlier in South Carolina, and beat Pat Buchanan here 46%–24%.

Congressional districting. Maine waited until 1994 to redistrict for the 1990s. It hardly mattered: the lines have been almost exactly the same since the state lost its 3d District in the 1960 Census. The Republican legislature then wanted to split areas of Democratic strength; the result is that there is not much partisan difference between the southern 1st District and the northern 2d. Maine is one of two states (Nebraska is the other) where the electoral vote can be divided if one congressional district votes for a candidate who loses statewide.

The People: Est. Pop. 1996: 1,243,000; Pop. 1990: 1,227,928, up 1.3% 1990–1996. 0.5% of U.S. total, 39th largest; 55% rural. Median age: 36.6 years. 14% 65 years and over. 98.0% White, 1% Asian, 1% Amer. Indian, 1% Hispanic origin. Households: 58.1% married couple families; 28% married couple fams. w. children; 42% college educ.; median household income: $27,854; per capita income: $12,957; 70.5% owner occupied housing median house value: $87,400; median monthly rent: $358. 5.1% Unemployment. 1996 Voting age pop.: 945,000. 1996 Turnout: 679,499; 72% of VAP. Registered voters (1996): 1,001,292; 317,886 D (32%), 287,933 R (29%), 395,473 unaffiliated and minor parties (39%).

Political Lineup: Governor, Angus S. King Jr. (I); Secy. of State, Dan A. Gwadosky (D); Atty. Gen., Andrew Ketterer (D); Treasurer, Dale McCormick (D); Comptroller, Carol F. Whitney; Auditor, Gail Chase (D). State Senate, 35 (19 D, 15 R and 1 I); Senate President, Mark Lawrence (D); State House, 151 (81 D and 69 R); House Speaker, Elizabeth Mitchell (D). Senators, Olympia J. Snowe (R) and Susan Collins (R). Representatives, 2 (2 D).

Elections Division: 207-287-4186; **Filing Deadline for U.S. Congress:** March 16, 1998.

1996 Presidential Vote

Clinton (D)	312,788	(52%)
Dole (R)	186,378	(31%)
Perot (I)	85,970	(14%)
Other(s)	20,752	(3%)

1996 Republican Presidential Primary

Dole (R)	31,147	(46%)
Buchanan (R)	16,478	(24%)
Forbes (R)	9,991	(15%)
Alexander (R)	4,450	(7%)
Other	5,214	(8%)

1992 Presidential Vote

Clinton (D)	263,420	(39%)
Perot (I)	206,820	(30%)
Bush (R)	206,504	(30%)

GOVERNOR

Gov. Angus S. King, Jr. (I)

Elected 1994, term expires Jan. 1999; b. Mar. 31, 1944, Alexandria, VA; home, Brunswick; Dartmouth Col., A.B. 1966; U. of VA Law Schl., J.D. 1969; Episcopalian; married (Mary).

Career: Staff Atty., Pine Tree Legal Assistance, 1969–72; Chief Cnsl., U.S. Sen. William Hathaway, 1972–75; Practicing atty., 1975–83; Vice Pres. & Gen. Cnsl., Swift River/Hafslund Co., 1983–89; TV talk show host, 1975–93; Founder & Pres., Northeast Energy Management Inc., 1989–94.

Office: State House, Sta. 1, Augusta 04333, 207-287-3531; Fax: 207-287-1034; Web site: www.state.me.us.

Election Results

1994 gen.	Angus S. King, Jr. (I)	180,829	(35%)
	Joseph E. Brennan (D)	172,951	(34%)
	Susan M. Collins (R)	117,990	(23%)
	Jonathan K. Carter (Green)	32,695	(6%)
	Others	6,843	(1%)
1990 gen.	John R. McKernan, Jr. (R)	243,766	(47%)
	Joseph E. Brennan (D)	230,038	(44%)
	Andrew Adam (I)	48,377	(9%)

SENATORS

Sen. Olympia J. Snowe (R)

Elected 1994, seat up 2000; b. Feb. 21, 1947, Augusta; home, Auburn; U. of ME, B.A. 1969; Greek Orthodox; married (John R. McKernan).

Career: Dir., Superior Concrete Co.; Auburn Bd. of Voter Registration, 1971–73; ME House of Reps., 1973–76; ME Senate, 1976–78; U.S. House of Reps., 1978–94.

DC Office: 250 RSOB 20510, 202-224-5344; Fax: 202-224-1946; e-mail: olympia@snowe.senate.gov.

State Offices: Auburn, 207-786-2451; Augusta, 207-622-8292; Bangor, 207-945-0432; Biddeford, 207-282-4144; Portland, 207-874-0833; Presque Isle, 207-764-5124.

Committees: *Armed Services* (9th of 10 R): Acquisition & Technology; Personnel; Sea Power. *Budget* (8th of 12 R). *Commerce, Science & Transportation* (7th of 11 R): Aviation; Manufacturing & Competitiveness; Oceans & Fisheries (Chmn.); Surface Transportation & Merchant Marine. *Small Business* (8th of 10 R).

Group Ratings

	ADA	ACLU	AFS	LCV	CFA	CON	NFIB	COC	ACU	NTLC	CHC
1996	35	22	14	54	57	77	93	77	70	83	38
1995	40	—	27	64	44	96	—	84	39	—	—

National Journal Ratings

	1995 LIB — 1995 CONS			1996 LIB — 1996 CONS		
Economic	48%	—	50%	47%	—	52%
Social	59%	—	37%	58%	—	41%
Foreign	38%	—	57%	38%	—	58%

Key Votes of the 104th Congress

1. Reduce Medicare Growth $	Y	5. Flag Amendment	Y	9. Anti-Missile Defense	Y
2. Lmt. Prod. Liab. Damages	Y	6. Endangered Species	N	10. Cuban Embargo	Y
3. Increase Min. Wage	Y	7. Gay Employment Rights	Y	11. Bar Bosnia Troop $	N
4. Welfare Reform	Y	8. Ovrd. Part. Birth Veto	N	12. Cut Vietnam Aid	Y

Election Results

1994 general	Olympia J. Snowe (R)	308,244	(60%)	($2,041,834)
	Thomas H. Andrews (D)	186,042	(36%)	($1,482,060)
	Others	17,447	(3%)	
1994 primary	Olympia J. Snowe (R)	unopposed		
1988 general	George J. Mitchell (D)	452,590	(81%)	($1,471,426)
	Jasper S. Wyman (R)	104,758	(19%)	($147,760)

Sen. Susan M. Collins (R)

Elected 1996, seat up 2002; b. Dec. 7, 1952, Caribou; home, Bangor; St. Lawrence U., B.A. 1975; Catholic; single

Career: Legis. Aide, U.S. Sen. Bill Cohen, 1975–87, Staff Dir., Oversight of Government Mgmt. Subcmte., 1981–87; Professional & Financial Regulation Commissioner, 1987–92; New England Regional Dir., US Small Business Admin., 1992; MA Dep. Treasurer, 1993; Exec. Dir., Center for Family Business, Husson Col., 1994–96.

DC Office: 171 RSOB 20510, 202-224-2523; Fax: 202-224-2693; e-mail: senator@collins.senate.gov.

State Offices: Augusta, 207-622-8414; Bangor, 207-945-0417; Biddeford, 207-283-1101; Lewiston, 207-784-6969; Portland, 207-780-3575; Presque Isle, 207-764-3266.

Committees: *Governmental Affairs* (2nd of 9 R): International Security, Proliferation & Federal Services; Permanent Subcommittee on Investigations (Chmn.). *Labor & Human Resources* (8th of 10 R): Children & Families; Public Health & Safety. *Aging (Special)* (9th of 10 R).

Group Ratings and Key Votes: Newly Elected

Election Results

1996 general	Susan M. Collins (R)	298,422	(49%)	($1,621,475)
	Joseph E. Brennan (D)	266,226	(44%)	($976,805)
	Others	42,129	(7%)	
1996 primary	Susan M. Collins (R)	53,339	(56%)	
	W. John Hathaway (R)	29,792	(31%)	
	Robert A.G. Monks (R)	12,943	(13%)	
1990 general	William S. Cohen (R)	319,167	(61%)	($1,628,292)
	Neil Rolde (D)	201,053	(39%)	($1,630,894)

FIRST DISTRICT

The 1st District of Maine stretches from southernmost Kittery and nearby Kennebunkport to the craggy-shored ancestrally Republican counties to the east. The historic center is Portland, birthplace of poet Henry Wadsworth Longfellow, and now Maine's largest city, home to the yuppies and lawyers that have revived and renovated its downtown landmarks. Most voters in the 1st District, except those far Down East, live within a couple hours drive of the Maine Mall—just off the Maine Turnpike and I-295 and near the airport—the state's heaviest concentration of retail and office space. Politically, the 1st votes very much like the state as a whole, quirkily, often for Independents, splitting tickets with abandon. From 1968–94 it elected three Democrats and three Republicans, with each side serving 14 years.

The congressman from the 1st District now is Tom Allen, a Democrat, who defeated freshman Republican James Longley in 1996. Allen is a native of Portland, where his grandfather and father served on the city council. He was class president in high school and college, and at Bowdoin challenged fraternities because they wouldn't admit blacks. He was a Rhodes Scholar in Oxford the same years as Bill Clinton, Robert Reich, and Strobe Talbott, and when he returned he got a job on the staff of Edmund Muskie. But he dropped out of politics, went to law school, practiced law in Portland, and worked on charities and community service. In 1989 he was elected to the Portland City Council, and in 1991 rotated into the position of mayor; he started a program of low-interest loans to businesses locating in downtown. In 1994 he ran for governor, and ran a distant second to Joseph Brennan in the Democratic primary, with 24%.

The 1st District race was an obvious next step, and an attractive opportunity. Freshman James Longley had a well-known name as son of the Independent elected governor in 1974, and he had won the 1994 race 52%–48%, though heavily outspent by Senate President Dennis Dutremble. Longley supported the Contract with America though overall he had a moderate voting record. But he was targeted by the AFL-CIO, which spent over $1 million on Portland TV ads charging, among other things, that he voted to "cut" Medicare. And the League of Conservation Voters, which gave him a 31% rating on their charts, named him as one of their "Dirty Dozen," because he had voted for Contract measures limiting EPA's powers and softening some provisions of the Clean Water Act. Yet even though he was under fierce attack, as late as October 1996 Longley said he was "hardly paying attention" to the looming campaign season.

Allen had competition in the Democratic primary from state Senator Dale McCormick, who is openly lesbian and brought her partner and their daughter to the podium at the state Democratic convention. Supported by feminist groups, talking about the Women Unlimited program she started to get women off welfare with job training, she held Allen to a 52%–48% win; only home town strength put him over. In the general, Allen sounded the themes already made familiar by the AFL-CIO and LCV. He favored "incremental steps" toward a single-payer healthcare finance system; he said Longley's votes "would have brought us dirtier air and dirtier water" and would have slowed the cleanup of Casco Bay. "Pure nonsense," Longley replied. Allen charged that the Republican followed Newt Gingrich rather than people in Maine, that he would cut college loans and education funding. The candidates took opposite stands on capital punishment, partial-birth abortions, term limits, the balanced budget amendment. Allen called for scaling back a Republican $10 billion increase in defense spending; Longley pointed out it included a Navy destroyer to be built at the Bath Iron Works, and Allen backtracked and said he would of course support Maine defense contracts.

Allen led by wide margins in polls throughout the campaign, and the biggest surprise may not have been that Longley lost but that the margin was only 10 points—a 55%–45% win for Allen. Many observers give credit for the result to the AFL-CIO or to environmentalists; and clearly they deserve some. But it should also be added that Longley, though an incumbent, allowed his opponent to raise more money, and that he may have allowed himself to become too preoccupied with legislating in Washington and not enough involved in campaigning in Maine. Allen seems likely to be one of the more liberal of the 1996 freshmen. Among his interesting proposals during the campaign were IRAs for education, a national bottle-return bill, a refundable deposit on batteries, and a bill banning discrimination against gays and lesbians.

The People: Pop. 1990: 636,528; 51% rural; 13% age 65+; 98% White; 1% Asian; 1% Hispanic origin. Households: 59% married couple families; 28% married couple fams. w. children; 47% college educ.; median household income: $30,952; per capita income: $14,362; median gross rent: $474; median house value: $106,400.

1996 Presidential Vote

Clinton (D)	165,053	(52%)
Dole (R)	100,851	(32%)
Perot (I)	39,845	(13%)
Other(s)	11,372	(4%)

1992 Presidential Vote

Clinton (D)	145,191	(40%)
Bush (R)	115,697	(32%)
Perot (I)	102,828	(28%)

Rep. Tom Allen (D)

Elected 1996; b. April 16, 1945, Portland; home, Portland; Bowdoin Col., B.A. 1967; Rhodes Scholar, Oxford U., B. Phil. 1970; Harvard U., J.D. 1974; Protestant; married (Diana)

Career: Intern, Gov. Kenneth B. Curtis, 1968; Staff, U.S. Sen. Edmund S. Muskie, 1970–71; Practicing atty., 1974–94; Portland City Cncl., 1989–95; Portland Mayor, 1991; Chmn., ME Clinton-Gore Campaign, 1992; Public Policy Consultant, 1995.

DC Office: 1630 LHOB 20515, 202-225-6116; Fax: 225-5590; e-mail: rep.tomallen@mail.house.gov.

District Offices: Portland, 207-774-5019.

Committees: *Government Reform & Oversight* (19th of 19 D): District of Columbia; Human Resources. *National Security* (17th of 25 D): Military Procurement; Military Research & Development.

Group Ratings and Key Votes: Newly Elected

Election Results

1996 general	Thomas H. Allen (D)	173,745	(55%)	($933,425)
	James B. Longley, Jr. (R)	140,354	(45%)	($906,432)
1996 primary	Thomas H. Allen (D)	26,182	(52%)	
	Dale McCormick (D)	24,527	(48%)	
1994 general	James B. Longley, Jr. (R)	136,316	(52%)	($196,048)
	Dennis L. Dutremble (D)	126,373	(48%)	($514,071)

SECOND DISTRICT

The 2d District covers the northern three-quarters of the acreage of Maine. The population is not evenly distributed, however: the district dips south to include the heavily Democratic mill town of Lewiston and reaches to Belfast on Penobscot Bay. There are several different Maines here: the bays of coastal Maine, with their small fishing towns, the potato fields of far northern

Aroostook County, the mill towns on the fast-running streams of western Maine, penned in between mountains. This was one of America's frontiers in the 1850s, when Bangor on the Penobscot River was the lumber capital of the world; today it is the largest city in the district. This part of Maine has had its economic troubles: potato production is only half what it was in 1980; Loring Air Force Base was closed in 1994. Politically this is protest country. This was Ross Perot's strongest district in the United States in 1992 and 1996: he finished a solid second here in 1992, with 33%, and a much reduced 16% in 1996.

The congressman from the 2d District is John Baldacci, a Democrat elected in 1994, indeed one of only four Democrats elected to replace a Republican that year (in his case, Olympia Snowe, who was elected to the Senate). Baldacci has deep local roots. He grew up in Bangor, where his family ran Momma Baldacci's, a restaurant started by his grandparents in 1933; he is of Italian and Lebanese descent, distantly related to former Senator George Mitchell, and the family restaurant used to get a daily delivery of rolls from former Senator William Cohen's father's bakery. He followed his father on the Bangor City Council in 1978, at 23; in 1982, he was elected to the state Senate, where he often dissented from Democrats, chairing the tax committee. He is unassuming, unbombastic, earnest; he campaigned for the House seat in 1994 by holding spaghetti dinners at $2 a head (children under 12 free) around the district. In a seven-candidate primary, with lots of support around Bangor, Baldacci won with 27% to 23% for former Democratic state chairman James Mitchell, George Mitchell's nephew. The Republican nominee was Richard Bennett, who won 30% in a four-way primary with a base in western Maine. Baldacci opposed the Clinton healthcare plan; Bennett was iffy about the Contract With America's defense spending increase; both were pressed by Green and Independent Party candidates, who ended up winning 5% and 9% respectively. Baldacci ran ads showing himself as manager of the restaurant and calling for more jobs ("I'm not going to skimp on the sauce or jobs for Maine"); he pledged to support no new taxes and was proud of running no negative ads. Baldacci won with 46% to Bennett's 41%. Bennett carried the western area and much of the coast, but Baldacci won solidly in Aroostook and carried the Bangor area as well.

In the House Baldacci compiled a mostly liberal record, though he voted for versions of the balanced budget amendment, line-item veto, term limits. He stirred debate on local editorial pages when he voted for repeal of the assault weapons ban. He sponsored a bill to help Maine exports. He worked on local projects—a second pier for Eastport, the Bates Complex in Lewiston, a magnet school at the former Loring Air Force Base. He brought the Agriculture Committee to Aroostook County for a hearing after Maine farmers were blocking the border to protest subsidized Canadian potato exports.

In the 104th Congress, a freshman Democrat had little clout. But Baldacci worked hard to get around the district, holding more spaghetti dinners and listening to constituents. In 1996 he was reelected by a huge margin—the first convincing win for anyone in this district in the 1990s.

The People: Pop. 1990: 591,400; 60% rural; 13% age 65+; 98% White; 1% Amer. Indian; 1% Hispanic origin. Households: 60% married couple families; 28% married couple fams. w. children; 36% college educ.; median household income: $24,672; per capita income: $11,446; median gross rent: $365; median house value: $66,500.

1996 Presidential Vote

Clinton (D)	147,735	(51%)
Dole (R)	85,527	(30%)
Perot (I)	46,125	(16%)
Other	9,380	(3%)

1992 Presidential Vote

Clinton (D)	118,229	(38%)
Perot (I)	103,992	(33%)
Bush (R)	90,807	(29%)

Rep. John Elias Baldacci (D)

Elected 1994; b. Jan. 30, 1955, Bangor; home, Bangor; U. of ME, B.A. 1986; Catholic; married (Karen).

Career: Restauranteur; Bangor City Cncl., 1978–81; ME Senate, 1982–94.

DC Office: 1740 LHOB 20515, 202-225-6306; Fax: 202-225-2943; e-mail: baldacci@hr.house.gov.

District Offices: Bangor, 207-942-6935; Lewiston, 207-782-3704; Presque Isle, 207-764-1036.

Committees: *Agriculture* (15th of 23 D): Forestry, Resource Conservation & Research; Risk Management & Specialty Crops. *Small Business* (6th of 16 D): Tax, Finance & Exports (RMM).

Group Ratings

	ADA	ACLU	AFS	LCV	CFA	CON	NFIB	COC	ACU	NTLC	CHC
1996	80	56	100	77	92	82	35	31	10	17	13
1995	90	—	—	75	85	16	—	33	20	—	—

National Journal Ratings

	1995 LIB	—	1995 CONS	1996 LIB	—	1996 CONS
Economic	71%	—	28%	79%	—	18%
Social	75%	—	23%	75%	—	24%
Foreign	84%	—	15%	70%	—	29%

Key Votes of the 104th Congress

1. Reduce Medicare Growth $	N	5. Flag Amendment	Y	9. Cuban Embargo	N
2. Ovrd. Product Liab. Veto	N	6. Drop EPA Limits	Y	10. Bar Bosnia Troop $	N
3. Increase Min. Wage	Y	7. Repeal Assault-Weap. Ban	Y	11. Cut Anti-Missile Defense	Y
4. Welfare Reform	N	8. Ovrd. Part. Birth Veto	N	12. Bar U.N. Uniforms	Y

Election Results

1996 general	John Elias Baldacci (D)	205,439	(72%)	($581,219)
	Paul R. Young (R)	70,856	(25%)	($154,653)
	Others	9,341	(3%)	
1996 primary	John Elias Baldacci (D)	unopposed		
1994 general	John Elias Baldacci (D)	109,615	(46%)	($442,226)
	Richard A. Bennett (R)	97,754	(41%)	($258,813)
	John M. Michael (I)	21,117	(9%)	($33,486)
	Charles FitzGerald (Green)	11,353	(5%)	($647)

MARYLAND

Maryland, at the midpoint of the 13 Colonies, just south of the Mason-Dixon Line and north of the lines between Union and Confederacy, can lay claim to being the typical American state, yet stands out for its particularities. This was the only one of the 13 colonies founded by Roman Catholics—the Calvert family—and its embrace of religious tolerance came less from abstract principle than from the Calverts' desire to protect their property from Protestant monarchs. It was one of the two big Chesapeake colonies, overshadowed by Virginia, but with the same tobacco economy—one that traded directly with Britain. In time, Virginia and Maryland went their separate ways, Virginia to become the capital of the Confederacy, Maryland to remain part of the Union, though grudgingly ("Maryland, My Maryland" condemns Abraham Lincoln's suppression of pro-Confederate rioters), and to become identified with the North.

The puritan impulse never was lively here: Prohibition was enforced only laxly in Baltimore, to the delight of its great journalist-cum-lexicographer, H.L. Mencken; slot machines were legal in the rural counties of the Western Shore. The state's law guaranteeing blacks equal access to public accommodations specifically excluded the Eastern Shore. By not pursuing any one course rigorously, Maryland could be many things at once: northern as well as southern, moralistic as well as libertine, industrial as well as rural, leaving people to their own devices yet with a heavy government presence. Perhaps as a result, much of Maryland's political history reads like a chronicle of rogues, from Luther Martin, the drunken haranguer at the Constitutional Convention, to Spiro Agnew, who took cash bribes as governor and vice president and resigned in 1973.

Maryland's genial tolerance may have given it a little too savory a history, but this state, perhaps because it is in so many ways typical, cherishes its sense of uniqueness. The Chesapeake Bay, for example, is the nation's largest estuary, with water saltier than a river but fresher than the ocean, with its unique watermen and shellfish. The terrapin and Chesapeake oyster may be so endangered as to be rare today, but Maryland blue crabs are still common, and the rockfish, once dwindling, can now be fished. Maryland likes its state bird (the Baltimore oriole), state flower (the black-eyed Susan), state dog (the Chesapeake Bay retriever), even if today's political correctness has made it convenient to forget the words to "Maryland, My Maryland."

Maryland also has some reason to be proud of the economy, or economies, it has built over the years. Half a century ago, half the state's population lived in the city of Baltimore and only one-fifth in suburbs. Now the proportions are the other way around, and then some: 15% Baltimore, 65% suburbs. And in 1992, the Census Bureau defined Washington and Baltimore as a single metropolitan area, the fourth largest in the country, with more than six million people. But this is a case of statistical definition at odds with practical reality. Baltimore and Washington are not fraternal, if sometimes quarrelsome, twins like Dallas and Fort Worth or Minneapolis and St. Paul; they are two quite separate cities, with different economic bases, and different attitudes toward public life. Baltimore started off as a port and an industrial city, and has managed to stay diversified and successful as it has spread out into the countryside from its new central core at the Inner Harbor and the solidly built edifices of its downtown grid streets. It has raised private money to rebuild the 142-year-old *U.S.S. Constellation*; it makes spices and writes insurance; it headquarters one of the nation's giant power tool makers, Black & Decker, and one of its great investment banks, Alex Brown & Sons. It has big government operations, the headquarters of the Social Security Administration and, quietly down the road, the National Security Agency. It is home to the Orioles in their new, intentionally old-fashioned Oriole Park at Camden Yards and to Johns Hopkins University in Georgian buildings along the affluent corridor that runs directly north from downtown all the way to the developing edge city of Hunt Valley. "Bawlmer" retains its local accent and a fierce local pride, and is celebrated by artists as vivid in

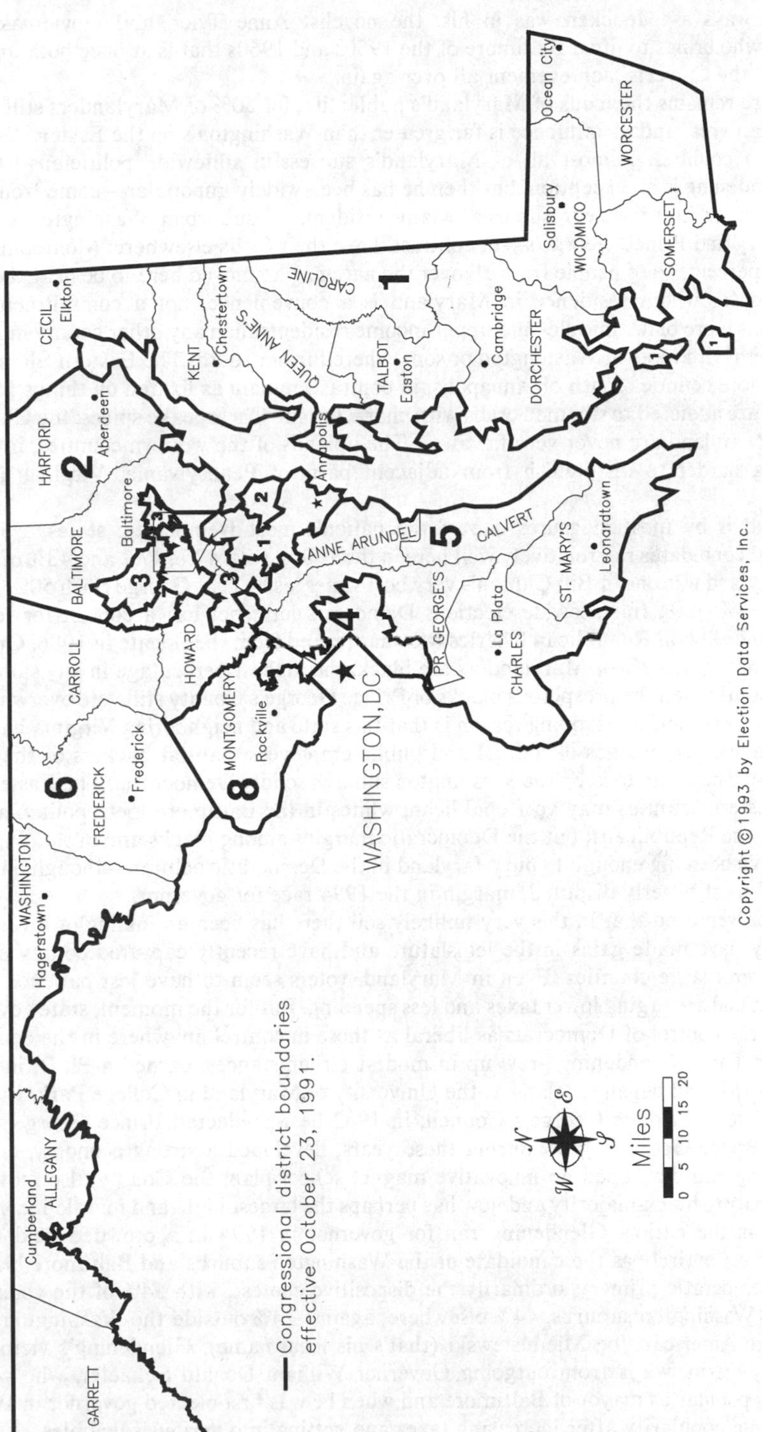

— Congressional district boundaries effective October 23, 1991.

their own ways as Mencken was in his: the novelist Anne Tyler, and moviemaker Barry Levinson, who brings to life a Baltimore of the 1950s and 1960s that is at once both unique and universal—the Calverts' achievement all over again.

Baltimore remains the focus of Maryland's public life, for 50% of Marylanders still live in its metropolitan area, and its influence is far greater than Washington's on the Eastern Shore or in the western counties. Almost all of Maryland's successful statewide politicians—Governor Parris Glendening is an exception, but then he has been widely unpopular—come from the city of Baltimore or its very near suburbs. Many residents of suburban Washington counties—Montgomery and Prince George's—in contrast, have their focus elsewhere: Montgomery has a very large percentage of people from all over the nation, who moved here to be near the nation's capital and for whom residence in Maryland is a convenience, not a commitment; Prince George's has more black middle- and upper-income residents than any other county in America, most of them with roots in Washington or somewhere farther south. The Eastern Shore and the Western Shore counties south of Annapolis, in contrast, remain as fixated on things Maryland-ish as they are addicted to steamed crabs with characteristic Chesapeake spices: the Chesapeake origins of Maryland are never very far away. The uplands of the western counties, in contrast, are getting harder to distinguish from adjacent parts of Pennsylvania, Virginia and West Virginia.

Maryland is by most measures one of the nation's most Democratic states. Democratic presidential candidates ran relatively well here in the 1980s, with 47%, 47% and 48% of the vote; twice, Maryland was one of Bill Clinton's very best states, as he beat George Bush 50%–36% and Bob Dole 54%–38%. In statewide elections Democrats have not lost a contest for senator or governor since liberal Republican Charles Mathias retired from the Senate in 1986. One reason for this is that some 27% of Marylanders are black, the highest percentage in any state outside the Deep South; even the prosperous blacks of Prince George's County still vote overwhelmingly Democratic. Another, overlapping reason is that this state and neighboring Virginia have by far the two highest percentages of federal and public employees, natural backers of the party of government. They help to keep the Washington suburbs solidly Democratic. The Eastern Shore and the western counties may go Republican; whites in the Baltimore metropolitan area may often favor the Republicans; but the Democratic margins among blacks and in the Washington suburbs have been big enough to put Maryland in the Democratic column—though only by the barest, and most bitterly disputed, margin in the 1994 race for governor.

It may be ventured that in this very unlikely soil there has been an inkling of a Republican trend. They have made gains in the legislature and have recently captured county executive posts in several large counties. Even in Maryland, voters seem to have lost patience with big government and are urging lower taxes and less spending. But for the moment, state government remains in the control of Democrats as liberal as those in control anywhere in the country.

Governor. Parris Glendening grew up in modest circumstances, earned a Ph.D. in political science in 1967, and began teaching at the University of Maryland in College Park. In 1974 he was elected to the Prince George's Council; in 1982 he was elected Prince George's County executive. Prince George's grew during these years, developed a strong economy, dealt with school busing and developed an innovative magnet school plan; the County also moved from white-majority to black-majority and now has perhaps the largest high- and middle-income black population in the nation. Glendening ran for governor in 1994 in a crowded field and won election almost entirely as the candidate of the Washington suburbs and Baltimore blacks. He took the Democratic primary, ordinarily the dispositive contest, with 54% of the vote; he won 75% in the Washington suburbs, 44% elsewhere, against 24% outside the Washington area for second-place American Joe Miedusiewski (that's his legal name). Glendening's victory came without any warm words from outgoing Governor William Donald Schaefer, who was overwhelmingly popular as mayor of Baltimore and when he was first elected governor in 1986, and who lost some popularity after increasing taxes and getting into various squabbles.

Indeed, Schaefer's favorite candidate was probably Republican Congresswoman Helen

Delich Bentley, a longtime reporter who covered the Baltimore docks, as tough as nails and something of a liberal on economic issues. But Bentley was upset in the Republican primary, 52%–38%, by Ellen Sauerbrey, House of Delegates minority leader for eight years, who called for a 24% tax cut, limiting state spending growth to the growth rate of the state's economy and passing a constitutional amendment to require a two-thirds vote to approve any sales or income tax increase. For four years she built support around the state, outside the range of most reporters. Her September primary victory and Republican legislative candidates' October Contract With Maryland pledge gave her candidacy oomph, and it failed only after extraordinary—some have charged illegal—political actions by Democrats. One was a purge of the Baltimore City polls directed at affluent and white voters. Another was an attorney general's ruling counting Republican Party spending against her total public financing. A third was quick reporting of some 9,000 votes that put Glendening over the top on election night, followed by a court decision blocking Republicans' access to the records for a week. Sauerbrey tried to gather evidence of fraud and appeared at the Republican Governors' Association meetings as governor-elect. Her findings fell well short of convincing evidence that the election was stolen, but did raise disturbing questions. Glendening won with 63% of the vote in metro Washington, while losing the rest of the state; metro Baltimore went 52% for Sauerbrey. Glendening won 90% among blacks, 75% in Baltimore City, 68% in Prince George's and 59% in Montgomery; Sauerbrey carried the other 19 counties.

In office Glendening has been the most pro-government governor in the country and, in 1996 polls at least, the least popular. He is also one of the most anti-tobacco, ironic considering Maryland's history as a tobacco colony. He proposed doubling the cigarette tax from 36 to 72 cents (which would probably send a lot of purchasers across state boundaries, which are seldom more than a few dozen miles away in any direction) and he aggressively and successfully promoted a ban on smoking in public places. One major project was funding construction of football stadiums in Baltimore for the Ravens (formerly Cleveland's Browns) and Prince George's County for the Washington Redskins. He promoted gun control by passing a law allowing purchase of one gun per month. He switched on one issue and opposed slot machines at race tracks. In fall 1996 Glendening continued welfare benefits for illegal aliens and called for a $170 million program to buy up open space to prevent urban sprawl. But he also called for a 10% income tax rate cut—a sharp change in position.

There was no electoral test of Glendening's popularity in 1996: Maryland elects its legislators as well as its governor for four-year terms. There has been talk that Speaker Casper Taylor, long an advocate of a tax cut, will run against him in the 1998 primary. And Ellen Sauerbrey seems likely to be the Republican nominee in the general.

Senior Senator. Paul Sarbanes was first elected to the Maryland House of Delegates in 1966, to the House in 1970, to the Senate in 1976: three decades as a legislator. His liberalism is rooted in his experience growing up in Salisbury on the Eastern Shore, the son of a Greek immigrant who owned the Mayflower Grill and taught himself enough on the side to discuss philosophy with his son's Princeton professors. As a big-firm lawyer in Baltimore, Paul Sarbanes got started in local politics campaigning in small groups, talking to voters and leaders, listening gravely to what they had to say. Tabbed early as a reformer, in the state legislature he voted against Marvin Mandel to replace Spiro Agnew as governor in 1969—not the most politic move. He beat a long-time incumbent in the primary to win a House seat in 1970 and in 1976 defeated former Senator Joseph Tydings in the primary and incumbent Senator Glenn Beall in the general by 59%–41%.

Since then Sarbanes has been one of the most durable champions of liberal politics: on the Budget Committee, as chair of the Joint Economic Committee from 1991–95, and on the Banking Committee, of which he would have become chairman in 1995 if Democrats had not lost their majority in the Senate. He long argued that the economic growth of the 1980s was illusory or confined to the rich and proposed countercyclical measures to the 1990–91 recession. He wants more political control of the Federal Reserve and to take the 12 regional bank presidents off the Open Market Committee. "We've been through 12 years of sheer torture," he said in 1992, but must have been disappointed by the sour reaction to the Clinton tax increase and the administration's acquiescence in the policies of the Greenspan Federal Reserve. He was one of just 21 senators who voted against the 1996 Welfare Reform Act. On foreign policy Sarbanes has been skeptical of foreign military involvement and eager for nuclear disarmament. He is second ranking Democrat on the Foreign Relations Committee, where he worked on reauthorizing foreign aid and has tilted toward Greece and away from aid to Turkey.

For many years Sarbanes seemed to be, in Republicans' words, a "stealth senator," sponsoring few bills and sending out few press releases. But he has always lived in Baltimore and after 1994 he started attending more civic and political events throughout Maryland. "If you're in the minority, you're getting frustrated a lot of the time, and you figure, [one] might as well get out in the state and really see sort of what's going on." In his quieter years he was reelected easily in 1982 and 1988 with 63% and 62%, carrying Baltimore area whites and blacks and running mostly on party lines elsewhere—stronger around his boyhood home of Salisbury. In 1994 he had an experienced opponent in former Senator Bill Brock, elected to the House in 1962 and the Senate in 1970 from Tennessee, later Republican National Committee chairman and U.S. trade representative. But Brock won his primary unimpressively over Montgomery County developer Ruthann Aron, 38%–26%, dodging complaints that he was a carpetbagger (he moved to Annapolis in 1988 and started paying Maryland taxes in 1990). Sarbanes won 59%–41%, slightly less than in the 1980s, but still convincingly. His 1994 margin was greatest in metro Washington, and he carried metro Baltimore as well.

Sarbanes has been mentioned as a possible Supreme Court nominee, but he seems happy serving out his term, which will make him the longest-serving Maryland senator ever, and he seems likely to run again. Competition could come from 2d District Congressman Bob Ehrlich, who must hope to cut into Sarbanes's Baltimore area strength.

Junior Senator. Barbara Mikulski came to the Senate with deep roots in immigrant, urban America and, more than most there, she seems fascinated by the new technology and jobs growing on the outer edges of the urban areas, many of which are held by people with backgrounds like her own. Her roots are in east Baltimore, where her Polish immigrant parents ran a bakery. She got her start in politics as a social worker, organizing in Highlandtown to stop a highway from going through. She won, and in the process was elected to the Baltimore City Council in 1971, in time to serve (and spar) with the then new mayor, Donald Schaefer. As a local official with genuine ethnic roots and a woman with genuine liberal impulses, she was chosen head of the Democratic National Committee's Commission on Delegate Selection in 1972. She ran for the Senate in 1974, and got a respectable 43% against incumbent Charles Mathias; when Paul Sarbanes ran for the other Senate seat in 1976, Mikulski ran for his 3d District seat and won. Ten years later, she gave up that seat for what seemed like a chancy Senate race, and won handily, with 50% in the primary to 31% for Montgomery County Congressman Michael Barnes and 14% for Governor Harry Hughes. In the general, she beat former White House aide Linda Chavez, 61%–39%.

Mikulski is loud and brash, humorous and warm, brusque and aggressive when she feels it is necessary, curious and thoughtful when encountering another new part of the world. She knows Baltimore well and still lives in the restored Fells Point neighborhood on the waterfront. Fells Point and Don Schaefer's Harborplace, she points out, stand where the highway she opposed was supposed to pass. But she also became, thanks to the Appropriations subcommittee chairmanship she held for six years and lots of hard work, the Senate's chief superintendent of the space program and an enthusiast for space exploration. An ardent backer of the manned Space Station *Freedom* often attacked by other liberals, she has battled to keep it alive, despite her sympathy for veterans' and housing programs also funded by her subcommittee which tend to compete for funds. On foreign policy, she usually votes with the doves and opposed the Gulf war resolution, but was attentive even in the Cold War years to human rights violations in left-wing as well as right-wing countries.

On domestic policy, Mikulski is a liberal who insists that "where there are rights there are responsibilities" and has criticized fellow Democrats for being "angst-addicted." "Being politically effective means helping those who are not middle class get there through hard work and practicing self-help." With Sam Nunn she was the major backer of the national service bill that produced AmeriCorps in 1993. Of housing programs she said, "A series of complicated rules and boutique programs have rewarded the wrong kind of behavior and made housing projects Zip Codes of pathology." She supported workfare in the 1980s and voted for the Welfare Reform Act of 1996. "Without this bill, would poor children be better off? I'm not so sure. The current welfare system is dysfunctional. It needs a big wake-up call. The very nature of the system encourages a culture of poverty."

Mikulski has been a strong adversary of sexual harassment, defending Anita Hill in 1991, opposing the retirement of Admiral Frank Kelso with four-star rank because of Tailhook, blocking reappointment of Architect of the Capitol George White because of alleged employment discrimination, staying on the Ethics Committee to judge the case of Bob Packwood. In November 1996 she was the first member of Congress to visit Aberdeen Proving Grounds, where 34 women filed sexual abuse and harassment charges against training instructors, and demanded that Joint Chiefs Chairman John Shalikashvili investigate sexual harassment throughout the military. But she is not concerned only with career women: with Republican Kay Bailey Hutchison she sponsored a bill to encourage homemaker IRAs.

Mikulski is part of the leadership, elected caucus secretary in 1994 and 1996. She has used her Appropriations seat to help Maryland projects, from the National Institutes of Health in Bethesda to the Baltimore Veterans Affairs program to the Goddard Space Flight Center in Prince George's County to a new $130 million marine biotechnology center in Baltimore. Mikulski's skills are not just political. She co-authored *Capitol Offense* with Marylouise Oates, a mystery novel describing freshman Senator Eleanor Gorzack of Pennsylvania, who is "somewhat younger, somewhat slimmer, but no less politically savvy than I am"—and also 5'4", five inches taller than the 4'11" Mikulski.

In 1992 Mikulski faced Republican Alan Keyes, a former Reagan appointee who ran against Sarbanes in 1988 and in 1996 ran for president. A fiery speaker who argues that American civilization is being destroyed by the disintegration of the American family, Keyes got little attention in Maryland, and Mikulski won with 71%. She is a heavy favorite to win reelection in 1998.

Presidential politics. Maryland is one of the most Democratic states in presidential elections. It voted for Jimmy Carter in 1980, came close to voting for Walter Mondale and Michael Dukakis in 1984 and 1988 and was one of Bill Clinton's best states in the 1990s. In 1992 it was his third best state, after Arkansas and New York; in 1996, his 5th best, tied with Illinois at 54%.

In 1992, Maryland held its primary a week before Super Tuesday, on March 3, to avoid being ignored as it mostly was on Super Tuesday 1988. Paul Tsongas led Bill Clinton 41%–33%, with all his margin and more coming from suburban Baltimore and Montgomery County. In 1996, Maryland again held its primary a week before Super Tuesday, on March 5. Republicans gave Bob Dole a victory with 53%; Pat Buchanan was a distant second at 21%. Marylander Alan Keyes finished a dismal fifth, with 5%.

Congressional districting. Population movements to the suburbs and the Voting Rights Act mandate to maximize the number of black-majority districts made 1992 redistricting a politically wrenching process for Maryland. The legislature worked hard to create a new black-majority Prince George's County seat and still leave a Democratic district for House power Steny Hoyer; so far it has succeeded. The loser was Democrat Tom McMillen, who was put in with 1st District Republican Wayne Gilchrest and lost. That and the defeat of Beverly Byron in the 6th District primary removed the last conservative Democrats from the Maryland delegation and created a House delegation evenly balanced between the two parties.

The People: Est. Pop. 1996: 5,072,000; Pop. 1990: 4,781,468, up 6.1% 1990–1996. 2.0% of U.S. total, 19th largest; 19% rural. Median age: 34.9 years. 11% 65 years and over. 69.6% White, 24.6% Black, 2.9% Asian, 2.6% Hispanic origin. Households: 54.2% married couple families; 26% married couple fams. w. children; 50% college educ.; median household income: $39,386; per capita income: $17,730; 65.0% owner occupied housing; median house value: $116,500; median monthly rent: $473. 4.9% Unemployment. 1996 Voting age pop.: 3,820,000. 1996 Turnout: 1,780,870; 47% of VAP. Registered voters (1996): 2,577,200; 1,511,430 D (59%); 774,161 R (30%); 291,609 unaffiliated and minor parties (11%).

Political Lineup: Governor, Parris N. Glendening (D); Lt. Gov., Kathleen Kennedy Townsend (D); Secy. of State, John T. Willis (D); Atty. Gen., J. Joseph Curran, Jr. (D); Treasurer, Richard Dixon (D); Comptroller, Louis L. Goldstein (D). State Senate, 47 (32 D and 15 R); Senate President, Thomas V. Mike Miller Jr. (D); State House, 141 (100 D and 41 R); House Speaker, Casper R. Taylor Jr. (D). Senators, Paul S. Sarbanes (D) and Barbara A. Mikulski (D). Representatives, 8 (4 R and 4 D).

Board of Elections: 410-974-3711; **Filing Deadline for U.S. Congress:** July 6, 1998.

1996 Presidential Vote

Clinton (D)	966,208	(54%)
Dole (R)	681,530	(38%)
Perot (I)	115,812	(7%)

1992 Presidential Vote

Clinton (D)	988,571	(50%)
Bush (R)	707,094	(36%)
Perot (I)	281,414	(14%)

1996 Republican Presidential Primary

Dole (R)	135,522	(53%)
Buchanan (R)	53,585	(21%)
Forbes (R)	32,207	(13%)
Alexander (R)	14,061	(6%)
Keyes (R)	13,718	(5%)
Other	5,153	(2%)

GOVERNOR

Gov. Parris N. Glendening (D)

Elected 1994, term expires Jan. 1999; b. June 11, 1942, Bronx, NY; home, University Park; FL St. U., B.A. 1964, M.A. 1965, Ph.D. 1967; Catholic; married (Frances).

Career: Prof., U. of MD, 1967–94; Hyattsville City Cncl., 1973–74; Prince George's Cnty. Council, 1974–82; Prince George's Cnty. Exec., 1982–94.

Office: State House, Annapolis 21401, 410-974-3901; Fax: 410-974-3275; Web site: www.mec.state.md.us/mec.

Election Results

1994 gen.	Parris N. Glendening (D)	708,094	(50%)
	Ellen R. Sauerbrey (R)	702,101	(50%)
1994 prim.	Parris N. Glendening (D)	293,314	(54%)
	American Joe Miedusiewski (D)	100,326	(18%)
	Melvin Steinberg (D)	82,308	(15%)
	Mary Boergers (D)	46,888	(9%)
	Others	24,567	(4%)
1990 gen.	William Donald Schaefer (D)	664,015	(60%)
	William S. Shepard (R)	446,980	(40%)

SENATORS

Sen. Paul S. Sarbanes (D)

Elected 1976, seat up 2000; b. Feb. 3, 1933, Salisbury; home, Baltimore; Princeton, A.B. 1954, Rhodes Scholar, Oxford U., B.A. 1957, Harvard, LL.B. 1960; Greek Orthodox; married (Christine).

Career: Law Clerk, Judge Morris A. Soper, U.S. 4th Circuit Crt. of Appeals, 1960–61; Practicing atty., 1961–62, 1965–70; A.A., Pres. Kennedy's Cncl. of Econ. Advisers, 1962–63; Exec. Dir., Baltimore Charter Revision Comm., 1963–64; MD House of Delegates, 1966–70; U.S. House of Reps., 1970–76.

DC Office: 309 HSOB 20510, 202-224-4524; Fax: 202-224-1651; e-mail: senator@sarbanes.senate.gov.

State Offices: Baltimore, 410-962-4436; Cobb Island, 301-259-2404; Cumberland, 301-724-0695; Salisbury, 410-860-2131; Silver Spring, 301-589-0797.

Committees: *Banking, Housing & Urban Affairs* (RMM of 8 D). *Budget* (4th of 10 D). *Foreign Relations* (2nd of 8 D): African Affairs; European Affairs; International Economic Policy, Export & Trade Promotion (RMM); Near Eastern & South Asian Affairs. *Joint Economic Committee* (8th of 10 Sens.).

Group Ratings

	ADA	ACLU	AFS	LCV	CFA	CON	NFIB	COC	ACU	NTLC	CHC
1996	95	44	100	100	93	4	28	23	0	3	7
1995	100	—	100	100	94	2	—	21	0	—	—

National Journal Ratings

	1995 LIB	—	1995 CONS	1996 LIB	—	1996 CONS
Economic	97%	—	0%	96%	—	0%
Social	75%	—	24%	80%	—	8%
Foreign	79%	—	15%	73%	—	24%

Key Votes of the 104th Congress

1. Reduce Medicare Growth $	N	5. Flag Amendment	N	9. Anti-Missile Defense	N
2. Lmt. Prod. Liab. Damages	N	6. Endangered Species	Y	10. Cuban Embargo	Y
3. Increase Min. Wage	Y	7. Gay Employment Rights	Y	11. Bar Bosnia Troop $	N
4. Welfare Reform	N	8. Ovrd. Part. Birth Veto	N	12. Cut Vietnam Aid	N

Election Results

1994 general	Paul S. Sarbanes (D)	809,125	(59%)	($2,767,187)
	William Brock (R)	559,908	(41%)	($3,201,650)
1994 primary	Paul S. Sarbanes (D)	382,115	(79%)	
	John B. Liston (D)	52,031	(11%)	
	Dennard A. Gayle (D)	30,665	(6%)	
	Leonard E. Trout (D)	19,393	(4%)	
1988 general	Paul S. Sarbanes (D)	999,166	(62%)	($1,466,477)
	Alan L. Keyes (R)	617,537	(38%)	($662,651)

Sen. Barbara A. Mikulski (D)

Elected 1986, seat up 1998; b. July 20, 1936, Baltimore; home, Baltimore; Mt. St. Agnes Col., B.A. 1958, U. of MD, M.S.W. 1965; Catholic; single.

Career: Social worker, admin., Baltimore Dept. of Social Svcs., 1965–70; Baltimore City Cncl., 1971–76; Adjunct prof., Loyola Col., 1972–76; Chmn., DNC Delegate Selection Comm., 1972; U.S. House of Reps., 1976–86.

DC Office: 709 HSOB 20510, 202-224-4654; Fax: 202-224-8858; e-mail: senator@mikulski.senate.gov.

State Offices: Annapolis, 410-263-1805; Baltimore, 410-962-4510; College Park, 301-345-5517; Hagerstown, 301-797-2826; Highlandtown, 410-563-4000; Salisbury, 410-546-7711.

Committees: *Appropriations* (8th of 13 D): Commerce, Justice, State & the Judiciary; Foreign Operations; Transportation; Treasury, Postal Service & General Government; VA, HUD & Independent Agencies (RMM). *Labor & Human Resources* (4th of 8 D): Aging (RMM); Public Health & Safety.

Group Ratings

	ADA	ACLU	AFS	LCV	CFA	CON	NFIB	COC	ACU	NTLC	CHC
1996	95	39	100	92	86	10	33	23	0	15	7
1995	90	—	100	86	75	16	—	39	4	—	—

National Journal Ratings

	1995 LIB — 1995 CONS	1996 LIB — 1996 CONS
Economic	83% — 16%	96% — 0%
Social	85% — 7%	80% — 8%
Foreign	64% — 35%	68% — 31%

Key Votes of the 104th Congress

1. Reduce Medicare Growth $	N	5. Flag Amendment	N	9. Anti-Missile Defense	N
2. Lmt. Prod. Liab. Damages	N	6. Endangered Species	Y	10. Cuban Embargo	Y
3. Increase Min. Wage	Y	7. Gay Employment Rights	Y	11. Bar Bosnia Troop $	N
4. Welfare Reform	N	8. Ovrd. Part. Birth Veto	N	12. Cut Vietnam Aid	N

Election Results

1992 general	Barbara A. Mikulski (D)	1,307,610	(71%)	($3,623,974)
	Alan L. Keyes (R)	533,688	(29%)	($1,175,682)
1992 primary	Barbara A. Mikulski (D)	376,444	(77%)	
	Thomas M. Wheatley (D)	31,214	(6%)	
	Walter Boyd (D)	26,467	(5%)	
	Don Allensworth (D)	19,731	(4%)	
	Others	36,621	(8%)	
1986 general	Barbara A. Mikulski (D)	675,225	(61%)	($2,097,216)
	Linda Chavez (R)	437,411	(39%)	($1,699,175)

FIRST DISTRICT

The largest estuary in North America, the Chesapeake Bay, was the central focus of the most thickly settled of the 13 colonies, and today it remains a central focus for much of modern Maryland—and a backwater where remnants of an older civilization live on. The first British here were amazed at the Chesapeake's oysters and terrapin turtles and crabs and rockfish; despite pollution, watermen still make hardy livings bringing them to shore. This was an estuary civilization in colonial days, every little hamlet tied to mother England by the highways of bays and creeks and inlets off the Chesapeake. Old settlements like Chestertown, Oxford, St. Michaels and Cambridge don't look much different from when George Washington slept there. On the Western Shore, Annapolis was laid out as a capital in 1694, with one circle planned for the State House and one for the Church; the marble-halled State House, built in 1772, where the Continental Congress ratified the Treaty of Paris, is the oldest state capitol in continuous use. Annapolis is the home of the United States Naval Academy and its waterfront, though gentrified, is a waterman's as well as a yachter's port.

In post-colonial times, when most Americans were caught up in the romance of westward movement, these estuaries and peninsulas were forgotten, off the main lines of railroads and highways. Some of the Chesapeake has been changed beyond recognition—Baltimore, for instance, or the condominiums and strip malls spread out along Kent Island at the eastern foot of the Bay Bridge. But much has evolved slowly and with a certain continuity. The Eastern Shore counties of Maryland in the 160 years between 1790 and 1950 only doubled in population, perhaps the slowest growth rate on the Eastern Seaboard; and if its towns are industrial today, with small factories and mechanized farms, they still seem antique and the landscape is not vastly different from a century or two ago. There is some change now, as northeastern metropolitan expansion reaches south from the northern end of the Bay or east across the Bridge, and the Eastern Shore becomes increasingly not only second-home but also commuter country, and businesses like Frank Perdue's chicken empire around Salisbury grow.

The 1st Congressional District of Maryland includes all of the Eastern Shore and a segment of Maryland west of the Bay, including Annapolis and a strip of four-lane highway suburbs up to the southern rowhouse tip of Baltimore. In national elections, this is a solidly Republican area, voting against Bill Clinton in both 1992 and 1996.

The congressman from the 1st District is Wayne Gilchrest, a Republican with an unusual political history and some unusual political views. Gilchrest served in the Marine Corps in Vietnam, taught high school for 13 years and painted houses in the summer. In 1988, Gilchrest ran for Congress and lost to incumbent Democrat Roy Dyson 50.4%–49.6%; Dyson spent vastly more money but was embarrassed by a *Washington Post* story on his personnel practices. In 1990, Gilchrest ran again, again was vastly outspent, but won 57%–43%. In 1992 redistricting placed him in the same district with Democratic incumbent Tom McMillen, former Rhodes Scholar and star basketball player for the University of Maryland and the NBA's Washington Bullets (now Wizards). McMillen raised vastly more money, and Gilchrest won his primary with an unimpressive 47%. But Gilchrest represented 53% of the new district, and the Eastern Shore has a certain clannishness. Gilchrest contrasted McMillen's foreign travel with Gilchrest's only trip, driving his pickup to Ocean City, to address fellow members of the Order of the Purple Heart. Gilchrest won 52%–48%, carrying 60% on the Eastern Shore.

In the House, Gilchrest has a compiled a moderate voting record, with an emphasis on environmental issues. He designates preserving the Chesapeake as one of his first priorities. He took issue with western Republicans when they sought to relax the Endangered Species Act, even threatening to resign his committee post when a Resources subcommittee chairmen wouldn't let him invite his scientists to testify in favor of the law at field hearings in the 1st district. He opposed the new majority's revisions of the Clean Water Act, despairing that "the environmental movement has to start all over again." His committee assignments—Resources and Transportation, with the chairmanship of the Coast Guard and Maritime Transportation Subcommittee, give him some leverage on these issues. Gilchrest is unorthodox in other ways: he was the only Maryland member to vote for D.C. statehood, and he voted for the assault weapons ban—in a district assumed to be vehemently opposed to gun control.

In 1994 Gilchrest was reelected with 68%. In 1996 much of his vehement opposition came from Republicans, usually conservatives who resented his stands on environment issues. In the primary he attracted no less than five opponents; none won more than 15%, and Gilchrest won with 65%. In the general he was endorsed by the Sierra Club in Annapolis and the League of Conservation Voters. Gilchrest does not accept PAC contributions, and his Democratic opponent Steven Eastaugh, a professor of public health at George Washington University, was able to raise about as much money. But Eastaugh was also hurt when he claimed to be an Eastern Shore "native" and it actually turned out he was born in Boston two weeks before his parents moved to Maryland. Gilchrest won 62%–38%, carrying every county but losing Baltimore City. He says that his priorities continue to be Chesapeake Bay and economic development, on a regional and not county-by-county basis.

The People: Pop. 1990: 597,821; 46% rural; 12% age 65+; 83% White; 15% Black; 1% Asian; 1% Hispanic origin. Households: 59% married couple families; 26% married couple fams. w. children; 42% college educ.; median household income: $35,115; per capita income: $16,104; median gross rent: $487; median house value: $100,500.

1996 Presidential Vote			1992 Presidential Vote		
Dole (R)	107,122	(47%)	Bush (R)	109,039	(44%)
Clinton (D)	97,338	(43%)	Clinton (D)	93,165	(37%)
Perot (I)	20,779	(9%)	Perot (I)	47,188	(19%)

Rep. Wayne T. Gilchrest (R)

Elected 1990; b. Apr. 15, 1946, Rahway, NJ; home, Kennedyville; Wesley Col., A.A. 1971, DE St. Col., B.A. 1973, Loyola Col., 1984; Methodist; married (Barbara).

Career: Marine Corps, 1964–67 (Vietnam); High schl. teacher, 1973–86.

DC Office: 332 CHOB 20515, 202-225-5311; Fax: 202-225-0254.

District Offices: Chestertown, 410-778-9407; Glen Burnie, 410-760-3372; Salisbury, 410-749-3184.

Committees: *Resources* (9th of 27 R): Fisheries Conservation, Wildlife & Oceans; National Parks & Public Lands. *Transportation & Infrastructure* (10th of 40 R): Coast Guard & Maritime Transportation (Chmn.); Water Resources & Environment.

Group Ratings

	ADA	ACLU	AFS	LCV	CFA	CON	NFIB	COC	ACU	NTLC	CHC
1996	20	6	0	46	62	34	86	100	80	81	60
1995	30	—	—	25	77	38	—	83	56	—	—

National Journal Ratings

	1995 LIB — 1995 CONS			1996 LIB — 1996 CONS		
Economic	41%	—	56%	42%	—	56%
Social	64%	—	36%	61%	—	38%
Foreign	36%	—	59%	36%	—	63%

Key Votes of the 104th Congress

1. Reduce Medicare Growth $	Y	5. Flag Amendment	N	9. Cuban Embargo	Y
2. Ovrd. Product Liab. Veto	Y	6. Drop EPA Limits	Y	10. Bar Bosnia Troop $	N
3. Increase Min. Wage	N	7. Repeal Assault-Weap. Ban	N	11. Cut Anti-Missile Defense	N
4. Welfare Reform	Y	8. Ovrd. Part. Birth Veto	Y	12. Bar U.N. Uniforms	Y

Election Results

1996 general	Wayne T. Gilchrest (R)	131,033	(62%)	($259,366)
	Steven R. Eastaugh (D)	81,825	(38%)	($229,073)
1996 primary	Wayne T. Gilchrest (R)	25,431	(65%)	
	Thomas E. Anderson (R)	5,739	(15%)	
	Bradlyn McClanahan (R)	3,224	(8%)	
	Robert Gawthrop (R)	2,875	(7%)	
	Others	2,075	(5%)	
1994 general	Wayne T. Gilchrest (R)	120,975	(68%)	($153,133)
	Ralph T. Gies (D)	57,712	(32%)	($30,612)

SECOND DISTRICT

The spokes of Baltimore's streets spread out in all directions from the downtown centered on the Inner Harbor, connecting the central city with the suburbs where most residents of metropolitan Baltimore now livc. The streets reach east to Dundalk and Essex, industrial suburbs where the tone of life was set for years by the giant Sparrows Point steel mill, long the biggest in the country. Northeast they extend to modest working class suburbs and the small towns of the Baltimore and Harford County countryside which are now speckled with suburban developments—Bel Air, Joppatowne, Aberdeen, Edgewood, the last two near the Aberdeen Proving Grounds and Edgewood Arsenal military installations. Straight north from downtown are the higher-income suburbs, the pleasant county seat of Towson, and farther north are Lutherville, Timonium, Cockeysville, Hunt Valley, all flanked by the Baltimore County hunt country.

The 2d Congressional District of Maryland takes up most of this territory. The Sparrows Point area political tradition is union and Democratic, but that has been tempered lately. The northeast suburbs are ancestrally Democratic, but culturally rather conservative; the suburbs to the north are solidly Republican. Legislative and local offices are mostly held by Democrats, but a Republican won the Baltimore County executive post in 1990, which the party had not held since Spiro Agnew became governor in 1966; and a Republican has represented the 2d in the House since 1984.

The congressman from the 2d District is Bob Ehrlich, a Republican first elected in 1994. Ehrlich grew up in a rowhouse in the modest suburb of Arbutus, the son of a car salesman. A six footer at 13, he got a football scholarship to the elite Gilman School in Baltimore and then to Princeton, where he was a linebacker; he went to law school at Wake Forest and practiced law in Baltimore. He volunteered in Republican campaigns and in 1986, at 28, was elected to the Maryland House of Delegates. There he worked on tough sentencing and child pornography laws, but also opposed some bills as unneeded or unconstitutional. In a heavily Democratic House, "I was successful because I built coalitions between Democrats and Republicans." When 2d District Congresswoman Helen Bentley ran for governor in 1994 (only to be upset in the primary by anti-tax legislator Ellen Sauerbrey), Ehrlich ran for the House. He campaigned as pro-business and an opponent of overregulation, a military hawk and a libertarian and beat an anti-abortion candidate in the primary, 57%–38%. Meanwhile, there was a close Democratic primary between Delegates Gerry Brewster and Connie Galiazzo DeJuliis. Brewster, the son of former Congressman and Senator Daniel Brewster, was more moderate; Dundalk-based DeJuliis, with labor support, portrayed herself as a fighter, and held Brewster to a 38%–35%

victory.

The Ehrlich-Brewster race was seen as close by the local press, and there were symmetries between the candidates, who were classmates at Gilman and Princeton, served together in the House of Delegates and on the Judiciary Committee, spent almost identical amounts in the campaign. But Ehrlich went to school on scholarship and could not contribute thousands as Brewster did to his own campaign. Also there were clear issue differences. Ehrlich campaigned against the House Democratic leadership and signed the Contract With America, though he opposed term limits. He was enthusiastic about tax cuts, which fit in with Ellen Sauerbrey's surprisingly successful gubernatorial campaign. He ran ads showing the rowhouse where he grew up and saying the most important lessons he learned were around the dining room table. The result was anything but close: Ehrlich won 63%–37%.

Ehrlich began the 104th Congress on Newt Gingrich's "corrections day" panel, producing a Reports Elimination Act which identified 200 federal reports as unnecessary. He showed a willingness to cast tough votes and fight back, as when he opposed the minimum wage and argued that it "will make some marginal workers happier and put a little money in their pockets, but you cost the other marginal workers their jobs. That's not the group we should do harm to." He broke with the Republican leadership on term limits, loser-pays legal reform, and trade sanctions against China. He worked on local projects like protecting Baltimore's Home Port status and financing Harford County sewers.

Ehrlich's biggest priority, he has said, is blocking the Baltimore/HUD housing plan agreed to by the Clinton HUD department to settle a lawsuit brought by the ACLU. The plan would give 1,342 poor families now living in housing projects vouchers to rent private apartments or houses, but only in non-poor or non-minority neighborhoods. To Ehrlich this sets constitutionally suspect limits on where the project residents can live and elevates racial criteria improperly. He attempted to block funding for the plan, but claimed his effort was stymied in a conference committee on which Barbara Mikulski served.

Ehrlich had a spirited opponent in 1996. Connie Galiazzo DeJuliis, the narrow loser in the 1994 primary, ran a well-funded campaign with aid from organized labor; she is a former legislator and labor-management consultant and her husband works for the International Union of Operating Engineers. She charged that Ehrlich voted with Newt Gingrich 93% of the time and supported Medicare "cuts." He defended House Republicans—"you finally have a group of people with the political guts to make tough decisions"—and dismissed the Medicare charges—"you've heard a lot of scare stuff and junk about Medicare." DeJuliis nearly equalled him in spending, but Ehrlich did much better with the voters, winning 62%–38%, just one point lower than in 1994.

Many Maryland Republicans see Ehrlich as their strongest statewide candidate, and he has made it no secret that he is considering running for the Senate. Combative and locally based, "smart and mirthful," as *The Baltimore Sun* called him, he could be a serious candidate indeed; the thinking is that he is more likely to seek Paul Sarbanes's seat in 2000 than Barbara Mikulski's in 1998.

The People: Pop. 1990: 597,450; 18% rural; 12% age 65+; 91% White; 6% Black; 2% Asian; 1% Hispanic origin. Households: 62% married couple families; 28% married couple fams. w. children; 47% college educ.; median household income: $40,120; per capita income: $17,931; median gross rent: $507; median house value: $110,500.

1996 Presidential Vote

Dole (R)	119,178	(50%)
Clinton (D)	95,112	(40%)
Perot (I)	22,412	(9%)

1992 Presidential Vote

Bush (R)	121,087	(44%)
Clinton (D)	98,267	(36%)
Perot (I)	52,668	(19%)

Rep. Robert L. Ehrlich, Jr. (R)

Elected 1994; b. Nov. 25, 1957, Arbutus; home, Timonium; Princeton U., B.A. 1979, Wake Forest U., J.D. 1982; Methodist; married (Kendel).

Career: Practicing atty., 1982–94; MD House of Delegates, 1986–94.

DC Office: 315 CHOB 20515, 202-225-3061; Fax: 202-225-3094; e-mail: ehrlich@hr.house.gov.

District Offices: Bel Air, 410-838-2517; Lutherville, 410-337-7222.

Committees: *Banking & Financial Services* (15th of 30 R): Financial Institutions & Consumer Credit; Housing & Community Opportunity. *Budget* (19th of 24 R).

Group Ratings

	ADA	ACLU	AFS	LCV	CFA	CON	NFIB	COC	ACU	NTLC	CHC
1996	10	0	0	15	23	42	89	94	100	93	73
1995	20	—	—	13	38	38	—	88	64	—	—

National Journal Ratings

	1995 LIB — 1995 CONS			1996 LIB — 1996 CONS		
Economic	49%	—	49%	20%	—	76%
Social	53%	—	46%	45%	—	55%
Foreign	15%	—	73%	0%	—	79%

Key Votes of the 104th Congress

1. Reduce Medicare Growth $	Y	5. Flag Amendment	Y	9. Cuban Embargo	Y
2. Ovrd. Product Liab. Veto	Y	6. Drop EPA Limits	Y	10. Bar Bosnia Troop $	Y
3. Increase Min. Wage	N	7. Repeal Assault-Weap. Ban	Y	11. Cut Anti-Missile Defense	N
4. Welfare Reform	Y	8. Ovrd. Part. Birth Veto	Y	12. Bar U.N. Uniforms	Y

Election Results

1996 general	Robert L. Ehrlich, Jr. (R)	143,075	(62%)	($844,918)
	Connie Galiazzo DeJuliis (D)	88,344	(38%)	($641,618)
1996 primary	Robert L. Enrlich, Jr. (R)	29,983	(83%)	
	Josef Thurston (R)	3,764	(10%)	
	Walter Boyd (R)	1,570	(4%)	
	Others	711	(2%)	
1994 general	Robert L. Ehrlich, Jr. (R)	125,162	(63%)	($562,892)
	Gerry L. Brewster (D)	74,275	(37%)	($550,471)

THIRD DISTRICT

In the 1990s Baltimore became one of America's star cities. Its Inner Harbor and new Camden Yards baseball stadium became national tourist attractions. Even its cuisine—steamed crabs with Chesapeake spices, crab cakes—became known beyond the watershed of the Chesapeake Bay. The central city of Baltimore certainly has its problems—high crime, poor schools, fiscal problems—but the greater Baltimore that slops over both sides of the Baltimore City and County lines retains a distinctive character. There is a patina of age, as on its Washington Monument, built in 1829 and now refurbished, and the townhouses of Mount Vernon Square and an atmosphere of tolerance and diversity nurtured by Maryland's founding Catholics in search of liberty; the nation's first Catholic diocese and cathedral were built here when America was overwhelmingly and militantly Protestant. And this is a city built solidly on commerce which has always known how to reap its pleasures.

The 3d Congressional District of Maryland is centered on Baltimore and consists of three portions that extend outward like spokes of a wheel from the focus of metropolitan Baltimore at the Inner Harbor. The three spokes are connected by narrow bridges of land, with boundaries designed to build a black-majority 7th District next door. From the harbor, the 3d extends northeast out into the Polish Highlandtown neighborhood and the mostly white Catholic northeast precincts and close-in suburbs of Overlea and Parkville. It extends northwest to the heavily Jewish suburbs of Pikesville and Owings Mills, past the array of temples and synagogues on Park Heights Avenue to the open subdivisions where the newest Jewish neighborhoods are being built. And it extends southwest, past old rowhouse neighborhoods overlooking Fort McHenry, where Francis Scott Key saw by the dawn's early light the star-spangled banner still there, out past Arbutus and Lansdowne into Linthicum and Fort Meade in Anne Arundel County and Elkridge and Columbia in Howard County. Here lies the cusp of the Baltimore-Washington boundary; for Columbia, now a 30-something "new town" draws from both metro areas. Ancestrally Democratic, this district is now contested territory. Pikesville and Columbia are solidly liberal on most issues; the northeast and close-in southeast areas are culturally more conservative.

The congressman from the 3d is Benjamin Cardin, former speaker of the Maryland House of Delegates and one of the many bright politicos produced by the Jewish neighborhoods of northwest Baltimore, where he grew up. He was elected to the House of Delegates in 1966, at 23, the first time he was eligible to run; after serving there for 20 years—for seven years as speaker—he was easily elected to Congress in 1986 when Barbara Mikulski ran for the Senate. In the House, Cardin has been an inside player. He got a seat on Ways and Means in October 1989, with the support of Chairman Dan Rostenkowski. On Ways and Means, he worked on complex and important issues—401(k) savings plan, pension rules, healthcare finance. His bill to restore the tax deduction for health insurance for the self-employed was quickly passed in the Republican Congress in 1995. His record is generally liberal, but sometimes moderate on economic issues; he opposed the labor unions and joined the Clinton Administration and Republican leadership in supporting NAFTA and opposed trial lawyers and supported a cap on medical malpractice damages. Even as other Democrats were hammering Republicans for proposing Medicare "cuts," Cardin in October 1996 was supporting a Medicare fix that sounded very much like the Republican plan: he would support "more options to voluntarily participate in managed-care options." He also abandons Democratic orthodoxy on Social Security. "Ultimately we should look carefully at the possibility of permitting younger working Americans to direct some part of their FICA taxes into private retirement-saving accounts."

Cardin's other major assignment has been on the Ethics Committee, dating back to the House bank scandal that flared in 1990; he was the ranking Democrat on the subcommittee that painstakingly investigated the charges against Newt Gingrich. Although Cardin is a party loyalist, he does not see himself as a partisan enthusiast. In comparing himself with his 1996 opponent, Pat McDonough, he said, "The biggest difference is I know how to get along with people. I work with Republicans. I work with Democrats. My number one priority is to tone down partisanship in Washington. I think it's obscene." He won that race 67%–33%, an unsurprising result. He has been mentioned many times as a candidate for governor, most recently in 1994, but has never run.

The People: Pop. 1990: 597,712; 2% rural; 13% age 65+; 79% White; 17% Black; 2% Asian; 2% Hispanic origin. Households: 52% married couple families; 23% married couple fams. w. children; 49% college educ.; median household income: $35,970; per capita income: $17,779; median gross rent: $506; median house value: $90,000.

1996 Presidential Vote			1992 Presidential Vote		
Clinton (D)	123,532	(58%)	Clinton (D)	136,829	(54%)
Dole (R)	72,017	(34%)	Bush (R)	82,494	(32%)
Perot (I)	13,872	(7%)	Perot (I)	34,973	(14%)

Rep. Benjamin L. Cardin (D)

Elected 1986; b. Oct. 5, 1943, Baltimore; home, Baltimore; U. of Pittsburgh, B.A. 1964, U. of MD, LL.B., J.D. 1967; Jewish; married (Myrna).

Career: MD House of Delegates, 1966–86, Speaker, 1979–86; Practicing atty., 1967–86.

DC Office: 104 CHOB 20515, 202-225-4016; Fax: 202-225-9219; e-mail: cardin@hr.house.gov.

District Offices: Baltimore, 410-433-8886.

Committees: *Budget* (12th of 19 D). *Ways & Means* (7th of 16 D): Health.

Group Ratings

	ADA	ACLU	AFS	LCV	CFA	CON	NFIB	COC	ACU	NTLC	CHC
1996	75	62	92	85	100	84	30	25	11	15	7
1995	89	—	—	75	100	25	—	25	12	—	—

National Journal Ratings

	1995 LIB — 1995 CONS			1996 LIB — 1996 CONS		
Economic	68%	—	31%	67%	—	32%
Social	80%	—	13%	72%	—	27%
Foreign	79%	—	17%	75%	—	25%

Key Votes of the 104th Congress

1. Reduce Medicare Growth $	N	5. Flag Amendment	N	9. Cuban Embargo	Y
2. Ovrd. Product Liab. Veto	N	6. Drop EPA Limits	Y	10. Bar Bosnia Troop $	N
3. Increase Min. Wage	Y	7. Repeal Assault-Weap. Ban	N	11. Cut Anti-Missile Defense	Y
4. Welfare Reform	N	8. Ovrd. Part. Birth Veto	N	12. Bar U.N. Uniforms	N

Election Results

1996 general	Benjamin L. Cardin (D)	130,204	(67%)	($577,270)
	Patrick L. McDonough (R)	63,229	(33%)	($49,459)
1996 primary	Benjamin L. Cardin (D)	34,496	(90%)	
	Dan Hiegel (D)	3,720	(10%)	
1994 general	Benjamin L. Cardin (D)	117,269	(71%)	($550,172)
	Robert Ryan Tousey (R)	47,966	(29%)	($10,439)

FOURTH DISTRICT

In 1696 the proprietors of the colony of Maryland created a new county between the Potomac and Patuxent Rivers and named it after the husband of the heir to the throne, Prince George of Denmark. From that time until its 300th birthday Prince George's County has not often won national fame—maybe briefly when investigators chased the plotters of Abraham Lincoln's murderer here—but it should now. Historically Prince George's was tobacco country, rural and heavily settled, with blacks and Catholics and big property-owners who pretty much ran things. Today Prince George's is or should be known as the home of America's largest black middle class, a place that gives a hopeful glimpse of the future. Prince George's is affluent by national standards, with one of the highest percentages of women in the work force in the nation (over 70%); if it has not had as much office and shopping mall growth as northern Virginia or next-door Montgomery County, it has also proved itself a far more commercially vibrant and culturally constructive community than the next-door District of Columbia. Prince George's has always had many black residents, since the first tobacco crop was planted, but that population grew as middle class blacks moved out from Washington into modest suburbs at the county's edge and affluent subdivisions far to the east. The black percentage here increased from 14% in 1970 to 37% in 1980; by the early 1990s it reached 50%.

The 4th Congressional District of Maryland includes most of Prince George's County and a portion of Montgomery County to the west; it is mostly, but not entirely, inside the Capital Beltway. The biggest industry here is still government: in 1990, 21.5% of its workers were employed by the federal government, the highest percentage of any congressional district in the nation. The district is 58% black and also 6% Hispanic; it is overwhelmingly Democratic.

The congressman from the 4th District is Albert Wynn, a Democrat effectively chosen in the 1992 primary. Wynn grew up in Prince Georges County, attending all black schools there until integration began in his sophomore year. He went to the University of Pittsburgh on a debate team scholarship and received a law degree from Georgetown University. He served a decade in the Maryland legislature, first as a member of the House and later the Senate, where he was deputy majority whip. Wynn entered the 1992 race better known than most of the 13 Democrats and seven Republicans running, with the exception of Prince George's State's Attorney Alex Williams. But Wynn was better funded, and his "put America first" platform, emphasizing domestic issues and attacks on George Bush overshadowed Williams's proclamation that he would be "a strong, independent voice for Congress." Wynn spent much effort in Montgomery County, while Williams seemed to be targeting primarily Prince George's blacks. Prince George's County Councilwoman Hilda Pemberton highlighted her pro-choice stand, and Montgomery state Delegate Dana Dembrow, one of four white Democrats in the race, attacked the concept of a mandatory black-majority district. Wynn was endorsed by the *Prince George's Journal* and *The Washington Post* and won the primary with 28% of the vote; Williams had 26%, Dembrow 15%, almost all from Montgomery, and Pemberton 13%. The general election was anticlimactic, with Wynn taking 75% of the vote against black businesswoman Michele Dyson.

Like many of the blacks elected from new black-majority districts, Wynn seems not to be making a monoracial appeal. He eschews expressions of contentiousnous for pronouncements on national issues. He was key in bringing about hearings in 1993 to investigate allegations of racial bias at the National Institutes of Health, at the close of which Congress and an NIH task force pledged to monitor the agency. In May 1994 the NAACP, along with NIH's chapter of Blacks in Government, called for the resignation of NIH Director Harold Varmus, citing lack of progress in racial equity since the hearings. Although Wynn did not advocate Varmus' removal, he did express frustration at the slow pace of change at NIH. Wynn's voting record remains solidly liberal, and he serves on the Commerce Committee.

In 1994 Wynn faced a rematch with Michele Dyson and again won with 75%. In October

1996 his Republican opponent offered to pose naked for *Playgirl* magazine, saying "I'll do whatever it takes to win the election." Wynn won with 85%.

The People: Pop. 1990: 597,791; 1% rural; 7% age 65+; 31% White; 58% Black; 4% Asian; 6% Hispanic origin. Households: 47% married couple families; 24% married couple fams. w. children; 56% college educ.; median household income: $41,081; per capita income: $17,251; median gross rent: $643; median house value: $122,600.

1996 Presidential Vote			1992 Presidential Vote		
Clinton (D)	152,396	(81%)	Clinton (D)	149,262	(74%)
Dole (R)	30,071	(16%)	Bush (R)	37,716	(19%)
Perot (I)	5,591	(3%)	Perot (I)	14,160	(7%)

Rep. Albert R. Wynn (D)

Elected 1992; b. Sept. 10, 1951, Philadelphia, PA; home, Largo; U. of Pittsburgh, B.S. 1973, Howard U., 1973–74; Georgetown U. Law Schl., J.D. 1977; Baptist; married (Jessie).

Career: Exec. Dir., PG Cnty. Consumer Protection Comm., 1977–81; Chmn., Metro Washington Cncl. of Consumer Agencies, 1980–81; Practicing atty., 1981–92; MD House of Delegates, 1982–87; MD Senate 1987–92.

DC Office: 407 CHOB 20515, 202-225-8699; Fax: 202-225-8714; e-mail: awynn@hr.house.gov.

District Offices: Landover, 301-773-4094; Oxon Hill, 301-839-5570; Silver Spring, 301-558-7328.

Committees: *Commerce* (19th of 23 D): Energy & Power; Telecommunications, Trade & Consumer Protection.

Group Ratings

	ADA	ACLU	AFS	LCV	CFA	CON	NFIB	COC	ACU	NTLC	CHC
1996	90	81	92	77	85	82	22	31	0	22	7
1995	95	—	—	88	100	25	—	21	12	—	—

National Journal Ratings

	1995 LIB		1995 CONS	1996 LIB		1996 CONS
Economic	78%	—	21%	67%	—	32%
Social	80%	—	13%	78%	—	21%
Foreign	88%	—	7%	82%	—	16%

Key Votes of the 104th Congress

1. Reduce Medicare Growth $	N	5. Flag Amendment	Y	9. Cuban Embargo	N
2. Ovrd. Product Liab. Veto	N	6. Drop EPA Limits	Y	10. Bar Bosnia Troop $	N
3. Increase Min. Wage	Y	7. Repeal Assault-Weap. Ban	N	11. Cut Anti-Missile Defense	Y
4. Welfare Reform	N	8. Ovrd. Part. Birth Veto	N	12. Bar U.N. Uniforms	N

Election Results

1996 general	Albert R. Wynn (D)	142,094	(85%)	($343,875)
	John B. Kimble (R)	24,700	(15%)	
1996 primary	Albert R. Wynn (D)	22,270	(85%)	
	Maria Turner (D)	4,044	(15%)	
1994 general	Albert R. Wynn (D)	93,148	(75%)	($358,607)
	Michele Dyson (R)	30,999	(25%)	($119,749)

FIFTH DISTRICT

Southern Maryland has a distinctive history, but not much of a national image. It was first settled by Catholics, the Calvert family of the Lords Baltimore, who founded their capital of St. Marys in 1634, not long after Jamestown and Plymouth Rock. Maryland became one of the two great tobacco colonies, and plantation houses grew up on every inlet off the broad Potomac and Patuxent Rivers, with docks where ships tied up straight from London. For years, none of these towns grew much, and even today many people here are directly descended from the old families. The biggest growth came from government installations like the Civil War Point Lookout prisoner-of-war camp or Patuxent Naval Air Test Center where many astronauts got their first training. This was never puritanical country: liquor flowed even during Prohibition and slot machines were specifically allowed by Maryland law until the 1940s.

The 5th Congressional District of Maryland, with lines redrawn completely in 1992, includes the three counties of southern Maryland, now attracting people who grew up in metro Washington and Baltimore, plus large slices of suburban Prince George's and Anne Arundel Counties between Washington and Annapolis. Its lines are drawn to make the adjacent 4th District in Prince George's majority-black, though with blacks moving outward in Prince George's and southern Maryland's historic black population, the 5th now is 19% black. Many of its people live north of Washington, in College Park, home of the University of Maryland, and Hyattsville, Greenbelt, Beltsville and Laurel. The 5th also includes southern Prince George's, from Clinton (heavily Democratic, unlike most Clinton Counties in the U.S.?) south, and the suburbs of Bowie, Crofton and Davidsonville just west of Annapolis. Historically, this is a Democratic area. But southern Maryland has been conservative on many issues and voted for George Bush over Bill Clinton, and many Prince George's and Anne Arundel whites are Republicans as well.

The congressman from the 5th District is Steny Hoyer, a veteran Democrat who in 1981 won a seat with a large black percentage based in Prince George's and then relocated following redistricting to this south Maryland seat. Hoyer was elected to the Maryland Senate in 1966, at 27, just after graduating from law school. He was Senate President from 1975–78; he made a misstep running for lieutenant governor on a losing ticket in 1978. But when the 5th District was declared vacant in 1981, after Representative Gladys Spellman went into an irreversible coma, Hoyer edged out Spellman's husband and several other Democrats in the primary and beat a well-financed, competent Republican candidate in the general.

Hoyer immediately became an accomplished, constituency service congressman and in very short order became one of the leaders of the Democratic Party in the House. He won a seat on the Appropriations Committee, where he became a key player not only for Prince George's County but for Maryland and the overall D.C. metropolitan area. When Democrats had control, Hoyer chaired the Treasury, Postal Service and General Government Appropriations Subcommittee, which oversees several major components of the federal work force—17% of 5th District workers are federal employees—and the White House budget. He used the panel to prohibit changes in federal workers' health plans, to get $6 million for flexiplace telecommuting centers to allow long-commuting feds to work closer to home, and to kill a Republican proposal to require federal employees to pay fair market value for parking. He pushed for completion of the Metro subway system, maintaining 3,300 civil service and 8,000 contract personnel jobs at the Goddard Space Flight Center, funding Chesapeake Bay cleanup, requiring the District of Columbia to spend more on the Blue Plains wastewater treatment plant, and funding ship self defense work at St. Inigoes. He has worked hard to maintain local military bases through the base-closing procedure, most recently keeping Indian Head naval base open with 5,000 new jobs.

Hoyer has also worked on national legislation, notably as the chief House sponsor of the Americans with Disabilities Act, skillfully shepherding it to passage in 1990. When Speaker Jim Wright and Whip Tony Coelho resigned from Congress in June 1989 because of ethics problems, Hoyer won a leadership position as chairman of the Democratic Caucus. In June 1991, when Democratic Whip William Gray retired, Hoyer tried to move up again. But his support from conservative Democrats was outweighed by David Bonior's coalition of liberals and committee chairmen, and Bonior won 160–109. Hoyer remains an integral part of the leadership, as chairman of the Democratic Steering Committee. He broke with party lines by supporting the balanced budget amendment in 1995, but worked hard in 1996 to raise and support Democratic stands on the minimum wage and health insurance portability.

Hoyer's stands on issues have reflected his changing constituency. Up through 1990, his Prince George's district had almost as many black as white residents; his liberal voting record helped him in the critical Democratic primary, and in 1990, against a candidate supported by Louis Farrakhan, he won 79% of the vote and carried every precinct. When the new black-majority 4th District was created in 1992, Hoyer ended up with only a part of Prince George's and most of the 5th District votes were cast in southern Maryland counties. His voting record became somewhat more moderate, and he weathered serious Republican challenges in 1992 and 1994. It helped that he is a champion fundraiser, spending $1.6 million and $1.3 million in those two races. In 1992 he beat Lawrence Hogan, Jr., whose father was a Prince George's congressman from 1968–74, voting for the impeachment of Richard Nixon; Hogan won 50%–45% in the half of the district outside Prince George's, but Hoyer's 60%–38% margin in Prince George's gave him a 53%–44% win. In 1994, against Donald Devine, director of the Office of Personnel Management in the first Reagan term, Hoyer led outside Prince George's County 53%–47% and in Prince George's 65%–35%, for a 59%–41% overall win. Hoyer was thus one of the few Democrats to increase his margin in the first two Clinton years. In 1996 Hoyer raised $1.2 million to $238,000 for Republican John Morgan. Once again he carried southern Maryland 53%–47%, which, with a 62%–38% margin in Prince George's, produced a 57%–43% victory. These numbers are testimony to Hoyer's political prowess, but also to the fact that this district cannot be counted as an utterly safe Democratic seat.

Interestingly, Hoyer is of Danish descent, like Attorney General Janet Reno and the original eponym of Prince George's County.

The People: Pop. 1990: 597,573; 30% rural; 8% age 65+; 76% White; 18% Black; 3% Asian; 2% Hispanic origin. Households: 62% married couple families; 31% married couple fams. w. children; 53% college educ.; median household income: $46,936; per capita income: $18,178; median gross rent: $674; median house value: $131,300.

1996 Presidential Vote

Clinton (D)	117,345	(51%)
Dole (R)	95,737	(42%)
Perot (I)	14,546	(6%)

1992 Presidential Vote

Clinton (D)	107,618	(45%)
Bush (R)	95,356	(39%)
Perot (I)	37,441	(15%)

Rep. Steny H. Hoyer (D)

Elected May 1981; b. June 14, 1939, New York, NY; home, Mitchellville; U. of MD, B.S. 1963, Georgetown U., J.D. 1966; Baptist; widowed.

Career: Practicing atty., 1966–80; MD Senate, 1966–78, Pres., 1975–78; MD Bd. of Higher Educ., 1978–81.

DC Office: 1705 LHOB 20515, 202-225-4131; Fax: 202-225-4300.

District Offices: Greenbelt, 301-474-0119; Waldorf, 301-843-1577.

Committees: *Appropriations* (10th of 26 D): Labor, Health & Human Services & Education; Military Construction; Treasury, Postal Service & General Government (RMM). *House Oversight* (2nd of 3 D). *Joint Committee on Printing* (4th of 5 Reps.).

Group Ratings

	ADA	ACLU	AFS	LCV	CFA	CON	NFIB	COC	ACU	NTLC	CHC
1996	85	56	92	85	69	91	27	13	5	17	13
1995	80	—	—	69	85	38	—	25	8	—	—

National Journal Ratings

	1995 LIB — 1995 CONS			1996 LIB — 1996 CONS		
Economic	70%	—	29%	76%	—	22%
Social	80%	—	13%	77%	—	23%
Foreign	61%	—	38%	61%	—	37%

Key Votes of the 104th Congress

1. Reduce Medicare Growth $	N	5. Flag Amendment	N	9. Cuban Embargo	Y
2. Ovrd. Product Liab. Veto	N	6. Drop EPA Limits	Y	10. Bar Bosnia Troop $	N
3. Increase Min. Wage	Y	7. Repeal Assault-Weap. Ban	N	11. Cut Anti-Missile Defense	Y
4. Welfare Reform	N	8. Ovrd. Part. Birth Veto	N	12. Bar U.N. Uniforms	N

Election Results

1996 general	Steny H. Hoyer (D)	121,288	(57%)	($1,155,840)
	John S. Morgan (R)	91,806	(43%)	($236,483)
1996 primary	Steny H. Hoyer (D)	22,598	(84%)	
	Thomas W. Defibaugh (D)	4,356	(16%)	
1994 general	Steny H. Hoyer (D)	98,821	(59%)	($1,295,542)
	Donald Devine (R)	69,211	(41%)	($581,198)

SIXTH DISTRICT

The long green sloping fields of western Maryland, cut through by the Appalachian ridges that diagonally cross the state, were America's first western frontier: wheat fields settled first by Pennsylvania Dutch and Scots-Irish hill people, not Chesapeake Bay tobacco growers. Maryland is where the fall line comes closest to an ocean port, where the 19th Century's great paths to the interior were staked out: first the National Road, then the nation's first railroad, the Baltimore & Ohio, crossed the wide valleys of bounteous farms and climbed over the Catoctin Mountains.

Towns grew up on narrow streets lined with rowhouses and today are overhung with telephone and streetcar wires, overlooking long vistas of cornfields, pasturelands and mountains of ancient stone rising above the plains. Across this placid land moved vast armies during the Civil War. In Frederick, city officials paid Confederates $200,000 to not burn down the town, and near Sharpsburg, blue- and gray-clad soldiers fought the Battle of Antietam, on the bloodiest day in American military history. Today, there is a new rush of settlement here, in Carroll and Howard Counties, long parts of metro Baltimore, and Frederick County, which grew 31% in the 1980s and is now classified as part of metro Washington; growth remains slow west of the Catoctins.

The 6th Congressional District of Maryland includes all of western Maryland, to mountainous Cumberland and Garrett County, and runs east to Carroll County northwest of Baltimore and the old town of Ellicott City in Howard County. The political tradition in most of this area, unlike the rest of Maryland, is Republican: this was Union country in the Civil War and has been mostly Republican ever since. The new rush of settlement seems to come from those seeking respite from metropolitan crime, strengthening the area's already conservative leanings. The 6th voted heavily for Republican state candidates in 1994 and for Bob Dole in 1996.

The congressman from the 6th District is a Republican who matches its current mood, Roscoe Bartlett. He is an interesting character, a descendant of a signer of the Declaration of Independence and a Seventh Day Adventist with 10 children. He invented life support equipment for pilots and astronauts, ran his own business and taught at Frederick Community College—old values and high tech. When he first ran for Congress in 1992, he was a 65-year-old retired University of Maryland physiology professor who seemed to have no chance of winning. Democrat Beverly Byron had represented the district for 14 years, had a conservative voting record, and chaired a subcommittee on National Security. But Byron was upset in the primary by Delegate Thomas Hattery, 56%–44%, who called for national health insurance and was pro-choice on abortion. Bartlett won his primary by only 42%–41%. But Bartlett's conservative views, campaign help from Oliver North and Tom Clancy, and his attacks on the Hattery for legislative perks won him a 54%–46% victory.

Bartlett has proved a surprisingly durable politician. Many in the press considered him an odd duck and made a big deal when he told an audience that not more than a third of scholarship winners have "normal American" names; he apologized later, explaining that he should have said "European" and added that he meant to compliment Americans of Asian background. They said he was squandering votes when he refused to back disaster relief after a 1993 blizzard. But he took advantage of Clinton Administration missteps from its healthcare plan to the May 1994 local newspaper photograph showing Clinton aide David Watkins boarding a helicopter at a Frederick County golf course: "The photo of two Marine guards saluting a golf bag as it was carried up the helicopter stairs is truly a picture that is worth a thousand words," he said. In 1994 he was reelected with 66% of the vote.

Bartlett's conservative voting record anticipated the Contract with America, and in the 104th Congress he was often in the majority, and pushed through a bill banning *Penthouse* and similar magazines from military post exchanges. He supported U.S. involvément in Bosnia, though he said we should not be the only show of force there. He wanted competition to Medicare from HMOs, Medical Savings Accounts, and Provider Service Networks. In 1996 Democrat Steve Crawford attacked him for taking contributions from Gun Owners of America and "smear poll" phone calls said he was part of a "secret militia group." But Bartlett's votes for repealing the assault weapons ban and his charge that the Democrat took $40,000 from labor unions connected with organized crime were evidently, as his slogan said, "mainstream for western Maryland." Bartlett, with a significant amount of his war chest left in tact, won 57%–43%.

The People: Pop. 1990: 597,660; 47% rural; 11% age 65+; 93% White; 4% Black; 1% Asian; 1% Hispanic origin. Households: 65% married couple families; 31% married couple fams. w. children; 44% college educ.; median household income: $36,883; per capita income: $15,979; median gross rent: $448; median house value: $113,100.

1996 Presidential Vote

Dole (R)	130,321	(52%)
Clinton (D)	96,185	(38%)
Perot (I)	21,205	(8%)

1992 Presidential Vote

Bush (R)	125,494	(48%)
Clinton (D)	88,196	(34%)
Perot (I)	46,376	(18%)

Rep. Roscoe G. Bartlett (R)

Elected 1992; b. June 3, 1926, Moreland, KY; home, Frederick; Columbia Union Col., B.A. 1947; U. of MD, M.S. 1949, Ph.D. 1952; Seventh Day Adventist; married (Ellen).

Career: Farmer; Prof., U. of MD, 1948–52; Asst. Prof., Loma Linda Schl. of Medicine, 1952–54; Asst. Prof., Howard U. Medical Schl., 1954–56; Research scientist, N.I.H., 1956–58; Research scientist, U.S. Naval Aerospace Medical Inst., 1958–62; Research scientist, Johns Hopkins U., 1962–67; Research Mgr., IBM, 1967–74; Pres., Roscoe Bartlett & Assoc., 1974–86.

DC Office: 322 CHOB 20515, 202-225-2721; Fax: 202-225-2193.

District Offices: Frederick, 301-694-3030; Frostburg, 301-689-0034; Hagerstown, 301-797-6043; Westminster, 410-857-1115.

Committees: *National Security* (15th of 30 R): Military Personnel; Military Research & Development. *Science* (10th of 25 R): Space & Aeronautics; Technology. *Small Business* (5th of 19 R): Government Programs & Oversight (Chmn.).

Group Ratings

	ADA	ACLU	AFS	LCV	CFA	CON	NFIB	COC	ACU	NTLC	CHC
1996	0	19	0	15	15	9	100	100	100	98	100
1995	0	—	—	0	8	38	—	100	100	—	—

National Journal Ratings

	1995 LIB — 1995 CONS			1996 LIB — 1996 CONS		
Economic	0%	—	74%	0%	—	82%
Social	0%	—	79%	24%	—	72%
Foreign	0%	—	85%	30%	—	65%

Key Votes of the 104th Congress

1. Reduce Medicare Growth $	Y	5. Flag Amendment	Y	9. Cuban Embargo	Y
2. Ovrd. Product Liab. Veto	Y	6. Drop EPA Limits	N	10. Bar Bosnia Troop $	Y
3. Increase Min. Wage	N	7. Repeal Assault-Weap. Ban	Y	11. Cut Anti-Missile Defense	N
4. Welfare Reform	Y	8. Ovrd. Part. Birth Veto	Y	12. Bar U.N. Uniforms	Y

Election Results

1996 general	Roscoe G. Bartlett (R)	132,853	(57%)	($253,966)
	Stephen Crawford (D)	100,910	(43%)	($383,127)
1996 primary	Roscoe G. Bartlett (R)	42,704	(85%)	
	John J. Kubricky (R)	4,183	(8%)	
	Fredric M. Parker (R)	3,216	(6%)	
1994 general	Roscoe G. Bartlett (R)	122,809	(66%)	($369,904)
	Paul Muldowney (D)	63,411	(34%)	($257,690)

SEVENTH DISTRICT

Baltimore, at the junction of North and South, terminus of America's first railroad and still the East Coast port closest to the great West, is one of the few American cities to have had large numbers of both blacks and European immigrants throughout its history. Its black community has a notable history: the *Afro-American* newspaper has been published here for more than 100 years; there was once a black symphony orchestra; and the city's black neighborhood west of downtown had a vital shopping district before World War II. Eubie Blake, the famous black musician and one of the founders of ragtime music, grew up here and now has a museum to honor him on Charles Street. Near downtown on the west side is the childhood home of Babe Ruth and the home of H.L. Mencken—two famous white Americans, and white Republicans like Mayor and Governor Theodore McKeldin once competed zestfully with Democrats for black votes.

Baltimore has been a black-majority city since the late 1970s, and most of its west side neighborhoods are heavily black. Black Republicanism has long since died out, and William Donald Schaefer, who carried west Baltimore for mayor as late as 1983, went on to become governor. Black Democrats are the key politicians here, notably Mayor Kurt Schmoke, first elected in 1987. Schmoke's abilities—he is a Rhodes Scholar—and good intentions sparked hopes he could help Baltimore lessen the pathologies of violent crime, single parenthood and labor force non-participation that plague cities elsewhere. Schmoke has launched controversial initiatives: in 1988, he called for a full debate on drug decriminalization, and in 1992, the city made available Norplant implants as a contraceptive to public school teenagers. One hopeful initiative was developer James Rouse's five-year project to rebuild a 72-block area called Sandtown. But in the meantime, middle- and upper-income blacks have left behind the marble-stepped rowhouses of the city and moved to the suburbs.

Maryland's 7th Congressional District includes almost all of Baltimore City's black neighborhoods and extends into the heavily black suburbs running west from the city, Catonsville along the old Baltimore National Pike and Randallstown out Liberty Heights Avenue; 79% of the people and 70% of the votes are in the city. From 1987 to February 1996 the congressman here was Kweisi Mfume, former councilman and radio talk show host, whose name ("Conquering Son of Kings") has echoes of the Black Power 1960s. He won the House seat in a spirited primary in 1986, became chairman of the Congressional Black Caucus in 1992, then resigned in February 1996 to become president of the troubled NAACP.

The new congressman is Elijah Cummings, effectively chosen in the special primary held March 5, 1996, the same day as Maryland's presidential and congressional primaries. Cummings grew up in Baltimore, graduated from Howard University and University of Maryland Law School, practiced law in Baltimore, and in 1982, at 31, was elected to the Maryland House of Delegates. Two years later he was chairman of the Legislative Caucus, the youngest in history, and he became known as a consensus builder and effective speaker. He chaired the governor's Commission on Black Males and founded the Maryland Bootcamp Aftercare program to address the self sufficiency of former youth offenders.

Cummings was one of 27 Democrats to jump into the race to succeed Mfume; there were five Republicans as well. It was probably one of the largest congressional fields in history; "every tenth person I talk to is a candidate," said Secretary of State John Willis. But only two or three turned out to have much backing, and relatively little money was raised. State Senator Delores Kelley represented a district straddling the city and county, and raised $180,000; she got 10% of the vote. The Reverend Frank Reid III, step-brother of Mayor Kurt Schmoke, raised $255,000; despite Schmoke's solid reelection win in September 1995, he won only 24%. Cummings had support from both community development organizations and from businessmen and lobbyists, from House Speaker Casper Taylor but not Mfume, who endorsed no one. He raised $450,000 and won 37% of the vote. His victories in the April special and November general elections were anticlimactic. Cummings still resides in his West Baltimore neighborhood, where his car has been broken into four times in the past year. As a first hand witness to the crime and drug dealing there, he is for strict gun control and has introduced a bill to establish a Commission on National Drug Policy. He is likely to have a strong liberal voting record; he was the only Marylander to vote against the 1996 Welfare Reform Act.

The People: Pop. 1990: 597,701; 1% rural; 12% age 65+; 27% White; 71% Black; 1% Asian; 1% Hispanic origin. Households: 34% married couple families; 14% married couple fams. w. children; 37% college educ.; median household income: $25,684; per capita income: $11,718; median gross rent: $432; median house value: $59,400.

1996 Presidential Vote

Clinton (D)	127,850	(81%)
Dole (R)	23,757	(15%)
Perot (I)	5,207	(3%)

1992 Presidential Vote

Clinton (D)	159,191	(77%)
Bush (R)	32,431	(16%)
Perot (I)	13,009	(6%)

Rep. Elijah E. Cummings (D)

Elected April 1996; b. Jan. 18, 1951, Baltimore; home, Baltimore; Howard U., B.S. 1973, U. of MD, J.D. 1976; Baptist; separated.

Career: Practicing atty., 1976–96; MD House of Delegates, 1982–96, Speaker Pro-Tem, 1995–96.

DC Office: 1632 LHOB 20515, 202-225-4741; Fax: 202-225-3178.

District Offices: Baltimore, 410-367-1900; Baltimore, 410-496-2010; Catonsville, 410-719-8777.

Committees: *Government Reform & Oversight* (13th of 19 D): Civil Service (RMM); National Security, International Affairs & Criminal Justice. *Transportation & Infrastructure* (24th of 33 D): Aviation; Surface Transportation.

Group Ratings (Only Served Partial Term)

	ADA	ACLU	AFS	LCV	CFA	CON	NFIB	COC	ACU	NTLC	CHC
1996	92	*	100	100	100	2	20	22	0	33	0
1995	*	—	—	*	*	*	—	*	*	—	—

National Journal Ratings (Only Served Partial Term)

	1995 LIB — 1995 CONS			1996 LIB — 1996 CONS		
Economic	*	—	*	82%	—	18%
Social	*	—	*	*	—	*
Foreign	*	—	*	84%	—	15%

Key Votes of the 104th Congress (Only Served Partial Term)

1. Reduce Medicare Growth $	*	5. Flag Amendment	*	9. Cuban Embargo	*
2. Ovrd. Product Liab. Veto	N	6. Drop EPA Limits	*	10. Bar Bosnia Troop $	*
3. Increase Min. Wage	Y	7. Repeal Assault-Weap. Ban	*	11. Cut Anti-Missile Defense	Y
4. Welfare Reform	N	8. Ovrd. Part. Birth Veto	N	12. Bar U.N. Uniforms	N

Election Results

1996 general	Elijah E. Cummings (D)	115,764	(83%)	($248,070)
	Kenneth Kondner (R)	22,929	(17%)	
1996 special	Elijah E. Cummings (D)	17,912	(81%)	($443,717)
	Kenneth Kondner (R)	4,131	(19%)	
1996 primary	Elijah E. Cummings (D)	23,156	(37%)	
	Frank Reid (D)	14,720	(24%)	
	Delores G. Kelley (D)	5,918	(10%)	
	A. Dwight Pettit (D)	4,384	(7%)	
	Mary W. Conaway (D)	3,003	(5%)	
	Others	10,609	(17%)	
1994 general	Kweisi Mfume (D)	97,016	(82%)	($161,285)
	Kenneth Kondner (R)	22,007	(18%)	

EIGHTH DISTRICT

One of America's most affluent and best-educated communities has grown up along an old road down which colonial farmers rolled barrels of tobacco to the port of Georgetown 200 years ago. The old road, now called Rockville Pike and Wisconsin Avenue, is the commercial spine of Montgomery County, Maryland. And this suburban jurisdiction just northwest of Washington, D.C., has for several decades ranked at or near the top of the list of counties in income and education. Today's Montgomery County is in large part a creation of the federal government, which has put huge facilities out here—Bethesda Naval Hospital, the National Institutes of Health, the Food and Drug Administration, the National Institute of Standards and Technology—to make it the center of America's fast-growing health industry. But the percentage of workers employed by government has been declining rapidly here, to about one in six in the mid-1990s—a figure only a percentage point or two above the national average. In the late 1970s or early 1980s, Montgomery seemed to have reached a critical mass, and started generating thousands of private sector health, high-tech, defense and service-industry jobs.

Wisconsin Avenue and Rockville Pike have become strip highways, with 1950s commercial development and 1960s shopping centers like so many in the country. But the stores are upscale, sometimes *very* upscale, and the new skyscrapers of downtown Bethesda and the office parks-cum-fitness centers of farther-out Gaithersburg are genuinely impressive. Not all of Montgomery County is exclusively high-income: there are some modest, mostly black and Jewish neighborhoods in Silver Spring and Wheaton. The 1980s saw a significant increase in foreign migration here, with the Asian population up 172% in the 1980s.

Historically, the typical Montgomery County voter was a high-ranking civil servant, but as private employment outpaces government work, the picture is changing. The fastest-growing parts of the county, out past Rockville in Gaithersburg and Germantown, are filling up with Republicans and conservatives more than Democrats and liberals.

The congresswoman from the 8th District is Connie Morella, a Republican first elected in 1986 when incumbent Democrat Michael Barnes ran for the Senate. Morella grew up in Massachusetts, taught school in Montgomery County in the 1950s. She raised nine children, six of them her late sister's, and at the same time earned a master's degree and taught English at American University and Montgomery College. In 1978, she was elected to the Maryland House of Delegates; after two four-year terms, she gave up the seat to run for Congress, and won with 53% against nursing home millionaire Stewart Bainum, who spent $1.5 million of his own money. She is hard-working, cooperative with colleagues, congenial with constituents, energetic enough to tend to 600,000 constituents who are only a local phone call away and to make a mark on national issues—a regimen exhausting enough that three of the last four congressmen here relinquished their seats to retire or run for the more restful Senate.

By almost any measure, Morella is one of the three or four most liberal Republicans in the House. Her votes against seven items of the Contract With America were three more than any other Republican. In the Montgomery County tradition, she takes liberal positions on cultural issues from abortion rights to gun control. Her record is more moderate on economics: the 8th has the second highest median household incomes of any district in the country (number one is the New Jersey 11th). She sponsored a tax credit for companies who take certain actions to reduce workplace violence and has been on the alert for retaliation against women who charge sexual harassment, whether at the Aberdeen Proving Ground or Mitsubishi. She opposed a moratorium on the Endangered Species Act and was one of two House Republicans (Tom Davis of northern Virginia was the other) who voted for a January 1996 measure to reopen the federal government which the House rejected 206–167. Morella chairs the Science Subcommittee on Technology and favors protecting software produced by federal scientists with limited copyrights. She is also the fourth-ranking Republican on Government Reform and Oversight, but she dodged an attempt by others to make her chairman to replace the conservative Dan Burton; they feared that he would not be as temperate and presentable an investigator of White House misdeeds as was Chairman Bill Clinger, who retired in 1996.

House Republican leaders understand that Morella represents a heavily Democratic district and are confident that she is not trying to undermine her party colleagues. Speaker Newt Gingrich has gone out of his way to praise her, even when she votes against the leadership, and he put her on the task force on the environment in an effort to come up with a Republican consensus on the issue. Still, some Montgomery County conservatives have been eager to oppose her; Ruthann Aron, who nearly won the 1994 Senate nomination, talked about running in the 1996 primary; she did not, but Morella did have competition and was held down to 65%. At the same time, her Republican label hurt. Montgomery County voted 59%–35% for Bill Clinton over Bob Dole, and Morella's percentage fell from 70% in 1994 to 61% in 1996. Morella may well have been the beneficiary of more split tickets than any other Republican House member, but despite her personal strengths and hard work she may well be the target of serious opposition, in the primary or in the general, in some future election.

The People: Pop. 1990: 597,760; 6% rural; 10% age 65+; 78% White; 8% Black; 8% Asian; 6% Hispanic origin. Households: 61% married couple families; 30% married couple fams. w. children; 75% college educ.; median household income: $56,789; per capita income: $26,900; median gross rent: $777; median house value: $205,500.

1996 Presidential Vote			**1992 Presidential Vote**		
Clinton (D)	156,450	(57%)	Clinton (D)	156,043	(53%)
Dole (R)	103,327	(38%)	Bush (R)	103,477	(35%)
Perot (I)	12,200	(4%)	Perot (I)	35,599	(12%)

Rep. Constance A. Morella (R)

Elected 1986; b. Feb. 12, 1931, Somerville, MA; home, Bethesda; Boston U., A.B. 1954; American U., M.A. 1967; Catholic; married (Anthony).

Career: Teacher, Montgomery Cnty. Pub. Schls., 1956–60; Instructor, American U., 1968–70; Prof., Montgomery Col., 1970–86; MD House of Delegates, 1978–86.

DC Office: 2228 RHOB 20515, 202-225-5341; Fax: 202-225-1389.

District Offices: Rockville, 301-424-3501.

Committees: *Government Reform & Oversight* (4th of 24 R): Civil Service; District of Columbia (Vice Chmn.). *Science* (4th of 25 R): Basic Research; Technology (Chmn.).

Group Ratings

	ADA	ACLU	AFS	LCV	CFA	CON	NFIB	COC	ACU	NTLC	CHC
1996	50	56	42	54	77	100	67	60	30	54	20
1995	45	—	—	44	92	99	—	65	25	—	—

National Journal Ratings

	1995 LIB — 1995 CONS			1996 LIB — 1996 CONS		
Economic	55%	—	45%	54%	—	45%
Social	75%	—	23%	84%	—	12%
Foreign	67%	—	32%	81%	—	19%

Key Votes of the 104th Congress

1. Reduce Medicare Growth $	Y	5. Flag Amendment	Y	9. Cuban Embargo	N
2. Ovrd. Product Liab. Veto	Y	6. Drop EPA Limits	Y	10. Bar Bosnia Troop $	N
3. Increase Min. Wage	Y	7. Repeal Assault-Weap. Ban	N	11. Cut Anti-Missile Defense	N
4. Welfare Reform	Y	8. Ovrd. Part. Birth Veto	N	12. Bar U.N. Uniforms	N

Election Results

1996 general	Constance A. Morella (R)	152,538	(61%)	($559,807)
	Donald Mooers (D)	96,229	(39%)	($196,858)
1996 primary	Constance A. Morella (R)	28,818	(65%)	
	Barrie S. Ciliberti (R)	11,845	(27%)	
	John C. Webb (R)	2,770	(6%)	
	Others	698	(2%)	
1994 general	Constance A. Morella (R)	143,449	(70%)	($306,968)
	Steven Van Grack (D)	60,660	(30%)	($10,802)

MASSACHUSETTS

It would be a city on a hill, John Winthrop wrote of the Massachusetts Bay colony his Puritans were building, an example to the entire world. And Massachusetts, in the more than three centuries since, has always assumed it has a lot to teach others. The New World Puritans' austere creed, stemming from English Puritan Oliver Cromwell, taught that only the select would be saved and that they must extirpate the forces of Satan—Indians, Papists, tolerationists. For 150 years, New England was partial to learning, but also insular, hostile to outsiders and economically stagnant. Then, after the American Revolution, the international war between royal Britain and revolutionary and Napoleonic France allowed New England shipowners to cross enemy lines to become the world's leading merchants. They made vast profits in just a few brief years, and plowed the money into textile mills, then railroads, then coal mining and steel-making: this was the capital that made industrial America.

Massachusetts made a new America in other ways. Intellectually, New England flowered: just a few writers from Boston and Concord—Ralph Waldo Emerson, Henry Wadsworth Longfellow, Henry David Thoreau, John Greenleaf Whittier, Nathaniel Hawthorne—created an American literary genre and popularized an American philosophy, more than 200 years after Plymouth Rock. Demographically, New England Yankees surged across the continent: long blocked from Upstate New York by natural impediments, they only reached Syracuse in the 1820s; by the 1850s they were in Iowa and Kansas and Oregon's Willamette Valley; by the 1880s they had settled Los Angeles. They built new cities and new colleges in the wilderness. They helped to start the Republican Party and did much to start—and win—the Civil War. They planted their economic system and their values, articulated in the *McGuffey Readers*, across the continent: a nation looking to Massachusetts for instruction.

But in the meantime, Massachusetts itself and Boston, the Hub of the Universe, were being remade. The potato famine of the 1840s and an economy that continued imploding for decades sent Irishmen across the Atlantic, and many came to Boston, looking for work in the mills, docks and factories. Yankee Protestants had seen Catholics as their great cultural enemy for 200 years and felt their commonwealth was under siege. As the Irish became a majority, first in Boston and then statewide, Protestants feared the Irish would use their political clout to ladle out government jobs and benefits to their own. And the Irish had a much better flair for politics than instinct for commerce; they yearned for the security of a government job. But they encountered such bigotry and rejection by the Yankees that even as successful an Irish Catholic as Joseph Kennedy felt obliged to move from Boston to New York in 1927. Politics in Massachusetts for years was a kind of cultural war between Yankee Republicans and Irish Democrats, an argument not so much over the distribution of income or the provision of services as over whose vision of Massachusetts should be honored, and whose version of history should be taught—not unlike battles being fought between liberals and conservatives today.

Sometimes, the stakes were concrete—control of patronage jobs, command of the Boston Police Department—but more often they were symbolic. Yankee Republicans tended to back activist government programs: public works and protective tariffs to help business, Civil War and Reconstruction to help suitably distant oppressed people like southern blacks, uplifting (and productivity-enhancing) social movements like temperance. The Irish found 19th Century Democrats—a party promoting *laissez-faire*—more congenial. The Irish had come from a place where the government was the enemy, and didn't want government spending money to help the rich or to stimulate commerce. They didn't want government to restrict immigration, to advance the blacks who might compete with them in the labor market, or to prohibit liquor.

Over the years, the percentage of Irish and Catholics slowly rose. Yankees had smaller

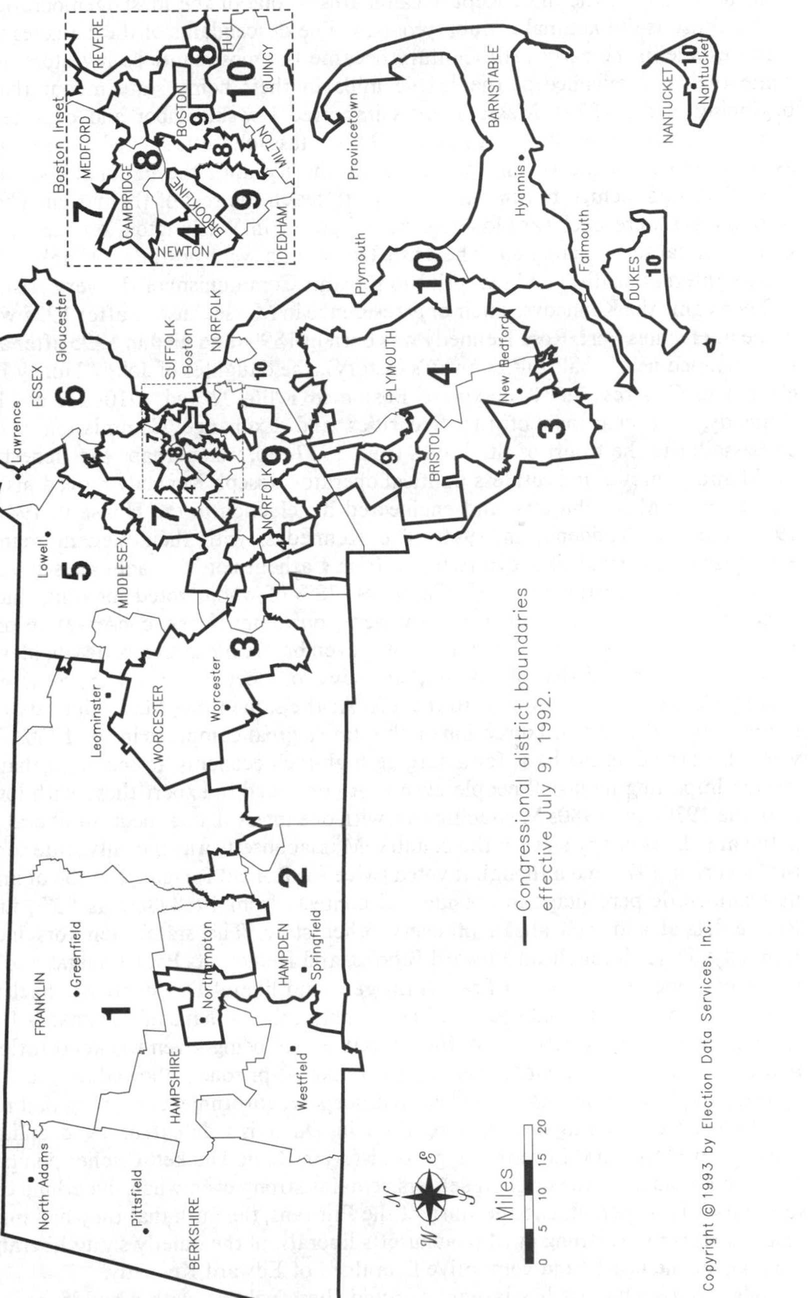
Boston Inset
REVERE
MEDFORD
CAMBRIDGE
BOSTON
BROOKLINE
NEWTON
DEDHAM
MILTON
QUINCY
HULL
7
8
4
9
10
ESSEX
Newburyport
Lawrence
Gloucester
6
SUFFOLK
Boston
NORFOLK
MIDDLESEX
Lowell
5
PLYMOUTH
Plymouth
New Bedford
BRISTOL
3
Provincetown
BARNSTABLE
Hyannis
Falmouth
DUKES
NANTUCKET
Nantucket
WORCESTER
Worcester
Leominster
FRANKLIN
Greenfield
HAMPSHIRE
Northampton
HAMPDEN
Springfield
Westfield
1
2
BERKSHIRE
Pittsfield
North Adams
Miles
0 5 10 15 20
— Congressional district boundaries
effective July 9, 1992.
Copyright © 1993 by Election Data Services, Inc.

families, moved west, intermarried with people of immigrant stock and lost their Yankee identity. The Irish mostly stayed put, raising large families and eventually Massachusetts moved from being one of the most Republican states to one of the most Democratic. Economically, Massachusetts did not make much progress. The descendants of the Yankees who had been so venturesome in the early 19th Century became the most cautious investors in the early 20th, while the predominance of the textile mills in their home state meant that for a century beginning in the 1820s, Massachusetts imported low-skill labor and exported highly skilled people. As textile mills fled south in the 1920s, Massachusetts started exporting low-skill people as well; and from the waning of Yankee authority until the national rise of the Kennedys, Massachusetts seemed to run out of things to teach the rest of the nation. The state's Yankee Republicans were backward-looking, out of power in Washington, on the defensive at home, without a cause to champion. The Irish Democrats were hostile to Franklin Roosevelt's pro-British internationalism and receptive to the anti-Communism of the very Irish Joe McCarthy.

Then came the Kennedys. Their only residence in Massachusetts after 1927 was their summer home in Hyannis Port. Rose Kennedy was born in 1890 (and died in 1995 after a remarkable life that spanned nearly half this country's history), the daughter of John "Honey Fitz" Fitzgerald, elected to Congress at 31, mayor of Boston in 1906–07 and 1910–14; her husband Joseph Kennedy, first chairman of the Securities and Exchange Commission in the 1930s and ambassador to the Court of St. James from 1937–40, was perhaps the richest Catholic in the world and a shrewd and ruthless political operator. Joseph Kennedy moved his oldest surviving son, John, to Massachusetts, and engineered his election to the House in 1946, the Senate in 1952 and the Presidency in 1960. The Kennedys, with their elegant manners and great achievements, seemed like royalty to the Irish Catholics of Massachusetts and John Kennedy's election in 1960 certified to U.S. Catholics, 78% of whom voted for him, that they too were Americans. Joseph and John Kennedy were, on many issues, conservative or skeptical. But Kennedy's Administration was increasingly, even before his untimely death, identified as liberal, and his example and that of his brother, Edward, elected to the U.S. Senate at 30 in 1962, moved Massachusetts Catholics to the left. At the same time, Massachusetts Protestants were influenced by the leftward direction on the state's great campuses in the 1960s. The universities were also providing the basis for a surging high-tech economy, to the point that Massachusetts started importing high-skill people even as it continued to export those with low skills.

In the 1970s and 1980s Massachusetts, with one interval, had the most liberal governance and national politics of any state in the country. Massachusetts was the only state to vote for George McGovern in 1972 and although it voted twice for Ronald Reagan, the son of an Irish Catholic, its Democratic percentage in presidential contests from 1968–88 was 53%, just 0.4% behind Rhode Island and well ahead of every other state. The state's senators included Edward Kennedy, liberal Republican Edward Brooke, and Democrats Paul Tsongas and John Kerry. Its governors, liberal Republican Francis Sargent and liberal Democrat Michael Dukakis, vastly increased spending and endorsed the inexplicable policies that sunk Dukakis's 1988 presidential campaign: prisoners sentenced to life without parole being given weekend furloughs—a policy that liberals in the press said it was racist to oppose—prisoners allowed to vote and be registered by state employees sent into prisons for that purpose, government spending that rose 9% a year in the 1980s. Rebellion against this resulted in Dukakis's defeat in 1978 and the election of conservative Democrat Edward King. As historian David Hackett Fischer points out in *Albion's Seed*, the mindset of the original settlers remains strong even when the ethnic origin of current residents is far different, and the spirit of the Puritans, the faith that they had much to teach the rest of the world, is strong in Massachusetts liberals: in the quietly smug liberalism of Michael Dukakis or the hearty and combative liberalism of Edward Kennedy.

Today, Massachusetts has largely rejected these politics, with a suddenness matched in its history by its merchants' sudden emergence as world traders in the 1790s and the appearance of Irish immigrants on Boston docks in the 1840s. It happened even as the country seemed to be going Massachusetts's way, as Michael Dukakis was winning the Democratic nomination for president and leading Massachusetts-born George Bush in the polls, and as "the Massachusetts miracle" was being celebrated by the *Boston Globe*, then as objective from the left as the old *Chicago Tribune* was on the right (although the *Globe* under its new editor, like the *Tribune* under its current leadership, comes closer to objectivity than most major dailies). But the state's financial problems were silently worsening as Dukakis campaigned across the country; he won only 53% of the vote in Massachusetts, running strong in the Berkshires and the Pioneer Valley in the west, but only running even in the Boston media market (which includes New Hampshire, a low-tax haven from high-tax Massachusetts since colonial times). Then in 1989, things fell apart. The state economy sagged badly: the slump in minicomputers hurt Massachusetts-based Wang and Digital; Cambridge's Lotus software was outflanked by Seattle's Microsoft; defense spending cutbacks, long sought by Massachusetts politicians, naturally produced job losses. More spectacular was the bursting of the Northeast real estate bubble and the resultant collapse of major New England banks: New Englanders relearned the old lesson that housing prices don't go up 25% a year indefinitely. The state government essentially went bankrupt, and Dukakis retired from office. It seemed that the rest of the country had something to teach Massachusetts.

In the decade since Massachusetts has learned some lessons and gone some distance toward forming a new consensus. It is a combination of fiscal austerity and cultural liberalism, best personified by Republican Governor William Weld whose self-confident persona and vision of a government that taxes and spends lightly, that is friendly to feminism and gay rights, that exerts some effort to protect the environment, that is tough on crime, proves to be enormously appealing. This combination also produced overwhelming majorities for Democrats. In 1992 Massachusetts, after backing native son Paul Tsongas in the Democratic primary, delivered a 48%–29% margin for Bill Clinton in November. Democrats won veto-proof majorities in the legislature, even as Republicans picked up two congressional seats and seriously contested three others, Democrats won the total vote cast for Congress by 57%–35%. In 1994 Edward Kennedy seemed momentarily threatened by businessman Mitt Romney. But Kennedy rallied and won by a solid 58%–41%, while Democrats held all statewide offices except treasurer, led by 72%–28% in popular vote in House races, and made gains in the legislature.

Meanwhile Bill Clinton, even in his 1994 national nadir, proved widely popular in Massachusetts. He had been careful to maintain close ties to the Kennedys, attending their commemorations and remembering his Rose Garden handshake with President Kennedy, appointing Jean Kennedy Smith Ambassador to Ireland and subcontracting Northern Ireland policy to her and former Edward Kennedy aide Nancy Soderberg. He evidently calculated early on that a leftish Democratic challenge in the 1996 primaries would not prosper if he could hold on to the Kennedys' support. They and other Massachusetts politicians like Barney Frank stuck with Clinton solidly in 1995 when others on the left were muttering curses and plotting mutiny. (There is a vivid contrast here with Jimmy Carter, who went out of his way to antagonize the Kennedys, and whose reelection campaign was gravely weakened by Edward Kennedy's 1980 primary challenge.) At the same time liberal campuses still kept generating talented young Democratic politicos in Massachusetts, as they did in most states in the 1970s but not in the 1990s. For his part, Weld was so desultory in building a Republican Party that there were fewer Republicans in the legislature after his big win in 1994 than there had been four years before; he declined to run for president, and watched wanly as the candidacy of his first choice, Pete Wilson, imploded. By the beginning of 1996, Clinton's popularity was so high in Massachusetts that it spread throughout New England, even into usually Massachusetts-hating New Hampshire. In November 1996 Massachusetts voted 61%–28% for Clinton, his best showing in the country; in the political dialogue that goes on endlessly in the state it was taken for granted that there was nothing to say for or even about the Republicans or Bob Dole.

Massachusetts's lesson was not absorbed everywhere. But it was followed in New England and in the Metroliner corridor from New York to Washington, where Clinton ran very strongly and Democrats walloped even Republican candidates who had previously run well. Clinton carried these states by a whopping 55%–34%, compared to only 47%–43% in the rest of the country;

Democratic House candidates won here 55%–43%, while losing 51%–47% in the rest of America. Why were Clinton and the Democrats so strong in Massachusetts and the Northeast? With tax increases now unthinkable, it was safe to vote on other issues, and on those this greater Massachusetts seemed to be closer to Western Europe than to large parts of America—the South, the Great Plains, the Rocky Mountains. But the spirit here is certainly not German or French or even British. It is closer to the new Irish immigrants who have been flocking to Massachusetts and to New York in the 1980s and 1990s—irreverent and not at all bound by the Catholic Church, disrespectful of big governments but determined to keep the benefits they have, with little sympathetic contact with the traditional values of the rest of America. Despite Clinton's victory, it is not clear that their lesson is taking hold in most of America.

Governor. William Weld is the first Yankee Massachusetts Republican governor determined to hold down taxes and government spending since Christian Herter left the State House on Beacon Hill in 1956. In Weld's office hangs a picture of James Michael Curley, the scampish mayor of Boston, congressman and one-term governor, who spent 50 years creating public jobs to help his friends and supporters. Though often called a Boston Brahmin, Weld technically is not: he grew up on Long Island, went to prep school and college in Massachusetts, and has stayed on except for a stint in Washington. He has more than a touch of the frayed-collar, patched-elbow WASP: he lives in a grand rambling house off Cambridge's Brattle Street; his wife is a great-granddaughter of Theodore Roosevelt; he majored in classics; he loves to hunt and play poker and at one public appearance suddenly dove into the Charles River. He would have been at home in the Boston of Henry Cabot Lodge, Sr., or the Washington of Henry Adams.

Weld's first issue was crime: as U.S. attorney in Massachusetts in the early 1980s, Weld prosecuted many local pols; as an assistant attorney general, he resigned in protest of the controversies surrounding Attorney General Edwin Meese; as candidate for governor, he lambasted the absurdly loose criminal justice policies of Michael Dukakis. His next issue was spending and taxes, and his posture was that of his predecessor Calvin Coolidge: NO. After a tumultuous campaign in 1990 that came as close as anything could to satisfying Massachusetts's appetite for political theater, he took control of the budget with juddering spending cuts and tax cuts; and Massachusetts's economy started to revive. At the same time, his outspoken pro-choice stand on abortion and his vehement support of gay rights—keep the government out of your pocketbook and your bedroom, he told the 1992 Republican National Convention—assuaged Massachusetts's articulate cultural liberals. His radical welfare proposal—replacing cash grants with services and giving applicants 90 days to find a job or work at community services—was only partially approved by the legislature and his charter schools were limited to 25. He has supported environmental measures and boasts of protecting 44,000 acres of open land from development. He changed his anti-gun control stand to back an assault weapons ban and waiting period for handgun purchases.

In 1990, Massachusetts was clearly ready to repudiate its high-tax, high-spending past, but Weld was anything but a sure winner for governor. He had competition in the sparse-voting Republican primary from an anti-abortion state legislator, and won 61%–39% only after spending $1.1 million of his own money. And in the general he faced John Silber, president of Boston University, who sounded back-to-basics themes on cultural issues while retaining ties to traditional Democratic politicians like Senate President Billy Bulger and refusing to support a tax-cutting ballot proposition. This was a sharply fought battle, which Weld won by only 50%–47%. The turning point came when Silber attacked working mothers ("We have a generation of abused children by women who have thought a third-rate day care center was just as good as a first-rate home"). Weld won with strong votes from women and baby boomers.

Weld was reelected easily in 1994, against liberal legislator Mark Roosevelt, a cousin of his wife's. Then his attention wandered to presidential politics. He propitiated legislators by approving a pay raise in December 1994, which hurt his standing in New Hampshire. In February 1995 he said he would not run for president and in April came out for California Governor Pete Wilson. With Wilson voiceless after throat surgery, Weld pretty much was the

Wilson campaign in New England. But then Wilson bowed out in September 1995, and Weld's attention turned to the Senate race against incumbent John Kerry. Previously they had worked together, but the race was fiercely fought, with many ads and many debates. Political reporters were fascinated by this atypical contest—the only one in the country in which most reporters could imagine voting for both candidates—and Weld seemed to be leading in September. But in November he lost 52%–45%, and met Kerry at McGann's Irish Pub for a concillatory, post-election beer.

In early 1997 Massachusetts's economy was in fine shape, with the lowest unemployment in the East and a high-tech, high-education base that seems headed for only better things; the burden of government is far lower even as the Central Artery/Third Harbor Tunnel, the largest public works project in the state's history, is under way in downtown Boston. Weld's main proposals were for more spending on early education, more charter schools, and cuts in taxes on insurance companies and investment incomes. There are still few Republicans in office, but Weld has set a course that even a Democratic successor would have to pay a high price to stray from. In 1996 Weld said he would not run for a third term, and though some thought he might reconsider, in April 1997, President Clinton offered Weld the ambassadorship to Mexico, which he accepted. And, Weld has been promoting the chances of Lieutenant Governor Paul Cellucci, whose name appears with Weld's in every press release and official sign. Cellucci has worked on downsizing state government, attracting jobs, the Central Artery—more than the usual lieutenant governor fare. Weld has said he will support Cellucci, even against the promised primary candidacy of state Treasurer Joe Malone: Weld like Bill Clinton seems to take some measure of success by naming his successor. On the Democratic side, two likely candidates are Congressman Joe Kennedy and Attorney General Scott Harshbarger. Kennedy leads in polls, except when paired against Weld, and has established in the House that he is something more than the dilettante he seemed when he was first elected in 1986, although the divorce from his first wife has become a thorn in his side. Harshbarger has gained wide publicity over the past eight years. Aficionados of Massachusetts politics are not likely to be denied a diverting spectacle.

Senior Senator. Edward Kennedy is now in his fourth decade as a national celebrity and a politician. He has had the highs and lows of his personal life followed by millions and criticized vitriolically by many; he has been a presidential candidate and, while still in his 30s, was widely assumed to be the next president. He is third in seniority in the Senate, behind Strom Thurmond and Robert Byrd. His reputation as an idealistic champion of the poor has been burnished by the praise of first-rate celebrators that no American political family has attracted before. To others, he is a symbol of personal immorality and unpunished criminal behavior, a man who has gotten away with things that would have ended anyone else's public career. There is some basis for both views, but neither is an entirely fair picture of this politician who was reelected by a smart margin in 1994 in a race whose outcome seemed by no means certain; Kennedy has been paid more attention in the 1990s as a scandal-beset celebrity than as a consistent and often effective advocate of a view of public policy.

For the luster of the Kennedys has worn off, in America and even in Massachusetts, and the percentage of Americans who look to the Kennedys for political leadership has grown small; most voters can't remember, or never knew, what made the Kennedys so exciting. Edward Kennedy was first elected in 1962, at age 30. "He can do more for Massachusetts" was his slogan, as it had been John Kennedy's 10 years before. After his brothers' assassinations, he was seen by many as their natural heir, and could have been nominated for president in 1968, at 36, or in 1972 had he chosen to run. Instead, in the latter year, he gave the first of several stirring convention speeches promoting his trademark liberalism. In 1980, he ran for president, and began the race against incumbent Jimmy Carter far ahead in the polls. But he was unable to articulate his reasons for running, and his candidacy was greeted with adverse reaction to him personally as well as to his policies. It ended in a crushing defeat, relieved only by another stirring convention speech, after which he pointedly refused to raise Carter's hand on the podium. In retrospect, it is plain that Edward Kennedy's presidential chances were ended in July 1969, with the accident at Chappaquiddick, even though the Kennedy family retainers managed to cast a cloud over the specifics in a way that would be considered outrageous if tried by anyone else. And after the Good Friday 1991 bar-hopping in Palm Beach and his nephew William Kennedy Smith's trial and acquittal for rape, Kennedy had to fight hard, with some low punches as well as fair hard lefts, to win reelection to represent in the Senate the Kennedy homeland of Massachusetts.

Kennedy has been a hardworking and practical politician who, after his brothers' deaths, took up the liberal causes and attention to the poor which had been the focus of Robert Kennedy in the last years of his life. He has worked hard for a quarter century on their behalf—until the election of Bill Clinton—without the friendship of a Democratic Administration and since 1994 without the backing of a Democratic majority. As chairman of the Labor and Human Resources Committee from 1987–94, Kennedy supported teachers' unions; on the Judiciary Committee he supported pro-choice and feminist groups with energy and enthusiasm. He immediately pounced on Judge Robert Bork's nomination in 1987, but was precluded from a similarly loud role in the Clarence Thomas hearings in October 1991 because of the Palm Beach incident.

In 1992 Kennedy supported Bill Clinton happily and basked as President Clinton gave repeated homage to the Kennedy family; he was also delighted when Clinton appointed his sister Jean Kennedy Smith Ambassador to Ireland. Legislatively Kennedy was productive, though not as much as he wished. Through his Labor and Human Resources Committee, he worked to pass direct student loans, AmeriCorps, Goals 2000 and the School-to-Work Opportunity Act. He sponsored the Family and Medical Leave Act which George Bush had vetoed and which was the first law Bill Clinton signed. He passed a bill criminalizing blocking access to abortion clinics. But he was gravely frustrated on other issues. He sought to prevent states from regulating abortions and to ban the death penalty when imposed disproportionately on criminals of different races; both efforts failed. Health care had been a Kennedy cause since the 1970s, when he backed a Canadian-style single-payer system. In May 1994 he got a healthcare bill resembling Clinton's through the Labor Committee. But that was as far as it went. Kennedy smelled the possibility of a bipartisan compromise, but the Clinton White House insisted on standing firm and trying to push a Democratic bill through, and got no result at all.

Kennedy entered the 1994 campaign popular but appeared tired and overweight. His opponent was businessman Mitt Romney, whose father was governor of Michigan and a presidential candidate in the 1960s; Romney fit the Massachusetts profile on issues: against 1960s-style big government, pro-choice on abortion, for the death penalty, for Clinton's don't-ask-don't-tell policy on gays in the military. "The 1960s liberal agenda hasn't worked. It is time to reform the reforms." To which Kennedy said, "I stand for the idea that public service can make a difference in the lives of people." This was the second most expensive campaign in the country—Kennedy spent $11.5 million, Romney $7.6 million, both dipping into their own money—and among the most sharply contested. A Romney ad showed Kennedy painfully sitting down, and Romney had a 43%–42% lead in a September poll. Astonishingly for a man whose brother won the presidency while appealing against religious bigotry, Kennedy echoed questions, first raised by his nephew Joe Kennedy, about Romney's Mormon faith, asking whether he had challenged that church's racially discriminatory beliefs before they were changed in 1978. The *Boston Globe* responded, "That line of attack makes no more sense than asking Kennedy how many times he has written to Rome demanding that the church change its stand on abortion." More damaging were Kennedy ads attacking Romney's business practices. Romney claimed his work at Bain Capital produced 10,000 jobs. But Kennedy investigators found an Indiana factory where 350 workers had gone out on strike after their pay and benefits were cut when it was bought by Bain Capital. Romney claimed he severed his ties with Bain before the purchase was complete, but the damage was palpable. Also, Kennedy performed above expectations in debate. By late October, a *Herald* poll had Kennedy ahead 50%–32%; he won 58%–41%.

Kennedy returned to a Republican Senate and shifted his focus from expanding government to protecting it from downsizing. In 1995 he defended Medicare and Medicaid from reductions and opposed changes in labor law— Davis-Bacon repeal, the TEAM Act and the flextime bill. He led the effort for a limited school choice experiment in Washington, D.C.—taking the side of teachers' unions and the wretched D.C. school system. On immigration, he successfully opposed the amendment to give states authority to expel children of illegal immigrants. In 1996 he went on the offensive. He pushed the minimum wage issue, ignored by Clinton and Kennedy when the Democrats were in control, and split the Republicans while developing a campaign issue. He pushed the Kassebaum-Kennedy healthcare bill, an incremental measure to provide portability of health insurance and to limit exclusions for preexisting conditions. Kennedy clearly saw this as an entering wedge for more government involvement, though not all his supporters did, and he wanted to keep Medical Savings Accounts out of the bill, stalling it for months until embarrassed by Republican charges he was sabotaging his own bill. He tried to add to the Defense of Marriage Act a provision to prohibit job discrimination against gays; this was rejected by only a narrow margin, indicating there may be a majority in the Senate for a gay rights bill some time soon. "If we become pale carbon copies of the opposition and try to act like Republicans, we will lose and we will deserve to lose," Kennedy said in January 1995. In 1996 Kennedy strongly supported Bill Clinton even after Clinton embraced a balanced budget and signed the Welfare Reform Act, and Kennedy had the pleasure of watching Clinton win and run strongest in Massachusetts. Kennedy campaigned actively for many Democrats, and in 1997 came roaring out with his latest health care bill, providing health insurance for children by raising cigarette taxes; but in May 1997 the Senate rejected his bill as part of the balanced budget resolution. He remains a very considerable force in the Senate.

Junior Senator. John Kerry first won fame as one of the organizers of Vietnam Veterans Against the War in 1971. His leadership attracted attention because of his background, unusual for a Vietnam veteran (he went to Yale and his mother is from the Brahmin Forbes family), and because of his record of genuine heroism in combat. "How do you ask a man to be the last to die for a mistake?" he asked in congressional testimony—a good question, and one which also suggested his future political ambitions. Yet his political career did not proceed straight ahead. He ran for Congress in 1972, after some widely observed district-shopping, and lost in a district carried by George McGovern. Chastened, Kerry went to law school, worked for a prosecutor, was elected lieutenant governor on the Dukakis ticket in 1982, and ran for senator in 1984; in both races, he upset a favored rival for the Democratic nomination. In 1982, Kerry won the general as part of a tied ticket with Dukakis; in the 1984 general, he beat Raymond Shamie, businessman and state Republican chairman, 55%–45%.

Kerry came to the Senate with a reputation as a strong liberal, and the similarity of his name to Kennedy's (his initials are J.F.K.) fed an assumption that the two Massachusetts senators would vote alike. They mostly have; but there have been differences of nuance and interest; Kerry has been more respectful of economic free markets and moved earlier than Kennedy toward supporting an expansive U.S. foreign and military policy. In the majority, Kerry made a name as an investigator, spending some time up blind alleys with klieg lights but also producing some important information regardless of political fallout. He used his Foreign Relations Terrorism, Narcotics and International Operations Subcommittee chairmanship to investigate the Bank of Credit & Commerce International—the now infamous BCCI scandal; his October 1992 report accused the Justice Department, British banking regulators and especially the CIA of "institutional failure" in recognizing the fraudulent nature of BCCI's operations. During that time, he did more than any American official except Manhattan District Attorney Robert Morgenthau to uncover what BCCI was up to. But the subcommittee also spent much time trying to pin drug-running charges on Central American rightists—convenient for American politicians supportive of Central American left-wingers. Kerry was on more solid ground, as later events made clear, in charging Manuel Noriega of Panama with drug-dealing.

Kerry's other great investigation was as chairman of the Select Committee on POW/MIA

Affairs, on whether Americans were left behind in Vietnamese hands in 1973. Kerry and Republican Bob Smith of New Hampshire went to Vietnam and attempted to dig up new evidence. Kerry grilled former Secretary of State Henry Kissinger, a bit unfairly, but overall this was a serious effort, with an appropriately hedged conclusion: there is evidence "that indicates the possibility of survival, at least for a small number," after 1973, but also said, "there is at this time no compelling evidence that any American remains alive in captivity in southeast Asia." By May 1995, Kerry and fellow Vietnam veteran Senator John McCain's efforts in this area had convinced them that Hanoi was fully cooperating and, aware that they had standing on this issue that Bill Clinton conspicuously lacked, they got him to normalize relations with Vietnam.

In the early 1990s, when big government was imploding in Massachusetts, Kerry took moderate tacks, supporting racial quotas but talking of the need for personal responsibility and the work ethic, opposing the Gulf war resolution but not in a nuanced way. He successfully worked with Richard Bryan of Nevada to eliminate the wool and mohair subsidy in 1993 and he won a fight to eliminate the Advanced Liquid Metal Reactor nuclear disposal in 1994. He has long called for campaign finance reform and has refused to take PAC contributions. In 1990, when Massachusetts was in revolt against Michael Dukakis, Kerry had a self-financing opponent who ran what is probably the first "morph spot" ever, showing Kerry changing into Dukakis. But Kerry won by a convincing 57%–43% margin.

Even as the Senate was captured by the Republicans in 1994, Massachusetts seemed to be moving toward the Democrats, and Kerry seemed to be in a secure political position, with a mostly liberal voting record and a mostly liberal constituency. In May 1995 he married Teresa Heinz, widow of Republican Senator John Heinz of Pennsylvania, who inherited his fortune of more than $600 million. But suddenly in late 1995 Kerry was faced with the one opponent who could give him real trouble, Governor William Weld. Weld had just been reelected with 71% of the vote, his job rating was as positive as Kerry's or more so and he was much more familiar to voters in Massachusetts. Earlier the two had worked together on some state problems and emphasized the similarity of their views: they were both pro-choice on abortion, even against the partial birth abortion ban; they were both for gay rights; they both supported the deployment of U.S. troops in Bosnia. But the campaign inevitably produced disagreements and some gentlemanly acrimony. Weld called Kerry a "tax-and-spend liberal who is soft on crime." Kerry charged that Weld would vote for budget cuts that would hurt Medicare, Medicaid, education and the environment. Weld tied Kerry to Michael Dukakis. Kerry tied Weld to Jesse Helms. Weld said he would change Washington. Kerry said Weld would tear down government. They held seven debates altogether, literate rounds of accusations and one-liners. They reached an agreement in August 1996 on a spending cap of $6.9 million a piece in overall spending with a maximum of $5 million on media expenditures. They both spent more, however: Kerry, $12.6 million, the second highest of any Senate candidate for 1996, including $1.9 million of his own; Weld, $8 million, including $152,000 of his own.

This was a race beloved of reporters, this battle of bluebloods, for the high verbal skills of the candidates. The rounds of ads and debate repartee were reported extensively, and great conclusions drawn about when and whether the tide was changing. But the polls showed relatively little change. Most showed Kerry ahead, some showed Weld leading, but for the most part this was a race fought out within the margin of error, with both candidates usually between 40% and 45%. Obviously many voters were split, and wobbled back and forth: Social Security, Medicare, education, environment worked for Kerry; crime, welfare, taxes worked for Weld. Kerry was hurt a bit by the revelation in mid-October that he had accepted free lodging at lobbyist and Democratic fundraiser Robert Farmer's Washington apartment in the late 1980s. But in the last debate Kerry framed the issues his way by asking Weld what programs he would cut; Weld declined to answer. The VNS exit poll suggested that most voters making their minds up in the last week chose Kerry: this may simply have been a matter of Democrats coming home. In heavily Republican states extremely popular Democratic governors were beaten in Senate races, in Wyoming in 1994 and Nebraska in 1996; in heavily Democratic Massachusetts, voting

61%–28% for Bill Clinton over Bob Dole, an extremely popular governor lost to a competent and popular senator by 52%–45%. The electorate was not split along historic lines: Catholics voted only 56%–40% for Kerry, Protestants by only 53%–42% for Weld, numbers a world away from what exit polls would have shown when John Kennedy beat Henry Cabot Lodge, Jr., in 1952, or when Kennedy's grandfather John Fitzgerald lost to Lodge's grandfather in 1916. Nor was there an especially large gender gap. Income didn't make much difference: Weld carried only the top bracket, and not by much.

The real split was along cultural lines. Jews and those voters with no religion voted about 75% for Kerry; and there was no significant bloc of conservative Protestants to balance them off. And Kerry's biggest margins among education groups was not among those with high school educations or less, the traditional bulwark of the Democratic Party, but among those with graduate degrees, who gave him a 62%–35% margin: teachers, social workers, lawyers, doctors and other credentialed professionals. Kerry got his biggest percentages in Boston and university towns like Cambridge and Amherst, and he carried—but not by large margins—old mill towns like Lowell and Lawrence. Kerry did just as well in high-tech and liberal-value suburbs like Lexington and Lincoln. Weld carried middle-income suburbs around Worcester and Springfield, the retirement towns of Cape Cod and many suburbs beyond Route 128 and around I-495, but not by impressive margins.

Presidential politics. Massachusetts is the most Democratic state in presidential elections with the arguable exception of Rhode Island. In 1996 it gave Bill Clinton his largest percentage and largest margin of victory (with the exception of the District of Columbia); in 1992 it also gave him his largest percentage margin. There was something approaching unanimity for Clinton in 1996 among many groups: he carried women 69%–22% and those with graduate school educations 67%–25%.

Massachusetts's presidential primary has long been in early March and is the leading northern Super Tuesday contest. In 1988 and 1992, victory in Massachusetts went to its native sons: Democrats Michael Dukakis and Paul Tsongas and Republican George Bush. In 1996, the primary was held on Junior Tuesday, March 5; Bob Dole won over Pat Buchanan 48%–25%.

Congressional districting. Massachusetts's convoluted congressional district lines deserve their own biographer, someone with a sure political instinct and a touch of whimsy. The state lost one seat in each of the last two reapportionments. It will probably lose another after the 2000 Census, which will be bad news for Democrats: they currently hold all 10 seats.

The People: Est. Pop. 1996: 6,092,000; Pop. 1990: 6,016,425, up 1.3% 1990–1996. 2.3% of U.S. total, 13th largest; 16% rural. Median age: 35.6 years. 14% 65 years and over. 87.8% White, 4.6% Black, 2.3% Asian, 4.8% Hispanic origin. Households: 52.1% married couple families; 24% married couple fams. w. children; 50% college educ.; median household income: $36,952; per capita income: $17,224; 59.3% owner occupied housing; median house value: $162,800; median monthly rent: $506. 4.3% Unemployment. 1996 Voting age pop.: 4,649,000. 1996 Turnout: 2,556,459; 55% of VAP. Registered voters (1996): 3,459,193; 1,318,753 D (38%); 476,581 R (14%); 1,661,035 unaffiliated and minor parties (48%).

Political Lineup: Governor, William F. Weld (R); Lt. Gov., Paul Cellucci (R); Secy. of the Commonwealth, William Galvin (D); Atty. Gen., L. Scott Harshbarger (D); Treasurer, Joseph Malone (R); Comptroller, William Kilmartin (D); Auditor, Joseph DeNucci (D). State Senate, 40 (33 D and 7 R); Senate President, Thomas F. Birmingham (D); State House, 160 (130 D, 29 R and 1 I); House Speaker, Thomas Finneran (D). Senators, Edward M. Kennedy (D) and John F. Kerry (D). Representatives, 10 (10 D).

Elections Division: 617-727-2828; **Filing Deadline for U.S. Congress:** May 5, 1998.

1996 Presidential Vote

Clinton (D)	1,571,755	(61%)
Dole (R)	718,104	(28%)
Perot (I)	226,787	(9%)
Other	39,347	(2%)

1996 Republican Presidential Primary

Dole (R)	135,946	(48%)
Buchanan (R)	71,688	(25%)
Forbes (R)	39,605	(14%)
Alexander (R)	21,456	(8%)
Other	16,138	(6%)

1992 Presidential Vote

Clinton (D)	1,318,639	(48%)
Bush (R)	805,039	(29%)
Perot (I)	630,731	(22%)

GOVERNOR

Gov. William F. Weld (R)

Elected 1990, term expires Jan. 1999; b. July 31, 1945, Smithtown, NY; home, Cambridge; Harvard, B.A. 1966, J.D. 1970, Oxford U., 1967; Episcopalian; married (Susan).

Career: Practicing atty., 1970–80, 1988–90; U.S. Atty. for MA, 1981–86; U.S. Asst. Atty. Gen., Criminal Div., 1986–88.

Office: State House, Boston 02133, 617-727-3600; Fax: 617-727-9725; Web site: www.magnet.state.ma.us.

Election Results

1994 gen.	William F. Weld (R)	1,533,380	(71%)
	Mark Roosevelt (D)	611,641	(28%)
1994 prim.	William F. Weld (R)	unopposed	
1990 gen.	William F. Weld (R)	1,175,817	(50%)
	John Silber (D)	1,099,878	(47%)
	Other	67,167	(3%)

SENATORS

Sen. Edward M. Kennedy (D)

Elected 1962, seat up 2000; b. Feb. 22, 1932, Boston; home, Hyannis Port; Harvard, B.A. 1956, The Hague Intl. Law Schl., 1958, U. of VA, LL.B. 1959; Catholic; married (Vicki).

Career: Army, 1951–53; Western states coordinator, John F. Kennedy Pres. Campaign, 1960; Asst. Dist. Atty., Suffolk Cnty., 1961–62.

DC Office: 315 RSOB 20510, 202-224-4543; Fax: 202-224-2417; e-mail: senator@kennedy.senate.gov.

State Offices: Boston, 617-565-3170.

Committees: *Armed Services* (2nd of 8 D): Acquisition & Technology; Personnel; Sea Power (RMM). *Judiciary* (2nd of 8 D): Constitution, Federalism & Property Rights; Immigration (RMM). *Labor & Human Resources* (RMM of 8 D): Employment & Training; Public Health & Safety (RMM). *Joint Economic Committee* (9th of 10 Sens.).

Group Ratings

	ADA	ACLU	AFS	LCV	CFA	CON	NFIB	COC	ACU	NTLC	CHC
1996	90	50	100	85	86	8	31	38	0	14	0
1995	100	—	100	100	88	19	—	33	4	—	—

National Journal Ratings

	1995 LIB — 1995 CONS			1996 LIB — 1996 CONS		
Economic	86%	—	11%	82%	—	14%
Social	93%	—	0%	92%	—	0%
Foreign	79%	—	15%	77%	—	17%

Key Votes of the 104th Congress

1. Reduce Medicare Growth $	N	5. Flag Amendment	N	9. Anti-Missile Defense	N
2. Lmt. Prod. Liab. Damages	N	6. Endangered Species	Y	10. Cuban Embargo	N
3. Increase Min. Wage	Y	7. Gay Employment Rights	Y	11. Bar Bosnia Troop $	N
4. Welfare Reform	N	8. Ovrd. Part. Birth Veto	N	12. Cut Vietnam Aid	N

Election Results

1994 general	Edward M. Kennedy (D)	1,265,997	(58%)	($11,493,735)
	W. Mitt Romney (R)..................	894,000	(41%)	($7,624,491)
1994 primary	Edward M. Kennedy (D)	unopposed		
1988 general	Edward M. Kennedy (D)	1,693,344	(65%)	($2,702,865)
	Joseph D. Malone (R).................	884,267	(34%)	($587,323)

Sen. John F. Kerry (D)

Elected 1984, seat up 2002; b. Dec. 11, 1943, Denver, CO; home, Boston; Yale, A.B. 1966, Boston Col., LL.B. 1976; Catholic; married (Teresa Heinz).

Career: Navy, 1966–70 (Vietnam), Naval Reserves, 1972–78; Organizer, Vietnam Veterans Against the War; Asst. Dist. Atty., Middlesex Cnty., 1976–81; Practicing atty., 1981–82; MA Lt. Gov., 1982–84.

DC Office: 421 RSOB 20510, 202-224-2742; Fax: 202-224-8525: e-mail: john—kerry@kerry.senate.gov.

State Offices: Boston, 617-565-8519; Fall River, 508-677-0522; Springfield, 413-785-4610; Worcester, 508-831-7380.

Committees: *Banking, Housing & Urban Affairs* (3rd of 8 D): Financial Services & Technology; Housing Opportunity & Community Development (RMM); Securities. *Commerce, Science & Transportation* (5th of 9 D): Communications; Oceans & Fisheries (RMM); Science, Technology & Space. *Foreign Relations* (4th of 8 D): East Asian & Pacific Affairs (RMM); International Operations; Western Hemisphere & Peace Corps Affairs. *Intelligence (Select)* (5th of 9 D). *Small Business* (RMM of 8 D).

Group Ratings

	ADA	ACLU	AFS	LCV	CFA	CON	NFIB	COC	ACU	NTLC	CHC
1996	95	47	86	100	86	14	34	31	5	17	7
1995	95	—	100	100	75	8	—	32	4	—	—

National Journal Ratings

	1995 LIB — 1995 CONS			1996 LIB — 1996 CONS		
Economic	77%	—	21%	74%	—	19%
Social	74%	—	25%	92%	—	0%
Foreign	79%	—	15%	77%	—	17%

Key Votes of the 104th Congress

1. Reduce Medicare Growth $	N	5. Flag Amendment	N	9. Anti-Missile Defense	N
2. Lmt. Prod. Liab. Damages	N	6. Endangered Species	Y	10. Cuban Embargo	Y
3. Increase Min. Wage	Y	7. Gay Employment Rights	Y	11. Bar Bosnia Troop $	N
4. Welfare Reform	Y	8. Ovrd. Part. Birth Veto	N	12. Cut Vietnam Aid	N

Election Results

1996 general	John F. Kerry (D)	1,334,135	(52%)	($12,619,152)
	William F. Weld (R)	1,143,120	(45%)	($8,002,123)
	Others	78,687	(3%)	
1996 primary	John F. Kerry (D)	unopposed		
1990 general	John F. Kerry (D)	1,321,712	(57%)	($8,040,970)
	Jim Rappaport (R)	992,917	(43%)	($5,177,801)

FIRST DISTRICT

The stony hills and green-clad mountains of western Massachusetts, with more trees today than when Henry David Thoreau was writing in the 1840s, where stone wall fencing now passing through thick forest once bounded one working farm from another, probably does not look much different from 300 years ago. This was the frontier in the 17th Century, where Puritan preachers formed new towns in the wilderness, farming the stony soil and preaching against declension. It was dangerous here as well, the site of the Indian uprising known as King Philip's War in 1676 and the Indian raid, supported by the French from Quebec, at Deerfield in 1704. This was Yankee New England's western frontier for nearly 200 years. In the 19th Century, western New England was the home of writers and artists, Emily Dickinson living quietly in Amherst, Edith Wharton grandly on her estate in Lenox, "The Mount," and the sculptor Augustus Saint Gaudens not far from where the Boston Symphony played in the Tanglewood Festival each summer. There were mill towns here as well, jammed in mountain crevasses or along the wide Connecticut River; but as the 20th Century went on, and trees grew up on stony land once farmed, western Massachusetts came to look less settled.

Western Massachusetts has also changed politically. For many years it was one of the heartlands of the Republican Party—flinty, thrifty and chilly just like the area's most famous politician, Calvin Coolidge, who worked his way up from mayor of Northampton to governor and president by lowering taxes and saying no to pleas for government action. But by the 1980s, western Massachusetts contained some of the most left-wing parts of America. A town like Stockbridge could attract liberal artist Norman Rockwell (a solid New Dealer and peacenik) and baby boom radical Arlo Guthrie, whose Alice's Restaurant is there. The concentration of colleges and universities in the Pioneer Valley, around Amherst, Northampton and South Hadley, brought together a critical mass of liberal scholars and an even more leftish graduate student proletariat, people defying their Marxist philosophy of economic determinism by remaining in places where they could make little money in order to be surrounded by culturally congenial people and places. The results show up in the election returns: Hampshire County, dominated by Pioneer Valley college towns, voted 64%–23% for Bill Clinton over Bob Dole in 1996; he carried Amherst, home of UMass, 75%–15%.

The 1st Congressional District of Massachusetts, like all the state's districts, has convoluted boundaries which defy easy description. It covers much but not all of western Massachusetts and stretches far to the northeast. It includes all of Berkshire and Franklin Counties and much of the Pioneer Valley: Amherst is in the 1st and so is the mill town of Holyoke on the Connecticut River, but the college towns of Northampton and South Hadley are in the 2d District. It includes New Braintree and Westfield, but not Springfield; it includes Fitchburg and Gardner, north of Worcester, but not Worcester. This is a Democratic district in most elections, but not overwhelmingly so. The Democratic base is split among the Amherst radicals, low-income factory workers of Holyoke and the descendants of ethnic mill and blue-collar workers in from Pittsfield in the Berkshires to Fitchburg. The Republican base is even more scattered, among small towns in the hills.

The congressman from the 1st is John Olver, a Democrat first chosen in a special election in June 1991. Olver was educated at Tufts and M.I.T. and came to UMass as a chemistry professor in 1961, at 25; his wife Rose is a professor of psychology and Women's and Gender Studies at Amherst College. John Olver was elected to the Massachusetts House in 1968 and to the Senate in 1972; altogether he served 23 years in Boston's State House. When longtime Republican Congressman Silvio Conte died in 1991, Olver ran for the seat, and his Pioneer Valley base helped him win 31% in the fragmented Democratic primary. In the June 1991 general he faced Steven Pierce, former state House Republican leader, Governor William Weld's conservative opponent in the 1990 primary and a Weld cabinet appointee. With Massachusetts liberalism in grave disrepute, the race was close; the election was scheduled after students' summer vacation began. But Olver was able to eke out a 50%–48% win.

Olver has had one of the most liberal voting records in the House. He sees his job as encouraging economic development and making the "federal government more responsive to people's needs by extending unemployment benefits, helping to ease the credit crunch on businesses and fighting to control the cost of health care." In his first term he passed a bill creating a network of Manufacturing Outreach Centers to help businesses tap into university resources—a bit of local pork?—and securing two-year funding for the Low-Income Home Energy Assistance Program. He was against NAFTA and for Canadian-style single-payer health insurance. He has called for a $6.50 minimum wage by 2000 and says Medicare can be saved by only cutting projected spending $90 billion rather than the $270 billion House Republicans called for. He has attacked the IRS for not collecting enough of taxes owed. In the face of the Republican House, he told a local labor group, "We need a positive program, a jobs strategy, a national minimum wage, a guarantee of jobs, increased money for research and development, universal health care and portability of health insurance." He won an Appropriations seat after the 1992 election, lost it to the downsizing of Democratic seats after the 1994 election, and got back on in 1997—the only Massachusetts congressman on the committee.

For a conscientious Democrat in a basically Democratic district, Olver has not had a dazzling electoral performance. In 1992, against former Conte staffer Patrick Larkin, he won 52%–43%, carrying Pittsfield and other Berkshire towns narrowly, winning big in the Pioneer Valley and carrying a plurality around Fitchburg. In 1994 he was unopposed. In 1996 he faced state Representative Jane Swift, a 31-year-old moderate, who spent an impressive sum ($693,000); business groups also targeted Olver with ads. Olver won 53%–47%, with big majorities in the Pioneer Valley (80% in Amherst), but running only even around Fitchburg and losing most towns in the Berkshires. This could be a targeted race again in 1998.

The People: Pop. 1990: 601,721; 36% rural; 14% age 65+; 92% White; 2% Black; 1% Asian; 5% Hispanic origin. Households: 55% married couple families; 25% married couple fams. w. children; 45% college educ.; median household income: $31,903; per capita income: $14,200; median gross rent: $479; median house value: $123,200.

1996 Presidential Vote			**1992 Presidential Vote**		
Clinton (D)	151,531	(61%)	Clinton (D)	130,308	(48%)
Dole (R)	63,998	(26%)	Bush (R)	72,238	(26%)
Perot (I)	29,116	(12%)	Perot (I)	68,545	(25%)
Other	4,718	(2%)			

Rep. John Olver (D)

Elected June 1991; b. Sept. 3, 1936, Homesdale, PA; home, Amherst; Rensselaer Polytechnic Inst., B.S. 1955, Tufts U., M.S. 1956, M.I.T., Ph.D. 1961; No religious affiliation; married (Rose).

Career: Prof., U. of MA, Amherst, 1961–69; MA House of Reps., 1968–72; MA Senate, 1972–91.

DC Office: 1027 LHOB 20515, 202-225-5335; Fax: 202-226-1224; e-mail: olver@hr.house.gov.

District Offices: Fitchburg, 508-342-8722; Holyoke, 413-532-7010; Pittsfield, 413-412-0946.

Committees: *Appropriations* (22nd of 26 D): Military Construction; Transportation.

Group Ratings

	ADA	ACLU	AFS	LCV	CFA	CON	NFIB	COC	ACU	NTLC	CHC
1996	95	94	100	92	100	87	22	19	0	7	0
1995	95	—	—	94	100	31	—	17	4	—	—

National Journal Ratings

	1995 LIB — 1995 CONS			1996 LIB — 1996 CONS		
Economic	85%	—	12%	85%	—	11%
Social	88%	—	0%	88%	—	0%
Foreign	88%	—	7%	90%	—	0%

Key Votes of the 104th Congress

1. Reduce Medicare Growth $	N	5. Flag Amendment	N	9. Cuban Embargo	N
2. Ovrd. Product Liab. Veto	N	6. Drop EPA Limits	Y	10. Bar Bosnia Troop $	N
3. Increase Min. Wage	Y	7. Repeal Assault-Weap. Ban	N	11. Cut Anti-Missile Defense	Y
4. Welfare Reform	N	8. Ovrd. Part. Birth Veto	N	12. Bar U.N. Uniforms	N

Election Results

1996 general	John Olver (D)	129,232	(53%)	($1,005,595)
	Jane Swift (R)	115,801	(47%)	($693,538)
1996 primary	John Olver (D)	unopposed		
1994 general	John Olver (D)	unopposed		($317,317)

SECOND DISTRICT

As American as apple pie, the place where basketball was invented, the city where the Webster's unabridged dictionaries (2d and 3d editions) were edited and published, the site of the Armory where M-1 rifles were manufactured in World War II, the city with the highest percentage of Puerto Ricans: this is Springfield, Massachusetts. Springfield is the third largest city in the Bay

State, but far from Boston; the second largest city in the Connecticut River Valley, but overshadowed by Hartford; a medium-sized American city built by New England Yankees, where immigrants from a dozen different countries have worked their way up.

Springfield is the largest city in the 2d Congressional District of Massachusetts, whose irregular boundaries stretch north to South Hadley and Northampton, college towns of the Pioneer Valley, and east across stony hills and the antique center of Brimfield to the factory towns of the Blackstone Valley just north of Woonsocket, Rhode Island. Historically, this was a Yankee Republican district for much of the 20th Century, then a solidly Catholic Democratic district; now it is more marginal, but still leans Democratic.

The congressman from the 2d District is Richard Neal, mayor of Springfield from 1984–88. Neal grew up in Springfield, went to work for the mayor in 1973, was elected to the Council in 1978, meanwhile teaching high school and college history. As mayor himself, he boasted of both downtown rehabilitation and neighborhood revitalization. Neal was essentially bequeathed the seat by his predecessor, 36-year incumbent Edward Boland, longtime friend of Tip O'Neill. In 1988 Boland announced his retirement just before the filing deadline, and after Neal had been making the rounds of the district for a year. Unopposed in the Democratic primary, Neal won 80% in the general.

Neal has a generally liberal voting record, with some exceptions; he voted for the final version of welfare reform, the partial birth abortion ban and the Defense of Marriage Act. On the Ways and Means Committee he refused to support the Clinton healthcare plan and in June 1994 offered an amendment to allow firms with more than 100 workers to self-insure. He co-sponsored an expansion of IRAs with Republican Bill Thomas. He tends to local matters, hailing additions to the Blackstone Valley National Heritage Corridor and pushing the Defense Center for Financial Management and Training at Southbridge. He has long had an interest in Ireland; in 1980, when he was a city council member, he sponsored a plank at the Democratic National Convention for the unification of Ireland. In 1993 he started one-hour special orders sessions on Irish issues, and in 1994 he personally lobbied Bill Clinton to grant a visa for Gerry Adams of Sinn Fein to visit the United States. He has since sponsored visits by Adams, who refused to condemn an IRA bombing in Britain.

Neal has had some serious challenges in Democratic primaries. In 1990 he beat Theodore DiMauro, who succeeded Neal as Springfield mayor, by 64%–36%. In 1992, he beat Springfield Councilwoman Kateri Walsh 48%–34%, with a third candidate getting 18%. That fall he won the general by 53%–31% over another Council member, Anthony Ravosa Jr.. But in 1994 he had no primary opposition and no serious opposition in the general. His 1996 Republican opponent, Mark Steele, had been convicted of arson in 1991. Massachusetts is the only state that allows felons to run, but it has been some time since it has given them enough votes to win; Neal won 72%–22%.

The People: Pop. 1990: 601,490; 21% rural; 14% age 65+; 88% White; 5% Black; 1% Asian; 6% Hispanic origin. Households: 56% married couple families; 25% married couple fams. w. children; 42% college educ.; median household income: $33,401; per capita income: $14,652; median gross rent: $497; median house value: $128,800.

1996 Presidential Vote			**1992 Presidential Vote**		
Clinton (D)	147,670	(61%)	Clinton (D)	121,759	(46%)
Dole (R)	66,344	(27%)	Bush (R)	76,277	(29%)
Perot (I)	25,252	(10%)	Perot (I)	65,935	(25%)

Rep. Richard E. Neal (D)

Elected 1988; b. Feb. 14, 1949, Springfield; home, Springfield; Amer. Intl. Col., B.A. 1972, U. of Hartford, M.A. 1976; Catholic; married (Maureen).

Career: Staff Asst., Springfield Mayor, 1973–78; High Schl. & Col. teacher, 1976–83; Springfield City Cncl., 1978–83; Springfield Mayor, 1984–88.

DC Office: 2236 RHOB 20515, 202-225-5601; Fax: 202-225-8112.

District Offices: Springfield, 413-785-0325; Milford, 508-634-8198.

Committees: *Ways & Means* (11th of 16 D): Social Security; Trade.

Group Ratings

	ADA	ACLU	AFS	LCV	CFA	CON	NFIB	COC	ACU	NTLC	CHC
1996	75	47	100	77	92	88	25	20	11	10	20
1995	75	—	—	75	92	9	—	25	16	—	—

National Journal Ratings

	1995 LIB — 1995 CONS	1996 LIB — 1996 CONS
Economic	80% — 18%	82% — 16%
Social	64% — 35%	70% — 30%
Foreign	79% — 17%	81% — 18%

Key Votes of the 104th Congress

1. Reduce Medicare Growth $	N	5. Flag Amendment	Y	9. Cuban Embargo	N
2. Ovrd. Product Liab. Veto	N	6. Drop EPA Limits	Y	10. Bar Bosnia Troop $	N
3. Increase Min. Wage	Y	7. Repeal Assault-Weap. Ban	N	11. Cut Anti-Missile Defense	Y
4. Welfare Reform	N	8. Ovrd. Part. Birth Veto	Y	12. Bar U.N. Uniforms	N

Election Results

1996 general	Richard E. Neal (D)	162,995	(72%)	($227,105)
	Mark Steele (R)	49,885	(22%)	($1,358)
	Scott Andrichak (I)	9,181	(4%)	
	Others	5,350	(2%)	
1996 primary	Richard E. Neal (D)	unopposed		
1994 general	Richard E. Neal (D)	117,178	(59%)	($318,582)
	John M. Briare (R)	72,732	(36%)	($60,685)
	Kate Ross (NL)	10,167	(5%)	

THIRD DISTRICT

Worcester (its name still pronounced with a particularly pungent Massachusetts accent making it sound as if it had no *R*s), although technically the second-largest city in Massachusetts, is often overlooked. People may drive in for concerts at the Centrum, but otherwise they zoom by on I-495 or the Turnpike. Worcester is one of the few major industrial cities not located on a river, lake or sea coast, and it is far from a commercial airport. A high-tech manufacturing haven before the term was invented, for 200 years the city has been one of the nation's centers of tinkering, contriving and inventing. But it hasn't always been smooth going; 50 years ago, Worcester's biggest industries were wire-making, textiles, grinding wheels and envelopes: not on the cutting edge even then and certainly not now. But in the 1970s and 1980s, electronics and computer firms sprouted up along Interstate 495—the circumferential highway located just 20 miles east of Worcester, as they had earlier around Route 128, closer to Boston. The high-tech boom brought prosperity, labor shortages, new residents and higher housing prices to central Massachusetts. Then, in the early 1990s, the minicomputer industry slumped, bringing recession and a collapse of real estate values. But Worcester's ingenious entrepreneurs and skilled labor force have hustled and in the middle 1990s the local economy again is perking up.

The 3d Congressional District of Massachusetts, grotesquely shaped, has Worcester as its largest city if not its geographic center. A little more than half its people live in Worcester and a cluster of towns all around. The other cluster of population is far away, in and around the old textile mill town of Fall River, east of Rhode Island, and Dartmouth and Westport on Buzzards Bay. The two are connected by a string of towns in some places only a few miles wide. Thus has the 3d District, if not quite Worcester, been made a seaport. The I-495 corridor and the towns around Worcester are Republican; Worcester itself is Democratic and Fall River and the area around even more so.

The congressman from the 3d District is Jim McGovern, a Democrat elected in 1996. McGovern grew up in Worcester, where his parents owned a small business; he went to American University in Washington, and while in graduate school worked in the office of former South Dakota Senator George McGovern, who is no relation. He ran McGovern's 1984 campaign in the Massachusetts presidential primary, where he finished third with 21% of the vote, and nominated him at the San Francisco convention. After that he got a job in Boston Congressman Joe Moakley's office, and moved up to chief of staff as Moakley moved up to Rules Committee chairman. McGovern got into the spotlight himself, leading a 1989 investigation of the murder of six Jesuits and two lay women in El Salvador, which led to a cutoff of aid. In 1994 he ran for the House, and lost in the Democratic primary 38%–30% to Kevin O'Sullivan, who in turn lost to incumbent Republican Peter Blute. In 1996 he ran again, this time with no primary opposition.

The 1996 campaign was targeted by both sides. Blute, a state Representative and sports promoter, had won the seat 50%–44% in 1992 thanks to the House Bank problems of incumbent Democrat Joe Early. In the House Blute made a moderate record by supporting gun control, family and medical leave and the minimum wage increase, and opposing abortion and NAFTA. In 1994 he beat O'Sullivan 55%–44%. In 1996 he stressed his "independence" from the House leadership and attacked McGovern for liberal stands on abortion and Cuba. The AFL-CIO targeted the district with TV ads, and McGovern ran a humorous spot that asked, "If you wouldn't vote for Newt, why would you ever vote for Blute?" Blute spent more than McGovern, but McGovern outraised him among PACs—an example of how well Democratic hill denizens can use the PAC system. Polling showed the race even, but the drag of the Dole-Kemp ticket was great even in the Worcester area. Blute ran slightly behind, 50%–45%, in the area around Worcester, and was clobbered 56%–45% in the Fall River area and the rest of the district, as McGovern won 53%–45%.

McGovern got some negative publicity in early 1997 for hiring a Philip Morris lobbyist as his chief aide after criticizing Blute for accepting tobacco PAC money. He echoed Bill Clinton in calling for increased aid to college students and government healthcare insurance for children. He also presented original proposals. He co-sponsored a bill with bipartisan support which called for requiring polltakers to disclose the funding of polls. As a member of the Transportation Committee, he promises to work for a favorable highway aid formula for Massachusetts, though it's not likely to be as favorable as at present; he also appeared at a hearing with Blute, now director of Massport, in support of a Logan Airport project. Mentioned as a possible opponent for 1998 is Worcester area state Senator Matthew Amorello.

The People: Pop. 1990: 601,852; 18% rural; 14% age 65+; 93% White; 2% Black; 2% Asian; 4% Hispanic origin. Households: 58% married couple families; 27% married couple fams. w. children; 48%

college educ.; median household income: $36,873; per capita income: $15,917; median gross rent: $515; median house value: $150,500.

1996 Presidential Vote			**1992 Presidential Vote**		
Clinton (D)	154,915	(60%)	Clinton (D)	123,724	(45%)
Dole (R)	76,413	(29%)	Bush (R)	85,047	(31%)
Perot (I)	24,690	(9%)	Perot (I)	62,667	(23%)
Other	4,096	(2%)			

Rep. James P. McGovern (D)

Elected 1996; b. Nov. 20, 1959, Worcester; home, Worcester; American U., B.A. 1981, M.P.A. 1984; Catholic; married (Lisa).

Career: Sr. Aide, U.S. Rep. John Joseph Moakley, 1981–96.

DC Office: 512 CHOB 20515, 202-225-6101; Fax: 202-225-5759; e-mail: james.mcgovern@mail.house.gov.

District Offices: Attleboro, 508-431-8025; Fall River, 508-677-0140; Worcester, 508-831-7356.

Committees: *Transportation & Infrastructure* (31st of 33 D): Surface Transportation; Water Resources & Environment.

Group Ratings and Key Votes: Newly Elected

Election Results

1996 general	James P. McGovern (D)	135,044	(53%)	($806,939)
	Peter I. Blute (R)	115,694	(45%)	($1,144,540)
	Others	4,359	(2%)	
1996 primary	James P. McGovern (D)	unopposed		
1994 general	Peter I. Blute (R)	115,810	(55%)	($977,107)
	Kevin O'Sullivan (D)	93,689	(44%)	($495,645)

FOURTH DISTRICT

The political transformation of Massachusetts is nowhere better illustrated than in the Boston suburbs of Brookline and Newton. These were Yankee enclaves a century ago, with avenues built by developers to resemble the sweep of Haussmann's Grand Boulevards in Paris, and villages of giant clapboard houses clustering within a few blocks of a commuter railroad station. Brookline was where The Country Club (the very first one) was established in 1882, and where Joseph Kennedy, as an Irish Catholic 20-something banker seeking respectability, moved his family in 1914. Brookline and Newton then were solidly Republican in politics, the political base of leading politicians like Christian Herter, governor of Massachusetts and U.S. secretary of state in the 1950s; as late as 1960, Brookline and Newton and adjacent wards of Boston were electing a Republican congressman. Then came the transformation, personified by the election in 1962 of Michael Dukakis at 29 to the Great and General Court (the legislature). As Massachusetts's university-educated classes became more liberal, and as Brookline's and Newton's Jewish population grew, and as young liberal-minded families refurbished the graceful old houses, these towns became liberal Democratic bastions. By the 1970s, the Brookline Town Meeting was opening each year with debates over whether they should recite the "Pledge of Allegiance"; against that background, it is easier to understand how Dukakis could fail so utterly to understand the cultural attitudes of most Americans. Brookline and Newton, more than Boston, are the liberal heart of Massachusetts: they voted 69%–29% for Dukakis in 1988, 68%–20% for Bill Clinton in 1992 and again for Clinton 75%–20% in 1996.

The 4th Congressional District of Massachusetts includes Brookline and Newton which are the political home bases for its congressman, Barney Frank. But they cast only 25% of the district's votes, and this grotesquely shaped district is not all of one piece: indeed, one setting out to canvass entirely the district's bounds might have to get off the road and step over fences and trudge through marshes. The shape results from successive redistrictings: in 1982, Frank's district was extended south to the old textile mill city of Fall River; in 1992, it lost much of Fall River and gained New Bedford, a great 19th Century whaling port and still home to one of the largest fishing fleets in the United States and with the largest percentage of Portuguese-Americans in the nation. The 4th also curves north to the interior of Plymouth County, around old towns like Bridgewater. This is a Democratic district in national politics, but not nearly so Democratic nor as uniformly culturally liberal as Brookline and Newton. There is a bit of most kinds of America here: high-income WASPy Wellesley, French Canadian mill worker Fall River, Foxboro with its football stadium, Sharon with a middle-income Jewish population, countrified Dover.

The congressman from the 4th District, Barney Frank, first elected in 1980, is one of the intellectual and political leaders of the Democratic Party in the House, political theorist and pit bull all at the same time. Frank grew up in Bayonne, New Jersey, went to Harvard, where he got to know local politicians as well as political scientists. In 1967, he went to work for newly elected Boston Mayor Kevin White; in 1971, he went to Washington to work for Congressman Michael Harrington. In 1972, Frank was elected to the Massachusetts House from the Back Bay of Boston, then just starting to be a liberal singles neighborhood. In 1980, when Congressman Robert Drinan retired after Pope John Paul II commanded Jesuits to leave elective office, Frank moved to Brookline and ran in the 4th District. With a strong base in Brookline and Newton he won and, keeping them together as redistricting moved the seat down to Fall River, beat Republican Margaret Heckler 60%–40% in 1982. He has been reelected by wide margins since.

In the House, Frank soon gained a reputation as one of the smartest talkers and best debaters in the chamber—he is surely the best floor debater in the House today, and may be one of the best of all time. At a time when so many members seem to rely on canned speeches produced by staffers and letterhead interest groups, Frank listens to others' arguments and engages them in his inimitable rapid-fire delivery. He has made many telling criticisms of conservatism over the years, and some of liberalism as well, especially in his 1992 book *Speaking Frankly* in which he criticized some stands beloved of some Brookline and Newton liberals. "Democratic positions are fully consistent with the values of patriotism, free enterprise, working hard for one's self and one's family, and holding people to a standard of behavior fully respectful of the person and property of others."

He has worked hard, often behind the scenes, on many substantive issues. He took over the subcommittee handling the bill to provide redress to Japanese Americans interned in World War II and got it through the House and signed into law. He has shaped immigration acts from 1986–96, to expand legal immigration, to allow HIV-positive people to enter the country, to bar states from excluding children of illegal aliens from school. On the Banking Committee, he has worked on housing issues, creating the HOME program of housing block grants to the states, shaping the RTC program that sold low-end housing units acquired by bankrupt S&Ls to low and moderate income people, barring housing discrimination against people with AIDS, blocking a Republican attempt to raise the 30% income cap on public housing rents.

But this was not how he made national headlines. In May 1987, in a seemingly casual answer to a reporter's question, Frank said he is gay. Then in August 1989 came the conservative *Washington Times*'s story that Frank had employed as a personal aide a male prostitute and convicted drug possessor, Steve Gobie, and let him live in his apartment where the man was allegedly carrying on his former trade. Frank admitted to paying Gobie, but was careful never to use official or campaign funds; he denied that he tolerated prostitution in his apartment and had thrown the man out when he suspected it was going on. The *Boston Globe* called on Frank to resign; his picture appeared on the cover of *Newsweek*; he called on the Ethics Committee to investigate. It did, and dismissed all but two minor charges. The committee recommended a reprimand but not censure; Frank agreed in a contrite appearance before the House in July 1990; the House voted 287–141 against censure (moved by Newt Gingrich); the vote for reprimand was 408–18. "I think members will agree that I have always had a reputation for honesty, not always tact or tolerance," Frank said to the House. That reputation was one reason he survived in the House; his brains, liberal stands, hard work and constituency service helped him survive in the 4th District.

In the early 1990s, Frank tended to work behind the scenes. He was active on the issue, raised by Bill Clinton and not by Frank or by gay rights groups in the 1992 campaign, of gays in the military. To the disappointment of many in the gay community, Frank admitted that allowing open homosexuals to serve in the military would not be accepted by most in Congress or the Pentagon. Taking Senator Sam Nunn's "Don't Ask, Don't Tell" compromise a step further, Frank suggested that gays be allowed to conduct an openly gay lifestyle when off-base without fear of reprisal; but Clinton eventually declined to go so far. On the Budget Committee in 1993, Frank worked to make the budget both liberal and passable; enough, it turned out, to pass by one vote. He tried unsuccessfully to break down the firewalls and cut defense to increase domestic spending; he made a start toward requiring European allies to share more of the burden of stationing U.S. troops abroad, a cause on which he and Republican Christopher Shays had more success in the Republican 104th Congress. He pressed to use trade agreements and the World Bank to force higher labor standards and environmental rules on Mexico and other less developed countries and voted against NAFTA.

After the Republican victory in November 1994, Minority Whip David Bonior asked Frank to be the Democrats' point man in floor debates; Frank asked whether Bonior wanted him to be such a visible symbol of the party, and Bonior said yes. So during the Contract With America debate, Frank prowled the floor, ready to take up a microphone and deliver stinging attacks on Republicans' hypocrisy or cross-examine a freshman with all the mercy of a Harvard Law professor questioning a not quite prepared first-year student. His strong and orderly mind, his ability to argue abstract principles in rapid-fire but comprehensible words, were on display—and made him the most feared adversary by the Republican side. It was a dazzling performance and a bit out of character: Frank, long known for candor, was taking a purely partisan tack. Like many House Democrats, he believes that the Republicans cannot succeed in fulfilling their campaign promises, that government spending simply cannot be cut without depriving voters of services and benefits they want, and that they will in time prefer Democratic majorities again. But the fury of his attacks on the other side suggest that he may subconsciously fear that their strategy might work politically, and that he is laboring hard to prevent the demolition of the liberal government he has spent his lifetime supporting. His partisan fervor, on display in the Banking Committee's 1994 hearings on Clinton scandals, came to the fore more often in 1995 and 1996. Even so, he had some bipartisan successes. With Republican Charles Canady, he managed the Lobbying Disclosure Act, barring all amendments so that the House would pass the Senate bill and no conference committee would be necessary. With Bob Dole, he was a lonely voice for auctioning off the digital TV spectrum rather than giving it away free, as most in Congress and the Clinton Administration favored. He passed a law, vital for the biotech industry, allowing companies to receive patents for processes for artificially manufacturing substances which exist naturally. In 1997 he became ranking Democrat on the Courts and Intellectual Property Subcommittee of Judiciary, and promises to work with the software and biotech industries and to fight censorship and deal with copyright on the Internet. He blocked Robert Dornan's amendment to require discharge of HIV-infected military personnel. He worked for a whaling park in New Bedford and assistance to the fishing industry.

Frank was reelected 72%–28% in 1996, winning Brookline and Newton 80%–20%.

The People: Pop. 1990: 601,392; 27% rural; 14% age 65+; 92% White; 2% Black; 2% Asian; 1% Other; 3% Hispanic origin. Households: 57% married couple families; 27% married couple fams. w. children; 51% college educ.; median household income: $39,005; per capita income: $18,963; median gross rent: $512; median house value: $170,200.

1996 Presidential Vote			1992 Presidential Vote		
Clinton (D)	169,078	(64%)	Clinton (D)	143,595	(51%)
Dole (R)	69,548	(26%)	Bush (R)	74,769	(26%)
Perot (I)	22,782	(9%)	Perot (I)	62,746	(22%)

Rep. Barney Frank (D)

Elected 1980; b. Mar. 31, 1940, Bayonne, NJ; home, Newton; Harvard, B.A. 1962, J.D. 1977; Jewish; companion, Herb Moses.

Career: Exec. Asst., Boston Mayor Kevin White, 1967–71; A.A., U.S. Rep. Michael Harrington, 1971–72; MA House of Reps., 1972–80; Lecturer, Harvard JFK Schl. of Govt., 1978–80.

DC Office: 2210 RHOB 20515, 202-225-5931; Fax: 202-225-0182.

District Offices: Bridgewater, 508-697-9403; Fall River, 508-674-3551; New Bedford, 508-999-6462; Newton, 617-332-3920.

Committees: *Banking & Financial Services* (5th of 25 D): Domestic & International Monetary Policy; Housing & Community Opportunity. *Judiciary* (2nd of 15 D): Courts & Intellectual Property (RMM).

Group Ratings

	ADA	ACLU	AFS	LCV	CFA	CON	NFIB	COC	ACU	NTLC	CHC
1996	100	88	92	92	100	60	19	13	0	7	0
1995	100	—	—	81	77	16	—	17	4	—	—

National Journal Ratings

	1995 LIB — 1995 CONS			1996 LIB — 1996 CONS		
Economic	78%	—	21%	89%	—	0%
Social	75%	—	25%	88%	—	0%
Foreign	88%	—	7%	90%	—	0%

Key Votes of the 104th Congress

1. Reduce Medicare Growth $	N	5. Flag Amendment	N	9. Cuban Embargo	N
2. Ovrd. Product Liab. Veto	N	6. Drop EPA Limits	Y	10. Bar Bosnia Troop $	N
3. Increase Min. Wage	Y	7. Repeal Assault-Weap. Ban	N	11. Cut Anti-Missile Defense	Y
4. Welfare Reform	N	8. Ovrd. Part. Birth Veto	N	12. Bar U.N. Uniforms	N

Election Results

1996 general	Barney Frank (D)	183,844	(72%)	($334,002)
	Jonathan Raymond (R)	72,701	(28%)	($108,348)
1996 primary	Barney Frank (D)	unopposed		
1994 general	Barney Frank (D)	unopposed		($208,936)

FIFTH DISTRICT

The Merrimack River Valley at the northern edge of Massachusetts has had an erratic history: high-tech boom, bust, boom, bust. When Massachusetts was a kind of maritime republic in the 19th Century, with a few farmers struggling to scratch out a living from the stony soil, a few clever Yankees used their profits from the sea trade to try to tame the rapidly flowing Merrimack and build cotton spinning mills. Creating the cities of Lowell and Lawrence, they built model dormitories and recreation programs for their women. Because of the textile industry, which lasted here for nearly a century, Massachusetts continued to grow even after the maritime industry faded. But in the 1920s, the price of labor rose here and newly built mills in the Carolinas—much closer to the cotton supply—decimated the industry that Lawrence and Lowell built. Many residents—by then rather elderly—waited forlornly for an upturn in the local economy.

It eventually improved, largely due to an unexpected source. High-tech industry drove the growth, beginning in the 1960s around MIT, then moving out to Route 128 ring road and then I-495, which passes through Lowell and Lawrence. Wang, headquartered in Lowell, grew spectacularly, and former Congressman and Senator Paul Tsongas spearheaded a national historical restoration of the old mill area. This was the Massachusetts miracle of the early 1980s. Then came the bust: Wang's word processors and minicomputers slumped as businesses purchased personal computers and hooked them together in networks. But Lowell revived again. Its new immigrants—mostly from Cambodia and Puerto Rico—provide vitality, and its entrepreneur creativity; the old Wang buildings were filled with health care, banking, telecommunications and Internet companies. Paul Tsongas died in January 1997, but lived long enough to see Lowell on the move again, rehabbing the River Place Towers, renovating the Bon Marche and building the Paul Tsongas Arena.

The 5th Congressional District of Massachusetts includes Lawrence and Lowell, which with next-door towns account for about half the district's population. The remainder of the district includes the troubled high-tech corridor further south on I-495, running from the stony hills of Lawrence and Lowell to Maynard (headquarters of Digital) and Marlborough. The district also includes fancy suburbs like Concord, aging mill towns like Ayer and the mountains along the New Hampshire state line. Except for Lowell and Lawrence, it is ancestrally Yankee Republican. It is culturally liberal and trended toward the Democrats in the early 1970s. But in the 1980s and 1990s, amid the high-tech boom, it went Republican in national and even statewide elections: a kind of Baja New Hampshire. In 1992 it went for Bill Clinton but with the lowest percentage in the state, and a big vote for high-tech pioneer Ross Perot; in 1996, unnerved by the Republican revolutionaries, it went more Democratic still.

The congressman from the 5th District is Martin Meehan, a Democrat first elected in 1992. Meehan grew up in Lowell, the son of a Lowell Sun compositor. He has been a lifelong politico: he was an aide to Congressman James Shannon while working on his masters degree, worked in the Massachusetts secretary of state's office after law school, was first assistant DA in Middlesex County from 1991 until he ran for Congress in 1992. He took on eight-year incumbent Democrat Chester Atkins. Atkins attacked an old ally, state Senate President Billy Bulger, and watched as Bulger and Governor William Weld kept Lawrence and Lowell, where Atkins was highly unpopular, in the district. Meehan beat Atkins by the astonishing margin of 65%–35%, winning the Lowell-Lawrence area 75%–25%. In the general, Meehan faced former Congressman Paul Cronin, who beat John Kerry in 1972 but lost to Paul Tsongas in 1974. Meehan called for a 50% defense cut, targeted capital gains tax cuts and income tax increases—and backed the balanced budget amendment and term limits, and won 52%–38%.

Meehan combines a pretty liberal voting record with distinctive stands on issues that have gotten him labeled a maverick. One of his crusades is against tobacco; his father, a smoker, had heart surgery when Marty was 11. In his first term he worked with Henry Waxman when he was conducting hearings with tobacco company heads and called for more prominent warnings on cigarette packages. After the 1994 election he assailed the new Commerce Committee Chairman Tom Bliley for taking tobacco money and for canceling further tobacco hearings, and asked Attorney General Janet Reno for a criminal investigation of the tobacco companies. In 1995 he offered his own budget plan, cutting Social Security and Medicare benefits for those with incomes over $50,000, cutting defense and corporate welfare and taxing cigarettes at 48 cents a pack. His other great cause is campaign finance reform. In 1997 with Christopher Shays and Senators Russ Feingold and John McCain, he co-sponsored the campaign finance plan which would outlaw soft money and foreign money, give free or discounted TV time to candidates who abide by spending caps and reduce the PAC contribution limit. Meehan serves on the National Security Committee; for all his talk of cutting defense spending, he boosts Raytheon and its upgrades of the Patriot missile.

Meehan was reelected easily in 1994 and without Republican opposition in 1996. In 1992 he committed himself to no more than four terms; if he keeps that pledge, 1998 will be his last House race. He has been mentioned as a candidate for attorney general; but Meehan has said he will not run against his old boss, Middlesex County DA Thomas Reilly.

The People: Pop. 1990: 601,527; 16% rural; 10% age 65+; 87% White; 2% Black; 4% Asian; 8% Hispanic origin. Households: 60% married couple families; 30% married couple fams. w. children; 52% college educ.; median household income: $42,701; per capita income: $18,293; median gross rent: $603; median house value: $174,100.

1996 Presidential Vote

Clinton (D)	143,122	(58%)
Dole (R)	76,605	(31%)
Perot (I)	24,079	(10%)
Other	4,070	(2%)

1992 Presidential Vote

Clinton (D)	113,073	(42%)
Bush (R)	85,366	(32%)
Perot (I)	70,474	(26%)

Rep. Martin T. (Marty) **Meehan (D)**

Elected 1992; b. Dec. 30, 1956, Lowell; home, Lowell; U. of MA, B.S. 1978, Suffolk U., M.A. 1981, J.D. 1986; Catholic; married (Ellen Murphy).

Career: Staff Asst., U.S. Rep. James Shannon, 1979–81; MA Dep. Secy. of State for Securities & Corps., 1986–90; Middlesex Cnty. 1st Asst. Dist. Atty., 1990–92.

DC Office: 2434 RHOB 20515, 202-225-3411; Fax: 202-226-0771; e-mail: mtmeehan@hr.house.gov.

District Offices: Lawrence, 508-681-6200; Lowell, 508-459-0101; Marlborough, 508-460-9292.

Committees: *Judiciary* (12th of 15 D): Commercial & Administrative Law; Crime. *National Security* (10th of 25 D): Military Readiness; Military Research & Development.

Group Ratings

	ADA	ACLU	AFS	LCV	CFA	CON	NFIB	COC	ACU	NTLC	CHC
1996	85	80	100	85	100	99	30	19	0	12	21
1995	80	—	—	69	92	95	—	38	16	—	—

National Journal Ratings

	1995 LIB — 1995 CONS	1996 LIB — 1996 CONS
Economic	66% — 33%	82% — 16%
Social	80% — 13%	88% — 0%
Foreign	88% — 7%	87% — 10%

Key Votes of the 104th Congress

1. Reduce Medicare Growth $	N	5. Flag Amendment	N	9. Cuban Embargo	N
2. Ovrd. Product Liab. Veto	N	6. Drop EPA Limits	Y	10. Bar Bosnia Troop $	N
3. Increase Min. Wage	Y	7. Repeal Assault-Weap. Ban	N	11. Cut Anti-Missile Defense	Y
4. Welfare Reform	N	8. Ovrd. Part. Birth Veto	N	12. Bar U.N. Uniforms	N

Election Results

1996 general	Martin T. (Marty) Meehan (D)	unopposed		($308,067)
1996 primary	Martin T. (Marty) Meehan (D)	23,405	(85%)	
	Patrick M. Raymond (D)	4,156	(15%)	
1994 general	Martin T. (Marty) Meehan (D)	140,725	(70%)	($803,523)
	David E. Coleman (R)	60,734	(30%)	

SIXTH DISTRICT

The North Shore of Massachusetts Bay has a number of times been at the leading edge of the nation's economy. In 1640, the Saugus Iron Works was built here—the beginning of American heavy industry. When Europe's great powers were convulsed in international war from 1792 to 1815, American ship owners suddenly became the richest in the world and traders from Boston accumulated the capital needed to build textile mills and railroads and to finance much of the American industrial revolution. From the small port of Salem, ships left for the China trade, bringing back porcelain and artifacts, which helped change American styles forever. Salem, first settled in 1626, had the nation's first millionaire, Elias Hasket Derby; in 1900 it was the richest per capita city in the nation. But the North Shore is a quiet place, from Boston harbor north to the mouth of the Merrimack River, a collection of ethnic factory towns from Lynn on up through next-door Peabody to Newburyport, alternating with the high-income enclaves of Marblehead with its yachts and Beverly with its estates, artsy Rockport and the fishing port of Gloucester. Lynn is the largest town and its General Electric jet engine plant the largest employer, though with far fewer jobs than during the defense buildup of the 1980s.

The 6th Congressional District of Massachusetts includes the North Shore from Lynn onward, plus towns and cities several miles inland. It is a varied area demographically and politically: its high-income Yankee towns are liberal Republican, while Lynn, Salem, Peabody and the Merrimack mill towns are still Irish working-class Democratic. The 6th has been a Democratic district on balance since the 1960s; but in the 1980s and in the 1990s only marginally so. While this district is the site of the original gerrymander—named after Elbridge Gerry—the current 6th District boundaries are less grotesque and politically determined than those of any other Massachusetts district.

The congressman from the 6th District is John Tierney, a Democrat elected in 1996 after coming close in 1994. Tierney grew up in Salem in modest circumstances; he worked his way through Salem State College and Suffolk University Law School as a janitor on the night shift. For nearly 20 years he practiced law in his family firm in Salem. In 1994 he spied a political opening and ran for Congress. The incumbent, Peter Torkildsen, was a Republican elected in 1992 by beating incumbent Nicholas Mavroulas, who had been indicted for tax evasion and bribery (he pled guilty in 1993); the district had otherwise been safely Democratic since liberal Michael Harrington won a special election in 1969 (his chief assistant was a graduate student named Barney Frank). In 1994 Tierney won a closely contested primary with 34% over two other

Democrats with 33% and 25%; he called for a single-payer health insurance plan and a ban on all handgun sales and attacked Torkildsen for voting against the crime bill and the ban on assault weapons. But Torkildsen won 51%–47%.

In the 104th Congress Torkildsen had a subcommittee chairmanship and a moderate voting record. But with his narrow margin he was an obvious target. The AFL-CIO ran ads against him and Tierney began running, winning the Democratic primary without serious opposition. Tierney ran a cookie-cutter Democratic campaign, assailing Republican Medicare "cuts" and Newt Gingrich, calling for "greater educational opportunities," government health care insurance for children and aid to college students, and criticized Torkildsen for not bringing enough defense dollars to the district. "Time and time again Peter Torkildsen voted with Newt and the gang," Tierney repeated during the campaign. Torkildsen talked of his independence, of getting funding for building helicopter engines; he took to voting against approving the minutes of the previous day to increase his anti-leadership score. Torkildsen raised and spent $1.1 million, while keeping to his promise to accept no PAC money, and led in early polls. But Tierney, aided by the early AFL-CIO ads, held his spending—$776,000 in total—mostly toward the end. The result was one of the closest races in the country. Tierney came out slightly ahead in initial returns and after several recounts, which stretched into December, Tierney had won by only 360 votes.

The transition was not entirely smooth. Tierney inherited Torkildsen's office, since he was not included in the lottery for offices because of the recount; then when he took possession claimed that the place had been vandalized. As his chief staffer he hired an employee of AFSCME, the public employees' union—testimony to the work labor had done for him—and called for the resignation of Newt Gingrich. Hc got a seat on Education and The Workforce, where he is likely to be a strong union vote. This being Massachusetts, Tierney must be favored for 1998; but there was talk of serious opposition, from Torkildsen again or Gloucester state Senator Bruce Tarr.

The People: Pop. 1990: 601,811; 10% rural; 14% age 65+; 94% White; 2% Black; 1% Asian; 3% Hispanic origin. Households: 57% married couple families; 26% married couple fams. w. children; 54% college educ.; median household income: $40,836; per capita income: $18,549; median gross rent: $617; median house value: $181,400.

1996 Presidential Vote			1992 Presidential Vote		
Clinton (D)	166,037	(59%)	Clinton (D)	134,424	(43%)
Dole (R)	86,306	(31%)	Bush (R)	96,857	(31%)
Perot (I)	26,273	(9%)	Perot (I)	75,893	(25%)

Rep. John F. Tierney (D)

Elected 1996; b. Sept. 18, 1951, Salem; home, Salem; Salem St. U., B.A. 1973; Suffolk U., J.D. 1976; No religious affiliation; single.

Career: Practicing atty., 1976–96.

DC Office: 120 CHOB 20515, 202-225-8020; Fax: 202-225-5915.

District Offices: Haverhill, 508-469-1942; Lynn, 617-595-7375; Peabody, 508-531-1669.

Committees: *Education & The Workforce* (16th of 20 D): Employer-Employee Relations; Postsecondary Education, Training & Life-Long Learning. *Government Reform & Oversight* (17th of 19 D): National Economic Growth, Natural Resources & Regulatory Affairs.

Group Ratings and Key Votes: Newly Elected

Election Results

1996 general	John F. Tierney (D)	133,002	(48%)	($776,359)
	Peter G. Torkildsen (R)	132,642	(48%)	($1,120,913)
	Others	10,735	(4%)	
1996 primary	John F. Tierney (D)	18,115	(85%)	
	John Gutta (D)	3,044	(14%)	
1994 general	Peter G. Torkildsen (R)	120,952	(51%)	($768,072)
	John F. Tierney (D)	113,481	(47%)	($497,570)
	Others	5,011	(2%)	

SEVENTH DISTRICT

The Yankee Protestants and Irish Catholics who settled Massachusetts arrived by boat, the Yankees to a cold stony land with a few Indians, the Irish to a crowded city with Yankees who seemed even less welcoming. The Yankees whose ancestors once farmed the soil had, by the early 20th Century, founded suburbs filled with solid brick and white frame houses, furnished in Early American furniture, with a view out the paned windows. As the years went on, their local public schools were emptied as young people with children had moved out, and attendance at Protestant churches went down. The Irish, for decades heavily concentrated in the crowded wards of Boston, started moving out into the Yankee suburbs 50 years ago. There were other ethnic groups here and there (Jews, Italians, French Canadians) but the major conflict—fought out in neighborhood playgrounds, in school committee meetings and not least in political campaigns—was between Protestant Yankee Republicans and Catholic Irish Democrats.

The 7th Congressional District of Massachusetts is made up of northern and western suburbs of Boston where vestiges of this conflict can still be seen. Geographically, it forms an arc around Boston, starting with the clapboard beach towns of Winthrop and Revere just beyond Logan Airport, going north as far as Wakefield, west past working class Woburn and Medford, home of Tufts University, to the patriot town of Lexington that spans Route 128 and Waltham, home of Brandeis University, through high-income Lincoln and Weston to modest-income Natick and Framingham. Most of these towns were Yankee Republican up through the 1950s, but by the late 1960s they were pretty solidly Democratic; the high-tech suburbs trended Republican again in the 1980s but swung against George Bush in 1992. The highest income areas seem to run across the grain of their ethnic experience: Weston, with many Catholics, is pretty solidly Republican; Lincoln, with Yankees like Thomas Boylston Adams and George Bush's sister Nancy Ellis, has been liberal since it voted for George McGovern in 1972.

The congressman in the 7th District is Edward Markey, first elected in 1976 at age 30, now one of the most powerful Democrats in the House. He grew up in Malden, where his father was a milkman; he went to Malden Catholic High, Boston College, Boston College Law, then immediately to the legislature, at 26. In 1976, he ran for the House and won a 12-candidate primary with 22% of the vote; he had never been to Washington. The Capitol he first laid eyes on was full of Democrats for whom Vietnam and Watergate were the paradigmatic events of all world history; Markey first made a name as a fierce opponent of nuclear power. In 1983 he was the leading political organizer for the nuclear freeze, which would have given away America's technological edge just as our defense buildup was starting to destabilize the Soviets' evil empire. Markey's enthusiastic certainty and his thirst for publicity infuriated many colleagues, who saw him as a self-righteous grandstander.

But seniority and events put Markey in position to become a productive and creative legislator. He is one of those lucky House members for whom the seniority system has clicked. With help from Tip O'Neill, he got on the Commerce Committee; impressed by the high-tech boom around Route 128, he got on the old Communications Subcommittee early. He flirted with running for the Senate in 1984, when Paul Tsongas retired, but he raised little money and when faced with a three-person primary, jumped back into the 7th District race and scrambled to win. Then, after only eight years in the House, he became chairman of the Energy Conservation and Power Subcommittee; after the 1986 election, with help from Chairman John Dingell, who liked aggressive and loyal younger Democrats, Markey became chairman of the Telecommunications Subcommittee. This is one of the plum positions in the House, with fabulous possibilities for campaign fund-raising (Markey doesn't take PAC money, but of course communications and securities executives can and do contribute, and for 1994 he got $956,000 in individual contributions) and with subject matter that is intellectually more demanding (and in lobbying terms more fiercely contested) than almost anything else in Congress. Markey received more than $657,000 in individual contributions in 1996, despite having minimal opposition.

As chairman and as ranking Democrat since 1994, Markey has been a major shaper of public policy, often working with Republicans, often coming up with original initiatives of his own, knowledgeable about the workings of these industries and inclined often toward deregulation, but also casting himself as the defender of consumers. His 1990 law responding to the 1987 market crash increased the power of the SEC to shut down markets or limit computer program trading in emergencies. Similarly, on derivatives, Markey sought not to shut the markets down but to provide more disclosure. In communications, Markey passed bills limiting dial-a-porn services, and requiring TVs to include decoder circuitry for close-captioned signals for the deaf. In 1992, he combined his penchant for regulation with political shrewdness to produce the cable TV reregulation bill on which both houses overrode President Bush's veto—the only bill passed over his veto in his four-year term. Another Markey achievement in 1993 was the law reallocating from public to private sector 200 megahertz of the radio frequency spectrum, four times as much as created the entire cellular phone industry, allocated by the most lucrative auction in history.

Markey's influence was not greatly reduced when he became ranking minority member; bills in these areas are hard to pass without bipartisan consensus, and he was in a key position to create or withhold it. Take telecommunications deregulation, the heart of which is opening up local phone service to long-distance companies and allowing the regional Bells into long-distance. A bill Markey co-sponsored with then ranking Republican Jack Fields passed the House in 1994 but was killed by Bob Dole in the Senate. In 1995 Fields introduced a similar bill, but Markey was one of five Democrats to oppose it. He felt its cable deregulation provisions left too many consumers without competition. On the floor in August 1995 he inserted one provision restricting networks to 35% of local audiences and to prohibit cross-ownership of broadcast and cable in the same market, thus preventing cable giants like TCI and Time Warner from broadcasting, and another establishing the V-chip, using the capacity of the decoder circuitry for the deaf to be used for the codes it required networks to place on all entertainment programming. Both passed, with significant Republican support. Markey described the V-chip as an upgraded off/on button, which allowed parents to make choices on their children's viewing. The House-passed bill foundered for a while in the Senate, then was revived by Ernest Hollings and others, and became law in 1996. Bill Clinton made the V-chip a talking point in his campaign; but the issue remains alive: after the campaign Markey criticized the broadcasters' movie-like single rating and called for specific information on violence, sex and language.

Another significant achievement was on securities reform, to eliminate overlapping state regulation of broker licenses and mutual fund prospectuses; Markey and SEC Chairman Arthur Levitt got Fields to drop provisions against lawsuits by big buyers like Orange County; the bill became law. Other Markey causes are ongoing. His requirement that broadcasters present three hours a week of educational programming for children got signatures from most House members, but didn't pass. Markey failed to change a Superfund reform provision repaying companies which had signed consent decrees; Superfund reform is still awaited. He won a close floor vote, beating the National Security Committee, against a bill to fund nuclear reactors using plutonium. He still pursues his "patient right-to-know" law, co-sponsored by Republican Greg Ganske, an Iowa physician, barring healthcare providers from failing to mention all medical options.

After the 1996 election, the subcommittee's jurisdiction was altered; it lost securities and gained consumer protection laws and was renamed. This was intra-party Republican politics: the chairmanship went to party-switcher Billy Tauzin, but party leaders felt they had to compensate Mike Oxley, next in line in seniority, and did so by giving his subcommittee more jurisdiction over financing issues. But Telecommunications retains jurisdiction over what is likely the most lobbied issue in the 105th Congress, electric utility deregulation. Markey says his goal is to demonopolize electric power, to give consumers a choice of electricity suppliers; he would repeal the 1935 Public Utility Holding Company restrictions and 1982 alternative energy requirements, but only for states which open up full retailing competition.

On other issues Markey has one of the most liberal voting records in the House, and continues to pummel Republicans with partisan attacks (GOP means "get old people," he declared in 1995). His 1986 report on experiments with biological radiation without consent was given national publicity when it was picked up by the *Albuquerque Journal* and Energy Secretary Hazel O'Leary. He has backed sanctions on China for ignoring nuclear export controls and opposes MFN for China. He has been easily reelected since 1984.

The People: Pop. 1990: 601,476; 1% rural; 15% age 65+; 92% White; 2% Black; 3% Asian; 3% Hispanic origin. Households: 53% married couple families; 22% married couple fams. w. children; 53% college educ.; median household income: $41,318; per capita income: $19,825; median gross rent: $685; median house value: $192,700.

1996 Presidential Vote

Clinton (D)	171,125	(64%)
Dole (R)	72,823	(27%)
Perot (I)	19,374	(7%)

1992 Presidential Vote

Clinton (D)	150,073	(50%)
Bush (R)	87,418	(29%)
Perot (I)	61,963	(21%)

Rep. Edward J. Markey (D)

Elected 1976; b. July 11, 1946, Malden; home, Malden; Boston Col., B.A. 1968, J.D. 1972; Catholic; married (Susan Blumenthal).

Career: Army Reserves, 1968–73; MA House of Reps., 1973–76.

DC Office: 2133 RHOB 20515, 202-225-2836.

District Offices: Medford, 617-396-2900.

Committees: *Commerce* (3rd of 23 D): Energy & Power; Finance & Hazardous Materials; Telecommunications, Trade & Consumer Protection (RMM). *Resources* (2nd of 23 D): National Parks & Public Lands.

Group Ratings

	ADA	ACLU	AFS	LCV	CFA	CON	NFIB	COC	ACU	NTLC	CHC
1996	95	88	100	77	100	53	22	6	0	5	7
1995	80	—	—	100	92	16	—	17	8	—	—

National Journal Ratings

	1995 LIB — 1995 CONS			1996 LIB — 1996 CONS		
Economic	85%	—	12%	89%	—	0%
Social	73%	—	26%	88%	—	0%
Foreign	88%	—	7%	90%	—	0%

Key Votes of the 104th Congress

1. Reduce Medicare Growth $	N	5. Flag Amendment	N	9. Cuban Embargo	N
2. Ovrd. Product Liab. Veto	N	6. Drop EPA Limits	Y	10. Bar Bosnia Troop $	N
3. Increase Min. Wage	Y	7. Repeal Assault-Weap. Ban	N	11. Cut Anti-Missile Defense	Y
4. Welfare Reform	N	8. Ovrd. Part. Birth Veto	N	12. Bar U.N. Uniforms	*

Election Results

1996 general	Edward J. Markey (D)	177,053	(70%)	($351,683)
	Patricia H. Long (R)	76,407	(30%)	($3,033)
1996 primary	Edward J. Markey (D)	24,560	(99%)	
1994 general	Edward J. Markey (D)	146,246	(64%)	($757,993)
	Brad Bailey (R)	80,674	(36%)	($360,370)

EIGHTH DISTRICT

A long generation ago, Cambridge, Massachusetts was a plainly aging city, with a grayness in the air matching its gray winter skies. Its two great universities, Harvard and MIT, were closely hemmed in by a not very friendly town of Irish Catholics, Italians and a few Portuguese, living generation after generation in three-decker houses with cracked walls letting in the cold in the long winters. Boston was the nation's slowest-growing metropolitan area, economically stagnant, still caught in a 17th Century Puritan-Papist rivalry. Students from suburbs across the country exploring Boston from their dormitories and campuses felt they were pawing through the living remnants of 1920s America, a quaint place where people called traffic circles rotaries and milk shakes frappes. Massachusetts has since changed, and nowhere more than in Cambridge. As universities and high tech have become driving forces of economic growth, Cambridge has gone glitzy, with trendy restaurants and high-priced hotels, boutiques and upscale condominiums. Greater Boston may well have the heaviest concentration of graduate students and post-graduate hangers-on of any major city, and their world is centered on Cambridge, with outposts in low-income Somerville, tenured-faculty haven Belmont, Boston's Back Bay and Allston and Brighton near the Harvard Business School.

Cambridge is the center, and the rest of these communities are part, of Massachusetts's 8th Congressional District, a district with great historic sites from the gold dome of the State House on Beacon Hill to the frigate *Constitution* in the Charlestown docks; the district, with MIT and the software concentration in Cambridge's once downscale Lechmere Square, is one of the high-tech capitals of America. The 8th also includes the impoverished suburb of Chelsea and much of the Roxbury black ghetto in Boston; this is by far the most Democratic district in Massachusetts.

Over the past 50 years the 8th District has had just three congressmen, John F. Kennedy, Thomas P. O'Neill and Joseph P. Kennedy II; one went on to become President of the United States, one became speaker of the House, and one quite possibly will become governor of Massachusetts. Joe Kennedy is the oldest son of Robert Kennedy, an object of affection and veneration in many Massachusetts homes, and of those who can remember how at 17 he shook hands with all the passengers on his father's funeral train. In the early 1980s, Joe was living on the South Shore and running the Citizens Energy Corporation he founded to buy oil in bulk for distribution to low-income citizens. When O'Neill announced his retirement, Kennedy came here and ran (his uncle's district residence was in a hotel). He faced half a dozen leftish candidates in the Democratic primary. His strongest competitor, Cambridge state senator George Bachrach made the mistake of charging Kennedy with having ties with Qaddafi's Libya, while O'Neill endorsed Kennedy; before that Kennedy had been running only even in the polls, but he beat Bachrach 52%–30%.

Like his uncle, Senator Edward Kennedy, Joe Kennedy seems to see himself as a tribune of the poor, and the three-decker house working-class as well; he tempers his liberalism with stands like supporting capital punishment and backing the balanced budget amendment. He oscillates between the boyish impulsiveness of a man who has never had to pay for his mistakes, and a determination to work hard and make a serious record as a mature politician; his admirers insist that he is now very little of the first and much of the second. He has in fact some respectable legislative achievements. On the Banking Committee he has worked on housing legislation such as the Community Reinvestment Act, seeking disclosure of the race and census tract of those who get mortgages; this has been used by the Clinton Administration to pressure banks to open branches in black neighborhoods and to grant more loans to blacks. He sponsored the 1990 Community Housing Partnership Act, funneling billions to community-based nonprofits, for loans to homebuyers—a law which has buoyed many distressed areas. With Barney Frank, he pushed the RTC to help low-income families purchase houses in the inventory of failed savings and loans. He has worked to reform flood insurance, to encourage private insurance and reduce federal outlays. He has held hearings on appealing and appalling subjects—credit ratings, a $25 annual fee for people who pay off their credit balance each month, Gulf war syndrome, and child labor abroad. He also has sponsored—good Cambridge causes—health warnings on alcohol bottles, indoor air quality standards and federal funding of bicycle paths. He supported the securities litigation reform law passed over Bill Clinton's veto and, with two high-tech-minded Republicans, has a bill to further restrict such suits in state courts.

On foreign policy, he sometimes takes an adversarial stand toward American policy. "Are we to be the international police force, the bully boys of the world?" he asked during the Gulf war debate. He has attacked the Army School of the Americas for fostering terrorism in Latin America. He has long been critical of Britain's policy in Northern Ireland, and joined his uncle Edward Kennedy in support of the mediation efforts of his aunt, Ambassador to Ireland Jean Kennedy Smith, and welcomed President Clinton's reception at the White House for Sinn Fein leader Gerry Adams, who could not bring himself to condemn IRA bombings in Britain. He worked to get humanitarian aid to Armenia (there's a big Armenian community in Watertown, west of Cambridge) and was a strong supporter of the Aristide government in Haiti.

Kennedy's interest in running for governor has not been camouflaged. In 1996 he was opposed by Philip Hyde, his first Republican opponent since 1990 (when Hyde mentioned he might run, Kennedy apparently replied, "Why would you ever want to do that?"); Kennedy took the opportunity to spend $1.9 million collected under federal rules, which are less restrictive than Massachusetts's; he still had more than a million dollars left over in December, enough to easily repay contributions from scandal-ridden John Huang and Johnny Chung. In early 1997 it was widely assumed he was running for governor, but not without competition. Attorney General Scott Harshbarger said he was running and predicted he would beat Kennedy in the primary; Governor William Weld, who accepted an appointment as Ambassador to Mexico, annointed Republican Lieutenant Governor Paul Cellucci as his successor; and also Republican Treasurer Joe Malone, who ran against Edward Kennedy in 1988, said he will run. But Kennedy's personal troubles may do more damage to his bid for governor than any opponent. Bad press about Kennedy's annulment from his former wife of 12 years, Sheila Rauch Kennedy, dropped Kennedy's favorability rating in April 1997 polls. And the much publicized saga of his brother and campaign director Michael Kennedy's alleged affair with a 14-year-old babysitter didn't help either. For the 8th District seat, there is no dearth of possibilities if Kennedy runs for governor, with at least four term-limited members of the state Senate. Possibilities include George Bachrach, Senate President Thomas Birmingham and Senators Warren Tolman and Dianne Wilkerson.

The People: Pop. 1990: 602,396; 11% age 65+; 61% White; 22% Black; 5% Asian; 1% Other; 11% Hispanic origin. Households: 32% married couple families; 13% married couple fams. w. children; 53% college educ.; median household income: $30,417; per capita income: $16,327; median gross rent: $636; median house value: $188,200.

1996 Presidential Vote

Clinton (D)	139,383	(77%)
Dole (R)	28,253	(16%)
Perot (I)	7,928	(4%)
Other	4,557	(3%)

1992 Presidential Vote

Clinton (D)	136,438	(67%)
Bush (R)	39,368	(19%)
Perot (I)	25,423	(13%)

Rep. Joseph P. Kennedy, II (D)

Elected 1986; b. Sept. 24, 1952, Brighton; home, Brighton; U. of MA, B.A. 1976; Catholic; married (Beth).

Career: Community Svcs. Admin., 1977–79; Founder & Pres., Citizens Energy Corp., 1979–86, Citizens Conservation Corp., 1981.

DC Office: 2242 RHOB 20515, 202-225-5111; Fax: 202-225-9322.

District Offices: Charlestown, 617-242-0200; Roxbury, 617-445-1281.

Committees: *Banking & Financial Services* (7th of 25 D): Domestic & International Monetary Policy; Housing & Community Opportunity (RMM). *Veterans' Affairs* (2nd of 13 D): Health.

Group Ratings

	ADA	ACLU	AFS	LCV	CFA	CON	NFIB	COC	ACU	NTLC	CHC
1996	95	69	100	85	100	71	24	13	0	5	7
1995	80	—	—	81	100	56	—	17	8	—	—

National Journal Ratings

	1995 LIB — 1995 CONS			1996 LIB — 1996 CONS		
Economic	71%	—	28%	85%	—	11%
Social	80%	—	13%	88%	—	0%
Foreign	93%	—	0%	90%	—	0%

Key Votes of the 104th Congress

1. Reduce Medicare Growth $	N	5. Flag Amendment	Y	9. Cuban Embargo	N
2. Ovrd. Product Liab. Veto	N	6. Drop EPA Limits	Y	10. Bar Bosnia Troop $	N
3. Increase Min. Wage	Y	7. Repeal Assault-Weap. Ban	N	11. Cut Anti-Missile Defense	Y
4. Welfare Reform	N	8. Ovrd. Part. Birth Veto	N	12. Bar U.N. Uniforms	N

Election Results

1996 general	Joseph P. Kennedy, II (D)	147,126	(84%)	($1,952,906)
	R. Philip Hyde (R)	27,303	(16%)	
1996 primary	Joseph P. Kennedy, II (D)	unopposed		
1994 general	Joseph P. Kennedy, II (D)	unopposed		($839,725)

NINTH DISTRICT

The "Hub of the Universe," the elder Oliver Wendell Holmes called it in the 19th Century, and so it seems again sometimes: when you reflect that Fidelity mutual funds and so many other big financial outfits are headquartered in modern towers built on streets laid out as 17th Century cowpaths; when you walk on the streets where Samuel Adams and Paul Revere plotted revolution or track down the sites of rallies and headquarters of the various Kennedy campaigns;

when you walk on Beacon Street past the Bull and Finch Pub which is the original for TV's *Cheers* (and whose name is a play on the architect of the State House, Thomas Bulfinch). Today's Boston is a different city from the Boston of John Kennedy's time. Boston then was a gray city with no new buildings and dust on every windowsill; the sky was dark with pollution and the air was thick with ancient Yankee and Irish animosity. The old office buildings were full of Yankees seeking safe investments for their antique family fortunes; the State House and City Hall were full of Irishmen, scampering after good patronage jobs and regaling each other with political battle stories. Today, that Boston is mostly gone. The new skyscrapers are full of venture capitalists and lawyers and management consultants, all working for high-tech companies radiating from Cambridge out into the countryside; the advertising slogans crackle with a sauciness and *double entendre* you can find only here and maybe in New York and London.

Most of Boston's neighborhoods have changed. There are still vestiges of the old Irish neighborhoods, as in South Boston, but the central city is increasingly populated by blacks and young singles; its population is down from 801,000 in 1950 to 574,000 in 1990; over 80% of the metropolitan area is in the suburbs. The 9th Congressional District, historically anchored in Boston, has followed the move, and today only one-third of its residents are in Boston, mostly in still-Irish areas of South Boston, Hyde Park and West Roxbury. From there, the 9th heads southwest to Easton and the old Patriots Stadium, southeast to Braintree, ancestral home of the presidential Adamses, Brockton, the old shoe manufacturing town, and the old textile mill town of Taunton. Ethnically it is probably the most heavily Irish congressional district in the nation; politically, it has been represented by only three members, all of them Democrats, for the last 70-plus years, the first of whom was Speaker of the House John McCormack.

The congressman from the 9th is Joe Moakley, first elected in 1972 as an Independent, but very much a Democrat. Moakley is a son of South Boston who has lived in the 7th Ward all his life. He was a high school football star who volunteered for the Navy in 1943, at 15, went to college in Miami after the war, then went to law school in Boston; in 1952, at 25, he was elected to the Massachusetts House. He was elected to the state Senate in the splendidly Democratic year of 1964, then to the Boston Council, with the highest vote, in 1971. He ran for the House when McCormack retired in 1970 and lost the primary to Louise Day Hicks, the anti-busing chairman of the Boston School Committee. In 1972 he ran again, this time as an Independent; in the primary, opposition to Hicks was divided among five other candidates, and she won with 37%, but Moakley won the general by 5,000 votes.

In the House Moakley got a seat on the Rules Committee in his second term. On the back benches in the 1970s, he moved up quickly in seniority and became chairman when Claude Pepper died in June 1989. As chairman of the Rules Committee, Moakley worked closely with Speaker Thomas Foley and Majority Leader Dick Gephardt; he helped David Bonior, also a Catholic deeply opposed to U.S. Central American policy, win his party whip leadership post. Under their lead, Rules increasingly passed closed rules, limiting amendments and debate, to the fury of the Republicans. His one headline cause was El Salvador. Acquainted with several nuns and priests murdered there, he sponsored a commission which looked into their deaths; its top staffer was Martin Meehan, now congressman from the 5th District. It found that high-ranking Salvadoran military officials were involved, and Moakley led a fight for cutoff of U.S. aid.

Moakley sees himself as a "bread and butter" politician and his voting record is liberal except on some cultural issues. He is proud of the federal money going into the rebuilding of Boston's Central Artery rebuilding, perhaps the largest public works project in U.S. history. He takes credit for the Boston Harbor cleanup and the third harbor tunnel and says he has created "countless jobs throughout the Commonwealth." Usually a humorous and gentle man, he abhors Newt Gingrich and the new Republican majority, especially on his Rules panel; "happy days aren't here again," he said on opening day in 1995. He found himself in the ironic position of criticizing Republicans for crafting restrictions on House debate, though arguably not as tight as the ones that he had backed—"I don't say we were fair and open all the way," he conceded.

Moakley has been reelected by wide margins, but not without drama. In June 1995 he stayed in South Boston to care for his wife, who was ill with a brain tumor; in July 1995 he had a liver transplant. In September 1995 he was about to announce his retirement, but decided to run instead. "Sending a new fellow to Congress in this kind of milieu is not really what is best for the citizens of this district. I've done a lot of work down there and I just happen to know where a lot of the bodies are buried." He returned to the House and his health sharply improved, and by January 1996 said,"The truth is I'm well. This may have killed the average guy, but I'm not the average guy. My [new] liver is perfect." He was reelected easily, despite his opponent's cautions about his health. Indeed, he remained as active as ever. In February 1997 he blocked New England Patriots' owner Robert Kraft's plans for a stadium in South Boston by talking the Army into refusing to turn over a key land parcel; then after a conversation with Moakley, Kraft appeared at a press conference in his office and dropped the plans. One tantalizing possibility for a successor, if Moakley decides not to run in 1998: Billy Bulger, who followed him in the state House and Senate, the longtime Senate President who is now head of the University of Massachusetts system. Another possibility is former Boston Mayor Ray Flynn, who spent three years as ambassador to the Vatican.

The People: Pop. 1990: 601,250; 2% rural; 15% age 65+; 86% White; 6% Black; 3% Asian; 1% Other; 5% Hispanic origin. Households: 51% married couple families; 22% married couple fams. w. children; 50% college educ.; median household income: $38,646; per capita income: $17,980; median gross rent: $616; median house value: $172,000.

1996 Presidential Vote			1992 Presidential Vote		
Clinton (D)	158,967	(62%)	Clinton (D)	131,644	(48%)
Dole (R)	76,202	(30%)	Bush (R)	85,901	(31%)
Perot (I)	19,168	(7%)	Perot (I)	56,431	(21%)

Rep. John Joseph (Joe) **Moakley (D)**

Elected 1972; b. Apr. 27, 1927, Boston; home, Boston; U. of Miami, Suffolk U., LL.B. 1956; Catholic; married (Evelyn).

Career: Navy, 1943–46 (WWII); MA House of Reps., 1952–62, Majority Whip, 1957; Practicing atty., 1957–72; MA Senate, 1964–70; Boston City Cncl., 1971–72.

DC Office: 235 CHOB 20515, 202-225-8273; Fax: 202-225-3984; e-mail: jmoakley@hr.house.gov.

District Offices: Boston, 617-565-2920; Brockton, 508-586-5555; Taunton, 508-824-6676.

Committees: *Rules* (RMM of 4 D): Legislative & Budget Process.

Group Ratings

	ADA	ACLU	AFS	LCV	CFA	CON	NFIB	COC	ACU	NTLC	CHC
1996	65	67	100	85	92	21	17	25	6	5	20
1995	35	—	—	75	46	2	—	13	0	—	—

National Journal Ratings

	1995 LIB — 1995 CONS			1996 LIB — 1996 CONS		
Economic	84%	—	16%	89%	—	0%
Social	*	—	*	67%	—	33%
Foreign	93%	—	0%	90%	—	0%

Key Votes of the 104th Congress

1. Reduce Medicare Growth $	N	5. Flag Amendment	*	9. Cuban Embargo	*
2. Ovrd. Product Liab. Veto	N	6. Drop EPA Limits	Y	10. Bar Bosnia Troop $	N
3. Increase Min. Wage	Y	7. Repeal Assault-Weap. Ban	*	11. Cut Anti-Missile Defense	Y
4. Welfare Reform	N	8. Ovrd. Part. Birth Veto	Y	12. Bar U.N. Uniforms	N

Election Results

1996 general	John Joseph (Joe) Moakley (D)	172,009	(72%)	($769,122)
	Paul V. Gryska (R)	66,079	(28%)	($232,527)
1996 primary	John Joseph (Joe) Moakley (D)	unopposed		
1994 general	John Joseph (Joe) Moakley (D)	146,287	(70%)	($981,247)
	Michael M. Murphy (R)	63,369	(30%)	($178,071)

TENTH DISTRICT

The South Shore of Massachusetts Bay, from Boston southward to Plymouth and then down Cape Cod (there is a lot of dispute about which way is up and down on the Cape), is Massachusetts's oldest-settled territory and the site of its fastest-growing new communities. The Pilgrims landed here at Plymouth Rock in 1620; this stony land was farmed by John Adams's father, who was anything but the aristocrat some later members of the Adams family would have you believe. Daniel Webster lived in the South Shore town of Marshfield, today a high-income suburb of Boston far out the usually clogged Southeast Expressway; Joseph P. Kennedy used to summer with his young family on Nantasket Beach in Hull, and then moved out of Massachusetts when the Yankees wouldn't let them into their beach club in Cohasset in the 1920s; the Kennedy family continues to summer at their Hyannis Port compound. The Plymouth area and Cape Cod were originally farming country, with some industry; a railroad, now long-gone, steamed along the middle of the Cape. Provincetown (at the tip of the Cape) is still a fishing port, and also now one of the major gay vacation areas in the country; the islands of Martha's Vineyard and Nantucket, rich whaling ports in the early 19th Century, are now favored summer resorts for the trendy liberal rich of New York and Washington. Cape Cod is the site of the bogs which still produce half of America's cranberries, but it is also filled increasingly with retirees and, to the dismay of some, is the fastest-growing part of Massachusetts.

The 10th Congressional District of Massachusetts, with grotesque boundaries like most other Bay State districts, follows the South Shore from Quincy to the Cape, jutting inland near Brockton, and including Martha's Vineyard and Nantucket. The South Shore and the Cape were once exclusively Protestant and Yankee, but in the Massachusetts way they have changed over the years, with Irish and Italian surnames as common as Yankee and the descendants of the Portuguese Azorean fishermen fanning out into the countryside. And trendy liberal politics, well established on the Vineyard and Nantucket, have spread inland as well.

The congressman from the 10th District is William Delahunt, a Democrat elected after tough contests in 1996. Delahunt is a lifelong resident of Quincy, who went to college at Middlebury and Boston College Law School and served in the Coast Guard. He practiced law and was elected to the Quincy Council. In 1972 he was elected to the legislature; in 1975 Governor Michael Dukakis appointed him district attorney of Norfolk County, which extends from Cohasset to Rhode Island and also includes non-contiguous Brookline. He was prompted to run by the retirement, announced in October 1995, of Congressman Gerry Studds, a Eugene McCarthy volunteer who was elected in 1972 and who worked hard on fishing issues; for one term Studds was chairman of the Merchant Marine and Fisheries Committee and was dismayed when Republicans abolished it in 1995. Delahunt had serious primary competition from former Marshfield state Representative Philip Johnston and self-financing environmentalist Ian

Bowles. Delahunt was the favorite; Johnston and Bowles attacked him for refusing to release his income tax returns and spending $100,000 of campaign money on meals. Johnston carried most of the Cape and Plymouth County; Bowles carried Martha's Vineyard and Falmouth, where you catch the ferry; Delahunt won nearly half his votes, and very big margins, in Quincy and next-door Weymouth.

The initial results of the September 17 primary showed 38% each for Delahunt and Johnston and 22% for Bowles, with Johnston ahead by 266 votes. A recount declared Johnston still ahead by 175 votes. But Delahunt sued, and on October 4 a judge ruled that more than 900 punch card votes in Weymouth had not been properly tabulated, and proceeded to count every ballot with an indentation, dimple or other mark. On October 10 Delahunt was declared the winner by 108 votes, even as Johnston was being hailed at a Quincy rally by Edward Kennedy and Hillary Rodham Clinton. Johnston called the result a "travesty," and Delahunt had less than a month to campaign for the general. The Republican primary had been won by conservative state House Minority Leader Edward Teague with 68% over liberal Francis Sargent, Jr., son of a former governor. Both ran million dollar campaigns, but Teague had been running ads against Johnston, and Delahunt's campaign was dormant. Eight years before George Bush had carried this district over Michael Dukakis, but reaction to the new Republican majority in the House was hostile, and Delahunt won 54%–42%. Teague ran only about even on Cape Cod, a bit behind in Plymouth County and lost the rest of the district by wide margins.

Delahunt pledged to wear Cape Cod ties in the House and has handed them out to colleagues of both parties. He serves on the Resources and Judiciary Committees and must deal with local problems like the Fore River Shipyard (Senator John McCain attacked its federal loan guarantees), the Greenbush rail line in Hingham (locals want a tunnel built), the Weymouth Naval Air Station (find new uses). Johnston, still bitter, said in early 1997 there was a 50–50 chance he would run again in 1998.

The People: Pop. 1990: 601,510; 27% rural; 16% age 65+; 94% White; 2% Black; 2% Asian; 1% Other; 1% Hispanic origin. Households: 56% married couple families; 24% married couple fams. w. children; 54% college educ.; median household income: $37,489; per capita income: $17,535; median gross rent: $651; median house value: $163,200.

1996 Presidential Vote			1992 Presidential Vote		
Clinton (D)	169,927	(56%)	Clinton (D)	133,601	(42%)
Dole (R)	101,612	(33%)	Bush (R)	101,798	(32%)
Perot (I)	28,125	(9%)	Perot (I)	80,654	(25%)

Rep. William D. Delahunt (D)

Elected 1996; b. July 18, 1941, Quincy; home, Quincy; Middlebury Col., B.A. 1963; Boston Col., J.D. 1967; Catholic; divorced.

Career: Coast Guard Reserves, 1963–71; Practicing atty., 1967–69; Asst. Clerk, Norfolk Superior Court., 1969–71; Quincy City Cncl., 1971; MA House of Reps., 1972–75; District Atty., Norfolk County, 1975–96.

DC Office: 1517 LHOB 20515, 202-225-3111; Fax: 202-225-5658.

District Offices: Hyannis, 508-771-0666; Quincy, 617-770-3700.

Committees: *Judiciary* (13th of 15 D): Commercial & Administrative Law; Courts & Intellectual Property. *Resources* (19th of 23 D): National Parks & Public Lands.

Group Ratings and Key Votes: Newly Elected

Election Results

1996 general	William D. Delahunt (D)	160,745	(54%)	($1,072,986)
	Edward B. Teague (R)	123,520	(42%)	($1,391,148)
	Others	11,658	(4%)	
1996 primary	William D. Delahunt (D)	17,385	(38%)	
	Philip W. Johnston (D)	17,277	(37%)	
	Ian A. Bowles (D)	10,289	(22%)	
	Others	1,317	(3%)	
1994 general	Gerry E. Studds (D)	172,753	(69%)	($639,313)
	Keith Jason Hemeon (R)	78,487	(31%)	($10,990)

MICHIGAN

Michigan is one of America's premier laboratories of reform and innovation, busy now with expanding high-skill small-scale manufacturing and reforming and downsizing government programs, just as it was once busy inventing the mass-production factory economy and then developing the giant industrial labor union and its version of the American welfare state. And in the middle 1990s, its latest experiment seems to be a success. Michigan's unemployment rate since 1994 has been below the national average for the first time in nearly 20 years. And Michigan voters in two elections in a row have given smashing majorities to two incumbent executives, Republican Governor John Engler in 1994 and Democratic President Bill Clinton in 1996. Michigan's task since the Big Three auto companies collapsed in the late 1970s has been to move from an industrial to a post-industrial economy, from domination by big units—big business, big labor, big government—to growth increasingly driven by small units—small businesses, individual workers, flexible government.

Michigan is arguably going back to its roots in the Tocquevillian decade of the 1830s. These two peninsulas, explored and named by French explorers (which explains why Mackinac is pronounced with a silent final c), were settled in a rush by Yankee migrants from Upstate New York, who cut down trees and built farms and neat New Englandish towns complete with schools and colleges. Politically, Michigan was full of reformers who hated slavery, manned the Underground Railroad, promoted temperance and in 1855 gave Michigan a constitution that bans (as it does to this day) capital punishment. Michigan was one of the birthplaces of the Republican Party, which was founded in Jackson in 1854 (Ripon, Wisconsin, also stakes a claim as the Republican Party birthplace) and swept the state in the elections later that year. Up through the 1920s, Michigan was one of the most Republican states in the nation.

Michigan also grew an industrial economy. Its Lower Peninsula was mostly covered with trees, and lumber was the first boom industry on which Michigan over-relied; forests were clear-cut or swept by blazes like the 1881 fire that burned out half the Thumb (look at the map). In the late 1800s huge copper deposits were discovered on the Keweenaw Peninsula, which juts from the Upper Peninsula into icy Lake Superior; immigrants from Italy and Finland, Cornwall and Croatia came to work in the mines. Then came the auto industry. A combination of accident and shrewdness, of bankers willing to finance auto startups and the prickly genius of Henry Ford, ensured that America's fastest-growing industry of the first 30 years of the 20th Century was centered in Michigan. Detroit became a boom town—the nation's fastest-growing metropolitan area after Los Angeles—zooming from 426,000 in 1900 to 2.2 million in 1930. The auto industry drew labor from the Outstate Michigan areas beyond Detroit, from southern Ontario and from the farms of Ohio and Indiana. During World War II and after, it brought whites from the

Kentucky and Tennessee mountains and blacks from Alabama and Mississippi. It attracted Poles and Italians, Hungarians and Belgians, Greeks and Jews. This influx of a polyglot proletariat eventually changed Michigan's politics. The catalyst was the Great Depression of the 1930s and the company managers' desire to use machines efficiently, treating employees as extensions of machines and with great distrust. The results were the 1937 sit-down strikes organized by the new United Auto Workers (UAW); management and labor fought, sometimes literally, for pieces of what both sides feared was a shrinking pie. The UAW won and organized most of the companies after Democratic Governor Frank Murphy refused to send in troops to break the illegal strikes. In the years that followed, auto workers became a heavily Democratic voting bloc.

Michigan politics, during its big-unit years, was a species of class warfare, conducted with a bitterness that split families and neighbors. The union mostly won, because demographics benefited the Democrats: auto workers and post-1900 immigrants produced more children than did Outstate Yankees or management. After Walter Reuther's election as UAW president in 1947, voters elected young, liberal G. Mennen Williams governor in 1948; by 1954 the Democrats, closely tied to the UAW, seemed to have become the natural majority in the state. And as growth continued, economic issues became less bitter; by the early 1960s, the class-warfare atmosphere had dissipated. Republican and former auto executive George Romney was narrowly elected governor in 1962, and Henry Ford II joined Walter Reuther in backing Lyndon Johnson in 1964. Romney and his successor, William Milliken, accepted the welfare-state policies endorsed by the UAW leadership and the Democrats. The state government was one of the nation's most generous, and not just to the poor and the unemployed; it supported one of the nation's most distinguished and extensive higher education systems, built state parks and recreation areas, and pioneered efforts to end racial discrimination.

This system which had seemed eternal came crashing down with the collapse of the domestic auto industry after the oil shock of 1979. Union-management relations had been static since 1941, and there had been no major technological changes in American autos since the automatic transmission in 1940. Michigan incomes had grown as Americans grew more affluent; the one-car household became the two-car household, and consumers enjoyed the tail fins and chrome of new car styling. Michigan was the fastest-growing state in the Midwest from 1940 to 1965; except for Illinois, with its big white-collar job base in Chicago, Michigan had the highest incomes in the Midwest. But in 1979, this big-unit economy went bust. It became startlingly clear that the Big Three and the UAW did not have a captive market, Americans did not have to buy a new full-sized American-made car every two or three years, and foreign competitors were producing better and cheaper cars more responsive to changes in consumer preference. Big business and labor, so well adapted for growth in the quarter century after World War II started, proved poorly adapted for the quarter century that followed. Auto employment in Michigan fell from 437,000 in October 1978 to 289,000 in October 1982. Chrysler nearly went bankrupt, Ford was in financial distress, General Motors had its first losses in years. As the recession passed, auto employment settled at 280,000, and wages and fringe benefits declined.

The collapse of the big-unit economy after 1979 forced the state to experiment. The first to try was Governor James Blanchard, a Democrat elected in 1982 with a record of supporting big units. His major achievement in eight years in Congress was managing the Chrysler bailout in the House. Blanchard worked to build a small-unit economy; he was proud of his efforts to stimulate high-skill, capital-intensive, flexible manufacturing, and he used $750 million of state pension funds as venture capital for manufacturers of items from tape drives for microcomputers to fiberglass coffins. Dodging his traditional labor allies, Blanchard made it clear that Michigan must learn how to nurture growth and that workers, instead of seeking more vacation and earlier retirement, would have to hustle and work harder than ever before. The second, and for the moment more successful, experiment came from John Engler, the Republican who beat Blanchard in 1990 and was resoundingly reelected in 1994. Engler believes in less government activism and industrial policy; he has cut or held the line on every state program but education.

KEWEENAW
KEWEENAW
HOUGHTON
ONTONAGON
BARAGA
Ironwood
GOGEBIC
IRON
MARQUETTE
Marquette
ALGER
LUCE
Sault Ste. Marie
CHIPPEWA
SCHOOLCRAFT
DICKINSON
MACKINAC
1
Iron Mountain
DELTA
Escanaba
MENOMINEE
Mackinaw City
Cheboygan
EMMET
CHEBOYGAN
CHARLEVOIX
PRESQUE ISLE
1
ANTRIM
OTSEGO
MONTMORENCY
ALPENA
LEELANAU
Traverse City
KALKASKA
CRAWFORD
Grayling
OSCODA
ALCONA
GR. TRAVERSE
BENZIE
Congressional district boundaries effective April 6, 1992.
MANISTEE
WEXFORD
MISSAUKEE
ROSCOMMON
OGEMAW
IOSCO
Au Sable
MASON
LAKE
OSCEOLA
CLARE
GLADWIN
ARENAC
HURON
Ludington
OCEANA
2
NEWAYGO
MECOSTA
4
ISABELLA
MIDLAND
Midland
BAY
Bay City
5
SANILAC
Miles
0 10 20 30 40
MUSKEGON
Muskegon
MONTCALM
GRATIOT
SAGINAW
Saginaw
TUSCOLA
KENT
Grand Rapids
OTTAWA
3
IONIA
CLINTON
SHIAWASSEE
GENESEE
Flint
LAPEER
9
P. Huron
ST. CLAIR
10
MACOMB
Holland
ALLEGAN
BARRY
EATON
Lansing
INGHAM
8
LIVINGSTON
Pontiac
OAKLAND
11
12
14
15
Kalamazoo
KALAMAZOO
Battle Creek
VAN BUREN
CALHOUN
JACKSON
Jackson
Ann Arbor
Detroit
Benton Harbor
13
WAYNE
BERRIEN
CASS
6
ST. JOSEPH
BRANCH
7
HILLSDALE
LENAWEE
MONROE
16
Monroe
WASHTENAW
Copyright © 1993 by Election Data Services, Inc.

He zeroed out general assistance to nonworkers without children, cut off funding for the museums and arts, and closed a state mental clinic—all actions that sparked fierce protest and hostile media coverage. In 1993, while Republicans controlled the legislature, Engler reduced the powers of his great adversaries, the teachers' unions; in 1994 he pushed through a tax reform, approved in a March referendum, cutting property taxes by raising sales taxes and prodding school districts to reform.

In his first years in office, Engler was bitterly attacked as mean-spirited by Democrats, union leaders and most of the press. He persevered. In 1992 Republicans beat the incumbent House speaker and won a 55–55 tie in the state House; in 1994, Engler was reelected 61%–38% and Republicans won both houses of the legislature. Engler pressed for more reforms: public school choice and charter schools and changing state pensions from defined benefits (which produce huge liabilities for the state and a sense of entitlement in employees) to defined contributions (which reduce the state's future expenses and empower employees to act as investors). In 1996, as Bill Clinton carried Michigan 52%–38%, Engler's Republicans were set back, losing control of the state House.

Historically, politics divided Michigan between labor and management and between the Detroit metro area and Outstate. Thus, in 1960 John Kennedy carried metro Detroit 62%–38% and Richard Nixon carried Outstate 60%–39%. Now that difference has diminished: George Bush in 1988 and then Bill Clinton in 1992 and 1996 carried both regions. New divisions have been created. In the Detroit metro area, the economically growing regions usually vote Republican—almost all of Oakland County, much of western Wayne County and about half of Macomb County, which is no longer as blue-collar as its reputation. Though it voted 63%–37% for Kennedy, Macomb County was carried by Bush in 1988 and 1992; it voted 49%–39% for Clinton in 1996 but 70%–30% for Engler two years before. Central city Detroit, 70% black and with a population half of its peak, and some close-in working class suburbs are solidly Democratic. Outstate, Democrats still run well in the old auto factory corridor from Flint through Saginaw and Bay City, in the university town of Ann Arbor, in the capital town of Lansing, and in the Upper Peninsula. Republicans run far ahead in the fast-growing western Michigan areas around Grand Rapids and Traverse City.

The final results of Michigan's experiments are not in. It has shown its economy can boom during a period of economic growth, as in the big unit days. But will it come crashing down in recession, as it did then, or has it developed a manufacturing expertise that can keep it producing for markets worldwide? Politically, the question is whether Engler's Republicans can continue to surge as in the early 1990s, or whether Michigan Democrats can develop the new Democrat stance that served Jim Blanchard well in the 1980s and Bill Clinton well in the 1990s. Meanwhile, welfare rolls decline, charter schools proliferate, once empty old factories are full of new machine tools and high-skill workers, and Detroit's airport sends out 747s every day straight to London and Tokyo.

Governor. John Engler grew up on a farm near Mount Pleasant, drove 60 miles south to go to Michigan State in East Lansing, then was elected to the state legislature in 1970, at 22, and remained there 20 years until he was elected governor: this downsizer of government has spent all his adult life in the public sector. He came to the fore in 1983, when Republicans, reacting to Jim Blanchard's tax increase, used recalls to seize control of the state Senate, and at 33 Engler became the state's most visible Republican. In a climate where liberals controlled most institutions, Engler was a skillful political player, capable of keeping on civil terms with opponents even as he gathered ideas from conservative think tanks and marshalled a fine political organization run by Spencer Abraham, now Senator, and Pete Secchia, George Bush's Ambassador to Italy. In 1990 Engler ran for governor and lagged behind Blanchard in polls leading up to November. But his call for increasing education spending and cutting property taxes was popular, and when Blanchard came forward with his own property tax cut, Engler effectively ridiculed it as saving a nickel a week per taxpayer. He won 50%–49%.

In office Engler relentlessly kept his campaign promises, ending general assistance (welfare for able-bodied non-parents) and aid to the arts; he privatized services and started seeking federal waivers for welfare reform. Democrats and the *Detroit Free Press* habitually called him "mean-spirited." His efforts to change school financing failed in 1992; in 1993, when Democratic state Senator Debbie Stabenow pushed through a bill to abolish the current education funding system by the end of the year, Engler unexpectedly accepted the dare. Engler's proposal was a major cut in property taxes plus a sales tax increase; the legislature agreed to put it before the voters, with an alternative: increasing the income taxes. Democrats and the teachers' unions backed a higher income tax, but Engler's stand was endorsed by Detroit's incoming Mayor Dennis Archer and approved by voters 70%–30%. "Promises made, promises kept," was Engler's theme in 1994. Michigan's unemployment rate was below the national average for the first time in years and the state was leading industrial states in creating new manufacturing jobs. Small-unit economic growth, seldom heralded in the news media, was making itself felt in people's lives. Engler's job rating, long low, zoomed up in 1994. Democrats had a seriously contested primary. Former Congressman Howard Wolpe, backed by the AFL-CIO, won with 35%, closely followed by Debbie Stabenow, running as a Blanchard Democrat, with 30%, and Larry Owen, backed by the teachers' union, with 26%. Under Michigan's public finance system, Wolpe could put as many ads on the air as Engler, but they did not prove helpful, and Engler won 61%–38%, carrying all but two counties.

In his second term, with a Republican legislature, Engler stepped up the pace of reform. More taxes were cut or abolished, education spending rose and charter schools were authorized, and a welfare reform requiring work was passed; by 1997 welfare rolls dropped more than 20%. Engler was also active nationally, as head of the Republican Governors Association, working with Speaker Newt Gingrich and Senate Majority Leader Bob Dole; his welfare director wrote much of the Republican welfare reform bill. In early 1997, even with a Democratic House, Engler plugged on, calling for state takeover of school districts with 80% failure rates on proficiency tests or 25% dropout rates and supporting demands for a gas tax increase to upgrade the state's pocked roads. Engler was mentioned as a candidate for vice president in 1996, but was subject to some ridicule when it was revealed he had been deferred from the draft for being two pounds overweight. He still has ambitions to affect national policy and perhaps to hold national office. In early 1997 he said he was not sure whether he would run for a third term in 1998; one mitigating factor is that he and his wife have triplet daughters born days after the 1994 election. Republicans who might run if Engler does not include state Senate Majority Leader Dick Posthumus and Congressman Joe Knollenberg. Already running were Democrats Larry Owen, hoping for union support, and Doug Ross, stressing his New Democrat policies as a Blanchard department head and Clinton Labor Department appointee, state legislators Karen Willard, James Berryman, James Agee and Chrysler executive Ed Hamilton. Other possible candidates include former Senator Donald Riegle and Detroit Mayor Dennis Archer.

Senior Senator. Carl Levin is a durable and likable liberal Democrat, a member of one of Michigan's most respected political families and a serious figure in Michigan politics for a quarter century. He is rumpled, unfashionable, speaks articulately but without apparent political artifice and takes unpopular stands on issues he cares about, without much regard for the political consequences. For these virtues, Michigan voters have been willing to forgive him for a few sins. He grew up in Detroit, worked for the state civil rights commissioner and the appellate public defender's office, and was elected to Detroit's city council in 1969 and 1973, practically the only member with substantial support from both blacks and whites. In 1978 he ran for the Senate and was helped when incumbent Robert Griffin got out of the race and then back in; Levin won 52%–48%. In 1984 he won by a similar margin against a former astronaut who had given a public testimonial for his Japanese car; in 1990 and 1996 Levin was reelected by wide margins.

Levin has spent much of his time on process issues. He was chief sponsor of the lobbying disclosure bill that passed the Senate early in 1993 but did not come to a vote in the then-Democratic House; in early 1995 Levin attacked House Speaker Newt Gingrich for not bringing the bill forward, but it passed both chambers and became law in December 1995. Levin also was the chief sponsor of the Senate gift rule, setting a limit of $50 on gifts to senators and staffers. He was the prime mover in reenacting the special counsel law, opposed by many Republicans and signed, perhaps to his later regret, by President Clinton. Levin later protested when the panel of federal judges set up by the law chose Kenneth Starr as independent counsel and tried to get him disqualified, though Starr had held the same job (Solicitor General) and had shown rather less partisanship than Archibald Cox, the special prosecutor appointed to investigate Watergate in 1973.

Levin generally has one of the most liberal records in the Senate. He opposed NAFTA and got Trade Representative Mickey Kantor to bring a Section 301 case against Japanese auto parts trade practices. One issue on which he is passionate is capital punishment: he began his public career as head of Detroit's public defender's office. He has not only opposed capital punishment, but many times has led the fight against it in the Senate: a position in line with tradition in Michigan, whose constitution has outlawed the death penalty since 1855. Levin fought hard against Republicans' unfunded mandates law, regulatory reform legislation and proposed moratorium on regulations.

With the retirement of Sam Nunn, Levin became the ranking Democrat on the Armed Services Committee. He characterizes his approach as supportive of basic, reliable weapons systems and conventional forces and skeptical of strategic weapons systems. He has favored buying fewer B-2s and F-16s than the Pentagon or Republicans have sought. He has strongly opposed efforts to speed up research and deployment of missile defense systems. He has worked hard to reduce the sometimes absurdly large Pentagon inventories, holding hearings and sponsoring laws of billion-dollar magnitude. He has worked for Senate ratification of the START II treaty and the Chemical Weapons Convention. His law created the Joint Simulation Center for Doctrine and Concept Development. Some of his votes became campaign issues in 1990. When a Levin ad showed him in the Persian Gulf on the battleship *Wisconsin*, Republican nominee Bill Schuette pointed out Levin had voted against the ship's recommissioning in 1985 as well as against the Maverick anti-tank missile used successfully in the Gulf. Levin responded by citing his support of many technologically more simple weapons, notably the M-1 tank produced in Chrysler's plant in Warren, just north of Detroit; he also ran an ad showing a retired Reagan Administration Pentagon official saluting Levin for critically assaying defense spending requests.

Levin has not been inattentive to Michigan projects either. He worked to get a $150 million grant for Detroit's Metro Airport, which is being vastly expanded, and he personally lobbied Bill Clinton in March 1996 to get approval of Northwest flights from Detroit nonstop to Beijing. He worked successfully to freeze CAFE car fuel mileage standards. He obtained a marketing order for tart cherry producers (Michigan is the nation's largest producer of tart cherries) and supported an invasive species act to combat the zebra mussel in the Great Lakes. He saved Michigan's six Manufacturing Technology Centers and three historic lighthouses on Lake Superior.

None of this hurt when Levin came up for reelection in 1996, but other things helped as well—his reputation for candor and hard work, his rumpled persona, the strength of Bill Clinton in Michigan and the revived spirits of Michigan Democratic activists after their rout in 1994. Plus, Republicans had a spirited primary in which PVS Chemical owner Jim Nicholson, pro-choice on abortion, came close to upsetting radio talk show host and 1994 primary contender Ronna Romney, pro-life, former daughter-in-law of the late Governor George Romney. Romney won 52%–48% but had to spend much time raising money while Levin, who ultimately spent $6.2 million, was on the air and, a bit awkwardly, in the papers: like most Democrats he had a policy of not speaking with *Detroit News* and *Free Press* reporters in support of strikers there, but suspended it in July to be able to communicate better with voters. The result was not in doubt: Levin won 58%–40%, a bit better than his 57%–41% margin in 1990; he carried Outstate Michigan as well as the Detroit metro area.

Junior Senator. Spencer Abraham, first elected in 1994, is the son of a Lansing "mom and pop" store owner and auto worker, and grandson of Lebanese immigrants, first elected in 1994. He grew up in Lansing, where he got the political bug early. While at Michigan State in 1974 he ran Clifford Taylor's nearly successful campaign against Democratic Congressman Bob Carr, and he became allies with a twenty-something legislator named John Engler. At Harvard Law School Abraham founded the Federalist Society and a conservative law review; in 1982, at 30, he became state Republican chairman. The party was then out of power throughout the state. He helped it regain the state Senate in 1983 and helped Engler win in 1990. His efforts to make Michigan an early presidential-caucus state in 1988 backfired when Pat Robertson's forces won a plurality of delegates, and Abraham had to hide out from Robertson's process-servers while his allies were cementing a George Bush-Jack Kemp alliance at the February 1988 state convention. In 1990 he joined Vice President Dan Quayle's staff and worked on the National Republican Congressional Committee. In 1993 he returned to Michigan and started running for the Senate, where he had anything but a clear field and trailed in initial polls for both the primary and general. But incumbent Donald Riegle, originally a young Republican and then a fiery liberal Democrat, retired after three terms and a brush with the Keating Five affair. In the primary Abraham faced Ronna Romney, also a Republican Party official; Abraham accused her of being less than strongly opposed to abortion and boasted of his endorsement by George Romney (made before Ronna entered the race). She lost 52%–48%, carrying metro Detroit but running far behind in western Michigan.

The Democratic primary was almost a dead heat. Lansing Congressman Bob Carr, with a moderate record and a history of winning nine races and losing one in marginal districts, won with 24%, to 23% for state Senator Lana Pollack, an Ann Arbor liberal; 20% for black businessman Joel Ferguson, who managed Jesse Jackson's 1988 presidential primary win here; 14% for former Congressman Bill Brodhead; 11% for state Senator John Kelly; and 8% for Macomb County Prosecutor Carl Marlinga. In the fall an Abraham ad showed footage of President Clinton saying he couldn't have gotten his budget and tax package through without Bob Carr; Carr sheepishly sat deep in the audience, not on the platform, at a Clinton appearance in Dearborn in October. Abraham ran a straightforward conservative candidacy, refusing even to rule out cuts in entitlements, opposing abortion, and favoring NAFTA and GATT, and he won by a solid 52%–43% margin.

Abraham quickly became an important conservative force in the Republican Senate, though his voting record was not completely conservative; he supported Carl Levin's lobbyist gift ban and research to curb the zebra mussel. But he took the lead role on several issues. Named to the Budget Committee, he managed the floor on the balanced budget. Named to Judiciary, he passed a bill to prevent the Sentencing Commission from lowering penalties for dealing crack cocaine, signed into law in October 1995. He sponsored what became the Prison Litigation Reform Act of 1996, seeking to bar frivolous civil lawsuits by inmates, and then complained the Clinton Justice Department was undercutting it. He pushed for a national database for stolen cars. He was one of the leaders on the bill to dismantle the Commerce Department. He lost that fight but became a member of the Commerce Committee after Bob Packwood resigned; in the 105th Congress he chairs its Manufacturing and Competitiveness Subcommittee, and promises to focus on how regulations, taxes and product and workplace standards affect economic efficiency.

Abraham's greatest impact came on immigration. Alan Simpson, in his final year in the Senate, was sponsoring a bill to restrict illegal immigration and reduce legal immigration. Abraham is a booster of immigration—"I really believe America was built, much of it, on the contributions of immigrants"—and he took the popular Simpson on. On March 7, 1996, Simpson removed from his bill provisions on verification (Abraham and others attacked it for putting civil liberties at risk) and restrictions on businesses importing workers with special job skills. But Abraham's coalition of liberal Democrats, business interests (notably Silicon Valley) and conservatives wanting to unite families held together, and on March 14 the Judiciary

Committee voted 12–6 to split the illegal immigration bill, which in a somewhat different form became law, from its legal immigration components, which went nowhere. It was a major decision on a policy that will shape the nation in the 21st Century, which probably wouldn't have happened but for this junior senator. Now Abraham chairs the Immigration Subcommittee.

Abraham had become, as journalist Paul Gigot put it, Dole's "favorite Senate freshman"; when Dole resigned, Abraham gave a nominating speech for the new Majority Leader, Trent Lott. It was Abraham who at a dinner in May 1996 first suggested the 15% across-the-board tax cut to Dole, adopted as part of Dole's campaign platform in August 1996. At the August 1996 Republican National Convention, Abraham chaired the Rules Committee, which produced rules to discourage early primaries by awarding more delegates to states with late primaries and required states to submit their delegate selection plans by July 1999: an attempt, perhaps futile, to reverse the frontloading which in 1996 meant that half the delegates were chosen within six weeks.

Abraham does not come up for reelection until 2000; one possible opponent is former Governor James Blanchard. Incidentally, like Governor John Engler, Abraham has a busy household, with twins born in 1993 and another baby born in 1996.

Presidential politics. In 1984, 1988 and 1992 Michigan voted within 1% of the national average for all major presidential candidates. But it lost its bellwether status in 1996, when it voted 52%–38% for Bill Clinton, 3% more Democratic and less Republican than the nation. Clinton targeted the state early, appeared there often, and clearly benefited from the good feeling about Michigan's economic prospects which also contributed to Republican Governor John Engler's 61%–38% victory in 1994. Special attention was devoted to Macomb County, where most voters have blue-collar roots and Democratic traditions but who now have more upscale jobs and weaker party ties. Macomb turned sharply Republican in the 1970s and 1980s, prompting 1992 Clinton pollster Stan Greenberg to study it closely; Clinton lost Macomb 42%–38% in 1992 but carried it 49%–39% in 1996, one of his biggest gains in the state. He turned around more upscale Oakland County next door as well, from a 44%–39% loss to a 48%–43% gain. In general Clinton gained most in cities with long-established blue-collar population—Muskegon, Saginaw—or areas with blue-collar migration fanning out from Detroit or other metro areas—the Thumb, central Michigan north of Lansing, downscale lake counties. These are signs of a hesitant emergence from slumber of the old blue collar, unionized Democratic voting bloc—not anything major yet, but enough to cheer Democrats and bother Republicans. The 1998 state elections should show whether this is the beginning of a new trend or the end of an old one.

In presidential primary races, Michigan has become a state where outsiders enter hoping support from disgruntled auto workers or some other constituency will give them victory—hopes that so far have been disappointed. Their hopes are further kindled because Michigan has kept switching from one defective selection system to another. In 1992 Michigan scheduled a regular primary for March 17, the same day as Illinois and a week after Super Tuesday. But the Illinois contest proved more crucial. Jerry Brown donned a UAW jacket and hoped to tap union activists who had been backing Tom Harkin, who had already withdrawn. But Clinton beat Brown 51%–26%. Meanwhile, Pat Buchanan had discovered the trade issue and on the Sunday before the primary motorcaded from Bay City to Saginaw and then to Flint, where he was jeered outside UAW Local 599. He lost to Bush 67%–25%. Undaunted, Buchanan was back again in 1996 for the March 19 primary, and took 34%. It was his best showing except for Wisconsin, and he seemed to be cracking that blue collar vote at least a little (it helped that Michigan does not have party registration). But he still lost to Bob Dole 51%–34%.

Congressional districting. Michigan, which lost one House seat after the 1980 Census and two after the 1990 Census, is now down to 16 House members, the same as after the 1930 Census. The current districting plan was drawn by a nonpartisan court and has rather regular lines. So far it has worked for Democrats. Republicans have six solid districts, more than Democrats have, but Democrats have won most marginal contests and two Outstate Democrats have proven popular enough to easily hold districts that without them might go the other way. As late as 1992, when Democrats were in control, Michigan had three committee chairmen and the House Majority Whip—one of the most powerful delegations in the House. But all those positions were lost when the Republicans won the House in 1994.

The People: Est. Pop. 1996: 9,594,000; Pop. 1990: 9,295,297, up 3.2% 1990–1996. 3.6% of U.S. total, 8th largest; 29% rural. Median age: 34.6 years. 12% 65 years and over. 82.3% White, 13.8% Black, 1.1% Asian, 1% Amer. Indian, 2.2% Hispanic origin. Households: 55.1% married couple families; 26% married couple fams. w. children; 44% college educ.; median household income: $31,020; per capita income: $14,154; 71.0% owner occupied housing; median house value: $60,600; median monthly rent: $343. 4.9% Unemployment. 1996 Voting age pop.: 7,072,000. 1996 Turnout: 3,848,844; 54% of VAP. Registered voters (1996): 6,674,827; no party registration.

Political Lineup: Governor, John M. Engler (R); Lt. Gov., Connie Binsfeld (R); Secy. of State, Candice Miller (R); Atty. Gen., Frank J. Kelley (D); Treasurer, Douglas B. Roberts (R). State Senate, 38 (16 D and 22 R); Senate President, Connie Binsfeld (R); State House, 110 (57 D, 52 R and 1 vacancy); House Speaker, Curtis Hertel (D). Senators, Carl Levin (D) and Spencer Abraham (R). Representatives, 16 (10 D and 6 R).

Elections Division: 517-373-2540; **Filing Deadline for U.S. Congress:** May 19, 1998.

1996 Presidential Vote

Clinton (D)	1,989,683	(52%)
Dole (R)	1,481,572	(39%)
Perot (I)	336,681	(9%)

1992 Presidential Vote

Clinton (D)	1,871,182	(44%)
Bush (R)	1,554,940	(36%)
Perot (I)	824,813	(19%)

1996 Republican Presidential Primary

Dole (R)	265,425	(51%)
Buchanan (R)	177,562	(34%)
Forbes (R)	26,610	(5%)
Other	54,564	(11%)

GOVERNOR

Gov. John M. Engler (R)

Elected 1990, term expires Jan. 1999; b. Oct. 12, 1948, Mount Pleasant; home, Mount Pleasant; MI St. U., B.A. 1971, Cooley Law Schl., J.D. 1981; Catholic; married (Michelle).

Career: MI House of Reps., 1970–76; MI Senate, 1978–1990.

Office: Olds Plaza, 111 S. Capitol, Lansing 48933, 517-373-3400; Fax: 517-335-6863; Web site: www.migov.state.mi.us.

Election Results

1994 gen.	John M. Engler (R)	1,899,101	(61%)
	Howard Wolpe (D)	1,188,438	(38%)
1994 prim.	John M. Engler (R)	unopposed	
1990 gen.	John M. Engler (R)	1,276,134	(50%)
	James J. (Jim) Blanchard (D)	1,258,539	(49%)

SENATORS

Sen. Carl Levin (D)

Elected 1978, seat up 2002; b. June 28, 1934, Detroit; home, Detroit; Swarthmore Col., B.A. 1956, Harvard, LL.B. 1959; Jewish; married (Barbara).

Career: Practicing atty., 1959–64, 1971–73, 1978–79; MI Asst. Atty. Gen. and Gen. Cnsl., MI Civil Rights Comm., 1964–67; Detroit Chief Appellate Defender, 1967–69; Detroit City Cncl., 1969–77, Pres., 1973–77.

DC Office: 459 RSOB 20510, 202-224-6221; Fax: 202-224-1388; e-mail: senator@levin.senate.gov.

State Offices: Alpena, 517-354-5520; Detroit, 313-226-6020; Escanaba, 906-789-0052; Grand Rapids, 616-456-2531; Lansing, 517-377-1508; Saginaw, 517-754-2494; Southgate, 313-285-8596; Traverse City, 616-947-9569; Warren, 810-573-9145.

Committees: *Armed Services* (RMM of 8 D). *Governmental Affairs* (2nd of 7 D): International Security, Proliferation & Federal Services (RMM); Permanent Subcommittee on Investigations. *Intelligence (Select)* (9th of 9 D). *Small Business* (3rd of 8 D).

Group Ratings

	ADA	ACLU	AFS	LCV	CFA	CON	NFIB	COC	ACU	NTLC	CHC
1996	85	44	86	85	86	51	25	23	5	7	0
1995	100	—	100	100	94	68	—	26	0	—	—

National Journal Ratings

	1995 LIB	—	1995 CONS	1996 LIB	—	1996 CONS
Economic	95%	—	3%	95%	—	4%
Social	93%	—	0%	70%	—	28%
Foreign	86%	—	7%	93%	—	0%

Key Votes of the 104th Congress

1. Reduce Medicare Growth $	N	5. Flag Amendment	N	9. Anti-Missile Defense	N
2. Lmt. Prod. Liab. Damages	N	6. Endangered Species	Y	10. Cuban Embargo	N
3. Increase Min. Wage	Y	7. Gay Employment Rights	Y	11. Bar Bosnia Troop $	N
4. Welfare Reform	Y	8. Ovrd. Part. Birth Veto	N	12. Cut Vietnam Aid	N

Election Results

1996 general	Carl Levin (D)	2,195,738	(58%)	($6,223,409)
	Ronna Romney (R)	1,500,106	(40%)	($3,208,968)
	Others	66,731	(2%)	
1996 primary	Carl Levin (D)	unopposed		
1990 general	Carl Levin (D)	1,471,753	(57%)	($7,066,832)
	Bill Schuette (R)	1,055,695	(41%)	($2,417,705)

Sen. Spencer Abraham (R)

Elected 1994, seat up 2000; b. June 12, 1952, East Lansing; home, Auburn Hills; MI St. U., B.A. 1974, Harvard U., J.D. 1979; Eastern Orthodox; married (Jane).

Career: Asst. Prof., Thomas Cooley Law Schl., 1981–83; MI Repub. Party Chmn., 1982–90; Dep. Chief of Staff, V.P. Dan Quayle, 1990–91; Co-Chair, Natl. Repub. Cong. Cmte., 1991–92.

DC Office: 329 DSOB 20510, 202-224-4822; Fax: 202-224-8834; e-mail: michigan@abraham.senate.gov.

State Offices: Grand Rapids, 616-975-1112; Lansing, 517-484-1984; Marquette, 906-226-9466; Saginaw, 517-752-4400; Southfield, 810-350-0510.

Committees: *Budget* (9th of 12 R). *Commerce, Science & Transportation* (10th of 11 R): Communications; Consumer Affairs, Foreign Commerce & Tourism; Manufacturing & Competitiveness (Chmn.); Science, Technology & Space; Surface Transportation & Merchant Marine. *Judiciary* (9th of 10 R): Constitution, Federalism & Property Rights; Immigration (Chmn.).

Group Ratings

	ADA	ACLU	AFS	LCV	CFA	CON	NFIB	COC	ACU	NTLC	CHC
1996	15	17	14	0	21	56	97	92	95	100	92
1995	5	—	0	7	6	88	—	100	87	—	—

National Journal Ratings

	1995 LIB — 1995 CONS			1996 LIB — 1996 CONS		
Economic	21%	—	74%	34%	—	63%
Social	31%	—	67%	28%	—	68%
Foreign	22%	—	67%	0%	—	74%

Key Votes of the 104th Congress

1. Reduce Medicare Growth $	Y	5. Flag Amendment	Y	9. Anti-Missile Defense	Y
2. Lmt. Prod. Liab. Damages	Y	6. Endangered Species	N	10. Cuban Embargo	Y
3. Increase Min. Wage	Y	7. Gay Employment Rights	N	11. Bar Bosnia Troop $	N
4. Welfare Reform	Y	8. Ovrd. Part. Birth Veto	Y	12. Cut Vietnam Aid	Y

Election Results

1994 general	Spencer Abraham (R)	1,578,770	(52%)	($4,437,038)
	Bob Carr (D)	1,300,960	(43%)	($3,040,416)
	Jon Coon (Lib)	128,393	(4%)	($303,369)
1994 primary	Spencer Abraham (R)	292,399	(52%)	
	Ronna Romney (R)	270,304	(48%)	
1988 general	Donald W. Riegle, Jr. (D)	2,116,865	(60%)	($3,383,849)
	Jim Dunn (R)	1,348,216	(39%)	($442,693)

FIRST DISTRICT

Michigan's Upper Peninsula, commonly known as the UP, is a land apart. Surrounded on three sides by frigid Lake Superior and Lake Michigan, it has its own flora, including the world's largest known-living object, a giant fungus that lives under 37 acres of a forest floor and is 1,500 years old. Although the UP is no farther north than Montreal or Seattle, it has one of the coldest climates in settled parts of North America."In October, usually, the first snow falls steady on the northland," writes Dixie Lee Franklin in *A Most Superior Land*, "whispering teasing promises of more to come"—for seven months or more. Far away from any major city, with ground too frozen and a growing season too short for most crops, the Upper Peninsula was explored by French voyagers more than 300 years ago but was never thickly settled until prospectors found rich veins of ore here. Through 1987 the mineral veins of the Keweenaw Peninsula produced 13.3 billion pounds of copper; the Marquette, Menominee and Gogebic iron ranges have more than one billion tons of iron ore. Starting in the 1880s, immigrants flocked here to work the mines—Irish, Italians, Swedes, Norwegians, miners' sons from Wales and Cornwall, and most prominently Finns, who must have found this cold land with its lakes and hills much like their home. By 1900, the UP was a northern industrial belt, with a few bosses and some absentee overlords and a work force disposed to radical ideas and union movements.

A major strike in 1913–14 and falling ore prices after World War I—events that would be long forgotten elsewhere—are remembered in the UP as the beginning of its decline: The UP's population peaked at 332,000 in 1920. The copper veins were mostly depleted by then, mining iron ore became less labor-intensive, and lumber and farming provided only a few thousand jobs. In the last half century, there has been great migration to Detroit, Chicago and the West Coast; the UP's population has hovered around 300,000, rising to 318,000 in 1980 and dropping back to 313,000 in 1990. But "Yoopers" who some say have their own dialect, "Yoopanese,"remain devoted to their land.

The 1st Congressional District of Michigan includes the Upper Peninsula and most of the three northern-tier counties in the Lower Peninsula. About half the people live in the UP; the other half live south of the breathtaking Mackinac Bridge. This is a vast area, geographically the second largest district east of the Mississippi and smaller than only 26 farther west; it is a 450-mile drive from Ironwood at the western end of the UP to the Sleeping Bear Dunes towering over Lake Michigan. The Lower Peninsula counties have two different personalities. On Lake Huron—the sunrise side—they are mostly industrial and slow growing. On Lake Michigan are affluent resort areas around Petoskey and Charlevoix, long summer places for people from Chicago (this is Ernest Hemingway's "up in Michigan"), and the boom area around Traverse City, with its burgeoning condominiums and resorts. Politically, the UP has long been Democratic, some parts more than others; the Lake Michigan shore of the Lower Peninsula is heavily Republican, the sunrise side marginal.

The congressman from the 1st District is Bart Stupak, a Democrat and a "Yooper" from Menominee on the Wisconsin border. He was a police officer in Escanaba, then became a Michigan state trooper in 1974 and also earned a law degree; in 1984 he was injured in the line of duty and retired from the force. In 1988 he was elected to the Michigan House; in 1990 he lost a race for the state Senate. Stupak got into the 1992 race when incumbent Republican Bob Davis, with 878 overdrafts on the House bank, decided to drop out in May 1992. Stupak won the three-way primary with 58% in the UP, which cast 70% of Democratic primary votes; overall he beat restauranteur Mike McElroy 49%–43%. In the general he beat Republican Philip Ruppe, who had represented the district from 1966–78, by 54%–44%.

In the House Stupak has a moderate and maverick voting record and has paid great attention to local issues. Angered by the closing of K.I. Sawyer Air Force Base, the biggest employer in Marquette County in the UP, he threatened to vote against the Clinton budget and tax package; after some muscling, he voted for it. He bucked Clinton by opposing NAFTA and the 1994 crime bill. He formed the Law Enforcement Caucus and has fought to prevent cuts in the Clinton COPS program. He sponsored a 1993 law limiting the sale of ephedrine, a legal drug that, when mixed with paint thinner, produces the addictive illegal drug methcathinone (CAT), much in use in northern Michigan. He boasted of obtaining $14 million in local disaster aid after the harsh winter of 1993–94. In 1994 he was opposed by Gil Ziegler, who made a fortune manufacturing "cold-formed" auto components; Ziegler spent $529,000 of his own money, criticizing Stupak for supporting Clinton's tax increase and contrasting his pro-choice position on abortion with Stupak's anti-abortion views (Stupak was one of the few visible abortion opponents at the 1996 Democratic convention). But Stupak matched him by raising $519,000 from PACs, and carried the UP and the sunrise side by large margins; Ziegler carried the Lake Michigan shore, but Stupak won a solid 57%–42% victory.

In his second term Stupak worked to redevelop the UP's two closed Air Force Bases, seeking development dollars for K. I. Sawyer and brownfield status for Kincheloe. He worked to find new uses for northern Michigan Coast Guard properties—giving land to the Great Lakes Shipwreck Historical Society near the wreck of the *Edmund Fitzgerald*, to the Michigan Audubon Society and to the Traverse City schools for a soccer field. In the telecommunications bill he inserted an amendment reducing a $115 fee for many boaters and aircraft operators. He got Navy tugboats about to be scrapped sold to a private operator. On repeal of the Delaney Clause, which prohibits any trace of cancer-causing pesticides in certain processes foods, he changed the pesticide standard from "adequate" to "necessary" for human health.

Stupak both showed strength and got a break in the 1996 election. That came when Dean Altobelli, the choice of Governor John Engler and a state football star, lost his primary 56%–44% to one Bob Carr—not the Democratic congressman who ran against Senator Spencer Abraham in 1994, but a local candidate who spent all of $5,800 on his campaign. Stupak won 71%–27%, carrying every county. In December 1996 he made news, though not history, when he proposed that the House elect Bob Dole as its Speaker; neither Democrats nor Republicans—nor for that matter Dole—were interested.

The People: Pop. 1990: 581,006; 69% rural; 16% age 65+; 96% White; 1% Black; 2% Amer. Indian; 1% Hispanic origin. Households: 60% married couple families; 27% married couple fams. w. children; 39% college educ.; median household income: $22,788; per capita income: $10,846; median gross rent: $328; median house value: $44,700.

1996 Presidential Vote

Clinton (D)	125,135	(47%)
Dole (R)	107,577	(40%)
Perot (I)	31,184	(12%)

1992 Presidential Vote

Clinton (D)	118,983	(41%)
Bush (R)	101,110	(35%)
Perot (I)	65,402	(23%)

Rep. Bart Stupak (D)

Elected 1992; b. Feb. 29, 1952, Milwaukee, WI; home, Menominee; NW MI Comm. Col., A.A. 1972, Saginaw Valley St. Col., B.S. 1977, Thomas Cooley Law Schl., J.D. 1981; Catholic; married (Laurie).

Career: Escanaba Police Officer, 1972–73; MI St. Trooper, 1974–84; Practicing atty., 1981–1992; MI House of Reps., 1988–90.

DC Office: 1410 LHOB 20515, 202-225-4735; Fax: 202-225-4744; e-mail: stupak@mail.house.gov.

District Offices: Alpena, 517-356-0690; Crystal Falls, 906-875-3751; Escanaba, 906-786-4504; Houghton, 906-482-1371; Marquette, 906-228-3700; Traverse City, 616-929-4711.

Committees: *Commerce* (16th of 23 D): Finance & Hazardous Materials; Health & the Environment; Oversight & Investigations.

Group Ratings

	ADA	ACLU	AFS	LCV	CFA	CON	NFIB	COC	ACU	NTLC	CHC
1996	75	62	100	69	62	63	35	25	20	17	33
1995	75	—	—	94	46	25	—	38	28	—	—

National Journal Ratings

	1995 LIB — 1995 CONS			1996 LIB — 1996 CONS		
Economic	71%	—	28%	70%	—	28%
Social	52%	—	47%	55%	—	43%
Foreign	77%	—	22%	82%	—	16%

Key Votes of the 104th Congress

1. Reduce Medicare Growth $	N	5. Flag Amendment	Y	9. Cuban Embargo	N
2. Ovrd. Product Liab. Veto	N	6. Drop EPA Limits	Y	10. Bar Bosnia Troop $	N
3. Increase Min. Wage	Y	7. Repeal Assault-Weap. Ban	Y	11. Cut Anti-Missile Defense	Y
4. Welfare Reform	N	8. Ovrd. Part. Birth Veto	Y	12. Bar U.N. Uniforms	N

Election Results

1996 general	Bart Stupak (D)	181,486	(71%)	($458,509)
	Bob Carr (R)	69,957	(27%)	($5,834)
	Others	5,348	(2%)	
1996 primary	Bart Stupak (D)	unopposed		
1994 general	Bart Stupak (D)	121,433	(57%)	($678,925)
	Gil Ziegler (R)	89,660	(42%)	($665,398)

SECOND DISTRICT

Lining the eastern shoreline of Lake Michigan, where the lake winds temper the frigid Michigan winters, are some of the nation's longest and highest sand dunes. In the late 19th Century, this shoreline was America's greatest lumber country; the ports on the small rivers were choked with logs and full of lumbermen from Norway and Sweden, Ireland and Scotland, Quebec and New England. During the lumber boom, the shoreline just to the south was the locus of America's largest migration from the Netherlands and still has the nation's largest concentration of Dutch-Americans. Wooden shoes are now seen only in the Tulip Festival in Holland, but here conscientious Dutch work habits have produced some of the most highly skilled workers in America, and major companies have grown up, like Gerber Foods in Fremont and Herman Miller furniture in Zeeland.

The 2d Congressional District of Michigan occupies the Lake Michigan shoreline counties, plus a tier of counties inland, from the lumber country around Manistee south to Holland and the resort town of Saugatuck. Some 25% of people here claim Dutch ancestry. Politically, the district is arguably Michigan's most Republican, roughly equal to the 3d and 11th. Its first Yankee settlers were part of the original Republican Party, and Dutch-Americans with their innate conservatism vie with Cuban-Americans for the title of America's most heavily Republican ethnic group.

The congressman from the 2d is Peter Hoekstra (pronounced HOOKstra), who immigrated from the Netherlands at 3, graduated from Hope College in Grand Rapids (with a semester in Washington during Watergate) and got an MBA at the University of Michigan. Hoekstra went to work at Herman Miller, where he helped develop the "Equa Chair" seat in the early 1980s and became a vice president. In 1992, he decided to run what seemed an improbable campaign for Congress against Guy Vander Jagt, 26-year incumbent and chairman of the National Republican Congressional Committee since 1975—but not a major presence in the district. Hoekstra saved up vacation time and in 1992 took a county-by-county bicycle tour of the district. With an earnestness that rang true, Hoekstra called for citizen, not career, politicians, refused PAC money and supported abolishing PACs, advocated 12-year term limits, and promised to uphold family values and to oppose abortion. He advocated balancing the budget, protecting the environment and upholding the Second Amendment. Hoekstra spent only $55,600 to Vander Jagt's $725,000. But on primary day, Hoekstra carried the heavily Dutch Ottawa and Allegan Counties, which were newly added to the district, 53%–31%, while Vander Jagt won just 53%–36% elsewhere; since Ottawa and Allegan cast 59% of the primary vote, Hoekstra won 46%–40%. He won the general election easily.

Hoekstra brought to the House the new participatory-management ideas he had developed at Herman Miller which, according to a *National Journal* profile, "caught the eye of Newt Gingrich and propelled him into the new Speaker's coterie of advisers." But Hoekstra has also voted against and sharply criticized Gingrich and the Republican leadership. On the Education and the Workforce Committee, as it is now called, he has worked for the TEAM Act and other measures to reduce adversity and rigidity in labor relations encouraged by unions; he tried to amend the Clinton healthcare plan with a 1% tax on employers with healthcare plans negotiated by unions; he strongly opposed the striker replacement ban.

Hoekstra worked closely with Gingrich throughout 1994 in planning how a Republican House—a prospect which many did not take seriously—would be managed. He led a task force which allowed C-SPAN cameras to pan across the sometimes empty House chamber. In October 1995 he cooperated with the leadership when then-freshman Mark Neumann infuriated Appropriations Chairman Bob Livingston by voting against one of his bills; Hoekstra gave up his seat on the Budget Committee so Neumann could move there from Appropriations after Livingston dismissed him. In return he got to chair the Republican Task Force on Reform. After his proposals were stalled in March 1996, he angrily confronted Gingrich. By July 1996 the leadership allowed some to go forward: Gingrich banned former members from lobbying members on the floor, but the campaign finance reform bill, reducing PAC contribution limits to $2,500 and allowing individual contribution limits to increase at the current $1,000 plus the rate of inflation, failed. Hoekstra's proposal to ban pensions to former members of Congress convicted of a felony while in office passed the House, but the Senate never acted on it. Some of his proposals are having better luck in the 105th Congress: the House banned check-giving on the House floor and the rule requiring constitutional justification for every law passed the House.

Hoekstra's voting record on foreign policy tends toward the liberal; he was one of 24 Republicans who voted against the Contract With America missile defense bill. On cultural issues, he is more conservative; he sponsored an amendment that became law banning discrimination—loss of federal funding—against medical schools that refuse to teach abortion procedures. He is an original reformer: he has called for a national referendum on term limits and has proposed enabling voters to choose "None of the Above." He is now chairman of the Oversight Subcommittee of Education and the Workforce: a fine perch to investigate wrongdoings of labor unions. Hoekstra was easily reelected in 1994 and 1996.

The People: Pop. 1990: 581,017; 52% rural; 12% age 65+; 91% White; 4% Black; 1% Asian; 1% Amer. Indian; 3% Hispanic origin. Households: 64% married couple families; 31% married couple fams. w. children; 39% college educ.; median household income: $28,905; per capita income: $12,305; median gross rent: $383; median house value: $58,100.

1996 Presidential Vote

Dole (R)	133,022	(50%)
Clinton (D)	108,242	(41%)
Perot (I)	23,512	(9%)

1992 Presidential Vote

Bush (R)	126,969	(45%)
Clinton (D)	95,351	(34%)
Perot (I)	58,238	(21%)

Rep. Peter Hoekstra (R)

Elected 1992; b. Oct. 30, 1953, Groningen, Netherlands; home, Holland; Hope Col., B.A. 1975, U. of MI, M.B.A. 1977; Christian Reformed; married (Diane).

Career: Furniture Exec., Herman Miller Co., 1977–92.

DC Office: 1122 LHOB 20515, 202-225-4401; Fax: 202-226-0779; e-mail: tellhoek@hr.house.gov.

District Offices: Cadillac; 616-775-0050; Holland, 616-395-0030; Muskegon, 616-722-8386.

Committees: *Budget* (13th of 24 R). *Education & The Workforce* (7th of 25 R): Oversight & Investigations (Chmn.); Workforce Protections.

Group Ratings

	ADA	ACLU	AFS	LCV	CFA	CON	NFIB	COC	ACU	NTLC	CHC
1996	10	25	8	23	31	96	100	88	95	98	93
1995	5	—	—	6	8	95	—	96	84	—	—

National Journal Ratings

	1995 LIB		1995 CONS	1996 LIB		1996 CONS
Economic	0%	—	74%	18%	—	80%
Social	36%	—	63%	24%	—	72%
Foreign	52%	—	46%	58%	—	42%

Key Votes of the 104th Congress

1. Reduce Medicare Growth $	Y	5. Flag Amendment	N	9. Cuban Embargo	Y
2. Ovrd. Product Liab. Veto	Y	6. Drop EPA Limits	N	10. Bar Bosnia Troop $	Y
3. Increase Min. Wage	N	7. Repeal Assault-Weap. Ban	Y	11. Cut Anti-Missile Defense	N
4. Welfare Reform	Y	8. Ovrd. Part. Birth Veto	Y	12. Bar U.N. Uniforms	Y

Election Results

1996 general	Peter Hoekstra (R)	165,608	(65%)	($185,831)
	Dan Kruszynski (D)	83,603	(33%)	($30,962)
	Others	4,488	(2%)	
1996 primary	Peter Hoekstra (R)	unopposed		
1994 general	Peter Hoekstra (R)	146,164	(75%)	($134,979)
	Marcus Peter Hoover (D)	46,097	(24%)	($9,792)

THIRD DISTRICT

Grand Rapids is Michigan's second largest city, the center of Michigan's most prosperous and confident metropolitan area. Grand Rapids has its roots in trees: it grew as a center for processing and turning into furniture the hardwood forests of northern Michigan. By the early 20th Century, Grand Rapids was the leading furniture manufacturer in the nation. But the Depression of the 1930s knocked the bottom out of the residential furniture market, and many manufacturers moved to cheaper-labor North Carolina. So Grand Rapids had to reinvent itself, and did. It went into office furniture, and today three of the nation's largest office furniture manufacturers (Steelcase, Haworth and Herman Miller) are located in or near here. It capitalized on a knack for sales. Rich DeVos and Jay Van Andel started Amway, the direct sales empire, which now has half of its sales abroad, and Frederik and Hendrik Meijer started Meijer's Thrifty Acres, combining supermarkets with discount stores in a way that even Wal-Mart has not been able to equal. Lumber is still important: Peter Secchia, ambassador to Italy during the Bush Administration, made his fortune in that business. Grand Rapids is also the center of a machine tool empire. Fifty years ago Grand Rapids and its up-and-coming businesses were outshined by Detroit and the auto industry. Today, the western Michigan region centered on Grand Rapids has been growing rapidly and is starting to rival Detroit in size and creativity.

One ingredient in Grand Rapids' success is its unique ethnic mix. It was founded by New England Yankees, but much of its character was set by the Dutch immigrants who began arriving in western Michigan in the 1870s, and are still coming today; 23% of people here claim Dutch ancestry (probably no other city has a high a proportion of "V" pages in the phone book). The Dutch brought with them a piety witnessed in their Reform and Christian Reform churches, and a culture of hard work and precision craftsmanship. Politically, Dutch-Americans have been the nation's most heavily Republican identifiable ethnic group, except perhaps for Cuban-Americans; their cultural conservatism and belief in market economics runs deep. Grand Rapids is the center of Michigan Republicanism, and over the years has produced major Republican politicians. One was Arthur Vandenberg, a newspaper editor who was U.S. senator from 1928–51; a one-time isolationist, he provided key support for the bipartisan internationalist foreign policies of Franklin Roosevelt and Harry Truman. Grand Rapids also produced Gerald Ford, backed by Vandenberg in the 1948 primary, who rose to become House Republican leader in 1965, vice president in 1973, and then president after Richard Nixon resigned in 1974. Nixon got a bit of a nudge from the Grand Rapids district when, in an early 1974 special election, it voted to replace Vice President Ford with a Democrat, a clear sign that the Republican heartland was turning on the president. In the 1980s, however, Grand Rapids became more Republican than ever and is now one of the most solidly Republican metro areas in the country.

The 3d Congressional District of Michigan includes all of Grand Rapids and surrounding Kent County, plus one and a half smaller counties east and southeast. It is one of the most Republican districts in Michigan, indeed in all the Midwest, and has produced many Michigan Republican leaders—state Senate Majority Leader Dick Posthumus, House Minority Leader Ken Sikkema, National Committeeman Chuck Yob and Betsy DeVos, a national committee-woman and state party chairman.

The congressman from the 3d District is Vern Ehlers, chosen in a December 1993 special election. Ehlers grew up in small-town Minnesota, the son of a Christian Reform minister, attended Calvin College in Grand Rapids, got a Ph.D. in physics at Berkeley and then returned to Calvin to teach for 17 years: he is the first research physicist in Congress. In 1974, concerned about local waste management, he ran for Kent County commissioner; in 1982 he was elected to the state House and in 1986 the state Senate. After Congressman Paul Henry died in July 1993, Ehlers ran to succeed him, as he had in both houses of the legislature. The key contest was the November 1993 primary. Ehlers finished first, with 33%, followed by 25% for Ken Sikkema, now Republican leader in the state House, 19% for state commerce official Marge Byington, and 16% for a furniture manufacturer. A month later Ehlers whipped the Democrat 67%–23%.

Ehlers brought to House Republicans, then entering their 40th year in the minority, a majority mindset, which brought him to the attention of Newt Gingrich. After the 1994 election Gingrich named him to the Republican transition team. He also assigned Ehlers to lead efforts to revamp the House's computer system. In 1995 Ehlers responded with a system making available to anyone vote tallies, public hearing transcripts and texts of amendments and bills. In 1996 he worked to provide each congressional office with easy-to-use computer software and hardware.

Ehlers has a middle-of-the-House voting record. He says his highest priority is balancing the budget, but he has also supported, since January 1995 as vice chairman of the Science Committee, scientific research. He brings his religious faith to his work as well: "I want to be a voice for justice. I try to analyze every piece of legislation from a Christian framework." Science and religion have both led him to a concern for the environment. He is the author of *Earthkeeping in the '90s: Stewardship of Creation* and *Earthkeeping: Christian Stewardship of Natural Resources.* His earlier record won him support when he ran for the House from both the Sierra Club and Consumers Power Company. In the House, he opposed Republicans' EPA riders on appropriations bills, supported the National Biological Survey, and opposed setting aside part of the Mojave National Reserve for hunting. His amendment converted from voluntary to mandatory the Great Lakes Water Quality Initiative standards in the 1996 Safe Drinking Water Act.

Ehlers refuses to take more than 30% of his campaign money from outside the district. He was reelected in 1994 and 1996 by very wide margins.

The People: Pop. 1990: 580,874; 24% rural; 11% age 65+; 88% White; 7% Black; 1% Asian; 1% Amer. Indian; 3% Hispanic origin. Households: 59% married couple families; 30% married couple fams. w. children; 47% college educ.; median household income: $31,917; per capita income: $13,924; median gross rent: $425; median house value: $65,600.

1996 Presidential Vote

Dole (R)	135,759	(53%)
Clinton (D)	99,698	(39%)
Perot (I)	17,583	(7%)

1992 Presidential Vote

Bush (R)	128,670	(46%)
Clinton (D)	94,715	(34%)
Perot (I)	52,773	(19%)

Rep. Vernon J. Ehlers (R)

Elected Dec. 1993; b. Feb. 6, 1934, Pipestone, MN; home, Grand Rapids; Calvin Col., 1952–55; U. of CA Berkeley, A.B. 1956, Ph.D. 1960; U. of Heidelberg, Germany, 1961–62; Christian Reformed; married (Johanna).

Career: Prof., Calvin Col., 1966–82; Kent Cnty. Comm. 1975–82, Chmn., 1978–81; MI House of Reps 1982–86; MI Senate, 1986–93; Pres. Pro-Tem, 1990–93.

DC Office: 1717 LHOB 20515, 202-225-3831; Fax: 202-225-5144; e-mail: congehlr@hr.house.gov.

District Offices: Grand Rapids, 616-451-8383.

Committees: *House Oversight* (4th of 6 R). *Science* (Vice Chmn. of 25 R): Energy & Environment; Technology. *Transportation & Infrastructure* (17th of 40 R): Aviation; Water Resources & Environment. *Joint Committee on the Library of Congress* (3rd of 5 Reps.).

Group Ratings

	ADA	ACLU	AFS	LCV	CFA	CON	NFIB	COC	ACU	NTLC	CHC
1996	25	25	17	31	38	86	91	94	79	82	80
1995	20	—	—	25	62	56	—	87	68	—	—

National Journal Ratings

	1995 LIB — 1995 CONS			1996 LIB — 1996 CONS		
Economic	47%	—	53%	45%	—	54%
Social	50%	—	50%	50%	—	48%
Foreign	58%	—	41%	67%	—	31%

Key Votes of the 104th Congress

1. Reduce Medicare Growth $	Y	5. Flag Amendment	N	9. Cuban Embargo	Y
2. Ovrd. Product Liab. Veto	Y	6. Drop EPA Limits	Y	10. Bar Bosnia Troop $	N
3. Increase Min. Wage	N	7. Repeal Assault-Weap. Ban	Y	11. Cut Anti-Missile Defense	N
4. Welfare Reform	Y	8. Ovrd. Part. Birth Veto	Y	12. Bar U.N. Uniforms	Y

Election Results

1996 general	Vernon J. Ehlers (R)	169,466	(69%)	($265,960)
	Betsy J. Flory (D)	72,791	(29%)	($13,042)
	Others	4,786	(2%)	
1996 primary	Vernon J. Ehlers (R)	unopposed		
1994 general	Vernon J. Ehlers (R)	136,711	(74%)	($203,428)
	Betsy J. Flory (D)	43,580	(24%)	($20,402)
	Others	4,786	(3%)	

FOURTH DISTRICT

Flat and treeless for miles, the central reaches of Michigan's Lower Peninsula are farm country, exposed to bitter winds and snow drifts in winter and shining sun for precious weeks in summer. Like the steppes of Eastern Europe, these are farmlands that produce hearty crops—potatoes, navy beans, sugar beets. The little cities here are often small factory towns, with neat tree-lined streets on a grid layout that suddenly end and turn to bare fields. Each city has some distinction. Midland in 1891 was a declining lumber town when Herbert Dow perfected an electrolytic process to extract chemicals from northern Michigan's extensive brine wells; that was the start of Dow Chemical, still headquartered in this now upscale town. Owosso in 1902 was the birthplace of Thomas E. Dewey, later New York governor and Republican candidate for president in 1944 and 1948. It was also the home of novelist James Oliver Curwood and his Curwood Castle writing studio; today it hosts the Curwood Festival, lovingly chronicled by Thomas Mallon in *Rockets and Rodeos*, and is the site of Mallon's novel *Dewey Defeats Truman*. Mount Pleasant, to the north, is the site of Central Michigan University, where parka-clad students stomp through snow to class; it is the home base of Governor John Engler.

The 4th Congressional District of Michigan includes much of this territory north of Lansing and Grand Rapids and west of Flint and Saginaw. It stretches north up the freeways, where thousands drive in fall to hunt and in winter to ski, into the rolling country around Houghton Lake, once lumber country and now a retirement and resort area, with trailers and condominiums between knotty-pine cottages clustered around icy green lakes. Politically, it remains mostly Republican territory, though retirees from the Detroit area and commuters to Flint and Saginaw have brought in some Democratic tendencies. The area gave small pluralities to Bill Clinton in 1992 and 1996.

The congressman from the 4th District is Dave Camp, a Republican first elected in 1990. Camp grew up in Midland, and returned there after school to practice law; he reports owning more than $500,000 in Dow stock. In 1984 he managed the successful congressional campaign of his boyhood friend Bill Schuette; in 1990 Schuette ran, unsuccessfully, against Senator Carl Levin (he now heads John Engler's Agriculture department), and Camp ran for Congress. Camp's key victory was in the Republican primary, where with 62% in Midland County he beat former legislator and Pat Robertson supporter Al Cropsey, 33%–30%. He has won since without difficulty.

Camp has a generally conservative voting record and, since 1992, has had a seat on Ways and Means where he played a key role in passing welfare reform in 1996. As the number two Republican on the Human Resources Subcommittee, he helped write the two welfare reform bills vetoed by Bill Clinton. In July 1996 he and Nevada freshman John Ensign circulated a letter signed ultimately by about 100 Republican congressmen urging that Republicans separate their welfare and Medicaid reforms, which had been passed as one bill, and vote on welfare reform alone, daring Bill Clinton to sign it and make history, or veto it and make it a campaign issue. Newt Gingrich and the Republican leadership decided to do this in July 1996, essentially disengaging House Republicans from the fate of the flagging Bob Dole presidential campaign. The bill passed, Clinton signed it, and the incumbent president and incumbent congressional Republicans got credit in November.

Camp has worked on other issues. In 1997 he proposed legislation to bar Medicare and Medicaid funding of assisted suicide: a response to Michigan's Dr. Jack Kevorkian. He co-sponsored legislation to speed up adoptions; he is one of the lead co-sponsors of the Adoption Promotion Act, making the safety and best interests of the child paramount to family preservation. He passed an amendment declaring it the sense of Congress to give states broad leeway on child support disbursement programs. He opposed a military appropriations bill for having too much pork.

Camp's name was mentioned as a possible candidate for senator in 1994 and 1996, but he did not run. He has worked hard on constituency services and has been reelected by wide margins.

The People: Pop. 1990: 580,890; 72% rural; 12% age 65+; 96% White; 1% Black; 1% Amer. Indian; 2% Hispanic origin. Households: 64% married couple families; 30% married couple fams. w. children; 38% college educ.; median household income: $25,898; per capita income: $11,549; median gross rent: $360; median house value: $49,100.

1996 Presidential Vote

Clinton (D)	112,625	(47%)
Dole (R)	98,215	(41%)
Perot (I)	28,350	(12%)

1992 Presidential Vote

Clinton (D)	104,228	(38%)
Bush (R)	102,284	(37%)
Perot (I)	67,263	(24%)

Rep. Dave Camp (R)

Elected 1990; b. July 9, 1953, Midland; home, Midland; Albion Col., B.A. 1975, U. of San Diego Law Schl., J.D. 1978; Catholic; married (Nancy).

Career: Practicing atty., 1978–90; MI Special Asst. Atty. Gen., 1980–84; A.A., U.S. Rep. Bill Schuette, 1984–87; MI House of Reps., 1988–90.

DC Office: 137 CHOB 20515, 202-225-3561; Fax: 202-225-9679; e-mail: davecamp@hr.house.gov.

District Offices: Houghton Lake, 517-366-4922; Midland, 517-631-2552; Owosso, 517-723-6759.

Committees: *Ways & Means* (10th of 23 R): Human Resources; Trade.

Group Ratings

	ADA	ACLU	AFS	LCV	CFA	CON	NFIB	COC	ACU	NTLC	CHC
1996	0	12	0	23	38	38	100	100	95	100	93
1995	5	—	—	13	8	87	—	100	84	—	—

National Journal Ratings

	1995 LIB		1995 CONS	1996 LIB		1996 CONS
Economic	26%	—	67%	27%	—	71%
Social	21%	—	72%	14%	—	77%
Foreign	42%	—	55%	52%	—	48%

Key Votes of the 104th Congress

1. Reduce Medicare Growth $	Y	5. Flag Amendment	Y	9. Cuban Embargo	Y
2. Ovrd. Product Liab. Veto	Y	6. Drop EPA Limits	N	10. Bar Bosnia Troop $	Y
3. Increase Min. Wage	N	7. Repeal Assault-Weap. Ban	Y	11. Cut Anti-Missile Defense	N
4. Welfare Reform	Y	8. Ovrd. Part. Birth Veto	Y	12. Bar U.N. Uniforms	Y

Election Results

1996 general	Dave Camp (R)	159,561	(65%)	($555,815)
	Lisa Donaldson (D)	79,691	(33%)	($13,284)
	Others	4,393	(2%)	
1996 primary	Dave Camp (R)	unopposed		
1994 general	Dave Camp (R)	145,176	(73%)	($444,419)
	Damion Frasier (D)	50,544	(25%)	($68,801)

FIFTH DISTRICT

Saginaw Bay, the inlet of Lake Huron that separates Michigan's Thumb (people really call it that) from the mitten of its Lower Peninsula, was for a moment in the 1870s the site of the greatest flow of lumber in the United States. There were 36 sawmills in Bay City then, and logs were piled high along both banks of the Saginaw River for miles. Bay City and Saginaw, 15 miles upstream, handled logs from the wide area on both sides of Saginaw Bay drained by the Saginaw River and its tributaries. Saginaw was also a center of precision machinery manufacturing, one reason General Motors put its huge power steering plants here. But starting in 1979 GM payrolls fell, and for a while the Saginaw area foundered. More recently, small high-skill manufacturing operations have grown up in old factory buildings once considered worthless; and this is part of the southern Michigan industrial belt with expertise needed to sustain just-in-time manufacturing. There also is agriculture here: the flat, broad fields around Saginaw Bay that once held so many trees are now the nation's leading producer of navy beans, the raw material of Senate bean soup.

The 5th Congressional District of Michigan includes Saginaw and Bay City and lands on both sides of Saginaw Bay. To the north it goes up past Oscoda on Lake Huron, where the 1993 closing of Wurtsmith Air Force Base resulted in a local economic boom rather than a bust as new employers were attracted and property sold readily. To the east it includes most of the Thumb. To the south it reaches to the city limits of Flint, including both black and white working-class townships just north of the city. Bay City, with its large Polish population, has long been Democratic and, since the auto industry woes of the 1980s, so are Saginaw and the Flint suburbs. While the Thumb historically is among the most Republican parts of Michigan, and the Oscoda area is Republican as well, both seem to be trending Democratic.

The congressman from the 5th District is Jim Barcia, a Democrat elected in 1992 when incumbent Bob Traxler retired. Barcia grew up in Bay City, went to Saginaw Valley State College, and has always lived in the area. He held political staff jobs until being elected to the state House in 1976, at age 24, and the state Senate in 1982. Barcia was known in the legislature for his whistleblower protection law, and he was not an automatic vote for unions or management; he bucked organized labor by backing a measure to cut the cost of workers' compensation and bucked others in his party by voting against abortion rights. In 1992 he had opposition from state Senator John Cherry of Saginaw, who had strong backing from organized labor, and from Don Hare, Traxler's district chief of staff. Barcia, with 72% in Bay County, won overall with 46%, to 29% for Cherry and 25% for Hare. Barcia won the general 60%–38%.

Barcia has a moderate, middle-of-the-House voting record. He supports the balanced budget constitutional amendment and the line-item veto; he opposed NAFTA and the 1994 Clinton healthcare plan. He serves on the Transportation and Infrastructure, and Science committees and tends closely to 5th district needs. He worked for disaster relief for farmers who suffered from quality losses in 1992 and floods in 1994 and 1996. In the 1994 highway bill he got the M-53 and M-25 state highways included in the U.S. highway system. He included water supply infrastructure earmarks for the town of Bad Axe, defending against charges of pork barrel spending by saying, "If this is pork, pass the platter." He hailed passage of the 1996 Safe Drinking Water Act by saying, "The next hurdle in solving the problem of clean drinking water for Bad Axe has been cleared." Outraged by an attack on a Bay City teenager, Barcia has been pressing for a requirement that all states make violent offender felons serve 85% of their sentences. He continues to press for a Farm Transportation Regulatory Relief Act.

He was reelected in 1994 and 1996 with 65% and 70% of the vote.

The People: Pop. 1990: 580,981; 51% rural; 13% age 65+; 87% White; 8% Black; 1% Amer. Indian; 3% Hispanic origin. Households: 60% married couple families; 28% married couple fams. w. children; 36% college educ.; median household income: $26,312; per capita income: $11,891; median gross rent: $366; median house value: $47,100.

1996 Presidential Vote			**1992 Presidential Vote**		
Clinton (D)	155,995	(57%)	Clinton (D)	119,086	(45%)
Dole (R)	90,107	(33%)	Bush (R)	85,603	(32%)
Perot (I)	27,477	(10%)	Perot (I)	61,544	(23%)

Rep. James A. Barcia (D)

Elected 1992; b. Feb. 25, 1952, Bay City; home, Bay City; Saginaw Valley St. U., B.A. 1974; Catholic; married (Vicki).

Career: Staff Asst., U.S. Sen. Philip Hart, 1971; Commun. Svc. Coord., MI Commun. Blood Ctr., 1974–75; A.A., MI Rep. Donald Albosta, 1975–76; MI House of Reps., 1976–82, Majority Whip, 1979–82; MI Senate, 1982–92.

DC Office: 2419 RHOB 20515, 202-225-8171; Fax: 202-225-2168; e-mail: jbarcia@hr.house.gov.

District Offices: Bay City, 517-667-0003; Flushing, 810-732-7501; Saginaw, 517-754-6075.

Committees: *Science* (7th of 21 D): Basic Research (RMM); Technology. *Transportation & Infrastructure* (18th of 33 D): Surface Transportation; Water Resources & Environment.

Group Ratings

	ADA	ACLU	AFS	LCV	CFA	CON	NFIB	COC	ACU	NTLC	CHC
1996	45	50	73	69	54	60	67	60	47	39	46
1995	70	—	—	56	38	75	—	63	52	—	—

National Journal Ratings

	1995 LIB	—	1995 CONS	1996 LIB	—	1996 CONS
Economic	61%	—	38%	59%	—	41%
Social	50%	—	50%	50%	—	48%
Foreign	66%	—	33%	55%	—	43%

Key Votes of the 104th Congress

1. Reduce Medicare Growth $	N	5. Flag Amendment	Y	9. Cuban Embargo	Y
2. Ovrd. Product Liab. Veto	Y	6. Drop EPA Limits	Y	10. Bar Bosnia Troop $	Y
3. Increase Min. Wage	*	7. Repeal Assault-Weap. Ban	Y	11. Cut Anti-Missile Defense	N
4. Welfare Reform	N	8. Ovrd. Part. Birth Veto	Y	12. Bar U.N. Uniforms	Y

Election Results

1996 general	James A. Barcia (D)	162,675	(70%)	($200,556)
	Lawrence Sims (R)	65,542	(28%)	($162,739)
	Others	4,234	(2%)	
1996 primary	James A. Barcia (D)	unopposed		
1994 general	James A. Barcia (D)	126,456	(65%)	($205,769)
	William Anderson (R)	61,342	(32%)	($5,856)
	Others	5,392	(3%)	

SIXTH DISTRICT

The southwest corner of Michigan is at the western end of the overland trail from Detroit, where the state's two southern tiers of counties were settled by New England Yankees and Upstate New Yorkers in the 1830s and 1840s. They built small towns with schools and churches and colleges, supported temperance and opposed capital punishment, and in 1854 started the Republican Party. There are towns in southwest Michigan that still recall proudly their past as termini of the Underground Railroad, and black families with ancestors who made their way north out of slavery to freedom (Dennis Archer, now mayor of Detroit, grew up here). Later, big industries transformed some of the small towns into large cities: Kalamazoo, started by Dutch-Americans who introduced celery to this country, became the home of Upjohn pharmaceuticals; Benton Harbor and St. Joseph, twin towns on Lake Michigan originally known for cherry and peach orchards, became the home of Whirlpool appliances. But this southwest corner is also where the influence of Michigan recedes: people here watch Chicago television and root for the Cubs or White Sox rather than the Tigers.

The 6th Congressional District of Michigan occupies this southwest corner of the state, with Kalamazoo and Benton Harbor-St. Joseph its two major urban areas, and three smaller counties besides. It was for many years arch-Republican territory, represented by a succession of congressmen who deplored federal spending and welfare state measures: New Deal opponent Clare Hoffman (1935–63), Nixon defender Edward Hutchinson (1963–77), and pork barrel critic and later Reagan Office of Management and Budget Director David Stockman (1977–81). More recently, Kalamazoo has trended toward the Democrats, and the 6th actually cast small pluralities for Bill Clinton in 1992 and 1996.

The current congressman from the 6th District is Fred Upton. The grandson of one of the founders of Whirlpool, Upton grew up in St. Joseph, attended the University of Michigan and worked for David Stockman, first on his House staff, then from 1981–85 at OMB. He returned home and challenged Congressman Mark Siljander, a conservative and evangelical Christian, in the 1986 Republican primary, and won 55%–45%. Upton is less like the congressional David Stockman, a scourge of federal spending, and more like the OMB Stockman, who rued the Reagan tax cuts. He has a moderate voting record and an impulse toward bipartisanship. He voted for the Brady bill and the national service bill, and in January 1993 resigned as deputy whip. He worked on the Commerce Committee for bipartisan bills on interstate waste shipments, Superfund and health care. He has worked with Democrat John Dingell on nuclear waste; their bill for an interim central waste disposal site in Nevada passed the Commerce Committee, but did not go to floor in 1996, because Newt Gingrich acceded to the pleas of the Nevada delegation; the Senate had passed a bill but Clinton threatened a veto. Upton has complained bitterly that the Department of Energy has missed deadlines for certifying Nevada's Yucca Mountain permanent disposal site which is supposed to come on line in the next century.

In 1995 Upton was anything but a Republican team player. He kept trying to lower the income limit on the $500-per-child tax credit, to as low as $50,000. He voted against some Republican environmental bills and called for a lifetime ban on members' lobbying for foreign governments. He called for making Republican tax cuts contingent on certification by the

(Clinton) OMB that the budget was on a realistic path to balance in 2002. Looking back at his experience with Stockman, Upton said, "We don't want to make the historic mistake we made in the '80s." In 1995 he became part of the Tuesday Lunch Bunch, now called the Tuesday Group, a band of 40 or so Republican moderates. In January 1996 he worked in vain with Democrat Tim Roemer of nearby Indiana to construct a bipartisan budget even as the government was shut down. He was successful later in 1996 with bipartisan action on welfare reform and the Safe Drinking Water Act. "Our group" he said, referring to the Tuesday Lunch Bunch, "was responsible for the positive agenda at the end of the Congress."

After the 1996 election, Upton decried the "shut-down, dark ages" approach taken by Republicans and said his party had come to be seen as "narrow" and "intolerant." He hailed Erskine Bowles' lack of "political baggage" after the new White House Chief of Staff met with the Lunch Bunch. He welcomed Newt Gingrich's disbanding of his Speaker's Advisory Group. But Upton did get partisan on one issue, saying proposed new EPA air standards could be disastrous for Michigan.

Upton considered running for the Senate in 1994 and 1996, but both times decided not to. He had one serious primary challenge from a conservative in 1990, but otherwise has won reelection easily.

The People: Pop. 1990: 580,973; 50% rural; 12% age 65+; 87% White; 10% Black; 1% Asian; 1% Amer. Indian; 2% Hispanic origin. Households: 57% married couple families; 26% married couple fams. w. children; 45% college educ.; median household income: $28,453; per capita income: $13,043; median gross rent: $385; median house value: $54,300.

1996 Presidential Vote

Clinton (D)	103,454	(46%)
Dole (R)	99,975	(44%)
Perot (I)	19,967	(9%)

1992 Presidential Vote

Clinton (D)	100,677	(39%)
Bush (R)	97,234	(38%)
Perot (I)	55,682	(22%)

Rep. Fred Upton (R)

Elected 1986; b. Apr. 23, 1953, St. Joseph; home, St. Joseph; U. of MI, B.A. 1975; Protestant; married (Amey).

Career: Project coord., U.S. Rep. David Stockman, 1975–80; Legis. Affairs, O.M.B., 1981–83, Dir., 1984–85.

DC Office: 2333 RHOB 20515, 202-225-3761; Fax: 202-225-4986; e-mail: talk2fsu@hr.house.gov.

District Offices: Kalamazoo, 616-385-0039; St. Joseph, 616-982-1986.

Committees: *Commerce* (8th of 28 R): Energy & Power; Health & the Environment; Telecommunications, Trade & Consumer Protection. *Education & The Workforce* (22nd of 25 R): Early Childhood, Youth & Families; Postsecondary Education, Training & Life-Long Learning.

Group Ratings

	ADA	ACLU	AFS	LCV	CFA	CON	NFIB	COC	ACU	NTLC	CHC
1996	10	12	8	31	62	63	95	94	85	93	66
1995	25	—	—	6	38	100	—	100	72	—	—

National Journal Ratings

	1995 LIB — 1995 CONS			1996 LIB — 1996 CONS		
Economic	0%	—	74%	33%	—	64%
Social	52%	—	47%	42%	—	58%
Foreign	52%	—	46%	72%	—	27%

Key Votes of the 104th Congress

1. Reduce Medicare Growth $	Y	5. Flag Amendment	Y	9. Cuban Embargo	Y
2. Ovrd. Product Liab. Veto	Y	6. Drop EPA Limits	Y	10. Bar Bosnia Troop $	Y
3. Increase Min. Wage	Y	7. Repeal Assault-Weap. Ban	Y	11. Cut Anti-Missile Defense	N
4. Welfare Reform	Y	8. Ovrd. Part. Birth Veto	Y	12. Bar U.N. Uniforms	Y

Election Results

1996 general	Fred Upton (R)	146,170	(68%)	($399,520)
	Clarence Annen (D)	66,243	(31%)	($12,089)
	Others	3,421	(2%)	
1996 primary	Fred Upton (R)	unopposed		
1994 general	Fred Upton (R)	121,923	(73%)	($575,406)
	David Taylor (D)	42,348	(26%)	($71,609)

SEVENTH DISTRICT

The small cities and towns spotting the southern-tier farmland counties of Michigan have been incubators of innovation since they were settled by Yankees from New England 150 years ago. The state's public school system was established by two politicians from Marshall, whose dashed hopes to make it the state capital resulted in the preservation of many of its 19th Century structures whose counterparts in Lansing, which won the contest, have long since been demolished. A few miles away, in Battle Creek, sanitarium operator W.K. Kellogg invented corn flakes as a health food; he and his one-time patient, C.W. Post, both established factories in the late 19th Century and created the American breakfast cereal industry. To the south is Hillsdale, where Hillsdale College has been proudly admitting blacks and women since the 1850s and refusing all federal aid. Politically, this area has been Republican territory since 1854, when the party was founded in the manufacturing and prison town of Jackson as a kind of reformist institution out of the same activist impulse that produced local support for women's rights and Prohibition and opposition to the death penalty. Southern Michigan mostly rejected New Deal tinkering and was hostile to the UAW, but the people here were receptive to moral claims made by later 20th Century reformers challenging racial segregation, the Vietnam war and the Watergate coverup.

The 7th Congressional District of Michigan covers all of six counties and parts of two others in Michigan's southern tier. It has typically voted Republican, but not always: Bill Clinton carried the district by small pluralities in 1992 and 1996.

The congressman from the 7th District is Nick Smith, a Republican who won the seat in 1992 after it was greatly altered by redistricting. Smith is a dairy farmer in Hillsdale County who was elected to the Somerset Township Board in 1962 and was involved in agriculture organizations;

he was elected to the state House in 1978 and state Senate in 1982. In 1992 he ran in the 7th District, which included much territory formerly represented by Republican Carl Pursell and Democrat Howard Wolpe. But Pursell's base was far distant and Wolpe found the district dauntingly Republican, and both retired from Congress. The 7th then had a brawling primary between Smith and fellow state Senator John Schwarz of Battle Creek, a physician accused by a third candidate of backing his car into a hospital security officer who had written him a ticket. Smith boasted of his 1992 property tax freeze and anti-abortion record and attacked Schwarz for raising money in Washington and from PACs while he took no PAC money. Smith won 43%–36%.

In the House Smith has had a conservative voting record on fiscal matters. He has taken on some daunting issues and others with clear local appeal. He wants two-year income averaging for farmers. He backed the Freedom to Farm Act and sponsored phase-downs of some dairy subsidies to make them competitive as exports. He also worked on revision of the Delaney clause in pesticide regulations. He is for the balanced budget amendment and tight budgets, but fought to save the Battle Creek Federal Center from the base-closing commission. He was the first co-sponsor of Dick Armey's flat tax, and he advanced his own Social Security Solvency Act. He would allow taxpayers to put 2.3% of their 12.4% FICA taxes into a private account that could be invested in stocks; he would raise the retirement age in steps to 69 without affecting current retirees; he would base benefits on average monthly earnings over 35 years; and he would stop borrowing from the Social Security trust fund. He also wants congressional oversight of administrative regulations.

Smith had little trouble in elections between the August 1992 primary and October 1996. His 1996 primary opponent, Doug Myers, a local newspaper columnist sympathetic to the militia movement, called him a tool of an international conspiracy to subjugate the United States to the United Nations. Smith won with 75%. For the general Smith proceeded to show his Social Security proposal charts to voters and encouraged supporters to write letters to the editor. Then around October 1, Democrat Kim Tunnicliff, head of the Gerald Ford Institute at Albion College, started campaigning heavily. Tunnicliff ran ads calling Smith a far right conservative, attacking his votes to "cut" Medicare, and charging that for all his opposition to big government he accepted $750,000 in farm subsidy payments. Smith, who wants to limit PAC contributions to $1,000 and doesn't take any PAC money himself, was not able to match Tunnicliff's broadcast spending, even though his budget was bigger.

Smith won 55%–43%, more narrowly than in 1994 and much less than in 1992 when he had no Democratic opponent. Tunnicliff carried Calhoun County, which includes Battle Creek, Marshall and Albion, 50%–48%. This result, and Smith's willingness to tackle the Social Security issue, suggests Democrats may try to seriously contest this district in 1998.

The People: Pop. 1990: 581,005; 52% rural; 12% age 65+; 91% White; 6% Black; 1% Asian; 2% Hispanic origin. Households: 60% married couple families; 28% married couple fams. w. children; 43% college educ.; median household income: $29,976; per capita income: $12,900; median gross rent: $382; median house value: $50,500.

1996 Presidential Vote

Clinton (D)	105,185	(46%)
Dole (R)	99,518	(43%)
Perot (I)	24,501	(11%)

1992 Presidential Vote

Clinton (D)	96,872	(38%)
Bush (R)	96,253	(37%)
Perot (I)	62,657	(24%)

Rep. Nick Smith (R)

Elected 1992; b. Nov. 5, 1934, Addison; home, Addison; MI St. U., B.A. 1957, U. of DE, M.S. 1959; Congregationalist; married (Bonnalyn).

Career: Air Force Intelligence, 1959–61; Businessman, farmer; Somerset Township Trustee, 1962–66, Supervisor, 1966–68; Hillsdale Cnty Bd. of Supervisors, 1966–68; Hillsdale Cnty. Repub. Chmn., 1966–68; MI Chmn., Agricultural Stabilization and Conservation Svc., 1969–72; Natl. Energy Dir., U.S. Dept. of Agriculture, 1972–74; MI Occup. Safety Standards Comm., 1975; MI House of Reps., 1978–82; MI Senate, 1982–92, Pres. Pro-Tem, 1983–90.

DC Office: 306 CHOB 20515, 202-225-6276; Fax: 202-225-6281; e-mail: repsmith@hr.house.gov.

District Offices: Adrian, 517-265-5012; Battle Creek, 616-965-9066; Charlotte, 517-543-0055; Jackson, 517-783-4486..

Committees: *Agriculture* (10th of 27 R): Department Operations, Nutrition & Foreign Agriculture; Forestry, Resource Conservation & Research; Livestock, Dairy & Poultry; Risk Management & Specialty Crops. *Budget* (9th of 24 R).

Group Ratings

	ADA	ACLU	AFS	LCV	CFA	CON	NFIB	COC	ACU	NTLC	CHC
1996	10	7	0	15	38	90	97	93	95	98	100
1995	0	—	—	6	0	98	—	96	100	—	—

National Journal Ratings

	1995 LIB — 1995 CONS			1996 LIB — 1996 CONS		
Economic	0%	—	74%	0%	—	82%
Social	35%	—	64%	35%	—	62%
Foreign	50%	—	49%	57%	—	43%

Key Votes of the 104th Congress

1. Reduce Medicare Growth $	Y	5. Flag Amendment	Y	9. Cuban Embargo	Y
2. Ovrd. Product Liab. Veto	Y	6. Drop EPA Limits	N	10. Bar Bosnia Troop $	Y
3. Increase Min. Wage	N	7. Repeal Assault-Weap. Ban	Y	11. Cut Anti-Missile Defense	N
4. Welfare Reform	Y	8. Ovrd. Part. Birth Veto	Y	12. Bar U.N. Uniforms	*

Election Results

1996 general	Nick Smith (R)	120,227	(55%)	($263,739)
	Kim Tunnicliff (D)	93,725	(43%)	($145,511)
	Others	4,592	(2%)	
1996 primary	Nick Smith (R)	40,019	(75%)	
	Doug Myers (R)	13,595	(25%)	
1994 general	Nick Smith (R)	115,621	(65%)	($289,573)
	Kim McCaughtry (D)	57,326	(32%)	($34,153)
	Others	4,553	(3%)	

EIGHTH DISTRICT

Lansing is Michigan's state capital, chosen in 1847 because of its geographic position halfway between Lake Huron and Lake Michigan and in ignorance of the fact that it has fewer days with sunshine than any place else in the state. But it is a tidy and pleasant city with more than its share of amenities. It has a beautifully restored Capitol and a fine state history museum and is neighbor to Michigan State University in East Lansing, started in 1855 as America's first land-grant college. Its Oldsmobile plant stimulated growth in the first half of this century, and state government has done the same in the second half. Politically, Lansing has tended to go with the party controlling state government. When the legislature was apportioned to stay Republican, as it was until 1964, the Lansing area was usually Republican; Democrats have had majorities in the state House in 28 of the 34 years since and Lansing has voted mostly Democratic.

The 8th Congressional District of Michigan includes Lansing and Ingham County but not the Lansing suburbs just across the line in Clinton and Eaton Counties, which are, respectively, in the 4th and 7th Districts. The 8th has two other very different population centers. One is the suburban fringe southwest of Flint, an area long Democratic and in deep trouble in the past two decades with the shutdown of General Motors operations there. The other is Livingston County, where I-96 crosses U.S. 23. Strewn with lakes and hills, this has been one of the fastest-growing counties in Michigan; its many new residents have left the Detroit area because they dislike its crime, high taxes and liberal politics. Livingston is very conservative and Republican; in 1992 and 1996 it was Bill Clinton's second and third worst county in Michigan, one of only five to give Bob Dole an absolute majority of the vote. Such politically disparate areas leave the 8th District precariously balanced, and it has switched parties in each of the last two elections.

The congresswoman from the 8th District is Debbie Stabenow, a Democrat elected in 1996. She grew up in the small Outstate town of Clare, went to Michigan State, where she got a master's degree in social work. Almost all her adult life she has been in politics. She was elected county commissioner before she finished her graduate degree; she was elected to the state House in 1978, at 28, making a record in family law and child abuse; she was elected to the state Senate in 1990. In 1994, while running for governor, she was at the storm center of state politics and policy. In response to Republican Governor John Engler's call for education finance reform, she proposed to zero out the existing property tax and start over, apparently calculating he would reject such a tax cut. Instead he accepted her proposal and his Republicans passed a plan reducing property taxes vastly and increasing the sales tax, which was approved by voters 70%–30% in March 1994. Meanwhile, in the August primary for governor, Stabenow was opposed by the two major forces in the Democratic Party, the Michigan Education Association, which backed Larry Owen, and the AFL-CIO and UAW, which backed former Congressman Howard Wolpe. Stabenow, comparing her politics to that of former Governor James Blanchard, won 30% of the vote, ahead of Owen's 26% but behind Wolpe's 35%. Eventually Wolpe chose her as his running mate, but the ticket lost to Engler 61%–38%.

Undaunted, Stabenow almost immediately started running for Congress. Her target in the 8th District was Dick Chrysler, a self-made millionaire (car customizing) who gave incumbent Democrat Bob Carr a 48%–46% scare in 1992, then won the district 52%–45% in 1994. Chrysler was a solid conservative, a follower of Newt Gingrich. While Chrysler spent $1.6 million of his own money in 1992, he was outspent by his opponent in 1994. And Stabenow outraised him from the start, getting more than $1 million in individual contributions, a tribute to her industriousness and the fundraising prowess of the feminist left; in mid-1995, when many potentially strong Democrats were declining to challenge Republican freshmen, she was already leading in public polls. Overall she spent $1.49 million, almost as much as his $1.51 million.

Stabenow was also a beneficiary of AFL-CIO ads charging Chrysler "cut" Medicare, and Sierra Club ads attacking his votes on the environment. Chrysler fought back by charging Stabenow voted to raise taxes 79 times in the state House, a number that turned out to be imprecise; she attacked his proposal for a 15% sales tax to replace the income tax and took credit for the property tax decrease resulting from Engler's referendum. On national issues Stabenow struck a thematic note similar to Bill Clinton's. She called for "balancing the budget in a way that does not shift the burden to middle-class families" and said she would produce "greater economic security for families" in three ways: "equipping our schools with computers and technology to prepare our students for good paying jobs and providing greater access to higher education and job training," "improving our nation's economic competitiveness through the creation of jobs based on new technologies and by supporting small business," and "addressing the health care needs of children and the needs of families caring for loved ones at home." Lots of good feeling, not much in the way of specific legislation.

Stabenow won impressively, 54%–44%, a decisive result in the 8th District. She gained nicely over previous years in Lansing and the traditionally Democratic Flint area; Chrysler's percentages in Livingston County were well below what he won in 1994, similar to when he lost narrowly in 1992. Stabenow has seats on the Science and Agriculture Committees. She was sought out by the moderate Democratic Blue Dogs but did not join. She has been mentioned as a candidate for statewide office, but is not thought likely to run for governor in 1998 or to oppose former Governor James Blanchard if he runs for the Senate in 2000.

The People: Pop. 1990: 581,072; 40% rural; 9% age 65+; 89% White; 6% Black; 2% Asian; 1% Amer. Indian; 3% Hispanic origin. Households: 58% married couple families; 29% married couple fams. w. children; 56% college educ.; median household income: $35,911; per capita income: $15,455; median gross rent: $435; median house value: $71,800.

1996 Presidential Vote

Clinton (D)	135,653	(49%)
Dole (R)	111,811	(40%)
Perot (I)	25,949	(9%)

1992 Presidential Vote

Clinton (D)	118,391	(40%)
Bush (R)	104,437	(36%)
Perot (I)	68,340	(23%)

Rep. Debbie Stabenow (D)

Elected 1996; b. April 29, 1950, Clare; home, Lansing; MI St. U., B.A. 1972, M.S.W. 1985; United Methodist; divorced.

Career: Ingham Cnty. Commission, 1975–78, Chair, 1976–78; MI House of Reps., 1979–90; MI Senate 1991–94; Consultant & Co-Founder, MI Leadership Inst., 1995–96.

DC Office: 1516 LHOB 20515, 202-225-4872; Fax: 202-225-5820.

District Offices: Flint, 810-230-8275; Howell, 517-545-2195; Lansing, 517-336-7777.

Committees: *Agriculture* (19th of 23 D): Forestry, Resource Conservation & Research; General Farm Commodities. *Science* (17th of 21 D): Technology.

Group Ratings and Key Votes: Newly Elected

Election Results

1996 general	Debbie Stabenow (D)	141,086	(54%)	($1,497,300)
	Dick Chrysler (R)	115,836	(44%)	($1,515,307)
	Others	5,499	(2%)	
1996 primary	Debbie Stabenow (D)	unopposed		
1994 general	Dick Chrysler (R)	109,663	(52%)	($356,924)
	Bob Mitchell (D)	95,383	(45%)	($474,437)
	Others	7,435	(4%)	

NINTH DISTRICT

General Motors was formed in 1918 as a merger of several smaller car companies; headquartered in Detroit, it had plants in small cities in Michigan and Ohio. Foremost among these cities were Flint and Pontiac, two industrial county seats on the old Woodward Avenue route that led northwest from Detroit. Pontiac, named for the 18th Century Indian chief who sparked a rebellion that spread all the way to what is now Pittsburgh, produced Pontiacs and GMC Trucks; Flint, named for the flint from which Indians made arrowheads, produced Buicks and Chevrolets. For five decades after 1918, Flint and Pontiac grew lustily, attracting new workers from the mountains of Kentucky and Tennessee and the Black Belt of Alabama; country and black music and Southern accents became common in towns originally settled by Yankees. There was turmoil, too. Flint was the scene in January 1937 of the great sitdown strike that, when Governor Frank Murphy refused to send the National Guard to enforce a court order, forced GM to recognize the United Auto Workers as the bargaining agent for all its workers. Yet in many ways these GM company towns built good lives for their citizens. The UAW-GM contracts produced the world's highest wages for industrial workers and lavish fringe benefits, including a generous healthcare plan. The Mott Foundation, started by GM's largest shareholder, Charles Stewart Mott, funded schools, including a university branch in Flint, and historical exhibitions—an exemplary plowing-back of money into a one-industry town. Workers who were laid off got 65 weeks of benefits amounting to 90% of regular wages—a real safety net.

Then disaster struck starting in the late 1970s. Auto sales plummeted with the oil shock of 1979, and imports, especially from Japan, that were higher in quality and cheaper in price than American cars were taking an increasing share of the market. GM managers and UAW leaders assumed that increased labor costs could be passed along to consumers, that buyers were indifferent to quality and eager for new models. Those assumptions proved vitally wrong: not even the cleverest advertising could persuade Americans to buy a new American car every two years. In 1979 GM employed more than 70,000 workers in its Flint plants, a huge share of the labor force in a metro area of 430,000 people; by the early 1990s GM employment was down significantly. Thousands left Flint. Those who stayed found their real estate values—the store of wealth for most Americans—stagnant, and government attempts to develop an upscale shopping mall, a Hyatt hotel and the AutoWorld theme park went bankrupt. Pontiac was also hurt in the late 1980s and early 1990s when GM closed plants there, but Pontiac has some advantages. The Detroit metro area has expanded, and surrounding Oakland County gained over 140,000 jobs in the 1980s, mainly in services and retail. Chrysler built its new headquarters along I-75 in Auburn Hills, and the freeway became the main street for a newly lean and efficient auto industry and its nimble just-in-time suppliers.

The 9th Congressional District of Michigan runs from Flint to Pontiac and takes in some diverse political territory. It includes the city of Flint and some of its suburbs to the southeast; this Genesee County portion has about one-third of the district's people and is heavily Democratic. Pontiac, about half black, is heavily Democratic but is only 12% of the district. Lake-strewn Waterford Township to the west, where many Pontiac whites moved when a school busing plan was ordered in the 1970s, is larger now and leans Republican. Auburn Hills and

Rochester Hills east of Pontiac are high-income and heavily Republican. Clarkston and other burgeoning communities to the north, where hills and lakes and large lots give new residents the advantages of Up North living with an easy commute on I-75, are heavily Republican. Similarly, Lapeer County, north of Pontiac and east of Flint, has been growing and has long been Republican. That means half the district is solidly Democratic, with a long union heritage; the other half is Republican, in some places very much so.

The congressman from the 9th District is Dale Kildee, a Democrat first elected in 1976, whose district until 1992 clustered closely around Flint. Kildee grew up in Flint, studied for the priesthood, taught at a Catholic high school in Detroit and at Flint Central. His door-to-door campaigning got him elected to a newly created state legislative seat in 1964, at 35, and enabled him to beat a 26-year veteran of the state Senate in 1974. He won the House seat in 1976, when it was solidly Democratic, without a primary opponent and held it easily for his first 16 years. Kildee brings to politics an intensity of conviction derived from the liberal tradition lively in the American Catholic church—a tradition with little regard for market economics and a strong obligation to care for the needy. He is solidly liberal on economics and always pro-union; he is against abortion and is something of a stickler on ethics.

Kildee is now a senior member of the Education and the Workforce and Resources Committees and claims credit for more legislation than any other Michigan congressman in the past six years. He is a strong ally of teachers' unions, a backer of increased federal aid for education and an opponent of school choice. He labored hard on the 1990 reauthorization of Head Start and on the 1990 child care bill. He worked on the 1994 elementary and secondary education reauthorization, downplaying President Clinton's proposal for national testing standards and promoting the "Opportunity to Learn" standards designed to ensure adequate learning resources for all, though he stops short of calling for equal funding for all schools. As ranking Democrat on the Postsecondary Education, Training and Lifelong Learning Subcommittee, he sponsored Goals 2000, the Star Schools Program and Head Start, and backed the Schools-to-Work Act of 1994 and magnet schools. He sponsored the first federal law on child pornography and backs stipends for Senior Companions and Foster Grandparents. He has fought against reducing federal standards on special education students.

He has worked on other issues as well. He was the first House member to argue imported minivans should be subject not to the 2.5% tariff for cars but to the 25% tariff for trucks, and was a strong opponent of NAFTA. He favors a strong Section 301 to require negotiations with countries that engage in discriminatory trade practices that result in trade deficits. He pressured Puerto Rico to stop taxing cars on weight: sales of hefty Flint-assembled cars went up. On Resources, he worked to produce a Michigan wilderness act and to designate local Wild and Scenic Rivers.

Kildee fit his old Flint-area district like a glove, but has had serious challenges in the 9th District since it was created in 1992. In 1992 and 1994 he was opposed by Megan O'Neill, a former Bush/Quayle advance staffer who called Kildee a "career politician" and "beholden to special interest groups." On the defensive, Kildee emphasized his opposition to congressional pay raises and his refusal to co-sponsor the Clinton healthcare plan. Also, he vastly outraised her, spending $795,000 in 1992 and $963,000 in 1994. Kildee won, but by 54%–45% in 1992 and only 51%–47% in 1994. In 1996 the anger at Democrats in Congress had died down, and Kildee faced an opponent who turned out to be less formidable than expected. Republican Pat Nowak was Michigan transportation director and a former aide to Oakland County Executive Brooks Patterson; but Michigan roads are in notoriously bad condition, and Kildee called him "Pothole Pat" and ran a radio ad commending Nowak for making money for auto repair shops. Nowak made some attacks which he proved unable to sustain—mailing a baby-food jar of mud to reporters to criticize the Superfund program and accusing Kildee of spending taxpayer money on sexually explicit material. Meanwhile, Kildee had been working Oakland County hard as he has Flint for so many years; and he outspent the Republican 2–1. The result was a solid 59%–39% Kildee victory; he won 78%–21% in Genesee County and even led in Oakland, 49%–48%.

The People: Pop. 1990: 580,908; 20% rural; 9% age 65+; 78% White; 18% Black; 1% Asian; 1% Amer. Indian; 3% Hispanic origin. Households: 54% married couple families; 26% married couple fams. w. children; 47% college educ.; median household income: $34,737; per capita income: $15,132; median gross rent: $448; median house value: $64,400.

1996 Presidential Vote			1992 Presidential Vote		
Clinton (D)	95,473	(46%)	Clinton (D)	117,872	(44%)
Dole (R)	89,538	(43%)	Bush (R)	92,262	(35%)
Perot (I)	21,567	(10%)	Perot (I)	55,077	(21%)

Rep. Dale E. Kildee (D)

Elected 1976; b. Sept. 16, 1929, Flint; home, Flint; Sacred Heart Seminary, B.A. 1952, U. of MI, M.A. 1961, Rotary Fellow, U. of Peshawar, Pakistan; Catholic; married (Gayle).

Career: High schl. teacher, 1954–64; MI House of Reps., 1964–74; MI Senate, 1974–75.

DC Office: 2187 RHOB 20515, 202-225-3611; Fax: 202-225-6393; e-mail: dkildee@hr.house.gov.

District Offices: Flint, 810-239-1437; Pontiac, 810-373-9337.

Committees: *Education & The Workforce* (3rd of 20 D): Early Childhood, Youth & Families; Postsecondary Education, Training & Life-Long Learning (RMM). *Resources* (5th of 23 D): Forests & Forest Health; National Parks & Public Lands.

Group Ratings

	ADA	ACLU	AFS	LCV	CFA	CON	NFIB	COC	ACU	NTLC	CHC
1996	75	50	100	85	85	30	24	31	15	10	33
1995	75	—	100	92	25	—	21	24	—	—	

National Journal Ratings

	1995 LIB — 1995 CONS			1996 LIB — 1996 CONS		
Economic	80%	—	18%	79%	—	18%
Social	57%	—	42%	62%	—	37%
Foreign	88%	—	7%	61%	—	37%

Key Votes of the 104th Congress

1. Reduce Medicare Growth $	N	5. Flag Amendment	Y	9. Cuban Embargo	N
2. Ovrd. Product Liab. Veto	N	6. Drop EPA Limits	Y	10. Bar Bosnia Troop $	N
3. Increase Min. Wage	Y	7. Repeal Assault-Weap. Ban	N	11. Cut Anti-Missile Defense	Y
4. Welfare Reform	N	8. Ovrd. Part. Birth Veto	Y	12. Bar U.N. Uniforms	Y

Election Results

1996 general	Dale E. Kildee (D)	136,856	(59%)	($816,337)
	Patrick Nowak (R)	89,733	(39%)	($443,415)
	Others	4,611	(2%)	
1996 primary	Dale E. Kildee (D)	unopposed		
1994 general	Dale E. Kildee (D)	97,096	(51%)	($963,249)
	Megan O'Neill (R)	89,148	(47%)	($302,174)
	Others	3,319	(2%)	

TENTH DISTRICT

Macomb County, Michigan, on the billiard-table-flat shore of Lake St. Clair just northeast of Detroit, has become one of the nation's most closely watched political battlegrounds, a place where the electoral fate of Michigan and even the entire country may be determined. Its reputation is not quite accurate: more people hold white-collar jobs than blue-collar these days and far fewer work in auto plants than in earlier generations; there are plenty of affluent subdivisions and boat ownership may well be the highest in the country. Macomb County is the product of the post-World War II boom: with just over 107,000 people in 1940, many in the old sulphur-water spa town of Mount Clemens, Macomb passed the 400,000 mark in 1960 and 600,000 by 1970; in 1990 it reached 717,000. Most people came here from Detroit: Polish-Americans marching out Van Dyke from Hamtramck to Warren; Italian-Americans heading out Gratiot from Detroit's east side to Roseville and Clinton Township; Belgian-Americans from the Mack corridor moving out farther to St. Clair Shores. These new suburbanites were heavily Catholic, often blue-collar, at least modestly affluent and ancestrally Democratic. They accepted the New Deal as part of their natural heritage but resented the efforts of Detroit politicians to tax them to pay for welfare, and they were fearful of the high crime rates in Detroit's black neighborhoods. Indeed, the suburb of East Detroit voted to change its name to Eastpointe to avoid any implication it is part of the central city.

In 1960, Macomb County was the most Democratic major suburban county in the United States, voting 63% for America's first Catholic president, John F. Kennedy. Since then, Macomb has been moving away from the national Democrats—in 1962, because they would let Detroit tax suburbanites, in 1972, because they didn't vehemently oppose a metropolitan school busing plan. From 1976 through 1992 no Democratic presidential candidate got more than 40% of the vote here; in 1996, after great effort and with the advice of his sometime pollster Stan Greenberg who has studied Macomb closely, Bill Clinton carried Macomb County by a 49%–39% margin. It was a solid win, but not as impressive as the 1994 margins for Republican Governor John Engler (70%–30%) or Senator Spencer Abraham (56%–36%). Democrats had a good year in 1996 and still hold most county and legislative offices in Macomb, but not all, and Republicans have one Macomb statewide officeholder, Secretary of State Candice Miller.

The 10th Congressional District of Michigan includes most of Macomb County, all but the southwest corner, and takes in Port Huron and St. Clair County to the northeast. Republican in most elections over the past decade, it swung sharply to Bill Clinton in 1996; in the House it has been represented for more than 20 years by David Bonior, now the House Democratic whip.

Bonior grew up in East Detroit (as it then was called), the grandson of Polish and Ukrainian immigrants; he became a seminarian in high school, had an athletic scholarship to the University of Iowa where he played football, worked as a probation officer and social worker in Mount Clemens and served in the Air Force stateside in the Vietnam era (he came to oppose the war). His father was a printer and auto worker who became mayor of East Detroit; it is his loss of that office in 1967 which Bonior refers to as his family's brush with unemployment. Bonior never became a priest, but he remains in accord with liberal strains of Catholic thought and liberation theology; he is against abortion, though he has voted with most Democrats against the anti-abortion "gag rule" and fetal tissue research. In 1972 he was elected to the Michigan House, and in 1976, when Congressman James O'Hara ran for the Senate, Bonior ran for the U.S. House. He had a knack for symbolism: that winter an ice storm killed many Macomb County trees, and in response he gave out thousands of pine seedlings as a campaign gimmick. This struck a chord with gun-toting sportsmen and baby-boomer environmentalists alike, and by now he has handed out more than 400,000 seedlings and featured them in his TV ads. He has done conspicuous work on local environmental problems—securing funds to study replacing the environmentally unsound Clinton River dam, taking credit for provisions in the Oil Spill Liability Act that subject foreign tanker pilots to the same operating standards as U.S. pilots.

Bonior brings to his work a great intensity and passion. "I think God's work should also be an expression of what you do on earth as much as what you strive for in heaven." Like many Catholic admirers of liberation theology, he opposed aid to the Nicaraguan Contras and El Salvador government. It was Bonior's deep convictions and determination that probably commended him to Speaker Jim Wright, who appointed him chief deputy whip in 1986. That appointment put Bonior on the leadership ladder. He did not move up immediately: William Gray beat him for whip in June 1989, 134–97, after Wright and Whip Tony Coelho resigned. But when Gray retired in June 1991, Bonior beat Maryland's Steny Hoyer 160–109. And after Speaker Thomas Foley lost his House seat in 1994, Dick Gephardt became Minority Leader and Bonior, winning the Minority Whip post by 145–60 over Charles Stenholm, got the number two position in his party's leadership.

If Bonior sees himself representing Latin American peasants oppressed by U.S.-supported rightist military leaders abroad, he also sees himself representing a forgotten and scorned blue-collar working class at home. With Marcy Kaptur of Ohio, he was one of the most passionate opponents of NAFTA, arguing it was "basically the sellout of [American] workers" and that "we can't let jobs be our number one export." He has opposed Most Favored Nation status for China because of its human rights violations. Some may argue the Sandinista defeat in the Nicaraguan elections and the well-above-national income figures in Macomb County prove Bonior's visions of the world are unrealistic. But he obviously feels a moral imperative to represent those who he believes need compassion and help from government, and that if many of his constituents have moved upscale he still has an obligation to those who have not. In that spirit he went to the White House in August 1995 after Bill Clinton pledged to seek a balanced budget by 2002 and had "a rough meeting with the president over Medicare and the budget issue and I expressed my displeasure."

His greatest animus seems to be reserved for Newt Gingrich. Bearded, serious, seldom smiling, Bonior has stalked Gingrich as Captain Ahab stalked Moby Dick. When Gingrich became speaker, Gephardt took care to speak in conciliatory tones; not Bonior. Asked if he had any respect for Gingrich, he said, "No, I don't." "I've watched him operate for a long time . . . I've watched him violate rules and laws, and I've watched him tear down the institution. And I've watched him really tear down things that I care about for my constituents." He led Democrats to file over 70 ethics charges against Gingrich, some arguably serious, many entirely without merit. Some had political repercussions, like his complaint about Gingrich's book deal, after which Gingrich gave up his $4 million advance. (Republicans filed a harassing complaint charging that Bonior had improperly used his staff to write a book about Vietnam veterans in 1984; one was listed as co-author.) One charge given serious consideration was that Gingrich improperly used political money to finance his tax-exempt college course. In fall 1996 Bonior angrily charged that Republicans on the Ethics Committee were stalling on the case, and he attacked them harshly for reelecting Gingrich Speaker on January 7, 1997, before the report on the independent counsel was made known. But Bonior was embarrassed when a Republican leadership conference call taped by Democratic activists from Florida was leaked to *The New York Times*; taping such calls is a federal crime, and the Floridians sent the tape to Florida Congresswoman Karen Thurman, who returned the tape to them, while suggesting that senior Bonior aides allegedly said they might get immunity from prosecution if they turned the tape over to the committee. Bonior chose not to speak the day Gingrich was reprimanded by the full House, and seemed muted in following weeks, perhaps stung as well by Bill Clinton's abjuration in his State of the Union address against "bickering."

Bonior's principled stands and political crusades have put him at risk in a district which has often voted Republican for other offices. He has had serious Republican challenges in each of the last three presidential years. In 1988 and 1992 he beat state Senator Doug Carl, a religious conservative, by 54%–45% and 53%–44, after spending immense sums—$1.34 million in 1992, with $934,000 from PACs—mostly on Detroit TV. In 1994, against nuisance opposition, he spent $1.12 million. In 1996, Republican Governor John Engler, who had been working closely with Gingrich on welfare reform, took great interest in the race. He recruited Republican state Chairman Susy Heintz, who in May 1996 decided to run; she had not lived in Macomb County for years, but had grown up in Mount Clemens where her father was mayor in the 1970s. Six feet tall, with white-blond hair and outsized glasses, she had attacked Bonior as a "whiny, wacky, wimpy, wasteful, worn-out, washed-up, windbag whip." Democrats tried to get her off the ballot for filing insufficient signatures, but she got on and beat former state Senator Gilbert DiNello in the primary. Bonior attacked Heintz for paying taxes late in 1991–93; she claimed it happened because of a disputed divorce. Heintz attacked Bonior for keeping his wife on his payroll; he said she had worked for him for four years before they were married in 1991 and was entitled to her previous salary. (A conservative foundation filed an ethics complaint on this, which was dismissed.) Michigan Right to Life endorsed Heintz, because of Bonior's vote on the use of fetal tissue research and against a ban on federal funds for clinics that offer abortion counseling. Bonior declined to participate in an October debate because Heintz refused to agree not to use video footage of the event in ads or mention his wife's job.

Once again Bonior had a huge financial advantage. He raised $862,000 from PACs and spent a total of $1.51 million; Bill Clinton was leading in Macomb and St. Clair Counties and by mid-October Bonior was leading 56%–30% in a public poll. But with Engler's and Gingrich's help Heintz raised a respectable $677,000, and became the first Bonior opponent to run TV ads. "Too liberal too long," her campaign said, and attacked him for his courageous vote against the 1996 welfare reform act (he was one of only three Michigan Democrats to vote against it, with the other two being from Detroit). The final result was a 54%–44% Bonior victory, almost identical to his wins in 1992 and 1988.

Bonior will surely continue to fight for his liberal policies as hard as ever. But questions remain. After his failure to bring down Gingrich and the fiasco over the Florida tapes, will he continue to attack the speaker as harshly? And will the Republicans take heart from his not overwhelming percentage to seriously challenge him again?

The People: Pop. 1990: 580,974; 17% rural; 12% age 65+; 96% White; 2% Black; 1% Asian; 1% Hispanic origin. Households: 62% married couple families; 29% married couple fams. w. children; 42% college educ.; median household income: $36,536; per capita income: $15,603; median gross rent: $471; median house value: $70,900.

1996 Presidential Vote		
Clinton (D)	120,921	(49%)
Dole (R)	96,592	(39%)
Perot (I)	27,083	(11%)

1992 Presidential Vote		
Bush (R)	115,849	(41%)
Clinton (D)	100,587	(36%)
Perot (I)	60,927	(22%)

Rep. David E. Bonior (D)

Elected 1976; b. June 6, 1945, Detroit; home, Mt. Clemens; U. of IA, B.A. 1967, Chapman Col., M.A. 1972; Catholic; married (Judy).

Career: Air Force, 1968–72; Probation officer, adoption caseworker, 1967–68; MI House of Reps., 1972–76.

DC Office: 2207 RHOB 20515, 202-225-2106; Fax: 202-226-1169.

District Offices: Mt. Clemens, 810-469-3232; Port Huron, 810-987-8889.

Committees: *Minority Whip.*

Group Ratings

	ADA	ACLU	AFS	LCV	CFA	CON	NFIB	COC	ACU	NTLC	CHC
1996	95	81	100	85	92	5	19	19	5	4.9	20
1995	95	—	—	88	85	4	—	13	12	—	—

National Journal Ratings

	1995 LIB — 1995 CONS			1996 LIB — 1996 CONS		
Economic	94%	—	0%	85%	—	11%
Social	65%	—	33%	69%	—	30%
Foreign	88%	—	7%	79%	—	19%

Key Votes of the 104th Congress

1. Reduce Medicare Growth $	N	5. Flag Amendment	N	9. Cuban Embargo	N
2. Ovrd. Product Liab. Veto	N	6. Drop EPA Limits	Y	10. Bar Bosnia Troop $	N
3. Increase Min. Wage	Y	7. Repeal Assault-Weap. Ban	N	11. Cut Anti-Missile Defense	Y
4. Welfare Reform	N	8. Ovrd. Part. Birth Veto	Y	12. Bar U.N. Uniforms	N

Election Results

1996 general	David E. Bonior (D)	132,829	(54%)	($1,513,432)
	Susy Heintz (R)	106,444	(44%)	($673,996)
	Others	5,008	(2%)	
1996 primary	David E. Bonior (D)	unopposed		
1994 general	David E. Bonior (D)	121,876	(62%)	($1,123,472)
	Donald J. Lobsinger (R)	73,862	(38%)	($18,084)

ELEVENTH DISTRICT

Oakland County, Michigan, long considered just a suburban adjunct of Detroit, is now the center of a giant, spread-out, affluent urban area. It is only minutes on the Lodge Freeway from the empty, abandoned blocks of inner-city Detroit, just north of Eight Mile Road; but here there are giant office buildings and multiplying small businesses, expensive houses on large lots and one shopping mall after another, high education levels and low crime rates. Even physically there is a distinction between the two areas: Detroit is on almost perfectly flat land, while many of the Oakland County suburbs run along a line of hills and lakes that marks the southernmost advance of an Ice Age glacier. Southfield, in southern Oakland County, is Michigan's largest office space center, far ahead of Detroit; Troy is another big office center, with upscale malls that compete with high-income Birmingham; new development proliferates around Novi and Northville, just south of Eight Mile Road in Wayne County; Bloomfield Hills has Michigan's highest incomes. Forty years ago, Detroit had 1.9 million people and Oakland County 396,000. In 1990 Oakland had over one million, and Detroit topped that mark only after Mayor Coleman Young pressured Census officials and presented names of people purportedly not counted.

The 11th Congressional District of Michigan includes almost half of Oakland County plus the comfortable suburbs of Redford Township and Livonia, west of Detroit. This is mostly high-income Republican territory, where people generally believe in free market economics and fiercely oppose higher taxes. It is also home to most of the Detroit area's Jewish community, which has moved out the Lodge first to Southfield and then to West Bloomfield and scattered in most of these suburbs. Jewish voters and affluent blacks who have moved to Southfield and other suburbs, form the district's chief Democratic bloc.

The congressman from the 11th District is Joe Knollenberg, a Republican first elected in 1992. Knollenberg grew up the fifth child in a family of 13 on a farm in Downstate Illinois, went to college in Illinois and became an insurance agent. He moved to Oakland County in 1967 and became involved in civic affairs and Republican politics. When Republican William Broomfield retired in 1992 after 36 years in office—and in the minority—Knollenberg ran. He had two colorful opponents in the Republican primary, David Honigman, a young and wealthy state Senator, and Alice Gilbert, who was pro-choice and a former judge. But they attacked one another, while Knollenberg, pro-life and supported by Broomfield, won with 43% to 30% for Honigman and 27% for Gilbert. He won the general election easily.

In the Democratic 103d Congress a freshman Republican like Knollenberg was easily overlooked; in the Republican 104th Congress he became something of a power. He got a seat on Appropriations, and besides the usual defending of local interests (getting $15 million to clean up the Rouge River, getting regular customs service for Oakland Airport, the nation's fourth busiest in corporate jets), he made policy on national issues. Knollenberg's proposals included one to allow HUD to give local housing authorities income data on tenants, one to require HUD to honor local English-only laws, and a third to zero out Transportation Department funding for the environmental impact statements necessary to raise CAFE standards for autos.

Knollenberg advanced another proposal of national import: a $500-per-person tax credit for contributions to charities that devote 75% of their spending to relieving poverty. "We want to get control of the welfare system in the hands of people locally. People could pick the charity down the street from their home, where they have some familiarity with their poverty-fighting experiences." The idea of supporting local personal over federal bureaucratic control of antipoverty spending attracted others: the amendment was co-sponsored by Arizona's Jim Kolbe, was picked up by Senators Dan Coats and John Ashcroft and was spoken of favorably by presidential candidate Bob Dole. It is some ways from this to enactment, of course, and CBO estimated it would cost $18 billion in revenue. But it seems obvious to many people in Oakland County that they might have better ideas and policies than the Washington policies which have resulted in the human misery seen every day in Detroit.

Knollenberg has been reelected without difficulty and has been mentioned as a candidate for governor in 1998 if Engler decides not to run.

The People: Pop. 1990: 580,934; 5% rural; 12% age 65+; 92% White; 4% Black; 2% Asian; 1% Hispanic origin. Households: 63% married couple families; 28% married couple fams. w. children; 63% college educ.; median household income: $49,021; per capita income: $24,466; median gross rent: $638; median house value: $110,300.

1996 Presidential Vote

Clinton (D)	134,344	(46%)
Dole (R)	131,571	(46%)
Perot (I)	19,322	(7%)

1992 Presidential Vote

Bush (R)	147,786	(47%)
Clinton (D)	116,266	(37%)
Perot (I)	50,385	(16%)

Rep. Joe Knollenberg (R)

Elected 1992; b. Nov. 28, 1933, Mattoon, IL; home, Bloomfield Township; E. IL U., B.S. 1955; Catholic; married (Sandie).

Career: Army, 1955–57; Insurance agent, 1958–92.

DC Office: 1221 LHOB 20515, 202-225-5802; Fax: 202-226-2356.

District Offices: Farmington Hills, 810-851-1366; Livonia, 313-425-7557.

Committees: *Appropriations* (19th of 34 R): Energy & Water Development; Foreign Operations, Export Financing & Related Programs; VA, HUD & Independent Agencies. *Education & The Workforce* (13th of 25 R): Employer-Employee Relations (Vice-Chmn.).

Group Ratings

	ADA	ACLU	AFS	LCV	CFA	CON	NFIB	COC	ACU	NTLC	CHC
1996	0	0	0	15	0	30	100	94	95	98	93
1995	0	—	—	0	0	38	—	100	88	—	—

National Journal Ratings

	1995 LIB — 1995 CONS	1996 LIB — 1996 CONS
Economic	0% — 74%	30% — 68%
Social	32% — 65%	29% — 68%
Foreign	15% — 73%	21% — 72%

Key Votes of the 104th Congress

1. Reduce Medicare Growth $	Y	5. Flag Amendment	Y	9. Cuban Embargo	Y
2. Ovrd. Product Liab. Veto	Y	6. Drop EPA Limits	N	10. Bar Bosnia Troop $	Y
3. Increase Min. Wage	N	7. Repeal Assault-Weap. Ban	Y	11. Cut Anti-Missile Defense	N
4. Welfare Reform	Y	8. Ovrd. Part. Birth Veto	Y	12. Bar U.N. Uniforms	Y

Election Results

1996 general	Joe Knollenberg (R)	169,165	(61%)	($608,882)
	Morris Frumin (D)	99,303	(36%)	($31,796)
	Others	8,150	(3%)	
1996 primary	Joe Knollenberg (R)	unopposed		
1994 general	Joe Knollenberg (R)	154,696	(68%)	($507,622)
	Mike Breshgold (D)	69,168	(30%)	($29,576)

TWELFTH DISTRICT

The flat expanse of land just north of Eight Mile Road, Detroit's northern city limit was mostly vacant in the years just after World War II. A string of suburbs in Oakland County ran along Woodward Avenue, Detroit's main street, already eight lanes wide, which led to the Shrine of the Little Flower church in Royal Oak. There, in the 1930s, Father Charles Coughlin made his radio broadcasts backing and then opposing Franklin Roosevelt and denouncing bankers and Jews. To the east in Macomb County was some industrial development along Van Dyke, but this was mostly empty land, too; Detroit's population was heading toward two million. Today, these areas are well-settled suburbs, long since built up, a few neighborhoods edging toward seediness, many others continually renovated and restored. Almost half of metro Detroit's population is now north of Eight Mile, in communities drawing on old traditions but crackling with economic creativity.

The 12th Congressional District of Michigan is in this suburban territory, with about half its population in the two suburban counties. On the Oakland County side are Royal Oak and other Woodward Avenue suburbs, now attracting singles and gays as well as families; Oak Park, heavily Jewish in the 1950s and now perhaps the only small city in America with sizable numbers of Jews, Arabs and blacks; Hazel Park and Madison Heights, mostly peopled with descendants of the Appalachian migrants of a few decades ago; and Troy, once blank fields and now a major office center, with the Kmart world headquarters across from the upscale Somerset Malls on Big Beaver Road. On the Macomb County side are Warren and Sterling Heights, the destination often of Polish-Americans moving out from Hamtramck and the East Side of Detroit, and site of the General Motors Technical Center, a big Chrysler plant and the M-1 tank plant where Michael Dukakis took his famous ride in the 1988 campaign. Historically, Macomb County is Democratic, and Oakland Republican, but Oak Park and Hazel Park have long been very Democratic, and Macomb has been trending Republican for years; both voted by similar percentages for George Bush in 1992 and Bill Clinton in 1996.

The congressman from the 12th District is Sander Levin. A member of one of Michigan's most respected political families, Levin, a Democrat, was first elected to the House in 1982. Levin grew up in Detroit, settled in the Woodward Avenue suburb of Berkley after school and was elected state senator in 1964; in 1970 and 1974 he ran for governor and lost narrowly each time to Republican William Milliken. In the Carter Administration he was a top appointee at the Agency for International Development. In 1982 a House seat suddenly opened up, even though Michigan lost a seat in redistricting, when incumbent James Blanchard ran for governor and incumbent William Brodhead retired. Levin won a spirited Democratic primary and held the seat without difficulty through 1990. The 1992 redistricting moved him east, into Macomb County, and placed him in the same district with Democrat Dennis Hertel, but Hertel, with 547 overdrafts on the House bank, retired, and Levin easily won the Democratic nomination.

Levin is a hard worker, a detail man, willing to spend endless hours with others working out a solution. He seems always to be seeking the mean between two extremes; he likes negotiations and dislikes issues that divide opponents on stark lines of principle. His voting record is mostly liberal, but he played a significant role in drafting the welfare reform act of 1996. In his first decade in the House he spent much time and energy on trade issues. While insisting he is not a protectionist, he formed the Congressional Auto Parts Task Force and in 1990 published in the *Congressional Record* the controversial anti-American article, *The Japan That Can Say No*, by Akio Morita and Shintaro Ishihara, when the Japanese authors refused to allow it to appear in translation. He pushed unsuccessfully for stringent measures—limits on Japanese car and truck sales, including those manufactured in U.S. plants, and a 25% rather than a 2.5% tariff on Japanese minivans. He was a strong opponent of NAFTA in 1993, arguing that Mexican environmental and labor standards were so far below those of the United States that the agreement did not make sense. But after it passed, he was one of the few House Democrats to back the original Mexican peso bailout proposed in early 1995 by the Clinton Administration.

Levin serves on the Ways and Means Committee, where he worked on health care in 1993 and 1994 and welfare in 1995 and 1996. He was a critical member of the Health Subcommittee which hammered out a healthcare bill in spring 1994. Levin withheld his vote for the bill until Democrats agreed to remove a payroll tax increase proposed by then-Subcommittee Chairman Pete Stark; needing his vote, Democrats dropped broad-based taxes and inserted a mix of smaller, health-related levies. He also got an agreement to lengthen the phase-in period for employer contributions to health insurance. On welfare, Levin stood between Democrats who opposed ending the welfare entitlement and Republicans who opposed health insurance and child care spending for former welfare beneficiaries. He did not support the first two welfare reform bills passed by Republicans, but he did work with them in July and August 1996 on the welfare reform bill which he voted for and which Bill Clinton, after much hesitation, signed in August 1996.

Levin emphasized that work in his campaign for reelection in 1996. The 1992 redistricting had removed much of metro Detroit's Jewish community from his district and added unfamiliar territory in Macomb County. Levin avoided primary opposition in 1992, but faced a serious challenge in the general from John Pappageorge, a retired Army colonel and M-1 tank executive who later was elected to the Oakland County Commission. Pappageorge attacked on health care, crime, welfare, and education; Levin campaigned in tandem with Bill Clinton. Levin spent \$1.18 million to his opponent's \$190,000, and won by just 53%–46%. Encouraged, Pappageorge tried again in 1994. This time Levin used his big financial edge (\$1.53 million to \$470,000) to tout his work obtaining local crime-fighting aid under the 1994 crime bill and on trade, and ignored Clinton. Levin won 52%–47%. In 1996 Pappageorge tried again, and again Levin had a huge financial edge: \$1.31 million to \$433,000. Pappageorge advertised on cable TV and hit Levin on taxes and partial-birth abortions. Levin, advertising on Detroit TV, stressed his work putting together the welfare reform act, and also called for stopping pension raids by companies, stopping crime, and making college tuition deductible. "I don't let partisan political games get in the way of sensible change. This past year I worked with Republicans and Democrats to significantly reform welfare to require all able-bodied individuals to work and place strict time limits on benefits. We also passed new laws to make it easier to keep health coverage for people who change jobs," his campaign literature said. He was endorsed by both the liberal *Detroit Free Press* and the conservative *Detroit News*. This above-politics appeal, plus Bill Clinton's greater strength locally, helped Levin win 57%–41%, his best showing in the current district. But with a significant Republican as well as Democratic base, this could still be a seriously contested district in the future.

The People: Pop. 1990: 580,987; 13% age 65+; 92% White; 4% Black; 2% Asian; 1% Hispanic origin. Households: 58% married couple families; 27% married couple fams. w. children; 48% college educ.; median household income: $38,760; per capita income: $16,796; median gross rent: $512; median house value: $75,300.

1996 Presidential Vote			1992 Presidential Vote		
Clinton (D)	128,820	(52%)	Clinton (D)	119,055	(42%)
Dole (R)	95,071	(38%)	Bush (R)	115,065	(40%)
Perot (I)	20,612	(8%)	Perot (I)	49,519	(17%)

Rep. Sander M. Levin (D)

Elected 1982; b. Sept. 6, 1931, Detroit; home, Royal Oak; U. of Chicago, B.A. 1952, Columbia U., M.A. 1954, Harvard, LL.B. 1957; Jewish; married (Victoria).

Career: Practicing atty., 1957–64, 1970–76; Oakland Bd. of Supervisors, 1961–64; MI Senate, 1965–70; Fellow, Harvard JFK Schl. of Govt., 1975; A.A., Agency for Intl. Devel., 1977–81.

DC Office: 2209 RHOB 20515, 202-225-4961; Fax: 202-226-1033; e-mail: slevin@hr.house.gov.

District Offices: Sterling Heights, 810-268-4444.

Committees: *Ways & Means* (6th of 16 D): Human Resources (RMM); Social Security.

Group Ratings

	ADA	ACLU	AFS	LCV	CFA	CON	NFIB	COC	ACU	NTLC	CHC
1996	85	69	100	85	92	84	19	19	0	5	7
1995	90	—	—	94	100	9	—	21	8	—	—

National Journal Ratings

	1995 LIB	—	1995 CONS	1996 LIB	—	1996 CONS
Economic	92%	—	6%	85%	—	11%
Social	80%	—	13%	79%	—	18%
Foreign	70%	—	28%	82%	—	16%

Key Votes of the 104th Congress

1. Reduce Medicare Growth $	N	5. Flag Amendment	N	9. Cuban Embargo	Y
2. Ovrd. Product Liab. Veto	N	6. Drop EPA Limits	Y	10. Bar Bosnia Troop $	N
3. Increase Min. Wage	Y	7. Repeal Assault-Weap. Ban	N	11. Cut Anti-Missile Defense	Y
4. Welfare Reform	N	8. Ovrd. Part. Birth Veto	N	12. Bar U.N. Uniforms	N

Election Results

1996 general	Sander M. Levin (D)	133,436	(57%)	($1,313,913)
	John Pappageorge (R)	94,235	(41%)	($432,894)
	Others	4,804	(2%)	
1996 primary	Sander M. Levin (D)	unopposed		
1994 general	Sander M. Levin (D)	103,508	(52%)	($1,536,445)
	John Pappageorge (R)	92,762	(47%)	($470,616)

THIRTEENTH DISTRICT

From Detroit's Metro Airport west to Ann Arbor runs what was once a key artery in the "arsenal of democracy." Now the I-94 expressway, it was built in 1942 so workers from Detroit could drive to the huge Willow Run bomber plant 30 miles west; later it was known by travelers for its pothole-pocked pavement and the giant Goodyear tire over the billboard with the digital counter showing the year's (American) car production. Today, it is still a key link between factories and suppliers, workers and workplaces, between the blue-collar neighborhoods of southwest Wayne County and Ann Arbor, home of the University of Michigan. But over the past two decades I-94 has seen a profound shift in Michigan's industrial economy: from an economy of many low-skill jobs assembling high-style but low-tech cars, to one with fewer but higher-skill jobs in higher-tech manufacturing, requiring precision work and computerized tools.

The 13th Congressional District of Michigan covers much of this unpicturesque landscape from the airport to Ann Arbor. A few of its suburbs are distinctly downscale, like Romulus, where poorer residents have worked a little at a time to build their own houses, on land so flat it oozes water after a rain. Others are proudly middle-income, like Westland, which was named after a shopping center, and Canton Township, which grew robustly in the 1980s; Plymouth and Northville just to the north are high-income and fast-growing. Southwest Wayne County has been Democratic since the UAW forced an unwilling Henry Ford to sign a collective bargaining contract in 1941, but as working-class wages went up and working-class consciousness declined it has become less so. In Washtenaw County the district's largest city, Ann Arbor, has a Republican history going back to its beginnings as a haven for German veterans of the failed revolutions of 1848, but undergraduates in the 1970s and graduate students in the 1980s swung it sharply to the left, making it one of the most dependably Democratic parts of Michigan. Ypsilanti, working class and home to Eastern Michigan University, is also Democratic. On balance the 13th leans Democratic but not overwhelmingly.

The congresswoman from the 13th District is Lynn Rivers, a Democrat first elected in 1994. Her story is an unusual one for an American politician. She was married and became a mother at 18; her husband is an auto worker and UAW member; she worked her way through school as her kids grew and got a bachelor's degree at University of Michigan in 1987 and a law degree in 1992. She entered politics as "a mom who got mad at the system" and was elected to the Ann Arbor school board in 1984. In 1992 she was elected to the state House. In 1994, 13th District incumbent William Ford decided to retire after 30 years in the House, and after winning by only 52%–43% over a serious Republican challenger in 1992. Rivers, with strong support from the leftist Democrats who dominate politics in Ann Arbor, easily won the Democratic primary. In the general election, with generous support from local and national unions as well as feminists, she outraised her Republican opponent, a Bush Administration appointee, and won 52%–45%.

In a House with 73 mostly conservative Republican freshmen, Rivers stood out. In Washington her voting record has been one of the most liberal in the House. She spoke out strongly against the partial birth abortion ban. She served on the Budget Committee and on the Science Committee, where she promised to expose "junk science" used to justify repeal of environmental protections. But she also worked with Republicans on some issues. With Ohio Republican Steve LaTourette she restored funding for the Great Lakes Environmental Research Laboratory in

Ann Arbor and supported more research in ridding the Great Lakes of the zebra mussel; she intervened to save the jobs of two chemists in another science center in Ann Arbor. She sought tougher gift bans, wanted to abolish many congressional perks, and sought to require members of Congress to pay out of their office allowance for special orders speeches—an odd position for one whose politics has long been associated with vigorous defense of free expression.

Rivers had a spirited challenge in 1996. Jim Fitzsimmons was a businessman who had turned around Ann Arbor-based University Microfilms Inc.; he also founded a Hands-on Children's Museum in Ann Arbor. He hoped to cut into Rivers's Ann Arbor base while carrying the often conservative-leaning Wayne County suburbs, and spent $1.22 million, including $566,000 of his own money, running ads calling for lower taxes and recounting his background. But Rivers raised $374,000 in PAC money and even more in individual contributions, again with help from feminist networks, and spent $1.1 million overall, running ads on her opposition to Republican policy, support of environmental protections and her personal background. Rivers won 57%–41%, carrying Ann Arbor and Washtenaw County by a resounding 65%–33% and running just barely ahead, 51%–47%, in Wayne County.

The People: Pop. 1990: 580,882; 7% rural; 9% age 65+; 84% White; 11% Black; 3% Asian; 2% Hispanic origin. Households: 53% married couple families; 26% married couple fams. w. children; 55% college educ.; median household income: $36,596; per capita income: $16,267; median gross rent: $519; median house value: $76,600.

1996 Presidential Vote

Clinton (D)	135,250	(58%)
Dole (R)	76,165	(33%)
Perot (I)	16,954	(7%)
Other	3,990	(2%)

1992 Presidential Vote

Clinton (D)	129,113	(49%)
Bush (R)	89,040	(34%)
Perot (I)	43,946	(17%)

Rep. Lynn N. Rivers (D)

Elected 1994; b. Dec. 19, 1956, Au Gres; home, Ann Arbor; U. of MI, B.A. 1987; Wayne St. U., J.D. 1992; Protestant; married (Joseph).

Career: Ann Arbor Schl. Bd., 1984–92; MI House of Reps., 1992–94.

DC Office: 1724 LHOB 20515, 202-225-6261; Fax: 202-225-3404; e-mail: lrivers@hr.house.gov.

District Offices: Ann Arbor, 313-741-4210; Wayne, 313-722-1411.

Committees: *Budget* (9th of 19 D). *Science* (11th of 21 D): Basic Research; Technology.

Group Ratings

	ADA	ACLU	AFS	LCV	CFA	CON	NFIB	COC	ACU	NTLC	CHC
1996	95	81	92	85	92	90	27	19	5	12	0
1995	95	—	—	94	100	16	—	25	16	—	—

National Journal Ratings

	1995 LIB		1995 CONS	1996 LIB		1996 CONS
Economic	76%	—	23%	85%	—	11%
Social	80%	—	13%	84%	—	12%
Foreign	79%	—	17%	82%	—	16%

Key Votes of the 104th Congress

1. Reduce Medicare Growth $	N	5. Flag Amendment	N	9. Cuban Embargo	N
2. Ovrd. Product Liab. Veto	N	6. Drop EPA Limits	Y	10. Bar Bosnia Troop $	Y
3. Increase Min. Wage	Y	7. Repeal Assault-Weap. Ban	N	11. Cut Anti-Missile Defense	Y
4. Welfare Reform	N	8. Ovrd. Part. Birth Veto	N	12. Bar U.N. Uniforms	Y

Election Results

1996 general	Lynn N. Rivers (D)	123,133	(57%)	($1,099,549)
	Joe Fitzsimmons (R)	89,907	(41%)	($1,223,433)
	Others	4,618	(2%)	
1996 primary	Lynn N. Rivers (D)	unopposed		
1994 general	Lynn N. Rivers (D)	89,573	(52%)	($610,394)
	John A. Schall (R)	77,908	(45%)	($348,322)
	Others	5,197	(3%)	

FOURTEENTH DISTRICT

Detroit's early auto factories—Packard, Hudson, Ford Highland Park, Dodge Main, Briggs, Ford Rouge, Cadillac, Kelsey-Hayes, Chrysler, Plymouth, DeSoto—were built between 1905 and 1925 in an arc about five miles from the city's center, in green fields at what was then the edge of urban development. Almost instantly the flat farmlands all around were platted in grid streets and filled with wooden bungalows and brick prairie-style houses, often with a driveway at the side and a single elm in front. Commercial strips lined the mile-square and radial main streets, stretching straight as far as the eye could see. Detroit was the nation's second fastest growing big city in those years, after Los Angeles, and like LA was built to automobile scale. Its neighborhoods filled up with factory workers and civil servants, professionals and maintenance men, corner store owners and management personnel, Catholics and Protestants and Jews: a middle-class melting pot. With one exception: Detroit in those days had few blacks, who did not begin their big migrations here from the South, especially Alabama, until around 1940, when defense plants began hiring in large numbers.

The history of black Detroit is one of conflict and uplift, inspiration and tragedy. The wartime mixture of Appalachian mountain whites and Deep South blacks proved volatile: there was a violent race riot in June 1943. During the war years, blacks were pent up in a few severely overcrowded neighborhoods like the Black Bottom, which is now the Chrysler Freeway. After 1945, when blacks began moving outward, real estate agents played on racial fears, and in the 1950s whole square miles of Detroit changed racial composition in just a few years. In the 1960s there was hope that the civil rights movement, encouraged by Walter Reuther's UAW, and antipoverty programs would improve blacks' lot, and in fact many black Detroiters found good jobs and made good incomes, bought their own homes and built community institutions. Then came the riot of July 1967, followed by extensive white flight and terrible increases in crime. Detroit's first black mayor, Coleman Young, elected in 1973, responded with policies that may have seemed appropriate in the 1960s but had disastrous results in the 1970s and 1980s: he pressured major employers like the Big Three auto companies to build facilities in Detroit, raised taxes to support a vast army of city employees, and attributed city problems to white racism. Violent crime became a part of everyday life and arson became common, especially on "devil's night" before Halloween, with never a criticism from the mayor—for, in his view, to criticize blacks who commit crimes would have been blaming the victim and playing into the hands of white racists.

Detroit took on a garrison atmosphere. Crime reduced the value of residential real estate to near zero, and the city's population dropped from 1.7 million in 1960 to an estimated 992,000 in 1994. Thousands of houses were abandoned to arsonists and drug dealers; in early 1993, the city's ombudsman proposed large stretches of property be purchased by the city, fenced off and abandoned. In political dialogue, most black politicians called for, and most black voters seemed to support, an ever-increasing public sector. Yet the existing public sector, which takes a larger share of residents' income than almost anywhere else in the country, serves citizens very poorly.

Turnaround has come agonizingly late in the 1990s, as Mayor Dennis Archer, elected in 1993, works to fight crime and encourage private-sector growth. Detroit made headlines when General Motors bought the Renaissance Center downtown for its headquarters. But more important is that crime rates are falling, housing values are rising, and commercial activity is picking up.

The 14th Congressional District of Michigan consists of the northern half of Detroit, including most neighborhoods just beyond the auto plants. It includes adjacent suburbs from high-income Grosse Pointe Woods and more modest Dearborn Heights to Highland Park, an enclave within the city, which had 52,000 people and fine city services in 1930 and 20,000 people and an essentially defunct government in 1990. There are some solid neighborhoods here, including high-income Palmer Woods and Sherwood Forest, and Rosedale Park. On many blocks homeowners bravely install the big front-lawn lights Detroit Edison sells and patrol their streets, trying to discourage thugs that have dominion over most blocks nearby. Too often those nearby blocks are pockmarked by burnt-out hulks and empty lots where houses used to be. Politically, this is one of the most Democratic areas in the nation, with many precincts turning in percentages between 90% and 98%.

The congressman from the 14th District is John Conyers, senior member (and one of the founders) of the Congressional Black Caucus, chairman of the Government Operations Committee for six years when Democrats controlled the House and now ranking Democrat on Judiciary. The son of a left-wing operative in the UAW, he grew up in Detroit, served in the Army in Korea, practiced law and worked as a staffer for a young congressman named John Dingell. Conyers was first elected to Congress in 1964—one of six blacks in the House at the time and the only one to take a militant approach to politics. He distanced himself from the Johnson Administration, criticizing the Vietnam war from the beginning and charging liberals were not doing enough for the poor. His response to the 1967 riot was to introduce the first bill for a guaranteed annual income. He supported reparations for the descendants of slaves. He stood by in disgust as his white Michigan Democratic colleagues opposed metropolitan school busing, and he has opposed most of the controversial parts of the crime bills of the 1970s, 1980s and 1990s, including the death penalty and abolishing the insanity defense after President Reagan was shot. He has one of the most liberal voting records in the House, calling for single-payer health plans and massive public works projects.

The 1994 election changed Conyers's standing in the House. With Chairman Jack Brooks' defeat, he was in line to be ranking Democrat on Judiciary; but he had to deflect a challenge from Patricia Schroeder. Conyers had criticized Attorney General Janet Reno's decision to storm the Branch Davidian compound in Waco and opposed the death penalty provisions of the 1994 crime bill, but he hailed the provisions calling for more cops on the beat. When the Clinton Administration proposed antiterrorism legislation after the Oklahoma City bombing, Conyers criticized Republicans for blocking wiretapping and explosive taggants provisions. He stressed his common stands with other Democrats on affirmative action, the assault weapons ban and intellectual property rights and, a bit defensively, called for reasonable tort reform and victims' rights legislation. He co-sponsored a bill prompted by a spate of racially motivated church burnings with Judiciary Chairman Henry Hyde in spring 1996. For 1997 his causes included a baseball antitrust bill, requiring states to criminalize sexual contact between prison guards and inmates, and banning "junk guns" (poorly made and cheap). Another cause is revision of the independent counsel statute he supported as recently as 1994, to curb what he considers abuses by Kenneth Starr. Some of these seem in tension if not conflict with many of his earlier stands, while others resemble the "little things" Clinton initiatives of 1996 and 1997.

For years Conyers coasted to reelection easily. But genuinely troubled by the decline of Detroit, he took grave political risks and ran for mayor in 1989 and 1993. The first race was against his old ally Coleman Young, but his campaign was glitch-ridden and light on specifics, and he finished a dismal third. In 1993, when Young retired, Conyers put his name on the ballot again, but did not run a serious campaign and got virtually no votes. In the 1994 House race he had two primary opponents, but won 51% of the votes to 28% for attorney Melvin Hollowell, a supporter of Mayor Dennis Archer, and 21% for city ombudsman Marie Farrell-Donaldson. In 1996 he was renominated and reelected easily.

The People: Pop. 1990: 580,977; 11% age 65+; 29% White; 69% Black; 1% Asian; 1% Hispanic origin. Households: 38% married couple families; 18% married couple fams. w. children; 40% college educ.; median household income: $25,079; per capita income: $11,462; median gross rent: $421; median house value: $29,400.

1996 Presidential Vote			1992 Presidential Vote		
Clinton (D)	160,009	(86%)	Clinton (D)	165,363	(79%)
Dole (R)	20,915	(11%)	Bush (R)	31,360	(15%)
Perot (I)	4,772	(3%)	Perot (I)	11,992	(6%)

Rep. John Conyers, Jr. (D)

Elected 1964; b. May 16, 1929, Detroit; home, Detroit; Wayne St. U., B.A. 1957, LL.B. 1958; Baptist; married (Monica).

Career: Army, 1950–54 (Korea); Legis. Asst., U.S. Rep. John Dingell, 1958–61; Practicing atty., 1959–61; Referee, MI Workmen's Compensation Dept., 1961–63.

DC Office: 2426 RHOB 20515, 202-225-5126; Fax: 202-225-0072; e-mail: jconyers@hr.house.gov.

District Offices: Detroit, 313-961-5670.

Committees: *Judiciary* (RMM of 15 D): Constitution; Courts & Intellectual Property.

Group Ratings

	ADA	ACLU	AFS	LCV	CFA	CON	NFIB	COC	ACU	NTLC	CHC
1996	90	100	100	85	77	21	11	13	0	5	0
1995	90	—	—	94	92	31	—	8	8	—	—

National Journal Ratings

	1995 LIB — 1995 CONS			1996 LIB — 1996 CONS		
Economic	94%	—	0%	89%	—	0%
Social	88%	—	0%	88%	—	0%
Foreign	93%	—	0%	90%	—	0%

Key Votes of the 104th Congress

1. Reduce Medicare Growth $	N	5. Flag Amendment	N	9. Cuban Embargo	N
2. Ovrd. Product Liab. Veto	N	6. Drop EPA Limits	*	10. Bar Bosnia Troop $	N
3. Increase Min. Wage	Y	7. Repeal Assault-Weap. Ban	N	11. Cut Anti-Missile Defense	Y
4. Welfare Reform	N	8. Ovrd. Part. Birth Veto	N	12. Bar U.N. Uniforms	N

Election Results

1996 general	John Conyers, Jr. (D)	157,722	(86%)	($267,039)
	William Ashe (R)	22,152	(12%)	
	Others	3,821	(2%)	
1996 primary	John Conyers, Jr. (D)	unopposed		
1994 general	John Conyers, Jr. (D)	128,463	(82%)	($575,696)
	Richard Charles Fournier (R)	26,215	(17%)	
	Others	2,953	(2%)	

FIFTEENTH DISTRICT

Few central cities in America have as vibrant a 20th Century history, and as sad a recent past, as Detroit. This was America's first automobile city, not just because it manufactured so many of the nation's cars but also because it was built to automobile scale. Detroit started the century as a second-rank city, no bigger than Milwaukee, with less than half a million people and extending no farther than four or five miles out from the site where the French built Fort Pontchartrain on the Detroit River in 1701. As the Motor City boomed, it grew outward along wide avenues and freeways; the auto companies put their factories and headquarters near the edge of urban settlement. As early as 1954, the nation's first big suburban shopping center, with parking for 10,000 cars, was drawing retail trade from downtown. Metro Detroit expanded to four million people, each generation moving out the roadways rapidly in many directions, leaving behind the previous generation's neighborhoods and civic institutions.

Today, that rapid movement has left large parts of Detroit literally empty. The central city, which had nearly 1.9 million people in 1950, was down to just over 1 million in 1990, and then only with the help of a city bureaucracy detailed to round up uncounted residents. It had the biggest rate of population loss of any 100,000-plus city in the 1980s except for Gary and Newark and was in the congressional district with the biggest population decline of the 1980s—23%; its estimated population in 1994 was 992,000. The reason is obvious: crime. Detroit has a murder rate drastically higher than in the suburbs, and over the years, whites and blacks who can afford to leave the city have done so. Downtown, the giant Hudson's department store is closed and several skyscrapers are all but empty, and while GM bought the 70-story Renaissance Center, it is inaccessible from the sidewalk (you can only get there by car). Vacant fields, where there were once five-story apartments or brick houses, are populated by pheasants.

Detroit's fate is all the more tragic because it comes in a city where liberal reformers hoped to create model anti-poverty and anti-discrimination programs. Instead, they seem to have undermined the sense of individual responsibility and confidence in the legitimacy of institutions. Metro area jobs rose from 1.5 million at the trough of the 1980s to 2.0 million: the problem is not so much a lack of jobs as the fact that too many people live by crime instead. Detroit's mayor for 20 years, Coleman Young, spent his energy on courting the Big Three, bulldozing the viable Poletown neighborhood for a new Cadillac plant. Meanwhile, high taxes and high crime—never denounced by Young—meant thousands of small-business jobs vanished. Dennis Archer, elected mayor in 1993, takes a more intelligent and judicious approach, and there are signs the city is turning around, with lower crime, more jobs, and a start at a growing private sector. But much of Detroit is still achingly vacant.

The 15th Congressional District of Michigan includes the southern half of Detroit, plus a few adjacent suburbs, from affluent Grosse Pointe Farms on Lake St. Clair to the Downriver town of Ecorse. The district also includes Hamtramck, America's fastest-growing city between 1910–20, the Polish-American enclave around the now demolished Dodge Main plant. The district is surely among the nation's top three or four in crime rate; median household income, at $15,264 in 1990, is lower than in all but three other districts nationwide. Politically, the 15th is overwhelmingly Democratic, but voter turnout is low—162,000 in 1996, compared with 276,000 in the high-income 11th District.

The congresswoman from the 15th District is Carolyn Cheeks Kilpatrick, a Democrat elected in 1996. She was raised in Detroit, became a teacher in Detroit public schools, and was elected to the state House in 1978. There she got a seat on the Appropriations Committee and worked on local projects, notably the highly successful River Place hotel and office complex in the old Stroh headquarters. She was a strong party loyalist, seeking the recall of Mayor Dennis Archer in March 1994 when he supported Governor John Engler's Proposition A to change school financing. Kilpatrick lost a race for the Detroit City Council, but won the 15th seat in the August 1996 Democratic primary against her one-time political ally, incumbent Barbara-Rose Collins, by a solid 51%–31% margin. Kilpatrick promises to work for a high-speed rail system and a new airport—rather distant goals in the Republican Congress one would think—and pledges, "I'm going to be working to build coalitions" with business, local government, churches, and community organizations.

Collins, an ally of Mayor Coleman Young, was one of the most flamboyant members of the House, a single mother elected to the legislature in 1974, the Detroit Council in 1981, and won the House seat with 34% in an eight-candidate primary in 1990. But, the Federal Elections Commission found reason to believe in June 1996, she violated campaign finance laws in 1990 by taking loan guarantees over the contribution limit. And (so said the Ethics Committee the day before her term expired in January 1997) there was good reason to assume she misused campaign, office, and scholarship funds for personal purposes or campaign work; the Justice Department was still investigating. Collins had the third-highest absentee rates in the House in 1995, missing one important vote, according to aides, because she refused to fly coach, and missing another while attending the opening of a casino in Indiana. In the weeks preceding her 1996 primary she scheduled a fundraiser at a bar featuring male and female strippers and was quoted in the *Detroit Free Press* as saying she had lots of white friends but "I hate the race." That quote, alas, was a misquote, apologized for after the primary: Collins was the victim of an injustice. But it also seems undeniable she was just not up to being a member of Congress.

The People: Pop. 1990: 580,933; 14% age 65+; 25% White; 70% Black; 1% Asian; 4% Hispanic origin. Households: 27% married couple families; 11% married couple fams. w. children; 33% college educ.; median household income: $15,264; per capita income: $9,650; median gross rent: $337; median house value: $22,900.

1996 Presidential Vote			1992 Presidential Vote		
Clinton (D)	146,357	(87%)	Clinton (D)	159,284	(82%)
Dole (R)	17,275	(10%)	Bush (R)	24,552	(13%)
Perot (I)	3,723	(2%)	Perot (I)	8,998	(5%)

Rep. Carolyn Cheeks Kilpatrick (D)

Elected 1996; b. June 25, 1945, Detroit; home, Detroit; Ferris St. U., 1968–70; W. MI U., B.S. 1972; U. of MI, M.S. 1977, African Methodist Episcopal; divorced.

Career: Teacher, Detroit public schls., 1970–78; MI House of Reps., 1978–96.

DC Office: 503 CHOB 20515, 202-225-2261; Fax: 202-225-5730.

District Offices: Detroit, 313-965-9003.

Committees: *Banking & Financial Services* (21st of 25 D): Financial Institutions & Consumer Credit; General Oversight & Investigations. *House Oversight* (3rd of 3 D). *Joint Committee on the Library of Congress* (4th of 5 Reps.).

Group Ratings and Key Votes: Newly Elected

Election Results

1996 general	Carolyn Cheeks Kilpatrick (D)	143,683	(88%)	($174,457)
	Stephen Hume (R)	16,009	(10%)	
	Others	2,908	(2%)	
1996 primary	Carolyn Cheeks Kilpatrick (D)	27,140	(52%)	
	Barbara Rose-Collins (D)	16,123	(31%)	
	Douglass Digg (D)	3,219	(6%)	
	George Hart (D)	2,440	(5%)	
	Others	3,681	(7%)	
1994 general	Barbara-Rose Collins (D)	119,442	(84%)	($177,120)
	John W. Savage II (R)	20,074	(14%)	
	Others	2,498	(2%)	

SIXTEENTH DISTRICT

One of America's great heavy-industry corridors is along the Detroit River, the choke point of the Great Lakes, in the Downriver communities below Detroit. Steel and chemical plants line the water, their dark and rusted hulks glaring across at Canada. A little ways up the sluggish Rouge River stands the giant Rouge complex, built by Henry Ford for $1 billion in the 1910s to take loads of iron ore, coal, limestone, and sand from Great Lake freighters and railroad cars and convert them into automobiles in 48 hours. This swampy, low-lying land, along the nation's most heavily trafficked waterway and within easy reach of the great East-West rail lines, was a natural place for industry in the early 20th Century. Around the older factories and well within range of their sulfurous odors, residential neighborhoods with neat, tightly packed houses were home to migrants who came for work—Polish, Hungarian, black, Italian, and more recently Mexican and Arab (the area has America's largest concentration of Arab-Americans). This industrial region has seen better times: many factories are dormant, and neighborhoods have been abandoned as the original migrants' children have moved outward. But there are also new factories, like Mazda's in Flat Rock, and smaller manufacturers are picking up the slack resulting from layoffs by corporate giants.

The 16th Congressional District of Michigan covers Dearborn and the Downriver communities, plus Monroe County directly to the south. The political tradition has been Democratic since the New Deal days, and while there is some cultural conservatism seen in top-of-the-ticket races, the basic preference remains much more Democratic here than in increasingly upscale Macomb County.

The congressman is John Dingell, the senior member of the House of Representatives. His father, John Dingell, Sr., was elected to the House in 1932, from a district created as a result of the Detroit area's auto boom. The first Congressman Dingell was one of the most productive urban liberals at that time, a sponsor of Social Security and, starting in 1943, of national health insurance. John Dingell, Jr., has been around Capitol Hill almost as long: he was a House page from 1938–43. After his father died, Dingell was elected to succeed him in December 1955, at 29, from a district with large Polish, black and Jewish populations. He had one serious fight, because of redistricting, in 1964, against a fellow Democrat who opposed the Civil Rights Act. But although most of the district was new to Dingell, he won, and has been reelected easily since. He has had an interesting personal life, raising his children after his divorce (his son Christopher was elected to the Michigan Senate in 1986) and marrying in 1981 a granddaughter of one of General Motors' Fisher brothers (his wife Debbie is active and popular in Washington and Michigan Democratic circles). He is now serving in his fifth decade in Congress—and his second term in the minority party.

Whatever else he does, Dingell will go down in history as one of the most powerful and effective committee chairmen ever. From 1981–95 he chaired the Energy and Commerce Committee (renamed Commerce) and its much-feared Investigations and Oversight Subcommittee. Dingell's committee, wrote *National Journal*'s Richard E. Cohen and Burt Solomon, "claims jurisdiction over anything that moves, burns or is sold"—clean air and securities markets, telecommunications and energy, railroads and toys, consumer protection and defense contracting. It handled up to 40% of all House bills, had the largest budget and staff of any House committee and for a decade was the House's most sought-after committee assignment. As institutions will, the committee took on the character of its leader: bright, pit-bull aggressive, domineering, determined. Commerce helped create many of the big stories in the 1980s: the indictment of Reagan White House aide Michael Deaver, the ousting of EPA Administrator Anne Burford, and the clamor over the Pentagon's $640 toilet seat and General Dynamics' bill to the government for dog kennel fees. Dingell and his committee superintended the breakup of AT&T and the sale of Conrail by public offering; studied insider trading, leveraged buyouts and hostile takeovers; and stimulated the growth of the generic drug industry and then swooped down to expose its misdeeds. After a decade of sparring with Health Subcommittee Chairman Henry Waxman over the clean air legislation, Dingell and Waxman worked together to produce the 1990 Clean Air Act. Commerce's cable regulation law of 1992 was the only bill on which Congress overrode George Bush's presidential veto. Dingell also worked to reduce trial lawyer leverage on product liability and to increase the Securities and Exchange Commission's oversight of bond sales. These were complex, heavily lobbied matters on which Dingell often had jurisdictional fights with Jack Brooks of Judiciary and Henry Gonzalez of Banking.

On other issues, Dingell backed organized labor's agenda against NAFTA and other trade agreements. A well-known sportsman, he long opposed gun control but voted for the 1994 crime bill and resigned from the National Rifle Association board. In many ways, he is an old-fashioned Franklin Roosevelt Democrat, supporting big government and strenuous regulation, taking a conservative line on some cultural issues and backing an assertive foreign policy: he was the only Michigan Democrat to vote for the Gulf War resolution.

With a Democratic administration in office, Dingell should have been at the peak of his power in the 103rd Congress, but the political forces that produced the Republican sweep of 1994 also frustrated him on legislation. For years he had introduced his father's national healthcare bill at the beginning of each session, and looked forward to passing some version of the Clinton healthcare plan. But for all his efforts he could not put together a majority on the committee for a bill with an employer mandate, and in June 1994 conceded that Commerce was hopelessly deadlocked on health care. The fact that Dingell couldn't break the deadlock is pretty good proof that nobody could have. Similarly, he was stymied in October 1994 when Superfund reform was killed under time pressure and House-passed telecommunications reform went down in the Senate.

Dingell was reelected in 1994 after spending $1,075,000 to his opponent's $8,000, but by a less-than-usual margin of 59%–40%; the 16th District voted for Republican Governor John Engler. Worse for Dingell was the new Republican majority. Republicans dismantled the Dingell staff and stripped Commerce of some of the jurisdiction Dingell had painstakingly amassed. But as the senior House member, he swore in new Speaker Newt Gingrich with good grace. Dingell took to his new place in the minority a remarkable good humor and sportsmanship and went after Republicans with unfeigned zest. He also did a lot of legislating, sometimes even in tandem with Republicans. He successfully opposed abolishing the Commerce Department and repeal of the Glass-Steagall Act separating commercial and investment banking. He worked with new Commerce Chairman Thomas Bliley to pass the Safe Drinking Water Act, and worked to keep out what he considered pork from Republicans on the Transportation and Infrastructure Committee; he worked out tough provisions on the pesticide regulation bill repealing the Delaney clause. With Bliley he opposed auctions of certain broadcast frequencies, and, dissatisfied with the way FCC Chairman Reed Hundt implemented the telecom act and provisions for local telephone competition in 1996, he proposed barring Hundt from official travel more than 50 miles outside Washington for two years. Unlike many Democrats, he supported the Republicans' wildlife refuge bill, a revision of an act he had pioneered many years before. Less successfully, he worked on Superfund revision, on which he remains skeptical of repealing retroactive liability, and he strove with Michigan Republican Fred Upton to open a central nuclear waste disposal site rather than let nuclear waste sit in storage near nuclear plants.

Dingell's bipartisan efforts did not prevent him from attacking Newt Gingrich with zest or from seeking to develop issues and inspire campaigns that would restore the Democratic majority. He proposed the healthcare portability preexisting conditions legislation that in somewhat different form was passed into law in August 1996. And he was among the first to propose the bill requiring 48-hour hospital stays for mothers of newborns. But even while he campaigned for other Democrats, Dingell had to campaign at home. Republicans recruited James DeSana, a former state legislator and mayor of Downriver Wyandotte. Dingell did not stint on fundraising, and spent $1.9 million to DeSana's $259,000. It paid off: Dingell improved on his 1994 showing and beat DeSana 62%–36%. Rumors in early 1997 were that Dingell would retire in 1998, and that he might want to pass his seat along to his son, state Senator Christopher Dingell. But Dingell snorts at such suggestions and continues to show great vitality and energy; no one should bet too heavily against him.

The People: Pop. 1990: 580,884; 13% rural; 13% age 65+; 95% White; 1% Black; 1% Asian; 2% Hispanic origin. Households: 60% married couple families; 28% married couple fams. w. children; 39% college educ.; median household income: $35,315; per capita income: $15,175; median gross rent: $456; median house value: $61,700.

1996 Presidential Vote

Clinton (D)	122,522	(54%)
Dole (R)	78,461	(34%)
Perot (I)	24,125	(11%)

1992 Presidential Vote

Clinton (D)	115,339	(43%)
Bush (R)	96,466	(36%)
Perot (I)	52,070	(20%)

Rep. John D. Dingell (D)

Elected Dec. 1955; b. July 8, 1926, Colorado Springs, CO; home, Dearborn; Georgetown U., B.S. 1949, J.D. 1952; Catholic; married (Deborah).

Career: Army, 1945–46 (WWII); Practicing atty., 1952–55; Wayne Cnty. Asst. Prosecuting Atty., 1953–55.

DC Office: 2328 RHOB 20515, 202-225-4071.

District Offices: Dearborn, 313-846-1276; Monroe, 313-243-1849.

Committees: *Commerce* (RMM of 23 D).

Group Ratings

	ADA	ACLU	AFS	LCV	CFA	CON	NFIB	COC	ACU	NTLC	CHC
1996	70	69	92	54	62	98	19	31	25	10	13
1995	90	—	—	81	100	37	—	17	8	—	—

National Journal Ratings

	1995 LIB — 1995 CONS			1996 LIB — 1996 CONS		
Economic	92%	—	6%	70%	—	28%
Social	78%	—	22%	66%	—	33%
Foreign	87%	—	12%	82%	—	16%

Key Votes of the 104th Congress

1. Reduce Medicare Growth $	N	5. Flag Amendment	N	9. Cuban Embargo	N
2. Ovrd. Product Liab. Veto	Y	6. Drop EPA Limits	Y	10. Bar Bosnia Troop $	N
3. Increase Min. Wage	Y	7. Repeal Assault-Weap. Ban	Y	11. Cut Anti-Missile Defense	Y
4. Welfare Reform	N	8. Ovrd. Part. Birth Veto	Y	12. Bar U.N. Uniforms	Y

Election Results

1996 general	John D. Dingell (D)	136,854	(62%)	($1,854,280)
	James DeSana (R)	78,723	(36%)	($259,035)
	Others	5,035	(2%)	
1996 primary	John D. Dingell (D)	unopposed		
1994 general	John D. Dingell (D)	105,849	(59%)	($1,075,063)
	Ken Larkin (R)	71,159	(40%)	($8,074)

MINNESOTA

Minnesota has long been a distinctive commonwealth, set far in America's frozen North, a state which in commerce, culture and politics has set one example after another for the rest of the nation. It is the node of transcontinental railroads that linked the winter wheat fields of the northern prairies to the greatest grain milling center in the world and the great Pacific ports of Puget Sound. It is also the birthplace of Scotch Tape, Betty Crocker and the Mall of America, the home base of chroniclers of small town America from Sinclair Lewis to Garrison Keillor. Politically, Minnesota over the last half century provided the nation with some of its most articulate and honorable leaders—Harold Stassen, Hubert Humphrey, Eugene McCarthy, Walter Mondale—and with traditions of probity, civic-mindedness and innovation which are second to none. Yet while commercially and culturally Minnesota has never been stronger, politically it has seen some hard times. Its recent electoral history has been one antic episode after another. Its two political parties, with their distinctive names—Democratic-Farmer-Labor and (until recently) Independent Republican—have been dominated by activists of left and right stubbornly out of touch with ordinary voters. Minnesota's two senators come from the extreme wings of their respective parties, former Carleton College political science professor Paul Wellstone on the Democratic-Farmer-Labor left and former KMSP-TV news anchor Rod Grams on the Independent-Republican right. Its primacy as a national policy-setter seems stuck in the past. But maybe these are signs of success, an indication that Minnesota and the nation are so secure that they no longer need the intense, impassioned, intellectually serious tutelage that Minnesota used to provide.

Minnesota's distinctive traditions come from a distinctive history. The far northern states were ignored by most Yankee immigrants, who headed straight west into Iowa, Nebraska and Kansas. But others saw opportunity in Minnesota's icy lakes and ferocious winters. James J. Hill, the builder of the Great Northern Railroad ("You can't interest me in any proposition in any place where it doesn't snow."), and others operating out of Minneapolis and St. Paul—already twin cities by 1860—worked to attract Norwegian, Swedish and German migrants who would find the terrain and climate congenial. By 1890, the Twin Cities—rivals that year in a Census competition—were the nerve center of a sprawling and rich agricultural empire stretching west from Minnesota through the Dakotas and eventually into Montana and beyond. Minneapolis and St. Paul became the termini of its rail lines and the site of its grain-milling companies.

The twin cities also became the center of a three-party politics and an economic radicalism reminiscent of the politics of Scandinavia. For our American regions seem a mirror image of the geography of Europe, with the East Coast resembling the British Isles and France, the industrial Midwest reminiscent of Germany and Poland, the relatively poor and always hawkish South a Baptist Mediterranean, and the Upper Midwest of Minnesota, Wisconsin and North Dakota as North American versions of Scandinavia. Like Scandinavia, these Upper Midwestern commonwealths pioneered their continent's welfare states, with an effect on public policy far out of proportion to their numbers. Alarmed by the unprecedented concentration of economic power and wealth into the hands of just a few identifiable millionaires who lived on St. Paul's Summit Avenue or the hill above Minneapolis's Hennepin Avenue, the immigrants drew on their native traditions of cooperative activity and bureaucratic socialism.

As in Wisconsin and North Dakota, a strong third party developed here in the years after the Populist era. This Farmer-Labor Party elected senators in the 1920s and dominated state politics in the 1930s. Hurt by their ties to Communists, the Farmer-Laborites were beaten by Harold Stassen's Republicans in 1938. But this was still a New Deal state and by 1944 the bedraggled local Democrats were merged with the anti-Communist faction of Farmer-Laborites to form the Democratic-Farmer-Labor Party. A key role was played by Hubert Humphrey—mayor of Minneapolis in 1945, and the dazzling advocate of the civil rights plank at the 1948 Democratic National Convention. Humphrey's DFL—clean, idealistic, closely tied to labor, backed by many farmers—attracted dozens of talented politicians, including Eugene McCarthy, Orville Freeman and Walter Mondale. In 1948, Humphrey's speech helped put the Democrats on record for civil rights, and he was elected to the Senate at age 37.

In the years following, the DFL dominated Minnesota politics, while a series of progressive companies led the development of a strong, diversified economy. The DFL stood for a generous, compassionate federal government, for strong labor unions and high wages, for an expansionist fiscal policy to encourage consumer-led economic growth, for civil rights, and for an anti-Communist but not bombastic foreign policy. Its base was among blue-collar workers in the Twin Cities, in Duluth and the Iron Range, and among farmers of Scandinavian origin. Minnesota's business leaders were conservative politically and innovation-minded in their work: 3M has been generating new products—more than 60,000 by 1995—since the abrasive material it was founded to sell proved a loser in 1903 (30% of 3M's sales is generated by products introduced after 1990). Control Data was an early high-tech pioneer; IDS was one of the first mass-marketers of mutual funds; the Dayton family retail empire helped invent the indoor shopping mall and the national bookstore chain. Both the political and the business innovators built on a high-skill work force and a squeaky-clean ethic of honesty and integrity, low levels of crime and aberrant behavior—children bearing children, substance abuse—with high wage levels and a high percentage of women working outside the home. Over several decades, Minnesota has grown robustly in prosperous years and has not fallen much behind during recessions.

On this solid economic base Minnesota has innovated in public policy, in the 1980s extending the scope of government, by the middle 1990s sometimes cutting it back. It produced the nation's first anti-smoking bill, one of the first public campaign financing schemes and the nation's first statewide educational choice plan and authorized charter schools. It was one of the first states to establish HMOs and boasts of its MinnesotaCare plan intended to hold down costs and provide healthcare coverage for the poor. It has tried industrial policy, pledging $840 million in credit and loan guarantees to Northwest Airlines in 1991, which in turn kept its Twin Cities hub and built a repair facility in the Iron Range. In 1995 it passed welfare reform, emphasizing work and providing child care. Most of these reforms were the product of DFL

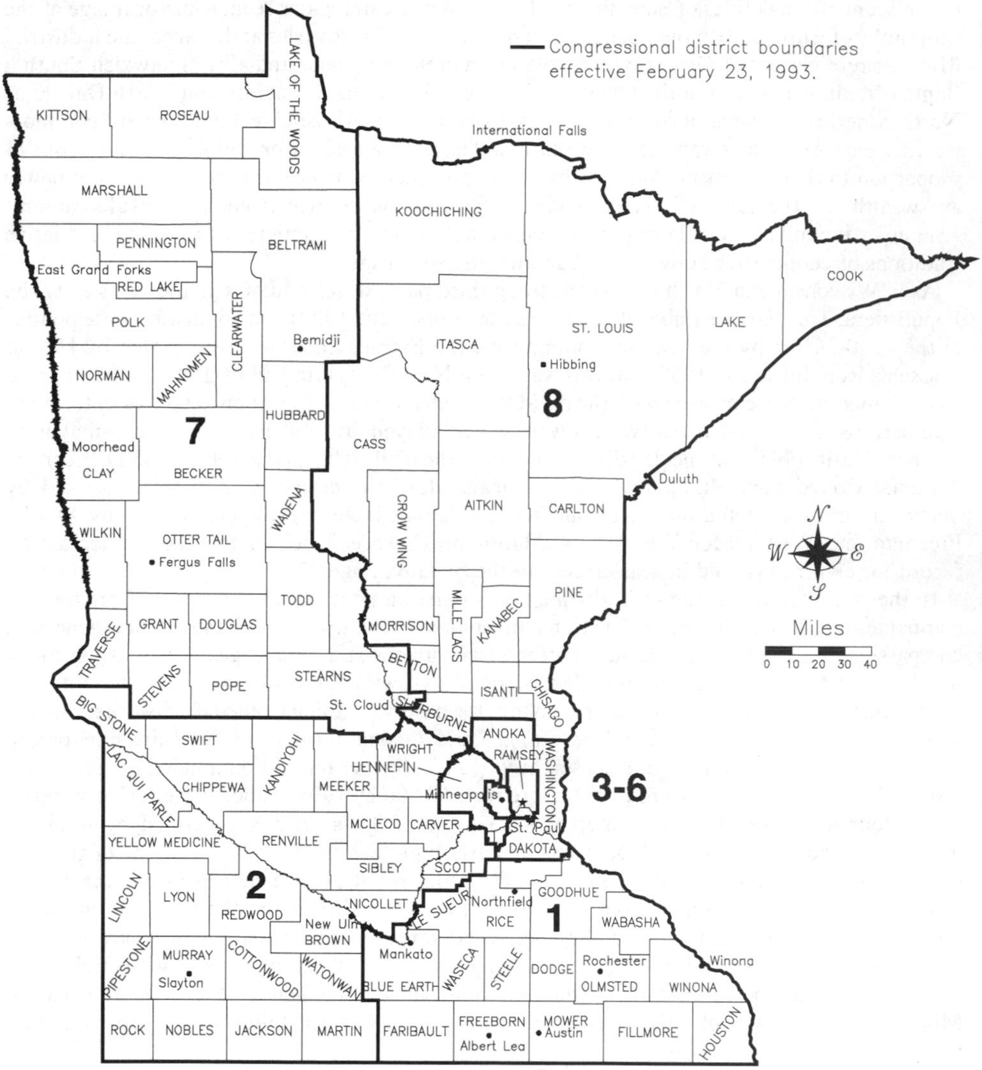

Congressional district boundaries
effective February 23, 1993.
KITTSON
ROSEAU
LAKE OF THE WOODS
International Falls
MARSHALL
KOOCHICHING
PENNINGTON
BELTRAMI
East Grand Forks
RED LAKE
COOK
POLK
CLEARWATER
ST. LOUIS
LAKE
Bemidji
ITASCA
Hibbing
NORMAN
MAHNOMEN
8
HUBBARD
7
CASS
Moorhead
CLAY
BECKER
Duluth
WADENA
CROW WING
AITKIN
CARLTON
WILKIN
OTTER TAIL
Fergus Falls
N
W
E
S
TODD
MILLE LACS
PINE
KANABEC
GRANT
DOUGLAS
MORRISON
Miles
TRAVERSE
BENTON
0 10 20 30 40
STEVENS
POPE
STEARNS
ISANTI
CHISAGO
BIG STONE
St. Cloud
SHERBURNE
SWIFT
ANOKA
KANDIYOHI
WRIGHT
RAMSEY
LAC QUI PARLE
HENNEPIN
WASHINGTON
CHIPPEWA
MEEKER
Minneapolis
3-6
MCLEOD
CARVER
St. Paul
YELLOW MEDICINE
RENVILLE
DAKOTA
SIBLEY
SCOTT
LINCOLN
LYON
2
NICOLLET
Northfield
GOODHUE
LE SUEUR
REDWOOD
New Ulm
RICE
1
WABASHA
BROWN
PIPESTONE
MURRAY
COTTONWOOD
Mankato
Rochester
Winona
Slayton
WATONWAN
WASECA
STEELE
DODGE
OLMSTED
WINONA
BLUE EARTH
ROCK
NOBLES
JACKSON
MARTIN
FARIBAULT
FREEBORN
Albert Lea
MOWER
Austin
FILLMORE
HOUSTON

legislatures and governors who were not liberal Democrats, such as DFLer Rudy Perpich, elected in 1982 and 1986. Their dominance even in this liberal state is an example of the declining appeal of economic redistributionist politics in a robust post-industrial economy. Workers and even (the much less numerous) farmers no longer feel at the mercy of a few big milling firms and railroads, young people starting out have many more career choices, and consumers have a much wider range of brand and product choices than they did 50 years ago. The need for New Deal-style intervention and regulation is less.

Not very effective, but definitely very noisy, are the activists who dominate both Minnesota parties' caucuses and nominating conventions. The early DFLers were proud of this system, which allowed plenty of political participation and ended control by party bosses. But in time the conventions came to be dominated not by laborite Humphrey followers or the wives of management Republicans, but by left-wingers and counterculturites and right-wing abortion opponents and religious hardliners. Much press attention was focused in 1994 on the supposedly fatal capture of the Republican Party by the religious right. But religious conservatives had dominated the convention process for some time, and in any case the convention's gubernatorial nominee was beaten easily by incumbent Arne Carlson in the primary. In 1995 the party convention decided to drop Independent from the party label saying, "Minnesota Republicans need to make a statement that . . . we are unabashedly and unambiguously part of the Republican revolution in the United States of America." The label had been adopted in 1975 in an effort to draw independent voters to the ranks following Watergate.

The party that has really been hurt by its extremists has been the DFL, who in 1994 nominated two idealistic but impractical liberals from leftish Twin Cities neighborhoods. As the DFL Chairman Mark Andrew said of them in 1995, "These people tend to be very, very liberal. The more outrageous the subcaucus, the more viable they become." The DFL nominee for governor, John Marty, called for higher taxes. "If that's not an example of a deaf ear, I don't know what is," said political scientist Steven Schier. Marty lost to Carlson 62%–33%. Senate nominee Ann Wynia, in a state where exit polls showed Bill Clinton's job rating higher than anywhere else but Massachusetts and Arkansas, managed to lose the Senate race to conservative Congressman Rod Grams, 49%–44%. The vote split according to opinion on abortion, opposition to which is not an anathema in this heartland state as it is said to be on the East and West Coasts. The left's major success has been the election of liberal Senator Paul Wellstone in 1990 and 1996. But he won with just 50% both times: neither of Minnesota's wings has shown itself able to win more than a bare majority.

Governor. Arne Carlson, elected governor twice without the support of a nominating convention and with the help of bizarre opposition, the son of Swedish immigrants, oddly enough grew up in New York. Some 30 years ago he was on the Minneapolis City Council; he spent eight years in the state legislature and 12 as elected state auditor until he ran for governor in 1990. He bypassed the convention, lost the September primary 49%–32%; then the nominee, John Grunseth, was charged with sexual improprieties and dropped out, and Carlson was named in his place. With just two weeks to go, Carlson scrambled to a 51%–47% victory over three-term DFL incumbent Rudy Perpich, carrying the Twin Cities metro area while losing the rest of the state. In his first term, he seemed to make a liberal record, signing MinnesotaCare, wetlands preservation and gay rights legislation. He succeeded in keeping the Minnesota Timberwolves basketball team in Minnesota by buying the Target Center arena for $55 million. But even then he was striving to cut taxes and control costs.

In 1994, Carlson was opposed by former legislator Allen Quist who was endorsed by the IR Party Convention. But Quist was twitted in the media for his ultra-conservative stands (men were "genetically predisposed" to head households), and Carlson won the primary 67%–33% In the general Carlson faced ultra-liberal state Senator John Marty, whose proposed tax hikes and big new spending programs, eased Carlson to another term with 62%–33%. Carlson seemed more conservative in his second term, with workmen's comp reform and a welfare reform package emphasizing return to the workforce and providing child care, and a veto of a temporary program which gave money for one month to able-bodied adults without children. He was proud of laws encouraging use of computers in schools. By November 1996 he was rebating income taxes and proposing more tax cuts and an education tax credit for tutoring, summer school, alternative learning or private school tuition.

Carlson has announced he will not run in 1998, and there will surely be a battle royal for the governorship. Lieutenant Governor Joanne Benson may run, and if so will likely face primary opposition from a more conservative candidate endorsed by the party convention, perhaps Allen Quist, the choice of strong conservatives who dominated the 1994 convention. The Democratic possibilities include "my three sons," the sons of three Democratic leaders of the 1950s and 1960s: Attorney General Skip Humphrey, Hennepin County Attorney Mike Freeman and state Senator Ted Mondale, a New Democrat who angered labor with some votes in the legislature. "My major interest is growing the economy," Mondale said. "If you don't care about economic opportunity, what do you care about?" Another possibility, and a favorite of party liberals, is Mark Dayton, the department store heir who ran for the Senate in 1982 and was finance chairman for Paul Wellstone in 1996; he has limited the amount of his own money he will spend. A wild card: St. Paul Mayor Norm Coleman, who switched to the Republican Party in 1996. Republicans have a chance to take over the closely divided (70–64) state House, but Democrats are far ahead in the Senate.

Senior Senator. Paul Wellstone is a happy warrior of the campus left, "the first 1960s radical elected to the U.S. Senate," in *Mother Jones*'s words. Wellstone grew up in northern Virginia, the son of Russian immigrants, more interested in wrestling than politics. He married young, quickly earned a Ph.D. at North Carolina, then went to teach at Carleton College in Minnesota in 1969. He was a "rock-the-boat professor" at Carleton, where he published little, taught the politics of protest. He made a name for himself in local politics by leading protesters in sympathy with Hormel meatpacker strikers in Austin and getting arrested while picketing a bank that had foreclosed on local farmers; he ran for state Auditor and co-chaired Jesse Jackson's 1988 presidential campaign in Minnesota.

Then in 1990 he ran for the Senate seat held by Republican Rudy Boschwitz. In the primary he beat Agriculture Commissioner Jim Nichols, populist on economics but anti-abortion, 60%–34%. For the general, he traveled around the state in a green bus and ran shrewd and humorous TV ads proclaiming that viewers wouldn't be seeing him as often as they saw Boschwitz (because he didn't accept PAC money) and made cute appeals ("I'm better looking"). In a takeoff on the film *Roger and Me*, one ad showed Wellstone in pursuit of a confrontation-shy Boschwitz; like the film, this was not entirely honest, since Boschwitz had agreed to a debate. But the ad's cleverness and the candidate's charm created an almost cuddly impression, while Boschwitz responded hamhandedly, needlessly involving himself in controversy over the Republican gubernatorial nominee, switching his stand on the voting rights renewal, sending out a letter to a Jewish mailing list suggesting that in this first Senate race between two Jewish candidates Boschwitz was the better Jew because Wellstone took no part in Jewish affairs and had not raised his children as Jews. Wellstone won 50%–48%, carrying metro Twin Cities 54%–45% while losing outstate Minnesota 51%–47%.

Wellstone has one of the most liberal voting records in Congress. "I still believe that government can be a force for good in people's lives. That won't change." At first he seemed awkward in the Senate, demanding roll call votes on all appropriations. But in time he learned to use Senate rules to achieve results. He successfully led opposition to the 1991 energy bill that would have opened the Arctic National Wildlife Refuge to oil drilling. He worked hard for years on lobbying reform and the gift ban, then finally got a vote on them in 1996 by threatening to attach the issue to telecommunications reform. He opposed U.S. military action in the Gulf war and, showing consistency, he criticized President Clinton for sending troops to Haiti without the consent of Congress. He had his lost causes—transferring defense money to job training, Canadian-style single-payer health insurance. But he also had considerable success. He and Pete Domenici pushed successfully in 1996 for mental health coverage in health insurance. And in

March 1996 he seized an opportune parliamentary moment to force a vote on a minimum wage increase—a measure that would have little effect in a prosperous economy but one which split the Republicans and hurt their morale.

Going into the 1996 campaign, Wellstone was not running much better than Boschwitz, who seemed interested in revenge and won the Republican primary easily. The National Republican Senatorial Committee ran ads calling Wellstone "embarrassingly liberal and decades out of touch." They called him "Senator Welfare" for his vote against the 1996 Welfare Reform Act and said he was a "1967 liberal" who wanted to "spend more." But the ads lacked the 1990 Wellstone ads' charm and Wellstone responded exuberantly, invoking Minnesota DFL tradition: "I am a Hubert Humphrey senator. I go to the floor of the Senate and I fight for children, I fight for senior citizens, I fight for health care. I'm a Minnesota senator!" Unlike 1990, he did not limit himself to $100 contributions, but proved himself a master of the current campaign finance system even as he denounced it, raising and spending $7.4 million, far more than Boschwitz's $4.3 million, ($1 million of which came from Boschwitz's own pocket). He attacked Boschwitz on the minimum wage and family and medical leave; he said the tobacco companies, pharmaceuticals and insurance companies already had good enough representation in Washington. "My job is to stand up for working families in Minnesota, and that's what I do." His welfare vote proved not to be disabling; he had more flak from his own supporters for voting for the Defense of Marriage Act. Boschwitz, evidently in desperation, ran ads citing issues on which he agreed with Bill Clinton, who was cruising to an easy victory in Minnesota; on the day before the election, without evidence Boschwitz accused Wellstone of burning an American flag in the 1960s. Wellstone won 50%–41%, carrying the Twin Cities heavily, 52%–39%, and running a bit ahead in the rest of the state, 49%–45%. Reform Party candidate Dean Barkley, a pro-choice lawyer who backs tough campaign reform and a flat tax, took 7%.

He has said that he is limiting himself to two terms.

Junior Senator. On the other side of the chamber, ideologically as well as on the seating chart, is Senator Rod Grams, elected in 1994. Grams grew up on a dairy farm 50 miles north of the Twin Cities, married early and went into broadcasting, working his way up as a TV reporter through small markets in Great Falls, Montana, Wausau, Wisconsin, and Rockford, Illinois to become an anchor on Channel 9 in Minneapolis-St. Paul in 1982. In 1985 he started a home building and land development business. Unlike most reporters, he was solidly conservative, a fervent opponent of abortion, an angry critic of government regulation, staunchly against higher taxes. "Families are under attack from all angles—the media, in schools and from all levels of government," he said. In 1991, Grams left his broadcast job and ran for Congress in the 6th District in the northern suburbs. The incumbent, Democrat Gerry Sikorski, had 697 overdrafts on the House bank and had just shifted from pro-life to pro-choice; an Independent calling for a national sales tax was also running. Grams was elected by 44%–33%–16%. In the House he pushed for the $500-per-child tax credit that became part of the Contract With America; he backed term limits and proposed sunset amendments to dozens of laws.

In 1993 a redistricting change made the 6th District more Democratic, and Grams decided to run for the Senate. The seat was being vacated by David Durenberger, a moderate Republican who was denounced by the Senate for ethics violations. Grams won a robust, multi-ballot fight at the Republican convention for the party endorsement. He was challenged in the primary by pro-choice Lieutenant Governor Joanell Dyrstad, who compared him to Ted Baxter, the mindless anchor on *The Mary Tyler Moore Show*, but the same voters who chose Governor Arne Carlson 2–1 over anti-abortion Allen Quist gave the anti-abortion Grams a 58%–35% victory. DFL leaders and activists were committed to running a woman, and their convention endorsed Ann Wynia, a serious-minded St. Paul liberal, teacher at a community college and longtime state representative from 1976–90. In the DFL primary she beat Ramsey County Attorney Tom Foley, local head of the moderate Democratic Leadership Council, by 62%–33%.

The general election was a battle of extremes. Grams was folksy, Wynia serious. Grams attacked her for voting 300 times for tax increases; she attacked him for opposing the Brady bill, family leave and single-payer healthcare reform. She also ran ads hitting Grams for not paying property taxes and not paying debts from his homebuilding business. He replied that he had not sought bankruptcy and had worked years to pay off $300,000 in debts; and it turned out that she also was late paying property taxes, which became the focus of Grams ads at the close of the campaign. Wynia was embarrassed at a press conference with retiring Congressman Tim Penny, when she admitted she would not have backed the Penny-Kasich budget cuts; Grams brandished a note from Penny thanking him for his vote and saying, "We did Minnesota proud!" At the beginning of the cycle this was the Republican seat Democrats targeted as the most likely pickup. But Wynia's liberalism was more of a handicap than Grams's conservatism. Wynia carried the Twin Cities area by only 46.4%–45.5%, while Grams carried the rest of the state 53%–42%, winning all but seven counties there, and won 49%–44%.

In the Senate Grams has had a solidly conservative voting record. Among the causes he has staked out is abolishing the Department of Energy, which he argues is simply a "patchwork quilt" of unrelated agencies, and has produced little worthwhile research. He has been a strong backer of the nuclear energy industry, demanding that the Energy Department find a waste disposal site by 1998; Minneapolis based Northern States Power Company is one of 80 plants in 41 states that is in need of permanent nuclear waste disposal. He has tried to cut funds to the Appalachian Regional Commission, without success. He has been the most prominent critic of the decision to close off Pennsylvania Avenue in front of the White House, and got a unanimous resolution to call for a plan to reopen the Avenue. He has questioned the intrusive security measures in federal buildings. "Where does it end? How much of Washington, D.C., are we going to have to rope off before the public figures out we simply do not want them there? As tragic as it sounds, that is the message we are sending to America." On the Foreign Relations Committee he opposed the Chemical Weapons Convention and with Connie Mack sponsored an amendment to require the Agency for International Development to report on the degree of economic freedom in the countries that receive its aid. He got a provision in the Safe Drinking Water Act to give states flexibility in regulating the amount of sulfates in community water systems and sponsored a bill for expedited EPA approval of products like disinfectants, bleaches and sanitizers. He sponsored an amendment for a taxpayer "lockbox" to devote budget savings to reducing the deficit and a bill to keep youthful troublemakers out of housing projects for the elderly.

Grams's conservative record, and the fact that he has never won 50% of the vote, leaves DFLers eager to run for his seat when it comes up in 2000; one possibility is Bill Luther, who succeeded him in the 6th District. But Grams seems no more deterred than Paul Wellstone by the opposition, and he has surprised his detractors before.

Presidential politics. Minnesota has the longest consecutive string going of voting Democratic for president of any state: the last time it voted Republican was in 1972, and even then it gave Richard Nixon his lowest percentage margin over George McGovern. So it is scarcely surprising that it gave large margins to Bill Clinton, 44%–32% in 1992 and 51%–35% in 1996. But Clinton's percentages were not especially high. Minnesota voted 24% for Ross Perot in 1992, 12% in 1996, among his best showings in the country: if voters here are by no means Republicans in presidential contests, they seem to have some qualms about Democrats.

Minnesota has a tradition of selecting national convention delegates in caucuses. In the March 1996 caucuses, Bob Dole won 41%; Buchanan finished second with 33%. It has sometimes run non-binding primaries as well, though not in 1996. When they were held, as in 1992, they were mostly ignored.

Congressional districting. Minnesota redistricted twice in the 1990s. A federal court set the lines for 1992; in 1993 the Supreme Court ruled that it should have deferred to a state court, whose plan was put into effect. That made for significant differences in the Twin Cities suburban 3d and 6th Districts, making the 3d even more heavily Republican and tilting the 6th toward the DFL; and in 1994 the DFL's Bill Luther captured the 6th which had been represented by Republican Rod Grams.

The People: Est. Pop. 1996: 4,658,000; Pop. 1990: 4,376,000, up 6.4% 1990–1996. 1.8% of U.S. total, 20th largest; 30% rural. Median age: 34.6 years. 12% 65 years and over. 93.7% White, 2.1% Black, 1.7% Asian, 1.1% Amer. Indian, 1.2% Hispanic origin. Households: 57.2% married couple families; 29% married couple fams. w. children; 49% college educ.; median household income: $30,909; per capita income: $14,389; 71.8% owner occupied housing; median house value: $74,000; median monthly rent: $384. 4.0% Unemployment. 1996 Voting age pop.: 3,422,000. 1996 Turnout: 2,192,640; 64% of VAP. Registered voters (1996): 2,730,505; no party registration.

Political Lineup: Governor, Arne H. Carlson (R); Lt. Gov., Joanne Benson (R); Secy. of State, Joan Anderson Growe (DFL); Atty. Gen., Hubert H. Humphrey, III (DFL); Treasurer, Michael McGrath (DFL); Auditor, Judith Dutcher (R). State Senate, 67 (42 DFL, 24 IR and 1 I); Senate President, Allan Spear (DFL); State House, 134 (70 DFL and 64 IR) House Speaker, Phil Carruthers (DFL). Senators, Paul D. Wellstone (DFL) and Rod Grams (R). Representatives, 8 (6 DFL and 2 IR).

Elections Division: 612-215-1440; **Filing Deadline for U.S. Congress:** July 21, 1998.

1996 Presidential Vote

Clinton (D)	1,120,279	(51%)
Dole (R)	766,476	(35%)
Perot (I)	257,704	(12%)
Other	48,425	(2%)

1992 Presidential Vote

Clinton (D)	1,020,997	(44%)
Bush (R)	747,841	(32%)
Perot (I)	562,506	(24%)

GOVERNOR

Gov. Arne H. Carlson (R)

Elected 1990, term expires Jan. 1999; b. Sept. 24, 1934, New York, NY; home, St. Paul; Williams Col., B.A. 1957, U. of MN; Protestant; married (Susan).

Career: Control Data Corp., 1962–64; Minneapolis City Cncl., Majority Ldr., 1965–67; MN House of Reps., 1970–78; MN St. Auditor, 1978–90.

Office: 130 State Capitol Bldg., Aurora Ave., St. Paul 55155, 612-296-3391; Fax: 612-296-2089; Web site: www.state.mn.us/mainmenu.html.

Election Results

1994 gen.	Arne H. Carlson (IR)	1,094,165	(62%)
	John Marty (DFL)	589,344	(33%)
	Others	82,081	(5%)
1994 prim.	Arne H. Carlson (IR)	321,084	(67%)
	Allen Quist (IR)	161,670	(33%)
1990 gen.	Arne H. Carlson (IR)	895,988	(51%)
	Rudy Perpich (DFL)	836,218	(47%)
	Others	45,016	(2%)

SENATORS

Sen. Paul D. Wellstone (DFL)

Elected 1990, seat up 2002; b. July 21, 1944, Washington, D.C.; home, St. Paul; U. of NC, B.A. 1965, Ph.D. 1969; Jewish; married (Sheila).

Career: Prof., Carleton Col., 1969–90.

DC Office: 136 HSOB 20510, 202-224-5641; Fax: 202-224-8438; e-mail: senator@wellstone.senate.gov.

State Offices: St. Paul, 612-645-0323; Virginia, 218-741-1074; Wilmar, 320-231-0001.

Committees: *Foreign Relations* (8th of 8 D): European Affairs; International Economic Policy, Export & Trade Promotion; Near Eastern & South Asian Affairs. *Labor & Human Resources* (6th of 8 D): Children & Families; Employment & Training (RMM). *Veterans' Affairs* (4th of 5 D). *Indian Affairs* (5th of 6 D). *Small Business* (6th of 8 D).

Group Ratings

	ADA	ACLU	AFS	LCV	CFA	CON	NFIB	COC	ACU	NTLC	CHC
1996	95	56	100	85	79	7	34	31	5	14	0
1995	100	—	100	100	94	8	—	32	4	—	—

National Journal Ratings

	1995 LIB — 1995 CONS	1996 LIB — 1996 CONS
Economic	80% — 17%	89% — 5%
Social	93% — 0%	80% — 8%
Foreign	86% — 7%	89% — 7%

Key Votes of the 104th Congress

1. Reduce Medicare Growth $	N	5. Flag Amendment	N	9. Anti-Missile Defense	N
2. Lmt. Prod. Liab. Damages	N	6. Endangered Species	Y	10. Cuban Embargo	N
3. Increase Min. Wage	Y	7. Gay Employment Rights	Y	11. Bar Bosnia Troop $	N
4. Welfare Reform	N	8. Ovrd. Part. Birth Veto	N	12. Cut Vietnam Aid	Y

Election Results

1996 general	Paul D. Wellstone (DFL)	1,098,493	(50%)	($7,459,878)
	Rudy Boschwitz (R)	901,282	(41%)	($4,385,982)
	Dean Barkley (Reform)	152,333	(7%)	($37,240)
1996 primary	Paul D. Wellstone (DFL)	194,699	(86%)	
	Dick Franson (DFL)	16,465	(7%)	
	Ed Hansen (DFL)	9,990	(4%)	
	Others	4,180	(2%)	
1990 general	Paul D. Wellstone (DFL)	911,999	(50%)	($1,338,708)
	Rudy Boschwitz (IR)	864,375	(48%)	($6,221,133)
	Other	29,820	(2%)	

Sen. Rod Grams (R)

Elected 1994, seat up 2000; b. Feb. 4, 1948, Princeton; home, Ramsey; Brown Inst., 1966–68, Anoka-Ramsey Jr. Col., 1970–72, Carroll Col., 1974–75; Lutheran; divorced.

Career: Engineering consultant, 1966–68, 1970–73; News Anchor: KFBB-TV, Great Falls, MT, 1976–78; WSAU-TV, Wausau, WI, 1978–81; WIFR-TV, Rockford, IL, 1981–83; Sr. News Anchor, KMSP-TV, Minneapolis, 1982–91; Pres. & CEO, Sun Ridge Builders, 1985–present; U.S. House of Reps., 1992–94.

DC Office: 261 DSOB 20510, 202-224-3244; Fax: 202-228-0956; e-mail: mail_grams@grams.senate.gov.

State Offices: Anoka, 612-427-5921.

Committees: *Banking, Housing & Urban Affairs* (7th of 10 R): Financial Institutions & Regulatory Relief; Financial Services & Technology; International Finance (Chmn.). *Budget* (11th of 12 R). *Energy & Natural Resources* (8th of 11 R): Energy Research, Development, Production & Regulation; National Parks, Historic Preservation & Recreation. *Foreign Relations* (7th of 10 R): African Affairs; International Operations (Chmn.); Near Eastern & South Asian Affairs. *Joint Economic Committee* (4th of 10 Sens.).

Group Ratings

	ADA	ACLU	AFS	LCV	CFA	CON	NFIB	COC	ACU	NTLC	CHC
1996	5	22	14	8	14	70	97	92	95	100	100
1995	0	—	0	0	0	88	—	100	96	—	—

National Journal Ratings

	1995 LIB	—	1995 CONS	1996 LIB	—	1996 CONS
Economic	18%	—	80%	18%	—	79%
Social	0%	—	88%	0%	—	72%
Foreign	22%	—	67%	26%	—	70%

Key Votes of the 104th Congress

1. Reduce Medicare Growth $	Y	5. Flag Amendment	Y	9. Anti-Missile Defense	Y
2. Lmt. Prod. Liab. Damages	Y	6. Endangered Species	N	10. Cuban Embargo	Y
3. Increase Min. Wage	Y	7. Gay Employment Rights	N	11. Bar Bosnia Troop $	N
4. Welfare Reform	Y	8. Ovrd. Part. Birth Veto	Y	12. Cut Vietnam Aid	N

Election Results

1994 general	Rod Grams (IR)	869,653	(49%)	($2,439,798)
	Ann Wynia (DFL)	781,860	(44%)	($2,659,423)
	Dean M. Barkley (I)	95,400	(5%)	($24,266)
1994 primary	Rod Grams (IR)	269,931	(58%)	
	Joanell M. Dyrstad (IR)	163,205	(35%)	
	Harold Edward Stassen (IR)	22,430	(5%)	
	Others	8,467	(2%)	
1988 general	Dave Durenberger (IR)	1,176,210	(56%)	($5,410,783)
	Hubert H. Humphrey, III (DFL)	856,694	(41%)	($2,477,068)

FIRST DISTRICT

The Mississippi River runs majestically southeast from Minneapolis and St. Paul, cutting a path through rolling hills and where it widens, forming calm lakes lapping at the bottomlands: one of the finest river landscapes of North America. This far north, the westward tide of Yankee migrants thinned out. After the Civil War, most settlers following the railroads on the floodplains west of the river were Germans and Scandinavians, bringing their families to this terrain so much like the Rhine, and to the rolling uplands beyond which resemble the northern European plain. Southeastern Minnesota is a borderland between Yankee and German settlements—politically, between Civil War Republicans and Farmer-Laborites favoring interventionist economic and isolationist foreign policies.

The 1st Congressional District of Minnesota occupies the state's southeastern corner. Within its compact bounds is considerable diversity. Rochester has been home of the Mayo Clinic since it was founded in 1863 when English-born physician William Mayo set up a practice to examine inductees into the Union Army—early government involvement in medicine. Today, Rochester, with its large professional population, is prosperous and growing. Austin, a county away, is headquarters of the Hormel meatpacking firm that beat a bitter strike in the 1980s; this is one place where class warfare politics seems alive. Rochester is a Republican stronghold; Austin is solidly DFL. The 1st District extends north to new subdivisions spreading out from the Twin Cities and to Northfield, home of Carleton College and former professor Senator Paul Wellstone. The 1st also includes the river towns of Red Wing, Wabasha and Winona, with their 19th Century stone storefronts and mountain-like rock outcroppings that overlook the river; this is dairy farming and small industrial country.

The congressman from the 1st District is Gil Gutknecht, a Republican elected in 1994. The name, he likes to explain, means "good hired hand," though "good indentured servant" might be closer to the mark. He grew up in Iowa, son of a union member, worked nine years as a school supply salesman, then became an auctioneer. He eventually handled large real estate auctions. He was elected to the legislature in 1982 from Rochester and became Republican floor leader. Partisan, ebullient, he once told Iron Range DFLers that the state motto *L'etoile du Nord* did not mean "send the money north." His legislation includes a whistleblowing law, ethics reforms and the 21-year-old drinking age. In 1993, he was aiming to run for the Senate in 1994. But 1st District Congressman Tim Penny, the very popular moderate Democrat who co-sponsored the Penny-Kasich budget cuts of 1993 and 1994, decided to retire, and Gutknecht ran for the House. (Penny, back in Minnesota teaching, continues to be an important political voice for entitlement reform.)

Gutknecht had plenty of competition. In the Republican primary he faced Arlen Erdahl, elected congressman in 1978 and defeated in 1982 after redistricting. Erdahl said he was closer to Garrison Keillor than Rush Limbaugh; Gutknecht said he was not conservative enough for the district, and won 57%–36%. The DFL nominated Mankato state Senator John Hottinger, who backed a single-payer healthcare system. Gutknecht attacked him for voting 98% of the time with the Democratic leadership and portrayed himself as "the Minnesota equivalent of Newt Gingrich." Hottinger had a 106-point budget-cutting plan; Gutknecht backed the balanced budget amendment. Hottinger carried Austin and ran even in Mankato. But Gutknecht won big in Rochester and in the river counties, for a 55%–45% victory.

Gutknecht was an enthusiastic member of the new House majority, with a mostly conservative voting record with some exceptions on foreign issues. He paid heed to district interests, sponsoring a Medicare formula that would pay more to rural hospitals and opposing changes in the sugar program (Minnesota is sugar beet country). He supported the Freedom to Farm Act, despite some concern about its dairy provisions. He was one of several Minnesota members to oppose the IRS ruling taxing in the current year income from futures contracts payable in the next. He sponsored and went on the talk radio circuit to boost a 12-year limit on congressional pension accrual—a pension term limit. In 1996, dismayed that the Republican leadership's budget was allowing an increase in non-defense discretionary spending and a 1.9% increase in the budget deficit, Gutknecht proposed amendments for a 1.9% reduction in every appropriations bill, with little success. It's like "cutting your hair an eighth of an inch," he argued.

Gutknecht's ebullient conservatism attracted Democratic opposition. He was targeted by AFL-CIO ads and had a serious Democratic opponent, Winona State economics professor Mary Rieder, who said she was a fiscal conservative like Penny. Gutknecht outspent her, but not overwhelmingly; she raised almost as much PAC and party money as the incumbent, a good example of Democrats' fundraising competence. Rieder's 47% closely tracked Clinton's 48% for the district, but Gutknecht won 53% (Dole lost with 37%). Again he won Rochester and lost Austin; he carried Mankato and the river counties but racked up high percentages nowhere. This could be a seriously contested seat again in 1998.

The People: Pop. 1990: 546,909; 48% rural; 14% age 65+; 97% White; 1% Asian; 1% Hispanic origin. Households: 62% married couple families; 30% married couple fams. w. children; 44% college educ.; median household income: $28,371; per capita income: $12,661; median gross rent: $342; median house value: $58,600.

1996 Presidential Vote			**1992 Presidential Vote**		
Clinton (D)	127,730	(48%)	Clinton (D)	109,829	(38%)
Dole (R)	97,050	(37%)	Bush (R)	98,384	(34%)
Perot (I)	35,408	(13%)	Perot (I)	75,227	(26%)

Rep. Gil Gutknecht (R)

Elected 1994; b. Mar. 20, 1951, Cedar Falls, IA; home, Rochester; U. of N. IA, B.A. 1973; Catholic; married (Mary).

Career: Sales Rep., Latta School Supply Co., 1973–82; Real Estate Auctioneer, 1979–present; MN House of Reps. 1982–94.

DC Office: 425 CHOB 20515, 202-225-2472; e-mail: gil@hr.house.gov.

District Offices: Rochester, 507-252-9841.

Committees: *Budget* (20th of 24 R). *Science* (15th of 25 R): Basic Research; Technology.

Group Ratings

	ADA	ACLU	AFS	LCV	CFA	CON	NFIB	COC	ACU	NTLC	CHC
1996	5	6	9	23	23	50	97	94	100	98	100
1995	0	—	—	0	0	75	—	100	96	—	—

National Journal Ratings

	1995 LIB — 1995 CONS			1996 LIB — 1996 CONS		
Economic	0%	—	74%	0%	—	82%
Social	21%	—	72%	0%	—	90%
Foreign	28%	—	65%	50%	—	50%

Key Votes of the 104th Congress

1. Reduce Medicare Growth $	Y	5. Flag Amendment	Y	9. Cuban Embargo	Y
2. Ovrd. Product Liab. Veto	Y	6. Drop EPA Limits	N	10. Bar Bosnia Troop $	Y
3. Increase Min. Wage	N	7. Repeal Assault-Weap. Ban	Y	11. Cut Anti-Missile Defense	N
4. Welfare Reform	Y	8. Ovrd. Part. Birth Veto	Y	12. Bar U.N. Uniforms	Y

Election Results

1996 general	Gil Gutknecht (R)	137,545	(53%)	($927,715)
	Mary Rieder (DFL)	123,188	(47%)	($625,244)
1996 primary	Gil Gutknecht (R)	unopposed		
1994 general	Gil Gutknecht (IR)	117,613	(55%)	($581,099)
	John C. Hottinger (DFL)	95,328	(45%)	($347,084)

SECOND DISTRICT

West of the Mississippi and Minnesota Rivers, where the plains rise above the gorges that the rivers have cut through them, is the great farming country of southwestern Minnesota. This is where Laura Ingalls Wilder's family came on the way west from their little house in the big woods in Wisconsin to the "Little House on the Prairie" in South Dakota, and stopped by the shores of Plum Creek, near Walnut Grove, Minnesota, not long after the Indians were forced out by U.S. troops following the Dakota rebellion of 1862. The creeks and rivers cut crevasses into these plains, spotted with occasional hills and towns settled 100 years ago by Yankee, German and Scandinavian farmers. This is a hard place to make a living; Laura's family, after all their struggles, left the farm for town as soon as they could. Even in the 1990s, farmers still toil against the elements to make a profitable living, and even their successes hurt; with higher productivity, fewer people live on the land, or even in town.

The 2d Congressional District of Minnesota takes in roughly the southwestern quadrant of the state. The farm counties over the decades slowly have become depopulated, as young people move off farms into small towns and, more often, to the Twin Cities or other big metro areas. But now there is movement in the other direction. The 2d District's boundaries were shifted eastward after the 1990 Census and now take in outlying counties and townships of the Twin Cities metro area. Some, around Chanhassen and Shakopee southwest of Minneapolis, are relatively high income areas. Others, farther out, like Waverly where Hubert Humphrey had his lakeside home, are more humble—places where modest-income young families are moving into what was once open countryside punctuated by small villages. It is almost as if the southwestern Minnesota farmers who saw their children go off to the big city are now seeing their grandchildren move back out toward the farmlands, or at least into the same political constituency.

The congressman from the 2d District is David Minge (pronounced with a hard *G*), a "common sense Democrat," as he puts it, first elected in 1992. Minge is close to a personification of "Minnesota nice," the quiet cheerfulness and pleasantness which permeates life in Minnesota. He grew up in Worthington, the son of a doctor who became a medical missionary, practiced law in Minneapolis, taught law for seven years in Wyoming and worked briefly on Capitol Hill. Then he returned to Minnesota to practice law in Montevideo, the town where Walter Mondale grew up, where he worked with community organizations to clean up the Minnesota river and resettle Vietnamese refugees and served on the school board. In 1992, he decided to run against Congressman Vin Weber, one of the leading-edge Republican conservatives in the House, a close ally of Newt Gingrich. But Weber had overdrafts on the House bank and decided to retire. Minge's opponent was conservative state legislator Cal Ludeman, the Republican nominee for governor in 1986. Ludeman started off with more money, but Minge had more energy, riding 500 miles on his bicycle and stopping in 47 towns in nine days. He attacked Ludeman for voting against minimum wages, drug abuse programs, and federal disaster relief, and called for handling the deficit with a commission like the one Congress used for military base closings and for a "unified" national healthcare plan. Bill Clinton carried the district 37%–35%, and Minge won 47.9%–47.7%. Ludeman was proclaimed the winner on election night but Minge, with Norwegian stoicism, went to sleep and woke up to find out he had won by 569 votes.

Minge opposed the Clinton budget and tax increase and NAFTA, supported the Clinton healthcare plan, voted for the Brady bill and assault weapons ban and worked for relief from the terrible floods of 1993. He returned part of his salary and office allowance to the Treasury and promised to serve no more than six terms. In 1994 he was reelected 52%–45% over Gary Revier, mayor of Redwood Falls.

In the Republican Congress Minge voted for the balanced budget amendment, the line-item veto, the congressional accountability act. He was one of the founding members of the moderate Blue Dog Democrats and helped draw up The Coalition budget. He helped form a Bipartisan Reform Team and favors eliminating PACs, though he received $353,000 from PACs in 1996. He supported the partial-birth abortion ban and took care to praise the National Rifle Association for its safety and training programs even as it opposed him. On the Agriculture Committee he worked to maintain the Conservation Reserve Program and praised the Freedom to Farm Act, though he voted against the House version and criticized the automatic payments. He was one of several Minnesota members to oppose the IRS ruling taxing in the current year income from futures contracts payable in the next. He amended the bill to take the highway trust fund off-budget to say that it would go back on-budget if any funds were used to earmark projects.

In 1996 Minge was again opposed by Revier. This time, as Clinton was carrying the district 45%–39%, Minge won 55%–41%, carrying all but Revier's home county. After the election, he got the Budget Committee seat being vacated by Minneapolis's Martin Sabo, an example of a liberal Democrat being replaced by a moderate.

The People: Pop. 1990: 546,874; 58% rural; 16% age 65+; 98% White; 1% Asian; 1% Hispanic origin. Households: 65% married couple families; 32% married couple fams. w. children; 37% college educ.; median household income: $27,024; per capita income: $12,159; median gross rent: $309; median house value: $55,000.

1996 Presidential Vote			1992 Presidential Vote		
Clinton (D)	120,652	(45%)	Clinton (D)	103,246	(37%)
Dole (R)	105,205	(39%)	Bush (R)	97,867	(35%)
Perot (I)	38,117	(14%)	Perot (I)	79,442	(28%)

Rep. David Minge (DFL)

Elected 1992; b. Mar. 19, 1942, Clarkfield; home, Montevideo; St. Olaf College, B.A. 1964, U. of Chicago, J.D. 1967; Lutheran; married (Karen).

Career: Practicing atty., 1967–70, 1977–90; Professor, U. of WY Law Schl., 1970–77; Montevideo School Bd., 1990–92.

DC Office: 1415 LHOB 20515, 202-225-2331; Fax: 202-226-0836; e-mail: dminge@hr.house.gov.

District Offices: Chaska, 612-448-6567; Montevideo, 320-269-9311; Windom, 507-831-0115.

Committees: *Agriculture* (7th of 23 D): Forestry, Resource Conservation & Research; General Farm Commodities (RMM). *Budget* (13th of 19 D).

Group Ratings

	ADA	ACLU	AFS	LCV	CFA	CON	NFIB	COC	ACU	NTLC	CHC
1996	70	69	75	77	85	98	54	38	15	32	26
1995	75	—	—	38	62	98	—	54	25	—	—

National Journal Ratings

	1995 LIB — 1995 CONS	1996 LIB — 1996 CONS
Economic	60% — 39%	62% — 36%
Social	67% — 32%	60% — 39%
Foreign	70% — 30%	90% — 10%

Key Votes of the 104th Congress

1. Reduce Medicare Growth $	N	5. Flag Amendment	N	9. Cuban Embargo	N
2. Ovrd. Product Liab. Veto	Y	6. Drop EPA Limits	N	10. Bar Bosnia Troop $	N
3. Increase Min. Wage	Y	7. Repeal Assault-Weap. Ban	N	11. Cut Anti-Missile Defense	Y
4. Welfare Reform	N	8. Ovrd. Part. Birth Veto	Y	12. Bar U.N. Uniforms	N

Election Results

1996 general	David Minge (DFL)	144,083	(55%)	($616,673)
	Gary B. Revier (R)	107,807	(41%)	($284,943)
	Others	10,463	(4%)	
1996 primary	David Minge (DFL)	unopposed		
1994 general	David Minge (DFL)	114,289	(52%)	($622,920)
	Gary B. Revier (IR)	98,881	(45%)	($325,853)
	Others	6,615	(3%)	

THIRD DISTRICT

Over the past half century, Minnesota's great twin metropolis has spread out from the neat streets inside the city limits of Minneapolis and St. Paul into the countryside all around. People have sorted themselves out geographically. In the lower lands along the Mississippi and Minnesota Rivers, where rail lines fan out from the Twin Cities heading toward the great farmlands of America, are the blue collar suburbs, with neat modest houses on grid streets and warehouses and factories near the tracks. Inland, around the lakes Minnesota is so proud of, in subdivisions with curved streets hugging the hills, are the Twin Cities' more affluent neighborhoods, quiet and unflashy in the Minnesota way, but comfortable whether blanketed with snow or when the lake is glinting in the summer sun. In between are the freeway interchanges where some of the Twin Cities' great innovations can be seen—Southdale Shopping Center in Edina, the first enclosed mall, and the site of the first B. Dalton store, the beginning of national book chains; and now the giant Mall of America, with its 4.2 million square feet, 400 stores, 45 restaurants, 14 theaters and 12,000 employees.

The 3d Congressional District of Minnesota takes in Hennepin County suburbs north, south and west of Minneapolis. On the north are working class Brooklyn Center and Brooklyn Park, still DFL strongholds; on the south is middle income Bloomington, home of the Mall of America; to the west are Edina, Plymouth, Wayzata and other towns around Lake Minnetonka, all heavily Republican. This is the largest lake and these are the most affluent communities in the Twin Cities area. The area also is home to headquarters of such diverse companies as Cargill and Radisson Hotels. The 3d also takes in fast-growing Burnsville across the Minnesota River from the airport and still vacant land northwest of Minneapolis. This is a district that usually votes Republican, though it gave pluralities to Bill Clinton in 1992 and 1996.

The congressman from the 3d District is Jim Ramstad, a Republican first elected in 1990. He has been in politics since childhood: raised in North Dakota, he used to go with his grandfather to visit Republican Senator Milton Young. He saw President Eisenhower in 1956 and met President Kennedy in 1963 at the same Rose Garden ceremony where a young Bill Clinton was photographed shaking Kennedy's hand (Ramstad is in the background of the now famous photo). He worked as an intern to Young and a staffer to Congressman Tom Kleppe while in his 20s. In 1980, at 34, he beat a Democratic state senator (spending the then record-breaking sum of $77,932) and worked on issues like chemical dependency in young people, "crack" babies and the handicapped, while favoring mandatory minimum sentences for drug dealers and boot camps for drug offenders. He used to spend time with police on all-night rounds.

In 1990, when 3d District Congressman Bill Frenzel retired after 20 years, Ramstad ran for the House. The crucial contest was the Republican convention. Ramstad was pro-choice on abortion while most delegates were anti-abortion, but he had good endorsements, from Senator Rudy Boschwitz and Congressman Vin Weber, both anti-abortion, and won on the eighth ballot. In the House, Ramstad's record recently has been moderate on most issues. He has taken on some environmental causes—trying to stop the Advanced Liquid Metal Reactor and scale down the proposed bridge over the St. Croix River—and voted against some appropriations riders scaling back environmental regulation. On the 1994 crime bill he sponsored a national tracking system for convicted child abusers released from prison. He attacks the FDA for stifling innovation and backs tort reform; his task force on legal reforms helped produce the securities litigation bill that was passed over Bill Clinton's veto. He demanded the firing of Surgeon General Joycelyn Elders long before other did.

Ramstad got a seat on the Ways and Means Committee in 1995 and passed a law reforming pensions for state and local public employees, making them more like 401(k)s. He also sponsored two important planks in the Republicans' January 1995 House rules reforms. One requires spending to be compared with spending the year before, not with the "current services" figure which allows every agency an increase for inflation and increased caseload, on the absurd premise that government operations have reached the maximum possible efficiency. The other, a response to the 1993 Clinton tax increase, was a ban on retroactive tax increases. A recovering alcoholic, he backed drug tests for released federal prisoners and sponsored a commission (named after the late Senator Harold Hughes) to study alcoholism. He opposed SSI cash benefits to alcoholics. "I can tell you that paying cash benefits to these people is not the kind of help they need. In fact, cash benefits only make the problem of alcoholism worse." Another achievement was a special immigration bill for Oscar Velazquez of Plymouth, who entered one sham marriage in the 1980s but then married an American and fathered two children and then was deported.

Ramstad has been easily reelected, and in 1994 had the third highest number of votes of any House candidate in the country. He was mentioned as a possible candidate against Senator Paul Wellstone in 1996, but made no move to run.

The People: Pop. 1990: 546,976; 2% rural; 8% age 65+; 95% White; 1% Black; 2% Asian; 1% Hispanic origin. Households: 63% married couple families; 32% married couple fams. w. children; 66% college educ.; median household income: $43,963; per capita income: $20,067; median gross rent: $577; median house value: $100,500.

1996 Presidential Vote

Clinton (D)	141,109	(47%)
Dole (R)	125,019	(41%)
Perot (I)	31,021	(10%)
Other	5,532	(2%)

1992 Presidential Vote

Clinton (D)	129,171	(39%)
Bush (R)	117,975	(36%)
Perot (I)	79,877	(24%)

Rep. Jim Ramstad (R)

Elected 1990; b. May 6, 1946, Jamestown, ND; home, Minnetonka; U. of MN, B.A. 1968, George Washington U., J.D. 1973; Protestant; single.

Career: Army Reserves, 1968–75; Special Asst., U.S. Rep. Tom Kleppe, 1970; Practicing atty., 1973–80; Adjunct Prof., American U., 1975–78; MN Senate, 1980–90.

DC Office: 103 CHOB 20515, 202-225-2871; Fax: 202-225-6351; e-mail: mn03@hr.house.gov.

District Offices: Bloomington, 612-881-4600.

Committees: *Ways & Means* (11th of 23 R): Oversight; Trade.

Group Ratings

	ADA	ACLU	AFS	LCV	CFA	CON	NFIB	COC	ACU	NTLC	CHC
1996	35	12	17	62	31	94	89	88	70	88	66
1995	30	—	—	19	77	96	—	92	64	—	—

National Journal Ratings

	1995 LIB — 1995 CONS			1996 LIB — 1996 CONS		
Economic	44%	—	53%	50%	—	49%
Social	53%	—	46%	48%	—	51%
Foreign	56%	—	43%	67%	—	31%

Key Votes of the 104th Congress

1. Reduce Medicare Growth $	Y	5. Flag Amendment	Y	9. Cuban Embargo	Y
2. Ovrd. Product Liab. Veto	Y	6. Drop EPA Limits	Y	10. Bar Bosnia Troop $	Y
3. Increase Min. Wage	Y	7. Repeal Assault-Weap. Ban	N	11. Cut Anti-Missile Defense	N
4. Welfare Reform	Y	8. Ovrd. Part. Birth Veto	Y	12. Bar U.N. Uniforms	Y

Election Results

1996 general	Jim Ramstad (R)	205,845	(70%)	($494,908)
	Stanley J. Leino (DFL)	87,359	(30%)	($22,600)
1996 primary	Jim Ramstad (R)	unopposed		
1994 general	Jim Ramstad (IR)	173,223	(73%)	($498,146)
	Bob Olson (DFL)	62,211	(26%)	($35,839)

FOURTH DISTRICT

Above the Mississippi River bluffs, forested when the first settlers arrived in the 1850s and one of America's great urban vistas today, stand the two great landmarks of St. Paul: the Minnesota Capitol and Archbishop Ireland's Cathedral. This is the older and smaller of the Twin Cities, settled mainly by Catholic Irish and German immigrants, while Minneapolis was attracting Protestant Swedes and Yankees. St. Paul became a major transportation hub, a railroad center and river port, while Minneapolis, farther up river at the Falls of St. Anthony, became the nation's largest grain milling center. St. Paul has a vibrant core. Beneath the Capitol and the cathedral, its skywalk-linked downtown is home to the Ordway Music Theater, the headquarters of Minnesota Public Radio and an active pop music industry. Beyond the cathedral is Summit Avenue, on which capitalists like the Great Northern Railway's James J. Hill built grandiose

Romanesque houses, and which, with Monument Avenue in Richmond and Meridian Street in Indianapolis, remains one of America's grand residential boulevards. In more modest neighborhoods are sturdy houses lined up on grid streets, and beyond are the close-in suburbs with more irregular street patterns and shopping nodes.

Minnesota's 4th Congressional District is made up of St. Paul, the Ramsey County suburbs to the north, West St. Paul and South St. Paul (which are right next to each other) to the south, and Lake Elmo and Woodbury to the east. St. Paul was one of the most Democratic parts of Minnesota even before the Democratic-Farmer-Labor Party was formed in 1944; St. Paul and Ramsey County have remained firmly DFL ever since, voting proudly in 1984 for Walter Mondale, who announced his candidacy in the State Capitol and lived during the campaign in the woodsy suburb of North Oaks just north of St. Paul. The 4th District has been held by the DFL since 1948, when it elected Eugene McCarthy.

The congressman from the 4th District is Bruce Vento who has held this seat since 1976. Vento grew up on the east side of St. Paul, where his father was an officer in the Machinist's Union. While in college he worked in the St. Paul Hotel restaurant and in the Hamm's Brewery and was a Machinist steward at Minnesota Plastics. He taught science and social studies in Minneapolis schools for 11 years and was elected to the state House in 1970, at 30, where he became a committee chairman. When the incumbent retired in 1976, Vento ran for the House and won the party endorsement at the DFL convention with union support, then won the primary and general elections easily.

In the House Vento has had an almost perfectly liberal voting record. He held one of the important second-line positions in the Democratic Congress, as chairman of the subcommittee on National Parks, Forests and Lands from 1985–94. This is the body which sorts through proposals for wilderness areas and national parks, national seashores, lakeshores and historic sites, wild and scenic rivers—attractive political plums for many members. Vento is a solid environmentalist, favoring severe restrictions on logging to protect the spotted owl in the Pacific Northwest, higher grazing fees on public lands, more money for urban parks. Now the subcommittee is under very different leadership, and Vento moved to a ranking position on the Banking Subcommittee on Financial Institutions and Consumer Credit. There his major interests include encouraging urban and community development—he is a big booster of the Community Reinvestment Act—and protecting ATM users from muggings. On bank deregulation issues he has disagreed sharply with committee Republicans, resulting in lack of action on repeal of the Glass-Steagall Act separating banks and investment firms. He has not been successful in his quest for the top post on the full Banking Committee. In December 1990 he challenged Chairman Henry Gonzalez and lost in the Democratic Caucus 163–89. In December 1996 Vento tried again, and so did John LaFalce, this time for the ranking minority position. Gonzalez made an impassioned speech, promising to give up the post after two years, and won with 82 votes, to 62 for LaFalce and 47 for Vento. The fact that the winning candidate got fewer votes than the loser six years before is testimony to the shrinkage of the Democratic Caucus; the fact that Vento finished third suggests he might not get the spot if Gonzalez steps down in 1998. Two other Vento causes are of interest. He passed through the House a bill to waive the English test for Hmongs and Laotians who served alongside U.S. soldiers as the Vietnam war spread to neighboring countries, and who now reside here and want to become citizens; it did not pass the Senate. And he supports campaign finance reform which would limit spending to $600,000 per district and limit candidates to spending $50,000 of their own money. He also has a bill to treat state and local public employees' pensions like Social Security benefits.

Vento was reelected with lackluster margins in 1992 and 1994, though he heavily outspent his opponents. In a 1996 rematch, Republican Dennis Newinski spent $307,000, but Vento spent $559,000 and got 57% of the vote—almost the same as Bill Clinton in the district.

The People: Pop. 1990: 546,812; 12% age 65+; 88% White; 4% Black; 5% Asian; 1% Amer. Indian; 3% Hispanic origin. Households: 51% married couple families; 24% married couple fams. w. children; 55%

college educ.; median household income: $32,670; per capita income: $15,863; median gross rent: $455; median house value: $83,700.

1996 Presidential Vote

Clinton (D)	152,555	(58%)
Dole (R)	77,704	(30%)
Perot (I)	23,566	(9%)
Other	7,688	(3%)

1992 Presidential Vote

Clinton (D)	147,266	(51%)
Bush (R)	79,137	(28%)
Perot (I)	58,850	(21%)

Rep. Bruce F. Vento (DFL)

Elected 1976; b. Oct. 7, 1940, St. Paul; home, St. Paul; U. of MN, A.A. 1961; WI St. U., B.S. 1965; Catholic; divorced.

Career: Teacher, 1965–76; MN House of Reps., 1970–76, Asst. Majority Ldr., 1974–76.

DC Office: 2304 RHOB 20515, 202-225-6631; Fax: 202-225-1968; e-mail: vento@hr.house.gov.

District Offices: St. Paul, 612-224-4503.

Committees: *Banking & Financial Services* (3rd of 25 D): Capital Markets, Securities & Government Sponsored Enterprises; Financial Institutions & Consumer Credit (RMM). *Resources* (4th of 23 D): Forests & Forest Health; National Parks & Public Lands.

Group Ratings

	ADA	ACLU	AFS	LCV	CFA	CON	NFIB	COC	ACU	NTLC	CHC
1996	95	88	100	85	92	97	16	13	0	5	7
1995	95	—	—	94	92	56	—	17	4	—	—

National Journal Ratings

	1995 LIB — 1995 CONS			1996 LIB — 1996 CONS		
Economic	85%	—	12%	89%	—	0%
Social	88%	—	0%	79%	—	18%
Foreign	88%	—	7%	90%	—	0%

Key Votes of the 104th Congress

1. Reduce Medicare Growth $	N	5. Flag Amendment	N	9. Cuban Embargo	N
2. Ovrd. Product Liab. Veto	N	6. Drop EPA Limits	Y	10. Bar Bosnia Troop $	N
3. Increase Min. Wage	Y	7. Repeal Assault-Weap. Ban	N	11. Cut Anti-Missile Defense	Y
4. Welfare Reform	N	8. Ovrd. Part. Birth Veto	N	12. Bar U.N. Uniforms	N

Election Results

1996 general	Bruce F. Vento (DFL)	145,831	(57%)	($559,370)
	Dennis Newinski (R)	94,110	(37%)	($315,410)
	Others	15,818	(6%)	
1996 primary	Bruce F. Vento (DFL)	unopposed		
1994 general	Bruce F. Vento (DFL)	115,638	(55%)	($339,703)
	Dennis Newinski (IR)	88,344	(42%)	($93,457)
	Others	6,648	(3%)	

FIFTH DISTRICT

From almost nowhere in Minneapolis today can you see the geographic feature that put the city here—the Falls of St. Anthony, the head of navigation on the Mississippi River, where waters rush in rapids beneath low downtown bridges. In olden days every riverboat had to stop here, and the waterpower generated by the falls was the energy source first for pioneers' grist mills and then for the giant grain mills that processed the wheat of the northern Great Plains into food for the United States and the world. By 1890, Minneapolis and St. Paul made up one of America's largest urban areas, living mainly off grain. Today, Minneapolis is a center of high-tech industry and of banking and finance. It is a regional railroad center, and the headquarters of Northwest Airlines; it is also the nerve center of an economic area that extends almost 1,000 miles west to the Rocky Mountains in Montana.

All of the city of Minneapolis, plus a few of its older suburbs directly west and south, make up the 5th District of Minnesota. In the southwest corner are part of the suburb of Edina and the gracefully aged Minneapolis neighborhoods around Lake Calhoun and Lake Harriet—affluent areas, long built-up and proudly maintained, not far from Minneapolis's skywalk-laced downtown skyscrapers and museum quarter up on the hill above Hennepin Avenue. But most of the 5th District is lower on the income scale. There are few blocks here as abandoned and ruined by crime as are some square miles of Chicago or Detroit. But many of the working-class neighborhoods of small frame houses on grid streets are now kept up by elderly homeowners, while new immigrants have built small communities of their own. North of the Mississippi is the University of Minnesota; to the northeast, behind the railroad and warehouse district along the Mississippi, is the home of many Hmongs from Laos. The 5th District is solidly Democratic. Minneapolis's political liberalism is drawn from the Yankee tradition of clean government, the Scandinavian tradition of cooperative enterprise and the industrial labor tradition of economic redistribution. To this has been added in recent years, by feminists and the graduate student proletariat, an antic cultural liberalism notable for its ignorance not only of any conservative heritage but of many of the liberal traditions here as well.

The congressman from the 5th District is Martin Olav Sabo, son of Norwegian immigrants, a DFL leader who has spent all his adult life in politics. He was elected to the Minnesota legislature in 1960 at age 22, was the minority leader at 30 and speaker at 34. In 1978, he was elected to the House and in his first year got a seat on the Appropriations Committee. It began as a quiet career: Sabo can be articulate, even humorous, and certainly is knowledgeable and averse to the cheap shot. But he pursued his career with a certain Scandinavian reticence and aversion to national publicity. Throughout the 1980s he delivered locally—new buses, bridges, and job training programs. On the Budget Committee, he wrote the 1990 budget summit agreement's "firewalls" between defense and domestic spending, intended by liberals as an attempt to save domestic programs and by conservatives as a way of protecting the Pentagon.

Sabo became more visible in the 1990s. After Leon Panetta was appointed OMB Director in January 1993, Sabo ran for Budget chairman, and won by 149–112 over the more moderate John Spratt of South Carolina. In that position it fell to Sabo to defend the first Clinton budget, which eventually passed by 218–216. Sabo then fought against the spending cut packages proposed by his Minnesota colleague Tim Penny and Budget ranking Republican John Kasich in late 1993 and early 1994. In 1994 the budget sledding was easier but the political sledding treacherous; Democrats lost their majority and Sabo became ranking minority member. Although he remained on pleasant terms with Kasich, this must have been frustrating work; in late 1995 Sabo said, "Throughout this budget process, Republicans engaged in a one-sided attack on lower-income Americans."

After the 1996 election Sabo rotated off Budget (Spratt became the ranking Democrat by 106–83) and concentrated more on his work on Appropriations, where he is an ally of ranking Democrat David Obey. Sabo is ranking member on the Transportation Subcommittee, and has strongly opposed the move of Transportation Committee Chairman Bud Shuster to take the transportation trust funds off-budget. Sabo pointed out accurately that this would vastly reduce Congress's discretion over the budget and that unspent trust fund monies currently accrue at an above-market interest rate. He backs mass transit and alternative modes of transportation and has fought for a national program to encourage bicycle riding. He also serves on the National Security Subcommittee, where his interests include arms control and military living standards. But he works on other issues as well. In early 1997 he endorsed the Blue Dog Medicare reform plan, and argued that the current formula, which the Clinton Administration would leave untouched, penalizes states like Minnesota, which have cut costs through HMOs, and hurts rural areas.

Sabo has been reelected by wide margins, by 64%–29% in 1996 against a Republican with impressive credentials. He once had a serious challenge from the left, in 1992 when Lisa Niebauer-Stall kept him from winning the party endorsement at the convention until the eighth ballot; he did better with voters than DFL activists and won the primary 67%–28%.

The People: Pop. 1990: 546,876; 14% age 65+; 83% White; 9% Black; 3% Asian; 2% Amer. Indian; 2% Hispanic origin. Households: 39% married couple families; 16% married couple fams. w. children; 57% college educ.; median household income: $28,634; per capita income: $15,794; median gross rent: $449; median house value: $77,900.

1996 Presidential Vote			1992 Presidential Vote		
Clinton (D)	159,018	(62%)	Clinton (D)	167,941	(58%)
Dole (R)	62,507	(25%)	Bush (R)	68,072	(23%)
Perot (I)	20,499	(8%)	Perot (I)	52,374	(18%)
Other	12,636	(5%)			

Rep. Martin Olav Sabo (DFL)

Elected 1978; b. Feb. 28, 1938, Crosby, ND; home, Minneapolis; Augsburg Col., B.A. 1959; Lutheran; married (Sylvia).

Career: MN House of Reps., 1961–78, Minority Ldr., 1969–73, Speaker, 1973–78.

DC Office: 2336 RHOB 20515, 202-225-4755; e-mail: msabo@hr.house.gov.

District Offices: Minneapolis, 612-664-8000.

Committees: *Appropriations* (6th of 26 D): District of Columbia; National Security; Transportation (RMM).

Group Ratings

	ADA	ACLU	AFS	LCV	CFA	CON	NFIB	COC	ACU	NTLC	CHC
1996	90	94	100	85	69	81	16	13	0	5	0
1995	100	—	—	94	92	37	—	17	4	—	—

National Journal Ratings

	1995 LIB — 1995 CONS			1996 LIB — 1996 CONS		
Economic	90%	—	8%	89%	—	0%
Social	88%	—	0%	88%	—	0%
Foreign	93%	—	0%	79%	—	19%

Key Votes of the 104th Congress

1. Reduce Medicare Growth $	N	5. Flag Amendment	N	9. Cuban Embargo	N
2. Ovrd. Product Liab. Veto	N	6. Drop EPA Limits	Y	10. Bar Bosnia Troop $	N
3. Increase Min. Wage	Y	7. Repeal Assault-Weap. Ban	N	11. Cut Anti-Missile Defense	Y
4. Welfare Reform	N	8. Ovrd. Part. Birth Veto	N	12. Bar U.N. Uniforms	N

Election Results

1996 general	Martin Olav Sabo (DFL)	158,272	(64%)	($515,970)
	Jack Uldrich (R)	70,115	(29%)	($66,821)
	Erika Anderson (GRT)	13,102	(5%)	
	Others	4,569	(2%)	
1996 primary	Martin Olav Sabo (DFL)	unopposed		
1994 general	Martin Olav Sabo (DFL)	121,515	(62%)	($333,075)
	Dorothy L. LeGrand (IR)	73,258	(37%)	($148,799)

SIXTH DISTRICT

The earliest settlers to the Twin Cities of Minneapolis and St. Paul came up the Mississippi River, or up the rail lines which were soon built on the bottomlands beside. They lived in their first generation within walking distance of the mills and factories and railyards; as first streetcars and then automobiles allowed them to live farther from work, they spread out in St. Paul and Minneapolis and then over the lake-strewn countryside all around. The flat lands are bleak here when the winter sun struggles to shine through grey clouds. The lakes are often surrounded by, sometimes indistinguishable from, swamps. The old lumber mill towns which pioneers built, like Stillwater on the St. Croix, were for years economic backwaters, their antique structures ill-tended. But the creativity and productivity of Minnesotans have turned this not especially attractive environment into some of the most pleasant suburbs in the world. They have taken maximum advantage of their lakes and have refurbished old towns and farmhouses and have built comfortable homes in new subdivisions. Here live today's typical American families. Busy at home and at the workplace, communicating with each other by Post-it notes (invented at St. Paul's 3M), exhausted at the end of each day, winning through their efforts a material standard of living that would have dazzled their grandparents but at a price that might well have appalled them.

The 6th Congressional District of Minnesota includes much of the Twin Cities metropolitan area, suburbs and townships north, east and south of St. Paul and Minneapolis. To the northwest, the Anoka County suburbs along the Mississippi River have attracted blue collar families. Incomes are below the high metro average, and politically this is a DFL area. Stillwater, facing Wisconsin on hills above the St. Croix River, with Victorian buildings from its days as a lumber port when it nearly became Minnesota's capital, and surrounding Washington County have attracted a mix of people and are politically marginal. South of St. Paul, the Dakota County towns along the Mississippi are blue collar and DFL; the newer, fast-growing Eagan and Apple Valley to the southwest are quite affluent and tend to vote Independent Republican. Altogether, this is perhaps Minnesota's most volatile district. Redistricting has affected the election results. The 1992 lines included some affluent suburbs west of Minneapolis and that year the 6th elected Republican Rod Grams, who went on to be elected U.S. Senator in 1994. The altered 1994 plan took those suburbs away and resulted in a DFL victory by 550 votes. This was one of only four districts which switched from Republican to Democrat in 1994, and would not have done so without redistricting.

The congressman from the 6th District is Bill Luther, the Democrat elected in 1994. He is another of Minnesota's talented career politicians. He grew up near Fergus Falls on a dairy farm owned by his family since 1882, went to college and law school, then was elected to the state House in 1974 at 29 and to the state Senate in 1976. He ran for the 6th District seat in 1982, and lost the DFL endorsement to fellow legislator Gerry Sikorski, whose 697 overdrafts on the House bank opened up the district to competition in the 1990s. Luther's life seems to be politics; his wife Darlene has served in the state House since 1992. He was Assistant Majority Leader in the state Senate, wrote the state's campaign finance laws, promoted a D.A.R.E. drug initiative for children. He worked hard, kept a low profile, developed shrewd strategies, and was strongly partisan. He had been eyeing the 6th District ever since Sikorski lost to Grams, and when redistricting removed his home base of Brooklyn Center, he bought a second house north of St. Paul; his base is now Stillwater. His Republican opponent, Tad Jude, was a career politician with a residence outside the new district lines. Jude was elected to the state House as a DFLer in 1972, at 20, ran for the 6th District as a pro-lifer and lost the DFL endorsement in 1980, was elected to the state Senate in 1982, then lost the 1992 primary to Sikorski 49%–46%.

The campaign was fiercely and expensively contested: Luther spent $1.1 million and Jude $699,000. Luther painted Jude as an extremist on abortion and compared him to losing Republican gubernatorial endorsee Allen Quist. Jude attacked Luther for voting against longer sentences for violent rapists and criminals attacking seniors. A late Jude ad attacked Luther for opposing a bill that would have prevented from being paroled a convict who had abducted and raped three women. Luther and local reporters said it was inaccurate, because the law would not have been retroactive. Luther won by 550 votes, carrying Washington and Anoka Counties and losing Dakota.

In the House Luther had a largely liberal voting record, but took up some reform causes with Republicans. He supported the Blue Dog budget and got a good rating from the Concord Coalition. With Gil Gutknecht he moved to reduce political appointees in the executive branch from 3200 to 2300, pointing out that Franklin Roosevelt licked the Depression and won World War II with 200; it passed the House 267–150, but was dropped in conference. With Jack Metcalf and Todd Tiahrt, he moved to deny COLAs to members of Congress; that went nowhere.

In 1996 Luther again faced Jude, who had been indicted under the state Fair Campaign Practices ad for the crime ad; a court dismissed the indictment in March 1996. Meanwhile, Luther raised the vast sum of $1.3 million and spent $851,000 to only $393,000 for Jude. Luther won 56%–44%, running well ahead of Bill Clinton. He served as ranking member of a Small Business Subcommittee in the 104th Congress, then moved to International Relations for 1996 after an unsuccessful bid for a seat on Commerce. His $524,000 left over in the bank will be a deterrent to serious opposition in 1998 and he could be a strong challenger against his predecessor in the House, Rod Grams, in the 2000 Senate race.

The People: Pop. 1990: 547,055; 10% rural; 6% age 65+; 96% White; 1% Black; 1% Asian; 1% Amer. Indian; 1% Hispanic origin. Households: 67% married couple families; 38% married couple fams. w. children; 56% college educ.; median household income: $42,346; per capita income: $16,970; median gross rent: $513; median house value: $90,900.

1996 Presidential Vote

Clinton (D)	154,333	(51%)
Dole (R)	107,560	(35%)
Perot (I)	37,111	(12%)
Other	5,201	(2%)

1992 Presidential Vote

Clinton (D)	120,759	(39%)
Bush (R)	102,265	(33%)
Perot (I)	82,587	(27%)

Rep. Bill Luther (DFL)

Elected 1994; b. June 27, 1945, Fergus Falls; home, Stillwater; U. of MN, B.S. 1967, J.D. 1970; Catholic; married (Darlene).

Career: Clerk, 8th Circuit U.S. Court of Appeals, 1970–71; Practicing atty., 1971–92; MN House of Reps., 1974–76; MN Senate, 1976–94.

DC Office: 117 CHOB 20515, 202-225-2271; Fax: 202-225-3368; e-mail: tellbill@mail.house.gov.

District Offices: Woodbury, 612-730-4949.

Committees: *International Relations* (21st of 22 D): International Economic Policy & Trade. *Science* (15th of 21 D): Basic Research; Space & Aeronautics.

Group Ratings

	ADA	ACLU	AFS	LCV	CFA	CON	NFIB	COC	ACU	NTLC	CHC
1996	80	62	92	92	92	98	32	19	0	17	20
1995	85	—	—	75	100	97	—	38	24	—	—

National Journal Ratings

	1995 LIB — 1995 CONS			1996 LIB — 1996 CONS		
Economic	66%	—	33%	73%	—	25%
Social	72%	—	27%	72%	—	27%
Foreign	68%	—	31%	84%	—	16%

Key Votes of the 104th Congress

1. Reduce Medicare Growth $	N	5. Flag Amendment	Y	9. Cuban Embargo	N
2. Ovrd. Product Liab. Veto	N	6. Drop EPA Limits	Y	10. Bar Bosnia Troop $	N
3. Increase Min. Wage	Y	7. Repeal Assault-Weap. Ban	N	11. Cut Anti-Missile Defense	Y
4. Welfare Reform	N	8. Ovrd. Part. Birth Veto	N	12. Bar U.N. Uniforms	N

Election Results

1996 general	Bill Luther (DFL)	164,921	(56%)	($850,638)
	Tad Jude (R)	129,989	(44%)	($392,953)
1996 primary	Bill Luther (DFL)	unopposed		
1994 general	Bill Luther (DFL)	113,740	(50%)	($1,133,977)
	Tad Jude (IR)	113,190	(50%)	($699,413)

SEVENTH DISTRICT

The lake-strewn country along the upper stretches of the Mississippi River, settled by Norwegian and German immigrants, is the source of some prime American literary and political traditions. Here a century ago in the town of Sauk Centre grew up Sinclair Lewis, whose *Main Street* and *Babbitt* were greeted as the definitive satires of small town life, though on rereading they show surprising affection for their subjects. Not far north of Sauk Centre is Little Falls, the boyhood home of Charles Lindbergh, whose father was a progressive and isolationist congressman who opposed declaring war on Germany in 1917. In those years this seemingly placid country was seething with rage, as WASPy nationalists banned German from schools, renamed sauerkraut liberty cabbage, and boycotted German-American businesses. The rage simmered and became the source of the bitter isolationism of the 1930s and 1940s, of which Lindbergh was a national leader, and of the bitter anti-Communism of the 1950s. This part of Minnesota is also the home—though the actual location has somehow disappeared from the map—of Garrison Keillor's Lake Wobegon, whose history has an authentic ring: founded by New England Yankees as New Albion in 1852, renamed when Norwegians got a majority on the council in 1880, where the Norwegian flag still flies on holidays but no one has seen a German flag since 1917.

The 7th Congressional District of Minnesota, covering the northwest corner of the state, includes just about all this territory. It takes in the wheat-farming plains up near North Dakota and the German Catholic country, strewn with farm villages named for saints, around Sauk Centre and St. Cloud. This is a mixed area politically: some wheat counties are heavily DFL; heavily Norwegian Otter Tail County leans Republican; St. Cloud and Stearns County are volatile, dovish and anti-abortion. The 7th's political history reads like something out of *Lake Wobegon Days*. Back in 1958, Congresswoman Coya Knutson lost reelection when her husband Andy issued a plaintive statement urging her to come home and make his breakfast again; she was the only incumbent Democrat to lose in heavily Democratic 1958. Other Scandinavian names followed: Odin Langen, Bob Bergland (later Jimmy Carter's Secretary of Agriculture), Arlan Stangeland. None except Bergland won by any great margin. For most of the last 40 years this has been one of America's prime marginal districts.

The congressman from the 7th District today is Collin Peterson, who has run for this seat eight times and won four times, the last one convincingly. Peterson grew up here, went to Moorhead State College across the Red River of the North from Fargo, North Dakota, then started a CPA office in Detroit Lakes. In 1976 he was elected to the state Senate, where he served 10 years, passing a 16% farm property tax reduction in 1985 and starting the Chickadee Checkoff which raises $900,000 a year for non-game wildlife fund. He also started running for the House. He lost a DFL caucus in 1982; he lost to Stangeland in 1984 and 1986 (by only 121 votes the second time; he declared victory and went to Washington to set up an office); he lost the DFL primary again in 1988. But in 1990, when the *St. Cloud Times* reported that Stangeland made 341 credit card calls to a woman not his wife, Peterson won with a robust 54%. In office, he continued to do things his way, acting as his own press secretary, campaign consultant, and pilot on flights within the district. He had a small staff, with community economic development professionals rather than Washington policy wonks. On the Agriculture Committee he pushed bills for rural economic development and wetland preservation and supported higher subsidies and price supports. He has rallied votes against changing the sugar program and vehemently opposed NAFTA. Moderate to conservative on cultural issues, he favors parental consent abortion laws and opposes gun control. In 1992 and 1994 he beat a young Republican legislator from Stearns County 51%–49% each time.

Ironically, the election of a Republican Congress has helped make this Democrat from a long-marginal district a nationally important figure. In February 1995, while voting for some parts of the Contract with America, Peterson and Gary Condit founded the Blue Dog Coalition Democrats, for "common sense legislation that embraces the ideas and values of mainstream America." He opposed what he considers overbearing environmental regulations and came up with a Blue Dog budget that moves toward balance with no tax cuts and less stringent spending cuts than the Republicans' budgets. In December 1995 he also criticized Senate Democrats on the budget: "They are not dealing with realistic numbers and are not dealing with where we have to be to get a budget deal." The Blue Dog budgets have not passed, but Peterson and the group were credited with organizing a political center with enough clout to propel the 1997 budget deal to completion. With fellow Blue Dog Dave Minge, Peterson also proposed a milder farm reform than the Freedom to Farm Act, which he believes will backfire when farm prices slump. "Farmers are going to be in Washington asking for help. And we'll help them. We always do."

Peterson's Blue Dog initiatives seemed a little risky for this district. There was talk of a primary challenge from a liberal Democrat but none materialized, and the National Resources Defense Council ran ads attacking Peterson for supporting restrictions on EPA. On the right, he was opposed by Republican Darrell McKigney, communications director of the Minnesota Family Council; but McKigney had no regional base and spent only $181,000 to Peterson's $532,000. Peterson won 68%–32%, carrying every county by a wide margin: a stirring endorsement of his independent course. He now stands as a force to be dealt with in a closely divided House.

The People: Pop. 1990: 547,021; 62% rural; 15% age 65+; 96% White; 1% Asian; 2% Amer. Indian; 1% Hispanic origin. Households: 61% married couple families; 30% married couple fams. w. children; 40% college educ.; median household income: $22,893; per capita income: $10,294; median gross rent: $316; median house value: $50,200.

1996 Presidential Vote

Clinton (D)	115,996	(45%)
Dole (R)	103,336	(40%)
Perot (I)	33,577	(13%)
Other	4,079	(2%)

1992 Presidential Vote

Clinton (D)	104,359	(38%)
Bush (R)	103,624	(38%)
Perot (I)	63,610	(23%)

Rep. Collin C. Peterson (DFL)

Elected 1990; b. June 29, 1944, Fargo, ND; home, Detroit Lakes; Moorhead St. U., B.A. 1966; Lutheran; divorced.

Career: Army Natl. Guard, 1963–69; Accountant, 1966–90; MN Senate, 1976–86.

DC Office: 2159 RHOB 20515, 202-225-2165; Fax: 202-225-1593; e-mail: tocollin.peterson@mail.house.gov.

District Offices: Detroit Lakes, 218-847-5056; Red Lake Falls, 218-253-4356; Waite Park, 320-259-0559.

Committees: *Agriculture* (4th of 23 D): Forestry, Resource Conservation & Research; Livestock, Dairy & Poultry (RMM). *Veterans' Affairs* (9th of 13 D): Health.

Group Ratings

	ADA	ACLU	AFS	LCV	CFA	CON	NFIB	COC	ACU	NTLC	CHC
1996	55	38	58	85	62	73	70	63	53	49	57
1995	45	—	—	13	15	97	—	63	60	—	—

National Journal Ratings

	1995 LIB — 1995 CONS		1996 LIB — 1996 CONS	
Economic	58% —	41%	60% —	40%
Social	36% —	64%	44% —	55%
Foreign	58% —	42%	78% —	21%

Key Votes of the 104th Congress

1. Reduce Medicare Growth $	N	5. Flag Amendment	Y	9. Cuban Embargo	Y
2. Ovrd. Product Liab. Veto	N	6. Drop EPA Limits	N	10. Bar Bosnia Troop $	Y
3. Increase Min. Wage	Y	7. Repeal Assault-Weap. Ban	Y	11. Cut Anti-Missile Defense	Y
4. Welfare Reform	Y	8. Ovrd. Part. Birth Veto	Y	12. Bar U.N. Uniforms	Y

Election Results

1996 general	Collin C. Peterson (DFL)	170,936	(68%)	($532,229)
	Darrell McKigney (R)	80,132	(32%)	($181,026)
1996 primary	Collin C. Peterson (DFL)	unopposed		
1994 general	Collin C. Peterson (DFL)	108,023	(51%)	($584,092)
	Bernie Omann (IR)	102,623	(49%)	($507,325)

EIGHTH DISTRICT

In the 1860s, prospectors in the Arrowhead region of the new state of Minnesota, northwest of Lake Superior in the low hills of the Mesabi Range, happened upon the nation's largest veins of iron ore; they moved on, looking for gold. But in the 1880s, Duluth banker George Stone and Philadelphia financier Charlemagne Tower started mining the Iron Range and created the northern end of the lifeline of American heavy industry. The range runs south alongside rail lines to the port of Duluth nestled on dramatic bluffs over the always cold and, every winter, frozen waters of Lake Superior—one of the most beautiful settings for a city in North America. Duluth was a grain-shipping rival of Chicago and the premier iron-ore port. Its city plan was drawn up by Daniel Burnham and its splendid turn-of-the-century buildings still celebrate the triumph of technology and civilization over wilderness and the elements. Millions of tons of ore have been dug out of the Range, loaded into rail cars for the ride down to Duluth, and into Great Lakes freighters for shipment to Cleveland, Gary, Detroit, Chicago, Pittsburgh and Buffalo.

For most of this century, in this land where the Arctic winds blow down over the Canadian Shield's thousands of inland lakes, about 100,000 people have lived on the Iron Range and another 100,000 in Duluth, most of them the products of America's 1880–1924 wave of immigration—Italians, Poles, Serbs and Croats, Jews, Swedes and Finns. In this punishing environment, they worked to the point of exhaustion, built solid houses with staunch central heating, and wore layers of warm clothing to survive the winter. Life was rough: the work was hard, the hours long, and the pay low. The churches, a separate one for each ethnic group, were the main community institutions. Living conditions improved vastly in the decades of great economic growth after World War II, but life remains rough-hewn today, and there is still economic distress. As the iron and steel industry got more efficient, fewer workers were needed. When the American steel industry collapsed after 1979, it needed even fewer, or none at all. Now steel and iron ore are profitable again, but with many fewer workers; northern Minnesota's biggest new employer is Northwest Airlines, with a repair facility in Duluth and reservations center in the Iron Range, located there in return for an $840 million investment by the state government when the airline was in trouble in the early 1990s.

The 8th Congressional District of Minnesota includes Duluth and the Iron Range, plus much of the north woods and lake country to the west and south; it moves all the way south to the boundaries of the Twin Cities metro area, to Isanti and Chisago Counties where young families are building new homes near pleasant old lakeside towns. The 8th District has been the bulwark of Minnesota's Democratic-Farmer-Labor Party since it was created in 1944, with turbulent convention and primary politics and solid DFL margins every November.

The congressman from the 8th District is Jim Oberstar, is from Chisholm in the Iron Range, where his father was a miner and union official. He studied French in college and in Belgium; for four years he was a civilian employee of the U.S. Naval Mission to Haiti, teaching French and Creole to Marines and French and English to Haitians. Then, in 1963, at 29, he landed a job as chief of staff to Congressman John Blatnik in Washington: he has been working for the 8th

District for a third of a century. When Blatnik retired in 1974, Oberstar won the seat, beating Tony Perpich, brother of former Governor Rudy Perpich. He won tough primaries in 1980 and 1984, the latter after briefly running for the Senate. His views are in the liberal Catholic tradition: he believes government has an obligation to help the poor and disadvantaged and to stimulate economic growth, and he has little faith in economic markets. He was long dubious about American military involvement abroad, especially in Central America, but favored involvement in Haiti. On many cultural issues his attitudes are traditional and he is an opponent of abortion.

On the Transportation and Infrastructure Committee, Oberstar was successfully following the tradition of Blatnik, who chaired the panel when it was called Public Works; following the October 1995 resignation of Norman Mineta, Oberstar became the ranking Democrat. For years he worked to bring projects into Duluth and the Iron Range and nurturing programs like EDA and UDAG, which did so. He claims credit for $80 million in highways, airports, high-tech research centers and the Voyageurs National Park visitor center. As chairman and ranking member of the Aviation Subcommittee, he worked hard for the state investment in Northwest and the Duluth and Iron Range facilities the airline built in return. He would like to make the FAA a separate agency outside the Transportation Department and opposes privatization of air traffic control; in alliance with unions, he held up the 1996 aviation bill for a time because of the FedEx provision which would have made it very difficult for FedEx workers to go on strike. With Transportation Chairman Bud Shuster, he sponsored the measure, passed in the House but not the Senate, to take the transportation trust funds off-budget.

Long a backer of big government, Oberstar has worked on deregulation, notably the measures to abolish the ICC and to deregulate ocean shipping (he, with the unions, wanted contracts published). The 8th District is on an international border, and Oberstar is alert to the fact that problems cross borders. He has proposed a single binational entity to manage the St. Lawrence Seaway; he opposes harmonization of truck safety standards with Canada and Mexico. On other issues, he opposed the Auburn Dam and the Union Pacific-Southern Pacific merger; he has a bill to allow states to recoup from tobacco companies the Medicaid dollars they spent on smokers.

Oberstar has ordinarily been reelected by very wide margins; his 1994 opponent, curiously, made a big issue of term limits in a district which has chosen to elect only two men to the House in 50 years. In 1996 Oberstar won 67%–25%, running 14% ahead of Bill Clinton.

The People: Pop. 1990: 546,576; 60% rural; 15% age 65+; 97% White; 2% Amer. Indian; 1% Hispanic origin. Households: 61% married couple families; 29% married couple fams. w. children; 40% college educ.; median household income: $24,667; per capita income: $11,302; median gross rent: $308; median house value: $49,000.

1996 Presidential Vote

Clinton (D)	148,886	(53%)
Dole (R)	88,095	(31%)
Perot (I)	38,405	(14%)
Other	6,147	(2%)

1992 Presidential Vote

Clinton (D)	138,426	(48%)
Bush (R)	80,517	(28%)
Perot (I)	70,539	(24%)

Rep. James L. Oberstar (DFL)

Elected 1974; b. Sept. 10, 1934, Chisholm; home, Chisholm; St. Thomas Col., B.A. 1956, Col. of Europe, Bruges, Belgium, M.A. 1957; Catholic; married (Jean).

Career: Navy civilian language teacher, Haiti, 1959–63; A.A., U.S. Rep. John Blatnik, 1963–74; A.A., U.S. House Public Works Cmte., 1971–74.

DC Office: 2366 RHOB 20515, 202-225-6211; Fax: 202-225-0699; e-mail: oberstar@hr.house.gov.

District Offices: Brainerd, 218-828-4400; Chisholm, 218-254-5761; Duluth, 218-727-7474; Fojo, 218-723-8813; Elk River, 612-241-0188.

Committees: *Transportation & Infrastructure* (RMM of 33 D).

Group Ratings

	ADA	ACLU	AFS	LCV	CFA	CON	NFIB	COC	ACU	NTLC	CHC
1996	80	88	100	77	54	40	22	20	20	5	26
1995	95	—	—	100	77	31	—	13	16	—	—

National Journal Ratings

	1995 LIB — 1995 CONS			1996 LIB — 1996 CONS		
Economic	94%	—	0%	89%	—	0%
Social	62%	—	38%	65%	—	35%
Foreign	88%	—	7%	79%	—	19%

Key Votes of the 104th Congress

1. Reduce Medicare Growth $	N	5. Flag Amendment	N	9. Cuban Embargo	N
2. Ovrd. Product Liab. Veto	N	6. Drop EPA Limits	Y	10. Bar Bosnia Troop $	N
3. Increase Min. Wage	Y	7. Repeal Assault-Weap. Ban	Y	11. Cut Anti-Missile Defense	Y
4. Welfare Reform	N	8. Ovrd. Part. Birth Veto	Y	12. Bar U.N. Uniforms	Y

Election Results

1996 general	James L. Oberstar (DFL)	185,333	(67%)	($538,159)
	Andy Larson (R)	69,460	(25%)	($26,951)
	Stan (The Man) Estes (RP)	16,639	(6%)	
1996 primary	James L. Oberstar (DFL)	unopposed		
1994 general	James L. Oberstar (DFL)	153,161	(66%)	($488,411)
	Phil Herwig (IR)	79,818	(34%)	($31,673)

MISSISSIPPI

Mississippi carries the weight of a tragic history as it takes hurried steps toward the future. This green land was settled in a rush in Jacksonian America, mostly by small farmers headed west from Georgia and south from Tennessee, and settled too by a small number of big planters, who made vast gains and great losses, built grand mansions and sent their sons to Civil War. For a century afterward, even as industrial farmers drained the Delta lands, Mississippi with its racial segregation, subsistence farmers and sharecroppers, and low wages, lived apart from most of America. It never developed great cities—its two commercial metropolises are Memphis and New Orleans. But if it did not excel at commerce, it did at art. Mississippi gave us the music of the blues and Elvis Presley. It gave the world William Faulkner and Eudora Welty, Walker Percy and Shelby Foote. Their work was informed by a sense of the tragic missing or forgotten in most of America, where life is a triumphant sales pitch or a labor-saving invention. As Anthony Walton, born in Illinois to Mississippi-born parents, put it, "In Mississippi I have learned to stop trying to evade and forget what I have seen and heard and understood and now must know, but rather to embrace the ghosts and cradle the bones and call them my own."

Mississippi has made much progress in the past three decades, but the past still hangs heavy. For years no other state had such a painful contrast between image and reality, between an ideal sincerely strived for and the tawdry facts of everyday life. Magnolia trees on the lawns of antebellum mansions, golden-haired young women in white dresses on the veranda, faithful black servants and retainers: this was once the ideal. And behind it stood loose-jointed frame houses and unpainted back-country stores, cabins without indoor plumbing and poor white crossroads clustered with askew advertising signs. Mississippi for years ranked 50th among states in income, literacy, health and education levels, despite the best efforts of civic, political and business leaders. As William Faulkner said of his state, "You don't love because: you love despite."

Today Mississippi still ranks 50th on many scales. But the gulf between Mississippi and the rest of America has narrowed enormously in the last half-century. In 1940 Mississippi had an economy based on low-wage, subsistence or sharecropper agriculture and a system of racial segregation enforced sometimes by violence. If history is, as Frederic Maitland wrote, the story of the progress from status to contract, then old Mississippi was still at the beginning, for status—race—meant just about everything. In the years since, Mississippi has moved, not always willingly, from status to contract, in its economy and in race relations. Per capita income in Mississippi was 36% of the national average in 1940; in 1995, it was 73%, well below average but, given the lower cost of living here, a level recognizably American. Daily life, thanks to cheap gas and air conditioning, national brands and the mechanization of farming, has changed drastically: most Mississippians of 50 years ago would be astonished by the physical comforts and mechanical marvels their grandchildren take for granted today. They would be astonished as well by relations between blacks and whites. As *The Washington Post's* William Raspberry, a Mississippi native, wrote, "There is an easiness to relationships, a mutual respect and a willingness to move beyond race that, quite frankly, didn't exist during my years in the state. Mississippi is finally a good place to be."

But everyone knows it should be better. The question is how. One answer, put forward by Democratic Governors William Winter and Ray Mabus in the 1980s, can be summarized by the single word "education." Winter finally made kindergarten mandatory and raised the dropout age to 14; Mabus proposed a major school reform policy. But the uncomfortable fact is that most high taxpayers are white and most public school children are black, because many white children attend private academies. About 40% of state spending goes to education, but those

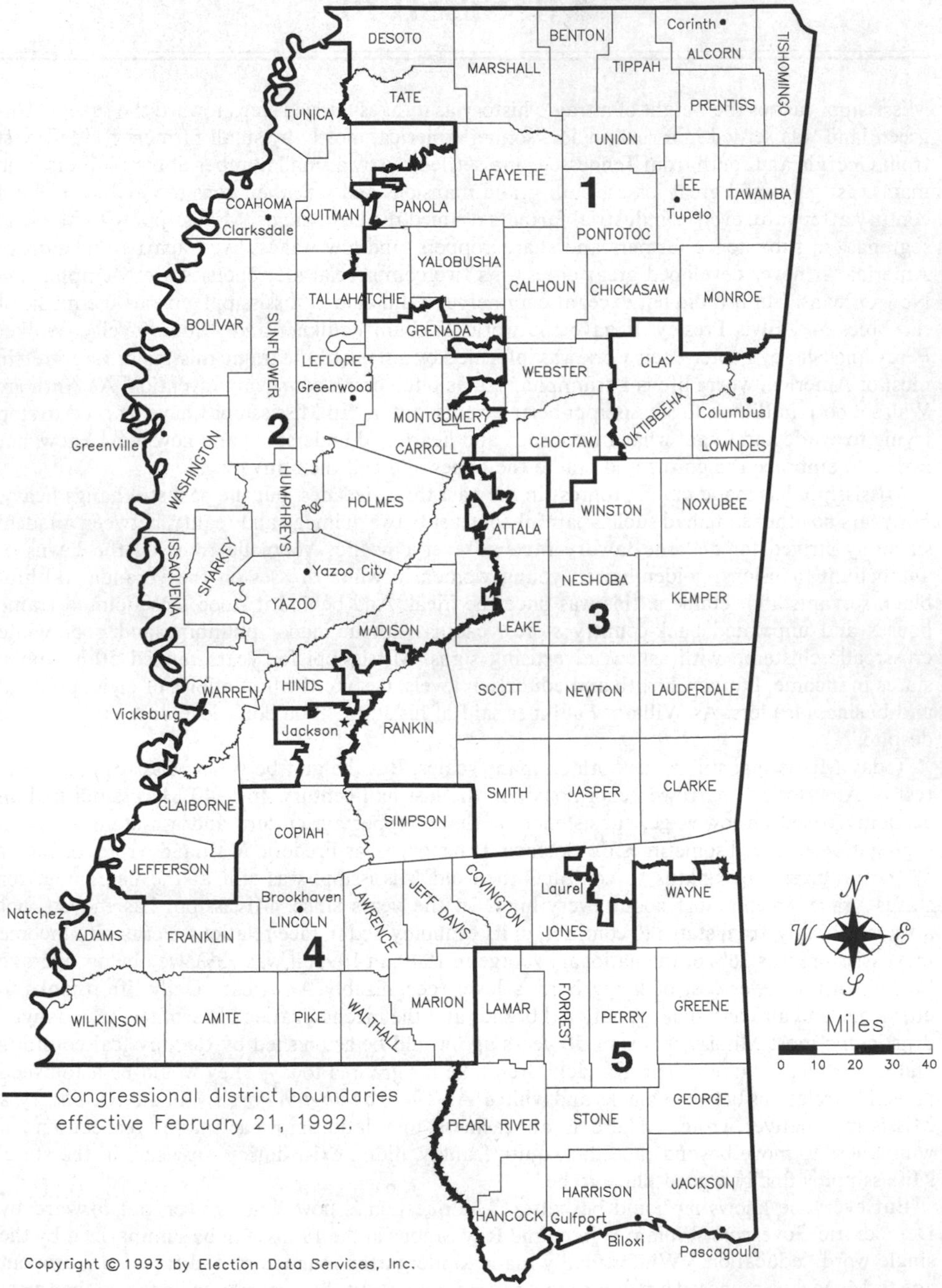

Congressional district boundaries effective February 21, 1992.

who oppose higher spending or taxes can point to the fact that there is no demonstrated correlation between higher education spending and improved test scores and learning. The other view, expressed in blunt terms by Governor Kirk Fordice, who beat Mabus in 1991 and was reelected in 1995, is that it is better to encourage private sector growth by holding down taxes and cutting regulation, by tort reform and by getting tough on crime and prisoners, and by boosting Mississippi's reputation: "Only positive Mississippi spoken here," say the signs Fordice has ordered put up on highways at the state line. Also important is encouraging traditional values, widely shared by blacks as well as whites. Fordice applauded when black Jackson high school principal Bishop Knox instituted school prayer; when Knox was fired by administrators, Mississippi passed a law authorizing student-initiated prayer in schools—which was promptly overturned by in federal court. Fordice also cheered when Jackson TV station owner Frank Melton, also black, went on the air and put up billboards calling on police to arrest certain named drug dealers; arrests were made and convictions followed.

The division between these views is rather close. Fordice won reelection by just 56%–44% in 1995, and in 1996 Bob Dole carried the state by just 49%–44%. Mississippi has two Republican senators, and three Republican congressmen in five districts, but Democrats are not entirely uncompetitive. The points of view of both sides are plausible. But both are in danger of being undercut by the culture. Greenville, which produced authors Hodding Carter (*Main Street Meets the River*) and William Alexander Percy (*Lanterns on the Levee*), where Shelby Foote and Walker Percy went to high school together, is now the nation's top media market in which people watch television more hours a day than any other. And, as Fordice does not like to mention, the biggest driver of economic growth in Mississippi is gambling. Mississippi approved riverboat gambling in 1989, when Mabus was governor, and 7 of 11 Mississippi River counties and two of the three Gulf counties have riverboat gambling now. Fordice has administered the law without serious scandal, but the fact is that crime, bankruptcy and divorce have risen in gambling counties. In the poorest county—Tunica near Memphis, once plantation country and now with four-lane roads jammed with casinogoers—few locals have been able to hold jobs at the casinos. But gambling is booming: in 1995 Mississippi was number three in gambling revenues, behind only Nevada and New Jersey, and in 1996 four 1,000-room casino hotels were rising on the Gulf coast. The original riverboats Mark Twain described in *Life on the Mississippi* were working vehicles, sooty and dangerous, taking chances on the treacherous river; but their captains showed how hard work could get people ahead. Mississippi's riverboat casinos are a form of entertainment, a diversion from gainful economic activity, which teach the lesson that those who get ahead depend on luck rather than talent and hard work. Is this really the lesson Mississippi wants to teach the nation?

Governor. Mississippi Governor Kirk Fordice, a businessman not entirely new to politics, is the first Republican governor elected here since 1874. He has the bluntness of an engineer and the self-assurance of a self-made man; he started his own construction company in Vicksburg at age 28 and in 1990 became head of the Associated General Contractors of America. He is capable of brusque and provocative language, such as his 1992 statement that the United States "is a Christian nation, which does not mean in any way to infer any kind of religious intolerance or any kind of particular dogma that is being forced on anyone." In 1995, while running for reelection, he said, "I'll tell you this. I don't believe we need to keep running this state by *Mississippi Burning* and apologizing for what happened 30 years ago. This is the '90s. This is now. We are on a roll. We've got the best race relations in all the United States of America." He won the governorship in 1991 by beating tough opponents, topping Auditor Pete Johnson, the grandson and nephew of governors, in the Republican primary, then beating incumbent Ray Mabus in the general. Mabus's policies were evidently just a little too liberal for Mississippians: his tax plan had been rejected by the legislature and a 24-hour waiting period on abortion passed over his veto; Mabus beat former Congressman Wayne Dowdy by only 50%–41% in the Democratic primary. Fordice campaigned against welfare abusers and racial quotas—veiled racism, Mabus supporters said. Fordice trailed in polls but won 51%–48%.

In office, Fordice helped pass a capital gains tax cut and tort reform, but a 1% increase in the sales tax was passed over his veto. He vowed to make Mississippi "the capital of capital punishment," and he eliminated air conditioning and television from prisons, required prisoners to wear stripes and to work more hours. He boasted that welfare rolls declined 33% and that K-12 funding went up $30 million. He claims to have attracted thousands of jobs by "CEO-to-CEO recruitment" of corporate executives, and to have cut state spending while Mississippi's riverboat casinos were generating much new revenue.

In 1995 Fordice was opposed by Secretary of State Dick Molpus, one of the young liberals associated with former Governors Winter and Mabus. It was a bitter campaign; when Fordice mocked Molpus's wife's speaking mannerisms in a campaign ad, Molpus said he would take him "to the woodshed" and Fordice said he would "whip his ass." But they also presented a clear contrast in philosophies in which many Mississippians believe, and Fordice won 56%–44%, carrying the Gulf coast and the Jackson area as well as most rural counties, posting respectable percentages in black-majority counties while Molpus carried some nearly all-white counties in northeast Mississippi. Fordice made news in December 1996 when his Jeep Cherokee overturned and caught fire; he was driving home from Memphis unaccompanied by any security, and it took him some months to recover from his injuries.

Fordice cannot succeed himself in 2000. While state House Republican Leader Charlie Williams and Democratic Lieutenant Governor Ronnie Musgrove are possible contenders for 1999, Democratic state Attorney General Mike Moore has the high-profile recognition to make him among the strongest; Moore filed the first suit (a move Fordice opposed), in 1994, against the major tobacco companies seeking reimbursement for state Medicaid expenditures, prompting 29 other states to follow his lead.

Senior Senator. Thad Cochran grew up in small towns in northern Mississippi, the son of a principal and a teacher, graduated with high grades from Ole Miss and its Law School, served in the Navy, spent a year abroad and practiced law in Jackson. In 1972, as Richard Nixon was sweeping Mississippi, he was elected as a Republican to the House from the Jackson area district with a plurality against a white Democrat and black Independent. After three terms, he was ready to retire, when Senator James Eastland retired; Cochran ran, and once again won with a plurality over a white Democrat and a black Independent. In the House and in the Senate he has managed to amass a solidly conservative record with little controversy or acrimony. His pleasant personal demeanor, his refusal to engage in racial politics, and his Republican Party label in a state where most whites have been voting Republican for president for three decades, have made him broadly acceptable to voters. His toughest race came in 1984, when he was opposed by popular former Governor William Winter. Winter could make a case for himself but not against Cochran; Cochran outraised him $2.7 million to $738,000, and won 61%–39%.

One Cochran specialty is farm policy: he serves on the Agriculture Committee and chairs the Appropriations Subcommittee on Agriculture and Rural Development. In 1996 he played a major role on the Freedom to Farm Act. He supported the move to phase out most crop subsidies over seven years, but insisted on maintaining the cotton marketing loan plan which he largely wrote in 1985, with farmers allowed to pay back loans at lower than the nominal interest rate if world prices drop below specified levels. He also pushed for open markets for farm exports. He worked with Vermont's James Jeffords on the complex dairy program. And he wrote the Senate version of the Wildlife Habitat Incentives Program, to give farmers an incentive to preserve habitat.

On other issues, he authored the Mississippi Wilderness Act and worked with Democratic Congressman George Miller on a National Writing Project to help teachers learn how to teach writing. He has worked for grants for historically black colleges and for vocational training for the disabled; he sponsored a bill to bring the latest computer technologies to the nation's schools. His voting record is tempered with respect for Mississippi interests. "I always voted against subsidies for the maritime industry," he explained in 1993. "It was the conservative position to take. Then I was campaigning for reelection at the gates of the Ingalls shipyard in Pascagoula. I was handing out my leaflets and the union guys showed up with their leaflets, saying 'A vote for Cochran is a vote against your job.' Ever since then, I've voted for maritime subsidies."

Cochran was part of the Republican leadership for six years. In 1990 he challenged the more moderate John Chafee of Rhode Island for the chairmanship of the Senate Republican Conference, the number three leadership position, and won 22–21. But in 1994 he pointedly endorsed Al Simpson, the Republican whip, when he was challenged for that number two position by his junior Mississippi colleague Trent Lott. Lott, with support from younger conservatives, won anyway, thus leapfrogging Cochran. And when Bob Dole announced in May 1996 that he would resign from the Senate in June, Cochran and Lott both entered the race for majority leader; Lott had the contest sewed up, but Cochran stayed in and lost 44–8. He has fared much better at the polls in Mississippi. In 1990 he was unopposed and for 1996 he spent $1.3 million and was reelected 71%–27%.

Junior Senator. Trent Lott is the Senate majority leader, elected to that position after less than a decade in the Senate (as was Lyndon Johnson in 1955). He grew up in Pascagoula, the son of a shipyard worker and a teacher, went to Ole Miss and worked his way through law school by running the Ole Miss alumni affairs office, accumulating good contacts along the way. After just a year of law practice, he got a job with Democratic Gulf Coast Congressman William Colmer, chairman of the Rules Committee. When Colmer retired in 1972, Lott ran for the House seat with Colmer's encouragement and endorsement—as a Republican. He was elected with 55% in what was the strongest Nixon district in the country that year. In 1974, Lott was the youngest member of the Judiciary Committee, loyally defending Richard Nixon in the impeachment hearings. In 1980, he was elected Republican whip, and he ran the Republican National Convention's platform committees in 1980 and 1984. He supported Jack Kemp for president in 1988, even as he was running for the Senate himself. In the House he was an ally of Kemp and the young Newt Gingrich, and his decision to run for the Senate opened the way for Newt Gingrich's rise: Lott was succeeded as whip by Dick Cheney; when Cheney became Defense secretary in March 1989, Gingrich was elected whip 87–85. Now these two conservatives who were part of one wing of the minority party a decade ago are the majority party's leaders in the two houses of Congress.

Lott gave up a safe seat and a chance at being speaker to run for the Senate in 1988, and he had something of a fight for it. Congressman Wayne Dowdy, who beat Secretary of State Dick Molpus in the primary 54%–42%, voiced populist themes and criticized Lott for having a chauffeur. Lott responded with an ad showing the employee in question, a black law enforcement professional named George Awkward, who explained he was guarding Lott because he was a member of the leadership: "I'm nobody's chauffeur, Mr. Dowdy." Lott outraised Dowdy and won a 61%–39% margin in the Jackson area, the Gulf Coast and other counties where turnout had increased 10% since 1980; in the rest of the state, Dowdy won only 51%–49%, giving Lott a 54%–46% win overall.

There is a discernible hard core of beliefs in Lott's career, and yet he is also an instinctive dealmaker, not much interested in quixotic gestures, an orderly and well-organized man who is dismayed by the dilatoriness of others. He has a visceral dislike of taxes and big government, and he has bucked party leaders on taxes at key junctures, opposing tax reform in 1986 and opposing the budget summit tax increase in 1990. He believes in traditional moral values and he wants people to believe that America is good to the core, not riddled with rottenness. He argues for an assertive foreign policy and plenty of defense spending. He can be sharp in debate, aggressively partisan and combative, but he is gregarious and personable, on good terms with most other members and careful to cultivate those whose support he needs. In the Senate he moved quickly into the leadership. After the 1992 election, he ran for conference secretary, the number four leadership post, and won, with 20 votes to 14 for Christopher Bond and five for Frank Murkowski. In 1993 he was chosen the Republican point man on Clinton appointments, but he mostly avoided confrontations; with the largest percentage of black constituents of any senator, he did not raise ethical questions against Commerce Secretary Ron Brown, just as he tried to smooth the way for Labor Secretary Alexis Herman (who once worked in Pascagoula) four years later.

After being reelected 69%–31% in 1994, he sought to move up again and challenged Republican Whip Alan Simpson. Bob Dole and most Republican moderates strongly supported Simpson, but Lott did well especially with younger conservatives elected in 1992 and 1994 who thought Simpson too moderate on some issues and insufficiently partisan. Lott won 27–26, which made him the first Republican ever elected whip in both houses. In the process he leapfrogged over his Mississippi colleague Thad Cochran, who held the number three leadership position. Lott's comment was typically unsentimental. "There comes a time in life, in politics as in baseball, when you seize the moment or it's gone forever. I ran and he didn't." Lott was careful not to usurp the prerogatives of Dole, who kept many decisions close to the chest. In public statements and in Capitol Hill back rooms, Lott presented a sharper partisan edge than Dole, but still showed a willingness to deal. In May 1996 Dole surprised almost everyone when he announced he would resign from the Senate in June. Lott immediately began canvassing for votes for majority leader and found himself far ahead of Cochran, who insisted on running anyway and lost 44–8. "The torch has been passed, but the flame is the same," he proclaimed on winning, and said he would follow the Dole agenda. He quickly found himself frustrated as Democrats and conservatives blocked action: "things are all balled up here—and it's not my fault." He departed from the Dole agenda by joining House Republicans and pushing for a vote on welfare reform; he also swiftly disposed of the minimum wage issue and pushed for the compromise healthcare bill and the Safe Drinking Water Act. He gave Republicans a solid record to run on—but left Dole with fewer issues on which to attack Clinton. He kept a back channel to the Clinton White House through pollster Dick Morris, who had worked for him as well as for Clinton in the past. He was solicitous to the new whip, Don Nickles, to freshmen and to party moderates and managed to work smoothly with Democratic Leader Tom Daschle.

After Dole lost and Newt Gingrich faced ethics charges that threatened to topple him, Lott was suddenly the most visible Republican leader in Congress. And his allies claimed that he was the most influential Republican, as well. Even as moderates worried that he would pursue a conservative agenda, conservatives worried that he would just be a deal-maker; both sides had something to fear. He helped junior members by limiting most senators to one committee or subcommittee chairmanship, and smoothed the way for Ben Nighthorse Campbell to chair the Indian Affairs Committee. After sending conciliatory signals that he would wait for the Clinton Administration to come forward with a budget in early 1997, he was a relentless advocate in closed-door negotiations that led the President and Republican leaders to announce in May a deal to balance the budget in 2002. Despite grumbling from a few on the Left and on the Right, and from budget experts who claimed that more should have been done and that the spending cuts were left mostly to the far out-years, the initial response was largely positive even though it would take many months of contentious debate to fill in all the details. But, as must happen for any Senate leader, some things will continue to go awry. "Counting senators is like getting bullfrogs in a wheelbarrow, two in and one jumps out." Lott's attempt to keep a narrow focus on Fred Thompson's investigation of campaign irregularities came undone as many reform-minded Republicans joined Democrats and forced a wider probe. Conservatives also griped about Lott joining Clinton to actively support ratification of the chemical-weapons treaty. His conservative and partisan instincts were by no means defunct: in early 1997 he joined the call to simplify the income-tax code, set a 25% ceiling on taxpayers' total payments to Washington and local governments, and to eliminate the IRS; and he walked out of his own office when Democrat Wendell Ford threatened to torpedo Republicans' investigation into the election results of the Louisiana Senate race. He was furious when the Navy passed over Pascagoula's Ingalls shipyard for Maine's Bath Iron Works and New Orleans's Avondale; he has long used his considerable influence to help Ingalls as well as Mississippi military bases. But conservative activists, still waiting for him to place his imprint on the Senate, complain that he has delivered little change from Dole as leader in style or substance.

Presidential politics. Mississippi voted 50%–41% for George Bush in 1992, his best percentage in the country; it was 49%–44% for Bob Dole in 1996, suggesting a tilt toward Democrats, or perhaps higher black turnout. On balance it is a Republican state, but not because of race; it is other issues—defense, crime, cultural attitudes, taxes—on which majorities here shunned Walter Mondale, Michael Dukakis and Bill Clinton.

Mississippi held its primary on Super Tuesday in 1996; Bob Dole easily beat Pat Buchanan.

Congressional districting. In 1984, Mississippi was the first state to get a redistricting plan dictated by the dominant interpretation of the 1982 Voting Rights Amendments. The result was the black-majority 2d District, which duly elected Mike Espy in 1986; he went on to become Bill Clinton's Agriculture secretary from 1993–94. Ironically, Espy wanted to hold down the black percentage in the 2d in the 1991 plan, because he was winning white votes and he wanted more black influence in other districts. But civil rights organizations said no. The result is that the other four districts vote heavily Republican in national politics. Democrats elected four congressmen here as recently as 1992. But one retired in 1994, one switched parties in 1995 and another retired in 1996, and the delegation is now 3–2 Republican.

The People: Est. Pop. 1996: 2,716,000; Pop. 1990: 2,573,216, up 5.5% 1990–1996. 1.0% of U.S. total, 31st largest; 53% rural. Median age: 32.9 years. 12% 65 years and over. 63.1% White, 35.4% Black, 1% Asian, 1% Hispanic origin. Households: 54.7% married couple families; 27% married couple fams. w. children; 37% college educ.; median household income: $20,136; per capita income: $9,648; 71.5% owner occupied housing; median house value: $45,600; median monthly rent: $215. 6.1% Unemployment. 1996 Voting age pop.: 1,967,000. 1996 Turnout: 893,857; 45% of VAP. Registered voters (1996): 1,715,913; no party registration.

Political Lineup: Governor, Kirk Fordice (R); Lt. Gov., Ronnie Musgrove (D); Secy. of State, Eric Clark (D); Atty. Gen., Mike Moore (D); Treasurer, Marshall Bennett (D); Auditor, Phil Bryant (R). State Senate, 52 (34 D and 18 R); Senate President, Ronnie Musgrove (D); State House, 122 (83 D, 36 R, 2 I, and 1 vacancy); House Speaker, Tim Ford (D). Senators, Thad Cochran (R) and Trent Lott (R). Representatives, 5 (3 R and 2 D).

Elections Division: 601-359-6359; **Filing Deadline for U.S. Congress:** March 1, 1998.

1996 Presidential Vote

Dole (R)	439,833	(49%)
Clinton (D)	394,020	(44%)
Perot (I)	52,221	(6%)

1996 Republican Presidential Primary

Dole (R)	91,639	(60%)
Buchanan (R)	39,324	(26%)
Forbes (R)	12,119	(8%)
Other	8,843	(7%)

1992 Presidential Vote

Bush (R)	487,793	(50%)
Clinton (D)	400,268	(41%)
Perot (I)	105,045	(9%)

GOVERNOR

Gov. Kirk Fordice (R)

Elected 1991, term expires Jan. 2000; b. Feb. 10, 1934, Memphis, TN; home, Vicksburg; Purdue U., B.S. 1956, M.S. 1957; Methodist; married (Pat).

Career: Army, 1957–59, Army Reserves, 1959–77; Engineer, Exxon Corp., 1956, 1959–62; Exec., Fordice Construction Co., 1962–92; Pres., Assoc. General Contractors of Amer., 1989–91.

Office: State Capitol, P.O. Box 139, Jackson 39205, 601-359-3100; Fax: 601-359-3022; Web site: www.state.ms.us.

Election Results

1995 gen.	Kirk Fordice (R)	455,261	(56%)
	Dick Molpus (D)	364,210	(44%)
1995 prim.	Kirk Fordice (R)	117,907	(94%)
	Wagonwheel Blair (R)	4,919	(4%)
	Other (R)	2,956	(2%)
1991 gen.	Kirk Fordice (R)	361,500	(51%)
	Ray Mabus (D)	338,459	(48%)
	Other	11,253	(2%)

SENATORS

Sen. Thad Cochran (R)

Elected 1978, seat up 2002; b. Dec. 7, 1937, Pontotoc; home, Jackson; U. of MS, B.A. 1959, J.D. 1965, Rotary Fellow, Trinity Col., Ireland, 1963–64; Baptist; married (Rose).

Career: Navy, 1959–61; Practicing atty., 1965–72; U.S. House of Reps., 1972–78.

DC Office: 326 RSOB 20510, 202-224-5054; e-mail: senator@cochran.senate.gov.

State Offices: Jackson, 601-965-4459; Oxford, 601-236-1018.

Committees: *Agriculture, Nutrition & Forestry* (3rd of 10 R): Marketing, Inspection & Product Promotion; Production & Price Competitiveness. *Appropriations* (2nd of 15 R): Agriculture, Rural Development & Related Agencies (Chmn.); Defense; Energy & Water Development; Interior; Labor, Health & Human Services & Education. *Governmental Affairs* (5th of 9 R): International Security, Proliferation & Federal Services (Chmn.); Permanent Subcommittee on Investigations. *Rules & Administration* (5th of 9 R). *Joint Committee on the Library of Congress* (3rd of 5 Sens.). *Joint Committee on Printing* (2nd of 5 Sens.).

Group Ratings

	ADA	ACLU	AFS	LCV	CFA	CON	NFIB	COC	ACU	NTLC	CHC
1996	5	11	0	0	7	76	92	91	94	97	100
1995	0	—	10	0	0	54	—	95	83	—	—

National Journal Ratings

	1995 LIB — 1995 CONS			1996 LIB — 1996 CONS		
Economic	34%	—	64%	24%	—	75%
Social	21%	—	78%	0%	—	72%
Foreign	22%	—	67%	32%	—	65%

Key Votes of the 104th Congress

1. Reduce Medicare Growth $	Y	5. Flag Amendment	Y	9. Anti-Missile Defense	Y
2. Lmt. Prod. Liab. Damages	Y	6. Endangered Species	N	10. Cuban Embargo	Y
3. Increase Min. Wage	*	7. Gay Employment Rights	N	11. Bar Bosnia Troop $	N
4. Welfare Reform	Y	8. Ovrd. Part. Birth Veto	Y	12. Cut Vietnam Aid	N

Election Results

1996 general	Thad Cochran (R)	624,154	(71%)	($1,305,680)
	James W. Hunt (D)	240,647	(27%)	
	Others	13,861	(2%)	
1996 primary	Thad Cochran (R)	138,813	(95%)	
	Richard O'Hara (R)	6,762	(5%)	
1990 general	Thad Cochran (R)	unopposed		($691,865)

Sen. Trent Lott (R)

Elected 1988, seat up 2000; b. Oct. 9, 1941, Grenada; home, Pascagoula; U. of MS, B.A. 1963, J.D. 1967; Baptist; married (Tricia).

Career: Practicing atty., 1967–68; A.A., U.S. Rep. William Colmer, 1968–72; U.S. House of Reps., 1972–1988.

DC Office: 487 RSOB 20510, 202-224-6253; Fax: 202-224-2262.

State Offices: Greenwood, 601-453-5681; Gulfport, 601-863-1988; Jackson, 601-965-4644; Oxford, 601-234-3774; Pascagoula, 601-762-5400.

Committees: *Majority Leader*. *Commerce, Science & Transportation* (5th of 11 R): Aviation; Communications. *Finance* (9th of 11 R): International Trade; Long-Term Growth, Debt & Deficit Reduction; Taxation & IRS Oversight. *Rules & Administration* (8th of 9 R). *Intelligence (Select)* (ex-officio).

Group Ratings

	ADA	ACLU	AFS	LCV	CFA	CON	NFIB	COC	ACU	NTLC	CHC
1996	5	17	0	0	7	64	100	85	100	100	100
1995	0	—	0	0	0	29	—	100	96	—	—

National Journal Ratings

	1995 LIB — 1995 CONS			1996 LIB — 1996 CONS		
Economic	12%	—	84%	0%	—	94%
Social	0%	—	88%	33%	—	62%
Foreign	8%	—	81%	0%	—	74%

Key Votes of the 104th Congress

1. Reduce Medicare Growth $	Y	5. Flag Amendment	Y	9. Anti-Missile Defense	Y
2. Lmt. Prod. Liab. Damages	Y	6. Endangered Species	N	10. Cuban Embargo	Y
3. Increase Min. Wage	N	7. Gay Employment Rights	N	11. Bar Bosnia Troop $	N
4. Welfare Reform	Y	8. Ovrd. Part. Birth Veto	N	12. Cut Vietnam Aid	Y

Election Results

1994 general	Trent Lott (R)	418,333	(69%)	($2,516,189)
	Ken Harper (D)	189,752	(31%)	($345,379)
1994 primary	Trent Lott (R)	72,543	(95%)	
	Others	3,476	(5%)	
1988 general	Trent Lott (R)	510,380	(54%)	($3,405,242)
	Wayne Dowdy (D)	436,339	(46%)	($2,355,957)

FIRST DISTRICT

The university town of Oxford, the center of William Faulkner's fictional Yoknapatawpha County, sits on a divide between the hill country of Mississippi and the flat farmlands of the Mississippi Delta. The mostly white hill counties run up to where the Tennessee River nicks the northeast corner of Tishomingo County. The Tennessee Valley Authority brought electricity here, the Tennessee-Tombigbee Waterway provided construction jobs for years and a new shipping canal when it was completed in 1985. A big Yellow Creek plant producing advanced solid rocket motors for the Space Shuttle seemed likely to guarantee local prosperity until it was canceled in 1994. The focus, though, is different in the hill-country metropolis, Tupelo, which is a stronghold of private enterprise and traditional values. It excels at corporate recruitment, attracting new jobs without giving away the store—"probably the best small city in the South" at it, says one corporate recruiter—and is a major furniture manufacturer. Tupelo is also the home of the Reverend Donald Wildmon, who organizes boycotts of products advertised on television shows that he thinks have excessive sex or violence. West of Oxford is Mississippi's Delta, the swampy land pioneered by large planters around the turn of the century, with large black work forces little removed—in the conditions of their daily lives or long-term economic chances—from slavery. Oxford, home of Ole Miss, is also the home today of the Center for the Study of Southern Culture.

The 1st Congressional District of Mississippi includes most of the hill country and a little bit of the Delta plus the Memphis suburban fringe that has run over the Mississippi line. This was the district that elected Jamie Whitten, first elected in November 1941, his last term ending in January 1995: 53 years and two months, the longest House service in history. Whitten served as chairman of the Agriculture Appropriations Subcommittee for 42 years and was Appropriations chairman from 1979–93.

The congressman from the 1st District now is Roger Wicker, a Republican elected in 1994. He grew up in Pontotoc, the son of a state senator and circuit judge, attended public schools and was a House page in 1967: the first of the 1994 freshmen to get on the floor of the House. He went to college and law school at Ole Miss, where he was student body president, served in the Air Force, and in 1980 became a staffer to Trent Lott on the House Rules Committee. In 1987, at 36, he was elected as a Republican to the state Senate and chaired the Elections, and Public Health and Welfare Committees where he sponsored a 24-hour waiting period for abortions. In 1994, when Whitten, disabled by a stroke, retired, Wicker was one of six Republicans and three Democrats to run for the seat. The spotlight at first was on Democratic House Speaker Tim Ford, a power in Jackson, but he trailed in the primary and lost the runoff to state Representative Bill Wheeler, who walked across the district and had support from blacks, labor and teachers.

Meanwhile Wicker, carrying his home base around Tupelo, led in the primary 27%–19% over Grant Fox, former aide to Senator Thad Cochran. In the runoff, Wicker campaigned as a conservative, but Fox, just 27, hit him hard for voting to override Governor Fordice's sales tax increase veto. Wicker won by just 53%–47%. Interestingly, Democratic turnout was not much higher than Republican in the primary (33,766 versus 26,607) or the runoff (29,871 versus 22,268). The general was easier. "If you want more Bill Clinton, maybe you should vote for my opponent," Wicker said, while Wheeler campaigned as the candidate of working people against a "country club Republican" and insisted he too was against abortion and gun control. The result wasn't even close: a district held for 53 years by a Democratic leader voted 63%–37% for the Republican.

In the House Wicker was elected president of the 73-member freshman class, one of the largest in the 20th Century. He also won Whitten's old seat on the Appropriations Committee. There was some tension between the two positions. Wicker had a very conservative voting record, and supported the Republican leadership in many tough corners: he rallied the freshman to support the budget when Newt Gingrich capitulated to Bill Clinton in January 1996. "We have fundamentally changed the debate in Washington," he said; even Clinton "is talking like a Republican." And he boosted the Republican record at home: "Contrary to what you hear in the media, it's not all gridlock in Washington." With Jay Dickey of Arkansas he sponsored the amendment which outlawed fetal tissue research, and he worked without success with Ernest Istook of Oklahoma on an amendment for voluntary school prayer.

But he also backed district projects on Appropriations and elsewhere. He worked to preserve the Appalachian Regional Commission and the Economic Development Administration. He supported funding of the Natchez Trace Parkway, started in the 1930s but never completed, and for Yalobusha River flood control. He and other Mississippi Republicans worked to transfer 1,200 acres of NASA land in Tishomingo County to the state of Mississippi. He got TVA to agree to buy power from a proposed lignite-burning plant in Choctaw County which will be one of the largest construction projects in Mississippi history, employing 9,000. "The model of New South conservatism," *CongressDaily* called him, generally very conservative but also alert, as Tip O'Neill might have predicted, to local needs. He was reelected 68%–31% in 1996.

The People: Pop. 1990: 515,196; 67% rural; 13% age 65+; 77% White; 23% Black; 1% Hispanic origin. Households: 61% married couple families; 30% married couple fams. w. children; 30% college educ.; median household income: $20,867; per capita income: $9,639; median gross rent: $277; median house value: $43,700.

1996 Presidential Vote		
Dole (R)	90,604	(48%)
Clinton (D)	78,894	(42%)
Perot (I)	13,695	(7%)
Other	3,864	(2%)

1992 Presidential Vote		
Bush (R)	101,252	(50%)
Clinton (D)	84,765	(42%)
Perot (I)	17,984	(9%)

Rep. Roger F. Wicker (R)

Elected 1994; b. July 5, 1951, Pontotoc; home, Tupelo; U. of MS, B.A. 1973, J.D. 1975; Baptist; married (Gayle).

Career: Air Force, 1976–80; Air Force Reserves, 1980–present; Staff, U.S. House Rules Cmte., 1980–82; Practicing atty., 1982–94; Lee Cnty. Public Defender, 1984–87; Tupelo City Judge Pro-Tem, 1986–87; MS Senate, 1987–94.

DC Office: 206 CHOB 20515, 202-225-4306; Fax: 202-225-3549; e-mail: rwicker@hr.house.gov.

District Offices: Southaven, 601-342-3942; Tupelo, 601-844-5437.

Committees: *Appropriations* (25th of 34 R): Labor, Health & Human Services & Education; Military Construction; VA, HUD & Independent Agencies.

Group Ratings

	ADA	ACLU	AFS	LCV	CFA	CON	NFIB	COC	ACU	NTLC	CHC
1996	0	0	0	15	0	17	95	100	100	98	93
1995	0	—	—	13	0	56	—	96	80	—	—

National Journal Ratings

	1995 LIB — 1995 CONS			1996 LIB — 1996 CONS		
Economic	26%	—	67%	0%	—	82%
Social	0%	—	79%	0%	—	90%
Foreign	28%	—	65%	21%	—	72%

Key Votes of the 104th Congress

1. Reduce Medicare Growth $	Y	5. Flag Amendment	Y	9. Cuban Embargo	Y
2. Ovrd. Product Liab. Veto	Y	6. Drop EPA Limits	N	10. Bar Bosnia Troop $	N
3. Increase Min. Wage	N	7. Repeal Assault-Weap. Ban	Y	11. Cut Anti-Missile Defense	N
4. Welfare Reform	Y	8. Ovrd. Part. Birth Veto	Y	12. Bar U.N. Uniforms	Y

Election Results

1996 general	Roger F. Wicker (R)	123,724	(68%)	($524,101)
	Henry Boyd Jr. (D)	55,998	(31%)	
	Others	3,244	(2%)	
1996 primary	Roger F. Wicker (R)	unopposed		
1994 general	Roger F. Wicker (R)	80,553	(63%)	($729,704)
	William R. Wheeler Jr. (D)	47,192	(37%)	($789,523)

SECOND DISTRICT

"The Mississippi Delta," wrote Delta native David Cohn, "begins in the lobby of the Peabody Hotel in Memphis and ends on Catfish Row in Vicksburg." For centuries, the flooding Mississippi and Yazoo Rivers left their sediments here, producing a fertile dark soil. Ironically, what may well be America's richest agricultural land has been home for more than a century of many of its poorest people. The Delta, criss-crossed by rivers and famously disease-ridden, wasn't much settled until after the Civil War; the tradition here is not of paternal masters and gracious mansions, but of sharp, profit-seeking operators who used 19th Century technology to drain the land, line the river with levees and build railroads on tracks above the rise of the river. Black sharecroppers and field hands worked here in conditions almost of bondage. From this episode of industrial farming came both great misery and great art: Clarksdale in Coahoma County was the home of W.C. Handy and Muddy Waters, the real birthplace of blues music; Greenville on the Mississippi has produced writers of the caliber of Walker Percy and Shelby Foote. Now Vicksburg's antebellum mansions, battlefield monuments and riverboat gambling bring in 1.5 million tourists annually from around the country.

Then 20th Century technology changed life in the Delta once again. The mechanical cotton-picking machine, invented in 1944, came along just as northern factories were seeking low-wage workers; the great exodus to Chicago and Memphis began, and the Delta's population has been declining ever since. Income levels remain very low, poverty is over 50% in some areas and infant mortality is at Third World levels; the crime and drugs of urban Chicago have been brought back by Delta migrants returning home. There are signs of hope: soybeans have become a big dollar crop here, although there is more acreage still in cotton; poultry farms have become a major enterprise, and the Delta produces 75% of the nation's catfish. Riverboat gambling was approved in 1992 in Tunica County, by some measures the nation's poorest county; in 1993 1.7 million people came in and spent $140 million in the casinos, which now have more square footage than Atlantic City's. There is still a gulf between the races, culturally and economically, but also positive signs: by 1990 a former state NAACP head was elected by a margin of 2–1 the mayor of Vicksburg, which is about half black; when Ku Klux Klansmen demonstrated in Greenwood and Clarksdale in 1994, they were promptly arrested and attracted no support. Still, the Delta has been unable to develop the self-propelling market economy that has brought growth to most of the nation.

The 2d Congressional District of Mississippi occupies the entire Mississippi Delta region, indeed the whole riverfront from Tunica almost to Natchez, plus black neighborhoods of Jackson. It is Mississippi's one black-majority (58% of voting population) district, first created as such in 1984, with modest changes in boundaries for 1992. Thirty years ago, when blacks were not allowed to vote in Mississippi, politics here was the domain of the big plantation owners, symbolized by James Eastland, U.S. senator from 1941–79, Judiciary chairman from 1955–79, an unyielding segregationist and conservative. Even after blacks got the vote, black registration was low and habits of deference in some places prevailed; voting was very racially polarized. In 1986, the district elected its first black congressman since Reconstruction, Mike Espy, whose grandfather and father built a chain of funeral homes and were among the biggest landowners in the state. He won narrowly, worked on farm issues, opposed gun control and courted white voters; he won reelection with 65%, 84% and 76% and in 1993 became secretary of Agriculture. In October 1994 he resigned amid charges of accepting Super Bowl tickets from Tyson Foods.

The congressman from the 2d District is Bennie Thompson, who grew up in Bolton, in Hinds County outside Jackson, graduated from Tougaloo College and receive a masters from Jackson State. He was elected alderman in Bolton in 1969, at 21, and mayor four years later; he named the first Mississippi street after Martin Luther King, Jr. In 1980 he became a Hinds County supervisor. He worked to encourage other blacks to run for office; Mississippi now has some 800 black officeholders; he was lead plaintiff in a suit, now in the remedy stage, charging that the state underfunded historically black state colleges. When Espy was appointed to the Cabinet, Thompson ran in the 2d District. In the March 1993 all-party primary, he won 28% to 20% for Henry Espy, Mike Espy's brother and mayor of Clarksdale. But the leader, with 34%, was Republican Hayes Dent, a 31-year-old aide to Governor Kirk Fordice. In the April runoff, voting was mostly along racial lines, and Thompson won 55%–45%. Most of his margin came from Jackson and Hinds County; elsewhere he led only 51%–49%.

Thompson, unlike Espy, made no particular attempt to win white votes and had a solidly liberal voting record, making as few concessions across the racial divide as had Eastland and his ilk in their day. He likes to quote Deuteronomy: "Thou shalt not harden thine heart, nor shut thine hand from thy poor brother: But thou shalt open thine hand unto him, and shalt surely lend him sufficient for his need." He worked for the empowerment zone which Bill Clinton established in six Delta counties; he got money for restoring buildings at Tougaloo and Rust Colleges; he got the Jackson and Ruleville Post Offices named for Medgar Evers and Fannie Lou Hamer; he got an exemption from EPA for a pesticide to kill the beet armyworm threatening cotton crops. He sought to add Mississippi counties to the Appalachian Regional Commission and wants restitution for black farmers who lost land because of Agriculture Department discrimination.

Thompson has had spirited opposition from black Republicans. In 1994 Ingalls Shipbuilding lawyer Bill Jordan ran against him and lost 54%–39%. In 1996 Danny Covington, a former aide to Republican Congressman Webb Franklin whom Espy beat in 1986, returned to the district and campaigned for school prayer and against welfare. This time Thompson won by a heftier 60%–38%.

The People: Pop. 1990: 514,469; 55% rural; 13% age 65+; 36% White; 63% Black; 1% Hispanic origin. Households: 47% married couple families; 23% married couple fams. w. children; 33% college educ.; median household income: $15,530; per capita income: $7,771; median gross rent: $267; median house value: $39,700.

1996 Presidential Vote

Clinton (D)	104,639	(62%)
Dole (R)	58,177	(34%)
Perot (I)	5,714	(3%)

1992 Presidential Vote

Clinton (D)	105,185	(58%)
Bush (R)	66,905	(37%)
Perot (I)	9,879	(5%)

Rep. Bennie G. Thompson (D)

Elected Apr., 1993; b. Jan. 28, 1948, Bolton; home, Bolton; Tougaloo Col., B.A. 1968, Jackson St. U., M.S. 1972; Methodist; married (London).

Career: Bolton Bd. of Aldermen, 1969–73; Bolton Mayor, 1973–79; Hinds Cnty. Supervisor, 1980–93.

DC Office: 1408 LHOB 20515, 202-225-5876; Fax: 202-225-5898; e-mail: ms2nd@hr.house.gov.

District Offices: Bolton, 601-866-9003; Greenwood, 601-455-9003; Greenville, 601-335-9003; Mound Bayou, 601-741-9003; Marks, 601-326-9003.

Committees: *Agriculture* (13th of 23 D): Department Operations, Nutrition & Foreign Agriculture; General Farm Commodities. *Budget* (11th of 19 D).

Group Ratings

	ADA	ACLU	AFS	LCV	CFA	CON	NFIB	COC	ACU	NTLC	CHC
1996	90	80	100	85	77	55	16	25	5	5	0
1995	95	—	—	94	100	4	—	8	8	—	—

National Journal Ratings

	1995 LIB — 1995 CONS			1996 LIB — 1996 CONS		
Economic	94%	—	0%	78%	—	21%
Social	80%	—	13%	88%	—	0%
Foreign	73%	—	24%	61%	—	37%

Key Votes of the 104th Congress

1. Reduce Medicare Growth $	N	5. Flag Amendment	Y	9. Cuban Embargo	N
2. Ovrd. Product Liab. Veto	N	6. Drop EPA Limits	Y	10. Bar Bosnia Troop $	N
3. Increase Min. Wage	Y	7. Repeal Assault-Weap. Ban	N	11. Cut Anti-Missile Defense	Y
4. Welfare Reform	N	8. Ovrd. Part. Birth Veto	N	12. Bar U.N. Uniforms	Y

Election Results

1996 general	Bennie G. Thompson (D)	102,503	(60%)	($361,452)
	Danny Covington (R)	65,263	(38%)	($215,943)
	Others	4,167	(2%)	
1996 primary	Bennie G. Thompson (D)	unopposed		
1994 general	Bennie G. Thompson (D)	68,014	(54%)	($396,502)
	Bill Jordan (R)	49,270	(39%)	($279,234)
	Vince Thornton (TXP)	9,408	(7%)	

THIRD DISTRICT

Mississippi, old and new: the old Mississippi is the Neshoba County fair, held every August since 1892 in the town of Philadelphia. This is traditionally the place where Mississippi politicians announce their candidacies, with the crowds watching to take their measure. When Ronald Reagan came here in 1980 and Michael Dukakis in 1988, neither mentioned what Philadelphia and Neshoba County are best known for in history, nor is there any memorial except engraved stones at two black churches: it was here during the "Freedom Summer" of 1964 that three civil rights workers, two white and one black, were murdered for the crime of urging black American citizens to register and vote. The new Mississippi is some 80 miles away, in Rankin and Madison County east and north of Jackson, where subdivisions and shopping centers are sprouting up on lands which only a few years ago seemed out in the country.

The 3d Congressional District of Mississippi includes the Rankin and the Madison County suburbs of Jackson and Neshoba County. It stretches north to Starkville, home of Mississippi State University, and south to Laurel, an hour's drive from the Gulf Coast. In the middle is Meridian, a small city that may go down in history as the site of departures of White House chiefs of staff: on the last two presidential trips here, President Nixon informed Bob Haldeman that he was out as chief of staff in April 1973 and in December 1991 John Sununu penned his letter of resignation to President Bush. The political tradition here is southern Democratic, but the area's recent preference has been Republican: Mississippi, old and new.

The congressman from the 3d District is Chip Pickering, a Republican elected in 1996. He grew up in Laurel where he attended public schools; his father was a state senator and state Republican chairman and is now a federal judge. But Pickering was not interested in politics at Ole Miss, and after college spent 18 months as a Baptist missionary in then-Communist Hungary. Then he worked at the Agriculture Department in the Bush Administration, promoting exports, and as a staffer for Senator Trent Lott. In the fall of 1995, Sonny Montgomery, congressman from the 3d District since 1966, a Democrat who mostly voted with Republicans, announced that he would retire after 30 years; he chaired the Veterans' Affairs Committee from 1981–95, and his great achievement was the 1985 veterans' bill, which provided generous education benefits which have helped the services maintain the high level of recruits that was on display in the Gulf war.

Pickering returned to Mississippi and started running for Congress. He was not without competition: nine Republicans and three Democrats ran. Pickering used his old parties ties: his father's executive director at the state party had been Haley Barbour, Republican National Committee chairman from 1993–97, and Pickering's campaign manager was his brother Henry Barbour. In the primary there was tough competition from candidates with regional bases in Meridian and in the Jackson suburbs; Pickering ran first in 13 of 19 counties, though in neither of the big population centers, and had 27% of the vote. Second was former state Representative Bill Crawford from Meridian, with 24%. Crawford had worked to save Meridian Naval Air Station and was vice president of the local community college, and attacked Pickering for having worked most of his adult life outside Mississippi. But Pickering attacked him strongly for resigning from the Republican state committee and supporting Democratic gubernatorial candidate Ray Mabus in 1987, and won the runoff 56%–44%; big margins in the Jackson suburbs were the key. The general election was a battle between the 32-year-old Pickering and 29-year-old John Arthur Eaves, Jr., son of a well-known lawyer and Democratic politician. Eaves spent $542,000 of his own money, and stressed his opposition to abortion and gun control and support of school prayer. But Pickering raised and spent more than $1 million. Boasting of his Republican label ("I consider politics a team sport"), he won in this heavily Republican district 61%–36%.

In the House Pickering won plum committee assignments; he is vice chairman of the Surface Transportation Subcommittee which will work on reauthorization of the ISTEA transportation bill. He also worked on completing Montgomery projects like improving Columbus Air Force Base and four-laning U.S. 45 from Columbus to Tuscaloosa, Alabama.

The People: Pop. 1990: 515,225; 61% rural; 12% age 65+; 67% White; 31% Black; 1% Amer. Indian; 1% Hispanic origin. Households: 57% married couple families; 28% married couple fams. w. children; 39% college educ.; median household income: $21,625; per capita income: $10,303; median gross rent: $324; median house value: $46,800.

1996 Presidential Vote			1992 Presidential Vote		
Dole (R)	107,292	(58%)	Bush (R)	116,973	(58%)
Clinton (D)	66,027	(36%)	Clinton (D)	67,411	(34%)
Perot (I)	9,733	(5%)	Perot (I)	16,049	(8%)

Rep. Chip Pickering (R)

Elected 1996; b. Aug. 10, 1963, Laurel; home, Laurel; U. of MS, B.A. 1986; Baylor U., M.B.A. 1988; Baptist; married (Leisha).

Career: Baptist missionary, Budapest, Hungary, 1986–87; Special Asst. to the Admin. & Asst. Coordinator, East European & Soviet Secretariat, U.S. Dept. of Agriculture, 1989–90; Legis. Aide, U.S. Sen. Trent Lott, 1990–94.

DC Office: 427 CHOB 20515, 202-225-5031; Fax: 202-225-5797.

District Offices: Golden Triangle, 601-327-2766; Meridian, 601-693-6681; Pearl, 601-932-2410.

Committees: *Agriculture* (23rd of 27 R): Forestry, Resource Conservation & Research; Livestock, Dairy & Poultry. *Science* (18th of 25 R): Basic Research; Space & Aeronautics. *Transportation & Infrastructure* (35th of 40 R): Aviation; Surface Transportation (Vice Chmn.).

Group Ratings and Key Votes: Newly Elected

Election Results

1996 general	Chip Pickering (R)	115,443	(61%)	($1,167,906)
	John Arthur Eaves, Jr. (D)	68,658	(36%)	($667,567)
	Others	4,043	(2%)	
1996 runoff	Chip Pickering (R)	23,947	(56%)	
	Bill Crawford (R)	18,467	(44%)	
1996 primary	Chip Pickering (R)	15,293	(27%)	
	Bill Crawford (R)	13,849	(24%)	
	Mike Gunn (R)	9,958	(18%)	
	Dutch Dabbs (R)	6,576	(12%)	
	Dean Kirby (R)	5,077	(9%)	
	Keith Heard (R)	2,671	(5%)	
	Others	3,298	(6%)	
1994 general	G. V. (Sonny) Montgomery (D)	83,163	(68%)	($571,635)
	Dutch Dabbs (R)	39,826	(32%)	($106,706)

FOURTH DISTRICT

A few decades ago, Jackson was a small town centered on the grand Beaux Arts 1901 state Capitol. Today, Jackson is clearly the metropolis of Mississippi, the pivot point between the Delta and the hills, the rivers flowing sluggishly to New Orleans and the Gulf of Mexico and the highways running north to Memphis and Chicago. Like Mississippi generally, it is racially divided, with a black, not-so-affluent south side and a white affluent north side; in its new subdivisions of pleasant, large colonial houses under huge, overhanging trees, you can get a sense of what growth has meant to Jackson—especially when you consider that at least some of the people in these neighborhoods came from humble rural Mississippi beginnings. This newer Mississippi contrasts with Natchez, where the finest collection of antebellum mansions sit on the bluffs overlooking the Mississippi River. Natchez had white millionaires and half the state's free blacks before the Civil War; it was content enough to oppose secession, and was spared major damage in the war because it was of no military importance. Both Jackson and Natchez went through an ugly decade during the civil rights revolution: Mississippi blacks were murdered for registering to vote or for seeking higher-paying jobs; today, the cities are more open, with more social contact between the races than in most northern metropolitan areas, but there is still yearning for economic growth and high-skill jobs.

The 4th Congressional District includes most of Jackson (excluding most black areas, which are in the black-majority 2d) and all of Natchez; it extends east to Laurel and south to the Louisiana line. This is an area that has trended Republican in national and state-wide elections, as newly affluent white Mississippians vote for a party they associate with economic growth and assertive foreign policy, while blacks remain pretty solidly Democratic. But in local contests, Democrats still win many races.

One example was 4th District Congressman Mike Parker, a Democrat elected in 1988 who switched to the Republican Party in November 1995. He hails from Brookhaven, where he owned a funeral home, a business that often provides a base for a political career, since everyone in town goes through your doors sooner or later. Parker entered the wide open race here when incumbent Wayne Dowdy ran for the Senate. Parker ran second in the Democratic primary with 19%, then more than doubled his votes and won the runoff 61%–39%. In the general Parker refused to endorse presidential nominee Michael Dukakis and criticized Dukakis's mandatory health insurance proposal; he vastly outspent his opponent and won 55%–45%.

Parker was clearly uncomfortable with the Democratic Party some time before his switch. In 1994 he was opposed in the primary by state Treasurer Marshall Bennett, who had support from labor unions and teachers' groups, and who attacked him for supporting NAFTA and opposing family leave and Head Start funding. Parker outspent Bennett and won 58%–35%. In January 1995 he voted "present" rather than vote for Dick Gephardt for speaker. In the 104th Congress Parker was fourth-ranking Democrat on the Budget Committee, but voted with Republicans on most budget issues. He was a member of "The Coalition," a group of conservative Democrats, until July 1995 when he resigned from the group. At one point he said in disgust, "I cannot find Democrats who are strong enough or who have the courage of their convictions to kick me out." Days after he was one of four Democrats to vote to abolish the ICC, he switched parties, to no one's surprise.

His voting record became even more conservative and in 1996 three Democrats vied to run against him. His own comments reveal a bitterness against House Democrats: "I think people understand the mendacity I had been through with the Democratic Party . . . things they had done, trying to censure me, slap me around." This was not a high-spending race, and Parker won 61%–36%, losing just one black-majority county. Although he insists that he does not agree with Republicans on everything, he is obviously more comfortable in their party.

The People: Pop. 1990: 513,715; 47% rural; 13% age 65+; 59% White; 41% Black. Households: 54% married couple families; 26% married couple fams. w. children; 42% college educ.; median household income: $20,234; per capita income: $10,411; median gross rent: $344; median house value: $47,500.

1996 Presidential Vote

Dole (R)	86,880	(48%)
Clinton (D)	83,425	(46%)
Perot (I)	9,648	(5%)

1992 Presidential Vote

Bush (R)	102,666	(50%)
Clinton (D)	84,089	(41%)
Perot (I)	16,758	(8%)

Rep. Mike Parker (R)

Elected 1988; b. Oct. 31, 1949, Laurel; home, Brookhaven; William Carey Col., B.A. 1970; Presbyterian; married (Rosemary).

Career: Funeral home owner, 1971–88.

DC Office: 2445 RHOB 20515, 202-225-5865; Fax: 202-225-5886.

District Offices: Brookhaven, 601-835-0706; Columbia, 601-731-1622; Jackson, 601-352-1355; Laurel, 601-425-4999; Mendenhall, 601-847-0873; Natchez, 601-446-7250.

Committees: *Appropriations* (23rd of 34 R): Energy & Water Development; Military Construction. *Budget* (18th of 24 R).

Group Ratings

	ADA	ACLU	AFS	LCV	CFA	CON	NFIB	COC	ACU	NTLC	CHC
1996	0	0	0	15	0	17	97	100	100	90	86
1995	10	—	—	13	0	75	—	88	63	—	—

National Journal Ratings

	1995 LIB — 1995 CONS			1996 LIB — 1996 CONS		
Economic	41%	—	56%	0%	—	82%
Social	21%	—	72%	0%	—	90%
Foreign	61%	—	38%	36%	—	63%

Key Votes of the 104th Congress

1. Reduce Medicare Growth $	Y	5. Flag Amendment	Y	9. Cuban Embargo	N
2. Ovrd. Product Liab. Veto	Y	6. Drop EPA Limits	N	10. Bar Bosnia Troop $	Y
3. Increase Min. Wage	N	7. Repeal Assault-Weap. Ban	Y	11. Cut Anti-Missile Defense	N
4. Welfare Reform	Y	8. Ovrd. Part. Birth Veto	Y	12. Bar U.N. Uniforms	Y

Election Results

1996 general	Mike Parker (R)	112,444	(61%)	($288,719)
	Kevin Antoine (D)	66,836	(36%)	($44,420)
	Others	4,383	(2%)	
1996 primary	Mike Parker (R)	unopposed		
1994 general	Mike Parker (D)	82,939	(68%)	($672,593)
	Mike Wood (R)	38,200	(32%)	($13,239)

FIFTH DISTRICT

The strand where Mississippi faces the Gulf of Mexico has gone through several transformations. French explorers here founded Biloxi in 1699, before New Orleans or St. Louis, and made it the capital of an empire extending to Yellowstone Park. In later decades, rich people from New Orleans came to this Gulf coast in summer to get away from yellow fever and to rest on Victorian verandas; six American presidents have vacationed here. More recently the Gulf Coast, with the help of riverboat casinos, has been gaining economically more than any other part of Mississippi; along much of the strand, new 1,000-room hotels are rising as part of Mississippi's boom. And Biloxi's Keesler Air Force Base is one of the four largest bases in the country. Pascagoula, once a small town, is now home of Litton's 16,000-worker Ingalls Shipyard, whose gray hangar-like buildings and skeletons of ships under construction loom over the flat landscape. To the west is the Stennis Space Center named for longtime (1947–88) Senator John Stennis, who died in 1995.

This is the heart of the 5th Congressional District of Mississippi, some 60% of whose people live on the Gulf Coast; the rest are inland, in farm counties or around Hattiesburg. This was mostly scrub land, not much good for plantations, and thus has never had many black residents. With its low black percentage and mostly booming economy, the 5th District has become prime Republican territory. It gave Richard Nixon his highest percentage in all 435 districts in 1972, it voted twice against fellow southerner Jimmy Carter, and it was represented for 16 years in the House by Trent Lott until he was elected to the Senate in 1988.

But the congressman from the 5th District now is Gene Taylor, a Democrat elected in an October 1989 special election. Taylor graduated from Tulane, served in the Coast Guard Reserves, worked as a boat salesman, then was on the Bay St. Louis Council. In 1983, at 30, he was elected to the state Senate. In 1988, when Lott left the House to run for the Senate, Taylor ran for Congress, beating Attorney General Mike Moore in the primary, but losing to Republican Larkin Smith 55%–45%. Smith died in an August 1989 plane crash, and Trent Lott brushed aside Smith's widow and backed his own longtime aide Tom Anderson, who had spent little time in the district and proved to be an abrasive candidate. Taylor, combining a barely reined-in aggressiveness with a down-home manner, won the special 65%–35%.

In the House, Taylor has had a conservative voting record and has criticized the leadership of his own party and the Republicans. He is a peppery populist ("what Mississippians think is usually the right answer") with a reasonably consistent view on issues. He is against abortion, gun control, free trade and foreign aid. He is strongly pro-defense and boasts of bringing defense contracts to the area. Feisty to the point of being belligerent, he is a kind of isolationist, opposed to any U.S. military commitment that stops short of assured and total victory: he opposed the Gulf war resolution, lifting the arms embargo on Bosnia, sending troops to Haiti. He is a protectionist, loudly opposing NAFTA and GATT. He voted against the Clinton economic package. He gives away his pay raise in local scholarships and cheers on lobbying reform. If there is anything that holds his record together, it is boats. He used to sell boats, he promotes Ingalls and other shipyards, he succeeded in widening and deepening the Gulfport shipping channel, he champions the seafood industry, and he wants to prohibit foreign-flag ships from conducting passenger "voyages to nowhere" from U.S. ports. His Washington residence is a 34-foot boat on the Anacostia River.

Taylor voted "present" rather than vote for Dick Gephardt for speaker in January 1995 and in 1996 announced he would not vote for Bill Clinton. But he had rebuffed all importunings to switch parties. "I personally would feel like a prostitute. I still believe the average working person's best interest is best served by the Democratic Party. If I switched, it certainly wouldn't be out of any moral conviction or professional conviction. It would just be to further my political situation and that is the wrong reason to do it." He is one of the Blue Dog Democrats, against any tax cut until the budget is balanced—and against federal spending on the arts until then too. He voted for welfare reform: "It's this or nothing. And this is better than nothing." He was furious that Republicans would not grant a rule allowing a floor vote on the Blue Dog Medicare plan in October 1995 and commended the Democratic leadership in May 1996 for no longer giving Rush Limbaugh sound bites on issues like gays in the military. Evidently this aggressive Mississippian sees that House Republicans are more cohesive and disciplined than Democrats, and he finds it easier to captain his own ship in the more choppy waters of the Democratic Party.

Taylor's Democratic allegiance may have been strengthened by the opposition he received from Republican Dennis Dollar in 1996. Dollar, a party-switcher himself in the legislature, argued for a tax cut and for party loyalty: "And in a world where you have to be either fish or fowl, nobody is going to follow a blue jay with gills." Taylor responded that he would keep fighting for defense spending and veterans' programs. He was against eliminating the Education and Transportation Departments or federal environmental standards; 40% of the money for the

University of Southern Mississippi, he said, came from the federal government, and he didn't want to see higher tuitions. These, plus Taylor's feisty demeanor, were evidently winning arguments. In a race where both candidates spent about equal amounts, Taylor won 58%–40%, down slightly from his 63% and 60% in 1992 and 1994, but still a solid win. But the inability of this stallion to submit to the reins of party discipline was still apparent in the 105th Congress: he was one of two Democrats to vote against reprimanding Newt Gingrich.

The People: Pop. 1990: 514,611; 35% rural; 11% age 65+; 78% White; 20% Black; 1% Asian; 1% Hispanic origin. Households: 59% married couple families; 29% married couple fams. w. children; 41% college educ.; median household income: $21,702; per capita income: $10,116; median gross rent: $329; median house value: $49,200.

1996 Presidential Vote

Dole (R)	96,880	(56%)
Clinton (D)	61,035	(35%)
Perot (I)	13,431	(8%)

1992 Presidential Vote

Bush (R)	99,997	(54%)
Clinton (D)	58,808	(32%)
Perot (I)	24,956	(14%)

Rep. Gene Taylor (D)

Elected Oct., 1989; b. Sep. 17, 1953, New Orleans, LA; home, Bay St. Louis; Tulane U., B.A. 1974; Catholic; married (Margaret).

Career: Coast Guard Reserves, 1971–84; Sales rep., Stone Container Corp., 1977–89; Bay St. Louis City Cncl., 1981–83; MS Senate, 1983–89.

DC Office: 2447 RHOB 20515, 202-225-5772; Fax: 202-225-7074.

District Offices: Gulfport, 601-864-7670; Hattiesburg, 601-582-3246; Ocean Spring, 601-872-7950.

Committees: *National Security* (8th of 25 D): Military Personnel (RMM); Military Readiness. *Transportation & Infrastructure* (22nd of 33 D): Surface Transportation; Water Resources & Environment.

Group Ratings

	ADA	ACLU	AFS	LCV	CFA	CON	NFIB	COC	ACU	NTLC	CHC
1996	30	12	50	46	31	45	76	63	80	59	78
1995	35	—	—	31	54	97	—	63	64	—	—

National Journal Ratings

	1995 LIB — 1995 CONS	1996 LIB — 1996 CONS
Economic	55% — 44%	54% — 45%
Social	40% — 60%	24% — 72%
Foreign	52% — 46%	49% — 50%

Key Votes of the 104th Congress

1. Reduce Medicare Growth $	N	5. Flag Amendment	Y	9. Cuban Embargo	N
2. Ovrd. Product Liab. Veto	Y	6. Drop EPA Limits	Y	10. Bar Bosnia Troop $	Y
3. Increase Min. Wage	Y	7. Repeal Assault-Weap. Ban	Y	11. Cut Anti-Missile Defense	Y
4. Welfare Reform	Y	8. Ovrd. Part. Birth Veto	Y	12. Bar U.N. Uniforms	Y

Election Results

1996 general	Gene Taylor (D)	103,415	(58%)	($451,833)
	Dennis Dollar (R)	71,114	(40%)	(462,252)
	Others	2,916	(2%)	
1996 primary	Gene Taylor (D)	14,249	(94%)	
	Arlon (Blackie) Coate (D)	861	(6%)	
1994 general	Gene Taylor (D)	73,179	(60%)	($182,381)
	George Barlos (R)	48,575	(40%)	($71,860)

MISSOURI

When Meriwether Lewis and William Clark set out on their expedition to the Pacific, they embarked from St. Louis in 1804. On high ground just below the point where the Missouri River swirls into the Mississippi, St. Louis was at the time the one well-established city in America's interior, with an aristocracy of French merchants, a brawling bourgeoisie of Yankee and southern frontiersmen and fur traders and a proletariat of black slaves. Part of the Louisiana Purchase in 1803, St. Louis by 1821 was part of the new state of Missouri and for the rest of the century St. Louis and Missouri were the gateway to the frontier. In Missouri, Daniel Boone finally found elbow room. Here were the eastern termini of the Pony Express, in St. Joseph, and the Santa Fe Trail, in Kansas City; here were railroads reaching across the continent, connecting the farmers of vast prairies with their markets. Here also were the Mississippi River steamboats, and here grew up their great chronicler, Mark Twain, and his creations Tom Sawyer and Huckleberry Finn and Jim.

For Missouri was not just the gateway to the frontier; it was also the focus of the furious battle over slavery. Missouri was the northernmost slave state at mid-century; it was Missouri ruffians crossing the border and killing antislavery settlers in the Kansas Territory that led proximately to the Civil War. In the 1860s, Missouri had its own mini-civil war in the hilly counties along the Missouri River. Throughout the 19th Century, both before and after the Civil War, Americans turned away from their oceans and headed inward to settle the great interior of the continent. They found Missouri at its heart, with farmland and mines, rivers and railroads, a major manufacturing state—and in the days before tractors, the nation's leading breeder and trader of mules. In 1874 the Eads Bridge opened, one of very few across the Mississippi, and St. Louis's Cupples Station was the largest rail hub in the world. At the turn of the 20th Century, Missouri was the fifth largest state. St. Louis was the fourth largest city, site of the 1904 World's Fair, and one of the few cities with two major league baseball teams, the Cardinals and the Browns; Missouri, after the 1900 Census, had 16 congressional districts.

Today Missouri does not loom as large in the national consciousness, yet it is in some sense still central. In the 20th Century, Americans—like the Browns who moved to Baltimore in the '50s and the football Cardinals who moved to Phoenix in the '80s—increasingly headed to the coasts, to the big cities of the East and to California, and eventually to Florida and Texas. Missouri has had below-average population growth since 1900, and today it is the 16th largest state, with just nine congressional districts. But Missouri, at once southern and northern, eastern and western, is the geographic center of the nation's population. Its airport is TWA's hub; next door is the former headquarters of McDonnell Douglas, which was bought by Boeing December 1996. Its Anheuser-Busch is the world's largest beer producer. And Missouri has again captured Americans' imaginations: if Americans in 1904 flocked to St. Louis on the banks of the

Mississippi, in the 1990s their vans and buses were jamming the two-lane road through the Ozarks to Branson, population 3,400, now America's number two tourist destination (with more than six million visitors annually), with country music stars and soft rock veterans, country violinist Shoji Tabuchi, more theater seats than Broadway, and more seats for regularly scheduled music than anywhere else in America.

Politically, Missouri has remained the nation's best bellwether states, having voted for every presidential winner but one (Eisenhower in 1956) in the 20th Century. From the 1960s to the 1980s it mirrored national trends by moving in its congressional politics from pretty solidly Democratic to leaning Republican. It votes for governor in presidential years and, since 1972, has voted for the same party for governor as the nation has for president. Missouri's ancient Civil War political divisions still hold in most rural areas: Little Dixie in the northeast, first settled by Virginians, and the northwest, settled by southerners, vote Democratic; the Ozarks in the southwest, which was pro-Union, is Republican; the southeast is split, like next-door Downstate Illinois. About one-third of the state's votes are cast in metro St. Louis, which is typically more Democratic than the state as a whole. About one-sixth are cast in metro Kansas City, which has been volatile in the 1980s and 1990s; it voted 25% for Ross Perot in 1992, giving him nearly as many votes as George Bush, and tilted Democratic in 1996, voting 66% for Democratic Governor Mel Carnahan. The rest of the state, which casts almost half the votes, went 41%–38% for Bill Clinton in 1992 and 45%–43% for Bob Dole in 1996—similar to trends in Downstate Illinois and rural Iowa.

Culturally, Missouri remains more conservative than most bigger states; it was Missouri's restrictions on abortion that were upheld by the Supreme Court in the 1989 Webster case. Even on economic issues it does not have an easy liberalism: voters in 1996 rejected a ballot initiative to raise the minimum wage to $6.25. And while its Republican Party has a strong Christian right presence, its Democrats tend to portray themselves as political moderates.

Governor. The governorship is central to Missouri politics, and Missourians have been partial to most of the recent governors: Republican Senators Christopher Bond and John Ashcroft both won two terms as governor, and Democratic Governor Mel Carnahan won in 1992 and 1996 with the biggest percentages any Democrat has won here since 1968. Carnahan grew up in Shannon and Carter Counties, in the midst of politics; his father, A.S.J. Carnahan, was a U.S. congressman (1945–47, 1949–61) and ambassador to Sierra Leone in the 1960s. After the Air Force and law school, Mel Carnahan was elected municipal judge in 1960 at age 26; he was elected to the legislature in 1962, then became majority leader in his second term, and returned to full-time law practice in Rolla two years later. In 1980, he was elected state treasurer and served four years; in 1988, he was elected lieutenant governor even while Republican Governor John Ashcroft was reelected by a wide margin. In 1992 Carnahan ran for governor and won the Democratic primary over then-Mayor Vince Schoemehl of St. Louis, 55%–34%. He focused on education, and went on to defeat Attorney General William Webster, 59%–41%, with 63% in the metro areas and 53% outside.

In his first term Carnahan got the legislature to act on his platform. In 1993, his Outstanding Schools Act was passed, complete with a $310 million tax increase: it sought to reduce class sizes in lower grades, raise state aid to low-revenue school districts, finance careers programs and apprenticeships for non-college-bound high schoolers, and fund a Parents as Teachers program. He had one major defeat: in 1994 the legislature rejected his attempt to require health insurers to disregard preexisting conditions and make policies portable between jobs. But he claims credit for a welfare program emphasizing work, for reorganizing state government, for lifetime sentences for sexual predators. He vetoed a concealed weapons law and a bill to further restrict abortion. He backed an initiative requiring voter approval of tax increases over $50 million, which passed in August 1996.

The record Carnahan brought to the voters in 1996 resembled the record Bill Clinton brought to the nation; and the economy in Missouri, as nationally, was humming. The Republican candidate, state Auditor Margaret Kelly, attacked Carnahan for his education tax increase and

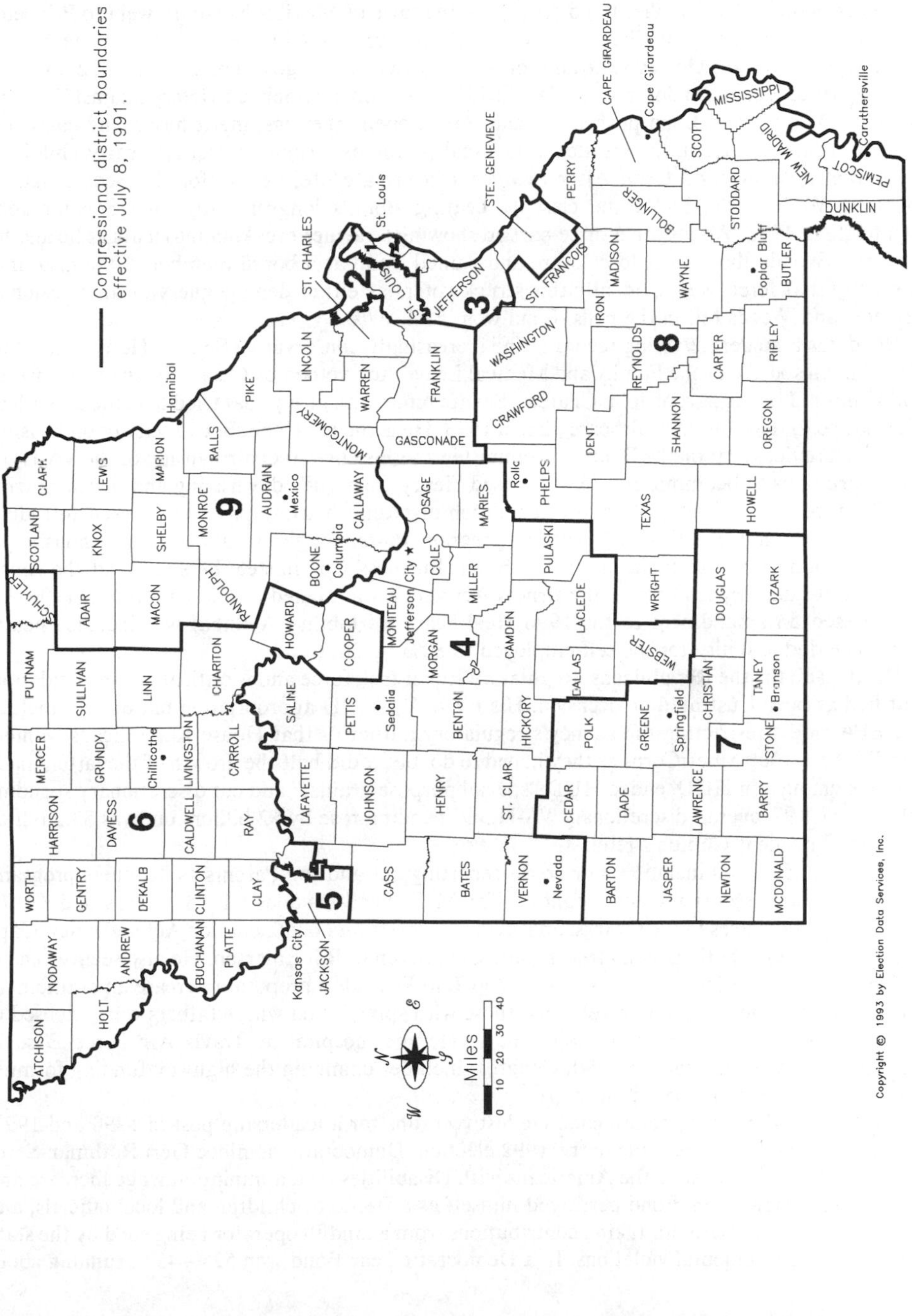
Congressional district boundaries
effective July 8, 1991.
1
2
3
4
5
6
7
8
9
ATCHISON
NODAWAY
WORTH
HOLT
ANDREW
GENTRY
HARRISON
MERCER
PUTNAM
SCHUYLER
SCOTLAND
CLARK
DEKALB
DAVIESS
GRUNDY
SULLIVAN
ADAIR
KNOX
LEWIS
BUCHANAN
CLINTON
CALDWELL
LIVINGSTON
LINN
MACON
SHELBY
MARION
PLATTE
CLAY
RAY
CARROLL
CHARITON
RANDOLPH
MONROE
RALLS
Hannibal
Chillicothe
Kansas City
JACKSON
LAFAYETTE
SALINE
HOWARD
BOONE
Columbia
AUDRAIN
Mexico
PIKE
LINCOLN
CASS
JOHNSON
PETTIS
Sedalia
COOPER
MONITEAU
Jefferson City
COLE
CALLAWAY
MONTGOMERY
WARREN
ST. CHARLES
ST. LOUIS
St. Louis
BATES
HENRY
BENTON
MORGAN
MILLER
OSAGE
MARIES
GASCONADE
FRANKLIN
JEFFERSON
STE. GENEVIEVE
VERNON
Nevada
ST. CLAIR
HICKORY
CAMDEN
PULASKI
PHELPS
Rolla
CRAWFORD
WASHINGTON
ST. FRANCOIS
PERRY
CAPE GIRARDEAU
Cape Girardeau
BARTON
CEDAR
POLK
DALLAS
LACLEDE
DENT
IRON
MADISON
BOLLINGER
JASPER
DADE
GREENE
Springfield
WEBSTER
WRIGHT
TEXAS
SHANNON
REYNOLDS
WAYNE
STODDARD
SCOTT
MISSISSIPPI
NEWTON
LAWRENCE
CHRISTIAN
DOUGLAS
HOWELL
OREGON
CARTER
BUTLER
Poplar Bluff
NEW MADRID
MCDONALD
BARRY
STONE
TANEY
Branson
OZARK
RIPLEY
DUNKLIN
PEMISCOT
Caruthersville
N
E
S
W
Miles
0 10 20 30 40
Copyright © 1993 by Election Data Services, Inc.

called for a $640 million tax cut. Carnahan said his agenda for a second term was a $1,500-a-year college tuition tax credit and elimination of the sales tax on food. At the polls Carnahan won almost as many votes as Clinton and Ross Perot combined, leading Kelly 57%–40%—a solid margin, though a bit under his 1992 mark. He ran very far ahead, 66%–32%, in the Kansas City area, and won non-metro Missouri with 55%, the best for a Democrat for some time. He obviously could be a candidate for the Senate in 1998 or some future year.

Senior Senator. Christopher Bond grew up in the town of Mexico, Missouri, went to Princeton and then the University of Virginia Law School, then ran for Congress in 1968, at age 29, and narrowly lost. He was elected state auditor in 1970, was elected governor at 33 in 1972, then lost in an upset to Democrat Joseph Teasdale in 1976 and won a comeback victory against Teasdale in 1980. As governor, Bond pushed reorganization, open meetings, merit hiring and campaign finance in his first term; he wrestled with fiscal problems, crime control and early childhood education in his second term. After two years in private life, he ran for the Senate against Harriett Woods, who had come close to beating Bond's longtime ally, then-Senator John Danforth, in 1982. Woods ran a three-part ad showing a farmer breaking into tears as he and his wife told Woods about their foreclosure and named Bond as a board member of the insurance company that foreclosed; evidently this struck voters as either demagoguery or an invasion of privacy, and Woods fell in the polls. Bond won, 53%–47%.

Bond has a moderate voting record in the increasingly conservative Senate. He was the chief Republican sponsor of the Family and Medical Leave Act, vetoed by George Bush and signed by Bill Clinton. He was part of John Chafee's Senate bipartisan group that tried to come up with an alternative to the Clinton healthcare plan in 1993. He is the lead Republican senator on housing, from his previous seat on the Banking Committee and his current chairmanship of the VA-HUD Appropriations Subcommittee. He supervised Henry Cisneros's downsizing and decentralizing of HUD, passed legislation to allow demolition of public housing projects, worked to reduce looming Section 8 multi-family housing program costs, fought to allow elderly housing to exclude youngsters. As chairman of the Small Business Committee, he sponsored the Small Business Regulatory Enforcement Fairness Act which was signed into law in March 1996. He also passed an amendment to the 1996 Healthcare Portability Act that will increase health insurance deductibility for the self-employed to 80% by 2006.

Bond co-chairs the Republicans' Regulatory Relief task force and is critical of overregulation. But he has been frustrated on occasion. His FY96 VA-HUD appropriation bill did not include the EPA riders restricting the agency's regulatory authority that House Republicans wanted, nor did it zero out AmeriCorps as they hoped to do; but it did half the growth of the latter, made massive changes in HUD, ended HUD "special purpose grants," and cut discretionary spending 10%. For FY97, overall discretionary VA-HUD spending rose by $2 billion, but was $3.2 billion less than President Clinton's request.

Other Bond causes include a fair credit reporting act and the Parents as Teachers program. He works on Missouri projects—funding for McDonnell-Douglas's F-18s, F-15s and C-17s, protecting wild horses in the Ozarks, and a Good Samaritan Food Donation Act and a new Cape Girardeau Bridge, both named after the late Congressman Bill Emerson. He also seems to have his pet peeves. He tried unsuccessfully to stop Tom Daschle's proposal to create an entitlement for the first time for children of veterans (those with spina bifida whose fathers were exposed to Agent Orange), and worked to stop a new veterans' hospital at Travis Air Force Base in California. His agenda for the 105th Congress includes changing the highway funding formula and tax relief for home-based businesses.

Bond has had his disappointments. He lost two runs for a leadership post in 1990 and 1992. And he did not have a free ride in the 1992 election. Democratic nominee Geri Rothman-Serot attacked Bond for opposing the Americans with Disabilities Act, a minimum wage increase and plant closing legislation. Bond portrayed himself as a friend of children and local officials, and attacked Rothman-Serot for taking contributions from a landfill operator being sued by the state for serious environmental violations. In a Democratic year Bond won 52%–45%, running about even in the big metro areas and ahead 56%–41% in the rest of the state. For 1998 the opponent most often mentioned is Attorney General Jay Nixon, who lost to John Danforth 68%–32% in 1988 but was reelected to his current post 57%–39%, in 1996. Other possibilities abound, including Governor Mel Carnahan. Given Democrats' recent strength in Missouri, this could be a close race.

Junior Senator. John Ashcroft was first elected in 1994, after a long political career. He grew up in Springfield, the son and grandson of ministers, graduated from Yale, met his wife when they were students at the University of Chicago Law School; they practiced law and wrote books together, raised a family and were active members of the Assemblies of God. Ashcroft is serious, hard-working, abstemious; he sings gospel hymns, plays the piano and is one of the four Singing Senators. He ran for Congress in 1972, at age 30, and lost the Republican primary 50%–45%; he was appointed state auditor in 1973, succeeding Christopher Bond when he became governor. Ashcroft went on to be elected attorney general in 1976 and 1980, and governor in 1984 and 1988. As governor he held tax rates down and concentrated on creating a favorable job environment, establishing 50 enterprise zones, building new prison cells and championing a Learnfare program and education reform.

After two terms in the Statehouse, Ashcroft left for a St. Louis law practice, but Danforth soon announced his retirement and Ashcroft was the obvious and best known candidate to succeed him. He raised vast sums and his conservative stands seemed increasingly in line with voters' views as the year went on. Democrats had a close primary between Kansas City Congressman Alan Wheat and Jackson County Executive Marsha Murphy, which Wheat eventually won 41%–38%. Wheat is black, and some speculated that his race hurt him against Ashcroft; a bigger problem was Wheat's solidly liberal voting record. Ashcroft ran ads against Wheat's votes on crime and welfare and about the House bank; Wheat had to pull one ad because it contained inaccuracies. Wheat raised plenty of money—$3.5 million to Ashcroft's $4 million—but Ashcroft won easily, 60%–36%, losing St. Louis City and Kansas City, but carrying all 115 counties.

In the Senate, Ashcroft soon established himself as a conservative activist with a very conservative voting record and a knack for original proposals. He sponsored the first term limits bill to reach the Senate floor in October 1995, the first in more than 50 years; he sponsored a constitutional amendment to reverse the Supreme Court decision overturning term limits. He has proposed other creative conservative solutions to difficult problems. While welfare reform languished, he proposed block grants specifically allowing states to use charities or faith-based organizations to provide services; that provision was included in the final welfare reform bill signed into law in August 1996. But Ashcroft tried unsuccessfully to pass amendments in the welfare reform bill requiring recipients to work toward obtaining a high school degree and giving states the authority to deny benefits to recipients who test positive for drugs. He has a flextime bill, opposed by labor unions, which would allow employers to give employees the option of compensatory time in place of overtime pay, and the TEAM Act, also opposed by labor and vetoed by Clinton, which would allow more worker-management cooperation in non-union shops.

Ashcroft's top priority is to make Social Security taxes deductible. It is a tax cut heavily pitched to lower brackets, and is already available to corporate taxpayers. He has worked for stricter prosecution of juvenile offenders and is a sharp critic of Clinton's drug policies. He is an Internet enthusiast and was one of the first senators with a home page; he developed a Gateway to Government program for students and responds to constituents' questions via e-mail. Ashcroft serves on the Foreign Relations, Commerce and Judiciary Committees and heads a Republican task force on workplace issues. He is not up for reelection until 2000, and seems to be in strong political shape.

Presidential politics. Missouri's peculiar balance of northern and southern, urban and rural, has helped to make it a presidential bellwether and explains its one deviation in the 20th Century: it voted for Adlai Stevenson in 1956, who capitalized on farmer discontent and whose patent lukewarmness about civil rights helped him carry traditional southern Democrats. In

1992, the economically hard-pressed northern part of the state has trended to the Democrats, and Bill Clinton won 44%–34%. In 1996, although the Dole campaign never targeted the state, rural Missouri moved toward Republicans while the Kansas City area moved toward Democrats, and Clinton's margin was a bit smaller, 48%–41%.

Missouri joined the Super Tuesday primary for 1988, then went back to multi-tiered caucuses to elect delegates. In 1992 the winners were Bill Clinton and George Bush. In 1996 Pat Buchanan won the March 9 Republican caucuses, thanks to support from many religious conservatives, including Phyllis Schlafly, longtime conservative networker, who had moved from Alton, Illinois, across the river to Missouri. After district caucuses and state conventions, the final delegation had 19 Dole, 11 Buchanan and 6 Alan Keyes delegates, the strongest anti-Dole and pro-Buchanan delegation beyond New Hampshire.

Congressional districting. Missouri did not lose any seats in the 1990 Census, but the loss of population in heavily Democratic areas forced new lines which have turned out to help Republicans, who are now down only 5–4 in the delegation.

The People: Est. Pop. 1996: 5,359,000; Pop. 1990: 5,117,073, up 4.7% 1990–1996. 2.0% of U.S. total, 16th largest; 31% rural. Median age: 35.2 years. 14% 65 years and over. 86.9% White, 10.7% Black, 1% Asian; 1.2% Hispanic origin. Households: 56.3% married couple families; 26% married couple fams. w. children; 41% college educ.; median household income: $26,362; per capita income: $12,989; 68.8% owner occupied housing; median house value: $59,800; median monthly rent: $282. 4.6% Unemployment. 1996 Voting age pop.: 3,995,000. 1996 Turnout: 2,158,065; 54% of VAP. Registered voters (1996): 3,339,852; no party registration.

Political Lineup: Governor, Mel Carnahan (D); Lt. Gov., Roger B. Wilson (D); Secy. of State, Rebecca Cook (D); Atty. Gen., Jay Nixon (D); Treasurer, Bob Holden (D); Auditor, Margaret Kelly (R). State Senate, 34 (19 D and 15 R); Senate President, Bill McKenna (D); State House, 163 (87 D, 75 R and 1 vacancy); House Speaker, Steve Gaw (D). Senators, Christopher S. (Kit) Bond (R) and John Ashcroft (R). Representatives, 9 (5 D and 4 R).

Elections Division: 573-751-2301; **Filing Deadline for U.S. Congress:** March 31, 1998.

1996 Presidential Vote

Clinton (D)	1,025,935	(48%)
Dole (R)	890,014	(41%)
Perot (I)	217,219	(10%)

1992 Presidential Vote

Clinton (D)	1,053,873	(44%)
Bush (R)	811,159	(34%)
Perot (I)	518,741	(22%)

GOVERNOR

Gov. Mel Carnahan (D)

Elected 1992, term expires Jan. 2001; b. Feb. 11, 1934, Birchtree; home, Rolla; George Washington U., B.A. 1954, U. of MO, J.D. 1959; Baptist; married (Jean).

Career: Air Force, 1954–56; Practicing atty., 1959–61, 1962–80, 1984–88; Rolla Municipal Judge, 1960–62; MO House of Reps., 1962–66, Maj. Leader, 1964–66; MO Treasurer, 1980–84; MO Lt. Gov., 1988–92.

Office: State Capitol Bldg., Jefferson City 65101, 314-751-3222; Fax: 314-751-1495; Web site: www.state.mo.us.

Election Results

1996 gen.	Mel Carnahan (D)	1,224,801	(57%)
	Margaret Kelly (R)	866,268	(40%)
	Others	51,449	(2%)
1996 prim.	Mel Carnahan (D)	347,488	(82%)
	Ruth Redel (D)	33,452	(8%)
	Edwin W. Howald (D)	29,890	(7%)
	Nicholas Clement (D)	14,940	(4%)
1992 gen.	Mel Carnahan (D)	1,375,425	(59%)
	William B. Webster (R)	968,574	(41%)

SENATORS

Sen. Christopher S. (Kit) **Bond (R)**

Elected 1986, seat up 1998; b. Mar. 6, 1939, St. Louis; home, Mexico; Princeton, B.A. 1960, U. of VA, LL.B. 1963; Presbyterian; divorced.

Career: Practicing atty., 1964–69, 1977–80; MO Asst. Atty. Gen., 1969–70; MO Auditor, 1970–72; MO Gov., 1972–76, 1980–84.

DC Office: 274 RSOB 20510, 202-224-5721; Fax: 202-224-8149; e-mail: kit_bond@bond.senate.gov.

State Offices: Cape Girardeau, 573-334-7044; Jefferson City, 573-634-2488; Kansas City, 816-471-7141; Springfield, 417-881-7068; St. Louis, 314-725-4484.

Committees: *Appropriations* (5th of 15 R): Agriculture, Rural Development & Related Agencies; Defense; Labor, Health & Human Services & Education; Transportation; VA, HUD & Independent Agencies (Chmn.). *Budget* (5th of 12 R). *Environment & Public Works* (7th of 10 R): Drinking Water, Fisheries & Wildlife; Transportation & Infrastructure. *Small Business* (Chmn.).

Group Ratings

	ADA	ACLU	AFS	LCV	CFA	CON	NFIB	COC	ACU	NTLC	CHC
1996	10	11	29	0	21	23	93	100	90	86	77
1995	5	—	9	0	13	81	—	100	91	—	—

National Journal Ratings

	1995 LIB — 1995 CONS			1996 LIB — 1996 CONS		
Economic	40%	—	59%	42%	—	56%
Social	33%	—	62%	0%	—	72%
Foreign	43%	—	56%	35%	—	63%

Key Votes of the 104th Congress

1. Reduce Medicare Growth $	Y	5. Flag Amendment	Y	9. Anti-Missile Defense	Y
2. Lmt. Prod. Liab. Damages	Y	6. Endangered Species	N	10. Cuban Embargo	Y
3. Increase Min. Wage	N	7. Gay Employment Rights	N	11. Bar Bosnia Troop $	N
4. Welfare Reform	Y	8. Ovrd. Part. Birth Veto	Y	12. Cut Vietnam Aid	N

Election Results

1992 general	Christopher S. (Kit) Bond (R)	1,221,901	(52%)	($5,048,333)
	Geri Rothman-Serot (D)	1,057,967	(45%)	($1,112,187)
	Other	75,048	(3%)	
1992 primary	Christopher S. (Kit) Bond (R)	337,795	(83%)	
	Wes Hummel (R)	70,626	(17%)	
1986 general	Christopher S. (Kit) Bond (R)	777,612	(53%)	($5,376,255)
	Harriet Woods (D)	699,624	(47%)	($4,397,780)

Sen. John D. Ashcroft (R)

Elected 1994, seat up 2000; b. May 9, 1942, Chicago, IL; home, Springfield; Yale U., B.A. 1964, U. of Chicago, J.D. 1967; Assembly of God; married (Janet).

Career: Practicing atty; Professor, 1968–73; MO Auditor, 1973–75; Asst. Atty. Gen. of MO. 1975–76; Atty Gen. of MO, 1976–84; MO Gov., 1984–92.

DC Office: 316 RSOB 20510, 202-224-6154; Fax: 202-228-0998; e-mail: john_ashcroft@ashcroft.senate.gov.

State Offices: Cape Girardeau, 573-334-7044; Jefferson City, 573-634-2488; Kansas City, 816-471-7141; Springfield, 417-881-7068; St. Louis, 314-725-4484.

Committees: *Commerce, Science & Transportation* (8th of 11 R): Aviation; Communications; Consumer Affairs, Foreign Commerce & Tourism (Chmn.); Manufacturing & Competitiveness; Surface Transportation & Merchant Marine. *Foreign Relations* (8th of 10 R): African Affairs (Chmn.); European Affairs; Near Eastern & South Asian Affairs. *Judiciary* (8th of 10 R): Constitution, Federalism & Property Rights (Chmn.); Youth Violence.

Group Ratings

	ADA	ACLU	AFS	LCV	CFA	CON	NFIB	COC	ACU	NTLC	CHC
1996	5	22	14	23	14	67	100	100	100	100	100
1995	0	—	10	0	0	65	—	100	70	—	—

National Journal Ratings

	1995 LIB — 1995 CONS			1996 LIB — 1996 CONS		
Economic	16%	—	82%	11%	—	86%
Social	0%	—	88%	0%	—	72%
Foreign	22%	—	67%	0%	—	74%

Key Votes of the 104th Congress

1. Reduce Medicare Growth $	Y	5. Flag Amendment	Y	9. Anti-Missile Defense	Y
2. Lmt. Prod. Liab. Damages	Y	6. Endangered Species	N	10. Cuban Embargo	Y
3. Increase Min. Wage	N	7. Gay Employment Rights	N	11. Bar Bosnia Troop $	N
4. Welfare Reform	Y	8. Ovrd. Part. Birth Veto	Y	12. Cut Vietnam Aid	Y

Election Results

1994 general	John Ashcroft (R)	1,060,149	(60%)	($4,063,927)
	Alan Wheat (D)	633,697	(36%)	($3,505,701)
	Bill Johnson (Lib)	81,264	(5%)	
1994 primary	John Ashcroft (R)	260,065	(83%)	
	Joyce Lea (R)	15,228	(5%)	
	Joseph A. Schwan (R)	14,713	(5%)	
	Others	22,642	(7%)	
1988 general	John C. Danforth (R)	1,407,416	(68%)	($4,060,441)
	Jeremiah W. Nixon (D)	660,045	(32%)	($880,160)

FIRST DISTRICT

For a century or more St. Louis seemed the center of America: the starting point for the Lewis and Clark expedition in 1804; the locus half a century later of the Dred Scott case, which produced a Supreme Court ruling that helped split the nation; the site of the 1904 World's Fair that introduced the hot dog and the ice cream cone and got 19 million people to "Meet Me in St. Louis." Its 630-foot-high Gateway Arch is just below the point where the waters of the Missouri surge into the Mississippi, about halfway between New Orleans and Lake Superior, the Atlantic and the Pacific. This first major American city west of the Mississippi River was the final resting place of Daniel Boone and for many years was Chicago's rival as the transportation hub of America. In 1904, St. Louis already had the Wainwright Building, one of Louis Sullivan's first skyscrapers, and Union Station, the world's largest passenger train station when it opened in 1894; some 600,000 people lived in densely-packed brick houses on old street grids radiating outward from downtown. This was a heavily German city, with a Teutonic solidity and orderliness which distinguished it from the surrounding southern-accented rural terrain; and from Mitteleuropa came the founders of St. Louis's great businesses—the Anheuser-Busch brewery, May Company department stores, Joseph Pulitzer's *St. Louis Post-Dispatch*—and its first great politician and a friend of Abraham Lincoln, Senator and Interior Secretary Carl Schurz. And there is almost a European aura to Forest Park, the site of the 1904 fair, and the dozen mansion-lined private streets nearby, like Portland Place.

St. Louis is still one of the nation's 20 largest metro areas, but today does not occupy as central a place in the national consciousness, and the central city itself has largely emptied out. The German order that made so many people comfortable living in close quarters and commuting by streetcar seems to have yielded to an American desire for Daniel Boone's wide open (suburban) spaces and the less restrictive automobile. St. Louis's population peaked at 856,000 in 1950; in 1990, it was 396,000, dwarfed by the one million in suburban St. Louis County. Downtown St. Louis has been spruced up admirably: the Gateway Arch was finished in 1965; Union Station has been redeveloped; Laclede's Landing is stocked with shops. But most of St. Louis's old factories have closed and its once tight neighborhoods are a memory.

Missouri's congressional districts have followed the people out of St. Louis. The 1st District, historically based on the north side of the city, now has more than two-thirds of its votes cast in suburban St. Louis County. It includes most of central and north St. Louis, the affluent and racially integrated suburbs of University City and Clayton just west of Forest Park, and the mostly black and mixed-race suburbs from the city limits north to Bellefontaine Neighbors, Florissant, and the airport. In 1990, this district was 52% black, a figure increasing since. This is easily Missouri's most Democratic district.

The congressman from the 1st District is the dean of the Missouri delegation, Bill Clay. He grew up in St. Louis, sold real estate and life insurance. In the 1960s he was a union staffer and firebrand civil rights activist known as "Wild Bill" (he served 105 days in jail in 1963 for participating in a civil rights demonstration). He was a House leader when Democrats were in control, and is now one of the angriest opponents of Newt Gingrich's Republicans. Clay was first elected to the House in 1968, when the black members of the House could be counted on two hands. He weathered some serious ethical charges in the 1970s, when he billed the government for numerous auto trips home though he was apparently traveling on cheaper airline tickets. In 1992, it was revealed he had 328 overdrafts on the House bank. Though there is a stubborn bloc against him in the suburbs, he has always won reelection.

Clay has just about a perfectly liberal voting record, and is an especially strong supporter of labor unions—of "workers' rights," he says. Before the Republicans won control in 1994, he was chairman of the now-abolished Post Office and Civil Service Committee and heir apparent to the then-Education and Labor Committee. One major Clay achievement was the Family and Medical Leave Act, vetoed by President Bush but signed by President Clinton in February 1993 as his first law. Hatch Act reform—allowing federal employees to be involved in politics—took only a bit longer; it passed the House in March 1993 and was signed by Clinton in October 1993. Less controversial was a Clay measure authorizing buyouts of senior federal employees, which passed the House 391–17 in February 1994 and became law in March. But Clay was not as successful in pushing striker replacement, which would revise the 1935 Wagner Act and give more leverage to unions; the bill passed the House in 1994, but in the Senate could not get the 60 votes required to break a promised Republican filibuster.

Since 1994 Clay, now ranking member of the renamed Education and the Workforce Committee, has been mostly frustrated. He opposed the Republicans' welfare reform plans vitriolically, predicting they would "potentially starve hundreds of thousands of children and impair the health of their mothers. This bill is not about welfare reform. This is a giant money laundering scheme. It's about writing blank checks to governors while imposing no standards or accountability." Despite his support of family and medical leave, he opposed the Republican bill to allow employees to choose between overtime pay and compensatory time, on the grounds that the choice can never be really voluntary. The one major bill he joined Republicans in supporting, Howard McKeon's CAREERS Act, consolidating job training programs, was passed in different forms in both houses; but the conference committee was unable to produce a version that made it back to the House floor. His biggest success was the bill increasing the minimum wage. His goals for the 105th Congress include expanding Family and Medical Leave to smaller employers and providing more redress in the Labor Department for sweatshop workers.

Clay expresses his views with great vehemence. He is the author of two books, *To Kill or Not to Kill*, on capital punishment, and *Just Permanent Interests*, on black members of Congress. He tried to block Republican Congressman Gary Franks' admittance to the Congressional Black Caucus and called on him to resign. When Franks was defeated in 1996, Clay sent him a six-page letter, calling him "a foot-shuffling, head-scratching 'Amos and Andy' brand of 'Uncle Tomism'" and a "Negro Dr. Kevorkian" who "gleefully assists in suicidal conduct to destroy his own race." Franks responded, "Obviously, Bill Clay is not a supporter of mine, but I wish him Godspeed."

Clay has generally been reelected easily. In 1994 he finished 53%–20% ahead of his nearest rival in a four-candidate primary; against the same man in the 1996 primary he won 78%–22%. The numbers were similar in the 1996 general election: Clay won 70%–28%, with 89% in St. Louis City and 61% in St. Louis County. During the campaign it was charged that Clay intends to resign in midterm in the hope of passing his seat on to his son, state Senator William Lacy Clay, but Bill Clay denied this.

The People: Pop. 1990: 568,472; 1% rural; 14% age 65+; 46% White; 52% Black; 1% Asian; 1% Hispanic origin. Households: 40% married couple families; 17% married couple fams. w. children; 44% college educ.; median household income: $24,963; per capita income: $12,632; median gross rent: $391; median house value: $55,200.

1996 Presidential Vote			1992 Presidential Vote		
Clinton (D)	145,586	(74%)	Clinton (D)	161,447	(68%)
Dole (R)	38,505	(20%)	Bush (R)	45,231	(19%)
Perot (I)	9,721	(5%)	Perot (I)	29,682	(13%)

Rep. William (Bill) Clay (D)

Elected 1968; b. Apr. 30, 1931, St. Louis; home, St. Louis; St. Louis U., B.S. 1953; Catholic; married (Carol).

Career: Real estate broker; Life insurance business, 1959–61; St. Louis City Alderman, 1959–64.

DC Office: 2306 RHOB 20515, 202-225-2406; Fax: 202-225-1725.

District Offices: Florissant, 314-839-9148; St. Louis, 314-367-1970.

Committees: *Education & The Workforce* (RMM of 20 D).

Group Ratings

	ADA	ACLU	AFS	LCV	CFA	CON	NFIB	COC	ACU	NTLC	CHC
1996	80	92	100	77	92	72	16	19	6	5	0
1995	100	—	—	88	100	9	—	13	4	—	—

National Journal Ratings

	1995 LIB — 1995 CONS			1996 LIB — 1996 CONS		
Economic	94%	—	0%	89%	—	0%
Social	88%	—	0%	88%	—	0%
Foreign	93%	—	0%	90%	—	0%

Key Votes of the 104th Congress

1. Reduce Medicare Growth $	N	5. Flag Amendment	N	9. Cuban Embargo	*
2. Ovrd. Product Liab. Veto	N	6. Drop EPA Limits	Y	10. Bar Bosnia Troop $	N
3. Increase Min. Wage	Y	7. Repeal Assault-Weap. Ban	*	11. Cut Anti-Missile Defense	Y
4. Welfare Reform	N	8. Ovrd. Part. Birth Veto	N	12. Bar U.N. Uniforms	N

Election Results

1996 general	William (Bill) Clay (D)	131,659	(70%)	($366,550)
	Daniel F. O'Sullivan Jr. (R)	51,857	(28%)	($77,978)
	Others	4,137	(2%)	
1996 primary	William (Bill) Clay (D)	44,971	(78%)	
	Patrick J. Cacchione (D)	12,537	(22%)	
1994 general	William (Bill) Clay (D)	97,061	(63%)	($349,528)
	Donald R. Counts (R)	50,303	(33%)	($7,408)
	Others	5,654	(4%)	

SECOND DISTRICT

Just as the U.S. population's geographic center has slowly crept westward into Missouri (the 1990 Census placed the axis just outside tiny Steelville), the greater St. Louis area continues to move farther west from the Gateway Arch on the Mississippi River. The fulcrum now rests in St. Louis County, established in 1876 when the city, tired of paying for dusty back roads, separated itself from the sticks. There were then about 350,000 people in the city and 31,000 in the county. In 1990, the city, which once had 856,000 people, was down to 396,000, while the county was about 1 million. By the 1960s, the center of office employment had moved from downtown across the county line to Clayton; now even many Clayton office buildings seem half-empty, and the focus is fast moving out the Daniel Boone Expressway (U.S. 40) to Chesterfield, west of the I-270 ring road.

The 2d Congressional District of Missouri is made up of central and western St. Louis County, plus some St. Charles County suburbs northwest across the Missouri River. It includes the blue collar areas around the Ford plant, the Airport and McDonnell Douglas (now owned by Boeing) in North County and the Chrysler plant in South County; these are mostly Democratic. It has fast-growing suburbs in and beyond St. Charles and historic suburbs like Webster Groves and Kirkwood; these are pretty solidly Republican. And in the center of St. Louis County, along the Daniel Boone Expressway, are elite Ladue and high-income Creve Coeur, Town and Country, Manchester and Chesterfield: Republican, even more so in the newer family-oriented subdivisions than in the leafy precincts of the old rich.

The congressman from the 2d District is Jim Talent, a Republican who first won the seat in 1992. Talent grew up in Des Peres and lives in Chesterfield; he was a law clerk to Judge Richard Posner, one of the great free market legal minds, and was a management lawyer in St. Louis. In 1984, at age 28, he was elected to the state legislature, where he opposed taxes and backed reform of House rules. He was House Minority Leader from 1989 to 1992. In 1992, Talent ran for the U.S. House, and in the primary beat George Bush's cousin, George Herbert Walker, by the unambiguous margin of 58%–32%. In the general, Talent faced incumbent Democrat Joan Kelly Horn, who in 1990 defeated Republican Jack Buechner by a grand total of 54 votes. But redistricting had made the district more Republican, and even in a Democratic year in Missouri, Talent won 50%–48%.

Talent has compiled a solidly conservative voting record and has emerged as a leader on conservative causes. In his first term he got a seat on what is now National Security and formed an ad hoc Hollow Forces Update Committee in the 103d Congress; he focused on military readiness and decried Clinton Administration defense budget cuts. Talent also introduced his own welfare reform, denying benefits for a second child born while the mother is on welfare and sending children with unfit parents to group homes. In 1996 Talent teamed with freshman J.C. Watts to sponsor the american community renewal act, to encourage enterprise zones, capital gains tax cuts, reduction of red tape, and public-private partnerships in central cities; it went nowhere legislatively. In 1997 Talent became chairman of the Small Business Committee, which Republicans spared from abolition in 1994 because it was the only committee headed by a woman (Jan Meyers); she retired in 1996, but it survives. Talent said he would use it to monitor how the 1995 Paperwork Reduction Act and the 1996 Small Business Regulatory Enforcement Fairness Act are actually administered. He is targeting regulations like OSHA's "fall protection standard" and the National Labor Relations Board's "single location bargaining units."

On local issues, Talent has been critical of dioxin testing at the Times Beach Superfund site, and got the EPA ombudsman to issue a report detailing irresponsible EPA testing practices there. He is highly skeptical of a St. Louis Airport plan to build a third runway in Bridgeton and demolish one-third of the town.

In 1994 Talent was reelected easily, 67%–31%. In 1996 he was opposed again by Joan Kelly Horn, who had been working in the Defense Department for reconversion of military plants to civilian use. The issues were squarely joined. Said Horn's ad of Talent, "He has continued to vote with Newt Gingrich against the environment, seniors, children, workers, consumers, education. The list goes on and on." Said Talent's, "The major issue is who wants to change Washington and who wants to keep the status quo." Talent outspent Horn, $1.1 million to $380,000. Talent won, 61%–37%, far better than his 50%–48% victory four years before.

The People: Pop. 1990: 568,449; 3% rural; 10% age 65+; 94% White; 4% Black; 2% Asian; 1% Hispanic origin. Households: 65% married couple families; 31% married couple fams. w. children; 61% college educ.; median household income: $43,957; per capita income: $20,654; median gross rent: $519; median house value: $94,900.

1996 Presidential Vote			1992 Presidential Vote		
Dole (R)	138,401	(49%)	Bush (R)	126,621	(40%)
Clinton (D)	115,698	(41%)	Clinton (D)	114,612	(36%)
Perot (I)	22,791	(8%)	Perot (I)	72,885	(23%)

Rep. James M. Talent (R)

Elected 1992; b. Oct. 18, 1956, Des Peres; home, Chesterfield; Washington U., B.S. 1978, U. of Chicago Law Schl., J.D. 1981; Presbyterian; married (Brenda).

Career: Practicing atty., 1981–92; Law Clerk, 7th Circuit Court of Appcals Judge Richard Posner, 1982–83; MO House of Reps., 1984–92, Minority Ldr., 1989–92.

DC Office: 1022 LHOB 20515, 202-225-2561; Fax: 202-225-2563; e-mail: rep.talent@mail.house.gov.

District Offices: St. Louis, 314-872-9561; St. Charles, 314-949-6826.

Committees: *Education & The Workforce* (11th of 25 R): Employer-Employee Relations. *National Security* (13th of 30 R): Military Personnel; Military Procurement. *Small Business* (Chmn. of 19 R).

Group Ratings

	ADA	ACLU	AFS	LCV	CFA	CON	NFIB	COC	ACU	NTLC	CHC
1996	10	0	0	15	23	43	100	100	100	100	100
1995	0	—	—	0	8	56	—	100	96	—	—

National Journal Ratings

	1995 LIB — 1995 CONS	1996 LIB — 1996 CONS
Economic	0% — 74%	24% — 73%
Social	0% — 79%	14% — 77%
Foreign	0% — 85%	0% — 79%

Key Votes of the 104th Congress

1. Reduce Medicare Growth $	Y	5. Flag Amendment	Y	9. Cuban Embargo	Y
2. Ovrd. Product Liab. Veto	Y	6. Drop EPA Limits	N	10. Bar Bosnia Troop $	Y
3. Increase Min. Wage	N	7. Repeal Assault-Weap. Ban	Y	11. Cut Anti-Missile Defense	*
4. Welfare Reform	Y	8. Ovrd. Part. Birth Veto	Y	12. Bar U.N. Uniforms	Y

Election Results

1996 general	Jim Talent (R)	165,999	(61%)	($1,165,814)
	Joan Kelly Horn (D)	100,372	(37%)	($381,873)
	Others	4,355	(2%)	
1996 primary	Jim Talent (R)	unopposed		
1994 general	Jim Talent (R)	154,882	(67%)	($773,953)
	Pat Kelly (D)	70,480	(31%)	($135,867)
	Others	4,925	(2%)	

THIRD DISTRICT

Middle America, it could be said, lies somewhere on the south side of metropolitan St. Louis. The geographical center of the country's population was here in 1980, just south of St. Louis in once rural and now half-suburban Jefferson County; and while that point has moved a few miles southwest, St. Louis is still the metro area nearest the midpoint of a country most of whose people live in million-plus metro areas. Geographically, this is a node where some of the nation's main arteries come together. The Missouri River flows into the Mississippi a few miles north of St. Louis's Gateway Arch; the National Road and its successors, U.S. 40 and Interstate 70, cross the Mississippi just below the Arch. And the great tides of southerners migrating west up the Mississippi and Germans migrating overland met here to create one of the nation's largest and most bustling cities out of a town founded by the French before the Revolutionary War. The south side of St. Louis is famous for its tight-knit, neat neighborhoods and pleasant parks; its most famous symbol is the Anheuser-Busch brewery just south of downtown and Grant's Farm, where Ulysses S. Grant lived in the 1850s and where Anheuser-Busch now keeps the Budweiser Clydesdales. But many more people now live in the suburbs heading out all directions, well into Jefferson County to the south.

The 3d Congressional District consists of the south side of St. Louis City, the southern St. Louis County suburbs, Jefferson County, and rural Ste. Genevieve County on the Mississippi to the south, the site of Missouri's oldest permanent settlement, founded near a salt mine in 1730. It is the descendant of districts dominated by St. Louis voters, but now the city casts only 25% of its votes, fewer than Jefferson County. Ethnically, this has been a heavily German-American area since the mid-19th Century. Politically, it has been Democratic since the New Deal of the 1930s.

The congressman from the 3d District is Dick Gephardt, first elected in 1976, the leader of the Democratic Party in the House, presidential candidate in 1988 and perhaps again in 2000. Gephardt grew up on the south side of St. Louis, the son of a milk truck driver who worked himself up into the middle class. A bit too old to be part of the generation of Vietnam-era student rebels, Gephardt returned home from law school in 1965 to work in a large downtown law firm, but was clearly intent on a traditional political career; he moved to the south side and was elected alderman in 1971. In 1976, when 3d District Congresswoman Leonor Sullivan announced her retirement, Gephardt jumped into the race as an anti-establishment candidate. He beat a labor union official in the primary and a former board of aldermen president in the general. Gephardt started off in the House as one of the newer breed of Democrats who did not automatically favor big government and higher taxes. With the help of Missouri's Richard Bolling, Gephardt got a seat on the Ways and Means Committee—rare for a freshman. He voted for the 1981 Reagan tax cut and was the House co-sponsor of New Jersey Senator Bill Bradley's bill that was the basis of the 1986 tax reform. Gephardt was one of the founders of the moderate Democratic Leadership Council and opposed many popular Democratic causes such as abortion, busing and raising the minimum wage.

But around the mid-1980s he began to shift, perhaps reflecting the increasingly liberal tenor of the Democratic Caucus, of which he was elected chairman over David Obey in 1984. Gephardt has always been a superb caucus politician and a good listener, working with small universes—caucuses—of colleagues and constituents. He is a hard-working detail man, eager to absorb information, with a gift for molding compromises, for coming up with positions that hold together the often unruly and fissiparous Democratic Caucus. When Gephardt started running for president in 1986, he had the enthusiastic support of dozens of House colleagues as he spent 144 days in Iowa campaigning for the February 1988 caucuses. Iowa was the biggest population-losing state in the 1980s, bitterly anti-Reagan; to Iowans, and to many House Democrats in Washington, there was a sense the Reagan era was over.

Gephardt adjusted to this new arena, sometimes to the dismay of his former allies. He played little role in the 1986 tax reform he had originally co-sponsored; he changed his stand on abortion to pro-choice. In Iowa, he supported mandatory agricultural production controls, a nonstarter even in a Democratic Congress; agricultural policy has since moved in the opposite direction. Even more prominently, he went on the offensive on trade issues. The United Auto Workers is a major factor in Iowa caucuses, and Gephardt, who had opposed the UAW's domestic content bill, came up with his amendment requiring retaliation against countries (read: Japan) running large trade surpluses with the United States. It passed the House in late 1987 by a 218–214 margin—a gift to Gephardt's presidential campaign, for the bill clearly was going nowhere in the Senate.

Gephardt won the Iowa caucuses with 31% of the vote, to 27% for Paul Simon and 22% for Michael Dukakis. In New Hampshire, Gephardt found himself under attack for switching positions in a prosperous state that hates taxes and government regulation; he finished second with 20% to Dukakis's 36%. On Super Tuesday, Gephardt had run out of money and won only Missouri, and was out of the race.

In the House Gephardt rebounded when another leadership position came his way. In June 1989 Speaker Jim Wright and Majority Whip Tony Coelho resigned, and as Thomas Foley was elected speaker, Gephardt ran for majority leader and defeated Georgian Ed Jenkins 181–76. Gephardt went to work creating a sense of camaraderie in a dispirited caucus. In the 1990 budget summit talks, Gephardt used OMB Director Richard Darman's desire for agreement to frame the issue as a choice between the Democrats' plan to tax the rich more and Bush's refusal to do so—a contrast that at least momentarily hurt Republican candidates and prevented them from making gains in the November 1990 elections. In September 1990, Gephardt supported Bush's dispatch of troops to the Persian Gulf, but in January 1991, he led the opposition to the Gulf war resolution and uncharacteristically stumbled by threatening to cut off funds for U.S. troops there. Gephardt decided not to run for president in 1992.

In the first Clinton years, Gephardt combined ardent support for the administration on most issues with carefully calibrated dissent on others. He fought for the Clinton economic stimulus plan and for the spending cuts and tax increase package which passed with exactly 218 votes in August 1993. His major dissent was on trade. He held off opposing NAFTA for several months as he sought more concessions from administration officials and he eventually came out against it, though critics said his efforts were too late. He called for side agreements on labor law, wage levels and the environment; but he did not get in the way as Clinton and his special aide William Daley and Republican Whip Newt Gingrich rounded up enough votes for NAFTA's passage in November 1993. In December 1993, Gephardt endorsed GATT; in February 1994, he came up with his own plan to force Japan to meet numerical goals in opening its markets or face retaliation.

Gephardt vigorously supported the Clinton healthcare plan in 1994, and tried to put together his own bill combining the Clinton and Ways and Means health reform plans and capable of winning 218 votes in the Democratic Caucus. But it was tough slogging and no bill came to the floor. Then in August 1994 the leadership lost the vote on the crime bill rule. To hold together the caucus, gun control amendments as well as tougher penalties were included; but gun control repelled too many moderate Democrats and Chairman Jack Brooks's highhandedness antagonized many moderate Republicans, and the rule failed. That delayed the crime bill two weeks and the healthcare bill forever.

Clinton had shaped his two major initiatives—the 1993 budget and tax increase and the 1994 healthcare bill—along the lines recommended by House Democratic leaders. In November 1994 they were all stunningly repudiated. Democrats lost 52 seats and control of the House. Speaker Thomas Foley was defeated and Gephardt lost his rank as majority leader and became minority leader instead. The strategy followed by Speakers Tip O'Neill, Jim Wright and Foley—hold the Democratic Caucus together enough to produce 218 votes—was now obsolete. There were only 205 Democrats altogether, and that number dropped to 199 with party switches and special election losses. Gephardt pushed aside a challenge by North Carolina's Charlie Rose for the party leadership, 150–58. But the day he handed over the gavel to Speaker Newt Gingrich, Gephardt later said, "was one of the worst days of my life." The Democratic president and Democrats in Congress started fending for themselves. In December 1994 Gephardt proposed a tax cut just days before Clinton was set to, and in January 1995 he said, "House Democrats are an independent organization, and we will present what we think is best for America's workers." In the debates on the Contract with America, Gephardt was far less visible than the rabidly anti-Gingrich Democratic Whip David Bonior. In June 1995 Gephardt and other Democrats were stunned when Clinton accepted the Republican goal of a balanced budget by 2002. Gephardt produced a "flat tax" plan in July 1995 under which most taxpayers would pay 10% and most deductions except for mortgage interest be abolished, and higher brackets ranging up to 34%; but it got just 119 votes on the floor.

Times got better for Democrats as support for Republicans and Gingrich plummeted during the government shutdown. Gephardt created a House Democratic Policy Committee to serve as a forum for developing a Democratic alternative to the Contract. By June 1996 Gephardt and Senate Minority Leader Tom Daschle came up with a united Democratic "Families First" platform—"modest and achievable ways to help every struggling family." It included tax deductions for child care, health insurance and higher education, a balanced budget, and tough anti-crime measures. "We're all new Democrats now," Gephardt said. "We have to be. Times change." And House Democrats scored a rousing success when they forced a vote on, and passage of, a minimum wage increase in summer 1996.

But the surging Clinton-Gore campaign ignored Gephardt and, though most polls started showing Democrats ahead of Republicans in the generic vote, ignored Democrats' efforts to win a majority in the House. Clinton never mentioned Families First, but instead unveiled a package of "little things" himself. When Gephardt spoke to the Democratic National Convention in August, the obedient crowd chanted "Four more years!"—although no member of Congress except the resident commissioner from Puerto Rico and the delegate from American Samoa has a four-year term. Clinton and Gore each devoted all of one sentence in their acceptance speeches to the need for Democratic majorities in Congress. Gore promoted himself with voters and Democratic insiders for president in 2000, much to Gephardt's chagrin. In October the Clinton campaign did raise impressive sums for Democratic congressional candidates, but Clinton avoided high-visibility appearances with most.

Gephardt's hopes to become speaker came crashing down in November 1996 as Democrats won only 207 House seats and Republicans 227, despite Newt Gingrich's unpopularity, despite the AFL-CIO $35 million ad campaign, despite Clinton's victory. Gephardt's hopes of forging majorities still depend on coalitions with Republicans whom Democratic leaders scorned and refused to deal with up through 1994 and with whom they made little contact in 1995 and 1996. Democrats have always tended to be a divided party, an uneasy alliance of disparate elements, and are today in the House. Most of the Black Caucus and perhaps 40 other members are dedicated social democrats, dismayed first at Clinton's and then at Gephardt's acceptance of the goal of a balanced budget, frustrated with downward pressure in discretionary spending, and determined not to give up the fading strength of the Medicare or Social Security issues. Then there are the 23 or so Blue Dogs, moderate on cultural issues, generally conservative and budget-balancing on economics, supportive of some Republican stands. And there are the many Democrats motivated most strongly by liberal views on cultural issues like abortion. Democrats of all stripes may be departing in 1998; no party in presidential power for six years has ever lost House seats. One response from Gephardt is campaign finance reform: he favors amending the First Amendment to allow limits on campaign spending. "What we have here is two important values in direct conflict: freedom of speech and our desire for healthy campaigns in a healthy democracy. You can't have both."

Gephardt is obviously giving serious consideration to running for president. He appeared before the AFL-CIO in February, the same day as Gore but immediately after a quick trip to Mexico—bringing to mind his and the AFL-CIO's opposition to NAFTA, which Gore supported. Gephardt clearly sees organized labor and House members as his base, and as Clinton and Gore kept proclaiming the era of big government was over and power was leaving Washington, Gephardt was positioned to be the alternative on the left. In May 1997, Gephardt denounced the balanced budget plan (which passed the House with support from 132 Democrats) as "a budget of many deficits—a deficit of principle, a deficit of fairness, a deficit of tax justice and, worst of all, a deficit of dollars." Gephardt also drew lines with Clinton when he declared his opposition to extending normal trade relations with China. Meanwhile, he has been mostly ignored by the Clinton-Gore White House, his relationship with Newt Gingrich is minimal, and House rules allow a determined and united majority—which Republicans have been and may be again—to have its way. Gephardt faces daunting challenges.

He also faced, briefly, an ethics problem. Republican leadership loyalist Jennifer Dunn filed a complaint in February 1996 that Gephardt made contradictory statements on disclosure forms and tax returns on a North Carolina beach house he traded for another in 1991. He claimed it as investment property on the tax forms, in order to make the exchange tax-free; but in House disclosure forms he had called it a vacation house and in some years disclosed no rental income. In September 1996 he amended his disclosure and the Ethics Committee found he had omitted some income: "The committee expects you will be more diligent in the future and adhere strictly to the requirements to file timely and accurate financial statements," it said in dismissing the case.

Gephardt has won reelection at home by solid but not enormous margins. He still goes door-to-door on occasion and work on local issues, like the McDonnell Douglas strike, overseas routes for TWA, bringing the Rams into and keeping the Defense Mapping Agency in the St. Louis area. But his strongest weapon is money. In 1990, he spent $1.4 million and won 57%–43%; in 1992 he spent $3.3 million and won 64%–33%. In 1994, with an opponent who actually spent a bit himself ($196,000), Gephardt spent $2.6 million and won 58%–40%. In 1996, against a candidate who spent $62,000, he spent $3.1 million and won 59%–39%. It was the costliest House campaign outside Newt Gingrich's district; Gephardt raised $1.1 million from PACs. While some of this campaigning is to promote his obvious national political interests, the numbers also suggest that Gephardt cannot take the 3d District for granted, even as he struggles with uniting a diffuse party caucus and running for president against a candidate backed by the White House.

The People: Pop. 1990: 568,105; 16% rural; 15% age 65+; 96% White; 2% Black; 1% Asian; 1% Hispanic origin. Households: 56% married couple families; 26% married couple fams. w. children; 41% college educ.; median household income: $30,863; per capita income: $14,272; median gross rent: $390; median house value: $71,500.

1996 Presidential Vote

Clinton (D)	115,141	(48%)
Dole (R)	93,190	(39%)
Perot (I)	25,643	(11%)
Other	3,604	(2%)

1992 Presidential Vote

Clinton (D)	121,213	(44%)
Bush (R)	87,155	(32%)
Perot (I)	64,415	(24%)

Rep. Richard A. Gephardt (D)

Elected 1976; b. Jan. 31, 1941, St. Louis; home, St. Louis; Northwestern U., B.S. 1962, U. of MI, J.D. 1965; Baptist; married (Jane).

Career: Air Natl. Guard, 1965–71; Practicing atty., 1965–71; St. Louis City Alderman, 1971–76. Dem. Candidate for Pres., 1988.

DC Office: 1226 LHOB 20515, 202-225-2671; Fax: 202-225-7452; e-mail: gephardt@hr.house.gov.

District Offices: St. Louis, 314-894-3400.

Committees: *Minority Leader. Democratic Policy Committee Chairman.*

Group Ratings

	ADA	ACLU	AFS	LCV	CFA	CON	NFIB	COC	ACU	NTLC	CHC
1996	85	47	100	85	77	1	26	27	6	10	14
1995	85	—	—	88	77	3	—	30	12	—	—

National Journal Ratings

	1995 LIB — 1995 CONS	1996 LIB — 1996 CONS
Economic	85% — 15%	78% — 22%
Social	71% — 28%	77% — 22%
Foreign	79% — 17%	73% — 27%

Key Votes of the 104th Congress

1. Reduce Medicare Growth $	N	5. Flag Amendment	Y	9. Cuban Embargo	Y
2. Ovrd. Product Liab. Veto	N	6. Drop EPA Limits	Y	10. Bar Bosnia Troop $	N
3. Increase Min. Wage	Y	7. Repeal Assault-Weap. Ban	N	11. Cut Anti-Missile Defense	Y
4. Welfare Reform	N	8. Ovrd. Part. Birth Veto	Y	12. Bar U.N. Uniforms	N

Election Results

1996 general	Richard A. Gephardt (D)	137,300	(59%)	($3,110,509)
	Deborah Lynn Wheelehan (R)	90,202	(39%)	($62,504)
	Others	5,253	(2%)	
1996 primary	Richard A. Gephardt (D)	45,619	(75%)	
	Joseph C. Keller (D)	12,390	(20%)	
	Leif O. Johnson (D)	2,690	(4%)	
1994 general	Richard A. Gephardt (D)	117,601	(58%)	($2,621,479)
	Gary Gill (R)	80,977	(40%)	($196,461)
	Others	5,362	(3%)	

FOURTH DISTRICT

Missouri was the first state settled west of the Mississippi, and the folks who settled it were a picture of pioneer diversity. Virginians and other southerners made their way to counties north of the Missouri River, while Germans settled around the still small capital city of Jefferson City. A taste of that variety can be found in the Capitol, with its mural by Thomas Hart Benton, great-grandnephew and eponym of Missouri's first senator, who championed hard money and westward expansion for 30 years and lost his seat for opposing the expansion of slavery. The painting shows dance hall girls, black coal miners, a mother diapering an infant—all reminders that pioneer life was less homogeneous than one might imagine.

The 4th Congressional District of Missouri occupies much of this early-settled part of central and western Missouri. It penetrates Kansas City's Jackson County and its metro overflow in Cass County, but the overall atmosphere here is rural and small town, with political traditions dating back to the community's early days. The rural counties around Kansas City were full of pro-slavery-expansion Bushwhackers who rode across the Kansas line to thwart the Yankee Jayhawks, and these areas today vote Democratic. The German area around Jefferson City was anti-slavery and remains among the most Republican parts of Missouri, and the new resort areas around Lake of the Ozarks are mixed. Party Cove, at the lake's western end, is an archetypical example of deregulation—no curfew, speed or size limits for boats on the water—although the drunken flotilla parties and nude sunbathing might not be what Republican regulatory reformers have in mind. But this entire region is also Truman country: Harry Truman was born just south of the district and lived just northwest of it, spanning the gaps between country and city, South and North; Truman's mother could remember her house being attacked by Yankee soldiers, and she remained pro-Confederate even when her son was in the White House.

The congressman from the 4th District is Ike Skelton, who in many ways can be called a Truman Democrat; indeed he says his family and Truman's have been friendly since 1928. Skelton grew up in Lexington, where he returned after college and law school to practice law; he became county prosecutor in 1957, at 25 and was elected to the Missouri Senate in 1970. In 1976 Skelton ran for Congress and won rather easily. Skelton looks and votes like an old-fashioned rural Missouri Democrat: his voting record puts him at the midpoint of this Republican House on economics and foreign issues, somewhat to the right on cultural issues. He supports the same expansive, assertive foreign and defense policies the preponderance of Democrats supported in the days of Truman.

Skelton serves on the National Security Committee where he has made great contributions to policy. He has long called for better strategic training in the armed services, particularly in the war colleges, and for improving the higher-level military educational programs. In the Democratic 103d Congress he warned against further cuts in military spending. In the Republican 104th he introduced a detailed five-year plan to fully fund national military strategy and meet shortfalls in modernization, readiness and quality of life for troops. Working bipartisanly, he got increases over the Clinton budget proposal for FY96 and FY97 defense spending, though not as much as his own plan called for. And though his work over the years has helped transform the American military into the high-performance force evident in the Gulf war, Skelton is cautious about engagement. He was reluctant to support sending troops to Bosnia in September 1995, and passed a resolution in the House, 287–141, which called for strict neutrality in the peacekeeping effort. He also warned against arming the Bosnian Muslims.

Skelton is not unaware of local issues. His Army Engineer school is located at Fort Leonard Wood, in Pulaski County, and Whiteman Air Force Base in his home county is the headquarters of the B-2 stealth bomber. Skelton worked to see that Leonard Wood was expanded rather than cut back in the 1995 base closing bill and convinced President Clinton to upgrade the B-2 as a deployable bomber. And in September 1996 the Navy christened the *U.S.S. Harry Truman*, a Nimitz-class aircraft carrier.

Skelton voted for some but not all of the Republicans' Contract with America, notably for the balanced budget amendment and the 1996 welfare reform. But when faced with a well-known Republican opponent in 1996, for the first time since he beat an incumbent he was redistricted with in 1982, he criticized the Republican proposals for Medicare and tax cuts. The opponent was Bill Phelps, Lieutenant Governor from 1973–1981, a Houston business executive since then. "Ike has become a professional politician. He's out of touch and it's time for him to go," Phelps said, and hit Skelton for accepting contributions from labor unions "with clear ties to organized crime." Skelton seemed genuinely unaware of the unions' record and attacked Phelps for leaving Missouri to make money in Texas. Skelton's percentage declined, but only a bit, from 68% in 1994 to a still safe and impressive 64%–34% victory in 1996; in a district Bob Dole carried in

1996 with a better margin than George Bush in 1992, Skelton carried every county but one.

In 1997, Skelton left his seat on Small Business when he was appointed to the Select Committee on Intelligence. He remains an influential member even in a Republican House and one of the last of a breed.

The People: Pop. 1990: 569,295; 61% rural; 15% age 65+; 95% White; 3% Black; 1% Asian; 1% Hispanic origin. Households: 64% married couple families; 30% married couple fams. w. children; 34% college educ.; median household income: $23,064; per capita income: $10,984; median gross rent: $319; median house value: $49,400.

1996 Presidential Vote			**1992 Presidential Vote**		
Dole (R)	111,172	(46%)	Bush (R)	96,770	(38%)
Clinton (D)	99,975	(41%)	Clinton (D)	94,948	(37%)
Perot (I)	29,011	(12%)	Perot (I)	65,233	(25%)

Rep. Ike Skelton (D)

Elected 1976; b. Dec. 20, 1931, Lexington; home, Lexington; Wentworth Military Academy Jr. Col., 1949–51, U. of MO, A.B. 1953, LL.B. 1956; Disciples of Christ; married (Susan).

Career: Lafayette Cnty. Prosecuting atty., 1957–60; MO Special Asst. Atty. Gen., 1961–63; Practicing atty., 1963–76; MO Senate, 1971–76.

DC Office: 2227 RHOB 20515, 202-225-2876.

District Offices: Blue Springs, 816-228-4242; Jefferson City, 314-635-3499; Lebanon, 417-532-7964; Sedalia, 816-826-2675.

Committees: *National Security* (2nd of 25 D): Military Personnel; Military Procurement (RMM). *Intelligence (Select)* (6th of 7 D): Technical & Tactical Intelligence.

Group Ratings

	ADA	ACLU	AFS	LCV	CFA	CON	NFIB	COC	ACU	NTLC	CHC
1996	40	31	73	69	31	17	67	60	50	58	69
1995	40	—	—	44	23	16	—	61	42	—	—

National Journal Ratings

	1995 LIB — 1995 CONS			1996 LIB — 1996 CONS		
Economic	56%	—	44%	59%	—	40%
Social	41%	—	58%	46%	—	52%
Foreign	52%	—	46%	52%	—	47%

Key Votes of the 104th Congress

1. Reduce Medicare Growth $	N	5. Flag Amendment	Y	9. Cuban Embargo	Y
2. Ovrd. Product Liab. Veto	N	6. Drop EPA Limits	N	10. Bar Bosnia Troop $	N
3. Increase Min. Wage	Y	7. Repeal Assault-Weap. Ban	Y	11. Cut Anti-Missile Defense	Y
4. Welfare Reform	Y	8. Ovrd. Part. Birth Veto	Y	12. Bar U.N. Uniforms	Y

Election Results

1996 general	Ike Skelton (D)	153,566	(64%)	($770,607)
	Bill Phelps (R)	81,650	(34%)	($316,989)
	Others	5,573	(2%)	
1996 primary	Ike Skelton (D)	unopposed		
1994 general	Ike Skelton (D)	137,876	(68%)	($427,184)
	James A. Noland Jr. (R)	65,616	(32%)	($15,666)

FIFTH DISTRICT

Kansas City, Missouri, named after a state it isn't in and a river that doesn't touch it, is the center of one of America's large metro areas, the biggest on the central Great Plains. The first pioneers here started little towns on the bluffs above the Missouri River—Independence, Kansas City, Westport—which coalesced a few decades later. Here the Santa Fe Trail set out to cross the Sand Hills of Kansas and reach Mexican territory; here Jayhawks and Bushwhackers set out to fight for control of Bleeding Kansas. It was a rail center and had one of the largest stockyards in the country, a major commercial center with lean skyscrapers and the Country Club Plaza, the first shopping center in America, in the 1920s. It is famous for Harry Truman, whose family lived on a farm now in the suburb of Grandview and who himself lived in Independence, the old county seat just to the east. It is famous also for its black community, and jazz musicians like Scott Joplin, Charlie Parker and Count Basie, and for its much-praised barbecue.

The 5th Congressional District of Missouri includes most of Kansas City in Jackson County, plus Grandview and the bulk of Independence; most of the city's landmarks, including the Truman home, are here. It includes all of Kansas City's black neighborhoods and was 24% black in 1990. Solidly but not overwhelmingly Democratic, for 34 years it was represented by Richard Bolling—a Truman ally first elected in the Truman wave of 1948, junior partner of Sam Rayburn in the 1950s, one of the real scholars of the House and ultimately chairman of the Rules Committee. Then, starting in 1983, for 12 years it was represented by Alan Wheat, a Democrat elected at age 31, one of the few black congressmen to represent a white-majority district; he gave up the seat for an unsuccessful run for the Senate in 1994.

The congresswoman from the 5th is Karen McCarthy, first elected in 1994, who seems to be one of those naturally gifted politicians of whom the Democrats have had so many over the years. She moved to Kansas City to teach school, and shortly thereafter, in 1976, at 29, was elected to the Missouri House. She served there 18 years, rising to become Chairman of Ways and Means in 1983 and president of the National Conference of State Legislators in 1994, working also as a government affairs consultant.

In 1994, she managed the not inconsiderable feat of winning 41% in an 11-candidate primary; the next two finishers also were women. McCarthy was supported by unions, environmentalists, black organizations, and Kansas City Mayor Emanuel Cleaver; she raised more than $350,000 for the primary. The Republicans had a serious candidate, Ron Freeman, a black who played professional football in the short-lived United States Football League and then worked with the Fellowship of Christian Athletes, and who attacked "a government which has refused to be accountable to the citizenship." McCarthy stressed her conciliatory skills. She was supported by business leaders and had a $250,000 edge in PAC money. She won 57%–43%, carrying Kansas City 2–1 but losing the suburban half of the district; not an overwhelming margin, but impressive enough for a non-incumbent in a Republican year against a candidate with potential appeal to the Democratic base.

In the House McCarthy called for bipartisan coalitions, and voted for the balanced budget amendment, the line-item veto and the law to end unfunded mandates. But overall she had a mostly liberal voting record—pro-gun control, pro-choice on abortion, against the flat tax and school vouchers. And she worked cooperatively with fellow Democrats. She lobbied successfully for a seat on the Transportation panel and met with then-White House Chief of Staff Leon Panetta to restore funding for a $100 million courthouse in Kansas City. She got $5 million to replace the 110-year-old Chouteau Bridge and $5 million in high-tech grants to local schools to use computers to study the Santa Fe Trail and put Truman Library documents on-line.

McCarthy's victory in Republican 1994 discouraged serious opposition in 1996. The Republican nominee dropped out after the primary and the party had to find another candidate. McCarthy raised nearly $280,000 from PACs, but didn't need it; she spent only $220,000 and ended the campaign with $286,000 in the bank. Her judgment was sound: she won 67%–29%. In the 105th Congress she is again seeking bipartisan solutions to difficult problems. She wants to work for campaign finance reform, and she has sponsored a bill to create a bipartisan commission of the long-term solvency of Medicare.

The People: Pop. 1990: 569,289; 1% rural; 14% age 65+; 72% White; 24% Black; 1% Asian; 1% Amer. Indian; 3% Hispanic origin. Households: 47% married couple families; 20% married couple fams. w. children; 46% college educ.; median household income: $26,968; per capita income: $13,650; median gross rent: $398; median house value: $56,300.

1996 Presidential Vote

Clinton (D)	127,691	(58%)
Dole (R)	71,453	(33%)
Perot (I)	17,489	(8%)

1992 Presidential Vote

Clinton (D)	134,862	(52%)
Bush (R)	67,511	(26%)
Perot (I)	55,799	(22%)

Rep. Karen McCarthy (D)

Elected 1994; b. Mar. 18, 1947, Haverhill, MA; home, Kansas City; U. of KS, B.A. 1969, M.B.A. 1986, U. of MO, M.A. 1976; Catholic; divorced.

Career: High Schl. teacher, 1969–76; MO House of Reps., 1976–94; Financial analyst, 1984–86; Govt. affairs consultant, Marion Merrill Dow, 1986–94; Pres., Natl. Conf. of State Legislatures, 1994.

DC Office: 1232 LHOB 20515, 202-225-4535; Fax: 202-225-4403.

District Offices: Independence, 816-833-4545; Kansas City, 816-842-4545.

Committees: *Commerce* (21st of 23 D): Energy & Power; Telecommunications, Trade & Consumer Protection.

Group Ratings

	ADA	ACLU	AFS	LCV	CFA	CON	NFIB	COC	ACU	NTLC	CHC
1996	80	75	100	85	92	87	40	25	5	22	20
1995	80	—	—	69	92	87	—	38	24	—	—

National Journal Ratings

	1995 LIB — 1995 CONS			1996 LIB — 1996 CONS		
Economic	69%	—	31%	85%	—	11%
Social	80%	—	13%	79%	—	18%
Foreign	66%	—	33%	85%	—	15%

Key Votes of the 104th Congress

1. Reduce Medicare Growth $	N	5. Flag Amendment	Y	9. Cuban Embargo	Y
2. Ovrd. Product Liab. Veto	N	6. Drop EPA Limits	Y	10. Bar Bosnia Troop $	N
3. Increase Min. Wage	Y	7. Repeal Assault-Weap. Ban	N	11. Cut Anti-Missile Defense	Y
4. Welfare Reform	N	8. Ovrd. Part. Birth Veto	N	12. Bar U.N. Uniforms	Y

Election Results

1996 general	Karen McCarthy (D)	144,223	(67%)	($220,339)
	Penny Bennett (R)	61,803	(29%)	
	Others	7,945	(4%)	
1996 primary	Karen McCarthy (D)	unopposed		
1994 general	Karen McCarthy (D)	100,391	(57%)	($866,808)
	Ron Freeman (R)	77,120	(43%)	($458,373)

SIXTH DISTRICT

The rolling, surging fields along the Missouri River in the northwest Missouri were settled in a rush in the late 19th Century, and have been losing people ever since. Fewer hands are needed on farms than half a century ago, far fewer than at the turn of the century; and even the biggest town in northwest Missouri, St. Joseph, has lost population. In 1940, this area had the fifth largest meat-packing operation in the world, but the meat-packing business has generated no more new jobs than farming, and St. Joseph has fewer people than in 1900. The counties of northwest Missouri, aside from those in the Kansas City metro area, had 508,000 people in 1900, 452,000 in 1940 and under 300,000 in 1990.

All these counties plus part of metro Kansas City—Clay and Platte Counties and a small portion of Jackson County east of Independence—make up Missouri's 6th Congressional District: greater Kansas City has gained people almost precisely to the extent that northwest Missouri has lost them. The Kansas City area casts almost half the district's votes. The historic political tradition here is mostly Democratic, tempered by dislike for national Democrats' cultural liberalism, but strengthened in the 1980s by anger at what people regard as neglect of this salt-of-the-earth farming area—an attitude similar to that found across the border in Iowa. This was strong Perot country in 1992: he got 27% of the vote in the 6th District, and Bill Clinton carried it with a solid 40%–32% plurality in 1992 and a narrower 46%–42% in 1996.

The congresswoman from the 6th District is Pat Danner, a Democrat first elected in 1992. Danner has been in politics much of her adult life. In the 1970s she was a staffer for 6th District Congressman Jerry Litton, who died in a plane crash the night he won the 1976 Democratic Senate nomination. Danner ran to succeed Litton that year, but placed second in the Democratic primary to Morgan Maxfield, who lost to Republican Tom Coleman when it was discovered Maxfield had falsified his life story. Following her defeat, Danner became co-chair of the Ozark Regional Planning Commission under President Carter; in 1982 she was elected to the state Senate. In 1990, her son Stephen was elected in an adjoining district, and they became the only mother-son team in a state Senate in America; he ran for state auditor in 1994, and lost 58%–39%. Things went better for Pat Danner in 1992, when she won an eight-candidate Democratic primary with 52% of the vote, and defeated the 16-year incumbent Republican Coleman, 55%–45%, in a spirited campaign.

Danner has a moderate, almost middle-of-the-House voting record, similar to the 4th District's Ike Skelton; she also works assiduously on local projects. She opposed the Clinton budget and tax increase in 1993 and pushed strongly for flood relief after the disastrous 1993 floods. She opposed nationalized health care, and, having voted for the Missouri abortion law upheld in the 1989 *Webster* case, she balked at the House version of the Freedom of Choice Act which gave states less leeway than the Senate version. She voted against NAFTA. She had attacked Coleman for sending out too much franked mail, and she spent far less, returning $100,000 of her office franking allowance to the Treasury. She contributed her pay raise to fund Danner Youth Awards for 6th District high school seniors.

She did not seem out of place in 1995 serving for the first time in a Republican-controlled legislative chamber. She joined the Blue Dogs, the moderate-to-conservative Democrats known as The Coalition, seeking bipartisan solutions for tough problems. She argued for restricting members' personal use of frequent flier miles, which Republicans balked at. And she was the one of the first members to use Speaker Newt Gingrich's Corrections Day procedure to get rid of outmoded or foolish regulations: she sponsored the Edible Oils Regulatory Reform Act, to require federal agencies to distinguish between petroleum and vegetable oils; 1970s legislation had mindlessly treated them the same. Danner formed a Missouri/Mississippi River Task Force, and convinced the Army Corps of Engineers to revise its flood control plans for the Missouri. Prompted by Harold Martin of the Patee Park Baptist Church Pantry in St. Joseph, she sponsored a uniform national law to protect good-faith donors of unused food; it was signed as the Bill Emerson Good Samaritan Food Donation Act in October 1996.

Danner's moderate voting record and attention to constituency have been rewarded with solid reelection margins. In Republican 1994 she won 66%–34% and in 1996 she won 69%–29%, both against lightly funded opposition; both times she ran well ahead of the Democratic ticket.

The People: Pop. 1990: 568,823; 37% rural; 14% age 65+; 96% White; 2% Black; 1% Asian; 2% Hispanic origin. Households: 62% married couple families; 29% married couple fams. w. children; 40% college educ.; median household income: $27,165; per capita income: $12,641; median gross rent: $362; median house value: $54,900.

1996 Presidential Vote

Clinton (D)	115,342	(46%)
Dole (R)	105,084	(42%)
Perot (I)	29,302	(12%)

1992 Presidential Vote

Clinton (D)	110,137	(40%)
Bush (R)	88,980	(32%)
Perot (I)	75,150	(27%)

Rep. Pat Danner (D)

Elected 1992; b. Jan. 13, 1934, Louisville, KY; home, Smithville; NE MO St. U., B.A. 1973; Catholic; married (Markt Meyer).

Career: Dist. Asst., U.S. Rep. Jerry Litton, 1973–76; Co-Chmn., Ozarks Regional Plng. Comm., 1977–81; MO Senate, 1982–92.

DC Office: 1207 LHOB 20515, 202-225-7041; Fax: 202-225-8221.

District Offices: Kansas City, 816-455-2256; St. Joseph, 816-233-9818.

Committees: *International Relations* (14th of 22 D): International Economic Policy & Trade. *Transportation & Infrastructure* (14th of 33 D): Aviation; Surface Transportation.

Group Ratings

	ADA	ACLU	AFS	LCV	CFA	CON	NFIB	COC	ACU	NTLC	CHC
1996	55	31	75	77	46	21	76	56	45	49	53
1995	70	—	—	25	15	31	—	67	48	—	—

National Journal Ratings

	1995 LIB — 1995 CONS			1996 LIB — 1996 CONS		
Economic	56%	—	43%	61%	—	39%
Social	49%	—	50%	42%	—	56%
Foreign	58%	—	42%	73%	—	26%

Key Votes of the 104th Congress

1. Reduce Medicare Growth $	N	5. Flag Amendment	Y	9. Cuban Embargo	Y
2. Ovrd. Product Liab. Veto	N	6. Drop EPA Limits	N	10. Bar Bosnia Troop $	Y
3. Increase Min. Wage	Y	7. Repeal Assault-Weap. Ban	Y	11. Cut Anti-Missile Defense	Y
4. Welfare Reform	Y	8. Ovrd. Part. Birth Veto	Y	12. Bar U.N. Uniforms	Y

Election Results

1996 general	Pat Danner (D)	169,006	(69%)	($112,970)
	Jeff Bailey (R)	72,064	(29%)	
	Others	5,212	(2%)	
1996 primary	Pat Danner (D)	42,450	(77%)	
	Larry E. Kinnamon Jr. (D)	12,782	(23%)	
1994 general	Pat Danner (D)	140,108	(66%)	($474,038)
	Tina Tucker (R)	71,709	(34%)	($42,378)

SEVENTH DISTRICT

The second biggest tourist destination in America today, after Orlando, Florida, is Branson, Missouri—a fact almost no one predicted 20 years ago. Even today Branson has only 3,400 residents, is served by two-lane roads, is nowhere near a major airport; but it thrives, paralleling the surging popularity of country and Western music. Branson was put on the map early in the century by Harold Bell Wright's novel, *The Shepherd of the Hills*, about the hardy people of the mountains, hills and meadows of southwest Missouri, just north of Arkansas. More tourists came in with completion of the Ozark Beach Dam which created Bull Shoals Lake in 1913, lured by the native bass and stocked trout. Then in the 1960s, new lakes were formed, a Shepherd of the Hills pageant and Silver Dollar City were started, and entertainers—the five Maybe brothers performing as "The Baldknobbers" and Box Car Willie from Grand Ole Opry—started performing. They were followed by others—Roy Clark, Glen Campbell, Charlie Pride, Mel Tillis, Louise Mandrell and the violinist Shoji Tabuchi. Today Branson has more than two dozen theaters with 55,000 seats—more than Broadway. Workers come in from as far away as Springfield, the biggest city in southwest Missouri, and headquarters of such Middle American institutions as the Mid-America Dairymen, the nation's largest milk producers' cooperative, and the Assemblies of God, one of the nation's largest and fastest-growing Protestant denominations. What do people like about Branson? The nonstop entertainment and fishing and boating; country music and family style entertainment; plenty of shopping and a safe atmosphere. These are also things that have made southwest Missouri the fastest growing part of the state in the last 20 years, generating new businesses and attracting retirees as well as vacationers.

The 7th Congressional District of Missouri includes Branson and Springfield and most of southwest Missouri. Historically, southwestern Missouri has been Republican—against secession in 1861: pro-Union Springfield changed hands several times during Missouri's own civil war. Its conservative response to the big-spending government of the 1960s and cultural liberalism of the 1970s reinforced its allegiance, and now this is the most Republican part of Missouri.

The congressman from the 7th District is Roy Blunt, a Republican first elected in 1996. Blunt grew up in southwest Missouri, taught high school and college history and government. In 1984, at 34, he was elected Missouri Secretary of State and was reelected with 60% in 1988. In 1992 he ran for governor, and lost the Republican primary to William Webster, 44%–39%. (Webster was defeated and disgraced, sent to jail because of his improper administration of the Second Injury Fund.) Blunt became president of Southwest Baptist University in Bolivar (Polk County). In 1996 Congressman Mel Hancock, author of Missouri ballot initiatives requiring voter approval of tax increases, kept his pledge to serve only four terms and retired. In the primary Blunt faced Gary Nodler, businessman and onetime staffer to Congressman Gene Taylor. Nodler charged Blunt's 1992 attacks on Webster caused the defeat of the entire Republican ticket. Blunt replied with an ad saying he would concentrate on the issues. Nodler carried his (and Webster's) home area around Joplin and Carthage, but Blunt carried everything else and won 56%–44%. There were 75,000 votes cast in the Republican primary and only 16,000 in the Democratic primary: a harbinger of the general election, which Blunt won 65%–32%, running ahead of the Republican ticket and carrying every county with at least 62% of the vote.

Blunt is likely to have a solidly conservative voting record. He favors the balanced budget amendment and term limits and opposes abortion, the family leave law and the minimum wage increase. He wants to reform Medicare and shrink the public sector. He has seats on the Agriculture, Transportation and International Relations Committees.

The People: Pop. 1990: 568,017; 48% rural; 16% age 65+; 97% White; 1% Black; 1% Asian; 1% Amer. Indian; 1% Hispanic origin. Households: 61% married couple families; 27% married couple fams. w. children; 38% college educ.; median household income: $21,712; per capita income: $11,029; median gross rent: $315; median house value: $48,200.

1996 Presidential Vote

Dole (R)	129,249	(51%)
Clinton (D)	93,537	(37%)
Perot (I)	27,580	(11%)

1992 Presidential Vote

Bush (R)	118,817	(45%)
Clinton (D)	96,621	(36%)
Perot (I)	48,824	(18%)

Rep. Roy Blunt (R)

Elected 1996; b. Jan. 10, 1950, Niangua; home, Strafford; SW Baptist U., B.A. 1970; SW MO St. U., M.A. 1972; Baptist, married (Roseann).

Career: Teacher, Marshfield H.S., 1970–73; Greene County Clerk, 1973–85; Adjunct Instructor, Drury Col., 1976–82; MO Secy. of State, 1984–93; Pres., SW Baptist U., 1993–96.

DC Office: 508 CHOB 20515, 202-225-6536.

District Offices: Joplin, 417-781-1041; Springfield, 417-889-1800.

Committees: *Agriculture* (22nd of 27 R): Livestock, Dairy & Poultry. *International Relations* (24th of 26 R): International Economic Policy & Trade; Western Hemisphere. *Transportation & Infrastructure* (29th of 40 R): Aviation (Vice-Chmn.).

Group Ratings and Key Votes: Newly Elected

Election Results

1996 general	Roy Blunt (R)	162,558	(65%)	($985,764)
	Ruth Bamberger (D)	79,306	(32%)	($103,747)
	Others	8,720	(3%)	
1996 primary	Roy Blunt (R)	42,401	(56%)	
	Gary Nodler (R)	33,426	(44%)	
1994 general	Mel Hancock (R)	112,228	(57%)	($218,098)
	James R. Fossard (D)	77,836	(40%)	($239,681)
	Others	5,852	(3%)	

EIGHTH DISTRICT

Mark Twain might not recognize life on the Mississippi below St. Louis today, where the land flattens out and the river is hidden behind levees, which ordinarily—except during the terrible flood of 1993—screen small towns and river roads from the sight of rows of barges tethered together, full of coal or soybeans. The Mississippi today is an industrial waterway. But it was never really all that romantic, for Twain's steamboats, as he is at pains to point out, were dangerous, noisy contraptions, forever blowing up or getting embedded in roots and branches in the swirling river currents. This is one of the older-settled parts of the United States: French settlers founded Missouri towns like Cape Girardeau in the late 1700s. But the big influx started just a few years after the 1811 earthquake centered on New Madrid; the spongy Mississippi valley land is also seismically very active, and this was the site of one of the most devastating earthquakes in U.S. history.

Outwardly, the southeast quadrant of Missouri—the river valley and the hills to the west, with coal and lead mines with their miles of tunnels, plus the Bootheel that hangs down in the far southeast—hasn't changed much in 50 years. The only big growth here in that time has been around Cape Girardeau and along the route of Interstate 44; there has been a big population outflow from the Bootheel, as machines replace low-wage farm workers, and from some mining communities, as ores give out or become uneconomical to extract.

The 8th Congressional District covers this southeast quadrant of Missouri. The political heritage is mixed. The Bootheel was as solidly Democratic as the Mississippi Valley around Memphis used to be, and some of the mining counties are Democratic. Cape Girardeau, the boyhood home of Rush Limbaugh but also the starting point of the 1996 Clinton-Gore bus tour, votes solidly Republican, as do surrounding counties. For many years this district was represented by moderate Democrats; since 1980, it has been represented by conservative Republicans.

The congresswoman from the 8th District is Jo Ann Emerson, elected in 1996 to replace her husband Bill Emerson, who was first elected in 1980 and died in June 1996. Jo Ann Emerson grew up in the Washington suburb of Bethesda, Maryland, in a Republican family but next door to Democrats Hale and Lindy Boggs, who served in Congress a total of 50 years; their daughter, Cokie Roberts, babysat for Jo Ann. In 1975 she married Republican Bill Emerson, then a Washington lobbyist with Capitol Hill experience: as a congressional page in 1954, he was on the House floor when it was fired upon by Puerto Rican terrorists, and later he was a staffer for Congressman Robert Ellsworth and Senator Charles Mathias. In 1979, spotting the personal vulnerability of the Democratic incumbent, Bill Emerson went back home to Missouri to run, and won with 55%. In time he moved up to second-ranking position on the House Agriculture Committee, where he prevented food stamps from being block-granted in 1995, and also served on Transportation. In 1995 he was diagnosed with cancer, but missed few votes during radiation therapy. Two pieces of legislation passed in 1996 memorialize him: the Bill Emerson Good Samaritan Food Donation Act, setting national standards to encourage donations of unused food, and the Bill Emerson Bridge across the Mississippi at Cape Girardeau.

After Bill's death on June 22, Jo Ann Emerson decided to run and announced July 10. "I was so totally focused on a mission to keep the seat and make it a living memorial to Bill," she said. She had political experience of her own: she worked for the American Insurance Association and had been a press aide at the National Republican Congressional Committee. Her views are conservative—for the balanced budget amendment, against gun control, for abortion restrictions, for property rights—and she was immediately endorsed by Senators Christopher Bond and John Ashcroft. But while she was named the Republican nominee in the contest for the remainder of her husband's term, to be held also on November 5, she could not run for the Republican nomination in the August 6 primary: Missouri law bars reopening filing for new candidates if an incumbent dies less than 11 weeks before the August primary. Emerson ran as an Independent in the general. Democrats turned out to have a serious candidate, Emily Firebaugh, a timber company owner and lifelong area resident, who attacked Jo Ann Emerson as a product of the Washington suburbs. Firebaugh eventually spent the impressive sum of $831,000, more than Emerson's $806,000. The Republican nominee was less trouble: one Richard Kline, who in 1995 had used pepper spray to try to place a Veterans Administration doctor under citizen's arrest.

Bill Emerson's record, Jo Ann Emerson's conservative views on issues, and the poignancy of the situation all worked in the same direction: toward an Emerson victory. For the full term she received 50% of the votes, with 37% for Firebaugh and 11% for Kline. A better gauge of opinion may have been the two-way contest for the short term, in which Emerson won 63%. That gave her a seniority advantage over incoming freshman. Like her husband, she has seats on the Agriculture and Transportation Committees in addition to Small Business.

The People: Pop. 1990: 568,385; 63% rural; 16% age 65+; 94% White; 4% Black; 1% Hispanic origin. Households: 61% married couple families; 28% married couple fams. w. children; 25% college educ.; median household income: $18,207; per capita income: $9,300; median gross rent: $268; median house value: $37,500.

1996 Presidential Vote

Clinton (D)	101,339	(45%)
Dole (R)	96,457	(43%)
Perot (I)	25,089	(11%)

1992 Presidential Vote

Clinton (D)	109,858	(46%)
Bush (R)	89,238	(37%)
Perot (I)	41,558	(17%)

Rep. Jo Ann Emerson (R)

Elected 1996; b. Sept. 16, 1950, Washington, DC; home, Cape Girardeau; Ohio Wesleyan U., B.A. 1972; Presbyterian; widowed.

Career: Deputy Communications Dir., Natl. Repub. Cong. Cmte., 1984–91; Dir., State Relations & Grassroot Programs, Natl. Restaurant Assn., 1991–94; Sr. Vice Pres., Pub. Affairs, American Insurance Assn., 1994–96.

DC Office: 132 CHOB 20515, 202-225-4404; e-mail: jemerson@hr.house.gov.

District Offices: Cape Girardeau, 573-335-0101; Farmington, 573-756-9755; Rolla, 573-364-2455.

Committees: *Agriculture* (20th of 27 R): Forestry, Resource Conservation & Research; General Farm Commodities. *Transportation & Infrastructure* (27th of 40 R): Surface Transportation; Water Resources & Environment. *Small Business* (16th of 19 R): Empowerment; Regulatory Reform & Paperwork Reduction.

Group Ratings and Key Votes: Newly Elected

Election Results

1996 general	Jo Ann Emerson (I)	112,472	(50%)	($806,205)
	Emily Firebaugh (D)	83,084	(37%)	($831,533)
	Richard Kline (R)	23,477	(11%)	
	Others	3,821	(2%)	
1996 special	Jo Ann Emerson (R)	132,804	(63%)	
	Emily Firebaugh (D)	71,625	(34%)	
	Others	5,326	(3%)	
1994 general	Bill Emerson (R)	129,320	(70%)	($396,967)
	James L. (Jay) Thompson (D)	48,987	(27%)	($3,752)
	Others	6,279	(3%)	

NINTH DISTRICT

Little Dixie, the swath of northeast Missouri along the Mississippi River, was settled by southerners from Kentucky and Virginia. Its most famous native son is Mark Twain, born Sam Clemens in Hannibal, then as now a little town on bluffs overlooking the river. Hannibal also was the thinly disguised St. Petersburg of Tom Sawyer and Huckleberry Finn, lovingly created years later complete with Pike County and other dialect by Twain, then living in New England. Little Dixie has always been Democratic politically and was pro-Confederate during the Civil War; Callaway County declared its independence from the Union. Twain's view of politics was different, both darker and more optimistic: he created a vision of America that transcended region and a view of antebellum society that identified slavery as an evil without ever saying so; Twain himself was a Republican and close friend of Union General and President Ulysses S. Grant. But whatever the author's feelings for his birthplace, Hannibal loves Twain; some quarter-million tourists pour in to visit his boyhood home each year.

Faithfully Democratic Little Dixie has reared some notable politicians as well. One was Champ Clark, speaker of the House from 1911–19 and presidential candidate in 1912; another was Clarence Cannon, author of the definitive text on the House's parliamentary procedure and chairman of the House Appropriations Committee until his death in 1964.

The 9th Congressional District is the descendant of the Little Dixie districts that elected Clark and Cannon, but declining population has required that it be expanded far to the south. Now it extends south to Columbia, home of the University of Missouri, and Fulton, home of Westminster College, where in 1946 Winston Churchill, accompanied by President Harry Truman, told the world that "from Stettin on the Baltic to Trieste on the Adriatic, an iron curtain has descended across the continent." Also it includes Franklin County and half of St. Charles County, formerly rural territory but now increasingly suburbanized. These suburban areas, which lean Republican, now cast one-third of the district's votes, and another one-third are cast in Columbia and two adjoining counties, leaving only one-third for the formerly dominant and still quite Democratic Little Dixie.

The congressman from the 9th District is Kenny Hulshof, a Republican first elected in 1996. Hulshof grew up on a farm in far southeast Missouri, near the confluence of the Mississippi and Ohio Rivers. After college and law school he joined the public defender's office in Cape Girardeau. In 1989 he became a special prosecutor for the Missouri Attorney General's office, and from his home in Columbia traveled to 53 Missouri counties eventually, getting 60 violent felony convictions and seven death sentences. In the midst of this, in 1994, he became the Republican nominee for Congress in the 9th District. This was a surprise: challenger Rick Hardy had held Democratic Congressman Harold Volkmer to a 48%–46% victory in 1992 and was running again; but after the primary filing deadline, he withdrew from the race due to depression and exhaustion. In August, party leaders named Hulshof as Hardy's replacement. He was far outspent, but even so made a respectable showing, carrying Columbia and Boone County, where the Libertarian candidate won 10% of the vote, and trailing 50%–45% overall.

In January 1996 Hulshof resigned as special prosecutor and started to run again. First elected in 1976, Volkmer had been known mainly as the House's leading opponent of gun control. But in 1995 his combative temperament and irritation with the new Republican majority made him one of its most persistent antagonists on the floor. Given Volkmer's narrow recent margins and the conservatism of even Democratic voters here, Volkmer was an attractive Republican target; and he lost 28% of the 1996 Democratic primary vote to a LaRouche follower. But Hulshof was not the only Republican competition. Ophthalmologist Harry Eggleston moved from Creve Coeur in St. Louis County to St. Charles County and began spending his own money, eventually $806,000. He carried St. Charles and Franklin Counties with big margins and ran just ahead of even in Little Dixie. But Hulshof won big in and around Columbia. Initial newspaper reports had Eggleston the winner by 827 votes; but the final results showed Hulshof 168 votes ahead out of 38,000 cast.

In the general Hulshof was the target of Volkmer's attacks on Republican Medicare and student loan "cuts" and Newt Gingrich. One cartoon ad showed a Porsche driven by Gingrich with Hulshof as a passenger. The ad continues with Hulshof asking Gingrich why he is driving his car, to which the Gingrich cartoon figure replies: "You signed the Contract On America, Kenny. There's a clause that says I get to drive." Hulshof replied that his Porsche was a used car sitting under a tarp in his yard. Hulshof charged Volkmer had voted to raise taxes 20 times in 20 years and had voted for 40% pay raises. Like Volkmer, Hulshof opposed gun control and abortion; unlike Volkmer, he championed property rights over environmental regulations. As a former prosecutor, he called for tougher limits on death row appeals. Hulshof actually outspent the incumbent, though much of his money was spent in the primary. The key moment came in October, when Volkmer, in response to a question, said voters were not overtaxed and that he would not mind paying $1 million in taxes. Hulshof ran radio ads quoting Volkmer all over the district, and this may have made the difference. Volkmer still carried Little Dixie 53%–46%, but Hulshof carried the Columbia area 54%–39% and St. Charles and Franklin Counties 49%–48%, for an overall 49%–47% margin.

House Republican leaders exulted in Volkmer's defeat. They were happy to see Hulshof named Republican Freshman Class President and got him a seat on the Ways and Means Committee. But with its Democratic base, this district could be seriously contested again.

The People: Pop. 1990: 568,238; 51% rural; 13% age 65+; 95% White; 4% Black; 1% Asian; 1% Hispanic origin. Households: 62% married couple families; 30% married couple fams. w. children; 38% college educ.; median household income: $26,055; per capita income: $11,741; median gross rent: $338; median house value: $55,200.

1996 Presidential Vote

Clinton (D)	111,626	(44%)
Dole (R)	106,503	(42%)
Perot (I)	30,593	(12%)

1992 Presidential Vote

Clinton (D)	110,175	(41%)
Bush (R)	90,836	(34%)
Perot (I)	65,195	(24%)

Rep. Kenny C. Hulshof (R)

Elected 1996; b. May 22, 1958, Sikeston; home, Columbia; U. of MO, B.S. 1980; U. of MS, J.D. 1983; Catholic, married (Renee).

Career: Asst. Pub. Defender, 32nd Judicial Circuit, 1983–86; Asst. Prosecuting Atty., Cape Girardeau, 1986–89; Special Prosecutor, MO Atty. General, 1989–96

DC Office: 1728 LHOB 20515, 202-225-2956; Fax: 202-225-7834.

District Offices: Columbia, 573-449-5111; Hannibal, 573-221-1200; Washington, 314-239-4001.

Committees: *Ways & Means* (23rd of 23 R): Oversight; Social Security.

Group Ratings and Key Votes: Newly Elected

Election Results

1996 general	Kenny Hulshof (R)	123,580	(49%)	($686,450)
	Harold L. Volkmer (D)	117,685	(47%)	($542,368)
	Others	8,965	(4%)	
1996 primary	Kenny Hulshof (R)	19,259	(50%)	
	Harry Eggleston (R)	19,091	(50%)	
1994 general	Harold L. Volkmer (D)	103,443	(50%)	($473,716)
	Kenny Hulshof (R)	92,301	(45%)	($185,418)
	Mitchell J. Moore (Lib)	9,198	(4%)	

MONTANA

"Montana is what America used to be," says Governor Marc Racicot. Physically, it is America's Big Sky Country, a land of great empty vistas, with mountains in the west and vast expanses of plateaus and plains in the east—the 4th largest state in area and 44th in population. To the casual observer, Montana still seems mostly empty yet is growing lustily once again, a place where you'll come across the Old West of 19th Century cowboys but whose recent growth owes much to 21st Century electronic communications—a financial advisor with a modem can live here as easily as in Los Angeles.

Montana sits atop America, spanning the Rockies so that on Interstate 15 you can cross the Continental Divide three times. Here in the mountains are the headwaters of the Missouri, from its source in Beaverhead County to its mouth in the Gulf of Mexico the longest river in North America, and of the Clark Fork which flows into the Columbia and eventually the Pacific. Not far away, at Egg Mountain near Choteau on the Deep Teton River, is the world's most plenteous source of dinosaur remains. But Montana's recorded history is recent: at its 1989 centennial, the son of one of its original cattleman-settlers watched 105 cowboys drive 4,000 cattle with 300 covered wagons trailing behind.

Statehood came less than a century after the first white Americans came here as agents of the government—the Lewis and Clark expedition in 1805. Next came the mountain men, seeking fur, and then came the miners seeking gold, silver, copper—sudden riches that would make them kings not of this barren land but of the metropolises back East. Raucous mining towns sprang up, complete with outlaws and vigilantes. The mining economy gave Montana a radical, class warfare politics. On one side was the Anaconda Mining Company, which until 1959 owned five of Montana's six daily newspapers, many of its utilities, and many of its politicians, and had strong allies in the Stockmen's Association and the Farm Bureau. On the other side were progressives like Senators Thomas Walsh, who exposed the Teapot Dome scandal, and Burton Wheeler, a New Dealer who broke with Franklin Roosevelt over court packing and isolationism, the labor unions (Montana has no right-to-work law and is the most pro-union state in the Rockies), and pork barrel beneficiaries (for a while in the 1930s, Montana received more federal money per capita than almost any other state). The locus of all this was Butte, with its gold and copper mines on "The Richest Hill on Earth," with its gamblers and bootleggers, company goons and union thugs, IWW organizers and Socialist mayor and millionaires who bought seats in the U.S. Senate. Today the mines are closed, the ore depleted, and the stone temples of commerce and grim looming mineheads are being restored to a cleanliness they never enjoyed in the boom days.

Slowly Montana has changed. Butte's population peaked in 1920, mines slowly closed all over the state, and agriculture—wheat-growing and cattle grazing—became the mainstays of the economy and class warfare died down. Other towns grew, though none is over 100,000 yet: Billings with its agricultural marketing in the east, the university town of Missoula, Great Falls just east of the Rockies, Kalispell near Lake Flathead, the university and resort town of Bozeman and the state capital of Helena. The muscular tone of a land settled by ranch hands, miners and railroad workers, of cowboy hats, boots and blue jeans, of men who do hard physical work and relax hard afterwards, remains a link with Montanans going back to the mountain men, miners and cowboys who drove herds of Texas longhorns across the open range. And there is still the sense of space. Hunting and fishing, as in *A River Runs Through It*, are never far away; development in the small cities and resort areas has not been enough to drive the game away. In the late 1970s, Montana started attracting affluent second home buyers, and by the mid-1990s they came in a rush, movie stars and Wall Street magnates but also just ordinary people buying small spreads near Big Sky or McLeod, near Bozeman, or around Flathead Lake or Big Timber or the Big Mountain ski resort in Whitefish, where grizzlies come down to forage and the bars hold mouse races. Computers, modems and fax machines make it possible for small businessmen and entrepreneurs to work here, far from their customers and clients, but in an environment they love. Montana has room too for misfits—for the Freemen, anti-tax protesters who holed up on the eastern plains for 81 days before surrendering to federal law enforcement officers, or the accused Unabomber Ted Kaczynski, who prepared his lethal bombs from a waterless shack in the mountains near Lincoln.

Politically, Montana is the most Democratic of the small Rocky Mountain states—which means pretty Republican by national standards. There are still Democratic strongholds—Butte with its union heritage, Missoula with its large university, various Indian reservations. But Billings and the grazing counties are Republican, and Montana, after voting 38%–35% for Bill Clinton over George Bush in 1992, with 26% for Ross Perot, swung sharply right and voted 44%–41% for Bob Dole over Bill Clinton in 1996. The same impulse was visible in the response to Initiative 122, which would have imposed stricter standards on mine wastes. Gold mine companies spent $2 million on ads arguing that water was safe under existing standards and that jobs would be lost if the initiative passed; it was rejected 57%–43%. Montanans also rejected an initiative to raise the minimum wage and passed one to permit lawsuits against those who file false liens against property—a jab at the militias and their ilk.

Governor. Marc Racicot (pronounced *roscoe*) is probably the nation's most popular governor; in December 1996, his job rating was 80%, higher that any of the other 49 governors. He grew up in the mining town of Libby, the son of the basketball coach. Racicot is famously unassuming, lobbying legislators himself, speaking at a high school commencement with just one graduate, corresponding with an 11-year-old concerned about guns in schools, keeping his phone number

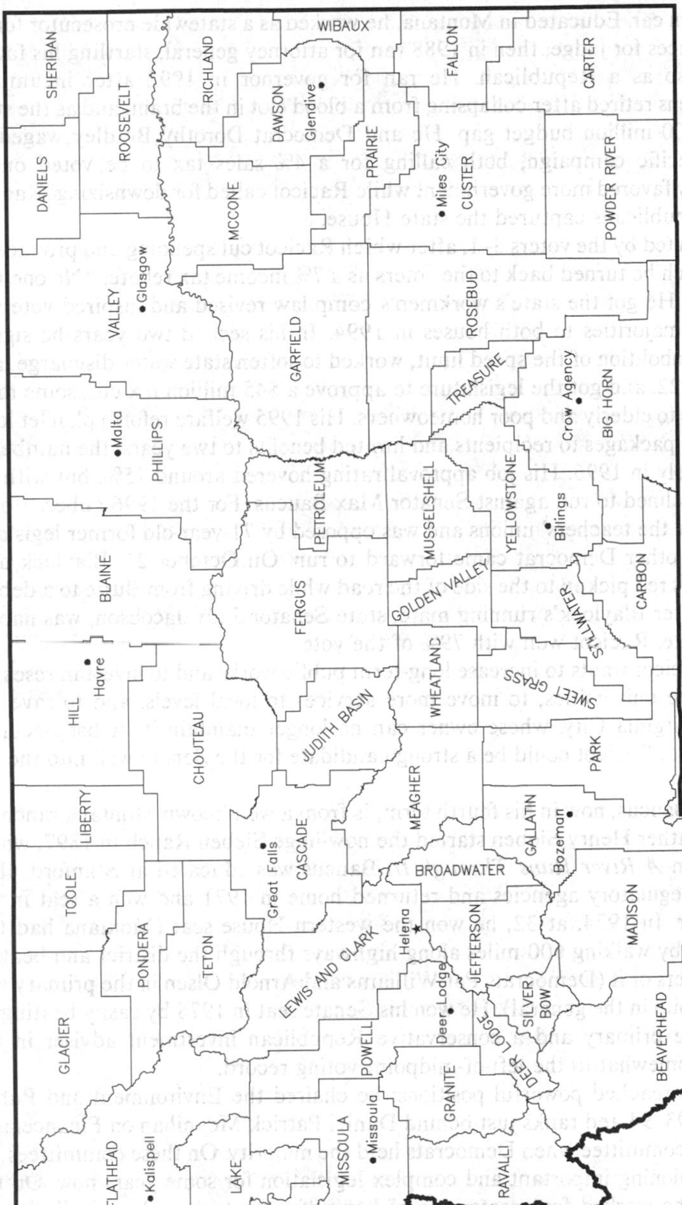

N E S W

Miles
0 10 20 30 40 50

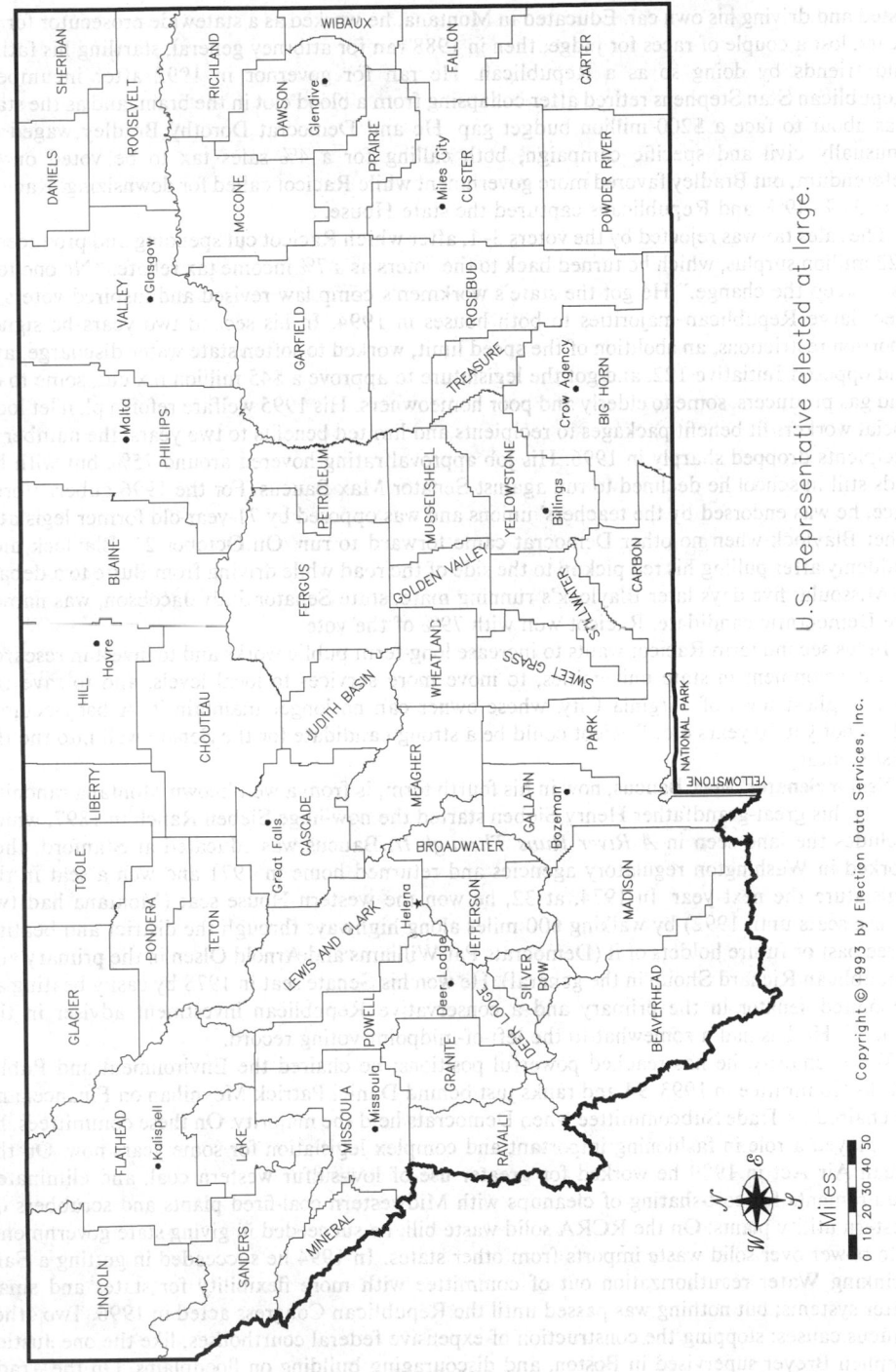

U.S. Representative elected at large.

listed and driving his own car. Educated in Montana, he worked as a statewide prosecutor for 12 years, lost a couple of races for judge, then in 1988 ran for attorney general, startling his father and friends by doing so as a Republican. He ran for governor in 1992 after incumbent Republican Stan Stephens retired after collapsing from a blood clot in the brain, and as the state was about to face a $200 million budget gap. He and Democrat Dorothy Bradley waged an unusually civil and specific campaign, both calling for a 4% sales tax to be voted on by referendum, but Bradley favored more government while Racicot called for downsizing. Racicot won 51%–49%, and Republicans captured the state House.

The sales tax was rejected by the voters 3–1, after which Racicot cut spending and produced a $22 million surplus, which he turned back to the voters as a 7% income tax rebate. "No one told us to keep the change." He got the state's workmen's comp law revised and inspired voters to elect large Republican majorities to both houses in 1994. In his second two years he signed abortion restrictions, an abolition of the speed limit, worked to soften state water discharge laws and opposed Initiative 122, and got the legislature to approve a $45 million tax cut, some to oil and gas producers, some to elderly and poor homeowners. His 1995 welfare reform plan let local social workers fit benefit packages to recipients and limited benefits to two years; the number of recipients dropped sharply in 1996. His job approval rating hovered around 75%, but with his kids still in school he declined to run against Senator Max Baucus. For the 1996 gubernatorial race, he was endorsed by the teachers' unions and was opposed by 71-year-old former legislator Chet Blaylock when no other Democrat came forward to run. On October 21, Blaylock died suddenly after pulling his red pickup to the side of the road while driving from Butte to a debate in Missoula; five days later Blaylock's running mate, state Senator Judy Jacobson, was named the Democratic candidate. Racicot won with 79% of the vote.

In his second term Racicot wants to increase long-term public works and to invest in research and development in state universities, to move more services to local levels, and to save the mining ghost town of Virginia City, whose owner can no longer maintain it. A baby-boomer who's not yet 50 years old, Racicot could be a strong candidate for the Senate well into the the 21st Century.

Senior Senator. Max Baucus, now in his fourth term, is from a well-known Montana ranching family; his great-grandfather Henry Sieben started the now-huge Sieben Ranch in 1897, which includes the land seen in *A River Runs Through It*. Baucus was educated at Stanford, then worked in Washington regulatory agencies and returned home in 1971 and won a seat in the legislature the next year. In 1974, at 32, he won the western House seat (Montana had two House seats until 1992) by walking 600 miles along highways through the district and beating three past or future holders of it (Democrats Pat Williams and Arnold Olsen in the primary and Republican Richard Shoup in the general). He won his Senate seat in 1978 by easily beating an appointed senator in the primary and a conservative Republican investment adviser in the general. He has had a somewhat to the left-of-midpoint voting record.

With seniority, he has reached powerful positions: he chaired the Environment and Public Works Committee in 1993–94 and ranks just behind Daniel Patrick Moynihan on Finance, and he chaired its Trade Subcommittee when Democrats held the majority. On these committees, he has played a role in fashioning important and complex legislation for some years now. On the Clean Air Act in 1989 he worked for greater use of low-sulfur western coal, and eliminated requirements for cost-sharing of cleanups with Midwestern coal-fired plants and scrubbers on western utility plants. On the RCRA solid waste bill, he succeeded in giving state governments veto power over solid waste imports from other states. In 1994 he succeeded in getting a Safe Drinking Water reauthorization out of committee with more flexibility for states and small water systems; but nothing was passed until the Republican Congress acted in 1996. Two other Baucus causes: stopping the construction of expensive federal courthouses, like the one Justice Stephen Breyer supervised in Boston, and discouraging building on floodplains. On the Trade Subcommittee, Baucus has taken the lead on preserving Most Favored Nation status for China, which is a major market for Montana products, especially wheat. He has kept his eye on other

Montana issues, seeking retaliation against Canada for its alleged subsidies of wheat, beef and lamb and for keeping U.S. products out of the Canadian market. He supported NAFTA and GATT, but tried without success to get the retaliatory Super 301 provision reenacted after it was effectively repealed by GATT.

Baucus says that his only philosophy is to "fight like the dickens for the average person of Montana," and he has shown himself sensitive to Montana opinion. He was at first considered a vote for the Clinton healthcare plan on Finance, but became part of the bipartisan group seeking a compromise, then withdrew from that in June 1994, saying he opposed new taxes to pay for reforms. Making what seemed like a local political calculation, he switched in 1995 and became a supporter of the balanced budget constitutional amendment. After initial qualms, he supported the Republican welfare reform in 1996. Perhaps his greatest success for his home state came in March 1993, when he led the effort against the Clinton Administration's proposals to increase grazing fees and impose a 12.5% royalty on mining in public lands. Clinton, needing Baucus's vote in the Finance Committee for his budget and tax package, immediately buckled, which undercut Interior Secretary Bruce Babbitt's chances for major reforms. Even after that, Baucus was one of the senators who insisted on a much smaller tax increase than in the original Clinton package.

Baucus was reelected by wide margins in 1984 and 1990, but in 1996 Republicans called him the most vulnerable Democratic incumbent. Baucus campaigned hard, as usual, shaking thousands of hands and walking 820 miles through the state. His opponent was Lieutenant Governor Dennis Rehberg, who backed term limits and promised to forego pay increases and pensions. The National Republican Senatorial Committee spent some $300,000 on ads labeling him, "Max Baucus—definitely a liberal." Rehberg attacked him for his 1993 tax increase vote and for changing his stand on the balanced budget amendment, the assault weapons ban (he voted for the 1994 crime bill), and welfare reform. "Max takes three sides of a two-sided issue," he said. Criticism was also vollied by environmentalists on the left, who were angry that the $1.4 billion McDonald mine was prospecting for gold on land along the Blackfoot River owned by the Sieben Ranch.

Baucus responded that Rehberg was a "special interest" candidate backing billions in tax breaks for the rich and that the Republican balanced budget would produce "cuts" in Medicare and student loans. For a time the two candidates pledged not to run negative ads, but eventually that deteriorated. Baucus complained to the Federal Election Commission that the National Republican Senatorial Committee ads violated rules because they advocated his defeat and that they violated the clean campaign pledge. Polls showed Baucus in the lead throughout, hovering around 50%, and he benefited from a huge money advantage: he had spent $4.2 million to Rehberg's $1.3. But in the end Baucus won by just 50%–45%, his closest showing ever. He will continue to be a pivotal vote in the Senate and on the Finance Committee. But his rather narrow victory and the apparent movement of Montana to the right—Republicans trailed by only 51%–48% in the last four Senate races here as compared to 57%–42% in the nine Senate races before that—suggest that he cannot take future elections for granted.

Junior Senator. Conrad Burns is almost a stereotypical Westerner, picking his teeth with a pocketknife, chewing tobacco, sporting pellets in his arm from a hunting accident, forever telling deadpan jokes. A native of Missouri, he started off as a livestock fieldman and auctioneer who became field representative of the *Polled Hereford World*; when he was reassigned back east (to Des Moines), he quit so he could stay in Billings where he set up a farm news radio network, which grew from four radio stations in 1975 to 29 radio and six TV stations in 1988. Piqued at a local politician, Burns ran for Yellowstone County Commissioner in 1986 and won; two years later, he ran against Democratic Senator John Melcher. Melcher had been in Congress for 19 years and Burns attacked him as "a liberal who is soft on drugs, soft on defense and very high on social programs." Melcher was hurt by a Reagan veto of a Melcher wilderness bill and by public opposition to the "let-it-burn" policy that resulted in the Yellowstone fires of summer 1988. Burns, who ended every speech with a Western "You bet!" won 52% of the vote.

In the Senate, Burns has made a mostly conservative voting record. His main issue is telecommunications—not so un-Montanan a cause when you think about it—and he has favored letting the regional Bells into cable and broadcast programming, which was accomplished in the 1996 Telecommunications Act. His ultimate goal is to encourage by 2015 a two-way interactive telecommunications information superhighway to every home, school and business. He chairs the Internet Caucus and also the Commerce Subcommittee on Communications. In 1995 he conducted the first congressional hearing on the Internet, with cybersurfers able to ask questions of witnesses and chat with subcommittee staffers. In November 1996 he ran for Republican Conference Secretary against Paul Coverdell and lost 41–14.

On Montana issues Burns is often critical of environmentalists. He opposed reintroduction of grey wolves into Yellowstone National Park, which he estimates will cost $123 million, or $1.8 million per wolf. And when the Clinton Administration and Max Baucus reached agreement limiting the Crown Butte New World gold mine near Yellowstone, Burns said, "By short-circuiting Montana's environmental-impact-statement process, Bill Clinton has told Montanans that they cannot be trusted to protect their own resources." He has blocked Democrats' plans for a Montana wilderness bill and they have blocked his.

Burns was targeted by Democrats when he came up for reelection in 1994. But they had as hard a time as Montana Republicans have often had in coming up with good candidates. Former Senator John Melcher ran, after spending the previous five years in Washington, but lost to University of Montana Law dean Jack Mudd in the primary. Mudd was poorly funded and his support of the 1993 Clinton tax increase and the 1994 crime bill with its gun control provisions were highly unpopular. Burns attacked Mudd as an advocate of higher taxes and was only briefly thrown on the defensive when he repeated to a reporter a conversation he had with a constituent that included a racial slur about living in the District of Columbia. He apologized the next day and said he was only repeating the rancher's comments. On election day 1994, Bill Clinton's job approval in Montana was only 36%, and Burns won by an impressive 62%–38%. That made him the first Republican senator to be reelected in Montana history, though as he likes to say, "I am not a career politician. Not even a skilled one."

Representative-At-Large. Montana lost one of its two House seats after the 1990 Census; population growth since will probably restore the second seat for the 2002 election. The congressman-at-large now, elected in 1996, is Republican Rick Hill. Hill owned a surety bond and insurance agency in Helena, then was made head of the state workmen's comp agency by Governor Marc Racicot. With legislative changes they sought, more attention to workplace safety and aggressive investigation of fraudulent claims, rates came way down; Hill reduced premiums 19% in 1996 alone, and businesses saved $75 million. He was one of four serious candidates who ran for the seat when the state was surprised by the retirement announcement of 18-year incumbent Democrat Pat Williams, an old-fashioned Montana liberal who believes that Montanans' real enemies are not bossy feds but eastern corporations eager to exploit their resources; as a goodbye gift Congress passed a boxing safety act, a reminder of the days when Williams put on the gloves in Butte. To succeed him Williams pushed hard for Bill Yellowtail, former state Senator and regional EPA administrator in Denver, who grew up on and still lives on the Crow Indian reservation. But in May 1996, the month before the primary, three startling revelations about Yellowtail came out. At a time when Democrats were proposing a waiting period for gun purchasers with a history of spouse abuse, it turned out that Yellowtail two decades ago had hit his wife hard enough to break her glasses and send her to the hospital. Also, at a time when politicians are denouncing deadbeat dads, it turned out that Yellowtail had failed to pay child support for five years in the mid-1980s and that his state legislative paycheck had been garnished. And at a time when all politicians denounce violent crime, it turned out he had burglarized a camera store while a sophomore at Dartmouth and had been found guilty of two felony counts. "I didn't have any money. I guess I wanted some camera stuff," he explained. Yellowtail held a press conference, complete with former wife, confessing error, expressing contrition, and concluding, "All I ask for is forgiveness." He seems to have gotten it all along: he was pardoned in New Hampshire, readmitted to Dartmouth, elevated from the state legislature to the EPA job, and in June 1996 he won the four-way Democratic primary with 56%, far ahead of the next highest candidate with 22%.

For a long time it seemed he might get forgiven in the general election too. The three Republican candidates were little known to the public. Hill, in something of an upset, won the primary with 44% to 36% for former Conrad Burns staffer Dwight MacKay and 20% for businessman Alan Mikkelsen. Yellowtail led Hill consistently in polls—42%–38% in July, 43%–30% in August, 39%–36% in September. The AFL-CIO came in with anti-Hill ads, the Republican campaign committee with anti-Yellowtail ads. Hill, after saying he would not use Yellowtail's personal problems, ran ads asking delphically, "Congressman Bill Yellowtail: Can we really afford to take the risk?" Hill turned out to have problems of his own. He had appeared at a militia gathering in spring 1996. "I believe in the politics of inclusion rather than exclusion." And he had left his first wife after an affair with a cocktail waitress and had an eight-year battle over finances and child custody. But he had paid his child support: "I lived up to my responsibilities every step of the way. Bill walked away. That's the difference."

Another difference was that Hill was far better financed. Hill outspent Yellowtail $943,000 to $635,000, a real edge even considering Yellowtail's support from unions and environmental organizations. The final outcome was not terribly close. Hill won 52%–43%, carrying all but nine counties—the old mining towns of Butte and Anaconda, the university town of Missoula, and the Indian reservations. The result raises the question of whether respondents in polls were reluctant, as Democratic politicians were, to say they were against a Native American politician who had some serious moral and character flaws despite some attractive personal accomplishments. In any case, Hill seems likely to be a solidly conservative member of the House, with a good prospect of holding this seat in a Republican-trending state.

Presidential politics. Montana, with only three electoral votes, can't expect to see much of presidential candidates, particularly because its presidential primary is in early June, the same day as New Jersey's. In the 1980s only Alaska, Idaho, Utah and North Dakota were farther out of the national political jetlanes. But in 1992 and 1996 Montana was closely divided and was visited by national candidates, though if it continues its Republican trend, and if environmentalist-friendly Al Gore is the Democratic nominee, it might not be in 2000. Ross Perot won 26% of the vote here in 1992, and as high as 36% in Phillips County up on the Canadian border; and he won 13.6% in Montana in 1996, just under Maine's 14.2% for his best showing.

The People: Est. Pop. 1996: 879,000; Pop. 1990: 799,065, up 10.1% 1990–1996. 0.3% of U.S. total, 44th largest; 47% rural. Median age 36.5 years. 13% 65 years and over. 91.8% White, 1% Asian; 5.8% Amer. Indian, 1.5% Hispanic origin. Households: 57.7% married couple families; 28% married couple fams. w. children; 48% college educ.; median household income: $22,988; per capita income: $11,213; 67.3% owner occupied housing; median house value: $56,600; median monthly rent: $251. 5.3% Unemployment. 1996 Voting age pop.: 656,000. 1996 Turnout: 407,083; 62% of VAP. Registered voters (1996): 590,751; no party registration.

Political Lineup: Governor, Marc Racicot (R); Lt. Gov., Judy Martz (R); Secy. of State, Mike Cooney (D); Atty. Gen., Joseph P. Mazurek (D); Auditor, Mark O'Keefe (D). State Senate, 50 (16 D and 34 R); Senate President, Gary Aklestad (R); State House, 100 (35 D and 65 R); House Speaker, John Mercer (R). Senators, Max Baucus (D) and Conrad Burns (R). Representative, 1 R at large.

Elections Division: 406-444-4732; **Filing Deadline for U.S. Congress:** March 19, 1998.

1996 Presidential Vote

Dole (R)	179,652	(44%)
Clinton (D)	167,922	(41%)
Perot (I)	55,229	(14%)

1992 Presidential Vote

Clinton (D)	154,507	(38%)
Bush (R)	144,207	(35%)
Perot (I)	107,225	(26%)

1996 Republican Presidential Primary

Dole (R)	72,176	(61%)
Buchanan (R)	28,581	(24%)
Forbes (R)	8,456	(7%)
Other	8,533	(7%)

GOVERNOR

Gov. Marc Racicot (R)

Elected 1992, term expires Jan. 2001; b. July 24, 1948, Thompson Falls; home, Helena; Carroll Col., B.A. 1970, U. of MT, J.D. 1973; Catholic; married (Theresa).

Career: Army Judge Advocate Corps, 1973–76; Dep. Missoula Cnty. Atty., 1976–77; MT Asst. Atty. Gen., 1977–89; MT Atty. Gen., 1988–92.

Office: Office of the Governor, State Capitol, Helena 59620, 406-444-3111; Fax: 406-444-4151; Web site: www.mt.gov.

Election Results

1996 gen.	Marc Racicot (R)	320,768	(79%)
	Judy Jacobson (D)	76,471	(19%)
	Others	7,936	(2%)
1996 prim.	Marc Racicot (R)	92,644	(76%)
	Rob Natelson (R)	28,672	(24%)
1992 gen.	Marc Racicot (R)	209,401	(51%)
	Dorothy Bradley (D)	198,421	(49%)

SENATORS

Sen. Max Baucus (D)

Elected 1978, seat up 2002; b. Dec. 11, 1941, Helena; home, Helena; Stanford U., B.A. 1964, LL.B. 1967; Protestant; married (Wanda).

Career: Staff atty., Civil Aeronautics Bd., 1967–69; Legal Asst., Securities and Exchange Comm., 1969–71; Practicing atty., 1971–74; MT House of Reps., 1973–74; U.S. House of Reps., 1975–78.

DC Office: 511 HSOB 20510, 202-224-2651; e-mail: max@baucus.senate.gov.

State Offices: Billings, 406-657-6790; Bozeman, 406-586-6104; Butte, 406-782-8700; Great Falls, 406-761-1574; Helena, 406-449-5480; Kalispell, 406-756-1150; Missoula, 406-329-3123.

Committees: *Agriculture, Nutrition & Forestry* (5th of 8 D): Forestry, Conservation & Rural Revitalization; Marketing, Inspection & Product Promotion (RMM). *Environment & Public Works* (RMM of 8 D): Transportation & Infrastructure (RMM). *Finance* (2nd of 9 D): Health Care; International Trade; Taxation & IRS Oversight (RMM). *Intelligence (Select)* (6th of 9 D). *Joint Committee on Taxation* (5th of 5 Sens.).

Group Ratings

	ADA	ACLU	AFS	LCV	CFA	CON	NFIB	COC	ACU	NTLC	CHC
1996	85	33	71	69	71	38	41	46	20	35	15
1995	75	—	82	86	56	2	—	47	13	—	—

National Journal Ratings

	1995 LIB — 1995 CONS	1996 LIB — 1996 CONS
Economic	58% — 40%	53% — 46%
Social	53% — 43%	63% — 34%
Foreign	72% — 24%	70% — 28%

Key Votes of the 104th Congress

1. Reduce Medicare Growth $	N	5. Flag Amendment	Y	9. Anti-Missile Defense	N
2. Lmt. Prod. Liab. Damages	N	6. Endangered Species	Y	10. Cuban Embargo	Y
3. Increase Min. Wage	Y	7. Gay Employment Rights	Y	11. Bar Bosnia Troop $	N
4. Welfare Reform	Y	8. Ovrd. Part. Birth Veto	N	12. Cut Vietnam Aid	Y

Election Results

1996 general	Max Baucus (D)	201,935	(50%)	($4,280,747)
	Dennis Rehberg (R)	182,111	(45%)	($1,358,165)
	Becky Shaw (Reform)	19,276	(5%)	
1996 primary	Max Baucus (D)	unopposed		
1990 general	Max Baucus (D)	217,563	(68%)	($2,568,899)
	Allen C. Kolstad (R)	93,836	(29%)	($747,661)
	Other	7,937	(2%)	

Sen. Conrad Burns (R)

Elected 1988, seat up 2000; b. Jan. 25, 1935, Gallatin, MO; home, Billings; U. of MO, 1952–54; Lutheran; married (Phyllis).

Career: Marine Corps, 1955–57; TWA and Ozark Airlines, 1958–61; Field rep., *Polled Hereford World*, 1962; Mgr., Billings Livestock Show, 1968; Radio & TV broadcaster, 1968–86; Yellowstone Cnty. Commissioner, 1986–88.

DC Office: 187 DSOB 20510, 202-224-2644; Fax: 202-224-8594; e-mail: conrad_burns@burns.senate.gov.

State Offices: Billings, 406-252-0550; Bozeman, 406-586-4450; Butte, 406-723-3277; Great Falls, 406-452-9585; Glendive, 406-365-2391; Helena, 406-449-5401; Kalispell, 406-257-3360; Missoula, 406-329-3528.

Committees: *Appropriations* (8th of 15 R): Agriculture, Rural Development & Related Agencies; Energy & Water Development; Interior; Military Construction (Chmn.); VA, HUD & Independent Agencies. *Commerce, Science & Transportation* (3rd of 11 R): Aviation; Communications (Chmn.); Consumer Affairs, Foreign Commerce & Tourism; Science, Technology & Space; Surface Transportation & Merchant Marine. *Energy & Natural Resources* (11th of 11 R): Forests & Public Land Management Subcommittee (Vice Chmn.); National Parks, Historic Preservation & Recreation. *Small Business* (2nd of 10 R). *Aging (Special)* (4th of 10 R).

Group Ratings

	ADA	ACLU	AFS	LCV	CFA	CON	NFIB	COC	ACU	NTLC	CHC
1996	5	22	0	0	14	32	97	85	100	97	100
1995	0	—	9	0	0	54	—	100	83	—	—

National Journal Ratings

	1995 LIB — 1995 CONS			1996 LIB — 1996 CONS		
Economic	31%	—	66%	22%	—	76%
Social	22%	—	74%	0%	—	72%
Foreign	34%	—	64%	0%	—	74%

Key Votes of the 104th Congress

1. Reduce Medicare Growth $	Y	5. Flag Amendment	Y	9. Anti-Missile Defense	Y
2. Lmt. Prod. Liab. Damages	Y	6. Endangered Species	N	10. Cuban Embargo	Y
3. Increase Min. Wage	N	7. Gay Employment Rights	N	11. Bar Bosnia Troop $	N
4. Welfare Reform	Y	8. Ovrd. Part. Birth Veto	Y	12. Cut Vietnam Aid	Y

Election Results

1994 general	Conrad Burns (R)	218,542	(62%)	($3,518,574)
	Jack Mudd (D)	131,845	(38%)	($1,107,591)
1994 primary	Conrad Burns (R)	unopposed		
1988 general	Conrad Burns (R)	189,445	(52%)	($1,076,010)
	John Melcher (D)	175,809	(48%)	($1,338,622)

REPRESENTATIVE

Rep. Rick Hill (R)

Elected 1996; b. Dec. 30, 1946, Grand Rapids, MN; home, Helena; St. Cloud St. U., B.A. 1968; Assembly of God; married (Betti).

Career: Pres., InsureWest Inc., 1984–96; Managing Partner, Hill Properties, 1988–present; Chmn., MT Mutual Compensation Insurance Fund, 1993–96.

DC Office: 1037 LHOB 20515, 202-225-3211; Fax: 202-225-5687.

District Offices: Billings, 406-256-1019; Helena, 406-443-7878.

Committees: *Banking & Financial Services* (25th of 30 R): Capital Markets, Securities & Government Sponsored Enterprises; Housing & Community Opportunity. *Resources* (24th of 27 R): Forests & Forest Health; National Parks & Public Lands. *Small Business* (17th of 19 R): Government Programs & Oversight.

Group Ratings and Key Votes: Newly Elected

Election Results

1996 general	Rick Hill (R)	211,975	(52%)	($943,062)
	Bill Yellowtail (D)	174,516	(43%)	($635,282)
	Jim Brooks (NL)	17,935	(4%)	
1996 primary	Rick Hill (R)	48,560	(44%)	
	Dwight MacKay (R)	39,651	(36%)	
	Alan Mikkelsen (R)	22,736	(20%)	
1994 general	Pat Williams (D)	171,372	(49%)	($734,121)
	Cy Jamison (R)	148,715	(42%)	($436,943)
	Steve Kelly (I)	32,046	(9%)	($17,440)

NEBRASKA

"The sea of Nebraska" is what the first settlers coming west called the Platte River—not actually a single river but a braid of streams that weave a silver chain around sandbars and islands, flooding the level floor of the great plain—a mile wide, as the saying goes, and six inches deep. Nebraska was formed in one rush of settlement in the 1880s, when its population increased from 452,000 to 1,062,000, more than in the century since (it was 1,652,000 in 1996). In the 1880s Omaha became a major railroad center, Lincoln the state capital and farming and food products became the main businesses. And for about 100 years, Nebraska remained pretty much that way. This is not what its founders intended: they hoped Nebraska would develop a diversified farming, industrial and commercial economy like Ohio, Illinois, Missouri or Minnesota. But while the 1880s were a time of plentiful rain here, the 1890s were a decade of drought, and Nebraska stopped growing. Many rural counties, and even Omaha, lost population and Nebraska has exported people ever since; 48% of Nebraskans in 1890 were children; in 1990, only 27% were. The creative energies in the economy seem to have skipped over the Great Plains and moved far to the West.

The sudden boom of the 1880s and the bust of the 1890s produced the most colorful—and atypical—politics of Nebraska's history: the populist movement and William Jennings Bryan, the "silver tongued orator of the Platte." Bryan was only 36 when he delivered the famous Cross of Gold speech at the 1896 Democratic National Convention and was swept to the Democratic nomination. He was thought so radical that Democratic President Grover Cleveland wouldn't support him, but he still won 47% of the vote in the first of three attempts. Nebraskans supported Bryan, whose program may have been forward-looking, but whose purpose was retrograde: to restore Nebraska to the prosperity it had enjoyed a few years before. Since Bryan's time, Nebraska's most notable politician has been George Norris, who led the House rebellion against Speaker Joseph Cannon in 1911, and in the 1930s pushed through the Norris-LaGuardia Anti-Injunction Act, the first national pro-union legislation, and the Tennessee Valley Authority. But most Nebraskans were repelled by the New Deal, which seemed to threaten their stable society. Although it often elects Democratic governors and Senators, Nebraska for half a century has been among the most Republican of states in national elections.

Now in the 1990s Nebraska seems to be growing and changing, after a century's pause. Omaha is the home base of the fast-growing ConAgra food combine and of mega-investor

Warren Buffett, whose down-home humor complements his knack for picking stocks that go up hundreds of percents. The nearby Strategic Air Command base brought the world's most advanced phone system to the Omaha area 40-odd years ago; starting in the 1980s hotel chains, credit card companies and telemarketers set up operations, making this the world's leading place to make a living by talking on the phone. Computers and fiber optics have made Nebraska, as one mayor said, "just another suburb of Chicago." In the 1990s, telemarketing and the big Nebraska Beef meat-processing plants, data-processing and dozens of little startup businesses have sent Nebraska's economy surging. There is now in-migration into the state, and population rose 5% between 1990–96; Nebraska businesses are trying to recruit high-skill workers from out of state while Nebraska Beef attracts workers from the Mexican border; unemployment was the lowest in the nation from 1993–96 (2.6%) and per capita income was just 7% below the national average. Growth is concentrated: most rural counties are losing population, while greater Omaha and Lincoln, Madison and Beatrice and the towns along I-80 and the Platte are growing rapidly. But the atmosphere has visibly changed. "If someone doesn't have a job in Omaha," said one Nebraskan with two jobs, "they don't want one."

Politically, Nebraska has remained a heavily Republican state with a proclivity for Democratic governors. Its senior senator, Democrat Bob Kerrey, served as governor from 1983–87 and was a candidate for president in 1992, and may be again in 2000; its current Democratic Governor Ben Nelson has one of the highest job ratings in the nation. But Nebraska cast the third-highest percentage for Bob Dole (after Kansas and Utah) and the second highest Dole-Clinton margin, and when Nelson tried to succeed former Democratic Governor Jim Exon in the Senate in 1996, he lost all but five counties to Republican Chuck Hagel; with Hagel's election, Nebraska became the only state represented in the Senate by two decorated Vietnam combat veterans.

Governor. Governor Ben Nelson, first elected in 1990, was the third Democrat in a row to beat an incumbent Republican associated with tax increases. The first two went on to become senators, Jim Exon in 1978 and Bob Kerrey in 1988; but Nelson lost his Senate bid in 1996. Nelson grew up in McCook, the home town of George Norris and novelist Willa Cather; he went to the University of Nebraska, practiced law, served as state insurance director and headed a major insurance company. In 1990 he ran for governor, taking on former Bob Kerrey staff aide Bill Hoppner in the primary, and won by all of 42 votes. In the general he beat Governor Kay Orr 50%–49% because she raised taxes and her political consultants failed to place many of her paid-for scheduled TV spots in October. Nelson pledged to serve "one Nebraska," spreading economic growth outward from Omaha and Lincoln, and to cut property taxes. He cut spending increases sharply and used his line-item veto to cut appropriations. He got the Senate to pass and voters to approve a lottery in 1992, with proceeds to go to creative education and environment projects. Nebraska voters, incidentally, have rejected most forms of gambling. He built more prisons, reformed workmen's comp and reorganized the Department of Aging. He pushed an Employment First welfare reform. Nationally, he was a leader against unfunded mandates. He pushed through a gradual reduction in property taxes and went to Japan to boost beef exports; he promoted ethanol and supported NAFTA. In 1994, he was reelected by a resounding 73%–26% margin, and promised during the campaign to serve out his entire term.

But in early 1995 Exon announced he was retiring from the Senate after three terms and Kerrey, the Democratic Senatorial Campaign Committee chairman, pressed Nelson to run. In September 1995, despite his pledge, Nelson announced. He led in polls throughout much of the campaign, but was hit by Republican nominee Chuck Hagel for not doing enough to cut property taxes. In an upset Hagel won 56%–42%—yet another example in the mid-1990s (Wyoming 1994, Massachusetts 1996) of how a state that strongly favors one party in national politics will not elect even the most popular governor of the other to the Senate.

Nelson returned to Lincoln determined to cut more taxes and get tougher on crime, with boot camps for young offenders. Term limits bar him from running in 1998. Possible successors include Democratic Lieutenant Governor Kim Robak, who herself was attacked as a liberal

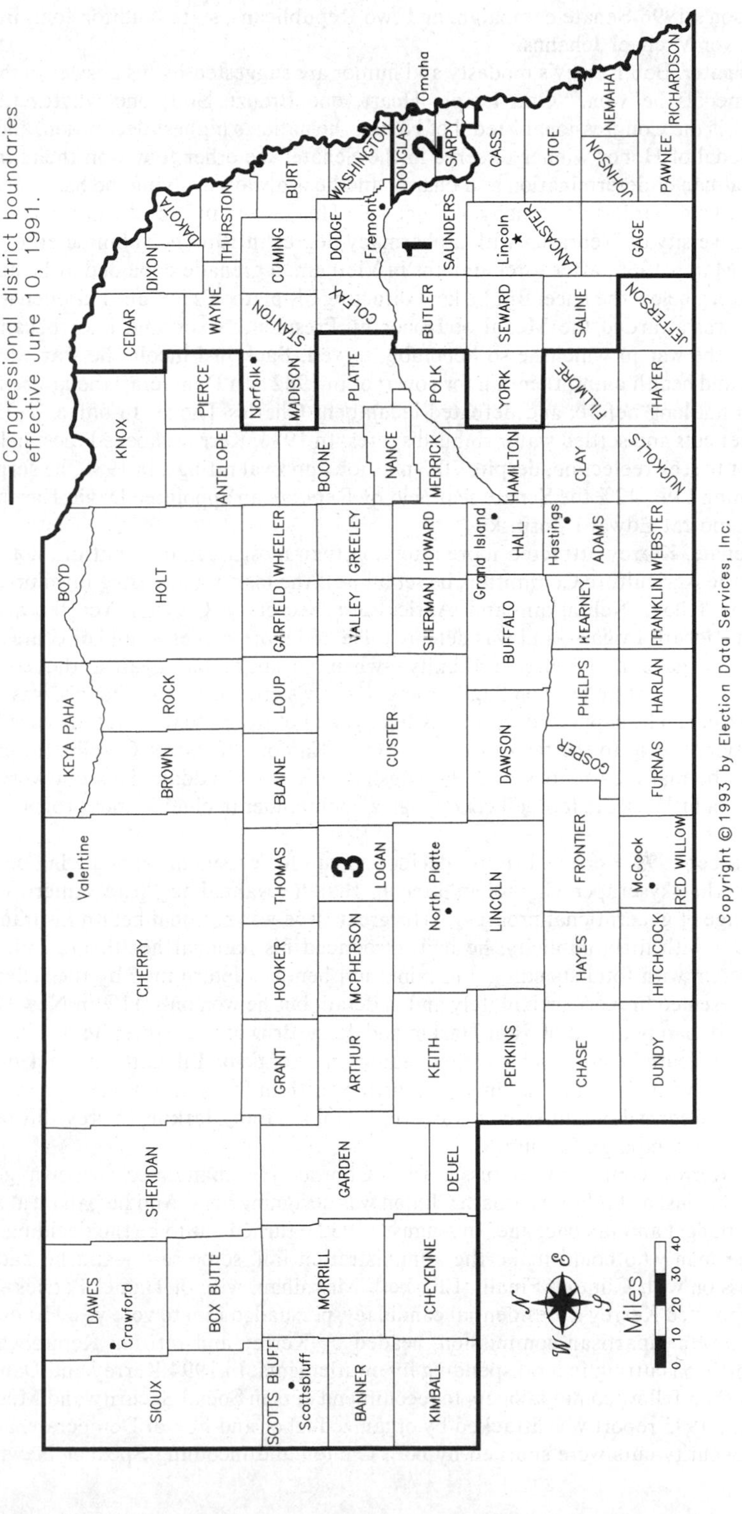
Congressional district boundaries effective June 10, 1991.
Copyright © 1993 by Election Data Services, Inc.
Miles
0 10 20 30 40
1
2
3
Omaha
Fremont
Lincoln
Norfolk
Grand Island
Hastings
North Platte
McCook
Valentine
Crawford
Scottsbluff
SIOUX
DAWES
SHERIDAN
CHERRY
KEYA PAHA
BOYD
BROWN
ROCK
HOLT
KNOX
CEDAR
DIXON
DAKOTA
THURSTON
WAYNE
PIERCE
ANTELOPE
BURT
CUMING
STANTON
MADISON
WASHINGTON
DODGE
COLFAX
PLATTE
BOONE
DOUGLAS
SARPY
SAUNDERS
BUTLER
POLK
NANCE
MERRICK
CASS
LANCASTER
SEWARD
YORK
HAMILTON
OTOE
JOHNSON
NEMAHA
RICHARDSON
PAWNEE
GAGE
JEFFERSON
SALINE
FILLMORE
THAYER
NUCKOLLS
CLAY
ADAMS
WEBSTER
HALL
HOWARD
GREELEY
WHEELER
GARFIELD
VALLEY
SHERMAN
BUFFALO
KEARNEY
FRANKLIN
PHELPS
HARLAN
LOUP
BLAINE
CUSTER
DAWSON
GOSPER
FURNAS
THOMAS
LOGAN
LINCOLN
FRONTIER
RED WILLOW
HOOKER
MCPHERSON
HAYES
HITCHCOCK
GRANT
ARTHUR
KEITH
PERKINS
CHASE
DUNDY
GARDEN
DEUEL
BOX BUTTE
MORRILL
CHEYENNE
SCOTTS BLUFF
BANNER
KIMBALL

during Nelson's 1996 Senate campaign, and two Republicans, state Auditor John Breslow and Lincoln Mayor Michael Johanns.

Senior Senator. Bob Kerrey's modesty and humor are suggested by his answer to the question of which medals he won. "One Purple Heart, one Bronze Star, one whatever," he said. "Whatever" is the Congressional Medal of Honor, the nation's highest decoration, and Kerrey is the fifth Medal of Honor winner to serve in the Senate; the other four won theirs in the Civil War. He is a man of determination and charm, and he is always evolving: he has never done any one thing for long, but has done many of them well. He grew up in Lincoln, and after graduating from the University of Nebraska with a pharmacy degree in 1966 he volunteered for the Navy SEALs. In March 1969, after three months in Vietnam, a grenade exploded at his feet, and he lost his right leg below the knee. But he kept directing his platoon's fire until his men were able to escape. He was awarded the Medal of Honor by President Nixon and later became an avid opponent of the war in which he so honorably served. Back in Lincoln, he started a chain of restaurants and health clubs, then ran for governor in 1982 as a Democrat, though he had been a Republican not long before, and defeated incumbent Charles Thone. In office, he made some tough budget cuts and settled water rights disputes. In 1986, Kerrey shocked most politicians by deciding not to seek reelection, despite 70%-plus job approval ratings; in 1988, he surprised very few by winning 57%–42% the Senate seat held by Republican appointee David Karnes after the death of Democrat Edward Zorinsky.

In the Senate, Kerrey attracted more attention than most freshmen, but did not always get results. On the Agriculture Committee, he set himself the task of increasing farm price supports and took on fellow Nebraskan and Agriculture Secretary Clayton Yeutter and Indiana Republican Richard Lugar—and was defeated. He had more success—and of course his record as a war hero gave him more credibility—when he spoke out against the constitutional amendment to allow state bans on flag burning. Kerrey's great crusade, though, was against the Gulf war. Although he supported the initial deployment of troops to the Gulf, he vocally opposed military action, taking to the floor often with Terry Sanford of North Carolina to predict that there would be many casualties and that Bush's threats to Saddam Hussein were more the language of "a little league football coach than a commander in chief"—not prognostications of great foresight.

In September 1991 Kerrey abruptly decided to run for president, announcing on a brilliant day outside the skyscraper Capitol in Lincoln that he wanted to "lead America's fearless, restless voyage of generational progress." His great issue was national health insurance reform. In July 1991, with little publicity, he had introduced his national healthcare bill, a publicly financed system with total spending and minimum benefits determined by the federal government. He presented his case articulately and in detail, but he won only 11% in New Hampshire, finishing third, barely ahead of Tom Harkin and Jerry Brown. Then, despite his 40%–25% win over Harkin in South Dakota and his harsh attacks in Georgia on Bill Clinton's lack of candor on his experiences with the draft, he finished fourth or fifth in five states a week later, and said "I just woke up Wednesday and said it was over." Unlike Tom Harkin, Kerrey did not endorse Clinton early or campaign for him.

In 1993 Kerrey continued to tussle with Clinton. He abandoned his own government healthcare plan just as Hillary Rodham Clinton was designing hers. And he balked at supporting the Clinton budget and tax package. In August 1993 he turned out to be the deciding vote in the Senate—the man who could make the administration fail, some said—and he had an angry shouting session with Clinton. Finally Elizabeth Moynihan, wife of Daniel Patrick Moynihan, who had supported Kerrey's presidential candidacy, persuaded him to vote yes. His quid pro quo was creation of a bipartisan commission, headed by Kerrey and retiring Republican Senator John Danforth, on cutting federal spending for entitlements. In 1994 Kerrey and Danforth tried to persuade their fellow commissioners to recommend cuts in Social Security and Medicare. But their January 1995 report was attacked by organized labor and liberal Democrats, and its calls for Social Security cuts were spurned by both Clinton and incoming Speaker Newt Gingrich.

The effort must be counted a failure, though it might have succeeded if the Democrats, as almost everyone expected, had retained control of Congress.

Kerrey has continued to question entitlements. In 1996 he and Wyoming Senator Alan Simpson proposed a Social Security reform—raising the retirement age to 70, adjusting the COLA downward and allowing workers to invest 2% of Social Security payments in personal investment plans in return for lower Social Security benefits. In January 1997 he said that entitlement increases might require $1.6 billion cuts in promised Agriculture Department spending. In a 1996 appropriation, Kerrey created a National Commission on Restructuring the Internal Revenue Service; he co-chairs the Commission with Republican Congressman Rob Portman of Ohio, and it is tasked with issuing a report in June 1997. Kerrey says his goal is for the agency to treat taxpayers like customers.

Kerrey has had a mostly, but not always predictably, liberal voting record, but his instinct is often toward the center. In May 1995 he voted for the Republicans' budget resolution and in December 1995 he supported the moderate Breaux-Chafee compromise budget. He serves on Agriculture and Finance, for which he left Appropriations in 1997, and is vice chairman of Intelligence. He has sometimes been tough on the CIA, calling for a determination in September 1995 of whether CIA employees broke the law when they withheld information from Congress about the murder of an American and disappearance of a rebel in Guatemala. He served with two persistent, even stubborn chairmen, Arlen Specter and Richard Shelby. Shelby's delays of hearings on CIA nominee Anthony Lake and then overbearing questions clearly troubled Kerrey. But in March 1997, Kerrey questioned whether Lake was properly in control of the National Security Council when it was pestered for White House invitations for a big Democratic contributor; Lake promptly withdrew his nomination.

Kerrey, writes George Will, "the most interesting senator not named Moynihan, has a flair for public-spirited impudence, uttering indiscreet facts." He has been willing to change positions when he changes his mind—on party identification, health care, gun control, abortion—and he sees no reason not to speak his mind when he sees a reason for a change in position. And so Kerrey predicts that Bill Clinton's much-ballyhooed tax credits for college tuition "will do for higher education what healthcare deductibility did for health care"—increase inflation. His humor and his willingness to say, quite openly and good-humoredly, what everyone in Washington knows must not be said aloud, could make him an explosive presidential candidate, one whose standing could rapidly rise—or fall.

Kerrey faced a serious challenge back home in 1994. Republican Jan Stoney, who rose from telephone company clerk to executive vice president of USWest, attacked him for supporting the Clinton budget and tax package and for switching to favor the assault weapons ban. One summer poll showed her trailing by only 48%–40%. Kerrey cited his attempts to cut Clinton budgets, and ran an ad showing himself at a target range picking up an AK-47 and saying, "Twenty-five years ago, in the war in Vietnam, people hunted me. They needed a good weapon, like this AK-47. But you don't need one of these to hunt birds." Most importantly, he outspent Stoney by more than 2–1. He won 55%–45%, lower than his 1988 win; he carried eastern Nebraska and the southern tier of the state, ran the strongest around Lincoln, and won 56% in greater Omaha.

Will Kerrey run for president again in 2000? His Senate seat comes up then, and Nebraska's May primary may cause him to choose between the two races; but he has never minded giving up office before. His attitude toward Bill Clinton is, if not adversarial, then very far short of reverent. He once said, "Clinton is an unusually good liar. Unusually good." The Clinton White House, perhaps to forestall a Kerrey primary challenge in 1996, urged him to chair the Democratic Senatorial Campaign Committee in 1995. It was a tough assignment: by April 1995 five Democratic incumbents announced their retirements and Republicans had several more plausible targets. Kerrey's strategy was to recruit rich moderate Democrats, rich enough to help finance their campaigns, moderate enough to appeal to voters; and he did so in Colorado, Idaho, Kansas, Oregon and Virginia. It was a good try, but none won, and Republicans gained a net two seats. But prospecting for money among big Democratic contributors is a useful exercise for a presidential candidate, and Kerrey volunteered to stay on the job through the 1998 cycle. After that, he has a big decision to make.

Junior Senator. Republican Chuck Hagel was elected in an upset over popular Governor Ben Nelson in a hard-fought race in 1996; but he was not phased by the rigors of the campaign. "I used to kid people, saying, 'What are you going to do? Send me to Vietnam?' I mean, I've been to hell, so I never saw anything I've done as a risk." Hagel grew up in the Sand Hills and small towns of Nebraska; his father died when he was 16; he became a radio DJ, then with his younger brother Tom volunteered for service in Vietnam. Promoted to sergeant because so many were dying, Chuck and Tom served together; when their armored personnel carrier was hit by a mine, Chuck, his body on fire, dragged Tom from the APC to safety. Chuck Hagel returned home, worked his way through the University of Nebraska, then got a job in Omaha Congressman John McCollister's office. He rose to administrative assistant; after McCollister lost a Senate race in 1976, Hagel became a lobbyist for Firestone. He got the number two position in the Reagan Veterans' Administration, but resigned after only one year on the job. He was one of two main speakers at the 1982 groundbreaking of the Vietnam Veterans' Memorial. Then he made his great break, putting all of his savings—$5,000—and starting Vanguard Cellular Systems; it became the second largest independent cell phone company in the nation. Hagel went back into government, as head of World USO and then deputy director of the 1990 G-7 Summit. In 1992 he returned to Omaha, to work in investment banking—and to prepare to run for the Senate.

In 1995 he started running, very much the underdog. In his first ad in January 1996, he said, "I fought in Vietnam where my brother and I were wounded. I served President Reagan. I started my own business, creating hundreds of new jobs. Now I'm running for the United States Senate because we don't need more career politicians in Washington. We need lower taxes, less government, a balanced budget and more personal responsibility." His platform was solidly conservative, sometimes riskily so: he backed school choice, opposed racial quotas and preferences, backed the Freedom to Farm Act ("less government and more open markets"), opposed the estate tax. In the primary he called Attorney General Don Stenberg a "career politician"; Stenberg hit him for living 20 years in Virginia and for contributing to Bob Kerrey's 1992 presidential campaign. Hagel won the May primary 62%–37%, losing only seven counties and tying Stenberg in four.

Ben Nelson was an even tougher opponent, a popular governor who held down spending and supported the balanced budget amendment and other conservative causes. He had just been reelected 73%–26%. But in the process he had pledged to serve his full term, and Hagel hammered him for that and for not cutting property taxes as much as he had promised. A woman in one Hagel ad said, "I'm not voting for Ben Nelson this time. He should stay here and do his job." Nelson led consistently in polls, though by lower margins in the fall. Nelson raised far more PAC money—$909,000, nearly half of his campaign funds—but Hagel spent $1 million of his own money and $3.5 million altogether. Hagel resisted advice from Republican campaign committee head Alfonse D'Amato to go negative; Nelson in the last weeks charged that Hagel had engaged in fraudulent franchising practices with Vanguard. Newspapers hit Nelson, and Hagel responded, "This is a guy who lies. This is a guy who cheats. This is a guy who will do anything."

The result was not even close. Hagel won 56%–42%, carrying all but five counties. Nelson's best county percentage in 1996 was lower than his percentages in all but seven counties in 1994. In the Senate Hagel got seats on the Banking and Foreign Relations Committee and became chairman of the International Economic Policy, Export and Trade Promotion Subcommittee—a good post for a state eager to export farm and food products. He and Kerrey, both decorated Vietnam war veterans, seem to have a friendly relationship; Hagel said he doesn't mind being compared with Kerrey and endorsed his Social Security plan. Some of Hagel's friends wonder whether he will some day, as Kerrey did in 1992 and may again, run for president.

Presidential politics. Over the last 50 years, Nebraska has voted more Republican in presidential elections than any other state—61% to Kansas' second place 57%. It was George Bush's best state outside the South in 1992, and Bob Dole's best state in 1996 except for Utah and his home state of Kansas. Greater Omaha usually goes Republican, Lincoln goes a few points less so, while the western counties are heavily Republican, much like neighboring Wyoming and eastern Colorado. In the 1996 exit polls elderly voters were for Bill Clinton, voters under 60 heavily for Dole: an indicator of future trends.

Nebraska has a presidential primary in May which once attracted attention; the whole national press followed Robert Kennedy and Eugene McCarthy out here in 1968 and took note when Frank Church won in 1976. No more: nominations are now sewn up long before May, and Nebraska has goes unnoticed.

Congressional districting. Nebraska has had three congressional districts since the 1960s. Redistricting made only marginal changes for the 1990s.

The People: Est. Pop. 1996: 1,652,000; Pop. 1990: 1,578,385, up 4.7% 1990–1996. 0.6% of U.S. total, 37th largest; 34% rural. Median age: 34.9 years. 14% 65 years and over. 92.5% White, 3.6% Black, 1% Asian, 1% Amer. Indian, 2.3% Hispanic origin. Households: 58.2% married couple families; 28% married couple fams. w. children; 47% college educ.; median household income: $26,016; per capita income: $12,452; 66.5% owner occupied housing; median house value: $50,400; median monthly rent: $282. 2.9% Unemployment. 1996 Voting age pop.: 1,211,000. 1996 Turnout: 677,415; 56% of VAP. Registered voters (1996): 1,015,056; 384,667 D (38%), 502,030 R (50%), 128,359 unaffiliated and minor parties (13%).

Political Lineup: Governor, E. Benjamin Nelson (D); Lt. Gov., Kim M. Robak (D); Secy. of State, Scott Moore (R); Atty. Gen., Donald Stenberg (R); Treasurer, David Heineman (R); Auditor, John Breslow (R). Unicameral Legislature, 49 (no party affiliation); Legislature President, Kim M. Robak (D). Senators, Robert Kerrey (D) and Chuck Hagel (R). Representatives, 3 (3 R).

Elections Division: 402-471-3229; **Filing Deadline for U.S. Congress:** Incumbents: February 15, 1998; Challengers: March 1, 1998.

1996 Presidential Vote

Dole (R)	363,467	(54%)
Clinton (D)	236,761	(35%)
Perot (I)	71,278	(11%)

1996 Republican Presidential Primary

Dole (R)	129,131	(76%)
Buchanan (R)	17,741	(10%)
Forbes (R)	10,612	(6%)
Other	13,107	(9%)

1992 Presidential Vote

Bush (R)	343,678	(47%)
Clinton (D)	216,864	(29%)
Perot (I)	174,104	(24%)

GOVERNOR

Gov. E. Benjamin Nelson (D)

Elected 1990, term expires Jan. 1999; b. May 17, 1941, McCook; home, Lincoln; U. of NE, B.A. 1963, M.A. 1965, LL.B. 1970; Methodist; married (Diane).

Career: Gen. Cnsl., Central Natl. Group Insurance, 1972–74, Pres. & CEO, 1977–81; NE Insurance Dir., 1975–76; Exec. V.P., Natl. Assn. of Insurance Commissioners, 1982–85; Practicing atty., 1985–90.

Office: State Capitol, P.O. Box 94848, Lincoln 68509, 402-471-2244; Fax: 402-471-6031; Web site: www.state.ne.us.

Election Results

1994 gen.	E. Benjamin Nelson (D)	423,270	(73%)
	Gene Spence (R)	148,230	(26%)
1994 prim.	E. Benjamin Nelson (D)	101,422	(88%)
	Robert Franklin Winingar (D)	6,993	(6%)
	Robb Nimic	6,373	(6%)
1990 gen.	E. Benjamin Nelson (D)	292,771	(50%)
	Kay A. Orr (R)	288,741	(49%)

SENATORS

Sen. Robert Kerrey (D)

Elected 1988, seat up 2000; b. Aug. 27, 1943, Lincoln; home, Omaha; U. of NE, M.S. 1966; Congregationalist; divorced.

Career: Navy, 1966–69 (Vietnam); Businessman, Restaurant owner, 1972–81; NE Gov., 1982–87.

DC Office: 141 HSOB 20510, 202-224-6551; Fax: 202-224-7645; e-mail: bob@kerrey.senate.gov.

State Offices: Lincoln, 402-437-5246; Omaha, 402-391-3411.

Committees: *Democratic Senatorial Campaign Committee Chairman. Agriculture, Nutrition & Forestry* (6th of 8 D): Marketing, Inspection & Product Promotion; Production & Price Competitiveness (RMM). *Finance* (9th of 9 D): Health Care; International Trade; Taxation & IRS Oversight. *Intelligence (Select)* (Vice Chmn. of 9 D).

Group Ratings

	ADA	ACLU	AFS	LCV	CFA	CON	NFIB	COC	ACU	NTLC	CHC
1996	85	47	100	69	79	59	41	23	5	18	8
1995	80	—	91	79	81	96	—	39	0	—	—

National Journal Ratings

	1995 LIB — 1995 CONS			1996 LIB — 1996 CONS		
Economic	68%	—	29%	96%	—	0%
Social	69%	—	29%	77%	—	22%
Foreign	79%	—	15%	69%	—	30%

Key Votes of the 104th Congress

1. Reduce Medicare Growth $	N	5. Flag Amendment	N	9. Anti-Missile Defense	N
2. Lmt. Prod. Liab. Damages	*	6. Endangered Species	Y	10. Cuban Embargo	Y
3. Increase Min. Wage	Y	7. Gay Employment Rights	Y	11. Bar Bosnia Troop $	N
4. Welfare Reform	N	8. Ovrd. Part. Birth Veto	N	12. Cut Vietnam Aid	N

Election Results

1994 general	Robert Kerrey (D)	317,297	(55%)	($5,009,792)
	Jan Stoney (R)	260,668	(45%)	($1,821,778)
1994 primary	Robert Kerrey (D)	unopposed		
1988 general	Robert Kerrey (D)	378,717	(57%)	($3,461,148)
	David Karnes (R)	278,250	(42%)	($3,411,361)

Sen. Chuck Hagel (R)

Elected 1996, seat up 2002; b. Oct. 4, 1946, North Platte; home, Omaha; U. of NE, B.A. 1971; Episcopalian; married (Lilibet).

Career: Army, 1968 (Vietnam), Newscaster & Talk Show Host, KBON & KLNG Radio, 1969–71; Admin. Asst., U.S. Rep. John Y. McCollister, 1971–77; Mgr., Govt. Affairs, Firestone Tire & Rubber Co., 1977–80; U.S. Dpty. Commissioner General, World's Fair, 1982; Dpty. Admin., Veterans' Admin., 1981; Pres., Collins, Hagel & Clarke Inc., 1983–84; Co-founder, Dir. & Exec. Vice Pres., Vanguard Cellular Systems Inc., 1984–87; Pres. & CEO, World USO, 1987–90; Pres. & CEO, Priv. Sector Cncl., 1990–92; Pres., McCarth & Co., 1992–95.

DC Office: 346 RSOB 20510, 202-224-4224; Fax: 202-224-5213; e-mail: chuck_hagel@hagel.senate.gov.

State Offices: Kearney, 308-237-5145; Lincoln, 402-476-1400; N. Platte, 308-534-2006; Omaha, 402-758-8981; Scottsbluff, 308-632-6295.

Committees: *Banking, Housing & Urban Affairs* (10th of 10 R): Financial Services & Technology; Housing Opportunity & Community Development; International Finance. *Foreign Relations* (4th of 10 R): East Asian & Pacific Affairs; European Affairs; International Economic Policy, Export & Trade Promotion (Chmn.). *Aging (Special)* (8th of 10 R).

Group Ratings and Key Votes: Newly Elected

Election Results

1996 general	Chuck Hagel (R)	379,933	(56%)	($3,564,316)
	E. Benjamin Nelson (D)	281,904	(42%)	($2,159,653)
	Others	14,952	(2%)	
1996 primary	Chuck Hagel (R)	112,953	(62%)	
	Don Stenberg (R)	67,974	(37%)	
1990 general	J. James Exon (D)	349,779	(59%)	($2,410,097)
	Hal Daub (R)	243,013	(41%)	($1,452,681)

FIRST DISTRICT

The eastern half of Nebraska, between the Missouri River and the 98th parallel, was laid out in remorseless Midwestern mile-square grids and became some of America's prime farmland in the single decade of the 1880s. The land here has contours just regular enough and weather just favorable enough to make farming economically viable. The plains here have completed most of their gentle decline from the Rockies to sea level; above the river bottoms the land is open to the winds. This land was settled by Yankee-descended Midwestern farmers and German immigrants. Politically it has long been Republican in national elections, but votes Democratic in seriously contested state races.

The 1st Congressional District of Nebraska includes 25 counties in eastern Nebraska. It does not include Omaha or its suburbs, which form the 2d District, but does take in Lincoln, the state capital and home of the University of Nebraska Cornhuskers. Lincoln, with the state government, the university and telemarketing, has been growing rapidly; big meatpacking operations have kept the population steady in smaller counties. Politically, Lincoln is fond of moderate-toned Republicans, and is more hospitable to Democrats than other parts of the state; Lincoln's Lancaster County stopped just short of giving Bill Clinton pluralities in 1992 and 1996, while almost every other Nebraska county voted more than 50% Republican.

The congressman from the 1st District is Douglas Bereuter (pronounced *BEEwriter*), a Republican first elected in 1978. He grew up in York, graduated from the University of Nebraska, served in the Army, then got degrees in planning and public policy from Harvard and worked as a planning consultant and part-time professor in Lincoln in the 1970s. He was elected to the Nebraska legislature in 1974. He is of the same vintage as Newt Gingrich, but not as confrontational: "Partisanship is not a compelling motive for service for me. I'm more interested in legislation." He has a rather moderate voting record and has been active in the North Atlantic Assembly and in exchanges with the European Parliament.

Bereuter is a senior member on Banking and International Relations, and chairman of the Asia and Pacific Subcommittee, where he is a strong supporter of eliminating trade barriers. He led the fight for renewing Most Favored Nation status for China, a possible large buyer of Nebraska products, in 1995 and 1996, authoring the China Policy Act of 1995; in March 1996, he toned down the resolution committing U.S. troops to defend Taiwan if attacked. "We don't need to make an enemy of China. I'm concerned we're pushing ourselves into an adversary relationship." In May 1996 he called for repealing the Jackson-Vanik law and abolishing the annual MFN process. He wrote the export promotion and food assistance sections of the 1996 Freedom to Farm Act: Nebraska of course is a great exporter of farm products. In January 1997 he introduced a fair trade opportunities bill which would give the president leverage by authorizing modest "snap-back" tariffs on countries not in the World Trade Organization, notably Russia and China. He led efforts to stop China, Taiwan, South Korea and Japan from keeping farm products off the APEC agenda. On other foreign issues, he passed an amendment in September 1995 placing strict limitations on the U.S.-North Korean nuclear deal; he was an orginal co-sponsor of the NATO Enlargement Act, and refocused his Farmer-to-Farmer AID program to the world's poorest countries.

On the Banking Committee he has backed regulatory relief and passed a loan guarantee program for developers and non-profits to construct low-cost rental housing. He worked to exempt from maximum driving times farm drivers within 100 miles of home carrying commodities or supplies during planting and harvesting season. He supports a coast-to-coast hiking and biking American Discovery Trail, following the Platte River through Nebraska.

Bereuter has been reelected with at least 60% since he first won the seat; in 1996 he won 70%. He argued: "I sway a lot of votes. People respect the way I make decisions. I reflect well upon you there." He has been mentioned as a Senate candidate but did not run for the open seat when Democrat Jim Exon retired in 1996.

The People: Pop. 1990: 526,291; 39% rural; 15% age 65+; 96% White; 1% Black; 1% Asian; 1% Amer. Indian; 1% Hispanic origin. Households: 59% married couple families; 28% married couple fams. w. children; 46% college educ.; median household income: $25,763; per capita income: $12,088; median gross rent: $338; median house value: $49,700.

1996 Presidential Vote			1992 Presidential Vote		
Dole (R)	114,563	(50%)	Bush (R)	107,081	(43%)
Clinton (D)	87,712	(38%)	Clinton (D)	80,696	(32%)
Perot (I)	25,974	(11%)	Perot (I)	59,974	(24%)

Rep. Doug Bereuter (R)

Elected 1978; b. Oct. 6, 1939, York; home, Lincoln; U. of NE, B.A. 1961, Harvard, M.C.P. 1966, M.P.A. 1973; Lutheran; married (Louise).

Career: Army, 1963–65; Urban planner, U.S. Dept. of HUD, 1965–66; Div. Dir., NE Econ. Devel. Dept., 1967–68; Dir., NE Office of Planning, 1968–70; NE Legislature, 1974–78.

DC Office: 2184 RHOB 20515, 202-225-4806.

District Offices: Fremont, 402-727-0888; Lincoln, 402-438-1598.

Committees: *Banking & Financial Services* (4th of 30 R): Domestic & International Monetary Policy; Financial Institutions & Consumer Credit; Housing & Community Opportunity. *International Relations* (5th of 26 R): Asia & the Pacific (Chmn.); International Economic Policy & Trade.

Group Ratings

	ADA	ACLU	AFS	LCV	CFA	CON	NFIB	COC	ACU	NTLC	CHC
1996	20	6	8	31	31	92	84	81	60	80	71
1995	20	—	—	25	46	87	—	92	58	—	—

National Journal Ratings

	1995 LIB		1995 CONS	1996 LIB		1996 CONS
Economic	26%	—	67%	45%	—	55%
Social	47%	—	52%	40%	—	59%
Foreign	42%	—	55%	45%	—	54%

Key Votes of the 104th Congress

1. Reduce Medicare Growth $	Y	5. Flag Amendment	Y	9. Cuban Embargo	N
2. Ovrd. Product Liab. Veto	Y	6. Drop EPA Limits	Y	10. Bar Bosnia Troop $	Y
3. Increase Min. Wage	Y	7. Repeal Assault-Weap. Ban	N	11. Cut Anti-Missile Defense	N
4. Welfare Reform	Y	8. Ovrd. Part. Birth Veto	Y	12. Bar U.N. Uniforms	N

Election Results

1996 general	Doug Bereuter (R)	157,108	(70%)	($394,292)
	Patrick J. Combs (D)	67,152	(30%)	($59,666)
1996 primary	Doug Bereuter (R)	unopposed		
1994 general	Doug Bereuter (R)	117,967	(63%)	($334,598)
	Patrick Combs (D)	70,369	(37%)	($178,046)

SECOND DISTRICT

Omaha, the commercial metropolis of Nebraska, the largest city on the Great Plains north of Kansas City and west of Minneapolis, the city that still produces one out of five American steaks, got its start from government: Abraham Lincoln picked it as the eastern terminus of the Union Pacific railroad, from which emerged the stockyards and livestock exchange that made it a top livestock town. Over the years, Omaha filled up with cattle hands from the West and European immigrants, especially Germans and Czechs; it developed fine civic institutions from the Joslyn Art Museum and the Ak-Sar-Ben (spell it backwards) Exhibition to the Boys Town of orphanage fame, founded by Father Flanagan in 1917. Though a major city by the 1880s, Omaha has remained small enough (and famous on Wall Street as the place where Warren Buffett lives and works) to be readily comprehensible; you don't feel distant, physically or psychologically, from the other side of town, and you usually know people from a broader range of backgrounds than you would in a large homogeneous neighborhood within a big metropolitan area. The older, less affluent part of Omaha is near the river and Iowa; to the west, the city has been quietly booming, with affluent neighborhoods and new shopping areas. All over, Omaha's economy has been changing. It still has many processors of food products, like the hard-charging ConAgra company, and the giant Peter Kiewit construction firm; but it is also the nation's telecommunications center, handling 100 million '800' and '900' calls annually and employing more than 10,000 people in 24 telemarketing centers.

The 2d Congressional District of Nebraska is metropolitan Omaha: Douglas County with Omaha and its western suburbs; Sarpy County with suburbs to the south and the old Strategic Air Command headquarters at Offutt Air Force Base; and a sliver of Cass County just to the south. Politically, Omaha has long had competitive politics, with Democrats strong on the south side around the stockyards and the northeast and Republicans strong in the area west of 72d Street; the 2d District has been competitive more often than not over the last two decades.

The congressman from the 2d District is Jon Christensen, a Republican elected in a bitter contest in 1994 and reelected in 1996. Christensen grew up in rural Nebraska, attended Midland Lutheran College on a basketball scholarship, went to law school in Texas, returned to Nebraska to work as an insurance agent and marketing director, and owned a company marketing organic fertilizer. In 1994, Christensen ran against Peter Hoagland, a Democratic congressman who had won by just 51%–49% in 1992. Christensen waged an active door-to-door campaign, backing school prayer, the option to teach creationism and a ban on abortion, and he won the May Republican primary with 53% to 25% for state Senator Brad Ashford, pro-choice and moderate, and 23% for Ron Staskiewicz, the 1992 Republican nominee. The general election was closely contested; Christensen led in the *Omaha World-Herald* poll after the primary—unusual for a challenger, and a harbinger of November 1994. In June 1994 Christensen sat in the front row at a Ways and Means hearing when Hoagland cast the decisive vote for employer mandates in health care; it passed 20–18, and Christensen was immediately on the phone to an Omaha radio station. Previously Hoagland had worked with Mutual of Omaha, the city's largest employer, to develop a managed competition plan; Christensen favored medical savings accounts. Some bizarre charges and countercharges followed, with lie detector tests about whether Christensen denounced school textbooks while campaigning door-to-door and death threats against a family featured in a Hoagland spot. Christensen attacked Hoagland as a Clinton clone; Hoagland called him a right-wing extremist. Christensen pounded again and again on the moderate Hoagland's vote for the Clinton budget and tax package in August 1993 and on his record of 81% support of Clinton. Hoagland, who spent a total of $2.5 million in three previous campaigns, spent $1.1 million in this one, raising $780,000 from PACs (the seventh highest in the country). Christensen raised $779,000; he ended the campaign with $150,000 cash-on-hand. In November Hoagland carried Omaha's Douglas County but lost suburban Sarpy County by a wider margin, giving Christensen a 50%–49% victory.

Christensen had a very conservative voting record and, with two other freshmen elected by narrow margins, got a seat on Ways and Means, the first Republican freshmen there since George Bush in 1968; all three won in 1996. There Christensen sponsored a bill to distinguish between independent contractors and employees, replacing the IRS's 20-factor test with a three-factor test; he added medical malpractice caps to the Republicans' tort reform bill; it passed the House but was vetoed by Clinton in May 1996. He voted against term limits because he thought them not stringent enough. He was unsuccessful in eliminating funding for the Capitol elevator operators. He had a bill to require prisoners to work 48 hours and study 12 hours a week, to ban televisions and weightlifting equipment in prisons and to end prisoner lawsuits. His big legislative success, ironically for a conservative, was increasing federal impact aid 8% for 1997, a big help to school districts in Sarpy County.

Democrats targeted Christensen in 1996 and found an attractive candidate in lawyer and Vietnam veteran James Martin Davis. Davis spoke out against "arrogant" government overregulation and emphasized family and faith over welfare. Davis charged that Republicans orchestrated a lawsuit against him by a former client, a convicted killer, who was a cousin of state Republican Party Director Andy Abboud. Abboud attacked Davis as a "dirt bag" for representing "the scum of the earth"; Davis replied that he had represented eight of Abboud's relatives. But the real campaign went on over the airwaves. Christensen raised $1.8 million, $627,000 from PACs, and starting in the spring, when his poll ratings were low (there were negative stories after the breakup of his marriage), ran positive spots about himself and called for less government, lower taxes and stiffer sentences. Davis, disheartened when his 16-year-old son died in a car crash in January, raised relatively little money, and spent $384,000 in all. The AFL-CIO ran ads against Christensen in May; he responded with a blitz accusing Davis of being controlled by "Washington union bosses." The Democratic Congressional Campaign Committee and the AFL-CIO ran ads again in September, but Davis had little money and the few ads he ran were positive; both organizations dropped this race from their target lists.

The result was that Christensen won 57%–40%, carrying Douglas County 55%–42% and Sarpy 65%–32%. In the 105th Congress Christensen was named to the Ways and Means bipartisan transportation tax task force.

The People: Pop. 1990: 526,573; 6% rural; 10% age 65+; 86% White; 10% Black; 1% Asian; 1% Amer. Indian; 3% Hispanic origin. Households: 55% married couple families; 28% married couple fams. w. children; 56% college educ.; median household income: $30,889; per capita income: $14,322; median gross rent: $405; median house value: $60,700.

1996 Presidential Vote			1992 Presidential Vote		
Dole (R)	116,889	(52%)	Bush (R)	115,255	(47%)
Clinton (D)	84,667	(38%)	Clinton (D)	78,701	(32%)
Perot (I)	18,934	(9%)	Perot (I)	48,657	(20%)

Rep. Jon Christensen (R)

Elected 1994; b. Feb. 2, 1963, St. Paul, NE; home, Omaha; Midland Lutheran Col., B.S. 1985; S. TX Col. of Law, J.D. 1989; Christian; divorced.

Career: Vice Pres., COMREP Inc., 1989–91; Mktg. Dir., CT Mutual Insurance Co., 1991–94.

DC Office: 413 CHOB 20515, 202-225-4155; Fax: 202-225-3032; e-mail: talk2jon@hr.house.gov.

District Offices: Omaha, 402-397-9944.

Committees: *Ways & Means* (19th of 23 R): Health; Social Security.

Group Ratings

	ADA	ACLU	AFS	LCV	CFA	CON	NFIB	COC	ACU	NTLC	CHC
1996	5	0	9	15	23	82	97	88	100	95	93
1995	0	—	—	6	0	87	—	96	92	—	—

National Journal Ratings

	1995 LIB — 1995 CONS	1996 LIB — 1996 CONS
Economic	0% — 74%	0% — 82%
Social	0% — 79%	14% — 77%
Foreign	15% — 73%	37% — 63%

Key Votes of the 104th Congress

1. Reduce Medicare Growth $	Y	5. Flag Amendment	Y	9. Cuban Embargo	Y
2. Ovrd. Product Liab. Veto	Y	6. Drop EPA Limits	N	10. Bar Bosnia Troop $	Y
3. Increase Min. Wage	N	7. Repeal Assault-Weap. Ban	Y	11. Cut Anti-Missile Defense	Y
4. Welfare Reform	Y	8. Ovrd. Part. Birth Veto	Y	12. Bar U.N. Uniforms	Y

Election Results

1996 general	Jon Christensen (R)	125,201	(57%)	($1,722,490)
	James Martin Davis (D)	88,447	(40%)	($384,582)
	Others	6,676	(3%)	
1996 primary	Jon Christensen (R)	43,396	(96%)	
	Others	1,652	(4%)	
1994 general	Jon Christensen (R)	92,516	(50%)	($953,163)
	Peter Hoagland (D)	90,750	(49%)	($1,105,892)

THIRD DISTRICT

West of Grand Island, Nebraska is wheat and livestock country. For miles on end you can see nothing but rolling brown fields, sectioned off here and there by barbed wire fences, and in the distance a grain elevator towering over a tiny town and its miniature railroad depot. The winds and rain and tornadoes that come suddenly out of the sky remind you that the original settlers likened this part of the country to an ocean and thought themselves in their wooden wagons almost as helpless as passengers at sea in a rowboat. Settlers passed through here on the Oregon Trail in the 1840s, then set down roots in the 1880s, but the rain they hoped for fell too unreliably, and wheatlands gave way to pasture and open range. It is a beautiful but hard land, exacting much from its people, as the novels of western Nebraska's Willa Cather make poignantly clear.

The 3d Congressional District of Nebraska has 33% of the state's people spread out over 82% of its acreage. And the land is emptying out: except along the interstate, the 3d has been losing population for decades; these 66 counties had 608,000 people in 1940, 525,000 in 1990. Geographically and politically, the 3d District is where the Midwest becomes the West. For years people here welcomed farm subsidies even as they angrily opposed federal interference. Politically, it is heavily Republican and sometimes ornery: George Bush and Bob Dole easily carried the district in the 1990s, and in 1992 Ross Perot got more votes than Bill Clinton.

The congressman from the 3d District is Bill Barrett, a Republican elected in 1990. He has lived all his life in Lexington, where he ran the insurance and real estate firm founded by his grandfather in 1924. He was Republican state chairman in 1973–75 and in 1978 he was elected to Nebraska's unicameral legislature. In 1987 he became speaker. In 1990 he ran for the House and won a five-candidate Republican primary with 30%, running well in his home area and in the eastern end of the district, in the Lincoln media market. In the general he had an unaccustomed hard time, as he was hammered for supporting Governor Kay Orr's 1987 tax package and for opposing abortion. Barrett won with 51% in a friends-and-neighbors contest, losing most of the western counties and carrying his home area.

In the House Barrett has compiled a solidly conservative voting record. He serves on the Agriculture Committee and after just four years became chairman of the General Farm Commodities Subcommittee. In 1995 and 1996 he worked with former House Agriculture Chairman Pat Roberts to write the Freedom to Farm Act, which phases out most farm subsidies over seven years. It "unleashes our nation's single largest industry from antiquated programs and overbearing federal intrusion. It allows producers to plant for the market, to make choices, to weigh risk, and to be in charge of their farms and their future." He got a National Fish Hatchery transferred to Crawford and worked to revise the boundaries of the North Platte Wildlife Reserve. His priority now is export market development.

Barrett has been reelected easily with 72%, 79% and 77% of the vote. In 1996 no Democrat filed against him, and Barrett actually received the most write-in votes in the Democratic primary. But he declined the nomination and Democrats named a candidate whom he ignored.

The People: Pop. 1990: 525,521; 56% rural; 18% age 65+; 96% White; 1% Amer. Indian; 3% Hispanic origin. Households: 62% married couple families; 29% married couple fams. w. children; 40% college educ.; median household income: $22,344; per capita income: $10,942; median gross rent: $284; median house value: $38,000.

1996 Presidential Vote

Dole (R)	132,015	(59%)
Clinton (D)	64,382	(29%)
Perot (I)	26,370	(12%)

1992 Presidential Vote

Bush (R)	121,342	(49%)
Perot (I)	65,473	(27%)
Clinton (D)	57,467	(23%)

Rep. Bill Barrett (R)

Elected 1990; b. Feb. 9, 1929, Lexington; home, Lexington; Hastings Col., B.A. 1951; Presbyterian; married (Elsie).

Career: Navy, 1951–52; Businessman, real estate and insurance, 1956–90; Chmn., NE Repub. Party, 1973–75; NE Legislature, 1978–90, Speaker, 1987–90.

DC Office: 2458 LHOB 20515, 202-225-6435; Fax: 202-225-0207.

District Offices: Grand Island, 308-381-5555; Scottsbluff, 308-632-3333.

Committees: *Agriculture* (3rd of 27 R): Forestry, Resource Conservation & Research (Vice Chmn.); General Farm Commodities (Chmn.). *Education & The Workforce* (6th of 25 R): Postsecondary Education, Training & Life-Long Learning; Workforce Protections.

Group Ratings

	ADA	ACLU	AFS	LCV	CFA	CON	NFIB	COC	ACU	NTLC	CHC
1996	0	0	0	15	8	87	100	94	95	100	93
1995	0	—	—	6	0	56	—	100	84	—	—

National Journal Ratings

	1995 LIB — 1995 CONS			1996 LIB — 1996 CONS		
Economic	0%	—	74%	0%	—	82%
Social	32%	—	65%	14%	—	77%
Foreign	36%	—	59%	30%	—	65%

Key Votes of the 104th Congress

1. Reduce Medicare Growth $	Y	5. Flag Amendment	Y	9. Cuban Embargo	N
2. Ovrd. Product Liab. Veto	Y	6. Drop EPA Limits	N	10. Bar Bosnia Troop $	Y
3. Increase Min. Wage	N	7. Repeal Assault-Weap. Ban	Y	11. Cut Anti-Missile Defense	N
4. Welfare Reform	Y	8. Ovrd. Part. Birth Veto	Y	12. Bar U.N. Uniforms	Y

Election Results

1996 general	William (Bill) Barrett (R)	167,758	(77%)	($203,582)
	John Webster (D)	48,833	(23%)	($15,190)
1996 primary	William (Bill) Barrett (R)	unopposed		
1994 general	William (Bill) Barrett (R)	154,919	(79%)	($232,013)
	Gil Chapin (D)	41,943	(21%)	($54,519)

NEVADA

Giant plinths, New York skyscrapers across the street from the sphinx-like lion, a flaming pirate ship next door to Roman ruins, a pyramid and obelisk, all rising in a bowl-shaped desert valley rimmed by barren peaks: welcome to Nevada! Nature left little here to encourage human settlement—lodes of gold and silver which attracted sudden agglomerations of miners and hangers-on for brief years, but almost no water or arable land. So Nevada is wholly the creation of post-industrial man. Its existence as a state is happenstance: the discovery of the Comstock Lode silver mine in 1859—$500 million worth was taken out in 20 years—brought settlers, and Abraham Lincoln's Republicans made it a state in 1864 even though Nevada did not meet the population requirement for statehood when Republicans thought they needed its 3 electoral votes. But Nevada's population dropped by the early 20th Century; in the early 1930s, there were only 91,000 Nevadans and the state government was about to go bankrupt. So Nevada decided to roll the dice. The state reduced its residency requirement for divorce to six weeks and legalized gambling. Catering to what most Americans considered sin—casinos, pawnshops, divorce mills, quick wedding chapels, even legal brothels—turned out to be good business. Nevada has been America's fastest growing state since 1960; in the 1980s its population rose 50%, from 800,000 to 1.6 million, adding 6,000 new residents every week; from 1990–96, it added another 401,000, growing 33% in just six years.

Las Vegas, a mere spot on the map when gambling was legalized, is now a metro area of 1.1 million and Reno, in the 1940s the divorce capital of America, is passing 400,000. Gaming—the Nevada word for gambling—generates most of this growth: Las Vegas's 99,000 hotel rooms house 30 million tourists who spend $22.5 billion a year, Reno's nearly five million tourists spend almost $4 billion; almost half Nevada's jobs are in services some way related to gambling or tourism. The 6.4% gambling receipts tax generates enough revenue so that Nevada has no income, corporate or inheritance tax, and the cost of living is low; half the houses in Las Vegas are valued at under $100,000 and many migrants from California cannot find a house that costs as much as the one they sold.

From mining to gaming, Nevada has been a second chance state, a place for outcasts to succeed and misfits to rebound. Some 11% of its adults are divorced, the highest rate in the nation. The four owners of the Comstock Lode—MacKay, Fair, Flood, O'Brien—were Irishmen; the first big hotel on the Las Vegas strip, the Flamingo, was built in 1946 by Jewish gangster Bugsy Siegel, later gunned down in his Beverly Hills home; most of the big casinos were owned by mobsters until Howard Hughes—a different kind of outcast—bought them up in the late 1960s. For years, the casinos catered to older tastes in entertainment, from Frank Sinatra to girlie shows, and depended on gamblers for all their trade. But in the early 1990s, Las Vegas became a family-friendly destination resort. Its huge and flashy hotels have glittering attractions: the 3,000-room Mirage with its tropical rainforest lobby has Siegfried and Roy's tiger-taming extravaganza; the MGM Grand, the largest hotel in the world, with its lion entry-hall, hosted Barbra Streisand's first live performance in decades in 1994; Caesars Palace has an upscale shopping center with Roman-style storefronts; the pyramid-shaped Luxor that looms over this desert has an amusement park and huge obelisk inside; New York New York imitates Gotham and the forthcoming Bellagio promises a taste of Italy. Slot machines no longer line every hallway, because that would mean keeping children out; Las Vegas has become decorous enough to attract the American Booksellers and Southern Baptist conventions. Will either political party ever dare to hold its national convention here?

There are other things going on in Nevada besides gambling and other places besides Las Vegas (though its Clark County contains more than 60% of Nevadans). The state's low taxes

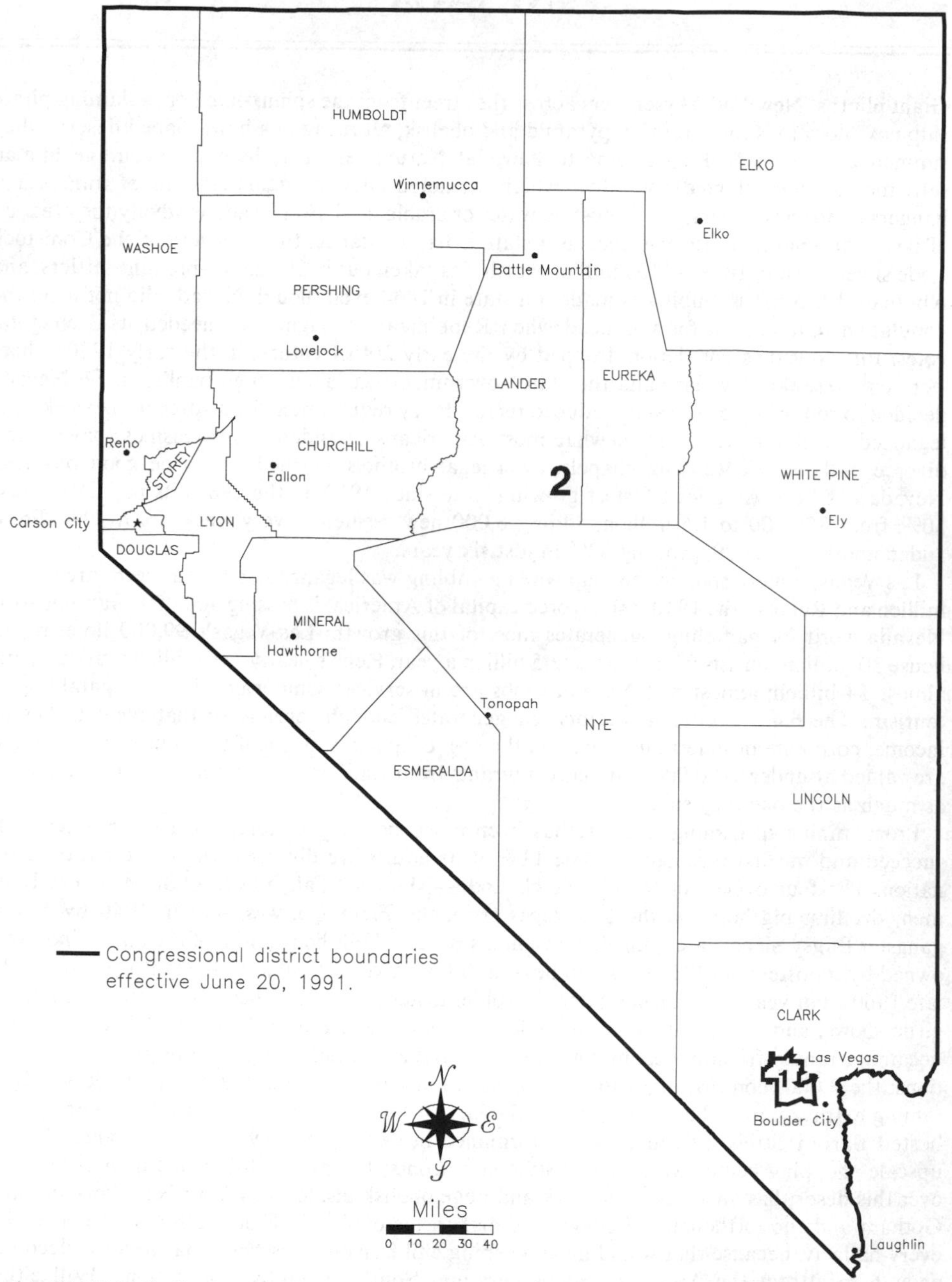
HUMBOLDT
ELKO
Winnemucca
Elko
WASHOE
Battle Mountain
PERSHING
Lovelock
LANDER
EUREKA
Reno
CHURCHILL
STOREY
Fallon
2
WHITE PINE
Carson City
LYON
Ely
DOUGLAS
MINERAL
Hawthorne
Tonopah
NYE
ESMERALDA
LINCOLN
Congressional district boundaries
effective June 20, 1991.
CLARK
Las Vegas
1
Boulder City
N
W
E
S
Miles
0 10 20 30 40
Laughlin

have made it a regional distribution and credit card operations center and it has attracted warehouses and factories from California. There is still some mining, a little gold and silver, plus less glamorous diatomaceous earth, used for swimming pool filters and kitty litter. And the Wild West atmosphere remains, especially in the "Cow Counties" beyond Las Vegas and Reno. Near Elko, a Canadian company's subsidiary in 1995 paid the federal government $9,765 for title to 1,949 acres of public lands with 30 million ounces of gold—all legal under the Mining Act of 1872. In Tonopah the federal government sued Nye County for claiming to own public lands and prosecuting federal officers enforcing federal land management laws.

For the past two decades, Nevada has had a volatile politics. Historically, it was Democratic, sending politically shrewd Democrats to Washington to protect the interests of a state always heavily dependent on the federal government. The most powerful were Key Pittman, chairman of the Senate Foreign Relations Committee, who backed FDR's foreign policy only after Roosevelt agreed to buy absurdly large amounts of silver, and penny-pinching Pat McCarran, author of the repressive McCarran Act, who shamelessly pushed aid for Reno and Las Vegas (the airport there is named for him) and became suddenly solicitous of civil liberties when mobsters and casino owners were called to testify before the Kefauver committee investigating crime and racketeering. In the 1980s Nevada trended sharply Republican, primarily because of newcomers. This came not out of devotion to family values, for Nevada is the least family-oriented state, with the nation's largest percentage of non-family households, but from people who think they are sharper than others, have a special angle, are a step ahead of the market, can and will beat the odds.

In the 1990s the dice have rolled both ways: Democrats tend to win the top races, Republicans most of those below. To the surprise of managers for both candidates, Bill Clinton carried Nevada in 1992, 37%–35%, and won again in 1996, 44%–43%, after promising to veto a nuclear waste depository bill and letting it be thought he would name Bill Bible, son of a former senator and head of Nevada Gaming Control Board, to the federal commission on gambling. Nevada has also elected and reelected two Democratic senators, Harry Reid and Richard Bryan. But in 1994 and 1996, Nevada elected two Republicans to the U.S. House. The parties split the top statewide offices; Republicans hold the state Senate 12–9 and Democrats control the Assembly 25–17, but before 1996 the Assembly was evenly split. Nevada may be vastly more populous than it used to be, but a few votes can still make a difference.

Politics can also make a difference, Nevadans have discovered, as they worry over the federal government's choice of Yucca Mountain, at the edge of the old Yucca Flats nuclear test site, as the nation's single high-level nuclear waste disposal site. This law was passed in 1987, when Nevada lacked political muscle in the traditional bulwark of small states, the Senate: Harry Reid was in his first year there and Chic Hecht seemed to be facing sure defeat. The plan is to bury the waste deep within the mountain, 1,000 feet above the water table, in reinforced steel containers in a 1,400-acre maze of storage tunnels, where presumably they will rest undisturbed for eternity, in all likelihood safe from contact with water. Nevada opinion is strongly opposed and Nevadans in Congress have tried to stop the project and have succeeded in delaying it. Governor Bob Miller did issue drilling permits for studies in 1992; by early 1997 they were still going on. An October 1992 filibuster attempt by Reid and Bryan was crushed 84–8. "We face this every time there is an opportunity to screw Nevada, there is an appetite to do so," Bryan said, but added, "I remain confident we will not have a nuclear waste dump at Yucca Mountain." In 1996 Idaho Senator Larry Craig, whose state agreed to temporarily take government nuclear waste, got a 63–37 vote for a bill setting up a temporary site near Yucca Mountain; but Bill Clinton threatened to veto it and Speaker Newt Gingrich pulled it in the House to help Congressman John Ensign's campaign. The bill passed the Senate again in April 1997, but fell two votes short of the margin needed to overcome Clinton's promised veto. Meanwhile the Clinton Energy Department says that Yucca Mountain won't open as a permanent depository until 2010 at the earliest, while nuclear waste is accumulating at 80 government and commercial sites around the country.

Governor. Bob Miller is approaching his tenth year as governor of Nevada, all he can serve under the state term limits. Miller's biography tracks much of the state's recent history. His father, Ross Miller, was a bookmaker in Chicago and owner of the Slots-A-Fun casino in Las Vegas. Bob Miller worked in the Las Vegas County Sheriff's office, was a deputy district attorney and justice of the peace. In 1978, he was elected district attorney in Las Vegas—a delicate position indeed—and was reelected in 1982; he was elected lieutenant governor in 1986 and became governor after Richard Bryan was elected senator in 1988. Miller represents a second generation in Nevada public life—knowledgeable about the gaming industry, but utterly clean ethically—and has been concerned about issues like education, workers' compensation reform and welfare. With a rising population, Nevada is one state that needs to build lots of new schools; Miller has worked to reduce class size to 16, to set tough standards and tests, and to establish a state Inquiry Team to take on poorly performing schools. He has been successful in avoiding tax increases and keeping Nevada's tax levels down and its business climate high, even while building governmental institutions which Nevada as a lightly populated state just didn't have. His hospital cost containment law slowed medical cost increases to a crawl. He has worked to make the best interest of the child the first consideration in adoptions and in parental abuse cases. He has called for a Family-to-Family network of services and set up a Baby Your Baby program. He has pushed for new prisons and longer sentences. He wants to establish a tuition trust fund and a law school. And of course he has tried to stop the nuclear waste depository in Yucca Mountain and opposed a federal gaming tax.

Miller has been a force on the national scene as well. As head of the National Governors' Association he worked to restore bipartisanship in 1996, after the Republican Governors' Association took over most lobbying of Congress in 1995. He was easily elected in 1990 and won over serious opposition in 1994, beating Las Vegas Mayor Jan Laverty Jones in the primary 63%–28% and in the general beating lawyer and airline pilot, and now congressman, Jim Gibbons by 53%–41%.

Senior Senator. Senator Harry Reid, who has held high office in Nevada for most of the last 30 years, looks mild-mannered but has proved he can be tough. He grew up in Searchlight, Nevada, in the scorching desert south of Las Vegas, was elected to the Assembly in 1968, at age 28, and in 1970 was elected lieutenant governor. In 1974, he came within 624 votes of beating Paul Laxalt in the race for senator, lost for mayor of Las Vegas in 1976, and then became head of the Gaming Commission from 1977–81—as sensitive a post as any in Nevada. In 1982, when Nevada got two House seats for the first time and Congressman Jim Santini ran for the Senate, Reid ran for the Las Vegas 1st District seat and won. Laxalt retired in 1986, and Reid ran for the Senate again; his opponent turned out to be Santini, who had switched parties at the last minute and was running as a Republican. Reid's ads depicted him as David to Santini's Goliath, and he won 50%–45%.

Reid combines a moderate-to-liberal voting record with a strong partisan commitment, tempered by a willingness to seek bipartisan solutions on occasion, working hard on the 1996 Safe Drinking Water Act, for instance. He is conservative on some issues—against abortion, for the Gulf war resolution, for some forms of regulatory reform. But he is also a party man, supporting the Clinton healthcare plan and the 1994 crime bill with its assault weapons ban. He considered running for the Democratic leadership in 1994, but instead endorsed Tom Daschle, and now works with him as co-chair. If reelected in 1998, Reid could move up the leadership ladder: he is already gathering commitments in the race to succeed retiring Minority Whip Wendell Ford. He argued that Social Security should not be counted in the balanced budget amendment, which he then voted against. He took on Ross Perot, then still highly popular, when he appeared before the Joint Committee on the Organization of Congress: "I think you should start checking your facts a little more and stop listening to the applause as much." After the 1994 election, he said, "We have to all swallow a little bit of our pride and go toward the middle." He called for piecemeal healthcare reform and tightening legal immigration. That same month he told Bill Clinton: "Our public lands policy is not working. You can't have a secretary of Interior who can't campaign for senators in the West."

As senator from a small state heavily impacted by the federal government, Reid has spent much time on local issues and has taken politically risky as well as popular stands. Through two years of negotiation he produced an agreement on allocating water from Lake Tahoe and the Truckee River between Nevada and California; Reid got the Pyramid Lake Paiute Indians to agree to return their fisheries to the state for $25 million, plus $40 million in economic aid. He pushed through a Nevada Wilderness Protection Act in 1990, over the objections of Republican Congresswoman Barbara Vucanovich.

He has successfully sponsored amendments to prohibit states from taxing pension income of non-residents. On the Mining Act of 1872 and grazing fees, he has sought middle positions between reforms sought by outsiders and total opposition by some Nevadans. On the Mining Act he has supported a revision requiring mining companies to pay market value for land they hold title to and a 3% royalty; he has supported a freeze of new claims but has pushed for the Interior Department to process existing claims promptly. On grazing fees, he has risked the ire of "Cow County" ranchers by negotiating with Interior Secretary Bruce Babbitt and members from non-grazing areas for some increase in the fees and opposing Pete Domenici's hard-line opposition, arguing that it would just produce a Clinton veto.

On Appropriations Reid is now the ranking member of the Energy and Water Development Subcommittee, which handles the budget for the Yucca Mountain nuclear waste disposal site and Colorado River water control issues: "Out of any position in the Senate, this is where I can be most helpful to Nevada." The great issue is Yucca Mountain and Reid, referring to his predecessor on the subcommittee, said "With Bennett Johnston out of the picture, Nevada stands a fighting chance to keep the nuke dump out of Nevada."

Electorally, Reid's great strength is in Las Vegas and Clark County, and he has won usually with little more than 50% of the vote. In 1992 he had both primary and general opposition. In the September primary, Charles Woods, a businessman severely scarred in World War II, who had run for governor of Alabama and other offices there in the 1960s and 1970s, ran TV ads that helped him win 39% to only 53% for Reid, who lost most of the Cow Counties. In the general, against rancher Demar Dahl, Reid won by a similar margin, 51%–40%. He approaches 1998 with substantial political assets but with the possibility of serious opposition; three potential Republican candidates are Congressmen John Ensign and Jim Gibbons, and retired millionaire Bruce James declared his candidacy in May 1997.

Junior Senator. Senator Richard Bryan has been governor or senator for over 14 years. He grew up in Las Vegas, was a deputy district attorney in Clark County in 1964, at 27, then became the county's first public defender. In 1968 he was elected to the Assembly (the same year as Harry Reid), in 1972 to the state Senate. In 1978, he was elected attorney general; in 1982, he defeated incumbent Governor Robert List; and in 1988, he defeated incumbent Senator Chic Hecht, by 50%–46%, after Hecht had failed to stop the 1987 law declaring Yucca Mountain as the nation's permanent nuclear waste disposal site.

Bryan combines a moderate-to-liberal voting record with an aggressive pursuit of particular causes. He has dissented from other Democrats on key issues, like the Gulf war resolution in 1991 and the Clinton budget and tax increase in 1993. His special causes include telemarketing fraud, on which he sponsored a law in his first term, and auto safety; his amendment required air bags in every new car. He was less successful in his efforts to raise the CAFE (Corporate Average Fuel Economy) standards on automakers to 40 miles per gallon by 2001. He was successful in eliminating the mohair subsidy and NASA's Search for Extraterrestrial Intelligence. He has sponsored fair credit reporting and toys labelling legislation. To combat illegal immigration, he worked to increase border patrols, restrict political asylum claims and expedite deportation proceedings. He wants to eliminate the special congressional pension and place members under the ordinary federal pension program. Bryan was most visible nationally as the chairman of the Ethics Committee in 1993 and 1994, when he chaired the investigation of Bob Packwood and led the successful fight for access to his diaries; Packwood resigned in 1995, and in 1996 Bryan rotated off the committee, on which his Nevada colleague Harry Reid now serves.

Bryan naturally looks out for Nevada interests. He is opposed to any further federal regulation of gaming, has sought to reduce the federal paperwork burden on the industry and has called for reform of the Indian Gaming Act. He has sought to put a solar energy plant and solar energy research center on the Nevada Test Site. But most important, he strongly opposes any nuclear waste disposal site, permanent or temporary, at Yucca Mountain or on the Test Site. "They want a toilet to flush their nuclear waste down," he says of the opposition. "And that toilet is Nevada." In July 1996 Bryan and Reid filibustered the bill for a temporary disposal site; although cloture was voted, 65–34, and the bill passed, 63–37, the Nevadans were pleased that it lacked the two-thirds vote necessary to overcome a promised Clinton veto, and it was not voted on in the House. But the battle continues in 1997, with many senators aware that nuclear waste is being piled up in their states and eager to implement the 1987 law naming Yucca Mountain as the permanent disposal site. The Energy department has acknowledged that the permanent site will not be ready by the law's January 1998 deadline; in response, the Senate passed a bill in April 1997 mandating that a temporary site be created at the test site. But the legislation only garnered 65 votes—two short of the total needed to overcome the veto promised by Clinton.

In 1994 Bryan won reelection in a Republican year. His opponent was Hal Furman, a staffer to Senator Paul Laxalt in the 1970s and an appointee in the Reagan Interior Department; in the private sector since 1985, he attacked Bryan for spending a lifetime in government. Bryan responded by calling Furman a lobbyist and asking what work the firm he was part of, public relations giant Hill and Knowlton, had done for the rogue international bank BCCI. Bryan campaigned as an independent voice and vastly outspent his opponent. He lost the Cow Counties narrowly, 46%–44%, but won by a solid 53%–40% in Las Vegas's Clark County, which cast 57% of the state's votes. That was enough for a 51%–41% victory, similar to Reid's margin two years before. It is too soon to make predictions for 2000.

Presidential politics. In the 1940s, Nevada was a Democratic state; in the 1960s, it was divided much as the nation was, voting narrowly for John Kennedy in 1960 and Richard Nixon in 1968. In the 1980s, it was heavily Republican, over 60% for Ronald Reagan and 59%–38% for George Bush in 1988. If it were bigger, it would have been a key battleground. In 1992 Nevada surprised everyone, including strategists for both campaigns, when it voted 37%–35% for Clinton. In 1996 there was less surprise, and an even narrower margin, as Clinton won 44%–43%. Undoubtedly his pledge to veto the bill to create temporary nuclear waste disposal site at Yucca Mountain made the difference.

Nevada's late March presidential primary has attracted little attention.

Congressional districting. Despite the most rapid population growth in the nation, Nevada did not gain a seat in the 1990 Census, and the two districts' boundaries were shifted only slightly. Nevada is expected to gain a seat after the 2000 Census.

The People: Est. Pop. 1996: 1,603,000; Pop. 1990: 1,201,833, up 33.4% 1990–1996. 0.6% of U.S. total, 38th largest; 12% rural. Median age: 34.8 years. 11% 65 years and over. 78.7% White, 6.4% Black, 3.0% Asian, 1.5% Amer. Indian, 10.4% Hispanic origin. Households: 51.4% married couple families; 23% married couple fams. w. children; 47% college educ.; median household income: $31,011; per capita income: $15,214; 54.8% owner occupied housing; median house value: $95,700; median monthly rent: $445. 5.4% Unemployment. 1996 Voting age pop.: 1,212,000. 1996 Turnout: 464,279; 38% of VAP. Registered voters (1996): 778,298; 325,501 D (42%), 329,730 R (42%), 96,624 unaffiliated and minor parties (16%).

Political Lineup: Governor, Bob Miller (D); Lt. Gov., Lonnie Hammargren (R); Secy. of State, Dean Heller (R); Atty. Gen., Frankie Sue Del Papa (D); Treasurer, Robert L. Seale (R); Controller, Darrell Daines (R). State Senate, 21 (9 D and 12 R); Senate President, Lonnie Hammargren (R); State Assembly, 42 (25 D and 17 R); Assembly Speaker, Joe Dini (D). Senators, Harry Reid (D) and Richard H. Bryan (D). Representatives, 2 (2 R).

Elections Division: 702-687-3176; **Filing Deadline for U.S. Congress:** June 2, 1998.

1996 Presidential Vote

Clinton (D)	203,974	(44%)
Dole (R)	199,244	(43%)
Perot (I)	43,986	(9%)
Other	17,130	(4%)

1992 Presidential Vote

Clinton (D)	189,148	(37%)
Bush (R)	175,828	(35%)
Perot (I)	132,580	(26%)

1996 Republican Presidential Primary

Dole (R)	72,932	(52%)
Forbes (R)	27,063	(19%)
Buchanan (R)	21,321	(15%)
Other	19,321	(15%)

GOVERNOR

Gov. Bob Miller (D)

Assumed office Jan. 1989, term expires Jan. 1999; b. Mar. 30, 1945, Chicago, IL; home, Carson City; U. of Santa Clara, B.A. 1967, Loyola U. Law Schl., J.D. 1971; Catholic; married (Sandy).

Career: Clark Cnty. Dep. Dist. Atty., 1971–73; Legal advisor, Las Vegas Metro. Police Dept., 1973–75; Justice of the Peace, Las Vegas Township, 1975–78; Clark Cnty. Dist. Atty., 1978–86; NV Lt. Gov., 1986–88; Chmn., Western Govs. Assn., 1992–94.

Office: Executive Chambers, Capitol Bldg., Carson City 89710, 702-687-5670; 702-687-4486; Web site: www.state.nv.us.

Election Results

1994 gen.	Bob Miller (D)	200,026	(53%)
	Jim Gibbons (R)	156,875	(41%)
	Others	22,775	(6%)
1994 prim.	Bob Miller (D)	75,311	(63%)
	Jan Laverty Jones (D)	33,566	(28%)
	Others	11,309	(9%)
1990 gen.	Bob Miller (D)	207,878	(66%)
	Jim Gallaway (R)	95,789	(31%)
	Other	8,984	(3%)

SENATORS

Sen. Harry Reid (D)

Elected 1986, seat up 1998; b. Dec. 2, 1939, Searchlight; home, Searchlight; Southern UT St. Col., A.S. 1959; UT St. U., B.S. 1961, George Washington U., J.D. 1964; U. of NV, 1969–70; Mormon; married (Landra).

Career: Practicing atty., 1969–82; Henderson City Atty., 1964–66; NV Assembly, 1968–70; NV Lt. Gov., 1970–74; Chmn., NV Gaming Comm., 1977–81; U.S. House of Reps., 1982–86.

DC Office: 528 HSOB 20510, 202-224-3542; Fax: 202-224-7327; e-mail: senator_reid@reid.senate.gov.

State Offices: Carson City, 702-882-7343; Las Vegas, 702-474-0041; Reno, 702-686-5750.

Committees: *Appropriations* (9th of 13 D): Energy & Water Development (RMM); Interior; Labor, Health & Human Services & Education; Military Construction; Transportation. *Environment & Public Works* (4th of 8 D): Drinking Water, Fisheries & Wildlife (RMM); Transportation & Infrastructure. *Ethics (Select)* (RMM of 3 D). *Indian Affairs* (3rd of 6 D). *Aging (Special)* (3rd of 8 D).

Group Ratings

	ADA	ACLU	AFS	LCV	CFA	CON	NFIB	COC	ACU	NTLC	CHC
1996	85	22	86	77	93	38	28	31	15	17	23
1995	80	—	100	93	69	2	—	37	9	—	—

National Journal Ratings

	1995 LIB — 1995 CONS			1996 LIB — 1996 CONS		
Economic	68%	—	29%	69%	—	30%
Social	47%	—	51%	52%	—	47%
Foreign	72%	—	24%	62%	—	36%

Key Votes of the 104th Congress

1. Reduce Medicare Growth $	N	5. Flag Amendment	Y	9. Anti-Missile Defense	N
2. Lmt. Prod. Liab. Damages	N	6. Endangered Species	Y	10. Cuban Embargo	Y
3. Increase Min. Wage	Y	7. Gay Employment Rights	Y	11. Bar Bosnia Troop $	N
4. Welfare Reform	Y	8. Ovrd. Part. Birth Veto	Y	12. Cut Vietnam Aid	Y

Election Results

1992 general	Harry Reid (D)	253,150	(51%)	($3,259,802)
	Demar Dahl (R)	199,413	(40%)	($471,371)
	Others	43,333	(9%)	
1992 primary	Harry Reid (D)	64,828	(53%)	
	Charles Woods (D)	48,364	(39%)	
	Others	9,551	(8%)	
1986 general	Harry Reid (D)	130,955	(50%)	($2,055,756)
	Jim Santini (R)	116,606	(45%)	($2,656,747)
	Others	14,271	(5%)	

Sen. Richard H. Bryan (D)

Elected 1988, seat up 2000; b. July 16, 1937, Washington, D.C.; home, Carson City; U. of NV, B.A. 1959, U. of CA, Hastings Col. of Law., LL.B. 1963; Episcopalian; married (Bonnie).

Career: Army, 1959–60; Clark Cnty. Dep. Dist. Atty., 1964–66; Clark Cnty. Public Defender, 1966–68; Cnsl., Clark Cnty. Juvenile Court, 1968–69; NV Assembly, 1968–72; NV Senate, 1972–78; NV Atty. Gen., 1978–82; NV Gov., 1982–1988.

DC Office: 269 RSOB 20510, 202-224-6244; Fax: 202-224-1867; e-mail: senator@bryan.senate.gov.

State Offices: Carson City, 702-885-9111; Las Vegas, 702-388-6605; Reno, 702-686-5770.

Committees: *Banking, Housing & Urban Affairs* (4th of 8 D): Financial Institutions & Regulatory Relief (RMM); Housing Opportunity & Community Development; Securities. *Commerce, Science & Transportation* (7th of 9 D): Aviation; Consumer Affairs, Foreign Commerce & Tourism; Manufacturing & Competitiveness (RMM); Science, Technology & Space; Surface Transportation & Merchant Marine. *Finance* (8th of 9 D): Health Care; Long-Term Growth, Debt & Defict Reduction; Taxation & IRS Oversight. *Intelligence (Select)* (3rd of 9 D).

Group Ratings

	ADA	ACLU	AFS	LCV	CFA	CON	NFIB	COC	ACU	NTLC	CHC
1996	85	35	71	85	86	95	31	38	10	17	15
1995	100	—	91	93	56	29	—	42	9	—	—

National Journal Ratings

	1995 LIB — 1995 CONS			1996 LIB — 1996 CONS		
Economic	73%	—	23%	61%	—	34%
Social	69%	—	29%	60%	—	38%
Foreign	62%	—	36%	77%	—	17%

Key Votes of the 104th Congress

1. Reduce Medicare Growth $	N	5. Flag Amendment	Y	9. Anti-Missile Defense	N
2. Lmt. Prod. Liab. Damages	N	6. Endangered Species	Y	10. Cuban Embargo	Y
3. Increase Min. Wage	Y	7. Gay Employment Rights	Y	11. Bar Bosnia Troop $	N
4. Welfare Reform	Y	8. Ovrd. Part. Birth Veto	N	12. Cut Vietnam Aid	N

Election Results

1994 general	Richard H. Bryan (D)	193,804	(51%)	($3,021,834)
	Hal Furman (R)	156,020	(41%)	($845,340)
	Others	30,706	(8%)	
1994 primary	Richard H. Bryan (D)	unopposed		
1988 general	Richard H. Bryan (D)	175,548	(50%)	($2,957,789)
	Jacob (Chic) Hecht (R)	161,336	(46%)	($3,007,864)
	Others	12,765	(4%)	

FIRST DISTRICT

Nevada's congressional districts, identical in 1990 population, differ vastly in size; the 1st consists of Las Vegas and its close-in suburbs; the 2d covers everything else, the other 99.8% of Nevada's land mass. The 1st, something like a nervously drawn circle in the center of Clark County, takes in all of Las Vegas, most of Henderson, part of heavily black North Las Vegas and just a bit of the Las Vegas Colony Indian Reservation. It also includes most of the Democratic precincts in the state.

The congressman from the 1st District is John Ensign, a Republican elected in an upset in 1994. Ensign grew up in northern Nevada and moved to Las Vegas at 16; his family owns the Gold Strike Hotel, which he managed for some years, and his father is an executive at Circus Circus. The younger Ensign opened an around-the-clock veterinary hospital in 1987. In 1994, he decided to run against Congressman James Bilbray, a Democrat, moderate on many issues. Ensign attacked Bilbray on the usual causes—the 1993 budget and tax bill, the 1994 healthcare plan and crime bill—and called for truth in sentencing and medical savings accounts and opposed government subsidized day care for welfare mothers. He was outspent, but with his gaming connections raised enough to be competitive. Then in October, the *Las Vegas Review-Journal* reported that a Bilbray political adviser stood to gain $7 million on a land investment if Bilbray's bill to expand the Red Rock Canyon National Conservation Area passed. It was signed into law six days before the election, and Ensign won 48.5%–47.5%.

Ensign had little political experience but showed signs of political competence. He got a seat on the Ways and Means Committee and formed a House Gaming Caucus, with Nevada's Barbara Vucanovich and Atlantic City, New Jersey's Frank LoBiondo. He voted for the Contract with America but cast many moderate votes on other issues. On Ways and Means he had considerable impact, altering the Medicare formula to help fast-growing areas, stopping a gaming tax, making long-term care expenses partly deductible, working to weaken the national commission on gaming. He and David Camp were the two Ways and Means members who urged Newt Gingrich to separate the welfare and Medicaid issues and pass a separate welfare bill in summer 1996—a bill which was signed by Bill Clinton. He also spoke out against the scheduled permanent and the proposed temporary nuclear waste disposal sites at Yucca Mountain, 95 miles from Las Vegas. He called it a budget-buster, a threat to private property rights, a contradiction of the Tenth Amendment, and he urged instead dry-cask storage of nuclear waste at reactor sites.

Ensign also raised money early, some from PACs, much from gaming interests, accumulating $1.3 million as early as June 1996, effectively deterring the candidacies of such well known Democrats as Las Vegas Mayor Jan Laverty Jones and Attorney General Frankie Sue Del Papa. His Democratic opponent, state Senator Bob Coffin, did not raise nearly as much, but Ensign had active opposition in, by his estimate, $700,000 worth of AFL-CIO television ads. Las Vegas is a big union town; most of the casinos are unionized, and there was a nasty strike going on at the Frontier. It also hurt that the editor of the largest local newspaper, *The Las Vegas Sun*, was a college friend of Bill Clinton. By early October Ensign led Coffin by only 43%–41% in a public poll. Ensign responded by spending his money on ads attacking the unions: "The unions who are saying John Ensign is cutting Medicare are the same people who are trying to persuade Washington to dump waste in Nevada." And he successfully persuaded the Republican leadership not to bring to the floor the nuclear waste bill to create a temporary disposal site in Nevada's Yucca Mountain; the bill had the votes to pass, and Clinton had promised to veto it. "I've been frank with the House leadership. It could potentially cost two Republican seats." Or at least one; every bit of the $1.9 million spent by Ensign was apparently necessary to eke out his narrow 50%–44% win over Coffin, who spent $592,000. Ensign has also been named as a possible challenger to Reid in 1998.

The People: Pop. 1990: 601,042; 11% age 65+; 73% White; 10% Black; 4% Asian; 1% Amer. Indian; 12% Hispanic origin. Households: 49% married couple families; 21% married couple fams. w. children; 44% college educ.; median household income: $29,611; per capita income: $14,837; median gross rent: $505; median house value: $88,900.

1996 Presidential Vote

Clinton (D)	91,307	(51%)
Dolc (R)	65,990	(37%)
Perot (I)	15,949	(9%)
Other	5,811	(3%)

1992 Presidential Vote

Clinton (D)	98,700	(43%)
Bush (R)	70,440	(31%)
Perot (I)	55,964	(24%)

Rep. John Ensign (R)

Elected 1994; b. Mar. 25, 1958, Roseville, CA; home, Las Vegas; OR St. U., B.S. 1981; CO St. U., D.V.M. 1985; Christian; married (Darlene).

Career: Practicing veternarian, 1987–93; Gen. Mgr., Gold Strike Hotel, 1991–93.

DC Office: 414 CHOB 20515, 202-225-5965; Fax: 202-225-3119; e-mail: ensign@hr.house.gov.

District Offices: Las Vegas, 702-731-1801.

Committees: *Resources* (19th of 27 R): National Parks & Public Lands; Water & Power. *Ways & Means* (18th of 23 R): Health; Human Resources.

Group Ratings

	ADA	ACLU	AFS	LCV	CFA	CON	NFIB	COC	ACU	NTLC	CHC
1996	5	40	8	38	46	66	97	88	85	98	100
1995	0	—	—	6	15	87	—	100	96	—	—

National Journal Ratings

	1995 LIB		1995 CONS	1996 LIB		1996 CONS
Economic	26%	—	67%	33%	—	64%
Social	41%	—	58%	38%	—	62%
Foreign	36%	—	59%	50%	—	48%

Key Votes of the 104th Congress

1. Reduce Medicare Growth $	Y	5. Flag Amendment	Y	9. Cuban Embargo	Y
2. Ovrd. Product Liab. Veto	Y	6. Drop EPA Limits	Y	10. Bar Bosnia Troop $	Y
3. Increase Min. Wage	Y	7. Repeal Assault-Weap. Ban	Y	11. Cut Anti-Missile Defense	N
4. Welfare Reform	Y	8. Ovrd. Part. Birth Veto	Y	12. Bar U.N. Uniforms	Y

Election Results

1996 general	John Ensign (R)	86,472	(50%)	($1,904,413)
	Bob Coffin (D)	75,081	(44%)	($592,726)
	Others	11,040	(6%)	
1996 primary	John Ensign (R)	unopposed		
1994 general	John Ensign (R)	73,769	(48%)	($687,194)
	James H. Bilbray (D)	72,333	(48%)	($913,708)
	Others	6,065	(4%)	

SECOND DISTRICT

The 2d District is the more Republican of Nevada's two districts, and includes 99.8% of the state's land area. Reno, smaller than Las Vegas, surrounded by wooded mountains, is the 2d's largest city, but one-quarter of the district's votes are cast in Las Vegas suburbs. These are mostly Republican, as is Reno ordinarily. And dislike of Interior Secretary Bruce Babbitt's proposed grazing fees and Mining Act reform have made the "Cow Counties" heavily Republican.

The congressman from the 2d District is Jim Gibbons, a Republican elected in 1996. Gibbons grew up near Reno, went to the University of Nevada and served in the Air Force in Vietnam. He went to law school and has practiced law, but he also was a mining geologist, a hydrologist and a pilot for Delta and Western Airlines and became Vice Commander of the Nevada Air National Guard. In 1988 he was elected to the Assembly; in 1990 he was called up to active duty in the Gulf war. While he was flying unarmed air reconnaissance missions, his wife was taking his place in the legislature. After his celebrated return, he proposed a Tax Initiative to require a 2/3 supermajority to raise any state tax; it passed with more than 70% of the votes in 1994 and by 1996 became law. In 1994 Gibbons ran for governor. He beat Secretary of State Cheryl Lau 52%–32% in the primary, but lost the general to Bob Miller, 53%–41%.

In 1996, 15 year Congresswoman Barbara Vucanovich, who did much to push the cause of breast cancer research and prevention, retired and Gibbons ran for the seat. He had serious competition in the primary from Lau, who returned from more than a year as counsel to the U.S. House, and Patty Cafferata, former state treasurer and Vucanovich's daughter. Gibbons carried the Reno area and Las Vegas suburbs to win with 42%, to 24% each for Lau and Cafferata. Meanwhile, in the Democratic primary, former state senator and former head of the state Ethics Commission Spike Wilson beat former Mustang Ranch brothel worker Jessi Winchester 62%–21%. Gibbons won in all the 16 "Cow Counties" and in the 2d's portion of Clark County as well, for a 59%–35% win.

In the House Gibbons serves on the Resources Committee, where he promises to vigorously oppose the Yucca Mountain nuclear waste disposal site, on National Security, and on Intelligence. Conservative on most issues, he is pro-choice on abortion. He attacked the Clinton defense budget for "dangerous cuts in vital military programs." In early 1997 Gibbons was considered a possible candidate for senator or governor in 1998; he said, "My preference is to serve and continue serving as the congressman from Congressional District 2. But you never shut the door."

The People: Pop. 1990: 600,791; 23% rural; 10% age 65+; 84% White; 3% Black; 2% Asian; 2% Amer. Indian; 9% Hispanic origin. Households: 56% married couple families; 26% married couple fams. w. children; 51% college educ.; median household income: $32,413; per capita income: $15,592; median gross rent: $515; median house value: $103,900.

1996 Presidential Vote			1992 Presidential Vote		
Dole (R)	133,254	(47%)	Bush (R)	105,388	(38%)
Clinton (D)	112,667	(39%)	Clinton (D)	90,448	(33%)
Perot (I)	28,037	(10%)	Perot (I)	76,616	(28%)
Other	11,319	(4%)			

Rep. Jim Gibbons (R)

Elected 1996; b. Dec. 16, 1944, Sparks; home, Reno; U. of NV, B.S. 1967, M.S. 1973; Southwestern U., J.D. 1979; Protestant; married (Dawn).

Career: Air Force, 1967–71 (Vietnam), NV Air Natl. Guard, 1975–95 (Persian Gulf); Pilot, Western Airlines, 1979–87, Delta Airlines, 1987–96; NV Assembly, 1988–94.

DC Office: 1116 LHOB 20515, 202-225-6155; Fax: 202-225-5679.

District Offices: Elko, 702-777-7920; Las Vegas, 702-255-1615; Reno, 702-686-5760.

Committees: *National Security* (30th of 30 R): Military Readiness; Military Research & Development. *Resources* (26th of 27 R): Energy & Mineral Resources; National Parks & Public Lands. *Intelligence (Select)* (9th of 9 R): Technical & Tactical Intelligence.

Group Ratings and Key Votes: Newly Elected

Election Results

1996 general	Jim Gibbons (R)	162,310	(59%)	($724,036)
	Thomas (Spike) Wilson (D)	97,742	(35%)	($606,227)
	Others	17,140	(6%)	
1996 primary	Jim Gibbons (R)	33,332	(42%)	
	Cheryl A. Lau (R)	19,243	(24%)	
	Patty Cafferata (R)	19,192	(24%)	
	Others	6,906	(9%)	
1994 general	Barbara F. Vucanovich (R)	142,202	(64%)	($692,936)
	Janet Greeson (D)	65,390	(29%)	($58,191)
	Thomas F. Jefferson (IA)	9,615	(4%)	
	Others	6,725	(3%)	

NEW HAMPSHIRE

New Hampshire, with four-tenths of 1% of the nation's population, in an odd corner of the country and with some most unusual public policies, has nonetheless done much to set the nation's political course over the last two decades. The lever by which this small state moves the world is New Hampshire's first-in-the-nation presidential primary, a device sanctioned by Democratic reformers in the 1970s which then did much to beat Democratic presidential candidates in the 1980s, and one embraced by Republicans in the 1980s which did much to beat their presidential nominees in the 1990s. For good reason, George Bush ended his victory speech in November 1988 by saying, "Thank you, New Hampshire." But New Hampshire did not say, "You're welcome" when the recession of 1990–91 sent real estate values plunging and unemployment rising. Pat Buchanan found the best possible turf to challenge Bush and destabilize his candidacy here, and Bush's drop from 63% of New Hampshire's vote in 1988 to 38% in 1992 was greater than in any other state in the nation. In 1994, Republicans' big win here was matched by their conquest of the Congress. But they took to squabbling in the 1996 primary even as Bill Clinton was perfecting his triangulating campaign that would in November give him a 49% victory nationally and in New Hampshire. What will New Hampshire do for, or to, America in 2000?

In a country that prides itself on its feistiness and freedom from outside direction, New Hampshire has always been even feistier and less fettered by authority. Before the Revolutionary War, New Hampshire was almost an outlaw colony, its great fortunes made by poachers in the king's forests and smugglers avoiding taxes. It was the first colony with an independent government and was fighting the British before the Minutemen stood at Lexington and Concord. In this free environment, 19th Century entrepreneurs built textile mills along fast-flowing rivers; the Amoskeag Mills in Manchester, lining the Merrimack River for a mile, were once the largest cotton mills on the globe, employing 17,000 people and producing enough cloth every two months to put a band around the world. Around the mills grew a city of red brick dormitories and three-family frame houses filled with immigrants from Quebec, Ireland, Poland and Greece, set down amid dirt-roaded villages of flinty Yankee farmers and mechanics. New Hampshire held to its traditions of local government and little external control, and for years its refusal to join most other states and enact an income or sales tax, or to provide statewide guidance of schools and social services, seemed to doom it to continued backwardness.

But low taxes proved to be New Hampshire's fortune. Starting in the 1960s, New Hampshire for 35 years had the fastest growth on the East Coast, attracting businesses from Massachusetts and other high-tax states. It became a location of choice for entrepreneurs and high-tech innovators, attracting an increasing number of people skeptical of government programs. From 1965–96, Massachusetts grew from 5.5 million to 6.1 million, up 11%; New Hampshire grew from 676,000 to 1,162,000, up 72%. The bedraggled New Hampshire of 50 years ago, of poor Yankee farmers and French Canadian mill hands, has largely disappeared, and in its place one of the nation's most prosperous economic communities has arisen. This "Nouvelle Hampshire," to use *Washington Post* writer Henry Allen's term, has none of the architectural purity of Amoskeag: its shopping centers and new subdivisions have a slap-dash, half-built look, as if there were no time for details in the hurry to build. The boom was feverish in the late 1980s, producing more jobs per capita than any other state and fabulous increases in real estate value. Descendants of Amoskeag mill hands and stone-poor farmers found themselves with high-income jobs and perhaps even substantial wealth, property and interests in businesses worth hundreds of thousands of dollars.

The low taxes that spurred this growth, making New Hampshire a tax haven in Governor John

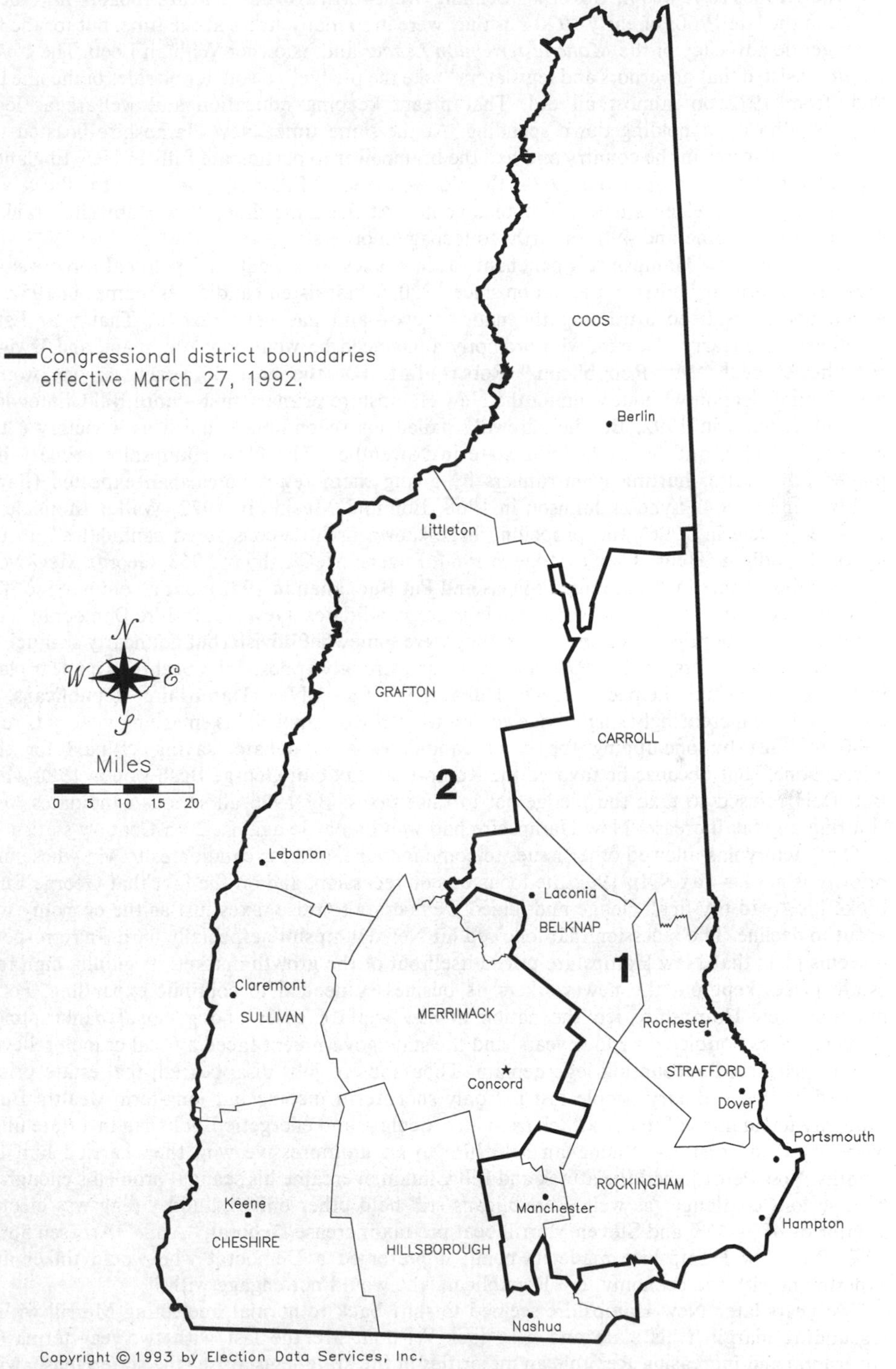
Congressional district boundaries effective March 27, 1992.
COOS
Berlin
Littleton
N
W
E
S
GRAFTON
CARROLL
Miles
0 5 10 15 20
2
Lebanon
Laconia
BELKNAP
1
Claremont
SULLIVAN
MERRIMACK
Rochester
STRAFFORD
Concord
Dover
Portsmouth
ROCKINGHAM
Keene
Manchester
Hampton
CHESHIRE
HILLSBOROUGH
Nashua

Sununu's 1980s as it was in Governor Benning Wentworth's 1760s, would probably have been raised in the late 1960s or early 1970s, as they were in so many states at the time, but for the far from gentle advocacy of the *Manchester Union Leader* and its owner William Loeb. The *Union Leader* insisted that governors and legislators "take the pledge" to vote for no sales or income tax and, from 1972 on, almost all did. That meant keeping education and welfare as local responsibilities and holding down spending. At the same time, New Hampshire boasted the highest SAT scores in the country and had the brainpower to participate fully in New England's high-tech boom for most of the 1980s: the old Amoskeag Mills were converted to offices, and once grimy Manchester is now a high-tech center. At the same time, New Hampshire ranked 48th in violent crime and 49th in births to teenage mothers.

Translating New Hampshire's penchant for low taxes into a national political force was its presidential primary. First in the nation since 1920, it first listed candidates' names in 1952, at which point it started attracting the nation's eye—and has never lost it. That year Estes Kefauver beat Harry Truman, who promptly announced he would not run again, and Dwight Eisenhower beat "Mr. Republican," Robert Taft. For the next 40 years, no one won a presidential election without winning the New Hampshire primary first—until Bill Clinton lost to Paul Tsongas in 1992. But he shrewdly hailed his second-place finish as a victory ("the comeback kid!"), and he carried the state in November. The New Hampshire primary has played other roles, hurting front-runners by giving them fewer votes than expected (Barry Goldwater in 1964, Lyndon Johnson in 1968, Edmund Muskie in 1972, Walter Mondale in 1984, Bob Dole in 1996) and propelling little-known or little-considered candidates into the national spotlight (Henry Cabot Lodge in 1964, Eugene McCarthy in 1968, George McGovern in 1972, Gary Hart in 1984, Paul Tsongas and Pat Buchanan in 1992): but a common motif in most of these surprises was an aversion to high-tax candidates. New Hampshire Democrats have shown signs of liberalism on some issues: they were somewhat dovish (but not nearly as much as Iowa caucus attenders) in the 1970s and 1980s and strongly opposed the Seabrook nuclear plant in the 1980s (which helped Michael Dukakis in 1988). New Hampshire Republicans, in contrast, were increasingly single-issue voters. Ronald Reagan won his smashing victory here in 1980 not just by one-upping the other candidates at a debate, saying "I paid for this microphone," but because he favored the Kemp-Roth tax cut; George Bush won in 1988 when Bob Dole refused to take the pledge not to raise taxes. By 1996 all serious candidates were abjuring any tax increase: New Hampshire had won its battle against 20th Century statism.

That victory has allowed other issues to come forward, and for candidates to win whose first priority is not low taxes. In 1992 the focus was on recession, and on the fact that George Bush broke his "read my lips" pledge and joined Democrats to raise taxes just as the economy was about to decline. The recession that followed hit New Hampshire especially hard. In retrospect, it seems plain that New Hampshire priced itself out of the growth market: its giddily high real estate prices kept out the new workers its businesses needed to continue expanding. For a moment New Hampshire led the nation in new welfare cases and personal bankruptcies. Property taxes doubled over four years, and the state government faced a fiscal crunch relieved only by Medicaid accounting legerdemain. Thousands of jobs disappeared; real estate prices crashed so that ordinary people lost not only short-term income but long-term wealth. Bush suddenly found himself under attack from an articulate and energetic Buchanan in a state filled with anger and distress. Buchanan held him to an unimpressive win, then harried him for months; Ross Perot joined the attack and Bill Clinton overcame his scandal problems enough to be a serious challenger as well. Republicans still held other offices; Judd Gregg was elected senator by 48%–45% and Steven Merrill beat pro-tax-increase Deborah "Arnie" Arnesen 56%–40%. But New Hampshire made its point: it preferred a Democrat who would tinker and experiment with the economy to a Republican who would not engage with it.

Two years later New Hampshire seemed to shift back to normal, reelecting Merrill with a resounding margin (this state and next-door Vermont are the last with two-year terms for governors) and increasing Republican majorities in the state legislature (the state House, with

400 members, is the world's largest legislature after the British House of Commons, the Indian Lok Sabha and the American House of Representatives). But the impulse of 1992 remained, even as the state's small-business-dominated economy took off again and unemployment fell under 4%. Even as the seven Republican candidates were debating in 1996 in the studio of Manchester's Channel 9, the state's only commercial TV station, George Stephanopoulos was spinning the press in a side room ("the President has kept the promises he meant to keep") and Clinton was running way ahead in New Hampshire polls. So it went up through November, as Senator Bob Smith and Republicans in the two congressional districts came close to losing and Democrat Jeanne Shaheen easily won election as governor—after taking the pledge early on. New Hampshire, having made the politics of Ronald Reagan possible in the 1980s, made the politics of Bill Clinton possible in the 1990s, across the country and at home.

Every four years in late February, within 24 hours after the primary returns are in, the national politicians and press switch off Channel 9, stuff the *Union Leader* into the wastebasket and clear out of the Sheraton Wayfarer parking lot, not to be seen again for the next three years. New Hampshire then has its politics to itself. For years the key issue has been taxes; now state politics has moved on to other things.

Governor. Jeanne Shaheen, the Democratic governor elected in 1996, like many in New Hampshire politics, is from somewhere else: she was born in Missouri, went to college in Pennsylvania and graduate school in Mississippi. She moved to New Hampshire in 1973, taught school, ran a silver and leather business with her husband and, most importantly, managed Gary Hart's campaign here in 1984, for which she received excellent notices; in 1988 she worked on Democrat Paul McEachern's gubernatorial campaign. In 1990 she ran for the state Senate, and served three terms. There she worked on New Hampshire's pioneering effort to open up electric utilities to competition and sponsored healthcare laws—stabilizing insurance rates, barring rejection for preexisting conditions, and trying to stop managed care insurers from denying access to physicians of choice. She sought to spend more on higher education and fought to create the first state-sponsored industrial research center.

In April 1996, two-term Governor Steve Merrill reversed course and announced he was not running. Merrill had cut taxes and spending, pushed workmen's comp reform and market-based healthcare reforms, and was reelected 70%–26% in 1994. He played a key role in Bob Dole's New Hampshire and national campaigns, and may have hoped for an appointment in Washington; in January 1997 he came close to being elected Republican National Committee chairman. Merrill's departure led to a Republican primary fight between 1st District Congressman Bill Zeliff and state Board of Education Chairman Ovide Lamontagne. They were old rivals: Zeliff beat Lamontagne 50%–35% in the 1992 House primary. Zeliff had a conservative record on economics but was moderate on cultural issues and pro-choice on abortion; Lamontagne was a strong conservative, very much against abortion and was supported vehemently by the *Manchester Union Leader*. Both started off better known than Shaheen, and proceeded to become more disliked. In July 1996 they became embroiled in controversy over ballot signatures. New Hampshire allows a candidate to escape a $500,000 spending limit if he files an extra number of signatures; Zeliff, with $300,000 in his campaign treasury at the start, sought to do this. But Lamontagne challenged the extra signatures on the grounds that not enough were notarized in the presence of a justice of the peace. A state election commission tossed Zeliff off the ballot; he appealed, and agreed to accept the spending limit. But the *Union Leader* denounced him as an incompetent manager and the moderate *Concord Monitor* portrayed him as the character Pigpen in "Peanuts." Lamontagne won an upset in the September primary, 47%–43%, largely from his margin in Manchester.

Meanwhile, Shaheen serenely campaigned on the anti-tax pledge and the record she had made in the legislature. As voters moved beyond the tax issue, they apparently saw Lamontagne as an extremist; free-and-easy New Hampshire has never had much of a religious right. As Clinton was carrying the state 49%–39%, Shaheen won by 57%–40%, carrying almost every county. In office, she reiterated her support for the pledge and submitted a balanced budget, while calling for a school building program to guarantee kindergarten for every five-year-old (New Hampshire is the one state which doesn't do this). She promises to work further on electricity deregulation, healthcare issues and tourism promotion. New Hampshire governors ordinarily win a second term, and in early 1997 there was no apparent reason why Shaheen should not.

Senior Senator. Bob Smith grew up in New Jersey, served in the Navy in Vietnam, taught high school and managed Yankee Pedlar Real Estate in Wolfeboro, New Hampshire. In 1980 he ran for the House and lost the primary; in 1982 he ran and lost the general 55%–45%; in 1984 he ran again, won the four-candidate primary with 42% and beat Democrat Dudley Dudley 59%–40%. In 1990, when Senator Gordon Humphrey honored a promise to retire after 12 years, Smith won the Republican nomination over a pro-choicer, 65%–29%, and in the general faced feisty former (1975–80) Senator John Durkin. Durkin attacked Smith for opposing abortion and supporting big oil companies, and called for $10 billion in new spending programs. Smith won 65%–32%.

Smith has had an almost perfectly conservative voting record in the Senate. From his seats on Armed Services and Environment and Public Works, he has taken the lead role on two major issues, Superfund reform and missile defense. Smith would like to repeal Superfund's retroactive liability for toxic wastes disposed of before the law was passed, but has been unable to come up with enough government money to pay for it. His bill did not pass in the 104th Congress; in the 105th, it was named by Majority Leader Trent Lott as one of his top ten in January 1997, and Smith seeks to exempt only small firms from retroactive liability. From the Environment post, Smith also worked on the 1996 Safe Drinking Water Act, drafting provisions on treatment mandates for radon in water and federal assistance to poor communities. He got unanimous consent for abolishing the pretreatment requirement in the Solid Waste Disposal Act. Smith believes in intensive research and development of missile defense, a program that does not have a strong institutional base in the Pentagon and has been opposed by the Clinton Administration; but Defense Secretary William Cohen did support it when he was in the Senate.

Smith has also pursued some distinctive issues of his own. One was the question of whether the United States left behind POWs and MIAs in Vietnam. In 1991 he became vice chairman of the Select Committee on POW/MIA Affairs, chaired by Massachusetts Senator John Kerry, also a Vietnam veteran; in 1993 Smith signed the final report concluding that there was "no compelling evidence" that POWs or MIAs are now in Southeast Asia, but the investigation brought to light disturbing evidence that some may have been left behind and could not rule out the possibility that some are still there against their will. In 1994, he opposed the Clinton Administration's lifting of the economic embargo against Vietnam. Smith was similarly skeptical of military authority when he pursued investigation of Gulf war syndrome and opposed U.S. troops in Bosnia in fall 1995. He has also shown concern over inhumane treatment of animals, backing dolphin-safe tuna fishing, zeroing out the subsidy for foreign marketing of mink furs and voting against the Bion mission with Rhesus monkeys in space capsules. He can be a stickler for principle: in March 1996 he voted against an appropriation's bill though it contained $20 million sought by Governor Steve Merrill to balance New Hampshire's Medicaid accounts. He said, "The bill added $3.5 billion in amendments which were offset by gimmicks—not real spending cuts." But he has worked for an access road from the Turnpike to Manchester's new Airport and the Broad Street Parkway in Nashua.

Smith had a close call in the 1996 election—indeed, a near-political-death experience on election night when the VNS exit poll declared him the loser. (New Hampshire exit polls have leaned Democratic since 1988; perhaps *Union Leader* faithful refuse to fill out their ballots.) The Democratic nominee was Dick Swett, elected to the 2d District House seat in 1990 and 1992 and defeated 51%–46% in 1994. Swett won the primary by only 53%–47% over John Rauh, the nominee against Senator Judd Gregg in 1992, even though Rauh took no PAC money and no contributions over $100; Swett ultimately spent some $1.6 million, much of it raised with the help of his father-in-law, California Congressman Tom Lantos. Before the September primary Swett painted himself as the moderate between two extremes. However, during the general campaign he hit Smith for voting for the congressional pay raise and moving his family to Washington. Smith attacked Swett as a liberal and for raising 90% of his money out of state. Both tried to play to their strengths: Smith ran ads showing him fishing in a pond flanked by moose and heron; Swett's mantra was "reward work, honor our families and make government work for us." Smith had only a narrow lead in most polls and was behind in some; he perhaps suffered from his heavy campaigning for Phil Gramm, who ended up withdrawing from the presidential campaign before he got to New Hampshire. In the end Smith won by just 49%–46%; he was later fined $95,000 for exceeding by $130,000 the state's voluntary campaign spending limit, which he described as "fatally flawed," but presumably does not regret doing so. Of late New Hampshire senators have a habit of retiring after two terms; the last to win a third full term was Norris Cotton, in 1968.

Junior Senator. Judd Gregg grew up in Nashua and in politics: his father, Hugh Gregg, was elected governor in 1952 and was a power in presidential primary politics up through 1988, when he backed George Bush. Judd Gregg was a student at Columbia during the student riots of 1968, but stayed true to New Hampshire Republicanism; after law school, he returned to Nashua and practiced law. In 1978 he was elected to the Executive Council, which dates to the colonial era and approves state appointments and expenditures. In 1980 he was elected to the House, where he was an eager participant in the Reagan revolution. In 1988, Gregg ran for governor and won handily; he was easily reelected in 1990. In 1992, he ran for the Senate when Warren Rudman retired, and in his taciturn way seemed sure he would win. But the New Hampshire economy had turned sour, and the race turned close. In the September primary he beat a construction company owner by only 50%–38%. In the general, he faced retired businessman John Rauh, who backed the line-item veto and balanced budget amendment and attacked Gregg for opposing abortion. Gregg was also attacked for having received a draft deferrment in 1969 for bad knees, sleepwalking and severe acne. Gregg won by an unimpressive 48%–45% margin.

In the Senate Gregg's *National Journal* ratings have become more moderate, probably because of the increasing number of very conservative Republicans. In June 1996, when Trent Lott became majority leader, Gregg became chief deputy whip. He served on the 1994 Entitlements Commission and in 1995 headed the Senate Republicans' working group on entitlement reform; he drafted a Medicare reform which would give seniors more choices, including the current system. "The status quo is not an option. We must save Medicare," he said in 1997. He also headed a task force on pension reform in 1997, and came forward with a proposal to eliminate $14 billion of "corporate welfare," notably the Power Marketing Administration, irrigation subsidies, the Advanced Technology program. He is not always an ally of western Republicans: he wants to reform the Mining Act of 1872 and, with Dale Bumpers of Arkansas, has sponsored higher grazing fees on federal lands. With Illinois' Carol Moseley-Braun, he passed a bill allowing states and localities to set retirement ages for public safety personnel. He has a special interest in the handicapped, and wants the federal government to fund 40% rather than 7% of special education. He was the sponsor of an OSHA reform bill which codified Clinton Administration policy, but a veto was threatened nevertheless. He passed an amendment barring states from regulating over-the-counter drugs without FDA permission.

Gregg comes up for reelection in 1998. His is regarded as one of the safer of Republican seats up, but New Hampshire's Democratic trend could produce a real contest. Possible candidates include Dick Swett, John Rauh or his wife Mary, and Joe Keefe, the 1996 nominee in the 1st District.

Presidential politics. Since 1920, New Hampshire has had the first-in-the-nation primary, and since 1952, when candidates' names were first put on the ballot, it has had extraordinary influence on the presidential selection process—a fact that 21st Century political scientists will surely regard as bizarre. To be sure, there are arguments for having early contests in small states which provide a venue for "retail politics," in which candidates meet voters in person, listening and talking to them, exchanging ideas and allowing them to gauge their character. In-person contact was one of the things that saved Bill Clinton in 1992, after the Gennifer Flowers charges;

exit polls showed he did much better than average with voters who had personally met one or more of the candidates. But New Hampshire is becoming large and metropolitan enough that the primary is increasingly fought out on television, in ads and on Channel 9's newscasts. And New Hampshire is increasingly an odd duck, one of the last states you would pick as typical.

In any case, New Hampshire retains its first-in-the-nation status not on its merits but because of threats. Democrats, who typically decide these things by nationally imposed rules, tried in the 1970s to confine primaries to a "window" period in which New Hampshire would have competition. But New Hampshire, with its outlaw tradition, insisted it would hold its primary before the window if necessary, confident that candidates and reporters would pay it heed even if its tiny delegation were threatened with not being seated at the national convention: the tradition of Benning Wentworth still lives. Republicans, who typically decide these things by letting the political marketplace work its will, made no such rules, but in 1996 let Iowa Governor Terry Branstad and New Hampshire Governor Steve Merrill threaten voter retaliation against candidates who took part in caucuses or primaries held before their states' or even during the week afterwards.

The victim was Phil Gramm, who tried to contrive early contests elsewhere. In May 1995 he dared to speak to a Delaware Republican convention without denouncing its plan to hold a primary four days after New Hampshire's; Merrill attacked him fiercely, and the campaign of this low-tax candidate in low-tax New Hampshire faltered. The top three finishers here in 1996—Buchanan, Bob Dole, and Lamar Alexander—were careful to give deference to New Hampshire tradition.

A word should be said about New Hampshire media. The *Manchester Union Leader* has one of the nation's sharpest conservative tongues. Its owner Nackey Loeb (the widow of William) and its editorials scold Republicans who stray from its gospel, which these days includes Pat Buchanan's opposition to free trade. Its insistence that politicians take the anti-tax pledge has set the course for New Hampshire state politics and government. But the *Union Leader* cannot automatically deliver votes on primary day—Buchanan won, but with just 27% of the votes—and its news coverage is more objective than that of many left-leaning national media outlets. New Hampshire's other great medium is Manchester's WMUR-TV, Channel 9, which also provides tons of information to a winter-bound audience. Channel 9's rule is to cover every candidate every day he or she is in New Hampshire, allowing each to present views and make arguments without the overlay of smirky, opinionated commentary that national network reporters use.

New Hampshire is ordinarily heavily Republican in general elections; when it is not, as in the 1990s, the Republicans are in deep trouble. Indeed, this is one of the few states which has more registered Republicans than Democrats. The Republican heart of the state is the Merrimack Valley, with the two biggest cities of Manchester and Nashua. Old Yankee towns farther north are also heavily Republican, and so are the suburbs just north of the Massachusetts line. More Democratic is the western edge of the state along the Connecticut River, which partakes a bit of the Ben & Jerry's Vermont liberalism, and Portsmouth and smaller old mill towns along the Maine border. The highest Democratic percentages in New Hampshire often come from Hanover, home of Dartmouth College; the highest Republican percentages from Dixville Notch in the far north, whose 28 voters troop in at one minute after midnight and cast the nation's first recorded votes every presidential year.

In 1996, New Hampshire Republicans dealt Bob Dole a crushing blow; he lost the Granite State primary 27%–26% to Pat Buchanan. Lamar Alexander came in third at 23%, and the results were widely perceived as the beginning of a wide-open race for the nomination.

Congressional districting. With only slight changes, New Hampshire's two congressional districts basically have had the same boundaries since 1881, neatly separating the Merrimack River mill towns of Manchester and Nashua, the state's largest cities. That was done originally to split the Catholic Democratic vote, but now both cities are high-tech Republican towns. So the split now gives Democrats a chance for upset victories in either seat.

The People: Est. Pop. 1996: 1,162,000; Pop. 1990: 1,109,252, up 4.8% 1990–1996. 0.4% of U.S. total, 42d largest; 49% rural. Median age: 35.1 years. 12% 65 years and over. 97.3% White; 1% Black; 1% Asian; 1% Hispanic origin. Households: 59.7% married couple families; 30% married couple fams. w. children; 50% college educ.; median household income: $36,329; per capita income: $15,959; 68.2% owner occupied housing; median house value: $129,400; median monthly rent: $479. 4.2% Unemployment. 1996 Voting age pop.: 871,000. 1996 Turnout: 499,053; 57% of VAP. Registered voters (1996): 713,236; 206,273 D (30%), 276,129 R (39%), 230,834 unaffiliated and minor parties (32%).

Political Lineup: Governor, Jeanne Shaheen (D); Secy. of State, William M. Gardner (D); Atty. Gen., Philip McLaughlin (D); Treasurer, Georgie A. Thomas (R); State Senate, 24 (9 D and 15 R); Senate President, Joseph Delahunty (R); State House, 400 (145 D, 253 R and 2 I); House Speaker, Donna Sytek (R). Senators, Bob Smith (R) and Judd Gregg (R). Representatives 2 (2 R).

Elections Division: 603-271-3242; **Filing Deadline for U.S. Congress:** June 12, 1998.

1996 Presidential Vote

Clinton (D)	246,166	(49%)
Dole (R)	196,486	(39%)
Perot (I)	48,387	(10%)
Other	8,014	(2%)

1996 Republican Presidential Primary

Buchanan (R)	56,921	(27%)
Dole (R)	54,840	(26%)
Alexander (R)	47,216	(23%)
Forbes (R)	25.535	(12%)
Lugar (R)	10,862	(5%)
Other	13,923	(8%)

1992 Presidential Vote

Clinton (D)	209,040	(39%)
Bush (R)	202,484	(38%)
Perot (I)	121,337	(23%)

GOVERNOR

Gov. Jeanne Shaheen (D)

Elected 1996, term expires Jan. 2001; b. Jan. 28, 1947, St. Charles, MO; home, Madbury; Shippensburg U., B.A. 1969; U. of MS, M.A. 1973; Protestant; married (William).

Career: Teacher, 1969–71; Admin. Asst., U. of NH, 1973–74, Parents' Assoc. Program Coordinator, 1982–86; Mgr., seasonal retail business, 1973–76; Campaign Mgr., Carter/Mondale NH Pres. Campaign, 1979–80, Hart NH Pres. Campaign, 1983–84, McEachern NH Gov. Campaign, 1986–88; NH Senate, 1990–96.

Office: State House, Concord 03301, 603-271-2121; Fax: 603-271-2130; Web site: www.state.nh.us.

Election Results

1996 gen.	Jeanne Shaheen (D)	284,131	(57%)
	Ovide Lamontagne (R)	196,278	(40%)
	Others	16,514	(3%)
1996 prim.	Jeanne Shaheen (D)	52,293	(86%)
	Sid Lovett (D)	4,289	(7%)
	Brian Woodworth (D)	2,613	(4%)
	Others	1,847	(3%)
1994 gen.	Steve Merrill (R)	218,134	(70%)
	Wayne D. King (D)	79,686	(26%)
	Steve Winter (Lib)	13,709	(4%)

SENATORS

Sen. Bob Smith (R)

Elected 1990, seat up 2002; b. Mar. 30, 1941, Trenton, NJ; home, Tuftonboro; Trenton Jr. Col., A.A. 1963, Lafayette Col., B.A. 1965, Long Beach St. Col., 1968–69; Catholic; married (Mary Jo).

Career: Navy, 1965–67 (Vietnam), Naval Reserves, 1962–65, 1967–69; High schl. teacher, 1975–84; Real Estate agent, 1975–84; Chmn., Gov. Wentworth Schl. Bd., 1978–83; U.S. House of Reps., 1984–90.

DC Office: 307 DSOB 20510, 202-224-2841; Fax: 202-224-1353; e-mail: opinion@smith.senate.gov.

State Offices: Berlin, 603-752-2600; Manchester, 603-634-5000; Portsmouth, 603-433-1667.

Committees: *Armed Services* (5th of 10 R): Acquisition & Technology; Sea Power; Strategic Forces (Chmn.). *Environment & Public Works* (3rd of 10 R): Superfund, Waste Control & Risk Assessment (Chmn.); Transportation & Infrastructure. *Ethics (Select)* (Chmn.). *Governmental Affairs* (8th of 9 R): International Security, Proliferation & Federal Services; Permanent Subcommittee on Investigations.

Group Ratings

	ADA	ACLU	AFS	LCV	CFA	CON	NFIB	COC	ACU	NTLC	CHC
1996	5	28	0	23	36	42	100	92	100	100	100
1995	0	—	0	7	0	29	—	100	100	—	—

National Journal Ratings

	1995 LIB		1995 CONS	1996 LIB		1996 CONS
Economic	0%	—	88%	18%	—	79%
Social	0%	—	88%	0%	—	72%
Foreign	0%	—	92%	0%	—	74%

Key Votes of the 104th Congress

1. Reduce Medicare Growth $	Y	5. Flag Amendment	Y	9. Anti-Missile Defense	Y
2. Lmt. Prod. Liab. Damages	Y	6. Endangered Species	N	10. Cuban Embargo	Y
3. Increase Min. Wage	N	7. Gay Employment Rights	N	11. Bar Bosnia Troop $	Y
4. Welfare Reform	Y	8. Ovrd. Part. Birth Veto	Y	12. Cut Vietnam Aid	Y

Election Results

1996 general	Bob Smith (R)	242,257	(49%)	($1,929,468)
	Dick Swett (D)	227,355	(46%)	($1,558,563)
	Ken Blevens (Lib)	22,261	(5%)	
1996 primary	Bob Smith (R)	85,223	(97%)	
	Others	2,354	(3%)	
1990 general	Bob Smith (R)	189,792	(65%)	($1,419,127)
	John A. Durkin (D)	91,299	(32%)	($319,879)
	Other	10,302	(3%)	

Sen. Judd Gregg (R)

Elected 1992, seat up 1998; b. Feb. 14, 1947, Nashua; home, Greenfield; Columbia U., A.B. 1969, Boston U., J.D. 1972, LL.M. 1975; Protestant; married (Kathleen).

Career: Practicing atty., 1976–80; NH Exec. Cncl., 1978–80; U.S. House of Reps., 1980–88; NH Gov., 1988–92.

DC Office: 393 RSOB 20510, 202-224-3324; Fax: 202-224-4952; e-mail: mailbox@gregg.senate.gov.

State Offices: Berlin, 603-752-2604; Concord, 603-225-7115; Manchester, 603-622-7979; Portsmouth, 603-431-2171.

Committees: *Appropriations* (10th of 15 R): Commerce, Justice, State & the Judiciary (Chmn.); Defense; Foreign Operations; Interior; Labor, Health & Human Services & Education. *Budget* (7th of 12 R). *Labor & Human Resources* (3rd of 10 R): Aging (Chmn.); Children & Families.

Group Ratings

	ADA	ACLU	AFS	LCV	CFA	CON	NFIB	COC	ACU	NTLC	CHC
1996	5	17	0	38	29	89	90	92	75	90	100
1995	0	—	0	21	6	86	—	95	87	—	—

National Journal Ratings

	1995 LIB		1995 CONS	1996 LIB		1996 CONS
Economic	21%	—	74%	34%	—	63%
Social	27%	—	71%	33%	—	62%
Foreign	47%	—	52%	38%	—	58%

Key Votes of the 104th Congress

1. Reduce Medicare Growth $	Y	5. Flag Amendment	Y	9. Anti-Missile Defense	N
2. Lmt. Prod. Liab. Damages	Y	6. Endangered Species	Y	10. Cuban Embargo	Y
3. Increase Min. Wage	Y	7. Gay Employment Rights	N	11. Bar Bosnia Troop $	Y
4. Welfare Reform	Y	8. Ovrd. Part. Birth Veto	Y	12. Cut Vietnam Aid	Y

Election Results

1992 general	Judd Gregg (R)	249,591	(48%)	($875,675)
	John Rauh (D)	234,982	(45%)	($1,109,467)
	Katherine Alexander (Lib)	18,214	(4%)	
	Others	15,629	(3%)	
1992 primary	Judd Gregg (R)	57,141	(50%)	
	Harold Eckman (R)	43,264	(38%)	
	Jean T. White (R)	10,642	(9%)	
	Others	3,690	(3%)	
1986 general	Warren Rudman (R)	154,090	(63%)	($831,098)
	Endicott Peabody (D)	79,222	(32%)	($307,760)

FIRST DISTRICT

The 1st Congressional District of New Hampshire includes Manchester, its suburbs and the seacoast. Manchester was once a heavily French Canadian textile mill town, which also had the nation's largest percentage of Greek-Americans; in the 1980s it became a fast-growing high-tech city. There are new shopping malls here and in towns on the Massachusetts border. Portsmouth has restored its downtown to some of its historic splendor; Wal-Mart, drawn by the combination of new affluence and down-home tastes, built its first New England stores in this area. There is a Democratic heritage here, especially in Manchester, but in general elections this is usually Republican territory.

The congressman from the 1st District is John Sununu Jr., a Republican elected in 1996, one of eight children of former New Hampshire Governor and White House Chief of Staff John Sununu. The younger Sununu grew up in Salem, became an engineer, worked for a microwave manufacturer, a high-tech consulting firm, the building automation manufacturer Teletrol and as a consultant for JHS Associates—high-tech, small-firm New Hampshire. In April 1996, when Congressman Bill Zeliff announced for governor, Sununu and seven other Republicans got into the House race. The best known was four-term Manchester Mayor Raymond "The Wiz" Wieczorek, builder of the new airport and endorsee of the *Manchester Union Leader*. But Wieczorek was 67 and did not carry much punch outside of Manchester. Another was Jack Heath, news director of WMUR-TV who often appeared on the station. He said he was concerned about his children's generation: the federal government "is working against them, not for them. The government was never meant to be this big." Heath was backed by heads of Cabletron Systems and New Hampshire International Speedway. He carried many towns in between Manchester and the coast and in the north country. Sununu called for tax simplification and a capital gains tax cut and a devolution of education programs to the states. This was an exceedingly close race: Sununu won with 28%, Wieczorek had 27% and Heath 26%.

In the general election Sununu faced Democratic state chairman Joe Keefe, who won 40% against Bob Smith in 1988 and 45% against Zeliff in 1990. Keefe raised more money than Sununu, with the help of PACs, and campaigned on "kitchen table" issues—college tuition tax credits, and opposition to cutting Head Start. Sununu contrasted his background as an engineer and businessman with Keefe's as a lawyer. Keefe made a strong race, but Sununu won 50%–47%. Keefe carried the eastern part of the district around Portsmouth, Rochester and Durham, and also won in Manchester, but Sununu won big in the Manchester suburbs and the north country.

In the House Sununu got a seat on the Budget Committee and also serves on Government Reform and Oversight, and Small Business. He started to work on local projects—the Portsmouth Naval Shipyard, the Manchester Airport Access Road, the Conway Bypass—and with Charlie Bass of the 2d District co-sponsored the Northern Forest Stewardship Act. In March 1997 Keefe said he would not run again; possible Democratic contenders for 1998 include state Senator Burt Cohen and Rockingham County attorney Bill Hart.

The People: Pop. 1990: 554,303; 45% rural; 11% age 65+; 97% White; 1% Black; 1% Asian; 1% Hispanic origin. Households: 60% married couple families; 29% married couple fams. w. children; 51% college educ.; median household income: $36,511; per capita income: $16,044; median gross rent: $555; median house value: $132,600.

1996 Presidential Vote

Clinton (D)	121,602	(48%)
Dole (R)	101,295	(40%)
Perot (I)	23,898	(10%)
Other	3,937	(2%)

1992 Presidential Vote

Bush (R)	104,653	(39%)
Clinton (D)	101,415	(38%)
Perot (I)	61,571	(23%)

Rep. John E. Sununu (R)

Elected 1996; b. Sept. 10, 1964, Boston, MA; home, Bedford; M.I.T., B.S. 1986, M.S. 1987; Harvard U., M.B.A. 1991; Catholic; married (Kitty).

Career: Design Engineer, Remec Inc., 1987–89; Mgr. & Operations Specialist, Pittiglio, Rabin, Todd & McGrath, 1990–92; C.F.O. & Dir. of Operations, Teletrol Systems Inc., 1993–95; Consultant, JHS Associates, 1995–96.

DC Office: 1229 LHOB 20515, 202-225-5456; Fax: 202-225-5822.

District Offices: Manchester, 603-641-9536.

Committees: *Budget* (23rd of 24 R). *Government Reform & Oversight* (19th of 24 R): Government Management, Information & Technology; National Economic Growth, Natural Resources & Regulatory Affairs (Vice Chmn.). *Small Business* (18th of 19 R): Government Programs & Oversight.

Group Ratings and Key Votes: Newly Elected

Election Results

1996 general	John E. Sununu (R)	123,939	(50%)	($545,865)
	Joseph F. Keefe (D)	115,462	(47%)	($580,749)
	Others	8,335	(3%)	
1996 primary	John E. Sununu (R)	14,768	(28%)	
	Raymond J. Wieczorek (R)	14,152	(27%)	
	Jack Heath (R)	13,678	(26%)	
	Tom Colantuono (R)	5,033	(9%)	
	Vivian Clark (R)	2,174	(4%)	
	Others	3,233	(6%)	
1994 general	William H. Zeliff, Jr. (R)	97,017	(66%)	($868,042)
	Bill Verge (D)	42,481	(29%)	($139,023)
	Others	8,324	(6%)	

SECOND DISTRICT

The 2d Congressional District includes Nashua, the state's second largest city, and Salem, both right on the Massachusetts line and solidly conservative: people came here to get away from "Taxachusetts." It also includes, farther from Boston and readier for taxes and government services, the state capital of Concord and towns in the Connecticut River Valley, from Keene near Mount Monadnock north to Hanover, home of Dartmouth College, an area of artists' retreats: from that of sculptor August Saint Gaudens a century ago to writer J. D. Salinger's today. The 2d runs to the farthest north country: Dixville Notch and the paper mill town of Berlin, the Mount Washington Hotel and cog railway and the resort of Bretton Woods where the world monetary system, and the basis for post-World War II prosperity, was established in a conference in 1944.

The congressman from the 2d District is Charles Bass, who has a long political pedigree: his grandfather Robert Bass was elected governor in 1910 and his father Perkins Bass served in the House from 1955–63. Charles Bass, after graduating from Dartmouth, worked for Maine Congressmen William Cohen and David Emery, then returned to New Hampshire to run for

Congress in 1980: he finished third in the primary, with 22%, to 34% for now-Senator Judd Gregg and 25% for liberal Susan McLane. With his two brothers, he ran a factory making architectural products and served in the state legislature—in the House from 1982 and the Senate from 1988—where he wrote the state's voluntary campaign spending law which called on U.S. House candidates to observe $500,000 total limit for both primary and general elections. But he angered many in 1990 when he helped elect a liberal Republican as Senate leader.

In 1994 Bass ran in the Republican primary for the right to oppose Democratic Congressman Dick Swett, elected in 1990 when party leaders and Nancy Sununu attacked the personal conduct of incumbent Chuck Douglas, and reelected as Bill Clinton carried the state in 1992. Bass ran as a moderate—pro-choice on abortion, but also a fiscal conservative, a supporter of welfare cuts and tougher sentencing. Bass ran only a few points better in the primary than he had in 1980, but his 29% this time was enough to beat former NRA consultant Mike Hammond (backed by the *Union Leader*) with 24%. Swett had a moderate voting record, but Bass attacked him for voting with Clinton 90% of the time and for supporting Democrats when his vote really mattered; Bass ran a TV spot of Swett and Clinton embracing. He also attacked Swett for switching on gun control and supporting the assault weapons ban and for raising most of his money out of state, much of it generated by his father-in-law, California Congressman Tom Lantos. Swett spent over $1 million, while Bass adhered to the voluntary spending limits and spent $448,000; but Bass won 51%–46%. Swett carried Concord, Hanover and other towns on the Connecticut River, the Keene area and the mill town of Berlin, but Bass carried practically everything else.

In the House Bass has a conservative record on economics and a moderate record on cultural and foreign issues. On campaign finance, he wants to allow states to set voluntary spending limits and to limit PAC contributions to $1,000. He co-sponsored the bipartisan Northern Forest Stewardship Act, to protect forestlands and timber-dependent jobs in northern New England and Upstate New York, where most land is privately owned. He also got passed unanimously a bill to ensure that the Fish and Wildlife Service work only with willing land sellers in New Hampshire and Vermont while assembling the Silvio Conte Refuge; this was vetoed by President Clinton. The House passed his amendment for an Inspector General in the White House, which would in effect hold the highest office to the same laws and regulations that ordinary American people and now also Congress must abide.

In 1996 Bass had primary opposition again from Hammond, who had chaired Pat Buchanan's New Hampshire campaign and attacked Bass on abortion and the environment. He attacked Bass on gun control as well, though Bass voted to repeal the assault weapons ban. But Senator Bob Smith and Majority Leader Dick Armey endorsed Bass, and he won by the much larger margin of 66%–27%. In the general election he was pressed hard by Deborah "Arnie" Arnesen, the Democratic gubernatorial candidate in 1992. Arnesen raised and spent more money than Bass and in September polls showed the race even. Bass called her a big-government liberal and recalled her backing of a 6% state income tax four years before. Arnesen said Bass was not the moderate she had known in the state Senate who usually voted with her. Bass won by 51%–43%, with the same configurations of support as in 1994.

After the election Bass got more committee assignments, staying on Budget (which now has both New Hampshire Republicans) and adding Transportation and Infrastructure and Intelligence. An instrument-rated pilot, he is on the Aviation Subcommittee. He reintroduced his Northern Forests and Conte Refuge bills. Possible 1998 opponents include Mary Rauh, wife of 1996 Senate candidate John Rauh, state Representative Peter Burling and state Senator Sylvia Larsen.

The People: Pop. 1990: 554,949; 53% rural; 11% age 65+; 97% White; 1% Black; 1% Asian; 1% Hispanic origin. Households: 61% married couple families; 30% married couple fams. w. children; 50% college educ.; median household income: $36,145; per capita income: $15,874; median gross rent: $541; median house value: $125,500.

1996 Presidential Vote

Clinton (D)	124,564	(50%)
Dole (R)	95,191	(38%)
Perot (I)	24,489	(10%)
Other	4,077	(2%)

1992 Presidential Vote

Clinton (D)	107,625	(40%)
Bush (R)	97,831	(37%)
Perot (I)	59,766	(22%)

Rep. Charles F. Bass (R)

Elected 1994; b. Jan. 8, 1952, Boston, MA; home, Peterborough; Dartmouth, A.B. 1974; Episcopalian; married (Lisa).

Career: Field worker, U.S. Rep. William Cohen, 1974; Legis. Asst., U.S. Rep. David Emery, 1975–76, Chief of Staff, 1976–79; Vice Pres., High Standard Inc., 1980–93; Chmn., Columbia Architectural Products, 1980–93; NH House of Reps., 1982–88; NH Senate, 1988–92.

DC Office: 218 CHOB 20515, 202-225-5206; Fax: 202-225-2946; e-mail: cbass@hr.house.gov.

District Offices: Concord, 603-226-0249; Keene, 603-358-4094; Littleton, 603-444-1271; Nashua, 603-889-8772.

Committees: *Budget* (16th of 24 R). *Transportation & Infrastructure* (24th of 40 R): Aviation; Surface Transportation. *Intelligence (Select)* (8th of 9 R): Human Intelligence, Analysis & Counterintelligence.

Group Ratings

	ADA	ACLU	AFS	LCV	CFA	CON	NFIB	COC	ACU	NTLC	CHC
1996	0	12	0	23	23	42	100	100	100	98	73
1995	15	—	—	6	38	87	—	96	72	—	—

National Journal Ratings

	1995 LIB		1995 CONS	1996 LIB		1996 CONS
Economic	0%	—	74%	0%	—	82%
Social	55%	—	43%	46%	—	52%
Foreign	45%	—	52%	38%	—	60%

Key Votes of the 104th Congress

1. Reduce Medicare Growth $	Y	5. Flag Amendment	Y	9. Cuban Embargo	Y
2. Ovrd. Product Liab. Veto	Y	6. Drop EPA Limits	Y	10. Bar Bosnia Troop $	Y
3. Increase Min. Wage	N	7. Repeal Assault-Weap. Ban	Y	11. Cut Anti-Missile Defense	N
4. Welfare Reform	Y	8. Ovrd. Part. Birth Veto	Y	12. Bar U.N. Uniforms	Y

Election Results

1996 general	Charles F. Bass (R)	122,957	(51%)	($625,147)
	Deborah (Arnie) Arnesen (D)	105,824	(43%)	($706,623)
	Carole Lamirande (I)	10,753	(4%)	($7,091)
	Others	3,961	(2%)	
1996 primary	Charles F. Bass (R)	30,403	(66%)	
	Mike Hammond (R)	12,073	(26%)	
	Others	3,254	(7%)	
1994 general	Charles F. Bass (R)	83,121	(51%)	($448,431)
	Dick Swett (D)	74,243	(46%)	($1,029,471)
	Others	4,209	(3%)	

NEW JERSEY

New Jersey has spent much of its history betwixt and between. It was named by King James II, then Duke of York, for the Channel Island on which he was sheltered during the English Civil War. It was plagued in its early years by rival claims from its neighbors and argues even today with New York over who owns the Statue of Liberty and Ellis Island; in early 1997 an arbitrator recommended giving New York Ellis Island's original five acres of bedrock and New Jersey the 22 acres of fill land. New Jersey's largest cities lie on the swampy sides of America's two greatest harbor rivers, overshadowed for years by the metropolises of New York and Philadelphia—"a valley of humility between two mountains of conceit," its neighbor Benjamin Franklin called it. But New Jersey has much to say for itself. It is "a sort of laboratory in which the best blood is prepared for other communities to thrive on," Woodrow Wilson said when he was governor, just a tad defensively; it is "the fighting center of the most important social questions of our time."

Today, New Jersey is the nation's ninth most populous state: it boomed in the 1980s, suffered sharply in the early 1990s recession and now has recovered more than its neighbors. This is high-tech country: New Jersey's pharmaceutical firms lead the nation in sophisticated research, and it is a leader in telecommunications as well. Within its close boundaries is great diversity, geographically from beaches to mountains, demographically from old Quaker stock to new Hispanics, economically from inner city slums to hunt country mansions. New York writers are inclined to look on New Jersey as a land of 1940s diners and 1950s pizza restaurants, but New Jersey comes far closer to resembling America than does Manhattan, even if some of its traffic signals are arrayed horizontally rather than vertically and its accents can be incomprehensible to outsiders. The Jersey City row houses seen on emerging from the Holland Tunnel, many renovated by Wall Street commuters and Latin immigrants, give way within a few miles to the lonely skyscrapers of Newark and comfortably packed middle-income suburbs. Nearby are the horse country around Far Hills, the university town of Princeton, old industrial cities like Paterson, and dozens of suburban towns and small factory cities where people work and raise families over generations; an hour from Philadelphia and two hours from Manhattan is Atlantic City, with more gambling revenues in 1995 ($3.7 billion) than the Las Vegas strip.

In the last 20 years, a new New Jersey has sprouted: many of the oil tank farms and swamplands of the Jersey Meadows have become sports palaces and office complexes; the intersection of I-78 and I-287 has become a major shopping and office edge city; U.S. 1 north from Princeton to North Brunswick has become one of the nation's high-tech centers; the flat vegetable fields once dotted with gas station junctions now have tourist attractions like Great Adventure amusement park. For the first census year since 1840, New Jersey in 1990 had more people (7.7 million) than New York City (7.3 million); it had far more than metropolitan Philadelphia (5.9 million), and it has been generating more new jobs than either New York or Pennsylvania. Growth is strongest in the interior away from New York City and Philadelphia, and New Jersey increasingly has an identity of its own. It is the home of Bruce Springsteen and of big league football, basketball and hockey franchises, of some of America's largest gambling casinos, of the world's longest expanse of boardwalks on the Jersey Shore from Cape May to Sandy Hook.

State government played an important role in building New Jersey identity and pride. Governor Brendan Byrne in the 1970s started the Meadowlands sports complex and got casino gambling legalized in Atlantic City. In the 1980s, Governor Tom Kean started education reforms and promoted the state shamelessly. The revolt against Governor Jim Florio's tax increase in 1990 was led by the first all-New Jersey talk radio station and took on national significance, and for the first time since Wilson New Jersey has produced politicians of national

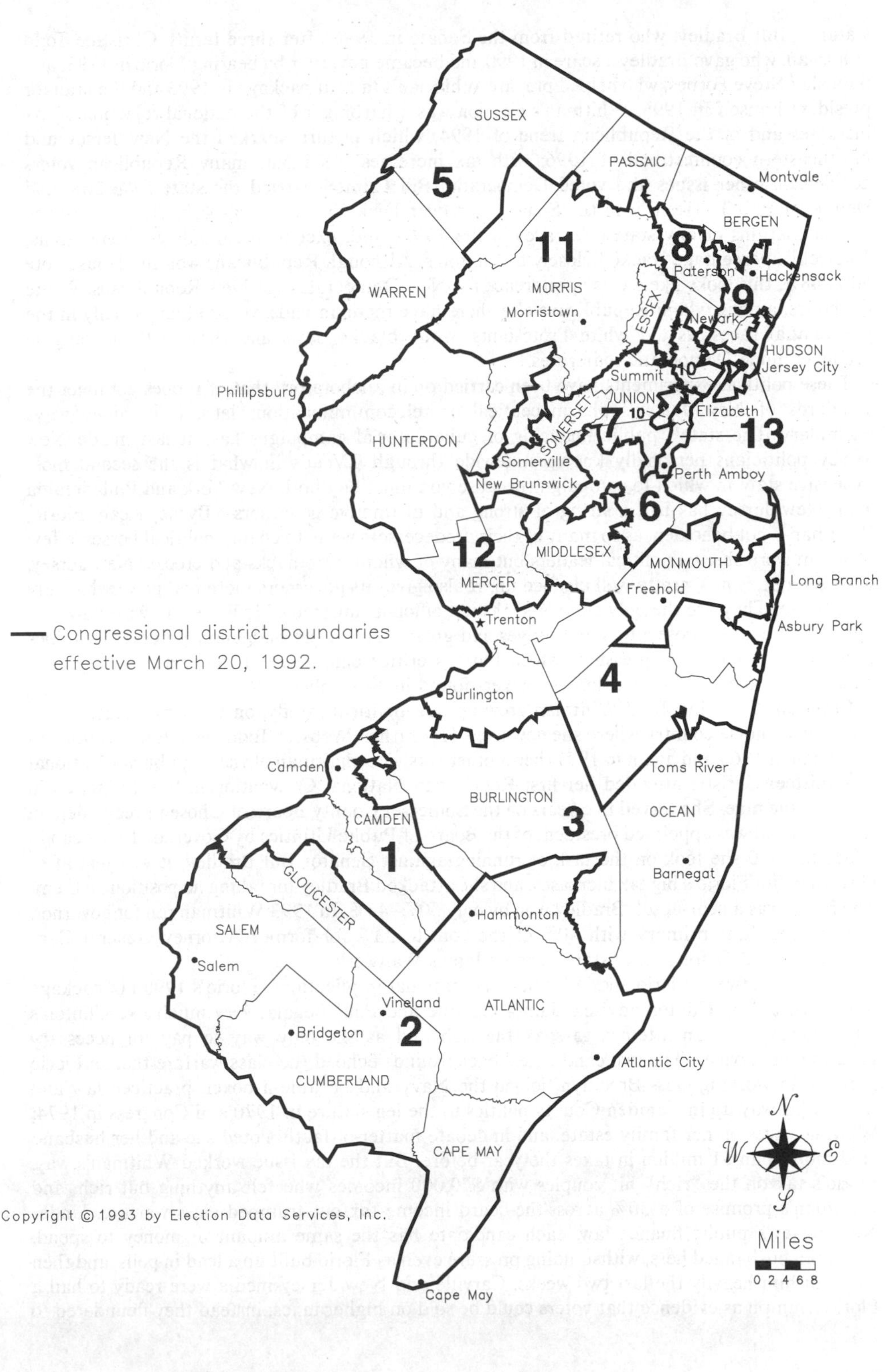
SUSSEX
PASSAIC
Montvale
5
BERGEN
11
8
Paterson
Hackensack
WARREN
MORRIS
9
Morristown
ESSEX
Newark
HUDSON
Jersey City
Summit
10
Phillipsburg
UNION
SOMERSET
7
10
Elizabeth
13
HUNTERDON
Somerville
Perth Amboy
New Brunswick
6
12
MIDDLESEX
MONMOUTH
MERCER
Long Branch
Freehold
Trenton
Asbury Park
Congressional district boundaries effective March 20, 1992.
4
Burlington
Toms River
Camden
BURLINGTON
OCEAN
CAMDEN
3
1
Barnegat
GLOUCESTER
Hammonton
SALEM
Salem
Vineland
ATLANTIC
Bridgeton
2
Atlantic City
CUMBERLAND
N
W
E
S
CAPE MAY
Miles
0 2 4 6 8
Cape May

stature—Bill Bradley, who retired from the Senate in 1996 after three terms, Christine Todd Whitman, who gave Bradley a scare in 1990 and became governor by beating Florio in 1993, and publisher Steve Forbes, who helped prepare Whitman's tax cut package in 1993 and then ran for president himself in 1996. Whitman's election was a harbinger of the national rejection of tax increases and of the Republican trend of 1994, which in turn sparked the New Jersey and Northeastern countertrend of 1996: with tax increases ruled out, many Republican voters decided on other issues and voted Democratic. Bill Clinton carried the state 54%–36% and Democrat Bob Torricelli won the Senate race over Dick Zimmer 53%–43%. These were the largest margins of any statewide races in the 1990s and, except in candidates' home areas, Torricelli's percentage tracked closely to Clinton's. Although Republicans won the House vote 50%–48%, this looks like a clear preference for New Democrats over New Republicans. White Catholics, among whom Republicans elsewhere have made inroads, voted almost evenly in the presidential races, as did white Protestants, while blacks, Jews and those with no religion produced huge Democratic majorities.

These political experiments have been carried on in a laboratory that, if it does not meet the standards of New Jersey's pharmaceutical or telecommunications labs, is in many ways exemplary. The state's public financing of gubernatorial campaigns has, at last, made New Jersey politicians personally known statewide through TV ads in what is the second most expensive state in which to campaign (because you must buy both New York and Philadelphia TV). New Jersey has had a string of strong and distinctive governors—Byrne, Kean, Florio, Whitman—not beholden, as so many of their predecessors were, to county political bosses, a few of whom were shrewd political leaders but many of whom were hacks and crooks. New Jersey, once corrupt, is now pretty well cleaned up. It also gives its governors more real power than any other state. They are the only statewide elected officials, unremovable by recall, with power to appoint all county prosecutors and judges and great clout in the budgetary process. This does insulate governors from pressure, which Florio's critics bemoaned in the early 1990s. But it makes them accountable, as Florio's backers found in November 1993.

Governor. Christine Todd Whitman grew up in a political family, on the same estate in the New Jersey horse country where she now lives. Her father, Webster Todd, was state Republican chairman in 1964 and again in 1977; her mother was vice chairman of the Republican National Committee. Christie attended her first Republican National Convention in San Francisco in 1956, at age nine. She served five years on the Somerset County Board of Chosen Freeholders in the 1980s and was appointed president of the Board of Public Utilities by Governor Tom Kean in 1988. In 1990 she took on the task of running against Senator Bill Bradley; it was just after Governor Jim Florio's big tax increases, and she attacked Bradley for taking no position on them. The result was a near-upset: Bradley won by only 50%–47%. In 1993 Whitman ran for governor, winning the June primary with 40% of the vote to 33% for former Attorney General Cary Edwards and 24% for former state Senator James Wallwork.

The race between Florio and Whitman had national implications. Florio's 1990 tax package was marketed by Clinton advisers James Carville and Paul Begala, very much like Clinton's 1993 package, as an attempt to soak the rich and as the only way to pay for necessary government services. The two candidates' backgrounds echoed the class warfare theme: Florio grew up in working class Brooklyn, joined the Navy and became a boxer, practiced law and worked his way up in Camden County politics to the legislature in 1970 and Congress in 1974; Whitman lives on her family estate, and in debate matter-of-factly noted she and her husband paid more than $1 million in taxes the year before. But the tax issue worked Whitman's way. Florio's tax on the "rich" hit couples with $70,000 incomes who felt anything but rich, and Whitman's promise of a 30% across-the-board income tax cut trumped class warfare. Under New Jersey's public finance law, each candidate has the same amount of money to spend; Whitman husbanded hers, withstanding pressure even as Florio built up a lead in polls, and then outspent him heavily the last two weeks. Carville and New Jersey media were ready to hail a Florio triumph as evidence that voters could be sold on higher taxes; instead they floundered to explain Whitman's 49%–48% victory.

As governor, Whitman delivered on her tax cuts a year ahead of schedule. Democrats charged that local governments would increase property taxes to make up for drops in state aid. Whitman argued that property taxes rose by an average of 4.2% in her first three years as compared to 5.4% in Florio's, and said she and the legislature made property taxes deductible on the state income tax and were aiding local governments in keeping costs down. Critics also charged she was underfunding state pensions; she said they were overfunded, and in February 1997 proposed a $2.9 billion bond issue—the largest in state history—to fund them to 2056 and offset lost tax revenues. On crime issues, Whitman signed the first Megan's Law—inspired by the case of a New Jersey girl murdered by a released sexual offender—plus the "three strikes and you're in" law which mandates a life sentence for any violent criminal convicted for the third time. She set up boot camps for juvenile offenders. She privatized health care for prison medical centers. On the environment she got dredging and environmental bond issues passed, as well as legislation providing $10 million for the preservation of Sterling Forest. Her 1996 Work First welfare reform bill limits benefits to five years and exacts tougher work requirements; it stalled in the legislature, which wanted to preserve local control of welfare programs, but was finally signed into law in March 1997. On education, Whitman opened charter schools and tried to satisfy a state Supreme Court ruling requiring equalized school funding by pushing through a plan that emphasized stricter curriculum standards; but in May 1997 the court struck down her proposal and ordered the state to increase spending for the poorest districts. On cultural issues Whitman is a liberal. She supports affirmative action programs and is outspokenly in favor of abortion rights and opposed the partial-birth abortion ban.

Whitman has become a national political figure. In January 1995 she delivered the Republican response to the President's State of the Union message—the first time a governor has done so. In 1996 there was speculation she might be the vice presidential nominee, or even run for president in 2000. But her stance on abortion—not just her position but her tone—would inspire rage among many delegates at any Republican convention.

In any case, Whitman is running for reelection in 1997. Her job rating was around 50% going into the election, and there was plenty of appreciation of her tax cuts. But New Jersey's lurch toward Bill Clinton in 1996 could signal more trouble for her than originally suggested. Her opponent is James McGreevey, Middlesex County state senator and mayor of Woodbridge, who edged out 1st District Congressman Rob Andrews and Morris County Prosecutor Michael Murphy in the June primary. McGreevey, during his primary campaign, attacked Whitman's plan to sell bonds to shore up the state pension system as "government by gimmickry," and proposed amending the state constitution to allow the election of an insurance commissioner to deal with New Jersey's highest-in-the-nation auto insurance costs. McGreevey also said he wants to "ultimately abolish" local property taxes as the primary funding for education, and proposed holding state-wide referenda on education plans. Both Whitman and McGreevey promised not to make personal attacks, but New Jersey has a tradition of rough campaigns. Whitman is certain to spotlight McGreevey's vote for former Governor Jim Florio's unpopular tax increase. This will be a race to see whether the Republican Party, Whitman version, still has vitality in the Northeast.

Senior Senator. Frank Lautenberg is one of a species common in the late 19th Century and the late 20th Century as well—the millionaire who becomes a senator. In 1980 he was a Democratic moneygiver and member of the board of the New York and New Jersey Port Authority; in 1994 he was reelected to a third term in the Senate at 70. He has shown he knows how to play the game—and that it helps to come in with a large pile of chips. Lautenberg grew up poor, the son of an immigrant silk worker in Paterson. He served in the Army Signal Corps in World War II and says he would never have gone to college without the G.I. Bill of Rights. In 1952, he started a company called Automatic Data Processing, which by the mid-1990s had almost 30,000 employees and processed the payroll for nearly 10% of private sector jobs in the United States—a brilliant success story. When an open Senate seat came up in 1982, Lautenberg ran, starting off as an unknown, but willing to spend $5 million of his own money spotlighting his high-tech experience. He beat several professional politicians in the primary and upset Republican Congresswoman Millicent Fenwick, 51%–48%, in the general. In 1994 he was a Republican target and was opposed by Assembly Speaker Chuck Haytaian, fresh from helping pass Governor Christie Whitman's tax cuts and backing a flat tax. Lautenberg campaigned on ocean dumping, the Brady handgun-control bill, college loans for middle-class students and opposition to Clinton's taxes; he got mileage from denouncing Haytaian for appearing on the program of WABC talk show host Bob Grant after Grant allegedly made racist remarks. Ross Perot, Lautenberg's fellow computer entrepreneur, endorsed him as "one of the few members of the Senate who know how the real world works." Money helped: Lautenberg spent $8 million to Haytaian's $5 million, and in a Republican year the Democrat won, 50%–47%.

Lautenberg believes government helped him and many others work their way up, and he has a solid liberal voting record; he was one of ten Senators to oppose the unfunded mandates bill in 1995. He has bucked party lines on occasion; when Jim Florio's tax increase was blazingly unpopular, Lautenberg obdurately refused to vote for the Clinton tax increase in 1993. As chairman (now ranking minority member) of the Transportation Appropriations Subcommittee, he sponsored the laws that banned smoking first on two-hour, then on all domestic flights. He has been the Senate's leader on anti-tobacco initiatives ever since; in 1994 he passed a bill banning smoking in all federally funded children's facilities and sponsored legislation that would force the tobacco industry to pay for states' costs associated with tobacco-caused illnesses. He was a pioneer on the lobbyist gift ban as well. He is a big booster of money for Amtrak and high-speed trains, and for maintaining highway formulas that help the Northeast. He was the author of the law pushing states to adopt the 21-year-old drinking age. As ranking Democrat on the Environment subcommittee on Superfund, he opposed the Republicans' 1996 bill limiting retroactive liability; he also worked on the Clean Air and Safe Drinking Water Acts. His first bill was for federal funding of computer instruction in schools. He wrote a law for trade retaliation against countries that steal U.S. inventions. He is a strong backer of gun control and author of the 1996 law barring those convicted of domestic abuse from possessing firearms.

The 1994 election cost Lautenberg his chairmanships, but his key vote for Tom Daschle as Democratic leader has increased his influence. In 1997 he became ranking Democrat on the Budget Committee, where he takes a harder and more adversarial role than some of his predecessors. He was a strong opponent of the balanced budget amendment and a strong critic of Republicans' reliance on Congressional Budget Office projections, yet he participated in the 1997 budget negotiations and helped shepherd the deal through the committee. In February 1996, when four F-16s nearly collided with civilian planes off New Jersey, he called two Air Force generals into his office and got them to change the Air Force flight patterns. Lautenberg comes up for reelection in 2000, when he turns 76. But don't count him out; with Bradley retired, he has been getting more air time from New York TV stations.

Junior Senator. The junior Senator from New Jersey is Bob Torricelli, elected after a furious contest in 1996. He grew up in Franklin Lakes in north Jersey, graduated from Rutgers and the Kennedy School at Harvard and in 1975, at 24, became an aide to New Jersey Governor Brendan Byrne. Three years later he was working for Vice President Walter Mondale; he managed the decisive Carter-Mondale victory over Edward Kennedy in the 1980 Illinois primary and argued party rules with Kennedy's Harold Ickes at the convention. He is aggressive, adversarial, articulate and never politically naive. In 1982, at 31, he returned home to New Jersey, raised lots of money and beat an incumbent Republican congressman in the 9th District. In the House, he took politically beneficial committee assignments: International Relations (many of his ethnic constituents had particular interest in Israel, Greece, Korea, the Philippines and Cuba) and Science (North Jersey is one of the biggest high-tech areas in the country). He is a tough party loyalist: he was one of Speaker Jim Wright's most outspoken defenders in 1989. But he can also take an independent stand: he was one of the most vocal supporters of the Gulf war resolution in 1991. He can also seize a leadership role, as he did on the 1992 Cuban

Democracy Act that tightened trade restrictions on Cuba. His ambitiousness caused him to be passed over for head of the Democratic Congressional Campaign Committee in 1990 and Democratic National Chairman in 1995—but if he had gotten either job he might not have run for the Senate.

In the Clinton years Torricelli continued to keep a high profile on foreign issues. On Haiti he favored tough sanctions: as on Cuba, the course Bill Clinton eventually took. He sought better protection of Taiwan from potential Chinese aggression; he challenged the labeling of the Iranian Mujahedin as terrorist; he opposed Clinton's 1995 agreement with Fidel Castro to restrict admission of Cuban refugees. On the House Intelligence Committee in 1995, he made national headlines when he announced that a Guatemalan military officer on the CIA payroll had been linked to the killings of an American innkeeper and a guerrilla leader in Guatemala. Colleagues charged that he broke his oath not to disclose confidential material; he said he got the information from outside sources, and in any case had an obligation to disclose a crime.

In August 1995 Bill Bradley announced his retirement, and Torricelli rushed into the race for Senate. He cleared away any Democratic opposition and raised money at a record-setting pace: $6.8 million by July 1996, spending $9 million in all, the most of any non-self-financing candidate in 1996. He had sponsored popular bills in the House—a handgun ban on those convicted of domestic violence, brokering a deal to end ocean dumping in the New Jersey Mud Dump Site, a mandated 48-hour hospital stay for childbirth, welfare reform requiring community service after two years of benefits. But Torricelli had serious opposition from 12th District Republican Congressman Dick Zimmer, a somewhat quieter but also ambitious and aggressive politician. Zimmer was solidly conservative on taxes, voting against tax increases in the New Jersey legislature and the House, but was more moderate on cultural issues—pro-choice on abortion, for environmental protection of greenfields. He led House opposition to the Space Station and the wool and mohair subsidy; he was chief sponsor of Megan's Law, requiring the disclosure of the whereabouts of released sexual offenders like the one who killed seven-year-old Megan Kanka in New Jersey. Zimmer also raised money, though more slowly than Torricelli, eventually spending $8 million; and he maneuvered deftly to keep former Governor Thomas Kean out of the Senate race.

There were some clear differences on issues here, but much of the ad campaign consisted of attacks on ethics. Torricelli hit Zimmer for supporting the assault weapons ban, Medicare "cuts," changes in student loans, renewal of ocean dumping, and constantly brought up Newt Gingrich. Zimmer attacked Torricelli for missing many votes, for liberal votes on crime, for increasing taxes; he ran ads showing Whitman endorsing him. On ethics, Zimmer attacked Torricelli for holding one fundraiser in the home of a convicted labor racketeer and another hosted by a man named as a drug user (but never prosecuted) in the Marion Barry case. Torricelli charged Zimmer with lying and said that his use of character issues showed that he had bad character. They both attacked each other for using their congressional offices for campaign purposes. Another odd story came forward, that Torricelli in the 1980s provided a home for a teenager whose father was a fugitive on charges of stealing $34 million from banks in California. Editorialists and commentators bemoaned all the attack ads, and in fact they were not terribly effective. Neither evidently were Zimmer's ads charging, sometimes in humorous style, that Torricelli was a liberal. Torricelli was going with the flow: opinion in New Jersey was clearly hostile to the Gingrich Republicans, and Zimmer did not emphasize enough the issues—abortion, environment, campaign finance—on which he disagreed with most House Republicans. After close polls during most of the campaign, Torricelli won 53%–43%, losing the western suburbs and the Jersey Shore, but piling up large margins in the counties within an hour's drive of New York and Philadelphia.

Torricelli's aggressiveness was already apparent in the Senate. Though a freshman, he was made vice chairman of the Democratic Senatorial Campaign Committee; an unusual position, evidently created to persuade Bob Kerrey to take a second term as chairman. In February 1997, he pleased many liberal Democrats by casting the deciding vote against the balanced budget amendment even though he had campaigned in favor of it. Even so, Torricelli showed himself independent of the White House by denouncing Vice President Al Gore for making fundraising calls from his office. He is a political force to be reckoned with.

Presidential politics. New Jersey has been a close state in close presidential elections most of this century, and has usually supported the winner—Kennedy in 1960, Nixon in 1968, Reagan in 1980, Bush in 1988—and only occasionally backing the loser—Dewey in 1948, Ford in 1976. Its demographic makeup is similar to New York's, but there is no huge central city here, and a lower percentage of Jews and fewer singles; hence New Jersey was closer to the national average. But in 1996 New Jersey seemed to move noticeably to the left of the nation, voting 54%–36% for Clinton. One reason is the relative absence of the new Republican base of the religious right; such voters are numerous in the vast interior of the country from the Appalachians to the Sierra Nevada and in the South Atlantic states as well, but not in the Northeast and New Jersey. Absent a change in the face the national Republican Party presents, New Jersey may find itself no longer the host of dozens of visits of presidential and vice presidential candidates.

For years, New Jersey's June presidential primary was overshadowed by California's on the same day. In 1996 California voted in March, and New Jersey did not get to the polls until two months after the nominations were sewed up. The last time New Jersey mattered much was 1984, when Walter Mondale seized on a quip by Gary Hart and took most of the state's delegates.

Congressional districting. New Jersey lost a seat in the 1990 Census and the Democrats, in control of the legislature and governor in 1991, fumbled the chance to draw new district lines before the Republicans unexpectedly won a veto-proof margin in both chambers in November 1991. Now Republicans, if Christie Whitman wins and they hold the legislature in 1997, will have a similar chance in 2001. The current plan is the product of a bipartisan commission and has produced some grotesquely-shaped districts, all for good and sufficient political reasons.

The People: Est. Pop. 1996: 7,988,000; Pop. 1990: 7,730,188, up 3.3% 1990–1996. 3.0% of U.S. total, 9th largest; 11% rural. Median age: 36.0 years. 14% 65 years and over. 74.0% White, 12.7% Black, 3.4% Asian, 9.6% Hispanic origin. Households: 56.5% married couple families; 26% married couple fams. w. children; 46% college educ.; median household income: $40,927; per capita income: $18,714; 64.9% owner occupied housing; median house value: $162,300; median monthly rent: $521. 6.2% Unemployment. 1996 Voting age pop.: 6,034,000. 1996 Turnout: 3,075,860; 51% of VAP. Registered voters (1996): 4,320,866; 1,099,722 D (26%), 866,873 R (20%), 2,354,271 unaffiliated and minor parties (55%).

Political Lineup: Governor, Christine Todd Whitman (R); Secy. of State, Lonna Hooks (D); Atty. Gen., Peter Vernier (R); Treasurer, Brian W. Clymer (R); Auditor, Richard L. Fair. State Senate, 40 (16 D and 24 R); Senate President, Donald T. DiFrancesco; General Assembly, 80 (30 D and 50 R); Assembly Speaker, Jack Collins (R). Senators, Frank R. Lautenberg (D) and Robert G. Torricelli (D). Representatives, 13 (6 D and 7 R).

Elections Division: 609-292-4251; **Filing Deadline for U.S. Congress:** April 9, 1998.

1996 Presidential Vote

Clinton (D)	1,651,019	(54%)
Dole (R)	1,102,577	(36%)
Perot (I)	261,932	(9%)
Other	59,424	(2%)

1996 Republican Presidential Primary

Dole (R)	180,412	(82%)
Buchanan (R)	23,789	(11%)
Keyes (R)	14,611	(7%)

1992 Presidential Vote

Clinton (D)	1,436,206	(43%)
Bush (R)	1,356,865	(41%)
Perot (I)	521,829	(16%)

GOVERNOR

Gov. Christine Todd Whitman (R)

Elected 1993, term expires Jan. 1998; b. Sept. 26, 1946, New York City, NY; home, Oldwick; Wheaton Col., B.A. 1968; Presbyterian; married (John).

Career: Staff Asst., Repub. Natl. Cmte., 1969–71; Somerset Cnty. Bd. of Chosen Freeholders, 1983–88; Pres., Public Utilities Bd., 1988–1990; U.S. Senate candidate, 1990.

Office: State House, 125 W. State St., #CN-001, Trenton 08625, 609-292-6000; Fax: 609-292-3454; Web site: www.state.nj.us.

Election Results

1993 gen.	Christine Todd Whitman (R)	1,236,124	(49%)
	Jim Florio (D)	1,210,031	(48%)
	Others	59,809	(2%)
1993 prim.	Christine Todd Whitman (R)	159,765	(40%)
	Cary Edwards (R)	131,578	(33%)
	Jim Wallwork (R)	96,034	(24%)
	Others	12,448	(3%)
1989 gen.	Jim Florio (D)	1,379,937	(61%)
	Jim Courter (R)	838,553	(37%)
	Others	34,563	(2%)

SENATORS

Sen. Frank R. Lautenberg (D)

Elected 1982, seat up 2000; b. Jan. 23, 1924, Paterson; home, Montclair; Columbia U., B.S. 1949; Jewish; separated.

Career: Army Signal Corps, 1942–46 (WWII); Co-founder, Automatic Data Processing, 1952–82; NY & NJ Port Authority Comm., 1978–82.

DC Office: 506 HSOB 20510, 202-224-4744; Fax: 202-224-9707; e-mail: frank_lautenberg@lautenberg.senate.gov.

State Offices: Barrington, 609-757-5353; Newark, 201-645-3030.

Committees: *Appropriations* (6th of 13 D): Commerce, Justice, State & the Judiciary; Defense; Foreign Operations; Transportation (RMM); VA, HUD & Independent Agencies. *Budget* (RMM of 10 D). *Environment & Public Works* (3rd of 8 D): Drinking Water, Fisheries & Wildlife; Superfund, Waste Control & Risk Assessment (RMM). *Intelligence (Select)* (8th of 9 D).

Group Ratings

	ADA	ACLU	AFS	LCV	CFA	CON	NFIB	COC	ACU	NTLC	CHC
1996	95	50	100	100	86	7	28	15	0	3	7
1995	100	—	100	100	94	54	—	16	0	—	—

National Journal Ratings

	1995 LIB — 1995 CONS			1996 LIB — 1996 CONS		
Economic	97%	—	0%	89%	—	5%
Social	85%	—	7%	80%	—	8%
Foreign	79%	—	15%	88%	—	11%

Key Votes of the 104th Congress

1. Reduce Medicare Growth $	N	5. Flag Amendment	N	9. Anti-Missile Defense	N
2. Lmt. Prod. Liab. Damages	N	6. Endangered Species	Y	10. Cuban Embargo	Y
3. Increase Min. Wage	Y	7. Gay Employment Rights	Y	11. Bar Bosnia Troop $	N
4. Welfare Reform	N	8. Ovrd. Part. Birth Veto	N	12. Cut Vietnam Aid	*

Election Results

1994 general	Frank R. Lautenberg (D)	1,033,487	(50%)	($8,217,716)
	Garabed (Chuck) Haytaian (R)	966,244	(47%)	($5,110,378)
	Others	55,156	(3%)	
1994 primary	Frank R. Lautenberg (D)	151,416	(81%)	
	Bill Campbell (D)	26,066	(14%)	
	Lynne A. Speed (D)	9,563	(5%)	
1988 general	Frank R. Lautenberg (D)	1,599,905	(54%)	($7,298,663)
	Peter M. Dawkins (R)	1,349,937	(46%)	($7,616,249)

Sen. Robert G. Torricelli (D)

Elected 1996, seat up 2002; b. Aug. 26, 1951, Paterson; home, Englewood; Rutgers U., B.A. 1974, J.D. 1977, Harvard JFK Schl. of Govt., M.P.A. 1980; United Methodist; divorced.

Career: Asst., NJ Gov. Brendan Byrne, 1975–77; Cnsl., Vice Pres. Walter Mondale, 1978–81; Practicing atty., 1981–82; U.S. House of Reps., 1982–96.

DC Office: 113 DSOB 20510, 202-224-3224; Fax: 202-224-8567.

State Offices: Newark, 201-624-5555.

Committees: *Democratic Senatorial Campaign Committee Vice Chairman. Governmental Affairs* (6th of 7 D): International Security, Proliferation & Federal Services; Permanent Subcommittee on Investigations. *Judiciary* (8th of 8 D): Antitrust, Business Rights & Competition; Constitution, Federalism & Property Rights; Youth Violence. *Rules & Administration* (7th of 7 D).

Group Ratings **(As Member of U.S. House of Representatives)**

	ADA	ACLU	AFS	LCV	CFA	CON	NFIB	COC	ACU	NTLC	CHC
1996	70	56	92	62	62	26	32	31	21	24	14
1995	80	—	—	75	100	7	—	25	13	—	—

National Journal Ratings **(as Member of U.S. House of Representatives)**

	1995 LIB — 1995 CONS			1996 LIB — 1996 CONS		
Economic	72%	—	27%	67%	—	33%
Social	78%	—	21%	69%	—	30%
Foreign	70%	—	28%	69%	—	30%

Key Votes of the 104th Congress (as Member of U.S. House of Representatives)

1. Reduce Medicare Growth $	N	5. Flag Amendment	N	9. Cuban Embargo	Y
2. Ovrd. Product Liab. Veto	*	6. Drop EPA Limits	Y	10. Bar Bosnia Troop $	N
3. Increase Min. Wage	Y	7. Repeal Assault-Weap. Ban	N	11. Cut Anti-Missile Defense	Y
4. Welfare Reform	N	8. Ovrd. Part. Birth Veto	N	12. Bar U.N. Uniforms	Y

Election Results

1996 general	Robert G. Torricelli (D)	1,519,154	(53%)	($9,134,854)
	Dick Zimmer (R)	1,227,351	(43%)	($8,238,181)
	Others	136,961	(5%)	
1996 primary	Robert G. Torricelli (D)	unopposed		
1990 general	Bill Bradley (D)	977,810	(50%)	($12,444,283)
	Christine Todd Whitman (R)	918,874	(47%)	($801,660)
	Others	41,770	(2%)	

FIRST DISTRICT

There are few urban spaces that have been more ravaged, yet now with some signs of hope, than Camden, New Jersey. Across the Delaware River from Philadelphia's skyline, its closely built streets were jammed with immigrants in the 19th Century, when poet Walt Whitman lived here. In 1894, a Camden machinist named Eldridge Johnson produced the Victor Talking Machine—the birth of the company that became RCA Victor in 1929. In 1897, Camden was the site of the invention of condensed soup, and the Campbell Soup Company was founded soon afterwards. Thus Camden became a major industrial locus on the Jersey side of the Delaware River, not the broadest and certainly not the most picturesque of our Atlantic estuaries, but probably the East Coast's premier industrial waterway, with a concentration of steel factories, chemical plants and oil tank farms equal to any in the country. The flat lands of South Jersey all around, ignored in the 19th Century, had easy access to cheap water transport and plenty of skilled labor from the Philadelphia area, making them one of the country's fastest-growing industrial areas for a quarter-century starting in the 1940s. Camden tended to empty out, many of its factories closed, its neighborhoods were beset by crime, its local government so incompetent the state has been moving toward taking it over. But the local Cooper's Ferry Development Corporation has developed a riverfront park, with the New Jersey Aquarium and the Sony Music/Pace amphitheater, that takes advantage of Camden's site and attracts multiracial crowds; an aerospace complex and a Campbell Soup office tower have gone up. But city government and crime are still major impediments to Camden coming farther back.

The 1st Congressional District of New Jersey is, more or less, greater Camden, the Delaware riverfront from Riverton south to a point across from the Delaware state line, and suburbs running southeast to the flat vegetable fields of South Jersey. Its boroughs and townships retain their separate identities; right next to Camden is Collingswood, with its middle-class porches still freshly painted and its shops prosperous. The district includes some underclass poor, but most people here are at some level of upward mobility from the grinding working-class life of 50 years ago, living in comfortable communities, worried that the petrochemical plants which have helped many of them move up may also be poisoning their land, water and air. Politically, this is an area with a Democratic heritage, the most Democratic district in South Jersey.

The 1st District is represented by Rob Andrews, one of the most interesting young Democratic congressmen. Andrews grew up in Bellmawr, the son of a shipyard worker, made a splendid record in college and law school, returned home and with then-Congressman Jim Florio's support was elected to the Camden County Board of Chosen Freeholders (wonderful name!) before he was 30. When Florio left Congress to become governor in January 1990, he postponed the special election to replace him until November; he supported Andrews, though Andrews was silent on his tax increase. Andrews had other help. He spent $541,000 on his campaign, and he had a Republican opponent who switched positions on abortion and claimed to have attended a college he hadn't. Even so, in the anti-Florio climate, Andrews won by only 54%–43%.

Andrews entered the House as its youngest Democrat and has proved to be one of its most aggressive and independent-minded reformers. One big initiative was direct student loans. Andrews felt banks were making college loans inefficiently and that direct government loans would "save money for students, families, schools and the federal treasury." Against strong lobbying opposition, he got the House to approve direct loan demonstration projects, got candidate Bill Clinton to endorse the idea in 1992 and then got it passed into law in 1993. He argues that it is a major success and it is one of the major achievements of the Clinton Administration. He had a rather conservative record on economics and foreign policy and was more liberal on cultural issues. He voted against tax increases, including the Clinton budget and tax package of 1993 and announced early he would oppose the Clinton healthcare program. To some of Andrews's Democratic critics in the New Jersey delegation and elsewhere, he is a grandstander who would cut needed government programs. But his record in Camden and on direct student loans shows that he supports government that is vigorous and serves real needs—but insists on pruning government that isn't working and on not forcing voters to pay more in taxes for the same low level of services they've been getting.

Andrews's other priority in the 103d Congress was the A-to-Z spending cut; its originator New Hampshire Republican Bill Zeliff looked for a Democratic co-sponsor whose name started with A and came up with Andrews. The idea was to set aside 56 hours of congressional debate during which any member could propose reducing or zeroing out spending on any program, with a guaranteed roll call vote. Speaker Thomas Foley strongly opposed it, and Andrews and Zeliff, with 228 co-sponsors, sought to come up with 218 signatures on a discharge petition to get it out of committee. This helped trigger the reform making discharge signatures public, but Foley twisted enough arms to keep it from the floor. Interest waned when Republicans took control; instead Speaker Newt Gingrich put his somewhat similar Corrections Day procedure into effect.

In the Republican House he has had less opportunity for such initiatives, and perhaps less interest: for his focus has remained on New Jersey, and on running for governor in 1997. He has been reelected to the House by overwhelming margins, and he has continued to live in Haddon Heights, commuting by train. Right after the November 1996 election he announced he was running for governor; he managed to get the endorsements of Jim Florio and Hudson County Executive Bob Janiszewski, who were both mentioned as candidates themselves. Andrews was initially favored to win the primary, but he ran into stiff competition from state Senator James McGreevey, who had the backing of more Democratic county organizations. Former Morris County Prosecutor Michael Murphy was the dark horse of the race, running, he said, as the "un-candidate." Andrews promised never to raise taxes, said he would force auto insurance costs down by requiring companies to lower rates if they wanted to continue issuing other policies, and called for combining the state's three toll road authorities. McGreevey said he would create a new insurance commissioner's office and proposed referenda on education issues. Near the end of the race, Andrews and McGreevey blasted each other on television and in debates, while Murphy chided them in humorous ads. Andrews swept south Jersey and took Hudson County, but McGreevey's big margins in Middlesex, Essex and Union Counties gave him a tight 39%–37% win, with Murphy taking 21% after a late surge. Both Andrews and Murphy lined up behind McGreevey after the primary.

Andrews was easily reelected to the House in 1994 and 1996, topping 70% both times. He seems assured of holding the seat in 1998 if he wants it. His close loss in the gubernatorial primary does not rule him out as a Democratic frontrunner in 2001, however, when Whitman would be term-limited.

The People: Pop. 1990: 594,494; 4% rural; 12% age 65+; 77% White; 15% Black; 2% Asian; 6% Hispanic origin. Households: 55% married couple families; 27% married couple fams. w. children; 38% college educ.; median household income: $35,250; per capita income: $14,502; median gross rent: $514; median house value: $93,700.

1996 Presidential Vote			1992 Presidential Vote		
Clinton (D)	132,715	(59%)	Clinton (D)	118,060	(48%)
Dole (R)	61,294	(27%)	Bush (R)	78,095	(32%)
Perot (I)	25,052	(11%)	Perot (I)	48,252	(20%)
Other	5,122	(2%)			

Rep. Robert E. Andrews (D)

Elected 1990; b. Aug. 4, 1957, Camden; home, Haddon Heights; Bucknell U., B.A. 1979, Cornell U., J.D. 1982; Episcopalian; married (Camille).

Career: Practicing atty., 1982–87; Adjunct Prof., Rutgers Col. of Law, 1985–86, 1989–90; Dir., Camden Cnty. Bd. of Chosen Freeholders, 1987–90.

DC Office: 2439 RHOB 20515, 202-225-6501; Fax: 202-225-6583; e-mail: randrews@hr.house.gov.

District Offices: Haddon Heights, 609-546-5100; Woodbury, 609-848-3900.

Committees: *Education & The Workforce* (8th of 20 D): Postsecondary Education, Training & Life-Long Learning; Workforce Protections. *International Relations* (9th of 22 D): Asia & the Pacific; Western Hemisphere.

Group Ratings

	ADA	ACLU	AFS	LCV	CFA	CON	NFIB	COC	ACU	NTLC	CHC
1996	65	53	92	92	100	24	34	31	25	38	30
1995	60	—	—	31	85	56	—	48	36	—	—

National Journal Ratings

	1995 LIB		1995 CONS	1996 LIB		1996 CONS
Economic	63%	—	37%	65%	—	33%
Social	72%	—	28%	72%	—	27%
Foreign	57%	—	42%	47%	—	52%

Key Votes of the 104th Congress

1. Reduce Medicare Growth $	N	5. Flag Amendment	Y	9. Cuban Embargo	Y
2. Ovrd. Product Liab. Veto	N	6. Drop EPA Limits	Y	10. Bar Bosnia Troop $	N
3. Increase Min. Wage	Y	7. Repeal Assault-Weap. Ban	N	11. Cut Anti-Missile Defense	N
4. Welfare Reform	N	8. Ovrd. Part. Birth Veto	N	12. Bar U.N. Uniforms	Y

Election Results

1996 general	Robert E. Andrews (D)	160,413	(76%)	($414,266)
	Mel Suplee (R)	44,287	(21%)	($9,010)
	Others	6,034	(3%)	
1996 primary	Robert E. Andrews (D)	unopposed		
1994 general	Robert E. Andrews (D)	108,155	(72%)	($674,366)
	James N. Hogan (R)	41,505	(28%)	($78,028)

SECOND DISTRICT

The builders of the Camden & Atlantic Railroad in 1852 may not have known it, but when they extended their line to the little inlet town of Absecon, they were starting America's biggest beach resort, Atlantic City. Like all resorts, it was a product of developments elsewhere: of industrialization and spreading affluence, of railroad technology and the conquest of diseases which used to make summer a time of terror for parents and doctors. In the years after the Civil War, first Atlantic City and then the whole Jersey Shore from Brigantine to Cape May became America's first seaside resort, and Atlantic City developed its characteristic features: the Boardwalk in 1870, the amusement pier in 1882, the rolling chair in 1884, salt water taffy in the 1890s, Miss America in 1921. By 1940, when 16 million Americans visited every summer, Atlantic City was a common man's resort of old traditions; it declined in the years after World War II as people could afford nicer vacations. By the early 1970s, Atlantic City was grim, with a bedraggled convention hall (site of the 1964 Democratic National Convention), empty hotels and bleak streets of rowhouses built in the ugliest Philadelphia style.

Then in 1977, New Jersey voters legalized casino gambling in Atlantic City and gleaming new hotels sprang up, big name entertainers came in and Atlantic City became more glamorous than it had been in 90 years. But not for all of its residents: casino and hotel jobs tend to be low-wage, and the slums begin just feet from the massive parking lots of the casinos. In the early 1990s Atlantic City seemed overbuilt; by early 1997, the casinos were thriving, and huge new casinos were planned on both Boardwalk and bayside. Atlantic City is growing into what Las Vegas has become, not just a collection of gaudy casinos but a gaggle of theme parks, with entertainment for the family as well as adults.

The Jersey Shore south of Atlantic City is a string of different resorts. There is the old Methodist town of Ocean City, where Gay Talese grew up the son of Italian immigrants, as he tells movingly in *Unto the Sons*. There is Wildwood, with its gritty boardwalk, and Cape May, with its beautifully preserved Victorian houses. Behind the Shore are swamp and flatland, the Pine Barrens and vegetable fields that gave New Jersey the name "Garden State." Growth has been slow in these small towns and gas station intersections, communities in whose eerie calmness in the summer you can hear mosquitoes whining. In the flatness, you can also find towns clustered around low-wage apparel factories or petrochemical plants on the Delaware estuary: the Northeast high-tech service economy has not reached this far south in Jersey yet.

This part of South Jersey makes up the 2d Congressional District. Politically, it was long marginal country, with strong Democratic presences in the chemical industry towns along the Delaware River and in Vineland and a strong Republican presence in Cape May; Democrats have carried the area in all 1990s statewide elections. Atlantic City often votes Democratic but has an antique Republican political machine which goes back generations. This is prime marginal territory, off the beaten track of Northeast politics.

In House elections, the 2d District for 20 years reelected William Hughes, a moderate Democrat who was an Ocean County prosecutor and who in the 1980s and 1990s superintended crime bills and worked on copyright and ocean dumping issues as well. In 1994, after a 1992 challenge from Vineland Assemblyman Frank LoBiondo held him to a 56%–42% victory, his lowest margin ever, Hughes decided to retire.

Since his victory in 1994, LoBiondo has been the congressman from the 2d District. He grew up in Vineland, went to college in Philadelphia and worked for the family trucking firm, LoBiondo Brothers Motor Express. In 1985 he was elected to a three-year term on the Cumberland County Board of Chosen Freeholders; in 1987 he was elected to the Assembly, where he stoutly opposed new taxes. LoBiondo also opposes gun control, and was backed by the National Rifle Association. When LoBiondo ran for Hughes's seat in 1994, he faced Atlantic County state Senator William Gormley in the Republican primary; LoBiondo attacked him as a taxer and NRA ads called him "a liberal in Republican clothing"; to the surprise of many,

LoBiondo won 54%–35%. LoBiondo easily won the general, 65%–35%.

In the House LoBiondo ranks among the lowest in office spenders and has a moderate voting record. He was one of six Republicans to vote against the Republican Medicare plan in October 1995 (four were from New Jersey); he voted against a veterans' appropriation as having insufficient medical care and against exempting small businesses from the minimum wage. With Susan Molinari and Sue Kelly, he introduced the bill against "drive-through" mastectomies. Much of his effort has been devoted to local issues. He is co-chair of the Congressional Gaming Caucus. In 1995 he organized a delegation letter to the President to keep the Coast Guard Training Center in Cape May. In 1996 he hailed passage of the water resources bill with major beach restoration for Atlantic City, saying, "We can't do enough for the protection of our beaches." In February 1997 he rallied local officials against a study recommending that the FAA's William J. Hughes Technical Center be moved from Egg Harbor Township to Oklahoma. "You are the heart and soul of the FAA nationwide. We will leave no stone unturned to make sure this misguided report does not ever get off the ground," he said.

In 1996 LoBiondo was opposed by Democrat Ruth Katz, who returned to the district after 15 years in Washington working on Capitol Hill and for a policy foundation, and who attacked him as a Newt Gingrich pawn. He won 60%–38%. In 1997 he switched from a seat on the Banking Committee to the Transportation and Infrastructure Committee, a fine place to handle local needs.

The People: Pop. 1990: 594,723; 30% rural; 15% age 65+; 78% White; 14% Black; 1% Asian; 7% Hispanic origin. Households: 54% married couple families; 24% married couple fams. w. children; 36% college educ.; median household income: $32,410; per capita income: $14,732; median gross rent: $525; median house value: $93,400.

1996 Presidential Vote			1992 Presidential Vote		
Clinton (D)	117,526	(50%)	Clinton (D)	101,718	(40%)
Dole (R)	84,043	(36%)	Bush (R)	97,696	(39%)
Perot (I)	27,589	(12%)	Perot (I)	50,773	(20%)
Other	4,464	(2%)			

Rep. Frank A. LoBiondo (R)

Elected 1994; b. May 12, 1946, Bridgeton; home, Vineland; St. Joseph's U., B.A. 1968; Catholic; married (Jan).

Career: Operations Mgr., LoBiondo Bros. Motor Express Inc., 1968–94; Cumberland Cnty. Bd. of Chosen Freeholders, 1985–88; NJ Assembly, 1987–94.

DC Office: 222 CHOB 20515, 202-225-6572; Fax: 202-225-3318; e-mail: lobiondo@hr.house.gov.

District Offices: Mays Landing, 609-625-5008.

Committees: *Small Business* (7th of 19 R): Empowerment; Regulatory Reform & Paperwork Reduction. *Transportation & Infrastructure* (39th of 40 R): Coast Guard & Maritime Transportation (Vice Chmn.); Water Resources & Environment.

Group Ratings

	ADA	ACLU	AFS	LCV	CFA	CON	NFIB	COC	ACU	NTLC	CHC
1996	25	19	42	46	85	55	84	81	70	88	80
1995	25	—	—	13	54	56	—	79	80	—	—

National Journal Ratings

	1995 LIB — 1995 CONS	1996 LIB — 1996 CONS
Economic	52% — 48%	50% — 49%
Social	45% — 54%	42% — 56%
Foreign	50% — 49%	64% — 35%

Key Votes of the 104th Congress

1. Reduce Medicare Growth $	N	5. Flag Amendment	Y	9. Cuban Embargo	Y
2. Ovrd. Product Liab. Veto	Y	6. Drop EPA Limits	Y	10. Bar Bosnia Troop $	Y
3. Increase Min. Wage	Y	7. Repeal Assault-Weap. Ban	Y	11. Cut Anti-Missile Defense	N
4. Welfare Reform	Y	8. Ovrd. Part. Birth Veto	Y	12. Bar U.N. Uniforms	Y

Election Results

1996 general	Frank A. LoBiondo (R)	133,131	(60%)	($890,526)
	Ruth Katz (D)	83,890	(38%)	($806,232)
	Others	3,697	(2%)	
1996 primary	Frank A. LoBiondo (R)	unopposed		
1994 general	Frank A. LoBiondo (R)	102,566	(65%)	($757,681)
	Louis N. Magazzu (D)	56,151	(35%)	($168,428)

THIRD DISTRICT

The Pine Barrens of New Jersey are one of the last vacant spots on the eastern seaboard; not quite *terra incognita*, but still not thickly populated. Encroached by the Philadelphia suburbs of South Jersey on the west and burgeoning retirement developments of the Jersey Shore on the east, they are crossed even today mostly by narrow two-lane roads; there are only a few small towns here, plus Fort Dix and McGuire Air Force Base. For years, the Barrens were seen as a barrier to civilization; only recently have environment-minded Jerseyites come to see them as a natural treasure.

The 3d Congressional District spans the Pine Barrens. Most of its residents live in the South Jersey suburbs of Philadelphia, in the spread-out suburb of Cherry Hill with its 1960s and 1970s shopping centers, or in the older towns along the Delaware River and newer ones inland toward McGuire. This is comfortable, but not hugely affluent, suburban country. East of the Pine Barrens is Ocean County, including the barrier islands from Normandy Beach south to Little Egg Harbor, with older beachfront communities and larger clusters of new subdivisions and condominium complexes inland. Ocean County grew rapidly in the 1980s, a kind of frost belt Florida, with many retirees from New York and north Jersey eager to leave the big cities' high crime and high taxes, but still jealous of their Social Security benefits and concerned about the local environment. Politically, both the west and east ends of this district are solidly Republican.

The congressman from the 3d District is James Saxton. He grew up in south Jersey, worked as a teacher for three years, then became a real estate broker. In 1975 he was elected to the New Jersey Assembly, when Republicans were struggling to stop Governor Brendan Byrne's income tax. In 1984 he ran to fill a vacancy in the House, won the Republican primary 45%–41%, and easily won the general.

In the House his record has been moderate on economic and cultural issues, conservative on foreign policy and defense. He co-sponsored the ocean dumping law of 1988, when medical wastes were washing up against the Jersey Shore. In 1995, he was given a seat with seniority on the Resources Committee, and became chairman of the new Fisheries Conservation, Wildlife and Oceans Subcommittee. But unlike most Republicans, he did not want to revise the Endangered Species Act to require compensation of property owners whose land value decreased as a result of federal regulations, and Resources Chairman Don Young turned the issue over to Californian Richard Pombo. With Republican Wayne Gilchrest, Saxton came up with a proposal for tax incentives for landowners who help protect endangered species before they are listed. With memories of the ocean dumping of 1988 still fresh, he opposed the House Republican changes to the Clean Water Act, and persuaded all but one New Jersey member to join him in opposing the bill in 1995. But he supported a revision of the Safe Drinking Water Act in 1996, and with Henry Waxman authored a "right to know" provision requiring water utilities to disclose pollutants. He also backed a Shore Protection Act and reauthorization of the Coastal Zone Management grants. He was one of four New Jersey Republicans to vote against the Republican Medicare plan in October 1995.

Saxton is a supporter of strong anti-terrorism efforts and of aid to Israel. With a seat on National Security he has worked to save local bases. When Fort Dix ended up on the 1991 base closing list, Saxton turned much of it into a federal prison and state police training center. When McGuire Air Force base was on the 1993 list, Saxton convinced the commission the base needed to be expanded as the East Coast air mobility hub for the armed forces.

Back home Saxton has been reelected by large margins.

The People: Pop. 1990: 594,667; 18% rural; 15% age 65+; 87% White; 8% Black; 2% Asian; 3% Hispanic origin. Households: 66% married couple families; 29% married couple fams. w. children; 47% college educ.; median household income: $41,257; per capita income: $18,138; median gross rent: $651; median house value: $128,300.

1996 Presidential Vote

Clinton (D)	134,326	(50%)
Dole (R)	101,100	(38%)
Perot (I)	28,212	(11%)
Other	4,914	(2%)

1992 Presidential Vote

Clinton (D)	114,503	(40%)
Bush (R)	113,583	(40%)
Perot (I)	54,996	(19%)

Rep. Jim Saxton (R)

Elected 1984; b. Jan. 22, 1943, Nicholson, PA; home, Mt. Holly; E. Stroudsburg St. Col., B.A. 1965, Temple U., 1967–68; United Methodist; divorced.

Career: Jr. High Schl. teacher, 1965–68; Real estate broker, 1968–84; NJ Assembly, 1975–82; NJ Senate, 1982–84.

DC Office: 339 CHOB 20515, 202-225-4765; Fax: 202-225-0778.

District Offices: Cherry Hill, 609-428-0520; Mt. Holly, 609-261-5800; Toms River, 908-914-2020.

Committees: *National Security* (9th of 30 R): Military Installations & Facilities; Military Procurement. *Resources* (4th of 27 R): Fisheries Conservation, Wildlife & Oceans (Chmn.). *Joint Economic Committee* (Chmn. of 10 Reps.).

Group Ratings

	ADA	ACLU	AFS	LCV	CFA	CON	NFIB	COC	ACU	NTLC	CHC
1996	15	6	0	54	62	11	92	94	84	83	86
1995	15	—	—	6	38	25	—	79	84	—	—

National Journal Ratings

	1995 LIB — 1995 CONS			1996 LIB — 1996 CONS		
Economic	44%	—	53%	37%	—	61%
Social	41%	—	58%	41%	—	58%
Foreign	0%	—	85%	0%	—	79%

Key Votes of the 104th Congress

1. Reduce Medicare Growth $	N	5. Flag Amendment	Y	9. Cuban Embargo	Y
2. Ovrd. Product Liab. Veto	Y	6. Drop EPA Limits	Y	10. Bar Bosnia Troop $	Y
3. Increase Min. Wage	N	7. Repeal Assault-Weap. Ban	N	11. Cut Anti-Missile Defense	N
4. Welfare Reform	Y	8. Ovrd. Part. Birth Veto	Y	12. Bar U.N. Uniforms	Y

Election Results

1996 general	Jim Saxton (R)	157,503	(64%)	($533,850)
	John Leonardi (D)	81,590	(33%)	($21,957)
	Others	6,185	(3%)	
1996 primary	Jim Saxton (R)	unopposed		
1994 general	Jim Saxton (R)	115,750	(66%)	($356,108)
	James B. Smith (D)	54,441	(31%)	
	Others	4,137	(2%)	

FOURTH DISTRICT

New Jersey, a state long thought to be split between a North Jersey that is an appanage of New York City and a South Jersey that has the distinctive accent of Philadelphia, is becoming a state with its own identity. In the 1980s, it bubbled over with pride at its growth and new civic institutions; in 1990, it raged with anger at Governor Jim Florio's tax increases. This showed a new unity: for the great medium of protest was the first New Jersey-oriented talk radio station, started in Trenton in 1989, and the symbolic event was the Hands Across New Jersey demonstration on a route approximating I-195, from the Jersey Shore west to the State House in Trenton overlooking the Delaware River. Trenton, an old manufacturing city ("Trenton Makes, The World Takes," the sign proclaims over the rooftops) where John Roebling of Brooklyn Bridge fame started making wire in 1848, and Walter Scott Lenox started making dishes in 1889. It is now the anomalously gritty capital—the only state capital with no large downtown hotel—of a mostly white-collar state.

The 4th Congressional District covers approximately the same span as Hands Across New Jersey, from Trenton to the Jersey Shore, roughly following I-195 to the Shore communities of Manasquan and Point Pleasant and Mantoloking. It includes the old colonial town of Burlington on the Delaware River and the Great Adventure Safari and Entertainment Park in the Pine Barrens. This is one part of America where population movement has been eastward, from the old neighborhoods of Trenton and its close-in suburbs to the new subdivisions of Ocean County and Wall Township. Trenton has long been a solidly Democratic town, but its suburbs are much less so, with the Jersey Shore parts of the district solidly Republican.

The congressman from the 4th District is Christopher Smith, a youthful-looking Republican with great seniority who has applied strong moral principles to practical politics with impressive results. Smith grew up in the Trenton area, worked in his family's sporting goods business, and was executive director of the New Jersey Right to Life Committee in the 1970s. In 1980 he ran for the House in a more Trenton-centered 4th District and beat 26-year incumbent Frank Thompson, a convicted Abscam defendant. A fluke, it seemed: but Smith proceeded to beat serious Democrats in the next five elections, with more than 60% each time.

His motivation comes from religion: "Christ said it in Matthew 25: 'Whatsoever you do to the least of my brethren, you do likewise to me.' That was my motivating scripture through all of my years in Right to Life, and it continues to be," he has said. He is concerned about children and about victims of human rights violations. If his anti-abortion stance comes from his Catholicism, his concern for victims also is part of a Catholic tradition.

On abortion, Smith got the House in 1995 to reinstate the ban, overturned by the Clinton Administration, on federal health insurance paying for abortion except when the woman's life is in danger, and he has worked to stop abortions in military hospitals. Smith has sought for years to reinstate the Reagan-era restrictions that would deny federal funds to family planning organizations that promote abortions abroad; the House finally passed his provision in February 1997, but the Senate voted to release international family planning funds without abortion restrictions. Smith was a prime mover of legislation to ban "partial-birth" abortions, which passed the House in 1996 and 1997, but failed to muster enough votes to overcome vetoes.

As chairman of the International Operations and Human Rights Subcommittee, he has criticized China for its forced sterilizations and abortions and its persecution of Christians and other religious minorities, and has opposed MFN status. "China has embarked on a Nazi-like eugenics program. People are being destroyed because they don't measure up to a certain standard of the government's." He has also pushed for money for pregnant women and neonatal care in the developing world. He has promised to fight slavery in Sudan and sponsored a provision to bar U.S. aid to Mauritania because of slavery there. His $5,000 tax credit for adoption was passed by the House as part of the Contract With America. He also serves on Veterans' Affairs, where he favored recognition of Gulf war syndrome and has worked on local VA facilities. He has also worked on other local projects—a wildlife refuge in Manasquan Inlet, a Catholic Charities mental health center, the Deborah Heart and Lung Center, the Hamilton train station.

Smith says he is "fiercely independent" and has a moderate voting record. He was one of four New Jersey Republicans to vote against the Republican Medicare plan in October 1995. He pushed to bar defense contractors from using government funds to finance mergers. In 1995 he scurried and got Lakehurst Naval Air Station removed from the base-closing list. In 1996 he backed former Congressman Joseph DioGuardi in his primary against New York incumbent Sue Kelly (Kelly is pro-choice); the leadership struck him from a congressional delegation to Bosnia in response.

Smith has been reelected by wide margins every two years.

The People: Pop. 1990: 594,673; 16% rural; 17% age 65+; 81% White; 12% Black; 2% Asian; 5% Hispanic origin. Households: 58% married couple families; 26% married couple fams. w. children; 41% college educ.; median household income: $36,888; per capita income: $16,107; median gross rent: $583; median house value: $129,800.

1996 Presidential Vote

Clinton (D)	127,489	(51%)
Dole (R)	92,845	(37%)
Perot (I)	26,880	(11%)
Other	4,709	(2%)

1992 Presidential Vote

Bush (R)	109,907	(41%)
Clinton (D)	105,335	(39%)
Perot (I)	50,721	(19%)

Rep. Christopher H. Smith (R)

Elected 1980; b. Mar. 4, 1953, Rahway; home, Washington Township; Trenton St. Col., B.S. 1975; Catholic; married (Marie).

Career: Sales exec., family-owned sporting goods business, 1975–80; Exec. Dir., NJ Right to Life, 1976–78.

DC Office: 2370 RHOB 20515, 202-225-3765; Fax: 202-225-7768.

District Offices: Hamilton, 609-585-7878; Whiting, 908-350-2300.

Committees: *International Relations* (6th of 26 R): International Operations & Human Rights (Chmn.); Western Hemisphere. *Veterans' Affairs* (2nd of 16 R): Health.

Group Ratings

	ADA	ACLU	AFS	LCV	CFA	CON	NFIB	COC	ACU	NTLC	CHC
1996	30	12	42	46	69	51	72	75	80	83	86
1995	20	—	—	19	54	16	—	63	64	—	—

National Journal Ratings

	1995 LIB — 1995 CONS	1996 LIB — 1996 CONS
Economic	52% — 47%	47% — 53%
Social	45% — 54%	35% — 62%
Foreign	15% — 73%	28% — 71%

Key Votes of the 104th Congress

1. Reduce Medicare Growth $	N	5. Flag Amendment	Y	9. Cuban Embargo	Y
2. Ovrd. Product Liab. Veto	Y	6. Drop EPA Limits	Y	10. Bar Bosnia Troop $	Y
3. Increase Min. Wage	Y	7. Repeal Assault-Weap. Ban	N	11. Cut Anti-Missile Defense	*
4. Welfare Reform	Y	8. Ovrd. Part. Birth Veto	Y	12. Bar U.N. Uniforms	Y

Election Results

1996 general	Christopher H. Smith (R)	146,404	(64%)	($284,776)
	Kevin John Meara (D)	77,565	(34%)	
	Others	6,145	(3%)	
1996 primary	Christopher H. Smith (R)	unopposed		
1994 general	Christopher H. Smith (R)	109,818	(68%)	($271,108)
	Ralph Walsh (D)	49,537	(31%)	($16,217)

FIFTH DISTRICT

The northern edge of New Jersey was first settled three centuries ago by the Dutch, for whom this plateau of land behind the Hudson River Palisades seemed a natural part of Nieuw Amsterdam. The Dutch influence is seen in old steep-roofed farmhouses and in many of the place names—Bergen County, Cresskill, Closter. But overall, northernmost New Jersey has the well-settled look of so many northeastern suburbs, with touches both of affluence and small town hominess, criss-crossed at its edges with limited access highways lined with shopping centers—with five million square feet in Paramus, the home of Toys "R" Us. Not far away are Saddle River, with million-dollar houses on multi-acre lots, and Park Ridge, with office buildings and condominiums, the last two retirement homes of the late President Richard Nixon. This area may look like WASP suburbia on the surface, but in fact it is home to successful people of all ethnic groups, many descended from those who first saw the Statue of Liberty from the steerage deck and passed through the inspection queues at Ellis Island.

The 5th Congressional District consists of most of northern Bergen County, plus a swath of North Jersey stretching west to the hill-enclosed upper reaches of the Delaware, crossing one ridge of mountains after another, running south along I-78. Three-fifths of its population is clustered in Bergen; to the west, little subdivisions set amid the lakes of western Passaic County are filling up with young families; farther west are once rural, now fast-growing Sussex and Warren Counties. Politically, this area is solidly Republican, more so in the rapidly growing areas to the west than in the older areas near the George Washington Bridge.

Since 1980, the congresswoman from this district has been Marge Roukema, a Republican whose Dutch name and Italian descent tell much of the district's ethnic history. She grew up in West Orange, settled with her psychiatrist husband in Ridgewood. She was a teacher who gave up her job to raise her children and was involved in community activities before becoming a political candidate; she brings to politics maturity and experience in the actual workings of civic institutions. She has a moderate, sometimes even liberal voting record and is not shy about frequently dissenting from some Republican leadership bills.

Before Republicans won the majority in 1994, Roukema was most conspicuously active on student loan programs and family and medical leave. She was the lead Republican sponsor of the Family and Medical Leave Act which was vetoed by President Bush in 1990 and 1992 and then passed and signed by President Clinton in February 1993. On student loans, Roukema in 1990 worked to make lenders and borrowers more accountable, and to crack down on for-profit trade schools that were generating many defaulted loans and in effect living off government guarantees. She did get a change so that home equity is not counted in determining loan eligibility, which helps in North Jersey, but her crackdown on trade schools was rejected by Democrats, and her reform was superseded by the direct student loan program boosted by New Jersey Democrat Rob Andrews and signed by President Clinton.

She voted against the Republican leadership to support the 1994 crime bill, opposed faster missile defense research, opposed the new funding formula for special education grants to states and opposed exempting small business from the minimum wage. She voted against term limits and the 1996 Welfare Reform Act, though she sponsored its child support provisions. She was the lead House sponsor of the 1996 healthcare portability bill to ban insurance rejections for pre-existing conditions, but was the only Republican to vote against it in March 1996 because of leadership-added malpractice liability limitations and Medical Savings Account provisions. She is a co-sponsor of measures to require 48-hour hospital stays for mastectomies and to pay for emergency room treatment according to patients' and not doctors' definitions of emergency. She backs the Shays-Meehan campaign finance reform plan.

Roukema chairs the Financial Institutions and Consumer Credit Subcommittee of Banking. She favors repeal of Glass-Steagall, which did not get far in the 104th Congress, and wants to combine the three bank insurance funds. She wants to abolish separate treatment of savings and loan institutions and has a bill for mandatory disclosure of ATM fees.

In November 1996 Roukema won reelection with more than 70%, as usual, and immediately started criticizing the Republican leadership. She called for more participation by moderates like herself and for different party positions on education, crime and Medicare. "We've got to get consensus or you're going to see many more going their own way." She called for delaying the election of the speaker until the Ethics Committee report on Newt Gingrich was released on January 21, but voted for Gingrich anyway; she later urged him to pay the Ethics Committee's $300,000 fine out of his own pocket.

The People: Pop. 1990: 594,581; 19% rural; 13% age 65+; 91% White; 1% Black; 4% Asian; 3% Hispanic origin. Households: 69% married couple families; 33% married couple fams. w. children; 55% college educ.; median household income: $53,433; per capita income: $23,942; median gross rent: $717; median house value: $213,100.

1996 Presidential Vote

Dole (R)	127,286	(47%)
Clinton (D)	115,060	(42%)
Perot (I)	23,642	(9%)
Other	5,090	(2%)

1992 Presidential Vote

Bush (R)	146,004	(49%)
Clinton (D)	99,733	(34%)
Perot (I)	48,661	(16%)

Rep. Marge Roukema (R)

Elected 1980; b. Sept. 19, 1929, W. Orange; home, Ridgewood; Montclair St. Col., B.A. 1951, Rutgers U.; Protestant; married (Richard).

Career: High schl. teacher, 1951–55; Ridgewood Board of Educ., 1970–73; Co-founder, Ridgewood Sr. Citizens Housing Corp., 1973.

DC Office: 2469 RHOB 20515, 202-225-4465; Fax: 202-225-9048.

District Offices: Hackettstown, 908-850-4747; Ridgewood, 201-447-3900.

Committees: *Banking & Financial Services* (3rd of 30 R): Domestic & International Monetary Policy; Financial Institutions & Consumer Credit (Chmn.). *Education & The Workforce* (3rd of 25 R): Employer-Employee Relations; Postsecondary Education, Training & Life-Long Learning.

Group Ratings

	ADA	ACLU	AFS	LCV	CFA	CON	NFIB	COC	ACU	NTLC	CHC
1996	50	38	42	62	77	100	59	56	53	65	46
1995	35	—	—	19	69	98	—	65	36	—	—

National Journal Ratings

	1995 LIB — 1995 CONS	1996 LIB — 1996 CONS
Economic	52% — 48%	53% — 46%
Social	61% — 38%	57% — 42%
Foreign	54% — 45%	67% — 33%

Key Votes of the 104th Congress

1. Reduce Medicare Growth $	Y	5. Flag Amendment	Y	9. Cuban Embargo	Y
2. Ovrd. Product Liab. Veto	Y	6. Drop EPA Limits	Y	10. Bar Bosnia Troop $	Y
3. Increase Min. Wage	Y	7. Repeal Assault-Weap. Ban	N	11. Cut Anti-Missile Defense	N
4. Welfare Reform	N	8. Ovrd. Part. Birth Veto	Y	12. Bar U.N. Uniforms	Y

Election Results

1996 general	Marge Roukema (R)	181,323	(71%)	($496,610)
	Bill Auer (D)	62,956	(25%)	($28,002)
	Others	10,054	(4%)	
1996 primary	Marge Roukema (R)	20,682	(75%)	
	George Matreyek (R)	5,076	(18%)	
	Roger Bacon (R)	1,820	(7%)	
1994 general	Marge Roukema (R)	139,964	(74%)	($497,345)
	Bill Auer (D)	41,275	(22%)	($160)
	Others	7,266	(4%)	

SIXTH DISTRICT

For generations great transportation arteries have brought people out of the huge central cities of New York and Philadelphia and into the long-empty flatlands and hills of New Jersey—to vacation, to raise families and to work toward affluence and build communities. The railroads of the late 19th Century created the towns of the Jersey Shore, from 1874, when the first train from New York City reached Long Branch, which quickly became the summer home of presidents from Grant to Wilson (Garfield, convalescing after he was shot, died there in 1881) and of New York race horse owners and socialites. The great freight rail lines in the New York-Philadelphia corridor sparked big electrical and chemical industries here—building on the inventions of Thomas Edison, many produced in his Menlo Park laboratory just off the rail lines. The same corridor was the site of America's first cloverleaf intersection, at the junction of U.S. 1 and U.S. 9, and the intersection of two of America's great post-World War II highways, the New Jersey Turnpike and the Garden State Parkway. The Turnpike, now 12 lanes wide, roars past oil tank farms and petrochemical plants, major rail lines and Newark Airport and the oily waters of Raritan Bay; the Parkway links leafy affluent suburbs a dozen miles west of the Hudson with the Jersey Shore.

The 6th Congressional District of New Jersey ties together these great transportation nodes and the upward mobility and economic progress that have taken place around them. It includes the central core of Middlesex County—New Brunswick and Edison Township and the surrounding communities—a heavy industry area that also, since the time of Thomas Edison, has housed some of America's great research and development facilities. Here, immigrant factory workers in modest frame houses have raised their families in small towns that seem as far removed from Manhattan as any place in the Midwest. The 6th District includes a strip of territory overlooking Lower New York Bay, with spacious estates on highlands above little port towns. It takes in a strip of beach towns from Sandy Hook south to Sea Girt: Long Branch, with its seedy boardwalk amusements; Deal's grand mansions, now being bought up by Syrian Jews; Allenhurst, with its renovated clapboard Victorians; Asbury Park, once the vital center of this beachfront; Irish-American Spring Lake, with streets of neat houses; and Ocean Grove, founded in 1869 as a Methodist resort "free from the dissipation and follies of fashionable watering places," still for teetotalers who throng to its 10,000-seat 1894 Great Hall. The Shore has remained a summer vacation area that attracts millions, but also has year-round communities, with their own upward-striving families, whose teenage energies have been expressed by the Shore's biggest celebrity, musician Bruce Springsteen.

The congressman from the 6th District is Frank Pallone, a Democrat who has faced severe political challenges to hold the seat. Pallone is the son of a disabled Long Branch policeman; he has been an environmentalist since 1969, when as a college freshman in Vermont he worked for that state's first-in-the-nation bottle deposit law. He was elected to the Long Branch City Council in 1982, at 31, and to the New Jersey Senate in 1983, where he did not always follow party lines and concentrated on environmental issues. When Congressman Jim Howard, chairman of the Transportation and Infrastructure Committee, died in March 1988, Pallone ran for the House. The district leaned Republican, but was angry about untreated sludge, plastic containers and medical waste washing up on the beach in 1987 and 1988. This was ruining the Jersey Shore economy, and Pallone's bumper sticker, without mentioning his party affiliation, said, "Stop Ocean Dumping." That, combined with his conservative stands on taxes and crime, helped him to a 52% win.

In the House, Pallone continued to be a maverick, speaking out against the congressional pay raise and distancing himself from Governor Jim Florio's 1990 tax increase. Still, in 1990 he beat Asbury Park Councilman Paul Kapalko by only 49%–46%. Redistricting nearly ended Pallone's career; he was the target of Republican redistricters, and Democrats did not do much to help him. For 1992, the new 6th combined much of Pallone's Shore district in Monmouth County with large parts of the Middlesex County seat held by 71-year-old Democrat Bernard Dwyer. Dwyer announced his retirement the day the district lines were made public, but Pallone still won the primary with only 55% against a Middlesex opponent. In the general, against Republican legislator Joseph Kyrillos, Pallone depended on a huge money advantage and Bill Clinton's edge in the district to win 52%–45%.

After that marginal victory, Pallone took care to continue his moderate voting record. He supported the Clinton Administration on many budget issues but voted against the budget and tax package in August 1993; he was one of nine non-southern Democrats to vote for the Contract with America's tax cut provision in 1995. Pallone had supported single-payer health insurance in the 1992 campaign, but steered clear of the Clinton healthcare plan in 1994, helping to stymie its progress through John Dingell's Commerce Committee. This record, plus $468,000 he raised from PACs, enabled him to win 60%–38% in 1994.

In 1995 Pallone became ranking Democrat on the Energy and Power Subcommittee on Commerce. He opposed repealing retroactive liability in Superfund and worked on the Safe Drinking Water Act. He attacked ocean dumping and similar practices in the East River, and got an agreement to stop ocean dumping at Sandy Hook. He formed a Save Our Fort Committee and tried to get defense technology commands consolidated at Fort Monmouth. In alliance with environmentalists and Public Service Electric and Gas, he called for revisiting the Clean Air Act before deregulating electric utilities. He courted ethnic groups, co-chairing the Armenian Issues Caucus and Indian Caucus. In 1996 he once again raised nearly $500,000 from PACs and outspent by 2–1 his opponent, Assemblyman Steven Corodemus, Governor Christie Whitman's point man on waste disposal. Pallone won by a handsome 61%–36%.

In November 1996 Pallone took leave of his seat on Commerce to make room for Ohio's Tom Sawyer. But he was promised the next vacancy and got it almost immediately when New Mexico's Bill Richardson was appointed Ambassador to the United Nations; but he lost the Energy and Power ranking post to Texas Congressman Ralph Hall. Pallone also serves on the House Resources Committee.

The People: Pop. 1990: 594,650; 12% age 65+; 78% White; 11% Black; 5% Asian; 6% Hispanic origin. Households: 57% married couple families; 26% married couple fams. w. children; 47% college educ.; median household income: $42,309; per capita income: $18,135; median gross rent: $645; median house value: $159,500.

1996 Presidential Vote

Clinton (D)	122,851	(54%)
Dole (R)	74,937	(33%)
Perot (I)	22,192	(10%)
Other	5,968	(3%)

1992 Presidential Vote

Clinton (D)	110,821	(44%)
Bush (R)	98,397	(39%)
Perot (I)	41,867	(17%)

Rep. Frank Pallone, Jr. (D)

Elected 1988; b. Oct. 30, 1951, Long Branch; home, Long Branch; Middlebury Col., B.A. 1973, Fletcher Schl. of Law & Diplomacy, M.A. 1974, Rutgers U., J.D. 1978; Catholic; married (Sarah).

Career: Asst. prof., Rutgers U., 1979–80; Practicing atty., 1981–83; Long Branch City Cncl., 1982–88; NJ Senate, 1983–88; Instructor, Monmouth Col., 1984–86.

DC Office: 420 CHOB 20515, 202-225-4671; Fax: 202-225-9665.

District Offices: Hazlet, 908-264-9104; Long Branch, 908-571-1140; New Brunswick, 908-249-8892.

Committees: *Commerce* (8th of 23 D): Energy & Power; Finance & Hazardous Materials; Health & the Environment. *Resources* (11th of 23 D): Fisheries Conservation, Wildlife & Oceans.

Group Ratings

	ADA	ACLU	AFS	LCV	CFA	CON	NFIB	COC	ACU	NTLC	CHC
1996	90	62	100	92	92	12	35	25	10	20	13
1995	85	—	—	75	100	31	—	33	24	—	—

National Journal Ratings

	1995 LIB — 1995 CONS			1996 LIB — 1996 CONS		
Economic	67%	—	32%	70%	—	28%
Social	72%	—	27%	78%	—	21%
Foreign	73%	—	24%	76%	—	22%

Key Votes of the 104th Congress

1. Reduce Medicare Growth $	N	5. Flag Amendment	Y	9. Cuban Embargo	Y
2. Ovrd. Product Liab. Veto	N	6. Drop EPA Limits	Y	10. Bar Bosnia Troop $	N
3. Increase Min. Wage	Y	7. Repeal Assault-Weap. Ban	N	11. Cut Anti-Missile Defense	Y
4. Welfare Reform	N	8. Ovrd. Part. Birth Veto	N	12. Bar U.N. Uniforms	N

Election Results

1996 general	Frank Pallone, Jr. (D)	124,635	(61%)	($658,357)
	Steven J. Corodemus (R)	73,402	(36%)	($319,354)
	Others	5,441	(3%)	
1996 primary	Frank Pallone, Jr. (D)	unopposed		
1994 general	Frank Pallone, Jr. (D)	88,922	(60%)	($672,626)
	Mike Herson (R)	55,287	(38%)	($252,307)
	Others	3,122	(2%)	

SEVENTH DISTRICT

The transportation arteries beneath the curve of the First Watchung Mountain are one of New Jersey's historic lines of development. The rail lines of the late 19th Century opened up commuter suburbs; in the 1940s the four lanes of U.S. 22 created an automobile civilization; and finally Interstate 78, completed in the mid-1980s, put Newark only an hour's distance from the Pennsylvania line. I-78 stimulated the development of an Edge City called Bridgewater Commons, where a huge shopping mall and office developments that included the new headquarters of AT&T rose up amid horse country around Far Hills and Bernardsville, where the likes of Malcolm Forbes and Charles Engelhard owned huge estates.

The 7th Congressional District of New Jersey covers these several generations of suburban development. It begins just west of Elizabeth, taking in affluent railroad commuter towns like Short Hills and Summit. It also includes more modest suburbs along U.S. 22, like Union and Westfield and the old city of Plainfield, with its large black community, plus the working class suburbs of Woodbridge and South Plainfield in Middlesex County. It then follows I-78 and the Watchung Mountains far into the countryside to the fields of Somerset County. Once this was all solidly Republican; now the closer-in suburbs are more mixed, with Democratic inner cities; the farther-out Edge City areas are, if anything, increasingly Republican. In the House, this area has been represented by Republicans for many years.

The congressman from the 7th is Bob Franks, who has been in politics most of his adult life. He grew up in New Jersey, went away to college and law school, worked as a political consultant, then in 1979, at 28, was elected to the New Jersey Assembly from a district including parts of all four counties now in the 7th. He served as state Republican chairman for all but one year from 1988–92 and one of the leaders of the revolt against Governor Jim Florio's 1990 tax increase. And he was a political ally of Matthew Rinaldo, the 7th District congressman for 20 years, who had a liberal voting record and a high-ranking spot on the Commerce Committee. When Rinaldo abruptly dropped out of the race in September 1992, after being renominated three months before, the local Republican organization chose Franks to take his place. But Franks had surprisingly serious competition from Democrat Leonard Sendelsky, a well-known local builder active in civic organizations. The two ran even in Middlesex, while Franks won 55% in the rest of the district, for a 53%–43% win.

In the House Franks has had a moderate record on economics and a rather liberal record on cultural and foreign issues. He serves on the Budget Committee and on Transportation and Infrastructure, where much of his work has a local angle. After the big pipeline explosion in Edison in March 1994 he worked on pipeline safety; after dredging for the port of New York and New Jersey was stopped because the waste could not be dumped in the ocean, he got a bill passed in October 1996 authorizing and financing an alternative disposal site; after complaints from those under the flight paths to Newark Airport, he proposed creating an FAA ombudsman on airplane noise. On ISTEA renewal he has promised to work to maintain the formula that favors New Jersey and to keep the programs paying for bridges, mass transit and air quality improvement. Franks has some interesting causes too. He wants to stop the unrestricted sale of personal information about children by commercial list brokers. He wants a bipartisan commission on campaign finance reform to recommend a package of reform, with Congress getting an up or down vote. He wants the government to stop subsidizing electric power produced by the Tennessee Valley Authority and transmitted by the Power Marketing Administrations.

Franks was reelected easily in 1994. In 1996 he had stronger opposition from Democrat Larry Lerner, who spent $490,000 of his own money. But Franks raised and spent $1.3 million, and won 55%–42%, running about even in Middlesex County but well ahead in the rest of the district.

The People: Pop. 1990: 594,844; 4% rural; 14% age 65+; 80% White; 10% Black; 5% Asian; 5% Hispanic origin. Households: 64% married couple families; 27% married couple fams. w. children; 53% college educ.; median household income: $50,996; per capita income: $23,253; median gross rent: $699; median house value: $186,200.

1996 Presidential Vote

Clinton (D)	129,773	(51%)
Dole (R)	101,538	(40%)
Perot (I)	19,769	(8%)
Other	4,710	(2%)

1992 Presidential Vote

Bush (R)	125,592	(44%)
Clinton (D)	115,846	(41%)
Perot (I)	40,690	(14%)

Rep. Bob Franks (R)

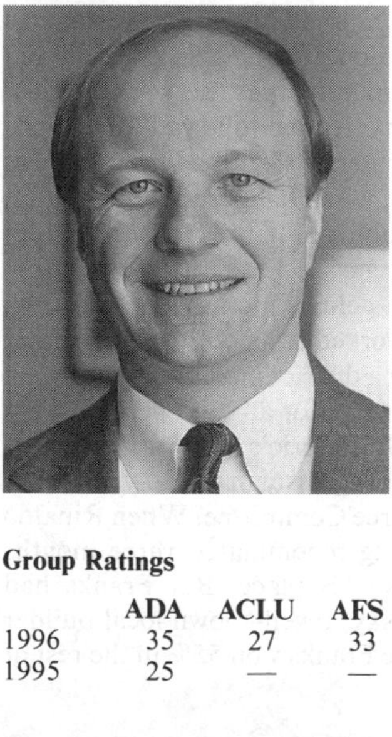

Elected 1992; b. Sept. 21, 1951, Hackensack; home, New Providence; DePauw U., B.A. 1973, S. Methodist U., J.D. 1976; Methodist; married (Fran).

Career: Political consultant, 1976–79; Med Data Inc., 1979–81; NJ Assembly, 1979–92; Co-owner, *County News*, 1982–84; NJ Repub. St. Chmn., 1988–89, 1990–92.

DC Office: 225 CHOB 20515, 202-225-5361; Fax: 202-225-9460; e-mail: franksnj@hr.house.gov.

District Offices: Union, 908-686-5576; Woodbridge, 908-602-0075.

Committees: *Budget* (8th of 24 R). *Transportation & Infrastructure* (13th of 40 R): Railroads; Surface Transportation; Water Resources & Environment.

Group Ratings

	ADA	ACLU	AFS	LCV	CFA	CON	NFIB	COC	ACU	NTLC	CHC
1996	35	27	33	62	77	55	86	81	63	85	66
1995	25	—	—	38	38	87	—	92	52	—	—

National Journal Ratings

	1995 LIB — 1995 CONS			1996 LIB — 1996 CONS		
Economic	44%	—	53%	49%	—	50%
Social	59%	—	40%	61%	—	39%
Foreign	55%	—	44%	67%	—	31%

Key Votes of the 104th Congress

1. Reduce Medicare Growth $	Y	5. Flag Amendment	Y	9. Cuban Embargo	Y
2. Ovrd. Product Liab. Veto	Y	6. Drop EPA Limits	Y	10. Bar Bosnia Troop $	N
3. Increase Min. Wage	Y	7. Repeal Assault-Weap. Ban	N	11. Cut Anti-Missile Defense	N
4. Welfare Reform	Y	8. Ovrd. Part. Birth Veto	Y	12. Bar U.N. Uniforms	Y

Election Results

1996 general	Bob Franks (R)	128,821	(55%)	($1,305,753)
	Larry Lerner (D)	97,285	(42%)	($801,815)
	Others	6,465	(3%)	
1996 primary	Bob Franks (R)	unopposed		
1994 general	Bob Franks (R)	98,814	(60%)	($542,563)
	Karen Carroll (D)	64,231	(39%)	($15,667)
	Others	2,812	(2%)	

EIGHTH DISTRICT

Paterson, New Jersey, is one of few American cities that has turned out pretty much as planned. The planner was Alexander Hamilton, who in the 1790s journeyed 20 miles from Manhattan into the interior of New Jersey to the Great Falls of the Passaic River. Watching the water surge down 72 feet—the highest falls along the East Coast—he predicted an industrial city would rise on this site. He formed the Society for Establishing Useful Manufactures, which opened a calico factory in 1794, and got Pierre L'Enfant, the designer of Washington, D.C., to design Paterson (named after then-Governor William Paterson). In 1836, Samuel Colt began manufacturing revolvers here; the first locomotive, the Sandusky, was built here in 1837, and a walkout of Paterson cotton workers in 1828 was America's first factory strike. Paterson ultimately became America's "Silk City," employing 25,000 silk mill workers before the great strike of 1913 led by the radical Industrial Workers of the World, at a time when the city fathers were erecting imposing public buildings and the narrow streets were buzzing with rumors of anarchist plots. Paterson kept producing locomotives and, after the silk mills started closing down following another unsuccessful strike in 1924, became a cloth-dying center. Throughout, it attracted immigrants from England, Ireland and, after 1890, Italy and Poland. But now Paterson is a kind of misfit in time and place: still a manufacturing center in a service-dominated economy, a blue-collar city set amid dozens of white-collar suburbs.

The 8th Congressional District includes Paterson as its largest city, plus much suburban territory west and south of Paterson and north and west of Newark. It includes the mixed factory and middle-class towns south of Paterson on the Passaic River—Clifton, Passaic, Nutley, Belleville. On higher ground are Bloomfield and, up on a ridge with views of New York City, part of Montclair. An affluent part of the Oranges is also included, as well as Wayne Township west of Paterson. The political heritage of the 8th District is Democratic, partly from its radical past, but more from the allegiances of its immigrant groups. But by the 1980s, the central cities were outvoted by increasingly Republican suburbs, and the district is now closely divided.

The congressman from the 8th District—the fourth the district has chosen in four elections—is Bill Pascrell, a Democrat elected in 1996. He grew up in Paterson, the grandson of Italian immigrants, graduated from Fordham, served in the Army, then taught high school for 12 years. From there he went into politics, first on the Paterson Board of Education, then in 1987 to the New Jersey Assembly. In 1990 he was elected mayor of Paterson, but continued to serve in the Assembly—a common practice in New Jersey. In these offices Pascrell showed a flair for sponsoring attractive government programs. In the statehouse he passed a bill for 2,000 additional street patrolmen in New Jersey, and got $14 million to renovate Paterson schools. He also sponsored a health program with preventive medicine and child immunizations and a housing program with new construction and help for first-time home-buyers. To stop drug dealers, he required permits for new pay phones and personally ripped out phones without permits. He started first-time drug offender boot camps and put city prisoners to work cleaning up streets.

Meanwhile, he watched as the 8th District seat changed hands. Democrat Robert Roe, first elected in 1969 and chairman of the Public Works Committee, retired in 1992. Liberal Democrat Herb Klein, who spent $580,000 of his own money, won the seat 47%–41%. Two years later Republican Bill Martini, active in politics in Clifton for years, beat Klein 50%–49%. In the House Martini supported the Contract with America 91% of the time, but also made a liberal record on the environment and other issues. He worked successfully on local issues, including funding for Sterling Forest on the New Jersey-New York border. He supported the minimum wage increase, the 1996 healthcare portability bill and welfare reform. He campaigned as an "independent congressman," and said, "In Washington, they can tell you where to sit, but they can't tell you where to stand." He got the endorsement of the Sierra Club and, with the help of his seat on Transportation and Infrastructure, of some transportation unions.

Pascrell nevertheless attacked him strenuously as the puppet of an "extremist" Republican leadership—one ad even showed Martini's face on a puppet operated by Speaker Gingrich. Pascrell echoed the AFL-CIO ad campaign's claim that Martini had voted to "cut" Medicare. Pascrell took liberal stands, opposing welfare reform and the partial birth abortion ban, and called for a middle class tax cut to be paid for by cutting corporate welfare. But he also echoed the soothing tone of the Clinton-Gore campaign. "People are very fed up with the partisan harping that led to the closure of the government." Martini called Pascrell a "double-dipper" for collecting two taxpayer salaries, and attacked him for allowing Paterson sewage to be dumped into the Passaic River and for raising property taxes 47% (only 38%, Pascrell said). This was an expensive campaign: Martini spent $1.4 million, Pascrell $953,000. In a district that gave nearly 60% to Clinton, the result was close: Pascrell won 51%–48%. He carried Paterson and Passaic County handily, but trailed a bit in the higher-income Essex County suburbs to the south.

Pascrell is likely to be an enthusiastic supporter of the House Democratic leadership. But this could be the scene of another close contest in 1998.

The People: Pop. 1990: 594,912; 15% age 65+; 67% White; 12% Black; 3% Asian; 18% Hispanic origin. Households: 55% married couple families; 24% married couple fams. w. children; 42% college educ.; median household income: $39,944; per capita income: $18,527; median gross rent: $595; median house value: $192,900.

1996 Presidential Vote

Clinton (D)	123,856	(58%)
Dole (R)	73,731	(34%)
Perot (I)	12,864	(6%)
Other	4,095	(2%)

1992 Presidential Vote

Clinton (D)	107,304	(45%)
Bush (R)	99,974	(42%)
Perot (I)	27,703	(12%)

Rep. Bill Pascrell, Jr. (D)

Elected 1996; b. Jan. 25, 1937, Paterson; home, Paterson; Fordham U., B.A. 1959; M.A. 1961; Catholic; married (Elsie).

Career: Army, 1961–67; High Schl. teacher, 1960–74; Dir., Paterson Dept. of Public Works, 1974–77; Dir., Paterson Dept. of Policy, 1977–87; Pres., Paterson Bd. of Educ., 1979–82; NJ Assembly, 1987–97; Paterson Mayor, 1990–97.

DC Office: 1722 LHOB 20515, 202-225-5751; Fax: 202-225-5782.

District Offices: Paterson, 201-523-5152.

Committees: *Small Business* (13th of 16 D): Empowerment. *Transportation & Infrastructure* (28th of 33 D): Surface Transportation; Water Resources & Environment.

Group Ratings and Key Votes: Newly Elected

Election Results

1996 general	Bill Pascrell, Jr. (D)	98,861	(51%)	($952,722)
	Bill Martini (R)	92,609	(48%)	($1,393,134)
1996 primary	Bill Pascrell, Jr. (D)	unopposed		
1994 general	Bill Martini (R)	70,494	(50%)	($851,781)
	Herb Klein (D)	68,661	(49%)	($1,116,614)
	Others	2,213	(2%)	

NINTH DISTRICT

The George Washington Bridge, one of several wondrous suspension bridges completed in America in the 1930s, strides across the Hudson, its west tower almost up against the green cliff of New Jersey's Palisades. It is one of the glories of modern engineering, enabling people and goods to be transported through the irregular terrain of metropolitan New York—tidal rivers and cliffs and broad expanses of swamp. For a century the dramatic beauty of the Palisades contrasted with the ugly sprawl of the Hackensack River Valley and the Jersey Meadowlands. This giant swamp was the image of New Jersey for many—a landscape of gas station signs, oil tank farms, truck terminals and 12 lanes of New Jersey Turnpike—a smelly, ugly place that meant you were still not where you wanted to go, full of garbage and pig farms, briefly famous when Secaucus tavern owner Henry Krajewski ran for president in 1956 and commemorated in today's New Jersey Garbage Museum. But the Meadowlands were the largest hunk of empty real estate near such a huge city center, and eventually they were developed. In the 1970s, the state built the Meadowlands Sports Complex—Giants Stadium (Giants and Jets now), the Meadowlands Racetrack, the Brendan Byrne Arena (now Continental Airlines Arena, home of the Nets and Devils). Private development followed—hotels, warehouses, light industry—whole small cities.

The 9th Congressional District of New Jersey includes much of the Palisades and the Meadowlands. It runs from the high-rise towers of Fort Lee and Cliffside Park, where apartment houses brag about their proximity to New York City, west and north to the leafy suburbs of Englewood and Teaneck, and southwest to the high land overlooking the Meadowlands and the Passaic River in old small towns like Rutherford, with Polish, German and Italian-Americans. Hackensack, an old industrial town and the Bergen County seat, and much of Fair Lawn, a planned town with a large Jewish population, also are in the 9th. This area grew in the 1950s and 1960s, as New Yorkers moved out of the City; it lost population in the 1970s and 1980s, as young people moved farther out and left empty nesters behind. Now there are new immigrants here: Englewood's schoolchildren are mostly black, Fort Lee's mostly Asian, many of Hackensack's Hispanic, though most of New Jersey's Cuban-American community is just to the south, around Union City in Hudson County. This was Republican country in the New Deal years, an area of white-collar enclaves. But the conservative families who grew up here are now being replaced by heavly Democratic immigrants and "tower dwellers."

The congressman from the 9th District is Steve Rothman, a Democrat elected in 1996. Rothman grew up in Englewood and Tenafly, went off to school at Syracuse University and then Washington University law school in St. Louis, then practiced law. From 1983–89 he was mayor of Englewood, where he claims to have cut taxes, reduced crime and led an economic renaissance. In 1993 he became a judge in the Bergen County Surrogate's Court. When 14-year 9th District Congressman Bob Torricelli ran for the Senate in 1996, Rothman resigned his judgeship and ran for the House. He won the party endorsement in March 1996, then faced former Fair Lawn Mayor Robert Gordon in the primary. Gordon spent $300,000 of his own money and called Rothman the "hand picked" candidate of the party bosses. But turnout is light in New Jersey primaries, and Rothman won 79% among the 21,000 who voted in June.

In the general Rothman faced Kathleen Donovan, Bergen County clerk, former assemblywoman, and from 1994–95 chairman of the New York-New Jersey Port Authority. Their positions on issues did not seem very different. Rothman was pro-choice on abortion, for the death penalty and gun control; so was Donovan. Rothman said he wanted to balance the budget, preserve open parcels of land, build new highways and mass transit. Donovan said much the same. But there were distinctions. Rothman took some strong liberal stands, against the welfare reform bill and the "partial-birth" abortion ban. He proposed an IRA-like higher education accumulation program, allowing parents to set aside tax-free $5,000 per year per child for college. Donovan spotlighted her record on environmental issues, and won the endorsement of the Sierra Club, the New Jersey Education Association and Cuban-American leader Jorge Mas Canosa. She was also endorsed by three northern New Jersey papers: *The Star-Ledger*, *The Record* and *The Herald and News*. Both made some sloppy charges. Rothman accused Donovan of a "lavish culture of waste" at the Port Authority for overusing its helicopter at taxpayer expense. Donovan charged that Rothman backed a compulsory merger of schools in Englewood with two nearby suburbs in the 1980s in an effort to integrate students. Both spent almost identical amounts of money: Rothman $798,000, Donovan $790,000.

Republicans had fond hopes for this race, but the district seems to have become too Democratic for a Republican win—after the Newark 10th and Jersey City 13th, the 9th District produced the third highest Clinton percentage in New Jersey. Rothman won by a solid 56%–42%. In the House he serves on Judiciary and International Relations. He pays attention to district interests: two of his first acts were to form a juvenile crime task force and to call for Israel to be grouped with the Western European bloc at the United Nations so it might have a chance for a Security Council seat.

The People: Pop. 1990: 594,790; 16% age 65+; 76% White; 6% Black; 6% Asian; 11% Hispanic origin. Households: 54% married couple families; 22% married couple fams. w. children; 44% college educ.; median household income: $40,816; per capita income: $20,012; median gross rent: $640; median house value: $194,500.

1996 Presidential Vote			**1992 Presidential Vote**		
Clinton (D)	138,242	(60%)	Clinton (D)	122,676	(47%)
Dole (R)	71,741	(31%)	Bush (R)	102,578	(40%)
Perot (I)	17,012	(7%)	Perot (I)	31,534	(12%)

Rep. Steven R. Rothman (D)

Elected 1996; b. Oct. 14, 1952, Englewood; home, Fair Lawn; Syracuse U., B.A. 1974; Washington U., J.D. 1977; Jewish; divorced.

Career: Practicing atty., 1977–93; Englewood Mayor 1983–89; Bergen Cnty. Surrogate Court Judge, 1993–96.

DC Office: 1607 LHOB 20515, 202-225-5061; Fax: 202-225-5851; e-mail: steven.rothman@mail.house.gov.

District Offices: Hackensack, 201-646-0808; Jersey City, 201-798-1366.

Committees: *International Relations* (19th of 22 D): International Economic Policy & Trade. *Judiciary* (15th of 15 D): Crime.

Group Ratings and Key Votes: Newly Elected

Election Results

1996 general	Steven R. Rothman (D)	117,646	(56%)	($797,632)
	Kathleen A. Donovan (R)	89,005	(42%)	($789,894)
	Others	4,279	(2%)	
1996 primary	Steven R. Rothman (D)	17,016	(79%)	
	Robert Gordon (D)	3,715	(17%)	
	Others	680	(3%)	
1994 general	Robert G. Torricelli (D)	99,984	(63%)	($744,648)
	Peter J. Russo (R)	57,651	(36%)	($21,811)

TENTH DISTRICT

Newark is the hollow core of New Jersey, the city to which main transportation arteries once led and whose corporate headquarters buildings were the tallest in the state. In 1930, 442,000 people lived here, one of every nine in New Jersey; in 1996, 275,000 did, one of every 28. Downtown Newark still has the Prudential and Public Service headquarters, there are still factories in the Ironbound district, the area around Newark airport has some industrial development, and the New Jersey Performing Arts Center is nearly complete with a grand opening scheduled for October 1997. But big corporate leaders and small businesses alike have not put new jobs here since the 1967 riot. The reason is obvious: high crime. Some neighborhoods of Newark have retained their vitality, but large parts are dominated by criminals and deserted by most law-abiding residents who can get out. In 1994 the state took over the public schools, abysmally run, while spending per pupil ranks among the nation's highest.

The 10th Congressional District of New Jersey is made up of most of Newark—the Central, South and West Wards—plus Irvington, most of the Oranges and part of Montclair to the west, and much of Elizabeth, Rahway, and Linden to the south. The 10th was 59% black in 1990, and overwhelmingly Democratic; its boundary lines wiggle around to include blacks in Jersey City, Montclair and Elizabeth, and leave Hispanics in the next-door 13th District.

The congressman from the 10th is Donald Payne. He grew up in Newark, was a teacher, worked for Prudential, served on the Essex Board of Chosen Freeholders in the 1970s and was vice president of Urban Data Systems for 13 years. In 1980 and 1986, he ran against Congressman Peter Rodino, chairman of the House Judiciary Committee when it voted to impeach President Richard Nixon; Payne lost, even as an African-American in a district with black majorities. But when Rodino retired in 1988, Payne got 73% in the Democratic primary and easily won the general, and has been reelected routinely ever since.

Payne has an impeccably liberal voting record. He supported the "opportunity to learn" standards in the 1994 education bill—actually, requirements for state spending on equipment, teachers' salaries and other inputs. He amended the Abandoned Infants Assistance Act to help "boarder babies." He called early for humanitarian assistance to Somalia. In December 1994 he was elected chairman of the Congressional Black Caucus, beating the more flamboyant Alcee Hastings 23–15, just as Republicans were defunding the caucuses and just as senior Democrats had to relinquish chairmanships to Republicans. Payne struggled to save affirmative action and racial quota programs as they were under attack, with varying success. He could not stop a law that eliminated race preferences in broadcast licenses nor could he stop the House from passing a bill outlawing "social investments" for pension funds. But he was successful in urging Bill Clinton not to abandon racial quotas and preferences and in urging Newt Gingrich not to bring such measures to the floor. He saved the Africa Subcommittee from abolition, and attacked cuts in aid to African countries; in 1995 he successfully restored $675 million to the Africa Development Fund. But he did not lionize all of Africa's leaders. He sponsored a resolution to cut off new investment in Nigeria because of the human rights abuses of the Abacha regime and in Sudan because of its practice of slavery. In a similar vein, he was one of only two House Democrats to criticize President Clinton for receiving China's General Chi, who suppressed the Tienanmen Square demonstrations in 1989. Payne rotated out of the CBC chairmanship in December 1996, but may still be an important voice in such issues.

On local issues, Payne has worked to bring millions of dollars in federal housing grants to his district, supported the Newark Riverfront project and secured grants to hire more police officers in Newark and Jersey City. Payne seems strong at home; in the 1996 primary he won 82% against two opponents; in the general Payne won 84%, as Bill Clinton carried the district with 82%—his best in the state.

The People: Pop. 1990: 593,876; 12% age 65+; 26% White; 59% Black; 2% Asian; 12% Hispanic origin. Households: 39% married couple families; 18% married couple fams. w. children; 34% college educ.; median household income: $28,849; per capita income: $12,833; median gross rent: $520; median house value: $136,100.

1996 Presidential Vote

Clinton (D)	138,128	(82%)
Dole (R)	21,911	(13%)
Perot (I)	5,774	(3%)

1992 Presidential Vote

Clinton (D)	126,415	(70%)
Bush (R)	36,299	(20%)
Perot (I)	14,887	(8%)

Rep. Donald M. Payne (D)

Elected 1988; b. July 16, 1934, Newark; home, Newark; Seton Hall, B.A. 1957; Baptist; widowed.

Career: Elem. & High Schl. teacher, 1957–64; Exec., Prudential Insurance Co., 1964–72; Pres., YMCAs of the U.S., 1970; Essex Cnty. Board of Chosen Freeholders, 1972–78, Dir. 1977–78; Vice Pres., Urban Data Systems Inc., 1975–88; Newark Municipal Cncl., 1982–89.

DC Office: 2244 RHOB 20515, 202-225-3436; Fax: 202-225-4160.

District Offices: Elizabeth, 908-629-0222; Newark, 201-645-3213..

Committees: *Education & The Workforce* (6th of 20 D): Early Childhood, Youth & Families; Employer-Employee Relations (RMM). *International Relations* (8th of 22 D): Africa; International Operations & Human Rights.

Group Ratings

	ADA	ACLU	AFS	LCV	CFA	CON	NFIB	COC	ACU	NTLC	CHC
1996	95	94	100	85	85	45	16	19	0	5	0
1995	100	—	—	94	100	16	—	8	4	—	—

National Journal Ratings

	1995 LIB — 1995 CONS			1996 LIB — 1996 CONS		
Economic	94%	—	0%	82%	—	16%
Social	88%	—	0%	88%	—	0%
Foreign	93%	—	0%	90%	—	0%

Key Votes of the 104th Congress

1. Reduce Medicare Growth $	N	5. Flag Amendment	N	9. Cuban Embargo	N
2. Ovrd. Product Liab. Veto	N	6. Drop EPA Limits	Y	10. Bar Bosnia Troop $	N
3. Increase Min. Wage	Y	7. Repeal Assault-Weap. Ban	N	11. Cut Anti-Missile Defense	Y
4. Welfare Reform	N	8. Ovrd. Part. Birth Veto	N	12. Bar U.N. Uniforms	N

Election Results

1996 general	Donald M. Payne (D)	127,126	(84%)	($404,017)
	Vanessa Williams (R)	22,086	(15%)	($20,902)
1996 primary	Donald M. Payne (D)	35,002	(82%)	
	Brian Connors (D)	4,421	(10%)	
	Cecil J. Banks (D)	3,062	(7%)	
1994 general	Donald M. Payne (D)	74,622	(76%)	($309,623)
	Jim Ford (R)	21,524	(22%)	($18,180)
	Others	2,222	(2%)	

ELEVENTH DISTRICT

New Jersey's Morris County, west of the Watchung Mountain ridges, was one of the first settled parts of the interior United States west of the Hudson. It has long been a place of comparative affluence, the home of skilled craftsmen during the Revolutionary War, with plenty of water mills and iron forges by the 19th Century. But only in the late 20th Century has it come into its own, as one of the most affluent quarters of the United States. And it is not just a collection of country estates with huddled small towns for the servants to live in, but a well-rounded community with all the appurtenances of urbanity except the high crime and poverty rates. The very rich have lived here for some time, connected to Manhattan by commuter rail lines, but in the 1970s and 1980s, more rushed out the newly completed I-80 and I-280 or the ring road I-287. Bayer was setting up a big operation down the road and hundreds of small businesses were quietly creating jobs more rapidly than highly-publicized big companies (AT&T had huge layoffs here in 1996) were downsizing.

The 11th Congressional District includes all of Morris County plus similar adjacent areas. It is one of the wealthiest districts in the country: number one in median household income in 1990, at $57,219, with the highest median housing value in New Jersey, $214,600—exceeded only by four districts in the New York area, 25 in California and one in Hawaii. It is family territory, with relatively few singles; not a strongly culturally conservative area, but not aggressively liberal either. Politically, it is heavily Republican, the most Republican district in New Jersey, and one of the most in the Northeast.

The congressman from the 11th District is Rodney Frelinghuysen, a Republican and member of one of New Jersey's most durable political families: four Frelinghuysens served as senator from New Jersey, starting in 1793 and as recently as 1923; Frederick Frelinghuysen was Chester Arthur's secretary of State; Peter Frelinghuysen, Rodney's father, was elected to the House in 1952 and served until his retirement in 1974. After college, Rodney Frelinghuysen served in the

Army in Vietnam and in 1972 was appointed an aide by then-Morris County Freeholder (and later 11th District congressman) Dean Gallo; he served as a freeholder himself from 1974–83 and was elected to the Assembly in 1983. There he supported one tax increase by Republican Governor Thomas Kean, but opposed Democratic Governor Jim Florio's 1990 tax increase and, as chairman of the Appropriations Committee, worked to control spending and roll back taxes as an ally of Governor Christie Whitman.

Frelinghuysen ran for Congress in the 12th District in 1990, when its boundaries were different, and lost the primary to Dick Zimmer. In August 1994, after that year's primary, Gallo retired because of illness; he died two days before the election. Frelinghuysen was chosen to be the Republican nominee at a September party convention and was elected with 71% of the vote. He showed his insider skills by winning a seat on the Appropriations Committee, where Gallo had served. On Appropriations Frelinghuysen worked to cut spending on many programs, while maintaining a moderate voting record and concentrating on New Jersey projects. He supported funds for "Urban Core" and "Midtown Direct" mass transit lines. He helped push Sterling Forest preservation into the 1996 parks bill President Clinton signed, and got $1 million to expand the Great Swamp National Wildlife Refuge by 79 acres. He boasted of a 700% increase in funds to combat domestic violence. He got more money for Picatinny Arsenal's infrastructure improvements. He got $2 million for trial of fast-track sediment decontamination technology, to help develop a disposal site for New York-New Jersey dredging waste—necessary if dredging is to continue. In 1997, he was one of three House Republicans to switch their vote to support a ban on "partial-birth" abortions; in 1996, he voted against the attempt to override President Clinton's veto of a similar bill.

Frelinghuysen was easily reelected in 1996. In 1997 he got a third Appropriations subcommittee assignment: Foreign Operations and Export Financing.

The People: Pop. 1990: 594,526; 13% rural; 11% age 65+; 89% White; 3% Black; 4% Asian; 4% Hispanic origin. Households: 67% married couple families; 31% married couple fams. w. children; 60% college educ.; median household income: $57,219; per capita income: $25,454; median gross rent: $730; median house value: $214,600.

1996 Presidential Vote

Dole (R)	135,972	(49%)
Clinton (D)	116,225	(42%)
Perot (I)	21,376	(8%)
Other	5,240	(2%)

1992 Presidential Vote

Bush (R)	153,731	(51%)
Clinton (D)	97,697	(33%)
Perot (I)	46,407	(16%)

Rep. Rodney P. Frelinghuysen (R)

Elected 1994; b. Apr. 29, 1946, New York City; home, Morristown; Hobart Col., B.A. 1969; Episcopalian; married (Virginia).

Career: Army, 1970–71 (Vietnam); Morris Cnty. Bd. of Freeholders, 1972–83, Aide, 1972–74; NJ Assembly, 1983–94.

DC Office: 228 CHOB 20515, 202-225-5034; Fax: 202-225-3186; e-mail: njeleven@hr.house.gov.

District Offices: Dover, 201-328-7413; Morristown, 201-984-0711; W. Caldwell, 201-228-9262.

Committees: *Appropriations* (24th of 34 R): Energy & Water Development; Foreign Operations, Export Financing & Related Programs; VA, HUD & Independent Agencies.

Group Ratings

	ADA	ACLU	AFS	LCV	CFA	CON	NFIB	COC	ACU	NTLC	CHC
1996	30	25	0	62	54	30	92	87	75	85	60
1995	15	—	—	13	46	56	—	88	60	—	—

National Journal Ratings

	1995 LIB — 1995 CONS			1996 LIB — 1996 CONS		
Economic	41%	—	56%	42%	—	56%
Social	55%	—	43%	65%	—	35%
Foreign	28%	—	65%	41%	—	59%

Key Votes of the 104th Congress

1. Reduce Medicare Growth $	Y	5. Flag Amendment	Y	9. Cuban Embargo	Y
2. Ovrd. Product Liab. Veto	Y	6. Drop EPA Limits	N	10. Bar Bosnia Troop $	N
3. Increase Min. Wage	N	7. Repeal Assault-Weap. Ban	N	11. Cut Anti-Missile Defense	N
4. Welfare Reform	Y	8. Ovrd. Part. Birth Veto	N	12. Bar U.N. Uniforms	Y

Election Results

1996 general	Rodney P. Frelinghuysen (R)	169,091	(66%)	($581,895)
	Chris Evangel (D)	78,742	(31%)	($181,050)
	Others	7,325	(3%)	
1996 primary	Rodney P. Frelinghuysen (R)	unopposed		
1994 general	Rodney P. Frelinghuysen (R)	127,868	(71%)	($243,923)
	Frank Herbert (D)	50,211	(28%)	($43,614)

TWELFTH DISTRICT

It was once the main East Coast arterial highway, carrying the nation's highest volume of truck traffic. Today it is crowded with cars taking high-salaried workers and clerical help to one of the East Coast's thickest concentrations of office buildings in one of the bigger Edge Cities spawned in the 1980s. This is U.S. 1, which once just connected the industrial cities of Trenton and New Brunswick on its way from Philadelphia to New York; now it is better thought of around here as connecting the university towns around Princeton and Rutgers, and is a locus of telecommunications and pharmaceutical research. This had been empty bucolic country, looked out on by F. Scott Fitzgerald's undergraduates from their Gothic Princeton towers; now it is filled with postmodern office campuses and hotels and restaurants clamoring for attention.

The 12th Congressional District of New Jersey extends several dozen miles on either side of U.S. 1. To the west, it takes in the rolling country of Hunterdon County, around the old county seat of Flemington, once the site of the Lindbergh kidnapping trial, now an outlet store center with many young families, affluent if not elite, modern but seeking traditional values. On the other side of U.S. 1, the 12th takes in modest-income suburbs like East Brunswick in Middlesex County and much of Monmouth County, almost to the beach resorts of the Jersey Shore. Some of these communities are long-settled, others are spanking new. Politically, the Princeton area and Middlesex County, in the center of the district, lean mildly Democratic. The two ends of the district—Monmouth County near the Shore and Hunterdon County inland—are usually heavily Republican. The balance is Republican, though Bill Clinton carried the district in 1996.

The congressman from the 12th District is Mike Pappas, a Republican elected in 1996. Pappas grew up in a small town in Somerset County and took to politics early: he was on the Franklin Township Planning Board in 1980, at 19. Two years later he was elected to the Township Council, and served five years, while also working in the family insurance agency; in 1984 he was elected to the Somerset County Board of Chosen Freeholders, where one of his colleagues was Christie Whitman. In 1996, when 12th District Congressman Dick Zimmer, a fiscal conservative and liberal on some cultural issues, ran for the Senate, Pappas was one of four Republicans and three Democrats to run for the seat. He was not the favorite at the start, but he was distinctive as the one candidate strongly against both abortion and gun control. The favorite in the Republican primary was state Senate Majority Leader John Bennett from Monmouth County, who raised lots of money and called for tax cuts; he was peppered with criticism from Hunterdon County Assemblyman Leonard Lance for having voting for tax increases. Meanwhile, Pappas was endorsed by 4th District Congressman Christopher Smith, a strong abortion foe. Each candidate carried his own local area, with the exception of Republican Luis De Agustin, who only won 2%. Although Pappas' county was the smallest, he finished second everywhere else and rolled up enough votes to win the primary with 38%, to 34% for Bennett and 26% for Lance.

Democrats suddenly became optimistic about winning the seat. Their nominee was David Del Vecchio, mayor of Lawrenceville, who won 45% of the vote, to 31% for Princeton Town Committeeman Carl Mayer and 24% for Princeton physicist Rush Holt (whose father was elected senator from West Virginia in 1934 but did not take his seat until June 1935 when he turned 30). Del Vecchio campaigned mostly on his record of cutting taxes as mayor and attacking Newt Gingrich. He quoted the National Rifle Association calling Pappas a "true believer"; Pappas said he had never owned or fired a gun but believed in the Second Amendment right to bear arms. Del Vecchio also quoted Republican activist Hazel Gluck, who called Pappas "extreme" for his views on abortion. But Pappas had support from Whitman and Zimmer, and insisted that his top goal was cutting taxes.

Press coverage cast a dim light on Pappas's chances; but he won anyway. His 50%–47% margin was far closer than Zimmer's 68%–30% in 1994. Del Vecchio carried the Princeton area and Middlesex County, but Pappas won more than 60% in Hunterdon and Somerset and carried Monmouth as well. In the House he serves on the National Security, Small Business, and Government Reform and Oversight Committees; he did not get Zimmer's seat on Ways and Means as he had hoped.

The People: Pop. 1990: 594,577; 34% rural; 11% age 65+; 88% White; 5% Black; 4% Asian; 3% Hispanic origin. Households: 67% married couple families; 32% married couple fams. w. children; 62% college educ.; median household income: $54,630; per capita income: $24,615; median gross rent: $696; median house value: $205,200.

1996 Presidential Vote

Clinton (D)	139,252	(48%)
Dole (R)	120,913	(42%)
Perot (I)	23,159	(8%)
Other	6,716	(2%)

1992 Presidential Vote

Bush (R)	130,651	(43%)
Clinton (D)	121,447	(40%)
Perot (I)	50,357	(17%)

Rep. Michael Pappas (R)

Elected 1996; b. Dec. 29, 1960, New Brunswick; home, Rocky Hill; Baptist; divorced.

Career: Insurance Exec., Pappas Insurance Agency, 1980–96; Franklin Twnshp. Planning Bd., 1980; Franklin Twnshp. Cncl., 1982–87; Franklin Mayor, 1983–84; Somerset Cnty. Bd. of Chosen Freeholders, 1984–96, Dir., 1988 & 1993.

DC Office: 1710 LHOB 20515; 202-225-5801.

District Offices: Flemington, 908-284-1138; Freehold, 908-462-8499.

Committees: *Government Reform & Oversight* (21st of 24 R): Civil Service (Vice Chmn.); Human Resources. *National Security* (28th of 30 R): Military Procurement; Military Research & Development. *Small Business* (13th of 19 R): Tax, Finance & Exports.

Group Ratings and Key Votes: Newly Elected

Election Results

1996 general	Michael Pappas (R)	135,811	(50%)	($591,536)
	David M. Del Vecchio (D)	125,594	(47%)	($475,370)
	Others	7,816	(3%)	
1996 primary	Michael Pappas (R)	11,069	(38%)	
	John Bennett (R)	9,894	(34%)	
	Leonard Lance (R)	7,630	(26%)	
	Others	481	(2%)	
1994 general	Dick Zimmer (R)	125,939	(68%)	($612,178)
	Joseph D. Youssouf (D)	55,977	(30%)	($49,395)

THIRTEENTH DISTRICT

The Statue of Liberty, standing in New York Harbor since 1886, has been the great symbol of America welcoming immigrants to its shores. Actually, the statue is on the New Jersey side of the Harbor, and the shore on which many immigrants first settle—in the old days when they came ashore by boat and today when they are more likely to disembark at Kennedy or Newark Airports—is in New Jersey. The towns sitting on the granite and gneiss ridge of Hudson County, New Jersey, overlooking the Harbor, have in particular been immigrant territory. Today, as a century ago, they are the most densely populated part of urban America except for Manhattan. When immigration was shut off by the laws of 1921 and 1924, many children and grandchildren of the Irish and Italian immigrants stayed in Hudson County, living in the same neighborhoods, working on the same docks or factories—Maxwell House and Palmolive were here—and voting the dictates of the same political machine.

Hudson County was the setting of one of America's classic political machines, undisciplined by any metropolitan elite. From 1917–49, the boss of Hudson County was Frank ("I am the law") Hague; his machine chose governors and U.S. Senators, prosecutors and judges, and had influence in the White House of Franklin D. Roosevelt. Hague collected high taxes from the industries clustered here—who then passed them on to consumers everywhere—and in return gave them an orderly city, free of most crime and vice, and a work force insulated against racketeers and militant unions. Hague's successor, John V. Kenny, was boss from 1949–71—continuous power for 54 years, a record beaten only in Albany.

But Hudson County began changing again, in ways little noticed by either the local machine or Manhattan sophisticates. New immigrants were coming in—refugees from Castro's Cuba, other Latinos and Asians after the 1965 immigration law changed the rules. Union City became predominantly Cuban, Jersey City neighborhoods became heavily Latino. Upscale young singles looking for lower rents moved into Hoboken's five-story Victorian apartments that sparkle with light off the Hudson, and are within a quick commute through the PATH tubes to Wall Street or Greenwich Village. The Jersey City waterfront is the scene of huge new condominium developments—Port Liberte, opposite the Statue of Liberty; Newport, with thousands of housing units and hundreds of thousands of square feet of office space; Liberty Place on the site of the old Colgate-Palmolive factory. This vibrant private sector contrasted with a somnolent public sector so incompetent and expensive that it gave an opening to Jersey City's Republican mayor, Bret Schundler, a former Wall Streeter who first won in 1992 after the incumbent went to jail and who was reelected in 1993 with 68%.

The 13th Congressional District of New Jersey includes most of Hudson County plus most of the immigrant entry ports along the water, from the Hackensack River and Newark Bay to Arthur Kill and Raritan Bay. It was designed in 1992 to be an "Hispanic influence" district; 42% of its residents in 1990 were Hispanic and 11% were black. With most of Jersey City and all of Union City and West New York and Weehawken, it includes 105,000 people in the old Ironbound area and North Ward of Newark, half of them Hispanic, and takes in the industrial city waterfront areas of Elizabeth, Linden, Carteret and Perth Amboy. It still votes Democratic, quite heavily in 1996.

The congressman from the 13th is Democrat Robert Menendez, a Cuban-American who grew up in Union City, America's most densely populated city (in 1990 it had 58,000 people in 1.3 square miles), and got into politics early: he was elected to the school board in 1974, at 20. He worked for Union City Mayor William Musto in the 1970s, but quit and testified against Musto in a corruption trial, and ran against him and lost in 1982. Menendez was elected mayor in 1986 and to the legislature in 1987, serving in both jobs until he was elected to Congress. When the new district lines were created and incumbent Congressman Frank Guarini retired, Menendez won his 1992 primary 68%–32% and the general 64%–31%.

In the House, Menendez serves on the International Relations Committee where he is now ranking minority member on the Africa Subcommittee. He supported Bob Torricelli's 1992 Cuban Democracy Act, and attacked Cuban oppression at the United Nations Commission on Human Rights in Geneva in April 1996. After the Brothers to the Rescue fliers were shot down in February 1996, he helped broker Clinton Administration acceptance of the Helms-Burton Act. He was disappointed when Clinton twice suspended lawsuits authorized by Helms-Burton against those who take title to expropriated property in Cuba, but he plugged on nonetheless. He shows sensitivity to ethnic sentiments: he called for receiving Sinn Fein's Gerry Adams in the United States and was a committee observer to the Sinn Fein Ard Fheis annual conference in Dublin; he called for sanctions on Turkey when that country signed a $23 billion natural gas deal with Iran. He is an ally of organized labor: he opposed NAFTA and, after the AFL-CIO attacked it, criticized the Republicans' Shipping Act deregulation as cartelization. He works on local projects—the Hudson-Bergen Light Rail Project, the Jersey City/MLK Partnership housing project, redevelopment of Linden Airport. Menendez will take a more high-profile role in upcoming years with his appointment in March 1997 to a leadership post. After New Mexico Congressman Bill Richardson was named U.N. Ambassador, Menendez was tapped as the Hispanic to fill the Chief Deputy Minority Whip position Richardson vacated.

Menendez has been reelected by large margins; his 1996 opponent called for English as the official language but could not speak it fluently himself and campaigned in Spanish. He is said to be interested in running for the Senate in 2000 if Frank Lautenberg retires.

The People: Pop. 1990: 594,875; 12% age 65+; 42% White; 11% Black; 4% Asian; 42% Hispanic origin. Households: 45% married couple families; 21% married couple fams. w. children; 31% college educ.; median household income: $28,721; per capita income: $13,028; median gross rent: $505; median house value: $142,700.

1996 Presidential Vote

Clinton (D)	115,576	(71%)
Dole (R)	35,266	(22%)
Perot (I)	8,411	(5%)
Other	2,764	(2%)

1992 Presidential Vote

Clinton (D)	94,651	(53%)
Bush (R)	64,358	(36%)
Perot (I)	14,981	(8%)

Rep. Robert Menendez (D)

Elected 1992; b. Jan. 1, 1954, New York, NY; home, Union City; St. Peter's Col., B.A. 1976, Rutgers Law Schl., J.D. 1979; Catholic; married (Jane Jacobsen-Menendez)

Career: Union City Bd. of Educ., 1974–82; Union City Mayor, 1986–92; NJ Assembly, 1987–91; NJ Senate 1991–92.

DC Office: 405 CHOB 20515, 202-225-7919; Fax: 202-226-0792.

District Offices: Bayonne, 201-823-2900; Jersey City, 201-222-2828; Perth Amboy, 908-324-6212.

Committees: *Chief Deputy Minority Whip. International Relations* (10th of 22 D): Africa (RMM); Western Hemisphere. *Transportation & Infrastructure* (15th of 33 D): Surface Transportation; Water Resources & Environment.

Group Ratings

	ADA	ACLU	AFS	LCV	CFA	CON	NFIB	COC	ACU	NTLC	CHC
1996	85	64	100	85	85	7	24	19	5	12	7
1995	90	—	—	94	92	16	—	21	17	—	—

National Journal Ratings

	1995 LIB — 1995 CONS			1996 LIB — 1996 CONS		
Economic	80%	—	18%	73%	—	25%
Social	75%	—	23%	84%	—	16%
Foreign	79%	—	17%	76%	—	22%

Key Votes of the 104th Congress

1. Reduce Medicare Growth $	N	5. Flag Amendment	Y	9. Cuban Embargo	Y
2. Ovrd. Product Liab. Veto	N	6. Drop EPA Limits	Y	10. Bar Bosnia Troop $	N
3. Increase Min. Wage	Y	7. Repeal Assault-Weap. Ban	N	11. Cut Anti-Missile Defense	Y
4. Welfare Reform	N	8. Ovrd. Part. Birth Veto	N	12. Bar U.N. Uniforms	Y

Election Results

1996 general	Robert Menendez (D)	115,459	(79%)	($379,469)
	Carlos E. Munoz (R)	25,427	(17%)	
	Others	5,587	(4%)	
1996 primary	Robert Menendez (D)	34,685	(93%)	
	Cristopher Curioli (D)	2,685	(7%)	
1994 general	Robert Menendez (D)	67,688	(71%)	($488,448)
	Fernando A. Alonso (R)	24,071	(25%)	($6,159)
	Others	3,708	(4%)	

NEW MEXICO

America's oldest settlements and its newest technologies can be found, in even surrealistic proximity, in New Mexico. For the oldest permanently inhabited city in the United States is not Plymouth, Massachusetts, or Jamestown, Virginia, or even St. Augustine, Florida; it is probably Acoma, New Mexico. Probably; because Acoma, inhabited by the Anasazi, "an agricultural, settled and architecturally sophisticated people," said historian Roger Kennedy in *Rediscovering America*, had perhaps 1,000 years of unrecorded history before Spanish conquistadors came upon them in 1540. Some 450 years later, much of what makes New Mexico distinctive derives from the people found here by the first European explorers—something true of no other state but Hawaii. While the Pilgrims built flimsy wood houses, the Indians in New Mexico were living in extensive dwellings hundreds of years old, made with the adobe that is still the characteristic building material here.

Other state cultures are generally based on what early white settlers brought to the land; natives have mostly disappeared or been killed off by diseases contracted from the first white settlers. Not in New Mexico. The English-speaking culture here is superimposed, at times rather lightly, on a society whose written history dates back to the Spanish settlement of Santa Fe in 1609, and to centuries long past when the Pueblo Indians set up stable agricultural societies on the sandy, rocky lands of northern New Mexico, using small pebbles as mulch to retain scarce moisture. Pueblo culture is still celebrated in the Indian pottery that commands premium prices in Santa Fe and in the annual Gathering of Nations pow-wow in Albuquerque which attracts 30,000 Indians. Today, a very substantial minority of New Mexicans are descendants of these Indians or the Spanish, or both. New Mexico had the highest percentage of Hispanics (38%) in the U.S. after the 1990 Census. Nearly one-third of the people in this state speak Spanish in everyday life, and only a few are recent migrants from Mexico. The Hispanic roots go very deep, as witnessed by the recent discovery of Hebrew symbols left on Christian gravestones by the *conversos*, Jews who hid their religion after it was outlawed by the Spanish in 1492; there are families here who have secretly maintained Jewish practices for centuries.

New Mexico is the northernmost salient of the great Indian-Spanish civilizations of the Cordillera, which extend along the mountain chain through Mexico and Central America to South America, as far away as Chile and Argentina. Yet New Mexico also is a civilization built on modern technology. It was to a remote mesa called Los Alamos that General Leslie Groves brought his Manhattan Project scientists during World War II to build a secret town and develop a secret weapon that would in two explosions end World War II and change the course of history. Los Alamos remains a government high-tech laboratory, and New Mexico has others as well—the White Sands Missile Range near Alamogordo, where the first atomic bomb was detonated, and the Sandia Laboratories near Albuquerque, run by Lockheed-Martin for the government, a non-nuclear high-tech weapons research facility, whose Intel computer, in early 1997, was the fastest in the world. And if New Mexico was in on the takeoff of nuclear power, it has also come in for part of the landing. Sandia's great mission now is maintaining nuclear weaponry know-how by using "pulsed power" research to simulate nuclear explosions. And New Mexico is a place where nuclear wastes will be buried beginning in May 1998: near Carlsbad is the federal Waste Isolation Pilot Project (WIPP), where the Energy Department plans to conduct a seven-year test of radioactive waste storage.

These two kinds of New Mexicos, very old and very young, intermingle with others of intermediate age in different proportions in this land of majestically vast vistas. The Hispanic-Indian culture predominates north and west of Albuquerque, with picturesque old towns and some still-functioning pueblos. "Little Texas," in the south and east, has small cities, plenty of oil

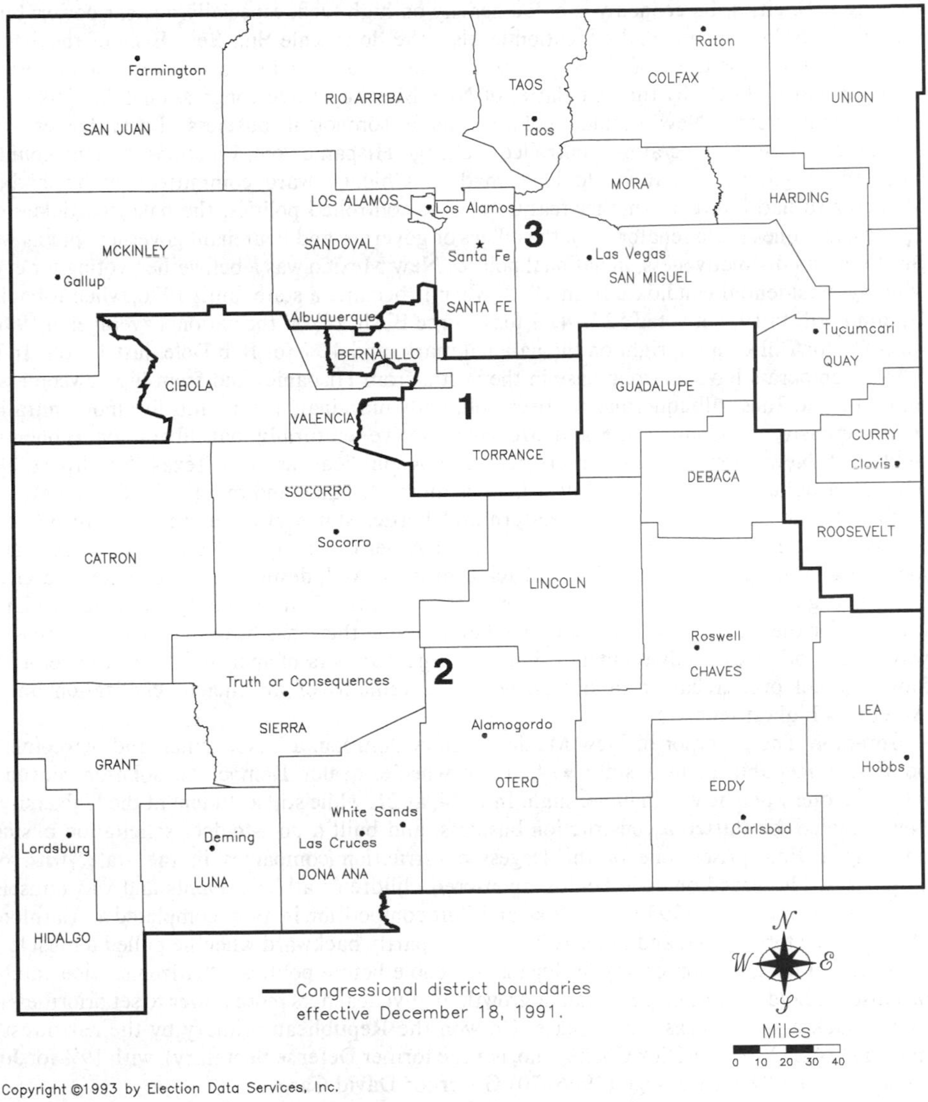

Farmington
SAN JUAN
RIO ARRIBA
TAOS
Taos
COLFAX
Raton
UNION
MORA
HARDING
LOS ALAMOS
Los Alamos
SANDOVAL
Santa Fe
3
Las Vegas
SAN MIGUEL
MCKINLEY
Gallup
Albuquerque
SANTA FE
BERNALILLO
Tucumcari
QUAY
CIBOLA
GUADALUPE
VALENCIA
1
CURRY
Clovis
TORRANCE
DEBACA
SOCORRO
Socorro
ROOSEVELT
CATRON
LINCOLN
Roswell
CHAVES
Truth or Consequences
2
SIERRA
Alamogordo
LEA
GRANT
OTERO
EDDY
Hobbs
White Sands
Deming
Las Cruces
Carlsbad
Lordsburg
LUNA
DONA ANA
HIDALGO
Congressional district boundaries effective December 18, 1991.
N
W
E
S
Miles
0 10 20 30 40

wells, vast cattle ranches and desolate military bases and resembles, economically and culturally, the adjacent west Texas High Plains. Here, as everywhere in New Mexico, government is a prime employer (accounting for 27% of jobs, one of the highest figures in the country) and often the moving force in the local economy. In the middle is Albuquerque which, with the arrival of airconditioning, grew from a small desert town of 35,000 in 1940 into a Sun Belt metropolis of 600,000 today. Albuquerque has a large Hispanic minority, as do many fast-growing U.S. cities. Its economy is based heavily on high tech, especially nuclear power; but it has relatively low income and education levels—the downscale Sun Belt. Each of these three areas has about one-third of the state's population, and their impressionistic boundaries are followed pretty closely by the boundaries of New Mexico's three congressional districts.

For many years, New Mexico politics was a somnolent business. Local bosses—first Republican, later Democratic—controlled the large Hispanic vote. Elections in many counties featured irregularities that would have made a Chicago ward committeeman blush. New Mexico also had for years another feature of boss-controlled politics, the balanced ticket: one Spanish and one Anglo senator, with the offices of governor and lieutenant governor split as well. But for all its distinctiveness, in national politics New Mexico was a bellwether, voting for every winning presidential candidate from 1912, when it became a state, until 1976, when it backed Gerald Ford. In 1988 it voted 52%–47% for George Bush, 1% off the national average; in 1996 it was 49% for Bill Clinton, right on the national mark, and 42% for Bob Dole, just 1% off. In the 1990s Democrats have a strong base in the north, from Hispanics and from hip newcomers in Santa Fe and Taos. Albuquerque has been politically marginal; its migrants live more in trailers than expensive condominiums, and are conservative culturally but liberal on economics. Southeast New Mexico is as conservative and Republican as west Texas. Southwest New Mexico, around Las Cruces and Silver City, is more Hispanic and marginally Democratic.

New Mexico differs from other western and border states in other ways. There has been relatively little migration from Mexico or Latin America; many of New Mexico's Hispanics have long family histories here that go back centuries. And, despite the emergence of a Green Party that got 10% of the vote for governor in 1994 and the Catron County ordinance declaring it illegal for the U.S. Forest Service to regulate grazing, there has been relatively little fuss one way or the other over environmental issues. Large numbers of merlin falcons and red-tailed hawks wheel over a barren landscape with live remains of an ancient civilization and of America's highest tech.

Governor. The governor of New Mexico is Gary Johnson, a businessman and newcomer to politics, a Republican in a state with many wheeler-dealer Democrats. Johnson moved to Albuquerque when he was in junior high. In 1974, at 21, while still a student at the University of New Mexico, he started a construction business, and built a door-to-door solicitation business into Big J Enterprises, one of the largest construction companies in the state, with 600 employees. He served on civic boards, sponsored children's athletic events and was himself a competitor: he won the 1993 Bump, Bike and Bolt competition in Taos, completed a Triathlon in Hawaii in October 1993, and ran a 100-mile race partly backward when he pulled a muscle. In 1994 he ran for governor, on vague slogans—"people before politics," "citizen service" and on promises to hold the line on government growth, to give teachers more power to set priorities and to roll back a six-cent gas tax increase. He won the Republican primary by the narrowest of margins, 34%–33% over Dick Cheney (no, not the former Defense Secretary), with 19% for John Dendahl and 13% for long-ago (1966–70) Governor David Cargo.

His Democratic opponent was a grizzled veteran of state politics, Santa Fe County rancher Bruce King, elected governor in 1970, 1978, and 1990, and now eligible for the first time for a second consecutive term. But he was pressed in the Democratic primary and won with only 39% over his own lieutenant governor, Casey Luna, with 36% and former Clinton Administration Interior Department official Jim Baca with 25%. In the general election the Green Party candidate, former Lieutenant Governor Roberto Mondragon, won 10%; Johnson beat King 50%–40%.

In office Johnson faced bitter opposition from Democratic legislative leaders. He did not get his proposed income tax cut and prescription tax abolition, but he did get the six-cent gas tax repealed. He vetoed some 200 bills, cut the state budget unilaterally (state employees sued), and after allowing a 5.5% spending increase, cut that to 2.8% for 1996 and zero for 1997. The Cato Institute ranked him sixth among governors on tax and fiscal policy. He cut the number of state employees—it has been far above the national average—and promised "the best possible service at the best possible cost." He instituted an "open door after four" on the third Thursday of every month during which citizens could get audiences with him for five minutes.

Johnson fared well in the 1996 legislative elections: Democrats hoped to pick up the one House and one Senate seat they needed to override Johnson's vetoes, but Republicans picked up three House seats and one Senate seat instead. In January 1997 Johnson proposed a $15 million tax cut and a $1.3 billion highway bond program, and called for devoting 30% of lottery proceeds to school computers. He presented a plan for two new prisons to be managed by private companies, and called for reducing the age at which juveniles could be tried as adults at 14. He favors legalizing Indian casino gambling and slot machines at racetracks. But Johnson's prospects for reelection are unclear as there are many potential Democratic candidates for 1998. Albuquerque Mayor Martin Chavez filed in May 1997, and former Governor Jerry Apodaca has also been mentioned as a possible candidate.

Senior Senator. Pete Domenici is in his third decade in the Senate and in his second decade as chairman of (or ranking Republican on) the Senate Budget Committee. Certainly he is the giant political figure in New Mexico. Domenici grew up in Albuquerque, the son of Italian immigrants who ran a grocery wholesale business. He played sports, practiced law, was elected to the city commission in 1966; he ran for governor in 1970, and lost to Bruce King, his only loss. In 1972, when a Senate seat opened up in a Republican year, he ran and won, beating a Democrat named Jack Daniels. Ever since he has been reelected by wide margins.

Domenici's great work in the Senate is on the budget. He chaired the Budget Committee from 1981–87, was ranking Republican from 1987–95, and now is chairman again: no other Republican need apply. In 1990 he turned down the ranking minority position on Energy and Natural Resources, an important committee for New Mexico, in order to keep Budget. For years he was frustrated in the Budget work. He was genuinely appalled at the deficits of the 1980s and was ready to recommend the bitterest of medicine—entitlement cuts, tax increases. But Democrats fought spending cuts and Republicans fought tax increases, and so Domenici's victories were few and hard won. In May 1985, Dole and Domenici got Republican senators to pass a freeze on Social Security cost of living adjustments; then President Reagan dropped the COLA freeze in a compromise with House Speaker Tip O'Neill and Senate Republicans, left exposed, lost their majority in 1986. Domenici backed the Gramm-Rudman Act, whose mechanisms, along with Reagan Budget Director Jim Miller's fixation on holding down spending, did in fact cut the deficit by about half; he backed the 1990 budget summit tax increase with its spending caps. Domenici opposed the Clinton budget and tax package in 1993. By 1994 he was cheered by the drop in the deficit, but pointed out that most of it was due to sales of savings and loan assets and unanticipated drops in medical costs.

After Republicans won control of Congress in 1994 Domenici was unable to push his own alternative, proposed with Sam Nunn—a 10-year plan to balance the budget, with $476 billion in tax increases and $1.4 trillion in spending cuts, plus a consumption-based tax to replace the income tax. Instead he worked in tandem, although some tension was present, with House Budget Chairman John Kasich, eschewing tax increases and supporting tax cuts he would have preferred to avoid. He supported cuts in domestic discretionary spending and worked to maintain the firewalls between defense and domestic spending. He favored a line-item veto that would allow a simple majority of one house to override the president, but most Republicans favored the House-passed two-thirds override. By 1996 Domenici surely could take comfort from the sharp drop in the deficit. But he kept looking ahead. He was pleased that the Clinton Administration and House Republicans were proposing budgets headed toward balance in 2002.

But he warned, "Our objective is not simply to balance the budget for a nanosecond in 2002. Our objective is to gain control of fiscal policy—to balance the budget in the year 2002 and to stay in balance in the years that follow." He said Clinton's "budget plan to take us into the next century . . . should be a solid bridge, and not one with weak spots, slick roads, secret compartments or trap doors."

Domenici is a passionate moderate, with a middle-of-the-road record passionately supported. He fears "the social fabric has broken down" and called on Hollywood and businesses to take responsibility for the morality of their products; his bill for character education grants became law in October 1994. He sponsored Small Business Regulatory Enforcement Fairness Act of 1996. He has argued strongly for including coverage of mental illness in health insurance, and talked of the severe mental illness of one of his daughters. Working with Democrat Paul Wellstone, he got the Senate to include mental illness in the 1996 health care bill and got the conference committee to accept coverage with a low cap. Domenici cited evidence that mental health treatments are increasingly rigorous and efficacious; opponents feared high and uncontrollable costs. This is a cause he is likely to pursue further.

Domenici also works for New Mexico causes. He looks after the Los Alamos and Sandia labs, and uses his Appropriations Subcommittee on Energy and Water Development chairmanship to promote local projects—a fish hatchery in Mora, a wastewater system near Espanola, the National Center for Genome Research in Santa Fe. He threatened a filibuster against a proposed 85% increase in grazing fees in October 1993.

Domenici was reelected with more than 70% of the vote in 1984 and 1990; in 1996, against a former Santa Fe mayor, he slipped a bit, but still won by an impressive 65%–30% even as Bill Clinton was carrying the state.

Junior Senator. Jeff Bingaman is a Democrat with good political lineage: his father was a professor at Western New Mexico University in Silver City, and his uncle was campaign manager for longtime Senator Clinton Anderson. A year out of law school, Bingaman was counsel to the state constitutional convention; a few years later, he went into law practice in Santa Fe with former Governor Jack Campbell. Bingaman's wife, Anne, started a highly successful law practice of her own that helped finance his first campaigns; she was assistant attorney general for antitrust in the first Clinton term. In a small state, bright young people like Jeff Bingaman rise fast. He ran for attorney general in 1978 and won; in 1982, he ran against Senator Harrison Schmitt, the former astronaut, also from Silver City, and won with 54%, partly because it was a recession year, but also because of Schmitt's misleading and negative ads.

Bingaman became a member of the Armed Services Committee and a protege of former Chairman Sam Nunn, who created a subcommittee tailored to his interests, now called Acquisition and Technology. In 1997, Bingaman traded his position there for the ranking Democratic spot on the Strategic Forces Subcommittee. From these seats Bingaman has had lots of say over New Mexico's Los Alamos and Sandia labs, which he has encouraged to enter into partnership with private firms, and a chance to make government research more accessible to the private sector. He has worked on procurement reform, superconductivity research and chartering the Technology Reinvestment Program. He sponsored a $1.6 billion defense conversion package which passed in 1992 and $100 million in seed money for regional partnerships of small technology firms. He helped to get Kirtland Air Force Base off the 1995 base-closing list.

Bingaman's voting record is fairly liberal. He is a strong booster of the Goals 2000 education plan and defended it during the 105th Congress. He sponsored the Technology for Education Act of 1994, which in 1996 distributed $48 million in grants; for the next year education technology programs were funded at $305 million. He inserted in the Telecom Act provisions for Internet access for schools and libraries. He wants to get tribally controlled Indian colleges treated the same as Historically Black Colleges. He serves on the Energy Committee, where he has worked to restore part of the Wheeler Peak Wilderness Area to the Taos Pueblo and restore the Rio Puerco watershed. He joined other western senators in opposing higher federal grazing fees but supports revision of the 1872 Mining Act. He was one of six Democrats who in 1995 switched their votes of the year before and opposed the balanced budget amendment, which lost by one vote. He opposed the 1996 Welfare Feform Act.

Bingaman had a serious challenge in 1994 from Republican Colin McMillan, a rancher and former assistant Defense secretary, and sponsor in the legislature of a 1981 "Big Mac" tax cut. McMillan spent over $1 million of his own money and attacked Bingaman's vote for the Clinton budget and tax increase and for what McMillan said was technically a vote to increase grazing fees. Bingaman ads boasted of his work on defense conversion, national education standards and education technology. The race tightened up in October, and Bingaman won 54%–46%, a decisive margin but a notable drop from 1988. He carried Albuquerque and won wide margins among Hispanics and Indians, but lost Little Texas.

Presidential politics. New Mexico, the most Democratic of the Rocky Mountain states and seriously contested in 1988, went for Bill Clinton in 1992 and 1996. Its bellwether status—it has voted for the winner in every presidential election since statehood in 1912, except for 1976—seems more accidental than anything else; it's hard to think of a state more atypical of the nation. Hoping to secure the support he had in 1992, Bill Clinton was heavily active in the Albuquerque television market in 1996; the Democratic National Committee channeled more than $1.1 million in 1995 and 1996 to New Mexico Democrats for party advertising that boosted the Clinton/Gore presidential ticket. Bob Dole won the Republican primary 75%–8% over Pat Buchanan.

Congressional districting. The boundaries of New Mexico's three congressional districts were slightly redesigned for 1992, with the apparent aim of making the Republican-held 1st and 2d both marginally more Democratic.

The People: Est. Pop. 1996: 1,713,000; Pop. 1990: 1,515,069, up 13.1% 1990–1996. 0.6% of U.S. total, 36th largest; 27% rural. Median age: 33.3 years. 11% 65 years and over. 50.4% White, 1.8% Black, 1% Asian, 8.5% Amer. Indian, 38.2% Hispanic origin. Households: 56.0% married couple families; 29% married couple fams. w. children; 46% college educ.; median household income: $24,087; per capita income: $11,246; 67.4% owner occupied housing; median house value: $70,100; median monthly rent: $312. 8.1% Unemployment. 1996 Voting age pop.:1,224,000. 1996 Turnout: 556,074; 45% of VAP. Registered voters (1996): 837,794; 457,678 D (55%), 281,895 R (34%), 98,221 unaffiliated and minor parties (12%).

Political Lineup: Governor, Gary E. Johnson (R); Lt. Gov., Walter Bradley (R); Secy. of State, Stephanie Gonzales (D); Atty. Gen., Thomas Udall (D); Treasurer, Michael A. Montoya (D); Auditor, Robert E. Vigil (D). State Senate, 42 (25 D and 17 R); Senate President, Walter Bradley (R); State House, 70 (42 D and 28 R); House Speaker, Raymond G. Sanchez (R). Senators, Pete V. Domenici (R) and Jeff Bingaman (D). Representatives, 3 (3 R).

Elections Division: 505-827-3620; **Filing Deadline for U.S. Congress:** February 10, 1998.

1996 Presidential Vote

Clinton (D)	273,495	(49%)
Dole (R)	232,751	(42%)
Perot (I)	32,271	(6%)
Other	17,566	(3%)

1996 Republican Presidential Primary

Dole (R)	53,300	(76%)
Buchanan (R)	5,679	(8%)
Forbes (R)	3,987	(6%)
Alexander (R)	2,676	(4%)
Other	4,822	(6%)

1992 Presidential Vote

Clinton (D)	261,617	(46%)
Bush (R)	212,824	(37%)
Perot (I)	91,895	(16%)

GOVERNOR

Gov. Gary E. Johnson (R)

Elected 1994, term expires Jan. 1999; b. Jan. 1, 1953, Minot, ND; home, Santa Fe; U. of NM, B.A. 1975; Lutheran; married (Dee).

Career: Pres. & CEO, Big J Enterprises, Inc., 1976–present.

Office: State Capitol, #417, Santa Fe 87503, 505-827-3000; Fax: 505-827-3026; Web site: www.state.nm.us.

Election Results

1994 gen.	Gary E. Johnson (R)	232,945	(50%)
	Bruce King (D)	186,686	(40%)
	Roberto Mondragon (Green)	47,990	(10%)
1994 prim.	Gary E. Johnson (R)	32,091	(34%)
	Dick Cheney (R)	30,811	(33%)
	John Dendahl (R)	18,007	(19%)
	David F. Cargo (R)	12,105	(13%)
1990 gen.	Bruce King (D)	224,564	(55%)
	Frank M. Bond (R)	185,692	(45%)

SENATORS

Sen. Pete V. Domenici (R)

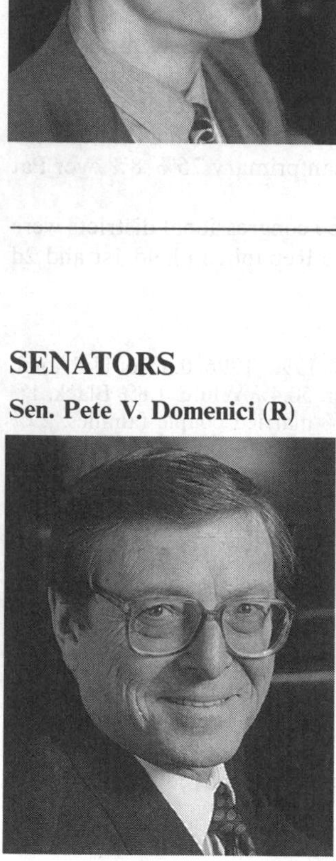

Elected 1972, seat up 2002; b. May 7, 1932, Albuquerque; home, Albuquerque; U. of NM, B.S. 1954, Denver U., LL.B. 1958; Catholic; married (Nancy).

Career: Practicing atty., 1958–72; Albuquerque City Comm., 1966–70, Mayor Ex-Officio, 1967–70.

DC Office: 328 HSOB 20510, 202-224-6621; e-mail: senator_domenici@domenici.senate.gov.

State Offices: Albuquerque, 505-766-3481; Las Cruces, 505-526-5475; Roswell, 505-623-6170; Santa Fe, 505-988-6511.

Committees: *Appropriations* (4th of 15 R): Commerce, Justice, State & the Judiciary; Defense; Energy & Water Development (Chmn.); Interior; Transportation. *Budget* (Chmn. of 12 R). *Energy & Natural Resources* (2nd of 11 R): Energy Research, Development, Production & Regulation Subcommittee (Vice-Chmn.); Forests & Public Land Management. *Governmental Affairs* (4th of 9 R): International Security, Proliferation & Federal Services; Permanent Subcommittee on Investigations. *Indian Affairs* (5th of 8 R).

Group Ratings

	ADA	ACLU	AFS	LCV	CFA	CON	NFIB	COC	ACU	NTLC	CHC
1996	20	13	14	8	21	24	93	83	85	86	84
1995	5	—	9	7	13	68	—	100	78	—	—

National Journal Ratings

	1995 LIB — 1995 CONS			1996 LIB — 1996 CONS		
Economic	41%	—	58%	38%	—	61%
Social	42%	—	57%	33%	—	62%
Foreign	44%	—	55%	37%	—	62%

Key Votes of the 104th Congress

1. Reduce Medicare Growth $	Y	5. Flag Amendment	Y	9. Anti-Missile Defense	Y
2. Lmt. Prod. Liab. Damages	Y	6. Endangered Species	N	10. Cuban Embargo	Y
3. Increase Min. Wage	Y	7. Gay Employment Rights	N	11. Bar Bosnia Troop $	Y
4. Welfare Reform	Y	8. Ovrd. Part. Birth Veto	Y	12. Cut Vietnam Aid	Y

Election Results

1996 general	Pete V. Domenici (R)	357,171	(65%)	($3,435,164)
	Art Trujillo (D)	164,356	(30%)	($155,213)
	Abraham J. Gutmann (Green)	24,230	(4%)	($12,025)
1996 primary	Pete V. Domenici (R)	unopposed		
1990 general	Pete V. Domenici (R)	296,712	(73%)	($2,250,086)
	Tom R. Benavides (D)	110,033	(27%)	($38,510)

Sen. Jeff Bingaman (D)

Elected 1982, seat up 2000; b. Oct. 3, 1943, El Paso, TX; home, Santa Fe; Harvard, B.A. 1965, Stanford, LL.B. 1968; United Methodist; married (Anne).

Career: Army Reserves, 1968–74; NM Asst. Atty. Gen., 1969; Practicing atty., 1970–78; NM Atty. Gen., 1979–82.

DC Office: 703 HSOB 20510, 202-224-5521; Fax: 202-224-2852; e-mail: senator_bingaman@bingaman.senate.gov.

State Offices: Albuquerque, 505-766-3636; Las Cruces, 505-523-6561; Roswell, 505-622-7113; Santa Fe, 505-988-6647.

Committees: *Armed Services* (3rd of 8 D): Acquisition & Technology; Airland Forces; Strategic Forces (RMM). *Energy & Natural Resources* (3rd of 9 D): Energy Research, Development, Production & Regulation; National Parks, Historic Preservation & Recreation (RMM). *Labor & Human Resources* (5th of 8 D): Children & Families; Public Health & Safety. *Joint Economic Committee* (7th of 10 Sens.).

Group Ratings

	ADA	ACLU	AFS	LCV	CFA	CON	NFIB	COC	ACU	NTLC	CHC
1996	95	44	100	69	86	27	34	15	0	14	0
1995	90	—	100	86	94	8	—	42	0	—	—

National Journal Ratings

	1995 LIB — 1995 CONS			1996 LIB — 1996 CONS		
Economic	73%	—	23%	89%	—	5%
Social	76%	—	18%	80%	—	8%
Foreign	72%	—	24%	76%	—	23%

Key Votes of the 104th Congress

1. Reduce Medicare Growth $	N	5. Flag Amendment	N	9. Anti-Missile Defense	N
2. Lmt. Prod. Liab. Damages	N	6. Endangered Species	Y	10. Cuban Embargo	N
3. Increase Min. Wage	Y	7. Gay Employment Rights	Y	11. Bar Bosnia Troop $	N
4. Welfare Reform	N	8. Ovrd. Part. Birth Veto	N	12. Cut Vietnam Aid	N

Election Results

1994 general	Jeff Bingaman (D)	249,989	(54%)	($3,652,899)
	Colin R. McMillan (R)	213,025	(46%)	($1,537,563)
1994 primary	Jeff Bingaman (D)	unopposed		
1988 general	Jeff Bingaman (D)	321,983	(63%)	($2,808,659)
	Bill Valentine (R)	186,579	(37%)	($659,624)

FIRST DISTRICT

The future and the past of New Mexico come together in its single metropolis, Albuquerque. Its Spanish and Indian past is memorialized in its name (for a 17th Century Spanish grandee) and age (founded in 1706) and its quaint Old Town; its high-tech future is symbolized by Sandia Laboratories and Kirtland Air Force Base, the government installations that are the city's biggest employers. When rocket scientist Robert Goddard moved here in 1930 and nuclear scientist J. Robert Oppenheimer reconnoitered the site in 1940, Albuquerque was still a town of 35,000 sitting at the junction of the Rio Grande and the old U.S. 66 that paralleled the Santa Fe Railroad—"a dirty red sod-hut tortilla desert highway city," Tom Wolfe wrote. Since then, Albuquerque has grown more than any place in New Mexico and, with a metro population of 600,000, has as many people as all New Mexico did when the scientists first arrived. Albuquerque's prosperous neighborhoods have climbed the gently rising heights to the east; poorer residents have spread north and south along the Rio Grande. To the northwest is the new town of Rio Rancho, with Intel, Olympus, U.S. Cotton and Pepsico installations. Albuquerque is counted as part of the Sun Belt, but its climate is closer to that of the High Plains of west Texas: hot in the summer, sometimes very cold in the winter, with high winds most of the time. Nor is its economy like that of other Sun Belt cities. It has lower income levels; its recent growth has lagged behind Phoenix, Dallas, and even El Paso. Albuquerque has some white-collar job growth and diversification and has become something of a tourist center (it is home of the International Balloon Fiesta), but it still depends primarily on government; that has worked out well, with Sandia and Intel running the world's fastest computer and Kirtland the site of one of four "superlabs."

The 1st Congressional District of New Mexico is, for all practical purposes, the city of Albuquerque and its suburbs; it also includes largely empty Torrance County and communities north and south along the Rio Grande. Albuquerque is one Sun Belt city which is not solidly Republican, and in 1992 it went by a decisive margin for Bill Clinton after voting Republican for president in the 1980s—not far off the national average. The 1st District in 1990 was 38% Hispanic, with both descendants of longtime New Mexicans and recent immigrants.

The congressman from the 1st District is Steven Schiff, a Republican first elected in 1988. Schiff grew up in Chicago and came to Albuquerque to attend law school. He is an unusual New Mexico figure. He is Jewish in a state made up mostly of Anglo Protestants and Hispanic Catholics; he is aggressive and a stickler for doing things by the book in a state often tolerant of lax practices. He served in the New Mexico Air National Guard, and is now a colonel in the Air Force Reserves: he participated in the Gulf war, briefing Americans on the intricacies of Muslim law, and in Turkey and northern Iraq afterward, working on the rules of engagement; in February 1996, though he opposed sending U.S. troops to Bosnia, he volunteered and served at the mission operation center in Aviano Air Force Base, Italy. After law school, he became a prosecutor and, after a few years of private practice, in 1980, at 33, he was elected district attorney of Albuquerque's Bernalillo County, where he was proud of the death penalty convictions he obtained. In 1988, when Congressman Manuel Lujan retired, Schiff ran for Congress. In the primary, he edged Lujan's brother Edward, 41%–37%; in the general, he beat Tom Udall, son of former Interior Secretary Stewart Udall and nephew of former House Interior Committee Chairman Morris Udall, and now New Mexico Attorney General, by 51%–47%.

Schiff is the sort of man who goes where his sense of right and wrong take him, regardless of politics; his voting record is middle-of-the-House on economic and cultural issues, very conservative on foreign policy. His major legislative achievements include the 1995 Sexual Crimes Against Children Prevention Act, which increased sentences for child pornography and prostitution, and a 1996 amendment to make healthcare fraud a federal crime. He opposed a bill allowing military personnel to sue military physicians for malpractice, because they may already qualify for disability. He opposed a bill to criminalize animal rights terrorism. Schiff is chairman of the Basic Research Subcommittee of the Science Committee, an important post for Albuquerque—and the nation. He led the fight to stop a national laboratory closure commission. "The national laboratories have to contribute to deficit reduction, they're not immune, but no one in the scientific community believes we should be closing the national labs." He worked to create the Petroglyph National Monument on the west side of Albuquerque and to buy land for the Tres Pistolas animal preserve.

From 1993 Schiff served on the House Ethics Committee, a hot seat given the charges Democrats filed against Newt Gingrich. Schiff was adamant that Gingrich's book deal not be investigated by an independent counsel, and worked with Democrat Ben Cardin to resolve the issue. Schiff also served on the task force, with Cardin, Democrat Nancy Pelosi and Republican Porter Goss, which handled the final charge against Gingrich in late 1996 and early 1997. All four members seem to have tried conscientiously to reach a decision on the merits, and were prevented by secrecy rules from refuting some of the more fabulous tales circulating. But Schiff and Goss did manage to signal Republicans who were queasy about reelecting Gingrich as speaker when on January 7 they issued a statement saying, "We know of no reason now, nor do we foresee any in the normal course of events in the future, why Newt Gingrich would be ineligible to serve as speaker."

Schiff, who had been reelected easily in 1992 and 1994, had tougher competition in 1996 from 28-year-old John Wertheim, campaign manager in 1994 for then-Governor Bruce King. Wertheim supported the Brady bill, the Clinton Medicare plan, a balanced budget that maintained education funding, and criticized Schiff for "cuts" in Medicare, student, loans, Head Start and Title I education money. Schiff replied that he didn't "cut" Medicare but funded it by the exact amount recommended by Clinton and that he voted against the assault weapons ban because they "aren't assault weapons and they aren't even banned." Schiff outspent Wertheim 2–1 and won by a solid but reduced 57%–37%.

The People: Pop. 1990: 505,329; 8% rural; 10% age 65+; 56% White; 2% Black; 1% Asian; 2% Amer. Indian; 38% Hispanic origin. Households: 53% married couple families; 26% married couple fams. w. children; 54% college educ.; median household income: $27,074; per capita income: $13,373; median gross rent: $400; median house value: $83,800.

1996 Presidential Vote			**1992 Presidential Vote**		
Clinton (D)	93,178	(48%)	Clinton (D)	95,754	(45%)
Dole (R)	82,613	(43%)	Bush (R)	81,038	(38%)
Perot (I)	9,520	(5%)	Perot (I)	33,034	(16%)
Other	7,212	(4%)			

Rep. Steven H. Schiff (R)

Elected 1988; b. Mar. 18, 1947, Chicago, IL; home, Albuquerque; U. of IL, B.A. 1968, U. of NM, J.D. 1972; Jewish; married (Marcia).

Career: Air Natl. Guard, 1969–91; Air Force Reserves, 1991–present; Asst. Dist. Atty., Bernalillo Cnty., 1972–77; Practicing atty., 1977–79; Asst. City Atty. and Cnsl., Albuquerque Police Dept., 1979–81; Dist. Atty., Bernalillo Cnty., 1981–89.

DC Office: 2404 RHOB 20515; 202-225-6316; Fax: 202-225-4975.

District Offices: Albuquerque, 505-766-2538.

Committees: *Government Reform & Oversight* (6th of 24 R): Human Resources; National Security, International Affairs & Criminal Justice. *Judiciary* (7th of 20 R): Commercial & Administrative Law; Crime. *Science* (7th of 25 R): Basic Research (Chmn.); Energy & Environment.

Group Ratings

	ADA	ACLU	AFS	LCV	CFA	CON	NFIB	COC	ACU	NTLC	CHC
1996	25	13	30	38	15	24	84	80	63	87	66
1995	16	—	—	25	31	75	—	92	64	—	—

National Journal Ratings

	1995 LIB — 1995 CONS	1996 LIB — 1996 CONS
Economic	51% — 49%	50% — 50%
Social	53% — 47%	59% — 40%
Foreign	15% — 73%	0% — 79%

Key Votes of the 104th Congress

1. Reduce Medicare Growth $	Y	5. Flag Amendment	Y	9. Cuban Embargo	Y
2. Ovrd. Product Liab. Veto	Y	6. Drop EPA Limits	Y	10. Bar Bosnia Troop $	Y
3. Increase Min. Wage	Y	7. Repeal Assault-Weap. Ban	Y	11. Cut Anti-Missile Defense	N
4. Welfare Reform	*	8. Ovrd. Part. Birth Veto	Y	12. Bar U.N. Uniforms	Y

Election Results

1996 general	Steven H. Schiff (R)	109,290	(57%)	($603,316)
	John Wertheim (D)	71,635	(37%)	($285,999)
	Others	12,153	(6%)	
1996 primary	Steven H. Schiff (R)	unopposed		
1994 general	Steven H. Schiff (R)	119,996	(74%)	($458,653)
	Peter Zollinger (D)	42,316	(26%)	($5,944)

SECOND DISTRICT

The plains of southern and eastern New Mexico are about as disparate a landscape as can be imagined: miles of sagebrush-strewn acreage, and then, suddenly, 9,000-foot mountain peaks rising in the distance. The eastern part of this region, Little Texas, is an extension of the Texas civilization that filled up empty counties when irrigation was developed. Oil has long been the economic mainstay here; cattle ranching is common; cotton is grown on irrigated land. The little cities are full of people with Texas twangs, not the lilt of northern New Mexico. West from Clovis and Portales, Lovington and Hobbs, the towns become fewer and farming mostly disappears. The scrub land shades into desert, and people are crammed into small cities, protected from an environment that is burning hot in the summer and sometimes deathly cold in winter.

The 2d Congressional District of New Mexico includes the entire southern half of the state—most of Little Texas, plus the desert on either side of the Rio Grande and the mining territory in the mountains just north of the Mexican border and just short of the Arizona line. The largest city here is Las Cruces, home of New Mexico State University and only 45 miles north of the million-plus metropolis of El Paso, Texas, and Chihuahua, Mexico. These places today vote the opposite of their partisan tradition: Little Texas, settled by yellow dog Democrats from the Lone Star state, is now solidly Republican; Las Cruces, long leaning Republican, has moved Democratic. The 2d District usually votes Republican, but Bill Clinton has carried it by 1% twice in a row; increased Indian turnout helped in 1996.

The congressman from the 2d District is Republican Joe Skeen. Skeen has been a sheep rancher for more than 40 years, when he bought his grandmother's ranch. He was elected to the New Mexico Senate in 1960, at 33, ran for lieutenant governor on a ticket with Pete Domenici and narrowly lost in 1970, and ran for governor in 1974 and 1978, losing by 1% each time. He was elected to the House in 1980, the hard way, as a write-in, with 61,000 votes, when Democratic incumbent Harold "Mud" Runnels died and the Democrats put Governor Bruce King's nephew on the ballot. Skeen got 38% of the vote to 34% for King and 28% for Runnels's widow, also a write-in; in 1986, Skeen beat Runnels's son Mike 63%–37%.

When Skeen became minority leader of the state Senate 30 years ago, there were only three other Republicans there. Since 1994, for the first time in his career, he is in the majority and a member of the House's "college of cardinals" as chairman of the House Appropriations Subcommittee on Agriculture. Skeen is something of an old-fashioned conservative, generally voting against domestic spending, but working to benefit his district. He has staunchly opposed efforts to increase grazing fees for livestock producers, so far successfully; he would like to see the Bureau of Land Management turn over its western lands to the states. He has worked for years, and finally with success, to revise the formula for federal Payments in Lieu of Taxes to local governments. He has used his seat on Appropriations and on the National Security and Agriculture Subcommittees, to help local projects, sometimes with national implications. He saved the underground lunchroom at Carlsbad Caverns and halted the FAA plan to remote-operate the Roswell radar. He helped preserve 200 jobs at Chaves County Home Health Services. He had worked for a lamb and wool checkoff program to promote sheep products and proposed a uniform national policy for fossil collecting on federal lands. He has worked to save the High Energy Laser Systems Test Facility at White Sands Missile Range, where short-range rockets, of the type fired by guerrillas around the world, were shot down with lasers. He has worked to open the WIPP nuclear waste disposal site in Carlsbad, over the noisy opposition of Democratic Attorneys General Tom Udall of New Mexico and Dan Morales of Texas, arguing that current conditions there are far more unsafe than the tested procedures that will be in place when WIPP is opened.

As chairman of the Agriculture Subcomittee of Appropriations, Skeen is responsible for significant cuts in domestic discretionary spending. His 1995 bill appropriated $62.5 billion, a $5.5 billion cut, and passed 313–78. It preserved WIC and children's nutrition funding but cut rural housing deeply and turned over research stations to local universities. But Skeen also cut 1.8% from direct payments to farmers, which aroused the ire of then-Agriculture Committee Chairman Pat Roberts, whose Freedom to Farm Act gave them guaranteed payments in return for a seven-year phaseout of subsidies. Skeen characterized Roberts's opposition as a "near volcanic eruption" and said it contributed to global warming, and Roberts gained stronger arguments when after conference the bill emerged with dozens of Senate-originated earmarks. Even so, Skeen's bill passed 288–132, with almost half the no votes coming from Republicans.

Skeen has won reelection by varying margins, by just 56%–44% in 1992, then by 63%–32% in 1994. In 1996, against a low-spending opponent, he won by a decisive but not impressive 56%–44%, winning nearly 2–1 in Little Texas but narrowly losing Las Cruces and the Indian areas.

The People: Pop. 1990: 504,767; 33% rural; 12% age 65+; 52% White; 2% Black; 1% Asian; 4% Amer. Indian; 42% Hispanic origin. Households: 61% married couple families; 31% married couple fams. w. children; 40% college educ.; median houschold income: $21,456; per capita income: $9,672; median gross rent: $325; median house value: $52,200.

1996 Presidential Vote

Clinton (D)	80,572	(46%)
Dole (R)	77,634	(45%)
Perot (I)	12,149	(7%)
Other	3,149	(2%)

1992 Presidential Vote

Clinton (D)	70,630	(41%)
Bush (R)	68,754	(40%)
Perot (I)	31,780	(18%)

Rep. Joe Skeen (R)

Elected 1980; b. June 30, 1927, Roswell; home, Picacho; TX A&M U., B.S. 1950; Catholic; married (Mary).

Career: Navy, 1945–46 (WWII), Air Force Reserves, 1949–52; Engineer, Zuni and Ramah Navajo Indian Reservations, 1950–51; Sheep rancher, 1951–present; NM Senate, 1960–70, Minority Ldr., 1965–70.

DC Office: 2302 RHOB 20515, 202-225-2365; Fax: 202-225-9599.

District Offices: Las Cruces, 505-527-1771; Roswell, 505-622-0055.

Committees: *Appropriations* (8th of 34 R): Agriculture, Rural Development, FDA & Related Agencies (Chmn.); Interior; National Security.

Group Ratings

	ADA	ACLU	AFS	LCV	CFA	CON	NFIB	COC	ACU	NTLC	CHC
1996	5	12	0	15	8	7	97	100	90	98	86
1995	0	—	—	13	0	53	—	96	76	—	—

National Journal Ratings

	1995 LIB — 1995 CONS			1996 LIB — 1996 CONS		
Economic	0%	—	74%	37%	—	61%
Social	32%	—	65%	33%	—	65%
Foreign	15%	—	73%	21%	—	72%

Key Votes of the 104th Congress

1. Reduce Medicare Growth $	Y	5. Flag Amendment	Y	9. Cuban Embargo	Y
2. Ovrd. Product Liab. Veto	Y	6. Drop EPA Limits	N	10. Bar Bosnia Troop $	Y
3. Increase Min. Wage	N	7. Repeal Assault-Weap. Ban	Y	11. Cut Anti-Missile Defense	N
4. Welfare Reform	Y	8. Ovrd. Part. Birth Veto	Y	12. Bar U.N. Uniforms	Y

Election Results

1996 general	Joe Skeen (R)	95,091	(56%)	($539,969)
	E. Shirley Baca (D)	74,915	(44%)	($191,794)
1996 primary	Joe Skeen (R)	17,520	(70%)	
	Gregory E. Sowards (R)	7,450	(30%)	
1994 general	Joe Skeen (R)	89,966	(63%)	($384,687)
	Benjamin Anthony Chavez (D)	45,316	(32%)	($221,676)
	Rex R. Johnson (Green)	6,898	(5%)	

THIRD DISTRICT

"The dancing ground of the sun" the Pueblo Indians called the land of northern New Mexico, where the long, empty vistas stretch for miles, detailed in pinpoint clarity in the cold light and clear air. For 100 years, artists have been coming here, attracted by the scenery and by a unique civilization that is part Indian, part Spanish, only a little Mexican (for northern New Mexico was Mexican only briefly, from 1821–46), part Anglo-American. The Spanish language, Indian pottery and dances, and the adobe pueblos give the impression that life on this rocky desert soil has gone on for centuries in much the same way. Actually, the civilization hasn't been so stable. The pueblos were built in sudden spurts; the Spanish conquistadors and priests brought the Catholic religion, the baroque accents of the adobe buildings and the Spanish language in a rush; successive waves of American settlement have changed New Mexico in different ways. The Indian crafts which are thriving today nearly died out in the 1880s, and the Palace of the Governors, built in Santa Fe 1610, had its Victorian balustrade torn off in 1913 to restore its original appearance. Yet up the back roads in Rio Arriba or Taos Counties, one can find a religion that mixes Catholicism with adaptations of Indian festivals, buildings not that much different from the old pueblos, and a standard of living reminiscent of the Indian past—quite a contrast to Santa Fe, with its thousands of affluent, bohemian migrants, its 300 restaurants, its local book publishers and the second-largest art market in the country.

The politics of northern New Mexico is a unique blend. For years, debate was conducted and votes bartered in Spanish, not by separatists, but by Republican and Democratic politicos, often cynically, sometimes corruptly; loyalties ran to families and communities more than to principles or parties. In the back country, you can still find more than just vestiges of the old communities and the old politics—though no one is going to let you in on them, even if you speak good Spanish. In Santa Fe and Taos, the affluent and hippie migrants have produced a politics of the cultural and environmental left, while in high-tech havens—the atomic laboratory town of Los Alamos, the huge new suburb of Rio Rancho, north of Albuquerque and centered on an Intel installation—favor free-market politics.

The 3d Congressional District of New Mexico contains most of the state's historic Spanish-speaking and Indian parts. Its largest and most dominant city is Santa Fe, but the district runs from the High Plains along the Texas border, past the haunting Sangre de Cristo Mountains, through the vast ridges and isolated buttes in the center, to the windy and dusty desert-like plains, dotted occasionally by mountains, with Indian reservations in the west. The population is 35% Hispanic origin and 20% Indian (with at least 6% overlap between the categories). Politically, it has long been heavily Democratic, and migrants to Santa Fe and Taos Counties in the 1980s made it more so. But it also has its Republican bastions at its east and west ends, in the mineral prospecting country in San Juan County around Farmington in the west, and on the dusty "Little Texas" plains around Clovis in the east. And Rio Rancho has supplied more conservative voters every year in the 1990s. The congressman from the 3rd since it was created in 1982 was Bill Richardson, a Democrat of Mexican background, who became a skilled international negotiator and was named ambassador to the United Nations in January 1997. But changes in the district plus local political machinations gave Republicans victory in the special election to succeed Richardson in May 1997.

The congressman from the 3d District now is Republican Bill Redmond, an Independent Christian minister from Los Alamos, who won just 31% against Richardson in November 1996, but was elected with 43% in a three-way special in May 1997. He was not the initial favorite. A half-dozen active Democratic politicians vied for the nomination. But under state law it was determined not by a primary but by vote of 89 members of the Democratic central committee, and in January 1997 the 11 Democratic county chairmen declared that Eric Serna, member of the state Corporation Commission since 1981, had the votes locked up. Other Democrats protested and demanded a primary; Santa Fe Mayor Debbie Jaramillo said of the chairmen's letter: "This kind of scare tactic just makes me get more pissed and makes me want to get out there and whip Eric's ass." But Republican Governor Gary Johnson said he would veto any primary bill, and Serna got the nomination.

This prompted healthcare consultant Carol Miller to run as the Green Party candidate and provided a basis for tough attacks by Redmond on Serna. The Greens had helped decide the 1994 gubernatorial race, when their candidate, former Lieutenant Governor Roberto Mondragon, got 10% of the vote, enabling Johnson to beat three-term Democratic Governor Bruce King 50%–40%. Although national environmental and abortion rights groups all endorsed Serna, Miller had great strength in Santa Fe and Taos Counties, which have large and active feminist communities. Meanwhile, Redmond said that Serna had a "seamy past," and that it was "no secret that Eric Serna is a corrupt politician." Redmond ran ads charging that Serna raised money from firms with interests before the Corporation Commission, used a state airplane for unofficial business, applied pressure on Commission employees to buy jewelry at a store he owned and used a state phone campaign purposes. In response, Serna ran ads attacking Redmond for backing school vouchers and favoring abolition of the Department of Education, and saying "Redmond is a radical right-wing preacher who wants to impose his extreme values and social agenda on all of us. He's against a woman's right to choose—even in cases of rape and incest."

Redmond also displayed some positive campaigning, courting Navajos in McKinley and Cibola Counties, and ran organizing drives in the high-tech areas—Los Alamos, Rio Rancho, San Juan County—and in the Little Texas counties in the east. Serna raised far more money, but Republican congressmen started sending Redmond money toward the end. The result was a shocker: Redmond beat Serna 43%–40%, with 17% for Miller. There were great regional splits. The four most heavily Hispanic counties, once the political heart of the district, voted 62%–12% for Serna over Redmond; but they cast only 16% of the district's votes. In Santa Fe and Taos Counties, which cast 30% of the votes, Serna won only 41% of the votes, not much ahead of Miller's 33% and Redmond's 25%. Redmond piled up big majorities over Serna in the high-tech counties, which cast 34% of district votes (60%–28%) and in Little Texas, with 11% (69%–27%). And he held down Serna's margin in the Indian counties, which cast 9% of the votes, to 57%–33%.

Redmond's victory gave House Republicans one more seat and a 228–207 edge over Democrats, just two votes less than their 1994 landslide. But can Redmond hold the seat in 1998? Presumably he will try to strengthen his backing in Hispanic and Indian areas with constituency services and organize the high-tech areas and Little Texas once again. But he must improve on his 43% to win if Democrats hold together and run a candidate capable of rebuffing an active Green Party candidacy. Possible Democratic candidates include Jaramillo, state Senator Roman Maes, Santa Fe County Commissioner Javier Gonzales, former state Supreme Court Justice Dan Sosa, former Santo Domingo Pueblo Governor Ernie Lovate and lawyer Francesca Lobato.

The People: Pop. 1990: 504,973; 40% rural; 10% age 65+; 44% White; 1% Black; 1% Asian; 20% Amer. Indian; 35% Hispanic origin. Households: 58% married couple families; 31% married couple fams. w. children; 45% college educ.; median household income: $23,610; per capita income: $10,689; median gross rent: $372; median house value: $68,400.

1996 Presidential Vote

Clinton (D)	99,745	(52%)
Dole (R)	72,504	(38%)
Perot (I)	10,602	(6%)
Other	7,205	(4%)

1992 Presidential Vote

Clinton (D)	95,233	(51%)
Bush (R)	63,032	(34%)
Perot (I)	27,081	(15%)

Rep. Bill Redmond (R)

Elected May 1997; b. Jan. 28, 1954, Chicago, IL; home, Los Alamos; Lincoln Christian Col., B.A. 1979; Lincoln Christian Seminary, M.Div. 1988; Independent Christian; married (Shirley).

Career: Army, 1985–93; Minister, 1978–97; Special educ. teacher, 1980–83; Group Home Admin., 1988–90; Mgr., Roller-skating rink, 1991–96.

DC Office: 2268 RHOB 20515, 202-225-6190; Fax: 202-226-1331 .

District Office: Santa Fe, 505-988-7230.

Committees: not assigned as of June 1, 1997.

Group Ratings and Key Votes: Newly Elected

Election Results

1997 special	Bill Redmond (R)	43,472	(43%)	($57,457)
	Eric P. Serna (D)	40,424	(40%)	($265,255)
	Carol A. Miller (Green)	17,079	(17%)	($7,443)
1996 general	Bill Richardson (D)	124,594	(67%)	($526,898)
	Bill Redmond (R)	56,580	(31%)	($56,442)
	Others	4,097	(2%)	
1996 primary	Bill Richardson (D)	unopposed		
1994 general	Bill Richardson (D)	99,900	(64%)	($579,737)
	F. Gregg Bemis Jr. (R)	53,515	(34%)	($110,575)
	Others	3,697	(2%)	

NEW YORK

New York is a place of miracles and disasters—and maybe more miracles to come. For all its recent woes, New York state still has America's largest city, its financial capital, its center of arts and letters and media, and the number one immigrant destination for more than 100 years. None of this was inevitable. These things happened because New Yorkers—and not least those people from elsewhere who opted to become New Yorkers—chose and worked to make them happen. They did it in a city that has a certain enduring character which goes back to its birth as the 17th Century Dutch colony of Nieuw Amsterdam. Simon Schama's *The Embarrassment of Riches* paints a picture of the old world Amsterdam: the richest city in the world; full of people who work hard all day and stay up late at night, smoke too much tobacco and drink too much coffee and gin, but are dazzlingly smart and shrewd; people who know their way around every corner of the globe and can make fine aesthetic discriminations, but are attached to their uncomfortable, crowded, bad-smelling city; merchants and manipulators with no aristocratic pedigree, welcoming any religious or ethnic group who can achieve and accumulate and show good taste, cherishing education and culture but indifferent to credentials. This could be a portrait of the New York of today, of Tom Wolfe and Tina Brown, or the New York of Alexander Hamilton and Aaron Burr, or the New York of Edith Wharton and Theodore Dreiser, or the New York of Harold Ross' *New Yorker* magazine and Henry Luce's early *Time*. Probably fewer than 2% of today's New Yorkers are descended from the Dutch of Nieuw Amsterdam, but the character of the place endures in daily life and in the workings of its great institutions, and helps explain its miraculous and entirely inevitable growth. Combine Amsterdam and America: Dutch character with British-born political freedoms and American military invulnerability—something the Dutch have never enjoyed except in the last half-century—and you have the opportunity to build a city-state that can lead the world.

New York was not always the nation's leader. In 1776, it was the seventh most populous colony. Only in the 19th Century did the descendants of Dutch patroons, Huguenot refugees, British West Indies traders and Yankee farmers become the nation's most successful merchants and capitalists, forging the first routes to the great American interior through the valleys of the Hudson and the Mohawk, over the Finger Lakes and the Great Lakes, and building grand brownstone mansions on broad midtown Manhattan avenues. That early diversity provides one clue to New York's success: if New York has been cynical, ready to cooperate with Loyalists and Revolutionaries, depending on who was ahead, it has also been tolerant, ready to accept anyone smart or rich enough to be counted a success. It has been propelled upward at each stage—forging ahead of London as a financial and manufacturing center by the First World War, and staying ahead of surging Chicago—by incorporating every wave of immigrants and consistently rewarding intelligence and hard work, unconcerned about preserving hierarchies.

New York's success has been a product not only of market economics, but of government—and politics. The Iroquois, the most deeply-rooted and militarily strong Native Americans, kept in place for 100 years by an alliance with British troops, were driven out of New York by the Revolution. The Erie Canal, which connected western New York state with the Hudson River, was the project of Governor DeWitt Clinton's state government. The railroads were subsidized by land grants and favorable laws. And New York led the nation in political innovation: Martin Van Buren's Albany Regency was the first state political machine, an ally of New York City's Tammany Hall, and Van Buren himself invented the Democratic Party, the national convention and the inaugural parade. His adversaries, Thurlow Weed and William Seward, formed the Whig Party and ultimately became Republicans; noting that Van Buren's Democrats were winning large margins from Irish Catholics and other immigrants, they too made bids for the newcomers' votes. Both parties served the function of mediating between the divergent interests of the New York City masses and Upstate New York's farmers and burghers, a conflict still evident in New York between city and country, immigrant and native, Catholic and Protestant, the Big Apple and the apple-knockers.

Both parties also worked to protect New Yorkers against the untrammeled workings of free economic and political markets. Mugwump Republicans, from Theodore Roosevelt through Elihu Root and Henry Stimson, worked to create civil service laws and bureaucratized purchasing and spending to protect taxpayers from corrupt party machines. And the Tammany machine led by Charles F. Murphy and the talented young men he advanced, Al Smith and Robert Wagner, responded to the shocking 1911 Triangle Shirtwaist fire (when hundreds of women jumped 11 floors to their death because fire escapes were blocked) by passing labor and safety measures. The results included minimum wages, maximum work hours, working-conditions regulations, encouragement of unions and state-owned electric utilities—the prototype 20 years later of the New Deal and the first American welfare state. In years after, New York pioneered public housing and fair housing laws, industry-wide unions (in the garment trades), increased minimum wages, rent control and dairy price controls to help both New York City tenants and Upstate farmers.

Statewide elections were exceedingly close, with Democrats carrying the New York City

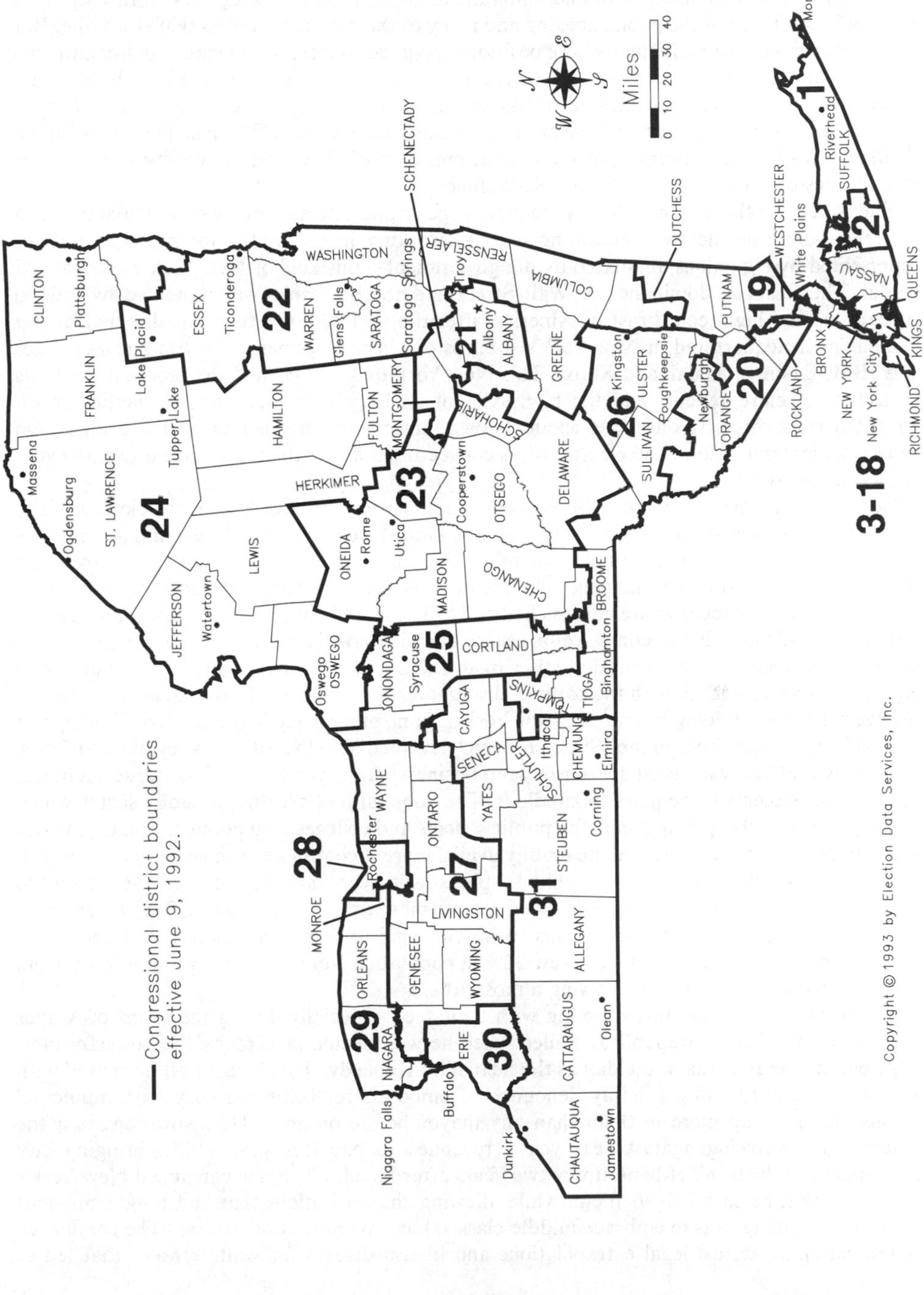
Congressional district boundaries effective June 9, 1992.
Miles
0 10 20 30 40
1
2
3-18
19
20
21
22
23
24
25
26
27
28
29
30
31
CLINTON
Plattsburgh
FRANKLIN
Lake Placid
ESSEX
Ticonderoga
Massena
Ogdensburg
ST. LAWRENCE
Tupper Lake
HAMILTON
WARREN
Glens Falls
WASHINGTON
SARATOGA
Saratoga Springs
SCHENECTADY
RENSSELAER
Troy
Albany
ALBANY
COLUMBIA
GREENE
DUTCHESS
Kingston
ULSTER
Poughkeepsie
Newburgh
ORANGE
PUTNAM
WESTCHESTER
White Plains
ROCKLAND
BRONX
NEW YORK
New York City
KINGS
QUEENS
RICHMOND
NASSAU
SUFFOLK
Riverhead
Montauk
SULLIVAN
DELAWARE
SCHOHARIE
MONTGOMERY
FULTON
HERKIMER
Cooperstown
OTSEGO
ONEIDA
Rome
Utica
LEWIS
JEFFERSON
Watertown
OSWEGO
Oswego
ONONDAGA
Syracuse
MADISON
CHENANGO
CORTLAND
BROOME
Binghamton
TIOGA
TOMPKINS
Ithaca
CAYUGA
SENECA
SCHUYLER
CHEMUNG
Elmira
WAYNE
ONTARIO
YATES
STEUBEN
Corning
MONROE
Rochester
LIVINGSTON
ALLEGANY
ORLEANS
GENESEE
WYOMING
NIAGARA
Niagara Falls
ERIE
Buffalo
CATTARAUGUS
Olean
CHAUTAUQUA
Dunkirk
Jamestown
Copyright © 1993 by Election Data Services, Inc.

Catholic vote and Republicans winning Protestants Upstate. Swing votes were cast by the 2 million Jewish immigrants and their children, who supported a generous welfare state but mistrusted the Tammany machine and valued civil rights. The politician who combined these appeals most cannily was Fiorello LaGuardia: a nominal Republican but almost a socialist, an Episcopalian who was half-Jewish and half-Italian, and who as mayor of New York City from 1933–45 built much of the public housing and many of the civic monuments that still stand. But both parties produced politicians whose positions appealed to these swing voters, politicians who became nationally prominent and often presidential candidates at a time when the national media was much more concentrated in Manhattan than today: Democrats Al Smith, Robert Wagner, Franklin Roosevelt and Averell Harriman; Republicans Thomas Dewey, Wendell Willkie, Dwight Eisenhower (a New Yorker as president of Columbia University when he was elected president in 1952) and Nelson Rockefeller.

The polity that these men built was productive, generous, tolerant and closely regulated. In an America where people were becoming used to working in big units—for big corporations, represented by big unions, regulated by big government—this kind of New York was a natural leader. The financial dominance of Wall Street and the big banks was protected by federal regulation. The high-tech thrust of America after the mid-20th Century was directed by big companies headquartered in New York's suburbs or Upstate: General Electric and Bell Labs and IBM, Eastman Kodak and Xerox. This New York took for granted the productivity of its thousands of entrepreneurs and the high skills of its largely immigrant-born, public school-educated work force. It was blase about its own miraculous infrastructure—the bridges and subways, electronic cables and electric wires connecting it better than any place else with every corner of the world.

But in the last quarter-century, New York's public strengths have become weaknesses. The state which was clearly the national leader of a big-unit America lost the leadership of a country where growth now occurs in small economic units, and flexibility and adaptability are more important than centralized planning. The institutions and practices and infrastructure which helped produce its successes are now ossified and brittle and likely, unless they are reformed and rebuilt, to lead to further decline. Welfare state benefits have become too expensive, measures meant to protect against corruption stifle innovation, and both have failed to achieve their objectives—ghettos throb with the pains of disorganization, and payoffs and rackets are part of the everyday cost of doing business in New York as in no other place in the country. The biggest new business in New York in the 1990s has been "new media"—the Silicon Alley of CD-ROMs, Web sites and software used for business-to-business sales; yet the city's antique technical infrastructure seems inadequate to handle it. The noble aim of creating a public sector which would guarantee cheap rents, topnotch public schools and colleges, and public hospitals, instead guarantees that none of these will be readily available: rent control keeps housing scarce, school bureaucracies stifle good teaching, public hospitals ration care down to nothing. The attempt to create a fail-safe government has produced a government that is sure to fail. The government that intended to aid growth now seems to be cutting it off—not completely, but enough to explain why New York state, which grew 32% in population from 1940–65, grew only 2% from 1965–95, while California was growing almost 70%.

People and businesses started voting with their feet, especially during the terms of Mayor John Lindsay, a liberal Republican hailed when he was elected in 1965 by the powerful New York-based liberal media of the day as the next John Kennedy, though about all he shared with Kennedy was good looks. Lindsay denounced Democrats for being too cozy with municipal unions, but gave up more to them than any mayor before or since. He institutionalized the practice of borrowing against next year's revenues to pay this year's bills, bringing city government to the brink of bankruptcy two years after he left office. He convinced New York's minorities that he cared about them, while allowing the institutions that had taught previous generations' immigrants to embrace middle-class values, to scorn those values. "The confluence of radical spite, absurd legal extrapolations and liberal disdain for white ethnics that led to forced busing, the bloating of welfare rolls and the mau-mauing of white teachers broke the spine of New York's civic culture," writes liberal Jim Sleeper in *The Closest of Strangers*. Antagonized middle-class New Yorkers fled not just to the suburbs, but by the hundreds of thousands to (then) low-tax New Jersey, Connecticut and Florida. In the 1970s, the population of New York, city and state, dropped by one million—an unprecedented hemorrhage of talent and productivity, a flight of the middle class away from a polity that seemed to be dying.

Retrenchment followed the mid-1970s bankruptcy crisis. Private financiers and the state government took control of city government, cut spending and negotiated cutbacks in jobs and salaries with public employees' unions. Citizens endured the loss of services and deterioration of streets, bridges and subways. With the financial boom of 1981–87, New York once again brimmed with confidence, and the buzzing of economic growth and cultural innovation could again be heard over the never-ending blare of car horns. Manhattan boomed as an office center and remained the center of America's financial, clothing, media and publishing industries. Its population was rising and it was attracting immigrants once again. The outer boroughs attracted migrants from Latin America, the eastern Mediterranean, East Asia, South Asia, even Russia, injecting youth and vitality into what had been aging, listless communities. Edward Koch, mayor from 1977–89, rationalized and disciplined city government in many ways; Mario Cuomo, governor from 1982–94, appointed some fine administrators and cut some taxes.

Yet all was not well. Koch succumbed to higher spending as revenues rolled in during the mid-1980s, and Cuomo allied himself with the public employee unions, many of which have been the most effective enemies of reform. New York's legislature—"the worst governmental institution in the western world," writes former city official William Stern—remains unusually tightly controlled by the two chambers' leaders, with the Assembly dominated by New York City Democrats and the state Senate by suburban and Upstate Republicans engaged in classic political logrolling, lavishing taxpayers' dollars on each other's pet projects, with no incentives to hold spending down or deliver services. Independent agencies set up to evade public scrutiny have borrowed huge sums and lavish them on politically connected contractors, with the taxpayers eventually paying the bill. Government and the public sector continued to grow robustly, but private sector job growth was all but invisible. New York's old welfare state measures left clever members of the middle class in comfortable niches, on public payrolls protected from accountability, in rent-controlled apartments paying a fraction of market value. These same measures left newcomers and the lower classes out in the cold.

But New York's decline was no more inevitable than its rise, and there are signs that the city and state that adapted so surely to the challenges of the 1830s and 1930s may be adapting well to the challenges of the 1990s. Leading the way to reform are two Republican executives, elected on similar government-cutting platforms, though not at all as political allies, Mayor Rudolph Giuliani, who beat Mayor David Dinkins in 1993, and Governor George Pataki, who beat Cuomo in 1994. Both are unsentimental men of little eloquence, without illusions, ambitious politicians who have unhesitatingly elbowed others aside, navigating with a clear eye on a lodestar of principle but willing to maneuver course to avoid political shoals and rapids. Giuliani was elected by just 51%–48%, a reversal of his 50%–48% defeat in 1989, after Dinkins outraged many New Yorkers by hesitating before denouncing a black boycott of a Korean-owned Brooklyn grocery store and visiting relatives of a suspected drug dealer shot by a policeman. Pataki won 49%–45% after falling behind in the polls, watching Giuliani endorse Cuomo, being snubbed by the patronage-rich Nassau County Republicans and being dismissed by most of the media, led by *The New York Times*, which cheered for "our governor." Both victories represented a judgment that what Cuomo and *New York Times* writers called "the New York tradition" was destroying jobs, communities and neighborhoods. The New York version of the welfare state, for all the attractiveness of its champions, was repudiated.

The results are not all in, but plainly policies—and life on the ground—have changed. In New York City, Giuliani and his first police commissioner, William Bratton employed the police tactics urged by James Q. Wilson and George Kelling: aggressively enforcing and prosecuting perpetrators of small crimes—the graffiti vandals, turnstile jumpers, squeegee men, aggressive panhandlers—and using computers to send large numbers of police to drug markets and violent crime locations. The result is that all crimes dropped by nearly one-third from 1993–96 and the murder rate alone has fallen to a 30-year low: a result that liberal criminologists had long declared impossible. Giuliani also succeeded in cutting the city's welfare rolls, swollen since John Lindsay's welfare commissioner announced that no applicant's eligibility would be checked. Giuliani also hacked away at bureaucracy and taxes, with little regard to the log-rolling Democratic majority on the city council or the constantly demonstrating public employee unions. In early 1997 Giuliani, though not especially liked by most New Yorkers, was leading his four little-known Democratic opponents (Manhattan Borough President Ruth Messinger, Bronx Borough President Fernando Ferrer, City Councilman Sal Albanese and the Reverend Al Sharpton) by wide margins in the polls. Meanwhile, in Albany Pataki got the death penalty reinstated, reformed the workmen's comp system, passed a $1.75 billion environmental bond referendum in November 1996 and in early 1997 announced a plan to cut the welfare spending by 45%. He sponsored tax cuts, including the estate and gift taxes, and stood by benignly as Republican Senate Majority Leader Joseph Bruno was blocking renewal of New York City's rent control laws before a June 15 deadline. The political results were encouraging. Pataki's job rating was over 50% in November 1996, he and Giuliani were working cooperatively together and in early 1997 Democratic Congressman Charles Schumer decided not to run against Pataki but against Senator Alfonse D'Amato instead.

New York City in once again evolving. There are islands of excellence, or at least good quality, in the public school system, unlike Chicago, and in city hospitals. Some neighborhoods, like Brownsville in Brooklyn, long considered irretrievable from the depths of drug-related crimes and murder, are starting to revive. Immigrants have been streaming into outer borough neighborhoods, creating new businesses, churches and neighborhood institutions—Caribbean blacks in Flatbush, Chinese in Flushing and Borough Park, Colombians in Corona, Pakistanis in Jackson Heights, Greeks in Astoria, Russians in Brighton Beach. For a quick look at the future, go and see the crowds of young people of dozens of ethnic backgrounds studying every day at the main Queens Library in Jamaica. The prospect of ending or limiting rent control may horrify the affluent elderly in Manhattan, but will mean more and better housing for the upwardly striving through much of the city. For the future of New York City depends less on what happens in already affluent Manhattan and far more on what happens in the could-go-either-way outer boroughs. As Fred Sigel points out in *The Future Once Happened Here*, one-third of jobs in Brooklyn and nearly half in the Bronx are in or directly dependent on the public sector, which is in necessary decline, and that the 1996 Welfare Reform Act which cuts off aid to legal immigrants will have a big impact on New York City which has so many of them. The question is whether the outer boroughs will develop the private sector jobs and housing which New York did in the earlier 20th Century surge of immigration and whether immigrants will be helped to assimilate into American society as they were then or shunted off into "multicultural" ghettos into which Manhattan-bound theorists and public sector union leaders want to confine them.

Not all of New York state is New York City, by any means. But the city's strengths and its problems flow beyond its limits. New York suburbs are still outvoted by the city because so much suburban overflow is in New Jersey or Connecticut. The suburbs have by national standards very large and well-paid local governments, with high property taxes and a hunger for state school aid that in the Cuomo years kept the suburban-dominated Republican state Senate a faithful ally in maintaining New York's big government apparatus. Beyond the New York City orbit is Upstate, with 45% of the state's voters, historically Protestant and Republican, now heavily Catholic and increasingly Republican. Upstate no longer has central transportation arteries as in the days of the New York Central's water level route, and so is off the beaten path; its population has not risen much since the 1950s. The largest city, Buffalo, is one of those Great Lakes factory cities where old steel mills have closed and is now growing as a low-wage back-office adjunct to Toronto. Upstate's biggest employer, IBM, lost money in the 1980s and laid off thousands, while healthier big Upstate companies—General Electric, Kodak, Xerox, Corning—have not been hiring in large numbers.

Upstate has great assets: a fine physical environment—green hills, majestic mountains, glistening lakes, a plentiful water supply—and winters are no colder than those in booming Minnesota or New Hampshire. It has a highly-skilled labor force and high-tech experience. The North American Free Trade Agreement put Upstate on the doorstep of the most prosperous part of Canada: the Golden Horseshoe of Ontario from Niagara Falls to Toronto is just across the river from Buffalo's Niagara Frontier, and Interstate 87 runs straight from Albany to Montreal. This was one of America's first frontiers, with fine colleges and cultural institutions going back to the early 1800s wave of Yankee settlements. It set the dominant cultural tone of the Yankee America that won the Civil War, settled the West and stretched the United States all the way to the Pacific Ocean. But now Upstate is struggling to adapt to a new economy and to reduce New York's strangling high taxes.

For 40 years New York has been counted as a Democratic state, and in presidential politics it certainly is: it was Bill Clinton's second best state in 1992, after Arkansas, and his third best in 1996, after Massachusetts and Rhode Island. Yet in the 1990s New York also seems to have trended Republican in state politics, electing Giuliani in 1993 and Pataki in 1994, reelecting Senator Alfonse D'Amato in 1992 and giving a reduced margin to the Democratic Party's wisest philosopher, Senator Daniel Patrick Moynihan, in 1994. These divergent trends can perhaps be reconciled. New York is happy to support Clinton, a Democrat who promised tax cuts not tax increases in both of his campaigns, and would keep more federal money flowing here than a Republican; but in state politics, in which the project is cutting back an overlarge and over-expensive welfare state, voters have been trending Republican.

Governor. George Pataki began 1994 as a state senator hardly recognized outside his Hudson Valley district, even in the Capitol complex in Albany. A year later he was governor of New York. He grew up in Peekskill, a small industrial city on the Hudson in northern Westchester County, at the cusp of metropolitan New York City and Upstate New York. His father was the son of Hungarian immigrants, his mother is of Italian and Irish ancestry; his parents had a farm in Peekskill and built it into a business. Pataki went to Yale and Columbia Law School, practiced law with a big Wall Street firm, then moved to a Westchester firm in 1974. In 1982 he was elected mayor of Peekskill, where he converted tax-exempt property to taxpaying housing, held taxes down, opened an industrial plant and approved 1,000 new housing units. In 1984 he ran against an incumbent Democratic assemblyman and won. In 1992, after eight years as a member of a powerless minority, he challenged an incumbent Republican state senator, and beat her by 558 votes. In the state Senate he chafed at the leadership of Nassau County's Ralph Marino, voted against the budget—a major rebellion in Albany—and was supported by a conservative group called Change/NY.

In 1993, the almost unknown Pataki began running for governor, taking on one of America's best-known politicians, Mario Cuomo. For all his national fame, and his feints at running for president in 1987 and 1991, Cuomo was in trouble in New York: he cut the top tax rates but also created other taxes and increased spending robustly; he claimed credit for a workfare program but tended to support the public employee unions; he resolutely opposed capital punishment. Cuomo portrayed himself as the champion of *The New York Idea*, the title of a book he published in 1994; but most voters wanted reform. Pataki provided a clear contrast on both taxes and capital punishment, and he also showed political skill. He got the support of Senator Alfonse D'Amato, inheriting his backers as well as his enemies. He easily won the May 1994 convention and prevented a primary challenge and a Conservative Party candidacy from 1990 Conservative nominee Herb London, who was nominated instead for comptroller. He chose as his running mate Elizabeth (Betsy) McCaughey Ross, a constitutional scholar whose devastating critique of the Clinton healthcare plan helped do it in. In the general election, Cuomo attacked Pataki for having raised taxes in Peekskill and Democrats charged that he was a puppet of D'Amato. But Pataki led in polls until Rudolph Giuliani in late October endorsed Cuomo and bitterly criticized

Pataki. Cuomo went into the lead but never reached 50%. He gained votes in New York City and in Nassau County, with its revenue-hungry Republican machine. Thomas Golisano, a Rochester businessman, was spending millions as an independent, advised by pro-Perot pollster Gordon Black; Perot endorsed him and polls showed him with 8%. But Golisano's share of the vote fell to 4%, and Cuomo got 45%, about where he was running in polls. Pataki won 49% of the vote, losing New York City 70%–28% but carrying the suburbs 54%–43% and Upstate (where Giuliani's endorsement hurt Cuomo) 59%–32%. 1994 was the best Republican year in recent New York history: Republican Dennis Vacco was elected attorney general over Democrat Karen Burstein by 49%–47%; Republicans won 47% of the votes for U.S. House as compared to Democrats' 48%; and Senator Daniel Patrick Moynihan's winning margin was reduced to 55%–42%.

As governor, Pataki has shown determination and even ruthlessness in seeking his goals. After the election, he declined to take a congratulatory phone call from Giuliani for three weeks and engineered a coup ousting Marino as Senate Leader that was executed (like an insurance fire in a failing store) while he was on vacation in Florida; Marino resigned from the legislature in February 1995. In office, Pataki called for a cut in the state income tax and an actual reduction in state spending, including a cut in AFDC payments and Medicaid. After bruising negotiations with Democratic Assembly Speaker Sheldon Silver, from the Lower East Side of Manhattan, Pataki got much of what he wanted; the Cato Institute called him the nation's most effective governor in cutting taxes and controlling spending. Pataki signed the death penalty into law in March 1995 and transferred to Oklahoma an inmate scheduled to be executed there. He forced his choice as head of the Port Authority over Republican Governor Christine Todd Whitman of New Jersey, appointing George Marlin, the Convservative Party's 1993 nominee for mayor of New York. In 1996 he got reform of workmen's comp. With D'Amato and almost all leading New York Republicans except Giuliani, he endorsed Bob Dole for the Republican nomination; but when the Dole campaign went nowhere in New York he coolly said in November, "I wasn't involved in the campaign."

Instead he spent much effort on a $1.75 billion bond issue, citing his longtime admiration for Theodore Roosevelt and gathering support from business, labor and environmental groups. The bond issue passed with large majorities from New York City and the suburbs, where it can be an asset for him in his 1998 reelection campaign; it lost Upstate, where he surely will remain strong against any New York City-based Democrat. He also switched and supported the state takeover of Lilco, the Long Island power company which charges some of the nation's highest utility rates. In early 1997 Pataki unveiled his welfare reform plan, cutting benefits to recipients who do not find work by 45% over four years; he called for a three-year phaseout of estate and gift taxes, which send many affluent New Yorkers to Florida. He stayed aloof from Senate President Joseph Bruno's crusade to end state wide rent controls, leaving himself the option of backing a compromise. In any case, he can not lose all that many votes in the New York City or in Manhattan, where support for rent control is strongest; he lost Manhattan 80%–18% and the outer boroughs 66%–31% in 1994, and won anyway.

Pataki entered the 1998 campaign cycle in strong shape. He had a 51% positive job rating in November 1996, even as Bill Clinton was carrying the state overwhelmingly, and got the endorsement of former Democratic Mayor Edward Koch. He had long had rocky relations with Lieutenant Governor Betsy McCaughey Ross, and in April 1997 dropped her from the ticket; she said she would run for another office, perhaps in a primary against D'Amato. Congressman Charles Schumer, long eyeing the governorship, announced in April 1997 that he was running against D'Amato instead. Possible gubernatorial opponents include state Comptroller Carl McCall, New York City Council Speaker Peter Vallone and Assembly Majority Leader Michael Bragman. In early 1997 some Pataki backers were even talking him up as a presidential candidate in 2000. Some of his stands—support of some abortion rights, opposition to cutoff of aid to legal immigrants—would not go over well with many Republican activists in other parts of the country; but Pataki is not to be underestimated.

Senior Senator. Daniel Patrick Moynihan, the nation's best thinker among politicians since

Lincoln and its best politician among thinkers since Jefferson, remains even in the minority at the summit of a long career in public life. He is New York's senior senator, the ranking Democrat on the Finance Committee, crucially positioned in a still closely balanced Senate to advance his own ideas and retard others. And for all his academic credentials, Moynihan has a range of experience in American government as broad as any member of Congress. He worked for Governor Averell Harriman in the 1950s, served as assistant secretary of labor in the Kennedy and Johnson Administrations, was chief domestic adviser to President Nixon and was ambassador to the United Nations under President Ford—the only person in American history, he likes to note, who has served in the cabinet or subcabinet of four successive presidents. As Finance chairman, he helped shepherd the 1993 budget and tax package to passage by one vote. And he advised Bill and Hillary Rodham Clinton early and often to give priority to welfare reform over healthcare reform. Had his advice been taken, it might have changed the course of their administration and the fortunes of the Democratic Party.

Moynihan is known rightly for his ability to spot emerging issues long before anyone else, qualities that were apparent at least as early as 1965, when he wrote "The Negro Family: The Case for National Action." The long expanse of his career has underlined the consistency of his ideas and interests and the persistence with which he has kept at his causes. Every summer Moynihan spends several weeks in an old one-room schoolhouse on his farm in Pindars Corners, deep in the hills of Upstate New York, writing in distinctive prose another book on any of a dozen subjects. This is the kind of philosopher-politician who the Founding Fathers hoped would people the Senate—although they would have been surprised to see one spring, as Moynihan did, from the Manhattan slum of Hell's Kitchen.

Moynihan's preoccupations are many and enduring. Three decades ago, he bemoaned the dilapidated state of Pennsylvania Avenue. A redevelopment corporation was set up, and now it is a splendid boulevard, with buildings restored and new, in one of which he keeps an apartment. He is also the father of the graceful Thurgood Marshall Federal Judiciary Center, next door to Union Station. For New York he worked to rebuild the Brooklyn courthouse (he can recite the history of all of New York's courthouses) and to get funding to make the Manhattan Post Office into a new Penn Station. From 1973–75, he was ambassador to India and he is an expert on things Indian. Tying these subjects together is his wife Elizabeth Moynihan's scholarly work on the gardens of the great Moguls. She has also managed his campaigns in New York.

In the early 1960s, before Ralph Nader, Moynihan was arguing that traffic deaths could be reduced by redesigning car interiors. Later he became almost the nation's transportation czar. As then-chairman of Environment and Public Works Subcommittee on Transportation and Infrastructure, he produced "Ice Tea," insider language for the Intermodal Surface Transportation Efficiency Act of 1991 (ISTEA), which provided vast new sums for transportation and gave states the choice of whether to use money for highways or mass transit. It made funding formulas more favorable to New York—a pet Moynihan cause on which he publishes yearly data to show how New York is shortchanged—and got New York reimbursed for building its Thruway and funded magnetic levitation trains, also a favorite cause. ISTEA comes up for reauthorization in 1997, and once again Moynihan will play a key role, as southern and western states vie for a greater piece of the pie.

In 1993 Moynihan became the first New Yorker to chair the Senate Finance Committee in 155 years. He also became a kind of senior tutor to Bill and Hillary Rodham Clinton, often counseling them privately and sometimes rebuking them publicly, treating them like bright but sometimes wayward students. The two major Clinton initiatives, the 1993 budget and tax package and the 1994 healthcare reform, had to go through Finance, and Moynihan played a pivotal role on each. Initially the Clinton White House was contemptuous. One staffer said to *Time* in early 1993, "He's not one of us. He can't control Finance like Bentsen did. He's cantankerous, but we'll roll right over him if we have to." But Moynihan got the budget and tax package through the Senate and in August when the White House needed one last vote it was Elizabeth Moynihan who persuaded Bob Kerrey (whose presidential candidacy Moynihan supported in 1992) to cast the critical vote. Under Moynihan's guidance, the nanny tax was reformed and the Social Security Administration was made an independent agency.

Health care went differently. In January 1993 Moynihan criticized HHS Secretary Donna Shalala sharply for not mentioning welfare reform in her opening statement to the committee, and for months he pressed the Clintons to emphasize welfare reform, but to no great avail. In January 1994, when the Clintons produced a vast healthcare bill, Moynihan called their puny efforts on welfare "boob bait for bubbas." On *Meet the Press* he insisted, "We don't have a healthcare crisis in this country. We do have a welfare crisis." He called the original Clinton financing mechanism "a fantasy," and he threatened to hold health care hostage to a welfare bill. He got Shalala to admit that the "few" who would pay more under the Clinton plan were actually 40% of insured families. Nonetheless Moynihan stood ready to cobble a compromise with Bob Dole, who seemed at the beginning of 1994 to be interested. But the Clintons, backed by Majority Leader George Mitchell and Finance member Jay Rockefeller, said it wasn't time to compromise yet. Finance did produce a bill, and Mitchell got ready to introduce his own version on the floor. But in August 1994, House Democrats lost a crucial procedural vote on the crime bill and had to delay action on health care, and the Mitchell effort ran out of steam.

Moynihan's great cause on health care was preserving teaching hospitals, and not just because New York has several of them. For him it was "a sin against the Holy Ghost" to threaten the existence of these institutions. In 1997 he proposed a Medical Education Trust Fund, with $17 billion from Medicare, Medicaid and the private sector to double federal spending on medical schools and teaching hospitals. One of his great causes on the Finance Committee was preserving the deductibility of gifts of appreciated property to nonprofit entities such as universities and museums. This was Moynihan using the tax code to become a Maecenas, channeling more money to America's Tocquevillian cultural institutions than the National Endowments for the Humanities and Arts will ever give.

Surprisingly, for one whose critique of society can be so radical, Moynihan's approach to some issues can be cautious and conservative. In 1981, he was the first Democrat to jump to defend Social Security from any Reagan Administration attack; he got the Senate to vote 96–0 against any cut in benefits. In the 1986 tax reform debate, his great cause was preserving the deductibility of state taxes, worth more in high-tax New York than any other state. In 1991, he got both Democrats and Republicans in a tizzy with his "Moyniplan" to cut the Social Security payroll tax 1%. In December 1996 he and Finance Chairman William Roth sponsored the Boskin Commission of economists who recommended adjusting the Consumer Price Index downward by 1.1% on the ground that it overstates inflation. His hope was that entitlement spending would grow more slowly. He sees government as afflicted by "Baumol's disease"—the condition noted by economist William Baumol of inevitably increasing costs of personal services—because "activities with cost disease tend to migrate to the public sector."

Welfare reform is the idea he has been most closely associated with since 1965, when he wrote "The Negro Family." He was harshly criticized for years for "blaming the victim"; in fact, he was blaming fatherlessness. Since then, family breakdown among blacks has reached harrowing proportions, and family breakdown overall is now about as common as it was among blacks in 1965. His response was the Welfare Reform Act of 1988, which recognized the responsibilities of fathers to provide for their children and encouraged workfare experiments. But enforcement of child support and work incentives produced disappointing results. The Clinton campaign promised to "end welfare as we know it." But the 1996 Welfare Reform Act, in ending the federal entitlement to welfare, in Moynihan's opinion went much too far. He feared that it would leave children hungry in the streets, and spoke out against it more than any other senator. "Shame on the President," he said when Clinton signed the bill, adding that if it had come before him 14 weeks after the election instead of 14 weeks before he would have vetoed it.

Moynihan has also been a force in foreign policy. In 1975 and 1976, as ambassador to the United Nations, he denounced the Soviet Union and some Third World nations, opposing their resolution declaring Zionism as racism. Once considered a foreign policy hawk, in the late 1970s he became convinced that the Soviet Union was not a strong enemy and would come apart through ethnic conflict. Moynihan believes ethnic allegiances and rivalries are more important in politics than economic differences: that is the theme of his and Nathan Glazer's *Beyond the Melting Pot*, a description of New York's ethnic groups that was published in 1963 and still rings true today, and it is the theme of his 1993 book *Pandemonium*, which describes how ethnic conflicts produce war and genocide. Though he came to be classed with foreign policy doves, there is a great difference between them: most doves believed that the Soviet Union was dangerous but not evil, while Moynihan believed that the Soviet Union was evil but, because it was economically weak and ethnically riven, not dangerous. Today, Moynihan believes the United States should have a far smaller military and should basically abolish the CIA. He opposed the NAFTA because of his feeling that Mexico remains a "Leninist" society, but he was very much for the new General Agreement on Tariffs and Trade and was one of the few members of Congress to support the Mexico bailout in early 1995.

Moynihan is not afraid to break with his fellow Democrats. In early 1995 he was the first Democratic senator to call for an independent counsel to investigate Whitewater; in early 1997 he was the first major Democrat to call for an independent counsel to investigate the Clinton-Gore campaign finance violations. He broke with liberals in 1996 when he supported the partial-birth abortion ban; the practice, he said, was too close to infanticide. And he broke with decades of bipartisan practice in 1997 when, as chairman of a Commission on Secrecy, he called for "a new way of thinking about secrecy," arguing that because government tries to keep too much information secret, it often fails to protect adequately the secrets most critical to national security. The unanimous report, supported by Senator Jesse Helms, former CIA Director John Deutsch and House Intelligence Committee Chairman Larry Combest, concluded, "The best way to ensure that secrecy is respected, and that the most important secrets remain secret, is for secrecy to be returned to its limited but necessary role." The Commission also released the Venona transcripts, records of Soviet spymasters which showed the impenetration of the U.S. government by Soviet spies in the 1940s.

Electoral politics has proved surprisingly congenial to Moynihan. After beating Bella Abzug in the 1976 primary, he won a party-line victory against incumbent James Buckley in a year when Republicans were hurt by President Ford's opposition to federal loan guarantees for New York City. For 1982, Moynihan's opposition to Reagan programs prevented the emergence of opposition from the left, and he eliminated the main Republican candidate, Bruce Caputo, when it became known that Caputo had falsified his military record. Moynihan won 65%–34% in 1982 and 67%–31% in 1988, both records for New York. In 1994 he insisted that the Democratic state convention not give perennial candidate Al Sharpton the 25% of its votes needed to put him on the primary ballot; it did not. His general election opponent was Bernadette Castro, heiress of the Castro convertible sofabed fortune. She was little known, but the election's last week surge toward Republicans almost made her a contender. Moynihan's share of the vote was sharply down from 1988. He carried New York City 73%–25%, but won in the suburbs by only 49%–48% and split the Upstate vote evenly, for a 55%–42% victory. Now Moynihan is in the minority again, with less institutional power but just as much moral stature.

Junior Senator. Alfonse D'Amato is an embattled but wily politician, a competent legislator and brilliant political maneuverer, a Republican who has won three terms in the Senate from a mostly Democratic state and who could very well win a fourth in 1998. He is not a quiet man: he is loud and persistent; he pinches cheeks and puts his arms around shoulders and stands just a little too close when he speaks; he uses lushly vulgar expressions and is utterly shameless in his bids for popularity. He grew up in the Long Island suburb of Island Park, went to college and law school in Syracuse, practiced law and became part of the Nassau County Republican machine in the 1960s. He was supervisor of the town of Hempstead, which has some 700,000 people, from 1971–77, and vice chairman of the Nassau County Board of Supervisors from 1977–80. These are big-spending governments and no place for the naive: "the dealmaking and politicking I witnessed in my own back yard equalled anything I have done in the U.S. Senate," he wrote in his 1995 book *Power, Pasta and Politics*. In 1980, he had the insight that he could win the Republican primary against Senator Jacob Javits, who was, as D'Amato's ads bluntly pointed out, 76, ailing and liberal, and that he could beat a liberal Democrat in a year when voters were turning against liberals. That is what happened: D'Amato first beat Javits 56%–44% and then beat Congresswoman (and later City Controller) Elizabeth Holtzman 45%–44%.

D'Amato quickly set out to establish a reputation as "Senator Pothole," with manically aggressive constituency service and shameless devotion to causes dear to New York constituencies—mass transit, AIDS funding, Israel, the death penalty for drug dealers, and protection for Wall Street brokerage firms in their fights against the big banks. Yet he gets along well enough with Pat Moynihan, and their interests overlap more than one might think: Moynihan really does care about getting New York reimbursed for the Thruway and D'Amato really does care about human rights in Lithuania. Indeed, D'Amato was prescient in condemning Saddam Hussein, and his speeches, sometimes with cameras rolling, for human rights in the former Soviet Union have been vindicated by history. But staying in favor by doing favors has downside risks. D'Amato is widely suspected of violating ethical standards—suspicions that have more basis in his personal style and background than in any proven facts. He has long since split with the Nassau County machine, yet as he showed when he backed George Pataki for governor in 1994 and Bob Dole for president in 1996, he can get the whole New York Republican Party moving in his direction. D'Amato was rebuked—the mildest sanction—by the Senate Ethics Committee for allowing his brother Armand to use his office while representing a defense contractor.

D'Amato was easily reelected in 1986 over Mark Green, now New York City public advocate (the post used to be council chairman). His tough race came in 1992, in a Democratic state in a Democratic year, against a strong field of Democrats. But D'Amato got some luck and made some luck. Geraldine Ferraro, who before her 1984 vice presidential nomination had been thinking about a race against D'Amato in 1986, ran in 1992 on a moderate platform (against single-payer health insurance, for the death penalty) and appealed to Manhattan feminists and outer borough Italian-Americans. But Elizabeth Holtzman, running again for the seat, attacked Ferraro in the primary for not throwing out a pornography distributor tenant from a building she and her husband owned in 1985, as they had promised, and a Holtzman ad showed a *Village Voice* headline, "What You Don't Know About Ferraro And The Mob." But if the charge hurt Ferraro, it rebounded against Holtzman, and the beneficiary was not Holtzman but Attorney General Robert Abrams. He won the September primary by some 11,000 votes, winning 37%, to 36% for Ferraro; Holtzman had 12% and the ever-telegenic black protester Al Sharpton 14%.

D'Amato, vastly better financed, attacked Abrams as "hopelessly liberal," and touted his constituency service with ads saying, "Gettin' it done. Makin' waves. Takin' 'em on." To pound home the point, he staged a 14-hour filibuster in mid-October to save 875 jobs at a Smith-Corona factory in the Upstate town of Cortland. Mid-October is also when Abrams made the mistake that cost him the election: after being heckled by D'Amato supporters in Binghamton, Abrams called D'Amato a "fascist." D'Amato demanded an apology; Abrams said his remark was "unfortunate" but for several days refused to apologize for calling D'Amato one of the few bad things he clearly is not. D'Amato took this, with some basis, as an anti-Italian slur and ran an ad attacking Abrams; Mario Cuomo, whom D'Amato had never striven to beat, evidently took umbrage, saying "Bobby's race is all negative." D'Amato called Abrams "Mudslide Bob" and a "sleazebag," citing a commission that criticized him for taking money from developers whom he regulated. When it was revealed that Abrams was late in paying taxes on a $400,000 country home, D'Amato said, "He wants to raise other people's taxes . . . Let him pay his own." Meanwhile, he highlighted issues—defense cuts, health insurance—where he was closer to Bill Clinton's positions than Abrams was. From all this D'Amato squeaked out a 49%–48% victory. Exit polls showed D'Amato with high percentages among Italian descent voters (66%: the fascist slur hurt), Irish descent (63%) and white Protestants (62%); Abrams did well with blacks (84%) and those with no religious affiliation (74%), but not as well with Jews (59%).

Having survived 1992, D'Amato thrived in 1993 and 1994. His voting record on non-economic issues grew more conservative; he pressed for death penalties in the crime bill for major drug dealers. As ranking Republican on the Banking Committee, he got Deputy Treasury Secretary Roger Altman to resign for giving the White House a "heads up" on Whitewater. Back home his relations for Cuomo soured as he perceived Cuomo's vulnerability on taxes and the death penalty. In early 1994 he supported George Pataki, a little-known state senator opposed by his former Nassau County allies, and got him nominated by the state convention. He accurately perceived that Pataki would be smart and cool enough not to wither under attacks from Cuomo and the media and would keep pressing his stands for tax cuts and the death penalty. Pataki did not falter when Cuomo was endorsed by Mayor Rudolph Giuliani, a fierce enemy of D'Amato since D'Amato supported Ron Lauder's primary race against him in 1989. As one shrewd New York politico put it, "The lesson of 1994 is never get in the way between Al D'Amato and what he wants."

In Washington D'Amato also took a lead role when Republicans won their majority. Bob Dole appointed him head of the Republicans' Senate campaign committee, and ingeniously took advantage of a Supreme Court decision allowing independent expenditures. D'Amato imposed on many candidates the strategy of his pollster Arthur Finkelstein, running against Democrats as "embarrassingly liberal," with mixed results; overall Republicans gained two seats. Oddly, he channeled $1 million to the New York Republican Party, though New York had no Senate race in 1996. As chairman of the Banking Committee, he was not able to produce Glass-Steagall reforms, letting banks into other financial businesses. He did conduct Whitewater hearings, which got a poor reception in the press; but D'Amato and his crack staff got top Clinton appointees to make admissions that would prove embarrassing or worse in 1997. D'Amato also showed adeptness at leading New York Republicans and reading tabloid-fed New York public opinion. He engineered a joint Dole endorsement by Pataki and all 14 New York Republicans in Congress—but, pointedly, not Giuliani. But, as Republican poll ratings plummeted in New York, D'Amato pointedly attacked Newt Gingrich and House Republicans for having "misread the 1994 election results . . . They voted for evolution, not revolution." And in 1996 Banking hearings he attacked Swiss banks for having held onto the property of Jewish victims of the Holocaust. He also pushed for a trade embargo on Iran, $15 million to fight Soviet organized crime, a law to help breast cancer detection and demands for a monthly accounting (and a demagogic denouncing) of the Mexican bailout: more than just potholes. He also made some gaffes, notably an imitation of Simpson trial Judge Lance Ito on "Imus in the Morning."

D'Amato's political obituary was being written after Dole's smashing defeat in New York; but it was written in the years running up to 1992 as well. His job rating was running below 50% in early 1997 and he was running behind Geraldine Ferraro in some polls. Ferraro is one possible candidate, though she expressed qualms about the difficulty of raising money; D'Amato at the time had $7 million in hand. Mark Green was also planning another candidacy. In April 1997 Congressman Charles Schumer, who had been looking at the race for governor, announced he was running for senator instead. Schumer has a substantial legislative record, considerable media savvy and $5 million in his campaign treasury, and would be as tough an opponent as D'Amato has faced. Also, it is possible that Lieutenant Governor Betsy McCaughey Ross, dumped as Pataki's running mate in April 1997, may run against D'Amato in the 1998 primary—though she would have to deal with New York's cumbersome petition and ballot access requirements.

Presidential politics. For more than 100 years, New York was a pivotal state in presidential politics: it was the nation's largest state and closely divided first between Whigs and Jacksonians, then Democrats and Republicans. But now California, with 54 electoral votes, is much larger than New York, with 33. California's moods are also more changeable, thus attracting candidates' attention, while New York typically is the most Democratic large state. Back in the 1960s New York's Democratic margins came from middle-income Jews and Catholics in the outer boroughs of New York City. Today they come primarily from blacks and Puerto Ricans in the outer boroughs and liberal whites in Manhattan. Manhattan liberals tend to be young singles, affluent childless couples, feminists, gays and the often underpaid highly-educated people who flock to this center of arts and letters—the nation's prime leftish voting bloc. Bill Clinton won New York by the onesided margin of 59%–31% in 1996, carrying New York City overwhelmingly (77%–17%) and winning impressively in the suburbs (55%–36%) and Upstate (50%–37%).

New York has had bossed politics for years, and it never had a presidential primary until 1968. Turnout is low—for Democrats 1.0 million in 1980 and 1992, 1.3 million in 1984 and 1.5 million 1988—and convoluted petition requirements make it hard for candidates to qualify; Pat Buchanan never made it on the ballot here in 1992. In 1996 Buchanan appeared on primary ballots in 23 of the 31 districts and Steve Forbes spent $1 million to overcome some heavyhanded tactics and become the only candidate to qualify against party leader-endorsed Bob Dole in 1996. The rules have been modified since, but one suspects only a little.

Such primaries as do occur have an ethnic cast. Jewish voters, turning out heavily, set the tone of Democratic primaries from 1976–84. Black voters, turning out heavily partly out of enthusiasm for Jesse Jackson but also because of anger at Mayor Edward Koch, set the tone in 1988. In 1992, the local press hyped the New York primary as a make-or-break test of Clinton, when in fact he had clinched the nomination in Illinois and Michigan three weeks before. Paul Tsongas had withdrawn, Jerry Brown was not going to win, Mario Cuomo was not running. Clinton played along with the charade, appearing on *Imus in the Morning* and parrying questions from Gabe Pressman: he won with 41% to 26% for Brown and 29% for the withdrawn Tsongas. New York's Republican primary electorate is made up almost entirely of suburbanites and Upstaters, with a large number of Italian-Americans.

New York's minor parties no longer much matter, except occasionally the Conservatives. The Liberal Party and its predecessor, the American Labor Party, were founded to give Jewish garment workers a line on which to vote for Franklin Roosevelt and against local Tammany Hall candidates; it won 1.8% of the gubernatorial vote in 1994. The Conservative Party was founded to withhold votes from liberal Republicans like Nelson Rockefeller and John Lindsay and encourage the Republican Party to nominate more conservative candidates; now it almost always does, though withdrawal of the Conservative line locally can hurt.

Congressional districting. When John Kennedy was elected president in 1960, New York elected 43 Congressmen and California 30. When Bill Clinton was elected in 1992, New York elected 31 and California 52. This is what happens when one state grows rapidly and another grows not at all. Redistricting is carnage time: New York lost five districts in the 1980 Census and another three in 1990 and is projected to lose two more in 2000. In 1992, New York was the last state to redistrict, in June. The plan has many districts with convoluted lines, all drawn for good political reasons. But after two Supreme Court rulings overturning district lines drawn using race as the predominant factor, a lawsuit was brought challenging New York's Hispanic-majority 12th District that snakes through Brooklyn, Manhattan and Queens, and borders on seven other congressional districts. In February 1997 a three-judge federal court ordered the legislature to redraw this "Bullwinkle district" by July 30. Congresswoman Nydia Velasquez went to Albany to try to save her light-voting district. But it surely must be changed considerably, which will require changing all surrounding districts, if not every one in the state; if the legislature fails to act, the court will, subject to appeal to the Supreme Court.

The People: Est. Pop. 1996: 18,185,000; Pop. 1990: 17,990,455, up 1.1% 1990–1996. 6.9% of U.S. total, 3d largest; 16% rural. Median age: 35.3 years. 13% 65 years and over. 69.3% White, 14.3% Black, 3.7% Asian, 12.3% Hispanic origin. Households: 49.9% married couple families; 23% married couple fams. w. children; 45% college educ.; median household income: $32,965; per capita income: $16,501; 52.2% owner occupied housing; median house value: $131,600; median monthly rent: $428. 6.2% Unemployment. 1996 Voting age pop.: 13,564,000. 1996 Turnout: 6,439,129; 48% of VAP. Registered voters (1996): 10,162,156; 4,738,254 D (47%); 2,998,511 R (30%); 2,435,394 unaffiliated and minor parties (24%).

Political Lineup: Governor, George E. Pataki (R); Lt. Gov., Elizabeth McCaughey Ross(R); Secy. of State, Alexander Treadwell (R); Atty. Gen., Dennis C. Vacco (R); Comptroller, H. Carl McCall (D). State Senate, 61 (26 D and 35 R); Senate President, Elizabeth McCaughey Ross(R); State Assembly, 150 (96 D and 54 R); House Speaker, Sheldon Silver (D). Senators, Daniel Patrick Moynihan (D) and Alfonse M. D'Amato (R). Representatives, 31 (18 D and 13 R).

Elections Division: 518-474-1953 **Filing Deadline for U.S. Congress:** July 16, 1998.

1996 Presidential Vote

Clinton (D)	3,756,455	(59%)
Dole (R)	1,932,894	(31%)
Perot (I)	503,356	(8%)
Other	128,915	(2%)

1996 Republican Presidential Primary

Dole (R)	599,748	(55%)
Forbes (R)	325,211	(30%)
Buchanan (R)	163,365	(15%)

1992 Presidential Vote

Clinton (D)	3,444,450	(50%)
Bush (R)	2,346,649	(34%)
Perot (I)	1,090,721	(16%)

GOVERNOR

Gov. George E. Pataki (R)

Elected 1994, term expires Jan. 1999; b. June 24, 1945, Peekskill; home, Garrison; Yale U., B.A. 1967, Columbia U. Law Schl., J.D. 1970; Roman Catholic; married (Libby).

Career: Practicing atty., 1970–89; Peekskill Mayor, 1982–84; NY Assembly, 1984–92; NY Senate, 1992–95.

Office: Executive Chamber, State Capitol, Albany 12224, 518-474-8390; Web site: www.state.ny.us.

Election Results

1994 gen.	George E. Pataki (R)	2,538,702	(49%)
	Mario M. Cuomo (D-L)	2,364,904	(45%)
	B. Thomas Golisano (INF)	217,490	(4%)
	Others	82,666	(2%)
1994 prim.	George E. Pataki (R)	273,620	(76%)
	Richard M. Rosebaum (R)	88,302	(24%)
1990 gen.	Mario M. Cuomo (D-L)	2,157,087	(53%)
	Pierre A. Rinfret (R)	865,948	(21%)
	Herbert I. London (C)	827,614	(20%)
	Others	206,247	(5%)

SENATORS

Sen. Daniel Patrick Moynihan (D)

Elected 1976, seat up 2000; b. Mar. 16, 1927, Tulsa, OK; home, Pindars Corners; City Col. of NY, 1943, Tufts U., B.A. 1948, M.A. 1949, Ph.D. 1961; Catholic; married (Elizabeth).

Career: Navy, 1944–47; Aide, NY Gov. Averell Harriman, 1955–58; U.S. Asst. Secy. of Labor, 1963–65; Dir., Joint Ctr. for Urban Studies, MIT and Harvard, 1966–69; Asst. to Pres. Nixon, Urban Affairs, 1969–71; Prof., Harvard, 1971–73; U.S. Ambassador to India, 1973–75; U.N. Ambassador, 1975–76.

DC Office: 464 RSOB 20510, 202-224-4451; Fax: 202-228-0406; e-mail: senator@dpm.senate.gov.

State Offices: Buffalo, 716-551-4097; Manhattan, 212-661-5150; Oneonta, 607-433-2310.

Committees: *Environment & Public Works* (2nd of 8 D): Superfund, Waste Control & Risk Assessment; Transportation & Infrastructure. *Finance* (RMM of 9 D): International Trade (RMM); Social Security & Family Policy; Taxation & IRS Oversight. *Rules & Administration* (4th of 7 D). *Joint Committee on the Library of Congress* (4th of 5 Sens.). *Joint Committee on Taxation* (4th of 5 Sens.).

Group Ratings

	ADA	ACLU	AFS	LCV	CFA	CON	NFIB	COC	ACU	NTLC	CHC
1996	90	53	100	77	93	72	28	31	10	7	7
1995	90	—	100	100	88	65	—	22	0	—	—

National Journal Ratings

	1995 LIB — 1995 CONS			1996 LIB — 1996 CONS		
Economic	90%	—	6%	82%	—	14%
Social	93%	—	0%	66%	—	33%
Foreign	69%	—	29%	77%	—	17%

Key Votes of the 104th Congress

1. Reduce Medicare Growth $	N	5. Flag Amendment	N	9. Anti-Missile Defense	N
2. Lmt. Prod. Liab. Damages	N	6. Endangered Species	Y	10. Cuban Embargo	N
3. Increase Min. Wage	Y	7. Gay Employment Rights	Y	11. Bar Bosnia Troop $	N
4. Welfare Reform	N	8. Ovrd. Part. Birth Veto	Y	12. Cut Vietnam Aid	N

Election Results

1994 general	Daniel Patrick Moynihan (D-L)	2,646,541	(55%)	($6,705,482)
	Bernadette Castro (R-C)	1,988,308	(42%)	($1,581,901)
	Others	155,487	(3%)	
1994 primary	Daniel Patrick Moynihan (D)	526,766	(75%)	
	Al Sharpton (D)	178,231	(25%)	
1988 general	Daniel Patrick Moynihan (D-L)	4,048,649	(67%)	($4,809,810)
	Robert R. McMillan (R-C)	1,875,784	(31%)	($528,989)

Sen. Alfonse M. D'Amato (R)

Elected 1980, seat up 1998; b. Aug. 1, 1937, Brooklyn; home, Island Park; Syracuse U., B.S. 1959, J.D. 1961; Catholic; divorced.

Career: Practicing atty., 1962–65; Nassau Cnty. Public Admin., 1965–68; Hempstead Town Receiver of Taxes, 1969; Hempstead Supervisor, 1971–77; Vice Chmn., Nassau Cnty. Bd. of Supervisors, 1977–80.

DC Office: 520 HSOB 20510, 202-224-6542; Fax: 202-224-5871; e-mail: senator_al@damato.senate.gov.

State Offices: Albany, 518-472-4343; Buffalo, 716-846-4111; Manhattan, 212-947-7390; Rochester, 716-263-5866; Syracuse, 315-423-5471.

Committees: *Banking, Housing & Urban Affairs* (Chmn. of 10 R). *Finance* (5th of 11 R): Health Care; International Trade; Taxation & IRS Oversight.

Group Ratings

	ADA	ACLU	AFS	LCV	CFA	CON	NFIB	COC	ACU	NTLC	CHC
1996	25	17	29	0	29	64	72	69	75	93	74
1995	15	—	9	7	13	29	—	89	78	—	—

National Journal Ratings

	1995 LIB — 1995 CONS			1996 LIB — 1996 CONS		
Economic	43%	—	54%	44%	—	54%
Social	33%	—	62%	38%	—	60%
Foreign	22%	—	67%	35%	—	63%

Key Votes of the 104th Congress

1. Reduce Medicare Growth $	Y	5. Flag Amendment	Y	9. Anti-Missile Defense	Y
2. Lmt. Prod. Liab. Damages	N	6. Endangered Species	N	10. Cuban Embargo	Y
3. Increase Min. Wage	Y	7. Gay Employment Rights	Y	11. Bar Bosnia Troop $	Y
4. Welfare Reform	Y	8. Ovrd. Part. Birth Veto	Y	12. Cut Vietnam Aid	Y

Election Results

1992 general	Alfonse M. D'Amato (R-C-RTL)	3,166,994	(49%)	($11,550,958)
	Robert Abrams (D-L)	3,086,200	(48%)	($6,408,981)
	Others	205,632	(3%)	
1992 primary	Alfonse M. D'Amato (R)	unopposed		
1986 general	Alfonse M. D'Amato (R-C-RTL)	2,378,197	(57%)	($12,914,822)
	Mark Green (D)	1,723,216	(41%)	($1,635,676)

FIRST DISTRICT

Long Island—the Island to most New Yorkers—is America's largest, most populous and in some ways most troubled island: 103 miles long, 12 to 20 miles wide, with gentle hills and cliffs above Long Island Sound and sandspit beaches fronting the Atlantic Ocean—a familiar sight in the summer of 1996 as searchers looked for wreckage of TWA Flight 800. Nearly seven million people live here, more than in all but nine states, 4.3 million in the New York City boroughs of Brooklyn and Queens and 2.6 million in the suburban counties of Nassau and Suffolk. Brooklyn, at the western end of the island, is urban and thickly settled, while the Hamptons at the east end are carefully manicured countryside, preserved by a stylish New York elite. The Hamptons and the old whaling village of Sag Harbor, originally settled by New Englanders, were left behind in the rush of westward migration; today they appear more comfortable than grand, a shingled and windmilled portion of middle America kept more pristine than workaday middle America ever was.

But demographically, the Hamptons are only a small (though growing) part of Long Island. More important are the (no longer growing) suburbs created in the rush eastward into what was once farmland after World War II. Developers looked for cheaper land for aircraft factories and shopping centers, subdivisions and office parks, and found them first in Nassau County just east of Queens and then in Suffolk County. Suffolk attracted young families, of Irish and Italian descent more often than Jewish or black, looking for more ground and trees and less crime and tension than in their city neighborhoods. Politically, Suffolk County is one of the most conservative parts of New York. It has also become turbulent political territory, as life in Long Island has turned sour in the last decade. Defense plants shut down and jobs evaporated as the defense buildup and then the Cold War ended. Lilco, the local utility, had cost overruns on its nuclear plant in Shoreham, and then went into bankruptcy after Governor Mario Cuomo shut the plant down, giving Long Island the nation's highest electric rates. But the partial state takeover of Lilco, brokered by Governor George Pataki in March 1996, is expected to cut rates by 17%.

The 1st Congressional District covers eastern Suffolk County, running east from Smithtown on the North Shore and Patchogue on the South Shore. It includes the Hamptons but, more important politically, the Brookhaven National Laboratory and the defense plants in the center of the Island. Politically, this is a Republican area willing in times of discontent to vote for Democrats with some special claim on support.

The congressman from the 1st District is Michael Forbes, a Republican elected in 1994. Forbes has roots in the East End, and a certain theatricalness. One grandfather founded *The News Review* in Riverhead, his other grandparents were a vaudeville song and dance team. Forbes was voted the "most spirited" member of his class at West Hampton Beach High School. Though he grew up in a Democratic household, he got the political bug early, as a Republican. In 1971, at 19, he started working in the Suffolk County legislature; he worked for Speaker Perry Duryea of Montauk in the mid-1970s, then for Senator Alfonse D'Amato, Upstate conservative Democrat Sam Stratton, Florida Congressman (now Senator) Connie Mack, and for the 1988 and 1992 Bush campaigns. He was a Small Business Administration regional director in the Bush Administration, then a New York area staffer for the U.S. Chamber of Commerce.

In 1994 Forbes ran against Democratic Congressman George Hochbrueckner, a four-term member of the National Security Committee who tried to save jobs at Grumman and other Long Island contractors. But in late September, Grumman announced another 3,500 layoffs, and voters turned to other issues. Forbes called for a 10% across-the-board cut in the federal government and campaigned against unfunded mandates. He said he wanted to connect the East End by wire with business opportunities in New York City and beyond, and to give tax incentives for small business and jobs. He was heavily outspent, but won 53%–47%, as national issues overcame local.

"I know my way around. I can hit the ground running," he claimed, and his 10-year acquaintance with Newt Gingrich proved that by helping him win a seat on the Appropriations Committee—an unusual feat for a freshman. Forbes proved his party loyalty to insiders by refusing to support Senator Pat Moynihan's pet project of building a new Penn Station in Manhattan's old Post Office. But he also voted with 23rd District Congressman Sherwood Boehlert to strip 17 EPA riders in 1995, and in 1996 he tried to get a vote on campaign finance reform. Forbes spent much time in the district and when the government shut down he furloughed nine staffers as "nonessential" and answered the telephone himself.

In 1996 Forbes found himself in a seat which Bill Clinton carried. But he heavily outspent his opponent, Suffolk County legislator Nora Bredes, a longtime opponent of the Shoreham nuclear plant whom he called a "sixties liberal" and denied that he was in lockstep with Newt Gingrich.

Near the end of the campaign he called her "anti-Catholic" for accusing Forbes of inflicting "his personal religious views on all of us," on abortion. Forbes won 55%–45%. Then came his biggest moment in the spotlight, in December 1996, when he was the first House Republican to announce he would not vote for Newt Gingrich for speaker on January 7. "Newt Gingrich, the talented visionary and tactician who brought Republicans to this historic moment, is not the man to lead the charge in the 105th Congress," he said. "His admissions and the ongoing investigations by the Ethics Committee and the IRS will distract us all from the important work at hand." Democrats and the press treated this as the beginning of the end for Gingrich; Republican leaders muttered that it was just personal ambition. Forbes ended up voting for Jim Leach for speaker, and eight other Republicans refused to vote for Gingrich; but he was reelected nevertheless.

Forbes's stand was evidently popular at home, but not in the House Republican Conference "It's very high school," he said when Susan Molinari walked past him in the House dining room without a word. "I haven't felt as comfortable" slapping a colleague on the back; "I'm afraid I'll do it to the wrong person." But there was no direct retaliation, and Forbes tried to repair his party credentials. He criticized the New York Democratic Party for receiving $105,000 in tainted funds from the Democratic National Committee, and he announced his opposition to any budget deal that failed to include "meaningful tax relief." Forbes cannot expect that this district will go uncontested in 1998. One possible candidate is actor Alec Baldwin, who holds fundraisers in his Hamptons house, said he was thinking about running. Forbes's reaction: "He is an artistic personality, and I think the world of him on that score. Of course, he is the polar opposite of me politically."

The People: Pop. 1990: 580,076; 8% rural; 12% age 65+; 89% White; 4% Black; 2% Asian; 5% Hispanic origin. Households: 67% married couple families; 33% married couple fams. w. children; 49% college educ.; median household income: $45,464; per capita income: $17,614; median gross rent: $782; median house value: $158,400.

1996 Presidential Vote

Clinton (D)	118,187	(51%)
Dole (R)	83,956	(36%)
Perot (I)	25,850	(11%)
Other	4,069	(2%)

1992 Presidential Vote

Bush (R)	101,160	(40%)
Clinton (D)	96,890	(38%)
Perot (I)	54,128	(21%)

Rep. Michael P. Forbes (R)

Elected 1994; b. July 16, 1952, Riverhead; home, Quogue; S.U.N.Y. Albany, B.A. 1983; Catholic; married (Barbara).

Career: Staff asst., U.S. Sen. Alfonse D'Amato, 1980–83; Staff asst., U.S. Rep. Sam Stratton, 1983–84; Admin. Asst., U.S. Rep. Connie Mack, 1984–87; Owner, Forbes & Co. PR firm, 1987–89; Regional Admin., Small Business Admin., 1989–93; Regional Dir., U.S. Chamber of Commerce, 1993–94.

DC Office: 416 CHOB 20515, 202-225-3826; Fax: 202-225-3143; e-mail: mpforbes@hr.house.gov.

District Office: Hampton Bays, 516-723-0017; Shirley, 516-345-9000; Smithtown, 516-724-4600.

Committees: *Appropriations* (26th of 34 R): Commerce, Justice, State & Judiciary; Foreign Operations, Export Financing & Related Programs; Treasury, Postal Service & General Government.

Group Ratings

	ADA	ACLU	AFS	LCV	CFA	CON	NFIB	COC	ACU	NTLC	CHC
1996	15	13	30	31	54	40	83	73	84	93	93
1995	15	—	—	6	54	38	—	79	80	—	—

National Journal Ratings

	1995 LIB — 1995 CONS			1996 LIB — 1996 CONS		
Economic	51%	—	49%	45%	—	55%
Social	43%	—	56%	40%	—	59%
Foreign	15%	—	73%	21%	—	72%

Key Votes of the 104th Congress

1. Reduce Medicare Growth $	Y	5. Flag Amendment	Y	9. Cuban Embargo	Y
2. Ovrd. Product Liab. Veto	Y	6. Drop EPA Limits	Y	10. Bar Bosnia Troop $	Y
3. Increase Min. Wage	Y	7. Repeal Assault-Weap. Ban	Y	11. Cut Anti-Missile Defense	N
4. Welfare Reform	*	8. Ovrd. Part. Birth Veto	Y	12. Bar U.N. Uniforms	Y

Election Results

1996 general	Michael P. Forbes (R-C-I-RTL)	116,620	(55%)	($918,162)
	Nora L. Bredes (D-SM)	96,496	(45%)	($394,083)
1996 primary	Michael P. Forbes (R)	unopposed		
1994 general	Michael P. Forbes (R-C-RTL)	90,491	(53%)	($265,930)
	George J. Hochbrueckner (D-LIF)	80,146	(47%)	($719,102)

SECOND DISTRICT

Following World War II, hundreds of thousands of New York City residents—people who had trouble imagining they would live anywhere but the close-packed city streets—moved to what had been the potato fields of central Long Island. The highways that Robert Moses built to connect Jones Beach with the city masses were the routes of that migration—and often the daily commuter paths back into New York—as young veterans and their families found they could afford to leave the row-house neighborhoods where they had grown up for the single-family houses of Levittown and other Long Island subdivisions. The first wave of postwar migration moved into Nassau County, and it was largely a cross-section of all but the poorest New Yorkers: about half Catholic, with the other half split almost evenly between Jews and Protestants. As Long Island developed its own employment base, another wave moved farther east into Suffolk County. This group was more Catholic and less Jewish than the first, and more blue-collar. It was ancestrally Democratic, but firmly traditional and culturally conservative.

The 2d Congressional District includes most of western Suffolk County. The bulk of the district's population is concentrated in the South Shore townships of Babylon and Islip, each of which contains numerous communities separated only by name. There are some spacious houses with views of Great South Bay and, across the bay—but still within the district—lie the beaches of Fire Island, where many of the homes are weekend retreats owned by affluent New York City residents. But, for the most part, the 2d is the lower-income part of Long Island, beyond the more fashionable and expensive commuter suburbs to the west and well south of the picturesque North Shore. This area filled up with people in the 1950s and 1960s but has grown little in the past quarter century. However, with some of the lowest-priced housing on the Island, it continues to attract young families. Ten percent of the 2d is Hispanic, the largest percentage of any of the Long Island districts.

The congressman from the 2d District is Rick Lazio, a Republican elected in 1992. Lazio grew up on the South Shore. After Vassar and law school in Washington, he was a prosecutor and, after 1989, a legislator in Suffolk County; he has been in the public sector since age 25. In 1992 he ran against Congressman Thomas Downey, a Democrat elected in 1974 at 25, the kind of natural politician who helped Democrats maintain majorities for 20 years. Lazio attacked Downey as part of the Washington culture out of touch with Long Island, for junketing and for his 151 overdrafts on the House bank. Downey spent $1.4 million to Lazio's $276,000, but Lazio won 53%–47%.

This was a presage of 1994 Republican victories, but Lazio was not exactly a Contract With America Republican, though he did call for congressional reform and promised to serve no more than six consecutive terms. His economic views are fairly conservative; he was named to the Budget Committee as a freshman after campaigning for a capital gains cut. On cultural issues he is moderate to liberal; he voted for family and medical leave, the Brady bill, the assault weapons ban and the striker replacement bill. He is one of the few Republicans to defend the National Endowment for the Arts, but he also calls on Hollywood to make a larger private commitment to arts funding.

When Republicans won their majority in 1994, Lazio dropped Budget and became chairman of Banking's Subcommittee on Housing and Community Opportunity. He worked for more local controls and community-based programs to give public-housing tenants incentives to move up the economic ladder. Liberals criticized his proposal to require unemployed public housing tenants to perform eight hours of community service a month. He also sought to repeal a 1970s requirement that caps public-housing tenants' rent at 30% of income; he contends that discourages many from getting better jobs. He successfully passed a "reverse mortgage" bill for senior citizens.

Lazio has been reelected easily, 68%–28% in 1994 and 64%–33% in 1996, when he was endorsed by the Sierra Club for his work on the Long Island shoreline. While his Long Island colleagues Michael Forbes and Peter King were publicly criticizing Newt Gingrich, Lazio was quietly supporting him. That helped him win a seat on the Commerce Committee in 1997. But he was not successful in getting appointed chairman of the National Republican Congressional Committee. Since Lazio has promised to serve no more than six terms in the House, some think he is interested in running for the Senate some day.

The People: Pop. 1990: 580,303; 10% age 65+; 79% White; 9% Black; 2% Asian; 10% Hispanic origin. Households: 68% married couple families; 33% married couple fams. w. children; 45% college educ.; median household income: $50,076; per capita income: $17,515; median gross rent: $817; median house value: $158,600.

1996 Presidential Vote

Clinton (D)	108,598	(54%)
Dole (R)	68,710	(34%)
Perot (I)	20,419	(10%)
Other	3,117	(2%)

1992 Presidential Vote

Bush (R)	92,762	(40%)
Clinton (D)	91,430	(40%)
Perot (I)	44,603	(19%)

Rep. Rick A. Lazio (R)

Elected 1992; b. Mar. 13, 1958, West Islip; home, Brightwaters; Vassar Col., B.A. 1980, American U., J.D. 1983; Catholic; married (Patricia Moriarty).

Career: Asst. Dist. Atty., Suffolk Cnty., 1983–88; Suffolk Cnty. legislator, 1989–92; Practicing atty., 1989–92.

DC Office: 2444 RHOB 20515, 202-225-3335; Fax: 202-225-4669; e-mail: lazio@hr.house.gov.

District Offices: Babylon, 516-893-9010.

Committees: *Banking & Financial Services* (6th of 30 R): Capital Markets, Securities & Government Sponsored Enterprises; Housing & Community Opportunity (Chmn.). *Commerce* (25th of 28 R): Finance & Hazardous Materials; Health & Environment.

Group Ratings

	ADA	ACLU	AFS	LCV	CFA	CON	NFIB	COC	ACU	NTLC	CHC
1996	15	6	18	38	69	78	89	87	75	90	66
1995	25	—	—	13	77	87	—	83	68	—	—

National Journal Ratings

	1995 LIB		1995 CONS	1996 LIB		1996 CONS
Economic	53%	—	47%	44%	—	56%
Social	55%	—	43%	59%	—	40%
Foreign	15%	—	73%	38%	—	60%

Key Votes of the 104th Congress

1. Reduce Medicare Growth $	Y	5. Flag Amendment	Y	9. Cuban Embargo	Y
2. Ovrd. Product Liab. Veto	Y	6. Drop EPA Limits	Y	10. Bar Bosnia Troop $	Y
3. Increase Min. Wage	Y	7. Repeal Assault-Weap. Ban	N	11. Cut Anti-Missile Defense	N
4. Welfare Reform	Y	8. Ovrd. Part. Birth Veto	Y	12. Bar U.N. Uniforms	Y

Election Results

1996 general	Rick A. Lazio (R-C)	112,135	(64%)	($574,460)
	Kenneth J. Herman (D-I)	57,953	(33%)	($14,487)
	Others	4,506	(3%)	
1996 primary	Rick A. Lazio (R)	unopposed		
1994 general	Rick A. Lazio (R-C)	100,107	(68%)	($484,133)
	James L. Manfre (D-LIF)	41,102	(28%)	($87,156)
	Others	5,567	(4%)	

THIRD DISTRICT

It was a pivotal moment in American suburban history: in September 1947, families moved into 300 tiny 750-square-foot houses, built in record time by mass production. They sold for $6,990, with no down payment for veterans. This was Levittown, and by the time the last new house was sold for $9,500 in November 1951, the name had become a synonym for rapid suburban development. Developer William Levitt recognized that many young veterans and their families were eager to move out of crowded New York City neighborhoods, so he bought a Nassau County potato field, planted trees, designed floor plans to allow easy additions and built a community of 65,000 people. As Levittown prepares to celebrate its 50th anniversary in 1997, few of the original four-room bungalows can be found, but homes are still in the affordable range. And if school enrollment has dropped here, and retiree workshops have cropped up, it only reflects the trend toward empty nesters that can be seen in the rest of Nassau County. In 1940 the county population was 450,000; by 1960 it was 1.3 million and 1.4 million in 1970; then it went back to around 1.3 million by 1990 as youngsters moved out.

Nassau County also is home to what may be the nation's premier county Republican machine. It was the creation of Nassau Republican Chairman J. Russell Sprague before the post-war population boom. Sprague managed to carry the county for Alf Landon in 1936 and that same year, persuaded the voters to adopt a county executive form of government in which control of political patronage would center in one man, responsible to the county Republican chairman. The result now is one of the most high-salaried local governments in America, and a Republican political machine that vies in size and power with the Democratic big city machines of old.

The 3d Congressional District includes nearly half of Nassau County. Most of the people in the district live in towns strung out on either side of Sunrise Highway or just off the Southern or Northern State Parkways from Levittown and Hicksville, east to the county line. The district also includes Bethpage, home to the old Grumman aircraft company, once a big employer here and now part of Northrop Grumman. The northern geographic half of the district, with about one-fifth of the population, includes the old estate areas around Oyster Bay, Old Westbury and Manhasset. Not many of greater New York's wealthiest live in the 3d, but the overall level of affluence is high, and the district has the third highest median income of any in the nation, just behind the New Jersey 11th and Maryland 8th. The 3d, which contains the Island Park home of New York Senator Alfonse D'Amato, tends to be pretty solidly Republican, although Democrats have been competitive here, most recently in 1992.

The congressman from the 3d is Peter King, a Republican elected by a narrow margin that year who has made a distinctive record in the House. King grew up in Nassau County and is a product of its Republican machine. He started working as a lawyer and staffer in county government in 1972, at 28; in 1981 he became Nassau County comptroller. When 22-year incumbent Republican Norman Lent announced his retirement in June 1992, King ran, emphasizing his record of holding down spending and of spotting the county government's fiscal crisis in 1991. He won the Republican primary 2–1. In the general he faced Democrat Steve Orlins, who grew up in Nassau County and started an Asian trading company and sold it to Lehman Brothers, and spent over $700,000 of his own money on this race. King campaigned as a political insider and fiscal conservative, Orlins as a reformer and supporter of abortion rights. King won, but by only 50%–46%.

King's voting record has been conventionally conservative, but he is best known on Capitol Hill for his involvement in a series of controversial causes and initiatives. His initial election to Congress was greeted with trepidation in Great Britain: during his years in Nassau County government, he was widely viewed as a one of the U.S.'s strongest supporters of the Irish Republican Army. Within days of his election, he flew to Belfast to meet with leaders of Sinn Fein, the IRA's political arm. He was pleased to see the Clinton Administration drop travel and fundraising restrictions on Gerry Adams, Sinn Fein's leader, and looked on approvingly on St. Patrick's Day 1995 as President Clinton greeted Adams in the White House. But Adams's refusal to criticize IRA bombings made him *persona non grata* at the White House, and the Irish talks stalled when the IRA refused to give up its arms. On the Banking Committee, King has gone after HUD's practice of contracting with firms associated with the Nation of Islam to provide security at housing projects. He also is pushing legislation to make English the country's official language. He was a strong partisan in the Banking Committee's hearings on Whitewater in 1995.

When Republican poll ratings dropped later in the year, he started criticizing his own party. In 1996, when Republican leaders initially resisted a minimum-wage increase, King said Republicans were driving working people toward Clinton. "We're going to turn ourselves into a party of barefoot hillbillies who go to revival meetings." He criticized party leaders for attacking unions—which are strong in Long Island—and said, "If I had to choose between having a drink with [AFL-CIO president] John Sweeney or any of these guys, I'd choose John Sweeney any day." The House Republicans' victory in 1996 didn't quiet him. In March 1997 he authored an article in the *Weekly Standard* on "Why I Oppose Newt." "As roadkill on the highway of American politics, Newt Gingrich cannot sell the Republican agenda. So instead of replacing Newt, the Republican leadership has replaced the agenda. Gone is the Contract With America . . . Congressional Republicans are adrift."

King has been opposed every two years by rich Democrats willing to spend their own money. In 1994 lawyer Norma Grill spent only $225,000 of her own, and King won 59%–40%. In 1996 tweezer and grooming instrument maker Dal LaMagna spent $1 million of his own money, and King won 55%–42%. King is said to be interested in following his Nassau County constituent Alfonse D'Amato to the Senate some day, but D'Amato gives no sign of quitting soon.

The People: Pop. 1990: 580,468; 13% age 65+; 91% White; 2% Black; 3% Asian; 4% Hispanic origin. Households: 70% married couple families; 30% married couple fams. w. children; 55% college educ.; median household income: $56,060; per capita income: $23,702; median gross rent: $811; median house value: $204,900.

1996 Presidential Vote

Clinton (D)	136,505	(53%)
Dole (R)	97,034	(38%)
Perot (I)	18,975	(7%)
Other	3,854	(2%)

1992 Presidential Vote

Clinton (D)	126,112	(44%)
Bush (R)	121,176	(42%)
Perot (I)	40,450	(14%)

Rep. Peter T. King (R)

Elected 1992; b. Apr. 5, 1944, Manhattan; home, Seaford; St. Francis Col., B.A. 1965, U. of Notre Dame, J.D. 1968; Catholic; married (Rosemary).

Career: Army Natl. Guard, 1968–73; Practicing atty., 1968–72, 1978–81; Dep. Atty., Nassau Cnty., 1972–74; Exec. Asst., Nassau Cnty. Exec., 1974–76, Gen. Cnsl., 1977; Hempstead Town Cncl., 1977–81; Nassau Cnty. Comptroller, 1981–92.

DC Office: 403 CHOB 20515, 202-225-7896; Fax: 202-226-2279; e-mail: peteking@hr.house.gov.

District Office: Massapequa Park, 516-541-4225.

Committees: *Banking & Financial Services* (9th of 30 R): Capital Markets, Securities & Government Sponsored Enterprises; Financial Institutions & Consumer Credit; General Oversight & Investigations. *International Relations* (14th of 26 R): Asia & the Pacific; International Operations & Human Rights.

Group Ratings

	ADA	ACLU	AFS	LCV	CFA	CON	NFIB	COC	ACU	NTLC	CHC
1996	20	25	36	38	8	26	81	69	79	98	93
1995	5	—	—	31	0	56	—	79	64	—	—

National Journal Ratings

	1995 LIB		1995 CONS	1996 LIB		1996 CONS
Economic	52%	—	47%	45%	—	55%
Social	0%	—	79%	44%	—	55%
Foreign	28%	—	65%	37%	—	62%

Key Votes of the 104th Congress

1. Reduce Medicare Growth $	Y	5. Flag Amendment	Y	9. Cuban Embargo	Y
2. Ovrd. Product Liab. Veto	N	6. Drop EPA Limits	N	10. Bar Bosnia Troop $	N
3. Increase Min. Wage	Y	7. Repeal Assault-Weap. Ban	N	11. Cut Anti-Missile Defense	N
4. Welfare Reform	Y	8. Ovrd. Part. Birth Veto	Y	12. Bar U.N. Uniforms	Y

Election Results

1996 general	Peter T. King (R-C-FR)	127,972	(55%)	($645,951)
	Dal A. LaMagna (D-I)	97,518	(42%)	($1,083,576)
	Others	5,936	(3%)	
1996 primary	Peter T. King (R)	7,593	(88%)	
	Robert Previdi (R)	1,014	(12%)	
1994 general	Peter T. King (R-C)	115,236	(59%)	($516,548)
	Norma Grill (D)	77,774	(40%)	($415,561)

FOURTH DISTRICT

Garden City is one of America's first suburbs, created more than a century ago by New York retailer A.T. Stewart at a time when reformers wanted to maintain the commercial vitality and social interaction of the city, but in a setting that preserved the healthful openness of the countryside. Garden City's wide avenues and single-family homes, connected to New York City by the Long Island Railroad, were intended to be middle-income territory, but its amenities have made it one of the highest-income parts of Long Island. In the century after its founding, the rest of Nassau County has changed from almost entirely rural to suburban. The big rush came after World War II, as one town ran into another, freeways replaced strip highways, and shopping centers sprang up at intersections. Today, many of the middle- and upper-income residents of the 4th Congressional District still depend on the Long Island Railroad to get them to jobs in New York City. But once-removed Garden City now sits amid Nassau County's civic institutions just south of the county seat of Mineola and the site of Roosevelt Field, where Charles Lindbergh took off for Paris. Almost 60 years later, Roosevelt Field is a large suburban shopping center, with the Nassau Coliseum—home to hockey's New York Islanders—nearby.

The 4th District includes Garden City and the civic center of Nassau County. It includes half of Levittown and the neat and conservative suburbs along the Queens line from New Hyde Park to Valley Stream; it takes in the "Five Towns"—Lawrence, Inwood, Cedarhurst, Hewlett and Woodmere—near Kennedy Airport's flight paths. Nassau County has traditionally been Republican, and Garden City and heavily Catholic suburbs like Elmont and East Meadow, are solidly Republican. But about one-quarter of the residents here are black or Hispanic, and the Five Towns are heavily Democratic. The 4th District has voted mostly Republican in local and state politics, but it has also voted twice for Bill Clinton. And its congressional politics has proved to be a bit quirky, as it has elected four different people to the House in the 1990s.

The congresswoman from the 4th District is Carolyn McCarthy, elected as a Democrat in 1996. She was born in Brooklyn, trained as a nurse, married and raised a family on Long Island; originally, she was a Republican. In 1993 her husband was killed and her son seriously injured in the "Long Island Railroad Massacre," when a black gunman opened fire on passengers as the train crossed the Nassau County line (he said he did not want to kill anyone in New York City lest he embarrass Mayor David Dinkins). McCarthy spoke movingly at Ferguson's trial and her strength in tragedy won her many admirers. "You took away my husband," she said directly to Ferguson. "You took away my best friend. You cannot take away my memories of him. Everything that I had wanted to say about my husband, I don't want you to hear it. You don't deserve to hear what a good man he was." She began campaigning for gun control, and in 1995 lobbied 4th District Congressman Daniel Frisa to vote against the repeal of the assault weapons ban. In fact, the vote was mostly symbolic, since weapons identical to those named in the ban were being manufactured legally. But Frisa, who won the seat in 1994 after defeating a Nassau County Republican rival in the primary, voted for the repeal nonetheless.

McCarthy made inquiry about running against Frisa in the primary, but Nassau County Republicans discouraged this. But Democrats wanted to recruit her; they had been eyeing this seat for some time, and in 1994 Phil Schiliro, a top aide to Henry Waxman and Long Island native, was their nominee here. McCarthy initially knew little about politics. When she was told that Minority Leader Dick Gephardt wanted to meet her, she reportedly asked, "Who's Dick Gephardt?" But she learned quickly. With the Democratic nomination in hand, she called for gun control and attacked Frisa as too close to Newt Gingrich. The political tide was clearly going her way, and Frisa disappeared in the last week of the campaign, did not show up at his election night party and never made a concession statement. On election day McCarthy won 57%–41%.

McCarthy was the biggest celebrity among freshman Democrats, but did not win the Commerce Committee seat she wanted. She said her top priorities were providing high-tech training for displaced defense workers and investigation into Long Island's high rate of breast cancer. In 1997 NBC was planning a made-for-TV movie on McCarthy's tragedy and subsequent political success. She certainly seems a strong candidate for reelection; her major problem may be avoiding a serious change in redistricting, either as a result of the challenge to the 12th District pending in 1997 or after the 2000 Census.

The People: Pop. 1990: 580,492; 15% age 65+; 74% White; 16% Black; 3% Asian; 8% Hispanic origin. Households: 65% married couple families; 28% married couple fams. w. children; 50% college educ.; median household income: $50,887; per capita income: $20,349; median gross rent: $705; median house value: $197,000.

1996 Presidential Vote

Clinton (D)	131,825	(56%)
Dole (R)	83,750	(36%)
Perot (I)	14,493	(6%)

1992 Presidential Vote

Clinton (D)	119,947	(47%)
Bush (R)	106,016	(41%)
Perot (I)	30,476	(12%)

Rep. Carolyn McCarthy (D)

Elected 1996; b. Jan. 5, 1944, Brooklyn; home, Mineola; Glen Cove Nursing Schl., L.P.N. 1964; Catholic; widowed.

Career: Nurse, 1964–93; Gun control activist, 1993–96.

DC Office: 1725 LHOB 20515, 202-225-5516.

District Office: Hempstead, 516-489-7066.

Committees: *Education & The Workforce* (15th of 20 D): Employer-Employee Relations; Postsecondary Education, Training & Life-Long Learning. *Small Business* (12th of 16 D): Government Programs & Oversight; Tax, Finance & Exports.

Group Ratings and Key Votes: Newly Elected

Election Results

1996 general	Carolyn McCarthy (D-I)	127,060	(57%)	($967,221)
	Dan Frisa (R-C-FR)	89,542	(41%)	($893,147)
	Others	4,414	(2%)	
1996 primary	Carolyn McCarthy (D)	unopposed		
1994 general	Dan Frisa (R)	87,815	(50%)	($231,931)
	Philip M. Schilro (D)	65,286	(37%)	($447,955)
	David A. Levy (C)	15,173	(9%)	($216,992)
	Others	6,689	(4%)	

FIFTH DISTRICT

The North Shore of Long Island is "Gatsby country," where peninsulas jutting out into the Sound are covered with vast green lawns leading to the mansions of America's great capitalists. Nineteenth century millionaires commuted by steam yacht from Manhattan to their estates in what now is Queens or Nassau County. In the early 20th Century the richest people in business and entertainment spent their leisure time here, playing croquet while their servants unloaded bootleggers' boats at their private docks during Prohibition. Inland, behind the expansive lawns, Long Island was still farm country, with little villages clustered at railroad stations, occasional colonial era houses, and acres of billboard-strewn wasteland on the highways to New York City. But The City grew out. Affluent neighborhoods developed in Douglaston and Bayside on the water, just beyond the middle-class Flushing area of Queens inland. The Great Neck peninsula became a very affluent, mostly Jewish suburb. Farther out, on Sands Point and Oyster Bay, old estates alternated with more modest homes, originally built for servants, and newer subdivision mansions. Further east, in Suffolk County, affluent subdivisions grew up on hilly land above the bays and points.

The 5th Congressional District ties together a disparate collection of New York City neighborhoods and suburbs on or within a few miles of the North Shore. At several points the district is connected across open water, and anyone wishing to traverse its boundaries from one end of it to the other better be a good swimmer. About one-third of its votes are cast in Suffolk County, where the political leanings are conservative on cultural and economic issues. In the middle, with about one-quarter of the votes, are the North Shore communities of Nassau: the Jewish areas Democratic and liberal, the WASPy areas Republican but also culturally liberal. Half the district's population and about 40% of its voters are in the borough of Queens. Here along the Sound are the affluent double-house Bayside neighborhood, and higher-income Douglaston and Little Neck, next to the Nassau border—all Republican territory. A few blocks inland is Flushing, an old Dutch settlement from the 17th Century, with the Queens numbered-street grid superimposed on old Dutch trails; once heavily Jewish, this has become one of the biggest Chinese (mostly Taiwanese) communities in the country. The 5th also goes south almost to the Long Island Expressway, to pleasant homeowner neighborhoods like Fresh Meadows and Oakland Gardens. But even here, far from Manhattan and in relatively affluent areas, there are plenty of high-rises.

The congressman from the 5th District is Gary Ackerman, a Democrat first elected in a March 1983 special election. Ackerman grew up in Flushing, taught junior high school, ran an advertising agency, started the *Queens Tribune* in 1970 and sold it to publisher Jerry Finkelstein in 1978. That same year he was elected to the New York Senate, where Democrats seem permanently in the minority. In 1983 he won his seat in the House, from a district centered in the heavily Jewish apartment complexes in central Queens. Ackerman is a colorful character, who always wears a white carnation and lives on a houseboat in Washington; he hosts an annual "Taste of New York" fundraiser, featuring pastrami sandwiches and stuffed cabbage, with waiters imported from New York. Acerbic but humorous, he is a pungent speaker: his comment on the Gulf war resolution (on which he voted yes) was "Slam, bam, thanks Saddam. You should have took the letter. Now take the loss, reverse the course, 'cause it ain't going to get no better." On the roll call for speaker in January 1995, when he was second in alphabetical order, after Neil Abercrombie of Hawaii voted for Dick Gephardt, Ackerman said, "Move to close the roll!"

Legislatively, Ackerman has been active on the International Relations Committee. He devoted much attention to the rescue of Ethiopian Jews and relieving government-caused famines in Ethiopia and Sudan. He was one of the few Americans ever to meet with North Korean dictator Kim Il Sung, in October 1993. He chaired the Asian and Pacific Affairs Subcommittee in 1993 and 1994, after Stephen Solarz lost his seat to redistricting; he switched to the ranking minority position on Western Hemisphere in 1997. In 1996 he steered to passage the "Baby AIDS" bill requiring HIV testing of newborns and disclosure of the results to the mother; the bill also bars insurers from terminating coverage because of AIDS test results. This measure had been opposed by Manhattan liberals, although many HIV-positive newborns can be saved if identified in time; it took some courage for Ackerman to brave the wrath of New York's left wing. But then he does not have a 100% liberal voting record, though he is careful to look after the interests of public employees, many of whom are in Queens.

The 1992 redistricting moved Ackerman from a Queens-based solidly Democratic district to this North Shore seat, where he started off unfamiliar and the Suffolk part of which is usually Republican. Two other incumbents had residences in the district; one, Bob Mrazek, was running for the Senate, and withdrew after it was revealed he had 920 overdrafts on the House bank; the other, James Scheuer, who in 28 years represented parts of the Bronx, Brooklyn, Queens and Nassau, decided to retire. Ackerman was caught up in the overdraft controversy; he was widely assumed to be the Ethics Committee member who leaked the list of worst offenders (which he, with 111 overdrafts, wasn't on), and he resigned from the committee in July 1992. He was opposed in the September primary by Rita Morris, who spent her lifetime savings of $500,000 and held Ackerman to a 60%–40% victory. That November Republican Allan Binder carried Suffolk and held Ackerman to a 52%–45% victory. In 1994 Grant Lally beat Binder in the Republican primary and waged a vigorous campaign. But Ackerman was better known and was one of the few Democrats to improve his showing that year, winning 55%–43%. In 1996 Lally ran again, spent less money and lost 64%–35%, with Ackerman carrying Suffolk for the first time.

The real threat to Ackerman's tenure is redistricting. A federal court has ordered a redrawing of the "Bullwinkle" Hispanic-majority 12th District by July 30, 1997, and that will surely force changes in boundaries of districts all around, including the 5th. Then there must be another redistricting after the 2000 Census, which will probably cost New York two districts. The 5th District, stretched thin across the North Shore, is geographically easy to eliminate, and Ackerman has not got great influence in the legislature in Albany. But he has survived some tough threats before.

The People: Pop. 1990: 581,073; 1% rural; 15% age 65+; 79% White; 3% Black; 11% Asian; 7% Hispanic origin. Households: 63% married couple families; 27% married couple fams. w. children; 58% college educ.; median household income: $50,103; per capita income: $24,296; median gross rent: $660; median house value: $255,000.

1996 Presidential Vote

Clinton (D)	132,588	(60%)
Dole (R)	71,194	(32%)
Perot (I)	13,354	(6%)
Other	4,040	(2%)

1992 Presidential Vote

Clinton (D)	131,042	(52%)
Bush (R)	88,505	(35%)
Perot (I)	30,459	(12%)

Rep. Gary L. Ackerman (D)

Elected Mar., 1983; b. Nov. 19, 1942, Brooklyn; home, Queens; Queens Col., B.A. 1965; Jewish; married (Rita).

Career: Jr. high schl. teacher, 1966–70; Editor and publisher, *Queens Tribune*, 1970–78; Pres., advertising agcy., 1972–78; NY Senate, 1978–83.

DC Office: 2243 RHOB 20515, 202-225-2601; Fax: 202-225-1589.

District Offices: Bayside, 718-423-2154; Huntington, 516-423-2154.

Committees: *Banking & Financial Services* (17th of 25 D): Capital Markets, Securities & Government Sponsored Enterprises; Financial Institutions & Consumer Credit. *International Relations* (5th of 22 D): International Operations & Human Rights; Western Hemisphere (RMM).

Group Ratings

	ADA	ACLU	AFS	LCV	CFA	CON	NFIB	COC	ACU	NTLC	CHC
1996	85	69	91	85	85	63	24	31	0	12	0
1995	90	—	—	69	92	25	—	25	13	—	—

National Journal Ratings

	1995 LIB		1995 CONS	1996 LIB		1996 CONS
Economic	78%	—	21%	70%	—	28%
Social	80%	—	13%	88%	—	0%
Foreign	77%	—	22%	71%	—	29%

Key Votes of the 104th Congress

1. Reduce Medicare Growth $	N	5. Flag Amendment	N	9. Cuban Embargo	Y
2. Ovrd. Product Liab. Veto	N	6. Drop EPA Limits	Y	10. Bar Bosnia Troop $	N
3. Increase Min. Wage	Y	7. Repeal Assault-Weap. Ban	N	11. Cut Anti-Missile Defense	Y
4. Welfare Reform	N	8. Ovrd. Part. Birth Veto	N	12. Bar U.N. Uniforms	N

Election Results

1996 general	Gary L. Ackerman (D-I-L)	125,918	(64%)	($1,123,926)
	Grant M. Lally (R-C-FR)	69,244	(35%)	($170,326)
1996 primary	Gary L. Ackerman (D)	unopposed		
1994 general	Gary L. Ackerman (D-L)	93,896	(55%)	($1,376,467)
	Grant M. Lally (R-C)	73,884	(43%)	($442,726)
	Others	2,862	(2%)	

SIXTH DISTRICT

New York City's largest middle-class black neighborhoods are not in Harlem or Brooklyn, but in the southeast corner of Queens. Here, in the "architectural monotony of block upon block of boxlike frame and brick houses," as one critic described them, built mostly from the 1920s to the 1950s, are the neighborhoods of Springfield, Laurelton, St. Albans and Rosedale, near Kennedy Airport and the tidal marsh of Jamaica Bay, just west of the Nassau County line. There was a small black community in South Jamaica half a century ago, and since then many black families have bought houses and raised their families in neighborhoods on the streets fanning east from Jamaica. They fought to maintain the relatively spacious streets, relishing unrefracted light in their windows, enjoying safe schools and parks and good neighborhood stores: people who, in Bill

Clinton's felicitous phrase, "work hard and play by the rules."

The 6th Congressional District contains all of these southeast Queens neighborhoods, plus others less affluent and orderly, in southern Queens, roughly south of the Interborough and Grand Central Parkways, including half of the Rockaway Peninsula across Jamaica Bay. It includes white ethnic Richmond Hill and Ozone Park as well as the heavily black neighborhoods in the southeast. In 1990, 53% of the people here were black, 17% Hispanic, 6% Asian and 23% non-Hispanic white. While there are pockets of poverty, the district is mostly middle-class country: the median income was $36,200, far ahead of the $23,000 to $26,000 of New York's other black-majority districts—indeed ahead of the $30,300 of Queens's white-majority 7th District.

The congressman from the 6th is Floyd Flake, a Democrat elected in 1986, who gained prominence by a different route than New York's other black congressmen. Flake, one of 13 children whose father was a janitor, went to college and then divinity school. In 1976, at 31, he became a minister at Allen A.M.E. Church in Queens. He built it up from 1,400 to 8,400 members and from three to over 700 employees, with a budget running up toward $20 million a year; it is the second largest employer in the 6th District, after JFK Airport. The Allen Church built a $12 million 300-unit housing project for the elderly, 48 two-family homes, a private school for 490 students (with 150 on the wait list) and a strip shopping and office center. Flake has creatively used federal loan guarantees and Fannie Mae loans to finance housing, has obtained an FDA testing center, has worked across party lines with Senator Alfonse D'Amato and has also attracted private investors (Flake virtually endorsed D'Amato in 1992). "I'm interested in investment," Flake said, "as a way to generate in those particular communities jobs, commercial strips, entrepreneurs, small businesses that can hire people who will not become welfare recipients, who will not become people who occupy these jail cells."

For all his success Flake has not always been welcomed by professional politicians. In 1986, when Congressman Joseph Addabbo died, Flake ran in a special primary against the Queens Democratic organization choice, Alton Waldon. Flake won by 167 votes at the polls, but lost the special primary by 276 votes because his name had been kept off the absentee ballots by one of New York's endless election law technicalities. Flake understandably felt cheated and, with strong local support and the endorsement of Mayor Edward Koch, beat Waldon in the September 1986 primary for the next full term and was easily elected in November. In the early 1990s Flake was the subject of a federal prosecution on charges—based on complaints by a disgruntled former church employee—that he embezzled funds from a church-sponsored housing project and from the church itself. In the middle of the April 1991 trial, prosecutors dropped the case after the judge suggested that the evidence against Flake was shaky: obviously this was a case that never should have been brought to trial. In 1992, the Queens Democratic organization endorsed Simeon Golar, an unsuccessful House candidate in 1982 and 1984 in Queens and in 1990 in the Bronx, who said Flake was using the church as a political machine that "evokes scary reminders of Jonestown." Flake won the primary 77%–23% and has not had serious competition since. To charges that he has unduly meshed church and state, Flake, who keeps three volumes entitled *God and Government* on his desk, said, "I don't think African-American communities can allow themselves to get caught in that trap while their communities are dying."

Flake voted against Dick Gephardt for minority leader in 1995 and criticized him for "nonproductive" parliamentary tactics. In 1996, in a traffic altercation, Flake was the object of racial epithets from White House security chief Craig Livingstone; Flake later said that it was wrong for Livingstone to be working in the White House "making the kind of decisions that led to the fiasco around the FBI files." In March 1997 Flake endorsed the American Community Renewal Act, sponsored by Republicans J.C. Watts and Jim Talent, and got four other Black Caucus members to join them. The bill would provide tax credits, home ownership incentives, regulatory relief and school choice for disadvantaged communities, costing $5.8 billion over five years. Flake thinks public schools will improve if they have competition and specifically wants parents to be entitled to use government funds to send their children to church schools, just as G.I. Bill of Rights and Pell grants can be used for tuition to church colleges; he points out that nearly all his Black Caucus colleagues send their children to private schools (the youngest member, Harold Ford, Jr., went to St. Alban's in Washington, the same school as Vice President Al Gore). Brooklyn Congressman Major Owens called Flake's stand "a betrayal," and NAACP chairman and former Black Caucus head Kweisi Mfume denounced the bill. But the Republican leadership has promised a floor vote, and it will be interesting to see if liberal Democrats want to deny black voters advantages they have enjoyed themselves for many years.

The People: Pop. 1990: 581,812; 11% age 65+; 23% White; 53% Black; 6% Asian; 1% Amer. Indian; 17% Hispanic origin. Households: 52% married couple families; 25% married couple fams. w. children; 38% college educ.; median household income: $36,223; per capita income: $13,150; median gross rent: $565; median house value: $157,900.

1996 Presidential Vote			1992 Presidential Vote		
Clinton (D)	128,071	(85%)	Clinton (D)	115,526	(75%)
Dole (R)	15,946	(11%)	Bush (R)	28,033	(18%)
Perot (I)	4,380	(3%)	Perot (I)	9,380	(6%)

Rep. Floyd H. Flake (D)

Elected 1986; b. Jan. 30, 1945, Los Angeles, CA; home, Rosedale; Wilberforce U., B.A., 1967, Payne Theological Seminary, M.A. 1970, Northeastern U., 1974–76; United Theological Sem., Ph.D., 1994; African Methodist Episcopal; married (Elaine).

Career: Social worker, Head Start, 1968–69; Mktg. analyst, Xerox Corp., 1969–70; Assoc. Dean of Students, Lincoln U. 1970–73; Boston U., Dean of Students and Chaplain, Dir., MLK Afro-American Ctr., 1973–76; Pastor, Allen A.M.E. Church, 1976–present; Founder and Chmn., Allen Christian Schl., 1982–present, Allen Home Care Agcy., 1983–present.

DC Office: 1035 LHOB 20515, 202-225-3461; Fax: 202-226-4169.

District Offices: Far Rockaway, 718-327-9791; St. Albans, 718-949-5600.

Committees: *Banking & Financial Services* (8th of 25 D): Capital Markets, Securities & Government Sponsored Enterprises; Domestic & International Monetary Policy (RMM). *Small Business* (3rd of 16 D): Empowerment.

Group Ratings

	ADA	ACLU	AFS	LCV	CFA	CON	NFIB	COC	ACU	NTLC	CHC
1996	80	81	100	92	69	97	23	8	6	5	13
1995	85	—	—	69	92	16	—	21	4	—	—

National Journal Ratings

	1995 LIB — 1995 CONS			1996 LIB — 1996 CONS		
Economic	83%	—	17%	82%	—	18%
Social	77%	—	23%	73%	—	26%
Foreign	93%	—	0%	84%	—	15%

Key Votes of the 104th Congress

1. Reduce Medicare Growth $	N	5. Flag Amendment	N	9. Cuban Embargo	N
2. Ovrd. Product Liab. Veto	N	6. Drop EPA Limits	Y	10. Bar Bosnia Troop $	N
3. Increase Min. Wage	Y	7. Repeal Assault-Weap. Ban	N	11. Cut Anti-Missile Defense	*
4. Welfare Reform	N	8. Ovrd. Part. Birth Veto	Y	12. Bar U.N. Uniforms	N

Election Results

1996 general	Floyd H. Flake (D)	102,799	(85%)	($165,311)
	Jorawar Misir (R-C-I-FR)	18,348	(15%)	($7,689)
1996 primary	Floyd H. Flake (D)	unopposed		
1994 general	Floyd H. Flake (D)	68,596	(80%)	($227,256)
	Denny D. Bhagwandin (R-C)	16,675	(20%)	

SEVENTH DISTRICT

The borough of Queens, home of Shea Stadium and Forest Hills Stadium, site of the 1939 and 1964 World's Fairs, home base of national politicians like Mario Cuomo and Geraldine Ferraro, doesn't get much attention or respect, even though this two million-person borough on its own would be the nation's fourth-largest city. But Queens does not have well-known history. It started as nondescript farmland in the 17th Century, with villages growing quickly into urban nodes as the subways reached the borough. It has no obvious center, unlike downtown Brooklyn or the Grand Concourse in the Bronx. Even Queens Boulevard is just another arterial street, starting in the industrial mishmash around the Queensborough Bridge (usually referred to by its Manhattan name, 59th Street) and ending near the unimpressive brick Borough Hall, sited by the Grand Central Parkway overpass, across from the Pastrami King and Crossroads Drugs.

Yet Queens is still growing with great vitality around dozens of small hubs, not from a central point outward or directly from Manhattan. More than any other area of New York City, this is a borough of neighborhoods and of ethnic diversity. It has high-income enclaves, like the old Tudor-mansioned Forest Hills. It has old ethnic communities, like Irish Sunnyside and College Point and German Ridgewood. Astoria, on the tip of Queens near the Triborough Bridge, is Greek-American and effervescently prosperous. Flushing, once mostly Jewish, is now heavily Chinese, the terminus of the number 7 subway line known as the Orient Express. Indian and Pakistani immigrants own stores and restaurants, Koreans own fruit stands, Colombians and Irish and Dominicans shop in the bustling streets of Jackson Heights and Corona. Sixty years ago the small frame houses and stolid brick apartments of Queens neighborhoods adjacent to subway lines were the homes of the immigrant wave of the early 20th Century; now they are the home again of late 20th Century immigrants. New York's high taxes, its burdensome regulations, its housing shortage created by rent control, all impose burdens on these immigrants that were not borne by their predecessors. But with the aid of public schools, by no means all of which are hopeless, and the entrepreneurial-minded Queens Library with its dozens of branches, they are learning to be successful Americans, not fenced-off "multicultural" groups dependent on government for quotas and welfare.

The 7th Congressional District, loosely connected by narrow corridors, is a collection of Queens neighborhoods plus, over the Bronx-Whitestone Bridge, a salient of land running far into the Bronx, the boundaries of which for the 1992, 1994 and 1996 elections are nearly indescribable. A federal court ruled that the boundaries of the adjacent "Bullwinkle" Hispanic-majority 12th District must be redrawn by July 1997, and so presumably the 7th's boundaries will be more regular for the 1998 and 2000 elections. Major landmarks in the 7th District include the Queensborough Bridge, LaGuardia Airport, Flushing Meadow, site of the still-remembered Trylon and Perisphere rising over the 1939 World's Fair and of Shea Stadium, the graceful Bronx-Whitestone Bridge and the giant Parkchester apartment complex and Yeshiva University in the Bronx. Fifty years ago most residents of Queens referred to Manhattan as "The City," and voted Republican, against the masters of Tammany Hall. Today, many still call Manhattan "The City" and, though they vote heavily Democratic in national elections, also gave a solid margin to Republican Mayor Rudolph Giuliani.

The congressman from the 7th District is Thomas Manton, a Democrat elected in 1984. He grew up in Queens, the son of Irish immigrants, became a police officer and IBM salesman who worked his way up to Queens Democratic chairman—a position that he continues to hold, in the long but dying tradition of urban politicians. He was first elected to the City Council in 1969, when he represented a conservative district opposed to liberal Republican Mayor John Lindsay. He first ran for Congress in 1972, unsuccessfully challenging conservative Democratic Congressman James Delaney in the primary. When Delaney retired in 1978, Manton ran and lost to Geraldine Ferraro. Ferraro had planned to represent Queens until she ran against Senator Alfonse D'Amato in 1986, but those plans were upset when she became the 1984 Democratic nominee for vice president. (Ferraro ran for the Senate in 1992 but narrowly lost the primary.) Manton was well prepared to move up when Ferraro moved out. He ran in the 1984 primary and won with 30% of the vote; three other candidates got 27%, 22% and 21%. In the general he beat Conservative Party stalwart (and now state Senator) Serphin Maltese 53%–47%.

Manton showed his skill as an insider early by winning a seat on the Commerce Committee. But his legislative initiatives often are geared toward solving local problems: an amendment to the hazardous waste law designed to stop the Long Island Railroad's plans to build a Long Island City waste transfer site, prohibition of sewage sludge composting plants in New York City, Clean Air Act amendments to help New York businesses. He opposed cable reregulation as a member of the Telecommunications Subcommittee; Time Warner is a big employer here. As a former cop, he worked to guarantee that disability payments to law enforcement personnel injured in the line of duty were on par with those killed on duty. In the 104th Congress, Manton sponsored an amendment to kill the "English rule" loser-pays plank from the Contract With America; that failed as well. Manton also serves as co-chairman of the Congressional Ad-Hoc Committee on Irish Affairs. As ranking Democrat on the Finance and Hazardous Materials Subcommittee, he may play an important part on Superfund reform; Republicans have sought and Democrats have resisted abolition of "retroactive liability" provisions to make polluters pay for cleanups. Manton may also play a part on securities issues, which are of course of great importance to New York. He is also backing legislation requiring taggants (identifying substances which show where and when a particular explosive material was made) in explosives, to help track down terrorists.

Manton has usually not had problems winning reelection. In 1992, Bob Dole aide Dennis Shea returned to the district and attacked Manton for overdrafts on the House bank, and held him to a 57%–43% win. But Newt Gingrich's Republican revolutionaries have proved highly unpopular in New York, and in 1996 Manton was reelected 71%–29%. The biggest threat to his tenure comes from redistricting. The court-ordered redrawing of the 12th District, which is intertwined with the 7th like two strands of DNA, must have some effect on the 7th; presumably it will increase its Hispanic percentage. At the moment that would help Manton in general elections and is unlikely to produce any large base of opposition for him in primaries.

The People: Pop. 1990: 580,116; 17% age 65+; 58% White; 9% Black; 11% Asian; 21% Hispanic origin. Households: 46% married couple families; 19% married couple fams. w. children; 36% college educ.; median household income: $30,324; per capita income: $14,905; median gross rent: $520; median house value: $205,900.

1996 Presidential Vote			1992 Presidential Vote		
Clinton (D)	99,813	(68%)	Clinton (D)	91,319	(56%)
Dole (R)	37,230	(25%)	Bush (R)	57,343	(35%)
Perot (I)	7,437	(5%)	Perot (I)	14,979	(9%)
Other	2,648	(2%)			

Rep. Thomas J. Manton (D)

Elected 1984; b. Nov. 3, 1932, New York City; home, Sunnyside; St. John's U., B.B.A. 1958, LL.B. 1962; Catholic; married (Diane).

Career: Marine Corps, 1951–53; NYC Police Officer, 1955–60; IBM salesman, 1960–64; Practicing atty., 1964–84; NYC Cncl., 1969–84; Queens Cnty. Dem. Party Chmn., 1986-present.

DC Office: 2235 RHOB 20515, 202-225-3965; Fax: 202-225-1909; e-mail: tmanton@hr.house.gov

District Offices: Bronx, 718-931-1400; Sunnyside, 718-706-1400.

Committees: *Commerce* (6th of 23 D): Finance & Hazardous Materials (RMM); Telecommunications, Trade & Consumer Protection.

Group Ratings

	ADA	ACLU	AFS	LCV	CFA	CON	NFIB	COC	ACU	NTLC	CHC
1996	65	38	100	85	77	42	27	33	26	13	28
1995	65	—	—	75	92	0	—	38	29	—	—

National Journal Ratings

	1995 LIB — 1995 CONS	1996 LIB — 1996 CONS
Economic	70% — 29%	78% — 21%
Social	50% — 49%	59% — 40%
Foreign	70% — 28%	64% — 35%

Key Votes of the 104th Congress

1. Reduce Medicare Growth $	N	5. Flag Amendment	Y	9. Cuban Embargo	Y
2. Ovrd. Product Liab. Veto	N	6. Drop EPA Limits	Y	10. Bar Bosnia Troop $	N
3. Increase Min. Wage	Y	7. Repeal Assault-Weap. Ban	N	11. Cut Anti-Missile Defense	Y
4. Welfare Reform	N	8. Ovrd. Part. Birth Veto	Y	12. Bar U.N. Uniforms	Y

Election Results

1996 general	Thomas J. Manton (D)	78,848	(71%)	($374,982)
	Rose Birtley (R-C-I)	32,092	(29%)	($62,209)
1996 primary	Thomas J. Manton (D)	unopposed		
1994 general	Thomas J. Manton (D)	58,935	(87%)	($360,940)
	Robert E. Hurley (C)	8,698	(13%)	

EIGHTH DISTRICT

For the last 200 years, New York has been a heavily Jewish city. New York's Dutch founders came from the European country most tolerant of Jews, and so Jews settled in Nieuw Amsterdam as they had in old. German Jews came in large numbers in the 19th Century, some insisting they were more German than they were Jewish; some founded great merchant banking dynasties. Around 1890, Ashkenazi Jews from Eastern Europe started coming from what were then the Romanov and Hapsburg Empires—now Poland, Lithuania, Belarus, Ukraine, Hungary and Romania. Then, after being persecuted in the years after World War I, as many as 400,000 Jews came past the Statue of Liberty to Ellis Island every year in the early 1920s, until a 1924 law virtually shut down immigration. Had a malapportioned, rural-dominated, nativist Congress not done that, perhaps two million of the six million who perished in the Holocaust would instead have become Americans.

Ashkenazi Jews initially lived on the Lower East Side but moved out to Brooklyn and the Bronx almost as soon as the subways were built. Their children moved up faster and farther than any new group in memorable history, rising despite prejudice to the top of almost every profession that would let them in. They invented new businesses from the rag trade to show biz: second-caste people from third-rate countries almost immediately becoming elite in the world's foremost country. Their descendants live all over the country, but New York remains America's most heavily Jewish city and has the largest Jewish population of any city in the world.

While there are no reliable figures, as the Census does not record religion, the 8th Congressional District of New York may be the most heavily Jewish district in the nation. About three-fifths of its population is in Manhattan, two-fifths in Brooklyn. Bizarre boundaries cordon off blacks and Hispanics in nearby majority-minority districts. One big voting area is the Upper West Side from 59th Street north to Morningside Heights and Columbia University: the venerable apartments along Central Park West and West End Avenue and Riverside Drive, and the brownstones on the cross streets which house some of America's most idealistic and dedicated liberal-to-radical voters. These professional people include the wealthy, as well as the struggling who enjoy the grittiness of the Upper West Side, the almost European atmosphere of boulevarded upper Broadway and the fierce struggle that is daily life in New York. People on the West Side took up the reform issue in the 1950s and eventually eviscerated the old Tammany Hall Democratic machine; in the 1960s they took up the struggle against the Vietnam war and helped oust a Democratic administration. By the late 1980s their dominant cause was feminism, from the preservation of abortion rights against all erosion to the eradication of gender-incorrect speech. Another big voting area is Greenwich Village, America's original Bohemia in the 1910s, now a neighborhood of expensive apartments and houses interlaced with much cheaper dwellings, and New York's most conspicuously gay community. Politically the Village has long had a taste for what it regards as radical. Then there are new Village-type residential areas to the south: SoHo, where old factory buildings have been refurbished as lofts; TriBeCa, where commercial space now houses artists; Battery Park City, the attractive modern apartments built on a landfill west of the now-crumbled West Side Highway.

The district includes two Brooklyn neighborhoods: Brighton Beach and Coney Island, with the biggest concentration of Russian Jewish immigrants in New York; and Borough Park, with many militantly pro-Israel Orthodox Jews. While they are connected to the heavily Jewish Manhattan neighborhoods by a narrow land bridge running along the Brooklyn waterfront and the massive Bush Terminal buildings, these areas are politically very different. The Russians favor free enterprise and are anti-socialist. Borough Park is extremely hostile to racial preferences and favors tough police treatment of crime. While people here are willing to vote Republican, Bill Clinton carried this district with 77% in 1996.

The congressman from the 8th District is Jerrold Nadler, a West Side liberal Democrat elected in 1992. He grew up in New York and was a veteran of the late 1960s antiwar movement; he was a junior at Columbia during the 1968 campus riots. He worked as a legislative staffer before being elected to the Assembly himself in 1976: politics has been his life. In the Assembly he was known as an expert on mass transit and advocate of rail freight into New York City. He voted there against the big tax cut of 1987. His election in 1992 was something of a surprise. Two incumbents' homes were in the redrawn district. Stephen Solarz, with his Brooklyn Jewish base, was at first expected to run here; but his strong positions for the Gulf war and U.S. engagement in Asia probably would have hurt him in Manhattan. He decided to run in the majority-Hispanic 12th District instead, where he narrowly lost. Ted Weiss, with his big Upper West Side base and his leftish voting record, was expected to win the seat, but he died the day before the September

1992 primary (which he won anyway). That left the nomination up to a convention of almost 1,000 county Democratic committee members, many of them involved in acerbic ideological and personal squabbles for decades. It was as tumultuous as can be imagined. Six candidates ran; former Congresswoman Bella Abzug (recently a candidate in Westchester County) withdrew in favor of Councilwoman Ronnie Eldridge; Assemblyman Richard Gottfried (elected in 1970 at 23) and state Senator Franz Leichter dropped out. The key vote was procedural, for a system of weighted voting under which Nadler won 62% of the votes and Eldridge 21%; opponents decried this system (after they lost), perhaps with some reason. Nadler became the Democratic nominee and thus congressman.

Nadler's voting record is among the most liberal in the House; not surprisingly he calls for large defense cuts and gay and lesbian rights. In the 1994 Democratic primary, he was opposed by City Councilman Thomas Duane, who is openly gay and announced in 1991 that he was HIV positive. Nadler won that contest 62%–29%, and then won the general election easily. In 1995 he called on Republicans to include in their tax cut bill a provision to cut taxes for people living in high cost-of-living areas like New York City. It is hard to imagine something that the Republican majority would be less likely to adopt. But Nadler proved effective on other fronts. Over the opposition of John Dingell, he pushed to passage the "Nadler rule" which restricted ranking members on full committees from taking any ranking subcommittee posts on their panels as well. He promised to block efforts by Donald Trump to relocate Manhattan's long-proposed, long-opposed Westway to accommodate Trump's luxury housing project.

Nadler entered the House with a two-month seniority advantage over other freshmen and immediately called for a comprehensive transportation bill, though Congress had just passed that in the form of Senator Pat Moynihan's ISTEA in 1991. In early 1997 Mayor Rudolph Giuliani endorsed a project which Nadler has made the centerpiece of his career, a rail freight tunnel under the Hudson River to allow trains to come directly into Manhattan and Brooklyn; currently they must offload in New Jersey. He has long pushed New York's claim to all of Ellis Island, which geographically is much closer to New Jersey; he must have been disappointed when a Supreme Court arbiter in April 1997 awarded the fill land, which is most of the island, to New Jersey, and left the original core, with the immigrants' arrival hall, to New York. As ranking Democrat on the Judiciary Subcommittee on Commercial and Administrative Law, Nadler will have a strong voice on bankruptcy and federal commercial law, of obvious interest to New York.

The People: Pop. 1990: 581,453; 15% age 65+; 74% White; 7% Black; 6% Asian; 13% Hispanic origin. Households: 32% married couple families; 13% married couple fams. w. children; 59% college educ.; median household income: $32,784; per capita income: $26,168; median gross rent: $544; median house value: $223,100.

1996 Presidential Vote

Clinton (D)	147,864	(77%)
Dole (R)	30,141	(16%)
Perot (I)	5,142	(3%)
Other	8,986	(5%)

1992 Presidential Vote

Clinton (D)	168,838	(77%)
Bush (R)	37,558	(17%)
Perot (I)	12,197	(6%)

Rep. Jerrold Nadler (D)

Elected 1992; b. June 13, 1947, Brooklyn; home, New York City; Columbia U., B.A. 1970, Fordham U., J.D. 1978; Jewish; married (Joyce Miller).

Career: Legis. Asst., NY Assembly, 1972; Law Clerk, 1976; NY Assembly, 1976–92.

DC Office: 2448 RHOB 20515, 202-225-5635; Fax: 202-225-6923; e-mail: nadler@hr.house.gov.

District Offices: Brooklyn, 718-373-3198; Manhattan, 212-334-3207.

Committees: *Judiciary* (6th of 15 D): Commercial & Administrative Law (RMM); Constitution. *Transportation & Infrastructure* (13th of 33 D): Railroads; Surface Transportation.

Group Ratings

	ADA	ACLU	AFS	LCV	CFA	CON	NFIB	COC	ACU	NTLC	CHC
1996	100	93	100	100	100	40	11	7	0	5	0
1995	100	—	—	94	100	16	—	8	0	—	—

National Journal Ratings

	1995 LIB — 1995 CONS			1996 LIB — 1996 CONS		
Economic	92%	—	6%	89%	—	0%
Social	80%	—	13%	88%	—	0%
Foreign	88%	—	7%	90%	—	0%

Key Votes of the 104th Congress

1. Reduce Medicare Growth $	N	5. Flag Amendment	N	9. Cuban Embargo	N
2. Ovrd. Product Liab. Veto	N	6. Drop EPA Limits	Y	10. Bar Bosnia Troop $	N
3. Increase Min. Wage	Y	7. Repeal Assault-Weap. Ban	N	11. Cut Anti-Missile Defense	Y
4. Welfare Reform	N	8. Ovrd. Part. Birth Veto	N	12. Bar U.N. Uniforms	*

Election Results

1996 general	Jerrold Nadler (D-L)	131,943	(82%)	($780,423)
	Michael Benjamin (R-FR)	26,028	(16%)	($121,422)
1996 primary	Jerrold Nadler (D)	28,466	(84%)	
	Brian W. Steel (D)	3,903	(11%)	
	Matthew W. Sperling (D)	1,668	(5%)	
1994 general	Jerrold Nadler (D-L)	109,946	(82%)	($791,767)
	David L. Askren (R)	21,132	(16%)	($16,172)
	Others	3,008	(2%)	

NINTH DISTRICT

Brooklyn. The single word used to arouse laughter in a comedian's monologue, applause when someone said they were from there. It evoked an accent that twisted the English language almost to non-recognition, a raucous and brusque confrontational style, a sense of humor with an edge, the chip-on-the-shoulder assertiveness of those sure they will always be in second place. Brooklyn would never be more important than Manhattan; the Dodgers would always lose the series to the Yankees or the playoffs to the Giants, and when they finally did win, in 1955, they moved to Los Angeles two years later. Brooklyn, as its Dutch name testifies, was a separate community from the 17th Century on, one of the largest cities in the country in the 19th Century, with its own celebrities (Henry Ward Beecher, Walt Whitman, John Roebling). By 1898, when the five boroughs were welded into Greater New York, one million people lived in Brooklyn, but the Brooklyn of the comedians really came into being as the subways were built in the early 20th Century. Suddenly workers in all the little Manhattan factories no longer had to live in Lower East Side tenements. They moved out the subway lines, into neighborhoods of three- to five-story apartments and four-family houses. Brooklyn grew from 1.1 million in 1900 to 1.6 million in 1910 to 2.0 million in 1920 and 2.6 million in 1930. The old Brooklynites were mostly Protestant—Dutch, Yankee, German—plus some Catholic Irish. The new Brooklynites were heavily Italian and Jewish, and peopled the sports and entertainment businesses for a long generation, making their home town and its impenetrable accent nationally famous. In 1940, as the nation was about to go to war, Brooklyn had 2.7 million people: one in every 49 Americans lived in this one borough.

Today, 2.3 million people, one in every 108 Americans, live in Brooklyn, and it is no longer a staple of national comedy. Some of its old neighborhoods—Jewish Brownsville, Italian East New York—have been ravaged by crime and stand empty and toothless. But there is great vitality in much of Brooklyn, among upwardly mobile Hispanic immigrants and a hard-working black middle class, and in neighborhoods of the grandchildren of the earlier Jews and Italians. The farther reaches of Ocean Parkway and the expanse of Flatlands and Canarsie, the quiet corners of Sheepshead Bay and Gerritsen are such places. Here young Orthodox Jews raise families within walking distance of school, and neighbors patrol the streets at night to keep down the crime which has wrecked neighborhoods just a few miles away.

The 9th Congressional District includes many such neighborhoods in Brooklyn and in the borough of Queens as well. Its geography is grotesque, its demography more comprehensible. This is where descendants of the 1890–1924 migrants live. In Brooklyn it extends from Prospect Park south along Ocean Parkway to Coney Island and Sheepshead Bay: still one of the most Jewish areas in the United States. It extends east over Flatlands and much of Canarsie and then across Jamaica Bay south to the Rockaway Peninsula and north to a collection of Queens neighborhoods: Howard Beach, next to Kennedy Airport; the old German neighborhoods of Glendale and Ridgewood, still orderly and spotlessly clean; Italian Woodhaven and Tudor-trimmed Forest Hills; much of the heavily Jewish high-rise area along Queens Boulevard. The political balance here is Democratic but not overwhelmingly so; Jewish portions of the 9th are heavily Democratic, but the other ethnic areas are often Republican.

The congressman from the 9th District is Charles Schumer, one of the most creative and active—if not hyperactive—members of the House. He has made important contributions to public policy without a traditional House power base, through energy, imagination, good humor and, not least, a certain amount of *chutzpah*: the old Brooklynite, de-rumpled a bit at Harvard. Schumer seems well aware that there is a country west of the Brooklyn Bridge. His outlook is optimistic but tempered by the memories of one just barely old enough to recall the Dodgers leaving town, and he has the brains and creativity that have enabled so many Brooklyn-born people to institute change.

The year he graduated from Harvard Law, 1974, Schumer was elected to the New York Assembly, at 23; in 1980, just before he turned 30, he was elected to the House. Immediately he raised a campaign treasury of over $1 million, lest he and Brooklyn neighbor Stephen Solarz be redistricted together in 1982; they weren't, and Schumer went on to concentrate on legislation. Similarly, by 1992 he had $2 million in the bank, for fear of a race against Solarz; but Solarz ran and lost in the neighboring Hispanic-majority 12th District. From the unlikely venue of the Banking Committee, a panel that most talented members lobby to get off of, Schumer spotted the perverse incentives set up by the combination of deposit insurance and letting S&Ls make risky investments. He fought Banking Chairman Fernand St Germain, calling early on for higher capital requirements, and helped shape the 1989 S&L bailout bill. He has also worked on housing programs, building on the success of the Nehemiah projects in Brooklyn. But he did even more work as a junior member of Judiciary and, eventually, chairman of its Crime

Subcommittee. He ranged far afield, coming up with a key compromise regarding farm laborers in the Immigration Reform Act of 1986, and another in 1990 on employment-sponsored immigration. With free marketeer (now Majority Leader) Dick Armey, he launched an unsuccessful 1990 effort to prohibit subsidy payments to farmers with adjusted gross incomes over $100,000. He worked hard to increase funding for tuberculosis control and amended the energy bill to phase out exports of highly enriched nuclear fuel. He wrote an auto theft law to reduce the market for resale of stolen parts. Other causes include the Violence Against Women Act and a federal law against impeding access to abortion clinics.

Schumer has managed several crime bills. Unlike many Democrats, he favors the death penalty; he also strongly backs gun control. He steered to passage the Brady bill, with its waiting period for handgun purchases, over strong opposition from the National Rifle Association. He supported the inclusion of the assault weapons ban in the 1994 crime bill, and also the provisions for crime prevention, from drug counseling to midnight basketball. But Schumer was caught short in August 1994 when on the crime bill rule vote, 59 Democrats voted no, many because of the gun control provisions, and all but 11 Republicans voted no as well. Many supporters of the bill were outraged by the heavyhanded tactics and pork-barrel projects of then-Judiciary chairman Jack Brooks. Schumer, who saw Brooks's conference report only when Republicans did, insisted that his bill was good legislation. The issue was caught up in the much greater partisan struggle that resulted in the Republican takeover in November 1994. But by then the bill was revised and passed, with the gun control measures.

In the Republican Congress Schumer had more trouble exerting leverage. He denounced Republicans and said "Newt Gingrich bent his knee and is kissing the ring of the NRA," after the House voted to repeal the assault weapons ban in March 1996. In April 1997, Schumer introduced legislation calling for tougher penalties on illegal sales of guns over state lines. He continued his battle against large farm subsidies, with Dick Zimmer of New Jersey; but it was overshadowed by the Republicans' Freedom to Farm Act which zeroed out most subsidies. His efforts with Dan Miller of Florida to end the sugar program were mostly unsuccessful. He did help crystallize opinion in New York and elsewhere against Newt Gingrich and his Republicans, but sometimes unfairly, as in his criticism of Christina Jeffrey, whom Gingrich appointed as House historian and then deserted after Schumer's attacks. Schumer spent much of his effort in 1995 and 1996 raising a record $3.3 million, not so much for his House campaign, on which he spent $487,000, but for his statewide ambitions. Had Mario Cuomo retired in 1994, Schumer would probably have run for governor, and in 1995 and 1996 he was considering running against Governor George Pataki. But in early 1997 Pataki's strong job rating and the difficulty for a New York City candidate of overcoming Pataki's Upstate lead evidently led him not to run for governor, and in April 1997 he announced he would run against Senator Alfonse D'Amato in 1998. But he will probably be tested in the primary first. Public Advocate (the title used to be Council Chairman) Mark Green, D'Amato's opponent in 1986, seemed certain to run; Geraldine Ferraro, who has eyed D'Amato's seat for more than a dozen years, seemed interested but not eager to raise the necessary funds. Schumer was already far ahead there, with $5 million in his campaign treasury after the 1996 election. A D'Amato-Schumer race would certainly be stimulating. Both are masters of communication in New York's tabloid-and-TV political culture, ready with the punchy riposte that can make a point better than a dozen TV ads or 100 position papers. "D'Amato will run a skillful campaign," Schumer told *National Journal*. "I will run just as good a campaign. People will choose me because I have a lot of good ideas that make peoples' lives better."

The 9th District is sure to remain Democratic, but not sure to remain within its current bounds. The Hispanic-majority 12th, with which it has a common boundary in Queens, must, a federal court ruled, be redistricted by July 1997, which could end up shifting more of the 9th to Brooklyn. Of potential candidates there is no dearth. Assemblyman Dov Hikind and Councilman Noach Dear, Democratic rivals from the Orthodox communities, are both likely to run and sure to raise lots of money. Former Schumer aides Jules Polonetsky and Daniel Feldman (now an

Assemblyman) could run also, as well as Assemblywomen Melinda Katz, Audrey Pheffer and Helen Weinstein, state Senator Carl Kruger, and Councilmen Anthony Weiner, Kenneth Fisher and Steve DeBrienza.

The People: Pop. 1990: 579,876; 20% age 65+; 82% White; 3% Black; 6% Asian; 9% Hispanic origin. Households: 52% married couple families; 21% married couple fams. w. children; 44% college educ.; median household income: $34,758; per capita income: $17,918; median gross rent: $534; median house value: $208,300.

1996 Presidential Vote

Clinton (D)	113,939	(66%)
Dole (R)	47,498	(27%)
Perot (I)	8,248	(5%)
Other	3,528	(2%)

1992 Presidential Vote

Clinton (D)	121,361	(59%)
Bush (R)	67,034	(32%)
Perot (I)	17,606	(9%)

Rep. Charles E. Schumer (D)

Elected 1980; b. Nov. 23, 1950, Brooklyn; home, Brooklyn; Harvard, B.A. 1971, J.D. 1974; Jewish; married (Iris).

Career: NY Assembly, 1974–80.

DC Office: 2211 RHOB 20515, 202-225-6616; Fax: 202-225-4183.

District Offices: Brooklyn, 718-627-9700; Forrest Hills, 718-268-8200; Rockaway, 718-945-9200.

Committees: *Banking & Financial Services* (4th of 25 D): Capital Markets, Securities & Government Sponsored Enterprises; Financial Institutions & Consumer Credit. *Judiciary* (3rd of 15 D): Crime (RMM); Immigration & Claims.

Group Ratings

	ADA	ACLU	AFS	LCV	CFA	CON	NFIB	COC	ACU	NTLC	CHC
1996	90	62	92	85	92	26	27	31	5	17	7
1995	80	—	—	75	100	16	—	32	4	—	—

National Journal Ratings

	1995 LIB — 1995 CONS			1996 LIB — 1996 CONS		
Economic	74%	—	26%	70%	—	28%
Social	80%	—	13%	76%	—	23%
Foreign	86%	—	14%	85%	—	14%

Key Votes of the 104th Congress

1. Reduce Medicare Growth $	N	5. Flag Amendment	N	9. Cuban Embargo	N
2. Ovrd. Product Liab. Veto	N	6. Drop EPA Limits	Y	10. Bar Bosnia Troop $	N
3. Increase Min. Wage	Y	7. Repeal Assault-Weap. Ban	N	11. Cut Anti-Missile Defense	Y
4. Welfare Reform	N	8. Ovrd. Part. Birth Veto	N	12. Bar U.N. Uniforms	N

Election Results

1996 general	Charles E. Schumer (D-L)	107,107	(75%)	($487,841)
	Robert J. Verga (R-I-FR)	30,488	(21%)	($36,351)
	Others	5,618	(4%)	
1996 primary	Charles E. Schumer (D)	unopposed		
1994 general	Charles E. Schumer (D-L)	95,139	(73%)	($157,108)
	James P. McCall (R-C)	35,880	(27%)	($13,831)

TENTH DISTRICT

Bedford, a century ago one of Brooklyn's fashionable neighborhoods, has given its name to half of what is Brooklyn's best known black neighborhood. It is not the most downtrodden. If Bedford's and Stuyvesant's brownstones looked bedraggled even before modern urban decay, they also remain solid and, on many streets, well-tended. The black community settled here well before World War II, but they were then one of the smaller of dozens of Brooklyn ethnic enclaves. It grew in the years after World War II as crime and crowding moved people out of Harlem and busloads of blacks came north from the Carolinas in the 1950s and early 1960s. Sluggish job growth has meant less migration, but Brooklyn's black community, with some of New York's highest birth rates, has grown rapidly and far beyond the original bounds of Bedford-Stuyvesant.

The 10th Congressional District of New York is centered on Bedford-Stuyvesant and is entirely contained within Brooklyn; there, regularity ends. It is shaped something like a set of barbells, with one end including gentrified Brooklyn Heights and downtown Brooklyn, plus part of the mixed Fort Greene and Williamsburg neighborhoods. To the east it extends to Jamaica Bay, including much of East New York and Canarsie and Brownsville. The landscape varies widely, from utterly bombed-out blocks to secure and hardy blocks of rowhouses or high-rise rent-supplemented apartments. The district in 1990 was 57% black and 20% Hispanic, with some blocks of Italians and Hasidic Jews. Politically, it is overwhelmingly Democratic; in 1996 it gave Bill Clinton his third highest vote percentage in the country, 90.2%.

The congressman from the 10th is Ed Towns, elected in 1982. He is a black Democrat from East New York who is as experienced in government as in politics. Towns has been a teacher, social worker and hospital administrator, and he is active in the civic affairs of this racially changing community. He served as Brooklyn's deputy borough president for six years and became widely popular. Towns's two best known legislative initiatives are the Student Athlete Right-to-Know Act, which requires colleges to report the graduation rates of student athletes, and strengthening the National Health Service Corps and the Minority Health Initiative, especially for Native Americans (not too many of them in Brooklyn). In 1990 he got a seat on the Commerce Committee, where he has quickly moved up in seniority. In 1993 he became chairman of the Government Reform and Oversight subcommittee on Human Resources; Towns has a long history of superintending the Food and Drug Administration and pressing for more-stringent regulation. He has kept the ranking position on the subcommittee, even though with his seniority he could have claimed the ranking position on Commerce's Health Subcommittee, the power base of Henry Waxman for 16 years; but evidently he did not relish taking the lead on issues like Medicaid reform, tobacco regulation and Clean Air legislation. Despite his very liberal voting record, he does not support every liberal cause. A native of North Carolina, he was part of an alliance of inner-city and tobacco-state members that has defended the tobacco industry against efforts led by Waxman to impose additional controls on cigarettes.

Towns ordinarily wins reelection without much trouble. He did face a vigorous primary challenge in 1992, after he had 408 overdrafts on the House bank, from Councilwoman Susan Alter; but he won 63%–28%. Towns moved rapidly to oppose any threat to divide his district as a result of the court-ordered redrawing of the Hispanic-majority 12th District, much of which is directly north of the 10th.

The People: Pop. 1990: 581,311; 10% age 65+; 21% White; 57% Black; 2% Asian; 20% Hispanic origin. Households: 34% married couple families; 16% married couple fams. w. children; 35% college educ.; median household income: $23,164; per capita income: $11,479; median gross rent: $441; median house value: $165,200.

1996 Presidential Vote

Clinton (D)	134,057	(90%)
Dole (R)	9,059	(6%)
Perot (I)	2,511	(2%)
Other	3,437	(2%)

1992 Presidential Vote

Clinton (D)	125,300	(83%)
Bush (R)	19,200	(13%)
Perot (I)	5,720	(4%)

Rep. Edolphus Towns (D)

Elected 1982; b. July 21, 1934, Chadbourn, NC; home, Brooklyn; NC A&T U., B.S. 1956, Adelphi U., M.S.W. 1973; Presbyterian; married (Gwendolyn).

Career: Army, 1956–58; Prof., Medgar Evers Col.; NY public schl. teacher; Dep. hospital admin., 1965–71; Brooklyn Dep. Borough Pres., 1976–82.

DC Office: 2232 RHOB 20515, 202-225-5936; Fax: 202-225-1018.

District Offices: Brooklyn, 718-387-8696; Brooklyn, 718-855-8018.

Committees: *Government Reform & Oversight* (5th of 19 D): Human Resources (RMM). *Commerce* (7th of 23 D): Energy & Power; Finance & Hazardous Materials; Health & the Environment.

Group Ratings

	ADA	ACLU	AFS	LCV	CFA	CON	NFIB	COC	ACU	NTLC	CHC
1996	85	93	100	92	100	76	18	20	0	5	0
1995	85	—	—	69	92	7	—	14	14	—	—

National Journal Ratings

	1995 LIB — 1995 CONS			1996 LIB — 1996 CONS		
Economic	77%	—	22%	89%	—	0%
Social	74%	—	26%	88%	—	0%
Foreign	86%	—	14%	90%	—	0%

Key Votes of the 104th Congress

1. Reduce Medicare Growth $	N	5. Flag Amendment	Y	9. Cuban Embargo	N
2. Ovrd. Product Liab. Veto	N	6. Drop EPA Limits	Y	10. Bar Bosnia Troop $	N
3. Increase Min. Wage	Y	7. Repeal Assault-Weap. Ban	N	11. Cut Anti-Missile Defense	Y
4. Welfare Reform	N	8. Ovrd. Part. Birth Veto	N	12. Bar U.N. Uniforms	N

Election Results

1996 general	Edolphus Towns (D-L)	99,889	(91%)	($533,824)
	Amelia Smith-Parker (R-C-FR)	8,660	(8%)	
1996 primary	Edolphus Towns (D)	unopposed		
1994 general	Edolphus Towns (D-L)	77,026	(89%)	($453,427)
	Amelia Smith Parker (R)	7,995	(9%)	($7,059)
	Others	1,489	(2%)	

ELEVENTH DISTRICT

When Jackie Robinson suited up for the Brooklyn Dodgers in 1947, becoming the first black major league baseball player, the borough didn't have many blacks. Manhattan's Harlem was the center of black life and entertainment in New York, though Brooklyn's Bedford-Stuyvesant, not far from Ebbetts Field, had a scattering of blacks in modest apartments. Then a subway line, built to replace the El, connected Bed-Stuy with Harlem, and inspired Duke Ellington's "Take the A Train."

Since then, Harlem has lost population and dozens of blocks have been emptied out, their brownstone townhouses vacant or vanished. But Brooklyn's black neighborhoods have grown and to a certain degree have prospered. Many of New York's black families came from the south, but large numbers, particularly in Flatbush, the area south of the Hasidic Jewish outposts in Crown Heights, come from what New Yorkers call "the Islands"—Jamaica, Haiti, the Dominican Republic, Barbados, Trinidad and Tobago. Speaking deeply accented English, French, Spanish or various forms of Creole, they bring spiced bread, peanut punch, Matouk's Special Hot Calypso Sauce, reggae and calypso music. These Caribbean immigrants tend to stay in family units more often than low-income American-born blacks; they work hard and are commercially and civically inclined. Coming from places where life and property are not always respected by governments, they are working, like so many other immigrants to America, to build new communities.

The 11th Congressional District extends from downtown Brooklyn and Prospect Park across Crown Heights—the scene of violent clashes between blacks and Hasidic Jews—and covers most of Flatbush, East Flatbush and Brownsville. This area had the largest concentration of Jews in America from the 1920s to the 1960s. But today, the 11th is 69% black, the highest percentage of any congressional district in the nation, with probably as many blacks with roots in the Islands as in the American South. Like depopulated Brownsville, some neighborhoods here are in dreadful shape, while others, like much of Flatbush, seem to have considerable strength.

The congressman from the 11th, Major Owens, started out as a librarian but has had a long career in New York politics and government. He is part of the district's southern-based tradition, growing up and attending school in the South before heading north for various public-sector and civil-rights jobs. He worked in the Brownsville Community Council and with CORE, and served in Mayor John Lindsay's Administration from 1968–73 as commissioner of the city's Community Development Agency. Critic Charles Morris called Owens "the most capable and canny" of New York's anti-poverty program directors. It was a high-pressure job with few guidelines, and Owens may have been relieved when he was elected to serve in the antique chamber of the New York Senate in 1974. When Congresswoman Shirley Chisholm, an immigrant from Barbados and presidential candidate in 1972, announced her retirement in 1982, Owens entered the primary to succeed her and beat Chisholm's choice. Since then Owens has had no serious electoral competition; in November 1996, he won 92% of the vote.

Owens has one of the most liberal voting records in the House. During the 103d Congress, he chaired Education's Subcommittee on Select Education and Civil Rights. He worked on the Americans With Disabilities Act and, fittingly for a librarian, the Literacy Corps and library funding in the child care bill. He shepherded legislation to reauthorize the Education Department's Office of Educational Research and Improvement, attempting to restructure the office to conduct research that responded to the needs of parents and teachers. He also pushed legislation that increased federal child abuse and domestic violence programs. He has been outspokenly critical of the Republican majority in the House, and of the Clinton Administration as well; he is often seen making long, vigorous floor speeches after the House has finished work for the day. "What troubles me most is that he only wants to take small steps," Owens said of Clinton after the 1996 election. Owens has been a strong opponent of the Republicans' plan to give employees the option of taking compensatory time rather than overtime pay; "The

Republicans are coming for your overtime pay," he said.

Owens speaks passionately of the need to support libraries, important institutions in the immigrant communities of New York's outer boroughs. His skill at writing rap lyrics led the *New York Observer* to name him "class bard" of the city's delegation. The only threat to his tenure is redistricting, ordered by a federal court for the nearby Hispanic-majority 12th District by July 1997. The 11th shares no boundary with the 12th, and it seems unlikely that a black-majority district would be seriously altered, but there is some danger from a domino effect and Owens rather gloomily noted, "Whenever there's a redistricting, I find I'm the one who's disadvantaged. I'm not in with the power brokers."

The People: Pop. 1990: 582,332; 9% age 65+; 16% White; 69% Black; 3% Asian; 12% Hispanic origin. Households: 36% married couple families; 20% married couple fams. w. children; 40% college educ.; median household income: $26,148; per capita income: $11,706; median gross rent: $482; median house value: $181,100.

1996 Presidential Vote

Clinton (D)	116,390	(90%)
Dole (R)	7,832	(6%)
Perot (I)	1,719	(1%)
Other	2,835	(2%)

1992 Presidential Vote

Clinton (D)	104,584	(86%)
Bush (R)	11,686	(10%)
Perot (I)	3,907	(3%)

Rep. Major R. Owens (D)

Elected 1982; b. June 28, 1936, Memphis, TN; home, Brooklyn; Morehouse Col., B.A. 1956, Atlanta U., M.L.S. 1957; Baptist; married (Maria).

Career: Brooklyn Public Library, 1958–65, Community Coord., 1964–65; V.P., Metro. Cncl. of Housing, 1964; Chmn., Brooklyn Congress on Racial Equality; Exec. Dir., Brownsville Community Cncl., 1966–68; NYC Community Devel. Commissioner, 1968–73, Dep. Admin., 1972–74; Dir., Community Media Library Program, Columbia U., 1973–74; NY Senate, 1974–82.

DC Office: 2305 RHOB 20515, 202-225-6231; Fax: 202-226-0112.

District Offices: Brooklyn, 718-773-3100; Brooklyn, 718-940-3213.

Committees: *Education & The Workforce* (5th of 20 D): Early Childhood, Youth & Families; Workforce Protections (RMM). *Government Reform & Oversight* (4th of 19 D): Government Management, Information & Technology; Postal Service.

Group Ratings

	ADA	ACLU	AFS	LCV	CFA	CON	NFIB	COC	ACU	NTLC	CHC
1996	95	100	100	92	100	21	15	19	0	3	0
1995	100	—	—	88	100	16	—	9	8	—	—

National Journal Ratings

	1995 LIB	—	1995 CONS	1996 LIB	—	1996 CONS
Economic	94%	—	0%	89%	—	0%
Social	88%	—	0%	88%	—	0%
Foreign	87%	—	13%	90%	—	0%

Key Votes of the 104th Congress

1. Reduce Medicare Growth $	N	5. Flag Amendment	N	9. Cuban Embargo	N
2. Ovrd. Product Liab. Veto	N	6. Drop EPA Limits	Y	10. Bar Bosnia Troop $	N
3. Increase Min. Wage	Y	7. Repeal Assault-Weap. Ban	N	11. Cut Anti-Missile Defense	Y
4. Welfare Reform	N	8. Ovrd. Part. Birth Veto	N	12. Bar U.N. Uniforms	N

Election Results

1996 general	Major R. Owens (D-L)	89,905	(92%)	($129,983)
	Claudette Hayle (R-C-I-FR)	7,866	(8%)	
1996 primary	Major R. Owens (D)	unopposed		
1994 general	Major R. Owens (D-L)	61,945	(89%)	($295,986)
	Gary S. Popkin (R)	6,605	(9%)	
	Others	1,150	(2%)	

TWELFTH DISTRICT

Amid a vast wave of migration that seemed destined to make Puerto Ricans the majority in New York, Leonard Bernstein in 1957 wrote his musical, *West Side Story*, with Romeo as an Italian-American and Juliet as a Manhattan Puerto Rican. While the inflow and outflow of Puerto Ricans balanced out by the early 1960s, ever since the 1965 Immigration Act, New York has had a vast influx of Hispanics from places not under the U.S. flag. They include Dominicans, most of whom are black; Colombians, largely of Indian ancestry; Panamanians, who like Puerto Ricans are products of a polyglot society; and those from other parts of Latin America.

The 12th Congressional District of New York, as drawn for 1992, 1994 and 1996, was designed to join these diverse people together. It is a serpentine-shaped entity in which, by Census definition, 58% of the residents are Hispanic. Insiders have called it the "Bullwinkle" district, because of its alleged resemblance to the cartoon character. Stitched together, often by the thinnest of threads, are the heavily Puerto Rican Sunset Park neighborhood in Brooklyn and on the other side of the borough, Bushwick, with a mixture of Latinos and a political machine run by Assemblyman Vito Lopez. The Dominican neighborhood of East Elmhurst and Corona, Queens are in the 12th, as are the Colombian areas several blocks west in Jackson Heights, plus some black neighborhoods in East New York. It also jumps across the Manhattan Bridge to include Puerto Rican parts of the Lower East Side. The district is connected by cemeteries or parks in at least three places. About one-half its voters are in Brooklyn, about one-quarter each in Manhattan and Queens.

The congresswoman from the 12th is Nydia Velazquez, elected when this district was created for the 1992 elections. Velazquez was born in Puerto Rico, taught at the University of Puerto Rico in the 1970s and at Hunter College in the 1980s, worked for Congressman Ed Towns in 1983 and served on the New York City Council in 1984. Then she worked for Puerto Rico's government offices in New York. When the 12th was created, she was one of three major candidates who ran; the others were liberal Elisabeth Colon and incumbent Congressman Stephen Solarz. But Solarz had 743 overdrafts on the House bank, and chose to run here rather than take on Charles Schumer in the 9th District or Ted Weiss in the 8th (ironically, Weiss died the day before the Democratic primary). Velazquez got the endorsements of Mayor David Dinkins and Jesse Jackson, and beat Solarz 34%–28%, with 26% for Colon.

After the primary, confidential hospital records were leaked to a New York tabloid showing that in September 1991, Velazquez had attempted suicide, was hospitalized and later underwent counseling. Evidently, that was of little concern to voters: she won in November with 77%. In the House she has had a solidly liberal voting record. In her first term, Velazquez used her seat on the Banking Committee to push legislation to require credit bureaus to let people talk with live operators and to provide consumers with a free copy of their credit report after information is corrected. She wanted insurance companies to disclose their investments so consumers could decide whether they were putting money in their neighborhoods. In 1996, she got $5 million to investigate and enforce labor law violations in the garment industry, in which many of her constituents work. She also claimed success in defeating proposals that would have added to the 1996 immigration law restrictions on children's access to immunization and healthcare services. She also complained about the numbers of Hispanic appointees in the Clinton Administration. "The President admitted the administration has to do better on giving Latinos fair representation at the highest levels of government," she said in early 1997.

After the Supreme Court in 1993 ruled in *Shaw v. Reno* that district lines drawn predominantly for racial reasons were unconstitutional, a lawsuit was brought against the 12th District. In February 1997, a three-judge federal court ruled the 12th District's boundaries were unconstitutional because race was used as the predominant factor; it added that there was no need for New York to create a seventh "majority-minority" district, especially one with such erose lines. Velazquez called the ruling "a sad day for equal justice for communities of color." The court ordered the legislature to draw new lines by July 30; otherwise, it would draw new lines itself. In Albany the Democratic Assembly had to come to agreement with the Republican Senate and governor, presumably in hard back-room negotiating. It is certainly possible to smooth out the lines, but it seems likely that any district that combines Borough Park, Bushwick, the Lower East Side and Corona would have such a convoluted shape the court would reject it. Velasquez has vowed to run in the new 12th, whatever the lines; low voter turnout in Hispanic areas, however, would make a race chancy if other ethnic groups got larger representation.

The People: Pop. 1990: 577,757; 8% age 65+; 14% White; 9% Black; 19% Asian; 1% Other; 58% Hispanic origin. Households: 42% married couple families; 23% married couple fams. w. children; 25% college educ.; median household income: $20,444; per capita income: $8,534; median gross rent: $454; median house value: $175,100.

1996 Presidential Vote

Clinton (D)	80,852	(85%)
Dole (R)	10,249	(11%)
Perot (I)	2,296	(2%)
Other	2,042	(2%)

1992 Presidential Vote

Clinton (D)	67,274	(68%)
Bush (R)	25,664	(26%)
Perot (I)	5,133	(5%)

Rep. Nydia M. Velazquez (D)

Elected 1992; b. Mar. 28, 1953, Yabucoa, PR; home, Brooklyn; U. of PR, B.A. 1974, N.Y.U., M.A. 1976; Catholic; divorced.

Career: Instructor, U. of PR, 1976–81; Adjunct prof., Hunter Col., 1981–83; Special Asst., U.S. Rep. Edolphus Towns, 1983; NYC Cncl., 1984; Migration Dir., PR Dept. of Labor & Human Resources, 1986–89; Secy., PR Dept. of Community Affairs in the U.S., 1989–92.

DC Office: 1221 LHOB 20515, 202-225-2361; Fax: 202-226-0327.

District Offices: Brooklyn, 718-599-3658; Manhattan, 212-673-3997; Queens, 718-699-2602.

Committees: *Banking & Financial Services* (14th of 25 D): Domestic & International Monetary Policy; Housing & Community Opportunity. *Small Business* (5th of 16 D): Empowerment (RMM).

Group Ratings

	ADA	ACLU	AFS	LCV	CFA	CON	NFIB	COC	ACU	NTLC	CHC
1996	100	100	100	85	85	53	11	6	0	5	0
1995	100	—	—	100	92	16	—	8	13	—	—

National Journal Ratings

	1995 LIB — 1995 CONS			1996 LIB — 1996 CONS		
Economic	94%	—	0%	89%	—	0%
Social	88%	—	0%	88%	—	0%
Foreign	76%	—	23%	90%	—	0%

Key Votes of the 104th Congress

1. Reduce Medicare Growth $	N	5. Flag Amendment	N	9. Cuban Embargo	N
2. Ovrd. Product Liab. Veto	N	6. Drop EPA Limits	*	10. Bar Bosnia Troop $	*
3. Increase Min. Wage	Y	7. Repeal Assault-Weap. Ban	N	11. Cut Anti-Missile Defense	Y
4. Welfare Reform	N	8. Ovrd. Part. Birth Veto	N	12. Bar U.N. Uniforms	N

Election Results

1996 general	Nydia M. Velazquez (D-L)	61,913	(85%)	($236,564)
	Miguel I. Prado (R-C-RTL)	9,978	(14%)	($23,991)
	Others	1,283	(2%)	
1996 primary	Nydia M. Velazquez (D)	unopposed		
1994 general	Nydia M. Velazquez (D-L)	39,929	(92%)	($11,360)
	Genevieve R. Brennan (C)	2,747	(6%)	

THIRTEENTH DISTRICT

Staten Island is part of New York City, yet a land apart; it is closer geographically to New Jersey, separated only by narrow Arthur Kill and Kill van Kull, than to Brooklyn, over the 5-mile-long span of the Verrazano Narrows Bridge. Its inclusion in Greater New York in 1898 was something of an afterthought, and for two-thirds of a century it was connected to the rest of The City only by ferry or through Bayonne, New Jersey, until the Verrazano was opened in 1965. It is far less densely populated than the rest of New York: With about as much acreage as Brooklyn has for 2.3 million people, Staten Island has about 400,000—and that's after recent robust population growth. Some of Staten Island is almost rural, though not bucolic. It has the highest point on the eastern seaboard, Todt Hill, and the vast Fresh Kills dump. Culturally, Staten Islanders are deeply conservative—more so than in most of New York's suburbs—quite a contrast from Manhattan at the other end of the ferry. New York City income taxes, the highest in the nation, pay for many programs opposed by most Staten Islanders; in November 1993, Staten Islanders voted for secession, but the legislature did not act; ironically Staten Island provided the key votes that year for the election of Mayor Rudolph Giuliani over incumbent David Dinkins.

The 13th Congressional District of New York is made up of Staten Island plus a couple of adjacent neighborhoods over the Verrazano Narrows Bridge in Brooklyn. The largest of these is Bay Ridge, heavily Catholic and Italian, mostly middle-class, with thick New York accents and resentment of high New York taxes and welfare payments: large single-family houses and small apartment buildings by the looming towers of the Bridge. The 13th also includes most of heavily Italian Bensonhurst, where in 1989 the murder of a black youth transfixed the city and altered its politics. This district may have more Italian-Americans and may also be home to more police officers than any other district in America.

The congresswoman from the 13th District—until August 1997—was Susan Molinari, a Republican who was the youngest member of Congress when she was chosen in a March 1990 special election. She quickly became one of the Republican leaders of the House, and was mentioned for statewide office, so it stunned some in Washington in May 1997 when she announced that she would resign her seat to anchor CBS's new Saturday morning news show. But Molinari had contemplated this move for some time, and already had some experience on CBS's New York affiliate Channel 2 in the "Chuck and Sue" debates with Brooklyn Democrat Charles Schumer.

Molinari entered the House with a political pedigree: her grandfather S. Robert Molinari was an assemblyman from Staten Island in the 1940s, and her father Guy Molinari represented the district from 1980 until he was elected Staten Island Borough president in November 1989. She became one of the most distinctive members of the House, combining her father's concentration on local issues with loyalty to the party leadership. Young, energetic, with postmodern style and perfect political pitch, Molinari in 1994 and 1995 became one of the most visible voices for her party. Locally and nationally, she was a prominent spokesman for the Contract with America. And she made news in July 1994 when, on neutral turf in Bucks County, Pennsylvania, she married Congressman Bill Paxon from Upstate New York, who is more conservative politically; they made dozens of party appearances for Republican candidates across the country. In December 1994, despite her views on cultural issues, she was elected Republican Conference vice chair over Cliff Stearns of Florida by 124–100. And in an effort to portray a party of inclusion and tolerance, Molinari was chosen to give the keynote address at the 1996 Republican National Convention during primetime network television coverage. As she delivered the speech, her husband sat among the delegates giving a bottle to their new baby girl, Susan Ruby, born in May 1996. Molinari generated the biggest applause with her one-liner, "Americans know that Bill Clinton's promises have the life span of a Big Mac on Air Force One."

Her departure set off a scramble for both her Staten Island House seat and her Republican Conference vice chair post, which Republican women seem to have made some claim on. Washington Congresswoman Jennifer Dunn, already Conference secretary, proclaimed her candidacy the day after Molinari's announcement; North Carolina's Sue Myrick also contemplated a bid, but decided instead to pursue the Conference secretary post Dunn was vacating. The special election to fill Molinari's seat will coincide with November 1997 New York City elections—a boon to the Republican who will run on the same ticket as popular incumbent Mayor Rudy Giuliani. With no time for a primary, candidates were chosen by the borough's party committees. Republicans quickly picked City Councilman Vito Fossella, who has close ties to the Molinari family. Democrats looked to veteran Assemblyman Eric Vitaliano, as well as Staten Island Democratic Chairman Robert Gigante, who Molinari beat in her first race for the House.

Molinari has not ruled out running for office again, but she is unlikely to run against fellow Republican incumbents D'Amato or Pataki in 1998, and Moynihan's seat doesn't come up until 2000. In the meantime, hosting a television program will give her more exposure to voters than her district seat. She wants the new show to be something like a "*60 Minutes* meets Rosie O'Donnell."

The People: Pop. 1990: 579,521; 14% age 65+; 82% White; 5% Black; 5% Asian; 8% Hispanic origin. Households: 57% married couple families; 26% married couple fams. w. children; 40% college educ.; median household income: $38,437; per capita income: $17,143; median gross rent: $553; median house value: $188,800.

1996 Presidential Vote

Clinton (D)	92,619	(51%)
Dole (R)	72,233	(40%)
Perot (I)	12,095	(7%)
Other	2,948	(2%)

1992 Presidential Vote

Bush (R)	100,761	(48%)
Clinton (D)	82,796	(39%)
Perot (I)	26,317	(12%)

Rep. Susan Molinari (R)

Elected Mar. 1990; b. Mar. 27, 1958, Staten Island; home, Staten Island; S.U.N.Y., B.A. 1980, M.A. 1981; Catholic; married (U.S. Rep. Bill Paxon).

Career: Finance asst., Natl. Repub. Govs. Assn. 1981–82; Ethnic Liaison, RNC, 1983–84; NYC Cncl., 1985–90.

DC Office: 2411 RHOB 20515, 202-225-3371; Fax: 202-226-1272; e-mail: molinari@hr.house.gov.

District Offices: Brooklyn, 718-630-5277; Staten Island, 718-987-8400.

Committees: *Republican Conference Vice Chairman. Budget* (11th of 24 R). *Transportation & Infrastructure* (8th of 40 R): Aviation; Railroads (Chmn.); Water Resources & Environment.

Group Ratings

	ADA	ACLU	AFS	LCV	CFA	CON	NFIB	COC	ACU	NTLC	CHC
1996	20	0	0	36	31	*	91	92	88	92	80
1995	10	—	—	19	8	56	—	96	68	—	—

National Journal Ratings

	1995 LIB	—	1995 CONS	1996 LIB	—	1996 CONS
Economic	0%	—	74%	27%	—	73%
Social	43%	—	56%	58%	—	42%
Foreign	36%	—	59%	30%	—	70%

Key Votes of the 104th Congress

1. Reduce Medicare Growth $	Y	5. Flag Amendment	Y	9. Cuban Embargo	Y
2. Ovrd. Product Liab. Veto	*	6. Drop EPA Limits	N	10. Bar Bosnia Troop $	N
3. Increase Min. Wage	*	7. Repeal Assault-Weap. Ban	N	11. Cut Anti-Missile Defense	*
4. Welfare Reform	Y	8. Ovrd. Part. Birth Veto	Y	12. Bar U.N. Uniforms	Y

Election Results

1996 general	Susan Molinari (R-C-FR)	94,660	(62%)	($557,586)
	Tyrone G. Butler (D-L)	53,376	(35%)	($53,459)
	Others	5,733	(4%)	
1996 primary	Susan Molinari (R)	unopposed		
1994 general	Susan Molinari (R-C)	96,491	(71%)	($481,588)
	Tyrone G. Butler (D-L)	32,060	(24%)	($21,618)
	Others	6,532	(5%)	

FOURTEENTH DISTRICT

Hardly any remnant can be found of early 19th Century New York, the city that diarists Philip Hone and George Templeton Strong said was continually being torn down and rebuilt, its earlier structures expendable after a generation or so on the high-priced real estate of this small, compact island. Yet the mayor of this quintessentially 20th Century city lives and works in two buildings of early 19th Century scale: City Hall, built in 1803–11, where his ground floor office, dwarfed by the Municipal and Woolworth Buildings, overlooks City Hall Park; and Gracie Mansion, built in 1799, which looks across East End Avenue to high-rise apartments and over the East River to the Triborough Bridge.

The 14th Congressional District, running irregularly from 14th Street north to 96th street, covers most of the East Side of Manhattan. The district also includes small salients on the Lower East Side and Upper West Side of Manhattan, although it gave up most of its black and Hispanic residents, especially on the Lower East Side; 5% of its votes are cast in the Brooklyn neighborhood of Greenpoint—Hispanic and industrial and polyglot—and about 8% in the Queens neighborhood of Astoria—Greek and boisterous and prosperous. The 14th is the direct descendant of the famous Silk Stocking District, originally created in 1918, then consisting of the few blocks east of Fifth Avenue along Central Park. In the years since, rich and articulate Manhattan, with its securities, publishing, advertising, entertainment, broadcasting and communications industries, has spread from this narrow enclave and taken over the greater part of the island. Meanwhile, the political leanings of this larger upper class—defined partly by income, but also by tastes in the arts, fashion, letters, all the things in which New York remains clearly the nation's capital—have changed, from elite Republican to culturally liberal.

Historically, the Silk Stocking tradition was Republican, and more tolerant than the rest of New York City and the rest of the nation—the politics of Theodore Roosevelt and the old *New York Herald-Tribune* and Henry Luce's *Time* magazine. While it did not trust union leaders and Democratic Party politicians, it accepted much of the New Deal. This district believed the nation should be led by the well-educated Protestant gentlemen one saw strolling down Madison Avenue to their clubs, who had continued to hold high government posts, though not the presidency, since the era of Franklin D. Roosevelt. But the district changed during the tenure of John Lindsay, who first served as a congressman from 1958–65 and then as mayor from 1965–73. Lindsay changed from being a liberal Republican to a radical Democrat. While mayor, he ran up the huge debts that led the city to the brink of bankruptcy in 1975, while neighborhoods deteriorated and the city lost one million people in the 1970s. He was succeeded as congressman and ultimately as mayor by Edward Koch, whose political travels were the reverse of Lindsay's. Koch started as a liberal and became more conservative, and in the process lost the support of Manhattan by backing capital punishment, opposing racial quotas and questioning poverty programs. But he left the city in far better shape, economically and fiscally and governmentally.

The Silk Stocking district proves that economics is not necessarily the basis of American politics. Its residents have the highest average household income in America, $74,780, but they also are solidly Democratic: 70% for Bill Clinton and 23% for Bob Dole in 1996. While the district is affluent, it also is full of gays, singles and others who consider anything past the canyons of Manhattan's east-west grid streets and the Hudson hostile country.

The congresswoman here is Carolyn Maloney, a liberal Democrat. Born and educated in North Carolina, she visited New York in 1970 at the age of 22, loved it and "just stayed." She worked on welfare education programs during the 1970s, and from 1977–82 she was a legislative staffer in Albany. She was elected to the New York City Council in 1982; one observer of her term there described her as "a little spacey" until she found a cause, but then she became "a pit bull." For 1992, redistricting created a Silk Stocking district even more Democratic than its predecessor and forced the veteran incumbent, Republican Bill Green, to sell himself to Democratic voters in Williamsburg and Astoria who had never heard of him. In the primary she faced Abe Hirschfeld, who in 1993 made a fool of himself when he briefly owned the *New York Post*, and beat him 66%–23%; she talked of running against millionaires, though her husband is an investment banker and they are millionaires themselves. Green, also rich, was a thoughtful legislator who shared Manhattan's cultural liberalism and won with 61% in 1988 and 1990. But he could not compete with the enthusiasm of a Democratic Party dominated by the feminist left for a woman candidate. And he was poorly positioned to appeal to voters in Astoria and

Greenpoint, who in city elections have favored Republicans who are culturally conservative and economically liberal. Green won the Manhattan part of the district, but only by 50%–44%, below his previous showings; Maloney carried Greenpoint 60%–34% and Astoria 64%–35%, for a 50%–48% upset victory.

Maloney brought a certain naivete to Washington, telling people she had no second choice to a seat on Appropriations and, when she didn't get it, ending up on Banking and Government Reform. She called for larger cuts in defense than almost any member and supported the balanced budget amendment. She alienated some western lawmakers in her first term, when she brought in singer Carole King to stump for her legislation to restrict development in the Northern Rockies; former Democratic Idaho Congressman Larry LaRocco wrote a bill designating Central Park and her district as a wilderness area. She also was not immune from criticism back home. *The New York Times* mentioned her reputation in the capital as a "lightweight." But Maloney was active on congressional and campaign finance reform, serving as a co-chair of freshman task forces on reform issues. She also pushed to eliminate wasteful spending, taking the lead in trying to slash spending for the controversial Civilian Marksmanship Program. Interestingly, she won approval in 1996 of an amendment excluding "kitchen cabinet" from a bill imposing conflict-of-interest requirements on White House advisers; many kitchen cabineters are from Manhattan. In 1997, representing the number one campaign contributor district in the country, she joined a bipartisan group calling for a commission on campaign finance, to produce a bill Congress must vote up or down.

Maloney showed her political strength in 1994 when she was opposed by Manhattan Councilman Charles Millard, a liberal Republican who raised almost $1 million. She blasted him for refusing to say he would not vote for Newt Gingrich for speaker, and even as most of the country was moving to the right, Manhattan was moving sharply to the left. The 14th District voted 78% for Mario Cuomo even as he was winning only 45% of the statewide vote, and Maloney won 64%–35%, a result that reportedly stunned both candidates. In 1996 Maloney ran even stronger, winning 72%–24%. Mayor Rudolph Giuliani may very well carry the East Side of Manhattan in his reelection campaign for mayor in November 1997, but Republican hopes for winning the 14th District seem pretty wan; the one well-known name circulating was Betsy McCaughey Ross, who was dumped as lieutenant governor by George Pataki in April 1997. But McCaughey Ross in April 1997 said she had no plans to challenge Maloney in 1998. What could change is the district's boundaries: in February 1997 a federal court ruled the lines of the Hispanic-majority 12th District were unconstitutional and must be redrawn by July 1997. One way to do that would be to take the Lower East Side from the 12th and put it in the 14th, while removing Williamsburg and Astoria. This would probably make the 14th even more safely Democratic.

The People: Pop. 1990: 578,639; 16% age 65+; 80% White; 4% Black; 5% Asian; 11% Hispanic origin. Households: 30% married couple families; 10% married couple fams. w. children; 69% college educ.; median household income: $42,184; per capita income: $41,151; median gross rent: $678; median house value: $242,500.

1996 Presidential Vote			**1992 Presidential Vote**		
Clinton (D)	144,885	(70%)	Clinton (D)	160,596	(69%)
Dole (R)	46,970	(23%)	Bush (R)	53,830	(23%)
Perot (I)	6,623	(3%)	Perot (I)	16,467	(7%)
Other	7,702	(4%)			

Rep. Carolyn B. Maloney (D)

Elected 1992; b. Feb.19, 1948, Greensboro, NC; home, Manhattan; Greensboro Col, A.B. 1968; Presbyterian; married (Clifton).

Career: NYC Bd. of Educ., 1970–77; Legis. aide, NY Assembly, NY Senate, 1977–82; NYC Cncl., 1982–92.

DC Office: 1330 LHOB 20515, 202-225-7944; Fax: 202-225-4709; e-mail: maloney@hr.house.gov.

District Offices: Brooklyn, 718-349-1260; Manhattan, 212-832-6531; Queens, 718-932-1804.

Committees: *Banking & Financial Services* (10th of 25 D): Domestic & International Monetary Policy; Financial Institutions & Consumer Credit. *Government Reform & Oversight* (8th of 19 D): Government Management, Information & Technology (RMM); National Security, International Affairs & Criminal Justice. *Joint Economic Committee* (10th of 10 Reps.).

Group Ratings

	ADA	ACLU	AFS	LCV	CFA	CON	NFIB	COC	ACU	NTLC	CHC
1996	85	80	100	92	100	79	24	20	5	5	0
1995	80	—	—	88	100	13	—	21	0	—	—

National Journal Ratings

	1995 LIB — 1995 CONS			1996 LIB — 1996 CONS		
Economic	83%	—	16%	85%	—	15%
Social	79%	—	20%	88%	—	0%
Foreign	87%	—	13%	85%	—	15%

Key Votes of the 104th Congress

1. Reduce Medicare Growth $	N	5. Flag Amendment	N	9. Cuban Embargo	N
2. Ovrd. Product Liab. Veto	N	6. Drop EPA Limits	Y	10. Bar Bosnia Troop $	N
3. Increase Min. Wage	Y	7. Repeal Assault-Weap. Ban	N	11. Cut Anti-Missile Defense	Y
4. Welfare Reform	N	8. Ovrd. Part. Birth Veto	N	12. Bar U.N. Uniforms	N

Election Results

1996 general	Carolyn B. Maloney (D-L)	130,175	(72%)	($599,406)
	Jeffrey E. Livingston (R)	42,641	(24%)	($152,503)
	Others	6,921	(4%)	
1996 primary	Carolyn B. Maloney (D)	unopposed		
1994 general	Carolyn B. Maloney (D-IDN)	98,479	(64%)	($1,032,181)
	Charles Millard (R-L)	54,277	(35%)	($988,112)

FIFTEENTH DISTRICT

Harlem, for many years America's most famous black ghetto, has fallen on grim times. Actually, Harlem was the central focus of black America for only a moment in history, and Harlem itself has not always been black. Its five-story tenements were built almost 100 years ago for working-class whites, and central Harlem became all black only around 1920—the beginning of the decade when black entertainers and night clubs on 125th Street became world-famous. This Harlem was a wondrous place, as the *WPA Guide* described 50 years ago: "To whites seeking amusement, it is an exuberant, original and unconventional entertainment center; to Negro college graduates, it is an opportunity to practice a profession among their own people; to those aspiring to racial leadership, it is a domain where they may advocate their theories unmolested; to the mass of Negro people, it is the spiritual capital of Black America." In 1944, Harlem got its own district and congressman, Adam Clayton Powell Jr., who won national fame for his Powell Amendments banning racial discrimination in government programs.

Today, Harlem's brownstones are often abandoned and empty, if they haven't been pulled down; family structure has deteriorated so much that the father-and-mother household is a rarity; drugs, crime, AIDS infection and infant mortality are at horrifying levels. Its population is down more than 200,000 since the 1940s. The boom in jobs and economic growth in the rest of Manhattan has not touched Harlem. Its high school graduates may get into City College because of its open admissions policy, but sadly, they seldom have the basic skills needed for white-collar work. There is some vitality now on 125th Street, with its state office building and Empowerment Zone designation, and perhaps some hope. But this is a community deeply wounded.

The 15th Congressional District includes all of Harlem, indeed almost all of northern Manhattan, from approximately East 96th Street and West 91st Street on up. That means the district takes in some of the white liberal Upper West Side and the precincts around Columbia University. It includes the once Irish and now Dominican Inwood neighborhood at the north tip of Manhattan; Washington Heights, with many Dominicans and Haitians; East Harlem, Italian in the days of Fiorello LaGuardia, now Puerto Rican and Latino. Overall the district is 37% black and 46% Hispanic—figures testifying to black flight from Harlem and the continuing rush of Western Hemisphere immigrants to fill it in.

The congressman from the 15th is Charles Rangel, first elected in 1970 when he narrowly beat the legendary but fading Adam Clayton Powell Jr.. Rangel is the senior member of the New York delegation and ranking Democrat on Ways and Means. He served in the Army in Korea, then went to college and law school, served as legal counsel in several government agencies and was elected to the Assembly in 1966; in 1970 he challenged Powell and won. Like most Harlem politicians, he has long argued that government aid and racial preferences are needed to solve Harlem's problems, and with more vehemence than ever since the Republicans won control of Congress. Yet much in his own career suggests otherwise. Rangel's main emphasis for at least ten years has been denunciation of the drug trade. From 1983 until it was abolished in 1993 with the other House select committees, Rangel chaired the Select Committee on Narcotics Abuse and Control, and seldom missed a chance to relate other problems to drugs; after all, he has seen how they can destroy a community. Rangel wants money spent on rehabilitation programs as much as interdiction and police work, and he was a scathing critic of Republican administrations' anti-drug efforts. But he also worked with the Bush Justice Department to create the Weed and Seed program, combining intensive law enforcement with social services. And he takes sharp issue with those who call for legalization of marijuana or provision of free needles to curtail AIDS, or giving heroin to terminal cancer patients.

Rangel does skillful work on other issues. He worked, with success, to protect state and local tax deductibility in the 1986 tax reform and was for years a prime defender of Section 936, the tax exemption that has created many jobs in Puerto Rico, now being phased out. He is an author of the Federal Empowerment Zone demonstration, the Low Income Housing tax credit (which he says financed 90% of affordable housing from 1984–94) and the Targeted Jobs tax credit.

For years Rangel had no serious competition at home and was in the majority in Washington. Not so in the mid-1990s. In 1994, he was opposed in the primary by Councilman Adam Clayton Powell IV, son of the man he beat 24 years earlier. Powell, who grew up in Puerto Rico hardly knowing his father, had a desultory record in the Council. But Rangel felt threatened enough to spend $1.4 million in the campaign, the 17th highest among House candidates. He won 61%–33%, a margin which may or may not deter serious challengers in the future. He returned to a House dominated by Republicans and a Ways and Means Committee that voted 26–10 to repeal a tax break for broadcast properties sold to minority owners; the repeal measure was prompted by a Viacom Inc. deal that would have cost the government $4 billion in lost revenues. Rangel's response was to lash out, in the same tones that he had used against Mayor Edward Koch and in support of Jesse Jackson. "Mr. Chairman, in America we cannot afford to be colorblind," he wrote in a letter to Ways and Means Chairman Bill Archer. "Just like under Hitler, people say they don't mean to blame any particular individuals and groups, but in the U.S. those groups always turn out to be minorities and immigrants." This of course was inaccurate—Hitler did single out Jews and other groups for persecution—but it also coarsened political discourse, as Archer noted. "Invoking the name of Adolf Hitler injects an utterly invalid and totally uncalled for extremism into a legitimate congressional debate."

That was not the only evidence of a chilly relationship between the buttoned-up, businesslike Archer and the garrulous, often genial but sometimes angry Rangel. Rangel accuses Archer of being too much under Newt Gingrich's control; an Archer aide said Rangel suffered from "gavel envy." However, in mid-1997, the two were at least making gestures in an attempt to better work together. Nor has Rangel gotten on well with the Clinton White House. He opposed the President's tax credit for college students as not germane to Harlem. He criticized as "a waste of my time" Clinton's call for task forces to reach common ground on budget issues between the White House and Congress. When those discussions produced a bipartisan deal, Rangel was not enthusiastic. "It's a Republican bill," he told CNN. He lashed out as well against Cardinal O'Connor when he criticized Catholic members who voted against the partial-birth abortion ban: "If the Church paid nearly as much attention to life after birth instead of life before birth, it would make a greater contribution." But as a House veteran, Rangel criticized the $300,000 fee imposed on Speaker Gingrich for his ethics violations. "A person's life and career should not be determined by vague penalties. You can't tell a guy from a poor background that he needs a nest egg if the Ethics Committee is going to fine him."

The People: Pop. 1990: 580,354; 12% age 65+; 14% White; 37% Black; 2% Asian; 46% Hispanic origin. Households: 26% married couple families; 12% married couple fams. w. children; 35% college educ.; median household income: $19,238; per capita income: $10,367; median gross rent: $402; median house value: $162,600.

1996 Presidential Vote

Clinton (D)	135,845	(91%)
Dole (R)	7,658	(5%)
Perot (I)	2,377	(2%)
Other	3,692	(2%)

1992 Presidential Vote

Clinton (D)	123,846	(85%)
Bush (R)	15,505	(11%)
Perot (I)	4,700	(3%)

Rep. Charles B. Rangel (D)

Elected 1970; b. June 11, 1930, New York City; home, New York City; N.Y.U., B.S. 1957, St. John's U., LL.B. 1960; Catholic; married (Alma).

Career: Army, 1948–52 (Korea); Asst. U.S. Atty., S. Dist. of NY, 1961; Legal Cnsl., NYC Housing and Redevel. Bd., Neighborhood Conservation Bureau, 1963–68; Gen. Cnsl., Natl. Advisory Comm. on Selective Svc., 1966; NY Assembly, 1966–70.

DC Office: 2354 RHOB 20515, 202-225-4365; Fax: 202-225-0816.

District Offices: Manhattan, 212-663-3900; Manhattan, 212-348-9630.

Committees: *Ways & Means* (RMM of 16 D): Trade. *Joint Committee on Taxation* (4th of 5 Reps.).

Group Ratings

	ADA	ACLU	AFS	LCV	CFA	CON	NFIB	COC	ACU	NTLC	CHC
1996	95	100	100	92	92	58	13	13	0	5	0
1995	85	—	—	63	69	24	—	14	8	—	—

National Journal Ratings

	1995 LIB — 1995 CONS			1996 LIB — 1996 CONS		
Economic	89%	—	11%	89%	—	0%
Social	88%	—	0%	88%	—	0%
Foreign	93%	—	0%	90%	—	0%

Key Votes of the 104th Congress

1. Reduce Medicare Growth $	N	5. Flag Amendment	N	9. Cuban Embargo	N
2. Ovrd. Product Liab. Veto	N	6. Drop EPA Limits	Y	10. Bar Bosnia Troop $	N
3. Increase Min. Wage	Y	7. Repeal Assault-Weap. Ban	N	11. Cut Anti-Missile Defense	Y
4. Welfare Reform	N	8. Ovrd. Part. Birth Veto	N	12. Bar U.N. Uniforms	N

Election Results

1996 general	Charles B. Rangel (D-L)	113,898	(91%)	($1,086,065)
	Edward R. Adams (R)	5,951	(5%)	
	Others	4,885	(4%)	
1996 primary	Charles B. Rangel (D)	unopposed		
1994 general	Charles B. Rangel (D-L)	77,830	(97%)	($1,437,297)
	Others	2,812	(3%)	

SIXTEENTH DISTRICT

It may not quite be "the beautiful Bronx," as borough historian Lloyd Utlan calls it, but the Bronx seems to be coming back. The beautiful days were in the 1930s and 1940s, when Presidents Roosevelt and Truman rode down 138th Street, when Babe Ruth and Lou Gehrig and Joe DiMaggio hit home runs in Yankee Stadium, when Art Deco apartment buildings went up along the Grand Concourse, when shoppers thronged Tremont Avenue stores and New Yorkers from all over flocked to the Bronx Zoo. This Bronx was built in a trice, starting in 1906 when the first subway came in, bringing the children of immigrants from dimly lit Lower East Side tenements to comparatively spacious quarters. The Bronx's population grew from 200,000 in 1900 to 430,000 in 1910, 732,000 in 1920, and 1.3 million in 1930—more than the 1.2 million of 1990.

The Bronx fell rapidly in the dozen years after John Lindsay was elected mayor in 1965. One reason was rent control, insisted on by tenants, which guarantees that owners of low-rent property won't maintain it: the result is empty vandalized shells and venues for drug deals. Another was the drop in low-income, low-skill jobs in Manhattan and the Bronx, abetted by high union and minimum wages, restrictive work rules and the tolls exacted by organized crime. A third reason was the disintegration of family structure: stable, law-abiding males became scarce in these parts. But most important was crime. With no community institutions and little parental supervision, poor teenagers here committed an alarming number of crimes, with seeming impunity. Arson became increasingly common, perpetrated by kids for kicks or on behalf of landlords who wanted to get insurance money for rent controlled buildings. A vicious cycle was created: crime drove away jobs, which drove away fathers, which produced more crime. A section of the South Bronx with 476,000 people in 1960 and 460,000 in 1970 dropped to 233,000 in 1980, a stunning change. As people left, presidents and presidential candidates came in—Jimmy Carter in 1977, Ronald Reagan in 1980—promising help.

Now the South Bronx seems to have turned around. It is still one of the lowest-income parts of America, but it is beginning to be possible for low-income families here to work their way up. Government has helped, particularly Mayor Edward Koch's housing subsidies and Mayor Rudolph Giuliani's police tactics. Rent control was phased out, criminals held in prison longer, pocket parks were built, graffiti painted over, crime vastly reduced. But citizens here did much of the work, forming community groups called Banana Kelly or Mid-Bronx Desperadoes (now MBD Housing) to build single-family pastel bungalows and small-scale apartment projects for the elderly, single-parent families and former homeless. Local institutions, notably Bronx-Lebanon Hospital, remained in operation, employing area residents and becoming a strong force for neighborhood stability; warehousing and truck terminals opened up as the streets became safer. Population rose in the South Bronx in the 1980s more than almost anywhere else in New York City. There are now $150,000 ranch houses on Charlotte Street, where Jimmy Carter spoke in 1977.

The 16th Congressional District includes most of the Bronx south of the Bronx Zoo. It includes the Art Deco apartments of the Grand Concourse and the narrow commercial strips of Westchester Avenue, Boston Road and the Hub. It includes the industrial flatlands of Bruckner Boulevard and Hunts Point and the hard-rock ridges through which the original subways bore. This is still a low-income district, with more residents below the poverty line than any other in the nation in 1990, with the lowest median family income, the second lowest per capita income and the third lowest median household income of any congressional district. The people here are 60% Hispanic—though not all are Puerto Rican, the district has New York City's largest Puerto Rican community—and 43% black (the categories aren't mutually exclusive). Politically, this was the most Democratic district in the country in 1996, 94% for Bill Clinton and 4% for Bob Dole.

The congressman from the 16th is Jose Serrano, chosen in a March 1990 special election. A native of Mayaguez, Puerto Rico, who grew up in the Millbrook project in the South Bronx, Serrano has moved up while other Bronx politicians have fallen by the wayside due to corruption. He was elected to the New York Assembly in 1974 and chaired its Education Committee beginning in 1983; in 1985, he ran for Bronx borough president, bucking the Bronx Democratic organization, and nearly won. His disparaging remarks about corruption in the Bronx were remembered in 1987 when the man who beat him had to be replaced after a criminal conviction in the scandal over the minority defense contractor Wedtech. Then, Congressman Robert Garcia, long the co-sponsor of Jack Kemp's enterprise zones, was convicted for accepting money from Wedtech and resigned in January 1990 (the conviction was later reversed but far too late to help him politically). Serrano was the obvious choice for the Democratic nomination and won the seat easily, and has held it without difficulty since.

Serrano has one of the most liberal voting records in the House and moved up rapidly when Democrats were in control. In the 103d Congress he got a seat on Appropriations and chaired the Hispanic Caucus. When the caucuses were defunded in 1995, Serrano said Republicans were trying to "silence" voices of opposition to their agenda. He sponsored amendments on bilingual education, victim counseling and conflict resolution in schools, pediatric AIDS and the School-to-Work Act. In 1995 he became a vice chairman of the Democratic Steering Committee. But the shrinkage of Democratic seats on Appropriations after the Republican takeover made Serrano the most senior of seven Democrats forced to relinquish their seat. He did, however, win a slot on Judiciary. And by March 1996, when the Republicans added Mississippi Congressman Mike Parker to the Appropriations roster, Serrano was given the newly created matching Democratic seat. But in January 1997, when Bill Richardson resigned from the House to become U.N. Ambassador, Minority Leader Dick Gephardt passed over Serrano for the less senior (but better fundraiser, with his Cuban-American connections) Robert Menendez of New Jersey to be chief deputy whip; "They sold the job to the highest bidder," an anonymous Democrat said. Serrano did get something of a victory when the House in April 1997 voted a Congressional Gold Medal for Frank Sinatra, of whom he is a longtime fan.

The People: Pop. 1990: 581,053; 7% age 65+; 4% White; 33% Black; 2% Asian; 1% Other; 60% Hispanic origin. Households: 28% married couple families; 15% married couple fams. w. children; 22% college educ.; median household income: $15,060; per capita income: $7,102; median gross rent: $398; median house value: $148,000.

1996 Presidential Vote			1992 Presidential Vote		
Clinton (D)	117,624	(94%)	Clinton (D)	101,195	(81%)
Dole (R)	4,825	(4%)	Bush (R)	19,029	(15%)
Perot (I)	1,862	(1%)	Perot (I)	4,123	(3%)

Rep. Jose E. Serrano (D)

Elected Mar. 1990; b. Oct. 24, 1943, Mayaguez, PR; home, Bronx; Lehman Col.; Catholic; married (Mary).

Career: Army Medical Corps, 1964–66; Banker 1961–69; Dist. 7 Schl. Bd., 1969–74; NY Assembly, 1974–90.

DC Office: 2342 RHOB 20515, 202-225-4361; Fax: 202-225-6001; e-mail: jserrano@hr.house.gov.

District Offices: Bronx, 718-538-5400.

Committees: *Appropriations* (19th of 26 D): Agriculture, Rural Development, FDA & Related Agencies; Legislative (RMM).

Group Ratings

	ADA	ACLU	AFS	LCV	CFA	CON	NFIB	COC	ACU	NTLC	CHC
1996	95	94	100	85	92	20	16	19	0	5	0
1995	100	—	—	88	92	16	—	13	4	—	—

National Journal Ratings

	1995 LIB — 1995 CONS			1996 LIB — 1996 CONS		
Economic	92%	—	6%	85%	—	11%
Social	88%	—	0%	88%	—	0%
Foreign	88%	—	7%	87%	—	10%

Key Votes of the 104th Congress

1. Reduce Medicare Growth $	N	5. Flag Amendment	N	9. Cuban Embargo	N
2. Ovrd. Product Liab. Veto	N	6. Drop EPA Limits	*	10. Bar Bosnia Troop $	N
3. Increase Min. Wage	Y	7. Repeal Assault-Weap. Ban	N	11. Cut Anti-Missile Defense	Y
4. Welfare Reform	N	8. Ovrd. Part. Birth Veto	N	12. Bar U.N. Uniforms	N

Election Results

1996 general	Jose E. Serrano (D-L)	95,568	(96%)	($149,752)
	Others	3,665	(4%)	
1996 primary	Jose E. Serrano (D)	unopposed		
1994 general	Jose E. Serrano (D-L)	58,572	(96%)	($125,441)
	Others	2,257	(4%)	

SEVENTEENTH DISTRICT

The Bronx, a product almost entirely of the first half of the 20th Century, was originally a collection of middle-class neighborhoods clustered around subway stops, a borough where children of immigrants left gloomy Manhattan for the sunlight of wide avenues and the vistas of a city where the street grid bent to adapt to nature's ridges and hills. Different ethnic groups were clustered here and there: Irish in Kingsbridge, in the valley between Riverdale and the Grand Concourse; Italians in Bedford Park, north of Fordham University and Bronx Park; well-to-do WASPs and Jews in Riverdale, on the palisades above the Hudson River; Jews with less education and advantages originally in the Art Deco apartments on the Grand Concourse, then in a rush to Co-op City, the giant union-built apartment complex, with 35 35-story buildings, built in 1965 on marshland between the Hutchinson River Parkway and I-95.

The 17th Congressional District includes much of these Bronx neighborhoods plus several in the Westchester County suburbs just to the north. Co-op City is one anchor, and perhaps the largest political bloc in the district. Just to the west is the heavily black, middle-income neighborhood of Williamsbridge. The 17th's portions of Yonkers, Mount Vernon and New Rochelle in Westchester are carefully drawn to include most blacks there. The district also dips south along the Harlem River to take in some housing projects in the South Bronx. The 17th is, in Voting Rights Act argot, a minority-influence district, 38% black and 29% Hispanic.

Eliot Engel, the congressman from the 17th District, is a son of the Bronx and a resident of Co-op City, a political junkie who memorized the names of the 100 senators when he was a boy, a teacher and guidance counselor who got elected to the New York Assembly in 1976, at 29. He was elected to the House in 1988 to replace Democrat Mario Biaggi, once the most decorated member of the New York Police Department, after he was convicted in two tawdry bribery cases. (Engel replaced a convicted incumbent in the Assembly, too; like Jose Serrano of the next-door 16th, he has risen politically when others fell.) Engel filed to run against Biaggi in June, giving up his Assembly seat; he won 48%, while Biaggi and Vincent Marchiselli each got 26%. In November, Biaggi was on the ballot again, this time as the Republican nominee, and Engel beat him 56%–27%. Biaggi ran again in the 1992 Democratic primary; Engel beat him yet again, 74%–26%.

Engel has one of the most liberal voting records in the House. On the Education and The Workforce Committee he backed the public sector programs that are part of the fabric of New York life—public housing, education spending, mental health services. On the International Relations Committee he supported policies popular among ethnic groups in the district—recognizing Jerusalem as the capital of Israel (he is the prime sponsor of this resolution), opposing British policy in Northern Ireland, watching Africa policy, and co-chairing the Albanian Issues Caucus. He can be aggressive: he supported the Gulf war resolution and wants a tough war on drugs. But his basic tendencies are liberal: he sponsored the Democrats' amendment to the Contract With America to allow U.S. troops to serve under United Nations commanders. In 1997 he won a seat on the Commerce Committee, where he can work on health and environmental issues.

Engel is a relentless constituency service congressman. In June 1996 *The Wall Street Journal* profiled him as "Revenge of a Nerd," telling how he is known as "the mayor" in the north Bronx because of his persistent attention to local problems from broken traffic lights to congested subway trains. "Even if they disagree with me on the issues, if they meet me, they'll vote for me. I want to meet people all the time." Engel also has gone on the talk show circuit in far-flung media markets, calling Republicans "mean-spirited extremists who are bent on destroying Medicare and Medicaid."

In 1994 Engel had serious primary opposition from salsa singer Willie Colon. Colon portrayed himself as a son of the streets (Engel grew up in a public housing project) and was supported by Reverend Al Sharpton and Assemblyman Larry Seabrook. Engel won 61%–39%, but that was not a reassuring margin for a primary and suggested he may have a serious challenge again. Colon considered running again in 1996 but withdrew from the race before the primary; against a weaker opponent Engel won with 77%. Incidentally, Engel's 1994 Republican opponent, Edward Marshall, was charged in July 1996 with grand larceny for allegedly stealing some $400,000 in state funds intended for residents of a public housing partnership, $100,000 of which went toward Marshall's race against Engel.

The People: Pop. 1990: 578,424; 14% age 65+; 29% White; 38% Black; 3% Asian; 29% Hispanic origin. Households: 38% married couple families; 18% married couple fams. w. children; 38% college educ.; median household income: $27,227; per capita income: $13,155; median gross rent: $483; median house value: $174,200.

1996 Presidential Vote

Clinton (D)	126,787	(85%)
Dole (R)	16,238	(11%)
Perot (I)	3,844	(3%)

1992 Presidential Vote

Clinton (D)	119,964	(75%)
Bush (R)	30,215	(19%)
Perot (I)	7,961	(5%)

Rep. Eliot L. Engel (D)

Elected 1988; b. Feb. 18, 1947, Bronx; home, Bronx; Hunter-Lehman Col., B.A. 1969; City U. of NY, Lehman Col., M.A. 1973; NY Law Schl., J.D. 1987; Jewish, married (Patricia).

Career: Teacher, guidance counselor, NYC public schl., 1969–77; NY Assembly, 1976–88.

DC Office: 2303 RHOB 20515, 202-225-2464; e-mail: engeline@hr.house.gov.

District Offices: Bronx, 718-796-9700.

Committees: *Commerce* (17th of 23 D): Finance & Hazardous Materials; Oversight & Investigations; Telecommunications, Trade & Consumer Protection.

Group Ratings

	ADA	ACLU	AFS	LCV	CFA	CON	NFIB	COC	ACU	NTLC	CHC
1996	95	100	100	85	92	2	19	25	0	7	0
1995	100	—	—	94	100	9	—	8	8	—	—

National Journal Ratings

	1995 LIB		1995 CONS	1996 LIB		1996 CONS
Economic	92%	—	8%	82%	—	16%
Social	88%	—	0%	88%	—	0%
Foreign	79%	—	17%	86%	—	13%

Key Votes of the 104th Congress

1. Reduce Medicare Growth $	N	5. Flag Amendment	N	9. Cuban Embargo	Y
2. Ovrd. Product Liab. Veto	*	6. Drop EPA Limits	Y	10. Bar Bosnia Troop $	N
3. Increase Min. Wage	Y	7. Repeal Assault-Weap. Ban	N	11. Cut Anti-Missile Defense	Y
4. Welfare Reform	N	8. Ovrd. Part. Birth Veto	N	12. Bar U.N. Uniforms	*

Election Results

1996 general	Eliot L. Engel (D-L)	101,287	(85%)	($374,074)
	Denis McCarthy (R-C-RTL)	15,892	(13%)	
	Others	2,008	(2%)	
1996 primary	Eliot L. Engel (D)	14,366	(77%)	
	Herbert Moreira-Brown (D)	4,314	(23%)	
1994 general	Eliot L. Engel (D-L)	73,321	(78%)	($464,001)
	Edward T. Marshall (R)	16,896	(18%)	($211,374)
	Others	4,262	(5%)	

EIGHTEENTH DISTRICT

The great granite ridges that form the spine of Manhattan and the Bronx move north into the thin peninsula of land between Long Island Sound and the Hudson River that is lower Westchester County. Blessed with some of America's loveliest scenery, easily accessible to Manhattan by train since the mid-19th Century, this became some of the country's first suburban terrain, with grand estates built by great millionaires, like Jay Gould's Gothic revival Lyndhurst or John D. Rockefeller's spectacular Kykuit, with villages for retainers clustered around the railroad stations.

Today, Westchester still looks suburban, perhaps more than ever now that it has a nice patina of age. It has little commuter railroad stations across from faux Tudor drugstores, soda fountains and cobblestone post offices; it also has shopping malls and gallerias and corporate headquarters. The county does have its share of homeless and racial ghettos, its seedy neighborhoods if not slums. Intensive development has not proceeded too far north of White Plains, for just to the north Westchester is crossed by the first of several mountain ridges—the closest the Appalachians come to the ocean. Historically Republican, Westchester is now intensely marginal political territory. More than Nassau or Suffolk County or northern New Jersey, it has attracted liberal-minded professionals, often Jews, who have made very high-income places like Scarsdale Democratic strongholds. In addition, blue-collar voters and blacks in places like Mount Vernon make this a mixed constituency. Westchester votes a lot like the comfortable central city neighborhoods it physically resembles—Cambridge's Brattle Street, Philadelphia's Chestnut Hill, Washington's Cleveland Park.

The 18th Congressional District contains the heart of suburban Westchester County but actually has less than half the county's population; it also includes a little territory in the Bronx and widely scattered areas in Queens. Politics, as one might expect, is at work here; this is a district designed for Congresswoman Nita Lowey, a Democrat first elected in 1988 and a favorite of then-Governor Mario Cuomo. The 18th includes most of southern Westchester, but not the black neighborhoods of Yonkers, Mount Vernon and New Rochelle, which are in the minority-influence 17th District. It includes the rich, Catholic and conservative suburbs of Pelham, Eastchester and Bronxville, and the more Jewish and liberal Scarsdale, plus some of the Long Island Sound towns. The 18th also contains the southern half of White Plains, the county seat-corporate headquarters-shopping mall center. From there the 18th goes on its odyssey, picking up a few thousand people in Bronx communities facing the Sound and the urban resort of City Island. Then it crosses the Throgs Neck Bridge and is connected by a block-wide land-bridge through Flushing to two distinct areas of Queens. One is Lefrak City and other high-rise apartments in Rego Park, along Queens Boulevard where the first condominium conversion in New York took place in 1966; this area is heavily Jewish and very Democratic. The other is the heavily Italian neighborhoods around St. John's University, including the longtime home of its most famous alumnus, Mario Cuomo, in the pleasant winding streets of Hollis Wood, a more politically mixed area.

Nita Lowey was born in the Bronx, raised her family in Queens, and now lives in upper-crust Harrison in Westchester. She went to work for Cuomo in 1975, after he was appointed secretary of state by Governor Hugh Carey; she was an assistant secretary of state when she decided to run for Congress in 1988. In the primary, she faced Hamilton Fish III, son and grandson of Republican Hudson River congressmen, and as a former publisher of *The Nation* considerably more liberal than Lowey; she won 44%–36%. Her opponent in the general was Joseph DioGuardi, a two-term incumbent who trumpeted his experience as a CPA but was dogged by charges of illicit contributions; she won 50%–47%. Each spent over $1 million, with Lowey spending $657,000 in personal funds. (In 1994, Fish and DioGuardi ran and lost in the 19th District, just to the north, where Fish's father was retiring from Congress after 26 years. DioGuardi ran in the 19th again in 1996 and lost the primary to Republican incumbent Sue Kelly.)

In the House Lowey has made a mostly liberal record. She has been a Clinton Administration loyalist when it was tough, voting for the 1993 budget and tax package in this high-income district, splitting with most New York Democrats and organized labor to support the North American Free Trade Agreement. On the Appropriations Committee she boosted biomedical and breast cancer research, worker retraining and aid to Israel. She has been one of the House's strongest advocates of abortion rights. In 1994 she organized 72 members, mostly Democrats, who pledged not to vote for a healthcare plan that did not cover abortions. In 1995 and 1997 she was a leading backer of funds for international family planning including abortion. She has been a leading speaker against the "partial-birth" abortion ban. She has called for stronger drunk driving laws, bans on foreign visitors buying guns, tax credits to companies with workplace programs to combat violence against women, college tuition tax credits, and improved train service in Westchester.

Since Lowey first won, the 18th District has been moving left, and she has proved a prodigious fundraiser, never spending less than $911,000 on a campaign. In 1992, DioGuardi came back for a rematch; she won 71% in the Queens portion just added to the district and won overall 56%–44%. In 1994, against a lawyer who put $247,000 of his own into the race, she won 57%–41%. In 1996 she won 64%–32%. Lowey has been mentioned as a Senate candidate in 1998, but she bowed out in early 1997, apparently deferring to Geraldine Ferraro. Redistricting, necessitated by the court decision outlawing the Hispanic-majority 12th District which comes within a block of the 18th in Queens, could change the boundaries; she would certainly not want to lose her portion of Queens.

The People: Pop. 1990: 581,021; 17% age 65+; 74% White; 7% Black; 8% Asian; 10% Hispanic origin. Households: 56% married couple families; 23% married couple fams. w. children; 54% college educ.; median household income: $43,754; per capita income: $24,392; median gross rent: $594; median house value: $286,000.

1996 Presidential Vote

Clinton (D)	121,501	(58%)
Dole (R)	73,399	(35%)
Perot (I)	10,215	(5%)
Other	3,715	(2%)

1992 Presidential Vote

Clinton (D)	117,572	(50%)
Bush (R)	94,652	(40%)
Perot (I)	21,986	(9%)

Rep. Nita M. Lowey (D)

Elected 1988; b. July 5, 1937, New York City; home, Harrison; Mt. Holyoke Col., B.A. 1959; Jewish, married (Stephen).

Career: Asst. for Econ. Devel. & Neighborhood Preservation, NY Secy. of St., Dep. Dir., Division of Econ. Opportunity, 1975–85; NY Asst. Secy. of St., 1985–87.

DC Office: 2421 RHOB 20515, 202-225-6506; Fax: 202-225-0546; e-mail: nitamail@hr.house.gov.

District Offices: Rego Park, 718-897-3602; White Plains, 914-428-1707.

Committees: *Appropriations* (18th of 26 D): Foreign Operations, Export Financing & Related Programs; Labor, Health & Human Services & Education.

Group Ratings

	ADA	ACLU	AFS	LCV	CFA	CON	NFIB	COC	ACU	NTLC	CHC
1996	90	69	92	85	92	24	22	31	0	12	7
1995	90	—	—	69	100	16	—	25	4	—	—

National Journal Ratings

	1995 LIB — 1995 CONS	1996 LIB — 1996 CONS
Economic	82% — 17%	73% — 25%
Social	80% — 13%	84% — 12%
Foreign	88% — 7%	90% — 0%

Key Votes of the 104th Congress

1. Reduce Medicare Growth $	N	5. Flag Amendment	N	9. Cuban Embargo	N
2. Ovrd. Product Liab. Veto	N	6. Drop EPA Limits	Y	10. Bar Bosnia Troop $	N
3. Increase Min. Wage	Y	7. Repeal Assault-Weap. Ban	N	11. Cut Anti-Missile Defense	Y
4. Welfare Reform	N	8. Ovrd. Part. Birth Veto	N	12. Bar U.N. Uniforms	N

Election Results

1996 general	Nita M. Lowey (D)	118,194	(64%)	($1,138,456)
	Kerry J. Katsorhis (R-C)	59,487	(32%)	($238,826)
	Others	8,041	(4%)	
1996 primary	Nita M. Lowey (D)	unopposed		
1994 general	Nita M. Lowey (D)	91,663	(57%)	($1,343,347)
	Andrew C. Hartzell Jr. (R-C)	65,517	(41%)	($427,491)
	Others	2,873	(2%)	

NINETEENTH DISTRICT

The great interior of America can be said to begin where the Hudson River squeezes through the chain of Appalachian ridges at the Hudson Highlands. This choke point was the barrier to British military power during the Revolutionary War, when American forces built a chain across the river to keep the British from sailing north. It was over control of this part of the Hudson that Benedict Arnold betrayed his country, and it was here that the new nation built its Military Academy high on the cliffs at West Point. The Hudson was the impetus for the builders of the Erie Canal and the water-level New York Central Railroad, the great projects that made New York City the port of the American interior, as well as the builders of the Croton Aqueduct not far away, which provided the water without which New York could not grow—and also provided a way for the first cockroaches to reach the city.

The lower Hudson was Dutch country, with Washington Irving country in Tarrytown and ancient estates like now restored Philipsburg Manor. In the late 19th Century, the ridges east of the Lower Hudson were first the site of great estates of New York's very rich and then became high-income suburbs: colonial-style Bedford, woodsy Chappaqua, John Cheever's Ossining. And in the mid-20th Century, these hills became home to some of America's leading corporations. *Reader's Digest* had built its colonial-style campus north of Pleasantville as early as the 1930s; General Foods moved to the north side of White Plains in the 1950s; soon after, not far from the Cross-Westchester Expressway, IBM, Pepsico, and Texaco built headquarters. Yet as woods have grown over what used to be farmland, this country has also become wilder: overpopulating deer have been eating gardens in northern Westchester and in May 1997 a black bear was captured running loose in White Plains.

The 19th Congressional District of New York covers much of the lower Hudson. It reaches south to take in part of White Plains and the corporate territory nearby, and includes northern Westchester County—now, for all its rural look, with almost as many people as the population-losing suburbs nearer New York City. The 19th runs north across towns filling up with middle-income public and corporate employees seeking reasonably priced housing in safe areas, up through Putnam County to Dutchess County and the old city of Poughkeepsie on the Hudson and the valleys of Millbrook and Amenia and the Innisfree gardens. It crosses the Hudson where the rebels' chain did, by West Point and the Storm King Highway, and runs inland in Orange County. IBM, with its headquarters in Armonk, a research center in Yorktown Heights, and key operations in Wappingers Falls, has been a major area employer, and its longtime policy of lifetime employment was a mainstay here; IBM's big layoffs in the mid-1990s came as an unnerving shock. Politically, sentiments here run counter to what might be expected. The older communities, with their well-educated and liberally inclined residents, have been historically Republican but now lean more to the Democrats. The newer communities, with upwardly striving people often disgusted by the crime and cultural disorder of New York City, may be filled with ancestral Democrats but are trending Republican.

The congresswoman from this district is Sue Kelly, a Republican elected in 1994. Kelly is not a Hudson Valley aristocrat but the daughter of a Lima, Ohio, doctor. She met her husband while she was a botany researcher at Harvard; they raised their family in Katonah, where she volunteered in many organizations, worked as a patient advocate, rape crisis counselor and educator, and sang in a church choir. She had a business renovating buildings and owned and ran a florist shop. She also had political experience as campaign manager for Assemblyman Jon Fossel in the 1970s. In March 1994, Congressman Hamilton Fish, a Hudson County aristocrat, son of another Congressman Hamilton Fish and descendant of Ulysses S. Grant's Secretary of State Hamilton Fish, decided to retire, and Kelly decided to use the $150,000 she had saved to buy a new business to help finance a campaign for Congress instead.

It was a crowded field, in which Kelly emerged as the only candidate who was both for lower taxes and "huge" budget cuts, and pro-choice on abortion. Her chief opponent in the primary was Joseph DioGuardi, elected in 1984 and 1986 in the Westchester district to the south and defeated there by Nita Lowey in 1988 and 1992. He said Kelly wasn't a real Republican, but he had to dodge charges of district-shopping. Kelly won with 23% to DioGuardi's 20%, with two other candidates at 19% and 18%. The Democratic nominee was Hamilton Fish, Jr., son of the retiring congressman but as publisher of the leftish and anti-Israel *The Nation*, with quite different politics; he was known as Hamilton Fish III until the death of his grandfather, Franklin

Roosevelt's least favorite congressman, in January 1991 at age 102. Kelly campaigned in her "Kellyvan," stressed her involvement in business and community life and insisted that "government should be both smaller and smarter." Fish talked of his work on Human Rights Watch and his support of healthcare reform and opposition to capital punishment. DioGuardi continued running as the nominee of the Conservative and Right-to-Life parties, and lobbed bitter criticisms at Kelly. This was expected to be a close race; but with good margins in the northern counties Kelly won 52%–37%, with 10% for DioGuardi. It helped perhaps that this district includes Peekskill and Garrison, the home bases of Governor George Pataki.

In the House Kelly supported the entire Contract With America, which brought her some criticism from local environmentalists, and voted to repeal the assault weapons ban, which enraged gun control advocates. But she also irritated many conservatives by being one of the few Republicans to vote against the "partial-birth" abortion ban. One of those outraged was DioGuardi, who never closed his 1994 campaign office; even a plea from Speaker Newt Gingrich not to oppose Kelly did not change DioGuardi's mind. DioGuardi challenged Kelly again in the 1996 Republican primary. He compared Kelly, who legally avoided tax payments in the early 1990s, with convicted tax evader Leona Helmsley. Congressmen Chris Smith of New Jersey and Robert Dornan of California, strong opponents of abortion, came to the district and backed DioGuardi, for which they were disciplined (by being excluded from foreign trips) by Gingrich. Kelly won the primary, but by a narrow 53%–42%. DioGuardi kept running as the Conservative candidate, even as Democrat Richard Klein assailed Kelly for supporting Gingrich and voting against gun control. Kelly won with just a plurality over Klein, 46%–39%, with 12% for DioGuardi.

In January 1997 Kelly became chairwoman of the Small Business Subcommittee on Regulatory Reform and Paperwork Reduction and promised to look for "new and innovative ways to create more high-paying and secure jobs" in the 21st Century; she also wants to let families keep 100% of capital gains from selling their primary residences. She made news in March 1997 when, after the executive director of the National Coalition of Abortion Providers admitted he lied about the frequency of "partial-birth" abortions, she changed her mind and came out for the partial-birth abortion ban. "When you get into doing it on a healthy woman, with a healthy fetus, very late term, what are we talking about here? . . . Because I can't get a clear reading from either side of the fence, I changed my vote." But it's still possible she will have fervent opposition from the right as well as the left in 1998.

The People: Pop. 1990: 580,386; 30% rural; 11% age 65+; 86% White; 7% Black; 2% Asian; 5% Hispanic origin. Households: 64% married couple families; 31% married couple fams. w. children; 57% college educ.; median household income: $50,239; per capita income: $22,458; median gross rent: $653; median house value: $198,300.

1996 Presidential Vote

Clinton (D)	116,697	(48%)
Dole (R)	98,597	(41%)
Perot (I)	20,803	(9%)
Other	5,089	(2%)

1992 Presidential Vote

Bush (R)	109,965	(42%)
Clinton (D)	104,949	(40%)
Perot (I)	45,088	(17%)

Rep. Sue W. Kelly (R)

Elected 1994; b. Sept. 26, 1936, Lima, OH; home, Katonah; Denison U., B.A. 1958, Sarah Lawrence Col., M.A. 1985; Presbyterian; married (Edward).

Career: Owner/Mgr., Kelly & Assoc. bldg. rehab., 1960–present; Researcher, Harvard, 1958–60; Owner/Mgr., Kelly Florist, 1980–83; Prof., Sarah Lawrence Col., 1988–91.

DC Office: 1222 LHOB 20515, 202-225-5441; Fax: 202-225-3289; e-mail: dearsue@hr.house.gov.

District Offices: Fishkill, 914-897-5200; Mt. Kisco, 914-241-6340.

Committees: *Banking & Financial Services* (18th of 30 R): Financial Institutions & Consumer Credit; Housing & Community Opportunity. *Small Business* (8th of 19 R): Regulatory Reform & Paperwork Reduction (Chmn.). *Transportation & Infrastructure* (20th of 40 R): Surface Transportation; Water Resources & Environment.

Group Ratings

	ADA	ACLU	AFS	LCV	CFA	CON	NFIB	COC	ACU	NTLC	CHC
1996	10	6	17	31	62	38	92	88	70	90	60
1995	30	—	—	13	54	56	—	92	64	—	—

National Journal Ratings

	1995 LIB — 1995 CONS			1996 LIB — 1996 CONS		
Economic	44%	—	53%	42%	—	56%
Social	62%	—	38%	57%	—	42%
Foreign	0%	—	85%	30%	—	65%

Key Votes of the 104th Congress

1. Reduce Medicare Growth $	Y	5. Flag Amendment	Y	9. Cuban Embargo	Y
2. Ovrd. Product Liab. Veto	Y	6. Drop EPA Limits	Y	10. Bar Bosnia Troop $	Y
3. Increase Min. Wage	Y	7. Repeal Assault-Weap. Ban	Y	11. Cut Anti-Missile Defense	N
4. Welfare Reform	Y	8. Ovrd. Part. Birth Veto	N	12. Bar U.N. Uniforms	Y

Election Results

1996 general	Sue W. Kelly (R-FR)	102,142	(46%)	($906,904)
	Richard S. Klein (D-L)	86,926	(39%)	($630,471)
	Joseph J. DioGuardi (C-RTL)	27,424	(12%)	
	Others	4,104	(2%)	
1996 primary	Sue W. Kelly (R)	11,693	(53%)	
	Joseph J. DioGuardi (R)	9,245	(42%)	
	Jim Russell (R)	1,198	(5%)	
1994 general	Sue W. Kelly (R)	100,173	(52%)	($570,821)
	Hamilton Fish, Jr. (D)	70,696	(37%)	($566,601)
	Joseph J. DioGuardi (C-RTL)	19,761	(10%)	($278,490)

TWENTIETH DISTRICT

From Sunnyside, the whimsical house that Washington Irving built in Tarrytown near the country he immortalized as Sleepy Hollow, you can see across the waters of the Tappan Zee, the widest point of the Hudson, and get a sense of how the land looked when first settled by Dutchmen. All around is Irving country—the old towns of Tarrytown, Irvington, Dobbs Ferry and Hastings-on-Hudson, now comfortably affluent suburbs. On the other side of the Tappan Zee is Rockland County, a stretch of suburbs between the Hudson and the Ramapos, the first Appalachian chain west of New York. First settled by Dutchmen, Rockland then was studded by little towns that grew up as if 1,000 miles from Gotham, but have thrived on the actual proximity: the town of Nyack here was the home of actress Helen Hayes; and James A. Farley, Franklin Roosevelt's chief political major domo and Democratic National Committee chairman, was from Stony Point just below the Hudson Highlands.

The 20th Congressional District of New York spans the Tappan Zee, connecting most of the Irving suburbs with Rockland County and stepping over the Ramapos 120 miles inland to the Pennsylvania border. Past the Ramapos is most of Orange County, New York's second-fastest-growing county in the 1980s, where old villages between mountains and farms on the nation's biggest deposit of muck soil outside the Everglades have been flanked with new modest-income subdivisions. Farther out, past the Shawangunk Mountains, is Sullivan County and the Catskills Borscht Belt district, a Jewish resort area with huge kosher hotels since the late 19th Century. Politically, this area has been trending Republican, as old Upstate-minded residents are joined by newcomers fleeing the city.

The 20th's congressman, Republican Benjamin Gilman, is chairman of the International Relations Committee. He grew up in Middletown; he traveled with his father to Nazi Germany in 1933, at 10, and remembers Hitler's storm troopers. After service in World War II, he became a lawyer, working for the state and bringing *habeas corpus* cases for mental hospital patients. In 1966 he was elected to the Assembly, and in 1972 to the U.S. House, which makes him the sixth ranking Republican in seniority today. Gilman is moderate on economics and cultural issues, but more conservative on foreign policy; he is pleasant and ordinarily arouses little animosity. In the 1970s he worked, often with East German lawyer Wolfgang Vogel, to arrange spy swaps. He visited Buenos Aires newspaper editor Jacobo Timmerman in jail in Argentina and helped secure his release; he championed the human rights of Pentecostals, Ukrainians, Poles and Jews in the Soviet empire. He has long been a supporter of Israel, and he strongly backed the Gulf war resolution.

Gilman became ranking Republican on International Relations in 1993, a position of potential influence since he could help bestow or withhold the "bipartisan" label on administration foreign policy. Despite his pleasant demeanor, he often withheld. He faulted Bill Clinton for not expanding NATO fast enough, for favoring Russia over the other former Soviet republics, and for not following through on threats to lift the Bosnian arms embargo and take action against the Bosnian Serbs. He opposed changing the mission of U.S. troops in Somalia, and he blocked the merger of the State Department counterterrorism office with the anti-drug unit just after the World Trade Center bombing. He wanted to delay full recognition of Vietnam pending a full accounting of American POWs. As he summed it up after the November 1994 election, "Instead of a strong, steady signal on foreign policy coming from Washington, regrettably the world has heard a series of wavering notes sounded by an uncertain trumpet, leaving our allies concerned and our adversaries confused." After the 1994 election, as chairman he seemed more moderate and bipartisan than his Senate counterpart, Jesse Helms. Some conservatives even wanted to pass over Gilman for someone else, but that was never in the cards. But he still dissented from Clinton policies in the Middle East and on North Korea and was critical of the procedure used in Bosnia. He sponsored the Contract With America provisions on foreign policy, including the ban on U.S. troops serving under United Nations commanders. But he took care to caution freshman conservatives—and Senate foreign-policy barons Jesse Helms and Mitch McConnell—that foreign aid serves good American purposes and to warn that "one-half of the Congress has less than four years of institutional memory and little experience in foreign affairs." His priorities continue to be peace in northern Ireland, democracy in Haiti and a reassessment of U.S. policy in Bosnia. Gilman also ranks second on the Government Reform and Oversight Committee, and was an early critic of John Huang's fundraising for the 1996 Clinton-Gore campaign. For a dozen years he was ranking Republican on the Select Committee on

Narcotics, until junior Republicans in 1993 launched a drive to eliminate four select committees, and in 1997 he opposed the recertification of Mexico as a drug-fighting ally, saying the administration's international narcotics control strategy is "in shambles."

After more than 20 years, Gilman continues to work his district hard, often spending Saturdays riding around in his mobile home-office. In March 1995 he marched next to Sinn Fein leader Gerry Adams in the St. Patrick's Day parade in Pearl River, the third largest St. Pat's parade in the world. He won the district fairly easily in 1972 against ultra-liberal John Dow, and he has had only one difficult reelection race since, in 1982 after redistricting, when he faced Republican-turned-Democrat Peter Peyser and won 53%–42%. He won in 1994 by 67%–29% and in 1996 by the lesser margin of 57%–38%.

The People: Pop. 1990: 580,025; 23% rural; 11% age 65+; 83% White; 8% Black; 3% Asian; 6% Hispanic origin. Households: 65% married couple families; 32% married couple fams. w. children; 54% college educ.; median household income: $47,107; per capita income: $19,680; median gross rent: $659; median house value: $193,500.

1996 Presidential Vote

Clinton (D)	130,550	(54%)
Dole (R)	89,214	(37%)
Perot (I)	18,216	(8%)
Other	4,329	(2%)

1992 Presidential Vote

Clinton (D)	116,694	(45%)
Bush (R)	107,107	(41%)
Perot (I)	37,014	(14%)

Rep. Benjamin A. Gilman (R)

Elected 1972; b. Dec. 6, 1922, Poughkeepsie; home, Middletown; U. of PA, B.S. 1946, NY Law Schl., LL.B. 1950; Jewish; married (Georgia).

Career: Army Air Corps, 1942–45 (WWII); Practicing atty., 1950–72; NY Asst. Atty. Gen., 1953–55; Atty., NY Temporary Comm. on the Courts; NY Assembly, 1966–72.

DC Office: 2449 RHOB 20515, 202-225-3776; Fax: 202-225-2541.

District Offices: Hastings-on-Hudson, 914-478-5550; Middletown, 914-343-6666; Monsey, 914-357-9000.

Committees: *Government Reform & Oversight* (2nd of 24 R): Human Resources; Postal Service. *International Relations* (Chmn. of 26 R).

Group Ratings

	ADA	ACLU	AFS	LCV	CFA	CON	NFIB	COC	ACU	NTLC	CHC
1996	35	19	33	46	62	2	81	63	45	83	53
1995	30	—	—	38	69	56	—	79	60	—	—

National Journal Ratings

	1995 LIB		1995 CONS	1996 LIB		1996 CONS
Economic	49%	—	49%	55%	—	45%
Social	65%	—	33%	70%	—	29%
Foreign	0%	—	85%	21%	—	72%

Key Votes of the 104th Congress

1. Reduce Medicare Growth $	Y	5. Flag Amendment	Y	9. Cuban Embargo	Y
2. Ovrd. Product Liab. Veto	N	6. Drop EPA Limits	Y	10. Bar Bosnia Troop $	Y
3. Increase Min. Wage	Y	7. Repeal Assault-Weap. Ban	Y	11. Cut Anti-Missile Defense	N
4. Welfare Reform	Y	8. Ovrd. Part. Birth Veto	N	12. Bar U.N. Uniforms	Y

Election Results

1996 general	Benjamin A. Gilman (R)	122,479	(57%)	($682,959)
	Yash P. Aggarwal (D-L)	80,761	(38%)	($210,670)
	Others	11,372	(5%)	
1996 primary	Benjamin A. Gilman (R)	unopposed		
1994 general	Benjamin A. Gilman (R)	120,334	(67%)	($547,731)
	Gregory B. Julian (D)	52,345	(29%)	($35,766)
	Others	5,612	(3%)	

TWENTY-FIRST DISTRICT

Albany, as readers of its novelist laureate William Kennedy know, is within living memory an antique city. Its solid rowhouses show its 19th Century prosperity; its once teeming lumberyards and railroad car shops, old restaurants and hotels, have the patina of age and the accumulated grime of decades of coal smoke burned during six-month-long winters. Its history is traceable to 1624, when the Dutch built Fort Orange on the banks of the Hudson so seagoing ships could dock at the edge of the great gloomy forests near the confluence of the Hudson and the Mohawk—the natural crossroads of Upstate New York even before the building of the Erie Canal and the New York Central Railroad. This was one of America's early industrial centers. Troy, a few miles upriver, was a steel town rivaling Pittsburgh in the 1840s, and later the leading producer of detachable collars; Cohoes, at the junction of the Hudson and the Mohawk, became a leading textile producer; Schenectady, a few miles up the Mohawk, was the site of Charles Steinmetz's fabled General Electric laboratories and has been a big GE town ever since. Albany was one of America's biggest lumber towns as well as the state capital.

Albany continues to have one of the nation's most famed Democratic political machines, dating back to 1921, when Daniel O'Connell and his brothers and local aristocrat Edwin Corning took control of City Hall. They never really relinquished it: Daniel O'Connell died in 1977 at age 91, still boss after 56 years, and his early partner's son, Erastus Corning II, was mayor from 1942 until his death in 1983. The machine was sustained by legions of city and county employees, by a certain creativity when it came to counting votes, and by the raffish atmosphere that was found in the speakeasies of so many cities during Prohibition and lingered in Albany for decades after. Curiously, the machine made possible the transformation of antique Albany into the shiny metropolis it is today. Mayor Corning provided financing for Nelson Rockefeller's monumental South Mall, expressways were built, the old Union Station was spruced up, and yuppies began buying and renovating old townhouses. These days, the Albany machine is battered in some elections and can't always control the suburbs as it once could Albany; but it clings to power in the H.H. Richardson City Hall facing the gaudy State House.

The 21st Congressional District includes all of Albany and Schenectady Counties, plus Troy on the Hudson's east bank, and the depressed factory town of Amsterdam on the Mohawk. More than half its votes are cast in Albany County, and it is a solidly Democratic district—and a solid Democratic machine district, though it may be in the throes of change.

The congressman from the 21st District is Michael McNulty, a Democrat first elected in 1988. McNulty's roots in Albany politics go back to his grandfather, who served as Albany County sheriff, as did his father, who was also a mayor. Michael McNulty was first elected to office in 1969, at 22, and served 13 years as town supervisor and mayor in the industrial suburb of Green Island; he was elected to the Assembly in 1982, at 35. The opening to Congress came without much warning. In 1988, four days after the July filing deadline and on the last day for withdrawal, 30-year incumbent Democrat Samuel Stratton announced he was retiring for health reasons, giving the Democratic machine a chance to name a replacement, which turned out to be McNulty. Serving in Congress was a fulfillment of his family's and his own ambition. McNulty won the 1988 general election by 62%–38% against a venture capital specialist who attacked him for avoiding the issues and for having been chosen by party bosses rather than primary voters. He has not had trouble in the general election since.

McNulty is hard-working, serious, abstemious, pleasant, and a conscientious campaigner. For a New York Democrat, his voting record is rather moderate on foreign and cultural issues; he is one of a handful of New York Democrats endorsed by the Conservative, not the Liberal, Party. He is pro-life on abortion and for the amendment allowing penalties for desecration of the flag. He had qualms about the Clinton Administration's healthcare and welfare plans. Still, given the strong performance of Democratic presidential candidates in his district, it was a bit surprising that he was the northern Democrat with the highest support for the Contract With America—voting for everything except welfare reform and the tax cut. But the Democrats' loss of control also hurt McNulty. He can no longer preside in the speaker's chair, where he performed ably—and where he announced the on-the-floor engagement of New York Republicans Bill Paxon and Susan Molinari. And, when the number of Democrats on Ways and Means was cut, McNulty temporarily lost the seat there he had won in 1993; in 1996 he got it back when Republicans increased the number of seats to accommodate party-switchers.

In 1996 McNulty suddenly faced a serious primary challenge. Lee Wasserman, the New York City-born head of Environmental Advocates, a statewide lobbying firm, accused McNulty of "voting for Newt Gingrich's extreme agenda more than any other northern Democrat." He opposed McNulty on abortion and environmental issues. McNulty was thrown on the defensive after running an ad saying: "What does Lee Wasserman have in common with us? Absolutely nothing." Critics charged that this was anti-Semitic; McNulty said that was "absurd," but pulled the ad nonetheless. He won but by only 57%–43%—not an overwhelming margin for an incumbent in a primary. Wasserman was still on the ballot in the general election as the Liberal nominee; McNulty won 66%–27%, with 7% for Wasserman.

That puts McNulty in an uncomfortable position. In a less-Democratic district, he might become a party-switcher, but his own family history and the district's partisan leanings make that unlikely. But as a Democrat he could face another serious primary challenge, with the Albany machine not what it used to be, unless he veers noticeably to the left.

The People: Pop. 1990: 580,320; 15% rural; 15% age 65+; 90% White; 6% Black; 2% Asian; 2% Hispanic origin. Households: 50% married couple families; 22% married couple fams. w. children; 48% college educ.; median household income: $31,489; per capita income: $15,304; median gross rent: $453; median house value: $98,800.

1996 Presidential Vote			**1992 Presidential Vote**		
Clinton (D)	151,701	(57%)	Clinton (D)	140,251	(48%)
Dole (R)	79,880	(30%)	Bush (R)	99,094	(34%)
Perot (I)	26,840	(10%)	Perot (I)	51,086	(17%)
Other	5,624	(2%)			

Rep. Michael R. McNulty (D)

Elected 1988; b. Sept. 16, 1947, Troy; home, Green Island; Holy Cross Col., B.A. 1969; Catholic; married (Nancy Ann).

Career: Green Island Supervisor, 1969–77; Green Island Mayor, 1977–83; NY Assembly, 1982–88.

DC Office: 2161 RHOB 20515, 202-225-5076; Fax: 202-225-5077; e-mail: mmcnulty@hr.house.gov.

District Offices: Albany, 518-465-0700; Amsterdam, 518-843-3400; Schenectady, 518-374-4547; Troy, 518-271-0822.

Committees: *Ways & Means* (12th of 16 D): Oversight; Trade.

Group Ratings

	ADA	ACLU	AFS	LCV	CFA	CON	NFIB	COC	ACU	NTLC	CHC
1996	60	40	100	69	100	5	58	33	22	18	40
1995	60	—	—	63	54	95	—	52	44	—	—

National Journal Ratings

	1995 LIB — 1995 CONS	1996 LIB — 1996 CONS
Economic	59% — 41%	72% — 28%
Social	54% — 45%	63% — 35%
Foreign	59% — 41%	59% — 40%

Key Votes of the 104th Congress

1. Reduce Medicare Growth $	N	5. Flag Amendment	Y	9. Cuban Embargo	Y
2. Ovrd. Product Liab. Veto	Y	6. Drop EPA Limits	Y	10. Bar Bosnia Troop $	N
3. Increase Min. Wage	Y	7. Repeal Assault-Weap. Ban	N	11. Cut Anti-Missile Defense	Y
4. Welfare Reform	N	8. Ovrd. Part. Birth Veto	Y	12. Bar U.N. Uniforms	Y

Election Results

1996 general	Michael R. McNulty (D-C-I)	158,491	(66%)	($628,000)
	Nancy Norman (R-FR)	64,471	(27%)	($6,953)
	Lee H. Wasserman (L)	16,794	(7%)	($392,588)
1996 primary	Michael R. McNulty (D)	23,842	(57%)	
	Lee H. Wasserman (D)	17,957	(43%)	
1994 general	Michael R. McNulty (D-C)	147,804	(67%)	($217,642)
	Joseph A. Gomez (R)	68,745	(31%)	($25,773)
	Others	4,125	(2%)	

TWENTY-SECOND DISTRICT

The Hudson River, an arm of the ocean and an avenue of commerce in colonial days, an inspiration to artists, is still one of America's great sights, though it is no longer central, as it was not so long ago, in the nation's consciousness and politics. The classic mansions overlooking the River, like Clermont, whose builder Robert Livingston financed Robert Fulton's first steamboat, and Montgomery Place, built by Janet Livingston Montgomery, the widow of the general who captured Quebec in 1775, are reminders of the cool serenity of the 18th Century mind and the daring nature of its spirit. Robert Livingston administered the first oath of office to George Washington in 1789 and helped negotiate the Louisiana Purchase in 1803. It was on a visit to his lands in the 1790s that James Madison and Aaron Burr welded the Virginia-New York alliance that set the course of American political history. The Hudson was also a center of America during the Romance Era: from Frederick Church's Moorish mansion, Olana, you can see the still unspoiled river landscape that inspired his art and that of others of the Hudson River school of painters.

The Hudson gave birth to our passionate party politics: nearby is Kinderhook, home of Martin Van Buren, the innkeeper's son who in alliance with Andrew Jackson invented the torchlight parade, the national party convention and, some argue, the Democratic Party itself. Later in the 19th Century, the Hudson was lined with the palaces of the nation's first great millionaires and the comfortable country houses of New York's gentry. In one of the latter, Springwood in Hyde Park, Franklin Roosevelt was born and lived; this politician, who expanded government at home and was the victorious commander-in-chief of American military forces throughout the world, was most comfortable looking out over his sloping lawn down to the river on which he remembered iceboating during the winters of the 1880s.

The 22d Congressional District of New York includes much of the Hudson Valley, the grand river south of Albany and the smaller river, freshly fed by the Adirondacks, to the north. After redistricting for 1992, it extends even further north to include most of Essex County and Lake Placid. Much of the district, just outside the old manufacturing city of Troy and the still grand 19th Century racing center Saratoga Springs, is essentially suburban Albany; Saratoga County has been one of the fastest-growing parts of New York state. Despite Van Buren and Roosevelt, this has been a Republican area since the birth of the Republican Party; indeed, Roosevelt never carried his home territory except when he ran for state Senate in 1910.

The congressman from the 22d, Gerald Solomon, is a Republican first elected in 1978. He grew up and was educated in Upstate New York, served in the Marine Corps, was an insurance agent in Glens Falls. He was elected Queensbury township supervisor in 1966, New York Assemblyman in 1972; now he is chairman of the House Rules Committee. Solomon is a strong partisan and an aggressive conservative, but not a free-market purist: in the 103d Congress he submitted a budget plan calling for higher taxes on incomes over $200,000, and he staunchly opposed the North American Free Trade Agreement and favored an end to China's most favored nation trade status. Tapped by then-Minority Leader Robert Michel as ranking Republican on the Rules Committee from 1991–94, he denounced the Democrats' plan to give floor votes to five representatives of territories and the District of Columbia; Democrats partially retreated, and the plan was summarily repealed in 1995 when Republicans took control. He has been sponsor of the line-item veto, which was rejected narrowly in 1994 when Democrats were in control, then passed in 1995; in April 1997 a federal court found it unconstitutional and the Supreme Court heard oral arguments on the case in late May 1997.

Solomon, who left college and enlisted in the Marine Corps when the Korean war began, fought to maintain the Selective Service System and sponsored several laws aimed at young people who flout their obligations: the Solomon Amendment in the early 1980s cut off college aid for young men who had not registered for the draft; a 1990 amendment cut off highway funding for states that don't suspend drug offenders' driver's licenses; a 1994 amendment prohibited federal grants to colleges that bar military recruiters. He is chief sponsor of the amendment to allow penalties for those who burn the flag. Solomon can be generous to those who do right. As ranking Republican on Veterans' Affairs in the 1980s, he helped pass the 1984 G.I. Bill of Rights, which creatively increased veterans' benefits and helped attract quality recruits to the volunteer military that performed so well in the Gulf.

When Robert Michel announced his retirement in October 1993, Solomon quickly stepped forward and ran for Republican leader. But he dropped his bid 10 days later, saying that Newt Gingrich had the votes. They seem to bear each other no ill will: Gingrich made no move to stop Solomon from becoming chairman of Rules, evidently prizing his aggressiveness, and Solomon has stepped forward to defend Gingrich when he has been under attack. When Long Island's Peter King wrote in March 1997 that Gingrich was "road kill on the highway of American politics," Solomon said that King "doesn't have the credibility to criticize a Speaker who has presided over one of the largest conservative shifts in American public policy in decades." Solomon's temper was also on display when Rhode Island Congressman Patrick Kennedy lectured the House on his family's knowledge of the dangers of assault weapons. "When he stands up and questions the integrity of those of us who have this bill on the floor, the gentleman ought to be a little more careful. And let me tell you why: because my wife lives alone five days a week in a rural area in upstate New York. She has a right to defend herself when I'm not there, son. And don't you ever forget it."

As Rules chairman, Solomon is involved in every serious piece of legislation. After criticizing Democrats for years over their increased number of closed rules and for their "king of the hill" procedure (in which the final majority vote of several alternatives prevails), he found himself sometimes under attack on similar grounds. The fact is that the ability to control the flow of business and determine which alternatives will be brought up for a vote are an essential part—the heart, really—of a majority party's control in the House. Solomon was also criticized by black members for hanging a portrait of former Rules Chairman Howard Smith, a Virginia segregationist and a Democrat (he later had it removed). He would have done better to hang Clarence Brown of Ohio, ranking Republican in Smith's day, and a supporter of civil rights.

Solomon has been reelected every two years by wide margins. In 1996 he was opposed in the general by an actor and dairy farmer who took umbrage at his comments about Kennedy; Solomon won 60%–40%.

The People: Pop. 1990: 580,522; 67% rural; 13% age 65+; 96% White; 2% Black; 1% Asian; 2% Hispanic origin. Households: 62% married couple families; 30% married couple fams. w. children; 46% college educ.; median household income: $33,306; per capita income: $14,646; median gross rent: $465; median house value: $99,600.

1996 Presidential Vote

Clinton (D)	117,831	(45%)
Dole (R)	105,106	(40%)
Perot (I)	34,415	(13%)
Other	5,119	(2%)

1992 Presidential Vote

Bush (R)	116,283	(41%)
Clinton (D)	99,984	(36%)
Perot (I)	62,533	(22%)

Rep. Gerald B. H. Solomon (R)

Elected 1978; b. Aug. 14, 1930, Okeechobee, FL; home, Queensbury; Siena Col., 1948–49, St. Lawrence U., 1953–54; Presbyterian; married (Freda).

Career: Marine Corps, 1951–52; Founding partner & Assoc., Glens Falls Insurance Co., 1964–78; Queensbury Town Supervisor, 1966–77; NY Assembly, 1972–78.

DC Office: 2206 RHOB 20515, 202-225-5614; Fax: 202-225-6234.

District Offices: Glens Falls, 518-792-3031; Hudson, 518-828-0181; Saratoga Springs, 518-587-9800.

Committees: *Rules* (Chmn. of 9 R): Legislative & Budget Process; Rules & Organization of the House.

Group Ratings

	ADA	ACLU	AFS	LCV	CFA	CON	NFIB	COC	ACU	NTLC	CHC
1996	5	7	25	31	8	42	92	81	95	100	100
1995	0	—	—	6	8	56	—	96	96	—	—

National Journal Ratings

	1995 LIB — 1995 CONS			1996 LIB — 1996 CONS		
Economic	40%	—	59%	24%	—	73%
Social	0%	—	79%	0%	—	90%
Foreign	0%	—	85%	0%	—	79%

Key Votes of the 104th Congress

1. Reduce Medicare Growth $	Y	5. Flag Amendment	Y	9. Cuban Embargo	Y
2. Ovrd. Product Liab. Veto	Y	6. Drop EPA Limits	N	10. Bar Bosnia Troop $	Y
3. Increase Min. Wage	Y	7. Repeal Assault-Weap. Ban	Y	11. Cut Anti-Missile Defense	N
4. Welfare Reform	Y	8. Ovrd. Part. Birth Veto	Y	12. Bar U.N. Uniforms	Y

Election Results

1996 general	Gerald B. H. Solomon (R-C-RTL-FR)	144,125	(60%)	($640,080)
	Steve James (D)	94,192	(40%)	($273,887)
1996 primary	Gerald B. H. Solomon (R)	unopposed		
1994 general	Gerald B. H. Solomon (R-C-RTL)	157,717	(73%)	($444,067)
	L. Robert Lawrence Jr. (D)	57,064	(27%)	($17,363)

TWENTY-THIRD DISTRICT

One of the first American frontiers was the Mohawk River Valley of Upstate New York, and it remained static for 150 years. From the establishment of Fort Orange in 1624 in what now is Albany until the Revolutionary War, white settlers did not dare move west along the Mohawk. The British used their Iroquois allies as a buffer against the French and in return kept New England Yankees from moving westward. Only after the French were driven from the colonies in 1759 did the pressures for westward settlement prevail; the British tried to keep their word to the Indians, but once the Revolutionary War started, the Iroquois dominion ended.

This is the background of *Drums Along the Mohawk* and of James Fenimore Cooper's *Leatherstocking Tales*. But there is little in these rolling hills today to evoke the bloody violence whose conclusion made possible the digging of the Erie Canal and the building of the New York Central Railroad. As migration slowed and trade increased, the Mohawk Valley became one of the nation's early industrial centers. The little Oneida County hamlets of Utica and Rome, where the canal builders had to dig through the route's highest ground, became sizable factory towns. Even the utopian Oneida Community, with its believers in plural marriage and communal ownership, kept open a stainless steel factory. First settled by New England Yankees, these towns attracted a new wave of immigration from the Atlantic coast in the early 20th Century. Today they are the most heavily Italian and Polish-American communities between Albany and Buffalo; politically, they are usually marginally Republican, but Bill Clinton won here in 1996, 46%–39%.

The 23d Congressional District, in the Mohawk Valley, is centered on Utica and Rome in Oneida County and includes a row of more sparsely settled counties to the south. Here the hilly land has an early 19th Century cast, in places like Cooperstown, certainly one of the loveliest and best-preserved small towns in America, and Pindars Corners, the crossroads where Senator Daniel Patrick Moynihan has a farm and a 19th Century schoolhouse office. Madison County here was one of the hotbeds of abolitionism in the 1850s. But this is also an area that feels bypassed by more recent economic growth and is in need of government assistance and sustenance.

The congressman from the 23d is Sherwood Boehlert, a Republican elected in 1982. He grew up and went to college in Utica, served in the Army, worked briefly in industry. For 15 years he worked for his two predecessors in Congress, then was elected Oneida County executive in 1978 and won the House seat in 1982. He has worked in government as much as politics, and does not share the free market economists' disdain for its works. He is a Republican partisan, but can dissent from much of the Republican program. He signed the Contract With America, but voted against more of it than any other Republican but Connie Morella of Maryland. Some of Boehlert's votes have a local angle: he supports dairy subsidies (the 23d is part of New York City's milkshed), he favors baseball's antitrust exemption (Cooperstown is where baseball was supposedly invented in 1839 and Boehlert is part owner of a minor league team); he sponsored Pledge of Allegiance Day (the Pledge was written by Francis Bellamy in Rome in 1892). His great success in the Democratic 103d Congress was leading the fight against the superconducting supercollider, a giant atom smasher that was to be built in Texas; he said it was "simply not affordable science," and in October 1993 the House voted 280–150 to kill it.

Boehlert's ties to Newt Gingrich go back a long way—he gave Gingrich crucial support when he was elected whip by two votes in March 1989—and Gingrich, as speaker, has stayed close to him. In 1995 he opposed the Republicans' EPA riders and attempts to limit wetlands regulations. After Boehlert blocked those efforts, which were led by Majority Whip Tom DeLay, Gingrich asked him to work with deregulatory Republicans to find middle ground on environmental issues. "If you didn't have me, you'd have to invent me," Boehlert said he told Gingrich. "You need someone up front on environmental issues, because quite frankly you're getting clobbered in the court of public opinion." But in mid-1997 the uneasy truce broke down; after Boehlert rallied votes to water down an attempt by western Republicans to exempt flood control projects from the Endangered Species Act, they complained bitterly to Gingrich that Boehlert has too much influence over Republican environmental policy. Boehlert has voted contrary to most Republicans on other issues. He was one of three Republicans to vote for the Clinton economic stimulus package in March 1993; he was one of the last undecideds on the North American Free Trade Agreement, ultimately voting yes; he voted for the Brady bill; he was an early advocate of the 1996 minimum wage increase; he opposed the "partial-birth" abortion ban. Yet with a 10-vote majority, Gingrich has little choice but to include Republicans like Boehlert if he is to assemble a governing majority; he showed his continuing loyalty in 1997 by giving Boehlert a seat on the Intelligence Committee.

Boehlert has been reelected easily by very large margins. He had primary opposition from two Republicans in 1996, but took 65% in the three-way race; he won the general 64%–26%.

The People: Pop. 1990: 580,259; 55% rural; 15% age 65+; 95% White; 3% Black; 1% Asian; 2% Hispanic origin. Households: 58% married couple families; 27% married couple fams. w. children; 40% college educ.; median household income: $26,155; per capita income: $11,792; median gross rent: $366; median house value: $67,800.

1996 Presidential Vote

Clinton (D)	102,854	(46%)
Dole (R)	88,120	(39%)
Perot (I)	29,172	(13%)
Other	3,686	(2%)

1992 Presidential Vote

Bush (R)	99,495	(40%)
Clinton (D)	92,554	(37%)
Perot (I)	55,887	(22%)

Rep. Sherwood Boehlert (R)

Elected 1982; b. Sept. 28, 1936, Utica; home, New Hartford; Utica Col., B.A. 1961; Catholic; married (Marianne).

Career: Army, 1956–58; P.R. Mgr., Wyandotte Chemicals Corp., 1961–64; A.A., U.S. Rep. Alexander Pirnie, 1964–72; A.A., U.S. Rep. Donald Mitchell, 1973–79; Oneida Cnty. Exec., 1978–82.

DC Office: 2246 RHOB 202-225-3665; Fax: 202-225-1891; e-mail: boehlert@hr.house.gov.

District Offices: Norwich, 607-336-7160; Oneonta, 607-432-5524; Utica, 315-793-8146.

Committees: *Transportation & Infrastructure* (4th of 40 R): Railroads; Water Resources & Environment (Chmn.). *Science* (2nd of 25 R): Basic Research. *Intelligence (Select)* (7th of 9 R): Technical & Tactical Intelligence.

Group Ratings

	ADA	ACLU	AFS	LCV	CFA	CON	NFIB	COC	ACU	NTLC	CHC
1996	50	27	42	69	62	63	62	69	50	68	33
1995	40	—	—	44	92	16	—	63	40	—	—

National Journal Ratings

	1995 LIB		1995 CONS	1996 LIB		1996 CONS
Economic	54%	—	45%	56%	—	43%
Social	65%	—	33%	68%	—	31%
Foreign	36%	—	59%	37%	—	63%

Key Votes of the 104th Congress

1. Reduce Medicare Growth $	Y	5. Flag Amendment	Y	9. Cuban Embargo	Y
2. Ovrd. Product Liab. Veto	Y	6. Drop EPA Limits	Y	10. Bar Bosnia Troop $	N
3. Increase Min. Wage	Y	7. Repeal Assault-Weap. Ban	N	11. Cut Anti-Missile Defense	N
4. Welfare Reform	Y	8. Ovrd. Part. Birth Veto	N	12. Bar U.N. Uniforms	N

Election Results

1996 general	Sherwood Boehlert (R-FR)	124,626	(64%)	($610,166)
	Bruce W. Hapanowicz (D)	50,436	(26%)	
	Thomas E. Loughlin Jr. (I)	10,835	(6%)	
	William Tapley (RTL)	7,790	(4%)	
1996 primary	Sherwood Boehlert (R)	15,115	(65%)	
	Francis A. Giroux (R)	5,824	(25%)	
	William Tapley (R)	2,206	(10%)	
1994 general	Sherwood Boehlert (R)	124,486	(71%)	($336,183)
	Charles W. Skeele Jr. (D)	40,786	(23%)	($12,774)
	Donald J. Thomas (RTL)	11,216	(6%)	

TWENTY-FOURTH DISTRICT

The North Country of Upstate New York, some early 19th Century visionaries thought, was the land of the future. Financier Gouverneur Morris, French slave trader James Leray, and Dutch silver speculator David Parish bought up thousands of acres between the Adirondacks and the St. Lawrence River and tried to unload them on farmers unaware of the shortness of the growing season and the unnavigability of the river. They left behind grand mansions, but their hopes for huge profits were frustrated when the Erie Canal turned the stream of settlement westward, and

Canadians built their new capital far north of the river and away from the Americans. But northern New York was not without its business successes: It was in Watertown in 1878 that 26-year-old Frank Woolworth put a sign over a table of odds and ends that read "Any Article 5 Cents," starting America's first retail chain and inventing the concept of discount stores.

More recently, the North Country has looked to government for help. The St. Lawrence Seaway proved too small for most ocean-going freighters and remains frozen three months of the year; the locks are slow and icebreakers would wreck the shoreline. The state government has built prisons in Ogdensburg and Cape Vincent, and private developers have built big malls in Watertown and Massena (attracting Canadians, as even New York has lower taxes than Ontario). But the biggest initiative has been the enlargement of Fort Drum, near Watertown, where despite the Army's preference for warm weather training sites, a 10,000-person light infantry division was stationed in 1985. The 24th Congressional District, covering most of the North Country, from Plattsburgh on Lake Champlain along the St. Lawrence Seaway and over the Adirondacks Forest Preserve to Watertown and Oswego on Lake Ontario, is geographically one of the largest districts in the East.

The congressman from the 24th is John McHugh, a Republican chosen almost without incident in 1992. McHugh has long been in government: he worked for the Watertown city manager in 1971, at 23; for eight years he was a staffer for state Senator Douglas Barclay; in 1984 he was elected to succeed Barclay in Albany. McHugh specialized in dairy issues (New York has long price-fixed dairy products to help farmers) and military bases—both part of the North Country's economic lifeblood. When incumbent David Martin announced his retirement in June 1992, just when the district lines were redrawn, McHugh ran, with plenty of financing plus Martin's endorsement. He won the Republican primary with 70%, then won the general 61%–24%. He has been reelected with more than 70% of the vote against token opposition.

McHugh combines a moderate, middle-of-the-House voting record with a concern about local economic needs, not surprising given his district's dependence on federal largess. In 1993 he got a seat on National Security and hired none other than Martin to monitor the Defense Base Closure and Realignment Commission. In that year's base closure round, McHugh found himself pitted in a fierce lobbying battle against his colleague to the south, Republican Sherwood Boehlert. Griffiss Air Force Base, a major employer in Boehlert's district, and Plattsburgh Air Force Base, in McHugh's, were competing for a similar mission. In the end, the commission voted to close both bases.

The 1994 Republican victory brought McHugh the chairmanship of the Government Reform and Oversight Subcommittee with jurisdiction over the Postal Service, a somewhat dubious honor since it gives him responsibility for one of Congress' perennial headaches. Then on National Security's Military Installations and Facilities Subcommittee he found himself siding with the tobacco industry against the Pentagon's plan to end discount pricing of cigarettes in military grocery stores. "These kinds of changes require congressional authorization and I'd be saying that whether it was tobacco or rosary beads," he told *The New York Times*. He is a member of the Tuesday Group and was elected Republican whip for the New York delegation; another mixed blessing perhaps, as New York Republicans are among the least party-line in the Gingrich House. In April 1997, he criticized the Republican leadership for being too cautious in the budget negotiations. "There doesn't seem to be any willingness to talk about areas of disagreement and that's the only way we're going to move ahead on balancing the budget," he told the Syracuse *Post-Standard*; a few weeks later congressional leaders and the White House announced a budget agreement.

The People: Pop. 1990: 580,376; 65% rural; 12% age 65+; 95% White; 2% Black; 1% Asian; 1% Amer. Indian; 2% Hispanic origin. Households: 60% married couple families; 31% married couple fams. w. children; 36% college educ.; median household income: $25,687; per capita income: $11,060; median gross rent: $368; median house value: $56,700.

1996 Presidential Vote			1992 Presidential Vote		
Clinton (D)	102,007	(49%)	Bush (R)	86,311	(38%)
Dole (R)	72,301	(35%)	Clinton (D)	85,078	(37%)
Perot (I)	30,047	(14%)	Perot (I)	54,537	(24%)

Rep. John M. McHugh (R)

Elected 1992; b. Sept. 29, 1948, Watertown; home, Pierrepont Manor; Syracuse U., B.A. 1970, S.U.N.Y., M.P.A. 1977; Catholic; separated.

Career: Confidential Asst., Watertown City Mgr., 1971–76; Research & Liaison Chief, NY Sen. Douglas Barclay, 1976–84; NY Senate, 1984–92.

DC Office: 2441 RHOB 20515, 202-225-4611; Fax: 202-226-0621.

District Offices: Watertown, 315-782-3150.

Committees: *Government Reform & Oversight* (9th of 24 R): National Security, International Affairs & Criminal Justice; Postal Service (Chmn.). *International Relations* (22nd of 26 R): Africa; Asia & the Pacific. *National Security* (12th of 30 R): Military Installations & Facilities; Military Research & Development.

Group Ratings

	ADA	ACLU	AFS	LCV	CFA	CON	NFIB	COC	ACU	NTLC	CHC
1996	10	19	42	38	31	26	84	81	79	90	86
1995	15	—	—	19	8	31	—	83	75	—	—

National Journal Ratings

	1995 LIB — 1995 CONS			1996 LIB — 1996 CONS		
Economic	47%	—	51%	52%	—	47%
Social	38%	—	60%	35%	—	62%
Foreign	0%	—	85%	29%	—	70%

Key Votes of the 104th Congress

1. Reduce Medicare Growth $	Y	5. Flag Amendment	Y	9. Cuban Embargo	Y
2. Ovrd. Product Liab. Veto	Y	6. Drop EPA Limits	N	10. Bar Bosnia Troop $	Y
3. Increase Min. Wage	Y	7. Repeal Assault-Weap. Ban	Y	11. Cut Anti-Missile Defense	N
4. Welfare Reform	Y	8. Ovrd. Part. Birth Veto	Y	12. Bar U.N. Uniforms	Y

Election Results

1996 general	John M. McHugh (R-C)	124,240	(71%)	($172,883)
	Donald Ravenscoft (D)	43,692	(25%)	
	Others	6,750	(4%)	
1996 primary	John M. McHugh (R)	unopposed		
1994 general	John M. McHugh (R-C)	124,645	(79%)	($53,187)
	Danny M. Francis (D)	34,032	(21%)	

TWENTY-FIFTH DISTRICT

Syracuse is a middle American city in the middle of Upstate New York, halfway between Albany and Buffalo on the Erie Canal and the old New York Central Railroad, for years the nation's major east-west transportation routes. Built on a swamp that was a salt spring, Syracuse is the home of many inventions: the dental chair, Stickley mission furniture, the drive-in bank teller, the foot measuring devices used in shoe stores. It was one of the first big manufacturers of typewriters and is the site of the New York State Fair. Its agricultural hinterland is rich with specialty crops like wine grapes, and its industrial jobs are mostly high-skill. Syracuse has spread out slowly across the countryside, but there is redevelopment of the Erie Canal waterfront where the city got its start.

The 25th Congressional District includes all of Syracuse and Onondaga County. It goes west to include part of Auburn, the home town of Governor, Senator and Secretary of State William Seward, and south to Cortland County and almost to Binghamton. Seward was the first great Republican politician of Upstate New York, and historically Syracuse is heavily Republican, partly out of antipathy to New York City. But it is also one of the most heavily Catholic cities in the United States and very ethnic, and has elected Democratic mayors and voted for Bill Clinton in 1992 and 1996.

The congressman from the 25th District is James Walsh, a Republican elected in 1988. He grew up in Syracuse, the son of a Syracuse mayor and former congressman. He came to the House as almost a professional civic activist: he was a Peace Corps volunteer, a social worker, then worked for New York Telephone and NYNEX, which detailed him to a local university. He was elected five times to the Syracuse Common Council, then ran for Congress in 1988 when a Republican incumbent nearly beaten two years earlier decided to retire. In the general, Walsh beat Democrat Rosemary Pooler by a solid 57%–42%. Like other Republicans from economically sluggish Upstate areas, he is open to government intervention in the economy; he voted for the Clinton stimulus package in March 1993, for the Americans with Disabilities Act and to maintain many food programs. But he also supports the balanced budget amendment and the line-item veto.

In the Republican 104th Congress, Walsh's most prominent position was chairman of the District of Columbia Appropriations Subcommittee, a position which made him virtually the surrogate mayor of the nation's capital. In the 103d Congress, his efforts to cut funds to the District government had mostly failed, but in 1994 the situation changed as Marion Barry returned to the mayor's office even as Republicans became the House majority. "Any progress we might have made with the District in recent years is now gone," was Walsh's initial reaction. But he worked with Northern Virginia Republican Tom Davis, chairman of the D.C. Subcommittee of Government Reform and Oversight, and District Delegate Eleanor Holmes Norton to create the financial control board to monitor District spending and to make the accountings and file the financial reports the D.C. government chronically failed to produce. Citing his own experience as council president in Syracuse, Walsh argued that the District government is too large and should concentrate on its core responsibilities, like garbage collection and policing, and get out of others like corrections, health and post-secondary education; and in fact the federal government took over some of these functions. Walsh also sponsored a limited school-choice experiment, to allow some small number of poor children options other than the wretched and mismanaged D.C. public schools. This aroused furious opposition from teachers' unions, and though it passed the House it was killed in the Senate.

In 1996, the AFL-CIO, 42% of whose members are public employees, targeted Walsh's district, running an estimated $500,000 in TV ads against Walsh and a vigorous organizing campaign for Democrat Marty Mack, former mayor of Cortland. By mid-October 1996, alarms suddenly sounded in Republican headquarters that Walsh's seat was in jeopardy. With a late-spending and organizational surge, Walsh won 55%–45%, down slightly from his last two contests.

Back in Washington, Walsh switched chairmanships from the D.C. to the Legislative Subcommittee, where he will face another challenge—living up to Republican promises to cut congressional staff and spending while keeping the new Republican majority contented.

The People: Pop. 1990: 580,233; 26% rural; 13% age 65+; 90% White; 7% Black; 1% Asian; 1% Amer. Indian; 1% Hispanic origin. Households: 54% married couple families; 25% married couple fams. w.

children; 48% college educ.; median household income: $31,080; per capita income: $14,148; median gross rent: $433; median house value: $77,600.

1996 Presidential Vote			1992 Presidential Vote		
Clinton (D)	121,304	(51%)	Clinton (D)	108,335	(41%)
Dole (R)	90,774	(38%)	Bush (R)	95,476	(36%)
Perot (I)	23,516	(10%)	Perot (I)	58,232	(22%)
Other	4,038	(2%)			

Rep. James T. Walsh (R)

Elected 1988; b. June 19, 1947, Syracuse; home, Syracuse; St. Bonaventure U., B.A. 1970; Catholic; married (Diane).

Career: Peace Corps, Nepal, 1970–72; Social worker, Onondaga Cnty. Dept. of Social Svcs., 1972–74; Marketing exec., NYNEX, 1974–88; Syracuse Common Cncl., 1978–88, Pres. 1986–88.

DC Office: 2351 RHOB 20515, 202-225-3701; Fax: 202-225-4042.

District Offices: Auburn, 315-255-0649; Cortland, 607-758-3918; Syracuse, 315-423-5657.

Committees: *Appropriations* (14th of 34 R): Agriculture, Rural Development, FDA & Related Agencies; Legislative (Chmn.); VA, HUD & Independent Agencies.

Group Ratings

	ADA	ACLU	AFS	LCV	CFA	CON	NFIB	COC	ACU	NTLC	CHC
1996	20	25	17	54	31	48	89	81	68	85	80
1995	10	—	—	13	8	38	—	96	76	—	—

National Journal Ratings

	1995 LIB — 1995 CONS			1996 LIB — 1996 CONS		
Economic	44%	—	53%	52%	—	47%
Social	32%	—	65%	42%	—	56%
Foreign	0%	—	85%	28%	—	71%

Key Votes of the 104th Congress

1. Reduce Medicare Growth $	Y	5. Flag Amendment	Y	9. Cuban Embargo	Y
2. Ovrd. Product Liab. Veto	Y	6. Drop EPA Limits	N	10. Bar Bosnia Troop $	Y
3. Increase Min. Wage	Y	7. Repeal Assault-Weap. Ban	Y	11. Cut Anti-Missile Defense	N
4. Welfare Reform	Y	8. Ovrd. Part. Birth Veto	Y	12. Bar U.N. Uniforms	Y

Election Results

1996 general	James T. Walsh (R-C-I-FR)	126,691	(55%)	($698,021)
	Marty Mack (D)	103,199	(45%)	($326,595)
1996 primary	James T. Walsh (R)	unopposed		
1994 general	James T. Walsh (R-C)	113,949	(58%)	($415,314)
	Rhea Jezer (D-CCP)	83,853	(42%)	($205,818)

TWENTY-SIXTH DISTRICT

New York's Southern Tier is territory not often explored by today's Americans. In colonial days, the Catskills looming over the Hudson were a great barrier, a mysterious zone in which phantom Dutchmen played nine pins and Indians lurked in the days of James Fenimore Cooper. The area then became part of a great pathway west, along the Erie Lackawanna and Delaware & Hudson Railroad lines, with engines steaming over giant viaducts and along narrow river valleys through these hills and mountains. But today, this quarter of Upstate New York has little passenger rail service and is bypassed by major air travel networks. Its interstates are lightly traveled, particularly as the once-famous kosher resorts in the "Borscht Belt" of the Catskills have lost their popularity in the past quarter century.

The sprawling 26th Congressional District includes much of the Southern Tier. The district stretches from the city of Beacon on the east side of the Hudson—where commuters board the train daily for jobs in New York City—west and north across the still-mysterious Catskills, past Bethel, site of the misnamed 1969 Woodstock music festival, to the industrial city of Binghamton in Broome County on the upper Susquehanna River, and finally to the university town of Ithaca, with Cornell University looming high above Cayuga Lake's waters. Along the west bank of the Hudson in Ulster County lies Kingston, settled by Dutchmen more than 300 years ago. This was Rip van Winkle country, and in the 19th Century was the political base of Governor and Vice President George Clinton. There are two population centers, widely separated: Binghamton-Ithaca in the west has about half the district's votes, and the Hudson Valley has about one-third. Politically, the heritage is Republican, but the Ithaca area, like so many university communities, is heavily Democratic, and Binghamton trends that way as well.

The congressman from the 26th is Maurice Hinchey, a liberal Democrat elected in 1992. Hinchey grew up in a humble background, enlisted in the Navy at 18, worked in a cement factory for five years, then worked his way through college as a New York State Thruway toll collector. He worked as an analyst for the state education department, then in the Democratic year of 1974, at 36, was elected from Ulster County to the Assembly. There he served for nine terms; he was proud of more than 600 bills passed—on, among other things, acid rain, toxic waste, illegal dumping (and organized crime's influence on it), groundwater and wetlands protection. When he ran for Congress in 1992, Hinchey called for national health insurance, a repeal of Reagan-Bush tax cuts for the rich and corporations, and "reindustrializating America." He put forth a plan to eliminate 2.6 million military and defense jobs and create 3.4 million civilian jobs. His Republican opponent Bob Moppert, a Binghamton moving company owner elected as a Broome County legislator in 1986, called for less government spending and bureaucracy. In a contest that was not only partisan but geographic, Hinchey beat Moppert 50%–47%. Hinchey carried Ulster and Moppert carried the Binghamton area; Ithaca and Tompkins County decided it, going for Hinchey by 30%.

In the House, Hinchey joined the Progressive Caucus and compiled one of the most liberal voting records. Assigned to the Resources and Banking Committees, he supported environmental measures and took potshots at the Federal Reserve. One issue that caused Hinchey both political and personal discomfort was gun control. He backed the Brady Bill on handguns. But, facing a tough reelection campaign in a heavily non-metropolitan district, he agonized over the assault weapons ban, deciding at the last minute to vote against it, despite a call from Bill Clinton. Then, just weeks after his 1994 reelection victory, Hinchey was boarding a plane at Washington's National Airport when his carry-on bag was found to contain a loaded handgun. Hinchey had a license to carry a gun in New York and said he was the subject of death threats while conducting probes of organized crime in the 1980s. He told a local court he had forgotten the gun was in his luggage; he pleaded no contest and was given a suspended sentence.

The 1994 campaign virtually began on election night 1992. Moppert spent much of 1993 attacking Hinchey, trying to tie him to Clinton while embracing the House Republicans'

Contract With America. If Moppert, like many Republicans in 1994, sought to nationalize the election, Hinchey, like many Democrats, sought to localize it. Hinchey boasted of his efforts at local economic development, such as his role in the successful transfer of a former Air Force facility in Broome County to private industry. Hinchey vastly outspent the challenger, but the result was one of the nation's closest races; Hinchey won 49%–48%, with the outcome uncertain until almost two weeks after the election. Ironically, the geographic breakdown was a reverse of 1992. Hinchey lost Ulster County and carried only the counties containing Ithaca and Binghamton. He spent almost $740,000, twice what he spent in 1992; Moppert spent just under $280,000.

Hinchey was again a Republican target in 1996. But this time Bill Clinton carried the district with 51%, and Hinchey's fundraising was as good as ever: he spent nearly $1 million. His Republican opponent, small businesswoman Sue Wittig, had an odd political background; she had smuggled guns to Afghan freedom fighters, and was once arrested for blocking an abortion clinic. Hinchey called her "a self-proclaimed foot soldier in the army of Newt Gingrich" and an extremist; it would be more accurate to say both were at the extremes of the not terribly broad spectrum of American electoral politicians. Hinchey won by the impressive margin of 55%–42%, carrying all parts of the district.

Whether he will be able to repeat that in 1998 is unclear. Governor George Pataki will be at the top of the ticket, and whatever his fate statewide, he seems likely to poll very well in this Upstate district. And a potential problem arose for Hinchey in March 1997, when a North American subsidiary of an Italian power plant construction company pleaded guilty in federal court of making $43,000 in illegal contributions to Hinchey's 1992 campaign. A lawyer representing Hinchey said that he had no knowledge of this, but the amount was sizable for any congressional campaign. Hinchey's name has been floated as a statewide candidate in 1998, for lieutenant governor or perhaps even governor. For his part, Hinchey has only said he hasn't ruled out a run for governor in 1998.

The People: Pop. 1990: 580,540; 43% rural; 13% age 65+; 88% White; 5% Black; 2% Asian; 4% Hispanic origin. Households: 54% married couple families; 25% married couple fams. w. children; 47% college educ.; median household income: $30,335; per capita income: $13,786; median gross rent: $449; median house value: $94,400.

1996 Presidential Vote

Clinton (D)	120,755	(51%)
Dole (R)	82,044	(35%)
Perot (I)	25,237	(11%)
Other	7,129	(3%)

1992 Presidential Vote

Clinton (D)	116,450	(44%)
Bush (R)	91,462	(35%)
Perot (I)	53,675	(20%)

Rep. Maurice D. Hinchey (D)

Elected 1992; b. Oct. 27, 1938, New York City; home, Saugerties; S.U.N.Y. New Paltz, B.S. 1968, M.A. 1970; Catholic; married (Ilene).

Career: Navy, 1956–59; Cement plant worker, 1959–1964; NY St. Thruway toll collector, 1959–68; Analyst, NY St. Dept. of Educ., 1971–74; NY Assembly, 1974–92.

DC Office: 2431 RHOB 20515, 202-225-6335; Fax: 202-226-0774; e-mail: hinchey@hr.house.gov.

District Offices: Binghamton, 607-773-2768; Ithaca, 607-273-1388; Kingston, 914-331-4466.

Committees: *Banking & Financial Services* (16th of 25 D): Domestic & International Monetary Policy; Housing & Community Opportunity. *Resources* (14th of 23 D): Forests & Forest Health (RMM); National Parks & Public Lands. *Joint Economic Committee* (9th of 10 Reps.).

Group Ratings

	ADA	ACLU	AFS	LCV	CFA	CON	NFIB	COC	ACU	NTLC	CHC
1996	95	94	100	92	100	9	16	19	5	5	0
1995	95	—	—	100	100	4	—	13	8	—	—

National Journal Ratings

	1995 LIB — 1995 CONS			1996 LIB — 1996 CONS		
Economic	94%	—	0%	85%	—	11%
Social	88%	—	0%	73%	—	26%
Foreign	84%	—	15%	87%	—	10%

Key Votes of the 104th Congress

1. Reduce Medicare Growth $	N	5. Flag Amendment	N	9. Cuban Embargo	N
2. Ovrd. Product Liab. Veto	N	6. Drop EPA Limits	Y	10. Bar Bosnia Troop $	N
3. Increase Min. Wage	Y	7. Repeal Assault-Weap. Ban	Y	11. Cut Anti-Missile Defense	Y
4. Welfare Reform	N	8. Ovrd. Part. Birth Veto	N	12. Bar U.N. Uniforms	N

Election Results

1996 general	Maurice D. Hinchey (D-L)	122,850	(55%)	($994,042)
	Sue Wittig (R-C-RTL-FR)	94,125	(42%)	($586,078)
	Others	5,531	(2%)	
1996 primary	Maurice D. Hinchey (D)	unopposed		
1994 general	Maurice D. Hinchey (D-L)	95,492	(49%)	($738,098)
	Bob Moppert (R-C)	94,244	(48%)	($278,962)
	Others	4,772	(2%)	

TWENTY-SEVENTH DISTRICT

Across the Finger Lakes of New York, the long, thin, deep-blue lakes in glacier-carved folds between rolling hillsides thick with grapevines, ran one of the first paths of westward migration. Originally cut off from white settlement by the British and the Iroquois, Upstate New York opened up after the Revolution, and streams of New England Yankees moved west. They followed the Mohawk River and the Erie Canal, dug by hand labor and finished in 1825, connecting the Hudson River and Lake Erie, the East Coast and the vast interior of America. The Finger Lakes region became one of the fastest-growing and most dynamic parts of America. Town squares here today have monuments to the enthusiasms of the 1830s and 1840s, when these new communities were full of young families on the rise, and religious revivals were so fervent that the area was known as the Burnt-Over district. Here in the village of Palmyra, near the Erie Canal, Joseph Smith had his vision of the angel Moroni and saw the golden tablets that led him to found the Mormon Church. Preachers fanned enthusiasm for abolition of slavery, greater here than anywhere else in the country. This was the birthplace of the women's movement: in Seneca Falls in 1848, Elizabeth Cady Stanton and Lucretia Mott produced a Declaration of Sentiments that started the women's suffrage movement. Upstate was also the birthplace of the temperance movement, another women's cause in those days.

The 27th Congressional District of New York covers much of this territory, now economically less dynamic and politically calmer than in its heyday. The district starts at Aurelius, one of the many Upstate towns with classical names, and includes Seneca Falls and Palmyra, then passes south of Rochester and through Batavia and Attica to the Buffalo suburb of Amherst. Most of this is part of America's Republican heartland, though the Buffalo area, with its historic industrial base, has leaned Democratic.

The congressman from the 27th is Bill Paxon, a Republican who is one of his party's best natural politicians. Paxon's roots are in Buffalo's Erie County, where his father was a family court judge. Paxon volunteered in 1970, at 15, in the first congressional campaign of Jack Kemp, then famous as a quarterback for the Buffalo Bills, and not yet known as an advocate of sweeping tax cuts. In 1974, Paxon saw his father and the Assembly candidate he was working for defeated in a Democratic landslide. But in 1977, the same year he graduated from Canisius College (almost a prerequisite for a Buffalo political career), Paxon was elected to the Erie County legislature at 23, the youngest member ever, and in 1982 he was elected to the New York Assembly. In 1988, when Kemp ran for president and left his House seat open, Paxon won the Republican nomination without opposition and then spent $688,000 and won the general election with 53%.

In the decade since, Paxon has moved from being an imperiled local politician to a triumphant national leader, from facing seeming political extinction in the redistricting process to chairing the National Republican Congressional Committee as they gained 52 seats and won control of the chamber for the first time in 40 years and then as they won their second majority in a row for the first time in 68 years. In the process, Paxon has played only a limited role on legislation. He fought against the gas tax increase in the 1991 energy bill and tried to stop imports of solid waste from Canada, but has resisted bans of waste exports across state lines (New York is a net exporter of waste). He started off with a seat on Banking and in 1993 moved to the plummier Commerce Committee. There he informally played a part in fashioning the 1996 Telecommunications Act and other highly lobbied legislation; he also found time to help preserve dairy subsidies in the 1996 Freedom to Farm Act. His redistricting crisis came back in 1992, when Upstate had to lose a district. He contributed to and lobbied Republican state senators and ended up with new Republican territory from the seat of a senior Republican who decided to retire in 1992; the result was a safe seat for Paxon for a decade.

At that point Paxon turned his love of campaigning and fundraising to the national scale. By lobbying hard, campaigning and raising money for fellow members, he undercut others interested in chairing the National Republican Congressional Committee and won the position unanimously in 1993. The NRCC was $4.5 million in debt, the staff (as is often the case with Republican committees) bloated and devoid of credibility after years of predicting Republican gains that never occurred. He installed young vice chairmen, fired scores of staffers, re-examined consulting contracts, worked to recruit candidates—and camouflaged the fact that the committee had much less money to contribute than in the past. He worked closely with Newt

Gingrich and Dick Armey in formulating the terms and the strategy for the Contract With America and getting near-unanimous support for it from Republican candidates.

On election night 1994, Paxon savored victory and looked forward to more gains in the future. He predicted further gains in 1996, and said that many Democrats would be discouraged and retire. He was right on the second count, wrong on the first. He did not foresee the decline in Republican popularity after the government shutdown in 1995–96, although he was correct in saying that public polls overstated the Democrats' lead in House voting intentions. With Republican National Chairman Haley Barbour, he agreed on the strategy of ignoring AFL-CIO ad campaigns early in 1996 and waiting until October for counterattack; it was successful, but only just. Paxon himself had spirited opposition in the 27th District from UAW regional director Tom Fricano. But Paxon spent $1.5 million, and other Democrats griped that the perverse effect of Fricano's challenge was to funnel money away from their better chance to beat Republican Jack Quinn in Buffalo. Paxon won 60%–40%, a solid result since Clinton and Dole were running even in the district and *The Buffalo News* endorsed the Democrat.

In August 1993, Paxon proposed on the floor of the House to his fellow New York Republican, Susan Molinari; they were married in July 1994. Young, energetic, enthusiastic, the couple went around the country recruiting candidates and campaigning for them, belying the image of Republicans as grim old fogies. Their daughter was born in May 1996, and as Molinari delivered the keynote address at the 1996 Republican National Convention, talking about family values and the pressures of working mothers in today's world, Paxon sat among the delegates, in camera's eye view, feeding little Susan Ruby a bottle—softening the Republican stereotype even further. But juggling two Congressional careers and a one-year-old might even be too much for this dynamic duo, and in May 1997, Molinari announced she would resign her seat in August to anchor a new CBS Saturday morning news show.

Paxon had pledged to serve only two terms as NRCC chairman, but he continues to have a leadership role. After the 1996 election, Newt Gingrich named him to an informal but powerful position as chairman of the Speaker's leadership operations. Gingrich and many other Republicans consider him one of the party's best political brains, and there was speculation when Gingrich's hold on the speakership seemed to be failing that Paxon might be the best successor. For the moment, he is evidently a conduit between Gingrich and other Republican members, one especially sensitive to their political situations and needs.

The People: Pop. 1990: 580,317; 55% rural; 13% age 65+; 95% White; 2% Black; 1% Asian; 1% Hispanic origin. Households: 63% married couple families; 30% married couple fams. w.children; 48% college educ.; median household income: $34,573; per capita income: $14,934; median gross rent: $434; median house value: $81,100.

1996 Presidential Vote

Clinton (D)	111,804	(43%)
Dole (R)	111,371	(43%)
Perot (I)	28,980	(11%)
Other	7,398	(3%)

1992 Presidential Vote

Bush (R)	115,432	(42%)
Clinton (D)	90,194	(33%)
Perot (I)	67,721	(25%)

Rep. Bill Paxon (R)

Elected 1988; b. Apr. 29, 1954, Buffalo; home, Amherst; Canisius Col., B.A. 1977; Catholic; married (U.S. Rep. Susan Molinari).

Career: Erie Cnty. Legislature, 1977–82; NY Assembly, 1982–88.

DC Office: 2412 RHOB 20515, 202-225-5265; Fax: 202-225-5910; e-mail: bpaxon@hr.house.gov.

District Offices: Victor, 716-742-1600, Williamsville, 716-634-2324.

Committees: *Commerce* (10th of 28 R): Energy & Power; Finance & Hazardous Materials.

Group Ratings

	ADA	ACLU	AFS	LCV	CFA	CON	NFIB	COC	ACU	NTLC	CHC
1996	0	6	0	23	8	36	97	100	100	100	100
1995	0	—	—	0	0	87	—	100	88	—	—

National Journal Ratings

	1995 LIB	—	1995 CONS	1996 LIB	—	1996 CONS
Economic	0%	—	74%	0%	—	82%
Social	0%	—	79%	14%	—	77%
Foreign	28%	—	65%	0%	—	79%

Key Votes of the 104th Congress

1. Reduce Medicare Growth $	Y	5. Flag Amendment	Y	9. Cuban Embargo	Y
2. Ovrd. Product Liab. Veto	*	6. Drop EPA Limits	N	10. Bar Bosnia Troop $	N
3. Increase Min. Wage	N	7. Repeal Assault-Weap. Ban	Y	11. Cut Anti-Missile Defense	*
4. Welfare Reform	Y	8. Ovrd. Part. Birth Veto	Y	12. Bar U.N. Uniforms	Y

Election Results

1996 general	Bill Paxon (R-C-RTL-FR)	142,568	(60%)	($1,553,754)
	Thomas M. Fricano (D-SM)	95,503	(40%)	($656,490)
1996 primary	Bill Paxon (R)	unopposed		
1994 general	Bill Paxon (R-C-RTL)	152,610	(75%)	($642,531)
	William A. Long Jr. (D)	52,160	(25%)	($62,746)

TWENTY-EIGHTH DISTRICT

Rochester, with a metro area just over one million, is one of the major cities of Upstate New York. Located where the Erie Canal, the backbone of Upstate, crosses the Genesee River, Rochester became a major industrial city, the "Flour City" in the 1830s, as it milled the wheat produced by western New York farmers, and then a high-tech city, when a bank clerk named George Eastman began making photographic dry plates and marketed the first still camera and film for Thomas Edison's motion picture camera in 1888 and 1889. Later, Bausch & Lomb developed its lens business here. Rochester, the home of Susan B. Anthony and Frederick Douglass, has lived on high-tech versions of the eye. Its great industries—Bausch & Lomb, Eastman Kodak, and Xerox, which started here as Haloid—have thrived on technical innovation, precision workmanship, high reliability and customer service, giving Rochester an affluent and well-educated population that maintains fine civic institutions and traditions. This was the city that in 1918 invented the Community Chest and still has the nation's highest United Way contributions; it is also the home of Wegman's, quite possibly the nation's best supermarket chain. A *Washington Post* 1996 profile of Rochester concluded that the city's growth proves that "the economic future of cities and states depends less on where the biggest companies chose to locate than where the best people chose to locate." Although Xerox and Kodak cut thousands of old jobs from 1988–93, the local work force grew and unemployment stayed low, as dozens of small companies produced even more new jobs.

The 28th Congressional District includes Rochester and most of its Monroe County suburbs—a compact district in a state where redistricting produced a dozen grotesqueries. In the 1990s, for the first time in 50 years, the heart of Monroe County wasn't separated into two districts. Traditionally Republican, the Rochester area moved toward Democrats in the 1970s and 1980s.

The congresswoman from the 28th District is Louise Slaughter, who is both a strong partisan Democrat and an assiduous worker for local interests. With an accent and occasional fieriness that are evidence of her roots in the Kentucky mountains ("I would wrestle alligators for a cause"), Slaughter has become a seasoned political professional. She worked as a local staffer for Mario Cuomo when he was lieutenant governor in the 1970s and won a seat on the Monroe County Legislature; she was elected to the New York Assembly in 1982 and 1984. In 1986, she beat a one-term conservative Republican congressman 51%–49%, by charging that he did nothing to free Lebanon hostage Terry Anderson, a reporter and native of Rochester. She has held the seat by tending carefully to local problems, by winning the support of area businessmen and the local *Democrat & Chronicle* newspaper—ironically, the flagship of Gannett, a chain founded by a diehard Upstate Republican—and by energizing core constituencies of the Democratic Party.

Slaughter was in her prime as a member of the majority party, an insider who used her skills to advance her cherished causes. She became a member of the Rules Committee, a proponent of her party's House reforms (and a disparager of the Republicans'). She worked to get funding for the Rochester International Airport and the harbor, for the Center for Integrated Manufacturing Studies, and for a high-tech business incubator. In 1993 she sponsored a permanent extension of industrial development bonds and in 1994 she got Rochester's pioneering managed care health plans exempted from the Clinton healthcare reform proposal. Slaughter also has tended to her party's core constituencies. The North American Free Trade Agreement might have helped Rochester exports, but she pleased organized labor by voting against it. She strongly backs feminist causes: in 1991 she was one of the seven women House members who marched on the Senate to protest its treatment of Anita Hill, in 1994 she sponsored the law to ban blockades of abortion clinics and in 1995 she spoke out loudly for surgeon general nominee Henry Foster. She chairs the Congressional Member Organization for the Arts, the current incarnation of the old Congressional Arts Caucus.

The Republican takeover of the Congress cost her seat on the Rules Committee for the 104th Congress—though she was back on it for the 105th—and she served on Budget in between. She got John Porter of Illinois, chairman of the House Appropriations subcommittee with jurisdiction over education, to block a rescission of the education program for homeless children she wrote, and she got Republicans to exempt a database on "sexual predators" from their unfunded mandates bill. But her amendment to the line-item veto bill that would have allowed the president to rescind all targeted tax benefits lost on party lines, 231–196. She is a leading advocate for requiring TV stations to give free advertising time for House candidates. And as head of the Congressional Caucus on Women's Health Care Issues, she has urged more health research and services for women.

Slaughter has been disappointed in seeking higher positions. In December 1994 she lost the race for vice chairman of the Democratic Caucus to Barbara Kennelly by a 93–90 margin. And despite appeals for more women Democrats in high positions, she lost the race for ranking

Democrat on the Budget Committee to the more moderate John Spratt by 106–83. That left Slaughter miffed with Minority Leader Dick Gephardt. And she was blunt in voicing her unhappiness with Bill Clinton's distancing of himself from House Democrats during the 1996 campaign. "The President is the smartest person I've ever met," she told *National Journal*. "But I don't understand how he can be persuaded to sit in the middle and play both sides."

Slaughter has won reelection by good but not overwhelming margins; in 1996 she was reelected 57%–43%.

The People: Pop. 1990: 580,347; 4% rural; 13% age 65+; 80% White; 14% Black; 2% Asian; 4% Hispanic origin. Households: 50% married couple families; 23% married couple fams. w. children; 53% college educ.; median household income: $33,899; per capita income: $16,205; median gross rent: $477; median house value: $90,000.

1996 Presidential Vote			**1992 Presidential Vote**		
Clinton (D)	136,424	(55%)	Clinton (D)	119,055	(44%)
Dole (R)	88,279	(36%)	Bush (R)	103,544	(38%)
Perot (I)	17,841	(7%)	Perot (I)	48,467	(18%)
Other	5,981	(2%)			

Rep. Louise M. Slaughter (D)

Elected 1986; b. Aug. 14, 1929, Harlan Cnty., KY; home, Fairport; U. of KY, B.S. 1951, M.S. 1953; Episcopalian; married (Robert).

Career: Monroe Cnty. Legislature, 1976–79; Regional Coord., Lt. Gov. Mario Cuomo, 1976–79; NY Assembly, 1982–86.

DC Office: 2347 RHOB 20515, 202-225-3615; Fax: 202-225-7822.

District Offices: Rochester, 716-232-4850.

Committees: *Rules* (4th of 4 D): Rules & Organization of the House.

Group Ratings

	ADA	ACLU	AFS	LCV	CFA	CON	NFIB	COC	ACU	NTLC	CHC
1996	90	88	100	85	100	48	24	25	5	2	0
1995	90	—	—	88	100	38	—	17	4	—	—

National Journal Ratings

	1995 LIB — 1995 CONS			1996 LIB — 1996 CONS		
Economic	78%	—	21%	73%	—	25%
Social	88%	—	0%	84%	—	16%
Foreign	88%	—	7%	86%	—	13%

Key Votes of the 104th Congress

1. Reduce Medicare Growth $	N	5. Flag Amendment	N	9. Cuban Embargo	N
2. Ovrd. Product Liab. Veto	Y	6. Drop EPA Limits	Y	10. Bar Bosnia Troop $	N
3. Increase Min. Wage	Y	7. Repeal Assault-Weap. Ban	N	11. Cut Anti-Missile Defense	Y
4. Welfare Reform	N	8. Ovrd. Part. Birth Veto	N	12. Bar U.N. Uniforms	N

Election Results

1996 general	Louise M. Slaughter (D)	133,084	(57%)	($868,969)
	Geoff H. Rosenberger (R-C-FR)	99,366	(43%)	($663,441)
1996 primary	Louise M. Slaughter (D)	unopposed		
1994 general	Louise M. Slaughter (D)	110,987	(57%)	($790,778)
	Renee Forgensi Davison (R-C)	78,516	(40%)	($165,922)
	Others	6,464	(3%)	

TWENTY-NINTH DISTRICT

The Niagara Frontier is the romantic name for the Buffalo metropolitan area and the northwest corner of Upstate New York facing Lake Ontario. This really was the frontier once, between the United States and British-held Upper Canada, when American troops crossed the raging Niagara River in the War of 1812 to fight the Battle of Lundys Lane. Not many years later, Niagara Falls became a prime vacation spot, a must-see sight for European tourists and American honeymooners. By the mid-20th Century, Niagara Falls vacations had become routine, and few tourists took notice of the huge water intakes farther up the river, the hydroelectric power lines strung out on giant pylons fanning out in every direction, providing cheap public power for the chemical and steel factories that made the Niagara Frontier one of the heavy industry capitals of America. Nor did they notice the school and the 200 frame houses which had been built on a toxic waste dump near Love Canal, land sold by Hooker Chemical to the city of Niagara Falls with a warning that no one should live there—and where children were born horrifying birth defects and some died.

The 29th Congressional District of New York includes the heart of the Niagara Frontier: the Falls; the Buffalo suburbs of Tonawanda and Kenmore; and the northwest one-third of Buffalo itself, with the city's downtown and its fine but financially beleaguered cultural institutions. The 29th also runs east to include towns and farm country along the southern shore of Lake Ontario to the Rochester suburb of Gates. Like most of Upstate New York, this was once Republican territory; as heavy industries declined, it trended Democratic. Its most famous congressman was William Miller, the Republican National Committee chairman from 1961–64 and Barry Goldwater's 1964 vice presidential nominee. But it hasn't elected a Republican since 1972.

The congressman from the 29th is John LaFalce, a son of Buffalo who attended Canisius College and was elected to the New York Senate in 1970, at 31, and to the Assembly in 1972. In 1974, when the Republican incumbent retired, he was elected to the House. He serves on the Banking and Small Business Committees, sponsoring a variety of legislation. "I introduce legislation when the spirit moves me," he told *The Buffalo News*. "I have tremendous intellectual curiosity, and that has made me legislatively versatile." Much of his work has been to get government to spur development of industrial areas. In the 1980s, LaFalce took up the banner of promoting competitiveness. He strongly backed the U.S.-Canada Free Trade Agreement, which enabled the Niagara Frontier, with its low land costs and rents, to partake of the prosperity of Ontario's Toronto-based Golden Horseshoe, but he voted against the North American Free Trade Agreement. As chairman of the Small Business Committee from 1987–95, he superintended the various Small Business Administration loan programs, which represent only a minuscule percentage of total lending to small business, and he has called for a government-sponsored enterprise, to be named Velda Sue, to provide a secondary market for SBA loans. LaFalce's small business interests led him to draw up his own family and medical leave, disabilities and civil rights bills, and he was a leader in the fight to repeal the Section 89 employee-benefits tax provisions that small business owners detested.

In 1994, LaFalce was weighing whether to give up the Small Business chair for the chairmanship of the Financial Institutions Subcommittee on Banking. Then Republicans won control of the House, and it mattered much less. He stuck with Small Business, working amicably with new Chairman Jan Meyers of Kansas. After the 1996 election, he decided to seek the ranking position on Banking by trying to oust the often autocratic and distracted 80-year-old Henry Gonzalez. Also in the race was Bruce Vento, a longtime Gonzalez adversary. In November 1996 the Democratic Steering Committee voted 29–12 to oust Gonzalez, and Banking Committee members voted 22–19 for LaFalce over Vento. But the next day Gonzalez made an emotional plea to the Democratic Caucus for just one more two-year term. He won only 82 votes on the first ballot, against a combined 109 for LaFalce and Vento, and it seemed likely Vento would drop out and LaFalce would prevail. But LaFalce unexpectedly dropped his challenge. "With Henry having that much support and having served so honorably, I didn't want it to end that way," he explained. It was a brilliant stroke: he won over Gonzalez's friends, including many Hispanics and blacks, and pretty much insured his spot in 1998.

In 1990, 1992 and 1994, the last two times against William Miller, Jr., LaFalce won with just 55%—not impressive for a longtime incumbent. But in 1996, as Bill Clinton was carrying the district 51%–35%, LaFalce won 62%–38%. His path was eased when Erie County Comptroller Nancy Naples unexpectedly abandoned her race for the Republican nomination. LaFalce is not assured of easy reelection or of the ranking post on Banking, but his prospects in the House look more inviting than they did just a few years ago. His current legislative projects include banking regulation modernization, urban revitalization via expanded home ownership, improved federal regulation of automobile leasing and prohibition on the use of credit cards for purchase of gambling chips.

The People: Pop. 1990: 579,831; 23% rural; 15% age 65+; 91% White; 4% Black; 1% Asian; 1% Amer. Indian; 3% Hispanic origin. Households: 54% married couple families; 24% married couple fams. w. children; 43% college educ.; median household income: $28,951; per capita income: $13,350; median gross rent: $383; median house value: $71,200.

1996 Presidential Vote

Clinton (D)	120,777	(51%)
Dole (R)	82,737	(35%)
Perot (I)	28,015	(12%)
Other	3,929	(2%)

1992 Presidential Vote

Clinton (D)	103,528	(40%)
Bush (R)	86,730	(33%)
Perot (I)	70,231	(27%)

Rep. John J. LaFalce (D)

Elected 1974; b. Oct. 6, 1939, Buffalo; home, Tonawanda; Canisius Col., B.S. 1961, Villanova U., J.D. 1964; Catholic; married (Patricia).

Career: Army, 1965–67; Law Clerk, U.S. Navy Gen. Cnsl., 1963; Lecturer, George Washington U., 1965–66; Practicing atty., 1967–74; NY Senate, 1970–72; NY Assembly, 1972–74.

DC Office: 2310 RHOB 20515, 202-225-3231.

District Offices: Buffalo, 716-846-4056; Niagara Falls, 716-284-9976; Spencerport, 716-352-4777.

Committees: *Banking & Financial Services* (2nd of 25 D): Financial Institutions & Consumer Credit; Housing & Community Opportunity. *Small Business* (RMM).

Group Ratings

	ADA	ACLU	AFS	LCV	CFA	CON	NFIB	COC	ACU	NTLC	CHC
1996	80	80	100	92	92	85	19	25	5	7	28
1995	75	—	—	94	85	53	—	25	16	—	—

National Journal Ratings

	1995 LIB — 1995 CONS	1996 LIB — 1996 CONS
Economic	74% — 25%	85% — 11%
Social	58% — 41%	65% — 35%
Foreign	72% — 27%	82% — 16%

Key Votes of the 104th Congress

1. Reduce Medicare Growth $	N	5. Flag Amendment	N	9. Cuban Embargo	N
2. Ovrd. Product Liab. Veto	N	6. Drop EPA Limits	Y	10. Bar Bosnia Troop $	N
3. Increase Min. Wage	Y	7. Repeal Assault-Weap. Ban	N	11. Cut Anti-Missile Defense	Y
4. Welfare Reform	N	8. Ovrd. Part. Birth Veto	Y	12. Bar U.N. Uniforms	N

Election Results

1996 general	John J. LaFalce (D-L)	132,317	(62%)	($443,052)
	David B. Callard (R-C-RTL-FR)	81,135	(38%)	($123,958)
1996 primary	John J. LaFalce (D)	unopposed		
1994 general	John J. LaFalce (D-L)	103,053	(55%)	($825,314)
	William E. Miller Jr. (R-C)	80,355	(43%)	($219,273)
	Others	3,296	(2%)	

THIRTIETH DISTRICT

Buffalo has hopes of being one of America's success stories of the 1990s. The city has had its successes before. The butt of many jokes about the snow that piles up at the eastern end of Lake Erie and that supposedly keeps it immobilized half the year, Buffalo also should be credited with building a heavy industrial base in the late 19th and early 20th Centuries, as America's number one grain milling center, and as a major steel producer. Today, the Lackawanna steel mills are cold, and grain milling waned when the St. Lawrence Seaway opened in the 1950s. Buffalo is eclipsed economically by the bigger Great Lakes industrial cities of Cleveland, Detroit and Chicago, and its architecturally bold 1920s City Hall and downtown skyscrapers are far overshadowed by the high-rise horizon of Toronto, not many miles away. And though it is still one of the nation's 50 largest municipalities, Buffalo's population plummeted by almost 30% during the 1970s and another 9% in the 1980s.

But Buffalo has considerable assets which went unnoticed until the late 1980s. It has a high-skill labor force that works for reasonably low wages; it has cheap real estate; it has spruced up and gentrified its rather handsome waterfront on what is now a clean Lake Erie. The key to Buffalo's recent resurgence in the 1980s and 1990s was Canada. For Canada is right across the Peace Bridge, and Buffalo is the major metropolitan area on the doorstep of the richest part of the nation whose free trade agreement with the United States was signed in late 1988. Then, Toronto's wages, real estate prices and taxes were much higher than Buffalo's, its labor market much tighter and its unions more militant, and Canadian investment flowed into Buffalo. But Buffalo's advantage has grown less as the Canadian dollar weakened and Ontario cut its sky-high taxes.

The 30th Congressional District of New York consists of the eastern and southern two-thirds of Buffalo, plus most of the Erie County suburbs east and south of the city, from working-class Cheektowaga and the steel-mill town of Lackawanna to higher-income Hamburg on Lake Erie. This is a solidly Democratic district, by any measure the most Democratic in Upstate New York, although some of the suburbs are Republican. But as Buffalo fitfully revived in the late 1980s and 1990s, it has been politically volatile, lashing out against some usual favorites. Ross Perot got a high 28% here in 1992, his best showing in a central city anywhere, and in 1994 Mario Cuomo, who had always run well in Buffalo, lost Erie County to George Pataki.

The congressman from the 30th District is Jack Quinn, a Republican elected in 1992. He is an authentic product of Buffalo, a graduate of Siena College who became a teacher and coach at Orchard Park Central High School, the Town of Hamburg supervisor (a full-time job) from 1983–92. Seeing his chance when 18-year Democratic incumbent Henry Nowak retired, Quinn created his own Change Congress Party, so his name would appear under this as well as the Republican Party label. In anti-incumbent 1992, he ran on an 11-point program of congressional reform, including term limits and a reduction in House staff. This was a vivid contrast with his Democratic opponent, Erie County Executive Dennis Gorski, an organization man who returned from service in Vietnam to be elected to the county legislature and the New York Assembly before becoming county executive in 1987. In a stunning upset, Quinn beat Gorski by 52%–46%; in effect, Quinn got the Perot vote while Gorski ran basically even with Bill Clinton's 45% plurality.

Quinn's fans and foes alike have compared him to another Republican who had strong appeal to working class Democrats: Ronald Reagan. The handsome Quinn is known for an affable personality that has made him well-liked on Capitol Hill as well as in Buffalo. And if critics suggest that, like Reagan, Quinn's grasp of the details of governing occasionally show some gaps, his first term demonstrated that he is highly skilled in the art of political survival. Tagged almost immediately by House Democratic strategists as their number one target for a while in 1994, Quinn worked to reach out to some key constituencies in his Democratic district. Despite the positive impact on Buffalo of the free trade agreement with Canada, Quinn in November 1993 split from most House Republicans and voted against the North American Free Trade Agreement. This, plus the fact that he was one of the few Republicans to support the 1993 striker replacement bill, won him the endorsement of the local AFL-CIO. Then, in August 1994, as most House Republicans were voting to kill the Clinton crime bill, Quinn proposed changes that helped attract support for the measure—meeting with Clinton once and talking with him twice on the phone. Meanwhile, local Democrats were split among several contenders. In the general election, Quinn rolled over his opponent, 67%–33%.

In his second term Quinn did even more to demonstrate his independence of the Republican leadership. He was the lead Republican pushing in 1996 for an increase in the minimum wage, opposed fiercely by party leaders like Majority Leader Dick Armey. Quinn took this initiative partly in response to the 1995–96 government shutdown, which looked like "gridlock all over again," as he put it. "Who's in charge down there? What are you guys doing?" Quinn said he was asked by voters. *The Buffalo News* effusively praised Quinn's stand for "mak[ing] work more attractive as an option to welfare." He also pressed for legislation to clean up brownfields—industrial sites unused because of the high cost of meeting governmental environmental regulations. Quinn was also helped because of his likability; he was one of the big boosters of the bipartisan "civility" retreat in Hershey, Pennsylvania, in March 1997. "I think we all would be better off if we got to know each other better," he said.

Against these assets Democratic Assemblyman Frank Pordum tried in 1996 to invoke the Republicans' leading liability. But his campaign sent out a signed card pledging to fight the "attack" on families by Speaker "Newyt" Gingrich; and Quinn's differences with him were well known. Even as Bill Clinton was carrying the 30th District 57%–29%, Quinn was winning 55%–45%—in a straight-ticket year, one of the outstanding examples of ticket-splitting in the country. Interestingly the AFL-CIO, which had endorsed Quinn in 1994 and which had pushed the minimum wage hard, nonetheless opposed him in 1996.

The People: Pop. 1990: 580,818; 13% rural; 15% age 65+; 81% White; 17% Black; 1% Asian; 1% Amer. Indian; 2% Hispanic origin. Households: 51% married couple families; 22% married couple fams. w. children; 39% college educ.; median household income: $26,263; per capita income: $12,176; median gross rent: $374; median house value: $68,000.

1996 Presidential Vote

Clinton (D)	137,557	(57%)
Dole (R)	69,341	(29%)
Perot (I)	28,166	(12%)
Other	5,070	(2%)

1992 Presidential Vote

Clinton (D)	119,115	(45%)
Perot (I)	73,333	(28%)
Bush (R)	68,174	(26%)

Rep. Jack Quinn (R)

Elected 1992; b. Apr. 13, 1951, Buffalo; home, Hamburg; Siena Col., B.A. 1969, S.U.N.Y., M.A. 1973; Catholic; married (Mary Beth).

Career: Teacher & coach, Orchard Park Central Schl., 1973–83; Hamburg Town Supervisor, 1983–92.

DC Office: 331 CHOB 20515, 202-225-3306; Fax: 202-226-0347.

District Offices: Buffalo, 716-845-5257.

Committees: *Transportation & Infrastructure* (15th of 40 R): Railroads; Surface Transportation; Water Resources & Environment. *Veterans' Affairs* (7th of 16 R): Benefits (Chmn.).

Group Ratings

	ADA	ACLU	AFS	LCV	CFA	CON	NFIB	COC	ACU	NTLC	CHC
1996	35	19	55	69	54	52	86	81	58	81	80
1995	20	—	—	13	31	87	—	92	72	—	—

National Journal Ratings

	1995 LIB — 1995 CONS			1996 LIB — 1996 CONS		
Economic	49%	—	49%	56%	—	43%
Social	47%	—	53%	50%	—	48%
Foreign	36%	—	59%	0%	—	79%

Key Votes of the 104th Congress

1. Reduce Medicare Growth $	Y	5. Flag Amendment	Y	9. Cuban Embargo	Y
2. Ovrd. Product Liab. Veto	Y	6. Drop EPA Limits	Y	10. Bar Bosnia Troop $	N
3. Increase Min. Wage	Y	7. Repeal Assault-Weap. Ban	N	11. Cut Anti-Missile Defense	N
4. Welfare Reform	Y	8. Ovrd. Part. Birth Veto	Y	12. Bar U.N. Uniforms	Y

Election Results

1996 general	Jack Quinn (R-C-I-FR)	121,369	(55%)	($752,713)
	Francis J. Pordum (D-PS)	100,040	(45%)	($520,826)
1996 primary	Jack Quinn (R)	unopposed		
1994 general	Jack Quinn (R-C)	124,738	(67%)	($488,083)
	David A. Franczyk (D-L)	61,392	(33%)	($193,717)

THIRTY-FIRST DISTRICT

The Southern Tier of New York is one of the nation's forgotten stretches of territory, yet it has an interesting and distinctive history. Elmira was the hometown of Mark Twain's beloved wife, Olivia, and where Twain is buried. On Lake Chautauqua, not far from Lake Erie, a training camp for Methodist Sunday school teachers was founded in 1874, where in summers, on wide green lawns and on porches and in gazebos decorated with Victorian gingerbread, some 25,000 people heard educational talks and inspirational lectures from the likes of William Jennings Bryan; Chautauqua lecture programs still thrive today. Corning is the headquarters of Corning Glass Works, one of America's long-successful and also artistically distinguished manufacturing companies, now specializing in high-tech products. In between are two small Indian reservations, miles and miles of dairy farms, and much of New York's wine country. Sheltered by hills, the lands at the edge of Upstate's deep lakes are the nation's largest grape-growing area outside California, and the leader in Concord grapes, with headquarters of prime New York State wineries and Welch's grape juice.

The Southern Tier's western half forms the 31st Congressional District. Politically, this has been Republican country since the party's founding. The towns and countryside are no longer homogeneously Protestant, but they remain solidly Republican in most elections—though occasionally willing to consider a Democrat (Bill Clinton increased his percentage here by 10% over 1992).

The 31st District's congressman carries his familiar name with considerable grace: He is Amory Houghton, scion of the very rich family that owns the Corning Glass Works, founded in 1851. He was a top executive at Corning for 25 years and had considered retiring to be a missionary in Africa, but instead ran for Congress. The Houghtons are not just rich folks in a small town, they are charter members of the American establishment: Houghton's father was an ambassador to France; his grandfather, a congressman in the 1920s, built one of the biggest mansions on Washington's Embassy Row; his family endowed the rare books library at Harvard; and this latest Houghton sat on boards of companies like IBM, Citicorp, and Procter and Gamble. Cheerful, articulate, used to being in comfortable command, Amo Houghton ran a chipper and well-financed campaign in 1986; he chatted with voters, competed with a serious Democratic opponent and won 60% of the vote. Houghton is not just a leader. He joined the Marine Corps in 1945, at 18, and in his campaigns did "work days" as a disc jockey at an Elmira radio station, as a cook at the Texas Hots restaurant in Wellsville, and as a man-on-the-street reporter for the *Olean Times-Herald*. He has been reelected by wide margins.

Houghton is the only former CEO of a *Fortune* 500 company in Congress, and he brings that perspective to government—he finds it wasteful and foolish, but also wants to preserve some programs with little public support. He dislikes adversariness (most CEOs hear little but praise) but is ready to listen to complaints (the up-to-date CEO had better know if the organization is not working). If he was not a typical freshman congressman in the 1980s, he may be more what the Founding Fathers had in mind than the politically adept youngsters who win in so many districts. By *Roll Call*'s estimate, he is the richest member of Congress, with $400 million; but that includes the wealth of many members of his rather large family. Anyway, he is the only member of Congress who pays for his foreign travel out of personal funds. He seems to have the cheerful unassuming nature of one to whom much is given, who has been living up to his responsibilities and has mostly enjoyed himself in the process.

Houghton's moderate attitude stands in contrast to most other Republicans on many issues. He is a staunch advocate of the National Endowment of the Arts and of public television. He supported the assault weapons ban, though he is a member of the National Rifle Association; he backed the plant closing law and spoke out for the beleaguered catastrophic healthcare program. He balks at declaring he will oppose new taxes and was prominent in early 1995 in demanding that his party leaders reduce to $95,000 the ceiling for families who could take advantage of the $500-per-child tax credit in the Contract With America. "When you look at the numbers, it will be a humongous problem to try to balance the budget and cut taxes. It will be difficult enough to balance the budget." His CEO experience also was in evidence during the crime bill fight in August 1994—the issue that broke the back of the Democratic majority—when he asked, "Why not try something different, the almost-unheard-of approach of working together? Who knows? It might just work." Yet his economic experience also led him to propose letting firms with 50 employees or less self-insure—a rend in the fabric of the Clinton healthcare plan—and to bitterly oppose New York state's community rating plan. With his seat on the Ways and Means Committee, he is a force for bipartisanship and consensus, seeking to season the inexperience of the many junior Republicans. On balance, likc most corporate CEOs, he has supported Newt Gingrich's Contract With America policies, despite economic qualms and a distaste for the Gingrichites' views on cultural issues.

Houghton's agenda for the 105th Congress includes "reseeding" the economy of the Southern Tier and balancing the federal budget through spending controls with tax incentives for business investment. In early 1997 he organized the Mainstreet Coalition, which he sees as a counterpart to the Democratic Leadership Council; he said the group's goal is to restore the "political strength and vitality of the political center in America."

The People: Pop. 1990: 580,400; 60% rural; 15% age 65+; 95% White; 2% Black; 1% Asian; 1% Amer. Indian; 2% Hispanic origin. Households: 58% married couple families; 27% married couple fams. w. children; 39% college educ.; median household income: $25,124; per capita income: $11,382; median gross rent: $341; median house value: $48,300.

1996 Presidential Vote

Clinton (D)	98,244	(44%)
Dole (R)	91,208	(41%)
Perot (I)	30,268	(14%)
Other	3,578	(2%)

1992 Presidential Vote

Bush (R)	97,447	(40%)
Clinton (D)	82,671	(34%)
Perot (I)	62,325	(25%)

Rep. Amo Houghton (R)

Elected 1986; b. Aug. 7, 1926, Corning; home, Corning; Harvard, B.A. 1950, M.B.A. 1952; Episcopalian; married (Priscilla).

Career: Marine Corps, 1945–46 (WWII); Corning Glass Works, 1951–86, Chmn. & CEO, 1964–86.

DC Office: 1110 LHOB 20515, 202-225-3161; Fax: 202-225-5574; e-mail: houghton@hr.house.gov.

District Offices: Corning, 607-937-3333; Jamestown, 716-484-0252; Olean, 716-372-2127.

Committees: *International Relations* (19th of 26 R): Africa. *Ways & Means* (7th of 23 R): Health; Trade.

Group Ratings

	ADA	ACLU	AFS	LCV	CFA	CON	NFIB	COC	ACU	NTLC	CHC
1996	20	13	36	54	15	90	81	63	60	81	53
1995	30	—	—	13	31	73	—	91	52	—	—

National Journal Ratings

	1995 LIB — 1995 CONS			1996 LIB — 1996 CONS		
Economic	44%	—	53%	52%	—	48%
Social	67%	—	33%	61%	—	38%
Foreign	48%	—	50%	45%	—	55%

Key Votes of the 104th Congress

1. Reduce Medicare Growth $	Y	5. Flag Amendment	Y	9. Cuban Embargo	Y
2. Ovrd. Product Liab. Veto	Y	6. Drop EPA Limits	Y	10. Bar Bosnia Troop $	N
3. Increase Min. Wage	Y	7. Repeal Assault-Weap. Ban	N	11. Cut Anti-Missile Defense	N
4. Welfare Reform	Y	8. Ovrd. Part. Birth Veto	Y	12. Bar U.N. Uniforms	N

Election Results

1996 general	Amo Houghton (R-C-FR)	139,734	(72%)	($699,270)
	Bruce D. MacBain (D)	49,502	(25%)	($1,849)
	Others	6,031	(3%)	
1996 primary	Amo Houghton (R)	unopposed		
1994 general	Amo Houghton (R-C)	121,178	(85%)	($356,525)
	Gretchen S. McManus (RTL)	21,747	(15%)	

NORTH CAROLINA

North Carolina in the 1990s, in its third century as a state, has become one of the leading-edge parts of the nation, a state whose growing economy, booming demography and vibrant culture are in many ways typical of the way the nation is going—or would like to go. This was mostly unanticipated. Few people 20 years ago picked North Carolina as a state that would chart a path to the future. It had no great central city, no Atlanta primed to become another Chicago or Los Angeles, but rather a series of small metropolitan areas spaced out over thickly-settled countryside. It did not have what seemed to be cutting-edge industries: the biggest employer was textiles, typically an underdeveloped nation's first industry, and the other two were stolid furniture and soon-to-be-disfavored tobacco. Geographically, it seemed to be off the nation's main lines of commerce; it seemed too steamy to be businesslike in the summer and too cold to be a resort in the winter. It did not seem socially advanced, with a population made up almost entirely of native-born Anglo-Saxons and African-Americans and with an attachment to traditional and sometimes fundamentalist religion.

Yet North Carolina has emerged as one of America's leading growth states. Its population grew by about 25% from 1980–96 (7,300,000 in 1996), and it vies with Georgia for the title of 10th largest state. Its economy has diversified and grown steadily. The number of textile and tobacco jobs is down, but Research Triangle Park, between Raleigh, Durham and Chapel Hill, has become one of the world's leading pharmaceutical and high-tech research centers; NationsBank, headquartered in Charlotte, is one of the nation's largest banks, and First Union down the street in Charlotte and Wachovia based in Winston-Salem are behemoths as well. Charlotte-headquartered Nucor became the nation's leading minimill steelmaker in the 1980s, even as Charlotte and Raleigh-Durham became major airport hubs. Not all of North Carolina's new businesses are upscale: the state is a big chicken-producer, and working conditions can be bad, as in the Hamlet chicken plant where 25 workers died in a fire in 1991.

But the overall picture is flexible, adaptive growth. While Carolina politicians were seeking protection for textiles, this more advanced economy was emerging so quietly and quickly that in many places the main economic problem is a labor shortage. But growth has not concentrated North Carolina's population in a few cities. This has always been thickly settled rural land, and if one is never out of sight of others there is also plenty of green space and reminders of rural roots, from barbecue stands to country Baptist churches. Tarheels can live surrounded by forests or farms and yet be within an hour's drive of huge shopping centers and thousands of workplaces: more than any other big state, North Carolina has had decentralized growth.

Change has not been directed from any single establishment; the forces that have produced it are diverse and sometimes hostile. North Carolina does have a small and articulate elite, which looks for guidance to the University of North Carolina at Chapel Hill and the historically progressive editors of the state's newspapers, most prominently the Raleigh *News & Observer* and the *Charlotte Observer*. Quite different attitudes are nurtured by tradition-minded churches in a state where churchgoing is deeply ingrained, endorsed for years through Sunday blue laws and strengthened periodically by religious revivals. North Carolina's Billy Graham remains a strong voice for revealed religion, appearing in Bill Clinton's inaugurations as he had in Dwight Eisenhower's 40 years before; Graham and his wife, Ruth, were awarded the Congressional Gold Medal in May 1996. In the economically backward state North Carolina was when infant mortality was common and indoor plumbing was not, religion was a fountain of hope and a source of discipline; and it is still, perhaps even more, in this now bustling air-conditioned, cable- and computer-wired commonwealth.

North Carolina has grown with the aid of both its progressive and tradition-minded citizens, and in spite of, sometimes because of, the polarized politics that has developed between the two sides. Tradition-minded religion has provided a discipline for many churchgoers that has made them steady workers and community leaders. Liberal progressivism has provided an impetus toward building good schools and universities and highways and amenities like the nation's only state symphony and the state high schools for science and mathematics and the arts. North Carolina's professionals tend to share progressive values; its businessmen and conservative Protestants tend to share tradition-minded values. Both groups have contributed to the state's economic dynamism and cultural energy.

From these two strands of North Carolina tradition developed a polarized, increasingly party-line politics that is pretty evenly balanced, waged partly on economic issues but even more on cultural attitudes. It is a politics in which Democrats and Republicans have been distinctive, sometimes bitter in their rivalries, for years not overlapping in their ideas but by the mid-1990s converging on at least some issues. This politics has built on historic partisan patterns: coastal North Carolina settlers tended to be British Anglicans who became Methodists, slaveholders who supported the Confederacy and voted Democratic; Piedmont settlers tended to be Scots-Irish Presbyterians, Union men in 1861 and Republicans ever after.

Today the two sides are differently but evenly balanced, as seen in the close margins in the last two presidential races: George Bush carried North Carolina 43.4%–42.7% in 1992, Bob Dole 49%–44% in 1996. The most effective paladins of both traditions, Republican Senator Jesse Helms and Democratic Governor Jim Hunt, have each been elected to statewide office five times over 25 years, and in 1984 waged what was then the most expensive Senate race in U.S. history (the record-breaker was in California in 1994); once bitter rivals, they have since reconciled, and work together on many issues. Since the 1970s, North Carolina has had more seriously contested House races than any other state, with results tending along straight party lines, and sharp reversals of fortune: Democrats controlled the delegation 8–4 after 1992, Republicans 8–4 after 1994, and it was 6–6 after 1996. This convergence of national and state politics came earlier than elsewhere in the South.

Bill Clinton's endorsement in 1995of the FDA's proposal to treat nicotine as a drug hurt Clinton and other Democrats in tobacco country in 1996, as Dole carried the state and the Republican margin increased (or Democratic margin decreased) in 10 of 12 congressional districts. Republicans won the vote for U.S. House 53%–45%; Democrats' two gains came in the pro-Clinton 4th District which had been a flukish gain for Republicans in 1994 and in the 2d

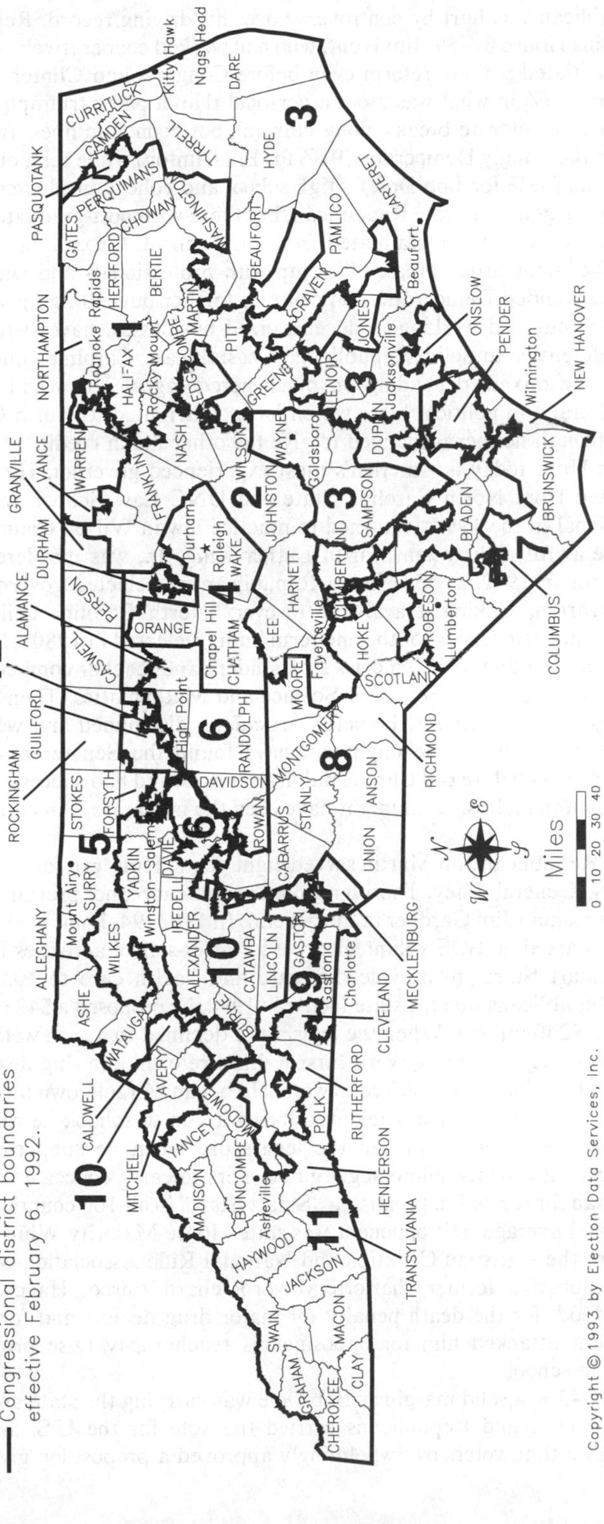
— Congressional district boundaries
effective February 6, 1992.
Copyright © 1993 by Election Data Services, Inc.
Miles
0 10 20 30 40
CURRITUCK
CAMDEN
PASQUOTANK
PERQUIMANS
GATES
HERTFORD
CHOWAN
TYRRELL
WASHINGTON
DARE
Kitty Hawk
Nags Head
HYDE
BEAUFORT
PAMLICO
CARTERET
Beaufort
CRAVEN
JONES
ONSLOW
Jacksonville
PENDER
NEW HANOVER
Wilmington
BRUNSWICK
COLUMBUS
BLADEN
SAMPSON
DUPLIN
LENOIR
GREENE
PITT
MARTIN
BERTIE
NORTHAMPTON
Roanoke Rapids
HALIFAX
Rocky Mount
EDGECOMBE
NASH
WILSON
WAYNE
Goldsboro
JOHNSTON
WAKE
Raleigh
Durham
FRANKLIN
WARREN
VANCE
GRANVILLE
DURHAM
PERSON
ALAMANCE
CASWELL
ORANGE
Chapel Hill
CHATHAM
LEE
HARNETT
CUMBERLAND
Fayetteville
HOKE
ROBESON
Lumberton
SCOTLAND
RICHMOND
MOORE
RANDOLPH
High Point
GUILFORD
ROCKINGHAM
STOKES
FORSYTH
Winston-Salem
DAVIDSON
MONTGOMERY
ANSON
STANLY
ROWAN
CABARRUS
UNION
MECKLENBURG
Charlotte
GASTON
Gastonia
LINCOLN
CATAWBA
IREDELL
DAVIE
YADKIN
SURRY
Mount Airy
ALLEGHANY
ASHE
WILKES
ALEXANDER
WATAUGA
CALDWELL
BURKE
CLEVELAND
RUTHERFORD
POLK
HENDERSON
TRANSYLVANIA
McDOWELL
AVERY
MITCHELL
YANCEY
MADISON
BUNCOMBE
Asheville
HAYWOOD
JACKSON
SWAIN
MACON
CLAY
GRAHAM
CHEROKEE
1
2
3
4
5
6
7
8
9
10
11
12

where the Republican was hurt by controversy over his driving record. Republicans held onto the North Carolina House 61–59. Jim Hunt, who had worked cooperatively with the Republican legislature and initiated welfare reform even before Congress and Clinton acted in 1996, won reelection by 56%–43% in what was more a personal than a party triumph.

North Carolina's electorate breaks along cultural, not economic lines. In the 1996 exit poll blacks were overwhelmingly Democratic (91% for Bill Clinton) while religious-right whites were heavily Republican (68% for Bob Dole). High school and college graduates, the middle of the education spectrum, generally vote Republican, but those with post-graduate degrees are just as Democratic as those who never graduated from high school. Geographically, this means the centers of the Piedmont urban areas, filling up with professionals and with significant black populations, have trended Democratic: the counties farther out, filling up with middle income families spreading out and working in decentralized businesses, have switched from historic Democratic preferences to solid Republican. Coastal east Carolina, once overwhelmingly Democratic, is now mixed, depending on black percentages. The result is a close balance between two cultural and political blocs which have contributed to North Carolina's unanticipated growth—though neither is inclined to give the other much credit.

Governor. Jim Hunt today is America's most experienced governor. He grew up in Wilson County, graduated from North Carolina State and UNC Law School, worked for the Ford Foundation in Nepal in the 1960s, returned to practice law in Wilson County and helped keep the peace on the awful night when Martin Luther King, Jr., was murdered. He was elected lieutenant governor in 1972, at 35, when a Republican was elected governor, and pushed for universal kindergarten, making it available to every North Carolina child. He was elected governor in 1976 and, after repeal of the one-term limit, reelected in 1980. He pushed education programs—primary reading, reduced class size, student and teacher competency tests, dropout prevention, the North Carolina School of Science and Mathematics. Then in 1984 he lost the hard-fought Senate race to Helms. Forceful, articulate, disciplined and well-organized, Hunt seems by nature an executive; he might not have found the Senate congenial. He became governor here two years before Bill Clinton did in Arkansas, and had successes much sooner than Clinton; had he beaten Helms, Hunt might have been the moderate Democrat elected president in the 1990s.

In 1992, after Republican Jim Martin served eight years, Hunt ran for governor again, easily beating Attorney General Lacy Thornburg in the primary and prevailing 53%–43% over Republican businessman Jim Gardner in the general. In 1993–94, Hunt pushed through tougher crime sentences, started an SOS volunteer drive for after-school activities for at-risk children, and initiated "Smart Start" to provide day care and health care to 10,000 children in 33 counties. After Republicans won the state House in 1994, he proposed a $483 million tax cut; the legislature passed $240 million. When the legislature declined to act on welfare, Hunt used his executive order privilege to start a Work First welfare reform, allowing flexibility for counties and moving 17,000 families from welfare to work. He began "Crackdown for Children," seeking overdue child support. He made it a felony to bring a gun to school; he required prisoners to work. He angered many Democrats in the legislature when he supported the Republican "conceal and carry" law which allows legal gun owners to carry concealed firearms in public.

In 1996 Hunt ran for reelection promising "Smart Start" in all 100 counties and a teacher pay raise to the national average. His opponent was state House Majority Whip Robin Hayes, who with support from the Christian Coalition and National Rifle Association won the Republican nomination 50%–46% over former Charlotte Mayor Richard Vinroot. Hayes called for repeal of the sales tax on food, for the death penalty for major drug dealers and for forcing people off welfare rolls. Hunt attacked him for opposing his teacher pay raise proposal and the law prohibiting guns in schools.

Hunt won 56%–43%, a solid margin as Bob Dole was carrying the state and Jesse Helms was being reelected senator and Republicans carried the vote for the U.S. and North Carolina House. At the same time voters overwhelmingly approved a proposition giving the governor a veto for the first time since the Revolutionary War. Hunt remains a national figure as chairman of the National Commission on Teaching and America's Future and is still involved at the ground level: he and his wife volunteer every week as mentors in Wake County schools. Behind the scenes, he took a lead role in the negotiations for a settlement between state attorneys general and the major tobacco companies in April 1997. While there has been much talk of New Democrats in Washington, Hunt has for many years now been a working New Democrat, setting a course for activist government informed by strong moral values in a state that often sets an example for America.

Senior Senator. No American politician is more controversial, beloved in some quarters and hated in others, than Jesse Helms, now beginning his fifth term in the Senate and chairman of the Foreign Relations Committee. Helms grew up the son of the police chief of Monroe, North Carolina, 15 miles from the birthplace of Andrew Jackson—a breeding ground, it seems, for true-believing, contentious leaders. With Jacksonian tenacity he has stuck to his early convictions—respect for elders and law and order, traditional religious faith and moral principles, patriotism, the order imposed by racial segregation—with the exception of the last, and his abandonment of it has often seemed grudging and halfhearted. In a time of relativism and ambiguity, Jesse Helms has stood out for the clarity of his views and his steadfast insistence on articulating them. Helms has always been an advocate, not a principal; a talker rather than a doer. Yet he has shown increasing openness to others as his responsibilities have increased, establishing warm working relationships with Secretary of State Madeleine Albright and his 1984 opponent Governor Jim Hunt.

Helms attended Wingate College and Wake Forest but did not graduate. He served in the Navy in World War II and became a journalist in Raleigh, worked for two U.S. senators from 1951–53, headed the state Banker's Association, served on the Raleigh Council and from 1960–72 was a commentator on Raleigh TV and the Tobacco Radio Network. So he was a familiar voice and a seasoned political operator when he ran for the Senate in 1972, and upset a moderate Democrat 54%–46%. Helms made then and makes now no attempt to win over everyone; he has a solidly conservative voting record, and can state his views pungently. Democrats and many in the press made much of his caustic 1994 comments on Bill Clinton—that the president was not respected by many in the military and, "jokingly," Helms insisted, that when visiting North Carolina, "Mr. Clinton had better watch out if he comes down here. He better have a bodyguard." He has had vigorous opposition every time he has run for reelection and his percentages have been in a narrow range—55%, 52%, 53%, 53%.

In his first 20 years in the Senate, Helms was mostly in the posture of opposition; in the mid-1990s he has been pursuing his own reform policies, with some success. He has long served on the Agriculture Committee, and chaired it in the 1980s; he supported tobacco programs there, but had to be bailed out of difficulties managing farm bills in the 1980s by Bob Dole. Helms was happier obtaining roll call votes on cultural issues—abortion and the fetal tissue research ban, school busing, Japanese American redress, AIDS funding, and the National Endowment for the Arts. He has been an adamant supporter of the flag-burning and school prayer amendments.

Helms has used his seat on Foreign Relations to conduct something like his own foreign policy. In the Reagan and Bush years he and aides James Lucier, Christopher Manion and Deborah DeMoss developed their own sources and attempted to manipulate State Department appointments to help the contras in Nicaragua and rightists in El Salvador. Helms's great cause in the 1970s was to defeat the Panama Canal treaties—a cause which helped defeat a dozen liberal senators and kept alive Ronald Reagan's candidacy when it threatened to die in the North Carolina primary in 1976. Helms became the ranking Republican on Foreign Relations in 1987 (he had promised not to take the chairmanship in the 1984 campaign, but did not feel bound when Republicans lost the majority in 1986) and chairman in 1995. But Helms had hired a new staff in the early 1990s and proceeded to exert influence adeptly. He favored lifting the arms embargo on Bosnia; he opposed the U.S. military intervention in Haiti; he opposes the use of U.S. troops as peacekeeping forces in the Golan Heights; he was leery of the U.S. agreement with North Korea; he looked askance at the operations of the United Nations. He promised not to obstruct most nominations. But when the White House rejected Secretary of State Warren Christopher's proposal to reorganize foreign policy agencies in 1995, Helms presented a similar plan of his own, holding up 18 ambassador nominations and approval of the START II and Chemical Weapons treaties; he ultimately passed $1.7 billion in spending cuts from State Department agencies over five years.

Helms succeeded in passing his Helms-Burton Act, signed by Bill Clinton in an election year, which codified the U.S. trade embargo against Cuba and allowed lawsuits against foreign companies who benefited by property expropriated from Americans by Fidel Castro's Communist dictatorship; the latter's implementation was delayed indefinitely by Clinton in 1996 and 1997. Helms was pleased to see Albright, then ambassador to the United Nations, exert pressure and block Boutros Boutros-Ghali from a second term as UN secretary general; in March 1997 Albright, as secretary of State, spent a day in North Carolina as Helms's guest. The Chemical Weapons Convention was finally passed in April 1997 over Helms's opposition, but with significant foreign policy concessions he negotiated.

In 1990 and 1996 Helms won reelection by beating Democrat Harvey Gantt in two strongly contested elections. The first contest, especially closely watched, was between an obdurate opponent of the Martin Luther King holiday and a black liberal who refused to trim on issues, proclaiming his support of more federal spending in TV spots and in personal appearances on the steps of each of North Carolina's 100 county courthouses. Gantt's personal story was inspiring: he was educated in segregated schools and was admitted to Clemson University by court order; he made a successful living as an architect; he was twice elected mayor of Charlotte; far from harboring resentments or seeking reparations, he seemed exuberant and optimistic. Rather than suggest whites were prejudiced, he sought their votes, and won a runoff primary against a white moderate, 57%–43%. In the general, Gantt did a superb job of framing the issues, dismissing Helms's preoccupation with the NEA and abortion as unimportant.

But Helms, armed with money raised by a nationwide direct mail campaign, seized the initiative in mid-October with three ads. One attacked racial quotas by showing white hands crumpling a rejection slip while the announcer said the man had lost his job to a minority though he was better qualified, and accused Gantt of supporting quotas. A radio spot attacked Gantt for "secret" campaigning because he ran ads on black radio stations (a similar charge could be made against most candidates in this segmented society). The third attacked Gantt for using "his office and minority status" to make a $450,000 profit on a $679 investment in a TV station license which was then sold to a white corporation—a charge Democrats and journalists cried was racist. But in fact Gantt had not resisted the temptation to take financial advantage of the law providing for racial preference in broadcast licenses, a law that when brought into light of day, most Democrats joined Republicans in repealing it in 1995. Gantt fell in the polls, and there was reason all along to think some of the Helms vote was hidden, concealed by conservative voters who would not speak openly to pollsters of the liberal media. Helms won 53%–47%. Gantt carried young voters and Helms the elderly, the opposite of partisan patterns elsewhere in the nation. Gantt won solidly in Charlotte but ran behind in much of east Carolina.

By 1996 Helms was visibly older and had split with his old campaign organizers. But he certainly did not give up. Gantt ran again, and had primary opposition from Charles Sanders, former CEO of the Glaxo pharmaceutical company, who ran as "the one Democrat who can beat Jesse Helms." During the primary campaign, Helms ran ads attacking both Gantt and Sanders for backing "racial preferences in hiring" and "extending health insurance to homosexual partners." Gantt won 52%–42%, but turnout was down 105,000 from six years before. Helms refused Gantt's challenge to debate (they have met only once, at a 1980s reception) and refused to let the press know his schedule. Gantt attacked Helms for voting to "cut" Social Security, and called for more student loans, a higher minimum wage, tax credits and deductions for day care and college tuition; Gantt said he supported the 1996 Welfare Reform Act. Helms ran ads accusing Gantt of using his minority status "to get preferential treatment on public school contracts" and raised the broadcast racial preference again. Gantt said Helms voted to cut Medicare while supporting tax breaks for Fortune 500 companies, and attacked Helms because the foundation that handles Helms's archives accepted contributions from corporations and the governments of Taiwan and Kuwait. Helms responded that Gantt has "raised millions from gay activists from New York to San Francisco." Gantt spent over $7 million; Helms spent a total of $14.5 million and won 53%–46%. Gantt ran almost even with Bill Clinton's minority showing in the state.

Junior Senator. Lauch Faircloth, a longtime Democrat, ran in 1992 as a Republican and an ally of Jesse Helms. (His first name is short for McLauchlin and pronounced *lock.*) Faircloth grew up in eastern North Carolina, started running his family's Sampson County farm at 19 when his father had a stroke, then served in the Army. In time he owned many hog farms in the nation's number one hog-producing county and began his own construction company as well. He also got involved in politics, and served as on the Highway Commission under Governors Terry Sanford and Dan Moore and was Jim Hunt's Commerce Commissioner for six years. In 1984, he ran third in the Democratic gubernatorial primary; there was talk he had wanted the 1986 Senate nomination and was angry it went to Sanford, who was then president of Duke University. Sanford won the seat narrowly, but his outspoken opposition to the Gulf war and his reluctance to condemn the Keating Five were clear liabilities. Faircloth switched parties in February 1991 and with the support of Helms allies ran against former Charlotte Mayor (and now Congresswoman) Sue Myrick for the Republican nomination. Myrick attacked Faircloth for his millionaire status and as a two-timer who backed both Helms and Hunt in 1984, but Faircloth won the primary by a 48%–30% margin (40% is enough to win without a runoff here), carrying even Charlotte. In the general Faircloth was a stealth candidate, making few appearances but running lots of ads, accusing Sanford of voting like Ted Kennedy, and for supporting welfare over workfare. In early October, Sanford, 75, had heart surgery. This raised the age issue against the incumbent, and in the end Faircloth, no youngster himself, won 50%–46%.

In the Senate Faircloth has proved his party switch wasn't insincere and has one of the most conservative voting records. He has been a thorn in the side of the Clinton Administration, although not always successfully: he failed to stop the Justice Department nomination of Duke law professor Walter Dellinger and the nomination of Arkansan Ricki Tigert-Helfer to head the FDIC. He was one of the harshest critics of the Clintons in the Banking Committee's Whitewater hearings, demanding that the Commodity Futures Trading Commission deliver records of Hillary Rodham Clinton's cattle-futures investments and criticizing independent counsel Robert Fiske for alleged leniency. Faircloth in turn was criticized for impropriety after he and Helms had lunch with Judge David Sentelle, a North Carolinian who headed the panel selecting independent counsels, although no rule was violated.

On other issues, he challenged U.S. loans to Mexico, sponsored legislation for state-set speed limits, worked to protect the free speech rights of citizens protesting addiction recovery homes. He opposed a full repeal of the Glass-Steagall act to open up banking and insurance services. He failed to end debate to get a Senate vote on his right-to-work bill which would have made union dues voluntary. He opposed the first Senate version of welfare reform because he wanted tougher restrictions for unwed teenage mothers, but voted for the final bill in July 1996. Faircloth has shown some moderate tendencies as well: he supported the Chafee-Breaux compromise budget in May 1996. With Ted Kennedy, he sponsored the Church Arson Act of 1996.

Faircloth got a seat in the 105th Congress on Appropriations (the first North Carolinian there since 1911) and the chair of the District of Columbia Subcommittee. He believes Congress has some obligation to the District but that home rule was a mistake. "There are many privileges of living in the capital of the U.S. Voting for mayor simply won't be one of them," he said; he wants instead for the fiscal control board to appoint a city manager. "My ability to run a city is exactly that of Marion Barry's: none at all." His major priority for 1997 is a $1,500 tax credit for two-year college or vocational school tuition. He also wants to deny DEA licenses to doctors in Arizona or California who prescribe or recommend marijuana under those states' 1996 referenda. And he seeks to tighten welfare reform by requiring drug tests of recipients and benefit losses for those who fail to meet work requirements on three occasions. He has worked for local North Carolina projects—Triangle regional rail, protecting tobacco farmers, the UNC-Chapel Hill telescope, the Lost Colony theater. He favors funding for the EPA Research Triangle complex which he once opposed.

Faircloth comes up for reelection in 1998 in a state which has trended Republican. Possible opponents include former Glaxo CEO Charles Sanders, who lost the 1996 Senate primary to Harvey Gantt; Crime Control and Public Safety Secretary Richard Moore; and state Senators Roy Cooper and Howard Lee.

Presidential politics. North Carolina has been the South's most straight-ticket state, which left it very much in play in 1992 and somewhat in 1996. But Bill Clinton's campaign against tobacco put it out of his reach in 1996, and makes it less likely to be seriously contested in the future.

North Carolina, which switched its primary to Super Tuesday in 1988, switched it back to May in 1992. It has been crucial only once: in 1976, when after five straight losses, Ronald Reagan started denouncing the Panama Canal Treaty and won his first victory over Gerald Ford. In 1988 Al Gore won here, after citing his credentials as a tobacco grower; his speech against tobacco at the 1996 convention will make it hard for him to win here in 2000, at least in the same way. One possible candidate with great strength here: North Carolina native Elizabeth Dole.

Congressional districting. North Carolina has had a raging controversy over districting ever since the 1990 Census gave it a 12th House seat, its first new seat in 60 years. The Justice Department, under the prevailing interpretation of the Voting Rights Act, required the state to create two black-majority districts—difficult because North Carolina has no large concentrations of blacks like Georgia or Texas. So the Democratic legislature drew a plan with a jagged-boundaried 1st District in east Carolina and a 12th extending, sometimes just along the median strip of I-85, from Gastonia through Charlotte, Winston-Salem and Greensboro. In June 1993 the Supreme Court in *Shaw v. Reno*, focusing on the 12th, ordered the plan reexamined. On remand a three-judge federal court upheld the plan in August 1994. But in June 1996 the Supreme Court declared the 12th unconstitutional. The three-judge panel in July ruled the 1996 election could go ahead under the old lines, but that they would have to be redrawn by April 1, 1997. On March 27, the divided legislature agreed on a new plan—veto-proof because North Carolina's new veto does not apply to redistricting.

The new plan, still subject to review by the Justice Department and the Supreme Court, smooths out the district lines but, in a spirit of bipartisan compromise, leaves the districts much as they were. The 1st and 12th districts, both formerly 57% black, are now 50% and 47% black, respectively (measuring by the 1990 Census), so that neither incumbent seems gravely endangered. The removal of some black precincts from the 1st and 12th will make some adjacent districts marginally more Democratic. But the plan is being challenged yet again in 1997, this time by African-American organizations and some state legislators, who are asking the three-judge panel to consider yet another alternative.

The People: Est. Pop. 1996: 7,323,000; Pop. 1990: 6,632,000, up 10.4% 1990–1996. 2.8% of U.S. total, 11th largest; 50% rural. Median age: 34.7 years. 13% 65 years and over. 75.0% White, 21.9% Black, 1% Asian, 1.2% Amer. Indian, 1.2% Hispanic origin. Households: 56.6% married couple families; 26% married couple fams. w. children; 41% college educ.; median household income: $26,647; per capita income: $12,885; 68.0% owner occupied housing; median house value: $65,800; median monthly rent: $284. 4.3% Unemployment. 1996 Voting age pop.: 5,519,000. 1996 Turnout: 2,515,807; 46% of VAP. Registered voters (1996): 4,318,008; 2,346,952 D (54%), 1,456,599 R (34%), 514,457 unaffiliated and minor parties (12%).

Political Lineup: Governor, James B. Hunt, Jr. (D); Lt. Gov., Dennis A. Wicker (D); Secy. of State, Elaine Marshall (D); Atty. Gen., Michael F. Easley (D); Treasurer, Harlan E. Boyles (D); Auditor, Ralph Campbell (D). State Senate, 50 (30 D and 20 R); Senate President, Dennis A. Wicker (D); State House, 120 (59 D and 61 R); House Speaker, Harold Brubaker (R). Senators, Jesse A. Helms (R) and Lauch Faircloth (R). Representatives, 12 (6 D and 6 R).

Board of Elections: 919-733-7173; **Filing Deadline for U.S. Congress:** February 2, 1998.

1996 Presidential Vote

Dole (R)	1,225,938	(49%)
Clinton (D)	1,107,849	(44%)
Perot (I)	168,059	(7%)

1996 Republican Presidential Primary

Dole (R)	202,863	(71%)
Buchanan (R)	37,126	(13%)
Keyes (R)	11,759	(4%)
Forbes (R)	11,588	(4%)
Other	20,876	(8%)

1992 Presidential Vote

Bush (R)	1,134,661	(43%)
Clinton (D)	1,114,042	(43%)
Perot (I)	357,864	(14%)

GOVERNOR

Gov. James B. Hunt, Jr. (D)

Elected 1992, term expires Jan. 2001; b. May 16, 1937, Greensboro; home, Rock Ridge; NC St., B.S. 1959, M.S. 1962, U. of NC at Chapel Hill, J.D. 1964; Presbyterian; married (Carolyn).

Career: Cattle rancher; Ford Foundation Econ. Advisor to Nepal, 1964–66; Practicing atty., 1966–92; NC Lt. Gov., 1972–77; NC Gov., 1976–85.

Office: State Capitol, Raleigh 27603, 919-733-4240; Fax: 919-733-5166; Web site: www.state.nc.us.

Election Results

1996 gen.	James B. Hunt Jr. (D)	1,436,638	(56%)
	Robin Hayes (R)	1,097,053	(43%)
1996 prim.	James B. Hunt Jr. (D) unopposed		
1992 gen.	James B. Hunt, Jr. (D)	1,368,246	(53%)
	Jim Gardner (R)	1,121,955	(43%)
	Scott McLaughlin (Lib)	104,983	(4%)

SENATORS

Sen. Jesse A. Helms (R)

Elected 1972, seat up 2002; b. Oct. 18, 1921, Monroe; home, Raleigh; Wingate Col., Wake Forest U.; Baptist; married (Dorothy).

Career: Navy, 1942–45 (World War II); City Editor, *Raleigh Times*; A.A., U.S. Sen. Willis Smith, 1951–53; A.A., U.S. Sen. Alton Lennon, 1953; Exec. Dir., NC Bankers Assn., 1953–60; Raleigh City Cncl., 1957–61; Exec. V.P., WRAL-TV & Tobacco Radio Network, 1960–72.

DC Office: 403 DSOB 20510, 202-224-6342; Fax: 202-228-1339; e-mail: jesse_helms@helms.senate.gov.

State Offices: Hickory, 704-322-5170; Raleigh, 919-856-4630.

Committees: *Agriculture, Nutrition & Forestry* (2nd of 10 R): Marketing, Inspection & Product Promotion; Production & Price Competitiveness. *Foreign Relations* (Chmn. of 10 R); Intl. Operations; Near Eastern & South Asian Affairs; Western Hemisphere & Peace Corps Affairs. *Rules & Administration* (2nd of 9 R).

Group Ratings

	ADA	ACLU	AFS	LCV	CFA	CON	NFIB	COC	ACU	NTLC	CHC
1996	5	18	0	8	7	42	100	85	100	100	100
1995	0	—	0	0	13	29	—	100	100	—	—

National Journal Ratings

	1995 LIB — 1995 CONS			1996 LIB — 1996 CONS		
Economic	31%	—	66%	11%	—	86%
Social	0%	—	88%	0%	—	72%
Foreign	0%	—	92%	0%	—	74%

Key Votes of the 104th Congress

1. Reduce Medicare Growth $	Y	5. Flag Amendment	Y	9. Anti-Missile Defense	Y
2. Lmt. Prod. Liab. Damages	Y	6. Endangered Species	N	10. Cuban Embargo	Y
3. Increase Min. Wage	N	7. Gay Employment Rights	N	11. Bar Bosnia Troop $	Y
4. Welfare Reform	Y	8. Ovrd. Part. Birth Veto	Y	12. Cut Vietnam Aid	Y

Election Results

1996 general	Jesse A. Helms (R)	1,345,833	(53%)	($14,589,266)
	Harvey B. Gantt (D)	1,173,875	(46%)	($7,992,980)
1996 primary	Jesse A. Helms (R)	unopposed		
1990 general	Jesse A. Helms (R)	1,088,331	(53%)	($17,761,579)
	Harvey B. Gantt (D)	981,573	(47%)	($7,811,520)

Sen. Lauch Faircloth (R)

Elected 1992, seat up 1998; b. Jan. 14, 1928, Concord; home, Clinton; Presbyterian; divorced.

Career: Army, 1954–55; Farmer, businessman; Owner, Faircloth Farms, Coharie Mills, Coharie Farms; NC Highway Commissioner, 1961–64, Chmn., 1967–73; NC Secy. of Commerce, 1977–83.

DC Office: 317 HSOB 20515, 202-224-3154; Fax: 202-224-7406; e-mail: senator@faircloth.senate.gov.

State Offices: Asheville, 704-244-3099; Charlotte, 704-375-1993; Raleigh, 919-856-4791; Winston-Salem, 919-631-5313.

Committees: *Appropriations* (14th of 15 R): District of Columbia (Chmn.); Labor, Health & Human Services & Education; Military Construction; Transportation; Treasury, Postal Service & General Government. *Banking, Housing & Urban Affairs* (5th of 10 R): Financial Institutions & Regulatory Relief (Chmn.); Housing Opportunity & Community Development; Securities. *Small Business* (9th of 10 R).

Group Ratings

	ADA	ACLU	AFS	LCV	CFA	CON	NFIB	COC	ACU	NTLC	CHC
1996	5	29	14	8	7	79	97	92	95	97	100
1995	0	—	0	0	13	54	—	95	100	—	—

National Journal Ratings

	1995 LIB — 1995 CONS			1996 LIB — 1996 CONS		
Economic	30%	—	69%	9%	—	89%
Social	0%	—	88%	0%	—	72%
Foreign	22%	—	67%	0%	—	74%

Key Votes of the 104th Congress

1. Reduce Medicare Growth $	Y	5. Flag Amendment	Y	9. Anti-Missile Defense	Y
2. Lmt. Prod. Liab. Damages	Y	6. Endangered Species	N	10. Cuban Embargo	Y
3. Increase Min. Wage	N	7. Gay Employment Rights	N	11. Bar Bosnia Troop $	Y
4. Welfare Reform	N	8. Ovrd. Part. Birth Veto	Y	12. Cut Vietnam Aid	Y

Election Results

1992 general	Lauch Faircloth (R)	1,297,892	(50%)	($2,952,102)
	Terry Sanford (D)	1,194,015	(46%)	($2,486,380)
	Others	85,984	(3%)	
1992 primary	Lauch Faircloth (R)	129,159	(48%)	
	Sue Myrick (R)	81,801	(30%)	
	Eugene (Gene) Johnston (R)	46,112	(17%)	
	Larry E. Harrington (R)	13,496	(5%)	
1986 general	Terry Sanford (D)	823,662	(52%)	($4,168,509)
	James T. Broyhill (R)	767,668	(48%)	($5,188,244)

FIRST DISTRICT

Eastern North Carolina in colonial days was a smaller version of the Chesapeake Bay colonies of Virginia and Maryland—a fertile land laced by dozens of rivers and inlets, with tobacco plantations and farms with docks on the water accessible to the ocean and so to London. North Carolina was settled later than the Chesapeake colonies, and was poorer, with smaller landholdings. But vestiges of its 18th Century past can still be seen in New Bern with its Tryon

Palace, the governor's house when this was the capital, and the tiny well-preserved town of Edenton on Albemarle Sound. Today, east Carolina is still tobacco country, indeed the major tobacco-producing land in the United States. It is inhabited almost entirely by the descendants of the original white settlers and black slaves of 250 years ago. They live in small towns and cities and in some of the most thickly-settled rural land in the United States. Tobacco is a labor-intensive crop which can produce yields of $4,000 an acre. A family can make a living off 40 acres of tobacco land and, with a tobacco allotment, many here do. But fewer than in the past. No-smoking laws and anti-smoking campaigns have cut cigarette sales, and many old east Carolina tobacco fields are planted with cucumbers, sweet potatoes and blueberries.

The 1st Congressional District of North Carolina, as redrawn in March 1997, covers much of the tobacco country of inland east Carolina. It touches Albemarle and Pamlico Sounds in the east and reaches rural counties north of Durham to the west. Although the old 1st District was not invalidated by the Supreme Court's June 1996 ruling, the redistricting changed the boundaries of every district, making the 1st much less irregularly shaped than before. It also reduced the black percentage of eligible voters from 57% to about 50%. The new 1st includes black-majority Northampton County and black neighborhoods in Rocky Mount, Greenville and New Bern. But the population is widely dispersed. Politically, this has long been Democratic country; some white voters here have been attracted to the Republicanism of Jesse Helms, but overall this remains a solid Democratic district.

The congresswoman from the 1st District is Eva Clayton, a Democrat with a long record in public life. She grew up in Savannah, Georgia, and has lived for many years in North Carolina. In the mid-1970s, she was director of the Soul City Foundation, civil rights leader Floyd McKissick's attempt to form a black "new town." That foundered, but Clayton backed Jim Hunt in 1976 and became an assistant secretary for community development in his first term as governor. She was elected to, and served as chairman of, the Warren County Board of Commissioners from 1982–91. She also ran her own consulting firm and in 1992 ran for the 1st District seat when the boundaries were drawn. The incumbent, 78-year-old Walter Jones, chairman of the Merchant Marine and Fisheries Committee since 1980 and chairman of the Peanuts and Tobacco Subcommittee before that, had decided to retire; he died in September 1992. His son, state legislator Walter Jones, Jr., ran and won 38% in the first Democratic primary—just 2% away from the 40% which under North Carolina law would have given him the nomination—ahead of Clayton, who had 31%. In the runoff in this 57% black district, Clayton won 55%–45%, and she won in November with 67%. Thus she—and 12th District Congressman Mel Watt—became the first black members of Congress from North Carolina since George White served in the late 1890s, and the first woman from North Carolina to serve a full term; Jones was elected in 1994 from the 3d District, as a Republican.

Clayton is part of the black middle class who have worked their way up in or close to government. In her 1992 campaign, she backed more public investment and job training and lower defense spending to cut the deficit; in office she earned one of the most liberal voting records, according to *National Journal*, in the House. Freshman Democrats elected her to chair their class. She was proud of working for WIC and food stamps extension, for crop disaster assistance, for the Section 515 affordable housing program. She amended the food stamps proposal in 1996 to reduce the 20-hour work requirement for those who receive food stamps worth less than what they would earn working 20 hours at the minimum wage. She has been alert to district interests, including defense contracts and bases outside district lines which employ many district residents, like the Newport News shipyard and Cherry Point Naval Aviation Depot. To urban Black Caucus members seeking her support for bills, she responds, "Does it include rural areas?" She has made reducing teen pregnancy a priority and has held forums in the district on that subject. In 1997 she got a seat on the Budget Committee; she also serves on Agriculture, where she got a waiver to sit as a non-voting member on the Risk Management and Specialty Crops Subcommittee so she can "monitor the subcommittee that oversees peanut and tobacco crops."

Clayton has been reelected easily. The March 1997 lines may reduce her percentage marginally but should not affect the safety of her seat.

The People: Pop. 1990: 553,426; 58% rural; 14% age 65+; 41% White; 57% Black; 1% Amer. Indian; 1% Hispanic origin. Households: 48% married couple families; 21% married couple fams. w. children; 28% college educ.; median household income: $18,226; per capita income: $8,918; median gross rent: $290; median house value: $45,600. *(Information does not reflect 1997 redistricting.)*

1996 Presidential Vote

Clinton (D)	105,563	(63%)
Dole (R)	53,582	(32%)
Perot (I)	8,229	(5%)

1992 Presidential Vote

Clinton (D)	109,657	(61%)
Bush (R)	53,019	(29%)
Perot (I)	18,266	(10%)

Rep. Eva M. Clayton (D)

Elected 1992; b. Sept. 16, 1934, Savannah, GA; home, Littleton; Johnson C. Smith U., B.S. 1955, NC Central U., M.S. 1962, U. of NC Law Schl., 1967–69; Presbyterian; married (Theaoseus).

Career: Exec. Dir., Soul City Foundation, 1974–76; NC Asst. Secy., Community Development, 1977–81; Pres. & Owner, Technical Resources Intl. Inc., 1981–92; Warren Cnty. Commission, Chmn., 1982–90.

DC Office: 2440 RHOB 20515, 202-225-3101; Fax: 202-225-3354.

District Offices: Greenville, 919-758-8800; Fayetteville, 910-323-9003; Warrenton, 919-257-4800.

Committees: *Agriculture* (6th of 23 D): Department Operations, Nutrition & Foreign Agriculture (RMM); Forestry, Resource Conservation & Research. *Budget* (19th of 19 D).

Group Ratings

	ADA	ACLU	AFS	LCV	CFA	CON	NFIB	COC	ACU	NTLC	CHC
1996	100	75	100	85	85	89	19	13	5	5	7
1995	100	—	—	100	100	31	—	13	8	—	—

National Journal Ratings

	1995 LIB — 1995 CONS			1996 LIB — 1996 CONS		
Economic	94%	—	0%	89%	—	0%
Social	80%	—	13%	84%	—	16%
Foreign	93%	—	0%	72%	—	28%

Key Votes of the 104th Congress

1. Reduce Medicare Growth $	N	5. Flag Amendment	Y	9. Cuban Embargo	N
2. Ovrd. Product Liab. Veto	N	6. Drop EPA Limits	Y	10. Bar Bosnia Troop $	N
3. Increase Min. Wage	Y	7. Repeal Assault-Weap. Ban	N	11. Cut Anti-Missile Defense	Y
4. Welfare Reform	N	8. Ovrd. Part. Birth Veto	N	12. Bar U.N. Uniforms	Y

Election Results

1996 general	Eva M. Clayton (D)	108,759	(66%)	($300,049)
	Ted Tyler (R)	54,666	(33%)	($26,248)
1996 primary	Eva M. Clayton (D)	unopposed		
1994 general	Eva M. Clayton (D)	66,827	(61%)	($417,700)
	Ted Tyler (R)	42,602	(39%)	($16,572)

SECOND DISTRICT

The coastal plain of North Carolina was long bypassed by history. It was settled after Virginia and South Carolina, and only filled in with English settlers as Scots-Irish families were streaming down the valley of Virginia to the western Piedmont. This has always been tobacco country, with life organized around a crop high-yield enough that a 40-acre plot of land can support a family (if it has a tobacco allotment). Tobacco was an important colonial crop, even more so after James B. Duke, a farmer from Durham County, created Bull Durham tobacco and Lucky Strike cigarettes. Cigarette factories grew up in Durham and eventually, from Duke's fortune, so did the Gothic buildings of Duke University. But otherwise this was a backward area. Its small farms and little cities were homes mainly to tenant farmers and mill hands, people raising families in thin-walled frame houses often with no electricity or running water.

Today, life is much better in the coastal plain. Not just because incomes are up, but because this is now one of America's fastest-growing metropolitan areas; Raleigh-Durham, with a dynamic economy, provides many counties around it with jobs. Most farmers here now own the land they farm and textile workers are better paid. And the four-lane roads and interstates enable people to live where they have family roots and church affiliations, and where traditional religion remains strong, and still partake of one of the nation's boom economies. Yet there remains a cultural divide. The Research Triangle area anchored by Durham, Raleigh and Chapel Hill has more Ph.D.s than almost any other area in the nation, and has been moving left politically despite rising incomes. The once rural counties, whose people are prosperous beyond their dreams but not highly educated, are moving to the right.

North Carolina's 2d Congressional District, as redrawn by the legislature in March 1997, covers much of the coastal plain around Raleigh. It stretches as far east as Rocky Mount, goes south into hog-producing Sampson County, spreads west to Sanford. Much of its population is in Johnston and Harnett Counties, south and east of Raleigh, where life is still rural in tone but where many new families have been moving; historically Democratic, these counties are now Republican. Before the 1997 redistricting, the 2d included Durham, which is heavily Democratic; that is now removed, but added was about half of Raleigh's Wake County including many black precincts in Raleigh. As a result, the district's black percentage rose from about 22% to 28%.

The congressman from the 2d District is Bob Etheridge, a Democrat elected in 1996. He was born in Sampson County, grew up in Johnston County, lives in Harnett County: he has the district pretty well covered. He is a hardware store owner and tobacco farmer, a pillar of his community and member of many boards; he served four years on the Harnett County Commission in the 1970s, was elected to the North Carolina House in 1978 and served 10 years, eventually chairing the Appropriations Committee. In 1988 and 1992 he was elected state Superintendent of Public Instruction, working on programs for educationally disadvantaged students and for a stronger curriculum. In the mid-1990s Governor Jim Hunt called for abolishing the superintendent post and transferred 300 employees to the State Board of Education. Etheridge, spying an opportunity, decided to run for the House.

The opportunity was to run against 1994 freshman David Funderburk, a longtime ally of Jesse Helms. Funderburk had a solid conservative voting record and the district seemed politically favorable; in 1996 it voted 52%–42% for Bob Dole. But in 1995, Funderburk was involved in an auto accident: his car forced another off the road, injuring three; witnesses said Funderburk was driving; the car went around the block, then appeared with Mrs. Funderburk at the wheel. The Funderburks contended she had been driving at the time of the accident, but he pleaded no-contest to crossing the center line.

For a time this incident wasn't an explicit subject of the campaign. Funderburk was a target of AFL-CIO ads; he attacked Etheridge for attending a conference at which homosexuality was discussed (in a seminar on "Unlearning Homophobia: The School's Role in Society"). He also tried to tie Etheridge to Bill Clinton's approval of FDA Commissioner David Kessler's announcement that tobacco could be regulated as a drug. A Funderburk commercial declared: "Bill Clinton and Bob Etheridge are running for office together. Bill Clinton has declared war on North Carolina tobacco farmers. If liberals like Henry Waxman and Bob Etheridge gain control of Congress, our tobacco farm families will be destroyed." Etheridge responded by citing his own tobacco credentials: "I'd be happy to match tobacco allotments with Mr. Funderburk. I own tobacco allotments and have for years. I'd like to know how many days Mr. Funderburk spent priming tobacco, setting tobacco, and how many days he spent under the hot sun in the tobacco fields." Then toward the end of the campaign, Etheridge ran an ad on the car accident, with the tag: "Congressman David Funderburk. Why won't he take responsibility?" This issue probably made the difference. Etheridge won 53%–46%, losing Johnston County only narrowly and carrying Harnett, both of which Funderburk swept in 1994.

For all his down-home image, Etheridge took some liberal stands in the campaign—against the House bill to ban "partial-birth" abortion, against term limits. He got a seat on the Agriculture Committee and called on members of Congress to imitate his "Give Teachers a Break" program of teaching a one-hour high school class twice a year. Redistricting probably helped him; if he lost Durham, he gained black votes in Raleigh. In the old boundaries, Etheridge would likely have had a strong Republican challenge in 1998, and in the new ones he may as well; but with his local strength and the advantages of incumbency, he will be tough to overtake.

The People: Pop. 1990: 552,529; 58% rural; 13% age 65+; 76% White; 22% Black; 1% Asian; 1% Amer. Indian; 1% Hispanic origin. Households: 58% married couple families; 26% married couple fams. w. children; 41% college educ.; median household income: $27,271; per capita income: $13,172; median gross rent: $376; median house value: $67,000. *(Information does not reflect 1997 redistricting.)*

1996 Presidential Vote

Dole (R)	111,155	(52%)
Clinton (D)	90,623	(42%)
Perot (I)	12,500	(6%)

1992 Presidential Vote

Bush (R)	99,256	(45%)
Clinton (D)	88,141	(40%)
Perot (I)	30,669	(14%)

Rep. Bob Etheridge (D)

Elected 1996; b. Aug. 7, 1941, Turkey; home, Lillington; Campbell U., B.S. 1965; Presbyterian; married (Faye).

Career: Army, 1965–67; Farmer, 1965–present; Vice Pres., Sales, Sorensen Industries, 1968–87; Harnett Cnty. Commissioner, 1973–76; Owner, Layton Hardware, 1973–90; NC House of Reps., 1978–88; Co-owner, WLLN Radio, 1979–91; NC Superintendent of Public Instruction, 1988–96.

DC Office: 1641 LHOB 20515, 202-225-4531; Fax: 202-225-5662.

DC Office: Durham, 919-383-7548; Lillington, 910-814-0335.

Committees: *Agriculture* (20th of 23 D): General Farm Commodities; Risk Management & Specialty Crops. *Science* (18th of 21 D): Basic Research.

Group Ratings and Key Votes: Newly Elected

Election Results

1996 general	Bob Etheridge (D)	113,820	(53%)	($730,969)
	David Funderburk (R)	98,951	(46%)	($1,037,080)
	Others	3,858	(2%)	
1996 primary	Bob Etheridge (D)	unopposed		
1994 general	David Funderburk (R)	79,207	(56%)	($725,357)
	Richard Moore (D)	62,122	(44%)	($918,909)

THIRD DISTRICT

Nearly 500 years ago, Giovanni de Verrazano sailed past the Gulf Stream and landed on a sandspit island he thought was the outer edge of China. He was wrong. It was the Outer Banks of North Carolina. These are probably America's most unstable barrier islands, constantly changing shape and cut by new inlets as they are battered by the ocean currents and storm winds. They were settled early by Europeans: Sir Walter Raleigh's Roanoke colony was founded here in 1587, then vanished shortly thereafter; Edward Teach—Blackbeard—and other pirates lurked in Pamlico and Albemarle Sounds behind the islets. History is still much with the Outer Banks: an antique form of English is spoken on Ocracoke Island, reachable only by ferry; the 208-foot lighthouse on Cape Hatteras looks out on some of the most treacherous currents in the Atlantic which have claimed a hundred ships; the sands along Kitty Hawk, with their constant winds, are where the Wright Brothers made mankind's first heavier-than-air flight in 1903.

Today, the Outer Banks have become vacation and retirement country, with affluent beachfront communities around Kitty Hawk, Nags Head and Duck and, much farther south, around Beaufort (*BOWfort*, not *BEWfort* as in South Carolina) and Morehead City. Inland, amid swamps, are some of America's biggest military bases, the Marine Corps's Camp Lejeune, the Army's Fort Bragg and Seymour Johnson Air Force Base. The flat lands of east Carolina have long been tobacco- and peanut-growing country, and now also hog-raising land.

The 3d Congressional District of North Carolina covers the Outer Banks and much of the coastal plain. Even after the March 1997 redistricting this remains an irregularly shaped district, with fingers of land going inland to include mostly white voters around Greenville and Goldsboro while leaving black majority areas in the 50% black 1st District. Before the 1997 redistricting, the boundaries here were even more bizarre; but in both cases the district was about 20% black.

The congressman from the 1st District is Walter Jones, Jr., a Republican elected in 1994. He grew up in eastern North Carolina, attended North Carolina State and Atlantic Christian College, and served in the National Guard. His father was Democratic congressman from the 1st District, which included most of northeast North Carolina, from February 1966 until his death in September 1992, and chairman of the Merchant Marine and Fisheries Committee for a dozen years. The younger Jones was elected in 1982 to the state legislature, where he voted to oust the Democratic speaker and often broke with Democratic leaders. In 1992, he ran as a Democrat in the new black-majority 1st District after his father retired, winning 38% in the first primary, just 2% shy of the 40% needed to avoid a runoff in North Carolina, then losing the runoff to Eva Clayton 55%–45%.

In April 1993, Jones switched to the Republican Party, and in May 1994, announced he was running for Congress in the 3d District: "My old party has changed and so has the world. Sadly, in my opinion, both are not for the best in far too many circumstances." This pitted Jones against four-term Congressman Martin Lancaster, a Democrat who had worked hard on local projects. But Lancaster had voted for the Clinton budget and tax package in 1993 and the crime bill in 1994, and hadn't been able to persuade the Clintons to drop the cigarette tax from their healthcare package. Jones ran an ad showing Lancaster jogging with Bill Clinton: "How'd Martin Lancaster get so out of touch? Well, look who he's running around with in Washington."

In a district which Clinton would lose 53%–40% in 1996, when he was more popular, Jones won 53%–47%. He ran especially strong in Greenville and Kinston and carried the areas around Camp Lejeune and Morehead City.

In the House, Jones got seats on National Security and on Resources, which absorbed his father's old Merchant Marine and Fisheries panel. His voting record was among the most conservative in the House. His major legislative accomplishment was passage of an original bill, the War Crimes Act of 1996, which authorizes future American prisoners of war to bring lawsuits against those who commit war crimes; this provides an enforcement mechanism for the Geneva Convention, which as a ratified treaty is the law of the land. Jones believes in sending U.S. troops abroad only when "there is a clear mission and an achievable goal," and "only under the flag and command of the United States"; he opposes gays and lesbians in the military. He also favors generous benefits and was one of the conservatives voting in November 1995 to send an appropriations bill back to conference to get more funds for veterans' health care. Jones opposes any efforts by the FDA to regulate tobacco. On abortion, he said: "I think abortion should be a political issue. All of the Founding Fathers acknowledged the existence of a supreme being. These issues are important, because unless we're morally and economically strong, we can't survive." He has worked on local projects, backing rock jetties on Oregon Inlet and funding to protect a herd of wild horses on Cape Lookout National Seashore.

In 1996 the best-known local Democrat, former state Senator Henson Barnes, declined to run against Jones. Instead, his opponent was George Parrott, who was once a volunteer for Jones in the state legislature. Parrott called Jones "the lyingest hypocrite I've ever seen in my life," because, Parrott said, Jones had broken a pledge to return $30,000 of his congressional salary to the government. Jones would not mention the Parrott's name in interviews. Jones won easily, 63%–37%, carrying every county. Redistricting should not change the political balance here much.

The People: Pop. 1990: 551,918; 62% rural; 12% age 65+; 76% White; 21% Black; 1% Asian; 2% Hispanic origin. Households: 61% married couple families; 28% married couple fams. w. children; 40% college educ.; median household income: $24,553; per capita income: $11,567; median gross rent: $359; median house value: $62,600. *(Information does not reflect 1997 redistricting.)*

1996 Presidential Vote

Dole (R)	100,123	(53%)
Clinton (D)	75,200	(40%)
Perot (I)	12,393	(7%)

1992 Presidential Vote

Bush (R)	89,877	(47%)
Clinton (D)	74,702	(39%)
Perot (I)	28,195	(15%)

Rep. Walter B. Jones, Jr. (R)

Elected 1994; b. Feb. 10, 1943, Farmville; home, Farmville; NC St. U., 1962–65, Atlantic Christian College, B.A. 1967; Catholic; married (Joe Anne).

Career: Mgr., Walter B. Jones Office Supply Co., 1967–73; Salesman, Dunn Assoc., 1973–82; NC House of Reps., 1982–92; Pres., Benefit Reserves Inc., 1989–94; Pres., Judson Co., 1990–94.

DC Office: 422 CHOB 20515, 202-225-3415; Fax: 202-225-3286.

District Offices: Goldsboro, 919-735-5382; Greenville, 919-931-1003.

Committees: *Banking & Financial Services* (30th of 30 R): Capital Markets, Securities & Government Sponsored Enterprises; Housing & Community Opportunity. *National Security* (24th of 30 R): Military Readiness; Military Research & Development. *Resources* (16th of 27 R): Fisheries Conservation, Wildlife & Oceans; National Parks & Public Lands.

Group Ratings

	ADA	ACLU	AFS	LCV	CFA	CON	NFIB	COC	ACU	NTLC	CHC
1996	5	12	0	8	8	9	100	94	100	100	100
1995	0	—	—	6	0	56	—	96	96	—	—

National Journal Ratings

	1995 LIB — 1995 CONS	1996 LIB — 1996 CONS
Economic	26% — 67%	0% — 82%
Social	21% — 72%	10% — 86%
Foreign	15% — 73%	0% — 79%

Key Votes of the 104th Congress

1. Reduce Medicare Growth $	Y	5. Flag Amendment	Y	9. Cuban Embargo	Y
2. Ovrd. Product Liab. Veto	Y	6. Drop EPA Limits	N	10. Bar Bosnia Troop $	Y
3. Increase Min. Wage	N	7. Repeal Assault-Weap. Ban	Y	11. Cut Anti-Missile Defense	N
4. Welfare Reform	Y	8. Ovrd. Part. Birth Veto	Y	12. Bar U.N. Uniforms	Y

Election Results

1996 general	Walter B. Jones, Jr. (R)	118,159	(63%)	($593,793)
	George Parrott (D)	68,887	(37%)	($37,255)
1996 primary	Walter B. Jones, Jr. (R)	unopposed		
1994 general	Walter B. Jones, Jr. (R)	72,464	(53%)	($477,463)
	H. Martin Lancaster (D)	65,013	(47%)	($941,901)

FOURTH DISTRICT

Back in the 1950s, few people would have predicted that the countryside around Raleigh and Durham, North Carolina, would be one of America's high-tech boom areas. But Governor Luther Hodges did, when he started Research Triangle Park as an R&D industrial park between the musty state capital of Raleigh, the Lucky Strike-manufacturing city of Durham and the tiny university town of Chapel Hill. With the drawing power of three universities (North Carolina State in Raleigh, Duke in Durham and the University of North Carolina in Chapel Hill), Research Triangle Park slowly began attracting big research outfits like Glaxo-Wellcome, IBM, Northern Telecom and the Environmental Protection Agency; today it has more than 37,000 people working for more than 96 major companies, stimulating hundreds of small startups and service businesses. Raleigh-Durham airport, which had four gates in the early 1970s, became a major national hub. Its metro area grew by more than 30% in the 1980s, the fastest metropolitan growth north and east of Atlanta, and for years had one of the lowest unemployment rates in the nation.

The 4th Congressional District of North Carolina includes most of the Research Triangle. In the 1992, 1994 and 1996 elections it included all of Raleigh's Wake County and Chapel Hill's Orange County, plus rural Chatham County; the legislature's March 1997 redistricting removed the eastern half of Wake County and added Durham and the Research Triangle Park itself. Politics here revolves around cultural issues; economic issues play little role in this booming environment where both tradition-minded and liberal-minded cultural views are vividly articulated by Jesse Helms, and university liberals and progressives like Jim Hunt. The two Democratic bases here are the black community and whites with post-graduate degrees. The big Republican base is whites with traditional religious beliefs. The balance in the 4th District, unlike that in North Carolina as a whole, has usually gone the Democrats' way: this is the only not heavily black North Carolina district that votes solidly against Jesse Helms and for Bill Clinton. Even so, there are some exceptions. Tom Fetzer, a longtime Helms supporter, was elected mayor of Raleigh in 1993 campaigning on an anti-crime platform and even winning some black votes. And in November 1994 Republican Fred Heineman won the 4th District House seat.

The congressman from the 4th District now, just as before 1994, is David Price, a Democrat first elected in 1986, who beat Heineman in 1996. Price grew up in east Tennessee, the son of a school principal and an English teacher. He came to North Carolina to go to college at Chapel Hill, earned a degree in divinity and a Ph.D. in Political Science at Yale and taught there four years, then became a political science professor at Duke in 1973. He was executive director of the North Carolina Democratic Party in the 1980 election cycle and chairman from 1983–84—both in effect appointments of Governor Jim Hunt; he helped develop North Carolina's robust straight-ticket two-party politics. In 1986 he ran for the House and beat a Republican who in 1984 had been swept in. In the House Price helped pass laws increasing the percentage of a home's value the FHA can insure, aiding technical education at community colleges, funding the EPA Research Triangle lab and raising the Falls Lake dam to ensure Raleigh's water supply. He is an interesting blend of political scientist and practical politician, and a lay Baptist preacher as well. He has written several books, including one on his experience in Congress.

In 1994 Price was upset by Fred Heineman, a former New York City cop and Raleigh police chief in the 1970s, who carried Wake County and won 50.4%–49.6%. Heineman had a solid conservative voting record in Congress and made the news most prominently in early 1995 when he was quoted by the strongly Democratic Raleigh *News & Observer* on his $133,600 salary and $50,000 police pension. "That does not make me rich . . . That makes me lower middle class . . . When I see someone who is making anywhere from $300,000 to $750,000 a year, that's middle class." Heineman said he was misquoted, but obviously the story did him damage: "Earth to Fred," said one Price ad, "Fred Heineman. He's out of touch with average families here. Way out." This was not an easy district for a Republican to hold. The AFL-CIO ran ads early against Heineman, and Price attacked him for his voting record on the environment and for backing a Clean Water Act revision that exempted hog producers from federal regulations. Heineman reprised his 1994 campaign, attacking Price for voting for a congressional pay raise and bouncing eight checks on the House bank; "Too liberal then, too liberal now," a Heineman ad said of Price. And Heineman trotted out 1994 video footage of Price saying, "We do have to cut Medicare." There was also a contrast in campaigning activity. Price walked precincts in north Raleigh and the suburb of Cary, while Heineman spent most of September in the hospital for repair of a torn intestine and then in October he avoided joint appearances and debates. Price outspent Heineman as well; the surprise perhaps was that the race was as close as it was: Price won 54%–44%.

Price now serves on Appropriations and says his major priorities are tax credits for college tuition and saving Medicare from insolvency. He wants to make scholarships and fellowships tax-exempt and to eliminate the 10% penalty on borrowing money from IRAs for education. Wake County Republican Chairman Tom Roberg announced in May 1997 that he will challenge Price in 1998.

The People: Pop. 1990: 552,441; 31% rural; 8% age 65+; 77% White; 20% Black; 2% Asian; 1% Hispanic origin. Households: 54% married couple families; 26% married couple fams. w. children; 62% college educ.; median household income: $34,569; per capita income: $16,708; median gross rent: $477; median house value: $95,500. *(Information does not reflect 1997 redistricting.)*

1996 Presidential Vote

Clinton (D)	141,051	(49%)
Dole (R)	130,642	(45%)
Perot (I)	14,401	(5%)

1992 Presidential Vote

Clinton (D)	126,577	(47%)
Bush (R)	105,612	(39%)
Perot (I)	38,878	(14%)

Rep. David E. Price (D)

Elected 1996; b. Aug. 17, 1940, Erwin, TN; home, Chapel Hill; U. of NC, B.A. 1961; Yale U., B.D. 1964, Ph.D. 1969; Baptist; married (Lisa).

Career: Legis. Aide, U.S. Sen. Bartlett, 1963–67; Prof., 1969–present, Yale U., 1969–73, Duke U., 1973–present; Exec. Dir., NC Dem. Party, 1979–80, Chmn., 1983–84; Staff Dir., DNC Comm. on Pres. Nominations, 1981–82; U.S. House of Reps., 1986–94.

DC Office: 2162 RHOB 20515, 202-225-1784; Fax: 202-225-2014; e-mail: david.price@mail.house.gov.

District Offices: Chapel Hill, 919-967-7924; Raleigh, 919-832-2456.

Committees: *Appropriations* (25th of 26 D): Treasury, Postal Service & General Government; VA, HUD & Independent Agencies.

Group Ratings and Key Votes: Newly Elected

Election Results

1996 general	David E. Price (D)	157,194	(54%)	($1,168,542)
	Fred Heineman (R)	126,466	(44%)	($980,249)
	Others	5,333	(2%)	
1996 primary	Davie E. Price (D)	unopposed		
1994 general	Fred Heineman (R)	77,773	(50%)	($264,869)
	David E. Price (D)	76,558	(50%)	($675,680)

FIFTH DISTRICT

From the coastal plain of North Carolina, the terrain rises slowly through modest hills cut by rivers in the Piedmont, until finally the first mountain ridges appear, their mysterious blue haze filling the crevasse valleys or clinging to the steep hillsides. The Piedmont, in between the plain and the mountains, was first settled by independent-minded Scots-Irish farmers and by followers of British and German sects like the Moravians. This was hardscrabble farm country at the time of the Civil War, with few slaves. By the late 19th Century, it was becoming industrialized, with textile mills alongside streams, furniture factories not far from hardwood forests and the R. J. Reynolds cigarette factories in Winston-Salem (the only city to be honored by the name of two cigarette brands). This Piedmont economy was hailed as the basis of a progressive New South, although textile mills paid low wages and tobacco employed few workers. In fact, only in the last two decades has the North Carolina economy taken off and grown substantially more affluent. Today this area has the country's most advanced tire recycling plant in Winston-Salem, a custom furniture making operation in Kernersville, the Hanes family's Moravian cookie business in Clemmons.

All these are within the boundaries of the 5th Congressional District of North Carolina, which sweeps along the northern edge of the state from the Piedmont to the main Appalachian chain, stopping along the way to include most of the Winston-Salem area. However, Winston-Salem casts only about one-third of the district's votes; the rest are sprinkled across the countryside and in small industrial cities like Reidsville, Eden and Mt. Airy (the setting for the Andy Griffith Show's fictional town of Mayberry). The legislature's March 1997 redistricting excised some of the 5th's eastern and western extremities, making it somewhat more compact but not changing the political balance; the black sections of Winston-Salem remain in the 12th District.

The congressman from the 5th District is Richard Burr, a Republican elected in 1994. Burr grew up in Winston-Salem, was a football player at Wake Forest, then worked for a wholesaling firm. In 1992 he ran against Congressman Steve Neal, a Democrat first elected in 1974, who usually won by close margins; Burr was outspent 3–1 and lost 53%–46%. Neal retired in 1994 and Burr ran again, with no opposition in the primary. His Democratic opponent was state Senator Sandy Sands, a rural trial lawyer who talked of "frustration with Washington taking action without concern for the impact on local government" and attacked Burr for using Jerry Falwell's Liberty University studios to produce his 1992 ads. Sands gained national publicity when he called on North Carolina to tax citrus crops in retaliation for Florida's cigarette tax. Burr headed North Carolina Taxpayers United and supported the Contract with America, and promised to make defense of tobacco his number one issue. He worked hard to tie Sands to the Clinton Administration. Burr won a solid 57%, carrying all but two counties and carrying the Winston-Salem area by nearly 2–1.

In the House he had a conservative voting record, was treasurer of the freshman class and won a seat on the Commerce Committee. His main cause there has been streamlining the FDA drug and medical device approval process, which he claims keeps valuable and life-saving products from patients; in March 1996 he introduced an FDA reform bill and held hearings, but no vote was taken in the full committee. He also attacked the FDA's move to regulate tobacco as a drug as a "witch hunt." "The tobacco industry currently spends millions of dollars to educate kids that smoking is an adult choice," he said. He helped to defeat an amendment to an agriculture appropriations bill that would have cut funding for crop insurance for tobacco; the vote was 212–210. On other issues, he worked to change the Medicaid formula, which got $900 million more for North Carolina over seven years, and he sought a crackdown on illegal textile imports, routed by China through other countries to evade quotas.

Burr has worked the district hard, with his 30-cup rule: he buys a cup of coffee everywhere he stops to talk to constituents and estimates he has bought as many as 30 in one day. He had underfunded opposition in 1996, and won easily, 62%–35%. He carried every county but Granville in the east, and it was removed by the March 1997 redistricting.

The People: Pop. 1990: 552,337; 60% rural; 14% age 65+; 84% White; 15% Black; 1% Hispanic origin. Households: 58% married couple families; 25% married couple fams. w. children; 36% college educ.; median household income: $25,543; per capita income: $12,716; median gross rent: $348; median house value: $59,000. *(Information does not reflect redistricting.)*

1996 Presidential Vote

Dole (R)	107,237	(51%)
Clinton (D)	87,100	(41%)
Perot (I)	15,376	(7%)

1992 Presidential Vote

Bush (R)	99,408	(43%)
Clinton (D)	98,056	(43%)
Perot (I)	30,631	(13%)

Rep. Richard M. Burr (R)

Elected 1994; b. Nov. 30, 1955, Charlottesville, VA; home, Winston-Salem; Wake Forest U., B.A. 1978; Presbyterian; married (Brooke).

Career: Natl. Sales Mgr., Carswell Distributing, 1978–95; NC Taxpayers United, Co-Chmn., 1993–present.

DC Office: 1513 LHOB 20515, 202-225-2071; Fax: 202-225-2995; e-mail: richard.burrnc05@hr.house.gov.

District Offices: Winston-Salem, 910-631-5125.

Committees: *Commerce* (18th of 28 R): Energy & Power; Health & the Environment; Oversight & Investigations.

Group Ratings

	ADA	ACLU	AFS	LCV	CFA	CON	NFIB	COC	ACU	NTLC	CHC
1996	5	6	0	8	0	55	100	88	100	100	93
1995	0	—	—	13	8	75	—	96	88	—	—

National Journal Ratings

	1995 LIB — 1995 CONS			1996 LIB — 1996 CONS		
Economic	26%	—	67%	0%	—	82%
Social	32%	—	65%	10%	—	86%
Foreign	36%	—	59%	0%	—	79%

Key Votes of the 104th Congress

1. Reduce Medicare Growth $	Y	5. Flag Amendment	Y	9. Cuban Embargo	Y
2. Ovrd. Product Liab. Veto	Y	6. Drop EPA Limits	N	10. Bar Bosnia Troop $	N
3. Increase Min. Wage	N	7. Repeal Assault-Weap. Ban	Y	11. Cut Anti-Missile Defense	N
4. Welfare Reform	Y	8. Ovrd. Part. Birth Veto	Y	12. Bar U.N. Uniforms	Y

Election Results

1996 general	Richard M. Burr (R)	130,177	(62%)	($697,067)
	Neil Grist Cashion Jr. (D)	74,320	(35%)	($185,998)
	Others	5,201	(2%)	
1996 primary	Richard M. Burr (R)	unopposed		
1994 general	Richard M. Burr (R)	84,741	(57%)	($741,986)
	A. P. (Sandy) Sands (D)	63,194	(43%)	($759,742)

SIXTH DISTRICT

For more than half a century furniture store managers and owners from all over the country twice a year have converged on the huge Furniture Mart in High Point, the center of the U.S. furniture business, for the giant trade show put on by manufacturers. High Point sits amidst rolling farmland originally settled by Quakers, the site of the Battle of Guilford Courthouse in the Revolutionary War, then slaveholding country in the years before the Civil War. The furniture business grew here early in the 20th Century because of the hardwoods in the mountains not far west and the abundance of low-wage labor in the flatlands not far east. Soon it was said of High Point that there were so many factories, "only a wise man knows his own factory whistle." Today, employment in furniture continues to grow, unlike in textiles and tobacco, and wages have risen. Race relations are now outwardly pleasant in the city where in 1960 black students at North Carolina A&T started the first lunch counter sit-in at a local Greensboro five-and-dime.

The 6th Congressional District of North Carolina covers most of Greensboro and High Point, about half of textile-producing Alamance County to the east, Quaker-settled Randolph County to the south and furniture-manufacturing Davidson County to the west. Alongside it snakes the heavily black 12th District, on its way from Greensboro and High Point southwest to Charlotte. This is a region which, even when it had the black areas now moved to the 12th, would lean Republican; without these areas, the 6th is now heavily Republican. The March 1997 redistricting smoothed out the borders so the 6th is no longer cut in half by the 12th.

The congressman from the 6th District is Howard Coble, a Republican first elected in 1984. He grew up in Guilford County, went to Guilford College, then after wrecking his father's car joined the Coast Guard, in which he started off collecting garbage and served five years. He was an insurance claims representative, went to law school and became an assistant U.S. attorney, state revenue commissioner and was elected to the state House in 1968 and 1978–82. In 1984 he was elected to Congress in a swing district; it was the third time the 6th had changed parties in three elections, and Coble won reelection in 1986 by just 79 votes. But his personal popularity and the 1990s redistrictings have made this a safe seat.

Coble is a friendly man who asks visitors if they mind if he smokes his cheap cigars; he likes bluegrass music and eats pork brains and eggs for breakfast. He is solidly conservative, with interesting twists. He is tightfisted, and since his first term he has tried to pass legislation to abolish congressional pensions; he boycotts the pension program himself, but hasn't found many co-sponsors. He was proud he didn't have a single overdraft on the House bank; "I'll wear a suit two years too long. I'll drive a car 10 years too long. I'm also very fastidious when it comes to maintaining my check balance." Like many of his constituents, he is leery of free trade. He opposed fast-track for NAFTA, but finally voted for it in 1993 (without visiting the White House or selling his vote, he said); but he opposed GATT. Naturally, he opposes FDA regulation of tobacco.

"I see my role more as one of keeping bad legislation off the books," he often says. But since Republicans took control he has been an active legislator. In December 1994 he turned down the chairs of the Immigration and Constitution Subcommittees on Judiciary for Coast Guard and Maritime Transportation on the Transportation and Infrastructure Committee. There he steered to House passage two major bills: an Ocean Shipping Reform Act, replacing cartels with free market pricing and eliminating the $19 million Federal Maritime Commission, and a Coast Guard authorization closing down 23 search and rescue stations and disposing of regulations that hurt U.S.-flagged ships in international competition. But neither went anywhere in the Senate.

After winning reelection easily in 1996, Coble moved to chair the Courts and Intellectual Property Subcommittee on Judiciary. He points out that copyright industries produce more GDP than any single manufacturing sector and that copyright and patent protection have been essential to the American biotechnology and software industries. On other issues, he sponsored a bill to stop illegal textile imports routed by China through other countries and supports the STEP-21 transportation formula to guarantee that states get a 95% return on payments made to the federal highway trust fund. The only threat to his tenure could come from future redistricting which would add black precincts to the 6th District and make it less heavily Republican.

The People: Pop. 1990: 552,663; 53% rural; 12% age 65+; 91% White; 7% Black; 1% Asian; 1% Hispanic origin. Households: 62% married couple families; 27% married couple fams. w. children; 42% college educ.; median household income: $30,628; per capita income: $14,942; median gross rent: $403; median house value: $72,900. *(Information does not reflect 1997 redistricting.)*

1996 Presidential Vote

Dole (R)	133,262	(58%)
Clinton (D)	75,904	(33%)
Perot (I)	18,412	(8%)

1992 Presidential Vote

Bush (R)	119,874	(51%)
Clinton (D)	75,651	(32%)
Perot (I)	38,180	(16%)

Rep. Howard Coble (R)

Elected 1984; b. Mar. 18, 1931, Greensboro; home, Greensboro; Appalachian St. U., 1949–50; Guilford Col., A.B. 1958, U. of NC, J.D. 1962; Presbyterian; single.

Career: Coast Guard, 1952–56, 1977–78, Coast Guard Reserves, 1956–81; NC House of Reps., 1968–70, 1978–84; Asst. U.S. Atty., NC Middle Dist., 1969–73; Commissioner, NC Dept. of Revenue, 1973–77; Practicing atty., 1979–83.

DC Office: 2239 RHOB 20515, 202-225-3065; Fax: 202-225-8611; e-mail: coblenc6@hr.house.gov.

District Offices: Asheboro, 919-626-3060; Graham, 919-228-0159; Greensboro, 919-333-5005; High Point, 919-886-5106; Lexington, 704-246-8230.

Committees: *Judiciary* (5th of 20 R): Courts & Intellectual Property (Chmn.); Crime. *Transportation & Infrastructure* (6th of 40 R): Coast Guard & Maritime Transportation; Surface Transportation.

Group Ratings

	ADA	ACLU	AFS	LCV	CFA	CON	NFIB	COC	ACU	NTLC	CHC
1996	15	6	0	23	15	55	92	88	90	100	100
1995	0	—	—	25	8	75	—	92	88	—	—

National Journal Ratings

	1995 LIB — 1995 CONS			1996 LIB — 1996 CONS		
Economic	41%	—	56%	27%	—	71%
Social	0%	—	79%	0%	—	90%
Foreign	45%	—	52%	47%	—	52%

Key Votes of the 104th Congress

1. Reduce Medicare Growth $	Y	5. Flag Amendment	Y	9. Cuban Embargo	Y
2. Ovrd. Product Liab. Veto	N	6. Drop EPA Limits	N	10. Bar Bosnia Troop $	Y
3. Increase Min. Wage	N	7. Repeal Assault-Weap. Ban	Y	11. Cut Anti-Missile Defense	N
4. Welfare Reform	Y	8. Ovrd. Part. Birth Veto	Y	12. Bar U.N. Uniforms	Y

Election Results

1996 general	Howard Coble (R)	167,828	(73%)	($498,224)
	Mark Costley (D)	58,022	(25%)	($32,829)
1996 primary	Howard Coble (R)	unopposed		
1994 general	Howard Coble (R)	unopposed		($350,981)

SEVENTH DISTRICT

Southernmost North Carolina, where the state boundary dips down along the Atlantic coast has been economically dependent on tobacco for more than 200 years. Tobacco can be cultivated profitably in only a few places in the world; it is labor intensive, requiring close tending and serial picking (one leaf on a stalk matures before the one above it); and it is valuable enough that North Carolina farmers today, if they have one of the tobacco allotments handed out in the 1930s or have bought the rights to one, can make a living off 40 acres. Tobacco produces more voters per federally assisted acre than any other crop. This tobacco country, it should be added, is racially diverse, the home of many blacks as well as the Lumbee Indians, whose origins have been lost in antiquity, but who were treated by state segregation laws—and still are treated by continuing custom—as a race distinct from whites and blacks; each race makes up about one-third of the population of Robeson County around Lumberton.

Southernmost North Carolina is also military country. The port city of Wilmington is home of the World War II battleship U.S.S. *North Carolina*. Eastward, in swampland, is Camp Lejeune, home base of one-fifth of the Marine Corps. Inland, near Fayetteville, is the huge complex of Fort Bragg and Pope Air Force Base, whence 39,000 troops left for the Persian Gulf in 1990. As the site of one of the biggest bases in the country, Fayetteville has developed the strip highway to an art form, with strip joints, fast food galore and the world's first Putt-Putt golf course.

North Carolina's 7th Congressional District covers much of this territory. From 1992 until March 1997, when the state legislature redrew the lines, it had astonishingly jagged boundaries, and took in Camp Lejeune and Fort Bragg; redistricting made it more compact, and removed the two military installations. Politically, the 7th consists of three areas: the coastal area around Wilmington, with hundreds of affluent condo-dwellers, now increasingly Republican; the area around Fayetteville, pretty evenly divided between the parties; and the Lumbee Indian country in and around Robeson County, very heavily Democratic. This was for many years a solidly Democratic district, but is now marginal. For 24 years it was represented by Democrat Charlie Rose, a smart political tactician who chaired the House Administration Committee; but he ran into severe ethical problems in the 1990s, was reelected by only 52%–48% in 1994 and retired from Congress in 1996.

The congressman from the 7th District is Mike McIntyre, a Democrat elected in 1996. McIntyre grew up in Lumberton, in Robeson County, graduated from college and law school at Chapel Hill and practiced law in Lumberton, where his family has been prominent for 200 years. He was active in civic affairs and in his church and was often asked to run for office. He had worked briefly after law school as an intern to Charlie Rose, and when Rose was first elected, McIntyre whispered to his father that he would succeed him. In 1995, when Rose announced his retirement, McIntyre decided to run. He was not alone: seven Democrats and four Republicans filed. McIntyre's chief opposition in the primary was Rose Marie Lowry-Townsend, a Lumbee and a liberal, who had support from the National Education Association, labor PACs and national women's groups; nearly half of her contributions came from outside North Carolina. Lowry-Townsend led McIntyre 30%–23% in the first contest, in which most of his support came from Robeson County. McIntyre called for smaller government and cited his close ties to the district and involvement in community activities. He won the runoff 52%–48%, carrying the Lumbee country and Fayetteville and trailing on the coast.

The Republican nominee was Bill Caster, a retired Coast Guard officer and New Hanover County commissioner, who beat Fayetteville-based Robert Anderson, the Republican nominee in the last three elections against Rose, 54%–46% in the runoff. McIntyre's platform was almost as conservative as Caster's—on some things, more so. McIntyre favored the balanced budget amendment, term limits, eliminating federal departments, and supported school prayer. He said he would vote for but would not campaign with Bill Clinton. He was moved by state labor leaders to withdraw his support for a national right-to-work law, but continued to favor right-to-work in North Carolina. He attacked Caster for backing two county tax increases, and signed the Americans for Tax Reform's anti-tax pledge months before Caster did. Caster ridiculed McIntyre's emphasis on his community ties—"While it's all well and good to coach Little League, that doesn't mean you're ready to go to Congress"—and attacked him for accepting a $3,000 campaign contribution and earlier buying signs from a Robeson County convicted cocaine seller; McIntyre said he didn't know the man's record, returned the contribution and said the sign payment was for legitimate services rendered. As in the primaries, there was a split between the coast and the interior. Caster carried the coastal counties 59%–39%; McIntyre carried the Fayetteville area 53%–46% and had a huge 81%–18% majority in Robeson County. Overall, he carried the district 53%–46%, even as Bill Clinton was losing it 48%–44%.

McIntyre immediately joined the conservative Blue Dog Democrats. "The pendulum is swinging," he said. "I feel the party has come home. I really feel the party has come back to where I've always been." He got a seat on the Agriculture Committee and the Risk Management and Specialty Crops Subcommittee that oversees the peanut and tobacco programs. He promises to oppose FDA regulation of tobacco. He said he was against cutting college loans, Medicare or Medicaid and that he would champion his "rock hard" values.

The People: Pop. 1990: 552,037; 41% rural; 9% age 65+; 70% White; 19% Black; 1% Asian; 7% Amer. Indian; 3% Hispanic origin. Households: 61% married couple families; 31% married couple fams. w. children; 43% college educ.; median household income: $24,708; per capita income: $11,663; median gross rent: $391; median house value: $63,600. *(Information does not reflect 1997 redistricting.)*

1996 Presidential Vote

Dole (R)	79,082	(48%)
Clinton (D)	71,377	(44%)
Perot (I)	11,917	(7%)

1992 Presidential Vote

Clinton (D)	71,334	(43%)
Bush (R)	70,159	(43%)
Perot (I)	22,194	(14%)

Rep. Mike McIntyre (D)

Elected 1996; b. Aug. 6, 1956, Lumberton; home, Lumberton; U. of NC, B.A. 1978, J.D. 1981; Presbyterian; married (Dee).

Career: Practicing atty., 1982–97.

DC Office: 1605 LHOB 20515, 202-225-2731; Fax: 202-225-5773.

District Offices: Fayetteville, 910-323-0260; Lumberton, 910-671-6223; Wilmington, 910-815-4959.

Committees: *Agriculture* (18th of 23 D): General Farm Commodities; Risk Management & Specialty Crops. *National Security* (24th of 25 D): Military Procurement.

Group Ratings and Key Votes: Newly Elected

Election Results

1996 general	Mike McIntyre (D)	87,487	(53%)	($490,063)
	Bill Caster (R)	75,811	(46%)	($332,746)
1996 runoff	Mike McIntyre (D)	16,285	(52%)	
	Rose Marie Lowry-Townsend (D)	14,868	(48%)	
1996 primary	Rose Marie Lowry-Townsend (D)	15,925	(30%)	
	Mike McIntyre (D)	12,327	(23%)	
	Glenn Jernigam (D)	9,920	(19%)	
	George W. Breece (D)	5,688	(11%)	
	Timothy Mark Dunn (D)	4,868	(9%)	
	Marcus W. Williams (D)	3,162	(6%)	
	Others	794	(2%)	
1994 general	Charlie Rose (D)	62,670	(52%)	($823,282)
	Robert C. Anderson (R)	58,849	(48%)	($91,027)

EIGHTH DISTRICT

From Atlanta to Durham in the Carolina Piedmont, along Interstate 85, is the thickest concentration of America's textile industry—so thick you can almost see the lint. Within North Carolina, I-85 passes through the nation's leading textile-producing area, past Salisbury, Concord and Kannapolis—named for its founding company, Cannon Mills. East Carolina was settled by Englishmen from the coast. This Piedmont land was settled primarily by Scots and diverse groups like Quakers and Moravian sects, coming down the Blue Ridge from Pennsylvania through Virginia. These migratory patterns were reflected in Civil War divisions and continue in current voting habits. The coastal counties all the way up through the Sand Hills were Confederate and are now Democratic. The textile mill towns along I-85 were anti-secession and are now Republican.

The 8th Congressional District of North Carolina, as redistricted, combines the area around Kannapolis and Concord with Sand Hill counties extending east almost to Fayetteville. In the district lines in effect for 1992, nearly two-thirds of the population was in the textile country or the Charlotte suburbs in Union County. Under the legislature's March 1997 redistricting plan, the textile counties of Rowan and Iredell were removed, and part of Charlotte and Mecklenburg County was added, raising the district's black percentage from 23% to about 28%. This had political effects: the textile counties were heavily Republican; the new areas Democratic, enough to raise the district's Democratic percentage by 3% to 5%.

The congressman from the 8th District is Bill Hefner, a Democrat first elected in the Watergate year of 1974. Hefner made his living singing in a gospel group called the Harvesters Quartet and owned a radio station in Kannapolis. He ran in a reform-minded year promising to "help restore Christian morality in the federal government" and protect "human-oriented programs." His voting record has been moderate to liberal; with other North Carolina Democrats, he stuck with the House Democratic leadership on most tough partisan issues. In return, North Carolina got leadership support on textiles and tobacco. Hefner also got a seat on Appropriations, which he unabashedly used to help the district. In 1982, after only eight years in the House, he became chairman of the Appropriations Military Construction Subcommittee and claims credit for funneling an average of $152 million a year into North Carolina between 1987 and 1995. Hefner is proud of his work for the $250 million Womack Medical Center at Fort Bragg, the Uwharrie National Forest and four different airport projects, and for sponsoring a "buy American" amendment for military clothing.

Hefner's formula for political success was threatened by the Republican takeover of the House. The shrunken Democratic Caucus was well to the left (and even in 1986 Hefner ran only a distant third in a race for whip) and in the minority he cannot deliver quite as much for the district. But the March 1997 redistricting came along, perhaps just in time for Hefner. With the large Republican vote in the textile counties, he has had serious competition in almost every election. He topped 60% of the vote only once, in 1976, and came close to losing in 1984 and 1988. In 1994 he beat auto dealer Sherrill Morgan by just 52%–48%. In 1996 Morgan was beaten in the Republican runoff by one-on-one campaigner Curtis Blackwood, but Republicans did not target this race and Blackwood spent only $151,000 to Hefner's $555,000. The 8th District voted 49%–43% for Bob Dole and also went for Jesse Helms in 1996. But Hefner won by a solid 55%–44%. He carried the Sand Hills by 68%–31% and lost the textile counties 51%–48%, the same margin as in 1994. In redistricting, the Democratic state Senate evidently insisted on strengthening Hefner's district, for partisan reasons and to keep his post on Military Construction (he is now ranking minority member); he will be a tougher target, if he is a target at all, in 1998.

The People: Pop. 1990: 552,039; 55% rural; 12% age 65+; 72% White; 23% Black; 1% Asian; 3% Amer. Indian; 1% Hispanic origin. Households: 61% married couple families; 29% married couple fams.

w. children; 34% college educ.; median household income: $26,180; per capita income: $11,462; median gross rent: $359; median house value: $56,700. *(Information does not reflect 1997 redistricting.)*

1996 Presidential Vote

Dole (R)	91,672	(49%)
Clinton (D)	80,296	(43%)
Perot (I)	14,607	(8%)

1992 Presidential Vote

Bush (R)	86,493	(44%)
Clinton (D)	81,736	(42%)
Perot (I)	27,296	(14%)

Rep. W. G. (Bill) **Hefner (D)**

Elected 1974; b. Apr. 11, 1930, Elora, TN; home, Concord; Baptist; married (Nancy).

Career: Entertainer, radio business, 1954–74.

DC Office: 2470 RHOB 20515, 202-225-3715; Fax: 202-225-4036.

District Offices: Concord, 704-786-1612; Rockingham, 910-997-2070; Salisbury, 704-636-0635.

Committees: *Appropriations* (9th of 26 D): Military Construction (RMM); National Security.

Group Ratings

	ADA	ACLU	AFS	LCV	CFA	CON	NFIB	COC	ACU	NTLC	CHC
1996	55	44	75	69	46	82	51	38	30	30	20
1995	75	—	—	69	38	16	—	42	9	—	—

National Journal Ratings

	1995 LIB — 1995 CONS	1996 LIB — 1996 CONS
Economic	63% — 37%	61% — 39%
Social	68% — 31%	67% — 32%
Foreign	73% — 24%	61% — 37%

Key Votes of the 104th Congress

1. Reduce Medicare Growth $	N	5. Flag Amendment	Y	9. Cuban Embargo	N
2. Ovrd. Product Liab. Veto	Y	6. Drop EPA Limits	Y	10. Bar Bosnia Troop $	N
3. Increase Min. Wage	Y	7. Repeal Assault-Weap. Ban	Y	11. Cut Anti-Missile Defense	Y
4. Welfare Reform	N	8. Ovrd. Part. Birth Veto	Y	12. Bar U.N. Uniforms	Y

Election Results

1996 general	W. G. (Bill) Hefner (D)	103,129	(55%)	($555,614)
	Curtis Blackwood (R)	81,676	(44%)	($151,081)
1996 primary	W. G. (Bill) Hefner (D)	unopposed		
1994 general	W. G. (Bill) Hefner (D)	62,845	(52%)	($669,622)
	Sherrill Morgan (R)	57,140	(48%)	($320,520)

NINTH DISTRICT

"An agreeable village but in a damn rebellious country," recorded General Cornwallis when, before the unpleasantness at Yorktown, he visited Charlotte, North Carolina. "A veritable nest of hornets." This town, settled by Scots-Irish and German colonists who came down the Blue Ridge from Pennsylvania, is now the biggest metro area between Washington and Atlanta, with 1.3 million people. Before the California gold rush, Charlotte was the gold mining capital of the country. Now, it is the headquarters of two of the nation's biggest banks: NationsBank and First Union; with $319 billion in assets, it is the second-largest financial center in the nation, behind only New York. It is the center of the nation's biggest textile manufacturing region and an airline hub for USAirways. It has become home to the NBA Hornets and NFL Panthers. Across from NationsBank's 60-story tower is a $50 million performing arts center. The rebelliousness Cornwallis noted can still be seen in this home of one of the nation's biggest stock car race tracks. But Charlotte has also built a boosterish pride in its capacity for accommodation. It is proud that it responded amicably to a busing order approved in a landmark Supreme Court case in 1971; that it uncovered the shenanigans of its nearby South Carolina neighbors Jim and Tammy Fae Bakker; that it elected Harvey Gantt, who is black, mayor several times and then replaced him with Sue Myrick, a Republican woman whose grievance wasn't race but traffic.

The 9th Congressional District of North Carolina includes most of Charlotte and Mecklenburg Counties—black precincts are in the black-majority 12th or the 8th Districts—and extends west to include most of Gaston and Cleveland Counties, with their many textile mills. If the 9th included whole counties, it would be politically marginal and in fact, with different boundaries, came close to electing a Democrat in 1984 and 1986. But with few blacks, the 9th is heavily Republican. The state legislature's March 1997 redistricting plan left the Republican majority here largely unchanged, although the new lines give the 9th all of Cleveland County.

Sue Myrick is now the congresswoman from the 9th District. A Republican elected in 1994, she grew up and went to college in Ohio, raised her family in Charlotte, owned an advertising agency and Amway distributorship. In 1981 she ran for the Charlotte Council and lost. She ran again and won in 1983, ran for mayor and lost in 1985, then beat Harvey Gantt in 1987. Despite nasty personal charges, she was reelected in 1989; she is proud of making infrastructure improvements, bringing the NFL Carolina Panthers to Charlotte and having no property tax increases in four years. Myrick ran for the Senate in 1992, but was beaten by Lauch Faircloth in the primary 48%–30%. In 1994 Charlotte Congressman Alex McMillan, passed over for the ranking position on Budget, retired. In the 1994 primary, against House Minority Leader David Balmer, a 31-year-old ambitious politician, Myrick led in the primary by just 34%–28%. But before the runoff three weeks later, it was revealed that Balmer had falsely claimed on his resume to have graduated in the top 20% of his law school class and to have played varsity soccer. Myrick won 68%–32%, then easily won the general.

Myrick has been a proud leader of the 1994 Republican freshman class, on Newt Gingrich's transition team and first freshman and then sophomore class liaison to the leadership; she is a likely candidate for the Republican Conference secretary position as leadership slots open up with the retirement of Conference Vice Chair Susan Molinari. She got a seat on the Budget Committee in 1995, and stood fast after the Republican budget was vetoed by Bill Clinton. She co-chaired a task force on privatizing HUD functions, supported a flat-rate income tax and sponsored a bill for civil monetary penalties for making false statements in political ads. In a 1997 response to a radio address by President Bill Clinton, she boosted the Republicans' flex-time bill to give workers a choice between overtime pay or time off. After the 1996 election, which she won easily, she was named to the Rules Committee; she took "on-leave" status on Banking, where she cannot vote but can build seniority to watch over her district's banking needs. She was one of 28 members who voted against reprimanding Newt Gingrich in January 1997.

The People: Pop. 1990: 552,490; 24% rural; 10% age 65+; 88% White; 9% Black; 1% Asian; 1% Hispanic origin. Households: 60% married couple families; 28% married couple fams. w. children; 55% college educ.; median household income: $35,346; per capita income: $17,234; median gross rent: $472; median house value: $83,200. *(Information does not reflect 1997 redistricting.)*

1996 Presidential Vote			1992 Presidential Vote		
Dole (R)	129,088	(55%)	Bush (R)	130,798	(52%)
Clinton (D)	89,400	(38%)	Clinton (D)	81,731	(33%)
Perot (I)	13,880	(6%)	Perot (I)	36,454	(15%)

Rep. Sue Myrick (R)

Elected 1994; b. Aug. 1, 1941, Tiffin, OH; home, Charlotte; Heidelberg Col., 1959–60; Methodist; married (Ed).

Career: Charlotte City Cncl., 1983–85; Pres. & CEO, Myrick Advertising, 1985–94; Charlotte Mayor, 1987–91; Pres. & CEO, Myrick Enterprises, 1992–94.

DC Office: 230 CHOB 20515, 202-225-1976; Fax: 202-225-3389; e-mail: myrick@hr.house.gov.

District Offices: Charlotte, 704-362-1060; Gastonia, 704-861-1976.

Committees: *Rules* (9th of 9 R): Rules & Organization of the House.

Group Ratings

	ADA	ACLU	AFS	LCV	CFA	CON	NFIB	COC	ACU	NTLC	CHC
1996	10	6	8	8	8	78	100	88	100	98	100
1995	0	—	—	6	0	73	—	100	96	—	—

National Journal Ratings

	1995 LIB — 1995 CONS			1996 LIB — 1996 CONS		
Economic	26%	—	67%	0%	—	82%
Social	0%	—	79%	14%	—	77%
Foreign	15%	—	73%	30%	—	65%

Key Votes of the 104th Congress

1. Reduce Medicare Growth $	Y	5. Flag Amendment	Y	9. Cuban Embargo	Y
2. Ovrd. Product Liab. Veto	Y	6. Drop EPA Limits	N	10. Bar Bosnia Troop $	Y
3. Increase Min. Wage	N	7. Repeal Assault-Weap. Ban	Y	11. Cut Anti-Missile Defense	N
4. Welfare Reform	Y	8. Ovrd. Part. Birth Veto	Y	12. Bar U.N. Uniforms	Y

Election Results

1996 general	Sue Myrick (R)	147,755	(63%)	($547,194)
	Michel C. Daisley (D)	83,078	(35%)	($63,598)
	Others	3,877	(2%)	
1996 primary	Sue Myrick (R)	unopposed		
1994 general	Sue Myrick (R)	82,374	(65%)	($663,405)
	Rory Blake (D)	44,379	(35%)	($85,458)

TENTH DISTRICT

Wreathed in the haze that gave them the name "Smoky," the heavily wooded mountains of North Carolina seem placid and ancient. Geologically, they are some of the oldest ranges in the world; economically, they are churning with activity. The North Carolina counties where the hills of the Appalachians rise from the Piedmont are not just countryside. Nestled in their valleys is perhaps the largest concentration of furniture factories in the world, where skilled craftsmen create, from the hardwoods of Carolina forests, both high quality and mass market furniture. Other industries are here as well—textiles, though not as much as in the I-85 corridor in the Piedmont, and chickens in the Holly Farms complex (acquired by Tyson) in Wilkes County.

The 10th Congressional District of North Carolina covers much of this hill and mountain country, roughly between I-85 and the Tennessee border. The district lines for 1992, 1994 and 1996 were very irregular; the March 1997 redistricting plan smooths out the lines and leaves the district more compact, bringing into the 10th the late Senator Sam Ervin's hometown of Morganton and the college town of Boone. Politically, this is a very Republican area, though the Republicans here tend not to be Jesse Helms fans, but rough-hewn hill Republicans, unsympathetic to government regulators, from factory inspectors to revenuers on the lookout for illegal stills.

The congressman from this district is Cass Ballenger, a Republican elected in 1986. Ballenger grew up in Hickory, enlisted in the Navy at 18, went to school in the East and headed a paper box company; in 1957 he founded Plastic Packaging Inc., to make plastic wrappings for J.C. Penney underwear. He served on the Catawba County Board of Commissioners for eight years and in the state legislature for 12. In 1986, after Congressman James Broyhill was appointed to the Senate (he lost in November), Ballenger ran for the House. He promised to be a "Broyhill Republican" and beat a primary opponent backed by Helms. Ballenger has won general elections by large margins.

Ballenger combines a solidly conservative voting record with a sense of civic responsibility. He and his wife have organized humanitarian trips to Central and South America, delivering donated medical supplies; in 1995 and 1996 Plastic Packaging sent a half-million plastic bags to Haiti to be used to grow eucalyptus seedlings to reforest the barren hills. When Democrats were in control of Congress, he opposed the Clinton healthcare plan, family and medical leave and striker replacement; he amended an OSHA law by exempting employers when violations are caused by employees breaking company work rules. Now that Republicans are in control, much of Ballenger's legislative work is done on the Workforce Protections Subcommittee which he chairs. He is the main sponsor of two major Republican initiatives: flex-time and OSHA reform. The flex-time bill would allow employees who work overtime to choose whether to receive overtime pay or compensatory time within the next year; federal employees have had this option since 1985. This measure passed the House in July 1996 but was fiercely opposed by the AFL-CIO, which argues that employers will coerce employees to take leave time. Ballenger worked to meet Democrats' objections, but almost all Democrats opposed the bill when it passed the House 222–210 in the 105th Congress.

On OSHA Ballenger has been pressed between subcommittee Republicans who would like to abolish the agency altogether and Democrats and labor leaders resisting any change. He produced a bill in 1996 that would have softened OSHA penalties on businesses and required a cost/benefit analysis for new regulations—provisions which had been supported by the White House. But the issue was not brought to a vote in the 104th Congress. In March 1997 he introduced a similar bill; one main feature is an increase from 16% to 50% of OSHA funds which must be spent on assisting businesses in complying with OSHA standards. "We ought to change the attitude of OSHA from being a Gestapo to being a teacher." Ballenger and his subcommittee may take up other labor issues. He would like to repeal the Davis-Bacon Act, which requires contractors on federal construction sites to pay workers "local prevailing wages," and in practice strengthens the building trades unions; that has been opposed by Clinton and most Democrats. Speaker Newt Gingrich has suggested Ballenger's subcommittee hold hearings on the power of unions, highlighting the fact that 42% of AFL-CIO members are public employees and that a Supreme Court decision banning involuntary use of dues money for political purposes has not been enforced by the Clinton Administration.

The People: Pop. 1990: 552,303; 71% rural; 12% age 65+; 93% White; 5% Black; 1% Hispanic origin. Households: 65% married couple families; 29% married couple fams. w. children; 35% college educ.; median household income: $28,511; per capita income: $13,434; median gross rent: $352; median house value: $63,700. *(Information does not reflect 1997 redistricting.)*

1996 Presidential Vote			1992 Presidential Vote		
Dole (R)	136,253	(60%)	Bush (R)	127,910	(53%)
Clinton (D)	70,751	(31%)	Clinton (D)	76,262	(32%)
Perot (I)	17,874	(8%)	Perot (I)	35,572	(15%)

Rep. Cass Ballenger (R)

Elected 1986; b. Dec. 6, 1926, Hickory; home, Hickory; U. of NC, Amherst Col., B.A. 1948; Episcopalian; married (Donna).

Career: Naval Air Corps, 1944–45; Businessman; Pres., Hickory Paper Box Co., 1948–70; Founder & Pres., Plastic Packaging Inc., 1957–present; Catawba Cnty. Bd. of Commissioners, 1966–74, Chmn. 1970–74; NC House of Reps., 1974–76; NC Senate, 1976–86.

DC Office: 2182 RHOB 20515, 202-225-2576; Fax: 202-225-0316; e-mail: cass.ballenger@mail.house.gov.

District Offices: Clemmons, 919-766-9455; Hickory, 704-327-6100.

Committees: *Education & The Workforce* (5th of 25 R): Employer-Employee Relations; Workforce Protections (Chmn.). *International Relations* (10th of 26 R): International Operations & Human Rights; Western Hemisphere.

Group Ratings

	ADA	ACLU	AFS	LCV	CFA	CON	NFIB	COC	ACU	NTLC	CHC
1996	0	0	0	8	8	30	100	100	100	100	93
1995	0	—	—	6	0	56	—	96	88	—	—

National Journal Ratings

	1995 LIB		1995 CONS	1996 LIB		1996 CONS
Economic	26%	—	67%	0%	—	82%
Social	32%	—	65%	14%	—	77%
Foreign	15%	—	73%	0%	—	79%

Key Votes of the 104th Congress

1. Reduce Medicare Growth $	Y	5. Flag Amendment	Y	9. Cuban Embargo	Y
2. Ovrd. Product Liab. Veto	Y	6. Drop EPA Limits	N	10. Bar Bosnia Troop $	Y
3. Increase Min. Wage	N	7. Repeal Assault-Weap. Ban	Y	11. Cut Anti-Missile Defense	N
4. Welfare Reform	Y	8. Ovrd. Part. Birth Veto	Y	12. Bar U.N. Uniforms	Y

Election Results

1996 general	Cass Ballenger (R)	158,585	(70%)	($244,447)
	Ben Neill (D)	65,103	(29%)	($17,993)
1996 primary	Cass Ballenger (R)	unopposed		
1994 general	Cass Ballenger (R)	107,829	(72%)	($221,536)
	Robert Wayne Avery (D)	42,939	(28%)	

ELEVENTH DISTRICT

Western North Carolina, the protrusion of the Tarheel state deep into the fastness of the eastern United States' highest and oldest mountains, is a land of long and ornery traditions. First settled by whites not long after the Revolutionary War, it still has tiny Indian communities and hollows where people are descended from the first white settlers. Its biggest city, Asheville, is memorialized in Thomas Wolfe's novels and was a retreat for lung patients in the early 20th Century. It was also the home of the brilliant eccentric George Vanderbilt, who built the chateau-like Biltmore mansion, and its vast forests, on which he pioneered scientific forestry. Over a ridge is the Smoky Mountains National Park, the nation's most heavily visited, 20 degrees cooler in the summer than the lowland towns an hour or so away. The climate and the forested, green, fog-wisped mountains have attracted millions of tourists and thousands of retirees to this area.

The 11th Congressional District is made up of the western end of North Carolina; its jagged boundaries in effect in 1992, 1994 and 1996 were smoothed out by a March 1997 redistricting plan. The orneriness of the mountain country has come out in its politics. This part of the state was reluctant to secede in the Civil War. There were few slaves and many small farmers loyal to the Union, and those who took up the Confederate cause did so out of loyalty to Governor Zebulon Vance, an Asheville native and reluctant secessionist himself. Ancestral party loyalties remain strong; local notables, like the Ponder family of Madison County, hold power for years; the retirees in the mountains south of Asheville haven't tipped things much. The partisan balance here has been close, and for a dozen years the 11th was one of the nation's most closely contested districts, throwing out incumbents in five of six elections between 1980 and 1990.

The current congressman is Charles Taylor, a Republican elected in 1990. He grew up in Brevard, where he has been a tree farmer and one of the biggest private landholders in the area. He served in the legislature from 1966–74, and ran for Congress in 1988 and narrowly lost. In 1990 he ran again and won. Taylor has a very conservative voting record and has spent much energy on district projects. He worked to delay draw-downs of area lakes each year by the TVA until August 1, and later until October 1, to keep waters high for tourist season. He worked to get the Asheville veterans' hospital refurbished and obtained funding for the I-26 highway. His major ongoing project he calls the Magnet Triangle economic development plan, to build three federal facilities which he says will double tourism in the area: the Blue Ridge Parkway headquarters, the Cradle of Forestry interpretive center near Brevard and the Oconaluftee museum and visitors' center.

Taylor has also been active on national issues. He was one of the members of 1991's Gang of Seven, Republican freshmen who pushed for full disclosure of overdrafts on the House bank and other congressional reforms. In the 104th Congress the House passed his property-rights protection amendments to the National Biological Survey and the Montana Wilderness Act. He sponsored the timber salvage bill that became law in July 1995. Also passed was his amendment to stop EEOC guidelines he believed would promote religious harassment in workplaces; in 1996 he sought to protect religious radio stations from unfair FCC licensing practices. He sponsored the Congressional Gold Medal for Ruth and Billy Graham, residents of western North Carolina, which was awarded in May 1996.

Taylor got a seat on Appropriations in 1993, and in 1997 became chairman of the District of

Columbia Subcommittee; his fellow North Carolinian Lauch Faircloth holds the same position in the Senate. He started out by saying, "No city can write its own checks and print its own bills." One of Taylor's first steps was to talk with Mayor Pat McCrory of Charlotte, which has almost as many people as Washington but a far smaller government, and which has seen some success in privatizing city services. He initially opposed the Bill Clinton's proposal for a federal takeover of D.C.'s prisons, tax collections, infrastructure repairs, and pensions. He admitted that his knowledge of the District is limited, but said he wanted to get to know the city; his approach may be suggested by the Earning by Learning reading program he personally finances for youngsters in his district.

Taylor has converted what used to be a marginal district into a safe seat. His 1994 opponent, Maggie Lauterer, was well-known and well-funded, but Taylor spent $999,000 and won 60%–40%. In 1996 he won 58%–40%. He ended the campaign with $288,000 in his treasury and has been urged to run for statewide office in 2000 or 2002.

The People: Pop. 1990: 552,497; 69% rural; 18% age 65+; 90% White; 7% Black; 1% Amer. Indian; 1% Hispanic origin. Households: 60% married couple families; 24% married couple fams. w. children; 38% college educ.; median household income: $23,564; per capita income: $11,923; median gross rent: $333; median house value: $59,500. *(Information does not reflect 1997 redistricting.)*

1996 Presidential Vote

Dole (R)	106,513	(47%)
Clinton (D)	97,073	(43%)
Perot (I)	20,681	(9%)

1992 Presidential Vote

Clinton (D)	105,006	(43%)
Bush (R)	103,849	(43%)
Perot (I)	34,643	(14%)

Rep. Charles H. Taylor (R)

Elected 1990; b. Jan. 23, 1941, Brevard; home, Brevard; Wake Forest U., B.A. 1963, J.D. 1966; Baptist; married (Elizabeth).

Career: Tree farmer; NC House of Reps., 1966–72, Minority Ldr., 1968–72; NC Senate, 1972–74, Minority Ldr., 1972–74.

DC Office: 231 CHOB 20515, 202-225-6401; e-mail: chtaylor@hr.house.gov.

District Offices: Asheville, 704-251-1988; Murphy, 704-837-3249; Shelby, 704-484-6971.

Committees: *Appropriations* (15th of 34 R): Commerce, Justice, State & Judiciary; District of Columbia (Chmn.); Interior.

Group Ratings

	ADA	ACLU	AFS	LCV	CFA	CON	NFIB	COC	ACU	NTLC	CHC
1996	5	7	0	15	15	45	97	87	100	100	100
1995	0	—	—	0	0	56	—	96	88	—	—

National Journal Ratings

	1995 LIB — 1995 CONS			1996 LIB — 1996 CONS		
Economic	0%	—	74%	0%	—	82%
Social	21%	—	72%	0%	—	90%
Foreign	0%	—	85%	21%	—	72%

Key Votes of the 104th Congress

1. Reduce Medicare Growth $	Y	5. Flag Amendment	Y	9. Cuban Embargo	Y
2. Ovrd. Product Liab. Veto	Y	6. Drop EPA Limits	N	10. Bar Bosnia Troop $	Y
3. Increase Min. Wage	N	7. Repeal Assault-Weap. Ban	Y	11. Cut Anti-Missile Defense	N
4. Welfare Reform	Y	8. Ovrd. Part. Birth Veto	Y	12. Bar U.N. Uniforms	Y

Election Results

1996 general	Charles H. Taylor (R)	132,860	(58%)	($481,658)
	James Mark Ferguson (D)	91,257	(40%)	($46,884)
	Others	3,908	(2%)	
1996 primary	Charles H. Taylor (R)	unopposed		
1994 general	Charles H. Taylor (R)................	115,826	(60%)	($999,467)
	Maggie Palmer Lauterer (D)	76,862	(40%)	($607,128)

TWELFTH DISTRICT

"This is perhaps the Negro's temporary farewell to Congress," said George White, a Tarboro, North Carolina lawyer and Republican, in his last days in the House of Representatives in 1901. Segregation was being imposed by law, and blacks informally but effectively were being stricken from the voting rolls in the rural South. It was 28 years until another black was elected to Congress and 70 years until another black won in the South. In North Carolina, although blacks have been politically influential since the Voting Rights Act of 1965, George White's prophecy was not overturned in North Carolina until 1992, when two blacks were elected. One, Eva Clayton, was from the mostly rural and small town 1st District—the kind of country where most blacks lived in George White's day. The other, Melvin Watt, represents the new 12th District, whose controversial boundaries connect blacks in several cities, and which were ruled unconstitutional by the Supreme Court.

The 12th District in effect for 1992, 1994 and 1996 was the most egregious example in the nation of the interpretation, urged by blacks and Republicans, that the 1982 revisions of the Voting Rights Act require the maximization of black percentages in congressional districts. It was called the I-85 district, because it consists of a series of urban black areas connected by a narrow line in some places no wider than I-85, splitting adjacent districts in two. A lawsuit was brought, and in June 1993 the Supreme Court in *Shaw v. Reno*, focusing on the 12th, ordered the plan reexamined. On remand a three-judge federal court upheld the plan in August 1994. But in June 1996 the Supreme Court declared the 12th unconstitutional. The three-judge court in July ruled that the 1996 election could go ahead under the old lines, but that they would have to be redrawn by April 1, 1997. On March 27 of that year, the divided legislature agreed on a new plan. The new 12th District no longer goes as far east as Durham and Burlington nor as far west as Gastonia, but it still follows I-85 pretty closely, linking black-majority areas of Charlotte, Statesville, Lexington, Winston-Salem, High Point and Greensboro. The black percentage is down from 57% to about 47%; it remains a heavily Democratic district. As of May 1997 it was still subject to review by the Justice Department and the courts.

Congressman Mel Watt, a Democrat first elected in 1992, grew up in a place called Dixie outside Charlotte, now overgrown with woods, in a tin-roofed house with no electricity or running water. His dream was to attend the University of North Carolina, and he was one of the first black students there; he made a fine academic record, went on to Yale Law School, and then to a civil rights law practice in Charlotte. He served one term in the state Senate, then decided not to seek office again until his sons completed high school. He managed Harvey Gantt's campaigns for city council and mayor in the 1980s and for U.S. Senate in 1990. In 1992 Watt decided to run in the 12th District. The contest turned out to be the kind of friends-and-neighbors Democratic primary common in the old segregated South. Watt took 47% of all votes in a four-way race, well over the 40% necessary for victory without a runoff in North Carolina. He won the general election easily, and on election night said he was "saddened that it took 92 years" to elect another black member to the state, "and I'm disappointed, because I know that thousands and thousands of people, but for the color of their skin, would have been just as qualified to fill this office."

In the House Watt has had a very liberal voting record, and he has often come forward to oppose popular measures on civil liberties grounds. He refused to oppose the tobacco tax in the Clinton healthcare plan and backed a Canadian-style single-payer system. He has voted against crime bills because of their death penalty provisions, against increased penalties for hate crimes, against gun bans in urban housing projects, against Megan's Law requiring registration of convicted sex offenders, against increased prison sentences for crimes against children because he said it would interfere with the U.S. Sentencing Commission's autonomy. On the 1996 terrorism bill, he said, "We can't sacrifice our constitutional principles because we're angry at people for bombing." He opposed the fence along the California-Mexico border, and tried to eliminate the immigration slots for immigrants with assets of $1 million who promise to create at least 10 jobs in the U.S.; "We are allowing rich people to buy their way into our country," he said. He passed an amendment to protect Legal Services lawyers' rights to federal legal aid money. He attacked the 1996 juvenile justice bill as "the most extreme piece of legislation this committee will have considered during this term of Congress." He vehemently opposed the 1996 Welfare Reform Act, and on the "partial-birth" abortion ban, he wanted to put the burden of proving a woman's life in danger on the state. In November 1995 he decided not to shave until the final budget bills for 1996 were passed; he finally shaved in May 1996.

When the *Shaw v. Reno* decision was announced in 1993, Watt was outraged. "You go down into North Carolina and you take a poll and 30% to 35% of the population will tell you under no circumstances, regardless of how qualified, would [they] vote for a black candidate. So there is a need for something that will equalize the playing field." But the existence of a bloc of opponents does not preclude victory, as Watt's own career showed. In 1990 Gantt won 47% of the votes in a state that was 22% black; in 1992 Watt was elected to the House with 70% of the votes in a district that was 57% black. There seems little doubt that he can be reelected in the March 1997 plan's 12th District, though his percentage may drop a bit from the 71% he won in 1996. But with his liberal views he might very well have difficulty in a compact district centered on Charlotte.

The People: Pop. 1990: 551,957; 14% rural; 12% age 65+; 41% White; 56% Black; 1% Asian; 1% Hispanic origin. Households: 43% married couple families; 19% married couple fams. w. children; 37% college educ.; median household income: $23,068; per capita income: $10,878; median gross rent: $381; median house value: $57,800. *(Information does not reflect 1997 redistricting.)*

1996 Presidential Vote

Clinton (D)	123,511	(69%)
Dole (R)	47,329	(26%)
Perot (I)	7,789	(4%)

1992 Presidential Vote

Clinton (D)	125,189	(66%)
Bush (R)	48,406	(25%)
Perot (I)	16,886	(9%)

Rep. Melvin L. Watt (D)

Elected 1992; b. Aug. 26, 1945, Mecklenburg; home, Charlotte; U. of NC, Chapel Hill, B.S. 1967, Yale U., J.D. 1970; Presbyterian; married (Eulada).

Career: Practicing atty., 1971–92; NC Senate, 1984–86; Co-owner, East Town Manor nursing home, 1989–present; Campaign Mgr., Harvey Gantt Senate Campaign, 1990.

DC Office: 1230 LHOB 20515, 202-225-1510; Fax: 202-225-1512; e-mail: melmail@hr.house.gov.

District Offices: Charlotte, 704-344-9950; Durham, 919-688-3004; Greensboro, 910-379-9403.

Committees: *Banking & Financial Services* (15th of 25 D): Capital Markets, Securities & Government Sponsored Enterprises; Financial Institutions & Consumer Credit. *Judiciary* (8th of 15 D): Constitution; Immigration & Claims (RMM).

Group Ratings

	ADA	ACLU	AFS	LCV	CFA	CON	NFIB	COC	ACU	NTLC	CHC
1996	90	93	100	85	92	91	8	19	0	2	0
1995	100	—	—	88	100	25	—	4	4	—	—

National Journal Ratings

	1995 LIB — 1995 CONS			1996 LIB — 1996 CONS		
Economic	90%	—	8%	89%	—	0%
Social	88%	—	0%	84%	—	16%
Foreign	93%	—	0%	90%	—	0%

Key Votes of the 104th Congress

1. Reduce Medicare Growth $	N	5. Flag Amendment	N	9. Cuban Embargo	N
2. Ovrd. Product Liab. Veto	N	6. Drop EPA Limits	Y	10. Bar Bosnia Troop $	N
3. Increase Min. Wage	Y	7. Repeal Assault-Weap. Ban	N	11. Cut Anti-Missile Defense	Y
4. Welfare Reform	N	8. Ovrd. Part. Birth Veto	N	12. Bar U.N. Uniforms	N

Election Results

1996 general	Melvin L. Watt (D)	124,675	(71%)	($148,001)
	Joseph A. Martino Jr. (R)	46,581	(27%)	($6,902)
	Others	3,143	(2%)	
1996 primary	Melvin L. Watt (D)	unopposed		
1994 general	Melvin L. Watt (D)	57,655	(66%)	($253,715)
	Joseph A. (Joe) Martino (R)	29,933	(34%)	($14,700)

NORTH DAKOTA

For more than a century after statehood, North Dakota remained as close to its roots as any other state. Yet in its second century there are signs of change ahead. North Dakota was settled and its farm economy developed in a short generation. There are North Dakotans alive today who knew the men and women that settled this land and saw the state enter the Union in 1889. As children, they walked in the ruts left by the early settlers' wagon trains; they saw the Indians, recently defeated, herded onto reservations; they saw still shining new the rails that brought the world's commerce to these desolate prairies. This was the frontier to which Teddy Roosevelt came in 1884, determined to shoot one of the fast-disappearing buffalo, a place where settlers were only then breaking the sod and plowing under the natural prairies that are still preserved in a few places. This was some of the best wheat land in the world, empty by then of Indians and buffalo, connected to markets by rail, ready to become a cog in the industrial world being created by entrepreneurs and to raise its living standards to unparalleled heights.

And so, in a sudden rush of settlement during the 20 years before World War I, North Dakota filled up to pretty much its present population. There were 632,000 people here in 1920 and in counts since, the number has fluctuated between 617,000 and 680,000. In 1990 it was 639,000, and cumulatively it was the state with the lowest growth rate since 1950; Governor Ed Schafer took great cheer in 1996 when the Census Bureau estimated that the state's population was going up. Wheat is not the only crop here, there are also pinto beans, and as the plains become more arid to the west, ranching and livestock grazing—along with strip mining and oil and natural gas production—are important, and hardy root crops like potatoes and sugar beets grow as well. But wheat is still number one. Typically the state produces about one-tenth of the U.S. crop, and a fair percentage of the world's; its durum wheat is the main ingredient of American pasta.

This dependence on agriculture shaped North Dakota's politics. Farmers, as much as they like to extol their way of life, are seldom content with the workings of the market. When prices are high, it may be due to low production; when they are low they seek protection. The boosterish optimism of the first settlers was soon followed by cries reverberating with varying intensity for government protection against market forces. Since commodity prices tend to fall during periods of economic growth, there has been a countercyclical element in North Dakota politics, a tendency to vote against the national trends, and a radical strain going back to the 1910s and still lively in recent years. That radical strain also owes much to the immigrant origins of so many of North Dakota's early settlers: Norwegians in the eastern part of the state, Canadians along the northern border, Volga Germans in the west, colonies of Poles and Czechs and Icelanders, and native Germans throughout the state. (Volga Germans are descendants of early 19th Century German migrants to Russia who kept their German language and character.)

These immigrants produced orderly small towns and grain and other cooperatives; they also provided support for the Non-Partisan League, which flourished from its founding in 1915 to its alliance with the Democratic Party around 1960. It appealed to marginal farmers, cut off in many cases from the wider American culture by language barriers and seemingly at the mercy of the grain millers in Minneapolis, the railroads of St. Paul, the banks of New York and the commodity traders of Chicago. The NPL's program was socialist—government ownership of railroads and grain elevators—and, like most North Dakota ethnics, it opposed going to war with Germany. The NPL often determined the outcome of the usually decisive Republican primary and sometimes swung its support to the otherwise heavily outnumbered Democrats, instituting reforms and creating a state-owned bank. By 1960, the NPL had more or less merged into the Democratic Party, a merger symbolized by the election of the late Democratic Senator Quentin

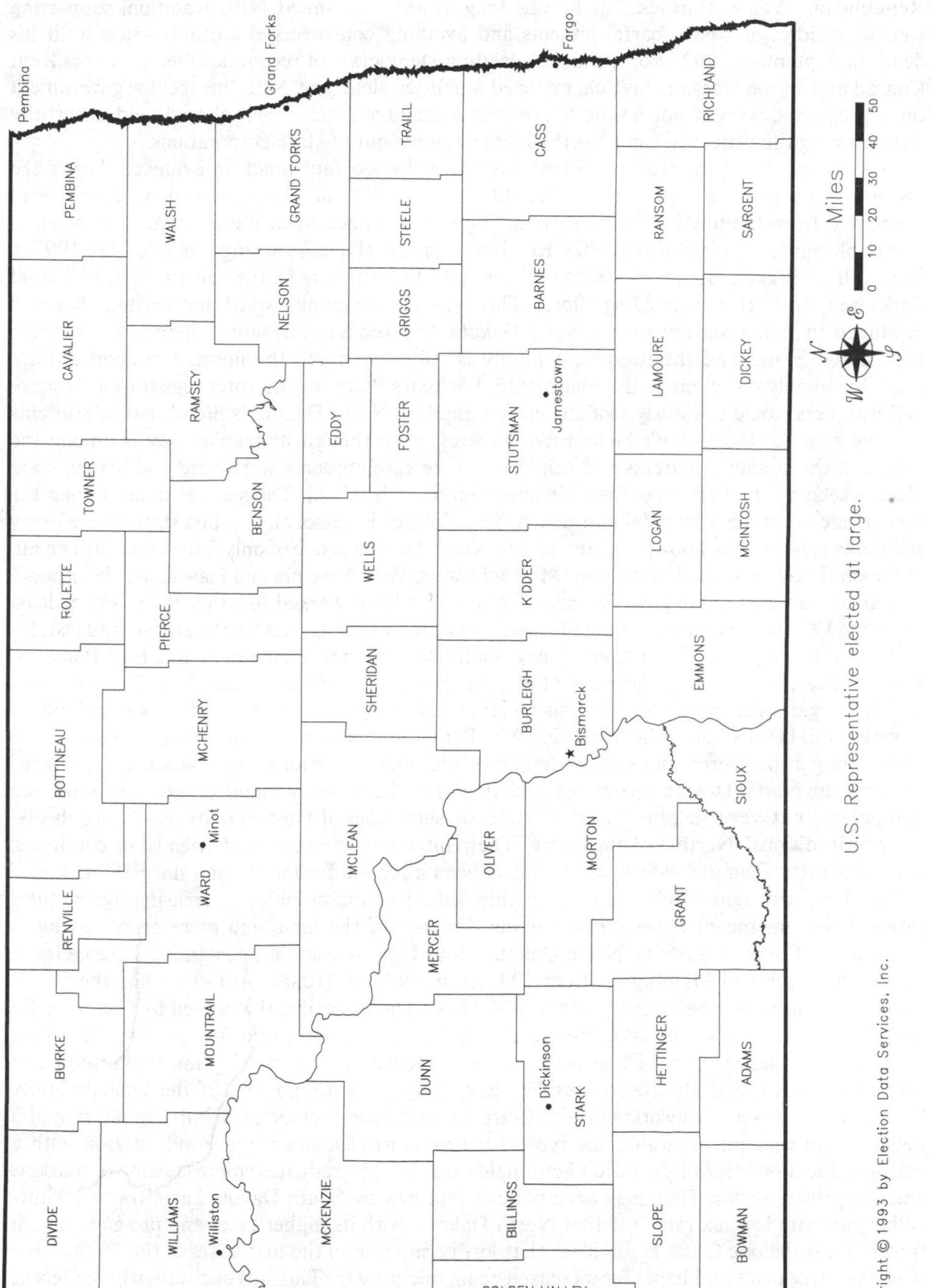
Pembina
Grand Forks
Fargo
PEMBINA
WALSH
GRAND FORKS
TRAILL
CASS
RICHLAND
NELSON
STEELE
GRIGGS
BARNES
RANSOM
SARGENT
CAVALIER
RAMSEY
EDDY
FOSTER
STUTSMAN
Jamestown
LAMOURE
DICKEY
TOWNER
BENSON
WELLS
KIDDER
LOGAN
MCINTOSH
ROLETTE
PIERCE
SHERIDAN
BURLEIGH
Bismarck
EMMONS
BOTTINEAU
MCHENRY
MCLEAN
OLIVER
MORTON
SIOUX
RENVILLE
WARD
Minot
MERCER
GRANT
BURKE
MOUNTRAIL
DUNN
STARK
Dickinson
HETTINGER
ADAMS
DIVIDE
WILLIAMS
Williston
MCKENZIE
BILLINGS
GOLDEN VALLEY
SLOPE
BOWMAN
Miles
0 10 20 30 40 50
U.S. Representative elected at large.
Copyright © 1993 by Election Data Services, Inc.

Burdick, whose father, Usher Burdick, served 20 years in the House as an NPL-endorsed Republican. "Young Burdick," as he was long known, continued NPL tradition, supporting wheat subsidies and pork barrel projects and avoiding controversial cultural issues until his death in September 1992. North Dakota's leading Democrats of recent decades, Senators Kent Conrad and Byron Dorgan, have championed a politics clearly of NPL lineage: for government farm programs, wary if not hostile to American military involvement abroad, and cheerfully championing the little guy from North Dakota against out-of-state corporations.

This is a place where everyone knows everyone else—a fact much in evidence during the disastrous flooding in 1997. Some 70,000 people—10% of the state's population—were evacuated from the town and area surrounding Grand Forks when the accumulation of eight winter blizzards melted and raised the Red River 26 feet above flood stage. In late May 1997, a state rally, "Bigger, Better & Stronger," was held to help benefit the townspeople of Grand Forks and aid in their rebuilding efforts. This type of community spirit and heritage has also produced an innate conservatism in North Dakota. Divorce is as uncommon here as anywhere in the United States and the two-parent family is still very much the norm, and abortions are available in only one clinic in the whole state. For years there was no voter registration because poll watchers would obviously spot anyone not eligible. North Dakota is proud that its students achieve some of the nation's highest math scores, even though its teacher pay is among the lowest in the country—parents and neighbors make sure students work hard and teachers are able to keep track of students from kindergarten to high school. The state also has among the lowest rates of student loan defaults and strikes. Politics is personal, too, in a state where every politician is personally known to many voters. North Dakota is one of only four states with an all-Democratic congressional delegation (Massachusetts, West Virginia and Hawaii are the others). The two senators and congressman are all allies who have worked together for years, at least since the 1974 campaign when Byron Dorgan, now junior senator, ran for the House, and lost; his campaign manager was Kent Conrad, now senior senator, and their driver was Earl Pomeroy, now congressman-at-large. The secret of their success was the office of state Tax Commissioner, which Dorgan held from 1969 until his election to Congress in 1980, which was then held by Conrad until his election to the Senate in 1986; Pomeroy was elected Insurance Commissioner in 1984. Dorgan pioneered and Conrad followed attempts to attribute out-of-state corporations' earnings to North Dakota operations and then tax them—very small potatoes to most big companies, but very helpful for thrift-minded, suspicious-of-big-corporations, farm-subsidy-hungry traditional North Dakota voters. Their interconnectedness and friendship continues: Lucy Calautti, Conrad's wife since 1986, has been a top staffer for Dorgan since 1974.

Yet there are signs of change even in this settled commonwealth. Increasing agricultural productivity has meant fewer farmers living directly off the land, and more people living in towns and off other industries. North Dakota's four biggest counties, containing Fargo, Grand Forks, Bismarck and Minot, grew from 134,000 in 1930 to 310,000 in 1996, while the state's other 48 counties dropped from 546,000 to 333,000. The diversification touted by Governor Ed Schafer has come along just as Congress passed the Freedom to Farm Act, phasing out wheat subsidies over seven years. These developments undermine the state's radical tradition and remove the advantage that farm subsidies have long given Democrats. If the typical elderly North Dakotan is a hard-working retired farmer, with fond memories of NPL agitation and a belief in government programs, the typical young North Dakotan is a family person with a college education (49% of the state's households are college graduates) more trusting of markets and the private sector. They may have noticed that nearby South Dakota has attracted white-collar jobs with low tax rates and that North Dakota, with its higher taxes and pro-government traditions, is the one Great Plains state that lost population in the first years of the 1990s—but now has lower taxes and hopes for increased economic growth. This was one state where George Bush and Bob Dole fairly easily beat Bill Clinton in 1992 and 1996, and the trend is for older North Dakotans voting heavily Democratic and younger North Dakotans Republican. It's too soon to say that North Dakota has moved away from its radical political roots, but a conservative

Dorgan was vastly popular as tax commissioner and congressman-at-large; his lowest percentage was in 1990, 65% against now-Governor Ed Schafer. But, having lost a House race to Mark Andrews in 1974, he declined to challenge Andrews for the Senate in 1986 or 80-year-old fellow-Democrat Quentin Burdick in 1988. Only with Conrad's surprise decision not to run for reelection in 1992 did he finally run for the Senate. He and his Republican opponent both backed most favored nation status for China (a major buyer of North Dakota wheat), but remained wary of free trade and supported relaxation of the regulations which have classified hundreds of seasonal puddles in North Dakota as protected wetlands. Dorgan won by a solid but not overwhelming 59%–39% margin—similar to Conrad's in 1994.

In the Senate Dorgan has worked for grants to aid economic development in for North Dakota, for restrictions on subsidized Canadian wheat imports, against NAFTA, and for requiring 400,000 federal vehicles to use ethanol fuel. He worked for tougher standards on federal construction contractors. He sponsored a law requiring a one-year expulsion of students who bring guns to school. Dorgan strongly backed fellow Dakotan Tom Daschle for Senate Democratic leader in 1994, and became an Assistant Floor Leader. He was the initial promoter of the move not to count Social Security revenues or outlays in the balanced budget amendment; this defeated the amendment in March 1995 and February 1997, although interestingly it would require deeper cuts in domestic discretionary spending than Dorgan surely wants. Some other Dorgan causes have proved so far quixotic: eliminating tax deductions for companies that build plants abroad and import products to the United States, imposing a fee on foreign airline overflights to subsidize air service in small airports. He sought to limit deregulation in the 1996 Telecommunications Act and to reduce the coverage of the product liability bill.

Dorgan comes up for reelection in 1998. His job ratings and past performance make him the obvious favorite. But there is talk of opposition from Governor Ed Schafer, who lost to Dorgan in 1990 but whose recent electoral performance has been very impressive. This would be an interesting battle between two quite different visions for North Dakota.

Representative-At-Large. North Dakota's single House member is Earl Pomeroy, a Democrat first elected in 1992. Pomeroy grew up in Valley City, North Dakota, and after college served as Byron Dorgan's driver during the 1974 campaign, then went to law school and practiced law in Valley City. In 1980, when Dorgan and Conrad won statewide elections, Pomeroy at 28 won a seat in the legislature; in 1984 and 1988 he was elected insurance commissioner. In 1992, he was planning to retire from politics and serve in the Peace Corps in Russia; then Dorgan ran for Conrad's seat in the Senate and Pomeroy ran for Dorgan's seat in the House. Articulate, cheerful and sincere, a critic of insurance companies yet unabrasive, he was the obvious choice for the House seat and was nominated unanimously by the Democratic convention. He won the general 57%–39%, almost exactly Dorgan's margin in the Senate race.

Pomeroy has compiled a moderate to liberal voting record, defending North Dakota interests and working with Republicans as well as Democrats on many issues. He served on the Budget Committee in his first term, and voted for both the Clinton budget and the Penny-Kasich spending cuts in 1993 and opposed the Clinton healthcare plan. In the Republican Congress he supported the Blue Dog budget and backed a $5,000 tax deduction for college tuition and job training. He formed a bipartisan, bicameral committee to seek consensus on retirement and pension issues; Pomeroy, with his experience as insurance commissioner, wants to help people on their lifelong project of accumulation of wealth. He strongly supported the adoption tax credit and brought his two-year-old daughter, adopted from Korea, onto the floor for the vote. "Children deserve families. Families are more important than political correctness." Pomeroy, though not averse to all change, opposed the Freedom to Farm Act. "I think Freedom to Farm is essentially a bait-and-switch proposition. By the year 2003, you've got nothing—no check, no protection against price collapse." He criticized the cutoff of farm loans after the 1996 bill passed; he authored the wetlands reform provisions of the act. On other local issues, he got the Clinton Administration to reverse its opposition to the Essential Air Services program and got $100 million in flood relief for overflowing Devils Lake and an Army Corps of Engineers study of an emergency outlet plan. During the devastating Grand Forks flooding in 1997, he helped man the dikes and slept in a nearby Air Force shelter in order to help residents deal with the disaster.

For all his strength Pomeroy has had serious Republican opposition. In 1994 businessman Gary Porter used his own money to match the incumbent's spending, attacking Pomeroy for supporting the 1994 crime bill with its gun control provisions. Pomeroy won 52%–45%, carrying the four largest counties by only 50%–48%. In 1996 Pomeroy with $604,000 in PAC contributions, outspent state Tourism director Kevin Cramer by more than 2–1 and increased his margin to 55%–43%, carrying the four largest counties 53%–45%. Pomeroy is now the only Democratic congressman in the belt of Great Plains states from North Dakota south to Oklahoma.

Presidential politics. Massachusetts, West Virginia and Hawaii, the other states with all-Democratic congressional delegations, are heavily Democratic in presidential elections; North Dakota is Republican. In 1996 Bob Dole carried the state by a respectable though not dazzling 47%–40%. North Dakota has been one of Ross Perot's strongest states; he got 23% here in 1992 and 12% in 1996. An echo of the Non-Partisan League?

With a tiny delegation, an out-of-the-way location and frigid weather in the early primary season, North Dakota does not loom large in choosing presidential nominees. The Democrats hold a caucus, the Republicans a primary, which was switched in 1996 from the latest in the country to February, just a week after New Hampshire. Fellow prairie man Bob Dole beat Steve Forbes 42%–20%.

The People: Est. Pop. 1996: 644,000; Pop. 1990: 638,800, up 0.7% 1990–1996. 0.2% of U.S. total, 47th largest; 47% rural. Median age: 34.9 years. 15% 65 years and over. 94.2% White, 1% Black, 1% Asian, 4% Amer. Indian, 1% Hispanic origin. Households: 59.1% married couple families; 30% married couple fams. w. children; 49% college educ.; median household income: $23,213; per capita income: $11,051; 65.6% owner occupied housing; median house value: $50,800; median monthly rent: $266. 3.1% Unemployment. 1996 Voting age pop.: 476,000. 1996 Turnout: 266,411; 56% of VAP. No state voter registration.

Political Lineup: Governor, Edward T. Schafer (R); Lt. Gov., Rosemarie Myrdal (R); Secy. of State, Alvin Jaeger (R); Atty. Gen., Heidi Heitkamp (D); Treasurer, Kathi Gilmore (D); Auditor, Robert W. Peterson (R). State Senate, 49 (19 D and 30 R); Senate President, Rosemarie Myrdal (R); State House, 98 (27 D and 71 R); House Speaker, Mike Timm (R). Senators, Kent Conrad (D) and Byron L. Dorgan (D). Representative, 1 D at large.

Elections Division: 701-328-4146; **Filing Deadline for U.S. Congress:** April 10, 1998.

1996 Presidential Vote

Dole (R)	125,050	(47%)
Clinton (D)	106,905	(40%)
Perot (I)	32,515	(12%)

1996 Republican Presidential Primary

Dole (R)	26,832	(42%)
Forbes (R)	12,455	(20%)
Buchanan (R)	11,653	(18%)
Gramm (R)	5,997	(9%)
Alexander (R)	4,008	(6%)
Other	2,789	(4%)

1992 Presidential Vote

Bush (R)	136,244	(44%)
Clinton (D)	99,168	(32%)
Perot (I)	71,084	(23%)

GOVERNOR

Gov. Edward T. Schafer (R)

Elected 1992, term expires Dec. 1996; b. August 8, 1946, Bismarck; home, Bismarck; U. of ND, B.A. 1969, U. of Denver, M.B.A. 1970; Episcopalian; married (Nancy).

Career: Gold Seal Co., 1971–86, Pres., 1978–86; Founder & Secy-Treasurer, American Eagle beverage distributorship, 1976–present; Pres. & owner, Dakota Classics auto dealership, and TRIESCO Properties real estate, 1986–present; Pres. & owner, Fish 'N Dakota aquaculture, 1990–94.

Office: State Capitol, 600 E. Boulevard, Bismarck 58505, 701-328-2200; Fax: 701-328-2205; Web site: www.state.nd.us.

Election Results

1996 gen.	Edward T. Schafer (R)........	174,937	(66%)
	Lee Kaldor (D)..............	89,349	(34%)
1996 prim.	Edward T. Schafer (R)........	unopposed	
1992 gen.	Edward T. Schafer (R)........	176,398	(58%)
	Nicholas Spaeth (D)..........	123,845	(41%)

SENATORS

Sen. Kent Conrad (D)

Elected 1986, seat up 2000; b. Mar. 12, 1948, Bismarck; home, Bismarck; Stanford U., B.A. 1971; George Washington U., M.B.A. 1975; Unitarian; married (Lucy Calautti).

Career: Asst., ND Tax Commissioner, 1974–80; Dir., Mgmt. Planning and Personnel, ND Tax Dept., 1980; ND Tax Commissioner, 1981–86.

DC Office: 530 HSOB 20510, 202-224-2043; Fax: 202-224-7776; e-mail: senator@conrad.senate.gov.

State Offices: Bismarck, 701-258-4648; Fargo, 701-232-8030; Grand Forks, 701-775-9601; Minot, 701-852-0703.

Committees: *Agriculture, Nutrition & Forestry* (3rd of 8 D): Forestry, Conservation & Rural Revitalization (RMM); Research, Nutrition & General Legislation. *Budget* (3rd of 10 D). *Finance* (5th of 9 D): Health Care; International Trade; Taxation & IRS Oversight. *Indian Affairs* (2nd of 6 D). *Ethics (Select)* (3rd of 3 D).

Group Ratings

	ADA	ACLU	AFS	LCV	CFA	CON	NFIB	COC	ACU	NTLC	CHC
1996	85	35	86	54	86	36	34	23	15	10	15
1995	90	—	100	79	81	68	—	42	9	—	—

National Journal Ratings

	1995 LIB — 1995 CONS			1996 LIB — 1996 CONS		
Economic	79%	—	20%	74%	—	19%
Social	57%	—	42%	56%	—	42%
Foreign	69%	—	29%	70%	—	28%

Key Votes of the 104th Congress

1. Reduce Medicare Growth $	N	5. Flag Amendment	N	9. Anti-Missile Defense	N
2. Lmt. Prod. Liab. Damages	N	6. Endangered Species	N	10. Cuban Embargo	Y
3. Increase Min. Wage	Y	7. Gay Employment Rights	Y	11. Bar Bosnia Troop $	N
4. Welfare Reform	Y	8. Ovrd. Part. Birth Veto	Y	12. Cut Vietnam Aid	Y

Election Results

1994 general	Kent Conrad (D)	137,157	(58%)	($1,927,866)
	Ben Clayburgh (R)	99,390	(42%)	($941,192)
1994 primary	Kent Conrad (D)	unopposed		
1992 special	Kent Conrad (D)	103,246	(63%)	($2,479,021)
	Jack Dalrymple (R)	55,194	(34%)	($282,104)
	Other	4,871	(3%)	

Sen. Byron L. Dorgan (D)

Elected 1992, seat up 1998; b. May 14, 1942, Dickinson; home, Bismarck; U. of ND, B.S. 1965, U. of Denver, M.B.A. 1966; Lutheran; married (Kimberly).

Career: Martin-Marietta Exec. Develop. Prog., 1966–68; ND Dep. Tax Commissioner, 1968–69, ND Tax Commissioner, 1969–80; U.S. House of Reps., 1980–92.

DC Office: 713 HSOB 20510, 202-224-2551; Fax: 202-224-1193; e-mail: senator@dorgan.senate.gov.

State Offices: Bismarck, 701-250-4618; Fargo, 701-239-5389.

Committees: *Appropriations* (12th of 13 D): Defense; Energy & Water Development; Interior; Legislative Branch (RMM). *Commerce, Science & Transportation* (8th of 9 D): Aviation; Communications; Manufacturing & Competitiveness; Science, Technology & Space; Surface Transportation & Merchant Marine. *Energy & Natural Resources* (5th of 9 D): Forests & Public Land Management (RMM); Water & Power. *Indian Affairs* (6th of 6 D).

Group Ratings

	ADA	ACLU	AFS	LCV	CFA	CON	NFIB	COC	ACU	NTLC	CHC
1996	85	44	86	69	71	14	45	38	20	17	15
1995	90	—	100	93	81	19	—	47	13	—	—

National Journal Ratings

	1995 LIB — 1995 CONS			1996 LIB — 1996 CONS		
Economic	67%	—	32%	61%	—	34%
Social	59%	—	37%	56%	—	42%
Foreign	76%	—	21%	84%	—	14%

Key Votes of the 104th Congress

1. Reduce Medicare Growth $	N	5. Flag Amendment	N	9. Anti-Missile Defense	N
2. Lmt. Prod. Liab. Damages	Y	6. Endangered Species	N	10. Cuban Embargo	Y
3. Increase Min. Wage	Y	7. Gay Employment Rights	Y	11. Bar Bosnia Troop $	N
4. Welfare Reform	Y	8. Ovrd. Part. Birth Veto	Y	12. Cut Vietnam Aid	Y

Election Results

1992 general	Byron L. Dorgan (D)	179,347	(59%)	($1,124,512)
	Steve Sydness (R)	118,162	(39%)	($498,107)
	Other	6,448	(2%)	
1992 primary	Byron L. Dorgan (D)	unopposed		
1986 general	Kent Conrad (D)	143,932	(50%)	($908,374)
	Mark Andrews (R)	141,797	(49%)	($2,270,557)

REPRESENTATIVE

Rep. Earl Pomeroy (D)

Elected 1992; b. Sept. 2, 1952, Valley City; home, Valley City; U. of ND, B.A. 1974, J.D., 1979; Presbyterian; married (Laurie Kirby).

Career: Practicing atty., 1979–84; ND House of Reps., 1980–84; ND Insurance Commissioner, 1984–92; VP, Natl. Assn. of Insurance Commissioners, 1989, Pres., 1990.

DC Office: 1533 LHOB 20515, 202-225-2611; Fax: 202-226-0893; e-mail: epomeroy@hr.house.gov.

District Offices: Bismarck, 701-224-0355; Fargo, 701-235-9760.

Committees: *Agriculture* (9th of 23 D): Forestry, Resource Conservation & Research; Risk Management & Specialty Crops. *Budget* (6th of 19 D).

Group Ratings

	ADA	ACLU	AFS	LCV	CFA	CON	NFIB	COC	ACU	NTLC	CHC
1996	80	44	92	69	54	78	46	31	11	20	14
1995	80	—	—	75	69	25	—	39	23	—	—

National Journal Ratings

	1995 LIB	—	1995 CONS	1996 LIB	—	1996 CONS
Economic	66%	—	34%	70%	—	28%
Social	65%	—	33%	65%	—	34%
Foreign	62%	—	36%	75%	—	25%

Key Votes of the 104th Congress

1. Reduce Medicare Growth $	N	5. Flag Amendment	Y	9. Cuban Embargo	Y
2. Ovrd. Product Liab. Veto	N	6. Drop EPA Limits	Y	10. Bar Bosnia Troop $	N
3. Increase Min. Wage	Y	7. Repeal Assault-Weap. Ban	N	11. Cut Anti-Missile Defense	Y
4. Welfare Reform	N	8. Ovrd. Part. Birth Veto	Y	12. Bar U.N. Uniforms	*

Election Results

1996 general	Earl Pomeroy (D)	144,833	(55%)	($971,332)
	Kevin Cramer (R)	113,684	(43%)	($434,082)
	Others	4,493	(2%)	
1996 primary	Earl Pomeroy (D)	unopposed		
1994 general	Earl Pomeroy (D)	123,134	(52%)	($813,900)
	Gary Porter (R)	105,988	(45%)	($818,392)
	Others	6,267	(3%)	

OHIO

Ohio was the first entirely American state, and one which ever since has seemed an epitome of American normalcy. The original 13 states started as British colonies, and the next three, Vermont, Kentucky and Tennessee, were spun off from them. But Ohio sprung Athena-like from the head of Congress, as the first state formed from the Northwest Territory of 1787. The Northwest Ordinance established 6 by 6 mile square townships, which imposed geometric order on diverse American landscapes west to the Pacific; it set aside one square mile per township for public schools, and the landscape was soon peppered with schoolhouses and small colleges, the foundation stones of a literate republic. The Ordinance prohibited slavery, opening the way for free labor to clear fields, raise crops, build mills and factories, and, in less than half a century, make this wilderness one of the most productive parts of western civilization. Ohio, in the years after the Civil War, became one of the great industrial states, the longtime headquarters of John D. Rockefeller's Standard Oil, the site of major steel mills along the narrow and languidly flowing Cuyahoga and Mahoning Rivers, and home of the biggest soap companies, machine tool makers, tire manufacturers and producers of safety glass. Settled by Virginians in the southwest around Cincinnati, by New Englanders in the northeast in the Western Reserve around Cleveland, Ohio has always been split between cultures: between the southern-accented counties south of the National Road and U.S. 40 and the northern-accented cities and towns to the north; between Butternut and Copperhead territory that didn't want to fight the Civil War and Yankee territory that fiercely prosecuted the War and Reconstruction afterwards.

This split heritage made Ohio politically a closely divided state—and a nationally pivotal one. Just a century ago it was Ohio that produced the candidate and campaign manager—Governor and former Ways and Means Chairman William McKinley and iron and coal industrialist Mark Hanna—who won the Presidency in 1896 and inaugurated a 34-year period of Republican national majorities. McKinley's Republicans were for high tariffs and hard money, had a friendly regard for workers and even some unions, but no patience with large union combinations and nascent socialism. They preached a nationalist Americanism tempered by a wariness about making major commitments abroad. Republicans were the majority in this increasingly industrial Ohio, losing rural Butternut counties but carrying the big industrial cities of the north.

Then came the Depression of the 1930s, and Ohio became the scene of something like class warfare, with sitdown strikes and victories for the CIO industrial unions in autos, steel and tires. CIO cities—Cleveland, Akron, Youngstown, Toledo—moved sharply toward the Democrats, while places with few CIO members—Cincinnati, Columbus, the dozens of small factory towns dotting the flat limestone plains of northern Ohio—stayed Republican. The political fighting was fierce and the stakes seemed big. CIO leaders hoped to organize the entire work force and build a Scandinavian-style welfare state; Republican leaders like Ohio Senator Robert Taft feared union control of business would imperil freedoms and throttle the economy. In the 1930s and 1940s, the unions made great gains. But Taft held them off, reducing union power with the Taft-Hartley Act of 1947, his own reelection to the Senate in 1950, and—his eventual rival—Dwight Eisenhower's presidential election in 1952.

In the years since, Ohio has oscillated and been courted by national campaigns. In the 1970s it seemed to swing toward the Democrats. Jimmy Carter won crucial electoral votes by carrying Ohio by 11,000 votes and Democrats controlled the state House throughout the 1970s and 1980s. Now in the 1990s Ohio seems to have veered Republican. Bill Clinton did carry the state twice, but by the narrowest of his margins in any megastate—40%–38% in 1992, 47%–41% in 1996. Also Ohio Republicans won a smashing victory in 1994 and, below the presidential level, held their own in 1996. The 1994 headline event was the reelection of Republican Governor

WILLIAMS
FULTON
LUCAS
Toledo
9
OTTAWA
Sandusky
WOOD
SANDUSKY
ERIE
DEFIANCE
HENRY
5
SENECA
Tiffin
HURON
PAULDING
Findlay
PUTNAM
HANCOCK
WYANDOT
CRAWFORD
RICHLAND
Mansfield
ASHLAND
VAN WERT
ALLEN
Lima
4
HARDIN
MARION
Marion
MORROW
MERCER
AUGLAIZE
LOGAN
SHELBY
UNION
DELAWARE
KNOX
12
LICKING
DARKE
CHAMPAIGN
MIAMI
8
CLARK
15
Columbus
Newark
7
FRANKLIN
MADISON
MONTGOMERY
Dayton
PREBLE
GREENE
Xenia
3
FAYETTE
PICKAWAY
FAIRFIELD
PERRY
BUTLER
Hamilton
2
WARREN
CLINTON
ROSS
Chillicothe
HOCKING
1
Cincinnati
HIGHLAND
2
PIKE
VINTON
6
HAMILTON
CLERMONT
BROWN
ADAMS
SCIOTO
Portsmouth
JACKSON
GALLIA
LAWRENCE
Ironton
Ashtabula
19
ASHTABULA
LAKE
CUYAHOGA
Cleveland
GEAUGA
11
10
19
13
Lorain
PORTAGE
LORAIN
13
14
Warren
MEDINA
SUMMIT
Akron
TRUMBULL
Youngstown
MAHONING
Alliance
WAYNE
STARK
Canton
COLUMBIANA
16
17
East Liverpool
HOLMES
CARROLL
TUSCARAWAS
JEFFERSON
Steubenville
COSHOCTON
HARRISON
18
MUSKINGUM
Zanesville
GUERNSEY
BELMONT
NOBLE
MONROE
MORGAN
WASHINGTON
Marietta
ATHENS
MEIGS
Pomeroy
N
W
E
S
Miles
0 5 10 15 20
Congressional district boundaries
effective March 27, 1992.

George Voinovich by a 72%–25% margin—by far the biggest margin since 1826, when neither Republican nor Democratic parties existed. And Republicans in 1994 won up and down the line: Mike DeWine was elected senator over Democrat Joel Hyatt 53%–39%, in a race that initially seemed even, and in a state that had not elected a Republican senator since 1970. Republicans won every one of the statewide offices, dominated by Democrats since 1970; they won large margins in both houses of the legislature, replacing the nation's longest-serving state House speaker, Vern Riffe, with Jo Ann Davidson; they gained four seats in the U.S. House. The new lieutenant governor, Nancy Putnam Hollister, a woman with an old Yankee pedigree, ran with the Serbo-Croatian Voinovich, who had served 10 years as mayor of Cleveland. Republicans also elected a woman Attorney General (Betty Montgomery), a black Treasurer (Kenneth Blackwell), and Ohio's first Hispanic legislator (John Garcia of Toledo). In 1996, Republicans lost two House seats, but held a majority of the House delegation and both houses of the legislature. Republicans ran only 3% behind their 1994 showing in seats contested both times; they won the voting for U.S. House 51%–46%, for state Senate (in which only half the seats were up) 57%–40%, and for state House 53%–46%.

The interesting question is whether this is a short-term blip or a long-run trend, a return to a McKinley-type Republican majority or a momentary interruption of New Deal voting patterns. It is a question of national significance, for in income levels, urban-rural balance, and ethnic mix, as well as presidential percentages, Ohio is close to the national average. One place to look for answers is in north-and-east Ohio, the traditionally Democratic area along Lake Erie and reaching south to the coal-mining counties across the Ohio River from West Virginia. This was the heartland of the CIO unions, the United Steelworkers in Youngstown and Cleveland, United Rubber Workers in Akron, United Mine Workers in the coal country, and United Auto Workers in Toledo and Lordstown. It is heavily ethnic, with hundreds of thousands of Poles, Hungarians, Slovaks, Serbs, and Croatians streaming in throughout the early 20th Century. When its auto, steel, rubber and glass factories lost hundreds of thousands of jobs in the five years after the oil shock of 1979, north-and-east Ohio was one of the most Democratic parts of the country; as a separate state, it would have come as close to voting against Ronald Reagan in 1980 and 1984 as Massachusetts or New York. It voted solidly for Michael Dukakis in 1988 (54%–46%) and Bill Clinton in 1992 (47%–31%). But as the shock of the early 1980s wore off, and it became clear that CIO industries' high-wage, low-skill jobs were gone for good, attitudes began changing. Voters gave up on trying to recreate the old factory economy and began building a new, more supple and adaptable manufacturing economy, with smaller factories, less rigid management and fewer union members, fewer low-skill jobs with high wages and more medium-skill, high-flexibility jobs with chances for advancement. They gave up on restricting trade, as steel and auto import quotas lapsed and NAFTA was approved, and began manufacturing goods for export markets. And so Ohio began to grow again. Cleveland's new downtown is gleaming, Akron is proud of the polymer technologies which have replaced tire manufacturing, the Cuyahoga River is clean and the valleys carved by rivers in the limestone are a source of pride.

George Voinovich, long familiar to the Cleveland TV market, carried north-and-east Ohio 55%–45% when he was elected governor in 1990; in 1994, against a little-known opponent, he won 69%–29%, the kind of Republican margin not seen in this area of Ohio since the 1920s. Even more startlingly, Republican Mike DeWine carried the area over Democrat Joel Hyatt 47%–45% in the 1994 Senate race. Then in 1996 the Democrats came partially back: Bill Clinton carried north-and-east Ohio 54%–33%. But his percentage was no higher than Dukakis's, and not enough for a statewide majority. The politics of union-management struggle, class warfare and economic redistribution seems less than vigorous, perhaps dying, in one of its American heartlands.

The rest of Ohio has long been a Republican area, a stronghold for Robert Taft and for James Rhodes, governor for 16 of the 20 years between 1962 and 1982, who favored low taxes in order to attract jobs. In the 1980s, this larger part of Ohio's cultural conservatism and patriotic nationalism, plus faith in a growing economy, made it heavily Republican: 67%–32% for Ronald

Reagan in 1984 and 63%–36% for George Bush (whose grandfather owned a steel factory in Columbus) in 1988. In 1992 and 1996 George Bush and Bob Dole won only pluralities here, but Republicans carried the area overwhelmingly in 1994.

The economy in both parts of Ohio has proved to be surprisingly robust in the 1990s. The unemployment rate, long high, fell below the national average; household incomes were up sharply; over half a million jobs were created. Ohioans' high-skill manufacturing is booming, and small entrepreneurs have created thousands of jobs in the shadows of huge steel mills long since shut down. Politically, this economic growth has benefited incumbents, George Voinovich in 1994, Bill Clinton in 1996. Voinovich attracted no serious competition and Democrats were unable to field winning candidates up and down the ticket, in vivid contrast to the 1970s and 1980s. Clinton increased his 1992 margin, and Democrats showed better morale, but their institutional base still seems weak; organized labor was more active than in 1994, but far less of an influence than in the 1960s and 1970s. A test for both parties comes in 1998. Senator John Glenn, the last major Ohio Democrat in office, who turns 77 in 1998, announced in February 1997 that he would not run again. Glenn, who started off his career disengaged from his party's liberals, has become an outspoken supporter of Bill Clinton and an increasing partisan in the Senate. George Voinovich announced in December 1996 that he would run for the seat, and early polls showed him to be a favorite. Whether Democrats can field a strong senatorial candidate is a major test for them; whether Voinovich can be followed by a like-minded candidate is a major test for the Republicans. 1998 is also a test of where Ohio stands in history. Is it New Deal Ohio, with ethnic factory workers ranged against small town businessmen, ethnic Catholics versus rural Protestants, all engaged in a contest to see how far and in what ways government should be enlarged? Or is it McKinley Ohio, with mechanical tinkerers and can-do manufacturers, adaptive businessmen and hard-working employees, striving to work hard, raise families and serve communities that feel little class conflict or economic envy? Ironically, the best-known figures of each party come from the other's heartland, Glenn from pious small town Guernsey County, Voinovich from a Serbo-Croatian ward in Cleveland.

Governor. In early 1997 George Voinovich stood at the summit of Ohio politics, in his seventh year as governor with very high job approval, a strong candidate for the Senate in 1998, with a like-minded Republican hoping to succeed him. Voinovich is a pleasant and unassuming man who can show temper—he was fined $1,500 for ordering his state plane to take off when the Secret Service shut down the Columbus airport for a Clinton visit—and has known tragedy—his young daughter was killed in an auto accident when he was running for mayor in 1979. He has been in government and politics most of his life. He grew up in Cleveland, an ethnic in an ethnic industrial metropolis; he practiced law, then was elected to the legislature in 1966, at 30. He was elected county auditor in 1971, county commissioner in 1977, and lieutenant governor in 1978. In 1979, after Mayor Dennis Kucinich bankrupted Cleveland, Voinovich was elected mayor. In 10 years in office, he fixed the budget and sparked the city's renaissance. His one defeat came in 1988, when he lost 57%–43% to Senator Howard Metzenbaum.

As governor, Voinovich slowed budget growth and claims he turned a $1.5 billion deficit into an $828 million rainy day fund. He backed one tax increase, in 1992; he accepted but did not initiate a small tax cut in 1996. He cut funding for higher education, but increased it for Head Start and K-12 schools; in early 1997 he called for more aid to poor districts, in response to a suit before the state Supreme Court in which 500 school districts were seeking to change school financing. He has proposed a $1 billion bond issue to finance school repairs and wants to put computers in every classroom. Voinovich boasts that his JOBS program enrolled more welfare recipients than any other state, and that he cut welfare rolls. He sponsored a managed healthcare plan, OhioCare, for Medicaid recipients and the uninsured, and continued Democratic Governor Richard Celeste's program for state investment in businesses. He is opposed to abortion but recognizes *Roe v. Wade* as the law and says, "Let's deal in the real world."

Voinovich has played a national role as well. In January 1995 he worked with Bob Dole and Newt Gingrich on the successful Republican move to limit unfunded mandates on the states, and at the same time urged a balanced budget amendment. He was the first governor to endorse Dole for president, though he seemed lukewarm to him in the summer of 1996. Voinovich was mentioned for the vice presidential nomination, but took himself out of the running. About the same time, in July 1996, his chief of staff resigned while the target of a state contract-steering investigation. He was chosen to lead the National Governors Association beginning in July 1997.

Voinovich is term-limited and by early 1997 the race to succeed him had begun. The likely Republican nominee is Secretary of State Robert A. Taft II, grandson of the senator, who stepped aside from a primary contest with Voinovich in 1990 at the urging of then-Republican Chairman Lee Atwater. Taft hails Ohio's leading the nation for three years in factory expansion, but he may face primary opposition from state Treasurer Kenneth Blackwell. Former Democratic Attorney General Lee Fisher, who narrowly lost in 1994, has announced his candidacy, and 13th District Congressman Sherrod Brown has been mentioned as a possibility.

Senior Senator. John Glenn is now the grand old man of Ohio politics. Many voters have no living memory of the event that thrust him into national fame, when he became the first American astronaut to orbit the earth in a space capsule in February 1962; almost forgotten is the movie *The Right Stuff*, whose release in October 1983 was expected to boost Glenn's presidential candidacy in 1984. His 22-year career in the Marine Corps, which included heroic service in World War II and Korea, has now been equalled in length by his career in the Senate. Glenn came to politics as the authentic embodiment of the small town virtues of family, God-fearing religion, duty, patriotism and hard work typical of his home town of New Concord, Ohio; he also brought the aggressiveness that made him a brilliant fighter pilot, earned him fame as an astronaut, and then propelled him into running for the Senate in 1964. He left that race after injuring himself in a household accident; in 1970, he ran again and lost in the primary to Howard Metzenbaum, the beginning of a long rivalry that ultimately became a friendship; in 1974, he beat Metzenbaum in the primary and then easily won the general.

In those days, Glenn was a moderate Democrat, with issue positions and a personal demeanor at odds with the liberal activists of the time—which helps account for the coolness of the response to his presidential candidacy in 1984. Glenn's difficulty that year was not just ideological. He did not shine in debates, and his decision to stay in the race one more week to compete in southern primaries helped pile up a campaign debt of some $3 million, the bulk of which he has never been able to pay off—and which became a liability in his 1992 Senate campaign.

Over the years Glenn has become less of an above-the-fray hero and more of a partisan politician, in Washington and with Ohio voters. His voting record is now quite liberal, and he has been one of the most enthusiastic boosters of the Clinton Administration on Capitol Hill and of candidate Bill Clinton on the stump in Ohio. "You don't help children," he proclaimed, mocking Newt Gingrich, "by taking Big Bird away from 5-year-olds, school lunches from 10-year-olds, summer jobs away from 15-year-olds, and student loans away from 20-year-olds." Much of Glenn's work over the years has come on the mechanics of government. He called for applying to Congress the laws Congress applies for others as early as 1978, a precursor of the Contract with America's Congressional Accountability Act. He questioned Vice President Dan Quayle's Competitiveness Council and supported Vice President Al Gore's "reinventing government." He sponsored Cabinet rank for the Environmental Protection Agency which failed in the House and Hatch Act repeal which Clinton signed into law. He co-sponsored the Republicans' unfunded mandates law in January 1995, of which George Voinovich was the most prominent advocate outside Congress. He sponsored the original Paperwork Reduction Act and the bill setting up inspectors general in each Cabinet department. He offered bipartisan substitutes to the Republicans' regulatory reform bills, which lost 48–50 in July 1995 and 48–52 in January 1996, after which he successfully filibustered the Republican version.

For two decades, Glenn has worked hard on the frustrating issue of nuclear proliferation. He has kept careful watch of, and has tried to reduce or eliminate, U.S. exports of nuclear technology and materials to Pakistan, Iraq and other countries. It is uphill work, for the violators are ingenious and foreign policy makers always have arguments why specific cases should be exempted from the anti-proliferation rules. In 1996 he accused China of proliferating, and pressed India not to conduct a nuclear test. Glenn has also been on the outlook for nuclear abuses at home. He spotlighted unsafe conditions in the government's nuclear materials plants, notably the Fernald plant just outside Cincinnati. And he worked for tough guidelines for obtaining consent for human radiation treatment. He has kept up his interest in space, urging the president of China to join multinational space exploration and volunteering to go up again himself to test the effects of weightlessness on aging.

In 1992 Glenn faced his strongest general election contest from Michael DeWine, who, given the obscurity of some of Glenn's legislative work, asked "What on earth has John Glenn done?" DeWine also brought up the Keating Five case. Glenn was one of five senators present at a meeting with federal regulators on the S&L case of Charles Keating, a former Ohioan, and he set up a meeting between Keating and then-Speaker Jim Wright. But Glenn had no further contact with Keating, and the Senate decided that he did nothing deserving discipline. Until September, DeWine's attacks held Glenn under 50% in polls. But then it turned out that DeWine had 31 overdrafts on the House bank and once fell asleep during the Iran-contra hearings, and Glenn won 51%–42%. For the first time, he needed his margin (58%–35%) in north-and-east Ohio, because he lost the rest of the state, which he once carried 65%–32%, by 47%–45%.

Glenn, who would turn 77 in 1998, announced in February 1997 he would not run again. Governor George Voinovich, with very high poll ratings, announced in December 1996 that he would run for the seat, and early polls show him to be a formidable candidate. On the Democratic side, former Cuyahoga County Commissioner Mary Boyle, who narrowly lost the Senate primary in 1994, has announced she will run. Both candidates would qualify under the rule long held in Ohio politics, that, before you can win an election for senator or governor, you must run once and lose: it applies to every governor or senator but one elected in the last 40 years.

Junior Senator. Michael DeWine is short, gap-toothed, bespectacled, and youthful looking; he is also past 50, the father of eight, and the holder of public office for nearly 20 years. DeWine grew up in Yellow Springs, Ohio, the home of liberal Antioch College, where his family owned a successful seed business; after finishing school, he and his wife moved to nearby Cedarville, in a part of the state with rolling hills, winding creeks and covered bridges, where they now host an annual ice cream social. There DeWine was elected Greene County Prosecutor at 29, where he resisted plea bargaining, and, in order to nail a drug dealer, once put up the collateral to get $50,000 cash to stage a buy. At 33 he was elected to the Ohio Senate; two years later, he won a six-candidate Republican primary with 69% of the vote and was elected to a U.S. House seat. He worked for tougher drunk driving penalties, mandatory sentencing, and aid to child crime victims, with more success in Republican Columbus than on Democratic Capitol Hill. Elected lieutenant governor in 1990, he sought better and more responsive teenage offender facilities and an Ohio DNA analysis lab.

In 1994 DeWine decided to run for the Senate, and had serious competition in both the primary and general. The contest was to succeed liberal Democrat Howard Metzenbaum, who hoped to be succeeded by his son-in-law, Joel Hyatt, founder of the storefront Hyatt Legal Services chain. But in the May primary, Hyatt defeated Cuyahoga County Commissioner Mary Boyle by only a 47%–43% margin, while DeWine by a 53%–32%–10% margin dispatched Dr. Bernadine Healy, former director of the National Institutes of Health, and state Senator Gene Watts. From then on, DeWine had solid leads in most polls. He spent much time in the Cleveland area, cutting into the Democrats' base; in a year of anti-politician rhetoric, he cited his experience and said, mimicking a Hyatt Legal Services TV ad, with Hyatt "all you have is his 'word on it.' " Hyatt was also hurt by his closeness to the Clintons, whom he knew at Yale Law School and whose healthcare plan he supported. Also, two incidents from his past hurt Hyatt with core Democratic constituencies. A Hyatt Legal Services office in Philadelphia in 1987 fired a lawyer with AIDS, and was one of the cases that inspired the movie *Philadelphia*, which premiered the spring of the primary. And while a student at Dartmouth, Hyatt had opposed admitting women to the college. DeWine's anti-crime planks, his backing of term limits and the line-item veto helped him. Also, DeWine's support of NAFTA did not hurt; in an exit poll voters thought it was good for Ohio by a 26%–23% margin, and in fact Ohio exports to Mexico and Latin America have boomed since NAFTA was ratified. Nor did it hurt that former Operation Rescue leader Joseph Slovenec ran as an Independent; Slovenec's highest percentages were in counties across from West Virginia, where he took Democratic votes. The 23% of voters in union households split evenly, while the 29% who were gun owners voted 58%–31% for the almost always plaid-shirt-clad DeWine. DeWine won statewide 53%–39%, by 47%–45% in north-and-east Ohio and 58%–35% in the rest of the state.

The common motif that runs through DeWine's career is a concern for children and the championing of legislation often prompted by tragedy striking a particular child, including his own: his daughter Becky died in an auto accident in 1993, at 22, and he and his wife decided to donate her organs. DeWine now spends much effort on donor programs and awareness. He has worked to change the family preservation emphasis in social work, trying to establish the best interest of the child as paramount, so that children can be taken away from abusive and violent parents. As a prosecutor, he said, "I've been to the autopsies. I've seen the dead children." Before Bill Clinton, he came out for banning hospitals from ejecting mothers in the 48 hours after delivery. Prompted by the death of a 13-year-old Greene County girl, he has crusaded for school bus safety and put incentives for the states to promote it in a 1996 appropriations bill. He moved to require the National Institutes of Health to spend more of its budget on problems of children, up from the current maximum of 14%. He wants to fix the "radical disparity" in funding between rich and poor school districts.

DeWine played an important role on the 1996 immigration bill. He opposed limiting family unification visas for siblings and adult children; he opposed federal standards for birth certificates and drivers' licenses; he was against raising the income requirement for sponsors of relatives from 125% to 200% of the poverty level; he opposed allowing INS agents to search open fields for illegals without a search warrant. Most important, he also prevailed in splitting the bill's legal and illegal immigration provisions apart, a move that defeated most attempts to lower levels of legal immigration. On all of these issues, this freshman opposed subcommittee Chairman Alan Simpson, who was seeking one last achievement before retiring, and on all the DeWine positions prevailed.

Now he is chairman of the Employment and Training Subcommittee. He wants to consolidate job training programs and cut back on the many that are ineffective. But he does not favor zeroing out Trade Adjustment Act aid to workers hurt by trade policies. Here, as on his overall voting record, his approach is conservative, but leavened very much by a concern for the helpless and a practical sensitivity to the problems of people in everyday life.

Presidential politics. With 21 electoral votes and a tradition of close partisan competition, Ohio is a crucial state in presidential politics. It matched the national average in 1984 and 1988 and came close to doing so in 1996. It cast the narrowest margins for Bill Clinton of any megastate in both 1992 and 1996. No Republican has ever been elected president without carrying Ohio; no Democrat, in the electoral vote arithmetic of the 1990s, can be sure of winning without it. Richard Nixon advised Reagan and Bush managers Ed Rollins and Lee Atwater to put extra money and special ads into Ohio, to make it a roadblock for Walter Mondale and Michael Dukakis. In 1992, that strategy was reversed, since the West Coast was lost to Bush and the South in jeopardy; then James Carville made Ohio a roadblock.

In 1996 Ohio switched its presidential primary from May to March 19, and voted on the same day as Illinois, Michigan, and Wisconsin. But even then, just four weeks after New Hampshire, the race was already over. George Voinovich was the first governor to endorse Bob Dole, and eventually the whole Republican leadership followed; Dole beat Pat Buchanan here 66%–22%.

Congressional districting. Ohio lost two districts in the 1990 Census and is likely to lose another one in 2000; this state that elected 24 congressmen in 1970 elected 19 in 1992. The contorted district lines, with at least three grotesque barbell-shaped districts, are the product of a late bipartisan compromise in 1992. But already six contests have been won by the party that redistricters thought would lose: so much for the plans of mice and men. A challenge to current lines brought by former Congressman Clarence Miller and the Libertarian Party filed suit in November 1994 was rejected.

The People: Est. Pop. 1996: 11,173,000; Pop. 1990: 10,847,115, up 3.0% 1990–1996. 4.2% of U.S. total, 7th largest; 26% rural. Median age: 35.3 years. 13% 65 years and over. 87.1% White, 10.6% Black, 1% Asian, 1.3% Hispanic origin. Households: 56.1% married couple families; 27% married couple fams. w. children; 39% college educ.; median household income: $28,706; per capita income: $13,461; 67.5% owner occupied housing; median house value: $63,500; median monthly rent: $296. 4.9% Unemployment. 1996 Voting age pop.: 8,347,000. 1996 Turnout: 4,534,434; 54% of VAP. Registered voters (1996): 6,644,803; 914,795 D (14%), 1,030,248 R (16%), 4,699,760 unaffiliated and minor parties (71%).

Political Lineup: Governor, George V. Voinovich (R); Lt. Gov., Nancy Hollister (R); Secy. of State, Robert A. Taft II (R); Atty. Gen., Betty D. Montgomery (R); Treasurer, J. Kenneth Blackwell (R); Auditor, James Petro (R). State Senate, 33 (12 D and 21 R); Senate President, Richard Finan (R); State House, 99 (39 D and 60 R); House Speaker, Jo Ann Davidson (R). Senators, John H. Glenn, Jr. (D) and Mike DeWine (R). Representatives, 19 (8 D and 11 R).

Elections Division: 614-466-2585; **Filing Deadline for U.S. Congress:** February 19, 1998.

1996 Presidential Vote

Clinton (D)	2,148,309	(47%)
Dole (R)	1,860,768	(41%)
Perot (I)	483,277	(11%)

1996 Republican Presidential Primary

Dole (R)	631,192	(66%)
Buchanan (R)	204,875	(22%)
Forbes (R)	57,358	(6%)
Other	55,823	(6%)

1992 Presidential Vote

Clinton (D)	1,984,942	(40%)
Bush (R)	1,894,310	(38%)
Perot (I)	1,036,426	(21%)

GOVERNOR

Gov. George V. Voinovich (R)

Elected 1990, term expires Jan. 1999; b. July 15, 1936, Cleveland; home, Columbus; Ohio U., B.A. 1958, Ohio State U., J.D. 1961; Catholic; married (Janet).

Career: OH Asst. Atty. Gen., 1963–64; OH House of Reps., 1967–71; Cuyahoga Cnty. Auditor, 1971–76; Cuyahoga Cnty. Commissioner, 1977–78; OH Lt. Gov., 1979; Cleveland Mayor, 1979–89.

Office: Office of the Governor, 77 S. High St., 30th Fl., Columbus 43266, 614-466-3555; Fax: 614-644-0951; Web site: www.ohio.gov.

Election Results

1994 gen.	George V. Voinovich (R)	2,401,572	(72%)
	Robert L. Burch, Jr. (D)	835,849	(25%)
	Others	108,817	(3%)
1994 prim.	George V. Voinovich (R)	unopposed	
1990 gen.	George V. Voinovich (R)	1,938,103	(56%)
	Anthony J. Celebrezze, Jr. (D). .	1,539,416	(44%)

SENATORS

Sen. John H. Glenn, Jr. (D)

Elected 1974, seat up 1998; b. July 18, 1921, Cambridge; home, Columbus; Muskingum Col., B.S. 1943; Presbyterian; married (Annie).

Career: Marine Corps, 1943–65 (WWII & Korea); NASA astronaut, 1959–65, first American to orbit the Earth, 1962; V.P., Royal Crown Cola Co., 1966–68, Pres., Royal Crown Intl., 1967–69.

DC Office: 503 HSOB 20510, 202-224-3353; Fax: 202-224-7983; e-mail: senator_glenn@glenn.senate.gov.

State Offices: Columbus, 614-469-6697; Cleveland, 216-522-7095; Cincinnati, 513-684-3265; Toledo, 419-259-7592.

Committees: *Armed Services* (4th of 8 D): Airland Forces (RMM); Readiness; Strategic Forces. *Governmental Affairs* (RMM of 7 D): Permanent Subcommittee on Investigations (RMM). *Intelligence (Select)* (2nd of 9 D). *Aging (Special)* (2nd of 8 D).

Group Ratings

	ADA	ACLU	AFS	LCV	CFA	CON	NFIB	COC	ACU	NTLC	CHC
1996	95	50	100	100	86	4	41	23	10	18	0
1995	80	—	100	100	81	8	—	37	5	—	—

National Journal Ratings

	1995 LIB — 1995 CONS			1996 LIB — 1996 CONS		
Economic	86%	—	11%	89%	—	5%
Social	76%	—	18%	80%	—	8%
Foreign	65%	—	31%	73%	—	24%

Key Votes of the 104th Congress

1. Reduce Medicare Growth $	N	5. Flag Amendment	N	9. Anti-Missile Defense	N
2. Lmt. Prod. Liab. Damages	Y	6. Endangered Species	Y	10. Cuban Embargo	Y
3. Increase Min. Wage	Y	7. Gay Employment Rights	Y	11. Bar Bosnia Troop $	N
4. Welfare Reform	N	8. Ovrd. Part. Birth Veto	N	12. Cut Vietnam Aid	N

Election Results

1992 general	John H. Glenn, Jr. (D)	2,444,419	(51%)	($4,974,109)
	Mike DeWine (R)	2,028,300	(42%)	($3,053,156)
	Martha Kathryn Grevatt (I)	321,670	(7%)	
1992 primary	John H. Glenn, Jr. (D)	unopposed		
1986 general	John H. Glenn, Jr. (D)	1,949,208	(62%)	($1,319,026)
	Thomas N. Kindness (R)	1,171,893	(38%)	($657,908)

Sen. Mike DeWine (R)

Elected 1994, seat up 2000; b. Jan. 5. 1947, Springfield; home, Cedarville; Miami U. of OH, B.S. 1969, OH Northern U., J.D. 1972; Catholic; married (Frances).

Career: Practicing atty; Greene Cnty. Asst. Prosecuting atty., 1973–75, Prosecuting atty., 1977–81; OH Senate, 1981–82; U.S. House of Reps., 1982–90; OH Lt. Gov., 1990–94.

DC Office: 140 RSOB 20510, 202-224-2315; Fax: 202-224-6519; e-mail: senator_dewine@dewine.senate.gov.

State Offices: Columbus, 614-469-6774; Cincinnati, 513-763-8260; Toledo, 419-259-7535; Cleveland, 216-522-7272; Marietta, 614-373-2317.

Committees: *Judiciary* (7th of 10 R): Antitrust, Business Rights & Competition (Chmn.); Youth Violence. *Labor & Human Resources* (5th of 10 R): Employment & Training (Chmn.); Public Health & Safety. *Intelligence (Select)* (4th of 10 R).

Group Ratings

	ADA	ACLU	AFS	LCV	CFA	CON	NFIB	COC	ACU	NTLC	CHC
1996	15	17	14	31	29	85	93	85	85	93	92
1995	0	—	9	7	31	54	—	89	70	—	—

National Journal Ratings

	1995 LIB — 1995 CONS			1996 LIB — 1996 CONS		
Economic	31%	—	66%	40%	—	58%
Social	33%	—	62%	40%	—	59%
Foreign	38%	—	57%	26%	—	70%

Key Votes of the 104th Congress

1. Reduce Medicare Growth $	Y	5. Flag Amendment	Y	9. Anti-Missile Defense	Y
2. Lmt. Prod. Liab. Damages	Y	6. Endangered Species	Y	10. Cuban Embargo	Y
3. Increase Min. Wage	Y	7. Gay Employment Rights	N	11. Bar Bosnia Troop $	N
4. Welfare Reform	Y	8. Ovrd. Part. Birth Veto	Y	12. Cut Vietnam Aid	N

Election Results

1994 general	Mike DeWine (R)	1,836,556	(53%)	($6,084,663)
	Joel Hyatt (D)	1,348,213	(39%)	($4,921,223)
	Joseph J. Slovenec (I)	252,031	(7%)	($192,867)
1994 primary	Mike DeWine (R)	422,366	(52%)	
	Bernadine Healy (R)	263,559	(32%)	
	Eugene J. Watts (R)	83,103	(10%)	
	George H. Rhodes (R)	42,633	(5%)	
1988 general	Howard M. Metzenbaum (D)	2,480,038	(57%)	($8,547,545)
	George V. Voinovich (R)	1,872,716	(43%)	($8,233,859)

FIRST DISTRICT

From its seven hills, Cincinnati, Ohio's first major metropolis, dubbed the Queen City of the West in the 19th Century, looks down on the curves of the Ohio River. This was the nation's fourth largest city at the outbreak of the Civil War, a heavily German beehive of riverboats and sausage factories, known as Porkopolis. Cincinnati has long given off an air of the recent past; Mark Twain said he'd like to be there for the apocalypse because everything in Cincinnati is 20 years behind. Today the city seems to be stepping, stylishly and gracefully, into the mid-1970s. Growing slowly over many decades, Cincinnati has long-settled good looks and an urbanity somehow consistent with its natural terrain: the bottomlands along the river, the hills and rolling terrain above. In the middle of Cincinnati is Mill Creek, lined with factories; on the hills to the west, above the restored Union Terminal with the children's, historic, and natural history museums, are the modest streetcar suburbs of the last century and the early years of this one. On Mount Adams and toward the northeast are set a string of affluent neighborhoods, with stately mansions like the William Howard Taft house, and the comfortable Tudors and colonials of the 20th Century bourgeoisie—Reform Jewish as well as WASP and German.

Cincinnati was the site of great innovations: the first iron suspension bridge, in 1867, connected Cincinnati to northern Kentucky and was designed by John Roebling who later built the Brooklyn Bridge; the first baseball team, the Red Stockings, in 1869; the country's leading Reform Jewish seminary, Hebrew Union College, in 1875. And if over the past century Cincinnati has not had the growth spurts of cities like Cleveland or Houston, neither has it had their sharp contractions. It has spawned not flashy but solid industries, like the Procter & Gamble soap business, now headquartered in a striking two-towered office complex at the edge of downtown, and it has America's biggest concentration of machine tool makers. Downtown Cincinnati's spruced-up Fountain Square shows off the well-maintained skyscrapers of the past, its first class restaurants still attract a dressy clientele. Old ethnic neighborhoods, crowded with brick row houses on steep hills, keep their thick local accents and special local foods, from German sauerbrauten to Cincinnati chili (try it "four way," served with spaghetti, onions and grated cheese).

The 1st Congressional District of Ohio includes almost all of Cincinnati, except for its affluent eastern edge, plus the middle-class suburbs that cling to the woody hills north and west, all the way to North Bend, the home of President William Henry Harrison, and the Indiana border. Ancestrally Republican, Cincinnati was a German anti-slavery island in a southern-stock pro-Confederate sea. City elections here have long been competitive between the old line Republicans and a combination of Democrats and Charterites (the latter started by Charles Taft, liberal brother of Senator Robert Taft, Sr.). Council members here become celebrities in the entire media market. One or both Cincinnati area congressional districts have been seriously contested in almost every election since 1964, and for 44 years were represented by nothing but former Cincinnati council members with the understandable exception of Robert Taft, Jr. (One former council member and mayor, Jerry Springer, has even become a national talk show host.)

The congressman from the 1st District is Steve Chabot, a Republican who first won in 1994. Like other congressmen here, he grew up in Cincinnati and served on the Council. After college he taught elementary school for a year, then went to law school and practiced law; he was elected to the Council in 1985, at 32, and to the Hamilton County Commission in 1990. In 1988 he ran for Congress and lost 56%–44% to longtime Democratic incumbent (1973–74, 1976–90) Tom Luken. Chabot stepped forward to run in 1994 amid an odd set of circumstances. In 1992, one-term incumbent Charles Luken (son of Tom) retired suddenly after the June primary. The special primary to replace him was fought by liberal state Senator William Bowen and moderate Council member David Mann, who won 33%–32%, by 416 votes. In the general Mann beat 51%–43% a Republican who ran as an Independent because no Republican had gotten on the ballot. In the House Mann voted against the Clinton tax package and for NAFTA, and infuriated local unions; Bowen ran again in 1994 and this time Mann won 49%–48%, by 667 votes. In the fall, Chabot backed the balanced budget amendment, strongly opposed abortion, and attacked Mann's support of Bill Clinton. Chabot was ahead in a September poll and won comfortably, 56%–44%.

In the House Chabot started off with a very conservative voting record, but moderated it somewhat in 1996. He showed himself willing to take political risks for principle. He voted against the Appalachian Regional Commission, which gives money to southern Ohio, and he opposed a $2 million study of light-rail in the Cincinnati area. Chabot believes that Cincinnati should look for ways to solve problems with local resources and not depend on Washington. He voted against funding for much basic research and the National Endowment for the Humanities. He opposed farm subsidies, and sponsored a losing amendment to abolish cotton marketing loans. He was also strongly against building another 20 B-2 bombers; his side lost 213–210 in September 1995. He voted against the Republican budget in June 1996, saying it was too liberal, despite leadership pleas. But he worked with Democrat Zoe Lofgren of California to allow counties as well as cities to apply for federal anti-crime aid.

On the Immigration Subcommittee and on the floor Chabot played a major role on the immigration bill, opposing major provisions backed by chairman Lamar Smith. He opposed Smith's procedure for employers to verify all employees' immigration status. "The goal of the scheme's backers is to prohibit any employee from holding his or her job unless the federal government has signed off on the arrangement," which he called "1-800-Big-Brother." The provision was beaten 159–260. Chabot was one of several Republican freshmen—with Dick Chrysler and Sam Brownback in the House and Spencer Abraham and Mike DeWine in the Senate—who worked hard and successfully to separate the legal and illegal immigration sections of the bill. They prevailed, and frustrated Smith's and Senate subcommittee chairman Alan Simpson's attempts to lower levels of legal immigration. Chabot also surprised some by attacking parts of the antiterrorism bill as violations of civil liberties.

In 1996 Chabot's Democratic opponent was Mark Longabaugh, a top aide in House Minority Leader Dick Gephardt's 1988 presidential campaign, a Clinton Administration staffer, and an unsuccessful Cincinnati Council candidate in 1995. But the real impetus against Chabot came from the AFL-CIO, which spent over $1 million, running nearly 2,000 television ads against him between January and November 1996. They attacked him for Medicare "cuts" and for supporting Speaker Newt Gingrich. Longabaugh also attacked him for backing tobacco and alcohol interests. A light moment came in October when Longabaugh ran an ad showing Chabot's yellow pages listing and noting that he took clients in DUI cases; Chabot responded with an ad showing the white pages and asking, "Where's Mark Longabaugh been listed for 15 years? Not here!" For all the sound and fury, the result was very much the same as in 1994: Chabot won 54%–43%. He seems likely to continue as one of the more original and outspoken of the Republican class of 1994.

The People: Pop. 1990: 571,052; 1% rural; 13% age 65+; 68% White; 30% Black; 1% Asian; 1% Hispanic origin. Households: 44% married couple families; 20% married couple fams. w. children; 43% college educ.; median household income: $25,405; per capita income: $12,616; median gross rent: $336; median house value: $64,300.

1996 Presidential Vote

Clinton (D)	110,166	(50%)
Dole (R)	96,103	(43%)
Perot (I)	12,842	(6%)

1992 Presidential Vote

Clinton (D)	104,494	(43%)
Bush (R)	104,339	(43%)
Perot (I)	34,531	(14%)

Rep. Steve Chabot (R)

Elected 1994; b. Jan. 22, 1953, Cincinnati; home, Cincinnati; Col. of William & Mary, B.A. 1975, N. KY U. Chase Col. of Law, J.D. 1978; Catholic; married (Donna).

Career: Elem. Schl. Teacher, 1975–76; Practicing atty., 1978–94; Cincinnati City Cncl., 1985–90; Hamilton Cnty. Comm., 1990–94.

DC Office: 129 CHOB 20515, 202-225-2216; Fax: 202-225-3012.

District Offices: Cincinnati, 513-684-2723.

Committees: *International Relations* (16th of 26 R): Africa; International Economic Policy & Trade. *Judiciary* (15th of 20 R): Commercial & Administrative Law; Crime. *Small Business* (10th of 19 R): Empowerment.

Group Ratings

	ADA	ACLU	AFS	LCV	CFA	CON	NFIB	COC	ACU	NTLC	CHC
1996	15	13	9	23	46	72	97	88	100	98	100
1995	0	—	—	0	8	87	—	96	100	—	—

National Journal Ratings

	1995 LIB — 1995 CONS	1996 LIB — 1996 CONS
Economic	0% — 74%	24% — 73%
Social	0% — 79%	14% — 77%
Foreign	28% — 65%	53% — 46%

Key Votes of the 104th Congress

1. Reduce Medicare Growth $	Y	5. Flag Amendment	Y	9. Cuban Embargo	Y
2. Ovrd. Product Liab. Veto	Y	6. Drop EPA Limits	N	10. Bar Bosnia Troop $	Y
3. Increase Min. Wage	N	7. Repeal Assault-Weap. Ban	Y	11. Cut Anti-Missile Defense	N
4. Welfare Reform	Y	8. Ovrd. Part. Birth Veto	Y	12. Bar U.N. Uniforms	Y

Election Results

1996 general	Steve Chabot (R)	118,324	(54%)	($983,163)
	Mark P. Longabaugh (D)	94,719	(43%)	($544,875)
	Others	5,381	(2%)	
1996 primary	Steve Chabot (R)	unopposed		
1994 general	Steve Chabot (R)	92,997	(56%)	($542,829)
	David Mann (D)	72,822	(44%)	($1,001,393)

SECOND DISTRICT

The most Republican major metro area in the nation over the longest time span has been Cincinnati. Back in the 1850s, when Harriet Beecher Stowe wrote *Uncle Tom's Cabin* here, Cincinnati was an island of German, pro-Union, Republican sentiment in a southern, Democratic, pro-slavery sea. Later Cincinnati attracted fewer southern and eastern European immigrants than Great Lakes industrial cities like Cleveland, Detroit and Chicago; its ethnic character (like its physical appearance) and its political preference have remained pretty well fixed. Even many of the Appalachians here are Republicans, from Civil War Republican counties in the hills. Democratic constituencies here never got very large: economically, it was never a strong CIO town; culturally, it is home to a strong anti-pornography movement that, among other things, canceled a Robert Mapplethorpe exhibit here. Cincinnati's Republican record remains intact in the 1990s: it was the only million-plus metro area which George Bush and Bob Dole carried with more than 50% in 1992 and 1996; in 1994 it voted 77%–20% for Republican Governor George Voinovich.

For 140 years after 1852, Cincinnati and surrounding Hamilton County were divided by a north-south line into two congressional districts. After the 1990 Census, redistricters created one mostly urban district which leaned a bit to the Democrats and a mostly suburban district that spread out into the countryside and was heavily Republican. This 2d Congressional District of Ohio includes the affluent eastern suburbs around elite Indian Hill and newer Montgomery, plus a few affluent precincts of Cincinnati itself; it includes recent growth areas like northeastern Hamilton County and Anderson Township south of the Little Miami River, plus the far west part of Hamilton County, all heavily Republican; it heads east along the Ohio River to include Clermont County, a fast-growth area for 20 years, plus two rural counties and an oddly-shaped sliver of Warren County between Cincinnati and Dayton.

The congressman from the 2d district is Rob Portman, a Republican first elected in May 1993, who by early 1995 was one of the most important legislators in the House. Portman has good connections both in Cincinnati and Washington. He grew up in Cincinnati, campaigned for his predecessor Bill Gradison before turning 21, went to work after law school for Patton Boggs & Blow in Washington and then for a Cincinnati law firm. In 1989 he went to work in the Bush White House, first in the counsel's office and then in legislative affairs; in 1992 he was U.S. representative to the United Nations Human Rights Council. He was back in Cincinnati in January 1993 when Gradison unexpectedly resigned from Congress to become head of the Health Insurance Association of America, which ran the famous "Harry and Louise" ads questioning the Clinton healthcare plan. Portman ran for the seat with Gradison's endorsement and impressive financial backing from the Cincinnati establishment, starting with mega-financier Carl Lindner. In the special primary he faced former Congressman Bob McEwen, who had represented the 6th District to the east for 12 years and then lost it after a contentious primary in 1992, and businessman Jay Buhert, a president of the National Association of Home Builders, who ran a vitriolic campaign against both Portman and McEwen. Portman won with 36% of the vote, to 30% for McEwen, who carried counties he had once represented, and 25% for Buchert. Portman won the special general with 70%.

In the House Portman compiled a conservative record well before the Contract with America and made himself an expert on unfunded mandates. He called the 1994 results a pronouncement for "a more accountable Congress and a leaner, more responsive federal government." In the first months of 1995 he helped floor-manage the unfunded mandates bill—a large responsibility for one who hadn't even been a member two years. His bill, signed by Bill Clinton, provides that unfunded mandates over $50 million would be subject to a point of order in the House or Senate, which could be overridden only by majority vote; it does not go as far as some would like, but much farther than a Democratic House would likely have gone. Portman also got a seat on Ways and Means, where he managed to passage two bills, one to help expand pension plans and the other to simplify rules governing Subchapter S corporations, a form used by many small businessmen. He is co-chairman of the National Commission on Restructuring the Internal Revenue Service, and says it will try to make the 100,000-plus employees agency more user friendly.

At home Portman sponsored a community-based anti-drug use effort, urging schools, businesses, churches, and local media to discourage drug abuse; he boasts that it takes no federal money. The 1996 election was not seriously contested; Portman won 72% of the vote, after which his Democratic opponent called him "a gentleman, a fine man. I think the district got a good man." Portman says the 105th Congress's main focuses should be on balancing the budget, preserving Medicare, simplifying the tax code, restructuring the IRS, and establishing a bipartisan commission on campaign finance reform.

The People: Pop. 1990: 570,779; 29% rural; 11% age 65+; 96% White; 2% Black; 1% Asian; 1% Hispanic origin. Households: 63% married couple families; 31% married couple fams. w. children; 46% college educ.; median household income: $34,688; per capita income: $16,813; median gross rent: $409; median house value: $79,000.

1996 Presidential Vote

Dole (R)	153,627	(58%)
Clinton (D)	90,571	(34%)
Perot (I)	19,894	(7%)

1992 Presidential Vote

Bush (R)	143,964	(52%)
Clinton (D)	78,117	(28%)
Perot (I)	51,356	(19%)

Rep. Rob Portman (R)

Elected May, 1993; b. Dec. 19, 1955, Cincinatti; home, Terrace Park; Dartmouth Col., B.A. 1979, U. of MI, J.D. 1984; Methodist; married (Jane).

Career: Practicing atty., 1984–88; Assoc. Cnsl., White House, 1989; Dep. Asst. and White House Legis. Affairs Dir., 1990–91; Alternate U.S. Rep. to UN Human Rights Comm., 1992.

DC Office: 238 CHOB 20515, 202-225-3164; Fax: 202-225-1992; e-mail: portmail@hr.house.gov.

District Offices: Batavia, 513-732-2948; Cincinatti, 513-791-0381.

Committees: *Government Reform & Oversight* (24th of 24 R): Government Management, Information & Technology. *Ways & Means* (16th of 23 R): Oversight; Social Security.

Group Ratings

	ADA	ACLU	AFS	LCV	CFA	CON	NFIB	COC	ACU	NTLC	CHC
1996	10	6	0	23	38	78	100	94	100	93	93
1995	0	—	—	6	23	87	—	100	80	—	—

National Journal Ratings

	1995 LIB		1995 CONS	1996 LIB		1996 CONS
Economic	0%	—	74%	20%	—	76%
Social	37%	—	63%	29%	—	68%
Foreign	45%	—	55%	30%	—	65%

Key Votes of the 104th Congress

1. Reduce Medicare Growth $	Y	5. Flag Amendment	Y	9. Cuban Embargo	Y
2. Ovrd. Product Liab. Veto	Y	6. Drop EPA Limits	N	10. Bar Bosnia Troop $	N
3. Increase Min. Wage	N	7. Repeal Assault-Weap. Ban	Y	11. Cut Anti-Missile Defense	N
4. Welfare Reform	Y	8. Ovrd. Part. Birth Veto	Y	12. Bar U.N. Uniforms	Y

Election Results

1996 general	Rob Portman (R)	186,853	(72%)	($256,544)
	Thomas R. Chandler (D)	58,715	(23%)	
	Kathleen M. McKnight (NL)	13,905	(5%)	
1996 primary	Rob Portman (R)	unopposed		
1994 general	Rob Portman (R)	150,128	(77%)	($250,860)
	Les Mann (D)	43,730	(23%)	($2,503)

THIRD DISTRICT

Dayton, once a medium-sized American city known as the home of the typical voter, is now the name of the international peace agreement reached in November 1995 that at least temporarily stopped the slaughter in the former Yugoslavia. Actually, the 21 days of negotiating took place at Wright-Patterson Air Force Base, outside the Dayton city limits; but the people of Dayton played a role. "From the time we landed at the airport," said U.S. negotiator Richard Holbrooke, "until the time we left, we felt that we were in a community that was literally praying for us. People were lighting candles in their windows, there were signs all over the airport and on the byways. That would never have happened in New York or in Washington. And it made a tremendous impression on people."

Dayton has made a difference in people's lives in America and around the world for many years. Here, just south of the old National Road that spans the Midwest, was the home of James Ritty, who in 1879 invented the cash register—that indispensable instrument of mass retail trade—and of John Henry Patterson, who bought it from Ritty for $6,500 in 1884 and established the National Cash Register company (NCR). It was home for a while of a former Patterson subordinate, Tom Watson Sr., who feuded with him and went off and founded IBM. It was in Dayton in the 1890s that Wilbur and Orville Wright, tinkering in their bicycle shop and observing the horseless carriages driven through Dayton's streets, experimented with kites and gliders and constructed the first wind tunnel in the world and the first heavier-than-air flying machine which they took to ever-windy Kitty Hawk, North Carolina, to fly in 1903. A few years later, Dayton's Charles Kettering would invent the automatic starter for cars. In the 1970s and 1980s, Dayton's economy seemed to be sputtering. General Motors, the area's largest employer, was in trouble; NCR was overtaken by others, and merged. But in the 1990s Dayton's unemployment rate is below the national average and its economic growth is faster. A General Motors strike in March 1996 was brief and evoked little passion; there are more scientists, engineers, and computer specialists and technicians here now than GM workers. Quietly and without much notice, the area's small manufacturers and suppliers have shown that Dayton's spirit of tinkering and innovation, practical organization and mechanical dreaming, are still thriving, as much as its neighborliness and compassion.

Politically, the Dayton area has been known as a bellwether since Richard Scammon and Ben Wattenberg's *The Real Majority* of 1970 profiled the Dayton housewife. In the 1980s and 1990s it has mostly voted for statewide and national winners. This is true as well of Ohio's 3d Congressional District, which includes Dayton and all but a small corner of surrounding Montgomery County.

The congressman from Dayton is Tony Hall, a Democrat first elected in 1978. Hall grew up in Dayton, where his father was once mayor; in 1966 and 1967 he served in the Peace Corps in Thailand, while the Vietnam war was raging not far away. He returned home and in 1968, at 26, was elected to the state legislature. When the 3d District came open in 1978, he was the obvious candidate, and easily won in a generally Republican year. In the early 1980s Hall became a born-again Christian. He opposes abortion, but his number one cause has been to alleviate world hunger. When Texas Congressman Mickey Leland died in a plane crash in Ethiopia, Hall succeeded him as chairman of the Select Committee on Hunger, and decried the civil wars and infrastructural deficiencies that obstructed food delivery throughout so much of Africa (he talks less about how African socialism has reduced food supplies). He has traveled to Somalia and Haiti, Uganda and Rwanda, North Korea and the former Yugoslavia, and obviously has been deeply moved by those suffering from hunger. He called for UN intervention in Somalia in February 1992, but was warier about Yugoslavia: he called for a 100-day cease-fire, to be used to immunize children, in August 1995 and said he would support the U.S. peacekeeping force after the Dayton agreements in November 1995. At home he has launched "gleaning" programs to use leftover hotel and restaurant food to feed the poor; he also applied these programs elsewhere—most notably at the Atlanta Olympics and both parties' 1996 convention cities. He set up the first 800 telephone number for food emergency assistance in 1995.

Institutionally, Hall has suffered setbacks, but he has been effective in getting results. In April 1993 the House voted not to reauthorize the Select Committee on Hunger, and Hall embarked on a 22-day fast. Then in early 1995 the Republican House voted to eliminate all funded caucuses, including his Hunger Caucus. But Hall's dedication, hard work, and obvious sincerity have probably made more difference than a staff structure. His 15-year-old son died of leukemia in July 1996, after a bone marrow transplant. But Hall worked on, urging the Democratic National Convention to adopt a "tolerance language" recognizing and welcoming those Democrats like Hall who oppose abortion, and traveling to North Korea in August 1996 and calling for food aid there. He continues to press for humanitarian foreign aid to "the poorest of the poor" and for American commitment to Africa. He opposed the 1996 welfare bill and called for banning "indecent material" on cable TV.

Hall has also tended to home issues. He fights hard to maintain Wright-Pat as the center for Air Force research and development and saved the Dayton Aviation Heritage National Historic Park in 1996; he worked for a smooth transition and clean up of the Energy Department's Mound Nuclear Weapons Plant and to maintain the Dayton Area Health Plan. In the 105th Congress he wants to lay the groundwork for the Wright Brothers 2003 celebration.

For most of 20 years, Hall has been reelected easily. Under harsh attack from a Gulf war veteran, he won 60%–40% in 1992; he won 59%–41% in Republican 1994 and 64%–33% in 1996. Possible future Republican contenders include state Representatives Jeff Jacobson and Don Mottley.

The People: Pop. 1990: 570,913; 5% rural; 13% age 65+; 80% White; 18% Black; 1% Asian; 1% Hispanic origin. Households: 53% married couple families; 23% married couple fams. w. children; 47% college educ.; median household income: $30,083; per capita income: $14,500; median gross rent: $403; median house value: $64,200.

1996 Presidential Vote

Clinton (D)	115,168	(50%)
Dole (R)	95,003	(41%)
Perot (I)	18,194	(8%)

1992 Presidential Vote

Clinton (D)	107,659	(41%)
Bush (R)	104,215	(40%)
Perot (I)	47,465	(18%)

Rep. Tony P. Hall (D)

Elected 1978; b. Jan. 16, 1942, Dayton; home, Dayton; Denison U., A.B. 1964; Presbyterian; married (Janet).

Career: Peace Corps, Thailand, 1966–67; Real estate broker, 1968–78; OH House of Reps., 1968–72; OH Senate, 1972–78.

DC Office: 1432 LHOB 20515, 202-225-6465.

District Offices: Dayton, 937-225-2843.

Committees: *Rules* (3rd of 4 D): Rules & Organization of the House (RMM).

Group Ratings

	ADA	ACLU	AFS	LCV	CFA	CON	NFIB	COC	ACU	NTLC	CHC
1996	65	79	78	83	77	73	35	33	15	12	23
1995	75	—	—	63	77	37	—	29	22	—	—

National Journal Ratings

	1995 LIB — 1995 CONS			1996 LIB — 1996 CONS		
Economic	71%	—	28%	64%	—	35%
Social	57%	—	43%	62%	—	38%
Foreign	77%	—	23%	64%	—	35%

Key Votes of the 104th Congress

1. Reduce Medicare Growth $	N	5. Flag Amendment	N	9. Cuban Embargo	N
2. Ovrd. Product Liab. Veto	Y	6. Drop EPA Limits	Y	10. Bar Bosnia Troop $	N
3. Increase Min. Wage	Y	7. Repeal Assault-Weap. Ban	N	11. Cut Anti-Missile Defense	Y
4. Welfare Reform	N	8. Ovrd. Part. Birth Veto	Y	12. Bar U.N. Uniforms	N

Election Results

1996 general	Tony P. Hall (D)	144,583	(64%)	($247,426)
	David A. Westbrock (R)	75,732	(33%)	($403,972)
	Others	6,888	(3%)	
1996 primary	Tony P. Hall (D)	unopposed		
1994 general	Tony P. Hall (D)	105,342	(59%)	($292,838)
	David A. Westbrock (R)	72,314	(41%)	($218,384)

FOURTH DISTRICT

Central Ohio looks mostly like farmland to the traveler. Yet this is manufacturing country, indeed one of America's premier manufacturing areas, where most people make their livings in factories in small towns and on rural highways. These places seem far from anywhere important, yet are on one of the great east-west routes—the old rail lines and newer highways—that cross the country. They seem old-fashioned and rooted in an older technological time, yet here, in Wapakoneta, a typically Ohioan-Indian name, is the home town of Neil Armstrong, first man on the moon. Politically, this crossroads on the flat limestone plains of northern Ohio is one of the Republican heartlands of the United States. On the B&O tracks from Dayton to Toledo that intersect the east-west rail lines used by Richard Nixon in 1968, Ronald Reagan in 1984, George Bush in 1992 and Bill Clinton in 1996 to make whistle-stop campaign tours, one can summon up memories of past campaign styles and loyalties.

Much of central Ohio makes up the 4th Congressional District, oddly regular in shape for an Ohio district. It includes Wapakoneta; Lima, whose name was pulled from a hat; Findlay, where a museum holds the captain's bathtub from the *U.S.S. Maine*, sunk in Havana harbor in 1898; Marion, where young Socialist-to-be Norman Thomas delivered newspapers edited by President-to-be Warren Harding; and Mansfield, home of John Sherman, one of Ohio's great 19th Century Republican statesmen, and his brother General William Tecumseh Sherman, who marched through Georgia for the Union and refused to be considered for president. This has been a Republican stronghold since the Civil War, industrial since the late 19th Century, quietly prosperous over most of the years since World War II, though shaken by the collapse of the auto-steel-coal industries after the oil shock of 1979. Through all this, it has remained mostly Republican, giving solid margins to George Bush in 1992 and Bob Dole in 1996.

The congressman here is Mike Oxley, first elected in June 1981, now holder of one of the most important subcommittee chairmanships. Oxley is from Findlay, worked for the local Republican congressman there, served three years in the FBI after law school, then came home and was elected to the legislature in 1972, at 28. In 1981, after the incumbent died, he ran for the House and won the special by the surprisingly narrow margin of 378 votes.

Oxley serves on the Commerce Committee where for years he was a minority vote on a panel run by Chairman John Dingell and a market-oriented conservative and critic of government regulation. Now he is in a position to call the shots; but these are complex issues, which often lap across party lines, and he showed ingenuity and had successes in the minority as well as in the majority. Oxley was a major player on the 1990 Clean Air Act, working with Ohioans of both parties to protect that state's high-sulfur power plants and big factories from being saddled with high costs. He successfully pushed his "auction" proposal, a market approach to pollution reduction, which, by allowing firms to sell polluting rights, lets supple and adaptive firms rather than rule-bound federal bureaucrats figure out how to best deal with pollution. On the Telecommunications Subcommittee, over opposition from Democrats, he also required that new frequencies of the radio spectrum be allocated not by lottery but by auction; the resulting auctions for personal communications systems, cell phones, and pagers have been the largest in history and have supplied the government with billions in revenue.

Oxley took a major part in the 1996 telecom act, the first rewrite of communications law since 1933, and helped break through deadlock to compromise in early 1996. As he proposed in 1991, the act allows regional Bell companies into long distance and manufacturing, and lets long distance carriers into local phone service; it also bans indecency on the Internet, authorizes the V-chip, and allows customized cable service. Oxley has also worked to open foreign markets to U.S. telecom manufacturers and to let foreigners own U.S. telephone and broadcasting companies. On Superfund ("super-scam," he calls it), Oxley was less successful; he promised to return to the issue in 1997. He is a supporter of the Resource Conservation and Recovery Act (RCRA), regulating interstate transport of solid waste, and has worked to give states more power to ban the import of out-of-state garbage (much New York garbage is trucked to Ohio). Oxley also worked on FTC reauthorization, the Storage Tank Trust Fund, and battery recycling legislation, achieving a bipartisan bill which, with voluntary recycling efforts from consumers, keeps nickel and cadmium from going into waste sites. He sponsored a bill regulating the sport of boxing, elimination of the Tourism and Travel Administration, and a crime victim's restitution proposal which made it into the anti-terrorism bill.

In late 1996 Oxley fought with Louisiana's Billy Tauzin for the chairmanship of the Telecommunications and Finance Subcommittee. Speaker Newt Gingrich promised the spot to Tauzin when he switched parties in August 1995 and Tauzin, who was first elected in May 1980, has 13 months more seniority. The solution was to split the subcommittee, whose jurisdiction in any case was perhaps greater than that of any in Congress. Tauzin got first choice and took Telecommunications, Trade and Consumer Protection; Oxley got Finance and Hazardous Materials.

Oxley has been reelected every two years without difficulty.

The People: Pop. 1990: 570,917; 46% rural; 13% age 65+; 94% White; 5% Black; 1% Hispanic origin. Households: 63% married couple families; 30% married couple fams. w. children; 31% college educ.; median household income: $27,312; per capita income: $12,009; median gross rent: $337; median house value: $50,300.

1996 Presidential Vote

Dole (R)	118,298	(50%)
Clinton (D)	88,758	(37%)
Perot (I)	28,248	(12%)

1992 Presidential Vote

Bush (R)	118,142	(46%)
Clinton (D)	77,975	(30%)
Perot (I)	58,900	(23%)

Rep. Michael G. Oxley (R)

Elected June 1981; b. Feb. 11, 1944, Findlay; home, Findlay; Miami U. of OH, B.A. 1966, OH St. U., J.D. 1969; Lutheran; married (Patricia).

Career: FBI Spec. Agent, 1969–71; OH House of Reps., 1972–81; Practicing atty., 1972–1981.

DC Office: 2233 RHOB 20515, 202-225-2676; e-mail: oxley@hr.house.gov.

District Offices: Lima, 419-999-6455; Findlay, 419-423-3210; Mansfield, 419-522-5757.

Committees: *Commerce* (3rd of 28 R): Finance & Hazardous Materials (Chmn.); Telecommunications, Trade & Consumer Protection (Vice Chmn.).

Group Ratings

	ADA	ACLU	AFS	LCV	CFA	CON	NFIB	COC	ACU	NTLC	CHC
1996	5	7	0	15	8	17	95	100	100	98	86
1995	0	—	—	6	0	38	—	96	76	—	—

National Journal Ratings

	1995 LIB — 1995 CONS			1996 LIB — 1996 CONS		
Economic	0%	—	74%	24%	—	73%
Social	0%	—	79%	29%	—	68%
Foreign	0%	—	85%	0%	—	79%

Key Votes of the 104th Congress

1. Reduce Medicare Growth $	Y	5. Flag Amendment	Y	9. Cuban Embargo	Y
2. Ovrd. Product Liab. Veto	Y	6. Drop EPA Limits	N	10. Bar Bosnia Troop $	Y
3. Increase Min. Wage	N	7. Repeal Assault-Weap. Ban	Y	11. Cut Anti-Missile Defense	N
4. Welfare Reform	Y	8. Ovrd. Part. Birth Veto	Y	12. Bar U.N. Uniforms	Y

Election Results

1996 general	Michael G. Oxley (R)	147,608	(65%)	($639,496)
	Paul McClain (D)	69,096	(30%)	($27,230)
	Michael McCaffery (I)	11,057	(5%)	
1996 primary	Michael G. Oxley (R)	unopposed		
1994 general	Michael G. Oxley (R)	unopposed		($279,829)

FIFTH DISTRICT

Undergirded by limestone, as flat and fertile as any place in America, northwest Ohio sits astride the land routes from the parts of the country which were economically the most productive in the years they were settled. Here were the "Firelands," reserved for Connecticut Yankees whose farms were burned in the Revolution, and the neat and substantial small towns built by German Protestants in the mid-19th Century. Northwest Ohio is the beginning of the great corn and hog belt that stretches through Indiana and Illinois into Iowa, and was long one of the heartlands of the Republican Party. Fremont, settled by abstemious Yankees, was the home of President Rutherford B. Hayes, whose wife Lucy served only lemonade in the White House; nearby Sandusky, settled by Germans who built big wineries and breweries, now has its own Merry-Go-Round Museum; Port Clinton, on Lake Erie, bills itself as the "Walleye Capital of the World" and drops a walleye on New Year's Eve to rival Times Square. Not far away is Milan, birthplace of the great inventor and capitalist Thomas Edison.

This is prime industrial country: its limestone, rail connections and location near the Great Lakes have spurred the growth of a factory economy which in dollar terms is far more important than agriculture. Since the first settlement, northwest Ohio hasn't had spectacular population growth, but it grew steadily for many decades, surging ahead in the 1950s and 1960s as its small factories supplied the big auto plants in Detroit and Ohio cities. Growth lagged noticeably in the early 1980s, when the domestic auto industry collapsed, but has returned in the 1990s as small firms sell not only to the Big Three but to foreign customers.

Ohio's 5th Congressional District sweeps across northwest Ohio, from Grafton, just beyond the westward expansion of metropolitan Cleveland, across the limestone plains through Sandusky, its harbor on Lake Erie, home of the giant Cedar Point amusement park. It continues through Milan and Fremont, past part of the university town of Bowling Green and the Toledo suburb of Perrysburg, to the western Ohio towns of Defiance and Napoleon (wonderful names!). It avoids Toledo and its suburbs directly east and west. Historically, this was a solidly Republican district from the Civil War through the New Deal and up through the 1970s. Recently it has been more competitive: the eastern counties here voted for Bill Clinton in 1996, the western counties for Bob Dole.

The current congressman from the 5th is Paul Gillmor, a Republican first elected in 1988. He grew up in northern Ohio, practiced law, and was elected to the state Senate in 1966, at 27. He is a professional, though not especially provocative, politician. For years Gillmor eyed this seat and waited for incumbent Delbert Latta to retire; he even passed a state law blocking the party from designating Latta's son as nominee if Latta resigned. In the 1988 primary Gillmor beat the junior Latta by exactly 27 votes out of 63,000 cast. Now Gillmor may be creating a family dynasty of his own. In 1992 his wife Karen was elected to the state Senate from the 26th District, which overlaps the 5th Congressional District in Sandusky and Seneca Counties. All the more strikingly, she had a baby (Paul Michael, known as Little P.M.) just before the primary. In June 1996, Karen Gillmor, by then 48, gave birth to twin boys; coincidentally (is it something in the water?) Paul Gillmor's House office was next door to that of Arkansan Blanche Lambert Lincoln, who announced in January 1996 that she was retiring because she was pregnant with twins. Gillmor's Democratic opponent attacked him for taking a leave of absence for the occasion; *The Hill* called it "one of the most ill-conceived campaign attacks in 1996."

Gillmor focused on internal reform in his first years in the House, working to freeze committee funding, and on local issues, repealing the Coast Guard recreational boating user fees. On the Commerce Committee, he backed limits on out-of-state solid waste and greater competition for cable TV and telephone companies. He has called for amending the Public Utility Holding Company Act to allow utilities to offer telecom services and wants to require corporations to disclose charitable contributions. He favors cost-benefit analysis and risk assessment and has a solidly conservative record on economics. He is more moderate on cultural and foreign issues, and is a member of both the Tuesday Group and the Leadership's Whip Team.

On recent local issues, he is proud of saving the National Rifle Matches at Camp Perry by creating a private non-profit corporation to conduct them; they were at peril from liberals in the appropriations process. He also got the National Weather Service to keep a radar facility in Fort Wayne so that tornado-prone northwest Ohio would not have to rely on Cleveland. Gillmor has been reelected easily, running very much ahead of his national ticket in 1996.

The People: Pop. 1990: 570,946; 54% rural; 13% age 65+; 94% White; 2% Black; 3% Hispanic origin. Households: 65% married couple families; 32% married couple fams. w. children; 32% college educ.; median household income: $30,117; per capita income: $12,755; median gross rent: $351; median house value: $57,800.

1996 Presidential Vote

Dole (R)	108,255	(44%)
Clinton (D)	102,862	(42%)
Perot (I)	32,365	(13%)

1992 Presidential Vote

Bush (R)	108,421	(41%)
Clinton (D)	88,773	(34%)
Perot (I)	66,051	(25%)

Rep. Paul E. Gillmor (R)

Elected 1988; b. Feb. 1, 1939, Tiffin; home, Old Fort; Ohio Wesleyan U., B.A. 1961, U. of MI, J.D. 1964; Methodist; married (Karen).

Career: Air Force, 1965–66; Practicing atty., 1965–88; OH Senate, 1966–88.

DC Office: 1203 LHOB 20515, 202-225-6405; Fax: 202-225-1985.

District Offices: Perrysburg, 419-872-2500; Port Clinton, 800-541-6446.

Committees: *Commerce* (Vice Chmn. of 28 R): Finance & Hazardous Materials; Telecommunications, Trade & Consumer Protection.

Group Ratings

	ADA	ACLU	AFS	LCV	CFA	CON	NFIB	COC	ACU	NTLC	CHC
1996	15	12	9	15	38	53	95	73	84	98	86
1995	5	—	—	13	23	53	—	100	80	—	—

National Journal Ratings

	1995 LIB — 1995 CONS			1996 LIB — 1996 CONS		
Economic	0%	—	74%	37%	—	61%
Social	41%	—	58%	10%	—	86%
Foreign	36%	—	59%	35%	—	64%

Key Votes of the 104th Congress

1. Reduce Medicare Growth $	Y	5. Flag Amendment	Y	9. Cuban Embargo	Y
2. Ovrd. Product Liab. Veto	Y	6. Drop EPA Limits	Y	10. Bar Bosnia Troop $	N
3. Increase Min. Wage	Y	7. Repeal Assault-Weap. Ban	Y	11. Cut Anti-Missile Defense	N
4. Welfare Reform	Y	8. Ovrd. Part. Birth Veto	Y	12. Bar U.N. Uniforms	Y

Election Results

1996 general	Paul E. Gillmor (R)	145,692	(61%)	($327,472)
	Annie Saunders (D)	81,170	(34%)	($23,710)
	David J. Schaffer (NL)	11,461	(5%)	($6,170)
1996 primary	Paul E. Gillmor (R)	unopposed		
1994 general	Paul E. Gillmor (R)	135,879	(73%)	($210,789)
	Jarrod Tudor (D)	49,335	(27%)	

SIXTH DISTRICT

The first settlers of Ohio came from the south, where the Ohio River was a superhighway through the forest. Yankee settlers came down the Ohio from Pittsburgh and founded Marietta in 1788 as Ohio's first town. About the same time, George Washington procured bounty lands for Revolutionary War veterans in the Virginia Military District of Ohio between the Scioto and Miami Rivers, centered on Chillicothe. In Marietta the Yankees built New England style churches; in Chillicothe the young Virginian Thomas Worthington, who became governor of Ohio, built his home, Adena, designed by architect Benjamin Latrobe. Virginians soon outnumbered New Englanders, and their traces remain on the landscape, which is laid out in irregular-shaped parcels as in Virginia, unlike the Northwest Ordinance's checkerboard grid imposed on most of the Midwest. There have been lasting political effects too. These rolling lands south of U.S. 40 have never attracted much industry; most people here speak with an accent that sounds southern to northern Ohioans; they retain, with conservative cultural attitudes, a Democratic heritage that manifests itself on occasion. It was one sign of the shrewdness of Bill Clinton's campaigning instincts that the 1992 Clinton-Gore bus trip out of the New York convention went through just this part of Ohio, and that Clinton returned in 1996, carrying Ohio both times in large part because of margins he won in many southern Ohio counties.

The 6th Congressional District of Ohio covers most of southern Ohio, from Marietta down the Ohio River to the gritty industrial towns of Ironton and Portsmouth; it runs across the hilly landscape to include part of Chillicothe and all of Piketon, and west over to the Warren County suburbs of Dayton and Cincinnati. It has no large central cities and almost entirely avoids metropolitan areas. Politically, this has been not just a battlefield but a killing ground: in the three elections held in the current boundaries of the 6th District, four incumbent congressmen have been defeated. The first two were Republicans, who were thrown together in 1992 by redistricting, Clarence Miller and Bob McEwen; the third was a Democrat elected in the wake of the Clinton bus tour, Ted Strickland; the fourth was a Republican elected in 1994, Frank Cremeans.

Today the congressman here is once again Ted Strickland, who ran unsuccessfully for this seat in 1976, 1978, and 1980, won in 1992, lost in 1994, and won again in 1996—the last three all being 51%–49% races. Strickland, son of a steelworker and eighth of nine children, is a Methodist minister, was director of a children's home, and then a prison psychologist (at Lucasville, site of an April 1993 riot) and psychology professor at Shawnee State College. He and his wife have both made their way up as counseling professionals. He once described his goal as "building communities where children are nurtured and educated and protected and cared for." On the third day of a hostage crisis, he said, "I'm concerned about guard hostages, but I'm really concerned about the inmates." Strickland and Cremeans, bitter opponents now in two close elections, provide an interesting contrast of their two parties' propensities toward therapy and discipline. Cremeans came from a poor family in rural Cheshire, worked as a teacher, principal and school superintendent, then started a concrete, crane, and rigging business and made millions. "I work six days a week," he once said. "My message is, hey, you can do it with your own hands. Don't look for handouts."

In 1992, Strickland campaigned for more highways and school spending, and for countering alcohol and drug abuse, school dropouts and teen pregnancy; he voted for the Clinton budget and tax package, but against the 1994 crime bill because of its gun control provisions and against NAFTA. In the 1994 campaign he was on the defensive, under attack for supporting the tax increase. In the last days of the campaign, Strickland suggested there might be a need to increase taxes to pay for healthcare finance reform; Cremeans seized on this and ran a last-minute ad that may have made the difference in his 51%–49% win. In 1995 and 1996 Cremeans compiled a conservative voting record, supporting the Contract with America. He was the first member of Congress to support Steve Forbes for president. Strickland, running again, attacked Cremeans for Medicare "cuts" and scaling down the Earned Income Tax Credit, which he called a tax increase on the poor. It was a bizarre campaign in many ways. Cremeans ran radio ads in which "Prisoners for Strickland" cheered him as a fighter for prisoners' rights, opponent of the death penalty, and "a crucial friend when the Republicans tried to take away our gym equipment and color televisions." Strickland claimed he supported the death penalty and had nothing to do with TVs and gyms. Strickland took to showing up at Cremeans appearances with a video camera, sometimes continuing to shoot after he had run out of tape. Cremeans was the target of AFL-CIO ads and some incredibly partisan journalism, such as an Associated Press article in October 1996 which reported that, "special interests and well-heeled backers were generous enough to reimburse Cremeans for all of the personal loans he extended to the campaign, and still have enough left over to run the campaign." In the end, Strickland won by the seemingly obligatory margin of 51%–49%, gaining crucial votes in the counties around Gallipolis.

In his second term, Strickland got a seat on the Commerce Committee. He promised to work for roads, sewers, and industrial parks ("good pork" is a phrase he once used) and to protect government contracts at a local Lockheed Martin plant.

The People: Pop. 1990: 570,804; 60% rural; 13% age 65+; 97% White; 2% Black; 1% Asian. Households: 61% married couple families; 29% married couple fams. w. children; 30% college educ.; median household income: $21,761; per capita income: $10,349; median gross rent: $315; median house value: $46,200.

1996 Presidential Vote			**1992 Presidential Vote**		
Clinton (D)	106,479	(44%)	Bush (R)	102,481	(40%)
Dole (R)	101,991	(43%)	Clinton (D)	99,761	(39%)
Perot (I)	28,942	(12%)	Perot (I)	50,532	(20%)

Rep. Ted Strickland (D)

Elected 1996; b. Aug. 4, 1941, Luccasville; home, Lucasville; Asbury Col., B.A. 1963, M.A., 1967; U. of KY, Ph.D. 1980; Methodist, married (Frances).

Career: Assoc. Minister, Trinity Methodist Church, 1967–68; Dir. of Soc. Svcs., KY Methodist Home, 1968–70; Consulting psychologist, Southern OH Correctional Facility, 1985–92, 1995–96; U.S. House of Reps., 1992 94; Prof , Shawnee St. U., 1988–92, 1994–96.

DC Office:336 CHOB 20515, 202-225-5705; 202-225-5907.

District Offices: Marrieta, 614-376-0868; Portsmouth, 614-353-5171.

Committees: *Commerce* (22nd of 23 D): Finance & Hazardous Materials; Health & the Environment.

Group Ratings and Key Votes: Newly Elected

Election Results

1996 general	Ted Strickland (D)	118,003	(51%)	($714,172)
	Frank A. Cremeans (R)	111,907	(49%)	($1,786,582)
1996 primary	Ted Strickland (D)	unopposed		
1994 general	Frank A. Cremeans (R)	91,263	(51%)	($862,015)
	Ted Strickland (D)	87,861	(49%)	($533,425)

SEVENTH DISTRICT

The hills and plains of central Ohio are dotted with towns and small cities that have been manufacturing centers almost since they were settled in the early 19th Century, when the dominant technologies were the waterwheel and the open forge. In the decades since, they have been replaced by one new technology after another, and the local manufacturing economy, sometimes with uncomfortable fits and starts, has adjusted and advanced. There were painful job losses here in the early 1980s, but there has been small business growth in the years since. As old factories are shut down, new ones open that are more productive; the result is higher incomes and, though not often remembered, far less of the backbreaking hard work and drudgery that were the lot of almost everyone in supposedly better times.

The 7th Congressional District of Ohio is made up of a capital G-shaped slice of the central part of the state. Its largest city is Springfield, where the Navistar truck plant, formerly International Harvester, is the biggest employer. To the south are the eastern suburbs of Dayton around Wright-Patterson Air Force Base, whose name recalls the Dayton-based fathers of the airplane and the cash register. In the northern end of the 7th District are Bellefontaine, site of the first concrete street in America, and, a few miles away, Marysville, the site of Honda's first U.S. plant, where Honda Accords are assembled by American workers.

The 7th District has always been Republican territory. It backed the policies of Ohio Republicans President William McKinley—tariff protection, railroad regulation, antitrust suits against monopolies, discouragement of labor unions—and Governor James Rhodes—low taxes, encouragement of new businesses and jobs. It is culturally conservative and economically mostly satisfied with free markets. Solidly Republican in 1994, it gave good margins to George Bush in 1992 and Bob Dole in 1996.

The 7th District's current congressman is David Hobson, a Republican from Springfield first elected in 1990 after eight years in the state Senate. Hobson sold real estate for many years and until 1993 owned two Japanese steakhouses. He has a moderate to conservative voting record. In the House his first bill was the National Child Abuser Registration Act, which established a registered network of convicted child abusers. After a 13-year-old Ohio girl was killed after her coat drawstring became caught in a school bus door, he got clothing manufacturers to agree voluntarily to remove drawstrings longer than three inches. He works on local issues, from advocating Wright-Pat as home for the Joint Strike Force research center to improving the U.S. 33 bypass. He worked with Dayton Democrat Tony Hall to secure a federal waiver for the Dayton Area Health Plan and to establish Dayton's National Aviation Historic Park.

Hobson is a member of both the Budget and Appropriations Committees. "The Budget Committee charts the course, the Appropriations Committee flies the plane," he says. Just behind his Ohio neighbor John Kasich on Budget, he supported Kasich's plans, but when Republicans backed down in January 1996 after Bill Clinton's vetoes, he said, "We wanted to prove to the country that we are reasonable people." He seemed more at home with the bipartisan cooperation on budget, health care, and welfare reform which prevailed later in the year, and felt that the successes of the 104th Congress would silence Democrats charges of an "extreme" Congress. Hobson worked on the Republican proposal for Medicare reform and sought support from the conservative Democratic Blue Dogs.

On Appropriations Hobson sought the Military Construction Subcommittee chair after the 1996 election, but lost it to the more senior Ron Packard of California. But he will continue to weigh in on military matters, and well beyond Wright-Pat; he serves on the National Security, Military Construction and VA, HUD and Independent Agencies Subcommittees. Hobson has also had a seat on the Ethics Committee, entrusted with the raft of cases brought by Democrats against Newt Gingrich; like many other members, he has been eager to leave the committee, and is not on it for the 105th Congress. He has been reelected with better than 2–1 margins.

The People: Pop. 1990: 570,939; 43% rural; 12% age 65+; 93% White; 5% Black; 1% Asian; 1% Hispanic origin. Households: 64% married couple families; 30% married couple fams. w. children; 37% college educ.; median household income: $30,364; per capita income: $12,919; median gross rent: $376; median house value: $62,400.

1996 Presidential Vote			1992 Presidential Vote		
Dole (R)	115,393	(47%)	Bush (R)	112,701	(45%)
Clinton (D)	100,509	(41%)	Clinton (D)	84,098	(33%)
Perot (I)	25,373	(10%)	Perot (I)	54,307	(22%)

Rep. David L. Hobson (R)

Elected 1990; b. Oct. 17, 1936, Cincinnati; home, Springfield; OH Wesleyan U., B.A. 1958, OH St. Col. of Law, J.D. 1963; Methodist; married (Carolyn).

Career: OH Natl. Guard, 1958–63; Real estate agent, 1969–present; Restaurant owner, 1977–93; OH Senate, 1982–90, Majority Whip, 1986–88, Pres. Pro Tem, 1988–90.

DC Office: 1514 LHOB 20515, 202-225-4324; Fax: 202-225-1984.

District Offices: Lancaster, 614-654-5149; Springfield, 937-325-0474.

Committees: *Appropriations* (16th of 34 R): Military Construction; National Security; VA, HUD & Independent Agencies. *Budget* (2nd of 24 R).

Group Ratings

	ADA	ACLU	AFS	LCV	CFA	CON	NFIB	COC	ACU	NTLC	CHC
1996	0	0	8	23	23	66	97	88	90	98	80
1995	10	—	—	13	15	38	—	96	68	—	—

National Journal Ratings

	1995 LIB	—	1995 CONS	1996 LIB	—	1996 CONS
Economic	26%	—	67%	33%	—	64%
Social	38%	—	60%	39%	—	61%
Foreign	36%	—	59%	21%	—	72%

Key Votes of the 104th Congress

1. Reduce Medicare Growth $	Y	5. Flag Amendment	Y	9. Cuban Embargo	Y
2. Ovrd. Product Liab. Veto	Y	6. Drop EPA Limits	N	10. Bar Bosnia Troop $	N
3. Increase Min. Wage	Y	7. Repeal Assault-Weap. Ban	Y	11. Cut Anti-Missile Defense	N
4. Welfare Reform	Y	8. Ovrd. Part. Birth Veto	Y	12. Bar U.N. Uniforms	Y

Election Results

1996 general	David L. Hobson (R)	158,087	(68%)	($620,093)
	Richard K. Blain (D)	61,419	(26%)	($9,824)
	Dawn Marie Johnson (NL)	13,478	(6%)	
1996 primary	David L. Hobson (R)	60,577	(86%)	
	Richard A. Herron (R)	10,142	(14%)	
1994 general	David L. Hobson (R)	unopposed		($191,660)

EIGHTH DISTRICT

The far west end of Ohio, where U.S. 40, the old National Road, heads straight as an arrow in its last miles across Ohio to Indiana, and the rail lines criss-cross the land from Cincinnati to Dayton, has since the early 20th Century been some of the nation's prime industrial country. Here the Great and Little Miami Rivers drain south into the Ohio; here U.S. 40 jogs southward twice to go over the Miami and Stillwater River dams, built after the great flood of 1913 that killed 361 people in Dayton and caused $1 billion in damage. Around Dayton and Cincinnati, in large factory towns like Middletown and Hamilton and smaller factory towns like Troy and Piqua, Ohioans, after the recession of the early 1980s, adapted to new conditions and began to produce for export to Europe and Latin America and Asia as well as for the American market. And if city centers were slowly emptying out, comfortable suburban tracts were growing up in what were once open fields.

The 8th Congressional District of Ohio covers much of this territory, including most of four counties north of Dayton and U.S. 40, Preble County west of Dayton, and Butler County between Dayton and Cincinnati. About half its people live in Butler, around Hamilton and Middletown and in suburbs north of Cincinnati—now a single metropolitan strip from northern Kentucky to U.S. 40 north of Dayton. Politically, this is solidly Republican territory, which Bob Dole carried with over 50%.

The congressman from the 8th District, John Boehner (pronounced *bayner*), was first elected in 1990 but has already become one of the leaders of the Republican Party in the House. He grew up in Cincinnati, one of 12 children, and after college moved just beyond the line to Butler County; he started a packaging company, served on the Union Township Board of Trustees, and in 1984, at 34, was elected to the Ohio State House. He won the U.S. House seat in the 1990 primary, by beating not one but two of his predecessors—incumbent Buz Lukens, who inexplicably ran after being convicted of having sex with a 16-year-old girl, and Thomas Kindness, who gave up the seat to run against Senator John Glenn in 1986 and then, as Boehner put it, deserted the district to become a Washington lobbyist. Boehner won 49%, to 32% for Kindness and 17% for Lukens. In the House, Boehner quickly became part of the Gang of Seven, young freshman Republicans who insisted on revealing the names of all 355 members who had overdrafts at the House bank, and then went on to assail Democratic leaders and Republican go-alongers on the pay raise and the House Post Office scandal. They also argued that members of Congress should be subject to the regulatory laws they impose on other citizens; in 1992 Boehner invited OSHA inspectors to his office, where they found what would have been 15 violations if Congress were covered by OSHA. That same month Boehner took the lead in adopting the 27th Amendment to the Constitution, proposed by James Madison with the original Bill of Rights in 1789, to prohibit Congress from varying its pay during its current term. Six states ratified it between 1789 and 1791, Ohio did so in 1873, and from 1978–92, 32 more states followed suit. Boehner argued that these 39 states were the three-quarters required for ratification; Archivist of the United States certified the amendment as ratified and Congress voted nearly unanimously to accept it.

Boehner and the Gang of Seven infuriated House veterans, but they struck a chord around the nation. All but Boehner had serious challenges in 1992, and all but one—Frank Riggs of California—won, and he came back to win in 1994. In the process Boehner became one of the top lieutenants of then-Minority Whip Newt Gingrich, raising money for Republican candidates, pressuring the U.S. Chamber of Commerce to oppose the Clinton healthcare plan, and managing Gingrich's campaign for the Republican leadership after Robert Michel announced his retirement. He was a major player in drafting and championing the 10-point Contract With America. After the 1994 election, he ran for chairman of the Republican Conference and, with Gingrich's backing, beat California's Duncan Hunter 122–102.

That made Boehner number four in the Republican leadership, with informal responsibility for encouraging PAC contributions to Republicans. At one point Boehner was handing out tobacco PAC checks on the floor, as Democrats had sometimes done; this was widely condemned and subsequently banned. Boehner worked hard to enforce disciplinc, on issues from the assault weapons ban repeal to the ethics charges against Gingrich; he sought in 1996 to avoid a vote on the minimum wage, which gave the Democrats an opening to keep raising the issue. But by any recent historic standard, Republicans held together exceedingly well, despite some disarray in 1996. Boehner also worked on legislation. With Agriculture Chairman Pat Roberts, he pushed for the Freedom to Farm bill which phased out most subsidies over seven years—the most important farm legislation since 1933, and one which deprives farm state Democrats of an issue they have long won on. Prompted by the difficulty of giving the closed Voice of America station house in West Chcster to Habitat for Humanity, he passed a repeal of the McKinney Act provision ("a well-intentioned mistake," he called it) giving homeless organizations an equal chance at bidding for closed federal facilities. In July 1996 Republicans held hearings on organized crime and labor unions, especially the Laborers, after the AFL-CIO had been running millions of dollars of ads against Republicans. "You're going to see a lot more serious oversight of the big labor bosses. It's a responsibility we've been overlooking," he said.

Boehner tempers his partisanship with courtesy: he urged Republicans to be civil toward President Clinton in January 1996 and after the election said, "You're going to see us work with the president to try to do the people's work." But in just three terms Boehner has played a major role in transforming the House and reshaping American politics. If he has misstepped and misjudged on occasion, he has also shown great skill and demonstrated how in the American political system someone who was just a few years ago a minority party legislator in one state can transform politics and government on the national stage.

The People: Pop. 1990: 570,837; 38% rural; 12% age 65+; 96% White; 3% Black; 1% Asian; 1% Hispanic origin. Households: 65% married couple families; 32% married couple fams. w. children; 36% college educ.; median household income: $31,171; per capita income: $13,355; median gross rent: $389; median house value: $65,900.

1996 Presidential Vote			**1992 Presidential Vote**		
Dole (R)	125,577	(52%)	Bush (R)	121,174	(47%)
Clinton (D)	89,331	(37%)	Clinton (D)	75,375	(29%)
Perot (I)	26,111	(11%)	Perot (I)	60,172	(23%)

Rep. John A. Boehner (R)

Elected 1990; b. Nov. 17, 1949, Cincinnati; home, West Chester; Xavier U., B.S. 1977; Catholic; married (Debbie).

Career: Navy, 1969; Pres., Nucite Sales, Inc., 1976–90; Union Township Bd. of Trustees, 1981–85, Pres., 1984; OH House of Reps., 1984–90.

DC Office: 1011 LHOB 20515, 202-225-6205; Fax: 202-225-0704.

District Offices: Hamilton, 513-870-0300; Troy, 513-339-1524.

Committees: *Republican Conference Chairman. Agriculture* (4th of 27 R): General Farm Commodities; Livestock, Dairy & Poultry (Vice Chmn.). *House Oversight* (3rd of 6 R).

Group Ratings

	ADA	ACLU	AFS	LCV	CFA	CON	NFIB	COC	ACU	NTLC	CHC
1996	0	6	0	8	0	61	100	94	100	100	100
1995	0	—	—	0	0	56	—	100	88	—	—

National Journal Ratings

	1995 LIB — 1995 CONS			1996 LIB — 1996 CONS		
Economic	0%	—	74%	0%	—	82%
Social	0%	—	79%	0%	—	90%
Foreign	28%	—	65%	0%	—	79%

Key Votes of the 104th Congress

1. Reduce Medicare Growth $	Y	5. Flag Amendment	Y	9. Cuban Embargo	Y
2. Ovrd. Product Liab. Veto	Y	6. Drop EPA Limits	N	10. Bar Bosnia Troop $	N
3. Increase Min. Wage	N	7. Repeal Assault-Weap. Ban	Y	11. Cut Anti-Missile Defense	N
4. Welfare Reform	Y	8. Ovrd. Part. Birth Veto	Y	12. Bar U.N. Uniforms	Y

Election Results

1996 general	John A. Boehner (R)	165,815	(70%)	($1,312,440)
	Jeffrey D. Kitchen (D)	61,515	(26%)	($20,853)
	Others	8,613	(4%)	
1996 primary	John A. Boehner (R)	unopposed		
1994 general	John A. Boehner (R)	unopposed		($713,223)

NINTH DISTRICT

In the 1920s Toledo was one of America's boom towns. This was "a decade of fabulous figures," Harlan Hatcher wrote: the Willys-Overland plant employed 25,000 workers and turned out an auto every 30 seconds; the city built $20 million coal and iron ore docks; the Libbey-Owens-Ford merger made Toledo, with good local supplies of natural gas and sand, the nation's biggest glass manufacturer; the city built a new museum and transcontinental airport. Toledo had long been well-situated, where the Maumee River empties into Lake Erie, where two dozen rail lines connected it with the East Coast and Chicago and the coal fields of Kentucky and West Virginia. It was also well-positioned to be one of the centers of the brash rising auto industry, a national leader when it first produced the Jeep in the 1940s. But by the late 1970s and early 1980s, auto company management had allowed the unions to bid wages and benefits too high while watching quality decline, to the point that consumers would not buy enough American-made cars for the industry to survive without vast subsidy or major shrinkage. Subsidy, beyond the temporary Chrysler loan and a few small trade barriers, was not forthcoming, and so Toledo and other auto-dependent cities went through tough times.

Yet revival is on its way. Toledo in the 1990s produces one of America's hottest vehicles, the Jeep Cherokee; the old plant will be closed, but Chrysler promises to build another within 50 miles by 2002. And Toledo's small manufacturers in search of markets here and abroad show the energy and ingenuity lacking in the big auto and glass companies 20 years prior. If Toledo's tough times were symbolized by the closing of the Portside Festival Marketplace in 1990, its rebound may be symbolized by the 1996 plans to rebuild the Toledo Sports Arena.

Ohio's 9th Congressional District is centered on Toledo, spreading east to the flatlands of Ottawa County, south to Bowling Green State University, and west to rural Fulton County. Toledo has been heavily Democratic since CIO unions organized the plants in the late 1930s; the collapse of the auto industry so unnerved the district that in 1980 it voted for Ronald Reagan and elected a Republican congressman. But in 1982, it became solidly Democratic again, electing Marcy Kaptur, who has held the seat ever since.

Kaptur is fervent and principled, hard-working and dedicated, always a loyal daughter of Toledo. She grew up there and has spent almost her entire career in the public sector. After eight years as an urban planner in Toledo, she got a job in the Carter White House; she was shrewd enough to return to Toledo in 1982 when no one else wanted to run for the House seat. She saw Toledo's economy nosedive, and feels intensely the pain of ordinary people who played by the rules but ended up losing because of the operation of larger economic forces.

Kaptur's great cause is trade. She has long been convinced that Toledo and places like it have lost jobs and industry because of unfair trade practices by the Japanese and low-wage competition in countries like Mexico. If "capitalism laughs at boundaries," as the historian Fernand Braudel wrote, Kaptur, with her faith in the public sector, has worked hard to make those boundaries stronger, and not something to be snickered at. She pressured the Japanese to buy more American auto parts, but is leery of Japanese investment in the United States. She has long proposed laws to prohibit top government officials from representing foreign corporations for five years and foreign governments forever after they leave office; she also would ban campaign contributions by foreign individuals or corporations, and hopes that the controversy over illegal foreign contributions to the Clinton campaign and the DNC would improve her bill's chances. She also favors a constitutional amendment to allow campaign spending limits.

Kaptur was probably Congress's most vocal and dedicated opponent of the North American Free Trade Agreement. She visited the Mexican border in spring 1993, and returned home with soil and water samples to demonstrate the pollution there. She argued that 100,000 jobs had been transferred from Ohio to Mexico, and cited the 1993 shutdown of a Toledo auto parts plant followed by the transfer of some of its jobs to Matamoros, Mexico. She criticized President Clinton for doing nothing for sagging U.S. industries and for not listening to her and other Democrats opposed to NAFTA. She brought to this issue a level of commitment that was genuinely moving, and did not drop trade issues even after NAFTA passed in November 1993. In early 1995, she argued forcefully against Clinton's proposal to bail out the Mexican peso with $40 billion of U.S. loan guarantees; the President was forced to abandon the legislation and proceed with an administrative rescue. In 1996 she sponsored a NAFTA Accountability Act, which would require renegotiation or withdrawal from NAFTA if certain performance standards are not met.

Kaptur weighs in on other issues as well. She took the lead in proposing the World War II Memorial now going up on the Mall. She opposes funding for abortion and favors the partial-birth abortion ban. She works on local projects, like restoring Toledo's Farmers' Market and the Central Union Terminal. She has set up Golden Eagle and Vulture Awards, for companies that are exemplary and poor corporate citizens. On the Agriculture Appropriations Subcommittee, of which she is now ranking minority member, she passed an amendment to the farm bill requiring farmers to plant or conserve land in order to receive transition payments.

Kaptur is exceedingly popular in Toledo, and has run far ahead of party lines in the 9th District. She has also become something of a national political figure. In August 1995 she appeared before Ross Perot's United We Stand and made a rousing speech, mostly on trade, that had the delegates cheering. Perot especially praised her, and offered her his vice presidential nomination in August 1996; she turned it down. She also declined to run for the Senate in 1994, and has not showed any interest in statewide office since. But she has published a book on women in Congress, has launched a weekly radio show, and shows no signs of discouragement in her work of representing the working class men and women of Toledo.

The People: Pop. 1990: 570,911; 14% rural; 13% age 65+; 83% White; 12% Black; 1% Asian; 3% Hispanic origin. Households: 53% married couple families; 25% married couple fams. w. children; 42% college educ.; median household income: $28,856; per capita income: $13,477; median gross rent: $392; median house value: $58,000.

1996 Presidential Vote			**1992 Presidential Vote**		
Clinton (D)	125,971	(55%)	Clinton (D)	118,713	(47%)
Dole (R)	76,613	(34%)	Bush (R)	81,784	(32%)
Perot (I)	22,960	(10%)	Perot (I)	50,151	(20%)

Rep. Marcy Kaptur (D)

Elected 1982; b. June 17, 1946, Toledo; home, Toledo; U. of WI, B.A. 1968, U. of MI, M.A. 1974, M.I.T., 1981–82; Catholic; single.

Career: Urban planner, Toledo, Lucas Cnty. Planning Comm., 1969–75; Urban planning consultant, 1975–77; White House Asst. Dir. for Urban Affairs, 1977–80; Dep. Secy., Natl. Consumer Coop. Bank, 1980–81; Author.

DC Office: 2311 RHOB 20515, 202-225-4146; Fax: 202-225-7711.

District Offices: Toledo, 419-259-7500.

Committees: *Appropriations* (12th of 26 D): Agriculture, Rural Development, FDA & Related Agencies (RMM); Legislative; VA, HUD & Independent Agencies.

Group Ratings

	ADA	ACLU	AFS	LCV	CFA	CON	NFIB	COC	ACU	NTLC	CHC
1996	75	67	100	69	77	48	32	33	15	13	20
1995	75	—	—	75	92	25	—	29	16	—	—

National Journal Ratings

	1995 LIB	—	1995 CONS	1996 LIB	—	1996 CONS
Economic	67%	—	32%	68%	—	31%
Social	67%	—	32%	63%	—	35%
Foreign	62%	—	36%	76%	—	22%

Key Votes of the 104th Congress

1. Reduce Medicare Growth $	N	5. Flag Amendment	N	9. Cuban Embargo	Y
2. Ovrd. Product Liab. Veto	Y	6. Drop EPA Limits	Y	10. Bar Bosnia Troop $	Y
3. Increase Min. Wage	Y	7. Repeal Assault-Weap. Ban	N	11. Cut Anti-Missile Defense	Y
4. Welfare Reform	N	8. Ovrd. Part. Birth Veto	Y	12. Bar U.N. Uniforms	N

Election Results

1996 general	Marcy Kaptur (D)	170,617	(77%)	($253,432)
	Randy Whitman (R)	46,040	(21%)	($44,641)
	Others	4,677	(2%)	
1996 primary	Marcy Kaptur (D)	unopposed		
1994 general	Marcy Kaptur (D)	118,120	(75%)	($309,247)
	Randy Whitman (R)	38,665	(25%)	($9,500)

TENTH DISTRICT

Cleveland, one of America's great cities at the beginning of the 20th Century, is on its way back as the century ends. It grew early in this century as a center of heavy industry: this was the original home base of John D. Rockefeller's Standard Oil; the city's twisting and deep Cuyahoga River was the site of several of the nation's largest steel mills; great industrial fortunes here built civic institutions like the museums in Wade Park, Case Western University and the Cleveland Symphony, and financed the campaigns of northeast Ohio Republican Presidents James Garfield and William McKinley. On the old Public Square, designed like a New England town green by the Yankees who settled this Western Reserve (the northeast corner of Ohio) in the early 19th Century, the two eccentric Van Sweringen brothers, trolley magnates of the early 20th Century, built the Terminal Tower, for many years the highest skyscraper in interior America. This yeasty, ethnic city, with more than 40 nationalities—Czechs, Hungarians, Poles, Italians, Germans: the Hapsburg Empire and more—and with many distinct ethnic neighborhoods, produced a robust two-party politics. Then, in the 1930s, after the New Deal and when CIO unions organized the steel factories and auto assembly plants, Cleveland became solidly Democratic, though with some affluent Republican suburbs.

But Cleveland never led the nation as it hoped: the nation's fourth largest city in 1910, it was overtaken in size first by Detroit, then by Los Angeles, eventually by the likes of Houston and Dallas; today, it's the center of the nation's 14th largest metropolitan area. The central city declined from 914,000 in 1950 to 493,000 in 1994, as the children who grew up in the tightly-packed neighborhoods made more money and moved to the suburbs. Movement was especially great in wards east of the Cuyahoga River, which were almost entirely ethnic in 1950 and almost entirely black by 1970. The 1970s were a bad decade for Cleveland, which became an object of ridicule by national sophisticates. Its heavy industries were fast declining, Lake Erie and the Cuyahoga River were badly polluted (the river caught fire in June 1969). City politics became racially polarized with the election of black Mayor Carl Stokes in 1967 and 1969, and in December 1978 the city defaulted on bank loans under 32-year-old Mayor Dennis Kucinich.

But the city government was rescued by George Voinovich, elected mayor in 1979 and governor in 1990. And the current mayor, Michael White, who is black, broke down racial polarization and first won municipal office in 1979 by carrying white wards west of the Cuyahoga while losing the black wards east of the river to black machine politician George Forbes. Downtown Cleveland revived, with a new headquarters for British Petroleum (here because it bought Standard Oil of Ohio), the fourth-largest performing arts center in the nation at Playhouse Square, the new Jacobs Field baseball stadium, a new basketball arena and the Rock and Roll Hall of Fame. Following the departure of the city's beloved Browns to Baltimore, a new football stadium is under construction to be financed with a $28 to $48 million NFL payment, $9 million in damages from Browns' owner Art Modell for breaking his lease, and public money from a sin tax voters approved in November 1995. The city has been promised a new or expansion team by 1999, and they have retained the Browns name and colors. People swim in now-clean Lake Erie, and restaurants and pleasure boat docks line the Cuyahoga where diners can sip Burning River pale ale. Cleveland continues to be headquarters of several of the nation's largest law firms, and some of its businesses, like iron-ore giant Cleveland-Cliffs, have sharply revived; the city's number one employer is now health services, and the Cleveland Clinic may be its best-known firm. Cleveland's revival became national news in 1995, when the Cleveland Indians went to the World Series for the first time since 1954.

The 10th Congressional District of Ohio includes most of the west side of Cleveland and the western suburbs in Cuyahoga County. Excluded is one salient of mostly black Cleveland precincts attached to the 11th District across the Cuyahoga; also several western suburbs—Brook Park, Middleburg Heights—are in the convoluted suburban 19th District. Suburbs in the 11th include Lakewood, well-established by the 1920s and still comfortable middle-class territory, and Rocky River and Bay Village, growing more affluent as one moves westward along the lake. Inland is Parma, a creation of the 1950s, when second- and third-generation ethnics moved out to subdivision houses set amid what was once calculated to be America's densest concentration of bowling alleys. The political tradition here is almost entirely Democratic, but George Voinovich, popular from his decade as mayor, carried the area in 1990 and 1994.

The congressman from the 10th District is Dennis Kucinich, elected in 1996, now 50, still unrepentant about the day nearly 20 years ago he plunged the city into default. Kucinich grew up as the oldest of 7 children whose family moved 21 times in different parts of Cleveland. He was a political prodigy who was elected to the City Council in 1969, at 23; he saw himself as the champion of the working man, eager for confrontations with Cleveland's business establishment. In 1977, at 31, he was elected mayor; one of his planks was maintaining municipal control of Muny Light, the electric utility for part of the city. But city government was in terrible financial straits, and Kucinich was unwilling or unable to balance the budget and meet obligations. When bankers demanded that he sell Muny Light, as other city-owned properties had been sold by the previous mayor, he refused, and they called their loans. "The city went into default on midnight of December 15, 1978, and I began my journey in the political wilderness," he said. The public verdict was negative: Kucinich lost in 1979 to Republican George Voinovich, who worked with business to redevelop downtown, and be elected governor in 1990. Kucinich taught at Cleveland State and Case Western Reserve, hosted a radio talk show, and was a TV reporter. In 1994 he staged a political comeback, arguing that he had saved utility ratepayers money, and was elected to the state Senate, defeating an incumbent Republican. In 1996 he ran for the House, celebrating his defense of Muny Light with the slogan "Light Up Congress."

The incumbent congressman was Martin Hoke, a Republican elected in 1992 and 1994 against Democrats with serious problems. Hoke made millions in business, with a firm providing auto repair service for air travelers and then a cellular phone company. In 1992 he faced incumbent Mary Rose Oakar, who had 213 overdrafts on the House bank; she barely won the Democratic primary against County Commissioner Tim Hagan, who may be one of the last true-believing white liberal Democrats in the country. Hoke called Oakar "the most persuasive argument for term limits" and won 57%–43%. In 1994 Hoke looked to be in trouble against Cuyahoga County Treasurer Francis Gaul, but Gaul had to deal with charges of investment mismanagement, and Hoke won 52%–39%.

The Hoke-Kucinich race was a rollicking one. Hoke called Kucinich a "demagogue," a "socialist," a "tax-dodger." He charged that "he would do to Medicare exactly what he did to Cleveland: he would throw it into default." Organized labor spent huge amounts—the AFL-CIO said $475,000, Hoke said $1.6 million—on ads claiming that Hoke voted to "cut" Medicare. And Hoke attacked Kucinich for accepting $5,000 from the mob-linked Laborers Union. Kucinich blasted Hoke for buying $50,000 in GTE stock before voting on the telecom bill and for reneging on a promise to put his holdings in a blind trust. Kucinich campaigned against NAFTA and GATT (though Ohio businesses have made money on exports to Mexico) and defended his ties with labor. "Are they my special interest? Yes . . . I am not a missionary for labor; I am from the house of labor, the family of labor." Democrats, many of them former Kucinich critics, rallied around him: the Cleveland council named a public power plant for him on the same day President Clinton came in to campaign for him in Parma. Hoke was not helped when 19th District Republican Steve LaTourette was quoted in the Cleveland *Plain Dealer* as saying that he didn't think Hoke would win.

Actually, given the Democratic leanings of the district, Hoke did very well. Kucinich won, but by only a 49%–46% margin. He says he wants to expand job training programs for skilled workers and for current welfare recipients. But his dreams of an ever-larger public sector are unlikely to be carried out immediately in the Republican Congress. But Kucinich's flair for publicity, zest for confrontation, and persistence should not be underestimated.

The People: Pop. 1990: 570,530; 15% age 65+; 92% White; 2% Black; 1% Asian; 4% Hispanic origin. Households: 52% married couple families; 23% married couple fams. w. children; 43% college educ.; median household income: $30,323; per capita income: $14,813; median gross rent: $388; median house value: $72,600.

1996 Presidential Vote			1992 Presidential Vote		
Clinton (D)	117,878	(51%)	Clinton (D)	107,465	(41%)
Dole (R)	83,055	(36%)	Bush (R)	92,846	(36%)
Perot (I)	26,952	(12%)	Perot (I)	58,092	(22%)

Rep. Dennis J. Kucinich (D)

Elected 1996; b. Oct. 6, 1946, Cleveland; home, Cleveland; Cleveland St. U., 1967–70; Case Western Reserve U., B.A., M.A., 1973; Catholic; single.

Career: Cleveland City Cncl., 1970–75, 1983–85; Clerk, Municipal Courts, 1976–77; Cleveland Mayor, 1977–79; Radio Talk Show Host, 1979, 1989; Lecturer, 1980–83; Consultant, 1986–94; TV Reporter, Channel 8, 1989–92; OH Senate, 1994–97.

DC Office: 1730 LHOB 20515, 202-225-5871.

District Offices: Lakewood, 216-228-6465.

Committees: *Education & The Workforce* (20th of 20 D): Early Childhood, Youth & Families. *Government Reform & Oversight* (14th of 19 D): Human Resources; National Economic Growth, Natural Resources & Regulatory Affairs.

Group Ratings and Key Votes: Newly Elected

Election Results

1996 general	Dennis Kucinich (D)	110,723	(49%)	($690,367)
	Martin R. Hoke (R)	104,546	(46%)	($1,480,181)
	Robert B. Iverson (NL)	10,415	(5%)	
1996 primary	Dennis Kucinich (D)	37,547	(77%)	
	Ed Boyle (D)	9,154	(19%)	
	Others	1,932	(4%)	
1994 general	Martin R. Hoke (R)	95,226	(52%)	($675,825)
	Francis E. Gaul (D)	70,918	(39%)	($494,467)
	Joseph J. Jacobs (I)	17,495	(10%)	

ELEVENTH DISTRICT

Like most great American cities, Cleveland grew in great bursts of migration, when capitalists' investments suddenly were paying off beyond their wildest dreams and low-wage workers were attracted from ready corners of the country and the world. Cleveland's greatest surge of growth started in the 1890s and lasted through the 1920s, as tens of thousands of immigrants from central and southern Europe arrived here, looking for jobs in steel and auto and other factories. Bohemians came to the tightly-packed neighborhoods along Broadway, Hungarians a bit to the northeast, Jews north of University Circle along East 105th Street, and Italians to Little Italy along Mayfield Road.

As the nation's heavy industries geared up for World War II and enjoyed years of unexpected prosperous growth afterward, a second surge of immigrants came, this time blacks from the American South. From Cleveland's old black ghetto, south of Carnegie Avenue downtown to East 105th, the rapidly increasing number of blacks covered most of the east side by the middle

1960s, with only a few Bohemian and Italian enclaves left east of the Cuyahoga and west of the city limits. Migration stopped around 1965, but blacks have continued to move out beyond the city limits to the east side suburbs, including modest East Cleveland and Warrensville Heights and upper-income Shaker Heights, laid out in 1905 on broad boulevards by streetcar magnates, the Van Sweringen brothers. These surges of migration led to political changes. A string of ethnic mayors—Frank Lausche, Anthony Celebrezze, Ralph Locher—was followed by the election in 1967 and 1969 of Carl Stokes, the nation's first big city black mayor, and Cleveland had racially polarized city politics for much of the 1970s. Ironically, Cleveland has never had a black majority and elected its second black mayor, Michael White, in 1989, because white voters preferred his accommodating politics to the more polarizing ways of longtime City Council Chairman George Forbes.

The 11th Congressional District of Ohio includes most of the east side of Cleveland, plus the suburbs just to the east, which together have about as many people as the city now. Some of these—East Cleveland, Warrensville Heights—are mostly black; some, notably Shaker Heights, have stable black percentages in carefully maintained neighborhoods. Others are the natural destination of blacks seeking low-crime neighborhoods and middle-class schools not often found on the city side of Cleveland's impressive set of museums and medical centers. This is a heavily Democratic district, with a solid black majority, and it has been represented since 1968 by Louis Stokes, Carl Stokes's brother. The Stokeses come from a humble background. Their mother stressed the importance of education. Louis Stokes served in the segregated Army in World War II, got a law degree when practically no law firm would hire blacks, and challenged the Ohio congressional district lines when it was considered unthinkable that a black could be elected to Congress.

1968 was the climactic political year for Louis Stokes: it was the first full year his brother was mayor, he argued the Terry v. Ohio stop-and-frisk case before the U.S. Supreme Court, and he was elected to the House, the first black ever from Ohio. It was not his last first, nor his last tough assignment. He was the first black member of Appropriations, on which he is now the third ranking Democrat. He was made chairman of the Select Committee on Presidential Assassinations in 1977, on which he supervised responsible hearings and produced a report that disputed the Warren Commission findings and concluded that President Kennedy "was probably assassinated as a result of a conspiracy." Following the chagrin caused by the film *J.F.K.*, Stokes returned to the subject in 1992, setting up a special commission to look into the matter and, despite Justice Department objections, was able to secure release of most of the still secret files on the assassination. In 1980, Stokes became chairman of the House Ethics Committee, and in 1987 and 1988 he chaired the House Intelligence Committee and was a member of the special committee investigating the Iran-contra scandal. In 1991, as all but one other member rotated off, Stokes was called again to head up ethics—just in time for the House Bank and Post Office scandals. Not unsinged himself, Stokes recused himself from investigating the bank and, as it turned out, he had 551 overdrafts.

Stokes is now ranking Democrat on the VA-HUD-Independent Agencies Appropriations Subcommittee, which he chaired in 1993 and 1994. This covers an odd hybrid of agencies, which inevitably get played off against one another: Stokes tends to favor housing over space, but in 1993 backed the space station in a crucial vote at the urging of the Clinton Administration. Stokes has shepherded minority set-aside programs, like his minority scholarship program for the CIA and NSA. He tried to keep earmarked projects off his bills, with some success in 1993 and less in other years. This does not mean he does not aid Cleveland projects: he boasts of funds for the Cleveland Federal Courthouse, a Veterans Medical Center Parking Component, aid to the Computer Assisted Minimally Invasive Surgery program at the Cleveland Clinic. Stokes has a very liberal voting record and detests the policies of Newt Gingrich's House Republicans. He hated the deep cuts in 1995 appropriations, and was less displeased with his subcommittee's 1996 bill, on which he worked to prevent cuts in Americorps and pushed for mental illness health insurance coverage, and aid to spina bifida babies born to soldiers exposed to Agent Orange.

1996 was nonetheless a difficult year for Stokes. In April his brother Carl Stokes, then ambassador to the Seychelles, died. And he seriously considered not running again; some said he would step aside for Cuyahoga County Prosecutor Stephanie Tubbs Jones. But Stokes yielded to pleas that he run again and, as usual, was reelected without difficulty.

The People: Pop. 1990: 571,295; 15% age 65+; 39% White; 58% Black; 1% Asian; 1% Hispanic origin. Households: 38% married couple families; 16% married couple fams. w. children; 41% college educ.; median household income: $22,459; per capita income: $12,629; median gross rent: $376; median house value: $58,100.

1996 Presidential Vote

Clinton (D)	155,895	(79%)
Dole (R)	28,938	(15%)
Perot (I)	9,553	(5%)

1992 Presidential Vote

Clinton (D)	169,870	(73%)
Bush (R)	37,886	(16%)
Perot (I)	23,428	(10%)

Rep. Louis Stokes (D)

Elected 1968; b. Feb. 23, 1925, Cleveland; home, Shaker Heights; Western Reserve U., 1946–48, Cleveland Marshall Law Schl., J.D. 1953; A. M. E. Zion; married (Jeanette).

Career: Army, 1943–46 (WWII); Practicing atty., 1954–68.

DC Office: 2365 RHOB 20515, 202-225-7032; Fax: 202-225-1339.

District Offices: Shaker Heights, 216-522-4900.

Committees: *Appropriations* (3rd of 26 D): Labor, Health & Human Services & Education; VA, HUD & Independent Agencies (RMM).

Group Ratings

	ADA	ACLU	AFS	LCV	CFA	CON	NFIB	COC	ACU	NTLC	CHC
1996	65	100	90	89	85	94	15	17	0	6	0
1995	90	—	—	94	85	9	—	17	9	—	—

National Journal Ratings

	1995 LIB — 1995 CONS		1996 LIB — 1996 CONS	
Economic	94%	0%	89%	0%
Social	88%	0%	88%	0%
Foreign	93%	0%	86%	13%

Key Votes of the 104th Congress

1. Reduce Medicare Growth $	N	5. Flag Amendment	N	9. Cuban Embargo	*
2. Ovrd. Product Liab. Veto	N	6. Drop EPA Limits	Y	10. Bar Bosnia Troop $	N
3. Increase Min. Wage	Y	7. Repeal Assault-Weap. Ban	*	11. Cut Anti-Missile Defense	Y
4. Welfare Reform	N	8. Ovrd. Part. Birth Veto	N	12. Bar U.N. Uniforms	N

Election Results

1996 general	Louis Stokes (D)	153,546	(81%)	($361,175)
	James J. Sykora (R)	28,821	(15%)	
	Others	6,672	(4%)	
1996 primary	Louis Stokes (D)	unopposed		
1994 general	Louis Stokes (D)	114,220	(77%)	($382,332)
	James J. Sykora (R)	33,705	(23%)	

TWELFTH DISTRICT

Columbus seems on the verge of becoming a major metropolis. With city limits stretching toward farmland at each point of the compass, Columbus is geographically the largest city in Ohio; its metropolitan area, though far less populous than Cleveland and a bit smaller than Cincinnati, is growing more rapidly and some time ago passed the magic million mark. Columbus has the advantages of being a state capital, the home of Ohio State University, and a major white-collar employment town: it is the home base of The Limited's Leslie Wexner and Wendy's Dave Thomas, of Nationwide Insurance and multistate giant Banc One. Columbus likes to brag of its airfreight operations at Port Columbus, the airport, among the best in the country, and about the $43 million Wexner Center for the Visual Arts, a post-post-modern structure by architect Peter Eisenman that has evoked vast controversy. This economic base and civic infrastructure has attracted the kind of upscale, enterprising people who have produced most of America's growth in recent years.

Politically, Columbus has always been a Republican city, with an even more Republican hinterland. It had few of the Eastern European immigrants and CIO unions that made Cleveland so Democratic; for most of the last 30 years, its mayor has been a Republican with support from a machine redolent of the era of William McKinley (whose statue sits in front of the flat-domed Capitol). Recently, local Republicans have had spirited competition from Democrats in the city, but the suburbs are heavily Republican and the countryside even more so. The Columbus area dominates two of Ohio's congressional districts: the 12th extends east to the small industrial town of Newark and north to bucolic Delaware County, and includes black areas and the affluent east side of the city around Bexley; the 15th includes most of the territory within the city limits and extends south and west to include Madison County.

The congressman from the 12th District is John Kasich, a Republican first elected in 1982, and a familiar figure nationally as the chairman of the House Budget Committee. Boyish-looking but hard-working, aggressive but ingratiating, with a command of fact and argument that can only come from perseverance together with a competitive drive colleagues see on the basketball court, Kasich puts a cheerful yet earnest face on Republican policies and priorities. Kasich has been in politics just about all his adult life. He is the son of a mail carrier who grew up in working class McKees Rocks, Pennsylvania, of Hungarian, Czech and Croatian descent; after graduating from Ohio State, he worked for a state legislator. In 1978, at 26, Kasich ran a strenuous door-to-door campaign and beat a Democratic state senator. In 1982, he ran for the House and, with the help of a favorable districting plan, beat a Democrat who had upset an incumbent in 1980. In the House he made his first commotion on National Security, where he was the leading Republican opponent of the B-2 bomber and succeeded in drastically reducing its production.

Kasich got on the Budget Committee in 1989 and won the ranking Republican spot in 1993 against seniority and with the help of Newt Gingrich. In the Democratic Congress he led the Republicans' charge to "cut spending first," which helped defeat the 1993 Clinton stimulus package. He advanced a Republican budget alternative with no tax increases or Social Security cuts, but means-testing of Medicare and serious cuts in discretionary spending: a preview of

1995. In October 1993 and April 1994, he and Democrat Tim Penny put together packages of spending cuts, which were defeated by only 219–213 and 216–202. Kasich had a few modest wins, like zeroing out the Interstate Commerce Commission. But the serious and detailed work he did in 1993 and 1994 was an indispensable ingredient of his successes in 1995 and 1996.

Kasich took the Budget chair determined to reduce the size and scale of government, and achieved partial success. He scotched the "current services" concept, which assumed that every agency was entitled to past appropriations plus more to serve larger populations plus inflation—a concept that insured that government would always grow faster than the economy. He was determined to start off with Republican rather than Clinton Administration proposals and present a plan that would plausibly balance the budget in seven years. He and other Republicans assumed that Clinton would eventually accept their budgets if they proved stubborn enough, but they underestimated how Clinton would attack them for "shutting the government down" (technically of course it was the president's veto that shut the government down; Congress had passed a budget to keep it going). Clinton won the public relations battle in the winter of 1995–96. But Republicans won on substance. The final budget for 1996 reduced domestic appropriations 9%, cutting some $53 billion from domestic discretionary spending. It reduced the deficit to about $100 billion.

Having done that, and with their popularity lower, Kasich and the Republicans concentrated on holding ground in 1996. He wanted to avoid another budget showdown and at the same time had no faith that Clinton was negotiating in good faith for a seven-year balanced budget. But Senate insistence on some $5 billion in spending increases meant that the 1997 budget Kasich presented to the House in June 1996 had both spending and deficit increases; conservatives balked, and only with intense lobbying was the leadership able to prevail 216–211. And Kasich initially balked at the maneuver that resulted in the biggest devolution of federal authority: he wanted to tie Medicaid cuts and welfare reform together, but other leaders, worried about Bob Dole's weakness in the polls, wanted to pass welfare reform alone. They prevailed in July 1996 and Bill Clinton, to the surprise of many, signed it in August. Other results include the line-item veto, small business tax cuts, and raising the Social Security earnings limit.

"Our budget efforts in Congress have been about sending your power and your money back to you in every city and town across America," Kasich said during the 1996 budget wars. They will surely continue into 1997 and 1998. Kasich seems to have no confidence in the promises of the Clinton Administration and he knows that the difficulty of curbing spending increases will be greater as we reach the outyears of the 1995–2002 seven-year period both sides set for balancing the budget. That will surely mean more Medicare reform and continued spending discipline: will Kasich and other Republicans have the nerve to continue, or will they treat their victory in 1996 as a defeat and let the Clinton Administration set the terms of argument and the levels of spending? He is keenly aware that Republicans will suffer if they cut programs for the poor and leave in place subsidies for the rich. And he will fight efforts like those of pork-barreling Infrastructure Chairman Bud Shuster to take large expenditures off-budget.

Kasich has been reelected by wide margins in the 12th District; Democrats took some comfort when they held him below 70%. His 1996 opponent attacked him for sharing a Washington house with a top staffer and asked for an accounting whether they shared the expenses 50–50; this attack backfired. Kasich was mentioned as a vice presidential candidate in 1996, and might have been an attractive one. He has also been mentioned as a Senate candidate. But he deferred to Mike DeWine, who ran and won in 1994, and he will surely support Governor George Voinovich for the Senate in 1998; Kasich is making his history in the House.

The People: Pop. 1990: 571,341; 15% rural; 9% age 65+; 74% White; 23% Black; 1% Asian; 1% Hispanic origin. Households: 52% married couple families; 26% married couple fams. w. children; 49% college educ.; median household income: $30,859; per capita income: $14,723; median gross rent: $417; median house value: $74,700.

1996 Presidential Vote		**1992 Presidential Vote**	
Clinton (D)	118,228 (47%)	Bush (R)	108,359 (41%)
Dole (R)	114,405 (46%)	Clinton (D)	105,852 (40%)
Perot (I)	16,426 (7%)	Perot (I)	47,080 (18%)

Rep. John R. Kasich (R)

Elected 1982; b. May 13, 1952, McKees Rocks, PA; home, Westerville; OH St. U., B.A. 1974; Christian; married (Karen).

Career: A.A., OH Sen. Donald Lukens, 1975–77; OH Senate, 1978–82.

DC Office: 1111 LHOB 20515, 202-225-5355.

District Offices: Columbus, 614-523-2555.

Committees: *Budget* (Chmn. of 24 R). *National Security* (4th of 30 R): Military Readiness; Military Research & Development.

Group Ratings

	ADA	ACLU	AFS	LCV	CFA	CON	NFIB	COC	ACU	NTLC	CHC
1996	15	6	0	31	46	78	97	94	95	100	100
1995	0	—	—	6	8	75	—	96	92	—	—

National Journal Ratings

	1995 LIB — 1995 CONS	1996 LIB — 1996 CONS
Economic	0% — 74%	20% — 76%
Social	0% — 79%	14% — 77%
Foreign	45% — 52%	0% — 79%

Key Votes of the 104th Congress

1. Reduce Medicare Growth $	Y	5. Flag Amendment	Y	9. Cuban Embargo	Y
2. Ovrd. Product Liab. Veto	Y	6. Drop EPA Limits	N	10. Bar Bosnia Troop $	Y
3. Increase Min. Wage	N	7. Repeal Assault-Weap. Ban	N	11. Cut Anti-Missile Defense	N
4. Welfare Reform	Y	8. Ovrd. Part. Birth Veto	Y	12. Bar U.N. Uniforms	Y

Election Results

1996 general	John R. Kasich (R)	151,667	(64%)	($1,578,812)
	Cynthia L. Ruccia (D)	78,762	(33%)	($273,184)
	Others	7,005	(3%)	
1996 primary	John R. Kasich (R)	47,107	(88%)	
	Ramona Whisler (R)	6,448	(12%)	
1994 general	John R. Kasich (R)	114,608	(67%)	($560,117)
	Cynthia L. Ruccia (D)	57,294	(33%)	($258,299)

THIRTEENTH DISTRICT

The imprint of the westward track of New England Yankee migration is still apparent today on the shores of Lake Erie in northern Ohio. The Yankees, cooped up in New England for 200 years, shot across the country through Upstate New York, west across Ohio and Michigan to Chicago, and then to Kansas and southern California in just two or three generations, providing inspiration, manpower and technical might for the Union victory in the Civil War, and leaving their impress along the way. One place they stopped was the Western Reserve, the northeast corner of Ohio along Lake Erie, created for the excess population of Connecticut, whose towns, colleges and cultural institutions were mostly established by Yankees. A prime example of Western Reserve Yankee-ism is Oberlin College, founded in 1832 as the first co-educational college in the world, though no women dared apply until 1837; it accepted black students a few years later, and the town of Oberlin became a center of the Underground Railroad. Or consider Hiram, home of another college and of James Garfield, who once represented the area in Congress when it was the most Republican part of Ohio, and who was the only president elected directly from the House, in 1880.

Politically, the lands of the Yankee diaspora, with their reformist ideas and dislike of slavery and the South, were naturally Republican territory. But the great masses of immigrants lured to Cleveland and the smaller industrial cities built by Yankee capital provided a base for labor unions and Progressive politics. After the New Deal and the bloody CIO organizing drives of the late 1930s, the Western Reserve had something like class-warfare politics for 30 years, with the Democrats usually winning. Northern Ohio, like New England, moved away from the Republicans and toward the Democrats. Now the Western Reserve may be moving toward a post-industrial economy as are Connecticut and Massachusetts. Factory employment has been falling, but total jobs are rising again; small, adaptive business units with highly skilled workers are the growth sectors. That leaves the Western Reserve, like New England, leaning Democratic—but not reliably so. Bill Clinton carried it in 1992 and 1996; but so did George Voinovich in 1990, and even more so in 1994, when it also favored Republican Mike DeWine over Democrat Joel Hyatt for senator.

The 13th Congressional District of Ohio is grotesquely shaped—something like a barbell—with two large segments of Western Reserve lands connected by a sort of land bridge between Cleveland and Akron. The western end includes the factory towns of Lorain and Elyria, plus Oberlin and Medina County, once rural and now filling up with outmigrants from Cleveland along I-71. The eastern, less heavily populated area includes all of Geauga County, high-income hilly townships with many reminders of New England origins, and rural parts of Trumbull and Portage Counties. This end of the district tends to vote Republican, while on the west end Lorain County is Democratic and Medina County Republican. This was an ungainly product of redistricting, represented until they retired in 1992 by two Democrats, Don Pease of Oberlin and Dennis Eckart of suburban Cleveland.

The congressman now is Sherrod Brown, one of the Democratic Party's remaining successful career politicians, who ran and won a seat in the state House the year he graduated from Yale, in 1974, and has never stopped running since. In 1982 he was elected secretary of state at 30 (while his brother, Charlie Brown, was elected attorney general of West Virginia) and worked hard to increase voter registration and turnout. He lost that office to Robert Taft in 1990, and Republican redistricters took care to keep Brown's home town of Mansfield outside the 13th. But in 1992 Brown moved into a rented lake cottage in Medina County and in the primary beat by 45%–22% a former aide to Cleveland Congresswoman Mary Rose Oakar. In the general Brown faced Republican Margaret Mueller, a millionaire social worker from Geauga County, who had run three times against Eckart. Brown showed great flair in the general election campaign, taking a 200-mile bicycle tour around the district; with solid labor support, he campaigned loud and hard against NAFTA and championed universal health care. Brown won

53%–35%, with 61% in Lorain County.

In the House Brown showed his usual political adeptness, winning a seat on the Commerce Committee. He supported the Clinton economic plan and supported a single-pay health care plan like that in Canada, across the Lake, but he did not sign onto the Clinton plan. On trade he was one of the most voluble liberal-labor members from the Great Lakes area attacking NAFTA and GATT. By fall 1994, Brown was relying on his work on local projects for local popularity. He had a serious Republican challenge in 1994, from Gregory White, Lorain County Prosecutor since 1980, who attacked him for raising taxes, opposing NAFTA and supporting the crime bill, and, as a Vietnam war hero, criticized Brown for attending Yale and studying in Russia. Brown won 49%–46%, with majorities in Lorain County and much of the east end of the district. This was one of several examples of a liberal-labor Democrat who survived because of business and labor PAC money: by mid-October White had outraised Brown in individual contributions, $400,000 to $269,000, but Brown had $571,000 in PAC contributions while White had $48,000.

Overall, Brown has one of the most liberal records in the House, though he did support the balanced budget amendment and line-item veto. From his election to the legislature at 21 until his statewide defeat in 1990, Brown was part of the majority, making public policy and benefiting from the perquisites of power. Now, as a junior member of the minority party, he has worked less on national issues than on local projects—a veterans' cemetery in Medina, a Coast Guard station on Lake Erie, an Export Assistance Center for Cleveland. He has supported federal guidelines for breast cancer treatment and called for an investigation of the sale of Blue Cross & Blue Shield of Ohio to hospital giant Columbia/HCA.

Against weak opposition he was easily reelected in 1996. He has been mentioned as a candidate for statewide office, but soon after John Glenn announced his retirement from the Senate, Brown declared "I absolutely am not interested in this race."

The People: Pop. 1990: 570,838; 36% rural; 11% age 65+; 92% White; 5% Black; 1% Asian; 3% Hispanic origin. Households: 66% married couple families; 32% married couple fams. w. children; 41% college educ.; median household income: $34,725; per capita income: $14,307; median gross rent: $403; median house value: $76,700.

1996 Presidential Vote

Clinton (D)	116,720	(46%)
Dole (R)	98,349	(39%)
Perot (I)	35,527	(14%)

1992 Presidential Vote

Clinton (D)	101,854	(38%)
Bush (R)	96,037	(35%)
Perot (I)	72,038	(27%)

Rep. Sherrod Brown (D)

Elected 1992; b. Nov. 9, 1952, Mansfield; home, Lorain; Yale U., B.A. 1974, OH St. U., M.A. 1979, M.A. 1981; Lutheran; divorced.

Career: OH House of Reps. 1974–82; Prof., Ohio State U. Mansfield, 1979–81; OH Secy. of State 1982–90.

DC Office: 328 CHOB 20515, 202-225-3401; Fax: 202-225-2266; e-mail: sherrod@hr.house.gov.

District Offices: Elyria, 216-934-5100; Medina, 330-722-9262; Middlefield, 216-632-5913.

Committees: *Commerce* (9th of 23 D): Energy & Power; Health & the Environment (RMM). *International Relations* (11th of 22 D): Asia & the Pacific.

Group Ratings

	ADA	ACLU	AFS	LCV	CFA	CON	NFIB	COC	ACU	NTLC	CHC
1996	95	88	92	92	100	85	35	13	0	20	13
1995	85	—	—	69	85	38	—	38	32	—	—

National Journal Ratings

	1995 LIB — 1995 CONS			1996 LIB — 1996 CONS		
Economic	70%	—	29%	85%	—	11%
Social	75%	—	23%	84%	—	12%
Foreign	79%	—	17%	86%	—	14%

Key Votes of the 104th Congress

1. Reduce Medicare Growth $	N	5. Flag Amendment	Y	9. Cuban Embargo	Y
2. Ovrd. Product Liab. Veto	N	6. Drop EPA Limits	Y	10. Bar Bosnia Troop $	N
3. Increase Min. Wage	Y	7. Repeal Assault-Weap. Ban	N	11. Cut Anti-Missile Defense	Y
4. Welfare Reform	N	8. Ovrd. Part. Birth Veto	N	12. Bar U.N. Uniforms	N

Election Results

1996 general	Sherrod Brown (D)	146,690	(60%)	($607,543)
	Kenneth C. Blair Jr. (R)	87,108	(36%)	($54,064)
	Others	8,707	(4%)	
1996 primary	Sherrod Brown (D)	unopposed		
1994 general	Sherrod Brown (D)	93,147	(49%)	($974,225)
	Gregory A. White (R)	86,422	(46%)	($570,331)
	Howard Mason (I)	7,777	(4%)	($11,593)

FOURTEENTH DISTRICT

Akron is the center of what at least some Ohioans today call the Polymer Valley, and formerly was known as Rubber Town. (Akron itself comes from the Greek word for high, the same root as Acropolis, because the city sits on a ridge between the Great Lakes and Mississippi watersheds.) Twenty years ago, Akron was as synonymous with tires as Detroit was with cars: Firestone, Goodyear, General Tire, and B. F. Goodrich all had their headquarters and big tire factories here; the United Rubber Workers had been the big union since the 1930s. But after the oil shocks of the 1970s, Akron's antiquated auto tire plants were closed, and the last truck and airplane tire plants closed in 1984 and 1985; several big firms were sold to out-of-town companies, though Goodyear remains as a leading employer. Akron began specializing in polymers, plastics and other hydrocarbons that can be formed or shaped like rubber into useful industrial products. The first polymer, polyvinyl chloride (PVC), was invented in 1926 when B. F. Goodrich chemist Waldo Semon, looking to make synthetic rubber, found a mysterious goo in the bottom of his test tube; the company did not bother to patent it until 1933, but now PVC is everywhere, in pipes and siding and shoes and toys and car tops and stadium covers. Polymers were a natural extension of the rubber companies' business, and now the Akron area and the Cuyahoga Valley north to Cleveland are called Polymer Valley. Ohio ships more plastic resins than any other state but Texas and employs more people in the field than any other state but California.

This change in the local economy has had political effects. Akron's population is largely descended from migrants from Eastern Europe and, especially, West Virginia, who thronged here in the 1910s and 1920s to snap up jobs in the tire factories for 10 or 12 hours a day at the price of smelling burning rubber for 24. In the 1930s, these people joined the new United Rubber Workers and started voting Democratic; they were courted in turn by Republicans with blue collar backgrounds fielded by local Republican Chairman Ray Bliss, who was also

Republican National chairman in the 1950s and 1960s. But as the smell of rubber vanished from Akron's air, the language of class conflict had mostly passed from its politics. Now Akron has more flexible businesses and a more upscale work force, and while greater Akron sometimes votes heavily Democratic, it can vote Republican as well.

Ohio's 14th Congressional District has long been made up of Akron and surrounding Summit County, with some variation in district boundaries; currently it also includes the area around Kent (and Kent State University) just to the east. The current congressman, Tom Sawyer, has spent most of his adult life in public office: he was elected to the state House in 1976, at 31, became mayor of Akron in 1984, and was elected in the 14th District when the incumbent retired in 1986. In that election and in 1994, he faced tough competition from Summit County Prosecutor Lynn Slaby.

In his first decade in the House, Sawyer had a mostly liberal voting record, ranking second to Speaker Thomas Foley in party loyalty in the 103d Congress and supporting Bill Clinton on some tough votes in the 104th. He denounced the Republicans loudly ("the Republican bill would balance the budget by unbalancing the nation," he said in October 1995) but also made some bipartisan initiatives. One was successful: with Ohio Republican David Hobson, he sponsored a common standard for electronic transmission of healthcare billing information, which was included in the healthcare bill passed in 1996. Another was stopped: a so-called CAREERS bipartisan reorganization of job training programs. On welfare reform he supported the bipartisan approach of Mike Castle and John Tanner. He joined The Coalition, a group of moderate Democrats, but not the mostly southern Blue Dogs. Representing a district where organized labor was historically strong, Sawyer does not necessarily vote the union line. After much public agonizing, he supported NAFTA in November 1993; as a result, he had opposition in the 1994 primary from plumber Kenneth Mack, whom he beat 69%–31%. In 1996 he did not oppose the Republicans' team worker bill outright, as unions did, but proposed an amendment asserting workers' right to independent representation.

Sawyer had seniority on the Education and The Workforce Committee, where he worked on literacy bills and federal aid formulas; in 1995 he urged colleagues to resist any cuts in federal education spending. In 1997 he got a seat on Commerce, where he is likely to focus on telecommunications issues and the efficiencies of utility services.

In 1994 Sawyer was one of the few Midwestern Democrats to welcome Bill Clinton in to campaign; whether he helped or hurt, Sawyer beat Slaby by 52%–48%, with most of the margin from Kent's Portage County rather than Akron's Summit County. In 1996 Republicans targeted the seat and touted their candidate, former Judge Joyce George. But this time Sawyer's closeness to Clinton may have paid off. Clinton carried the 14th by a wide margin, and Sawyer won 54%–42%. The question now is whether this talented politician who has been in elective office most of his adult life can find satisfaction and accomplishments in the minority party.

The People: Pop. 1990: 570,987; 8% rural; 13% age 65+; 87% White; 11% Black; 1% Asian; 1% Hispanic origin. Households: 55% married couple families; 24% married couple fams. w. children; 44% college educ.; median household income: $28,184; per capita income: $13,931; median gross rent: $394; median house value: $59,800.

1996 Presidential Vote

Clinton (D)	121,635	(53%)
Dole (R)	76,083	(33%)
Perot (I)	30,312	(13%)

1992 Presidential Vote

Clinton (D)	118,715	(45%)
Bush (R)	81,232	(31%)
Perot (I)	60,000	(23%)

Rep. Tom Sawyer (D)

Elected 1986; b. Aug. 15, 1945, Akron; home, Akron; U. of Akron, B.A. 1968, M.A. 1970; Presbyterian; married (Joyce).

Career: OH House of Reps., 1976–82; Akron Mayor, 1984–86.

DC Office: 1414 LHOB 20515, 202-225-5231; Fax: 202-225-5278.

District Offices: Akron, 330-375-5710; Ravenna, 330-296-9810.

Committees: *Commerce* (18th of 23 D): Finance & Hazardous Materials; Oversight & Investigations; Telecommunications, Trade & Consumer Protection.

Group Ratings

	ADA	ACLU	AFS	LCV	CFA	CON	NFIB	COC	ACU	NTLC	CHC
1996	90	62	92	92	92	94	24	25	0	13	7
1995	95	—	—	81	100	31	—	29	0	—	—

National Journal Ratings

	1995 LIB — 1995 CONS			1996 LIB — 1996 CONS		
Economic	80%	—	18%	73%	—	25%
Social	88%	—	0%	79%	—	18%
Foreign	79%	—	17%	75%	—	24%

Key Votes of the 104th Congress

1. Reduce Medicare Growth $	N	5. Flag Amendment	N	9. Cuban Embargo	N
2. Ovrd. Product Liab. Veto	N	6. Drop EPA Limits	Y	10. Bar Bosnia Troop $	N
3. Increase Min. Wage	Y	7. Repeal Assault-Weap. Ban	N	11. Cut Anti-Missile Defense	Y
4. Welfare Reform	N	8. Ovrd. Part. Birth Veto	N	12. Bar U.N. Uniforms	N

Election Results

1996 general	Tom Sawyer (D)	124,136	(54%)	($523,412)
	Joyce George (R)	95,307	(42%)	($279,210)
	Others	8,992	(4%)	
1996 primary	Tom Sawyer (D)	32,024	(80%)	
	Ken Mack (D)	4,350	(11%)	
	John B. Nicholas (D)	3,831	(10%)	
1994 general	Tom Sawyer (D)	96,274	(52%)	($595,448)
	Lynn Slaby (R)	89,106	(48%)	($256,758)

FIFTEENTH DISTRICT

Columbus, smack in the center of Ohio, was founded in 1812 to be the state capital. By the early 20th Century it became a regional mid-sized city and, in the last couple of decades, has become the center of a major metropolitan area, and headquarters to major research centers like the Batelle Memorial Institute and Ohio State University, to financial powers like Nationwide Insurance and Banc One, and to retailers like The Limited and fast food chains like Wendy's. Its flat-domed Capitol at Broad and High, with the statue of William McKinley out front, is surrounded by high-rises, public and private, while the city grows out in all directions into the countryside.

Ohio's 15th Congressional District is made up of most of Columbus, all but the east side, plus southern and western Franklin County and rural Madison County directly to the west. The 15th includes most of Columbus's black population, some white working-class areas on the south side of the city and in nearby Grove City, and the Ohio State University campus area. Politically, these Democratic areas are more than balanced by the heavily Republican suburb of Upper Arlington, across the Olentangy River from Ohio State, and by Republican subdivisions sprouting up in rural land between the old villages.

The 15th District is represented in the House by Deborah Pryce, a Republican first elected in 1992. Pryce graduated from law school in Columbus in 1976, worked in state government and as a city prosecutor, and became an elective municipal court judge in 1985. In 1992, when incumbent Chalmers Wylie retired after 26 years, Pryce ran for the office. She was unopposed in the primary but had tough competition in the general, from Democrat Richard Cordray and from pro-life Independent Linda Reidelbach, who became angry when Pryce announced after the primary she would support a Freedom of Choice Act which would restrict states' power to limit abortions. Pryce talked much about congressional reform—term limits, rotating chairmanships, line-item veto—and called for limiting spending increases to 3%. She won with 44% of the vote to Cordray's 38% and Reidelbach's 18%.

In the House Pryce has been pretty conservative on economic and foreign issues, sometimes liberal on cultural matters. She was elected interim president of her freshman Republican class, cast votes in fall 1993 against the Superconducting Supercollider and for the Penny-Kasich spending cuts. She supported term limits, the balanced budget amendment, and the line-item veto. She has served on the Rules Committee since 1995, and on the subcommittee handling legislative reforms and budget procedures. She is "on leave with seniority" from the Banking Committee, and on Rules played a key role in April 1996 in siding with banks to block a plan, backed by the administration and the Republican leadership, to shore up a thrift insurance fund. Perhaps Pryce's greatest cause is reform of the Indian Child Welfare Act governing outside-the-tribe adoptions. She was prompted by the case of a Columbus couple whose adoption of twins was challenged after four years because the father had, despite his assurance otherwise, Indian blood; the children, he said, were 3/32 Indian and must be turned back to him. Other adoptions have been voided and children sent back to the tribe to live in foster care. Pryce would exempt from the ICWA children whose parents had no significant affiliation with the tribe. In May 1996 she prevailed 212–195 against an Indian-tribe-backed amendment sponsored by Don Young of Alaska; but her version was changed in the Senate by Indian Affairs Committee Chairman John McCain, and the two were not reconciled. Pryce promises to return to the issue in 1997.

Pryce has won reelection easily, by identical 71%–29% margins in 1994 and 1996, defeating a lawyer that focused on campaign reform in 1996. In June 1997, Pryce announced she would run for Republican Conference secretary, as leadership positions opened up following the retirement of Conference Vice Chair Susan Molinari.

The People: Pop. 1990: 570,740; 10% rural; 10% age 65+; 92% White; 5% Black; 2% Asian; 1% Hispanic origin. Households: 52% married couple families; 24% married couple fams. w. children; 51% college educ.; median household income: $31,020; per capita income: $15,076; median gross rent: $438; median house value: $73,000.

1996 Presidential Vote

Dole (R)	114,183	(48%)
Clinton (D)	105,947	(44%)
Perot (I)	17,324	(7%)

1992 Presidential Vote

Bush (R)	119,588	(45%)
Clinton (D)	94,232	(35%)
Perot (I)	52,316	(20%)

Rep. Deborah Pryce (R)

Elected 1992; b. July 29, 1951, Warren; home, Columbus; Ohio State U., B.A. 1973, Capital U. Law Schl., J.D. 1976; Presbyterian; married (Randy Walker).

Career: Admin. Law Judge, OH Dept. of Insurance, 1976; Sr. Asst. Columbus City Prosecutor, 1978; Franklin Cnty. Munic. Court Judge, 1985–1992; Practicing atty., 1992.

DC Office: 221 CHOB 20515, 202-225-2015; e-mail: pryce15@hr.house.gov.

District Offices: Columbus, 614-469-5614.

Committees: *Rules* (5th of 9 R): Legislative & Budget Process.

Group Ratings

	ADA	ACLU	AFS	LCV	CFA	CON	NFIB	COC	ACU	NTLC	CHC
1996	5	6	0	38	23	69	100	94	85	98	73
1995	10	—	—	13	15	56	—	100	72	—	—

National Journal Ratings

	1995 LIB — 1995 CONS			1996 LIB — 1996 CONS		
Economic	0%	—	74%	37%	—	61%
Social	51%	—	49%	55%	—	43%
Foreign	28%	—	65%	0%	—	79%

Key Votes of the 104th Congress

1. Reduce Medicare Growth $	Y	5. Flag Amendment	Y	9. Cuban Embargo	Y
2. Ovrd. Product Liab. Veto	Y	6. Drop EPA Limits	Y	10. Bar Bosnia Troop $	Y
3. Increase Min. Wage	N	7. Repeal Assault-Weap. Ban	N	11. Cut Anti-Missile Defense	N
4. Welfare Reform	Y	8. Ovrd. Part. Birth Veto	Y	12. Bar U.N. Uniforms	Y

Election Results

1996 general	Deborah Pryce (R)	156,776	(71%)	($384,780)
	Cliff Arnebeck (D)	64,665	(29%)	($9,629)
1996 primary	Deborah Pryce (R)	35,034	(86%)	
	Craig V. Lortz (R)	5,920	(14%)	
1994 general	Deborah Pryce (R)	112,912	(71%)	($443,007)
	Bill Buckel (D)	46,480	(29%)	

SIXTEENTH DISTRICT

A century ago Canton, Ohio, was at the center of American politics. Canton was already an industrial city then, though not with the huge steel factories being built in Youngstown or Cleveland; its high-skill workers were fashioning new kinds of plows and reapers and making watches and, beginning in 1899, roller bearings. Canton did not attract masses of immigrants; its factories did not run on harsh stopwatch discipline; there was none of the class-warfare politics here that would be seen later in other northern Ohio industrial cities. Instead, Canton was united a century ago in admiring its first citizen, William McKinley, who rose to the rank of major at 22 in the Civil War, was elected congressman and governor, and was chairman of the House Ways and Means Committee. As the Republican candidate for president in 1896, McKinley conducted his campaign from his front porch in Canton, meeting with delegations brought in by train from all over the country. This spectacle, with its display of technological virtuosity and personal modesty, sounds an appealing and reverberating note in American politics, as does the McKinley platform—the "full dinner pail," the gold standard, the enforcement of law and order in labor relations—which had long been seen as antiquated but still provides useful instruction.

Canton a century later is no longer at the center of American politics, though Canton and surrounding Stark County, which have voted much like the nation as a whole for the last 30 years, were the subject of a year-long series of stories by Michael Winerip in *The New York Times*. What he found was a community still based on manufacturing—mostly high-skill, with companies like Timken, Diebold, Republic Engineered Steels, and Hoover—economically prosperous but uneasy because of downsizing and decisions by some local companies to build new plants elsewhere, politically ambivalent about both major party candidates, worried about the young House Republicans but mostly opposed to old liberal Democrats. Stark County turned out to be not quite a bellwether: in 1992 the 46%–38%–15% Clinton margin was the same as nationally, but in 1996 Bill Clinton and Bob Dole each ran 3% behind and Ross Perot 6% ahead of their national percentages.

The 16th Congressional District of Ohio includes all of Stark County, plus three-and-a-half more Republican counties to the west: Wayne, site of the College of Wooster and the headquarters of Rubbermaid; Holmes, with its Amish communities; and Ashland and part of Knox. The district has been mostly Republican since McKinley's time, and has elected only Republican congressmen since 1950.

The congressman from the 16th is Ralph Regula, first elected in 1972 and one of the senior Republicans in the House. He grew up in outer Stark County, the son of a farmer and coal mine operator; he served in the Navy in World War II, worked his way through the William McKinley School of Law teaching school, and was elected to the Ohio legislature in 1964, just before turning 40. When the incumbent retired in 1972, he ran for the House and was easily elected. He is a senior member of Appropriations, and became ranking Republican on the Interior Subcommittee in 1985; since 1994 he has been chairman. That subcommittee serves as a counterweight to the Resources Committee, chaired by Don Young of Alaska and with many western Republicans who resent federal management of and restriction on their lands; Regula, with a middle-of-the-House voting record, is more supportive of environmental regulations. He has long sought to reform the Mining Act of 1872 and is an advocate of higher grazing fees—positions that infuriate the westerners—though he is dubious about some Clean Air provisions and bans on offshore oil drilling. After the 1994 election, some conservatives wanted to keep Regula out of the subcommittee chairmanship, but Newt Gingrich saw that he got the job; he was, however, passed over for full committee chairman for the more junior Bob Livingston. In 1995, he was one of 51 Republicans who voted against the Contract With America restrictions on EPA enforcement powers.

The 1995 Interior Appropriations bill stirred much controversy. It cut increases in spending on the National Endowment for the Arts—a source of principled controversy far out of proportion to the dollars it spends—and banned restrictions on the Tongass National Forest in Alaska and the Mohave desert in California. But eventually, after a Clinton veto, it was passed shorn of some of these provisions. In 1996 Regula tried to avoid controversy, but had to work hard to meet overall spending cut goals. The solution was to cut deeply into energy research and land acquisition; Regula believes it is more important to properly fund current parks rather than to designate new ones. To that he makes some exception. One was for Everglades restoration, which was generously funded, and is important to the 15 Florida House Republicans. Another was for the Ohio and Erie Canal Heritage Corridor, which he finally succeeded in authorizing in the omnibus parks bill in October 1996. Nor does Regula forget McKinley: every Congress he introduces a bill to name Alaska's highest peak Mount McKinley, despite efforts to rename it Denali, the Indian-inspired name of the surrounding park.

Regula has been reelected by wide margins. For the 105th Congress he wants federal aid to develop "brownfield" industrial sites and seeks renegotiation of NAFTA to correct for trade imbalances and currency differentials.

The People: Pop. 1990: 570,705; 37% rural; 14% age 65+; 94% White; 5% Black; 1% Hispanic origin. Households: 62% married couple families; 29% married couple fams. w. children; 33% college educ.; median household income: $27,524; per capita income: $12,413; median gross rent: $353; median house value: $58,000.

1996 Presidential Vote

Clinton (D)	100,293	(43%)
Dole (R)	98,786	(42%)
Perot (I)	33,255	(14%)

1992 Presidential Vote

Bush (R)	98,824	(39%)
Clinton (D)	95,157	(37%)
Perot (I)	60,639	(24%)

Rep. Ralph S. Regula (R)

Elected 1972; b. Dec. 3, 1924, Beach City; home, Navarre; Mt. Union Col., B.A. 1948, William McKinley Schl. of Law, LL.B. 1952; Episcopalian; married (Mary).

Career: Navy, 1944–46 (WWII); Teacher and schl. principal, 1948–52; Practicing atty., 1952–73; OH Bd. of Educ., 1960–64; OH House of Reps., 1964–66; OH Senate, 1966–72.

DC Office: 2309 RHOB 20515, 202-225-3876; Fax: 202-225-3059.

District Offices: Canton, 330-489-4414.

Committees: *Appropriations* (4th of 34 R): Commerce, Justice, State & Judiciary; Interior (Chmn.); Transportation.

Group Ratings

	ADA	ACLU	AFS	LCV	CFA	CON	NFIB	COC	ACU	NTLC	CHC
1996	15	6	17	38	15	55	92	81	75	95	73
1995	10	—	—	31	23	56	—	100	71	—	—

National Journal Ratings

	1995 LIB — 1995 CONS			1996 LIB — 1996 CONS		
Economic	26%	—	67%	50%	—	49%
Social	45%	—	54%	40%	—	59%
Foreign	45%	—	52%	41%	—	56%

Key Votes of the 104th Congress

1. Reduce Medicare Growth $	Y	5. Flag Amendment	Y	9. Cuban Embargo	Y
2. Ovrd. Product Liab. Veto	Y	6. Drop EPA Limits	Y	10. Bar Bosnia Troop $	Y
3. Increase Min. Wage	Y	7. Repeal Assault-Weap. Ban	Y	11. Cut Anti-Missile Defense	N
4. Welfare Reform	Y	8. Ovrd. Part. Birth Veto	Y	12. Bar U.N. Uniforms	Y

Election Results

1996 general	Ralph S. Regula (R)	159,314	(69%)	($154,379)
	Thomas E. Buckhart (D)	64,902	(28%)	($3,552)
	Others	7,611	(3%)	
1996 primary	Ralph S. Regula (R)	54,606	(84%)	
	Vince Yambrovich (R)	10,576	(16%)	
1994 general	Ralph S. Regula (R)	137,322	(75%)	($120,279)
	J. Michael Finn (D)	45,781	(25%)	

SEVENTEENTH DISTRICT

On a relief map the Mahoning River is just a thin line in the lowlands of eastern Ohio. But on an economic map it is, or was, one of the major waterways of the United States. For the Mahoning was one of America's prime steel valleys. The first coal mine here opened in 1826, canals followed, and in 1892 the first steel mill was built in Youngstown. "Soon," writes historian Harlan Hatcher, "the banks of the river were lined with Bessemer converters, open-hearth furnaces, strip and rolling mills, pipe plants, and manufacturers of steel accessories and products." For nearly a century, the Mahoning Valley, centered on Youngstown, between the Lake Erie docks that unload iron ore from Great Lakes freighters and the coalfields of western Pennsylvania and West Virginia, was one of the steel capitals of the United States. Now, in the late 20th Century, the steel mills stand empty and smokeless and silent—except those that have been dynamited and torn down. Big steel management allowed foreign producers to gain a technological edge back in the 1950s and 1960s; worldwide overcapacity in steel grew as almost every developing country decided it needed its own steel mills, while cooperation between the United Steelworkers and management after the 119-day strike in 1959 boosted wages and fringe benefits to price domestic steel out of the market. Import restrictions kept the furnaces hot for a while, but the oil shock of 1979 produced sharply higher energy prices and a collapse in the U.S. auto and steel market. Every plant in Youngstown and the Mahoning Valley closed and in the early 1980s metro Youngstown—Mahoning and Trumbull Counties—had one of the nation's highest unemployment rates.

Steel has since revived, but elsewhere: in decentralized minimills or in huge new rolling plants in northern Indiana. The biggest business headquartered in Youngstown is not steel, but the shopping center empire of Edward DeBartolo. The high-wage standard of living of the 1970s has vanished; young people looking for opportunities routinely leave; population has declined. Politically, the Mahoning Valley writhed in anger. Republican in the 1920s, solidly Democratic for years after the United Steelworkers organized the plants following sometimes bloody skirmishes in the late 1930s, the area wobbled toward Republicans in the Carter 1970s, and now has become one of the most Democratic parts of the country in the Reagan 1980s and the Clinton 1990s.

The 17th Congressional District of Ohio includes all of the Mahoning Valley, running south from Youngstown to the Ohio River across from West Virginia and north past Warren halfway to Lake Erie. The congressman from the 17th is a Democrat who speaks in the authentic demotic accents of the Mahoning Valley. James Traficant is loud and angry and earthy—and, in his own way, creative and consistent and compassionate. Traficant grew up in Mahoning County, directed a drug program from 1971–81, and was elected Mahoning County Sheriff in 1980, where he met controversy. He admitted taking large bribes from mobsters to overlook gambling, loan-sharking, drug trafficking and prostitution in Mahoning County and argued, when presented with tapes of some of these transactions, that this was part of his own sting operation. He was tried on criminal charges in 1983 and, acting as his own lawyer, he persuaded the jury to find him not guilty. In 1984 he ran against a Republican incumbent and won 53%–46%.

Traficant has a middle-of-the-House voting record, but a distinctive one: like Youngstown Republicans of the 1920s he is protectionist and isolationist; he is vitriolically opposed to aid to Israel and to NAFTA and GATT; he has been a harsh critic of "lying, thieving, stealing CIA nincompoops." He is familiar to C-SPAN viewers for his loud speeches—tirades, some say—against foreign aid, free trade, the Federal Reserve and the oppression visited on citizens by the Internal Revenue Service. But he also has some accomplishments. His "Made in America" amendments, which he offers to all spending legislation, often pass. He has advanced his Taxpayer Bill of Rights measures by such tactics as standing on the floor for 10 hours and raising points of order against every section of the Treasury bill. He amended the crime bill to require a net gain in street cops, amended an immigration bill to require monitoring of federal efforts to stop illegal immigration, and amended the Taxpayer Bill of Rights to impose penalties on IRS agent misconduct of up to $1 million. He joined 14 Republicans and Patrick Buchanan to hail Michael New, the soldier court-martialed for refusing to wear the United Nations insignia: "He like Rosa Parks and other people in our history, took a stand."

Traficant has also secured a raft of local projects for the Youngstown area, from a $13 million air cargo facility to restoring Amtrak service to Youngstown. Some of his other proposals remain unenacted, and perhaps always will be—a flat tax bill coupled with a consumption tax, an 800 number for information on American-made products, a ban on bareheaded boxing, public meetings of the Federal Reserve Open Market Committee. Loud and abrasive on the floor, he is one of the kindest and most thoughtful members to House employees and pages.

Traficant survived redistricting nicely in 1992. His district could have been carved up, but evidently no one wanted to take him on. His popularity was such that in 1988, when he ran in the Ohio presidential primary, he won 18% of the vote in the 17th District, running just behind Jesse Jackson.

The People: Pop. 1990: 570,963; 26% rural; 16% age 65+; 88% White; 10% Black; 1% Hispanic origin. Households: 58% married couple families; 25% married couple fams. w. children; 33% college educ.; median household income: $25,220; per capita income: $11,938; median gross rent: $337; median house value: $48,400.

1996 Presidential Vote			**1992 Presidential Vote**		
Clinton (D)	142,121	(58%)	Clinton (D)	131,983	(50%)
Dole (R)	67,705	(28%)	Bush (R)	67,858	(26%)
Perot (I)	31,494	(13%)	Perot (I)	64,339	(24%)

Rep. James A. Traficant, Jr. (D)

Elected 1984; b. May 8, 1941, Youngstown; home, Poland; U. of Pittsburgh, B.S. 1963; Youngstown St. U., M.S. 1973, M.S. 1976; Catholic; married (Patricia).

Career: Dir., Mahoning Cnty. Drug Program, 1971–81; Mahoning Cnty. Sheriff, 1980–85.

DC Office: 2446 RHOB 20515, 202-225-5261; Fax: 202-225-3719; e-mail: telljim@hr.house.gov.

District Offices: Youngstown, 330-743-1914; Niles, 330-652-5649; E. Liverpool, 330-385-5921.

Committees: *Science* (4th of 21 D): Space & Aeronautics. *Transportation & Infrastructure* (6th of 33 D): Aviation; Public Buildings & Economic Development (RMM).

Group Ratings

	ADA	ACLU	AFS	LCV	CFA	CON	NFIB	COC	ACU	NTLC	CHC
1996	55	31	67	77	15	0	62	44	50	51	46
1995	55	—	—	38	15	0	—	63	48	—	—

National Journal Ratings

	1995 LIB — 1995 CONS			1996 LIB — 1996 CONS		
Economic	60%	—	39%	60%	—	40%
Social	53%	—	47%	52%	—	47%
Foreign	54%	—	45%	41%	—	56%

Key Votes of the 104th Congress

1. Reduce Medicare Growth $	N	5. Flag Amendment	Y	9. Cuban Embargo	Y
2. Ovrd. Product Liab. Veto	N	6. Drop EPA Limits	N	10. Bar Bosnia Troop $	Y
3. Increase Min. Wage	Y	7. Repeal Assault-Weap. Ban	N	11. Cut Anti-Missile Defense	Y
4. Welfare Reform	Y	8. Ovrd. Part. Birth Veto	Y	12. Bar U.N. Uniforms	Y

Election Results

1996 general	James A. Traficant, Jr. (D)	218,283	(91%)	($156,597)
	James M. Cahaney (NL)	21,685	(9%)	
1996 primary	James A. Traficant, Jr. (D)	unopposed		
1994 general	James A. Traficant, Jr. (D)	149,004	(77%)	($145,793)
	Mike G. Meister (R)	43,490	(23%)	($8,522)

EIGHTEENTH DISTRICT

From their earliest settlement in the 1790s, the hills of east central Ohio have been industrial country. The local clay was used to make pottery, the coal that lies near the surface was dug up, a green vitriol works was built, and a nail factory went into operation, all before 1814. For more than 100 years, this area has been part of the great coal and steel belt that centers on Pittsburgh and Cleveland and stretches from the coal mines of West Virginia to Lake Erie, the destination of Great Lakes freighters filled with iron ore from Minnesota's Mesabi Range. This area is filled with small cities, each with its little steel mill or factory, most of them old towns whose storefronts and wooden, working-class houses bear the unmistakable imprint of the early 20th Century. For a time the pay was good, but after the oil shock of 1979, the coal and steel economy went into collapse; the impact here was cushioned by continuing demand for coal from electric utilities, but that threatens to be reduced by the 1990 Clean Air Act. Wage levels have sagged and the hopes many had of getting ahead have been disappointed.

The 18th Congressional District of Ohio covers much of this land along the Ohio River, just west of West Virginia, and spreads west over hilly farmland pockmarked by strip mines, from Steubenville on the Ohio, which used to have the nation's worst air quality, to New Rumley, the birthplace of General Custer, and Zanesville, the birthplace of writer Zane Grey and architect Cass Gilbert and home of a famous Y-shaped bridge, and Newark—almost all the way across the old National Road and U.S. 40 to Columbus. As one goes west, the territory is less industrial, but overall the 18th is, sociologically and politically, a kind of ethnic working-class neighborhood. For 40 years since the New Deal and World War II, it has leaned Democratic in most elections.

The congressman from the 18th District is Bob Ney, a Republican elected in 1994 and reelected in 1996 in this Democratic territory. Ney grew up in Belleaire, just across the Ohio from Wheeling, West Virginia, worked as a teacher and safety director for the city of Belleaire, was elected to the state House in 1980, at 26, in quite an upset, beating Wayne Hays, the and longtime (1948–76) congressman from the 18th and power in the House who lost his seat due to scandal in 1976 and then won a state House seat in 1978. Ney lost that seat in the Democratic year of 1982, but in 1984 was elected to the state Senate. There, he backed a bill encouraging electric power plants to install scrubbers so they could use high-sulfur Ohio coal and sponsored a bill to help people get or keep health insurance. When Douglas Applegate, the practical-minded Democrat who had replaced Hays, announced he would not run again in 1994, Ney ran for Congress, giving up his chair of the Finance Committee in Columbus. Democrats had a serious primary, in which state Representative Greg DiDonato beat Applegate aide James Hart 49%–36%; 1994 was not a good year to have Capitol Hill connections. DiDonato criticized Ney for accepting honoraria from lobbyists; Ney criticized DiDonato for sharing an apartment with a cable TV lobbyist. Most unions backed DiDonato, except for teachers' unions who backed ex-teacher Ney. Ney's home base of Belmont County turned out to be the key; only 35% for Republican Senate candidate Mike DeWine, it voted 67% for Ney, enough to clinch a 54%–46% victory.

In the House Ney made a record that was often at odds with the Republican leadership and clearly aimed at the folks back home. His voting record was moderate or even conservative, especially on cultural issues. His first legislative action came on the House Oversight Committee, where he moved to cut each member's mail allowance by one-third. He worked successfully to prevent the zeroing out of the Appalachian Regional Commission and the Development Disabilities Councils. He removed language eliminating the reachback provisions of the Coal Industry Retiree Health Benefits Act, to make former employers pay for retirees' health care. He worked for criminal penalties for disarming a federal law enforcement officer and Internet access for schools and libraries. He helped organized labor by amending the transportation appropriations to protect the bargaining rights of unionized bus drivers. With Ohio neighbor Frank Cremeans, he stopped additional land purchases by the Wayne National Forest. With Joe Kennedy, he barred from elderly public housing those "disabled" whose only disability is alcohol or drug abuse. With John Kasich, he toughened work requirements for able-bodied food stamp recipients under 50. He worked for construction of the Pike Island Project hydroelectric dam on the Ohio River. He fought against what he called EPA's "overregulation" under the Clean Air Act, and voted to cut the EPA budget by one-third and to stop EPA from making policy by rule-making.

Ney was opposed by state Senator Robert Burch, a favorite of organized labor and the 1994 Democratic nominee who won 25% against Governor George Voinovich. Burch brought up the honoraria issue from 1994 (after an investigation, other legislators, but not Ney, were indicted in February 1996) and otherwise tried to make the election a referendum on Newt Gingrich. But Ney's pro-labor record got him the NEA endorsement and kept him from being an AFL-CIO target. Ney did not run so well in Belmont County this time, but he did gain ground in the west and in Tuscarawas County, south of Canton, enough for a 50%–46% win, even as Bob Dole was losing badly in the district. "I have defied the odds for years," Ney proclaimed, and so he has; though quite possibly Democrats will target this district again.

The People: Pop. 1990: 570,784; 60% rural; 15% age 65+; 97% White; 2% Black. Households: 61% married couple families; 28% married couple fams. w. children; 25% college educ.; median household income: $22,808; per capita income: $10,531; median gross rent: $298; median house value: $44,000.

1996 Presidential Vote			1992 Presidential Vote		
Clinton (D)	112,851	(47%)	Clinton (D)	110,491	(43%)
Dole (R)	86,305	(36%)	Bush (R)	87,512	(34%)
Perot (I)	36,143	(15%)	Perot (I)	58,605	(23%)

Rep. Bob Ney (R)

Elected 1994; b. July 5, 1954, Wheeling, WV; home, St. Clairsville; OH St. U., B.S. 1976; Catholic; divorced.

Career: Teacher, Iran, 1978; Bellaire Safety Dir.; OH House of Reps., 1980–82; OH Senate, 1984–94.

DC Office: 1024 LHOB 20515, 202-225-6265; Fax: 202-225-3394; e-mail: bobney@hr.house.gov.

District Offices: Bellaire, 614-676-1960; New Philadelphia, 330-364-6380; Steubenville, 614-283-3716; Zanesville, 614-452-7023.

Committees: *Banking & Financial Services* (14th of 30 R): Domestic & International Monetary Policy; General Oversight & Investigations; Housing & Community Opportunity (Vice Chmn.). *House Oversight* (2nd of 6 R). *Transportation & Infrastructure* (25th of 40 R): Surface Transportation; Water Resources & Environment. *Joint Committee on the Library of Congress* (2nd of 5 Reps.). *Joint Committee on Printing* (2nd of 5 Reps.).

Group Ratings

	ADA	ACLU	AFS	LCV	CFA	CON	NFIB	COC	ACU	NTLC	CHC
1996	10	12	17	23	15	30	92	88	85	100	93
1995	10	—	—	0	8	75	—	88	84	—	—

National Journal Ratings

	1995 LIB — 1995 CONS			1996 LIB — 1996 CONS		
Economic	44%	—	53%	39%	—	58%
Social	0%	—	79%	29%	—	68%
Foreign	28%	—	65%	47%	—	52%

Key Votes of the 104th Congress

1. Reduce Medicare Growth $	Y	5. Flag Amendment	Y	9. Cuban Embargo	Y
2. Ovrd. Product Liab. Veto	Y	6. Drop EPA Limits	N	10. Bar Bosnia Troop $	Y
3. Increase Min. Wage	Y	7. Repeal Assault-Weap. Ban	Y	11. Cut Anti-Missile Defense	N
4. Welfare Reform	Y	8. Ovrd. Part. Birth Veto	Y	12. Bar U.N. Uniforms	Y

Election Results

1996 general	Bob Ney (R)	117,365	(50%)	($879,110)
	Robert L. Burch, Jr. (D)	108,332	(46%)	($263,417)
	Others	8,146	(3%)	
1996 primary	Bob Ney (R)	unopposed		
1994 general	Bob Ney (R)	103,115	(54%)	($600,426)
	Greg A. DiDonato (D)	87,926	(46%)	($434,905)

NINETEENTH DISTRICT

The Western Reserve—the northeast corner of Ohio that belonged to Connecticut until 1800—still bears a distinctive New England Yankee imprint. This land was on the direct westward trail of Yankee settlement in the years before the Civil War; here, amid the low hills which produced the steel streams of the Cuyahoga and the Mahoning, they established New England-style townships, churches and schools. This area produced some of the strongest opposition to slavery and support of the Union armies and the Republican Party in the nation. Its thrifty, hard-working, well-educated citizens built communities with fine schools and, with their accumulated savings, invested in what became some of the nation's leading industries. That brought great masses of immigrants to Cleveland and the other cities of northeast Ohio, which remained solidly Republican until the Great Depression and the bloody CIO organizing drives of the late 1930s; then, for 30 years, the Western Reserve was Democratic during Ohio's class-warfare politics. In the early 1980s, when the auto and steel industries lost thousands of jobs, northeast Ohio went heavily Democratic; in the early 1990s, as the economy diversified and recovered, it hovered between the parties.

The 19th Congressional District of Ohio takes in an irregularly-shaped hunk—a very irregularly-shaped hunk—of northeast Ohio and the old Western Reserve. It includes all of Lake County, with mixed middling-to-affluent suburbs and industrial Ashtabula County in the northeast corner of the state. It also includes a motley collection of the Cuyahoga County suburbs of Cleveland. East of Cleveland are affluent Italian, Jewish and WASP suburbs, Beachwood, Pepper Pike and Chagrin Falls. Directly south of Cleveland are more working-class suburbs on either side of the Cuyahoga River gorge and west to Brook Park around the convention center and airport.

The congressman from the 19th District is Steve LaTourette, a Republican elected in 1994 and reelected in 1996. LaTourette grew up and went to law school in the Cleveland area; in the 1980s he worked as a public defender and a private lawyer in Lake County, and became Lake County District Attorney in 1988, at 34. Well-known and well-liked, he won a three-candidate 1994 Republican primary with 54%. In the general he faced Eric Fingerhut, a 35-year-old political prodigy who in 1992 was elected to replace not one but two retiring Democratic incumbents who were prodigies themselves: Dennis Eckart, who at 42 had served 12 years, and Ed Feighan, who at 45 had served 10. Fingerhut had come to Capitol Hill as an aggressive reformer, but was unable to produce a promised lobby reform and gift ban. LaTourette attacked Fingerhut for backing the Clinton budget and tax increase, for being soft on crime, and for hypocritically using the frank. Fingerhut attacked LaTourette for opposing gun control and said, "Washington will never change me." But evidently some voters thought it already had. LaTourette won 48%–43%, even though he did not raise nearly as much PAC money as Fingerhut, carrying Lake County 58%–33%.

In the House LaTourette had a moderate voting record, and showed more irreverence than one might expect from a former prosecutor or a Republican. The only bearded freshman, in his first weeks, he invited humorist Dave Barry to spend several days on his press staff, with predictably funny results. Later he was quoted as saying that being a congressman "sucks." He was one of 10 Republicans to vote against the party's seven-year balanced budget plan in October 1995. He worked with Democrat Carl Stokes to protect EPA enforcement powers and with Democrat Sherrod Brown to keep Coast Guard stations open on Lake Erie.

In 1996 LaTourette faced Democrat Tom Coyne, Mayor of Brook Park since 1982, and the second-place finisher in the 10th District Democratic primary in 1994. For several months the AFL-CIO ran ads against LaTourette, but quit in June, to concentrate on Martin Hoke, the Republican representing the more Democratic 10th. LaTourette did Hoke no favors: in early October, when asked why he should be reelected, he told the Cleveland Plain Dealer, "With all due respect to my colleague Martin Hoke, I don't think he's going to win this race. I don't think the Democrats will take control of the House, and I think it's important for northeast Ohio to have a member of the majority party in power." Such a characteristically candid answer rather than the usual ritual dishonesty naturally angered Hoke and didn't especially help LaTourette. But his base in Lake County again came through, 63%–32%. LaTourette also won 50% in the rest of the district, for a 55%–41% margin overall.

The People: Pop. 1990: 570,834; 12% rural; 15% age 65+; 96% White; 2% Black; 1% Asian; 1% Hispanic origin. Households: 62% married couple families; 26% married couple fams. w. children; 43% college educ.; median household income: $34,385; per capita income: $16,609; median gross rent: $464; median house value: $77,200.

1996 Presidential Vote			1992 Presidential Vote		
Clinton (D)	126,926	(48%)	Clinton (D)	114,358	(40%)
Dole (R)	102,099	(39%)	Bush (R)	106,947	(37%)
Perot (I)	31,362	(12%)	Perot (I)	66,424	(23%)

Rep. Steven C. LaTourette (R)

Elected 1994; b. July 22, 1954, Cleveland; home, Madison Village; U. of MI, B.A. 1976, Cleveland St. U., J.D. 1979; Methodist; married (Susan).

Career: Lake Cnty. Asst. Public Defender, 1980–83; Practicing atty., 1983–88; Lake Cnty. Prosecuting atty., 1988–94.

DC Office: 1239 LHOB 20515, 202-225-5731; Fax: 202-225-3307.
District Offices: Painesville, 216-352-3939.

Committees: *Banking & Financial Services* (27th of 30 R): Domestic & International Monetary Policy; General Oversight & Investigations. *Government Reform & Oversight* (17th of 24 R): National Economic Growth, Natural Resources & Regulatory Affairs; National Security, International Affairs & Criminal Justice; Postal Service. *Transportation & Infrastructure* (19th of 40 R): Public Buildings & Economic Development; Surface Transportation; Water Resources & Environment.

Group Ratings

	ADA	ACLU	AFS	LCV	CFA	CON	NFIB	COC	ACU	NTLC	CHC
1996	15	6	25	38	46	34	92	88	80	93	73
1995	15	—	—	25	23	31	—	96	80	—	—

National Journal Ratings

	1995 LIB — 1995 CONS			1996 LIB — 1996 CONS		
Economic	44%		53%	42%		56%
Social	45%	—	54%	33%	—	65%
Foreign	15%	—	73%	46%	—	53%

Key Votes of the 104th Congress

1. Reduce Medicare Growth $	Y	5. Flag Amendment	Y	9. Cuban Embargo	Y
2. Ovrd. Product Liab. Veto	Y	6. Drop EPA Limits	Y	10. Bar Bosnia Troop $	Y
3. Increase Min. Wage	Y	7. Repeal Assault-Weap. Ban	Y	11. Cut Anti-Missile Defense	N
4. Welfare Reform	Y	8. Ovrd. Part. Birth Veto	Y	12. Bar U.N. Uniforms	Y

Election Results

1996 general	Steven C. LaTourette (R)	135,012	(55%)	($1,025,247)
	Thomas J. Coyne, Jr. (D)	101,152	(41%)	($568,352)
	Thomas A. Martin (NL)	10,655	(4%)	
1996 primary	Steven C. LaTourette (R)	unopposed		
1994 general	Steven C. LaTourette (R)	99,997	(48%)	($712,925)
	Eric D. Fingerhut (D)	89,701	(43%)	($981,882)
	Ronald E. Young (I)	11,364	(6%)	($42,785)
	Others	5,180	(3%)	

OKLAHOMA

After the horrible shock of the bombing in Oklahoma City in April 1995, the first response of many was to wonder how this happened "in the middle of nowhere," where nothing ever seems to happen; and then Americans began to marvel at how the people of Oklahoma City helped and coped. But Oklahoma is not in the middle of nowhere, but in the middle of America, and the idea that nothing ever seems to happen there is wrong—Oklahoma has had exhilarating highs and sickening lows several times in its history—and misleading: the very creation of an orderly yet energetic society in which ordinary people can do great things, can recover from tragedy as Oklahoma City did, is an achievement often taken for granted in this country, yet yearned for throughout the course of human history.

Oklahoma's success has come from a most improbable history. It was settled in a rush, first by the Five Civilized Tribes driven west by Andrew Jackson's troops over the Cherokees' Trail of Tears in the 1830s. Then came white settlers one morning in April 1889 when, in the great land rush memorialized in an Edna Ferber novel, the Rodgers and Hammerstein musical and half a dozen Hollywood movies, thousands of would-be homesteaders drove their wagons across the territorial line at the sound of a gunshot, the most adventurous or unscrupulous of them literally jumping the gun—the Sooners. The heritage of these rushes remains. Oklahoma has the second largest Indian population in the U.S. (California has the largest), 253,000 in the 1990 Census, though there is just one reservation and the status of many other tribal entities is often disputed. Some Indian tribes here have unsuccessfully sought a return of native lands and face high unemployment rates. But there has been much intermarriage over the years, and many Oklahomans proudly claim some Indian blood; assimilation into everyday life plus commemoration of historic traditions and efforts to keep the Cherokee, Choctaw, Chickasaw and Seminole languages from dying out seem to have provided a better life for most Native Americans here than approaches elsewhere.

Statehood came to Oklahoma late, in 1907, at which point it filled up with farmers, rising from 1.5 million people in 1907 to 2.4 million in 1930. Oil helped: the first well was drilled here in 1897 and by 1920 Tulsa was an oil boom town. Then, a decade of bust. Oklahoma went up in smoke, or rather dust, as soil loosened by erosion was whipped into giant swirling clouds: the Dust Bowl. "On a single day, I heard, 50 million tons of soil were blown away," John Gunther reported later. "People sat in Oklahoma City, with the sky invisible for three days in a row, holding dust masks over their faces and wet towels to protect their mouths at night, while the farms blew by." Okies headed in droves west out U.S. 66 to the green land of California and Oklahoma's population sank to 2.3 million in 1940 and 2.2 million in 1950, not to reach its 1930 level again until 1970.

Eventually, oil brought another boom: as the oil shocks of 1973 and 1979 sent oil prices up, Oklahoma's population rose from 2.5 million in 1970 to 3 million in 1980 and 3.3 million in 1983. Then, with the collapse of oil prices and of Oklahoma's farm economy as well, bust again. A giddy rise was followed by a giddier fall: the rig count fell from 882 in January 1982 to 232 in February 1983, and 105 in 1997. Just as the dust cloud symbolized Oklahoma's 1930s bust, so the auction of oil drilling equipment was a symbol of the 1980s calamity. The 1990 Census reported just 3.1 million Oklahomans.

In the 1990s, with a more diversified and high-skill economy, Oklahoma has prospered and grown (the population is up 4.9% from 1990–96), and has performed well in other ways, with rising test scores in its tradition-minded schools. And with the help of a 1993 tax law which gives tax breaks and accelerated depreciation to any business located on current or "former" Indian reservation land—nearly the entire state—Oklahoma is getting its share of Fortune 500

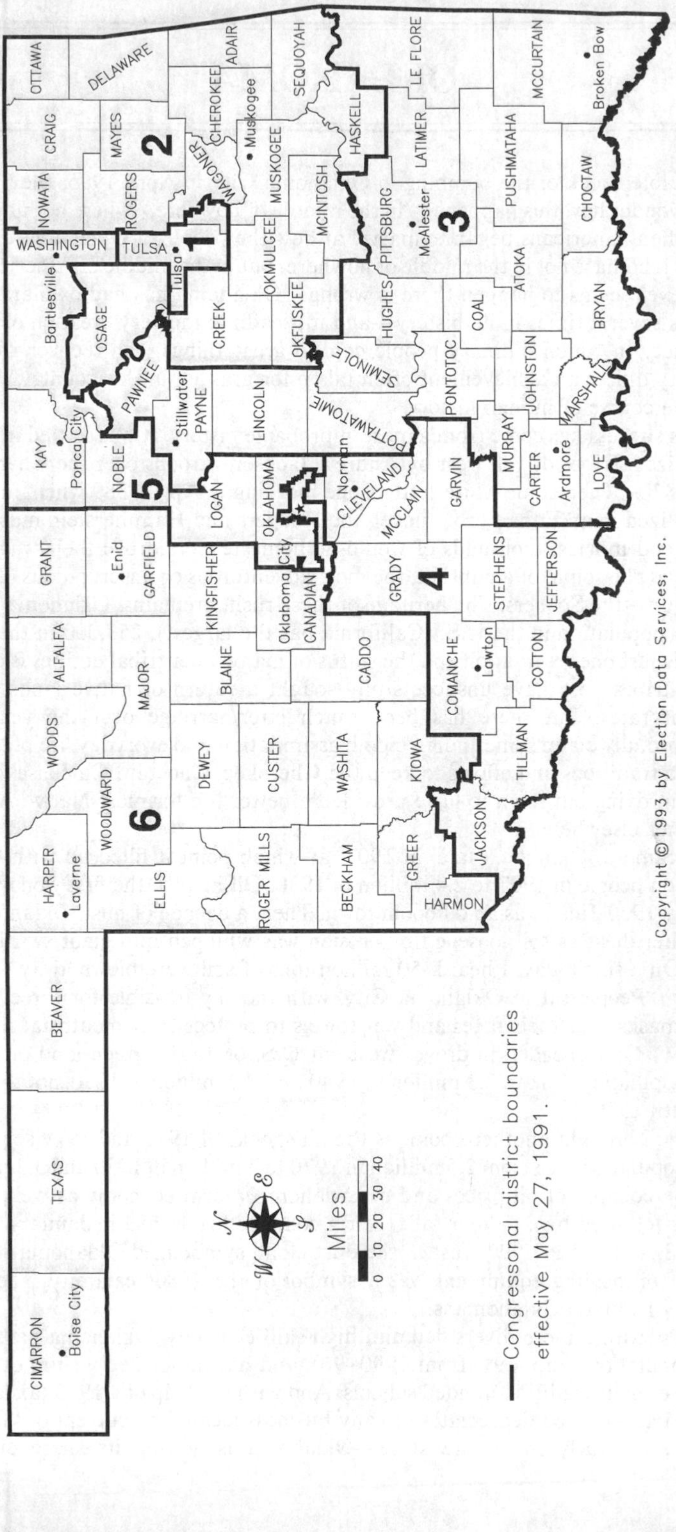
1
2
3
4
5
6
OTTAWA
DELAWARE
ADAIR
SEQUOYAH
LE FLORE
MCCURTAIN
Broken Bow
CRAIG
MAYES
CHEROKEE
Muskogee
HASKELL
LATIMER
PUSHMATAHA
NOWATA
ROGERS
WAGONER
MUSKOGEE
MCINTOSH
PITTSBURG
McAlester
CHOCTAW
WASHINGTON
TULSA
Tulsa
OKMULGEE
HUGHES
COAL
ATOKA
Bartlesville
OSAGE
CREEK
OKFUSKEE
SEMINOLE
PONTOTOC
JOHNSTON
BRYAN
PAWNEE
PAYNE
Stillwater
LINCOLN
POTTAWATOMIE
MURRAY
MARSHALL
KAY
Ponca City
NOBLE
LOGAN
OKLAHOMA
Oklahoma City
Norman
CLEVELAND
MCCLAIN
GARVIN
CARTER
Ardmore
LOVE
GRANT
Enid
GARFIELD
KINGFISHER
CANADIAN
GRADY
STEPHENS
JEFFERSON
ALFALFA
MAJOR
BLAINE
CADDO
COMANCHE
Lawton
COTTON
WOODS
DEWEY
CUSTER
WASHITA
KIOWA
TILLMAN
WOODWARD
ELLIS
ROGER MILLS
BECKHAM
GREER
JACKSON
HARMON
HARPER
Laverne
BEAVER
TEXAS
CIMARRON
Boise City
Miles
0 10 20 30 40
— Congressional district boundaries
effective May 27, 1991.
Copyright © 1993 by Election Data Services, Inc.

companies such as American Airlines, General Motors and Hitachi American Ltd.

In partisan politics Oklahoma has seen similarly turbulent changes, leaving it—for the moment anyway—with a split political personality. The historical political patterns were set in the early years: most of the first settlers were southerners and so Oklahoma leaned to the Democrats. They were especially strong in Little Dixie in the south, while the wheat counties of the northwest leaned Republican; Tulsa, originally Republican, and Oklahoma City, originally Democratic, both lean Republican today. Oklahoma has had more than its share of scandal-tarred governors. One in the 1970s went to jail, and was replaced by David Boren, later U.S. senator. More recently, Democrat David Walters, elected in 1990, was charged with campaign finance violations and pleaded guilty in October 1993.

That scandal, plus negative reaction to the first two years of the Clinton Administration, produced a Republican takeover of Oklahoma's top offices. Republican Frank Keating was elected governor in 1994, and Tulsa Congressman Jim Inhofe was elected to Boren's Senate seat over 4th District Congressman Dave McCurdy, who once harbored presidential ambitions. The House delegation underwent almost total turnover in just a few years. In January 1994 it consisted of four Democrats and two Republicans; then Republicans won a special election in 1994, captured two Democratic seats that fall and even won the Little Dixie seat in 1996, as Bob Dole carried the state over Bill Clinton. So now the governor, both senators, and all six congressmen are Republicans. But Democrats retain wide margins in both houses of the state legislature, despite a concerted campaign by Keating in 1996.

Governor. Frank Keating won the governorship in 1994. He grew up in Tulsa, in comfortable circumstances, went to Georgetown—where he overlapped with Bill Clinton—and University of Oklahoma Law School, then in 1969 became an FBI agent, investigating new left terrorists on the West Coast. He worked as a prosecutor in Tulsa and was elected to the Oklahoma House in 1972, at 28, and the state Senate in 1974. In 1981 he became U.S. Attorney in Tulsa; during Reagan's second term served as assistant secretary of the Treasury and then as associate attorney general under Bush; he was general counsel of HUD when Jack Kemp was secretary. After Senate Democrats refused to act on his nomination for a federal judgeship, Keating returned to Oklahoma in 1993 and began running for governor. He was clearly the party leaders' choice and won the 1994 Republican primary 57%–29%.

He presented an image of competent conservatism while the Democrats were in disarray. Incumbent David Walters, after pleading guilty of campaign finance violations, still hesitated before dropping out of the race. Lieutenant Governor Jack Mildren got 49% in the August primary and so was forced into a September runoff. And former Democratic Congressman Wes Watkins, from Little Dixie, who had lost the 1990 runoff to Walters 51%–49%, was running as an Independent. Keating campaigned for business and other tax cuts and rose in the polls. In November he won with 47% of the vote, to 30% for Mildren and 23% for Watkins. Watkins carried 22 counties in the southern part of the state and Mildren carried 12 others, but Keating had wide margins in the metropolitan areas—58%–27% over Mildren in Oklahoma City, 60%–27% in Tulsa. (Watkins won the 3d District seat in 1996 as a Republican.)

In office Keating encountered vehement opposition from Democrats. "I was booed during my inaugural speech. The governor was booed, and the Democratic leadership did nothing to stop it." The legislature rejected his proposed business tax cuts, workmen's comp reform and right-to-work law; he vetoed education and other spending bills. Keating constantly complained of Oklahoma's low income levels. "Our goal is a basic one: it's time to make Oklahoma rich." Democrats complained that he was badmouthing the state on speaking tours. But Keating performed with aplomb after the April 1995 Oklahoma City bombing, supervising the search for survivors and comforting victims and their families; his wife helped raise $7 million for them and compiled a commemorative book which made the bestseller lists. As Timothy McVeigh was convicted of all 11 counts in a Denver courtroom in June 1997, Oklahoma City prosecutors still planned to charge him with 160 additional murder counts locally.

Keating and the legislature did reach agreement on some bills, including welfare reform, a victims' bill of rights, a limit on punitive damages and higher spending on higher education. But the partisan battling continued. Keating campaigned strenuously for Republican candidates for the legislature, but with little success. Republicans gained two seats in the Senate, but Democrats emerged with a 33–15 edge, enough to override a veto or pass emergency legislation. In the House, Republicans and Democrats each lost two seats, leaving the 65–36 balance as before. Nevertheless, Keating again called for business tax cuts, workmen's comp reform, school choice and teacher performance awards.

Keating appears to be in strong shape for reelection, but it is not clear if he can translate his popularity into more Republican legislative seats. Possible Democratic opponents in 1998 include Mildren, Attorney General Drew Edmondson, Treasurer Robert Butkin, Auditor Cliff Scott and Tulsa Mayor Susan Savage.

Senior Senator. Don Nickles, senior member of the Oklahoma delegation and the Senate majority whip, was first elected in 1980. He grew up in Ponca City, and, after his father died when he was 13, worked his way through Oklahoma State as a janitor making the minimum wage; then he returned to Ponca City and helped run the family machine business. In 1978, at age 29, he was elected to the Oklahoma Senate; two years later, he ran for the U.S. Senate seat being vacated by Republican Henry Bellmon. With support from Christian conservatives, he won 35% in a multicandidate primary and 65% in the runoff; in the general he won 53%–44%—at 31 the youngest Republican ever elected to the Senate. It was a signal that Oklahoma was now a basically Republican state, and that a culturally conservative Catholic like Nickles could make a political alliance with Protestant evangelicals. For many years now, Nickles has had one of the most conservative voting records in the Senate and has been a stalwart Republican in partisan controversy. He chaired the Republican Senate campaign committee during the 1990 cycle and, as an opponent of the 1990 budget summit tax increase, in December 1990 beat Pete Domenici for Republican Conference chairman by 23–20. He won the whip post without opposition when Bob Dole resigned in June 1996, and Trent Lott moved up.

Several threads run through his record. One is opposition to energy taxes and regulations; he backed the successful fights to deregulate oil and natural gas prices, to repeal the windfall profits tax and to repeal the 55-mile-per-hour speed limit. He strongly opposed the Clinton Btu and gasoline taxes in 1993, and in 1996 tried to repeal the law requiring power companies to buy electricity from generators using renewable sources. Another thread is conservative stands on health and lifestyle issues. He got the Senate to go on record 76–23 in 1993 against allowing HIV-positive immigrants into the U.S. and introduced a bill in 1997 requiring AIDS testing for indicted sex offenders and partner notification of HIV-positive results. He led opposition to surgeon general nominees Joycelyn Elders and Henry Foster. He pushed to cut the Earned Income Tax Credit, saying it had been widely abused. He has worked successfully against government funding of abortion and to limit abortion coverage for federal employees. He passed a bill stopping research grants to universities that bar military recruiters from on-campus visits. He sponsored the Defense of Marriage Act in 1996.

Nickles was calling for congressional reform long before the Contract With America: in 1991 he introduced an amendment applying to Congress the same laws it applies to others. He was one of the backers of the 27th Amendment, finally ratified in 1992 after having been proposed by James Madison in 1789, which bans mid-term changes in congressional pay. He has sponsored victim's rights bill requiring restitution to victims and blocking criminals from using bankruptcy to avoid it. With Nevada's Harry Reid, he won Senate passage of a bipartisan regulatory reform bill in March 1995—a more realistic and effective version of the moratorium on new regulations in the House's Contract With America. Nickles was also the chief sponsor of the Republicans $500-per-child tax credit included in the 1995 budget reconciliation bill vetoed by President Clinton; the tax credit was part of the FY98 budget resolution endorsed by The White House.

When Bob Dole announced that he would resign from the Senate in June 1996, Nickles stood by his side. He considered running for majority leader against Trent Lott, but decided not to. "It was possible to win leader. But it was more probable to win whip. It looked very, very doable, maybe without a race. The other one was going to be a knockdown, drag-out fight." The Senate's Republicans were a much more conservative group than in 1990, when he just edged out Domenici, and Nickles gained a reputation of being true to conservative principles and politically shrewd, easy to work with and reliable. Lott has given him key committee assignments—Governmental Affairs, when it was set to investigate Clinton campaign misdeeds—and made him head of a task force on campaign finance reform in 1997. Nickles has little interest in quixotic battles; in December 1996 he said he was "not really interested in passing a bill just to have it vetoed." But he also spoke favorably of adjusting the Consumer Price Index and partially privatizing Social Security—signs that he has not abandoned the advocacy of bold conservative proposals he has shown earlier in his career.

Nickles's one tough reelection race came in 1986, when he faced Tulsa Congressman Jim Jones, Ways and Means member and Budget chairman in the first Reagan term. But Jones's ad campaign misfired and Nickles showed greater strength than many in Washington expected and won 55%–45% in a year when several other southern Republicans elected in 1980 lost. Incidentally, Nickles supported Jones's nomination to be ambassador to Mexico in 1993. In 1992 Nickles won 59%–38%; in early 1997 he seemed to be in very strong shape for 1998.

Junior Senator. Republican James Inhofe was elected in 1994 to fill the vacancy created by the resignation of David Boren, who became president of the University of Oklahoma. Inhofe grew up in Tulsa, served in the Army, worked in real estate, insurance and aviation, has for years regularly flown planes and is one of Congress's few certified commercial pilots; he flew around the world following Wiley Post's route. He was elected to the Oklahoma House as long ago as 1966, at 31, and to the Oklahoma Senate in 1969; he ran for governor in 1974 and lost to David Boren, 64%–36%. In 1976, Inhofe ran for the U.S. House against Jim Jones and lost; from 1979–84 Inhofe was mayor of Tulsa. He won the heavily Republican 1st District House seat in 1986, but held it with uninspiring margins. He was hurt by negative publicity about a family business lawsuit (he eventually was awarded $3.6 million), charges of campaign finance irregularities, an order to pay the FDIC $588,000 on promissory notes to an insurance company and for misstating the date he received his college degree; the liberal-leaning *Tulsa World* made sure to pepper him with criticism.

In Washington, Inhofe has had a very conservative voting record. One great achievement was to reform the arcane House discharge petition rule. For years House rules kept secret the names of signers of petitions to discharge bills stuck in committees; members could lie and claim they had worked to bring legislation to the floor when they hadn't. One of the first bills to benefit from the new rules was the aviation liability reform bill, co-sponsored by Inhofe, which limited the liability of small airplane manufacturers in lawsuits resulting from crashes.

When Boren announced his retirement in 1994, Inhofe jumped into the race. He faced the toughest possible Democrat, Dave McCurdy, congressman since 1980 from southwest Oklahoma, chairman of the moderate Democratic Leadership Council, expert on military and intelligence affairs, critic of the House Democratic leadership. An extrapolation from their past electoral showings would put Inhofe far behind: he had won by small margins in a heavily Republican district, while McCurdy had won by large margins in a district that gave Bill Clinton only one-third of its votes in 1992. But in Oklahoma in 1994 the Clinton burden was too heavy for even McCurdy to carry. He had voted for the Clinton budget and tax package with its original Btu tax and for the 1994 crime bill with its assault weapons ban. "Dave McClinton," as Republicans called him, was beaten, one Democrat said, by "God, guns and gays." Inhofe won by a solid 55%–40%, carrying the Tulsa area by a higher percentage that ever before (60%–37%) and Oklahoma City by even more (61%–35%); he also bested McCurdy in the rest of Oklahoma (52%–42%), carrying even McCurdy's old congressional district.

In the Senate Inhofe was president of the conservative 11-member freshman class. He introduced a bill to limit Congressional pensions and worked to secure funding for Oklahoma's military bases. He had the satisfaction of seeing the Congressional Medal of Honor awarded to seven black soldiers for their service in World War II; since 1990 he had been championing the cause of Ruben Rivers, a Hotulka, Oklahoma, soldier who after being gravely wounded refused evacuation and continued attacking Germans, and was killed trying to save his unit. Inhofe in the House and the Senate pushed to see that the Army reviewed the cases and sponsored legislation authorizing the Medals.

Because he had been elected to serve the last two years of Boren's term, he had to run again in 1996. The atmosphere proved less Republican, but his competition was much weaker. After former Governor George Nigh refused to run, Democrats nominated James Boren, David Boren's cousin, who years ago had written an amusing book about bureaucrats. (Boren also once ran for president promising "bold, reckless, arrogant, ignorant leadership" and attempted to race against the Postal Service across country with a team of turtles and backward-facing joggers.) Boren refused to accept PAC money, but probably would not have gotten much anyway. Inhofe spent $2.5 million to Boren's $301,000 and won 57%–40%.

In the 105th Congress Inhofe chairs two subcommittees with important jurisdiction. One is the Readiness Subcommittee of Armed Services, relevant to Oklahoma's military bases. Inhofe is a strong supporter of missile defense and is troubled that American force strength is only half what it was before the Gulf war. He also chairs the interestingly-named Clean Air, Wetlands, Private Property and Nuclear Safety Subcommittee of Environment. It has jurisdiction over the EPA's newly proposed air quality standards for ozone and particulate matter, which Inhofe strongly questions.

Presidential politics. Oklahoma has been a solidly Republican state in presidential elections for a very long time. There are no large blocs of voters here who back national Democrats and almost everyone finds national Republicans acceptable. Oklahoma is thus not on anyone's list of target states in October, nor is it the subject of much attention as one of the southern Super Tuesday primaries. In recent primaries it voted in 1996 for Bob Dole, in 1992 for George Bush and Bill Clinton and in 1988 for Al Gore (a distant relation of onetime Oklahoma Senator Thomas Gore, grandfather of writer Gore Vidal).

Congressional districting. For the 1990s, Oklahoma narrowly missed losing a seat. State Democrats drew up an "incumbent protection plan," which was supposed to strengthen the four Democratic congressmen by concentrating Republican votes in the other two districts. But retirements and anti-Clinton animus have made all six districts Republican now.

The People: Est. Pop. 1996: 3,301,000; Pop. 1990: 3,145,585, up 4.9% 1990–1996. 1.2% of U.S. total, 27th largest; 32% rural. Median age: 34.9 years. 13% 65 years and over. 81% White, 7.4% Black, 1% Asian, 7.8% Amer. Indian, 2.7% Hispanic origin. Households: 57.7% married couple families; 28% married couple fams. w. children; 44% college educ.; median household income: $23,577; per capita income: $11,893; 68.1% owner occupied housing; median house value: $48,100; median monthly rent: $259. 4.1% Unemployment. 1996 Voting age pop.: 2,426,000. 1996 Turnout: 1,206,713; 50% of VAP. Registered voters (1996): 1,979,017; 1,169,526 D (59%), 690,611 R (35%), 118,880 unaffiliated and minor parties (6%).

Political Lineup: Governor, Frank Keating (R); Lt. Gov., Mary Fallin (R); Secy. of State, Tom Cole (R); Atty. Gen., Drew Edmondson (D); Treasurer, Robert Butkin (D); Auditor, Clifton Scott (D). State Senate, 48 (33 D and 15 R); Senate President, Mary Fallin (R); State House, 101 (65 D and 36 R); House Speaker, Loyd Benson (D). Senators, Don Nickles (R) and James M. Inhofe (R). Representatives, 6 (6 R).

Elections Division: 405-521-2391; **Filing Deadline for U.S. Congress:** July 8, 1998.

1996 Presidential Vote

Dole (R)	582,315	(48%)
Clinton (D)	488,105	(40%)
Perot (I)	130,788	(11%)

1996 Republican Presidential Primary

Dole (R)	156,829	(59%)
Buchanan (R)	56,949	(22%)
Forbes (R)	37,213	(14%)
Other	13,551	(5%)

1992 Presidential Vote

Bush (R)	592,929	(43%)
Clinton (D)	473,066	(34%)
Perot (I)	319,878	(23%)

GOVERNOR

Gov. Frank Keating (R)

Elected 1994, term expires Jan. 1999; b. Feb. 10, 1944, St. Louis, MO; home, Oklahoma City; Georgetown U., B.A. 1966, U. of OK, J.D. 1969; Catholic; married (Catherine).

Career: FBI Agent, 1969–71; Asst. Dist. Atty. Tulsa Cnty., 1971–72; OK House of Reps., 1972–74; OK Senate, 1974–81; US Atty., N. OK Dist., 1981–84; U.S. Asst. Secy. of Treasury., 1986–88; U.S. Assoc. Atty. Gen., 1988–89; Gen. Cnsl. & Acting Dpty. Secy. of HUD, 1989–93; Practicing atty., 1993–95;

Office: 212 State Capitol Bldg., Oklahoma City 73105, 405-521-2342; Fax: 405-521-3353; Web site: www.state.ok.us.

Election Results

1994 gen.	Frank Keating (R)	466,740	(47%)
	Jack Mildren (D)	294,936	(30%)
	Wes Watkins (I)	233,336	(23%)
1994 prim.	Frank Keating (R)	117,265	(57%)
	Jerry Pierce (R)	60,280	(29%)
	Virginia Hale (R)	15,229	(7%)
	Others	13,173	(6%)
1990 gen.	David Walters (D)	523,196	(57%)
	Bill Price (R)	297,584	(33%)
	Thomas Ledgerwood (I)	90,534	(10%)

SENATORS

Sen. Don Nickles (R)

Elected 1980, seat up 1998; b. Dec. 6, 1948, Ponca City; home, Ponca City; OK St. U., B.A. 1971; Catholic; married (Linda).

Career: OK Natl. Guard, 1970–76; Vice Pres. & Gen. Mgr., Nickles Machine Co., 1976–80; OK Senate, 1978–80.

DC Office: 133 HSOB 20510, 202-224-5754; Fax: 202-224-6008; e-mail: senator@nickles.senate.gov.

State Offices: Lawton, 405-357-9878; Oklahoma City, 405-231-4941; Ponca City, 405-767-1270; Tulsa, 918-581-7651.

Committees: *Majority Whip. Budget* (3rd of 12 R). *Energy & Natural Resources* (3rd of 11 R): Energy Research, Development, Production & Regulation (Chmn.); National Parks, Historic Preservation & Recreation. *Finance* (7th of 11 R): Health Care; Social Security & Family Policy; Taxation & IRS Oversight (Chmn.). *Governmental Affairs* (6th of 9 R): International Security, Proliferation & Federal Services; Permanent Subcommittee on Investigations. *Rules & Administration* (7th of 9 R).

Group Ratings

	ADA	ACLU	AFS	LCV	CFA	CON	NFIB	COC	ACU	NTLC	CHC
1996	0	22	0	15	14	70	100	100	100	100	100
1995	0	—	0	7	0	29	—	100	100	—	—

National Journal Ratings

	1995 LIB — 1995 CONS			1996 LIB — 1996 CONS		
Economic	12%	—	84%	0%	—	94%
Social	0%	—	88%	0%	—	72%
Foreign	0%	—	92%	0%	—	74%

Key Votes of the 104th Congress

1. Reduce Medicare Growth $	Y	5. Flag Amendment	Y	9. Anti-Missile Defense	Y
2. Lmt. Prod. Liab. Damages	Y	6. Endangered Species	N	10. Cuban Embargo	Y
3. Increase Min. Wage	N	7. Gay Employment Rights	N	11. Bar Bosnia Troop $	Y
4. Welfare Reform	Y	8. Ovrd. Part. Birth Veto	Y	12. Cut Vietnam Aid	Y

Election Results

1992 general	Don Nickles (R)	757,876	(59%)	($3,492,603)
	Steve Lewis (D)	494,350	(38%)	($1,455,848)
	Others	42,197	(3%)	
1992 primary	Don Nickles (R)	unopposed		
1986 general	Don Nickles (R)	493,436	(55%)	($3,252,965)
	James R. Jones (D)	400,230	(45%)	($2,564,982)

Sen. James M. Inhofe (R)

Elected 1994, seat up 2002; b. Nov. 17, 1934, Des Moines, IA; home, Tulsa; U. of Tulsa, B.A. 1973; Presbyterian; married (Kay).

Career: Army, 1955–56; Businessman, land developer, 1962–86; OK House of Reps., 1966–69; OK Senate, 1969–77, Repub. Ldr., 1975–77; Repub. nominee for Gov., 1974; Tulsa Mayor, 1978–84; U.S. House of Reps., 1986–94.

DC Office: 453 RSOB 20510, 202-224-4721; Fax: 202-228-0380.

State Offices: Oklahoma City, 405-231-4381; Tulsa, 918-748-5111.

Committees: *Armed Services* (7th of 10 R): Airland Forces; Readiness (Chmn.); Strategic Forces. *Environment & Public Works* (5th of 10 R): Clean Air, Wetlands, Private Property & Nuclear Safety (Chmn.); Superfund, Waste Control & Risk Assessment; Transportation & Infrastructure. *Indian Affairs* (8th of 8 R). *Intelligence (Select)* (6th of 10 R).

Group Ratings

	ADA	ACLU	AFS	LCV	CFA	CON	NFIB	COC	ACU	NTLC	CHC
1996	0	24	0	0	7	51	100	100	100	100	100
1995	0	—	0	7	0	27	—	100	100	—	—

National Journal Ratings

	1995 LIB — 1995 CONS			1996 LIB — 1996 CONS		
Economic	16%	—	82%	0%	—	94%
Social	0%	—	88%	0%	—	72%
Foreign	0%	—	92%	0%	—	74%

Key Votes of the 104th Congress

1. Reduce Medicare Growth $	Y	5. Flag Amendment	Y	9. Anti-Missile Defense	Y
2. Lmt. Prod. Liab. Damages	Y	6. Endangered Species	N	10. Cuban Embargo	Y
3. Increase Min. Wage	N	7. Gay Employment Rights	N	11. Bar Bosnia Troop $	Y
4. Welfare Reform	Y	8. Ovrd. Part. Birth Veto	Y	12. Cut Vietnam Aid	Y

Election Results

1996 general	James M. Inhofe (R)	670,610	(57%)	
	James Boren (D)	474,162	(40%)	
	Others	38,378	(3%)	
1996 primary	James M. Inhofe (R)	116,241	(75%)	
	Dan Lowe (R)	38,044	(25%)	
1994 general	James M. Inhofe (R)	542,390	(55%)	($1,920,227)
	Dave McCurdy (D)	392,488	(40%)	($1,872,160)
	Danny Corn (I)	47,552	(5%)	

FIRST DISTRICT

Tulsa was one of America's oil boom towns in the early 20th Century, settled not just by people from the immediate hinterland but by Midwesterners and New Englanders of Yankee stock. In the 1920s, as its skyscrapers rose in downtown on heights above the Arkansas River, it was a raw town, but intent on culture. It was optimistic and ready to seek economic change, yet culturally and politically conservative—with a Yankee elite and an Indian heritage recalled today in the Gilcrease Museum, left by one-eighth Creek Indian oil millionaire Thomas Gilcrease, and an ethnic variety suggested by the Gershon & Rebecca Fenster Museum of Jewish Art. In the decades since, Tulsa has boomed and occasionally busted; it has remained cosmopolitan and conservative; it is one of America's leading petroleum centers, and also is the headquarters of Oral Roberts and his university and 60-story City of Faith hospital.

The 1st Congressional District of Oklahoma includes all of Tulsa County plus a bit of Wagoner County to the southeast: essentially metropolitan Tulsa. The political tradition here is heavily Republican, even more so than in Oklahoma City, and accentuated in recent decades by national Democrats' cultural liberalism and penchant for petroleum taxes. Even during the collapse of oil prices in the 1980s, Tulsa remained full of a contagious enthusiasm for new business enterprises and innovations. Ordinary people here do not resent the oil companies or the new rich; they identify with them. They see not class conflict, but a coincidence of economic interests. They see government as interfering with efforts to produce desired goods and services—although Tulsans are pleased that the federal government built the McClellan-Kerr Waterway that has made the Catoosa suburb a seaport.

The congressman from the 1st District is Steve Largent, a Republican elected in 1994, one of four freshmen and two football players elected from Oklahoma that year. Largent is a native of Tulsa, who played football for the University of Tulsa in the mid-1970s; he went on to be a record-setting wide receiver with the Seattle Seahawks, retiring after 14 years in 1989, at age 34. Back in Tulsa he worked in his own advertising and consulting firm. Largent is an active Christian conservative, and when incumbent Congressman Jim Inhofe decided to run for David Boren's Senate seat, Largent ran for Congress. He won the Republican nomination with an impressive 51% in the six-candidate primary. His Democratic opponent, Bill Clinton's state finance chairman in 1992, spent almost as much money as Largent, but Largent won 63%–37%.

1995 was a big year for Largent: he was sworn in as a member of Congress and inducted into the National Football Hall of Fame. At the latter, he said: "I thank my Lord and Savior, Jesus Christ. Football is what he gave me the physical gifts to do for a time. But my faith really defines who I am, as a husband, a father and a man." The son of divorced parents, he wants to strengthen the family and enforce child support. "The root problems that we face as a nation are the moral deficit not necessarily the economic deficit." Troubled by condom distribution, directives outlawing grounding and intrusive psychological testing in schools, he introduced a Parental Rights and Responsibilities Act; and he sees signs of a revival in the National Fatherhood Initiative and the Promise Keepers movement. He supports a flat tax, a radical overhaul and eventual end of Social Security.

Largent has one of the most conservative voting records in the House, and he has bucked the leadership when he thought it soft, voting against the continuing resolution in January 1996 and against the budget resolution which came within five votes of losing in June 1996. He is also a stickler for ethics. In July 1996 he considered running against Conference Chairman John Boehner, who had handed out tobacco PAC checks on the floor; but he did not run. Instead he has campaigned and raised money for many colleagues on the road. After the 1996 election he was quoted as saying that Newt Gingrich should step aside as speaker until the ethics charges were resolved; he claimed his remarks were taken out of context. For all his maverick tendencies, Largent has a plum committee assignment—Commerce and its Energy and Telecommunications and Finance Subcommittees; United Video and LDDS/WorldCom are two fast-growing telecommunications firms in his district.

Largent says he doesn't know where his career will lead. "I feel like that you sort of bloom where you are planted. I feel like this is where I was planted for a season. I don't know how long. This is where I feel, beyond a shadow of a doubt, I'm supposed to be right now." In 1996 he was opposed by a paralegal and pizza deliverer who spent $9,300. Largent won 68%–28%.

The People: Pop. 1990: 524,135; 6% rural; 11% age 65+; 82% White; 10% Black; 1% Asian; 5% Amer. Indian; 2% Hispanic origin. Households: 55% married couple families; 26% married couple fams. w. children; 54% college educ.; median household income: $27,472; per capita income: $14,695; median gross rent: $366; median house value: $60,700.

1996 Presidential Vote			**1992 Presidential Vote**		
Dole (R)	115,997	(54%)	Bush (R)	122,137	(49%)
Clinton (D)	79,518	(37%)	Clinton (D)	73,509	(30%)
Perot (I)	19,087	(9%)	Perot (I)	52,077	(21%)

Rep. Steve Largent (R)

Elected 1994; b. Sept. 28, 1954, Tulsa; home, Tulsa; Tulsa U., B.S. 1976; Protestant; married (Terry).

Career: Pro football player, Seattle Seahawks, 1976–89; Owner, adv. & mktg. co., 1989–present;

DC Office: 426 CHOB 20515, 202-225-2211; Fax: 202-225-9187.

District Offices: Tulsa, 918-749-0014.

Committees: *Commerce* (17th of 28 R): Energy & Power; Finance & Hazardous Materials; Telecommunications, Trade & Consumer Protection.

Group Ratings

	ADA	ACLU	AFS	LCV	CFA	CON	NFIB	COC	ACU	NTLC	CHC
1996	10	12	17	15	23	90	100	86	100	95	100
1995	0	—	—	0	0	95	—	100	100	—	—

National Journal Ratings

	1995 LIB — 1995 CONS	1996 LIB — 1996 CONS
Economic	0% — 74%	37% — 63%
Social	0% — 79%	0% — 90%
Foreign	15% — 73%	0% — 79%

Key Votes of the 104th Congress

1. Reduce Medicare Growth $	Y	5. Flag Amendment	Y	9. Cuban Embargo	Y
2. Ovrd. Product Liab. Veto	Y	6. Drop EPA Limits	N	10. Bar Bosnia Troop $	Y
3. Increase Min. Wage	N	7. Repeal Assault-Weap. Ban	Y	11. Cut Anti-Missile Defense	N
4. Welfare Reform	Y	8. Ovrd. Part. Birth Veto	Y	12. Bar U.N. Uniforms	Y

Election Results

1996 general	Steve Largent (R)	143,415	(68%)	($345,612)
	Randolph John Amen (D)	57,996	(28%)	($9,377)
	Karla Condray (I)	8,996	(4%)	
1996 primary	Steve Largent (R)	unopposed		
1994 general	Steve Largent (R)	107,085	(63%)	($610,211)
	Stuart Price (D)	63,753	(37%)	($546,570)

SECOND DISTRICT

The land that is now northeast Oklahoma a century ago was the Indian Territory, the place where in the 1830s, the Five Civilized Tribes were driven from Georgia and Alabama over the Trail of Tears. More than one in six people here report their race as American Indian, and in some counties over 40% claim they are at least partly of Native American descent. The Indian percentage is highest in the hilly counties just west of the Ozarks of Arkansas, where county names—Cherokee, Delaware, Sequoyah—recall the Civilized Tribes. The northeast is the one non-metropolitan part of Oklahoma that has been growing rapidly since 1980, from overspill from Tulsa, but even more from retirees and young families moving onto land around the area's large man-made lakes and into peaceful hills where crime and the cost of living are low.

The 2d Congressional District of Oklahoma is made up of the northeast corner of the state, minus Tulsa County. Its geographic enter is Muskogee, subject of Merle Haggard's song, "Okie from Muskogee." It includes Will Rogers's home town of Claremore in Rogers County. It reaches far northeast where the TV signal is from Joplin, Missouri, not Oklahoma; it reaches west of Tulsa to include Osage County, still an Indian reservation and site of a revived tallgrass prairie where buffalo again roam. Most of this area is ancestrally Democratic, especially the Little Dixie counties south of Muskogee; but it is now conservative on many cultural, foreign and most economic issues.

The congressman from the 2d District is Tom Coburn, a Republican elected in 1994. Coburn grew up in Muskogee, graduated from Oklahoma State; in the 1970s he managed the Virginia branch of the family business, Coburn Optical Industries, which grew to 35% of the U.S. lens manufacturing market; when the firm was sold, he went to University of Oklahoma Medical School and graduated in 1983, at 35. He returned to Muskogee, practicing family medicine and obstetrics, delivering more than 3,000 babies and embarking on medical missionary trips to Haiti and Iraq. He is a deacon in the Southern Baptist Church, anti-abortion and a strong conservative on most issues. In 1994 he decided to run against Congressman Mike Synar, a liberal Democrat first elected in 1978, at 28, and a battler for gun control and higher grazing fees, for public financing of campaigns and against the Gulf war resolution—not popular stands here. But Synar lost the Democratic runoff 51%–49%, and died in January 1996 of a brain tumor. Coburn, who beat Synar's 1992 opponent 64%–31% in the Republican primary, found himself facing Virgil Cooper, a 71-year-old retired principal and conservative. Coburn vastly outspent the Democrat, but Cooper's folksy humor and Little Dixie's Democratic heritage held the Republican's margin to 52%–48%. Coburn ran strong in the northeast part of the district and his local popularity enabled him to carry Muskogee County with 58%, the key to his win.

Coburn was one of the few Republicans not to sign the Contract With America in September 1994; he supported most conservative positions, but showed independence from the party leadership, opposing the B-2 bomber and describing the Republican veterans' health care budget as inadequate. He won a seat on the Commerce Committee and its Health Subcommittee, good spots from which to make a mark on medical issues. His first achievement here was a bill, signed into law, requiring testing of infants for HIV if their mothers had not been tested. He also proposed an HIV Prevention Act, with confidential national reporting, partner notification and protection for patients and providers in risky invasive medical procedures. He opposed Henry Foster's nomination as surgeon general. He favored the Republican Medicare plan, as giving seniors more choices, and backed Medical Savings Accounts. He got amendments through the House to deny punitive damages on makers of products approved by the FDA and to encourage use of debit cards rather than coupons in the food stamp program.

He founded the Congressional Family Caucus and opposed the V-Chip on grounds that it required government ratings; he favored technologies to allow families to make their own decisions. In February 1997, Coburn was reprimanded by Republican colleagues for criticizing NBC's decision to broadcast the uncut version of *Schindler's List* during family viewing time;

Coburn later apologized for his comments. On local issues, he restored $12 million for Oklahoma schools which was lost in committee when the Office of Indian Education was eliminated, and funded a $1.5 million study of flooding in the Grand Neosho Basin in Ottawa and Delaware Counties.

With his close margin in 1994, Coburn became a prime Democratic target. Party leaders recruited Oklahoma House Speaker Glen Johnson, elected to that post at 36 in 1990, to challenge Coburn, while the AFL-CIO ran a huge barrage of ads against him. Johnson campaigned as a conservative and claimed his Quality Jobs Act created thousands of jobs in Oklahoma; he also boasted of his work on drug-free school zones and education funding bills vetoed by Governor Frank Keating. But Coburn also had strengths. He had pledged to serve just three terms and turned down his congressional pension. He dismissed Johnson's charges of Republican cuts in student lunch, school loan and veterans' programs as "pure foolishness," and he attacked Johnson for deficits in the teachers' retirement fund. Coburn was endorsed by 1994 opponent Virgil Cooper: "He went to Congress and did the things he said he would do. He's a man of his word." Coburn featured his medical practice on TV; he continues to deliver babies while in the district. This was a heavy-spending race: Coburn spent $1.3 million, with $622,000 raised from PACs, to $1 million for Johnson, plus there was heavy spending by the AFL-CIO and, later, from business groups for Coburn. Coburn won 55%–45%, an improvement on 1994. He ran well ahead of Dole, especially in the northern counties, and carried the heavily populated areas around Claremore and Muskogee handily while losing in four southern counties. "The political pundits are wrong more often than they are right," he declared on election night. Coburn must be counted the favorite to win his third and presumably last term in 1998.

The People: Pop. 1990: 524,389; 63% rural; 15% age 65+; 77% White; 5% Black; 17% Amer. Indian; 1% Hispanic origin. Households: 63% married couple families; 29% married couple fams. w. children; 35% college educ.; median household income: $20,633; per capita income: $9,914; median gross rent: $289; median house value: $40,800.

1996 Presidential Vote

Clinton (D)	97,284	(47%)
Dole (R)	81,558	(40%)
Perot (I)	25,928	(13%)

1992 Presidential Vote

Clinton (D)	96,486	(42%)
Bush (R)	81,432	(36%)
Perot (I)	49,124	(22%)

Rep. Tom Coburn (R)

Elected 1994; b. Mar. 14, 1948, Casper, WY; home, Muskogee; OK St. U., B.S. 1970; OK U., M.D. 1983; Southern Baptist; married (Carolyn).

Career: Mgr., Coburn Optical Industies, 1970–1978; Practicing physician, 1983–present.

DC Office: 429 CHOB 20515, 202-225-2701; Fax: 202-225-3038.

District Offices: Muskogee, 918-687-2533.

Committees: *Commerce* (24th of 28 R): Energy & Power; Health & Environment; Oversight & Investigations. *Science* (24th of 25 R): Energy & Environment.

Group Ratings

	ADA	ACLU	AFS	LCV	CFA	CON	NFIB	COC	ACU	NTLC	CHC
1996	10	13	8	23	23	6	100	80	89	95	100
1995	0	—	—	13	8	87	—	96	100	—	—

National Journal Ratings

	1995 LIB — 1995 CONS			1996 LIB — 1996 CONS		
Economic	0%	—	74%	39%	—	61%
Social	0%	—	79%	23%	—	77%
Foreign	45%	—	55%	45%	—	54%

Key Votes of the 104th Congress

1. Reduce Medicare Growth $	Y	5. Flag Amendment	Y	9. Cuban Embargo	Y
2. Ovrd. Product Liab. Veto	Y	6. Drop EPA Limits	N	10. Bar Bosnia Troop $	Y
3. Increase Min. Wage	N	7. Repeal Assault-Weap. Ban	Y	11. Cut Anti-Missile Defense	N
4. Welfare Reform	Y	8. Ovrd. Part. Birth Veto	Y	12. Bar U.N. Uniforms	Y

Election Results

1996 general	Tom Coburn (R)	112,273	(55%)	($1,354,299)
	Glen D. Johnson (D)	90,120	(45%)	($1,053,616)
1996 primary	Tom Coburn (R)	unopposed		
1994 general	Tom Coburn (R)	82,479	(52%)	($604,924)
	Virgil R. Cooper (D)	75,943	(48%)	($75,202)

THIRD DISTRICT

West of Arkansas and just north of Texas, Little Dixie is the most recognizably southern part of Oklahoma. It was settled between 1889 and 1907 by white southerners, most of them poor; some county names (Leflore, Pontotoc) were taken directly from Mississippi. It remains mostly rural today but no longer poor. A private economy that has produced jobs is one reason; another is government, which built interstate highways and turnpikes connecting many people to jobs in more vibrant metropolitan areas. Dam-made lakes have spurred the creation of resort and retirement communities. But traditional cultural attitudes are still strong here: people listen to religious radio and read the Bible twice as frequently as the average American, they serve more often in the military, they stay married and raise large families more than most.

The 3d Congressional District of Oklahoma includes most of the Little Dixie counties, and juts up into the center of the state into the old university town of Stillwater, which is Republican territory, to include enough people to meet the population standard. It has long been solidly Democratic and voted for Bill Clinton in the 1990s; its conservative cultural attitudes, however, have been helping Republicans in other races. For 30 years, from 1946–76, it was represented by Carl Albert, speaker of the House his last six years and majority leader during the Kennedy-Johnson years. Until 1996 it had never elected a Republican congressman.

Today the congressman from the 3d is Wes Watkins, elected as a Republican in 1996, but also with a Democratic background: he was elected as a Democrat to replace Albert in 1976 and held the district until he ran unsuccessfully for governor in 1990 and in 1994 as an Independent. Watkins grew up in a family that moved around, from Arkansas to California and back again. He graduated from Oklahoma State, worked for the university and for a local development agency, then ran his own real estate and homebuilding firm for nine years. In 1974, at 36, he was elected to the state Senate. In 1976, when Albert retired, he ran for Congress and won the Democratic nomination by beating Albert aide Charles Ward. In the House he served on Appropriations for 10 years and concentrated on encouraging rural development, including advanced technology and international trade centers at Oklahoma State. He had a middle-of-the-House voting record and headed the House Rural Caucus and the Congressional Prayer Breakfast Group.

In 1990 Watkins ran for governor and lost the Democratic runoff to David Walters, 51%–49%. He served as president of a Stillwater investment firm and in 1992 he supported Ross Perot for president. In 1994 he ran for governor as an Independent, finishing third with a respectable 23% of the vote and carrying the 3d District. In December 1995, when conservative Democratic Congressman Bill Brewster announced his retirement, Watkins plunged into the race as a Republican because he was for a balanced budget amendment and against gun control—a risky move in a district where Democrats outnumber Republicans 4 to 1. "The national Democratic Party is controlled by extreme liberals and does not represent Oklahoma's traditional and conservative moral values," he said. In May 1996 the best-known local Democrat, former Lieutenant Governor Robert Kerr III, decided not to run.

"I'm the same Wes Watkins," he said, adding that he had been promised a seat on Ways and Means (which he got) and would work hard for local projects again. The Democratic nominee, state Senator Darryl Roberts, former Carter County District Attorney and Vietnam veteran, attacked Watkins for party disloyalty, flipflopping on issues and avoiding debates. He stressed his own work for education and law enforcement and accused Watkins of switching from pro-choice to anti-abortion. Watkins replied that he had "quite a transition in my life" after the birth of a premature grandson who "basically was lifeless." Watkins said that Roberts had voted 50 times to raise taxes and fees, and a Watkins ad showed Roberts letting criminals out on the street, a reference to his support of a Specialized Supervision Program to relieve overcrowding in prisons.

Watkins raised and spent far more money, $1.1 million to Roberts's $542,000. Although polls showed the race even, in November Watkins won 51%–45%, with large margins in the northern counties around Stillwater, but also carrying Little Dixie. He boasted that he had never lost the 3d District, as a Democrat, an Independent and a Republican. With his Democratic past and his priority on district needs, he will probably not be a completely loyal Republican. But he appears strong in this long-Democratic district.

The People: Pop. 1990: 524,287; 56% rural; 16% age 65+; 83% White; 4% Black; 1% Asian; 11% Amer. Indian; 1% Hispanic origin. Households: 60% married couple families; 27% married couple fams. w. children; 35% college educ.; median household income: $18,394; per capita income: $9,635; median gross rent: $294; median house value: $35,800.

1996 Presidential Vote

Clinton (D)	92,007	(47%)
Dole (R)	77,287	(40%)
Perot (I)	24,580	(13%)

1992 Presidential Vote

Clinton (D)	94,753	(41%)
Bush (R)	77,040	(34%)
Perot (I)	55,973	(24%)

Rep. Wes Watkins (R)

Elected 1996; b. Dec. 15, 1938, DeQueen, AR; home, Stillwater; OK St. U., B.S. 1960, M.S. 1961; Presbyterian; married (Lou).

Career: Dir., High School Relations, OK State U., 1963–66; Exec. Dir., Kiamichi Econ. Development Dist., 1966–67; Residential construction, 1967–77; OK Senate, 1974–76; U.S. House of Reps., 1976–90; Pres. & CEO, World Export Services, 1990–96.

DC Office: 2312 RHOB 20515, 202-225-4565; Fax: 202-225-5966.

District Offices: Ada, 405-436-1980; McAlester, 918-423-5951; Stillwater, 405-743-1400.

Committees: *Ways & Means* (20th of 23 R): Human Resources; Oversight.

Group Ratings and Key Votes: Newly Elected

Election Results

1996 general	Wes Watkins (R)	98,526	(51%)	($1,106,300)
	Darryl Roberts (D)	86,647	(45%)	($542,286)
	Others	6,335	(3%)	
1996 primary	Wes Watkins (R)	12,740	(79%)	
	Evelyn L. Rogers (R)	1,262	(8%)	
	Ken B. Privett (R)	1,045	(6%)	
	Others	1,051	(7%)	
1994 general	Bill Brewster (D)	115,731	(74%)	($833,456)
	Darrel DeWayne Tallant (R)	41,147	(26%)	

FOURTH DISTRICT

Early in this century the brown hills west of Oklahoma City and north of the Red River filled up rapidly with farmers, riding north from Texas, past the well-watered green lands of the east toward the bare brown pasturelands of the southwest. These were young people with large families, and in the years since, this land has emptied out, as children have grown up and moved elsewhere and fewer hands are needed for farming. People in southwest Oklahoma instead have accumulated around major government institutions: the state capital of Oklahoma City; Norman, home of the University of Oklahoma; Lawton, to the southwest, home of the Army's Fort Sill.

These are major landmarks for the 4th Congressional District of Oklahoma, which begins a few miles from the oil-derrick-surrounded state Capitol in Oklahoma City, smack dab in the middle of the state, and proceeds south and west to cover half of Oklahoma's Red River Valley. Demographically, this seat is becoming more suburban, but the cultural tone remains rural. That is true even in Oklahoma City suburbs, stretching out over the midwestern mile grid roads, where in new subdivisions dust still gets tracked indoors, and people still prefer chicken-fried steak to stir-fried chicken (though they eat both). Politically, this country is ancestrally Democratic, but Norman, Lawton and the Oklahoma City fringe now tend to vote Republican, and the 4th District has voted twice against Bill Clinton.

The congressman from the 4th District is J. C. Watts, a Republican, former college and professional football player, conservative Christian and African-American. He won the seat in 1994 when 14-year incumbent Dave McCurdy, one of the Democrats' most competent and politically skillful moderates, ran for the Senate and lost. Watts grew up in Eufaula, Oklahoma (named after the largest town in the Alabama county where George Wallace grew up), son of a Baptist minister who was also a policeman and traded cattle; he was one of two children who integrated his elementary school. "My thinking was formed in Eufaula, Oklahoma, under the roof of Buddy and Helen Watts, where you were going to work and be responsible. We were in church on Sunday morning for Bible study. In that home you understood the meaning of sacrifice, commitment, sticking with it. I didn't know growing up if this was conservative or liberal." J. C. Watts was a quarterback at the University of Oklahoma and led the team to Big Eight championships and Orange Bowl wins in 1980 and 1981. From 1981–86, he played in the Canadian Football League. In Oklahoma, Watts owned real estate and petroleum marketing companies and was a youth minister at the Sunnylane Southern Baptist Church in Del City. He became a Republican in 1989, "because I think the Democratic Party leadership—not the Democrats but their party leadership—has totally deserted the values of Buddy and Helen Watts." In 1990 he ran for state corporation commissioner and won.

In 1994, Watts decided to run for Congress, and had plenty of competition. He led in the Republican primary, 49%–35%, but was forced into a runoff in which he was accused of business improprieties. He won that race by just 757 votes. In October Democrat David Perryman ran an ad opening with a picture of Watts in high school with an Afro haircut, followed by Perryman as a Future Farmer of America holding a pig: an ad that some in the national press suggested was racist. Watts won by a comfortable 52%–43%; though he lost most of the rural counties, he won 60% in Norman's Cleveland County and 58% in Oklahoma County.

Watts inevitably attracted attention as one of two black Republicans in the House. Newt Gingrich asked him to respond to Bill Clinton's Saturday radio address right after the election, and Watts declined to join the Congressional Black Caucus ("I didn't come to Congress to be a black leader or a white leader, but a leader"). In the House his voting record was conservative, with some exceptions; he supported more spending on veterans health than other Republicans and counseled going slow on repealing racial quotas and preferences. On the National Security Committee he worked successfully to save Tinker Air Force Base from the base closing list and opposed "privatization in place" of military depots. He pushed to allow the military to provide health care to military retirees over 65. His major legislative project, co-sponsored with Jim Talent, was a community renewal bill, to encourage investment and savings, allow school choice and allow use of faith-based programs in poor areas. "Let's allow the neighborhood and faith-based organizations, the people who have the same zip code as those who need the help, to help solve some of the problems. The faith-based organizations are the ones really getting results."

Watts was a featured and inspirational speaker at the 1996 Republican National Convention. "Character is simply doing right when nobody is looking," he said. But the old-line networks which spotlight Jesse Jackson, who has never been elected to any serious public office, didn't seem to take much notice of this black politician elected in a 7% black district. In February 1997 he gave the response to Clinton's State of the Union, a polished performance obscured for some by the verdict in the O.J. Simpson civil trial which was announced just minutes before Watts began his address, and in the capital by a *Washington Post* article that spliced together an interview with Watts in a way that suggested he called Jesse Jackson and Washington Mayor Marion Berry "race-hustling poverty pimps"; Watts later said he used the phrase in reference to "some of the leadersip in the black community" but angrily denied he connected it specifically to Barry and Jackson. At home he had vehement opposition in 1996 from state Representative Ed Crocker, who accused Watts of defaulting on a bank loan and pointing out he had fathered two children out of wedlock in 1976. Watts admitted the latter but denied the former. He won by the increased margin of 58%–40%, carrying all but three rural counties along the Red River.

The People: Pop. 1990: 524,407; 26% rural; 11% age 65+; 83% White; 7% Black; 2% Asian; 5% Amer. Indian; 4% Hispanic origin. Households: 62% married couple families; 31% married couple fams. w. children; 47% college educ.; median household income: $25,391; per capita income: $11,554; median gross rent: $364; median house value: $50,800.

1996 Presidential Vote			1992 Presidential Vote		
Dole (R)	92,011	(49%)	Bush (R)	90,975	(42%)
Clinton (D)	75,291	(40%)	Clinton (D)	72,551	(33%)
Perot (I)	20,376	(11%)	Perot (I)	53,894	(25%)

Rep. J. C. Watts, Jr. (R)

Elected 1994; b. Nov. 18, 1956, Eufaula; home, Norman; U. of OK, B.A. 1981; Baptist; married (Frankie).

Career: Pro football player, Canadian League, 1981–86; Businessman, 1986–94; OK Corp. Comm., 1990–94, Chmn., 1992–94.

DC Office: 1210 LHOB 20515, 202-225-6165; Fax: 202-225-3512.

District Offices: Lawton, 405-357-2131; Norman, 405-329-6500.

Committees: *National Security* (18th of 30 R): Military Personnel (Vice Chmn.); Military Procurement. *Transportation & Infrastructure* (40th of 40 R): Surface Transportation.

Group Ratings

	ADA	ACLU	AFS	LCV	CFA	CON	NFIB	COC	ACU	NTLC	CHC
1996	0	20	0	15	8	36	100	100	100	95	100
1995	0	—	—	6	8	56	—	100	96	—	—

National Journal Ratings

	1995 LIB — 1995 CONS			1996 LIB — 1996 CONS		
Economic	0%	—	74%	0%	—	82%
Social	32%	—	65%	14%	—	77%
Foreign	15%	—	73%	36%	—	63%

Key Votes of the 104th Congress

1. Reduce Medicare Growth $	Y	5. Flag Amendment	Y	9. Cuban Embargo	Y
2. Ovrd. Product Liab. Veto	Y	6. Drop EPA Limits	N	10. Bar Bosnia Troop $	Y
3. Increase Min. Wage	N	7. Repeal Assault-Weap. Ban	Y	11. Cut Anti-Missile Defense	Y
4. Welfare Reform	Y	8. Ovrd. Part. Birth Veto	Y	12. Bar U.N. Uniforms	Y

Election Results

1996 general	J.C. Watts, Jr. (R)	106,923	(58%)	($1,363,291)
	Ed Crocker (D)	73,950	(40%)	($350,073)
	Others	4,500	(2%)	
1996 primary	J.C. Watts, Jr. (R)	unopposed		
1994 general	J.C. Watts, Jr. (R)	80,251	(52%)	($568,942)
	David Perryman (D)	67,237	(43%)	($222,946)
	Bill Tiffee (I)	7,913	(5%)	

FIFTH DISTRICT

Oklahoma City, suddenly the center of the nation's attention in April 1995 when a bomb destroyed the Alfred P. Murrah federal building, killing 168 and injuring more than 500, has for a century been the center of Oklahoma. Oklahoma City, like many state capitals, was not the spontaneous creation of commerce but the deliberate creation of government, sited in the geographic center of the state, on what turned out to be oil lands; oil rigs were pumping crude on the grounds of the domeless Capitol until 1989. The land here is browner and more eroded by creeks than the greener, rolling Oklahoma farmland farther east. From its center Oklahoma City has grown far out into the countryside, followed, as in so many southwestern cities, by expanding city limits so that it extends into five counties and four congressional districts and covers 624 square miles.

The 5th Congressional District of Oklahoma includes most of Oklahoma City, but it is a carefully chosen part: the most Democratic sections of the city, including its black areas, were chopped off and put in the 6th District. This is a solidly Republican area as a result. The 5th proceeds north through wheat country, to the onetime state capital of Guthrie and the market town of Ponca City, areas as Republican as any similar place in nearby Kansas. Connected by a strip of mostly uninhabited Osage County is Bartlesville, headquarters of Phillips Petroleum, solidly conservative in the Oil Patch manner. The 5th is by far Oklahoma's most Republican district: a constituency created by Democratic legislatures to corral solidly Republican precincts and give Democrats a chance to win the five other districts, as they did at one time or another in the 1980s though they hold none of them now.

The congressman from the 5th District is Ernest Istook, first elected in 1992, in his views and attitudes a forerunner of the Republican freshmen of 1994. With heavy turnover he became in just two terms the most senior of the state's House Republicans. Istook is the grandson of Hungarian immigrants; after graduating from Baylor, he was a radio reporter in Oklahoma City and went to law school at night. He attracted attention as Governor David Boren's head of the alcohol control board, where he refused to stop an investigation of liquor distributors; the state Senate denied him confirmation to complete his term in that post. He practiced law and was elected to the Oklahoma House in 1986. In 1992 he ran for the House, taking on 16-year incumbent Republican Mickey Edwards, a member of the House leadership who had 386 overdrafts on the House bank. Edwards finished third in the primary, with 26% to 32% for Istook and 37% for 1990 gubernatorial nominee Bill Price, who harshly criticized Edwards. Istook ran on conservative issues and won the runoff 56%–44%. He won the general election by only 53%–47% over oil and gas lawyer Laurie Williams, who attacked Istook for his anti-abortion stance.

In the House Istook has a conservative voting record and has used his seat on Appropriations to press for conservative policies; he "brings a physical intensity and nervous energy to his work," writes *National Journal*'s Richard Cohen. He has even voted against local pork: against a bill with money for Oklahoma City's Tinker Air Force Base, against the MAPS light-rail trolley. He pressed to learn the cost of Hillary Rodham Clinton's healthcare task force and the role of Treasury Secretary Robert Rubin in the Mexico bailout.

On three major initiatives he has been frustrated but plugs on. One is his effort to ban organizations that receive federal funds from using more than 5% of their money for lobbying: welfare reform for lobbyists. This was fought vociferously by nonprofits eager to use taxpayers' dollars as somehow an infringement on their freedom of speech. Different forms of the Istook amendment were passed by both houses, and a Labor-HHS appropriation bill was held up for a time by this issue, but no limit was passed. Another cause was Istook's amendment to allow states to refuse to use federal funds to pay for abortions in cases of rape and incest, without any penalty; the amount of money was small, but the principle was important to many on both sides for non-trivial reasons. "Life is about a lot more than just financial issues," Istook said; but again his side lost. A third Istook cause was to require parental permission for condom distribution and birth control advice, just as permission is required for a pupil to take aspirin; this was opposed by the Clinton Administration and dropped as too controversial to pass. Istook also backed legislation to crack down on Indian small businesses that fail to pay state sales taxes, and he introduced a school prayer constitutional amendment in both the 104th and 105th Congresses.

But Istook was successful in limiting direct lending to 40% of all student loans, banning Centers for Disease Control research on gunshot wounds, eliminating the Young American Chef at the White House and (after bringing the issue to the Supreme Court) stopping the Clinton Administration's imposition of a striker replacement law that failed to pass even in the Democratic Congress. As a co-chair of the Conservative Action Team, Istook is sure to pursue these and other original causes in the 105th Congress. He was easily reelected in 1994 and 1996.

The People: Pop. 1990: 523,729; 13% rural; 13% age 65+; 85% White; 6% Black; 2% Asian; 5% Amer. Indian; 3% Hispanic origin. Households: 57% married couple families; 26% married couple fams. w. children; 56% college educ.; median household income: $28,348; per capita income: $15,024; median gross rent: $370; median house value: $58,200.

1996 Presidential Vote			1992 Presidential Vote		
Dole (R)	128,792	(59%)	Bush (R)	129,379	(51%)
Clinton (D)	68,222	(31%)	Clinton (D)	62,251	(25%)
Perot (I)	20,668	(9%)	Perot (I)	59,542	(24%)

Rep. Ernest J. Istook, Jr. (R)

Elected 1992; b. Feb. 11, 1950, Ft. Worth, TX; home, Warr Acres; Baylor U., B.A. 1971, Oklahoma City U. Law Schl., J.D. 1976; Mormon; married (Judy).

Career: Political reporter, Oklahoma City KOMA Radio, 1972–73, WKY Radio, 1973–76; Dir., OK Alcohol Beverage Control Bd., 1977; Practicing atty., 1977–92; OK House of Reps., 1986–92.

DC Office: 119 CHOB 20515, 202-225-2132; Fax: 202-226-1463; e-mail: istook@hr.house.gov.

District Offices: Bartlesville, 918-336-5546; Oklahoma City, 405-942-3636; Ponca City, 405-762-6778.

Committees: *Appropriations* (17th of 34 R): Labor, Health & Human Services & Education; National Security; Treasury, Postal Service & General Government.

Group Ratings

	ADA	ACLU	AFS	LCV	CFA	CON	NFIB	COC	ACU	NTLC	CHC
1996	10	6	8	15	23	38	92	94	100	98	100
1995	0	—	—	13	0	85	—	96	96	—	—

National Journal Ratings

	1995 LIB		1995 CONS	1996 LIB		1996 CONS
Economic	36%	—	60%	20%	—	76%
Social	0%	—	79%	0%	—	90%
Foreign	15%	—	73%	0%	—	79%

Key Votes of the 104th Congress

1. Reduce Medicare Growth $	Y	5. Flag Amendment	Y	9. Cuban Embargo	Y
2. Ovrd. Product Liab. Veto	Y	6. Drop EPA Limits	N	10. Bar Bosnia Troop $	Y
3. Increase Min. Wage	N	7. Repeal Assault-Weap. Ban	Y	11. Cut Anti-Missile Defense	N
4. Welfare Reform	Y	8. Ovrd. Part. Birth Veto	Y	12. Bar U.N. Uniforms	Y

Election Results

1996 general	Ernest J. Istook, Jr. (R)	148,362	(70%)	($306,411)
	James L. Forsythe (D)	57,594	(27%)	($40,483)
	Others	6,835	(3%)	
1996 primary	Ernest J. Istook, Jr. (R)	unopposed		
1994 general	Ernest J. Istook, Jr. (R)	136,877	(78%)	($274,179)
	Tom Keith (I)	38,270	(22%)	($9,666)

SIXTH DISTRICT

First settled just a century ago, western Oklahoma is a fertile land forever at the mercy of the elements. The western plains are scorching hot under the summer sun and snow-blown in winter; this is one of the windiest parts of America. The rural counties here have far fewer people than before the dust bowl of the 1930s. Oil and natural gas drilling in the Anadarko basin and nearby areas was a boom industry in the late 1970s, then collapsed in the 1980s.

The 6th Congressional District of Oklahoma is made up of the western plains of Oklahoma, plus blue-collar and black neighborhoods in Oklahoma City. A few of its counties in the south, settled by farmers crossing the Red River from Texas, have been heavily Democratic ever since. But most of these plains were settled by farmers coming south from Kansas, and these have long been heavily Republican. These divisions are as permanent as if Oklahoma had been split down the middle during the Civil War, even though there were no whites in the state at the time. The bigger fact here is depopulation: counties wholly within the 6th Congressional District had 423,000 people in 1930 and 282,000 in 1990. Some 40% percent of the district's votes are cast in metropolitan Oklahoma City.

The congressman from the 6th District is Frank Lucas, a Republican chosen in the May 1994 special election. Lucas's roots are in western Oklahoma; he owns a farm and cattle ranch in Roger Mills County and was elected to the Oklahoma House in 1988, at 28. The vacancy arose when Glenn English, a conservative Democrat who had represented the 6th for 19 years, resigned to head the National Rural Electric Cooperative Association—in effect, to lobby the subcommittee he chaired for years. Lucas had serious competition in both the primary and general elections. In the primary he trailed 36%–34% state Senator Brooks Douglass, who had witnessed the murder of his parents as a child, and was campaigning from his Oklahoma City base with a western accent. In the runoff Lucas ridiculed "some Johnny-come-lately dressed up like a drugstore cowboy" and carried all the rural areas to win 56%–44%. In the general he faced Dan Webber, 27-year-old press secretary to outgoing Senator David Boren. Lucas ran an ad showing the U.S. Capitol ("this is where Dan Webber has worked his entire adult life") and Oklahoma farmland ("this is where Frank Lucas has worked his entire adult life") and benefited from Oklahoma Taxpayers Union ads and Christian Coalition voting guides, and won 54%–46%.

Lucas has seats on the Agriculture and Banking Committees and has a solidly conservative voting record. As a harbinger of the freshman class of 1994, he enthusiastically supported the Contract With America. Representing the site of the Oklahoma City bombing, he introduced the resolution condemning it and the bill for relief spending. He supported the anti-terrorism bill and, after the Oklahoma City trial was moved to Denver, sponsored the amendment for closed-circuit broadcasting of out-of-town trials, whereupon Oklahoma City residents were able to listen as Timothy McVeigh was convicted on all 11 counts of murder and conspiracy. He hailed the base-closing commission decision to close two other maintenance depots and keep open Oklahoma City's Tinker Air Force Base. He supported the SBA loan program citing how his family got an SBA loan in the 1970s.

The most important—in Washington and at home—legislation he worked on was the Freedom to Farm Act, which he backed. "We have to get Uncle Sam out of the farm business and give farmers the ability to produce for markets. This bill will help farmers, by breaking the bonds of the old and ringing in a market-oriented program which will guide us into the next century." He backed reform of the Endangered Species Act and hit the Fish and Wildlife Service for considering listing the Arkansas River shiner fish as an endangered species. He sponsored a bill to prevent the IRS from taxing income that farmers defer for a year through commodity contracts.

Lucas was elected to a full term in November 1994 with an impressive 70%. In 1996 he was opposed by oil and gas businessman Paul Barby, who before his campaign announced he was gay. Barby's brother announced several family members were endorsing Lucas, for policy not personal reasons. Barby spent $417,000 of his own money and carried Oklahoma County narrowly. But Lucas carried even the heavily Democratic rural counties north of I-70 and won 64% of the vote.

The People: Pop. 1990: 524,638; 30% rural; 15% age 65+; 77% White; 13% Black; 1% Asian; 5% Amer. Indian; 4% Hispanic origin. Households: 57% married couple families; 26% married couple fams. w. children; 38% college educ.; median household income: $21,797; per capita income: $10,540; median gross rent: $323; median house value: $39,500.

1996 Presidential Vote

Dole (R)	86,670	(47%)
Clinton (D)	75,783	(41%)
Perot (I)	20,149	(11%)

1992 Presidential Vote

Bush (R)	91,966	(43%)
Clinton (D)	73,516	(34%)
Perot (I).	49,268	(23%)

Rep. Frank D. Lucas (R)

Elected May 1994; b. Jan. 6, 1960, Cheyenne; home, Cheyenne; OK St. U., B.S. 1982; Baptist; married (Lynda).

Career: Farmer & rancher; OK House of Reps., 1988–1994.

DC Office: 107 CHOB 20515, 202-225-5565; Fax: 202-225-8698.

District Offices: Enid, 405-237-9224; Oklahoma City, 405-231-5511; Woodward, 405-256-5752.

Committees: *Agriculture* (12th of 27 R): Forestry, Resource Conservation & Research; General Farm Commodities; Livestock, Dairy & Poultry. *Banking & Financial Services* (12th of 30 R): Capital Markets, Securities & Government Sponsored Enterprises (Vice Chmn.); Domestic & International Monetary Policy.

Group Ratings

	ADA	ACLU	AFS	LCV	CFA	CON	NFIB	COC	ACU	NTLC	CHC
1996	0	12	0	8	0	34	100	100	100	100	100
1995	0	—	—	0	0	38	—	100	88	—	—

National Journal Ratings

	1995 LIB — 1995 CONS			1996 LIB — 1996 CONS		
Economic	0%	—	74%	0%	—	82%
Social	0%	—	79%	14%	—	77%
Foreign	0%	—	85%	0%	—	79%

Key Votes of the 104th Congress

1. Reduce Medicare Growth $	Y	5. Flag Amendment	Y	9. Cuban Embargo	Y
2. Ovrd. Product Liab. Veto	Y	6. Drop EPA Limits	N	10. Bar Bosnia Troop $	Y
3. Increase Min. Wage	N	7. Repeal Assault-Weap. Ban	Y	11. Cut Anti-Missile Defense	N
4. Welfare Reform	Y	8. Ovrd. Part. Birth Veto	Y	12. Bar U.N. Uniforms	Y

Election Results

1996 general	Frank D. Lucas (R)	113,499	(64%)	($439,969)
	Paul M. Barby (D)	64,173	(36%)	($476,471)
1996 primary	Frank D. Lucas (R)	unopposed		
1994 general	Frank D. Lucas (R)	106,961	(70%)	($146,806)
	Jeffrey S. Tollett (D)	45,399	(30%)	($22,760)

OREGON

Oregon is an experimental commonwealth and laboratory of reform on the Pacific Rim, a maker of national trends. It is far removed from where most Americans live, but closer in touch with the rest of America than sometimes appears: within minutes after a tree branch brushed a power line in Oregon in August 1996, the entire western power grid—"the largest machine man has ever made," in one expert's words—shut down all the way from the Canadian border to San Diego, where the Republican National Convention was opening two days later. Oregon has led the nation with bike trails and Nike sneakers, light rail trams and Pendleton shirts; ordinary Oregonians have made the national news from the nine volunteer firefighters from Prineville who died fighting a Colorado forest fire to Tonya Harding and her thuggish entourage. Oregon is an affluent high-tech civilization where one can still see much the same land and water—and rain—that Lewis and Clark saw in 1805 when they came down the Columbia River gorge, past what is now Portland, to the vast Pacific Ocean.

This Oregon was settled by Americans when John Jacob Astor set up his fur trading post at Astoria in 1811 and when New England Yankees rode the Oregon Trail and down the Columbia to the well-watered Willamette Valley. In this remote land, nearly 2,000 miles from the Mississippi River frontier and 700 miles from the small settlements of California, the orderly, productive society of Oregon—a kind of western New England—was built. It grew steadily over the years, with a few booms—when timber, always its first industry, surged in 1900–10, during the war and after in the 1940s, and in the 1970s when home building skyrocketed and Oregon's natural environment began to be widely appreciated. Too widely for some, like Governor Tom McCall (1966–74), who used to urge people to visit Oregon, "but for heaven's sake don't come to live here."

Today's Oregon is more confident it can live comfortably with growth. In the 1990s it has been the nation's ninth-fastest growing state, adding nearly 400,000 new residents. The newcomers are highly educated, sparkplugs of the economic growth that leaves employers begging for workers, the reason half of Oregon households have personal computers. The newcomers fill Portland's postmodern skyscrapers and high-tech offices in Silicon Forest to the west, and they prosper and invent in the smaller cities and towns of the green Willamette Valley and the sere lands of eastern Oregon as well.

They come to a state which has a distinctive culture. Founded by New England churchmen, Oregon today is America's most unchurched state, with the lowest rate of church membership, with large numbers of believers in astrology, New Age lore and the like. To the innovations of this cultural left the public voices of Oregon's big institutions, like those of New England, have been friendly. Oregon a generation ago produced one of the first bottle-deposit laws, decriminalized marijuana, legalized most abortions before *Roe v. Wade*, and backed limits on development and use of property. More recently, it has produced an Oregon Health Plan which rations medical care, denying specified low-priority treatments to Medicaid recipients, and in 1994 adopted a measure legalizing physician-assisted suicide. A gun control law passed banning semi-automatic weapons, and weekly betting on professional sports games was legalized. More recently Oregon, quite unlike New England, seems to be moving a bit in the other direction. Voters in 1996 rejected an expansion of the bottle bill and bonds for Portland's light rail, and while Democrats hold most high offices here, Republicans control both houses of the state legislature.

It seems the articulate liberalism based in Portland and university towns is being challenged by an increasingly vocal conservatism in the rest of the state. One spark was lit in the early 1990s when the federal government and a federal judge banned logging of old-growth forests to protect the spotted owl. Loggers protested, Bill Clinton convened a timber summit in Portland in 1993, legislators in Washington moved to pass timber salvage and other bills that kept the logging industry going, even while the rest of the economy expanded. Other sparks came from the Oregon Citizens' Alliance (OCA), which backed referenda from 1990–94 limiting abortion, denouncing homosexuality and repealing gay rights laws; all lost, but some by only narrow margins. Voting on all these measures followed similar patterns, with Portland and the university towns taking liberal positions and counties east of the Cascades and outside the metro reach taking more conservative stands. But in daily life, each region goes its own way. Portland is as proud of its Metropolitan Greenspaces and light rail lines as it is of its Rose Festival, and Mayor Vera Katz is an innovative and politically shrewd liberal. But two dozen other cities and counties have passed measures prohibiting "special rights" for gays.

These cultural gaps are reflected increasingly in Oregon's partisan politics. Back in the 1960s this state showed only the mildest of regional variations in partisan preference, disposed to support articulate moderate Republicans, like its two long-term senators, Mark Hatfield and Bob Packwood, first elected in 1966 and 1968, both now no longer in Congress. But in the 1980s and 1990s cultural splits have favored first Portland-oriented Democrats and now rather conservative Republicans. Presidentially Oregon has voted Democratic in the last three elections, but Bill Clinton's margin narrowed slightly. In gubernatorial elections Oregon has elected three Portland-backed Democrats in a row. But they have emphasized different issues. Neil Goldschmidt, former Portland mayor, won 52%–48% and emphasized transportation and land use planning, and did not seek reelection. Barbara Roberts, elected 46%–40% in 1990 as an OCA-backed candidate split the Republican vote, had low job ratings and did not seek a second term. John Kitzhaber, elected 51%–42% in 1994, a physician and the author of the Oregon Health Plan, has worked with the Republican legislature which came in with him, though they have fought bitterly at times.

And in 1996 Oregon had two open-seat Senate contests, one in January to replace Bob Packwood after his fall 1995 resignation, the other in November to replace Mark Hatfield, who retired after 30 years. Both were decided by narrow margins. In the January election, the nation's first election conducted by mail-in ballots—another Oregon innovation—Democrat Ron Wyden beat Republican Gordon Smith 48%–47%, carrying the Portland area, university towns, and northwest coastal counties 56%–40%. In November Smith beat Democrat Tom Bruggere 50%–46%, carrying the areas outside of Portland, 60%–37%.

Behind these geographical divisions are cultural attitudes; as Americans become more affluent they can afford to choose places to live that are culturally sympathetic. For much of the 1980s growth in Oregon was concentrated in metro Portland, which tended to attract bright young people of a liberal bent. In the 1990s the balance has shifted in the other direction: voter turnout between 1992 and 1996 fell most sharply in the city of Portland and the university towns, the state's liberal bastions, even while it was rising east of the Cascades in the counties

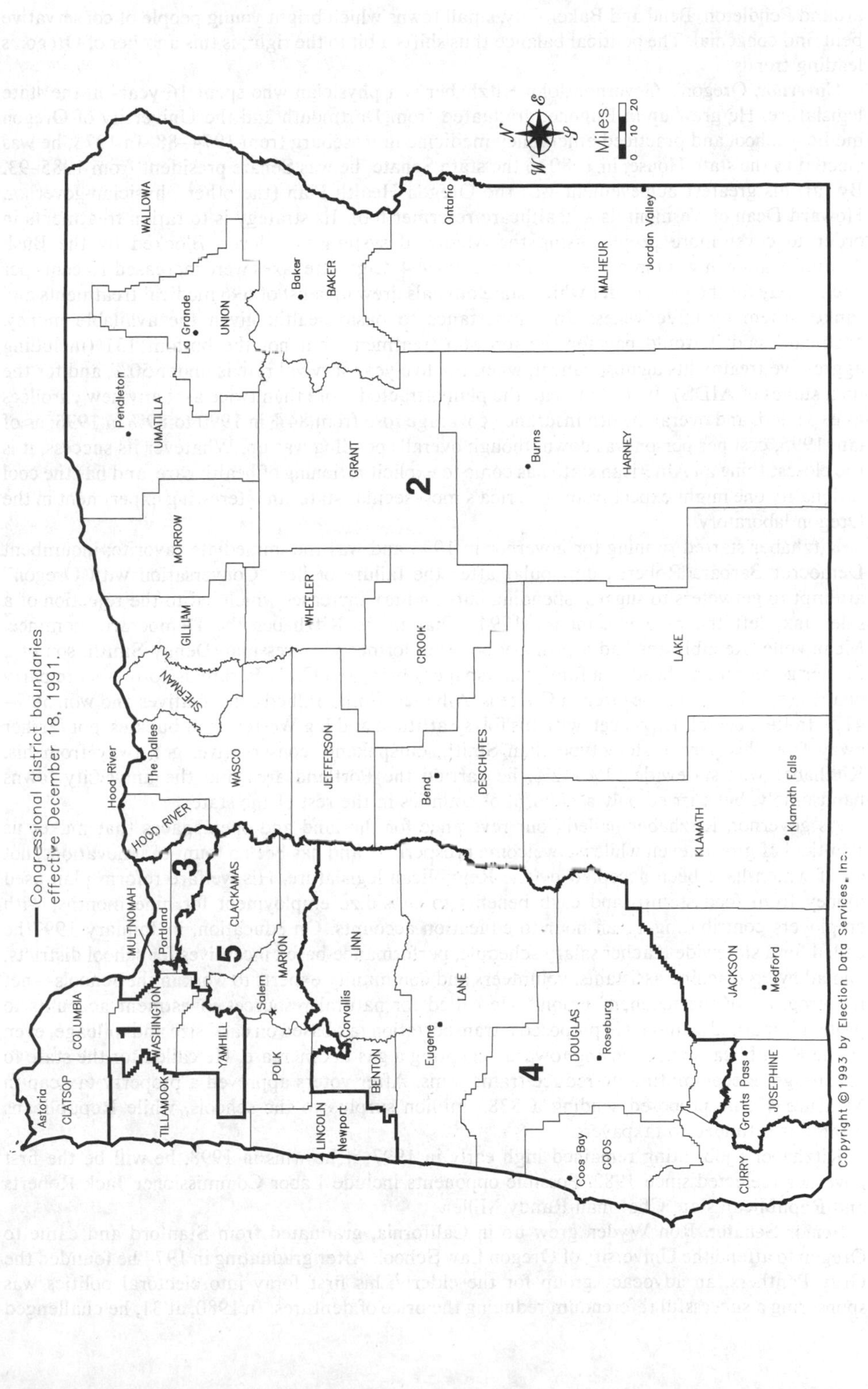
Congressional district boundaries effective December 18, 1991.
Miles
0 10 20
Astoria
CLATSOP
COLUMBIA
TILLAMOOK
WASHINGTON
YAMHILL
MULTNOMAH
Portland
CLACKAMAS
HOOD RIVER
Hood River
The Dalles
WASCO
SHERMAN
GILLIAM
MORROW
UMATILLA
Pendleton
UNION
La Grande
WALLOWA
BAKER
Baker
Ontario
MALHEUR
Jordan Valley
GRANT
WHEELER
JEFFERSON
CROOK
HARNEY
Burns
DESCHUTES
Bend
LAKE
KLAMATH
Klamath Falls
MARION
Salem
POLK
LINN
BENTON
Corvallis
LINCOLN
Newport
LANE
Eugene
DOUGLAS
Roseburg
COOS
Coos Bay
CURRY
JOSEPHINE
Grants Pass
JACKSON
Medford
1
2
3
4
5
Copyright © 1993 by Election Data Services, Inc.

around Pendleton, Bend and Baker City, small towns which bright young people of conservative bent find congenial. The political balance thus shifts a bit to the right; is this another of Oregon's leading trends?

Governor. Oregon's Governor John Kitzhaber is a physician who spent 16 years in the state legislature. He grew up in Eugene, graduated from Dartmouth and the University of Oregon medical school and practiced emergency medicine in Roseburg from 1974–88. In 1978, he was elected to the state House, in 1980 to the state Senate; he was Senate president from 1985–93. By far, his greatest achievement was the Oregon Health Plan (the other physician-governor, Howard Dean of Vermont, is a healthcare reformer too). Its strategy is to ration treatments in order to cover more people, using the Medicaid system as a lever. Blocked by the Bush Administration, it went into effect in February 1994. Cigarette taxes were increased 10 cents per pack to pay for the plan, under which state officials drew up a list of 696 medical treatments and ranked them by effectiveness and importance to basic health; given the available money, Medicaid said it would pay for the top 565 treatments but not the bottom 131 (including aggressive treatments against cancer, when the five-year survival rate is under 50%, and for the final stages of AIDS). In its first year, the plan attracted more than twice as many new enrollees as expected, and overall health insurance coverage rose from 84% in 1990 to 89% in 1996; as of late 1995, cost per person was down, though overall spending was up. Whatever its success, it is the closest thing an American state has come to explicit rationing of health care, and has the cool rationality one might expect from America's most secular state: an interesting experiment in the Oregon laboratory.

Kitzhaber started running for governor in 1993 and was the immediate favorite; incumbent Democrat Barbara Roberts, unpopular after the failure of her "Conversation with Oregon" attempt to get voters to suggest spending cuts and tax increases which led to the rejection of a sales tax, left the race in January 1994. That made Kitzhaber the Democratic nominee. Meanwhile, Republicans had a primary between former Congressman Denny Smith, son of a former governor and head of a family newspaper chain, and Craig Berkman, former state party chairman and critic of the Oregon Citizens' Alliance; Smith rallied conservatives and won 50%–41%. In the general, Kitzhaber, with his folksy attitude and big Western belt buckles, got farther away from his party's stereotype than Smith, outspokenly conservative, got away from his. Kitzhaber won statewide 51%–42%; he carried the Portland area and the university towns handsomely, but carried only a handful of counties in the rest of the state.

As governor, Kitzhaber hailed "our reverence for the land and open spaces that makes us skeptical of growth even while we welcome prosperity," and has been a fount of innovations, not all of which have been accepted by the Republican legislature. His welfare reform plan used money from food stamps and cash benefits to subsidize employment for nine months, with employers contributing $1 an hour to education accounts. On education, in January 1997 he called for a statewide teacher salary schedule, performance-based incentives for school districts, and allowing teaching assistants, volunteers and community experts to work in the schools—not the program of the teachers' unions. He called for natural resources investment accounts to protect imperiled salmon. He proposed a transportation tax based on cars' size and mileage, even as the Republicans were moving toward accepting a gas tax increase. He called for the state to encourage telecommuting, to reduce traffic jams. After voters approved a property tax cap in Measure 47, he proposed sending a $383 million surplus to the schools, while Republicans wanted it refunded to taxpayers.

Kitzhaber's job rating remained high early in 1997; if he wins in 1998, he will be the first governor reelected since 1982. Possible opponents include Labor Commissioner Jack Roberts and Republican state Chairman Randy Miller.

Senior Senator. Ron Wyden grew up in California, graduated from Stanford and came to Oregon to attend the University of Oregon Law School. After graduating in 1974 he founded the Gray Panthers, an advocacy group for the elderly; his first foray into electoral politics was sponsoring a successful referendum reducing the price of dentures. In 1980, at 31, he challenged an incumbent in the heavily Democratic 3d District, which covers most of Portland, and won the primary 60%–40%. In his first term in the House, he got a seat on Commerce Committee and became an ally of both Chairman John Dingell and Health Subcommittee Chairman Henry Waxman. Wyden has a genius for coming up with sensible-sounding ideas no one else has thought of and a knack for making the counter-intuitive political alliances which are so helpful in passing unfamiliar measures through the House. His achievements include a law, co-sponsored with Connecticut Republican Nancy Johnson, reducing federally funded community health clinics' malpractice insurance premiums by requiring the Justice Department to defend them in malpractice cases. He also passed a law to conserve the Pacific yew, a rare tree needed to produce a cancer-fighting drug, and an infant formula bill to prohibit manufacturers from engaging in anti-competitive bidding practices. He passed a law to allow some unemployed workers to use part of their benefit checks to start small businesses. He worked hard to get a waiver for John Kitzhaber's Oregon Health Plan and to bring the abortifacient drug RU-486 to the United States. He teamed up with Waxman to orchestrate the 1994 hearings at which top executives of tobacco companies were excoriated.

Wyden did not respond confrontationally when Republicans won the House majority in November 1994. He voted for their unfunded mandates bill and for the line-item veto. He opposed adjusting the Consumer Price Index. He proposed a targeted capital gains tax cut and partial tax-free cash benefits for workers who achieve specific company targets. He tried to stop the Energy Department from listing 10 ports as entry points for the return of nuclear waste from foreign reactors.

Then in September 1995 the Senate Ethics Committee recommended the expulsion of Bob Packwood for sexual harassment and Packwood announced he would resign. Packwood had in many ways a distinguished Senate career: he was its leading supporter of abortion rights in the 1970s and as Finance chairman put together the Tax Reform Act of 1986. In the special election to fill his seat, Oregon experimented with a new system—election by mail ballot; though originally a one-time experiment, it may be repeated. Wyden, with his base in Portland (whose TV stations cover most of the state) was a natural candidate. But he had spirited opposition in the primary, for which voting ended December 5, from Eugene-based Congressman Peter DeFazio. They differed on some issues—DeFazio opposed NAFTA, GATT and gun control—and DeFazio was helped when Wyden, taking a quiz on KOIN TV, could not name the prime minister of Canada or locate Bosnia on a globe. DeFazio carried his own district overwhelmingly, holding Wyden to a 50%–44% win. Meanwhile, the Republican nominee was state Senate President Gordon Smith, a frozen vegetable tycoon from eastern Oregon, who ultimately spent $2 million of his own money. With conservative views on cultural issues and far more money, he overwhelmed moderate longtime statewide official Norma Paulus 63%–25% in the primary.

Most polls had the race in a dead heat as Smith adroitly avoided identification with House Republicans' intransigent stands on the budget and won the support of the respected Mark Hatfield (an abortion opponent himself). But organized labor and environmental groups ran heavy flights of ads against him, including a Sierra Club spot that charged spills from his plant had polluted a local creek. Early in January, after balloting started, Wyden said he would stop all negative campaigning; Smith, noting the Sierra Club ad was continuing, refused to join him. Wyden seemed to pick up strength the week before the January 30 deadline and won 48%–47%. This was hailed as a rejection of Newt Gingrich and a victory for abortion rights, but most voters deciding on abortion picked Smith, and Wyden, with his considerable strengths, had just barely managed to win in a state carried by Bill Clinton and Michael Dukakis.

Wyden did not remain quiet long in the Senate. In April he called for disclosure of the names of senators who place "holds" on legislation. Over the summer he worked with California Congressman Christopher Cox to push their amendment prohibiting government censorship of the Internet and urging on-line providers to offer technologies to help parents control their children's access to Internet materials. In September he sponsored an amendment barring HMOs from restricting physicians from mentioning treatment options outside the plan's scope of coverage; this did not pass but got much publicity and prompted an HMO group to promise a voluntary ban. Similarly, a Wyden call for disclosure of airline safety records resulted in FAA action to putting that information on the Internet in January 1997. That month Wyden and Cox introduced a bill to ban state and local taxes on the Internet and content providers. Wyden criticized the Clinton Medicare reform for relying on command and price controls. He proposed his own plan, to cut $100 billion over five years and encourage more managed care for seniors, as in Oregon; he wants more competition in the system while maintaining patients' rights. He argues persuasively that it is necessary to make such reforms now to be prepared for the demographic crunch Medicare faces around 2010. Since Wyden won only the remaining three years of Packwood's term, he comes up for reelection in 1998. He will not be opposed by Smith, who won the other seat in November 1996, and in early 1997 had only one declared opponent, Korean American state Senator John Lim.

Junior Senator. Gordon Smith was born in Pendleton and grew up, after his father sold his food processing business to serve as an aide to Eisenhower Agriculture Secretary Ezra Taft Benson, lived in the Washington suburbs; he is a cousin of former Congressmen Morris and Stewart Udall. He served two years as a Mormon missionary in New Zealand, then graduated from Brigham Young and from law school in Los Angeles, was a law clerk in New Mexico and practiced law in Arizona. Then he bought a frozen vegetable processing company in Pendleton, and guided it out of debt to profitability; Smith Frozen Foods is now one of largest private label packers of frozen vegetables in the country. In 1992 he was elected to the state Senate and in 1995 became Senate president and ran for Bob Packwood's U.S. Senate seat, losing to Ron Wyden 48%–47% in January 1996. In December 1995, Mark Hatfield announced his retirement after 30 years; deeply religious, close to a pacifist on foreign affairs, he was also a practical politician who as Appropriations chairman looked after Oregon interests. At first Smith was reluctant to run again—indeed, he is the first candidate to run in two Senate races in the same year—but Republicans urged him to run even after he insisted he would not spend $2 million of his own money as he did in the earlier race. Another difference was that he positioned himself closer to the center. Attacked during the Wyden race for being endorsed by the conservative Oregon Citizens' Alliance, he turned down the OCA endorsement this time; when OCA head Lon Mabon ran against him in the primary, Smith beat him 78%–8%.

Smith's opponent was Tom Bruggere, another self-made millionaire, who started Mentor Graphics near Portland and, like Smith, owned a Ferrari. Bruggere had not run for office before, but won his primary 50%–25% over Harry Lonsdale, Hatfield's opponent in 1990; two candidates backed by labor and far-out environmental groups got only 10% and 9%. Smith continued to oppose abortion, but promised not to back a constitutional amendment and at the end of the campaign said he would vote for Medicaid to cover abortions in cases of rape, incest or threat to life of the mother; he promised to work for a balance of environment, economic development and job creation. "What gets me up in the morning is the belief that we can be fiscally responsible, reduce taxes and we can reform government," he said. But he also ran an ad in which Hatfield praised his work in the legislature for education, the Oregon Health Plan and Portland's light rail.

Like many campaigns, this started out positive but didn't stay that way. Bruggere had an attractive history: he worked his way through college by pumping gas and is a Vietnam veteran; he started off running positive ads on education. He attacked Smith on abortion and the environment, and he and environmental groups charged that Smith's plant polluted the water. Bruggere touted his firm's day care program and contribution of 1% of profits to charity. But Smith ran an ad attacking Bruggere for taking $2.5 million in stock options while laying off 500 employees in 1991 and 1992. And he called Bruggere "your classic, extremist Democratic liberal" supported by "extreme preservationist organizations." In this campaign Smith spent $3.5 million, for a total of over $9 million in both campaigns, but only $306,000 of his own money this time. Bruggere spent $3.3 million, $1.4 million of it his own. The result was apparent only when Oregon's large number of absentee ballots were counted: Smith won 50%–46%, carrying every county but Portland, two university towns and two northeast counties; he lost metro Portland and those areas by only 52%–43% and carried the rest of the state 60%–37%. Bruggere's vote closely tracked Bill Clinton's 47%, not enough to win a two-way race.

Smith and Wyden are not the first two senators from the same state to have run against each other, but are the first to have run against each other so recently; they seem to get along satisfactorily, if only because each knows the other will never run against him again. Smith serves on Budget, Energy and Foreign Relations, and chairs the European Affair Subcommittee; he (and Wyden) have vowed they will never consent to the privatization of the Bonneville Power Administration. Smith's other goals include reform of the Endangered Species Act, forest health legislation, and reduced taxes. His seat does not come up until 2002.

Presidential politics. Oregon was once the most Republican state in the West, voting for Thomas Dewey over Harry Truman in 1948, and recently it has been one of the most Democratic, voting for Michael Dukakis over George Bush in 1988. It has voted twice for Bill Clinton by solid margins, although his percentage went down from 1992's 43%–33% to 1996's 47%–39%; one reason was that Ralph Nader won 4% here, his best showing in any state. But it had large votes for Ross Perot and, in 1996, Ralph Nader have kept Clinton under the 50% mark here—significant in 1996 when Democratic House candidates' vote tended to closely track Clinton's. The closeness of Oregon's two Senate contests in 1996 suggests neither party can take Oregon for granted in 2000.

Oregon once had an important presidential primary, scheduled in May. In 1948 Oregon ended Harold Stassen's serious presidential career, when he lost 52%–48% to Dewey; in 1968 Oregon gave Robert Kennedy his only defeat when it voted 44%–38% for Eugene McCarthy. Oregon in those days was part of a West Coast campaign swing, just before the California primary; at a time when campaigners were not used to flying all over the country they, like National Football League teams in the 1950s, scheduled West Coast contests together to minimize travel time. For 1992 and 1996, Oregon scheduled its primary for Super Tuesday in March, but it was overshadowed by bigger contests in the South.

Congressional districting. Congressional politics in Oregon has a certain volatility, because distance and the sparsity of nonstop flights make it hard for even the most conscientious congressman to get back to the district very often. The 1990s districting plan created two safe Democratic seats, the 3d in Portland and the 4th centered on Eugene, and one safe Republican, the eastern 2d. The 1st and 5th, centered on Portland suburbs, are marginal; both are currently held by Democrats who won by narrow margins.

The People: Est. Pop. 1996: 3,204,000; Pop. 1990: 2,842,321, up 12.7% 1990–1996. 1.2% of U.S. total, 29th largest; 30% rural. Median age: 36.3 years. 13% 65 years and over. 90.8% White, 1.6% Black, 2.4% Asian, 1.3% Amer. Indian, 4% Hispanic origin. Households (1980): 55.6% married couple families; 25% married couple fams. w. children; 53% college educ.; median household income: $27,250; per capita income: $13,418; 63.1% owner occupied housing; median house value: $67,100; median monthly rent: $344. 5.9% Unemployment. 1996 Voting age pop.: 2,411,000; 1996 Turnout: 1,377,760; 57% of VAP. Registered voters (1996): 1,962,155; 805,286 D (41%); 714,548 R (36%); 442,321 unaffiliated and minor parties (23%).

Political Lineup: Governor, John A. Kitzhaber (D); Secy. of State, Phil Keisling (D); Atty. Gen., Hardy Myers (D); Treasurer, Jim Hill (D). State Senate, 30 (10 D and 20 R); Senate President, Brady Adams (R); State House, 60 (29 D and 31 R); House Speaker, Lynn Lundquist (R). Senators, Ron Wyden (D) and Gordon H. Smith (R). Representatives, 5 (4 D and 1 R).

Elections Division: 503-986-1518; **Filing Deadline for U.S. Congress:** March 10, 1998.

1996 Presidential Vote

Clinton (D)	649,631	(47%)
Dole (R)	538,155	(39%)
Perot (I)	121,218	(9%)
Other	68,746	(5%)

1996 Republican Presidential Primary

Dole (R)	206,938	(51%)
Buchanan (R)	86,987	(21%)
Forbes (R)	54,121	(13%)
Alexander (R)	28,332	(7%)
Keyes (R)	14,340	(4%)
Other	16,796	(4%)

1992 Presidential Vote

Clinton (D)	621,314	(43%)
Bush (R)	475,757	(33%)
Perot (I)	354,091	(24%)

GOVERNOR

Gov. John A. Kitzhaber (D)

Elected 1994, term expires Jan. 1999; b. Mar. 5, 1947, Colfax, WA; home, Eugene; Dartmouth Col., B.S. 1969; U. of OR Med. Schl., M.D. 1973; no religious affiliation; married (Sharon).

Career: Practicing physician, 1974–88; Health & environment consultant, 1988–93; OR House of Reps., 1978–80; OR Senate, 1980–94, Senate Pres., 1985–93.

Office: State Capitol, #254, Salem 97310, 503-378-3111; Fax: 503-378-6827; Web site: www.state.or.us.

Election Results

1994 gen.	John A. Kitzhaber (D)	622,083	(51%)
	Denny Smith (R)	517,874	(42%)
	Ed Hickman (American)	58,449	(5%)
	Others	22,604	(2%)
1994 prim.	John A. Kitzhaber (D)	250,514	(88%)
	Paul Damian Wells (D)	30,052	(11%)
1990 gen.	Barbara Roberts (D)	508,749	(46%)
	Dave Frohnmayer (R)	444,646	(40%)
	Al Mobley (I)	144,062	(13%)

SENATORS

Sen. Ron Wyden (D)

Elected Jan. 1996; seat up 1998; b. May 3, 1949, Wichita, KS; home, Portland; Stanford U., B.A. 1971, U. of OR, J.D. 1974; Jewish; married (Laurie).

Career: Co-Dir. & Co-Founder, OR Gray Panthers, 1974–80; Dir., OR Legal Svcs. for the Elderly, 1977–79; Prof. of Gerontology, U. of OR, 1976, Portland St. U., 1979, U. of Portland, 1980; U.S. House of Reps., 1980–96.

DC Office: 717 HSOB 20510, 202-224-5244; Fax: 202-228-2717; e-mail: senator@wyden.senate.gov.

State Offices: Bend, 541-330-9142; Eugene, 541-431-0229; La Grande, 541-962-7691; Medford, 541-858-5122; Portland, 503-326-7525; Salem, 503-589-4555.

Committees: *Budget* (7th of 10 D). *Commerce, Science & Transportation* (9th of 9 D): Aviation; Communications; Surface Transportation & Merchant Marine. *Energy & Natural Resources* (7th of 9 D): Energy Research, Development, Production & Regulation; Forests & Public Land Management; Water & Power. *Environment & Public Works* (8th of 8 D): Drinking Water, Fisheries & Wildlife. *Aging (Special)* (7th of 8 D).

Group Ratings (1995-House, 1996-Senate)

	ADA	ACLU	AFS	LCV	CFA	CON	NFIB	COC	ACU	NTLC	CHC
1996	95	42	86	92	85	18	33	38	15	20	0
1995	90	—	—	81	100	25	—	29	12	—	—

National Journal Ratings (1995-House, 1996-Senate)

	1995 LIB — 1995 CONS			1996 LIB — 1996 CONS		
Economic	76%	—	23%	73%	—	26%
Social	71%	—	28%	72%	—	26%
Foreign	77%	—	22%	83%	—	16%

Key Votes of the 104th Congress (1996 Senate Votes Only)

1. Reduce Medicare Growth $	*	5. Flag Amendment	*	9. Anti-Missile Defense	*
2. Lmt. Prod. Liab. Damages	N	6. Endangered Species	Y	10. Cuban Embargo	*
3. Increase Min. Wage	Y	7. Gay Employment Rights	Y	11. Bar Bosnia Troop $	*
4. Welfare Reform	Y	8. Ovrd. Part. Birth Veto	N	12. Cut Vietnam Aid	Y

Election Results

1996 spec. gen.	Ron Wyden (D)	571,739	(48%)	($4,237,134)
	Gordon H. Smith (R)	553,519	(47%)	($5,542,482)
	Others	56,392	(5%)	
1995 spec. prim.	Ron Wyden (D)	212,532	(50%)	
	Peter A. DeFazio (D)	187,411	(44%)	
	Others	21,820	(5%)	
1992 general	Bob Packwood (R)	717,455	(52%)	($8,034,249)
	Les AuCoin (D)	639,851	(47%)	($2,629,397)

Sen. Gordon H. Smith (R)

Elected 1996, seat up 2002; b. May 25, 1952, Pendleton; home, Pendleton; Brigham Young U., B.A. 1976; Southwestern U., J.D. 1979; Mormon; married (Sharon).

Career: Law Clerk, NM Supreme Court, 1979–80; Practicing atty., 1980–81; Pres., Smith Frozen Foods, 1980–96; OR Senate, 1992–96, Pres., 1994–96.

DC Office: 359 DSOB 20510, 202-224-3753; Fax: 202-228-3997.

State Offices: Eugene, 541-465-6750; Medford, 541-608-9102; Pendleton, 541-278-1129; Portland, 503-326-3386.

Committees: *Budget* (12th of 12 R). *Energy & Natural Resources* (9th of 11 R): Energy Research, Development, Production & Regulation; Forests & Public Land Management; Water & Power Subcommittee (Vice Chmn.); *Foreign Relations* (5th of 10 R): European Affairs (Chmn.); International Operations; Near Eastern & South Asian Affairs.

Group Ratings and Key Votes: Newly Elected

Election Results

1996 general	Gordon H. Smith (R)	677,336	(50%)	($3,527,252)
	Tom Bruggere (D)	624,370	(46%)	($3,301,736)
	Others	58,524	(4%)	
1996 primary	Gordon H. Smith (R)	224,428	(78%)	
	Lon Mabon (R)	23,479	(8%)	
	Kirby Brumfield (R)	15,744	(5%)	
	Jeff Lewis (R)	13,359	(5%)	
	Others	10,490	(4%)	
1990 general	Mark O. Hatfield (R)	590,095	(54%)	($2,714,661)
	Harry Lonsdale (D)	507,743	(46%)	($1,479,099)

FIRST DISTRICT

Postmodern skyscrapers rising above the riverfront and below a range of hills: this is downtown Portland. The city—which would have been named Boston if a coin toss had gone the other way—started here, along the Willamette River just before it flows into the Columbia, and downtown was built on the narrow margin of land west of the river and below the hills, not on the flat expanse that stretches east to the snow-capped peak of Mount Hood. Downtown Portland was once a dowdy place, proper in a New Englandish way, with a few formal buildings above the warehouses and factories.

But in the last decade there has been an explosion of creativity here, symbolized by handsome postmodern high-rises—the pyramid-crested brick KOIN Tower, the wedge-shaped Justice Center—restored Victorian storefronts, a downtown transit trolley and a new light rail line know as MAX (Metropolitan Area Express), and just across the river the new Oregon Museum of Science and Industry. The affluent neighborhoods in the hills overlooking downtown are full of old lumber barons' mansions with splendid views, and postmodern houses with hot tubs. Just over the hills are the valleys and interstices between green mountains of suburban Washington County.

Not so long ago, this was farm county, with 39,000 people in 1940; now it has 311,000 and is an integral part of metro Portland. This is an affluent area with a high-tech, healthy-lifestyle aura, with clusters of towns and protected forest areas; the biggest employers here are Tektronix, Intel, Nike and Sequent Computer Systems. Like Silicon Valley, the Silicon Forest has an environment—at the foot of mountains, woodsy and even rustic but outfitted with all the comforts and services of modern civilization—that appeals to a high-skill work force.

The 1st Congressional District of Oregon includes downtown Portland and its western hills, plus a bit of the residential areas east of the Willamette, and all of Washington County. The 1st also proceeds northwest along the Columbia to Astoria and the Pacific Coast, and southwest to Yamhill County, where metro growth is spreading. Like Oregon, the 1st District is historically New England Republican, electing only Republican congressmen from 1892 to 1972; like New England, it then trended sharply left on cultural issues, even as its high-tech economy brought new affluence, and since 1974 it has elected leftish Democrats. But the political balance is close here: there are Republican blocs, to some extent in high-income Lake Oswego and west Portland, even more so in middle-income Beaverton and Hillsboro, and the appeal of Portland-style liberalism thins as one heads down the Columbia to the sea.

The congresswoman from the 1st District is Elizabeth Furse, a Democrat elected in 1992. Furse was born a colonist, the daughter of British parents in Kenya; she grew up in South Africa, and at 15 marched as a member of Black Sash, an anti-apartheid group founded by her mother. She became a U.S. citizen in 1972, and taught self-sufficiency to women in Watts, California and volunteered for the United Farm Workers. She moved to Oregon in 1978, where she and her husband own a vineyard in Washington County. For six years, she lobbied Congress to restore legal status to three Oregon Indian tribes. In 1985, she co-founded the Peace Institute and in 1988, lead a 300-person "Citizens' Train" to lobby Congress for a more liberal budget. These are not perhaps conventional credentials but they were assets in 1992, when 18-year Congressman Les AuCoin left to run against Senator Bob Packwood. In this "year of the woman" Furse was able to raise more money and rally more enthusiasm than a former AuCoin staffer and won 60%–40%. She also outraised her Republican opponent, state Treasurer Tony Meeker, and made her support of legal abortion her key issue. As Bill Clinton was carrying the district, Furse won 52%–48%.

Furse is far to the left in the House on foreign and cultural issues, a bit more moderate on economics. She was proud of getting funding for the Westside Light Rail Project and authorization for a Hillsboro extension, for putting together community teams to deal with domestic violence in the 1994 crime bill, for sponsoring national "Year of the Girl Child." She peppers Pentagon spending bills with amendments, some of which pass—a $22 million cut in aircraft procurement in July 1995, a $35 million cut to force streamlining of the Transportation Command in June 1996. She is a founder of the Congressional Diabetes Caucus, and wants Medicare to cover the strips used to test blood and self-management training for diabetics. She supports maritime subsidies and opposes timber salvage laws, seeks funding for watershed restoration, protecting salmon and the Marine Environmental Research Training Station at Tongue Point.

Furse was opposed in both 1994 and 1996 by Republican Bill Witt, owner of an office supply company and founder of the Oregon Christian Coalition. Furse painted Witt's views in sinister tones—"Oregon has become a real test case for the religious right. If they can do it here, they can do it anywhere"—but in fact both candidates occupy the not too-far extreme positions on the conventional American electoral spectrum. Furse survived both times by heavily outspending her opponents: $1.1 million in 1994, $431,000 of it raised from PACs, to Witt's $541,000. But Furse won by only 319 votes on the initial count, and 301 on recount; she carried the Portland portion of the district 67%–30%, but lost every other county. In 1996, after flirting with the idea of running for the Senate, Witt ran in the 1st District again, and unimpressively won his six-candidate Republican primary by 32%–22% over conservative Molly Bordonaro. Witt attacked Furse on taxes, defense cuts and timber salvage laws; she attacked him for his office supply company's $40,000 fine for setting back the counters on copiers. In the last days of the campaign Witt, on the basis of a "casual conversation," accused Furse of using congressional influence to get a bank loan; he admitted he lacked any substantiation, and Governor John Kitzhaber and Senator Mark Hatfield stood by Furse at a press conference when she denounced the charge and announced she was suing Witt for defamation (under Oregon law a successful suit could be grounds for overturning the election result if she had lost the election).

Furse won 52%–45%, with the help of a 68%–29% edge in Multnomah County; Witt narrowly carried the rest of the district. Furse has promised to serve only four terms, so the 1998 election will presumably be her last. She is likely to face stiff competition from Molly Bordonaro again, and from John Kivastad, a local metro government official.

The People: Pop. 1990: 568,501; 18% rural; 12% age 65+; 91% White; 1% Black; 3% Asian; 1% Amer. Indian; 4% Hispanic origin. Households: 56% married couple families; 26% married couple fams. w. children; 64% college educ.; median household income: $33,227; per capita income: $17,120; median gross rent: $453; median house value: $84,500.

1996 Presidential Vote

Clinton (D)	145,540	(50%)
Dole (R)	112,152	(38%)
Perot (I)	21,304	(7%)
Other	14,310	(5%)

1992 Presidential Vote

Clinton (D)	136,630	(44%)
Bush (R)	99,304	(32%)
Perot (I)	73,134	(24%)

Rep. Elizabeth Furse (D)

Elected 1992; b. Oct. 13, 1936, Nairobi, Kenya; home, Hillsboro; Evergreen St. Col., B.A. 1974; Protestant; married (John Platt).

Career: Owner, Helvetia Vineyards, 1983-present; Founder & Dir., Oregon Peace Instit., 1985–1991; Oregon Legal Services, 1980–86.

DC Office: 316 CHOB 20515, 202-225-0855; Fax: 202-225-9497; e-mail: furseor1@hr.house.gov.

District Offices: Portland, 503-326-2901.

Committees: *Commerce* (11th of 23 D): Energy & Power; Finance & Hazardous Materials; Health & the Environment.

Group Ratings

	ADA	ACLU	AFS	LCV	CFA	CON	NFIB	COC	ACU	NTLC	CHC
1996	80	67	92	85	85	98	27	33	5	20	13
1995	90	—	—	75	100	56	—	33	20	—	—

National Journal Ratings

	1995 LIB		1995 CONS	1996 LIB		1996 CONS
Economic	72%	—	27%	62%	—	36%
Social	88%	—	0%	79%	—	18%
Foreign	88%	—	7%	90%	—	0%

Key Votes of the 104th Congress

1. Reduce Medicare Growth $	N	5. Flag Amendment	N	9. Cuban Embargo	N
2. Ovrd. Product Liab. Veto	N	6. Drop EPA Limits	Y	10. Bar Bosnia Troop $	N
3. Increase Min. Wage	Y	7. Repeal Assault-Weap. Ban	N	11. Cut Anti-Missile Defense	Y
4. Welfare Reform	Y	8. Ovrd. Part. Birth Veto	*	12. Bar U.N. Uniforms	N

Election Results

1996 general	Elizabeth Furse (D)	144,588	(52%)	($1,370,710)
	Bill Witt (R)	126,146	(45%)	($874,271)
	Others	7,870	(3%)	
1996 primary	Elizabeth Furse (D)	47,893	(99%)	
1994 general	Elizabeth Furse (D)	121,147	(48%)	($1,132,394)
	Bill Witt (R)	120,846	(48%)	($541,456)
	Others	11,996	(5%)	

SECOND DISTRICT

The Cascade Mountains that wall eastern Oregon off from the rest of the state are a magnificent chain of once (and quite possibly still) active volcanic mountains that drain almost every drop of moisture out of the air coming in from the Pacific, and thus separate green, wet western Oregon from the brown, parched east. Eastern Oregon has 70% of the state's land, but less than 400,000 of its 3.2 million people, most of whom still make their living off the land: beef and dairy cattle, timber and lumber, fish from the Columbia River and wheat from the irrigated plains. The effect of the Cascades can be felt in the one place they are breached—by the Columbia River Gorge. Here, surrounded by brown hills on both sides, funneled winds pound in steadily from the west, making the confluence of the Columbia and Hood Rivers the best windsurfing site in the United States.

The 2d Congressional District of Oregon covers all of the state east of the Cascades and the southernmost valley between the Cascades and the Coast Range. Population concentrations here are far apart: Pendleton in the northeastern wheat fields; La Grande in the rich Grande Ronde Valley; The Dalles where the Columbia River Gorge begins; Bend in the center of the state, near Crook County, which until it voted for George Bush in 1992 was the only county in the country to have voted for the winning presidential candidate in every election (it went for Bob Dole in 1996). In the southwestern corner, separated from other areas by the Cascades and the once huge volcano whose blown-off cone is now 2,000-foot deep Crater Lake, is the lumber and pear orchard country around Medford, Ashland, Klamath Falls and Grants Pass.

Politically, the 2d District has grown increasingly Republican. Many people here are furious with intrusions from the federal government—which owns three quarters of the district's land—particularly with the designation of the spotted owl as an endangered species, which shut much of Oregon's timber industry out of federal lands, forcing the businesses to resort to heavily logging state and private lands. They are unhappy as well with the cultural liberalism of Portland and the East Coast; politically, this is more a part of the leave-us-alone Rocky Mountain basin than of the culturally hip West Coast.

The congressman from the 2d District is Bob Smith, a Republican elected in 1996 under odd circumstances, who was first elected to the House in 1982 and retired in 1994. He grew up in sparsely populated Harney County, the son of a physician and a nurse, graduated from Willamette University and became a successful cattle rancher. In 1960, at 29, he was elected to the Oregon House and from 1969–73 served as speaker. In 1973 he was elected to the state Senate, where he became Republican leader. In 1982 he was elected to the U.S. House, where he served on the Agriculture and Resources Committee, a quiet solid conservative in a noisy Democratic chamber, and was co-chairman of the Congressional Beef Caucus.

In November 1993, long before a Republican House seemed likely, Smith announced his retirement. Smith's successor was Wes Cooley, owner of a firm selling nutritional supplements, who after two years in the Oregon legislature called himself "the most conservative state senator" and won the seven-candidate Republican primary for Smith's House seat with 23% of the vote. He won the general 57%–39% and made a conservative record in the House.

Then, in April 1996, damaging charges came out. The *Medford Mail Tribune* claimed Cooley had never served in the Army in Korea as he claimed on the 1994 state voter guide; Army documents said he had never gone overseas. His wife had received benefits as a Marine widow until 1994, but in a 1985 bank loan they claimed to be married—which would have made her ineligible for the benefits. He was accused of paying an employee illegally low wages and then claiming the man as a dependent on his income tax form. No one had filed against Cooley for the May 21 primary, and he did not come up with documents he promised on May 18 to prove his case. On May 28 he claimed that fire had destroyed the Army personnel records that would prove his innocence, but refused to answer questions about his marriage and blamed "character assassination" by the "liberal media." But other Republicans began to fear the Democratic nominee, Deschutes County District Attorney Mike Dugan, could win (he led by 30% in a summer poll), and called on Cooley to withdraw. State Senator Greg Walden got the signatures for a third party candidacy and religious broadcaster Perry Atkinson angled for the Republican nomination. Bob Smith, at the time a lobbyist in Medford, rebuffed pleas to run, but denounced Cooley, saying, "So we're going to destroy the opportunity to elect a conservative, maybe adding to the demise of a House of Representatives controlled by the Republicans, because we have a politically deaf and dumb candidate." He added: "Do you turn around and support someone who lied to you? It's impossible. We have enough people in America criticizing our government without proving to them that it is corrupt by electing a liar."

Still Cooley stubbornly stayed in. Finally Republican National Chairman Haley Barbour urged him to get out, and House Republican leaders promised Smith the chairmanship of the Agriculture Committee if he would run. (Chairman Pat Roberts was running for the Senate, second-ranking member Bill Emerson died in June, third-ranking Republican Steve Gunderson was retiring and fourth-ranking Larry Combest was Chairman of Intelligence.) On August 6 Cooley said he would step aside, then hesitated, then after motorcycling to the Republican National Convention in San Diego and hiding out from the Oregon delegation, withdrew August 13. He was indicted for making a false statement on the voter guide in December and convicted in March 1997.

Smith then received the Republican nomination. He said the Clinton Administration was "declaring war on the West" by trying to control water and to shut down logging, grazing and mining; Dugan said the war was being waged on Medicare and school lunches by Newt Gingrich. "We have to keep this seat in conservative hands," Smith said. "Eastern people don't understand how we live out there. They think that the last tree has been cut down and grazing is ravaging the land." Smith outspent his opponent, and won 62%–37%, carrying every county. In the House he got the promised Agriculture Committee chair. Its workload, after the Freedom to Farm Act of 1996, was much reduced; and Smith seems likely to concentrate on forest issues. "Throughout Oregon," he said in January 1997, "federal forests are suffering from dead and dying trees, disease and insect infestation, frequent and uncontrollable wildfires, and, unfortunately at times, neglectful federal management." He also vowed to oppose privatizing the Bonneville Power Administration. Whether he will run again in 1998, at 67, is unclear, though this seat is likely to remain Republican unless Cooley is somehow nominated again.

The People: Pop. 1990: 568,437; 50% rural; 16% age 65+; 91% White; 1% Asian; 2% Amer. Indian; 5% Hispanic origin. Households: 61% married couple families; 26% married couple fams. w. children; 44% college educ.; median household income: $23,949; per capita income: $11,704; median gross rent: $363; median house value: $62,400.

1996 Presidential Vote

Dole (R)	130,408	(48%)
Clinton (D)	103,116	(38%)
Perot (I)	30,093	(11%)
Other	10,362	(4%)

1992 Presidential Vote

Bush (R)	106,696	(38%)
Clinton (D)	97,458	(35%)
Perot (I)	74,346	(27%)

Rep. Robert F. (Bob) Smith (R)

Elected 1996; b. June 16, 1931, Portland; home, Medford; Willamette U., B.A. 1953; Presbyterian; married (Kaye).

Career: Cattle Rancher; OR House of Reps., 1960–73, Speaker, 1969–73; OR Senate, 1973–82; U.S. House of Reps., 1982–94.

DC Office: 1126 LHOB 20515, 202-225-6730; Fax: 202-225-5774; e-mail: smith.oregon@hr.house.gov.

District Offices: Burns, 541-573-3607; Medford, 541-776-4646.

Committees: *Agriculture* (Chmn. of 27 R). *Resources* (20th of 27 R): National Parks & Public Lands; Water & Power.

Group Ratings and Key Votes: Newly Elected

Election Results

1996 general	Robert F. (Bob) Smith (R)	164,062	(62%)	($412,394)
	Mike Dugan (D)	97,195	(37%)	($264,902)
	Others	4,799	(2%)	
1996 primary	Wes Cooley (R)	31,528	(82%)	
	Others (R)	6,942	(18%)	
1994 general	Wes Cooley (R)	134,255	(57%)	($298,053)
	Sue C. Kupillas (D)	90,822	(39%)	($369,790)
	Others	9,304	(4%)	

THIRD DISTRICT

Postmodern Portland, the Rose City set between Mount Hood to the east and the Tualatin Mountains to the west, spanning the Willamette River with its airport and industrial back to the Columbia, is still one of America's least known major cities. It has its own style, a light rail system that runs down the middle of the Banfield Freeway and shining buildings set amid classic masonry piles in the downtown area west of the Willamette. It has a Metropolitan Greenspaces program expanding its inventory of natural areas. Portland is proud of its New England beginnings (it almost was called Boston) and its traditional Rose Festival. It boasts of its local microbreweries and its bicycle paths. Much of the central city of Portland has a middle-class, white-bread look; but it has attracted the hip and the culturally liberal people who want an urban atmosphere.

Portland's economy, to be sure, is more basic than boutique: it is in many ways a muscular, blue-collar town where Oregon unloaded autos from Japan on the docks or supplies from the east in rail yards, and where it shipped out Oregon's products, mainly lumber and fruit. Portland has been particularly conscious for the last two decades that it is on the Pacific Rim, living more and more on foreign trade, seeing East Asians as customers rather than competitors.

The 3d Congressional District of Oregon takes in most of Portland and Multnomah County east of the Willamette River, extending over suburban plains and hills to the splendid scenery of the Bonneville Dam in the Columbia River Gorge and Mount Hood high in the Cascades. It is middle income, largely white, not a glaringly ethnic place, but it also reflects a cultural liberalism which sets Portland apart even from its suburbs and the rest of Oregon. In 1996 Portland's Multnomah County voted 59%–26% for Bill Clinton, and gave Ralph Nader more votes (7%) than Ross Perot (6%); while the rest of Oregon gave Clinton a bare 44%–42% margin, with 9% for Perot and 3% for Nader.

The congressman from the 3d District is Earl Blumenauer, elected in May 1996 to replace Ron Wyden, who was elected to the Senate in January. Blumenauer grew up in Portland, graduated from Lewis and Clark College and its Northwestern Law School, and has been involved in politics since his teens when he was inspired by the civil rights and anti-Vietnam War movements. In 1969, in college, he headed a statewide campaign to lower Oregon's voting age. He worked two years as assistant to the president of Portland State University. In 1972, at 23, he was elected to the Oregon House; in 1978 he was elected to the Multnomah County Board of Commissioners; in 1986 he was elected to the Portland City Council. In these offices he has pushed some of the policies which have made Portland distinctive—regional light rail transit, curbside recycling, land use planning. He successfully fought the Mount Hood Freeway and neighborhood school closures. He worked for more jail space and health programs for teens. He initiated a law taking away the cars of repeat drunk driving offenders. He encouraged bike riding—Portland has many bike paths and its buses have bicycle racks—and a Clean Rivers program. Shy and cerebral, he loves to study issues before making decisions.

Blumenauer has had his name on the ballot 24 times and has had some setbacks. He lost a city commission race in 1981 after staying in a Hawaii condo owned by a lobbyist who never cashed his check for payment. And in 1992 he lost a race for mayor to Vera Katz. But when Wyden was elected to the Senate, Blumenauer was the obvious candidate. A mail-in primary was scheduled for March and April, with the special election the same day as the May 21 primary for the two-year term. Blumenauer was supported by prominent Democrats including former Governors Neil Goldschmidt and Barbara Roberts and even by Republican Senator Mark Hatfield (Blumenauer headed Democrats for Hatfield in 1990); his slogan in these multiple races was "Vote Earl, Vote Often." Blumenauer won the mail-in primary 72%–24% over state Senator Shirley Gold, a labor stalwart, and won the special election 68%–25%; he won the primary for the full term 78%–21% and the general in November 67%–26%.

"I'm choked up with nostalgia," said Blumenauer as he left for Washington. "Leaving the city I knew would be hard, but I didn't realize it would be this hard." He promised to fight for the same programs he had pushed in Portland—light rail, ride-sharing, recycling, bike paths, land use planning. He started off by backing shower facilities and discount Metro passes for House employees, by requiring the Post Office to obey local land use regulations and giving local fans a chance to buy sports teams. With a safe seat, he saw his task as long term: "That is not short term. It's going to span the next two presidents, and it's going to span two or three or four Congresses. And I'm prepared to put the time and energy and commitment into it for six or eight or 10 or 12 years. And then somebody else needs to do the job."

The People: Pop. 1990: 568,276; 6% rural; 13% age 65+; 86% White; 6% Black; 4% Asian; 1% Amer. Indian; 3% Hispanic origin. Households: 49% married couple families; 22% married couple fams. w. children; 53% college educ.; median household income: $27,150; per capita income: $13,167; median gross rent: $414; median house value: $59,300.

1996 Presidential Vote

Clinton (D)	147,056	(58%)
Dole (R)	72,124	(28%)
Perot (I)	18,553	(7%)
Other	17,884	(7%)

1992 Presidential Vote

Clinton (D)	146,835	(53%)
Bush (R)	72,338	(26%)
Perot (I)	58,900	(21%)

Rep. Earl Blumenauer (D)

Elected May 1996; b. Aug. 16, 1948, Portland; home, Portland; Lewis & Clark Col., B.A. 1970, J.D. 1976; no religious affiliation; divorced.

Career: Asst. to Pres., Portland St. U., 1970–77; OR House of Reps., 1972–78; Multnomah Cnty. Commissioner, 1978–86; Portland City Cncl., 1986–96.

DC Office: 1113 LHOB 20515, 202-225-4811; Fax: 202-225-8941; e-mail: write.earl@mail.house.gov.

District Offices: Portland, 503-231-2300.

Committees: *Transportation & Infrastructure* (25th of 33 D): Railroads; Water Resources & Environment.

Group Ratings (Only Served Partial Term)

	ADA	ACLU	AFS	LCV	CFA	CON	NFIB	COC	ACU	NTLC	CHC
1996	78	75	100	100	89	*	0	20	0	0	0
1995	*	—	—	*	*	*	—	*	*	—	—

National Journal Ratings (Not Available)

Key Votes of the 104th Congress (Only Served Partial Term)

1. Reduce Medicare Growth $	*	5. Flag Amendment	*	9. Cuban Embargo	*
2. Ovrd. Product Liab. Veto	*	6. Drop EPA Limits	*	10. Bar Bosnia Troop $	*
3. Increase Min. Wage	*	7. Repeal Assault-Weap. Ban	*	11. Cut Anti-Missile Defense	*
4. Welfare Reform	N	8. Ovrd. Part. Birth Veto	N	12. Bar U.N. Uniforms	N

Election Results

1996 general	Earl Blumenauer (D)	165,922	(67%)	($196,703)
	Scott Bruun (R)	65,259	(26%)	($11,823)
	Others	16,728	(7%)	
1996 primary	Earl Blumenauer (D)	50,747	(78%)	
	Shirley Gold (D)	13,812	(21%)	
1996 spec. gen.	Earl Blumenauer (D)	73,656	(68%)	($310,711)
	Mark Brunelle (R)	26,735	(25%)	($3,258)
	Others	7,317	(7%)	
1996 spec. prim.	Earl Blumenauer (D)	53,275	(72%)	
	Shirley Gold (D)	17,674	(24%)	
	Others	3,149	(4%)	
1994 general	Ron Wyden (D)	161,624	(73%)	($437,586)
	Everett Hall (R)	43,211	(19%)	
	Mark Brunelle (I)	13,550	(6%)	($29,516)
	Others	4,437	(2%)	

FOURTH DISTRICT

Eugene is nestled in the southernmost bit of lowland at the end of Oregon's Willamette Valley, surrounded by mountains on three sides. It is a farming center, lumber metropolis and, most notably, an university town. Settlers first arrived here in 1846, farming in the valley and cutting timber in the hills. In 1876, the University of Oregon was established, a symbol of Oregon's strong Yankee cultural ethic and sparse settlement: its first graduating class had just five students. Thousands of miles from most Americans, Eugene and next-door Springfield have grown steadily into the comfortable middle-sized towns in which many Americans would like to live. The university gives this part of Oregon a special bean-sprout tone. Eugene has bicycle paths along the river banks and on main streets and likes to bill itself as the Running Capital of the Universe. This is where Phil Knight and his former University of Oregon track coach, Bill Bowerman, started Nike—the first soles formed on a waffle iron.

Beyond the Eugene city limits is a different atmosphere. This is timber country: surrounded by green-clad mountains, southwestern Oregon around Eugene and the southwest coast cuts more timber than any other place in the country. But demand for wood is volatile, dependent on the vagaries of interest rates; and the demand from East Asia is increasingly for unprocessed logs rather than milled lumber, which means fewer jobs for Oregon. The early 1980s, when recession reduced the demand for housing, were tough on southern Oregon; the late 1980s, when cutting of old-growth forests was banned to protect the endangered spotted owl, was even worse. In between, many big lumber companies switched their major operations to the pinelands of the Southeastern U.S., while sawmills ran short of work because of log exports to the Far East. In the early 1990s, it seemed federal restrictions on logging would destroy the area's economy. But an otherwise robust local economy and active job retraining has resulted in local job gains and far less unemployment than forecast.

The 4th Congressional District of Oregon includes Eugene and Springfield and surrounding Lane County; it goes south to include Roseburg in Douglas County, once perhaps the premier logging county in the United States; it extends north to Albany and part of Corvallis, home of Oregon State University; and includes two counties on the southwest coast. Eugene is now heavily Democratic, and so is Corvallis. Roseburg and Albany tend to be Republican, but the overall balance here is toward the cultural left.

The congressman from the 4th District is Peter DeFazio, a Democrat first elected in 1986. He grew up in Massachusetts, came to Oregon for graduate school and in 1977 went to work for 4th District Congressman Jim Weaver; in 1982, he moved to Springfield and won a seat on the county commission. When Weaver retired in 1986, DeFazio won the House seat in a three-way race. In the House, DeFazio has compiled a record that seems to satisfy both Eugene and the rest of the district—liberal on some issues, moderate or even conservative on others. On foreign policy he vociferously opposed the Gulf War, and has called for an end to draft registration. He opposed the Mexican financial bailout, NAFTA and GATT. He supports the balanced budget amendment and is a co-author of the Black Caucus/Progressive Caucus budget. He has taken aim at what he considers unjustifiable spending, from the Pentagon's operational support aircraft ("generals' jets") to the Animas-La Plata irrigation project in Colorado. He moved to prevent short maternity hospital stays ("drive-through deliveries") and government financing of defense contractor mergers. He sought increased spending on chemical weapons disposal. He pushed the FAA to change its mission to safety only, not promoting civil aviation. He has a bill, with interesting support from right and left, to allow patients greater access to alternative medical treatments.

On local forest issues, he supported log export restrictions in the 1980s, pushed for a no-logging buffer zone in return for more sensitive management during the spotted owl crisis of the early 1990s and more recently has engineered a timber replacement plan allowing trading rights to log other forests for local old-growth forests. He has backed refinancing of Bonneville Power Administration debt at prevailing rates, and opposed power rate increases.

DeFazio has won reelection by impressive margins in a district which before him was often marginal. After Bob Packwood resigned in 1995, DeFazio ran for the Senate in the special mail-in primary ending December 5. He had far less money than Portland Congressman Ron Wyden, whom he attacked for receiving money from Packwood contributors; in an ad, DeFazio made the best of this: "[DeFazio's] '63 Dodge tells the lobbyists and special interests he's not for sale." His opposition to gun control, NAFTA and GATT provided clear contrasts with Wyden. He ran very strongly in the 4th District and the two counties just to the south, leading Wyden 72%–22%

there. But Wyden ran ahead 61%–32% in the rest of the state, for a 50%–44% victory, and went on to win the seat in January. In February DeFazio, daunted by the financial prowess of millionaire candidates Gordon Smith and Tom Bruggere, decided not to run for the Senate seat Hatfield was vacating.

The People: Pop. 1990: 568,395; 39% rural; 15% age 65+; 95% White; 1% Black; 1% Asian; 1% Amer. Indian; 2% Hispanic origin. Households: 58% married couple families; 25% married couple fams. w. children; 49% college educ.; median household income: $24,593; per capita income: $11,919; median gross rent: $390; median house value: $60,400.

1996 Presidential Vote

Clinton (D)	122,392	(45%)
Dole (R)	108,780	(40%)
Perot (I)	26,826	(10%)
Other	15,087	(6%)

1992 Presidential Vote

Clinton (D)	123,593	(42%)
Bush (R)	94,032	(32%)
Perot (I)	74,640	(25%)

Rep. Peter A. DeFazio (D)

Elected 1986; b. May 27, 1947, Needham, MA; home, Springfield; Tufts U., B.A. 1969, U. of OR, M.S. 1977; Catholic; married (Myrnie).

Career: Air Force, 1967–71; Dist. Office Dir., U.S. Rep. James Weaver, 1977–82; Lane Cnty. Bd. of Commissioners, 1982–86.

DC Office: 2134 RHOB 20515, 202-225-6416; Fax: 202-225-0373; e-mail: pdefazio@hr.house.gov.

District Offices: Coos Bay, 541-269-2609; Eugene, 541-465-6732; Roseburg, 541-440-0511.

Committees: *Resources* (6th of 23 D): Water & Power (RMM). *Transportation & Infrastructure* (7th of 33 D): Aviation; Surface Transportation.

Group Ratings

	ADA	ACLU	AFS	LCV	CFA	CON	NFIB	COC	ACU	NTLC	CHC
1996	95	81	100	85	77	34	24	19	5	10	7
1995	90	—	—	81	100	56	—	25	16	—	—

National Journal Ratings

	1995 LIB — 1995 CONS			1996 LIB — 1996 CONS		
Economic	72%	—	27%	79%	—	18%
Social	88%	—	0%	77%	—	23%
Foreign	62%	—	36%	87%	—	10%

Key Votes of the 104th Congress

1. Reduce Medicare Growth $	N	5. Flag Amendment	N	9. Cuban Embargo	N
2. Ovrd. Product Liab. Veto	N	6. Drop EPA Limits	Y	10. Bar Bosnia Troop $	N
3. Increase Min. Wage	Y	7. Repeal Assault-Weap. Ban	N	11. Cut Anti-Missile Defense	Y
4. Welfare Reform	N	8. Ovrd. Part. Birth Veto	N	12. Bar U.N. Uniforms	Y

Election Results

1996 general	Peter A. DeFazio (D)	177,270	(66%)	($301,211)
	John D. Newkirk (R)	76,649	(28%)	($10,609)
	Others	15,937	(6%)	
1996 primary	Peter A. DeFazio (D)	unopposed		
1994 general	Peter A. DeFazio (D)	158,981	(67%)	($221,178)
	John D. Newkirk (R)	78,947	(33%)	(10,767)

FIFTH DISTRICT

The Willamette Valley was the great promised land at the end of the Oregon Trail, one of America's most fertile valleys, shielded by the Coast Range from the cold storms of the Pacific but squeezing most of the moisture out of the clouds in the form of rain, fog and persistent mist. Here, New England Yankees planted small towns they called Salem and Albany and Oregon City, founded schools and colleges, built high-spired churches and eventually Salem's cylindrical-domed Art Deco state Capitol. This was one of the few valleys in the West which settlers found readily suitable for agriculture. California's great valleys depend on irrigation as does the cultivation of wheat in eastern Washington. In the Willamette Valley the soil is fertile, the plain created by the waters of the Willamette sweeping down from the mountains is broad, and the rains everyone hears about in Oregon are dependable. But this is not only farming country now: metro Portland is spreading south and young people seeking a pleasant environment are moving into the neat little cities and towns between the two mountain ranges.

The 5th Congressional District of Oregon includes much of the northern Willamette Valley. Near Portland it has the old pioneer town of Oregon City, and spreads south to the state capital of Salem (rather conservative) and Corvallis (home of Oregon State University and quite liberal). Then the district hops over the Coast Range to take in Lincoln and Tillamook Counties, fishing and logging and cheesemaking communities (strongly Democratic) and now also includes all of Polk County. Historically, the Willamette Valley was Republican, like the New England whence most of its settlers came, but, also like New England, it has been trending Democratic, and now is prime marginal territory.

The congresswoman from the 5th District is Darlene Hooley, a Democrat elected in 1996. She was born in North Dakota, moved with her family to Salem at age 8. She worked as a reading and physical education teacher in rural Woodburn Gervais and raised her family in West Linn, on the Willamette north of Oregon City. Angry when council members wouldn't replace the rugged asphalt after her son fell off a playground swing and cut his head, she served on the Park District board and then was elected to the City Council in 1976, at 37. In 1980 she was elected to the Oregon House, where she worked on recycling, land use and equal pay laws. In 1987 she was appointed to the Clackamas County Board of Supervisors, where she worked on roads, welfare reform and police and claimed credit for creating 10,000 private sector jobs.

Rather late in the 1996 campaign cycle Hooley decided to run for Congress. Incumbent Republican Jim Bunn, elected 50%–47% in 1994 after Democrat Mike Kopetski abruptly retired, combined religious conservatism with a moderate record on some issues; he opposed the Republicans' welfare reform because he feared it would encourage abortions. He also worked on Appropriations to get money for the Oregon Health Plan and Portland light rail, supported the minimum wage increase and defense spending cuts.

Hooley had two Democratic primary opponents, but with help from EMILY's List had far more money—ultimately she spent $1.1 million, twice as much as the incumbent. She won the three-way primary with 51% and launched into attacks on Bunn for supporting Newt Gingrich and Medicare "cuts." She also supported college tuition tax deductions and juvenile crime prevention programs. But working most strongly against Bunn was his divorce and marriage to his 31-year-old chief of staff, whom he was paying $97,500—more than any other staffer in the

Oregon House delegation. After some criticism, she quit, but the issue lingered; without it, Bunn's surprisingly moderate record might have got him reelected. Hooley won 51%–46%, carrying all but one county, though most by narrow margins.

In the House Hooley did not get the seat on Appropriations she wanted and serves on the Banking and Science Committees instead. In this marginal seat, which has been represented by two Republicans and two Democrats in the last decade, she may well have serious competition in 1998.

The People: Pop. 1990: 568,712; 35% rural; 13% age 65+; 91% White; 1% Black; 2% Asian; 1% Amer. Indian; 5% Hispanic origin. Households: 60% married couple families; 27% married couple fams. w. children; 53% college educ.; median household income: $28,608; per capita income: $13,180; median gross rent: $403; median house value: $69,100.

1996 Presidential Vote

Clinton (D)	131,527	(47%)
Dole (R)	114,691	(41%)
Perot (I)	24,442	(9%)
Other	11,103	(5%)

1992 Presidential Vote

Clinton (D)	116,798	(40%)
Bush (R)	103,387	(35%)
Perot (I)	73,071	(25%)

Rep. Darlene Hooley (D)

Elected 1996; b. April 4, 1939, Williston, ND; home, West Linn; OR St. U., B.S. 1961; Lutheran; married (John).

Career: Teacher, 1961–75; West Linn City Cncl., 1977–80; OR House of Reps., 1980–86; Clackamas Cnty. Commissioner, 1987–96.

DC Office: 1419 LHOB 20515, 202-225-5711; Fax: 202-225-5699.

District Office: Salem, 503-588-9100.

Committees: *Banking & Financial Services* (23rd of 25 D): General Oversight & Investigations; Housing & Community Opportunity. *Science* (20th of 21 D): Energy & Environment.

Group Ratings and Key Votes: Newly Elected

Election Results

1996 general	Darlene Hooley (D)	139,521	(51%)	($1,109,312)
	Jim Bunn (R)	125,409	(46%)	($553,726)
	Others	7,706	(3%)	
1996 primary	Darlene Hooley (D)	27,930	(51%)	
	Loren W. Collins (D)	14,899	(27%)	
	Sharon Scott (D)	11,461	(21%)	
1994 general	Jim Bunn (R)	121,369	(50%)	($362,620)
	Catherine Webber (D)	114,015	(47%)	($668,534)
	Others	8,232	(3%)	

PENNSYLVANIA

Pennsylvania started off as the center of America: Philadelphia was the 13 colonies' largest city when it hosted the Continental Congress in 1776 and the Constitutional Convention in 1787. This was one of the newer colonies, founded 50 years after Massachusetts and 70 years after Virginia. Under the benevolent rule of the early Penns and with its Quaker traditions, Pennsylvania soon became the major settlement in the Middle Colonies: its tolerance attracted Englishmen of all religious sects and thousands of Germans as well. The rich green farmlands west to the first Appalachian chain filled rapidly. Bordermen from Scotland, Yorkshire and Northern Ireland crossed the corduroy-like ridges and settled the mountainous interior where General Braddock had been beaten by the French and Indians not long before, and where a decade later George Washington would again lead troops when the Whiskey Rebellion flared up. On the banks of a wide estuary, with its thriving commerce and rich hinterland, Philadelphia was, after London and Dublin, the largest Georgian city in the late 18th Century. It seemed destined to be the London of America, the metropolis of government and commerce and culture.

But Philadelphia, and Pennsylvania, failed to hold the central position the Founders had expected. The nation's capital was put on the Potomac rather than the Delaware as part of a political deal, and the Erie Canal and the water-level railroad from the Hudson to Lake Erie channeled trade away from Philadelphia to New York. And Philadelphia lost its chance to be the nation's financial capital when Andrew Jackson in righteous rage vetoed the rechartering of the Second Bank of the United States. Philadelphia's Quaker tradition, tolerant of diversity and indifferent to others' behavior, was overshadowed in intellectual life by New England's Puritan tradition, angrily intolerant and ready to use the state to impose cultural values from abolitionism to prohibition. In antebellum America, Philadelphia was eclipsed by Washington in government, New York in commerce and Boston in education and literature.

Instead, Pennsylvania became America's energy and heavy industry capital. The key was coal. Northeast Pennsylvania was the nation's primary source of anthracite, the hard coal used for home heating, and western Pennsylvania was laced with bituminous coal, the soft coal used in steel production. Connected with Philadelphia by the Pennsylvania Railroad, Pittsburgh, where the Allegheny and Monongahela rivers join to become the Ohio, was the center of the nation's steel industry by 1890. Immigrants poured in from Europe and from the surrounding hills to work in the mines and factories there. Pittsburgh became synonymous with industrial prosperity, the inspiration behind the civic pride that celebrated chuffing smokestacks. In 1900, Pennsylvania was the nation's second-largest state and growing rapidly. But the boom ended conclusively with the Depression of the 1930s, and in parts of Pennsylvania it has never returned. After World War II, both home heating and industry switched away from coal. John L. Lewis's United Mine Workers traded higher pay and benefits for payroll cuts. Even when coal prices boomed in the 1970s, strip mining created relatively few new jobs. Similarly, Pennsylvania steel ceased to be a growth industry three decades ago, when big company management made bad technological decisions and agreed to big wage and benefit increases with the mistaken confidence they could pass the costs along. Big steel got import quotas in 1969—Pennsylvania has been the nation's most protectionist state since the first Bessemer converter furnaces were lit—but they didn't create jobs. By the time quotas lapsed in the 1990s, the industry had modernized, but mostly in huge new Indiana mills and small mini-mills scattered far from the factories that once lined the Monongahela.

The result has been the slowest population growth in the nation: there were 9.5 million Pennsylvanians in 1930, 12.0 million in 1996. Pennsylvania cast 36 electoral votes for Franklin Roosevelt in 1940 and 23 for Bill Clinton in 1996; it had as many congressmen (30) as California

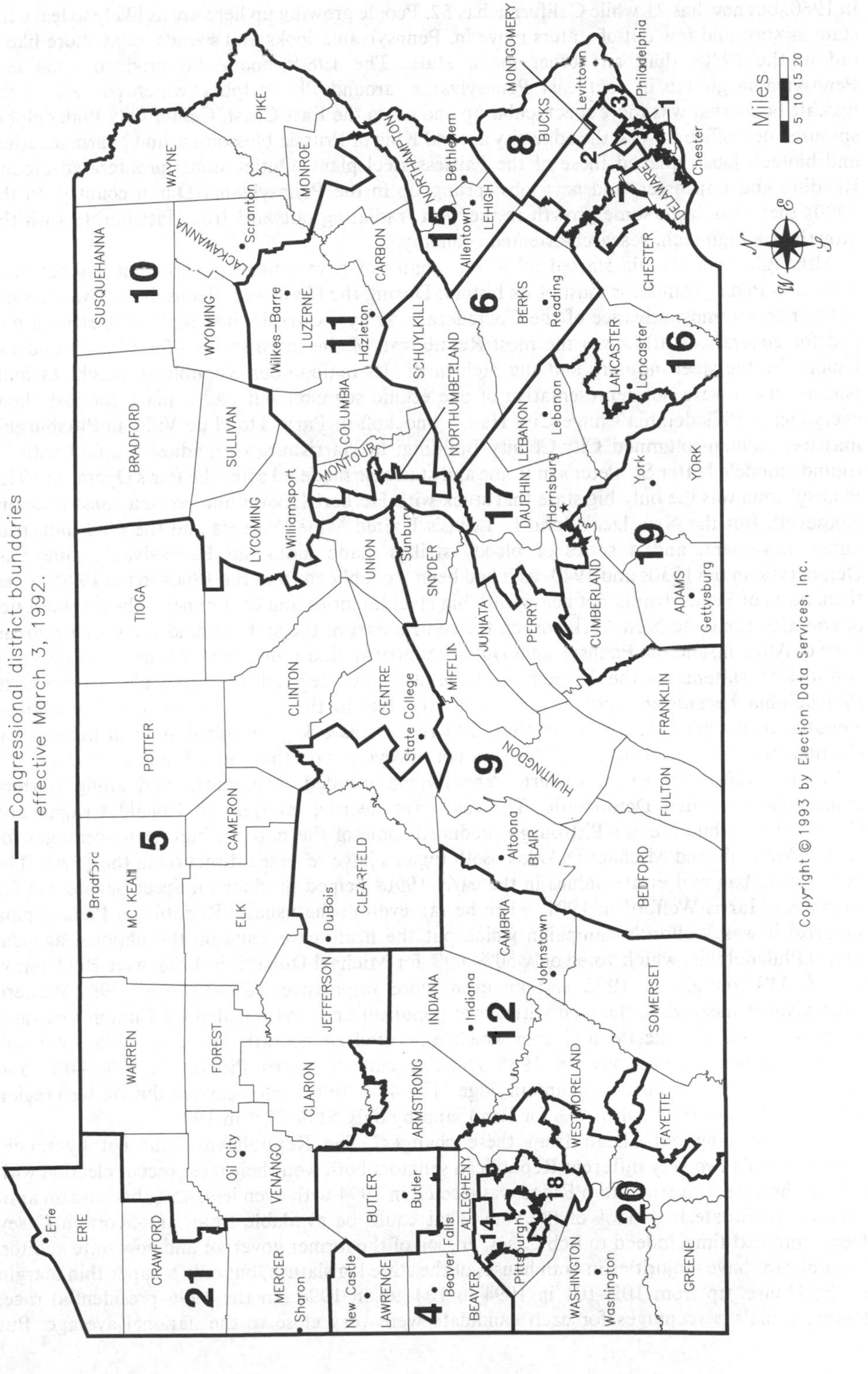
Congressional district boundaries effective March 3, 1992.
Miles
0 5 10 15 20
Copyright © 1993 by Election Data Services, Inc.
ERIE
Erie
CRAWFORD
WARREN
MC KEAN
Bradford
POTTER
TIOGA
BRADFORD
SUSQUEHANNA
WAYNE
PIKE
LACKAWANNA
Scranton
WYOMING
SULLIVAN
LYCOMING
Williamsport
CLINTON
CAMERON
ELK
FOREST
VENANGO
Oil City
MERCER
Sharon
LAWRENCE
New Castle
BUTLER
Butler
BEAVER
Beaver Falls
ALLEGHENY
Pittsburgh
WASHINGTON
Washington
GREENE
FAYETTE
WESTMORELAND
SOMERSET
INDIANA
Indiana
ARMSTRONG
CLARION
JEFFERSON
CLEARFIELD
DuBois
CAMBRIA
Johnstown
BLAIR
Altoona
BEDFORD
FULTON
HUNTINGDON
CENTRE
State College
MIFFLIN
JUNIATA
PERRY
FRANKLIN
ADAMS
Gettysburg
CUMBERLAND
YORK
York
DAUPHIN
Harrisburg
LEBANON
Lebanon
LANCASTER
Lancaster
CHESTER
Chester
DELAWARE
Philadelphia
MONTGOMERY
BUCKS
Levittown
BERKS
Reading
LEHIGH
Allentown
NORTHAMPTON
Bethlehem
CARBON
MONROE
LUZERNE
Wilkes-Barre
Hazleton
SCHUYLKILL
NORTHUMBERLAND
Sunbury
COLUMBIA
MONTOUR
UNION
SNYDER
1
2
3
4
5
6
7
8
9
10
11
12
14
15
16
17
18
19
20
21

in 1960, but now has 21 while California has 52. People growing up here are as likely to leave the state as stay, and few out-of-staters move in. Pennsylvania looks and sounds today more like it did in the 1940s than any other major state. The 1980s boom did produce some new Pennsylvania growth in southeast Pennsylvania, around Philadelphia, which partook of the upscale boom that was more spectacular up and down the East Coast. Center City Philadelphia sprouted new office towers, the edge city around King of Prussia blossomed, and pharmaceutical and biotech jobs replaced those of the Fairless steel plant. Outlet stores proliferated around Reading and Lancaster, and new jobs sprung up in the Pennsylvania Dutch country. In the 1990s there has been some growth in the west, radiating outward from Pittsburgh, with the growth of a high-tech, research-oriented economy.

Although Pennsylvania started off as our center of government, government has not been central to Pennsylvania for most of its history. During the Civil War, Pennsylvania was the site of the northernmost advance of the Confederate Army—Carlisle, just north of Gettysburg—and for generations after was the most Republican of the large states—for Lincoln and the Union, for the steel industry and the high tariff. Its malodorous Republican machines built parties which were not representative of one ethnic segment but had a place for just about everyone: in Philadelphia's huge City Hall, a knockoff of Paris' Hotel de Ville; in Pittsburgh's massive, Roman-columned City-County Building; in Harrisburg's grandiose Capitol with its rotunda modeled after St. Peter's in Rome and staircase modeled after the Paris Opera. In 1932, Pennsylvania was the only big state that stuck with Herbert Hoover and voted against Franklin Roosevelt. But the New Deal, John L. Lewis's United Mine Workers and the CIO industrial union movement, and a series of bloody strikes made industrial Pennsylvania almost as Democratic in the 1930s and 1940s as it had been Republican from the 1860s to the 1920s. Even then, parts of Pennsylvania not heavy with big steel factories and coal mines—the northern tier of counties along the New York border, the central part of the state around the Welsh railroad town of Altoona, and the Pennsylvania Dutch country around Lancaster—an area referred to by political consultants as the T—remained the strongest Republican voting bloc in the East. Philadelphia became a mostly Democratic city, but in the suburban counties the antique Republican machines stayed in control. The result was a key marginal state in presidential elections from the 1950s to the 1980s, and not always a state that moved in one direction.

In the 1980s, prosperous eastern Pennsylvania trended Republican and ailing western Pennsylvania trended Democratic. The east gave decisive margins to Ronald Reagan and George Bush while greater Pittsburgh produced some of the nation's highest percentages for Walter Mondale and Michael Dukakis. Both regions have reversed direction in the 1990s. The fall in suburban real estate values in the early 1990s helped produce an upset Senate win for Democrat Harris Wofford in 1991, when he ran even in the usually Republican Philadelphia suburbs; it was Wofford's campaign which put the healthcare issue on the national agenda. Metro Philadelphia, which voted only 50%–49% for Michael Dukakis in 1988, gave Bill Clinton a 51%–33% margin in 1992 and an even more impressive 58%–33% in 1996. Western Pennsylvania meanwhile dabbled with Perot populism and was repelled by Clinton's cultural liberalism. This was the Pennsylvania which supported Democratic Governor (1986–94) Bob Casey's abortion restrictions. In 1988 Dukakis carried metro Pittsburgh 59%–40%, and Pennsylvania west of the first mountain ridge 51%–48%. Bill Clinton carried this western region only 45%–35% in 1992, with 20% for Perot, and by only 51%–39% in 1996.

Who is coming out ahead from these changes? The Republicans—but not by much. Pennsylvania's two very different Republican senators both won their most recent election with 49% of the vote. Governor Tom Ridge was elected in 1994 with even less, 45%, because an anti-abortion candidate took 13% of the vote. That could be available to an anti-abortion Casey Democrat next time, indeed to Bob Casey, Jr., son of the former governor and now state auditor. Republicans have majorities in both houses of the state legislature, but only a paper-thin margin in the House, up from 102–101 in 1994 to 104–99 in 1996. In the 1996 presidential race, Pennsylvania's percentages for each candidate were very close to the national average. But

Democrats here tend to be culturally more conservative than those in most states and Republicans sometimes culturally more liberal; the balance is more like the America of the 1950s than the America of the 1990s, and strategies that work nationally can be counterproductive here. If Pennsylvania is a bellwether, it strikes an atypical note.

Governor. Tom Ridge, elected governor of Pennsylvania in 1994, is from Erie, off in the far northwestern corner of the state, where he grew up in a Catholic, Slovak-Irish, working-class family and once lived in a housing project. He went to Harvard and then served as a sergeant in Vietnam—an unusual combination. He returned to Erie, practiced law for 10 years and was elected to the House in 1982, at 37. There he had a mixed voting record by the lights of almost every rating group—not always market-oriented on economics, sometimes dovish on defense and foreign policy, liberal on some cultural issues and tradition-minded on others. He worked on banking and home finance legislation; he favored more spending for homeless veterans and treatment of Post Traumatic Stress Disorder. In February 1993 he announced he would run for governor. Outside his 21st District he was hardly known, though the addition of a new county in his 1992 district race gave him an excuse to run ads on Pittsburgh TV.

This turned out to be a crowded race. Ridge's best known opponent in the Republican primary was Attorney General Ernie Preate, a statewide winner in 1990 who was hurt when, a month before the primary, the Crime Commission said he had taken money from illegal video poker operators. Ridge, with backing from party leaders, won the May primary with 35% to 29% for Preate, 16% for Philadelphia businessman Sam Katz, campaigning as tough on crime and for school vouchers, and 14% for Pittsburgh legislator Mike Fisher, an opponent of abortion and gun control. The Democrats had an even more crowded primary, but Lieutenant Governor Mark Singel, who acting governor for six months while Governor Bob Casey recovered from a heart and liver transplant, won with 31%.

In the general, Ridge campaigned for tough crime measures, citizens rights' to statewide initiatives and referenda, less-strict environmental regulation and a lower corporate tax. "I have not been part of the Harrisburg problem," he said. Both Ridge and Singel were pro-choice on abortion, which probably hurt them: Singel, because Casey was lukewarm to him; Ridge, because of the independent candidacy of anti-abortion Peg Luksik, who won 13% of the vote, with more than 20% in heavily Republican Lancaster and other Republican counties in western Pennsylvania. But the defining issue was probably crime. Ridge attacked Singel for his votes as chairman of the Pardons Board recommending the release of 55 prisoners serving life sentences. Casey approved only eight releases, but one of them kidnapped, raped and robbed a woman in New York, and Ridge made that a major issue. Singel apologized, but Ridge won 45%–40%, continuing Pennsylvania's 40-year practice of alternating the two parties in the governorship every eight years.

As governor, Ridge has moved to cut taxes, expand school choice, reform welfare, and hold down spending, with mixed success at midterm. His first two budgets increased spending at less than the rate of inflation and he got the legislature to cut corporate taxes by $280 million a year; in early 1997 he sought even more cuts, as well as bigger personal exemptions for the working poor. He got significant changes in workmen's comp. He forced through a cut of 250,000 from the rolls of government-funded health care programs and an expansion of a lottery-funded program for drug prescriptions for the elderly. He reformed welfare with a work requirement and a time limit for certain benefits. Electric utilities were opened to competition. His plan for school vouchers failed narrowly in the legislature in 1995; in 1997 he sought to authorize charter schools. His failure to get a German shipbuilding firm to set up shop in the closed Philadelphia Navy Yard was highly publicized. Other Ridge proposals include state initiative and referendum legislation and privatizing state liquor stores.

Ridge's policies have brought him wide popularity and strenuous opposition. Democrats charge his business tax cuts produced slashes in welfare and ignored the need for more funds for basic and higher education. A November 1996 labor rally attracted 10,000 angry workers, and state Senate Minority Leader Robert Mellow said, "He's the best governor Wall Street ever had." Ridge in turn has worked hard to raise money for himself and other Republicans, and in 1996, despite the Clinton victory, picked up legislative seats. He was mentioned as a possible vice presidential nominee in 1996, and some of his friends later spoke of him as a presidential candidate; but first he faces reelection in 1998.

A few words should be said about Bob Casey, who remains an important voice in Pennsylvania and national politics. Casey, with his deep-held Catholic beliefs, is the lineal descendant of those practical New Dealers who believed in a government compassionate to the helpless and supportive of traditional values. He is best known for his fervent opposition to abortion, which produced Pennsylvania's abortion restrictions and got him barred from speaking at the 1992 Democratic National Convention. In the spring of 1995, he considered running for president, but decided not to; his son Bob Casey Jr. is now state auditor and could be a candidate for governor himself some day.

Senior Senator. Arlen Specter, one of the nation's most durable career politicians, has held public office and has been an important national figure off and on for three decades. Specter grew up in Russell, Kansas—also the home town of Bob Dole—and came to Philadelphia at 17 to attend the University of Pennsylvania. After college he served in the Air Force, went to Yale Law School and practiced law in Philadelphia. In 1964 he was a top staffer for the Warren Commission investigating the Kennedy assassination, where he helped develop the Single-Bullet theory. After the Warren Commission, he returned to his law practice, switched to the Republican Party, and was elected district attorney in Democratic Philadelphia in 1965 and again in 1969. He lost the race for D.A. in 1973, for the Senate in 1976, and for governor in 1978, before narrowly edging a former state Republican chairman in the 1980 primary and beating a low-spending Democrat 50%–48% in the general for his Senate seat. In 1986, he won reelection by a 56%–43% margin against a low-profile House Democrat; in 1992 he was reelected 49%–46% after he became a target of feminists for his questioning of Anita Hill during the confirmation hearings of Clarence Thomas. He ran for president in 1995, but withdrew before the first caucus and primary.

Throughout this career of narrow victories and numerous defeats, Specter's assets have been brains and hard work. He is respected by colleagues and constituents, though not always well-liked. He sides with conservatives on some divisive issues, with liberals on others, building up no permanent credit with either. He is aggressive and prosecutorial, well-prepared and persuasive once he takes a stand. These traits are both his strengths and weaknesses: they explain why he was vulnerable in 1992, and why he won; why he ran for president, and why his campaign foundered. His voting record is almost precisely at the midpoint of the Senate, and he has played key roles on a variety of issues. Though he switched and voted to override President Clinton's "partial-birth" abortion veto, he is generally pro-choice on abortion—an issue he featured in his presidential campaign, infuriating many Republican activists. He pushes tough penalties for crime and supports capital punishment. He argued persuasively for the Gulf war resolution. On a closely divided and rancorous Judiciary Committee, he has played a key role on several Supreme Court nominations. More than anyone else, he defeated Robert Bork in 1987 and, more than anyone but John Danforth, he confirmed Clarence Thomas in 1991.

In the latter case he caught the nation's attention. When Anita Hill came before the committee with charges against Thomas that were both serious and unsubstantiated, he questioned her with the rigor that Senators skeptical or disbelieving of the truth of testimony are ordinarily entitled to use. Politically, this evoked a firestorm from people enraged that Hill's testimony had not been received earlier and was not being accepted without demur—responses that were emotionally understandable but blithely ignorant of the lessons taught by the history of Joe McCarthy and Titus Oates. Specter's most aggressive moment in the hearings came when he accused Hill of committing perjury. Interestingly, he declined to defend his eminently defensible questioning a few years later, saying simply that the hearings enabled him to learn a lot about sexual harassment: which raises the question whether his campaign for president and his persistence in confronting and attacking the religious right were forms of expiation for what were regarded as sins by those close to him.

Specter is just as capable of confronting the left. His devastatingly complex chart describing the Clinton healthcare plan played no small part in defeating it. He has worked aggressively to expedite death penalty appeals. He voted to override the Clinton veto of the partial birth abortion ban. He called for a 20% flat tax in 1995, while preparing to run for president. He also takes some liberal stands, voting with Democrats to bar Social Security surpluses from being counted in the balanced budget amendment, strongly supporting a minimum wage increase, voting to ban discrimination against gays, supporting Goals 2000. He can be a tough-as-nails negotiator, as he showed in the conference committee considering the 1996 Immigration Reform Act, when he questioned the Gallegly amendment which allows states to deny free public schooling to children of illegal immigrants. As chairman of the Appropriations Labor Subcommittee, he has charge of funding many large domestic spending programs.

As chairman of the Intelligence Committee from 1995–96, he sought to reorganize the intelligence agencies, giving the CIA director greater authority over the NSA budget and the power to reallocate intelligence funds during the year even within Pentagon agencies; this was scotched by the Armed Services Committee. He would also have made theft of "proprietary economic information" a crime; he still has a prosecutorial frame of mind. In December 1996 he questioned whether CIA nominee Anthony Lake was sensitive to the need to keep Congress informed, given his approval of the decision to let Iran secretly arm the Bosnian Muslims. He backs amending the First Amendment to let Congress and the states limit campaign spending. As chairman of the Veterans' Affairs Committee in 1997, he called for doing more to investigate whether there is a Gulf war syndrome and what was known about chemical hazards in the region.

Specter lives in Philadelphia, where his wife used to serve on the City Council, but he has labored hard at keeping in touch with all parts of Pennsylvania and worked on local issues from the Philadelphia Navy Yard—he argued a case before the Supreme Court trying to overturn the base-closing law and lost 9–0 to Lake Erie. That served him well in 1992, when he was challenged by an anti-abortion legislator in the Republican primary and by feminist Democrat Lynn Yeakel in the general election. Specter won the primary 65%–35%, attacked Yeakel's ethics problems and proceeded to out-debate her. He won 49%–46%, running about even in metro Philadelphia and Pittsburgh, far ahead of usual Republican showings, and carried most smaller areas.

Specter's presidential campaign seems to have started in June 1994, when he attended an Iowa straw poll and confrontationally attacked the religious right. He called himself a fiscal conservative and cultural moderate—not quite accurately, since he has been economically more liberal than almost all other Republicans in the Senate. But in March 1995 he called for a 20% flat tax with limited mortgage interest and charitable deductions. His strategy was to try to win Iowa or New Hampshire with pluralities in a multi-candidate field, then target Florida and the big northern states that vote immediately afterward. But this candidate who has made such a point of how he differs from most Republicans on important issues was never able to galvanize the support of party moderates—even Pennsylvania Governor Tom Ridge endorsed Bob Dole—and he withdrew from the presidential race in late November.

At that point many Pennsylvania Republicans were angry at him for his adversarial approach to party activists, and his wife lost her Council seat to another Republican back home. But Specter labored on, revisiting the state's 67 counties and raising $1 million by early 1997. His vote to override the "partial-birth" abortion ban veto reduced the likelihood of primary competition; so did the heart attack of likely opponent, former Attorney General Tom Corbett; so did his support from Senator Rick Santorum, whose campaign Specter helped greatly in 1994, and Governor Tom Ridge. Possible Democratic opponents for 1998 include former 1994 gubernatorial candidate state Representative Dwight Evans, Congressman Ron Klink and state Senator Allyson Schwartz. Interestingly, since 1962 Pennsylvania has elected a Democratic senator only once, in the 1991 special election after the death of John Heinz.

Junior Senator. Rick Santorum is the youngest senator, elected from one of the oldest states, a hard-sell conservative elected in a state that still has many New Deal voters. Santorum is the son of an Italian immigrant who was a clinical psychologist for the Veterans' Administration; he was born in Virginia and moved to Butler, Pennsylvania, at age 7. He started in politics working for John Heinz's first Senate campaign, in 1976; he went to Penn State and Pitt Business School and worked his way through Dickinson Law School as a staffer for state Senate Republicans in Harrisburg; he worked for a blue chip law firm in Pittsburgh for four years. In 1990, at 32, he challenged seven-term incumbent Doug Walgren, who outspent him $717,000 to $251,000. But Santorum knocked on 25,000 doors, amassed an army of volunteers including many right-to-lifers, attacked Walgren for voting "for a pay raise seven times" and for living in the Washington suburbs. Santorum opposed the congressional pay raise, backed the line-item veto and came out for limits on PAC contributions. He won 51%–49%.

In the House he had a solid conservative voting record and was one of the "Gang of Seven" freshman Republicans who helped expose the House bank scandal. Redistricting gave him a seat shorn of many Republican suburbs and centered on the industrial Monongahela Valley, historically very Democratic. George Bush got only 30% in this new district, but Santorum beat a state Senator 61%–38%—an astonishing victory. Brash and confident, Santorum immediately started running for the Senate. His opponent was Harris Wofford, elected in November 1991 to replace John Heinz, who died in a plane crash. Wofford was a civil rights activist in the 1960s, the adviser who persuaded John Kennedy to phone Coretta Scott King when her husband was jailed during the 1960 campaign, one of Sargent Shriver's top aides at the Peace Corps. Appointed to the Senate by Bob Casey in May 1991, he upset former Governor Dick Thornburgh 55%–45% by emphasizing health care: "If criminals have the right to a lawyer, I think working Americans should have a right to a doctor." In the Senate Wofford sponsored the AmeriCorps bill. But he was politically hurt when the Clinton healthcare bill failed to pass.

This was a race of sharp contrasts in issues and style: Santorum, brashly eager to chop government, backing medical savings accounts, opposing gun control; Wofford, earnestly working for government healthcare financing, backing the 1994 crime bill and gun control, supporting Clinton. Wofford appealed to a long liberal tradition; Santorum scoffed at him for championing 1960s ideas in the 1990s. Wofford was helped in the last week of the campaign by Teresa Heinz, widow of John Heinz, who called Santorum part of a "worrisome breed" of politicians who "mock, belittle and vilify those who disagree with them"; she later married Democratic Senator John Kerry. But with home town appeal, Santorum ran behind only 50%–47% in metro Pittsburgh, where Wofford had won 61% in 1991. Santorum did not go over so well in metro Philadelphia, which Wofford carried 54%–42%. But in the rest of the state—where half the votes are cast and where gun control hurt Wofford—Santorum won 55%–41%, for a statewide victory of 49%–47%.

Santorum was not cowed by the traditions of the Senate. In his first full month there he argued about the balanced budget amendment with Robert Byrd, who was elected to the Senate the year Santorum was born. Then, when senior Republican Mark Hatfield cast a decisive vote against the amendment, Santorum and Florida Republican Connie Mack called on Hatfield to be removed as Appropriations chairman. Santorum said, "I have a lot of respect for Mark Hatfield and the service he's provided for this country, but he is an equal to me—in that we're both United States Senators. I have every right to be heard and make things happen as much as anybody else." Senior senators and Washington insiders tut-tutted. Although Hatfield wasn't removed, he retired in 1996, and Senate Republicans changed the rules, limiting chairmen to six years and calling for secret ballot elections of chairmen starting in 1997. That will inevitably produce more party discipline and cohesion, as secret ballot elections by House Democrats have done since they were instituted by Phillip Burton in 1974. Later in 1995 Santorum took to the floor a dozen times with a "Where's Bill?" sign, asking where the President's balanced budget was. On the Agriculture Committee and on the floor he conducted a campaign against the peanut and sugar subsidies—a sop to Hershey, cynics suggested—which threatened to undercut the Republicans' farm bill aimed at zeroing out the wheat, corn, and soybean subsidies. But his vote was needed on the Agriculture Committee, and he got the sugar subsidy cut a bit and the peanut program limited to five years.

At the same time Santorum was floor-managing the welfare reform bill, pending Bob Packwood's resignation. Even while showing himself capable of working with Barbara Boxer on amendments, he stood tough on the heart of the bill. In reponse to claims he was hurting children, he said, "All of this concern here expressed for children has not panned out in reality as a cure for the problems of children." But he was calm rather than brash when the bill passed, recognizing that many people's lives would be affected and that no one could be sure what would happen, though he was convinced it was better than the status quo. "This is not reforming welfare. This is a replacement of the entire welfare culture. That is a big deal." On other issues Santorum had a perfectly conservative record—he sponsored a "partial-birth" abortion ban bill that passed the Senate in May 1997 by 64–36, but may not have the votes to override Clinton's expected veto. As a former congressman from the Mon Valley, he has a middle-of-the-road record on economic issues. He voted against NAFTA in the House and for the minimum wage increase in the Senate. He is part of the Renewal Alliance: conservative Republicans who want to encourage private sector, especially faith-based, organizations to care for the poor and helpless, even as they repeal government programs originally intended to help them. He is a member of the Armed Services Committee and chairman of its Acquisitions and Technology Subcommittee.

Santorum has moved fast: from a 32-year-old ringing doorbells in 1990 to the floor manager of the law which has changed a 61-year-old welfare system in 1996. He has not forgotten politics, however, and has formed his own Fight PAC to help Republicans get to the 60-member veto-proof majority he would like to see in the Senate. His own seat comes up again in 2000.

Presidential politics. Pennsylvania, with its 23 electoral votes, has been a swing state in every close presidential election, and even some that were not close; it voted near the national average in 1996. However, it is not typical of the country. With its older, deeply-rooted population, it tends to be culturally conservative; with its long-dying blue-collar communities, it tends to be economically more liberal—though both tendencies are being muted with time.

Pennsylvania's late April presidential primary has not been crucial since 1976, when Jimmy Carter clinched the Democratic nomination here by beating Henry Jackson and Morris Udall. Bill Clinton and Bob Dole easily won the unremarkable 1996 primaries.

Congressional districting. Pennsylvania lost three congressional districts in the 1950 Census and two in each of the following four decades, reducing its delegation to 21. Control of redistricting was split between the parties, but the new plan seemed to eliminate two Republican seats. In fact, anticipations here, as in many other states, were confounded as both parties in 1992 and 1994 lost seats they were expected to win and won some they seemed sure to lose. But enough veteran Republicans have survived in safe seats so the state has four committee chairmen and would have a fifth had not one incumbent been removed from his post because of a criminal indictment.

The People: Est. Pop. 1996: 12,056,000; Pop. 1990: 11,881,643, up 1.5% 1990–1996. 4.5% of U.S. total, 5th largest; 31% rural. Median age: 36.9 years. 16% 65 years and over. 87.7% White, 9% Black, 1.1% Asian, 2% Hispanic origin. Households: 55.7% married couple families; 25% married couple fams. w. children; 36% college educ.; median household income: $29,069; per capita income: $14,068; 70.6% owner occupied housing; median house value: $69,700; median monthly rent: $322. 5.3% Unemployment. 1996 Voting age pop.: 9,197,000. 1996 Turnout: 4,506,118; 49% of VAP. Registered voters (1996): 6,805,612; 3,336,933 D (49%), 2,910,614 R (43%), 558,065 unaffiliated and minor parties (8%).

Political Lineup: Governor, Tom Ridge (R); Lt. Gov., Mark Schwieker (R); Secy. of Commonwealth, Yvette Kane (R); Atty. Gen., D. Michael Fisher (R); Treasurer, Barbara Hafer (R); Auditor General, Robert P. Casey Jr. (D). State Senate, 50 (20 D and 30 R); Senate President, Mark Schwieker (R); State House, 203 (99 D and 104 R); House Speaker, Matthew J. Ryan (R). Senators, Arlen Specter (R) and Rick Santorum (R). Representatives, 21 (11 D and 10 R).

Elections Division: 717-787-5280; **Filing Deadline for U.S. Congress:** March 10, 1998.

1996 Presidential Vote

Clinton (D)	2,215,819	(49%)
Dole (R)	1,801,169	(40%)
Perot (I)	430,984	(10%)

1992 Presidential Vote

Clinton (D)	2,239,164	(45%)
Bush (R)	1,791,841	(36%)
Perot (I)	902,667	(18%)

1996 Republican Presidential Primary

Dole (R)	435,031	(64%)
Buchanan (R)	123,011	(18%)
Forbes (R)	55,018	(8%)
Keyes (R)	40,025	(6%)
Lugar(R)	31,119	(5%)

GOVERNOR

Gov. Tom Ridge (R)

Elected 1994, term expires Jan. 1999; b. Aug. 26, 1945, Munhall; home, Erie; Harvard, B.A. 1967, Dickinson Law Sch., J.D. 1972; Catholic; married (Michele).

Career: Army, 1968–70 (Vietnam); Practicing atty., 1972–82; Erie Cnty. Asst. Dist. Atty., 1979–81; U.S. House of Reps., 1982–94.

Office: 225 Capitol Bldg., Harrisburg 17120, 717-787-2500; Fax: 717-772-8284; Web site: www.state.pa.us.

Election Results

1994 gen.	Tom Ridge (R)	1,627,976	(45%)
	Mark S. Singel (D)	1,430,099	(40%)
	Peg Luksik (Constitutional)	460,269	(13%)
	Others	67,182	(2%)
1994 prim.	Tom Ridge (R)	344,708	(35%)
	Ernie Preate (R)	287,400	(29%)
	Sam Katz (R)	156,895	(16%)
	Mike Fisher (R)	139,712	(14%)
	John F. Perry (R)	68,069	(7%)
1990 gen.	Robert P. Casey (D)	2,065,244	(68%)
	Barbara Hafer (R)	987,516	(32%)

SENATORS

Sen. Arlen Specter (R)

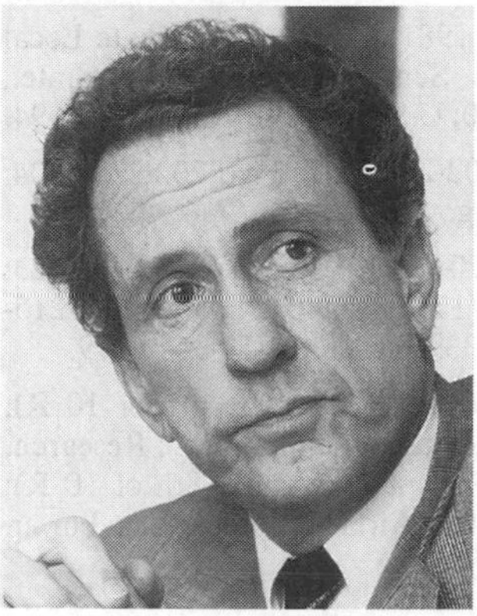

Elected 1980, seat up 1998; b. Feb. 12, 1930, Wichita, KS; home, Philadelphia; U. of PA, B.A. 1951, Yale, LL.B. 1956; Jewish; married (Joan).

Career: Air Force, 1951–53; Practicing atty., 1955–56, 1974–80; Asst. Cnsl., Warren Comm., 1964; PA Asst. Atty. Gen., 1964–65; Philadelphia Dist. Atty., 1965–73.

DC Office: 711 HSOB 20510, 202-224-4254; Fax: 202-228-1229; e-mail: senator_specter@specter.senate.gov.

State Offices: Allentown, 610-434-1444; Harrisburg, 717-782-3951; Philadelphia, 215-597-7200; Pittsburgh, 412-644-3400; Erie, 814-453-3010; Scranton, 717-346-2006.

Committees: *Appropriations* (3rd of 15 R): Agriculture, Rural Development & Related Agencies; Defense; Foreign Operations; Labor, Health & Human Services & Education (Chmn.); Transportation. *Governmental Affairs* (7th of 9 R): International Security, Proliferation & Federal Services; Oversight of Government Management, Restructuring & the District of Columbia; Permanent Subcommittee on Investigations. *Judiciary* (4th of 10 R): Antitrust, Business Rights & Competition; Immigration; Terrorism, Technology & Government Information. *Veterans' Affairs* (Chmn. of 7 R).

Group Ratings

	ADA	ACLU	AFS	LCV	CFA	CON	NFIB	COC	ACU	NTLC	CHC
1996	50	33	29	54	57	85	76	77	50	79	38
1995	55	—	45	50	44	29	—	79	36	—	—

National Journal Ratings

	1995 LIB	—	1995 CONS	1996 LIB	—	1996 CONS
Economic	50%	—	49%	50%	—	48%
Social	59%	—	37%	59%	—	40%
Foreign	38%	—	57%	47%	—	51%

Key Votes of the 104th Congress

1. Reduce Medicare Growth $	Y	5. Flag Amendment	Y	9. Anti-Missile Defense	Y
2. Lmt. Prod. Liab. Damages	N	6. Endangered Species	Y	10. Cuban Embargo	Y
3. Increase Min. Wage	Y	7. Gay Employment Rights	Y	11. Bar Bosnia Troop $	N
4. Welfare Reform	Y	8. Ovrd. Part. Birth Veto	Y	12. Cut Vietnam Aid	N

Election Results

1992 general	Arlen Specter (R)	2,358,125	(49%)	($10,454,793)
	Lynn Yeakel (D)	2,224,966	(46%)	($5,028,669)
	John F. Perry (Lib)	219,319	(5%)	($53,690)
1992 primary	Arlen Specter (R)	683,118	(65%)	
	Stephen F. Freind (R)	366,608	(35%)	
1986 general	Arlen Specter (R)	1,906,537	(56%)	($5,993,230)
	Robert W. Edgar (D)	1,448,219	(43%)	($3,968,994)

Sen. Rick Santorum (R)

Elected, 1994, seat up 2000; b. May 10, 1958, Winchester, VA; home, Penn Hills; PA St. U., B.A. 1980, U. of Pittsburgh, M.B.A. 1981, Dickinson Law Sch., J.D. 1986; Catholic; married (Karen).

Career: A.A., PA Sen. J. Doyle 1981–86; Dir., PA Senate Local Govt. Cmte., 1981–84; Dir., PA Senate Transportation Cmte., 1984–86; Practicing atty., 1986–90; U.S. House of Reps., 1990–94.

DC Office: 120 RSOB 20510, 202-224-6324; Fax: 202-228-0604; e-mail: senator@santorum.senate.gov.

State Offices: Allentown, 610-770-0142; Altoona, 814-946-7023; Erie, 814-454-7114; Harrisburg, 717-231-7540; Philadelphia, 215-864-6900; Pittsburgh, 412-562-0533, Scranton, 717-344-8799.

Committees: *Agriculture, Nutrition & Forestry* (6th of 10 R): Forestry, Conservation & Rural Revitalization (Chmn.); Research, Nutrition & General Legislation. *Armed Services* (8th of 10 R): Acquisition & Technology (Chmn.); Airland Forces; Sea Power. *Rules & Administration* (6th of 9 R). *Aging (Special)* (6th of 10 R).

Group Ratings

	ADA	ACLU	AFS	LCV	CFA	CON	NFIB	COC	ACU	NTLC	CHC
1996	15	17	14	31	29	91	97	77	95	97	92
1995	5	—	0	0	13	29	—	100	83	—	—

National Journal Ratings

	1995 LIB	—	1995 CONS	1996 LIB	—	1996 CONS
Economic	0%	—	88%	44%	—	54%
Social	19%	—	79%	0%	—	72%
Foreign	8%	—	81%	0%	—	74%

Key Votes of the 104th Congress

1. Reduce Medicare Growth $	Y	5. Flag Amendment	Y	9. Anti-Missile Defense	Y
2. Lmt. Prod. Liab. Damages	Y	6. Endangered Species	N	10. Cuban Embargo	Y
3. Increase Min. Wage	Y	7. Gay Employment Rights	N	11. Bar Bosnia Troop $	N
4. Welfare Reform	Y	8. Ovrd. Part. Birth Veto	Y	12. Cut Vietnam Aid	Y

Election Results

1994 general	Rick Santorum (R)	1,735,691	(49%)	($6,732,849)
	Harris Wofford (D)	1,648,481	(47%)	($6,300,560)
	Others	129,189	(4%)	
1994 primary	Rick Santorum (R)	667,115	(82%)	
	Joe Watkins (R)	150,969	(18%)	
1991 special	Harris Wofford (D)	1,860,760	(55%)	($3,241,556)
	Dick Thornburgh (R)	1,521,986	(45%)	($3,993,070)

FIRST DISTRICT

In Center City Philadelphia, the 1680s look out on the 1780s, 1880s and 1980s. The statue of William Penn, who founded the city in 1682, stands 37 feet high atop the 548-foot tower of the 1880s Second Empire-style City Hall at Market and Broad; east, is Independence Hall, where Americans in the 1780s drew up the nation's Constitution; west, is the tower of One Liberty Place, with its "romantic modernist" spire, the 1980s building that broke tradition to rise above City Hall. Philadelphia is built on a certain order. Earlier American colonies were settled by practical men, out to make money or replicate a farm settlement back home. But Penn was a

Quaker, a member of one of those rationalizing sects of the 17th Century, who intended to impose order on his new environment, and did: no cowpath street patterns here, like those in Boston or Charleston, but a grid of numbered and named streets, with occasional open squares.

Penn's city of brotherly love has turned out to be a commercial and industrial metropolis that has grown steadily over the years, spreading out over the countryside. Yet there are still places in which you can see the distant past: in the restored townhouses of Society Hill and the tree-shaded public buildings around Independence Hall and, on the way to the ornate City Hall, the Federal and Greek Revival buildings and the temples of commerce, built when Philadelphia was the nation's largest city. Interspersed are I.M. Pei's modernist Society Hill Towers (though the rich in Philadelphia, unlike New York or Chicago, don't much like apartments) and the 1920s masonry-faced skyscrapers and 1970s glass-and-steel towers built around City Hall and in Center City farther west.

For all the grandness of City Hall, Philadelphia has seldom had a city government of which to be proud. Corruption has reigned here off and on for more than a century, and so has incompetence. While the city's private economy grew robustly in the 1980s, the city government, swollen with overpaid employees, committed to a costly, union-run health plan and mismanaged with ferocious ineptitude, lurched unknowingly toward bankruptcy under Mayor Wilson Goode. Then in 1991 Democrat Ed Rendell was elected mayor. Ebullient and energetic, he immediately set to work, literally scrubbing City Hall's grimy steps. He cut spending sharply, privatized government functions and faced down unions in a strike threat. At the same time, he improved performance and sponsored innovative new programs, took over the closed-down Philadelphia Navy Yard and found new employers to save at least half the jobs there. Rendell, overwhelmingly reelected in 1995, showed national Democrats the viable future for their politics: not increasing spending and defending public employees against constituents, but cutting spending and producing more and better services for less money.

City Hall lies at the geographic center of Pennsylvania's 1st Congressional District. The 1st runs north on both sides of the Broad Street corridor to include much of black North Philadelphia and south through most of heavily Italian South Philadelphia, where Italian families and their grocery stores and restaurants have been pressed tightly into narrow English and Indian-named streets under a tangle of overhead wires; this is the neighborhood where the various *Rockys* were filmed and the original Philadelphia cheesesteaks are sold. The district also includes the oil tank farms where the Schuylkill River flows into the Delaware River, the Navy Yard, the Philadelphia airport, and the swath of industrial suburbs along the river to the black-majority city of Chester. This was created as a black-majority district, in the argot of the Voting Rights Act, but also includes many Hispanics, and is overwhelmingly Democratic.

The 1st is represented by Democrat Thomas Foglietta, whose long career embodies Philadelphia's traditions of family politics and party switching. Foglietta, whose father was a Republican politician, was once a Republican himself during the 20 years he served as a councilman from South Philadelphia. He first won his House seat in 1980 as an independent, beating a convicted Abscam defendant. He held the seat as a Democrat in the 1982 primary against another incumbent, Joseph Smith, 52%–48%, and in 1984 and 1986 weathered serious primary challenges from South Philadelphia politico James Tayoun.

Foglietta has one of the most liberal voting records in Congress. He is head of the Congressional Urban Caucus and works closely with Black Caucus members. He attacked the Contract With America harshly, claiming Philadelphia would lose $15 billion over seven years, and wants a three-fifths supermajority for cuts in "safety net programs." He has called for a base-closing-type commission to produce $50 billion to $100 billion in cuts in corporate welfare—and has tried to work with Republicans like Budget Committee Chairman John Kasich as well as Democrats on this. He has a bill for a more "holistic" approach to enterprise zones, creating "more empowerment zones in more cities, new financing tools for zone infrastructure, new education, transportation and environmental programs, and expanded and more flexible tax incentives for business." He has used his seat on Appropriations' Transportation Subcommittee to bring more funds to Philadelphia area mass transit.

Foglietta is the only white representing a black-majority district and has won impressive margins over black primary opponents: 69%–31% over Harvey Clark in 1994, 73%–27% over Judge John Braxton in 1996. Both times he was endorsed by Black Clergy of Philadelphia and Vicinity and the *Philadelphia Tribune*. The latter victory came after Braxton accused him of being a slumlord and he had to take out a $40,000 loan to pay back taxes and delinquent sewer fees on an apartment building he co-owns. In early 1997 Foglietta was tapped to become the next Ambassador to Italy. His likeliest successor is city Democratic Chairman Bob Brady, who is also white and who has the support of leading blacks and Mayor Ed Rendell. A host of others, including former Congressman Lucien Blackwell, who represented the 2d District from 1991–94, are thinking of entering the race.

The People: Pop. 1990: 566,133; 13% age 65+; 36% White; 52% Black; 2% Asian; 10% Hispanic origin. Households: 35% married couple families; 15% married couple fams. w. children; 25% college educ.; median household income: $20,372; per capita income: $9,703; median gross rent: $404; median house value: $36,700.

1996 Presidential Vote			1992 Presidential Vote		
Clinton (D)	148,850	(83%)	Clinton (D)	150,091	(72%)
Dole (R)	21,845	(12%)	Bush (R)	39,086	(19%)
Perot (I)	7,519	(4%)	Perot (I)	17,052	(8%)

Rep. Thomas M. Foglietta (D)

Elected 1980; b. Dec. 3, 1928, Philadelphia; home, Philadelphia; St. Joseph's Col., B.A. 1949, Temple U., J.D. 1952; Catholic; single.

Career: Practicing atty., 1952–80; Philadelphia City Cncl., 1955–75; Reg. Dir., U.S. Dept. of Labor, 1976.

DC Office: 242 CHOB 20515, 202-225-4731; Fax: 202-225-0088; e-mail: mailtom@hr.house.gov.

District Offices: Philadelphia, 215-925-6840; Philadelphia, 215-463-8702; Philadelphia, 215-236-5430.

Committees: *Appropriations* (16th of 26 D): Foreign Operations, Export Financing & Related Programs; Transportation.

Group Ratings

	ADA	ACLU	AFS	LCV	CFA	CON	NFIB	COC	ACU	NTLC	CHC
1996	85	88	100	85	69	85	17	20	5	2	7
1995	100	—	—	100	100	13	—	17	4	—	—

National Journal Ratings

	1995 LIB	—	1995 CONS	1996 LIB	—	1996 CONS
Economic	94%	—	0%	89%	—	0%
Social	78%	—	22%	82%	—	17%
Foreign	84%	—	15%	90%	—	0%

Key Votes of the 104th Congress

1. Reduce Medicare Growth $	N	5. Flag Amendment	N	9. Cuban Embargo	N
2. Ovrd. Product Liab. Veto	N	6. Drop EPA Limits	Y	10. Bar Bosnia Troop $	N
3. Increase Min. Wage	Y	7. Repeal Assault-Weap. Ban	N	11. Cut Anti-Missile Defense	Y
4. Welfare Reform	N	8. Ovrd. Part. Birth Veto	Y	12. Bar U.N. Uniforms	N

Election Results

1996 general	Thomas M. Foglietta (D)	145,210	(88%)	($485,748)
	James Cella (R)	20,734	(12%)	($4,603)
1996 primary	Thomas M. Foglietta (D)	36,426	(73%)	
	John L. Braxton (D)	13,237	(27%)	
1994 general	Thomas M. Foglietta (D)	99,669	(82%)	($486,812)
	Roger F. Gordon (R)	22,595	(18%)	

SECOND DISTRICT

Looking out over the Schuylkill River north of Center City Philadelphia, you can still see the landscape painted 100 years ago by Philadelphia artist Thomas Eakins—the tightly-packed but formidable rowhouses, the old fieldstone houses of Germantown, the grey-blue water flowing past boat houses below the small Greek temples of the Water Works and the larger temple of the Museum of Art and the skyscraper towers looming behind. On both sides of this romantic scene are some of Philadelphia's long-established black neighborhoods—West Philadelphia, across the Schuylkill on either side of Market Street; North Philadelphia, on either side of Broad Street; to the northwest, off the narrow diagonal of Germantown Avenue that ran through open fields in Benjamin Franklin's time.

The 2d Congressional District of Pennsylvania is centered on this part of Philadelphia, following the Schuylkill north and south. It includes Center City skyscrapers, affluent Chestnut Hill, upper-class Rittenhouse Square, and the University of Pennsylvania. Pennsylvania never had slavery—thanks to William Penn's Quaker legacy—and Philadelphia had a large black community even before the Civil War. As redistricted for the 1990s, the 2d District is 62% black, and overwhelmingly Democratic. There are occasional reminders of Philadelphia's historic Republicanness: Senator Arlen Specter, who has a long record of support for civil rights, won enough black votes here to make the difference in his 49%–47% reelection in 1992.

The congressman from the 2d District is Chaka Fattah, first elected in 1994. Fattah grew up in Philadelphia, and in 1982, at 25, was elected to the state House—the youngest member ever. In 1988 he was elected to the state Senate, where he worked to fend off bankruptcy for Philadelphia. In 1991, much to everyone's surprise, 2d District Congressman William Gray resigned to become head of the United Negro College Fund. Gray was a shining star in the political firmament, first elected in 1978, chairman of the Budget Committee from 1982–88, majority whip since 1989: no serious candidate thought of running against him. But the vacancy invited competition. Local ward leaders nominated Councilman Lucien Blackwell. Blackwell was a former longshoreman and boxer, a labor union stalwart who lived in West Philadelphia for decades; he attended to parochial neighborhood concerns while leaders like Gray were concerned about the world beyond. Fattah ran under the Consumer Party label and state welfare secretary John White ran as an Independent. Blackwell won the 1991 special election with 39% to 28% for Fattah and 27% for White.

In 1992 Fattah did not run, but Blackwell won the primary by only 54%–46% over former Secretary of State C. Delores Tucker. In 1994 Fattah ran again. He challenged Blackwell's petitions, but dropped the suit rather than reveal the name of his informant. Blackwell was endorsed by Mayor Ed Rendell and Council President John Street, but relied mostly on ward politicians. Fattah was endorsed by the Black Clergy of Philadelphia and Vicinity and by state

Senator Hardy Williams and produced position papers on education, crime, housing, and the plight of the inner city. In this rematch Fattah was successful, winning 58%–42%. He did not have serious primary opposition in 1996.

Fattah shares with several others the most liberal voting record in the House. He voted against Contract With America measures more often than all but one other member. "Dark clouds are gathering," he told constituents. "A new cast of characters has taken over Congress" who would spend money on "smart bombs, but nothing on smart children." He attended the Million Man March in fall 1995 and said he hoped it would lead to higher voter turnout by black men. Fattah has a checklist of legislative initiatives—guaranteed Pell grants for students in poverty areas who stay in high school and maintain the necessary grades, a federal law to get states to equalize school district funding, expanding HUD lending to community development—but none seems likely to pass in a Republican or even in a narrowly Democratic House. Fattah is articulate and telegenic, and could be an attractive candidate for higher office, though his liberal stands on some issues would be a handicap.

The People: Pop. 1990: 565,242; 15% age 65+; 34% White; 62% Black; 2% Asian; 2% Hispanic origin. Households: 32% married couple families; 12% married couple fams. w. children; 40% college educ.; median household income: $24,880; per capita income: $13,121; median gross rent: $479; median house value: $42,300.

1996 Presidential Vote			**1992 Presidential Vote**		
Clinton (D)	173,723	(86%)	Clinton (D)	183,758	(79%)
Dole (R)	20,675	(10%)	Bush (R)	31,878	(14%)
Perot (I)	5,981	(3%)	Perot (I)	14,514	(6%)

Rep. Chaka Fattah (D)

Elected 1994; b. Nov. 21, 1956, Philadelphia; home, Philadelphia; U. of PA, M.A. 1986; Baptist; married (Patricia).

Career: PA House of Reps., 1982–1988; PA Senate, 1988–1994.

DC Office: 1205 LHOB 20515, 202-225-4001; Fax: 202-225-5392; e-mail: cfattah@hr.house.gov.

District Offices: Philadelphia, 215-387-6404; Philadelphia, 215-848-9386.

Committees: *Education & The Workforce* (13th of 20 D): Employer-Employee Relations; Postsecondary Education, Training & Life-Long Learning. *Government Reform & Oversight* (11th of 19 D): National Economic Growth, Natural Resources & Regulatory Affairs; Postal Service (RMM).

Group Ratings

	ADA	ACLU	AFS	LCV	CFA	CON	NFIB	COC	ACU	NTLC	CHC
1996	95	94	100	85	77	60	18	25	0	3	0
1995	95	—	—	94	100	16	—	13	4	—	—

National Journal Ratings

	1995 LIB	—	1995 CONS	1996 LIB	—	1996 CONS
Economic	94%	—	0%	89%	—	0%
Social	88%	—	0%	88%	—	0%
Foreign	93%	—	0%	90%	—	0%

Key Votes of the 104th Congress

1. Reduce Medicare Growth $	N	5. Flag Amendment	N	9. Cuban Embargo	N
2. Ovrd. Product Liab. Veto	N	6. Drop EPA Limits	Y	10. Bar Bosnia Troop $	N
3. Increase Min. Wage	Y	7. Repeal Assault-Weap. Ban	N	11. Cut Anti-Missile Defense	Y
4. Welfare Reform	N	8. Ovrd. Part. Birth Veto	N	12. Bar U.N. Uniforms	N

Election Results

1996 general	Chaka Fattah (D)	168,887	(88%)	($412,478)
	Larry G. Murphy (R)	23,047	(12%)	
1996 primary	Chaka Fattah (D)	unopposed		
1994 general	Chaka Fattah (D)	120,553	(86%)	($492,348)
	Lawrence R. Watson II (R)	19,824	(14%)	($2,828)

THIRD DISTRICT

North and east of Center City Philadelphia, stretching more than a dozen miles along the Delaware River and back along the parklands by Frankford, Tacony and Pennypacker Creeks, are most of the white residential neighborhoods of Philadelphia. They start off in the closely packed 19th Century homes of Kensington, where descendants of Irish and Italian immigrants live in inelegant frame houses and often earn less than the residents in many black neighborhoods. Farther out is northeast Philadelphia, a more suburban area itself the size of a major city. Here, when the alley-wide streets of North and South Philadelphia and the river wards were already teeming with houses and people and the Main Line suburbs were already well-settled, the workers of Philadelphia's docks and factories and Center City offices were just starting to move out and fill up vacant land. They settled in neighborhoods like the one near Pennypack Park, where Philadelphia's hero Sylvester Stallone grew up. Unlike much of Philadelphia, with its high crime rate and struggling city government, northeast Philadelphia is still new urban territory, with more than half of its dwellings built after 1950, and is still growing.

Politically the district appears to be a throwback to an earlier era, when you would expect to see ward heelers walking through the neighborhoods of Kensington and Frankford, distributing coal for the winter. Most people here are Catholic, but there are also many Jews, living in neighborhoods like neither Brooklyn nor Scarsdale. The houses are pleasant, but modest. Many residents are part of the hard-pressed lower middle-class and are Democrats, but also are conservative on many cultural issues, and there is a Republican tradition in some wards. Northeast Philadelphia recoiled from the national Democrats and voted for Mayor Frank Rizzo in the 1970s; now it seems to have returned to its Democratic allegiance.

The congressman from the 3d District is Robert Borski, a Democrat first elected in 1982. He grew up in Northeast Philadelphia, and first distinguished himself as an athlete: he was captain of the Frankford High basketball and baseball teams in 1966 and became a coach after graduating from college with an athletic scholarship. Contacts made as an athlete helped him get a job as a floor manager at the Philadelphia Stock Exchange, and in 1976 he was elected to the state House of Representatives, where he served until his election to Congress in 1982. He won the seat by beating a Republican who had won in 1980 over a Democrat who had been indicted in 1978: thus is a career shaped by events of long ago. He has won easily ever since.

Borski is a party loyalist, favorable to organized labor, with a voting record a bit to the conservative side on cultural issues. But most of all, he is concerned about Philadelphia, and about using his seat on the Transportation and Infrastructure Committee to help it. In December 1996 he served unhappily on the Ethics Committee, painstakingly and soberly judging the case against Speaker Newt Gingrich: at the eye of the Washington political hurricane. But his thoughts were of home. "I do need to be talking to the people in Philadelphia. I normally spend this time talking to the airport folks and the port people about what their legislative wishes are." He does work on national legislation, like his bills to ban backhauling of toxic chemicals and to ban triple-trailer trucks. He sponsored a bill, backed by the Teamsters, to stop the FAA from certifying foreign aircraft repair stations and to make all repair stations play by the same operating rules, saying the foreign stations have lower standards than U.S. facilities. He objects to Republican Superfund changes as reimbursing polluters. He sponsored an amendment, partially drafted by the National Governors' Association, to protect wetlands, and has also sponsored a brownfields law.

But Philadelphia seems to come first. He worked to get an $800,000 reconstruction of the river wall at Glen Foerd on the Delaware River. He got $20 million to overhaul the hopper dredge *McFarland* at the Philadelphia Navy Yard; he felt the dredge was essential to maintaining the port. By 29–25 on the committee, he beat a provision in the Amtrak privatization law which would have required SEPTA to pay Amtrak higher fees for use of its tracks. He has superintended the Superfund toxic waste cleanup at the Metal Bank property in Tacony. He led a delegation to get more nonstop flights from Philadelphia to Europe.

He considers one of his greatest personal accomplishments the reversal of a base-closing commission plan to close the Aviation Supply Office on Robbins Avenue in Northeast Philadelphia, which would have cost 8,000 jobs; Borski united the Philadelphia delegation, Mayor Ed Rendell, and Pennsylvania's two senators on this issue. Borski takes his responsibilities seriously. He was a force for calm when on the Ethics Committee, and evidently would not have voted for censure of Gingrich: a sign Gingrich might have survived even if the Democrats had won the House. He will never be a philosophical national leader, but seems likely to remain for some time a congressman from Philadelphia.

The People: Pop. 1990: 565,884; 18% age 65+; 87% White; 5% Black; 3% Asian; 5% Hispanic origin. Households: 51% married couple families; 22% married couple fams. w. children; 29% college educ.; median household income: $29,157; per capita income: $13,429; median gross rent: $472; median house value: $64,900.

1996 Presidential Vote

Clinton (D)	114,680	(61%)
Dole (R)	51,781	(28%)
Perot (I)	18,878	(10%)
Other	2,870	(2%)

1992 Presidential Vote

Clinton (D)	125,078	(52%)
Bush (R)	75,388	(31%)
Perot (I)	39,582	(16%)

Rep. Robert A. Borski (D)

Elected 1982; b. Oct. 20, 1948, Philadelphia; home, Philadelphia; U. of Baltimore, B.A. 1971; Catholic; married (Karen).

Career: Asst. Coach, U. of Baltimore, 1971–72; Stockbroker, 1972–76; PA House of Reps., 1976–82.

DC Office: 2267 RHOB 20515, 202-225-8251; Fax: 202-225-4628.

District Offices: Philadelphia, 215-335-3355; Philadelphia, 215-426-4616.

Committees: *Transportation & Infrastructure* (3rd of 33 D): Coast Guard & Maritime Transportation; Railroads; Water Resources & Environment (RMM).

Group Ratings

	ADA	ACLU	AFS	LCV	CFA	CON	NFIB	COC	ACU	NTLC	CHC
1996	80	56	100	92	85	34	19	20	10	5	20
1995	84	—	100	92	2	—	22	16	—	—	

National Journal Ratings

	1995 LIB — 1995 CONS	1996 LIB — 1996 CONS
Economic	84% — 15%	89% — 0%
Social	60% — 39%	63% — 35%
Foreign	79% — 17%	79% — 19%

Key Votes of the 104th Congress

1. Reduce Medicare Growth $	N	5. Flag Amendment	N	9. Cuban Embargo	Y
2. Ovrd. Product Liab. Veto	N	6. Drop EPA Limits	Y	10. Bar Bosnia Troop $	N
3. Increase Min. Wage	Y	7. Repeal Assault-Weap. Ban	N	11. Cut Anti-Missile Defense	Y
4. Welfare Reform	N	8. Ovrd. Part. Birth Veto	Y	12. Bar U.N. Uniforms	N

Election Results

1996 general	Robert A. Borski (D)	121,120	(69%)	($317,799)
	Joseph M. McColgan (R)	54,681	(31%)	($95,008)
1996 primary	Robert A. Borski (D)	26,211	(91%)	
	John R. Kates (D)	2,687	(9%)	
1994 general	Robert A. Borski (D)	92,702	(63%)	($323,957)
	James C. Hasher (R)	55,209	(37%)	($120,616)

FOURTH DISTRICT

For a century one of America's great industrial zones was along the banks of the Beaver and Ohio Rivers, near where they join in westernmost Pennsylvania. This was steel country, with mills rising black and brooding from the bottomlands and filling the narrow river valleys with smoke. The sinewy sons of immigrant families worked hard in the hot mills. Looking down on riverscapes lined with piles of iron ore, limestone and coal, and littered with cranes, stocks and furnaces, families lived in small frame houses on the hillsides. Although not an environmentalist's idea of perfection, this was a land of opportunity for thousands whose lives were far worse before moving to steel country. For a few heady years, the high union wages and early retirement plans seemed to make working in the mills the way to affluence. But the industry crashed after the oil shock of 1979, when mills were closed and jobs vanished. Today, thousands of workers who long ago exhausted their unemployment benefits have given up and left the Beaver and Ohio valleys. Forty years ago, the western Pennsylvania steel country had 11 House Members; it now has six.

The congressman from the 4th District is Ron Klink, a Democrat first elected in 1992. Klink grew up in Myersdale, Pennsylvania, and has been a jack of many trades. In his 20s he was a restaurant owner; in 1978 he became a reporter and anchor for Pittsburgh's KDKA-TV. In 1992, he decided to run for the House. The incumbent, Democrat Joe Kolter, was lightly regarded and drew no fewer than three primary opponents; after years of supporting union positions, he missed a key vote on unemployment benefits and in March lost the AFL-CIO endorsement, which went to another Democrat. But Klink, from his years on the air, was much better known, and his "Ron Klink Plan for Jobs" struck a chord in an area long suffering from high unemployment. Klink won the primary with a rousing 35%, two state legislators got 22% and 13%, and the hapless Kolter 20%. Klink won the general election handily.

In the House Klink has had a liberal voting record on economics and been more moderate on cultural and foreign issues. He supported the Clinton budget and tax plan but vigorously opposed NAFTA in 1993 and, on the then-Education and Labor Committee, worked on the Schools-to-Work Transition Act. Unlike most Democrats, he favors restrictions on abortion and proposed that no healthcare plan should require insurers to cover abortions. He sponsored the Uniform Adoption Act, to make adoption more secure. Switching to the Commerce Committee in his second term, he worked to get FDA approval of home drug-testing kits. By 1997 he was ranking Democrat on Commerce's Oversight and Investigations Subcommittee, once one of John Dingell's power bases.

Much of Klink's work is bolstering the 4th District's local economy. He got an extension of Trade Readjustment Assistance benefits for Rockwell International employees in New Castle. He worked to get approval of the USAirways-British Airways agreement (USAirways' Pittsburgh hub is nearby). He worked to strengthen pilot and air traffic controller training at Community College of Beaver County. He got a moratorium on zinc sales from the strategic stockpile, to save 700 jobs at Zinc Corporation of America's Monaca plant. He got an abandoned federal facility in Hopewell Township transferred to the Beaver County Corporation for Economic Development.

Klink was reelected by wide margins in 1994 and 1996. His agenda for the 105th Congress includes the Individual Training Accounts Act, the Crows Run Road Connector in Beaver County and a resolution recognizing the heroic struggle of the people of Crete for their battle with Germany for the island in World War II.

The People: Pop. 1990: 565,809; 33% rural; 16% age 65+; 96% White; 3% Black; 1% Hispanic origin. Households: 63% married couple families; 27% married couple fams. w. children; 36% college educ.; median household income: $26,792; per capita income: $12,684; median gross rent: $332; median house value: $55,400.

1996 Presidential Vote

Clinton (D)	107,017	(47%)
Dole (R)	96,511	(42%)
Perot (I)	23,375	(10%)

1992 Presidential Vote

Clinton (D)	118,701	(48%)
Bush (R)	76,291	(31%)
Perot (I)	50,654	(21%)

Rep. Ron Klink (D)

Elected 1992; b. Sept. 23, 1951, Canton, OH; home, Jeannette; Protestant; married (Linda).

Career: Businessman; Restaurant Owner; Reporter & Anchor, KDKA-TV, Pittsburgh, 1978–92.

DC Office: 125 CHOB 20515, 202-225-2565; Fax: 202-226-2274.

District Offices: Beaver, 412-728-3005; Cranberry Township, 412-772-6080; Lower Burrell, 412-335-4518; N. Huntingdon, 412-864-8681; New Castle, 412-654-9036.

Committees: *Commerce* (15th of 23 D): Oversight & Investigations (RMM); Telecommunications, Trade & Consumer Protection.

Group Ratings

	ADA	ACLU	AFS	LCV	CFA	CON	NFIB	COC	ACU	NTLC	CHC
1996	65	62	100	69	54	50	27	20	30	12	20
1995	75	—	—	94	62	16	—	29	16	—	—

National Journal Ratings

	1995 LIB — 1995 CONS			1996 LIB — 1996 CONS		
Economic	76%	—	23%	89%	—	0%
Social	57%	—	42%	50%	—	48%
Foreign	68%	—	31%	67%	—	31%

Key Votes of the 104th Congress

1. Reduce Medicare Growth $	N	5. Flag Amendment	N	9. Cuban Embargo	N
2. Ovrd. Product Liab. Veto	*	6. Drop EPA Limits	Y	10. Bar Bosnia Troop $	N
3. Increase Min. Wage	Y	7. Repeal Assault-Weap. Ban	Y	11. Cut Anti-Missile Defense	Y
4. Welfare Reform	N	8. Ovrd. Part. Birth Veto	Y	12. Bar U.N. Uniforms	Y

Election Results

1996 general	Ron Klink (D)	142,621	(64%)	($506,560)
	Paul T. Adametz (R)	79,448	(36%)	($17,028)
1996 primary	Ron Klink (D)	unopposed		
1994 general	Ron Klink (D)	119,115	(64%)	($467,285)
	Ed Peglow (R)	66,509	(36%)	($88,576)

FIFTH DISTRICT

North central Pennsylvania—isolated from the rest of the country by chains of mountains, off the main east-west rail and highway lines until the 1970s—is one of those empty spaces that make even the northeastern states seem lightly populated to someone used to the densely packed terrain of Western Europe or East Asia. In narrow valleys, pressed tightly by mountains and fast-flowing rivers, connected by roads that switch back and wind precariously over mountains, there are few population concentrations. The largest is in the Nittany Valley, the home of Pennsylvania State University, long known for its powerful football teams coached by Joe Paterno. To the west are Titusville, where Colonel Edwin Drake sunk the first successful oil well in 1859, and Oil City, headquarters of Quaker State Oil from 1931 until it left for Texas in 1995. To the east, near the Susquehanna River, is Lewisburg, home of Bucknell University and the Lewisbury federal penitentiary. The solidly built courthouses and banks in the center of each county seat testify to the long history of hard work and thrift in this part of the country. Yet today, even with the main east-west truck line, Interstate 80, it is a low-wage area.

The 5th Congressional District of Pennsylvania includes a very wide swath of north central Pennsylvania, and has somewhat irregular boundaries. Its largest city is State College in the Nittany Valley; it sweeps west to Oil City and east to Lewisburg. The political heritage here is Republican, with few exceptions, from the Civil War through the New Deal and the Great Society, in Ronald Reagan's 1980s and Bill Clinton's 1990s.

The congressman from the 5th District is John Peterson, a Republican elected in 1996. Peterson grew up in Titusville, the son of a steelworker; he went to Penn State, served in the Army as a cook, then opened a grocery store that eventually became Peterson's Golden Dawn Supermarket chain. He served on the Pleasantville Borough Council for eight years, then in 1977, at 39, was elected to the state House. In 1984 he was elected to the state Senate, where he chaired the Public Health and Welfare Committee, concentrating on rural health issues, and working on Pennsylvania's welfare reform. Then in 1996 Congressman Bill Clinger announced his retirement after 18 years in the House. He was well known nationally for heading the investigation into the Clinton White House travel office firings and misuse of FBI files; in the 5th District he was affectionately known as "Mr. Sewer" for his work on the Transportation and Infrastructure Committee. Peterson was an obvious candidate; his state Senate district included eight of the 5th's 17 counties. Three other Republicans ran. The one who attracted the most attention was Bob Shuster, the 31-year-old son of 9th District Congressman Bud Shuster, chairman of the Transportation and Infrastructure Committee and an unashamed builder of roads in his home district (including the Bud Shuster Freeway). "What a one-two punch we could be for central Pennsylvania," Bud Shuster said on announcement day, and his son had controversial fundraising help from Ann Eppard, a lobbyist and former Shuster aide with whom the chairman has stayed while in Washington. Bob Shuster had worked briefly for Clinger and moved into Centre County in the Nittany Valley, the largest county in the district. However, the county Republican chairman called him a "carpetbagger" and endorsed another 31-year-old candidate, Patrick Conway, a longtime aide to Shuster and then to Governor Tom Ridge. "The Honest Way is Conway," he proclaimed. The fourth candidate was Daniel Gordeuk, a Centre County surgeon with strong local roots, and who ended up as Peterson's chief competition, carrying Centre County and three others nearby. But that local vote was split, and Peterson won with 38%, to 28% for Gordeuk, 18% for Shuster and 16% for Conway.

Peterson was the clear favorite in the general. One prominent moderate Democrat, state Representative Mike Hanna, declined to run. Peterson attacked the nominee, state Representative (and former Centre County Prothonotary) Ruth Rudy as "an old-fashioned liberal" and touted his work in the legislature, his support for a "flatter tax" and his opposition to abortion and gun control. But Rudy ran a spirited campaign. She spent time in each county working at different jobs through "work days"—literally working her way through the district, imploring voters to "Do their duty, vote for Rudy." Then in mid-October, the Harrisburg *Patriot News* reported charges that six women accused Peterson of inappropriate sexual advances; a seventh soon spoke up. Peterson denied the charges. "I may have been an excessive hugger," he said, and admitted he was a "too friendly person." But "it was never a sexual advance—never, ever, ever." This was evidently not devastating at a time when the president of the United States stands accused of similar conduct. Peterson won 60%–40%. Rudy carried Centre County and next-door Clinton County; Peterson carried most of the rest by 2–1 or better.

In the House Peterson was assigned to the Education and The Workforce, and Resources Committees, neither of which has jurisdiction over his special interest of rural health care. But his interest continues. "The federal government is the greatest threat to rural health care, and that's because of the current bias against rural America when it comes to health programs and spending," he repeatedly said, citing the Health Care Financing Administration as the chief culprit. "I am going to be in their face as soon as I can figure out the best way to do that." He also promised to promote economic development and adult education and to work to keep interstate waste out of Pennsylvania.

The People: Pop. 1990: 565,736; 66% rural; 14% age 65+; 97% White; 1% Black; 1% Asian; 1% Hispanic origin. Households: 60% married couple families; 27% married couple fams. w. children; 31% college educ.; median household income: $23,934; per capita income: $10,946; median gross rent: $334; median house value: $47,800.

1996 Presidential Vote

Dole (R)	91,619	(46%)
Clinton (D)	80,003	(40%)
Perot (I)	25,687	(13%)

1992 Presidential Vote

Bush (R)	89,385	(41%)
Clinton (D)	78,057	(36%)
Perot (I)	48,100	(22%)

Rep. John E. Peterson (R)

Elected 1996; b. Dec. 25, 1938, Titusville; home, Pleasantville; PA St. U., 1974–76; Methodist; married (Sandy).

Career: Army, 1958–64; Owner, Peterson's Golden Dawn Food Market, 1958–84; Pleasantville Borough Council, 1969–77; PA House of Reps, 1977–84; PA Senate, 1984–96.

DC Office: 1020 LHOB 20515, 202-225-5121; Fax: 202-225-5796. **District Offices:** State College, 814-238-1776; Titusville, 814-827-3985; Warren, 814-726-3910.

Committees: *Education & The Workforce* (21st of 25 R): Early Childhood, Youth & Families; Postsecondary Education, Training & Life-Long Learning. *Resources* (23rd of 27 R): Fisheries Conservation, Wildlife & Oceans; Forests & Forest Health.

Group Ratings and Key Votes: Newly Elected

Election Results

1996 general	John E. Peterson (R)	116,303	(60%)	($858,637)
	Ruth C. Rudy (D)	76,627	(40%)	($446,613)
1996 primary	John E. Peterson (R)	22,000	(38%)	
	Daniel S. Gordeuk (R)	16,230	(28%)	
	Bob Shuster (R)	10,734	(18%)	
	Patrick Conway (R)	9,334	(16%)	
1994 general	William F. (Bill) Clinger, Jr. (R)	unopposed		($340,709)

SIXTH DISTRICT

The gentle hills of southeastern Pennsylvania, settled in the 18th Century by Quaker townsmen, Welsh farmers, German peasants, and members of pietistic sects who became known as the Pennsylvania Dutch, were America's first polyglot interior. A diverse lot looking for tolerance in the area above Philadelphia and the Delaware River and below the first chains of the Appalachians, they found a land that yielded riches, first in crops, then in ironworking and other industry. In time this civilization poured over the mountain chains, where the farmers were rough-hewn and more violence-prone, and where the towns existed solely to mine rich veins of anthracite and bituminous coal, the primary energy source of late 19th and early 20th Century America. These mountain towns were less orderly, filled with tough-talking miners and factory workers who stayed menacingly in the background unless a character stumbled into the wrong roadhouse at night or the wrong diner at dawn: this was the Pennsylvania John O'Hara grew up in and described in his 1930s and 1940s novels and stories.

The area was linked together by the Reading Railroad in 1842 and became one of America's prime industrial sites for a century after. But the anthracite country around Pottsville and the hat and textile mills of Reading were left behind by the economic growth of the late 20th Century. The anthracite country, nestled amid mountains, has never rebounded from the switch from coal to oil and natural gas for home heating: Schuylkill County around Pottsville had 228,000 people in 1940 and 153,000 in 1990. But Reading has come back, starting in 1970, when a company called Vanity Fair began selling seconds and overruns of stockings and lingerie at wholesale prices in what had been the Berkshire Knitting Mills; this was the first of the factory outlets. Reading was home to some 300 outlets by the mid-1990s, selling deeply-discounted goods on the polished wood floors of converted brick mills, bringing in more than half a billion dollars a year, generating 5,000 jobs and spawning 2,000 motel rooms.

The 6th Congressional District includes Berks and Schuylkill Counties centered on Reading and Pottsville, plus an almost unconnected sliver of Northumberland County, an industrial area between mountains and the upper Susquehanna River. It is politically divided between the rough mining tradition of the anthracite country and the quietism of the Pennsylvania Dutch, between Democratic Schuylkill County and Republican Berks County.

The congressman from the 6th District is Tim Holden, a Democrat first elected in 1992. Holden comes from a political family from the coal mining hamlet of St. Clair; his great-grandfather was a coal miner who founded the forerunner to the United Mine Workers, and his father served four terms as Schuylkill County commissioner. Holden gained fame as a football player; he says he has been around athletics all his life. He is a regular church-goer and likes to attend fire company block parties. In 1985, at age 28, after selling insurance and real estate for five years, he was elected Schuylkill County sheriff, and reelected with 75%. Holden's opponent in the 1992 Congressional race was John Jones III, a lawyer who ran a family business operating golf courses: two characters out of O'Hara. Jones called Holden "clueless" and called for term limits and congressional salary cuts; Holden said he represented "the hardworking men and women" of the district. In culturally conservative but economically polarized Schuylkill County, this appeal sold, and Holden won 52%–48%.

Holden has a moderate voting record, in 1996 he voted near the middle of the House on economic, cultural and foreign issues. He is one of the centrist Blue Dog Democrats. He opposed NAFTA and the Clinton healthcare plan, but backed welfare reform and healthcare portability. He serves on the Agriculture Committee, where he looks after dairy programs; he wants the government to buy more cheese, increase the flow of dairy products in international food aid and resume a dairy export subsidy program, idle since 1995. He seeks new roads in Schuylkill County and wants to increase black lung benefits for miners. Most of all, he works the district hard, talking issues and solving constituents' problems. As the Pottsville *Republican & Evening Herald* wrote, "It would be hard to imagine a legislator more precisely in tune with his county on virtually any and every issue that has come before Congress in the past four years."

That work has paid off at election time. In 1994 Republicans had to substitute a candidate, as the winner of their primary had left the race because of illness. Holden won 68% in Schuylkill County, plus narrow margins elsewhere, for a 57%–43% victory. In 1996 Holden faced Christian Leinbach, a staffer for Senator Rick Santorum and a former Berks County Republican chairman. Holden outspent Leinbach, largely because of PAC contributions, and won 69%–31% in Schuylkill County and 59%–41% district wide.

After the election Holden said, "The problems our country is facing need to be solved in a bipartisan manner. There's about 70 liberals and 70 ultraconservatives still in the House. They need to be left behind." His own goals were a balanced budget, protection of Medicare and Medicaid and 100% deductibility of health insurance for the self-employed.

The People: Pop. 1990: 565,923; 44% rural; 17% age 65+; 94% White; 2% Black; 1% Asian; 3% Hispanic origin. Households: 59% married couple families; 25% married couple fams. w. children; 28% college educ.; median household income: $28,766; per capita income: $13,349; median gross rent: $367; median house value: $65,900.

1996 Presidential Vote

Dole (R)	89,695	(45%)
Clinton (D)	83,779	(42%)
Perot (I)	25,139	(13%)

1992 Presidential Vote

Bush (R)	90,140	(41%)
Clinton (D)	78,776	(36%)
Perot (I)	50,333	(23%)

Rep. Tim Holden (D)

Elected 1992; b. Mar. 5, 1957, Pottsville; home, St. Clair; U. of Richmond, 1976–78, Bloomsburg St. U., B.A. 1980; Catholic; married (Gwen).

Career: Insurance broker/real estate agent, Holden Insurance Agency, 1980–85; Schuylkill Cnty. Sheriff, 1985–92.

DC Office: 1421 LHOB 20515, 202-225-5546; Fax: 202-226-0996.

District Offices: Pottsville, 717-662-4212; Reading, 610-371-9931; Sunbury, 717-988-1902.

Committees: *Agriculture* (10th of 23 D): Forestry, Resource Conservation & Research; Livestock, Dairy & Poultry. *Transportation & Infrastructure* (32nd of 33 D): Public Buildings & Economic Development.

Group Ratings

	ADA	ACLU	AFS	LCV	CFA	CON	NFIB	COC	ACU	NTLC	CHC
1996	45	31	67	69	46	57	57	63	47	38	42
1995	60	—	—	63	38	9	—	46	46	—	—

National Journal Ratings

	1995 LIB	—	1995 CONS	1996 LIB	—	1996 CONS
Economic	65%	—	35%	58%	—	41%
Social	47%	—	52%	48%	—	52%
Foreign	52%	—	46%	54%	—	45%

Key Votes of the 104th Congress

1. Reduce Medicare Growth $	N	5. Flag Amendment	Y	9. Cuban Embargo	Y
2. Ovrd. Product Liab. Veto	Y	6. Drop EPA Limits	Y	10. Bar Bosnia Troop $	N
3. Increase Min. Wage	Y	7. Repeal Assault-Weap. Ban	Y	11. Cut Anti-Missile Defense	*
4. Welfare Reform	Y	8. Ovrd. Part. Birth Veto	Y	12. Bar U.N. Uniforms	Y

Election Results

1996 general	Tim Holden (D)	115,193	(59%)	($609,346)
	Christian Y. Leinbach (R)	80,061	(41%)	($419,013)
1996 primary	Tim Holden (D)	unopposed		
1994 general	Tim Holden (D)	90,023	(57%)	($675,274)
	Fred Levering (R)	68,610	(43%)	($132,889)

SEVENTH DISTRICT

The close-in suburbs of the great eastern cities are homes to some of the most curious and most long-lasting political machines in America. They are Republican; they conduct business in the accents of ordinary people, ethnic as well as WASP; they have a tolerance for patronage, and for what city reform liberals would call corruption, that is sharply at odds with their embodiment of middle-class morality; they are old, going back to the days when political machines were as much a part of the urban landscape as trolley lines or overhead electrical wires; and, unlike most big-city Democratic machines, they are still in business. One such machine is the War Board of Pennsylvania's Delaware County. This is a diverse area, mostly but not entirely white, predominantly Catholic where it was predominantly Protestant two generations ago. Its housing is aging but well-maintained; its population is above average in income but differs from the affluent Main Line commuter towns. People here treasure traditional cultural values but also feel pinched by family obligations and worry about retirement; they have deep roots in greater Philadelphia, but also deep fears about crime in nearby city neighborhoods.

The 7th Congressional District includes almost all of Delaware County, except for a few towns appended to Philadelphia districts, and extends north to include Main Line suburbs and King of Prussia, the edge city where the Schuylkill Expressway intersects the Pennsylvania Turnpike. This remains a solidly Republican district in most elections, although it gave a narrow margin to Bill Clinton in 1996.

The congressman from the 7th is Curt Weldon, a Republican backed by the War Board and with anything but an aristocratic pedigree. A teacher and personnel trainer, he first came to public attention as mayor of Marcus Hook, Pennsylvania's southernmost town on the Delaware River, the home of oil tank farms and a rusty-looking steel mill. Weldon was elected to the county council, ran for the House in 1984 against liberal Democrat Bob Edgar (who got to Congress when the War Board split 10 years before), lost by 412 votes, and ran again (with no primary opposition) in 1986, this time successfully, when Edgar ran unsuccessfully for the Senate.

Weldon is a local congressman first of all, attending every Eagle Scout induction in the district, seeking out work for the closed Philadelphia Navy Yard, and promoting the V-22 Osprey tilt-rotor aircraft much of which is made in these parts. But he also works on national issues. As chairman of the National Security Subcommittee on Military Research and Development, he favors faster development of missile defense. He attacked the Clinton Administration for slowing down missile defense by fudging intelligence estimates and ignoring statutes passed by law; he warns that the SS-25 missiles Russia is selling could be used to drop payloads on the United States. A Russian studies major in college, he has initiated a U.S. Congress-Duma Study Group, and hopes to establish direct internet communication with instantaneous translation; he wants to do the same with China's People's Congress. He is concerned about ocean dumping, especially dumping of nuclear waste by Russia; he announced he is hosting a multi-nation conference on oceans in 1997. As a former volunteer fireman, he founded the Congressional Fire Services Caucus (Weldon once put out a fire in Speaker Jim Wright's office). More recently, he has worked on reforming FEMA, has tried to set aside 40% of the spectrum between channels 60 and 69 for public safety notices, and had provided other members with materials on how to prevent church arson.

Weldon is a partisan Republican but not always a free-market enthusiast; like Pennsylvanian Republicans of yore, he supports trade restrictions and voted against NAFTA. Although he has supported unions on some issues, he is a co-sponsor of Davis-Bacon reform and favors the flextime law which would let workers take compensatory time off rather than higher overtime pay. Nor is he as thorough a budget-cutter as some Republicans. In the 104th Congress, he urged Speaker Newt Gingrich to back $3.5 billion in education block grants to the states, and they were included in the final budget deal. He strongly backs the partial-birth abortion ban. He co-sponsored the Animal Drug Availability Act, to allow lower regulatory thresholds for drugs used to treat animals, and he and Tom Lantos have sponsored a bill to discourage product testing on animals when other methods are deemed more reliable.

Weldon has been reelected by robust margins, 67%–32% in 1996. His one moment of political peril came when redistricting put him and 18-year veteran Richard Schulze in the same district in 1992, but Schulze retired.

The People: Pop. 1990: 565,815; 5% rural; 15% age 65+; 93% White; 4% Black; 2% Asian; 1% Hispanic origin. Households: 60% married couple families; 26% married couple fams. w. children; 53% college educ.; median household income: $41,710; per capita income: $20,175; median gross rent: $568; median house value: $133,000.

1996 Presidential Vote

Clinton (D)	116,654	(45%)
Dole (R)	112,429	(44%)
Perot (I)	23,647	(9%)
Other	4,338	(2%)

1992 Presidential Vote

Bush (R)	124,751	(43%)
Clinton (D)	111,511	(39%)
Perot (I)	49,798	(17%)

Rep. Curt Weldon (R)

Elected 1986; b. July 22, 1947, Marcus Hook; home, Aston; West Chester St. Col., B.A. 1969; Protestant; married (Mary).

Career: Elem. schl. teacher, Vice principal, 1969–76; Dir., Training and Manpower Devel., CIGNA Corp., 1976–81; Marcus Hook Mayor, 1977–82; Delaware Cnty. Cncl., 1981–86, Chmn. 1985–86.

DC Office: 2452 RHOB 20515, 202-225-2011; Fax: 202-225-8137; e-mail: curtpa7@hr.house.gov.

District Offices: Paoli, 610-640-9064; Upper Darby, 610-259-0700.

Committees: *National Security* (7th of 30 R): Military Readiness; Military Research & Development (Chmn.). *Science* (5th of 25 R): Energy & Environment; Technology.

Group Ratings

	ADA	ACLU	AFS	LCV	CFA	CON	NFIB	COC	ACU	NTLC	CHC
1996	15	8	36	31	54	14	88	85	84	87	86
1995	15	—	—	25	54	95	—	83	78	—	—

National Journal Ratings

	1995 LIB — 1995 CONS			1996 LIB — 1996 CONS		
Economic	41%	—	56%	47%	—	53%
Social	44%	—	56%	29%	—	68%
Foreign	15%	—	73%	30%	—	65%

Key Votes of the 104th Congress

1. Reduce Medicare Growth $	Y	5. Flag Amendment	Y	9. Cuban Embargo	Y
2. Ovrd. Product Liab. Veto	*	6. Drop EPA Limits	*	10. Bar Bosnia Troop $	Y
3. Increase Min. Wage	Y	7. Repeal Assault-Weap. Ban	Y	11. Cut Anti-Missile Defense	N
4. Welfare Reform	Y	8. Ovrd. Part. Birth Veto	Y	12. Bar U.N. Uniforms	Y

Election Results

1996 general	Curt Weldon (R)	165,087	(67%)	($362,252)
	John F. Innelli (D)	79,875	(32%)	($50,252)
1996 primary	Curt Weldon (R)	49,999	(84%)	
	Rob McMonagle (R)	9,882	(17%)	
1994 general	Curt Weldon (R)	137,480	(70%)	($349,639)
	Sara Nichols (D)	59,845	(30%)	($149,028)

EIGHTH DISTRICT

One of William Penn's three original settlements, Bucks County had a split personality from the beginning: it was a paradise of bucolic hills and creeks running into the Delaware River and, after Penn's secretary James Logan built the Durham Furnace iron works in 1727, one of the nation's major industrial sites. In the 1920s, Bucks County's well-settled farmland, old fieldstone houses and covered bridges in its northern parts captured the imagination of writers and artists, attracting a theatrical crowd—Oscar Hammerstein, Moss Hart, Dorothy Parker, S. J. Perelman. After World War II, its location between Philadelphia and industrial Trenton, New Jersey, brought industrial Bucks to the forefront. The ocean-navigable Delaware River and several rail lines resulted in huge new developments: U.S. Steel's Fairless Works, one of the few big postwar steel plants, down by the river, and the Levitt organization's second Levittown, in what had been farmland and swamp between U.S. 13 and U.S. 1. But Bucks County's economy now depends more on small businesses; the biggest new operation here came when Lockheed Martin bought 52 acres from Holy Name College in Newtown and built a communications center with 1,200 jobs in 1997.

Bucks County's political tradition was heavily Republican and protectionist; more recently it has been marginally Republican and environmentalist. This was the home of Senator Joseph Grundy, longtime head of the Pennsylvania Manufacturers Association, who opposed the 1930 Smoot-Hawley tariff as not protectionist enough. Development in Bucks came after the New Deal, unlike other suburban Philadelphia counties where most blue-collar immigration occurred years ago, when county political organizations were ready to enroll new residents in their party. So Lower Bucks, around the Fairless Works and Levittown, with its tightly-packed homes filled with blue collar workers, became Democratic. And Upper Bucks, fast-growing in the 1980s and still attracting trendy New Yorkers, is Republican but environment-conscious.

The 8th Congressional District of Pennsylvania includes all of Bucks County plus Horsham Township in Montgomery County. One of the few districts in the country with boundaries almost entirely unchanged for the last two decades, it was marginal in congressional elections between 1976 and 1992, and voted for Bill Clinton in 1992 and 1996. But it has gone back to its Republican roots in House races.

The congressman from the 8th is James Greenwood, a Republican elected in 1992. Greenwood grew up in Newtown, on the margin between Lower Bucks and Upper Bucks. After college he worked for a state legislator, then was a social worker in Langhorne. He was elected to the state House in 1980 and the state Senate in 1986. In 1992 he ran against Peter Kostmayer, an environment-minded, defense-cutting liberal, who first won the seat in 1976, lost it in 1980 but won it back in 1982, by spotlighting environmental issues at home and raising large sums nationally from admirers of his leftish foreign and environmental stands. But Kostmayer had 50 overdrafts on the House bank and other financial problems, and Greenwood won 52%–46%.

In the House Greenwood's voting record has been conservative on economic issues and moderate-to-liberal on cultural issues. In early 1997 he was the moderate Tuesday Group's representative at Republican leadership meetings. He supported the 1994 crime bill and was one of 24 Republicans to oppose a higher priority for missile defense. He sought a bipartisan healthcare alternative, in vain. One of his big causes has been to maintain funding of international family planning; he successfully led the House on this in February 1997, insisting the issue wasn't abortion. Greenwood serves on the Commerce Committee, and on its Health and Environment, Finance and Hazardous Materials, and Oversight Subcommittees. He has sought more funds for study of traumatic brain injuries.

Another goal is Superfund reform. Greenwood is dismayed that Superfund's liability clauses make brownfield sites in older cities unmarketable and held hearings in Bristol Township on how this could be changed. Commerce Chairman Thomas Bliley asked Greenwood to work on speeding up FDA approval of drugs. Greenwood said he wanted something the President would sign, but the only legislation passed in the 104th Congress concerned drugs for animals. He wants to give states and local governments power to control the disposal of out-of-state solid waste. Greenwood has worked on local projects—the Lockheed Martin facility in Newtown, reuse of the former NAWC Warminster site by Penn State and VEDA as a new technology center; he wants an I-95 southbound exit at Bristol and an interchange between I-95 and the Pennsylvania Turnpike (astonishingly, there isn't one).

Greenwood's political formula seems to suit the 8th District well. He was reelected by 66%–27% in 1994 and 59%–35% in 1996. Indeed, his bigger problem may be conservative Republicans: in 1996 he defeated Democrat-turned-Republican Tom Lingenfelter by 60%–40%, not a comfortable margin in a primary.

The People: Pop. 1990: 565,820; 18% rural; 11% age 65+; 94% White; 3% Black; 2% Asian; 2% Hispanic origin. Households: 66% married couple families; 32% married couple fams. w. children; 49% college educ.; median household income: $43,483; per capita income: $18,374; median gross rent: $608; median house value: $139,700.

1996 Presidential Vote

Clinton (D)	107,500	(45%)
Dole (R)	99,458	(42%)
Perot (I)	25,570	(11%)
Other	4,771	(2%)

1992 Presidential Vote

Clinton (D)	101,630	(39%)
Bush (R)	99,269	(38%)
Perot (I)	56,261	(22%)

Rep. Jim Greenwood (R)

Elected 1992; b. May 4, 1951, Philadelphia; home, Erwinna; Dickinson Col., B.A. 1973; Protestant; married (Christina).

Career: Legis. Asst., PA Rep. John Renninger, 1972–76; Caseworker, Bucks Cnty. Child & Youth Social Svcs., 1977–80; PA House of Reps., 1980–86; PA Senate, 1986–93.

DC Office: 2436 RHOB 20515, 202-225-4276; Fax: 202-225-9511.

District Offices: Doylestown, 215-348-7511; Langhorne, 215-752-7711.

Committees: *Commerce* (13th of 28 R): Finance & Hazardous Materials; Health & the Environment; Oversight & Investigations. *Education & The Workforce* (12th of 25 R): Early Childhood, Youth & Families; Postsecondary Education, Training & Life-Long Learning.

Group Ratings

	ADA	ACLU	AFS	LCV	CFA	CON	NFIB	COC	ACU	NTLC	CHC
1996	25	13	17	46	38	38	84	88	60	85	57
1995	20	—	—	13	77	75	—	88	60	—	—

National Journal Ratings

	1995 LIB — 1995 CONS			1996 LIB — 1996 CONS		
Economic	41%	—	56%	42%	—	56%
Social	64%	—	36%	68%	—	32%
Foreign	45%	—	52%	41%	—	56%

Key Votes of the 104th Congress

1. Reduce Medicare Growth $	Y	5. Flag Amendment	N	9. Cuban Embargo	Y
2. Ovrd. Product Liab. Veto	Y	6. Drop EPA Limits	Y	10. Bar Bosnia Troop $	Y
3. Increase Min. Wage	Y	7. Repeal Assault-Weap. Ban	N	11. Cut Anti-Missile Defense	N
4. Welfare Reform	Y	8. Ovrd. Part. Birth Veto	N	12. Bar U.N. Uniforms	Y

Election Results

1996 general	Jim Greenwood (R)	133,749	(59%)	($614,221)
	John P. Murray (D)	79,856	(35%)	($67,321)
	Others	12,717	(6%)	
1996 primary	Jim Greenwood (R)	18,376	(60%)	
	Tom Lingenfelter (R)	12,088	(40%)	
1994 general	Jim Greenwood (R)	110,499	(66%)	($360,600)
	John P. Murray (D)	44,559	(27%)	($29,945)
	Jay Russell (Lib)	7,925	(5%)	
	Others	4,191	(3%)	

NINTH DISTRICT

Like a series of vertebrae through central Pennsylvania, the Appalachian mountain chain has been a formidable barrier throughout most of the state's history. Up close the mountains look tantalizingly low: you imagine that you could hike over them in an hour or so. But they are much more daunting than they seem. The colonials and British regulars (led by General Braddock to defeat near Pittsburgh in 1754) found it hard going, despite guidance from George Washington; 19th Century pioneers in Conestoga wagons found it not much easier, for there are few gaps in the ridges and, unless you build a tunnel, you have to climb over the top.

During the 18th Century, the mountains provided Quaker Pennsylvania with a rampart against Indian attacks and allowed the commonwealth to become the richest and most populous of the colonies. But in the 19th Century, when people wanted to open up and trade with the vast interior, the mountains proved to be a barrier, and people travelled via New York's Erie Canal and New York Central Railroad instead. It took the aggressive capitalists who built the Pennsylvania Railroad to get trains over these ridges, and a nation facing war in 1940 to build the first highway, the Pennsylvania Turnpike, that could dependably get trucks over them. Today, the old towns look much as they did 60 years ago; the farmhouses and red barns still sit on rolling hills in the shadow of the ridges, isolated and out of touch with the pulsing rhythms of 1990s America.

Pennsylvania's 9th Congressional District lies wholly within these mountains. This part of the Alleghenies (the term is often used interchangeably with Appalachians in Pennsylvania) was settled by poor Scottish and Ulster Irish farmers just after the Revolutionary War. They were fiercely independent and proud, as the Whiskey Rebellion demonstrated—corn was not an article of commerce out here unless distilled into easily portable, if not very potable, alcohol. The settlers worked their hardscrabble farms and built little towns. The 9th is mostly not coal country and was thus spared the boom-bust cycles of northeastern Pennsylvania and West Virginia. This was an important area for the Pennsylvania Railroad, however. Near Altoona was the railroad's famous Horseshoe Curve, and in Altoona the nation's largest car yards were built. As rail transportation became less important and the prosperous Pennsylvania Railroad became the bankrupt Penn Central, Altoona's population fell from 82,000 in 1930 to 52,000 in 1990; it is 99% white, the highest percentage of any metro area. This part of Pennsylvania has been solidly Republican since the election of 1860 and has not come close to electing a Democrat to Congress for years.

The congressman from the 9th District is Bud Shuster, a Republican first elected in 1972 and now chairman of the House Transportation and Infrastructure Committee. Shuster grew up in western Pennsylvania, made a fortune building a computer business, then settled in the southern Pennsylvania mountains. He became interested in local affairs, ran for Congress and beat the favorite, a local state senator, in the 1972 Republican primary. In the 1970s, Shuster was a hard-driving partisan and conservative firebrand, the House's most vociferous opponent of the automobile air bag, and chairman of the Republican Policy Committee until 1980. Then he ran for minority whip against Trent Lott and lost. He abruptly shifted course and spent most of his time on Public Works, as the committee was then called, working to craft bipartisan highway and water project bills with national scope—and with plenty of pork for the 9th District. In the 1990s he has had a solidly conservative voting record but has concentrated on committee work. Shuster has obviously taken a long journey from market conservatism, although his work is arguably in line with the 19th Century Republican tradition of subsidizing canals and railroads and the World War II subsidies for the Pennsylvania Turnpike—transportation arteries that made most commerce possible in these mountains. There are plenty of local monuments to him in central Pennsylvania, from U.S. 220 between Altoona and the Turnpike, christened the Bud Shuster Highway by Democratic Governor Bob Casey, to the nation's first federally funded bus testing center, in Blair County.

But Shuster is not just a generous local benefactor but a serious national policymaker. Even before he was chairman, he was instrumental in passing the 1991 Intermodal Surface Transportation Efficiency Act (ISTEA), the revolutionary bill giving states much more leeway in transportation projects, in deregulating interstate trucking and abolishing the Interstate Commerce Commission. More recently, Shuster has been working to get Amtrak in shape for privatization, to pass a revision of the 1972 Water Pollution Act, and to reform Superfund; these went nowhere in the Senate, but he did reauthorize the 161,000-mile National Highway System, and passed a National Invasive Species Act to combat the zebra mussel in the Great Lakes. To his work Shuster brings energy and efficiency; he runs the committee according to a "pert card" schedule, and keeps up with it by the day, even if Democrats complain sometimes that he doesn't take time to build consensus. So his National Highway bill was ready right after the Contract With America in 1995, and he was ready to act on ISTEA reauthorization in early 1997.

Shuster's two great challenges in the 105th Congress are likely to be ISTEA and his effort to take the four transportation trust funds off-budget. He wants to revise ISTEA to give the states even more leeway. He predicts "blood on the floor" over the formula, with growing states in the South and West seeking revised formulas and Northeastern states with aging highways wanting to keep the current one; Shuster says, "I am open to revising" the formula. Shuster's great crusade is to take the trust funds (highway, aviation, inland waterways, harbor maintenance) off-budget. He argues that appropriators have held back the money and cheated users of their fair spending, that in effect the trust funds are being raided to balance the budget. Other House leaders—Ways and Means Chairman Bill Archer, Appropriations Chairman Bob Livingston, and Budget Chairman John Kasich—vociferously oppose this, arguing it would remove Congress's discretion over spending and would increase the budget deficit; Federal Reserve Chairman Alan Greenspan chimed in with his concern. Livingston, Archer and Kasich attacked Shuster's "misinformation campaign" and said Shuster's proposal would create a budget "shell game." Even so, in April 1996 the House voted to take them off-budget, to Shuster's delight; the Senate, however, never acted on the bill. In May 1997, a Shuster amendment to add $12 billion in highway spending would have upset the budget deal brokered by Clinton and Republican leaders; it failed by the slimmest of margins, 214–216.

One problem he may have to face is ethics charges. In February 1996 *Roll Call* reported Shuster repeatedly stayed overnight without paying rent at the home of his former aide and current campaign fundraiser Ann Eppard. She is a transportation lobbyist who has reportedly earned more than $1 million a year and in 1996 raised money both for Shuster and for his son Bob Shuster, who was running for the Republican nomination in the 5th District (he finished third with 22%). Shuster said he had an verbal O.K. from the Ethics staff in December 1995; he wrote the committee for advice in May 1996 and received a letter with guidelines but without the usual official approval. An outside group filed charges with the committee in September 1996. Questions also were raised about Shuster's intervention with HUD for a developer who is a business partner of two of his sons in a Chrysler dealership.

None of this seems to have hurt Shuster within driving distance of the Bud Shuster Highway. He had no opposition in primary or general elections between 1988 and 1994. In 1996, facing a Democrat who spent $113,000, he took no chances and spent $1.2 million. He won 74%–26%.

The People: Pop. 1990: 565,858; 70% rural; 15% age 65+; 98% White; 1% Black. Households: 63% married couple families; 28% married couple fams. w. children; 23% college educ.; median household income: $24,309; per capita income: $11,229; median gross rent: $305; median house value: $49,200.

1996 Presidential Vote			1992 Presidential Vote		
Dole (R)	102,847	(53%)	Bush (R)	97,764	(48%)
Clinton (D)	70,206	(36%)	Clinton (D)	66,923	(33%)
Perot (I)	21,239	(11%)	Perot (I)	40,200	(20%)

Rep. E. G. (Bud) **Shuster (R)**

Elected 1972; b. Jan. 23, 1932, Glassport; home, Everett; U. of Pittsburgh, B.S. 1954, Duquesne U., M.B.A. 1960, American U., Ph.D. 1967; United Church of Christ; married (Patricia).

Career: Army, 1954–56; Vice Pres., Electronic Computer Div., RCA, 1965–8; Founder and Chmn., computer software co., 1968–72.

DC Office: 2188 RHOB 20515, 202-225-2431.

District Offices: Altoona, 814-946-1653; Chambersburg, 717-264-8308; Clearfield, 814-765-9106.

Committees: *Transportation & Infrastructure* (Chmn. of 40 R). *Intelligence (Select)* (4th of 9 R): Human Intelligence, Analysis & Counterintelligence.

Group Ratings

	ADA	ACLU	AFS	LCV	CFA	CON	NFIB	COC	ACU	NTLC	CHC
1996	0	0	0	15	8	30	97	100	100	100	100
1995	0	—	—	6	0	85	—	96	87	—	—

National Journal Ratings

	1995 LIB — 1995 CONS		1996 LIB — 1996 CONS	
Economic	34%	64%	0%	82%
Social	21%	72%	0%	90%
Foreign	15%	73%	0%	79%

Key Votes of the 104th Congress

1. Reduce Medicare Growth $	Y	5. Flag Amendment	Y	9. Cuban Embargo	Y
2. Ovrd. Product Liab. Veto	Y	6. Drop EPA Limits	N	10. Bar Bosnia Troop $	Y
3. Increase Min. Wage	N	7. Repeal Assault-Weap. Ban	Y	11. Cut Anti-Missile Defense	N
4. Welfare Reform	Y	8. Ovrd. Part. Birth Veto	Y	12. Bar U.N. Uniforms	Y

Election Results

1996 general	E.G. (Bud) Shuster (R)	142,105	(74%)	($1,213,304)
	Monte Kemmler (D)	50,650	(26%)	($113,294)
1996 primary	E.G. (Bud) Shuster (R)	unopposed		
1994 general	E.G. (Bud) Shuster (R)	unopposed		($776,175)

TENTH DISTRICT

"Coal is the theme song of this city in the hills," the *WPA Guide* said of Scranton in the middle of this century. But as those words were written, the anthracite kingdom was dying. Demand for hard coal as a home heating fuel started falling in the 1920s and plummeted in the 1940s; the three major anthracite counties in Pennsylvania had 991,000 people in 1930 and 699,000 in 1990; Scranton's Lackawanna County fell from 310,000 to 219,000. In the process, the coal dust and air pollution vanished, the ethnic groups—Irish and Poles, Ukrainians and Welsh—became less distinctive, and what had been boom towns full of young families became time-worn communities of senior citizens. In the 1960s and 1970s, there was an influx of textile and apparel mills, bringing low-wage, non-union jobs to what had once been a high-wage, unionized area. But the anthracite kingdom, created by unbridled free enterprise, was looking to government for sustenance.

That is the basis of the politics of the 10th Congressional District, which is centered on Scranton and includes most of the northeast corner of Pennsylvania—green hills with little towns in crevassed river valleys, criss-crossed by giant viaducts built for the railroads linking coal and iron mines with great cities' factories, the outer-borough New Yorkers' resorts of the Poconos and, in the three counties closest to New York and New Jersey, new subdivisions for refugees from high taxes. Historically, this is very Republican territory, while Scranton from the 1930s on has been Democratic, producing a roughly equal balance in the 10th District. But congressional politics here depends less on party than on pork. In the 1970s the benefactor of the anthracite kingdom was Daniel Flood of neighboring Wilkes-Barre, an Appropriations subcommittee chairman. When scandal forced him to resign in 1980, the new benefactor was Joseph McDade, senior Republican on Appropriations and ranking member on its National Security Subcommittee.

McDade is short, chunky, white-haired, good-humored. He comes from a Scranton Irish family and was city solicitor when he was first elected to the House in 1962. Those were the days when Republicans could hold such seats only by propitiating organized labor with liberal votes. McDade's predecessor, William Scranton, had done so and was elected governor in 1962. On Appropriations, McDade naturally worked with members of both parties to bring home the bacon. He and fellow Pennsylvanian John Murtha, with the top seats on the National Security Subcommittee, continued Flood's law requiring the military to buy tons of expensive Pennsylvania coal. He funded the McDade Center for Technology at the University of Scranton and got $10 million for a Military Family Institute at Marywood College. He claims credit for funding the Tobyhanna Army Depot, now the district's biggest employer. His biggest and most controversial monument is Steamtown, where the locomotive collection of a Vermont millionaire is housed in a restored railyard at a total cost of $66 million. McDade snuck funds into a 1986 omnibus appropriations bill and has nursed it along ever since, commanding the Park Service to spend money on a project that specialists think has no historic merit or relevance to Scranton.

For most of the 1990s McDade's career has been under the shadow of an indictment. It was issued in 1992, after a long investigation beginning in December 1988 when *The Wall Street Journal* detailed how he had received $45,000 in campaign contributions and speaking fees from officials of United Chem-Con, a company with a plant in Lancaster for which he helped get a Defense Department minority set-aside contract. It was charged that some of the employees were illegally reimbursed by the company for contributions to McDade, and later that McDade accepted gifts and gratuities—jet trips, a scholarship for his son at Georgetown Law School, a green golf jacket—from United Chem-Con and other defense contractors. McDade protested the charges vigorously, accusing the prosecutor, a protege of Senator Arlen Specter, of political bias, attacking the RICO anti-racketeering law as being applied to situations Congress never contemplated and arguing the indictment violated his constitutional immunity from prosecution for words and acts on the House floor. In 1992 House Republicans (unlike Democrats) did not require members to step down from top committee positions, and McDade did not do so. The Republican Conference passed such a rule in August 1993, but exempted McDade. Even so, junior Republicans were appalled by the prospect of McDade as Appropriations chairman, partly because he had always got along well with committee Democrats and tended to favor more spending than some other Republicans, and incoming Speaker Newt Gingrich declared the new chairman would be the fourth-ranking Bob Livingston, who promised to step down if McDade were acquitted.

Meanwhile, McDade's problems did not hurt him in the 10th District. In 1992, he not only was renominated but won the Democratic primary as a write-in; in 1994, he beat a Democrat 66%–31%. But in March 1996 he lost his last appeal, and the case was scheduled for trial in Philadelphia in June. In the May 1996 primary, McDade beat a former aide to Governor Robert Casey named Errol Flynn by only 53%–47%. "If his name was Bob Hope, he would have won," McDade quipped. McDade lost the three eastern counties, which have grown more than any other in the state, and was saved only by his big margin in Lackawanna County.

Then in August 1996, after a seven-and-a-half-week trial during which he was hospitalized twice, McDade was acquitted by a jury after 12 hours of deliberation. Memories were dim of the now 12-year-old transactions, two witnesses were dead, some of the offenses seemed trivial (the green golf jacket was the subject of indictment because it was worth over $100) and jurors evidently accepted the defense that McDade was just a congressman doing his job. Democrat Joe Cullen, who had promised not to attack him on ethics, hit McDade for missed votes and votes on Medicare, and failure to debate. The state AFL-CIO, which had long backed McDade, endorsed Cullen. But McDade won by a solid 60%–36%.

Immediately he said he wanted the Appropriations chair. Livingston offered to resign as chairman, but Gingrich said no: "The core question is, if Livingston had run the team brilliantly for two years, did everything we asked him to, saved $53 billion and got the spending bills through on time this year, how could you demote him?" Then McDade demanded the chair of the National Security Subcommittee on which he had served so long. Livingston vetoed that, saying Florida's Bill Young had performed well in that post for two years and that his ouster would touch off a highly disruptive domino effect on the subcommittees. So Livingston named McDade vice chairman of Appropriations and of the National Security Subcommittee, and chairman of the Energy and Water Development Subcommittee. This was not one of McDade's subcommittees for all those years, but does allow opportunities to help the district. McDade, vindicated in court, but disappointed in Washington and suffering from a mild form of Parkinson's disease, is soldiering on and can obviously be reelected if he likes, but he must have mixed feelings about his situation.

The People: Pop. 1990: 565,777; 54% rural; 17% age 65+; 98% White; 1% Black; 1% Asian; 1% Hispanic origin. Households: 60% married couple families; 26% married couple fams. w. children; 33% college educ.; median household income: $25,648; per capita income: $12,005; median gross rent: $339; median house value: $70,100.

1996 Presidential Vote

Clinton (D)	95,712	(45%)
Dole (R)	91,629	(43%)
Perot (I)	24,303	(11%)

1992 Presidential Vote

Bush (R)	95,803	(41%)
Clinton (D)	88,193	(38%)
Perot (I)	46,881	(20%)

Rep. Joseph M. McDade (R)

Elected 1962; b. Sept. 29, 1931, Scranton; home, Clarks Summit; U. of Notre Dame, B.A. 1953, U. of PA, LL.B. 1956; Catholic; married (Sarah).

Career: Clerk, Chief Fed. Judge John W. Murphy, 1956–57; Practicing atty., 1957–62; Scranton City Solicitor, 1962.

DC Office: 2107 RHOB 20515, 202-225-3731; Fax: 202-225-9594.

District Offices: Scranton, 717-346-3834; Williamsport, 717-327-8161.

Committees: *Appropriations* (Vice Chmn. of 34 R): Energy & Water Development (Chmn.); Interior; National Security.

Group Ratings

	ADA	ACLU	AFS	LCV	CFA	CON	NFIB	COC	ACU	NTLC	CHC
1996	5	18	50	15	8	*	91	67	75	95	80
1995	5	—	—	13	0	38	—	91	65	—	—

National Journal Ratings

	1995 LIB — 1995 CONS			1996 LIB — 1996 CONS		
Economic	47%	—	53%	47%	—	52%
Social	40%	—	59%	40%	—	60%
Foreign	35%	—	64%	30%	—	70%

Key Votes of the 104th Congress

1. Reduce Medicare Growth $	Y	5. Flag Amendment	Y	9. Cuban Embargo	Y
2. Ovrd. Product Liab. Veto	Y	6. Drop EPA Limits	N	10. Bar Bosnia Troop $	Y
3. Increase Min. Wage	Y	7. Repeal Assault-Weap. Ban	N	11. Cut Anti-Missile Defense	N
4. Welfare Reform	*	8. Ovrd. Part. Birth Veto	Y	12. Bar U.N. Uniforms	Y

Election Results

1996 general	Joseph M. McDade (R)	124,670	(60%)	($724,776)
	Joe Cullen (D)	75,536	(36%)	($204,185)
	Others	8,334	(4%)	
1996 primary	Joseph M. McDade (R)	17,155	(53%)	
	Errol Flynn (R)	15,043	(47%)	
1994 general	Joseph M. McDade (R)	106,992	(66%)	($263,752)
	Daniel J. Schreffler (D)	50,635	(31%)	($12,395)
	Others	5,196	(3%)	

ELEVENTH DISTRICT

One of the major industrial centers of America grew up in the 19th Century, nestled in the valley of the East Branch of the Susquehanna River, surrounded by mountain ridges. The mountains were laced with anthracite coal, the main home-heating fuel of the time. Thousands of immigrants, attracted by the high wages paid to scrape out the coal, flocked to this valley, in the chain of little cities north and south of Wilkes-Barre, named for two backers of the American revolution. While the supply was endless—the area produced 40% of the world's hard coal—the demand was not. The peak year of anthracite production was 1917, and long strikes in 1922 and 1925 quickened the conversion to oil and gas. By the 1930s, the valley around Wilkes-Barre was in decline; surrounding Luzerne County's population, 445,000 in 1930, was 328,000 in 1990.

This is Pennsylvania's 11th Congressional District, including all of Luzerne County and similar land east to the town of Jim Thorpe and the Poconos, and west almost to the Susquehanna. A large Democratic voting bloc—consisting of miners—has been here since the 1930s, but there also were a lot of white-collar and rural Republicans. In presidential politics this was a Republican district in the 1980s, Democratic in the 1990s. It is a district which long has hungered for federal aid and subsidy, much of which was delivered by longtime Congressman Daniel Flood, a theatrical Democrat who used his seat on Appropriations to bring millions of dollars into the anthracite country; but in 1980 he resigned amid scandal and in six years the 11th had three different congressmen.

The congressman from the 11th District now is Paul Kanjorski, first elected in 1984. Kanjorski grew up in Nanticoke, near Wilkes-Barre. After college, the Army Reserves and law school, he returned home to practice law; for nine years he was a workmen's compensation administrative law judge and for 12 Nanticoke city solicitor. In 1984 he ran for Congress and beat the incumbent in the May Democratic primary by pointing out the incumbent was in Central America while flood-soaked Wilkes-Barre area residents had to boil tap water because of contamination. Kanjorski has won the seat easily ever since.

In the House, Kanjorski's voting record has been liberal on economics and moderate on cultural issues. He is anti-abortion but voted for international family planning aid in 1997. He is skeptical about foreign commitments and Washington lobbyists. He is also a tough partisan. While chairing a subcommittee with jurisdiction over White House operations, he sharply attacked the Bush White House for lavish spending; Bush once apologized at a breakfast meeting for the skimpy meal and blamed Kanjorski's investigations. But with Bill Clinton in the White House, Kanjorski vitriolicly attacked fellow Pennsylvania Bill Clinger's investigation of the White House travel office firings, delaying issuance of the report and then saying, "Like horses, we should take it out and shoot it."

Most important to Kanjorski is helping his long economically ailing district. *The New York Times* called him "a master of earmarking" for capturing millions of dollars for the Earth Conservancy Applied Research Center, a public-private project for developing new technologies to reclaim mine-ravaged northeastern Pennsylvania. Other Kanjorski projects include a Social Security claims processing center in Plains Township, renovation of a VA hospital, and the Stegmaier Brewery project. When President Clinton called for 10 more National Historic Rivers in his 1997 State of the Union address, Kanjorski summoned local leaders to help make the Susquehanna one of them.

The People: Pop. 1990: 565,802; 40% rural; 19% age 65+; 98% White; 1% Black; 1% Hispanic origin. Households: 57% married couple families; 24% married couple fams. w. children; 29% college educ.; median household income: $24,310; per capita income: $11,937; median gross rent: $327; median house value: $57,600.

1996 Presidential Vote

Clinton (D)	97,393	(48%)
Dole (R)	76,969	(38%)
Perot (I)	25,597	(13%)

1992 Presidential Vote

Clinton (D)	91,616	(42%)
Bush (R)	84,199	(38%)
Perot (I)	42,950	(20%)

Rep. Paul E. Kanjorski (D)

Elected 1984; b. Apr. 2, 1937, Nanticoke; home, Nanticoke; Temple U., 1957–61, Dickinson U., 1962–65; Catholic; married (Nancy).

Career: Army Reserves, 1960–61; Practicing atty., 1966–85; Nanticoke City Solicitor, 1969–81; Admin. Law Judge, 1971–80.

DC Office: 2353 RHOB 20515, 202-225-6511; e-mail: paul.kanjorski@mail.house.gov.

District Offices: Wilkes-Barre, 717-825-2200.

Committees: *Banking & Financial Services* (6th of 25 D): Capital Markets, Securities & Government Sponsored Enterprises (RMM); Domestic & International Monetary Policy. *Government Reform & Oversight* (6th of 19 D): Government Management, Information & Technology; National Economic Growth, Natural Resources & Regulatory Affairs.

Group Ratings

	ADA	ACLU	AFS	LCV	CFA	CON	NFIB	COC	ACU	NTLC	CHC
1996	65	50	92	85	69	68	22	25	30	10	20
1995	80	—	—	88	85	16	—	29	16	—	—

National Journal Ratings

	1995 LIB — 1995 CONS			1996 LIB — 1996 CONS		
Economic	80%	—	18%	85%	—	11%
Social	58%	—	41%	55%	—	43%
Foreign	73%	—	24%	76%	—	22%

Key Votes of the 104th Congress

1. Reduce Medicare Growth $	N	5. Flag Amendment	Y	9. Cuban Embargo	N
2. Ovrd. Product Liab. Veto	N	6. Drop EPA Limits	Y	10. Bar Bosnia Troop $	N
3. Increase Min. Wage	Y	7. Repeal Assault-Weap. Ban	Y	11. Cut Anti-Missile Defense	Y
4. Welfare Reform	N	8. Ovrd. Part. Birth Veto	Y	12. Bar U.N. Uniforms	Y

Election Results

1996 general	Paul E. Kanjorski (D)	128,258	(68%)	($342,141)
	Stephen A. Urban (R)	60,339	(32%)	($43,761)
1996 primary	Paul E. Kanjorski (D)	unopposed		
1994 general	Paul E. Kanjorski (D)	101,966	(67%)	($304,520)
	J. Andrew Podolak (R)	51,295	(33%)	($57,006)

TWELFTH DISTRICT

The mountains and valley within a 100-mile radius of Pittsburgh are one of America's most beautiful areas—and have also been one of the most economically troubled. This has been tough, hard-working country ever since Scots-Irish farmers settled here in the 1790s. Their first big product was whiskey—this was the site of the Whiskey Rebellion of 1794—but historically the most important product was bituminous coal. Discovered in the 19th Century, it was the basic energy source for the production of iron and steel, and in the 19th Century, local farmers were joined by thousands of immigrants to work the mines and the blast furnaces. Politically, this was one of the most Republican parts of America from the Civil War up to the Depression of the 1930s. Republican policies, including high tariffs and discouragement of labor unions, were seen as protecting jobs and increasing growth in the steel economy centered on Pittsburgh. But with the coming of the New Deal, and the successes of the United Mine Workers and the United Steelworkers, people here began voting mostly Democratic. But they have not followed the national Democratic Party on all issues. As employment in coal collapsed in the 1950s and employment in steel collapsed in the 1980s, people here sought trade restrictions to protect the remaining jobs, even as Democrats elsewhere favored free trade. And they maintained their conservative views on cultural issues and foreign policy, even as Democrats elsewhere embraced various forms of liberation. Today those traditions continue in muted form, as unemployment has dropped and the area has perked up. First Pittsburgh and now perhaps the mountain areas all around are fighting to develop a more diverse and supple economy.

The 12th Congressional District of Pennsylvania includes much of this coal and steel country. Its best known community is Johnstown, the steel town that was ravaged by the disastrous flood of May 31, 1889, when a dam broke and a 75-foot wall of water half a mile wide swept through the town killing more than 2,200 people. Johnstown had 67,000 people in 1920, and about 27,000 in 1996. From Johnstown, the 12th reaches south to the West Virginia border and west to take in Armstrong and Indiana Counties northeast of Pittsburgh. It also includes the hills around Ligonier, green with prosperity, where Mellons and others of Pittsburgh's elite have vast estates. On balance this is a Democratic district, though one troubled by some of the tendencies of the Democratic Party.

The congressman from the 12th District is John Murtha, a Democrat first elected in one of those 1974 special elections that signalled the political weakness of Richard Nixon. Murtha grew up in this area, served in the Marine Corps, then graduated from the University of Pittsburgh and reenlisted in the Marines in 1966, at 34, and served in Vietnam. He is a member of the Appropriations Committee and the ranking Democrat on the National Security Subcommittee, his party's man on the defense budget. His voting record—hawkish and patriotic on foreign policy, interventionist on economics and usually tradition-minded on cultural issues—seems perfectly suited to the steel and coal country. Murtha is also one of those old-time politicians who operates best in secret, standing at the back of the House chamber and trading gossip and votes, avoiding speaking for attribution to national and local reporters and appearing on television only when presiding over the chamber.

On foreign issues, Murtha voted for the Gulf war resolution and opposed intervention in Bosnia and deployment in Somalia, arguing that U.N. officials lacked the know-how to command U.S. troops. He also pushed a proposal that would have barred funds for U.N. peacekeeping missions unless the president gave Congress 15 days advance notice of deployment; that was added as non-binding language to a defense appropriations bill. He calls for "more clear rules on when the United States will intervene on humanitarian missions in other countries." He argues that we need to have a "clear national interest, achievable goals and a clear timetable and plan for getting out—before we get into any troop deployment." He has stood up for the Nunn-Lugar program to decommission former Soviet nuclear weapons. He favors technology that provides "force multipliers" and has focused recently on quality-of-life for service men and women, recognizing that it's harder for the military to attract and retain good volunteers when the economy is humming along. He is caught sometimes between Democratic demands for lower defense spending to make more money available for domestic programs and Republican desires to spend even more on defense, but he seeks to come up with appropriations that will be sustained on a bipartisan basis in the House. Murtha might have become chairman of Appropriations in March 1994, after William Natcher died. Instead he supported the senior Democrat, Neal Smith of Iowa, who lost in the Democratic Caucus to David Obey. Now Murtha ranks number four.

In 1990 Murtha had an uncomfortably close primary race, and since then his interests in the district have taken interesting turns. He hired a press secretary, who concentrated on local, not national press, and he traveled around the district, staying whole days in communities. From these visits has come a conviction that environmental cleanup and amenities could be the key to the area's economic growth in the post-steel era. He has pushed for passive treatment systems to clean up creeks, inspired river improvement projects, urged groups to develop processes to extract minerals from mine draining so that restoring the environment will become a business itself. Interestingly, he seems to be relying less on providing federal dollars, though he does some of that, than in stimulating imaginative ideas and community action.

He has been reelected in recent years by very wide margins.

The People: Pop. 1990: 565,760; 70% rural; 17% age 65+; 98% White; 1% Black. Households: 61% married couple families; 27% married couple fams. w. children; 25% college educ.; median household income: $22,024; per capita income: $10,586; median gross rent: $293; median house value: $44,300.

1996 Presidential Vote

Clinton (D)	93,532	(46%)
Dole (R)	81,122	(40%)
Perot (I)	25,755	(13%)

1992 Presidential Vote

Clinton (D)	102,768	(47%)
Bush (R)	72,664	(33%)
Perot (I)	44,846	(20%)

Rep. John P. Murtha (D)

Elected Feb., 1974; b. June 17, 1932, New Martinsville, WV; home, Johnstown; U. of Pittsburgh, B.A. 1962, Indiana U. of PA, 1963–64; Catholic; married (Joyce).

Career: Marine Corps, 1952–55, 1966–67 (Vietnam), Marine Corps Reserves, 1955–65, 1968–90; Owner, Johnstown Minute Car Wash; PA House of Reps., 1969–74.

DC Office: 2423 RHOB 20515, 202-225-2065; Fax: 202-225-5709; e-mail: murtha@hr.house.gov.

District Offices: Johnstown, 814-535-2642.

Committees: *Appropriations* (4th of 26 D): Interior; National Security (RMM).

Group Ratings

	ADA	ACLU	AFS	LCV	CFA	CON	NFIB	COC	ACU	NTLC	CHC
1996	55	56	100	69	31	86	28	25	25	20	26
1995	65	—	—	75	69	16	—	33	24	—	—

National Journal Ratings

	1995 LIB		1995 CONS	1996 LIB		1996 CONS
Economic	70%	—	29%	79%	—	18%
Social	55%	—	45%	53%	—	45%
Foreign	59%	—	39%	50%	—	48%

Key Votes of the 104th Congress

1. Reduce Medicare Growth $	N	5. Flag Amendment	Y	9. Cuban Embargo	Y
2. Ovrd. Product Liab. Veto	N	6. Drop EPA Limits	Y	10. Bar Bosnia Troop $	N
3. Increase Min. Wage	Y	7. Repeal Assault-Weap. Ban	Y	11. Cut Anti-Missile Defense	N
4. Welfare Reform	N	8. Ovrd. Part. Birth Veto	Y	12. Bar U.N. Uniforms	N

Election Results

1996 general	John P. Murtha (D)	136,815	(70%)	($785,486)
	Bill Choby (R)	58,643	(30%)	($22,867)
1996 primary	John P. Murtha (D)	unopposed		
1994 general	John P. Murtha (D)	117,825	(69%)	($913,004)
	Bill Choby (R)	53,147	(31%)	($35,782)

THIRTEENTH DISTRICT

Montgomery County, Pennsylvania, is the hinterland of Philadelphia: rolling hills cut on one side by the Schuylkill River and at intervals by the Pennsylvania and Reading Railroad lines radiating outward from Center City. Older suburbs, the rich Main Line towns and more modest places like Glenside and Ambler, grew up around rail stations, with comfortable houses within walking distance for commuters. Here and there are the old Schuylkill River factory towns, Conshohocken and Norristown and towns established 200 years ago by German sects; near the big shopping malls around King of Prussia is Valley Forge, where George Washington wintered in 1778 and Ross Perot was nominated by the Reform Party in 1996. Farther out are 18th and 19th Century villages, once surrounded by farm fields, now encroached on by subdivisions where people depend on cars, not rail lines, to get to work, and office complexes in places like Blue Bell, the headquarters of Unisys. Statistically, Montgomery County is the most affluent part of metro Philadelphia, but as in most suburban counties there is much variety here—economically, with high income enclaves like Gladwyne, and ethnically, with Jewish suburbs out York Road.

The 13th Congressional District of Pennsylvania is made up of most of Montgomery County; parts of the county are nibbled off by four other districts. Historically it was a quintessentially Republican seat, where the style of politics was set for years by Ivy-educated Republican men, and where Republicans with more modest and sometimes ethnic backgrounds manned the local precincts and staffed local offices. But now the suburbs are as multi-ethnic as the central city, if not more so, and with varied cultural attitudes. The suburbs were a land of discontent in the recession of the early 1990s, which hit harder at residential real estate and other forms of wealth than incomes, and which saw more permanent layoffs of white-collar and professional workers than temporary layoffs of blue-collar and factory workers. This remained a land of discontent in the mid-1990s economic recovery as well, as taxes seemed to increase and government provided services poorly and in ways that seemed to undercut hard work and traditional values. Montgomery County cast huge margins for Ronald Reagan and George Bush in the 1980s but voted for Bill Clinton in the 1990s.

The congressman from the 13th District is Jon Fox, a Republican defeated in 1992, elected in 1994 and reelected in 1996 by small margins emblematic of this uneasiness. Fox is in many ways a typical suburban Republican politician. He was class president at Penn State, worked in Washington while attending law school, became a Montgomery County assistant DA in 1976, at 29. He was elected Abington Township commissioner in 1980, state representative in 1984, member of the Montgomery County Board of Commissioners in 1990. Fox is Jewish and won in constituencies with many Jewish Democratic voters; the *Philadelphia Inquirer* called him a "zen master of constituency service." In 1992, when Congressman Lawrence Coughlin retired after 24 years, Fox ran for Congress. He won the Republican primary with 37%, to 25% for state legislator Ellen Harley and 18% for self-financing businessman Jack Murray. In the general election he faced Marjorie Margolies-Mezvinsky, a longtime television news reporter, mother of 11 and wife of former Iowa Congressman Edward Mezvinsky. MMM (as she is called) was inspired to run by the Clarence Thomas hearings and was helped by her TV fame and appealing personal story. In one of 1992's closest races, she won by 1,373 votes. In the House, she gained her greatest fame by her vote on the 1993 Clinton budget package and tax increase. After taping an interview with a Philadelphia TV station explaining why she would vote against it, she responded to pleadings by Democratic leaders and switched her vote, casting the deciding 218th vote, as Republicans chanted, "Goodbye, Marjorie." In 1994, Fox ran again, contrasting his tax cutting in Montgomery County with her vote for a tax increase that cut heavily in one of the dozen most high-income districts in the country. This time Fox won 49%–45%; incidentally, in both races the candidate who spent most lost.

In the House Fox voted for most of the Contract With America but also became part of the moderate Tuesday Group. He passed one original piece of legislation: a jury tampering bill which provided penalties as harsh as those of the crime in question (except for the death penalty) on those who use violence to influence jurors. On many issues he took moderate stances: he was careful to vote with environmentalist Republican Sherwood Boehlert on environmental issues and co-sponsored an amendment to spend nearly double what conservative Republicans were seeking on the Legal Services Corporation. He sponsored, without success, an FDA reform bill providing for third-party approval of drugs and medical devices by FDA-approved reviewers and easing restrictions on export of unapproved drugs.

With his narrow 1994 margin, Fox was an obvious target for Democrats; for 15 months the AFL-CIO ran ads against him on expensive Philadelphia media outlets. Fox himself raised and spent $1.7 million, $1.1 million in individual contributions and $483,000 from PACs. Altogether he has spent $3.4 million on three House elections; his opponents have spent $2.9 million. "I'm an independent Republican," he proclaimed, and his brochures ("Jon Fox. Independent. Effective. Fighting for us.") did not include the word Republican. His opponent was County Commissioner Joseph Hoeffel, who ran strong races against Coughlin in 1984 and 1986. Hoeffel attacked Fox for voting 91% of the time with Newt Gingrich—the lowest of any House freshman, Fox responded—and said: "This is not Newt Gingrich country. This is a moderate, progressive community in both political parties. And this is the home of the proverbial soccer moms." Both candidates campaigned indefatigably, the backslapping Fox with his wife and mother and Adlai Stevenson-style holes in his shoes, the practical joker Hoeffel accompanied by his wife and teenage children in layered clothing in chilly shopping center parking lots. Both sides sensed this was a bellwether race that would determine who would control the House, and they were very close to right: this was the closest House race in the country. The unofficial tally showed Fox ahead by 10 votes; only nine days after the election was Fox clearly declared the winner, by 84 votes. In three elections Fox has won 49% of the votes, his Democratic opponents 48%.

After the election, while still hailing the tax and spending cuts and welfare and telecommunications reforms of the 104th Congress, Fox was calling for a different, less partisan atmosphere in the 105th. "Neither party holds the patent on good ideas and both Republicans and Democrats want to act in the best interests of the people they are sworn to serve." He called for bipartisan commissions on both campaign finance and on Medicare and Social Security. His priorities include FDA reform, the $500-per-child tax credit and a capital gains tax cut, putting the burden of proof in tax cases on the IRS rather than the taxpayer. Locally, he calls for repairing Route 309, widening Route 202 and creating a Cross County Metro and Schuylkill Valley Metro light-rail system. It would be astonishing if this were not a seriously contested district again in 1998.

The People: Pop. 1990: 565,663; 8% rural; 15% age 65+; 90% White; 6% Black; 3% Asian; 1% Hispanic origin. Households: 61% married couple families; 27% married couple fams. w. children; 55% college educ.; median household income: $44,764; per capita income: $22,786; median gross rent: $600; median house value: $146,600.

1996 Presidential Vote

Clinton (D)	125,364	(50%)
Dole (R)	103,461	(41%)
Perot (I)	19,922	(8%)
Other	4,179	(2%)

1992 Presidential Vote

Clinton (D)	118,579	(44%)
Bush (R)	107,439	(39%)
Perot (I)	44,148	(16%)

Rep. Jon D. Fox (R)

Elected 1994; b. Apr. 22, 1947, Abington; home, Abington; PA St. U., B.A. 1969, DE Law Schl., J.D. 1975; Jewish; married (Judithanne).

Career: Air Force Reserves, 1969–75; Montgomery Cnty. Asst. Dist. Atty., 1976–80; Abington Township Bd. of Commissioners, 1980–84; PA House of Reps., 1984–91; Montgomery Cnty. Bd. of Commissioners, 1991–94.

DC Office: 435 CHOB 20515, 202-225-6111; Fax: 202-225-3155; e-mail: jonfox@hr.house.gov.

District Offices: Abington, 215-885-3500; Norristown, 610-272-8400.

Committees: *Banking & Financial Services* (17th of 30 R): Capital Markets, Securities & Government Sponsored Enterprises; Domestic & International Monetary Policy (Vice Chmn.); Housing & Community Opportunity. *International Relations* (21st of 26 R): Asia & the Pacific. *Transportation & Infrastructure* (38th of 40 R): Railroads.

Group Ratings

	ADA	ACLU	AFS	LCV	CFA	CON	NFIB	COC	ACU	NTLC	CHC
1996	35	6	42	54	54	9	86	81	65	90	86
1995	20	—	—	25	54	56	—	83	80	—	—

National Journal Ratings

	1995 LIB — 1995 CONS	1996 LIB — 1996 CONS
Economic	49% — 49%	51% — 48%
Social	47% — 52%	53% — 45%
Foreign	28% — 65%	47% — 52%

Key Votes of the 104th Congress

1. Reduce Medicare Growth $	Y	5. Flag Amendment	Y	9. Cuban Embargo	Y
2. Ovrd. Product Liab. Veto	Y	6. Drop EPA Limits	Y	10. Bar Bosnia Troop $	Y
3. Increase Min. Wage	Y	7. Repeal Assault-Weap. Ban	N	11. Cut Anti-Missile Defense	N
4. Welfare Reform	Y	8. Ovrd. Part. Birth Veto	Y	12. Bar U.N. Uniforms	Y

Election Results

1996 general	Jon D. Fox (R)	120,304	(49%)	($1,659,723)
	Joseph M. Hoeffel (D)	120,220	(49%)	($697,490)
	Others	5,455	(2%)	
1996 primary	Jon D. Fox (R)	unopposed		
1994 general	Jon D. Fox (R)	96,254	(49%)	($1,015,330)
	Marjorie Margolies-Mezvinsky (D)	88,073	(45%)	($1,620,110)
	Others	10,461	(5%)	

FOURTEENTH DISTRICT

The Golden Triangle is the inevitable focus of Pittsburgh, the tip of land where the Allegheny and Monongahela Rivers come together to form the Ohio, and has been a strategic site for more than 200 years. It was there, to Fort Duquesne in the French and Indian war, that Braddock's army was headed (with George Washington helping lead the way) when it was ambushed and defeated in 1754. A few years later, the first American city west of the Appalachian chain was carved out of the wilderness here and named after the English statesman William Pitt. Pittsburgh grew rapidly in those days when most of the nation's commerce moved over water.

When traffic switched to railroads, Pittsburgh still did nicely, since rail lines run at riverside rather than scale the mountains. Then came Andrew Carnegie—and steel. A Scottish immigrant working as a telegrapher for the Pennsylvania Railroad, he saw that steel would replace iron for railroad bridges and built a steel factory in Pittsburgh—then a rail junction with large deposits of coal nearby and ready access to iron ore from the Great Lakes. With associates like Henry Clay Frick and Henry Phipps, Carnegie built his capacity to the point that when he sold out in 1901, the resulting U.S. Steel Corporation had a near-monopoly of the business.

The Pittsburgh that Carnegie and his steel men built is one of giant mills in the bottomlands along the rivers and massive buildings downtown, like the classic City-County Building next to the Richardsonian jail. There were 12 cable cars going up the Duquesne Incline and other routes, connecting mills with neighborhoods above, and the ever-present grime of coal smoke in the air. The Pittsburgh smog—a word used here before it was in Los Angeles—was so bad that street lights stayed on all day downtown; a 1947 photograph shows a midnight-like darkness at nine in the morning. In the years after World War II, Pittsburgh's business leaders and Mayor David Lawrence were determined to clean up the smog and did so: Pittsburgh is one of our cleaner-aired cities today. They also cleaned up the riverfront and created a grand park at the junction of the three rivers. Pittsburgh ranks high, though not as high as it used to, as a headquarters of major corporations (USX, Westinghouse, Heinz, Alcoa, Koppers, PPG) and has fine cultural institutions, from Carnegie-Mellon University and the University of Pittsburgh with its "cathedral of learning" to its public television station (home of *Mr. Rogers' Neighborhood*) and the Andy Warhol museum. In the early 1980s, Pittsburgh formed a high-tech council to encourage start-up businesses. By the early 1990s, it had a robust high-tech, white-collar sector, replacing the manufacturing jobs which had declined in the metropolitan area from 265,000 in the mid-1970s to 133,000 by 1996. The old millworker towns in the outer metro ring continued to lose population and jobs, but much of the central city is vital, with yuppie-like growth in Mount Washington and Manchester and fine homes still maintained in Shadyside and Squirrel Hill.

The 14th Congressional District includes all of the city of Pittsburgh plus suburban territory to the west and north. It takes in the city's black neighborhoods and Shadyside and its depopulated white working-class areas. To the west it goes out along a new expressway up to the airport, which is USAir's major hub; to the north, through middle-income townships and northeast along the Ohio River to some of the hilly high-income precincts of Sewickley. The 14th has its Republican neighborhoods and a Republican heritage, but that has not been very lively since the New Deal, and this is a solidly Democratic district today. Though unhappy with the Democrats' cultural liberalism in the 1970s, it became more Democratic in the years of the steel industry's collapse in the 1980s.

The congressman from the 14th District is William Coyne, a Democrat first elected in 1980. He grew up in an Irish-American family in Pittsburgh, served in the Army, worked as an accountant, graduated from Robert Morris College. With a characteristic Irish-American knack for politics, he went to the legislature in 1970, at 34, then to the City Council in 1973, to the chairmanship of the Democratic Party in Pittsburgh in 1978, and to Congress in 1980 when he beat the son of his predecessor in the Democratic primary by a 65%–35% margin. After the 1984 election, he won a seat on the Ways and Means Committee, where he is now the fifth-ranking Democrat. His voting record is one of the most liberal in the House. He wants the government to spend more on transportation, education and energy conservation, which he sees as producing economic growth. In the 103d Congress, he successfully opposed the proposed $1 increase in the federal fuel tax for inland waterways and supported paying the earned income tax credit on a monthly basis. He worked to make the earned income tax credit payable monthly rather than yearly. He has secured funding for many local projects—the Software Engineering Institute, Children's Hospital, restructuring the former Hays Ammunition Plant. In the minority in the 104th Congress, he was less successful in seeking incentives to clean up urban brownfields, expanding workers' rights in trade agreements and seeking federal monitoring of fatal medication errors.

For years Coyne worked quietly, not seeking publicity as most congressmen do. That changed in 1996, when he was challenged in the primary by 38-year-old Pittsburgh Councilman Dan Cohen, a graduate of Yale and Stanford Law. By January 1996 Cohen had raised more money than the incumbent, and charged him with not looking out for the local economy and being soft on crime. Coyne, who had never spent more than $323,000, spent $1 million this time. "Results. Not Talk," was his slogan, making his taciturnity an asset, and he worked to knock on 25,000 doors by the April primary. He was endorsed by the local Democratic Party, the AFL-CIO, the Sierra Club; District Attorney Bob Colville cut an ad praising Coyne's record against crime. The result was a thumping 66%–34% victory for Coyne. He was reelected easily in the fall, and he is now ranking Democrat on the Ways and Means Oversight Subcommittee.

The People: Pop. 1990: 565,838; 17% age 65+; 80% White; 18% Black; 1% Asian; 1% Hispanic origin. Households: 44% married couple families; 17% married couple fams. w. children; 42% college educ.; median household income: $24,751; per capita income: $14,255; median gross rent: $379; median house value: $50,900.

1996 Presidential Vote

Clinton (D)	126,704	(59%)
Dole (R)	70,466	(33%)
Perot (I)	15,417	(7%)
Other	3,690	(2%)

1992 Presidential Vote

Clinton (D)	145,419	(58%)
Bush (R)	66,016	(26%)
Perot (I)	38,460	(15%)

Rep. William J. Coyne (D)

Elected 1980; b. Aug. 24, 1936, Pittsburgh; home, Pittsburgh; Robert Morris Col., B.S. 1965; Catholic; single.

Career: Army, 1955–57; Accountant, 1957–70; PA House of Reps., 1970–72; Pittsburgh City Cncl., 1973–80; Chmn., Pittsburg Dem. Party, 1978–84.

DC Office: 2455 RHOB 20515, 202-225-2301; Fax: 202-225-1844.

District Offices: Pittsburgh, 412-644-2870.

Committees: *Ways & Means* (5th of 16 D): Human Resources; Oversight (RMM).

Group Ratings

	ADA	ACLU	AFS	LCV	CFA	CON	NFIB	COC	ACU	NTLC	CHC
1996	100	94	100	92	85	13	16	19	0	2	0
1995	100	—	—	100	92	16	—	13	4	—	—

National Journal Ratings

	1995 LIB — 1995 CONS			1996 LIB — 1996 CONS		
Economic	90%	—	8%	89%	—	0%
Social	88%	—	0%	84%	—	12%
Foreign	84%	—	15%	87%	—	10%

Key Votes of the 104th Congress

1. Reduce Medicare Growth $	N	5. Flag Amendment	N	9. Cuban Embargo	N
2. Ovrd. Product Liab. Veto	N	6. Drop EPA Limits	Y	10. Bar Bosnia Troop $	N
3. Increase Min. Wage	Y	7. Repeal Assault-Weap. Ban	N	11. Cut Anti-Missile Defense	Y
4. Welfare Reform	N	8. Ovrd. Part. Birth Veto	N	12. Bar U.N. Uniforms	N

Election Results

1996 general	William J. Coyne (D)	122,922	(61%)	($1,027,674)
	Bill Ravotti (R)	78,921	(39%)	($212,284)
1996 primary	William J. Coyne (D)	47,334	(66%)	
	Dan Cohen (D)	24,364	(34%)	
1994 general	William J. Coyne (D)	105,310	(64%)	($185,539)
	John Robert Clark (R)	53,221	(32%)	($9,747)
	Others	5,645	(3%)	

FIFTEENTH DISTRICT

Allentown, Pennsylvania, has long been derided by show biz songwriters, from "42nd Street" back in 1933, in which it is scorned as nowhere, the polar opposite of Broadway, to Billy Joel's "Allentown" in 1982, with its grim picture of closed factories and unemployment. Neither is an entirely fair portrait of Allentown, the largest city in Pennsylvania's Lehigh Valley, though both have nuggets of truth. Allentown and next-door Bethlehem are off the Metroliner corridor that is the big population center of the Northeast, and both have suffered from industrial shutdowns—Allentown, when Mack Truck moved one of its main assembly plants to non-union South Carolina, and Bethlehem, when Bethlehem Steel announced it was shutting down its last blast furnace in its headquarters city since 1857. But the rolling hills of the Lehigh Valley today are economically productive and creative, with big new installations from AT&T and Nestle, long-surviving businesses like Crayola Crayons and Dixie cups, and dozens of small startups which never get the visibility of the big closedowns but which together have produced more new jobs than have been lost. If the Lehigh Valley is off the main lines of traffic, it is connected by I-78 to New York and by the Turnpike Extension to Philadelphia, and its lower living costs and taxes make it attractive to newcomers from both big metro areas.

The 15th Congressional District of Pennsylvania consists of the Lehigh Valley plus a small adjacent portion of Montgomery County. This has been a marginal political area for years, the intersection of heavily Democratic industrial precincts with the Republican farmlands of the Pennsylvania Dutch Country. Yet it has had only four congressmen since 1933—three Democrats and a Republican—three of whom lasted at least 14 years.

The congressman from the 15th today is Paul McHale, a Democrat elected in 1992. McHale grew up in the Lehigh Valley, graduated from Lehigh University in Bethlehem, volunteered for the Marine Corps in 1972 and served two years overseas. He returned to the Lehigh Valley, practiced law, and stayed active in the Marine Corps Reserves. In 1982, at 32, he was elected to the state House. After the invasion of Kuwait in 1990, he volunteered for active duty in the Gulf War; he resigned from the legislature, and his wife won his seat; he served two tours of duty in Saudi Arabia and Kuwait. In 1992, he ran for Congress against incumbent Republican Don Ritter. McHale supported the balanced budget amendment and the line-item veto and healthcare finance reform. As Bill Clinton was carrying the Lehigh Valley, McHale won by a similar margin, 52%–47%.

In the House McHale has had a moderate voting record, supporting liberal positions on about two-thirds of votes. He eventually came out against the Clinton healthcare plan, which didn't suit Bethlehem Steel or the United Steelworkers, who often looked to government for help even with their generous medical plans. McHale also criticized Pentagon plans that he believed would reduce combat readiness. He opposed plans by the Joint Chiefs of Staff to create "pre-positioning" ships loaded with tanks and supplies for quick-response Army divisions on the grounds that the Marine Corps was already equipped to carry out that function. But McHale did little to raise money for the 1994 election, in which he was outspent by Republican Jim Yeager. With a Perot-ist Patriot Party candidate winning 5% of the vote, McHale won by only 48%–47%; there was a recount before he was officially declared the winner by 471 votes.

In his second term, McHale continued to steer his centrist course, calling for means-testing entitlements except for veterans' disability payments, backing lobby disclosure successfully, opposing tobacco advertising subsidies, calling for deductibility of college tuition even before it became a Clinton priority. He also had his quixotic causes, like reducing the number of House members by one-third. He worked on getting federal money for industrial parks and the Ben Franklin Partnership, and on the missing link of Route 33 and the U.S. 222 bypass. He sought brownfields legislation, to make saleable abandoned industrial sites, like Bethlehem's steel plants. He continues to be active on military affairs, on the National Security Committee, as a Marine Reserve lieutenant colonel, on the board of visitors at the Naval Academy, as co-founder with Steve Buyer of the National Guard and Reserve Components Caucus.

With his close 1994 margin, McHale was naturally a Republican target in 1996. But this time he raised money earlier and had more success in framing the issues. It was widely expected that Bethlehem Mayor Ken Smith would win the Republican primary. But realtor Bob Kilbanks, with support from the Christian right, a strong opponent of gun control and abortion, beat Smith 39%–33%. This time McHale outspent his opponent, running ads promising to protect education, the environment, Medicare and Social Security, and attacking Kilbanks as a follower of Newt Gingrich. McHale won 55%–41%, running slightly ahead of Clinton; the Reform Party candidate got 3%. "I'm a moderate representing a moderate district," McHale said after winning. "I very clearly had what I think was a proper campaign strategy of requiring [Kilbanks] to run in the fall on the same issues that got him the nomination in the spring."

The People: Pop. 1990: 565,818; 26% rural; 15% age 65+; 92% White; 2% Black; 1% Asian; 5% Hispanic origin. Households: 61% married couple families; 26% married couple fams. w. children; 37% college educ.; median household income: $33,049; per capita income: $15,073; median gross rent: $458; median house value: $101,400.

1996 Presidential Vote			1992 Presidential Vote		
Clinton (D)	96,380	(46%)	Clinton (D)	92,363	(41%)
Dole (R)	85,736	(41%)	Bush (R)	81,349	(37%)
Perot (I)	22,125	(11%)	Perot (I)	47,740	(21%)
Other	3,130	(2%)			

Rep. Paul McHale (D)

Elected 1992; b. July 26, 1950, Bethlehem; home, Bethlehem; Lehigh U., B.A. 1972, Georgetown U. Law Sch., J.D. 1977; Catholic; married (Katherine).

Career: Marine Corps, 1972–74, 1990–91 (Persian Gulf); Marine Reserves, 1974–80, 1984–present; Practicing atty., 1977–92; PA House of Reps., 1982–91.

DC Office: 217 CHOB 20515, 202-225-6411; Fax: 202-225-5320; e-mail: mchale@hr.house.gov.

District Offices: Allentown, 610-439-8861; Bethlehem, 610-866-0916; Pennsburg, 215-541-0614.

Committees: *National Security* (13th of 25 D): Military Readiness; Military Research & Development. *Science* (8th of 21 D): Energy & Environment; Technology.

Group Ratings

	ADA	ACLU	AFS	LCV	CFA	CON	NFIB	COC	ACU	NTLC	CHC
1996	70	44	75	92	92	95	32	38	20	20	20
1995	75	—	—	75	85	87	—	38	12	—	—

National Journal Ratings

	1995 LIB — 1995 CONS			1996 LIB — 1996 CONS		
Economic	69%	—	30%	62%	—	36%
Social	68%	—	31%	63%	—	37%
Foreign	58%	—	42%	67%	—	31%

Key Votes of the 104th Congress

1. Reduce Medicare Growth $	N	5. Flag Amendment	N	9. Cuban Embargo	N
2. Ovrd. Product Liab. Veto	N	6. Drop EPA Limits	Y	10. Bar Bosnia Troop $	N
3. Increase Min. Wage	Y	7. Repeal Assault-Weap. Ban	N	11. Cut Anti-Missile Defense	Y
4. Welfare Reform	Y	8. Ovrd. Part. Birth Veto	Y	12. Bar U.N. Uniforms	N

Election Results

1996 general	Paul McHale (D)	109,812	(55%)	($366,847)
	Bob Kilbanks (R)	82,803	(41%)	($263,747)
	Others	7,748	(4%)	
1996 primary	Paul McHale (D)	unopposed		
1994 general	Paul McHale (D)	72,073	(48%)	($284,930)
	Jim Yeager (R)	71,602	(47%)	($325,713)
	Victor Mazziotti (Patriot)	7,227	(5%)	

SIXTEENTH DISTRICT

The Pennsylvania Dutch Country, settled by Germans in the 18th Century when it was Pennsylvania's frontier, remains a distinctive part of America. These Germans were Amish and Mennonites, members of pietistic sects seeking religious liberty and determined to farm rich lands in the same intensive way they had in Germany. Today, many of their descendants—the Eisenhower family is the most famous example—have blended into mainstream America, but in the Dutch area around Lancaster, many "Plain People" still live. Tourists can still see Amish families clad in black, clattering over the back roads in horse-drawn carriages, with scrupulously tended farms set amid rolling hills, the barns decorated with hex signs. Farmers here continue to produce some of the highest per-acre yields on earth, with simple equipment and limited use of chemicals. But efficient farming is not all that is happening here economically. Lancaster is the headquarters of Armstrong, and nearby Hershey is where Milton Hershey built his chocolate firm back in 1903—the main street is Chocolate Avenue and the lampposts are topped with ceramic Hershey Kisses; this was perhaps appropriately the site of the bipartisan House of Representatives family get-together and "civility retreat" in March 1997. The Dutch area also has many small firms and many new outlet malls; new startups prosper, profiting from the skills and work habits of the labor force. Lancaster County grew robustly in the 1980s, and so did western Chester County, technically part of metro Philadelphia, but with its own Pennsylvania Dutch communities.

The 16th Congressional District includes most of Lancaster County and part of Chester County, ranging east from the Dutch Country through the small towns and spreading suburbs of greater Philadelphia, including America's leading mushroom-growing center around Kennett Square (fragrant with the compost needed for the crop) and on to the Wyeth country around Chadds Ford. By most measures this is the most Republican district in Pennsylvania and perhaps the whole Northeast. It has favored the party of Lincoln since it abandoned the party of

Pennsylvania's only president, Lancaster resident James Buchanan, in the years just before the Civil War.

The congressman from the 16th District is Joe Pitts, a Republican elected in 1996 after the retirement of 20-year Congressman Bob Walker, one of the reform conservatives who, with Newt Gingrich, helped revolutionize the House and produce the Republican majority of 1994. Pitts grew up in Kentucky, joined the Air Force after college, and served three tours of duty and flew 116 B-52 combat missions in Vietnam. He returned to become a math and science teacher in Malvern, in Chester County, and later owned a nursery near Kennett Square. In 1972, at 33, was elected to the Pennsylvania House. Pitts became a leader in Harrisburg, a "champion of traditional values," in his words, and staunchly anti-abortion. In 1989 he became chairman of the Appropriations Committee, and was proud of balancing budgets and also of starting a program in which low-income neighborhood leaders met regularly with legislators to discuss how government could "support and not hinder" their organizations. He also oversaw the restoration of the Pennsylvania Capitol.

In December 1995, when Walker cited the "Pennsylvania Dutch tradition" of not serving over 20 years, Pitts ran for the 16th District seat. He was one of five Republicans, each with some political base. Pat Sellers of Chester County was an admirer of Pat Buchanan, Brad Fischer of Lancaster County was a former Democrat, Stephen Gibble used to chair the Lancaster Republican Party and got its endorsement. But the race boiled down to a contest between Pitts and Chester County Commissioner Karen Martynick. She was for family leave and gun control and called herself a fiscal conservative; he spoke favorably of home-schooling and unfavorably of gambling, and ran as a "true conservative." She called him a political insider; he called her an opportunist. Pitts raised the most money and won the most votes: in Chester he beat Martynick 54%–35% and in Lancaster he beat Gibble 38%–35%; districtwide the score was 45% for Pitts, 26% for Martynick, 20% for Gibble.

In the general Pitts faced newspaper publisher James Blaine, a descendant of James G. Blaine, the "Plumed Knight" of late 19th Century politics and Republican presidential nominee in 1884. Blaine spent $251,000 of his own money on the campaign, which about equalized general election spending. But in this safe Republican district—Bob Dole got 60% of the vote in Lancaster County—Pitts won 59%–38%.

In the House Pitts won his desired committee slots, Transportation and Infrastructure and Budget. His first bills were to require identifying disclaimers on candidates' "push polls"—when candidates level charges about their opponents in the guise of a telephone poll—and to abolish the estate tax, which he says breaks up family businesses and produces little net revenue. He is a member of the Renewal Alliance, seeking ways to encourage local and faith-based groups in low-income neighborhoods to work on the needs of the poor. Unlike Walker, Pitts has no scruples against earmarking local highway projects, and seeks major improvements on U.S. 30 in Chester County and Route 41 in Lancaster County; he is also attendant to the woes of the mushroom industry.

The People: Pop. 1990: 565,908; 44% rural; 12% age 65+; 90% White; 5% Black; 1% Asian; 4% Hispanic origin. Households: 64% married couple families; 31% married couple fams. w. children; 42% college educ.; median household income: $37,553; per capita income: $16,321; median gross rent: $500; median house value: $115,300.

1996 Presidential Vote

Dole (R)	114,164	(53%)
Clinton (D)	80,476	(37%)
Perot (I)	18,010	(8%)

1992 Presidential Vote

Bush (R)	109,019	(48%)
Clinton (D)	72,724	(32%)
Perot (I)	43,271	(19%)

Rep. Joseph R. Pitts (R)

Elected 1996; b. Oct. 10, 1939, Lexington, KY; home, Kennett Square; Asbury Col., A.B. 1961; West Chester U., M.Ed. 1972; Protestant; married (Virginia).

Career: Air Force, 1963–69 (Vietnam); High schl. teacher, 1969–72; PA House of Reps., 1972–96; Owner, Landscape & Nursery Co., 1974–90.

DC Office: 504 CHOB 20515, 202-225-2411; Fax: 202-225-2013; e-mail: pa16@hr.house.gov.

District Offices: Downingtown, 610-518-5823; Kennett Square, 610-429-1540; Lancaster, 717-393-0667.

Committees: *Budget* (24th of 24 R). *Transportation & Infrastructure* (30th of 40 R): Aviation; Railroads; Surface Transportation.

Group Ratings and Key Votes: Newly Elected

Election Results

1996 general	Joseph R. Pitts (R)	124,511	(59%)	($616,874)
	James G. Blaine (D)	78,598	(38%)	($405,264)
	Others	6,493	(3%)	
1996 primary	Joseph R. Pitts (R)	26,515	(45%)	
	Karen Martynick (R)	15,314	(26%)	
	Stephen R. Gibble (R)	11,777	(20%)	
	Pat Sellers (R)	2,696	(5%)	
	Brad S. Fischer (R)	2,386	(4%)	
1994 general	Robert S. Walker (R)	109,759	(70%)	($242,192)
	Bill Chertok (D)	47,680	(30%)	($71,547)

SEVENTEENTH DISTRICT

Through the center of Pennsylvania flows the Susquehanna, the longest river in the East if you include the Chesapeake Bay, which is actually the flooded lower Susquehanna Valley. Starting in Cooperstown, New York, emptying into the Chesapeake next to the antique town of Havre de Grace, Maryland, the Susquehanna is the one river strong enough to break through the Appalachian chains of central Pennsylvania. But few songs are written to celebrate the Susquehanna; it has not given a name to a fever (Potomac), a school of painting (Hudson) or economics (Charles), or to a state (Delaware, Connecticut, Ohio, Mississippi, Alabama, Illinois, Missouri, Colorado).

The 17th Congressional District of Pennsylvania covers much of the lower Susquehanna Valley, where the river breaks through the mountains and drains the fertile plains of the Pennsylvania Dutch Country, one of colonial America's great frontiers. Its big population center is Harrisburg, the central city huddled around the marvelous restored Capitol building—its dome is modeled after St. Peter's in Rome, its stairway on the Paris Opera—the metro area spreading over various valleys, not far upstream from the Three Mile Island nuclear power plant. From there the district spreads east to the Pennsylvania Dutch Country, including Lebanon

County and part of Lancaster County. Here the black buggies of the "Plain People" click-clack over the roads of some of the most fertile farmland in the world.

This is a solidly Republican area. Harrisburg has been a Republican town from the days when the party seemed to conquer all in Pennsylvania; Republicans held the governorship for all but eight years from 1860 to 1934 and filled the ornate halls of the Capitol with Republican patronage hacks. The Pennsylvania Dutch Country is even more Republican.

The congressman from the 17th District is George Gekas who, as state senator from Harrisburg, helped draw the district boundaries and won the seat easily in 1982. Gekas grew up in Harrisburg, went to Dickinson College in nearby Carlisle, served in the Army, graduated from Dickinson Law. Within two years he was in the public sector, as Dauphin County Assistant district attorney. He was elected to the Pennsylvania House in 1966, at 36, to the Pennsylvania Senate in 1976, and to the U.S. House in 1982: an interesting example of a conservative who has spent most of his life in government.

Gekas is fourth-ranking Republican on the Judiciary Committee, an active and sometimes creative legislator, with a solidly conservative voting record leavened by some moderate votes on cultural issues. For years he has sponsored the death penalty for various heinous crimes. Prompted by constituents' experiences he sponsored a law preventing international kidnapping of children and another preventing evictions of the elderly. He sponsored the law, which took effect in 1992, barring congressmen from converting leftover campaign funds for personal use. He has worked to keep Legal Services Corporation lawyers from taking abortion cases and, more recently, has proposed block-granting legal aid funds to the states and abolishing the Legal Services Corporation—a solution not entirely satisfactory to House conservatives or liberals; in 1996 he went along with House Republicans' small cuts but promises to phase out LSC. He sponsored an International Child Adoption Act signed by President Clinton. He is interested in biomedical research, forming a caucus on it, calling for increases in funding for the National Institutes of Health. He seeks limited protection from lawsuits for suppliers of raw materials for biomedical implantation devices. He got passed a law punishing animal rights "terrorism."

Gekas's major bill in the 104th Congress was regulatory reform. He sought impact analyses of new regulations, placing on government the same burden it places on enterprise. He sought to bar government fines when defendants could prove they had not been given "fair warning" they might be in violation of government regulations. He has authored a Government Shutdown Protection Act, providing enough funds if appropriations bills aren't signed to "keep the government's lights on." He seeks state rather than EPA enforcement of auto emissions standards. He has a "Plastic Pork Bill" to get rid of government-issued credit cards. On local issues, Gekas has worked to save Fort Indiantown Gap military base and to clean up the Harrisburg Airport Superfund site.

Gekas has been reelected with large majorities every two years against low-spending opponents.

The People: Pop. 1990: 565,702; 39% rural; 13% age 65+; 90% White; 7% Black; 1% Asian; 2% Hispanic origin. Households: 59% married couple families; 27% married couple fams. w. children; 33% college educ.; median household income: $31,841; per capita income: $14,434; median gross rent: $415; median house value: $76,500.

1996 Presidential Vote

Dole (R)	116,473	(54%)
Clinton (D)	81,205	(37%)
Perot (I)	17,997	(8%)

1992 Presidential Vote

Bush (R)	114,245	(50%)
Clinton (D)	72,594	(32%)
Perot (I)	40,495	(18%)

Rep. George W. Gekas (R)

Elected 1982; b. Apr. 14, 1930, Harrisburg; home, Harrisburg; Dickinson Col., B.A. 1952, Dickinson Law Sch., J.D. 1958; Greek Orthodox; married (Evangeline).

Career: Army, 1953–55; Asst. Dist. Atty., Dauphin Cnty., 1960–66; PA House of Reps., 1966–75; PA Senate, 1976–83.

DC Office: 2410 RHOB 20515, 202-225-4315; Fax: 202-225-8440. **District Offices:** Elizabethtown, 717-367-6731; Harrisburg, 717-541-5507; Lebanon, 717-273-1451.

Committees: *Judiciary* (4th of 20 R): Commercial & Administrative Law (Chmn.); Crime.

Group Ratings

	ADA	ACLU	AFS	LCV	CFA	CON	NFIB	COC	ACU	NTLC	CHC
1996	0	0	0	23	8	9	97	100	100	98	86
1995	5	—	—	0	0	38	—	100	76	—	—

National Journal Ratings

	1995 LIB — 1995 CONS			1996 LIB — 1996 CONS		
Economic	0%	—	74%	0%	—	82%
Social	37%	—	63%	33%	—	65%
Foreign	41%	—	58%	0%	—	79%

Key Votes of the 104th Congress

1. Reduce Medicare Growth $	Y	5. Flag Amendment	Y	9. Cuban Embargo	Y
2. Ovrd. Product Liab. Veto	Y	6. Drop EPA Limits	N	10. Bar Bosnia Troop $	N
3. Increase Min. Wage	N	7. Repeal Assault-Weap. Ban	Y	11. Cut Anti-Missile Defense	N
4. Welfare Reform	Y	8. Ovrd. Part. Birth Veto	Y	12. Bar U.N. Uniforms	Y

Election Results

1996 general	George W. Gekas (R)	150,678	(72%)	($110,578)
	Paul Kettl (D)	57,911	(28%)	($1,476)
1996 primary	George W. Gekas (R)	unopposed		
1994 general	George W. Gekas (R)	unopposed		($86,839)

EIGHTEENTH DISTRICT

Pittsburgh is surely the hilliest of the large metropolitan areas of the United States—indicative of the nerve of its founders that they were willing to build on such steep terrain. In its years of great growth, from the mid-1800s to the early 1900s, with the steel mills lining the riverbanks, Pittsburgh and its suburbs spread up and down hills, through the interstices of river valleys and over gaps to the next nearly level spot. Then, as growth resumed in the mid-20th Century, the spreading-out process continued. One result is that there are no clusters of rich and poor suburbs, no one middle-class zone: they are spread out around the irregular terrain. The richest Pittsburghers, for example, live in Fox Chapel and Sewickley to the northeast and northwest; there are upper-middle-income suburbs like Mount Lebanon south of the Golden Triangle, but also some north of the Allegheny; working class enclaves, now greatly depopulated, are strung along the Monongahela River near the mostly cold steel mills, but are found in other pockets as well. Pittsburgh does not yet have an edge city, though there are new housing and a few office developments to the north and to the west around the airport, now a major hub for USAirways.

When John Kennedy was elected president, there were four congressional districts in Pittsburgh's Allegheny County, numbered 27th through 30th; now all of Pennsylvania has only 21 districts, and there are only two fully in Allegheny County. One, the 14th, is made up primarily of the city of Pittsburgh; the other, the 18th, includes suburbs to the north, south and east, plus most of the industrial Mon Valley to the southeast. This is the creation of 1990s redistricting, containing much of the old Republican-leaning suburban 18th and some of the heavily Democratic Mon Valley 20th. It was expected to be a Democratic district, but in fact has been seriously contested.

The congressman from the 18th is Mike Doyle, a Democrat who won in 1994 when the 18th District's Republican incumbent, 36-year-old brash conservative Rick Santorum, was elected to the U.S. Senate. Of Irish and Italian descent, Doyle grew up in the Mon Valley town of Swissvale, returned there after Penn State, worked as an insurance agent and for a nonprofit agency and was elected to the Swissvale Borough Council in 1977, at 24. In 1978 he became chief of staff to state Senator Frank Pecora, a Republican who had switched parties and run in the 18th District against Santorum in 1992, and lost 61%–38%. When Santorum ran for the Senate, Doyle was one of seven Democrats and four Republicans to seek the open seat. The Democrats were close to evenly matched: all won between 10% and 20% of the vote. Doyle, who had switched to the Democratic Party only recently, was helped by endorsements from unions and community leaders; he, like Santorum in his first campaign, knocked on 40,000 doors. In the general, he faced John McCarty, a former aide to the late Senator John Heinz; interestingly, McCarty is pro-choice and Doyle anti-abortion. Doyle campaigned for sweeping healthcare reform, against the new General Agreement on Tariffs and Trade, and for rebuilding the Mon Valley's industrial base, and won 55%–45%.

In the House Doyle had a mixed voting record, toward the right on cultural issues, toward the left on economics. But he did support the Blue Dog Coalition budget, welfare reform and regulatory reform. He opposed tax cuts and called for higher Medicare co-payments for high-income recipients. He serves on the Science and Veterans' Affairs Committees, where he worked for the Supercomputer and the Pittsburgh Energy Technology Center and the Oakland veterans hospital.

In 1996 Doyle had serious opposition from Republican Dave Fawcett, but outspent him with the help of $284,000 in PAC and party contributions. In the last weeks Fawcett attracted notice with two mailings. One showed the late pianist Liberace in flamboyant attire and attacked Doyle for party-switchings ("more changes than Liberace's wardrobe"). Another argued that Doyle was against utility deregulation because he was influenced by Duquesne Light ("DuPain Light"), and showed a picture of him holding money bags in both hands. Doyle objected vociferously to doctored photos of himself, but he might just as well have lightened up; the mailings didn't seem to make much difference. Doyle won 56%–40%, with 3% for Richard Caligiuri, a perennial candidate with the same name as the late Pittsburgh Mayor.

House Democratic leaders have promised Doyle the next Pennsylvania seat on Appropriations. But with Republicans in control, they had no new seats, and Doyle remains on Science and Veterans' Affairs.

The People: Pop. 1990: 565,771; 2% rural; 19% age 65+; 91% White; 8% Black; 1% Asian; 1% Hispanic origin. Households: 55% married couple families; 21% married couple fams. w. children; 43% college educ.; median household income: $29,003; per capita income: $15,251; median gross rent: $394; median house value: $55,000.

1996 Presidential Vote			**1992 Presidential Vote**		
Clinton (D)	119,943	(52%)	Clinton (D)	137,507	(52%)
Dole (R)	89,580	(39%)	Bush (R)	80,795	(30%)
Perot (I)	19,689	(8%)	Perot (I)	46,754	(18%)

Rep. Mike Doyle (D)

Elected 1994; b. Aug. 5, 1953, Pittsburgh; home, Swissvale; PA St. U., B.S. 1975; Catholic; married (Susan).

Career: Insurance agent, 1975–77; Exec. Dir., Turtle Creek Valley Citizens Union, 1977–79; Swissvale Borough Cncl., 1977; Chief of Staff, PA Sen. Frank Pecora, 1978–94; Co-Founder, Eastgate Insurance Agency, 1983–present.

DC Office: 133 CHOB 20515, 202-225-2135; Fax: 202-225-3084; e-mail: rep.doyle@mail.house.gov.

District Offices: McKeesport, 412-664-4049; Pittsburgh, 412-241-6055.

Committees: *Science* (13th of 21 D): Energy & Environment; Technology. *Veterans' Affairs* (7th of 13 D): Health.

Group Ratings

	ADA	ACLU	AFS	LCV	CFA	CON	NFIB	COC	ACU	NTLC	CHC
1996	55	50	75	92	46	45	49	44	32	32	40
1995	75	—	—	75	38	38	—	50	36	—	—

National Journal Ratings

	1995 LIB — 1995 CONS	1996 LIB — 1996 CONS
Economic	63% — 37%	62% — 38%
Social	54% — 45%	48% — 52%
Foreign	70% — 28%	74% — 25%

Key Votes of the 104th Congress

1. Reduce Medicare Growth $	N	5. Flag Amendment	Y	9. Cuban Embargo	Y
2. Ovrd. Product Liab. Veto	N	6. Drop EPA Limits	Y	10. Bar Bosnia Troop $	N
3. Increase Min. Wage	Y	7. Repeal Assault-Weap. Ban	N	11. Cut Anti-Missile Defense	Y
4. Welfare Reform	Y	8. Ovrd. Part. Birth Veto	Y	12. Bar U.N. Uniforms	Y

Election Results

1996 general	Mike Doyle (D)	120,410	(56%)	($528,291)
	David B. Fawcett (R)	86,829	(40%)	($343,898)
	Others	7,751	(4%)	
1996 primary	Mike Doyle (D)	45,967	(74%)	
	Joseph Rudolph (D)	15,822	(26%)	
1994 general	Mike Doyle (D)	101,784	(55%)	($381,733)
	John McCarty (R)	83,881	(45%)	($362,091)

NINETEENTH DISTRICT

The Mason-Dixon Line, the historic boundary between Maryland and Pennsylvania, runs through some of the country's most pleasant rolling farmlands, west of the Susquehanna River up through the first of the Appalachian chains. It was over this invisible line that Robert E. Lee's confederate troops crossed and were then repulsed in the Battle of Gettysburg in July 1863. Nearby was the westernmost capital of the United States during the Revolutionary War, the small city of York, capital from September 1777 to June 1778. This is where the Continental Congress passed the Articles of Confederation, received word from Benjamin Franklin in Paris that the French would help the colonies with money and ships and issued the first proclamation calling for a national day of thanksgiving. Little today recalls it was once frontier and later fiercely fought over: the rolling green farmland looks peaceful, prosperous and mostly undisturbed by the commercial trappings and stylistic excesses of the late 20th Century.

Some 50 miles of the Mason-Dixon Line is the southern boundary of the 19th Congressional District of Pennsylvania, which is centered on York, including the suburbs of Harrisburg across the Susquehanna, the old town of Carlisle with Dickinson College, the Carlisle Barracks, the U.S. Army War College, and President Eisenhower's retirement home near Gettysburg. Eisenhower was of Pennsylvania Dutch stock himself; his father migrated in the late 19th Century, with a group of Mennonite brethren, to Kansas and Texas. The district has the look of deeply contented land and has been, with occasional exceptions, heavily Republican.

The congressman from the 19th District is Bill Goodling, chairman of the Education and The Workforce Committee (renamed for the second consecutive Congress), a Republican first elected in 1974. Goodling was a public school teacher, coach and principal in a small town in York County for 22 years; his father was 19th District congressman for 12 years, elected every two years from 1960–72 except in 1964. When George Goodling retired in 1974, Bill Goodling ran and won the primary and general by rather narrow margins. His toughest election since was in 1992, after it was revealed he had 430 overdrafts on the House bank totalling $188,000. Both a Democrat and a former Jack Kemp aide running as an Independent campaigned aggressively; Goodling, with campaign appearances by Newt Gingrich and Dan Quayle, won with 45% to 34% for Paul Kilker and 20% for Thomas Humbert—almost the same percentages as in the presidential race here.

Goodling has labored long and hard over the years on the baroque edifice of federal education laws, until 1994 as a minority member with limited influence on the Education and Labor Committee, then as chairman of the renamed Economic and Educational Opportunities Committee in 1995–97, now the Education and The Workforce Committee. Since the 1950s, when a bipartisan coalition wanted to limit labor union powers, organized labor saw to it the committee had a majority of pro-labor members, including Republicans; as the focus shifted to education programs in the 1970s and 1980s, they strove to use the not terrifically strong lever of federal spending—on the order of 8% of all government spending in America—to steer school systems and other social agencies in liberal directions they might not seek if left up to states and localities. Now Goodling and the Republicans are attempting to move things in the other direction, so far with limited success. One reason is that the basic elementary and secondary school aid laws were reauthorized in 1994, with Democrats in control. Another is that Goodling is not a backer of total local control: he wants to shrink, not abolish, the federal Department of Education and to make a sympathetic review of education programs, not just zero them out. A third reason is that these programs have built constituencies of their own, people whose livelihood depends on them and who often believe in them deeply. And with their complexity, any change is a fiendishly complex business.

Such was the experience with the complex gaggle of job training programs. It was the impulse of Goodling and the Republicans to give states a block grant and let them decide how to use it, and such bills passed both House and Senate by wide margins in 1995. But conservatives objected to some provisions, and Republican responses to them made the bill unpalatable to Democrats, especially repeal of Bill Clinton's school-to-work law and the de-earmarking of aid to workers affected by trade agreements, a favorite of organized labor. So the measure languished in conference committee, sure to be blocked in the Senate or vetoed by Clinton. In early 1997 Goodling proposed a different approach that received significant bipartisan support and would consolidate over 60 job training and adult education programs into three block grants, including one aiding dislocated workers. Similarly, on school loans, the Republican bills passed in 1995 were harshly attacked as cuts; and so the bill was modified sharply to mollify Democrats. Goodling was more successful in molding his Individuals with Disabilities Education Improvement Act (IDEA); it contained some provisions to make it easier to discipline and remove disruptive pupils and at the same time contained provisions supported by disability advocates. But the full Senate never took it up. Early in the 105th Congress, Goodling and his Senate counterpart, Vermont's Jim Jeffords, worked out a compromise measure that gave states slightly more flexibility to discipline students but left most protections intact; it passed both houses of Congress by near-unanimous margins in May.

Goodling over the years has spent less time on labor issues and has taken a tougher conservative line on them. In the 104th Congress Republicans made limited progress, partly because it was not a priority to move measures like Davis-Bacon repeal that would surely be vetoed by Clinton. They did come up with some interesting initiatives, however. One was the TEAM Act, to encourage worker-management teams in non-union companies. Opponents charge this would allow management to oppress workers; proponents say it would allow management and workers to be more creative and productive. But this was furiously opposed by Democrats and Clinton vetoed it. The other initiative was the flextime bill pushed by North Carolina Republican Cass Ballenger, to allow non-union workers to agree to take compensatory time rather than work overtime at higher rates. Again, unions were solidly against, but the bill passed the House, after union workers (only 10% of the private sector work force) were exempted. Union backers in the Senate will surely try to block this, but Bill Clinton spoke favorably of the idea in his 1997 State of the Union speech. Much of Goodling's time in 1996 was grappling with the minimum wage increase, a policy whose economic arguments are so weak it was not advanced when Democrats had a majority in 1993 and 1994, but which they revived in 1995 as an attractive issue with which to batter and divide Republicans. That is what happened in 1996; a key Goodling amendment exempting employers with annual sales under $500,000 from any minimum wage was defeated in May, and the bill passed in the summer. But it was not much mentioned in the fall campaign.

In April 1996 Goodling faced tough primary competition from Charles Gerow, head of the state Citizens Against Government Waste. He called Goodling an insider, attacked him on term limits and ran as a cultural conservative. Goodling was renominated by only 55%–45%, losing one of the 19th's three counties. Goodling won easily in the fall, 63%–36%.

The People: Pop. 1990: 565,789; 50% rural; 13% age 65+; 95% White; 3% Black; 1% Asian; 1% Hispanic origin. Households: 63% married couple families; 28% married couple fams. w. children; 33% college educ.; median household income: $32,424; per capita income: $14,539; median gross rent: $416; median house value: $80,200.

1996 Presidential Vote

Dole (R)	112,221	(52%)
Clinton (D)	81,319	(38%)
Perot (I)	18,972	(9%)

1992 Presidential Vote

Bush (R)	105,647	(47%)
Clinton (D)	75,515	(33%)
Perot (I)	44,373	(20%)

Rep. Bill Goodling (R)

Elected 1974; b. Dec. 5, 1927, Loganville; home, Jacobus; U. of MD, B.S. 1953, Western MD Col., M.A. 1957; Methodist; married (Hilda).

Career: Army, 1946–48; Public schl. teacher, admin., 1952–74; Pres., Dallastown School Bd., 1966–67.

DC Office: 2263 RHOB 20515, 202-225-5836; Fax: 202-226-1000.

District Offices: Camp Hill, 717-763-1988; Carlisle, 717-243-5432; Gettysburg, 717-334-3430; Hanover, 717-632-7855, 800-631-1811; York, 717-843-8887.

Committees: *Education & The Workforce* (Chmn. of 25 R): Early Childhood, Youth & Families; Employer-Employee Relations; Postsecondary Education, Training & Life-Long Learning. *International Relations* (2nd of 26 R): International Operations & Human Rights.

Group Ratings

	ADA	ACLU	AFS	LCV	CFA	CON	NFIB	COC	ACU	NTLC	CHC
1996	10	12	0	31	23	38	100	94	95	100	93
1995	5	—	—	6	15	85	—	96	84	—	—

National Journal Ratings

	1995 LIB — 1995 CONS			1996 LIB — 1996 CONS		
Economic	0%	—	74%	0%	—	82%
Social	45%	—	54%	38%	—	61%
Foreign	28%	—	65%	38%	—	60%

Key Votes of the 104th Congress

1. Reduce Medicare Growth $	Y	5. Flag Amendment	Y	9. Cuban Embargo	Y
2. Ovrd. Product Liab. Veto	Y	6. Drop EPA Limits	Y	10. Bar Bosnia Troop $	Y
3. Increase Min. Wage	N	7. Repeal Assault-Weap. Ban	Y	11. Cut Anti-Missile Defense	N
4. Welfare Reform	Y	8. Ovrd. Part. Birth Veto	Y	12. Bar U.N. Uniforms	Y

Election Results

1996 general	Bill Goodling (R)	130,716	(63%)	($305,541)
	Scott L. Chronister (D)	74,944	(36%)	($63,803)
	Others	3,303	(2%)	
1996 primary	Bill Goodling (R)	24,014	(55%)	
	Charles R. Gerow (R)	19,700	(45%)	
1994 general	Bill Goodling (R)	unopposed		($50,718)

TWENTIETH DISTRICT

The area south of Pittsburgh and next to the deceptively straight-edged West Virginia state line is one of the industrial backlands of America. The Scots and Irish bordermen who came here 200 years ago were wild settlers who were never tamed by townsmen in their native countries or here; this was the land of the Whiskey Rebellion of 1794. In the 19th Century, more or less never-ending seams of bituminous coal were discovered under these never-ending ridges. The offspring of the original settlers were joined by immigrants from Italy, Poland and Czechoslovakia, living in little frame houses packed into the towns on interstices between hills and rivers, within walking distance of steel factories, foundries and coal mine shafts. Life was never easy here; after some prosperous years in the 1960s and 1970s, the coal country was hit hard by the recession that followed the 1979 oil shock. Young people have been leaving the area for years, and it has a disproportionate elderly population. Only in recent years has the revived high-tech economy of greater Pittsburgh radiated outward into these hills, so far with limited effect.

The 20th Congressional District of Pennsylvania consists of most of this southwest corner of the state, where the population fell 7% in the 1980s. It includes Washington, Fayette, and Greene Counties, which have been heavily Democratic since the United Mine Workers backed the New Deal and established the United Steelworkers as the bargaining agent in the steel mills. But there is political balance: the 20th also includes some high- and middle-income suburbs of Pittsburgh in Allegheny County and a corner of Westmoreland County.

The congressman from the 20th District is Frank Mascara, a Democrat who won the seat in 1994 after coming close in 1992. Mascara grew up in this rough industrial country and knows its risks personally: his father was injured and suffered for years from the aftermath of a steel mill accident in Monessen and his grandfather was killed in a mining accident in Fayette County. Frank Mascara served in the Army as a teenager and was an accountant and small businessman before being elected Washington County controller in 1973; he was elected chairman of the county board of commissioners in 1980 and held that post through 1994. There he helped create

Southpointe industrial park, a magnet for business development and new communities. In 1992 he ran for Congress and lost to scandal-tarred incumbent Austin Murphy in the Democratic primary by only 36%–34%. In 1994, after Murphy retired, Mascara ran again, winning a three-candidate primary with 54%, and in the general beating financial consultant Mike McCormick by 53%–47%.

In the House Mascara did not get his desired committee assignments—Education and The Workforce or Transportation and Infrastructure—because Democrats had no seats open for freshmen; so he served on the Government Reform and Oversight and Veterans' Affairs Committees. He had on balance a moderate voting record. He vociferously attacked the Contract With America, but he also voted for many of its provisions—the line-item veto, the unfunded mandates bill, welfare reform. He calls himself "pro-life and pro-gun." But he vociferously opposed Republicans' labor legislation. One of the few congressmen with vivid memories of the hardships of the 1930s, when his injured father supported a family of seven as a WPA worker, he called the Republican plans "class warfare" and proclaimed, "I believe in workplace safety and do not want it diluted!" He also worked on local issues, keeping the 911th Air Wing at Pittsburgh Airport and Charles E. Kelly Army Support facility off the base-closing list and seeking funding for the proposed Mon-Fayette Freeway. He helped to authorize the coin commemorating General George C. Marshall, a native of Fayette County, and sought flexibility for meeting air quality standards.

In 1996 Mascara again faced McCormick in what became a bitter campaign. Once again, he outspent the Republican, with help from PACs, for which McCormick criticized him. Rather than steer clear of Newt Gingrich, McCormick invited him to a breakfast fundraiser and pledged to cut taxes and spending. He favored allowing people under 50 to opt out of the current Social Security and said in a debate, "Miracles lie in the hearts of people, not in the bureaucratic bowels of government." He also pledged to build the Mon-Fayette Freeway, and said that as a member of the majority party he would better be able to do it. In October McCormick ran an ad showing C-SPAN footage of a committee hearing on congressional pensions, in which Mascara said: "I'm not going to apologize for anything I might get. I work hard. And I am different. So don't tell me I should be treated on an even keel with everybody." C-SPAN holds a copyright on its broadcasts of hearings (though not on its broadcasts of the House floor) and demanded McCormick stop airing the ads; he ignored that. Mascara was enraged at what he considered unfair and misleading tactics, and at the end of the campaign ran a spot charging McCormick had not paid his corporate taxes for three years.

This turned out to be almost a carbon copy of 1994. Mascara won 57% in Washington County and 35% in Fayette, but McCormick took 59% in the Allegheny County suburbs of Pittsburgh; the final result was a 54% Mascara win. Mascara hopes to plug the Mon-Fayette Freeway on the Transportation and Infrastructure Committee, and has said he will work for term limits and campaign finance reform.

The People: Pop. 1990: 565,789; 40% rural; 17% age 65+; 96% White; 3% Black; 1% Asian; 1% Hispanic origin. Households: 61% married couple families; 26% married couple fams. w. children; 36% college educ.; median household income: $26,294; per capita income: $13,349; median gross rent: $332; median house value: $56,600.

1996 Presidential Vote

Clinton (D)	109,299	(50%)
Dole (R)	85,040	(39%)
Perot (I)	23,652	(11%)

1992 Presidential Vote

Clinton (D)	121,823	(51%)
Bush (R)	69,811	(29%)
Perot (I)	48,251	(20%)

Rep. Frank R. Mascara (D)

Elected 1994; b. Jan. 19, 1930, Belle Vernon; home, Charleroi; CA U. of PA., B.S. 1972; Catholic; married (Delores).

Career: Army, 1946–47; Businessman, 1956–74; Washington Cnty. Controller, 1973–80; Chmn., Bd. of Cnty. Commissioners, 1980–94.

DC Office: 314 CHOB 20515, 202-225-4665; Fax: 202-225-3377.

District Offices: Greensburg, 412-834-6441; N. Charleroi, 412-483-9016, 800-213-5570; Uniontown, 412-437-5078; Washington, 412-228-4326; Waynesburg, 412-852-2182.

Committees: *Transportation & Infrastructure* (21st of 33 D): Surface Transportation; Water Resources & Environment. *Veterans' Affairs* (8th of 13 D): Benefits; Oversight & Investigations.

Group Ratings

	ADA	ACLU	AFS	LCV	CFA	CON	NFIB	COC	ACU	NTLC	CHC
1996	60	31	75	85	46	38	41	38	35	20	33
1995	80	—	—	88	54	25	—	42	40	—	—

National Journal Ratings

	1995 LIB — 1995 CONS			1996 LIB — 1996 CONS		
Economic	69%	—	30%	65%	—	33%
Social	54%	—	45%	50%	—	50%
Foreign	62%	—	36%	70%	—	29%

Key Votes of the 104th Congress

1. Reduce Medicare Growth $	N	5. Flag Amendment	Y	9. Cuban Embargo	Y
2. Ovrd. Product Liab. Veto	N	6. Drop EPA Limits	Y	10. Bar Bosnia Troop $	N
3. Increase Min. Wage	Y	7. Repeal Assault-Weap. Ban	Y	11. Cut Anti-Missile Defense	Y
4. Welfare Reform	Y	8. Ovrd. Part. Birth Veto	Y	12. Bar U.N. Uniforms	Y

Election Results

1996 general	Frank R. Mascara (D)	113,394	(54%)	($577,217)
	Mike McCormick (R)	97,004	(46%)	($381,404)
1996 primary	Frank R. Mascara (D)	unopposed		
1994 general	Frank R. Mascara (D)	95,251	(53%)	($489,508)
	Mike McCormick (R)	84,156	(47%)	($363,080)

TWENTY-FIRST DISTRICT

The best natural harbor on Lake Erie is in a state that few think of as a Great Lakes state. It is the harbor of Erie, Pennsylvania, protected by the Presque Isle peninsula, up in the remotest corner of Pennsylvania, 428 miles from Center City Philadelphia. This is heavy industry country: there is farmland here, and even some woods, but this land between the Great Lakes and the basin of the Ohio River has been prime heavy industry territory for more than 100 years.

The 21st Congressional District occupies this corner of Pennsylvania. About half its people are in Erie County. To the south are the farming areas of Crawford County, the steel-producing town of Sharon in Mercer County—on the Ohio border and part of the Youngstown-Warren area—and Butler County, a suburban area directly north of Pittsburgh. Politically this is closely balanced territory: Erie and Mercer Counties usually vote Democratic, and Butler and Crawford Counties usually vote Republican. The result was one of the classic marginal seats in the nation from 1964–82 and again 1994–96. The exception came during the tenure of Tom Ridge, a Republican from a Catholic working class family in Erie, a Harvard graduate and Vietnam veteran, first elected here in 1982, who won easily until he was elected governor in 1994.

The congressman from the 21st now is Phil English, a Republican elected in 1994 and reelected after a fierce battle in 1996. English grew up in Erie and has worked at little else but politics and government. At 20, he was an alternate to the 1976 Republican National Convention, and he worked during the early 1980s as a Republican staffer in Harrisburg. In 1985 he became Erie controller; in 1988, he was the Republican nominee for state treasurer, losing to Democrat Catherine Baker Knoll. In 1990 he helped produce Rick Santorum's upset win in the Pittsburgh-area 18th District, the first step on Santorum's path to the Senate, and went on to other Republican staff jobs. In 1994, when Ridge ran for governor, English ran for the House and won 66% in the Republican primary—which attracted almost as many voters (61,000) as the Democratic primary (62,000). Nonetheless, the attention was on the Democratic primary, in which five candidates competed, four from Erie, two of them the men beaten by Ridge in 1982 and 1984. The winner was the one candidate from outside Erie, Bill Leavens, who won 70% in Mercer, 40% in Butler and 6% in Erie. He campaigned as a moderate Democrat and against abortion. English promised to reform welfare, cut wasteful spending and create jobs for northwestern Pennsylvania with an 18-point plan for revitalizing small business and manufacturing. Three of the four counties voted on party lines. But Erie, English's home—and probably more important, Tom Ridge's—voted for the Republican, giving English a 49%–47% victory.

In the House the obviously vulnerable English was given a seat on Ways and Means, an excellent spot from which to both legislate and to raise money. Early on, English made a record on local issues, getting the Army Corps of Engineers to dredge and replenish the beach at Presque Isle, co-sponsoring a Rural Telemedicine Act, working to stop Korea's dumping of pipe and tubing (the Shenango Valley is the leading U.S. producer), preserving spending on low-income heating, saving an Erie bus project, and protecting Erie Forge & Steel from the IRS. While he supported the Contract With America and the Republican leadership on most votes, he had a moderate record on economic and foreign issues and dissented prominently on occasion. He was one of three Republicans who publicly supported the minimum wage increase early on and voted against the budget resolution in 1996. He took a tough line on welfare in 1995 and urged a compromise in 1996. He wrote an amendment to bar insurers from treating victims of domestic violence as suffering from a preexisting condition. With Allegheny County Auditor Frank Lucchino, he got HUD to bar Section 8 subsidized housing landlords from renting to relatives. Most important, he wrote the "Lockbox Amendment" purporting to guarantee that Medicare savings are not spent on anything else.

All this might have been enough for reelection in a low-visibility House race. But not this one. The campaign started very early—in April 1995, when the Democratic Congressional Campaign Committee ran an ad showing English morphing into Newt Gingrich. This ad convinced Democrats that attacking Gingrich was a winning tactic; its impact convinced English he would need to raise more than twice the $450,000 he spent in 1994. The AFL-CIO began running ads that spring and sent in the first of ultimately five organizers in July; they and Citizens Action staged an event in which a steamroller ridden by a dummy labelled English was shown rolling over mannequins labeled as senior citizens. English saw the danger: "If people see a false picture painted repeatedly and it isn't checked as aggressively as it has to be, the message will sometimes stick." He set up a task force of district residents with different views on Medicare and conducted more than 100 "coffee hours" on issues.

English's early activity scared off some Democratic opponents, but he had a serious challenger. Ron DiNicola is the son of an immigrant bricklayer who grew up in Erie, went to Harvard, served in the Marine Corps, went to Georgetown Law; he had a law practice in Los Angeles, which he maintained even when he returned to Erie to run in the 1994 Democratic primary. He kept running, encouraged by the campaign others were running, and started raising money himself, though not nearly as much as English. In January 1996 the AFL-CIO started running Medicare "cuts" ads, and English responded with a heavy buy. In April English released his tax return and challenged DiNicola to do the same; DiNicola had asked for an extension, and English pounded him for six weeks. "California office. California driver's license . . . And a great tan." By late spring a U.S. Chamber of Commerce-led business coalition was running ads, and the National Republican Congressional Committee spent $340,000 on TV here. In the summer of 1996 English ran positive spots on helping a local couple adopt a child from Russia, getting an electric wheelchair for an Erie senior, pushing the dredging of Presque Isle. "Independent Voice. Pennsylvania Values," English proclaimed, one English brochure used the word "Republican" just once, when mentioning his opposition to the leadership on the minimum wage. English even showed Bill Clinton in a TV spot, and praised his proposal for tax deductions for college tuition.

In the fall the going got tougher. AFL-CIO and DiNicola ads hammered English for his closeness to Newt. The American Hospital Association ran ads praising English's attempts to save Medicare. The National Republican Congressional Committee ran one spot applauding English for backing welfare reform and another bashing "big labor bosses" and for trying to buy the House seat. During one 20-hour stretch in November, more than 500 political ads aired on Erie television. Altogether English spent $1.3 million and DiNicola $479,000; other organizations appear to have spent at least $1.4 million, and quite possibly more. All of this has been attacked as wretched excess, and it certainly sounds exhausting. Undoubtedly in this barrage there were attacks that were tendentious, inaccurate, misleading, and beside the point. But it can also be said that the voters of the 21st District were exposed to more information about public policy and political differences than voters in the large majority of American districts over the past decades, and that in a free and competitive electoral system much of that information will be presented in adversarial terms. Would people make better decisions if they had less or biased information?

The result was what it might very well have been if this had been a much less furiously contested campaign. English won 51%–49%. He ran behind in Erie County, but his 48% there was 11% ahead of Bob Dole; he carried Butler County with 59% and Crawford County with 55% and lost Mercer County with 47%. English has shown great political survival skills, but this is very likely to be a seriously contested district in 1996.

The People: Pop. 1990: 565,806; 44% rural; 15% age 65+; 95% White; 4% Black; 1% Hispanic origin. Households: 58% married couple families; 26% married couple fams. w. children; 33% college educ.; median household income: $25,845; per capita income: $11,884; median gross rent: $326; median house value: $50,200.

1996 Presidential Vote

Clinton (D)	106,080	(49%)
Dole (R)	87,448	(40%)
Perot (I)	22,510	(10%)

1992 Presidential Vote

Clinton (D)	105,538	(45%)
Bush (R)	80,902	(34%)
Perot (I)	48,004	(20%)

Rep. Philip S. English (R)

Elected 1994; b. June 20, 1956, Erie; home, Erie; U. of PA., B.A. 1978; Catholic; married (Christiane).

Career: Staff aide, PA Senate; 1980–84; Erie City Controller, 1985–89; Chief of Staff, PA Sen. Melissa Hart 1990–92; Exec. Dir., PA Senate Finance Cmte., 1990–94.

DC Office: 1721 LHOB 20515, 202-225-5406; Fax: 202-225-3103.

District Offices: Butler, 412-285-7005; Erie, 814-456-2038; Hermitage, 412-342-6132; Meadville, 814-724-8414.

Committees: *Science* (22nd of 25 R): Energy & Environment. *Small Business* (14th of 19 R): Empowerment; Tax, Finance & Exports. *Ways & Means* (17th of 23 R): Human Resources; Oversight.

Group Ratings

	ADA	ACLU	AFS	LCV	CFA	CON	NFIB	COC	ACU	NTLC	CHC
1996	10	19	50	31	46	6	92	88	74	90	100
1995	15	—	—	6	31	75	—	92	84	—	—

National Journal Ratings

	1995 LIB — 1995 CONS			1996 LIB — 1996 CONS		
Economic	44%	—	53%	48%	—	52%
Social	43%	—	57%	29%	—	68%
Foreign	15%	—	73%	48%	—	51%

Key Votes of the 104th Congress

1. Reduce Medicare Growth $	Y	5. Flag Amendment	Y	9. Cuban Embargo	Y
2. Ovrd. Product Liab. Veto	Y	6. Drop EPA Limits	Y	10. Bar Bosnia Troop $	Y
3. Increase Min. Wage	Y	7. Repeal Assault-Weap. Ban	Y	11. Cut Anti-Missile Defense	N
4. Welfare Reform	Y	8. Ovrd. Part. Birth Veto	Y	12. Bar U.N. Uniforms	Y

Election Results

1996 general	Philip S. English (R)	106,875	(51%)	($1,262,645)
	Ronald A. Dinicola (D)	104,004	(49%)	($478,871)
1996 primary	Philip S. English (R)	unopposed		
1994 general	Philip S. English (R)	89,439	(49%)	($450,795)
	Bill Leavens (D)	84,796	(47%)	($465,191)
	Others	6,588	(4%)	

RHODE ISLAND

The tiny little city-state with a mouthful of an official name, Rhode Island and Providence Plantations, has as turbulent a political history as any state in the Union. A successful trading community since the 1600s, a leader in manufacturing since Samuel Slater replicated from memory an English water-powered cotton textile mill in Pawtucket in 1791, Rhode Island also had its beginning as an upstart community, a refuge for religious dissenters, "the sewer of New England," as the orthodox Cotton Mather put it. Rhode Island profited from slavery (two-thirds of America's slaves arrived on ships owned by Rhode Islanders) and war (the state boomed during the Civil War), and carried its tradition of tolerating just about anything into its politics. Rhode Island refused to pay its share for the Revolutionary War, declined to send delegates to the 1787 Constitutional Convention, and delayed joining the Union until the other 12 states had, prompting George Washington to say, "Rhode Island still perseveres in that impolitic, unjust—and one might add without much impropriety—scandalous conduct, which seems to have marked all her public counsels of late." Later the new nation's first bank failure occurred here in 1809, when a bank capitalized at $45 issued $800,000 in bank notes. In the 1840s, conflict between hard money merchants and soft money farmers resulted in two state governments and a conflict known as Dorr's War, with the outcome determined when merchant Dorr's two ancient cannons failed to fire.

Then, in the 1930s, Rhode Island had something resembling a political revolution. Thousands of immigrants from French Canada, Ireland and Italy had come to Rhode Island to work in the textile mills; by the early 1900s, this colony of dissident Protestants had become the most heavily Catholic state in the nation. Yankee Republicans tried to appeal to Catholics by running French Canadians for office. But national events—Al Smith's candidacy in 1928, when he carried Rhode Island, and Franklin Roosevelt's New Deal—moved the Catholics toward the Democrats. Then came the revolution: in 1935, the Democrats under Governor Theodore Green, although they had won only 20 of the 42 state Senate seats, refused to seat two Republicans. With the lieutenant governor's tie-breaker, they voted Democrats into the seats, and proceeded in 14 minutes to declare the state Supreme Court seats vacant, abolish state boards that controlled Democratic cities, strengthen the power of the governor and reorganize state government to purge Republicans. This ended the direct political control of Rhode Island's "Five Families"—the Browns, Metcalfs, Goddards, Lippitts and Chafees—who owned or ran many of the textile mills, the Rhode Island Hospital Trust (long the largest bank), the Providence *Journal-Bulletin*, Brown University, the Rhode Island School of Design and the state Republican Party; they ultimately lost the leadership of Rhode Island politics to the heirs of the 1935 Green revolution. The Democrats have won most elections with the lion's share of votes from Rhode Island's 64% Catholic majority, starting with Green's election in 1936 at age 69 to the first of his four terms as U.S. senator. From 1940–80, Democrats won every election for U.S. House seats; its Democratic percentages in presidential elections from 1968–92 were rivalled only by Massachusetts. Republicans have won when they've been able to capitalize on scandal or Democratic disarray, as Governor Lincoln Almond did in 1994. But the only really durable Republican politician has been John Chafee, elected governor in 1962, 1964 and 1966, senator in 1976, 1982, 1988 and 1994; and even he has lost twice statewide, in 1968 and 1972.

But if Rhode Island's national politics are mostly stable and Democratic, its state politics have been bipartisan and antic. The state's economy was transformed, not without some distress, from blue collar to white collar, from textiles to high tech. The recession of the early 1990s hit hard here, and Rhode Island lost population, falling below the one million mark in 1996; but that year the unemployment rate was under the national average and tourism was booming in southern

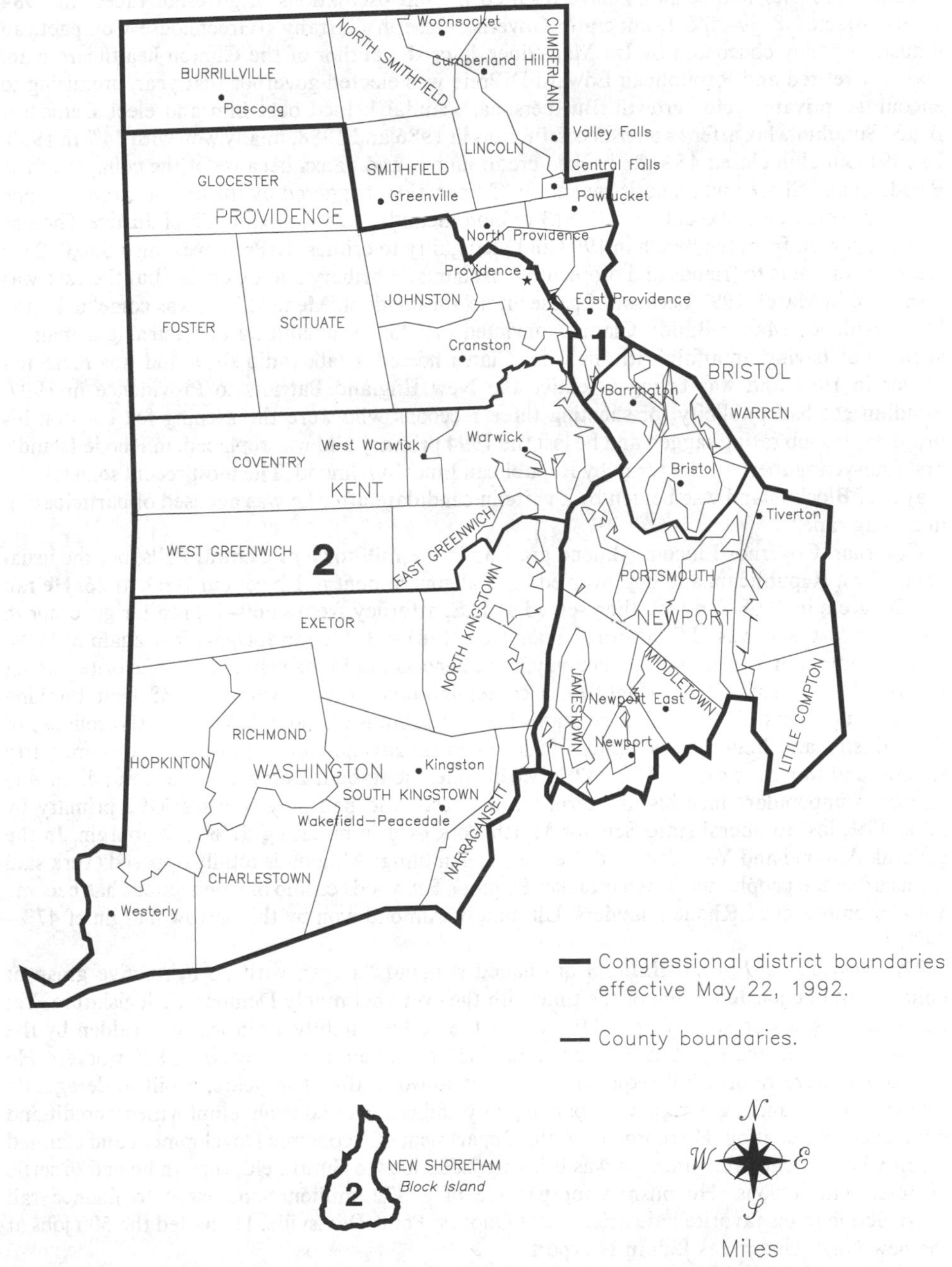
Woonsocket
NORTH SMITHFIELD
CUMBERLAND
Cumberland Hill
BURRILLVILLE
Pascoag
Valley Falls
LINCOLN
Central Falls
GLOCESTER
SMITHFIELD
Greenville
Pawtucket
PROVIDENCE
North Providence
Providence
JOHNSTON
East Providence
FOSTER
SCITUATE
Cranston
1
BRISTOL
Barrington
WARREN
West Warwick
Warwick
COVENTRY
Bristol
KENT
Tiverton
EAST GREENWICH
WEST GREENWICH
2
PORTSMOUTH
NORTH KINGSTOWN
NEWPORT
EXETOR
MIDDLETOWN
JAMESTOWN
Newport East
LITTLE COMPTON
Newport
RICHMOND
HOPKINTON
WASHINGTON
Kingston
SOUTH KINGSTOWN
Wakefield-Peacedale
NARRAGANSETT
CHARLESTOWN
Westerly
Congressional district boundaries effective May 22, 1992.
County boundaries.
N
W
E
S
NEW SHOREHAM
Block Island
2
Miles
0 1 2 3 4

Rhode Island. Unions remained politically powerful, though they lost many members, and the legislature remains the most Democratic in the nation: 41–9 in the Senate, 84–16 in the House.

Policy debacles and scandals have resulted in wild oscillations in governor races. In 1984 voters rejected 80%–20% Democratic Governor Joseph Garrahy's Greenhouse Compact, an industrial policy concocted by Ira Magaziner, later the author of the Clinton healthcare plan. Garrahy retired and Republican Edward DiPrete was elected governor that year, promising to encourage private sector growth. But personal scandal helped oust him and elect Democrat Bruce Sundlun who, after two unsuccessful runs in 1986 and 1988, finally won with 74% in 1990. In 1991 Sundlun closed 45 state-backed credit unions and banks because of the collapse of the Rhode Island Share and Deposit Indemnity Corporation, triggered by the disappearance of one mob-connected bank executive with $13 million. Scandal was rampant: Chief Justice Thomas Fay was forced from the bench in 1993 and pled guilty to crimes; DiPrete was fined $30,000 for steering contracts to friends and prosecuted on counts of bribery and extortion, but the case was dismissed in March 1997 because of prosecutors' misconduct. Meanwhile it was comeback time for Providence Mayor Buddy Cianci, convicted in 1984 of assaulting and burning a man he accused of having an affair with his wife; Cianci hosted a talk radio show and was reelected mayor in 1994 and was trying to entice the New England Patriots to Providence in 1997. Sundlun got bad publicity for shooting three raccoons who were threatening fox cubs on his property; his job rating sagged and he lost the 1994 primary and was replaced, in Rhode Island's first four-year gubernatorial term, by Republican Lincoln Almond. The most recent scandal: the mayor of Block Island was beaten by a write-in candidate after he was accused of participating in a gang rape.

Governor. Governor Lincoln Almond grew up in the mill town of Central Falls, not the usual venue for a Republican, and got involved in local government in Lincoln in 1963, at 26. He ran for Congress in 1968 and lost, then served as U.S. attorney from 1969–78, ran for governor in 1978 and lost, and was U.S. attorney again from 1981–93. He ran for governor again in 1994, and this time won. It was an upset not only in the general but in the primary. The favorite was 1st District Congressman Ron Machtley, a career military veteran who in 1988 beat Banking Chairman Fernand St Germain, the man whose lax savings and loan laws led to the collapse of the industry and hundreds of billions in losses to taxpayers. But Almond rallied more party support and won the primary 58%–42%. Meanwhile, incumbent Democrat Bruce Sundlun, who had been unpopular since his first-term tax increases and had only won his 1992 primary by 52%–48%, lost to liberal state Senator Myrth York by a humiliating 57%–27% margin. In the general, Almond and York disputed over casino gambling: Almond is totally opposed, York said it was up to the people; the Mashantucket Pequot's Foxwoods casino in Connecticut has become a major employer of Rhode Islanders. Ultimately, Almond won by the narrow margin of 47%–44%.

The Providence *Journal-Bulletin* has called Almond "a man with no instinctive grasp of politics" and he jousted much of the time with the overwhelmingly Democratic legislature. Yet he made progress on some fronts. His veto of the budget in July 1996 was overridden by the legislature, but he managed to reduce the number of state employees by about 800 workers. He signed a welfare reform bill requiring recipients to work after two years, a bill to deregulate electric utilities and a gay rights bill banning discrimination in housing, employment, credit and public accommodation. He reorganized the Department of Economic Development and claimed credit when Fidelity announced it was bringing 2,500 jobs to Smithfield, though he had to settle disputes with unions. He pushed for passage of a $72 million bond issue to finance rail construction to his favorite industrial site at Quonest Point-Davisville. He hailed the 500 jobs at the new Navy Underseas Lab in Newport.

Almond's FY98 budget provided for a 9% income tax cut over five years, an R&D investment tax credit, and a new formula for distributing state educational aid. Whether Democrats would accept that was unclear. Spending has not always produced results: Rhode Island is one of the top per-capita spenders on education, but ranks 45th in SAT scores. In January 1997 Democrats angered Almond when they rejected Supreme Court appointee Margaret Curran and they argued that he had no right to appoint a new lieutenant governor when incumbent Robert Weygand retired to serve in Congress; Almond appointed Bernard Jackvony anyway and the state Supreme Court upheld him. Almond has announced he is running for reelection in 1998. Possible opponents include 1994 nominee Myrth York and Senate Majority Leader Paul Kelly.

Senior Senator. John Chafee was first elected governor in 1962 and senator in 1976. He grew up a scion of one of Rhode Island's Five Families, left Yale to enlist in the Marine Corps and served at Guadalcanal, was recalled to active duty in 1951 and commanded a rifle company in Korea. He was elected to the legislature as a young lawyer, in 1956; ran for governor in 1962, and beat a Democratic incumbent by 398 votes; was reelected by wide margins in 1964 and 1966. For all his popularity, this Republican has had electoral setbacks in this Democratic state: he was defeated for a fourth term as governor in 1968 and, after three years as Richard Nixon's secretary of the Navy, he lost the 1972 Senate race to Pell. But he won an open Senate seat in 1976, was reelected with just 51% in the recession year of 1982, won with 55% in 1988 over Lieutenant Governor Richard Licht, whose uncle had defeated him 20 years before, and was reelected with 65% in 1994, carrying every city and town.

Chafee's voting record is roughly at midpoint in the Senate, a bit more liberal on cultural issues, a bit more conservative on foreign and defense policy. But he can also be a tough and stubborn Republican partisan. He is knowledgeable, thoughtful, widely respected, an unassuming hard worker not given to political cheap shots. When he started in politics, Rhode Island was a heavy union state, and he has supported measures like family and medical leave; he sided with the Clinton Administration on some early budget votes, but joined with relish the Republican filibuster against the 1993 Clinton stimulus package. He backed the 1996 Welfare Reform Act after working to preserve federal child welfare and adoption assistance programs. He supported the 1995 Republican Medicaid reform, but pushed to continue it as an entitlement for pregnant women, children and the disabled. His impulse, in a Senate increasingly populated by conservative Republicans and liberal Democrats, is toward bipartisan compromise. His Chafee-Breaux compromise budget failed in May 1996, but by only a 53–46 margin, winning the support of 22 Republicans and 24 Democrats; it had a smaller tax cut than the Republican package and included an adjustment of the Consumer Price Index. On foreign policy he was cautious about intervening in Bosnia; a combat veteran, he favored repealing the ban on gays in the military. From a part of the country where Catholics have large families and Protestants preach birth control, he is pro-choice and was a vehement opponent of the "gag rule." He has worked to build the third Seawolf submarine, produced just over the line in Connecticut, and to fund the new attack submarine. He worked to repeal the luxury tax which has destroyed Rhode Island's boat-building industry (boatbuilders are not themselves rich: see John Casey's Rhode Island novel *Spartina*).

Chafee has been a leader on health care throughout the 1990s. He produced a Republican package in 1991 and co-sponsored a bill with then-Finance Committee Chairman Lloyd Bentsen in 1992, with small group insurance reform, more portability, managed care and 100% deductibility for the self-employed. This was swept aside by the Clinton healthcare bill in 1993 and 1994; there was widespread expectations that Chafee's proposals would be at the center of a bipartisan compromise. But the Clintons held fast to their approach long past the time when a compromise on this complex issue could be worked out, and Bob Dole in early 1994 switched from interest in compromise to a determination to stop the Clinton plan. But the 104th Congress saw a return to bipartisanship and Chafee worked to pass the Kassebaum-Kennedy Healthcare Portability Act in 1996. And in 1997, with Jay Rockefeller, Chafee introduced a bill to expand children's health insurance through Medicaid.

On the environment Chafee is a Republican in the conservationist tradition that goes back to Theodore Roosevelt; and he is well positioned to influence such issues, as chairman of the Environment and Public Works Committee since 1994 and ranking Republican for eight years before that. He supported the 1987 water projects bill passed over Ronald Reagan's veto, the

1988 ocean dumping law, the 1989 oil spill law and, especially, the 1990 Clean Air Act. He has been a major force for protection of wetlands and barrier islands. He has also backed billboard control, commercial fishing safety, state partnerships for wildlife preservation and the Rio treaties on global climate change and biodiversity. But he is not a down-the-line supporter of liberal environmental groups. He took the lead on reforming the Safe Drinking Water Act in 1995 and 1996, requiring cost-benefit analysis for EPA regulations and revoking its authority to set water contaminant standards every three years; the bill also provided for a $7.6 billion revolving fund for states to improve their water treatment facilities. This was passed with strong bipartisan support. On the Endangered Species Act, he favored incentives for property owners who comply with regulations but contrary to many other Republicans opposed compensation for landowners whose property value decreases as a result of regulations; no bill was passed in the 104th Congress. He opposed requiring a new nuclear waste dump in Nevada, helping to produce enough votes to uphold a Clinton veto. Although his parochial interest as chairman is to the contrary, he opposed efforts to take the transportation trust funds off-budget; this passed by a wide margin in the House but went nowhere in the Senate.

In early 1997 he called for reauthorizing the ISTEA transportation law by the fall: a mammoth project, over which there are great fights regarding funding formulas. He also is pushing legislation on the interstate transportation of solid waste. He urged his fellow Republicans to take a "realistic" approach on Superfund reform. He surprised some in late 1996 and early 1997 when he circulated letters critical of the proposed EPA air quality standards. He said that costs should be taken into account, and questioned the science behind the EPA's conclusions. He warned that regulations requiring extremely expensive steps to meet dangers not clearly visible might provoke a "revolt" against the Clean Air Act. "You overload the horse . . . and you get the whole program in jeopardy," he said.

Chafee is now considerably to the left of most Senate Republicans, and with the retirement of some moderates must feel quite lonely at times. He won the leadership post of Conference chairman back in 1984 by 28–25 vote over Jake Garn, but lost it in 1990 to Thad Cochran, 22–21. But Chafee's candor and expertise command respect even among those who disagree, and a move to deny him the Environment chairmanship in 1994 came to nothing. And in many ways the 104th Congress produced good results for his kind of bipartisanship. Chafee also had accomplishments on local issues, securing funds for the Blackstone River Valley National Heritage Corridor and the Pettaquamscutt Cove National Wildlife Refuge. He obtained $7 million for the Rhode Island freight rail project and, following the North Cape oil spill, he passed oil pollution amendments to prevent future spills. He passed bills to modify copyright requirements to expand the availability of books for the blind and for a memorial on the Mall to African-American Revolutionary War patriots. He got a reassertion of the Rhode Island Indian Claims Settlement Act of 1978, requiring state voter approval for Indian gaming; Chafee was sharply criticized on that issue by Congressman Patrick Kennedy, who has pointedly not ruled out running for Chafee's seat in 2000. But Chafee has said he has every intention of running again, and it would be unwise to bet heavily against him.

Junior Senator. Jack Reed is a Democrat elected in 1996 after six years in the House. Reed is from working-class Cranston, the son of a school custodian, a graduate of West Point who served in the 82d Airborne and taught at West Point; in 1979 he retired from the Army and went to Harvard Law School. In 1984, at 35, he beat an incumbent in the primary for state Senate, where he served for six years, was close to the party leadership and built a good reputation. When Republican Claudine Schneider left the House to run against Senator Claiborne Pell in 1990, Reed ran for the House seat, overcoming several better known candidates in the primary, and winning with 59% over Save the Bay Executive Director Trudy Coxe in the general.

Reed compiled a substantially, though not quite totally, liberal record in the House. In 1991 he worked successfully for a $180 million loan guarantee package for Rhode Island during its banking crisis. On the Education and The Workforce Committee he worked for the Goals 2000 Act, insisting on a requirement that states show gradual progress in meeting educational standards; on reauthorization of the Elementary and Secondary Education Act, he backed the "opportunity to learn" standards—spending requirements— backed by teachers' unions. He sees the federal role as "not only a matter of doing the right thing but doing the necessary thing in terms of individual opportunity but also for the competitiveness of the nation." He tried to amend the 1996 Welfare Reform Act to have block grants increase when national unemployment is over 6%. He amended the immigration reform bill to bar reentry of those who renounce U.S. citizenship to avoid taxes. Using his military experience, he criticized UN efforts in the Balkans as trying to be "all things to all people" and, before American Rangers were killed, said the Somalia mission was hampered by "poor intelligence" and "an awkward command structure." In summer 1994, after a trip to Haiti, he called for tougher economic sanctions and no military involvement; in March 1995 he said he was "pleasantly surprised" about Aristide's "apparent commitment to democratic reform." On local issues, Reed worked for the freight rail connection at Quonset Point-Davisville port and introduced legislation to require indelible country of origin markings on foreign made jewelry and jewelry boxes; Rhode Island's jewelry industry, which produces about a third of the costume jewelry in the United States, has been in decline for the past 20 years as it increasingly competes with foreign imports.

When Senator Claiborne Pell announced his retirement after 36 years in the Senate, where he chaired the Foreign Relations Committee for eight years and sponsored the Pell grants, Reed almost immediately started running. His most formidable Democratic opponent, former Providence Mayor Joseph Paolino, ran for the House instead, and lost his primary. Reed was easily nominated and faced state Treasurer Nancy Mayer in the general. National Republicans spent nearly $1 million on ads attacking Reed as a liberal for opposing workfare and for supporting labor unions; in liberal, unionized Rhode Island these did not hurt him, and may have helped. Mayer's support for campaign finance reform and opposition to soft money were parried when Reed in debate asked her why she didn't call off the Republican soft money campaign against him. She attacked him as a supporter of "pension giveaways" when he was a legislator and for being too close to teacher unions. She wanted both of them to pull all TV ads and debate in every part of the state.

But Mayer's campaign was overshadowed by Reed's: she spent $773,000 and he spent $2.7 million. His biography was his message: he launched his campaign in a school conference room named after his late father, he stressed how he came up from humble beginnings by hard work, he called for education spending to help others rise as he had. That message, and his own pleasant, unassuming demeanor evidently touched a chord. He won 63%–35%, an impressive first Senate victory. Pell, first elected at 41, served 36 years; Reed, elected just before turning 47, has every prospect of a long Senate career.

Presidential politics. Rhode Island is always among the most Democratic states in presidential elections—over the last generation, the most Democratic on average: it voted 60%–27% for Bill Clinton in 1996. Rhode Island's Catholic majority is heavily Democratic and, interestingly, pro-choice on abortion: in states where Catholics are beleaguered minorities they may stand together and strongly oppose abortion; here, where they're the strong majority and where the mostly Mediterranean Catholics have never paid much attention to the mostly Irish priests anyway, they come out against the church position—the same as Catholics in Italy.

Rhode Island holds a presidential primary the same day as Massachusetts, usually with the lowest turnout rate in the nation. It has not won much attention. In 1992 only 66,000 of the one million Rhode Islanders voted in both parties' primaries; in 1996 only 14,000 voted in the Republican primary.

Congressional Districting. The boundaries of Rhode Island's two congressional districts were altered only slightly for 1992. Providence is split and both districts are overwhelmingly Democratic.

The People: Est. Pop. 1996: 990,000; Pop. 1990: 1,003,464, down 1.3% 1990–1996. 0.4% of U.S. total, 43d largest; 14% rural. Median age: 35.8 years. 16% 65 years and over. 89.3% White, 3.4% Black, 1.8% Asian, 1% Other, 4.6% Hispanic origin. Households: 53.5% married couple families; 24% married couple fams. w. children; 43% college educ.; median household income: $32,181; per capita income: $14,981; 59.5% owner occupied housing; median house value: $133,500; median monthly rent: $416. 5.1% Unemployment. 1996 Voting age pop.: 751,000. 1996 Turnout: 390,247; 52% of VAP. Registered voters (1996): 602,692; no party registration.

Political Lineup: Governor, Lincoln Almond (R); Lt. Gov., Bernard A. Jackvony (R); Secy. of State, James Langevin (D); Atty. Gen., Jeffrey B. Pine (R); General Treasurer, Nancy J. Mayer (R). State Senate, 50 (41 D and 9 R); Senate President, Bernard A. Jackvony (R); State House, 100 (84 D and 16 R); House Speaker, John Harwood (D). Senators, John H. Chafee (R) and Jack Reed (D). Representatives, 2 (2 D).

Elections Division: 401-277-2340; **Filing Deadline for U.S. Congress:** June 24, 1998.

1996 Presidential Vote

Clinton (D)	233,050	(60%)
Dole (R)	104,683	(27%)
Perot (I)	43,723	(11%)
Other	8,674	(2%)

1996 Republican Presidential Primary

Dole (R)	9,664	(64%)
Alexander (R)	2,859	(19%)
Other	2,486	(17%)

1992 Presidential Vote

Clinton (D)	213,299	(47%)
Bush (R)	131,601	(29%)
Perot (I)	105,045	(23%)

GOVERNOR

Gov. Lincoln Almond (R)

Elected 1994, term expires Jan. 1999; June 16, 1936, Pawtucket; home, Lincoln; U. of RI, B.S. 1958, Boston U., J.D. 1961; Episcopalian; married (Marilyn).

Career: Naval Reserves, 1953–61; Practicing atty., 1962–94; Lincoln Town Admin., 1963–68; Rep. Nominee, U.S. House, 1968; U.S. Atty. for RI, 1969–78, 1981–93; Repub. nominee for Gov., 1978; Pres., Blackstone Valley Land Develop. Foundation, 1982–94.

Office: The State House, #222, Providence 02903, 401-277-2080; Fax: 401-272-0860; Web site: www.state.ri.us.

Election Results

1994 gen.	Lincoln Almond (R)	171,194	(47%)
	Myrth York (D)	157,361	(44%)
	Robert J. Healey, Jr. (I)	32,822	(9%)
1994 prim.	Lincoln Almond (R)	24,873	(58%)
	Ronald K. Machtley (R)	18,150	(42%)
1992 gen.	Bruce Sundlun (D)	261,484	(62%)
	Betty Leonard (R)	145,590	(34%)
	Others	17,744	(4%)

SENATORS

Sen. John H. Chafee (R)

Elected 1976, seat up 2000; b. Oct. 22, 1922, Providence; home, Warwick; Yale, B.A. 1947, Harvard, LL.B. 1950; Episcopalian; married (Virginia).

Career: Marine Corps, 1942–45 (WWII), 1951–53 (Korea); Practicing atty., 1952–63, 1973–75; RI House of Reps., 1956–63, Minority Ldr., 1959–63; RI Gov., 1962–69; Secy. of the Navy, 1969–72; Repub. nominee for U.S. Senate, 1972.

DC Office: 505 DSOB 20510, 202-224-2921; e-mail: senator_chafee@chafee.senate.gov.

State Offices: Providence, 401-528-5294.

Committees: *Environment & Public Works* (Chmn. of 10 R). *Finance* (2nd of 11 R): Health Care; International Trade; Social Security & Family Policy (Chmn.). *Intelligence (Select)* (2nd of 10 R). *Joint Committee on Taxation* (2nd of 5 Sens.).

Group Ratings

	ADA	ACLU	AFS	LCV	CFA	CON	NFIB	COC	ACU	NTLC	CHC
1996	40	50	29	85	50	81	86	92	60	83	23
1995	30	—	9	57	25	88	—	89	35	—	—

National Journal Ratings

	1995 LIB — 1995 CONS			1996 LIB — 1996 CONS		
Economic	51%	—	48%	52%	—	47%
Social	67%	—	32%	63%	—	34%
Foreign	50%	—	48%	43%	—	54%

Key Votes of the 104th Congress

1. Reduce Medicare Growth $	Y	5. Flag Amendment	N	9. Anti-Missile Defense	N
2. Lmt. Prod. Liab. Damages	Y	6. Endangered Species	Y	10. Cuban Embargo	Y
3. Increase Min. Wage	Y	7. Gay Employment Rights	Y	11. Bar Bosnia Troop $	N
4. Welfare Reform	Y	8. Ovrd. Part. Birth Veto	N	12. Cut Vietnam Aid	N

Election Results

1994 general	John H. Chafee (R)	222,856	(65%)	($2,086,236)
	Linda J. Kushner (D)	122,532	(35%)	($805,867)
1994 primary	John H. Chafee (R)	27,906	(69%)	
	Thomas Post (R)	12,517	(31%)	
1988 general	John H. Chafee (R)	217,273	(55%)	($2,841,985)
	Richard A. Licht (D)	180,717	(45%)	($2,735,917)

Sen. Jack Reed (D)

Elected 1996, seat up 2002; b. Nov. 12, 1949, Cranston; home, Cranston; U.S. Military Acad., West Point, B.S. 1971, Harvard, M.P.P. 1973, J.D. 1982; Catholic; single.

Career: Army, 1967–79; Assoc. Prof., U.S. Military Acad., West Point, Dept. of Soc. Sciences, 1978–79; Practicing atty., 1982–90; RI Senate, 1984–90; U.S. House of Reps., 1990–96.

DC Office: 320 HSOB 20510, 202-224-4642; Fax: 202-224-4680.

State Offices: Providence, 401-528-5200.

Committees: *Banking, Housing & Urban Affairs* (8th of 8 D): Financial Institutions & Regulatory Relief; Housing Opportunity & Community Development; International Finance. *Labor & Human Resources* (8th of 8 D): Children & Families; Public Health & Safety. *Aging (Special)* (8th of 8 D).

Group Ratings (as Member of U.S. House of Representatives)

	ADA	ACLU	AFS	LCV	CFA	CON	NFIB	COC	ACU	NTLC	CHC
1996	80	75	100	85	92	78	27	31	5	12	7
1995	90	—	—	88	100	9	—	25	12	—	—

National Journal Ratings (as Member of U.S. House of Representatives)

	1995 LIB — 1995 CONS			1996 LIB — 1996 CONS		
Economic	80%	—	18%	70%	—	28%
Social	80%	—	13%	73%	—	26%
Foreign	73%	—	24%	79%	—	19%

Key Votes of the 104th Congress (as Member of U.S. House of Representatives)

1. Reduce Medicare Growth $	N	5. Flag Amendment	N	9. Cuban Embargo	N
2. Ovrd. Product Liab. Veto	Y	6. Drop EPA Limits	Y	10. Bar Bosnia Troop $	N
3. Increase Min. Wage	Y	7. Repeal Assault-Weap. Ban	N	11. Cut Anti-Missile Defense	Y
4. Welfare Reform	N	8. Ovrd. Part. Birth Veto	N	12. Bar U.N. Uniforms	N

Election Results

1996 general	Jack Reed (D)	230,676	(63%)	($2,732,011)
	Nancy J. Mayer (R)	127,368	(35%)	($773,789)
1996 primary	Jack Reed (D)	59,336	(86%)	
	Don Gil (D)	9,554	(14%)	
1990 general	Claiborne Pell (D)	225,105	(62%)	($2,363,904)
	Claudine Schneider (R)	138,947	(38%)	($2,056,923)

FIRST DISTRICT

The 1st Congressional District is the eastern half of Rhode Island, east of Narragansett Bay, a line that cuts through Providence and then proceeds west and north to the Massachusetts-Connecticut-Rhode Island border. It includes much of Providence (including elite College Hill around Brown University) and all of next-door Pawtucket whose Slater Mill is known as the birthplace of the American Industrial Revolution. The onetime textile mill towns of the Blackstone Valley, Woonsocket and Central Falls are also in the 1st, along with high income Barrington and Bristol and, south on the ocean, the old city of Newport, with its restored 18th Century houses and the summer "cottages" that are really palaces. Newport was once home to the America's Cup races and now hosts its famous jazz festival. It is also the site of the oldest synagogue in North America. Ethnically, this district is the more French Canadian and less Italian of the two Rhode Island districts; politically, it is strongly Democratic in most elections.

The congressman from the 1st District is Patrick Kennedy, elected in 1994, one of the growing number of grandchildren of Joseph P. Kennedy who are seeking political constituencies in corners of New England. Patrick Kennedy was born in 1967, his father Ted Kennedy's fifth year in the Senate; a week after his second birthday came the terrible accident at Chappaquiddick. He had a somewhat troubled youth, spending time in a drug rehabilitation clinic in 1986 before enrolling at Providence College, at 20, in 1987. Almost immediately, in 1988, he ran for a seat in the legislature and, in one of Rhode Island's tiny districts beat the longtime incumbent with the help of his name recognition. He became chairman of the Rules Committee in 1992, a year after spending the now-infamous Easter weekend in Palm Beach with his father and cousin William Kennedy Smith. In 1994, when the 1st District's Congressman Ron Machtley ran for governor, Kennedy decided to run for Congress. Kennedy had an attractive and energetic Republican opponent, Kevin Vigilante, a doctor who worked with handicapped orphans in Romania and with female prison inmates infected with HIV. Vigilante was a moderate on issues, and raised enough to spend $803,000. But Kennedy had the advantages of money and of his family name, and won 54%–46% in a Republican year.

Rather awkwardly Kennedy took his place in the Republican 104th Congress. In a Republican House, he has had a harder time demonstrating that he is something more than one of the minor players in a family dedicated politically to redistributing others' income. He started off by avoiding national media and working on local issues, from the Naval Undersea Warfare Center in Newport to visas for Portuguese immigrants. He became co-chairman of the Portuguese-American Caucus and brought the president of Portugal to Rhode Island and visited the former Portuguese colony of East Timor. He worked to save funding for Meals on Wheels and sought tax deductibility for interest on student loans. He sponsored a bill to fund public-private partnerships on ocean research. He had a somewhat conservative record on foreign issues and voted for the Helms-Burton Act. He aggressively raised money across the country and he spent $1 million on his 1996 reelection campaign, winning 69%–28%.

Kennedy could not run for Claiborne Pell's Senate seat in 1996, since he was only 29. But he has not denied an interest in running for John Chafee's seat in 2000, and attacked Chafee sharply for supporting the Defense of Marriage Act and for blocking the Narragansett Indians from building a gambling casino without a popular vote.

The People: Pop. 1990: 501,696; 9% rural; 16% age 65+; 91% White; 3% Black; 1% Asian; 1% Other; 4% Hispanic origin. Households: 55% married couple families; 24% married couple fams. w. children; 42% college educ.; median household income: $31,675; per capita income: $15,224; median gross rent: $482; median house value: $136,400.

1996 Presidential Vote

Clinton (D)	114,858	(61%)
Dole (R)	48,964	(26%)
Perot (I)	20,287	(11%)
Other	4,304	(2%)

1992 Presidential Vote

Clinton (D)	107,141	(48%)
Bush (R)	62,758	(28%)
Perot (I)	50,842	(23%)

Rep. Patrick J. Kennedy (D)

Elected 1994; b. July 14, 1967, Brighton, MA; home, Providence; Providence Col., B.A. 1991; Catholic; single.

Career: RI House of Reps., 1988–94.

DC Office: 312 CHOB 20515, 202-225-4911; Fax: 202-225-3290.

District Offices: Pawtucket, 401-729-5600.

Committees: *National Security* (14th of 25 D): Military Personnel; Military Research & Development. *Resources* (17th of 23 D): Fisheries Conservation, Wildlife & Oceans; National Parks & Public Lands.

Group Ratings

	ADA	ACLU	AFS	LCV	CFA	CON	NFIB	COC	ACU	NTLC	CHC
1996	85	81	100	92	92	68	22	13	10	5	7
1995	90	—	—	81	100	4	—	25	16	—	—

National Journal Ratings

	1995 LIB — 1995 CONS			1996 LIB — 1996 CONS		
Economic	78%	—	21%	85%	—	11%
Social	70%	—	29%	82%	—	17%
Foreign	64%	—	34%	58%	—	42%

Key Votes of the 104th Congress

1. Reduce Medicare Growth $	N	5. Flag Amendment	N	9. Cuban Embargo	Y
2. Ovrd. Product Liab. Veto	N	6. Drop EPA Limits	Y	10. Bar Bosnia Troop $	N
3. Increase Min. Wage	Y	7. Repeal Assault-Weap. Ban	N	11. Cut Anti-Missile Defense	Y
4. Welfare Reform	N	8. Ovrd. Part. Birth Veto	Y	12. Bar U.N. Uniforms	N

Election Results

1996 general	Patrick J. Kennedy (D)	121,781	(69%)	($1,051,719)
	Giovanni D. Cicione (R)	49,199	(28%)	($23,237)
	Others	4,445	(3%)	
1996 primary	Patrick J. Kennedy (D)	unopposed		
1994 general	Patrick J. Kennedy (D)	89,832	(54%)	($1,065,597)
	Kevin Vigilante (R)	76,069	(46%)	($803,371)

SECOND DISTRICT

The 2d Congressional District is the western half of Rhode Island. While the 1st includes many mill towns, the 2d has most of its population in working and middle-class towns like Cranston and Warwick which, despite their Anglo-Saxon names, are inhabited mostly by people with Irish, Italian, French and Portuguese surnames. The 2d also has the affluent suburbs to the south along Narragansett Bay and the area around Westerly, where many residents work at the Electric Boat shipyards in Groton, Connecticut.

The congressman from the 2d District is Robert Weygand, a Democrat elected in 1996. Weygand grew up in Rhode Island, received arts and engineering degrees at the University of Rhode Island, and became a landscape architect and started his own architectural firm. He served on the East Providence Planning Board in 1978, at 30, and in 1984 was elected to the state House, where he chaired the Corporations Committee and worked on land use, lead poisoning and nursing home legislation. In 1992 and 1994 he was elected lieutenant governor, where he worked on small business and elderly care programs. But he made his political name in 1991 as a state representative, when he was offered a city architectural contract for a $1,750 kickback by Pawtucket Mayor Brian Sarault; Weygand immediately went to the FBI, was fitted with a listening device, went back to Sarault's office where the offer was repeated—and the FBI agents stormed in and arrested the mayor, who was sent to prison. In 1996 Weygand looked to have an easy run of it in the usually decisive Democratic primary, when Joseph Paolino, former Providence mayor and recently resigned ambassador to Malta, left the Senate race and ran in the 2d District. Paolino called for a crackdown on illegal immigration, a phasing out of bilingual education and making English the official language. He outmaneuvered Weygand to get the party endorsement at the state convention, partly because of Weygand's opposition to abortion, and was backed by Providence Mayor Buddy Cianci, Congressman and Senate candidate Jack Reed, Congressman Patrick Kennedy and 1994 gubernatorial nominee Myrth York. Paolino spent liberally of his own money and seemed well ahead. But Weygand had resources of his own. He was supported by Rhode Island's usually outnumbered right-to-lifers and by many labor unions. He ran an ad in which actors portraying figures in *The Maltese Falcon* made fun of Paolino for giving up his ambassadorship. He accused Paolino of hiring relatives in his last days as mayor. In something of a shocker, Weygand won the primary 48%–38%. Paolino carried Providence and next-door Johnston, plus heavily Italian-American Westerly, but Weygand carried everything else.

In the general Weygand had spirited opposition from Republican Rick Wild, but Weygand's constant averrals of opposition to Newt Gingrich and his advocacy of affordable education and long-term health care propelled him far ahead. Wild called him a "lackey of the union bosses"—not a negative in Rhode Island. Weygand won 64%–32%, carrying every city and town. He is likely to be a strong liberal vote in the House, except on abortion and Indian casino gambling. In 1997, Weygand pressed for reauthorization of the Older Americans Act, which provides funding for social and nutritional programs for the low-income elderly, and he introduced a bill to expand home-based business tax deductions.

The People: Pop. 1990: 501,768; 19% rural; 14% age 65+; 88% White; 4% Black; 2% Asian; 1% Amer. Indian; 5% Hispanic origin. Households: 55% married couple families; 25% married couple fams. w. children; 43% college educ.; median household income: $32,729; per capita income: $14,739; median gross rent: $498; median house value: $129,500.

1996 Presidential Vote

Clinton (D)	118,192	(59%)
Dole (R)	55,719	(28%)
Perot (I)	23,436	(12%)
Other	4,370	(2%)

1992 Presidential Vote

Clinton (D)	106,158	(46%)
Bush (R)	68,843	(30%)
Perot (I)	54,203	(23%)

Rep. Bob Weygand (D)

Elected 1996; b. May 10, 1948, Attelboro, MA; home, N. Kingstown; U. of RI, B.A. 1971, B.S. 1976; Catholic; married (Frances).

Career: Landscape Architect, 1973–93; RI House of Reps., 1984–1992; RI Lt. Gov., 1992–96.

DC Office: 507 CHOB 20515, 202-225-2735; Fax: 202-225-9580.

District Offices: Warwick, 401-732-9400.

Committees: *Budget* (18th of 19 D). *Small Business* (9th of 16 D): Government Programs & Oversight; Tax, Finance & Exports.

Group Ratings and Key Votes: Newly Elected

Election Results

1996 general	Bob Weygand (D)	118,827	(64%)	($785,547)
	Rick Wild (R)	58,458	(32%)	($416,771)
	Others	7,033	(4%)	
1996 primary	Bob Weygand (D)	19,898	(48%)	
	Joseph R. Paolino (D)	15,689	(38%)	
	Kathryn O'Hare (D)	4,876	(12%)	
	Others	904	(2%)	
1994 general	Jack Reed (D)	119,659	(68%)	($604,267)
	A. John Elliot (R)	56,348	(32%)	($224,743)

SOUTH CAROLINA

South Carolina, at times beleaguered and under attack, stands proud as one of America's great success stories. Not so long ago this state looked like an underdeveloped country: beneath a thin veneer of rich people, it was among the poorest of states in the union, with income levels less than half the national average and with high levels of illiteracy and disease. South Carolina was founded by planters from Barbados and even today there are reminders of the West Indies—the semitropical climate, the lush foliage and trademark palmettos, and the billions of damage from hurricanes, like Hugo in September 1989. But economically and culturally, South Carolina is now securely part of the booming South Atlantic region from Maryland to Florida, filling up with new retirement condominiums, factories and office buildings, giant shopping centers, and leading the nation's economic growth in the 1990s.

In South Carolina, this growth occurs atop the plantation economy built on the swampy Low Country below the Fall Line, where the great 18th and 19th Century planters built rice paddies and cultivated exotic crops like indigo in the days before cotton was king. The great wealth of these Low Country planters was destroyed by the Civil War which they, more than any other southerners, provoked. But their pride and way of life continued as did that of former slaves. As late as 1940, 43% of South Carolinians were black, most living in conditions inconceivable today. South Carolina's economic growth had started only in the 1920s, with that lowest-wage of industries, textiles. Mills were built in the Up Country above Columbia, hiring poor whites (never blacks) from the hardscrabble farms in the area. Politics remained a rough business, with harsh appeals to racial fear and economic envy, and with limited participation: in 1940, just 99,000 South Carolinians voted for president, 96% of them Democratic—the highest Democratic percentage in the nation. In the 1946 Democratic primary, the year Strom Thurmond ran for governor, only 271,000 people voted in this state of more than two million.

Now this once underdeveloped country has joined the First World. Personal incomes are near national levels; health standards are as good as those in the rest of the nation; educational achievement in some ways exceeds the national average. South Carolina was helped for some years by the military bases clustered around Charleston, by the big textile mills around Greenville and Spartanburg, and by the outmigration of Low Country blacks to big cities of the northeast. Then, starting in the 1970s, South Carolina became the most aggressive state in the South in attracting new industry. It advertised its business climate (one of the lowest rates of unionization), its taxes (low), and its willingness to meet local employers' needs (very high). It enticed French and German firms to set up major operations in the Piedmont and the Low Country, a process capped when BMW in 1992 built its first U.S. assembly plant off I-85 in Spartanburg. But even more typical are the decisions of hundreds of small employers to open plants, rent offices and create jobs in what has become one of America's more vibrant economic environments. This has happened even as federal support has diminished: the Navy pretty much pulled out of the port of Charleston in the 1980s; the Savannah River nuclear plant, including the only tritium plant in the country, closed down in 1993.

All this progress has happened even as South Carolina has been overcoming its heritage of slavery and racial segregation. Starting in the 1950s, fewer people were kept from voting by the poll tax, and turnout surged as South Carolina became competitive in the presidential elections of 1952, 1956 and 1960. Then the Civil Rights Act of 1964 and the Voting Rights Act of 1965 ended legal segregation of public accommodations and workplaces and brought blacks suddenly into the electorate. This naturally shook up South Carolina politics, though not in the way widely expected: Democrats hoped to build biracial majorities, and sometimes did, but overall South Carolina moved, more than any other state in the South, toward the Republicanism exemplified by its native son, the late Republican National Chairman Lee Atwater. Republicans now hold the governorship and one Senate seat and came close to winning the other in 1992; they hold four of the state's six House seats, and have seriously contested the fifth; they won six of eight downballot state offices in 1994 and elected a Republican speaker of the House in 1995. South Carolina was one of the most heavily Republican states in presidential races in the 1980s and, thanks to a pre-Super Tuesday primary Atwater set up, was the key state in determining the Republican nominees in 1988 and 1996.

Republicans understand that they are not likely to win many votes from the 30% of South Carolinians who are black, but their most successful leaders have avoided confrontation and have sought to bring blacks within their coalition. Leading the way was Senator Strom Thurmond, the once fierce segregationist who left the Democratic Party in 1964 to become a Republican; in the early 1970s he became the first southern senator to hire black staffers and make black patronage appointments. Another was Carroll Campbell, an Atwater ally elected congressman in 1978 and governor in 1986 and 1990, a policy activist who stressed race-free issues. He sought black votes while gaining near-unanimous white support by emphasizing economic growth and education reform, against a background of a relaxed acceptance of patriotism and traditional values in a world that, even in South Carolina, has been moving away from old traditions.

Some of these traditions are hard to break away from however, as illustrated by Shannon Faulkner's two and a half years of legal wrangling to attend the all male Citadel military college, her subsequent withdrawal, and the departure of two other women because of illegal hazing and relentless harassment. And Republican Governor David Beasley's toughest issue has been whether to continue flying the Confederate battle flag over the state Capitol, as it has been since

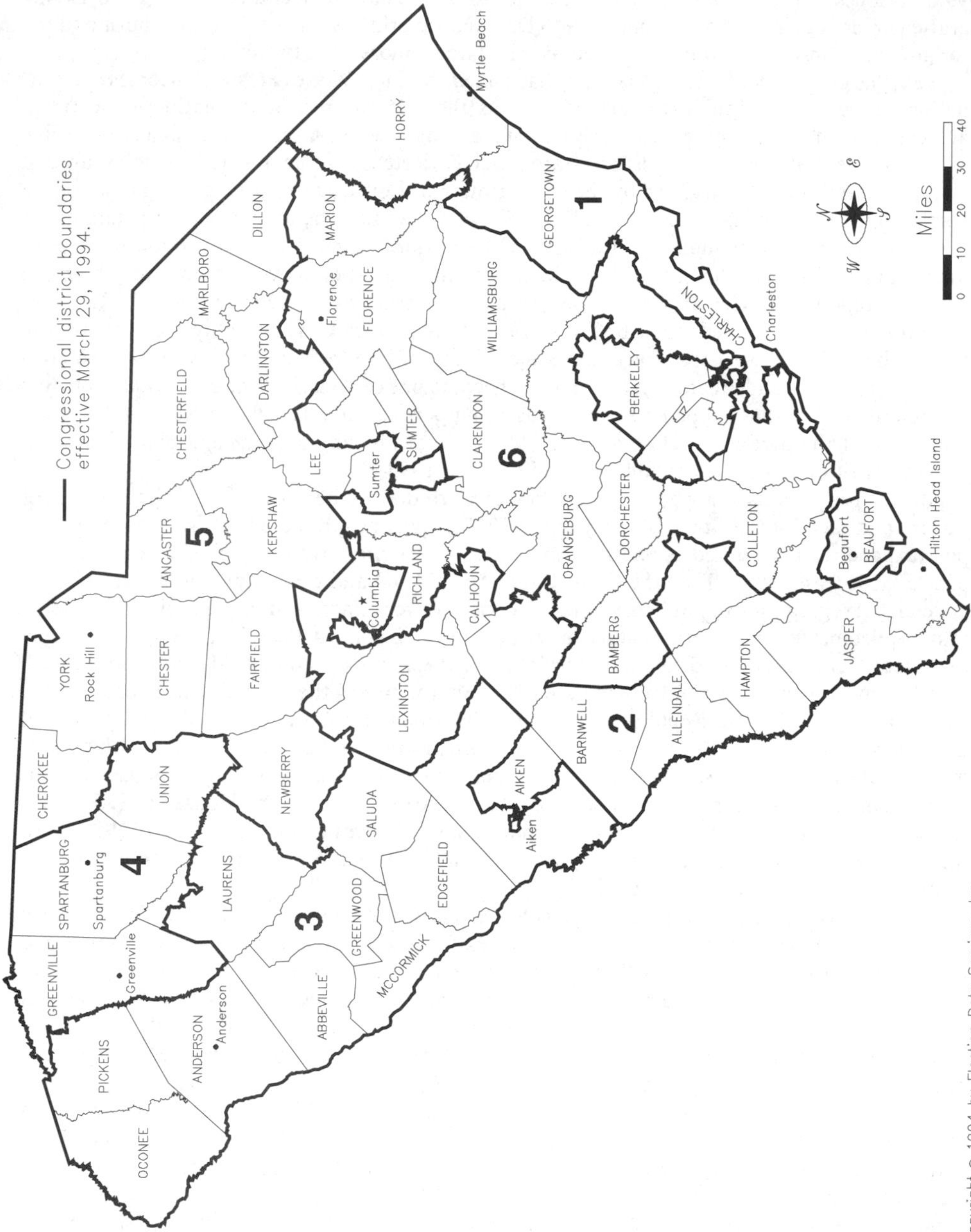
Congressional district boundaries
effective March 29, 1994.
HORRY
Myrtle Beach
GEORGETOWN
1
DILLON
MARION
MARLBORO
FLORENCE
Florence
WILLIAMSBURG
CHARLESTON
Charleston
BERKELEY
CHESTERFIELD
DARLINGTON
LEE
SUMTER
Sumter
CLARENDON
6
LANCASTER
5
KERSHAW
RICHLAND
Columbia
CALHOUN
ORANGEBURG
DORCHESTER
COLLETON
BEAUFORT
Beaufort
Hilton Head Island
YORK
Rock Hill
CHESTER
FAIRFIELD
LEXINGTON
BAMBERG
BARNWELL
2
ALLENDALE
HAMPTON
JASPER
CHEROKEE
UNION
NEWBERRY
AIKEN
Aiken
SALUDA
SPARTANBURG
Spartanburg
4
LAURENS
3
GREENWOOD
EDGEFIELD
MCCORMICK
GREENVILLE
Greenville
ANDERSON
Anderson
ABBEVILLE
PICKENS
OCONEE
N
S
E
W
Miles
0
10
20
30
40

1962. In 1994 he called for keeping it there and that position was supported 3–1 by Republican primary voters in a referendum that same year. But in November 1996 Beasley went on TV and called for moving the battle flag to a separate Confederate memorial on the Capitol grounds, a compromise which had passed the state Senate in 1994. Beasley said his mind had been changed by reflecting in prayer on church arsons, the drive-by shooting of three black teenagers and KKK scrawls on walls, and he denounced "hate-filled cowards" who dishonored the heritage the flag commemorates. Beasley's move united Democrats and blacks and split Republicans and whites; statewide polls showed a plurality for moving the flag, but a majority of Republican voters against. In January 1997 the state House passed a bill calling for a November 1997 referendum; the state Senate ignored that proposal and passed a bill that protected Confederate monuments. The state House, in turn, shelved that bill, ending any legislative attempt to deal with the issue for 1997.

Whatever the result, it can be said that South Carolina is facing the tensions between its traditions more squarely than any other southern state. And in some ways more gracefully. It is the host to all sorts of gatherings, from Charleston's Spoleto Festival to Darlington's Southern 500 stock car race to Renaissance Weekend at Hilton Head, where Bill and Hillary Rodham Clinton spend every New Year's with hundreds of friends in gatherings hosted by onetime Democratic gubernatorial candidate and now a labor management consultant, Phil Lader. It is pulsing with economic activity and its students' test scores are rising above national averages. If it still argues with vehemence about the past, it is also entitled to look forward with some confidence to the future.

Governor. South Carolina's governor is David Beasley, a Democrat-turned-Republican elected in 1994. Beasley grew up in Lamar, in Darlington County. As a Clemson junior in 1978, at 20, he was elected to the state House and served 14 years, rising to majority leader and becoming chairman of the Education and Public Works Committee. But the key event in his life, as he tells it, was his born-again religious experience in 1984—not a political liability in a state where 55% of voters said they shared those views. In 1994, he ran for governor, with the clear support of outgoing incumbent Carroll Campbell and open support from the Christian right. In the Republican primary, Beasley faced flamboyant Charleston Congressman Arthur Ravenel and former Congressman Tommy Hartnett, who had won 47% against Senator Ernest Hollings in 1992. In a Republican primary that attracted 253,000 voters, almost as many as the Democrats' 261,000, Beasley won 47% to 32% for Ravenel and 21% for Hartnett. Ravenel called the runoff a battle "for the soul" of the Republican Party; Beasley said this was "Christian-bashing," and won the runoff 58%–42%. Among Democrats, former Lieutenant Governor Nick Theodore had 49.6% to 38% for Charleston Mayor Joe Riley, Jr. In the general election, the affable, mature Theodore carried Charleston County and Columbia—cities where Republicans usually run strong—but the fervent, young Beasley made inroads in rural areas and carried the Greenville-Spartanburg I-85 corridor solidly. This was a battle along cultural lines: Theodore carried 92% of blacks, Beasley 80% of the white religious right; Beasley carried young voters, while Theodore won those with graduate school degrees. Beasley's margin may have been only 50%–48%, but the Republican tide extended to most statewide offices and resulted in the election of Republican House Speaker David Wilkins.

Despite his narrow margin, Beasley embarked on an ambitious program. He cut spending, from Campbell's already tough levels, on everything but education and commerce; passed an enterprise zone act; passed tough sentences and two-strikes-you're-out for violent offenders; passed welfare reform with a time limit on benefits and mandatory job training. He attempted to change the culture of welfare social workers from check-cutting to career counseling, and for 1997 wants to pass a statewide education technology plan. He hailed South Carolina for creating 50,000 new jobs, cutting 11,000 families from the welfare rolls and cutting crime sharply. His program for 1997 included higher teacher pay, raising credit requirements for high school graduation, a commission for school accountability, and tuition accounts for college.

But Beasley got the most attention in November 1996 when in an eloquent address he switched positions and called for moving the Confederate battle flag from the state Capitol and flying it in a separate Confederate memorial on the Capitol grounds. He strongly condemned racists, and insisted that the Confederate flag stood for nobler ideas. His proposal proved controversial. Blacks and most Democrats favored it, and a similar proposal passed the state Senate in 1994. But Republicans voted 3–1 in a referendum during the 1994 primary for keeping the flag on the Capitol, and Attorney General Charlie Condon and other Republican politicians spoke out angrily at Beasley. In January 1997 the House rejected Beasley's plan and voted to place it on the ballot in November 1997; the Senate opposed that, and the issue died for the year.

Polls showed pluralities of South Carolinians favoring Beasley's stand. But it splits Republicans, and raises the possibility that Beasley will have primary opposition from Condon or some other Republican—a split which may help the Democratic nominee in 1998. Democratic possibilities include Nick Theodore and House Minority Leader Jim Hodges.

Senior Senator. The most enduring figure in American politics today is Strom Thurmond. The man who was elected to his eighth term in the Senate in 1996 as a Republican was elected to the legislature as a Democrat in 1932. Thurmond grew up in the small town of Edgefield, was a teacher, coach and school superintendent, studied law under his father and was elected to the legislature at 29. In his youth he knew "Pitchfork Ben" Tillman, South Carolina governor and senator, who was born in 1847; more than half a century ago Thurmond parachuted into Normandy on D-Day having received an exemption for his age. He attended the Democratic National Convention in 1932 and voted for Franklin D. Roosevelt, and he attended the Republican National Convention in 1996 and voted for Bob Dole—64 years later. Thurmond was elected governor in 1946, ran for president in 1948 as a "States' Rights Democrat" and won 39 electoral votes. He was elected senator as a write-in in 1954, resigned and ran for the seat again in 1956. In March 1996, at 93, he became the oldest person ever to serve in Congress; on May 25, 1997, he became the longest-serving senator in history.

Thurmond switched to the Republican Party to support Barry Goldwater in 1964, which means that by 1996 he had been a Democrat 32 years and a Republican 32 years in his political career. His party switch seemed unwise at the time but proved sentient about the direction of opinion; in 1968, Thurmond provided key backing to hold the South for Richard Nixon at the Republican National Convention. Thurmond has combined a reputation for steadfastness with a flexibility and adroitness that have enabled this onetime symbol of racial segregation to prosper politically in an era of integration. In 1957, he set a record, filibustering for over 24 hours against a fair housing bill. But when South Carolina blacks started voting in large numbers after the Voting Rights Act of 1965, Thurmond shifted gears and became the first Southern senator to hire black staffers and appoint blacks to high positions (including a federal judgeship). He voted for renewal of the Voting Rights Act and the Martin Luther King Holiday. He gets more votes from blacks than most Republicans.

Thurmond has been a proud teetotaler and physical fitness buff all his life, always an appreciator of beautiful women, and still seems in surprisingly good physical health. . His first wife was 23 years his junior; after she died, he married a South Carolina beauty queen 44 years younger; the first of his four children was born when he was 69. In hearings and on the Senate floor, as well as on the campaign trail, Thurmond usually seems heavily scripted and has slowed some physically, but he responds aptly to arguments and interjections and is polite and courtly. In any case, he has never been much for subtlety or nuance; his mind is simple and strong, and if he increasingly relies on staff he does so with confidence that they understand where he wants to go and will help him get there by the most direct course.

As the senior Republican in the Senate, Thurmond is president pro tempore, which puts him fourth in line for the presidency. He is chairman of the Armed Services Committee, where he works in traditional fashion with an expert staff to pass bipartisan bills. He believes that it is important to maintain high defense spending, quality of life for members of the military and speedy development of missile defense. He was ranking member of the Judiciary Committee during the fights over Supreme Court nominees Robert Bork and Clarence Thomas. He has sponsored many bills to extend the death penalty and reduce federal courts' jurisdiction over collateral attacks on state criminal convictions. He has supported some gun control measures endorsed by police, such as bans on cop-killer bullets and plastic guns. He is a stickler for ethics, supporting outside income limits for senators, bans on lobbying for federal projects on a contingent fee basis and lobbying for foreign countries by former federal officials. He backs the use of fetal tissue in research; one of his daughters has diabetes, research on which requires such material.

Thurmond's popularity remained high in South Carolina as he sought reelection in 1996 at age 93, but polls also showed that a majority thought it was time for him to retire. His last tough challenge was from businessman Charles Ravenel in 1978, when he got 56%; Thurmond won with 67% and 64% in 1984 and 1990. In the 1996 primary he had opposition from Harold Worley, a state legislator and developer from the Grand Stand along Myrtle Beach. Worley spent $600,000 of his own money and said that Thurmond was "simply too old." Thurmond won 61%–30%, carrying everything but Worley's home base of Horry County. In the general, Thurmond faced Elliott Close, 43-year-old scion of the Springs Mills textile family. Thurmond campaigned actively, shaking hands and speaking from note cards; he has refused to debate since 1950. He got a bit tough with Close. "It might have been more in order for him to run for the town council of Fort Mill," he said. "It would take my opponent 60 years to catch up with what I can do in the next six years." And "I'm a conservative and he's a liberal, from all I hear about him. He's got the money, but I've got the experience." Close spent $944,000 of his own money on a stumbling campaign that had three different managers. He boasted that his family's mill never laid off workers during the Depression, just one week before it closed three mills and laid off 850 workers. Close focused on Thurmond's age and alleged infirmness: "Is Strom Thurmond still up to the job? . . . Vote for our future, not for our past." Thurmond supporters like Carroll Campbell bellowed in rage, but the attacks on age didn't seem to have a huge impact. During the fall Thurmond was running in the low 50s in polls, and on election day he won 53%–44%. He carried all the bigger metropolitan areas and lost mainly low-income rural counties. He has said he will not run again, and if he serves out his term he will turn 100 one month before he retires.

Junior Senator. Ernest Hollings, approaching 30 years in the Senate, is still the junior senator from South Carolina—the longest-serving junior senator in history. Hollings grew up in Charleston, in moderate not aristocratic circumstances, graduated from The Citadel and served in the Army in World War II. Returning home, he worked as a trial lawyer and was elected to the legislature in 1948, at 26, was a member of the leadership two years later; he was elected governor in 1958 at 36, serving as South Carolina first faced school desegregation, and then spent four years out of office until he beat another former governor in the 1966 Senate race. Hollings has one of the quickest and sharpest tongues in the Senate and his instinct for zeroing in on others' weaknesses can be directed at the strong as well as the weak. Hollings has had his disappointments. His campaign for president fell flat in 1984, and after he was the only South Carolinian to vote against the Gulf war, he suddenly found himself with a sharply lowered job rating after enjoying years of top-level, positive visibility.

In the 1980s Hollings concentrated on budget issues, arguing for a budget freeze in the early 1980s and co-sponsoring in 1985 the Gramm-Rudman-Hollings deficit-cutting bill, which did in fact lead to lower deficits. He strongly backs the line-item veto and was one of 19 Senate Democrats to vote for it in 1995. In 1993 he argued for a value-added tax as an alternative to the Clinton tax increases. Overall, Hollings believes in an activist but disciplined government, disagreeing with Republicans on the former and Democrats on the latter. In the Democratic Senate, his voting record was usually middle-of-the-road; in the Republican Senate, it is off some distance to the left.

In the 1990s Hollings has concentrated on telecommunications issues, as chairman or ranking minority member on the Commerce Committee and its Communications Subcommittee.

Telecom issues were probably the most intellectually demanding and certainly the most heavily lobbied issues in Congress during those years, and Hollings managed to keep an even keel—and to get legislation passed. Hollings's instinct is to regulate at the federal level, which puts him at odds with many trends of the times. He was the major opponent of deregulating broadcasting and a major proponent of the 1992 Cable Reregulation Act, the one law on which Congress overrode President Bush's veto. But he has also been the most persistent backer of telecommunications reform, for more competition between long distance companies and the regional Bells. He first raised the issue in the early 1990s, then worked hard as a bill passed the House in 1994; but it died in the Senate because Hollings insisted that regional Bell companies get actual competition in local service before they were permitted to enter the long distance or cable markets. In 1995 and 1996, Hollings worked with new Chairman Larry Pressler to produce a bipartisan bill, which was signed into law in February 1996; at one point the measure seemed clearly dead, but Hollings helped to revive it. After that, Hollings and other leading sponsors insisted on FCC rather than state regulation of the rates regional Bells could charge long distance companies for interconnecting their wires. Hollings will now have to work on these issues with new Chairman John McCain, who favors a more deregulatory approach.

Other Hollings causes include education funding, on which he has sharply opposed Republicans, and trade, on which he proclaims himself a "hawk." He shepherded a textile bill to passage in 1990, only to see it vetoed; he opposed NAFTA and caused GATT to be postponed until after the 1994 elections over the objections of then-Majority Leader George Mitchell, and then voted against. He opposes using federal tax money for private and religious schools and for counting Social Security surpluses toward the budget deficit. He has passed laws on ocean dumping and climate change. Since 1987 he has called for amending the First Amendment to allow Congress to set "reasonable limits" on campaign spending; his approach was taken up in early 1997 by Minority Leaders Tom Daschle and Dick Gephardt, but was soundly defeated in a Senate vote.

Hollings comes up for reelection in 1998, when he turns 76. In early 1997 he seemed interested in running again but faced a daunting race. South Carolina has trended Republican for years, and in 1992 Hollings won by only 50%–47% over former Congressman Tommy Hartnett, widely considered a weak opponent. Hollings could easily face a stronger one this time, notably Carroll Campbell, elected governor in 1986 and 1990, leading backer of George Bush in 1988 and Bob Dole in 1996; Campbell claims a record of activist government on education, reducing infant mortality and attracting the BMW plant to Spartanburg and has continued to have high poll ratings. In a December 1996 poll Campbell led Hollings 52%–35%. But Campbell is widely thought to be waiting for Strom Thurmond's seat instead. Already declared candidates in early 1997 were Congressman Bob Inglis, a term-limits advocate highly popular in the Greenville-Spartanburg area, and Secretary of State Jim Miles, who said he would run regardless of what Campbell does. If Hollings does not run, one possible Democrat is Congressman John Spratt.

Presidential politics. South Carolina can be said to have led the South into the Republican Party. It was the only Deep South state to vote for Richard Nixon over George Wallace in 1968 and since then has voted Democratic only once, for Jimmy Carter in 1976. It was one of the top three Republican states in 1988 and 1992; among southern states, only Mississippi in 1992 and Alabama in 1996 gave Republican nominees higher percentages. Traditional values and a booming, non-union private sector have reinforced the Republican trend.

South Carolina has also turned out to be pivotal in Republican nomination contests. In 1987 Lee Atwater purposefully scheduled the Republican primary here for the Saturday before Super Tuesday, and in 1988, George Bush won a smashing victory over Bob Dole and Pat Robertson, forecasting the southern sweep that clinched his nomination. In 1992, Bush won with two-thirds of the vote, squashing Pat Buchanan's claims to represent the South. And in 1996, former Governor Carroll Campbell and Governor David Beasley led a grass-roots campaign that gave Bob Dole, after his disappointing showings elsewhere, an impressive 45%–29% victory over Buchanan March 9. Steve Forbes and Lamar Alexander trailed with 13% and 10%, essentially ending their candidacies, and Dole was able to follow up with victories over Buchanan everywhere else.

The Democrats in contrast have sought to deflect attention from a primary whose turnout can be more than 50% black. Their 1988 caucus, scheduled after Super Tuesday, was won by Jesse Jackson, who was born in South Carolina and was briefly registered to vote there after his 1984 campaign. In 1992, Democrats voted the same day as Republicans, and gave Bill Clinton a huge margin.

Congressional districting. The Voting Rights Act amendments of 1982 were interpreted to require creation of a black-majority district in South Carolina, and the plan adopted in May 1992 stitches together black majority areas in the Low Country (but not the condominium-glutted coast) and in Columbia and Charleston to create the 6th District. The plan made the 1st, 2d, 3d and 5th Districts more Republican. After the Supreme Court's *Shaw v. Reno* case, that plan was overturned by a federal court in July 1993; the legislature passed a plan the following March with only minor changes for 1994. That version came under scrutiny in 1997, but no major changes are expected even if the current lines are overturned.

The People: Est. Pop. 1996: 3,699,000; Pop. 1990: 3,486,703, up 6.1% 1990–1996. 1.4% of U.S. total, 26th largest; 45% rural. Median age: 34.4 years. 12% 65 years and over. 68.5% White, 29.7% Black, 1% Asian, 1% Hispanic origin. Households: 56.4% married couple families; 27% married couple fams. w. children; 39% college educ.; median household income: $26,256; per capita income: $11,897; 69.8% owner occupied housing; median house value: $61,100; median monthly rent: $276. 6.0% Unemployment. 1996 Voting age pop.: 2,771,000. 1996 Turnout: 1,151,689; 42% of VAP. Registered voters (1996): 1,814,776; no party registration.

Political Lineup: Governor, David M. Beasley (R); Lt. Gov., Bob Peeler (R); Secy. of State, Jim Miles (R); Atty. Gen., Charles M. Condon (R); Treasurer, Richard Eckstrom (R); Comptroller General, Earle E. Morris (D). State Senate, 46 (26 D and 20 R); Senate President, Bob Peeler (R); State House, 124 (53 D, 69 R, 1 I and 1 vancancy); House Speaker, David Wilkins (R). Senators, Strom Thurmond (R) and Ernest F. (Fritz) Hollings (D). Representatives, 6 (4 R and 2 D).

Elections Division: 803-734-9060; **Filing Deadline for U.S. Congress:** March 30, 1998.

1996 Presidential Vote

Clinton (D)	506,283	(44%)
Dole (R)	573,458	(50%)
Perot (I)	64,386	(6%)

1992 Presidential Vote

Bush (R)	577,508	(48%)
Clinton (D)	479,514	(40%)
Perot (I)	138,782	(12%)

1996 Republican Presidential Primary

Dole (R)	124,904	(45%)
Buchanan (R)	80,824	(29%)
Forbes (R)	35,039	(13%)
Alexander (R)	28,647	(10%)
Other	7,327	(3%)

GOVERNOR

Gov. David M. Beasley (R)

Elected 1994, term expires Jan. 1999. b. Feb. 26, 1957, Lamar; home, Society Hill; Clemson U., 1975–78; U. of SC, B.A. 1979, J.D. 1983; Baptist; married (Mary).

Career: Practicing atty., 1983–94; SC House of Reps., 1978–92

Office: P.O. Box 11369, The State House, Columbia 29211, 803-734-9818; Fax: 803-734-1598; Web site: www.state.sc.us.

Election Results

1994 gen.	David M. Beasley (R)	470,756	(50%)
	Nick A. Theodore (D)	447,002	(48%)
	Others	17,128	(2%)
1994 runoff	David M. Beasley (R)	134,297	(58%)
	Arthur Ravenel, Jr. (R)	98,915	(42%)
1994 prim.	David M. Beasley (R)	119,724	(47%)
	Arthur Ravenel, Jr. (R)	81,129	(32%)
	Tommy Hartnett (R)	52,866	(21%)
1990 gen.	Carroll A. Campbell, Jr. (R)	528,831	(69%)
	Theo Mitchell (D)	212,034	(27%)
	Others	20,100	(3%)

SENATORS

Sen. Strom Thurmond (R)

Elected 1956, seat up 2002; b. Dec. 5, 1902, Edgefield; home, Aiken; Clemson U., B.S. 1923; Baptist; separated.

Career: Army, 1942–46 (WWII), Army Reserves, 1923–59; Teacher & coach, 1923–29; Edgefield Cnty. Supervisor of Educ., 1929–33; Practicing atty., 1930–38, 1951–55; SC Senate, 1933–38; Circuit Judge, 1938–42; SC Gov., 1947–51; States' Rights candidate for U.S. Pres., 1948; U.S. Senate, 1954–56; Pres. Pro Tem, U.S. Senate, 1981–87.

DC Office: 217 RSOB 20510, 202-224-5972; Fax: 202-224-1300; e-mail: senator@thurmond.senate.gov.

State Offices: Aiken, 803-649-2591; Charleston, 803-727-4282; Columbia, 803-765-5494; Florence, 803-662-8873.

Committees: *President Pro-Tempore. Armed Services* (Chmn. of 10 R). *Judiciary* (2nd of 10 R): Administrative Oversight & the Courts; Antitrust, Business Rights & Competition; Constitution, Federalism & Property Rights. *Veterans' Affairs* (2nd of 7 R).

Group Ratings

	ADA	ACLU	AFS	LCV	CFA	CON	NFIB	COC	ACU	NTLC	CHC
1996	5	17	0	0	14	32	97	92	95	100	100
1995	0	—	0	0	0	52	—	100	96	—	—

National Journal Ratings

	1995 LIB — 1995 CONS			1996 LIB — 1996 CONS		
Economic	12%	—	84%	26%	—	69%
Social	0%	—	88%	0%	—	72%
Foreign	8%	—	81%	0%	—	74%

Key Votes of the 104th Congress

1. Reduce Medicare Growth $	Y	5. Flag Amendment	Y	9. Anti-Missile Defense	Y
2. Lmt. Prod. Liab. Damages	Y	6. Endangered Species	N	10. Cuban Embargo	Y
3. Increase Min. Wage	Y	7. Gay Employment Rights	N	11. Bar Bosnia Troop $	N
4. Welfare Reform	Y	8. Ovrd. Part. Birth Veto	Y	12. Cut Vietnam Aid	Y

Election Results

1996 general	Strom Thurmond (R)	619,739	(53%)	($2,632,682)
	Elliott Springs Close (D)	510,810	(44%)	($1,913,574)
	Others	30,419	(3%)	
1996 primary	Strom Thurmond (R)	132,157	(61%)	
	Harold Worley (R)	65,670	(30%)	
	Charlie Thompson (R)	20,188	(9%)	
1990 general	Strom Thurmond (R)	482,032	(64%)	($2,333,689)
	Robert H. Cunningham (D)	244,112	(33%)	($6,232)
	Others	24,122	(3%)	

Sen. Ernest F. (Fritz) **Hollings (D)**

Elected 1966, seat up 1998; b. Jan. 1, 1922, Charleston; home, Charleston; The Citadel, B.A. 1942, U. of SC, LL.B. 1947; Lutheran; married (Peatsy).

Career: Army, 1942–45 (WWII); Practicing atty., 1947–55, 1963–66; SC House of Reps., 1948–54, Speaker Pro Tem, 1951–54; SC Lt. Gov., 1954–58; SC Gov., 1958–62.

DC Office: 125 RSOB 20510, 202-224-6121; Fax: 202-224-4293; e-mail: senator@hollings.senate.com.

State Offices: Charleston, 803-727-4525; Columbia, 803-765-5731, Greenville, 864-233-5366; Spartanburg, 864-585-3702

Committees: *Appropriations* (3rd of 13 D): Commerce, Justice, State & the Judiciary (RMM); Defense; Energy & Water Development; Interior; Labor, Health & Human Services & Education. *Budget* (2nd of 10 D). *Commerce, Science & Transportation* (RMM of 9 D): Aviation; Communications (RMM); Manufacturing & Competitiveness.

Group Ratings

	ADA	ACLU	AFS	LCV	CFA	CON	NFIB	COC	ACU	NTLC	CHC
1996	70	29	71	77	79	12	38	46	20	17	7
1995	75	—	91	86	69	19	—	37	35	—	—

National Journal Ratings

	1995 LIB — 1995 CONS			1996 LIB — 1996 CONS		
Economic	60%	—	38%	87%	—	12%
Social	53%	—	43%	67%	—	30%
Foreign	56%	—	43%	60%	—	39%

Key Votes of the 104th Congress

1. Reduce Medicare Growth $	N	5. Flag Amendment	Y	9. Anti-Missile Defense	Y
2. Lmt. Prod. Liab. Damages	N	6. Endangered Species	Y	10. Cuban Embargo	Y
3. Increase Min. Wage	Y	7. Gay Employment Rights	Y	11. Bar Bosnia Troop $	N
4. Welfare Reform	Y	8. Ovrd. Part. Birth Veto	N	12. Cut Vietnam Aid	N

Election Results

1992 general	Ernest F. (Fritz) Hollings (D)	591,030	(50%)	($4,188,829)
	Tommy Hartnett (R)	554,175	(47%)	($886,816)
	Other	35,233	(3%)	
1992 primary	Ernest F. (Fritz) Hollings (D)	unopposed		
1986 general	Ernest F. (Fritz) Hollings (D)	456,500	(63%)	($2,233,843)
	Henry D. McMaster (R)	262,886	(36%)	($584,288)

FIRST DISTRICT

Looking out across the harbor to Fort Sumter are the glorious mansions of the Battery, gazing on the same view that the hot-blooded young swells of Charleston saw in April 1861 when they fired the shots that began the Civil War. Today there are few more beautiful urban scenes in America than the pastel "single houses" of Charleston, built flush with the sidewalk, turning their shoulders to the streets, with open piazzas inside their gateways facing south to catch the breeze, lovingly restored and maintained. Charleston, founded in 1670, was blessed with one of the finest harbors on the Atlantic, at the point where, Charlestonians say, the Ashley and Cooper Rivers meet to form the Atlantic Ocean. It was one of the South's two leading cities through the Civil War. Across its docks went cargoes of rice, indigo and cotton—all cultivated by black slaves, enriching the white planters and merchants who dominated the state's economic and political life. In the years following the Civil War, Charleston became an economic backwater, enabling the old buildings to survive; now the prosperity of recent years has financed their restoration.

This old society, descended from Barbados planters and French Huguenots, Sephardic Jews and English gentry second sons, was once a leading force in American political life. The hotheads in the gallery disrupted the 1860 Democratic National Convention here so boisterously that it was adjourned and reconvened in Baltimore, while southern Democrats split off and nominated their own candidate, enabling Abraham Lincoln to win with 38% of the popular vote. South Carolina's blacks also have a lively history. There were free blacks here before the Civil War (some even owned slaves themselves), and Charleston's historic black culture was memorialized in George Gershwin's *Porgy and Bess*. The local accent, which seems to outsiders to have a touch of New Jersey and which can be incomprehensible when rapidly spoken, is best appreciated in the speech of Charlestonian Senator Ernest Hollings.

Some 25 years ago, the Charleston area depended heavily on its big Navy and Air Force bases, which accounted for 20% of regional payrolls. In the years since, Charleston has lost most of the bases, but far from languishing it has built a vibrant private economy with lots of small companies. The tourist attractions of Charleston and beach communities have helped. Overall, the South Carolina beach from the high rises of the Grand Strand around Myrtle Beach through the eponymous hammocks of Pawleys Island south to Hilton Head with its tasteful condos, has become one of the South's favorite vacation and second home areas.

The 1st Congressional District of South Carolina, includes most of the Charleston area and much of the Low Country district. Its lines were drawn to maximize the black population of the next-door 6th; but, given the plantation heritage here, it is still 20% black. It includes the old houses of the Battery of Charleston and the beachfront and affluent suburbs strung out on high ground in all directions. It proceeds north past Pawleys Island to the Grand Strand; it runs south to Kiawah Island, but stops short of Hilton Head. About two-thirds of the voters are in metropolitan Charleston, which has produced notable leaders like Mayor Joe Riley, Jr., and Police Chief Reuben Greenberg, who is both black and Jewish and who has had legendary success fighting crime. Politically, it is solidly Republican, the more so as more new people move to the Charleston area and the Grand Strand.

The congressman from the 1st District is Mark Sanford, a Republican who was a surprise winner in 1994. Sanford grew up on a family farm in Beaufort County, went to Furman and business school, then worked in real estate finance and investment in New York City and Charleston. When 1st District incumbent Arthur Ravenel ran for governor in 1994, Sanford, with no political experience, decided at 34 to run for Congress. Sanford gave his own campaign $100,000 and ran against Congress. He called for term limits and cutting the deficit; he said citizen-legislators needed to replace career politicians; he pledged to serve only three terms, to take no PAC money, to vote for no tax increases and to refuse any salary increase until the budget was balanced. In the first primary he trailed Van Hipp, former Pentagon official and state Republican chairman, with strong political backing, by 31% to 19%; two other candidates had 17% each and Mendel Rivers, Jr., son of a former congressman and Armed Services chairman, had 12%. In the runoff Sanford emphasized his outsider status, copying some of the spots that helped elect Bob Inglis in an upset win in the 4th District in 1992. It was close, but with 55% in Charleston County, Sanford won the runoff 52%–48%. Even before the general election, Inglis and 3d District Republican nominee Lindsey Graham started holding conference calls with Sanford each week. It was a good formula: Sanford won 66% of the vote, Graham 60% and Inglis 74%.

In Congress Sanford supported the Contract with America but had a somewhat moderate record on other issues and dared to oppose the Republican leadership when he thought it was in the wrong. On Newt Gingrich's ethics problems, Sanford thought that the leaders wrongly forced a vote before the full report was released and was dismayed at the sum levied against speaker. He felt that the leadership had betrayed him into believing the amount would be akin to a "speeding ticket." "I have yet to see a $300,000 speeding ticket," Sanford said. He strongly advocated term limits and made a point of sleeping in his office and returning to his family in Charleston as soon as possible. Sanford had no Democratic opponent in 1996, and took the opportunity to advance his own alternative to Social Security, a Thrift Investment Plan. Under its terms, people receiving retirement benefits by December 1999 would continue to receive them, those then over 35 but not retired would have the option of the current system or Sanford's SSTIP, and those under 35 would go into SSTIP. That system would allow workers to choose between various safe investments and to have unlimited choice once they have accumulated enough capital to finance a minimum-wage retirement. They could choose when to retire, how much of their money to take out and whom to leave the unspent excess to after death. Social Security has long been known as the third rail in American politics—touch it and you die—but there is no evidence Sanford is in trouble in the 1st District. He seems in excellent shape to win his third and presumably last term in 1998.

The People: Pop. 1990: 581,445; 25% rural; 9% age 65+; 77% White; 20% Black; 1% Asian; 1% Hispanic origin. Households: 60% married couple families; 30% married couple fams. w. children; 48% college educ.; median household income: $28,705; per capita income: $13,112; median gross rent: $441; median house value: $75,400.

1996 Presidential Vote

Dole (R)	107,221	(55%)
Clinton (D)	74,150	(38%)
Perot (I)	11,491	(6%)

1992 Presidential Vote

Bush (R)	101,830	(53%)
Clinton (D)	63,318	(33%)
Perot (I)	26,620	(14%)

Rep. Marshall (Mark) **Sanford, Jr. (R)**

Elected 1994; b. May 28, 1960, Ft. Lauderdale, FL; home, Charleston; Furman U. B.A. 1983; U. of VA, M.B.A. 1988; Episcopalian; married (Jenny).

Career: Owner, Norton & Sanford real estate investment firm, 1992–present.

DC Office: 1223 LHOB 20515, 202-225-3407; e-mail: sanford@hr.house.gov.

District Offices: Charleston, 803-727-4175; Conway, 803-248-2660; Georgetown, 803-527-6868.

Committees: *International Relations* (17th of 26 R): Africa; Western Hemisphere. *Government Reform & Oversight* (18th of 24 R): Government Management, Information & Technology; Postal Service (Vice Chmn.). *Joint Economic Committee* (3rd of 10 Reps.).

Group Ratings

	ADA	ACLU	AFS	LCV	CFA	CON	NFIB	COC	ACU	NTLC	CHC
1996	10	25	25	23	62	89	92	81	95	88	100
1995	15	—	—	6	62	97	—	92	88	—	—

National Journal Ratings

	1995 LIB — 1995 CONS			1996 LIB — 1996 CONS		
Economic	34%	—	64%	30%	—	68%
Social	38%	—	60%	41%	—	58%
Foreign	42%	—	55%	45%	—	54%

Key Votes of the 104th Congress

1. Reduce Medicare Growth $	Y	5. Flag Amendment	Y	9. Cuban Embargo	Y
2. Ovrd. Product Liab. Veto	Y	6. Drop EPA Limits	Y	10. Bar Bosnia Troop $	Y
3. Increase Min. Wage	N	7. Repeal Assault-Weap. Ban	Y	11. Cut Anti-Missile Defense	N
4. Welfare Reform	Y	8. Ovrd. Part. Birth Veto	Y	12. Bar U.N. Uniforms	*

Election Results

1996 general	Marshall (Mark) Sanford, Jr. (R)	138,467	(96%)	($97,231)
	Others	5,226	(4%)	
1996 primary	Marshall (Mark) Sanford, Jr. (R)	unopposed		
1994 general	Marshall (Mark) Sanford, Jr. (R)	97,803	(66%)	($544,574)
	Robert Barber (D)	47,769	(32%)	($437,530)

SECOND DISTRICT

Soon after the Revolutionary War, in 1786, the South Carolina legislature decided to move the state's capital away from the Charleston aristocracy and into the Up Country interior, away from a city named after a king to a new city named after a discoverer of America: so began Columbia. The State House was built on high ground above the Congaree River in a town of one-and-a-half story houses with first floor porticoes, dormers and raised brick basements—"Columbia cottages." In 1865, General William Tecumseh Sherman's army burned everything here but the State House. In the post-Sherman years, Columbia grew slowly, with state government and the university, the Army's Fort Jackson and local insurance companies proving steady employers. In the 1970s and 1980s, it started to boom, attracting plants such as Michelin, Allied Chemical, United Technologies, FN of Belgium, DuPont and Square D. Approaching half a million in metro area population in the 1990s, Columbia is becoming a true city, and not just a village-capital.

The Columbia to which Jimmy Byrnes, after years in top posts in Democratic Washington, returned as governor to lament the *Brown v. Board of Education* decision in 1954, has trended Republican in the years since. Upwardly mobile South Carolinians, transplanted from underdeveloped rural areas to comfortable subdivisions with two-car garages, preferred Republicans first in national and then in state and local elections. Columbia voted for Eisenhower in the 1950s; in the late 1960s and 1970s, blacks were usually outnumbered by increasingly Republican whites in Columbia's Richland County and fast-growing Lexington County across the river.

South Carolina's 2d Congressional District includes most of metropolitan Columbia, except for black neighborhoods lopped off in 1992 to create a black-majority 6th District. It contains the city's affluent white neighborhoods and the spread-out towns of Richland and Lexington Counties, with their shopping centers and many churches and the Army's huge training center, Fort Jackson. The district extends south through the horse-farm area around Aiken and several lightly populated black-majority rural counties, and then includes Beaufort and Hilton Head on the coast—the former is an old town, with wonderful mansions and a history intertwined with slave plantations and the Marine Corps's Parris Island training base; the latter, made famous by Pat Conroy's novel, *The Prince of Tides*, has been developed with much meticulous attention to its natural environment, a model now for Atlantic coast condominium and vacation communities. This is a heavily Republican district: few whites vote Democratic, and since this new 2d is only 25% black, Republicans carry it almost every time.

The congressman from the 2d District is Floyd Spence, a Republican first elected in 1970 who is now chairman of the National Security Committee. Spence was a star football player and student body president at the University of South Carolina; he served as an officer in the Navy and was in the Naval Reserve until 1985. When he graduated from law school in 1956, he was elected to the state House; he switched parties and became a Republican in 1962, two years before Strom Thurmond. He narrowly lost a House race that year to a Democrat who later switched parties; then Spence was elected to the state Senate as a Republican in 1966. When the incumbent ran for governor in 1970, Spence ran again for the House seat and won. He is now tied for third in seniority among House Republicans, trailing only Joseph McDade and Philip Crane (neither of whom is a committee chairman) and tied with Bill Archer and Bill Young.

Spence has had a solidly conservative voting record. He was the first House member to sponsor the balanced budget constitutional amendment, in 1971; he served for 13 years as ranking Republican on the Ethics Committee. But his greatest energy has been devoted to military issues. He favored the defense buildup of the 1980s and called for "responsible downsizing of defense expenditures rather than drastic cuts" in the 1990s. He probes in great detail into readiness and charged in late 1994 that one-quarter of units had readiness problems. Spence became ranking Republican on National Security in 1993, and chairman in 1995. Spence of course uses his committee slots to service local bases and installations, but—as Strom Thurmond has also learned—the base closing law limits his ability to keep bases open; he may have an easier time helping the local veterans' hospital and historically black colleges and the Congaree Swamp National Monument.

As chairman, Spence has peppered the Clinton Administration with criticism even as he has managed the complex and lengthy defense authorization bills. He argues that defense cuts have been too deep, twice as deep as Clinton promised in 1992. He is worried about the erosion of the nuclear stockpile. He argues that cuts in procurement have jeopardized the technological superiority so apparent in the Gulf war. He criticized the administration for not withdrawing from Bosnia after the promised period of one year and issued a tough report on the June 1996 bombing of the Khobar Towers troop facility in Saudi Arabia. He has decried the administration policy of selling high-tech devices to China. He seized on CIA Director John Deutch's September 1996 statement that Clinton's bombings in northern Iraq left Saddam Hussein stronger than before. He has sought to increase the pace of developing missile defense, though he felt forced to drop language on that from the committee's bill after a Clinton veto.

Spence received a double lung transplant in 1988, but has seemed in fine health in the years since. He has been reelected easily, indeed has not had a Democratic opponent, since 1988.

The People: Pop. 1990: 580,624; 40% rural; 10% age 65+; 72% White; 25% Black; 1% Asian; 1% Hispanic origin. Households: 59% married couple families; 28% married couple fams. w. children; 50% college educ.; median household income: $30,500; per capita income: $13,807; median gross rent: $435; median house value: $73,400.

1996 Presidential Vote			1992 Presidential Vote		
Dole (R)	117,261	(53%)	Bush (R)	119,658	(52%)
Clinton (D)	90,871	(41%)	Clinton (D)	82,652	(36%)
Perot (I)	10,827	(5%)	Perot (I)	25,853	(11%)

Rep. Floyd D. Spence (R)

Elected 1970; b. Apr. 9, 1928, Columbia; home, Lexington; U. of SC, A.B. 1952, LL.B. 1956; Lutheran; married (Deborah).

Career: Navy, 1952–54, Naval Reserves, 1947–52, 1954–88; SC House of Reps., 1956–62; Practicing atty., 1956–70; SC Senate, 1966–70, Minority Ldr., 1966–70.

DC Office: 2405 RHOB 20515, 202-225-2452; Fax: 202-225-2455.

District Offices: Beaufort, 803-521-2530; Columbia, 803-254-5120; Estill, 803-625-3177; Hilton Head Island, 803-842-7212; Orangeburg, 803-536-4641.

Committees: *National Security* (Chmn. of 30 R): Military Procurement. *Veterans' Affairs* (4th of 16 R): Oversight & Investigations.

Group Ratings

	ADA	ACLU	AFS	LCV	CFA	CON	NFIB	COC	ACU	NTLC	CHC
1996	5	7	0	15	0	45	100	88	100	100	100
1995	0	—	—	0	8	38	—	96	92	—	—

National Journal Ratings

	1995 LIB — 1995 CONS			1996 LIB — 1996 CONS		
Economic	0%	—	74%	0%	—	82%
Social	28%	—	72%	14%	—	77%
Foreign	15%	—	73%	21%	—	72%

Key Votes of the 104th Congress

1. Reduce Medicare Growth $	Y	5. Flag Amendment	Y	9. Cuban Embargo	Y
2. Ovrd. Product Liab. Veto	Y	6. Drop EPA Limits	N	10. Bar Bosnia Troop $	Y
3. Increase Min. Wage	N	7. Repeal Assault-Weap. Ban	Y	11. Cut Anti-Missile Defense	N
4. Welfare Reform	Y	8. Ovrd. Part. Birth Veto	Y	12. Bar U.N. Uniforms	Y

Election Results

1996 general	Floyd D. Spence (R)	158,229	(90%)	($303,421)
	Maurice T. Raidford (NL)	17,713	(10%)	
1996 primary	Floyd D. Spence (R)	unopposed		
1994 general	Floyd D. Spence (R)	unopposed		($149,321)

THIRD DISTRICT

The South Carolina Up Country, many days' travel by wagon from the Low Country plantations, was first settled by Scots-Irish farmers, like the family of John C. Calhoun in the years around the Revolutionary War. The pioneers wanted to make big plantations of these forests, but the land did not always cooperate: it was often too hilly for the labor-intensive rice crop grown in the Low Country and sometimes too cold for cotton. So relatively few slaves were brought here, and the land was mostly small farms owned by whites. Today, the racial and cultural tone of Up Country South Carolina shows traces of these roots. This is a mostly white part of the South, with a hell-of-a-fella tone to daily life, an economically growing and culturally tradition-minded slice of Middle America.

The 3d Congressional District of South Carolina covers much of this territory, following the Georgia border from the government's troubled Savannah River Site all the way north to mountains on the North Carolina border. In the southern part of the 3d are a few heavily black communities, like Edgefield, where Strom Thurmond grew up and first won public office in the 1930s. But the major population center here is the increasingly affluent suburban strip linking Aiken and Augusta, Georgia. In the northern part of this district, Calhoun had his mansion and his son-in-law created Clemson University nearby. Here today, the Savannah River intersects Interstate 85, the main street of America's textile belt, one of the nation's prime economic growth areas. The politics of this area, ancestrally Democratic, has been trending Republican for years. Yankified Aiken started voting Republican for Dwight Eisenhower in the 1950s, well before Thurmond switched parties in 1964; Anderson skittered around, supporting Jimmy Carter for a while but then veering Republican again; Pickens and Oconee Counties around Clemson and the mountains are heavily Republican. The 3d District in presidential elections voted Republican not only in the 1980s but also in the 1990s.

The congressman from the 3d District is Lindsey Graham, a Republican first elected in 1994. Graham grew up in Oconee County, went to college and law school, then served in the Air Force as a prosecutor; in 1988 he returned home and practiced law, also serving as judge advocate at McEntire Air National Guard base. He was called up to active duty and served in the Gulf war. In 1992 he was elected state representative. In 1994, with the retirement of 20-year Congressman Butler Derrick, a member of the Democratic leadership who came under tough criticism in South Carolina, Graham ran for Congress. Both parties here had contested primaries, but the Republican contest attracted more voters—41,000 versus 35,000—and Graham emerged as a clear winner, with 52% of the vote. In the general he faced state Senator Jim Bryan, who won the Democratic runoff against Deborah Dorn, daughter of Derrick's predecessor in the House. Graham called for term limits, supported more defense spending and was against gays in the military. His attitude toward the Clinton Administration and the House Democratic leadership was unequivocal: "I'm one less vote for an agenda that makes you want to throw up." Bryan also campaigned as a conservative—pro-life, anti-gays in the military, against employer mandates in health care, against defense cuts, and boasted of his experience in the legislature. But Graham modeled his campaign after Bob Inglis's successful 1992 race in the next-door 4th District and won 60%–40%—a smashing victory in a district represented only by Democrats since Reconstruction.

In the House Graham made a strong though not entirely conservative voting record. He supported the Contract with America and called for lifting the tax burden on individuals and removing onerous regulations on business. He continued to be an enthusiast for term limits. But his chief legislative efforts were devoted to the Savannah River Site (SRS). This huge installation was once used to manufacture tritium for nuclear weapons. At its peak it had 35,000 jobs and, while still among the largest employers in South Carolina, it was overtaken by Westinghouse as the single largest employer in the state. Now the nuclear plant is shut down and SRS is used as a holding site for foreign nuclear waste while the government works on developing a long-term disposal. Graham strongly criticized Energy Secretary Hazel O'Leary for not developing plans for SRS and for her foreign travels, though he cheered her procurement reforms. Graham would like SRS to be used as a disposal site for surplus weapons-grade plutonium and highly-enriched uranium and as a base for the nation's nuclear stockpile, and hopes it will maintain some 15,000 jobs.

In 1996 Graham was opposed by Deborah Dorn, loser of the 1994 primary. He won 60%–39%, an almost identical margin. He is a solid favorite to be reelected in 1998.

The People: Pop. 1990: 580,873; 58% rural; 13% age 65+; 78% White; 21% Black; 1% Hispanic origin. Households: 60% married couple families; 27% married couple fams. w. children; 34% college educ.; median household income: $25,897; per capita income: $11,813; median gross rent: $326; median house value: $54,100.

1996 Presidential Vote

Dole (R)	100,390	(54%)
Clinton (D)	71,755	(39%)
Perot (I)	13,220	(7%)

1992 Presidential Vote

Bush (R)	101,962	(51%)
Clinton (D)	69,161	(35%)
Perot (I)	26,424	(13%)

Rep. Lindsey Graham (R)

Elected 1994; b. July 9, 1955, Central; home, Seneca; U. of SC, B.A. 1977, J.D. 1981; Baptist; single.

Career: Air Force, 1982–88; Air Force Reserves, 1988–present (Persian Gulf), Air Natl. Guard, 1989–present; Air Force Chief Prosecutor, 1984–88; Asst. Oconee Cnty. Atty., 1988–92; Practicing atty., 1988–94; Judge Advocate, McEntire Air Natl. Guard Base, 1989–94; Central SC City Atty., 1990–94; SC House of Reps., 1992–94.

DC Office: 1429 LHOB 20515, 202-225-5301.

District Offices: Aiken, 803-649-5571; Anderson, 864-224-7401; Greenwood, 864-223-8251.

Committees: *Education & The Workforce* (15th of 25 R): Postsecondary Education, Training & Life-Long Learning (Vice Chmn.); Workforce Protections. *International Relations* (23rd of 26 R): International Economic Policy & Trade; International Operations & Human Rights. *National Security* (25th of 30 R): Military Personnel; Military Procurement.

Group Ratings

	ADA	ACLU	AFS	LCV	CFA	CON	NFIB	COC	ACU	NTLC	CHC
1996	0	12	0	31	8	17	92	100	100	98	100
1995	5	—	—	19	0	38	—	96	96	—	—

National Journal Ratings

	1995 LIB — 1995 CONS			1996 LIB — 1996 CONS		
Economic	26%	—	67%	0%	—	82%
Social	21%	—	72%	10%	—	86%
Foreign	0%	—	85%	0%	—	79%

Key Votes of the 104th Congress

1. Reduce Medicare Growth $	Y	5. Flag Amendment	Y	9. Cuban Embargo	Y
2. Ovrd. Product Liab. Veto	Y	6. Drop EPA Limits	N	10. Bar Bosnia Troop $	Y
3. Increase Min. Wage	N	7. Repeal Assault-Weap. Ban	Y	11. Cut Anti-Missile Defense	N
4. Welfare Reform	Y	8. Ovrd. Part. Birth Veto	Y	12. Bar U.N. Uniforms	Y

Election Results

1996 general	Lindsey Graham (R)	114,273	(60%)	($644,451)
	Deborah Dorn (D)	73,417	(39%)	($128,230)
1996 primary	Lindsey Graham (R)	unopposed		
1994 general	Lindsey Graham (R)	90,123	(60%)	($551,212)
	James E. Bryan Jr. (D)	59,932	(40%)	($443,965)

FOURTH DISTRICT

A century ago, northern investors looking for sites for textile mills, looked at the Up Country of South Carolina and "were attracted by the mild climate, abundant water power, proximity to the cotton fields and plenty of native [white] labor already accustomed to a low standard of living." As mills fled New England, the textile industry became concentrated along the Southern Railway and Seaboard Coast Line tracks between Charlotte and Atlanta, especially in the Piedmont of South Carolina. The textile country might look bucolic, but Greenville, Spartanburg and the dozens of mill towns thick in the surrounding countryside were as industrial as Lancashire or the Ruhr, with mills rising up on what were once twisting woodland paths.

Today, this same stretch of land along South Carolina's Interstate 85, which parallels the Southern Railway, remains the number one textile-producing area in the United States. But it is much more than that. The number of textile and apparel jobs declined from 57,000 in the early 1970s to 42,000 in the late 1980s, from 27% of all jobs to 14%, but many more jobs were created by big companies and small. And often by foreign employers: Michelin's North American headquarters is near Greenville and BMW's one American plant is next to the airport and just off I-85. What attracts these businesses? Sometimes big tax concessions do, as with BMW. More important, overall tax levels are low, with good state-built infrastructure—the airport, the Interstate highways, the port of Charleston, now one of the busiest on the East Coast. Unions are almost nonexistent. The work ethic here is strong; as public schools elsewhere in America seem to concentrate on inculcating multiculturalism and self-esteem, South Carolina public schools strive to teach reading, mathematics and good work habits. Culturally this area ranges from conservative to very conservative, with a strong influence by Greenville's Bob Jones University and many evangelical and fundamentalist churches. But the culture of mainstream churches and civic boosters has a certain bedrock conservatism to it as well.

South Carolina's 4th Congressional District fits almost perfectly around the Greenville-Spartanburg area. It has voted Republican in national elections for many years now, and Republican voting habits have spread to downballot races as well. Indeed, the real contest here is between evangelical and economic conservatives.

The congressman from the 4th District is Bob Inglis, a Republican first elected in 1992. Inglis grew up in the Low Country, then excelled at Duke and the University of Virginia law school, and moved to Greenville to practice commercial law; he started a family and became involved in civic and church affairs. In 1992, at 33, he decided to run for Congress. The incumbent was Liz Patterson, a Democrat with a political pedigree (her father was governor and senator) and a moderate reputation. Inglis campaigned hard for term limits and against PAC contributions; he pledged to serve only three terms and to never take PAC money. He inspired a huge door-to-door effort, targeting key precincts with many volunteers; volunteers hung tens of thousands of doorknob fliers attacking the House bank and post office scandals. He benefited as well from a 200,000-person mailing of comparative issue stands by the Christian Coalition. Inglis won 57% in Greenville County and 43% in Spartanburg County, for a 50%–48% upset victory.

In the House Inglis kept his promises. His calls for reform went mostly unheeded in his first term, but when Republicans won the House they voted to apply all laws to Congress, cut staff, and pass a gift ban; he saw the House vote for the balanced budget amendment and a majority vote for term limits—though not for his six-year limit. He resisted acclimatization to Washington, sleeping in his office on an air mattress, refusing to take PAC money, voting against funding for the Southern Connector between I-85 and I-385 because it was part of what he considered a pork-laden bill. He explained, "It reflects a change in South Carolina's situation. There was a day when we were the nation's redheaded step-child and we had to depend on seniority to bring us goodies. Now the situation has changed, dramatically. What we need is a sound economy and the key to that is right-sizing the federal government." To that end he was able to contribute as a member of the Budget Committee. Inglis also worked for the tort reform bill vetoed by President Clinton and an Emergency Assistance Compact authorizing states to cooperate on disaster relief. He co-sponsored the Church Arson Prevention Act.

Inglis was reelected in 1994 and 1996 with more than 70% of the vote. In January 1997 he announced he was running for the Senate seat held by Democrat Ernest Hollings. "This really isn't a campaign against an incumbent. It is a campaign for a new Senate with a new point of view," he said, one that "rather than condescending to govern us, responds to the ideal that we govern ourselves." He called for lightening the burden of taxation, regulation, and litigation, adding, "From the very first day of this campaign, I want to say, 'Welcome,' to black South Carolinians. I share an appreciation of the historic civil rights struggle, and I passionately agree that economic empowerment is the key to completing that work." Inglis has at least one primary opponent for the Senate seat, Secretary of State Jim Miles, and it is also possible that former Governor and 4th District Congressman Carroll Campbell might run. After Inglis backed Beasley's Confederate Flag proposal, Attorney General Charlie Condon, who vocally opposed the plan, said he is "looking seriously" at the race. The Republican primary for this 4th District seat will attract a host of current and former state legislators.

The People: Pop. 1990: 581,385; 36% rural; 12% age 65+; 79% White; 20% Black; 1% Asian; 1% Hispanic origin. Households: 58% married couple families; 26% married couple fams. w. children; 39% college educ.; median household income: $27,703; per capita income: $13,011; median gross rent: $367; median house value: $58,900.

1996 Presidential Vote

Dole (R)	111,699	(56%)
Clinton (D)	74,208	(37%)
Perot (I)	11,496	(6%)

1992 Presidential Vote

Bush (R)	107,970	(54%)
Clinton (D)	65,106	(33%)
Perot (I)	24,131	(12%)

Rep. Bob Inglis (R)

Elected 1992; b. Oct. 11, 1959, Bluffton; home, Greenville; Duke U., B.A. 1981, U. of VA Law Schl., J.D. 1984; Presbyterian; married (Mary Anne).

Career: Practicing atty., 1984–92.

DC Office: 320 CHOB 20515, 202-225-6030; Fax: 202-226-1177; e-mail: binglis@hr.house.gov.

District Offices: Greenville, 864-232-1141; Spartanburg, 864-582-6422; Union, 864-427-2205.

Committees: *Budget* (10th of 24 R). *Judiciary* (10th of 20 R): Commercial & Administrative Law; Constitution.

Group Ratings

	ADA	ACLU	AFS	LCV	CFA	CON	NFIB	COC	ACU	NTLC	CHC
1996	10	12	0	23	46	80	97	87	100	100	100
1995	0	—	—	6	0	87	—	96	92	—	—

National Journal Ratings

	1995 LIB — 1995 CONS	1996 LIB — 1996 CONS
Economic	26% — 67%	0% — 82%
Social	0% — 79%	14% — 77%
Foreign	0% — 85%	30% — 65%

Key Votes of the 104th Congress

1. Reduce Medicare Growth $	Y	5. Flag Amendment	Y	9. Cuban Embargo	Y
2. Ovrd. Product Liab. Veto	Y	6. Drop EPA Limits	N	10. Bar Bosnia Troop $	Y
3. Increase Min. Wage	N	7. Repeal Assault-Weap. Ban	Y	11. Cut Anti-Missile Defense	N
4. Welfare Reform	Y	8. Ovrd. Part. Birth Veto	Y	12. Bar U.N. Uniforms	Y

Election Results

1996 general	Bob Inglis (R)	138,165	(71%)	($143,966)
	Darrell E. Curry (D)	54,126	(28%)	($15,643)
1996 primary	Bob Inglis (R)	unopposed		
1994 general	Bob Inglis (R)	109,626	(73%)	($184,079)
	Jerry L. Fowler (D)	39,396	(26%)	($6,311)

FIFTH DISTRICT

Some of the fiercest battles of the Revolutionary War were fought in South Carolina's Up Country, on hilly lands just being settled by Scots-Irish farmers moving up from the Low Country or down the Virginia Piedmont valley. This was a country of violent passions and unclear lines; Carolinians have long argued over which side of the North and South Carolina boundary Andrew Jackson was born in 1767. Ever since, the fighting spirit and Calvinist faith of Up Country Carolinians have never wavered. This "Olde English District" remains intensely religious and pro-military. But it is no longer impoverished. For many years, the dominant industry here was textiles, traditionally the first factory enterprise of industrializing countries, with low pay and poor working conditions. But in the 1980s the number of textile jobs declined, and small-business prosperity more recently has been barreling out the interstates from Greenville-Spartanburg and Columbia and Charlotte, to transform counties once dependent on tobacco fields and textile mills.

The 5th Congressional District of South Carolina consists of all or part of 13 counties, mostly in the Up Country. It includes none of the state's three large metropolitan centers, but much of their growing fringe. In the east, the 5th includes Darlington, site of the Southern 500 stock car race every Labor Day, and verges on lowland tobacco country, including Marlboro and Chesterfield Counties, although heavily black areas here have been lopped off and placed in the black-majority 6th District. In the west, it includes Fort Mill and Rock Hill in York County, just south of Charlotte, ready for fast development now that a land settlement with the Catawba Indians has been reached. Politically, this homeland of Andrew Jackson is ancestrally Democratic. But in recent years, first the more affluent towns and then the countryside have been trending Republican.

The congressman from the 5th District is John Spratt, one of the leading Democrats in the House, first elected in 1982. He comes from a prominent York County family and has degrees from Davidson, Yale Law and Oxford; he first got involved in politics in Charles Ravenel's unsuccessful 1974 campaign for governor. In 1982 the 5th District incumbent announced his retirement a week before the filing deadline; Spratt put a campaign together fast and won 38% in the primary, 55% in the runoff against a candidate who spent $929,000, and 68% in the general. For 10 years he was reelected easily; then in 1994 and 1996 he had tough races, winning by 52%–48% and 54%–45%, carrying the rural counties and running even in York County. It is a measure of the strength of the Republican tide that a Democrat with so many political assets could be so hard pressed.

Spratt's two major specialties are military issues and the budget. He served in the Pentagon during the Vietnam war and is the fourth ranking Democrat on the National Security Committee. In the 1980s, he worked with then-Chairman Les Aspin and, in his thick Carolina accent and with impressive knowledge of details, stitched together compromises on the MX missile, binary nerve gas weapons, the Strategic Defense Initiative, and the Savannah River and other nuclear plants—keeping military projects flowing through the House, many of whose members were constantly looking to cut military spending. In the 1990s he has worked on the details of defense budgets, concentrating on maintaining troop levels and equipment in good condition. Although he says the ABM Treaty will some day have to be abandoned, he is opposed to rapid development and deployment of missile defense; on this issue his amendment prevailed in February 1995 by 218–212, the first significant defeat of a Contract with America promise in the Republican House.

Spratt's other major preoccupation is the budget deficit. In 1990 he proposed a bill requiring both the administration and the Congress to submit balanced budgets. Starting in 1991 he served on the Budget Committee for two years, and in 1992 ran for Budget chairman, losing to Martin Sabo in the Democratic Caucus 149–112. He rotated off the committee in 1992, then ran for the ranking Democrat position on Budget again in December 1996, proclaiming his "determination" to balance the budget. His opponent, Louise Slaughter, had a more liberal voting record, but Spratt was nominated by Appropriations ranking Democrat David Obey, and he won 106–83; he actually had fewer votes than four years before, but apparently the tenor of opinion in the Caucus had changed. On Budget Spratt will work with Chairman John Kasich, who has served with him on National Security; just months into the job, Spratt was thrust into a key role in the negotiations that ended in a balanced budget deal. His goal, he says, is to "reclaim our reputation for fiscal responsibility without renouncing our heritage as the party that has a heart and cares about average Americans."

On other issues Spratt has a moderate to liberal record. He voted for the Clinton budget and tax increase in 1993 and the crime bill in 1994; he voted for the balanced budget amendment and the line-item veto in 1995. He co-sponsored the Democratic welfare alternative with Georgia's Nathan Deal in March 1995, which came close to passing; he voted for the Welfare Reform Act of 1996. He has been co-chair of the Textile Caucus, and pressed in various ways to get the Clinton Administration to enforce rules against illegal textile imports; he attacked the Caribbean Basin Initiative proposal to allow textile imports without reciprocity; he voted against Most Favored Nation status for China. He is co-chair of the Congressional Ball Bearing Caucus, and sponsored an amendment requiring the Defense Department to buy ball and roller bearings in the United States. He criticized the FDA's attempts to regulate tobacco as unjustified by law, and sponsored a bill to prohibit FDA regulation. He sponsored the V-chip legislation adopted in 1996. He has pressed measures against foreign counterfeiting. He opposed sale of Power Marketing Administrations. He has worked to keep Shaw Air Force Base near Sumter off the base-closing list, and he settled a 15-year controversy just before a 1992 deadline which would have triggered an Indian lawsuit against 62,000 landowners.

In 1994 and 1996 Spratt was opposed by Republican Larry Bigham, graduate of The Citadel, owner of Thursday's Too restaurant in Rock Hill, school board member for 10 years. Bigham denounced government mandates and pledged, "I will work to get government out of our lives, out of our schools, out of our homes, out of our businesses" and argued that "a vote for John Spratt is a vote for Bill Clinton." He made some clumsy errors—wrongly charging that the Indian settlement would allow new forms of gambling—but in the climate of 1994 his support of term limits and pledge to serve only four terms struck a chord. Spratt outraised Bigham and spent $180,000 of his own money, but ended up winning by only 52%–48%. In 1996 Bigham ran again. This time the angry tone of 1994 was less apparent, and Bill Clinton ran about even with Bob Dole in the district. Spratt won by the slightly greater margin of 54%–45%, after outspending Bigham more than 2–1, with the help of $427,000 in PAC contributions. This is a seat that could be targeted again; much will depend on Spratt's performance in his high-visibility position on budget issues.

The People: Pop. 1990: 581,174; 63% rural; 12% age 65+; 68% White; 31% Black; 1% Hispanic origin. Households: 59% married couple families; 28% married couple fams. w. children; 32% college educ.; median household income: $25,215; per capita income: $11,009; median gross rent: $327; median house value: $52,800.

1996 Presidential Vote			**1992 Presidential Vote**		
Dole (R)	83,273	(47%)	Bush (R)	86,118	(45%)
Clinton (D)	82,203	(46%)	Clinton (D)	81,192	(42%)
Perot (I)	11,827	(7%)	Perot (I)	23,462	(12%)

Rep. John M. Spratt, Jr. (D)

Elected 1982; b. Nov. 1, 1942, Charlotte, NC; home, York; Davidson Col., A.B. 1964, Oxford U., M.A. 1966, Yale U., LL.B. 1969; Presbyterian; married (Jane Stacy).

Career: Army Operations, U.S. Dept. of Defense, 1969–71; Practicing atty., 1971–82; Pres., Bank of Ft. Mill, 1973–82; Pres., Spratt Insurance Agcy., 1973–82.

DC Office: 1536 LHOB 20515, 202-225-5501; Fax: 202-225-0464; e-mail: jspratt@hr.house.gov.

District Offices: Darlington, 803-393-3998; Rock Hill, 803-327-1114; Sumter, 803-773-3362.

Committees: *Budget* (RMM of 19 D). *National Security* (4th of 25 D): Military Procurement.

Group Ratings

	ADA	ACLU	AFS	LCV	CFA	CON	NFIB	COC	ACU	NTLC	CHC
1996	60	33	83	77	77	85	43	31	25	20	20
1995	65	—	—	63	77	38	—	46	16	—	—

National Journal Ratings

	1995 LIB — 1995 CONS			1996 LIB — 1996 CONS		
Economic	63%	—	36%	64%	—	36%
Social	65%	—	33%	63%	—	35%
Foreign	59%	—	39%	70%	—	29%

Key Votes of the 104th Congress

1. Reduce Medicare Growth $	N	5. Flag Amendment	Y	9. Cuban Embargo	Y
2. Ovrd. Product Liab. Veto	Y	6. Drop EPA Limits	Y	10. Bar Bosnia Troop $	N
3. Increase Min. Wage	Y	7. Repeal Assault-Weap. Ban	N	11. Cut Anti-Missile Defense	Y
4. Welfare Reform	N	8. Ovrd. Part. Birth Veto	Y	12. Bar U.N. Uniforms	Y

Election Results

1996 general	John M. Spratt, Jr. (D)	97,174	(54%)	($855,622)
	Larry L. Bigham (R)	81,360	(45%)	($373,117)
1996 primary	John M. Spratt, Jr. (D)	unopposed		
1994 general	John M. Spratt, Jr. (D)	77,311	(52%)	($643,947)
	Larry L. Bigham (R)	70,967	(48%)	($213,775)

SIXTH DISTRICT

South Carolina was first settled by planters from Barbados, bringing with them a tropical plantation economy, which they transferred to the not quite tropical climate of the Carolina coastal lowlands. Here the flat Low Country and many islands are laced with sluggish-flowing rivers and swamps, and here the planters brought thousands of slaves directly from Africa. Colonial South Carolina was one of the richest parts of North America, with dazzling Georgian architecture in Charleston and classic plantation gardens; the planters built great irrigation systems and grew rice and cotton and the dye-plant indigo, all heavily in demand in Britain and elsewhere. And of course all this wealth was built on the slave labor of thousands of African-Americans, many of them still speaking their ancestral languages, or a patois mixing them with English. A majority of colonial South Carolinians were black slaves; so were most residents of the lowlands when the Civil War started with the bombardment of Fort Sumter in Charleston Harbor, although by that time there were also many free blacks in Charleston, some of whom owned slaves themselves.

South Carolina's black heritage has left an imprint on American culture, still apparent in the lowlands today. The special accents and dialects of lowland blacks were long retained: traces of Gullah and others still can be found on lowland islands and in the Charleston accent, which to outsiders seems often incomprehensible (should C-SPAN run subtitles when Senator Hollings speaks?). The poverty that was the almost universal lot of lowland blacks after the Civil War has only in the last generation been alleviated, as development comes to the coast and the long cultural isolation of people here is dissipated. But many blacks who grew up here have long since left, leaving after high school graduation on the bus for New York, nicknamed "the chicken-bone special" because of the fried chicken their families packed for the journey.

The 6th Congressional District of South Carolina, created for 1992 to have a black majority, and modified slightly for 1994, includes very little of the coast, now mostly lined with affluent condominium communities; but it does include most of the geographic expanse of Low Country South Carolina. Its erose and irregular boundaries are designed to include the black central city neighborhoods of Charleston and Columbia but leave in the adjacent 1st and 2d Districts their affluent white city and suburban areas. The 6th district includes much of Orangeburg, home of the historically black South Carolina State University, and Florence, at the center of the Pee Dee tobacco-growing country in eastern South Carolina.

The congressman from the 6th is James Clyburn, a Democrat elected in 1992. Clyburn grew up in Sumter, the son of a minister; he worked as a teacher, in government antipoverty programs, and on the staff of Governor John West. In 1974 he became state Human Affairs Commissioner; twice he ran for Secretary of State, losing narrowly. Clyburn effectively won the seat in the 1992 Democratic primary, with 56% of the vote against four black opponents, all with serious claims for the nomination; the white incumbent in the old 6th District, Robin Tallon, at the last minute decided not to run. Each of the others had regional strengths. But Clyburn, well known statewide, ran first or second in each major center and piled up huge margins in others (88% in his home county of Sumter).

Clyburn is the first black to represent South Carolina in Congress since 1897. He has been active in the civil rights movement since his youth and also has good working relationships with leading businessmen and Republicans. He has a generally liberal voting record, but supported the balanced budget amendment and term limits. He has worked on local projects like airport funding and the South Carolina Heritage Corridor and has pushed for funds for restoring buildings at historically black colleges and universities. He won a fight with Strom Thurmond to get the new courthouse in Columbia named after Matthew Perry, South Carolina's first black federal judge. He sponsored a bill, before the ValuJet crash, to protect whistleblowers in the aviation industry. Against reformers in his own party, he has defended PACs as the voice of the little guy. Though he lamented the occasion of the visit, Clyburn was honored to accompany President Clinton on a personal inspection of the Mount Zion A.M.E. Church, one of two burned by local KKK members, in June 1996. But Clyburn attacked Republican colleague Bob Inglis for visiting another burned church in his district without notifying him, and accused Inglis of grandstanding.

Clyburn was easily reelected in 1994 and 1996. The district lines were challenged in 1997 as racially gerrymandered, but even if they are thrown out the new lines are not expected to significantly change.

The People: Pop. 1990: 581,202; 51% rural; 12% age 65+; 37% White; 62% Black; 1% Hispanic origin. Households: 49% married couple families; 24% married couple fams. w. children; 30% college educ.; median household income: $19,254; per capita income: $8,628; median gross rent: $314; median house value: $47,900.

1996 Presidential Vote

Clinton (D)	113,096	(65%)
Dole (R)	53,614	(31%)
Perot (I)	5,525	(3%)

1992 Presidential Vote

Clinton (D)	118,085	(62%)
Bush (R)	59,970	(31%)
Perot (I)	12,292	(6%)

Rep. James E. Clyburn (D)

Elected 1992; b. July 21, 1940, Sumter; home, Columbia; SC St. U., B.A. 1962; African Methodist Episcopal; married (Emily).

Career: Teacher, 1962–66; Dir., Charleston Neighborhood Youth Corps, 1966–68; Exec. Dir., SC Commission for Farm Workers, 1968–71; Asst., SC Gov. West, 1971–74; SC Human Affairs Commissioner, 1974–92.

DC Office: 319 CHOB 20515, 202-225-3315; Fax: 202-225-2313; e-mail: jclyburn@hr.house.gov.

District Offices: Columbia, 803-799-1100; Florence, 803-622-1212; N. Charleston, 803-965-5578.

Committees: *Transportation & Infrastructure* (16th of 33 D): Aviation; Surface Transportation. *Veterans' Affairs* (5th of 13 D): Oversight & Investigations (RMM).

Group Ratings

	ADA	ACLU	AFS	LCV	CFA	CON	NFIB	COC	ACU	NTLC	CHC
1996	95	75	100	77	85	63	27	25	5	15	20
1995	90	—	—	81	100	16	—	29	16	—	—

National Journal Ratings

	1995 LIB — 1995 CONS			1996 LIB — 1996 CONS		
Economic	80%	—	18%	76%	—	22%
Social	80%	—	13%	79%	—	18%
Foreign	73%	—	24%	61%	—	37%

Key Votes of the 104th Congress

1. Reduce Medicare Growth $	N	5. Flag Amendment	Y	9. Cuban Embargo	N
2. Ovrd. Product Liab. Veto	N	6. Drop EPA Limits	Y	10. Bar Bosnia Troop $	N
3. Increase Min. Wage	Y	7. Repeal Assault-Weap. Ban	N	11. Cut Anti-Missile Defense	Y
4. Welfare Reform	N	8. Ovrd. Part. Birth Veto	N	12. Bar U.N. Uniforms	Y

Election Results

1996 general	James E. Clyburn (D)	120,132	(69%)	($196,440)
	Gary McLeod (R)	51,974	(30%)	($39,395)
1996 primary	James E. Clyburn (D)	48,807	(88%)	
	Ben Frasier Jr. (D)	6,950	(12%)	
1994 general	James E. Clyburn (D)	88,635	(64%)	($445,461)
	Gary McLeod (R)	50,259	(36%)	($13,047)

SOUTH DAKOTA

When the Census Bureau proclaimed the closing of the American frontier in 1890, one of the last places to close was the southern part of the Dakota Territory, just admitted to the Union in 1889 as the state of South Dakota. For years this land had been the home of the Oglala Sioux, one of the largest Native American tribes, who had built a buffalo hunting civilization by becoming masters of the horses the Spaniards had imported to North America 350 years earlier. It was the Sioux warrior chief Sitting Bull, now buried on a bluff above the Missouri River, who destroyed Custer at Little Big Horn in 1876; it was Oglala Sioux who were the victims at the massacre of Wounded Knee in 1890. After half a century of horrifying disease and a decade of defeat, the Sioux were a traumatized people, and still are today, living on reservations with proud traditions but in terrible poverty. Out there they are isolated far from the mainstream economic marketplace, beset by high rates of alcoholism and suicide, which may be the after-effects of the traumas of 100 years ago. There have been clashes between the civilizations in recent memory—the killings of government agents by Indian rebels at Wounded Knee in 1975—but also moves in the other direction, as when Governor George Mickelson declared 1990 a Year of Reconciliation. And the Indians are in the process of getting a great monument, the late Korczak Ziolkowski's Crazy Horse sculpture, which—when and if finished—will dwarf Mount Rushmore; by 1996 the chief's full mouth and cleft chin have begun to emerge.

Less tragic and more successful, though not without its moments of violence, has been the whites' settlement of South Dakota. It was a rapid process: the first gold strikes in the Black Hills came in 1876, and soon the mountains swarmed with settlers; Deadwood became a city of 20,000 where Calamity Jane ruled the saloons and Wild Bill Hickock was shot in the back while holding two pair—aces and eights. Ranchers, knowing that the buffalo could not be contained by barbed wire fences, massacred them so thoroughly that when Teddy Roosevelt got to the Dakota Territory in 1884, he had a hard time finding one to shoot. It was not long before the railroad came through, and before long settlers, many of them German and Scandinavian immigrants recruited by the railroads, had built sodhouses, broken the land and set down enough roots to justify making both the two Dakota states.

Geographically, South Dakota has never entirely filled up. In the 25 years between statehood and World War I, the eastern third of the state, sectioned off Midwestern style into 640 acre square miles, was settled by farmers. But moving westward, before a traveler reaches the Missouri River in the middle of the state, green turns to brown, cultivation grows sparse and then stops; the plains are open grazing land, scarcely touched by the white men who were so eager to establish dominion over them a century ago. The land is punctuated, not by roads meeting every mile at precise angles, but by buttes, gullies and grasslands sweeping to the horizon with no sign of human habitation except the occasional missile silos which once were pointed at the Soviet Union and which by 1994 were all empty.

South Dakota's political patterns were fairly well set by the early 1900s. Its early settlers were mostly Midwesterners who brought their Republicanism with them. Voters here never had much use for the Non-Partisan League, which caught on in the more Scandinavian soil of North Dakota, and there was never anything here comparable to the Farmer-Labor Party of Minnesota. But the nature of the farm economy—its dependence on the great railroads and milling companies, and on the vagaries of international markets—meant that South Dakota was subject to periodic farm revolts. It voted for Populists and William Jennings Bryan in the 1890s; it supported the early New Deal; it revolted against the Eisenhower Administration in the 1950s by electing a young congressman named George McGovern. South Dakota also shared the isolationist impulse of much of the Great Plains, and McGovern's opposition to the Vietnam war in the late 1960s was not a liability here. In the early 1970s, Democrats seemed on the verge of becoming the majority party.

Instead, it moved to the Republicans, with party registrations making significant increases. This began with the angry response to Wounded Knee in 1975. And it was perpetuated by the economic policies of Republican Governor William Janklow, elected in 1978 and 1982 and then again in 1994. It was Janklow who invited Citicorp to move its credit card operations to Sioux Falls, where they had the advantages of a high usury rate, no state corporate or personal income taxes, and a literate low-wage work force. The Citibank operation here grew from 50 employees to 2,700 in 1981 to 3,200 in 1996, replacing the meatpacker John Morrell as the biggest employer; other banks followed, and telemarketing, and NordicTrak and high-tech firms like Gateway computers shopping centers burgeoned as Sioux Falls grew and shoppers started driving more than 200 miles for the selection a big mall could provide; medical centers grew, as South Dakotans sought the better care large hospitals could provide. Metro Sioux Falls grew 13% in the 1980s and another 10% by 1997—amazing growth in a state which often lost population between censuses—and in the 1990s had the nation's lowest unemployment rate, down to 1.7% in Sioux Falls in 1996; Rapid City, with a similar economic boost plus tourism, grew 16%; Watertown and Brookings, mid-sized freeway towns, grew as well, even as most small counties lost population. There are still some 34,000 farms in South Dakota, but population patterns here on the Plains now look more like those in the Rockies, with most people concentrated in a few areas, while vast acreage remains vacant, punctuated with infrequent ranches and resort areas—a landscape that would not have been totally alien to Sitting Bull.

South Dakota also works hard to court tourists. The lure of natural attractions in the Black Hills and the huge and varyingly unfinished sculptures of Mount Rushmore and the Crazy Horse Memorial are augmented by such commercial enterprises as gold-panning creeks and gambling casinos in Deadwood and on Indian reservations. And Wall Drug, the 46,000-square foot emporium between the Badlands and Rapid City snares three-quarters of the freeway traffic.

Politically, these successes have helped to reestablish South Dakota's Republican heritage. True, the state elected a second Democratic senator in 1996, but Tim Johnson was elected in part because of his opponent's perceived weaknesses, and his and Tom Daschle's hold may be weakened because of the 1996 Freedom to Farm Act, which phases out the farm subsidies whose continuance has been the Democrats' strongest issue for 60 years. Republicans have won almost everything else—the governorship and the legislature, the state's lone House seat and the presidential race, for both George Bush and Bob Dole. And conservative stands are popular: South Dakota passed a law (overturned by the courts) requiring parental consent for abortions; in 1996 voters passed 74%–26% an initiative requiring a two-thirds majority vote to increase taxes. And lastly, people are voting for South Dakota with their U-Hauls: low-tax, small-

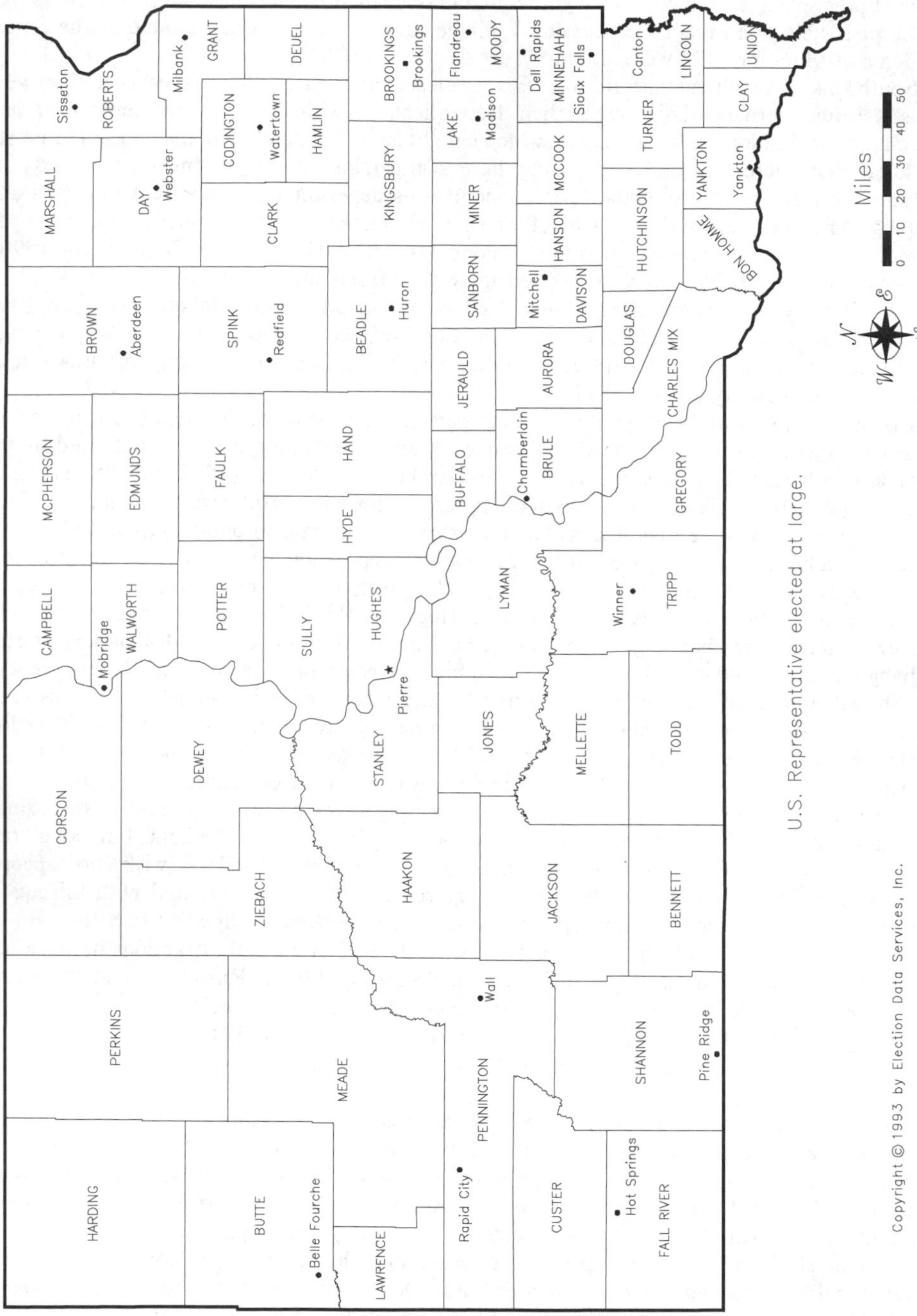

U.S. Representative elected at large.

government South Dakota has seen its population increase smartly the last 15 years, while the population of higher-tax, larger-government North Dakota has been stagnant.

Governor. Bill Janklow has had more impact on state government and the South Dakota economy than any other South Dakota governor. He grew up in Chicago, then after the death of his father, a prosecutor at the Nuremburg war crimes trial, the family moved to his mother's home town, Flandreau, South Dakota. Janklow dropped out of high school and joined the Marines; he returned in 1960, married, and without a high school diploma talked his way into the University of South Dakota. After law school, he worked in the legal aid program at the Rosebud Indian Reservation. But he did not sympathize with the Indian rebels of the 1970s. He was elected state attorney general in 1974, with 67% of the vote, getting tough on Indian violence and compiling a high conviction record. In 1978 he was elected governor with 56%; in 1982, reelected with 71%. During this time, he attracted Citicorp to the state, reduced agricultural and residential property taxes, cut state payrolls, stimulated new business, and converted a state college into a prison. Term-limited, in 1986 Janklow ran against incumbent Republican Senator Jim Abdnor and lost 55%–45% in the primary.

Janklow's successor, Republican George Mickelson, took a different course, with a revolving economic development fund financed by a temporary one-cent sales tax increase. He died in a plane crash in April 1993, and was succeeded by 67-year-old Walter Dale Miller, a rancher from near Rapid City who served 20 years in the legislature and six as lieutenant governor. Janklow challenged him in the 1994 Republican primary and won by a 54%–46% margin, carrying most of eastern South Dakota and losing much of the west. In the general election he won easily, 55%–41%, over Jim Beddow, the former president of George McGovern's alma mater, Dakota Wesleyan University.

In his latest term Janklow seems even more aggressive. He cut the state payroll, cut state spending except education, rolled back property taxes, established state standards for student learning and gave school districts the leeway to achieve them. He welcomed more new businesses including the headquarters of IBP meatpackers to South Dakota and reduced EPA hazardous waste reporting forms from 155 pages to four. He has reduced foster care by encouraging adoption and has worked to increase child immunizations.. He changed the name "correctional facility" to "prison" and "client" to "inmate," to reflect a change in attitude, and agreed, along with Governor Branstad of Iowa and Governor Nelson of Nebraska, to coordinate law enforcement among the three states by cross-deputizing officers.

Senior Senator. Tom Daschle, the Senate minority leader since January 1995, grew up in Aberdeen, graduated from South Dakota State, served in the Air Force in the years George McGovern was running for president. In 1972 he became a Washington staffer for Senator James Abourezk. In 1978, as Abourezk was about to retire, Daschle returned to South Dakota, ran for the eastern House district that Larry Pressler was vacating to run for the Senate, and won by exactly 139 votes over former P.O.W. Leo Thorsness, who had come close to beating George McGovern in 1974. Daschle was a generally faithful follower of the Democratic leadership in the House, trapped far behind others in seniority; his political highlight came in 1982, when South Dakota lost one of its two House seats and he had to run against Republican Cliff Roberts; Daschle won 52%–48%.

Already representing the entire state, it was natural for Daschle to run in 1986 for the Senate seat held by Republican Jim Abdnor. Daschle had the additional good luck that Governor Bill Janklow was opposing Abdnor in the primary, putting Abdnor on the defensive and forcing him to use much of his money for the June primary. Daschle again won 52%–48%, in one of the key victories that returned control of the Senate to the Democrats for eight years. Two years later, in January 1989, new Senate Majority Leader George Mitchell named Daschle co-chairman of the Senate Democratic Policy Committee—in effect, though not in title, the number two man in the Senate leadership. When Mitchell announced his retirement in March 1994, Daschle immediately started running for majority leader—too soon to suit some traditionalists. His opponent Jim Sasser seemed to have enough votes to win, but Sasser lost to Republican Bill Frist in Tennessee in November. That was the good news for Daschle; the bad news was that Democrats had lost enough seats that the race was for minority rather than majority leader. Connecticut's Christopher Dodd immediately entered the race, with encouragement from some older committee chairmen; but Daschle relinquished his seat on the Finance Committee to Carol Moseley-Braun of Illinois, whose vote gave him a 24–23 victory—one that brings to mind his first election to the House.

As minority leader, Daschle has not been especially effective legislatively—but he could hardly hope to be, and he was successful in stopping some Republican initiatives. The first big test was on the balanced budget amendment. Here he was upstaged by former Democratic Leader Robert Byrd as the measure's leading opponent. But Daschle segued smoothly from his former support of the amendment to opposition, with the politically effective but rather imprudent argument that any such amendment should exclude Social Security. This would actually make it more difficult to balance budgets over the next several years, and would not make Social Security more viable in the 21st Century, but it provided cover for him and five other Democrats, who had previously supported balanced budget amendments, to switch and defeat the issue by one vote in March 1995. To this achievement he added other successes in 1996: passage of the minimum wage and the bipartisan healthcare portability bill. Congress also passed a law declaring children born with spina bifida to Vietnam veterans exposed to Agent Orange to be entitled to VA benefits—the first entitlement ever for children of veterans, and a follow-up to Daschle's long advocacy of compensation for Agent Orange victims. Daschle also had some success in getting Democrats to unite in support of specific platforms—the "Work First" welfare alternative he put together with John Breaux and Barbara Mikulski and the "Families First" platform he announced with House Minority Leader Richard Gephardt. Neither came close to passage, but both were arguably constructive efforts by a minority party.

Probably Daschle's greatest disappointment in the 104th Congress came on Agriculture. For years he was a "prairie populist," resisting cuts in farm subsidies, which were nonetheless cut in the farm bills of 1985 and 1990—big losses, compared to his gains in getting reformulated gas included in the 1990 Clean Air Act and subsidizing ethanol. But in 1996 he was not able to stop the Republicans and Democrats, including ranking Agriculture Committee Democrat Patrick Leahy, from supporting the Freedom to Farm Act, which phases out farm subsidies for most crops over seven years. This is a long-term political loss for Dakota Democrats, who have run for years, and with considerable success, with the implicit promise of raising federal payments.

Through all this, Daschle's soft-spoken style, about which many Democrats had qualms, proved effective on television. He continued his rather liberal voting record, modulated a bit on economic issues; a strong backer of the Clinton healthcare plan in 1994, he sought an increased role for government by urging it take over responsibility for healthcare for children. Once rather skeptical of American foreign involvements, and an opponent of the Gulf war resolution, he supported the Clinton Administration on Bosnia and MFN status for China. But following the 1996 election, after Republicans gained two seats in the Senate, Daschle distanced himself somewhat from the administration and announced his own priorities. The first was campaign finance reform: he backs a constitutional amendment to limit spending by candidates, parties and independent groups; second was a children's health insurance tax credit. On some issues he called for an end to partisanship: he wanted a "partial-birth" abortion ban capable of winning 100 votes, but his proposed compromise only garnered 36 votes; he called for Congress—not a bipartisan commission—to address Medicare; he said that a portion of Social Security payroll taxes should be invested in the stock market; and he backed the budget deal hammered out in early 1997.

Daschle was reelected comfortably in 1992, by 65%–33%, over Republican Charlene Haar, with the help of a huge financial edge. He certainly would not accept Republican proposals to limit out-of-state fundraising; most of his money comes from outside South Dakota. He has worked the state hard, trying to visit all 66 counties once a year, dressing casually and listening to voters; he works on local projects, like a $13 million waste treatment facility for Watertown or

Port of Entry status for Sioux Falls.

Daschle's seat comes up for reelection in 1998, and he is considered a clear favorite to win. Republican state Senator Alan Aker has promised a challenge.

Junior Senator. In 1996 Democrat Tim Johnson defeated three-term Senator Larry Pressler, the only incumbent Republican senator to lose that year. Johnson has spent most of his life in the southeast corner of South Dakota, where he grew up and went to the University of South Dakota, and in Washington, D.C. He did go to graduate school at Michigan State and worked as a staffer in the Michigan Senate, then he returned home to practice law in Vermillion. He was elected to the legislature in 1978, at 31, and served in the House and Senate until he ran for Congress in 1986, when Daschle ran for the Senate. Like Daschle, Johnson won his House seat by a narrow margin, 48%–45%, by edging a fellow state senator in the primary, with big margins in his southeastern home area and in Sioux Falls and Rapid City. He won the general by 59%–41%, and ran even better every two years thereafter.

In the House he compiled a pretty liberal voting record, though he voted for the balanced budget amendment and was the only Democrat to switch his vote to support lifting the Bosnia arms embargo. He worked on South Dakota water and public works projects and tried to maintain farm subsidies. He successfully managed reauthorization of crop insurance as a subcommittee chairman in the 103d Congress and, in the 104th, helped relax the "swampbuster" provisions penalizing farmers who violated wetlands regulations in the 1996 Freedom to Farm Act; but he warned that the phasing out of farm supports would hurt in drought years. Johnson championed the state's elderly population as well, opposing any cuts in or taxes on Social Security benefits, and favoring penalties for drug companies that charge seniors high prices for drugs.

Johnson's race against Pressler had been a long time contemplated. Pressler won election to the House in 1974 and the Senate in 1978 as a constituency-service, ear-to-the-ground Republican, in tune with South Dakota opinion; in the late 1980s, and after 1994 when he became chairman of the Commerce Committee, he became consistently more conservative. To some he seemed, in *Time*'s words, "occasionally clueless," and was often under attack from the Sioux Falls *Argus Leader*.

When TV ads began running in August 1995 the race was about even, and it stayed that way for 15 months. Pressler raised almost $4.7 million, over $1.7 million from PACs; Johnson raised nearly $850,000 from PACs. Since South Dakota TV is cheap, that meant one barrage of ads after another—plus seven debates. Pressler attacked Johnson as too liberal, going back to a 1981 vote in the legislature against workfare. Johnson attacked Pressler as a Newt-oid Medicare cutter and charged that he switched from opposition to support of maritime subsidies after receiving $29,000 from maritime PACs. Johnson was assisted by collateral attacks from others. The *Argus Leader* charged that Pressler didn't properly itemize some campaign expenses, and left-wing columnist Alexander Cockburn was brought to South Dakota in October 1996 by former Senator James Abourezk to broadcast a charge in his book that Pressler is gay. There was no evidence to support that and Johnson called on Abourezk to apologize. But the key role may have been played by national issues. Pressler spent much time in 1995 and 1996 on the telecommunications bill, the most-lobbied and arguably most complex bill before the 104th Congress. In negotiations he held out for deregulation, and to South Dakotans he promised lower telephone and cable TV rates. Pressler succeeded in passing the bill, the first major rewrite of communications law in 63 years, but back home Johnson was charging that phone and cable rates were going up.

The final result was a 51%–49% Johnson victory, narrower than final month's polls suggested, but nonetheless decisive. The state split almost precisely along the 100th meridian that is often taken as the dividing line between farm land and grazing land. Johnson carried almost every county east of the 100th, except for a couple of ethnic Republican counties; Pressler carried almost everything west of the 100th, except for a few Indian counties.

In the Senate, Johnson serves on the Agriculture, Banking, Budget and Energy Committees, though the farm subsidies and energy price controls which were the staple of Dakota Democrats when he got started are no longer live issues. He backs Tom Daschle's proposal to amend the First Amendment to allow limits on campaign spending and contributions.

Representative-at-Large. South Dakota has had only one seat in the House since 1982; for the first time since then he is a Republican, John Thune, elected in 1996 to replace successful Senate candidate Tim Johnson. Thune grew up on the dusty plains west of the Missouri River, went to college and business school, and got a job on Senator Jim Abdnor's staff in Washington in 1985. After four years in Washington, he returned to South Dakota in 1989, at 28, to become executive director of the state Republican Party. In 1991 he became state railroad director under Governor George Mickelson and in 1993 director of the state Municipal League. In his early 30s he had plenty of contacts in Pierre, the nation's smallest state capital, and all around the state.

Thune nevertheless entered the 1996 race as very much an underdog. The favorite in the Republican primary was Lieutenant Governor Carole Hillard, who seemed to have Governor Bill Janklow on her side and was endorsed by the 1994 Republican nominee. A poll released in May 1996 showed her ahead of Thune 69%–15%. But Thune was escorted around main streets by Abdnor, he attracted the support of religious conservatives and presidential campaign leaders, fresh from organizing for the February 27 presidential primary. Hillard lent her campaign $140,000 but didn't raise much money, and Janklow eventually announced he was neutral on the candidates. It turned out to be no contest. Thune carried 54 counties, Hillard 12; Thune won 59%–41%; it would have been more except that Hillard carried Rapid City.

The Democrats had more competitors. The early favorite was cable TV executive Jim Abbott. But Rick Weiland, a former state director for Senator Tom Daschle, attacked Abbott for giving money to Republicans. Weiland carried 46 counties and led Abbott 42%–28%, well above the 35% needed in South Dakota to avoid a runoff.

After the primary the Sioux Falls *Argus Leader* summarized the race: "November's option is crystal clear: choose a liberal or a conservative." Thune was for term limits, against all tax increases (and against Bob Dole's tax cut pending a balanced budget), and pledged to refuse the congressional pension; he had the support of Christian conservatives and cattlemen's organizations. Weiland attacked Newt Gingrich and Medicare "cuts" and called for an "impact fee" on big hog producers to build a loan fund for small hog producers. On agriculture, Thune called not for farm subsidies, but for increasing exports and promoting value-added goods: "market solutions that can help keep prices high." The two raised similar amounts, but from different sources: Thune raised more from individuals, $580,000 to $500,000, while Weiland, with strong labor support, led in PAC money, $346,000 to $176,000. In response to which Thune attacked him for taking contributions from a union (the Laborers) connected with organized crime.

It turned out to be not much of a contest: Weiland carried only six counties (his home, a university county, and four Indian counties), and Thune won 58%–37%. On election night Thune promised, "I won't forget that the tax dollars you pay to the government isn't their money. It's your money. No matter how hard it tries, government can never be a substitute for personal initiative and it can never take the place of the family." Thune serves on the Agriculture and Transportation Committees and was chosen the freshman class representative to the Republican leadership. In 1997 Thune first turned to local issues, requesting eight transportation projects for the state. He also became embroiled in the battle over the emergency flood relief bill, criticizing Republican leaders for leaving on the Memorial Day recess before passing the package. Thune also blasted the AFL-CIO for running anti-"corporate welfare" advertisements targeting him and 18 other House members in April 1997, 20 months before the 1998 election.

Presidential politics. With only three electoral votes, South Dakota is not a glittering prize in presidential contests. Nevertheless, it has been close in five of the last seven elections. With typical Farm Belt contrariness, it has tilted against the party in power, giving good, though losing, votes to Democrats in 1972, 1976, 1988 and 1992 and going heavily Republican in 1980. George Bush narrowly won here twice, 53%–47% in 1988 and 41%–37% in 1992; Bob Dole won

46%–43% in 1996.

South Dakota's presidential primary for years was held on the same day as California's, and eclipsed by it. Since 1988 it has been held in February, just one week after New Hampshire. So far it has been not a trendsetter, but a booster of Great Plains candidates who do not fare well elsewhere: Bob Dole and Dick Gephardt in 1988, Bob Kerrey and Tom Harkin in 1992. In 1996 Bob Dole beat Pat Buchanan here 45%–29%.

The People: Est. Pop. 1996: 732,000; Pop. 1990: 696,004, up 5.2% 1990–1996. 0.3% of U.S. total, 45th largest; 50% rural. Median age: 34.5 years. 14% 65 years and over. 91.2% White, 1% Black, 7.1% Amer. Indian, 1% Hispanic origin. Households (1980): 58.9% married couple families; 29% married couple fams. w. children; 43% college educ.; median household income: $22,503; per capita income: $10,661; 66.1% owner occupied housing; median house value: $45,200; median monthly rent: $242. 3.2% Unemployment. 1996 Voting age pop.: 535,000. 1996 Turnout: 323,826; 61% of VAP. Registered voters (1996): 459,971; 184,262 D (40%); 223,932 R (49%); 51,777 unaffiliated and minor parties (11%).

Political Lineup: Governor, William J. Janklow (R); Lt. Gov., Carole Hillard (R) Secy. of State, Joyce Hazeltine (R); Atty. Gen., Mark Barnett (R); Treasurer, Richard Butter (D); Auditor, Vernon L. Larson (R). State Senate, 35 (13 D and 22 R); Senate President, Harold Halverson (R); State House, 70 (22 D and 48 R); House Speaker, Rex Hagg (R). Senators, Thomas A. Daschle (D) and Tim Johnson (D). Representative, 1 R at large.

Elections Division: 605-773-5002; **Filing Deadline for U.S. Congress:** April 7, 1998.

1996 Presidential Vote

Dole (R)	150,543	(46%)
Clinton (D)	139,333	(43%)
Perot (I)	31,250	(10%)

1996 Republican Presidential Primary

Dole (R)	30,918	(45%)
Buchanan (R)	19,780	(29%)
Forbes (R)	8,831	(13%)
Alexander (R)	6,037	(9%)
Other	3,604	(5%)

1992 Presidential Vote

Bush (R)	136,718	(41%)
Clinton (D)	124,888	(37%)
Perot (I)	73,295	(22%)

GOVERNOR

Gov. William J. Janklow (R)

Elected 1994, term expires Jan. 1999; b. Sept. 13, 1939, Chicago, IL; home, Brandon; U. of SD, B.S. 1964, LL.B 1966; Lutheran; married (Mary).

Career: Marine Corps, 1956–59; Legal Aid, Rosebud Indian Reservation, 1966–73; SD Special Prosecutor, 1973–75; SD Atty. Gen., 1974–78; SD Gov., 1978–86; Practicing atty., 1987–94;

Office: Executive Office, State Capitol, Pierre 57501, 605-773-3212; Fax: 605-773-5844; Web site: www.state.sd.us.

Election Results

1994 gen.	William J. Janklow (R)	172,515	(55%)
	Jim Beddow (D)	126,273	(41%)
	Nathan A. Barton (Lib)	12,825	(4%)
1994 prim.	William J. Janklow (R)	57,221	(54%)
	Walter D. Miller (R)	48,754	(46%)
1990 gen.	George S. Mickelson (R)	151,198	(59%)
	Bob L. Samuelson (D)	105,525	(41%)

SENATORS

Sen. Thomas A. Daschle (D)

Elected 1986, seat up 1998; b. Dec. 9, 1947, Aberdeen; home, Aberdeen; SD St. U., B.A. 1969; Catholic; married (Linda).

Career: Air Force, 1969–72, Air Force Reserves, 1975–78; Legis. Asst., U.S. Sen. James Abourezk, 1972–77; U.S. House of Reps., 1978–86.

DC Office: 509 HSOB 20510, 202-224-2321; Fax: 202-224-2047; e-mail: tom_daschle@daschle.senate.gov.

State Offices: Aberdeen, 605-225-8823; Rapid City, 605-348-7551; Sioux Falls, 605-334-9596.

Committees: *Minority Leader. Democratic Policy Committee Chairman. Agriculture, Nutrition & Forestry* (4th of 8 D): Forestry, Conservation & Rural Revitalization; Production & Price Competitiveness. *Intelligence (Select)* (ex-officio).

Group Ratings

	ADA	ACLU	AFS	LCV	CFA	CON	NFIB	COC	ACU	NTLC	CHC
1996	90	44	100	69	79	1	34	38	0	21	7
1995	95	—	100	100	81	2	—	37	4	—	—

National Journal Ratings

	1995 LIB	—	1995 CONS	1996 LIB	—	1996 CONS
Economic	73%	—	23%	70%	—	27%
Social	85%	—	7%	80%	—	8%
Foreign	86%	—	7%	73%	—	24%

Key Votes of the 104th Congress

1. Reduce Medicare Growth $	N	5. Flag Amendment	N	9. Anti-Missile Defense	N
2. Lmt. Prod. Liab. Damages	N	6. Endangered Species	Y	10. Cuban Embargo	Y
3. Increase Min. Wage	Y	7. Gay Employment Rights	Y	11. Bar Bosnia Troop $	N
4. Welfare Reform	N	8. Ovrd. Part. Birth Veto	N	12. Cut Vietnam Aid	N

Election Results

1992 general	Thomas A. Daschle (D)	217,095	(65%)	($3,981,548)
	Charlene Haar (R)	108,733	(33%)	($478,421)
	Others	8,667	(3%)	
1992 primary	Thomas A. Daschle (D)	unopposed		
1986 general	Thomas A. Daschle (D)	152,657	(52%)	($3,485,870)
	James Abnor (R)	143,173	(48%)	($3,410,387)

Sen. Tim Johnson (D)

Elected 1996, seat up 2002; b. Dec. 28, 1946, Canton; home, Vermillion; U. of SD, B.A. 1969, M.A. 1970, J.D. 1975; MI St. U., 1970–71; Lutheran; married (Barbara).

Career: Budget Analyst, MI Senate, 1971–72; Practicing atty., 1975–85; Clay Cnty. Dep. State Atty., 1985; SD House of Reps., 1978–82; SD Senate, 1982–86; U.S. House of Reps., 1986–96.

DC Office: 502 HSOB 20510, 202-224-5842; Fax: 202-228-0368; e-mail: tim@johnson.senate.gov.

State Offices: Aberdeen, 605-226-3440; Rapid City, 605-341-3990; Sioux Falls, 605-332-8896.

Committees: *Agriculture, Nutrition & Forestry* (8th of 8 D): Production & Price Competitiveness; Research, Nutrition & General Legislation. *Banking, Housing & Urban Affairs* (7th of 8 D): Financial Institutions & Regulatory Relief; Financial Services & Technology; Securities. *Budget* (9th of 10 D). *Energy & Natural Resources* (8th of 9 D): Energy Research, Development, Production & Regulation; Forests & Public Land Management.

Group Ratings (as Member of U.S. House of Representatives)

	ADA	ACLU	AFS	LCV	CFA	CON	NFIB	COC	ACU	NTLC	CHC
1996	55	27	75	69	69	20	46	33	37	28	26
1995	85	—		63	54	38	—	50	28	—	—

National Journal Ratings (as Member of U.S. House of Representatives)

	1995 LIB — 1995 CONS	1996 LIB — 1996 CONS
Economic	65% — 35%	62% — 38%
Social	65% — 33%	57% — 43%
Foreign	88% — 7%	75% — 24%

Key Votes of the 104th Congress (as Member of U.S. House of Representatives)

1. Reduce Medicare Growth $	N	5. Flag Amendment	Y	9. Cuban Embargo	N
2. Ovrd. Product Liab. Veto	N	6. Drop EPA Limits	Y	10. Bar Bosnia Troop $	N
3. Increase Min. Wage	Y	7. Repeal Assault-Weap. Ban	Y	11. Cut Anti-Missile Defense	Y
4. Welfare Reform	Y	8. Ovrd. Part. Birth Veto	Y	12. Bar U.N. Uniforms	Y

Election Results

1996 general	Tim Johnson (D)	166,533	(51%)	($2,990,554)
	Larry Pressler (R)	157,954	(49%)	($5,138,298)
1996 primary	Tim Johnson (D)	unopposed		
1990 general	Larry Pressler (R)	135,682	(52%)	($2,124,359)
	Ted Muenster (D)	116,727	(45%)	($1,323,770)
	Other	6,567	(3%)	

REPRESENTATIVE

Rep. John Thune (R)

Elected 1996; b. Jan. 7, 1961, Pierre; home, Pierre; Biola U., B.A. 1983; U. of SD, M.B.A. 1985; Protestant; married (Kimberley).

Career: Legis. Asst., U.S. Sen. James Abdnor, 1985–87; Special Asst., U.S. Small Business Admin., 1987–89; Exec. Dir., SD Republican Party, 1989–91; SD Railroad Dir., 1991–93; Exec. Dir., SD Municipal League, 1993–96.

DC Office: 506 CHOB 20515, 202-225-2801; Fax: 202-225-5823.

District Offices: Rapid City, 605-342-5135; Sioux Falls, 605-331-1010.

Committees: *Agriculture* (25th of 27 R): Department Operations, Nutrition & Foreign Agriculture; General Farm Commodities. *Transportation & Infrastructure* (34th of 40 R): Surface Transportation; Water Resources & Environment.

Group Ratings and Key Votes: Newly Elected

Election Results

1996 general	John Thune (R)	186,393	(58%)	($773,125)
	Rick Weiland (D)	119,547	(37%)	($890,708)
	Others	17,263	(5%)	
1996 primary	John Thune (R)	41,322	(59%)	
	Carole Hillard (R)	28,139	(41%)	
1994 general	Tim Johnson (D)	183,036	(60%)	($480,230)
	Jan Berkhout (R)	112,054	(37%)	($144,356)
	Others	10,832	(4%)	

TENNESSEE

Tennessee is a battleground state, with a fighting temperament since it was settled 200 years ago by the likes of Andrew Jackson and produced so many soldiers it was labeled the Volunteer State. This was a frontier battleground in the 1790s, from which Jackson launched his wars on the Indians and the British. It was a military battleground in the 1860s, when Yankee troops swept down the Tennessee and Cumberland Rivers on their way to Mississippi and through Chattanooga's Lookout Mountain on their way to Atlanta and the sea. It has been a cultural battleground for much of this century. On one side were the Fugitives, writers like John Crowe Ransom and Allen Tate, who contributed to "I'll Take My Stand," a manifesto calling for retaining the South's rural economy and heritage. On the other side have been business leaders and politicians who have made Tennessee the fastest-growing state of the interior South: Tennessee has given birth to the first supermarket, the Holiday Inn, Federal Express and Kentucky Fried Chicken. And Tennessee has been—if not a battleground—then at least a marshaling ground for the music traditions which have vied for a large place in Americans' lives.

East Tennessee is one of the homes of bluegrass music and mountain fiddling, with string bands and vocal harmony; Knoxville's Tennessee Barn Dance has been broadcast since 1942. Gospel music has long been centered in Nashville, which is also the nation's leading center of religious publishing. Country music got its commercial start in Nashville, with broadcasts of the Grand Ole Opry from Ryman Auditorium starting in 1925 and now the Opryland U.S.A. theme park; and Nashville remains indisputably the capital of this ever-popular music form. The Mississippi lowlands around Memphis, economically and culturally the metropolis of the Mississippi Delta, gave birth to the blues in the years from 1890s to 1920; and the blues were in turn the inspiration for the jazz musicians of Beale Street in the 1920s and Elvis Presley, whose Graceland mansion is now a major tourist destination, in the 1950s and 1960s.

Tennessee also is and has long been a political battleground. Its political divisions have the roots in the Civil War, and most counties today still vote their 1860s loyalties: the Union counties, mainly in the east but with a scattering to the west, vote solidly Republican, while the Confederate counties in middle and west Tennessee have long been heavily Democratic. Within the limits of these enduring party loyalties, political entrepreneurs have set the tone for the state. From the 1920s to 1948, Edward Crump, longtime mayor of Memphis, used his total control of Democratic primary votes there to elect governors and senators. The Tennessee Valley Authority and the cheap electric power it generated provided an institutional base for reform liberal Democrats Estes Kefauver and Albert Gore, Sr., elected to the Senate in 1948 and 1952. They were soon national figures, with reliable enough backing from Tennessee's yellow-dog Democratic majority to vote for civil rights bills and to refuse to sign the segregationist Southern Manifesto, and still thrive electorally. Tennessee has never had a large black population—about 16% in the 1990s, half of whom live in and around Memphis—and the state was not riven by the racial animosity that seared so much of the South in the 1950s and 1960s, thanks in large part to the actions of its leading politicians, but also to the continuing hold of ancestral partisan preferences.

Eventually, the Democrats' cultural liberalism on issues other than race moved west Tennessee voters away from their ancestral party, and moderate east Tennessee Republicans Howard Baker and Bill Brock, elected to the Senate in 1966 and 1970, set the state's tone; Baker protege and 1996 Republican presidential candidate Lamar Alexander, elected governor in 1978, instituted education reforms and attracted Japanese investment that have changed and strengthened the state over the last dozen or so years. But Jimmy Carter carried Tennessee solidly, and Democrats were elected to both Senate seats—Jim Sasser in 1976 and Albert Gore, Jr., in 1984. Tennessee voted 47%–42% for the Clinton-Gore ticket in 1992. But by 1994 it turned against the Clinton Administration and produced a kind of political revolution. Republican Fred Thompson, famous as a Watergate investigator and movie actor, won the remainder of Gore's Senate term by a landslide, surgeon Bill Frist beat Sasser, and Republican Don Sundquist was elected governor. They won a majority of the vote for the U.S. House, gaining two seats and coming close in a third. In 1996, as the Clinton-Gore ticket was sweeping nationally, Republicans remained strong in Tennessee. The Clinton-Gore campaign poured money, into Tennessee, and Gore made 16 campaign appearances in the state; Clinton made six, Bob Dole nine and Jack Kemp four). The Clinton-Gore ticket won, but by just 48%–46%, and Republicans maintained their 5–4 majority in the House. Young voters here did not embrace Clinton as they did nationally; the exit poll shows the vote almost even among voters under 45, with Democrats winning their biggest margin among the elderly—not a good augury for the future.

Tennessee's swing toward Republicans in the early 1970s resulted mainly from switches in west Tennessee; its apparent swing toward Republicans in the middle 1990s is centered in middle Tennessee. This has been the most rapidly growing and changing part of the state. It grew first in manufacturing: in the 1980s Nissan built a huge plant in Smyrna, in Rutherford County, and General Motors put its Saturn plant in Spring Hill, in Maury County, both within an hour's drive of Nashville; both have specialized in the new style of team cooperation between

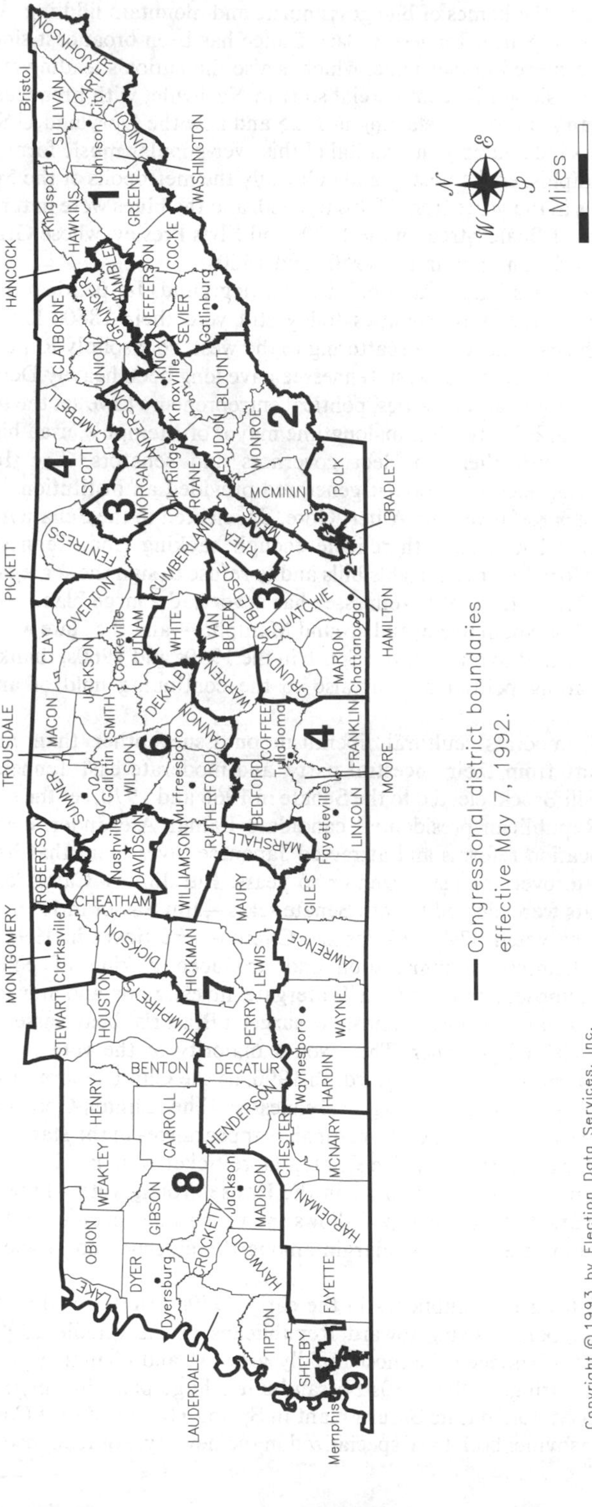

—Congressional district boundaries
effective May 7, 1992.

workers and management. Nashville has also become "the Silicon Valley" of health care, according to Thomas F. Frist Jr., Senator Bill Frist's brother and vice chairman of Columbia/HCA, one of the largest hospital companies in the nation, headquartered in Nashville. Politically, the core of Nashville-Davidson remains Democratic, but the counties all around have grown faster and most are now Republican. One result: the two districts (6th and 7th) that contain many of the counties Al Gore once represented in the House voted for the Dole-Kemp ticket over Clinton-Gore in 1996. The Nashville establishment traditionally supported Democrats in Tennessee politics. But now Nashville money has become heavily Republican: the presidential campaign of Nashville's Lamar Alexander raised so much money locally that 37205 and 37215 became two of the Republican presidential candidates' top five fundraising zip codes in 1996.

There seems to be economic change in east Tennessee as well. For years east Tennessee Republicans vied with middle Tennessee Democrats in supporting the Tennessee Valley Authority. But in 1997 TVA Chairman Craven Crowell Jr., a Clinton appointee, proposed eliminating TVA's $106 million in federal funding by 1999, so that TVA could concentrate on electricity sales in the increasingly competitive market and spin off its navigation and flood control functions to state or federal agencies. Tennessee has grown, attracting and spawning new businesses, in part because its institutions were mostly untouched by the labor union strife of the 1930s and the civil rights strife of the 1960s. The lack of strong unions and racial divisions attracted the many Japanese companies here, which in turn attracted General Motors. If Tennessee's economy lagged behind the nation's through much of the 20th Century, its respect for tradition and hard work and its open climate for entrepreneurism have enabled it to grow mightily in its last decades.

Tennessee in the late 1990s seemed to be a hotbed of political candidates. The most prominent of course is Vice President Al Gore, whose poll ratings held up well in 1997 even after revelations that he was present at a Buddhist temple fundraiser where legally questionable contributions appear to have been made and himself made improper fundraising phone calls from the White House. Like all vice presidents since Walter Mondale, and perhaps even more than some, he has been a working and influential part of the administration, running the Reinventing Government program, superintending the space program, regularly conducting sensitive foreign policy talks with leaders like Russia's Prime Minister Viktor Chernomyrdin and being involved in most of Bill Clinton's important policy and political decisions. Another Tennessee presidential candidate was—and apparently still is—Lamar Alexander, elected governor in 1978 and 1982, and Education secretary under George Bush. Alexander instituted merit pay for teachers and teacher competency tests in Tennessee, and later endorsed school choice. His 1996 campaign was disciplined and well-organized, raised large amounts of money and was based on a coherent theme of devolving power from the federal government, expecting "less from Washington and more from ourselves." It came closer than is generally thought to winning; Alexander finished just behind Bob Dole in New Hampshire, and if 7,600 votes had switched and he had come out ahead, he might have replaced Dole as Pat Buchanan's main competitor and the Republican nominee. Clinton pollster Dick Morris has said that Alexander was the only Republican candidate Clinton and especially Gore feared. Alexander seems clearly to be running in 2000; he held a fundraising conference call the morning of November 6, 1996. A third possible candidate is Senator Fred Thompson, like Alexander an early protege of Senator Howard Baker. Thompson's genuine country roots, his performances on television and his role investigating the Clinton scandals have led many to view him as a strong candidate, though in early 1997 he, unlike Alexander, seemed to be making no moves to run.

Governor. Tennessee's governor is Don Sundquist, a Republican elected in 1994, who quite unusually for this state is not from Tennessee at all. He was born in Illinois, the son of a welder, was the first in his family to go to college and served in the Navy. He worked for Jostens, a college and high school ring maker, in Shelbyville, Tennessee, for 10 years; in 1972, he started his own graphics and printing firm in Memphis. He volunteered for Howard Baker as early as

1964, when Baker lost a Senate race, and became active in the national Young Republicans organization. In 1982, Sundquist ran for Congress from the 7th District, which stretched from Memphis all the way to Nashville; he won 51%–49% over current 5th District Congressman Bob Clement, carrying the white Memphis suburbs but losing the rural counties. Sundquist served on the Ways and Means Committee and opposed tax increases; he worked his rural counties with 100 "community days" a year. He was reelected easily.

In 1994 Sundquist ran for governor. The Democratic nominee was Nashville Mayor Phil Bredesen, also a migrant from the North, who made a fortune in health care. Bredesen was popular in Nashville, center of the state's largest media market, and rich enough to self-finance his campaign generously. Moreover, the record of Democratic incumbent Ned McWherter was impressive: the passage of TennCare; 21st Century Schools, with teacher salary raises and more leeway for superintendents and principals in choosing teachers; no income tax (Tennessee is one of seven states without one). Sundquist was boosted by Alexander, Baker and east Tennessee Congressman Jimmy Quillen, and won by a solid 54%–45% margin, losing Nashville but carrying the other big metro areas handily.

Sundquist worked on a bipartisan basis with the state legislature to pass a 20-bill crime package and Families First, a plan to move welfare recipients to work in 18 months; by early 1997 the rolls were down 13,000. He put all children's programs in one department and eliminated the Public Service Commission. In early 1997 he promised to make TennCare coverage available to all uninsured children. His main negative publicity came when he questioned high spending at the University of Tennessee, and gave substantial raises to members of his staff. Sundquist had a good job rating in early 1997. Possible opponents include Bredesen, Congressman Bob Clement, state House Majority Leader Bill Purcell, and businessman Clayton McWhorter.

Senior Senator. Fred Thompson has been a familiar face on television and movie screens for many years. He grew up in Lawrenceburg, Tennessee, son of a used car dealer, worked his way through school rearing a young family. After Vanderbilt Law, he became an assistant U.S. attorney in Nashville, handling moonshine and stolen car cases. In 1973, Howard Baker made Thompson chief Republican counsel to the Senate Watergate Committee, where he helped uncover the scandal that drove a Republican president from office. Back in Tennessee, incoming Governor Lamar Alexander appointed Thompson special counsel to investigate clemency-selling by outgoing Governor Ray Blanton, who went to jail. In the process, Thompson defended parole board chairman Marie Ragghianti, whose plight was the subject of the movie *Marie*, Thompson's first movie role. He took a couple more special counsel assignments in Washington and acted in 16 movies, including box office hits like *The Hunt for Red October*. His roles included a CIA chief, FBI director, a White House chief of staff and a senator, as well as some explicit villains. But he spent most of his time practicing law and lobbying, never running for office.

Then Al Gore resigned his Senate seat to become vice president, and Governor Ned McWherter passed over the Democrat who seemed the most likely candidate—Congressman Jim Cooper—to appoint his own aide Harlan Mathews, who did not run in the election to fill the last two years of Gore's term in 1994. Instead, Thompson and Cooper did. Cooper seemed well positioned for the race. The son of a former governor, he had represented the elongated 4th District for 12 years and was conspicuously a New Democrat and chief sponsor of a managed care health bill, which was vigorously opposed by the Clinton White House. With a seat on Commerce, he raised plenty of money and ultimately spent slightly more than Thompson.

But Thompson stressed some issues which caught voters' attention and found a device to symbolize his message. One of his issues has long been advocated by Howard Baker and was featured by Lamar Alexander: limiting congressional sessions to half the year and allowing lawmakers to make their livings in their home communities. To this he coupled strong advocacy of term limits. The symbol—gimmick, Democrats said—for this was the red pickup truck which Thompson leased in August 1994 and drove all around Tennessee, speaking to small groups over coffee or fried chicken. Ads also captured a personal contrast between the candidates: the six foot five Thompson appeared in workshirts, speaking confidently to the camera while walking up porch stairs (not so easy to do: his acting experience helped); the much shorter and youthful-looking Cooper appeared before a church in starched white shirt and tie. In early October, Thompson zoomed to a lead. Cooper responded by citing his opposition to the Clinton healthcare plan. But Cooper got squeezed out of the middle ground he had long worked to occupy. Tennesseans decided to vote against the Clinton Administration and career politicians, and Thompson won 60%–39%.

He quickly became a political star in Washington. Bob Dole named him to respond on television to Clinton's 1994 speech urging a tax cut. Thompson's strong words and delivery made him seem the more presidential: "We welcome the President to help us lead America in a new direction, but if he will not, we will welcome the President to follow—because we are moving ahead." Thompson voted for most of the Contract with America provisions. He soft-pedalled issues like abortion, but emphasized campaign finance reform, sponsoring a measure to save the current presidential checkoff system and becoming one of the few Republicans to endorse the McCain-Feingold bill. He sponsored the 1996 amendment to freeze congressional pay and spoke out strongly for term limits. He had objections to the Republicans' tort reform proposals. He sponsored a two-year budget and a bipartisan juvenile justice bill giving more flexibility to the states. He attacked corporate welfare and aggressively questioned the performance of Solicitor General Drew Days III. Thompson was strongly favored to win a full term in 1996, and Democrats had to scramble before they came up with a respectable candidate to oppose him, lawyer Houston Gordon. Thompson ran an ad saying, "I want you to meet my number one adviser on Social Security and Medicare," and introduced his mother. Thompson won 61%–37%, winning nearly 1.1 million votes, more than anyone ever has in Tennessee.

Thompson then became chairman of the Governmental Affairs Committee, and as such inherited the duty of investigating the Clinton scandals. He started off uncertainly, irritating Democrats when he asked for a $6.5 million budget for the investigation, then irritating Republicans when he promised a broad investigation of congressional and Republican campaigns as well as the Clinton-Gore operation. With his memories of providing bipartisan cooperation on the Watergate Committee, he seemed a bit startled at Democrats' partisanship and attempts to limit his initial budget to $1.8 million: "At every step of the way, I've been met with resistance, resistance on big things, resistance on little things. The only consistent thing they've done is resistance," he said in February 1997. Meanwhile he resisted Republican pressure that he narrow his scope. Ultimately, Thompson got $4.35 million and the broader mandate he had originally sought. But he also got saddled with a December 31, 1997, deadline which led to accusations of stalling by The White House and increasing partisanship on the committee.

Junior Senator. Bill Frist is a heart and lung transplant surgeon elected in 1994. He is from a medical family famous in Tennessee: his father practiced medicine for 50 years, was internist and cardiologist to seven successive governors; his brother, Tom Frist, Jr., and his father started HCA and is now vice chairman of Columbia/HCA, one of the nation's leading owners of hospitals, with stock worth hundreds of millions; his brother Bob is a cardiac surgeon in Nashville. Bill Frist graduated from Harvard Medical School, studied at Mass General, in England and at Stanford, and in 1986 started the heart and lung transplant program at Vanderbilt. He wrote a book, *Transplant*, on the social and ethical issues of these surgeries; he has performed 250 transplants. He was not, however, politically active: he did not vote until he returned to Nashville at age 34, and never voted in a Republican primary until 1994; the Frists were not known as Republicans, and Democratic Governor Ned McWherter appointed Bill Frist in 1992 to chair a task force on Medicaid.

In 1994, Frist decided to challenge Jim Sasser, then chairman of the Budget Committee and running for majority leader. Frist had tough primary opposition from east Tennessee businessman Bob Corker, who attacked him for not voting for years and for obtaining cats from animal shelters for experiments as a medical student. But Frist, spending liberally, carried the Nashville and Memphis media markets and beat Corker 44%–32% (Tennessee is the one former Confederate state without a runoff primary). In the fall campaign, Frist said he wanted to "give communities and individuals the freedom to solve problems and return to our basic conservative values," and backed term limits, welfare reform, federal spending cuts and school prayer. "Term limits for career politicians and the death penalty for career criminals," one ad said. Sasser emphasized school prayer, the balanced budget amendment and cracking down on illegal immigrants, and he ridiculed Frist as a bored, rich surgeon. Frist charged that Sasser "never met a tax he didn't like" and as majority leader would be "the official water boy to Bill Clinton." Frist outspent Sasser, with $7 million total, $3.7 million of it his own money to $5 million for Sasser. Sasser led in polls up through October, but in November Frist won 56%–42%, carrying all the large metro areas and losing only scattered traditionally Democratic rural counties.

In the Senate Frist has had a solidly conservative voting record. He played a key role on the 1996 healthcare bill on portability and preexisting conditions, working to include Medical Savings Accounts: "the goal of this bill has always been to insure that people who play by the rules will not be denied access to health insurance." He also helped to write the provision guaranteeing insurance coverage for 48-hour hospital maternity stays. He worked to reauthorize the Ryan White CARE Act for the treatment and support of AIDS patients. He put on the income tax form a box to checkoff to get information on organ donor cards. He worked to make sure Tennessee was not penalized for extending TennCare to uninsured children. He favors FDA reform. In the 105th Congress Frist became chairman of the Public Health and Safety and the Science, Technology and Space Subcommittees. In January 1997, Frist was elected vice chairman of the Alliance for Health Reform, a group founded and chaired by Jay Rockefeller. Together, they sponsored a bill that would allow provider service organizations to contract directly with Medicare to offer medical care, bypassing state regulation and insurance companies. "The mother-may-I mentality that has emerged has frustrated both parties and providers and led them to question who is in charge," said Frist.

Frist also worked on the IDEA special education act, which was passed the Senate in May 1997 after two years of dispute over, among other things, how special education students could be disciplined. He favors a two-year budget and argued that administration spending increases for welfare should go to schools instead. He sought to block the merger of the bank and thrift insurance funds until the thrift charter is eliminated. He has worked for Tennessee flood control and defense projects. Frist has used his medical credentials in political debate. In 1996 he called the "partial-birth" abortion procedure "indefensible from a medical standpoint," and he cut a spot challenging labor unions attacks on Republican proposals for Medicare.

Presidential politics. The existence of two strong partisan traditions, with the Democrats' base somewhat larger over the years, has made for unusual stability in Tennessee presidential politics. While other southern states went Republican, Tennessee stayed about evenly divided—in the Eisenhower 1950s and the Carter-Reagan race of 1980—with similar percentages in almost every county. When southern Democrats have run strong races, they have carried Tennessee handily, as in 1964, 1976 and 1992. And when Republicans are strong, they have won similarly: Ronald Reagan and George Bush both won 58% here in 1984 and 1988, and the Republican percentage in the three major statewide races in 1994 ranged between 54% and 60%. In 1996 Tennessee was almost dead even: with more than its share of presidential contenders, Tennessee could be closely contested again in 2000.

Tennessee's presidential primary is held on Super Tuesday; the easy winners in 1992 were those two southern moderates, Bill Clinton and George Bush. Native son Lamar Alexander had already withdrawn from the race and endorsed and campaigned with Bob Dole by the time the Super Tuesday Republican contest rolled around in 1996; Dole won handily.

Congressional districting. Tennessee needed only minor changes to get its districts back to equal population after the 1990 Census. Democrats controlled the process, and tried to help their prospects marginally, but the 1994 Republican revolution swept most of their advantage away.

The People: Est. Pop. 1996: 5,320,000; Pop. 1990: 4,877,185, up 9.1% 1990–1996. 2.0% of U.S. total, 17th largest; 39% rural. Median age: 35.3 years. 13% 65 years and over. 82.6% White, 15.9% Black, 1% Asian, 1% Hispanic origin. Households: 57.2% married couple families; 26% married couple fams. w. children; 37% college educ.; median household income: $24,807; per capita income: $12,255; 68.0% owner occupied housing; median house value: $58,400; median monthly rent: $273. 5.2% Unemployment. 1996 Voting age pop.: 4,035,000. 1996 Turnout: 1,894,105; 47% of VAP. Registered voters (1996): 3,011,195; no party registration.

Political Lineup: Governor, Don Sundquist (R); Lt. Gov., John Wilder (D); Secy. of State, Riley C. Darnell (D); Atty. Gen., John Knox Walkup (D); Treasurer, Steve Adams (D); Comptroller, William Snodgrass (D). State Senate, 33 (18 D and 15 R); Senate President, John Wilder (D); State House, 99 (61 D and 38 R); House Speaker, Jimmy Naifeh (D). Senators, Fred Thompson (R) and William H. Frist (R). Representatives, 9 (4 D and 5 R).

Elections Division: 615-741-7956; **Filing Deadline for U.S. Congress:** May 21, 1998.

1996 Presidential Vote

Clinton (D)	909,146	(48%)
Dole (R)	863,530	(46%)
Perot (I)	105,918	(6%)

1992 Presidential Vote

Clinton (D)	933,521	(47%)
Bush (R)	841,300	(42%)
Perot (I)	199,968	(10%)

1996 Republican Presidential Primary

Dole (R)	148,063	(51%)
Buchanan (R)	72,929	(25%)
Alexander (R)	32,742	(11%)
Forbes (R)	22,171	(8%)
Other	13,138	(5%)

GOVERNOR

Gov. Don Sundquist (R)

Elected 1994, term expires Jan. 1999; b. Mar. 15, 1936, Moline, IL; home, Memphis; Augustana Col., B.A. 1957; Lutheran; married (Martha).

Career: Navy, 1957–59; Jostens, Inc., 1961–72; Pres. & Partner, Graphic Sales of Amer., 1972–82; Co-founder, Red, Hot & Blue Restaurant, 1989; U.S. House of Reps., 1982–94.

Office: State Capitol, 7th Ave. & Charlotte, Nashville 37243, 615-741-2001; Fax: 615-741-1416; Web site: www.state.tn.us.

Election Results

1994 gen.	Don Sundquist (R)	807,104	(54%)
	Phil Bredesen (D)	664,252	(45%)
1994 prim.	Don Sundquist (R)	386,696	(83%)
	David Y. Copeland (R)	69,773	(15%)
	Others	7,978	(2%)
1990 gen.	Ned McWherter (D)	480,885	(61%)
	Dwight Henry (R)	289,348	(37%)
	Other	20,148	(3%)

SENATORS

Sen. Fred Thompson (R)

Elected 1994; seat up 2002; b. Aug. 19, 1942, Sheffield, AL; home, Nashville; Memphis St. U., B.S. 1964; Vanderbilt U. Schl. of Law, J.D. 1967; Church of Christ; divorced.

Career: Practicing Atty,. 1967–94; Asst. US Atty., Middle TN Dist., 1969–72; Minority Cnsl., U.S. Sen. Watergate Cmte., 1973–74; Special Cnsl., TN Gov. Lamar Alexander, 1980; Special Cnsl., U.S. Sen. Foreign Relations Cmte., 1980–81; Special Cnsl., U.S. Sen. Intelligence Cmte., 1982; TN Appellate Court Nom. Comm., 1985–87; Author; Actor.

DC Office: 523 DSOB 20515, 202-224-4944; Fax: 202-228-3679; e-mail: senator_thompson@thompson.senate.gov.

State Offices: Jackson, 901-423-9344; Knoxville, 423-545-4253; Memphis, 901-544-4224; Nashville, 615-736-5129.

Committees: *Governmental Affairs* (Chmn. of 9 R). *Judiciary* (5th of 10 R): Constitution, Federalism & Property Rights; Terrorism, Technology & Government Information; Youth Violence.

Group Ratings

	ADA	ACLU	AFS	LCV	CFA	CON	NFIB	COC	ACU	NTLC	CHC
1996	0	11	0	31	36	70	90	100	85	97	92
1995	5	—	0	7	25	54	—	89	83	—	—

National Journal Ratings

	1995 LIB — 1995 CONS			1996 LIB — 1996 CONS		
Economic	18%	—	80%	26%	—	69%
Social	26%	—	73%	38%	—	60%
Foreign	0%	—	92%	0%	—	74%

Key Votes of the 104th Congress

1. Reduce Medicare Growth $	Y	5. Flag Amendment	Y	9. Anti-Missile Defense	Y
2. Lmt. Prod. Liab. Damages	Y	6. Endangered Species	Y	10. Cuban Embargo	Y
3. Increase Min. Wage	Y	7. Gay Employment Rights	N	11. Bar Bosnia Troop $	Y
4. Welfare Reform	Y	8. Ovrd. Part. Birth Veto	Y	12. Cut Vietnam Aid	Y

Election Results

1996 general	Fred Thompson (R)	1,091,554	(61%)	($3,469,369)
	Houston Gordon (D)	654,937	(37%)	($795,969)
	Others	32,173	(2%)	
1996 primary	Fred Thompson (R)	266,549	(94%)	
	Jim F. Counts (R)	16,715	(6%)	
1994 general	Fred Thompson (R)	885,998	(60%)	($3,793,813)
	Jim Cooper (D)	565,930	(39%)	($3,979,425)

Sen. William H. Frist (R)

Elected 1994, seat up 2000; b. Feb. 22, 1952, Nashville; home, Nashville; Princeton U., A.B. 1974; Harvard Medical Schl., M.D. 1978; Presbyterian; married (Karyn).

Career: Practicing surgeon, 1978–94; Dir., Vanderbilt Medical Ctr. Heart-Lung Transplant Program, 1986–93.

DC Office: 565 DSOB 20510, 202-224-3344; Fax: 202-228-1264; e-mail: senate_frist@frist.senate.gov.

State Offices: Chattanooga, 423-894-2203; Jackson, 901-424-9655; Kingsport, 423-323-1252; Knoxville, 423-602-7977; Memphis, 901-683-1910; Nashville, 615-352-9411.

Committees: *Budget* (10th of 12 R). *Commerce, Science & Transportation* (9th of 11 R): Aviation; Communications; Manufacturing & Competitiveness; Science, Technology & Space (Chmn.); Surface Transportation & Merchant Marine. *Foreign Relations* (9th of 10 R): African Affairs; East Asian & Pacific Affairs; International Economic Policy, Export & Trade Promotion. *Labor & Human Resources* (4th of 10 R): Children & Families; Public Health & Safety (Chmn.). *Small Business* (7th of 10 R).

Group Ratings

	ADA	ACLU	AFS	LCV	CFA	CON	NFIB	COC	ACU	NTLC	CHC
1996	0	17	0	15	29	85	97	100	95	100	92
1995	0	—	0	0	13	29	—	100	83	—	—

National Journal Ratings

	1995 LIB — 1995 CONS			1996 LIB — 1996 CONS		
Economic	0%	—	88%	31%	—	68%
Social	31%	—	67%	28%	—	68%
Foreign	22%	—	67%	0%	—	74%

Key Votes of the 104th Congress

1. Reduce Medicare Growth $	Y	5. Flag Amendment	Y	9. Anti-Missile Defense	Y
2. Lmt. Prod. Liab. Damages	Y	6. Endangered Species	N	10. Cuban Embargo	Y
3. Increase Min. Wage	Y	7. Gay Employment Rights	N	11. Bar Bosnia Troop $	N
4. Welfare Reform	Y	8. Ovrd. Part. Birth Veto	Y	12. Cut Vietnam Aid	Y

Election Results

1994 general	William H. Frist (R)	834,226	(56%)	($7,017,424)
	James R. (Jim) Sasser (D)	623,164	(42%)	($5,020,515)
	Others	23,001	(2%)	
1994 primary	William H. Frist (R)	197,734	(44%)	
	Bob Corker (R)	143,808	(32%)	
	Steve Wilson (R)	50,274	(11%)	
	Harold Sterling (R)	28,425	(6%)	
	Others	25,410	(6%)	
1988 general	James R. (Jim) Sasser (D)	1,020,061	(65%)	($3,069,615)
	Bill Andersen (R)	541,033	(35%)	($612,421)

FIRST DISTRICT

Between the corduroy-like ridges of the Appalachian chains, as they bend west and then south, the valley of Virginia extends far into northeastern Tennessee. The communities of this region—a hilly patchwork of industrial centers, small farms and federal land—were largely shaped by the building of railroads in the 1850s. The land rush immediately after the Revolutionary War populated the area; here in tiny Jonesborough the early settlers established the free state of Franklin in 1784, and many pioneer cabins, federal mansions and Greek Revival churches are lovingly preserved. It was the railroads, however, that determined the winners and losers. Other Appalachian areas were cut off from the rest of America, with tracks running only to the coal mines, but the small industrial cities that had grown up here—Johnson City, Kingsport, Bristol—were on the main lines of national commerce even before the Civil War. The War had a different political effect here than in most of the South: northeast Tennessee, the home of wartime Governor and then Vice President Andrew Johnson, had few slaves and with its connection to northern industry was Union territory. It remains heavily Republican to this day.

The political continuity is all the more surprising because this area has had continuous economic growth and has developed the sort of industrial economy which produced unions and Democrats in the North. Its growth has been helped by modest wage levels, a skilled and hard-working labor force, low electric power rates because of the TVA and good transportation routes (rail lines and now Interstate 81). Its small cities boast major paper and printing plants, and have the look of comfortable, clean, 1920s factory towns. Growth has been rapid only in Sevier County, where Gatlinburg and Pigeon Forge are the main tourist centers—5,000 motel rooms and numerous attractions—for travelers to the Great Smoky Mountains National Park. And even there, the small-town flavor lingers: Pigeon Forge's big scandal of 1994 was the mysterious killing of some 80 rabbits at Bunnyland Mini Golf.

The far northeastern end of the state forms the 1st Congressional District of Tennessee, a district so heavily Republican that it has not elected a Democrat to the House for more than 100 years. Nonetheless, it has had turbulent politics on occasion. For almost 40 years (1921–61, with one four-year and one two-year hiatus), the seat was held by B. Carroll Reece, a fierce mountain politician who was once Republican National Committee chairman. After Reece died in 1961, and his widow was elected to fill out his term, there was a hotly contested primary here. The winner, Jimmy Quillen, a bread-and-butter politician, a former owner of the *Johnson City Times*, represented the 1st for the next 34 years. His crowning achievements were the building of the James H. Quillen College of Medicine at East Tennessee State University and the James H. and Cecile C. Quillen Center for Rehabilitative Medicine, both in Johnson City. In 1995, Quillen was named the first-ever House committee chairman emeritus—of Rules—but he announced his retirement in April 1996, saying, "Let's face it. Younger people are emerging as leaders in Washington and those with long records of service are stepping aside."

The new congressman is Bill Jenkins, the winner by 331 votes in the Republican primary. Jenkins is a lawyer from Rogersville in Hawkins County, and a farmer who raises beef cattle and grows burley tobacco. He was elected to the state House in 1962, at 25. In 1969, the state House was evenly split between Democrats and Republicans, and Jenkins was elected Speaker, the only Republican to serve in that position in the 20th Century. In 1971 he was named to the Tennessee Valley Authority Board of Directors; he served as commissioner of the state Department of Conservation; in 1990 he was elected Circuit Court Judge. In May 1996 he resigned to run for Congress.

Jenkins was just one of 11 Republicans—the Quillen 11—filed to run in the August primary. Tennessee has no runoff, and this was what political scientist V.O. Key called a "friends and neighbors" primary: there were few perceptible differences on issues, and candidates struggled to get enough votes out in their home areas to win. Jenkins won with just 18% of the votes, including 74% in Hawkins County. In second, state Senator Jim Holcomb, who had conservative

Christian activist support, also won 18%, with 37% in Sullivan County, the highest-voting county in the district. Sevierville District Attorney Al Schmutzer was third with 15%; he got 83% in Sevier County and 51% in next-door Cocke County. Medical supply millionaire David Davis won 13%, with 57% in Unicoi County. Quillen's second cousin, state Representative Richard Venable, whom Quillen endorsed late in the race, won 13% district-wide, with 27% in Sullivan County and 26% in Johnson County. David Crockett, who ran an ad saying race driver Richard Petty was supporting him, but which Petty promptly denied, won 12%., with 30% in Carter County. Kingsport businesswoman Anne Pope won 10%. The general election was anticlimactic; Jenkins won 65%–32%.

In the House Jenkins serves on the Judiciary and Agriculture Committees and seemed to have a strong conservative voting record. Two Johnson City legislators have introduced a runoff bill in the state legislature, and Holcomb did not rule out a 1998 candidacy. But Jenkins should be in a strong position: this district has been represented by only two men for all but seven of the last 76 years. He began tending to local needs in early 1997, pressing the EPA to deny a wastewater discharge permit and variance to Champion International's Canton, North Carolina, paper mill just across the Pigeon River from the 1st District, and closely watched a proposal to spin off some of EPA's functions. Jenkins also plans to host an economic summit in 1998 modeled on ones held by other east Tennessee members. Nonetheless, he will be hard pressed to match Quillen's legendary record of constituent service.

The People: Pop. 1990: 541,978; 53% rural; 14% age 65+; 97% White; 2% Black. Households: 63% married couple families; 27% married couple fams. w. children; 31% college educ.; median household income: $21,952; per capita income: $11,024; median gross rent: $295; median house value: $51,200.

1996 Presidential Vote

Dole (R)	107,668	(54%)
Clinton (D)	73,681	(37%)
Perot (I)	14,532	(7%)

1992 Presidential Vote

Bush (R)	107,515	(51%)
Clinton (D)	76,113	(36%)
Perot (I)	24,358	(12%)

Rep. William L. (Bill) Jenkins (R)

Elected 1996; b. Nov. 29, 1936, Detroit, MI; home, Rogersville; TN Tech., B.B.A. 1957; U. of TN, J.D. 1961; Baptist; married (Kathryn).

Career: Army Military Police, 1960–62; Farmer, 1961–present; Practicing atty., 1961–90; TN Assembly, 1962–71, Speaker, 1969–71; Commissioner, TN Dept. of Conservation, 1971–72; Dir., TN Valley Authority, 1972–78; TN Circuit Court Judge, 1990–96.

DC Office: 1708 LHOB 20515, 202-225-6356; Fax: 202-225-5714.

District Offices: Kingsport, 423-247-8161.

Committees: *Agriculture* (26th of 27 R): Forestry, Resource Conservation & Research; Livestock, Dairy & Poultry. *Judiciary* (17th of 20 R): Constitution; Immigration & Claims.

Group Ratings and Key Votes: Newly Elected

Election Results

1996 general	William L. (Bill) Jenkins (R)	117,676	(65%)	($457,975)
	Kay C. Smith (D)	58,657	(32%)	($32,296)
	Others	5,375	(3%)	
1996 primary	William L. (Bill) Jenkins (R)	15,532	(18%)	
	Jim Holcomb (R)	15,201	(18%)	
	Al Schmutzer (R)	12,908	(15%)	
	David Davis (R)	10,787	(13%)	
	Richard S. Venable (R)	10,604	(13%)	
	David Crockett (R)	10,263	(12%)	
	Anne Pope (R)	8,247	(10%)	
1994 general	James H. (Jimmy) Quillen (R)	102,947	(73%)	($1,117,126)
	J. Carr (Jack) Cristian (D)	34,691	(25%)	
	Others	3,589	(3%)	

SECOND DISTRICT

Knoxville, the largest city in east Tennessee, is nestled between mountain ridges where the Holston and French Broad Rivers join to form the Tennessee. It was established not long after the first wave of pioneers came through the gaps and down between the mountains of the Appalachian chain. During the Civil War it was Union territory, and has remained Republican in allegiance ever since: the ancestral tug of Tennessee politics. But its Republican heritage is tempered by another tradition, that of the Tennessee Valley Authority. A venturesome program when created in the 1930s, it is now part of the fabric of life in east Tennessee, sometimes criticized as its cheap hydroelectric power capacity was filled and more of its production came from expensive and sometimes poorly functioning nuclear plants. But TVA has cut its payroll sharply in the last 10 years and held down rates; and in a newly competitive electricity market, its director has proposed abandoning federal subsidies and spinning off navigation and flood control functions to state or federal agencies.

The 2d Congressional District of Tennessee, which includes Knoxville and several mountainous counties to the south, is one of the most reliably Republican districts in the nation—but also one of the more practical-minded. The congressman from the district, Jimmy Duncan, is similarly inclined; his father represented the district from 1964 until his death in 1988. John Duncan, Jr.—his formal name—was educated in Knoxville and Washington, practiced law and was a trial judge in the 1980s. When his father died, he won the seat despite a spirited challenge from Democrat Dudley Taylor, also from a family long prominent in east Tennessee politics, who attacked Duncan for signing up with the National Guard in 1970 and for his ties to convicted banker Jake Butcher. Duncan won anyway with 57% in the special and 56% in November. He has been reelected easily in the 1990s.

Duncan is now chairman of the Aviation Subcommittee of Transportation and Infrastructure, dealing with issues like the airline tax and airline safety. The subcommittee passed a bill in September 1996 prohibiting unsolicited lawyers from contacting air crash victims' relatives for 30 days, and the House in July 1996 passed Duncan's bill—inspired by the death of 7-year-old pilot Jessica Dubroff—barring anyone without a valid pilot's license from flying to break a record. Duncan has been named by the National Taxpayers' Union as one of the top five fiscally conservative members of Congress, and he likes to point out questionable projects like NASA's $12 million to search for extraterrestrial intelligence and the Army Corps of Engineers proposal to restore Florida's Kissimmee River to its original shape after spending millions to straighten it out. "What really lacks compassion is for the federal government to take so much money from families that they don't have enough money left to support their children in the way they should," said Duncan. But Duncan has sought funding for local projects—resurfacing the

Foothills Parkway in the Great Smoky Mountains National Park, a $40 million federal judicial center in Knoxville, a $1.25 million grant to help Kimberly-Clark expand its operation in Loudon County, a $1 million grant to help put local public TV Channel 15 on the air. Duncan opposed the U.S. troop deployment to Bosnia, questioned the Mexico bailout in 1995 and criticized Alan Greenspan for actions to prop up Japanese banks. "I'm not saying we should be isolationist, but we can't solve every problem," Duncan remarked. He is chief sponsor of a National Parks checkoff on the income tax form, which would provide more funding for U.S. parks and, of course, the Great Smoky Mountains National Park.

The People: Pop. 1990: 541,780; 36% rural; 13% age 65+; 92% White; 7% Black; 1% Asian; 1% Hispanic origin. Households: 59% married couple families; 26% married couple fams. w. children; 41% college educ.; median household income: $25,267; per capita income: $13,118; median gross rent: $337; median house value: $59,400.

1996 Presidential Vote

Dole (R)	117,248	(51%)
Clinton (D)	95,810	(42%)
Perot (I)	12,522	(5%)

1992 Presidential Vote

Bush (R)	107,920	(48%)
Clinton (D)	92,752	(41%)
Perot (I)	25,157	(11%)

Rep. John J. Duncan, Jr. (R)

Elected 1988; b. July 21, 1947, Lebanon; home, Knoxville; U. of TN, B.S. 1969, George Washington U., J.D. 1973; Presbyterian; married (Lynn).

Career: Army Natl. Guard & Army Reserves, 1970–87; Practicing atty., 1973–81; St. Trial Judge, 1981–88.

DC Office: 2400 RHOB 20515, 202-225-5435; Fax: 202-225-6440; e-mail: jjduncan@hr.house.gov.

District Offices: Athens, 615-745-4671; Knoxville, 615-523-3772; Maryville, 615-984-5464.

Committees: *Resources* (6th of 27 R): Energy & Mineral Resources; National Parks & Public Lands. *Transportation & Infrastructure* (7th of 40 R): Aviation (Chmn.); Public Buildings & Economic Development.

Group Ratings

	ADA	ACLU	AFS	LCV	CFA	CON	NFIB	COC	ACU	NTLC	CHC
1996	30	20	17	38	31	95	95	88	85	98	100
1995	5	—	—	31	0	100	—	96	96	—	—

National Journal Ratings

	1995 LIB — 1995 CONS			1996 LIB — 1996 CONS		
Economic	26%	—	67%	32%	—	67%
Social	28%	—	70%	0%	—	90%
Foreign	52%	—	46%	55%	—	43%

Key Votes of the 104th Congress

1. Reduce Medicare Growth $	Y	5. Flag Amendment	Y	9. Cuban Embargo	Y
2. Ovrd. Product Liab. Veto	Y	6. Drop EPA Limits	*	10. Bar Bosnia Troop $	Y
3. Increase Min. Wage	Y	7. Repeal Assault-Weap. Ban	Y	11. Cut Anti-Missile Defense	N
4. Welfare Reform	Y	8. Ovrd. Part. Birth Veto	Y	12. Bar U.N. Uniforms	Y

Election Results

1996 general	John J. Duncan, Jr. (R)	150,953	(71%)	($260,818)
	Stephen Smith (D)	61,020	(29%)	($53,820)
1996 primary	John J. Duncan, Jr. (R)	unopposed		
1994 general	John J. Duncan, Jr. (R)	128,937	(90%)	($200,332)
	Randon J. Krieg (I)	6,854	(5%)	
	Greg Samples (I)	6,682	(5%)	

THIRD DISTRICT

Through some of the most vivid scenery of the Appalachian chain, etching its way through the serrated ridges of east Tennessee, is the river that gave Tennessee its name. From Knoxville, the river cuts through a ridge and then plunges down a long valley to the city of Chattanooga at the Georgia line. There it switches course again, winding around the table-top Lookout Mountain and then moving into northern Alabama. Chattanooga, the city at the base of Lookout Mountain, was just a village when it was a Civil War battlefield; it grew into an industrial city after the War. A quarter-century ago it was labeled America's most polluted city. But it has cleaned up its air with the use of smokestack scrubbers and battery-powered buses, and it has spruced up its river banks. It is now the proud home of the 12-story-high Tennessee Aquarium, the world's largest fresh water aquarium, with an exhibit in which you can follow the course of a drop of rain from the headwaters of the Tennessee until it flows out the Mississippi River into the ocean.

The 3d Congressional District of Tennessee is centered on Chattanooga, with an irregular shape that has a political provenance. It reaches far north to take in the Democratic area around Oak Ridge, site of the nuclear laboratory, but avoids heavily Republican counties on either side of this salient; it reaches east to the North Carolina line and west to the Cumberland Plateau to take in more Democratic areas. These lines were drawn by Democrats eager to keep the 3d Democratic; Chattanooga has been trending Republican in recent years, evidently pinning its hopes for growth more on the private sector, which developed the Aquarium among other attractions, and less on public sector institutions like the Tennessee Valley Authority, which has laid off more than a third of its work force and whose chairman wants to zero out federal subsidies.

The congressman from the 3d District is Zach Wamp, a Republican elected in 1994. Wamp left college before graduating to become a real estate developer back in Chattanooga, selling $22 million in real estate in five years. In 1987, at 30, he was county Republican chairman. In 1992 he ran for Congress against 20-year Democrat Marilyn Lloyd in a high-voltage race. At the start, Wamp revealed he had used cocaine and had treatment for it 10 years before. Lloyd referred to Wamp's "criminal" past (two bad checks for $20 written while he was in college) and litigation against his real estate firm; Wamp called these "vicious, personal attacks." Wamp carried Chattanooga and Hamilton County 51%–44%; overall Lloyd won by just 49%–47%, the closest margin of her career, and she decided to retire in 1994.

In 1994, Wamp ran again as a strong conservative; one proposal was to pay members of Congress the same as a lieutenant colonel and billet them in officer housing. Democrat Randy Button, winner of a close primary, attacked Wamp's character, bringing up his past cocaine use and accusing him of lying when he said he had a "Q" security clearance at the Oak Ridge Reservation and only had a "Secret" clearance instead. Wamp accused Button of flip-flopping on issues and attacked him for taking PAC money. Like many Republicans, Wamp ran an ad showing his opponent's face morphing into Bill Clinton's. Button complained, saying his six-year-old daughter was upset: "She said it turned her father into a monster." Wamp ran behind the statewide Republican ticket, but still won, carrying Hamilton County 54%–43% and losing the Oak Ridge area only narrowly, for an overall win of 52%–46%.

In the House, Wamp was elected the freshman representative on the Republican Steering Committee and was made the number two Republican on the subcommittee overseeing the Tennessee Valley Authority. He got $25 million for flood control in East Ridge, funding for a NEXRAD weather radar station to serve southeast Tennessee, funding for natural gas lines to Meigs County; he promises to work to develop an East Tennessee Technology Corridor and to complete the Spallation Neutron Source installation in Oak Ridge. He urged creative action to get more airline flights—perhaps buying arrival and departure slots at larger airports, perhaps financing a startup carrier—for Chattanooga's spiffy airport, which recently opened a new terminal. He became chairman of the TVA Caucus, even as TVA was moving away from reliance on government and toward market competition. He has made a conservative record laced with stands of great appeal locally. He has never accepted PAC money and supports the McCain-Feingold campaign finance reform bill. In December 1995 Marilyn Lloyd endorsed him for reelection; he said that most people "yearn for more statesmanship and less partisanship."

In 1996 Wamp had spirited opposition from Chuck Jolly, second-place finisher in the 1994 Democratic primary. Democrats were furious that Wamp mass-mailed through a local vendor newsletters to nearly 6,500 black households touting his record on civil rights; but harping on this issue may not have won many votes. Wamp conducted a mostly positive campaign but hit Jolly for accepting $3,000 from the Laborers' Union, which the U.S. Justice Department and the union agreed has "ties to organized crime, according to federal records." Wamp won 56%–43%, an improvement on 1994, and ahead of party lines; Bob Dole carried the district by just 47%–46%. On election night Wamp said, "Angels have found their way to my path over the last two years in Washington and here in this district, but tonight I genuinely want to humble myself in service to you to recognize that God Almighty has given me this opportunity, and I'm grateful so very much for it." In the House he got a seat on the Appropriations Committee, the first Tennessee Republican there since 1910—a fine spot from which to work on East Tennessee projects.

The People: Pop. 1990: 542,065; 35% rural; 14% age 65+; 87% White; 12% Black; 1% Asian; 1% Hispanic origin. Households: 59% married couple families; 26% married couple fams. w. children; 38% college educ.; median household income: $24,687; per capita income: $12,338; median gross rent: $348; median house value: $55,000.

1996 Presidential Vote

Dole (R)	93,799	(47%)
Clinton (D)	92,780	(46%)
Perot (I)	13,284	(7%)

1992 Presidential Vote

Clinton (D)	97,112	(44%)
Bush (R)	97,073	(44%)
Perot (I)	25,719	(12%)

Rep. Zach Wamp (R)

Elected 1994; b. Oct. 28, 1957, Fort Benning, GA; home, Chattanooga; U. of NC, 1976–77, 1979–80; U. of TN, 1978–79; Baptist; married (Kim).

Career: Regional Sales Super., 1981–82; Partner, Wamp Alliance Architectural Development Co., 1983–89; Real estate broker, 1989–94.

DC Office: 423 CHOB 20515, 202-225-3271; Fax: 202-225-3494.

District Offices: Chattanooga, 423-894-7400; Oak Ridge, 423-483-3366.

Committees: *Appropriations* (31st of 34 R): Interior; Legislative; Military Construction.

Group Ratings

	ADA	ACLU	AFS	LCV	CFA	CON	NFIB	COC	ACU	NTLC	CHC
1996	15	19	0	15	23	71	100	88	100	90	100
1995	0	—	—	6	8	87	—	96	100	—	—

National Journal Ratings

	1995 LIB — 1995 CONS			1996 LIB — 1996 CONS		
Economic	0%	—	74%	39%	—	58%
Social	0%	—	79%	10%	—	86%
Foreign	28%	—	65%	30%	—	65%

Key Votes of the 104th Congress

1. Reduce Medicare Growth $	Y	5. Flag Amendment	Y	9. Cuban Embargo	Y
2. Ovrd. Product Liab. Veto	Y	6. Drop EPA Limits	N	10. Bar Bosnia Troop $	Y
3. Increase Min. Wage	N	7. Repeal Assault-Weap. Ban	Y	11. Cut Anti-Missile Defense	N
4. Welfare Reform	Y	8. Ovrd. Part. Birth Veto	Y	12. Bar U.N. Uniforms	Y

Election Results

1996 general	Zach Wamp (R)	113,408	(56%)	($942,237)
	Charles N. Jolly (D)	85,714	(43%)	($420,390)
1996 primary	Zach Wamp (R)	unopposed		
1994 general	Zach Wamp (R)	84,583	(52%)	($704,220)
	Randy Button (D)	73,839	(46%)	($502,668)
	Others	3,431	(2%)	

FOURTH DISTRICT

The invisible line between Civil War Republican and Civil War Democratic territory runs along the Cumberland Plateau, the westernmost upswelling of the Appalachians, west of the valley where the Tennessee River runs south from Knoxville to Chattanooga. It separates the Tennessee valley, which had few slaves and whose economic ties were with the North, from the rolling farmlands of middle Tennessee, first settled by Andrew Jackson in the 1790s and resolutely Democratic from the time he became the first president to call himself a Democrat in the 1830s. And not only is this line invisible, it is also irregular: some counties in west Tennessee, where the Tennessee River runs north from Alabama to Kentucky, are Union Republican.

The 4th Congressional District of Tennessee runs across this line and crosses the state northeast to southwest, from Lee County, Virginia, all the way to Tishomingo County, Mississippi. It is some 300 miles long, yet seldom more than one county wide, and contains such spots as Lynchburg, home of the Jack Daniels distillery since 1860, and Dayton, where in 1925 John Scopes was prosecuted by William Jennings Bryan and defended by Clarence Darrow for teaching Darwin's theory of evolution.

The congressman from the 4th District is Van Hilleary, a Republican elected in 1994. Hilleary grew up in Spring City, where he helped start the family textile company; after college he served in the Air Force, went to law school and volunteered for duty in the Persian Gulf, where he flew 24 missions on a C-130. In 1992, at 33, he ran for the state Senate against 18-year incumbent Anna Belle Clement O'Brien, sister of former Governor Frank Clement, and lost by only 52%–48% despite her much greater fame and financing. In 1994, when 4th District incumbent Democrat Jim Cooper, sponsor of a major managed care bill, ran for the Senate, Hilleary was one of three Republicans to file for the primary. He easily won the Republican primary with 58%. Hilleary argued for term limits, welfare reform with a two-year limit, tougher crime sentences and limiting PACs to the same amount as individual contributions and 10% of a candidate's total campaign funds. In the general the Democratic nominee was Jeff Whorley, at 34 a veteran of Democratic campaigns since he was 18 and former aide to 6th District Democrat Bart Gordon. He won his five-person primary with 31% and favored the death penalty, school vouchers, school prayer, gun control: mostly a conservative platform. Whorley spent over $225,000 more than Hilleary, who took no PAC money. Hilleary carried the eastern Republican counties by wide margins; he carried the far western counties, where Whorley was hurt by the harsh aftereffects of the primary campaign, and he lost the middle Tennessee counties rather narrowly, for a 57%–42% victory.

In his second full month in the House, Hilleary was in the spotlight as the sponsor of a term limits constitutional amendment, the first freshman to put an amendment to a vote since 1897; his version would limit members to 12 years or less if required by state law. The measure was caught between advocates of six- and 12-year term limits, and was beaten 164–265. Hilleary was more successful on a quieter issue: an amendment to kill a $1,000 docking fee imposed by the Tennessee Valley Authority's Shoreline Management Initiative on anyone who builds or improves a dock on TVA's lakes. Hilleary's amendment passed, but was killed in conference by pro-TVA Republican Jimmy Quillen. However, Hilleary snuck his dock deposit ban into the October 1996 continuing resolution and it became law, foiling TVA's plans.

In 1996 Hilleary had spirited opposition from Democrat Mark Stewart, whose grandfather A. Tom Stewart served as U.S. senator from 1939–49. Stewart blasted Hilleary for his ties to Newt Gingrich's Contract With America; Hilleary asserted that he had done what he promised, working for a balanced budget and welfare reform. A Stewart ad said "Van Hilleary and Newt Gingrich have hurt Tennessee families" and "taken food away from the elderly," citing a $23 million cut in Meals on Wheels which Hilleary said was just a cut in bureaucracy. A Hilleary ad said, "Fact is, Van Hilleary's been in Congress fighting for senior citizens and working families. What's Mark Stewart been doing? He's a trial lawyer. Defended criminals convicted of child abuse. He defended child molesters, drunk drivers, even a man accused of attempted murder." There was much talk that this was a close race, and Bill Clinton carried the district 46%–45%. But Hilleary this time outspent his opponent and won by a wider margin than in 1994, 58%–41%, carrying every county but two.

In the 105th Congress Hilleary got a seat on the Budget Committee. But he still showed independence of the leadership when he refused to back reinstatement of the airline ticket tax without an offsetting tax cut.

The People: Pop. 1990: 541,650; 74% rural; 14% age 65+; 96% White; 4% Black. Households: 65% married couple families; 29% married couple fams. w. children; 24% college educ.; median household income: $20,685; per capita income: $9,886; median gross rent: $277; median house value: $44,400.

1996 Presidential Vote			1992 Presidential Vote		
Clinton (D)	92,106	(46%)	Clinton (D)	100,292	(48%)
Dole (R)	90,135	(45%)	Bush (R)	83,923	(40%)
Perot (I)	14,816	(7%)	Perot (I)	23,838	(11%)

Rep. Van Hilleary (R)

Elected 1994; b. June 20, 1959, Dayton; home, Grandview; U. of TN, B.S. 1981; Samford U. Cumberland Schl. of Law, J.D. 1990; Presbyterian; single.

Career: Air Force, 1982–84; Air Force Reserves, 1984–present (Persian Gulf); Dir., Planning & Business Devel., SSM Industries, Inc, 1984–86, 1992–94.

DC Office: 114 CHOB 20515, 202-225-6831; Fax: 202-225-3272; e-mail: hilleary@hr.house.gov.

District Offices: Crossville, 615-484-1114; Morristown, 423-587-0396; Tullahoma, 615-393-4764.

Committees: *Budget* (21st of 24 R). *Education & The Workforce* (24th of 25 R): Early Childhood, Youth & Families; Oversight & Investigations. *National Security* (22nd of 30 R): Military Installations & Facilities; Military Research & Development.

Group Ratings

	ADA	ACLU	AFS	LCV	CFA	CON	NFIB	COC	ACU	NTLC	CHC
1996	0	19	8	31	15	38	97	94	95	100	100
1995	0	—	—	0	8	75	—	100	100	—	—

National Journal Ratings

	1995 LIB — 1995 CONS			1996 LIB — 1996 CONS		
Economic	0%	—	74%	20%	—	76%
Social	0%	—	79%	10%	—	86%
Foreign	15%	—	73%	0%	—	79%

Key Votes of the 104th Congress

1. Reduce Medicare Growth $	Y	5. Flag Amendment	Y	9. Cuban Embargo	Y
2. Ovrd. Product Liab. Veto	Y	6. Drop EPA Limits	N	10. Bar Bosnia Troop $	Y
3. Increase Min. Wage	Y	7. Repeal Assault-Weap. Ban	Y	11. Cut Anti-Missile Defense	N
4. Welfare Reform	Y	8. Ovrd. Part. Birth Veto	Y	12. Bar U.N. Uniforms	Y

Election Results

1996 general	Van Hilleary (R)	103,091	(58%)	($1,183,570)
	Mark Stewart (D)	73,331	(41%)	($586,987)
1996 primary	Van Hilleary (R)	unopposed		
1994 general	Van Hilleary (R)	81,539	(57%)	($613,648)
	Jeff Whorley (D)	60,489	(42%)	($842,445)

FIFTH DISTRICT

Nashville is the home of country music, the buckle of the Bible Belt, and in almost every way the heart of Tennessee. This was one of the first American cities established west of the Appalachians; Andrew Jackson built his Hermitage nearby above the banks of the Cumberland River, and his political home base has remained Democratic ever since. It was the capital of Tennessee early on, just as it was—and still is—the center of the state's political life and discourse: the *Tennessean* and the *Nashville Banner* still present more or less Democratic and Republican views of Tennessee politics, and Nashville is the biggest television market in the state. Nashville is proud of its universities and of its columned Capitol and its Parthenon; this is perhaps the greatest center of Greek Revival architecture in America. Nashville is also firmly established as the religious publishing center of the country, producing more Bibles probably than any city in the world. And of course, Nashville is headquarters to a $2 billion nationwide country music industry centered on the Country Music Hall of Fame and the Grand Ole Opry, now broadcast from the giant theme park on the banks of the Cumberland in Opryland U.S.A.

Nashville has been one of the boom cities of the South in the 1980s and 1990s, the fastest growing metropolitan area between Atlanta and Dallas-Fort Worth. Country music and Bible publishing flourished, Ingram grew as the nation's largest book wholesaler, the Goo-Goo Cluster candy factory churned out its product, Nissan built a big plant in nearby Smyrna and General Motors set its Saturn plant in nearby Spring Hill, and many smaller businesses started up. There were commercial and apartment real estate booms as well, though followed as booms usually are by some busts. But the overall picture is of growth and, for those who can remember back more than a generation, a lifestyle of comfort mostly undreamed of—air conditioning everywhere, shopping malls and supermarkets overflowing with affordable goods. An agreeable quality of life, plenty of medium-wage, high-skill labor, a central location, and absence of urban strife and militant unions have all helped Nashville grow.

The 5th District of Tennessee includes all but one precinct of Nashville and Davidson County plus the bulk of increasingly suburban Robertson County to the north—but this is not all of metropolitan Nashville now that development has spread into once rural areas. The 5th is usually reliably Democratic in statewide elections, and to Congress it has long elected rather liberal Democrats: this is, after all, the home of the first Democratic president. It was also for several years the home of Al Gore, when he was a divinity student at Vanderbilt and reporter for the *Tennessean*, and as much his home base as is his ancestral home near Carthage in Smith County.

The congressman from the 5th District is Bob Clement, a Democrat whose father was a three-term governor of Tennessee and memorably keynoted the 1956 Democratic National Convention. Bob Clement grew up in Tennessee, was elected to the Public Service Commission in 1972, at 29, served six years, including two as chairman, and went into private business, was on the Tennessee Valley Authority board from 1979–81, and in 1982 lost a House race in the 7th District to Don Sundquist, now governor, by 51%–49%. He then went into real estate and became president of Cumberland University. In 1987, after incumbent Bill Boner resigned one step ahead of an ethics investigation, Clement ran in a special election in the 5th, winning the Democratic primary with 40% (Tennessee has no runoff) and easily winning the January 1988 special election.

In the House, Clement has compiled a moderate voting record, voting for welfare reform and English as the official language. He has worked on airport noise abatement and getting Nashville $1 million from the Intelligent Transportation Systems account for downtown parking and a traffic guidance system; he pushed to replace the Bordeaux railroad bridge over the Cumberland River and to finish the Natchez Trace Parkway into Nashville; he has worked hard on nuclear plant design standards and increasing penalties for drug sales at truck stops. He has supported music and arts education and has won funding for the restoration of buildings at historically black colleges and universities. He has proposed to eliminate soft money contributions: "I'm weary of the negative politics." He supported the unsuccessful nomination of Nashville's Henry Foster to be surgeon general.

Clement has been reelected by wide margins in the 5th District. He considered running for governor in 1994, but decided not to do so; he has been mentioned as a candidate in 1998.

The People: Pop. 1990: 541,878; 5% rural; 12% age 65+; 75% White; 23% Black; 1% Asian; 1% Hispanic origin. Households: 48% married couple families; 21% married couple fams. w. children; 47%

college educ.; median household income: $28,208; per capita income: $14,874; median gross rent: $430; median house value: $74,200.

1996 Presidential Vote			1992 Presidential Vote		
Clinton (D)	116,987	(55%)	Clinton (D)	112,795	(53%)
Dole (R)	82,053	(39%)	Bush (R)	79,398	(37%)
Perot (I)	9,727	(5%)	Perot (I)	21,531	(10%)

Rep. Bob Clement (D)

Elected Jan. 1988; b. Sept. 23, 1943, Nashville; home, Nashville; U. of TN, B.S. 1967, Memphis St. U., M.B.A. 1968; United Methodist; married (Mary).

Career: Army, 1969–71, Army Natl. Guard, 1971–present; TN Public Svc. Comm., 1972–79; Bd. of Dir., TN Valley Authority, 1979–81; Founder and owner, Bob Clement & Assoc., 1981–83; Owner and partner, Charter Equities real estate, 1981–83; Pres., Cumberland U., 1983–87.

DC Office: 2229 RHOB 20515, 202-225-4311; Fax: 202-226-1035; e-mail: clement@hr.house.gov.

District Offices: Nashville, 615-736-5295; N. Nashville, 615-320-1363; Springfield, 615-384-6600.

Committees: *International Relations* (20th of 22 D): International Economic Policy & Trade. *Transportation & Infrastructure* (8th of 33 D): Coast Guard & Maritime Transportation (RMM); Railroads.

Group Ratings

	ADA	ACLU	AFS	LCV	CFA	CON	NFIB	COC	ACU	NTLC	CHC
1996	60	40	83	77	69	66	65	50	30	32	33
1995	75	—	—	56	62	25	—	63	32	—	—

National Journal Ratings

	1995 LIB — 1995 CONS	1996 LIB — 1996 CONS
Economic	60% — 39%	58% — 41%
Social	61% — 39%	55% — 43%
Foreign	66% — 33%	57% — 42%

Key Votes of the 104th Congress

1. Reduce Medicare Growth $	N	5. Flag Amendment	Y	9. Cuban Embargo	N
2. Ovrd. Product Liab. Veto	Y	6. Drop EPA Limits	*	10. Bar Bosnia Troop $	N
3. Increase Min. Wage	Y	7. Repeal Assault-Weap. Ban	Y	11. Cut Anti-Missile Defense	Y
4. Welfare Reform	N	8. Ovrd. Part. Birth Veto	Y	12. Bar U.N. Uniforms	N

Election Results

1996 general	Bob Clement (D)	140,264	(72%)	($299,403)
	Steven L. Edmondson (R)	46,201	(24%)	
	Others	7,318	(4%)	
1996 primary	Bob Clement (D)	unopposed		
1994 general	Bob Clement (D)	95,953	(60%)	($486,214)
	John Osborne (R)	61,692	(39%)	($102,251)

SIXTH DISTRICT

The rolling countryside of middle Tennessee, west of the Cumberland Plateau and the last chain of Appalachians, has been called "the dimple of the universe." This is hilly and fertile land, cut by deep rivers ambling along in S-curves. The terrain here was never much suited for plantation crops; this has long been a land of small farmers and small county seat towns, nestled amid what people here regard as some of the loveliest scenery on earth. Middle Tennessee has also been one of the heartlands of the Democratic Party. It was the political home base of Andrew Jackson and supported him nearly unanimously; during the Civil War, though it had very few slaves, it resisted the invading Union armies. For 140 years after Jackson, it voted solidly Democratic and elected as its congressmen some of the luminaries of the national Democratic Party: James K. Polk (1825–39), speaker of the House and later president; Cordell Hull (1907–21, 1923–31), later senator and secretary of State; Albert Gore Sr., (1939–53), later senator; and Albert Gore Jr., (1977–85), later senator and now vice president.

The 6th Congressional District of Tennessee includes 14 middle Tennessee counties east and south of Nashville, plus a bit of Nashville itself. The heritage here is old and rural, but economic growth has fanned out into the farmland from Nashville—symbolized most vividly by the huge Nissan plant in Smyrna and General Motors's Saturn plant in Spring Hill (actually a mile outside the district), but also evident in thousands of jobs created by Japanese companies and American startups, firms fleeing the North and entrepreneurs fleeing Texas. Many new voters here are Republican, not only in the affluent suburbs of Williamson County just south of Nashville, but in the more modest suburbs spreading to the east. The 6th District voted for the Clinton-Gore ticket by 47%–40% in 1992, a margin that was decisive but which would not have impressed Andrew Jackson. In 1996 it voted for the Dole-Kemp ticket 47%–45%, which would have impressed General Jackson very negatively indeed.

The congressman from the 6th District is Bart Gordon, a Democrat first elected in 1984 when Al Gore left the House seat to run for the Senate. Gordon grew up in Murfreesboro in Rutherford County and went to college there. He practiced law and became Tennessee Democratic chairman in 1981: politics is most of his life. In 1984, he ran a computerized fund-raising operation and voter contact system—then a novelty in this district where a personal handshake from a candidate was the norm. He won a multi-candidate primary with 28% of the vote—there is no runoff in Tennessee—and won the general election 63%–37%.

In the House, Gordon used his insider skills to build a close relationship with the Democratic leadership, and got a seat on the Rules Committee in 1987. Gordon went after trade schools with high student loan default rates, even posing in 1991 as a student (though he was 42 at the time) with an NBC investigative unit. He passed new accountability provisions for the federal financial aid system in 1992 and claims that defaults have dropped from 22% of loans in 1990 to 12% in 1993—a significant saving for taxpayers. Gordon also got passed a proposal to ban Pell grants to prison inmates, which amazingly enough has saved between $70 million and $200 million a year. In the Democratic 103d Congress he passed a bill to require phone companies to make available free blocking of 900 lines, so that parents could keep their children from pornography services. He also worked in the Republican 104th Congress, in which he lost his seat on Rules and moved to Commerce, for the V-chip in the Telecommunications Act and to bar charges for 800 number pornographic services without parents' permission, and he supported the Communications Decency Act to apply obscenity standards to the Internet. With a similar ear for constituents' complaints, he has opposed construction of a temporary nuclear waste dump in middle Tennessee. He has also opposed Republican proposals to sell the South Eastern Power Administration, which he says will put the dam-created lakes on the Tennessee and Cumberland Rivers up for auction.

But Gordon's moderate-to-liberal voting record and his support of the Democratic leadership in this Republican-trending district have caused him trouble in the 1990s. In 1992, after winning four races with over 60%, Gordon was reelected 57%–41%. In 1994 he faced Steve Gill, a lawyer from Williamson County, better known as a member of a championship basketball team at the University of Tennessee. Gill dressed in his trademark maroon shirt, and spread his anti-Clinton message—balanced budget amendment, tougher sentences, term limits—around the district. Gordon spent $1,386,000, with $608,000 of it from PACs, more than Gill spent altogether. Gill ran ahead in the ring of counties around Nashville, where most of the votes are cast, 52%–48%. But Gordon carried the smaller rural counties 58%–42%, for a slim overall victory margin of 51%–49%.

After the election, Gill never stopped running, and for that matter neither did Gordon. Much of the dialogue stayed the same: Gill hit Gordon as a liberal who voted 40 times for tax increases in 12 years and voted himself a $45,000 pay increase. Travelling the district in an 18-wheel tractor-trailer, Gill complained that Gordon voted for welfare reform just to neutralize a campaign issue and said he used House staff for personal affairs. Gordon counterattacked on two fronts. On the one hand, he ran an ad charging that Gill used campaign money to get his personal car back after it was repossessed and that he failed to pay property taxes on time. On the other hand, Gordon called for serenity by offering to pull his ad off the air: "When I was a boy, my grandfather told me that there would be times in life when I could choose to take the high road or the low road, and I believe this is one of those times." Gordon also courted local tobacco farmers, even as former local tobacco farmer Al Gore was pummeling the tobacco industry at the Chicago convention. Gordon had more money: Gill spent an impressive $1.1 million, but Gordon spent $1.6 million, raising—despite Republican control of the House—$743,000 from PACs. Gordon raised his percentage from 51% in 1994 to 54% in 1996, for a 54%–42% win; with a big margin in his home county he won 51% in the counties outside Nashville and 64% in the rural counties. This could very well be a seriously contested race in 1998.

The People: Pop. 1990: 542,002; 54% rural; 11% age 65+; 93% White; 6% Black; 1% Asian; 1% Hispanic origin. Households: 66% married couple families; 33% married couple fams. w. children; 38% college educ.; median household income: $29,234; per capita income: $13,286; median gross rent: $378; median house value: $71,300.

1996 Presidential Vote

Dole (R)	112,827	(47%)
Clinton (D)	107,821	(45%)
Perot (I)	15,375	(6%)

1992 Presidential Vote

Clinton (D)	109,895	(47%)
Bush (R)	93,036	(40%)
Perot (I)	28,151	(12%)

Rep. Bart Gordon (D)

Elected 1984; b. Jan. 24, 1949, Murfreesboro; home, Murfreesboro; Middle TN St. U., B.S. 1971, U. of TN, J.D. 1973; United Methodist; single.

Career: Practicing atty., 1974–84; Chmn., TN Dem. Party, 1981–83.

DC Office: 2201 RHOB 20515, 202-225-4231; Fax: 202-225-6887; e-mail: bart@hr.house.gov.

District Offices: Cookeville, 615-528-5907; Murfreesboro, 615-896-1986.

Committees: *Commerce* (10th of 23 D): Energy & Power; Telecommunications, Trade & Consumer Protection. *Science* (3rd of 21 D): Space & Aeronautics; Technology (RMM).

Group Ratings

	ADA	ACLU	AFS	LCV	CFA	CON	NFIB	COC	ACU	NTLC	CHC
1996	45	38	67	69	69	38	70	56	50	46	40
1995	75	—	—	38	54	16	—	63	40	—	—

National Journal Ratings

	1995 LIB — 1995 CONS			1996 LIB — 1996 CONS		
Economic	59%	—	40%	55%	—	44%
Social	64%	—	36%	55%	—	43%
Foreign	64%	—	34%	70%	—	29%

Key Votes of the 104th Congress

1. Reduce Medicare Growth $	N	5. Flag Amendment	Y	9. Cuban Embargo	Y
2. Ovrd. Product Liab. Veto	Y	6. Drop EPA Limits	Y	10. Bar Bosnia Troop $	Y
3. Increase Min. Wage	Y	7. Repeal Assault-Weap. Ban	Y	11. Cut Anti-Missile Defense	Y
4. Welfare Reform	Y	8. Ovrd. Part. Birth Veto	Y	12. Bar U.N. Uniforms	Y

Election Results

1996 general	Bart Gordon (D)	123,846	(54%)	($1,609,419)
	Steve Gill (R)	94,599	(42%)	($1,107,850)
	Jim Coffer (I)	9,125	(4%)	($1,113)
1996 primary	Bart Gordon (D)	37,324	(89%)	
	Jessie R. Bly (D)	4,673	(11%)	
1994 general	Bart Gordon (D)	90,933	(51%)	($1,385,995)
	Steve Gill (R)	88,759	(49%)	($533,704)

SEVENTH DISTRICT

Rural Tennessee north of Mississippi is one of the most sparsely settled areas in the state. Along each side of the Tennessee River, as it flows north and widens out into Kentucky Lake amid heavy forests, are small rural communities that go back to pre-Civil War days and have not grown much since. Farther west the land is flatter and more open, a northward extension economically and demographically of the northern Mississippi farmlands, with cotton fields and a large black rural population. This mostly empty land is bounded on two sides by large metropolitan areas, Nashville to the east and Memphis to the west.

The 7th Congressional District of Tennessee spans this territory, from the Cheatham County suburban fringe of Nashville, west across the Tennessee River and south to the Mississippi border and finally to the white neighborhoods on the east side of Memphis and Shelby County. It is a mixed district politically. Most of the rural counties are traditionally Democratic, with a few Republican exceptions, while the fringe of Nashville is mixed and the 7th District's portion of Memphis is, like all white parts of Memphis, heavily Republican. The balance has usually tipped toward Republicans, though the lines in Memphis and Shelby County were altered by 1990s redistricting to help the Democrats.

The congressman from the 7th District is Ed Bryant, a Republican elected in 1994 to replace Republican Don Sundquist, who was elected governor. Bryant is from Jackson in west Tennessee, went to school at Ole Miss, served six years in the Army and practiced law in Tennessee since 1978. In 1991, President Bush, on the recommendation of Don Sundquist, made him U.S. attorney in West Tennessee; Bryant left that post in 1993 in a dispute over jury selection in the bank fraud trial of then-Memphis Democratic Congressman Harold Ford Sr. This was a hugely visible and controversial case, which gave him celebrity all over the area. In the 1994 Republican primary, Bryant lost Shelby County to Germantown Mayor Charles Salvaggio. But he won in all but one of the rural counties by enough votes to win overall 35%–

33% (Tennessee has no runoff). The Democratic nomination went to Harold Byrd, former state legislator and former aide to Senator Jim Sasser, owner of a family farm, travel agency, bank and mortgage company.

One omen for the general election is that more votes were cast in the Republican primary (62,000) than in the Democratic (57,000), not the usual pattern in Tennessee. Bryant called for converting closed military bases into prisons, term limits and cuts in congressional staff; he proposed that half of all congressional campaign contributions must be from in-state. Byrd called for market-oriented healthcare reform, the balanced budget amendment and line item veto: a pretty conservative platform. This was a close race, 51%–48% for Bryant outside Shelby County. But Bryant carried Shelby County with 72%, for an overall solid 60%–39% win.

In the House Bryant was a visible co-sponsor of Contract With America crime bills, and also sponsored bills for doubling the penalty for prison escapes from 5 to 10 years, for a life without parole sentence in military law, for trying federal judges in different circuits from where they served. He was especially strong for *habeas corpus* reform, but he also argued that measures like midnight basketball were useful when properly administered. In response to a bill which was blocking the move of the Houston Oilers to Nashville, Bryant proposed the Sports Relocation Reform Act, which would balance the interests of professional sports leagues and the communities affected by franchise relocation.

The 1996 race was still close in the rural areas; Bryant lost seven counties, including the area around Clarksville and Fort Campbell. But he carried the Shelby County portion of the district 81%–17%, for a 65%–33% victory.

The People: Pop. 1990: 542,270; 43% rural; 10% age 65+; 86% White; 12% Black; 1% Asian; 1% Hispanic origin. Households: 65% married couple families; 32% married couple fams. w. children; 42% college educ.; median household income: $29,242; per capita income: $13,758; median gross rent: $412; median house value: $69,500.

1996 Presidential Vote

Dole (R)	122,177	(54%)
Clinton (D)	92,802	(41%)
Perot (I)	10,965	(5%)

1992 Presidential Vote

Bush (R)	114,544	(50%)
Clinton (D)	91,644	(40%)
Perot (I)	22,486	(10%)

Rep. Ed Bryant (R)

Elected 1994; b. Sept. 7, 1948, Jackson; home, Henderson; U. of MS, B.A. 1970, J.D. 1972; Protestant; married (Cyndi).

Career: Army, 1973–78; Instructor, West Point Military Acad., 1977–1978; Practicing atty., 1978–90; US Atty. for West TN, 1991–93.

DC Office: 408 CHOB 20515, 202-225-2811; Fax: 202-225-2989.

District Offices: Clarksville, 615-503-0391; Columbia, 615-381-8100; Memphis, 901-382-5811.

Committees: *Agriculture* (16th of 27 R): Risk Management & Specialty Crops. *Judiciary* (14th of 20 R): Commercial & Administrative Law; Constitution; Immigration & Claims.

Group Ratings

	ADA	ACLU	AFS	LCV	CFA	CON	NFIB	COC	ACU	NTLC	CHC
1996	0	6	0	15	0	17	100	100	100	100	100
1995	0	—	—	0	0	75	—	100	100	—	—

National Journal Ratings

	1995 LIB — 1995 CONS			1996 LIB — 1996 CONS		
Economic	0%	—	74%	0%	—	82%
Social	0%	—	79%	0%	—	90%
Foreign	28%	—	65%	0%	—	79%

Key Votes of the 104th Congress

1. Reduce Medicare Growth $	Y	5. Flag Amendment	Y	9. Cuban Embargo	Y
2. Ovrd. Product Liab. Veto	Y	6. Drop EPA Limits	N	10. Bar Bosnia Troop $	Y
3. Increase Min. Wage	N	7. Repeal Assault-Weap. Ban	Y	11. Cut Anti-Missile Defense	N
4. Welfare Reform	Y	8. Ovrd. Part. Birth Veto	Y	12. Bar U.N. Uniforms	Y

Election Results

1996 general	Ed Bryant (R)	126,737	(65%)	($649,783)
	Don Trotter (D)	64,512	(33%)	($315,501)
1996 primary	Ed Bryant (R)	unopposed		
1994 general	Ed Bryant (R)	102,587	(60%)	($493,712)
	Harold Byrd (D)	65,851	(39%)	($608,768)

EIGHTH DISTRICT

West of Nashville and the TVA lakes along the Tennessee River and north of Memphis, the rivers roll lazily through flat or gently rolling land that almost could be the northern end of Mississippi. Cotton and soybeans are the main crops; more blacks remain in rural areas here than in any other part of Tennessee, a reminder of its old plantation economy. The towns here are small, edged in by farm fields; the river bottoms, often flooded, are heavily forested. Here is Henning, the home town of Alex Haley, where he used to sit on his porch and listen to his aunts tell him stories about slave ships and the Civil War that in time became *Roots*.

The 8th Congressional District of Tennessee includes much of this west Tennessee farmland, from the TVA lakes west to the Mississippi; its largest city is Jackson, but it includes the northern fringe of Memphis. Historically, this is Democratic country; Republicans haven't represented most of the counties that make up the 8th since the end of Reconstruction. The region trended Republican in national races in the 1960s and 1970s, then turned back toward the Democrats with the help of some smart local politicians. One of them is Ned McWherter, first elected to the legislature from Weakley County in 1968, speaker from 1973–86, then governor until 1994; another was Congressman Ed Jones, elected in a 1969 special election over a Republican and a George Wallace-supported Independent in a race which presaged the survival of conservative Democrats in rural southern districts for another quarter century.

The congressman from the 8th District is John Tanner, a Democrat elected in 1988. Tanner grew up in Obion County, went to college and law school at the University of Tennessee, served four years in the Navy, then practiced law in Union City: exactly the sort of local notable who traditionally runs things in southern politics, combining political shrewdness with a country demeanor. At 32, he successfully ran for the Tennessee House in 1976, where he served 12 years. In 1988, when Jones retired, he ran for Congress and won the seat with a whopping 66% in a four-candidate primary and 62% in the general. Tanner's voting record put him solidly in the middle of the Democratic House, a little to the left of midpoint in the Republican House. He has worked on local issues, promoting the City of Millington and then getting a grant to redevelop its Naval Air Station's surplus property. He successfully opposed a 1995 move to end federal payments to the Tennessee Valley Authority, which would have cut funding for the Land Between the Lakes park; in 1997 the TVA director called for an end to federal payments and spinning off of such functions to state governments and federal agencies. He has sponsored research on the New Madrid Fault, which produced three great earthquakes in 1811–12. He stopped the killing of Commerce's Manufacturing Extension Partnership program in 1995 and was co-sponsor of a successful Technologies Transfer bill in 1996. He wants to eliminate estate taxes on family-owned farms and small businesses and in early 1997 opposed the IRS's current-year taxation of farmers' income from deferred payment contracts. He has long supported the balanced budget amendment and line-item veto, though has opposed some Republican versions. In 1992, Tanner could have been a senator for the asking. Governor McWherter was ready to appoint him to succeed Al Gore, but Tanner refused the post and chose instead to stay in the House. If he had accepted he might have become a more nationally prominent figure, but he would also have had to defend the seat in what turned out to be the very Republican year of 1994.

Instead Tanner has become a major force in the House. He is one of the founders and co-chairman of The Coalition, known more often as the Blue Dogs, a group of conservative Democrats who have advanced their own budget and welfare reform proposals. The Blue Dog budget has no tax cuts until the budget is balanced, and would cut spending sooner than either Democratic or Republican budgets; it got 130 votes in May 1996, including 20 from Republicans: the closest thing to a bipartisan budget in the partisanly divided House. Tanner was also co-sponsor (after the original co-sponsor, Nathan Deal, switched parties) of the Blue Dogs' welfare reform proposal. This, he claims with some basis, was "the genesis for the broad welfare reform plan that the President signed in August" 1996. When House Republicans revived the welfare issue in July 1996, Tanner passed amendments allowing states to provide non-cash assistance like baby formula and diapers and providing that no one loses Medicaid because of federally-imposed time limits; he also grandfathered in time limits of the states' currently approved reform plans, like Tennessee's bipartisan Families First. These provisions helped win the support of half the House's Democrats—including Tanner—and went into the final Welfare Reform Act that was signed by Bill Clinton in August 1996.

In the 8th District Tanner has held nearly 1,000 town hall meetings and has been reelected by very wide margins. In 1996 he carried the Shelby County (Memphis) portion of the district by only 51%–43%, but carried the rest of the district 71%–27%, for a 67%–30% victory. After the election he was named to the Ways and Means Committee; his 8th District predecessor Jere Cooper served there from 1932–57, the last three years as chairman.

The People: Pop. 1990: 541,852; 52% rural; 14% age 65+; 79% White; 20% Black; 1% Hispanic origin. Households: 60% married couple families; 27% married couple fams. w. children; 30% college educ.; median household income: $22,622; per capita income: $10,712; median gross rent: $311; median house value: $47,200.

1996 Presidential Vote		
Clinton (D)	98,925	(50%)
Dole (R)	85,856	(44%)
Perot (I)	10,835	(6%)

1992 Presidential Vote		
Clinton (D)	101,328	(48%)
Bush (R)	89,533	(42%)
Perot (I)	19,328	(9%)

Rep. John Tanner (D)

Elected 1988; b. Sept. 22, 1944, Halls; home, Union City; U. of TN, B.S. 1966, J.D. 1968; Disciples of Christ; married (Betty Ann).

Career: Navy, 1968–72; TN Natl. Guard, 1974–present; Practicing atty., 1973–88; TN House of Reps., 1976–88.

DC Office: 1127 LHOB 20515, 202-225-4714; Fax: 202-225-1765.

District Offices: Jackson, 901-423-4848; Memphis, 901-382-3220; Union City, 901-885-7070.

Committees: *Ways & Means* (14th of 16 D): Oversight; Social Security.

Group Ratings

	ADA	ACLU	AFS	LCV	CFA	CON	NFIB	COC	ACU	NTLC	CHC
1996	45	40	67	54	31	61	73	56	47	55	46
1995	35	—	—	31	31	38	—	67	29	—	—

National Journal Ratings

	1995 LIB		1995 CONS	1996 LIB		1996 CONS
Economic	56%	—	43%	57%	—	42%
Social	58%	—	41%	52%	—	47%
Foreign	55%	—	44%	57%	—	43%

Key Votes of the 104th Congress

1. Reduce Medicare Growth $	N	5. Flag Amendment	N	9. Cuban Embargo	N
2. Ovrd. Product Liab. Veto	*	6. Drop EPA Limits	Y	10. Bar Bosnia Troop $	N
3. Increase Min. Wage	Y	7. Repeal Assault-Weap. Ban	Y	11. Cut Anti-Missile Defense	Y
4. Welfare Reform	N	8. Ovrd. Part. Birth Veto	Y	12. Bar U.N. Uniforms	Y

Election Results

1996 general	John Tanner (D)	123,681	(67%)	($395,726)
	Tom Watson (R)	55,024	(30%)	($14,478)
	Others	5,193	(3%)	
1996 primary	John Tanner (D)	unopposed		
1994 general	John Tanner (D)	97,951	(64%)	($251,431)
	Neal R. Morris (R)	55,573	(36%)	($14,906)

NINTH DISTRICT

Memphis, the largest city in Tennessee, is in the far southwestern corner of the state, 500 miles from Tennessee's Appalachian border with Virginia and only 20 miles from Mississippi cotton fields. Memphis is symbolized by its musical tradition, entirely separate from Nashville's country music: Beale Street, near downtown Memphis, gave birth to jazz in the 1920s, rooted in the blues music of the lower Mississippi Valley, particularly the Delta; Elvis Presley, Mississippi-born but a Memphis resident most of his adult life, drew on both blues and black music to produce the rock-and-roll which made him a star in his lifetime and a strong presence years after his death. Some 41% of metropolitan Memphis's residents are black—one of the highest percentages in the country and evidence of the city's economic heritage as a capital of the

Cotton Kingdom. Today it still has the world's largest spot cotton market. For some years Memphis tried to live this heritage down, redeveloping Beale Street; now it recognizes its history as an asset, and is proud of its old fountains and the courtyard of the Peabody Hotel, where you can get a sense of the days when big Mississippi planters came north to sell their crop and make financial arrangements for the next growing season. Memphis's heritage also includes the Lorraine Motel, where Martin Luther King was assassinated in 1968, now site of a civil rights museum; Graceland, the grandiosely decorated mansion where Elvis Presley lived and, contrary to sightings, died August 16, 1977, is now one of the nation's biggest tourist attractions.

Memphis has become more than a cotton center and it has more than just history. Geographically central in the U.S., it is the home of the first supermarket (Piggly Wiggly) and the first Holiday Inn. Home of the world's top cargo airport in metric tons, Memphis calls itself "America's distribution center": by far its biggest employer is Federal Express, which ships all of its domestic packages in and out of Memphis Airport every night. Just north of Mud Island in the Mississippi, near the old downtown, is the 32-story Great American Pyramid sports and events arena. Like Mississippi, Memphis has not had an entirely happy political life. The hard edge of racial animosity may have now worn off, but racial polarization, to most people's discomfort, remains. Blacks still vote almost unanimously Democratic; whites vote by percentages almost as high for Republicans in seriously contested races. The 9th Congressional District of Tennessee consists of most of the city of Memphis and a bit of its suburban fringe; in 1992, 54% of its residents were black.

The congressman from the 9th District is Harold Ford Jr. elected in 1996. He is the youngest member of the 105th Congress, elected at 26, and his father Harold Ford Sr. first elected at 29, represented the 9th District for 22 years before him. Harold Ford Jr. was born in 1970, grew up in Memphis until 1979, when the family moved to Washington. He graduated from the elite St. Albans School, classmate of Jesse Jackson's son Yusef, then graduated from the University of Pennsylvania in 1992. He worked on his father's 1992 and 1994 campaigns and on the Clinton transition team and as a special assistant in the Economic Development Administration (and thus technically worked for late Commerce Secretary Ron Brown, whom he has praised as a "profound influence.") In 1993 he went off to the University of Michigan Law School. In April 1996, one month before graduation, Harold Ford Sr. announced his retirement and Harold Ford Jr. announced his candidacy. He said he has wanted to be like his father since he was four. "I took advantage of my opportunities. If I went out and said I'm Harold Ford Jr. and I couldn't construct a sentence, nobody would vote for me. You can't inherit it. You've got to go out and earn it."

The Ford family have been prominent morticians in Memphis for years, and went into electoral politics soon after the civil rights revolution; Harold Ford Sr. was elected to the legislature in 1970, at 25, and to Congress, beating a white Republican incumbent, in 1974. In the House he became chairman of the Ways and Means subcommittee handling welfare in 1981, but lost the post when he was indicted in April 1987 for receiving allegedly illegal loans from political backers; a Memphis jury hung 8–4 along racial lines for acquittal in April 1990, and a jury of 11 whites and 1 black acquitted him in April 1993, at which point he became chairman again. All the while he remained active in Memphis politics. When he announced his retirement, W.W. Herenton, elected Memphis's first black mayor in 1991 and a Ford rival, looked for a candidate to run against Harold Ford Jr., but city housing official Ricky Wilkins and state legislator Lois DeBerry declined to run. This left as Ford's main rival liberal state Senator Steve Cohen, who ran an ad showing the famous news footage of a single man standing up to tanks in Tiananmen Square. But the public employee unions which Cohen had always backed endorsed Ford, and Ford rolled on to a 60%–34% primary win; Herenton endorsed a candidate who won 5%, and there is talk that Harold Ford Sr. will run against him for mayor in 1999. In the general election Ford, whose campaign buttons read "Jr.," brought Congressmen Patrick Kennedy and Jesse Jackson Jr. in to campaign for him and attacked Newt Gingrich. He won 61%–37%, slightly better than the 58% his father won in the last three general elections.

In the House Harold Ford Jr. formed a Congressional Children's Caucus and said that his goal was to give every child access to a high-quality education. "Instead of public policy makers focusing solely on ways to punish and sentence kids, we should expand our attention to develops ways to challenge, inspire and motivate our people for the 21st Century." He added, "I don't buy the notion that kids who attend inner-city schools or urban schools can't learn and can't achieve. If they can master Nintendo and Sega, I am confident they can achieve." He opposed teaching in Ebonics: "You can't communicate with this kind of English." He spoke for reauthorization of the TRIO program and offered an amendment to the Republicans' flextime bill that aimed to protect employees who choose monetary compensation over comp time. After an explosion in south Memphis, he called for banning construction or expansion of hazardous waste facilities within 5,000 feet of any residential community, school, day care center or church. "I am part of the first generation not to know codified segregation," he said in explaining his approach to public policy. "We are the first to really be able to live where we want to live, go to school where we choose. There are still barriers that have to be brought down, but I tell young people all the time that my generation, our generation, complains so very much about things . . . but by and large, our generation has not faced greater challenges than the generations in the past."

The People: Pop. 1990: 541,710; 12% age 65+; 39% White; 59% Black; 1% Asian; 1% Hispanic origin. Households: 40% married couple families; 18% married couple fams. w. children; 42% college educ.; median household income: $22,117; per capita income: $11,296; median gross rent: $362; median house value: $54,900.

1996 Presidential Vote

Clinton (D)	138,234	(71%)
Dole (R)	51,767	(27%)
Perot (I)	3,862	(2%)

1992 Presidential Vote

Clinton (D)	151,590	(66%)
Bush (R)	68,358	(30%)
Perot (I)	9,400	(4%)

Rep. Harold E. Ford, Jr. (D)

Elected 1996; b. May 11, 1970, Memphis; home, Memphis; U. of PA, B.A. 1992; U of MI, J.D. 1996; Baptist; single.

Career: Staff Aide, U.S. Senate Budget Cmte., 1992; Spec. Asst., Clinton/Gore Transition Team, 1992; Spec. Asst., DNC Chairs Ron Brown & Alexis Herman, 1993; Spec. Asst., U.S. Dept. of Commerce, 1993.

DC Office: 1523 LHOB 20515, 202-225-3265; Fax: 202-225-5663.

District Offices: Memphis, 901-544-4131.

Committees: *Education & The Workforce* (19th of 20 D): Oversight & Investigations; Postsecondary Education, Training & Life-Long Learning. *Government Reform & Oversight* (19th of 19 D): Civil Service.

Group Ratings and Key Votes: Newly Elected

Election Results

1996 general	Harold E. Ford, Jr. (D)	116,345	(61%)	($679,843)
	Rod DeBerry (R)	70,951	(37%)	($95,687)
	Others	3,118	(2%)	
1996 primary	Harold E. Ford, Jr. (D)	63,888	(60%)	
	Steve Cohen (D)	35,844	(34%)	
	Rufus E. Jones (D)	5,244	(5%)	
1994 general	Harold E. Ford, Sr. (D)	94,805	(58%)	($366,683)
	Rod DeBerry (R)	69,226	(42%)	($181,980)

TEXAS

Texas is a country-sized state, one of three to have been an independent republic, but the only one to have had national ambitions throughout its history. Texas has been the second largest state in area since Alaska was admitted to the Union in 1959; it became the second largest in population in 1994, when it passed New York. The key to Texas's history is that this is a place with no aristocratic past, a state not formed by plantation owners or plutocrats but by dirt farmers. Texas was founded by Southerners, mainly Tennesseans, who wanted to establish their own republic in what were empty spaces within the borders of Mexico, a republic with Anglo-Saxon freedoms and black slavery. They defended their dream to the death at the Alamo and to a bloody victory at San Jacinto; they entered the Union willingly in 1845 and left it enthusiastically in 1861. The Texas that emerged from that war was still young and poor; it was only in 1901 that oil was discovered at Spindletop, and the first Texas wildcatters made their first fortunes.

Without the underpinnings and burdens of tradition, 20th Century Texas has produced fabulous wealth, generously rewarding success while unforgiving of error. It has respect for learning and style—think of its great universities, or of Neiman Marcus—but it revels in rough manners and western wear. Texans are prone to wild swings in fortune—think of Sam Houston, or the great wildcatters, or Lyndon Johnson. And Texans, for all their history of slavery and segregation, have proved open to immigrants and friendly with their neighbors in Mexico. NAFTA, the opening up of the border and the coming together of these two countries which are at such different economic levels and have such different cultures, is a project mainly of Texans of both political parties, of President George Bush and Treasury Secretary Lloyd Bentsen, Governors Ann Richards and George W. Bush. At the same time, Texas has become a high-tech powerhouse, a country with some of the nation's most creative businesses. But its success is not just economic. There are large elements of heroism—some mythical, some genuine—in the Texas history that every high school student here learns. "What Texans dream, Texans can do," as Governor George W. Bush likes to say.

Their dreams, sometimes seemingly unrealistic, have taken them far. Texas started off as a marchland on the border of the Third World, with an economy based on commodities, mainly cotton, whose prices were in long-term decline. Its farmers felt like part of a colonial economy controlled by bankers and Wall Street financiers. After Spindletop Texas became the nation's—and for a time the world's—leading producer of oil. But oil prices, too, fell in free markets, and were propped up by politicians—the 1936 "hot oil" act that Sam Rayburn, as chairman of the Commerce Committee, pushed through and the oil depletion allowance maintained for years by Rayburn when he was speaker, Senate Majority Leader Johnson, Senate Finance Chairman Lloyd Bentsen and others. These politicians also got subsidies for cotton growers and defense plants and space facilities in World War II and through the long years of the Cold War. Most Texas voters stayed Democratic up to the middle 1960s because of Confederate memories, New Deal affections and the clout and competence of Texas's Democratic politicians.

But as Texas's economy became complex and creative, Texas's politics changed from a mostly Democratic move to prop up the price of commodities to an increasingly Republican push to open up markets. By the 1970s Texas's economy was no longer dependent on raw commodities. The "awl bidness" here is less a matter of extracting oil from Texas; instead, Texas has the greatest concentration of experts and high-skill specialists in extracting oil and natural gas in any part of the world. Also, beginning in the 1960s Texas has become a center for high tech, with the critical mass of knowledge and finance needed to produce firms like Texas Instruments and Ross Perot's Electronic Data Systems, and a university infrastructure in the University of Texas and

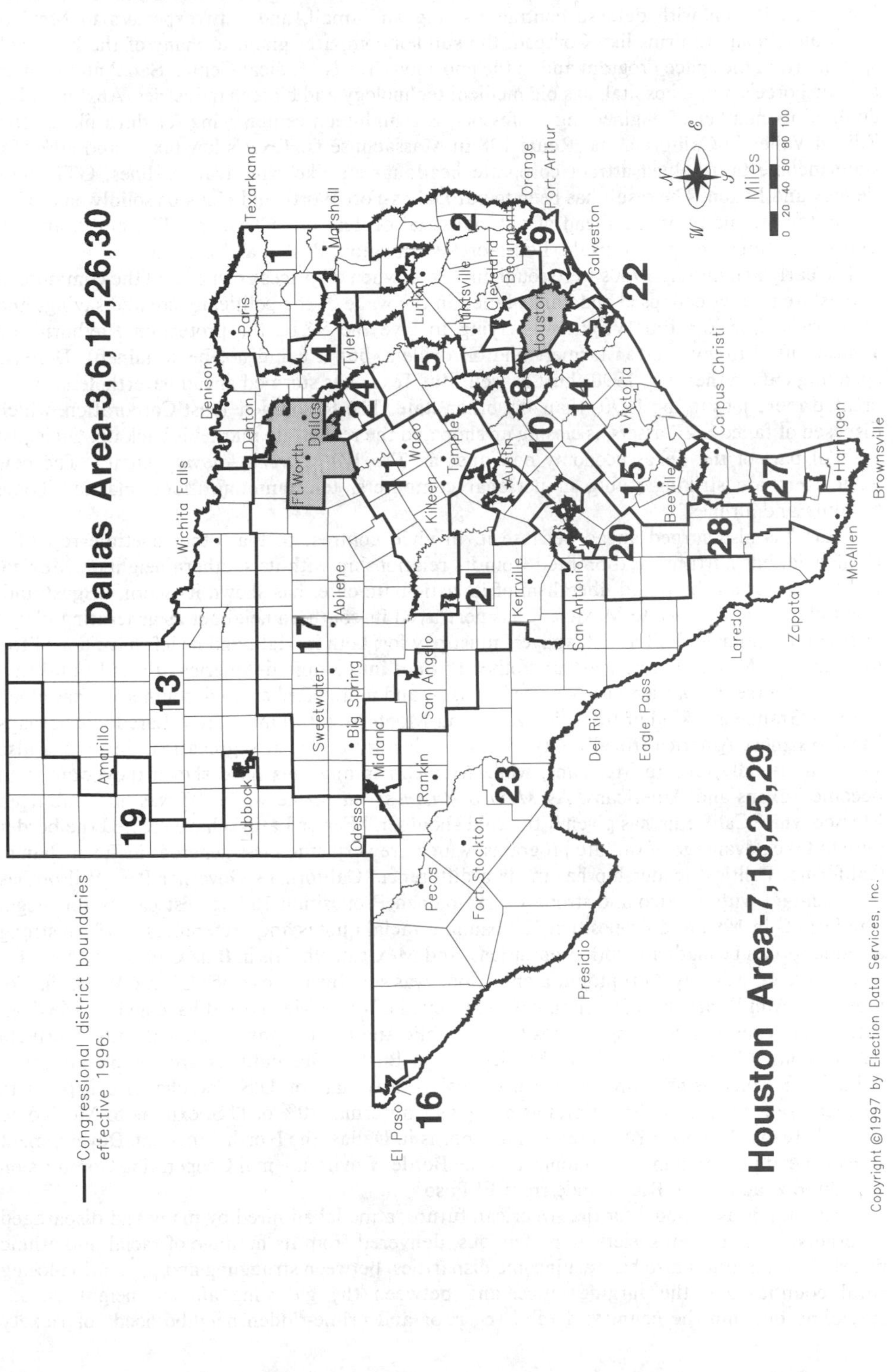
Dallas Area-3,6,12,26,30
Houston Area-7,18,25,29
Congressional district boundaries effective 1996.
Copyright ©1997 by Election Data Services, Inc.
Miles
0 20 40 60 80 100
Amarillo
Lubbock
Wichita Falls
Denison
Denton
Paris
Texarkana
Marshall
Tyler
Lufkin
Huntsville
Cleveland
Beaumont
Orange
Port Arthur
Galveston
Houston
Dallas
Ft. Worth
Waco
Temple
Killeen
Austin
Victoria
Corpus Christi
Beeville
Harlingen
Brownsville
McAllen
Zapata
Laredo
San Antonio
Kerrville
Abilene
Sweetwater
Big Spring
Midland
Odessa
San Angelo
Rankin
Eagle Pass
Del Rio
Fort Stockton
Pecos
Presidio
El Paso
1
2
4
5
8
9
10
11
13
14
15
16
17
19
20
21
22
23
24
27
28

Texas A&M to match the highway system that ties the state together. The Dallas-Fort Worth Metroplex is rich with defense contractors, big and small, and with exporters to Mexico. Houston is home to firms like Compaq, the sudden computer giant, to many of the high-tech spinoffs from the space program and to the enormous Texas Medical Center. San Antonio, with the Air Force's prime hospital, has big medical technology and biotech industries. Austin, as UT doubled its number of engineering professors, is a high-tech center vying for third place after Silicon Valley in California and Route 128 in Massachusetts. Texas's low taxes (and lack of a state income tax) helped attract corporate headquarters like American Airlines, GTE, J.C. Penney and Exxon. The result has been to put Dallas-Fort Worth and Houston solidly on the list of the top ten metro areas, ahead of old industrial centers like Cleveland, Pittsburgh and St. Louis, and threatening to overtake Baltimore-Washington, Boston and Detroit.

The early and middle 1980s were rough in Texas, when oil prices crashed and the commercial real estate market collapsed and banks failed in the wake of the politically-created savings and loan crisis (Speaker Jim Wright was trying to give the S&Ls the protection Rayburn and Johnson used to give cotton farmers and oil drillers, but it could not be sustained). Defense spending cuts in the early 1990s hurt as well. But Texas has stormed ahead nevertheless. It has created more jobs in the 1990s than any other state. The Resolution Trust Corporation, which disposed of failed S&L assets, is closing up shop and the real estate market is back up. Oil is just a small part of the Texas economy now and, as *The Wall Street Journal* put it, "The new wildcatters are striking it big in personal computers, telecommunications, plastics, home building and airlines."

Texas has also surged ahead because it, in vivid contrast to that other onetime republic, California, has nurtured and profited from its relationship with its southern neighbor, Mexico. California, for all the proud liberalism of its articulate elite, has shown its scorn, disgust and, worst of all, indifference to Mexico; it has portrayed its southern neighbor as generating illegal aliens and criminals California taxpayers must pay for; both its right and its left have done little to assimilate Mexican-Americans and other Latinos into a united America. Texas has taken a different course. Its border with Mexico is longer, and more often crossed; southern Texas along the Rio Grande is a kind of transition zone, and Monterrey, 140 miles from Laredo, is perhaps Mexico's most America-friendly city; despite a history of racial segregation, Texas has also shown a friendly face to Mexicans, while Mexican immigrants have shown they wanted to become Texans and Americans. As *Mexico Business* magazine wrote, "Texas has embraced Mexico while California has given it the cold shoulder." Fewer Latinos have crossed the border here to take advantage of welfare programs, which are very much less generous in Texas than in California. Political leadership has made a difference. California's Governor Pete Wilson has little contact with Mexico and strongly championed Proposition 187 against paying for illegal immigrants in 1994 and Proposition 209 banning racial quotas and preferences in 1996; strong arguments can be made for both propositions, and Mexican officials in Baja California Norte for years were egregiously corrupt: but a chilly tone was set. Texas Governor George W. Bush, like Governor Ann Richards before him, have journeyed often to Mexico and have invited Mexican leaders to Texas, emphasizing the positive in public and leaving any negative details to private negotiations. "You cannot wall off Mexico," says Bush. "Our cultures are completely intertwined." So increasingly are their economies. Nearly half of U.S. merchandise exports to Mexico are from Texas, three times as many as California; 70% of U.S. exports to Mexico go through Texas. The NAFTA secretariat of labor is in Dallas, the North American Development Bank is headquartered in San Antonio, and the Border Environmental Cooperation Commission is in Juarez, across the Rio Grande from El Paso.

Texas stands as a model for the American future, a model admired by many and disparaged by others. It is an open society, unpretentious, delivered from its heritage of racial and ethnic discrimination. But it also has vast income disparities, between struggling and population-losing rural counties and the surging cities, and between the gleaming affluent neighborhoods spreading out into the countryside and the poor and crime-ridden neighborhoods of rickety frame houses around the urban cores. Texas presents a contrast with and a challenge to the traditions of other megastates New York which pioneered the American welfare state, California which used high taxes to build highways and schools, the Great Lakes industrial states with their big labor unions. For Texas has some of the lowest taxes in the country and some of the lowest welfare levels; it has few union members and a relatively small public sector; it has resisted court-ordered moves to equalize spending among school districts; it continues to be a violent state, with a high crime rate and the nation's most executions. For years, out-of-state elites and liberals in Texas have called on the state to become more like New York or California or Michigan. But most Texans prefer their own model. Indeed, in important respects New York and California and Michigan are choosing to become more like Texas; so is Mexico: the last 25 years can be seen as—at least the beginnings of—the Texafication of North America. Low taxes and high tech, few barriers to opportunity but a less elaborate safety net, moving away from reliance on agriculture and oil, bypassing the era of big factories and big unions of the Great Lakes and eschewing the liberal cultural values of the two coasts: this is Texas's way, and increasingly North America's.

Politically, Texas is now an indisputably Republican state. This was not always so: its three major officeholders, George W. Bush, Phil Gramm and Kay Bailey Hutchison each lost an election before they started winning, though now each seems unbeatable. One-party Democratic dominance ended in the 1960s, and for two decades Democratic victories were largely the product of Lloyd Bentsen, when he was on the ballot in 1976, 1982 and 1988 and when he exerted his influence for Ann Richards for governor in 1990. The old Democratic strength in the Texas countryside is gone—in 1994 George W. Bush carried 189 counties to Richards's 65—and the Republican hold on the big cities is solid—Bush carried 55% in the Dallas-Fort Worth Metroplex and in greater Houston, which together cast 45% of the state's votes. Democrats still have a majority in the Texas U.S. House delegation, but that is only because of the cleverest Democratic redistricting plan of the 1990s: in 1994 Republicans won the House vote 56%–42% but took only 11 of 30 seats; in 1996, for which the plan was slightly revised, Republicans won the House votes 54%–44%, winning 13 of 30 seats. In 1994 Republicans won three of seven downballot offices and, in races sharply contested by trial lawyers and their adversaries, all the contested statewide judgeships in 1994. Inexorably, Republicans have rolled toward majorities in the state legislature. The state Senate was 18–13 Democratic after 1992, 17–14 Democratic after 1994, and 17–14 Republican after 1996. The state House was 92–58 Democratic after 1992, 81–69 after 1994, and 82–68 after 1996. The Democratic primary electorate has shrunk, from 1.8 million in 1978 to 890,000 in 1996, a more liberal, minority-dominated constituency. The Republican primary electorate has grown, from 158,000 in 1978 to just over one million in 1996: more Republicans than Democrats for the first time in history. Bob Dole carried Texas 49%–44%, his best showing in a large state.

Pockets of Democratic strength in Texas are increasingly isolated. Their best vote is in the Border counties, which cast 8% of the state's votes; they voted 60%–39% for Richards in 1994, 62%–32% for Clinton in 1996. Hispanics were the one group among which Clinton gained, from 58% in 1992 to 75% in 1996. Another traditionally Democratic area is the urban strip from San Antonio to Austin. But the cultural liberals who hang out in Austin's Sixth Street are now being joined by high-tech engineers and hard-charging entrepreneurs in the new subdivisions and office centers running north of the pink marble Capitol and the UT campus, and this area voted only 48%–45% for Clinton in 1996. George W. Bush carried rural Texas 57%–43% in 1994, Bob Dole 51%–40% in 1996, both against the toughest competition Democrats are likely to present for a while. Cultural attitudes are conservative here, and there is little of the economic populism of Sam Rayburn's day. In East Texas, once the home of yellow dog Democrats, most counties voted for Bush and Dole. In West Texas, Richards and Clinton carried only sparsely populated ranch territory. In the vast triangle from Waco (Richards's home town) to Midland (Bush's) and Victoria near the Gulf of Mexico, Bush carried practically every county.

Nearly half of Texas's votes are cast in the two big metro areas. Dallas-Fort Worth, with an increasingly Democratic core city but burgeoning heavily Republican edge cities, has been volatile, supplying the votes that elected Ann Richards in 1990 and giving native son Ross Perot 28% of its votes in 1992, nearly as many as Bill Clinton. But Bush won in DFW 55%–45% and Dole beat Clinton 52%–40%, with only 7% for Perot in 1996. Metro Houston, slightly less Republican, also voted 55%–45% for Bush and 51%–43% for Dole.

The prospect for Texas Democrats is bleak. They have their enclaves of control, but few statewide prospects. Their two large political figures, capable of rallying statewide majorities and governing ably, are absent from the scene: Lloyd Bentsen spends much of his time in San Diego and Ann Richards much of hers in Washington. Lieutenant Governor Bob Bullock is the only statewide Democrat of stature, but he is unlikely to run against Bush. Texas's national political figures are almost all Republicans—Senators Phil Gramm and Kay Bailey Hutchison, House Majority Leader Dick Armey, House Majority Whip Tom DeLay, House Ways and Means Committee Chairman Bill Archer. On the major issues, and on the overriding question of whether to continue Texas's traditions of cultural conservatism and minimalist government, Bush and the Republicans seem very much on the majority side. The future in Texas appears to be theirs and, if this state is as attractive a model as it thinks, perhaps in the nation as well.

Governor. George W. Bush is governor of the nation's second largest state, arguably the most popular governor of any big state, well positioned to become a presence and perhaps a candidate in national office; yet he is still known outside Texas's borders as the former president's son and managing director of the Texas Rangers baseball team. Bush was raised in a modest ranch house in Midland, when it was a rough and tumble Permian Basin oil boom town. Soon after his parents moved to Houston in 1960, he went east to school, where he was uncomfortable with the radicalism of late 1960s Yale College and the trendy leftism of mid-1970s Harvard Business School. He returned to Texas, became a fighter pilot in the National Guard, got into the oil business in Midland and ran for Congress in 1978. He lost that race 53%–47% to Kent Hance, then a Democrat from Lubbock: rural West Texas wasn't yet ready for a Midland Republican. Bush's business career wasn't especially successful. He did better as a political adviser to his father in 1988 and after, and as the 2% owner and managing director of the Rangers.

After his father's defeat in 1992, the younger Bush decided to run for governor. He brought his nervous intensity to the race and a determination to discuss specifics of state issues in a way that illustrated sensitivity to the texture of everyday life—just the opposite of his father's perceived disinterest in domestic issues and distance from ordinary life. In heavy personal campaigning he consistently called for tougher sentences for criminals, adult prison for violent offenders as young as 14, limiting welfare benefits to two years and requiring job training and limiting punitive damages in lawsuits. He did not pick an easy opponent. Ann Richards, first known nationally for her keynote speech attacking George Bush in 1988 ("born with as silver foot in his mouth"), had been elected in 1990 after a grueling campaign and had proved popular in office. Richards pushed through a state lottery and a corporate income tax, but stoutly opposed any income tax; she got increased minimum sentences for murder and a new school finance formula to respond to court orders. She hosted Mexico's President Carlos Salinas and campaigned for NAFTA. Yet Richards unaccountably failed to sound the positive, triumphalist note she might have. In public she called George W. Bush "shrub" and referred to him as "some jerk who's running for public office," while he was careful always to refer to her as Governor Richards. While Richards launched late attacks on Bush and was endorsed by Ross Perot, Bush stuck with his message, "Take a stand for Texas values." The opinion polls were close from spring on, so it was a bit of a surprise when Bush won 53%–46%.

Texas's legislature meets for 140 days every two years, with key roles being played by the speaker, Democrat Pete Laney, and lieutenant governor, Democrat Bob Bullock, who remained leader of the Senate even after Republicans won a majority there in 1996. In his 1995 session Bush, working closely with Bullock and Laney, was exceedingly successful in enacting his programs. Bush got the legislature to pass tort reform, limiting punitive damages and changing some rules, though not imposing loser-pays. He passed a bill giving much more autonomy to local school districts, though initially none took advantage of it. He got welfare reform limiting benefits and requiring job training, though it did include his proposal for a cutoff after two children, and the Clinton Administration denied a waiver in May 1997 to allow privatization of welfare services. And he got tougher juvenile justice laws. The legislature also passed a law enabling law-abiding citizens to get a permit to carry concealed weapons. In his second session, in 1997, Bush was not so successful. He started off with an ambitious plan to cut property taxes by 40% and to raise the sales tax and business taxes. Court rulings have been threatening Texas, like many other states, with drastic action because of school districts' widely varying property tax bases. But Bush could not put the different sides together, and in May 1997 settled for a $1 billion property tax cut funded by budget savings.

Bush's ratings in polls have been exceedingly high and in early 1997 he was an overwhelming favorite to win reelection. Possible Democratic opponents include Controller John Sharp and Land Commissioner Gary Mauro. Early in his term as governor, he abjured any interest in national politics, and stayed mostly in Texas; but it will surprise very few if in 1999 he decides to run for president. He has a wide base of support, in Texas and nationally, and a secure base. Presumably he would approach a 2000 campaign as he did in 1994, concentrating on just a few issues, setting out his positions in soothing rhetoric, but taking a sharp stand against what he regards as the failed liberal culture of so much of his own generation. Initial polls suggest his chances of winning are as good as anyone's.

Senior Senator. Phil Gramm is the product of adverse circumstances who makes his own considerable success sound like a hard grind. His father was an Army sergeant who died young; his mother, as he remembered in a grim-looking presidential campaign ad, sat him and his brother around the kitchen table and decided which bills they would pay. He flunked third, seventh and ninth grades, but his mother made him work hard and he went on to earn his Ph.D. from the University of Georgia. His field was economics, the one discipline that has moved to the right since the 1960s, due to the growing belief in the efficacy of free markets; and Gramm certainly is a believer in free markets. He moved to Texas in 1967 to teach economics at Texas A&M. There he met and married his second wife, Wendy Lee, granddaughter of Korean immigrants and also an economics Ph.D. In the Texas of Lyndon Johnson's time, where Democrats held almost all offices and while preaching conservatism concentrated on funneling federal money into what was then considered an underdeveloped economy, Gramm conceived political ambitions, though he had no local connections, no personal money and little to none of the good ol' boy charm which was long an ingredient of political success in the state.

Seething with energy and conviction, he started giving speeches around the state, boosting free market economics and decrying the grasping hand of government. One of his first fans was Dicky Flatt, a print shop owner in Mexia who became a staple in Gramm speeches, the hard-working American whose money the government was taking away to spend on someone else. In 1976, at 34, Gramm ran as a Democrat in the primary against Senator Lloyd Bentsen and lost 64%–28%. Undaunted, Gramm ran for an open House seat in 1978, making the runoff by 115 votes over current Congressman Chet Edwards, and then winning the primary runoff 53%–47% and easily beating the Republican in the general. One sign of future races: he spent the very considerable sum of $480,000. Within three years, Gramm was a major national figure. He got a seat on the Budget Committee, promising Majority Leader Jim Wright to be a team player. But, while he kept attending Democratic strategy meetings, he became co-sponsor of the Gramm-Latta budget resolution, the 1981 Reagan budget cuts, which passed the House over the opposition of the Democratic leadership.

For that apostasy and because Democrats decided that they could not trust him with confidential information, Speaker Tip O'Neill kicked Gramm off the Budget Committee in 1983. But Gramm turned that to his advantage by switching parties, resigning and triumphantly running in a special election campaign that gave him exposure in both the Houston and Dallas-Fort Worth media markets. "I had to choose between Tip O'Neill and y'all," he said, showing his capacity for attractively framing issues, "and I decided to stand with y'all." He won with 55%

and in 1984 easily won the Republican Senate nomination when John Tower announced his retirement from Congress. The Democratic winner in an epic three-way primary was Lloyd Doggett, then a liberal state senator from Austin and now congressman from the 10th District, whom Gramm attacked for holding a fundraiser at a gay male strip joint in San Antonio. Gramm won 59%–41%.

In his first year in the Senate Gramm had two major initiatives. First, he engineered a vacancy in the east Texas 1st District seat by securing a federal judgeship for the incumbent Democrat and, with the aid of a young operative named Lee Atwater, came close to having his Republican candidate win in that yellow dog Democratic territory. His idea was to encourage Republicans to run in rural southern districts. If he had succeeded, they might have captured the House in 1988 or 1990, rather than 1994. Gramm's second initiative, advanced immediately after his first, was the Gramm-Rudman deficit reduction law requiring automatic budget cuts if the deficit was not reduced to specific levels. Politically, Gramm-Rudman swept all before it and passed both houses. Fiscally, under the lead of OMB Director James Miller (who earned his economics Ph.D. from the University of Georgia at the same time as Phil Gramm), it did in fact result in lowering the deficit.

Gramm was one of the Republican negotiators at the 1990 budget summit, but did not resist a tax increase, as some conservatives had hoped. After George Bush caved in on the issue, Gramm ended up negotiating the final package of budget cuts, spending caps and tax increases. Texas loyalty, perhaps: Gramm gave the nominating speech for Bush in New Orleans in 1988 and the keynote speech in Houston in 1992. Texas loyalty works other ways too: critics on both sides of the aisle also noted that he has worked hard to keep money for big government projects flowing into Texas—Houston's space program, Waxahachie's now-canceled Supercollider, Austin's Sematech research center, Ingleside's Navy base. But Gramm's government-cutting initiatives kept coming. In 1991, he joined with Newt Gingrich to propose a series of tax cuts; in 1992, he held up Senate business to press for the balanced budget amendment; in 1995, he saw abolition of "baseline" and "current services" budgeting which he had long opposed.

Gramm was also all business at politics. In 1991, he was elected chairman of the National Republican Senatorial Committee by 26–17; he hoped initially to gain seats, but despite the Clinton victory and the press ballyhoo about "the year of the woman" (there were no such articles when most women candidates were Republicans in 1990) Republicans picked up one seat on election day and then another weeks later in the Georgia runoff. Gramm sought an unusual second term as campaign chairman, and beat Mitch McConnell (who now holds the job) by 20–19. Gramm ended up with a splendid record: Republicans gained seven seats on November 8, 1994, and an eighth a day later when Richard Shelby of Alabama switched parties, and won control of the Senate.

Gramm was also running for president, and was not shy about it. "I love raising money," he said, and put out the theory that any candidate would have to spend $20 million to win the 1996 Republican nomination. That kept several candidates out of the field. He also tried to define the terms of the debate. "I have always felt on budget issues the party that defines the parameters of the debate almost always wins the debate," he once said, and he is as good as anyone in American politics at tightly defining issues to steer the public his way. Gramm preached root-and-branch opposition to the Clinton healthcare plan in 1993 and 1994; he supported the House Republicans' tough line on the budget in 1995. A strong free trader, he took on Pat Buchanan on trade issues when others counseled quiet.

To his presidential campaign he brought a bullish aggressiveness, a strong and well-disciplined mind, a gift for pungent phrase, the ability to frame issues favorably for his cause. But he also insisted on doing things his way, even when it did not help him. His commercials and his stump speech projected an angry, even pessimistic tone; there was nothing of the geniality and uplift of his fellow party-switcher Ronald Reagan. Gramm raised vast sums of money, but also spent vast sums on staff and in contests like the August 1995 straw poll in which he tied Bob Dole. He angered James Dobson of Focus on the Family by insisting that he would not stress cultural issues, even though his stands were almost identical to Dobson's. He tried to engineer contests earlier than the Iowa caucuses and New Hampshire primary, in order to get a lead on others with lesser resources. But that infuriated the Governors of Iowa and New Hampshire, and cast a pall over his campaigns in those states. Then Pat Buchanan took up his challenge in a Gramm-engineered firehouse primary in Louisiana February 6. Gramm, confident that his party backers would triumph, spent little time there, while Buchanan criss-crossed the state, calling talk radio hosts on his cell phone and getting interviewed by country editors. Gramm predicted he would win all 21 delegates; instead Buchanan won 13, and Gramm's campaign was effectively over. He finished fifth eight days later in Iowa, and pulled out of the race two days later, when it was obvious he would get nowhere in New Hampshire. In contrast to his high visibility in 1988 and 1992, he was quiet the rest of the year; "when you lose, you sit down," he said.

Anyway, Gramm was also running for reelection in Texas and, under a law written by Democrats first for Lyndon Johnson and used by Lloyd Bentsen, he was allowed to run for both offices. Two Democratic congressmen ran against him, John Bryant of Dallas and Jim Chapman of east Texas, but the lead in the March 1996 primary went to Victor Morales (with the same last name as state Attorney General Dan Morales), a civics teacher at Poteet High School in Mesquite, who campaigned driving his pickup truck around the state. Bryant carried the Dallas-Fort Worth area with 62% of the vote, but it cast only 10% of primary votes; in the areas outside the big metropolitan areas and the border, which cast half the primary vote, Chapman had a lead, but it was only 38%–28% over Morales; in the border counties, which cast 19% of the vote, far more than their share of population, Morales won 60% of the vote. Statewide he had 36% to 30% for Bryant and 27% for Chapman. In the runoff Morales's ingenuous stands on issues and his Hispanic name got him past Bryant 51%–49%.

Gramm, reelected six years before with 60%, now seemed beleaguered. But Morales was hurt by the fact that his wife had not repaid delinquent student loans. And he was hurt by his stands against the balanced budget amendment and welfare reform and for affirmative action and same-sex marriage. Gramm won 55%–44%, losing the border counties which he had carried in 1990 but winning 60% again in rural Texas. In the big metropolitan areas Morales's percentages tracked Clinton's losing performance. Back in the Senate, Gramm is now chairman of the informal Steering Committee and of the Finance Subcommittee on Health Care. He was sharply critical of the budget deal announced by Clinton and Republican congressional leaders in late April 1997, charging it would "open the floodgates for new spending."

Junior Senator. Republican Kay Bailey Hutchison won a stunning June 1993 victory to win Lloyd Bentsen's Senate seat and then was reelected to the full term in 1994 to become Texas's junior senator. Kay Bailey grew up in LaMarque, near the refinery town of Texas City, a prom queen who went to college and then law school at the University of Texas and then, unable to get a law job, in 1967 worked for a Houston TV station as a reporter. In 1972, she won a seat in the legislature, its first Republican woman. In 1976 she went to Washington to fill the number two position at the National Transportation Safety Board. She married, moved to Dallas and went into banking and became a small business owner in 1978. In 1982, she lost a House race to Steve Bartlett, later mayor of Dallas. But she stayed active in Republican politics and in 1990 was elected state treasurer, a breakthrough race for state Republicans. Hutchison has been mocked by liberals for her tight-lipped good manners, but she remembers when being a woman was much more of a career handicap than today's younger generation has ever encountered, and she has passed through political ordeals as searing as those endured by her predecessor as treasurer—and political non-friend—former Governor Ann Richards.

Hutchison quickly became one of four major candidates for the Senate seat vacated by Treasury Secretary Lloyd Bentsen and to which Richards appointed former Congressman Bob Krueger. Krueger, a Shakespeare-quoting former professor and congressman, worked to deregulate energy prices in the 1970s, nearly beat Senator John Tower in 1978, then ran third in a three-way Senate primary in 1984 and was elected Railroad Commissioner (actually, oil regulator) in 1990. A market conservative, he opposed the Clinton budget and tax plan. Even so, the Democratic label was so deadly that he took only 29% of the vote in the May 1993 open general, and finished second to Hutchison, who also had 29%. Krueger's cause was obviously doomed, and his campaign flailed around, running absurd ads in which Krueger, dressed in an Arnold Schwarzenegger Terminator outfit, claimed to be a lousy politician. Meanwhile, Hutchison weathered charges she had hit a Treasury employee (the daughter of former Governor John Connally), and kept the focus on Bill Clinton, whose Texas job rating was 73% negative. Hutchison won the runoff by an astonishing 67%–33%, ahead of any Senate candidate here since the 1950s, when Republicans did not put up serious candidates. She won the Dallas-Fort Worth Metroplex 71%–29% and greater Houston 70%–30%, carried the usually Democratic San Antonio-Austin corridor and the Border counties; rural Texas, once heavily Democratic, went for Hutchison 68%–32%. Yellow dog Democratic counties went Republican in droves: Krueger carried 15 counties, Hutchison 239. Her victory echoed with greater resonance the defeat of the last Texas senator appointed by a Democratic governor to replace a Texan taking a high position in Washington: the 1961 loss of conservative Democrat "Dollar Bill" Blakeley to Republican John Tower, replacing then-Vice President Lyndon Johnson. Tower's victory was a sign that Republicans could be competitive in Texas; Hutchison's victory was a sign that they were the majority.

Hutchison started her Senate career articulate and pleasant but willing to be partisan; pro-choice on abortion but opposing taxpayer funding and a Freedom of Choice Act that would wipe out state parental consent laws; opposing the Clinton tax increase and supporting NAFTA; and voting with two other women senators to deny Admiral Frank Kelso retirement with his four-star rank. But immediately after her win in 1993, Austin District Attorney Ronnie Earle, a liberal Democrat, worked to indict Hutchison for using office employees for political purposes and for destroying some records. It was a rotten prosecution from the beginning: the law imposes limits on state elected officials, which at times seem absurd, and Hutchison had purged mailing lists from her Texas computer on the advice of the Democratic attorney general. Then, in February 1994, Earle dropped the charges when the trial judge refused to rule on the admissibility of evidence seized in a June 1993 raid on Hutchison's office, in effect admitting he had no case.

Hutchison's job rating had declined, but not disastrously, and she avoided any serious Republican primary opposition. Three serious Democrats were running for her seat. The potentially strongest candidate, moderate Houston Congressman Mike Andrews, was eliminated in the March primary with 16%. In the April runoff, former Attorney General and bitter Richards enemy Jim Mattox lost 54%–46% to Richard Fisher, a free-spending moderate who campaigned extensively in the Border counties in Spanish. In the general, Fisher's credentials seemed a bit fishy—he claimed to have been an adviser to former British Prime Minister Margaret Thatcher, though Thatcher said their acquaintance was minor—and Hutchison cruised to a solid 61%–38% victory. This time she lost the Border, but won the San Antonio-Austin corridor and took over 60% in the big metro areas and the rural counties.

In the Senate she worked on welfare reform, helping to write a funding formula helpful to Texas and getting funding for colonias and other border infrastructure. She supported the partial-birth abortion ban but was still the target of conservatives who wanted to keep her off the delegation to the Republican National Convention in San Diego. But as a delegate there she presented the toughest criticism of Bill Clinton, mocking his changing schedule for balancing the federal budget. In 1997 she co-sponsored the Republican flextime bill, allowing employees to get compensatory time instead of overtime pay.

Presidential politics. Texas can hardly be ignored in presidential politics: it is too big, with 32 electoral votes; it has too many leading politicians, too many fundraisers. But there is little suspense about the outcome here. Texas voted Republican 56%–43% in 1988, when Lloyd Bentsen was on the Democratic ticket; it voted 41%–37% Republican in 1992, when Bill Clinton was sweeping to victory over George Bush; it voted 49%–44% for Bob Dole in 1996, when Sun Belt states like Florida and California went Democratic. Texas is a sort of counterpoint to New

York, which it surpassed in size in 1993 but which still has one more electoral vote: just as New York is safely Democratic and has generated dozens of major Democratic national politicians, so Texas is safely Republican and is generating dozens of major national politicians. The campaign of Senator Phil Gramm, its Republican presidential candidate in 1996, fizzled early; Gramm's ambition may not be extinguished, but it is generally assumed he will not run in 2000. Attention is focused instead on Governor George W. Bush, who must decide on whether to make a national race by mid-1999; many Texans are betting he will. And then there is that other Texan, Ross Perot, whose appetite for national attention may not be sated. But his vote-getting ability has waned: his share of the vote went down from 19% in 1992 to 8% in 1996. In Texas the drop was sharper, from 22% to 7%, and from 28% to 7% in the Dallas-Fort Worth metro area.

Texas's presidential primary, originally in May, was moved to March for Super Tuesday in 1988; attempts to move it back to May for 2000 failed in 1997. Its results have mostly been unsurprising; Bill Clinton and George Bush both won twice, easily; Bob Dole won easily in 1996. It is interesting to look back on the 1988 Democratic primary here, with an eye on 2000. The winner then was Michael Dukakis, with 33%, who did well with Hispanics; Jesse Jackson had 25%; two possible 2000 contenders trailed: Al Gore with 20% and 14% for Dick Gephardt. But that was with a turnout of 1.7 million, nearly twice the 900,000 Democrats who turned out in the 1996 primary. A smaller Democratic turnout means that Hispanic voters and committed liberals will be a larger percentage of the total; Texas could be important, though scarcely typical.

Congressional districting. Texas's congressional districting has had as complicated a history—and as complicated a set of lines—as any in the country in the 1990s. The original redistricting plan was the product of Bob Mansker, aide to Democratic Congressman Martin Frost, drawn in 1991 when Democrats controlled the legislature and held the governorship. While modified by court ruling, it is still in effect for 17 of the 30 districts. This was a Democratic gerrymander, and its partisan effect has been clear and effective—though not entirely availing against the clear Republican trend in Texans' voting. In 1992 Democrats carried the popular vote for House by only 50%–48% but won 21 of 30 seats. In 1994 they lost the popular vote 56%–42%, but won 19 seats. In 1996 they lost the popular vote 54%–44% and still won 17 seats.

The court-required redistricting has made little partisan difference. In August 1994 a federal court ruled that three districts, all with incredibly convoluted boundaries, the 30th in Dallas and the 18th and 29th in Houston, were racially gerrymandered and therefore unconstitutional. But the boundaries were left in place for 1994. In June 1996 the Supreme Court agreed and sent the case back to the district court. In August 1996 that court redrew the lines of 13 districts—those held unconstitutional and 10 more adjacent to them, all in the Dallas-Fort Worth and Houston areas. Throwing out their March 1996 primary results, state officials set an August 30 filing deadline for a November 5 special election, with anyone getting 50% winning the seat. Otherwise, the top two candidates regardless of party would face off in a December 10 runoff. As it happened, runoffs were necessary in only three districts, and only one incumbent lost, for reasons having nothing to do with the redistricting. In May 1997 the state House and state Senate approved slightly different plans, both similar to the court-adopted plan; legislative leaders said they would submit both to the court by the June 30 deadline, and so it appeared that the 1998 elections would be conducted with similar if not identical district lines to those in effect in 1996.

Looking ahead, redistricting after the 2000 Census could provide quite a jolt for Texas incumbents—and perhaps for Democrats nationally. There is at least a possibility that Republicans will be in total control of the process and a very strong likelihood they will have a veto. That probably means an end to several contorted districts whose only rationale is to elect Democrats. There will probably be more districts radiating out into the countryside from heavily Republican suburban territory. In the meantime, retirements and defeats have left a Texas delegation with many new members—after the 1996 election, 10 freshmen and four sophomores in the 30 districts.

The People: Est. Pop. 1996: 19,128,000; Pop. 1990: 16,986,510, up 12.6% 1990–1996. 7.2% of U.S. total, 2d largest; 20% rural. Median age: 32.6 years. 10% 65 years and over. 60.6% White, 11.6% Black, 1.8% Asian, 25.5% Hispanic origin. Households: 56.6% married couple families; 30% married couple fams. w. children; 47% college educ.; median household income: $27,016; per capita income: $12,904; 60.9% owner occupied housing; median house value: $59,600; median monthly rent: $328. 5.6% Unemployment. 1996 Voting age pop.: 13,597,000. 1996 Turnout: 5,611,644; 41% of VAP. Registered voters (1996): 10,540,678; no party registration.

Political Lineup: Governor, George W. Bush (R); Lt. Gov., Bob Bullock (D); Secy. of State, Antonio Garza (R); Atty. Gen., Dan Morales (D); Comptroller, John Sharp (D); Auditor, Lawrence Alwin (D). State Senate, 31 (14 D and 17 R); Senate President, Bob Bullock (D); State House, 150 (81 D, 68 R, and 1 vacancy); House Speaker, Pete Laney (D). Senators, Phil Gramm (R) and Kay Bailey Hutchison (R). Representatives, 30 (17 D and 13 R).

Elections Division: 512-463-5650; **Filing Deadline for U.S. Congress:** January 2, 1998.

1996 Presidential Vote

Dole (R)	2,736,119	(49%)
Clinton (D)	2,459,616	(44%)
Perot (I)	378,429	(7%)

1996 Republican Presidential Primary

Dole (R)	567,164	(56%)
Buchanan (R)	217,974	(21%)
Forbes (R)	130,938	(13%)
Other	103,727	(10%)

1992 Presidential Vote

Bush (R)	2,496,060	(41%)
Clinton (D)	2,281,890	(37%)
Perot (I)	1,354,740	(22%)

GOVERNOR

Gov. George W. Bush (R)

Elected 1994, term expires Jan. 1999; b. July 6, 1946, New Haven, CT; home, Austin; Yale U., B.A. 1968; Harvard U., M.B.A. 1975; Methodist; married (Laura).

Career: TX Air Natl. Guard, 1968–73; Founder & CEO, Bush Exploration Oil & Gas Co., 1975–87; Sr. Advisor, Bush Presidential Camp., 1988; Managing General Partner, Texas Rangers baseball org., 1989–94.

Office: State Capitol, P.O. Box 12428, Austin 78711, 512-463-2000; Fax: 512-463-1849; Web site: www.state.tx.us.

Election Results

1994 gen.	George W. Bush (R)	2,350,994	(53%)
	Ann W. Richards (D)	2,016,928	(46%)
1994 prim.	Geroge W. Bush (R)	520,130	(93%)
	Ray Hollis (R)	37,210	(7%)
1990 gen.	Ann W. Richards (D)	1,925,670	(49%)
	Clayton Williams (R)	1,826,431	(47%)
	Twenty Others	140,645	(4%)

SENATORS

Sen. Phil Gramm (R)

Elected 1984, seat up 2002; b. July 8, 1942, Ft. Benning, GA; home, College Station; U. of GA, B.A. 1964, Ph.D. 1967; Episcopalian; married (Wendy).

Career: Prof., TX A&M U., 1967–78; U.S. House of Reps., 1978–84.

DC Office: 370 RSOB 20510, 202-224-2934; Fax: 202-228-2856.

State Offices: Dallas, 214-767-3000; Harlingen, 210-423-6118; Houston, 713-718-4000; El Paso, 915-534-6897; Lubbock, 806-472-7533; San Antonio, 210-366-9494; Tyler, 903-593-0902.

Committees: *Agriculture, Nutrition & Forestry* (9th of 10 R): Production & Price Competitiveness; Research, Nutrition & General Legislation. *Banking, Housing & Urban Affairs* (2nd of 10 R): Financial Institutions & Regulatory Relief; International Finance; Securities (Chmn.). *Budget* (4th of 12 R). *Finance* (8th of 11 R): Health Care (Chmn.); International Trade; Social Security & Family Policy.

Group Ratings

	ADA	ACLU	AFS	LCV	CFA	CON	NFIB	COC	ACU	NTLC	CHC
1996	0	20	0	8	7	58	100	100	100	100	100
1995	0	—	0	7	0	86	—	100	100	—	—

National Journal Ratings

	1995 LIB — 1995 CONS			1996 LIB — 1996 CONS		
Economic	0%	—	88%	0%	—	94%
Social	0%	—	88%	0%	—	72%
Foreign	22%	—	67%	0%	—	74%

Key Votes of the 104th Congress

1. Reduce Medicare Growth $	Y	5. Flag Amendment	Y	9. Anti-Missile Defense	Y
2. Lmt. Prod. Liab. Damages	Y	6. Endangered Species	N	10. Cuban Embargo	Y
3. Increase Min. Wage	N	7. Gay Employment Rights	N	11. Bar Bosnia Troop $	Y
4. Welfare Reform	Y	8. Ovrd. Part. Birth Veto	Y	12. Cut Vietnam Aid	Y

Election Results

1996 general	Phil Gramm (R)	3,027,680	(55%)	($14,078,131)
	Victor M. Morales (D)	2,428,776	(44%)	($978,862)
1996 primary	Phil Gramm (R)	838,339	(85%)	
	David Young (R)	75,463	(8%)	
	Henry C. Grover (R)	72,400	(7%)	
1990 general	Phil Gramm (R)	2,302,357	(60%)	($12,349,397)
	Hugh Parmer (D)	1,429,986	(37%)	($1,677,087)
	Other	89,814	(2%)	

Sen. Kay Bailey Hutchison (R)

Elected June 1993, seat up 2000; b. July 22, 1943, Galveston; home, Dallas; U of TX, B.A. 1992, J.D. 1967; Episcopalian; married (Ray).

Career: Political & legal corresp., KPRC-TV, 1967–70; TX House of Reps., 1972–76; Vice Chmn., Natl. Transp. Safety Bd., 1976–78; V.P. & Gen. Cnsl., RepublicBank Corp., 1978–82; Owner, McCraw Candies, 1984–88; TX Treasurer, 1990–93.

DC Office: 283 RSOB 20510, 202-224-5922; Fax: 202-224-0776; e-mail: senator@hutchison.senate.gov.

State Offices: Abilene, 915-676-2839; Austin, 512-916-5834; Dallas, 214-361-3500; Houston, 713-653-3456; San Antonio, 210-340-2885.

Committees: *Appropriations* (15th of 15 R): Commerce, Justice, State & the Judiciary; Defense; District of Columbia; Labor, Health & Human Services & Education; Military Construction. *Commerce, Science & Transportation* (6th of 11 R): Aviation; Communications; Oceans & Fisheries; Science, Technology & Space; Surface Transportation & Merchant Marine (Chmn.). *Rules & Administration* (9th of 9 R).

Group Ratings

	ADA	ACLU	AFS	LCV	CFA	CON	NFIB	COC	ACU	NTLC	CHC
1996	5	12	0	15	14	60	100	92	100	100	100
1995	0	—	0	0	0	54	—	100	87	—	—

National Journal Ratings

	1995 LIB — 1995 CONS			1996 LIB — 1996 CONS		
Economic	26%	—	71%	11%	—	86%
Social	29%	—	70%	0%	—	72%
Foreign	8%	—	81%	0%	—	74%

Key Votes of the 104th Congress

1. Reduce Medicare Growth $	Y	5. Flag Amendment	Y	9. Anti-Missile Defense	Y
2. Lmt. Prod. Liab. Damages	Y	6. Endangered Species	N	10. Cuban Embargo	Y
3. Increase Min. Wage	N	7. Gay Employment Rights	N	11. Bar Bosnia Troop $	N
4. Welfare Reform	Y	8. Ovrd. Part. Birth Veto	Y	12. Cut Vietnam Aid	Y

Election Results

1994 general	Kay Bailey Hutchison (R)	2,604,218	(61%)	($6,114,755)
	Richard Fisher (D)	1,639,615	(38%)	($3,360,850)
1994 primary	Kay Bailey Hutchison (R)	467,975	(84%)	
	Stephen Hopkins (R)	34,703	(6%)	
	Others	52,660	(9%)	
1993 runoff	Kay Bailey Hutchison (R)	1,188,716	(67%)	($6,255,765)
	Bob Krueger (D)	576,538	(33%)	($4,582,323)
1993 special	Kay Bailey Hutchison (R)	593,338	(29%)	
	Bob Krueger (D)	593,239	(29%)	
	Joe L. Barton (R)	284,135	(14%)	
	Jack M. Fields, Jr. (R)	277,560	(14%)	
	Richard Fisher (D)	165,564	(8%)	
	Nineteen Others	131,923	(6%)	

FIRST DISTRICT

Texarkana, with a population of 50,000 and a rural and small town hinterland somewhat larger, for years was noteworthy mainly because its neat grid streets cross the Texas-Arkansas state line. The downtown post office straddles the boundary, with the west wing serving Texarkana TX 75501 and the east wing Texarkana AR 75502. Yet this small city and its hinterland produced not one but two presidential candidates in 1992: Ross Perot grew up in Texarkana, while Bill Clinton's boyhood home of Hope, Arkansas, is only 30 miles east on Interstate 30. Both grew up in comfortable but not lavish circumstances: Perot's father was a cotton broker, Clinton's stepfather a Buick dealer. Both lived in town, where the houses were shaded from the pounding summer sun by trees and most people had electricity and indoor plumbing—a vivid contrast with the countryside when Perot was growing up in the 1930s and even when Clinton was young in the late 1940s.

Did the particular atmosphere of the Texarkana area have an effect on these men's politics? Maybe. Both were taught that they had obligations to those less fortunate, even while they were obliged themselves to work hard to get ahead. Texarkana was populist country then, a place where farmers producing cotton and crops felt themselves at the mercy of Dallas cotton brokers, Wall Street financiers and railroad magnates who were grabbing all the gains of their hard work. Outside Texarkana, in landscape littered with small houses amid lazily winding rivers, there was little protection from the sun and wind, and precious little ornament. The politics here was always Democratic: Clinton, who remembers his grandfather as a FDR fan, has never been anything else, while Perot seems more at ease with moderate Democrats Lloyd Bentsen and Ann Richards than with Republicans. And in Texarkana this politics was surely affected by Wright Patman, congressman from the 1st District of Texas from 1928 until his death in 1976, a populist who began his career in the House by moving to impeach Treasury Secretary Andrew Mellon, punctuated it by calling constantly for low interest rates and ended it after years as Banking Committee chairman. But culture here was always traditional: this is an area of heavy churchgoing and proud patriotism. Traces of that can be seen in Perot's military bearing and Clinton's religious cadences.

The 1st Congressional District of Texas includes most of the northeastern corner of the state—east Texas from Texarkana west to within two counties of Dallas and south almost to Lufkin. Politically, it is traditionally Democratic but has been trending toward Republicans in the 1980s and 1990s. In 1985 it was the scene of an epic special election, contrived by Phil Gramm, fought on the other side by Jim Wright and Tony Coelho; the result was a narrow 51%–49% win for Democrat Jim Chapman and a stop to Gramm's plans to contest rural southern seats in the 1980s.

The congressman from the 1st District now is Max Sandlin, a Democrat elected in 1996 to replace Chapman, who ran for the Senate and finished third with 27% in the Democratic primary. Sandlin grew up in east Texas, went to Baylor, practiced law in Marshall and got involved in oil and gas exploration. He was Harrison County judge, an elected administrative position, when he ran for the House in 1996. This campaign was far less dramatic and politically meaningful than the 1985 contest. The Democratic primary attracted four times as many voters as the Republican—a vestige of tradition—and Sandlin led lawyer Jo Ann Howard, wife of a longtime opponent of Chapman, 42%–34%. In the runoff Sandlin, spending his own money and using his oil business connections to raise more, out-polled Howard 56%–44%. Sandlin pointed to his tax-cutting experience in Harrison County and promised to find "common sense" solutions to Medicare and education. Also, he attacked Republican Ed Merritt, an insurance attorney with no political experience, for backing Medicare "cuts." Merritt attacked him for appearing with Bill Clinton. Overall Sandlin spent $1.7 million, including $784,000 of his own money—a campaign budget almost four times Merritt's. Sandlin won 52%–47%, carrying all the counties around Texarkana and Marshall and losing counties only in the periphery of the district, perhaps out of range of local media.

In the House Sandlin was a freshman whip, but failed to get a seat on the coveted Commerce Committee; he serves on Transportation and Infrastructure, which must reauthorize ISTEA. He announced himself as a Blue Dog Democrat and a supporter of the balanced budget amendment. But he also backed the STEP-21 highway funding formula, which would bring more highway money to Texas.

The People: Pop. 1990: 565,594; 56% rural; 16% age 65+; 78% White; 18% Black; 3% Hispanic origin. Households: 60% married couple families; 27% married couple fams. w. children; 37% college educ.; median household income: $21,697; per capita income: $10,785; median gross rent: $334; median house value: $43,600.

1996 Presidential Vote

Dole (R)	94,433	(46%)
Clinton (D)	91,721	(45%)
Perot (I)	17,237	(8%)

1992 Presidential Vote

Clinton (D)	85,868	(39%)
Bush (R)	84,529	(38%)
Perot (I)	50,526	(23%)

Rep. Max A. Sandlin, Jr. (D)

Elected 1996; b. Sept. 29, 1952, Texarkana; home, Marshall; Baylor U., B.A. 1975, J.D. 1978; Baptist; married (Leslie).

Career: Practicing atty., 1978–96; Harrison Cnty. Judge, 1986–89; Judge, Harrison County Court, 1989–96; Vice Pres., Howell & Sandlin Inc., 1989–96; Pres., E. TX Fuels, Inc., 1992–96.

DC Office: 214 CHOB 20515, 202-225-3035; Fax: 202-225-5866.

District Offices: Marshall, 903-938-8386; New Boston, 903-628-5594; Sulphur Springs, 903-885-8682.

Committees: *Transportation & Infrastructure* (26th of 33 D): Railroads; Surface Transportation.

Group Ratings and Key Votes: Newly Elected

Election Results

1996 general	Max A. Sandlin, Jr. (D)	102,697	(52%)	($1,691,255)
	Ed Merritt (R)	93,105	(47%)	($467,750)
	Others	3,368	(2%)	
1996 runoff	Max A. Sandlin, Jr. (D)	31,659	(56%)	
	Jo Ann Howard (D)	25,063	(44%)	
1996 primary	Max A. Sandlin, Jr. (D)	36,142	(42%)	
	Jo Ann Howard (D)	28,962	(34%)	
	Tommy Kessler (D)	19,948	(23%)	
1994 general	Jim Chapman, Jr. (D)	86,480	(55%)	($752,189)
	Mike Blankenship (R)	63,911	(41%)	($519,586)
	Others	6,001	(4%)	

SECOND DISTRICT

East Texas is thick with landmarks of Lone Star history. There's still an Indian reservation in Polk County and the Big Thicket National Preserve to remind you of what this land once looked like. Over near Beaumont is the site of Spindletop, where the world's first gusher spewed out in 1901 and started the Texas oil boom. Not far away is the huge oil field that wildcatter H. L. Hunt found in 1931, the foundation of a billion-dollar fortune. Much of east Texas looks little different from the wildcat days of 50 years ago: the town squares with courthouses and churches; the stands of cheap, quick-growing pine; the rough farmland. Yet much has changed. Real incomes have tripled over 50 years, endemic diseases have been wiped out and racial segregation has been abolished, despite vestiges found in tiny Vidor. Small-town isolation has been ended by television, the interstate highway and the regional shopping mall, and metropolitan growth, sprinting outward from Houston's loop freeways, is spreading in between the pine forests and reservoirs.

The 2d Congressional District of Texas includes all or part of 19 east Texas counties, most of them still seemingly rural; it runs from the oil port of Orange past Lufkin and Nacogodoches to Jacksonville. The political tradition here is Democratic and populist, devoted to traditional values but with a taste for military posture and a certain Texas rowdiness. This is the kind of district Democrats must carry to win Texas: Ann Richards won it in 1990 and Bill Clinton in 1992—but barely in 1996, and it voted for George W. Bush in 1994.

The congressman from the 2d District is Jim Turner, a Democrat elected in 1996. He grew up in east Texas, went to college and law school in Austin, served in the Army, then returned to Crockett in Houston County, practiced law and was active in church and community organizations. In 1980 he was elected to the Texas House and served four years; he was mayor of Crockett for two years; in 1990 he was elected to the Texas Senate in a district that includes four of the 18 counties in the 2d District. His opportunity to run for the House came in 1996, when Congressman Charlie Wilson decided to retire after 24 years; Wilson was long known as one of Washington's *bon vivants*, but also channeled critical aid to the Afghan *mujaheddin* in the 1980s, which helped them defeat the Soviets. Wilson characteristically said that he wanted to resign in August, so he could start lobbying after the required one-year hiatus; but media criticism about walking away from the job convinced Wilson to delay his resignation until October, which would also avoid the need for a special election. Turner's legislative work against crime and for patient protection against HMOs, plus Wilson's support helped him win a three-candidate Democratic primary with 59%, carrying everything but his opponents' home counties. The Republican primary was something of a surprise. Running again was Donna Peterson, a West Point graduate who was Wilson's well-publicized opponent in 1990, 1992 and 1994. She led in the five-candidate primary, but with only 35% to 31% for dentist Brian Babin, who was supported by Christian conservatives. In the runoff turnout fell from 22,000 to 11,000, and with a motivated constituency Babin won 67%–33%, although he won fewer votes than before. In the general Babin charged that Turner was an "elitist liberal," who voted for an income tax on small businesses and tried to weaken the carrying concealed weapons law. Turner charged that Babin backed the Republican budget and Medicare "cuts," and he called for more police and college tuition deductions. Turner outspent Babin by nearly 2–1 and won 52%–46%. Babin carried the three counties closest to Houston and ran about even in several nearby. But Turner carried the more distant counties, some by 2–1.

In the House Turner serves on the National Security Committee and joined the Blue Dog Democrats. He lined up with other conservative Democrats calling for a bipartisan deal on the budget, and when Bill Clinton announced the agreement in May 1997 Turner was there beaming right behind the president in the photograph. The biggest threat to Turner in the long term is redistricting: a seat with more Houston area precincts could make the district more Republican.

The People: Pop. 1990: 565,906; 61% rural; 14% age 65+; 77% White; 17% Black; 6% Hispanic origin. Households: 61% married couple families; 28% married couple fams. w. children; 32% college educ.; median household income: $21,216; per capita income: $10,113; median gross rent: $333; median house value: $41,800.

1996 Presidential Vote			**1992 Presidential Vote**		
Clinton (D)	90,379	(45%)	Clinton (D)	91,678	(43%)
Dole (R)	89,817	(45%)	Bush (R)	76,337	(35%)
Perot (I)	19,136	(10%)	Perot (I)	47,137	(22%)

Rep. Jim Turner (D)

Elected 1996; b. Feb. 6, 1946, Fort Lewis, WA; home, Crockett; U. of TX, B.B.A. 1968, M.B.A. 1971, J.D. 1971; Baptist; married (Ginny).

Career: Army, 1970–78; TX House of Reps., 1981–84; Exec. Asst., Gov. Mark White, 1984–86; Practicing atty., 1986–96; Crockett Mayor, 1989–91; TX Senate, 1991–96; Chmn., TX Commission on Children & Youth, 1993–94.

DC Office: 1508 LHOB 20515, 202-225-2401; Fax: 202-225-5955.

District Offices: Crockett, 409-544-8414; Lufkin, 409-637-1770; Orange, 409-883-4990.

Committees: *Government Reform & Oversight* (18th of 19 D): National Economic Growth, Natural Resources & Regulatory Affairs; National Security, International Affairs & Criminal Justice. *National Security* (19th of 25 D): Military Procurement; Military Research & Development.

Group Ratings and Key Votes: Newly Elected

Election Results

1996 general	Jim Turner (D)	102,908	(52%)	($919,505)
	Brian Babin (R)	89,838	(46%)	($595,410)
	Others	4,225	(2%)	
1996 primary	Jim Turner (D)	45,453	(59%)	
	Fred Hudson (D)	16,068	(21%)	
	Edgar J. (Bubba) Groce (D)	15,171	(20%)	
1994 general	Charles Wilson (D)	87,709	(57%)	($848,019)
	Donna Peterson (R)	66,071	(43%)	($136,188)

THIRD DISTRICT

North Dallas's history is full of irony. This is one of America's most famous affluent, educated and Republican areas, famed as the locus of the most successful television program of the 1980s and the eponymous football novel of the 1970s, but in its youth was one of the poorest, least educated and most Democratic parts in the nation. Dallas, named for the Philadelphia lawyer who was James K. Polk's vice president, got its commercial start as the place where the first railroad in Texas stopped at the three forks of the Trinity River, surrounded by dirt-poor farm country. "Its wealth originally came from cotton," John Gunther wrote in 1946, "but primarily it is a banking and jobbing and distributing center, the headquarters of railroads and utilities." Then Dallas became one of the nation's leading high-tech cities, the home of Texas Instruments and Ross Perot's EDS, and one of the nation's major defense centers. As Dallas's private sector has demanded and rewarded expertise, it has attracted high-skill people from all over the world, and they tend to move to the north side.

On the rolling, scrub-covered hills north of downtown Dallas, this growth has built a vast affluent metropolis, extending now 30 miles out into the countryside, far from the mansion-lined streets of Highland Park and Southern Methodist University's larger-than-life copy of Thomas Jefferson's University of Virginia. These landmarks in long-established prestigious neighborhoods are well-known; less known are the somewhat more modest neighborhoods that have spread out into the countryside: a *new* North Dallas *north* of North Dallas. Outside the LBJ Freeway have grown up middle-income Mesquite east of Dallas, higher-income Garland and Richardson northeast of Dallas, and the almost entirely new city of Plano in Collin County, now a corporate headquarters as well as bedroom community, and the highest-income section of the Dallas-Fort Worth Metroplex.

The 3d Congressional District, with its lines redrawn by a federal court for the 1996 election, no longer includes the Park Cities and North Park Center—the heart of historic North Dallas. Instead, inside much more regular boundaries, it includes most of Mesquite, and all of Garland, Richardson and Plano. This is a very Republican district, 60% for Bob Dole in 1996, though not as Republican as it was in its 1992 and 1994 boundaries.

The congressman from the 3d District is Republican Sam Johnson, former Air Force fighter pilot and prisoner of war in Vietnam for seven years. Johnson grew up in Dallas, graduated from SMU and George Washington University, then began his career in the Air Force, fighting in combat in both Korea and Vietnam, where he was imprisoned from 1966–73. On his return he started a home-building company and was elected to the Texas House in 1984. He won the 3d District seat in a May 1991 special election when incumbent Steve Bartlett, frustrated with being in the minority, became mayor of Dallas. Johnson ran second in the primary, with 20%, to 28% for two-time 5th District House candidate and former Peace Corps head Tom Pauken. In the runoff Johnson emphasized his war record, tended to stay above the fray and, although he showed limited knowledge of issues in debate, won by a 53%–47% margin over Pauken, who is now Texas Republican chairman and a sometime critic of Governor George W. Bush.

In the House, Johnson has had a strong conservative record, opposing pork barrel projects of all kinds, voting for more IRAs and against extending unemployment benefits. He chairs the Conservative Action Team, which tries to press the leadership to stick with conservative goals from budget targets to elimination of the National Endowment for the Arts. Every Congress he offers a constitutional amendment to repeal the 16th Amendment which authorized the income tax. As a member of the Ways and Means Committee, he staunchly supports Chairman Bill Archer and shares his goal of replacing the income tax with something in the nature of a consumption tax and abolishing the IRS. Johnson also sponsored a successful amendment to require school districts to permit voluntary prayer. For months he led opposition to the disgraceful and distorted *Enola Gay* exhibit at the National Air and Space Museum, and then was appointed to the Board of Regents, where he led the move to replace the exhibit and get rid of the current museum director. Unlike some other former POWs in Congress, Johnson strongly opposed the Clinton decision to give diplomatic recognition to Vietnam; "the President is giving away the store for nothing in return." He successfully opposed the immigration bill provision for a tamper-proof Social Security card as a federal identification card.

Redistricting gave Johnson his first Democratic opponent ever; he won 73%–24%.

The People: Census data not available due to 1996 redistricting.

1996 Presidential Vote			1992 Presidential Vote		
Dole (R)	133,044	(60%)	Bush (R)	110,744	(45%)
Clinton (D)	72,217	(32%)	Perot (I)	80,152	(33%)
Perot (I)	17,778	(8%)	Clinton (D)	53,280	(22%)

Rep. Sam Johnson (R)

Elected May 1991; b. Oct. 11, 1930, San Antonio; home, Dallas; Southern Methodist U., B.B.A. 1951, George Washington U., M.S. 1974; Methodist; married (Shirley).

Career: Air Force, 1950–79 (Korea & Vietnam); Home Builder; TX House of Reps., 1984–91.

DC Office: 1030 LHOB 20515, 202-225-4201; Fax: 202-225-1485; e-mail: samtx03@mail.house.gov.

District Office: Richardson, 972-470-0892.

Committees: *Education & The Workforce* (10th of 25 R): Early Childhood, Youth & Families. *Ways & Means* (13th of 23 R): Health; Social Security.

Group Ratings

	ADA	ACLU	AFS	LCV	CFA	CON	NFIB	COC	ACU	NTLC	CHC
1996	5	19	0	15	0	66	100	94	100	100	100
1995	0	—	—	0	0	38	—	100	96	—	—

National Journal Ratings

	1995 LIB — 1995 CONS			1996 LIB — 1996 CONS		
Economic	0%	—	74%	20%	—	76%
Social	0%	—	79%	14%	—	77%
Foreign	0%	—	85%	0%	—	79%

Key Votes of the 104th Congress

1. Reduce Medicare Growth $	Y	5. Flag Amendment	Y	9. Cuban Embargo	Y
2. Ovrd. Product Liab. Veto	Y	6. Drop EPA Limits	N	10. Bar Bosnia Troop $	Y
3. Increase Min. Wage	N	7. Repeal Assault-Weap. Ban	Y	11. Cut Anti-Missile Defense	N
4. Welfare Reform	Y	8. Ovrd. Part. Birth Veto	Y	12. Bar U.N. Uniforms	Y

Election Results

1996 spec. prim.	Sam Johnson (R)	142,325	(73%)	($625,107)
	Lee Cole (D)	47,654	(24%)	($7,968)
	Others	5,047	(3%)	
1994 general	Sam Johnson (R)	157,011	(91%)	($417,039)
	Tom Donahue (Lib)	15,611	(9%)	

FOURTH DISTRICT

The Red River Valley is just one of the hearts of Texas. It is hardscrabble farm country along an unnavigable river. First settled in the 1830s, in the days of the Texas Republic, many counties here reached their population peak around 1900, when every 160 acres was worked by a large farm family with skads of children and aunts and grandparents. This was the part of Texas that first sent Speaker Sam Rayburn to Congress in 1912. The Red River then was one of the strongest Democratic parts of the country, with a sentimental regard for Confederate veterans and a seething hatred of Wall Street bankers. Today, that economic populism is muted, but traditional religious values remain strong, even as people head for work on the interstate, listen to country music on their "Walkmans" and shop at Wal-Marts.

The 4th Congressional District of Texas is the lineal descendant of the seat represented by Sam Rayburn for 49 years, and still includes his home town of Bonham in Fannin County. But about one-quarter of the district's people now live in the Dallas-Fort Worth Metroplex, with one-third in the small oil cities of Tyler and Longview. These are the homes of upwardly mobile families, still conservative in their cultural values, far more trusting of free markets than of government regulation. Politics here has changed as well. In 1940, when Rayburn first became speaker, his 4th Congressional District voted 90% for Franklin Roosevelt. In 1992, Bill Clinton finished third here, with 28%, behind George Bush and Ross Perot, and in 1996 he lost to Bob Dole 56%–35%.

The congressman from the 4th is Ralph Hall, a conservative Democrat of the old Tory mold, one of the few left in the House. He was first elected in 1980 after a 30-year career in local politics and business; he was a county judge as long ago as 1950 and from 1962–72 was in the Texas Senate. He has one of the most conservative voting records of any House Democrat, and usually does not back the leadership except on purely party matters, and not always on these: he once declined to vote for Tip O'Neill for speaker. He opposed the Clinton budget and tax package in 1993 and supported just about everything in the Contract with America in 1995. But he is not a pure free marketeer: he voted against NAFTA. On the Commerce Committee he was skeptical about allowing the regional Bells into long distance and favored cable reregulation.

Those views are perhaps one reason why Hall, unlike five other conservative Democrats—some with voting records actually less conservative than his, did not switch parties in the 104th. "I think it's my duty to stay [a Democrat] and try to pull them back toward the middle," he said. Hall is a hunting pal of Commerce's ranking Democrat John Dingell, and he is now the ranking Democrat himself on the Energy and Power Subcommittee, which is handling electric utility deregulation, likely to be the most heavily lobbied issue in the 105th Congress and perhaps in the 106th and 107th as well. Previously he chaired a space subcommittee, and emphasized the use of space for biomedical research: "I fully and firmly believe that we're going to find some cures for the dreaded diseases, cancer and diabetes, there, because we can't find them on Earth." He authored the bill passed in 1997 to ban federal assistance to doctors like Jack Kevorkian to assist suicides.

Despite speculation about his retirement, Hall ran again in 1996 and won handily, by a significantly better margin than in 1992 or 1994. He may have been helped when the favored candidate of Republican Party insiders lost the primary 54%–46% to a newcomer from Houston whose last name happened to be Hall. At the same time Hall endorsed Republican Senator Phil Gramm for reelection. Political observers—and most everyone else—agree that the 4th will elect a Republican when Hall retires. But it's also possible that this rather ungainly-shaped district will be altered beyond recognition after the 2000 Census, thus sparing "Mister Sam" the pain of seeing his former district in Republican hands.

The People: Pop. 1990: 567,231; 49% rural; 14% age 65+; 86% White; 8% Black; 1% Amer. Indian; 4% Hispanic origin. Households: 63% married couple families; 30% married couple fams. w. children;

45% college educ.; median household income: $26,974; per capita income: $12,724; median gross rent: $385; median house value: $57,100.

1996 Presidential Vote			**1992 Presidential Vote**		
Dole (R)	117,895	(56%)	Bush (R)	95,182	(41%)
Clinton (D)	73,873	(35%)	Perot (I)	69,647	(30%)
Perot (I)	18,693	(9%)	Clinton (D)	65,520	(28%)

Rep. Ralph M. Hall (D)

Elected 1980; b. May 3, 1923, Fate; home, Rockwall; U. of TX, TX Christian U., Southern Methodist U., LL.B. 1951; United Methodist; married (Mary Ellen).

Career: Navy, 1942–45 (WWII); Rockwall Cnty. Judge, 1950–62; TX Senate, 1962–72; Practicing atty.; Pres. and CEO, TX Aluminum Corp.; Spec. Cnsl., Howmet Corp.

DC Office: 2221 RHOB 20515, 202-225-6673; Fax: 202-225-3332.

District Offices: Gainesville, 817-668-6370; Rockwall, 214-771-9118; Sherman, 903-892-1112; Tyler, 903-597-3729.

Committees: *Commerce* (4th of 23 D): Energy & Power (RMM); Finance & Hazardous Materials; Health & the Environment. *Science* (2nd of 21 D): Energy & Environment; Space & Aeronautics.

Group Ratings

	ADA	ACLU	AFS	LCV	CFA	CON	NFIB	COC	ACU	NTLC	CHC
1996	15	19	8	23	31	82	97	94	90	85	100
1995	10	—	—	6	0	87	—	100	76	—	—

National Journal Ratings

	1995 LIB — 1995 CONS			1996 LIB — 1996 CONS		
Economic	41%	—	56%	42%	—	56%
Social	21%	—	72%	14%	—	77%
Foreign	36%	—	59%	41%	—	56%

Key Votes of the 104th Congress

1. Reduce Medicare Growth $	Y	5. Flag Amendment	Y	9. Cuban Embargo	Y
2. Ovrd. Product Liab. Veto	Y	6. Drop EPA Limits	N	10. Bar Bosnia Troop $	Y
3. Increase Min. Wage	N	7. Repeal Assault-Weap. Ban	Y	11. Cut Anti-Missile Defense	N
4. Welfare Reform	Y	8. Ovrd. Part. Birth Veto	Y	12. Bar U.N. Uniforms	Y

Election Results

1996 general	Ralph M. Hall (D)	132,126	(64%)	($527,260)
	Jerry Ray Hall (R)	71,065	(34%)	($30,156)
	Others	3,986	(2%)	
1996 primary	Ralph M. Hall (D)	unopposed		
1994 general	Ralph M. Hall (D)	99,303	(59%)	($559,157)
	David L. Bridges (R)	67,267	(40%)	($46,375)

FIFTH DISTRICT

Not all of Dallas is glitz and postmodern marble. From each side of downtown, on one of the three street grids that run skew to each other, is an older Dallas, with neighborhoods of high-ceilinged old mansions, modest bungalows and shotgun houses running out toward the old airport at Love Field or the State Fair Grounds and the Cotton Bowl in east Dallas, or south to the desolate treeless parks along the cement-lined Trinity River. Some of this older Dallas is being renovated and rebuilt, with chic cafes and trendy stores serving those who make their livings catering to the rich farther north. Other once middle-class neighborhoods are filling up with immigrants from Mexico and other parts of Latin America, once again noisy with children as they were in the 1950s when people moved here not from Mexico or Central America but from the almost all-Anglo counties of north and central Texas.

Texas's 5th Congressional District, as redistricted in 1996, includes such neighborhoods just north and east of downtown Dallas. Added in the redistricting was the affluent Lakewood and Lake Highlands areas around and beyond White Rock Lake, out to the LBJ Freeway. Then, following the same lines used in the Democrats' creative 1991 redistricting, the 5th proceeds through a narrow corridor through the suburbs to combine this part of Dallas County with seven rural and small town counties about halfway between Dallas and Houston, plus black neighborhoods in Tyler and Bryan. But the political balance in 1996 was a bit different than before redistricting. The affluent precincts added are heavily Republican and mostly white, reducing the 5th's black and Hispanic percentages, and changing a district Bill Clinton carried in 1992 by 40%–34% to one that voted 37%–37% that year and 46%–46% in 1996.

The congressman from the 5th District is Pete Sessions, a Republican elected in 1996. Sessions grew up in Waco, graduated from Southwestern University, then worked at Southwestern Bell in Dallas for 16 years; his father William Sessions, a federal judge, served as FBI director from 1987–93. Pete Sessions ran in the 1991 special election in the 3d District, and finished sixth, far behind eventual winner Sam Johnson. In 1993 he resigned his job to run against 5th District Democratic Congressman John Bryant. A liberal and an active legislator, Bryant was one of the prime beneficiaries of Texas's Democratic districting plan, and he won easily in 1992. But in 1994, Sessions ran a vigorous campaign, making a two-day, 12-city tour of the rural portions of the district with a livestock trailer full of horse manure with a sign saying, "the Clinton healthcare plan stinks worse than this trailer." "A vulgar thing," Bryant sniffed. Although he outspent Sessions 2–1, Bryant was closely pressed and won by just 50%–47%. Bryant had a 51%–46% lead in Dallas County and ran only 735 votes ahead in the rest of the district. In 1996, even before redistricting, Bryant decided to run for the Senate against Phil Gramm; he was taken by surprise by the pickup truck campaign of high school teacher Victor Morales; Bryant trailed in the March primary 36%–30%, and lost the April runoff 51%–49%.

Sessions ran again in 1996 and won the March primary; that result was thrown out in the redistricting case in the summer, but only Sessions and the winner of the Democratic primary, John Pouland, a former regional GSA administrator, filed to run in November. Sessions was pleased that his home area in east Dallas was now included in the district. Sessions took some venturesome stands: for partially privatizing Social Security and proclaiming his support of Newt Gingrich. He charged that Pouland was a big government liberal and would abandon U.S. military bases overseas; Pouland criticized subsidizing the foreign bases while pursuing Medicare "cuts." Pouland charged that Sessions had changed to an anti-abortion stance since his 1991 race; Sessions sent out brochures graphically describing partial-birth abortions. Sessions attacked Pouland for taking money from the Laborers Union which the Clinton Justice Department found to be mob-connected and attacking him for defending criminals in his law practice. This was a seriously contested race: Sessions spent $1 million, Pouland $600,000. Redistricting probably made the difference. Sessions won 56%–44% in Dallas County, 10% ahead of his 1994 showing there. Pouland carried the rest of the district by 507 votes, nearly a carbon copy of Bryant's showing there. Overall Sessions won 53%–47%.

In the House Sessions serves on the Banking, Science and Government Reform Committees. He predicted Democrats and Republicans "are going to work together" on reforming government, and looked forward to perusing the "annual performance plans" of federal agencies required by the 1993 Government Performance and Results Act—part of Vice President Al Gore's Reinventing Government project.

The People: Census data not available due to 1996 redistricting.

1996 Presidential Vote			1992 Presidential Vote		
Clinton (D)	78,249	(46%)	Bush (R)	73,805	(37%)
Dole (R)	77,002	(46%)	Clinton (D)	73,076	(37%)
Perot (I)	13,355	(8%)	Perot (I)	50,147	(25%)

Rep. Pete Sessions (R)

Elected 1996; b. March 22, 1955, Waco; home, Dallas; Southwestern U., B.A. 1978; Methodist; married (Juanita).

Career: District Mgr., Southwestern Bell Telephone Co., 1978–93; Vice Pres., Public Policy, Natl. Center for Policy Analysis, 1995–96.

DC Office:1318 LHOB 20515, 202-225-2231; Fax: 202-225-5878.

District Offices: Dallas, 214-349-9996.

Committees: *Banking & Financial Services* (26th of 30 R): Capital Markets, Securities & Government Sponsored Enterprises; Housing & Community Opportunity. *Government Reform & Oversight* (20th of 24 R): Civil Service; Government Management, Information & Technology (Vice Chmn.); Postal Service. *Science* (25th of 25 R): Basic Research.

Group Ratings and Key Votes: Newly Elected

Election Results

1996 spec. prim.	Pete Sessions (R)	80,196	(53%)	($1,091,122)
	John Pouland (D)	70,922	(47%)	($602,884)
1994 general	John Bryant (D)	61,877	(50%)	($799,511)
	Pete Sessions (R)	58,521	(47%)	($394,401)
	Others	3,218	(3%)	

SIXTH DISTRICT

The Dallas-Fort Worth Metroplex—yes, the name is part of everyday speech there—has spread outward from its two, different-sized historic nodes in downtown Dallas and Fort Worth and although the larger population center is in the east, in Dallas, much of the development has moved west, across the dusty plains where one crosses the barely perceptible Balcones Escarpment, the geologist's boundary between green and grassy east Texas and the brown and barren West. This was empty territory a few decades ago; now it has mostly been filled in, with subdivisions and shopping centers that leave some feeling of the shape of this land under the enormous Texas sky.

The 6th Congressional District takes in much of this territory. It is the descendant of a district that stretched across rural territory from Dallas-Fort Worth to Houston and was represented from 1978–84 by Phil Gramm, who shifted from Boll Weevil Democrat to Reagan Republican even as the population balance shifted from rural to urban. Now the 6th, under the complex lines drawn and changed marginally for 1996, is entirely within the Metroplex. It includes much of Dallas-Fort Worth Airport and cargo-servicing Alliance Airport, developed by Ross Perot. Jr.. In between are rapidly growing and increasingly affluent suburbs—Colleyville, Grapevine, Euless, Bedford—and to the south is Arlington, home of Texas Stadium and Six Flags Over Texas. Essentially the 6th is a ring of middle-income to affluent suburban territory around Fort Worth, wrapping around the 12th District and part of the 24th. The boundaries were only a little smoothed out by the federal court. The original Democratic redistricters were trying to concentrate Republican votes in this heavily Republican district; as to the court's motivation, others may share the view of 6th District Congressman Joe Barton, "I'd like to be able to talk to the federal judges and ask what the heck they were trying to accomplish."

Barton grew up in Ennis, graduated from Texas A&M, worked in business and was a White House Fellow. When Gramm ran for the Senate in 1984, Barton ran for the House, and won the Republican runoff by only 10 votes and the general with 57%. In 1986, against the well-financed Democrat Pete Geren, who from 1989–96 represented the Fort Worth-based 12th District, Barton won with 56%. Barton has had two great causes, one defunct, the other hanging fire. The first was the Superconductor Supercollider, an enormous scientific laboratory that was to have been built in Waxahachie, south of Dallas, part of which is in the District. In retrospect this was a Texas project, alive only so long as George Bush was president; despite all Barton's efforts the House voted 282–143 to zero it out in October 1993. Barton's other great cause has been the constitutional balanced budget amendment. He has been the chief House sponsor of the version requiring a three-fifths vote to raise taxes. When the House took up the issue in early 1995, the issue threatened to cause a schism among House Republicans; many freshmen complained that party leaders were not doing enough to support Barton's version, while leaders whispered there was no way the three-fifths measure could win the needed 290 votes. In fact it got 253, and the plain balanced budget amendment passed with 300; Barton played a vital role in getting all but two Republicans to vote for that, and in return Newt Gingrich promised to schedule the three-fifths amendment for a vote on April 15, 1996, and on subsequent April 15ths until it passed. It got 243 votes in 1996, 233 in 1997—not an encouraging trajectory. But Barton did get the House to vote a rule requiring a two-thirds vote for a tax increase. And he has sponsored a bill to reform the budget process drastically, by creating a biennial budget cycle that the president would have to sign into law.

Barton is chairman of the Commerce Oversight and Investigations Subcommittee, once a great vehicle of publicity for John Dingell and his proteges. Barton has conducted extensive hearings on the 1990 Clean Air Act and the Food and Drug Administration and has sponsored reform bills on each. He also gained considerable attention with hearings that explored millions of dollars of travel expenses by Energy Secretary Hazel O'Leary; the review helped ensure her departure from office. Barton can be stubborn and original. He has voted against a ban on education spending for children of illegal immigrants, against compromise budgets backed by the Republican leadership and against changing the District of Columbia domestic partners ordinance, but only because he opposed federal intervention over a local ordinance.

Barton has had some political disappointments outside Congress. He ran for the Senate in 1993 after Lloyd Bentsen resigned to be Treasury Secretary. Despite the support of former Governor Bill Clements and Barton's strong opposition to the then-hot issue of gays in the military, he finished third with just 14% of the vote in the May all-party primary. In June 1994 he was outgoing Republican state Chairman Fred Meyer's choice to succeed him. But Clements (in a move he has since regretted) opposed his candidacy, and Barton lost at the convention to Tom Pauken. And in 1995 he was the House chairman of Phil Gramm's hapless presidential campaign. He has been more fortunate in his own House races: in 1996 he was reelected with 77% of the vote.

The People: Census data not available due to 1996 redistricting.

1996 Presidential Vote			1992 Presidential Vote		
Dole (R)	144,773	(60%)	Bush (R)	123,783	(46%)
Clinton (D)	78,617	(33%)	Perot (I)	81,458	(30%)
Perot (I)	17,483	(7%)	Clinton (D)	66,250	(24%)

Rep. Joe L. Barton (R)

Elected 1984; b. Sept. 15, 1949, Waco; home, Ennis; Texas A&M U., B.S. 1972, Purdue U., M.S. 1973; United Methodist; married (Janet).

Career: Asst. to V.P., Ennis Business Forms, 1973–81; White House Fellow, U.S. Dept. of Energy, 1981–82; Consultant, Atlantic Richfield Co., 1982–84.

DC Office: 2264 RHOB 20515, 202-225-2002; Fax: 202-225-3052; e-mail: barton06@hr.house.gov.

District Offices: Arlington, 817-543-1000; Ennis, 972-875-8488.

Committees: *Commerce* (6th of 28 R): Health & the Environment; Oversight & Investigations (Chmn.); Telecommunications, Trade & Consumer Protection. *Science* (8th of 25 R): Basic Research; Space & Aeronautics.

Group Ratings

	ADA	ACLU	AFS	LCV	CFA	CON	NFIB	COC	ACU	NTLC	CHC
1996	15	6	20	8	0	71	89	88	89	93	93
1995	0	—	—	6	0	31	—	96	80	—	—

National Journal Ratings

	1995 LIB — 1995 CONS			1996 LIB — 1996 CONS		
Economic	0%	—	74%	24%	—	73%
Social	30%	—	68%	33%	—	65%
Foreign	28%	—	65%	30%	—	65%

Key Votes of the 104th Congress

1. Reduce Medicare Growth $	Y	5. Flag Amendment	Y	9. Cuban Embargo	Y
2. Ovrd. Product Liab. Veto	Y	6. Drop EPA Limits	N	10. Bar Bosnia Troop $	Y
3. Increase Min. Wage	N	7. Repeal Assault-Weap. Ban	Y	11. Cut Anti-Missile Defense	N
4. Welfare Reform	Y	8. Ovrd. Part. Birth Veto	Y	12. Bar U.N. Uniforms	Y

Election Results

1996 spec. prim.	Joe L. Barton (R)	160,800	(77%)	($890,468)
	Janet Carroll Richardson (I)	26,713	(13%)	($123,291)
	Catherine A. Anderson (Lib)	14,456	(7%)	
	Others	6,547	(3%)	
1994 general	Joe L. Barton (R)	152,038	(76%)	($574,897)
	Terry Jesmore (D)	44,286	(22%)	($33,383)
	Others	4,688	(2%)	

SEVENTH DISTRICT

When George Bush moved from Midland in West Texas to Houston in 1960, he bought a house in Briarwood, in what was then near the western edge of the fast-growing city, beyond Memorial Park and Loop 610, long before the Galleria and high-rises went up around the intersection of Post Oak and Westheimer. Bush returned to Houston in 1993 and built a new house a mile from his old one. The territory is familiar: Memorial Park, the largest in Houston, is just to the east. Bush's favorite shopping mall is nearby on Sage and San Felipe and his favorite barbecue joint a mile east on Memorial; his new office is atop the Park Laureate building at 10000 Memorial. But now all these landmarks are not at the edge of the vastly bigger Houston metropolitan area, but near its epicenter, certainly its retail center and not far from its commercial center, though the industrial center of gravity remains far to the east, near the Ship Channel.

The 7th Congressional District of Texas is the lineal descendant of the district that elected George Bush its first member of the House in 1966 and 1968. It occupied far more territory then, and its boundaries have been pared back as the population of the west side of Houston has skyrocketed. There are more than 1.5 million people today in the area that had 350,000 when Bush was first elected. Indeed, in 1990 the then-7th District had 784,000 people, the second most in Texas. The district was pared back for 1992, and it was not much changed by the 1996 court redistricting, so that it now starts just outside Memorial Park and extends west on Westheimer and the Katy Freeway and occupies part of Harris County west of Hillcroft and Bingle. It remains hyper-Republican, arguably the most Republican district in the nation.

The congressman from the 7th District is Bill Archer, chairman of the House Ways and Means Committee, who was elected to the House in 1970 when Bush ran for the Senate. Archer is a native Houstonian, who after service in the Air Force ran a feed business and participated in civic affairs. He was elected to the state House in 1966 as a Democrat, a very conservative one; in 1968 he switched parties and in 1970 was easily elected to the House as a Republican. His devotion to free market economics, cultural conservatism and an assertive foreign policy give him one of the most conservative voting records in the House. He joined Ways and Means in 1973, when Chairman Wilbur Mills let Republicans participate as much as Democrats. From 1975–94, when Al Ullman and Dan Rostenkowski were chairmen, Archer was given little say on most issues. Sometimes he was even a minority within his party. He opposed the 1983 Social Security bailout and was one of the Republicans who nearly scuttled the 1986 tax reform in December 1985. He opposed the budget summit agreement of 1990. He is a scrupulous man, who insists on preparing his own income tax every year because he wants to understand the burdens it imposes, who refuses to take PAC contributions though in a position to command millions, and he stays punctiliously loyal to his convictions.

As chairman, Archer has behaved courteously and worked hard, has cooperated with the Republican leadership on many major issues but has also moved strategically to put his own imprint on long-term policy. Through much of the 104th Congress, Archer's leeway on issues was sharply circumscribed by the Republican leadership. The Contract with America specified what tax cuts Republicans would seek, and Budget Chairman John Kasich pressed other tasks on Archer and his committee, including what Kasich considers cuts in corporate welfare and what Archer considers tax increases on business. On two other major issues in which Ways and Means passed major reforms—welfare and Medicare—subcommittee chairmen, Clay Shaw on welfare and Bill Thomas on Medicare, did much of the detail work, and several governors made large contributions as well. But Archer also showed a mastery of specifics and strategy as well. And he played a major role in keeping medical savings accounts in the healthcare bill passed in August 1996. Archer managed to do this while leaving committee meetings and legislative drafting much more open than they had been under longtime Chairman Dan Rostenkowski, though Democrats still complained, sometimes in extravagant terms. Of course not all of Archer's legislation was signed by Bill Clinton.

The May 1997 balanced budget agreement gave Archer the task of coming up with a package of tax cuts that were left vaguely defined and limited to specific sums. In June he proposed $135 billion in tax cuts over five years (minus $50 billion in some tax increases), but the Clinton Administration bellowed that the plan betrayed accords agreed to by Republican leaders the month before. Archer's plan offered per-child and higher-eduction tuition tax credits, higher estate tax credits, reductions in taxes on capital gains and on gains on the sale of homes up to $500,000, "American Dream" IRAs for home purchases, and income tax reductions in Washington, D.C., "enterprise zones." Administration officials complained that the package moved toward higher-income people and away from those less well-off in its benefits, and that the education relief fell short of their proposed $35 billion objective.

Temperamentally, Archer is pleased to work in a courteous, bipartisan fashion; ideologically, he is strongly committed to many goals which are anathema to most Democrats. But the bill gave him an opportunity to shape policy—and to move forward his long-range tax strategy. Archer's long-term goal is to replace the income tax with a broad-based consumption tax. He tends to favor something like a value-added tax, while Majority Leader Dick Armey favors a flat 17% income tax; Archer seems to be trying to come up with a unified Republican position which is capable of being passed. He probably will not be there to see it accomplished. House Republican rules limit chairmanships to six years, and Archer has announced that after his term is up in 2000 he will not seek reelection to the House, and thus will not serve with a Republican president. But he may affect those who do.

Archer is not quite so outward-looking as some other free market Republicans. He has on occasion been cautious about a fast-track bill authorizing negotiations of free trade agreements with Latin American countries beyond Mexico, and he has supported reducing legal immigration levels by half. But he has said that advancing free trade is one of his top goals for the 105th Congress.

Back home Archer is not handicapped at all by his policy of not taking contributions from PACs or from outside Texas. With a Democratic opponent for the first time since 1988, he was reelected with 81% of the vote.

The People: Census data not available due to 1996 redistricting.

1996 Presidential Vote

Dole (R)	145,637	(67%)
Clinton (D)	61,834	(28%)
Perot (I)	10,338	(5%)

1992 Presidential Vote

Bush (R)	132,053	(58%)
Clinton (D)	50,805	(22%)
Perot (I)	46,165	(20%)

Rep. Bill Archer (R)

Elected 1970; b. Mar. 22, 1928, Houston; home, Houston; Rice U., 1945–46, U. of TX, B.B.A. 1949, LL.B. 1951; Catholic; married (Sharon).

Career: Air Force, 1951–53; Pres., Uncle Johnny Mills Inc., 1953–61; Hunters Creek Village Cncl., Mayor Pro Tem, 1955–62; TX House of Reps., 1966–70; Dir., Heights State Bank, Houston, 1967–70; Practicing atty., 1968–71.

DC Office: 1236 LHOB 20515, 202-225-2571; Fax: 202-225-4381.

District Office: Houston, 713-682-8828.

Committees: *Ways & Means* (Chmn.). *Joint Committee on Taxation* (Chmn. of 5 Reps.).

Group Ratings

	ADA	ACLU	AFS	LCV	CFA	CON	NFIB	COC	ACU	NTLC	CHC
1996	5	0	0	15	8	66	95	94	100	98	93
1995	0	—	—	6	0	73	—	96	80	—	—

National Journal Ratings

	1995 LIB — 1995 CONS	1996 LIB — 1996 CONS
Economic	0% — 74%	20% — 76%
Social	0% — 79%	0% — 90%
Foreign	28% — 65%	0% — 79%

Key Votes of the 104th Congress

1. Reduce Medicare Growth $	Y	5. Flag Amendment	Y	9. Cuban Embargo	Y
2. Ovrd. Product Liab. Veto	Y	6. Drop EPA Limits	N	10. Bar Bosnia Troop $	Y
3. Increase Min. Wage	N	7. Repeal Assault-Weap. Ban	Y	11. Cut Anti-Missile Defense	N
4. Welfare Reform	Y	8. Ovrd. Part. Birth Veto	Y	12. Bar U.N. Uniforms	Y

Election Results

1996 spec. prim.	Bill Archer (R)	152,024	(81%)	($298,951)
	Al J.K. Siegmind (D)	28,187	(15%)	
	Others	6,620	(4%)	
1994 general	Bill Archer (R)	unopposed		($215,637)

EIGHTH DISTRICT

When Houston Intercontinental Airport opened in 1969, it was located far north of the city, in vacant ground near the small town of Humble (named for the oil company that was the predecessor of Exxon)—much too far, said many, from downtown Houston or from just about any other concentration of population. Today, Intercontinental is still a long way from downtown Houston, but it is no longer in the middle of nowhere. It's in the middle of a zone of rapid metropolitan expansion and growth, of commercial office space and upscale residential subdivisions rising on land that once held roadside stands and barbecues and unpainted farmhouses with water pooling on low swampy fields. Greater Houston has spread far out into the countryside, past Loop 610 in the inner city, past the Sam Houston Tollway, past the now mislabeled Farm-Market 1960, out past Conroe and Woodbranch Village in once rural Montgomery County.

The 8th Congressional District occupies most of this territory. A district that once covered the docks along the Houston Ship Channel has moved out with the people, so that its southern boundary runs roughly along FM 1960, sometimes dipping south to the Sam Houston Tollway. In its current boundaries, with minor changes made by the court-ordered redistricting in 1996, the 8th includes almost all of Montgomery County and two still mostly rural counties to the west and takes in College Station, home of Texas A&M University. This institution deserves more notice than it usually gets: it is one of Texas's two major state universities, with quite a different atmosphere from the University of Texas at Austin. A&M has an agricultural and military tradition, but it is a major university whose students' achievement roughly match those at its great rival the University of Texas. Senator Phil Gramm used to teach economics at A&M and it is the site of the George Bush Presidential Library. College Station, and almost all the rest of the 8th District, is staunchly Republican: defiantly free market on economics, respectful of tradition on cultural issues, firmly hawkish on military policy.

The congressman from the 8th District is Kevin Brady, a Republican elected after running in four separate elections in 1996—surely a record. Brady grew up and went to college in South Dakota. Then he moved to Montgomery County and worked as a chamber of commerce executive. In 1990 he was elected to the Texas House, where he sponsored sunset laws. In 1995 8th District Congressman Jack Fields announced he was retiring. First elected in 1980, Fields was chairman of the Telecommunications Subcommittee and one of the prime fathers of the 1996 Telecommunications Act; he had run for the Senate in the 1993 special election and finished fourth with 14%. Brady's main rival in this Republican district was Eugene Fontenot, a physician who wants "to restore America to its Christian heritage." Fontenot spent $4.7 million, a good portion of it his own money, running in the open 25th District seat in 1994; he won the primary 56%–44% but lost the general to Ken Bentsen 52%–45%. In 1996 Fontenot moved his campaign operation to the north side 8th District, and he and Brady ran against each other no less than four times. Brady had the support of Governor George W. Bush, Senators Phil Gramm and Kay Bailey Hutchison and Fields; Fontenot was endorsed by Patrick Buchanan, Pat Robertson and Phyllis Schlafly. Brady touted the sunset law he had passed in the legislature. Fontenot attacked him for being one of the two Republicans to vote against the carrying-concealed-weapons law. Brady opposed most gun control bills, but not this; his father had been shot and killed while trying a case in a South Dakota courtroom in the 1960s.

In their first faceoff, in the March primary, Fontenot beat Brady 36%–22% in a six candidate field. Then in the April runoff Brady won 53%–47%. In all but name Brady was congressman-elect. Then in August a three-judge federal court, following a Supreme Court order, redrew the boundaries of three invalid congressional districts and 10 of those adjoining, including the 8th. The court mandated an all-party primary November 5, with a runoff if no one got 50% between the two top candidates regardless of party December 10. Fontenot started spending liberally again, though less than in 1994—$1.3 million in all, and Brady nearly matched him, with $1.1 million. While the district seemed sure to remain Republican, suddenly Brady's victory was in doubt. In November Brady won 41% of the votes and Fontenot 39%; two Democrats got 14% and 6%. Brady's lead came because of his big margin in Montgomery County; Fontenot carried College Station and the Harris County part of the district. In December turnout was sharply down, from 193,000 to 51,000. This evidently helped party-regular Brady, who won 59%–41%, carrying every county.

Because House Republicans handed out most of their committee assignments before Brady was even elected, he ended up with a short straw, the Science Committee, that gives him an opportunity to work on local NASA issues. Perhaps as a consolation he was asked to give the response to President Clinton's Saturday radio address—the party's first public speech of the new year; he urged bipartisanship. His most distinctive priority is sunset reform of ineffective government agencies.

The People: Census data not available due to 1996 redistricting.

1996 Presidential Vote

Dole (R)	155,593	(67%)
Clinton (D)	62,641	(27%)
Perot (I)	14,892	(6%)

1992 Presidential Vote

Bush (R)	134,968	(55%)
Clinton (D)	55,702	(23%)
Perot (I)	55,357	(23%)

Rep. Kevin Brady (R)

Elected 1996; b. April 11, 1955, Vermillion, SD; The Woodlands, TX; U. of SD, B.S. 1990; Catholic; married (Kathy).

Career: Exec., Chamber of Commerce, 1978–96; TX House of Reps., 1990–96.

DC Office: 1531 LHOB 20515, 202-225-4901; Fax: 202-225-5524.

District Offices: College Station, 409-846-6068; Houston, 281-895-8892.

Committees: *International Relations* (26th of 26 R): International Economic Policy & Trade; Western Hemisphere. *Resources* (22nd of 27 R): Energy & Mineral Resources. *Science* (20th of 25 R): Space & Aeronautics; Technology.

Group Ratings and Key Votes: Newly Elected

Election Results

1996 spec. runoff	Kevin Brady (R)	30,366	(59%)	($1,094,498)
	Gene Fontenot (R)	21,004	(41%)	($1,379,749)
1996 spec. prim.	Kevin Brady (R)	80,325	(41%)	
	Gene Fontenot (R)	75,399	(39%)	
	Cynthia Newman (D)	26,246	(14%)	
	Robert Musemeche (D)	11,689	(6%)	
1994 general	Jack M. Fields, Jr. (R)	148,473	(92%)	($709,896)
	Russ Klecka (I)	12,831	(8%)	

NINTH DISTRICT

The spongy land of the Texas Gulf Coast, where the French explorer LaSalle and the Spanish colonizer Galvez dreamed of thriving settlements, remained mostly unsettled until well into the 20th Century. The elements here are not gentle, as Galveston learned when a hurricane in 1900 destroyed this city on a sandspit; the summer heat is ferocious and the rains torrential; few crops grow well here. But this is a land of oil. Ever since the Spindletop strike in Beaumont in 1901, southeast Texas has grown. First oil exploration, then petroleum refining, then petrochemicals: the straight-edged metal of oil rigs and the intricate curving metalwork of refineries shine through the swampy landscape of southeast Texas. And the rig workers and mechanical engineers they brought here have given a kind of permanent roughneck air to the region.

The 9th Congressional District of Texas occupies much of this territory. About half its people live in and around Beaumont and Port Arthur, still very much oil country, and one of the few places in Texas where labor unions have ever had much strength. The other half live south of Houston—in Galveston, now restoring its grand historic buildings (and the unlikely site of a

Dickensian Christmas celebration every year); and the refinery town of Texas City, where more than 500 died in a huge liquefied natural gas tanker explosion in 1947; and the Lyndon B. Johnson Space Center, where America's probes into space are planned, brought here originally by then-Vice President Lyndon Johnson and longtime Houston Congressman Albert Thomas.

The congressman from the 9th District is Nick Lampson, a Democrat elected in December 1996. Lampson grew up in Beaumont; he got his first job when his father died when he was 12; after graduating from Lamar University, he taught science in Beaumont schools, leading the first local Earth Day celebration in 1969, and then a real estate management course at Lamar; he also headed a home healthcare company. In 1977, at 32, he was elected Jefferson County Tax Assessor. He claims to have cut the costs of tax collections and was easily reelected. In 1996 Lampson decided to run against Steve Stockman, one of the most controversial members of the Republican freshman class of 1994, who won the seat by upsetting 32-year incumbent Jack Brooks. Stockman had a rocky youth, arrived in Texas looking for a job and living in his car, then found first religion and then politics, running twice against Brooks before winning. Stockman stirred controversy in Washington for writing a letter to Attorney General Janet Reno expressing concern about raids allegedly planned on militias and for garbling reporting about a threatening fax from a militia group his office received the day of the Oklahoma City bombing; in fact Stockman immediately turned the fax over to the FBI. Still, he was in trouble in the 9th, if only because of the Democratic leanings of the district.

Lampson had solid backing for the Democratic nomination, and won the five-candidate March primary with 69%. But then the Supreme Court ruled three Texas districts unconstitutional, and the redistricting plan adopted by a three-judge federal court marginally shifted the 9th's boundaries. The court said that required holding a whole new election (even though the changes could not conceivably have changed the primary results), with an all-party primary November 5 and a runoff, if no one got 50%, on December 10. The going got nasty: Stockman said Lampson's home health care company was accused of defrauding Medicare, while Lampson accused Stockman of failing to repay his college loans on time. Democrats, fearing diluted support for Lampson, cried foul when one of the losing primary candidates, Geraldine Sam, and a west Texan named Jack Brooks (high name recognition, but no relation) filed to run in the open November election; party leaders ostentatiously endorsed Lampson and Brooks dropped out. But the Democratic vote was split, and on November 5 Stockman led Lampson 46%–44%. Then Sam endorsed Stockman: more screams from Democrats. The numbers suggested that Stockman would lose if turnout was proportionate. Labor unions worked Beaumont hard to get Lampson votes out, and its county turnout fell only 29% compared to 50% in the rest of the district. Lampson won 53%–47%, winning more than his entire margin in the Beaumont area.

In the House, Lampson promised to promote the Johnson Space Center and local rice-growing. He is working to rebuild Route 87 near Sea Rim Park, improving the hurricane evacuation route on U.S. 69 and deepening the Sabine-Neches Ship Channel.

The People: Census data not available due to 1996 redistricting.

1996 Presidential Vote

Clinton (D)	97,268	(48%)
Dole (R)	89,942	(45%)
Perot (I)	14,144	(7%)

1992 Presidential Vote

Clinton (D)	98,785	(44%)
Bush (R)	80,631	(36%)
Perot (I)	47,273	(21%)

Rep. Nick Lampson (D)

Elected 1996; b. Feb. 14, 1945, Beaumont; home, Beaumont; Lamar U., B.S. 1968, M.Ed. 1971; Catholic; married (Susan).

Career: Public schl. teacher, 1968–71; Instructor, Lamar U., 1971–76; Jefferson Cnty. Assessor, 1977–95; Pres., Jefferson Cnty. Home Health Care, 1993–95.

DC Office: 417 CHOB 20515, 202-225-6565; Fax: 202-225-5547.

District Offices: Beaumont, 409-838-0061; Galveston, 409-762-5877.

Committees: *Science* (19th of 21 D): Space & Aeronautics. *Transportation & Infrastructure* (33rd of 33 D): Public Buildings & Economic Development; Water Resources & Environment.

Group Ratings and Key Votes: Newly Elected

Election Results

1996 spec. runoff	Nick Lampson (D)	59,225	(53%)	($1,379,749)
	Steve Stockman (R)	52,870	(47%)	($1,898,778)
1996 spec. prim.	Steve Stockman (R)	88,171	(46%)	
	Nick Lampson (D)	83,782	(44%)	
	Geraldine Sam (D)	17,887	(9%)	
1994 general	Steve Stockman (R)	81,353	(52%)	($245,547)
	Jack Brooks (D)	71,643	(46%)	($1,202,868)
	Others	3,801	(2%)	

TENTH DISTRICT

Austin, the capital of the second largest state in the United States and site of its largest Capitol building, is also the southernmost capital in the continental 48 states. It is one of many capitals with a first-rate university, the University of Texas, but one of the few (Nashville is the obvious other) with its own musical tradition, symbolized by Willie Nelson. Not so long ago Austin seemed as laid-back and countrified as Nelson himself. There has never been much commerce here, and for much of the year the Capitol basked in a sun that seemed to ban gainful employment. Its skies were untainted with the smoke of industry, its ground unpocked with pumping oil rigs, its main street lined not with business offices but with buildings holding a few lobbyists and the antique Driskill Hotel.

Today Austin is quite different: if not bustling, it is busy; if it is still laid-back, it is everywhere air-conditioned; the Driskill still stands, but glass high-rises also have popped up all over downtown, to the south and far to the north in what was once lonely hill country. Sparking the change is the University of Texas. Endowed with thousands of west Texas acres that turned out to sit on top of oil, the nation's largest single university campus is here in Austin. With some 50,000 students, it has a tower at its symbolic center that looms high over the campus, and houses the exemplary LBJ Presidential Library with its 35 million documents. The University has spawned a community of liberal intellectuals since the 1950s and a high-tech industry that started booming in the 1980s, symbolized when Austin was selected in 1983 as the site of the Microelectronics and Computer Technology Corporation research consortium. Austin is now one of America's four or five leading high-tech centers; in the mid-1990s Motorola and Advanced Micro Devices built $1 billion facilities here, and the number of manufacturing jobs rose more than 30%. The Austin area has had some of the fastest population growth in the country, and the city limits have expanded, with vast new tracts of houses have been built north of the old town, far beyond the Capitol and the University, and south of the Colorado River. Bergstrom Air Force Base, now closed, has been suggested as the site for a larger, much needed new airport, and may start cargo flights there as early as 1998.

Historically Democratic, Austin moved toward the Republicans in the 1980s, but not all the way. The new subdivisions in the high-tech north and south vote Republican, though less than similar places in Houston or Dallas. The University area is still heavily Democratic. In 1992, Austin's Travis County voted for Bill Clinton over George Bush by a 52%–40% margin. The new affluent techie residents have built a bigger Republican base than in the old Austin. But as in other high-tech areas, Research Triangle and Silicon Valley, the cultural politics of the 1990s has driven voters back to the Democrats.

The 10th District of Texas, which once spread over the Hill Country to the west and south, now is entirely within Travis County: essentially Austin and its suburban fringe. It is the descendant of the 10th District which in April 1937 elected a gangly-looking 29-year-old New Dealer named Lyndon Johnson. Johnson gave up the seat to make his second, and successful, run for the Senate in 1948. His friend Homer Thornberry won the seat and held it until he became a federal judge in December 1963. Another LBJ backer, Jake Pickle, was elected that month and served until he retired in 1994—57 years of representation from three political allies, all born between 1908 and 1913.

Today the congressman from the 10th is Lloyd Doggett, a liberal Democrat with a dream resume and an up-and-down political career. Doggett grew up in Austin, finished first in his class and was president of the student body at UT in 1967. In 1972, he was elected to the state Senate at 26: he is the same age as Bill Clinton, who spent that fall in Austin as the Texas McGovern coordinator. Doggett was part of a surprisingly large bloc of liberals in the Texas Senate in the 1970s and pushed laws against job discrimination and copkiller bullets and for generic drugs. He had a certain flair. He was one of the "killer bees" who hid out to prevent a quorum on changing the rules in the Democratic primary and filibustered—wearing sneakers—against what he called an anti-consumer bill.

Doggett, vastly popular in Austin, is somewhat less so in the rest of the state. In 1984 he ran for the U.S. Senate, narrowly edging out future Senator Bob Krueger in the primary and conservative Congressman Kent Hance in the runoff. Then, despite the campaign help of James Carville, Doggett lost the general by a resounding 59%–41% to party-switching Congressman Phil Gramm, who attacked him sharply for holding a fund raiser at a San Antonio gay strip bar. Doggett came back and, with strong support from trial lawyers, was elected to the Texas Supreme Court in 1988. When Pickle retired, Doggett left that position and ran for Congress. He won the Democratic primary with only token opposition and in the general outpolled black Republican Jo Baylor. Campaigning strongly on the 1994 crime bill, endorsing its death penalties and assault weapons ban, Doggett won by the solid, but not quite overwhelming, margin of 56%–40%.

This made Doggett one of the 13 House Democratic freshman, vastly outnumbered by the 73 Republican freshmen. Doggett's voting record was mostly but not totally liberal; he voted for the final version of welfare reform and voted to bring the Blue Dog budget to the floor (but not for it). He defended the COPS program, called for campaign finance reform, compiled a rather stingy record on spending. With Tom Davis, he formed an Information Technology Working Group. He emerged as a vocal critic of Speaker Newt Gingrich and a close ally of Minority Whip David Bonior. "He's like a first-round draft choice," Bonior told National Journal.

At home Doggett holds neighborhood office hours in front of shopping centers and he often reads constituents' letters on the floor of the House. In 1996 his Republican opponent was Teresa Doggett, small business owner and unsuccessful candidate for state Controller in 1994. Lloyd Doggett won 56%–41%, spending less money than he took in and leaving $972,000 in his treasury afterwards, which miffed some Democrats who would have liked contributions. That may have been the reason he failed to get a high-profile committee assignment.

The People: Pop. 1990: 566,357; 8% rural; 7% age 65+; 65% White; 11% Black; 3% Asian; 21% Hispanic origin. Households: 45% married couple families; 23% married couple fams. w. children; 64% college educ.; median household income: $27,280; per capita income: $14,978; median gross rent: $415; median house value: $76,700.

1996 Presidential Vote			1992 Presidential Vote		
Clinton (D)	126,855	(54%)	Clinton (D)	128,816	(48%)
Dole (R)	93,219	(40%)	Bush (R)	84,562	(32%)
Perot (I)	13,453	(6%)	Perot (I)	54,307	(20%)

Rep. Lloyd Doggett (D)

Elected 1994; b. Oct. 6, 1946, Austin; home, Austin; U. of TX, B.B.A. 1967, J.D. 1970; Methodist; married (Libby).

Career: Practicing atty., 1970–89; TX Senate, 1973–85; Adjunct Prof., U. of TX Law Schl., 1989–94; TX Supreme Ct. Justice, 1989–94.

DC Office: 126 CHOB 20515, 202-225-4865; Fax: 202-225-3073; e-mail: doggett@hr.house.gov.

District Offices: Austin, 512-916-5921.

Committees: *Budget* (10th of 19 D). *Resources* (23rd of 23 D): National Parks & Public Lands; Water & Power.

Group Ratings

	ADA	ACLU	AFS	LCV	CFA	CON	NFIB	COC	ACU	NTLC	CHC
1996	80	81	100	92	92	96	27	19	0	10	7
1995	90	—	—	81	100	9	—	29	8	—	—

National Journal Ratings

	1995 LIB — 1995 CONS			1996 LIB — 1996 CONS		
Economic	76%	—	23%	73%	—	25%
Social	80%	—	13%	79%	—	18%
Foreign	66%	—	33%	87%	—	10%

Key Votes of the 104th Congress

1. Reduce Medicare Growth $	N	5. Flag Amendment	N	9. Cuban Embargo	N
2. Ovrd. Product Liab. Veto	N	6. Drop EPA Limits	Y	10. Bar Bosnia Troop $	Y
3. Increase Min. Wage	Y	7. Repeal Assault-Weap. Ban	N	11. Cut Anti-Missile Defense	Y
4. Welfare Reform	N	8. Ovrd. Part. Birth Veto	N	12. Bar U.N. Uniforms	N

Election Results

1996 general	Lloyd Doggett (D)	132,066	(56%)	($410,302)
	Teresa Doggett (R)	97,204	(41%)	($402,904)
	Others	5,721	(2%)	
1996 primary	Lloyd Doggett (D)	unopposed		
1994 general	Lloyd Doggett (D)	113,738	(56%)	($567,552)
	A. Jo Baylor (R)	80,382	(40%)	($374,706)
	Others	7,866	(4%)	

ELEVENTH DISTRICT

Waco, at the intersection of lines from Dallas to Austin and Houston to Amarillo, is arguably the geographic and cultural heart of Texas. The accent here may be the purest Texas accent around: listen to former Governor Ann Richards, a Waco native. Waco is now a city of over 100,000, but the farm fields and small towns all around recall the state as it was years ago, before the growth of the oil industry transformed Texas from a rural backwater into one of the centers of western capitalism, while the latest extravagances of affluent metropolitan Texas can be sampled at gallerias of the Dallas-Fort Worth Metroplex, a little more than an hour away on I-35. Some of Texas's characteristic institutions cluster around Waco: Baylor University, the oldest college in Texas and the largest Baptist university in the world, and Fort Hood, the Army's second largest installation, which occupies much of next-door Bell and Coryell Counties and employs just under 50,000 military personnel and civilians. The odd-duck violence which is also part of Texas's history flared here in February 1993 when, in a dreadful misuse of government power, agents of the Bureau of Alcohol, Tobacco and Firearms moved in on David Koresh's Branch Davidian compound, Ranch Apocalypse, near Waco, until agents stormed the compound and Koresh and his followers immolated themselves.

The 11th Congressional District of Texas is centered on Waco and the Fort Hood area. It includes all or most of 12 counties, most of them still pretty rural, all of them ancestrally Democratic. But that loyalty has slowly waned. Ann Richards carried the 11th with 51% in 1990, but lost it to George W. Bush 52%–47% in 1994. It voted 41%–36% for George Bush in 1992 and 50%–42% for Bob Dole in 1996.

The congressman from the 11th is Chet Edwards, a Democrat elected in 1990, and only the third congressman from the district since 1936. Edwards is one of those highly skilled and motivated Democrats who has made politics his life—and who made the House ever Democratic until 1994. He graduated from Texas A&M, where he studied economics under Phil Gramm, then a conservative Democrat; Edwards went to work directly after as district director for 6th District Congressman Olin Teague. In 1978, at 27, he ran for the 6th District seat when Teague retired. In the first Democratic primary, Edwards wound up in third place, just 115 votes behind Phil Gramm, who went on to win the seat; if Edwards had won just 116 more votes, a lot of Texas and national political history would be different. Edwards went off to Harvard to get an M.B.A., returned and moved to Duncanville in southwest Dallas County, and at age 31 ran for the state Senate in 1982 and won. There he made a moderate-to-liberal record, helping to incorporate Texas into the Super Tuesday primary and working to attract the Supercollider, bucking the unions and trial lawyers on workmen's compensation reform.

In 1990 when 11th District Congressman Marvin Leath retired, Edwards dropped his race for lieutenant governor, moved his residence to Waco (the Senate district overlapped), and ran for the 11th District seat unopposed in the Democratic primary. Bell County legislator Hugh Shine, who beat two former Waco mayors in the Republican primary, emphasized his military experience and attacked Edwards for attending a gay and lesbian fund raiser. Edwards got a promise of a National Security Committee slot from Speaker Thomas Foley and strong support from Leath. Shine carried Bell County, but Edwards got 56% in Waco's McLennan County and carried all the rural counties for a 53%–47% victory.

In the House Edwards got his promised committee seat. He worked on National Security for Fort Hood and claims credit for $245 million in construction there; he also opposed Republicans on missile defense. He bucked the Democratic leadership quickly on the Gulf war resolution and the balanced budget amendment and he voted against the Clinton tax increase. In 1992, from his seat on Veterans' Affairs, he managed the campaign of Sonny Montgomery to retain the Veterans' chair over the younger Lane Evans. He worked successfully to stop the designation of 33 Texas counties as a critical habitat for the allegedly endangered golden-cheeked warbler and supported the Private Property Owners Bill of Rights. He voted against the Brady bill but for the assault weapons ban and the 1994 crime bill.

In previous decades Edwards might have been a credible statewide candidate; in the 1990s he did well to win reelection by comfortable margins. In previous decades he might have become part of the majority party leadership in the House; instead, in December 1994, after Democrats lost their majority, Dick Gephardt asked him to serve as one of four chief deputy whips. He accepted, adding, "I did not ask for this job and I will not change my political independence to keep it." He promptly voted for the Contract with American balanced budget amendment and line-item veto. Also in 1995, he moved from National Security to Appropriations, but continued to look after Fort Hood.

In 1996 Edwards faced his toughest electoral competition in six years. Republican Jay Mathis, an insurance agent whose father had run unsuccessfully in the 1990 Republican primary, won the Republican nomination and raised over $500,000. Mathis peppered Edwards with criticism, citing his "liberal vote of the day" each day during the campaign. Edwards won by 57%–42%, running well ahead of his party's ticket, but not so far ahead of 50% as to justify the conclusion that this is an utterly safe seat.

The People: Pop. 1990: 566,280; 29% rural; 13% age 65+; 70% White; 16% Black; 2% Asian; 12% Hispanic origin. Households: 60% married couple families; 30% married couple fams. w. children; 43% college educ.; median household income: $22,283; per capita income: $10,630; median gross rent: $362; median house value: $49,700.

1996 Presidential Vote

Dole (R)	88,429	(50%)
Clinton (D)	74,063	(42%)
Perot (I)	14,671	(8%)

1992 Presidential Vote

Bush (R)	75,760	(41%)
Clinton (D)	66,619	(36%)
Perot (I)	42,465	(23%)

Rep. Chet Edwards (D)

Elected 1990; b. Nov. 24, 1951, Corpus Christi; home, Waco; TX A&M U., B.A. 1974, Harvard, M.B.A. 1981; Methodist; married (Lea Ann).

Career: Legis. and Dist. Dir., U.S. Rep. Olin Teague, 1975–77; Marketing rep., Trammell Crow Co., 1981–85; TX Senate, 1982–90; Pres., Edwards Communications, 1985–90.

DC Office: 2459 RHOB 20515, 202-225-6105; Fax: 202-225-0350.

District Offices: Belton, 817-933-2904; Waco, 817-752-9600.

Committees: *Chief Deputy Minority Whip. Appropriations* (26th of 26 D): Energy & Water Development; Military Construction.

Group Ratings

	ADA	ACLU	AFS	LCV	CFA	CON	NFIB	COC	ACU	NTLC	CHC
1996	60	50	75	77	38	4	62	50	20	45	13
1995	45	—	—	44	31	4	—	63	25	—	—

National Journal Ratings

	1995 LIB — 1995 CONS			1996 LIB — 1996 CONS		
Economic	56%	—	44%	62%	—	36%
Social	61%	—	38%	66%	—	33%
Foreign	59%	—	39%	53%	—	46%

Key Votes of the 104th Congress

1. Reduce Medicare Growth $	N	5. Flag Amendment	Y	9. Cuban Embargo	Y
2. Ovrd. Product Liab. Veto	Y	6. Drop EPA Limits	N	10. Bar Bosnia Troop $	N
3. Increase Min. Wage	Y	7. Repeal Assault-Weap. Ban	N	11. Cut Anti-Missile Defense	Y
4. Welfare Reform	Y	8. Ovrd. Part. Birth Veto	N	12. Bar U.N. Uniforms	N

Election Results

1996 general	Chet Edwards (D)	99,990	(57%)	($844,126)
	Jay Mathis (R)	74,549	(42%)	($565,402)
1996 primary	Chet Edwards (D)	unopposed		
1994 general	Chet Edwards (D)......................	76,667	(59%)	($420,832)
	Jim Broyles (R)........................	52,876	(41%)	($52,992)

TWELFTH DISTRICT

Fort Worth, Texas, has a fair claim to being the quintessential mid-American city: halfway across the continent, midway between the oceans, just west of the Balcones Escarpment that divides the dry treeless grazing lands of west Texas from the humid green croplands of the east. It is southern in heritage and northern in its advanced post-industrial economy. It has the nation's biggest row of Western wear shops and one of the nation's richest families, the Basses, whose steel-sheen skyscrapers, outlined at night by lights, dominate the skyline. This is where the West begins, Fort Worth boosters say, adding, as Will Rogers said, that Dallas is "where the East peters out." This is not a primitive West. Fort Worth has a high-tech economy, though one hard hit by defense cuts. The big General Dynamics plant that produced so many U.S. bombers has been sold to Lockheed; next-door Carswell Air Force Base, the home of B-52s for years, was slated for closure in 1993 but was turned into a Joint Reserve Base in late 1994. The assembly lines at Bell Helicopter's nearby plant were kept going only when the Texas delegation and others overruled the cancellation of the V-22 Osprey. Fort Worth also has some of the nation's premier small museums, the Amon Carter Museum of Western Art, Louis Kahn's gem The Kimbell Museum and the Will Rogers Coliseum with exhibits of Texas history. Other cities have their claims, but the visitor from abroad who wants to see what is quintessentially American would be well advised to head to Fort Worth.

The 12th District of Texas is still centered on Fort Worth. Its highly convoluted boundaries drawn in 1991 (and not changed in the 1996 redistricting case) include much of the city, though not the poor black southeast or rich white southwest areas, which are in the 24th and 6th Districts. It also extends south and west in a whorl around Fort Worth, taking in much of rural Johnson and Parker Counties, including Weatherford, where Speaker Jim Wright got his start in politics. Fort Worth's political heritage is Democratic, but lately it has been trending Republican. For 34 years the 12th District was represented by Wright, speaker of the House from January 1987 until he resigned in June 1989. Wright was first elected to Congress in 1954 after a primary victory over an anti-labor Democrat in this still dusty blue-collar town, in contrast to white-collar Dallas, which was electing its first Republican congressman the same year. Now Fort Worth is more diverse, with extensive rich as well as poor neighborhoods, and Tarrant County, with a population boom in Arlington between Fort Worth and Dallas and in the north around Dallas-Fort Worth Airport and Ross Perot Jr.'s cargo airport, has become more Republican than Dallas County.

The congresswoman from the 12th District is Kay Granger, elected in 1996, and the first Republican woman elected to the House from Texas. Granger went to college at Texas Wesleyan in Fort Worth, raised three children and started her own insurance agency. In 1989 she was elected to the Fort Worth Council; in 1991 she became mayor. She became very popular for her "Code: Blue" anti-crime initiatives and encouragement of citizen patrols, as violent crime dropped 49%. She also formed the Vision Coalition, a community-wide consensus-building organization, and attracted new business facilities from FedEdx, Motorola, Intel and the Texas Motor Speedway. In late 1995 Congressman Pete Geren, a conservative Democrat elected to replace Wright in 1989, announced his retirement, and both Republican and Democratic leaders tried to recruit Granger. After being elected to the U.S. Conference of Mayors board of trustees, she said she was a Republican, and ran in the March 1996 Republican primary. Attacked there as a liberal, partly for her pro-choice stand on abortion, she won 69% in a three-candidate race.

The Democratic candidate was Hugh Parmer, also a former Fort Worth mayor; he served only one term in the 1970s. He was also elected to the state Senate and was the Democratic nominee against Senator Phil Gramm in 1990. That turned out to be a liability when it was revealed that he had large unpaid debts left over from that campaign, which he lost 60%–37%. Granger raised much more money and outspent Parmer by more than 2–1. He attacked Republican Medicare plans and Newt Gingrich. She called for a balanced budget and tax cuts for business and ran on her record as mayor. Granger won 58%–41%, a stunning victory in a district represented a decade ago by a Democratic Speaker of the House.

On the opening day of the 105th Congress, Granger called a press conference with California Democrat Gary Condit backing a balanced budget. She pushed for the Republican flextime bill to give more options for working families. She has seats on the Budget and the Transportation and Infrastructure Committees, and is part of the I-35 Caucus, working with other members from the Dallas-Fort Worth Metroplex to get some $3.4 billion for the I–35 corridor from Mexico to Canada in the reauthorized ISTEA up in 1997.

The People: Pop. 1990: 565,988; 13% rural; 12% age 65+; 74% White; 8% Black; 2% Asian; 1% Amer. Indian; 16% Hispanic origin. Households: 57% married couple families; 28% married couple fams. w. children; 43% college educ.; median household income: $27,366; per capita income: $12,641; median gross rent: $402; median house value: $57,200.

1996 Presidential Vote

Clinton (D)	80,709	(46%)
Dole (R)	79,299	(46%)
Perot (I)	14,187	(8%)

1992 Presidential Vote

Clinton (D)	76,639	(38%)
Bush (R)	70,520	(35%)
Perot (I)	55,954	(28%)

Rep. Kay Granger (R)

Elected 1996; b. Jan. 18, 1943, Greenville; home, Fort Worth; TX Wesleyan U., B.S. 1965; Methodist; divorced.

Career: Teacher, 1965–78; Life Insurance Agent, 1978–85; Founder & Pres., Kay Granger Insurance Co., Inc., 1985–present; Chmn., Fort Worth Zoning Commission, 1981–88; Fort Worth City Council, 1989–91; Fort Worth Mayor, 1991–96.

DC Office: 515 CHOB 20515, 202-225-5071; Fax: 202-225-5683.

District Offices: Fort Worth, 817-338-0909.

Committees: *Budget* (22nd of 24 R). *House Oversight* (5th of 6 R). *Transportation & Infrastructure* (36th of 40 R): Aviation; Railroads (Vice Chmn.); Surface Transportation. *Joint Committee on Printing* (3rd of 5 Reps.).

Group Ratings and Key Votes: Newly Elected

Election Results

1996 general	Kay Granger (R)	98,349	(58%)	($1,001,836)
	Hugh Parmer (D)	69,859	(41%)	($455,703)
1996 primary	Kay Granger (R)	21,774	(69%)	
	Ernest J. Anderson Jr. (R)	6,355	(20%)	
	Bill Burch (R)	3,355	(11%)	
1994 general	Pete Geren (D)	96,372	(69%)	($345,739)
	Ernest J. Anderson Jr. (R)	43,959	(31%)	($20,471)

THIRTEENTH DISTRICT

Heading west in Texas, the population thins out, the land becomes browner, until you can travel through a whole county with only a few hundred people—plus quite a few more head of cattle. And then the land rises nearly 1,000 feet in elevation, up steep hillsides from the gullies that surround the rivers which for most of the year are just tiny trickles, to the tilted tableland that is the High Plains of west Texas. The winds here sweep down from the Rockies, the land is barren except where irrigated, often with the now dangerously depleted waters of the Ogallala Aquifer. But here and there in this demanding environment—sticky-hot in the summer, swept by north winds from Canada in winter, always threatened here in "Tornado Alley"—comfortable cities have been built to house the people and businesses that bring forth oil, natural gas, helium and other elements from the earth.

The 13th Congressional District of Texas spans much of this territory. Population declined here in the 1980s, in some rural counties by as much as 30%, with only small gains in and around two of the three biggest cities, Wichita Falls and Amarillo. Around Wichita Falls, in the eastern part of the district, is the agricultural land of the Red River Valley—dusty land with empty skylines, like Archer City, the boyhood home of novelist Larry McMurtry, chronicled in *The Last Picture Show* and *Texasville* and where he lives now in the biggest mansion in town. This is white Anglo Texas: few blacks got this far west and few Mexican-Americans go this far north. Up on the High Plains, the economy is different: it is based on minerals. The largest city here is Amarillo, the helium capital of North America and, *not* Chicago, the windiest city in the United States. Just outside town is the Pantex Plant that made thousands of nuclear warheads—the epicenter of American defense in the Cold War, and its 16,000 acres are now scheduled (pending lawsuits) to be used to store the disarmed weapons. The political traditions here differ. The Red River Valley, settled by Confederate veterans, was until very recently Democratic. The High Plains, settled overland from Kansas wheatlands, is more Republican. The lines were changed for the 1990s: not all of Amarillo is in the 13th any more, and black portions of Lubbock have been added, in an effort to help Democrats, though it turned out to be not enough.

For the congressman from the 13th District is Mac Thornberry, a Republican elected in 1994. His great-great-grandfather Amos Thornberry, a Union Army veteran and staunch Republican, moved to Clay County, just east of Wichita Falls, in the 1880s; a year after he died, in 1925, his great-grandfather bought the cattle ranch which Mac Thornberry, his brothers and father now run. From the window of his ranch house, writes *The Texas Techsan*, "as far as the eye can see is the Golden Spread of Texas for which this part of the state is named. There are no buildings, no roadways, no signs of life. Gaze out long enough and you begin to think you can actually see the curvature of the earth." And, as the writer goes on, you can get a sense of why Thornberry is so unhappy with federal government intrusion into people's lives. But Thornberry is not just a local farmer: after college and law school in Texas he worked for Congressman Tom Loeffler and Larry Combest and at the State Department in Washington. Then he returned to practice law in west Texas.

In 1994 the well-connected Thornberry decided to take on Democratic Congressman Bill Sarpalius. He won the Republican primary with 75% of the vote. He attacked Sarpalius for voting for the Clinton budget and tax package. He also profited from a series of stories about how Sarpalius did not pay a moving company that moved his furniture to Washington, then accepted a fee for speaking at the company's convention in Las Vegas; the FBI investigated in October 1994: not helpful for Sarpalius's campaign. Thornberry won a solid 55%–45% victory, carrying the northern panhandle by wide margins and carrying Wichita Falls as well, trailing only in sparsely populated ranching counties.

In the House Thornberry had an almost perfectly conservative voting record. He pressed especially hard for estate tax repeal and tax credits for energy production to encourage production in marginal wells. But he was not loath to seek drought assistance for parched west Texas. He got the National Security Committee to pass his proposal barring transfer of Pantex Plant explosives work elsewhere by a 49–2 margin. He wants to reform the Endangered Species Act and to allow state-inspected meat to be sold in other states the same as foreign-inspected meat which does not have to go through USDA approval. After a 1996 visit, he said it was a "mistake" to send U.S. troops to Bosnia. "Militaries will be demobilizing, people will be going home to bombed-out homes. If they don't have something productive to do, they will most likely go back to their old ways of fighting each other."

Thornberry was easily reelected in 1996, by 67%–32%, as Bob Dole carried the district 53%–39%. This seems to be a safe Republican seat.

The People: Pop. 1990: 566,682; 27% rural; 14% age 65+; 71% White; 8% Black; 1% Asian; 1% Amer. Indian; 19% Hispanic origin. Households: 58% married couple families; 28% married couple fams. w. children; 37% college educ.; median household income: $20,907; per capita income: $10,344; median gross rent: $334; median house value: $38,100.

1996 Presidential Vote			**1992 Presidential Vote**		
Dole (R)	92,815	(53%)	Bush (R)	87,492	(43%)
Clinton (D)	69,149	(39%)	Clinton (D)	73,454	(36%)
Perot (I)	14,030	(8%)	Perot (I)	41,186	(20%)

Rep. Mac Thornberry (R)

Elected 1994; b. July 15, 1958, Clarendon; home, Clarendon; TX Tech. U., B.A. 1980, U. of TX Schl. of Law, J.D. 1983; Presbyterian; married (Sally).

Career: Legis. Cnsl., U.S. Rep. Tom Loeffler, 1983–85; Chief of Staff, U.S. Rep. Larry Combest, 1985–88; Dep. Asst. Secy. of State for Legis. Affairs, 1988–89; Practicing atty., 1989–94.

DC Office: 412 CHOB 20515, 202-225-3706; Fax: 202-225-3486.

District Offices: Amarillo, 806-371-8844; Wichita Falls, 817-767-0541.

Committees: *National Security* (19th of 30 R): Military Personnel; Military Procurement. *Resources* (17th of 27 R): Energy & Mineral Resources; Water & Power. *Joint Economic Committee* (4th of 10 Reps.).

Group Ratings

	ADA	ACLU	AFS	LCV	CFA	CON	NFIB	COC	ACU	NTLC	CHC
1996	0	0	0	8	0	55	97	94	100	100	100
1995	0	—	—	6	0	56	—	100	96	—	—

National Journal Ratings

	1995 LIB — 1995 CONS			1996 LIB — 1996 CONS		
Economic	0%	—	74%	0%	—	82%
Social	0%	—	79%	0%	—	90%
Foreign	0%	—	85%	30%	—	65%

Key Votes of the 104th Congress

1. Reduce Medicare Growth $	Y	5. Flag Amendment	Y	9. Cuban Embargo	Y
2. Ovrd. Product Liab. Veto	Y	6. Drop EPA Limits	N	10. Bar Bosnia Troop $	Y
3. Increase Min. Wage	N	7. Repeal Assault-Weap. Ban	Y	11. Cut Anti-Missile Defense	N
4. Welfare Reform	Y	8. Ovrd. Part. Birth Veto	Y	12. Bar U.N. Uniforms	Y

Election Results

1996 general	Mac Thornberry (R)	116,098	(67%)	($565,578)
	Samuel Brown Silverman (D)	56,066	(32%)	($16,126)
1996 primary	Mac Thornberry (R)	unopposed		
1994 general	Mac Thornberry (R)	79,466	(55%)	($442,237)
	Bill Sarpalius (D)	63,923	(45%)	($540,096)

FOURTEENTH DISTRICT

Retreating east from the Alamo, the ragtag army led by Sam Houston passed over what would become, after their bloody and conclusive victory at San Jacinto, some of the prime cropland in the new Republic and later the state of Texas. The hilly and river-crossed land between Houston and Austin, both named after Texas' first leaders, was settled early. The flat coastal plains, steamy and humid so much of the year, were settled later when the railroads came in. The Gulf of Mexico coastline, though it has plenty of inlets, never had any important ports in the stretch between Houston and Corpus Christi until the discovery of oil here made it worthwhile to build channels to ship the oil out.

This is the land of the 14th Congressional District of Texas. Made up of rural countrysides, small towns and a couple of small cities, it runs along the Gulf coast and inland toward the old Texas German country. Its eastern and northern edges bring it within metropolitan range of Houston, Austin and San Antonio; more than one-third of its people live in these areas. Redistricting in 1991 changed its shape somewhat, adding Blanco County in the Hill Country west of Austin, the birthplace and first political base of Lyndon B. Johnson. This country is ancestrally Democratic except for a couple of counties settled by Texas Germans, who were pro-Union in the Civil War and have remained Republican ever since. But it voted Republican in the 1980s and twice rejected the candidacy of Bill Clinton.

The congressman from the 14th District is Ron Paul, a Republican elected in 1996, but also the Libertarian candidate for president in 1988 and Republican congressman from the 22d District in the 1970s and 1980s. Paul grew up in Pennsylvania, went to Duke Medical School, served as a flight surgeon in the Air Force, then moved to Texas to practice obstetrics and gynecology in Brazoria County, on the Gulf coast just southwest of Houston. Paul was dismayed when Richard Nixon cut the connection between the dollar and gold in August 1971, and started getting interested in politics. He ran in a special election in April 1976 in the 22d District, then extending from southwest Houston out into Fort Bend and Brazoria Counties, upset the Democrat and won, then lost the seat in November 1976 and won it back in 1978 and served three terms. In 1984 he ran for the Senate and lost the primary to Phil Gramm 73%–16%. In 1988, as the Libertarian candidate for president, he ran third with 432,000 votes, 0.47% of the total. In Congress, Paul advanced some ideas which have become more widespread since—term limits, which a majority of House members have voted for, and abolition of the income tax, a project of the chairman of the Ways and Means Committee. Other Paul ideas remain outside the political pale—endorsing a group that wants to end all government funding of education and compulsory attendance laws, cutting $150 million from the defense budget and returning to the gold standard. It should be added that Paul practices what he preaches. He will not accept payment by Medicare or Medicaid, he wouldn't let his children accept federal student loans and he refuses his congressional pension.

What prompted Paul to reenter congressional politics was the party switch by Congressman Greg Laughlin in June 1995. Elected as a Democrat in 1988 after losing one race, Laughlin had a moderate voting record, by no means the most conservative even of Texas Democrats; he served in an Army Reserve unit in the Gulf war. In 1994 he had spirited opposition from Republican Jim Deats, who attacked him for accepting moving services without paying from a firm that did most of its business moving the military; in 1990 he supported a bidding system that benefited the firm and the firm's head was indicted for illegally funneling money into his campaign. Laughlin still won 56%–44%. In spring 1995 Republicans offered him a seat on Ways and Means if he switched, and he did so. "I tried to be part of the Democratic team, but I was miserable on some of the votes I cast," he said later. "Since I've been a Republican, I haven't cast one hard vote. I'm really comfortable where I am." But others weren't so comfortable. Speaker Newt Gingrich, Governor George W. Bush and 50 House Republicans who sent Laughlin contributions rallied to his side. But some local Republicans were not impressed. "These guys in Washington want us to go and support a guy who backed Tom Foley [for speaker] all those years," one local Republican told *The Wall Street Journal*. "What planet are they on?" Deats ran again as "the real Republican choice": "I am a solid conservative and I have been a Republican for 25 years. He is, at best, a moderate with a voting record that I think the people of the 14th District will find quite interesting." And Paul ran again as—well, as Ron Paul, raising money from his nationwide network of libertarians, gold bugs and subscribers to the *Ron Paul Political Report*. He may not have always been a Republican, but his convictions came through. "The [federal] government perpetually takes our money, lies to us and makes our lives worse."

Laughlin backers worried that he would be swamped in a low-turnout March primary, but turnout was up from 18,000 to 34,000 and he finished first with 43%, carrying all but four counties. Paul was second, with 32%, and the underfinanced Deats was third with 24%. But in the April runoff turnout was down, to 20,700, and Paul won 54%–46%. This set up an excruciating situation for Republican leaders. They did not want to lose the seat to the Democrat, Charles "Lefty" Morris, a trial lawyer who ran as a "conservative Democrat" and omitted from his resume the fact that he was president of the state trial lawyers' association in 1983–84. But they didn't want to get associated with Paul's wackier-seeming views either. Morris ("Lefty is right") hit Paul for favoring abolition of the minimum wage, repealing federal anti-drug laws (Paul said that would leave states to ban drugs, but he was against that too) and anti-prostitution laws, cutting defense spending $150 million. Researchers reported that Paul's newsletter in 1992 said that 95% of black men in Washington, D.C., are "semi-criminal or entirely criminal" and that black teenagers are "unbelievably fleet of foot." "Ron Paul wants to abandon the federal government. I want to fix it," said Morris.

But Paul had his own arguments and resources. His fundraising networks came through: Morris, an advocate of banning PACs (trial lawyers don't need them; they have lots of money themselves), spent $977,000, but Paul spent $1.9 million. He said that Morris was a "liberal lawyer lobbyist" who "made millions on frivolous lawsuits" and would raise taxes. Paul ran 1% ahead of Bob Dole, Morris 6% ahead of Bill Clinton, and Paul won 51%–48%, in a race that was pretty close throughout the district.

In Washington Paul made a bit of a sensation, not through his work on the Banking and Education Committee, but by saying on C-SPAN, "I fear and there's alot of people in the country who fear that they may be bombed by the federal government at another Waco." Chet Edwards, 11th District Democrat, who represents Waco, on the floor called Paul's comments "sheer lunacy at best"; Republican Whip Tom DeLay, who followed Paul in representing the

22d District, rebuked Edwards for not having the "courtesy" to alert Paul about his intended remarks, so he could reply on the floor; but he did not bother when he had the chance.

It is hard to imagine how this could avoid being a seriously and interestingly contested district in 1998.

The People: Pop. 1990: 566,008; 51% rural; 13% age 65+; 65% White; 10% Black; 1% Asian; 24% Hispanic origin. Households: 61% married couple families; 30% married couple fams. w. children; 37% college educ.; median household income: $23,812; per capita income: $11,127; median gross rent: $344; median house value: $52,300.

1996 Presidential Vote			1992 Presidential Vote		
Dole (R)	100,319	(50%)	Bush (R)	86,247	(41%)
Clinton (D)	84,317	(42%)	Clinton (D)	78,751	(37%)
Perot (I)	15,696	(8%)	Perot (I)	47,125	(22%)

Rep. Ron Paul (R)

Elected 1996; b. Aug. 20, 1935, Pittsburg, PA; home, Surfside; Gettysburg Col., B.A. 1957; Duke U., M.D. 1961; Protestant; married (Carol).

Career: Flight Surgeon, Air Force, 1963–68; Practicing physician, 1968–96; U.S. House of Reps., 1976, 1978–84.

DC Office: 203 CHOB 20515, 202-225-2831; Fax: 202-226-4871; e-mail: rep.paul@mail.house.gov.

District Offices: Freeport, 409-230-0000; San Marcos, 512-396-1400; Victoria, 512-576-1231.

Committees: *Banking & Financial Services* (19th of 30 R): Domestic & International Monetary Policy; Financial Institutions & Consumer Credit. *Education & The Workforce* (19th of 25 R): Early Childhood, Youth & Families; Workforce Protections.

Group Ratings and Key Votes: Newly Elected

Election Results

1996 general	Ron Paul (R)	99,961	(51%)	($1,927,756)
	Charles (Lefty) Morris (D)	93,200	(48%)	($977,888)
1996 runoff	Ron Paul (R)	11,244	(54%)	
	Greg Laughlin (R)	9,555	(46%)	
1996 primary	Greg Laughlin (R)	14,777	(43%)	
	Ron Paul (R)	11,112	(32%)	
	Jim Deats (R)	8,466	(24%)	
1994 general	Greg Laughlin (D)	86,175	(56%)	($789,201)
	Jim Deats (R)	68,793	(44%)	($271,551)

FIFTEENTH DISTRICT

The Lower Rio Grande Valley of south Texas is one of America's 20th Century frontiers. A century ago, there was little here but desert wilderness. Only a handful of people lived anywhere near the shallow, sluggish Rio Grande; there was no Border patrol, because in this desert land no one bothered to cross it. Then in the early days of this century came pioneers like Lloyd Bentsen, Sr., father of the former Senator and Treasury secretary, who arrived after World War I with five dollars in his pocket and became one of the biggest Valley landowners, remaining active in his business until he died in an auto accident in 1989 at age 95. Bentsen and others cleared the land and dug canals, hired Mexican and Mexican-American workers, planted citrus groves and cornfields and palm windbreaks, ran cattle and drilled for oil and gas. Along U.S. 83 north of the Rio Grande these pioneers built a string of towns with Anglo names and storefronts. But most of the people here were Latino in culture and language. Wage levels higher than in Mexico (though low by U.S. standards) brought more Mexicans over the border. But if wages are low, so is the cost of living—which makes this a haven for low-income "winter Texan" retirees, coming down from the North in their RVs. The days are past when ranchers and oil men wielded absolute political power here. There is instead a robust, mostly Hispanic politics, with results not always what you would expect from the rhetoric of the self-appointed spokesmen who head Hispanic organizations in Washington.

The 15th Congressional District of Texas is one of three districts dividing up the Lower Rio Grande Valley. Some two-thirds of its residents and about 60% of its voters live in Hidalgo County, in or near the string of towns from Mercedes through McAllen to Los Ebanos, just north of the river. The 15th then moves north through a narrow corridor of land between Corpus Christi and San Antonio to include Goliad, where 352 captured Texans were massacred by Santa Ana's troops in 1836, and Bee County, where George Bush goes to hunt quail at each year's end. The 15th's population is 75% Hispanic and mostly Democratic. This is the descendant of a district that in 1948, 1950 and 1952 elected Lloyd Bentsen, Jr., to the House, before he went to Houston to make his fortune and then on to national office.

The congressman from the 15th District is Ruben Hinojosa, a Democrat elected in 1996. His background is not in politics but in business and civic affairs. He grew up in Mercedes, between McAllen and Harlingen, where his family owns H & H Foods, which produces Mexican foods and beef patties and has 400 employees—one of the largest employers in the Valley. Hinojosa graduated from the University of Texas, then went into the family business and was active in civic affairs, primarily in education and regional development. He served on the state Board of Education, serving from 1974–84, and led an effort to create the South Texas School for Health Professions, a magnet high school; he also worked to establish two other regional magnet schools, the Academy for Math and Science and the Teachers' Academy. In the early 1990s he was on a steering committee to create South Texas Community College.

Then in December 1995 Congressman Kika de la Garza announced he was not running for reelection. First elected in 1964, de la Garza was chairman of the Agriculture Committee from 1981–95, presiding over the passage of three farm bills; he did not play a major part in the 1996 farm bill which phased out most crop subsidies, and evidently did not relish being in the minority. Hinojosa was one of three major candidates in the Democratic primary, and his main political assets were his civic activities and cash—he spent $431,000 of his own money on the campaign. In the March primary he won 34% to 33% for lawyer Jim Selman and 22% for Renato Cuellar. Selman, an Anglo lawyer, ran as a reformer; he promised to fight corruption and ensure that federal dollars weren't misused by local officials. He questioned Hinojosa's Democratic credentials and for profiting from government contracts. Hinojosa talked more of his interest in improving educational opportunities in the Lower Rio Grande Valley and getting I-69 extended to the Valley; he called for reducing the capital gains tax and giving investment tax credits for those making capital improvements. He also attacked Selman for hiring a campaign worker who had past legal problems. This was an exceedingly close election, which Hinojosa won 52%–48%. He carried Hidalgo County 51%–49% and the rest of the district 55%–45%. In effect the more conservative of the two candidates won; none of the Lower Valley districts are represented by the sort of liberals who lead most national and Texas Hispanic organizations. Hinojosa won the general election over a Mennonite minister 62%–37%.

In the House Hinojosa serves on the Education and the Workforce Committee. He wants to protect benefits for legal immigrants and to promote NAFTA; he wants to work for more and better educational opportunities in the Lower Valley; he wants to promote I-69 and also to improve other local roads. As befits his business and civic background, he was an enthusiastic supporter of the House's March 1997 bipartisan "civility" retreat.

The People: Pop. 1990: 566,805; 29% rural; 11% age 65+; 24% White; 1% Black; 75% Hispanic origin. Households: 66% married couple families; 38% married couple fams. w. children; 29% college educ.; median household income: $17,866; per capita income: $7,407; median gross rent: $290; median house value: $36,900.

1996 Presidential Vote			1992 Presidential Vote		
Clinton (D)	86,707	(60%)	Clinton (D)	80,246	(53%)
Dole (R)	49,595	(35%)	Bush (R)	52,168	(34%)
Perot (I)	7,093	(5%)	Perot (I)	20,004	(13%)

Rep. Ruben Hinojosa (D)

Elected 1996; b. Aug. 20, 1940, Mercedes; home, Mercedes; U. of TX, B.B.A. 1962, M.B.A. 1980; Catholic; married (Marty).

Career: Pres. & CEO, H & H Foods Inc., 1962–present; TX St. Board of Educ., 1974–84.

DC Office: 1032 LHOB 20515, 202-225-2531; Fax: 202-225-2534; e-mail: ruben.hinojosa@mail.house.gov.

District Office: McAllen, 210-682-5545.

Committees: *Education & The Workforce* (14th of 20 D): Employer-Employee Relations; Postsecondary Education, Training & Life-Long Learning. *Small Business* (15th of 16 D): Tax, Finance & Exports.

Group Ratings and Key Votes: Newly Elected

Election Results

1996 general	Ruben Hinojosa (D)	86,347	(62%)	($715,391)
	Tom Haughey (R)	50,914	(37%)	($39,345)
1996 runoff	Ruben Hinojosa (D)	24,940	(52%)	
	Jim Selman (D)	22,983	(48%)	
1996 primary	Ruben Hinojosa (D)	21,726	(34%)	
	Jim Selman (D)	21,138	(33%)	
	Renato Cuellar (D)	13,832	(22%)	
	Tony Dominguez (D)	5,008	(8%)	
	Others	1,877	(3%)	
1994 general	E (Kika) de la Garza (D)	61,527	(59%)	($701,528)
	Tom Haughey (R)	41,119	(39%)	($30,193)
	Others	1,720	(2%)	

SIXTEENTH DISTRICT

El Paso, Texas, and Juarez, Mexico, sit across from each other on the narrow Rio Grande, their tree-shaded streets spread out below the rough brown face of Comanche Peak, two border cities surrounded by hundreds of miles of some of the most desolate landscape in the country, 400 miles from Phoenix and 600 from Dallas-Fort Worth. There is much history here: Texas claims the first Thanksgiving took place in San Elizario near El Paso in 1598. Fifty years ago, there were still only 140,000 people in both cities; now there are over two million, 700,000 in El Paso, 1.6 million in Juarez. This is a bilingual, bicultural pair of cities, where most people have a Mexican heritage; the thrust of growth is from Spanish-speaking people and an English-speaking economy. El Paso is one of the lowest wage cities in the U.S., Juarez one of the highest wage in Mexico; *maquiladora* plants pioneered a cross-border economy and the North American Free

Trade Agreement has strengthened it. But free trade doesn't necessarily mean porous borders. In September 1993, El Paso Immigration and Naturalization Service leader Silvestre Reyes started Operation Hold the Line, wangling $300,000 extra and positioning 400 officers on the border instead of trying to intercept illegals after they have crossed into El Paso (amazingly enough, this was firmly-rooted INS policy). Before that, 8,000 illegals had crossed the border each day; that was drastically reduced by more than half. Mexico complained about threats to its sovereignty, merchants worried about loss of sales, a few homeowners fretted about finding domestic help. But auto thefts were down 30%, burglaries and robberies were down, beggars were absent from the streets, fewer Mexicans were having babies in El Paso hospitals; the move was almost universally popular. The law was finally being enforced, by an agency which had long said it was impossible; Californians began asking why the INS couldn't hold the line in their state.

The 16th Congressional District of Texas is made up of most of the city of El Paso and communities up and down the Rio Grande, and giant Fort Bliss to the north. A full 70% of the people here are Latino, and for many years politics divided people on ethnic lines, with most Anglos Republican and Latinos Democratic. Republicans made some inroads among Latinos in the early 1990s and hope to again, although Latino turnout and Democratic percentages surged in 1996.

The congressman from the 16th District now is Silvestre Reyes, the architect of Operation Hold the Line, elected in 1996 as a Democrat. He grew up on a farm in Canutillo, just five miles north of El Paso, on the Rio Grande, the oldest of 10 children; he went to college in El Paso and Austin. He served in the Army in Vietnam, then "took as many civil service tests as I could, and the Border Patrol called" in 1969. He worked for the INS in four cities in Texas and Glynco, Georgia, and returned to El Paso in 1993 as chief patrol agent. When he got there he found that "people could basically cross the border at any time, wherever they wanted to." More than 40 boatmen ran "what were essentially international ferries" across the Rio Grande. So he instituted Operation Hold the Line almost immediately, getting around INS standard procedures and against the wishes of many border agents, eager to get credit for apprehending aliens which would be impossible if they never got across the border at all.

By 1995 Reyes's name recognition was 65%, higher than most elected officials, and in November 1995 he resigned from the INS and started running for Congress as a Democrat. He talked of the need for integrity and common sense; his target was Ron Coleman, a Democrat first elected in 1982, around whom scandals lurked—he had 673 overdrafts on the House bank, he was accused by Texas Attorney General Dan Morales on *60 Minutes* of trying to block prosecution of a local developer, there were reports a local businessman had assumed $65,000 of his debts. "My message is one of change," said Reyes. "I'm giving voters an option to change what they've had for a decade and a half." In December 1995 Coleman announced he was retiring, but he remained a factor in the race: his legislative assistant for 13 years, Jose Luis Sanchez, ran, backed by Coleman and labor unions. Also running was Delores Briones, public relations director for Thomason Hospital, who was supported by EMILY's List and national feminist and Hispanic groups.

Sanchez attacked Reyes harshly as a crypto-Republican, pointing out that his campaign treasurer had worked for Republicans in the past and that he had the support of Republican former Mayor Jonathan Rogers, and attacking him for backing a capital gains tax cut. One Sanchez mailing read, "Two of a kind: Gingrich and Reyes." Reyes hewed to his moderate platform, calling for water conservation research, a capital gains tax cut (but not entitlement cuts, as Sanchez charged), promoting high-tech jobs, developing more highways and border crossings. Reyes stumbled when he said he wouldn't support creating a Department of Education on a National Education Association questionnaire; he didn't realize the department had been created in 1979 (though perhaps that is an assessment of the department's work). And he waffled on abortion. He came out for repeal of the assault weapons ban and was endorsed by the National Rifle Association. Nonetheless Reyes won the Democratic nomination. He led

Sanchez in the March primary 42%–28%, with 22% for Briones. In the runoff Sanchez and the unions pressed hard, but Reyes won 51%–49%. He won the general election 71%–28%.

Reyes's victory goes against some political stereotypes. "The one thing I find curious," Reyes told *George* magazine, "is that people are amazed that Hispanics react like other groups. We're concerned about crime, taxes, education. I remember a reporter writing a story about me, coming over to our house and asking, 'How do you guys celebrate Independence Day?' We said, well, with fireworks, a picnic. 'Really! I had no idea that you celebrated the sixteenth of September [Mexico's Independence Day] that way.' I said, We're talking about the Fourth of July." On border issues, he admits that Operation Hold the Line is "not a permanent solution. The permanent solution is the economic stabilization of Mexico." He says a border fence is unnecessary, because electronic monitoring can work over most of its distance, and opposes a national identification card. He spoke out against the resolution to decertify Mexico for its drug enforcement record, saying it would upset the Mexican economy. He seeks retraining for workers displaced by NAFTA, though he says that overall it is a great success, and he wants to work on border environmental problems and water conservation, and to promote high-tech jobs and Fort Bliss.

The People: Pop. 1990: 566,238; 2% rural; 8% age 65+; 25% White; 3% Black; 1% Asian; 70% Hispanic origin. Households: 61% married couple families; 36% married couple fams. w. children; 41% college educ.; median household income: $22,632; per capita income: $9,195; median gross rent: $345; median house value: $57,000.

1996 Presidential Vote

Clinton (D)	80,475	(63%)
Dole (R)	40,983	(32%)
Perot (I)	5,902	(5%)

1992 Presidential Vote

Clinton (D)	65,578	(51%)
Bush (R)	45,333	(35%)
Perot (I)	18,760	(14%)

Rep. Silvestre Reyes (D)

Elected 1996; b. Nov. 10, 1944, Canutillo; home, El Paso; El Paso Com. Col., A.A. 1977; Catholic; married (Carolina).

Career: Army, 1966–68 (Vietnam); Border Patrol Agent, 1969–1995; Canutillo Schl. Board, 1968–70.

DC Office: 514 CHOB 20515, 202-225-4831; Fax: 202-225-2016.

District Office: El Paso, 915-534-4400.

Committees: *National Security* (16th of 25 D): Military Installations & Facilities; Military Research & Development. *Veterans' Affairs* (11th of 13 D): Benefits.

Group Ratings and Key Votes: Newly Elected

Election Results

1996 general	Silvestre Reyes (D)	90,260	(71%)	($587,193)
	Rick Ledesma (R)	35,271	(28%)	($110,765)
	Others	2,253	(2%)	
1996 runoff	Silvestre Reyes (D)	21,161	(51%)	
	Jose Luis Sanchez (D)	20,157	(49%)	
1996 primary	Silvestre Reyes (D)	22,119	(42%)	
	Jose Luis Sanchez (D)	14,698	(28%)	
	Dolores Briones (D)	11,583	(22%)	
	Tom Peterson (D)	3,095	(6%)	
1994 general	Ronald D. Coleman (D)	49,815	(57%)	($704,186)
	Bobby Ortiz (R)	37,409	(43%)	($324,335)

SEVENTEENTH DISTRICT

West from Fort Worth, the West Texas plains stretch miles beyond the horizon, thousands and thousands of acres of rolling grazing land punctuated occasionally by oases of irrigated farmland (often in circles that show the reach of the sprinklers). This is primarily cattle country, although there is some oil here, and cotton and grain. On the interstate straight west of Fort Worth, settlements start thinning out quickly. Before long, you are on open plains, with enormous skies and no people to be seen. Then in the distance is a good-sized town, an oasis of busyness. The largest town here is Abilene, with a high concentration of bankers, lawyers and professionals. Settled by Confederate veterans suspicious of eastern bankers and Yankee businessmen, this was one of the Democratic heartlands of America up through the 1970s; now it is voting Republican in major statewide races. In the sparsely populated counties that seem utterly left behind, the few hundred voters may tilt crazily left and resoundingly right.

The 17th Congressional District of Texas takes up much of this "God's country," starting a few miles from Fort Worth and including most of three tiers of counties westward almost to New Mexico. This is ancestral Democratic country, but it voted 51%–39 for Bob Dole over Bill Clinton in 1996.

The congressman from the 17th District is Charles Stenholm, one of several conservative Texas Democrats elected in 1978, and the only one still a Democratic member of the House. Stenholm is a farmer from a small town settled by Swedes near Abilene, a natural politician who went to Congress after running the Rolling Plains Cotton Growers Association and the Stamford Electric Co-op (Stamford is the home town also of Democratic super-lobbyist Robert Strauss). He became a Democrat because in the 1970 Senate race Lloyd Bentsen was interested in his issues and George Bush wasn't. In 1978, when 32-year incumbent Omar Burleson retired, Stenholm ran for the seat and won, easily beating a Republican. In the House, he and Phil Gramm were leaders of the "Boll Weevils" backing the 1981 Reagan budget and tax cuts. He threatened momentarily to run against Speaker Tip O'Neill in 1985, but desisted when conservatives were promised more attention. His voting record is conservative, especially on cultural issues, but not always market-oriented. On the Agriculture Committee, where he is now ranking minority member, he has worked on farm credit, disaster relief, animal product safety and pesticide bills; he is for relaxing environmental restrictions and against caps on subsidies. He favored a "better safety net" than the Republicans' Freedom to Farm Act and a government insurance program to protect farmers against price risk in "the volatile global marketplace."

Stenholm used to be the lead conservative Democrat on budget issue, as head of the Conservative Democratic Forum and on the Budget Committee. But that is no longer the case since Republicans won their majority; Newt Gingrich and other party leaders view Stenholm as a conservative talker but a partisan Democratic doer, and the action has passed to the Democratic Blue Dogs, with other members taking the lead. "I think maybe people felt I was getting too much attention," he told *National Journal*. "I needed to step back and let others take some credit." In the Democratic House, Stenholm was a crucial vote for Republicans; in the Republican House, he usually is not. But he was the co-author of the balanced budget amendment which passed with 300 votes in January 1995. He supported the Blue Dog budget and worked closely with Budget ranking Democrat Martin Sabo on preparing a budget both Blue Dogs and liberals could back. On welfare reform, he pushed to allow school to be counted as work for people over 20 and voted for the final measure. He worked to save the Legal Services Corporation but voted against increasing the minimum wage. He worked to fund construction at Dyess Air Force Base and to bring more Border Patrol officers to San Angelo.

Unlike some other Democrats with similar voting records, Stenholm did not switch parties. Instead in December 1994 he ran for minority whip, predictably losing to David Bonior 145–60. One reason is that he does not entirely believe in free market economics, on farm issues in particular. He has plenty of seniority, and the ranking position on Agriculture; Republicans have never been ready to offer him anything comparable. A third reason, at least when he was starting out, was that it was politically safer to be a Democrat: Democratic incumbents were never beaten by Republicans in central Texas, and seldom lost in primaries, while Republicans were guaranteed an opponent every time, often a seasoned and popular local officeholder. But that is no longer the case in the 17th District. Stenholm was unopposed in general elections from 1980–90 and won in 1992 with 66% of the vote. But in 1994 Republican Phil Boone, though vastly outspent, carried Abilene and seven other counties and held Stenholm to a 54%–46% win. In 1996 Republican Rudy Izzard, a dentist and former San Angelo Councilman, carried Abilene and eight other counties and held Stenholm to a 52%–47% win. Again, Stenholm raised and spent far more money. If Stenholm does not run in 1998, Republicans must be favored to win this district; if he does run, look for a seriously contested race.

The People: Pop. 1990: 566,255; 38% rural; 16% age 65+; 79% White; 3% Black; 1% Asian; 17% Hispanic origin. Households: 62% married couple families; 29% married couple fams. w. children; 36% college educ.; median household income: $21,532; per capita income: $10,642; median gross rent: $329; median house value: $38,400.

1996 Presidential Vote

Dole (R)	98,804	(51%)
Clinton (D)	76,057	(39%)
Perot (I)	19,182	(10%)

1992 Presidential Vote

Bush (R)	86,491	(40%)
Clinton (D)	73,388	(34%)
Perot (I)	55,835	(26%)

Rep. Charles W. Stenholm (D)

Elected 1978; b. Oct. 26, 1938, Stamford; home, Avoca; TX Tech. U., B.S. 1961; M.S. 1962; Lutheran; married (Cynthia).

Career: Farmer; Vocational educ. teacher, 1962–65; Exec. V.P., Rolling Plains Cotton Growers, 1965–68; Mgr., Stamford Electric Co-op., 1968–76.

DC Office: 1211 LHOB 20515, 202-225-6605; Fax: 202-225-2234; e-mail: texas17@hr.house.gov.

District Offices: Abilene, 915-673-7221; San Angelo, 915-655-7994; Stamford, 915-773-3623.

Committees: *Agriculture* (RMM of 23 D).

Group Ratings

	ADA	ACLU	AFS	LCV	CFA	CON	NFIB	COC	ACU	NTLC	CHC
1996	50	31	42	54	15	97	67	63	65	49	66
1995	35	—	—	19	15	75	—	63	44	—	—

National Journal Ratings

	1995 LIB — 1995 CONS			1996 LIB — 1996 CONS		
Economic	56%	—	44%	57%	—	43%
Social	21%	—	72%	14%	—	77%
Foreign	56%	—	43%	58%	—	41%

Key Votes of the 104th Congress

1. Reduce Medicare Growth $	N	5. Flag Amendment	Y	9. Cuban Embargo	Y
2. Ovrd. Product Liab. Veto	Y	6. Drop EPA Limits	N	10. Bar Bosnia Troop $	N
3. Increase Min. Wage	N	7. Repeal Assault-Weap. Ban	Y	11. Cut Anti-Missile Defense	Y
4. Welfare Reform	N	8. Ovrd. Part. Birth Veto	Y	12. Bar U.N. Uniforms	Y

Election Results

1996 general	Charles W. Stenholm (D)	99,678	(52%)	($804,936)
	Rudy Izzard (R)	91,429	(47%)	($192,082)
1996 primary	Charles W. Stenholm (D)	unopposed		
1994 general	Charles W. Stenholm (D)	83,497	(54%)	($712,156)
	Phil Boone (R)	72,108	(46%)	($192,079)

EIGHTEENTH DISTRICT

Houston contains, within its vast bounds, disparities of income and wealth as striking as any city in the United States. This is what one must expect in an expanding city with dynamic economic growth, vast immigration, absence of centralized planning and openness to cultural diversity. The contrast is most glaringly apparent at the edge of Houston's gleaming downtown with its keynote Pennzoil, Heritage Plaza and NationsBank buildings; only a few blocks away are the slums where blacks and Mexican-Americans live in unpainted frame houses full of cracks wide enough to let in Houston's humid, smoggy air. But the contrasts are less obvious as one moves out from Houston's historic center. Half a century ago, when Houston pioneers like Jesse Jones, millionaire cotton broker and newspaper publisher, started building downtown skyscrapers, they were operating in a town with a Third World economy, a low-skill producer of basic commodities, where a few got rich and many lived near subsistence level. Today, Houston has a high-tech advanced economy which offers myriads of opportunities and a wide range of economic outcomes. One result is that as Houston's blacks and Hispanics have moved outward from the city center, increasingly they are living in comfortable middle-class neighborhoods.

The 18th Congressional District of Texas contains central Houston and many of these outlying neighborhoods, to the northeast, the south and especially the northwest. Its boundaries for 1996 were drawn by a three-judge federal court in August 1996, after the Supreme Court ruled the previous boundaries, drawn in 1991, as unconstitutional because racially motivated. Those 1991 boundaries were convoluted, perhaps the most irregular in American history. The aim was to maximize the black percentage in the 18th and the Hispanic percentage in the interlocking 29th District. But was it worth all the trouble? Within the 1991 boundaries the 18th District was 50% black and 15% Hispanic; in the 1996 boundaries it was 45% black and 23% Hispanic: not really much difference in the overall balance. The 1996 redistricting added the Heights, just north of downtown Houston, and dropped Pleasantville and North Forest. The new district can be thought of as having three spokes running out from Loop 610, a northeast spoke along the Eastex Freeway, a southern spoke between the South Freeway and Telegraph Road and a long northwest spoke between the Northwest Freeway and Route 249.

The congresswoman from the 18th District is Sheila Jackson Lee, a Democrat first elected in 1994. Jackson Lee was educated at Yale and Virginia Law School, worked on Capitol Hill and practiced law in Houston, served as a local judge and won two terms in an at-large seat on the Houston Council. After a local term limits law took effect, in January 1994, she ran for Congress in the March Democratic primary. The incumbent was Craig Washington, a talented but storm-tossed legislator, elected to the legislature in 1972 and to Congress in 1989 to replace Mickey Leland after he was killed in a plane crash in Ethiopia. Washington had the worst attendance record in Congress (absent on 24% of roll calls in 1993), was sentenced at one point to 30 days in jail for leaving two legal clients "in the lurch," and filed for personal bankruptcy, claiming to owe $205,000 in federal taxes. He often was an iconoclast: He voted against thanking U.S. military personnel for serving in Operation Desert Storm, and against the Space Station and NAFTA, both of which are big pluses for the Houston area economy. Jackson Lee supported NAFTA and raised lots of money from business interests who favored it. Jackson Lee won by the unambiguous margin of 63%–37%. She was reelected with 77% in the all-party primary held November 5, 1996.

Like many new legislators of both parties, Jackson Lee did not move her family to Washington. Her husband is a vice president at the University of Houston and her children remain in local schools. She did not get her first choice of a seat on the Commerce Committee—always a popular slot for a Texan, no matter their party or ideology; it went instead to Gene Green of the 29th District. In the House Jackson Lee won approval of one amendment to restore $1.5 million in funding to the African Development Foundation and another on human-rights concerns in Ethiopia. More often than not, her liberal proposals—on NASA funding and abortion—were defeated. She voted "present" on the Defense of Marriage Act, the only Texan not to vote for it. *Roll Call* in 1996 identified her as having some of the highest staff turnover on Capitol Hill. She suggested an ombudswoman for the Army after revelations of sexual harassment at the Aberdeen Proving Ground. In 1997 she was named whip of the Congressional Black Caucus and was an organizer of the Congressional Children's Caucus.

The People: Census data not available due to 1996 redistricting.

1996 Presidential Vote

Clinton (D)	116,059	(73%)
Dole (R)	37,280	(23%)
Perot (I)	5,515	(3%)

1992 Presidential Vote

Clinton (D)	119,386	(66%)
Bush (R)	40,422	(22%)
Perot (I)	21,472	(12%)

Rep. Sheila Jackson Lee (D)

Elected 1994; b. Jan. 12, 1950, Queens, NY; home, Houston; Yale U., B.A. 1972, U. of VA Law Schl., J.D. 1975; Seventh Day Adventist; married (Elwyn).

Career: Practicing atty., 1975–77, 1978–87; Staff Cnsl., U.S. House Select Assassinations Cmte., 1977–78; Houston Assoc. Municipal Judge, 1987–90; Houston City Cncl., 1990–94.

DC Office: 410 CHOB 20515, 202-225-3816; Fax: 202-225-3317; e-mail: tx18@lee.house.gov.

District Office: Houston, 713-655-0050.

Committees: *Judiciary* (10th of 15 D): Commercial & Administrative Law; Crime. *Science* (14th of 21 D): Basic Research; Space & Aeronautics.

Group Ratings

	ADA	ACLU	AFS	LCV	CFA	CON	NFIB	COC	ACU	NTLC	CHC
1996	90	93	100	85	62	68	22	27	5	7	0
1995	100	—	—	88	100	16	—	21	0	—	—

National Journal Ratings

	1995 LIB — 1995 CONS	1996 LIB — 1996 CONS
Economic	83% — 16%	79% — 18%
Social	88% — 0%	88% — 0%
Foreign	84% — 15%	79% — 21%

Key Votes of the 104th Congress

1. Reduce Medicare Growth $	N	5. Flag Amendment	N	9. Cuban Embargo	N
2. Ovrd. Product Liab. Veto	N	6. Drop EPA Limits	Y	10. Bar Bosnia Troop $	N
3. Increase Min. Wage	Y	7. Repeal Assault-Weap. Ban	N	11. Cut Anti-Missile Defense	Y
4. Welfare Reform	N	8. Ovrd. Part. Birth Veto	N	12. Bar U.N. Uniforms	Y

Election Results

1996 spec. prim.	Sheila Jackson Lee (D)	106,111	(77%)	($477,866)
	Larry White (R)	13,956	(10%)	($124,166)
	Jerry Burley (R)	7,877	(6%)	($29,151)
	Others	9,744	(7%)	
1994 general	Sheila Jackson Lee (D)	84,790	(73%)	($593,740)
	Jerry Burley (R)	28,153	(24%)	($113,182)
	Others	2,447	(2%)	

NINETEENTH DISTRICT

Up on the High Plains of Texas, separated from the dusty cattlelands further east by rising gullies astride wide river courses, is some of the most productive cotton and wheat land in the United States, centered around the city of Lubbock. This fertility is a triumphant work of man. For this is irrigated land, which gets its water from the giant Ogallala Aquifer that undergirds so much of the western Great Plains, making this part of Texas a sort of green island in a vast brown sea of arid grazing land. The area was settled relatively late, with most growth after World War II. Lubbock grew from 31,000 in 1940 to 128,000 in 1960 and 191,020 in 1994. But the 1980s and 1990s were tough on the High Plains. The aquifer seemed to be going dry, populations declined in almost every rural county, hospitals were closed in small towns. Lubbock, with an economy that includes Texas Tech University as well as agribusiness, has continued to grow. Politically this was once Democratic territory, and Lubbock elected George Mahon, chairman of the House Appropriations Committee from 1964–79. Now Lubbock has indeed become heavily Republican, so much so that George Bush always liked to refer to it as a bellwether of public opinion. Lubbock County, which voted against George W. Bush when he ran for Congress in 1978, voted for him for governor over Ann Richards 63%–37% in 1994.

The 19th Congressional District of Texas covers the western edge of the High Plains of Texas, from the northern edge of the Panhandle south to the Permian Basin. Tantalizingly, it includes only part of each of its four widely separated major cities. In 1992, the Democratic legislature took the black area of Lubbock and the lower income areas of Amarillo and put them in the 13th District to help the incumbent Democrat there; the Permian Basin oil towns of Midland and Odessa, where George and Barbara Bush moved in the pre-airconditioning days of 1948, were split to help another incumbent Democrat. Now both incumbents are gone, one beaten in 1992 and one in 1994, but the lines remain, helping to make the 19th Texas's most Republican district in 1996, when it gave Bob Dole a 67%–26% margin over Bill Clinton.

The congressman from the 19th District is Larry Combest, a Republican first elected in 1984. He graduated from West Texas State University, worked as a teacher and farmer and for the Soil Conservation Service; from 1971–78 he worked on Senator John Tower's staff, specializing in farm issues. He moved back to Lubbock in 1978, where he owned an electronics company. In 1984, when conservative Democratic Congressman Kent Hance ran for the Senate, Combest ran for the House. He had a tough primary, runoff and general election, and has since won easily.

In the House Combest has had a solidly conservative voting record. Much of his work has been on farm issues. On these he has tended to favor not oppose government subsidies. He opposed cutting target prices and ending subsidies in the 1990 farm bill. In 1995 he and three other southern Republicans opposed the Republicans' original Freedom to Farm Act and killed it in committee, because of its changes in the cotton marketing program. He argued that cotton farmers needed the protection because world prices are manipulated by Third World governments, much more than the prices of commodities like wheat and corn. Chairman Pat Roberts was forced to concede to the "cottonmouth moccasins," as he called them, and leave it pretty much as is. Immediately after passage of the bill, he got its farm credit terms softened when farmers in the 19th District were unable to get crop loans. He supports the Conservation Reserve Program to retain topsoil in areas exposed to wind erosion and research funding for the Plant Stress and Water Conservation Laboratory at Texas Tech. But he insists that the prime farm issue is protecting property rights against government intervention to enforce environmental laws. As chairman of the Resource Conservation Subcommittee, he plans to monitor closely Clinton Administration efforts to remove millions of acres from farm production.

In the summer of 1996 it appeared that Combest was in line to be the next Agriculture chairman. Of senior members, Roberts was running for the Senate, Bill Emerson died in June and Steve Gunderson (after considering a write-in candidacy) was retiring. But the House leadership, desperate to get scandal-tarred Wes Cooley of Oregon out of his race, got Cooley's predecessor, Bob Smith, to run in his place by promising him the chairmanship. Smith had been senior to Combest on the committee, and Gingrich and others may not have felt as beholden to Combest, given his opposition to Roberts's original bill; Combest became vice chairman.

Combest's disappointment may have been greater because he was giving up a chairmanship, of the Intelligence Committee. He had served on the committee since 1989, and Gingrich had already extended the usual six-year limit in 1995 to enable him to be chairman after serving two years as ranking minority member. Combest was generally favorable to the enterprise of intelligence; "I believe we need more intelligence, not less," he said in 1996. But he was also critical of the CIA's handling of the Aldrich Ames case and "the compartmented culture of the intelligence community." He worries about the effects of secret budget cuts and laments that secret successes cannot be known: he said that budget cuts forced the withdrawal of American intelligence from Somalia six months before Marines hit the beach, while after the World Trade Center bombing in New York intelligence agencies foiled a plan to set off five simultaneous bombs elsewhere. In March 1996 he unveiled his "fairly radical" CIA reforms—combine the CIA's Directorate of Operations with the Defense Department Clandestine Service, with the new agency separate from CIA and Defense, and meld the National Security Agency into a new Technical Collection Agency also embodying non-Directorate of Operations parts of the CIA. But this was vastly scaled back in committee, further altered in the National Security Committee, and the bill passed in September 1996 made only modest changes.

Combest has been active on two other diverse projects. He was vice chairman of the Commission on Protecting and Reducing Government Secrecy (chaired by Daniel Patrick Moynihan) which produced a unanimous report in March 1997 calling for both more and less secrecy. "The government must be made to discharge its superfluous secrets and behave in a more open manner. Government officials must be more subject to limits on what they can classify. But in our rush to widen access, we must not compromise vital secrets, nor betray those who have risked their lives and fortunes to confide in us." Combest's other project is to increase the availability of two-way tele-medicine treatment between a doctor's office and a patient's home—of special interest to rural citizens. In 1994 he and three others established a Senate-House Ad Hoc Committee on Tele-medicine and Informatics, which has about 40 members.

The People: Pop. 1990: 565,925; 18% rural; 10% age 65+; 77% White; 3% Black; 1% Asian; 20% Hispanic origin. Households: 62% married couple families; 32% married couple fams. w. children; 50% college educ.; median household income: $27,267; per capita income: $13,184; median gross rent: $366; median house value: $55,000.

1996 Presidential Vote			1992 Presidential Vote		
Dole (R)	133,397	(67%)	Bush (R)	130,637	(60%)
Clinton (D)	51,996	(26%)	Clinton (D)	50,814	(23%)
Perot (I)	12,323	(6%)	Perot (I)	36,067	(17%)

Rep. Larry Combest (R)

Elected 1984; b. Mar. 20, 1945, Memphis; home, Lubbock; W. TX St. U., B.B.A. 1969; United Methodist; married (Sharon).

Career: Farmer; Teacher, 1970–71; Dir., U.S. Agric. Stabilization and Conservation Svc., Graham TX, 1971; Aide, U.S. Sen. John Tower, 1971–78; Founder & Pres., Combest Distrib. Co., 1978–1985.

DC Office: 1026 LHOB 20515, 202-225-4005.

District Offices: Amarillo, 806-353-3945; Lubbock, 806-763-1611; Odessa, 915-550-0743.

Committees: *Agriculture* (Vice Chmn. of 27 R): Forestry, Resource Conservation & Research (Chmn.); General Farm Commodities (Vice Chmn.); Risk Management & Specialty Crops (Vice Chmn.). *Small Business* (2nd of 19 R): Regulatory Reform & Paperwork Reduction.

Group Ratings

	ADA	ACLU	AFS	LCV	CFA	CON	NFIB	COC	ACU	NTLC	CHC
1996	0	6	0	15	0	17	97	100	95	100	100
1995	0	—	—	0	0	56	—	100	96	—	—

National Journal Ratings

	1995 LIB — 1995 CONS			1996 LIB — 1996 CONS		
Economic	0%	—	74%	0%	—	82%
Social	0%	—	79%	0%	—	90%
Foreign	15%	—	73%	0%	—	79%

Key Votes of the 104th Congress

1. Reduce Medicare Growth $	Y	5. Flag Amendment	Y	9. Cuban Embargo	Y
2. Ovrd. Product Liab. Veto	Y	6. Drop EPA Limits	N	10. Bar Bosnia Troop $	Y
3. Increase Min. Wage	N	7. Repeal Assault-Weap. Ban	Y	11. Cut Anti-Missile Defense	N
4. Welfare Reform	Y	8. Ovrd. Part. Birth Veto	Y	12. Bar U.N. Uniforms	Y

Election Results

1996 general	Larry Combest (R)	156,910	(80%)	($440,379)
	John W. Sawyer (D)	38,316	(20%)	($46,000)
1996 primary	Larry Combest (R)	unopposed		
1994 general	Larry Combest (R)	unopposed		($148,894)

TWENTIETH DISTRICT

San Antonio, with its antique past and theme park future, its Hispanic heritage, its military superstructure and its high-tech hopes, is unlike any other city in the United States. Here on a plaza is the Alamo, preserved by the Daughters of the Republic of Texas, where Davy Crockett, Jim Bowie and 184 others were wiped out in 1836 (Crockett was a Tennessee congressman for three terms; if he had not lost his bid for reelection in 1835, he never would have left Tennessee for Texas). The Spanish architecture, recalling San Antonio's days as the most important town in Texas when the state was part of Mexico, contrasts with the 31-story Tower Life Building, which contrasts with the armadillo-like Alamodome; the stark terrain contrasts with the lushness of the Paseo, the 1970s-redeveloped Riverwalk along the tiny San Antonio River. The city also includes old neighborhoods redolent of the Texas Germans who were its chief Anglo citizens for many years. For most of this century, San Antonio's economy has been built on the military: this is the home of three Air Force bases and the Brooks Army Medical Center at Fort Sam Houston, contributing some $3 billion to the local economy; San Antonio also has 30,000 military retirees, second highest in the country. Behind them as a local employer is the medical complex centered on the Health Science Center. And San Antonio is also becoming a tourist center: for generations Texas schoolchildren have made pilgrimages to the Alamo, and in recent decades, they stop at the nearby HemisFair, preserved from the 1968 World's Fair, and the Riverwalk.

With almost a million people, San Antonio is the third largest city in Texas, though its metro area is barely more than one third the size of metro Houston or the Dallas-Fort Worth Metroplex. San Antonio is also notable as the only Hispanic-majority major city in the country, and it has the low education and income levels one might expect from a city whose economy is affected by the proximity of the Mexican border. Yet it has avoided the polarized politics and ethnic anger that was manifested in the urban black-white tensions of the 1960s and has made notable progress as a kind of low-wage, high-tech center, making some linkage with nearby Austin. Much of the credit is due Henry Cisneros, mayor from 1981–89, educated at Texas A&M and Harvard, who sparked high-tech and tourism growth but dropped out of Texas politics in 1989 over bad publicity from an extramarital affair, then served from 1993–96 as secretary of Housing and Urban Development.

The 20th Congressional District of Texas includes most of central San Antonio and its west side. Its boundaries on the north are irregular, since affluent Anglo neighborhoods are set off and placed in the 21st District. On the west it extends beyond I-410 to Loop 1604 and in some places beyond. This is one of Texas's six Hispanic-majority districts, and the first to elect a Hispanic congressman. It is also solidly Democratic.

The congressman from the 20th District is Henry B. Gonzalez, first elected in a 1961 special election, and for six years chairman of the Banking Committee. Gonzalez grew up in San Antonio, learned to speak English by reading Carlyle and Stevenson, went to the University of Texas and got a law degree at St. Mary's University; he served in military intelligence in World War II. San Antonio in the post-World War II years did not have many places for Mexican-American professionals and politicians, and Gonzalez worked as a probation officer and housing director. Gonzalez was elected to the San Antonio Council in 1953 and to the Texas Senate in 1956, and had the nerve to run for governor in 1958 and for the Senate in the 1961 special election (against John Tower and Jim Wright, among others). Gonzalez ran poorly in those races, but later in 1961, when Congressman Paul Kilday, part of a long-successful San Antonio machine, was appointed to a federal judgeship, Gonzalez got into the race for Congress—and won. In his early days in Congress, he was the patron saint of Texas liberalism, as he compiled a record of support for the administration and civil rights. Gonzalez has brought a determination to do right and an indifference to what others may think. He is not afraid to show his temper: in 1963, he took a swing at Texas Republican Congressman Ed Foreman who accused him of being a Communist; in 1986, he punched a man in a San Antonio restaurant for the same offense.

From 1989–95, Gonzalez was chairman of the Banking Committee, the lone-wolf head of a fractious, divisive pack. His first major task was the savings and loan bailout bill, made necessary by the failures of his predecessor Fernand St Germain. Gonzalez hammered out a version that may have cracked down too hard on some S&L investments but which enabled regulators to wind up most of their work by 1993. Gonzalez also held hearings on the Charles Keating scandal. Gonzalez's first love has been housing programs, and after some tussles with HUD Secretary Jack Kemp he passed a housing bill that included his National Housing Trust proposal. Gonzalez's go-it-alone style can prompt opposition.

Perhaps in response to legislative disappointments, Gonzalez started investing more energy in partisan responses to alleged scandal. In 1991 he started probing "Iraqgate." Gonzalez went so far out on a limb as to call for Bush's impeachment on the issue. In late 1993 he angrily blocked any investigation of the Whitewater scandals and accused ranking Republican Jim Leach, who like Gonzalez had proved his nonpartisan bona fides on S&Ls, of acting as a shill for the Republican Conference. Gonzalez canceled a March 1994 hearing at which Leach would have raised Whitewater and refused to endorse Leach's efforts to get government documents, accusing Republicans of a "witch hunt." In June 1994 he agreed to hearings, but under absurd conditions. In the meantime, the committee's big legislative issue—consolidating bank regulators—went nowhere.

Thrust into the minority in 1995, Gonzalez seemed to founder. He often missed committee meetings, and committee members began taking charge on issues themselves. But Gonzalez's absence made it hard to get bipartisan agreement on anything or to forge united Democratic initiatives. After the November 1996 election, the 80-year-old Gonzalez was challenged for the ranking minority position by the next two Democrats in seniority, Bruce Vento (who ran against him in December 1990 and lost 163–89) and John LaFalce. Minority Leader Dick Gephardt declined to endorse Gonzalez, and the Steering Committee voted 29–12 to make him ranking member emeritus. But Gonzalez bridled. In a letter he offered to serve just one more term and then take emeritus status. In the Democratic Caucus meeting he made a stirring speech. "I have served with honor and integrity and success. I have never failed myself and I have never failed you," Gonzalez orated. "I appeal to your sense of justice: one last term as ranking member, and I will not disappoint you." That may have changed some votes: Gonzalez got 82, LaFalce 62 and Vento 47. Then, though it looked like he would win on the second ballot, LaFalce withdrew. "I think there's a way to win and a way not to win. With Henry having that much support and having served so honorably, I didn't want it to end that way."

Whether Gonzalez would be more active in those two years was unclear. Nor is it clear whether he will wish to run again, to serve in emeritus status, though there is little doubt that he can win in the 20th District.

The People: Pop. 1990: 564,865; 3% rural; 10% age 65+; 32% White; 6% Black; 1% Asian; 61% Hispanic origin. Households: 51% married couple families; 28% married couple fams. w. children; 44% college educ.; median household income: $22,372; per capita income: $9,672; median gross rent: $362; median house value: $48,500.

1996 Presidential Vote			**1992 Presidential Vote**		
Clinton (D)	82,892	(60%)	Clinton (D)	81,368	(48%)
Dole (R)	48,488	(35%)	Bush (R)	57,961	(34%)
Perot (I)	7,285	(5%)	Perot (I)	28,962	(17%)

Rep. Henry B. Gonzalez (D)

Elected Nov. 1961; b. May 3, 1916, San Antonio; home, San Antonio; San Antonio Jr. Col., A.A. 1937, U. of TX, St. Mary's U., LL.B., J.D. 1943; Catholic; married (Bertha).

Career: Military Intelligence, 1941–44; Bexar Cnty. Chief Probation Officer, 1946; Dpty. Dir., San Antonio Housing Authority, 1950–51; San Antonio City Cncl., 1953–56, San Antonio Mayor Pro Tem, 1955–56; TX Senate, 1956–61.

DC Office: 2413 RHOB 20515, 202-225-3236.

District Office: San Antonio, 210-472-6195.

Committees: *Banking & Financial Services* (RMM of 25 D).

Group Ratings

	ADA	ACLU	AFS	LCV	CFA	CON	NFIB	COC	ACU	NTLC	CHC
1996	80	75	100	77	62	1	19	38	15	18	7
1995	85	—	—	88	69	2	—	20	4	—	—

National Journal Ratings

	1995 LIB — 1995 CONS			1996 LIB — 1996 CONS		
Economic	88%	—	11%	76%	—	22%
Social	80%	—	13%	75%	—	24%
Foreign	73%	—	24%	52%	—	47%

Key Votes of the 104th Congress

1. Reduce Medicare Growth $	N	5. Flag Amendment	N	9. Cuban Embargo	N
2. Ovrd. Product Liab. Veto	N	6. Drop EPA Limits	Y	10. Bar Bosnia Troop $	N
3. Increase Min. Wage	Y	7. Repeal Assault-Weap. Ban	N	11. Cut Anti-Missile Defense	Y
4. Welfare Reform	N	8. Ovrd. Part. Birth Veto	N	12. Bar U.N. Uniforms	Y

Election Results

1996 general	Henry B. Gonzalez (D)	88,190	(64%)	($86,231)
	James Walker (R)	47,616	(34%)	($138,735)
	Others	2,603	(2%)	
1996 primary	Henry B. Gonzalez (D)	unopposed		
1994 general	Henry B. Gonzalez (D)	60,114	(63%)	($55,382)
	Carl Bill Colyer (R)	36,035	(37%)	

TWENTY-FIRST DISTRICT

The Texas German country, on the gently rolling plains between San Antonio and Austin and west into the Hill Country, is one of America's lesser known ethnic enclaves. First settled by refugees from the failed democratic revolutions of 1848, the German country has always been a set of orderly communities in riproaring Texas, economically prosperous in a state that considered itself poor until it struck oil. It has been antislavery and politically Republican in a state whose enthusiasm for the Democratic party had roots in Confederate loyalties and populist rebellions. The Texas Germans in political history are entwined with the career of Lyndon Johnson: the death of Republican Congressman Harry Wurzbach of Guadalupe County enabled the Democrats to elect John Nance Garner of Uvalde speaker in 1931, while Wurzbach's replacement in the House, Democrat Richard Kleberg (of the King ranch family) hired the then 23-year-old Johnson to his first Washington job. And, though Johnson never emphasized this, his LBJ Ranch was not in Blanco County or near poor Johnson City, where he grew up, but west in Gillespie County near the prosperous town of Fredericksburg, historically Texas German and heavily Republican.

The 21st Congressional District has its demographic center in the old Texas German country, where the San Antonio and Austin metropolitan areas are now growing together. As with so many Texas districts under the 1991 redistricting, its boundaries are quite complex. About 40% is on the north side of San Antonio and Bexar County (pronounced like a drawn-out *bear*), mostly Anglo neighborhoods around Alamo Heights and out I-35, and in Guadalupe and Comal Counties just beyond—Texas German country now classified as part of metro San Antonio; all this is heavily Republican. Another 20% is in Williamson County, just north of Austin—suburban overspill subdivisions full of high-tech and white-collar workers who are much more Republican than the liberals who live in older neighborhoods near downtown Austin and UT. These two areas are connected by sparsely populated Hill Country and Texas German counties, including Fredericksburg and the LBJ Ranch, the almost mountainous country around Kerrville, sheep and goat ranching country reaching west to San Angelo, the mohair capital of America, all the way to Midland, headquarters of the high-income, oil-rich Permian Basin, where George Bush lived from 1949–60.

The congressman from the 21st District is Lamar Smith, a Republican first elected in 1986, now chairman of the Judiciary Committee's Immigration Subcommittee and member of the Budget Committee. Smith is from an old San Antonio and south Texas ranching family; he went to Yale and SMU Law School, worked as a reporter and a lawyer, was elected to the Texas House in 1980 and the Bexar County Commission in 1982. In 1986, when Congressman Tom Loeffler ran for governor, Smith ran for the House; at that time the 21st ranged far wider and had more acreage than Ohio. Smith won by beating two other San Antonio-based candidates in the primary 31%–25%–20% and then winning the runoff, with help from Senator Phil Gramm, against a religious conservative. He has been reelected easily since.

In his first three terms, Smith earned a conservative record and pursued some original initiatives. One Smith bill added 100,000 acres to Big Bend National Park along the Rio Grande; another sponsored the Bush Administration's government-wide ethics act. By 1991, Smith was proposing cuts in every appropriations bill, with special emphasis on cutting government overhead costs, especially travel; often Democrats prevented them from coming to a vote. Appointed to Budget in 1993, he worked on now-Chairman John Kasich's alternative budget and has pointed out that the budget could be balanced with a one-year spending freeze and inflation rate increases only thereafter. In April 1993 he was appointed head of the Republicans' "theme team," organizing more than 800 one-minute speeches by Republican members. Meanwhile, he pursued other interests: stopping designation of part of Texas as "critical habitat" for the golden-cheeked warbler, funding programs to promote teen abstinence, stopping HIV-positive aliens from attending the Gay Games.

In 1995, Smith became chairman of the Immigration Subcommittee, on which he had been ranking Republican since 1991. Smith has long believed in stronger action to stop illegal immigration and lower levels of legal immigration. "While we welcome immigrants who see America as a land of opportunity to make good through their own efforts, we should not subsidize immigration through the welfare system," he said. Working carefully but steadily, he steered his bill through subcommittee and Judiciary Committee in 1995 largely unchanged, although he did make telephone verification of immigrant status by employers a pilot project rather than a national requirement and dropped a provision preventing businesses from sponsoring foreign workers with specific skills. On the House floor in March several provisions were challenged. A move by Sam Brownback, Dick Chrysler and Howard Berman to strip out almost all provisions on legal immigration passed 238–183. Moves to cut the verification pilot project and to require a tamperproof identification card were both beaten. And the House agreed to Elton Gallegly's amendment allowing states to bar children illegally in the country from public schools. The bill passed by a wide margin, but more negotiations were ahead. In the fall the White House threatened veto if the bill included the Gallegly amendment; the Republican leadership, eager for legislative accomplishment, dropped it. The bill as amended removed almost all aid for illegals, even as the welfare bill barred states from aiding legal immigrants; it had tougher deportation proceedings, including for legals who go on welfare; it doubled the Border Patrol and mandated a 14-mile fence on the California-Mexico border.

Smith played a minor role in the Gingrich ethics case. When Jim Bunning resigned from the Ethics Committee in January 1997, Smith was appointed by the leadership to fill out the remaining term. Smith found the charges largely without merit and the bipartisan call for a reprimand to be excessive. He became the only committee member to vote against the penalties, and he led the debate against the measure on the House floor.

The People: Pop. 1990: 566,105; 29% rural; 13% age 65+; 82% White; 2% Black; 1% Asian; 14% Hispanic origin. Households: 63% married couple families; 29% married couple fams. w. children; 59% college educ.; median household income: $32,103; per capita income: $16,086; median gross rent: $434; median house value: $79,400.

1996 Presidential Vote

Dole (R)	174,072	(63%)
Clinton (D)	81,940	(30%)
Perot (I)	18,474	(7%)

1992 Presidential Vote

Bush (R)	143,833	(52%)
Clinton (D)	70,448	(25%)
Perot (I)	63,289	(23%)

Rep. Lamar S. Smith (R)

Elected 1986; b. Nov. 19, 1947, San Antonio; home, San Antonio; Yale, B.A. 1969, Southern Methodist U., J.D. 1975; Christian Scientist; married (Beth).

Career: U.S. Small Business Admin., 1969–70; Business writer, *Christian Science Monitor*, 1970–72; Practicing atty., 1975–76; TX House of Reps., 1981–82; Bexar Cnty. Commissioner, 1982–85.

DC Office: 2231 RHOB 20515, 202-225-4236; Fax: 202-225-8628.

District Offices: Kerrville, 210-895-1414; Midland, 915-687-5232; Round Rock, 512-218-4221; San Angelo, 915-653-3971; San Antonio, 210-821-5024.

Committees: *Budget* (6th of 24 R). *Judiciary* (6th of 20 R): Commercial & Administrative Law; Immigration & Claims (Chmn.).

Group Ratings

	ADA	ACLU	AFS	LCV	CFA	CON	NFIB	COC	ACU	NTLC	CHC
1996	10	7	0	15	8	46	97	93	100	100	100
1995	0	—	—	0	0	53	—	100	84	—	—

National Journal Ratings

	1995 LIB		1995 CONS	1996 LIB		1996 CONS
Economic	0%	—	74%	24%	—	73%
Social	0%	—	79%	0%	—	90%
Foreign	0%	—	85%	0%	—	79%

Key Votes of the 104th Congress

1. Reduce Medicare Growth $	Y	5. Flag Amendment	Y	9. Cuban Embargo	Y
2. Ovrd. Product Liab. Veto	Y	6. Drop EPA Limits	N	10. Bar Bosnia Troop $	Y
3. Increase Min. Wage	N	7. Repeal Assault-Weap. Ban	Y	11. Cut Anti-Missile Defense	N
4. Welfare Reform	Y	8. Ovrd. Part. Birth Veto	Y	12. Bar U.N. Uniforms	Y

Election Results

1996 general	Lamar S. Smith (R)	205,830	(76%)	($443,571)
	Gordon H. Wharton (D)	60,338	(22%)	($18,844)
1996 primary	Lamar S. Smith (R)	unopposed		
1994 general	Lamar S. Smith (R)	165,595	(90%)	($538,347)
	Kerry L. Lowry (I)	18,480	(10%)	

TWENTY-SECOND DISTRICT

Spreading out in all directions from its historic center at Allen's Landing on Buffalo Bayou, Houston has become one of the great metropolises of North America. A half-century ago, the steaming flatlands south of Houston running down to the Gulf of Mexico did not seem a likely site of one of the world's most advanced civilizations. But they are today. It was Houston where most of the scientific work was done that put the first man on the moon: the first word spoken on the moon was "Houston." Houston is the undisputed center of expertise in the oil business; the greatest concentration of experts in the world, within a few miles of each other. Houston has also become one of the great medical centers of the world, with the giant Texas Medical Center looming as impressively massive as any great office skyscraper. All this success and sophistication are testimony to human—and Texan—creativity, and to the triumph of air conditioning. For who supposed that all these people would move here if they had to sweat through Houston's steamy five-month summer?

The 22d Congressional District of Texas is made up of the southwest quadrant of metropolitan Houston, starting near Loop 610 and heading out into Fort Bend and Brazoria Counties. It also has a spur heading westward to a point near the Johnson Space Center and Galveston Bay. Much of the district's shape derives from the 1991 redistricting, but its lines in Houston and Harris County were very much smoothed out by the court-ordered redistricting plan of August 1996 adopted after the Supreme Court ruled the 18th and 29th Districts unconstitutional because racially motivated. The new lines raised the 22d's black percentage from 8% to 13%; not much changed were its Hispanic and Asian percentages, the latter the highest in Texas. The 22d is a heavily Republican district. You will be hard pressed to find many national Democrats among the people who have come from other parts of Texas and the nation to live in these new, mostly affluent subdivisions. Even in local elections the historic Democratic leanings of the rural areas are usually overwhelmed by the strong Republican allegiance of the newcomers.

The congressman from the 22d District is Tom DeLay, the House Majority Whip, number three member of the House Republican leadership—an aggressive political operator, strong ideological conservative and key member of the new leadership team. DeLay was born in the border town of Laredo and spent much of his childhood in Venezuela, where his father drilled oil wells. Settling in Sugar Land, DeLay built a pest control business and was elected to the state legislature in 1978, the first Republican legislator from Fort Bend County this century. DeLay easily won the 1984 Republican primary and the general election for this seat; the previous congressman, Ron Paul, now represents the 14th District and was then running for the Senate. DeLay's voting record is almost purely conservative, but he sought posts that usually appeal to more practical pols.

In his first term, he was the freshman representative on the Republican Committee on Committees. In his second term he got a seat on the Appropriations Committee, where he has been known to seek money for his district, including grants for a bus system to ease traffic on the choked Southwest Freeway. But he opposed a $1.2 billion monorail, a sure clunker in this auto town. More recently he has pushed the designation of a new I-69 heading southwest from Houston and has backed the STEP-21 highway formula which would give more dollars to Texas. DeLay is an ardent booster of the space program and has worked mightily to save the Space Station from demise. Partly through his efforts this scientifically unadventurous venture survived in 1994, winning 278–155 in the House, while the scientifically much more interesting Supercollider was killed in October 1993. He also has maintained close ties to the Christian Coalition and to cultural conservatives like organizer Paul Weyrich.

Much of DeLay's energy has been devoted to working in and running for leadership positions. Not all of his moves proved to be well-plotted. In March 1989, in his third term, he managed the campaign of moderate Edward Madigan to replace Dick Cheney as minority whip; Madigan was backed by his Illinois neighbor, Minority Leader Robert Michel, but he was beaten 87–85 by Newt Gingrich. That didn't stop DeLay from running in December 1992 against incumbent Bill Gradison for the post of Republican Conference secretary and won 95–71; Gradison left Congress to head the Health Insurance Association, the organization that ran the "Harry and Louise" ads against the Clinton healthcare plan. It soon became known that Michel would retire and Gingrich would run for Republican leader; DeLay ran for whip, to replace Gingrich, and leapfrogging Dick Armey, who had described him as his best friend. That was when almost no one assumed Republicans would win the 1994 elections. When they did, Gingrich was easily elected speaker and Armey majority leader. DeLay was opposed by Robert Walker, Gingrich's best friend in the House, and Bill McCollum, but he had campaigned in 25 states and contributed $2 million to Republican candidates. DeLay showed his vote-counting acumen by proclaiming that he was not interested in the second-ballot votes he would need if no one had a majority: "We are locked into winning this outright." He won with 119 votes to 80 for Walker and 28 for McCollum. "I'm very aggressive. I'm a hard-working, aggressive, persistent whip. That's why I'm whip."

Given all this, there has been a pretty good working relationship between these ambitious politicians, even when Gingrich cut DeLay's budget while increasing his own. DeLay spent much of 1995 and 1996 pursuing his great policy interest, regulatory reform. In early 1995, working with committee leaders on Capitol Hill and with lobbyists from downtown, he led to passage bills and appropriations riders designed to halt and reverse the steady growth and power of the federal bureaucracy, especially as it affects corporate decisions in the free market. Through increased use of risk assessment and cost-benefit analyses and a moratorium on new regulations, DeLay's goal has been to change the culture of federal regulatory agencies—a tall order—and the way they treat small businesses. In doing that, he also has sought to make the downtown lobbyists more sympathetic to what he considers their natural allies among Republicans and to end their alliance of convenience with Democrats. But much of his legislative product was vetoed by Bill Clinton, and his attempts to cut back environmental regulations spurred protests from many including Republicans in parts of the country unfamiliar with the regulatory excess DeLay likes to chronicle. Moderate Republicans led Sherwood Boehlert of New York took to opposing DeLay's EPA riders, and by summer 1995 DeLay was having more trouble winning majorities. In response, he tried to show that he was not opposed to the environment, but simply wanted to improve cumbersome regulation.

In December 1996 and January 1997, when Newt Gingrich was scrambling to win reelection as speaker, DeLay emerged as his most ardent defender within the leadership team. He was one of 28 Members who voted against the reprimand and $300,000 fine recommended by the Ethics Committee, claiming that he was defending not Gingrich but "the speaker and his office and this institution." Some thought DeLay was just trying to keep Armey from moving up into Gingrich's spot, or that DeLay was dubious about whether he had the votes to succeed Armey; possibly the explanation was the one he offered, that he thought the case against Gingrich was weak on the merits.

The People: Census data not available due to 1996 redistricting.

1996 Presidential Vote			1992 Presidential Vote		
Dole (R)	119,341	(56%)	Bush (R)	105,885	(48%)
Clinton (D)	79,683	(38%)	Clinton (D)	66,839	(30%)
Perot (I)	12,213	(6%)	Perot (I)	47,796	(22%)

Rep. Tom DeLay (R)

Elected 1984; b. Apr. 8, 1947, Laredo; home, Sugar Land; U. of Houston, B.S. 1970; Baptist; married (Christine).

Career: Owner, Albo Pest Control, 1973–84; TX House of Reps., 1978–84.

DC Office: 341 CHOB 20515, 202-225-5951; Fax: 202-225-5241.

District Office: Stafford, 281-240-3700.

Committees: *Majority Whip. Appropriations* (10th of 34 R): Transportation; VA, HUD & Independent Agencies.

Group Ratings

	ADA	ACLU	AFS	LCV	CFA	CON	NFIB	COC	ACU	NTLC	CHC
1996	0	6	0	15	8	55	94	93	100	98	93
1995	0	—	—	6	0	38	—	96	83	—	—

National Journal Ratings

	1995 LIB — 1995 CONS		1996 LIB — 1996 CONS	
Economic	0%	74%	0%	82%
Social	0%	79%	0%	90%
Foreign	0%	85%	0%	79%

Key Votes of the 104th Congress

1. Reduce Medicare Growth $	Y	5. Flag Amendment	Y	9. Cuban Embargo	Y
2. Ovrd. Product Liab. Veto	Y	6. Drop EPA Limits	N	10. Bar Bosnia Troop $	Y
3. Increase Min. Wage	N	7. Repeal Assault-Weap. Ban	Y	11. Cut Anti-Missile Defense	N
4. Welfare Reform	Y	8. Ovrd. Part. Birth Veto	Y	12. Bar U.N. Uniforms	Y

Election Results

1996 spec. prim.	Tom DeLay (R)	126,056	(68%)	($1,621,708)
	Scott Douglas Cunningham (D)	59,030	(32%)	($28,383)
1994 general	Tom DeLay (R)	120,302	(74%)	($701,245)
	Scott Douglas Cunningham (D)	38,826	(24%)	($149,385)
	Others	4,016	(2%)	

TWENTY-THIRD DISTRICT

The border country of Texas is a zone all its own. It is part of the United States but its culture and economy are not entirely Yanqui or Latino, a local economy that fluctuates depending on, among other things, the strength of the peso and the aggressiveness of INS patrols. Years ago, movements like La Raza Unida—which got its beginnings here in 1969 when Hispanic youngsters wanted to elect high school cheerleaders in Crystal City—wanted the border country to become more like Mexico, with its union and party apparatchiks. More recently, with its economic reforms and NAFTA, Mexico has been trying to become more like the United States, and particularly like Texas, with open markets and privatized companies, less controlled by political or labor bosses. Border towns like Laredo have seen great booms and then busts, as Mexico starts to grow and then, as in 1982 and 1994, devalues the peso. In the early 1990s Laredo was the second fastest-growing U.S. metro area, with one of the largest Wal-Marts and the busiest railroad crossing on the border. Bustling also, but more steadily, is San Antonio and the smaller cities 100 miles or so from the border. In between is quiet ranching and oil country and places like Loving County, the smallest U.S. county with 141 people in 1990.

The 23d Congressional District of Texas includes the longest portion of the 2,500-mile U.S.-Mexico border, following the Rio Grande almost from El Paso south past Laredo. The 23d begins in the Anglo neighborhoods on the north side of San Antonio and goes all the way to the Big Bend territory, where 7,000-foot peaks tower over stony desert. It covers miles of arid hills and rugged desert, of cattle grazing, sheep ranching and oil well country. Yet most of its people live in a few widely scattered metropolitan areas, about one-third in or near San Antonio, with others in Laredo, Midland and Odessa, and the fringes of El Paso. Politically, the border counties around Laredo and Eagle Pass are heavily Democratic, while many of the grazing counties inland are Republican. Some 63% of the residents here in 1990 were Hispanic, as were something approaching 50% of its voters.

The congressman from the 23d is Henry Bonilla, a Republican who beat a scandal-tarred incumbent in 1992 and has been reelected impressively in 1994 and 1996. He was brought up in a Latino neighborhood in San Antonio; his grandmother worked as a maid and his father worked two jobs. Bonilla went to the University of Texas and then worked as a TV reporter, news producer and executive at local stations in San Antonio, New York, Philadelphia and in 1986 San Antonio again, where he appeared on TV as did his wife, news anchor Deborah Knapp Bonilla. In 1991, Bexar County Republican leaders recruited Bonilla to run for Congress against incumbent Democrat Albert Bustamante, who reportedly was being investigated by the FBI for racketeering, who had 30 overdrafts on the House bank and who after the election was convicted of two counts of misuse of office for racketeering and bribery. Bonilla, who has said that "Newt inspired me to run for office," backed standard conservative planks—term limits, the line-item veto and a congressional ethics committee made up of private citizens. But he made his own issues as well. He opposed two new hazardous waste dumps near Del Rio, backed tax and environmental policies more favorable to the oil industry and sided with water users over the allegedly endangered fountain darter fish in a dispute over Comal Springs. Bustamante called Bonilla "a eunuch for the plantation owners," for opposing a minimum wage bill, but Bonilla won by a whopping 59%–38%, with most of his margin in San Antonio's Bexar County, which he won 81%–16%.

Republicans gave their first Mexican-American member a seat on Appropriations, where he has shown talent at putting deregulatory riders on appropriations bills, eliminating funding for enforcing a rule on cardboard balers, for example, or blocking the Labor Department from developing ergonomic standards. Bonilla has a mostly conservative voting; he voted enthusiastically for NAFTA and against gun control. He readily praises the 104th Congress's "common sense accomplishments." He also bragged of getting $800 million for health centers and attacked the Clinton Administration for diverting funds from bilingual education to administration. He is cautious about banning racial quotas and preferences. Bonilla was a visible presence at the 1996 Republican National Convention, delivering a seconding speech for Bob Dole.

Back home Bonilla has been reelected by handsome margins. In 1994 voting rights attorney Rolando Rios attacked Bonilla for opposing the Clinton budget, the earned income tax credit and gun control. Bonilla called him "one of those pseudo-intellectuals who think that all Mexican-American voters want to hear about is food stamps and welfare." Bonilla won 63%–37%, winning 76% in Bexar County but, more important for the longer run, carrying most of the border counties and losing Laredo by only 59%–41%. In 1996 he almost precisely duplicated this showing, winning 62%–36% while Bob Dole was losing the district 50%–44%, carrying 77% in Bexar and losing Laredo by only 51%–48%. The *San Antonio Express-News* headlined that Bonilla was "strong as [an] acre of garlic." His political potential seems great.

The People: Pop. 1990: 566,736; 25% rural; 9% age 65+; 34% White; 3% Black; 1% Asian; 63% Hispanic origin. Households: 66% married couple families; 38% married couple fams. w. children; 39% college educ.; median household income: $21,555; per capita income: $9,764; median gross rent: $322; median house value: $47,900.

1996 Presidential Vote			1992 Presidential Vote		
Clinton (D)	83,965	(50%)	Clinton (D)	72,511	(42%)
Dole (R)	73,282	(44%)	Bush (R)	70,638	(41%)
Perot (I)	9,372	(6%)	Perot (I)	28,873	(17%)

Rep. Henry Bonilla (R)

Elected 1992; b. Jan. 2, 1954, San Antonio; home, San Antonio; U. of TX, B.A. 1976; Baptist; married (Deborah).

Career: TV reporter, 1976–80; Asst. Press Secy., PA Gov. Thornburgh, 1981; Writer/producer, WABC, New York, 1982–85; Asst. News Dir., WATF-TV, Philadelphia, 1985–86; KENS-TV, San Antonio, Exec. News Producer, 1986–89, Public Affairs, 1989–92.

DC Office: 1427 LHOB 20515, 202-225-4511; Fax: 202-225-2237.

District Offices: Del Rio, 210-774-6547; Laredo, 210-726-4682; Midland, 915-686-8833; San Antonio, 210-697-9055.

Committees: *Appropriations* (18th of 34 R): Agriculture, Rural Development, FDA & Related Agencies; Labor, Health & Human Services & Education; National Security.

Group Ratings

	ADA	ACLU	AFS	LCV	CFA	CON	NFIB	COC	ACU	NTLC	CHC
1996	0	25	0	23	8	30	100	94	85	100	93
1995	0	—	—	0	0	38	—	100	88	—	—

National Journal Ratings

	1995 LIB		1995 CONS	1996 LIB		1996 CONS
Economic	0%	—	74%	30%	—	68%
Social	35%	—	64%	46%	—	52%
Foreign	0%	—	85%	0%	—	79%

Key Votes of the 104th Congress

1. Reduce Medicare Growth $	Y	5. Flag Amendment	Y	9. Cuban Embargo	Y
2. Ovrd. Product Liab. Veto	Y	6. Drop EPA Limits	N	10. Bar Bosnia Troop $	Y
3. Increase Min. Wage	N	7. Repeal Assault-Weap. Ban	Y	11. Cut Anti-Missile Defense	N
4. Welfare Reform	Y	8. Ovrd. Part. Birth Veto	Y	12. Bar U.N. Uniforms	Y

Election Results

1996 general	Henry Bonilla (R)	101,332	(62%)	($779,893)
	Charles P. Jones (D)	59,596	(36%)	($74,755)
	Others	2,911	(2%)	
1996 primary	Henry Bonilla (R)	unopposed		
1994 general	Henry Bonilla (R)	73,815	(63%)	($758,591)
	Rolando L. Rios (D)	44,101	(37%)	($426,042)

TWENTY-FOURTH DISTRICT

The geographical heart of the Dallas-Fort Worth Metroplex was open country as late as the 1950s, when the Dallas-Fort Worth Turnpike was built to link the two downtowns. Then, over the next three decades, the bottomlands of the West Fork of the Trinity River and the barren hills overlooking them filled up. Whole new Dallases and Fort Worths, with as many people as the central cities had in the 1940s—Grand Prairie and Arlington and Irving—grew up in these once impoverished lands and became central to one of America's richest and most productive metropolitan areas. Major landmarks have arisen here as well, from Six Flags Over Texas to The Ballpark in Arlington, the new old-style major league baseball stadium that replaced the old modern Turnpike Stadium. New subdivisions are going up here, but one can still see barren hills above the Metroplex. These new towns are taking on a graceful aging air, as trees grow and houses are renovated and added onto and commercial buildings are adapted to new and unexpected uses. Not that the oldest areas are all left behind: there are slums in the Metroplex, but also neighborhoods like Oak Cliff, across the Trinity River south of Dallas, large parts of which are being redeveloped by Texans appreciating their prairie architectural heritage.

When the Mid-Cities area, as it is sometime known, started filling up in the 1950s, Dallas was Republican and Fort Worth Democratic; in the years since, the white Anglo majority in the Metroplex has tilted heavily Republican, and most Democratic votes have come from blacks and Hispanics. But there still are a few pockets of blue-collar whites who give Democrats at least sizeable minorities—in the lower income areas of Grand Prairie or around the GM assembly plant in Arlington.

The 24th Congressional District of Texas contains much of this area. The first 24th District was established in 1972; its boundaries have changed several times, most recently in August 1996, following the June 1996 Supreme Court decision declaring the adjacent 30th District unconstitutional; the lines used in the 1996 election were much more regular than those used in 1992 and 1994, though the basic outline and character of the districts were similar. The 24th now includes Grand Prairie and part of Arlington, the older part of Oak Cliff and most of southern Dallas County, the heavily black southeast side of Fort Worth and parts of rural Ellis and Navarro Counties south of Dallas. The 24th is 20% black and 21% Hispanic. Politically, it is pretty solidly Democratic, 54%–39% for Bill Clinton in 1996.

The congressman from the 24th District is Martin Frost, first elected in 1978 and the winner in a series of 24th Districts; the 1991 redistricting was the work of Frost and his staffer Bob Mansker, and managed to create a majority-black 30th District in Dallas for Eddie Bernice Johnson while compensating Frost for his loss of blacks in Dallas by annexing blacks in Fort Worth. Frost grew up in Fort Worth, went to the University of Missouri and Georgetown Law, was a commentator on public TV and practiced law. But politics has been most of his professional life. He first ran in the 24th in 1974, at 32, and lost the primary 3–2; he ran again in 1978 and reversed the result, ousting a conservative Democrat. As a freshman he got a seat on the Rules Committee, thanks to then-Majority Leader Jim Wright of Fort Worth. Frost was a stalwart supporter of Wright to the end and has been a Democratic leadership man ever since. He worked in tandem with Wright to kill measures that would have tightened lending and investment requirements for S&Ls and would have increased capital requirements. He lost two leadership bids in the 1980s, backing off a bid to chair the Budget Committee in 1984 and losing the race for Caucus vice chairman to Vic Fazio in 1989 by 147–74. But he came back to chair the IMPAC 2000 redistricting panel from 1991–94 and, as a loyal backer of Minority Leader Dick Gephardt, he was appointed chairman of the Democratic Congressional Campaign Committee after the debacle of 1994.

Frost has worked on local causes, including funding the V-22 Osprey at Bell Helicopter in Fort Worth, expanding DFW Airport, building a Dallas area light rail; he worked to keep the General Motors plant in Arlington open. He is proud of having sponsored the Amber Hagerman Child Protection Act, tacked onto an appropriation bill and passed in October 1996 and named for an Arlington nine-year-old who was kidnapped and murdered; it mandates life in prison for anyone twice convicted of a sex offense against a child. In 1997 he switched his vote and voted for the partial-birth abortion ban.

Despite all his strengths, Frost has had tough competition in the 1990s. He has raised and spent $1.5 million in 1992 and 1994, nearly $2 million in 1996. Against a low-spending opponent in 1992, he won with 60%. In 1994 he was opposed by home builder Ed Harrison, who attacked Frost for voting with Bill Clinton 91% of the time. Frost scampered on the crime issue (switching to oppose the assault weapon ban, then voting for the crime bill rule) and had the chutzpah, after years of loyalty to leadership loyalty, to accuse Harrison of kowtowing to Newt Gingrich. He ended up losing Dallas County 54%–46% but carried Tarrant 62%–38%, for a 53%–47% victory—his lowest general election percentage ever. In 1996 Harrison ran again. This time Frost was more on the attack, hitting Harrison as a clone of the now highly unpopular Gingrich and attacking him for backing Medicare "cuts" and tax breaks for the wealthy: the same tactics he was counseling for Democrats all across the country. Because of the redistricting, the November contest was an all-party primary in which one other Democrat and one Independent filed; Frost won 56%–39%, in a vote that came close to echoing the presidential result; this time Frost carried Dallas as well as Tarrant.

But he was disappointed when Democrats narrowly missed their goal of retaking the House. But they gained at least a few seats rather than lost—the first Democratic House gains since 1990—and Minority Leader Dick Gephardt prevailed on him to take the job for another two years. He will try to hold down the number of Democratic retirees and keep the flow of PAC money coming into Democratic incumbents and open seat candidates, as it did in 1996. He may also keep money flowing into Texas: Roll Call in a critical article said that 30% of DCCC soft money in 1996 was sent by Frost to Texas, much of it to Tarrant and Dallas County, where it could help his campaign; but Frost could reply that Texas had many open seats that year and that his own race was a legitimate target for Democratic spending. His best case scenario is winning control and moving up in the leadership; his worst case scenario is national losses and a tough opponent again in the 24th.

The People: Census data not available due to 1996 redistricting.

1996 Presidential Vote

Clinton (D)	80,626	(54%)
Dole (R)	59,125	(39%)
Perot (I)	10,681	(7%)

1992 Presidential Vote

Clinton (D)	74,392	(42%)
Bush (R)	58,857	(33%)
Perot (I)	45,530	(25%)

Rep. Martin Frost (D)

Elected 1978; b. Jan. 1, 1942, Glendale, CA; home, Dallas; U. of MO, B.A., B.J., 1964, Georgetown U., J.D. 1970; Jewish; married (Valerie).

Career: Army Reserves, 1966–72; Legal commentator, KERA-TV, Dallas, 1971–72; Practicing atty., 1972–78.

DC Office: 2256 RHOB 20515, 202-225-3605; Fax: 202-225-4951; e-mail: frost@hr.house.gov.

District Offices: Corsicana, 903-874-0760; Dallas, 214-948-3401; Ft. Worth, 817-293-9231.

Committees: *Democratic Congressional Campaign Committee Chairman. Rules* (2nd of 4 D): Legislative & Budget Process (RMM).

Group Ratings

	ADA	ACLU	AFS	LCV	CFA	CON	NFIB	COC	ACU	NTLC	CHC
1996	65	44	92	69	62	12	40	38	10	21	14
1995	85	—	—	56	69	4	—	41	14	—	—

National Journal Ratings

	1995 LIB — 1995 CONS	1996 LIB — 1996 CONS
Economic	67% — 33%	72% — 27%
Social	75% — 23%	72% — 27%
Foreign	70% — 28%	55% — 43%

Key Votes of the 104th Congress

1. Reduce Medicare Growth $	N	5. Flag Amendment	Y	9. Cuban Embargo	Y
2. Ovrd. Product Liab. Veto	N	6. Drop EPA Limits	Y	10. Bar Bosnia Troop $	N
3. Increase Min. Wage	Y	7. Repeal Assault-Weap. Ban	Y	11. Cut Anti-Missile Defense	Y
4. Welfare Reform	N	8. Ovrd. Part. Birth Veto	N	12. Bar U.N. Uniforms	N

Election Results

1996 spec. prim.	Martin Frost (D)	77,847	(56%)	($1,963,529)
	Ed Harrison (R)	54,551	(39%)	($868,345)
	Others	7,239	(5%)	
1994 general	Martin Frost (D)	65,019	(53%)	($1,589,612)
	Ed Harrison (R)	58,062	(47%)	($562,260)

TWENTY-FIFTH DISTRICT

Houston is, among other things, a blue-collar city: the Ship Channel which made it a great port is lined with petrochemical plants and refineries and surrounded by port facilities, factories, truck terminals and railroad offloading platforms. And many of the neighborhoods that have sprouted up in and around Houston's wide city limits in the last three decades, with their plain, contemporary houses and commercial strip highways, could be called working class. Some of these neighborhoods have been close-knit places for decades, but others have sprouted up recently, moved into by whites as Mexican-Americans fill their former streets. After all, physical mobility is easy in spread-out Houston and many people keep in touch through churches though they are miles apart.

The 25th District of Texas includes many such neighborhoods on the east and south sides of

Houston. Its boundaries, now that they have been smoothed out by the August 1996 federal court redistricting, can be described more easily. On the east it includes Baytown and the industrial corridor to the north, Deer Park and Pasadena south of the Ship Channel, Highlands on the north. It includes the southern edge of Houston from Hobby Airport west to the Southwest Freeway. It includes Bellaire and the affluent neighborhoods just west of the Texas Medical Center and Rice University. The 1996 redistricting removed some black precincts; the black percentage went down from 27% to 23% but the Hispanic percentage went up from 16% to 19%. The political complexion was changed more than any other Texas district. The district under the old lines voted 47%–36% for Bill Clinton in 1992; the district under the new lines was 42%–39% for Clinton.

The congressman from the 25th District is Ken Bentsen, a Democrat elected in 1994. He grew up in Houston, where his father is an architect; his grandfather was the fabled Rio Grande Valley pioneer Lloyd Bentsen, Sr., and his uncle is former Senator and Treasury Secretary Lloyd Bentsen, Jr. After college in Houston, Ken Bentsen worked four years as a staffer on Capitol Hill for Ron Coleman, spending much of his time at the Appropriations Committee; then, he joined an investment banking firm in Houston and was elected Harris County Democratic chairman in 1990 and 1992. In 1994, when incumbent Democrat Mike Andrews ran for the Senate (he finished third in the primary), Bentsen ran for the House. In a light-turnout Democratic primary, Bentsen had only 26% to 37% for Beverley Clark, a black former Houston Council member, anti-abortion and supported by the Christian right, 23% for former legislator Paul Colbert and 13% for high-spending Carrin Patman, daughter and granddaughter of Texas congressmen. In the runoff, Bentsen, pro-choice on abortion, concentrated on crime issues, supporting boot camps and more death penalties, and won 64%–36%. Meanwhile, the Republican nomination was won by Dr. Eugene Fontenot, a Christian conservative, who spent $853,000 of his own money in the primary to beat pro-choice 1992 nominee Dolly Madison McKenna by 56%–44%. In the general election Fontenot spent more than any other candidate in the country that year, $4.7 million. Bentsen, spending a comparatively modest $973,000, attacked Fontenot as "radical right," and called for a budget freeze with a pledge of universal healthcare coverage.

Bentsen won 52%–45%, getting only 50% in Harris County but adding nearly 6,000 votes to his margin from the heavily black portion of Fort Bend County then in the district. He was just to the left of the middle of the House in his voting record. He supported the moderate Blue Dog budget; he sought more money for medical research, space exploration, education—Houston priorities. In the March 1996 primary Bentsen won the right to face Republican Brent Perry. The August 1996 court-ordered redistricting threw Bentsen for a loop, and reintroduced a cast of familiar characters—though not Fontenot, who was busy running in the heavily Republican 8th, where he managed to lose in the December runoff. The new rules were: an all-party primary on November 5, with a runoff if no one got 50% on December 10. The chances of avoiding a runoff were reduced toward zero when Beverley Clark and Dolly Madison McKenna entered the race—two women at odds with most of their fellow party members on the hot-button issue of abortion. Bentsen easily led in November, but won just 34%; Perry, for five months the Republican nominee with a chance of winning, finished fourth with 13%; Clark and McKenna had 17% each, with McKenna ahead by 199 votes. Clark challenged the results, citing ballot irregularities; after a court dismissed her challenge, she endorsed McKenna two days before the runoff. Meanwhile, McKenna had been spending much time and psychic energy trying to mollify abortion opponents. It failed to work. "The last thing Republicans need is a high-profile woman parading around Congress being the darling of the pro-abortion forces," Al Clements of the Texas Right to Life Committee told the *Houston Chronicle*. Democrats had only a 51%–49% lead in total votes in the November primary. But in the December runoff Bentsen won 57%–43%.

In the 105th Congress Bentsen called for bipartisanship and cuts in corporate welfare. He called for ending the ethanol subsidy (not popular in oil-producing territory) and for indexing capital gains.

The People: Census data not available due to 1996 redistricting.

1996 Presidential Vote			1992 Presidential Vote		
Clinton (D)	81,482	(51%)	Clinton (D)	77,200	(42%)
Dole (R)	70,344	(44%)	Bush (R)	71,294	(39%)
Perot (I)	8,331	(5%)	Perot (I)	33,228	(18%)

Rep. Ken Bentsen (D)

Elected 1994; b. June 3, 1959, Houston; home, Houston; U. of St. Thomas., B.A. 1982, American U., M.P.A., 1985; Presbyterian; married (Tamra).

Career: Legis. Asst., U.S. Rep. Ronald Coleman, 1983–87; Staff Assoc., U.S. House Appropations Cmte., 1985–87; Investment Banker, 1987–94.

DC Office: 128 CHOB 20515, 202-225-7508; Fax: 202-225-2947; e-mail: bentsen@hr.house.gov.

District Offices: Houston, 713-718-4100; Baytown, 281-837-8225; Pasadena, 713-473-4334.

Committees: *Banking & Financial Services* (18th of 25 D): Domestic & International Monetary Policy; Financial Institutions & Consumer Credit. *Budget* (15th of 19 D).

Group Ratings

	ADA	ACLU	AFS	LCV	CFA	CON	NFIB	COC	ACU	NTLC	CHC
1996	75	50	83	77	62	75	32	31	10	20	7
1995	85	—	—	75	77	25	—	29	8	—	—

National Journal Ratings

	1995 LIB — 1995 CONS	1996 LIB — 1996 CONS
Economic	72% — 27%	65% — 33%
Social	72% — 27%	71% — 28%
Foreign	64% — 34%	70% — 29%

Key Votes of the 104th Congress

1. Reduce Medicare Growth $	N	5. Flag Amendment	Y	9. Cuban Embargo	Y
2. Ovrd. Product Liab. Veto	N	6. Drop EPA Limits	Y	10. Bar Bosnia Troop $	N
3. Increase Min. Wage	Y	7. Repeal Assault-Weap. Ban	N	11. Cut Anti-Missile Defense	Y
4. Welfare Reform	N	8. Ovrd. Part. Birth Veto	N	12. Bar U.N. Uniforms	Y

Election Results

1996 spec. runoff	Ken Bentsen (D)	29,396	(57%)	($1,654,345)
	Dolly Madison McKenna (R)	21,892	(43%)	($649,716)
1996 spec. prim.	Ken Bentsen (D)	43,701	(34%)	
	Dolly Madison McKenna (R)	21,898	(17%)	
	Beverley Clark (D)	21,699	(17%)	
	Brent Perry (R)	16,737	(13%)	
	John Devine (R)	9,070	(7%)	
	John M. Sanchez (R)	8,984	(7%)	
	Others	6,304	(5%)	
1994 general	Ken Bentsen (D)	61,959	(52%)	($972,688)
	Gene Fontenot (R)	53,321	(45%)	($4,658,585)
	Others	3,249	(3%)	

TWENTY-SIXTH DISTRICT

On the northern edge of the Dallas-Fort Worth Metroplex, one of America's most affluent and fastest-growing metropolitan areas heads out into hardscrabble countryside. Here is a clash of cultures, the advance of one set of values and beliefs with another. On one side are the values of North Dallas, of the entrepreneurs who have so often created fortunes, starting from scratch with a good idea, a willingness to work, a determination to find good luck. They work in the dozens of high-rises that line the freeways of north Dallas or in smaller offices in industrial areas, they live in the affluent areas starting with the superwealthy Park Cities not far north of downtown Dallas or in any one of dozens of comfortable neighborhoods running dozens of miles north. They believe in free markets, in personal responsibility, in traditional values, in the Republican Party: this is one of the most heavily Republican areas in the nation. And it is advancing into what used to be one of the most Democratic.

The tiers of Texas counties south of the Red River were the home of Sam Rayburn, speaker of the House and author of New Deal regulations, always suspicious of bankers and big corporations and eager to have government weigh in on the side of the little guy. Rayburn and his colleagues were sometimes infected with the pessimism of the farmer for whom there is always something that can go wrong, and not much protection against it, and their spirit was held down by the sheer physical effort needed to scratch a living from these hills. They believed in economic redistribution, regulations and usury ceilings, and the Democratic Party. It is fairly clear which of these views is winning in north Texas. Forty years ago the Republican vote here was limited to affluent neighborhoods within a few miles of the Park Cities. Now it has spread out far into the countryside into counties which once voted near-unanimously for Mr. Sam's Democrats.

The 26th Congressional District of Texas covers much of the northern part of the Dallas-Fort Worth Metroplex. Its boundaries were substantially changed by the August 1996 court-ordered redistricting which followed the June 1996 Supreme Court decision declaring the boundaries of the adjacent 30th District unconstitutional because of racial gerrymandering. It now includes the Park Cities and the affluent quadrant of North Dallas between the Central Expressway and the Stemmons Freeway. It includes Carrollton and Farmers Branch to the northwest and the wonderfully named Grapevine just north of the Dallas-Fort Worth Airport. It also includes half of Denton County, once rural and Democratic, now suburban and affluent and very heavily Republican. Overall, this is a very Republican district, with little partisan effect from the boundary changes. A little more than half its voters are in Dallas County and about one-third in Denton County.

The congressman from the 26th District is Dick Armey, first elected in 1984, now the House majority leader. He is a free market economist who a decade ago was a political nonentity who did not even attend the 1984 Republican National Convention in nearby Dallas where Ronald Reagan was renominated. His political career could never have happened before the 1980s. He grew up on a farm in Cando, North Dakota—pronounced affirmatively as *can do*. At 18, working atop an electric pole at night when it was 30 below zero, he decided to become the first in his family to go to college. By 1984, Armey was an economics professor at North Texas State University in Denton, a northern-accented academic in the Red River Valley of Texas: not a likely candidate for anything. But as he was watching the House sessions on C-SPAN, it occurred to him that he could do as well as or better than the people he was watching on the screen. He got the Republican nomination in the 26th in 1984 unopposed, because no one thought incumbent Tom Vandergriff, the longtime mayor of Arlington, then the largest city in the 26th, could be unseated. But Armey won 51%–49%.

Armey arrived in Washington in modest circumstances—"When I came to Washington, the only congressman I'd known or spent much time with was the man I beat"—and he saved money by sleeping first in the House gym and, when forced to stop, on his office couch—a practice that has since been abandoned by Armey but was okayed for others by Speaker Newt Gingrich in 1995.

Armey brought to the House a sometimes impolitic bluntness but also fine political instincts and an appreciation of how to sell his principles to his colleagues. His first major achievement was the military base closing bill. In 1987, Armey proposed a base closing commission operating outside of politics, but neither Congress nor then-Defense Secretary Caspar Weinberger were ready to delegate such power. After a long debate, Armey worked with the Pentagon, the Joint Chiefs of Staff and then-Armed Services Chairman Les Aspin to create an independent commission that would draw up a list of base closings which Congress would have to approve or reject in its entirety. The result: in 1988 Congress approved the first base closings in 12 years. The 1990 round of closings was rejected, but in 1993 the second round of base closings was approved. In 1995, a more modest third round was proposed by the Clinton Administration and subsequently was approved. Armey's bill had changed political incentives so that they ratcheted government spending down, not up. Rather than compete for House committee positions which would allow them to save uneconomic bases, members are forced to maneuver to make bases economically defensible.

Armey has had less immediate success with his next target, farm subsidies. He argued persuasively that subsidies are no more needed to maintain supplies of the six large subsidized crops than they are for the hundreds of crops which manage to be produced without subsidies and that farmers no more deserve subsidies than any other small businessmen. He forged an alliance on the issue with Brooklyn Democrat Charles Schumer, but was never able to prevail on the floor. But in 1996 the Republican Congress passed the Freedom to Farm Act, phasing out most of the subsidies over seven years.

Armey had little success for his first decade as a minority back-bencher on the Economic & Educational Opportunities or Budget Committees, where he was outvoted by committed partisans of expanded domestic programs, which he attacked. But he found more sympathizers in the Republican Conference. He strongly opposed President Bush's budget summit tax increase and determined he wanted "a seat at the table." So after the 1992 election, Armey ran for Republican Conference chairman against incumbent Jerry Lewis, who had supported the budget summit. Armey won the number-three leadership position 88–84, winning the lion's share of the 47 freshman Republicans and gaining crucial support from Lewis's California delegation as well. This put Armey into leadership meetings at the White House, at one of the first of which he told President Clinton that passage of his budget and tax plan would make him a "one-term president"—not the first or last Armey breach of Washington's collegial etiquette. He is capable of bitter riposte: during the 1994 crime bill debate, when Democrats talked of the need to support President Clinton, Armey said, "Your president is just not that important for us"—for which he soon apologized, and Minority Leader Bob Michel took him to task.

But when Newt Gingrich came up with the idea of having all Republican incumbents and candidates sign a pledge on the steps of the Capitol in September 1994, Armey spearheaded the effort to draw up and then sell—including to some doubters within his own party, let alone other parts of Washington's political class—many of the specifics of the Contract with America. Along with Gingrich, he then travelled virtually non-stop across the nation in the month before the election to raise money and enthusiasm for Republican candidates. After they won control in November, Armey gained his just reward of being elected majority leader without opposition. And he then surprised many with his legislative skill in commanding the 100-day schedule that delivered on the Republicans' campaign promise to debate each item of the Contract, with the House passing everything except for term limits. Later scheduling got more ragged, and members complained about votes scheduled at odd hours or business put off until inconvenient times. Some of this was blunders, some was the inevitable inefficiency of a process never designed to be efficient: in fact the Republicans, with Gingrich plotting long-range strategy in his office overlooking the Washington Monument and Armey operating more on the floor as "the chief operating officer," performed more competently than their utter lack of experience managing a legislative majority gave warrant to imagine. Of tensions between Gingrich and Armey, little more public evidence appeared than of tensions between Tip O'Neill and Jim Wright a decade before. During the 1996–97 controversy over the Gingrich ethics complaint, Armey was careful to stay supportive in public but presumably made some preparation in private to succeed to the speakership should that have been necessary.

There was some tension between Armey's personal stands and his leadership responsibilities. He would have liked to see all farm subsidies cut, but realized that southern Republicans from cotton districts would block such a bill. He said that he would oppose a minimum wage increase "with every fiber of my being," but became reconciled when Gingrich and others realized they had to let it go through. And he acquiesced in the 1997 budget deal, with its complicated tax incentives, which run entirely contrary to the thrust of his current favorite proposal, for a flat tax. Armey's flat tax would start at 20%, then fall to 17% after two years, and would cover all personal and corporate income, with no deductions but generous personal allowances ($11,600 for individuals, $23,200 for married couples, $5,300 deduction per child). There would be no taxes on capital gains, dividends, interest or inheritances. But Ways and Means Committee Chairman Bill Archer has his own tax reform idea; he prefers a consumption-based tax. Gingrich has urged the two of them to go on the road and have a national debate. Each would like to set the stage for a major tax reform, although Archer has announced he will retire in 2000 and Armey hopes he will be about to serve his fourth term as majority leader then, with a Republican President. But that is far in the future, and Armey if anyone should know that in politics things don't always turn out as expected.

Armey still has a rough and ready style. He drives a red pickup truck, wears cowboy boots, quotes country music lyrics, and loves to go fishing, often with Justice Clarence Thomas (whose wife Virginia is an Armey staffer). He said that he has never tried to bring home pork, and in fact his base-closing law closed Carswell Air Force Base in Fort Worth. He has been reelected by overwhelming margins, with 74% of the vote in 1996.

The People: Census data not available due to 1996 redistricting.

1996 Presidential Vote			**1992 Presidential Vote**		
Dole (R)	153,691	(63%)	Bush (R)	127,008	(48%)
Clinton (D)	73,675	(30%)	Perot (I)	79,921	(30%)
Perot (I)	17,802	(7%)	Clinton (D)	57,098	(22%)

Rep. Richard K. (Dick) Armey (R)

Elected 1984; b. July 7, 1940, Cando, ND; home, Cooper Canyon; Jamestown Col., B.A. 1963, U. of ND, M.A. 1964, U. of OK, Ph.D. 1969; Presbyterian; married (Susan).

Career: Prof., West TX St. U., 1967–68, Austin Col., 1968–72, North TX St. U., 1972–77, Chmn., Dept. of Economics, 1977–83.

DC Office: 301 CHOB 20515, 202-225-7772.

District Office: Irving, 972-556-2500.

Committees: *Majority Leader.*

Group Ratings

	ADA	ACLU	AFS	LCV	CFA	CON	NFIB	COC	ACU	NTLC	CHC
1996	0	0	0	15	8	73	97	94	100	100	100
1995	0	—	—	0	0	56	—	100	92	—	—

National Journal Ratings

	1995 LIB — 1995 CONS			1996 LIB — 1996 CONS		
Economic	0%	—	74%	0%	—	82%
Social	0%	—	79%	29%	—	68%
Foreign	0%	—	85%	0%	—	79%

Key Votes of the 104th Congress

1. Reduce Medicare Growth $	Y	5. Flag Amendment	Y	9. Cuban Embargo	Y
2. Ovrd. Product Liab. Veto	Y	6. Drop EPA Limits	N	10. Bar Bosnia Troop $	Y
3. Increase Min. Wage	N	7. Repeal Assault-Weap. Ban	Y	11. Cut Anti-Missile Defense	N
4. Welfare Reform	Y	8. Ovrd. Part. Birth Veto	Y	12. Bar U.N. Uniforms	Y

Election Results

1996 spec. prim.	Richard K. (Dick) Armey (R)	163,708	(74%)	($1,673,388)
	Jerry Frankel (D)	58,623	(26%)	($56,094)
1994 general	Richard K. (Dick) Armey (R)	135,398	(76%)	($900,871)
	LeEarl Ann Bryant (D)	39,763	(22%)	($13,131)

TWENTY-SEVENTH DISTRICT

South from Corpus Christi, the southernmost natural port on Texas's Gulf Coast, with its big petrochemical plants, to the Rio Grande and the Mexican border, are two Texan versions of dreamland. One, fronting the Gulf of Mexico, is the sandspit of Padre Island, for most of its length a national seashore, at the southern tip of which is a high-rise resort to which college students throng for Spring break. Remains of a 1554 Spanish shipwreck have been found here, and it is here that Portuguese settlers began cattle ranching. The other, inland from the Laguna Madre, are the vast grazing and oil lands of the 825,000-acre (that's 1,289 square miles, partner) King Ranch. This still seemingly vacant land between the Nueces and the Rio Grande was the territory in contention in the Mexican-American War. The United States won that war and established its sovereignty. But today most of the people here are of Mexican ancestry, and if their culture and economy are, ultimately, thoroughly Norteamericano, they also have a pronounced Mexican accent.

The 27th Congressional District of Texas includes this land from Corpus Christi south to the Rio Grande. The population is not spread out evenly here. Over half the 27th's voters live in and around Corpus (as it is called locally). Most of the other half live some 150 miles south in the Lower Rio Grande Valley around Brownsville and Harlingen. With a 66% Hispanic majority, the 27th is a Democratic district, though not quite so Democratic as some may suspect, since many Hispanics here are not citizens and those who are by no means vote solidly Democratic.

The congressman from the 27th, since its creation following the 1982 redistricting, has been Solomon Ortiz. He grew up in the Canta Ranas (singing frogs) neighborhood of Robstown, inland from Corpus. His father died when he was 14, leaving him the eldest of four children who scratched out a living as migrant farm workers, sometimes as far away as Colorado and Michigan. "I know what it is being poor, going home and nothing to eat," he says. As a boy he shined policemen's shoes, and wanted to be a policeman himself. When his father died, his employer at the local newspaper raised his wage, and then urged him to join the Army. Ortiz worked as an Army investigator and translator, using his Spanish to learn French, then took a correspondence course in police work and returned home to run for constable. "If it wasn't for the military, I wouldn't be here today," he has said. In 1976 he was elected Nueces County Sheriff. In 1982, when the new 27th lines were drawn, he ran for Congress; after receiving 26% in the initial primary, he made a propitious alliance with party leaders in the Brownsville area and won the runoff with 52% and the general with 64%.

Ortiz's voting record has been moderate; he said he was "probably the only Democrat who did not have to sit down in horror" when Republicans won their majority in 1994. Ortiz is now the fifth ranking Democrat on the National Security Committee. He watches out for the four military installations in the Coastal Bend, as he calls the area; they came out of the 1995 base closing procedure with more jobs than before. Looking after the Corpus Christi Army Depot, he is the author of the provision requiring 60% of military maintenance to be performed at military depots rather than by private contractors; noting that privatization has been sought by the Clinton White House, the Pentagon, major defense contractors and important senators, he said, after the 60–40 formula survived the 1996 conference committee, "I often felt like David going up against Goliath. In both cases, the Philistines went down." Ortiz is proud also of the public-private Navy housing being built in Portland and Kingsville. Ortiz is an enthusiastic supporter of NAFTA, made a rare floor speech against decertification of Mexico as a partner in good standing in the drug war and fought successfully to get an I-69 corridor ("the free trade highway") dedicated from Houston to the Lower Rio Grande Valley. He has also passed bills for the Palo Alto Battlefield, the Lower Rio Grande wildlife range and the Brownsville wetlands bill.

Ortiz has generally won reelection without difficulty; it was noteworthy when his percentage dipped to 56% in 1992. In 1996 he had primary opposition from Mary Helen Berlanga, whose husband is a state senator representing part of the district (Texas Senate districts are just slightly smaller than congressional districts), his first primary opposition since 1982. He won 70%–30% and won in November 65%–34%—pretty convincing stuff.

The People: Pop. 1990: 565,992; 14% rural; 10% age 65+; 31% White; 2% Black; 1% Asian; 66% Hispanic origin. Households: 61% married couple families; 34% married couple fams. w. children; 38% college educ.; median household income: $21,552; per capita income: $9,366; median gross rent: $343; median house value: $47,000.

1996 Presidential Vote

Clinton (D)	87,511	(57%)
Dole (R)	57,533	(38%)
Perot (I)	8,094	(5%)

1992 Presidential Vote

Clinton (D)	78,330	(48%)
Bush (R)	58,714	(36%)
Perot (I)	27,459	(17%)

Rep. Solomon P. Ortiz (D)

Elected 1982; b. June 3, 1937, Robstown; home, Corpus Christi; Del Mar Col., Natl. Sheriffs Training Inst., 1977; Methodist; divorced.

Career: Army, 1960–62; Nueces Cnty. Constable, 1965–68, Commissioner, 1969–76, Sheriff, 1976–82.

DC Office: 2136 RHOB 20515, 202-225-7742; Fax: 202-226-1134.

District Offices: Brownsville, 210-541-1242; Corpus Christi, 512-883-5868.

Committees: *National Security* (5th of 25 D): Military Installations & Facilities (RMM); Military Readiness. *Resources* (9th of 23 D): Energy & Mineral Resources; Fisheries Conservation, Wildlife & Oceans.

Group Ratings

	ADA	ACLU	AFS	LCV	CFA	CON	NFIB	COC	ACU	NTLC	CHC
1996	60	53	91	77	38	12	50	43	37	39	60
1995	50	—	—	50	15	25	—	46	32	—	—

National Journal Ratings

	1995 LIB — 1995 CONS			1996 LIB — 1996 CONS		
Economic	62%	—	38%	67%	—	32%
Social	36%	—	64%	53%	—	45%
Foreign	59%	—	39%	50%	—	48%

Key Votes of the 104th Congress

1. Reduce Medicare Growth $	N	5. Flag Amendment	Y	9. Cuban Embargo	Y
2. Ovrd. Product Liab. Veto	N	6. Drop EPA Limits	N	10. Bar Bosnia Troop $	N
3. Increase Min. Wage	Y	7. Repeal Assault-Weap. Ban	Y	11. Cut Anti-Missile Defense	Y
4. Welfare Reform	N	8. Ovrd. Part. Birth Veto	Y	12. Bar U.N. Uniforms	Y

Election Results

1996 general	Solomon P. Ortiz (D)	97,350	(65%)	($407,316)
	Joe Gardner (R)	50,964	(34%)	($96,900)
	Others	2,286	(2%)	
1996 primary	Solomon P. Ortiz (D)	37,434	(70%)	
	Mary Helen Berlanga (D)	16,097	(30%)	
1994 general	Solomon P. Ortiz (D)	65,325	(59%)	($469,694)
	Erol A. Stone (R)	44,693	(41%)	($42,282)

TWENTY-EIGHTH DISTRICT

The Mexican-American tradition in the part of south Texas radiating from San Antonio is anchored in two culturally conservative but adaptive institutions, the Roman Catholic Church and the United States military. They are a major presence in San Antonio, which for many years had the largest Mexican-American population of any American city, a place just 150 miles north of the border where Spanish was widely spoken and political refugees from Mexico's revolution could be sure of freedom. The church in San Antonio was led for years by liberal bishops who also ran St. Mary's University, which educated many Hispanic politicians and leaders, including two longtime House committee Chairmen, Henry B. Gonzalez and Kika de la Garza. Just as visible a presence in San Antonio are the Army and Air Force, with huge Fort Sam Houston, Lackland Air Force Base, Randolph Air Force Base, and the Brooks Air Medical Center, all in or near the city limits. Mexican-Americans have long volunteered for military service in numbers far higher than most ethnic groups, and for many years Mexican-Americans in San Antonio worked in civilian jobs for the military service—Uncle Sam was long an equal opportunity employer. San Antonio's Mexican-American community has produced many politicians who are liberal on economic issues and on civil rights and civil liberties. But it has not produced many who are hostile to the military or to traditional religious and cultural values.

The 28th Congressional District of Texas stretches from the southern half of San Antonio to the Mexican border. Some 63% of its people are in San Antonio and Bexar County, on the south and east sides of the city. It has a salient north to Hispanic precincts in Guadalupe County and also heads south, through thinly settled ranch and oil well country, to the Lower Rio Grande. There it includes Starr County, home of many blatant and wealthy drug smugglers, and, not far north, Duval County, often the most Democratic county in the United States, whose then-boss George Parr provided the key votes Lyndon Johnson needed for his disputed 87-vote victory in the 1948 Democratic Senate runoff. This was a new district for 1992, 60% Hispanic and solidly Democratic.

The congressman from the 28th District is Ciro Rodriguez, chosen in the special election in April 1997 to replace Frank Tejeda, who died of a brain tumor in January. Tejeda joined the Marines at 17 ("I was a grunt, and proud of it"), was awarded the Bronze Star, won the highest grades ever at Marine Officer Candidate School, was elected to the legislature in 1976; he helped design the 28th District and won the 1992 Democratic primary without opposition. After his death, many prominent local politicians decided not to run: his successor in the state Senate, Frank Madla, his cousin Bexar County Commissioner Robert Tejeda, Councilman Frank Wing, state Representative John Longoria, 1996 U.S. Senate nominee Victor Morales (though he is from the Dallas suburb of Mesquite). But Ciro Rodriguez was soon up and running (too soon, some opponents charged). He grew up in San Antonio, was a social worker, teacher and educational consultant, spent 12 years on the Harlandale school board. In 1986 he was elected to the Texas House, where he had a liberal record, working on equalizing education funding and private development of Kelly Air Force Base. Critical in the campaign was his endorsement by the San Antonio Central Labor Council; he raised $280,000 from PACs, mostly union PACs, more than half of his $505,000 total.

The only serious competition came from San Antonio Councilman Juan Solis, who was supported by Robert Tejeda and Justice of the Peace Edmund Zaragoza. Solis, like Tejeda, was pro-life on abortion and against gun control; he backed term limits and school vouchers; he called Rodriguez "more of a wild-eyed liberal, and that's not what we need in Congress." Rodriguez was backed by more prominent politicians—Madla, Wing, Longoria and Congressmen Ruben Hinojosa, Lloyd Doggett, Sheila Jackson Lee, Chet Edwards and Gene Green—and was promised Tejeda's seat on the National Security Committee by House Democratic leaders (which he got). Even more important, he had the money to go on television and Solis didn't. In the March 15 all-party primary, Rodriguez led Solis 46%–27%, leaving little doubt about the outcome; Rodriguez won the April 12 runoff 67%–33%. As he went off to the House and the National Security Committee, Rodriguez said, "District 28 has a lot of diversity and a lot of poverty . . . It's a district that's hungry to make things happen, and I'm going to work to make things happen."

The People: Pop. 1990: 566,447; 21% rural; 11% age 65+; 30% White; 8% Black; 1% Asian; 60% Hispanic origin. Households: 61% married couple families; 34% married couple fams. w. children; 30% college educ.; median household income: $20,276; per capita income: $8,050; median gross rent: $328; median house value: $39,900.

1996 Presidential Vote

Clinton (D)	93,147	(63%)
Dole (R)	47,338	(32%)
Perot (I)	8,211	(6%)

1992 Presidential Vote

Clinton (D)	94,106	(55%)
Bush (R)	51,279	(30%)
Perot (I)	27,199	(16%)

Rep. Ciro Rodriguez (D)

Elected April, 1997; b. Dec. 9, 1946, Piedras Negras, Coah., Mexico; home, San Antonio; St. Mary's U., B.A. 1973; Our Lady of the Lake U., M.S.W., 1978; Catholic; married (Carolina).

Career: Substance Abuse Counselor, 1971–74, 1978–80; Harlandale ISD Schl. Bd., 1975–87; Educ. Consultant, 1980–87; Faculty, Our Lady of the Lake U., 1987–97; TX House of Reps., 1986–97.

DC Office: 323 CHOB 20515, 202-225-1640; Fax: 202-225-1641.

District Offices: San Antonio, 210-924-7383; San Diego, 512-279-3907.

Committees: *National Security* (25th of 25 D): Military Readiness. *Veterans' Affairs* (13th of 13 D): Benefits.

Group Ratings and Key Votes: Newly Elected

Election Results

1997 runoff	Ciro Rodriguez (D)	19,992	(67%)	($504,945)
	Juan Solis (D)	9,990	(33%)	($91,552)
1997 special	Ciro Rodriguez (D)	14,018	(46%)	
	Juan Solis (D)	8,056	(27%)	
	Mark L. Cude (R)	2,452	(8%)	
	Carlos Uresti (D)	1,345	(4%)	
	John Kelly (R)	1,229	(4%)	
	Others	3,294	(11%)	
1996 general	Frank M. Tejeda (D)	110,148	(75%)	($222,182)
	Mark L. Cude (R)	34,191	(23%)	($9,476)
1996 primary	Frank M. Tejeda (D)	unopposed		
1994 general	Frank M. Tejeda (D)	73,986	(71%)	($224,124)
	David C. Slatter (R)	28,777	(28%)	
	Others	1,612	(2%)	

TWENTY-NINTH DISTRICT

"What built Houston," wrote John Gunther in *Inside U.S.A.*, "was a combination of cotton, oil, and the ship canal." The cotton and oil were gifts of nature, though they require much human effort and ingenuity to produce in commercial quantities; the Houston Ship Channel was almost totally man's creation. After the sand-spit port of Galveston was destroyed by a hurricane and tidal wave in 1900, Houston's town fathers decided to dredge out Buffalo Bayou and make their inland city a seaport, and they succeeded: today it is the eighth busiest port in the world, generating 200,000 jobs and $5.5 billion a year to the local economy. And so a sluggish creek became a harbor and this small city built on a swamp became a major port by the 1940s and a world-class metropolis of four million people in the 1990s. On the west side of town, Houston seems entirely a white-collar, office-bound city. But on the east and north, around the turning basin in the port and through the maze of refinery towers and tubing, Houston is plainly blue collar, with blacks, Mexican-Americans and large numbers of whites from the rural South and even Michigan and California, who came here to move up in the world.

The 29th Congressional District of Texas covers much of the Ship Channel area and working class Houston. It is one of three Texas districts declared unconstitutional by the Supreme Court as racially gerrymandered (the other two are the 18th and 30th); it was created in 1991 to be the Houston area's Hispanic-majority district, but ironically has not elected a Hispanic congressman. Its boundaries in effect for the 1992 and 1994 elections were well described by Paul Burka in *Texas Monthly*: "The 29th District looks like a sacred Mayan bird, with its body running eastward along the Ship Channel from downtown Houston until the tail terminates in Baytown. Spindly legs reach south to Hobby Airport, while the plumed head rises northward almost to Intercontinental Airport. In the western extremity of the district, an open beak appears to be searching for worms in Spring Branch. Here and there, ruffled feathers jut out at odd angles." The district lines for 1996, drawn by a three-judge federal court in August 1996 are much more regular. Removed from the 29th are Baytown, Spring Branch and the Heights neighborhood in Houston. Added is much area on Houston's Northside, between the Eastex and North Freeways all the way out to Houston Intercontinental Airport and FM 1960, and blue collar neighborhoods in northeast Houston. The old district was 55% Hispanic and 10% black; the new 29th is about 45% Hispanic and 15% black: not an enormous change.

The congressman from the 29th District is Gene Green, a Democrat elected since the district was created in 1992. Green grew up in Houston, worked as a printer's apprentice and was admitted to the bar at age 30; he was elected to the state House in 1972, at 25, and to the state Senate in a special election in 1985. He has been a faithful union and trial-lawyer man in Austin and Washington, and also an opponent of gun control—a politician whose natural base is Texas's small union, blue-collar class. He is a compulsive campaigner who goes door to door, with lawn signs and a hammer in his trunk; and a good thing, for him anyway, since otherwise he never would have won in the 29th. In the 1992 Democratic primary he faced Houston Councilman Ben Reyes, a tempestuous character; to protest official inaction, he and friends demolished a crack house, after which they carted off a magnolia tree from its front yard and planted it on Reyes's property. In this district of 566,000 people, only 30,989 voters showed up; Reyes led with 34% to 28% for Green. In the April runoff, Green ran ads showing Reyes's face with "GUILTY" pasted over it; Reyes attacked Green for switching from anti-abortion to pro-choice just before filing. Green came out ahead by 180 votes out of 31,508 cast. Then Reyes went to court and charged that Republican voters had illegally crossed over and voted in the runoff. That got him a July re-runoff, but to no avail. This time Green won with 52%, by 1,132 votes out of 36,722 cast. Green won the general election with 65%.

In the House, Green cast two controversial votes: against NAFTA and against the Brady bill. That got him strong support from unions and the National Rifle Association, and he campaigned at *panchagas*, political gatherings that include as part of the festivities tamales, guacamole and mariachi bands. Reyes ran again in 1994, pro-NAFTA and pro-gun control, supported by downtown business money and most Latino politicians. Only 30,726 voted in the Democratic primary. Green won 55%–45%, winning 80% of Anglos and 30% of Latinos. In the fall, he won with 73%. In 1996 Green was challenged by Houston Councilman Felix Fraga, who was charged with accepting illegal campaign contributions in an FBI sting operation. With a turnout of 11,000 Green won with 63%. That result was mooted by the redistricting court, which ordered an all-party primary on November 5 with a runoff if necessary in December. Neither Fraga nor any other Democrat ran, and Green won with 68% of the vote.

Green has worked on local issues, to keep the Coast Guard Marine Safety Offices open in Houston and Galveston, to get a $17.6 million grant for the Coalition for the Homeless, to help keep Anchor Glass Company open in Jacinto City. By far his biggest such accomplishment was authorization, in the Water Resources Act of September 1996, of a $286 million project to dredge the Houston Ship Channel, widening it from 400 to 530 feet and increasing its depth from 40 to 45 feet. He also, after a spirited fight with other Texas Democrats, got a seat on the Commerce Committee.

The People: Census data not available due to 1996 redistricting.

1996 Presidential Vote			**1992 Presidential Vote**		
Clinton (D)	65,794	(61%)	Clinton (D)	60,033	(49%)
Dole (R)	35,809	(33%)	Bush (R)	40,890	(33%)
Perot (I)	6,331	(6%)	Perot (I)	22,606	(18%)

Rep. Gene Green (D)

Elected 1992; b. Oct. 17, 1947, Houston; home, Houston; U. of Houston, B.A., 1971, Bates College of Law at U. of Houston, 1973–77; Methodist; married (Helen).

Career: TX House of Reps., 1972–84; Practicing atty., 1977–92; TX Senate, 1985–92.

DC Office: 2429 RHOB 20515, 202-225-1688; Fax: 202-225-9903; e-mail: ggreen@hr.house.gov.

District Offices: Houston, 281-999-5879; Houston, 281-477-0761.

Committees: *Commerce* (20th of 23 D): Health & the Environment; Telecommunications, Trade & Consumer Protection.

Group Ratings

	ADA	ACLU	AFS	LCV	CFA	CON	NFIB	COC	ACU	NTLC	CHC
1996	60	67	100	69	54	0	36	38	28	24	13
1995	90	—	—	75	62	4	—	35	21	—	—

National Journal Ratings

	1995 LIB — 1995 CONS	1996 LIB — 1996 CONS
Economic	68% — 31%	72% — 28%
Social	68% — 32%	71% — 29%
Foreign	61% — 38%	73% — 26%

Key Votes of the 104th Congress

1. Reduce Medicare Growth $	N	5. Flag Amendment	Y	9. Cuban Embargo	Y
2. Ovrd. Product Liab. Veto	N	6. Drop EPA Limits	Y	10. Bar Bosnia Troop $	N
3. Increase Min. Wage	Y	7. Repeal Assault-Weap. Ban	Y	11. Cut Anti-Missile Defense	Y
4. Welfare Reform	N	8. Ovrd. Part. Birth Veto	N	12. Bar U.N. Uniforms	Y

Election Results

1996 spec. prim.	Gene Green (D)	61,751	(68%)	($552,655)
	Jack Rodriguez (R)	28,381	(31%)	($58,181)
1994 general	Gene Green (D)	44,102	(73%)	($594,375)
	Harold (Oilman) Eide (R)	15,952	(27%)	($10,065)

THIRTIETH DISTRICT

Dallas is, among other things, the westernmost city of the Deep South. Cotton was the major crop originally in this part of Texas, and many of Dallas's first enterprising businessmen, when the railroad reached the Trinity River here in the 1870s, were cotton brokers. Geographically, Dallas is directly west of the Black Belt of Alabama and the Mississippi Delta, both heavy cotton-producing areas in the days before the boll weevil. Many blacks and whites came west on U.S. 80—and now Interstate 20—to this metropolis, which is now the largest metro area in the South. The south side of Dallas, not much visited by tourists or conventioncers, is predominately black, and black neighborhoods are scattered through other parts of the city and suburbs as well.

The 30th Congressional District of Texas, originally intended to be the Dallas-Fort Worth Metroplex's black-majority district, includes most of Dallas's predominantly black neighborhoods. Its creation in 1991 was insisted on by Eddie Bernice Johnson, then chairwoman of the Texas Senate's committee on redistricting, and the precise lines were drawn by Bob Mansker, aide to 24th District Congressman Martin Frost, who made them exceedingly complex in order to create safe districts for Frost and 5th District Democrat (now retired) John Bryant. The result was one of the most grotesquely-shaped districts in the country: attached to the central body in south and east Dallas are tentacles that appear as complex and attenuated as a series of DNA molecules. Not surprisingly, a lawsuit was filed by Republicans, claiming racial gerrymandering; Democrats contended the lawsuit was politically motivated. The Supreme Court disagreed, and in June 1996 ruled the 30th and two other Texas districts unconstitutional. In August 1996 a three judge federal court drew new lines for the 1996 election, and ordered an all-party primary to be held November 5 with a runoff if no candidate got 50% in December. The new 30th consists of two compact geographic units, connected by downtown Dallas. One consists of the south side of Dallas; the other runs northwest out Stemmons Freeway and includes most of Irving. The old 30th was 50% black and 17% Hispanic; the new 30th was 44% black and 18% Hispanic. The new boundaries reduced the 1992 Clinton percentage by 3%—not an earthshaking change in a heavily Democratic district.

The congresswoman from the 30th District is its creator, Eddie Bernice Johnson. She grew up in Texas and graduated from college as a Registered Nurse—the only professional nurse in Congress. She worked at St. Paul Hospital and was Chief Psychiatric Nurse at the VA Hospital in Dallas. In 1972 she was elected to the Texas House—the first black woman elected to anything in Dallas. She became a regional HEW director in the Carter Administration and then was elected to the state Senate in 1986. She has never had any effective opposition in the 30th District: she won the 1992 Democratic primary with 92% of the vote. After 1996 redistricting, she won comfortably with 55% against seven opponents in the November special election and avoided a December runoff.

In the House Johnson has had a mostly liberal voting record. But she has been attentive as well to business interests in Dallas. Though she once pledged to unions to vote against NAFTA, she changed her mind and voted for it; Dallas probably exports more to Mexico than does any other American city, and many jobs depend on exports to Mexico. She has worked to get NAFTA Superhighway status for I-35. Dallas also is big in aerospace and interested in exports: Johnson strongly favors MFN status for China. She is concerned that "in too many high school classrooms, the world of work is distant and removed," and praises School to Work programs for involving industry in education. She serves on the Transportation and Infrastructure Committee, and on the Surface Transportation Subcommittee which reauthorizes ISTEA. In 1997 she got a seat on the Aviation Subcommittee, of great importance here: the 30th District includes Dallas-Fort Worth Regional Airport, the nation's second busiest, and three others, Love Field, Red Bird Airport and Lancaster Airport.

The People: Census data not available due to 1996 redistricing.

1996 Presidential Vote			**1992 Presidential Vote**		
Clinton (D)	95,715	(70%)	Clinton (D)	94,910	(59%)
Dole (R)	34,820	(25%)	Bush (R)	38,037	(24%)
Perot (I)	6,527	(5%)	Perot (I)	28,840	(18%)

Rep. Eddie Bernice Johnson (D)

Elected 1992; b. Dec. 3, 1935, Waco; home, Dallas; St. Mary's at Notre Dame, B.A. 1955, Texas Christian U., B.S. 1967, Southern Methodist U., M.B.A. 1976; Baptist; divorced.

Career: Registered nurse; TX House of Reps., 1972–1977; Regional Dir., U.S. Dept. of HEW, 1977–80; Mgmt. consultant, Sammons Corp., 1979–1981; Owner, Eddie Bernice Johnson & Assoc., 1981–present; TX Senate, 1986–92.

DC Office: 1123 LHOB 20515, 202-225-8885; Fax: 202-226-1477; e-mail: ejohnson@hr.house.gov.

District Offices: Dallas, 214-922-8885; Dallas, 972-253-8885.

Committees: *Science* (9th of 21 D): Energy & Environment; Technology. *Transportation & Infrastructure* (20th of 33 D): Aviation; Surface Transportation.

Group Ratings

	ADA	ACLU	AFS	LCV	CFA	CON	NFIB	COC	ACU	NTLC	CHC
1996	80	75	100	77	54	55	22	25	0	5	7
1995	95	—	—	88	100	1	—	17	8	—	—

National Journal Ratings

	1995 LIB	—	1995 CONS	1996 LIB	—	1996 CONS
Economic	85%	—	12%	85%	—	11%
Social	80%	—	13%	84%	—	12%
Foreign	79%	—	17%	65%	—	34%

Key Votes of the 104th Congress

1. Reduce Medicare Growth $	N	5. Flag Amendment	Y	9. Cuban Embargo	N
2. Ovrd. Product Liab. Veto	N	6. Drop EPA Limits	Y	10. Bar Bosnia Troop $	N
3. Increase Min. Wage	Y	7. Repeal Assault-Weap. Ban	N	11. Cut Anti-Missile Defense	Y
4. Welfare Reform	N	8. Ovrd. Part. Birth Veto	N	12. Bar U.N. Uniforms	N

Election Results

1996 spec. prim.	Eddie Bernice Johnson (D)	61,723	(55%)	($416,694)
	John Hendry (R)	20,664	(18%)	($101,948)
	James L. Sweatt (D)	9,909	(9%)	($112,343)
	Marvin E. Crenshaw (D)	7,765	(7%)	
	Lisa Kitterman (R)	7,761	(7%)	($18,467)
	Others	5,250	(5%)	
1994 general	Eddie Bernice Johnson (D)	73,166	(73%)	($240,577)
	Lucy Cain (R)	25,848	(26%)	($1,060)
	Others	1,728	(2%)	

UTAH

Utah is a triumph of man over nature, the creation of a productive and orderly civilization in a remote expanse of desert and mountain, arrayed around a desolate salt sea. Today's Utah and Mormonism have their roots in a very different landscape of more than 150 years ago, when a wave of religious enthusiasm, prophecy and utopianism swept across the "burnt-over district" of Upstate New York in the 1820s and 1830s. There Joseph Smith, a young farmer, experienced a vision in which the angel Moroni appeared and told him where to unearth several golden tablets inscribed with hieroglyphic writings. With the aid of special spectacles, Smith translated the tablets and published them as the Book of Mormon in 1831. He later declared himself a prophet and founded the Church of Jesus Christ of Latter-day Saints.

The Mormons, as they were called, attracted thousands of converts and created their own communities; persecuted for their beliefs, they moved west to Ohio, Missouri and then Illinois. In 1844, the Mormon colony at Nauvoo, Illinois, had some 15,000 members living under the strict theocratic rule of Joseph Smith. It was here that Smith received a revelation sanctioning the practice of polygamy, which led to his death at the hands of a mob in 1844. After the murder, the new church president Brigham Young, decided to move the faithful, "the saints," farther west into territory that was still part of Mexico and far beyond white settlement. In 1847 Young led a well-organized march across the Great Plains and into the Rocky Mountains, on a path where Mormons reenacted the march 150 years later in 1997. In 1847, they stopped on the western slope of the Wasatch Range and, as Brigham Young gazed over the valley of the Great Salt Lake spread out below, he uttered the now famous words, "This is the place."

The place was Utah. Young was governor of the territory for many years, and it is the only state that largely continues to live by the teachings of a church. The early pioneers laid out towns foursquare to the points of the compass, with huge city blocks, built sturdy houses and planted dozens of trees. Brigham Young's home still stands a block away from Temple Square, where the Temple, closed to non-Mormons, stands in gleaming marble, topped by the golden angel Moroni, across from the oval Mormon Tabernacle where its great choir sings. For 150 years this "Zion" has attracted thousands of converts from the Midwest, the north of England and Scandinavia. The object of religious fear and prejudice, Utah was not granted statehood until 1896, after the church renounced polygamy. Utah has grown steadily since then, and remains heavily Mormon, its basic character is stamped on the desert, mountain-shadowed, often surrealistic landscape which would have been, without the Mormons, mostly unpopulated.

The Church remains distinctive in many ways. It cares deeply about its past: in caves in the mountains of Utah, the Church preserves America's most complete genealogical records. It tries to spread the faith: young Mormons spend missionary years abroad, and their experiences in turn give Utah the biggest inventory of people with knowledge of obscure foreign languages of any state in the union, a nice commercial advantage. It prohibits the consumption of tobacco, alcohol and caffeine; it encourages hard work and large families, and Utah has by far the nation's highest birth rates and the nation's lowest median age; its members are healthier than the average American; better educated, they work longer hours and earn more money. In an individualist country, it fosters communitarian attitudes: the LDS Church has no clergy, but members serve in positions for which they are chosen, conducting religious services but also keeping in touch with members and counseling them when they need help. And the Church also maintains its own social service organizations. It evidently works. While American mainline denominations are losing members, the Mormon Church is growing, with more members than either the Presbyterian or Episcopalian churches. There were 2.9 million Mormon in 1970 and 10 million by 1997, about half in the United States and half abroad.

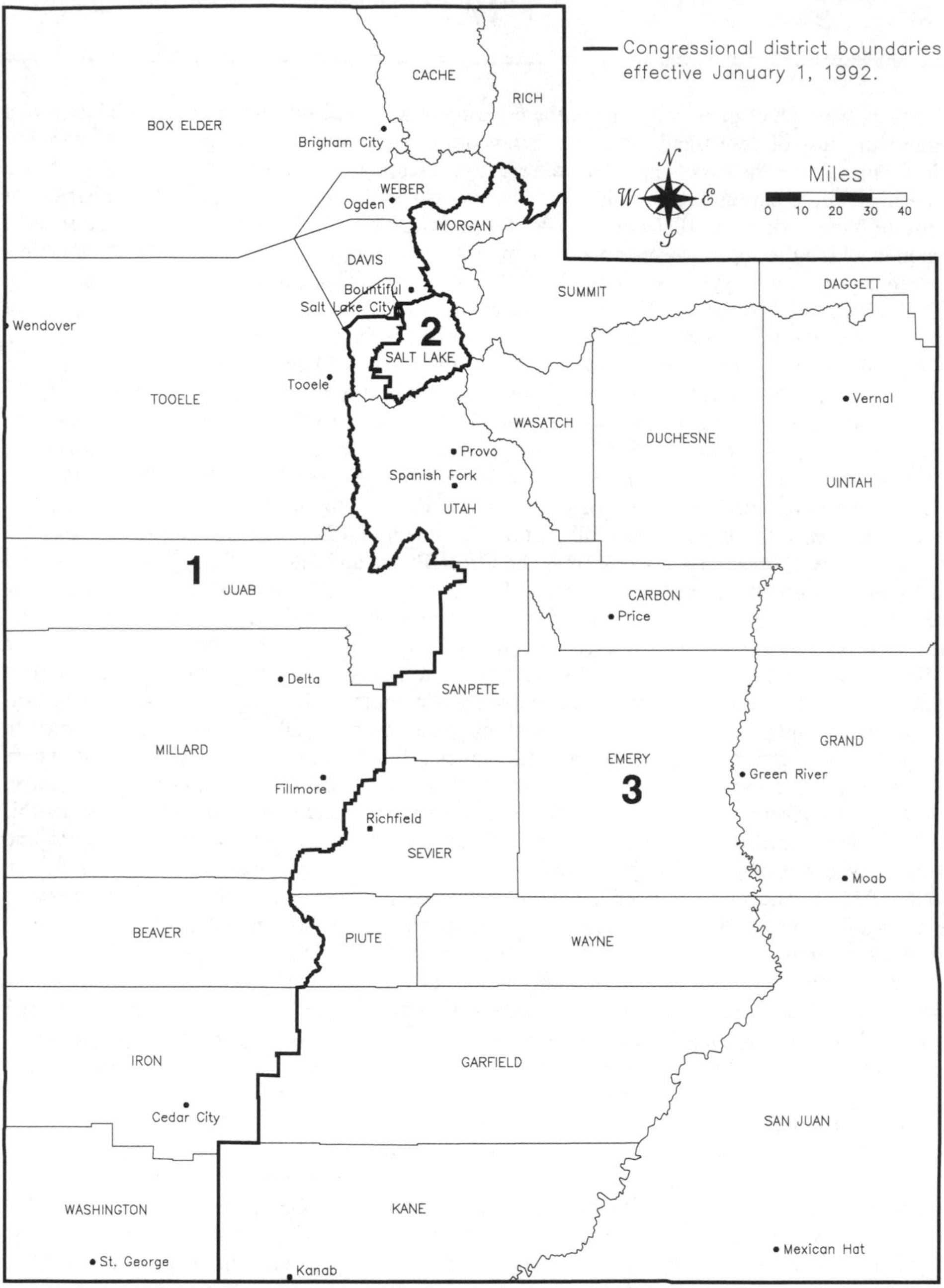
Congressional district boundaries effective January 1, 1992.
N
W
E
S
Miles
0 10 20 30 40
CACHE
RICH
BOX ELDER
Brigham City
WEBER
Ogden
MORGAN
DAVIS
Bountiful
Salt Lake City
SUMMIT
DAGGETT
Wendover
2
SALT LAKE
Tooele
TOOELE
WASATCH
Vernal
DUCHESNE
Provo
Spanish Fork
UTAH
UINTAH
1
JUAB
CARBON
Price
Delta
SANPETE
MILLARD
GRAND
EMERY
Green River
3
Fillmore
Richfield
SEVIER
Moab
BEAVER
PIUTE
WAYNE
IRON
GARFIELD
Cedar City
SAN JUAN
WASHINGTON
KANE
Mexican Hat
St. George
Kanab

The Church's influence in Utah is great—it owns one of the two leading Salt Lake City newspapers and a TV station, it has holdings in an insurance company, several banks, real estate and owns ZCMI, the largest department store in Salt Lake City—and it is sometimes resented. The conservative hold that the Church has over the state can appear in political issues. In 1991 Utah passed the strictest abortion law of any state, banning abortion except in cases of rape and incest, or if the mother's life is endangered. Also in 1990, it became the first state to ban the sale of vending machine cigarettes, although earlier in the year it became the last state to abolish the provision which stated that hard liquor could not be served in public. And the Church itself, financed by the tradition of tithing, runs its own high-quality welfare programs: this is a society that favors market economics and free enterprise, but also has a lively tradition of communal effort and responsibility. Utah's state workfare program, started in 1983, requires one adult in a welfare family to spend 32 hours a week in community service or training, plus job search, and benefits are paid only after performance; social workers here seem to strengthen middle-class values rather than rebel against them.

But if the moral underpinnings of life in Utah have not changed in 50 years, Utah's view of its place in the nation has. Before World War II, Utah saw itself as a colonial victim of East Coast bankers and financiers and Mormons saw themselves as suffering religious discrimination and bigotry—all with some cause. Its income levels were well below the national average, its cost of living higher, the prices paid for the things it produced seemed to be controlled elsewhere. Politically, this perspective translated into a Democratic allegiance: in 1940, Utah was represented by staunch New Dealers in Congress and cast 62% of its votes for Franklin Roosevelt. Today, Utah is more likely to see itself as a busy generator of wealth, with a raft of successful businesses and a knack for high-tech innovation. It has the youngest and highest-productivity work force of any in the nation, second in the nation in job creation (Nevada was first), with more than 5% job growth every year since 1992. Its population has grown 16% in the 1990s, the fourth highest rate in the nation. Workers here work an average of 48 hours a week, more than Japan, far more than the 39 elsewhere in America. It has fast-rising incomes and America's fastest-rising house prices. And Utah has the second largest concentration of information technology firms, after California. WordPerfect, long the favorite word processing software, was invented in Orem; Novell is headquartered in Provo; the University of Utah in Salt Lake City and Brigham Young University in Provo are producing hundreds of computer engineers. Utah has over 39,000 jobs in information technology; the state government has a Centers of Excellence program to fund small high-tech startups. In 1997 the Salt Lake City-Provo area was rated the number one entrepreneurial hot spot, with lots of "baby gazelles," small companies with the potential to be the Intels or Microsofts of the future. Utah is also a place with community spirit: it looks forward to putting itself on display when it hosts the 2002 Winter Olympics, for which it has already built some of the winter sports facilities.

Politically, this perspective now translates into a strong Republican preference; Utah was pretty solidly Republican by the middle 1960s. In the last 20 years, as traditional values thriving in Utah have come under attack elsewhere, it has become arguably the most Republican of states—standing out in national statistics politically just as it does demographically. In 1960, Richard Nixon carried Utah with 55% of the vote; by 1972, he won with 72%. Ronald Reagan won 73% and 75% of Utah's votes; George Bush won 66% here in 1988: for four presidential elections in a row, Utah was the nation's most Republican state. In five of the last six presidential elections, Utah has been the nation's most Republican state, and in the other, 1992, it was the least Democratic: Ross Perot finished ahead of Bill Clinton, 27% to 25%. In 1996 Utah voted 54%–33% for Bob Dole. Democrats are competitive in some races, but only if they show themselves to be consistent with Utah values and attitudes, and even then are in jeopardy; after Bill Clinton in September 1996 declared 1.7 million acres of southern Utah as the Grand Staircase-Escalante National Monument, against local opinion and in order to court environmentalists, without consultation with Utah representatives, the 3d District's conservative Democratic Congressman Bill Orton was beaten for reelection. The state's entire delegation is now Republican, as are the governor and 75 of 104 state legislators. New residents may be occasionally more liberal, and Utah is less heavily Mormon than it was, but the basic character of the state has not changed.

Governor. Mike Leavitt, governor of Utah, grew up in Cedar City in southern Utah, ran an insurance business and managed the campaigns of two-term Governor Norman Bangerter and Senator Jake Garn. In 1992, when Bangerter retired after two terms, Leavitt ran himself. He won the Republican primary 56%–44% over Richard Eyre, author of *Utah in the Year 2000* and 20 other books, who backed a $1,200 school choice voucher. Leavitt had his own Strategic Plan for Education and opposed vouchers. In the general, liberal Democrat Stewart Hanson ran third, with only 23%; second was anti-tax crusader and now 2nd District Congressman Merrill Cook, with 34%; Leavitt won with 42%.

In office Leavitt cut taxes in 1994, 1995 and 1996, as the state's economy surged, and pushed activist programs with catchy labels. One was the 1994 Healthprint insurance reforms; he boasted that Utah had lower healthcare costs than all but one other state. Another was a $120 million, seven-year Technology 2000 initiative. In 1995 he convened a Growth Summit which came up with a 10-year, $2.6 billion highway-building program, with half the money to make I-15 in Salt Lake County a 10-lane highway by 2001, in time for the Winter Olympics; for that he raised gas taxes while cutting the sales tax. In 1996 he proposed a Legacy project, to build a north-south highway west of I-15. He also called for water conservation measures and dam repairs. He has sponsored a Centennial Charter schools program and Highly Impacted Schools program for disadvantaged children. He wants to start, with other western states, a Western Virtual University and is completing UtahLINK giving Internet access to all Utah schools. He sought a less adversarial approach to wilderness issues, even as Bill Clinton without warning created a new and locally highly unpopular Grand Staircase-Escalante National Monument in southern Utah. He opposed the Goshute Indians' plans to build a nuclear waste disposal site on their lands. On cultural issues, he enforced the state's strict abortion law and backed the Salt Lake City school board when it banned all high school clubs rather than sanction a gay students club. But he criticized Utah's method of execution, the firing squad.

Leavitt's policies have been widely popular, and his conciliatory, open, consensus-seeking style has been attractive. In 1996 his job approval was as high as 85%. Democrats had to scrounge to find a candidate against him. Leavitt won 75%–23%.

Senior Senator. Orrin Hatch, who never planned a political career, is now beginning his third decade in the Senate. Hatch grew up in Pittsburgh, where his father was a metal lather; he worked his way through Brigham Young, then Pittsburgh law school, practiced law there and then moved to Salt Lake City. He got into the 1976 Senate race late, filing the last day; an endorsement from Ronald Reagan helped him win the Republican nomination and in the general he upset three-term Democrat Frank Moss 54%–45%. His toughest reelection fight came in 1982, when he was opposed by popular Salt Lake City Mayor Ted Wilson; Hatch won 58%–41%.

Hatch's Senate career has been shaped by two impulses, which are sometimes in tension with each other: a strong conservative philosophy and a sense of responsibility for the superintendency of legislation. In a Senate dominated by Democrats, Hatch startled observers by successfully filibustering the AFL-CIO's labor law reform which had been expected to pass. He worked to convert federal programs to block grants to states, but became fans of some programs, like the Job Corps. On the Labor Committee, where he served as chairman from 1981–86, he worked for bipartisan compromise on child care, family and medical leave, immunizations, the WIC program and AIDS babies. He backed the Americans With Disabilities Act. But he remained a strong opponent of the striker replacement law sought by unions and eventually passed a subminimum wage for teens. On the Judiciary Committee, he fought abortion and civil rights bill which produce racial quotas and preferences, and staunchly defended Supreme Court nominees Robert Bork and Clarence Thomas. Hatch has spent much time on technical rather than headline issues: railway labor disputes, bankruptcy reform, sovereign immunity of states for patents and trademarks, patent protection for pharmaceuticals under GATT and compensation for people exposed to radiation during nuclear tests (which affects southern Utah). He worked on home health care, food safety, organ transplants, orphan drugs and smoking bans. He has worked hard to get a user fee for drug companies seeking quick FDA approval of new drugs and sought to allow exports of FDA-regulated products regardless of their FDA status; former FDA Commissioner David Kessler, appointed by George Bush and retained for four years by Bill Clinton, a *bete noire* of many Republicans, is a former Hatch staffer.

In 1993 Hatch switched from ranking Republican on Labor to the same post on Judiciary, when it was vacated by Strom Thurmond, and took a seat on Finance; in 1995 he became chairman of Judiciary and left Labor altogether. There he worked on tort reform and regulatory reform and managed the balanced budget amendment to one-vote defeats in 1995 and 1997. He worked also on the flag amendment, the anti-terrorism law and the Religious Freedom Restoration Act. In early 1996 he criticized the administration on drugs, saying that Bill Clinton "has abandoned the bully pulpit, overemphasized treatment of hard-core users and—most importantly—deemphasized core law enforcement and interdiction activities." Later in the year he defended Whitewater independent counsel Kenneth Starr, decrying "a rising tide of name-calling and diversionary attacks on Judge Starr's integrity." In March 1997 he revealed that the FBI had warned some members of Congress that China was planning to make illegal campaign contributions, and in April 1997 he held hearings attacking Attorney General Janet Reno for not appointing an independent counsel on Clinton illegal fundraising practices. On judicial appointments, Hatch promised in 1995 to cooperate with the Clinton Administration; by early 1997 some Democrats were charging that he was stalling approval of nominees while some Republicans were complaining that he was allowing too many liberal, activist judges on the bench. Hatch was also caught in the middle on Utah wilderness: while environmentalists wanted 5.7 million acres set aside, Hatch called for 2 million to be protected with another 18 million permanently set aside for mining, recreation and other non-wilderness use; much of this argument was mooted by Clinton's campaign year decision to create the Grand Staircase-Escalante National Monument in southern Utah. In 1997 Hatch again surprised some on both sides of the aisle when he joined Ted Kennedy in sponsoring a $20 billion program to get states to provide health insurance for children of low-income working parents who don't qualify for Medicaid; for Hatch, a tobacco opponent, one attraction must have been that the money would come from increasing the cigarette tax from 24 to 67 cents a pack. They tried to attach their measure to the budget, but it failed 55–45.

Hatch has been reelected three times now. In 1993 he was dogged by stories that he had tried to help a business associate get a loan from the scandal-plagued BCCI and that he defended the bank on the Senate floor following its guilty plea on charges of laundering drug money, and for a time he was only running even in polls against 3d District Congressman Bill Orton. But in November 1993 Hatch was cleared by the Senate Ethics Committee on all the BCCI charges, and Orton and other prominent Democrats passed on the race. His opponent was Pat Shea, former Democratic state chairman and in 1997 Clinton's nominee to head the Bureau of Land Management; but his campaigned was underfinanced, and Hatch won 69%–28%.

Junior Senator. Bob Bennett was first elected in 1992, but was no stranger to the Senate. He grew up in Salt Lake City, and was 17 when his father Wallace Bennett was elected in 1950 to the first of four terms in the Senate. Bob Bennett worked as a congressional staffer and was the Transportation Department's chief lobbyist during the Nixon Administration. He also headed the public relations firm (and CIA front) that employed Watergate burglar Howard Hunt, but was involved in no wrongdoing himself; author Bob Woodward has denied that Bennett was his "Deep Throat" source. Back in Utah, he headed Microsonics Corporation, which makes audio discs for talking toys, for three years and then became head of Franklin Quest, which produces the Franklin day planners and organizers; he increased it from four to 700 employees and sales of $80 million; he sold his interest in 1991 for a reported $25 million. He headed a commission that produced Utah's Strategic Plan for Education and wrote *Gaining Control*, a book on the forces that control daily life.

In 1992, when Jake Garn retired from the Senate, Bennett decided to run for the seat his father once held. He was not the only millionaire in the race. The initial favorite was Republican Joseph Cannon, who had taken over the old Geneva Steel plant and made it profitable, and who spent $5 million of his own money. But Bennett spent $1.4 million of his own and effectively attacked Geneva's environmental record, and won 51%–49%. The Democratic nominee, Congressman Wayne Owens, was a familiar face; he was elected to the House from Salt Lake City in 1972 and ran for the Senate in 1974, then after Mormon missionary work in Canada was elected to the House again in 1986. His record in Washington was moderate, but perhaps too liberal for Utah; Bennett won 55%–40%, with exit polls showing Owens carrying only the elderly—not a good omen for Utah Democrats.

Bennett's voting record in the Senate has been conservative on economics, more moderate on cultural and foreign issues. He was a favorite of Bob Dole, and when Dole's presidential campaign was foundering in February 1996, Bennett started flying around the country with him and helped formulate his tax plan. Dole appointed Bennett head of a task force on health care in August 1994; he worked on the Healthcare Portability Act that passed in 1996. With Vermont's Patrick Leahy, he has sponsored a bill to protect the confidentiality of medical records. In 1997 he announced support for, and later voted against, the Kennedy-Hatch bill to provide health insurance for low-income children. In 1995 Dole named him liaison to the Clinton Administration and the Federal Reserve on the devaluation of the peso. In 1997 Majority Leader Trent Lott appointed him head of a task force on Senate restructuring. "Just because something is old doesn't mean it's an anachronism," Bennett said, saying he seeks "common sense changes that will not destroy the unique nature of the institution."

Bennett has also tended to Utah issues. He wants to consolidate, not abolish, the National Endowments for the Arts and Humanities because he says without them arts programs in rural Utah would dry up. To help the Winter Olympics, he arranged an exchange of land with the Forest Service to help the Snowbasin resort near Ogden. He worked to get a Full Funding Agreement on mass transit in Salt Lake City's I-15 corridor. Like most other Utahans, he was appalled that Bill Clinton without consultation created the Grand Staircase-Escalante National Monument. He wrote a bill codifying the promises Clinton made in his Arizona announcement, but the White House in 1996 said Clinton would veto it; Bennett brought this forward again in 1997.

Bennett comes up for reelection in 1998. By early 1997, no Democratic opponent had appeared.

Presidential politics. Utah has been the most Republican state in five of the last six presidential elections. It sees few candidates in presidential years; Bill Clinton's 1996 announcement that he was establishing a national monument in southern Utah was made in Arizona. Utah's relatively few delegates to national conventions are chosen in caucuses; in the last serious contest, in 1992, Democrats preferred Paul Tsongas and Jerry Brown to Bill Clinton.

Congressional districting. The Republican legislature drew new lines for Utah's three congressional districts for 1992. Salt Lake County, the most Democratic part of the state now, had to be split between districts, and the legislature gave some of the less Republican portions to the 1st and 3d Districts.

The People: Est. Pop. 1996: 2,000,000; Pop. 1990: 1,722,850, up 16.1% 1990–1996. 0.8% of U.S. total, 34th largest; 13% rural. Median age: 26.8 years. 9% 65 years and over. 91.2% White, 1% Black, 1.9% Asian, 1.3% Amer. Indian, 4.9% Hispanic origin. Households: 64.8% married couple families; 38% married couple fams. w. children; 58% college educ.; median household income: $29,470; per capita income: $11,029; 68.1% owner occupied housing; median house value: $68,900 median monthly rent: $300. 3.5% Unemployment. 1996 Voting age pop.: 1,333,000. 1996 Turnout: 665,629; 50% of VAP. Registered voters (1996): 1,050,452; no party registration.

Political Lineup: Governor, Michael O. Leavitt (R); Lt. Gov., Olene S. Walker (R); Atty. Gen., Jan Graham (D); Treasurer, Edward T. Alter (R); Auditor, Austin Johnson (R). State Senate, 29 (9 D and 20 R); Senate President, Lane Beattie (R); State House, 75 (20 D and 55 R); House Speaker, Melvin R. Brown (R). Senators, Orrin G. Hatch (R) and Robert F. Bennett (R). Representatives, 3 (3 R).

Elections Division: 801-538-1041; **Filing Deadline for U.S. Congress:** March 17, 1998.

1996 Presidential Vote

Dole (R)	361,911	(54%)
Clinton (D)	221,633	(33%)
Perot (I)	66,461	(10%)
Other	15,623	(2%)

1992 Presidential Vote

Bush (R)	322,632	(43%)
Perot (I)	203,400	(27%)
Clinton (D)	183,429	(25%)
Other	34,607	(5%)

GOVERNOR

Gov. Michael O. Leavitt (R)

Elected 1992, term expires Jan. 2001; b. Feb. 11, 1951, Cedar City; home, Salt Lake City; S. UT U., B.A. 1976; Mormon; married (Jacalyn).

Career: Army Natl. Guard, 1969–78; Pres. & CEO, Leavitt Group Insurance Co., 1984–92; Chmn., S. UT U. Bd. of Trustees, 1985–89; UT Board of Regents, 1989–92.

Office: 210 State Capitol, Salt Lake City 84114, 801-538-1000. Fax: 801-538-1528; Web site: www.state.ut.us.

Election Results

1996 gen.	Michael O. Leavitt (R)	503,693	(75%)
	Jim Bradley (D)	156,616	(23%)
	Others	11,570	(2%)
1996 prim.	Michael O. Leavitt (R)	unopposed	
1992 gen.	Michael O. Leavitt (R)	321,713	(42%)
	Merrill Cook (I)	255,733	(34%)
	Stewart Hanson(D)	177,181	(23%)

SENATORS

Sen. Orrin G. Hatch (R)

Elected 1976, seat up 2000; b. Mar. 22, 1934, Pittsburgh, PA; home, Salt Lake City; Brigham Young U., B.S. 1959, U. of Pittsburgh, J.D. 1962; Mormon; married (Elaine).

Career: Practicing atty., 1962–76.

DC Office: 131 RSOB 20510, 202-224-5251; Fax: 202-224-6331; e-mail: senator_hatch@hatch.senate.gov.

State Offices: Cedar City, 801-586-8435; Ogden, 801-625-5672; Provo, 801-375-7881; Salt Lake City, 801-524-4380; St. George, 801-634-1795.

Committees: *Finance* (4th of 11 R): Health Care; International Trade; Taxation & IRS Oversight. *Indian Affairs* (7th of 8 R). *Judiciary* (Chmn.); Antitrust, Business Rights & Competition; Constitution, Federalism & Property Rights; Terrorism, Technology & Government Information. *Intelligence (Select)* (7th of 10 R).

Group Ratings

	ADA	ACLU	AFS	LCV	CFA	CON	NFIB	COC	ACU	NTLC	CHC
1996	5	17	0	0	14	77	100	92	100	100	92
1995	0	—	9	0	0	29	—	100	83	—	—

National Journal Ratings

	1995 LIB — 1995 CONS			1996 LIB — 1996 CONS		
Economic	0%	—	88%	26%	—	69%
Social	33%	—	62%	28%	—	68%
Foreign	8%	—	81%	0%	—	74%

Key Votes of the 104th Congress

1. Reduce Medicare Growth $	Y	5. Flag Amendment	Y	9. Anti-Missile Defense	Y
2. Lmt. Prod. Liab. Damages	Y	6. Endangered Species	N	10. Cuban Embargo	Y
3. Increase Min. Wage	N	7. Gay Employment Rights	N	11. Bar Bosnia Troop $	N
4. Welfare Reform	Y	8. Ovrd. Part. Birth Veto	Y	12. Cut Vietnam Aid	Y

Election Results

1994 general	Orrin G. Hatch (R)	357,297	(69%)	($4,209,993)
	Pat Shea (D)	146,938	(28%)	($311,491)
	Others	15,088	(3%)	
1994 primary	Orrin G. Hatch (R)	unopposed		
1988 general	Orrin G. Hatch (R)	430,089	(67%)	($3,706,381)
	Brian H. Moss (D)	203,364	(32%)	($153,475)

Sen. Robert F. Bennett (R)

Elected 1992, seat up 1998; b. Sept. 18, 1933, Salt Lake City; home, Salt Lake City; U. of UT, B.S. 1957; Mormon; married (Joyce).

Career: Chaplain, Army Natl. Guard, 1957–60; Staff Aide, U.S. Rep. Sherm Lloyd, 1962; Staff Aide, U.S. Sen. Wallace F. Bennett, 1963; Cong. Liaison, U.S. Dept. of Transportation, 1969–70; Pres., Robert Mullen P.R., 1970–74; P.R. Dir., Summa Corp., 1974–78; Pres., Osmond Communications, 1978–79; Chmn., American Computers Corp., 1979–81; Pres., Microsonics Corp., 1981–84; Chmn., UT Educ. Strategic Plng. Comm., 1988; CEO, Franklin Quest Co., 1984–91.

DC Office: 431 DSOB 20510, 202-224-5444; e-mail: senator@bennett.senate.gov

State Offices: Ogden, 801-625-5676; Provo, 801-379-2525; Salt Lake City, 801-524-5933; St. George, 801-628-5514.

Committees: *Appropriations* (11th of 15 R): Energy & Water Development; Foreign Operations; Interior; Legislative Branch (Chmn.); Transportation. *Banking, Housing & Urban Affairs* (6th of 10 R): Financial Services & Technology (Chmn.); International Finance; Securities. *Government Affairs* (9th of 9 R): Oversight of Government Management, Restructuring & the District of Columbia; Permanent Subcommittee on Investigations. *Small Business* (5th of 10 R). *Joint Economic Committee* (3rd of 10 Sens.).

Group Ratings

	ADA	ACLU	AFS	LCV	CFA	CON	NFIB	COC	ACU	NTLC	CHC
1996	5	24	0	0	14	83	100	92	95	97	92
1995	0	—	9	0	0	29	—	100	81	—	—

National Journal Ratings

	1995 LIB — 1995 CONS			1996 LIB — 1996 CONS		
Economic	12%	—	84%	17%	—	82%
Social	40%	—	59%	32%	—	67%
Foreign	33%	—	66%	42%	—	57%

Key Votes of the 104th Congress

1. Reduce Medicare Growth $	Y	5. Flag Amendment	N	9. Anti-Missile Defense	Y
2. Lmt. Prod. Liab. Damages	Y	6. Endangered Species	N	10. Cuban Embargo	Y
3. Increase Min. Wage	N	7. Gay Employment Rights	N	11. Bar Bosnia Troop $	N
4. Welfare Reform	Y	8. Ovrd. Part. Birth Veto	Y	12. Cut Vietnam Aid	N

Election Results

1992 general	Robert F. Bennett (R)	420,069	(55%)	($3,339,325)
	Wayne Owens (D)	301,228	(40%)	($1,904,750)
	Others	37,182	(5%)	
1992 primary	Robert F. Bennett (R)	135,514	(51%)	
	Joe Cannon (R)	128,125	(49%)	
1986 general	Edwin Jacob (Jake) Garn (R)	314,608	(72%)	($752,944)
	Craig S. Oliver (D)	115,523	(27%)	($24,508)

FIRST DISTRICT

In May 1869, a motley crowd of Irish and Chinese laborers, teamsters, engineers, train crews, officials and guests from California and Salt Lake City gathered in Promontory Point, Utah, to watch the opening of the transcontinental railroad. The Union Pacific train was late and Leland Stanford raised his hammer and totally missed the golden spike, but an alert telegrapher mimicked the sound over the wire and a photographer recorded the scene for posterity: united at last were the civilized East and the mostly untamed West. Here, beyond sight of the snow-capped mountains crossed by the Mormon pioneers, the salt flats still stretch out endlessly; the rail lines now pass north of here, and Promontory Point lies on uninhabited flat land beside the rising Great Salt Lake. The lake kept rising into the middle 1980s, despite state legislation forbidding it from going above a certain level. The local county commissioners called for a day of prayer for drought in May 1986, the lake finally obeyed the law, and the state didn't have to pump water through canals which would have formed a vast new lake in the salt flats to the west.

The 1st Congressional District of Utah includes the western half of the state, from Promontory Point down to the Arizona and Nevada borders near Las Vegas, where the Colorado River flows south through Glen Canyon into Arizona; Zion National Park is in the south, there is mining country in the center and the desert lies west of the lake. But 75% of the people in this district live along the Wasatch Front, a thin strip of land on the east side of the Lake between the salt flats and the Wasatch Mountains. It takes in Brigham City and Logan near the Idaho border, goes south through Ogden, an old working-class town on the Union Pacific line and the nearest station stop to Promontory Point, and then proceeds through a strip of suburbs to the salt flats northwest of downtown Salt Lake City near the airport. The rest of the 1st's voters live in small communities, many entirely Mormon, in central and southern Utah.

The congressman from this district is James Hansen, a Republican with a solidly conservative record. He grew up in Farmington, Utah, served in the Navy, worked as an insurance agent and head of a land development company. He was elected to the City Council in Farmington, just north of Salt Lake City, and then to the Utah House in 1972, at 40; he was Speaker in 1979 and 1980. In 1980 he ran against incumbent Democrat Gunn McKay and won 52%–48%; he has won usually by wide margins ever since. Hansen describes himself as a "common kid from Utah" and seems unpretentious, but he holds important positions in the House. He is on the Resources Committee and chairman of the National Parks and Public Lands Subcommittee. He worked to complete the Central Utah Project to bring Colorado River water to the Wasatch Front in 1992 and helped crack down on cheap water rates in the Central Valley of California. He favors "multiple uses" of public land, including mining, timber, ranching and grazing. He was outraged when Bill Clinton created the Grand Staircase-Escalante National Monument in September 1996: "Without any public input, without any consideration under the National Environmental Policy Act and any consultation with Utah's elected officials, President Clinton with one stroke of the pen made a decision that will steal over $1 billion from Utah's school children and end up costing the state of Utah over $6.5 billion." The reference was to a proposed coal mine on Utah School lands; Hansen has sponsored bills to limit the president's power to create monuments and to allow the Bureau of Land Management to turn over lands to state governments to manage. He is chairman of the Western Caucus, fighting the "sagebrush rebellion" against what he consider's Clinton's "war on the West," but he can also be bipartisan: he and ranking Democrat Bruce Vento in 1996 co-sponsored a bill to require the National Park Service to produce a management plan for the next century.

On the National Security Committee, he fought successfully to save Hill Air Force Base, Utah's number two employer, from the base closing commission in 1995. He chairs the House Depot Caucus and objects to Clinton efforts to privatize depot bases in California and Texas; he wants to keep Hill and the two other depots in Oklahoma and Georgia. In January 1997 Hansen was tapped to be chairman of the House Ethics Committee. "I've lost out," he said. "It's the absolute last thing I want to do." He had already spent 12 years as a member of the committee (from 1980–92) and refers to its basement meeting room as "the dungeon." He wants to bounce off the committee anyone who leaks anything; but that wasn't a problem in early 1997, as the committee temporarily consisted only of Hansen and Ranking Democrat Howard Berman. There was a moratorium on filing new ethics complaints until a bipartisan task force charged with reforming the ethics process finished its work mid-year, and only then would appointments be made to fill out the committee membership. Hansen is also co-chairman, with Joe Kennedy, of the Congressional Task Force on Tobacco and Health; he wants to end all tobacco advertising. One last Hansen cause: disclosure of the terms of private mortgage insurance, which is required on low-down-payment mortgages but which, as Hansen found out with his Crystal City, Virginia, condominium, is very hard to cancel when the borrower has built up the required equity.

Hansen was reelected 68%–30% in 1996.

The People: Pop. 1990: 574,205; 16% rural; 9% age 65+; 92% White; 1% Black; 2% Asian; 1% Amer. Indian; 5% Hispanic origin. Households: 69% married couple families; 40% married couple fams. w. children; 57% college educ.; median household income: $30,563; per capita income: $10,856; median gross rent: $364; median house value: $68,800.

1996 Presidential Vote

Dole (R)	129,273	(59%)
Clinton (D)	64,104	(29%)
Perot (I)	22,893	(10%)
Other	4,548	(2%)

1992 Presidential Vote

Bush (R)	115,627	(47%)
Perot (I)	68,884	(28%)
Clinton (D)	50,622	(20%)
Other	12,989	(5%)

Rep. James V. Hansen (R)

Elected 1980; b. Aug. 14, 1932, Salt Lake City; home, Farmington; U. of UT, B.A. 1960; Mormon; married (Ann).

Career: Navy, 1951–55; Insurance agent; Land developer; Farmington City Cncl., 1962–72; UT House of Reps., 1972–80, Speaker, 1978–80.

DC Office: 2466 RHOB 20515, 202-225-0453; Fax: 202-225-5857.

District Offices: Ogden, 801-625-5677; St. George, 801-628-1071.

Committees: *National Security* (6th of 30 R): Military Procurement; Military Readiness. *Resources* (3rd of 27 R): Forests & Forest Health; National Parks & Public Lands (Chmn.). *Standards of Official Conduct* (Chmn. of 5 R).

Group Ratings

	ADA	ACLU	AFS	LCV	CFA	CON	NFIB	COC	ACU	NTLC	CHC
1996	0	6	0	23	15	11	97	100	100	100	93
1995	0	—	—	0	0	53	—	100	92	—	—

National Journal Ratings

	1995 LIB		1995 CONS	1996 LIB		1996 CONS
Economic	0%	—	74%	0%	—	82%
Social	32%	—	65%	14%	—	77%
Foreign	0%	—	85%	21%	—	72%

Key Votes of the 104th Congress

1. Reduce Medicare Growth $	Y	5. Flag Amendment	Y	9. Cuban Embargo	Y
2. Ovrd. Product Liab. Veto	Y	6. Drop EPA Limits	N	10. Bar Bosnia Troop $	Y
3. Increase Min. Wage	N	7. Repeal Assault-Weap. Ban	Y	11. Cut Anti-Missile Defense	N
4. Welfare Reform	Y	8. Ovrd. Part. Birth Veto	Y	12. Bar U.N. Uniforms	*

Election Results

1996 general	James V. Hansen (R)	150,126	(68%)	($274,156)
	Gregory J. Sanders (D)	65,866	(30%)	($72,989)
	Others	3,787	(2%)	
1996 primary	James V. Hansen (R)	unopposed		
1994 general	James V. Hansen (R)	104,954	(65%)	($348,036)
	Bobbie Coray (D)	57,664	(35%)	($276,892)

SECOND DISTRICT

The center of Utah and of the Mormon Church is Temple Square, illuminated by 300,000 lights during Christmas week, and nestled beneath the towering, snow-capped mountains that flank Salt Lake City. Here you can find the Mormon Tabernacle, home of the famous choir, and the Temple itself, crowned with the golden angel Moroni. Two long blocks north is the state Capitol, four blocks south is City Hall and all around are Salt Lake City's impressive skyscrapers. Ironically, Salt Lake City is the least Mormon and most cosmopolitan part of Utah, with the state university and businesses bringing in outsiders. Some think it now has a non-Mormon majority, but most likely it doesn't; it grew nearly 18% in the 1980s, and the metro area has 1.1 million people now, but that growth is in large part internally generated by Utah's large Mormon families.

Utah's 2d Congressional District, which includes most of Salt Lake County, has somewhat fewer families and children than the other two Utah districts. Its boundaries exclude the western suburbs on the flats out toward the Great Salt Lake, which lean toward the Democrats—an attempt by the Republican legislature to help Republican chances. The 2d has most of Utah's affluent people, living in Salt Lake City and suburbs like East Millcreek, Holladay and Cottonwood, right next to the Wasatch Mountains which rise at that point to 9,000 feet. It's just a 20-minute drive—well, 30—from offices to ski slopes, as Utah boosters like to tell prospective new residents. The district also includes a string of suburbs south of Salt Lake City—West Jordan, South Jordan, Murray, Sandy, Draper, Riverton, Bluffdale. By national standards, this is a Republican district, but it is the most Democratic of Utah's three House seats, and in fact has been seriously contested in 12 of the last 14 elections.

The congressman from the 2d District is Merrill Cook, a Republican elected in 1996. Cook grew up in Salt Lake City, served as a missionary in Britain, graduated from the University of Utah and Harvard Business School, then worked two years in Cambridge. He returned to Salt Lake City in 1973 and founded Cook Slurry Company, an explosives manufacturer. A conservative Republican, Cook was angered when Republican Governor Norman Bangerter raised taxes; he put a tax rollback and property tax freeze proposition on the ballot and in 1988 ran against Bangerter as an Independent, finishing third with 21% of the vote. He put two more propositions on the ballot, a removal of the sales tax on food in 1990 and term limits in 1994; the latter was defeated after the legislature passed 12-year limits for state officials. He also ran for governor again in 1992, finishing second to Republican Mike Leavitt with 34% of the vote. In 1994 he ran in the 2d District, coming in third with 18%, behind incumbent Democrat Karen Shepherd (36%) and Republican Enid Greene Waldholtz (46%). By early 1995 it seemed Cook's running days were over: he had said he would not run again if he lost, Leavitt had become an exceedingly popular governor, and there seemed no way to oust an attractive Republican like Waldholtz from the 2d District seat.

But Waldholtz turned out to have problems—to say the least. She had run (as Enid Greene) and lost in 1992, spending $446,000; in August 1993 she married Joe Waldholtz, reportedly a rich political operative from Pennsylvania, and in 1994 she spent $1,976,000, some $1.6 million of it supposedly her own money. She made news in Congress when she got a seat on the Rules Committee and when she announced in March 1995 that she was pregnant. But she could not answer questions about her personal finances and how she had paid for the campaign, and in November 1995 Joe Waldholtz disappeared for several days before turning himself over to the police; she announced she was seeking a divorce. It became clear that he had embezzled the money from her father; she said he had passed it off as his own. Enid Greene—she changed her name back—held a five-hour televised press conference to apologize and answer questions. In March 1996, she finally bowed to pressure from Utah and Washington and announced she would not seek reelection. Joe Waldholtz was charged with bank fraud and falsifying campaign spending reports in May 1996 and pleaded guilty in June.

Given this opening, Cook ran again despite his pledge to the contrary. Many Republicans resented Cook's previous Independent candidacy, and he got just barely enough votes at the May 1996 party convention to make it onto the primary ballot. His primary opponent Todd Neilson, a forensic accountant who worked on the case against savings and loan magnate Charles Keating, charged that Cook would cut Social Security; Cook had written his Harvard Business School thesis on how to make Social Security fiscally sound, and favored restructuring and portable private pensions. Cook, spending liberally of his own money, just barely beat Neilson, 52%–48%. "To anybody who ever flunked a test or got fired from a job or lost a political race—lost six races—my message is try once more." In the Democratic primary state legislator Kelly Atkinson lost 56%–44% to Ross Anderson, who opposed the death penalty and said he would vote against the Defense of Marriage Act—a sign of how liberal the Democratic core constituency is in Salt Lake City. In the general election Cook again peppered the district with

TV ads and mailings, spending $1 million altogether, $866,000 of it his own. Cook emphasized taxes, Social Security, and the death penalty. He ran ads charging that Anderson once referred to Utahns as murderers for executing a black man and said that Anderson backed same-sex marriage. In the last week Anderson ran a defensive ad, saying he wouldn't go to Congress advocating same-sex marriages; Cook was running ads showing Senator Bob Bennett and former Senator Jake Garn speaking highly of him. Cook won 55%–42%, and in 1998 will try to be the first member reelected here since 1990.

In the House Cook serves on the Transportation and Infrastructure Committee, important because Utah wants to enlarge I-15 in Salt Lake County in time for the 2002 Winter Olympics, and also on Banking and Science. He backs Dick Armey's 17% flat tax and making IRS agents personally responsible for mistreating taxpayers.

The People: Pop. 1990: 574,412; 9% age 65+; 92% White; 1% Black; 2% Asian; 1% Amer. Indian; 5% Hispanic origin. Households: 60% married couple families; 34% married couple fams. w. children; 62% college educ.; median household income: $30,960; per capita income: $12,971; median gross rent: $379; median house value: $76,700.

1996 Presidential Vote			**1992 Presidential Vote**		
Dole (R)	111,166	(47%)	Bush (R)	101,169	(38%)
Clinton (D)	96,037	(41%)	Clinton (D)	81,233	(31%)
Perot (I)	22,143	(9%)	Perot (I)	75,921	(29%)
Other	6,619	(3%)			

Rep. Merrill Cook (R)

Elected 1996; b. May 6, 1946, Philadelphia, PA; home, Salt Lake City; U. of UT, B.A. 1969; Harvard U., M.B.A. 1971; Mormon, married (Camille).

Career: Mgmt. Consultant & Budget Analyst, Arthur D. Little Inc., 1971–73; Pres. & Founder, Cook Slurry Co., 1973–96.

DC Office: 1431 LHOB 20515, 202-225-3011; Fax: 202-225-5638; e-mail: merrill.cook@mail.house.gov.

District Offices: Salt Lake City, 801-524-4394.

Committees: *Banking & Financial Services* (22nd of 30 R): Capital Markets, Securities & Government Sponsored Enterprises; Domestic & International Monetary Policy; Housing & Community Opportunity. *Science* (21st of 25 R): Space & Aeronautics; Technology. *Transportation & Infrastructure* (32nd of 40 R): Aviation; Surface Transportation.

Group Ratings and Key Votes: Newly Elected

Election Results

1996 general	Merrill Cook (R)	129,963	(55%)	($1,061,793)
	Ross Anderson (D)	100,283	(42%)	($491,738)
	Others	6,075	(3%)	
1996 primary	Merrill Cook (R)	18,507	(52%)	
	R. Todd Neilson (R)	17,257	(48%)	
1994 general	Enid Greene Waldholtz (R)	85,507	(46%)	($1,976,289)
	Karen Shepherd (D)	66,911	(36%)	($1,009,176)
	Merrill Cook (I)	34,167	(18%)	($878,528)

THIRD DISTRICT

The heartland of the Mormon Church in America is in a geographically isolated valley between 11,000-foot peaks of the Wasatch Range and the shores of Utah Lake. Here is Provo, the home of Brigham Young University, an institution long known for the rigorously conservative views of its faculty, the old-fashioned moral standards it encourages and its welcoming of technological innovation. The Mormon commonwealth, after all, started off with a terrific shortage of both labor and water and was eager to use technology to make up for this and prosper in this fearsome terrain. Today this is one of America's high-tech centers, the home of WordPerfect and Novell and hundreds of other firms, some fleeing California's high taxes and cultural liberalism.

The 3d Congressional District of Utah includes Provo and Utah County and most of the west side of Salt Lake City and its suburb of West Valley. These two urban areas cast more than two-thirds of the district's votes; the rest are cast in towns scattered amid huge mountains, florid rock formations and deep canyons from Wyoming down to the Arizona border. Its northernmost point is in the Wasatch Range, and it includes the depressed uranium country in eastern Utah around Moab and the surreal rock formations of Canyonlands and Capitol Reef National Parks. Utah County is one of the most heavily Republican areas in the United States, and the 3d District was the number one Republican district in the 1980 presidential election. Republican redistricters for 1992, however, added the Democratic west side of Salt Lake County to make the 2d District more Republican, which strengthened Democrats marginally in the 3d.

The congressman from the 3d District is Chris Cannon, a Republican elected in 1996—with a big boost from Bill Clinton. Cannon is a great-grandson of Utah's first territorial delegate and counselor to Church President Brigham Young, George Q. Cannon, who had five wives and a lot of progeny. He grew up in Salt Lake City, practiced law, and from 1983–86 worked, sometimes controversially, in the Reagan Interior and Commerce Departments, on coal surface mining and other issues. In 1987, with his brother Joe, he purchased and reopened the Geneva Steel plant near Provo, restoring 2,500 jobs. In 1988 they had a dispute about modernizing the plant. In 1990 Chris Cannon was bought out and set up his own venture capital investment firm, which invested in Onyx Graphics (imaging software), Unibase (data processing, data entry, software), Kyzen (environmentally sensitive high-tech cleaning chemicals), Premium Beef of Nebraska (slaughterhouse). He was active in Republican politics, as was Joe, who ran for the Senate in 1992 and lost the primary 51%–49% to Bob Bennett.

In 1996 Cannon ran for the 3d District seat held by Democrat Bill Orton. Orton first won the seat in 1990, by 58%–36%, after a fractious Republican primary. His voting record was moderate to conservative, close to the most conservative of any Democrat; he opposed the 1993 tax increase and the Brady bill and supported means-testing entitlements and the Blue Dog budget. "I've worked hard to be an independent voice of reason for Utah. I've always put principle before politics," he said. In the Republican primary, Cannon faced Tom Draschil who called Cannon (a backer of Lamar Alexander for president) too moderate; Cannon said that Draschil was an extremist and had a lawn sign backing militia favorite Bo Gritz for president in 1992. Cannon won by only 56%–44%—a sign of how conservative the Republican core vote is here.

In the general election, Cannon was helped by his wealth: he spent $1.8 million altogether, $1.5 million of it his own money, against Orton's $709,000. He was helped also when in September 1996, speaking in Arizona and without consultation with Utah officials (including Orton), Bill Clinton announced that he was establishing a 1.7 million-acre Grand Staircase-Escalante National Monument in southern Utah. This was heartily opposed in the area: much of the land is owned by a state school fund, which wanted to lease it for coal mining, and now would not get the revenue; and locals were busy turning trails into roads which federal officials legally couldn't close. Cannon ran an ad showing himself denim-clad, leading a horse, attacking Clinton, "I feel like I'm back in the 1850s again with the federal government encamped all around us."

Orton responded, "It doesn't facilitate working toward solutions to use the rhetoric of a war on government." But he said the designation was "a monumental blunder—pun intended." Polls showed Orton ahead, and but the downdraft of the Clinton candidacy was powerful: Bob Dole carried the district 58%–29%. Orton proclaimed that he had never voted a straight-party ticket in his life, but very many of his constituents did. Orton still carried the Salt Lake County portion, but Cannon won solidly in the Provo area and carried most of the rural counties, winning 51%–47%.

In the House Cannon serves on the Resources, Judiciary and Science Committees. He favors limiting the financial impact of the new Monument and narrowing the law under which it was declared, and says that Conoco should be able to prospect for oil there under an existing lease. He called for a two-year moratorium on a proposal for a 5.7 million acre wilderness bill, and pointed out that it would cover an area three times the size of chief sponsor Maurice Hinchey's Upstate New York district, but Hinchey said no. But Cannon did favor adding 3,500-acre Lost Spring Canyon to Arches National Park. In January 1997 Cannon was attacked because some of his companies paid their taxes late, but a spokesman said he was no Enid Greene.

The People: Pop. 1990: 574,233; 23% rural; 8% age 65+; 90% White; 2% Asian; 3% Amer. Indian; 5% Hispanic origin. Households: 68% married couple families; 41% married couple fams. w. children; 54% college educ.; median household income: $26,570; per capita income: $9,259; median gross rent: $358; median house value: $59,800.

1996 Presidential Vote

Dole (R)	121,472	(58%)
Clinton (D)	61,492	(29%)
Perot (I)	21,425	(10%)
Other	4,456	(2%)

1992 Presidential Vote

Bush (R)	105,836	(46%)
Perot (I)	58,595	(25%)
Clinton (D)	51,574	(22%)
Other	14,245	(6%)

Rep. Christopher B. Cannon (R)

Elected 1996; b. Oct. 20, 1950, Salt Lake City; home, Mapleton; Brigham Young U., B.S. 1974, J.D. 1980; Mormon; married (Claudia).

Career: Practicing atty., 1980–83; Dpty. Assoc. Solicitor, Dept. of Interior, 1983–84, Assoc. Solicitor, 1984–86; Co-owner, Geneva Steel, 1987–90; Founder, Cannon Industries Inc., 1990–96.

DC Office: 118 CHOB 20515, 202-225-7751; Fax: 202-225-5629; e-mail: cannonut03@mail.house.gov.

District Offices: Provo, 801-379-2500.

Committees: *Judiciary* (20th of 20 R): Courts & Intellectual Property; Immigration & Claims. *Resources* (21st of 27 R): Energy & Mineral Resources; Water & Power. *Science* (19th of 25 R): Space & Aeronautics; Technology.

Group Ratings and Key Votes: Newly Elected

Election Results

1996 general	Christopher B. Cannon (R)	106,220	(51%)	($1,826,849)
	Bill Orton (D)	98,178	(47%)	($708,778)
	Others	3,317	(2%)	
1996 primary	Christopher B. Cannon (R)	27,738	(56%)	
	Tom Draschil (R)	22,178	(44%)	
1994 general	Bill Orton (D)	91,505	(59%)	($278,477)
	Dixie Thompson (R)	61,839	(40%)	($114,884)

VERMONT

Maple syrup, snowy tracks through the woods, tiny clapboard villages, mountains seemingly carpeted in green: this is the image of Vermont. This is an antique state, almost as carefully preserved as its Shelburne Museum, with a barn and jail, railroad station and blacksmith shop and covered bridge and 37 buildings of folk art. Vermont, wrote native Dorothy Canfield Fisher half a century ago, "represents the past, is a piece of the past in the midst of the present and future." Today, reverence for that past has made Vermont, for many Americans approaching the 21st Century, a guide to a congenial future. Vermont's closeness to nature, the intimacy of its small communities, its 114 covered bridges, its lack of unattractive accoutrements of early 20th Century industrialism have all made it a kind of promised land for urban expatriates: the state that missed out on U.S. Steel now produces Ben & Jerry's Ice Cream. By the 1980s, for the first time in nearly 200 years, Vermont became a growth area: in an era when Americans are increasingly ill-served by the rigidities of big organizations and repelled by big-city congestion, small businesses and computers enable more and more Americans to make their livings where they want, which often means Vermont.

Vermont was first settled by flinty Yankees from Connecticut, and showed an independent streak from the beginning. After Ethan Allen's Green Mountain Boys repulsed the British in 1777, this was an independent republic for 14 years, claimed by New York and New Hampshire without avail, their argument settled when Vermont was admitted as the 14th state in 1791. The economy at first was agricultural, as second sons and daughters from small New England farms struggled to scratch out livings from the rocky soil. In time they quit struggling and raised dairy cows instead, producing milk for the masses of New York City. But Vermont developed commerce as well. With its legendary thriftiness, it accumulated capital that, invested wisely, was used to build the solid stone office buildings and courthouses, the thick-timbered houses and gold-topped state Capitol that have remained long after ramshackle wooden buildings of the 19th Century have crumbled into dust. But Vermont never developed labor-intensive industry, and so over the years it exported people, and aged. Today, millions of Americans have Vermont blood—far more than the half million who live here now, many of whom have no Vermont roots at all. Two presidents were born here, but both made their careers elsewhere—Chester Arthur in New York, Calvin Coolidge in Massachusetts—while Vermont made no visible impression on two great writers who lived here for years—Rudyard Kipling and Aleksander Solzhenitsyn. From 1850 to the 1960s, as a result of continuous outmigration, Vermont's population hovered between 300,000 and 400,000.

Since then—perhaps the key date was 1963, when people started outnumbering cows—Vermont has changed rapidly. Its economy has boomed, led by leisure-time industries—ski resorts, summer homes—and IBM, with several big high-tech facilities around the Burlington area on the mostly undeveloped shores of glorious Lake Champlain. Vermont's tradition of cottage industries continues, with knitters seeking to overturn union-inspired federal bans on home production. Home-grown firms started by erstwhile Baby Boom rebels—Ben & Jerry's Ice Cream is the archetype—have flourished. The population rose from 390,000 in 1960 to 444,000 in 1970, 511,000 in 1980 and 589,000 in 1996, and it hasn't been random settlement. While next-door New Hampshire, trumpeting its low taxes and aversion to government, has attracted right-leaning migrants from Massachusetts happy to live in spanking-new developments and ravenous for low taxes, Vermont, proclaiming its desire to preserve the environment and the past, has attracted left-leaning migrants from New York and elsewhere, willing to pay higher taxes and higher prices for the privilege of living in a seemingly pristine setting where the governor tries to confine Wal-Marts to the existing tiny downtowns. The result has been growth, not as lusty as

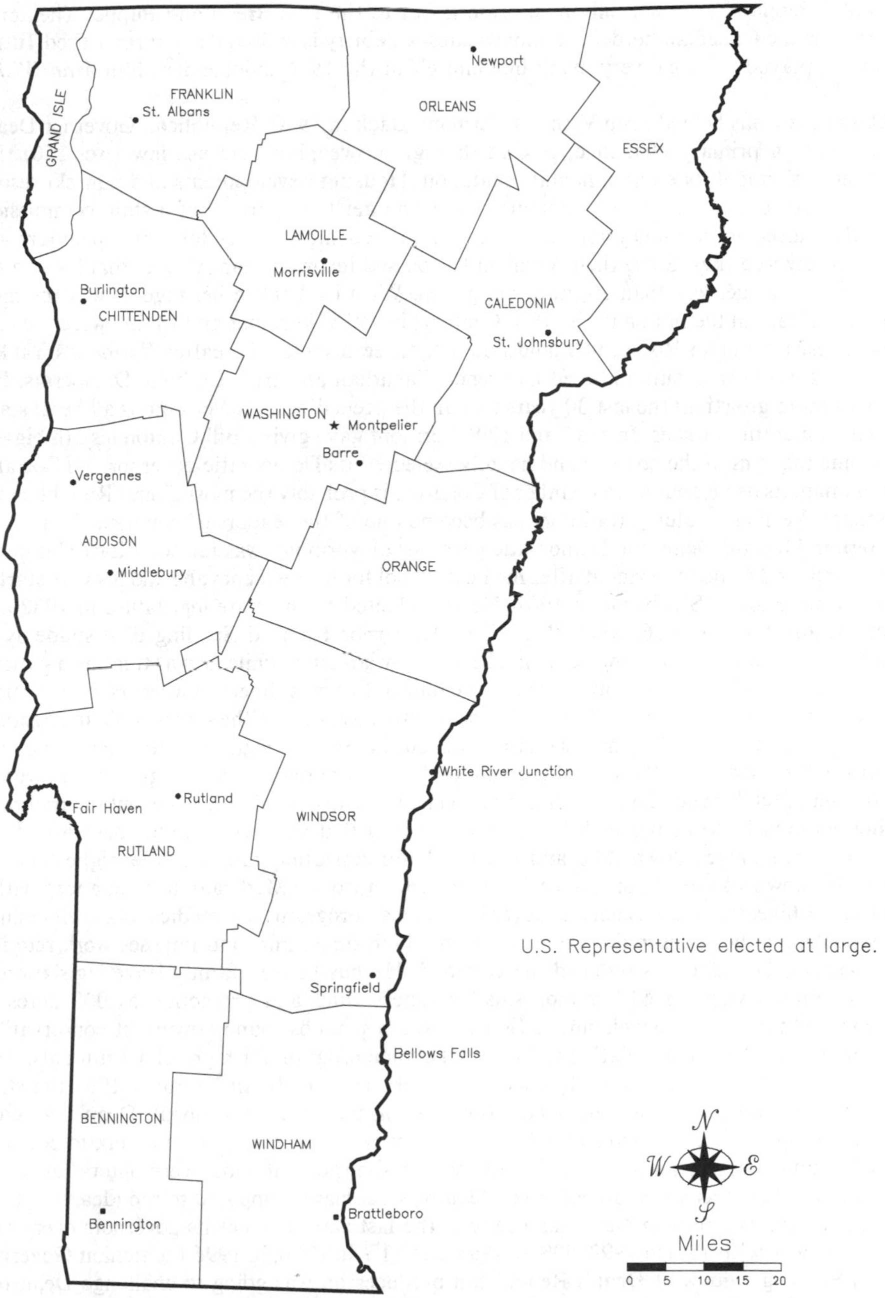
GRAND ISLE
FRANKLIN
St. Albans
ORLEANS
Newport
ESSEX
LAMOILLE
Morrisville
CALEDONIA
St. Johnsbury
Burlington
CHITTENDEN
WASHINGTON
Montpelier
Barre
Vergennes
ADDISON
Middlebury
ORANGE
White River Junction
Fair Haven
Rutland
RUTLAND
WINDSOR
Springfield
Bellows Falls
BENNINGTON
Bennington
WINDHAM
Brattleboro
U.S. Representative elected at large.
N
W
E
S
Miles
0 5 10 15 20

New Hampshire's but also without as big a recession in the early 1990s. There is high-tech growth around Burlington but also a high dependence on tourism; as Vermont Preservation Trust Director Paul Bruhn says, "At least 30% of our economy is based upon Vermont being Vermont." People throng not only to ski resorts but to the free Bread and Puppet Theater in Glover, near the Canadian border. Vermont's latest celebrity is retired dairy farmer Fred Tuttle, who at 77, played someone very much like himself in the 1996 independent film *Man With a Plan.*

Public policy has helped keep Vermont Vermont. Back in 1970, Republican Governor Deane Davis, facing a primary challenge, pushed through a sweeping land use law (Act 250) that helped give Vermont its environmental reputation. Housing developments and new ski resorts were required to meet ten environmental criteria and get the approval of a state commission. Davis also raised more money for education, authorized higher fines for water polluters and liberalized divorce laws. Since then, Vermont has passed its own Clean Air Act that levies a tax on new cars that get less than 20 miles per gallon. With its Yankee heritage, it was the most Republican state in the nation in the 19th Century; in 1936, Vermont and Maine were the only states to resist Franklin Roosevelt's landslide. For three decades thereafter Vermont's Yankee Protestant Republicans outnumbered its French Canadian and Irish Catholic Democrats. But now, with more growth in the last 30 years than in the preceding 110, Vermont is a liberal state, especially on cultural issues. In 1992 and 1996 Vermont gave giving Bill Clinton his 5th biggest percentage margins in the country and handily reelected its Democratic governor and Socialist congressman; its one Republican member of Congress is probably the most liberal Republican in the Senate. Vermont, valuing tradition, has become one of the leaders of America's left.

Governor. Howard Dean, the Democratic governor of Vermont, was raised in East Hampton, Long Island, and came to Vermont after medical school for his residency; he and his wife started a medical practice in Shelburne in 1981. He was elected to the state legislature in 1982 and lieutenant governor in 1986; when Republican Governor Richard Snelling died suddenly in August 1991, Dean was given the news that he was now governor while he was treating a patient. Pleasant and articulate, he is probably one of the four or five most liberal governors in the nation.

Not surprisingly, Dean's major issue has been health care. In 1992 he signed a bill to negotiate with insurance companies for universal insurance; but in 1993 his legislation was rejected by the legislature, foreshadowing the fate of the Clinton healthcare plan in Washington. He moved to promote early childhood development, and pushed a Success By Six prevention program, offering home visits to homes with babies, and claimed that as a result child abuse was down 30%, teen pregnancies down 20% and the child immunization rate was the highest in the country. He now seeks health insurance for all children, through Medicaid, to be financed with a cigarette tax hike. But Dean is not a believer in giveaway programs: his medical plans all include co-payments, and he sponsored a welfare reform which time-limits and imposes work requirements on recipients and has reduced the caseload. He has backed family leave legislation, a higher minimum wage, a $14 million small business fund and protecting 51,000 acres of farmland and forest from development. Some of Dean's stands sound downright conservative. He supports electricity deregulation and a school choice program for high school students; 25% of them, in rural areas with no high schools, have choice already. In February 1997 the state Supreme Court declared the state school funding formula unconstitutional; Dean favored a state-wide property tax on non-residential property over an increase in income tax to equalize school funding. Despite an authorized study which showed that most Vermonters favor the legalization of hemp as an industrial crop, Dean was adamantly opposed to the idea.

Vermont with its non-twin New Hampshire is the last state to elect its governors every two years. Dean won with 75% in 1992, 69% in 1994 and 71% in 1996; in 1996 Lieutenant Governor Barbara Snelling, widow of Dean's Republican predecessor, was going to challenge Dean but withdrew in June for health reasons. Democrats elected a Democratic lieutenant governor, Douglas Racine, and took control of the state Senate, 17–13, and widened their lead in the state House to 89–57. In May 1997, the legislature passed a campaign finance reform bill, backed by

Dean, to create a publicly-funded campaign finance system and set mandatory spending limits on state races. Dean could be a strong candidate for Jim Jeffords's Senate seat in 2000.

Senior Senator. Patrick Leahy has held public office for most of his adult life. He grew up in Burlington, went to Georgetown Law School, returned home to Burlington to practice law. He was elected Chittenden County State's Attorney in 1966, at 26, and, after eight years in that post—and few public officials are scrutinized as closely as a local prosecutor—he was elected to the U.S. Senate at 34, the first and so far only Democratic senator elected in Vermont history. Now he is in his third decade in the Senate and his second stint in the minority party.

Leahy's major legislative achievement in the 104th Congress was enactment of the 1996 Freedom to Farm Act. As chairman of Agriculture from 1987–95 and ranking Democrat from 1995–97 he worked closely with Indiana Republican Richard Lugar. Unlike Farm Belt senators, Leahy had no major subsidy program to defend except dairy, which is *sui generis* and has far fewer farmers than it has had in the past. He helped pass the 1990 farm bill, which pared subsidies and sought to promote environmental causes, a 1994 crop insurance reform and the 1994 Leahy-Lugar Act that closed down 1100 USDA offices and promises to save $3.5 billion over the next several years—the first of Vice President Al Gore's Reinventing Government initiatives to be passed. On the Freedom to Farm Act, he accepted the seven-year phaseout of most farm subsidies and transitional payments, but in a deal brokered in February 1996 got the conservation, rural development and nutrition provisions he wanted, including reauthorization of food stamps; he also got the Northeast Dairy Compact, allowing a commission to set milk prices in the six New England states. Separately the Senate passed Leahy's Northern Forests bill, to protect privately owned New England and Upstate New York forests; the House did not act and Leahy will try again in the 105th Congress.

On two other major issues Leahy left a distinctive mark. A gadgeteer and fine amateur photographer, he was one of the first senators to go on-line and use the Internet—a "cyber-Senator," as he is often described, who early on conducted electronic town meetings with Vermonters on the Internet. On the Judiciary Committee, he opposed the Clinton Administration's Clipper Chip encryption, which he thought might violate property rights, and with Montana's Conrad Burns favored relaxing controls on exports of encryption technology. He was the Senate's leading opponent of the Communications Decency Act censoring the Internet. He also sponsored a bill signed in October 1996 to update the Freedom of Information Act to provide on-line access to government documents. The other distinctive Leahy issue is landmines. Since 1989, he has been crusading against the export and use of landmines, which are easy and cheap to implant and difficult and expensive to remove, and which injure thousands of civilians long after hostilities have ended. In 1992 he got a one-year moratorium on U.S. export of landmines, since renewed; in 1994 he got the United Nations to approve unanimously their eventual elimination. In February 1997 the Clinton Administration refused to join a Canadian-led treaty banning landmines because China and Russia had not signed on, but Secretary of State Madeleine Albright and Secretary of Defense William Cohen have supported restrictions, and Leahy will be pressing for an international agreement and U.S. ratification.

Leahy is now the ranking Democrat on the Judiciary Committee. As he said in 1996, "I didn't think much of the seniority system when I first got here. But now that I've had a chance to study it for 22 years I understand it a whole lot better." He is part of the liberal bloc on the Committee, voting against Republican nominees for the Supreme Court and criticizing Republicans for not acting on Clinton judicial appointees. He successfully moved to get rid of the $1 per person border crossing fee in the 1996 Immigration Act. He got a Justice for Victims of Terrorism Act included in the anti-terrorism bill and is sponsoring a juvenile crime bill and one to extend the racketeering law to cover counterfeiting of goods and copyright infringement. On the Appropriations Committee, he has moved to deny aid or arms sales to governments which violate human rights and pushed for continued federal funding of international family planning programs.

To his record, among the most liberal in the Senate in some years, Leahy brings the parsimony consonant with Vermont tradition, and a quiet, thoughtful temperament. But he also has a zest for life and a puckish sense of humor, part of the Yankee heritage of Vermont, though his Irish and Italian ethnic origin is certainly not standard Yankee. His standing in Vermont has been strong over the years: he survived the Republican sweep in 1980 and beat popular Governor Richard Snelling 63%–35% in 1986. In 1992, against Republican state Treasurer Jim Douglas, who attacked him for voting for the congressional pay raise and for the loss of dairy jobs, he won 54%–43%—a decisive margin, but no landslide. But his job approval rating in early 1997 was high and one potential opponent, state Senator Susan Sweetser, ran poorly in the 1996 House race. Possible 1998 challengers include Rutland Mayor Jeff Wennberg, former state Senator Sara Gear, state Representative Walter Freed and former Lieutenant Governor Barbara Snelling.

Junior Senator. Jim Jeffords is known, since he was first elected to the House in 1974, for having one of the most liberal records of all Republicans. Jeffords grew up in Rutland, son of a Vermont chief justice, went to Yale, served in the Navy, went to Harvard Law School and then returned to Shrewsbury in the Green Mountains and practiced law. He was elected state senator in 1966, at 32, and then state attorney general in 1968 and 1970. In 1974, he was elected to the House and in 1988, when Senator Robert Stafford retired, to the Senate. There he has had a record somewhat to the left of midpoint of the Senate, especially on cultural issues, and has usually voted more often with Democrats than any other Republican senator. In the Clinton years he voted for family and medical leave, motor voter, national service, the Brady bill and the 1994 crime package, despite anti-gun control feeling in Vermont; in July 1993 he announced he was supporting the not-yet-written Clinton healthcare plan—the only Republican member of Congress who ever did. He pushed for more funding for the National Endowment for the Arts, supported raising the minimum wage, supports abortion rights, favors banning discrimination against gays and lesbians. As chairman of the District of Columbia Subcommittee on Appropriations in the 104th Congress, Jeffords opposed the Republican plan for a limited number of school vouchers for students in the District, thus sentencing them to continue in the dreadful D.C. public schools, which with he must be familiar; he volunteers in the Everyone Wins! program in Capitol Hill schools to encourage kids to read.

In 1997 Jeffords became chairman of the Labor and Human Resources Committee. Some conservatives wanted to substitute the less senior and more conservative Dan Coats; but Majority Leader Trent Lott, desirous of party unity and part of a singing quartet with Jeffords, persuaded Coats not to oppose Jeffords. Of his approach, Jeffords said, "The country demands that we be bipartisan. They're more involved in solving difficult situations we have for individuals, more than they are with political posturing and all. So, that's me. I'm independent, these are all well-known facts." But he also was careful not to block Republican initiatives: "I have told the members if we disagree, I won't hold up legislation that all Republicans except me want." His own stated policy goals seem almost quixotic: raising dollar limits on health insurance policies (he tried and failed to do that in the 1996 Healthcare Portability Act), increasing the percentage of the nation's workforce covered by company pensions, getting more people health insurance. But as chairman he took the lead on the Republican-backed TEAM Act to allow worker-management consultation, vehemently opposed by labor unions. On health care he promised "to go slow" on regulating managed care and said that micromanagement, such as the 48-hour maternity stay he backed in 1996, should be approached with caution. He promised to move ahead on OSHA reform, a Republican goal. He worked on rauthorization of the bipartisan IDEA special education bill, which passed in May 1997, and promised to work on reauthorizing the Higher Education Act. He supported the Kennedy-Hatch child health insurance bill and tobacco tax, but advanced his own bill, making the program optional for states.

Jeffords also tends to Vermont issues and his own special causes. In 1996 he maintained support for Vermont wind and solar energy projects, and he passed an amendment to increase food stamp eligibility for recipients of federal heating assistance. A history buff, he had a bill to catalogue and study unprotected Civil War sites, has sponsored a Revolutionary War and War of 1812 historic preservation study act and backs an historic corridor along the New York-

Vermont border.

In 1988 Jeffords's toughest hurdle in winning the seat in 1988 was the Republican primary, in which a conservative opponent attacked him on gun control, abortion, and church and family issues, but Jeffords won 61%–39%. In 1994 his serious competition was in the general. State Senator Jan Backus clearly benefited from being a woman in this culturally liberal state and, though little known and not well financed, held Jeffords to a 50%–41% win. Jeffords's seat does not come up until 2000, too long to allow any worthwhile predictions here; one serious Democratic opponent could be Governor Howard Dean.

Representative-At-Large. The 1990s will go down as the decade in which socialism was rejected all over the world—except in Vermont. At least in House elections: for Vermont has four times now elected Bernie Sanders, self-proclaimed Socialist, to Congress. Sanders is not just a Socialist, but also very much a modern Vermonter: the son of a Flatbush paint salesman, he came here as part of the hippie invasion of 1968. His rumpled, tieless, sincere persona helped him win election as mayor of Burlington in 1981 by 10 votes, after losing four statewide races. There he governed ably for eight years, using the city's prosperity to start a municipal day-care center, expand low- and moderate-income housing, put a pollution control facility on Lake Champlain and switch the tax base from property to hotel and restaurant fees and a utility tax on companies using certain public facilities. In 1990, he ran for Congress and reversed his defeat by Republican Peter Smith two years before, by capitalizing on Smith's support of the 1990 budget summit agreement and his vote for the ban on semiautomatic weapons. The National Rifle Association came out against Smith, and Sanders' opposition to gun control—Vermont is the only state with no limits on gun ownership at all—helped this urban-based Socialist carry 227 of Vermont's 251 cities and towns, and three gores and one grant. Sanders became only the third Socialist elected to the House, after Victor Berger of Milwaukee (1911–13, 1923–29) and Meyer London of Manhattan's Lower East Side (1915–23), and the only Socialist elected by an entire state.

Sanders's Socialist label doesn't matter much in the House. Initially Democrats balked at accepting him in their caucus, but they have granted him seniority as a Democrat since 1991, gave him ranking minority position on a Governmental Affairs subcommittee in 1997 over the objections of Elijah Cummings and, when a Democrat had the effrontery to run against him in 1996, none less than George Stephanopoulos came to Burlington to speak at a Sanders fundraiser. But Sanders adds to an almost perfectly liberal voting record his own particular stamp. He formed a Progressive Caucus, with 58 members in the 104th Congress, with what is for the moment a quixotic agenda: progressive tax reform, a Canadian-style single-payer healthcare system, a 50% cut in military spending over five years, a national energy policy and—here Vermont speaks—support for family farms (including opposition to bovine growth hormone). But Sanders has also been a practical and sometimes successful legislator, gaining Republican allies in targeting what they consider corporate welfare. With Chris Smith of New Jersey, for example, he passed an amendment barring Defense spending for defense contractor mergers ("payoffs for layoffs"), and he passed another barring defense spending on bonuses for defense contractor executives. With Budget Chairman John Kasich, he got the House to pass a three-year phaseout of OPIC, which provides risk insurance for foreign investments. He passed another amendment, which turned out to be moot, limiting taxpayer liability for the Mexican peso bailout. With Gerald Solomon, whose Upstate New York district borders Vermont, he battled Wisconsin's Steven Gunderson who was trying to end the milk marketing system; and he was the House's leading backer of the Northeast Dairy Compact which Senator Patrick Leahy got into the 1996 Freedom to Farm Act. Sanders also backed the Indoor Air Quality Act of 1993, retention of low-income heating assistance and the 1996 measure guaranteeing 48-hour maternity stays. He got Majority Leader Dick Armey to agree to a vote in the 105th Congress on the "gag rules"—HMO directives to doctors not to mention procedures not covered by insurance; Sanders has a patient right-to-know bill to prevent "gag rules" in HMOs.

Sanders was reelected 58%–31% in 1992, and considered running against Republican Senator

Jim Jeffords in 1994, but decided not to do so. In 1994, after voting for the assault weapons ban and the crime bill with its gun control provisions, Sanders was opposed by the National Rifle Association-backed Vermont Sportsmen's Coalition. Sanders outspent state Senator John Carroll, but won by only 50%–47%. His gun control stand evidently hurt in rural areas; Sanders carried only 136 cities and towns. In 1996 Republican state Senator Susan Sweetser was expected to be a strong challenger. But the candidacy of moderate Democrat Jack Long, an attorney and former state commissioner of environmental conservation, may have hurt her more than Sanders, given the national Democrats' insistence that Sanders was their candidate against Newt Gingrich, not a popular figure here. And Sweetser had to apologize in September when her opposition researcher contacted Sanders's former wife asking about Sanders' past. Sanders outspent Sweetser $942,000 to $572,000 and won 55%–33%. His rural support seems to have returned; he got 50% or more in every county but Bennington and Essex.

Presidential politics. James A. Farley had a good laugh on Vermont in 1936 when he updated an adage to say "As goes Maine, so goes Vermont." But today's Vermont, liberal on cultural and foreign issues, not tremendously conservative on economics, has little use for conservative Republicans and seems solidly Democratic. Back in 1980, Ronald Reagan got his seventh lowest percentage here and John Anderson his best, 15%; in 1984 and 1988 Vermont was more Democratic than the nation, and in 1992 and 1996 it gave Bill Clinton his fifth largest percentage margins.

The Vermont presidential primary, abolished for 1992, reappeared in 1996. Richard Lugar made this state his last stand, hoping that Vermont's traditions of thoughtful town meeting discourse would enable him to deliver his message. Not enough, it seems: Bob Dole won with 40%, Pat Buchanan had 17%, Steve Forbes had 16%, and Lugar 14%, ahead of Lamar Alexander with 11%.

The People: Est. Pop. 1996: 589,000; Pop. 1990: 562,758, up 4.6% 1990–1996. 0.2% of U.S. total, 49th largest; 68% rural. Median age: 35.7 years. 12% 65 years and older. 98.1% White; 1% Asian; 1% Hispanic origin. Households: 56.4% married couple families; 28% married couple fams. w. children; 46% college educ.; median household income: $29,792; per capita income: $13,527; 69.0% owner occupied housing; median house value: $95,500; median monthly rent: $378. 4.6% Unemployment. 1996 Voting age pop.: 445,000. 1996 Turnout: 258,449; 58% of VAP. Registered voters (1996): 385,328; no party registration.

Political Lineup: Governor, Howard Dean (D); Lt. Gov., Douglas A. Racine (D); Secy. of State, James Milne (R); Atty. Gen., William H. Sorrell (D); Treasurer, James H. Douglas (R); Auditor, Edward S. Flanagan (D). State Senate, 30 (17 D and 13 R); Senate President, Peter Schumlin (D); State House, 150 (89 D, 57 R, 1 I, and 3 Progressive); House Speaker, Michael Obuchowski (D). Senators, Patrick J. Leahy (D) and James M. Jeffords (R). Representative, 1 I at large.

Elections Division: 802-828-2464; **Filing Deadline for U.S. Congress:** July 20, 1998.

1996 Presidential Vote

Clinton (D)	137,894	(53%)
Dole (R)	80,352	(31%)
Perot (I)	31,024	(12%)
Other	9,179	(4%)

1996 Republican Presidential Primary

Dole (R)	23,419	(40%)
Buchanan (R)	9,730	(17%)
Forbes (R)	9,066	(16%)
Lugar (R)	7,881	(14%)
Alexander (R)	6,145	(11%)
Other	1,872	(3%)

1992 Presidential Vote

Clinton (D)	133,592	(46%)
Bush (R)	88,122	(30%)
Perot (I)	65,991	(23%)

GOVERNOR

Gov. Howard Dean (D)

Assumed office, Aug. 1991, term expires Jan. 1999; b. Nov. 17, 1948, New York, NY; home, Burlington; Yale., B.A. 1977, Albert Einstein Col. of Medicine, M.D. 1978; Congregationalist; married (Judith).

Career: Practicing physician, 1981–91; VT House of Reps, 1982–86; VT Lt. Gov., 1986–91.

Office: Pavilion State Office Bldg., 109 State St., Montpelier 05609, 802-828-3333. Fax: 802-828-3339.
Web site: www.state.vt.us.

Election Results

1996 gen.	Howard Dean (D)	179,544	(71%)
	John L. Gropper (R)	57,161	(22%)
	Others	17,943	(7%)
1996 prim.	Howard Dean (D) . unopposed		
1994 gen.	Howard Dean (D)	145,661	(69%)
	David F. Kelley (R)	40,292	(19%)
	Thomas J. Morse (I)	15,000	(7%)
	Others	11,093	(5%)

SENATORS

Sen. Patrick J. Leahy (D)

Elected 1974, seat up 1998; b. Mar. 31, 1940, Montpelier; home, Burlington; St. Michael's Col., B.A. 1961, Georgetown U., J.D. 1964; Catholic; married (Marcelle).

Career: Practicing atty., 1964–74; VT St. Atty., Chittenden Cnty., 1966–74.

DC Office: 433 RSOB 20510, 202-224-4242; e-mail: senator_leahy@leahy.senate.gov.

State Offices: Burlington, 802-863-2525; Montpelier, 802-229-0569.

Committees: *Agriculture, Nutrition & Forestry* (2nd of 8 D): Forestry, Conservation & Rural Revitalization; Research, Nutrition & General Legislation (RMM). *Appropriations* (4th of 13 D): Agriculture, Rural Development & Related Agencies; Defense; Foreign Operations (RMM); Interior; VA, HUD & Independent Agencies. *Judiciary* (RMM of 8 D): Antitrust, Business Rights & Competition.

Group Ratings

	ADA	ACLU	AFS	LCV	CFA	CON	NFIB	COC	ACU	NTLC	CHC
1996	90	59	100	85	93	45	29	23	5	3	7
1995	100	—	100	100	94	54	—	16	0	—	—

National Journal Ratings

	1995 LIB — 1995 CONS			1996 LIB — 1996 CONS		
Economic	97%	—	0%	82%	—	14%
Social	93%	—	0%	67%	—	30%
Foreign	94%	—	3%	93%	—	0%

Key Votes of the 104th Congress

1. Reduce Medicare Growth $	N	5. Flag Amendment	N	9. Anti-Missile Defense	N
2. Lmt. Prod. Liab. Damages	N	6. Endangered Species	Y	10. Cuban Embargo	N
3. Increase Min. Wage	Y	7. Gay Employment Rights	Y	11. Bar Bosnia Troop $	N
4. Welfare Reform	N	8. Ovrd. Part. Birth Veto	Y	12. Cut Vietnam Aid	N

Election Results

1992 general	Patrick J. Leahy (D)	154,762	(54%)	($1,202,445)
	James H. Douglas (R)	123,854	(43%)	($195,737)
	Other	7,123	(2%)	
1992 primary	Patrick J. Leahy (D)	unopposed		
1986 general	Patrick J. Leahy (D)	124,123	(63%)	($1,705,099)
	Richard Snelling (R)	67,798	(35%)	($1,502,304)

Sen. James M. Jeffords (R)

Elected 1988, seat up 2000; b. May 11, 1934, Rutland; home, Shrewsbury; Yale U., B.S. 1956, Harvard, LL.B. 1962; Congregationalist; married (Elizabeth).

Career: Navy, 1956–59, Naval Reserves, 1959–90; Law clerk, 1962–63; Practicing atty., 1963–69, 1973–75; Shrewsbury Repub. Chmn., 1963–74, Town Agent, Grand Juror, 1964; VT Senate, 1966–68; VT Atty. Gen., 1968–72; U.S. House of Reps. 1974–1988.

DC Office: 728 HSOB 20515, 202-224-5141; e-mail: vermont@jeffords.senate.gov.

State Offices: Burlington, 802-658-6001; Montpelier, 802-223-5273; Rutland, 802-773-3875.

Committees: *Finance* (10th of 11 R): Health Care; Social Security & Family Policy; Taxation & IRS Oversight. *Labor & Human Resources* (Chmn. of 10 R); Employment & Training; Public Health & Safety. *Veterans' Affairs* (4th of 7 R). *Aging (Special)* (2nd of 10 R).

Group Ratings

	ADA	ACLU	AFS	LCV	CFA	CON	NFIB	COC	ACU	NTLC	CHC
1996	50	33	29	46	50	96	77	62	45	86	30
1995	55	—	36	64	25	88	—	76	23	—	—

National Journal Ratings

	1995 LIB — 1995 CONS			1996 LIB — 1996 CONS		
Economic	52%	—	47%	50%	—	48%
Social	72%	—	27%	62%	—	37%
Foreign	59%	—	40%	64%	—	34%

Key Votes of the 104th Congress

1. Reduce Medicare Growth $	Y	5. Flag Amendment	N	9. Anti-Missile Defense	N
2. Lmt. Prod. Liab. Damages	Y	6. Endangered Species	Y	10. Cuban Embargo	N
3. Increase Min. Wage	Y	7. Gay Employment Rights	Y	11. Bar Bosnia Troop $	N
4. Welfare Reform	Y	8. Ovrd. Part. Birth Veto	N	12. Cut Vietnam Aid	N

Election Results

1994 general	James M. Jeffords (R)	106,505	(50%)	($1,174,973)
	Jan Backus (D)	85,868	(41%)	($308,069)
	Gavin T. Mills (I)	12,465	(6%)	
	Others	6,834	(3%)	
1994 primary	James M. Jeffords (R)	unopposed		
1988 general	James M. Jeffords (R)	163,183	(70%)	($876,877)
	Bill Gray (D)	71,460	(30%)	($549,908)

REPRESENTATIVE

Rep. Bernard Sanders (I)

Elected 1990; b. Sept. 8, 1941, New York, NY; home, Burlington; U. of Chicago, B.A. 1964; Jewish; married (Jane).

Career: Writer; Dir., Amer. People's History Soc.; Burlington Mayor, 1981–89; Lecturer, Harvard, 1989; Prof., Hamilton Col., 1989–90.

DC Office: 2202 RHOB 20515, 202-225-4115; Fax: 202-225-6790; e-mail: bernie@hr.house.gov

District Offices: Burlington, 802-862-0697.

Committees: *Banking & Financial Services* (1st of 1 I): Domestic & International Monetary Policy; Housing & Community Opportunity. *Government Reform & Oversight* (1st of 1 I): Human Resources; National Economic Growth, Natural Resources & Regulatory Affairs (RMM).

Group Ratings

	ADA	ACLU	AFS	LCV	CFA	CON	NFIB	COC	ACU	NTLC	CHC
1996	100	100	100	85	92	9	19	19	0	10	0
1995	100	—	—	94	100	25	—	13	8	—	—

National Journal Ratings

	1995 LIB — 1995 CONS	1996 LIB — 1996 CONS
Economic	94% — 0%	85% — 11%
Social	88% — 0%	84% — 12%
Foreign	88% — 7%	90% — 0%

Key Votes of the 104th Congress

1. Reduce Medicare Growth $	N	5. Flag Amendment	N	9. Cuban Embargo	N
2. Ovrd. Product Liab. Veto	N	6. Drop EPA Limits	Y	10. Bar Bosnia Troop $	N
3. Increase Min. Wage	Y	7. Repeal Assault-Weap. Ban	N	11. Cut Anti-Missile Defense	Y
4. Welfare Reform	N	8. Ovrd. Part. Birth Veto	N	12. Bar U.N. Uniforms	N

Election Results

1996 general	Bernard Sanders (I)	140,678	(55%)	($942,438)
	Susan W. Sweetser (R)	83,021	(33%)	($572,021)
	Jack Long (D)	23,830	(9%)	($8,504)
	Others	7,177	(3%)	
1996 primary	Bernard Sanders (I)	unopposed		
1994 general	Bernard Sanders (I)	105,502	(50%)	($622,351)
	John Carroll (R)	98,523	(47%)	($387,767)
	Others	7,424	(4%)	

VIRGINIA

In Virginia, traditions endure. Through nearly 400 years of history, Virginians have honored, and sometimes been fixated by, traditions going back to the Revolution and before. For half a century Virginia has been growing lustily, but the first state in the nation to elect a black governor still hews to a course close to its roots. In the first years after World War II, Virginia's growth came mainly from an expanding government, but in recent decades it has come more from a vibrant private sector. The first Virginia was a commonwealth ruled by a landed gentry which was, in the words of historian David Hackett Fischer, "elitist and libertarian." From the tobacco-growing counties emerged in the 1770s a group of leaders—George Washington, Patrick Henry, Thomas Jefferson, Richard Henry Lee, James Madison, James Monroe—who in learning, wisdom and strength of character, equal any such group from any similarly sized polity since Periclean Athens or republican Rome. They were slaveholders who insisted on liberty, armed men living on the marches of civilization who insisted on the rule of law, believers in racial inequality who set forth principles of equality to form the basis of a non-racist society. The Virginia they led into the American Revolution was not only the most populous and richest of the 13 colonies, it also was the indispensable creator of the Republic and the Constitution that has held together the world's greatest democracy.

After the Revolutionary War, gentry control continued even as Virginia was eclipsed in population and wealth by Pennsylvania and New York and, its tobacco fields all but exhausted, became a breeding ground for slaves. But Virginia had two more great heroes, Robert E. Lee and Stonewall Jackson, both of whom reluctantly and brilliantly fought for their state rather than their country. The state's leadership class was impoverished and embittered by the Civil War, so much of which was fought on Virginia soil. Industrialization was haphazard: railroads were constructed to ship cotton up from the South and coal east to the seaports; textile mills were built in Southside towns and tobacco factories in Richmond; the giant Newport News Shipbuilding & Drydock Company was built by railroad magnate Collis Huntington.

But most of Virginia remained agricultural, sunk in a low-wage economy and ruled by a local gentry who had become a small class of landowners, bankers and lawyers worshipping their Revolutionary past and their Lost Cause. They were pessimists, looking not for economic growth but for stability, bent on maintaining Virginia's segregation and content with its second-class economy, determined that the poor masses not use government to pillage the rich as Yankee troops once had done. County courthouse organizations became the political machine of Harry Byrd, who ran Virginia politics from 1925, when he was elected governor, until 1965, when he retired from the Senate. In national politics, this machine lost battles more often than Lee lost on the field, and less gallantly. But the machine succeeded in keeping most vestiges of the welfare state and racial equality out of Virginia, to the point of closing public schools in the 1950s rather than obeying federal court desegregation orders. This "massive resistance," however, generally collapsed in the late 1950s, and Governor Mills Godwin, though a Byrd loyalist, accepted integration and reformed state government in the late 1960s.

Meanwhile, demographics changed the Old Dominion. As the 20th Century progressed, the peripheral parts of the state grew: the coal-mining counties of the southwest, the Tidewater area around the Navy bases in Norfolk and the shipbuilding yards in Newport News, and the government employee-filled suburbs across the Potomac from Washington, D.C. Courthouse politicians no longer carried the vote for the Byrd machine by the middle 1960s: Harry Byrd Jr., appointed to his father's Senate seat, was nearly beaten in the 1966 Senate primary, and 20-year Senate veteran A. Willis Robertson—father of 1988 presidential candidate and televangelist Pat Robertson—was beaten in his primary. There began a quarter-century of political flux. The Byrd Democrats were beaten in primaries and ran as Independents (Senator Harry Byrd Jr. in 1976) or became Republicans (Mills Godwin in 1973). In the 1970s conservative Republicans won most statewide races, while Democrats still held the legislature. In the 1980s three moderate Democrats were elected governor—Charles Robb in 1981, Gerald Baliles in 1985, Douglas Wilder in 1989—because they no longer represented an attempt to impose a labor-liberal agenda on an unwilling Virginia, and because they argued they could use government effectively to improve education and build Virginia's economy. Wilder's election was a national breakthrough, an attempt by a black politician to campaign and govern on equal terms; he won largely because of his margins in the Tidewater and Northern Virginia, where his pro-choice stand on abortion clearly helped, but he also ran solidly across the state. His fiscal conservatism, which resulted in sharp spending cuts in the early 1990s, like his elegant manners and thick Richmond accent, echoed Virginia's elitist and libertarian tradition.

Now Virginia seems to have developed ideological politics along party lines. George Allen, elected governor by a wide margin in 1993, is a Republican who believes in lower taxes, traditional cultural values, longer prison terms, and teaching basic skills. He succeeded in passing most of his programs through the Democratic legislature, which traditionally favors more spending over discipline in the areas of education, welfare and crime. But his Republicans have narrowly failed to achieve other goals—they lost a Senate race they could easily have won in 1994 due to the unpopularity of their nominee, Oliver North, and they came up just short in their attempt to control the legislature in 1995. They took no great satisfaction from the reelection of Republican Senator John Warner in 1996, since he had opposed North in the 1994 Senate race, and Michael Farris, the 1993 Republican lieutenant governor candidate, and beat a conservative primary opponent, Jim Miller, in 1996. The great contest for 1997 is for the governorship. Democratic Lieutenant Governor Donald Beyer of Northern Virginia and Republican Attorney General James Gilmore from the Richmond suburbs began the race little known and about even in the polls. Beyer's election would be a repudiation of much of Allen's politics, Gilmore's a confirmation. But this serious argument over cultural values should not obscure the elements of consensus which has developed out of Virginia's last quarter-century of political flux. Virginia has more faith in growth through market economics than the Byrd machine did, more commitment to racial equality than the Founders imagined possible and more confidence that it can be a national leader than it has had since Appomattox.

Governor. George Allen came into Virginia politics with a congenial manner and hard-line conservative proposals. He grew up in California, son of the football coach fondly remembered in Virginia for his winning seasons with the Washington Redskins. During those years, the younger George Allen was at college and law school at the University of Virginia. He moved to a home in the country near Charlottesville and practiced law—wearing boots and chewing tobacco. In 1982, he was elected to the Virginia Assembly, where he was a conservative backbencher; in a 1991 special election, he won a seat in the U.S. House, which was promptly redistricted out from under him. So he started running for governor.

The initial favorite was Democratic Attorney General Mary Sue Terry, a moderate from Southside Virginia, who backed some forms of gun control (like Governor Douglas Wilder's one-

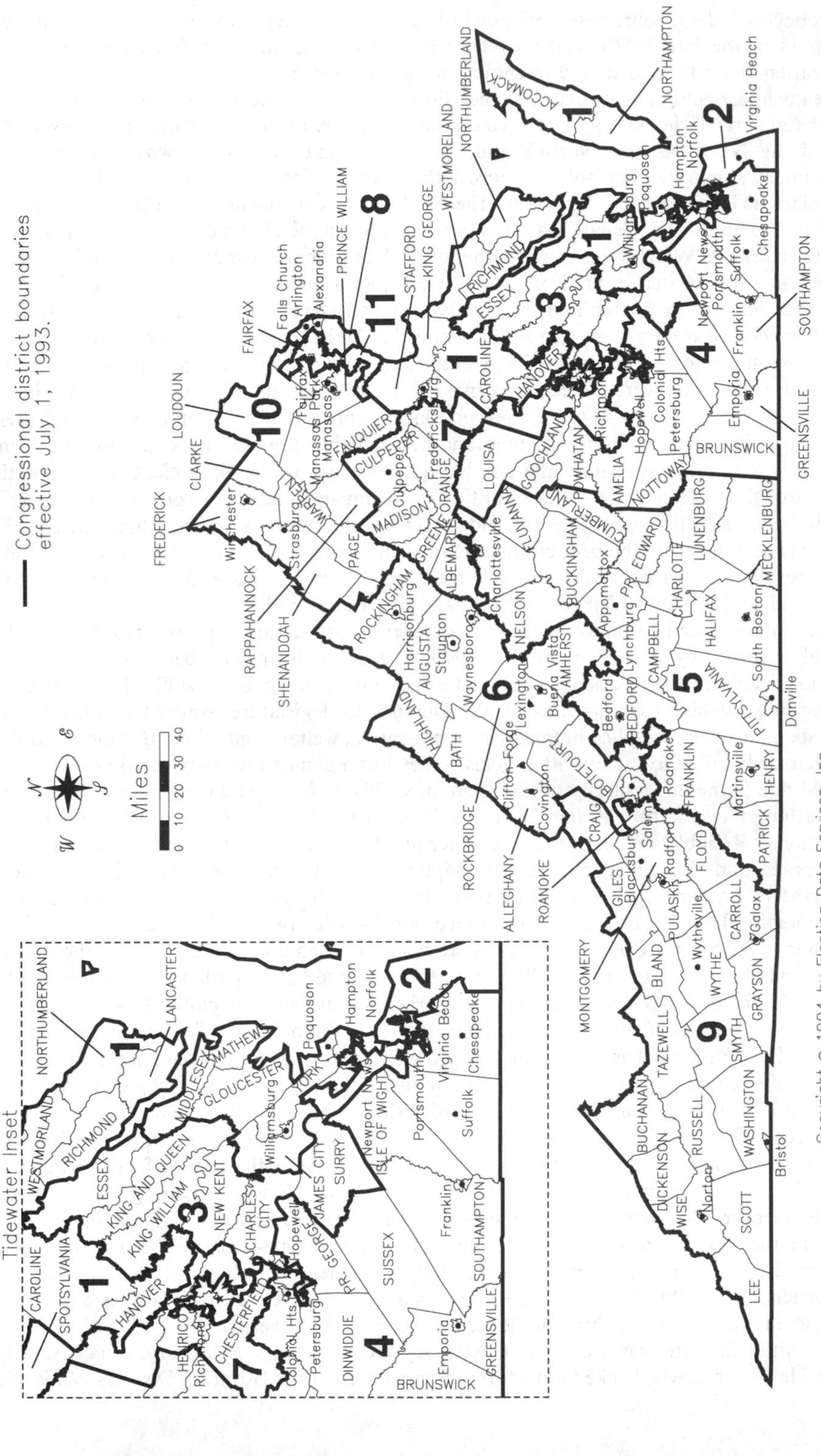
Congressional district boundaries
effective July 1, 1993.
Miles
0 10 20 30 40
Tidewater Inset
CAROLINE
SPOTSYLVANIA
WESTMORLAND
NORTHUMBERLAND
LANCASTER
RICHMOND
ESSEX
KING AND QUEEN
KING WILLIAM
NEW KENT
HANOVER
HENRICO
Richmond
CHESTERFIELD
CHARLES CITY
Hopewell
Colonial Hts.
Petersburg
PR. GEORGE
DINWIDDIE
SUSSEX
BRUNSWICK
Emporia
GREENSVILLE
SOUTHAMPTON
Franklin
SURRY
JAMES CITY
Williamsburg
ISLE OF WIGHT
Newport News
Portsmouth
Suffolk
Chesapeake
Virginia Beach
Norfolk
Hampton
Poquoson
YORK
GLOUCESTER
MATHEWS
MIDDLESEX
FREDERICK
Winchester
CLARKE
LOUDOUN
FAIRFAX
Falls Church
Arlington
Alexandria
Fairfax
Manassas Park
Manassas
PRINCE WILLIAM
STAFFORD
KING GEORGE
WESTMORELAND
NORTHUMBERLAND
NORTHAMPTON
ACCOMACK
FAUQUIER
CULPEPER
Culpeper
Fredericksburg
MADISON
ORANGE
GREENE
LOUISA
GOOCHLAND
POWHATAN
AMELIA
NOTTOWAY
FLUVANNA
CUMBERLAND
BUCKINGHAM
PR. EDWARD
Appomattox
CHARLOTTE
LUNENBURG
MECKLENBURG
HALIFAX
South Boston
CAMPBELL
Lynchburg
PITTSYLVANIA
Danville
WARREN
Strasburg
PAGE
RAPPAHANNOCK
SHENANDOAH
ROCKINGHAM
Harrisonburg
AUGUSTA
Staunton
Waynesboro
ALBEMARLE
Charlottesville
NELSON
AMHERST
Buena Vista
Lexington
HIGHLAND
BATH
ROCKBRIDGE
Clifton Forge
Covington
ALLEGHANY
BOTETOURT
Bedford
BEDFORD
Roanoke
FRANKLIN
Martinsville
HENRY
PATRICK
FLOYD
CRAIG
ROANOKE
Salem
Radford
Blacksburg
GILES
MONTGOMERY
PULASKI
CARROLL
Galax
GRAYSON
WYTHE
Wytheville
BLAND
TAZEWELL
SMYTH
WASHINGTON
Bristol
RUSSELL
BUCHANAN
DICKENSON
WISE
Norton
SCOTT
LEE
1
2
3
4
5
6
7
8
9
10
11
Copyright © 1994 by Election Data Services, Inc.

handgun-a-month purchase limit) and was pro-choice on abortion. Allen opposed abortion and gun control and called for abolishing parole. Allen maneuvered smartly to get the support of religious conservatives at the 13,000-delegate June 1993 state convention, perhaps the largest deliberative body in the history of democracy (and whose real enthusiasm was reserved for its lieutenant governor nominee, home schooling advocate Michael Farris). Democrats thought gun control and the religious right would hurt Republicans. But Allen won by a whopping 58%–41% margin, Republican James Gilmore was elected attorney general and Farris lost to Democratic Lieutenant Governor Donald Beyer, who outspent him 10–1, by only 54%–45%.

Allen's agenda proved more successful than many had expected. His achievements included a more permissive concealed weapons law, abolition of parole, parental notification for abortions and welfare reform that requires recipients to work after 90 days and cuts off benefits after two years—which resulted in a decline in welfare rolls. His education program included tougher graduation requirements, state takeovers of troubled schools and a focus on basics; his social sciences guide, requiring students to learn facts and dates, was scorned by some educators but copied in other states. But in 1995 the legislature rejected Allen's proposed tax cuts, and Allen's Republicans fell just short of winning legislative majorities, ending up with a 20–20 tie in the Senate which could be broken by Beyer and a 53–46 deficit (and one Independent) in the House of Delegates.

Virginia limits its governors to one term, so the candidates in 1997 were Democratic Lieutenant Governor Donald Beyer, owner of a car dealership in Northern Virginia, and Republican Attorney General James Gilmore, a former prosecutor in suburban Richmond. Beyer concentrated on education, promising to bring Virginia teachers' salaries up to the national average by 2002, and at one point declining to rule out a tax increase to do so. Gilmore promised to phase out most of the state's unpopular personal property taxes and to hire 4,000 new elementary school teachers, both to be paid for by Virginia's booming economy. The race began to heat up in March, when Gilmore was criticized for retaining his position as attorney general during the campaign; some felt the dual role represented a conflict of interest, while Republicans wanted Gilmore to focus on the race and hand. Gilmore agreed to resign after the Republican primary in June and become a full-time candidate.

Senior Senator. John Warner, now in his fourth Senate term, has been lucky in politics, but has also worked to make his luck. If he is sometimes prone to cliche, he does have a stubbornness and strength of character. He grew up in Washington, D.C., and volunteered for the Navy in 1944, at age 17. He went to college at Washington & Lee and then interrupted his years at the University of Virginia Law School to serve in the Marine Corps in Korea. He worked as an assistant U.S. Attorney and then practiced law in Washington and had a house in the horse country in Middleburg, Virginia. During the Nixon Administration he was secretary of the Navy. He ran for the Senate in 1978 with few political assets other than his then-wife, Elizabeth Taylor. Finishing second at the huge Republican state convention, he graciously supported winner Richard Obenshain; then, when Obenshain died in a plane crash, Republican leaders reluctantly named Warner to fill his place. Warner won the general over Democrat Andrew Miller by a 4,721-vote margin. For many years he made few enemies, and was easily reelected over a liberal Democrat in 1984 and had no serious opposition in 1990.

Warner can be grandiloquent and showy, yet he works hard on important issues and has shown steadfastness in his beliefs. His voting record is moderate on economics and occasionally on cultural issues, conservative on foreign policy and defense. He has voted for government funding of abortions in some cases, but favors parental consent laws and the "partial-birth" abortion ban. He voted for the Brady gun control bill. He backed Bob Dole's 1996 presidential candidacy warmly but did not endorse the Dole tax cut. He opposes term limits but would back sending a constitutional amendment to the states for a "national referendum." Representing a state which still has a large number of public employees (though the proportion is dropping), he favors higher federal pay and supported repeal of the Hatch Act.

Much of his work has been on defense issues. He was the ranking Republican on Armed

Services from 1987–93, when he was bumped by the more senior Strom Thurmond, who thus became chairman in 1995. Warner obviously would like the 95-year-old Thurmond to step aside. In 1996 he said: "I want very much to some day be chairman. Not in any way to damage his career or reputation—but I would hope that some time, maybe in the next six years, that opportunity could arise." A strong supporter of the Gulf war resolution, he warned against U.S. military involvement in Bosnia. He backs a strong missile defense and has said that the continuing controversy over the Tailhook incident is "debilitating to the morale of naval aviation."

Virginia is the number one state in defense spending per capita, and Warner looks out for its interests. In 1996 he helped get an immediate, rather than eventual, $1.1 billion for a nuclear reactor and other components of an aircraft carrier being built at Newport News Shipbuilding & Drydock. In 1997 he moved from chairman of the AirLand Forces Subcommittee to chairman of the Sea Power Subcommittee: as a Virginian, and a Navy and Marine veteran, he is very much a Navy man. His 1995 Republican blueprint for defense spending would have cut funds for the B-2 bomber, National Guard expansion and some construction in order to fully fund military readiness.

Warner has taken care not to offend other senators—but not other Virginia Republicans. In 1993, he refused to endorse lieutenant governor candidate Michael Farris, who was seen by some in the party as too conservative and who still blames Warner for his loss. In 1994 Warner announced he could not support Senate nominee Oliver North, whose conviction on Iran-contra charges was overturned on the grounds of inadmissibility of some critical evidence. Instead Warner backed Independent (and twice Republican gubernatorial candidate) Marshall Coleman, and many blamed Warner for North's loss. "My conscience is clear, and I'm just not going to change. I'm going to fight for what I think is correct. And I'm not spending one second a day thinking about '96," Warner said. Farris and North were both nominees of the state's large Republican convention, dominated by conservative activists, and they hoped to defeat Warner in 1996. They had a candidate in James Miller, budget director under President Ronald Reagan who lost narrowly to North at the 1994 convention and then supported him. But under Virginia law, Warner had the right to insist on a primary rather than a convention because he had filed primary papers in 1990. While some conservatives wanted to challenge the law, state Republicans quite sensibly reasoned that a convention nomination would not help Miller much because Warner would run as an Independent, which would only hurt the party. Activists vowed to stop Warner in a primary. But Miller raised little money, while Warner ran ads trumpeting his record. Turnout was high, and Warner won 66%–34%.

The Democratic nominee was Alexandria businessman Mark Warner, former state party chairman, a native of Connecticut who was criticized by John Warner for using his Democratic connections to win cellular phone licenses, amassing a personal fortune of over $100 million. "Putting phones in cars—people thought that was a crazy idea," he said of his success. Mark Warner crushed former Congresswoman Leslie Byrne at the party convention and proceeded to spend liberally—$11.6 million in all, $10.3 million of it his own money, far more per capita than what Michael Huffington spent in California in 1994, though the Democratic Warner was never attacked in the press as the Republican Huffington was. "MARKNOTJOHN" read one bumper sticker, and Mark Warner argued that John Warner "talks like Mr. Independent but votes like Mr. Gingrich." Mark Warner expressed support for cautious reductions in Medicare spending, the federal Goals 2000 funding to improve education, federal regulation of wetlands, and had a pro-choice stance on abortion. John Warner called himself a "common sense conservative" and, in the primary race, cited his seniority as better protecting the state's defense facilities: "Virginia's got an investment in me."

John Warner led in public polls, but still hovered around 50%—a danger sign for an incumbent. And he was placed on the defensive in October 1996 when his media consultant ran an ad superimposing Mark Warner's face on a picture of Charles Robb shaking hands with Douglas Wilder, as Bill Clinton looked on. John Warner fired the consultant and apologized for the deception, but did not repudiate the ad's quotation of a *Richmond Times-Dispatch* editorial calling Mark Warner "dirty, stupid, reckless, dangerous." John Warner won, but only narrowly, 52%–47%. His biggest margins were in high-income suburbs and in the Navy-dependent Hampton Roads area around Norfolk and Newport News; he lost the mountainous 9th District. Mark Warner's ads in Virginia, like Republican Michael Huffington's in California, seem to have been most effective in non-metropolitan areas.

As chairman of the Senate Rules Committee, Warner presided at the inaugural ceremonies in January 1997, a task for which his style is perfectly suited. In an April 1997 move that angered Democrats, this position allowed Warner to propose broadening the scope of the investigation into the contested 1996 Louisiana Senate race, won by Democrat Mary Landrieu. Warner got a seat on the Labor and Human Resources Committee, where he is likely to be a solid management man (Virginia has never been a pro-union state). He also chairs the Public Works Subcommittee on Transporation and Infrastructure where he promised to back the STEP-21 highway formula that would guarantee each state a near-match between federal transportation funding and federal gas taxes the state paid; and he also has aimed to develop a funding source for the Woodrow Wilson Bridge on the Capitol Beltway.

Junior Senator. Senator Charles Robb, one of only four Virginians to serve as governor and senator (the others were James Monroe, Claude Swanson and Harry Byrd Sr.) has had a roller coaster of a career in the public spotlight for more than 30 years by proving himself on the battlefield and on the political battleground. He grew up in various parts of the country, went to high school in Virginia, college in Wisconsin, then served in the Marines. He became one of the Marine Guards in the White House, and there met Lynda Byrd Johnson, whom he married in 1967. Then he went off to command an infantry company in Vietnam and was awarded the Bronze Star.

Robb began his political career in 1977 when, working in Washington and living across the river in McLean, he ran for lieutenant governor and won, while Republicans were carrying other offices. In 1981, he ran for governor and beat Republican Marshall Coleman 54%–46%. As governor, he was widely popular and was given credit for much of Virginia's dynamic growth; he added $1 billion to the education budget, worked to boost Virginia's coal export industry and appointed blacks and women to top posts in large numbers. Out of office, he was the second chairman of the Democratic Leadership Council, after Dick Gephardt. He was easily elected to the Senate in 1988: incumbent Paul Trible decided to retire at age 42, and Robb's only opponent was a hapless Republican black minister.

In the Senate Robb had a fairly conservative record while remaining something of a partisan Democrat, voting for the Gulf war resolution and Clarence Thomas while chairing the Democratic Senatorial Campaign Committee in 1991 and 1992. In 1993 and 1994 Robb moved to support the Clinton Administration on gays in the military, the 1993 budget and tax package and the 1994 crime bill. But he had other troubles. In August 1988, newspaper stories reported that, while governor, he was present at parties in Virginia Beach where cocaine was used. Charges of a sexual encounter with a former Miss Virginia were aired by NBC in April 1991. That same month, Robb aides played for reporters a tape of Governor Douglas Wilder in a car phone conversation gloating over Robb's problems; Robb was the object of a grand jury investigation related to the phone incident, but the grand jury voted in January 1993 not to indict him.

All of which left him vulnerable to almost any Republican in 1994, except the eventual nominee, Oliver North. North stirred more emotions, pro and con, than any other candidate in the 1994 cycle: his believers saw him as a man who struggled to save the West from effete liberals, his detractors saw him as a man who lied to even his own associates in government as well as to Congress and broke the law. Scorn for inside-the-Beltway elites annealed his support in far-beyond-the-Beltway hinterlands in Virginia, which produced the votes enabling him to beat conservative James Miller 55%–45% at the state convention; in remote zip codes all over the country, direct mail recipients helped North raise and spend over $20 million. Robb was fortunate that the sharp-tongued Wilder did not run against him, and in the primary he beat conservative Delegate (and now Congressman) Virgil Goode 58%–34%. Marshall Coleman, who narrowly lost the 1981 and 1989 governor races, ran as an Independent and got 11% of the vote, including Senator John Warner's. In the end, Robb won 46%–43%. Northern Virginia's Washington suburbs voted overwhelmingly for Robb (55%–33%) and so did the black-majority 3d Congressional District (72%–22%); the rest of the state went for North (48%–40%). North wisely retired from electoral politics and became a talk radio host; Robb went back to the Senate, chastened but politically alive.

There he was the only Democrat to vote for all six of the Republicans' major initiatives in early 1995, but he staked out a position independent of either party. He supported the Republican budget resolution in 1995, but in 1996 opposed it, saying it was certain to be vetoed, and instead was one of 46 senators of both parties who backed the rejected Chafee-Breaux budget bill in May 1996. He supported the balanced budget amendment, favored an adjustment of the Consumer Price Index and opposed tax cuts. He voted against ending the filibuster on the product liability bill in March 1996; he voted against the Defense of Marriage Act and for a ban on job discrimination against gays and lesbians in September 1996. Robb also became the first senator in history to serve on the Armed Services, Foreign Relations and Intelligence Committees, and some looked to him in 1997 as a replacement for Sam Nunn as a leader of Southern Democratic centrists. But he demurred. He did oppose the Clinton Administration defense posture, saying that "defense spending has fallen to a level that will not meet the national military strategy for fighting and winning in two major regional conflicts." Another Robb project was wiring all Virginia schools for the Internet: in 1996 he announced a public-private partnership, Net Day East, to do so by 2000, and he and his staff volunteered Saturdays to wire individual schools.

How will Robb fare when his seat comes up in 2000? Memories of the early 1990s scandals will probably have faded. But he could face serious opposition from Governor George Allen, who leaves office after 1997 but undoubtedly remains interested in politics.

Presidential politics. Virginia remains one of the most Republican states in presidential races, though it came close to voting for Bill Clinton in 1996. Virginia's national convention delegates are chosen at state conventions. Virginia, so near the White House and the Capitol, sees relatively little presidential politicking.

Congressional districting. Virginia's districting plan in effect for 1992 and modified slightly for 1994 and 1996 was a partisan Democratic contraption, with an odd-shaped black-majority 3d District and a similarly grotesque 7th District designed to end the brief House career of Republican George Allen. It did, but Allen had the revenge of being elected governor. Actually Bill Clinton carried only two districts, the 3d and the Northern Virginia 8th, by significant margins in 1996; Democrats hold four other districts by personal appeal. But all this may change. In February 1997 a three-judge federal panel ruled the 3d District unconstitutional because race was the primary factor in drawing the lines. Virginia Attorney General and Republican gubernatorial candidate James Gilmore announced in May that he would appeal the decision to the Supreme Court. The three-judge panel instructed legislators to redraw the 3d before the 1998 elections, and that will affect at least the 1st, 2d and 7th and perhaps all other districts as well.

The People: Est. Pop. 1996: 6,675,000; Pop. 1990: 6,187,358, up 7.9% 1990–1996. 2.5% of U.S. total, 12th largest; 31% rural. Median age: 34.5 years. 11% 65 years and over. 76% White, 18.6% Black, 2.5% Asian, 2.6% Hispanic origin. Households: 56.8% married couple families; 27% married couple fams. w. children; 49% college educ.; median household income: $33,328; per capita income: $15,713; 66.3% owner occupied housing; median house value: $91,000; median monthly rent: $411. 4.4% Unemployment. 1996 Voting age pop.: 5,083,000. 1996 Turnout: 2,416,642; 48% of VAP. Registered voters (1996): 3,322,135; no party registration.

Political Lineup: Governor, George F. Allen (R); Lt. Gov., Donald S. Beyer Jr. (D); Secy. of Commonwealth, Betsy Davis Beamer (D); Atty. Gen., Richard Cullen (R) ; Treasurer, Susan Dewey; Comptroller, William E. Landsidle. State Senate, 40 (20 D and 20 R); Senate President, Donald S. Beyer Jr. (D); State House, 100 (52 D, 46 R, 1 I and 1 vacancy); House Speaker, Thomas Moss (D). Senators, John W. Warner (R) and Charles S. Robb (D). Representatives, 11 (6 D and 5 R).

Elections Division: 804-786-6551; **Filing Deadline for U.S. Congress:** April 10, 1998.

1996 Presidential Vote			**1992 Presidential Vote**		
Dole (R)	1,138,350	(47%)	Bush (R)	1,150,517	(45%)
Clinton (D)	1,091,060	(45%)	Clinton (D)	1,038,650	(41%)
Perot (I)	159,861	(7%)	Perot (I)	348,639	(14%)

GOVERNOR

Gov. George F. Allen (R)

Elected 1993, term expires Jan. 1998; b. Mar. 8, 1952, Whittier, CA; home, Earlysville; U. of VA, B.A. 1974, J.D. 1977; Presbyterian; married (Susan).

Career: Practicing atty., 1977–91; VA House of Delegates, 1982–91; U.S. House of Reps., 1990–92.

Office: State Capitol, Richmond 23219, 804-786-2211; Fax: 804-371-6351; Web site: www.state.va.us.

Election Results

1993 gen.	George F. Allen (R)	1,045,319	(58%)
	Mary Sue Terry (D)	733,527	(41%)
1993 prim.	George F. Allen (R), nom. by convention		
1989 gen.	L. Douglas Wilder (D)	896,936	(50%)
	J. Marshall Coleman (R)	890,195	(50%)

SENATORS

Sen. John W. Warner (R)

Elected 1978, seat up 2002; b. Feb. 18, 1927, Washington, D.C.; home, Middleburg; Washington & Lee U., B.S., 1949, U. of VA, LL.B. 1953; Episcopalian; divorced.

Career: Navy, 1944–46 (WWII), Marine Corps, 1950–52 (Korea); Law Clerk, U.S. Court of Appeals Chief Judge Barrett Prettyman, 1953–54; Practicing atty., 1954–56, 1960–69; Asst. U.S. Atty., 1956–60; U.S. Navy, Undersecy., 1969–72, U.S. Navy, Secy., 1972–74; Dir., Amer. Rev. Bicentennial Comm., 1974–76.

DC Office: 225 RSOB 20510, 202-224-2023; Fax: 202-224-6295; e-mail: senator@warner.senate.gov.

State Offices: Abingdon, 540-628-8158; Norfolk, 757-441-3079; Richmond, 804-771-2579; Roanoke, 540-857-2676.

Committees: *Armed Services* (2nd of 10 R): Airland Forces; Sea Power (Chmn.); Strategic Forces. *Environment & Public Works* (2nd of 10 R): Drinking Water, Fisheries & Wildlife; Superfund, Waste Control & Risk Assessment; Transportation & Infrastructure (Chmn.). *Labor & Human Resources* (9th of 10 R): Aging; Employment & Training. *Rules & Administration* (Chmn. of 9R). *Small Business* (6th of 10 R). *Aging (Special)* (7th of 10 R). *Joint Committee on the Library of Congress* (2nd of 5 Sens.). *Joint Committee on Printing* (Chmn. of 5 Sens.).

Group Ratings

	ADA	ACLU	AFS	LCV	CFA	CON	NFIB	COC	ACU	NTLC	CHC
1996	5	22	0	8	21	56	93	85	95	97	100
1995	5	—	0	7	6	54	—	100	91	—	—

National Journal Ratings

	1995 LIB — 1995 CONS	1996 LIB — 1996 CONS
Economic	37% — 61%	42% — 56%
Social	22% — 74%	0% — 72%
Foreign	0% — 92%	0% — 74%

Key Votes of the 104th Congress

1. Reduce Medicare Growth $	Y	5. Flag Amendment	Y	9. Anti-Missile Defense	Y
2. Lmt. Prod. Liab. Damages	Y	6. Endangered Species	N	10. Cuban Embargo	Y
3. Increase Min. Wage	Y	7. Gay Employment Rights	N	11. Bar Bosnia Troop $	Y
4. Welfare Reform	Y	8. Ovrd. Part. Birth Veto	Y	12. Cut Vietnam Aid	Y

Election Results

1996 general	John W. Warner (R)	1,235,744	(52%)	($5,819,157)
	Mark R. Warner (D)	1,115,982	(47%)	($11,600,424)
1996 primary	John W. Warner (R)	323,520	(66%)	
	James C. (Jim) Miller (R)	170,015	(34%)	
1990 general	John W. Warner (R)	876,782	(81%)	($1,219,726)
	Nancy B. Spannaus (I)	196,755	(18%)	

Sen. Charles S. Robb (D)

Elected 1988, seat up 2000; b. June 26, 1939, Phoenix, AZ; home, McLean; U. of WI, B.B.A. 1961, U. of VA, J.D. 1973; Episcopalian; married (Lynda).

Career: Marine Corps, 1961–1970 (Vietnam), Marine Corps Reserves, 1970–91; Law Clerk, Judge John Butzner, U.S. Court of Appeals, 1973–74; Practicing atty., 1974–77, 1986–88; VA Lt. Gov., 1977–82; VA Gov., 1981–86.

DC Office: 154 RSOB 20510, 202-224-4024; Fax: 202-224-8689; e-mail: senator@robb.senate.gov.

State Offices: Clintwood, 540-926-4104; Danville, 804-791-0330; Norfolk, 757-441-3124; Richmond, 804-771-2221; Roanoke, 540-985-0103.

Committees: *Armed Services* (6th of 8 D): Personnel; Readiness (RMM); Sea Power. *Foreign Relations* (5th of 8 D): East Asian & Pacific Affairs; Near Eastern & South Asian Affairs (RMM); Western Hemisphere & Peace Corps Affairs. *Intelligence (Select)* (7th of 9 D). *Joint Economic Committee* (10th of 10 Sens.).

Group Ratings

	ADA	ACLU	AFS	LCV	CFA	CON	NFIB	COC	ACU	NTLC	CHC
1996	80	39	71	77	71	88	48	46	20	31	7
1995	95	—	82	100	50	96	—	58	13	—	—

National Journal Ratings

	1995 LIB — 1995 CONS	1996 LIB — 1996 CONS
Economic	57% — 42%	61% — 34%
Social	76% — 18%	78% — 20%
Foreign	53% — 44%	58% — 40%

Key Votes of the 104th Congress

1. Reduce Medicare Growth $	N	5. Flag Amendment	N	9. Anti-Missile Defense	N
2. Lmt. Prod. Liab. Damages	N	6. Endangered Species	Y	10. Cuban Embargo	Y
3. Increase Min. Wage	Y	7. Gay Employment Rights	Y	11. Bar Bosnia Troop $	N
4. Welfare Reform	Y	8. Ovrd. Part. Birth Veto	N	12. Cut Vietnam Aid	N

Election Results

1994 general	Charles S. Robb (D)	938,376	(46%)	($5,501,697)
	Oliver L. (Ollie) North (R)	882,213	(43%)	($20,607,367)
	J. Marshall Coleman (I)	235,324	(11%)	($813,409)
1994 primary	Charles S. Robb (D)	154,561	(58%)	
	Virgil H. Goode Jr. (D)	90,547	(34%)	
	Sylvia L. Clute (D)	17,329	(6%)	
	Others	4,507	(2%)	
1988 general	Charles S. Robb (D)	1,474,086	(71%)	($2,881,666)
	Maurice A. Dawkins (R)	593,652	(29%)	($282,229)

FIRST DISTRICT

When the first British settlers sailed up the estuaries that flow into the Chesapeake Bay, they were searching for gold, hoping to sail back soon with fortunes. But they couldn't help noticing that the spot where the James River feeds into the Bay, now Hampton Roads, was a fine natural harbor, with calm, deep water and good anchorages. There they established a civilization whose elegance is recalled in the craftsmanship of restored Williamsburg and whose coarseness and brutality is brought to life by the story of Jamestown and the other beleaguered settlements. Tidewater Virginia brought slavery to America and tobacco to the world, and slave-raised tobacco was the center of its economy in the colonial era and in the years afterward, when its most talented sons left its depleted soil for better opportunities elsewhere.

Now the economy and tone of life in Tidewater Virginia are set by the American military. Nearly 60 years ago, as America was on the brink of world war, the Navy base at Norfolk and the shipbuilding centers in Newport News across Hampton Roads became the center of American naval might in the Atlantic. There were less than 370,000 people living then on both sides of Hampton Roads. Today there are 1.5 million—a population collected from all over the country, making this a metropolitan area that is not so much southern in atmosphere as it is, in the manner of military bases abroad, national. But you can still see this area's origins in the Newport News Shipbuilding and Drydock Company that lies over the flat neighborhoods lining the baysides, with ships looming larger than life, their turrets and superstructures bristling with armored might. This is the biggest private employer in Virginia. At the height of 1980s naval expansion, 30,000 people worked here, and defense spending here has topped $1 billion a year.

Virginia's 1st Congressional District—America's First District, Congressman Herb Bateman calls it—contains much of this territory. Its boundaries are convoluted in order to accommodate the black-majority 3d District, although they may be smoothed out in response to a February 1997 federal court decision that ruled the 3d unconstitutional. Nearly half the district's residents live on the Peninsula, in and around Newport News, Williamsburg and other Hampton Roads area towns. It also includes the southern tip of the Delmarva Peninsula—Virginia's Eastern Shore, site of the annual roundup of wild Chincoteague ponies—and much of the Northern

Neck between the Rappahannock and Potomac Rivers, where Robert "King" Carter, one of the great landowners of colonial Virginia, reigned, and where George Washington and Robert E. Lee were born; the Northern Neck is now growing lustily again for the first time in two centuries. The 1st also dips south to the Hanover County suburbs outside of Richmond. Ancestrally, most of this area is Democratic, but with black precincts shorn away, the 1st now is reliably Republican, 52% for Bob Dole in 1996.

Congressman Herb Bateman has deep roots in the area—deeper indeed than many Hampton Roads area locals, who were brought here by the military. He grew up in Newport News, went to William and Mary, enlisted in the Air Force during the Korean war, practiced law and was elected to the Virginia Senate as a Democrat in 1967. He switched parties in 1976, and was outmaneuvered for the congressional nomination that year. But when the district became open again in 1982, he easily won the nomination and then won the general. Bateman has moderate voting record; he opposed term limits and voted for the Brady bill and the assault weapons ban.

Most of Bateman's work has been on the National Security Committee, where he now chairs the Readiness Subcommittee. In 1989, he led the effort to build two new Nimitz-class aircraft carriers at Newport News—the *U.S.S. John C. Stennis* and *Harry S Truman*, built at a cost of $6.3 billion. In the 103d Congress, he led the effort to build a third carrier, the *U.S.S. Ronald Reagan*, now under construction with a cost of $4.5 billion. In 1995 and 1996 he worked to reverse a Pentagon decision to build all future nuclear submarines at the Electric Boat plant in Connecticut; instead, two subs will be built there and two at Newport News, and the yards will compete again in 2003. He is chairman of a special Merchant Marine panel, and passed in 1993 a bill to encourage commercial ship construction in the U.S.; Newport News is now working on four double-hulled tankers for a Greek company. Bateman also sponsored the 1995 law granting subsidies to U.S. shipping lines, which suffer higher taxes and operating costs than foreign ships, in return for a commitment to make all their ships available to the Defense Department in case of war. Bateman brags no military base has been closed in this area during the four rounds of closings since the 1980s; he worked hard to save Fort Monroe, Fort Eustis and Fort A.P. Hill.

On the Transportation and Infrastructure Committee, he has worked to fund the Chesapeake Bay cleanup at $21 million a year, to fund a $10 million program to protect oysters and crabs and to impose a ban on tributyltin-based paints to save oyster beds. He also worked to set up telecommuting centers for federal workers near Fredericksburg.

In 1994 Bateman promised to retire in 1996, but when Republicans won control of the House he reconsidered. In the past he had some tough challenges from Democrats: Bobby Scott, now congressman from the 3d District, held him to 56% in 1986 and former TV anchorman Andy Fox held him to 51% in 1990. More recently, Bateman has been opposed by conservatives angry at his votes for gun control. In 1996, when he was opposed by a former housing director for Governor George Allen, he opted for a primary, rather than a convention where conservative activists might dominate; he won the primary 80%–20%. The Democratic nominee promptly dropped out and Bateman was reelected with 99% of the vote.

The People: Pop. 1990: 563,126; 44% rural; 11% age 65+; 79% White; 18% Black; 1% Asian; 2% Hispanic origin. Households: 63% married couple families; 30% married couple fams. w. children; 47% college educ.; median household income: $33,285; per capita income: $14,675; median gross rent: $491; median house value: $92,700.

1996 Presidential Vote			**1992 Presidential Vote**		
Dole (R)	125,080	(52%)	Bush (R)	120,131	(49%)
Clinton (D)	95,853	(40%)	Clinton (D)	81,826	(34%)
Perot (I)	17,435	(7%)	Perot (I)	39,307	(16%)

Rep. Herbert H. Bateman (R)

Elected 1982; b. Aug. 7, 1928, Elizabeth City, NC; home, Newport News; William and Mary, B.A. 1949, Georgetown U., LL.B. 1956; Protestant; married (Laura).

Career: Air Force, 1951–53; Teacher, Hampton Schl., 1949–51; Law Clerk, Judge Bastian, 1956–57; Practicing atty., 1957–82; VA Senate, 1967–82.

DC Office: 2350 RHOB 20515, 202-225-4261; Fax: 202-225-4382.

District Offices: Accomac, 757-787-7836; Fredericksburg, 703-898-2975; Newport News, 757-873-1132.

Committees: *National Security* (5th of 30 R): Military Readiness (Chmn.); Military Research & Development. *Transportation & Infrastructure* (5th of 40 R): Surface Transportation; Water Resources & Environment.

Group Ratings

	ADA	ACLU	AFS	LCV	CFA	CON	NFIB	COC	ACU	NTLC	CHC
1996	15	7	0	23	0	21	83	94	85	88	76
1995	5	—	—	13	0	56	—	88	62	—	—

National Journal Ratings

	1995 LIB — 1995 CONS			1996 LIB — 1996 CONS		
Economic	49%	—	51%	37%	—	61%
Social	0%	—	79%	29%	—	68%
Foreign	35%	—	64%	36%	—	63%

Key Votes of the 104th Congress

1. Reduce Medicare Growth $	Y	5. Flag Amendment	Y	9. Cuban Embargo	Y
2. Ovrd. Product Liab. Veto	Y	6. Drop EPA Limits	N	10. Bar Bosnia Troop $	N
3. Increase Min. Wage	N	7. Repeal Assault-Weap. Ban	N	11. Cut Anti-Missile Defense	N
4. Welfare Reform	Y	8. Ovrd. Part. Birth Veto	Y	12. Bar U.N. Uniforms	N

Election Results

1996 general	Herbert H. Bateman (R)	unopposed		($534,156)
1996 primary	Herbert H. Bateman (R)	49,548	(80%)	
	David L. Caprara (R)	12,636	(20%)	
1994 general	Herbert H. Bateman (R)	142,930	(74%)	($423,501)
	Mary F. Sinclair (D)	45,173	(23%)	($80,435)
	Others	4,393	(2%)	

SECOND DISTRICT

The United States Navy Atlantic fleet berthed in its home port of Norfolk is one of the great awe-inspiring sights in America, or anywhere. The aggregation of destructive power in the line of towering gray ships is probably greater than in any other single port in history—over 100 ships are based here, with some 100,000 sailors and Marines, some $2 billion in annual spending. Norfolk has been a Navy port since 1801, and has long been recognized as one of the best natural harbors on the East Coast, one that never freezes, has a channel 50 feet deep and is within 750 miles of three-quarters of U.S. manufacturing capacity.

Norfolk, once a small city, is now the center of a metropolitan area on both sides of Hampton Roads with over 1.5 million people. Nearly one-third of the total workforce here is employed by the military, but with its skilled labor force and lack of unions the Hampton Roads area has also attracted a lot of private employment; the port has taken a great deal of business away from the labor-torn piers of Baltimore. To the Hampton Roads area, this growth over the last 45 years has brought a wider cross-section of people than usually found in the South. There is no heavy accent here: the brothy Tidewater accent is heard more often farther up the rivers toward Richmond. And Norfolk preserves its antique past more carefully now, developing cultural institutions and commercial amenities appropriate to a major metro area. Older parts of Norfolk have the look and feel of a working-class town, with shipyard workers and many blacks (39% in the city of Norfolk), but most of it is white middle-class suburbia, except perhaps for Virginia Beach's string of oceanfront motels.

The 2d Congressional District of Virginia is made up of most of Norfolk and Virginia Beach, with boundaries carefully drawn to put heavily black neighborhoods in the black-majority 3d District; a February 1997 federal court decision ruling the 3d unconstitutional may require a change for 1998. The politics here has changed as the area has become more heavily suburban, and the Democrats more associated with defense policy critics. In 1968, the 2d District voted for Hubert Humphrey, as Norfolk cast 65,000 votes and Virginia Beach 37,000. In 1996, the 2d District voted 48%–44% for Bob Dole, as its portion of Norfolk cast 40,000 votes and Virginia Beach 123,000.

The congressman from the 2d District is Owen Pickett, a Democrat first elected in 1986. With old Virginia roots, he became an accountant and lawyer, was elected to the Virginia House of Delegates in 1971, at 41, where he was known as a fiscal conservative and for his hard work restructuring the state retirement system. He was state Democratic chairman in 1981, when Charles Robb won the governorship, beginning a string of Democratic victories. In 1982, he was Robb's choice for the Senate but withdrew after Douglas Wilder, then state senator and later governor, threatened to run as an independent. But by the time he ran for Congress in 1986, the quiet and methodical Pickett had Wilder's support and that of Jesse Jackson's Norfolk coordinator. Pickett carried Norfolk heavily, and won 49%–42%.

In the House, Pickett showed his political acumen by getting a new seat created for him on the National Security Committee and getting a seat on the old Merchant Marine Committee as well—two crucial spots for any Norfolk congressman. His voting record is a bit to the left of the House as a whole. But he did vote for the Gulf war resolution and against family and medical leave, and he opposed the Clinton budget and tax package in 1993. He is a member of The Coalition—the Blue Dogs, as they are generally known—who have proposed their own budget with no tax cuts until the budget is balanced and faster spending cuts than either Democratic or Republican versions. Much of Pickett's work has been in supporting Hampton Roads military bases and defense contractors, and revitalizing the shipbuilding industry and merchant marine. That work has mostly been successful. Newport News Shipbuilding and Drydock across the bay has been building three Nimitz-class aircraft carriers in the 1990s, at a cost over $10 billion, and has kept Electric Boat Companyin Connecticut from getting a monopoly on building nuclear submarines. With subsidies for operating costs and new contract terms, U.S.-flag shipping firms have thrived and Newport News is building commercial ships too. The Norfolk Navy Shipyard has survived four rounds of base-closings and calls for privatization. Pickett has opposed the Clinton Pentagon on items from aircraft (he wants to go ahead with the Super Hornet and F-22 and delay the joint strike fighter), to increases on cigarette prices at military commissaries.

Pickett continues to be reelected in a Republican-leaning district. He won 56% and 59% against a vocal conservative in 1992 and 1994; in a quieter race in 1996 he won 65%–35%, running 21% ahead of Bill Clinton, who lost the district to Bob Dole. He had been mentioned as a candidate against Senator John Warner in 1996, but made no move to run.

The People: Pop. 1990: 562,789; 1% rural; 7% age 65+; 77% White; 16% Black; 4% Asian; 3% Hispanic origin. Households: 60% married couple families; 31% married couple fams. w. children; 55%

college educ.; median household income: $32,576; per capita income: $14,492; median gross rent: $528; median house value: $92,500.

1996 Presidential Vote			1992 Presidential Vote		
Dole (R)	77,943	(48%)	Bush (R)	85,773	(48%)
Clinton (D)	71,683	(44%)	Clinton (D)	62,946	(35%)
Perot (I)	11,905	(7%)	Perot (I)	30,587	(17%)

Rep. Owen B. Pickett (D)

Elected 1986; b. Aug. 31, 1930, Richmond; home, Virginia Beach; VA Polytechnic Inst., B.S. 1952, U. of Richmond, LL.B. 1955; Baptist; married (Sybil).

Career: Accountant; Practicing atty., 1955–86; VA House of Delegates, 1972–86; Chmn., VA Dem. Party, 1980–82.

DC Office: 2430 RHOB 20515, 202-225-4215; Fax: 202-225-4218; e-mail: opickett@hr.house.gov.

District Offices: Norfolk, 757-583-5892; Virginia Beach, 757-486-3710.

Committees: *National Security* (6th of 25 D): Military Personnel; Military Readiness; Military Research & Development (RMM). *Resources* (10th of 23 D): Water & Power.

Group Ratings

	ADA	ACLU	AFS	LCV	CFA	CON	NFIB	COC	ACU	NTLC	CHC
1996	45	38	50	69	8	24	59	63	50	46	13
1995	55	—	—	38	15	4	—	46	28	—	—

National Journal Ratings

	1995 LIB — 1995 CONS			1996 LIB — 1996 CONS		
Economic	62%	—	37%	58%	—	41%
Social	63%	—	36%	61%	—	38%
Foreign	51%	—	48%	50%	—	48%

Key Votes of the 104th Congress

1. Reduce Medicare Growth $	N	5. Flag Amendment	Y	9. Cuban Embargo	Y
2. Ovrd. Product Liab. Veto	N	6. Drop EPA Limits	N	10. Bar Bosnia Troop $	N
3. Increase Min. Wage	Y	7. Repeal Assault-Weap. Ban	Y	11. Cut Anti-Missile Defense	Y
4. Welfare Reform	Y	8. Ovrd. Part. Birth Veto	N	12. Bar U.N. Uniforms	Y

Election Results

1996 general	Owen B. Pickett (D)	106,215	(65%)	($266,059)
	John F. Tate (R)	57,586	(35%)	($194,912)
1996 primary	Owen B. Pickett (D)	nominated by convention		
1994 general	Owen B. Pickett (D)	81,372	(59%)	($386,469)
	J.L. (Jim) Chapman (R)	56,375	(41%)	($433,587)

THIRD DISTRICT

The history of African-American slavery literally began along the tidal expanse of the James River. In 1607, the first English colonists chose one of the marshiest, least healthy spots along the broad river as the site of their settlement at Jamestown. Only a dozen years later, the first slave ship sailed up the James and offloaded its human cargo, giving birth to the biracial society of the American South. In the 20th Century, the great plantation houses of the Tidewater, entire communities once adorned by the most impressive architecture of the day and attended by hundreds of slaves, still dot the banks of the James. Charles City County, the site of William Byrd II's Westover, Benjamin Harrison III's Berkeley, and John Carter's Shirley, also was the birthplace of two successive presidents, William Henry Harrison and John Tyler. The county's population continues to be heavily black—the demography of the plantation remains.

The 3d Congressional District of Virginia is the black-majority district formed in 1991, slightly redrawn in 1993 and threatened with change by a February 1997 federal court decision ruling its boundaries unconstitutional. It strings together black precincts and communities along the James River from Norfolk and Newport News upriver on the Peninsula past Jamestown and Charles City County, with spindly extensions into black neighborhoods of Richmond and Petersburg and their suburban fringes. It also includes several rural counties to the north with high black percentages. Overall, the district's population is 64% black. Politically, the 3d is by far the most Democratic in Virginia—72% for Bill Clinton in 1996. But it also is sensitive to the needs of the businesses that supply its economic base—notably Newport News Shipbuilding and Drydock Company, the state's largest private employer, and to the ravages of crime on its urban core. Voters in Richmond, one-quarter of the district, ousted most of its Council in 1994 because of high homicide rates and a dwindling job base, installing a different generation of black officeholders.

The congressman here is Bobby Scott, a Democrat elected when the new 3d District was created in 1992. He grew up in Newport News, the son of a doctor, went to Harvard, where he was a classmate of Al Gore, and then to Boston College Law School. He served in the National Guard and Army Reserves and returned home to practice law in 1973. In 1977, he was elected to the Virginia House of Delegates and in 1983 to the state Senate, representing a multi-racial district in a community where, because of the military tradition of integration, biracial politics comes more naturally than in other places. In 1986 he ran a creditable race for Congress in the 1st District and lost to Republican Herb Bateman, 56%–44%. In 1992 he ran in the 3d. With his base in the Peninsula, and against two Richmond-based candidates, Scott won the crucial Democratic primary with 67% of the vote. The general election made him the first black Member of Congress to be elected from Virginia since Reconstruction.

In his first year in Congress, Scott seemed cautious on economic and foreign policy issues; since then he has had a solidly liberal voting record, easily the most liberal in the Virginia delegation. On the Education and The Workforce Committee, he jumped into the healthcare debate: remembering how his father had been denied staff privileges in a Newport News hospital, he vowed that any healthcare bill would prohibit racial discrimination against patients and healthcare providers. He opposes the death penalty and supports a requirement that it not be applied disproportionately by race; he has voted against many bills that contain capital punishment, from the Democrats' 1994 crime bill, when they desperately needed the votes, to the noncontroversial adoption of the Geneva Conventions in July 1996. In the Republican 104th Congress, Scott spoke out frequently against Republican welfare and crime bills, and his passion showed no sign of cooling. On many issues he seems to focus on the rights of the wrongdoer, almost to the exclusion of any consideration for victims. He opposed Megan's law, requiring public disclosure of released sexual predators, and he opposed expelling problematic special needs students in the IDEA debate: "the child still needs an education," he said. He succeeded in removing the age limit of 20 for welfare recipients seeking a high school diploma as a work requirement. He says his long-term goals are affordable health care for all, extending the opportunity to attend college, improving the education system and "to prevent crime before it occurs."

In each election Scott has won about 80% of the vote, but his tenure could be imperiled if the 3d is drastically redrawn. A lawsuit was filed against it in November 1995 and in February 1997 a three-judge federal panel ruled it unconstitutional, because race was the primary factor in drawing the lines. Factually, that can hardly be denied; indeed, that is what the Bush Justice Department drove the Virginia legislature to do. In May 1997, Attorney General and Republican gubernatorial candidate Jim Gilmore announced he would appeal the decision to the Supreme Court, though the federal panel did not set a timetable for redistricting. Scott said he would run again in 1998 no matter what happens to the boundaries. But there are only so many black-majority neighborhoods in Virginia, and to draw a black-majority district requires creating something that looks very much like the current 3d. Scott's chances would not be zero in a district with a large black minority, but his liberal voting record might be a liability.

The People: Pop. 1990: 560,640; 11% rural; 12% age 65+; 33% White; 64% Black; 1% Asian; 1% Hispanic origin. Households: 42% married couple families; 19% married couple fams. w. children; 36% college educ.; median household income: $22,556; per capita income: $10,558; median gross rent: $398; median house value: $61,700.

1996 Presidential Vote			**1992 Presidential Vote**		
Clinton (D)	117,357	(72%)	Clinton (D)	124,857	(65%)
Dole (R)	36,099	(22%)	Bush (R)	48,843	(25%)
Perot (I)	7,643	(5%)	Perot (I)	16,779	(9%)

Rep. Robert C. (Bobby) Scott (D)

Elected 1992; b. Apr. 30, 1947, Washington, D.C.; home, Newport News; Harvard U., B.A. 1969, Boston Col. Law Schl., J.D. 1973; Episcopalian; divorced.

Career: Army Natl. Guard, 1970–73; Army Reserves, 1973–76; Practicing atty., 1973–91; VA House of Delegates, 1977–82; VA Senate, 1983–92.

DC Office: 2464 RHOB 20515, 202-225-8351; Fax: 202-225-8354.

District Offices: Newport News, 757-380-1000.

Committees: *Education & The Workforce* (10th of 20 D): Early Childhood, Youth & Families. *Judiciary* (7th of 15 D): Constitution (RMM).

Group Ratings

	ADA	ACLU	AFS	LCV	CFA	CON	NFIB	COC	ACU	NTLC	CHC
1996	90	81	100	85	69	63	24	31	0	13	0
1995	95	—	—	100	92	25	—	13	4	—	—

National Journal Ratings

	1995 LIB	—	1995 CONS	1996 LIB	—	1996 CONS
Economic	83%	—	16%	76%	—	22%
Social	88%	—	0%	88%	—	0%
Foreign	73%	—	27%	59%	—	40%

Key Votes of the 104th Congress

1. Reduce Medicare Growth $	N	5. Flag Amendment	N	9. Cuban Embargo	*
2. Ovrd. Product Liab. Veto	N	6. Drop EPA Limits	Y	10. Bar Bosnia Troop $	N
3. Increase Min. Wage	Y	7. Repeal Assault-Weap. Ban	N	11. Cut Anti-Missile Defense	Y
4. Welfare Reform	N	8. Ovrd. Part. Birth Veto	N	12. Bar U.N. Uniforms	N

Election Results

1996 general	Robert C. (Bobby) Scott (D)	118,603	(82%)	($176,104)
	Elsie Goodwyn Holland (R)	25,781	(18%)	($1,856)
1996 primary	Robert C. (Bobby) Scott (D)	nom. by convention		
1994 general	Robert C. (Bobby) Scott (D)	108,532	(79%)	($252,350)
	Thomas E. (Tom) Ward (R)	28,080	(21%)	($77,642)

FOURTH DISTRICT

The clash of arms resounds through much of the history of Tidewater Virginia. This was the scene of the first permanent English settlement in North America, at Jamestown, and of its first revolution, Bacon's Rebellion, in 1676. In 1781, George Washington's tattered and exhausted army finally pushed General Cornwallis to the sea, where the French Navy waited at Yorktown: the final victory of the Revolutionary War. The Tidewater also was the scene of bitter fighting more than 80 years later in the Civil War, as Union troops invested the battlements of the small industrial city of Petersburg, 25 miles south of Richmond. Today, the Tidewater region boasts one of the densest concentrations of military power in the world: the Hampton Roads area has the United States' largest accumulation of Navy bases, while Fort Lee, the big Army base near Petersburg, provides an estimated 17,000 local jobs.

The 4th Congressional District of Virginia includes much of the Tidewater. Nearly half its people are in the Hampton Roads area, in Portsmouth—a Navy port and industrial town with a charming old section—and in the suburban expanse of Chesapeake and Suffolk Counties. The district also takes in the flat lands of Southside Virginia fanning south from the James River. These were tobacco lands when the English first settled them in the 17th Century; today they also produce Virginia's peanut crop and its Smithfield hams. The district then loops around most of Petersburg and Hopewell, with its Allied Chemical plant facing 18th Century plantations, and juts to the growing suburbs north and west of Richmond. Historically, this was a solidly Democratic area, and the 4th's Democratic percentages are buoyed up by the 32% of its residents who are black. But in national and increasingly in state elections, this area has been trending Republican: it voted 61% for Governor George Allen in 1993 and was almost precisely even in the 1996 presidential race.

The congressman from the 4th District is Norman Sisisky, a Democrat elected in 1982. Sisisky is a Richmond native who transformed a small Pepsi bottling company in Petersburg into one of the largest soft drink bottling operations in the South. In 1973, when he had owned his firm 24 years, Sisisky was elected to the Virginia House of Delegates. He ran for Congress in 1982, financing a solid campaign with his own money. Once in the House, he immediately got a seat on the National Security Committee and compiled a moderate voting record. He is a member of the Blue Dogs, moderate Democrats whose budget has no tax cuts until the budget reaches balance, and cuts spending more quickly than others. In the 104th Congress, he co-sponsored a paperwork reduction act for small business. In 1993 he joined six other House Democrats calling themselves "Democrats for a Strong Defense" who mobilized against further defense cuts. He opposed the 1980s homeporting proposal which would have dispersed the Navy fleet out from Hampton Roads, and played a major role in an all-hands-on-deck lobbying effort by the Tidewater's congressional delegation. In 1994, he helped win approval of the $4.5 billion Nimitz-class aircraft carrier, the *U.S.S. Ronald Reagan*, now being built in Hampton Roads. He is the ranking Democrat on the Military Readiness Subcommittee (Charles Robb holds the corresponding position in the Senate); he took a lead role in reforming the Defense Business Operating Fund and has opposed further privatization plans. Another favorite Sisisky project: promoting Medicare coverage for colon cancer screening; he had surgery in 1995 and underwent 52 weeks of chemotherapy.

Sisisky's moderate views and work for local bases have made him highly popular in a marginal district. Against the minister of a Baptist church, Sisisky spent $290,000 of his own money and won 62%–38% in 1994. In 1996 he won 79%–21%.

The People: Pop. 1990: 563,206; 37% rural; 12% age 65+; 66% White; 32% Black; 1% Asian; 1% Hispanic origin. Households: 61% married couple families; 29% married couple fams. w. children; 38% college educ.; median household income: $30,425; per capita income: $12,887; median gross rent: $424; median house value: $72,900.

1996 Presidential Vote

Dole (R)	103,368	(46%)
Clinton (D)	101,686	(46%)
Perot (I)	15,879	(7%)

1992 Presidential Vote

Bush (R)	106,392	(46%)
Clinton (D)	90,641	(39%)
Perot (I)	31,467	(14%)

Rep. Norman Sisisky (D)

Elected 1982; b. June 9, 1927, Baltimore, MD; home, Petersburg; VA Commonwealth U., B.A. 1949; Jewish; married (Rhoda).

Career: Navy, 1945–46; Pres., Pepsi-Cola Bottling Co. of Petersburg, 1949–82; VA House of Delegates, 1973–82.

DC Office: 2371 RHOB 20515, 202-225-6365; Fax: 202-226-1170.

District Offices: Emporia, 804-634-5575; Petersburg, 804-732-2544; Portsmouth, 757-393-2068.

Committees: *National Security* (3rd of 25 D): Military Installations & Facilities; Military Readiness (RMM). *Small Business* (2nd of 16 D): Regulatory Reform & Paperwork Reduction.

Group Ratings

	ADA	ACLU	AFS	LCV	CFA	CON	NFIB	COC	ACU	NTLC	CHC
1996	35	25	55	54	25	60	69	67	55	51	28
1995	45	—	—	19	15	87	—	52	22	—	—

National Journal Ratings

	1995 LIB — 1995 CONS			1996 LIB — 1996 CONS		
Economic	57%	—	42%	55%	—	44%
Social	60%	—	39%	55%	—	45%
Foreign	59%	—	41%	47%	—	52%

Key Votes of the 104th Congress

1. Reduce Medicare Growth $	N	5. Flag Amendment	Y	9. Cuban Embargo	*
2. Ovrd. Product Liab. Veto	Y	6. Drop EPA Limits	N	10. Bar Bosnia Troop $	N
3. Increase Min. Wage	Y	7. Repeal Assault-Weap. Ban	Y	11. Cut Anti-Missile Defense	Y
4. Welfare Reform	Y	8. Ovrd. Part. Birth Veto	Y	12. Bar U.N. Uniforms	Y

Election Results

1996 general	Norman Sisisky (D)	160,100	(79%)	($223,771)
	Anthony J. Zevgolis (R)	43,516	(21%)	($2,878)
1996 primary	Norman Sisisky (D)	nominated by convention		
1994 general	Norman Sisisky (D)	115,055	(62%)	($741,224)
	A. George Sweet III (R)	71,678	(38%)	($329,607)

FIFTH DISTRICT

Southside Virginia is a geographic name which for years was shorthand for a state of mind. Here is Appomattox Court House, in the serene little hamlet where Robert E. Lee surrendered to his onetime subordinate Ulysses S. Grant; here is Danville, where the tobacco auction originated in 1858; here also is Prince Edward County, where Harry Byrd's massive resistance shut down public schools in 1957 rather than obey a federal court desegregation order. This land north of the dividing line Colonel William Byrd surveyed in 1728 has some variety. Its eastern counties are flat and humid—frontier in the late colonial period, plantation country by 1800, now peanut fields and pine forests. To the west, into the Piedmont, the land gradually gets hillier. Here are textile mill towns and furniture manufacturing centers—Danville, Martinsville and a dozen smaller towns. Westward, nearer to the mountains, is more livestock and less tobacco, and the thick syrupy tones of the Southside Virginia accent turn to mountain twangs.

The 5th Congressional District consists of much of Southside Virginia, west of metropolitan Richmond and at some points up to the Blue Ridge. It includes Charlottesville and much of surrounding Albemarle County, but skirts around Lynchburg; the boundaries could change as a result of a February 1997 court decision invalidating the 3d District. Historically, politics here were Democratic, segregationist and conservative, run by chain-smoking local bankers and courthouse lawyers, personified by the late Virginia House of Delegates Speaker A. L. Philpott. But those Democrats are a rare breed these days, and younger and sleeker politicians are now competing for office in Southside; Southside Virginia voted for George Bush and Bob Dole in 1992 and 1996.

The Congressman from the 5th District is Virgil Goode, a Democrat from Rocky Mount elected in 1996. A lifelong resident of Franklin County, Goode (rhymes with "mood") went to college at the University of Richmond. He graduated from the University of Virginia law school in 1973, and the same year was elected to the Virginia Senate, at age 27. In 1994, Goode ran against scandal-beleaguered Senator Charles Robb in the Democratic primary; he lost 58%–34%, but showed local strength. In 1995, his reelection in a Republican-leaning state Senate district enabled Democrats to hold control of the Senate with a 20–20 tie that could be broken by Democratic Lieutenant Governor Donald Beyer.

In 1996 conservative Democratic Congressman L.F. Payne, developer of the Wintergreen resort, announced his retirement after eight years in the House, and promptly began running for lieutenant governor in 1997. The only Democrat to run here in the 5th—and probably the only Democrat with a strong chance to win the district—was Goode, who emphasized bipartisan cooperation with the slogan on the pencils and emery boards he handed out to voters: "Work together in Congress." Republicans had a convention in which Delegate Frank Ruff, recruited by 7th District Congressman Thomas Bliley, lost to George Landrith, a former Albemarle County school board member who lost 53%–47% to Payne in 1994. This time it was no contest. Goode carried Franklin County 87%–10%; Landrith carried only two counties, one by a single vote. Overall, Goode won 61%–36%, an impressive margin indeed.

In the House Goode serves on the Agriculture and Small Business Committees. His swing-vote position in Congress has given him remarkable clout for a freshman, enabling him to work both sides of the aisle: "If I agree with them, I'll vote Democrat. If I agree with Republicans on an issue, I'll vote with them." He joined the Blue Dogs, conservative Democrats who produced a no-tax-cut, early-spending-cuts balanced budget plan; he was disappointed by Clinton's opposition to the balanced budget amendment. He supported campaign finance reform, as well as the STEP-21 transportation funding plan that aims to match funding to each state's federal gas tax payments. In Washington, he runs a low-budget operation that defies the sometimes opulent culture of Capitol Hill; lobbyists who visit must sit on a oak stump he has had since his days as a state senator, and during off-hours, he answers his own phone and takes messages for his aides. He seems strongly entrenched in the 5th District.

The People: Pop. 1990: 562,273; 67% rural; 14% age 65+; 74% White; 25% Black; 1% Asian; 1% Hispanic origin. Households: 58% married couple families; 24% married couple fams. w. children; 32% college educ.; median household income: $24,807; per capita income: $11,675; median gross rent: $325; median house value: $55,400.

1996 Presidential Vote			1992 Presidential Vote		
Dole (R)	104,325	(48%)	Bush (R)	104,236	(46%)
Clinton (D)	93,040	(43%)	Clinton (D)	90,769	(40%)
Perot (I)	16,914	(8%)	Perot (I)	26,978	(12%)
Other	3,844	(2%)			

Rep. Virgil H. Goode, Jr. (D)

Elected 1996; b. Oct. 17, 1946, Richmond; home, Rocky Mount; U. of Richmond, B.A. 1969; U. of VA, J.D. 1973; Baptist; married (Lucy).

Career: VA Natl. Guard, 1969–75; VA Senate, 1973–96; Practicing atty., 1973–96.

DC Office: 1520 LHOB 20515, 202-225-4711; Fax: 202-225-5681.

District Offices: Charlottesville, 804-295-6372; Danville, 804-792-1280.

Committees: *Agriculture* (17th of 23 D): Forestry, Resource Conservation & Research; Risk Management & Specialty Crops. *Small Business* (14th of 16 D): Regulatory Reform & Paperwork Reduction.

Group Ratings and Key Votes: Newly Elected

Election Results

1996 general	Virgil H. Goode, Jr. (D)	120,323	(61%)	($485,1194)
	George C. Landrith III (R)	70,869	(36%)	($392,152)
	Others	6,731	(3%)	
1996 primary	Virgil H. Goode, Jr. (D)	nominated by convention		
1994 general	L. F. Payne (D)	95,308	(53%)	($915,224)
	George C. Landrith III (R)	83,555	(47%)	($356,574)

SIXTH DISTRICT

The sturdy men and women who settled the Valley of Virginia west of the Blue Ridge could hardly have differed more from the "second sons" of the European aristocracy who cleared the marshy forests of the Tidewater and built grand plantations there. Even before the Revolutionary War, Englishmen and Scots, German Protestants and Mennonites and Moravians—members of religious communities and fiercely independent farmers—poured down the great Wagon Road from Pennsylvania to the Valley. They were looking not for the flat, mahogany-brown land that eastern tobacco growers sought, but for fields which could support wheat, corn and hay, crops which could be rotated and which an individual farmer and his family could handle. That same independent spirit nurtured the growth of higher education here. In Lexington alone are Washington and Lee University, which Robert E. Lee headed, and the Virginia Military Institute, where Stonewall Jackson taught philosophy and artillery tactics, and which began admitting women in 1996 under pressure from the U.S. Supreme Court. A quartet of the South's most distinguished women's private colleges are only a short drive away: Mary Baldwin College at Staunton, Randolph-Macon Woman's College at Lynchburg, Sweet Briar College at Sweet Briar, and Hollins College at Roanoke, farther south in the Valley. Meanwhile, industry flourished here more than in most of Virginia east of the Blue Ridge. In the 19th Century the Norfolk and Southern Railroad established its chief junction at Roanoke; as the years passed the city became the railroad's headquarters, and many major companies have plants here.

The 6th Congressional District of Virginia covers the heart of the Valley of Virginia, from Harrisonburg south to Roanoke, and crosses over the Blue Ridge to take in Lynchburg. Politically, this area has a Republican tradition hospitable to economic assistance for the little guy, and fiercely opposed to Byrd Democrats. But in more recent years, the ancestral conservatism of Byrd Democrats and the feisty politics of the mountain rebels have melded into a single conservative Republicanism, more populist than elite in tone, as concerned with moral values as economic freedom, prickly about interference from Washington or even Richmond.

The congressman from the 6th District is Bob Goodlatte, a Republican first elected in 1992. Goodlatte grew up in Massachusetts, attended college in Maine and then law school at W&L, and went to work in Congressman Caldwell Butler's office in Roanoke. Goodlatte then practiced law and stayed active in politics; in 1992, when Democratic Congressman Jim Olin retired, Goodlatte was nominated by convention and won the general 60%–40%.

Goodlatte compiled a mostly conservative voting record and early in his first term was one of the Republican freshmen who pushed successfully for term limits on committees' ranking minority members—which now applies to committee chairmen. When Republicans took control in the 104th Congress, Goodlatte rushed to confront OMB Director Alice Rivlin on the administration's unbalanced budget and was floor leader for the "loser pays" provision in Contract With America litigation reform legislation. Goodlatte is an enthusiast for the Internet and other new communications technologies, which he believes can put out-of-the-way places like the 6th District on the same commercial level as major cities. On the Judiciary Committee he was chief House Republican sponsor of the bill liberalizing export control of encryption technology; he argued commerce would thrive only if it could keep secrets, while the Clinton Administration wanted governments to have access to codes, citing the Aldrich Ames spy case as an example of how encryption can threaten national security. At the same time he supported the Communications Decency Act, allowing censorship of obscene material on the Internet. He sponsored a law imposing tougher penalties on commercial counterfeiters, especially important in the software industry; he sought tougher penalties for telemarketing fraud. He amended the Telecommunications Act to give local governments more say over the location of cellular phone towers. He also serves on Agriculture, where he became the Department Operations, Nutrition and Foreign Agriculture Subcommittee chairman in July 1996. He worked to impose a cap on the number of foreign guest workers to be let in under a proposed temporary farm workers program; this became moot when the House rejected setting up the program. He sought to prevent families from receiving food stamps benefits for members in prison.

Goodlatte was reelected without opposition in 1994 and by 67%–31% in 1996.

The People: Pop. 1990: 562,426; 34% rural; 15% age 65+; 87% White; 11% Black; 1% Asian; 1% Hispanic origin. Households: 57% married couple families; 24% married couple fams. w. children; 39% college educ.; median household income: $27,155; per capita income: $13,017; median gross rent: $358; median house value: $64,600.

1996 Presidential Vote

Dole (R)	108,757	(50%)
Clinton (D)	87,883	(41%)
Perot (I)	16,116	(7%)
Other	3,471	(2%)

1992 Presidential Vote

Bush (R)	111,405	(49%)
Clinton (D)	84,037	(37%)
Perot (I)	29,207	(13%)

Rep. Bob Goodlatte (R)

Elected 1992; b. Sept. 22, 1952, Holyoke, MA; home, Roanoke; Bates Col., B.A. 1974, Washington & Lee Law Schl., J.D. 1977; Christian Scientist; married (Maryellen).

Career: Dist. Dir., U.S. Rep. Caldwell Butler, 1977–79; Practicing atty., 1979–92.

DC Office: 123 CHOB 20515, 202-225-5431; Fax: 202-225-9681; e-mail: talk2bob@hr.house.gov.

District Offices: Harrisonburg, 540-432-2391; Lynchburg, 804-845-8306; Roanoke, 703-857-2672; Staunton, 540-885-3861.

Committees: *Agriculture* (7th of 27 R): Department Operations, Nutrition & Foreign Agriculture (Chmn.); Livestock, Dairy & Poultry. *Judiciary* (11th of 20 R): Constitution; Courts & Intellectual Property.

Group Ratings

	ADA	ACLU	AFS	LCV	CFA	CON	NFIB	COC	ACU	NTLC	CHC
1996	5	0	0	31	23	38	97	100	95	100	93
1995	0	—	—	6	15	87	—	96	88	—	—

National Journal Ratings

	1995 LIB	—	1995 CONS	1996 LIB	—	1996 CONS
Economic	0%	—	74%	33%	—	64%
Social	21%	—	72%	0%	—	90%
Foreign	42%	—	55%	41%	—	56%

Key Votes of the 104th Congress

1. Reduce Medicare Growth $	Y	5. Flag Amendment	Y	9. Cuban Embargo	Y
2. Ovrd. Product Liab. Veto	Y	6. Drop EPA Limits	N	10. Bar Bosnia Troop $	N
3. Increase Min. Wage	N	7. Repeal Assault-Weap. Ban	Y	11. Cut Anti-Missile Defense	N
4. Welfare Reform	Y	8. Ovrd. Part. Birth Veto	Y	12. Bar U.N. Uniforms	Y

Election Results

1996 general	Bob Goodlatte (R)	133,576	(67%)	($566,763)
	Jeffrey W. Grey (R)	61,485	(31%)	($92,744)
	Others	4,300	(2%)	
1996 primary	Bob Goodlatte (R)	nominated by convention		
1994 general	Bob Goodlatte (R)	unopposed		($211,653)

SEVENTH DISTRICT

In the center of Virginia, on a hill in downtown Richmond above the James River, is Thomas Jefferson's Capitol, one of the first classical-style buildings in North America, chaste and simple in the Jefferson style. Monument Avenue, Richmond's grand 140-foot-wide boulevard, is punctuated by circles, each with a statue of a Confederate hero—Robert E. Lee (62 feet tall, dedicated Memorial Day 1890), Jeb Stuart, Jefferson Davis, Stonewall Jackson, Matthew Fountain Maury, "the Pathfinder of the Sea." On the grid streets of Church Hill, on the other side of the Capitol, Douglas Wilder grew up in a segregated neighborhood, working as a waiter in a hotel he could not check into, looking up the downtown streets at office buildings he could only dream of working in, staring at the Capitol where it was assumed he could never hold office.

It is not surprising that there eventually was a clash between the whites who occupied the leading places in Richmond's great institutions—the Virginia Electric and Power Company, the big Main Street banks and the big law firms, the Philip Morris tobacco company and the Richmond newspapers—and the blacks who have become a majority within the Richmond city limits. When blacks first won a majority on the Richmond council in the 1970s, the outgoing administration feared the newcomers would tear down the statue of Lee, and so deeded it to the state. Now, the state has had a black governor, the Martin Luther King holiday law pays homage to Confederate heroes as well as to the civil rights leader, and a statue of Richmond-born African-American tennis champion Arthur Ashe has been added to Monument Avenue. But there remains a gulf between these two separate cultures, connected but still not unified.

That gulf now has been reflected in the boundaries of Richmond area congressional districts. In the 1991 and slightly changed 1993 plans, most black precincts, including downtown Richmond and the Capitol, were collected in the black-majority 3d District, which extended downriver along the James to Newport News and Norfolk. The mostly white precincts on the west side of Richmond, most of suburban Henrico, Chesterfield and Hanover Counties were put in the 7th District, which extends north past James Madison's home at Montpelier to Culpeper County and the Blue Ridge Mountains. But some 80% of the 7th's population is in metro Richmond. These boundaries may change for 1998 or 2000, since a three-judge federal panel in February 1997 ruled the 3d District lines unconstitutional; in May, state Attorney General and Republican gubernatorial candidate James Gilmore said he would appeal the decision to the Supreme Court. Any change in the Richmond area would make the overwhelmingly Democratic 3d less Democratic and the overwhelmingly Republican 7th less Republican.

The congressman from the 7th District is Thomas Bliley, elected in 1980, now chairman of the Commerce Committee. Bliley grew up in Richmond, where his family owned a funeral home; he started off in politics as a conservative Democrat and was mayor of Richmond from 1970–77. In 1980, he was elected to this seat as a Republican by a 53%–33% margin, and has been reelected easily; in 1992, one-year incumbent George Allen was redistricted in with him, but Allen decided to leave the House and run for governor—and of course won. Bliley got on Commerce in his first term, became ranking Republican on John Dingell's Oversight Committee in 1989, then in 1993 became ranking Republican on Henry Waxman's Health and Environment Subcommittee. Bliley early on showed legislative skill dealing with issues from the electric utility grid and Medicaid formulas to home medical services and drug discounts for veterans. He showed he could stand up to tough partisans like Dingell and Waxman and also work for bipartisan solutions.

When Republicans won their House majority, Speaker Newt Gingrich, impressed by Bliley's skills, passed over more senior Republican Carlos Moorhead of California to make Bliley chairman of Commerce. The press initially focused on tobacco: Waxman had hauled tobacco company executives before TV cameras in 1994 and Bliley, representing a city that has been a tobacco center for 250 years and one of whose largest employers is Philip Morris, obviously would have none of that. But other issues proved more important, and Bliley, keeping a tight rein on the power of subcommittee chairmen, compiled an impressive record of legislative achievement. Not all Republican priorities were accomplished, if only because of the threat of Clinton's veto—though one, securities litigation reform, got bipartisan support and was passed over Clinton's veto. Bipartisan agreement was hammered out on many important bills, including some where it initially seemed improbable. For all his strong conservative views, Bliley understands that on complex regulatory bills, compromise is usually necessary for passage: "You can stand like the oak or you can bend like the pine. If you choose to stand like the oak, you'll probably fall like the oak. If you stand like the pine and bend a little bit, you'll usually come out of the storm in pretty good shape."

A striking example of bipartisan agreement came on the pesticide bill in July 1996. Republicans wanted to repeal the Delaney clause, which bans any substance with any provable carcinogenic effect; modern instruments are so sensitive that many harmless substances would have to be banned. Bliley and Waxman hammered out a bill which replaced Delaney and limited stricter state regulations, but which would make safety rules for certain foods more stringent and established a "no reasonable risk of harm" standard. Similarly, the Safe Drinking Water Act, after some tussles, was signed by Bill Clinton in August 1996. Bliley was not successful in getting agreement on Superfund reform; most money now goes to lawyers, and Bliley blamed the trial lawyers lobby for opposing changes. A major committee priority for 1997 and 1998 is electric utility deregulation; Bliley is supportive, but this is a complex matter that may need more than one Congress to be settled. Bliley also worked on a capital markets securities bill. The giant legislative achievement of Commerce was the Telecommunications Act, passed in February 1996. Bliley also worked on local issues, producing a Virginia National Parks Act limiting local park boundaries and protecting battlefield sites in the Shenandoah Valley, a National Ground Intelligence Center in Charlottesville, and money for Richmond water projects. He favors a national sales tax and requiring a two-thirds vote for any tax increase.

The People: Pop. 1990: 562,729; 26% rural; 11% age 65+; 87% White; 10% Black; 2% Asian; 1% Hispanic origin. Households: 59% married couple families; 29% married couple fams. w. children; 56% college educ.; median household income: $38,865; per capita income: $18,360; median gross rent: $520; median house value: $91,300.

1996 Presidential Vote			**1992 Presidential Vote**		
Dole (R)	155,466	(58%)	Bush (R)	154,575	(54%)
Clinton (D)	93,025	(35%)	Clinton (D)	85,357	(30%)
Perot (I)	16,607	(6%)	Perot (I)	42,724	(15%)

Rep. Tom Bliley (R)

Elected 1980; b. Jan. 28, 1932, Chesterfield Cnty.; home, Richmond; Georgetown U., B.A. 1952; Catholic; married (Mary Virginia).

Career: Navy, 1952–55; Funeral home Dir., 1955–80; Richmond City Cncl. 1968–77, Vice Mayor 1968–70, Mayor, 1970–77.

DC Office: 2409 RHOB 20515, 202-225-2815; Fax: 202-225-0011.

District Offices: Culpeper, 540-825-8960; Richmond, 804-771-2809.

Committees: *Commerce* (Chmn. of 28 R).

Group Ratings

	ADA	ACLU	AFS	LCV	CFA	CON	NFIB	COC	ACU	NTLC	CHC
1996	0	0	0	15	8	30	97	100	100	98	93
1995	0	—	—	6	0	38	—	96	80	—	—

National Journal Ratings

	1995 LIB — 1995 CONS	1996 LIB — 1996 CONS
Economic	0% — 74%	0% — 82%
Social	0% — 79%	0% — 90%
Foreign	28% — 65%	0% — 79%

Key Votes of the 104th Congress

1. Reduce Medicare Growth $	Y	5. Flag Amendment	Y	9. Cuban Embargo	Y
2. Ovrd. Product Liab. Veto	Y	6. Drop EPA Limits	N	10. Bar Bosnia Troop $	N
3. Increase Min. Wage	N	7. Repeal Assault-Weap. Ban	Y	11. Cut Anti-Missile Defense	N
4. Welfare Reform	Y	8. Ovrd. Part. Birth Veto	Y	12. Bar U.N. Uniforms	Y

Election Results

1996 general	Tom Bliley (R)	189,644	(75%)	($1,092,570)
	Roderic H. Slayton (D)	51,206	(20%)	($28,328)
	Bradley E. Evans (I)	11,527	(5%)	($195)
1996 primary	Tom Bliley (R)	nominated by convention		
1994 general	Tom Bliley (R)	176,941	(84%)	($572,427)
	Gerald E. (Jerry) Berg (I)	33,220	(16%)	

EIGHTH DISTRICT

Some two hundred years ago, when George Washington trod the brick sidewalks of Alexandria, Virginia, on his way to market or court or church, this was the largest city in northern Virginia, and dwarfed Georgetown, Maryland, just up the Potomac River; what is now Capitol Hill and downtown Washington were just hills above the river's mud flats. As Washington grew, Northern Virginia seemed left behind. The District of Columbia retroceded its land south of the Potomac—now Alexandria and Arlington—to Virginia in 1846 because it seemed obvious that the federal government would never need it, and it was 97 years before the first federal building was built on the Virginia side—the Pentagon; Franklin Roosevelt wondered out loud what they would do with all that space after the war. When the Pentagon was built, Alexandria and the rural countryside of Northern Virginia were represented in Congress by Judge Howard W. Smith, a Byrd Democrat, who saw as his mission the maintenance of the standards of George Washington, Thomas Jefferson and Robert E. Lee. Yet by the 1960s, even as Judge Smith kept his law offices in Old Town, Alexandria, the area was changing around him. New subdivision dwellers with white-collar jobs and lots of children wanted schools with good academic programs—not the segregated schoolhouses Judge Smith's friends were willing to finance. The new generation wanted freeways and traffic lights, planning instituted to regulate development, parks and recreation facilities. Smith's district was moved farther out into the countryside, two-party politics came to the suburbs, and local governments got to work. The congressional seat here, though often bitterly contested, was held from 1952–74 by Republican Joel Broyhill, a real estate developer who ran a fine constituency service operation in a district more than one-third of whose residents were federal employees. Democrats still held many legislative and local offices.

Now the onetime suburbs of Arlington and Alexandria have become central cities of a sort—"edge cities," in Joel Garreau's term—themselves. Giant office developments sprang up from rail yards in Crystal City and from used car lots in Rosslyn. Vietnamese and other Asian-

Americans have moved into these neighborhoods, and one of America's biggest Vietnamese commercial districts is in Clarendon, about a mile from Arlington National Cemetery and Fort Myer. Politically, once hotly contested Alexandria and Arlington are now solidly Democratic.

The 8th Congressional District of Virginia consists of Arlington County and the cities of Alexandria and Falls Church. It also takes in two separate parts of Fairfax County—the portion of high-income McLean inside the Capital Beltway and several areas south of Alexandria's Old Town: the gentle landscapes of Mount Vernon, lower-income Groveton along the old U.S. 1, suburban Springfield and the more rural areas around Lorton prison and Fort Belvoir. This district was designed for the 1990s by a Democratic legislature and governor to be solidly Democratic. Where formerly there had been two marginal Northern Virginia districts, now there is the safely Democratic 8th, the safely Republican 10th and the toss-up 11th (Democratic in 1992, Republican in 1994 and 1996).

The congressman from the 8th District is Jim Moran, an oft-embattled Alexandria politician with traces in his accent of his Massachusetts roots. He was elected to the Alexandria City Council in 1979 and vice mayor in 1982; in 1984 he pleaded no contest to a conflict of interest charge and resigned from the Council. The charges were eventually dropped (the law he supposedly violated was even changed), and in 1985 Moran was elected mayor. In 1990, he ran for Congress in what had become one of the most populous districts in the country, stretching from Alexandria south almost to Fredericksburg; the incumbent was Stanford Parris, elected congressman in 1972 and again throughout the 1980s, candidate for governor of Virginia in 1989. It was a nasty race: Parris said Moran was a supporter of Saddam Hussein; Moran said he wanted to "break [Parris's] nose," and called him "a deceitful, fatuous jerk." The major substantive issue was abortion, on which Moran ran a pro-choice ad portraying Lady Liberty behind bars. With a big margin in Alexandria, Moran won 52%–45%.

In the House, Moran was freshman class whip, but flip-flopped on his first big vote, the Gulf war resolution, which he ultimately voted against. He has engaged in a long and mostly unsuccessful fight to stop 11,000 Navy employees from being relocated out of Crystal City but he successfully fought Redskins owner Jack Kent Cooke's plan to build a football stadium at Potomac Yards in Alexandria. In 1993 he voted for the Clinton budget and tax package, despite its one-year pay freeze on federal employees—a tough vote in a district where 21% of workers are federal employees, the second highest in the country. He switched his vote at the last minute in June 1994 to save NASA's space station. But he balked at the Clinton healthcare reform because it threatened federal employees' plan, and he blasted as "politically expedient" and based on "sound bites" the reinventing government plan as threatening the most talented federal employees. In the 104th Congress he had a moderate to liberal voting record. He was the only Democrat to vote for a Republican program to allow local governments to consolidate federal grants into more flexible spending plans: his Alexandria experience counted. He jousted with Chairman John Mica of the subcommittee handling civil service, concerned that strengthening veterans' preferences would give them too much of an advantage over other workers. Moran also worried about streamlining the civil service appeals process with language that would have excluded the EEOC. He jousted—literally—with other Republicans, shoving Californian Randy Cunningham off the floor and out the House chamber doors in November 1995 after Cunningham said that Moran had "turned his back on Desert Storm." Moran later apologized and said, "I would prefer to be known as a statesman rather than a fighter in the literal way."

Since the 1990s redistricting Moran has been in good electoral shape. In 1992 and 1994 he was opposed by conservative Kyle McSlarrow in races which sometimes became acerbic; but Moran won by comfortable margins, 56%–42% in 1992 and 59%–39% in 1994. McSlarrow went on to become a top aide to Senate Majority Leaders Bob Dole and Trent Lott. In 1996 Moran won 66%–28% in a district Bill Clinton was carrying 55%–40%; Moran had more cash on hand at the end of the campaign than he spent on it. In March 1997 he and Calvin Dooley and Tim Roemer created the centrist "New Democratic Coalition" to work for alternatives to "traditional Democratic policies." They differed from the usually more rural Blue Dogs, being more pro-business on economics and more liberal on cultural issues; they could play an important part on close votes.

The People: Pop. 1990: 562,808; 9% age 65+; 71% White; 13% Black; 7% Asian; 9% Hispanic origin. Households: 48% married couple families; 21% married couple fams. w. children; 71% college educ.; median household income: $48,839; per capita income: $24,799; median gross rent: $729; median house value: $210,200.

1996 Presidential Vote			1992 Presidential Vote		
Clinton (D)	130,177	(55%)	Clinton (D)	133,183	(51%)
Dole (R)	95,839	(40%)	Bush (R)	96,799	(37%)
Perot (I)	9,439	(4%)	Perot (I)	28,967	(11%)

Rep. James P. Moran, Jr. (D)

Elected 1990; b. May 16, 1945, Buffalo, NY; home, Alexandria; Col. of Holy Cross, B.A. 1967, City U. of NY, 1968, U. of Pittsburgh, M.P.A. 1970; Catholic; married (Mary).

Career: Budget analyst, auditor, U.S. Dept. of H.E.W., 1968–74; Fiscal policy spec., Library of Congress, 1974–76; Staff, U.S. Senate Approp. Cmte., 1976–80; Alexandria City Cncl., 1979–82; Alexandria Vice Mayor, 1982–84, Alexandria Mayor, 1985–90; Investment broker, 1980–88.

DC Office: 1214 LHOB 20515, 202-225-4376; Fax: 202-225-0017; e-mail: repmoran@hr.house.gov.

District Offices: Alexandria, 703-971-4700.

Committees: *Appropriations* (21st of 26 D): District of Columbia (RMM); Interior.

Group Ratings

	ADA	ACLU	AFS	LCV	CFA	CON	NFIB	COC	ACU	NTLC	CHC
1996	65	56	83	69	100	92	38	31	20	22	20
1995	65	—	—	63	77	56	—	42	8	—	—

National Journal Ratings

	1995 LIB — 1995 CONS			1996 LIB — 1996 CONS		
Economic	66%	—	34%	58%	—	42%
Social	71%	—	28%	69%	—	30%
Foreign	88%	—	7%	70%	—	29%

Key Votes of the 104th Congress

1. Reduce Medicare Growth $	N	5. Flag Amendment	Y	9. Cuban Embargo	N
2. Ovrd. Product Liab. Veto	Y	6. Drop EPA Limits	Y	10. Bar Bosnia Troop $	N
3. Increase Min. Wage	Y	7. Repeal Assault-Weap. Ban	N	11. Cut Anti-Missile Defense	Y
4. Welfare Reform	N	8. Ovrd. Part. Birth Veto	Y	12. Bar U.N. Uniforms	N

Election Results

1996 general	James P. Moran, Jr. (D)	152,334	(66%)	($319,334)
	John E. Otey (R)	64,562	(28%)	($71,267)
	Others	12,525	(5%)	
1996 primary	James P. Moran, Jr. (D)	nominated by convention		
1994 general	James P. Moran, Jr. (D)	120,281	(59%)	($910,239)
	Kyle E. McSlarrow (R)	79,568	(39%)	($643,979)

NINTH DISTRICT

One of the first areas to be settled from the seacoast to the great American interior was what is now southwest Virginia. As early as 1765, settlements were carved out in the great Valley of Virginia, which bends westward and south toward Tennessee and the Cumberland Gap. Most settlers were of Scots-Irish lineage, and the mountainous area where they moved developed almost apart from the rest of Virginia. The fiercely independent settlers were first farmers, later often coal miners, as in West Virginia, which wasn't a separate state until 1863. Politically, this virtually all-white area opposed slavery and was skeptical if not hostile to the Confederacy. Out of the crucible of struggle between secessionists and unionists, southwest Virginia developed a robust two-party politics after the Civil War, with both parties resembling their national counterparts more closely than in the rest of Virginia.

The 9th Congressional District of Virginia covers all of southwest Virginia west of Roanoke. Over the years, the district became known as the "Fighting Ninth," because of its taste for raucous politics, culturally conservative and economically populist. It is becoming somewhat more like the rest of Virginia, as development has moved down Interstate 81 to, and even past, Blacksburg, home of Virginia Tech. But mountain counties farther west have lost population and otherwise not changed much, and a bitter coal strike in 1990 showed that the old economic order and antagonisms had not entirely vanished.

The congressman from the 9th is Rick Boucher, a Democrat first elected in 1982. Boucher grew up in the antique town of Abingdon, went to Roanoke College and then the University of Virginia for law school; he practiced law in Abingdon and was elected to the Virginia Senate in 1975, at 29. In 1982 he ran for the U.S. House against veteran incumbent William Wampler and won with big margins in the coal counties on the Kentucky border. Boucher, like other "Fighting Ninth" Democrats, tends to vote with House Democrats most but not all of the time.

But the bulk of Boucher's work is on the Commerce Committee and its Telecommunications Subcommittee. Back in 1988 he co-sponsored with Al Gore a bill to allow phone companies to offer cable TV and sponsored the 1988 Satellite Home Viewers Act, so viewers without over-the-air network reception could subscribe to satellite services carrying network channels: the beginning of the now booming satellite TV business. Cable TV had its start in mountainous areas where network TV signals were weak, and Boucher sees new technologies, from satellite TV to the Internet, as a means for out-of-the-way places like the 9th to compete on an equal commercial basis with urban areas. The 1988 bill was a precursor of the 1996 Telecommunications Act, on which Boucher also worked, and which opens up the local telephone and long distance markets. He was a co-founder of the Internet Caucus in April 1996 with Vermont's Patrick Leahy, South Dakota's Larry Pressler and Washington's Rick White—three of the four from rural areas. He worked on the Judiciary Subcommittee on Courts and Intellectual Property with Bob Goodlatte of the 6th District to update copyright laws for the digital age and for a consensus on a National Information Infrastructure. He seeks more funding for advanced research in high performance computing. With Republican Fred Upton he worked, so far unsuccessfully, for compromises on two partisan issues: for binding arbitration to decide liability for costs in Superfund suits and for allowing state or local governments to ban or limit interstate shipment of municipal solid waste. In 1997 he switched from the Trade and Hazardous Materials Subcommittee to Energy and Power to work on electric utility deregulation, which he hopes will benefit the coal industry and stimulate investment in mine facilities. At home he has sponsored since 1989 a Showcasing Southwest Virginia program which he claimed has attracted $150 million in investments, and has worked to encourage "electronic villages" in local communities.

In this usually partisan district, Boucher has become highly popular. His Commerce Committee seat helps him to raise large sums of money; in 1996 he spent $576,709 and had $418,164 cash on hand afterwards. He was reelected 65%–31% in a district which Bill Clinton carried by just 46%–43%.

The People: Pop. 1990: 562,508; 71% rural; 13% age 65+; 96% White; 3% Black; 1% Asian; 1% Hispanic origin. Households: 62% married couple families; 28% married couple fams. w. children; 30% college educ.; median household income: $20,857; per capita income: $10,097; median gross rent: $315; median house value: $49,100.

1996 Presidential Vote			1992 Presidential Vote		
Clinton (D)	91,469	(46%)	Clinton (D)	99,099	(45%)
Dole (R)	85,531	(43%)	Bush (R)	93,673	(42%)
Perot (I)	20,603	(10%)	Perot (I).	26,676	(12%)
Other	3,103	(2%)			

Rep. Rick Boucher (D)

Elected 1982; b. Aug. 1, 1946, Abingdon; home, Abingdon; Roanoke Col., B.A. 1968, U. of VA, J.D. 1971; United Methodist; single.

Career: Practicing atty., 1971–83; VA Senate, 1975–1983.

DC Office: 2329 RHOB 20515, 202-225-3861; Fax: 202-225-0442; e-mail: ninthnet@hr.house.gov.

District Offices: Abingdon, 540-628-1145; Big Stone Gap, 540-523-5450; Pulaski, 540-980-4310.

Committees: *Commerce* (5th of 23 D): Energy & Power; Telecommunications, Trade & Consumer Protection. *Judiciary* (5th of 15 D): Courts & Intellectual Property.

Group Ratings

	ADA	ACLU	AFS	LCV	CFA	CON	NFIB	COC	ACU	NTLC	CHC
1996	65	71	92	77	77	24	33	44	15	23	7
1995	75	—	—	63	92	1	—	33	4	—	—

National Journal Ratings

	1995 LIB — 1995 CONS			1996 LIB — 1996 CONS		
Economic	74%	—	25%	65%	—	35%
Social	77%	—	22%	71%	—	29%
Foreign	64%	—	34%	76%	—	22%

Key Votes of the 104th Congress

1. Reduce Medicare Growth $	N	5. Flag Amendment	N	9. Cuban Embargo	N
2. Ovrd. Product Liab. Veto	Y	6. Drop EPA Limits	Y	10. Bar Bosnia Troop $	N
3. Increase Min. Wage	Y	7. Repeal Assault-Weap. Ban	Y	11. Cut Anti-Missile Defense	Y
4. Welfare Reform	N	8. Ovrd. Part. Birth Veto	N	12. Bar U.N. Uniforms	N

Election Results

1996 general	Rick Boucher (D)	122,908	(65%)	($576,709)
	Patrick C. Muldoon (R)	58,055	(31%)	($71,662)
	Thomas I. Roberts (VA Reform)	8,080	(4%)	($5,110)
1996 primary	Rick Boucher (D)	nominated by convention		
1994 general	Rick Boucher (D)	102,876	(59%)	($779,616)
	S. H. (Steve) Fast (R)	72,133	(41%)	($209,235)

TENTH DISTRICT

Even as the Constitution was being hammered out in Philadelphia, the rolling green Piedmont of northern Virginia and the fertile mountain-bound lands of the Shenandoah Valley were buzzing with new settlers. They came up the rivers that flow into the Chesapeake, into the Valley from the great Wagon Road south from Pennsylvania, moving onto lands speculated on by George Washington and his peers. During the Civil War, this was some of the most heavily contested land on the continent; afterwards, the surge of movement having propelled new settlers much farther west, this part of Virginia was well-settled and became prime fox hunting country. Now subdivisions have sprouted up on fields, and the horse farms of the Piedmont, long first or second homes of some of the richest people in America, are attracting a growing population of Washington, D.C., commuters and weekend residents. What looked like marginal farmlands to the settlers of the early 19th Century now looks like heaven for city-dwellers: bucolic green hills with views of the Blue Ridge and other mountains, antique houses and tiny crossroads communities. There is still an old-fashioned air in the narrow streets of the old county seat towns, but a McDonald's culture has developed on the bypass roads on their outskirts.

The 10th Congressional District of Virginia covers much of this territory. The 10th has expanded as people have moved outward; today it is entirely, in the familiar phrase, outside the Beltway. About one-third of its people live in suburban Fairfax County, by many measures the most affluent county in the United States: 61% of its households had incomes over $50,000 in 1989, number one in the country, though it was only number seven in percentage of over $100,000 households. Also, 49% of its adults over 25 were college graduates, more than double the national figure. Fairfax, and especially the 10th's portion of it—affluent and woodsy Great Falls and parts of McLean, the new subdivisions around the old crossroads of Centreville and the upscale Fair Oaks shopping mall area—is full of high-salaried, two-earner families, young and well-educated, employed more often by the private sector than by government, frazzled by commuting on clogged roads. Beyond Fairfax, another one-third of district residents live in Loudoun County and parts of Prince William County, once rural—the Manassas battlefield is here—but now heavily settled, not as high-income or well-educated as Fairfax nor as culturally liberal. The last third of the 10th's residents are in smaller, still rural-appearing Fauquier and Rappahannock Counties, and west of the Blue Ridge in the Shenandoah Valley. Politically, this is a very Republican district. The Shenandoah tradition of Harry Byrd Democrats switched seamlessly to Republicanism, as indeed many local politicians switched parties themselves; the new suburbanites are if anything more determinedly Republican. This was the second most Republican Virginia district in the 1996 presidential election.

The congressman from the 10th District is Frank Wolf, elected in 1980, now chairman of the Appropriations' Transportation Subcommittee. Wolf is a native of Philadelphia who went to law school at Georgetown, was an appointee in the Nixon and Ford Administrations, then ran for Congress in 1980, when most of the 10th District was inside the Beltway. He beat a Democratic incumbent and as the 10th has moved outward, and as he has worked hard on federal employee, transportation and other issues, he has become unbeatable. His overall voting record is moderately conservative. He has long maintained a crackerjack constituency service operation and has been key in promoting federal employee causes. He has promoted on-site child care centers at federal workplaces and pushed federal telecommuting (the first center was in Winchester). He opposed Hatch Act repeal, saying it would politicize the federal workforce. He opposed the Clinton healthcare reform in 1994 because it would have gutted the federal employee health plan, and he opposed the Contract With America tax cut in 1995 because it would have required higher pension payments by federal employees; he and 11th District Congressman Tom Davis and Maryland's Connie Morella were three of only 11 Republicans to vote against the tax cut.

Wolf has used his seat to improve transportation in traffic-choked northern Virginia. He got full funding for the 103-mile Metro subway system, for widening I-66 from the Beltway to Gainesville, for the Route 234 interchange in Manassas, and for express buses in the Dulles Airport corridor. He led the move to put National and Dulles Airports under a regional authority and pushed to get the National Air and Space Museum annex located at Dulles. But he has consistently opposed earmarking funds for members' pet transportation projects in appropriations bills as "immoral," offending House Transportation and Infrastructure Chairman Bud Shuster and West Virginia Senator Robert Byrd. As subcommittee chairman, Wolf has worked for bipartisan consensus, and his bills have passed and been signed with relatively little controversy. His bill for fiscal year 1996 cut spending for Amtrak, mass transit and the FAA and zeroed out the Interstate Commerce Commission; it increased spending for highways and restructured the Coast Guard. His bill for fiscal 1997 had a big increase for highways, a slight increase for public transit grants and an increase for the FAA to hire more air traffic control personnel.

On other issues Wolf has been motivated by deep moral concerns. Disturbed by the fighting in the former Yugoslavia, he got MFN status for Serbia revoked in 1992 and zeroed-out a Croatian-American Enterprise Fund in 1996. With California's Nancy Pelosi, he has led moves to withdraw MFN status for China because of human right violations. In 1996 his bill to establish a national commission to study gambling was passed, though it did not have the subpoena powers to call witnesses which he initially proposed. He is offended by what he considers political wrongdoing, from whatever quarter. In 1994 he worked doggedly to find out how many non-employees had White House passes and to get campaign consultants with passes to make financial disclosures. In 1997, when the embattled Newt Gingrich needed every vote he could get to be reelected speaker, Wolf voted "present."

Wolf has been reelected by wide margins, 72%–25% in 1996.

The People: Pop. 1990: 562,257; 44% rural; 7% age 65+; 89% White; 6% Black; 3% Asian; 2% Hispanic origin. Households: 67% married couple families; 35% married couple fams. w. children; 55% college educ.; median household income: $46,205; per capita income: $20,065; median gross rent: $657; median house value: $155,000.

1996 Presidential Vote

Dole (R)	140,684	(54%)
Clinton (D)	99,510	(38%)
Perot (I)	16,476	(6%)

1992 Presidential Vote

Bush (R)	124,783	(50%)
Clinton (D)	83,214	(33%)
Perot (I)	41,228	(16%)

Rep. Frank R. Wolf (R)

Elected 1980; b. Jan. 30, 1939, Philadelphia, PA; home, Vienna; PA St. U., B.A. 1961; Georgetown U., LL.B. 1965; Presbyterian; married (Carolyn).

Career: Army, 1962–63, Army Reserves 1963–67; Legis. Asst., U.S. Rep. Edward Biester, 1968–71; Asst., U.S. Interior Secy. Rogers Morton, 1971–74; Dep. Asst. Secy., U.S. Dept. of Interior, 1974–75; Practicing atty., 1975–80.

DC Office: 241 CHOB 20515, 202-225-5136; Fax: 202-225-0437.

District Offices: Herndon, 703-709-5800; Winchester, 540-667-0990.

Committees: *Appropriations* (9th of 34 R): Foreign Operations, Export Financing & Related Programs; Transportation (Chmn.); Treasury, Postal Service & General Government.

Group Ratings

	ADA	ACLU	AFS	LCV	CFA	CON	NFIB	COC	ACU	NTLC	CHC
1996	5	12	8	31	23	87	89	81	95	85	93
1995	10	—	—	25	38	75	—	92	64	—	—

National Journal Ratings

	1995 LIB — 1995 CONS	1996 LIB — 1996 CONS
Economic	47% — 51%	39% — 58%
Social	43% — 56%	33% — 67%
Foreign	52% — 46%	21% — 72%

Key Votes of the 104th Congress

1. Reduce Medicare Growth $	Y	5. Flag Amendment	Y	9. Cuban Embargo	Y
2. Ovrd. Product Liab. Veto	Y	6. Drop EPA Limits	Y	10. Bar Bosnia Troop $	N
3. Increase Min. Wage	N	7. Repeal Assault-Weap. Ban	Y	11. Cut Anti-Missile Defense	N
4. Welfare Reform	Y	8. Ovrd. Part. Birth Veto	Y	12. Bar U.N. Uniforms	Y

Election Results

1996 general	Frank R. Wolf (R)	169,266	(72%)	($251,763)
	Robert L. Weinberg (D)	59,145	(25%)	($61,881)
	Others	6,602	(3%)	
1996 primary	Frank R. Wolf (R)	nominated by convention		
1994 general	Frank R. Wolf (R)	153,311	(87%)	($222,532)
	Alan R. Ogden (I)	13,687	(8%)	
	Robert L. (Bob) Rilee (I)	8,267	(5%)	

ELEVENTH DISTRICT

When author and *Washington Post* reporter Joel Garreau coined the term "edge city" to describe the autonomous urban centers developing on the rims of some of the nation's oldest municipalities, his prime example was Tysons Corner, Virginia. Rising on a hill west of Washington, Tysons Corner was a back-country intersection 50 years ago and a junction of several suburban roads 25 years ago; today it is home to the largest concentration of office space to be found anywhere between Washington and Atlanta, with a modern skyline and busy multi-lane avenues that serve as arteries to the nearby Capital Beltway. Fairfax County, which includes all of Tysons Corner, has changed just as dramatically since the end of World War II. At first only a few District of Columbia residents seeking breathing room in the suburbs trickled into Northern Virginia; initially they went to Arlington and Alexandria. But that trickle became a rush as young marrieds with large families and whites avoiding the increasingly high-crime District pushed farther out into Fairfax. Now Fairfax County is no longer Washington's country cousin. It has the nation's highest median household income—$59,284 in 1990, almost half its residents have a bachelor's degree or more, and nearly 70% of its households have two or more vehicles. Gradually but inexorably, Fairfax has been transformed from a suburban county where people commute to government jobs in Washington, to a 21st Century urban county where people work somewhere around the Beltway and mostly for private sector employers.

The 11th Congressional District, the seat Virginia gained in the 1990 Census, went to fast-growing Fairfax County and its neighbor just to the south, Prince William County. The 11th straddles the Beltway; its inner portion includes older comfortable areas like Annandale, which has an increasing Asian-American population, while the outer portion spans Tysons Corner and the office corridor out the Dulles Access Road, to Dulles Airport. The 11th runs south through comfortable subdivision areas like Burke and covers the somewhat lower-income Woodbridge and Dale City areas of Prince William. This is a cosmopolitan district: 8% black, 7% Hispanic, 8% Asian; 19% of residents speak a language other than English at home. The district is made up largely of two-income families, with at least one spouse employed in one of the many divisions of high-tech companies that dot Fairfax County. Politically, the 11th's educated, mobile electorate produces a robust two-party politics. In the 1980s, it voted Republican for president, with both Democratic and Republican state legislators; in the 1990s it voted 43%–42% for George Bush in 1992 and 48%–46% for Bill Clinton in 1996.

The congressman from the 11th District is Thomas Davis III, a Republican elected in 1994. Davis grew up in northern Virginia, was a friend of David Eisenhower at Amherst College, and served on active duty in the Army before earning a law degree. He was first elected to the Fairfax County Board of Supervisors, a high visibility position here, in 1979. Over the years, he gained a reputation for financial savvy in municipal matters and for seeking compromise over confrontation. In 1991 he was elected Board Chairman, something in the nature of a mayor of a jurisdiction with more diversity and over 200,000 more people than the District of Columbia.

In 1994 Davis ran for the 11th District seat against Democrat Leslie Byrne, who had won 50%–45% in 1992. Byrne had voted solidly for Clinton Administration positions and called for discipline against members of the Democratic Caucus who did not; she had strong support from labor and feminist groups, and spent $1.1 million. But Davis, with his connections, was able to raise and spend even more, $1.4 million. Davis won 53%–45%, even as Republican Oliver North fell to Democratic Senator Charles Robb in the 11th by 51%–36%.

As soon as he arrived on Capitol Hill, Davis was handed by Speaker Newt Gingrich one of the hottest potatoes of the new Congress: dealing with the affairs of the troubled District of Columbia government and its mayor, Marion Barry. As chairman of the House Government Reform and Oversight Committee's District of Columbia Subcommittee, Davis first rejected Barry's request for massive federal aid, working closely with Gingrich and District Delegate Eleanor Holmes Norton to cut District spending. Together they passed in April 1995 a law establishing a five-member control board to oversee the D.C. government. Davis's years in local government, including many dealings with Barry, gave him a reputation as "Mr. Conciliation," and he tried not to be confrontational with the District, playing "good cop" to D.C. Appropriations Subcommittee Chairman James Walsh's "bad cop." Davis even avoided the term "control board" officially, but understood that a D.C. government unwilling to make cuts and indeed ignorant of its actual fiscal status could not be trusted to balance its own budget. Davis tended to oppose the detailed policy objectives passed by Walsh—"Congress can't micromanage the city," Davis said—and in October 1995 he, Gingrich, control board Chairman Andrew Brimmer and Walsh got rid of most of them. The District's progress has been rocky, but the control board's efforts continue to lurch forward. In January 1997, President Clinton proposed the federal government assume responsibility for general city functions, including tax collection, infrastructure and prison maintenence, and Medicaid in exchange for eliminating the annual federal payment to the District. Working with the administration, Republican leaders and Norton, in June 1997 Davis developed a bill similar to Clinton's proposal, with added regulatory reform and a place for Ways and Means Chairman Bill Archer to insert tax cuts for economically depressed areas of the city.

On other issues, Davis has a moderate voting record, near the midpoint of the House. He opposed the Contract With America tax cut in 1995 because it would have required higher pension payments by federal employees; he and suburban Washington's Frank Wolf and Connie Morella were three of only 11 Republicans who voted against the tax cut. He supported the Democratic Blue Dogs' budget as well as the Republicans'. He also worked on unfunded mandate reform, federal acquisition policy and the securities litigation reform which was passed over Clinton's veto. He has looked out for the interests of federal employees and contractors and was one of four co-chairmen of the Information Technology Working Group.

In the 1996 election Davis spent over $1.3 million, and won by 64%–35% in a district often evenly divided in presidential races.

The People: Pop. 1990: 562,596; 2% rural; 6% age 65+; 76% White; 8% Black; 8% Asian; 7% Hispanic origin. Households: 62% married couple families; 33% married couple fams. w. children; 71% college educ.; median household income: $54,369; per capita income: $22,202; median gross rent: $797; median house value: $190,400.

1996 Presidential Vote			1992 Presidential Vote		
Clinton (D)	109,377	(48%)	Bush (R)	103,907	(43%)
Dole (R)	105,258	(46%)	Clinton (D)	102,721	(42%)
Perot (I)	10,844	(5%)	Perot (I)	34,719	(14%)

Rep. Tom Davis (R)

Elected 1994; b. Jan. 5, 1949, Minot, ND; home, Falls Church; Amherst Col. B.A. 1971; U. of VA, J.D. 1975; Christian Scientist; married (Peggy).

Career: Army, 1971–72; Army Reserves, 1972–79; Vice Pres. & Gen. Cnsl., PRC Inc., 1977–94; Fairfax Cnty. Bd. of Supervisors, 1979–94, Chmn., 1991–94.

DC Office: 224 CHOB 20515, 202-225-1492; Fax: 202-225-3071; e-mail: tomdavis@hr.house.gov.

District Offices: Annandale, 703-916-9610; Herndon, 703-437-1726; Woodbridge, 703-590-4599.

Committees: *Government Reform & Oversight* (12th of 24 R): District of Columbia (Chmn.); Government Management, Information & Technology. *Science* (14th of 25 R): Space & Aeronautics; Technology. *Transportation & Infrastructure* (37th of 40 R): Public Buildings & Economic Development.

Group Ratings

	ADA	ACLU	AFS	LCV	CFA	CON	NFIB	COC	ACU	NTLC	CHC
1996	15	12	0	46	46	96	89	94	79	88	66
1995	15	—	—	13	38	97	—	88	60	—	—

National Journal Ratings

	1995 LIB — 1995 CONS			1996 LIB — 1996 CONS		
Economic	47%	—	51%	48%	—	52%
Social	47%	—	53%	53%	—	45%
Foreign	48%	—	50%	37%	—	62%

Key Votes of the 104th Congress

1. Reduce Medicare Growth $	Y	5. Flag Amendment	Y	9. Cuban Embargo	Y
2. Ovrd. Product Liab. Veto	Y	6. Drop EPA Limits	N	10. Bar Bosnia Troop $	N
3. Increase Min. Wage	N	7. Repeal Assault-Weap. Ban	N	11. Cut Anti-Missile Defense	N
4. Welfare Reform	Y	8. Ovrd. Part. Birth Veto	Y	12. Bar U.N. Uniforms	Y

Election Results

1996 general	Tom Davis (R)	138,758	(64%)	($1,333,607)
	Thomas J. Horton (D)	74,701	(35%)	($290,492)
1996 primary	Tom Davis (R)	nominated by convention		
1994 general	Tom Davis (R)	98,216	(53%)	($1,430,272)
	Leslie L. Byrne (D)	84,104	(45%)	($1,136,669)
	Others	3,360	(2%)	

WASHINGTON

From Starbucks coffee to grunge music, from America's leading exporter Boeing to America's leading software maker Microsoft, Washington—the state at the far northwest corner of the continental United States, not the city back east—has become a national trend-setter. An unusual environment and human creativity have combined to produce these achievements: Seattle's cold misty air and 225 overcast days a year stimulate the appetite for strong aromatic coffee and the shapeless blue jeans and sweatshirts worn year-round in this moist climate by professionals and teenage runaways alike created a trend made famous by Nirvana and Soundgarden and other grunge groups. Boeing's airframe business took off during World War II because of the Pacific Northwest's abundant hydroelectric power made cheap aluminum possible, and through booms and busts Boeing has just kept growing. Microsoft, founded by the usually tieless and tousle-haired Bill Gates and based in Redmond, Washington, became one of America's great success stories as its software business boomed, while the hardware business faced increasing problems and IBM, with its white shirts and plain ties, laid off thousands. With flannel shirts and umbrellas, blue-collar types working off a hangover as if in a Raymond Carver story and professionals relaxing on woodsy acreage, Washington has set a tone for the 1990s, a style plainly Middle American but with attitude, an ordinariness so apt it is no longer ordinary.

All this comes to a state barely a century old, which in the two decades after statehood in 1889 built a new civilization, as transcontinental railroads reached the great ports of Puget Sound, the wheat-processing city of Spokane inland, orchard towns and fishing ports and lumber settlements. Shielded from the heavy rains and storms of the Pacific by the Olympic Mountains and the Sound, Seattle quickly became a serious American city, a lusty town full of lumbermen and railroad workers. When gold was struck in the Klondike and Alaska, Seattle became a metropolis of miners, prospectors and get-rich-quick operators, the site of the original "Skid Road" (skid row is a corruption propagated by a 1937 magazine article), where logs were rolled downhill to the port; today it's the focus of the restored Pioneer Square area. Booming, young Seattle had a turbulent class-warfare politics in the years before World War I, pitting the Industrial Workers of the World (the IWW, or Wobblies) against city business and civic leaders; the businessmen, brutally, prevailed. Adding to the area's distinctiveness was its large numbers of Scandinavian immigrants, more favorable to cooperative enterprises and government ownership than other Americans.

Over time, Washington was transformed by a series of national decisions which set its course for decades. One was government development of hydroelectric power. The Columbia River and its tributary, the Snake, falling thousands of feet in a relatively short distance, had far greater hydroelectric potential than any other American river system, and Franklin Roosevelt was always interested in these river valley projects. In 1937, Bonneville Dam was completed on the lower Columbia; in 1940, Grand Coulee Dam, the largest man-made structure in the world at the time, was opened where the Columbia cuts through the arid, surrealistically contoured plains of eastern Washington. Washington proved hospitable to the industrial union movement of the 1930s and became one of the nation's most heavily unionized states. When war came, Washington's hydroelectric power—the cheapest electricity in the country—made it the natural site for huge aluminum production plants, which require vast amounts of electricity, and the Seattle area became the home not only of shipbuilders, but of the biggest aircraft manufacturer in the country, Boeing. After the war, the Hanford plant on the Columbia was one of the government's main nuclear weapons manufacturing sites. Cheap power, aluminum, aircraft, nuclear weapons and high unionized wages: these became Washington's economic foundations in the post-World War II years.

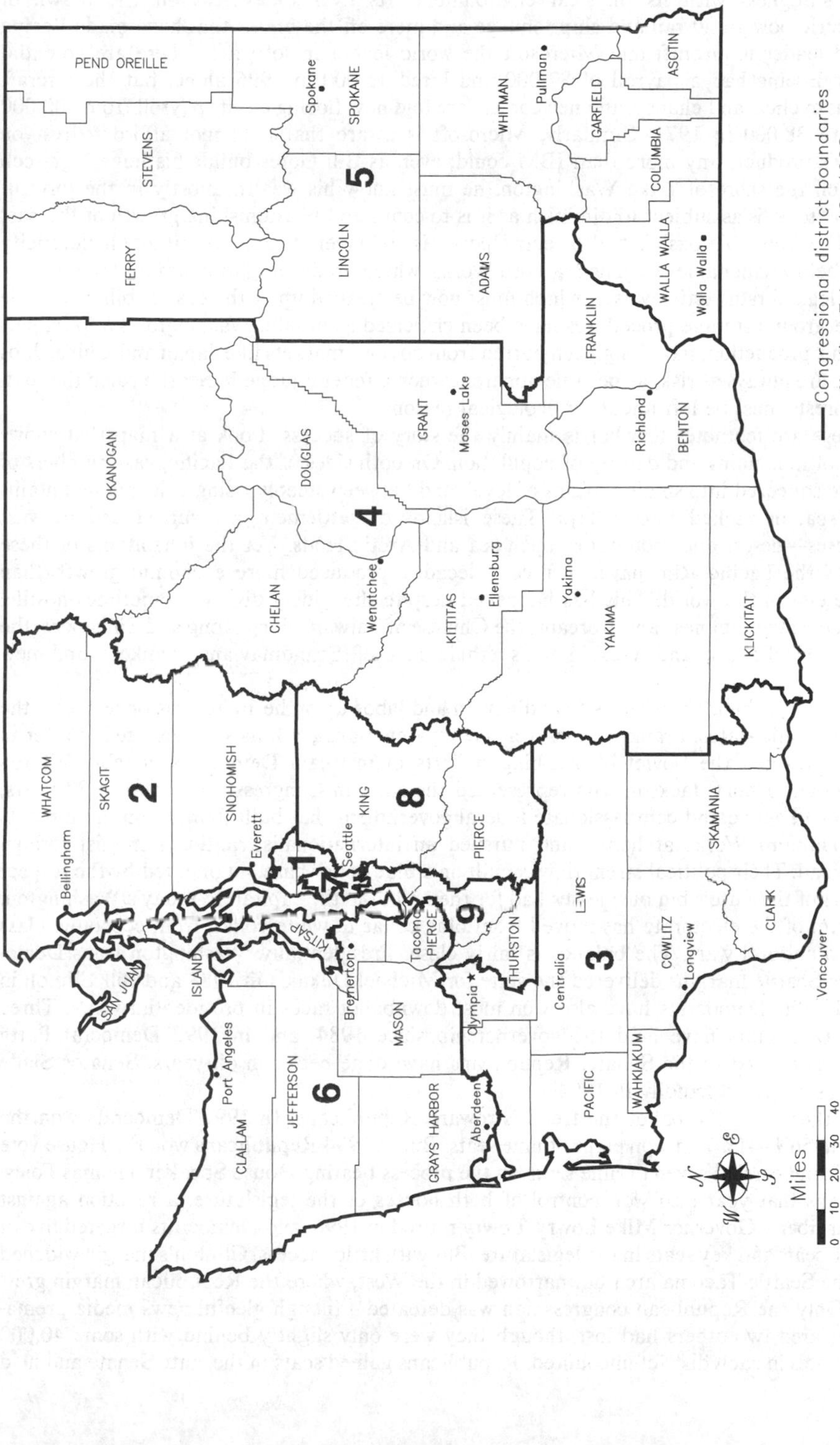
PEND OREILLE
STEVENS
FERRY
OKANOGAN
WHATCOM
SKAGIT
SNOHOMISH
KING
CHELAN
DOUGLAS
GRANT
LINCOLN
SPOKANE
WHITMAN
ADAMS
FRANKLIN
GARFIELD
COLUMBIA
ASOTIN
WALLA WALLA
BENTON
KITTITAS
YAKIMA
KLICKITAT
PIERCE
LEWIS
THURSTON
SKAMANIA
CLARK
COWLITZ
WAHKIAKUM
PACIFIC
GRAYS HARBOR
MASON
KITSAP
JEFFERSON
CLALLAM
ISLAND
SAN JUAN
Spokane
Pullman
Walla Walla
Moses Lake
Richland
Wenatchee
Ellensburg
Yakima
Seattle
Everett
Bellingham
Bremerton
Tacoma
Olympia
Centralia
Longview
Vancouver
Port Angeles
Aberdeen
1
2
3
4
5
6
7
8
9
Congressional district boundaries effective February 12, 1992.
Miles
0 10 20 30 40
Copyright © 1993 by Election Data Services, Inc.

Today, Washington is a commonwealth of 5.5 million, economically booming, pleased to the point of smugness with its physical environment. Its lives today less off the brawn of hydroelectric power and rail and ship tonnage and more off the brains that have made Boeing the world leader in aircraft and Microsoft the world leader in software. There are potential problems: Boeing had a payroll of 87,000 and hired 15,000 in 1996 alone; but the aircraft business is cyclical and chancy, and newcomers are told how Boeing cut its payroll from 100,000 in 1967 to 38,000 in 1971. Similarly, Microsoft is aware that it cannot afford to rest on yesterday's products any more than IBM could; even as Bill Gates builds his huge high-tech mansion on the shore of Lake Washington, he must know his wealth, mostly in the form of Microsoft stock, is as subject to diminish as it is to continue the astonishing growth of the past decade. The Columbia basin's hydroelectric power is no longer at capacity, although electricity rates are below national levels. The Hanford Works, which produced plutonium for the military, for years leaked radioactive waste, which must now be cleaned up at the cost of billions, while new underground storage procedures have been criticized as unsafe. Washington's apples, half the nation's production, have long been barred from obvious markets like Japan and China. Jobs in logging are always at risk, as became apparent when a federal judge in Seattle ruled that old-growth forests must be left uncut for ecological reasons.

Yet these are footnotes to what is mainly the story of success. Look at a map that shows elevation of mountains and density of population. On both sides of the Pacific, vast numbers of people are squeezed into small margins of level land between steeply rising volcanic mountains and the sea, or tucked into valleys. These islands of settlement are surrounded by vast wildernesses—desert and mountains, open sea and Arctic lands. Yet the inhabitants of these pockets of the Pacific Rim have, in recent decades, produced more economic growth than anywhere else in the world. This has happened despite the widely diverse, sometimes hostile, ethnic groups: the Japanese and Koreans, the Chinese of Taiwan, Hong Kong and Singapore, the Malays and Filipinos; and Washington's ethnic mix of Scandinavians, Yankees and new migrants.

Politically, Washington, with its Scandinavian and labor union heritage, was once one of the most Democratic states: Franklin Roosevelt's campaign manager James Farley used to refer to "the 47 states and the Soviet of Washington." Its mainstream Democrats, notably Warren Magnuson and Henry Jackson who represented the state in Congress for a total of 87 years, believed in an active and compassionate federal government that built dams, aluminum plants and the Hanford Works at home, and pursued an internationalist, anti-Communist foreign policy abroad. Their political strength was built on a blue-collar base, augmented by the respect the leaders of the state's big businesses had for their clout in the capital. In today's Washington, the fulcrum of the electorate has moved from blue collar to white collar, from economic class warfare to cultural wars. The balance is fairly close. Presidentially, Washington leans Democratic: big Seattle margins delivered the state for Michael Dukakis in 1988 and Bill Clinton in 1992 and 1996. Democrats have also won most downballot races in presidential years. Three different Democrats have held the governorship since 1984, and in 1992 Democrat Patty Murray was elected to the Senate. Republicans have done better in off-years: Senator Slade Gorton was reelected handily in 1994.

But farther down the ballot the trend is toward Republicans. In 1992 Democrats won the House vote 56%–41% and won eight of nine seats. But in 1994 Republicans won the House vote 51%–49% and carried seven of nine seats, in the process beating House Speaker Thomas Foley. Republicans that year also won control of both houses of the legislature, a reaction against unpopular liberal Governor Mike Lowry. Lowry retired in 1996, and Democrats targeted five of the House seats and key seats in the legislature. But with little success. Clinton's margin widened a bit in the Seattle-Tacoma area but narrowed in the West, where the Republican margin grew slightly. Only one Republican congressman was defeated—though gleeful news media prematurely declared two others had lost, though they were only slightly behind with some 40,000 absentee votes in each district uncounted. Republicans gained seats in the state Senate and held their losses down enough in the state House to retain control.

The political lines are fairly clear. The central city of Seattle is increasingly the liberal bastion, while old blue-collar lumber country strongholds have soured on many Democrats. Republicans run best, but not way ahead, in the arid country east of the Cascades. Culture wars also are fought out in referenda. Washington rejected a "death with dignity" assisted suicide measure in 1991 by 54%–46%. It voted for term limits, opposed by most liberals, 52%–48% in 1992; it was this measure as applied to congressmen against which Tom Foley filed a lawsuit; he won in the Supreme Court but was defeated at the polls. One effect of term limits has been to increase the number of women in the legislature; they are now 22 of 49 in the state Senate, the national high. In 1996 voters rejected bear baiting 63%–37% and rejected video poker on Indian reservations 56%–44%—a victory each for cultural liberals and conservatives.

Governor. The governor of Washington is Gary Locke, a Democrat elected in 1996, the first governor of Chinese descent elected in American history. Locke grew up in Seattle, the son of immigrants from Guandong and Hong Kong; he lived six years in a housing project and worked in his father's restaurant and grocery store. He graduated from Yale and Boston University Law School, returned to Seattle and worked as a deputy prosecutor and community relations manager for US West. In 1982, at 32, he was elected to the state House and rose to chair the Appropriations Committee; he supported the 1993 tax increases that helped to make Democratic Governor Mike Lowry unpopular. That same year, Locke was elected King County Executive where he cut the budget, established a savings incentive program and produced a growth management plan.

In February 1996 Lowry, a liberal and former congressman who was staggering under charges of sexual harassment, announced his retirement, and Locke decided to run for governor. It was a crowded field in Washington's all-party primary. Locke's main opponent, Seattle Mayor Norm Rice, shared the same base; they also faced former Congressman Jay Inslee from east of the mountains. Locke won with 24% of the total votes to 18% for Rice and 10% for Inslee. The Republican field was more fragmented, and the nomination was won by former state Senator Ellen Craswell, who emphasized her religious faith. Altogether Democrats won 52% of votes, Republicans 48%, indicating a close race in November. Republicans had lost some good campaign issues by repealing much of Lowry's tax increases and healthcare employer mandates and insurance premium caps, though the mandates for portability and increased coverage of the poor that were not repealed resulted in steep increases in health insurance premiums. Craswell emphasized not these issues, but what she called "God's plan" to cut state taxes 30% (later modified to 15%) and to privatize state universities, which evidently struck many voters as bizarre. Republican ads accusing Locke of supporting prostitution, because of a county prostitute-counseling service may have added to the impression. Locke, despite his liberal record in the legislature, took a moderate tack, abjuring tax increases and calling for more spending on education, with higher standards and accountability. Although some polls showed a close race, Locke won 58%–42%, fortified by a 62%–38% lead in the Seattle area; Craswell just barely carried the east.

In office Locke faced a Republican legislature. In his first months, Locke vetoed more bills than any previous governor, though he and the legislature came to agreement on a no-new-taxes budget.

Senior Senator. Slade Gorton, a Republican first elected in 1980, defeated in 1986, then elected again in 1988 and 1994, is Washington's senior senator. Gorton grew up in Chicago, served in the Army and went to school in the east, and moved to Seattle in 1953. He was elected to the state House in 1958, at 30, and was elected attorney general for 12 years starting in 1968. In 1980 he challenged and beat 75-year-old Senator Warren Magnuson. During that time Gorton had a reputation as a liberal Republican, with a political base in Seattle. In the past decade, as Washington's Democrats have moved well to the left, Gorton has maintained a moderate voting record generally, but taken conservative stands on high-visibility local issues like timber harvesting and Indian fishing rights. His political base has shifted to eastern

Washington. On timber, he opposed the court decision outlawing cutting of old-growth timber to save the spotted owl, and in 1995 passed a law allowing clear-cutting in some old-growth forests. After clashes with Native American tribes over fishing rights in the 1970s, he has decried alleged Indian violations of property rights. In 1995, as an Appropriations subcommittee chairman, he passed a bill that cut funding to tribes that violated the property rights of non-Indians living on their reservations; Native Americans were happy when he allowed himself to be passed over for the chairmanship of the Indian Affairs Committee in favor of Colorado's Ben Nighthorse Campbell. On other state issues, Gorton has sought funding for cleanup of the Hanford nuclear facilities (which he had tried to keep in operation), he opposes privatization of the Bonneville Power Administration, and he has promised to work for fish restoration on dammed rivers. He has argued for a different Medicaid funding formula for Washington. He defended the Market Promotion Program and opposed Airbus unfair trading practices (a concern of Boeing). But he did not join Boeing in urging permanent MFN status for China, arguing instead for annual renewals to pressure China into fair trading practices. When the NFL's Seattle Seahawks threatened to leave the city in 1995, he sponsored a law requiring such teams to offer themselves to local investors; in 1996 he served as a "bridge" between baseballs's Seattle Mariners' owners and the city council and mayor.

On national issues, Gorton supports a balanced budget and is not an avid tax-cutter; he supported the Breaux-Chafee compromise budget proposal which got 46 votes in May 1996. On crime, he is a hard-liner, and worked to get a *habeas corpus* reform amendment in the 1996 anti-terrorism bill. He sponsors the Edward Byrne Memorial Grants to help localities fight drug-related crime. With Jay Rockefeller, he was the lead sponsor of the product liability reform bill which passed both houses but was vetoed by Bill Clinton in May 1996. In early 1997 Gorton, Rockefeller and other Senators were working with the Clinton Administration to develop a compromise bill that Clinton would sign. He supported the V-chip provision of the Telecommunications Reform Act and criticized the broadcasters' program rating code as insufficient. He has worked to change the special education law to make it easier to remove violent children from classrooms. A sometime critic of liberal judges and with considerable legal expertise of his own, he became Republican point man on judicial nominees in 1997. Gorton is not afraid to stand up for principle: in September 1996 he was the only senator to vote against a resolution praising the bombing raids on Iraq which even CIA Director John Deutsch admitted left Saddam Hussein stronger than before.

In 1986 Gorton was upset for reelection by Democrat Brock Adams, who ended up retiring in 1992 after a charge of sexual harassment. In 1988, when Republican Senator Daniel Evans retired, Gorton came back and beat Democrat Mike Lowry, then a Seattle congressman and later governor. In 1994 Gorton was seeking a third Senate term at a time when Washington seemed headed well to the left, having given Bill Clinton and Senator Patty Murray big margins in 1992. But the best-known Democrats—former Governor Booth Gardner, Seattle Mayor Norm Rice—declined to run. Gorton ran as "an independent voice," an implicit concession that his views were by no means universally popular. Washington's all-party primary often gives a good forecast of the general election: Gorton, with only nuisance Republican opposition, won 53% of total vote, while the Democratic nomination went to King County Councilman Ron Sims over talk show host Mike James by 17%–14%. Sims is black, a New Democrat, a fiscal conservative who would not close the county budget until all "adds" were matched by "deletes"; he claimed hands-on experience with social problems from street kids to day care. But he was no match for Gorton in debate and the incumbent outspent him, $4.8 million to $1.2 million. Gorton won 56%–44%, losing King County but carrying working class enclaves in most of the rest of the state and running strong in the east.

Junior Senator. Washington's junior senator is Patty Murray, one of those Democrats whose election made 1992 "the year of the woman." Murray grew up in Bothell, the daughter of a disabled veteran, graduated from Washington State in 1972, married and stayed home to raise her children. "Our culture needs to value parents who stay at home much more than they do," she said in 1996. In 1980, when she was in Olympia trying to save a parent education class she was teaching at Shoreline Community College from being cut from the budget, a state legislator told her gruffly, "You're just a mom in tennis shoes; you can't make a difference." But, like many committed public employees, she won her fight; then she ran for the school board, lost, was appointed and then elected, and served as president. In 1988, she challenged a Republican state senator, knocked on 17,000 doors, and won the seat. Her first great cause there was extending a family leave bill to include leave for a parent whose child is sick or dying; she threatened to put the proposal on the ballot, and won the issue; she worked on school bus safety, "negative option" mail orders, accidental pesticide exposure—the warp and woof of everyday life. Then in late 1991, she decided to run against U.S. Senator Brock Adams, who was under a cloud from charges of sexual harassment; but he decided not to run.

Amid a crowd of better-known conventional male politicians, Murray, with her flat accent and "mom in tennis shoes" line, attracted most of the attention and most of the votes. In the all-party primary, her main Democratic opponent was former Congressman Don Bonker, who had run and narrowly lost a Senate nomination in 1988. But Murray won 28% to Bonker's 19% of the total vote. Meanwhile, three well-known Republicans vied: Congressman Rod Chandler won 20% to 16% for state Senator (and former opponent of George McGovern in South Dakota) Leo Thorsness and 11% for King County Executive Tim Hill. The two nominees were quite a contrast: Murray is short with a squeaky voice, Chandler tall with the booming voice of a former TV reporter. Murray sprinted to a big lead in polls, and in November won 54%–46%, carrying 60% in King County and winning Puget Sound and the west. Her margins over Chandler were similar to Bill Clinton's over George Bush, except in eastern Washington, which Clinton nearly carried but where Murray ran 10% behind.

In the Senate Murray has had a very liberal voting record and an unconventional approach. In her first years, she refused to see Washington industry lobbyists; in a scathing *Seattle Times* profile in 1996, Robert Nelson wrote of Murray, "Colleagues, lobbyists and former staff members view her as indifferent to issues that can't be explained through anecdotes about her family and neighbors." When Democrats were in control, she did not stake out areas of expertise, though she did get a seat on Appropriations. She attracted attention instead by demanding that the Senate Ethics Committee subpoena Oregon Senator Bob Packwood's diaries (he later resigned under threat of expulsion). In time she worked on Washington issues: seeking funding for cleanup of the Hanford reactor, trying to preserve the undammed Hanford Reach of the Columbia as a Wild and Scenic River, delaying with Slade Gorton the Alaska fisheries bill until a provision hurting Washington fishermen was removed. She opposed Gorton and Oregon's Mark Hatfield on timber cutting issues; their measure to allow some clear-cutting of old-growth forests passed in March 1995, and her plan to allow environmentalists to challenge timber sales in court failed.

On national issues, Murray pledges to oppose cuts in Medicare, Medicaid, education, health care and housing programs. She sought abortion coverage in federal workers' health insurance in 1993 and moved to overturn the policy on not allowing privately funded abortions in military hospitals in 1996. She pledges a "Commitment to Children," with money for children's health care, child care, and technology in the classroom. She formed a Senate Advisory Youth Involvement Team (SAY IT!) to meet with kids via her computer. She wants to include under the family leave bill 24 hours of leave for parent-teacher conferences, interviews for a new school and participation in family literacy training. She pushed an amendment to waive from the new welfare rules battered women and children.

Murray is one of the Senate's strongest proponents of permanent MFN for China—a position strongly backed by Boeing; "I honestly believe that not having MFN for China will not affect human rights issues. The best way we can affect human rights in China is to have a good conversation going with them," she said in 1996. She also favors relaxing export restrictions on encryption technology.

Murray is a prime Republican target in 1998. Congresswoman Linda Smith, a maverick on campaign finance and other issues, announced her candidacy in May 1997. Congresswoman Jennifer Dunn, a former state party chairman and party leader in the House, might run if she does not succeed New York's Susan Molinari as vice chair of the House Republican Conference. If Dunn does not run, other possiblities are Pierce County Executive Doug Sutherland and Congressmen Rick White and George Nethercutt.

Presidential politics. Washington has been one of the most contrarian states in presidential politics, voting for Richard Nixon in 1960, Hubert Humphrey in 1968, Gerald Ford in 1976 and Michael Dukakis in 1988. In the 1990s it has been in sync with the nation, voting for Bill Clinton twice, but there has been an increasing divergence between coastal and interior voting patterns. In 1996 Clinton carried the state 50%–37%, winning by solid margins in the Seattle area (54%–34%) and the West (48%–39%). In the eastern part of Washington, which Clinton carried narrowly in 1992, Bob Dole won 44%–42%.

Washington switched from a caucus system to primaries after 1988, when Pat Robertson won among Republicans and Jesse Jackson finished a solid second among Democrats. Counting the results from the 1992 primary as they would be in Washington's all-party primary for state office, George Bush had 43% of the votes to Clinton's 31% and Perot's 27%: perhaps a measure of opinion at the time, but not a good forecast of November. Bob Dole easily beat Pat Buchanan here in March 1996.

Congressional districting. Washington gained a seat in each of the last two censuses, and both new districts went to fast-growing suburban areas east and south of Seattle. A nonpartisan commission drew the district lines for the 1990s and most districts are evenly balanced—Democrats won eight of nine districts in 1992 and Republicans seven of nine in 1994 and six of nine in 1996. All but the heavily Democratic 6th and 7th and the heavily Republican 8th have been in play in the 1990s.

The People: Est. Pop. 1996: 5,533,000; Pop. 1990: 4,866,692, up 13.7% 1990–1996. 2.1% of U.S. total, 15th largest; 24% rural. Median age: 34.9 years. 12% 65 years and over. 86.7% White, 3% Black, 4.2% Asian, 1.6% Amer. Indian, 4.4% Hispanic origin. Households: 55.0% married couple families; 26% married couple fams. w. children; 56% college educ.; median household income: $31,183; per capita income: $14,923; 62.6% owner occupied housing; median house value: $93,400; median monthly rent: $383. 6.5% Unemployment. 1996 Voting age pop.: 4,115,000. 1996 Turnout: 2,253,837; 55% of VAP. Registered voters (1996): 3,078,208; no party registration.

Political Lineup: Governor, Gary Locke (D); Lt. Gov., Brad Owen (D); Secy. of State, Ralph Munro (R); Atty. Gen., Christine Gregoire (D); Treasurer, Mike Murphy (D); Auditor, Brian Sonntag (D). State Senate, 49 (23 D and 26 R); Senate President, Brad Owen (D); State House, 98 (42 D and 56 R); House Speaker, Clyde Ballard (R). Senators, Slade Gorton (R) and Patty Murray (D). Representatives, 9 (3 D and 6 R).

Elections Division: 360-753-7121; **Filing Deadline for U.S. Congress:** July 31,1998.

1996 Presidential Vote

Clinton (D)	1,123,323	(50%)
Dole (R)	840,712	(37%)
Perot (I)	201,003	(9%)
Other	90,465	(4%)

1996 Republican Presidential Primary

Dole (R)	76,155	(63%)
Buchanan (R)	25,247	(21%)
Forbes (R)	10,339	(9%)
Keyes (R)	5,610	(5%)
Other	3,333	(3%)

1992 Presidential Vote

Clinton (D)	993,037	(43%)
Bush (R)	731,234	(32%)
Perot (I)	541,780	(24%)

GOVERNOR

Gov. Gary Locke (D)

Elected 1996, term expires Jan. 2001; b. Jan. 21, 1950, Seattle; home, Olympia; Yale U., B.A. 1972; Boston U., J.D. 1975; Protestant; married (Mona).

Career: Dpty. King Cnty. Prosecuting atty., 1976–80; Staff atty., WA Senate, 1981; Legal Advisor, Seattle Human Rights Dept., 1981–82; WA House of Reps., 1982–93; Community Relations Mgr., U.S. West, 1988–92; Chief Exec., King Cnty., 1994–97.

Office: Office of the Governor, P.O. Box 40002, Olympia 98504, 360-753-6780; Fax: 360-753-4110; Web site: www.wa.gov.

Election Results

1996 gen.	Gary Locke (D)	1,296,492	(58%)
	Ellen Craswell (R)	940,538	(42%)
1996 prim.	Gary Locke (D)	287,762	(24%)
	Norm Rice (D)	212,888	(18%)
	Ellen Craswell (R)	185,680	(15%)
	Dale Foreman (R)	162,615	(13%)
	Jay Inslee (D)	118,571	(10%)
	Norm Maleng (R)	109,088	(9%)
	Jim Waldo (R)	63,854	(5%)
	Others	76,219	(6%)
1992 gen.	Michael Lowry (D)	1,184,315	(52%)
	Ken Eikenberry (R)	1,086,216	(48%)

SENATORS

Sen. Slade Gorton (R)

Elected 1988, seat up 2000; b. Jan. 8, 1928, Chicago, IL; home, Bellevue; Dartmouth, A.B. 1950, Columbia U., LL.B. 1953; Episcopalian; married (Sally).

Career: Army, 1946–47, Air Force, 1953–56, Air Force Reserves, 1956–81; WA House of Reps., 1958–68, Majority Ldr., 1966–68; WA Atty. Gen., 1968–80; Pres., Natl. Assn. of Attys. Gen., 1976–78; U.S. Senator, 1980–86.

DC Office: 730 HSOB 20510, 202-224-3441; Fax: 202-224-9393; e-mail: senator_gorton@gorton.senate.gov.

State Offices: Bellevue, 206-451-0103; E. Wenatchee, 509-884-3447; Kennewick, 509-783-0640; Lakewood, 206-581-1646; Spokane, 509-353-2507; Vancouver, 360-696-7838; Yakima, 509-248-8084.

Committees: *Appropriations* (6th of 15 R): Agriculture, Rural Development & Related Agencies; Energy & Water Development; Interior (Chmn.); Labor, Health & Human Services & Education; Transportation. *Budget* (6th of 12 R). *Commerce, Science & Transportation* (4th of 11 R): Aviation (Chmn.); Communications; Consumer Affairs, Foreign Commerce & Tourism; Oceans & Fisheries. *Energy & Natural Resources* (10th of 11 R): Energy Research, Development, Production & Regulation; Water & Power. *Indian Affairs* (4th of 8 R).

Group Ratings

	ADA	ACLU	AFS	LCV	CFA	CON	NFIB	COC	ACU	NTLC	CHC
1996	15	11	29	8	36	70	86	100	85	83	69
1995	10	—	0	0	31	68	—	89	74	—	—

National Journal Ratings

	1995 LIB — 1995 CONS	1996 LIB — 1996 CONS
Economic	43% — 54%	39% — 60%
Social	43% — 55%	33% — 62%
Foreign	38% — 57%	38% — 58%

Key Votes of the 104th Congress

1. Reduce Medicare Growth $	Y	5. Flag Amendment	Y	9. Anti-Missile Defense	Y
2. Lmt. Prod. Liab. Damages	Y	6. Endangered Species	N	10. Cuban Embargo	Y
3. Increase Min. Wage	Y	7. Gay Employment Rights	N	11. Bar Bosnia Troop $	N
4. Welfare Reform	Y	8. Ovrd. Part. Birth Veto	Y	12. Cut Vietnam Aid	N

Election Results

1994 general	Slade Gorton (R)	947,821	(56%)	($4,792,764)
	Ron Sims (D)	752,352	(44%)	($1,228,098)
1994 primary	Slade Gorton (R)	492,251	(53%)	
	Ron Sims (D)	162,382	(17%)	
	Mike James (D)	138,005	(15%)	
	Others	136,965	(15%)	
1988 general	Slade Gorton (R)	944,359	(51%)	($2,851,591)
	Michael Lowry (D)	904,183	(49%)	($2,191,187)

Sen. Patty Murray (D)

Elected 1992, seat up 1998; b. Oct. 11, 1950, Seattle; home, Seattle; WA St. U., B.A. 1972; no religious affiliation; married (Rob).

Career: Shoreline Schl. Bd., 1985–89, Pres., 1985–86; WA Senate, 1988–92.

DC Office: 111 RSOB 20510, 202-224-2621; Fax: 202-224-0238; e-mail: senator_murray@murray.senate.gov.

District Offices: Everett, 206-259-6515; Seattle, 206-553-5545; Spokane, 509-624-9515; Vancouver, 206-696-7797; Yakima, 509-453-7462.

Committees: *Appropriations* (11th of 13 D): Energy & Water Development; Foreign Operations; Labor, Health & Human Services & Education; Military Construction (RMM); Transportation. *Budget* (6th of 10 D). *Labor & Human Resources* (7th of 8 D): Aging; Children & Families. *Veterans' Affairs* (5th of 5 D). *Ethics (Select)* (2nd of 3 D).

Group Ratings

	ADA	ACLU	AFS	LCV	CFA	CON	NFIB	COC	ACU	NTLC	CHC
1996	90	59	100	85	71	27	36	17	0	13	0
1995	95	—	100	100	88	8	—	33	0	—	—

National Journal Ratings

	1995 LIB — 1995 CONS			1996 LIB — 1996 CONS		
Economic	90%	—	6%	96%	—	0%
Social	93%	—	0%	80%	—	8%
Foreign	76%	—	21%	93%	—	0%

Key Votes of the 104th Congress

1. Reduce Medicare Growth $	N	5. Flag Amendment	N	9. Anti-Missile Defense	N
2. Lmt. Prod. Liab. Damages	N	6. Endangered Species	Y	10. Cuban Embargo	N
3. Increase Min. Wage	Y	7. Gay Employment Rights	Y	11. Bar Bosnia Troop $	N
4. Welfare Reform	N	8. Ovrd. Part. Birth Veto	N	12. Cut Vietnam Aid	N

Election Results

1992 general	Patty Murray (D)	1,197,973	(54%)	($1,342,038)
	Rod Chandler (R)	1,020,829	(46%)	($2,504,777)
1992 primary	Patty Murray (D)	318,455	(28%)	
	Rod Chandler (R)	228,083	(20%)	
	Don Bonker (D)	208,321	(19%)	
	Leo K. Thorsness (R)	185,498	(16%)	
	Tim Hill (R)	128,232	(11%)	
	Six Others	56,042	(5%)	
1986 general	Brock Adams (D)	677,471	(51%)	($1,912,307)
	Slade Gorton (R)	650,937	(49%)	($3,290,072)

FIRST DISTRICT

In the last 20 years metropolitan Seattle has spread out to the north and the east, as a tidal wave of newcomers have arrived seeking this area's distinctive blend of natural environmental beauty, free-wheeling culture and briskly expanding economy. With growth, Seattle has lost a bit of its distinctiveness: the fishy odor of its docks does not permeate the new subdivisions built on what were once vegetable fields or vineyards; the Scandinavian heritage of old neighborhoods like Ballard has been mixed into a Pacific Northwest blend; the hoboes who used to hang around Yesler Way, the original "Skid Road," with its cast iron buildings and its street clocks, aren't allowed in the shopping malls off I-5 or I-405. The heart of the new Seattle is east of Lake Washington, in Redmond, where the turquoise, pine-shaded low-rise buildings of the Microsoft campus house one of America's most innovative and successful corporations, the creator of the standard for computer software, still working hard to stay ahead of the technological and economic curve. Not far away, in Medina on the eastern shore of Lake Washington, is the mansion Microsoft's founder Bill Gates has been building since 1991—a 37,000-square-foot complex with a trampoline room with vaulted ceilings, video walls that can be electronically programmed with art from the world's great museums, and a garage large enough to hold 20 cars: from across the lake you can see it rising, Seattle's Xanadu.

The 1st Congressional District of Washington includes Redmond, Medina and a small part of Seattle, then stretches north to take in much of the northern and eastern suburbs of Seattle in Snohomish and King counties. It also runs west across Puget Sound, to Kitsap County, and gathers in Bainbridge Island, where you can commute by ferry to downtown Seattle each day and return home to what looks like the perfect American small town in the evening. Politically, this is an area torn by forces of roughly equal strength between the two parties. Most Seattle-area residents appreciate, and want to preserve, the region's unique natural aura: the evergreen smell of a well-watered land; the subtle cultural patterns that are plainly American yet geographically distant from most of the nation. But it is impossible not to recognize the spectacular success of market economics in the 1st District—and to predict which way the district will lean if that success goes sour, as recent events indicate it could.

The congressman from the 1st District is Rick White, one of six freshman Republicans from Washington in 1994 and perhaps the biggest surprise winner. He grew up in Indiana, went to college and law school in the east, then joined Seattle's largest law firm in 1983—a typical 1980s migrant to the area. Not quite so typically, he soon became active in local Republican politics. In 1990 White helped found the "Farm Team" to recruit young professionals to the party, and worked on a 1992 campaign for governor. In 1994 he decided to run for Congress. The incumbent was Maria Cantwell, a Democrat elected in 1992 with a moderate record that seemed well suited to the district. In the all-party primary White had competition from King County prosecutor Anthony Lowe and minister Bill Tinsley. White won with 28%, to 14% and 10% for the others; but even more important, in a primary where an incumbent's percentage is usually a good forecast for the general election, Cantwell got only 44% of the total vote. In the general, White emphasized his extensive involvement in church and community activities, and contrasted his own attractive family—he and his wife have four children and a home on Bainbridge Island—against the fact that Cantwell was single and had no family in the district. Cantwell ran a widely criticized ad insinuating that because White took money from oil interests and his father is an oil executive, voters could expect to see drilling platforms in Puget Sound. But White matched the incumbent in spending, and won 52%–48%.

In the House White's voting record was conservative on economic and foreign policy issues and moderate-to-liberal on cultural issues. He supported repeal of the assault weapons ban and opposed the flag amendment. He supported most of the Contract With America and pledged to serve no more than five terms. He got a seat on the Commerce Committee, and played a key role on some important issues. He was the only freshman on the telecommunications reform bill conference committee, where he worked for maximum deregulation. He formed an Internet Caucus, with nearly 100 members, and worked to keep the federal government from regulating content on the Internet; on the Communications Decency Act, he sought a compromise mechanism for parents to regulate their children's exposure to undesirable material, while exempting material with literary, cultural or scientific value. He worked on the securities litigation reform, strongly sought by high-tech companies plagued by trial lawyers' suits; this was the only bill passed over Bill Clinton's veto.

He was a member of the Enterprise for the Environment group trying to update laws while spending money only on protection and cleanup; he opposes the current Superfund law, where much of the money goes to lawyers. He got provisions for allowing Seattle flexibility in the Safe Drinking Water Act. He sought funding to purchase two old dams on the Elwha River on the Olympic Peninsula so they could be dismantled to allow free migration of salmon. With Peter Hoekstra of Michigan, he started an Education Crossroads project to identify problems in the current education system and permit more local control. He called for an independent commission on campaign finance reform, whose recommendations Congress would have to vote up or down as a whole.

White was the subject of a series of articles in *The Wall Street Journal*, which used him as a sort of measure on how Republians elected in 1994 might fare in 1996. He was heavily targeted by the Democrats and the AFL-CIO and two Democrats ran against him. Former King County deputy prosecutor Jeffrey Coopersmith, whose mother is a well-known Democrat in Washington, D.C., took the more liberal stands: for banning all semi-automatic weapons, including many hunting guns, and for a single-payer health insurance system. He was opposed by lawyer and fisherman Don Stuart, who charged Coopersmith's late filing of court documents in 1994 resulted in the reversal of a conviction of a defendant found guilty of illegal possession of firearms. In the all-party September primary, Coopersmith beat Stuart 26%–23%, while White got almost exactly 50%, indicating a very close race in November. But White was helped by the attacks on Coopersmith's record, and charged him with voting against tougher sentences for crimes committed with firearms, and for moving into the district (from another residence in Seattle) just before running. White also outspent Coopersmith, raising $705,000 from PACs and spending nearly $1.7 million to the Democrat's $1.1 million. The result was a 54%–46% White victory, a pretty solid margin in a district where Newt Gingrich has little popularity, but not one which insulates White from serious challenge in 1998. White is considering a bid for Senator Patty Murray's seat in 1998, but would likely defer to fellow Representatives Jennifer Dunn and George Nethercutt, should either decide to run.

The People: Pop. 1990: 540,315; 10% rural; 9% age 65+; 90% White; 1% Black; 5% Asian; 1% Amer. Indian; 2% Hispanic origin. Households: 60% married couple families; 29% married couple fams. w. children; 67% college educ.; median household income: $40,390; per capita income: $18,687; median gross rent: $587; median house value: $147,900.

1996 Presidential Vote

Clinton (D)	140,182	(51%)
Dole (R)	103,002	(37%)
Perot (I)	21,352	(8%)
Other	10,527	(4%)

1992 Presidential Vote

Clinton (D)	118,386	(42%)
Bush (R)	90,537	(32%)
Perot (I)	70,340	(25%)

Rep. Rick White (R)

Elected 1994; b. Nov. 6, 1953, Bloomington, IN; home, Bainbridge Island; Dartmouth Col., B.A. 1975, Georgetown U., J.D. 1980; Presbyterian; married (Vikki).

Career: Practicing atty., 1980–94.

DC Office: 116 CHOB 20515, 202-225-6311; Fax: 202-225-3524; e-mail: repwhite@mail.house.gov.

District Offices: Mountlake Terrace, 206-640-0233.

Committees: *Commerce* (23rd of 28 R): Energy & Power; Finance & Hazardous Materials; Telecommunications, Trade & Consumer Protection.

Group Ratings

	ADA	ACLU	AFS	LCV	CFA	CON	NFIB	COC	ACU	NTLC	CHC
1996	0	19	0	31	31	84	100	88	95	98	80
1995	15	—	—	13	31	75	—	100	72	—	—

National Journal Ratings

	1995 LIB		1995 CONS	1996 LIB		1996 CONS
Economic	0%	—	74%	18%	—	80%
Social	63%	—	37%	53%	—	47%
Foreign	36%	—	59%	0%	—	79%

Key Votes of the 104th Congress

1. Reduce Medicare Growth $	Y	5. Flag Amendment	N	9. Cuban Embargo	Y
2. Ovrd. Product Liab. Veto	Y	6. Drop EPA Limits	Y	10. Bar Bosnia Troop $	N
3. Increase Min. Wage	N	7. Repeal Assault-Weap. Ban	Y	11. Cut Anti-Missile Defense	N
4. Welfare Reform	Y	8. Ovrd. Part. Birth Veto	Y	12. Bar U.N. Uniforms	*

Election Results

1996 general	Rick White (R)	141,948	(54%)	($1,671,909)
	Jeff Coopersmith (D)	122,187	(46%)	($1,079,648)
1996 primary	Rick White (R)	67,241	(50%)	
	Jeff Coopersmith (D)	35,006	(26%)	
	Don Stuart (D)	31,254	(23%)	
1994 general	Rick White (R)	100,554	(52%)	($877,570)
	Maria Cantwell (D)	94,110	(48%)	($875,756)

SECOND DISTRICT

The 172 San Juan Islands, in the waters of Puget Sound at the far northwest corner of Washington, were the last part of the continental United States to be turned over to this country; these waters were great whaling ground, and not until 1860 did the British relinquish the islands. Today, ferry boats ply the waters of the Sound, connecting the islands to mainland Washington, and to British Columbia directly to the west. This is some of the most beautiful land and water of North America, the steely blue Sound with green forested hills rising behind; it is wet country, shielded from the full force of Pacific rains by the Olympic Mountains, but still seldom dry. The little towns, on bits of level land between the water and mountains, have the look of pristine New England villages or Midwestern historic towns, but are better preserved than the originals; the stores are full of fresh produce and local seafood. Here the Seattle metropolitan area has marched north along the shore of Puget Sound, to and beyond the old lumber port and railroad terminus of Everett, with the huge Boeing plant—the largest building in the world—where 747s, 767s and 777s are built. Far to the north is the small city of Bellingham and the town of Blaine on the 49th parallel, with America's most attractively landscaped border crossing and International Peace Arch, just south of British Columbia.

The 2d Congressional District of Washington includes the San Juan Islands, Whidbey Island and most of Puget Sound from Everett north, plus the margin of mainland along the Sound and the huge mountains, topped by snow-capped Mount Baker, behind. The political tradition in most of the lumbering and fishing areas here is Democratic, while the rich agricultural areas, like the flower-bulb-growing Skagit Valley, are more Republican. Overall, this is a pretty evenly balanced district which tends to vote as the state does.

The congressman from the 2d District is Jack Metcalf, a Republican elected in 1994, successful at last in getting elected to Congress 26 years after his first attempt. Metcalf grew up in Washington, served in the Army and was a high school history teacher in Everett for 29 years. He was first elected to the legislature in 1960, at 33. He lost his seat in the anti-Goldwater landslide of 1964, was elected to a four-year term to the Washington Senate in 1966, then was the Republican candidate against Senator Warren Magnuson in 1968 and 1974. Metcalf was again elected to the state Senate in 1980, and after his retirement from teaching he and his wife started the Log Castle Bed and Breakfast on Whidbey Island. He was known for his opposition to court decisions curbing limits on Indian fishing rights, and to the money-creating powers of the Federal Reserve. In 1992 he ran for Congress again, and lost 52%–42% to incumbent Democrat Al Swift, the last in a line of Democrats who represented the district for 52 of 54 years going back to the election of 28-year-old Henry Jackson in 1940.

In 1994 Swift retired and Metcalf ran again. His attacks on congressional corruption, his promise to serve no more than three terms, his opposition to gun control and Indian fishing rights resonated with the Republican themes of that year; he easily beat a state legislator in the primary. His Democratic opponent, state Senator Harriet Spanel, sounded Clintonesque notes, calling for "a more holistic approach to these needs, recognizing that our country's problems cannot be overcome by repairing just one link in a chain." Metcalf won 55%–45%.

Metcalf was the oldest member of the freshman class, and by no means typical. His voting record was more moderate than expected, but not predictable on standard lines. He supported Linda Smith's campaign finance reform bill in 1996 and the Shays-Meehan bill in 1997. He sponsored the 1996 amendment barring automatic pay increases for members of Congress and other federal officials. He tried to get a congressional vote on the deployment of U.S. troops to Bosnia and sponsored bills to help homeless veterans, and in 1997 was pushing for further investigation of Gulf war syndrome. He fought Newt Gingrich to get Boeing's 747 considered as a supplemental cargo plane to McDonnell Douglas's C-17. He spent much time on local issues, in 1995 killing a Forest Service project to spend $37,000 to paint rocks along US-2, which the Forest Service claimed was necessary "because it could take up to five years for the rock to weather naturally," and opposing a White House plan to tax northern border crossings. He lobbied the FCC to lower licensing fees for VHF radios used by Puget Sound boat owners and protected the Magnuson Act Northwest halibut and sablefish quota program from revision. He got a provision requiring local government participation and congressional approval of NOAA's proposed designation of Puget Sound as a marine sanctuary.

On all these Metcalf was thrusting against federal regulation; but on other issues he pushed the other way. He introduced a bill to bar the federal government from selling timber below cost—an anathema to Alaskan Don Young who chairs the Resources Committee. He wanted to expand the Endangered Species Act to protect habitat as well as the species themselves. In 1996 he worked with liberal Californian George Miller and the Canadian Sea Shepherd Conservation Society to fight an administration plan to allow the Makah Indians to kill five gray whales a year in Washington waters. Metcalf remembered as a boy of eight seeing 100 orcas swimming in the waters off Whidbey Island, and they are still seen sometimes from his bed and breakfast. "People ask me whether I'm comfortable associating with some of these groups, and I admit some of them are very radical environmentalists. But I have always been a free spirit in politics. I do what I want to do, and I don't see how anyone could not want to protect those wonderful creatures."

In 1996 Metcalf had vigorous opposition from Kevin Quigley, a state Senator with a Harvard law degree and deep roots in the district: he lives in the log house built in Lake Stevens, near Everett, by his grandfather, who as a physician delivered Scoop Jackson back in 1912. Quigley attacked Medicare "cuts" and called for more spending on higher education but backed the balanced budget amendment and the 1996 welfare reform. Similarly, in the legislature he voted for Governor Mike Lowry's tax increase in 1993, then joined Republicans to repeal business tax increases in 1995. Quigley ran an energetic door-knocking campaign, and called Metcalf an extremist. But Quigley had been reprimanded by an ethics board for writing a memo to his former law firm offering to introduce clients to state legislators; a Metcalf ad asked, "Is this the kind of person we want to represent us in Congress?" Metcalf got 52% in the September all-party primary, a good sign for victory; but Quigley's campaigning cut into his margin. Quigley came out of the election night counting 2,200 votes ahead, and news media proclaimed Metcalf the loser. But there were 40,000 absentee votes still uncounted, and Quigley's lead disappeared. Metcalf finally won 49%–48%. His promise to seek no more than three terms means that 1998 will be his last race; but the 1996 campaign shows the result cannot be taken for granted, by anyone.

The People: Pop. 1990: 540,861; 42% rural; 12% age 65+; 92% White; 1% Black; 2% Asian; 2% Amer. Indian; 3% Hispanic origin. Households: 60% married couple families; 28% married couple fams. w. children; 52% college educ.; median household income: $31,305; per capita income: $14,419; median gross rent: $468; median house value: $100,100.

1996 Presidential Vote

Clinton (D)	123,729	(47%)
Dole (R)	103,901	(39%)
Perot (I)	27,177	(10%)
Other	11,055	(4%)

1992 Presidential Vote

Clinton (D)	103,405	(39%)
Bush (R)	85,876	(33%)
Perot (I)	71,794	(27%)

Rep. Jack Metcalf (R)

Elected 1994; b. Nov. 30, 1927, Marysville; home, Marysville; Pacific Lutheran U., B.A. 1951, U. of WA, M.A. 1966; Protestant; married (Norma).

Career: Army 1946–47; U.S. Marshal Patrol Boat Skipper, 1947–48; High Schl. Teacher, 1951–81; WA House of Reps., 1960–64; Repub. nominee, U.S. Senate, 1968 & 1974; WA Senate, 1966–74, 1980–92; Owner, Log Castle Bed & Breakfast, 1978–present.

DC Office: 1510 LHOB 20515, 202-225-2605; Fax: 202-225-4420.

District Offices: Bellingham, 360-733-4500; Everett, 206-252-3188.

Committees: *Banking & Financial Services* (13th of 30 R): Domestic & International Monetary Policy; Financial Institutions & Consumer Credit; Housing & Community Opportunity. *Transportation & Infrastructure* (26th of 40 R): Aviation; Surface Transportation.

Group Ratings

	ADA	ACLU	AFS	LCV	CFA	CON	NFIB	COC	ACU	NTLC	CHC
1996	0	6	33	31	31	85	89	75	90	95	100
1995	5	—	—	6	15	56	—	92	100	—	—

National Journal Ratings

	1995 LIB — 1995 CONS			1996 LIB — 1996 CONS		
Economic	44%	—	53%	39%	—	58%
Social	38%	—	60%	24%	—	72%
Foreign	15%	—	73%	41%	—	56%

Key Votes of the 104th Congress

1. Reduce Medicare Growth $	Y	5. Flag Amendment	Y	9. Cuban Embargo	Y
2. Ovrd. Product Liab. Veto	Y	6. Drop EPA Limits	Y	10. Bar Bosnia Troop $	Y
3. Increase Min. Wage	Y	7. Repeal Assault-Weap. Ban	Y	11. Cut Anti-Missile Defense	N
4. Welfare Reform	Y	8. Ovrd. Part. Birth Veto	Y	12. Bar U.N. Uniforms	Y

Election Results

1996 general	Jack Metcalf (R)	124,655	(49%)	($797,442)
	Kevin Quigley (D)	122,728	(48%)	($447,812)
	Others	9,561	(4%)	
1996 primary	Jack Metcalf (R)	67,603	(52%)	
	Kevin Quigley (D)	30,635	(24%)	
	Joe Bowen (D)	14,267	(11%)	
	Ann Weinzierl (D)	10,630	(8%)	
	Others	6,487	(5%)	
1994 general	Jack Metcalf (R)	107,430	(55%)	($407,902)
	Harriet A. Spanel (D)	89,096	(45%)	($613,063)

THIRD DISTRICT

From the Pacific Ocean to the majestic row of active and inactive volcanoes from Mount Rainier to Mount St. Helens to Oregon's Mount Hood, southwest Washington is one of America's most productive lumber areas. The moist air and almost constant rains blown in from the Pacific keep the trees on the coast growing rapidly; in the valleys just past the Coast Range, there is still plenty of precipitation and fast-growing forest. Then come the high mountains: the Cascades are a genuine divide, wrenching almost all precipitation out of the air so the climate eastward for a thousand miles is arid. Americans were reminded of the force of the volcanoes when Mount St. Helens, dormant for 123 years, erupted in 1980, killing 65 people and ruining the land in its path. But nature has repaired itself, as it must have done many times before.

Lewis and Clark came here in 1805, down the Columbia River to a rainy and foggy winter by the ocean, and for many years this part of Washington was sparsely settled, with lumber mill and fishing boat towns interspersed between mountains and water. It was flannel shirt country, Democratic since the New Deal days. In recent years, its resource-based economy was threatened by the environmental movement, which got a court decision shutting down old-growth forest logging to save the spotted owl and restricted fishing practices. This roiled local politics, and gave Republicans an opening.

More important recently has been the growth of the Pacific Northwest's great metropolitan areas into these valleys. Clark County across the Columbia from Portland, Oregon, has filled up with new residents, eager to avoid Oregon's income tax; the Seattle-Tacoma metro area has been moving down from the north past the small state capital of Olympia. This is one of America's great international trading areas, with big exports of logs and timber and vast imports on the docks of Portland and the Puget Sound. The political result has been to make this area more marginal and volatile.

The 3d Congressional District of Washington covers the land between the ocean and the Cascades, from the state capital of Olympia on an inlet of Puget Sound, south to Vancouver in Clark County, site of the Hudson Bay company headquarters in the 19th Century. Politically, this was long a solidly Democratic district, indeed sometimes the most Democratic district in Washington. But economic growth and diversification and the coming of many new residents with no roots in the old industries have made the 3d now a politically marginal district.

The congresswoman from the 3d District is Linda Smith, a Republican elected in 1994 and one of the most distinctive members of the House. Smith grew up poor in Colorado; her father abandoned the family and her stepfather worked as a fruit picker and mechanic. She met her husband in their Assembly of God church and married two weeks before she turned 18. She raised a family and worked in a tax preparation business in Vancouver, eventually managing seven offices; her husband is a locomotive engineer on Burlington Northern trains. Her religious faith and small business experience made her a strong conservative. In 1983, at 32, she was elected to the Washington House, beating an appointed Democratic incumbent in a special election. In 1987 she beat another appointed Democrat for the state Senate, giving Republicans control of the chamber. There she became known for her strong opposition to gay rights and gay adoption laws. Frustrated in efforts to promote campaign ethics and tax reforms, she sponsored ballot measures: Initiative 134 on campaign ethics, cutting campaign spending and big-group contributions, passed in 1992; Initiative 601 on requiring voter approval for tax increases passed in 1993, after Governor Mike Lowry's tax increase.

As late as August 1994 Smith was not a candidate for Congress. The incumbent was Jolene Unsoeld, a favorite of the environmentalist and feminist left, who had spent $1.3 million in the heavily contested 1990 race. The leading Republican was businessman Timothy Moyer, who spent $1.5 million of his own money. Then a newspaper report accused Moyer of dodging taxes on his luxury automobiles, and on August 31 he dropped out of the race. Local Republican activists opposed the other active Republican candidate, chiropractor Paul Phillips, and drafted

Smith. In less than three weeks her write-in campaign called 50,000 voters and sent out 145,000 mailers. In the September 20 all-party primary, Unsoeld won the Democratic nomination with 40% of the total vote—not impressive, since incumbents' totals are often good forecasts of their general election percentages. Smith won 34,038 write-in votes (did it help that her name is easy to spell?), 29% of the total, well ahead of Phillips's 15%.

In the general Smith had the enthusiastic support of the Christian right and of opponents of the Endangered Species Act, and some renown for her work on ballot initiatives. "We're the people of Washington, taking back our government," she proclaimed in one ad. Unsoeld spent nearly twice as much money, charging that Smith would means-test Social Security and stressing her own opposition to gun control and NAFTA. Unsoeld carried the heavily Democratic counties on and near the Pacific coast and, though only narrowly, the state capital of Olympia. But Smith carried the ordinarily Democratic Vancouver area and the inland lumbering area around Centralia, for a 52%–45% victory overall.

Smith was one of the most distinctive members of the 1994 Republican freshman class—"the cage rattler," as *National Journal* called her. Democrats tried to tar her as a supporter of militias after the April 1995 Oklahoma City bombing, but she clashed with Washington state militia members who chastised her for voting for a Republican-backed bill easing restrictions on federal prosecutors' use of evidence found in searches. Her voting record was strongly conservative. She voted against Medicaid funding for abortion in cases of rape and incest: "We don't kill children because their father is a jerk." She also looked after district interests. When some Republicans suggested privatizing the Bonneville Power Administration, which is required to sell hydroelectric power for cost in the Pacific Northwest, Smith strongly opposed it. "I've always supported privatization, but not if it's going to destroy the economy of our region." She proposed amendments to allow private vessels conducting fish surveys to keep part of the catch as a fee and to provide aid for shipbuilding and ship repair yards on the West Coast after Alaska oil exports were allowed. She got approval of the Fort Vancouver National Historic Reserve, money to stop erosion of Route 105 near Tokeland and for dredging the mouth of Wind River in Skamania County. With Illinois Democrat Richard Durbin she sponsored an amendment to take $23 million from the tobacco program and give it to rural water projects.

But Smith made her name nationally as a supporter of campaign finance reform, presenting her own bill and then supporting the Shays-Meehan bill (better known for its Senate sponsors as McCain-Feingold). She angrily attacked Newt Gingrich and the Republican leadership for stalling on the lobbyist gift ban ("The institution, under your leadership, is truly on trial"), and pushed for the proposal which passed in November 1995. She made a stirring speech for campaign finance reform at Ross Perot's United We Stand meeting in Dallas in August 1995. Furious with Republicans for preventing a vote on the issue, in June 1996 she declared, "I get called 'girlie' one more time by those old guys and I'm going to sock them in the nose." The *Seattle Times* said that "Smith can wear the Speaker's scorn as a badge of honor."

None of this protected her against serious opposition in 1996 from Democrat Brian Baird, head of the psychology department at Pacific Lutheran University. He attacked Smith for supporting Medicare "cuts" and called her a "95% Newt vote." She responded that Baird was "blood brothers with Newt Gingrich" for refusing to stop fundraising from special interests. "Mr. Baird has been bought by the special interests; Linda Smith is owned only by the people from the district." She called him an environmental radical, charging he wanted to ban logging on federal lands and shut down the Asarco smelter in Tacoma, and said he wanted to raise taxes to pay for health care. Smith declared she was ahead 70%–30% in the summer, but overestimated her support. Baird held Smith to a 52%–48% lead in the September all-party primary—usually a good predictor of the incumbent's performance in November.

In fact the result was closer. On election night Baird was ahead by 2,400 votes and was pronounced the winner by the overeager media. But when the more than 40,000 absentee votes outstanding were counted, Smith won by 887 votes, 50.2%–49.8%. The closeness of this race had little effect on Smith; she seems fearless of defeat. In January 1997 she voted against Newt

Gingrich for speaker and for former Congressman Robert Walker. She lost her Small Business subcommittee chairmanship, but not in response to her speaker vote, or so both she and Republican leaders said.

In May 1997, Smith announced she will run against Senator Patty Murray in 1998, and would be a strong contender—although she may first have to fend off a primary challenge from fellow members of her state delegation as Jennifer Dunn, George Nethercutt and Rick White are each thinking of running. In the now-open 3d District, Baird will run again and appears to have unified the party behind him. Paul Phillips, who lost to Smith in the 1994 primary, and real estate developer and former school superintendent candidate Ron Taber will seek the Republican nomination, as may state Senator Don Benton and state Representative John Pennington.

The People: Pop. 1990: 540,658; 38% rural; 13% age 65+; 93% White; 1% Black; 2% Asian; 1% Amer. Indian; 3% Hispanic origin. Households: 59% married couple families; 28% married couple fams. w. children; 50% college educ.; median household income: $29,154; per capita income: $13,328; median gross rent: $414; median house value: $70,300.

1996 Presidential Vote			1992 Presidential Vote		
Clinton (D)	124,864	(49%)	Clinton (D)	104,682	(42%)
Dole (R)	97,985	(38%)	Bush (R)	82,648	(33%)
Perot (I)	24,407	(9%)	Perot (I)	61,609	(25%)
Other	9,895	(4%)			

Rep. Linda Smith (R)

Elected 1994; b. July 16, 1950, LaJunta, CO; home, Vancouver; Assembly of God; married (Vern).

Career: Mgr., Tax Consulting firm, 1968–82; WA House of Reps., 1983–87; WA Senate, 1987–94.

DC Office: 1317 LHOB 20515, 202-225-3536; Fax: 202-225-3478; e-mail: asklinda@hr.house.gov.

District Office : Olympia, 360-753-3073; Vancouver, 360-695-6292.

Committees: *Resources* (14th of 27 R): National Parks & Public Lands; Water & Power. *Small Business* (6th of 19 R): Government Programs & Oversight; Tax, Finance & Exports (Vice Chmn.).

Group Ratings

	ADA	ACLU	AFS	LCV	CFA	CON	NFIB	COC	ACU	NTLC	CHC
1996	5	27	9	38	23	46	97	79	84	95	100
1995	0	—	—	0	0	87	—	100	96	—	—

National Journal Ratings

	1995 LIB — 1995 CONS			1996 LIB — 1996 CONS		
Economic	0%	—	74%	45%	—	55%
Social	0%	—	79%	33%	—	65%
Foreign	28%	—	65%	30%	—	65%

Key Votes of the 104th Congress

1. Reduce Medicare Growth $	Y	5. Flag Amendment	Y	9. Cuban Embargo	Y
2. Ovrd. Product Liab. Veto	Y	6. Drop EPA Limits	*	10. Bar Bosnia Troop $	Y
3. Increase Min. Wage	Y	7. Repeal Assault-Weap. Ban	Y	11. Cut Anti-Missile Defense	N
4. Welfare Reform	Y	8. Ovrd. Part. Birth Veto	Y	12. Bar U.N. Uniforms	Y

Election Results

1996 general	Linda Smith (R)	123,117	(50%)	($1,216,368)
	Brian Baird (D)	122,230	(50%)	($718,322)
1996 primary	Linda Smith (R)	69,291	(52%)	
	Brian Baird (D)	62,778	(48%)	
1994 general	Linda Smith (R)	100,188	(52%)	($515,316)
	Jolene Unsoeld (D)	85,826	(45%)	($987,242)
	Others	6,620	(3%)	

FOURTH DISTRICT

The rugged peaks of the Cascade Mountains divide Washington state into two starkly different climate zones and two almost as starkly different political cultures. West of the Cascades, Washington is moist, green, full of watery inlets; to the east, it is barren and brown, except where irrigation ditches feed the waters of the Columbia River into thirsty valleys, or where mountaintop waters fall east, as they do to water the apple orchards in the Yakima Valley. The federal government has been a presence in the East-of-the-Cascades since the 1930s, when it began to build dams that provided cheap power and boosted economic development in this forbidding, often surreal, landscape: a giant bust of Franklin Roosevelt gazes from a bluff on the Columbia out over 550-foot-high Grand Coulee Dam, which Roosevelt initiated and which was one of his favorite projects. Other dams are strung along downriver, like beads on the necklace of the Columbia, along most of the way to Bonneville Dam near Portland, where the river breaks through the Cascades.

The one exception is the Hanford Reach, the last undammed, undeveloped stretch of the upper Columbia River, near the 560-square mile Hanford Nuclear Reservation, north of the Tri-Cities of Richland, Kennewick and Pasco. Hanford was built by the Army to manufacture plutonium for the Manhattan Project and was where the Nagasaki bomb was constructed. After the war the Hanford Works became the primary producer of materials for America's nuclear weapons and eastern Washington's largest employer. Then in 1988 Hanford's plutonium plant was shut down because of hazardous leaks and contaminated waste. Now about 55 million gallons of hazardous waste lie in concrete holding pools near the Columbia, while in the next decade the government spent close to $8 billion on a not-yet-successful cleanup.

The 4th Congressional District covers the western half of Washington east of the Cascades, running from the Canadian border past Grand Coulee and through the Hanford Works down to the Dalles Dam. Sentiment toward the federal government has soured in other parts of the district almost as much as around the Tri-Cities. The Yakima Valley, which produces more than half of the nation's apples, was angry that the apparently groundless Alar scare in 1989 hurt sales. Lumber towns in the Cascades are furious that those who want to preserve the spotted owl may shut down logging businesses. In an area once pretty evenly divided between the parties, opinion has shifted away from Democrats and toward Republicans; the cultural liberalism of Seattle seems very far away here.

The congressman from the 4th District is Doc Hastings, a Republican elected in 1994. Hastings grew up in the Tri-Cities, went to college in Ellensburg, served in the Army Reserves and for 27 years ran the Columbia Basin Paper and Supply Company in Pasco. In 1979 he was elected to the legislature, served as a Republican leader, then retired after eight years in 1987. In 1992 he ran for Congress, won the Republican nomination, but was beaten 51%–49% by moderate Democrat Jay Inslee. But Inslee voted for the Clinton budget and tax package in 1993 and the crime bill with its gun control provisions in 1994—big liabilities when Hastings ran again in 1994. Hastings led with 50% in the September all-party primary, to only 41% for Inslee. Hastings had support from Bob Dole, Newt Gingrich and the National Rifle Association; Inslee had to make do with Special Trade Representative Mickey Kantor. Inslee attacked Hastings for opposing abortion and being backed by conservative religious groups. Hastings campaigned heavily in three counties in the north of the district where Inslee had eked out his victory margin in 1992. This time Hastings carried all three, swept the Tri-Cities and, despite losing Yakima, won overall 53%–47%.

In the House Hastings has had a solidly conservative voting record, even opposing a $24 million remodeling of the Richland federal building. Much of his time was spent on Hanford. With Senator Slade Gorton, he sponsored a bill in 1995 to make the state of Washington responsible for the cleanup, allowing privatization of cleanup work and avoiding the plethora of often impractical and duplicative federal regulations; this was supported also by Democratic Congressman Norman Dicks and Senator Patty Murray. Hastings also worked closely with Dicks, a high-ranking and politically savvy member of Appropriations, to stop a proposal by Lloyd Doggett of Texas to zero out the nearly-completed $230 million Environmental and Molecular Sciences Laboratory at Hanford; they even enlisted support from scientists in Austin, Doggett's home town. Hastings and Gorton were pleased in summer 1996 when a new contractor, Fluor Daniel, was chosen to take over the Hanford cleanup, saying its plans were similar to those in their bill. On another Hanford issue, Hastings opposed Murray's proposal to designate the Hanford Reach a Wild and Scenic River, preferring that local officials keep control of land use and owners be compensated for any lessening of value; ironically, the area looks pristine because the Hanford Works kept everyone else out. Hastings is also opposed to the Columbia Basin Ecosystem Management Project, which seeks uniform forest regulations for an area of the Northwest equivalent to the size of Texas.

In 1996 Hastings's 1992 and 1994 opponent Jay Inslee ran for governor, and finished third to two Seattle-based Democrats in the primary. Hastings instead faced Rick Locke, who won the Democratic nomination with backing from unions including the Washington Education Association. Locke ran an ad in which a menacing voice said Hastings's vote was controlled by "someone back east named Newtie." In another he said, "Hastings gets his marching orders every morning from the Speaker's office." Hastings retaliated with an ad with a Robin Leach-like voice saying: "Today we'll meet political candidate Rick Locke, the Seattle millionaire who just moved to central Washington to buy a seat in Congress. Of course, buying things comes naturally to Rick Locke. He still maintains several luxurious homes in Seattle and a 38-foot sailing yacht on nearby Puget Sound. Rick also likes to unwind at his exclusive resort home hideaway in the chic San Juan Islands." Even so, Locke spent only $121,000 of his own money and $409,000 overall, far behind Hastings's $735,000. Hastings won 55% of the total vote in the September all-party primary and 53% in the general; Locke carried Yakima and Kittitas Counties narrowly and Hastings carried everything else.

In the 105th Congress Hastings moved from the Resources and National Security Committees to Rules. He promised to keep working for a speedy and inexpensive cleanup at Hanford and to help Boeing and other Washington defense contractors.

The People: Pop. 1990: 540,701; 39% rural; 12% age 65+; 79% White; 1% Black; 1% Asian; 3% Amer. Indian; 16% Hispanic origin. Households: 59% married couple families; 29% married couple fams. w. children; 44% college educ.; median household income: $25,055; per capita income: $11,578; median gross rent: $333; median house value: $60,100.

1996 Presidential Vote

Dole (R)	101,963	(48%)
Clinton (D)	84,157	(40%)
Perot (I)	20,516	(10%)
Other	4,868	(2%)

1992 Presidential Vote

Bush (R)	87,995	(42%)
Clinton (D)	71,914	(35%)
Perot (I)	45,256	(22%)

Rep. Doc Hastings (R)

Elected 1994; b. Feb. 7, 1941, Spokane; home, Pasco; Columbia Basin Col., 1959–61; Central Washington U., 1963–64; Catholic; married (Claire).

Career: Army Reserves, 1964–69; Pres., Columbia Basin Paper & Supply, 1967–present; WA House of Reps., 1979–87; Repub. Nominee, US House of Reps., 1992.

DC Office: 1323 LHOB 20515, 202-225-5816; Fax: 202-225-3251.

District Offices: Kennewick, 509-783-0310; Wenatchee, 509-662-4294; Yakima, 509-452-3243.

Committees: *Rules* (8th of 9 R): Legislative & Budget Process.

Group Ratings

	ADA	ACLU	AFS	LCV	CFA	CON	NFIB	COC	ACU	NTLC	CHC
1996	0	12	0	8	0	9	97	100	100	100	100
1995	0	—	—	0	0	56	—	100	92	—	—

National Journal Ratings

	1995 LIB — 1995 CONS			1996 LIB — 1996 CONS		
Economic	0%	—	74%	0%	—	82%
Social	0%	—	79%	10%	—	86%
Foreign	0%	—	85%	30%	—	65%

Key Votes of the 104th Congress

1. Reduce Medicare Growth $	Y	5. Flag Amendment	Y	9. Cuban Embargo	Y
2. Ovrd. Product Liab. Veto	Y	6. Drop EPA Limits	N	10. Bar Bosnia Troop $	Y
3. Increase Min. Wage	N	7. Repeal Assault-Weap. Ban	Y	11. Cut Anti-Missile Defense	N
4. Welfare Reform	Y	8. Ovrd. Part. Birth Veto	Y	12. Bar U.N. Uniforms	Y

Election Results

1996 general	Doc Hastings (R)	108,647	(53%)	($734,640)
	Rick Locke (D)	96,502	(47%)	($408,772)
1996 primary	Richard Hastings (R)	65,939	(55%)	
	Rick Locke (D)	33,987	(28%)	
	Joe Walkenhauer (D)	11,704	(10%)	
	Glenn Phipps (D)	8,238	(7%)	
1994 general	Doc Hastings (R)	92,828	(53%)	($619,963)
	Jay Inslee (D)	81,198	(47%)	($496,638)

FIFTH DISTRICT

Eastern Washington is a land of great rivers and bare parched land, where the Columbia, Spokane and Snake Rivers wind among vast plateaus, bringing water from the Rockies to the desert. Spokane grew up at the falls of the Spokane River when the railroads first came through, and became a major wheat, mining, electrical and railroad center early in this century, the center of the so-called "Inland Empire"; it celebrated with the 1974 World's Exposition on the downtown riverfront. Nearby are some of the most fascinating landscapes in the United States: surreally undulating yellow wheatfields, the ridges of the Palouse where the topsoil is 200 feet deep, the bare-rock coulees rising above dammed-up lakes and barren desert. This is remote and inhospitable land: the summers are blazing hot and winters bitter cold; the rivers run wildly. But it has been tamed by man, and the water from the Grand Coulee and other dams irrigates some of the richest farmland in the country.

The 5th Congressional District covers the easternmost part of Washington. About two-thirds of the people here live in greater Spokane, a city whose voting habits are a fairly good proxy of the nation's. Its heritage leans toward the Republicans, but it is not as Republican as most of the nearby Rocky Mountain states, though it veers toward them angrily at times; it is open also to Democrats, and Spokane County voted for Bill Clinton in 1992 and 1996.

The congressman from the 5th District is George Nethercutt, a Republican elected in 1994 when he defeated Speaker of the House Thomas Foley—the first time a speaker of the House has been defeated in his home district since Galusha Grow lost in Pennsylvania in 1862. Nethercutt grew up in Spokane, graduated from Washington State in Pullman and Gonzaga Law School in Spokane, served four years on the staff of Alaska Senator Ted Stevens in the 1970s, then returned home and practiced law. He was involved in civic work, representing clients in adoptions, heading the local Diabetes Foundation (his daughter was diagnosed with the disease), and starting a crisis nursery for abused children. In 1994 he decided to run for Congress. Foley had served the district for 30 years and had wide personal popularity. But in 1992 his margin was not much larger than that of Bill Clinton, whose popularity had plummeted since, and many in the state were angry at Foley for filing a lawsuit against congressional term limits imposed by the voters in 1992. Nethercutt announced his candidacy in April 1994; in May two former Foley opponents also announced—Duane Alton, owner of a chain of tire stores who ran in 1976 and 1978, and John Sonneland, a physician who ran in 1980, 1982 and 1992, when he spent $400,000 of his own money and won 45% of the vote. For a time the contest among Republicans seemed more intense than the race against Foley; Nethercutt won with 29% of the total vote, to 20% for Alton and 15% for Sonneland. But the big news was that in the all-party primary, which often forecasts the November results, Foley took only 35% of the votes. Immediately Foley began spending heavily, emphasizing the work he had done for the district and what he could do in the future. However, he had to buck not only Nethercutt's ads but campaigns by the National Rifle Association (furious that Foley, a longtime gun control opponent, backed the 1994 crime bill) and the National Taxpayers Union. Nethercutt in an ad promised never to sue the people of Washington—a swipe at Foley's lawsuit against the term limits initiative. When attacked for his conservatism and support for the Kasich budget cuts, Nethercutt responded with sensitive ads showing him walking out of a crisis nursery holding a baby and one with his family walking in a park; he was helped also by a November 4th campaign appearance by Ross Perot. This was one of the most expensive House races in the nation: Foley spent $2.1 million; Nethercutt, $1.1 million. Foley did carry Spokane County, but not by much, and lost all but one of the smaller counties; that gave Nethercutt a 51%–49% win.

In the House Nethercutt got a seat on Appropriations and supported most of the Contract With America. Initially noncommittal, he supported the Freedom to Farm Act, including the fixed payments to formerly subsidized farmers in its seven-year phaseout. He opposed the Interior Columbia Basin Ecosystem Management Project, which he feared might lead to restrictions on logging, mining and grazing on private lands; he pushed a measure to authorize a scientific survey of forests, but bar any environmental impact statement that could impose broad restrictions on land use. He pushed for spending on local projects—the Bureau of Mines in Spokane, Fairchild Air Force Base, the wheat research building at Washington State. On his general course, he said in 1995: "I'd rather be known as a work horse than a show horse. I thought it best to work behind the scenes rather than play to the cameras."

In 1996 three Democrats vied to run against him. The winner, with 25% of the total in the September all-party primary, was Judy Olson, former president of National Association of Wheat Growers. She accused him of supporting Medicare "cuts" and said, "His priority was marching in the Republican revolution." She also attacked him on the shutdown of federal government, the minimum wage and student loans. She criticized him for buying a $400,000 house in the Washington, D.C. suburbs; Nethercutt replied that he had two mortgages and added, "Don't criticize my kids for wanting a stable home." Joining in the attack were the AFL-CIO and environmental groups. Nethercutt attacked Olson for potentially putting the military "in jeopardy through lack of funding" and for getting most of her contributions from unions. He called for balancing the budget and restricting illegal immigration. In response to the Medicare charges, he featured his mother in ads and said, "I resent people thinking I would do anything to hurt my own mother." Nethercutt spent $1.1 million, compared to Olson's $616,000. He won 51% in the all-party primary, suggesting a very close general election, and won 56%–44% in the general election, carrying Spokane County smartly and every smaller county.

After the election, Nethercutt (perhaps with an eye on the AFL-CIO ads) called for a truth in advertising law. "The First Amendment can be abused in this country. There is more protection for a can of Pepsi than for the truth." When the IRS started taxing farmers on deferred income from futures contracts, he proposed a $40,000 income tax deferral account and introduced a bill preventing the alternative minimum tax from applying to sales of farm property. He got a seat on the Science Committee. Nethercutt had pledged to serve no more than six years in the House, but seemed to be backing away from that in early 1997. He may not need to renege on his pledge in order to stay in Congress, however, since he is considering running against Senator Patty Murray in 1998.

The People: Pop. 1990: 540,865; 29% rural; 13% age 65+; 92% White; 1% Black; 2% Asian; 2% Amer. Indian; 3% Hispanic origin. Households: 55% married couple families; 26% married couple fams. w. children; 54% college educ.; median household income: $25,107; per capita income: $12,177; median gross rent: $345; median house value: $57,400.

1996 Presidential Vote

Clinton (D)	104,052	(44%)
Dole (R)	102,384	(43%)
Perot (I)	25,250	(11%)
Other	6,826	(3%)

1992 Presidential Vote

Clinton (D)	99,676	(40%)
Bush (R)	90,294	(36%)
Perot (I)	56,472	(23%)

Rep. George R. Nethercutt, Jr. (R)

Elected 1994; b. Oct. 7, 1944, Spokane; home, Spokane; WA St. U., B.A. 1967; Gonzaga U. Schl. of Law, J.D. 1971; Presbyterian; married (Mary Beth).

Career: Law Clerk, Fed. Judge Ralph Plumer, 1971–72; Chief of Staff & Cnsl., U.S. Sen. Ted Stevens, 1972–76; Practicing atty., 1976–94.

DC Office: 1527 LHOB 20515, 202-225-2006; Fax: 202-225-3392; e-mail: grnwa05@hr.house.gov.

District Offices: Colville, 509-684-3481; Spokane, 509-353-2374; Walla Walla, 509-529-9358 .

Committees: *Appropriations* (27th of 34 R): Agriculture, Rural Development, FDA & Related Agencies; Interior; National Security. *Science* (23rd of 25 R): Space & Aeronautics.

Group Ratings

	ADA	ACLU	AFS	LCV	CFA	CON	NFIB	COC	ACU	NTLC	CHC
1996	0	19	0	23	8	66	100	93	95	95	86
1995	0	—	—	13	0	56	—	100	88	—	—

National Journal Ratings

	1995 LIB — 1995 CONS			1996 LIB — 1996 CONS		
Economic	36%	—	60%	37%	—	61%
Social	21%	—	72%	35%	—	62%
Foreign	0%	—	85%	0%	—	79%

Key Votes of the 104th Congress

1. Reduce Medicare Growth $	Y	5. Flag Amendment	Y	9. Cuban Embargo	Y
2. Ovrd. Product Liab. Veto	Y	6. Drop EPA Limits	N	10. Bar Bosnia Troop $	Y
3. Increase Min. Wage	N	7. Repeal Assault-Weap. Ban	Y	11. Cut Anti-Missile Defense	N
4. Welfare Reform	Y	8. Ovrd. Part. Birth Veto	Y	12. Bar U.N. Uniforms	Y

Election Results

1996 general	George R. Nethercutt, Jr. (R)	131,618	(56%)	($1,071,823)
	Judy Olson (D)	105,166	(44%)	($615,636)
1996 primary	George R. Nethercutt, Jr. (R)	61,893	(51%)	
	Judy Olson (D)	30,666	(25%)	
	Susan Kaun (D)	16,317	(13%)	
	Don McCloskey (D)	13,039	(11%)	
1994 general	George R. Nethercutt, Jr. (R)	110,057	(51%)	($1,067,185)
	Thomas S. Foley (D)	106,074	(49%)	($2,144,579)

SIXTH DISTRICT

The rainiest part of the continental United States is at its far northwest corner, where the Olympic Mountains of Washington thrust into the Pacific Ocean. The waters of the Pacific evaporate, condense and then mist or rain down on the hills and mountains that jut up from the ocean and Puget Sound. The mountains here are always green, the trees that line the inlets towering, and during heavy rainfalls the rivers can rise six feet a day. This has long been lumbering and fishing country, where men go out to work at 6 a.m. in air cold enough to see your breath year round, and where dependence on the vagaries of nature and the unpredictable requirements of environmentalists—like the ban on old-growth logging to protect the habitat of the spotted owl—have strengthened a traditional surly independence and suspicion of authority.

The inlets of Puget Sound, winding sinuously through the mountains, are among America's most picturesque waterways and strategically quite important. Here during World War II, shipyards built and sheltered much of the U.S. Navy's Pacific fleet, and here during the Cold War much of the nuclear submarine fleet anchored at the giant Bremerton Navy base. To the south is the Tacoma Straits Bridge, the replacement of the narrow span that, in a scene preserved on newsreel (and still viewed by civil engineering students), started vibrating on the wrong harmonic in high winds and collapsed in 1940. On the other side is Tacoma, long the second ranking city on Puget Sound, with its impressive massive docks and pleasant hilly residential neighborhoods.

The 6th Congressional District of Washington contains the Olympic Peninsula, Bremerton and most of surrounding Kitsap County amid various inlets of Puget Sound and about half of Tacoma. Politically, the Olympic Peninsula and Bremerton are working-class Democratic. Tacoma also is traditionally Democratic, though the 6th's portion of it is the more white-collar side of town. On balance the 6th is, after the central Seattle 7th, Washington's most Democratic district.

The congressman from the 6th District is Norman Dicks, a onetime University of Washington football player who was on Senator Warren Magnuson's staff when it was one of the best staffs ever seen on Capitol Hill. Dicks returned home to Kitsap County to run for Congress in 1976, when the 6th District incumbent got the judgeship for which he had been hankering for 12 years.

Dicks was elected easily that year, and in every year since except 1980, when Magnuson lost. He has passed up several chances to run for the Senate, and seems firmly committed to the House.

Dicks has brought to the House the aggressiveness and political shrewdness that were the hallmarks of the Magnuson staff in its golden days, plus an interest in defense and intelligence reminiscent of Magnuson's colleague for 40 years, Henry Jackson. These talents would be deployed, he long assumed, from a place in the majority; in 1995 he said: "In 27 years I never once thought about being in the minority. It never, ever occurred to me until about noon on Election Day" in November 1994. But he has adapted smoothly to being part of the minority party, helped by the fact that on some issues, though not all, his goals are more congenial to many Republicans than Democrats. "I still feel it's worth doing. And with Speaker Foley gone now, we've got to have a couple of people who know how to operate. I've got to be the person who takes the lessons of 27 years and puts it to use." Dicks has a seat on the Appropriations Committee and on the National Security Subcommittee—a vital post for Kitsap County, where most workers depend on Pentagon payrolls, and for Washington generally, because of Boeing. He is also ranking Democrat on the Select Committee on Intelligence. In these posts Dicks, even in the minority can exert pivotal influence on important policies, usually operating quietly and behind the scenes. For example, in the early 1980s, Dicks took the lead on restoring Export-Import Bank loan authority—Boeing is America's biggest exporter and user of the loans—when the Reagan Administration wanted to cut it, and led a campaign that switched 80 House votes overnight. In the middle 1980s, he helped keep the MX missile alive in return for arms control commitments from the Reagan Administration. During the post-Cold War downsizing of the Pentagon, he has looked out for the F-117 Stealth aircraft and the B-2 Stealth bomber. In the 105th Congress, he led the fight for more B-2s than the administration requested, arguing that their stealth capability might have deterred Saddam Hussein from invading Kuwait and prevented Scott O'Grady from being shot down over Bosnia. Dicks lobbied colleagues persistently at Camden Yards Stadium in September 1995, on the day Cal Ripken was setting his consecutive-games-played record, pausing only for the long fifth-inning ovation. The next day the B-2s were authorized, over the opposition of many Democrats and Budget Chairman John Kasich, by a 213–210 vote; Dicks told Kasich he had six or seven votes in reserve.

Dicks has also used his Appropriations seat to help Washington communities, funneling money to lumber mill towns when logging in old-growth forests was banned, passing timber salvage riders to keep mills going, dealing with the cost of maintaining salmon runs in dammed rivers. In 1997 he called for consideration of introducing grey wolves into Olympic National Park, traveling to Canada's Algonquin Park and hearing them howl in response to his simulated howls. Naturally he looks after the interests of the Bremerton waterfront and has pushed for funding of a Tacoma waterfront development from which visitors can gaze upon Mount Rainier; when the Navy decided to send the *U.S.S. Missouri* to Honolulu, he promised to try to get another battleship for Bremerton. He is also a strong supporter of MFN status for China; Washington accounts for one-quarter of U.S. exports to China, and Boeing foresees a great market there. But Dicks knows there are problems: "We're trying to have a constructive engagement with China, and they just get worse and worse . . . I think we're in some trouble here," he said in March 1996. On the Intelligence Committee Dicks has operated quietly, knowledgeably and in a bipartisan manner—quite an accomplishment in the House of the mid-1990s.

Dicks has been reelected easily every two years, with a solid 66% in 1996.

The People: Pop. 1990: 540,836; 26% rural; 14% age 65+; 86% White; 5% Black; 4% Asian; 2% Amer. Indian; 3% Hispanic origin. Households: 55% married couple families; 24% married couple fams. w. children; 51% college educ.; median household income: $27,882; per capita income: $13,403; median gross rent: $415; median house value: $74,400.

1996 Presidential Vote		
Clinton (D)	122,342	(50%)
Dole (R)	87,961	(36%)
Perot (I)	23,830	(10%)
Other	8,968	(4%)

1992 Presidential Vote		
Clinton (D)	106,370	(43%)
Bush (R)	77,539	(31%)
Perot (I)	60,582	(25%)

Rep. Norm Dicks (D)

Elected 1976; b. Dec. 16, 1940, Bremerton; home, Bremerton; U. of WA, B.A. 1963, J.D. 1968; Lutheran; married (Suzanne).

Career: Legis. Asst., U.S. Sen. Warren Magnuson, 1968–73, A.A., 1973–76.

DC Office: 2467 RHOB 20515, 202-225-5916; Fax: 202-226-1176.

District Offices: Bremerton, 360-479-4011; Tacoma, 453-593-6536.

Committees: *Appropriations* (5th of 26 D): Interior; Military Construction; National Security. *Intelligence (Select)* (RMM of 7 D): Technical & Tactical Intelligence.

Group Ratings

	ADA	ACLU	AFS	LCV	CFA	CON	NFIB	COC	ACU	NTLC	CHC
1996	65	69	91	85	54	71	27	19	0	17	7
1995	80	—	—	81	85	25	—	33	0	—	—

National Journal Ratings

	1995 LIB — 1995 CONS			1996 LIB — 1996 CONS		
Economic	72%	—	27%	75%	—	24%
Social	75%	—	23%	72%	—	28%
Foreign	64%	—	34%	61%	—	37%

Key Votes of the 104th Congress

1. Reduce Medicare Growth $	N	5. Flag Amendment	N	9. Cuban Embargo	N
2. Ovrd. Product Liab. Veto	N	6. Drop EPA Limits	Y	10. Bar Bosnia Troop $	N
3. Increase Min. Wage	Y	7. Repeal Assault-Weap. Ban	N	11. Cut Anti-Missile Defense	Y
4. Welfare Reform	N	8. Ovrd. Part. Birth Veto	*	12. Bar U.N. Uniforms	N

Election Results

1996 general	Norm Dicks (D)	155,467	(66%)	($477,269)
	Bill Tinsley (R)	71,337	(30%)	($16,384)
	Others	9,106	(4%)	
1996 primary	Norm Dicks (D)	94,755	(67%)	
	Bill Tinsley (R)	14,603	(10%)	
	Ken Lund (R)	11,159	(8%)	
	Richard Meyer (R)	8,299	(6%)	
	Steve Whitaker (R)	5,980	(4%)	
	Others	7,323	(5%)	
1994 general	Norm Dicks (D)	105,480	(58%)	($629,161)
	Benjamin Gregg (R)	75,322	(42%)	($60,721)

SEVENTH DISTRICT

Seattle is America's hot city of the 1990s. It first zoomed into the national consciousness with the 1897 Klondike gold strike, has been a major American city since around 1910, had its own World's Fair in 1962. But only in the last decade has its combination of economic growth and creativity and its physical beauty and distinctive style made it a national leader. Seattle rises from the Puget Sound harbor of Elliott Bay on steep hills, once covered with 300-foot-high Douglas firs; behind the hills and buildings you can see on a clear day, from almost anywhere, the nimbus of Mount Rainier. On the waterfront, below gleaming high-rises, is the Pike Place market, where you can get fresh salmon and Dungeness crab; nearby is Pioneer Square, where stores and warehouses from the turn of the century have been restored and renovated; and Yesler Way, America's original "Skid Road," now has upscale shops but still some homeless too. Seattle's upper class, like San Francisco's, continues to be anchored downtown, with its upscale stores and busy sidewalks; but the most remarkable growth has come east of Lake Washington, where Microsoft has dominated computer software from its turquoise-building campus. Seattle still has its old ethnic neighborhoods, like Scandinavian Ballard, and comfortable working-class frame houses on steep hillsides. But it also has a new ethnic mix, with thousands of Asian immigrants, and the Capitol Hill neighborhood with grunge-clad shoppers jamming busy stores and clubs. Yet the downtown office district and the affluent quarter along Lake Washington and Queen Anne overlooking Puget Sound have a certain formality. Generally, blue-collar workers live on the south side of the city and in valleys, or midway between Puget Sound and Lake Washington; the factories, warehouses and railroad yards are concentrated in a flat plain near Puget Sound and south of downtown. The big Boeing factories are located farther south, and younger blue-collar workers have followed them into the suburban areas directly south of the city: Burien, Tukwila, Kent and Renton, which lie at the southern end of Lake Washington.

All this is knit together by infrastructure that was high-tech for its time: the pontoon bridge across Lake Washington, the Lake Washington Ship Canal, connecting the Sound and the Lake, whose Chittenden Locks are the second-largest locks in this hemisphere, behind the Panama Canal. Seattle has been booming, and exporting its own institutions—Boeing airplanes have been the world's best sellers for many years; Nordstrom department stores with their famously polite service (even in the New York area); Seattle espresso bars—especially Starbucks, named after the coffee-crazed first mate in Herman Melville's *Moby Dick*—have been bringing cafe latte across America.

The 7th Congressional District of Washington includes almost all the city of Seattle, a little industrial suburban fringe to the south, plus rural-looking Vashon Island in Puget Sound. This is the Seattle area's minority district, 10% black and 11% Asian. The 7th has the highest education levels of any Washington district (37% of adults are college grads), but not at all the highest household income; it has the oldest housing and by far the highest percentage of householders living alone (39%) and the fewest households with families (49%). Central Seattle, in other words, shares more with central San Francisco than hills and scenery: it is heavily populated by singles and gays, young professionals and elderly pensioners. A generation ago, the city of Seattle was roughly split between the parties; today, it is heavily Democratic and liberal, proud of having had a black mayor, Norm Rice, and a Chinese-American County Executive, Gary Locke, now governor.

The congressman from the 7th District is Jim McDermott, one of the most liberal members of the House and its only (credentialed) psychiatrist. McDermott was the first in his family to attend college, and went to conservative religious Wheaton College; after service in the Navy and stints in New York and Illinois hospitals, he came to the University of Washington Hospital in Seattle. Almost immediately, he was elected to the state House in 1970 and state Senate in 1974, where he worked on issues from clean water to health care. He ran for governor in 1980, beat incumbent Dixy Lee Ray in the primary, then lost to Republican John Spellman. In 1987 he retired from the legislature and went to Zaire (now Congo) as a medical officer in the Foreign Service. But when Congressman Mike Lowry ran for the Senate in 1988 (he lost, but in 1992 was elected governor), McDermott returned home and ran for the 7th District seat and easily won, beating Norm Rice 38%–29% in the primary and winning 76% in the general. He has been reelected without difficulty.

In the House his great cause has been health care and his greatest publicity has come from ethics investigations; he has had some frustrations on both. He did pass an AIDS Housing Opportunity Act in 1990, in his first term, and remains head of the Congressional Task Force on International HIV-AIDS. He has long backed a single-payer, Canadian-style national health insurance program and had a bill, with some 90 co-sponsors in 1993, financed by a $2 cigarette tax and 50-cent handgun and ammunition excise. But he deferred to the Clinton healthcare plan, even while making the point that his was simpler to administer and more comprehensible to voters. Then in August 1994, as the Clinton plan was failing and Democratic leaders George Mitchell and Richard Gephardt were scrambling to come up with an alternative, McDermott urged Congress to abandon all healthcare bills for the year. He evidently expected a more favorable political environment after the 1994 elections, and, like many, was surprised by the result. After Republicans took control, he said: "A lot of people around here have never been in the minority. I have. I know what to do: attack." He criticized Republicans for abandoning the refundability of their $500-per-child tax credit, so that those with low income tax liabilities or receiving the Earned Income Tax Credit didn't get a payment. He sponsored his own bill to reduce payments to hospitals and doctors and set up a commission to study Medicare's needs after 2010 (which got nowhere), and put together a bill in 1997 for a 30% tax credit for health insurance costs for families without insurance from their employers. Another quixotic but interesting initiative is his plan for free trade negotiations with Africa, supported by free market Republican Philip Crane; the problem is that the Agency for International Development is not interested in subsidizing private investment and few private investors, even Africans, want to put their money there. But McDermott is thinking long-term, and many African countries have been turning to democracy, so there may be hope.

McDermott joined the Ethics Committee in 1991 and was made chairman in 1993 by Speaker Thomas Foley; for some time he called for nonpartisan investigations and got along with his successor in the chair, Nancy Johnson. But that changed during the long hearings on charges against Newt Gingrich. McDermott was frustrated with what he considered Republican dilatoriness and successfully pressed for the appointment of special counsel James Cole, a former prosecutor, rather than a tax lawyer to conduct a more limited review. McDermott was angry that Johnson would not make public Cole's report before the House voted for speaker on January 7, 1997, and he attacked Johnson for canceling a series of committee hearings after a meeting with Majority Leader Dick Armey. During the public hearings on January 17, the full committee approved the proposed sanctions of a House reprimand and a $300,000 penalty, which the House approved a few days later.

Then on January 10 *The New York Times* printed an excerpt of a tape made by Florida Democratic activists John and Alice Martin of a phone conversation between Gingrich and Republican leaders and advisers. It was presented as evidence that Gingrich was violating an agreement not to orchestrate response to the committee's action, but much of it was taken up by discussions as to how to comply with the agreement. In any case it quickly became apparent that taping the call was a felony. The Martins said they ultimately gave the tape to McDermott, and it was widely assumed he was the *Times*' source; McDermott denied he ever possessed or knew anything about the tape, then avoided the press in his office in Seattle. On January 14 the FBI announced it was investigating, and McDermott announced he was conditionally excusing himself from the case against Gingrich, blasting the Republicans in the process. In ensuing days McDermott, long known as intellectually honest and candid, said he wouldn't give an explanation of the incident and said of the investigation, "Nobody has come out pure."

The tape incident damaged McDermott's credibility in the House and raised the possibility of prosecution; the Martins pleaded guilty to intercepting the call and were ordered to pay a small fine in April 1997. That and his frustration on health care raise the question of whether McDermott will want to stay in the House. In January 1996 he told *National Journal*'s Richard Cohen he expected that Bill Clinton, if reelected, would send Congress a major healthcare reform to which even a Republican House would have to respond, and said, "I want to keep working here as long as I can have an impact on health care." But as of mid-1997 Clinton gave no sign of producing a major healthcare bill, and even a sympathetic observer must wonder whether McDermott will want to stay.

The People: Pop. 1990: 541,202; 2% rural; 15% age 65+; 74% White; 10% Black; 11% Asian; 1% Amer. Indian; 4% Hispanic origin. Households: 38% married couple families; 14% married couple fams. w. children; 66% college educ.; median household income: $29,707; per capita income: $18,021; median gross rent: $462; median house value: $132,100.

1996 Presidential Vote

Clinton (D)	182,671	(67%)
Dole (R)	53,437	(20%)
Perot (I)	13,671	(5%)
Other	23,267	(9%)

1992 Presidential Vote

Clinton (D)	191,781	(65%)
Bush (R)	54,478	(18%)
Perot (I)	45,167	(15%)

Rep. Jim McDermott (D)

Elected 1988; b. Dec. 28, 1936, Chicago, IL; home, Seattle; Wheaton Col., B.S. 1958; U. of IL, M.D. 1963; Episcopalian; divorced.

Career: U.S. Navy Medical Corps., 1968–70; Asst. Prof., U. of WA, Practicing psychiatrist, 1970–83; WA House of Reps., 1970–72; WA Senate, 1974–87; Dem. Nominee, Gov., 1980; Medical Officer, U.S. Foreign Svc., Zaire, 1987–88.

DC Office: 2349 RHOB 20515, 202-225-3106.

District Offices: Seattle, 206-553-7170.

Committees: *Budget* (2nd of 19 D). *Ways & Means* (8th of 16 D): Human Resources; Trade.

Group Ratings

	ADA	ACLU	AFS	LCV	CFA	CON	NFIB	COC	ACU	NTLC	CHC
1996	95	100	100	85	100	36	22	27	0	2	0
1995	100	—	—	94	92	24	—	13	4	—	—

National Journal Ratings

	1995 LIB — 1995 CONS			1996 LIB — 1996 CONS		
Economic	90%	—	8%	89%	—	0%
Social	88%	—	0%	88%	—	0%
Foreign	93%	—	0%	90%	—	0%

Key Votes of the 104th Congress

1. Reduce Medicare Growth $	N	5. Flag Amendment	N	9. Cuban Embargo	N
2. Ovrd. Product Liab. Veto	N	6. Drop EPA Limits	Y	10. Bar Bosnia Troop $	N
3. Increase Min. Wage	Y	7. Repeal Assault-Weap. Ban	N	11. Cut Anti-Missile Defense	Y
4. Welfare Reform	N	8. Ovrd. Part. Birth Veto	N	12. Bar U.N. Uniforms	N

Election Results

1996 general	Jim McDermott (D)	209,753	(81%)	($190,250)
	Frank Kleschen (R)	49,341	(19%)	($6,680)
1996 primary	Jim McDermott (D)	106,613	(79%)	
	Frank Kleschen (R)	29,138	(21%)	
1994 general	Jim McDermott (D)	148,353	(75%)	($275,259)
	Keith Harris (R)	49,091	(25%)	

EIGHTH DISTRICT

The land east of Seattle's Lake Washington half a century ago was quiet countryside. Orchards and vineyards flourished in the rich, moist soil just below the rise of the Cascades Mountains, while farms and broad pasturelands spread toward 14,410-foot Mount Rainier like a living green quilt. But as Seattle has grown over the years, people have crossed the pontoon bridge across Mercer Island to Bellevue and have made this Overlake area one of the most vibrant part of metropolitan Seattle. Bellevue now has more than 100,000 people and enough office space to make it an edge city. While downtown Seattle specialized in banks and law firms and trading companies, Bellevue and other communities in Overlake specialized in high-tech startups. Redmond, just to the north, is the headquarters of Microsoft, and there are dozens of other firms here that make this one of America's leading high-tech centers.

The 8th Congressional District of Washington includes most of the eastern edge of metro Seattle, plus the scarcely inhabited territory of the Cascades. It includes most of Bellevue and all of Mercer Island, Issaquah at the edge of the Cascades and Renton at the south edge of Lake Washington. It spreads south along Kent, Auburn and Puyallup to include the countryside and suburban fringe east of Tacoma, and includes Mount Rainier itself. This is the most affluent district in Washington, rivaled only by the 1st, politically, market-oriented on economics, more liberal on the environment, mixed on cultural issues. In partisan terms, it is also one of the two most Republican districts in the state.

The congresswoman from the 8th District is Jennifer Dunn, a Republican elected in 1992. Dunn grew up in Bellevue, went to Stanford, worked as a systems engineer for IBM in the 1960s, then stayed home to raise her children. In 1981 she became Washington Republican Party chairwoman and served for 12 years. She is a peppery partisan, vigorous and knowledgeable about issues, persevering through bad times for her party and working to make them better. In 1992, when Congressman Rod Chandler ran for the Senate, she ran for the House and won in a walkaway. In the House she was a vocal deficit hawk, backing the Penny-Kasich budget cuts and the A-to-Z spending cut procedure. With Georgia's Nathan Deal she passed a Dunn-Deal bill to allow local communities to track convicted sex offenders. She served as the only freshman on the Joint Committee on the Organization of Congress. Her voting record has been conservative on economic and foreign policy, moderate on cultural issues.

When Republicans won the majority in 1994, Dunn was put on the transition team and the speaker's task force on committee review, and given a seat on Ways and Means. She was appointed to the three-member task force on the contested Connecticut 2d District race. On Ways and Means, she worked on the child support provisions of the welfare reform bill and pushed for medical savings accounts in the 1996 healthcare bill. She sponsored an IRAs for homemakers amendment, which was vetoed, a small business tax relief package, a rise in the earning limits for seniors, and estate tax reductions. She backed a pension plan for employees of small companies with no plan of their own. She worked on the Medicaid formula for Washington state and on the preventive medicine provisions of Medicare reform. She sought to privatize the Government Printing Office and to cut its payroll. She worked to allow software firms to lower their taxes by setting up foreign sales corporations as other businesses can. She got an extra $850,000 for Mount Rainier National Park to repair storm damage and $8 million for Puyallup area levee repair. She worked against privatization of the Bonneville Power Administration and sought lower BPA power rates.

Dunn, as one might expect of a longtime state party chairman, took political initiatives as well. She has been a loyal supporter of Newt Gingrich through his travails. In February 1996 she filed an ethics complaint against Democratic Leader Dick Gephardt, arguing that he reported his interest in a North Carolina vacation home inconsistently on his disclosure forms, tax returns and bank loan documents; it was dismissed in September, after Gephardt was allowed to amend his disclosure forms. Dunn raised and spent $1.1 million in her easy 1996 reelection campaign. Late in November 1996 she was elected secretary of the Republican Conference. In May 1997, Dunn decided run for Conference vice chair—the post being vacated by retiring New York Congresswoman Susan Molinari. With the tacit approval of the leadership, Dunn seemed to be the favorite for the July election, but she faced competition from Jim Nussle of Iowa and possibly others. Prior to Molinari's departure Dunn had considered running against Senator Patty Murray in 1998, but the opportunity to continue her rise in the House leadership seemed to good to pass up.

The People: Pop. 1990: 540,735; 21% rural; 8% age 65+; 91% White; 2% Black; 5% Asian; 1% Amer. Indian; 2% Hispanic origin. Households: 65% married couple families; 33% married couple fams. w. children; 63% college educ.; median household income: $42,379; per capita income: $18,432; median gross rent: $550; median house value: $142,100.

1996 Presidential Vote

Clinton (D)	130,472	(47%)
Dole (R)	112,463	(41%)
Perot (I)	23,994	(9%)
Other	8,593	(3%)

1992 Presidential Vote

Clinton (D)	102,859	(38%)
Bush (R)	92,274	(34%)
Perot (I)	72,523	(27%)

Rep. Jennifer B. Dunn (R)

Elected 1992; b. July 29, 1941, Seattle; home, Bellevue; U. of WA, 1960–62, Stanford, B.A. 1963; Episcopalian; divorced.

Career: Systems Engineer, IBM, 1964–69; P.R., King Cnty. Assessors Office, 1978–80; Delegate, U.N. Comm. on Status of Women, 1984, 1990; Chmn., WA Repub. Party, 1981–92.

DC Office: 432 CHOB 20515, 202-225-7761; Fax: 202-225-8673; e-mail: dunnwa08@hr.house.gov.

District Office: Bellevue, 206-450-0161.

Committees: *Republican Conference Secretary. Ways & Means* (14th of 23 R): Oversight; Trade.

Group Ratings

	ADA	ACLU	AFS	LCV	CFA	CON	NFIB	COC	ACU	NTLC	CHC
1996	0	0	0	25	15	30	100	100	100	100	84
1995	5	—	—	0	8	56	—	100	80	—	—

National Journal Ratings

	1995 LIB — 1995 CONS			1996 LIB — 1996 CONS		
Economic	0%	—	74%	0%	—	82%
Social	42%	—	57%	50%	—	50%
Foreign	0%	—	85%	0%	—	79%

Key Votes of the 104th Congress

1. Reduce Medicare Growth $	Y	5. Flag Amendment	Y	9. Cuban Embargo	Y
2. Ovrd. Product Liab. Veto	Y	6. Drop EPA Limits	N	10. Bar Bosnia Troop $	Y
3. Increase Min. Wage	N	7. Repeal Assault-Weap. Ban	Y	11. Cut Anti-Missile Defense	N
4. Welfare Reform	Y	8. Ovrd. Part. Birth Veto	Y	12. Bar U.N. Uniforms	Y

Election Results

1996 general	Jennifer B. Dunn (R)	170,691	(65%)	($1,146,933)
	Dave Little (D)	90,340	(35%)	($6,838)
1996 primary	Jennifer B. Dunn (R)	86,662	(65%)	
	Dave Little (D)	46,961	(35%)	
1994 general	Jennifer B. Dunn (R)	140,409	(76%)	($685,083)
	Jim Wyrick (D)........................	44,165	(24%)	

NINTH DISTRICT

The misty shores of Puget Sound have seen some of America's most vibrant economic growth over the last decade. It has spread south from Seattle, over the mixed suburban territory, south and west to the once industrial city of Tacoma. The subdivisions along the Sound, which have some of the loveliest views in America, tend to be high-income. But much of greater Seattle's prime industrial territory lies between the ridges that run north and south inland. Weyerhaeuser, the world's largest private owner of softwood timber, has its headquarters here in Federal Way. Boeing is also a major presence in Renton, on the south end of Lake Washington; its aircraft and electronic components plants and its business services division, employing more than 14,000 people, have helped make the company America's number one exporter. A host of smaller factories cluster near the rail lines that run from Minneapolis-St. Paul across the Great Plains to Puget Sound. The military has influenced this area too. Fort Lewis is just west of Tacoma and active-duty and retired military personnel and their families make up perhaps one-fifth of the population in this area.

The 9th Congressional District of Washington covers much of this area. It is a new seat created after the 1990 Census and confirmed by a June 1992 Supreme Court decision that upheld the counting of servicemen abroad in their state of residence (otherwise, this seat would have gone to Massachusetts). The 9th District's northern end wraps around Sea-Tac International Airport and Renton, then winds south past Kent, Auburn and Federal Way, and reaches the shipyards and docks of Tacoma. It covers half of Tacoma, including McChord Air Force Base, and proceeds west, taking in the Army's vast Fort Lewis in Pierce County and stopping just shy of the boundaries of the state capital of Olympia. Politically, this is a district balanced almost at equipoise: it went Democratic in 1992, Republican in 1994, Democratic in 1996.

The congressman from the 9th District is Adam Smith, a Democrat elected in 1996. He grew up in the Sea-Tac area; his father, a baggage handler for United Airlines and active in the Machinists' Union, died when Smith was 17. The family went on welfare; Smith worked his way through Fordham driving trucks for UPS, then went to the University of Washington Law School. He worked as a lawyer, then as a Seattle prosecutor, handling drunk driving and domestic abuse cases. In 1990, at 25, he was elected to the state Senate, beating an incumbent Republican by doorbelling the district twice. He was reelected in 1994 and in July 1995 decided to run against Congressman Randy Tate. In many ways they were similar: born the same year to families of modest backgrounds: Tate's father owned and managed a mobile home park, and he was elected to the state House in 1988, at 22, by doorbelling his district. In 1994 Tate ran against Democrat Mike Kreidler, and beat him 52%–48%, becoming at 28 the youngest member of the 1994 Republican freshman class. Tate was a religious conservative and strong supporter of Speaker Newt Gingrich. He was an immediate target of the AFL-CIO in 1996, which spent somewhere between $500,000 and $1 million on ads against him; he was also a favorite of conservative activists like Grover Norquist of Americans for Tax Reform, and raised and spent $1.6 million on his reelection campaign.

Smith portrayed himself as a moderate Democrat, a supporter of the death penalty and three strikes legislation—a believer in a more efficient and responsive government. "I've worked very hard in my life, overcome some personal adversity. I can't stand it when people don't want to be responsible for their action. If you don't have a great life handed to you by wealth or a parent, you have to work hard, but government can make sure the rules of the game are fair." But the brunt of his campaign was his attacks on Tate for supporting Gingrich on 96% of House votes and for backing Medicare "cuts." Tate argued that the Medicare plan increased spending and said: "I make no apologies for trying to cut taxes. It's your money." He attacked Smith for opposing a bill giving homeowners additional rights to defend themselves against intruders and another channeling youthful offenders to adult courts and prisons and for voting for Governor Mike Lowry's $1.2 billion tax increase in 1993. Each could argue his record was tempered with moderation: Smith voted to repeal some of those tax increases in 1995 and for a bill to bar the sale of sexually explicit material to minors; Tate voted for the minimum wage increase and campaigned hard against the enlargement of Sea-Tac airport. And if Smith campaigned as a moderate, most of the money backing his candidacy—a large percentage of his own contributions plus the independent expenditures campaign—came from unions. This was one of the closest races in the country. In the September all-party primary, usually a good indicator of the final result in Washington, Smith led 49%–48%. The result in November was not as close: 50%–47% for Smith.

In the House Smith showed political acumen, winning good committee assignments—Resources and National Security—and stationing his top staffers in the district. He announced he would not accept contributions from PACs or individuals outside Washington state in 1997, and kept doorbelling constituents. But the closeness of this result virtually guarantees a seriously contested race in 1998, and turn this very closely divided district over once again. Tate, out of public office for the first time since age 23, was chosen in June 1997 to head up the Christian Coalition after Ralph Reed departs in September.

The People: Pop. 1990: 540,519; 9% rural; 9% age 65+; 84% White; 5% Black; 6% Asian; 1% Amer. Indian; 4% Hispanic origin. Households: 57% married couple families; 27% married couple fams. w. children; 52% college educ.; median household income: $32,194; per capita income: $14,264; median gross rent: $478; median house value: $93,300.

1996 Presidential Vote

Clinton (D)	110,854	(51%)
Dole (R)	77,616	(36%)
Perot (I)	20,806	(10%)
Other	6,466	(3%)

1992 Presidential Vote

Clinton (D)	93,964	(42%)
Bush (R)	69,593	(31%)
Perot (I)	58,037	(26%)

Rep. Adam Smith (D)

Elected 1996; b. June 15, 1965, Washington, DC; home, Kent; Fordham U. B.A. 1987; U. of WA, J.D. 1990; Christian; married (Sara).

Career: WA Senate, 1990–96; Practicing atty., 1991–92; Seattle Prosecutor, 1992–95.

DC Office: 1505 LHOB 20515, 202-225-8901; Fax: 202-225-5893.
District Offices: Tacoma, 206-926-6683.

Committees: *National Security* (21st of 25 D): Military Installations & Facilities; Military Procurement. *Resources* (18th of 23 D): Water & Power.

Group Ratings and Key Votes: Newly Elected

Election Results

1996 general	Adam Smith (D)	105,236	(50%)	($711,722)
	Randy Tate (R)	99,199	(47%)	($1,578,748)
	Others	5,432	(3%)	
1996 primary	Adam Smith (D)	56,668	(49%)	
	Randy Tate (R)	55,462	(48%)	
	Others	3,450	(3%)	
1994 general	Randy Tate (R)	77,833	(52%)	($617,127)
	Mike Kreidler (D)	72,451	(48%)	($880,262)

WEST VIRGINIA

Things are finally looking up for West Virginia. It's about time: this is a state that has had more than its share of tragedy and heartbreak, but whose people have never lost their sense of hope or their affection for the hills and mountains that make this the most unhorizontal state in the nation. West Virginia was born out of the tragedy of the Civil War, when 55 mountain counties with few slaves seceded from Virginia, and made its living most of the years since on that cruelest of commodities, coal. Coal kept the sons of large mountaineer families here for much of the 20th Century, men who would otherwise have left for big cities; coal brought immigrants in, a few from odd corners of Europe, but more from adjacent areas of the South where the local farming economies were stagnant when West Virginia's coal economy was booming. Coal and local rock salt and brines brought the large concentration of chemical plants 50 years ago to the Kanawha Valley around Charleston; it built steel mills and glass factories in the panhandle and the Monongahela River valley, not far south of Pittsburgh.

Coal did not build a self-sustaining economy. When America was beleaguered abroad, demand for coal increased and energy prices rose, and West Virginia boomed, during World War II (the state reached its all-time population peak of two million in 1950) and the oil shocks of the 1970s. Coal changed West Virginia's politics too. West Virginia's heritage from the Civil War days was Republican, though some counties tilted toward the Confederacy and the Democrats. But after John L. Lewis's United Mine Workers organized most of the West Virginia mines, the coal country shifted toward the New Deal Democrats, and West Virginia for half a century has been one of the most Democratic states, deserting the ticket only in Republican landslide years (1956, 1972, 1984).

But neither Democratic administrations nor the pensions and medical benefits the UMW negotiated for retired miners have been able to provide the economic growth to keep thousands of West Virginians from leaving their mountains to find work elsewhere—now more often south on I-77 to the booming Carolinas than north to the Great Lakes' industrial cities. As underground miners were replaced by strip-mining machines, coal tonnage went way up but coal mine employment dropped from 22% of the state's work force in 1950 to 10% in 1980 and 5% in 1990, and was only 39% in March 1997. The state's population, 1.95 million in 1980, fell to about 1.8 million in 1990—the largest decrease, absolutely and in percentage terms, of any state. But West Virginians have a strong attachment to this unique state, where the accent sounds southern and the early 20th Century factories and houses look northern, where the landscape is rural and the economy industrial.

Now in the 1990s West Virginia is on the rebound, and not because of upward spikes of energy prices. Population rose nearly 2% from 1990–96, and the number of jobs rose 6%; unemployment was the lowest since the 1970s, averaging 7% in 1996. And this despite a continuing drop in coal mining jobs, as machines replace men and the Clean Air Act of 1990 reduces demand for West Virginia's high-sulfur coal. Government has played a role. Senator Robert Byrd, chairman for six years and now ranking Democrat on the Appropriations Committee, achieved his career goal of channeling $1 billion of federal projects into West Virginia, and more: over $1.5 billion. They include offices for the FBI and Fish and Wildlife Service, NASA and the National Institute of Occupational Safety; federal jobs in West Virginia have grown 20% since 1988. State tax breaks promoted by Governor Gaston Caperton (1989–97) attracted investments from Georgia Pacific, Swearingen Aircraft, NGK Sparkplugs and Toyota. West Virginia's plastics and chemicals industries have been expanding, forest products are replacing coal in rural counties, health care is growing as everywhere and telemarketing is growing as well. West Virginia has finally completed its Interstate highway network and in a computer age it is no longer isolated; with low wages, good work habits, low land costs, West Virginia has even developed a software industry in the corridor between Morgantown and Clarksburg. Governor Cecil Underwood, elected in 1956 and then again in 1996, notes that he started building the Interstate highway system 40 years ago and now is building a "technology superhighway system." In Caperton's two terms, the state moved from 46th to 33d in teachers' salaries and the legislature approved more than $60 million to put a computer in every school classroom. In 1996, his last year in office, Caperton sponsored a Homecoming '96 program, with 300 communities scheduling street fairs, parades, motorcycle rallies and other commemorative events, celebrating West Virginia. An estimated 40% of West Virginians who leave the state come back, very often to retire. Now for the first time in 50 years West Virginia has reason to be hopeful about its economic future and its young people have reason to stay.

Governor. Cecil Underwood was the nation's youngest governor when he was first elected in 1956 at 34 and its oldest governor when he was elected in 1996 at 74: surely the longest-spanning gubernatorial career in American history. In between terms, he ran for office unsuccessfully (for senator in 1960 and governor in 1964 and 1976), ran businesses and was president of Bethany

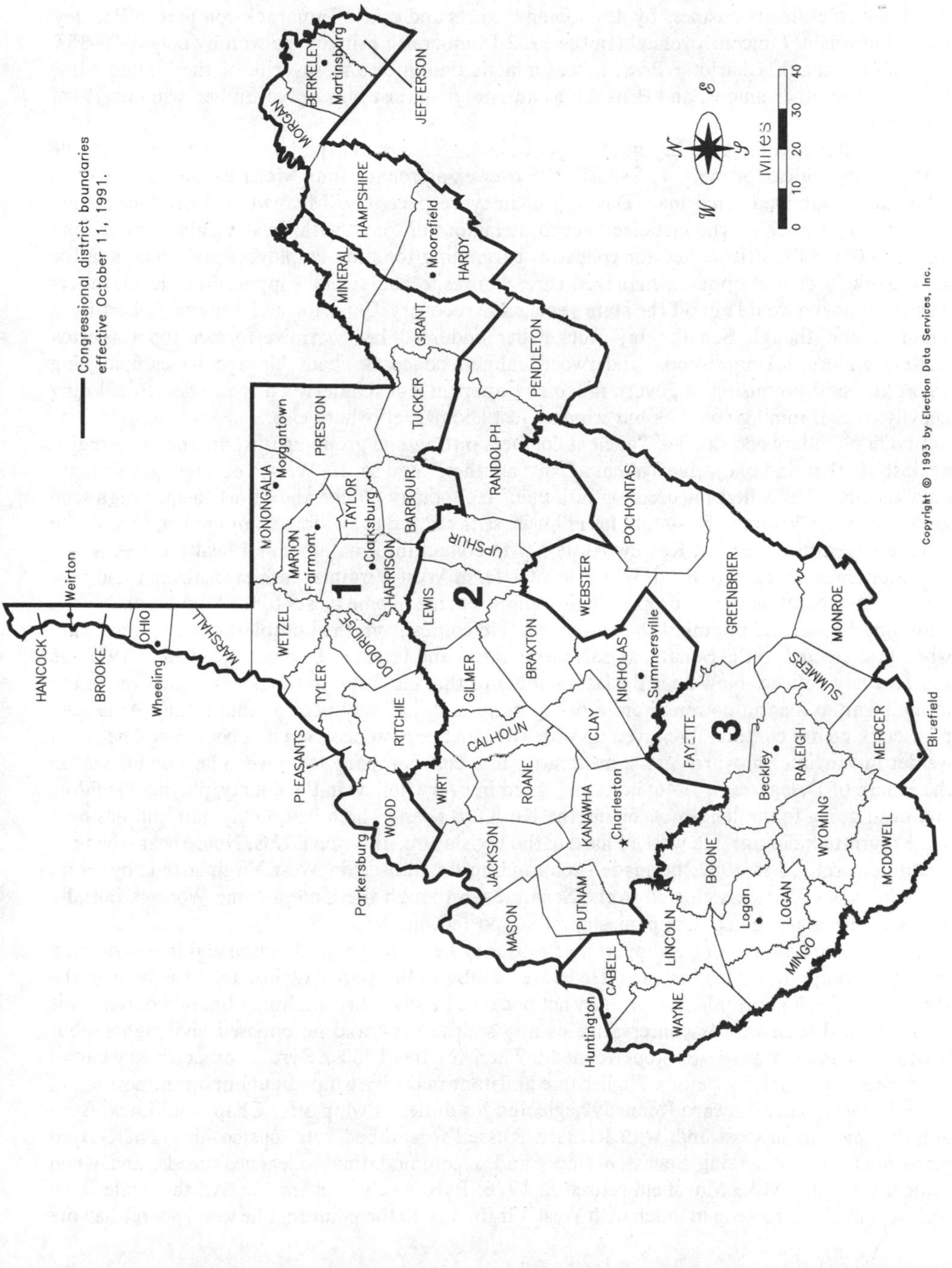
Congressional district boundaries effective October 11, 1991.
HANCOCK
Weirton
BROOKE
OHIO
Wheeling
MARSHALL
WETZEL
MONONGALIA
Morgantown
MARION
Fairmont
TAYLOR
PRESTON
TUCKER
GRANT
MINERAL
HAMPSHIRE
Moorefield
HARDY
MORGAN
BERKELEY
Martinsburg
JEFFERSON
PENDLETON
RANDOLPH
BARBOUR
HARRISON
Clarksburg
DODDRIDGE
TYLER
PLEASANTS
RITCHIE
LEWIS
UPSHUR
POCHONTAS
WEBSTER
BRAXTON
GILMER
CALHOUN
WIRT
WOOD
Parkersburg
ROANE
JACKSON
CLAY
NICHOLAS
Summersville
GREENBRIER
MONROE
SUMMERS
FAYETTE
RALEIGH
Beckley
MERCER
Bluefield
KANAWHA
Charleston
MASON
PUTNAM
BOONE
WYOMING
MCDOWELL
LINCOLN
LOGAN
Logan
MINGO
CABELL
Huntington
WAYNE
1
2
3
Miles
0 10 20 30 40
Copyright © 1993 by Election Data Services, Inc.

College in the 1970s. He is a Republican, but in many ways he represents continuity with his Democratic predecessor, Gaston Caperton. Caperton, from a wealthy Charleston family, spent $2 million of his own money to be elected in 1988, immediately raised taxes and cut spending to fill a budget gap; but he also used tax incentives to attract jobs, raised teacher pay, started a $500 million school construction plan, began a program to put computers in every classroom and, passed brownfields legislation to redevelop cleaned up industrial sites. He even put the state into the wholesale art business by developing the arts and crafts Tamarack complex in Beckley. Caperton was not uncontroversial. In the 1992 Democratic primary he won by only 43%–35% over state Senator Charlotte Pritt, a coal miner's daughter and favorite of the United Mine Workers and other unions, and Pritt ran as a write-in against him in November, winning 7% of the votes.

The specter of a Pritt victory in 1996 got business leaders to urge Underwood to run, and he won the Republican primary 41%–33%–26% over ex-astronaut John McBride and former West Virginia Republican Chairman David McKinley respectively. Meanwhile Pritt faced state Senator Joe Manchin, who criticized her for being out of touch with West Virginia values, and won by 40%–33%. Pritt called for collective bargaining for state employees and no cuts in the state work force and opposed managed care; while she had strong support from labor, others worried that she would cut off the state's economic recovery. Caperton and Senator Robert Byrd shunned her, though Senator Jay Rockefeller endorsed her warmly; former top Caperton staffers endorsed Underwood. Underwood calmed concerns about his age by campaigning vigorously and promising to govern much as Caperton had. Underwood won 52%–46%, losing heavily in coal mining counties but winning just about everywhere else.

In office Underwood decried "ancient conflicts pitting one group against another, one region against another and one value system against another," and said, "We see obsolete government all about us." He called for creation of a chief technology officer and effort to spur high-tech growth in West Virginia; he sought lower business taxes and even more computers in schools; he sought a Health Care Cost Review Authority to collect information about health care costs.

Senior Senator. Robert Byrd, senior senator from West Virginia, former chairman and now ranking Democrat on the Appropriations Committee, may come closer to the kind of senator the Founding Fathers had in mind than any other. He comes from the humblest of beginnings, and when first elected to the Senate, as part of the large and talented Democratic class of 1958, he was scarcely noticed. Now he is the last member of that class still in the Senate, and even in the minority an authentic power. From a background as grindingly poor as that of any American politician, he has continually moved up with awesome persistence. Son of a coal miner, he was a welder in wartime shipyards and a meatcutter in a coal company town when he won his seat in the House of Delegates in 1946; he campaigned in every hollow in the county, playing his fiddle and even going to the length of joining the Ku Klux Klan (which he quickly quit and has ever since regretted joining). He worked hard in the legislature, and won a U.S. House seat when the incumbent retired in 1952; he made such a name for himself in West Virginia that by 1958, when he was 40, he was elected to the Senate even though the United Mine Workers initially opposed him and the coal companies never supported him.

In the Senate, he became a supporter of Majority Leader Lyndon Johnson and in return got a seat on Appropriations his first year. He backed Hubert Humphrey against John Kennedy in the 1960 West Virginia presidential primary not because he shared Humphrey's liberal politics—his voting record then was as conservative as any southerner's and he opposed civil rights—but because Johnson wanted to stop Kennedy. Then, in the 1960s, Byrd's career took what in retrospect was a helpful detour. He became assistant majority whip, an unimportant position in 1965; in 1971, when Edward Kennedy neglected his duties as whip after Chappaquiddick, Byrd quietly lined up support and, with Richard Russell's deathbed vote, ousted him. There Byrd performed ably, managing Senate business and accommodating colleagues' needs, and when Majority Leader Mike Mansfield retired in 1976, Byrd easily won the job. All the while Byrd was working hard to keep in touch with West Virginians, to the point that he won 78% of the vote in 1970, becoming the first candidate to carry all 55 counties.

Byrd did not like being majority leader. Contrary to most people's assumptions, the post carries little power, because Senate rules requiring unanimous consent or supermajorities allow individual senators to block action; the office gained its reputation in the six years Lyndon Johnson held it, when his extraordinary abilities and compulsive personality enabled him temporarily to become a national leader. No majority leader has since, and Byrd was aware that his power came from meeting other senators' needs and did not have a national issues agenda of his own, though his voting record became notably less conservative. His formal manner did not project well on television, and when Democrats were in the minority, Byrd was challenged in 1984 for the minority leader post by then-Florida Senator (now Governor) Lawton Chiles. In 1987, with Democrats back in the majority after six years out of power, Byrd established some legislative priorities and then announced he would leave the post after the 1988 election.

So in 1989 Byrd got the position he had been aiming for all along, chairman of the Appropriations Committee. "I want to be West Virginia's billion dollar industry," he announced in 1990, and in six years as chairman succeeded handsomely. An FBI office went to Clarksburg, Treasury and IRS offices to Parkersburg, the Fish and Wildlife Training Center in Harper's Ferry, a Bureau of Alcohol, Tobacco and Firearms in Martinsburg, a NASA Research center in Wheeling. "All roads, they say, lead to Rome," he said in 1994 in Logan, West Virginia. "They haven't seen anything yet. All roads lead to Logan." Byrd does not always deliver: a GAO report helped defeat his attempt to build a $1.2 billion CIA facility in Jefferson County; and he lost by one vote, despite personally lobbying every senator, his amendment to compensate coal miners who lose their jobs because of the Clean Air Act. But Byrd usually wins. And, while he insists that he does not retaliate against those who oppose his projects, no one doubts he remembers how every senator voted. "You might as well slap my wife as take the highway money from West Virginia."

It should be added that Byrd's positions are not just parochial but are the product of serious study of the Constitution and of history. With the assistance of Senate historian Richard Baker, he wrote *The Senate 1789–1989*, a two-volume history, plus two volumes of classic speeches and statistics; based on impressive research, gracefully written, full of arresting anecdotes and sound insights, it surpasses any previous work on the subject. In 1995 he published *The Senate of the Roman Republic: Addresses on the History of Roman Constitutionalism*. Byrd earned his law degree while in the Senate and had his diploma presented to him by President Kennedy at the 1963 American University commencement where Kennedy delivered his most important foreign policy speech; in 1994 he was awarded his B.A. summa cum laude by Marshall University, which he had attended for one semester 43 years before and could not afford to continue, and where he earned As in all eight courses he took. Byrd has been educating himself as well, systematically reading the classics, and takes to quoting Shakespeare, Thucydides or Cato the Younger in debates on the balanced budget amendment and the line-item veto. In December 1995, in the budget crisis, he decried "insolence" and "harsh and severe" speeches, referring to the partisan climate on Capitol Hill. "Little did I know when I came here that I would live to see pygmies stride like Colossus while marveling, like Aesop's fly, sitting on the axle of a chariot, 'My, what a dust I do raise.' " He said the balanced budget amendment "would rudely disrupt the carefully balanced powers of the three branches so assiduously planned by the Framers." He said passage of the line-item veto in 1996 was "one of the darkest moments in the history of the republic," and with five other members of Congress brought suit against it; a federal judge ruled it unconstitutional in April 1997, and the Supreme Court heard arguments to the Justice Department appeal in May.

Byrd's insistence on Senate prerogatives have not always worked well. His practice of earmarking West Virginia projects in appropriations bills has come under attack; his response was to denounce critics for hypocrisy when the Senate passed a FY96 appropriations bill with no earmarks for highways but dozens for rail and bus projects. He is a stickler for Senate rules and is known to have studied them meticulously on weekends. When a blind aide to freshman Ron

Wyden wanted to bring her leader dog onto the floor in 1997, Byrd raised an objection. "Matters such as this ought to go to the Committee on Rules and Administration for any change in regulations or rules deemed necessary. Senator Wyden's resolution may pass with flying colors, but the proper procedure should be followed." Byrd may not be easy to deal with, but he is open to persuasion. He switched and voted for the "partial-birth" abortion ban in May 1997 after an abortion clinic lobbyist admitted he lied in arguing against the ban in 1995 and after the American Medical Association endorsed the bill.

In 1994 Byrd was reelected with 69% of the vote, repeating his 1970 victory of carrying all 55 counties. He became the third senator to be elected to seven six-year terms (the others were Carl Hayden of Arizona and Strom Thurmond of South Carolina); he has served longer than any senator but those two and John Stennis, whose tenure he will surpass in March 2000. In July 1995 he became the first senator to cast 14,000 votes; before Governor Caperton left office in 1997, he unveiled a bronze statue of Byrd in the state Capitol.

Junior Senator. West Virginia's junior senator is Jay Rockefeller. His full name, John D. Rockefeller IV, has a familiar ring to most older voters, who remember his great-grandfather as the oil billionaire who was America's richest man and his grandfather as the heir who had more than enough money to build New York's Rockefeller Center, restore Colonial Williamsburg and found the Museum of Modern Art during the Depression. Jay Rockefeller's father and uncles were men of impressive achievement in different fields, in two cases in politics. His uncle Winthrop Rockefeller moved to an impoverished state in the southern hills—in his case Arkansas—ran for governor and lost, ran again and won two terms and ran an honest and reforming administration: the same could be said of Jay Rockefeller's career in West Virginia. There are interesting comparisons between the careers of Jay Rockefeller and his other governor-uncle: Nelson Rockefeller, in his 30s, became head of Franklin Roosevelt's Latin American policy program; Jay Rockefeller, in his 20s, studied for three years in Japan. Nelson Rockefeller became governor of the nation's then-biggest state and spent money expansively on generous welfare and gigantic monuments; Jay Rockefeller became governor of what turned out to be America's number one population-losing state of the 1980s, leaving behind a network of roads and highways and a progressive tax structure. Nelson Rockefeller was a Republican at a time when the party's Ivy League establishment believed it was in the minority and had to move left to win votes. Jay Rockefeller broke family tradition and became a Democrat at a time when the party's Ivy League ideologues believed it would always retain the majority party even as it was losing that status. Both Rockefellers were mentioned early on as presidential candidates: Nelson, never very shy about running, finally did so in 1964 at 56, and again in 1968 (he ultimately served briefly as vice president under Gerald Ford); Jay for years avoided projecting his name forward, then almost decided to run in the summer of 1991 at 54, but now as an ally of Bill Clinton and Al Gore seems unlikely to run in 2000.

The parallels stop here, for Jay Rockefeller lacks the aloof, imperial bearing of his Uncle Nelson; he is affable, full of self-deprecating humor, tall enough so that he stoops to get through doorways and uses hearing aids because of noise damage from frequent helicopter travel. He was careful to work his way up the political ladder. He first came to West Virginia as a VISTA volunteer, was elected to the House of Delegates in Kanawha County in 1966 and as secretary of State in 1968, and then had the chastening experience of losing the gubernatorial race to Arch Moore in 1972. He served three years as president of West Virginia Wesleyan College in Buckhannon, and became more practical, dropping his opposition to strip mining. He was not shy about spending his own millions and was elected governor in 1976 and, against Moore, in 1980, after which the state was plunged into deep recession. In 1984, he ran for the U.S. Senate and beat Republican businessman John Raese by just 52%–48% after spending $12 million. Every penny helped, especially the huge sums needed to air ads on Washington and Pittsburgh TV: in most counties in the state, Rockefeller ran between 1% and 7% ahead of Walter Mondale's 45% showing; in all but one of the dozen or so panhandle counties in these hugely expensive media markets, he ran 12% to 18% ahead of Mondale.

Initially in the Senate Rockefeller deferred to Robert Byrd, compiled a conventional liberal voting record, somewhat more inclined to free trade because of his experience in East Asia. Then he began his concentration on health care. With a seat on the Finance Committee, he got a place on the Pepper Commission on long-term health care and became chairman when Pepper died in June 1989. He got majorities on the commission to back long-term care for all Americans regardless of age and, by 8–7, universal medical insurance coverage. But getting others to agree was harder. Rockefeller talked mostly about healthcare financing when he was mulling a presidential race; but he warmly endorsed Clinton and applauded his emphasis on health care. He was motivated in part by anger at his mother's treatment during a long terminal illness—an experience that would be much worse for people of ordinary incomes, he thought—and he worked to increase the number of general practitioners, especially in states like West Virginia and Arkansas, at the risk of harming the major teaching hospitals. He resisted efforts at any compromise. "We're going to push through healthcare reform regardless of the views of the American people," he said at one point, sounding like his uncle Nelson. Poor political judgment: efforts at compromise came far too late, after voters had turned against a government takeover of health care, and the healthcare bill crashed and burned in September 1994.

Rockefeller has worked on other health care issues since. Perhaps his biggest legislative achievement was his 1992 law, passed over furious opposition from western coal states, which forced union and non-union coal companies and "reachback" companies that had gone out of the coal business to pay for the exploding cost of the United Mine Workers' healthcare trust funds; he successfully defended it against Republican attacks in 1995. He also opposed the Republicans' Medicare reform, worked to save Medicaid for pregnant women, children and the disabled, and backed compensation for veterans suffering from the vaguely-defined Gulf war syndrome. He is lead sponsor of a bipartisan Medigap bill, which would require insurers to issue policies to people with preexisting conditions who don't qualify for Medicaid. In related areas, he supported the adoption tax credit, raising it to $6,000 for special needs children. With three Republicans, he has sponsored a SAFE Act, to make the interest and safety of the child, rather than family preservation, central in child placement.

Rockefeller's voting record is mostly but not entirely liberal. He was one of 14 Democrats, along with Robert Byrd, who voted for the flag burning amendment. He supported the 1996 Welfare Reform Act, working to maintain programs for abused and neglected children. And one of his major causes has been a uniform federal product liability law, to reduce the burden of expensive lawsuit settlements on manufacturers. A product liability bill passed the House in March 1995; a similar bill was filibustered in the Senate, but Rockefeller scaled it down, dropping controversial medical malpractice provisions, to get 61 votes for passage in May 1995. After a nearly year-long conference, it was vetoed by Bill Clinton in May 1996. Rockefeller has said he will not undertake all that work again until Clinton sets out what kind of bill he would sign. On telecommunications reform, he worked to assure discounts for schools, libraries and rural health providers, so that West Virginia, so isolated by its mountains, could have equal access to the world. Rockefeller has left funding local West Virginia projects mostly in the capable hands of Robert Byrd. Rockefeller specializes in attracting industry to the state. He has led two Project Harvest trade missions to Japan and Taiwan, and has brokered negotiations for the Wheeling-Nisshin Steel, NGK Sparkplugs, and Sino-Swearingen Aircraft plants in the state and the Toyota engine plant in Buffalo in Putnam County.

Rockefeller is in strong shape politically, strong enough that he no longer spends any of his own money and wins handsomely. In 1990 he won 68%–32%; in 1996, against a nurse's aide who didn't like to see the ballot space empty, he won 77%–23%, duplicating Byrd's feat of winning all 55 counties.

Presidential politics. West Virginia is one of the nation's most Democratic states in presidential elections; it has voted Republican only three times in the last 65 years. West Virginia's presidential primary, held in May, has not attracted much attention in years. But in 1960 it was the focus of the nation's attention when John Kennedy, reportedly fortified with large injections of cash from his father, took on Hubert Humphrey and beat him, proving that a Catholic could carry a virtually all-Protestant state.

Congressional districting. West Virginia lost one of its four House seats for 1992, and so one of its four Democratic congressmen had to go. This game of musical chairs was played out lustily in the legislature, and the loser turned out to be Harley Staggers, whose 2d District was divided up among the other three; he ran against Alan Mollohan in the 1st District primary and lost. West Virginia has had an all-Democratic congressional delegation since 1982.

The People: Est. Pop. 1996: 1,826,000; Pop. 1990: 1,793,477, up 1.8% 1990–1996. 0.7% of U.S. total, 35th largest; 64% rural. Median age: 37.7 years. 15% 65 years and over. 95.8% White, 3.1% Black, 1% Hispanic origin. Households: 59.0% married couple families; 28% married couple fams. w. children; 29% college educ.; median household income: $20,795; per capita income: $10,520; 74.1% owner occupied housing; median house value: $47,900; median monthly rent: $221. 7.5% Unemployment. 1996 Voting age pop.: 1,417,000. 1996 Turnout: 636,459; 45% of VAP. Registered voters (1996): 970,743; 616,205 D (63%); 288,199 R (30%); 66,339 unaffiliated and minor parties (7%).

Political Lineup: Governor, Cecil H. Underwood (R); Secy. of State, Ken Hechler (D); Atty. Gen., Darrell V. McGraw Jr. (D); Treasurer, John Perdue (D); Auditor, Glen B. Gainer III (D). State Senate, 34 (24 D and 10 R); Senate President, Earl Ray Tomblin (D); State House, 100 (74 D and 26 R); House Speaker, Robert Kiss (D). Senators, Robert C. Byrd (D) and John D. (Jay) Rockefeller IV (D). Representatives, 3 D.

Elections Division: 304-558-6000; **Filing Deadline for U.S. Congress:** February 7, 1998.

1996 Presidential Vote

Clinton (D)	327,812	(52%)
Dole (R)	233,946	(37%)
Perot (I)	71,639	(11%)

1992 Presidential Vote

Clinton (D)	331,001	(48%)
Bush (R)	241,974	(35%)
Perot (I)	108,829	(16%)

1996 Republican Presidential Primary

Dole (R)	87,534	(69%)
Buchanan (R)	20,928	(16%)
Forbes (R)	6,222	(5%)
Keyes (R)	4,822	(4%)
Other	7,948	(6%)

GOVERNOR

Gov. Cecil H. Underwood (R)

Elected 1996, term expires Jan. 2001; b. Nov. 5, 1922, Joseph's Mills; home, Huntington; Salem Col., A.B. 1943; WV U., M.A. 1952; Methodist; married (Hovah).

Career: Army Reserves, 1942–43; Teacher, 1943–46; WV House of Delegates, 1944–57; Faculty, Marietta Col., 1946–50; Vice Pres., Salem Col., 1950–56; WV Governor, 1956–61; Repub. nominee, U.S. Senate, 1960; Vice Pres., Island Creek Coal Co., 1961–64; Repub. nominee, WV Gov., 1964, 1976; Vice Pres., Gov. & Civic Affairs, Monsanto Co., 1965–68; Pres., Bethany Col., 1972–75; Pres., Princess Coals, Inc., 1978–81, Chmn., 1981–83; Pres., Morgantown Industrial Research Park, 1983–89, Chmn., 1989–96; Pres., Software Valley, 1989–93; Pres., Mon View Heights of WV, 1993–96.

Office: State Capitol, Charleston 25305, 304-558-2000; Fax: 304-558-2722; Web site: www.state.wv.us.

Election Results

1996 gen.	Cecil H. Underwood (R)	324,518	(52%)
	Charlotte Pritt (D)	287,870	(46%)
	Others	16,171	(3%)
1996 prim.	Cecil H. Underwood (R)	54,628	(41%)
	Jon McBride (R)	44,255	(33%)
	David McKinley (R)	35,089	(26%)
1992 gen.	Gaston Caperton (D)	368,302	(56%)
	Cleve Benedict (R)...........	240,390	(37%)
	Charlotte Jean Pritt (I)	48,501	(7%)

SENATORS

Sen. Robert C. Byrd (D)

Elected 1958, seat up 2000; b. Nov. 20, 1917, North Wilkesboro, NC; home, Sophia; American U., J.D. 1963; Baptist; married (Erma).

Career: WV House of Delegates, 1946–50; WV Senate, 1950–52; U.S. House of Reps., 1952–58; U.S. Senate Majority Whip, 1971–76, Majority Ldr., 1977–80, Minority Ldr., 1981–86, Pres. Pro-tem, 1989–94; Book Author.

DC Office: 311 HSOB 20510, 202-224-3954; Fax: 202-228-0002; e-mail: senate_byrd@byrd.senate.gov.

State Office: Charleston, 304-342-5855.

Committees: *Appropriations* (RMM of 13 D): Agriculture, Rural Development & Related Agencies; Defense; Energy & Water Development; Interior (RMM); Transportation. *Armed Services* (5th of 8 D): Airland Forces; Sea Power; Strategic Forces. *Rules & Administration* (2nd of 7 D).

Group Ratings

	ADA	ACLU	AFS	LCV	CFA	CON	NFIB	COC	ACU	NTLC	CHC
1996	70	33	86	77	86	5	24	23	15	10	30
1995	85	—	100	86	88	8	—	26	26	—	—

National Journal Ratings

	1995 LIB — 1995 CONS	1996 LIB — 1996 CONS
Economic	80% — 17%	74% — 19%
Social	53% — 43%	67% — 30%
Foreign	86% — 7%	66% — 33%

Key Votes of the 104th Congress

1. Reduce Medicare Growth $	N	5. Flag Amendment	Y	9. Anti-Missile Defense	N
2. Lmt. Prod. Liab. Damages	N	6. Endangered Species	Y	10. Cuban Embargo	N
3. Increase Min. Wage	Y	7. Gay Employment Rights	N	11. Bar Bosnia Troop $	N
4. Welfare Reform	Y	8. Ovrd. Part. Birth Veto	N	12. Cut Vietnam Aid	Y

Election Results

1994 general	Robert C. Byrd (D)	290,495	(69%)	($1,550,354)
	Stan Klos (R)	130,441	(31%)	($267,165)
1994 primary	Robert C. Byrd (D)	190,061	(85%)	
	John M. Fuller (D)	20,057	(9%)	
	Paul Nuchims (D)	12,381	(6%)	
1988 general	Robert C. Byrd (D)	410,983	(65%)	($1,282,746)
	M. Jay Wolfe (R)	223,564	(35%)	($115,284)

Sen. John D. (Jay) Rockefeller IV (D)

Elected 1984, seat up 2002; b. June 18, 1937, New York, NY; home, Charleston; Harvard, B.A. 1961, Intl. Christian U., Tokyo, Japan, 1957–60; Presbyterian; married (Sharon).

Career: Natl. Advisory Cncl., Peace Corps, 1961; Asst., Peace Corps Dir. Sargent Shriver, 1962–63; VISTA worker, 1964–66; WV House of Delegates, 1966–68; WV Secy. of State, 1968–72; Dem. nominee, WV Gov., 1972; Pres., WV Wesleyan Col., 1973–75; WV Gov., 1976–84.

DC Office: 531 HSOB 20510, 202-224-6472; Fax: 202-224-7665; e-mail: senator@rockefeller.senate.gov.

State Offices: Beckley, 304-253-9704; Charleston, 304-347-5372; Fairmont, 304-367-0122.

Committees: *Commerce, Science & Transportation* (4th of 9 D): Aviation; Communications; Manufacturing & Competitiveness; Science, Technology & Space (RMM). *Finance* (3rd of 9 D): Health Care (RMM); International Trade; Social Security & Family Policy. *Veterans' Affairs* (RMM of 5 D).

Group Ratings

	ADA	ACLU	AFS	LCV	CFA	CON	NFIB	COC	ACU	NTLC	CHC
1996	85	28	86	92	71	10	39	46	16	10	7
1995	90	—	100	100	69	8	—	42	9	—	—

National Journal Ratings

	1995 LIB — 1995 CONS			1996 LIB — 1996 CONS		
Economic	68%	—	29%	74%	—	19%
Social	65%	—	34%	75%	—	24%
Foreign	85%	—	14%	72%	—	27%

Key Votes of the 104th Congress

1. Reduce Medicare Growth $	N	5. Flag Amendment	Y	9. Anti-Missile Defense	N
2. Lmt. Prod. Liab. Damages	Y	6. Endangered Species	Y	10. Cuban Embargo	Y
3. Increase Min. Wage	Y	7. Gay Employment Rights	Y	11. Bar Bosnia Troop $	N
4. Welfare Reform	Y	8. Ovrd. Part. Birth Veto	N	12. Cut Vietnam Aid	N

Election Results

1996 general	John D. (Jay) Rockefeller IV (D)	456,526	(77%)	($5,819,157)
	Betty A. Burks (R)	139,088	(23%)	
1996 primary	John D. (Jay) Rockefeller IV (D)	280,303	(88%)	
	Bruce Barilla (D)	36,637	(12%)	
1990 general	John D. (Jay) Rockefeller IV (D)	276,234	(68%)	($2,709,665)
	John Yoder (R)	128,071	(32%)	($22,904)

FIRST DISTRICT

The northern part of West Virginia is in many ways an extension of the Pittsburgh metropolitan area. People here are Steelers and Pirates fans, they drink Iron City and Rolling Rock beer, they watch Pittsburgh TV, they live in the crevasses between hills cut by the Monongahela and Ohio Rivers, on terrain that seems forbidding to industrial and urban development. Yet this has been one of America's prime industrial areas; northern West Virginia is part of the same coal-and-steel economy that made Pittsburgh one of the nation's largest cities and filled the narrow bottomlands along the rivers with steel and glass factories, foundries and coal yards. In the 1980s and 1990s these have been declining industries, or rather industries becoming far less labor-intensive. Replacing them are Japanese factories and high-tech startups, as well as federal office complexes obtained by Senator Robert Byrd.

The 1st Congressional District of West Virginia includes the northern third of the state. On the panhandle along the Ohio River are Victorian Wheeling, once one of the richest cities in the country with its steel and glass company investors and executives, and where the radio show "Jamboree U.S.A." has been broadcast every Saturday night for more than 50 years, and Weirton, a steel company town and site of one of the most visible experiments in employee ownership, where steelworkers decided to cut their own pay in order to produce profits. South of Pittsburgh on the Monongahela are Morgantown, site of West Virginia University, and Clarksburg and Fairmont. Far to the west, the district includes Parkersburg and the surrounding hills on the Ohio River. To the east, it extends to the upper Potomac River opposite Cumberland, Maryland. Politically, most of this territory is solidly Democratic, except for some mountain countries never heavily industrialized which have remained Republican since the Civil War.

The congressman from the 1st District is Alan Mollohan, a Democrat whose father Robert Mollohan was elected congressman in 1952 and 1954, ran for governor and lost in 1956, and then won the House seat again when Arch Moore was elected governor in 1968 and kept it until he retired in 1982. Alan Mollohan, a Washington lawyer for Consolidation Coal among other clients, returned home in 1982 and won the seat. His one major challenge came in the 1992 primary, after he was redistricted in with another congressman who was also the son of a congressman, Harley Staggers, Jr. The younger Staggers made his name as chief sponsor of the National Rifle Association-supported substitute for the Brady bill seven-day handgun purchase waiting period, to establish a computerized list of felons which gun sellers could check before sales. The younger Mollohan made his name as a member of the Appropriations Committee who hustled to bring jobs to northern West Virginia. But the key was that only 20% of the Democratic primary vote here was cast in Staggers's old district. He carried that part with 73%, but Mollohan won 70% in his old district and won overall, 62%–38%.

Mollohan has compiled a moderately liberal voting record and concentrated on bringing projects to the district. He claims credit for a First District Federal Procurement Team and a West Virginia High-Technology Consortium, headquartered in the Alan B. Mollohan Innovation Center and spurring a computer software testing center in Fairmont. Mollohan secured $5 million for the Consortium to manage a national weather project. He has worked to fund waterways, education projects, a flight simulator for Fairmont State College and a defense procurement center in Parkersburg, historic sites, the Morgantown federal prison, the Orbital Science Corporation's satellite tracking station. In April 1994 Mollohan moved up to the "college of cardinals" when he became chairman of the Commerce, Justice, State, and Judiciary Appropriations Subcommittee; now he is ranking minority member. Even in the minority, Mollohan got an SBA Business Information Center in Fairmont, $750,000 to combat acid mine drainage problems in the Tygart River valley, favorable language on the use of high-sulfur coal for the Kammer power plant in Marshall County. He helped get an expansion of Morgantown's federal prison and community-based outpatient clinics in Wood and Tucker Counties. On national issues, he sponsored a successful amendment in July 1996 to increase Legal Services spending by $109 million, over the opposition of House conservatives.

Mollohan was reelected without opposition in 1996.

The People: Pop. 1990: 598,056; 55% rural; 16% age 65+; 97% White; 2% Black; 1% Asian; 1% Hispanic origin. Households: 59% married couple families; 27% married couple fams. w. children; 32% college educ.; median household income: $21,903; per capita income: $10,920; median gross rent: $307; median house value: $46,400.

1996 Presidential Vote			**1992 Presidential Vote**		
Clinton (D)	107,835	(49%)	Clinton (D)	113,756	(46%)
Dole (R)	83,306	(38%)	Bush (R)	86,131	(35%)
Perot (I)	28,900	(13%)	Perot (I)	45,856	(19%)

Rep. Alan B. Mollohan (D)

Elected 1982; b. May 14, 1943, Fairmont; home, Fairmont; Col. of William & Mary, A.B. 1966, WV U., J.D. 1970; Baptist; married (Barbara).

Career: Army, 1970, Army Reserves, 1970–83; Practicing atty., 1970–82.

DC Office: 2346 RHOB 20515, 202-225-4172; Fax: 202-225-7564.

District Offices: Clarksburg, 304-623-4422; Morgantown, 304-292-3019; Parkersburg, 304-428-0493; Wheeling, 304-232-5390.

Committees: *Appropriations* (11th of 26 D): Commerce, Justice, State & Judiciary (RMM); VA, HUD & Independent Agencies. *Budget* (3rd of 19 D).

Group Ratings

	ADA	ACLU	AFS	LCV	CFA	CON	NFIB	COC	ACU	NTLC	CHC
1996	65	62	90	77	23	2	35	25	15	18	33
1995	60	—	—	69	8	2	—	38	33	—	—

National Journal Ratings

	1995 LIB — 1995 CONS			1996 LIB — 1996 CONS		
Economic	69%	—	31%	78%	—	21%
Social	48%	—	51%	62%	—	38%
Foreign	59%	—	39%	52%	—	48%

Key Votes of the 104th Congress

1. Reduce Medicare Growth $	N	5. Flag Amendment	Y	9. Cuban Embargo	Y
2. Ovrd. Product Liab. Veto	N	6. Drop EPA Limits	N	10. Bar Bosnia Troop $	N
3. Increase Min. Wage	Y	7. Repeal Assault-Weap. Ban	Y	11. Cut Anti-Missile Defense	N
4. Welfare Reform	N	8. Ovrd. Part. Birth Veto	Y	12. Bar U.N. Uniforms	N

Election Results

1996 general	Alan B. Mollohan (D)	unopposed		($195,128)
1996 primary	Alan B. Mollohan (D)	unopposed		
1994 general	Alan B. Mollohan (D)	103,177	(70%)	($315,389)
	Sally Rossy Riley (R)	43,590	(30%)	($7,245)

SECOND DISTRICT

Not all of West Virginia is coal country, not all of its valleys are industrial hollows choked with workingmen's homes and small factories, not all of its hills are scarred with strip mining wounds or piled with tailings. For miles you can see gentle hills and rugged mountains, stands of green trees and vistas stretching to far horizons. Yet over another hill you may find, amid scenery primeval and rural, sudden evidence of industrialization: a pulp mill or charcoal factory in a clearing scraped out of the forest; a small factory town, built close to a river in a cleft bordered with hills, its houses built in the same 1910s style as in the factory towns of Pittsburgh; the entrance to an underground coal mine or the exposed brown earth of a strip minc scar. Large parts of this naturally beautiful state look as verdant and unchanged as they must have when George Washington was speculating in land here or taking the waters in Berkeley Springs, or when John Brown launched his assault at the federal arsenal at Harper's Ferry, or when the Civil War pitted brother against brother.

The 2d Congressional District of West Virginia is the central part of the state, a belt of land from Berkeley Springs and Harper's Ferry all the way west to the Ohio River town of Point Pleasant where the Kanawha River (pronounced *kaNAW*) flows into the Ohio. It could easily take a full day to drive through this district which, if ironed out, would probably spread across the country. The 2d District includes Putnam County, where Toyota will open its new $400 million engine plant in 1998. The major urban center here is Charleston, where on the banks of the Kanawha rises West Virginia's Capitol, built in 1932 and designed by Cass Gilbert with a dome higher than the U.S. Capitol and a chandelier with 10,000 pieces of cut glass. Charleston, with its two partisan newspapers, the Democratic *Gazette* and the Republican *Daily Mail*, is the state capital and the center of the state's political culture. Charleston is also a major industrial center, with coal in the hills all around and, downriver from the Capitol, huge petrochemical plants that convert coal tar and other feedstocks into everyday products. This was a center of American high tech in the 1940s, when it produced all the nation's lucite, polyethylenes and nylon as well as much of its artificial rubber and antifreeze. More recently, these factories are seen as heavy polluters in a valley that has well above average rates of cancer. Yet Charleston is also West Virginia's white-collar and professional center, with a few downtown skyscrapers and some pleasant affluent residential districts. Politically, the 2d has some mountain Republican counties, and Charleston's Kanawha County sometimes goes Republican too; but in national terms this is a solidly Democratic seat.

The congressman from the 2d District is Bob Wise, a Democrat from an affluent Charleston family, who returned home after law school to start a law practice geared to low- and middle-income clients and led a movement to force coal companies to pay higher taxes. A strong advocate of West Virginia culture he urges West Virginia students to make their careers, as he did, in their home state. But he is not a total traditionalist. In a state where past politicians got ahead by relying on ancestral loyalties and smoothing relations with big economic institutions, he has made his way by emphasizing issues on which he opposes the big interests. Wise, elected to the state Senate in 1980, was shrewd and popular enough to beat the state House majority leader and a former Kanawha County sheriff in the 1982 primary for the 2d District House seat, and then to beat a Republican incumbent soundly in November. He has been reelected easily ever since.

In the House Wise is an enthusiastic and articulate partisan Democrat. Early in his career he bucked local power, taking to the floor in 1983 to oppose a dam favored by the rest of the West Virginia delegation; he is a booster of alternative fuels and has championed compressed natural gas as an auto fuel; he got the Postal Service to use it for their fleet of vehicles and has had two CNG-powered cars himself (though one broke down on I-64 with transmission problems). His biggest legislative success was his 1990 amendment, adopted 274–146, to provide benefits for workers displaced by compliance with the Clean Air Act, with a $250 million cap. He sponsored the Community Right to Know Act, requiring disclosure by chemical companies. He favors a capital budget and sponsored his own version of a balanced budget amendment with a separate capital budget in 1995. He wants to develop what he calls Transpark in west central West Virginia, a combined hub for air, rail and barge shipping. He leads "Project Europe" trade missions, focusing on Germany, to attract jobs to West Virginia.

Early in the 104th Congress, Wise, with his witty and cheerful demeanor, joined Barney Frank and a few others, prowling the floor and opposing almost every Republican proposal; but he was not reluctant to support conservative policies on occasion. He strongly opposed sending U.S. troops to Bosnia. He voted to repeal the assault weapons ban, and vowed at the same time not to accept campaign contributions from the National Rifle Association or tobacco PACs. He voted for the flag amendment. He voted for the final version of welfare reform in August 1996 after voting against it earlier. Moreover, unlike most Democrats, he did not automatically defend the Clinton White House against any scandal charge; in June 1996 he backed hearings on the White House's wrongful acquisition of 400 FBI files and in March 1997 he called for an independent counsel to investigate Clinton campaign finance improprieties.

The People: Pop. 1990: 597,921; 62% rural; 14% age 65+; 96% White; 3% Black; 1% Hispanic origin. Households: 61% married couple families; 28% married couple fams. w. children; 30% college educ.; median household income: $22,253; per capita income: $11,083; median gross rent: $321; median house value: $55,200.

1996 Presidential Vote

Clinton (D)	108,503	(49%)
Dole (R)	88,930	(40%)
Perot (I)	23,238	(10%)

1992 Presidential Vote

Clinton (D)	104,257	(45%)
Bush (R)	90,375	(39%)
Perot (I)	36,813	(16%)

Rep. Robert E. (Bob) Wise, Jr. (D)

Elected 1982; b. Jan. 6, 1948, Washington, D.C.; home, Clendenin; Duke U., B.A. 1970, Tulane U., J.D. 1975; Episcopalian; married (Sandy).

Career: Practicing atty., 1975–80; Dir., WV for Fair and Equitable Assessment of Taxes, 1977–80; WV Senate, 1980–82.

DC Office: 2367 RHOB 20515, 202-225-2711; Fax: 202-225-7856; e-mail: bobwise@hr.house.gov.

District Offices: Charleston, 304-965-0865; Martinsburg, 304-264-8810.

Committees: *Government Reform & Oversight* (3rd of 19 D): National Security, International Affairs & Criminal Justice. *Transportation & Infrastructure* (5th of 33 D): Railroads (RMM); Water Resources & Environment.

Group Ratings

	ADA	ACLU	AFS	LCV	CFA	CON	NFIB	COC	ACU	NTLC	CHC
1996	70	62	92	69	54	91	24	25	10	10	7
1995	90	—	—	94	100	2	—	29	16	—	—

National Journal Ratings

	1995 LIB — 1995 CONS			1996 LIB — 1996 CONS		
Economic	78%	—	21%	82%	—	16%
Social	69%	—	31%	72%	—	28%
Foreign	73%	—	24%	69%	—	31%

Key Votes of the 104th Congress

1. Reduce Medicare Growth $	N	5. Flag Amendment	Y	9. Cuban Embargo	N
2. Ovrd. Product Liab. Veto	N	6. Drop EPA Limits	Y	10. Bar Bosnia Troop $	Y
3. Increase Min. Wage	Y	7. Repeal Assault-Weap. Ban	Y	11. Cut Anti-Missile Defense	Y
4. Welfare Reform	N	8. Ovrd. Part. Birth Veto	N	12. Bar U.N. Uniforms	Y

Election Results

1996 general	Robert E. (Bob) Wise, Jr. (D)	141,551	(69%)	($376,555)
	Greg Morris (R)	63,933	(31%)	($49,732)
1996 primary	Robert E. (Bob) Wise, Jr. (D)	81,340	(86%)	
	Howard Swint (D)	13,762	(14%)	
1994 general	Robert E. (Bob) Wise, Jr. (D)	90,757	(64%)	($271,315)
	Sam Cravotta (R)	51,691	(36%)	($43,897)

THIRD DISTRICT

Early in this century, the coalfields of southern West Virginia were one of America's boom areas. Into rural farmland and hollows, inhabited by the same families since they first arrived at these mountains 100 years before, came coal company lawyers with mineral rights' leases to sign, coal company engineers to design and sink the mineshafts, and men from other mountain counties, as well as Europe, to work the mines. Company houses were built, company stores stocked with goods as the company dictated and company paymasters kept close tabs on the finances of every employee. These conditions bred dull discontent, ignited into the fire of industrial unionism by the tongue of John L. Lewis, president of the United Mine Workers, who organized most of the mines in the 1930s. Lewis was not only a militant unionist, but an isolationist, and during and after World War II he called out his coal miners on strikes, to the fury of Franklin Roosevelt and Harry Truman. The entire national war effort and postwar economic recovery seemed gravely threatened by these labor stoppages involving perhaps 300,000 workers, centered in back corners of the country like southern West Virginia.

All that is history now. Coal is no longer central to the U.S. economy and there are only a few thousand coal miners left in southern West Virginia—and many are not UMW members anymore. In 1950, when coal area population peaked, there were 579,000 people in the eight counties that made up the heart of southern West Virginia's coal country. Their population fell to 437,000 in 1970, then spurted up after energy prices were raised by the two oil shocks of the 1970s to 487,000 in 1980, but went down by 1990 to only 421,000. Most of the old underground mines have been abandoned, leaving behind mineshafts and piles of tailings—and lives that were snuffed out by cave-ins or simple carelessness in America's deadliest industry.

The 3d Congressional District of West Virginia includes most of the coal country in the southern part of the state, the mountainous counties directly south of Charleston that are among America's most heavily Democratic—and in some cases most politically corrupt—jurisdictions: Mingo County, where in the 1980s a sheriff bought his job for $100,000 and other politicos bought votes for $2 or a half-pint of bourbon. But the coal mining counties are no longer populous enough for a full congressional district and now make up about half the 3d District. About one-quarter is in and around the industrial city of Huntington on the Ohio River, and another quarter is to the east, in the farming uplands around the resort of White Sulphur Springs, where President John Tyler honeymooned in 1844, and the interstate junction at Beckley, which has become a popular whitewater rafting area. These two areas as a whole are much less Democratic than the coal counties.

The congressman here is Nick Joe Rahall, a Democrat first elected in 1976, at 27; he was the youngest member of the 95th Congress. He comes from the thin economic upper crust of the coal country; his family owns radio and TV stations in Beckley and in St. Petersburg, Florida. Rahall has concentrated on bringing public works projects and jobs to his district. He got a seats on Transportation and Infrastructure and Resources early on, and is now high-ranking on both; he is ranking Democrat on the Surface Transportation Subcommittee. He was the chief sponsor in the House of the 1992 law requiring union and non-union coal operators to bail out the United Mine Workers healthcare funds. He has worked for flood control in the Greenbrier River basin, for $25 million for southern West Virginia water and wastewater systems, a Lower Mud River flood control project in Milton, and the Hatfield-McCoy Trail System. He was a lead House sponsor of a bill establishing a new National Highway System comprised of Interstate Highways, leading arterial roads and other corridors designated by Congress. In West Virginia they include the I-73 Corridor (Route 52 replacement), Route 2, Appalachian Corridors G and L, the Coalfields Expressway and the proposed Shawnee Parkway, all of which became eligible for federal highway trust funds when the bill was signed into law in November 1995. Rahall also passed laws creating a National Coal Heritage Area and expanding the boundaries of the New River Gorge National River. Another project was seeking $200 million to reclaim abandoned mines in coalfield states.

On national issues, Rahall was successful in opposing Cass Ballenger's revisions of the 1969 Coal Mine Health and Safety Act and Barbara Cubin's move to make enforcement of the Surface Mining Control and Reclamation Act a state rather than federal and state responsibility. With Scott Klug, he got the House to vote to continue a moratorium on mining claim patents under the Mining Act of 1872; western mining interests have prevented repeal of this law, which allows minerals to be mined for $2.50 an acre, but the amendment prevents the law from operating. In a 1995 bill which terminated the Interstate Commerce Commission, Rahall succeeded in retaining rail pricing protections (or captive coal provisions) for coal shippers. But he failed in his attempt to maintain a 65 mile per hour federal speed limit.

Rahall has mostly won reelection easily. In 1990, after negative publicity for gambling debts and a drunk driving arrest, he had close calls. His predecessor, then 75-year-old Secretary of

State (and onetime Adlai Stevenson speechwriter) Ken Hechler, won 43% of the vote in the primary; an underfinanced Republican in the general won 48%. But Rahall worked hard on district projects and recovered politically. He is criticized sometimes for taking lavish lobbyist-paid trips, but in 1996 he was reelected easily, after his only opponent, former state Commissioner of Human Services Sharon Lord, withdrew for medical reasons.

The People: Pop. 1990: 597,500; 74% rural; 15% age 65+; 95% White; 4% Black. Households: 60% married couple families; 29% married couple fams. w. children; 26% college educ.; median household income: $18,166; per capita income: $9,557; median gross rent: $284; median house value: $41,700.

1996 Presidential Vote			**1992 Presidential Vote**		
Clinton (D)	111,474	(58%)	Clinton (D)	112,988	(55%)
Dole (R)	61,710	(32%)	Bush (R)	65,468	(32%)
Perot (I)	19,501	(10%)	Perot (I)	26,160	(13%)

Rep. Nick J. Rahall, II (D)

Elected 1976; b. May 20, 1949, Beckley; home, Beckley; Duke U., B.A. 1971; Presbyterian; divorced.

Career: Civil Air Patrol, 1977–88; Staff Asst., U.S. Sen. Robert Byrd, 1971–74; Bd. of Dir., Rahall Communications Corp. 1974–76; Pres., Mountaineer Tour & Travel Agency, 1974–76; Pres., WV Broadcasting Corp. 1980–present.

DC Office: 2307 RHOB 20515, 202-225-3452; Fax: 202-225-9061; e-mail: nrahall@hr.house.gov.

District Offices: Beckley, 304-252-5000; Bluefield, 304-325-6222; Huntington, 304-522-6425; Lewisburg, 304-647-3228; Logan, 304-752-4934.

Committees: *Resources* (3rd of 23 D): Energy & Mineral Resources. *Transportation & Infrastructure* (2nd of 33 D): Aviation; Surface Transportation (RMM); Water Resources & Environment.

Group Ratings

	ADA	ACLU	AFS	LCV	CFA	CON	NFIB	COC	ACU	NTLC	CHC
1996	75	69	92	77	77	6	24	19	20	10	33
1995	70	—	—	81	85	4	—	25	28	—	—

National Journal Ratings

	1995 LIB — 1995 CONS			1996 LIB — 1996 CONS		
Economic	85%	—	12%	76%	—	22%
Social	48%	—	52%	55%	—	45%
Foreign	73%	—	24%	66%	—	34%

Key Votes of the 104th Congress

1. Reduce Medicare Growth $	N	5. Flag Amendment	Y	9. Cuban Embargo	Y
2. Ovrd. Product Liab. Veto	N	6. Drop EPA Limits	Y	10. Bar Bosnia Troop $	N
3. Increase Min. Wage	Y	7. Repeal Assault-Weap. Ban	Y	11. Cut Anti-Missile Defense	Y
4. Welfare Reform	N	8. Ovrd. Part. Birth Veto	Y	12. Bar U.N. Uniforms	Y

Election Results

1996 general	Nick J. Rahall, II (D)	unopposed		($145,980)
1996 primary	Nick J. Rahall, II (D)	unopposed		
1994 general	Nick J. Rahall, II (D)	74,967	(64%)	($389,323)
	Ben Waldman (R)	42,382	(36%)	($41,838)

WISCONSIN

Wisconsin, tucked off north of the main east-west routes across the country and squeezed between Lake Michigan and the Mississippi River, almost a century ago was one of America's premier "laboratories of reform," in Justice Louis Brandeis's phrase—and is again today: a state originating new public policies, seeing how they work, serving as an example for others. Wisconsin's first fame as a laboratory came during the Progressive era that began around 1900, and its primacy was due to an extraordinary governor, Robert LaFollette, Sr., and to the state's unique history and German heritage. For Wisconsin is the first state of the Old Northwest, that vast stretch of the United States reaching all the way to the Pacific, settled first by New England Yankees but even more by immigrants from Germany and Scandinavia. The German language is seldom heard now, the once plainly German beer brands now seem quintessentially American and few ties remained with the old country after two world wars. But in the late 19th and early 20th Centuries, Germans were among America's most numerous immigrants and until the 1890s probably the most distinctive. They established, on the rolling dairyland of Wisconsin and the orderly streets of Milwaukee, their separate religions, often keeping their language and maintaining old customs, from country weddings to drinking beer—a source of friction in temperance-minded America—to eating bratwurst.

Politically, the Germans were not monolithic. Their origins were diverse and they were spread too widely across the nation. But where they were concentrated, there was a distinctive politics, basically American, but with echoes of progressive ideas current in German-speaking countries in Europe. Nowhere was the politics of German-Americans more apparent than in Wisconsin. This is one of the two states that gave birth to the Republican Party in 1854 (the other is Michigan), and Germans, then arriving in America in vast numbers, heavily favored it. They abhorred slavery and welcomed the free lands Republicans advocated in the Homestead Act, the free education promised by setting up land grant colleges and the transportation routes constructed by subsidizing railroad builders. Then came the Progressive movement of Robert LaFollette, elected governor of Wisconsin in 1900. Up to that time a conventional Republican politician, LaFollette completely revamped the state government before going to the Senate in 1906. At a time when Germany was Europe's leader in graduate education and the application of science to government, LaFollette had professors from the University of Wisconsin, just across town in Madison, help develop the state workmen's compensation system and income tax. The Progressive movement favored rational use of government to improve the lot of the ordinary citizen—an idea borrowed partly from German liberals and adopted by the New Dealers a generation later. All these programs were an attempt to bring bureaucratic rationality—Germanic systematization—to the seemingly disordered America of free markets and multiple cultures, gigantic fortunes and vast open spaces.

LaFollette became a national figure. He tried to run for president in 1912 as a Progressive, but was shoved aside by Theodore Roosevelt. He did run in 1924 on his Progressive ticket and won 18% of the votes, the best third-candidate showing between 1912 and 1992. He was strongest in the northern tier of states from Wisconsin west and along the West Coast—the same area of strength of later liberals George McGovern, Walter Mondale and Michael Dukakis. After LaFollette died in 1925, his sons carried on his tradition, progressive at home and isolationist abroad: Robert LaFollette, Jr., for 22 years in the Senate; Philip, elected governor in 1930, 1934 and 1936. Philip created his own Progressive Party in 1934, with ominous overtones: with a "Cross in Circle" symbol his critics called a circumcised swastika, huge rally-like parades reminiscent of some in Europe at the time and a call for the governor to propose all legislation. But Philip lost in 1938 and did not run again, and Robert, Jr., decided to run for reelection in

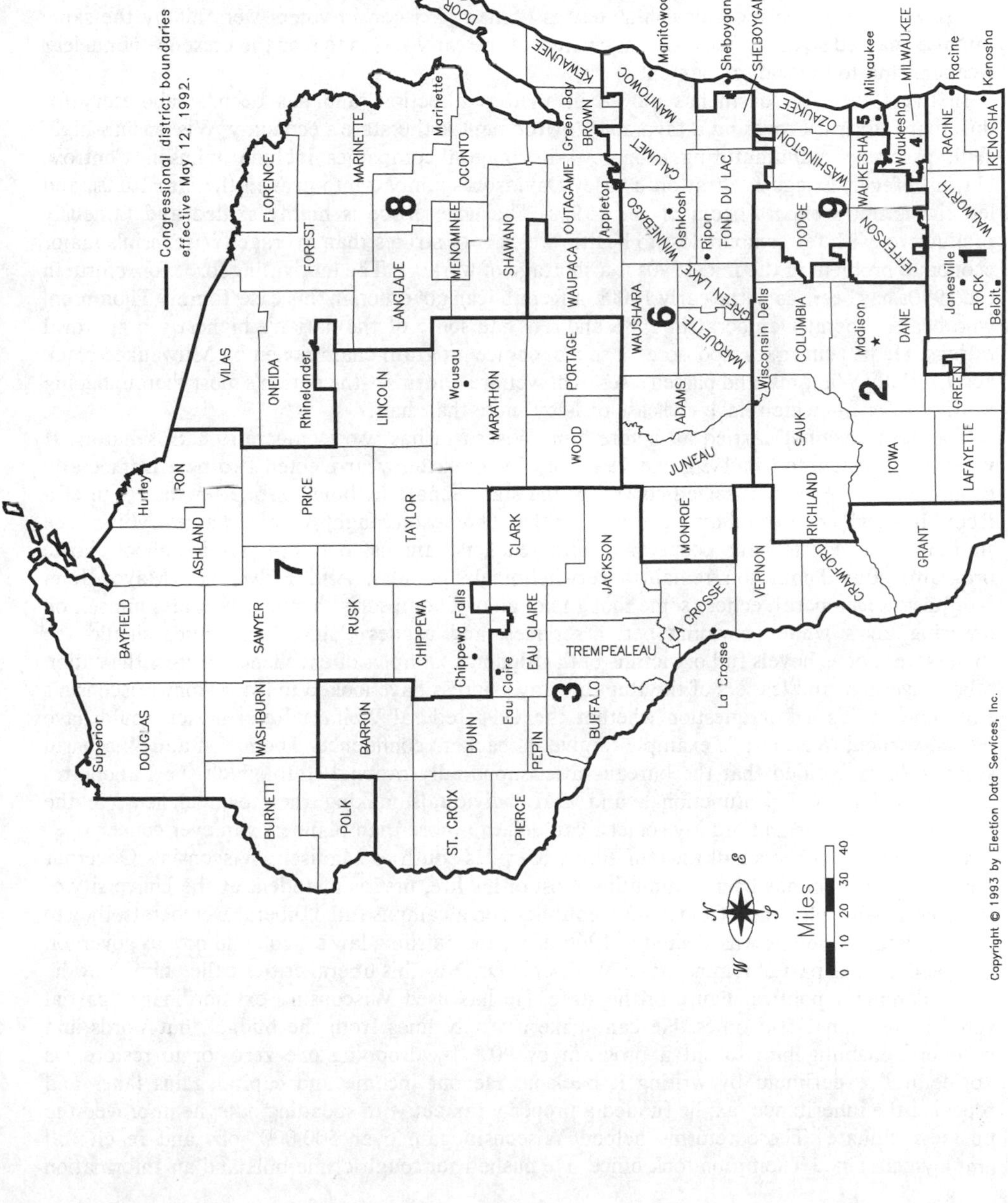
Congressional district boundaries effective May 12, 1992.
Miles
0 10 20 30 40
Copyright © 1993 by Election Data Services, Inc.
1
2
3
4
5
6
7
8
9
DOUGLAS
Superior
BAYFIELD
ASHLAND
IRON
Hurley
VILAS
FLORENCE
FOREST
MARINETTE
Marinette
OCONTO
DOOR
KEWAUNEE
BROWN
Green Bay
MANITOWOC
Manitowoc
SHEBOYGAN
Sheboygan
OZAUKEE
MILWAUKEE
Milwaukee
RACINE
Racine
KENOSHA
Kenosha
WALWORTH
WAUKESHA
Waukesha
WASHINGTON
CALUMET
FOND DU LAC
Ripon
WINNEBAGO
Oshkosh
OUTAGAMIE
Appleton
MENOMINEE
SHAWANO
LANGLADE
ONEIDA
Rhinelander
LINCOLN
MARATHON
Wausau
WAUPACA
PORTAGE
WOOD
WAUSHARA
GREEN LAKE
MARQUETTE
ADAMS
JUNEAU
Wisconsin Dells
COLUMBIA
DODGE
JEFFERSON
DANE
Madison
ROCK
Janesville
Beloit
GREEN
LAFAYETTE
IOWA
SAUK
RICHLAND
GRANT
CRAWFORD
VERNON
LA CROSSE
La Crosse
MONROE
JACKSON
TREMPEALEAU
BUFFALO
PEPIN
PIERCE
ST. CROIX
POLK
BURNETT
WASHBURN
SAWYER
PRICE
TAYLOR
RUSK
BARRON
DUNN
CHIPPEWA
Chippewa Falls
EAU CLAIRE
Eau Claire
CLARK

1946 as a Republican but lost the primary to Joseph McCarthy. McCarthy's charges that Communists were influencing American foreign policy fed on the inarticulate convictions of many in Wisconsin and elsewhere that the U.S. should have been fighting Russia as well as Germany in World War II.

McCarthy's national prominence made Wisconsin seem like a Republican state. But he won by narrow margins and the LaFollette Progressive tradition was taken up by liberal Democrats like Senators William Proxmire and Gaylord Nelson and Governor Patrick Lucey. Like most liberals of their era, these progressives saw Washington rather than Madison as the main site of their laboratory of reform. Wisconsin, a mostly Republican state in the mostly Democratic years from 1944–64, became a mostly Democratic state in the mostly Republican years from 1968–88. It was one of the most dovish states, as if many Wisconsin voters were hit by the same impulse that led so many West German voters in the early 1980s to fear the presence of nuclear weapons and to favor disarmament.

In the 1990s Wisconsin has moved in another direction, and has been a laboratory for different reforms. Providing a favorable environment is the state's economy. Wisconsin's high-skill, precision manufacturing economy—its biggest companies include Johnson Controls, Harnischfeger, Briggs & Stratton, Harley-Davidson—jumped into gear in the late 1980s, and led the nation's export boom of the 1990s. The labor force is highly skilled and famously productive, with fewer hours lost to health, weather or strikes than average; Wisconsin's major economic problem in the mid-1990s is a shortage of workers. The motivating force for reform in the 1990s has been, as in the early 1900s, a Republican governor, in this case Tommy Thompson, who beat a liberal Democrat in 1986 and has had some of the nation's highest job approval ratings. He has cut taxes, sponsored a school choice program championed by Milwaukee black activist Polly Williams, and passed a series of welfare reforms—the nation's most thoroughgoing welfare reform—which have cut caseloads by more than half.

Thompson has not carried all before him. Wisconsin has two Democratic U.S. senators. It voted for Bill Clinton in 1992 and 1996 and in the latter year elected two new Democratic congressmen. Democrats seized control of the state Senate in June 1996, after the recall of a Republican who had voted for a tax increase that Thompson sought to finance a new Milwaukee stadium. The courts have cooperated with teachers' unions to try to stymie school choice programs. But Thompson remains overwhelmingly popular. And Milwaukee Mayor John Norquist, a Democrat, echoes some though not all of Thompson's themes. He prides himself on lowering taxes while providing better services, and argues that central cities should see themselves not as hovels full of victims but as shining examples of excellence. Across the nation other governors and leaders of the Republican Congress have looked to learn from Wisconsin's experiments: it's a fair question whether the 1996 federal Welfare Reform Act would have passed without Wisconsin's example to give its backers confidence. Thompson and Wisconsin seem to have decided that the bureaucratic, supposedly rational state which the LaFollettes championed is now dysfunctional, and that individuals making their own choices, in the framework of a fair and orderly society, can achieve more than planners can ever conceive.

Governor. From the small town of Elroy, 85 miles south to Madison, Wisconsin's Governor Tommy Thompson has been commuting most of his life, first as a student at the University of Wisconsin, where he was a Goldwater Republican on a campus full of liberal Democrats, then to the legislature when he was elected in 1966 just after finishing law school, and now as governor. For years he was part of a minority in Madison; "Dr. No," his liberal critics called him. Now he is the dominant political figure in the state. He has used Wisconsin's extraordinary "partial veto" more than 1,500 times. He can strike not only lines from the budget, but words and numbers, enabling him to cut a program by 90% by dropping one zero, or to restore his "bridefare" experiment by writing it back in. He cut income and capital gains taxes and repealed the inheritance tax; he funded a property tax cut with spending cuts; he improved the business climate. Those reforms helped Wisconsin gain over 500,000 jobs and reach full employment since Thompson took office. He pushed for tough crime bills and an Information

Technology Fund which will make government services more efficient and cost effective through expanded technology. He has backed school choice programs in Milwaukee and elsewhere.

Thompson is best known, however, for having instituted the nation's most thoroughgoing welfare reform. This was not a single piece of legislation, but an ongoing process, in which Thompson sought not only new laws from the legislature but worked to reshuffle agencies and create new incentives for government agencies and employees so as to change the culture of the caregiving institutions—from one favoring continual dependence to one favoring work and independence. Thompson started with "learnfare" in 1987 tying grants to children's school attendance, then "bridefare" in 1992 with incentives for marriage and against more children, "work not welfare" in 1995 requiring work and scouting for jobs for recipients. His "Wisconsin Works," (known as W-2) ending welfare grants altogether and requiring recipients to either work or perform community service, goes into effect at different times around the state, in March 1997 in Fond du Lac and Pierce Counties and in September 1997 in Milwaukee, which was divided into six districts, with government agencies, nonprofit organizations and profit-making businesses each able to bid on contracts.

The secrets of Thompson's success have been hard work, good political instincts and a common touch. He refers constantly to his home town of Elroy, and refers to the rest of the state as "greater metropolitan Elroy." "Let's face it," he likes to say, "It's hard to be humble when you're from Wisconsin." He has had some disappointments: he lost the primary for a vacant congressional seat to Tom Petri in 1979, and he has not always been taken as seriously at the national level as he thinks he deserves. He has been mentioned as a presidential candidate, and has a record that would entitle him to serious attention. In the meantime, he seems a strong candidate for reelection in 1998. Mentioned as possible opponents are Mayor John Norquist, Attorney General Jim Doyle and former senatorial candidate Ed Garvey.

Senior Senator. Democrat Herb Kohl is one of the richest members of Congress, and one of the least flamboyant, a mild-mannered but stubborn and politically successful politician. His parents immigrated to Milwaukee from Russia and Poland in the 1920s and opened a food store. Kohl's ultimately became a Wisconsin supermarket chain and was sold in 1979, for great profit; Kohl's fortune has been estimated at $250 million. In 1985 he became a local celebrity, in a city smarting from sports franchises with lousy records and eager to move elsewhere, when he bought the Milwaukee Bucks basketball team to keep it from moving out of the city. When Senator William Proxmire retired in 1988, Kohl decided to run. He spent his own money liberally, running an extensive ad campaign with the theme, "Nobody's senator but yours." He won 47% in the primary to 38% for former Governor Tony Earl. In the general, against moderate Republican Susan Engeleiter, Kohl stressed his support of defense cuts—popular in dovish Wisconsin—and for requiring businesses to provide medical insurance; Engeleiter stressed her environmental stands, her legislative experience and her status as a wife and mother—in contrast to Kohl, a bachelor. This turned out to be one of the closest Senate races in the country, with Kohl winning 52%–48%, after spending $7 million of his own money.

Kohl is a pleasant, shy, almost painfully earnest man, of transparent good will and seemingly little guile. He has a liberal record on cultural and foreign issues and is more moderate on economics; he dislikes the clash of partisan fighting. "I try not to be a, quote, political kind of person. You might see me with one group on one issue, another group on another issue." He favors the balanced budget amendment and voted for the Chafee-Breaux bipartisan budget in May 1996. He exerted great leverage when Democrats had a narrow majority in 1993 by insisting on paying for the Clinton stimulus package with spending cuts and by refusing to support a gas tax increase over 4.3 cents. He opposed the Supercolider, the space station, and Trident II missiles and has tried to keep defense spending increases down to Clinton budget levels. In 1994, prompted by Tommy Thompson's welfare reforms in Wisconsin, he sponsored a welfare-to-work bill, one of the predecessors of 1996's welfare reform. He has sponsored a tax credit limited to 50% for businesses that build child care facilities at or near worksites.

Kohl has been active on crime and gun issues. He was a sponsor of the Brady bill, and wrote the 1990 law banning guns in schools; when that was overturned by the Supreme Court in 1995 (on the ground it had nothing to do with interstate commerce), he wrote another bill limiting guns within 1,000 feet of schools; it passed in 1996. He has sponsored a bill to require child safety locks on guns. As ranking Democrat on the Terrorism Subcommittee in the 104th Congress, he tried to conduct nonpartisan hearings after Oklahoma City and about Ruby Ridge. He voted against the "partial-birth" abortion ban in May 1997, which led to a statewide recall effort, sponsored by a Milwaukee-based organization called First Breath Alliance, that fell just 50,000 signatures short.

Kohl also supports Wisconsin causes. As a subcommittee chairman, he stood stoutly against adjustment of the 1990 Census figures—a worthy stand against a measure that, as it happens, would have cost Wisconsin a congressional seat. He has worked on Great Lakes issues, from farm commodity shipping to the zebra mussel. On the 1996 Freedom to Farm Act he got the Senate to vote 50–46 against the Northeast Dairy Compact, intended to cartelize New England dairy markets; but it was slipped in during conference and passed. He personally funds the Herb Kohl Educational Foundation which has given $1.4 million in scholarships and grants to students, teachers and schools, and in April 1995 gave $25 million to his alma mater, the University of Wisconsin.

In his 1994 reelection campaign, Kohl stressed his work against spending and crime and also his own sincere, unprepossessing demeanor. He was able to get his message across: with far less press criticism than in 1988, he spent $6.5 million of his own money on the campaign (far more per voter, incidentally, than the much-ridiculed Michael Huffington was spending in California). His Republican opponent, Robert Welch, a land surveyor and a young conservative firebrand in the state legislature, raised many of the issues Republicans were winning on elsewhere, but did not have the funds to get much of a hearing. Meanwhile, Kohl joked with voters by asking them to contribute to meet basketball player Glenn Robinson's demands for the Bucks to give him a $100 million contract. Kohl won 58%–41%.

Junior Senator. Russ Feingold was first elected in 1992 at age 39 after a riproaring and sometimes amusing campaign. Feingold wanted to be a senator when he was growing up in Janesville. He nurtured his ambition at the University of Wisconsin, as a Rhodes Scholar, and at Harvard Law School; he moved to Middleton, a not-so-academic suburb of Madison, and beat an incumbent state senator in 1982, at 29. Feingold has a flair for publicity, and for political reform issues and novel arguments. His great goal in the legislature was to ban bovine growth hormone, a luddite measure aimed at keeping in business Wisconsin's numerous and overly subsidized dairy farmers (their problem is that Americans drink less milk today than in the 1950s). Feingold also opposed Governor Tommy Thompson's welfare reforms and tax cuts and opposed capital punishment. Feingold's goal for 1992 was the Senate seat held by Bob Kasten, a free-market conservative who pushed tort reform and capital gains tax cuts, and had won by narrow margins in 1980 and 1986. In the Democratic primary, while Milwaukee businessman Joseph Checota and Congressman Jim Moody battered each other with negative ads, Feingold ran clever, humorous spots: one showing Elvis, alive and endorsing Feingold; another showing Feingold at home, opening up a closet and saying, "No skeletons"; another showing his three key pledges written out on his garage door. He also had detailed position papers, including an 82-point plan for reducing the deficit. Near primary day, Checota apologized for his ads and asked voters to vote for Feingold if they didn't vote for him. Feingold, already ahead in polls, zoomed to an astonishing 70% win in this three-way primary. Feingold also bounced way ahead of Kasten, who ran his own Elvis ads attacking Feingold on issues; Feingold attacked Kasten's negativity and avoided engaging on specifics. The race narrowed, but Feingold won 53%–46%.

In the Senate, Feingold made a very liberal record on cultural and foreign issues, more moderate on economics. He pushed through a moratorium and study on bovine growth hormone, worked to dispatch the wool and mohair subsidy and forced a consolidation of government overseas broadcasting. He attacked spending virtually wherever he could find it: the Pentagon's medical school, helium subsidies and the Supercollider; he moved to eliminate the Extremely Low Frequency radio system—"a cold war relic" in his words—embedded in northern Wisconsin. He attacked the national milk-marketing system as anti-Midwest and opposed the Northeast Dairy Compact, though it got through on conference committee, and he has been monitoring the National Cheese Exchange. He worked against the CVN-76 aircraft carrier, western water subsidies, TVA overheads and tax breaks for asbestos, lead, mercury and uranium mining. He was one of the crusaders against lobbyists' gifts to lawmakers. His most widely publicized reform has been the McCain-Feingold campaign finance law, which would attempt to hold down campaign spending and contributions; it was debated on the Senate floor in July 1996, and filibustered; Feingold and Arizona's John McCain appeared at rallies backing it in March 1997, but Republicans like Mitch McConnell seemed determined to keep it off the floor. Feingold called for an independent counsel on Clinton fundraising scandals in February 1997.

Feingold comes up with original and interesting positions and votes. He worked to link military sales to Indonesia to human rights progress in East Timor, and opposes MFN status for China. He opposed the Communications Decency Act and with Michigan's Spencer Abraham opposed the cumbersome worker verification provisions of the immigration bill. He wants to prohibit Members of Congress from using frequent flyer miles earned on business trips and to establish a long-term healthcare program like Wisconsins' Community Options. He worked to deauthorize the La Farge Dam and return the land to the state for the Kickapoo Valley Reserve.

Feingold comes up for reelection in 1998. Despite his visits each year to each of Wisconsin's 72 counties, his poll ratings have been unspectacular. But he works hard and is skillful at framing issues. One almost certain opponent is 1st District Congressman Mark Neumann, former homebuilder and strong conservative. Neumann urged Feingold to vote for the "partial-birth" abortion ban in May 1997, to no avail, which led Neumann to encourage a recall effort, sponsored by the Milwaukee-based First Breath Alliance, that failed by just 50,000 signatures. Another opponent will be state Senator Alberta Martin, who will attempt to become the first woman ever elected to Congress from Wisconsin.

Presidential politics. For all the distinctiveness of its history, Wisconsin has come pretty close to voting the national average for president in the last two elections, a little light for Clinton in 1992 and a little light for Dole in 1996. It has been seriously contested in five of the last six elections, and may well be again. There are not huge regional differences in Wisconsin. Bob Dole, who never targeted Wisconsin, carried only one of the state's nine congressional districts, and Bill Clinton carried only two with more than 50%; the other six voted pretty much all alike.

Wisconsin once had one of the nation's most influential presidential primaries. It knocked Wendell Willkie out of the race in 1944, helped John Kennedy establish his lead over Hubert Humphrey in 1960, and prompted Lyndon Johnson to withdraw as Eugene McCarthy was about to beat him here in 1968. But now Wisconsin's primary, even moved from April to March 19 for 1996, tends to get lost. The national Democrats, incidentally, have allowed Wisconsin to continue its open primary (that is, there is no party registration), one of Bob LaFollette's reforms.

Congressional districting. Wisconsin did not lose a congressional district in the 1990 Census, and its population grew evenly enough that no major changes were needed in the current district lines to meet the equal-population standard. The Democratic legislature's plan, signed by Thompson, shifted a few dozen townships between districts.

The People: Est. Pop. 1996: 5,160,000; Pop. 1990: 4,891,769, up 5.5% 1990–1996. 1.9% of U.S. total, 18th largest; 34% rural. Median age: 35.1 years. 13% 65 years and over. 91.3% White, 4.9% Black, 1.1% Asian, 1% Amer. Indian, 1.9% Hispanic origin. Households: 57.5% married couple families; 28% married couple fams. w. children; 42% college educ.; median household income: $29,442; per capita income: $13,276; 66.7% owner occupied housing; median house value: $62,500; median monthly rent: $331. 3.5% Unemployment. 1996 Voting age pop.: 3,824,000. 1996 Turnout: 2,196,169; 57% of VAP. No state voter registration.

Political Lineup: Governor, Tommy G. Thompson (R); Lt. Gov., Scott McCallum (R); Secy. of State, Douglas LaFollette (D); Atty. Gen., James E. Doyle (D); Treasurer, Jack C. Voight (R). State Senate, 33 (17 D, and 16 R); Senate President, Fred Risser (D). State Assembly, 99 (47 D and 52 R); Assembly Speaker, Ben Brancell (R). Senators, Herb Kohl (D) and Russell D. Feingold (D). Representatives, 9 (5 D and 4 R).

Board of Elections: 608-266-8005; **Filing Deadline for U.S. Congress:** July 7, 1998.

1996 Presidential Vote

Clinton (D)	1,071,970	(49%)
Dole (R)	845,028	(38%)
Perot (I)	227,310	(10%)
Other	51,881	(2%)

1996 Republican Presidential Primary

Dole (R)	301,628	(53%)
Buchanan (R)	194,733	(34%)
Forbes (R)	32,205	(6%)
Other	45,203	(8%)

1992 Presidential Vote

Clinton (D)	1,041,066	(41%)
Bush (R)	930,855	(37%)
Perot (I)	544,479	(22%)

GOVERNOR

Gov. Tommy G. Thompson (R)

Elected 1986, term expires Jan. 1999; b. Nov. 19, 1941, Elroy; home, Elroy; U. of WI, B.A. 1963, J.D. 1966; Catholic; married (Sue Ann).

Career: Practicing atty; WI Assembly, 1966–86, Asst. Minority Ldr., 1973–81, Floor Ldr., 1981–86; Chmn., Repub. Govs. Assn., 1991–92; Chmn., Natl. Govs. Assn., 1995–present.

Office: State Capitol, 115 E. State Capitol, Madison 53707, 608-266-1212. Fax: 608-267-8983; Web site: www.state.wi.us.

Election Results

1994 gen.	Tommy G. Thompson (R)	1,051,326	(67%)
	Chuck Chvala (D)	482,850	(31%)
	Others	29,659	(2%)
1994 prim.	Tommy G. Thompson (R)	unopposed	
1990 gen.	Tommy G. Thompson (R)	802,321	(58%)
	Thomas Loftus (D)	546,280	(42%)

SENATORS

Sen. Herb Kohl (D)

Elected 1988, seat up 2000; b. Feb. 7, 1935, Milwaukee; home, Milwaukee; U. of WI, B.A. 1956, Harvard, M.B.A. 1958; Jewish; single.

Career: Army Reserves, 1958–64; Businessman; Pres., Kohl Corp., 1970–79; Chmn., WI St. Dem. Party, 1975–77; Pres., Herbert Kohl Investments, 1979–88; Owner, Milwaukee Bucks basketball team, 1985-present.

DC Office: 330 HSOB 20510, 202-224-5653; Fax: 202-224-9787; e-mail: senator_kohl@kohl.senate.gov.

State Offices: Appleton, 414-738-1640; Eau Claire, 715-832-8424; Madison, 608-264-5338; Milwaukee, 414-297-4451.

Committees: *Appropriations* (10th of 13 D): Agriculture, Rural Development & Related Agencies; Energy & Water Development; Labor, Health & Human Services & Education; Transportation; Treasury, Postal Service & General Government (RMM). *Judiciary* (4th of 8 D): Administrative Oversight & the Courts; Antitrust, Business Rights & Competition (RMM); Youth Violence. *Aging (Special)* (4th of 8 D).

Group Ratings

	ADA	ACLU	AFS	LCV	CFA	CON	NFIB	COC	ACU	NTLC	CHC
1996	75	35	71	92	64	100	52	69	20	24	15
1995	95	—	91	100	63	88	—	47	17	—	—

National Journal Ratings

	1995 LIB — 1995 CONS			1996 LIB — 1996 CONS		
Economic	60%	—	38%	61%	—	34%
Social	82%	—	15%	80%	—	8%
Foreign	76%	—	21%	84%	—	14%

Key Votes of the 104th Congress

1. Reduce Medicare Growth $	N	5. Flag Amendment	N	9. Anti-Missile Defense	N
2. Lmt. Prod. Liab. Damages	Y	6. Endangered Species	Y	10. Cuban Embargo	Y
3. Increase Min. Wage	Y	7. Gay Employment Rights	Y	11. Bar Bosnia Troop $	N
4. Welfare Reform	Y	8. Ovrd. Part. Birth Veto	N	12. Cut Vietnam Aid	Y

Election Results

1994 general	Herb Kohl (D)	912,662	(58%)	($8,249,531)
	Robert T. Welch (R)	636,989	(41%)	($1,180,382)
1994 primary	Herb Kohl (D)	135,982	(90%)	
	Edmond Galileo Hou-Seye (D)	15,579	(10%)	
1988 general	Herb Kohl (D)	1,128,625	(52%)	($7,491,600)
	Susan Engeleiter (R)	1,030,440	(48%)	($2,853,842)

Sen. Russell D. Feingold (D)

Elected 1992, seat up 1998; b. Mar. 2, 1953, Janesville; home, Middleton; U. of WI, B.A. 1975, Rhodes Scholar, Oxford U., 1977, Harvard Law Schl., J.D. 1979; Jewish; married (Mary).

Career: Practicing atty., 1979–83; WI Senate, 1982–92;

DC Office: 716 HSOB 20510, 202-224-5323; Fax: 202-224-2725; e-mail: senator@feingold.senate.gov.

State Offices: Green Bay, 414-465-7508; LaCrosse, 608-782-5585; Middleton, 608-828-1200; Milwaukee, 414-276-7282; Wausau, 715-848-5660.

Committees: *Budget* (8th of 10 D). *Foreign Relations* (6th of 8 D): African Affairs (RMM); East Asian & Pacific Affairs. *Judiciary* (6th of 8 D): Administrative Oversight & the Courts; Constitution, Federalism & Property Rights (RMM). *Aging (Special)* (5th of 8 D).

Group Ratings

	ADA	ACLU	AFS	LCV	CFA	CON	NFIB	COC	ACU	NTLC	CHC
1996	95	82	86	100	93	27	38	31	10	14	0
1995	100	—	100	100	94	68	—	42	13	—	—

National Journal Ratings

	1995 LIB — 1995 CONS			1996 LIB — 1996 CONS		
Economic	71%	—	27%	74%	—	19%
Social	93%	—	0%	92%	—	0%
Foreign	79%	—	15%	89%	—	7%

Key Votes of the 104th Congress

1. Reduce Medicare Growth $	N	5. Flag Amendment	N	9. Anti-Missile Defense	N
2. Lmt. Prod. Liab. Damages	N	6. Endangered Species	Y	10. Cuban Embargo	N
3. Increase Min. Wage	Y	7. Gay Employment Rights	Y	11. Bar Bosnia Troop $	Y
4. Welfare Reform	Y	8. Ovrd. Part. Birth Veto	N	12. Cut Vietnam Aid	Y

Election Results

1992 general	Russell D. Feingold (D)	1,290,662	(53%)	($2,056,079)
	Robert W. Kasten, Jr. (R)	1,129,599	(46%)	($5,427,163)
1992 primary	Russell D. Feingold (D)	367,746	(70%)	
	Jim Moody (D)	74,472	(14%)	
	Joseph Checota (D)	71,570	(13%)	
	Other	14,056	(3%)	
1986 general	Robert W. Kasten, Jr. (R)	1,754,537	(51%)	($3,433,870)
	Edward Garvey (D)	1,702,963	(47%)	($1,702,963)

FIRST DISTRICT

Rolling dairy country, blanketed by snow during most of the winter, gloriously green under sunny blue skies in summer, the southern tier of Wisconsin from Lake Michigan inland to the Rock River Valley is some of America's prime industrial country. Settled by Yankee and

German farmers 150 years ago, it was once primarily dairyland. By the early 20th Century, the steady habits and high skills of the local dairy farmers provided a good labor pool for factories. Today, there are still major plants here: the operations center for Johnson Wax (and its Frank Lloyd Wright-designed tower and Wingspread Center) in Racine; and the Parker Pen operation in Janesville. In between on lakes are resorts, most notably Lake Geneva, a favorite of rich Chicagoans. To the untrained eye, this part of southern Wisconsin looks much the same as nearby northern Illinois; but politically there is a vast difference. The dotted line on the map is the boundary between the corruption-prone machine politics of Illinois and squeaky-clean progressive politics of Wisconsin.

This is the land of the 1st District of Wisconsin, from Lake Michigan west to the Rock River and beyond, a politically marginal area in Wisconsin politics and a marginal district in congressional politics from 1958–70 and then again since 1993. In between, it was the district represented by the late Les Aspin, chairman of the House Armed Services Committee from 1985–93 and secretary of Defense from 1993–94.

The congressman from the 1st District is Mark Neumann, a Republican elected in 1994. He is emblematic, if not exactly typical, of the Republican freshmen of that year. Neumann grew up in southern Wisconsin, worked his way through college washing dishes and tending bar, became a math teacher, then decided to become a homebuilder on the side in 1980. In 1986 he started his own business and made a fortune by using computers to make quick and accurate estimates on custom-built houses. He sold the business in 1992 and, deciding that he must do something about the national debt and high taxes, he ran for Congress. He had support from the Christian right, spent more than $700,000 of his own money, and held Aspin to a 58%–41% win. When Aspin left for the Defense post, Neumann ran again in the special, but spent less of his own money and minimized his connection with the religious right and sharply attacked the Clinton budget and tax package. One Democrat, former state party chairman Jeff Neubauer, came forward and defended it, but he lost the primary 49%–34% to Peter Barca, a state legislator with a solid base in Kenosha and strong labor union support. Barca said he would not vote for many of the new taxes proposed by Clinton, but backed healthcare and welfare reform, while labor unions conducted a heavy "negative persuasion" phone bank campaign against Neumann, especially against his proposal to invest some Social Security trust funds. Barca won 50%–49%; Neumann demanded a recount, which delayed Barca's swearing in until June, allowing him to skirt the first tough vote on Clinton's tax-increase proposal.

Neumann was reluctant to run again in 1994, but was pressed by national Republican leaders. Again he argued that taxes and regulations were strangling small companies like his; he attacked Barca for voting for the Clinton budget and tax package after having pledged to vote against the gas tax it contained. Although Barca voted against some spending measures, Neumann responded, "When his vote doesn't count, he votes conservative," and attacked him for getting most of his campaign money from PACs. Neumann ran ads featuring Governor Tommy Thompson and supported the Contract With America. Barca carried Kenosha County and led in Rock County, Neumann's home area. But Neumann carried Racine and the area around Lake Geneva, for a narrow 49.4%–48.8% victory.

To the House Neumann brought his almost religious zeal for cutting spending and balancing the budget. He got a seat on Appropriations, which leaders thought would be helpful in a marginal district. But Neumann disapproved of pork barrel projects even at home and yelled at Walworth County officials seeking money for a sewer project. Neumann's voting record was maverick also, rather moderate on economics and isolationist-prone on foreign issues. He wrote his own budget which would be balanced by 1999 and cut corporate welfare; it got 89 votes on the floor in May 1995. In September 1995 he tried to amend an appropriations bill to require congressional approval of the dispatch of any U.S. troops to Bosnia. When his amendment lost, he refused to vote for the bill, saying he was acting out of "conscience" and did not want to "play the Washington game." Chairman Bob Livingston was furious and Speaker Newt Gingrich kicked him off the National Security Subcommittee. After other freshmen squawked, a seat was found for him (Peter Hoekstra gave up his) on Budget. And so it went. "Every once in a while, he has his moments," Gingrich said of him. "If it's a matter of conscience, you should never give in . . . But there are a lot of times, frankly, when you just get to be a pain in the neck," Gingrich added. Neumann, sure of answers, decries partisanship: "This Republican-Democrat thing—it's just so destructive."

At first defiance of powers in Washington made Neumann look like an easy winner. But Wisconsin has a late filing deadline, and he got serious opposition. Kenosha Council President Lydia Spottswood was one of several rich and hitherto unknown women who ran strong Democratic races in 1996. She beat Secretary of State Douglas LaFollette in the September primary 46%–37%; LaFollette, of Wisconsin's founding Progressive family, ran a closer race against Les Aspin in 1970. This was a contest of styles as well as issues. Neumann on the stump would continually get into harsh arguments with constituents, then sometimes pull back. "He's a creep," Spottswood told a *New York Times* reporter. "This is a man who doesn't like serving his constituents . . . Have you ever seen a more rigid person than Mark Neumann?" She went on to tell what the reporter found to be baseless stories about Neumann's business dealings and parenting skills.

The campaigning was rough. The AFL-CIO spent over $300,000 on ads attacking Neumann for backing Medicare "cuts" and lifting pension fund protections. Neumann, who spent $1.2 million, none of it his own, ran an ad accusing Spottswood of voting in 1990 for a Kenosha redevelopment project that boosted the value of an apartment partly owned by her husband, a successful physician (she spent $223,000 of her own money in her $709,000 campaign). "This is the kind of action that got Dan Rostenkowski in jail," the ad said; Spottswood was cleared by the city district attorney, and Neumann had to pull his ads. Neumann won, in a district Bill Clinton was carrying 50%–38%, by 51%–49%, a narrow margin though the widest one in the 1st District since Aspin resigned.

After the election Neumann voted "present" in the election for speaker; he wanted to vote for Dick Armey, but Armey talked him out of it. Neumann attacked Senators Herb Kohl and Russ Feingold for opposing the "partial-birth" abortion ban and called on them to switch. Neumann also hit Feingold for opposing the balanced budget amendment and supporting the 1993 tax increase, and said he might run against Feingold in 1998. He argued that he would be more effective in the Senate with its less restrictive rules. Meanwhile, in March 1997 he helped beat a budget resolution 213–210, objecting because it increased the budget of the House itself.

The People: Pop. 1990: 543,380; 29% rural; 12% age 65+; 90% White; 5% Black; 1% Asian; 3% Hispanic origin. Households: 60% married couple families; 28% married couple fams. w. children; 39% college educ.; median household income: $31,431; per capita income: $13,567; median gross rent: $401; median house value: $61,200.

1996 Presidential Vote

Clinton (D)	117,308	(50%)
Dole (R)	88,599	(38%)
Perot (I)	25,957	(11%)
Other	4,353	(2%)

1992 Presidential Vote

Clinton (D)	109,790	(41%)
Bush (R)	94,712	(35%)
Perot (I)	62,465	(23%)

Rep. Mark W. Neumann (R)

Elected 1994; b. Feb. 27, 1954, Mukwonago; home, Janesville; U. of WI, B.S. 1975, M.S., 1977; Lutheran; married (Sue).

Career: High Schl. teacher, 1977–80; Realtor, 1980–86; Home-builder, 1986–92; Owner, Neumann Corp. Real Estate & Devel., 1992–93.

DC Office: 415 CHOB 20515, 202-225-3031; Fax: 202-225-3393; e-mail: mneumann@hr.house.gov.

District Offices: Janesville, 608-752-4050; Kenosha, 414-654-1901.

Committees: *Appropriations* (28th of 34 R): District of Columbia; VA, HUD & Independent Agencies. *Budget* (17th of 24 R).

Group Ratings

	ADA	ACLU	AFS	LCV	CFA	CON	NFIB	COC	ACU	NTLC	CHC
1996	15	25	42	31	38	93	92	69	95	90	100
1995	0	—	—	0	8	53	—	100	100	—	—

National Journal Ratings

	1995 LIB — 1995 CONS	1996 LIB — 1996 CONS
Economic	34% — 64%	42% — 56%
Social	0% — 79%	10% — 86%
Foreign	42% — 55%	55% — 43%

Key Votes of the 104th Congress

1. Reduce Medicare Growth $	Y	5. Flag Amendment	Y	9. Cuban Embargo	Y
2. Ovrd. Product Liab. Veto	Y	6. Drop EPA Limits	N	10. Bar Bosnia Troop $	Y
3. Increase Min. Wage	Y	7. Repeal Assault-Weap. Ban	Y	11. Cut Anti-Missile Defense	N
4. Welfare Reform	Y	8. Ovrd. Part. Birth Veto	Y	12. Bar U.N. Uniforms	Y

Election Results

1996 general	Mark W. Neumann (R)	118,408	(51%)	($1,211,134)
	Lydia C. Spottswood (D)	114,148	(49%)	($708,825)
1996 primary	Mark W. Neumann (R)	unopposed		
1994 general	Mark W. Neumann (R)	83,937	(49%)	($512,091)
	Peter W. Barca (D)	82,817	(49%)	($671,438)
	Others	3,101	(2%)	

SECOND DISTRICT

On a narrow isthmus between Lakes Mendota and Monona is the center of Madison and, in many ways, the center of Wisconsin. Here the state Capitol rises at the one end of State Street; at the other end of several commercial blocks is the main campus of the University of Wisconsin, on a beautiful, parklike, sometimes windswept setting above Lake Mendota. For most of this century, Wisconsin politics was dominated by the Madison-based LaFollettes and their liberal Democratic successors. And the traffic on State Street was two-way, with university faculty devoted to Bob LaFollette's "Wisconsin idea" of an apolitical bureaucracy, his Wisconsin Tax Commission and workmen's compensation law—both firsts in the nation. Now there is more division, with the liberal campus at odds with the welfare reform and school choices reforms of Governor Tommy Thompson. But there is a steady debate carried on here between the liberal *Madison Capital-Times* and its Republican rival, the *Wisconsin State Journal*, with a much larger circulation; the two newspapers practice the kind of partisan journalism still seen in only a few major cities and state capitals (Nashville, Sacramento, Boston, Detroit). Meanwhile, Madison's varied economy is thriving, with unemployment in 1996 hovering around 1.5%.

Madison is the center of Wisconsin's 2d Congressional District, and with surrounding Dane County casts about 70% of the district's votes. The rest are in several rural dairy counties which are more Republican and conservative; they include such picturesque Wisconsin scenes as Frank Lloyd Wright's home, Taliesin, the Swiss-settled town of New Glarus, and the headquarters of Lands' End in Dodgeville. Madison was LaFollette country for the first half of the century, and very liberal and Democratic for most of the second, enough so that despite the Republican leanings of the rural counties, the 2d District voted for George McGovern in 1972 and Walter Mondale in 1984. It also spawned an activist and sometimes violent student movement (during the Vietnam war, a graduate student was killed in a laboratory by a bomb set off by a protester) and a permanent postgraduate proletariat. But there has been some mellowing out. Grad students stuck in the sixties may have left, but there are now plenty of Republicans as well as Democrats among undergraduates. And Madison has even been known to vote Republican, for Governor Tommy Thompson in 1994 and in the 2d District House race in the 1990s.

The congressman from the 2d District is Scott Klug, a Republican elected in 1990. Klug grew up in Wisconsin, and after college went to work as an investigative TV reporter in Washington. In 1988 he returned to Madison to work as an anchor at Channel 27. In 1990 he ran against Congressman Robert Kastenmeier, one of the most liberal members of the House, first elected in 1958. Klug's campaign was deft. He treated Kastenmeier respectfully but said his ideas were "stuck in the '60s" and he ran as his campaign logo the number 32 in a circle with a line drawn through it (indicating 32 years in Congress is enough). He showed candor in calling for means-testing Social Security and moderation in calling for early intervention programs for at-risk children. Klug lost Madison's Dane County by only 52%–48% and won 63% in the smaller counties, for a 53%–47% victory, slightly ahead of Republican Governor Tommy Thompson's strong showing there.

Klug has had a moderate, even liberal voting record, and at the same time has cooperated with Republican reformers and often the leadership. In his first term he was part of the freshman "Gang of Seven" who insisted on full disclosure of House bank overdrafts. He joined the Porkbusters' Coalition identifying $1 billion in recommended cuts. But he also worked on preserving details of federal dairy programs, tried to restrict cheese imports, boosted ethanol fuels and supported University of Wisconsin Chancellor Donna Shalala as Bill Clinton's secretary of Health and Human Services. He got a law changed so that U.S. soldiers killed by friendly fire can receive the Purple Heart.

In his second term he successfully sponsored amendments to kill the Advanced Solid Rocket Motor (passed 379–43) and against experiments that he referred to as "pigs in space" (333–98). He opposed the Haiti invasion and called for lifting the Bosnian arms embargo. He opposed the Clinton vaccine program and supported the healthcare plan sponsored by Tennessee Representative Jim Cooper, working with a bipartisan group of House members on the issue. With Oregon's Ron Wyden, he proposed a national data bank on medical malpractice. He also bucked most of his party by supporting the assault weapons ban and the 1994 crime bill. He got new regulations to protect against the ticket fraud that many Wisconsin fans complained about at the Rose Bowl in 1994.

After the 1994 election Klug found himself in the majority, and still sometimes at odds with his party. He was one of Speaker Newt Gingrich's main liaisons with moderate Republicans. On the Commerce Committee he worked on the Telecommunications Act. He tried to zero out the Appalachian Regional Commission. "Appalachia needed help. My friends, 30 years of help is enough," he said sarcastically. He also took an assignment from Gingrich to head the House Republicans' effort to identify federal programs that are ripe for privatization—from the Government Printing Office to public power agencies. One juicy target was the Tennessee Valley Authority, which will soon compete with private utilities, enjoys tax advantages and in the Clinton budget was to get $140 million a year in federal money. Klug tried to zero that out in July 1995 and was beaten badly. But he predicted at the time, "Money will get so tight there will be no way to defend TVA." In January 1997 TVA head Craven Crowell, a longtime staffer for former Tennessee Senator Jim Sasser, proposed zeroing out TVA's federal subsidy and spinning off TVA's navigation and flood control functions to the Army Corps of Engineers or local agencies, leaving TVA free to compete in the about-to-be-deregulated electricity market.

Klug has been reelected handily three times. In 1992 he faced Ada Deer, a Menominee Indian organizer. She said she was not sure if she would have voted for declaring war against Germany and Japan in 1941 and held a fundraiser at an abortion clinic with a basket of condoms next to her bumper stickers. Klug won 63%–37%, with 60% of the vote in Dane County. In 1994 even the *Cap Times* endorsed Klug, and he won 69%–29%, with 66% in Dane County. In 1996 he faced the avatar of 1960s student liberalism, Paul Soglin, elected to the Madison Council in 1968 and mayor from 1973–79 and from 1989 on. Soglin criticized Wisconsin's welfare reform and said it would leave people "dying in the streets"; he said Klug voted with Newt Gingrich 84% of the time and, desperate for coattails, ended a TV ad with "Clinton Soglin." Klug ran an ad campaign with a picture that morphed from a black-and-white Gingrich to an in-color Klug, ticking off how he differed from Gingrich on defense, environment, corporate welfare and education. He attacked Soglin's financial record as mayor and defended his own votes on student loans. Klug spent well over $1 million and won 57%–41%, carrying Dane County with 53%.

Klug began his fourth term by voting "present" on the ballot for speaker. In February 1997 he announced that he would not run for reelection in 1998. While his own vote-getting record shows a Republican can win, the 2d District seems likely to elect a Democrat to replace him. The Democrats could have a crowded field as former Dane County Executive Rick Phelps and state legislators Joe Wineke and Tammy Baldwin will probably run in the primary.

The People: Pop. 1990: 543,625; 36% rural; 11% age 65+; 95% White; 2% Black; 2% Asian; 1% Hispanic origin. Households: 55% married couple families; 26% married couple fams. w. children; 53% college educ.; median household income: $30,625; per capita income: $14,319; median gross rent: $441; median house value: $69,800.

1996 Presidential Vote

Clinton (D)	146,819	(55%)
Dole (R)	88,072	(33%)
Perot (I)	21,682	(8%)
Other	12,743	(5%)

1992 Presidential Vote

Clinton (D)	149,340	(50%)
Bush (R)	94,368	(32%)
Perot (I)	52,552	(18%)

Rep. Scott Klug (R)

Elected 1990; b. Jan. 16, 1953, Milwaukee; home, Madison; Lawrence U., B.A. 1975, Northwestern U., M.S.J. 1976, U. of WI, M.B.A. 1990; Catholic; married (Theresa).

Career: Investigative reporter, WJLA-TV Washington, D.C., 1976–88; News anchor, WKOW-TV Madison, 1988–90.

DC Office: 2331 RHOB 20515, 202-225-2906; Fax: 202-225-6942; e-mail: badger02@hr.house.gov.

District Offices: Madison, 608-257-9200.

Committees: *Commerce* (12th of 28 R): Finance & Hazardous Materials; Health & the Environment; Telecommunications, Trade & Consumer Protection.

Group Ratings

	ADA	ACLU	AFS	LCV	CFA	CON	NFIB	COC	ACU	NTLC	CHC
1996	40	25	17	54	69	99	92	81	75	81	73
1995	25	—	—	19	62	100	—	88	72	—	—

National Journal Ratings

	1995 LIB	—	1995 CONS	1996 LIB	—	1996 CONS
Economic	49%	—	49%	51%	—	48%
Social	57%	—	42%	59%	—	40%
Foreign	56%	—	43%	67%	—	31%

Key Votes of the 104th Congress

1. Reduce Medicare Growth $	Y	5. Flag Amendment	Y	9. Cuban Embargo	Y
2. Ovrd. Product Liab. Veto	Y	6. Drop EPA Limits	Y	10. Bar Bosnia Troop $	Y
3. Increase Min. Wage	N	7. Repeal Assault-Weap. Ban	N	11. Cut Anti-Missile Defense	N
4. Welfare Reform	Y	8. Ovrd. Part. Birth Veto	Y	12. Bar U.N. Uniforms	Y

Election Results

1996 general	Scott Klug (R)	154,557	(57%)	($1,261,546)
	Paul R. Soglin (D)	110,467	(41%)	($506,513)
	Others	4,350	(2%)	
1996 primary	Scott Klug (R)	unopposed		
1994 general	Scott Klug (R)	133,734	(69%)	($689,215)
	Thomas C. Hecht (D)	55,406	(29%)	($281,783)
	Others	4,109	(2%)	

THIRD DISTRICT

On the rolling land of western Wisconsin, in the knobby hills just east of the Mississippi River, on some of the most beautiful river landscape in the country, is where Laura Ingalls Wilder's family built the "little house in the big woods" in the 1870s, before the first railroad came steaming up the narrow floodplain alongside the Mississippi River. Today, it is hard to imagine the big woods: the trees have long since been cut and the hillsides are covered with grass grazed by placid dairy cattle. Where pioneers tried to scratch out diversified crops, farmers soon made America's premier dairying region, producing milk, butter and especially cheese. Today the dairy industry is in trouble. Cows are more productive, while demand for milk has decreased because there are fewer children in America today than in the 1950s, and fewer Americans are descended exclusively from the northern European stock that carries the genes for the enzymes adults need to effectively digest milk. And Wisconsin has trouble competing against the European Common Market's hugely subsidized cheese and butter. Many communities here lost population, as did the factory town of La Crosse, where the locally owned Trane Company and Heileman Brewing were bought by outsiders. But there is also growth in these beautiful hills, evidence of mobility and prosperity despite problems in the dairy industry.

The 3d Congressional District of Wisconsin follows the Mississippi and St. Croix River counties from the southern border of the state almost to Lake Superior, and here and there reaches east a county or two. This is probably the nation's number one dairy district, with more cows than people. It was settled largely by German and Scandinavian immigrants (Laura's Yankee family moved away as Swedes were moving into the area), and it once voted for LaFollette Progressives. More recently, it has been sharply contested partisan territory.

The congressman from the 3d District is Ron Kind, a Democrat elected in 1996. He grew up in a large family in La Crosse, the son of a telephone repairman and a secretary. He went to Harvard on scholarship and played quarterback and worked as a summer intern for Senator William Proxmire, doing research for his Golden Fleece awards. He attended the London School of Economics and Minnesota Law School, practiced law in a big firm in Milwaukee, then returned home to La Crosse to work as an assistant prosecutor on rape and sexual abuse cases. Kind started running for Congress soon after Congressman Steve Gunderson announced during the 1994 campaign that he would not run again in 1996. Gunderson was known nationally as the Republican revealed to be gay in an October 1994 *New York Times Magazine* article; in the district he was known as a hard-working young politician, first elected at 29 in 1980, who was the top Republican on the Agriculture subcommittee handling dairy programs. Early in the race to succeed him was Republican former state Senator Jim Harsdorf, from the northern part of the district up near Minneapolis-St. Paul. Kind was one of five Democrats running. He set a tone for the primary election by renting the Hollywood Theater in La Crosse for a special showing of *Mr. Smith Goes to Washington.* Kind's leading opponent, Lee Rasch, president of a La Crosse technical college, had run before and called for farmers to wean themselves from federal price supports. Kind talked of cutting corporate welfare and aiding the poor, and won the September primary 46%–29%. But before that there was much commotion on the Republican side. Gunderson was third-ranking Republican on Agriculture; Chairman Pat Roberts was running for the Senate, and in June 1996 second-ranking Republican Bill Emerson died. That put Gunderson in line for the chairmanship, and many Wisconsin dairy people urged him to run for reelection. He said in June that he would only if he had no primary opponent, but Harsdorf refused to leave the race, and Gunderson did not file. In July a Gunderson write-in movement was launched. In late July Newt Gingrich called Gunderson and told him that conservative activist (and Wisconsin native) Paul Weyrich was planning an independent expenditure effort against him and that four of the five other Wisconsin Republicans were against the write-in. On July 31 in Eau Claire, Gunderson asked the write-in organizers "to not go forward" and added, "It has been explained to me bluntly that if you, as an openly gay person, became chairman of the Agriculture Committee, you would legitimatize homosexuality."

In the general election, Harsdorf took hard-edged, well-defined stands, for the balanced budget and Governor Tommy Thompson's "Wisconsin Works" welfare reform (known as W-2). Kind complained the ads were misleading and called for an end to such campaigning, though the ads accurately set out the candidates' differences on two important issues: Kind said he was concerned whether W-2 provided enough job training and child care and wanted to see how Congress tackled the budget in 1997 before considering an amendment. He talked instead of campaign finance reform and presented his own balanced budget proposal. On November 1 Gunderson announced he was neutral on the candidates because he didn't agree with Harsdorf's views on civil rights and human rights and thought him too close to the Christian Coalition. In a district that Bill Clinton carried 50%–34%, Kind won 52%–48%. Harsdorf won over some Clinton voters in his northeast base and in southern Grant County, but Kind ran 8% ahead of

Clinton in his base of La Crosse and 6% ahead in Eau Claire.

In the House, Kind promised to work for a campaign finance reform commission and a balanced budget. He promised to address the dairy farmers' chief complaints that the 1996 farm bill didn't get rid of the Eau Claire-based pricing formula, which puts Midwesterners at a disadvantage, and that the basic price formula for cheese is not accurately determined from the market; and he warned that he would be vigilant as the National Cheese Exchange moved from Green Bay to the Chicago Merc. Kind did not get a seat on the Agriculture Committee, but said the farm bill left these decisions up to Agriculture Secretary Dan Glickman and that he would try to work with him. Also he promised to protect the Mississippi River from environmental degradation and, in a bipartisan move, hired Gunderson's press secretary and one of his district staffers. He said he would ask Proxmire for permission to revive the Golden Fleece award, spotlighting wasteful government spending. He sponsored a bill to relax the English language requirement for citizenship for Hmong immigrants, some of whom fought for the United States in Vietnam, and will lose their welfare benefits from the 1996 Immigration Act. Possible opponents in 1998 include Harsdorf, state Senator Brian Rude and Steve Gunderson's brother Matt Gunderson.

The People: Pop. 1990: 543,447; 56% rural; 14% age 65+; 98% White; 1% Asian; 1% Hispanic origin. Households: 60% married couple families; 30% married couple fams. w. children; 39% college educ.; median household income: $25,758; per capita income: $11,505; median gross rent: $336; median house value: $52,400.

1996 Presidential Vote

Clinton (D)	120,717	(50%)
Dole (R)	82,678	(34%)
Perot (I)	33,325	(14%)
Other	5,274	(2%)

1992 Presidential Vote

Clinton (D)	119,721	(43%)
Bush (R)	90,813	(33%)
Perot (I)	67,134	(24%)

Rep. Ron Kind (D)

Elected 1996; b. March 16, 1963, La Crosse; home, La Crosse; Harvard U., B.A. 1985; London Schl. of Econ., 1986; U. of MN, J.D. 1990; Lutheran; married (Tawni).

Career: Practicing atty., 1990–92; Asst. St. Prosecutor, La Crosse Cnty., 1992–96.

DC Office: 1713 LHOB 20515, 202-225-5506; Fax: 202-225-5739.

District Offices: Eau Claire, 715-831-9214; La Crosse, 608-782-2558.

Committees: *Education & The Workforce* (17th of 20 D): Oversight & Investigations; Postsecondary Education, Training & Life-Long Learning. *Resources* (22nd of 23 D): National Parks & Public Lands; Water & Power.

Group Ratings and Key Votes: Newly Elected

Election Results

1996 general	Ron Kind (D)	121,967	(52%)	($497,919)
	James E. Harsdorf (R)	112,146	(48%)	($507,175)
1996 primary	Ron Kind (D)	13,685	(46%)	
	Lee Rasch (D)	8,582	(29%)	
	Tim Bakken (D)	5,370	(18%)	
	Others	2,254	(8%)	
1994 general	Steve Gunderson (R)	89,338	(56%)	($658,181)
	Harvey Stower (D)	65,758	(41%)	($217,460)
	Others	5,217	(3%)	

FOURTH DISTRICT

The world's largest four-sided clock faces outward from all sides of the tower on the Allen-Bradley factory, looking out over the manufacturing city of Milwaukee. It is an apt symbol, a piece of precision engineering, in this high-skill manufacturing town, with its skyline of smokestacks and church steeples, the closest thing in America to the factory cities of the Germany whence so many Milwaukeeans' ancestors came. Chicago, just 90 miles away, provides much of the banking, advertising, insurance, accounting and legal services Milwaukee businesses need, and the retail and entertainment base as well, and Madison has the big research university. But Milwaukee leads the nation in industrial control equipment, mining gear, cranes and independent foundries. The work force, with German, Polish, Mitteleuropean work habits, is highly skilled and hard-working. German-Americans made Milwaukee the nation's major beer brewer for years, though brewing employs fewer than 4,000 here today. Milwaukee lost 60,000 manufacturing jobs in the 1979–82 recession years, but it stuck to its high-skill manufacturing strength and eventually prospered. Since that recession, Allen-Bradley has spent millions on improvements and new facilities, Rockwell International doubled sales to $1.5 billion, and Harnischfeger has recovered nicely to regain its status as a leader in mining equipment and papermaking machinery, after nearly going bankrupt in 1983.

Prospering quietly from this growth, for this is still a union, high-wage town, are the residents of Milwaukee's traditionally blue-collar south side. Here, in neighborhoods with sturdy houses that withstand northern winters and streets lined with bars emblazoned with beer signs, are Milwaukee's prototypical Polish neighborhoods and its even larger number of German-Americans. The 4th Congressional District of Wisconsin, which has been the south-side district since 1892, has spread out with the population into the suburbs. Now, over 100 years later, only one-third of its voters are in Milwaukee, another 40% in the Milwaukee County suburbs and one-quarter farther west in suburban Waukesha County. Historically this was the only securely Democratic part of Wisconsin. But Waukesha County is solidly Republican, and the 4th District is now far less Democratic than the north side 5th. In 1996 it went for Bill Clinton by only 49%–40%, less than some rural Wisconsin districts.

The congressman from the 4th District is Jerry Kleczka, a Democrat elected in April 1984. Kleczka is a product of the south side, the sort of man who has remodeled his house from top to bottom and maintains the best lawn in the neighborhood. He was elected to the Wisconsin Assembly in 1968 at 24, to the state Senate in 1974 where he chaired several committees, and to the U.S. House in April 1984, after the death of Clement Zablocki, who represented the district for 35 years and chaired the Foreign Affairs Committee.

In the House Kleczka has had a moderate to liberal voting record. He supported both family and medical leave in 1993 and welfare reform in 1996. He has criticized SSI for providing benefits for children who are not in any serious way disabled and for drug addicts and alcoholics. He favors tax-free withdrawals from IRAs for first-time home-buying, college education, medical expenses, and during long-term unemployment. With Barney Frank, he has a bill to prohibit adjustment of the Consumer Price Index without a vote of Congress. Inspired by Pabst Brewery closure in early 1997, he has sponsored a CARE Act to require employers to give six months' notice before changing health benefits and granting retirees between 55 and 65 the right to keep their group health insurance.

In 1994 Republican Tom Reynolds, a Christian conservative printer whose backyard print shop churned out anti-abortion as well as campaign literature, held him to a 54%–45% victory. In May 1995, after a second drunk driving arrest, Kleczka gave up drinking. In 1996 Reynolds ran again, and beat former Judge Mac Davis, son of former Congressman Glenn Davis, in the Republican primary. Reynolds favored creating medical savings accounts and complained when Kleczka charged he was against requiring employers to provide health insurance, but the attack stung. This time Kleczka won convincingly, 58%–42%. But the presence of a Republican base in Waukesha County means that this could someday be a seriously contested district.

The People: Pop. 1990: 543,482; 2% rural; 13% age 65+; 91% White; 1% Black; 1% Asian; 1% Amer. Indian; 6% Hispanic origin. Households: 56% married couple families; 25% married couple fams. w. children; 43% college educ.; median household income: $32,260; per capita income: $14,177; median gross rent: $448; median house value: $71,400.

1996 Presidential Vote			**1992 Presidential Vote**		
Clinton (D)	115,466	(49%)	Clinton (D)	116,048	(41%)
Dole (R)	94,003	(40%)	Bush (R)	108,761	(38%)
Perot (I)	21,373	(9%)	Perot (I)	59,263	(21%)
Other	5,032	(2%)			

Rep. Jerry Kleczka (D)

Elected Apr. 1984; b. Nov. 26, 1943, Milwaukee; home, Milwaukee; U. of WI; Catholic; married (Bonnie).

Career: Air Natl. Guard, 1963–69; Accountant; Milwaukee Cnty. Cncl., 1965–68; WI Assembly, 1968–74; WI Senate, 1974–84, Asst. Majority Ldr., 1977–82.

DC Office: 2301 RHOB 20515, 202-225-4572; Fax: 202-225-8135; e-mail: jerry4wi@hr.house.gov.

District Offices: Milwaukee, 414-297-1140; Waukesha, 414-549-6360.

Committees: *Ways & Means* (9th of 16 D): Health; Oversight.

Group Ratings

	ADA	ACLU	AFS	LCV	CFA	CON	NFIB	COC	ACU	NTLC	CHC
1996	75	56	83	77	77	11	31	44	10	13	26
1995	70	—	—	63	77	37	—	41	25	—	—

National Journal Ratings

	1995 LIB	—	1995 CONS	1996 LIB	—	1996 CONS
Economic	65%	—	34%	70%	—	28%
Social	67%	—	33%	70%	—	30%
Foreign	77%	—	23%	87%	—	10%

Key Votes of the 104th Congress

1. Reduce Medicare Growth $	N	5. Flag Amendment	N	9. Cuban Embargo	N
2. Ovrd. Product Liab. Veto	N	6. Drop EPA Limits	Y	10. Bar Bosnia Troop $	Y
3. Increase Min. Wage	Y	7. Repeal Assault-Weap. Ban	N	11. Cut Anti-Missile Defense	Y
4. Welfare Reform	Y	8. Ovrd. Part. Birth Veto	Y	12. Bar U.N. Uniforms	N

Election Results

1996 general	Jerry Kleczka (D)	134,470	(58%)	($862,686)
	Tom Reynolds (R)	98,438	(42%)	($253,357)
1996 primary	Jerry Kleczka (D)	30,199	(86%)	
	Roman R. Blenski (D)	4,962	(14%)	
1994 general	Jerry Kleczka (D)	93,789	(54%)	($495,371)
	Tom Reynolds (R)	78,225	(45%)	($111,356)
	Others	2,675	(2%)	

FIFTH DISTRICT

Milwaukee is America's most German city, with an ethnic heritage noticeable not just in the names of its beers and its old German restaurants but in the solidness of its houses and the orderliness of its streets. Until the World Wars made this German character seem un-American, German was spoken on the streets and read in newspapers, German beer was produced in dozens of breweries and German cultural traditions breathed in churches, union halls and parlors. There was a German-type politics, with a Socialist mayor and an efficient, honest city government. Wisconsin's 5th Congressional District, which since 1892 has included the north side of Milwaukee, elected Socialist Victor Berger to Congress in 1910 and again from 1918–20 and 1922–26, even though he was denied his House seat after the 1918 election because of his opposition to World War I; in 1919, he was sentenced to 20 years in prison for writing antiwar articles, but that was later reversed by the Supreme Court. Though some ghetto neighborhoods here are beset by crime and drug use, most of Milwaukee is solid and upstanding, and some of it—Brewers Hill near the old Schlitz brewery—is gentrifying. There is an Oktoberfest (as well as an Irish Fest, summerfest, etc.), and there are large and efficiently run factories that pay high wages to highly-skilled and well-disciplined workers. This is also the place where state legislator Polly Williams, a Jesse Jackson backer in 1988, joined forces with Republican Governor Tommy Thompson to oppose the Democratic education bureaucracy and enact a school choice program, bitterly attacked by teachers' unions but now perceptibly raising the testing scores of disadvantaged students.

The 5th Congressional District of Wisconsin includes the northern half of Milwaukee and Milwaukee County, including its black neighborhoods and the high-income suburbs on Lake Michigan. Overall, its tone is sturdily blue and white collar. Once Socialist and LaFollette Progressive, the 5th is now the most heavily Democratic district in Wisconsin.

The congressman from the 5th District is Tom Barrett, who has spent most of his adult life in politics. He grew up in Milwaukee, went to college and law school in Madison, practiced law and was elected to the state Assembly in 1984, at 30; in 1988 he was overwhelmingly elected to the state Senate in a district that conveniently was one of only two entirely within the 5th District. His legislation included bringing 911 emergency call service to Milwaukee and passing a state version of the Brady bill. Running for the House in 1992 when the 5th District's Jim Moody ran for the Senate, Barrett presented detailed position papers on the economy and healthcare reform. He also called for large defense cutbacks, a national police corps and federal encouragement of direct investment in "microenterprises" in depressed city neighborhoods. He won his primary with 41% over a black county supervisor, a former circuit judge who spent $200,000 of his own money and a former Marquette basketball star; the general election was easy.

Barrett has a moderate to liberal voting record; he supported the Blue Dog budget. He was a strong supporter of lobbying reform and the gift ban; he has a bill to prohibit congressmen from using frequent flier miles from official travel for personal vacations. In response to local concerns, he worked to save the Summer Youth Employment Program in 1995 and to require HUD to give owner-occupants preference in resales of HUD-owned houses. His provision to prohibit Community Development Block Grants from being used to attract business from one part of the country to another was incorporated into the Republican housing bill in early 1997. Inspired by the Pabst Brewery closure in early 1997, he sponsored a bill to require companies that wish to terminate retiree benefits to notify employees and face a court hearing within 14 days if someone objects. He has sought unsuccessfully to extend the Republicans' line-item veto to targeted tax breaks. With David Obey and Jerry Kleczka, he tried to stop Mark Neumann's bill for waivers for Governor Tommy Thompson's W-2 welfare reform. That became moot when national welfare reform passed in July 1996; Barrett was one of two Wisconsin votes against it (David Obey was the other), arguing that there isn't enough child care capacity in Milwaukee County.

Barrett is ranking Democrat on the Government Reform and Oversight Subcommittee on National Security, International Affairs and Criminal Justice. In early 1997 he opposed the certification of Mexico's drug-fighting efforts, but said that penalties should be waived; the Clinton Administration certified them anyway. Another issue before the Committee is Census sampling; from one of the states with the highest response rate, Barrett is likely to oppose Census sampling.

The People: Pop. 1990: 543,607; 13% age 65+; 60% White; 35% Black; 2% Asian; 1% Amer. Indian; 3% Hispanic origin. Households: 41% married couple families; 18% married couple fams. w. children; 49% college educ.; median household income: $26,267; per capita income: $13,277; median gross rent: $435; median house value: $62,400.

1996 Presidential Vote			1992 Presidential Vote		
Clinton (D)	126,179	(63%)	Clinton (D)	142,047	(56%)
Dole (R)	58,560	(29%)	Bush (R)	76,935	(30%)
Perot (I)	10,182	(5%)	Perot (I)	32,138	(13%)
Other	5,603	(3%)			

Rep. Thomas M. Barrett (D)

Elected 1992; b. Dec. 8, 1953, Milwaukee; home, Milwaukee; U. of WI, B.A. 1976, J.D., 1980; Catholic; married (Kristine).

Career: FDIC bank examiner, 1977; Law Clerk, Fed. Dist. Judge Robert Warren 1980–82; Practicing atty., 1982–84; WI Assembly, 1984–88; WI Senate, 1988–92.

DC Office: 1224 LHOB 20515, 202-225-3571; Fax: 202-225-2185; e-mail: telltom@hr.house.gov.

District Office: Milwaukee, 414-297-1331.

Committees: *Banking & Financial Services* (13th of 25 D): Capital Markets, Securities & Government Sponsored Enterprises; Financial Institutions & Consumer Credit. *Government Reform & Oversight* (9th of 19 D): Human Resources; National Security, International Affairs & Criminal Justice (RMM).

Group Ratings

	ADA	ACLU	AFS	LCV	CFA	CON	NFIB	COC	ACU	NTLC	CHC
1996	85	69	92	85	100	93	24	25	5	5	13
1995	90	—	—	81	92	75	—	29	12	—	—

National Journal Ratings

	1995 LIB — 1995 CONS			1996 LIB — 1996 CONS		
Economic	72%	—	27%	85%	—	11%
Social	80%	—	13%	78%	—	21%
Foreign	70%	—	28%	90%	—	0%

Key Votes of the 104th Congress

1. Reduce Medicare Growth $	N	5. Flag Amendment	N	9. Cuban Embargo	N
2. Ovrd. Product Liab. Veto	N	6. Drop EPA Limits	Y	10. Bar Bosnia Troop $	N
3. Increase Min. Wage	Y	7. Repeal Assault-Weap. Ban	N	11. Cut Anti-Missile Defense	Y
4. Welfare Reform	N	8. Ovrd. Part. Birth Veto	Y	12. Bar U.N. Uniforms	N

Election Results

1996 general	Thomas M. Barrett (D)	141,179	(73%)	($153,139)
	Paul D. Melotik (R)	47,384	(25%)	($13,315)
	Others	4,006	(2%)	
1996 primary	Thomas M. Barrett (D)	unopposed		
1994 general	Thomas M. Barrett (D)	87,806	(62%)	($239,418)
	Stephen B. Hollingshead (R)	51,145	(36%)	($115,791)

SIXTH DISTRICT

Central Wisconsin is solid country, a producer of basic commodities—milk, butter and cheese, paper and paper products, Mirro pots and pans and Mercury outboard motors and Kleenex. Settled first by Yankee Protestants, it was one of the birthplaces of the Republican Party in February 1854, when a group of Whigs, Free Soilers and Democrats met in a small white schoolhouse in Ripon, Wisconsin, and proclaimed themselves Republicans; Jackson, Michigan, also claims to be the birthplace of the party. Whichever, the party grew rapidly, winning a near-majority in the House in the 1854 elections. But Republican roots here are not just Yankee. The 1850s brought the first surge of German migration into the United States, and central Wisconsin was a favorite destination. Here they built the dairy farms and factory towns that seemed steadfastly prosperous 50 years ago, and are now part of a manufacturing boom. Here also is the testing ground, in Fond du Lac County, of Governor Tommy Thompson's W-2 welfare reform; the rolls there have fallen by 55% in less than three years.

The 6th Congressional District of Wisconsin, which cuts a swath across the state from Manitowoc on Lake Michigan through Oshkosh and Ripon west almost to the Mississippi River, includes country which has voted Republican almost without interruption since that first meeting in Ripon. It has also elected Republican congressmen who have come up with thoughtful and original solutions to problems. One was William Steiger, first elected in 1966, whose chief monuments are the all-volunteer military and the 1978 Steiger amendment cutting capital gains tax rates—considerable accomplishments for a member of the minority party, and for one who died at age 40 in 1978. Another is Thomas Petri, who won the 1979 special election to succeed Steiger by a narrow margin and has also specialized in proposals that cut across ideological and party lines.

Petri grew up in Fond du Lac. He went to Harvard, was a Peace Corps volunteer in Somalia and was elected to the state Senate in 1972, at 32. In April 1979, after Steiger died, Petri ran for the House, beating Tommy Thompson (now governor) in the primary 35%–19% and then winning the special with 50.4%. Some of Petri's ideas have been adopted. He long boosted the Earned Income Tax Credit, which results in payments to low-income people who work, targeting aid to families much better than the minimum wage; the Clinton Administration agreed and increased the EITC when Democrats were in control, then dragged out the tattered arguments for the minimum wage when they wanted an issue to bash Republicans with in 1996. Petri would like to expand the EITC concept to provide a $1,000 tax credit per child, in place of the current deduction; but neither party seems interested. Petri favors making college loans repayable in amounts regulated by post-college earnings; this was adopted in the Clinton direct student loan program, which he supports. Petri would also like the amount of the subsidy based on post-college income. Another Petri success has been stopping the Auburn Dam near Sacramento, which he says is too expensive. Other Petri reforms have been pretty much ignored. He would withdraw the deductibility of healthcare insurance and substitute "Multicare," a fixed subsidy for catastrophic coverage, allowing people or employers to buy more insurance if they like. His campaign finance reform bill would include a 50% tax credit for up to $200 in contributions. He would privatize deposit insurance, on the theory that private insurers are better at spotting risks than government regulators. He wants to maintain the Census by actual enumeration, as provided in the Constitution, not by sampling, which could be politically manipulated; he also wants to give people the option of saying they are multi-racial.

Petri is chairman of the Surface Transportation Subcommittee, responsible for the reauthorization of ISTEA, the multi-modal transportation bill. On this committee he has taken less venturesome positions: he wants a spending formula favorable to Wisconsin, and he supports Transportation Chairman Bud Shuster's move to take the transportation trust funds off-budget. He has worked for more funding for recreational trails for bicycles and snowmobiles. Petri is definitely not a fan of "the outdated relic of Soviet-style central planning that is our federal dairy program." He is dismayed by the Northeast Dairy Compact's cartel and the exclusion of Wisconsin milk from other markets by the Eau Clair pricing system.

Petri, usually reelected easily, had a tough race in 1992; Democratic District Attorney Peggy Lautenschlager ran a vigorous race and held him to 53%–47%. In 1994 he was unopposed and in 1996 he won 73%–24%.

The People: Pop. 1990: 543,531; 47% rural; 15% age 65+; 98% White; 1% Asian; 1% Hispanic origin. Households: 63% married couple families; 29% married couple fams. w. children; 34% college educ.; median household income: $28,038; per capita income: $12,400; median gross rent: $349; median house value: $54,800.

1996 Presidential Vote

Clinton (D)	108,004	(45%)
Dole (R)	99,650	(41%)
Perot (I)	28,459	(12%)
Other	4,280	(2%)

1992 Presidential Vote

Bush (R)	114,517	(41%)
Clinton (D)	97,121	(34%)
Perot (I)	69,339	(25%)

Rep. Thomas E. Petri (R)

Elected Apr. 1979; b. May 28, 1940, Marinette; home, Fond du Lac; Harvard U., B.A. 1962, J.D. 1965; Lutheran; married (Anne).

Career: Peace Corps, Somalia, 1966–67; Law Clerk, Fed. Judge James Doyle, 1965–66; White House aide, 1969; Practicing atty., 1970–79; WI Senate, 1972–79.

DC Office: 2262 RHOB 20515, 202-225-2476; Fax: 202-225-2356; e-mail: tompetri@hr.house.gov.

District Offices: Fond du Lac, 414-922-1180; Oshkosh, 414-231-6333.

Committees: *Education & The Workforce* (Vice Chmn.): Employer-Employee Relations; Postsecondary Education, Training & Life-Long Learning. *Transportation & Infrastructure* (3rd of 40 R): Surface Transportation (Chmn.); Water Resources & Environment.

Group Ratings

	ADA	ACLU	AFS	LCV	CFA	CON	NFIB	COC	ACU	NTLC	CHC
1996	20	31	25	23	62	78	95	88	100	88	93
1995	5	—		13	31	87	—	92	75	—	

National Journal Ratings

	1995 LIB	—	1995 CONS	1996 LIB	—	1996 CONS
Economic	36%	—	60%	39%	—	58%
Social	32%	—	65%	23%	—	77%
Foreign	54%	—	45%	55%	—	43%

Key Votes of the 104th Congress

1. Reduce Medicare Growth $	Y	5. Flag Amendment	N	9. Cuban Embargo	Y
2. Ovrd. Product Liab. Veto	Y	6. Drop EPA Limits	N	10. Bar Bosnia Troop $	Y
3. Increase Min. Wage	N	7. Repeal Assault-Weap. Ban	Y	11. Cut Anti-Missile Defense	N
4. Welfare Reform	Y	8. Ovrd. Part. Birth Veto	Y	12. Bar U.N. Uniforms	Y

Election Results

1996 general	Thomas E. Petri (R)	169,213	(73%)	($364,660)
	Al Lindskoog (D)	55,377	(24%)	
	Others	7,129	(3%)	
1996 primary	Thomas E. Petri (R)	unopposed		
1994 general	Thomas E. Petri (R)	unopposed		($326,635)

SEVENTH DISTRICT

In the late 19th Century, on the rail lines radiating northwest from Chicago and Milwaukee, came thousands of migrants whose descendants have made the northern reaches of Wisconsin the most thickly settled land this far north in the United States and east of the Mississippi. What brought people up so far was not cropland—there are no industrial-sized wheat farms as in the Red River Valley of North Dakota—but trees and iron and cows. This was one of America's largest virgin timberlands, and the river towns are still dotted with paper mills. Farther north, iron brought Finns and Italians to the port of Superior, Wisconsin, right next to Duluth, Minnesota, and to smaller towns on the chilly lake. Then, on the cleared forestlands, came dairy farms. Dairy cattle, properly cared for, thrive in these northern uplands and the sons of Wisconsin dairymen, many of them immigrants from Germany and Norway, moved their dairy herds even farther north. On this base, small cities grew, some with big enterprises. Wausau has paper mills and Wausau Insurance, Wisconsin Rapids has Georgia-Pacific and Stevens Point has Sentry Insurance.

All these places are in Wisconsin's 7th Congressional District, which stretches from a point not far from Green Bay and Madison in the south up to Lake Superior in the north. The politics of northern Wisconsin and the 7th District has a rough-hewn quality, a certain lumberjack populist flavor. Ancestrally Republican, this area favored the progressivism of the LaFollettes. Today Superior and Stevens Point are heavily Democratic, while much of the country in between leans Republican.

The congressman from the 7th District is David Obey, a Democrat first elected in April 1969. Chairman of the Appropriations Committee from March 1994 to January 1995, he is now one of the ablest and mostly strongly motivated legislators on the minority side of the aisle. He grew up in Wausau, where his father worked in a roofing factory. Obey is a natural politician, who in 1962, the year he got his master's degree, was elected to the Wisconsin Assembly, at 24. When Melvin Laird resigned his House seat to become Richard Nixon's Defense secretary, Obey won an upset in the April 1969 special election. In the state legislature he was inspired by older New Deal Democrats who fought hard for the little guy. In the House Obey entered, the driving energy came from liberal Democrats opposed to the Vietnam war. Obey preserves something of the force of each. He is not a sentimental liberal: he has a prickly personality and a vigorous temper and does not suffer gladly those he considers fools or knaves. Even as he has moved to the top of the seniority ladder, he has retained his sense of outrage and his eagerness to fight for what he believes in—a quality that even some Democrats complain has been too intense. But he continues to display abundant energy and leadership on a host of fronts. In the mid-1970s he chaired a special committee on ethics, pushing through a code requiring detailed disclosure of personal finances and limiting outside income: this was not forgiven by some of the oldtimers. From 1979 well into the 1980s he was the chief sponsor of campaign finance bills to limit PAC contributions, reduce individual donations and provide public financing. In 1991 the office of House Administrator was created—something Obey proposed 16 years before, and a recommendation which might have saved a lot of House Democrats and some House Republicans much trouble if it had been followed earlier. He had his disappointments. He lost the Budget Committee chairmanship to Oklahoma's Jim Jones in 1980 by 121–116. In 1984 he wanted to become Caucus chairman, but demurred when it became clear that Dick Gephardt had the votes. Even so, informally Obey became a key leader of liberal Democrats, in 1989 pushing Gephardt for majority leader when Jim Wright and Tony Coelho were resigning, in 1990 pushing a rules change requiring Ways and Means subcommittee chairmen to be elected by the whole caucus.

Obey remains a true believer in traditional liberalism, in Keynesian economics and economic redistribution. He thinks that government should provide economic security, create jobs and build infrastructure through public investment, that it should control healthcare costs and guarantee coverage with choice of physician for everyone. In 1994 he wanted to give the president power to lower taxes to counterbalance Federal Reserve interest rate increases and stood ready to back middle-class tax cuts even as the economy by some measures was growing smartly. In two stints as chairman of the Joint Economic Committee, he prepared studies arguing that Reagan-Bush policies enriched the rich and hurt the middle class. He has bucked the Democratic leadership on behalf of principle, leading the opposition to the 1990 budget summit package. He also has bucked the Clinton Administration, vocally opposing NAFTA and, when Clinton seemed to be backing away from universal healthcare coverage in July 1994, said "then I will walk away from the Clinton healthcare plan" and support his real preference, a single-payer system. In June 1995, when Clinton accepted the Republicans' goal of a budget balanced in seven years, Obey issued a written statement reading. "I think most of us learned some time ago that if you don't like the President's position on a particular issue you simply need to wait a few weeks." Or months—Obey was much more pleased when Clinton started vetoing

Republican appropriations bills in the fall. Obey also opposes some administration positions from the right. He has long opposed abortion, and backs the "partial-birth" abortion ban; he opposes gun control, and pointed out that one of the guns singled out in the assault weapons ban is owned by 23,000 residents of the 7th District, including two sheriffs.

Obey is above all an appropriator, and takes some justifiable pride in his skill at this work. He first got his seat on Appropriations in August 1969, when he was just 30; when he became chairman, in March 1994, he was the youngest man to hold the post since James Good of Iowa in 1919. A good appropriator needs to be a master of detail, a tough and far-sighted negotiator, but also a deal-maker, able to work with those with whom he disagrees. Obey has shown these all these skills, plus a determination to get things done on time—which is not always how appropriating works. Much of his work came on the Foreign Operations Subcommittee, which he chaired from 1985–95. This subcommittee handles rather small sums of money but deals with some very sensitive issues, and it was often rocked in disputes about aid to the Nicaraguan contras, the pace of negotiations in the Middle East, the treatment of the liberated nations of Eastern Europe. Obey was inclined to think the Camp David agreements committed too much aid to Egypt and Israel and wanted to see more spent on humanitarian assistance. He opposed aid to El Salvador and the Nicaraguan contras and voted against the Gulf war resolution; he supported the dispatch of troops to Somalia in 1992 and Haiti in March 1994. Obey has not always gotten his way, but in each case he worked to move appropriations bills forward in an orderly manner. When Obey became chairman of the Foreign Operations Subcommittee, he passed separate foreign operations appropriation bills nine out of 10 years, something that had only been accomplished twice in 10 years by his predecessors. Similarly, when Obey became chairman of the full committee, all 13 appropriations bills were signed into law prior to the beginning of the new fiscal year for the first time in 47 years.

Obey's climb to the chairmanship was sudden. In January 1993 Jamie Whitten, whose health was visibly impaired, was voted out after 14 years as chairman. William Natcher, holder of the record for consecutive roll call votes, performed ably for a year, then visibly failed in January 1994. When he died in March 1994, Obey challenged the next Democrat in line, 74-year-old Neal Smith of Iowa. Smith had the support of other "cardinals," but Obey had more from non-committee liberals and less senior members, and won in the Democratic Caucus 152–106. But Obey was not as partisan as some may have hoped. "Our mission has been fairly well defined by circumstances," he said. "We've been trying to dig out of the Reagan-era deficits and manage the downsizing of programs while freeing up a tiny bit for the president's programs, and I want to do that in the most collegial and bipartisan way."

Looking back on the first two Clinton years, it was obvious that the President foundered when he failed to unite Democrats on issues with no possible bipartisan strategy—on tax increases, gun control, the healthcare proposal. Obey in fashioning party positions took care not just to express his own views but to take stands that could unify Democrats and put them in a position to prevail if they could win just a few Republican votes—as they did on occasions that became more numerous in 1996 than in 1995. This approach was exemplified by Obey's support for South Carolina's John Spratt for ranking Democrat on the Budget Committee in late 1996. And despite some loud arguments—both men are known for their tempers—Obey and Chairman Bob Livingston managed to work together on numerous occasions, sometimes to reach agreement, often to frame disagreement in orderly choices for other members.

The 7th is a pretty solidly Democratic district—it voted for Michael Dukakis in the 1980s as well as Bill Clinton in the 1990s—and for years Obey won with little difficulty. But in Republican 1994 his opponent, Scott West, a 32-year-old admissions counselor at UW-Stevens Point, though outspent by a wide margin, held him to a 54%–46% victory—a bit too close for comfort. Obey even lost the southern part of the district, his home base, by 52%–48%. That created some interest in the 1996 race and Eau Claire state Senator David Zien was touted as the strongest Republican. But he lost the primary to West, who was again vastly outspent. West said Obey was aloof and out of touch and that he had a bad temper. Obey said that he certainly was angry at the way working families were being treated by Republican policies and continually pounded away at Newt Gingrich. "A new direction or a Newt direction?" he asked. The answer came in: 57% for Obey, 43% for West. This is a solid margin, but not an overwhelming one; Republicans, if they think there is a tide of opinion in their direction, might more aggressively contest this district some day.

The People: Pop. 1990: 543,569; 59% rural; 15% age 65+; 97% White; 1% Asian; 2% Amer. Indian; 1% Hispanic origin. Households: 62% married couple families; 29% married couple fams. w. children; 34% college educ.; median household income: $25,277; per capita income: $11,427; median gross rent: $327; median house value: $48,400.

1996 Presidential Vote

Clinton (D)	119,984	(49%)
Dole (R)	86,374	(35%)
Perot (I)	34,328	(14%)
Other	5,257	(2%)

1992 Presidential Vote

Clinton (D)	117,203	(42%)
Bush (R)	93,156	(33%)
Perot (I)	67,558	(24%)

Rep. David R. Obey (D)

Elected Apr. 1969; b. Oct. 3, 1938, Okmulgee, OK; home, Wausau; U. of WI, B.S. 1960, M.A., 1962; Catholic; married (Joan).

Career: Asst., family run supper club & motel, 1962–68; WI Assembly, 1962–69.

DC Office: 2462 RHOB 20515, 202-225-3365.

District Offices: Wausau, 715-842-5606.

Committees: *Appropriations* (RMM of 26 D): Labor, Health & Human Services & Education (RMM).

Group Ratings

	ADA	ACLU	AFS	LCV	CFA	CON	NFIB	COC	ACU	NTLC	CHC
1996	75	67	100	69	69	55	27	19	25	15	21
1995	80	—	—	88	69	25	—	25	8	—	—

National Journal Ratings

	1995 LIB — 1995 CONS			1996 LIB — 1996 CONS		
Economic	80%	—	18%	82%	—	16%
Social	69%	—	31%	68%	—	32%
Foreign	79%	—	17%	82%	—	16%

Key Votes of the 104th Congress

1. Reduce Medicare Growth $	N	5. Flag Amendment	N	9. Cuban Embargo	N
2. Ovrd. Product Liab. Veto	N	6. Drop EPA Limits	Y	10. Bar Bosnia Troop $	N
3. Increase Min. Wage	Y	7. Repeal Assault-Weap. Ban	Y	11. Cut Anti-Missile Defense	Y
4. Welfare Reform	N	8. Ovrd. Part. Birth Veto	Y	12. Bar U.N. Uniforms	Y

Election Results

1996 general	David R. Obey (D)	137,428	(57%)	($862,370)
	Scott West (R)	103,365	(43%)	($161,402)
1996 primary	David R. Obey (D)	unopposed		
1994 general	David R. Obey (D)	97,184	(54%)	($607,058)
	Scott West (R)	81,706	(46%)	($98,781)

EIGHTH DISTRICT

In 1673, the French explorer and priest Father Marquette sailed from the open waters of Lake Michigan into what is now Green Bay. He had hoped to find the Northwest Passage to the Pacific. He actually found the Fox River, which leads to Lake Winnebago and, after a not-too-difficult portage, the Wisconsin River that flows into the Mississippi. Green Bay and the Fox River Valley remained mostly wilderness and Indian country for more than 150 years. But once settled by Europeans, they became, as Father Marquette would have liked, one of the most heavily Catholic parts of the United States, though Indians still remain a presence; there was a long dispute over Chippewa Indians spearfishing rights and Green Bay's best hotel is now next to the Oneida Indians' casino. This is a thriving area economically, with traditional paper mills joined by high-skill manufacturing in Green Bay and the Fox River Valley. And it is thriving even more psychically, after the January 1997 Super Bowl victory of the Green Bay Packers, the only community-owned franchise in the National Football League. The Lombardi trophy returns home to "Titletown."

The 8th Congressional District of Wisconsin includes Green Bay and the Fox River Valley south to Appleton. It also includes several north woods and dairy counties inland, plus the Door County peninsula that juts out into Lake Michigan, a favorite summer vacation spot for Chicago and Milwaukee families. Politically, this has often been malleable country. Democrats, especially Catholics, can win here: John Kennedy carried the Fox River Valley in the primary and general election in 1960, and Bill Clinton carried it in 1996. But the 8th District can turn almost ferociously Republican: Appleton was the home of Senator Joseph McCarthy, who did much to tar the good names of politics, Congress, conservatism and the Republican Party in the early 1950s.

The congressman from the 8th District is Jay Johnson, a Democrat elected in 1996. He grew up in the mining country of Michigan's Upper Peninsula (interestingly, Bart Stupak, the congressman from the Upper Peninsula grew up in the 8th District of Wisconsin), where his parents ran a hardware store and his mother was a teacher. After Northern Michigan University and the Army, he majored in broadcasting at Michigan State, worked as a TV reporter in several states and came to Green Bay in 1981, first at WFRV-TV, then at WLUK-TV. Long interested in politics, he considered running against Congressman Toby Roth in 1996, but the race did not look particularly inviting; Roth, first elected in 1978, usually won by large margins. Then in March 1996 Roth announced he was retiring and Johnson jumped into the race. The favored candidate was Republican Assembly Speaker David Prosser, who was first elected to the Assembly in 1978 and had lost a 1972 Assembly primary to Roth.

But Johnson brought his TV-familiar face to the Democratic primary, arguing that education was the number one issue; former legislator Stan Gruszynski, the 1994 nominee, said campaign finance reform was the most important issue. Johnson won 59%–41%, losing three western counties which receive Wausau rather than Green Bay TV. Meanwhile, in the Republican primary businessman Chuck Dettman spent over $200,000 of his own money and biked and jogged through the district. He attacked Prosser for the proposal he and Governor Tommy Thompson backed to raise the sales tax in the five-county Milwaukee area to pay for a new baseball stadium, and for pressuring legislators into supporting a gas tax. Prosser gave the lawyer-like response that the gas tax wasn't his idea, he didn't threaten anyone and anyway it didn't pass. Dettman also questioned Prosser's commitment to family values because he was unmarried. "I keep asking David what his core beliefs are. But because he's involved with lobbyists, he can't have core beliefs. He owes too many people," he said. Prosser won, but by only 58%–42%, and his candidacy took on some water.

In the general, Johnson attacked Prosser as an out-of-touch politician who mishandled the stadium, but Prosser defended his support of the stadium. Prosser ran an ad showing a bunch of cows, ridiculing Johnson for proposing a 25 cents a hundred weight tax on milk (in Wisconsin!) to pay for education. Johnson said he had made the proposal after misreading a pamphlet. With similar naivete, he said of the 1996 welfare reform, "It's not the best bill, but it's what the people want. Now we'll see how it works." He supported NAFTA and opposed the "partial-birth" abortion ban, the balanced budget amendment and Roth's English-as-the-official-language bill. Prosser spent nearly twice as much money, but Johnson won 52%–48%. He ran behind Bill Clinton's showing here in the western counties where he was not a familiar face, but in the Green Bay media market, he ran between 7% and 10% ahead of Clinton's 46%.

Despite his expressed interest in education, Johnson was assigned to the Agriculture and Transportation Committees. A possible 1998 opponent is Brown County (Green Bay) Executive Nancy Nusbaum.

The People: Pop. 1990: 543,526; 44% rural; 14% age 65+; 96% White; 1% Asian; 3% Amer. Indian; 1% Hispanic origin. Households: 62% married couple families; 30% married couple fams. w. children; 37% college educ.; median household income: $28,169; per capita income: $12,628; median gross rent: $357; median house value: $57,800.

1996 Presidential Vote

Clinton (D)	116,073	(46%)
Dole (R)	105,131	(41%)
Perot (I)	28,567	(11%)
Other	3,862	(2%)

1992 Presidential Vote

Bush (R)	115,128	(40%)
Clinton (D)	101,493	(35%)
Perot (I)	69,373	(24%)

Rep. Jay W. Johnson (D)

Elected 1996; b. Sept. 30, 1943, Bessemer, MI; home, New Franken; Gogebic Comm. Col., A.A. 1963; Northern MI U., B.A. 1965; MI St. U., M.A. 1970; Presbyterian; married (JoLee).

Career: Army, 1966–68; Broadcast Journalist, 1970–96: WOWO Radio, Fort Wayne, IN, 1970–74; WPTV, W. Palm Beach, FL, 1974–76; WPLG-TV, WVCG Radio, W. Palm Beach, FL, 1976–77; WPEC-TV, W. Palm Beach, FL, 1977–80; WOTV, Grand Rapids, MI, 1980–81; WFRV-TV, Green Bay, WI, 1981–87; WLUK-TV, Green Bay, WI, 1987–96; Pres., Family Violence Center, 1982–87.

DC Office: 1313 LHOB 20515, 202-225-5665; Fax: 202-225-5729.

District Offices: Appleton, 414-731-7586; Green Bay, 414-430-1776.

Committees: *Agriculture* (22nd of 23 D): General Farm Commodities; Livestock, Dairy & Poultry. *Transportation & Infrastructure* (29th of 33 D): Coast Guard & Maritime Transportation; Water Resources & Environment.

Group Ratings and Key Votes: Newly Elected

Election Results

1996 general	Jay W. Johnson (D)	129,551	(52%)	($289,624)
	David Prosser (R)	119,398	(48%)	($556,074)
1996 primary	Jay W. Johnson (D)	18,293	(59%)	
	Stan Gruszynski (D)	12,681	(41%)	
1994 general	Toby Roth (R)	114,319	(64%)	($683,149)
	Stan Gruszynski (D)	65,065	(36%)	($215,831)

NINTH DISTRICT

For decades, the orderly, heavily German-American factory city of Milwaukee has been spreading slowly, mostly west and north, into Wisconsin dairy country. There are high-income enclaves here, like close-in Elm Grove and Oconomowoc spread out around its lakes. There is office development in Brookfield; subdivisions spread out in Mequon and Menomonee Falls and farther, to reach small towns with roots deep in the 19th Century. This is comfortable but not fancy territory, and the economy here is still based heavily on skilled manufacturing. Not far from Milwaukee are Sheboygan, home of Kohler plumbing fixtures; Port Washington, with Allen-Edmonds shoes; West Bend, with West Bend kitchen appliances; Pewaukee, with Quad/Graphics printing.

The 9th Congressional District of Wisconsin includes most of the western, northwestern and northern suburbs of Milwaukee and spreads out into rich dairy farm country and to these factory towns. Almost every precinct here votes Republican, and this is usually the most Republican district in the state—the only Wisconsin district for Bob Dole in 1996.

The congressman from the 9th District, James Sensenbrenner, first elected in 1978, is one of the most senior Republicans in the House. His Wisconsin roots are strong—his great-grandfather was a top executive at Kimberly-Clark—and Sensenbrenner is one of the richest members of Congress and the most scrupulous (he discloses a complete list of his investments). After Stanford and University of Wisconsin Law School, he has spent most of his adult life in politics, briefly as a U.S. House staffer, and then serving 10 years in the Wisconsin legislature from 1968–78. For almost all that time, Sensenbrenner has been in the minority, gamely undertaking the Sisyphean task of moving amendments certain to lose. But he has persevered out of a dogged sense of principle. But his voting record is not entirely conservative: he supported the Brady bill, but led the fight against the assault weapons ban. He was an original co-sponsor and floor manager of the Defense of Marriage Act, to keep states from undermining federal law that does not recognize same-sex marriages. He sponsored a Fairness in Music Licensing Act, which would reduce royalty fees for small business owners playing home-style radio or TV in their establishments; he was aroused when auditors from the American Society of Composers, Authors and Publishers converged on Pewaukee Lake bars and demanded payments. He has spoken out strongly for Milwaukee's school choice experiment. He has introduced a bill to repeal the Northeast Dairy Compact authorized by the 1996 farm bill.

Sensenbrenner now is chairman of the House Science Committee, after serving a term as chairman of its Space Subcommittee. On those bodies he has worked in a bipartisan manner with ranking Democrat George Brown. He supports the Space Station, which survived by a one-vote margin in 1993 and by larger margins since. he has raised questions about whether Russia is fulfilling its obligations under the U.S.-Russia space agreement, and in early 1997, after Russia failed to produce a Service Module on time, was pressing the Clinton Administration to remove Russia from the critical path schedule. Sensenbrenner wants to promote opportunities for private businesses in space, such as remote sensing satellites which can assess soil, timber and mineral resources. But in early 1997 he was also persuaded to seek funding increases for science research and development.

Sensenbrenner is a stickler for rules and ethics, one of the first to urge that Congress apply to itself the laws it imposes on the rest of the country. He has insisted on impeachment action against federal judges convicted of crimes. He prepared motions to censure or expel Dan Rostenkowski if he had pleaded guilty to any crimes—one reason, perhaps, why he did not. Sensenbrenner upholds the principle of colorblindness, opposing race-based standards in crime bills and arguing strongly against racial quotas until George Bush negotiated the issue away in 1991.

Sensenbrenner's only tough race was the 1978 primary. He was unopposed in 1994 and reelected by 74%–25% in 1996.

The People: Pop. 1990: 543,602; 36% rural; 12% age 65+; 98% White; 1% Asian; 1% Hispanic origin. Households: 69% married couple families; 33% married couple fams. w. children; 46% college educ.; median household income: $37,579; per capita income: $16,187; median gross rent: $430; median house value: $82,500.

1996 Presidential Vote			1992 Presidential Vote		
Dole (R)	141,961	(52%)	Bush (R)	142,465	(48%)
Clinton (D)	101,420	(37%)	Clinton (D)	88,303	(30%)
Perot (I)	23,437	(9%)	Perot (I)	64,657	(22%)
Other	5,477	(2%)			

Rep. F. James Sensenbrenner, Jr. (R)

Elected 1978; b. June 14, 1943, Chicago, IL; home, Menomonee Falls; Stanford U., A.B. 1965, U. of WI, J.D. 1968; Episcopalian; married (Cheryl).

Career: Practicing atty., 1968–69; Staff asst., U.S. Rep. Arthur Younger, 1965; WI Assembly, 1968–74; WI Senate, 1974–78.

DC Office: 2332 RHOB 20515, 202-225-5101; e-mail: sensen09@hr.house.gov.

District Offices: Brookfield, 414-784-1111.

Committees: *Judiciary* (2nd of 20 R): Courts & Intellectual Property. *Science* (Chmn. of 25 R).

Group Ratings

	ADA	ACLU	AFS	LCV	CFA	CON	NFIB	COC	ACU	NTLC	CHC
1996	20	19	17	15	46	80	95	81	100	93	93
1995	5	—	—	13	31	87	—	88	80	—	—

National Journal Ratings

	1995 LIB — 1995 CONS			1996 LIB — 1996 CONS		
Economic	34%	—	64%	39%	—	58%
Social	21%	—	72%	0%	—	90%
Foreign	48%	—	50%	55%	—	43%

Key Votes of the 104th Congress

1. Reduce Medicare Growth $	Y	5. Flag Amendment	Y	9. Cuban Embargo	Y
2. Ovrd. Product Liab. Veto	Y	6. Drop EPA Limits	N	10. Bar Bosnia Troop $	Y
3. Increase Min. Wage	N	7. Repeal Assault-Weap. Ban	Y	11. Cut Anti-Missile Defense	N
4. Welfare Reform	Y	8. Ovrd. Part. Birth Veto	Y	12. Bar U.N. Uniforms	Y

Election Results

1996 general	F. James Sensenbrenner, Jr (R)	197,910	(74%)	($261,644)
	Floyd Brenholt (D)	67,740	(25%)	($13,781)
1996 primary	F. James Sensenbrenner, Jr (R)	unopposed		
1994 general	F. James Sensenbrenner, Jr (R)	unopposed		($161,986)

WYOMING

Wyoming is "the land of the cowboy" the *WPA Guide* proclaimed 50 years ago. "Its mountains, plains, and valleys are essentially livestock country. A cowboy astride a bucking bronco greets the visitor from enameled license plates, from newspapers, magazines and painted signs." The cowboy is still on the license plates, and Wyoming remains the most western of states in spirit—largely unsettled, the least populous state, a thin veneer of civilization stretched over a forbidding and beautiful land. Wyoming "has a 'lean-to' look," writes Gretel Ehrlich. "Instead of big, roomy barns and Victorian houses, there are dugouts, low sheds, log cabins, sheep camps and fence lines that look like driftwood blown haphazardly into place. People here still feel pride because they live in such a harsh place, part of the glamorous cowboy past." "What you see now in Wyoming is the promotion of things we used to apologize for," says the state Commerce Department director. "Wide open spaces, a huge expansive sky with no pollution, uncluttered clean rivers with maybe a lone fly fisherman, a cowboy and his dog and a herd of cattle."

But the economic life of Wyoming now depends less on cowboys and more on mining and minerals. The mining bust and population losses of the 1980s have been succeeded by new mining and job growth in the 1990s. The Clean Air Act has put a premium on Wyoming's low-sulfur coal, and Wyoming is now the number-one coal-producing state, with enough reserves to last 500 years. It is also the number four oil and number six natural gas producer, and the nation's top producer of the mineral bentonite (used in oil drilling and cosmetics) and the world's largest reserve of trona (used in glass and baking soda). Wyoming has also had glamour growth around Jackson Hole, which made headlines during the Bush Administration as the vacation home of Secretary of State James Baker and Secretary of Defense and former Wyoming Congressman Dick Cheney. And there has been growth in the scenic and pastoral country on the eastern slope of the Big Horn mountains around Buffalo and Sheridan. Meanwhile, tourists still flock to Yellowstone and Grand Teton National Parks: tourism is Wyoming's second industry. The third is agriculture: Wyoming is second in the nation in wool production, third in sheep inventory and also produces sugar beets, barley, pinto beans and beef cattle.

For all its Old West atmosphere, Wyoming has always depended on new technology to tame age-old nature. Cattle ranches after the open-range era were made possible only by the barbed wire that could fence in roaming herds, and the steam locomotives that could carry cattle to market back east. This 19th Century high tech was brought to Wyoming by large capitalist operators, some of them onetime Texas cowhands or second sons of English landed gentry, who started the first big operations and consolidated their power in the Johnson County land war of 1890. More recently, Wyoming has boomed and busted as geologists and engineers have discovered and developed minerals in demand on world markets. The 1970s spikes in energy prices brought in big operators who found oil and natural gas in the Overthrust belt near Evanston. Huge deposits of coal in the north became economically feasible to mine when transportation improved and clean air laws were changed to remove the advantage for high-sulfur West Virginia coal. The result was not always a pretty picture. Workers who flocked here lived in grimy trailers, linked only precariously to civilization's utilities and unprotected against the winds and snows that come out of the enormous sky; these communities had an atmosphere redolent of 19th Century mining camps like Virginia City, Nevada, or Deadwood, South Dakota. In the 1990s, grey wolves were returned, despite local ranchers' objections, to the Yellowstone area and were seen elsewhere—nature edging man back just a little bit. Wyoming still is a kind of frontier: it was until recently one of the few states with more men than women—the reason it was the first part of the United States, when it was a territory in 1869, to give women the vote.

There is a settled part of Wyoming as well, in the medium-sized towns that are the state's largest cities, and among sheep and cattle ranches, sugar beet and malting barley farms and denizens of tiny settlements. This is a small state, a single community really, where people remember who played what position, when and how well, for what high-school football team; where because all locals know who your father's cousins married, you mostly live on the straight and narrow. Yet there is a sharp economic and regional split traditionally reflected in partisan politics. The big economic interests—cattle ranchers, organized in the Wyoming Stock Growers' Association, and the Union Pacific Railroad management always favored the Republicans, as do the wildcatters, independent producers and oil company geologists. The main Democratic constituency has been the Union Pacific Railroad workers who built the first transcontinental line across southern Wyoming in the 1860s and have maintained it ever since; the southern tier of counties, from Cheyenne through Laramie to Evanston, often votes Democratic. The population balance favors the Republicans, and Wyoming has been one of the most Republican states since the 1970s; it hasn't elected a Democrat to the Senate since 1970 or the House since 1976, but has had mostly Democratic governors over that time. In presidential elections it is safely Republican, but with a large Perot vote—the nation's fourth highest in 1996.

Wyoming's Republican strength has been tested in the 1990s, and has prevailed. The Clinton Administration's environmental policies, from proposed grazing fee increases to reintroduction of grey wolves into Yellowstone—have not been popular here, indeed are often referred to as the "war on the West." That has hobbled even Democrats who have won state office and do well in the personal campaigning which has always remained important here: there aren't many people—not even half a million, less than the size of an average congressional district, in 1996—and Wyoming voters expect to talk person-to-person with their governors, senators and congressmen every few years. Democrat Mike Sullivan was elected governor twice and had high job ratings. But nonetheless in 1994 he lost the Senate race 59%–39% to Congressman-at-Large Craig Thomas. Democrat Kathy Karpan became popular as Secretary of State. But she lost the governorship to Jim Geringer in 1994 59%–40% and a Senate race to Mike Enzi in 1996 54%–42%. And in 1994 Barbara Cubin won the House seat 53%–41% despite the big spending of Democrat Bob Schuster.

Governor. Jim Geringer, the governor of Wyoming, grew up in Wheatland, where his father, a Volga German, had emigrated early in the century. That was his Old West background; his high-tech experience came from service in the Air Force, where he worked on Air Force and NASA space boosters for 10 years. In 1977, Geringer returned to Wyoming, starting from scratch and buying his own farm. He was elected to the state legislature in 1982. In 1994, when incumbent Mike Sullivan ran for the Senate, Geringer ran for governor. He won the four-way Republican primary with 43%, then beat Secretary of State Kathy Karpan by 59%–40%, carrying all but one county. He called for Wyoming to use its mineral resources and low taxes to build a more diversified, higher-tech economy. But he adds, "We don't define economic growth the way other states do. If the alternative is high growth, high anxiety, crime and pollution, then what we are doing is worth the gamble. When the dust settles and urbanization is complete in other states, we will be envied. Wyoming will be seen as the true new West, the last state standing with wide open spaces, clean air and a healthy public attitude." With revenues exceeding estimates, the problem is to plan ahead, although a court case may require new taxes to equalize school district resources. Simmering controversies include whether to allow Indian

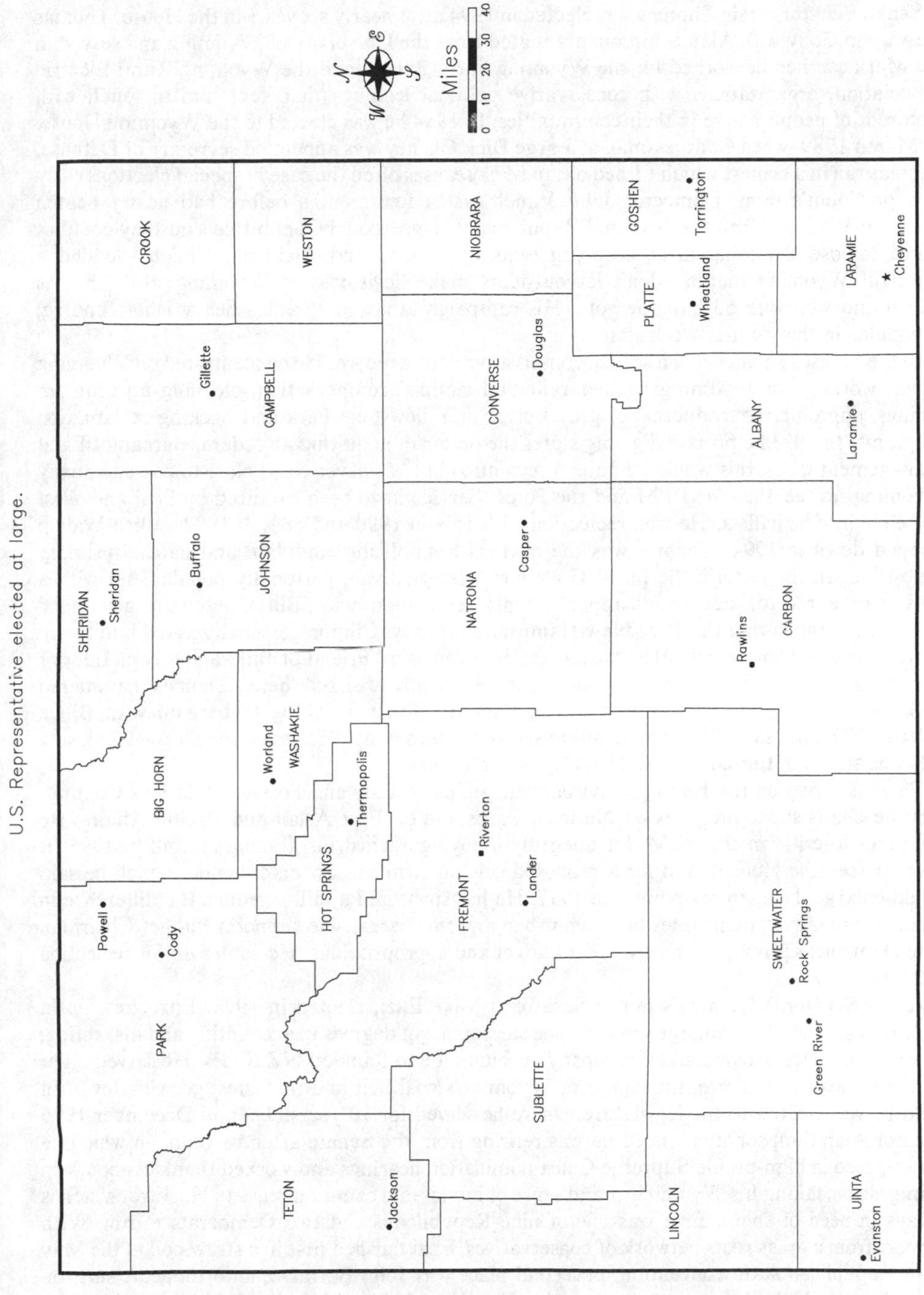
U.S. Representative elected at large.
Miles
0 10 20 30 40
N E S W
SHERIDAN
Sheridan
CROOK
CAMPBELL
Gillette
WESTON
JOHNSON
Buffalo
BIG HORN
WASHAKIE
Worland
PARK
Powell
Cody
HOT SPRINGS
Thermopolis
NIOBRARA
CONVERSE
Douglas
NATRONA
Casper
FREMONT
Riverton
Lander
TETON
Jackson
SUBLETTE
LINCOLN
GOSHEN
Torrington
PLATTE
Wheatland
LARAMIE
Cheyenne
ALBANY
Laramie
CARBON
Rawlins
SWEETWATER
Rock Springs
Green River
UINTA
Evanston

gambling and a lawsuit with Nebraska over Platte River water. The legislature is heavily Republican. Geringer appears to be in strong shape for reelection in 1998.

Senior Senator. Craig Thomas was elected in 1994 after nearly six years in the House. Thomas grew up in Cody with Alan Simpson, graduated from the University of Wyoming and served in the Marines; then he worked for the Wyoming Farm Bureau and the Wyoming Rural Electric Association, organizations with conservative political leanings that kept him in touch with hundreds of people active in their communities. In 1984 he was elected to the Wyoming House. In March 1989, when Congressman-at-Large Dick Cheney was appointed secretary of Defense, Thomas ran in a contest which turned out to be close, as is often the case in special elections early in a president's term. Democrat John Vinich just a few months before had nearly beaten Malcolm Wallop. When the National Republican Congressional Committee said they couldn't afford to lose Wyoming after dropping seats in Indiana and Alabama, Vinich sounded a powerful Wyoming theme—don't let outsiders make decisions for Wyoming. But Thomas rallied and won with 53% of the vote. His campaign attacked Vinich's heavy labor funding, unpopular in this right-to-work state.

In the House, Thomas had a solidly conservative voting record. He concentrated on Wyoming issues: working for Wyoming nuclear radiation victims' compensation, cleaning up uranium tailings, opposing reintroduction of grey wolves in Yellowstone Park and backing reclamation programs. In 1993 he proposed giving states the option of acquiring all federal Bureau of Land Management lands: this would be quite a revolution but has never come close to passage; many Wyomingites feel that the BLM and the Forest Service have been captured by East and West coase environmentalists. He won reelection with 55% in 1990 and 58% in 1992. When Wallop stepped down in 1994, Thomas was the obvious Republican candidate and had no primary opposition. In the general, he faced Governor Mike Sullivan, personally popular and with a conservative record, but handicapped by his association with Bill Clinton at governors' conferences and during the 1992 New Hampshire primary; Clinton personally asked him to run for the Senate. Thomas relentlessly attacked Sullivan as a "Friend of Bill" and ally of Interior Secretary Bruce Babbitt, whose policies are especially disliked here. Thomas hammered Sullivan for being willing to bargain with Babbitt. "I'm not willing to bargain with Bruce Babbitt," Thomas said. "I'm not afraid to stand up and say no." Thomas won 59%–39%, losing only one southern tier county, and that by only six votes.

Thomas serves on the Energy, Environment, Indian Affairs and Foreign Relations Committees; he chairs subcommittees on National Parks and on East Asian and Pacific Affairs. He continues to criticize the BLM, for allegedly lobbying against his grazing fee bill in 1995 (it never passed the House), and for a proposed rule on criminal law enforcement which he said would enlarge the agency's powers in 1997. He has sponsored a bill to reduce the difference in Medicare reimbursement rates between urban and rural areas. He supports Budget Chairman Pete Domenici's proposal for a two-year budget and appropriations. He comes up for reelection in 2000.

Junior Senator. Wyoming's junior Senator is Mike Enzi, elected in 1996. Enzi grew up in Thermopolis and Sheridan, the son of a shoe salesman, got degrees in accounting and marketing, moved to Gillette became an oil company accountant and founded NZ Shoes. He served eight years as mayor of Gillette, the center of Wyoming's coal belt and its fastest-growing town. In 1986 he was elected to the legislature, where he served for 10 years. Then in December 1995 Senator Alan Simpson announced he was retiring from the Senate after 18 years, in which he participated in high-profile Supreme Court nomination hearings and worked thankless hours on immigration, taking his Wyoming-brand sense of humor and common sense to Harvard, which is always in need of them. Enzi was one of nine Republicans and two Democrats to run. With support from a grass roots network of conservatives, Enzi finished first in a straw poll at the May 1996 Republican state convention; in second place was John Barrasso, an orthopedic surgeon from Casper who had appeared on statewide TV discussing health issues for 12 years; his chief difference on issues was his support of abortion rights. A third candidate, state Senator Curt

Meier, spent over $200,000 of his own money, but this was basically a two-man race. Barrasso had more money, but Enzi won 32%–30%, with a big majority in his home area in northeast Wyoming and narrow margins in the Casper and Cheyenne areas.

The Democratic nominee was Kathy Karpan, secretary of State from 1986–94, gubernatorial candidate in 1994, who beat a man who called for construction of a 22,000-mile-high tower into space to promote world peace. Karpan had an appealing story—she helped raise her siblings when her mother died, she worked her way through school and then was a prosecutor—and moderate stances on many issues: she called herself "a DLC Democrat." Her opposition to gun control led the National Rifle Association to stay neutral; her opposition to federally funded abortions kept her off EMILY's List. But she had the liabilities of having supported the presidential candidacies of Bill Clinton in 1992 and Bruce Babbitt in 1988. She appeared in one ad in hunting gear, toting a shotgun. "She's all in camouflage, but you can see right through her," was Enzi's reply. She opposed the balanced budget amendment and Senator Craig Thomas's bill to turn over BLM lands to state governments; Enzi favored both. The National Republican Senatorial Committee chimed in with ads claiming Karpan was "way too liberal for Wyoming." "When I get to Washington, I'm going to help make the whole United States more like Wyoming," Enzi said. It was a game effort by Karpan, but Enzi led in polls all the way and won 54%–42%. She carried the southern counties and ran nearly even in Cheyenne and Casper; he won big just about everywhere else.

In the Senate Enzi serves on the Banking, Labor and Small Business and Aging Committees. He has sponsored a bill to modernize OSHA and he has co-sponsored a home-based business fairness bill, providing deductibility for home offices and health insurance for the self-employed and clarifying the status of independent contractors: an accountant at work. He favors the Republican flextime bill and compensation to property owners harmed by the Endangered Species Act.

Representative-At-Large. Wyoming, the nation's least populous state, has elected one congressman-at-large since it was admitted to the Union in 1890. The current incumbent is Barbara Cubin, a Republican elected in 1994. The great-great-granddaughter of one of Wyoming's original homesteaders, she grew up in Casper, where she worked as a teacher, social worker, chemist and realtor; for 19 years she managed her husband's medical practice. She was divorced after an early first marriage, worked as a single mother, was subjected to sexual harassment, but insists: "I am not a feminist. I am not gender sensitive." She worked in Casper charities and was elected to the legislature in 1986, where she was prime sponsor of a 1994 ballot measure authorizing life without parole sentences.

In 1994, when Congressman Craig Thomas ran for the Senate, Cubin was one of five Republicans and two Democrats to run for the House. She sharply attacked "the Clinton-Babbitt war on the West," though she said she would accept an increase in some grazing fees and slightly higher mining royalties. In the Republican primary, she won 39% to 25% for House staffer Rob Wallace, 18% for sheep farmer Jim Magagna and 17% for state House Speaker Doug Chamberlain. The Democratic nominee was Bob Schuster, a law partner of high-profile Wyoming trial lawyer Gerry Spence, who spent $2.4 million, most of it his own money, on what was the third-highest spending campaign in the country. Schuster's big issue in the general was abortion; he was pro-choice, Cubin anti-abortion, and he hammered her even as the anti-abortion initiative was going down to defeat. She called him a "a slick trial-lawyer Clinton Democrat." That was epithet enough in Wyoming in 1994: Schuster carried only four counties, three in the southern tier and the other in Jackson Hole, and Cubin won 53%–41%.

Cubin initially got seats on the Resources and Science Committees and compiled a very conservative voting record. She worked on the detail of many bills, with varying results. She opposed allowing volunteers to conduct environmental surveys, arguing they tend to overcount "in their zeal to protect and preserve the resource"; she lost after Newt Gingrich came out on the other side. She angrily criticized his removal of a provision authorizing sales of power marketing administrations after she had take an political risk by voting for it. She complains that "AIDS is getting all the research money" and squeezing out research on diabetes and Alzheimer's and Parkinson's diseases. She was one of four members to switch their votes at the last minute and pass the budget resolution in June 1996.

When Senator Al Simpson announced his retirement in December 1995, Cubin quickly decided not to run for the Senate. Her 1996 opponent for the House was state Senator and law professor Pete Maxfield, who attacked her for "cuts" in Medicare and education. She was a target of AFL-CIO ads and in public polls her pairing numbers stayed well below 50. But she outspent Maxfield by more than 2–1 and won 55%–41%, an uptick from two years before in a year when most Republicans' percentages went down.

Presidential politics. Wyoming is one of the least likely states in the nation to be seriously contested in presidential general elections: it is too Republican, too remote and has only three electoral votes. But with a high Perot vote, Wyoming looked close enough that Bill Clinton vacationed here in August 1996, the first presidential campaign visit in a long time. He still lost 50%–37%, with 12% for Perot, his fourth best showing in the country. Clinton support was highest among older voters—not a good augury for Wyoming Democrats.

Wyoming holds presidential caucuses in early March, to which candidates' organizations pay some attention. Interestingly for 2000, this was one of the few non-southern states where Al Gore won in the 1988 presidential primary.

The People: Est. Pop. 1996: 481,000; Pop. 1990: 453,588, up 6.1% 1990–1996. 0.2% of U.S. total, 51st largest; 35% rural. Median age: 34.9 years. 11% 65 years and over. 91% White, 1% Black, 1% Asian, 2% Amer. Indian; 5.7% Hispanic origin. Households: 59.7% married couple families; 31% married couple fams. w. children; 50% college educ.; median household income: $27,096; per capita income: $12,311; 67.8% owner occupied housing; median house value: $61,600; median monthly rent: $270. 5.0% Unemployment. 1996 Voting age pop.: 356,000. 1996 Turnout: 211,571; 59% of VAP. Registered voters (1996): 240,711; 74,673 D (31%), 140,438 R (58%), 25,600 unaffiliated and minor parties (11%).

Political Lineup: Governor, Jim Geringer (R); Secy. of State, Diana Ohman (R); Atty. Gen., William U. Hill (R); Treasurer, Stan Smith (R); Auditor, David Ferrari (R). State Senate, 30 (9 D and 21 R); Senate President, Robert Grieve (R); State House, 60 (17 D and 43 R); House Speaker, Bruce Hinchey (R). Senators, Craig Thomas (R) and Michael B. Enzi (R). Representative, 1 R at large.

Elections Division: 307-777-5333; **Filing Deadline for U.S. Congress:** June 5, 1998.

1996 Presidential Vote

Dole (R)	105,388	(50%)
Clinton (D)	77,934	(37%)
Perot (I)	25,928	(12%)

1992 Presidential Vote

Bush (R)	79,347	(40%)
Clinton (D)	68,160	(34%)
Perot (I)	51,263	(26%)

GOVERNOR

Gov. Jim Geringer (R)

Elected 1994, term expires Jan. 1999; b. Apr. 24, 1944, Wheatland; home, Wheatland; KS St. U., B.S. 1967; Lutheran; married (Sherri).

Career: Air Force, 1967–77, Air Force Reserves, 1977–91; Contract Admin., Missouri Basin Power Project, 1977–79; Farmer, Rancher; WY House of Reps., 1982–88; WY Senate, 1988–94.

Office: State Capitol Bldg., #124, Cheyenne 82002, 307-777-7434; Fax: 307-632-3909; Web site: www.state.wy.us.

Election Results

1994 gen.	Jim Geringer (R)	118,016	(59%)
	Kathy Karpan (D)	80,747	(40%)
1994 prim.	Jim Geringer (R)	37,847	(43%)
	John Perry (R)	28,019	(32%)
	Charles K. Scott (R)	19,305	(22%)
	Others	3,442	(4%)
1990 gen.	Michael J. Sullivan (D)	104,638	(65%)
	Mary Mead (R)	55,471	(35%)

SENATORS

Sen. Craig Thomas (R)

Elected 1994, seat up 2000; b. Feb. 17, 1933, Cody; home, Casper; U. of WY, B.S. 1954, LaSalle U., LL.B. 1968; Methodist; married (Susan).

Career: Marine Corps, 1955–59; V.P., WY Farm Bureau, 1960–66; Legis. staff, Amer. Farm Bureau, 1966–75; Gen. Mgr., WY Rural Electric Assn., 1975–89; WY House of Reps., 1984–89; U.S. House of Reps., 1989–94.

DC Office: 109 HSOB 20515, 202-224-6441; Fax: 202-224-1724; e-mail: craig@thomas.senate.gov.

State Offices: Casper, 307-261-6413; Cheyenne, 307-772-2451; Riverton, 307-856-6642; Rock Springs, 307-362-5012; Sheridan, 307-672-6456.

Committees: *Energy & Natural Resources* (6th of 11 R): Forests & Public Land Management; National Parks, Historic Preservation & Recreation (Chmn.). *Environment & Public Works* (6th of 10 R): Drinking Water, Fisheries & Wildlife; Transportation & Infrastructure. *Foreign Relations* (6th of 10 R): East Asian & Pacific Affairs (Chmn.); European Affairs; International Economic Policy, Export & Trade Promotion. *Indian Affairs* (6th of 8 R).

Group Ratings

	ADA	ACLU	AFS	LCV	CFA	CON	NFIB	COC	ACU	NTLC	CHC
1996	5	28	0	8	7	74	97	92	100	97	100
1995	5	—	9	14	6	68	—	100	83	—	—

National Journal Ratings

	1995 LIB — 1995 CONS			1996 LIB — 1996 CONS		
Economic	21%	—	74%	9%	—	89%
Social	33%	—	62%	0%	—	72%
Foreign	8%	—	81%	0%	—	74%

Key Votes of the 104th Congress

1. Reduce Medicare Growth $	Y	5. Flag Amendment	Y	9. Anti-Missile Defense	Y
2. Lmt. Prod. Liab. Damages	Y	6. Endangered Species	N	10. Cuban Embargo	Y
3. Increase Min. Wage	N	7. Gay Employment Rights	N	11. Bar Bosnia Troop $	Y
4. Welfare Reform	Y	8. Ovrd. Part. Birth Veto	Y	12. Cut Vietnam Aid	Y

Election Results

1994 general	Craig Thomas (R)	118,754	(59%)	($1,068,335)
	Mike Sullivan (D)	79,287	(39%)	($712,991)
	Others	3,669	(2%)	
1994 primary	Craig Thomas (R)	unopposed		
1988 general	Malcolm Wallop (R)	91,143	(50%)	($1,344,185)
	John P. Vinich (D)	89,821	(50%)	($490,230)

Sen. Michael B. Enzi (R)

Elected 1996, seat up 2002; b. Feb. 1, 1944, Bremerton, WA; home, Gillette; George Washington U., B.S. 1966, Denver U., M.B.A. 1968; Presbyterian; married (Diana).

Career: WY Natl. Guard, 1967–73; Owner, NZ Shoes, 1969–95; Gillette Mayor, 1975–82; Dir. & Chmn., First WY Bank of Gillette, 1978–88; Accounting Mgr. & Computer Programmer, Dunbar Well Service, 1985–97; WY House of Reps., 1986–90; Education Commission of States, 1989–93; WY Senate, 1990–1996; Dir., Black Hills Corp., 1992–1996; Western Interstate Commission for Higher Education, 1995–96.

DC Office: 290 RSOB 20510, 202-224-3424; e-mail: senator@enzi.senate.gov.

State Offices: Casper, 307-261-6572; Cheyenne, 307-772-2477; Cody, 307-527-9444; Gillette, 307-682-6268; Jackson, 307-739-9507.

Committees: *Banking, Housing & Urban Affairs* (9th of 10 R): Financial Institutions & Regulatory Relief; Financial Services & Technology; Housing Opportunity & Community Development. *Labor & Human Resources* (6th of 10 R): Employment & Training; Public Health & Safety. *Small Business* (10th of 10 R). *Aging (Special)* (10th of 10 R).

Group Ratings and Key Votes: Newly Elected

Election Results

1996 general	Michael B. Enzi (R)	114,116	(54%)	($953,572)
	Kathy Karpan (D)	89,103	(42%)	($814,258)
	Others	7,858	(4%)	
1996 primary	Michael B. Enzi (R)	27,056	(32%)	
	John Barrasso (R)	24,918	(30%)	
	Curt Meier (R)	14,739	(18%)	
	Nimi McConigley (R)	6,005	(7%)	
	Kevin P. Meenan (R)	6,000	(7%)	
	Others	4,610	(6%)	
1990 general	Alan K. Simpson (R)	100,784	(64%)	($1,435,814)
	Kathy Helling (D)	56,848	(36%)	($6,243)

REPRESENTATIVE

Rep. Barbara Cubin (R)

Elected 1994; b. Nov. 30, 1946, Salinas, CA; home, Casper; Creighton U., B.S. 1969; Episcopalian; married (Frederick).

Career: Office Mgr., Dr. Frederick Cubin, 1975–94; WY House of Reps., 1986–92; WY Senate, 1992–94.

DC Office: 1114 LHOB 20515, 202-225-2311; Fax: 202-225-3057.

District Offices: Casper, 307-261-5595; Cheyenne, 307-772-2595; Rock Springs, 307-362-4095.

Committees: *Commerce* (26th of 28 R): Finance & Hazardous Materials; Health & the Environment. *Resources* (12th of 27 R): Energy & Mineral Resources (Chmn.).

Group Ratings

	ADA	ACLU	AFS	LCV	CFA	CON	NFIB	COC	ACU	NTLC	CHC
1996	0	12	0	8	0	30	100	100	100	100	93
1995	0	—	—	0	0	53	—	100	92	—	—

National Journal Ratings

	1995 LIB — 1995 CONS			1996 LIB — 1996 CONS		
Economic	0%	—	74%	0%	—	82%
Social	21%	—	72%	29%	—	68%
Foreign	0%	—	85%	0%	—	79%

Key Votes of the 104th Congress

1. Reduce Medicare Growth $	Y	5. Flag Amendment	Y	9. Cuban Embargo	Y
2. Ovrd. Product Liab. Veto	Y	6. Drop EPA Limits	N	10. Bar Bosnia Troop $	Y
3. Increase Min. Wage	N	7. Repeal Assault-Weap. Ban	Y	11. Cut Anti-Missile Defense	N
4. Welfare Reform	Y	8. Ovrd. Part. Birth Veto	Y	12. Bar U.N. Uniforms	Y

Election Results

1996 general	Barbara Cubin (R)	116,004	(55%)	($679,599)
	Pete Maxfield (D)	85,724	(41%)	($273,881)
	Others	8,255	(4%)	
1996 primary	Barbara Cubin (R)	unopposed		
1994 general	Barbara Cubin (R)	104,426	(53%)	($511,119)
	Bob Schuster (D)	81,022	(41%)	($2,429,346)
	Dave Dawson (Lib)	10,749	(5%)	

PUERTO RICO, VIRGIN ISLANDS, GUAM, AMERICAN SAMOA

Four American insular territories—Puerto Rico, Virgin Islands, Guam, American Samoa—are represented in Congress by elected delegates who, like the District of Columbia's delegate, have floor privileges, votes on committees but not votes on the floor (though House Democrats let them vote in committee of the whole proceedings in the 103d Congress). Each territory's status—its relationship to the United States—is different, governed by a separate law, and status is often the pivot around which territorial politics turn.

PUERTO RICO

Puerto Rico has a unique history. For four centuries, from Columbus's landing here in 1493 until the Spanish-American War of 1898, Puerto Rico was a Spanish colony and the port of San Juan the gathering place for its annual convoy of gold and silver from the Americas to Spain. Today, with 3.6 million people, it is the largest American territory—about the same population as South Carolina (with perhaps an additional two million Puerto Ricans on the mainland). Fifty years ago, it was "the poorhouse of the Caribbean," heavily populated, devoted almost entirely to sugar cultivation. It has elected a resident commissioner to Congress since 1900 and its residents have been American citizens since 1917, but it didn't elect its own governor until 1948. Then in the 1940s, 1950s and early 1960s, Puerto Rico was transformed by Governor Luis Munoz Marin and his Popular Democratic Party. Munoz initiated "Operation Bootstrap" to lure businesses to Puerto Rico with promises of low-wage labor and government assistance. Munoz also developed Puerto Rico's commonwealth form of government—better understood in Spanish, Estado Libre Asociado (ELA): Free Associated State—approved by plebiscite in 1952. Under commonwealth, Puerto Rico is part of the United States for purposes of international trade, foreign policy and war, but has its own separate laws, taxes and representative government, and is not subject to federal income taxes. Puerto Rico has also developed its own political parties: Munoz's Popular Democrats, the New Progressives who favor statehood, and two Independence parties.

But the commonwealth solution, by its own terms, was open to amendment; and ever since Munoz's voluntary retirement in 1964, the central issue in Puerto Rico's politics has been status:

should this island continue or modify ELA, should it seek statehood, should it seek independence? Over time there clearly has been slow movement toward statehood. In the July 1967 referendum, conducted when the Popular Democrats were in power, Puerto Ricans voted for ELA over statehood by 60%–39%; in the November 1993 referendum, conducted with New Progressives Governor Pedro Rosello in office, the vote was 48% for ELA, 46% for statehood. Independence has negligible support—4% in 1993—primarily from university students; nor are there many pro-independence abstentions, for voter turnout in the enthusiastic politics of Puerto Rico is the highest under the American flag, higher than in even the most affluent, long-settled suburbs of the mainland.

Possibly accelerating the trend toward statehood, certainly weakening the support for ELA, is Congress's decision in 1996 to phase out Section 936, the provision that shelters earnings of some Puerto Rico manufacturing from federal taxes and allows their products into the U.S. duty-free. Pharmaceutical companies in particular have set up highly visible plants in Puerto Rico, and ELA supporters have claimed that the island's economy depends on the tax exemptions. Rosello argues that the number of Section 936 jobs, estimated at about 130,000, has remained static, and that Puerto Rico gained rather than lost jobs after Congress passed a partial phaseout in 1993. And it can be argued that growing an economy through manufacturing is the wave of the past, and that with greater political stability in the Caribbean, other countries can vastly underprice Puerto Rico; job increases here have been in tourism, services, commerce and exports. In Washington, House Republican Budget Chairman John Kasich attacked 936 as $3 billion of corporate welfare, and in September 1995 Ways and Means Chairman Bill Archer decided to get rid of it. That was done in August 1996 in the minimum wage bill: no new businesses can qualify for 936, and it will be phased out for current businesses by 2006. The move was supported by Rosello and by New Progressive Resident Commissioner Carlos Romero Barcelo, who declared, "The Archer legislation guts the commonwealth." Rosello predicted that the higher minimum wage would help Puerto Ricans and the 936 phaseout wouldn't hurt.

Their views prevailed in the 1996 election, in which status and the phaseout of 936 were the chief issues. Rosello, opposed by Popular Democrat San Juan Mayor Hector Luis Acevedo, won 51%–44%, a slight improvement on his 50%–46% victory in 1992. Rosello was also helped by his "mano dura" stand against crime; he has fought the drug trade by sending National Guard troops into 76 housing projects, arresting drug dealers, then putting fences around them enabling police to control who enters and leaves. He made English Puerto Rico's second official language again (as it was during the first half of the century) and took steps to increase teaching in English in schools by September 1997. Romero was opposed by Celeste Benitez, who in 1995 took over control of the local Democratic Party apparatus and Democratic National Convention delegation (many New Progressives used to affiliate with the national Republicans, but none do now). She criticized him harshly for allowing 936 to be phased out, but he won 50%–46%. The New Progressives also maintained control of the legislatures and most municipios, though Popular Democrat Sila Calderon was elected mayor of San Juan.

It is commonly expected that another plebiscite on status will be held in 1998. Previous plebiscites have been conducted on terms framed by the Puerto Rico legislature, but there is a move in Congress to define the terms, since a vote for statehood would send a very hot potato to Capitol Hill. Previous Republican Presidents Gerald Ford and George Bush, moved by their New Progressive Party supporters, promised they would support statehood if Puerto Ricans voted for it; but today's congressional Republicans (and many if not most Democrats) would not vote for statehood on terms most voters in Puerto Rico seem to expect. House Resources Chairman Don Young sponsored a bill in the 104th Congress that would have set the terms of the plebiscite and, if statehood won, would have required the U.S. president, if statehood won, to draw up a 10-year transition plan which would have to be approved by Puerto Rico's voters before statehood would be granted. The bill was dropped in September 1996 after an amendment was passed requiring Puerto Rico schools to teach in English; but an effort will probably be made again in the 105th Congress.

Governor Pedro Rosello is the son of a psychiatrist, educated at Notre Dame and Yale Medical School, trained at Harvard and Boston teaching hospitals; he returned to Puerto Rico in 1976, specialized in surgery and wrote scholarly articles, played championship tennis. In 1988 he ran for resident commissioner and lost 49%–47%; in 1992 he ran for governor against Senator Victoria "Melo" Munoz, the daughter of Luis Munoz Marin, and won 50%–46%. Puerto Rico's straight ticket voting swept his party to large majorities in both the Senate and House. Rosello wants to free Puerto Rico from its old-style Latin American-style centralized bureaucratic regulations which, though often unenforced nonetheless choke off small business growth. He sees this as the way to free Puerto Rico from its persistently high unemployment rate and dependence on welfare programs such as food stamps, for which most Puerto Ricans are eligible. He points out that Puerto Rico's gross domestic product has been stuck for a generation at one-third the level of the mainland United States and one-half that of the lowest state, Mississippi; to raise that, he wants vibrant free enterprise, stimulated by "status-neutral" enterprise zones and a wage credit of up to 60% on federal taxes.

Carlos Romero-Barcelo, two-term governor, was elected resident commissioner in 1992, in a party-line vote; he is the only member of Congress with a four-year term. He was educated at Exeter and Yale and earned a law degree in Puerto Rico; he was elected mayor of San Juan in 1968 and 1972 and governor in 1976 and 1980; he lost to his longtime rival Rafael Hernandez Colon in 1984. He has worked to get federal funding for Puerto Rico projects: nutritional programs, Medicaid, Tren Urbano, drug-fighting projects, El Portal de El Yunque tropical research center at the Caribbean National Forest.

Puerto Rico does not vote for president in November, but it does choose delegates to the parties' national conventions. It elects only a few Republicans, but its Democratic delegation is larger than that of 25 other states and, since it is usually made up of backers of a single leader, it casts a bigger margin for its candidate than all but a few large states.

Del. Carlos A. Romero-Barcelo (D)

Elected 1992; b. Sept. 4, 1932, San Juan; home, San Juan; Yale U., B.A. 1951, U. of PR Law Schl., LL.B. 1956; Catholic; married (Kathleen).

Career: Practicing atty., 1956–68, 1985–92; San Juan Mayor, 1968–76; PR Gov., 1976–84; Pres., New Progressive Party, 1989–91.

DC Office: 2443 RHOB 20515, 202-225-2615; Fax: 202-225-2154.
District Offices: Ponce, 809-841-3300; San Juan, 809-723-6333.

Committees: *Education & The Workforce* (12th of 20 D): Postsecondary Education, Training & Life-Long Learning. *Resources* (13th of 23 D): Energy & Mineral Resources (RMM); National Parks & Public Lands.

VIRGIN ISLANDS

The United States' other insular territory in the Caribbean is the Virgin Islands, a very different sort of place than Puerto Rico. It is much smaller, with a resident population of only 101,000, mainly on the three islands of St. Thomas, St. John and St. Croix; 50 acres of the federal government's Water Island officially became part of the Virgin Islands in December 1996.

Puerto Rico is multiracial and not self-conscious about it; most Virgin Islanders are black, with a clear divide between the races much resented by the blacks. While Puerto Rico has attracted all kinds of light industry, the Virgin Islands live off tourism and refineries, industries that have produced higher income levels for its few citizens but have not provided the basis for a mature economy. Tourism can be tenuous: Hurricanes Luis and Marilyn in September 1995 caused terrible damage and the shooting of three tourists in January 1996 has attracted unwanted negative publicity.

The Virgin Islands was the scene in 1994 of a minor political revolution, the replacement by Independents of two longtime Democratic officeholders—Governor Alexander Farrelly, first elected in 1986, and Congressional Delegate Ron de Lugo, first elected in 1968 and in office since except for one two-year interval. The new governor is Roy Schneider, an oncologist, a Virgin Island native who worked at Howard Medical School and Sloan-Kettering Institute, then came back to be Governor Cyril King's health director in 1977. In 1994 Farrelly stepped down, and Schneider ran against his protege Lieutenant Governor Derek Hodge. He called for smaller government and getting tough on drugs; he was accused of accepting money to testify that smoking does not cause cancer, but was elected anyhow. In office Schneider said the deficit was far worse than he thought, and called for spending cuts, a war against drugs and an enterprise zone in St. Croix. He called for reducing the Virgin Islands' dependence on ad hoc appropriations from Congress, given its desire for spending cuts, and to rely instead on local revenues.

The delegate from the Virgin Islands is Donna Christian-Green, a Democrat elected in 1996, when she beat Victor Frazer, an Independent and the upset winner in 1994. Christian-Green is from an old St. Croix family; her father was Virgin Islands Chief District Court Judge Almeric Christian. She graduated from St. Mary's College and George Washington Medical School; she practiced medicine for more than 20 years in the Virgin Islands, in a family practice and in several public positions. She was elected Democratic National Committeewoman in 1984 and ran one losing race for delegate in 1994. In 1996 she attacked Frazer, who after some hesitation caucused with the Democrats, for foreign travel (11 trips to four continents), and for inaction in opposing the welfare reform bill. Frazer, who spent far less money, said, "What they don't realize is, these things are not possible," in reference to Christian-Green's promise that she would get the floor vote back for delegates. Christian-Green led Frazer 38%–34% on November 5; in the runoff two weeks later she won 52%–48%. It was a regional race: Christian-Green won 69% on St. Croix, Frazer 64% on St. Thomas and St. John.

Del. Donna M. Christian-Green (D)

Elected 1996; b. Sept. 19, 1945, Teaneck, NJ; home, St. Croix; St. Mary's Col., B.S. 1966; George Washington U., M.D. 1970; Moravian; single.

Career: Practicing physician, 1975–97; Territorial Asst., Commissioner of Health, 1988–94; Acting Commissioner of Health, 1994–95.

DC Office: 1711 LHOB 20515, 202-225-1790; Fax: 202-225-5517.

District Offices: St. Croix, 809-778-5900; St. Thomas, 809-774-4408.

Committees: *Resources* (21st of 23 D): Energy & Mineral Resources; National Parks & Public Lands.

GUAM

Some 3,700 miles west of Hawaii, 19 hours of flying time to Washington, D.C., is Guam, the place where, as viewers of political conventions over the years have been informed, America's day begins. Guam lies just west of the International Date Line, and it is indeed the early hours of Tuesday there when the rest of us are just trying to get through Monday afternoon. Geographically in the center of the Mariana Islands, Guam is legally separate: the Northern Marianas were administered by the U.S. as a trust territory until they became a commonwealth in 1978. Guam was ruled by a Navy captain from 1898 to 1950, except for years of Japanese occupation during World War II; in 1950 the Organic Act made Guamanians U.S. citizens and allowed them to elect a local government, but Congress still retained final power over the territory; it started electing a delegate to Congress in 1972. Guam is 30 miles long by five miles wide, with 150,000 people; in 1990, 47% were Chamorro, descendants of the original islanders, 25% Filipino, 18% other Asian and 10% Caucasian; almost everyone is Catholic. There are about 20,000 U.S. military personnel here and some 6,000 refugees, mostly Kurds from Iraq. In 1990 Guam passed a law banning almost all abortions, which was overturned by a federal court in April 1992, as clearly contrary to *Roe v. Wade*; in November 1992 the Supreme Court declined to review the case, thus dodging a direct challenge to that landmark decision. Economically, Guam depended for years on American military bases; now its economy is diversifying, with tourism from Japan, although Guamanians cautioned against a Base Closing Commission decision to phase out Agana Naval Air Station.

The major issue in Guam's politics is status. In a 1982 plebiscite, Guamanians voted for commonwealth status and later in the 1980s a Commission on Self-Determination drafted a bill proposing a commonwealth with two major provisions. One is immigration control. Chamorros say they want to block others from coming in and becoming citizens and making them a minority. But others suspect they want to allow foreigners in as guestworkers, like those in the Commonwealth of the Northern Marianas, where they have been exploited and abused, as Henry Hurt reported in the June 1997 *Reader's Digest*; Guamanians replied that U.S. labor laws would apply, but the Guam commonwealth act would transfer enforcement of those provisions from the federal to the Guamanian government.

The other provision is "mutual consent," which would bar Congress from changing laws and treaties that affect Guam without Guam's consent. Guamanians remembered that its just-created watch and garment industries were destroyed by congressional action in the 1970s and 1980s. The bill was endorsed by Republican Governor Joseph Ada and introduced in Congress by Guam's Delegate Robert Underwood, a Democrat first elected in 1992. The Bush Administration had rejected this as inconsistent with the Constitutional provision giving Congress full powers over territories. The Clinton Interior Department, perhaps sympathetic to native claims and perhaps alert to implied threats to U.S. military bases in Guam which have become our major forward staging point in the western Pacific with the shutdown of Clark Air Force Base and the Subic Bay Navy base in the Philippines, appointed former University of California Chancellor Michael Heyman as its negotiator. In October 1994 Heyman and Ada agreed on "mutual consent," and prepared a bill that, as Underwood pointed out, would establish a relation similar to that of New Zealand and the Cook Islands. But the election of the Republican Congress abruptly changed its prospects. The new House Territories Subcommittee chairman, Elton Gallegly of California, announced in January 1995 that he would block any mutual consent bill that seeks to bind future Congresses; in February 1995, Heyman, newly appointed head of the Smithsonian Institution, resigned his negotiating post.

It did not soothe feelings when in November 1994 Clinton top advisers Anthony Lake and Robert Rubin laughed out loud (they later apologized) when they heard a suggestion that Guam take part in the APEC summit. But when seeking reelection funds, Clintonites were much more sympathetic. In August Democratic national chairman Donald Fowler wrote to Guam Governor

Carl Gutierrez requesting $250,000 in donations. Fifteen days later Hillary Rodham Clinton stopped in Guam on her way to the UN women's conference in Beijing and attended a buffet hosted by Gutierrez. Three weeks later Guamanians arrived in Washington with more than $250,000 in contributions for Clinton and other Democrats; within six months Guamanians had given the Clinton-Gore campaign and the Democratic National Committee $892,000—the largest amount per capita anywhere under the U.S. flag. In December 1996, Deputy Interior Secretary John Garamendi, in charge of Guam policy, circulated a report supporting key provisions of the Guam commonwealth bill, including giving Guam a right to take over lands relinquished by the military. Whether congressional Republicans—or Democrats—will move in the same direction is unclear.

The governor of Guam is Carl Gutierrez, a Democrat elected in 1994. He went to high school in California, served in the Air Force, then set up the first data processing center in Guam and started a construction business; he was elected to the Guam Senate for all but four years starting in 1972. He campaigned for commonwealth status, for return of federal lands to Guam and for exemption from the Jones Act requirement that goods from the U.S. be shipped in U.S.-registered ships; only two lines serve Guam, and Gutierrez wants foreign competition. After the election he attacked, Republican-style, the high-handedness of federal bureaucrats: "Guam has to survive with minor federal luminaries who operate with no apparent adult supervision," he said, and complained that the Fish and Wildlife Service seized 20% of Guam's land for a wildlife refuge. And when California Republican Dana Rohrabacher called Guam and other territories "economic basket cases" that are "backward and economically depressed," Gutierrez attacked "this ignorance and lack of sensitivity which run counter to our country's democratic traditions and which ensures the continuation of our status as second-class citizens in the American family."

Delegate Robert Underwood was also educated in California. He started teaching at the University of Guam in 1976 and was known for his efforts promoting and preserving Chamorro culture. By 1990 he had become the university's academic vice president, and he ran against Republican Delegate Ben Blaz, a former Marine general. Personal connections are often more important than party in Guam, and Underwood explained his victory thus: "I have a lot of relatives. His grandfather and my great-grandfather are first cousins. So I cut into his action when I ran—more of the relatives are closer to me." He was reelected in 1994 and 1996 without opposition; evidently no one has more relatives. In January 1994 he pushed through the House a bill transferring 3,200 acres from federal to GovGuam control; he called for a land summit, not the Interior Department, to parcel out the territory. He has made some progress in getting reparations for Guamanians harmed by Japanese during their occupation in World War II.

In 1995 Underwood bucked efforts to lower his seniority on the National Security and Resources Committees, and questioned whether Republicans who wanted to devolve power to the states wanted to devolve it to territories as well. He cheered with Republicans when the head of Interior's OTIA, unpopular in Guam, announced her agency would be terminated by September 1995. He seeks help in eradicating the brown tree snake, which has ravaged indigenous species and has no predators; he wants the Endangered Species Act amended to allow Guamanians to bring in predators, and he criticized a $1.6 million appropriation in 1996 for eradication programs because he said the designated funds, which come from the Department of Interior's Office of Insular Affairs, will mean less money available for other territorial programs. "The way it's been handled, it sounds like we need St. Patrick more than $1.6 million." Underwood has also shown a keen sense of humor; to Toby Roth's bill declaring English our official language, Underwood responded with a "ketchup-only" proposal to name ketchup the national condiment. But he can also show indignation: he denounced France for nuclear tests in the Pacific, boycotting Jacques Chirac's speech in the Capitol in 1996.

Del. Robert A. Underwood (D)

Elected 1992; b. July 13, 1948, Tamuning; home, Yona; CA St. U., B.A. 1969, M.A. 1971, U. of S. CA, Ed.D. 1988; Catholic; married (Lorraine Aguilar).

Career: Teacher, Admin., Guam Public Schls., 1972–76; Prof., U. of Guam, 1976–88, Dean, 1988–90, Academic Vice Pres., 1990–92.

DC Office: 424 CHOB 20515, 202-225-1188; Fax: 202-226-0341; e-mail: guamtodc@hr.house.gov.

District Offices: Agana, 671-477-4272.

Committees: *National Security* (11th of 25 D): Military Installations & Facilities; Military Personnel; Military Readiness. *Resources* (15th of 23 D): National Parks & Public Lands.

AMERICAN SAMOA

American Samoa, the only American territory south of the Equator, has been little influenced by western settlers and remains almost as Polynesian as it was when the United States took possession in 1900. American Samoa has 53,000 people, 89% of them Polynesian, mostly Christian (50% Congregationalist, 20% Catholic); it is an unincorporated territory administered by the Interior Department. Its islands of Ofu, Tau and Tutuila are the site of our 50th national park, the National Park of American Samoa, opened in April 1997, preserving the fruit bat habitat, tropical forest and coral reefs. The governor is Tauese Sunia, elected in 1996, the son of Congregationalist ministers; Sunia taught high school in Nebraska and American Samoa and was the first Samoan television teacher. He headed the local department of education and the bar association and is the father of 10 children. He was elected lieutenant governor in 1992, serving with then-Governor A. P. Lutali, then was elected in his own right as a Democrat; Lutali finished third in the first election and in the runoff Sunia won by a 51%–49% margin over Lealaifuaneva Peter Reid.

American Samoa has elected a delegate to Congress since 1980. The current Delegate is Eni F. H. Faleomavaega, a Democrat first elected in 1988; he won reelection in 1994 with 63% of the vote. He went to high school in Hawaii, to Brigham Young University, then to law school in Houston and Berkeley; he served in Vietnam in the Army. In the 1970s he worked on the Insular subcommittee staff. In 1981 he became deputy attorney general in American Samoa, in 1985 lieutenant governor. He serves on the Resources Committee where in 1995 he became ranking Democrat on the Native Americans and Insular Affairs Subcommittee—Indians and Islands, insiders called it; that subcommittee was abolished in the 105th Congress and Faleomavaega became ranking Democrat on the National Parks and Public Lands Subcommittee. He worked to improve conditions at the StarKist plant and to get BCTC to make the largest investment there since the canneries were built decades ago. He worked to warm up the frosty relations between the United States and New Zealand. He led the congressional protest against the French nuclear tests in the Pacific and boycotted President Jacques Chirac's speech on Capitol Hill; he tried to bring the issue of French nuclear waste shipments in the Pacific before the UN Security Council. He and Hawaii Senator Daniel Inouye got $2 million to repair and certify the *Ataata o Samoa*, a vessel to provide transportation for people in Manu'a.

In 1996 Faleomavaega fell just short of winning reelection on November 5, 1996, with 49.6%, to 26% for Independent Gus Hanneman and 24% for Republican Aumua Amata Coleman.

Faleomavaega won the November 19 runoff 56%–44%. American Samoa staged a Democratic presidential primary in 1988, but only 36 people actually voted. None of the candidates campaigned in person.

Del. Eni F. H. Faleomavaega (D)

Elected 1988; b. Aug. 15, 1943, Vailoatai; home, Pago Pago; Brigham Young U., B.A. 1972, U. of CA, LL.M. 1973; Mormon; married (Hinanui).

Career: Army, 1966–69 (Vietnam); A.A., U.S. Del. from AS, 1973–75; Cnsl., U.S. House Interior Cmte., 1975–81; AS Dep. Atty. Gen., 1981–84; AS Lt. Gov., 1984–89.

DC Office: 2422 RHOB 20515, 202-225-8577; Fax: 202-225-8757.

District Offices: Pago Pago, 684-633-1372.

Committees: *International Relations* (6th of 22 D): Asia & the Pacific; International Operations & Human Rights. *Resources* (7th of 23 D): Forests & Forest Health; National Parks & Public Lands (RMM).

GUBERNATORIAL ELECTION CYCLE

1997, 2 States

New Jersey (R)
Virginia (R)

1998, 36 States

Alabama (R)
Alaska (D)
Arizona (R)
Arkansas (D)
California (R)
Colorado (D)
Connecticut (R)
Florida (D)
Georgia (D)
Hawaii (D)
Idaho (R)
Illinois (R)
Iowa (R)
Kansas (R)
Maine (I)
Maryland (D)
Massachusetts (R)
Michigan (R)
Minnesota (R)
Nebraska (D)
Nevada (D)
New Hampshire (D)
New Mexico (R)
New York (R)
Ohio (R)
Oklahoma (R)
Oregon (D)
Pennsylvania (R)
Rhode Island (R)
South Carolina (R)
South Dakota (R)
Tennessee (R)
Texas (R)
Vermont (D)
Wisconsin (R)
Wyoming (R)

1999, 3 States

Kentucky (D)
Louisiana (R)
Mississippi (R)

2000, 11 States

Delaware (D)
Indiana (D)
Missouri (D)
Montana (R)
New Hampshire
North Carolina (D)
North Dakota (R)
Utah (R)
Vermont
Washington (D)
West Virginia (R)

32 Republicans, 17 Democrats, 1 Independent

New Hampshire and Vermont have two year terms. All others are four year.
Boldface indicates governors who may not suceed themselves in the election that year.

SENATE SEATS

1998 ELECTION CYCLE

Republicans (16)

Robert F. Bennett (UT)
Christopher S. (Kit) Bond (MO)
Sam Brownback (KS)
Ben Nighthorse Campbell (CO)
Daniel R. Coats (IN)*
Paul Coverdell (GA)
Alfonse M. D'Amato (NY)
Lauch Faircloth (NC)
Charles E. Grassley (IA)
Judd Gregg (NH)
Dirk Kempthorne (ID)
John McCain (AZ)
Frank H. Murkowski (AK)
Don Nickles (OK)
Richard C. Shelby (AL)
Arlen Specter (PA)

Democrats (18)

Barbara Boxer (CA)
John B. Breaux (LA)
Dale Bumpers (AR)
Thomas A. Daschle (SD)
Christopher J. Dodd (CT)
Byron L. Dorgan (ND)
Russell D. Feingold (WI)
Wendell H. Ford (KY)*
John H. Glenn Jr. (OH)*
Bob Graham (FL)
Ernest F. (Fritz) Hollings (SC)
Daniel K. Inouye (HI)
Patrick J. Leahy (VT)
Barbara A. Mikulski (MD)
Carol Moseley-Braun (IL)
Patty Murray (WA)
Harry Reid (NV)
Ron Wyden (OR)

**will not seek reelection in 1998*

2000 ELECTION CYCLE

Republicans (19)

Spencer Abraham (MI)
John D. Ashcroft (MO)
Conrad Burns (MT)
John H. Chafee (RI)
Mike DeWine (OH)
William H. Frist (TN)
Slade Gorton (WA)
Rod Grams (MN)
Orrin G. Hatch (UT)
Kay Bailey Hutchison (TX)
James M. Jeffords (VT)
Jon Kyl (AZ)
Trent Lott (MS)
Richard G. Lugar (IN)
Connie Mack III (FL)
William V. Roth Jr. (DE)
Rick Santorum (PA)
Olympia J. Snowe (ME)
Craig Thomas (WY)

Democrats (14)

Daniel K. Akaka (HI)
Jeff Bingaman (NM)
Richard H. Bryan (NV)
Robert C. Byrd (WV)
Kent Conrad (ND)
Dianne Feinstein (CA)
Edward M. Kennedy (MA)
Robert Kerrey (NE)
Herb Kohl (WI)
Frank R. Lautenberg (NJ)
Joseph I. Lieberman (CT)
Daniel Patrick Moynihan (NY)
Charles S. Robb (VA)
Paul S. Sarbanes (MD)

CONGRESSIONAL LEADERSHIP

U.S. SENATE

Republicans

Majority Leader	Trent Lott (MS)
Majority Whip	Don Nickles (OK)
President Pro-Tempore	Strom Thurmond (SC)
Republican Conference Chairman	Connie Mack III (FL)
Republican Conference Secretary	Paul Coverdell (GA)
Republican Policy Committee Chairman	Larry Craig (ID)
NRSC Chairman	Mitch McConnell (KY)

Democrats

Minority Leader	Thomas A. Daschle (SD)
Minority Whip	Wendell H. Ford (KY)
Democratic Policy Committee Chairman	Thomas A. Daschle (SD)
DSCC Chairman	Robert Kerrey (NE)
DSCC Vice Chairman	Robert G. Torricelli (NJ)

U.S. HOUSE OF REPRESENTATIVES

Republicans

Speaker of the House	Newt Gingrich (GA-6)
Majority Leader	Richard K. (Dick) Armey (TX-26)
Majority Whip	Tom DeLay (TX-22)
Chief Deputy Majority Whip	J. Dennis Hastert (IL-14)
Republican Conference Chairman	John A. Boehner (OH-8)
Republican Conference Vice Chairman	Susan Molinari (NY-13)*
Republican Conference Secretary	Jennifer B. Dunn (WA-8)
Republican Policy Committee Chairman	Christopher Cox (CA-47)
NRCC Chairman	John Linder (GA-11)

Democrats

Minority Leader	Richard A. Gephardt (MO-3)
Minority Whip	David E. Bonior (MI-10)
Chief Deputy Minority Whip	Rosa L. DeLauro (CT-3)
Chief Deputy Minority Whip	Chet Edwards (TX-11)
Chief Deputy Minority Whip	John Lewis (GA-5)
Chief Deputy Minority Whip	Robert Menendez (NJ-13)
Democratic Caucus Chairman	Vic Fazio (CA-3)
Democratic Caucus Vice Chairman	Barbara B. Kennelly (CT-1)
Democratic Policy Committee Chairman	Richard A. Gephardt (MO-3)
DCCC Chairman	Martin Frost (TX-24)

**Retiring August 1997.*

COMMITTEE CHAIRMEN

COMMITTEE CHAIRMEN

Senate Committees	Chairman	Ranking Member
Aging (Special)	Charles E. Grassley (IA)	John B. Breaux (LA)
Agriculture, Nutrition & Forestry	Richard G. Lugar (IN)	Tom Harkin (IA)
Appropriations	Ted Stevens (AK)	Robert C. Byrd (WV)
Armed Services	Strom Thurmond (SC)	Carl Levin (MI)
Banking, Housing & Urban Affairs	Alfonse M. D'Amato (NY)	Paul S. Sarbanes (MD)
Budget	Pete V. Domenici (NM)	Frank R. Lautenberg (NJ)
Commerce, Science & Transportation	John McCain (AZ)	Ernest F. (Fritz) Hollings (SC)
Energy & Natural Resources	Frank H. Murkowski (AK)	Dale Bumpers (AR)
Environment & Public Works	John H. Chafee (R)	Max Baucus (MT)
Ethics (Select)	Bob Smith (NH)	Harry Reid (NV)
Finance	William V. Roth Jr. (DE)	Daniel Patrick Moynihan (NY)
Foreign Relations	Jesse A. Helms (NC)	Joseph R. Biden Jr. (DE)
Governmental Affairs	Fred Thompson (TN)	John H. Glenn Jr. (OH)
Indian Affairs	Ben Nighthorse Campbell (CO)	Daniel K. Inouye (HI)
Intelligence (Select)	Richard C. Shelby (AL)	Robert Kerrey (NE)
Judiciary	Orrin G. Hatch (UT)	Patrick J. Leahy (VT)
Labor & Human Resources	James M. Jeffords (VT)	Edward M. Kennedy (MA)
Rules & Administration	John W. Warner (VA)	Wendell H. Ford (KY)
Small Business	Christopher S. (Kit) Bond (MO)	John F. Kerry (MA)
Veterans' Affairs	Arlen Specter (PA)	John D. (Jay) Rockefeller IV (WV)

House Committees	Chairman	Ranking Member
Agriculture	Robert F. (Bob) Smith (OR-2)	Charles W. Stenholm (TX-17)
Appropriations	Robert L. (Bob) Livingston (LA-1)	David R. Obey (WI-7)
Banking & Financial Services	James A. Leach (IA-1)	Henry B. Gonzalez (TX-20)
Budget	John R. Kasich (OH-12)	John M. Spratt (SC-5)
Commerce	Tom Bliley (VA-7)	John D. Dingell (MI-16)
Education & The Workforce	Bill Goodling (PA-19)	William (Bill) Clay (MO-1)
Government Reform & Oversight	Dan Burton (IN-6)	Henry A. Waxman (CA-29)
House Oversight	William M. Thomas (CA-21)	Samuel Gejdenson (CT-2)
Intelligence (Select)	Porter Johnston Goss (FL-14)	Norm Dicks (WA-6)
International Relations	Benjamin A. Gilman (NY-20)	Lee H. Hamilton (IN-9)
Judiciary	Henry J. Hyde (IL-6)	John Conyers Jr. (MI-14)
National Security	Floyd D. Spence (SC-2)	Ronald V. Dellums (CA-9)
Resources	Don Young (AK-AL)	George Miller (CA-7)
Rules	Gerald B.H. Solomon (NY-22)	John Joseph (Joe) Moakley (MA-9)
Science	F. James Sensenbrenner Jr. (WI-9)	George E. Brown Jr. (CA-42)
Small Business	James M. Talent (MO-2)	John J. LaFalce (NY-29)
Standards of Official Conduct	James V. Hansen (UT-1)	Howard L. Berman (CA-26)
Transportation & Infrastructure	E.G. (Bud) Shuster (PA-9)	James L. Oberstar (MN-8)
Veterans' Affairs	Bob Stump (AZ-3)	Lane Evans (IL-17)
Ways & Means	Bill Archer (TX-7)	Charles B. Rangel (NY-15)

SENATE COMMITTEES

AGING (Special) **G-31 Dirksen**
http://www.senate.gov/committee/aging.html **202-224-5364**

Majority (10 R): Grassley (IA), Chmn.; Jeffords (VT), Craig (ID), Burns (MT), Shelby (AL), Santorum (PA), Warner (VA), Hagel (NE), Collins (ME), Enzi (WY).
Minority (8 D): Breaux (LA), RMM; Glenn (OH), Reid (NV), Kohl (WI), Feingold (WI), Moseley-Braun (IL), Wyden (OR), Reed (RI).

NO SUBCOMMITTEES

AGRICULTURE, NUTRITION & FORESTRY **328-A Russell**
http://www.senate.gov/committee/agriculture.html **202-224-2035**

Majority (10 R): Lugar (IN), Chmn.; Helms (NC), Cochran (MS), McConnell (KY), Coverdell (GA), Santorum (PA), Roberts (KS), Grassley (IA), Gramm (TX), Craig (ID).
Minority (8 D): Harkin (IA), RMM; Leahy (VT), Conrad (ND), Daschle (SD), Baucus (MT), Kerrey (NE), Landrieu (LA), Johnson (SD).

SUBCOMMITTEES

FORESTRY, CONSERVATION & RURAL REVITALIZATION
Majority (5 R): Santorum, Chmn.; Grassley, Coverdell, Roberts, Craig.
Minority (4 D): Conrad, RMM; Leahy, Daschle, Baucus.

MARKETING, INSPECTION & PRODUCT PROMOTION.
Majority (4 R): Coverdell, Chmn.; Helms, Cochran, McConnell.
Minority (3 D): Baucus, RMM; Kerrey, Landrieu.

PRODUCTION & PRICE COMPETITIVENESS
Majority (5 R): Roberts, Chmn.; Cochran, Helms, Grassley, Gramm.
Minority (4 D): Kerrey, RMM; Daschle, Johnson, Landrieu.

RESEARCH, NUTRITION & GENERAL LEGISLATION
Majority (4 R): McConnell, Chmn.; Gramm, Craig, Santorum.
Minority (3 D): Leahy, RMM; Conrad, Johnson.

APPROPRIATIONS **S-128 The Capitol**
http://www.senate.gov/committee/appropriations.html **202-224-3471**

Majority (15 R): Stevens (AK), Chmn.; Cochran (MS), Specter (PA), Domenici (NM), Bond (MO), Gorton (WA), McConnell (KY), Burns (MT), Shelby (AL), Gregg (NH), Bennett (UT), Campbell (CO), Craig (ID), Faircloth (NC), Hutchison (TX).
Minority (13 D): Byrd (WV), RMM; Inouye (HI), Hollings (SC), Leahy (VT), Bumpers (AR), Lautenberg (NJ), Harkin (IA), Mikulski (MD), Reid (NV), Kohl (WI), Murray (WA), Dorgan (ND), Boxer (CA).

SUBCOMMITTEES

AGRICULTURE, RURAL DEVELOPMENT & RELATED AGENCIES

Majority (6 R): Cochran, Chmn.; Specter, Bond, Gorton, McConnell, Burns.
Minority (5 D): Bumpers, RMM; Harkin, Kohl, Byrd, Leahy.

COMMERCE, JUSTICE, STATE & THE JUDICIARY

Majority (6 R): Gregg, Chmn.; Stevens, Domenici, McConnell, Hutchison, Campbell.
Minority (5 D): Hollings, RMM; Inouye, Bumpers, Lautenberg, Mikulski.

DEFENSE

Majority (9 R): Stevens, Chmn.; Cochran, Specter, Domenici, Bond, McConnell, Shelby, Gregg, Hutchison.
Minority (8 D): Inouye, RMM; Hollings, Byrd, Leahy, Bumpers, Lautenberg, Harkin, Dorgan.

DISTRICT OF COLUMBIA

Majority (2 R): Faircloth, Chmn.; Hutchison.
Minority (1 D): Boxer, RMM.

ENERGY & WATER DEVELOPMENT

Majority (7 R): Domenici, Chmn.; Cochran, Gorton, McConnell, Bennett, Burns, Craig.
Minority (6 D): Reid, RMM; Byrd, Hollings, Murray, Kohl, Dorgan.

FOREIGN OPERATIONS

Majority (7 R): McConnell, Chmn.; Specter, Gregg, Shelby, Bennett, Campbell, Stevens.
Minority (6 D): Leahy, RMM; Inouye, Lautenberg, Harkin, Mikulski, Murray.

INTERIOR

Majority (8 R): Gorton, Chmn.; Stevens, Cochran, Domenici, Burns, Bennett, Gregg, Campbell.
Minority (7 D): Byrd, RMM; Leahy, Bumpers, Hollings, Reid, Dorgan, Boxer.

LABOR, HEALTH & HUMAN SERVICES, & EDUCATION

Majority (8 R): Specter, Chmn.; Cochran, Gorton, Bond, Gregg, Faircloth, Craig, Hutchison.
Minority (7 D): Harkin, RMM; Hollings, Inouye, Bumpers, Reid, Kohl, Murray.

LEGISLATIVE BRANCH

Majority (3 R): Bennett, Chmn.; Stevens, Craig.
Minority (2 D): Dorgan (RMM), Boxer.

MILITARY CONSTRUCTION

Majority (4 R): Burns, Chmn.; Hutchison, Faircloth, Craig.
Minority (3 D): Murray, RMM; Reid, Inouye.

TRANSPORTATION

Majority (7 R): Shelby, Chmn.; Domenici, Specter, Bond, Gorton, Bennett, Faircloth.
Minority (6 D): Lautenberg, RMM; Byrd, Mikulski, Reid, Kohl, Murray.

TREASURY, POSTAL SERVICE & GENERAL GOVERNMENT

Majority (3 R): Campbell, Chmn; Shelby, Faircloth.
Minority (2 D): Kohl, RMM; Mikulski.

VA, HUD & INDEPENDENT AGENCIES

Majority (6 R): Bond, Chmn.; Burns, Stevens, Shelby, Campbell, Craig.
Minority (5 D): Mikulski, RMM; Leahy, Lautenberg, Harkin, Boxer.

ARMED SERVICES — 228 Russell

http://www.senate.gov/committee/armed_services.html — 202-224-3871

Majority (10 R): Thurmond (SC), Chmn.; Warner (VA), McCain (AZ), Coats (IN), Smith (NH), Kempthorne (ID), Inhofe (OK), Santorum (PA), Snowe (ME), Roberts (KS).
Minority (8 D): Levin (MI), RMM; Kennedy (MA), Bingaman (NM), Glenn (OH), Byrd (WV), Robb (VA), Lieberman (CT), Cleland (GA).

SUBCOMMITTEES

ACQUISITION & TECHNOLOGY
Majority (4 R): Santorum, Chmn.; Smith, Snowe, Roberts.
Minority (3 D): Lieberman, RMM; Kennedy, Bingaman.

AIRLAND FORCES
Majority (6 R): Coats, Chmn.; Warner, Kempthorne, Inhofe, Santorum, Roberts.
Minority (5 D): Glenn, RMM; Bingaman, Byrd, Lieberman, Cleland.

PERSONNEL
Majority (4 R): Kempthorne, Chmn; McCain, Coats, Snowe.
Minority (3 D): Cleland, RMM; Kennedy, Robb.

READINESS
Majority (4 R): Inhofe, Chmn.; McCain, Coats, Roberts.
Minority (3 D): Robb, RMM; Glenn, Cleland.

SEA POWER
Majority (5 R): Warner, Chmn; McCain, Smith, Santorum, Snowe.
Minority (4 D): Kennedy, RMM; Byrd, Robb, Lieberman.

STRATEGIC FORCES
Majority (4 R): Smith, Chmn.; Warner, Kempthorne, Inhofe.
Minority (3 D): Bingaman, RMM; Glenn, Byrd.

BANKING, HOUSING & URBAN AFFAIRS — 534 Dirksen

http://www.senate.gov/committee/banking.html — 202-224-7391

Majority (10 R): D'Amato (NY), Chmn.; Gramm (TX), Shelby (AL), Mack (FL), Faircloth (NC), Bennett (UT), Grams (MN), Allard (CO), Enzi (WY), Hagel (NE).
Minority (8 D): Sarbanes (MD), RMM; Dodd (CT), Kerry (MA), Bryan (NV), Boxer (CA), Moseley-Braun (IL), Johnson (SD), Reed (RI).

SUBCOMMITTEES

FINANCIAL INSTITUTIONS & REGULATORY RELIEF
Majority (7 R): Faircloth, Chmn; Allard, Enzi, Shelby, Mack, Grams, Gramm.
Minority (5 D): Bryan, RMM; Johnson, Boxer, Moseley-Braun, Reed.

FINANCIAL SERVICES & TECHNOLOGY
Majority (5 R): Bennett, Chmn.; Hagel, Mack, Grams, Enzi.
Minority (4 D): Boxer, RMM; Kerry, Dodd, Johnson.

HOUSING OPPORTUNITY & COMMUNITY DEVELOPMENT
Majority (6 R): Mack, Chmn.; Faircloth, Enzi, Shelby, Allard, Hagel.
Minority (5 D): Kerry, RMM; Reed, Dodd, Bryan, Moseley-Braun.

INTERNATIONAL FINANCE

Majority (4 R): Grams, Chmn; Hagel, Gramm, Bennett.

Minority (3 D): Moseley-Braun, RMM; Boxer, Reed.

SECURITIES

Majority (5 R): Gramm, Chmn.; Shelby, Allard, Bennett, Faircloth.

Minority (4 D): Dodd, RMM; Johnson, Kerry, Bryan.

BUDGET — 621 Dirksen

http://www.senate.gov/committee.budget.html — 202-224-0642

Majority (12 R): Domenici (NM), Chmn.; Grassley (IA), Nickles (OK), Gramm (TX), Bond (MO), Gorton (WA), Gregg (NH), Snowe (ME), Abraham (MI), Frist (TN), Grams (MN), Smith (OR).

Minority (10 D): Lautenberg (NJ), RMM; Hollings (SC), Conrad (ND), Sarbanes (MD), Boxer (CA), Murray (WA), Wyden (OR), Feingold (WI), Johnson (SD), Durbin (IL).

NO SUBCOMMITTEES

COMMERCE, SCIENCE & TRANSPORTATION — 508 Dirksen

http://www.senate.gov/committee/commerce.html — 202-224-5115

Majority (11 R): McCain (AZ) Chmn.; Stevens (AK), Burns (MT), Gorton (WA), Lott (MS), Hutchison (TX), Snowe (ME), Ashcroft (MO), Frist (TN), Abraham (MI), Brownback (KS).

Minority (9 D): Hollings (SC), RMM; Inouye (HI), Ford (KY), Rockefeller (WV), Kerry (MA), Breaux (LA), Bryan (NV), Dorgan (ND), Wyden (OR).

SUBCOMMITTEES

AVIATION

Majority (9 R): Gorton, Chmn.; Stevens, Burns, Lott, Hutchison, Ashcroft, Frist, Snowe, Brownback.

Minority (8 D): Ford, RMM; Hollings, Inouye, Bryan, Rockefeller, Breaux, Dorgan, Wyden.

COMMUNICATIONS

Majority (9 R): Burns, Chmn.; Stevens, Gorton, Lott, Ashcroft, Hutchison, Abraham, Frist, Brownback.

Minority (8 D): Hollings, RMM; Inouye, Ford, Kerry, Breaux, Rockefeller, Dorgan, Wyden.

CONSUMER AFFAIRS, FOREIGN COMMERCE & TOURISM

Majority (5 R): Ashcroft, Chmn.; Gorton, Abraham, Burns, Brownback.

Minority (3 D): Breaux, RMM; Ford, Bryan.

MANUFACTURING & COMPETITIVENESS

Majority (5 R): Abraham, Chmn.; Snowe, Ashcroft, Frist, Brownback.

Minority (4 D): Bryan, RMM; Hollings, Dorgan, Rockefeller.

OCEANS & FISHERIES

Majority (4 R): Snowe, Chmn.; Stevens, Gorton, Hutchison.

Minority (3 D): Kerry, RMM; Inouye, Breaux.

SCIENCE, TECHNOLOGY & SPACE

Majority (5 R): Frist, Chmn.; Burns, Hutchison, Stevens, Abraham.

Minority (4 D): Rockefeller, RMM; Kerry, Bryan, Dorgan.

SURFACE TRANSPORTATION & MERCHANT MARINE

Majority (7 R): Hutchison, Chmn.; Stevens, Burns, Snowe, Frist, Abraham, Ashcroft.

Minority (5 D): Inouye, RMM; Breaux, Dorgan, Bryan, Wyden.

ENERGY & NATURAL RESOURCES — 304 Dirksen
http://www.senate.gov/committee/energy.html — 202-224-4971

Majority (11 R): Murkowski (AK), Chmn.; Domenici (NM), Nickles (OK), Craig (ID), Campbell (CO), Thomas (WY), Kyl (AZ), Grams (MN), Smith (OR), Gorton (WA), Burns (MT).

Minority (9 D): Bumpers (AR), RMM; Ford (KY), Bingaman (NM), Akaka (HI), Dorgan (ND), Graham (FL), Wyden (OR), Johnson (SD), Landrieu (LA).

SUBCOMMITTEES

ENERGY RESEARCH, DEVELOPMENT, PRODUCTION & REGULATION

Majority (7 R): Nickles, Chmn.; Domenci, Vice Chmn.; Craig, Grams, Gorton, Campbell, Smith.

Minority (6 D): Ford, RMM; Bingaman, Graham, Wyden, Johnson, Landrieu.

FORESTS & PUBLIC LAND MANAGEMENT

Majority (6 R): Craig, Chmn.; Burns, Vice Chmn.; Domenici, Thomas, Kyl, Smith.

Minority (5 D): Dorgan, RMM; Graham, Wyden, Johnson, Landrieu.

NATIONAL PARKS, HISTORIC PRESERVATION, & RECREATION

Majority (5 R): Thomas, Chmn.; Campbell, Vice Chmn.; Grams, Nickles, Burns.

Minority (4 D): Bingaman, RMM; Akaka, Graham, Landrieu.

WATER & POWER

Majority (5 R): Kyl, Chmn.; Smith, Vice Chmn.; Gorton, Campbell, Craig.

Minority (4 D): Akaka, RMM; Ford, Dorgan, Wyden.

ENVIRONMENT & PUBLIC WORKS — 410 Dirksen
http://www.senate.gov/committee/environment.html — 202-224-6176

Majority (10 R): Chafee (RI), Chmn.; Warner (VA), Smith (NH), Kempthorne (ID), Inhofe (OK), Thomas (WY), Bond (MO), Hutchinson (AR), Allard (CO), Sessions (AL).

Minority (8 D): Baucus (MT), RMM; Moynihan (NY), Lautenberg (NJ), Reid (NV), Graham (FL), Lieberman (CT), Boxer (CA), Wyden (OR).

SUBCOMMITTEES

CLEAN AIR, WETLANDS, PRIVATE PROPERTY & NUCLEAR SAFETY

Majority (4 R): Inhofe, Chmn.; Hutchinson, Allard, Sessions.

Minority (3 D): Graham, RMM; Lieberman, Boxer.

DRINKING WATER, FISHERIES & WILDLIFE

Majority (5 R): Kempthorne, Chmn.; Thomas, Bond, Warner, Hutchinson.

Minority (4 D): Reid, RMM; Lautenberg, Lieberman, Wyden.

SUPERFUND, WASTE CONTROL, & RISK ASSESSMENT

Majority (5 R): Smith, Chmn.; Warner, Inhofe, Allard, Sessions.

Minority (4 D): Lautenberg, RMM; Moynihan, Boxer, Graham.

TRANSPORTATION & INFRASTRUCTURE

Majority (6 R): Warner, Chmn.; Smith, Kempthorne, Bond, Inhofe, Thomas.

Minority (5 D): Baucus, RMM; Moynihan, Reid, Graham, Boxer.

ETHICS (Select) **220 Hart**
http://www.senate.gov/committee/ethics.html **202-224-2981**

Majority (3 R): Smith (NH), Chmn; Roberts (KS), Sessions (AL).
Minority (3 D): Reid (NV), RMM; Murray (WA), Conrad (ND).

NO SUBCOMMITTEES

FINANCE **219 Dirksen**
http://www.senate.gov/committee/finance.html **202-224-4515**

Majority (11 R): Roth (DE), Chmn.; Chafee (RI), Grassley (IA), Hatch (UT), D'Amato (NY), Murkowski (AK), Nickles (OK), Gramm (TX), Lott (MS), Jeffords (VT), Mack (FL).
Minority (9 D): Moynihan (NY), RMM; Baucus (MT), Rockefeller (WV), Breaux (LA), Conrad (ND), Graham (FL), Moseley-Braun (IL), Bryan (NV), Kerrey (NE).

SUBCOMMITTEES

HEALTH CARE
Majority (8 R): Gramm, Chmn.; Roth, Chafee, Grassley, Hatch, D'Amato, Nickles, Jeffords.
Minority (7 D): Rockefeller, RMM; Baucus, Conrad, Graham, Moseley-Braun, Bryan, Kerrey.

INTERNATIONAL TRADE
Majority (9 R): Grassley, Chmn.; Roth, Chafee, Hatch, D'Amato, Murkowski, Gramm, Lott, Mack.
Minority (8 D): Moynihan, RMM; Baucus, Rockefeller, Breaux, Conrad, Graham, Moseley-Braun, Kerrey.

LONG-TERM GROWTH, DEBT & DEFICIT REDUCTION
Majority (3 R): Mack, Chmn.; Murkowski, Lott.
Minority (2 D): Graham, RMM; Bryan.

SOCIAL SECURITY & FAMILY POLICY
Majority (4 R): Chafee, Chmn.; Nickles, Gramm, Jeffords.
Minority (4 D): Breaux, RMM; Moynihan, Rockefeller, Moseley-Braun.

TAXATION & IRS OVERSIGHT
Majority (9 R): Nickles, Chmn.; Roth, Grassley, Hatch, D'Amato, Murkowski, Lott, Jeffords, Mack.
Minority (6 D): Baucus, RMM; Moynihan, Breaux, Conrad, Bryan, Kerrey.

FOREIGN RELATIONS **450 Dirksen**
http://www.senate.gov/committee/foreign.html **202-224-4651**

Majority (10 R): Helms (NC), Chmn.; Lugar (IN), Coverdell (GA), Hagel (NE), Smith (OR), Thomas (WY), Grams (MN), Ashcroft (MO), Frist (TN), Brownback (KS).
Minority (8 D): Biden (DE), RMM; Sarbanes (MD), Dodd (CT), Kerry (MA), Robb (VA), Feingold (WI), Feinstein (CA), Wellstone (MN).

SUBCOMMITTEES

AFRICAN AFFAIRS

Majority (3 R): Ashcroft, Chmn.; Grams, Frist.
Minority (2 D): Feingold, RMM; Sarbanes.

EAST ASIAN & PACIFIC AFFAIRS

Majority (5 R): Thomas, Chmn.; Frist, Lugar, Coverdell, Hagel.
Minority (4 D): Kerry, RMM; Robb, Feingold, Feinstein.

EUROPEAN AFFAIRS

Majority (5 R): Smith, Chmn.; Lugar, Ashcroft, Hagel, Thomas.
Minority (4 D): Biden, RMM; Wellstone, Sarbanes, Dodd.

INTERNATIONAL ECONOMIC POLICY, EXPORT & TRADE PROMOTION

Majority (4 R): Hagel, Chmn.; Thomas, Frist, Coverdell.
Minority (3 D): Sarbanes, RMM; Biden, Wellstone.

INTERNATIONAL OPERATIONS

Majority (4 R): Grams, Chmn.; Helms, Brownback, Smith.
Minority (3 D): Feinstein, RMM; Dodd, Kerry.

NEAR EASTERN & SOUTH ASIAN AFFAIRS

Majority (5 R): Brownback, Chmn.; Smith, Grams, Helms, Ashcroft.
Minority (4 D): Robb, RMM; Feinstein, Wellstone, Sarbanes.

WESTERN HEMISPHERE & PEACE CORPS AFFAIRS

Majority (4 R): Coverdell, Chmn.; Helms, Lugar, Brownback.
Minority (3 D): Dodd, RMM; Kerry, Robb.

GOVERNMENTAL AFFAIRS — 340 Dirksen

http://www.senate.gov/committee/governmental_affairs.html — 202-224-4751

Majority (9 R): Thompson (TN), Chmn.; Collins (ME), Brownback (KS), Domenici (NM), Cochran (MS), Nickles (OK), Specter (PA), Smith (NH), Bennett (UT).
Minority (7 D): Glenn (OH), RMM; Levin (MI), Lieberman (CT), Akaka (HI), Durbin (IL), Torricelli (NJ), Cleland (GA).

SUBCOMMITTEES

INTERNATIONAL SECURITY, PROLIFERATION & FEDERAL SERVICES

Majority (6 R): Cochran, Chmn.; Collins, Domenici, Nickles, Specter, Smith.
Minority (5 D): Levin, RMM; Akaka, Durbin, Torricelli, Cleland.

OVERSIGHT OF GOVERNMENT MANAGEMENT, RESTRUCTURING & THE DISTRICT OF COLUMBIA

Majority (3 R): Brownback, Chmn.; Specter, Bennett.
Minority (2 D): Lieberman, RMM; Cleland.

PERMANENT SUBCOMMITTEE ON INVESTIGATIONS

Majority (8 R): Collins, Chmn.; Brownback, Domenici, Cochran, Nickles, Specter, Smith, Bennett.
Minority (7 D): Glenn, RMM; Levin, Lieberman, Akaka, Durbin, Torricelli, Cleland.

INDIAN AFFAIRS **838 Hart**
http://www.senate.gov/committee/indian_affairs.html **202-224-2251**

Majority (8 R): Campbell (CO), Chmn.; Murkowski (AK), McCain (AZ), Gorton (WA), Domenici (NM), Thomas (WY), Hatch (UT), Inhofe (OK).
Minority (6 D): Inouye (HI), Vice Chmn.; Conrad (ND), Reid (NV), Akaka (HI), Wellstone (MN), Dorgan (ND).

NO SUBCOMMITTEES

INTELLIGENCE (Select) **211 Hart**
http://www.senate.gov/committee/intelligence.html **202-224-1700**

Majority (10 R): Shelby (AL), Chmn.; Chafee (RI), Lugar (IN), DeWine (OH), Kyl (AZ), Inhofe (OK), Hatch (UT), Roberts (KS), Allard (CO), Coats (IN), Lott (MS), ex-officio.
Minority (9 D): Kerrey (NE), Vice Chmn.; Glenn (OH), Bryan (NV), Graham (FL), Kerry (MA), Baucus (MT), Robb (VA), Lautenberg (NJ), Levin (MI), Daschle (SD), ex-officio.

NO SUBCOMMITTEES

JUDICIARY **224 Dirksen**
http://www.senate.gov/committee/judiciary.html **202-224-5225**

Majority (10 R): Hatch (UT), Chmn.; Thurmond (SC), Grassley (IA), Specter (PA), Thompson (TN), Kyl (AZ), DeWine (OH), Ashcroft (MO), Abraham (MI), Sessions (AL).
Minority (8 D): Leahy (VT), RMM; Kennedy (MA), Biden (DE), Kohl (WI), Feinstein (CA), Feingold (WI), Durbin (IL), Torricelli (NJ).

SUBCOMMITTEES

ADMINISTRATIVE OVERSIGHT & THE COURTS
Majority (4 R): Grassley, Chmn.; Thurmond, Sessions, Kyl.
Minority (3 D): Durbin, RMM; Feingold, Kohl.

ANTITRUST, BUSINESS RIGHTS & COMPETITION
Majority (4 R): DeWine, Chmn.; Hatch, Thurmond, Specter.
Minority (3 D): Kohl, RMM; Torricelli, Leahy.

CONSTITUTION, FEDERALISM & PROPERTY RIGHTS
Majority (5 R): Ashcroft, Chmn.; Hatch, Abraham, Thurmond, Thompson.
Minority (3 D): Feingold, RMM; Kennedy, Torricelli.

IMMIGRATION
Majority (4 R): Abraham, Chmn.; Grassley, Kyl, Specter.
Minority (3 D): Kennedy, RMM; Feinstein, Durbin.

TERRORISM, TECHNOLOGY & GOVERNMENT INFORMATION
Majority (4 R): Kyl, Chmn.; Hatch, Specter, Thompson.
Minority (3 D): Feinstein, RMM; Biden, Durbin.

YOUTH VIOLENCE
Majority (5 R): Sessions, Chmn.; Thompson, DeWine, Ashcroft, Grassley.
Minority (4 D): Biden, RMM; Torricelli, Kohl, Feinstein.

LABOR & HUMAN RESOURCES — 835 Hart
http://www.senate.gov/committee/labor.html — 202-224-6770

Majority (10 R): Jeffords (VT), Chmn.; Coats (IN), Gregg (NH), Frist (TN), DeWine (OH), Enzi (WY), Hutchinson (AR), Collins (ME), Warner (VA), McConnell (KY).
Minority (8 D): Kennedy (MA), RMM; Dodd (CT), Harkin (IA), Mikulski (MD), Bingaman (NM), Wellstone (MN), Murray (WA), Reed (RI).

SUBCOMMITTEES

AGING

Majority (3 R): Gregg, Chmn.; Hutchinson, Warner.
Minority (2 D): Mikulski, RMM; Murray.

CHILDREN & FAMILIES

Majority (6 R): Coats, Chmn.; Gregg, Frist, Hutchinson, Collins, McConnell.
Minority (5 D): Dodd, RMM; Bingaman, Wellstone, Murray, Reed.

EMPLOYMENT & TRAINING

Majority (5 R): DeWine, Chmn.; Jeffords, Enzi, Warner, McConnell.
Minority (4 D): Wellstone, RMM; Kennedy, Dodd, Harkin.

PUBLIC HEALTH & SAFETY

Majority (6 R): Frist, Chmn.; Jeffords, Coats, DeWine, Enzi, Collins.
Minority (5 D): Kennedy, RMM; Harkin, Mikulski, Bingaman, Reed.

RULES & ADMINISTRATION — 305 Russell
http://senate.gov/committee/rules.html — 202-224-6352

Majority (9 R): Warner (VA), Chmn.; Helms (NC), Stevens (AK), McConnell (KY), Cochran (MS), Santorum (PA), Nickles (OK), Lott (MS), Hutchison (TX).
Minority (7 D): Ford (KY), RMM; Byrd (WV), Inouye (HI), Moynihan (NY), Dodd (CT), Feinstein (CA), Torricelli (NJ).

NO SUBCOMMITTEES

SMALL BUSINESS — 428-A Russell
http://www.senate.gov/committee/small_business.html — 202-224-5175

Majority (10 R): Bond (MO), Chmn.; Burns (MT), Coverdell (GA), Kempthorne (ID), Bennett (UT), Warner (VA), Frist (TN), Snowe (ME), Faircloth (NC), Enzi (WY).
Minority (8 D): Kerry (MA), RMM; Bumpers (AR), Levin (MI), Harkin (IA), Lieberman (CT), Wellstone (MN), Cleland (GA), Landrieu (LA).

NO SUBCOMMITTEES

VETERANS' AFFAIRS — 412 Russell
http://www.senate.gov/committee/veterans.html — 202-224-9126

Majority (7 R): Specter (PA), Chmn.; Thurmond (SC), Murkowski (AK), Jeffords (VT), Campbell (CO), Craig (ID), Hutchinson (AR).
Minority (5 D): Rockefeller (WV), RMM; Graham (FL), Akaka (HI), Wellstone (MN), Murray (WA).

NO SUBCOMMITTEES

HOUSE COMMITTEES

AGRICULTURE **1301 Longworth**
http://www.house.gov/agriculture/ **202-225-2171**

Majority (27 R): Smith (OR), Chmn.; Combest (TX), Vice Chmn.; Barrett (NE), Boehner (OH), Ewing (IL), Doolittle (CA), Goodlatte (VA), Pombo (CA), Canady (FL), Smith (MI), Everett (AL), Lucas (OK), Lewis (KY), Chenoweth (ID), Hostettler (IN), Bryant (TN), Foley (FL), Chambliss (GA), LaHood (IL), Emerson (MO), Moran (KS), Blunt (MO), Pickering (MS), Schaffer (CO), Thune (SD), Jenkins (TN), Cooksey (LA).

Minority (23 D): Stenholm (TX), RMM; Brown (CA), Condit (CA), Peterson (MN), Dooley (CA), Clayton (NC), Minge (MN), Hilliard (AL), Pomeroy (ND), Holden (PA), Baesler (KY), Bishop (GA), Thompson (MS), Farr (CA), Baldacci (ME), Berry (AR), Goode (VA), McIntyre (NC), Stabenow (MI), Etheridge (NC), John (LA), Johnson (WI), Boswell (IA).

SUBCOMMITTEES

DEPARTMENT OPERATIONS, NUTRITION & FOREIGN AGRICULTURE

Majority (7 R): Goodlatte, Chmn.; Ewing, Vice Chmn.; Canady, Smith (MI), Foley, LaHood, Thune.

Minority (5 D): Clayton, RMM; Thompson, Berry, Brown, Bishop.

FORESTRY, RESOURCE CONSERVATION, & RESEARCH

Majority (18 R): Combest, Chmn.; Barrett, Vice Chmn.; Doolittle, Pombo, Smith (MI), Everett, Lucas, Lewis, Chenoweth, Hostettler, Chambliss, LaHood, Emerson, Moran, Pickering, Schaffer, Jenkins, Cooksey.

Minority (15 D): Dooley, RMM; Brown, Farr, Stabenow, John, Peterson, Clayton, Minge, Hilliard, Pomeroy, Holden, Baesler, Baldacci, Berry, Goode.

GENERAL FARM COMMODITIES

Majority (9 R): Barrett, Chmn.; Combest, Vice Chmn.; Boehner, Lucas, Chambliss, Emerson, Moran, Thune, Cooksey.

Minority (7 D): Minge, RMM; Thompson, McIntyre, Stabenow, Etheridge, John, Johnson.

LIVESTOCK, DAIRY & POULTRY

Majority (10 R): Pombo, Chmn.; Boehner, Vice Chmn.; Goodlatte, Smith (MI), Lucas, Lewis, Hostettler, Blunt, Pickering, Jenkins.

Minority (8 D): Peterson, RMM; Hilliard, Holden, Johnson, Condit, Dooley, Farr, Boswell.

RISK MANAGEMENT & SPECIALTY CROPS

Majority (11 R): Ewing, Chmn.; Combest, Vice Chmn.; Doolittle, Pombo, Smith (MI), Everett, Lewis, Bryant, Foley, Chambliss, Moran.

Minority (9 D): Condit, RMM; Baesler, Bishop, Pomeroy, Baldacci, Goode, McIntyre, Etheridge, Boswell.

APPROPRIATIONS **H-218 The Capitol**
http://www.house.gov/appropriations/ **202-225-2771**

Majority (34 R): Livingston (LA), Chmn.; McDade (PA), Vice Chmn.; Young (FL), Regula (OH), Lewis (CA), Porter (IL), Rogers (KY), Skeen (NM), Wolf (VA), DeLay (TX), Kolbe (AZ), Packard (CA), Callahan (AL), Walsh (NY), Taylor (NC), Hobson (OH), Istook (OK), Bonilla (TX), Knollenberg (MI), Miller (FL), Dickey (AR), Kingston (GA), Parker (MS), Frelinghuysen (NJ), Wicker (MS), Forbes (NY), Nethercutt (WA), Neumann (WI), Cunningham (CA), Tiahrt (KS), Wamp (TN), Latham (IA), Northup (KY), Aderholt (AL).

Minority (26 D): Obey (WI), RMM; Yates (IL), Stokes (OH), Murtha (PA), Dicks (WA), Sabo (MN), Dixon (CA), Fazio (CA), Hefner (NC), Hoyer (MD), Mollohan (WV), Kaptur (OH), Skaggs (CO), Pelosi (CA), Visclosky (IN), Foglietta (PA), Torres (CA), Lowey (NY), Serrano (NY), DeLauro (CT), Moran (VA), Olver (MA), Pastor (AZ), Meek (FL), Price (NC), Edwards (TX).

SUBCOMMITTEES

AGRICULTURE, RURAL DEVELOPMENT, FDA & RELATED AGENCIES

Majority (7 R): Skeen, Chmn.; Walsh, Dickey, Kingston, Nethercutt, Bonilla, Latham.
Minority (4 D): Kaptur, RMM; Fazio, Serrano, DeLauro.

COMMERCE, JUSTICE, STATE & JUDICIARY

Majority (6 R): Rogers, Chmn.; Kolbe, Taylor, Regula, Forbes, Latham.
Minority (3 D): Mollohan, RMM; Skaggs, Dixon.

DISTRICT OF COLUMBIA

Majority (6 R): Taylor, Chmn.; Neumann, Cunningham, Tiahrt, Northup, Aderholt.
Minority (3 D): Moran, RMM; Sabo, Dixon.

ENERGY & WATER DEVELOPMENT

Majority (7 R): McDade, Chmn.; Rogers, Knollenberg, Frelinghuysen, Parker, Callahan, Dickey.
Minority (4 D): Fazio, RMM; Visclosky, Edwards, Pastor.

FOREIGN OPERATIONS, EXPORT FINANCING & RELATED PROGRAMS

Majority (8 R): Callahan, Chmn.; Porter, Wolf, Packard, Knollenberg, Forbes, Kingston, Frelinghuysen.
Minority (5 D): Pelosi, RMM; Yates, Lowey, Foglietta, Torres.

INTERIOR

Majority (8 R): Regula, Chmn.; McDade, Kolbe, Skeen, Taylor, Nethercutt, Miller, Wamp.
Minority (5 D): Yates, RMM; Murtha, Dicks, Skaggs, Moran.

LABOR, HEALTH & HUMAN SERVICES, & EDUCATION

Majority (8 R): Porter, Chmn.; Young, Bonilla, Istook, Miller, Dickey, Wicker, Northup.
Minority (6 D): Obey, RMM; Stokes, Hoyer, Pelosi, Lowey, DeLauro.

LEGISLATIVE

Majority (5 R): Walsh, Chmn.; Young, Cunningham, Wamp, Latham.
Minority (3 D): Serrano, RMM; Fazio, Kaptur.

MILITARY CONSTRUCTION

Majority (8 R): Packard, Chmn.; Porter, Hobson, Wicker, Kingston, Parker, Tiahrt, Wamp.
Minority (5 D): Hefner, RMM; Olver, Edwards, Dicks, Hoyer.

NATIONAL SECURITY

Majority (9 R): Young, Chmn.; McDade, Lewis, Skeen, Hobson, Bonilla, Nethercutt, Istook, Cunningham.

Minority (6 D): Murtha, RMM; Dicks, Hefner, Sabo, Dixon, Visclosky.

TRANSPORTATION

Majority (8 R): Wolf, Chmn.; DeLay, Regula, Rogers, Packard, Callahan, Tiahrt, Aderholt.

Minority (5 D): Sabo, RMM; Foglietta, Torres, Olver, Pastor.

TREASURY, POSTAL SERVICE & GENERAL GOVERNMENT

Majority (6 R): Kolbe, Chmn.; Wolf, Istook, Forbes, Northup, Aderholt.

Minority (3 D): Hoyer, RMM; Meek, Price.

VA, HUD & INDEPENDENT AGENCIES

Majority (8 R): Lewis, Chmn.; DeLay, Walsh, Hobson, Knollenberg, Frelinghuysen, Neumann, Wicker.

Minority (5 D): Stokes, RMM; Mollohan, Kaptur, Meek, Price.

BANKING & FINANCIAL SERVICES — 2129 Rayburn
http://www.house.gov/banking/ — 202-225-7502

Majority (30 R): Leach (IA), Chmn.; McCollum (FL), Roukema (NJ), Bereuter (NE), Baker (LA), Lazio (NY), Bachus (AL), Castle (DE), King (NY), Campbell (CA), Royce (CA), Lucas (OK), Metcalf (WA), Ney (OH), Ehrlich (MD), Barr (GA), Fox (PA), Kelly (NY), Paul (TX), Weldon (FL), Ryun (KS), Cook (UT), Snowbarger (KS), Riley (AL), Hill (MT), Sessions (TX), LaTourette (OH), Manzullo (IL), Foley (FL), Jones (NC).

Minority (25 D): Gonzalez (TX), RMM; LaFalce (NY), Vento (MN), Schumer (NY), Frank (MA), Kanjorski (PA), Kennedy (MA), Flake (NY), Waters (CA), Maloney (NY), Gutierrez (IL), Roybal-Allard (CA), Barrett (WI), Velazquez (NY), Watt (NC), Hinchey (NY), Ackerman (NY), Bentsen (TX), Jackson (IL), McKinney (GA), Kilpatrick (MI), Maloney (CT), Hooley (OR), Carson (IN), one vacancy.

Independent (1): Sanders (I-VT)

SUBCOMMITTEES

CAPITAL MARKETS, SECURITIES & GOVT. SPONSORED ENTERPRISES

Majority (14 R): Baker, Chmn.; Lucas, Vice Chmn.; Cook, Snowbarger, Riley, Hill, Sessions, Lazio, Bachus, King, Campbell, Royce, Fox, Jones.

Minority (10 D): Kanjorski, RMM; Schumer, Flake, Waters, Gutierrez, Vento, Roybal-Allard, Barrett, Watt, Ackerman.

DOMESTIC & INTERNATIONAL MONETARY POLICY

Majority (14 R): Castle, Chmn.; Fox, Vice Chmn.; LaTourette, Lucas, Metcalf, Ney, Barr, Paul, Weldon, Roukema, Bereuter, Cook, Manzullo, Foley.

Minority (9 D): Flake, RMM; Frank, Kennedy, Kanjorski, Velazquez, Maloney (NY), Hinchey, Bentsen, Jackson.

Independent (1): Sanders.

FINANCIAL INSTITUTIONS & CONSUMER CREDIT

Majority (13 R): Roukema, Chmn.; McCollum, Vice Chmn.; Bereuter, King, Campbell, Royce, Metcalf, Ehrlich, Barr, Kelly, Paul, Weldon, Ryun.

Minority (11 D): Vento, RMM; LaFalce, Schumer, Maloney (NY), Barrett, Watt, Roybal-Allard, Ackerman, Bentsen, McKinney, Kilpatrick.

GENERAL OVERSIGHT & INVESTIGATIONS

Majority (6 R): Bachus, Chmn.; Riley, LaTourette, King, Ney, Foley.
Minority (4 D): Waters, RMM; McKinney, Kilpatrick, Hooley.

HOUSING & COMMUNITY OPPORTUNITY

Majority (13 R): Lazio, Chmn.; Ney, Vice Chmn.; Bereuter, Baker, Castle, Ehrlich, Fox, Kelly, Cook, Hill, Sessions, Metcalf, Jones.
Minority (10 D): Kennedy, RMM; Gutierrez, Velazquez, Frank, Hinchey, Jackson, LaFalce, Maloney (CT), Hooley, Carson.
Independent (1): Sanders

BUDGET

309 Cannon

http://www.house.gov/budget/

202-226-7270

Majority (24 R): Kasich (OH), Chmn.; Hobson (OH), Shays (CT), Herger (CA), Bunning (KY), Smith (TX), Miller (FL), Franks (NJ), Smith (MI), Inglis (SC), Molinari (NY), Nussle (IA), Hoekstra (MI), Shadegg (AZ), Radanovich (CA), Bass (NH), Neumann (WI), Parker (MS), Ehrlich (MD), Gutknecht (MN), Hilleary (TN), Granger (TX), Sununu (NH), Pitts (PA).
Minority (19 D): Spratt (SC), RMM; McDermott (WA), Mollohan (WV), Costello (IL), Mink (HI), Pomeroy (ND), Woolsey (CA), Roybal-Allard (CA), Rivers (MI), Doggett (TX), Thompson (MS), Cardin (MD), Minge (MN), Baesler (KY), Bentsen (TX), Davis (FL), Sherman (CA), Weygand (RI), Clayton (NC).

NO SUBCOMMITTEES

COMMERCE

2125 Rayburn

http://www.house.gov/commerce/welcome.html

202-225-2927

Majority (28 R): Bliley (VA), Chmn.; Tauzin (LA), Oxley (OH), Bilirakis (FL), Schaefer (CO), Barton (TX), Hastert (IL), Upton (MI), Stearns (FL), Paxon (NY), Gillmor (OH), Vice Chmn.; Klug (WI), Greenwood (PA), Crapo (ID), Cox (CA), Deal (GA), Largent (OK), Burr (NC), Bilbray (CA), Whitfield (KY), Ganske (IA), Norwood (GA), White (WA), Coburn (OK), Lazio (NY), Cubin (WY), Rogan (CA), Shimkus (IL).
Minority (23 D): Dingell (MI), RMM; Waxman (CA), Markey (MA), Hall (TX), Boucher (VA), Manton (NY), Towns (NY), Pallone (NJ), Brown (OH), Gordon (TN), Furse (OR), Deutsch (FL), Rush (IL), Eshoo (CA), Klink (PA), Stupak (MI), Engel (NY), Sawyer (OH), Wynn (MD), Green (TX), McCarthy (MO), Strickland (OH), DeGette (CO).

SUBCOMMITTEES

ENERGY & POWER

Majority (15 R): Schaefer, Chmn.; Crapo, Vice Chmn.; Bilirakis, Hastert, Upton, Stearns, Paxon, Largent, Burr, Whitfield, Norwood, White, Coburn, Rogan, Shimkus.
Minority (12 D): Hall, RMM; Furse, Rush, McCarthy, Wynn, Markey, Boucher, Towns, Pallone, Brown, Gordon, Deutsch.

FINANCE & HAZARDOUS MATERIALS

Majority (14 R): Oxley, Chmn.; Tauzin, Vice Chmn.; Paxon, Gillmor, Klug, Greenwood, Crapo, Deal, Largent, Bilbray, Ganske, White, Lazio, Cubin.
Minority (11 D): Manton, RMM; Stupak, Engel, Sawyer, Strickland, DeGette, Markey, Hall, Towns, Pallone, Furse.

HEALTH & ENVIRONMENT

Majority (15 R): Bilirakis, Chmn.; Hastert, Vice Chmn.; Barton, Upton, Klug, Greenwood, Deal, Burr, Bilbray, Whitfield, Ganske, Norwood, Coburn, Lazio, Cubin.
Minority (12 D): Brown, RMM; Waxman, Towns, Pallone, Deutsch, Eshoo, Stupak, Green, Strickland, DeGette, Hall, Furse.

OVERSIGHT & INVESTIGATIONS

Majority (8 R): Barton, Chmn.; Cox, Vice Chmn.; Greenwood, Crapo, Burr, Bilbray, Ganske, Coburn.
Minority (6 D): Klink, RMM; Waxman, Deutsch, Stupak, Engel, Sawyer.

TELECOMMUNICATIONS, TRADE & CONSUMER PROTECTION

Majority (15 R): Tauzin, Chmn.; Oxley, Vice Chmn.; Schaefer, Barton, Hastert, Upton, Stearns, Gillmor, Klug, Cox, Deal, Largent, White, Rogan, Shimkus.
Minority (12 D): Markey, RMM; Boucher, Gordon, Engel, Sawyer, Manton, Rush, Eshoo, Klink, Wynn, Green, McCarthy.

EDUCATION & THE WORKFORCE — 2181 Rayburn

http://www.house.gov/eeo/ — 202-225-4527

Majority (25 R): Goodling (PA), Chmn.; Petri (WI), Vice Chmn.; Roukema (NJ), Fawell (IL), Ballenger (NC), Barrett (NE), Hoekstra (MI), McKeon (CA), Castle (DE), Johnson (TX), Talent (MO), Greenwood (PA), Knollenberg (MI), Riggs (CA), Graham (SC), Souder (IN), McIntosh (IN), Norwood (GA), Paul (TX), Schaffer (CO), Peterson (PA), Upton (MI), Deal (GA), Hilleary (TN), Scarborough (FL).
Minority (20 D): Clay (MO), RMM; Miller (CA), Kildee (MI), Martinez (CA), Owens (NY), Payne (NJ), Mink (HI), Andrews (NJ), Roemer (IN), Scott (VA), Woolsey (CA), Romero-Barcelo (PR), Fattah (PA), Hinojosa (TX), McCarthy (NY), Tierney (MA), Kind (WI), Sanchez (CA), Ford (TN), Kucinich (OH).

SUBCOMMITTEES

EARLY CHILDHOOD, YOUTH & FAMILIES

Majority (11 R): Riggs, Chmn.; Castle, Vice Chmn.; Johnson, Souder, Paul, Goodling, Greenwood, McIntosh, Peterson, Upton, Hilleary.
Minority (9 R): Martinez, RMM; Miller, Kildee, Owens, Payne, Mink, Roemer, Scott, Kucinich.

EMPLOYER-EMPLOYEE RELATIONS

Majority (7 R): Fawell, Chmn.; Talent, Knollenberg, Vice Chmn.; Petri, Roukema, Ballenger, Goodling.
Minority (5 D): Payne, RMM; Fattah, Hinjosa, McCarthy, Tierney.

OVERSIGHT & INVESTIGATIONS

Majority (6 R): Hoekstra, Chmn.; Norwood, Vice Chmn.; Hilleary, Scarborough, McKeon, Fawell.

Minority (4 D): Mink, RMM; Kind, Sanchez, Ford.

POSTSECONDARY EDUCATION, TRAINING & LIFE-LONG LEARNING

Majority (15 R): McKeon, Chmn.; Graham, Vice Chmn.; Goodling, Petri, Roukema, Barrett, Greenwood, McIntosh, Schaffer, Peterson, Castle, Riggs, Souder, Upton, Deal.

Minority (12 D): Kildee, RMM; Andrews, Roemer, Woolsey, Romero-Barcelo, Fattah, Hinojosa, McCarthy, Tierney, Kind, Sanchez, Ford.

WORKFORCE PROTECTIONS

Majority (7 R): Ballenger, Chmn.; Fawell, Vice Chmn.; Barrett, Hoekstra, Graham, Paul, Schaffer.

Minority (5 D): Owens, RMM; Miller, Martinez, Andrews, Woolsey.

GOVERNMENT REFORM & OVERSIGHT — 2157 Rayburn

http://www.house.gov/reform/ — 202-225-5074

Majority (24 R): Burton (IN), Chmn.; Gilman (NY), Hastert (IL), Morella (MD), Shays (CT), Schiff (NM), Cox (CA), Ros-Lehtinen (FL), McHugh (NY), Horn (CA), Mica (FL), Davis (VA), McIntosh (IN), Souder (IN), Scarborough (FL), Shadegg (AZ), LaTourette (OH), Sanford (SC), Sununu (NH), Sessions (TX), Pappas (NJ), Snowbarger (KS), Barr (GA), Portman (OH).

Minority (19 D): Waxman (CA), RMM; Lantos (CA), Wise (WV) Owens (NY), Towns (NY), Kanjorski (PA), Condit (CA), Maloney (NY), Barrett (WI), Norton (DC), Fattah (PA), Cummings (MD), Kucinich (OH), Blagojevich (IL), Davis (IL), Tierney (MA), Turner (TX), Allen (ME), Ford (TN).

Independent (1): Sanders (VT).

SUBCOMMITTEES

CIVIL SERVICE

Majority (5 R): Mica, Chmn.; Pappas, Vice Chmn.; Morella, Cox, Sessions.

Minority (3 D): Cummings, RMM; Norton, Ford.

DISTRICT OF COLUMBIA

Majority (4 R): Davis, Chmn.; Morella, Vice Chmn.; Ros-Lehtinen, Horn.

Minority (2 D): Norton, RMM; Allen.

GOVERNMENT MANAGEMENT, INFORMATION & TECHNOLOGY

Majority (7 R): Horn, Chmn.; Sessions, Vice Chmn.; Davis, Scarborough, Sanford, Sununu, Portman.

Minority (5 D): Maloney, RMM; Kanjorski, Owens, Blagojevich, Davis.

HUMAN RESOURCES

Majority (7 R): Shays, Chmn.; Snowbarger, Vice Chmn.; Gilman, McIntosh, Souder, Pappas, Schiff.

Minority (5 D): Towns, RMM; Kucinich, Allen, Lantos, Barrett.

Independent (1): Sanders

NATIONAL ECONOMIC GROWTH, NATURAL RESOURCES & REGULATORY AFFAIRS

Majority (9 R): McIntosh, Chmn.; Sununu, Vice Chmn.; Hastert, Scarborough, Shadegg, LaTourette, Snowbarger, Barr, one vacancy.
Minority (6 D): Tierney, Turner, Kanjorski, Condit, Kucinich, Fattah.
Independent (1): Sanders, RMM.

NATIONAL SECURITY, INTERNATIONAL AFFAIRS & CRIMINAL JUSTICE

Majority (10 R): Hastert, Chmn.; Souder, Vice Chmn.; Shays, Schiff, Ros-Lehtinen, McHugh, Mica, Shadegg, LaTourette, Barr.
Minority (8 D): Barrett, RMM; Lantos, Wise, Condit, Blagojevich, Maloney, Cummings, Turner.

POSTAL SERVICE
Majority (5 R): McHugh, Chmn.; Sanford, Vice Chmn.; Gilman, LaTourette, Sessions.
Minority (3 D): Fattah, RMM; Owens, Davis.

HOUSE OVERSIGHT — 1309 Longworth
http://www.house.gov/cho/ — 202-225-8281

Majority (6 R): Thomas (CA), Chmn.; Ney (OH), Boehner (OH), Ehlers (MI), Granger (TX), Mica (FL).
Minority (3 D): Gejdenson (CT), RMM; Hoyer (MD), Kilpatrick (MI).

NO SUBCOMMITTEES

INTELLIGENCE (Select) — H-405 The Capitol, 202-225-4121

Majority (9 R): Goss (FL), Chmn.; Young (FL), Lewis (CA), Shuster (PA), McCollum (FL), Castle (DE), Boehlert (NY), Bass (NH), Gibbons (NV).
Minority (7 D): Dicks (WA), RMM; Dixon (CA), Skaggs (CO), Pelosi (CA), Harman (CA), Skelton (MO), Bishop (GA).

SUBCOMMITTEES

HUMAN INTELLIGENCE, ANALYSIS & COUNTERINTELLIGENCE

Majority (4 R): McCollum, Chmn.; Shuster, Castle, Bass
Minority (4 D): Dixon, RMM; Skaggs, Pelosi, Bishop.

TECHNICAL & TACTICAL INTELLIGENCE

Majority (4 R): Lewis, Chmn.; Young, Boehlert, Gibbons.
Minority (4 D): Skaggs, RMM; Dicks, Harman, Skelton.

INTERNATIONAL RELATIONS **2170 Rayburn**
http://www.house.gov/international_relations/ **202-225-5021**

Majority (26 R): Gilman (NY), Chmn.; Goodling (PA), Leach (IA), Hyde (IL), Bereuter (NE), Smith (NJ), Burton (IN), Gallegly (CA), Ros-Lehtinen (FL), Ballenger (NC), Rohrabacher (CA), Manzullo (IL), Royce (CA), King (NY), Kim (CA), Chabot (OH), Sanford (SC), Salmon (AZ), Houghton (NY), Campbell (CA), Fox (PA), McHugh (NY), Graham (SC), Blunt (MO), Moran (KS), Brady (TX).
Minority (22 D): Hamilton (IN), RMM; Gejdenson (CT), Lantos (CA), Berman (CA), Ackerman (NY), Faleomavaega (AS), Martinez (CA), Payne, (NJ), Andrews (NJ), Menendez (NJ), Brown (OH), McKinney (GA), Hastings (FL), Danner (MO), Hilliard (AL), Capps (CA), Sherman (CA), Wexler (FL), Rothman (NJ), Clement (TN), Luther (MN), Davis (FL).

SUBCOMMITTEES

AFRICA

Majority (6 R): Royce, Chmn.; Houghton, Chabot, Sanford, Campbell, McHugh.
Minority (4 D): Menendez, RMM; Payne, Hastings, Davis.

ASIA & THE PACIFIC

Majority (10 R): Bereuter, Chmn.; Leach, Rohrabacher, King, Kim, Salmon, Fox, McHugh, Manzullo, Royce.
Minority (8 D): Berman, RMM; Faleomavaega, Andrews, Brown, Martinez, Hastings, Capps, Wexler.

INTERNATIONAL ECONOMIC POLICY & TRADE

Majority (10 R): Ros-Lehtinen, Chmn.; Manzullo, Chabot, Campbell, Graham, Blunt, Moran, Brady, Bereuter, Rohrabacher.
Minority (8 D): Gejdenson, RMM; Danner, Hilliard, Sherman, Rothman, Clement, Lantos, Luther.

INTERNATIONAL OPERATIONS & HUMAN RIGHTS

Majority (9 R): Smith, Chmn.; Goodling, Hyde, Burton, Ballenger, King, Salmon, Graham, Ros-Lehtinen.
Minority (7 D): Lantos, RMM; McKinney, Ackerman, Faleomavaega, Payne, Hilliard, Wexler.

WESTERN HEMISPHERE

Majority (9 R): Gallegly, Chmn.; Ballenger, Sanford, Smith, Burton, Ros-Lehtinen, Kim, Blunt, Brady.
Minority (7 D): Ackerman, RMM; Martinez, Andrews, Menendez, McKinney, Capps, Sherman.

JUDICIARY
http://www.house.gov/judiciary/

2138 Rayburn
202-225-3951

Majority (20 R): Hyde (IL), Chmn.; Sensenbrenner (WI), McCollum (FL), Gekas (PA), Coble (NC), Smith (TX), Schiff (NM), Gallegly (CA), Canady (FL), Inglis (SC), Goodlatte (VA), Buyer (IN), Bono (CA), Bryant (TN), Chabot (OH), Barr (GA), Jenkins (TN), Hutchinson (AR), Pease (IN), Cannon (UT).

Minority (15 D): Conyers (MI), RMM; Frank (MA), Schumer (NY), Berman (CA), Boucher (VA), Nadler (NY), Scott (VA), Watt (NC), Lofgren (CA), Jackson Lee (TX), Waters (CA), Meehan (MA), Delahunt (MA), Wexler (FL), Rothman (NJ).

SUBCOMMITTEES

COMMERCIAL & ADMINISTRATIVE LAW

Majority (6 R): Gekas, Chmn.; Schiff, Smith, Inglis, Bryant, Chabot.
Minority (4 D): Nadler, RMM; Jackson Lee, Meehan, Delahunt.

CONSTITUTION

Majority (8 R): Canady, Chmn.; Hyde, Inglis, Bryant, Jenkins, Goodlatte, Barr, Hutchinson.
Minority (5 D): Scott, RMM; Waters, Conyers, Nadler, Watt.

COURTS & INTELLECTUAL PROPERTY

Majority (9 R): Coble, Chmn.; Sensenbrenner, Gallegly, Goodlatte, Bono, Pease, Cannon, McCollum, Canady.
Minority (6 D): Frank, RMM; Conyers, Berman, Boucher, Lofgren, Delahunt.

CRIME

Majority (8 R): McCollum, Chmn.; Schiff, Buyer, Chabot, Barr, Hutchinson, Gekas, Coble.
Minority (5 D): Schumer, RMM; Jackson Lee, Meehan, Wexler, Rothman.

IMMIGRATION & CLAIMS

Majority (7 R): Smith, Chmn.; Gallegly, Bono, Jenkins, Pease, Cannon, Bryant.
Minority (5 D): Watt, RMM; Schumer, Berman, Lofgren, Wexler.

NATIONAL SECURITY
http://www.house.gov/nsc/

2120 Rayburn
202-225-4151

Majority (30 R): Spence (SC), Chmn.; Stump (AZ), Hunter (CA), Kasich (OH), Bateman (VA), Hansen (UT), Weldon (PA), Hefley (CO), Saxton (NJ), Buyer (IN), Fowler (FL), McHugh (NY), Talent (MO), Everett (AL), Bartlett (MD), McKeon (CA), Lewis (KY), Watts (OK), Thornberry (TX), Hostettler (IN), Chambliss (GA), Hilleary (TN), Scarborough (FL), Jones (NC), Graham (SC), Bono (CA), Ryun (KS), Pappas (NJ), Riley (AL), Gibbons (NV).

Minority (25 D): Dellums (CA), RMM; Skelton (MO), Sisisky (VA), Spratt (SC), Ortiz (TX), Pickett (VA), Evans (IL), Taylor (MS), Abercrombie (HI), Meehan (MA), Underwood (GU), Harman (CA), McHale (PA), Kennedy (RI), Blagojevich (IL), Reyes (TX), Allen (ME), Snyder (AR), Turner (TX), Boyd (FL), Smith (WA), Sanchez (CA), Maloney (CT), McIntyre (NC), Rodriguez (TX).

SUBCOMMITTEES

MILITARY INSTALLATIONS & FACILITIES

Majority (10 R): Hefley, Chmn.; McHugh, Hostettler, Hilleary, Scarborough, Stump, Saxton, Buyer, Fowler, Everett.
Minority (8 D): Ortiz, RMM; Sisisky, Abercrombie, Underwood, Reyes, Snyder, Boyd, Smith.

MILITARY PERSONNEL

Majority (9 R): Buyer, Chmn.; Talent, Bartlett, Lewis, Watts, Vice Chmn., Thornberry, Graham, Bono, Ryun.
Minority (7 D): Taylor, RMM; Skelton, Pickett, Underwood, Harman, Kennedy, Maloney.

MILITARY PROCUREMENT

Majority (15 R): Hunter, Chmn.; Spence, Stump, Hansen, Saxton, Talent, Everett, McKeon, Lewis, Watts, Thornberry, Graham, Bono, Ryun, Pappas.
Minority (12 D): Skelton, RMM; Dellums, Spratt, Evans, Blagojevich, Allen, Snyder, Turner, Boyd, Smith, Maloney, McIntyre.

MILITARY READINESS

Majority (11 R): Bateman, Chmn.; Kasich, Fowler, Chambliss, Jones, Riley, Gibbons, Hunter, Hansen, Weldon, McKeon.
Minority (9 D): Sisisky, RMM; Ortiz, Pickett, Evans, Taylor, Meehan, Underwood, McHale, Rodriguez.

MILITARY RESEARCH & DEVELOPMENT

Majority (14 R): Weldon, Chmn.; Bartlett, Kasich, Bateman, Hefley, McHugh, Hostettler, Chambliss, Hilleary, Scarborough, Jones, Pappas, Riley, Gibbons.
Minority (11 D): Pickett, RMM; Abercrombie, Meehan, Harman, McHale, Kennedy, Blagojevich, Reyes, Allen, Turner, Sanchez.

RESOURCES — 1324 Longworth

http://www.house.gov/resources/ — 202-225-2761

Majority (27 R): Young (AK), Chmn.; Tauzin (LA), Hansen (UT), Saxton (NJ), Gallegly (CA), Duncan (TN), Hefley (CO), Doolittle (CA), Gilchrest (MD), Calvert (CA), Pombo (CA), Cubin (WY), Chenoweth (ID), Smith (WA), Radanovich (CA), Jones (NC), Thornberry (TX), Shadegg (AZ), Ensign (NV), Smith (OR), Cannon (UT), Brady (TX), Peterson (PA), Hill (MT), Schaffer (CO), Gibbons (NV), Crapo (ID).
Minority (23 D): Miller (CA), RMM; Markey (MA), Rahall (WV) Vento (MN), Kildee (MI), DeFazio (OR), Faleomavaega (AS), Abercrombie (HI), Ortiz (TX), Pickett (VA), Pallone (NJ), Dooley (CA), Romero-Barcelo (PR), Hinchey (NY), Underwood (GU), Farr (CA), Kennedy (RI), Smith (WA), Delahunt (MA), John (LA), Christian-Green (VI), Kind (WI), Doggett (TX).

SUBCOMMITTEES

ENERGY & MINERAL RESOURCES

Majority (8 R): Cubin, Chmn.; Tauzin, Duncan, Calvert, Thornberry, Cannon, Brady, Gibbons.
Minority (7 D): Romero-Barcelo, RMM; Rahall, Ortiz, Dooley, John, Christian-Green, one vacancy.

FISHERIES CONSERVATION, WILDLIFE & OCEANS

Majority (6 R): Saxton, Chmn.; Tauzin, Gilchrest, Jones, Peterson, Crapo.
Minority (5 D): Abercrombie, RMM; Ortiz, Pallone, Farr, Kennedy.

FORESTS AND FOREST HEALTH

Majority (7 R): Chenoweth, Chmn.; Hansen, Doolittle, Radanovich, Peterson, Hill, Schaffer.
Minority (6 D): Hinchey, RMM; Vento, Kildee, Faleomavaega, two vacancies.

NATIONAL PARKS & PUBLIC LANDS

Majority (15 R): Hansen, Chmn.; Gallegly, Duncan, Hefley, Gilchrest, Pombo, Chenoweth, Smith (WA), Radanovich, Jones, Shadegg, Ensign, Smith (OR), Hill, Gibbons.
Minority (13 D): Faleomavaega, RMM; Markey, Vento, Kildee, Romero-Barcelo, Hinchey, Underwood, Kennedy, Delahunt, Christian-Green, Kind, Doggett, one vacancy.

WATER & POWER

Majority (12 R): Doolittle, Chmn.; Calvert, Pombo, Chenoweth, Smith (WA), Radanovich, Thornberry, Shadegg, Ensign, Smith (OR), Cannon, Crapo.
Minority (10 D): DeFazio, RMM; Miller, Pickett, Dooley, Farr, Smith, Kind, Doggett, two vacancies.

RULES — H-312 The Capitol

http://www.house.gov/rules/ — 202-225-9191

Majority (9 R): Solomon (NY), Chmn.; Dreier (CA), Goss (FL), Linder (GA), Pryce (OH), Diaz-Balart (FL), McInnis (CO), Hastings (WA), Myrick (NC).
Minority (4 D): Moakley (MA), RMM; Frost (TX), Hall (OH), Slaughter (NY).

SUBCOMMITTEES

LEGISLATIVE & BUDGET PROCESS

Majority (5 R): Goss, Chmn.; Linder, Pryce, Hastings, Solomon.
Minority (2 D): Frost, RMM; Moakley.

RULES & ORGANIZATION OF THE HOUSE

Majority (5 R): Dreier, Chmn.; Diaz-Balart, McInnis, Myrick, Solomon.
Minority (2 D): Hall, RMM; Slaughter.

SCIENCE — 2320 Rayburn

http://www.house.gov/science/ — 202-225-6371

Majority (25 R): Sensenbrenner (WI), Chmn.; Boehlert (NY), Fawell (IL), Morella (MD), Weldon (PA), Rohrabacher (CA), Schiff (NM), Barton (TX), Calvert (CA), Bartlett (MD), Ehlers (MI) Vice Chmn.; Weldon (FL), Salmon (AZ), Davis (VA), Gutknecht (MN), Foley (FL), Ewing (IL), Pickering (MS), Cannon (UT), Brady (TX), Cook (UT), English (PA), Nethercutt (WA), Coburn (OK), Sessions (TX).
Minority (21 D): Brown (CA), RMM; Hall (TX), Gordon (TN), Traficant (OH), Roemer (IN), Cramer (AL), Barcia (MI), McHale (PA), Johnson (TX), Hastings (FL), Rivers (MI), Lofgren (CA), Doyle (PA), Jackson Lee (TX), Luther (MN), Capps (CA), Stabenow (MI), Etheridge (NC), Lampson (TX), Hooley (OR), Tauscher (CA).

SUBCOMMITTEES

BASIC RESEARCH

Majority (8 R): Schiff, Chmn.; Boehlert, Morella, Barton, Gutknecht, Ewing, Pickering, Sessions.
Minority (6 D): Barcia, RMM; Etheridge, Rivers, Jackson Lee, Luther, Capps.

ENERGY & ENVIRONMENT

Majority (10 R): Calvert, Chmn.; Fawell, Weldon (PA), Rohrabacher, Schiff, Ehlers, Salmon, Foley, English, Coburn.
Minority (8 D): Roemer, RMM; McHale, Doyle, Hooley, Hall, Johnson, Lofgren, Hastings.

SPACE & AERONAUTICS

Majority (13 R): Rohrabacher, Chmn.; Barton, Calvert, Bartlett, Weldon (FL) Vice Chmn.; Salmon, Davis, Foley, Pickering, Cannon, Brady, Cook, Nethercutt.
Minority (10 D): Cramer, RMM; Hall, Traficant, Hastings, Jackson Lee, Luther, Lofgren, Capps, Lampson, Gordon.

TECHNOLOGY

Majority (10 R): Morella, Chmn.; Weldon (PA), Bartlett, Ehlers, Davis, Gutknecht, Ewing, Cannon, Brady, Cook.
Minority (8 D): Gordon, RMM; Johnson, Rivers, Stabenow, Barcia, McHale, Doyle, Tauscher.

SMALL BUSINESS — 2361 Rayburn
http://www.house.gov/smbiz/ — 202-225-5821

Majority (19 R): Talent (MO), Chmn.; Combest (TX), Hefley (CO), Manzullo (IL), Bartlett (MD), Smith (WA), LoBiondo (NJ), Kelly (NY), Souder (IN), Chabot (OH), Ryun (KS), Snowbarger (KS), Pappas (NJ), English (PA), McIntosh (IN), Emerson (MO), Hill (MT), Sununu (NH), one vacancy.
Minority (16 D): LaFalce (NY), RMM; Sisisky (VA), Flake (NY), Poshard (IL), Velazquez (NY), Baldacci (ME), Jackson (IL), Millender-McDonald (CA), Weygand (RI), Davis (IL), Boyd (FL), McCarthy (NY), Pascrell (NJ), Goode (VA), Hinojosa (TX), Berry (AR).

SUBCOMMITTEES

EMPOWERMENT

Majority (6 R): Souder, Chmn.; LoBiondo, Chabot, English, Emerson, one vacancy.
Minority (5 D): Velazquez, RMM; Flake, Millender-McDonald, Davis, Pascrell.

GOVERNMENT PROGRAMS & OVERSIGHT

Majority (6 R): Bartlett, Chmn.; Manzullo, Smith, Hill, Sununu, one vacancy.
Minority (5 D): Poshard, RMM; Weygand, Boyd, McCarthy, Davis.

REGULATORY REFORM & PAPERWORK REDUCTION

Majority (6 R): Kelly, Chmn.; Combest, LoBiondo, Ryun, McIntosh, Emerson.
Minority (5 D): Jackson, RMM; Sisisky, Goode, Boyd, one vacancy.

TAX, FINANCE & EXPORTS

Majority (6 R): Manzullo, Chmn.; Smith, Vice Chmn.; Snowbarger, Pappas, English, one vacancy.
Minority (5 D): Baldacci, RMM; Hinojosa, Berry, Millender-McDonald, Weygand.

STANDARDS OF OFFICIAL CONDUCT HT-2 The Capitol, 202-225-7103

Majority (5 R): Hansen (UT), Chmn.; four vacancies.
Minority (5 D): Berman (CA), RMM; four vacancies.

NO SUBCOMMITTEES

TRANSPORTATION & INFRASTRUCTURE 2165 Rayburn
http://www.house.gov/transportation/ 202-225-9446

Majority (40 R): Shuster (PA), Chmn.; Young (AK), Petri (WI), Boehlert (NY), Bateman (VA), Coble (NC), Duncan (TN), Molinari (NY), Ewing (IL), Gilchrest (MD), Kim (CA), Horn (CA), Franks (NJ), Mica (FL), Quinn (NY), Fowler (FL), Ehlers (MI), Bachus (AL), LaTourette (OH), Kelly (NY), LaHood (IL), Baker (LA), Riggs (CA), Bass (NH), Ney (OH), Metcalf (WA), Emerson (MO), Pease (IN), Blunt (MO), Pitts (PA), Hutchinson (AR), Cook (UT), Cooksey (LA), Thune (SD), Pickering (MS), Granger (TX), Davis (VA), Fox (PA), LoBiondo (NJ), Watts (OK).

Minority (33 D): Oberstar (MN), RMM; Rahall (WV), Borski (PA), Lipinski (IL), Wise (WV), Traficant (OH), DeFazio (OR), Clement (TN), Costello (IL), Poshard (IL), Cramer (AL), Norton (DC), Nadler (NY), Danner (MO), Menendez (NJ), Clyburn (SC), Brown (FL), Barcia (MI), Filner (CA), Johnson (TX), Mascara (PA), Taylor (MS), Millender-McDonald (CA), Cummings (MD), Blumenauer (OR), Sandlin (TX), Tauscher (CA), Pascrell (NJ), Johnson (WI), Boswell (IA), McGovern (MA), Holden (PA), Lampson (TX).

SUBCOMMITTEES

AVIATION

Majority (15 R): Duncan, Chmn.; Blunt, Vice Chmn.; Molinari, Ewing, Ehlers, LaHood, Bass, Metcalf, Pease, Pitts, Hutchinson, Cook, Cooksey, Pickering, Granger.

Minority (14 D): Lipinski, RMM; Boswell, Poshard, Rahall, Traficant, DeFazio, Costello, Cramer, Danner, Clyburn, Brown, Johnson (TX), Millender-McDonald, Cummings.

COAST GUARD & MARITIME TRANSPORTATION

Majority (4 R): Gilchrest, Chmn.; LoBiondo, Vice Chmn.; Young, Coble.
Minority (3 D): Clement, RMM; Johnson (WI), Borski.

PUBLIC BUILDINGS & ECONOMIC DEVELOPMENT

Majority (5 R): Kim, Chmn.; Cooksey, Vice Chmn.; Duncan, LaTourette, Davis.
Minority (4 D): Traficant, RMM; Norton, Holden, Lampson.

RAILROADS

Majority (10 R): Molinari, Chmn.; Granger, Vice Chmn.; Boehlert, Franks, Mica, Quinn, Fowler, Bachus, Pitts, Fox.

Minority (8 D): Wise, RMM; Blumenauer, Borski, Lipinski, Clement, Nadler, Filner, Sandlin.

SURFACE TRANSPORTATION

Majority (27 R): Petri, Chmn.; Pickering, Vice Chmn.; Bateman, Coble, Ewing, Horn, Franks, Mica, Quinn, Fowler, Bachus, LaTourette, Kelly, LaHood, Baker, Riggs, Bass, Ney, Metcalf, Emerson, Pease, Pitts, Hutchinson, Cook, Thune, Granger, Watts.

Minority (21 D): Rahall, RMM; DeFazio, Cramer, Danner, Clyburn, Brown, Barcia, Filner, Johnson (TX), Mascara, Millender-McDonald, Costello, Norton, Nadler, Menendez, Taylor, Cummings, Sandlin, Tauscher, Pascrell, McGovern.

WATER RESOURCES & ENVIRONMENT

Majority (19 R): Boehlert, Chmn.; Thune, Young, Petri, Bateman, Molinari, Gilchrest, Kim, Horn, Franks, Quinn, Ehlers, LaTourette, Kelly, Baker, Riggs, Ney, Emerson, LoBiondo.
Minority (15 D): Borski, RMM; Johnson (WI), Wise, Poshard, Menendez, Barcia, Mascara, Taylor, Blumenauer, Tauscher, Pascrell, Boswell, McGovern, Rahall, Lampson.

VETERANS' AFFAIRS — 335 Cannon

http://www.house.gov/va/ — 202-225-3527

Majority (16 R): Stump (AZ), Chmn.; Smith (NJ), Bilirakis (FL), Spence (SC), Everett (AL), Buyer (IN), Quinn (NY), Bachus (AL), Stearns (FL), Schaefer (CO), Moran (KS), Cooksey (LA), Hutchinson (AR), Hayworth (AZ), Chenoweth (ID), LaHood (IL).
Minority (13 D): Evans (IL), RMM; Kennedy (MA), Filner (CA), Gutierrez (IL), Clyburn (SC), Brown (FL), Doyle (PA), Mascara (PA), Peterson (MN), Carson (IN), Reyes (TX), Snyder (AR), Rodriguez (TX).

SUBCOMMITTEES

BENEFITS

Majority (5 R): Quinn, Chmn.; Schaefer, Hayworth, LaHood, one vacancy.
Minority (4 D): Filner, RMM; Mascara, Reyes, Rodriguez.

HEALTH

Majority (8 R): Stearns, Chmn.; Smith, Bilirakis, Bachus, Moran, Cooksey, Hutchinson, Chenoweth.
Minority (6 D): Gutierrez, RMM; Kennedy, Brown, Doyle, Peterson, Carson.

OVERSIGHT & INVESTIGATIONS

Majority (4 R): Everett, Chmn.; Stump, Spence, Buyer.
Minority (3 D): Clyburn, RMM; Snyder, Mascara.

WAYS & MEANS — 1102 Longworth

http://www.house.gov/ways_means/ — 202-225-3625

Majority (23 R): Archer (TX), Chmn.; Crane (IL), Thomas (CA), Shaw (FL), Johnson (CT), Bunning (KY), Houghton (NY), Herger (CA), McCrery (LA), Camp (MI), Ramstad (MN), Nussle (IA), Johnson (TX), Dunn (WA), Collins (GA), Portman (OH), English (PA), Ensign (NV), Christensen (NE), Watkins (OK), Hayworth (AZ), Weller (IL), Hulshof (MO).
Minority (16 D): Rangel (NY), RMM; Stark (CA), Matsui (CA), Kennelly (CT), Coyne (PA), Levin (MI), Cardin (MD), McDermott (WA), Kleczka (WI), Lewis (GA), Neal (MA), McNulty (NY), Jefferson (LA), Tanner (TN), Becerra (CA), Thurman (FL).

SUBCOMMITTEES

HEALTH

Majority (8 R): Thomas, Chmn.; Johnson (CT), McCrery, Ensign, Christensen, Crane, Houghton, Johnson (TX).
Minority (5 D): Stark, RMM; Cardin, Kleczka, Lewis, Becerra.

HUMAN RESOURCES

Majority (8 R): Shaw, Chmn.; Camp, McCrery, Collins, English, Ensign, Hayworth, Watkins.
Minority (5 D): Levin, RMM; Stark, Matsui, Coyne, McDermott.

OVERSIGHT

Majority (8 R): Johnson (CT), Chmn.; Portman, Ramstad, Dunn, English, Watkins, Weller, Hulshof.
Minority (5 D): Coyne, RMM; Kleczka, McNulty, Tanner, Thurman.

SOCIAL SECURITY

Majority (8 R): Bunning, Chmn.; Johnson (TX), Collins, Portman, Christensen, Hayworth, Weller, Hulshof.
Minority (5 D): Kennelly, RMM; Neal, Levin, Jefferson, Tanner.

TRADE

Majority (9 R): Crane, Chmn.; Thomas, Shaw, Houghton, Camp, Ramstad, Dunn, Herger, Nussle.
Minority (6 D): Matsui, RMM; Rangel, Neal, McDermott, McNulty, Jefferson.

JOINT COMMITTEES

JOINT ECONOMIC COMMITTEE G-01 Dirksen

http://www.senate.gov/committee/jec.html 202-224-5171

House (10): Saxton (NJ), Chmn.; Manzullo (IL), Sanford (SC), Thornberry (TX), Doolittle (CA), McCrery (LA), Stark (CA), Hamilton (IN), Hinchey (NY), Maloney (NY).
Senate (10): Mack (FL), Vice Chmn.; Roth (DE), Bennett (UT), Grams (MN), Brownback (KS), Sessions (AL), Bingaman (NM), Sarbanes (MD), Kennedy (MA), Robb (VA).

JOINT COMMITTEE ON THE LIBRARY OF CONGRESS 1309 Longworth

http://www.senate.gov/committee/jcloc.html 202-225-8281

House (5): Thomas (CA), Chmn.; Ney (OH), Ehlers (MI), Kilpatrick (MI), Gejdenson (CT).
Senate (5): Stevens (AK), Vice Chmn.; Warner (VA), Cochran (MS), Moynihan (NY), Feinstein (CA).

JOINT COMMITTEE ON PRINTING — 818 Hart

http://www.senate.gov/committee/jcp.html — 202-224-5241

Senate (5): Warner (VA), Chmn.; Cochran (MS), McConnell (KY), Ford (KY), Inouye (HI).
House (5): Thomas (CA), Vice Chmn,; Ney (OH), Granger (TX), Hoyer (MD), Gejdenson (CT).

JOINT COMMITTEE ON TAXATION — 1015 Longworth

http://www.senate.gov/committee/jct.html — 202-225-3621

House (5): Archer (TX), Chmn.; Crane (IL), Thomas (CA), Rangel (NY), Stark (CA).
Senate (5): Roth (DE), Vice Chmn.; Chafee (RI), Grassley (IA), Moynihan (NY), Baucus (MT).

CAMPAIGN FINANCE

All data are derived from candidate and party reports as well as other official studies available from the Federal Election Commission (FEC) located at 999 E Street, N.W., Washington, DC 20463. Telephone 202-219-4140 (or toll-free 800-424-9530). Individuals listed in italics were losing candidates in that election.

U.S. SENATE

The following charts show the top 15 1996 Senate candidates in terms of the highest total net receipts, net expenditures, political action committee (PAC) contributions, individual contributions, cash on hand and debts owed during the 1990–96 election cycle.

1996 Senate: Top Raisers

1.	*Mark R. Warner (D-VA)*	$11,625,483
2.	John F. Kerry (D-MA)	10,342,115
3.	*Guy W. Millner (R-GA)*	9,917,102
4.	Robert G. Torricelli (D-NJ)	9,211,508
5.	*Dick Zimmer (R-NJ)*	8,212,612
6.	*Harvey Gantt (D-NC)*	8,128,548
7.	*William F. Weld (R-MA)*	8,074,417
8.	Jesse A. Helms (R-NC)	7,808,820
9.	Carl Levin (D-MI)	6,021,723
10.	Paul D. Wellstone (DFL-MN)	5,991,013
11.	*James B. Nicholson (R-MI)*	5,909,261
12.	Gordon H. Smith (R-OR)	5,543,520
13.	John W. Warner (R-VA)	5,433,390
14.	Richard J. Durbin (D-IL)	4,767,940
15.	*Al Salvi (R-IL)*	4,754,916

1996 Senate: Top Spenders

1.	*Mark R. Warner (D-VA)*	$11,600,424
2.	John F. Kerry (D-MA)	10,962,607
3.	*Guy W. Millner (R-GA)*	9,858,955
4.	Robert G. Torricelli (D-NJ)	9,134,854
5.	*Dick Zimmer (R-NJ)*	8,238,181
6.	*Harvey Gantt (D-NC)*	8,012,980
7.	*William F. Weld (R-MA)*	8,002,123
8.	Jesse A. Helms (R-NC)	7,798,520
9.	Phil Gramm (R-TX)	6,289,591
10.	Paul D. Wellstone (DFL-MN)	5,979,224
11.	Carl Levin (D-MI)	5,965,017
12.	*James B. Nicholson (R-MI)*	5,908,415
13.	John W. Warner (R-VA)	5,596,061
14.	Gordon H. Smith (R-OR)	5,542,482
15.	Tom Harkin (D-IA)	5,276,708

1996 Senate: Top PAC Recipients

1.	John W. Warner (R-VA)	$1,601,460
2.	*Larry Pressler (R-SD)*	1,513,835
3.	Max Baucus (D-MT)	1,352,466
4.	Mitch McConnell (R-KY)	1,293,151
5.	Pat Roberts (R-KS)	1,216,831
6.	Ted Stevens (R-AK)	1,203,797
7.	*Dick Zimmer (R-NJ)*	1,197,917
8.	Pete V. Domenici (R-NM)	1,154,329
9.	Richard J. Durbin (D-IL)	1,153,210
10.	James M. Inhofe (R-OK)	1,117,944
11.	Phil Gramm (R-TX)	1,107,961
12.	Fred Thompson (R-TN)	1,080,345
13.	Wayne Allard (R-CO)	1,061,594
14.	Tom Harkin (D-IA)	1,061,573
15.	*Rudy Boschwitz (R-MN)*	1,035,527

1996 Senate: Top Individual Contributions

1.	John F. Kerry (D-MA)	$7,843,781
2.	*Harvey Gantt (D-NC)*	7,619,519
3.	*William F. Weld (R-MA)*	7,062,001
4.	Jesse A. Helms (R-NC)	6,614,683
5.	Robert G. Torricelli (D-NJ)	6,112,877
6.	*Dick Zimmer (R-NJ)*	5,525,662
7.	Paul D. Wellstone (DFL-MN)	5,288,600
8.	Carl Levin (D-MI)	4,937,261
9.	Richard J. Durbin (D-IL)	3,394,275
10.	Tom Harkin (D-IA)	3,390,007
11.	*Rudy Boschwitz (R-MN)*	3,286,786
12.	*Al Salvi (R-IL)*	3,249,981
13.	John W. Warner (R-VA)	2,955,543
14.	Fred Thompson (R-TN)	2,923,085
15.	Jeff Sessions (R-AL)	2,878,517

1996 Senate: Top Cash-on-Hand

1.	John D. (Jay) Rockefeller (D-WV)	$980,751
2.	Fred Thompson (R-TN)	836,460
3.	Thad Cochran (R-MS)	600,518
4.	Phil Gramm (R-TX)	598,108
5.	Ted Stevens (R-AK)	328,540
6.	Pete V. Domenici (R-NM)	253,282
7.	James M. Inhofe (R-OK)	208,283
8.	*Dick Swett (D-NH)*	198,526
9.	Bob Smith (R-NH)	190,341
10.	Mitch McConnell (R-KY)	189,324
11.	*Roger Hugh Bedford (D-AL)*	128,828
12.	*Harvey Gantt (D-NC)*	125,749
13.	Pat Roberts (R-KS)	109,499
14.	Carl Levin (D-MI)	109,381
15.	*James Clifford Miller II (R-VA)*	109,057

1996 Senate: Top Debts Owed

1.	*Guy W. Millner (R-GA)*	$6,340,850
2.	Gordon H. Smith (R-OR)	2,422,459
3.	*Robert A. G. Monks (R-ME)*	2,085,000
4.	John F. Kerry (D-MA)	2,074,461
5.	*William Henry Linder (R-LA)*	1,885,937
6.	*F. Charles McMains Jr. (R-LA)*	1,775,149
7.	*Charles Addison Sanders (D-NC)*	1,737,654
8.	*Al Salvi (R-IL)*	1,458,923
9.	*Thomas H. Bruggere (D-OR)*	1,399,500
10.	*David W. Cuddy (R-AK)*	1,168,257
11.	Chuck Hagel (R-NE)	1,052,107
12.	*Clinton M. Day (R-GA)*	923,700
13.	*Walter Clifford Minnick (D-ID)*	740,421
14.	Jesse A. Helms (R-NC)	508,004
15.	*Harold Gene Worley (R-SC)*	425,000

U.S. HOUSE OF REPRESENTATIVES

The following charts show the top 25 1996 House candidates in terms of the highest total net receipts, net expenditures, political action committee (PAC) contributions, individual contributions, cash on hand and debts owed during the 1994–96 election cycle.

1996 House: Top Raisers

1.	Newt Gingrich (R-GA)	$6,252,069
2.	*Michael J. Coles (D-GA)*	3,327,354
3.	Charles E. Schumer (D-NY)	3,318,153
4.	Richard A. Gephardt (D-MO)	3,309,642
5.	Ellen O. Tauscher (D-CA)	2,573,780
6.	Joseph P. Kennedy II (D-MA)	2,414,369
7.	Vic Fazio (D-CA)	2,412,373
8.	Greg Ganske (R-IA)	2,337,935
9.	John Ensign (R-NV)	1,989,386
10.	Martin Frost (D-TX)	1,964,330
11.	Ron Paul (R-TX)	1,933,263
12.	Tom Campbell (R-CA)	1,904,564
13.	*Steve Stockman (R-TX)*	1,899,173
14.	John R. Kasich (R-OH)	1,882,613
15.	Christopher B. Cannon (R-UT)	1,827,718
16.	*Frank A. Cremeans (R-OH)*	1,788,241
17.	Jon Christensen (R-NE)	1,771,220
18.	Max A. Sandlin Jr. (D-TX)	1,706,389
19.	Jane Harman (D-CA)	1,703,775
20.	Ken Bentsen Jr. (D-TX)	1,692,979
21.	Charlie Norwood Jr. (R-GA)	1,681,950
22.	Rick White (R-WA)	1,679,748
23.	Jon D. Fox (R-PA)	1,663,100
24.	Nick Lampson (D-TX)	1,643,257
25.	Tom DeLay (R-TX)	1,620,227

1996 House: Top Spenders

1.	Newt Gingrich (R-GA)	$5,577,715
2.	*Michael J. Coles (D-GA)*	3,325,030
3.	Richard A. Gephardt (D-MO)	3,110,509
4.	Ellen O. Tauscher (D-CA)	2,571,595
5.	Greg Ganske (R-IA)	2,334,251
6.	Vic Fazio (D-CA)	2,320,330
7.	Martin Frost (D-TX)	1,963,529
8.	Joseph P. Kennedy II (D-MA)	1,952,906
9.	Ron Paul (R-TX)	1,927,756
10.	John Ensign (R-NV)	1,904,413
11.	*Steve Stockman (R-TX)*	1,898,778
12.	John D. Dingell (D-MI)	1,854,280
13.	Christopher B. Cannon (R-UT)	1,826,849
14.	*Frank A. Cremeans (R-OH)*	1,786,582
15.	Jon Christensen (R-NE)	1,722,490
16.	Max A. Sandlin Jr. (D-TX)	1,691,255
17.	Richard K. (Dick) Armey (R-TX)	1,673,388
18.	Rick White (R-WA)	1,671,909
19.	Jon D. Fox (R-PA)	1,659,723
20.	Ken Bentsen Jr. (D-TX)	1,654,345
21.	Tom Campbell (R-CA)	1,650,740
22.	Charlie Norwood Jr. (R-GA)	1,622,486
23.	Tom DeLay (R-TX)	1,621,708
24.	Nick Lampson (D-TX)	1,612,625
25.	Bart Gordon (D-TN)	1,609,419

1996 House: Top PAC Recipients

1.	Vic Fazio (D-CA)	$1,348,260
2.	Richard A. Gephardt (D-MO)	1,169,422
3.	Martin Frost (D-TX)	1,112,737
4.	Newt Gingrich (R-GA)	1,098,746
5.	Tom DeLay (R-TX)	1,066,875
6.	Ken Bentsen Jr. (D-TX)	910,734
7.	John D. Dingell (D-MI)	879,060
8.	David E. Bonior (D-MI)	862,148
9.	Bart Gordon (D-TN)	742,511
10.	Charles B. Rangel (D-NY)	711,089
11.	Rick White (R-WA)	705,106
12.	John Ensign (R-NV)	698,949
13.	Tom Bliley (R-VA)	697,582
14.	Steny H. Hoyer (D-MD)	696,267
15.	Philip S. English (R-PA)	672,296
16.	Bill Paxon (R-NY)	668,971
17.	Greg Ganske (R-IA)	668,464
18.	Charlie Norwood Jr. (R-GA)	664,419
19.	William M. Thomas (R-CA)	650,824
20.	*Randy Tate (R-WA)*	645,900
21.	Robert L. (Bob) Livingston (R-LA)	642,295
22.	Joe L. Barton (R-TX)	634,813
23.	Jon Christensen (R-NE)	627,125
24.	Tom Coburn (R-OK)	622,794
25.	Earl Pomeroy (D-ND)	604,261

1996 House: Top Individual Contributions

1.	Newt Gingrich (R-GA)	$5,094,260
2.	Charles E. Schumer (D-NY)	2,672,010
3.	Joseph P. Kennedy II (D-MA)	2,040,525
4.	Ron Paul (R-TX)	1,774,209
5.	John R. Kasich (R-OH)	1,388,377
6.	Tom Campbell (R-CA)	1,262,932
7.	*Steve Stockman (R-TX)*	1,251,102
8.	Richard A. Gephardt (D-MO)	1,220,900
9.	*Martin Hoke (R-OH)*	1,202,660
10.	Van Hilleary (R-TN)	1,197,858
11.	John Ensign (R-NV)	1,189,784
12.	Linda Smith (R-WA)	1,153,291
13.	Rod R. Blagojevich (D-IL)	1,152,958
14.	Jon D. Fox (R-PA)	1,132,013
15.	Nita M. Lowey (D-NY)	1,100,757
16.	Debbie Stabenow (D-MI)	1,088,363
17.	Jon Christensen (R-NE)	1,084,923
18.	*Peter G. Torkildsen (R-MA)*	1,062,367
19.	Greg Ganske (R-IA)	1,034,374
20.	Tom Davis (R-VA)	1,022,016
21.	Vic Fazio (D-CA)	1,014,510
22.	Jane Harman (D-CA)	997,937
23.	Charlie Norwood Jr. (R-GA)	961,230
24.	Nick Lampson (D-TX)	955,580
25.	*William P. Baker (R-CA)*	954,444

1996 House: Top Cash-on-Hand

1.	Charles E. Schumer (D-NY)	$5,052,292
2.	David Dreier (R-CA)	2,741,564
3.	Joseph P. Kennedy II (D-MA)	1,247,271
4.	Lloyd Doggett (D-TX)	972,924
5.	Dan Burton (R-IN)	961,370
6.	Nick J. Rahall II (D-WV)	957,731
7.	Newt Gingrich (R-GA)	894,499
8.	Jerry Lewis (R-CA)	827,480
9.	Jim Ramstad (R-MN)	825,054
10.	Rick A. Lazio (R-NY)	757,524
11.	Peter Deutsch (D-FL)	720,642
12.	Robert Menendez (D-NJ)	690,692
13.	Edward J. Markey (D-MA)	689,402
14.	Jim Saxton (R-NJ)	678,012
15.	W. J. (Billy) Tauzin (R-LA)	663,894
16.	Christopher Cox (R-CA)	663,039
17.	Scott McInnis (R-CO)	659,098
18.	Bill Archer (R-TX)	647,303
19.	Ileana Ros-Lehtinen (R-FL)	639,899
20.	John Lewis (D-GA)	624,137
21.	William M. Thomas (R-CA)	579,140
22.	Clifford B. Stearns (R-FL)	570,105
23.	Harold D. Rogers (R-KY)	549,207
24.	John J. LaFalce (D-NY)	540,509
25.	Joe L. Barton (R-TX)	539,454

1996 House: Debts Owed

1.	*Eugene J. Fontenot (R-TX)*	$3,479,347
2.	*Michael J. Coles (D-GA)*	2,785,707
3.	Ellen O. Tauscher (D-CA)	1,677,609
4.	Christopher B. Cannon (R-UT)	1,644,509
5.	*Dick Chrysler (R-MI)*	1,613,568
6.	*Dal Anthony Lamagna (D-NY)*	993,879
7.	Max A. Sandlin Jr. (D-TX)	843,436
8.	Terry Everett (R-AL)	675,873
9.	*Richard P. Sybert (R-CA)*	670,554
10.	Norman Sisisky (D-VA)	639,183
11.	Brad Sherman (D-CA)	623,989
12.	*Peter James Tsakanikas (D-FL)*	573,851
13.	*Joseph J. Fitzsimmons (R-MI)*	520,000
14.	*Michela A. Alioto (D-CA)*	506,310
15.	Greg Ganske (R-IA)	501,583
16.	*Brian Dodd Pardo (R-TX)*	498,437
17.	*Irwin Savodnik (R-CA)*	492,692
18.	*Lawrence Irwin Lerner (D-NJ)*	488,625
19.	*Joseph R. Paolino Jr (D-RI)*	477,875
20.	*David Lee Davis (R-TN)*	467,584
21.	Rodney P. Frelinghuysen (R-NJ)	441,079
22.	*Jo Ann Howard (D-TX)*	439,054
23.	*Paul M. Barby (D-OK)*	410,000
24.	Newt Gingrich (R-GA)	384,975
25.	Ruben Hinojosa (D-TX)	381,000

DEMOGRAPHICS

Population. All population figures are from the Bureau of the Census, U.S. Department of Commerce, Washington, D.C. 20233, 301-457-3030. Figures for 1970, 1980 and 1990 are final Census Bureau population counts as of April 1 of those years. Figures for 1996 are estimates as of July 1. (The District of Columbia is included as a state in all the following charts.)

Voting Age Population. This figure indicates all persons at least 18 years of age who are eligible to vote, including the Armed Forces, aliens and institutional members.

Chart I shows the total U.S. population and total U.S. voting age population for 1996, 1990, 1980 and 1970.

Chart I

Total U.S. Population		Total U.S. Voting Age Population	
July 1, 1996 (est.)	265,284,000	July 1, 1996 (est.)	196,511,000
April 1, 1990	248,709,873	April 1, 1990	185,105,441
April 1, 1980	226,545,805	April 1, 1980	163,997,000
April 1, 1970	203,302,031	April 1, 1970	135,290,000

Chart II indicates the range of highest and lowest state population changes in percentage growth and absolute change for 1980–90.

Chart II

1980–90 Population Change
(National Avg.: up 9.8%)

State	*Highest*		*State*	*Lowest*	
Nevada	50.1%	401,340	West Virginia	−8.0%	−156,167
Alaska	36.9	148,192	District of Columbia	−4.9	−31,433
Arizona	34.8	947,013	Iowa	−4.7	−137,053
Florida	32.7	3,191,602	Wyoming	−3.4	−15,969
California	25.7	6,092,119	North Dakota	−2.1	−13,917

Chart III shows the ten highest and the ten lowest state populations.

Chart III

1996 (Est.) U.S. Population: Ten Highest and Lowest States

State	*Highest*	*State*	*Lowest*
California	31,878,000	Wyoming	481,000
Texas	19,128,000	District of Columbia	543,000
New York	18,185,000	Vermont	589,000
Florida	14,400,000	Alaska	607,000
Pennsylvania	12,056,000	North Dakota	644,000
Illinois	11,847,000	Delaware	725,000
Ohio	11,173,000	South Dakota	732,000
Michigan	9,594,000	Montana	879,000
New Jersey	7,988,000	Rhode Island	990,000
Georgia	7,353,000	New Hampshire	1,162,000

Chart IV lists the states with the highest and lowest median age.

Chart IV

1990 Median Age
(National Avg.: 34.6 years)

State	*Highest*	*State*	*Lowest*
West Virginia	37.7 years	Utah	26.8 years
Florida	37.6	Alaska	31.9
Pennsylvania	36.9	Texas	32.6
Maine	36.6	California	32.7
Montana	36.5	Mississippi	32.9

Chart V illustrates the states with the highest and lowest average percentages of married-couple family households.

Chart V

1990 Married-Couple Family Households
(National Avg.: 55.9%)

State	*Highest*	*State*	*Lowest*
Utah	64.8%	District of Columbia	25.3%
Idaho	62.2	New York	49.9
Wyoming, New Hampshire	59.7	Nevada	51.4
Arkansas, Iowa, Kentucky	59.2	Massachusetts	52.1
North Dakota	59.1	California	52.7

Chart VI illustrates the states with the highest and lowest average percentages of population over 65 years of age.

Chart VI

1990 Population Over 65 Years of Age

(National Avg.: 12.8%)

State	*Highest*	*State*	*Lowest*
Florida	18.5%	Alaska	5.2%
Pennsylvania	15.9	Utah	8.8
Rhode Island	15.8	Georgia	9.9
West Virginia, Iowa	15.2	Colorado	10.1
North Dakota	14.5	Texas	10.2

Chart VII illustrates the states with the highest and lowest average percentages of Owner Occupied Housing.

Chart VII

1990 Owner Occupied Housing

(National Avg.: 65.4%)

State	*Highest*	*State*	*Lowest*
West Virginia	74.1%	District of Columbia	38.9%
Minnesota	71.8	New York	52.2
Mississippi	71.5	Hawaii	53.9
Michigan	71.0	Nevada	54.8
Pennsylvania	70.6	California	55.6

Chart VIII illustrates the states with the highest and lowest median house value.

Chart VIII

1990 Median House Value

(National Avg.: $84,209)

State	*Highest*	*State*	*Lowest*
Hawaii	$245,300	South Dakota	$45,200
California	195,500	Mississippi	45,600
Connecticut	177,800	Iowa	45,900
Massachusetts	162,800	Arkansas	46,300
New Jersey	162,300	West Virginia	47,900

Chart IX illustrates the states with the highest and lowest median monthly rent.

Chart IX

1990 Median Monthly Rent

(National Avg.: $350)

State	*Highest*	*State*	*Lowest*
Hawaii	$599	Mississippi	$215
California	561	West Virginia	221
New Jersey	521	Alabama	229
Connecticut	510	Arkansas	230
Massachusetts	506	South Dakota	242

Chart X shows the states with the highest and lowest per capita income.

Chart X

1990 Per Capita Income

(National Avg.: $18,685)

State	*Highest*	*State*	*Lowest*
Connecticut	$25,358	Mississippi	$12,735
New Jersey	24,968	West Virginia	13,747
District of Columbia	23,491	Utah	14,083
Massachusetts	22,642	Arkansas	14,218
New York	21,975	New Mexico	14,228
Maryland	21,864	Louisiana	14,391
Alaska	21,761	Alabama	14,826
California	20,795	Kentucky	14,929
New Hampshire	20,789	South Carolina	15,099
Illinois	20,303	Montana	15,110

Chart XI shows the states with the highest and lowest average unemployment rates for 1996. These figures are from the U.S. Department of Labor, Bureau of Labor Statistics, and were compiled independently of the Census Bureau figures.

Chart XI

1996 Average Unemployment Rate

(National Avg: 5.4%)

Highest		*Lowest*	
District of Columbia	8.5%	Nebraska	2.9%
New Mexico	8.1	North Dakota	3.1
Alaska	7.8	South Dakota	3.2
West Virginia	7.5	Utah	3.5
California	7.2	Wisconsin	3.5
Louisiana	6.7	Iowa	3.8
Washington	6.5	Minnesota	4.0
Hawaii	6.4	Indiana	4.1
New York	6.2	Oklahoma	4.1
New Jersey	6.2	Colorado	4.2

Ethnic Breakdown. The racial and ethnic breakdowns illustrate the potential ethnic vote as opposed to the overall population. The concepts of race and ethnicity as defined by the Census Bureau reflect self-identification and not clear-cut biological definitions.

Chart XII lists voting age and total state population figures for the fourteen states with black populations above the national average of 12.1% in 1990. Black ethnic classification refers to those persons who indicated their race as Black on the Census questionnaire.

Chart XII

1990 Black Population: Total State Population

State	*% of voting age pop.*	*% of total state pop.*	*State*	*% of voting age pop.*	*% of total state pop.*
District of Columbia	62.4%	65.8%	North Carolina	20.1%	22.0%
Mississippi	31.6	35.6	Virginia	17.6	18.8
Louisiana	27.9	30.8	Delaware	15.3	16.9
South Carolina	26.9	29.8	Tennessee	14.4	16.0
Georgia	24.6	27.0	New York	14.7	15.9
Alabama	22.7	25.3	Arkansas	13.7	15.9
Maryland	23.5	24.9	Illinois	13.4	14.8

Chart XIII illustrates the voting age and total population figures for the fourteen states with American Indian concentrations above the national average of 0.8% in 1990. The American Indian classification includes persons who classified themselves as American Indian, Eskimo, or Aleut.

Chart XIII

1990 American Indian: Total State and Voting Age Population

State	*% of voting age pop.*	*% of total state pop.*	*State*	*% of voting age pop.*	*% of total state pop.*
Alaska	13.5%	15.6%	Wyoming	1.8%	2.1%
New Mexico	7.5	8.9	Washington	1.4	1.7
Oklahoma	6.9	8.0	Nevada	1.5	1.6
South Dakota	5.4	7.3	Utah	1.2	1.4
Montana	4.8	6.0	Oregon	1.2	1.4
Arizona	4.4	5.6	Idaho	1.2	1.4
North Dakota	3.1	4.1	North Carolina	1.1	1.2

Chart XIV illustrates the voting age and total state population figures for the eight states with Asian concentrations at or above the national average of 2.9% in 1990. The Asian classification includes persons who classified themselves as Asian or Pacific Islander.

Chart XIV

1990 Asian Origin: Total State and Voting Age Population

State	*% of voting age pop.*	*% of total state pop.*	*State*	*% of voting age pop.*	*% of total state pop.*
Hawaii	61.3%	61.8%	Alaska	3.6%	3.6%
California	9.2	9.6	New Jersey	3.2	3.5
Washington	4.1	4.3	Nevada	3.1	3.2
New York	3.8	3.9	Maryland	2.8	2.9

Chart XV illustrates voting age and total state population figures for the eight states with Hispanic origin concentrations above the national average of 9.0% in 1990. The Hispanic origin classification includes three specific categories—Mexican, Puerto Rican and Cuban—as well as those who indicated that they were of other Spanish or Hispanic origin (origin can be viewed as ancestry, nationality group, lineage or country of birth of the person or the person's parents or ancestors prior to their arrival in the United States). Persons of Hispanic origin may be of any race.

Chart XV

1990 Hispanic Origin: Total State and Voting Age Population

State	*% of voting age pop.*	*% of total state pop.*	*State*	*% of voting age pop.*	*% of total state pop.*
New Mexico	33.0%	38.2%	Colorado	11.2%	12.9%
California	22.5	25.8	New York	11.2	12.3
Texas	22.4	25.5	Florida	11.7	12.2
Arizona	15.8	18.8	Nevada	9.1	10.4

INDEX

The 50 States and the names of all the Governors, Senators and Representatives appear in boldface type. The number of the page that includes Members' corresponding biographical, voting and campaign finance information also appears in bold.

A

C

D

E

F

H

I

J

K

L

N

Q

R

T

U

V

W

X

Y

Z

THE AUTHORS

MICHAEL BARONE, senior staff editor for *Reader's Digest*, is a graduate of Harvard College and Yale Law School. He has been affiliated with the polling group of Peter D. Hart Research Associates, Inc. and was an editorial writer and columnist for *The Washington Post* and senior editor at *U.S. News and World Report*. Barone is also author of *Our Country: The Shaping of America from Roosevelt to Reagan*, and has appeared as an analyst/commentator on various television and radio shows. He lives with his daughter Sarah in Washington, DC.

GRANT UJIFUSA is a senior editor at *Reader's Digest* in Pleasantville, New York. A native of Worland, Wyoming, Ujifusa received an A.B. from Harvard College in 1965, and did graduate work at Brandeis and Brown Universities. He lives in Chappaqua, New York, with his wife Amy and sons Steven and Andrew.

THE PUBLISHER

"The nation's most respected nonpartisan source of information about how Washington policymaking machinery really works."

That's how *Newsweek* described *National Journal*. For more than 25 years, *National Journal* has reached subscribers with an award-winning weekly magazine noted for its dedication to "facts only" reporting. *National Journal* speaks to people who make it their business to know what's going on in the world's largest business—the United States Government.

Only *National Journal* is exclusively devoted to the coverage and analysis of what the government is doing today, what it's going to do tomorrow, and how its actions affect every facet of our lives.

This 1998 edition of *The Almanac of American Politics* marks the eighth volume to be published by National Journal Inc. In addition to the *Almanac* and *National Journal*, National Journal Inc. publishes the monthly *Government Executive* magazine; *CongressDaily*, a daily fax newsletter covering Congress; *The Hotline*, a daily briefing on American politics; *American Health Line*, *Greenwire*, and *The Abortion Report*, daily news briefings for political professionals; the semi-annual directory, *The Capital Source*; and the *National Journal Convention Daily*, in conjunction with the Democratic and Republican Conventions. A new World Wide Web service, National Journal's "Cloakroom," debuted in July 1997.

National Journal

1501 M Street, NW, Washington, DC 20005 Telephone (202) 739-8400